CHAMBERS
BOOK OF
FACTS

Editors
Trevor Anderson
Una McGovern
Hazel Norris

CHAMBERS

CHAMBERS
An imprint of Chambers Harrap Publishers Ltd
7 Hopetoun Crescent
Edinburgh, EH7 4AY

www.chambers.co.uk

Previously published as *The Chambers Encyclopedia* 2001
This edition published by Chambers Harrap Publishers Ltd 2003

A CIP catalogue record for this book is available from the British Library.

ISBN 0550 10103 9

Designed and typeset by Chambers Harrap Publishers Ltd, Edinburgh
Printed and bound in Italy

Introduction

Since its first edition over a decade ago, *Chambers Book of Facts* has established itself as an authoritative and indispensable reference work. This new edition has been extensively updated and expanded to provide even more facts, figures and useful information from a diverse range of fields.

As in previous editions, all material relating to specific fields is grouped under individual sections and subsections, enabling the user to find information on any particular topic with great ease. There are fourteen major subject areas: Space, Earth, Climate and Environment, Nations of the World, Social Structure, History, Time, Natural History, Human Body, Health and Nutrition, Communication, Science and Technology, Arts and Culture, Sports and Games, and Thought and Belief. Within these broad areas are clearly-labelled subsections to guide the user quickly to the relevant material. Tables, lists, diagrams, illustrations and maps complement the text.

The thematic arrangement means that it is easy to satisfy a specific query, and then broaden one's knowledge in a particular field by browsing around the section or subsection. Where material could be categorized under more than one heading, every effort has been made to locate the information in the place the reader would be most likely to look first. However, the detailed contents pages at the front and extensive index at the back of the book can also be used to go straight to the information you want.

Whether you are seeking an answer to an urgent enquiry or dipping in at leisure, we hope you find this new edition useful and stimulating.

The Editors

Contributors

Editors
Trevor Anderson
Hazel Norris

Managing Editor
Una McGovern

Contributors
Gary Dexter
Michael Munro

Prepress
Clair Cameron
David Reid
Kirsteen Wright

Abbreviations

AD	Anno Domini	K	Kelvin
admin	administration	kcal	kilocalorie(s)
b.	born	kg	kilogram(s)
BC	Before Christ	kJ	kilojoules
b.c.	born circa	l	litre(s)
c	century	L	Lake
c.	circa	Lat	Latin
C	Celsius (Centigrade)	lb	pound(s)
cc	cubic centimetre(s)	l y	light year(s)
Chin	Chinese	m	metre(s)
CIS	Commonwealth of	min	minute(s)
	Independent States	mi	mile(s)
cm	centimetre(s)	mm	millimetre(s)
Co	County	Mt	Mount(ain)
cont.	continued	Mts ·	Mountains
cu	cubic	N	north(ern)
cwt	hundredweight	n/a	not applicable
d.	died	no.	number
d.c.	died circa	oz	ounce(s)
e	estimate	p(p)	page(s)
E	east(ern)	pop	population
eg	for example	Port	Portuguese
Eng	English	Pt	pint(s)
F	Fahrenheit	r.	reigned
fl oz	fluid ounce(s)	R	River
fl	flourished (floruit)	Russ	Russian
Fr	French	S	south(ern)
ft	foot (feet)	sec	second(s)
g	gram(s)	Span	Spanish
gal	gallons	sq	square
Ger	German	St	Saint
Gr	Greek	Sta	Santa
h	hour(s)	Ste	Sainte
ha	hectare(s)	Swed	Swedish
Hung	Hungarian	TV	television
I(s)	Island(s)	UT	Unified Team
ie	that is (id est)	v.	versus
in	inch(es)	vols.	volumes
Ir	Irish	W	west(ern)
Ital	Italian	yd	yard(s)
Jap	Japanese		

See also

Other conventions

Months are abbreviated to the first three letters (3 Jan 1817)

Contents

SOCIAL STRUCTURE

HISTORY

TIME

NATURAL HISTORY

HUMAN BODY, HEALTH AND NUTRITION

COMMUNICATION

SCIENCE AND TECHNOLOGY

ARTS AND CULTURE

SPORTS AND GAMES

THOUGHT AND BELIEF

SPACE

Planetary data

Planet	Distance from Sun (million km/mi)				Sidereal period	Axial rotation period (equatorial)	Diameter (equatorial)	
	Maximum		Minimum				km	mi
Mercury	69.4	43.0	46.8	29.0	88 d	58 d 16 h	4 878	3 031
Venus	109.0	67.6	107.6	66.7	224.7 d	243 d	12 104	7 521
Earth	152.6	94.6	147.4	91.4	365.256 d	23 h 56 m	12 756	7 927
Mars	249.2	154.5	207.3	128.5	687 d	24 h 37 m 23 s	6 794	4 222
Jupiter	817.4	506.8	741.6	459.8	11.86 y	9 h 50 m 30 s	142 800	88 700
Saturn	1 512	937.6	1 346	834.6	29.46 y	10 h 14 m	120 536	74 900
Uranus	3 011	1 867	2 740	1 699	84.01 y	16–28 h[1]	51 118	31 765
Neptune	4 543	2 817	4 466	2 769	164.79 y	18–20 h[1]	49 492	30 754
Pluto	7 364	4 566	4 461	2 766	247.7 y	6 d 9 h	2 300	1 429

y: years   d: days   h: hours   m: minutes   s: seconds   km: kilometres   mi: miles
[1] Different latitudes rotate at different speeds.

Major planetary satellites

	Year discovered	Distance from planet		Diameter	
		km	mi	km	mi
Earth					
Moon	—	384 000	239 000	3 476	2 160
Mars					
Phobos	1877	9 380	5 830	27	17
Deimos	1877	23 460	14 580	15	9
Jupiter					
Io	1610	422 000	262 000	3 630	2 260
Europa	1610	671 000	417 000	3 138	1 950
Ganymede	1610	1 070 000	665 000	5 260	3 270
Callisto	1610	1 883 000	1 170 000	4 800	3 000
Saturn					
Mimas	1789	186 000	116 000	390	240
Enceladus	1789	238 000	148 000	500	310
Tethys	1684	295 000	183 000	1 050	650
Dione	1684	377 000	234 000	1 120	700
Rhea	1672	527 000	327 000	1 530	950
Titan	1655	1 222 000	759 000	5 150	3 200
Hyperion	1848	1 481 000	920 000	300	190
Iapetus	1671	3 560 000	2 212 000	1 460	900
Uranus					
Miranda	1948	130 000	81 000	470	290
Ariel	1851	191 000	119 000	1 160	720
Umbriel	1851	266 000	165 000	1 170	725
Titania	1787	436 000	271 000	1 580	980
Oberon	1787	583 000	362 000	1 520	945
Neptune					
Triton	1846	355 000	221 000	2 700	1 675
Nereid	1949	5 515 000	3 427 000	340	210
Proteus	1989	117 600	73 000	400	249
Pluto					
Charon	1978	19 700	12 240	1 200	750

Comets

The solid nucleus of a comet is usually several kilometres in diameter; it consists of ice, dust and solid particles like a large, dirty snowball. When the comet passes close to the Sun, a cloud of gas and dust is ejected from the nucleus, forming a huge head or coma, many thousands of kilometres in diameter. The radiations from the Sun elongate the gas and dust to form one or more tails, often extending millions of kilometres in space. These tails point away from the Sun, but as the comet recedes, the tail will decrease in length until the comet returns to its latent dirty snowball state.

Information for selected comets is given below.

Comet	First seen	Period of orbit (years)
Halley	240BC	76.1
Tycho	1577	*not known*
Kirch[1]	1680	8 814
De Chéseaux	1744	*not known*
Lexell	1770	5.6
Encke	1786	3.3
Flauergues	1811	3 094
Pons-Winnecke	1819	6.34
Great Comet	1843	512.6
Donati	1858	1 950
Tebbutt	1861	409.1
Swift-Tuttle	1862	125
Cruls	1882	758.4
Wolf	1884	8.4
Morehouse	1908	*not known*
Daylight Comet	1910	*not known*
Schwassmann-Wachmann 1	1925	15
Arend-Roland	1957	*not known*
Mrkos	1957	*not known*
Humason	1961	3 000
Seki-Lines	1962	*not known*
Ikeya-Seki	1965	880
Tago-Sato-Kosaka	1969	420 000
Bennett	1970	1 680
Kohoutek	1973	75 000
West	1975	500 000
IRAS-Araki-Alcock	1983	*not known*
Hale-Bopp	1995	2 400
Hyakutake	1996	18 000

[1] Kirch also known as Newton.

Annual meteor showers

Meteors appear to radiate from named star region.

Shower	Dates	Maximum activity	Notes
Quadrantids	1–6 Jan	3–4 Jan	swift
Lyrids	19–25 Apr	22 Apr	
Alpha-Scorpiids	20 Apr–19 May	28 Apr–10 May	S Hemisphere
Eta Aquariids	1–8 May	5 May	
Delta Aquariids	15 Jul–10 Aug	28 Jul–5 Aug	S Hemisphere
Perseids	27 Jul–17 Aug	11–14 Aug	very reliable
Orionids	15–25 Oct	21 Oct	
Taurids	25 Oct–25 Nov	4–14 Nov	
Leonids	14–20 Nov	17–18 Nov	
Geminids	8–14 Dec	13–14 Dec	very reliable
Ursids	19–24 Dec	22–23 Dec	

Sun data

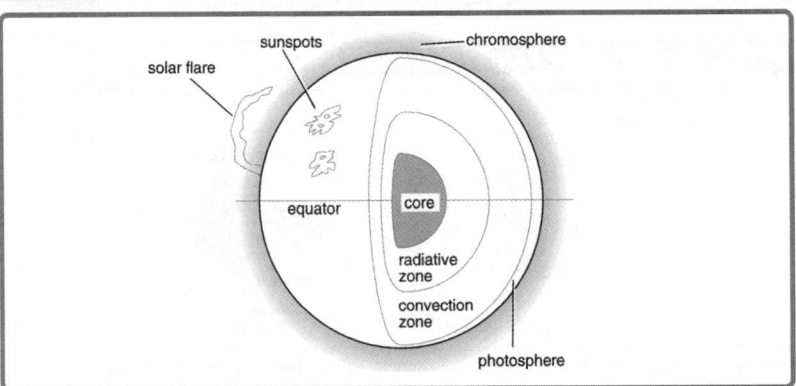

Physical characteristics of the Sun
Diameter 1392530km;   Volume $1.414 \times 10^{18}\,\mathrm{km}^3$;   Mass $1.9891 \times 10^{30}\,\mathrm{kg}$

Density (water = 1)

Mean density of entire Sun	$1.410\mathrm{g\,cm}^{-3}$
Interior (centre of Sun)	$150\mathrm{g\,cm}^{-3}$
Surface (photosphere)	$10^{-3}\mathrm{g\,cm}^{-3}$
Chromosphere	$10^{-6}\mathrm{g\,cm}^{-3}$
Low corona	$1.7 \times 10^{-16}\mathrm{g\,cm}^{-3}$

Temperature

Interior (centre)	15 000 000K
Surface (photosphere)	6 050K
Sunspot umbra (typical)	4 240K
Penumbra (typical)	5 680K
Chromosphere	4 300 to 50 000K
Corona	800 000 to 5 000 000K

Rotation (as seen from Earth)

Of solar equator	26.8 days
At solar latitude 30°	28.2 days
At solar latitude 60°	30.8 days
At solar latitude 75°	31.8 days

Chemical composition of photosphere

Element	% weight
Hydrogen	73.46
Helium	24.85
Oxygen	0.77
Carbon	0.29
Iron	0.16
Neon	0.12
Nitrogen	0.09
Silicon	0.07
Magnesium	0.05
Sulphur	0.04
Other	0.10

Space

Solar system

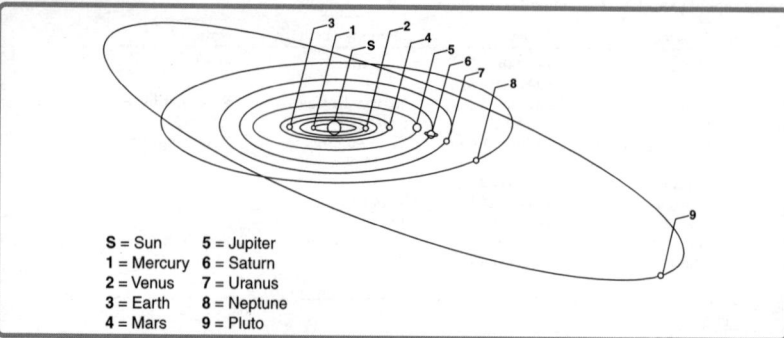

S = Sun	**5** = Jupiter
1 = Mercury	**6** = Saturn
2 = Venus	**7** = Uranus
3 = Earth	**8** = Neptune
4 = Mars	**9** = Pluto

Total and annular solar eclipses 1995–2020

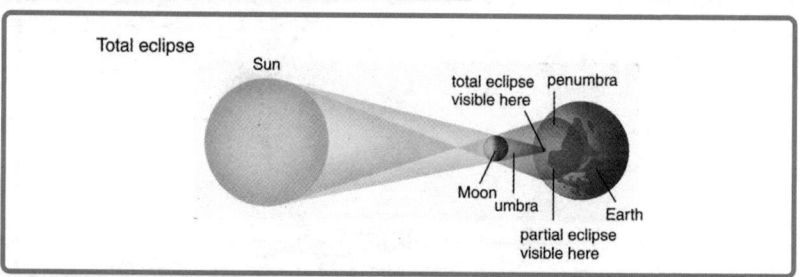

The eclipse begins in the first country named. In an annular eclipse, part of the Sun remains visible.

Date	Type of eclipse	Visibility path
29 Apr 1995	Annular	S Pacific, S America
24 Oct 1995	Total	Middle East, S Asia, S Pacific
9 Mar 1997	Total	C and N Asia, Arctic
26 Feb 1998	Total	Mid-Pacific, C America, N Atlantic
22 Aug 1998	Annular	Indonesia, S Pacific, Indian Ocean
16 Feb 1999	Annular	Indian Ocean, Australia
11 Aug 1999	Total	N Atlantic, N Europe, Middle East, N India
21 Jun 2001	Total	S Atlantic, S Africa, Madagascar
14 Dec 2001	Annular	Pacific, C America
10 Jun 2002	Annular	Indonesia, Pacific, Mexico
4 Dec 2002	Total	S Africa, Indian Ocean, Australia
31 May 2003	Annular	Iceland, Greenland
23 Nov 2003	Total	Antarctic
8 Apr 2005	Annular/Total	Pacific, Panama, Venezuela
3 Oct 2005	Annular	Atlantic, Spain, Libya, Indian Ocean
29 Mar 2006	Total	Atlantic, Libya, Turkey, Russia
22 Sep 2006	Annular	Guyana, Atlantic, Indian Ocean
7 Feb 2008	Annular	Antarctic
1 Aug 2008	Total	Arctic, Siberia, China
26 Jan 2009	Annular	S Atlantic, Indian Ocean, Borneo
22 Jul 2009	Total	India, China, Pacific
15 Jan 2010	Annular	Africa, Indian Ocean, China
11 Jul 2010	Total	Pacific, S Chile
20–21 May 2012	Annular	China, N Pacific, N America
13 Nov 2012	Total	N Australia, Pacific
9–10 May 2013	Annular	Australia, Pacific
3 Nov 2013	Total	Atlantic, C Africa, Ethiopia
20 Mar 2015	Total	N Atlantic, Arctic
9 Mar 2016	Total	Indonesia, Pacific
1 Sep 2016	Annular	Atlantic, Africa, Madagascar, Indian Ocean
26 Feb 2017	Annular	Pacific, S America, Atlantic, Africa
21 Aug 2017	Total	Pacific, N America, Atlantic

Date	Type of eclipse	Visibility path
2 Jul 2019	Total	Pacific, S America
26 Dec 2019	Annular	Middle East, Sri Lanka, Indonesia, Pacific
21 Jun 2020	Annular	Africa, Middle East, China, Pacific
12 Dec 2020	Total	Pacific, S America, Atlantic

Lunar eclipses 1995–2020

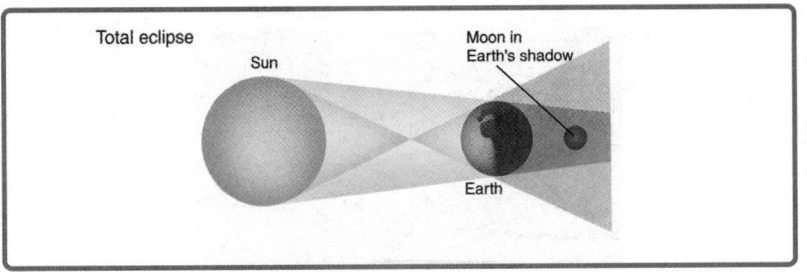

Date	Type of eclipse	Time of mid-eclipse UT[1]	Where visible
15 Apr 1995	Partial	12.19	Pacific, Australia, SE Asia
4 Apr 1996	Total	00.11	Africa, SE Europe, S America
27 Sep 1996	Total	02.55	C and S America, part of N America, W Africa
24 Mar 1997	Partial	04.41	C and S America, part of N America, W Africa
16 Sep 1997	Total	18.47	S Africa, E Africa, Australia
28 Jul 1999	Partial	11.34	Pacific, Australia, SE Asia
21 Jan 2000	Total	04.45	N America, part of S America, SW Europe, W Africa
16 Jul 2000	Total	13.57	Pacific, Australia, SE Asia
9 Jan 2001	Total	20.22	Europe, Asia, Africa
5 Jul 2001	Partial	14.57	Asia, Australia, Pacific
16 May 2003	Total	03.41	Americas, Europe, Africa
9 Nov 2003	Total	01.20	Americas, Europe, Africa, W Asia
4 May 2004	Total	20.32	Europe, Africa, Asia
28 Oct 2004	Total	03.05	Americas, Europe, Africa
17 Oct 2005	Partial	12.05	E Asia, Pacific, N America
7 Sep 2006	Partial	18.53	Australia, Asia, E Africa
3 Mar 2007	Total	23.22	Europe, Asia, Africa
28 Aug 2007	Total	10.39	Australia, Pacific, part of N America
21 Feb 2008	Total	03.27	Americas, Europe, Africa
16 Aug 2008	Partial	21.12	Europe, Asia, W Asia
31 Dec 2009	Partial	19.23	Asia, Africa, Europe
26 Jun 2010	Partial	11.39	Pacific Rim
21 Dec 2010	Total	08.17	N and S America
15 Jun 2011	Total	20.12	Asia, Africa, Europe
10 Dec 2011	Total	14.32	Pacific, Australia, E Asia
4 Jun 2012	Partial	11.03	Pacific, Australasia
25 Apr 2013	Partial	20.09	Asia, Australia, Europe
14 Apr 2014	Total	07.47	N and S America
8 Oct 2014	Total	10.54	Pacific, Australia, W Americas
4 Apr 2015	Partial	12.01	Pacific, Australasia
28 Sep 2015	Total	02.47	Africa, Europe, Americas
7 Aug 2017	Partial	18.21	Asia, Africa, Australia
31 Jan 2018	Total	13.30	Pacific, Australia, Asia
27 Jul 2018	Total	20.22	Asia, Africa, part of Europe
21 Jan 2019	Total	05.12	Americas, part of Europe
16 Jul 2019	Partial	21.31	Asia, Africa, Europe

[1] Universal Time, equivalent to Greenwich Mean Time (GMT).

Space

The lunar 'seas'

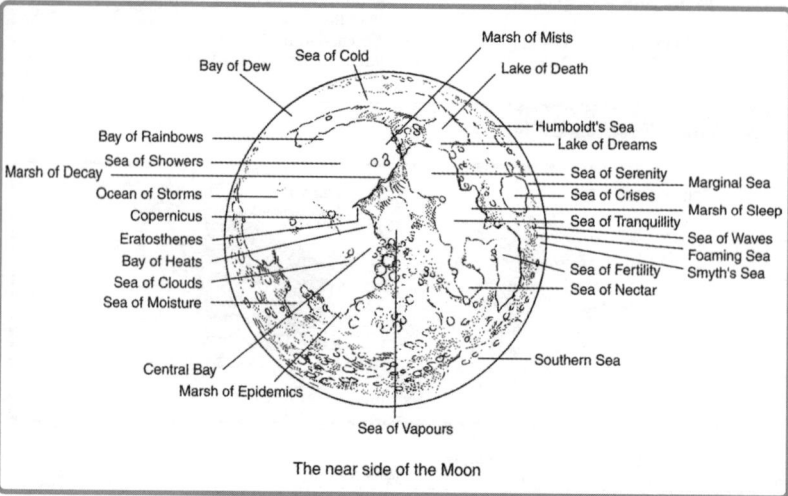

The near side of the Moon

Latin name	English name	Latin name	English name
Lacus Mortis	Lake of Death	Mare Serenitatis	Sea of Serenity
Lacus Somniorum	Lake of Dreams	Mare Smythii	Smyth's Sea
Mare Australe	Southern Sea	Mare Spumans	Foaming Sea
Mare Crisium	Sea of Crises	Mare Tranquillitatis	Sea of Tranquillity
Mare Fecunditatis	Sea of Fertility	Mare Undarum	Sea of Waves
Mare Frigoris	Sea of Cold	Mare Vaporum	Sea of Vapours
Mare Humboldtianum	Humboldt's Sea	Oceanus Procellarum	Ocean of Storms
Mare Humorum	Sea of Moisture	Palus Epidemiarum	Marsh of Epidemics
Mare Imbrium	Sea of Showers	Palus Nebularum	Marsh of Mists
Mare Ingenii[1]	Sea of Geniuses	Palus Putredinis	Marsh of Decay
Mare Marginis	Marginal Sea	Palus Somnii	Marsh of Sleep
Mare Moscoviense[1]	Moscow Sea	Sinus Aestuum	Bay of Heats
Mare Nectaris	Sea of Nectar	Sinus Iridum	Bay of Rainbows
Mare Nubium	Sea of Clouds	Sinus Medii	Central Bay
Mare Orientale[1]	Eastern Sea	Sinus Roris	Bay of Dew

[1] On the far side of the Moon.

Phases of the Moon

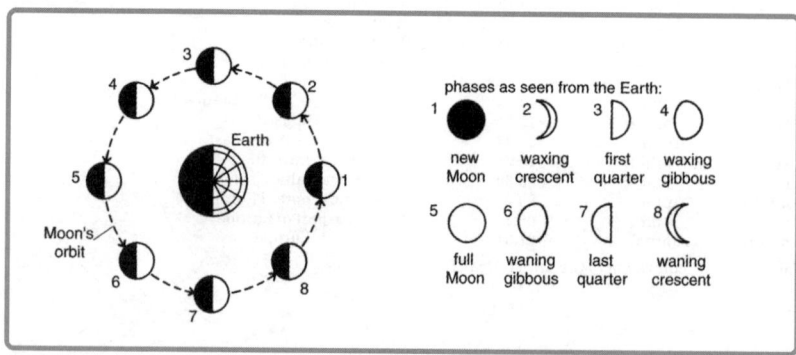

phases as seen from the Earth:

1 new Moon
2 waxing crescent
3 first quarter
4 waxing gibbous
5 full Moon
6 waning gibbous
7 last quarter
8 waning crescent

The constellations

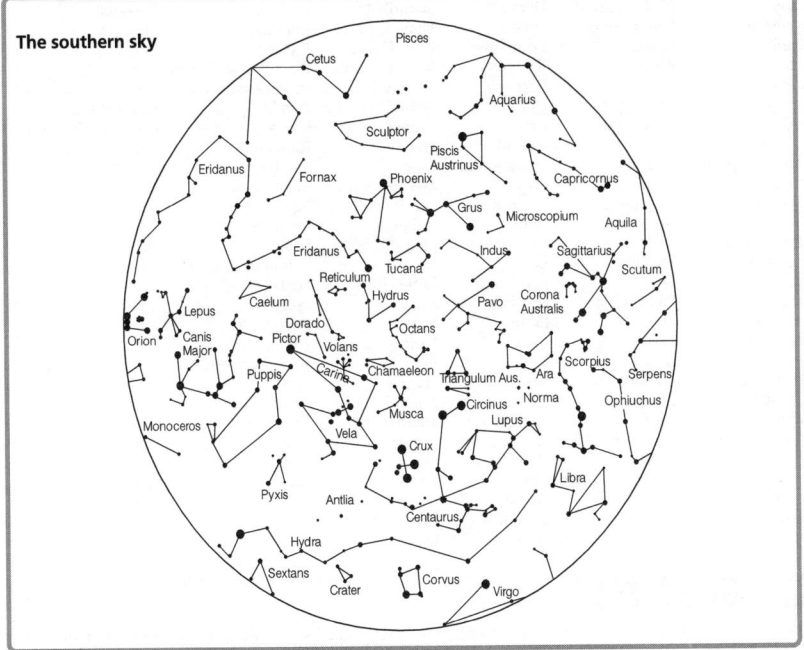

The southern sky

The northern sky

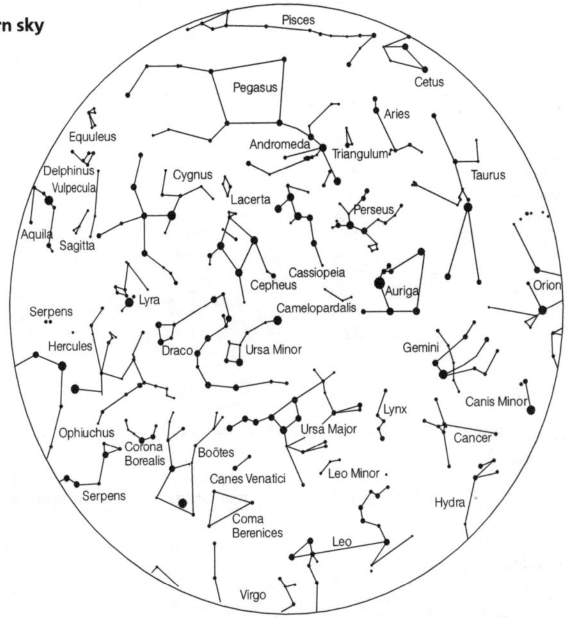

Space

Space

Latin name	English name	Latin name	English name	Latin name	English name
Andromeda	Andromeda	Cygnus	Swan	Pavo	Peacock
Antlia	Air Pump	Delphinus	Dolphin	Pegasus	Winged Horse
Apus	Bird of Paradise	Dorado	Swordfish	Perseus	Perseus
Aquarius	Water Bearer	Draco	Dragon	Phoenix	Phoenix
Aquila	Eagle	Equuleus	Little Horse	Pictor	Easel
Ara	Altar	Eridanus	River Eridanus	Pisces	Fishes
Aries	Ram	Fornax	Furnace	Piscis Austrinus	Southern Fish
Auriga	Charioteer	Gemini	Twins	Puppis	Ship's Stern
Boötes	Herdsman	Grus	Crane	Pyxis	Mariner's Compass
Caelum	Chisel	Hercules	Hercules	Reticulum	Net
Camelopardalis	Giraffe	Horologium	Clock	Sagitta	Arrow
Cancer	Crab	Hydra	Sea Serpent	Sagittarius	Archer
Canes Venatici	Hunting Dogs	Hydrus	Water Snake	Scorpius	Scorpion
Canis Major	Great Dog	Indus	Indian	Sculptor	Sculptor
Canis Minor	Little Dog	Lacerta	Lizard	Scutum	Shield
Capricornus	Sea Goat	Leo	Lion	Serpens	Serpent
Carina	Keel	Leo Minor	Little Lion	Sextans	Sextant
Cassiopeia	Cassiopeia	Lepus	Hare	Taurus	Bull
Centaurus	Centaur	Libra	Scales	Telescopium	Telescope
Cepheus	Cepheus	Lupus	Wolf	Triangulum	Triangle
Cetus	Whale	Lynx	Lynx	Triangulum Australe	Southern Triangle
Chamaeleon	Chameleon	Lyra	Harp	Tucana	Toucan
Circinus	Compasses	Mensa	Table	Ursa Major	Great Bear
Columba	Dove	Microscopium	Microscope	Ursa Minor	Little Bear
Coma Berenices	Berenice's Hair	Monoceros	Unicorn	Vela	Sails
Corona Australis	Southern Crown	Musca	Fly	Virgo	Virgin
Corona Borealis	Northern Crown	Norma	Level	Volans	Flying Fish
Corvus	Crow	Octans	Octant	Vulpecula	Fox
Crater	Cup	Ophiuchus	Serpent Bearer		
Crux	Southern Cross	Orion	Orion		

The 20 brightest stars

The apparent brightness of a star is represented by a number called its magnitude. The larger the number, the fainter the star. The faintest stars visible to the naked eye are slightly fainter than magnitude 6. Only about 6 000 of the billions of stars in the sky are visible to the naked eye.

Star name	Distance (light years)	Apparent magnitude	Absolute magnitude
Sirius A	8.6	−1.46	+1.4
Canopus	98	−0.72	−8.5
Arcturus	36	−0.06	−0.3
Alpha Centauri A	4.3	−0.01	+4.4
Vega	26.5	+0.04	+0.5
Capella	45	+0.05	−0.7
Rigel	900	+0.14	−6.8
Procyon A	11.2	+0.37	+2.6
Betelgeuse	520	+0.41	−5.5
Achernar	118	+0.51	−1.0
Beta Centauri	490	+0.63	−5.1
Altair	16.5	+0.77	+2.2
Aldebaran	68	+0.86	−0.2
Spica	220	+0.91	−3.6
Antares	520	+0.92	−4.5
Pollux	35	+1.16	+0.8
Fomalhaut	22.6	+1.19	+2.0
Deneb	1 500	+1.26	−6.9
Beta Crucis	490	+1.28	−4.6
Alpha Crucis	120	+0.83	−4.0

The 20 nearest stars

Star name	Distance (light years)	Apparent magnitude	Absolute magnitude
Proxima Centauri	4.3	+11.05	+15.5
Alpha Centauri A	4.3	−0.01	+4.4
Alpha Centauri B	4.3	+1.33	+5.7
Barnard's Star	5.9	+9.54	+13.3
Wolf 359	7.6	+13.53	+16.7
Lalande 21185	8.1	+7.50	+10.5
Sirius A	8.6	−1.46	+1.4

Star name	Distance (light years)	Apparent magnitude	Absolute magnitude
Sirius B	8.6	+8.68	+11.6
Luyten 726-8A	8.9	+12.45	+15.3
UV 726-8B	8.9	+12.95	+15.3
Ross 154	9.4	+10.60	+13.3
Ross 248	10.3	+12.29	+14.8
Epsilon Eridani	10.8	+3.73	+6.1
Ross 128	10.8	+11.10	+13.5
Luyten 789-6	10.8	+12.18	+14.6
61 Cygni A	11.1	+5.22	+7.6
61 Cygni B	11.1	+6.03	+8.4
Epsilon Indi	11.2	+4.68	+7.0
Procyon A	11.2	+0.37	+2.7
Procyon B	11.2	+10.70	+13.0

Space

Largest ground-based telescopes

Telescope name	Type	Observatory	Site (altitude m/ft)	Mirror/ dish size	Founded
Anglo-Australian Telescope (AAT)	optical	Anglo-Australian Observatory	Siding Spring Mountain, NSW, Australia (1 165 m/3 820ft)	3.9 m	1974
Arecibo Telescope	radio	National Astronomy and Ionosphere Centre	Puerto Rico (496 m/1 625ft)	304.8 m	1963
Australia Telescope	radio	Commonwealth Scientific and Industrial Research Organization	Throughout NSW, Australia	7 × 22 m, 1 × 64 m	1990
Bol'shoi Teleskop Azimutal'nyi	optical	Special Astrophysical Observatory	Mt Pastukhov, Zelenchukskaya, Russia (2 100 m/6 900ft)	6 m	1976
—	optical	Byurakan Astrophysical Observatory	Mt Aragatz, Armenia (1 500 m/5 000ft)	2.6 m	1976
C Donald Shane Telescope	optical	Lick Observatory	Mt Hamilton, California, USA (1 277 m/4 190ft)	3.05 m	1959
California Submillimetre Observatory	submilli-metre	California Institute of Technology	Mauna Kea, Hawaii, USA (4 160 m/13 650ft)	10.4 m	1986
Canada-France-Hawaii Telescope (CFHT)	optical	Canada-France-Hawaii Telescope Corporation	Mauna Kea, Hawaii, USA (4 180 m/13 720ft)	3.6 m	1979
—	optical	Cerro Tololo Inter-American Observatory	Cerro Tololo, Chile (2 160 m/7 100ft)	4 m	1976
Effelsberg Radio Telescope	radio	Max Planck Institut für Radioastronomie	Effelsberg, nr Bonn, Germany	100 m	1971
ESO New Technology Telescope,	optical	European Southern Observatory	Cerro Tololo, Chile (2 160 m/7 100ft)	3.6 m	1990
ESO 3.6 m	optical	European Southern Observatory	Cerro La Silla, Chile (2 400 m/7 850ft)	3.6 m	1976
—	radio	Five College Radio Astronomy	New Salem, Massachusetts, USA	14 m	1969
Gemini North Telescope, Gemini South Telescope	optical/ infrared	various	Mauna Kea, Hawaii, USA (4 160 m/13 650ft), Cerro Pachón, Chile (2 715 m/8 907ft)	2 × 8.1m	1999
George Ellery Hale Telescope	optical	Palomar Observatory	Palomar Mountain, California, USA (1 700 m/5 600ft)	5.08 m	1948
—	optical	German-Spanish Astronomical Centre	Calar Alto, Spain (2 160 m/7 100ft)	3.5 m	1985
Harlan J Smith Telescope	optical	McDonald Observatory	Mt Locke, Texas, USA (2 070 m/6 791ft)	2.7 m	1968
Hobby-Eberly Telescope	optical	McDonald Observatory	Mt Fowlkes, Texas, USA (2100m/6 900ft)	11 m	1997
Irénée du Pont Telescope	optical	Mt Wilson and Las Campanas Observatories	Cerro Las Campanas, Chile (2 510 m/8 235ft)	2.57 m	1977

Telescope name	Type	Observatory	Site (altitude m/ft)	Mirror/ dish size	Founded
IRAM Array	milli-metre	Institut de Radio Astronomie Millimétrique	Plateau de Bure, France (2 552 m/8 373ft)	4 × 15 m	1979
Isaac Newton Telescope	optical	Observatory Roque de los Muchachos	La Palma, Canary Is (2 336 m/7 660ft)	2.54 m	1984
James Clerk Maxwell Telescope (JCMT)	submilli-metre	Royal Observatory, Edinburgh	Mauna Kea, Hawaii, USA (4 160 m/13 650ft)	15 m	1987
Keck Telescope	optical/ infrared	California Association for Research and Astronomy (CARA)	Mauna Kea, Hawaii, USA (4 160 m/13 650ft)	2 × 10 m	1990
Lovell Telescope	radio	Nuffield Radio Astronomy Laboratory (Jodrell Bank), University of Manchester	Jodrell Bank, Cheshire, UK	76 m	1957
MERLIN (Multi-Element Radio-Linked Interferometer Network)	radio	Nuffield Radio Astronomy Laboratory (Jodrell Bank), University of Manchester	UK (Midlands and Wales)	5 × 25 m, 1 × 32 m, 1 × 76 m	1980
Multiple Mirror Telescope	optical	Whipple Observatory	Mt Hopkins, Arizona, USA (2 606 m/8 550ft)	6.5 m	1979
NASA Infrared Telescope Facility (IRTF)	infrared	NASA	Mauna Kea, Hawaii, USA (4 160 m/13 650ft)	3 m	1979
—	milli-metre	National Radio Astronomy Observatory (NRAO)	Kitt Peak, Arizona, USA (1 920 m/6 300ft)	12 m	1982
Nicholas U Mayall Telescope	optical	Kitt Peak National Observatory	Kitt Peak, Arizona, USA (2 100 m/6 900ft)	4 m	1973
Nobeyama Millimetre Array	milli-metre	Nobeyama Radio Observatory	Nobeyama, Japan (1 300 m/4 265ft)	5 × 10 m	1986
Nobeyama Radio Telescope	radio	Nobeyama Radio Observatory	Nobeyama, Japan (1 300 m/4 265ft)	45 m	1970
Parkes Radio Telescope	radio	Australian National Radio Observatory	Nr Parkes, NSW, Australia (392 m/1 285ft)	64 m	1961
Shajin Telescope	optical	Crimean Astrophysical Observatory	Simeis, Ukraine (680 m/2 230ft)	2.6 m	1961
Subaru Telescope	optical/ infrared	National Astronomical Observatory of Japan	Mauna Kea, Hawaii, USA (4 160 m/13 650ft)	8 m	1999
Swedish/European Submillimetre Telescope	submilli-metre	European Southern Observatory	Cerro Tololo, Chile (2 160 m/7 100ft)	10 m	1987
United Kingdom Infrared Telescope (UKIRT)	infrared	Royal Observatory, Edinburgh	Mauna Kea, Hawaii, USA (4 180 m/13 720ft)	3.8 m	1979
Very Large Array (VLA)	radio	National Radio Astronomy Observatories	Socorro, New Mexico, USA	27 × 25 m	1980–1
William Herschel Telescope	optical	Observatory Roque de los Muchachos	La Palma, Canary Is (2 332 m/7 650ft)	4.2 m	1987

Significant space missions

Mission	Nation/ Agency	Launch date	Event description
Sputnik 1	USSR	4 Oct 57	Earth satellite
Sputnik 2	USSR	3 Nov 57	Dog Laika
Explorer 1	USA	1 Feb 58	Discovered radiation belt (Van Allen)
Luna 1	USSR	2 Jan 59	Escaped Earth gravity
Vanguard 2	USA	17 Feb 59	Earth photo
Luna 2	USSR	12 Sept 59	Lunar impact
Luna 3	USSR	4 Oct 59	Lunar photo (far side)
TIROS 1	USA	1 Apr 60	Weather satellite
Transit 1B	USA	13 Apr 60	Navigation satellite
ECHO 1	USA	12 Aug 60	Communications satellite
Sputnik 5	USSR	19 Aug 60	Two dogs recovered alive
Vostok 1	USSR	12 Apr 61	Manned orbital flight
Mariner 2	USA	26 Aug 62	Venus flyby
Vostok 6	USSR	16 Jun 63	Woman in orbit

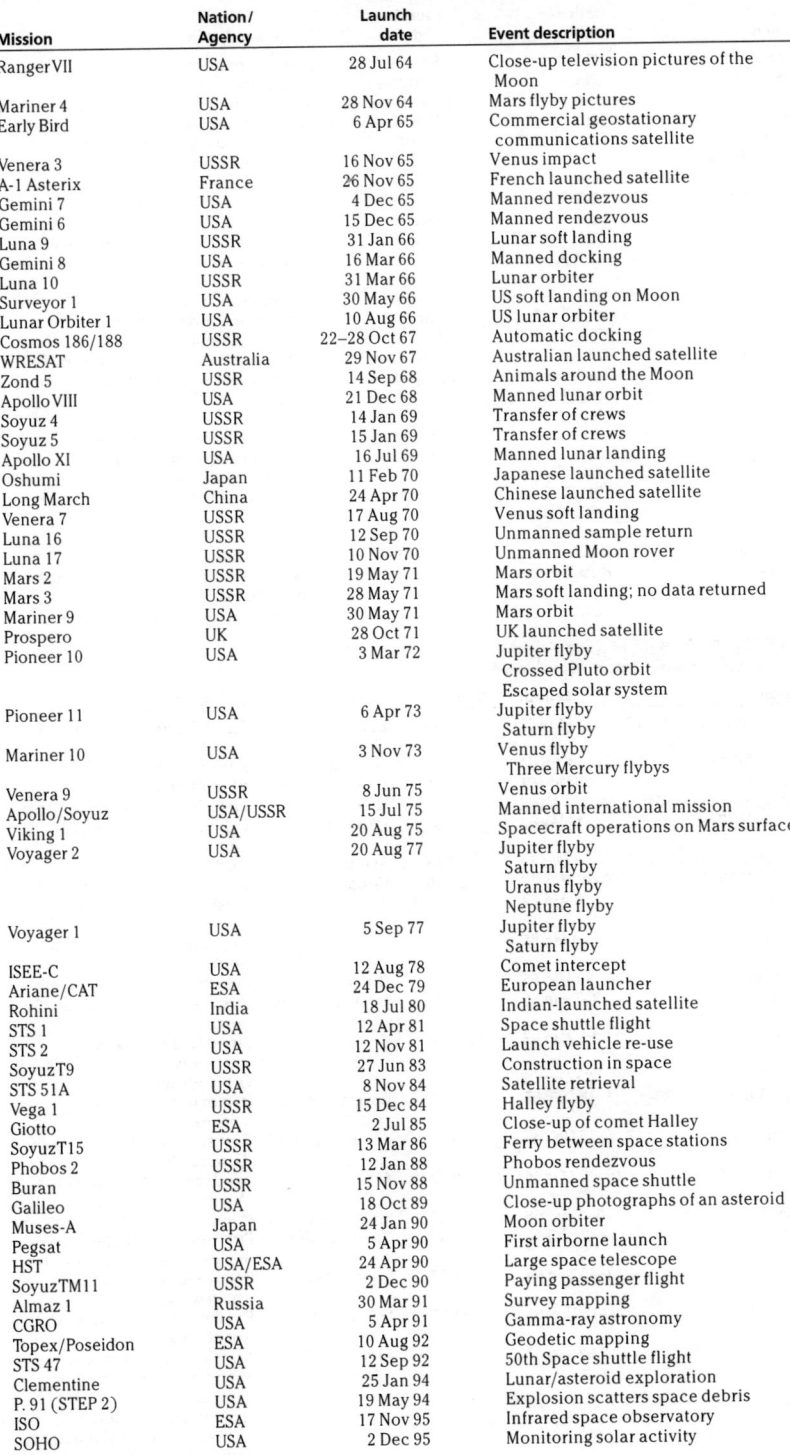

Mission	Nation/ Agency	Launch date	Event description
Ranger VII	USA	28 Jul 64	Close-up television pictures of the Moon
Mariner 4	USA	28 Nov 64	Mars flyby pictures
Early Bird	USA	6 Apr 65	Commercial geostationary communications satellite
Venera 3	USSR	16 Nov 65	Venus impact
A-1 Asterix	France	26 Nov 65	French launched satellite
Gemini 7	USA	4 Dec 65	Manned rendezvous
Gemini 6	USA	15 Dec 65	Manned rendezvous
Luna 9	USSR	31 Jan 66	Lunar soft landing
Gemini 8	USA	16 Mar 66	Manned docking
Luna 10	USSR	31 Mar 66	Lunar orbiter
Surveyor 1	USA	30 May 66	US soft landing on Moon
Lunar Orbiter 1	USA	10 Aug 66	US lunar orbiter
Cosmos 186/188	USSR	22–28 Oct 67	Automatic docking
WRESAT	Australia	29 Nov 67	Australian launched satellite
Zond 5	USSR	14 Sep 68	Animals around the Moon
Apollo VIII	USA	21 Dec 68	Manned lunar orbit
Soyuz 4	USSR	14 Jan 69	Transfer of crews
Soyuz 5	USSR	15 Jan 69	Transfer of crews
Apollo XI	USA	16 Jul 69	Manned lunar landing
Oshumi	Japan	11 Feb 70	Japanese launched satellite
Long March	China	24 Apr 70	Chinese launched satellite
Venera 7	USSR	17 Aug 70	Venus soft landing
Luna 16	USSR	12 Sep 70	Unmanned sample return
Luna 17	USSR	10 Nov 70	Unmanned Moon rover
Mars 2	USSR	19 May 71	Mars orbit
Mars 3	USSR	28 May 71	Mars soft landing; no data returned
Mariner 9	USA	30 May 71	Mars orbit
Prospero	UK	28 Oct 71	UK launched satellite
Pioneer 10	USA	3 Mar 72	Jupiter flyby Crossed Pluto orbit Escaped solar system
Pioneer 11	USA	6 Apr 73	Jupiter flyby Saturn flyby
Mariner 10	USA	3 Nov 73	Venus flyby Three Mercury flybys
Venera 9	USSR	8 Jun 75	Venus orbit
Apollo/Soyuz	USA/USSR	15 Jul 75	Manned international mission
Viking 1	USA	20 Aug 75	Spacecraft operations on Mars surface
Voyager 2	USA	20 Aug 77	Jupiter flyby Saturn flyby Uranus flyby Neptune flyby
Voyager 1	USA	5 Sep 77	Jupiter flyby Saturn flyby
ISEE-C	USA	12 Aug 78	Comet intercept
Ariane/CAT	ESA	24 Dec 79	European launcher
Rohini	India	18 Jul 80	Indian-launched satellite
STS 1	USA	12 Apr 81	Space shuttle flight
STS 2	USA	12 Nov 81	Launch vehicle re-use
Soyuz T9	USSR	27 Jun 83	Construction in space
STS 51A	USA	8 Nov 84	Satellite retrieval
Vega 1	USSR	15 Dec 84	Halley flyby
Giotto	ESA	2 Jul 85	Close-up of comet Halley
Soyuz T15	USSR	13 Mar 86	Ferry between space stations
Phobos 2	USSR	12 Jan 88	Phobos rendezvous
Buran	USSR	15 Nov 88	Unmanned space shuttle
Galileo	USA	18 Oct 89	Close-up photographs of an asteroid
Muses-A	Japan	24 Jan 90	Moon orbiter
Pegsat	USA	5 Apr 90	First airborne launch
HST	USA/ESA	24 Apr 90	Large space telescope
Soyuz TM11	USSR	2 Dec 90	Paying passenger flight
Almaz 1	Russia	30 Mar 91	Survey mapping
CGRO	USA	5 Apr 91	Gamma-ray astronomy
Topex/Poseidon	ESA	10 Aug 92	Geodetic mapping
STS 47	USA	12 Sep 92	50th Space shuttle flight
Clementine	USA	25 Jan 94	Lunar/asteroid exploration
P. 91 (STEP 2)	USA	19 May 94	Explosion scatters space debris
ISO	ESA	17 Nov 95	Infrared space observatory
SOHO	USA	2 Dec 95	Monitoring solar activity

Space

Mission	Nation/ Agency	Launch date	Event description
NEAR	USA	17 Feb 96	Asteroid rendezvous
MGS	USA	7 Nov 96	Mars global survey
MPF	USA	4 Dec 96	Mars Pathfinder explored surface
Haruka	Japan	12 Feb 97	Radio astronomy
Iridium	USA	5 May 97	Communication constellation
Cassini/Huygens	USA	15 Oct 97	Saturn/Titan study in 2004
Lunar Prospector	USA	6 Jan 98	Lunar surface investigation
Deep Space 1	USA	24 Oct 98	Ion propulsion spacecraft
STS 95	USA	29 Oct 98	John Glenn's return to space
Zarya	USA/Russia/ ESA/Canada/ Japan	20 Nov 98	First launch in International Space Station assembly
MCO	USA	11 Dec 98	Mars climate survey
MPL	USA	3 Jan 99	Mars surface investigation
Stardust	USA	7 Feb 99	Capture and analysis of comet particles
Shenzhou	China	22 Nov 99	China launches manned spacecraft
Zvezda	USA/Russia/ ESA/Canada/ Japan	12 Jul 00	International Space Station command module
Cluster II	ESA	16 Jul 00	Earth's magnetosphere survey
Cluster II	ESA	9 Aug 00	Earth's magnetosphere survey
STS 92	USA	11 Oct 00	100th Space shuttle flight
Expedition 1	USA/Russia/ ESA/Canada/ Japan	31 Oct 00	First residents of International Space Station
Progress M1	Russia	24 Jan 01	Bringing Mir back to earth
Soyuz TM32	Russia	28 Apr 01	First space tourist goes to International Space Station
STS109	USA	1 Mar 02	Hubble space telescope overhaul

NASA launches (Crew-related)

Mission	Launch	Duration[1]	Crew	Comment
Mercury MR3 (Freedom 7)	5 May 61	0:15	Shepard	First US manned suborbital flight
Mercury MR4 (Liberty Bell 7)	21 Jul 61	0:16	Grissom	Suborbital flight
Mercury MA5	29 Nov 61	3:16	Enos	Chimpanzee
Mercury MA6 (Friendship 7)	20 Feb 62	4:55	Glenn	First US manned orbital flight
Mercury MA7 (Aurora 7)	24 May 62	4:56	Carpenter	Orbital flight; manual re-entry
Mercury MA8 (Sigma 7)	3 Oct 62	9:13	Schirra	6 orbits
Mercury MA9 (Faith 7)	15–16 May 62	34:20	Cooper	22 orbits; last Mercury flight
Gemini I	8 Apr 64			Test of launch vehicle compatability
Gemini II	19 Jan 65			Unmanned suborbital test flight
Gemini III	23 Mar 65	4:53	Grissom/Young	First manned Gemini flight
Gemini IV	3–7 Jun 65	97:56	McDivitt/White	First spacewalk (by White, 36 min)
Gemini V	21–29 Aug 65	190:56	Cooper/Conrad	Simulated rendezvous manoeuvres
Gemini VI	25 Oct 65			Orbit not achieved
Gemini VII	4–18 Dec 65	330:35	Borman/Lovell	Part of mission without spacesuits
Gemini VII-A	15–16 Dec 65	25:51	Schirra/Stafford	First space rendezvous (with Gemini VII)
Gemini VIII	16–17 Mar 66	10:42	Armstrong/Scott	Rendezvous/docking with Agena target vehicle
Gemini IX-A	3–6 Jun 66	72:21	Stafford/Cernan	Docking not achieved
Gemini X	18–21 Jul 66	70:47	Young/Collins	First docked vehicle manoeuvres and spacewalks
Gemini XI	12–15 Sep 66	71:17	Conrad/Gordon	Rendezvous/docking and spacewalks
Gemini XII	11–15 Nov 66	94:35	Lovell/Aldrin	Rendezvous/docking and spacewalks
Apollo I	27 Jan 67		Grissom/White/ Chaffee	Astronauts killed in command module in fire at launch site
Apollo IV	9 Nov 67			First launch by Saturn V rocket; successful launch of unmanned module

Mission	Launch	Duration[1]	Crew	Comment
Apollo V	22–24 Jan 68			Flight test of lunar module in Earth orbit
Apollo VII	11–22 Oct 68	260:09	Schirra/Eisele/ Cunningham	First manned Apollo flight in Earth orbit
Apollo VIII	21–27 Dec 68	147:01	Borman/Lovell/ Anders	First manned orbit of Moon (10 orbits)
Apollo IX	3–13 Mar 69	241:01	McDivitt/Scott/ Schweickart	First manned lunar module flight in Earth orbit
Apollo X	18–26 May 69	192:03	Stafford/Young/ Cernan	First lunar module orbit of Moon
Apollo XI	16–24 Jul 69	195:18	Armstrong[2]/ Aldrin[2]/Collins	First men on Moon, 20 Jul, Sea of Tranquillity
Apollo XII	14–24 Nov 69	244:36	Conrad[2]/ Bean[2]/Gordon	Moon landing, 19 Nov, Ocean of Storms
Apollo XIII	11–17 Apr 70	142:54	Lovell/Swigert/ Haise	Mission aborted, ruptured oxygen tank
Apollo XIV	31 Jan–9 Feb 71	216:02	Shepard[2]/ Mitchell[2]/Roosa	Moon landing, 5 Feb, Fra Mauro area
Apollo XV	26 Jul–7 Aug 71	295:12	Scott[2]/Irwin[2]/ Worden	Moon landing, 30 Jul, Hadley Rille; Lunar Roving Vehicle used
Apollo XVI	16–27 Apr 72	265:51	Young[2]/Duke[2]/ Mattingly	Moon landing, 20 Apr, Descartes
Apollo XVII	7–19 Dec 72	301:52	Cernan[2]/ Schmitt[2]/Evans	Longest Apollo mission, 11 Dec, Taurus-Littrow
Skylab 1	14 May 73		Unmanned space station	Launched unmanned, uncontrolled re-entry 1979
Skylab 2	25 May 73	672:50	Conrad/Kerwin/ Weitz	Repairs in orbit, duration record (28 days)
Skylab 3	28 Jul 73	1427:09	Bean/Garriott/ Lousma	New duration record (59 days)
Skylab 4	16 Nov 73	2017:15	Carr/Gibson/ Pogue	Final visit (84 days)
Apollo–Soyuz Test Project	15–24 Jul 75	217:28	Stafford/Brand/ Slayton	Rendezvous/docking with Soyuz 19 (▸ p15)

[1] (h:min).

[2] Astronauts who landed on the Moon; the remaining astronaut was the pilot of the command module.

Shuttle flights 1992–2002

Flight/Name	Launch	Landing	Commander/Pilot/ Number of other crew	Payload
STS 42 (D)	22 Jan 92	30 Jan 92	Grabe/Oswald/5	International microgravity laboratory[1]
STS 45 (A)	24 Mar 92	2 Apr 92	Bolden/Duffy/5	ATLAS[1] (Earth observation)
STS 49 (E)	7 May 92	16 May 92	Brandenstein/Chilton/5	Satellite reorientation
STS 50 (C)	25 Jun 92	9 Jul 92	Richards/Bowersox/5	Spacelab USML 1
STS 46 (A)	31 Jul 92	8 Aug 92	Shriver/Allen/5	Eureca, TSS 1
STS 47 (E)	12 Sep 92	20 Sep 92	Gibson/Brown/5	Spacelab
STS 52 (C)	22 Oct 92	1 Nov 92	Wetherbee/Baker/4	Lageos 2
STS 53 (D)	2 Dec 92	9 Dec 92	Walker/Cabana/3	USA 87, ODERACS
STS 54 (E)	13 Jan 93	19 Jan 93	Casper/McMonagle/3	TDRS-6
STS 56 (D)	8 Apr 93	17 Apr 93	Cameron/Oswald/3	ATLAS 2, Spartan 201
STS 55 (C)	26 Apr 93	6 May 93	Nagel/Henricks/5	Spacelab D2
STS 57 (E)	21 Jun 93	1 Jul 93	Grabe/Duffy/4	Spacehab, Eureca retrieval
STS 51 (D)	12 Sep 93	22 Sep 93	Culbertson/Readdy/3	ACTS, Orfeus-SPAS
STS 58 (C)	18 Oct 93	1 Nov 93	Blaha/Searfoss/5	Spacelab Life Sciences 2
STS 61 (E)	2 Dec 93	13 Dec 93	Covey/Bowersox/5	Hubble Telescope refurbishment
STS 60 (D)	3 Feb 94	11 Feb 94	Bolden/Reightler/4	Spacehab 2, WSF, Bremsat, ODERACS
STS 62 (C)	4 Mar 94	18 Mar 94	Casper/Allen/3	OAST 2, USMP 2
STS 59 (E)	9 Apr 94	20 Apr 94	Gutierrez/Chilton/4	SRL 1
STS 65 (C)	8 Jul 94	23 Jul 94	Cabana/Halsell/5	Spacelab IML-2
STS 64 (D)	9 Sep 94	20 Sep 94	Richards/Hammond/4	Spartan 201, SAFER, LITE
STS 68 (E)	30 Sep 94	11 Oct 94	Baker/Wilcutt/4	SRL 2
STS 66 (A)	3 Nov 94	14 Nov 94	McMonagle/Brown/4	Atlas, CRISTA-SPAS

Space

Flight/Name	Launch	Landing	Commander/Pilot/ Number of other crew	Payload
STS 63 (D)	3 Feb 95	11 Feb 95	Wetherbee/Collins/4	Spartan, Spacehab, MIR formation
STS 67 (E)	2 Mar 95	18 Mar 95	Oswald/Gregory/5	Astro 2
STS 71 (A)	27 Jun 95	7 Jul 95	Gibson/Precourt/5-6	MIR docking, Spacelab
STS 70 (D)	13 Jul 95	22 Jul 95	Henricks/Kregel/3	TDRS-7
STS 69 (E)	7 Sep 95	18 Sep 95	Walker/Cockrell/3	Spartan, Wake Shield Facility 2
STS 73 (C)	20 Oct 95	5 Nov 95	Bowersox/Rominger/5	Spacelab, USML 2
STS 74 (A)	12 Nov 95	20 Nov 95	Cameron/Halsell/3	MIR docking
STS 72 (E)	11 Jan 96	20 Jan 96	Duffy/Jett/4	Spartan 206, OAST, SFU retrieval
STS 75 (C)	22 Feb 96	9 Mar 96	Allen/Horowitz/5	USMP 3, TSS 1R
STS 76 (A)	22 Mar 96	31 Mar 96	Chilton/Searfoss/4	MIR docking
STS 77 (E)	19 May 96	29 May 96	Casper/Brown/4	Spacehab, Spartan 207
STS 78 (C)	20 Jun 96	7 Jul 96	Henricks/Kregel/5	LMS 1, Spacelab
STS 79 (A)	16 Sep 96	26 Sep 96	Readdy/Wilcutt/4	MIR docking, Spacehab
STS 80 (C)	19 Nov 96	7 Dec 96	Cockrell/Rominger/3	Wake Shield 3, Orfeus-SPAS
STS 81 (A)	12 Jan 97	22 Jan 97	Baker/Jett/4	MIR docking
STS 82 (D)	11 Feb 97	21 Feb 97	Bowersox/Horowitz/5	Hubble Telescope refurbishment
STS 83 (C)	4 Apr 97	8 Apr 97	Halsell/Still/5	Microgravity Science Lab-1
STS 84 (A)	15 May 97	24 May 97	Precourt/Collins/5	MIR docking
STS 94 (C)	1 Jul 97	17 Jul 97	Halsell/Still/5	Microgravity Science Lab-1 reflight
STS 85 (D)	7 Aug 97	19 Aug 97	Brown/Rominger/4	MPESS, CRISTA-SPAS
STS 86 (A)	26 Sep 97	6 Oct 97	Wetherbee/Bloomfield/5	MIR docking
STS 87 (C)	19 Nov 97	5 Dec 97	Kregel/Lindsey/4	Spartan 201/USMP 4
STS 89 (E)	22 Jan 98	31 Jan 98	Wilcutt/Edwards/5	MIR docking
STS 90 (C)	17 Apr 98	3 May 98	Searfoss/Altman/5	Neurolab, GAS
STS 91 (D)	2 Jun 98	12 Jun 98	Precourt/Pudwill/Gorie/4	MIR docking, Spacehab
STS 95 (D)	29 Oct 98	7 Nov 98	Brown/Lindsey/5	Spacehab, Spartan 201
STS 88 (E)	4 Dec 98	15 Dec 98	Cabana/Sturckow/4	International Space Station assembly
STS 96 (D)	27 May 99	6 Jun 99	Rominger/Husband/5	International Space Station assembly
STS 93 (C)	23 Jul 99	27 Jul 99	Collins/Ashby/3	AXAF, MSX
STS 103 (D)	19 Dec 99	27 Dec 99	Brown/Kelly/5	Hubble servicing
STS 99 (E)	11 Feb 00	22 Feb 00	Kregell/Pudwill/Gorie/4	SRTM, EarthKAM
STS 101 (A)	19 May 00	29 May 00	Halsell/Horowitz/5	International Space Station assembly
STS 106 (A)	8 Sep 00	19 Sep 00	Wilcutt/Altman/5	International Space Station assembly
STS 92 (D)	11 Oct 00	24 Oct 00	Duffy/Melroy/5	International Space Station assembly
STS 97 (E)	30 Nov 00	11 Dec 00	Jett/Bloomfield/3	International Space Station assembly
STS 98 (A)	7 Feb 01	20 Feb 01	Cockrell/Polansky/3	International Space Station assembly
STS 102 (D)	8 Mar 01	21 Mar 01	Wetherbee/Kelly/5	International Space Station crew exchange
STS 100 (E)	19 Apr 01	1 May 01	Rominger/Ashby/5	International Space Station assembly
STS 104 (A)	12 Jul 01	24 Jul 01	Lindsey/Hobaugh/3	International Space Station assembly
STS 105 (D)	10 Aug 01	22 Aug 01	Horawitz/Sturckow/2	International Space Station crew exchange
STS 108 (E)	5 Dec 01	17 Dec 01	Gorie/Kelly/5	International Space Station crew exchange
STS 109 (C)	1 Mar 02	12 Mar 02	Altman/Carey/5	Hubble servicing
STS 110 (A)	8 Apr 02	19 Apr 02	Bloomfield/Frick/5	International Space Station assembly
STS 111 (E)	5 Jun 02	19 Jun 02	Cockrell/Lockhart/2	International Space Station crew exchange
STS 112 (A)	7 Oct 02	16 Oct 02	Ashby/Melroy/4	International Space Station assembly
STS 113 (E)	23 Nov 02	7 Dec 02	Wetherbee/Lockhart/5	International Space Station crew exchange

A: Atlantis Ch: Challenger C: Columbia D: Discovery E: Endeavour
[1] Not separated from shuttle.

Major Russian launches (Crew-related)[1]

Mission	Launch	Duration[2]	Crew	Comment
Vostok 1	12 Apr 61	01:48	Gagarin	First space flight (1 orbit)
Vostok 2	6 Aug 61	25:18	Titov	Day-long mission
Vostok 3	11 Aug 62	94:22	Nikolayev	First dual mission
Vostok 4	12 Aug 62	71:00	Popovich	First dual mission
Vostok 6	16 Jun 63	70:50	Tereshkova	First woman in space
Voshkod 1	12 Oct 64	24:17	Komarov/Feoktistov/ Yegorov	Three man flight
Voshkod 2	18 Mar 65	26:02	Belyayev/Leonov	First spacewalk (EVA)
Soyuz 1	23 Apr 67	27:00	Komarov	Cosmonaut killed on re-entry
Soyuz 4	14 Jan 69	71:14	Shatalov	Khrunov and Yeliseyev transferred from Soyuz 5
Soyuz 5	15 Jan 69	72:46	Volynov/Khrunov/ Yeliseyev	Docked with Soyuz 4
Soyuz 10	22 Apr 71	48:00	Shatalov/Yeliseyev/ Rukavishnikov	Docked with Salyut 1 space station but did not enter for undisclosed reason
Soyuz 11	6 Jun 71	23 days	Dobrovolsky/Volkov/ Patsayev	Docked with Salyut 1; crew killed on re-entry
Salyut 3	25 Jun 74	214 days	Soyuz 14	Operational military space station
Soyuz 14	4 Jul 74	16 days	Popovich/Artyukhin	Docked with Salyut 3
Salyut 4	26 Dec 74	769 days	Soyuz 17/Soyuz 18/Soyuz 20	Space station; re-entered 2 Feb 77
Soyuz 17	9 Jan 75	30 days	Gubarev/Grechko	Docked with Salyut 4
Soyuz 19 (Apollo–Soyuz Test Project)	15 Jul 75	6 days	Kubasov/Leonov	First international space mission with USA; crew transfer
Salyut 5	22 Jun 76	412 days	Soyuz 21/Soyuz 24	Space station; re-entered 8 Aug 77
Soyuz 21	6 Jul 76	49 days	Volynov/Zholobov	Docked with Salyut 5
Soyuz 23	14 Oct 76	2 days	Zudov/Rozhdestivensky	Attempted docking with Salyut 5
Soyuz 24	7 Feb 77	18 days	Gorbatko/Glazkov	Docked with Salyut 5
Salyut 6	29 Sep 77	1 764 days	Soyuz 25 through Soyuz 40	Space station; re-entered 29 Jul 82
Soyuz 26	10 Dec 77	96 days	Romanenko/Grechko	First prime crew Salyut 6; broke endurance record
Soyuz 27	10 Jan 78	65 days	Dzhanibekov/Makarov	First visiting crew to Salyut 6
Soyuz 28	2 Mar 78	8 days	Gubarev/Remek	Second visiting crew to Salyut 6
Soyuz 29	15 Jun 78	140 days	Kovalenok/Ivanchenko	Second prime crew of Salyut 6
Soyuz 32	25 Feb 79	108 days	Lyakhov/Ryumin	Third prime crew of Salyut 6; broke endurance record
SoyuzT1	16 Dec 79	100 days		Redesigned Soyuz craft
SoyuzT4	12 Mar 81	75 days	Kovalenok/Savinykh	Last prime crew of Salyut 6
Soyuz 39	22 Mar 81	8 days	Dzhanibekov/Gurragcha	Mongolian cosmonaut
Soyuz 40	14 May 81	8 days	Popov/Prunariu	Last visiting crew to Salyut 6
Salyut 7	19 Apr 82	9 years	Soyuz T5 through Soyuz T15	Space station; re-entered 7 Feb 91
SoyuzT5	14 May 82	106 days	Berezovoy/Ledebev	Crew broke endurance record
SoyuzT7	19 Aug 82	113 days	Popov/Serebrov/Savitskaya	Savitskaya, second woman in space
SoyuzT9	27 Jun 83	149 days	Lyakhov/Alexandrov	Docked with Salyut 7
SoyuzT10-1	27 Sep 83		Titov/Strekalov	Exploded on launch pad; crew safe
SoyuzT10	8 Feb 84	263 days	Kizim/Solovyov/Atkov	Crew broke endurance record
SoyuzT12	17 Jul 84	12 days	Dzhanibekov/Savitskaya/Volk	Docked with Salyut 7; first female EVA
SoyuzT14	17 Sep 85	65 days	Vasyutin/Volkov/Grechko	Docked with Salyut 7; mission terminated when Vasyutin fell ill
MIR 1	19 Feb 86	Projected 13 years	Soyuz T15 onwards	Space station; designed for orbit; modular construction
SoyuzT15	13 Mar 86	125 days	Kizim/Solovyov	Docked with both MIR and Salyut 7
SoyuzTM1	21 May 86	9 days		Redesigned Soyuz T craft

Space

Mission	Launch	Duration[2]	Crew	Comment
Kvant 1	31 Mar 87	in orbit		Astrophysical module attached to MIR
SoyuzTM3	22 Jul 87	160 days	Viktorenko/Alexandrov/Faris	Docked with MIR
SoyuzTM4	21 Dec 87	179 days	Titov/Manarov/Levchenko	Docked with MIR; Titov and Manarov completed 365-day flight
Kvant 2	26 Nov 89	in orbit		Module attached to MIR on 6 Dec 89
Kristall	31 May 90	in orbit		Material processing module added to MIR
SoyuzTM11	2 Dec 90	175 days	Afanasyev/Manarov/Akiyama	Docked with MIR; Japanese journalist on board
SoyuzTM12	18 May 91	311 days	Artsebarsky/Krikalev/Sharman	Docked with MIR; first British cosmonaut
SoyuzTM13	2 Oct 91	175 days	Volkov/Aubakirov/ Vietiboeck (Austria)	Docked with MIR; partial crew rotation (Artsebarsky down)
SoyuzTM14	17 Mar 92	146 days	Viktorenko/Kaleri/Flade (Germany)	Docked with MIR; crew rotation (Volkov, Krikalev down)
SoyuzTM15	27 Jul 92	189 days	A Solovyov/Avdeyev	[3]
SoyuzTM16	24 Jan 93	179 days	Manakov/Poleshchuk	[3]
SoyuzTM17	1 Jul 93	197 days	Tsibliev/Serebrov	[3]
SoyuzTM18	8 Jan 94	182 days	Afanasyev/Usachyov/ Polyakov	[3]
SoyuzTM19	1 Jul 94	126 days	Malenchenko/Musabayev	[3]
SoyuzTM20	3 Oct 94	170 days	Viktorenko/Kondakova/ Merbold	[3]
SoyuzTM21	14 Mar 95	181 days	Dezhurov/Strekalov/Thagard	[3]
Spektr Module	20 May 95	in orbit		Module attached to MIR
SoyuzTM22	3 Sep 95	179 days	Gidzenko/Avdeyev/Reiter	[3]
SoyuzTM23	21 Feb 96	194 days	Onufrienko/Usachyov	[3]
Priroda Module	23 Apr 96	in orbit		Module attached to MIR
SoyuzTM24	17 Aug 96	197 days	Korzun/Kaleri	[3]
SoyuzTM25	10 Feb 97	185 days	Tsibliev/Lazutkin/Ewald	[3]
SoyuzTM26	5 Aug 97	197 days	A Solovyov/Vinogradov	[3]
SoyuzTM27	29 Jan 98	207 days	Musabayev/Budarin/Eyharts	[3]
SoyuzTM28	13 Aug 98	198 days	Padalka/Avdeyev/Baturin	[3]
SoyuzTM29	20 Feb 99	188 days	Afanasyev/Haigneré/Bella	[3]
SoyuzTM30	6 Apr 00	71 days	Zalyotin/Kaleri	Mir maintenance
SoyuzTM31	31 Oct 00	186 days	Krikalyov/Gidzenko/ Shepherd (USA)[5]	Docked with International Space Station; delivered first crew
SoyuzTM32	28 Apr 01	185 days	Musabayev/Baturin/ Tito (USA)[5]	Docked with International Space Station; first space tourist
SoyuzTM33	21 Oct 01	195 days	Afanasyev/Kozeyev/ Haigneré (France)[5]	[4]
SoyuzTM34	25 Apr 02	198 days	Gidzenko/Vittori (Italy)/ Shuttleworth (South Africa)[5]	[4]
SoyuzTMA-1	29 Oct 02	ongoing[6]	Zalyotin/De Winne (Belgium)/ Lonchakov[5]	[4]

[1] USSR until 1990.

[2] (h:min).

[3] The purpose was basically the same for all the Soyuz spacecraft: they were all 'ferry' craft which were used to take crews to and from MIR, acting as 'lifeboats' in case of emergencies.

[4] The Soyuz spacecraft have served the International Space Station since late 2000 as 'lifeboats' in case of emergencies. A new craft is delivered approximately every six months and left at the Station while the crew return to Earth in the previous craft.

[5] Crews given are for the outward journey; each craft remains at the Station for six months and returns with a different crew.

[6] SoyuzTMA-1 scheduled to return to Earth in May 2003.

Space

Space launchers

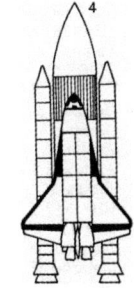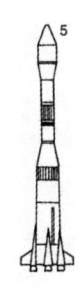

1. Vostok, USSR 1961
2. Mercury-Atlas, USA 1962
3. Apollo-Saturn V, USA 1968
4. US shuttle, 1981
5. Ariane, Europe 1981

Some satellites in geostationary orbit (1965–92)

Satellites	Years of Launch	Satellites	Years of Launch	Satellites	Years of Launch
Anik	1972–91	Eutelsat	1990–1	Meteosat	1977–88
Apple 1	1981	Fleetsatcom 1–8	1978–89	MOP 1–2	1989–91
Arabsat 1A, 1B	1985	Galaxy 1, 2, 3, 6	1983–90	Morelos 1–2	1985
Asiasat 1	1990	GMS 1–4	1977–89	NATO 1–4A	1970–91
Astra	1988–91	GOES 1–7	1975–87	Palapa	1976–90
Aurora 2	1991	Gorizont 1–24	1978–91	Panamsat	1988
Aussat 1–3	1985–7	Gstar 1–4	1985–90	Raduga 1–28	1975–91
Ayama 1–2	1979–80	Himawari 1–3	1977–84	RCA Satcom	1975–90
Brasilsat 1–2	1985–6	IMEWS	1970–87	Sakura 2, 3	1983–8
China 15, 18, 22	1984–8	Inmarsat 2	1990–1	SBS 1–6	1980–90
China 25–6	1988–90	Insat 1A, B, C, D	1982–90	Skynet 1A– 4C	1969–90
Comstar 1	1976–81	Intelsat 1–2	1965–7	SMS 1–3	1974–5
Cosmos	1987–91	Intelsat 3	1968–70	Superbird 1	1989
CS-2, CS-3	1983–8	Intelsat 4	1971–5	Symphonie 1–2	1974–5
DFS-Kopernicus	1989–90	Intelsat 4A	1975–8	Tactical comsat	1969
DSCS 1–16	1971–82	Intelsat 5	1980–9	TDF	1988–90
DSCS-3	1985	Intelsat 5A	1985–9	TDRS 1, 3, 4, 5	1983–91
DSP	1990–2	Intelsat 6	1989–91	Telecom 1A–2A	1984–91
Early Bird	1965	JCSat 1–2	1989–90	Telesat 1–9	1972–85
ECS 1–2	1979–80	Leasat 1–5	1984–90	Telstar 3A, C, D	1983–5
ECS 1–5	1983–8	LES 6, 8, 9	1968–76	TV-Sat 1–2	1987–9
Ekran 1–19	1976–88	Marcopolo 1	1989	USA 7, 11, 12, 20, 28, 48	1984–8
ESA GEOS 2	1978	Marecs 1–2	1981–4	Westar 1–5	1974–82
ETS 2, 3, 5	1977–87	Marisat 1–3	1976	Yuri 3A	1990

Some satellites in geostationary orbit (1992–2000)

Satellite	Launch date	Satellite	Launch date	Satellite	Launch date
USA 78	10 Feb 1992	Satcom C3	10 Sep 1992	Gorizont 29	18 Nov 1993
Superbird B1	27 Feb 1992	DFS 3	12 Oct 1992	Meteosat 6	20 Nov 1993
Arabsat 1C	27 Feb 1992	Galaxy 7	28 Oct 1992	Solidaridad 1	20 Nov 1993
Galaxy 5	14 Mar 1992	Ekran 20	30 Oct 1992	USA 97	28 Nov 1993
Gorizont 25	2 Apr 1992	Gorizont 27	27 Nov 1992	Nato 4B	8 Dec 1993
Telecom 2B	15 Apr 1992	Superbird A1	1 Dec 1992	Telstar 401	16 Dec 1993
Inmarsat 2 F-4	15 Apr 1992	Cosmos 2224	17 Dec 1992	DBS 1	18 Dec 1993
Palapa 7	18 May 1992	TDRS 6	13 Jan 1993	Thaicom 1	18 Dec 1993
Intelsat K	10 Jun 1992	Raduga 29	25 Mar 1993	Gals 1	20 Jan 1994
USA 82	2 Jul 1992	Astra 1C	12 May 1993	Raduga 1-3	5 Feb 1994
Insat 2A	9 Jul 1992	Galaxy 4	25 Jun 1993	Milstar DFS 1	7 Feb 1994
Eutelsat 2 F-4	9 Jul 1992	Hispasat 1B	22 Jul 1993	Raduga 31	18 Feb 1994
Gorizont 26	14 Jul 1992	Insat 2B	22 Jul 1993	Galaxy 7	19 Feb 1994
Aussat B1	13 Aug 1992	ACTS	12 Sep 1993	GOES 8	13 Apr 1994
Satcom C4	31 Aug 1992	Raduga 30	30 Sep 1993	Gorizont 30	19 May 1994
Cosmos 2209	10 Sep 1992	Intelsat 7F1	22 Oct 1993	Intelsat 702	17 Jun 1994
Hispasat 1A	10 Sep 1992	Gorizont 28	28 Oct 1993	UHF FO 3	24 Jun 1994

Space

SOME SATELLITES IN GEOSTATIONARY ORBIT (1992–2000)

Satellite	Launch date	Satellite	Launch date	Satellite	Launch date
Cosmos 2282	6 Jul 1994	Palapa C-1	1 Feb 1996	Cakrawarta	12 Nov 1997
PAS 2	8 Jul 1994	N-Star b	5 Feb 1996	JCSat 5	2 Dec 1997
BS-3N	8 Jul 1994	Intelsat 707	14 Mar 1996	Astra 1G	2 Dec 1997
Apstar 1	21 Jul 1994	Inmarsat 3F-1	3 Apr 1996	Galaxy 8i	8 Dec 1997
Brasilsat B1	10 Aug 1994	Astra 1F	8 Apr 1996	Intelsat 804	21 Dec 1997
Turksat 1B	10 Aug 1994	MSAT 1	20 Apr 1996	Skynet 4D	10 Jan 1998
USA 105	27 Aug 1994	USA 118	24 Apr 1996	Brasilsat B3	4 Feb 1998
Optus B3	27 Aug 1994	Palapa	6 May 1996	Inmarsat 3F-5	4 Feb 1998
Cosmos 2291	21 Sep 1994	AMOS	6 May 1996	Hot Bird 4	27 Feb 1998
Intelsat 703	6 Oct 1994	Galaxy 9	24 May 1996	Intelsat 806	28 Feb 1998
Solidaridad 2	8 Oct 1994	Gorizont 34	25 May 1996	UHF FO 8	16 Mar 1998
Thaicom 2	8 Oct 1994	Intelsat 709	15 Jun 1996	B-Sat 1B	28 Apr 1998
Ekspress	13 Oct 1994	Apstar 1A	3 Jul 1996	Nilesat 1	28 Apr 1998
Elektro	31 Oct 1994	Arabsat 2A	9 Jul 1996	Cosmos 2350	29 Apr 1998
Astra 1D	1 Nov 1994	Turksat 1C	9 Jul 1996	Echostar 4	7 May 1998
Orion 1	29 Nov 1994	UHF FO 7	25 Jul 1996	Zhongwei 1	30 May 1998
DFH 3	29 Nov 1994	Italsat 2	8 Aug 1996	Thor 3	10 Jun 1998
Luch	16 Dec 1994	Telecom 2D	8 Aug 1996	Intelsat 805	18 Jun 1998
DSP F17	22 Dec 1994	Inmarsat 3F-2	6 Sep 1996	Sinosat	18 Jul 1998
Raduga 32	28 Dec 1994	GE-1	8 Sep 1996	ST-1	25 Aug 1998
Intelsat 704	10 Jan 1995	Echostar 2	11 Sep 1996	Astra 2A	30 Aug 1998
UHF FO 4	29 Jan 1995	Ekspress	26 Sep 1996	Panamsat 7	16 Sep 1998
SFU	17 Mar 1995	Arabsat 2B	13 Nov 1996	Sirius 3	5 Oct 1998
GMS	17 Mar 1995	Measat 2	13 Nov 1996	Eutelsat W2	5 Oct 1998
Intelsat 705	22 Mar 1995	Hot Bird 2	21 Nov 1996	Hot Bird 5	9 Oct 1998
Brasilsat B2	28 Mar 1995	Inmarsat 3F-3	18 Dec 1996	UHF FO 9	20 Oct 1998
Hot Bird 1	28 Mar 1995	GE-2	30 Jan 1997	Afristar	28 Oct 1998
AMSC-1	7 Apr 1995	Nahuelsat	30 Jan 1997	GE-5	28 Oct 1998
USA 110	4 May 1995	JCSat 4	17 Feb 1997	PAS 8	4 Nov 1998
Intelsat 706	17 May 1995	USA 130	23 Feb 1997	BONUM-1	22 Nov 1998
GOES 9	23 May 1995	Intelsat 801	1 Mar 1997	SatMex 5	6 Dec 1998
UHF FO 5	31 May 1995	Tempo	8 Mar 1997	PAS 6B	22 Dec 1998
DBS 3	10 Jun 1995	Thaicom 3	16 Apr 1997	Telstar 6	15 Feb 1999
TDRS 7	13 Jul 1995	B-Sat 1A	16 Apr 1997	JCSAT 6	16 Feb 1999
DSCS III-9	31 Jul 1995	GOES 10	25 Apr 1997	Arabsat 3A	26 Feb 1999
PAS 4	3 Aug 1995	DFH 3	11 May 1997	Skynet 4E	26 Feb 1999
Mugunghwa	5 Aug 1995	Thor 2	21 May 1997	Raduga-1	28 Feb 1999
JCSat 3	29 Aug 1995	Telstar 5	24 May 1997	Asiasat 3S	21 Mar 1999
N-Star a	29 Aug 1995	Inmarsat 3F-4	3 Jun 1997	Insat 2E	2 Apr 1999
Cosmos 2319	30 Aug 1995	Insat 2D	3 Jun 1997	Nimiq 1	20 May 1999
Telstar 402	24 Sep 1995	FengYung	10 Jun 1997	Telkom 1	12 Aug 1999
Luch	11 Oct 1995	Intelsat 802	25 Jun 1997	Koreasat 3	4 Sep 1999
Astra 1E	19 Oct 1995	Superbird 3	28 Jul 1997	Yamal 101	6 Sep 1999
UHF FO 6	22 Oct 1995	Panamsat 6	8 Aug 1997	Yamal 102	6 Sep 1999
Milstar DFS 2	6 Nov 1995	Cosmos 2345	14 Aug 1997	Telstar 7	25 Sep 1999
Gals 2	17 Nov 1995	Agila 2	19 Aug 1997	Orion 2	19 Oct 1999
Asiasat 2	28 Nov 1995	Panamsat 5	28 Aug 1997	GE-4	13 Nov 1999
Telecom 2C	6 Dec 1995	Hot Bird 3	2 Sep 1997	Galaxy XI	21 Dec 1999
Insat 2C	6 Dec 1995	Meteosat 7	2 Sep 1997	Galaxy XR	24 Jan 2000
Galaxy 3R	15 Dec 1995	Intelsat 803	23 Sep 1997	Superbird 4	17 Feb 2000
Echostar 1	28 Dec 1995	Echostar 3	5 Oct 1997	Asiastar	21 Mar 2000
Panamsat 3R	2 Jan 1996	Apstar 2R	16 Oct 1997	Insat 3B	21 Mar 2000
Measat 1	12 Jan 1996	DSCS III B-13	25 Oct 1997	Galaxy IVR	18 Apr 2000
Koreasat 2	14 Jan 1996	Kupon	12 Nov 1997	Echostar 6	14 Jul 2000
Gorizont 33	25 Jan 1996	Sirius 2	12 Nov 1997	PAS 9	27 Jul 2000

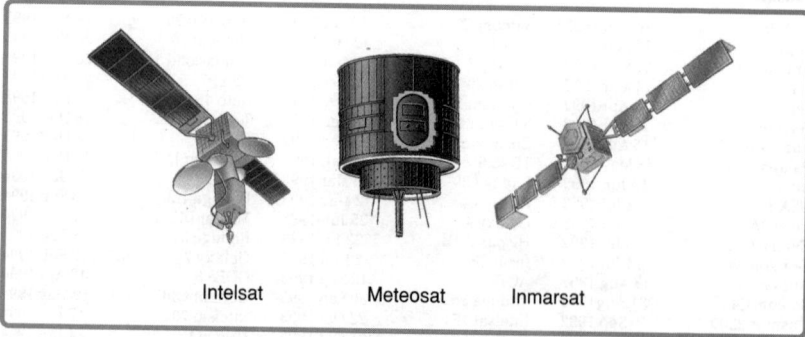

Intelsat   Meteosat   Inmarsat

EARTH

There are no universally agreed estimates of the natural phenomena given in this section. Surveys make use of different criteria for identifying natural boundaries, and use different techniques of measurement. The sizes of continents, oceans, seas, deserts, and rivers are particularly subject to variation.

Age 4 500 000 000 years (accurate to within a very small percentage of possible error)
Area 509 600 000 sq km/197 000 000 sq mi
Mass $5\,976 \times 10^{27}$ grams
Land surface 148 000 000 sq km/57 000 000 sq mi
(c.29% of total area)
Water surface 361 600 000 sq km/140 000 000 sq mi
(c.71% of total area)
Circumference at equator 40 076km/24 902mi
Circumference of meridian 40 000km/24 860mi

Atmosphere

The Earth's atmosphere is composed of air, generally containing 78% nitrogen, 21% oxygen and 1% argon, together with carbon dioxide, hydrogen, ozone and methane, and traces of the other rare gases. The amount of water vapour present depends on the temperature and humidity. The atmosphere is divided into several layers, the lowest being the *troposphere*, which contains almost all of the clouds. Above it is the *stratosphere*, which extends up to 48km/30mi above the Earth, and contains very few clouds. Aircraft usually fly in this layer above the weather disturbances in the troposphere. The ozone layer is between the stratosphere and the *mesosphere*. The latter extends to 80km/50mi above the Earth, and above it lies the *thermosphere* where the air is very thin. The lower part of the thermosphere, the *ionosphere*, reflects radio waves back to Earth, enabling signals to be transmitted around the curved surface of the Earth. The outermost layer of the atmosphere, from which light gases can escape, is known as the *exosphere*.

Temperature and pressure of atmosphere

The temperature of the atmosphere is the balance between convection and radiation. The amount of heat contained at any level depends on the pressure or density as well as the temperature. In the thermosphere the temperature may be as high as 2 000°C/3 600°F,.but the pressure is only a millionth of a billionth of that at sea-level. The temperature falls steadily as the influence of solar radiation lessens, reaching a minimum about 80km/50mi above the ground; then it increases again. Temperatures decrease down through the stratosphere, where typical pressures are still only a hundredth of those on the surface, but down through the troposphere temperatures increase again.

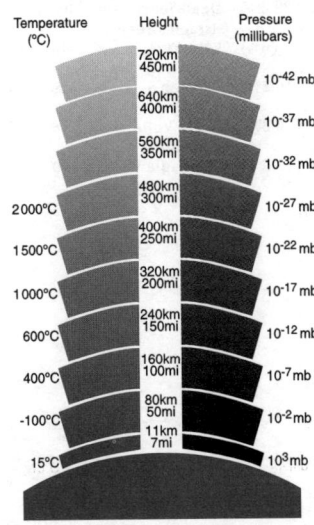

Temperature (°C)	Height	Pressure (millibars)
	720km / 450mi	10^{-42} mb
	640km / 400mi	10^{-37} mb
	560km / 350mi	10^{-32} mb
2000°C	480km / 300mi	10^{-27} mb
1500°C	400km / 250mi	10^{-22} mb
1000°C	320km / 200mi	10^{-17} mb
600°C	240km / 150mi	10^{-12} mb
400°C	160km / 100mi	10^{-7} mb
-100°C	80km / 50mi	10^{-2} mb
	11km / 7mi	
15°C		10^{3} mb

Earth

Structure of the Earth

At the centre of the Earth there is a molten metallic core of iron and nickel, possibly with a solid core at the very centre at a temperature of around 4 000°C/7 200°F. A silicate mantle overlies the core. The outermost crust is about 10km/6mi thick under the oceans and 30km/19mi thick where there are continents. A dozen or so crustal plates—the *lithosphere*—slide over the less rigid *asthenosphere*. Collisions between the plates produce folded mountains, and zones of seismic activity are concentrated along the plate boundaries.

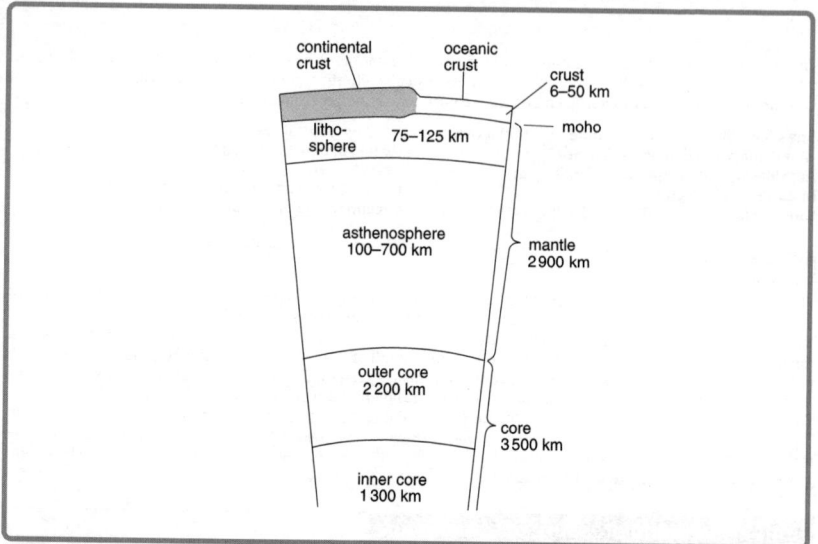

Continents

Name	Area sq km	sq mi		Lowest point below sea level	m	ft	Highest elevation	m	ft
Africa	30 293 000	11 696 000	(20.2%)	Lake Assal, Djibouti	156	512	Mt Kilimanjaro, Tanzania	5 895	19 340
Antarctica	13 975 000	5 396 000	(9.3%)	Bently sub-glacial trench	2 538	8 327	Vinson Massif	5 140	16 864
Asia	44 493 000	17 179 000	(29.6%)	Dead Sea, Israel/Jordan	400	1 312	Mt Everest, China-Nepal	8 848	29 028
Oceania	8 945 000	3 454 000	(6%)	Lake Eyre, S Australia	15	49	Puncak Jaya (Ngga Pulu)	5 030	16 500
Europe[1]	10 245 000	3 956 000	(6.8%)	Caspian Sea, SW Asia	29	94	Mt El'brus, Russia	5 642	18 510
North America	24 454 000	9 442 000	(16.3%)	Death Valley, California	86	282	Mt McKinley, Alaska	6 194	20 320
South America	17 838 000	6 887 000	(11.9%)	Península Valdés, Argentina	40	131	Aconcagua, Argentina	6 960	22 831

[1] Including the former western USSR.

Plate tectonics

Plate tectonics is a geological theory, developed in the late 1960s, according to which the Earth's crust is composed of a small number of large plates of solid rock, whose movements in relation to one another are responsible for continental drift. According to the theory, the plates of the Earth's crust are floating on the moving molten rock of the mantle which lies beneath the crust. It is believed that the plates move as a result of convection currents which occur deep within the mantle. New crust is formed at the edges of the plates where rising convection currents bring up new material from the mantle. Some plates may be 'sliding' in relation to one another along margins where there are huge fault systems, eg the San Andreas fault system off the coast of California. It is thought that mountain ranges are formed when one crustal plate pushes into another, forcing the land upward under great pressure.

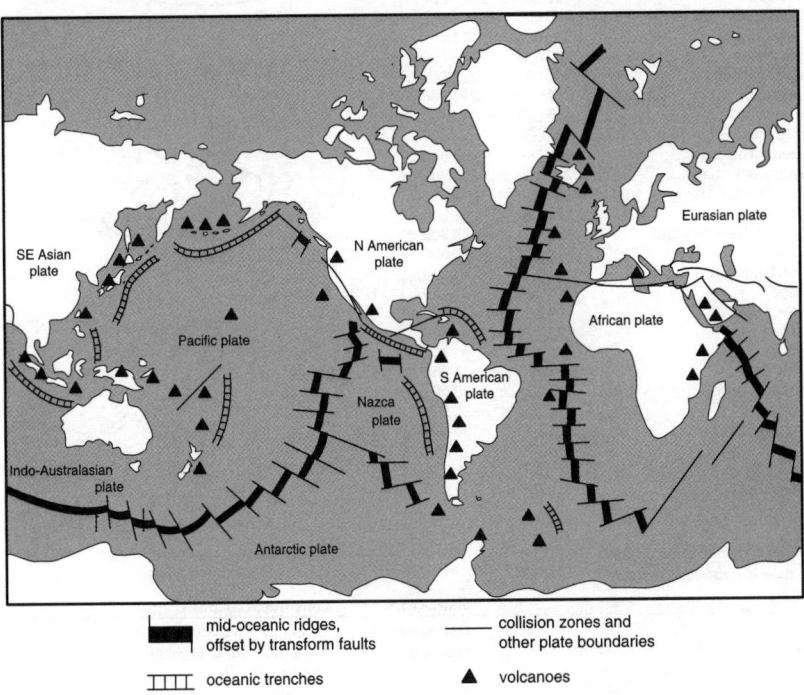

mid-oceanic ridges, offset by transform faults

oceanic trenches

collision zones and other plate boundaries

▲ volcanoes

Earth

Earth

Continental drift

Continental drift is the theory that the continents were formed as a result of the breaking up of a single land mass into several smaller land masses, which slowly drifted apart across the Earth's surface.

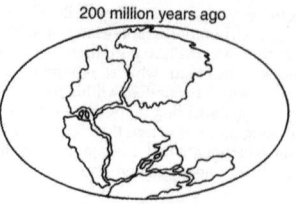

200 million years ago

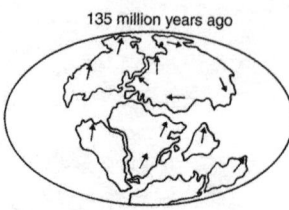

135 million years ago

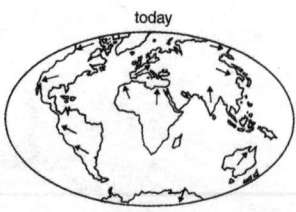

today

← direction of drift

Largest islands

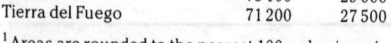

Name	Area[1] sq km	Area[1] sq mi
Australia	7 692 300	2 970 000
Greenland	2 175 600	840 000
New Guinea	790 000	305 000
Borneo	737 000	285 000
Madagascar	587 000	226 600
Baffin	507 000	195 800
Sumatra	425 000	164 100
Honshu (Hondo)	228 000	88 000
Great Britain	219 000	84 600
Victoria, Canada	217 300	83 900
Ellesmere, Canada	196 000	75 700
Celebes	174 000	67 200
South I, New Zealand	151 000	58 300
Java	129 000	49 800
North I, New Zealand	114 000	44 000
Cuba	110 900	42 800
Newfoundland	109 000	42 100
Luzon	105 000	40 500
Iceland	103 000	39 800
Mindanao	94 600	36 500
Novaya Zemlya (two islands)	90 600	35 000
Ireland	84 100	32 500
Hokkaido	78 500	30 300
Hispaniola	77 200	29 800
Sakhalin	75 100	29 000
Tierra del Fuego	71 200	27 500

[1]Areas are rounded to the nearest 100 sq km/sq mi.

Major island groups

Name	Country	Sea/Ocean	Constituent islands
Aeolian	Italy	Mediterranean	Stromboli, Lipari, Vulcano, Salina
Åland	Finland	Gulf of Bothnia	Ahvenanmaa, Eckero, Lemland, Lumparland, Vardo
Aleutian	USA	Pacific	Andreanof, Adak, Atka, Fox, Umnak, Unalaska, Unimak, Near, Attu, Rat, Kiska, Amchitka
Alexander	Canada	Pacific	Baranof, Prince of Wales
Antilles, Greater	—	Caribbean	Cuba, Jamaica, Haiti and the Dominican Republic, Puerto Rico
Antilles, Lesser	—	Caribbean	Windward, Leeward, Netherlands Antilles
Andaman	India	Bay of Bengal	over 300 islands including N Andaman, S Andaman, Middle Andaman, Little Andaman
Azores	Portugal	Atlantic	nine main islands: Flores, Corvo, Terceira, Graciosa, São Jorge, Faial, Pico, Santa Maria, Formigar, São Miguel
Bahamas, The	The Bahamas	Atlantic	700 islands including Great Abaco, Acklins, Andros, Berry, Cat, Cay, Crooked, Exuma, Grand Bahama, Inagua, Long, Mayaguana, New Providence, Ragged
Balearic	Spain	Mediterranean	Ibiza, Majorca, Menorca, Formentera, Cabrera
Bay	Honduras	Caribbean	Utila, Roatan, Guanja
Bismarck Archipelago	Papua New Guinea	Pacific	c.200 islands including New Britain, New Ireland, Admiralty, Lavonga, New Hanover
Bissagos	Guinea-Bissau	Atlantic	15 islands including Orango, Formosa, Caravela, Roxa
Canadian Arctic Archipelago	Canada	Arctic	main islands: Baffin, Victoria, Queen Elizabeth, Banks

Name	Country	Sea/Ocean	Constituent islands
Canary	Spain	Atlantic	Tenerife, Gomera, Las Palmas, Hierro, Lanzarote, Fuerteventura, Gran Canaria
Cape Verde	Cape Verde	Atlantic	10 islands divided into 1. Barlavento (windward) group: Santo Antão, São Vicente, Santa Luzia, São Nicolau, Boa Vista, Sal and 2. Sotavento (leeward) group: São Tiago, Maio Fogo, Brava
Caroline	USA	Pacific	c.680 islands including Yap, Ponape, Truk, Kusac, Palau
Chagos	UK	Indian	Diego Garcia, Peros, Banhos, Salomon
Channel	UK	English	Jersey, Guernsey, Alderney, Sark
Chonos Archipelago	Chile	Pacific	main islands: Chaffers, Benjamin, James, Melchior, Victoria, Luz
Commander	Russia	Bering Sea	main islands: Bering, Medny
Comoros	Comoros (excluding French Mayotte)	Mozambique Channel	Grand Comore, Anjouan, Mohéli, Mayotte
Cook	New Zealand	Pacific	main islands: Rarotonga, Palmerston, Mangaia
Cyclades	Greece	Aegean	c.220 islands including Andros, Mikonos, Milos, Naxos, Paros, Kithnos, Sérifos, Tinos, Siros
Denmark	Denmark	Baltic	main islands: Zealand, Fyn, Lolland, Falster, Bornholm
Desolation	France	Indian	Kerguélen, Grande Terre, and 300 islets
Dodecanese	Greece	Aegean	12 islands including Kásos, Kárpathos, Rhodes, Sámos, Khalki, Tilos, Simi, Astipalaia, Kós, Kálimnos, Léros, Pátmos
Ellice	Tuvalu	Pacific	main islands: Funafuti, Nukefetau, Nukulailai, Nanumea
Falkland	UK	Atlantic	over 200 islands including W Falkland, E Falkland, S Georgia, S Sandwich
Faroe	Denmark	Atlantic	22 islands including Stromo, Ostero
Fiji	Fiji	Pacific	main islands: Viti Levu, Vanua Levu
Frisian, East	Germany and Denmark	North Sea	main islands: Borkum, Juist, Norderney, Langeoog, Spiekeroog, Wangerooge
Frisian, North	Germany and Denmark	North Sea	main islands: (German) Sylt, Föhr, Nordstrand, Pellworm, Amrum; (Danish) Rømø, Fanø, Mandø
Frisian, West	Netherlands	North Sea	main islands: Texel, Vlieland, Terschelling, Ameland, Schiermonnikoog
Galapagos	Ecuador	Pacific	main islands: San Cristóbal, Santa Cruz, Isabela, Floreana, Santiago, Fernandina
Gilbert	Kiribati	Pacific	main islands: Tarawa, Makin, Abaiang, Abemama, Tabiteuea, Nonouti, Beru
Gotland	Sweden	Baltic	main islands: Gotland, Fårö, Karlsö
Greenland	Denmark	N Atlantic/Arctic	main islands: Greenland, Disko
Hawaiian	USA	Pacific	eight main islands: Hawaii, Oahu, Maui, Lanai, Kauai, Molokai, Kahoolawe, Niihau
Hebrides, Inner	UK	Atlantic	main islands: Skye, Eigg, Coll, Tiree, Mull, Iona, Staffa, Jura, Islay
Hebrides, Outer	UK	Atlantic	Lewis, Harris, N and S Uist, Benbecula, Barra
Indonesia	Indonesia	Pacific	13 677 islets and islands including Java, Sumatra, Kalimantan, Celebes, Lesser Sundas, Moluccas, Irian Jaya (Papua)
Ionian	Greece	Aegean	Kerkira, Kefallinia, Zakinthos, Levkas
Japan	Japan	Pacific	main islands: Hokkaido, Honshu, Shikoku, Kyushu, Ryuku
Juan Fernandez	Chile	Pacific	Más á Tierra, Más Afuera, Santa Clara
Kuril	Russia	Pacific	56 islands including Shumsu, Iturup, Urup, Paramushir, Onekotan, Shiaskhotan, Shikotanto, Kunashir, Shimushir
Laccadive	India	Arabian Sea	27 islands including Amindivi, Laccadive, Minicoy, Androth, Kavaratti
Line	Kiribati	Pacific	main islands: Christmas, Fanning, Washington
Lofoten	Norway	Norwegian Sea	main islands: Hinnøy, Austvågøy, Vestvågøy, Moskenes
Madeira	Portugal	Atlantic	Madeira, Ilha do Porto Santo, Ilhas Desertas, Ilhas Selvagens

Earth

Earth

Name	Country	Sea/Ocean	Constituent islands
Malay Archipelago	Indonesia, Malaysia, Philippines	Pacific/Indian	main islands: Borneo, Celebes, Java, Luzon, Mindanao, New Guinea, Sumatra
Maldives	Maldives	Indian	19 clusters, main island: Male
Malta	Malta	Mediterranean	main islands: Malta, Gozo, Comino
Mariana	Mariana Islands	Pacific	14 islands including Saipan, Tinian, Rota, Pagan, Guguan
Marquesas	France	Pacific	10 islands including Nukultiva, Ua Pu, Ua Huka, Hiva Oa, Tahuata, Fatu Hiva, Eïao, Hatutu
Marshall	Marshall Islands	Pacific	main islands: Bikini, Wotha, Kwajalein, Eniwetok, Maiura, Jalut, Rogelap
Mascarenes	—	Indian	main islands: Réunion, Mauritius, Rodrigues
Melanesia	—	Pacific	main groups of islands: Solomon Islands, Bismarck Archipelago, New Caledonia, Papua New Guinea, Fiji, Vanuatu
Micronesia	—	Pacific	main groups of islands: Caroline, Gilberts, Marianas, Marshalls, Guam, Kiribati, Nauru
New Hebrides	Vanuatu	Pacific	main islands: Espíritu Santo, Malekula, Efate, Ambrim, Eromanga, Tanna, Epi, Pentecost, Aurora
New Siberian	Russia	Arctic	main islands: Kotelny, Faddeyevski
Newfoundland	Canada	Atlantic	Prince Edward, Anticosti
Nicobar	India	Bay of Bengal	main islands: Great Nicobar, Camorta with Nancowry, Car Nicobar, Teressa, Little Nicobar
Northern Land	Russia	Arctic	main islands: Komsomolets, Bolshevik, October Revolution
Novaya Zemlya	Russia	Arctic	two main islands: North, South
Orkney	UK	North Sea	main islands: Mainland, South Ronaldsay, Sanday, Westray, Hoy, Stronsay, Shapinsay, Rousay
Pelagian	Italy	Mediterrannean	Lampedusa, Linosa, Lampione
Philippines	Philippines	Pacific	over 7 100 islands and islets including Luzon, Mindanao, Samar, Palawan, Mindoro, Panay, Negros, Cebu, Leyte, Masbate, Bohol
Polynesia	—	Pacific	main groups of islands: New Zealand, French Polynesia, Phoenix Islands, Hawaii, Line, Cook Islands, Pitcairn, Tokelau, Tonga, Society, Easter, Samoa, Kiribati, Ellice
Queen Charlotte	Canada	Pacific	150 islands including Prince Rupert, Graham, Moresby, Louise, Lyell, Kunghit
São Tomé and Príncipe	São Tomé and Príncipe	Atlantic	main islands: São Tomé, Príncipe
Scilly	UK	English Channel	c. 150 islands including St Mary's, St Martin's, Tresco, St Agnes, Bryher
Seychelles	Seychelles	Indian	115 islands including Praslin, La Digue, Silhouette, Mahé, Bird
Shetland	UK	North Sea	100 islands including Mainland, Unst, Yell, Whalsay, West Burra
Society	France	Pacific	island groups: Windward, Leeward; main island: Tahiti
Solomon	Solomon Islands	Pacific	main islands: Choiseul, Guadalcanal, Malaita,
South Orkney	UK	Atlantic	main islands: Coronation, Signy, Laurie, Inaccessible
South Shetland	UK	Atlantic	main islands: King George, Elephant, Clarence, Gibbs, Nelson, Livingstone, Greenwich, Snow, Deception, Smith
Sri Lanka	Sri Lanka	Indian	main islands: Sri Lanka, Mannar
Taiwan	Taiwan	China Sea/Pacific	main islands: Taiwan, Lan Hsü, Lü Tao, Quemoy, the Pescadores
Tasmania	Australia	Tasman Sea	main islands: Tasmania, King, Flinders, Bruny
Tierra del Fuego	Argentina/Chile	Pacific	main islands: Tierra del Fuego, Isla de los Estados, Hoste, Navarino, Wallaston, Diego Ramírez, Desolación, Santa Inés, Clarence, Dawson

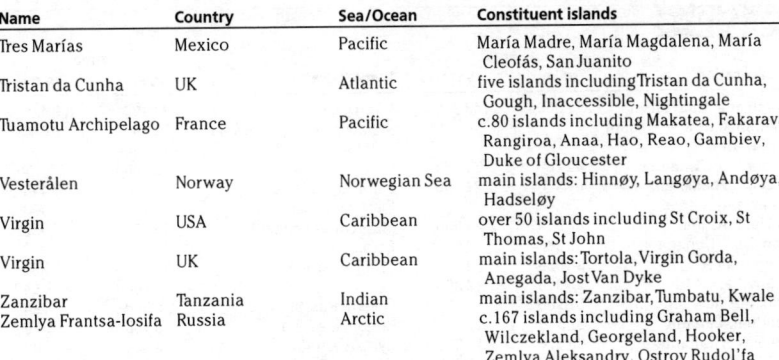

Name	Country	Sea/Ocean	Constituent islands
Tres Marías	Mexico	Pacific	María Madre, María Magdalena, María Cleofás, San Juanito
Tristan da Cunha	UK	Atlantic	five islands including Tristan da Cunha, Gough, Inaccessible, Nightingale
Tuamotu Archipelago	France	Pacific	c.80 islands including Makatea, Fakarava, Rangiroa, Anaa, Hao, Reao, Gambiev, Duke of Gloucester
Vesterålen	Norway	Norwegian Sea	main islands: Hinnøy, Langøya, Andøya, Hadseløy
Virgin	USA	Caribbean	over 50 islands including St Croix, St Thomas, St John
Virgin	UK	Caribbean	main islands: Tortola, Virgin Gorda, Anegada, Jost Van Dyke
Zanzibar	Tanzania	Indian	main islands: Zanzibar, Tumbatu, Kwale
Zemlya Frantsa-Iosifa	Russia	Arctic	c.167 islands including Graham Bell, Wilczekland, Georgeland, Hooker, Zemlya Aleksandry, Ostrov Rudol'fa

Earth

Oceans

Name	Area sq km	sq mi			Greatest depth m	ft	Average depth m	ft
Arctic	13 986 000	5 400 000	(3%)	Eurasia Basin	5 122	16 804	Arctic 1 330	4 400
Atlantic	82 217 000	31 700 000	(24%)	Puerto Rico Trench	8 648	28 372	Atlantic 3 700	12 100
Indian	73 426 000	28 350 000	(20%)	Java Trench	7 725	25 344	Indian 3 900	12 800
Pacific	181 300 000	70 000 000	(46%)	Mariana Trench	11 040	36 220	Pacific 4 300	14 100

Largest seas

Name	Area[1] sq km	sq mi	Name	Area[1] sq km	sq mi
Coral Sea	4 791 000	1 850 000	Arafura Sea	1 037 000	400 000
Arabian Sea	3 863 000	1 492 000	Philippine Sea	1 036 000	400 000
S China (Nan) Sea	3 685 000	1 423 000	Sea of Japan	978 000	378 000
Mediterranean Sea	2 516 000	971 000	E Siberian Sea	901 000	348 000
Bering Sea	2 304 000	890 000	Kara Sea	883 000	341 000
Bay of Bengal	2 172 000	839 000	E China Sea	664 000	256 000
Sea of Okhotsk	1 590 000	614 000	Andaman Sea	565 000	218 000
Gulf of Mexico	1 543 000	596 000	North Sea	520 000	201 000
Gulf of Guinea	1 533 000	592 000	Black Sea	508 000	196 000
Barents Sea	1 405 000	542 000	Red Sea	453 000	175 000
Norwegian Sea	1 383 000	534 000	Baltic Sea	414 000	160 000
Gulf of Alaska	1 327 000	512 000	Arabian Gulf	239 000	92 000
Hudson Bay	1 232 000	476 000	St Lawrence Gulf	238 000	92 000
Greenland Sea	1 205 000	465 000			

Oceans are excluded.

[1] Areas are rounded to the nearest 1 000 sq km/sq mi.

Earth

Largest lakes

Name/Location	Area[1] sq km	sq mi	Name/Location	Area[1] sq km	sq mi
Caspian Sea, Iran/Russia/ Turkmenistan/Kazakhstan/ Azerbaijan	371 000	143 240[2]	Winnipeg	24 390	9 420
			Malawi/Nyasa, E Africa	22 490	8 680
			Balkhash, Kazakhstan	17 000– 22 000	6 560– 8 490[2]
Superior, USA/Canada	82 260	31 760[3]			
Aral Sea, Uzbekistan/ Kazakhstan	64 500	24 900[2]	Ontario, Canada	19 270	7 440[3]
			Ladoga, Russia	18 130	7 000
Victoria, E Africa	62 940	24 300	Maracaibo, Venezuela	13 010	5 020[4]
Huron, USA/Canada	59 580	23 000[3]	Patos, Brazil	10 140	3 920[4]
Michigan, USA	58 020	22 400	Chad, W Africa	10 000– 26 000	3 860– 10 040
Tanganyika, E Africa	32 000	12 360			
Baikal, Russia	31 500	12 160	Onega, Russia	9 800	3 780
Great Bear, Canada	31 330	12 100	Rudolf, E Africa	9 100	3 510
Great Slave, Canada	28 570	11 030	Eyre, Australia	8 800	3 400[4]
Erie, USA/Canada	25 710	9 930[3]	Titicaca, Peru	8 300	3 200

The Caspian and Aral Seas, being entirely surrounded by land, are classified as lakes.

[1] Areas are rounded to the nearest 10 sq km/sq mi.
[2] Salt lakes.
[3] Average of areas given by Canada and USA.
[4] Salt lagoons.

Longest rivers

Name	Outflow	Length[1] km	mi
Nile-Kagera-Ruvuvu-Ruvusu-Luvironza	Mediterranean Sea (Egypt)	6 690	4 160
Amazon-Ucayali-Tambo-Ene-Apurimac	Atlantic Ocean (Brazil)	6 570	4 080
Mississippi-Missouri-Jefferson- Beaverhead-Red Rock	Gulf of Mexico (USA)	6 020	3 740
Chang Jiang (Yangtze)	E China Sea (China)	5 980	3 720
Yenisey-Angara-Selenga-Ider	Kara Sea (Russia)	5 870	3 650
Amur-Argun-Kerulen	Tartar Strait (Russia)	5 780	3 590
Ob-Irtysh	Gulf of Ob, Kara Sea (Russia)	5 410	3 360
Plata-Parana-Grande	Atlantic Ocean (Argentina-Uruguay)	4 880	3 030
Huang He (Yellow)	Yellow Sea (China)	4 840	3 010
Congo-Lualaba	S Atlantic Ocean (Angola- Democratic Republic of Congo)	4 630	2 880
Lena	Laptev Sea (Russia)	4 400	2 730
Mackenzie-Slave-Peace-Finlay	Beaufort Sea (Canada)	4 240	2 630
Mekong	S China Sea (Vietnam)	4 180	2 600
Niger	Gulf of Guinea (Nigeria)	4 100	2 550

[1] Lengths are given to the nearest 10km/mi, and include the river plus tributaries comprising the longest watercourse.

Largest deserts

Name/Location	Area[1] sq km	sq mi
Sahara, N Africa	8 600 000	3 320 000
Arabian, SW Asia	2 330 000	900 000
Gobi, Mongolia and NE China	1 166 000	450 000
Patagonian, Argentina	673 000	260 000
Great Victoria, SW Australia	647 000	250 000
Great Basin, SW USA	492 000	190 000
Chihuahuan, Mexico	450 000	174 000
Great Sandy, NW Australia	400 000	154 000
Sonoran, SW USA	310 000	120 000
Kyzyl Kum, Kazakhstan	300 000	116 000
Takla Makan, N China	270 000	104 000
Kalahari, SW Africa	260 000	100 000
Kara Kum, Turkmenistan	260 000	100 000
Kavir, Iran	260 000	100 000
Syrian, Saudi Arabia/Jordan/Syria/Iraq	260 000	100 000
Nubian, Sudan	260 000	100 000
Thar, India/Pakistan	200 000	77 000
Ust'-Urt, Kazakhstan	160 000	62 000
Bet-Pak-Dala, S Kazakhstan	155 000	60 000

Name/Location	Area[1]	
	sq km	sq mi
Simpson, C Australia	145 000	56 000
Dzungaria, China	142 000	55 000
Atacama, Chile	140 000	54 000
Namib, SE Africa	134 000	52 000
Sturt, SE Australia	130 000	50 000
Bolson de Mapimi, Mexico	130 000	50 000
Ordos, China	130 000	50 000
Alashan, China	116 000	45 000

[1] Desert areas are very approximate, because clear physical boundaries may not occur.

Earth

Highest waterfalls

Name	Height[1]		Name	Height[1]	
	m	ft		m	ft
Angel (upper fall),Venezuela	807	2 648	Pilao, Brazil	524	1 719
Itatinga, Brazil	628	2 060	Ribbon, USA	491	1 611
Cuquenán, Guyana-Venezuela	610	2 001	Vestre Mardola, Norway	468	1 535
Ormeli, Norway	563	1 847	Kaieteur, Guyana	457	1 500
Tysse, Norway	533	1 749	Cleve-Garth, New Zealand	450	1 476

[1] Height denotes individual leaps.

Deepest caves

Name/Location	Depth		Name/Location	Depth	
	m	ft		m	ft
Jean Bernard, France	1 494	4 902	Dachstein-Mammuthöhle, Austria	1 174	3 852
Snezhnaya, Caucasus	1 340	4 396	Zitu, Spain	1 139	3 737
Puertas de Illamina, Spain	1 338	4 390	Badalona, Spain	1 130	3 707
Pierre-Saint-Martin, France	1 321	4 334	Batmanhöhle, Austria	1 105	3 625
Sistema Huautla, Mexico	1 240	4 068	Schneeloch, Austria	1 101	3 612
Berger, France	1 198	3 930	G E S Malaga, Spain	1 070	3 510
Vqerdi, Spain	1 195	3 921	Lamprechtsofen, Austria	1 024	3 360

Highest mountains

Name	Height[1]		Location
	m	ft	
Everest	8 850	29 030	China-Nepal
K2	8 610	28 250	Kashmir-Jammu
Kangchenjunga	8 590	28 170	India-Nepal
Lhotse	8 500	27 890	China-Nepal
Kangchenjunga S Peak	8 470	27 800	India-Nepal
Makalu I	8 470	27 800	China-Nepal
Kangchenjunga W Peak	8 420	27 620	India-Nepal
Lhotse E Peak	8 380	27 500	China-Nepal
Dhaulagiri	8 170	26 810	Nepal
Cho Oyu	8 150	26 750	China-Nepal
Manaslu	8 130	26 660	Nepal
Nanga Parbat	8 130	26 660	Kashmir-Jammu
Annapurna I	8 080	26 500	Nepal
Gasherbrum I	8 070	26 470	Kashmir-Jammu
Broad Peak I	8 050	26 400	Kashmir-Jammu
Gasherbrum II	8 030	26 360	Kashmir-Jammu
Gosainthan	8 010	26 290	China
Broad Peak Central	8 000	26 250	Kashmir-Jammu
Gasherbrum III	7 950	26 090	Kashmir-Jammu
Annapurna II	7 940	26 040	Nepal
Nanda Devi	7 820	25 660	India
Rakaposhi	7 790	25 560	Kashmir
Kamet	7 760	25 450	India
Ulugh Muztagh	7 720	25 340	China (Tibet)
Tirich Mir	7 690	25 230	Pakistan
MuzTag Ata	7 550	24 760	China
Communism Peak	7 490	24 590	Tajikistan
Pobedy Peak	7 440	24 410	China-Kyrgyzstan
Aconcagua	6 960	22 830	Argentina
Ojos del Salado	6 910	22 660	Argentina-Chile

[1] Heights are given to the nearest 10 m/ft.

Earth

Major volcanoes

Name	Height m	ft	Major eruptions (years)	Last eruption (year)
Aconcagua (Argentina)	6 959	22 831	extinct	—
Ararat (Turkey)	5 137	16 853	extinct	—
Awu (Sangihe Is, Indonesia)	1 327	4 355	1711, 1856, 1892, 1968	1992
Bezymianny (Russia)	2 800	9 186	1955–6, 1981, 1997	2000
Coseguina (Nicaragua)	847	2 779	1835	1835
Cotopaxi (Ecuador)	5 897	19 347	1877	1975
El Chichón (Mexico)	1 350	4 430	1982	1982
Erebus (Antarctica)	4 023	13 200	1947, 1972, 1980, 1986, 1991	1995
Etna (Italy)	3 239	10 625	122, 1169, 1329, 1536, 1669, 1928, 1964, 1971, 1981, 1986, 1992, 1994, 2000	2001
Fuji (Japan)	3 776	12 388	1707	1707
Galunggung (Java)	2 181	7 155	1822, 1918	1984
Hekla (Iceland)	1 500	4 920	1693, 1845, 1947–8, 1970, 1981, 1991	2000
Helgafell (Iceland)	215	706	1973	1973
Hudson (Chile)	1 750	5 742	1971, 1973	1991
Jurullo (Mexico)	1 330	4 255	1759–74	1774
Katmai (Alaska)	2 047	6 715	1912, 1920, 1921, 1931, 1962	1974
Kilauea (Hawaii)	1 250	4 100	1823–1924, 1952, 1955, 1960, 1967–8, 1968–74, 1983–7, 1988, 1991, 1992, 1994, 1995, 2001	2002
Kilimanjaro (Tanzania)	5 928	19 450	extinct	Pleistocene
Klyuchevskoy (Russia)	4 850	15 910	1700–1966, 1984, 1985, 1993, 1997	2001
Krakatoa (Sumatra)	818	2 685	1680, 1883, 1927, 1952–3, 1969, 1980, 1995, 1999	2001
La Soufrière (St Vincent)	1 234	4 048	1718, 1812, 1902, 1971–2	1997
Laki (Iceland)	500	1 642	1783, 1784, 1938	1996
Lamington (Papua New Guinea)	1 781	5 844	1951	1956
Lassen Peak (USA)	3 186	10 453	1914–15	1921
Mauna Loa (Hawaii)	4 171	13 685	1750, 1859, 1880, 1887, 1919, 1950, 1984	1987
Mayon (Philippines)	2 464	8 084	1616, 1766, 1814, 1897, 1968, 1978, 1993	2000
Nyamuragira (Democratic Republic of Congo)	3 056	10 026	1884, 1921–38, 1971, 1980, 1984, 1988, 1995, 2000	2002
Paricutín (Mexico)	3 188	10 460	1943–52	1952
Pelée, Mont (Martinique)	1 397	4 584	1902, 1929–32	1932
Pinatubo, Mt (Philippines)	1 759	5 770	1391, 1991	1992
Popocatèpetl (Mexico)	5 483	17 990	1347, 1920, 1998, 2000	2001
Rainier, Mt (USA)	4 394	14 416	1c BC, 1820, 1825	1882
Ruapehu (New Zealand)	2 797	9 175	1945, 1953, 1969, 1975, 1986	1995
St Helens, Mt (USA)	2 549	8 364	1800, 1831, 1835, 1842–3, 1857, 1980, 1982, 1987	1991
Santoriní/Thíra (Greece)	566	1 857	1470BC, 197BC, AD46, 1570–3, 1707–11, 1866–70, 1950	1950
Soufrière Hills (Montserrat)	914	3000	1995, 1997, 1998	2000
Stromboli (Italy)	931	3 055	1768, 1882, 1889, 1907, 1930, 1936, 1941, 1950, 1952, 1975, 1986, 1990, 1996	2002
Surtsey (Iceland)	174	570	1963–7	1967
Taal (Philippines)	1 448	4 752	1906, 1911, 1965, 1969, 1977	1988
Tambora (Sumbawa, Indonesia)	2 868	9 410	1815	1880
Tarawera (New Zealand)	1 149	3 770	1886	1973
Unzen (Japan)	1 360	4 461	1360, 1791, 1991	1996
Vesuvius (Italy)	1 289	4 230	79, 472, 1036, 1631, 1779, 1906	1944
Vulcano (Italy)	503	1 650	antiquity, 1444, 1730–40, 1786, 1873, 1888–90	1890

Major tsunamis

Tsunamis are long-period ocean waves associated with earthquakes, volcanic explosions, or landslides. They are also referred to as *seismic sea waves* and popularly, but incorrectly, as *tidal waves*.

Location of source	Year	Height m	ft	Location of deaths/damage	Deaths
Papua New Guinea	1998	10	33	Papua New Guinea	2 200+
Peru	1996	4.9	16	Peru	12
Irian Jaya, Indonesia	1996	7	23	Indonesia	161
Makassar Straits, Indonesia	1996	4.9	16	Indonesia	9
Mindoro I	1994	15	49	Philippines	41
Skagway, Alaska[1]	1994	11	36	Skagway, Alaska	1
Java trench (Indian Ocean)	1994	11	36	Java	223
Sea of Japan	1993	30.5	100	Japan, Russia	202
Flores I (Indonesia)	1992	26	85	Indonesia	400
Nicaragua	1992	9	30	Nicaragua	167
Sea of Japan	1983	15	49	Japan, Korea	103

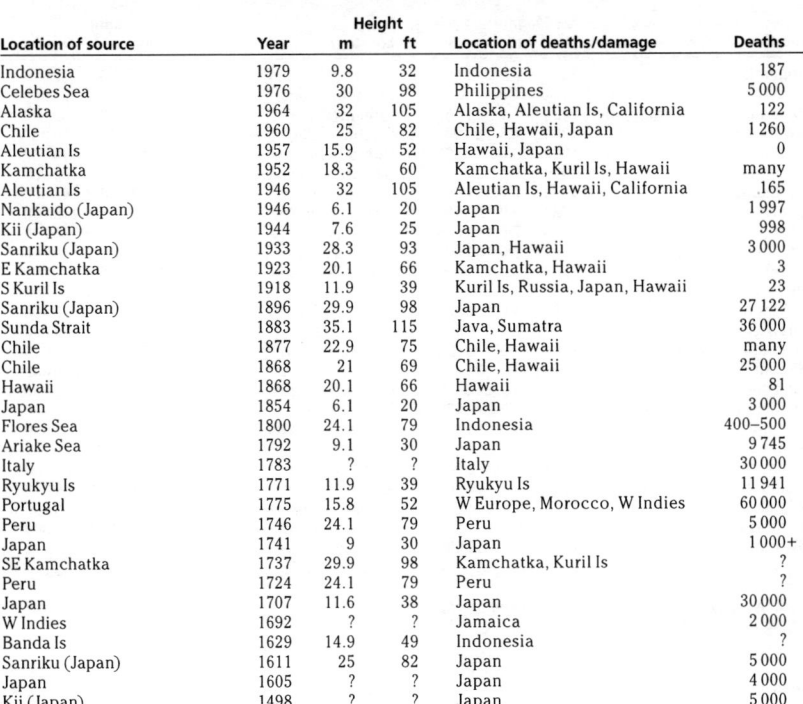

Location of source	Year	Height m	Height ft	Location of deaths/damage	Deaths
Indonesia	1979	9.8	32	Indonesia	187
Celebes Sea	1976	30	98	Philippines	5 000
Alaska	1964	32	105	Alaska, Aleutian Is, California	122
Chile	1960	25	82	Chile, Hawaii, Japan	1 260
Aleutian Is	1957	15.9	52	Hawaii, Japan	0
Kamchatka	1952	18.3	60	Kamchatka, Kuril Is, Hawaii	many
Aleutian Is	1946	32	105	Aleutian Is, Hawaii, California	165
Nankaido (Japan)	1946	6.1	20	Japan	1 997
Kii (Japan)	1944	7.6	25	Japan	998
Sanriku (Japan)	1933	28.3	93	Japan, Hawaii	3 000
E Kamchatka	1923	20.1	66	Kamchatka, Hawaii	3
S Kuril Is	1918	11.9	39	Kuril Is, Russia, Japan, Hawaii	23
Sanriku (Japan)	1896	29.9	98	Japan	27 122
Sunda Strait	1883	35.1	115	Java, Sumatra	36 000
Chile	1877	22.9	75	Chile, Hawaii	many
Chile	1868	21	69	Chile, Hawaii	25 000
Hawaii	1868	20.1	66	Hawaii	81
Japan	1854	6.1	20	Japan	3 000
Flores Sea	1800	24.1	79	Indonesia	400–500
Ariake Sea	1792	9.1	30	Japan	9 745
Italy	1783	?	?	Italy	30 000
Ryukyu Is	1771	11.9	39	Ryukyu Is	11 941
Portugal	1775	15.8	52	W Europe, Morocco, W Indies	60 000
Peru	1746	24.1	79	Peru	5 000
Japan	1741	9	30	Japan	1 000+
SE Kamchatka	1737	29.9	98	Kamchatka, Kuril Is	?
Peru	1724	24.1	79	Peru	?
Japan	1707	11.6	38	Japan	30 000
W Indies	1692	?	?	Jamaica	2 000
Banda Is	1629	14.9	49	Indonesia	?
Sanriku (Japan)	1611	25	82	Japan	5 000
Japan	1605	?	?	Japan	4 000
Kii (Japan)	1498	?	?	Japan	5 000

[1] Tsunami caused by the dock collapsing into the sea.

Major earthquakes

All magnitudes on the Richter scale. The energy released by earthquakes is measured on the logarithmic Richter scale. Thus:

2 Barely perceptible;　5 Rather strong;　7+ Very strong

Location	Year	Magnitude	Deaths	Location	Year	Magnitude	Deaths
Pacific Ocean (near Papua New Guinea)	2003	7.8	—	Kuril Is (Russia)	1995	7.9	0
Xinjiang Region (China)	2003	6.3	250+	Manzanillo (Mexico)	1995	7.6	66
Colima (Mexico)	2003	7.6	21+	S Mexico	1995	7.3	
Vanuatu	2002	7.2	0	Sakhalin I (E Russia)	1995	7.5	2 000
Alaska (USA)	2002	7.9	0	Kobe (Japan)	1995	7.2	6 300
Papua New Guinea	2002	7.6	5+	Hokkaido I (Japan) and	1994	8.2	16+
Qazvin (Iran)	2002	6.0	500+	Kuril Is (Russia) (undersea)			
Hindu Kush (Afghanistan)	2002	6.1	1800+	Bolivia (617km underground)	1994	8.2	5
Gujarat (India)	2001	6.9	20 000+	Paez River Valley	1994	6.8	269
El Salvador	2001	7.7	675+	(SW Colombia)			
Bengkulu (Sumatra)	2000	7.9	115+	Java (Indonesia)	1994	7.7	200
Nantou Province (Taiwan)	1999	7.6	2 400+	Sumatra I (Indonesia)	1994	7.2	215
Izmit (NW Turkey)	1999	7.4	17 000+	Halmahera I (Indonesia)	1994	6.8	7+
Armenia (Colombia)	1999	6.0	1 100+	Los Angeles, California (USA)	1994	6.8	61
Badakhshan Province (Afghanistan)	1998	7.1	5 000+	Maharashtra State (India)	1993	6.5	22 000
Rustaq (Afghanistan)	1998	6.1	4 000+	Guam (Mariana Is)	1993	8.1	—
Qayen (E Iran)	1997	7.1	2 400	Okushiri and Hokkaido Is	1993	7.8	185
Ardabil (NW Iran)	1997	5.5	965+	(N Japan)			
Xinjiang Region (China)	1996	6.9	26	Papua New Guinea	1993	6.8	60
Biak I (Indonesia)	1996	7.9	108	Maumere, Flores I (Indonesia)	1992	7.5	1 232
Flores Sea (near Indonesia)	1996	7.9	—	Joshua Tree and Yucca Valley,	1992	7.4	2
Samar (Philippines)	1996	7.9	—	California (USA)			
Andreanof Is (off Alaskan coast)	1996	7.9	—	Erzincan (Turkey)	1992	6.8	500
				Nusa Tenggara Is (Indonesia)	1992	6.8	2 500
Lijiang, Yunan Province (China)	1996	7.0	304	Uttar Pradesh (India)	1991	6.1	1 000
				Costa Rica/Panama	1991	7.5	80
				Georgia	1991	7.2	100

Earth

Location	Year	Magni- tude	Deaths	Location	Year	Magni- tude	Deaths
Afghanistan	1991	6.8	1 000	Agadir (Morocco)	1960	5.8	12 000
Pakistan	1991	6.8	300	Erzincan (Turkey)	1939	7.9	23 000
Cabanatuan City (Philippines)	1990	7.7	1 653	Chillan (Chile)	1939	7.8	30 000
NW Iran	1990	7.5	40 000	Quetta (India)	1935	7.5	60 000
N Peru	1990	5.8	200	Gansu (China)	1932	7.6	70 000
Romania	1990	6.6	70	Nan-shan (China)	1927	8.3	200 000
Philippines	1990	7.7	1 600	Kwanto (Japan)	1923	8.3	143 000
San Francisco (USA)	1989	6.9	100	Gansu (China)	1920	8.6	180 000
Armenia	1988	7.0	25 000	Avezzano (Italy)	1915	7.5	30 000
SW China	1988	7.6	1 000	Messina (Italy)	1908	7.5	120 000
Nepal/India	1988	6.9	900	Valparaiso (Chile)	1906	8.6	20 000
Mexico City (Mexico)	1985	8.1	7 200	San Francisco (USA)	1906	8.3	500
N Yemen	1982	6.0	2 800	Ecuador/Colombia	1868	*	70 000
S Italy	1980	7.2	4 500	Calabria (Italy)	1783	*	50 000
El Asnam (Algeria)	1980	7.3	5 000	Lisbon (Portugal)	1755	*	70 000
NE Iran	1978	7.7	25 000	Calcutta (India)	1737	*	300 000
Tangshan (China)	1976	8.2	242 000	Hokkaido (Japan)	1730	*	137 000
Guatemala City (Guatemala)	1976	7.5	22 778	Catania (Italy)	1693	*	60 000
Kashmir (India)	1974	6.3	5 200	Caucasia (Caucasus)	1667	*	80 000
Managua (Nicaragua)	1972	6.2	5 000	Shensi (China)	1556	*	830 000
S Iran	1972	6.9	5 000	Chihli (China)	1290	*	100 000
Chimbote (Peru)	1970	7.7	66 000	Silicia (Asia Minor)	1268	*	60 000
NE Iran	1968	7.4	11 600	Corinth (Greece)	856	*	45 000
Anchorage (USA)	1964	8.5	131	Antioch (Turkey)	526	*	250 000
NW Iran	1962	7.1	12 000				

*Magnitude not available

Earthquake severity measurement

Modified Mercalli intensity scale (1956 Revision)

Intensity value	Description
I	Not felt; marginal and long-period effects of large earthquakes.
II	Felt by persons at rest, on upper floors or favourably placed.
III	Felt indoors; hanging objects swing; vibration like passing of light trucks; duration estimated; may not be recognized as an earthquake.
IV	Hanging objects swing; vibration like passing of heavy trucks, or sensation of a jolt like a heavy ball striking the walls; standing cars rock; windows, dishes, doors rattle; glasses clink; crockery clashes; in the upper range of IV, wooden walls and frames creak.
V	Felt outdoors; direction estimated; sleepers awoken; liquids disturbed, some spilled; small unstable objects displaced or upset; doors swing, close, open; shutters, pictures move; pendulum clocks stop, start, change rate.
VI	Felt by all; many frightened and run outdoors; persons walk unsteadily; windows, dishes, glassware break; knick-knacks, books, etc, fall off shelves; pictures off walls; furniture moves or overturns; weak plaster and masonry D crack; small bells ring (church, school); trees, bushes shake visibly, or heard to rustle.
VII	Difficult to stand; noticed by drivers; hanging objects quiver; furniture breaks; damage to masonry D, including cracks; weak chimneys broken at roof line; fall of plaster, loose bricks, stones, tiles, cornices, also unbraced parapets and architectural ornaments; some cracks in masonry C; waves on ponds, water turbid with mud; small slides and caving in along sand or gravel banks; large bells ring; concrete irrigation ditches damaged.

Intensity value	Description
VIII	Steering of cars affected; damage to masonry C and partial collapse; some damage to masonry B; none to masonry A; fall of stucco and some masonry walls; twisting, fall of chimneys, factory stacks, monuments, towers, elevated tanks; frame houses move on foundations if not bolted down; loose panel walls thrown out; decayed piling broken off; branches broken from trees; changes in flow or temperature of springs and wells; cracks in wet ground and on steep slopes.
IX	General panic; masonry D destroyed; masonry C heavily damaged, sometimes with complete collapse; masonry B seriously damaged; general damage to foundations; frame structures, if not bolted, shift off foundations; frames racked; serious damage to reservoirs; underground pipes break; conspicuous cracks in ground; in alluviated areas sand and mud ejected, earthquake fountains, sand craters.
X	Most masonry and frame structures destroyed with their foundations; some well-built wooden structures and bridges destroyed; serious damage to dams, dykes, embankments; large landslides; water thrown on banks of canals, rivers, lakes, etc; sand and mud shifted horizontally on beaches and flat land; rails bent slightly.
XI	Rails bent greatly; underground pipelines completely out of service.
XII	Damage nearly total; large rock masses displaced; lines of sight and level distorted; objects thrown into the air.

Earth

Notes:

Masonry A   Good workmanship, mortar and design; reinforced, especially laterally, and bound together by using steel, concrete etc; designed to resist lateral forces.

Masonry B   Good workmanship and mortar; reinforced, but not designed in detail to resist lateral forces.

Masonry C   Ordinary workmanship and mortar; no extreme weakness like failing to tie in at corners, but neither reinforced nor designed against horizontal forces.

Masonry D   Weak materials, such as adobe; poor mortar; low standards of workmanship; weak horizontally.

Mohs' hardness scale

The relative hardness of solids can be expressed using a scale of numbers from 1 to 10, each relating to a mineral (1 representing talc, 10 representing diamond). The method was devised by Friedrich Mohs (1773–1839), a German mineralogist. Sets of hardness pencils are used to test specimens to see what will scratch them; other useful instruments include: fingernail (2.5), copper coin (3.5), steel knife (5.5), glass (6.0).

Talc	1	Calcite	3	Apatite	5	Quartz	7	Corundum	9
Gypsum	2	Fluorite	4	Orthoclase	6	Topaz	8	Diamond	10

Properties of common minerals

Name	Type	Mohs of hardness	Specific gravity	Crystal	Optical	Fracture
Talc	Silicate	1	2.6–2.8	Monoclinic	Pale green or grey, pearly lustre	Uneven
Graphite	Element	1–2	2.1–2.3	Trigonal/ hexagonal	Grey metallic lustre	Perfect basal cleavage
Gypsum	Sulphate	2	2.32	Monoclinic	White to transparent	Splintery
Calcite	Carbonate	3	2.71	Trigonal/ hexagonal	Double refraction	Perfect rhombic cleavage
Barytes	Sulphate	3–3.5	4.5	Orthorhombic	Pale, translucent	Perfect cleavage
Aragonite	Carbonate	3.5–4	2.95	Orthorhombic	Translucent white streak	Subconchoidal
Dolomite	Carbonate	3.5–4	2.85	Trigonal/ hexagonal	Pale, translucent	Rhombohedral cleavage
Fluorite	Halide	4	3.18	Cubic	Many colours, fluorescent	Perfect octahe-dral cleavage
Apatite	Phosphate	5	3.1–3.2	Trigonal/ hexagonal	Usually green	Uneven
Sodalite	Silicate	5.5–6	2.2–2.4	Cubic	Blue	Uneven
Pyrite	Sulphide	6–6.5	5.0	Cubic	'Fool's Gold'	Uneven
Quartz	Oxide	7	2.65	Trigonal/ hexagonal	Translucent, also microcrystalline	Uneven
Garnet	Silicate	7	3.5–4.3	Cubic	Various forms, often plum red	Uneven
Tourmaline	Silicate	7–7.5	3.0–3.2	Trigonal/ hexagonal	Often pink or green	Uneven
Zircon	Silicate	7.5	4.3	Tetragonal	Often brown	Uneven
Beryl	Silicate	7–8	2.6–2.9	Trigonal/ hexagonal	Many colours, emerald green	Uneven
Spinel	Oxide	7.5–8	3.5–4.1	Cubic	Many colours, vitreous lustre	Uneven
Corundum	Oxide	9	4.0–4.1	Trigonal/ hexagonal	Various forms including ruby and sapphire	Uneven
Diamond	Element	10	3.52	Cubic	Transparent, sparkles if cut	Octahedral cleavage

Properties of gemstones

Nearly all gemstones are minerals, as are those in this table. The four non-mineral gems are amber, coral, jet and pearl. The hardness of solid substances is expressed on the Mohs' scale.

Mineral	Colour	Mohs of hardness
agate	brown, red, blue, green, yellow	7.0
alexandrite	green, red	8.5
amethyst	violet	7.0
aquamarine	sky blue, greenish blue	7.5
beryl	green, blue, pink	7.5
bloodstone	green with red spots	7.0

Earth

Mineral	Colour	Mohs of hardness
chalcedony	all colours	7.0
chrysoprase	apple green	7.0
citrine	yellow	7.0
diamond	colourless, tints of various colours	10.0
emerald	green	7.5
garnet	red and other colours	6.5–7.25
jade	green, whitish, mauve, brown	7.0
jasper	dark red, multi-coloured	7.0
lapis lazuli	deep blue	5.5
malachite	dark green banded	3.5
moonstone	whitish with blue shimmer	6.0
onyx	various colours with straight coloured bands	7.0
opal	black, white, orange-red, rainbow coloured	6.0
peridot	green	6.5
ruby	red	9.0
sapphire	blue and other colours	9.0
serpentine	red and green	3.0
soapstone	white, may be stained with impurities	2.0
sunstone	whitish red-brown flecked with golden particles	6.0
topaz	blue, green, pink, yellow, colourless	8.0
tourmaline	brown-black, blue, pink, red, violet-red, yellow, green	7.5
turquoise	greenish grey, sky blue	6.0
zircon	all colours	7.5

Classification of sedimentary rocks

Sedimentary rocks result from the deposition of materials transported by water, wind or ice. Clastic rocks are the eroded remnants of earlier rocks; chemical sediments are formed from precipitation out of solution; organic sediments are formed from living material.

Clastic

Conglomerate	Large, rounded, cemented
Breccia	Coarse, angular, cemented
Gritstone	Coarse
Sandstone	Medium
Greensand	With glauconite
Greywacke	Deep ocean sediments
Siltstone	Fine, with more quartz than shale
Loess	Fine, angular particles
Marl	Fine silt or clay with limestone cement
Shale	Very fine laminated clay and detritus
Mudstone	Clay and very fine grains cemented with iron or calcite
Clay	Very fine; absorbs water

Chemical

Limestone	Calcium carbonate
Chalk	Soft white limestone, mostly microfossils
Tufa	Calcium carbonate; precipitated from fresh water
Dolomite	Calcium and magnesium carbonate
Ironstone	Limestone or chert enriched in iron, often Pre-Cambrian
Chert and flint	Hard silicatious nodules or sheets in chalk or limestone

Organic

Peat	Plant material
Lignite	Soft, carbonaceous
Coal	Hard, brittle, carbonaceous
Jet	Hard, black, coal-like

Principal metamorphic rocks

Metamorphic rocks are produced when pressure and heat cause changes in existing rocks.

Name	Texture	Origin
Slate	Aligned minerals produce perfect cleavage; not necessarily aligned with bedding	Sedimentary shale and clay
Phyllite	As slate, but coarser, with small-scale folding	Medium grain sediments
Schist	Flaky minerals such as mica give glittery, foliated texture	Sediments buried deep in mountain belts, eg siltstones

Name	Texture	Origin
Gneiss	Medium/coarse grain; quartz, feldspar and mica with darker layers or lines	High pressure and temperature, from sediment or granite; abundant deep under continents
Migmatite	Mixture of dark schist and light granitic rock; highly folded	Extensive deep metamorphism of sediments
Eclogite	Coarse grain; mostly green pyroxene and red garnet	Very high temperature and pressure close to mantle
Amphibolite	Coarse grain; often foliated; mostly hornblende	Highly metamorphosed igneous dolerite
Marble	Crystalline, soft and sugary; made of calcium carbonate	Limestone heated by igneous intrusion
Hornfels	Fine grain; dark coloured with quartz, mica and pyroxene	Sediments closest to hot igneous intrusion
Quartzite	Medium grain; of even texture with fused quartz crystals; very hard	Sandy sediment heated by intrusion or regional metamorphism
Serpentenite	Coarse grain; green serpentine minerals	Intense metamorphism of olivine-rich rock

Principal igneous rocks

Igneous rocks result from volcanic activity in the Earth's crust and upper mantle.

Rock	Texture	Type	Composition	Origin	Features	Varieties
Granite	Coarse	Acid	>20% quartz, K-feldspars, mica	Intrusive batholiths	Occasional phenocrysts	Pink, white and microgranite
Pegmatite	Coarse	Acid	>20% quartz, mica and feldspar	Deep batholiths and dykes	Very large crystals	Occasional rare minerals
Diorite	Coarse	Intermediate	Plagioclase feldspar and hornblende	Dykes associated with granite	Biotite and pyroxene	Granodiorite with quartz
Syenite	Coarse	Intermediate	Little or no quartz, otherwise like granite	Dykes and sills near granite	Often pink	Nepheline syenite, quartz syenite
Gabbro	Coarse	Basic	Plagioclase, pyroxene and olivine	Large layered intrusions	Layers of magnetite	Olivine gabbro
Larvikite	Coarse	Intermediate	Feldspar crystals with pyroxene, mica and amphibolite banks	Small sills	Popular for cladding banks	None
Anorthosite	Coarse	Basic	>90% plagioclase feldspar	Layered intrusions, on Moon	Aligned mineral grains	Can include olivine and pyroxene
Dolerite	Medium	Basic	<10% quartz with plagioclase and pyroxene	Dykes and sills near basalt	Dark colour	None
Dunite	Medium	Ultrabasic	Almost entirely olivine	Deep sourced intrusions	Can contain chromite	None
Kimberlite	Coarse	Ultrabasic	Dense ferromagnesian minerals	Pipes of deep ancient volcanoes	Sometimes contains diamonds	None
Peridotite	Coarse	Ultrabasic	No quartz or feldspar, mostly olivine and garnet	Caught up in intrusions	Possibly derived from mantle	With pyroxene and hornblende
Rhyolite	Fine	Acid	As granite	Explosive volcanic eruptions	Phenocrysts and gas bubbles	Banded form
Obsidian	Glassy	Acid	Silica-rich glass	Rapid cooling of acid lava	Black, glassy	Snowflake obsidian
Lamprophyre	Medium	Acid to basic	Amphibole pyroxene and biotite	Dykes and sills around granite	Phenocrysts of biotite and hornblende	None
Andesite	Fine	Intermediate	Mainly plagioclase	Volcanoes above subduction zones	Dark with white phenocrysts	With vesicles of zeolite
Trachyte	Fine	Intermediate	<10% quartz, rich in alkali feldspar	Lava flows, dykes and sills	Not many	Sometimes porphyritic
Basalt	Fine	Basic	Plagioclase and pyroxene	Volcanic eruptions	Dark — the commonest lava	Bubbles and vesicles
Tuff	Fine	Acid to basic	Consolidated volcanic fragments	Thrown out by volcanic vents	Variable	Tuff-breccia, lapilli-tuff
Pumice	Fine	Acid to basic	Glass and minute silicate crystals	Rapidly quenched frothy lava	Can sometimes float	Bubbles and vesicles

Earth

Earth

Fossils

Fossils are produced when animals and plants decompose and become preserved within sedimentary rock.

Period	Fossil type
Cenozoic	Foraminifera (plankton)
Upper Cretaceous	Foraminifera, echinoderms, bivalves and belemnites
Lower Cretaceous	Ammonites
Jurassic	Ammonites plus ostracods (tiny crustacea) and bivalves
Triassic	Ammonites
Permian	Foraminifera, ammonites and goniatites (ammonite ancestors)
Carboniferous	Foraminifera, goniatites, fresh-water bivalves and plants
Lower Carboniferous	Corals and brachiopods
Devonian	Goniatites, fish and plants
Silurian	Graptolites (thin, branching, free-swimming, coral-like)
Ordovician	Graptolites, trilobites (small crustacea)
Cambrian	Trilobites and brachiopods

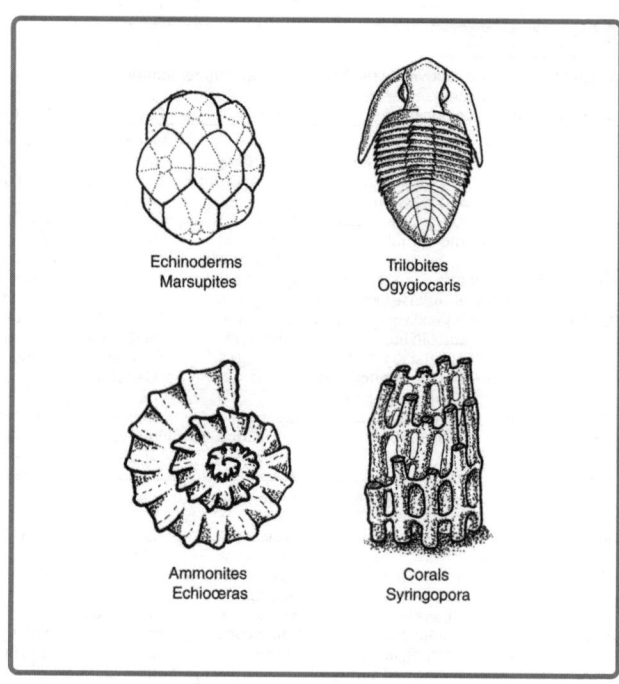

Echinoderms
Marsupites

Trilobites
Ogygiocaris

Ammonites
Echioceras

Corals
Syringopora

Geological time scale

Cenozoic

This Era is divided into two sub-eras or periods, Tertiary and Quaternary. In the early part of the former, the flora and fauna of the Cretaceous gave way to more modern forms, with the mammals replacing the reptiles as the dominant fauna. Later, in the Miocene, large-scale earth movements built many of the mountain ranges of the world, followed by wide-scale volcanic activity.

In the much shorter Quaternary, modern landscape and geography were laid down. The many stages were much influenced by the ice ages, and differ in name and typical climate around the world.

Quaternary sub-era

The Quaternary is completely different from any previous period. It has had a much shorter time span than any earlier period, less than two million years, but the period has exerted a profound influence on mankind: its processes and deposits mould the modern landscape and geography. The British Isles, north of a line from the Bristol Channel to the mouth of the Thames, and much of Europe were affected by glaciation which also markedly influenced sea levels. The record of past climatic fluctuations and the history of modern faunas, floras and the human race during and since the last glaciation lie in the Quaternary deposits.

In all previous periods it is possible to establish correlations based on the evolution and disappearance of species, but this method is of limited use in the Quaternary where climatic fluctuations are predominantly used in its chronology. The enormous variations between different regions at any one time, involving latitude and altitude, frequently render precise correlations of deposits and events difficult, and impossible over longer distances. The table shows the stage names that are widely used for the British Quaternary although there is no complete agreement on their use or validity.

Throughout the world, differently named, locally based, stages have been established, with which the British stages cannot be firmly correlated. The most recent stage, the Flandrian, is correlated by general agreement with the Holocene of the Continent, and the Devensian cold stage with the Weichselian of north-west continental Europe. In the Alps, successive glaciations are named as Günz (oldest), Mindel, Riss and Würm (youngest). The Würm glaciation can be correlated with the Devensian.

Era	Period	Series	British stages	Climate	Age
Cenozoic	Quaternary	Holocene or Recent	Flandrian	temperate	10 000 years
		Pleistocene	Devensian	last glacial	
			Ipswichian	temperate	
			Wolstonian	cold, glacial	
			Hoxnian	temperate	
			Anglian	glacial	
			Cromerian	temperate	
			Beestonian	glacial	
			Pastonian	temperate	
			Baventian	cold	
			Antian	temperate	
			Thurnian	cold	
			Ludhamian	temperate	
			Waltonian	variable	1.64 Ma

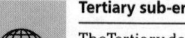

Earth

Tertiary sub-era

TheTertiary derives its name from an old and disused division of all geological time into three parts. It forms the lower part of the Cenozoic era (also *Cainozoic, Kainozoic*, meaning 'recent life') and consists of five epochs or series: Palaeocene, Eocene, Oligocene, Miocene and Pliocene.

There was a very marked change from the flora and fauna of the Cretaceous to plants and animals of more modern aspect. On land there was a reversal of roles of reptiles and mammals, the latter becoming predominant.

During the Eocene, lavas, mainly basaltic, erupted from a series of fissures in many parts of the world including north-east Ireland and western Scotland, and plutonic centres developed at a number of localities including Skye, Rhum, Ardnamurchan, Mull, Arran, the Mourne Mountains and Rockall in the North Atlantic. There were also extensive dyke swarms.

Era	Sub-era, Period		Series	Stage	Age, Ma
Cenozoic		Quaternary	Holocene		
			Pleistocene		
					1.64
	Tertiary	Neogene	Pliocene	Piacenzian	3.4
				Zanclian	5.2
			Miocene	Messinian	6.7
				Tortonian	10.4
				Serravallian	14.2
				Langhian	16.3
				Burdigalian	21.5
				Aquitanian	23.3
		Palaeogene	Oligocene	Chattian	29.3
				Rupelian	35.4
			Eocene	Priabonian	38.6
				Bartonian	42.1
				Lutetian	50.0
				Ypresian	56.5
			Palaeocene	Thanetian	60.5
				Danian	65.0

The Palaeogene had a temperate to warm climate and forests became widespread in theTertiary. Lamellibranchs, gastropods and echinoderms were abundant. In the Neogene (Miocene and Pliocene), the climate was temperate and warm, cooling in the Pliocene of more northern latitudes.

Following earlier Palaeogene tremors, earth-movements during the Miocene built many of the mountain ranges of the world (Himalayas, Rockies, Alps etc). Britain was on the edge of the area affected and folding occured in southern England, including the anticline of theWealden axis and the syncline of the London basin.

Mesozoic

The Mesozoic ('middle life') was characterized by ammonites and reptiles, together with brachiopods, lamellibranchs, gastropods and corals. The first period, the Triassic, had an impoverished fauna and flora that followed the extinctions at the end of the Palaeozoic era. During the second period, the Jurassic, there was a rich flora in the warm climate, when reptiles, notably dinosaurs, were dominant on land. In the Cretaceous, flowering plants spread and many large reptiles, ammonites, most belemnites and many brachiopod species became extinct, and chalk was the most important formation.

Era	Period	Series	Stage		Age, Ma
Mesozoic	Cretaceous	Upper		Maastrichtian	74
			Senonian	Campanian	83
				Santonian	87
				Coniacian	89
			Turonian		90
			Cenomanian		97
		Lower	Albian		112
			Aptian		125
			Barremian		132
			Hauterivian		135
			Valanginian		141
			Ryazanian		146
	Jurassic	Upper (Malm)	Portlandian		152
			Kimmeridgian		155
			Oxfordian		157
			Callovian		161
		Middle (Dogger)	Bathonian		166
			Bajocian		174
			Aalenian		178
		Lower (Lias)	Toarcian		187
			Pliensbachian		194
			Sinemurian		204
			Hettangian		208
	Triassic	Upper	Rhaetian		210
		Middle			235
					241
		Lower			245

Earth

Palaeozoic

Earth

The oldest of the Phanerozoic eras. The Palaeozoic ('ancient life') began with the Cambrian period, when there was a great expansion of animal life, now recorded by the fossils, especially trilobites, brachiopods, graptolites and molluscs, as well as early plant life. Graptolites and trilobites reached their acme in the Ordovician, and in the Silurian lamellibranchs became abundant. Amphibians evolved by the end of the Devonian when the graptolites had become extinct. During the Carboniferous there was a rich flora in Coal Measure forests, but a glacial climate existed in Gondwana continents. The trilobites died out in the Permian, a period of desert conditions in Britain.

Era	Period	Series	Stage	Age, Ma
Palaeozoic	Permian	Zechstein		256
		Rotliegendes		290
	Carboniferous — Pennsylvanian, Silesian	Stephanian		
		Westphalian		318
		Namurian		333
	Carboniferous — Mississippian, Dinantian	Viséan		350
		Tournaisian		362
	Devonian	Upper	Famerinian	367
			Frasnian	377
		Middle	Givetian	381
			Eifelian	386
		Lower	Emsian	390
			Siegenian	398
			Gedinnian	408
	Silurian	Ludlow		424
		Wenlock		430
		Llandovery		439
	Ordovician	Ashgill		443
		Caradoc		464
		Llandeilo		469
		Llanvirn		476
		Arenig		493
		Tremadoc		510
	Cambrian	Upper		517
		Middle		536
		Lower		570

Precambrian

All rocks which were formed before the Cambrian. They consist of two divisions, the older a series of highly metamorphosed rocks, crystalline schists and gneisses with intrusive rocks, largely of Archaean age, eg the Lewisian Complex. Unconformably overlying this basement complex are Proterozoic sediments, eg the Torridonian (of Riphean age). There is little agreement on how Precambrian rocks should be divided, and almost no formal divisions. The table below shows a number of the more widely used terms.

In the highest Proterozoic there are impressions of soft-bodied animals and trace fossils (burrows and tracks) indicating a long period of earlier evolution. Primitive plant life existed well back into the Archaean, and bacteria may have existed 3 800 Ma ago. The algae are the only fossil group to have had a widespread development in the Precambrian.

Eon		Era	Age, Ma
Phanerozoic			570
Precambrian	Proterozoic	Vendian	610
		Riphean	1 650
		Aphebian	2 500
	Archaean		4 600

Earth

CLIMATE AND ENVIRONMENT

Climatic zones

The earth may be divided into zones, approximating to zones of latitude, such that each zone possesses a distinct type of climate.

The principal zones are:

- **Tropical** One zone of wet climate near the equator (either constantly wet or monsoonal with wet and dry seasons, tropical savannah with dry winters); the average temperature is not below 18°C;
  - Amazon forest
  - Malaysia
  - S Vietnam
  - India
  - Africa
  - Congo Basin
  - Indonesia
  - S E Asia
  - Australia
- **Subtropical** Two zones of steppe and desert climate (transition through semi-arid to arid);
  - Sahara
  - Central Asia
  - Mexico
  - Australia
  - Kalahari
- **Mediterranean** Zones of rainy climate with mild winters; coolest month above 0°C but below 18°C;
  - California
  - S Africa
  - S Europe
  - parts of Chile
  - SW Australia

- **Temperate** Rainy climate (includes areas of temperate woodland, mountain forests, and plains with no dry season; influenced by seas — rainfall all year, small temperate changes); average temperature between 3°C and 18°C;
  - Most of Europe
  - Eastern Asia
  - NW/NE USA
  - New Zealand
  - Southern Chile
- **Boreal** Climate with a great range of temperature in the northern hemisphere (in some areas the most humid month is in summer and there is ten times more precipitation than the driest part of winter. In other areas the most humid month is in winter and there is ten times more precipitation than in the driest part of summer); in the coldest period temperatures do not exceed 3°C and in the hottest do not go below 10°C;
  - Prairies of USA
  - parts of S Africa
  - parts of Russia
  - parts of Australia
- **Polar caps** Snowy climate (tundra and ice-cap) with little or no precipitation. There is permafrost in the tundra and vegetation includes lichen and moss all year, and grass in the summer; the highest annual temperature in the polar region is below 0°C and in the tundra the average temperature is 10°C;
  - Arctic regions of Russia and N America
  - Antarctica

Great ice ages

Precambrian era	Early Proterozoic
Precambrian era	Upper Proterozoic
Palaeozoic era	Upper Carboniferous
Cenozoic era	Pleistocene[1]
	(Last 4 periods of glaciation)
	Günz (Nebraskan or Jerseyan) 520 000–490 000 years ago
	Mindel (Kansan) 430 000–370 000 years ago
	Riss (Illinoian) 130 000–100 000 years ago
	Würm (Wisconsin and Iowan) 40 000–18 000 years ago

[1] The Pleistocene epoch is synonymous with 'The Ice Age'.

Wind force and sea disturbance

Beaufort number	m/ sec	Windspeed kph	mph	Wind name	Observable wind characteristics	Sea disturbance number	Average wave ht. m	ft	Obervable sea characteristics
0	1	<1	<1	Calm	Smoke rises vertically	0	0	0	Sea like a mirror
1	1	1–5	1–3	Light air	Wind direction shown by smoke drift, but not by wind vanes	0	0	0	Ripples like scales, without foam crests

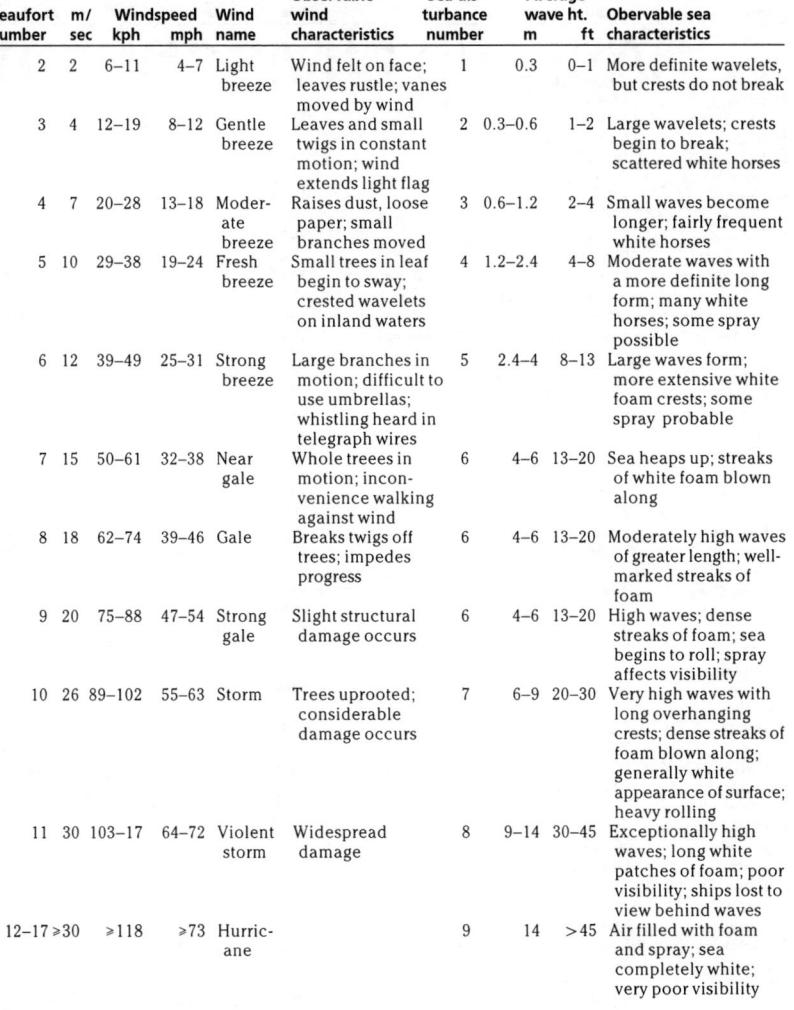

Beaufort number	m/ sec	Windspeed kph	mph	Wind name	Observable wind characteristics	Sea disturbance number	Average wave ht. m	ft	Obervable sea characteristics
2	2	6–11	4–7	Light breeze	Wind felt on face; leaves rustle; vanes moved by wind	1	0.3	0–1	More definite wavelets, but crests do not break
3	4	12–19	8–12	Gentle breeze	Leaves and small twigs in constant motion; wind extends light flag	2	0.3–0.6	1–2	Large wavelets; crests begin to break; scattered white horses
4	7	20–28	13–18	Moder- ate breeze	Raises dust, loose paper; small branches moved	3	0.6–1.2	2–4	Small waves become longer; fairly frequent white horses
5	10	29–38	19–24	Fresh breeze	Small trees in leaf begin to sway; crested wavelets on inland waters	4	1.2–2.4	4–8	Moderate waves with a more definite long form; many white horses; some spray possible
6	12	39–49	25–31	Strong breeze	Large branches in motion; difficult to use umbrellas; whistling heard in telegraph wires	5	2.4–4	8–13	Large waves form; more extensive white foam crests; some spray probable
7	15	50–61	32–38	Near gale	Whole treees in motion; incon- venience walking against wind	6	4–6	13–20	Sea heaps up; streaks of white foam blown along
8	18	62–74	39–46	Gale	Breaks twigs off trees; impedes progress	6	4–6	13–20	Moderately high waves of greater length; well-marked streaks of foam
9	20	75–88	47–54	Strong gale	Slight structural damage occurs	6	4–6	13–20	High waves; dense streaks of foam; sea begins to roll; spray affects visibility
10	26	89–102	55–63	Storm	Trees uprooted; considerable damage occurs	7	6–9	20–30	Very high waves with long overhanging crests; dense streaks of foam blown along; generally white appearance of surface; heavy rolling
11	30	103–17	64–72	Violent storm	Widespread damage	8	9–14	30–45	Exceptionally high waves; long white patches of foam; poor visibility; ships lost to view behind waves
12–17	≥30	≥118	≥73	Hurric- ane		9	14	>45	Air filled with foam and spray; sea completely white; very poor visibility

Windstorms

A **cyclone** is a circulation of winds in the atmosphere which rotates anticlockwise round a depression in the northern hemisphere and clockwise in the southern.

A **hurricane** is a windstorm originating over tropical oceans in the N hemisphere, with winds in excess of 74mph. Hurricanes are named by the National Hurricane Center, USA, in alphabetical sequence as they occur each year. Since 1978 names given have been alternately male/female. In the N Pacific they are known as **typhoons**. Abbrev H. and T.

A **tornado** is a column of air rotating rapidly around a very low pressure centre.

Information on selected windstorms to 2000 is given.

Name	Location	Year	Deaths	Damage in US $ million[1]
C. Gloria	Madagascar, Mozambique	2000	*	*
C. Eline	Madagascar, Mozambique	2000	*	*
Cyclone	Orissa	1999	10 000+	2 300
H. Floyd	Florida, N Carolina, The Bahamas	1999	57	3 000–6 000
H. Mitch	C America (Honduras, Nicaragua), Florida	1998	10 000+	5 500
H. Georges	NE Caribbean, Mississippi	1998	602	5 900
T. Linda	Vietnam, Thailand	1997	453	400

Climate and Environment

Name	Location	Year	Deaths	Damage in US $ million[1]
H. Fran	N Carolina	1996	34	3 200
H. Opal	NW Florida	1995	19	3 000
H. Marilyn	Virgin Is, Puerto Rico	1995	9	1 500
H. Gordon	Florida, Alabama	1994	4	400
H. Andrew	S Florida, The Bahamas	1992	88	26 500
H. Iniki	Kauai, Hawaii	1992	3	1 800
H. Bob	NE USA	1991	17	1 500
Cyclone	Bangladesh	1991	200 000	—
H. Hugo	S Carolina	1989	49	7 000
H. Gilbert	Caribbean, Mexico	1988	318	5 000
H. Joan	Caribbean	1988	216	—
Winter Storm	S England, NW France	1987	17	1 700
T. Vera	Korea, Democratic People's Republic of (North Korea)	1986	—	40
H. Juan	Louisiana	1985	12	1 500
H. Elena	Mississippi, Alabama, NW Florida	1985	2	1 250
H. Gloria	E USA	1985	15	900
H. Kate	Florida (Keys), NW Florida	1985	16	300
Cyclone	Bangladesh	1985	11 000	—
Ts. Ike and June	Philippines (Mindanao)	1984	1 000	220
H. Alicia	N Texas	1983	18	2 000
H. Allen	S Texas	1980	235	300
H. David	Florida, E USA	1979	2 400	320
H. Frederic	Alabama, Mississippi	1979	31	2 300
H. Eloise	NW Florida	1975	100	490
H. Carmen	Louisiana	1974	1	150
Tornadoes	C USA	1974	322	1 000
H. Fifi	C America (Honduras)	1974	10 000	1 000
Cyclone Tracy	Australia (Darwin)	1974	65	1 000
H. Agnes	E Coast, USA	1972	122	2 100
Cyclone	Bangladesh	1970	300 000	86
H. Camille	Mississippi, Louisiana	1969	256	1 420.7
H. Beulah	S Texas	1967	15	200
H. Betsy	SE Florida, SE Louisiana, Mississippi	1965	75	1 420.5
T. Louise	Philippines (Mindanao)	1964	58	600
H. Hilda	C Louisiana	1964	38	125
H. Dora	NE Florida	1964	5	250
H. Cleo	SE Florida	1964	154	128.5
H. Flora	Haiti, Cuba, Dominican Republic	1963	7 000	625
H. Carla	Texas	1961	46	408
H. Donna	Florida, E USA	1960	50	387
T. Vera	Ise Bay, Japan	1959	5 098	600
H. Audrey	Louisiana, N Texas	1957	390	150
H. Diane	NE USA	1955	184	831.7
H. Hazel	S Carolina, N Carolina	1954	95	281
H. Carol	NE USA	1954	60	461
Typhoon	Japan (Toyama, N Honshu)	1954	3 000	—
Hurricane	SE Florida, Louisiana, Mississippi	1947	51	110
Typhoon	Japan (Makurazaki)	1945	3 756	400
Hurricane	NE USA	1944	390	100
Cyclone	Bangladesh	1942	61 000	—
Hurricane	Georgia, S Carolina, N Carolina	1940	50	5
Hurricane	New England	1938	600	306
Hurricane	Florida (Keys)	1935	408	12
Hurricane	S Texas	1933	40	—
Hurricane	Texas (Freeport)	1932	40	—
Hurricane	Cuba	1932	2 500	—
Hurricane	Belize	1931	2 000	—
Hurricane	San Zenon, Santo Domingo, Dominican Republic	1930	2 000	60
Hurricane	Florida (Lake Okeechobee)	1928	1 836	25
Hurricane	Florida (Miami)	1926	243	112
Typhoon	China (Shantou)	1922	28 000	—
Hurricane	Florida (Keys), S Texas	1919	600–900	22
Typhoon	Japan (Honshu)	1917	4 000	50
Hurricane	N Texas (Galveston), Louisiana (New Orleans)	1915	550	63
Tornado	Ohio, Indiana	1913	700	200
Typhoon	China (Wenchang)	1912	50 000	—
Hurricane	Louisiana (Grand Isle)	1909	350	—
Typhoon	Hong Kong	1906	10 000	20

Name	Location	Year	Deaths	Damage in US $ million[1]
Hurricane	SE Florida	1906	164	—
Hurricane	Mississippi, Alabama, Florida (Pensacola)	1906	134	—
Hurricane	N Texas (Galveston)	1900	6 000	30
Hurricane	San Ciriaco	1899	3 369	20
Typhoon	Philippines (Leyte)	1897	10 000	10
Hurricane	S Carolina, Georgia	1893	1 000	—
Typhoon	W Coast, Japan	1884	2 000	—
Cyclone	India (Bombay)	1882	100 000	—
Typhoon	China	1881	300 000	—
Cyclone	Bangladesh (Bakarganj)	1876	215 000	—
Cyclone	India (Calcutta)	1864	50 000	—
Cyclone	Bangladesh (Bakarganj)	1822	50 000	—
Hurricane	Cuba	1791	3 000	—
Hurricane	West Indies, Barbados, Martinique, St Vincent, Guadeloupe	1780	24 000	—
Cyclone	India (Calcutta)	1737	300 000	—
Winter Storm	UK (sinking of the Spanish Armada)	1588	20 000	—

[1] No adjustment has been made for inflation.
* Indeterminate, due to severe flooding prior to cyclone.

World temperatures

The maps below show the average world temperatures for January and July.

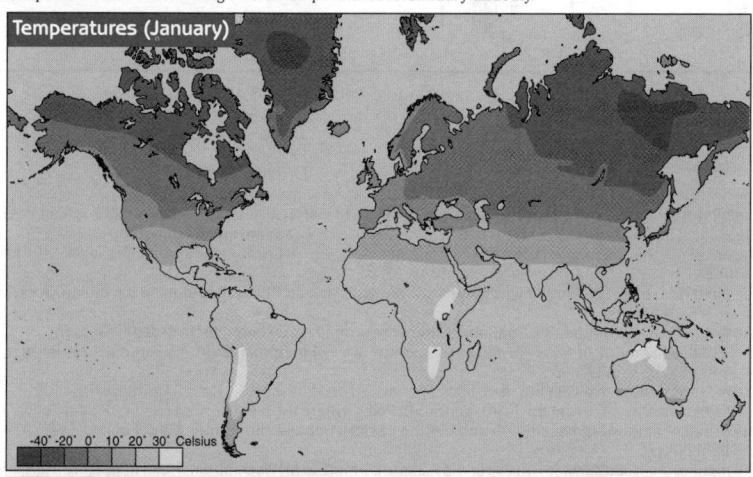

Temperatures (January)

-40° -20° 0° 10° 20° 30° Celsius

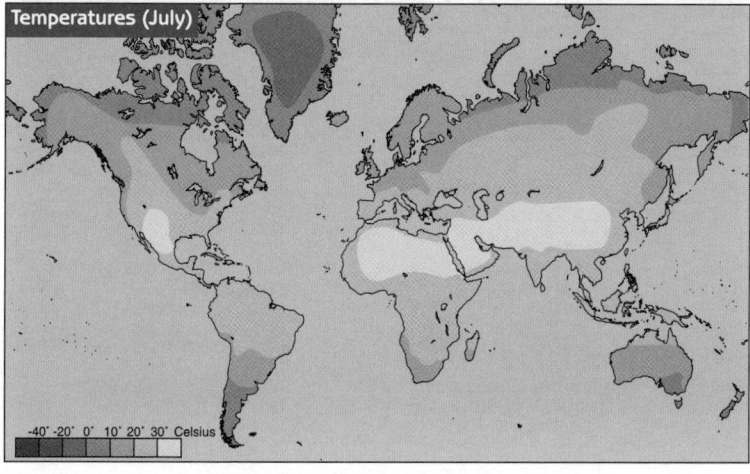

Temperatures (July)

-40° -20° 0° 10° 20° 30° Celsius

Climate and Environment

World temperature change

Climate and Environment

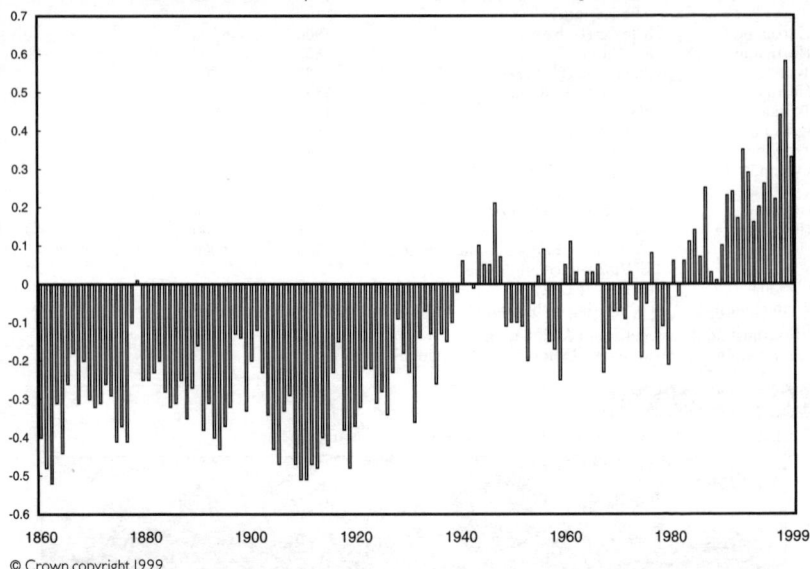

Global Near-Surface Temperatures 1860–1999, relative to the average for 1961–90

© Crown copyright 1999

Meteorological extremes

- The hottest place is Dallol, Ethiopia, at 34.4°C/93.9°F (annual mean temperature).
- The highest recorded temperature in the shade is 58°D/136°4F at al'Aziziyah, Libya, on 13 September 1922.
- The coldest place is Pole of Cold, Antarctica, at −57.8°C/−72°F (annual mean temperature).
- The driest place is the Atacama desert near Calama, Chile, where no rainfall was recorded in over 400 years to 1972.
- The most rain to fall in 24 hours was 1 870mm/74in. which fell on Cilaos, Réunion, in the Indian Ocean, on 15–16 March 1952.
- The wettest place is Tutunendo, Colombia, where the rainfall is 11 770mm/464in (annual average).
- The greatest amount of snow to fall in 12 months was 31 102mm/1 225in, at Paradise, Mt Rainier, in Washington, USA, in 1971–2.
- The most rainy days in a year are the.c.350 experienced on Mt Waialeale, Kauai, Hawaii, USA.
- The least sunshine occurs at the North and South Poles, where the Sun does not rise for 182 days of winter.
- The greatest amount of sunshine occurs in the eastern Sahara: more than 4 300 hours a year (97% of daylight hours).
- The highest recorded surface wind speed is 371kph/231mph, at Mt Washington, New Hampshire, USA, on 12 April 1934.

Acid rain

A term generally used for polluted rainfall associated with the burning of fossil fuels. It is implicated in damage to forests and the stonework of buildings, and increases the acid content of soils and lakes, harming crops and fish.

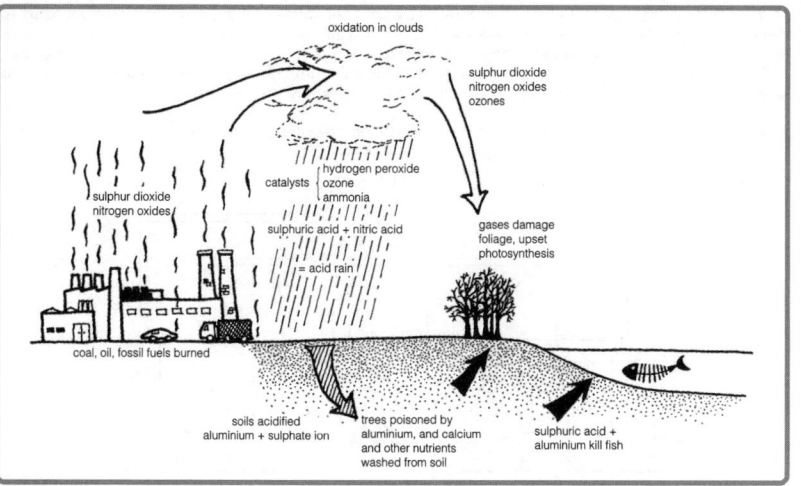

oxidation in clouds

sulphur dioxide
nitrogen oxides
ozones

hydrogen peroxide
catalysts ozone
ammonia

sulphur dioxide
nitrogen oxides

sulphuric acid + nitric acid

= acid rain

gases damage
foliage, upset
photosynthesis

coal, oil, fossil fuels burned

soils acidified
aluminium + sulphate ion

trees poisoned by
aluminium, and calcium
and other nutrients
washed from soil

sulphuric acid +
aluminium kill fish

Clouds

Clouds are formed by the condensation or freezing of water vapour on minute particles in the atmosphere when air masses move upward as a result of convection currents, unstable conditions, etc, and in so doing cool rapidly. Clouds are usually classified according to their height and shape.

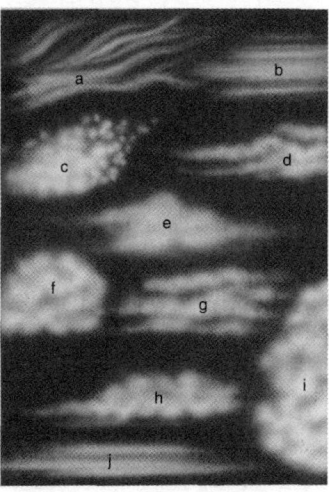

a. cirrus
b. cirrostratus
c. cirrocumulus
d. altocumulus
e. altostratus

f. cumulus
g. stratocumulus
h. nimbostratus
i. cumulonimbus
j. stratus

Climate and Environment

Climate and Environment

Nitrogen cycle

The diagram below illustrates the continuous circulation of nitrogen and its compounds between the atmosphere and the biosphere as a result of the activity of living organisms.

Nitrogen taken up by plants is incorporated into proteins, and when such plants are subsequently eaten by animals, it is incorporated into animal protein. The excreta of animals, together with the decomposing remains of dead plants and animals, are broken down by nitrifying bacteria to form ammonia, which is oxidized first to nitrites and then to nitrates in a process known as *nitrification*. The ammonia and nitrates may be used as plant nutrients, and nitrates are also converted to molecular nitrogen (which is released back to the atmosphere) by bacteria that live in waterlogged soils, in a process known as *denitrification*.

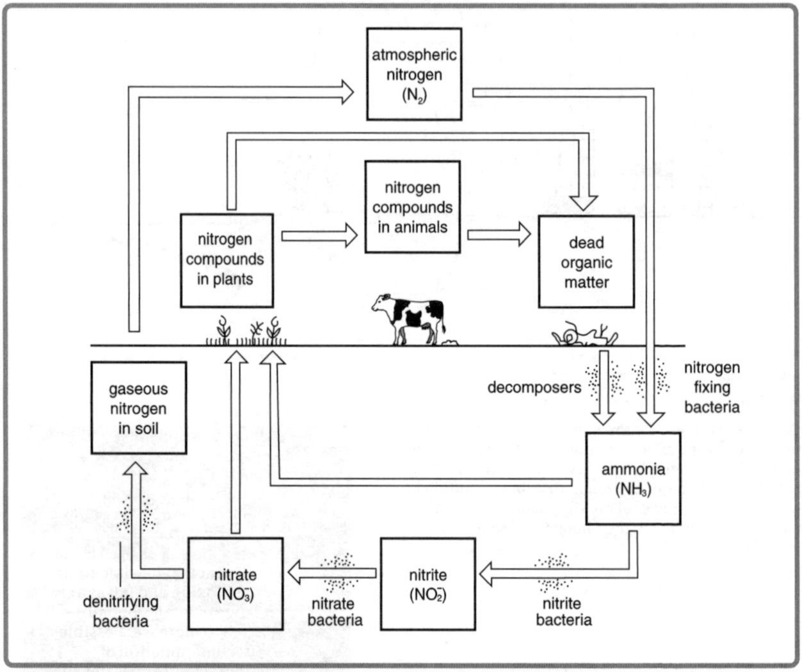

atmospheric nitrogen (N_2)

nitrogen compounds in animals

nitrogen compounds in plants

dead organic matter

decomposers

nitrogen fixing bacteria

gaseous nitrogen in soil

ammonia (NH_3)

denitrifying bacteria

nitrate (NO_3^-)

nitrate bacteria

nitrite (NO_2^-)

nitrite bacteria

Environmental disasters on land

Location	Event	Date	Consequence
Basle, Switzerland	Fire in Sandoz factory warehouse resulted in major chemical spill.	Nov 1980	River Rhine rendered lifeless for 200km/124mi.
Beirut	Toxic waste dumped by Italian company.	Jul–Sep 1988	Italy forced to take back its poison drums.
Bhopal, India	Toxic gas leaked from a Union Carbide pesticide plant and enveloped a nearby slum area housing 200 000 people.	Dec 1984	Possibly 10 000 people died (officially 2 352). Survivors suffer ravaged lungs and/or blindness. 100km² /39mi² affected by the gas.
Camelford, Cornwall	20 tonnes of aluminium sulphate were flushed down local rivers after an accident at a water treatment works.	Jul 1988	60 000 fish killed. Local people suffered from vomiting, diarrhoea, blisters, mouth ulcers, rashes and memory loss.
Chernobyl, Ukraine	Nuclear reactor exploded, releasing a radioactive cloud over Europe.	Apr 1986	Fewer than 50 people were killed, but the radioactive cloud spread as far as Britain, contaminating farmland. 100 000 Soviet citizens may die of radiation-induced cancer, a further 30 000 fatalities are possible worldwide. 250 000 people evacuated from the area in five years.

Location	Event	Date	Consequence
Cubatão, Brazil	Uncontrolled pollution from nuclear industry.	1980s	Local population suffer serious ailments and genetic deformities. 30% of deaths are caused by pollution-related diseases and damage to respiratory systems.
Cumbria, England	Fire in Windscale plutonium production reactor burned for 24 hours and ignited 3 tonnes of uranium.	Oct 1957	Radioactive material spread throughout the countryside. In 1983 the British government said 39 people probably died of cancer as a result. Unofficial sources say 1 000.
Decatur, Alabama, USA	Fire at Browns Ferry reactor caused by a technician checking for air leaks with a lighted candle.	Mar 1975	$100 million damage. Electrical controls burned out, lowering cooling water to dangerous levels.
Detroit, Michigan, USA	Malfunction in sodium cooling system at the Enrico Fermi demonstration breeder reactor.	Oct 1966	Partial core meltdown. Radiation was contained.
Erwin, Tennessee, USA	Highly enriched uranium released from top-secret nuclear fuel plant.	Aug 1979	1 000 people contaminated (with up to 5 times as much radiation as would normally be received in a year).
Flixborough, England	Container of cyclohexane exploded.	June 1974	28 people died.
Goiânia, Brazil	Major radioactive contamination incident involving an abandoned radiotherapy unit containing radioactive caesium chloride salts.	Sep–Oct 1987	People evacuated; homes demolished; 249 people affected by sickness or death.
Gore, Oklahoma, USA	Cylinder of nuclear material burst after being improperly heated at Kerr-McGee plant.	Jan 1986	1 worker died, 100 hospitalized.
Idaho Falls, Idaho, USA	Accident at experiment reactor.	Jan 1961	3 workers killed. Damage contained, despite high radiation levels at the plant.
Kasli, Russia	Chemical explosion in tanks containing nuclear waste.	Sep 1957	Radioactive material spread. Major evacuation of area.
Kuwait	Iraqi forces set alight 600 oil wells.	Feb 1991	Air pollution consisted of clouds of soot and oil particles which obscured the sun and fell as 'black rain'. Threat that it would turn into sulphur dioxide and fall as acid rain. Incidence of fatal bronchitis expected to increase. Possible serious contamination of agricultural land and water supplies particularly in Iraq's Tigris and Euphrates valleys.
Love Canal, near Niagara Falls, New York, USA	Dumping of drums containing hazardous waste at Love Canal, which by the 1970s were leaking toxic chemicals.	1940s to 1952	More than 240 families evacuated, countryside contaminated.
Lucens Vad, Switzerland	Coolant malfunction in an experimental underground reactor.	Jan 1969	Large amount of radiation released into cavern, which was then sealed.
Minimata Bay, Japan	Dumping of chemicals, including methyl mercury.	1953	Minimata disease, characterized by cerebral palsy, had killed more than 300 people by 1983. Thousands more suffered genetic abnormalities, brain disease and nervous disorders.
Monongahela River, Pennsylvania, USA	Storage tank ruptured and spilled 3 800 000 gallons of diesel oil into the Monongahela River.	Jan 1988	Water supply to 23 000 residents of Pittsburgh cut off. Oil slick spread into W Virginia, growing to 77km/48mi, and reached Steubenville, Ohio.
Monticello, Minnesota, USA	Water-storage space at Northern States Power Company's reactor overflowed.	Nov 1971	50 000 gallons of radioactive waste water dumped in Mississippi River. St Paul water system contaminated.
Rochester, New York, USA	Steam-generator pipe broke at the Rochester Gas & Electric Company's plant.	Jan 1982	Small amounts of radioactive steam escaped.

Climate and Environment

Location	Event	Date	Consequence
Seveso, N Italy	Leak of toxic TCDD gas containing the poison dioxin.	Jul 1976	Local population still suffering; in worst contaminated area, topsoil had to be removed and buried in a giant plastic-coated pit.
Tennessee, USA	100 000 gallons of radioactive coolant leaked into the containment building of the TVA's Sequoyah 1 plant.	Feb 1981	8 workers contaminated.
Three Mile Island, Harrisburg, Pennsylvania, USA	Water pump broke down releasing radioactive steam.	Mar 1979	Pollution by radioactive gases. Some authorities claimed regional cancer, child deformity. Massive clean-up operation resulted in 150 tonnes of radioactive rubble and 250 000 gallons of radioactive water.
Tsuruga, Japan	Accident during repairs of a nuclear plant.	Apr 1981	100 workers exposed to radioactive material.

Major oil spills at sea

Name	Location	Date	Consequence
Aegean Sea, Greek-registered tanker, grounded and spilled 16 000 000 gallons and caught fire	La Coruña, Spain	Dec 1992	marine pollution; 80km/50mi of Spanish coast polluted.
Amoco Cadiz, Cyprus-registered tanker, grounded and spilled 65 562 000 gallons	near Portshall, France	Mar 1978	marine pollution; 160km/99mi of French coast polluted.
Aragon spilled 7 350 000 gallons	off Madeira Is	Dec 1989–Jan 1990	marine pollution
Atlantic Empress and *Aegean Captain*; collision between tankers caused spillage of 88 200 000 gallons	off Trinidad and Tobago	Jul 1979	marine pollution
Braer tanker, broke up and spilled 26 000 000 gallons	Shetland, Scotland	Jan 1993	marine pollution
Burmah Agate collided and spilled 10 700 000 gallons	Galveston Bay, Texas	Nov 1979	marine pollution
Castillo de Beliver tanker; fire caused spillage of 73 500 000 gallons	off Cape Town, South Africa	Aug 1983	marine pollution
Diamond Grace, Panamanian-registered tanker, grounded and spilled 4 000 000 gallons	off Yokohama, Japan	Jul 1997	marine pollution
Ekofisk oil field; blow-out caused spillage of 8 200 000 gallons	North Sea	Apr 1977	marine pollution
Exxon Valdez, US tanker, grounded on Bligh Reef and spilled 10 080 000 gallons	Prince William Sound, Alaska	Mar 1989	1 770km/1 162mi of Alaskan coastline polluted. More than 3 600 sq km/1 390 sq mi of water fouled. Thousands of animals killed.
Gulf; Iraq pumped oil at a rate of 4 200 000 gallons a day into the sea	16km/10mi off coast near Kuwait City	Jan–Feb 1991	Threat to desalination plants and therefore to water supply. Devastating effect on all areas of marine environment.
Hawaiian Patrol; fire caused spillage of 29 106 000 gallons	N Pacific	Feb 1977	marine pollution
Ixtoc oil well; blow-out caused spillage of 176 400 000 gallons	Gulf of Mexico	Jun 1979	marine pollution
Keo; hull failure caused spillage of 88 200 000 gallons	off Massachusetts, USA	Nov 1969	marine pollution
Kharg 5, Iranian supertanker, spilled 19 000 000 gallons of light crude oil after an explosion in its hull	700km/435mi N of the Canary Is, Atlantic Ocean	Dec 1989	370km/230mi oil slick almost reached Morocco. About 40% evaporated and much sank to ocean floor, endangering fish and oysters.
Kirki, Greek tanker, broke up and spilled 5 880 000 gallons of light crude oil	off Cervantes, W Australia	Jul 1991	Pollution of conservation zones and lobster fishery.
Nowruz oil field; blow-out caused spillage of about 176 400 000 gallons	Persian Gulf	Feb 1983	marine pollution

Name	Location	Date	Consequence
Othello collided and spilled 17 640 000–29 400 000 gallons	Tralhavet Bay, Sweden	Mar 1970	marine pollution
Prestige; hull cracked in storm, sinks, begins to leak cargo of 20 500 000 gallons at rate of 33 000 gallons a day	off north-western Spain	Dec 2002	marine pollution; Spanish coast polluted
Sea Empress, Liberian-registered tanker, grounded and spilled 21 500 000 gallons	Milford Haven, Wales	Feb 1996	marine pollution
Sea Star collided and spilled 33 810 000 gallons	Gulf of Oman	Dec 1972	marine pollution
Sewaren storage tank rupture caused spillage of 8 400 000 gallons	New Jersey	Nov 1969	marine pollution
Torrey Canyon grounded and spilled 34 986 000 gallons	off Land's End, England	Mar 1967	marine pollution
Urquiola grounded and spilled 29 400 000 gallons	La Coruña, Spain	May 1976	marine pollution
World Glory; hull failure caused spillage of 13 524 000 gallons	off South Africa	Jun 1968	marine pollution

World Heritage sites

This list is up-to-date to December 2000. It comprises the 630 sites in 118 countries selected by UNESCO as being of such outstanding natural, environmental or cultural importance that they merit exceptional international efforts to make them more widely known and to save them from damage and destruction.

- **Albania**
  Butrinti
- **Algeria**
  Algiers (Casbah)
  Al Qal'a of Beni Hammad
  Djémila (Roman ruins)
  M'Zab Valley
  Tassili N'Ajjer
  Timgad (Roman ruins)
  Tipasa (archaeological site)
- **Argentina**
  Iguazú National Park
  Jesuit Missions of the Guaranis (shared with Brazil)
  Los Glaciares National Park
  Península Valdés
  Río Pinturas (The Cueva de las Manos)
- **Armenia**
  Haghpat Monastery
- **Australia**
  Central Eastern Australian Rainforest
  Fraser I
  Great Barrier Reef
  Heard and McDonald Is
  Kakadu National Park
  Lord Howe I
  Macquarie I
  Queensland (wet tropics)
  Riversleigh/Naracoorte (mammal fossil sites)
  Shark Bay
  Tasmanian Wilderness
  Uluru-Kata Tjuta National Park
  Willandra Lakes region
- **Austria**
  Graz (historic centre)
  Hallstatt-Dachstein Salzkammergut cultural landscape
  Salzburg (historic city centre)
  Schönbrunn palace and gardens
  Semmering Railway
- **Bangladesh**
  Bagerhat (historic mosque city)
  Paharpur (ruins of the Buddhist Vihara)
  Sundarbans (mangrove forest)
- **Belarus**
  Belovezhskaya Pushcha/Bialowieza Forest (shared with Poland)
- **Belgium**
  Belfries of Flanders and Wallonia
  Brussels (Grand-Place)
- **Belize**
  Barrier Reef Reserve System
- **Benin**
  Dahomey (royal palaces)
- **Bolivia**
  Jesuit Missions of the Chiquitos
  Potosi (mining town)
  Sucre (historic city)
- **Brazil**
  Bom Jesus do Congonhas (sanctuary)
  Brasilia
  Diamantina (historic centre)
  Discovery Coast Atlantic Forest Reserves
  Iguaçu National Park
  Jesuit Missions of the Guaranis (shared with Argentina)
  Olinda (historic centre)
  Ouro Preto (historic town)
  Salvador da Bahia (historic centre)
  São Luis (historic centre)
  Serra da Capivara National Park
  South-East Atlantic Forest Reserves
- **Bulgaria**
  Boyana Church
  Ivanovo rock-hewn churches
  Kazanlak (Thracian tomb)
  Madara Rider
  Nessebar (old city)
  Pirin National Park
  Rila Monastery
  Srebarna Nature Reserve
  Sveshtari (Thracian tomb)
- **Cambodia**
  Angkor
- **Cameroon**
  Dja Faunal Reserve
- **Canada**
  Anthony I
  Canadian Rocky Mountain Parks

Climate and Environment

Climate and Environment

Dinosaur Provincial Park
Gros Morne National Park
Head-Smashed-In Buffalo Jump complex
L'Anse aux Meadows Historic Park
Lunenburg (old city)
Miguasha Park
Nahanni National Park
Quebec (historic area)
Tatshenshini-Alsek, Kluane National Park,
Wrangell St Elias National Park and Reserve,
  and Glacier Bay National Park (shared with USA)
Waterton Glacier International Peace Park
  (shared with USA)
Wood Buffalo National Park

■ **Central African Republic**
Manovo-Gounda St Floris National Park

■ **Chile**
Rapa Nui National Park (Easter I)

■ **China**
Beijing (Imperial Palace of the Ming and Qing
  dynasties, Summer Palace and Temple of Heaven)
Chengde (mountain resort and outlying temples)
Dazu (rock carvings)
Great Wall
Huanglong area
Mt Huangshan
Jiuzhaigou Valley area
Lhasa (Potala Palace)
Lijiang (old town)
Lushan National Park
Mausoleum of the first Qin emperor
Mogao caves
Mt Emei scenic area including Leshan giant
  Buddha scenic area
Mt Taishan
Mt Wuyi
Ping Yao (ancient city)
Qufu (temple and cemetery of Confucius and
  the K'ung family mansion)
Suzhou (classical gardens)
Wudang mountains (ancient building complex)
Wulingyuan area
Zhoukoudian (Peking Man site)

■ **Colombia**
Cartagena (port, fortress and monuments)
Los Katios National Park
San Agustín Archaeological Park
Santa Cruz de Mompox (historic centre)
Tierradentro National Archaeological Park

■ **Congo, Democratic Republic of**
Garamba National Park
Kahuzi-Biega National Park
Okapi Faunal Reserve
Salonga National Park
Virunga National Park

■ **Costa Rica**
Area de Conservación Guanacaste
Cocos I National Park
La Amistad National Park (shared with Panama)

■ **Côte d'Ivoire**
Comoé National Park
Mt Nimba Nature Reserve (shared with Guinea)
Taï National Park

■ **Croatia**
Dubrovnik (old city)
Plitvice Lakes National Park
Porec (episcopal complex of the Euphrasian
  basilica in the historic centre)
Split (historic centre with Diocletian's Palace)
Trogir (historic city)

■ **Cuba**
Desembarco del Granma National Park

Old Havana and its fortifications
Santiago de Cuba, San Pedro de la Roca Castle
Trinidad and the Valley de los Ingenios
Viñales Valley

■ **Cyprus**
Choirokoitia
Paphos (archaeological site)
Troödos (painted churches)

■ **Czech Republic**
Cesky Krumlov (historic centre)
Kutna Hora (historic centre) with Church of St
  Barbara and the Cathedral of Our Lady at Sedlec
Holašovice (historical village reservation)
Kromeríz (gardens and castle)
Litomysl Castle
Lednice-Valtice cultural landscape
Prague (historic centre)
Telc (historic centre)
Zelena Hora (pilgrimage church of St John of
  Nepomuk)

■ **Denmark**
Jelling (mounds, runic stones and church)
Roskilde Cathedral

■ **Dominica**
Morne Trois Pitons National Park

■ **Dominican Republic**
Santo Domingo

■ **Ecuador**
Galapagos Is National Park
Quito (old city)
Sangay National Park
Santa Ana de los Rios de Cuenca (historic centre)

■ **Egypt**
Abu Mena (Christian ruins)
Abu Simbel to Philae (Nubian monuments)
Cairo (Islamic sector)
Memphis and its Necropolis with the Pyramid fields
Thebes and its Necropolis

■ **El Salvador**
Joya de Cerén (archaeological site)

■ **Estonia**
Tallinn (historic centre, old town)

■ **Ethiopia**
Aksum (archaeological site)
Awash Lower Valley
Fasil Ghebbi and Gondar monuments
Lalibela rock-hewn churches
Omo Lower Valley
Simien National Park
Tiya (carved steles)

■ **Finland**
Old Rauma
Petäjävesi (old church)
Sammallahdenmäki (Bronze Age burial site)
Suomenlinna (fortress)
Verla groundwood and board mill

■ **France**
Amiens Cathedral
Arc-et-Senans (royal saltworks)
Arles (Roman and Romanesque monuments)
Avignon (historic centre)
Bourges Cathedral
Canal du Midi
Carcassonne (historic fortified city)
Chambord (château and estate)
Chartres Cathedral
Corsica (Cape Girolata, Cape Porto, Scandola
  Natural Reserve and the Piana Calanches)
Fontainebleau (palace and park)
Fontenay (Cistercian abbey)
Lyons (historic site)
Mont St Michel and its bay

Nancy (Place Stanislas, Place de la Carrière and Place d'Alliance)
Orange (Roman theatre and triumphal arch)
Paris (banks of the Seine)
Pont du Gard (Roman aqueduct)
Pyrenees, Mt Perdu landscape (shared with Spain)
Rheims (Cathedral of Notre-Dame, St Remy Abbey and Palace of Tau)
Routes of Santiago de Compostela
St Emilion (jurisdiction)
St Savin-sur-Gartempe (church)
Strasbourg (Grande Île)
Versailles (palace and park)
Vezelay (basilica and hill)
Vézère (decorated caves)

■ **Georgia**
Bagrati Cathedral and Gelati Monastery
Mtskheta (historic church ensemble)
Upper Svaneti

■ **Germany**
Aachen Cathedral
Bamberg
Bauhaus and its sites in Weimar and Dessau
Brühl (Augustusburg and Falkenlust castles)
Cologne Cathedral

Cologne Cathedral

Eisleben and Wittenberg, the Luther memorials
Hildesheim (St Mary's Cathedral and St Michael's Church)
Lorsch (abbey and Altenmünster)
Lübeck (Hanseatic city)
Maulbronn (monastery)
Messel Pit (fossil site)
Museum Island
Potsdam and Berlin palaces and parks
Quedlinburg (collegiate church, castle and old town)
Rammelsberg mines and historic town of Goslar
Speyer Cathedral
Trier (Roman monuments, cathedral and Liebfrauen church)
Völklingen ironworks
Wartburg Castle
Weimar (classical sites)
Wies (pilgrimage church)
Würzburg Residence

■ **Ghana**
Ashante traditional buildings
Forts and castles of Ghana

■ **Greece**
Athens (Acropolis)

Acropolis, Athens

Bassae (temple of Apollo Epicurius)
Chorá (historic centre, with the monastery of St John 'the Theologian' and the cave of the Apocalypse on Pátmos)
Daphni, Hossios Luckas and Nea Moni of Chios monasteries
Delos
Delphi (archaeological site)
Epidaurus (archaeological site)
Meteora
Mt Athos
Mycenae (archaeological site)
Mystras
Olympia (archaeological site)
Rhodes (medieval city)
Samos (Pythagoreion and Heraion)
Thessalonika (Paleochristian and Byzantine monuments)
Tiryns (archaeological site)
Vergina (archaeological site)

■ **Guatemala**
Antigua Guatemala
Quirigua (archaeological site and ruins)
Tikal National Park

■ **Guinea**
Mt Nimba Nature Reserve (shared with Côte d'Ivoire)

■ **Haiti**
Citadel, Sans-Souci and site of Ramiers National Historic Park and Palace

■ **Honduras**
Maya ruins of Copan
Río Plátano Biosphere Reserve

■ **Hungary**
Aggtelek caves and the Slovak Karst (shared with Slovakia)
Budapest (banks of the Danube and the Buda Castle quarter)
Hollókő (traditional village)
Hortobágy National Park
Pannonhalma, Millenary Benedictine Abbey and its natural environment

■ **India**
Agra Fort
Ajanta caves
Darjeeling Himalayan Railway
Elephanta caves
Ellora caves
Fatehpur Sikri (Moghul city)
Goa (churches and convents)
Hampi (monuments)
Humayun's Tomb
Kaziranga National Park
Keoladeo National Park
Khajuraho (monuments)
Konarak (Sun Temple)
Mahabalipuram (monuments)
Manas Wildlife Sanctuary
Nanda Devi National Park
Pattadakal (monuments)
Qutb Minar
Sanchi Buddhist monuments
Sundarbans National Park
Taj Mahal
Thanjavur (Brihadisvara Temple)

■ **Indonesia**
Borobudur Temple compounds
Komodo National Park
Lorentz National Park
Prambanan Temple compounds
Sangiran (early man site)
Ujung Kulon National Park

Climate and Environment

Climate and Environment

- **Iran**
  Esfahan (Meidan Emam)
  Persepolis
  Tchogha Zanbil Ziggurat and complex
- **Iraq**
  Hatra
- **Ireland**
  Skellig Michael
  Valley of the Boyne
- **Israel**
  Jerusalem (old city and its walls)

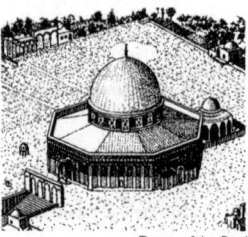

Dome of the Rock, Jerusalem

- **Italy**
  Agrigento (archaeological area)
  Alberobello (the trulli)
  Amalfi (the coast)
  Aquileia (archaelogical area and the patriarchal basilica)
  Barumini, Sardinia (the nuraghi)
  Casale (Villa Romana)
  Caserta (18c palace, park, aqueduct of Vanvitelli and the San Leucio complex)
  Cilento and Vallo di Diano National Park with archaeological sites of Paestum and Velia, and the Certosa di Padula
  Castel del Monte
  Crespi d'Adda
  Ferrara (Renaissance city)
  Florence (historic centre)
  I Sassi di Matera
  Modena (cathedral, Torre Civica and Piazza Grande)
  Naples (historic centre)
  Padua (botanical garden)
  Pienza (historic city centre)
  Pisa (Piazza del Duomo)
  Pompeii, with Herculaneum and Torre Annunziata archaeological areas
  Portovenere, Cinque Terre and the islands of Palmaria, Tino and Tinetto
  Ravenna, early Christian monuments and mosaics
  Rome (historic centre)
  San Gimignano (historic centre)
  Santa Maria delle Grazie with *The Last Supper* by Leonardo da Vinci
  Siena (historic centre)
  Turin (royal houses of Savoy)
  Urbino (historic centre)
  Valcamonica (rock drawings)
  Venice and its lagoon
  Vicenza (city and Palladian villas of the Veneto)
  Villa Adriana

Rialto Bridge, Venice

- **Japan**
  Ancient Kyoto (Kyoto, Uji and Otsu cities)
  Ancient Nara (historic monuments)
  Himeji-jo
  Hiroshima Peace Memorial (Genbaku Dome)
  Horyu-ji (Buddhist monuments)
  Itsukushima Shinto shrine
  Nikko (shrines and temples)
  Shirakami-Sanchi
  Shirakawa-go and Gokayama (historic villages)
  Yakushima
- **Jordan**
  Petra
  Quseir Amra
- **Kenya**
  Mt Kenya (national park and natural forest)
  Sibiloi and Central I national parks
- **Korea, Republic of (South Korea)**
  Ch'angdokkung Palace complex
  Chongmyo Shrine
  Haeinsa Temple, including woodblocks of the Tripitaka Koreana
  Hwasong Fortress
  Sokkuram Grotto
- **Laos**
  Luang Prabang
- **Latvia**
  Riga (historic centre)
- **Lebanon**
  Anjar (archaeological site)
  Baalbek
  Byblos
  Ouadi Qadisha and the Forest of the Cedars of God
  Tyre (archaeological site)
- **Libya**
  Cyrene (archaeological site)
  Ghadamès (old town)
  Leptis Magna (archaeological site)
  Sabratha (archaeological site)
  Tadrart Acacus (rock-art sites)
- **Lithuania**
  Vilnius (historic centre)
- **Luxembourg**
  City of Luxembourg, old quarters and fortifications
- **Macedonia**
  Ohrid and its lake
- **Madagascar**
  Tsingy Bemaraha Nature Reserve
- **Malawi**
  Lake Malawi National Park
- **Mali**
  Cliffs of Bandiagara (land of the Dogons)
  Djenné (old towns)
  Timbuktu
- **Malta**
  Hal Saflieni Hypogeum
  Megalithic temples
  Valetta (old city)
- **Mauritania**
  Ancient ksour of Ouadane, Chinguetti, Tichitt and Oualata
  Banc d'Arguin National Park
- **Mexico**
  Campeche (historic fortified town)
  Chichen Itza (pre-Hispanic city)
  El Tajín (pre-Hispanic city)
  El Vizcaino Whale Sanctuary
  Guadalajara (Hospicio Cabañas)
  Guanajuato (historic town) and adjacent mines
  Mexico City (historic centre and Xochimilco)
  Morelia (historic centre)

Oaxaca (historic zone) and Monte Alban
  (archaeological site)
Palenque (pre-Hispanic city and national park)
Paquimé, Casas Grandes (archaeological zone)
Popocatepetl (16c monasteries on the slopes)
Puebla (historic centre)
Queretaro (historic monuments zone)
Sian Ka'an (Biosphere reserve)
Sierra de San Francisco (rock paintings)
Teotihuacán (pre-Hispanic city)
Tlacotalpan (historic monuments zone)
Uxmal (pre-Hispanic town)
Xochicalco (archaeological monuments zone)
Zacatecas (historic centre)

- **Morocco**
Aït-Ben-Haddou (fortified village)
Fez (Medina)
Marrakesh (Medina)
Meknes (historic city)
Tétouan (Medina)
Volubilis (archaeological site)

- **Mozambique**
Island of Mozambique

- **Nepal**
Chitwan National Park
Kathmandu Valley
Lumbini (birthplace of Lord Buddha)
Sagarmatha National Park

- **The Netherlands**
Amsterdam defence line
D F Wouda Steam Pumping Station
Beemster Polder
Kinderdijk-Elshout (mill network)
Schokland and its surroundings
Willemstad (historic area, inner city and harbour)

- **New Zealand**
Sub-Antarctic Islands
Te Wahipounamu
Tongariro National Park

- **Niger**
Air and Ténéré (nature reserves)
'W' National Park

- **Nigeria**
Sukur (cultural landscape)

- **Norway**
Alta (rock drawings)
Bergen (Bryggen area)
Røros (mining town)
Urnes Stave Church

- **Oman**
Arabian Oryx Sanctuary
Bahla Fort
Bat, Al-Khutm and Al-Ayn (archaeological sites)

- **Pakistan**
Lahore (fort and Shalamar gardens)
Mohenjo Daro (archaeological site)
Rohtas Fort
Takht-i-Bahi Buddhist ruins
Taxila (archaeological remains)
Thatta (historical monuments)

- **Panama**
Darien National Park
La Amistad National Park (shared with Costa Rica)
Panama (historic district, with Salón Bolívar)
Portobelo and San Lorenzo fortifications

- **Paraguay**
Jesuit Missions

- **Peru**
Chan Chan (archaeological site)
Chavin (archaeological site)
Cuzco (old city)
Huascarán National Park

Lima (historic centre)
Machu Picchu (historic sanctuary)
Manu National Park
Nasca and Pampas de Jumana (lines and
  geoglyphs)
Rio Abiseo National Park

- **Philippines**
Baroque churches of the Philippines
Puerto-Princesa Subterranean River National Park
Rice terraces of the Philippine Cordilleras
Tubbataha Reef Marine Park
Vigan (historic town)

- **Poland**
Auschwitz concentration camp
Belovezhskaya Pushcha/Bialowieza Forest
  (shared with Belarus)
Cracow (historic centre)
Kalwaria Zebrzydowska (mannerist architectural
  and park landscape complex, and pilgrimage
  park)
Malbork (castle of the Teutonic order)
Torun (medieval town)
Warsaw (historic centre)
Wieliczka saltmines
Zamosc (old city)

- **Portugal**
Alcobaça (monastery)
Angra do Heroismo (Azores)
Batalha (monastery)
Belém Tower and Monastery of the Hieronymites
Côa Valley (rock-art sites)
Evora (historic centre)
Madeira (Laurisilva)
Oporto (historic centre)
Sintra (cultural landscape)
Tomar (Convent of Christ)

Belém Tower

- **Romania**
Biertan and its fortified church
Danube Delta
Horezu Monastery
Maramures (wooden churches)
Orastie Mountains (Dacian fortresses)
Painted churches of northern Moldavia
Sighisoara (historic centre)

- **Russia**
Altai (golden mountains)
Kamchatka volcanic region

Red Square, Moscow

Climate and Environment

Kizhi Pogost
Kolomenskoye (Church of the Ascension)
L Baikal
Moscow (Kremlin and Red Square)
Novgorod (historic monuments)
St Petersburg (historic centre)
Sergiev Posad
Solovetsky Is
Virgin Komi forests
Vladimir and Suzdal monuments
Western Caucasus

■ **St Kitts and Nevis**
Brimstone Hill Fortress National Park

■ **Senegal**
Djoudj Bird Sanctuary
Gorée I
Niokolo-Koba National Park

■ **Serbia and Montenegro** ► Yugoslavia

■ **Seychelles**
Aldabra Atoll
Vallée de Mai Nature Reserve

■ **Slovakia**
Aggtelek caves and the Slovak Karst (shared with
  Hungary)
Banska Stiavnica
Spissky Hrad
Vlkolinec

■ **Slovenia**
Skocjan caves

■ **Solomon Islands**
East Rennell

■ **South Africa**
Greater St Lucia Wetland Park
Robben Island
Sterkfontein, Swartkrans Kromdraai and environs
  (fossil hominid sites)

■ **Spain**
Alcalá de Henares (university and historic precinct)
Altamira Cave
Avila (old town) with its Extra-Muros churches
Barcelona (Parque and Palacio Güell, Casa Milá,
  Palau de la Musica Catalana and Hospital de Sant
  Pau)
Burgos Cathedral
Caceres (old town)
Córdoba (historic centre)
Cuenca (historic walled town)
Doñana National Park
El Escurial (monastery and site)
Garajonay National Park (Canary Is)
Granada (Alhambra, Generalife and Albayzin)
Ibiza (biodiversity and culture)
Kingdom of Asturias (its churches)
Las Médulas
Mediterranean Basin (rock art)
Merida
Poblet Monastery
Pyrenees, Mt Perdu landscape (shared with
  France)
Salamanca (old city)

San Cristóbal de La Laguna
San MillánYuso and Suso monasteries
Santa Maria de Guadalupe (royal monastery)
Santiago de Compostela (old town and route)
Segovia (old town and its aqueduct)
Seville (cathedral, Alcazar and Archivo de Indias)
Teruel (Mudejar architecture)
Toledo (historic city)
Valencia, 'La Lonja de la Seda'

■ **Sri Lanka**
Anuradhapura (sacred city)
Dambulla (Golden RockTemple)
Galle (old town and its fortifications)
Kandy (sacred city)
Polonnaruwa (ancient city)
Sigiriya (ancient city)
Sinharaja Forest Reserve

Temple of the Tooth, Kandy

■ **Sweden**
Birka and Hovgården
Drottningholm Palace
Engelsberg ironworks
Gammelstad (church town)
Karlskrona (naval port)
Laponian area
Skogskyrkogården
Tanum (rock carvings)
Visby (Hanseatic town)

■ **Switzerland**
Berne (old city)
Müstair (Benedictine convent)
St Gall (convent)

■ **Syria**
Aleppo (old city)
Bosra (ancient city)
Damascus (old city)
Palmyra (archaeological site)

■ **Tanzania**
Kilimanjaro National Park
Kilwa Kisiwani and Songa Mnara ruins
Ngorongoro area
Selous Game Reserve
Serengeti National Park

■ **Thailand**
Ayutthaya (historic city) and associated towns
Ban Chiang (archaeological site)
Sukhothai (historic city) and associated towns
Thungyai-Huai Kha Khaeng (wildlife sanctuaries)

■ **Tunisia**
Carthage (archaeological site)
Dougga/Thugga
El Djem (amphitheatre)
Ichkeul National Park
Kairouan
Kerkuane (Punic town and necropolis)
Sousse (Medina)
Tunis (Medina)

■ **Turkey**
Divrigi (Great Mosque and hospital)

Casa Milá, Barcelona

Göreme National Park and rock sites of
  Cappadocia
Hattusha (Hittite city)
Hierapolis-Pamukkale
Istanbul (historic areas)
Nemrut Dag (archaeological site)
Safranbolu (old city)
Troy (archaeological site)
Xanthos-Letoon

- **Turkmenistan**
Ancient Merv (state historical and cultural park)
- **Uganda**
Bwindi Impenetrable National Park
Rwenzori Mountains National Park
- **Ukraine**
L'viv (ensemble of the historic centre)
St Sophia and Lavra of Kiev-Pechersk
- **UK**
Bath
Blenheim Palace
Canterbury Cathedral, St Augustine's Abbey and St
  Martin's Church
Durham (castle and cathedral)
Edinburgh (old town and new town)
Giant's Causeway and its coast
Gough Island Wildlife Reserve (South Atlantic
  Ocean)
Greenwich (maritime buildings and park)
Gwynedd (castles and towns of King Edward I)
Hadrian's Wall
Henderson I (Pacific Ocean)
Ironbridge Gorge
Orkney (Neolithic areas)
St Kilda I
Stonehenge, Avebury and related megalithic
  sites

Stonehenge

Studley Royal Park and the ruins of Fountains
  Abbey
Tower of London
Westminster (palace and abbey) and St Margaret's
  Church
- **USA**
Cahokia Mounds site
Carlsbad Caverns National Park
Chaco Culture National Historical Park

Everglades National Park
Grand Canyon National Park
Great Smoky Mountains National Park
Hawaii Volcanoes National Park
Independence Hall, Philadelphia
Mammoth Cave National Park
Mesa Verde National Park
Monticello and the University of Virginia in
  Charlottesville
Olympic National Park
Pueblo de Taos
Puerto Rico (La Fortaleza and San Juan historic
  site)
Redwood National Park
Statue of Liberty
Tatshenshini-Alsek, Kluane National Park,
  Wrangell St Elias National Park and Reserve, and
  Glacier Bay National Park (shared with Canada)
Waterton Glacier International Peace Park (shared
  with Canada)
Yellowstone National Park
Yosemite National Park
- **Uruguay**
Colonia del Sacramento (historic quarter)
- **Uzbekistan**
Bukhara
Itchan Kala (historic city)
- **Vatican City**
Vatican City
- **Venezuela**
Canaima National Park
Coro and its port
- **Vietnam**
Ha Long Bay
Hoi An (ancient town)
Hué (complex of monuments)
My Son Sanctuary
- **Yemen**
San'a (old city)
Shibam (old walled city)
Zabid (historic town)
- **Yugoslavia***
Durmitor National Park
Kotor and its gulf
Stari Ras and Sopocani
Studenica Monastery
- **Zambia**
Victoria Falls/Mosi-oa-Tunya (shared with
  Zimbabwe)
- **Zimbabwe**
Khami ruins
Great Zimbabwe National Monument
Mana Pools, National Park and Sapi and Chewore
  safari areas
Victoria Falls/Mosi-oa-Tunya (shared with Zambia)

*now Serbia and Montenegro

Climate and Environment

National parks and nature reserves

The first national park was Yellowstone, Wyoming, which was obtained by the US government during the 1870s for the use and enjoyment of the people. By the late 1980s there were more than 3 000 national parks and wildlife reserves scattered around the world. All together, they covered approximately 4 million km^2/1.5 million mi^2. Below is a selection of the best known.

Name	Country	Area (km^2) [1]	Special features
Altos de Campana	Panama	48	Great variety of plant zones
Amazonia	Brazil	9 940	Rainforest
Badlands	USA	985	Prehistoric fossils; dramatically eroded hills
Banff	Canada	6 640	Spectacular glaciated scenery; hot springs
Beinn Eighe	UK	48	Original Scottish pine forest
Bialowieski	Poland	53	Largest remnant of primeval forest; European bison
Burren	Ireland	15	Limestone pavement with remarkable plants
Camargue	France	131	Wetland; many rare birds, especially flamingoes
Canaima	Venezuela	30 000	World's highest waterfall, Angel Falls
Canyonlands	USA	1 365	Deep gorges, colourful rock, spectacular landforms
Carlsbad Caverns	USA	189	Huge limestone caverns with millions of bats
Carnarvon	Australia	2 980	Bush-tailed rock wallabies; aboriginal cave paintings
Chitwan	Nepal	932	Royal Bengal tigers, gavials (type of Indian crocodile), Gangetic dolphins
Corbett	India	520	Indian tigers; gavials, muggers (both types of Indian crocodile)
Dartmoor	UK	954	Wild ponies
Death Valley	USA	8 368	Lowest point in W hemisphere; unique flora, fauna
Doñana	Spain	507	Wetland; rare birds and mammals; Spanish lynx
Everglades	USA	5 929	Swamp, mangrove; subtropical wildlife refuge
Etosha	Namibia	22 270	Swampland and bush; rare and abundant wildlife
Fiordland	New Zealand	12 570	Kiwis, keas, wekas, takahe, kakapo (all flightless birds, except for the kea)
Fuji-Hakone-Izu	Japan	1 232	Mt Fuji; varied animal and plant life
Galapagos Islands	Ecuador	6 937	Giant iguanas, giant tortoises
Gemsbok	Botswana	24 305	Desert, grassland; lions and large herds of game
Gir	India	258	Asiatic lions
Glacier	USA	4 102	Virgin coniferous forest; glaciers
Gran Paradiso	Italy	702	Alpine scenery; chamois, ibex
Grand Canyon	USA	4 834	Mile-deep canyon, colourful walls; many life zones
Great Smoky Mountains	USA	2 094	Varied wildlife including wild turkey, black bear
Hardangervidda	Norway	3 422	Plateau of ancient rock; large wild reindeer herd
Hawaii Volcanoes	USA	920	Active volcanoes, rare plants and animals
Heron Island	Australia	0.17	Part of Great Barrier Reef; corals, invertebrates, fish
Hoge Veluwe	Netherlands	54	Largely stabilized dunes; wet and dry heath
Iguazú/Iguaçu	Argentina/Brazil	6 900	Iguazú/Iguaçu Falls
Ixtacihuatl-Popocatépetl	Mexico	257	Snow-capped volcanoes
Kafue	Zambia	22 400	Numerous animals and birds; black rhinoceros refuge
Kakadu	Australia	20 277	Aboriginal rock art; crocodiles, water birds
Kaziranga	India	430	Indian one-horned rhinoceros, swamp deer
Khao Yai	Thailand	2 169	Large caves and waterfalls; many bird species
Kilimanjaro	Tanzania	756	Africa's highest peak, Mt Kilimanjaro; colobus monkeys
Kinabalu	Malaysia	754	Orchids; South-East Asia's highest peak, Mt Kinabalu
Kosciusko	Australia	6 469	Australia's highest peak, Mt Kosciusko; mountain pygmy possum
Kruger	South Africa	19 485	Wide range of animals and birds; rare white rhinoceros
Lainzer Tiergarten	Austria	25	Ancient forest and meadow; wild boar, deer, moufflon (wild sheep)
Lake District	UK	2 292	Lake and mountain scenery
Los Glaciares	Argentina/Chile	1 618	Glacial landforms

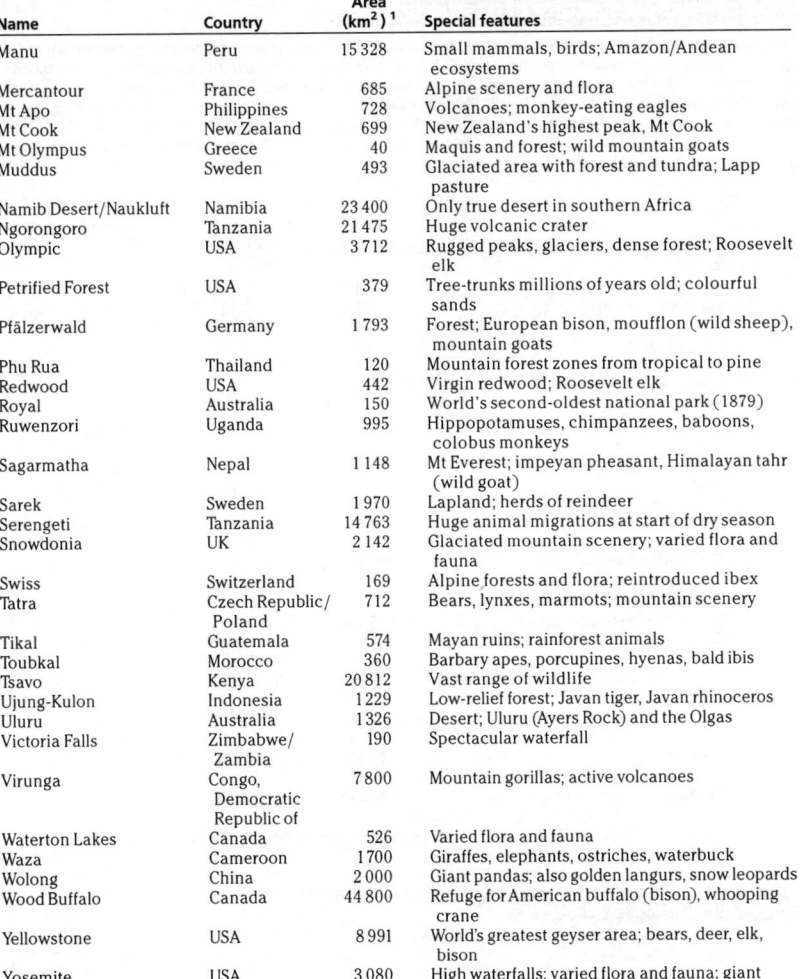

Name	Country	Area (km²)¹	Special features
Manu	Peru	15 328	Small mammals, birds; Amazon/Andean ecosystems
Mercantour	France	685	Alpine scenery and flora
Mt Apo	Philippines	728	Volcanoes; monkey-eating eagles
Mt Cook	New Zealand	699	New Zealand's highest peak, Mt Cook
Mt Olympus	Greece	40	Maquis and forest; wild mountain goats
Muddus	Sweden	493	Glaciated area with forest and tundra; Lapp pasture
Namib Desert/Naukluft	Namibia	23 400	Only true desert in southern Africa
Ngorongoro	Tanzania	21 475	Huge volcanic crater
Olympic	USA	3 712	Rugged peaks, glaciers, dense forest; Roosevelt elk
Petrified Forest	USA	379	Tree-trunks millions of years old; colourful sands
Pfälzerwald	Germany	1 793	Forest; European bison, moufflon (wild sheep), mountain goats
Phu Rua	Thailand	120	Mountain forest zones from tropical to pine
Redwood	USA	442	Virgin redwood; Roosevelt elk
Royal	Australia	150	World's second-oldest national park (1879)
Ruwenzori	Uganda	995	Hippopotamuses, chimpanzees, baboons, colobus monkeys
Sagarmatha	Nepal	1 148	Mt Everest; impeyan pheasant, Himalayan tahr (wild goat)
Sarek	Sweden	1 970	Lapland; herds of reindeer
Serengeti	Tanzania	14 763	Huge animal migrations at start of dry season
Snowdonia	UK	2 142	Glaciated mountain scenery; varied flora and fauna
Swiss	Switzerland	169	Alpine forests and flora; reintroduced ibex
Tatra	Czech Republic/ Poland	712	Bears, lynxes, marmots; mountain scenery
Tikal	Guatemala	574	Mayan ruins; rainforest animals
Toubkal	Morocco	360	Barbary apes, porcupines, hyenas, bald ibis
Tsavo	Kenya	20 812	Vast range of wildlife
Ujung-Kulon	Indonesia	1 229	Low-relief forest; Javan tiger, Javan rhinoceros
Uluru	Australia	1 326	Desert; Uluru (Ayers Rock) and the Olgas
Victoria Falls	Zimbabwe/ Zambia	190	Spectacular waterfall
Virunga	Congo, Democratic Republic of	7 800	Mountain gorillas; active volcanoes
Waterton Lakes	Canada	526	Varied flora and fauna
Waza	Cameroon	1 700	Giraffes, elephants, ostriches, waterbuck
Wolong	China	2 000	Giant pandas; also golden langurs, snow leopards
Wood Buffalo	Canada	44 800	Refuge for American buffalo (bison), whooping crane
Yellowstone	USA	8 991	World's greatest geyser area; bears, deer, elk, bison
Yosemite	USA	3 080	High waterfalls; varied flora and fauna; giant sequoias

¹ To convert km² to mi², multiply by 0.386.

Climate and Environment

Climate and Environment

Tropical rainforests (rate of destruction)

The destruction of the world's rainforests has taken place largely as a result of economic pressures for more agricultural land and products. This destruction has led to a huge increase in the amount of carbon dioxide being released into the atmosphere. It also causes the degradation and erosion of top-soil, increasing the risk of rivers silting up and flooding. Rainforests are home to half the world's plant and animal species, many of which are now in imminent danger of extinction. The following data are 1997 FAO estimates for 87 tropical countries, taken from *State of the World's Forests 1997* published by the Food and Agriculture Organization of the United Nations.

Region	Forest area 1995 (1 000 ha)[1]	Annual forest loss 1990–5 (1 000 ha)	Annual rate of destruction (%)
Africa			
West Sahelian Africa	39 827	295	0.7
East Sahelian Africa	57 542	420	0.7
West Moist Africa	46 324	492	1.0
Central Africa	204 677	1 201	0.6
Tropical Southern Africa	141 311	1 158	0.8
Insular East Africa	15 220	131	0.8
Total Tropical Africa	*504 901*	*3 695*	*0.7*
Asia			
South Asia	77 137	141	0.2
Continental Southeast Asia	70 163	1 164	1.6
Insular Southeast Asia	132 466	1 750	1.3
Total Tropical Asia	*279 766*	*3 055*	*1.1*
North and Central America			
Central America and Mexico	75 018	959	1.2
Caribbean	4 425	78	1.7
Total Tropical North and Central America	*79 443*	*1 037*	*1.3*
South America	827 946	4 655	0.6
Oceania	41 903	151	0.4
TOTAL	**1 733 959**	**12 593**	**0.7**

[1] One hectare (ha) = 10 000 sq m. To convert ha to sq km, divide by 100; to convert ha to sq mi, multiply by 0.003861.

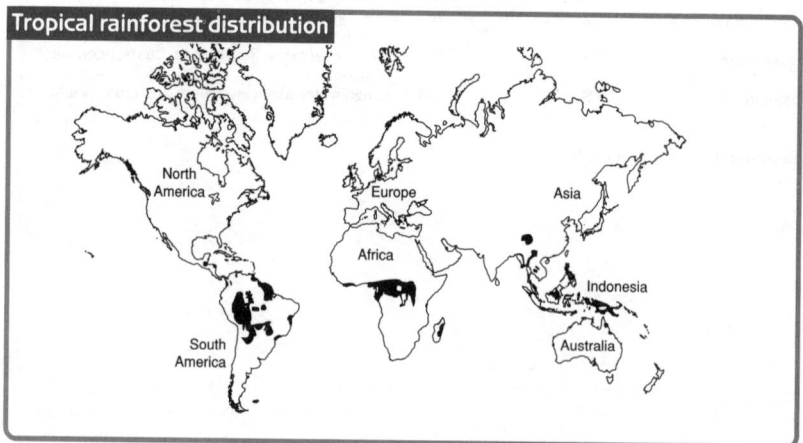

Tropical rainforest distribution

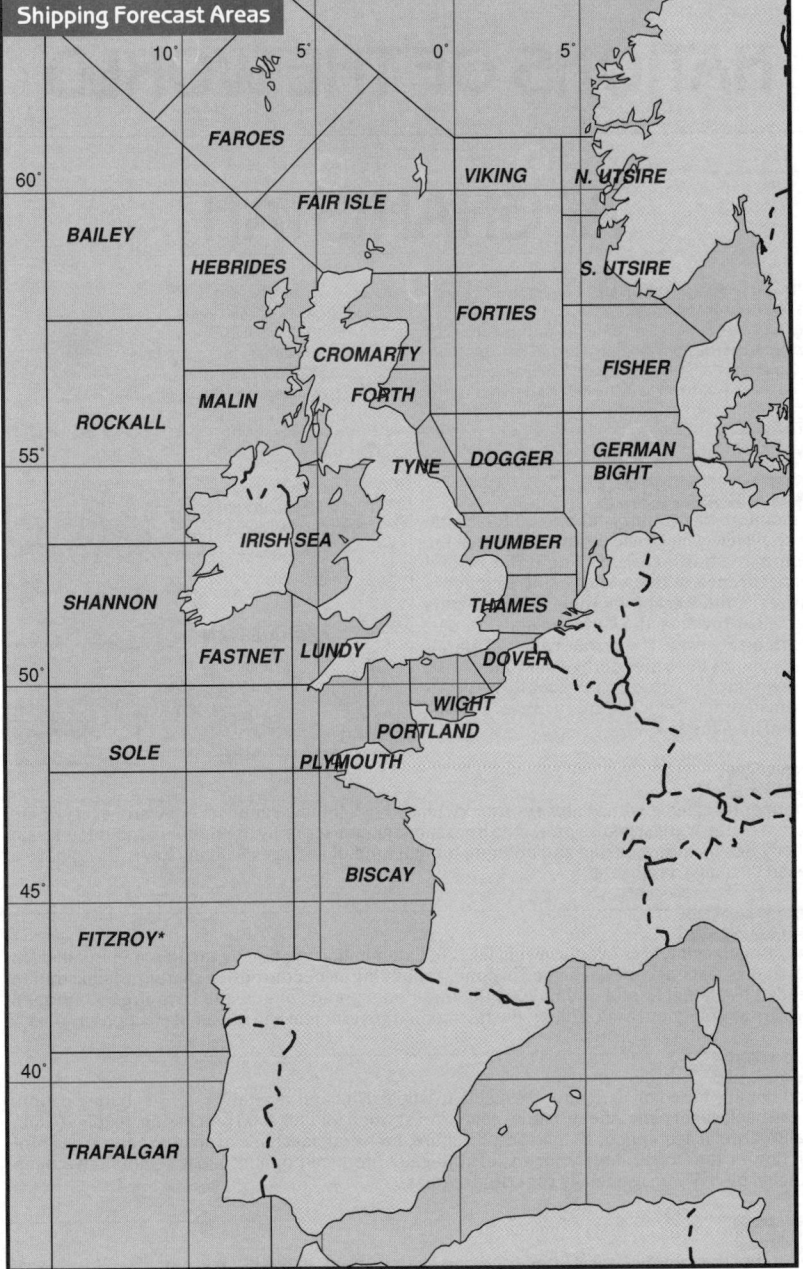

Shipping Forecast Areas

Climate and Environment

*Formerly Finisterre (renamed 2002)   Reproduced with data supplied by the Met Office.

NATIONS OF THE WORLD

AFGHANISTAN

Official name Islamic State of Afghanistan
Local name Afghānestān
Location A landlocked, mountainous republic in south-central Asia, bounded to the north by Turkmenistan, Uzbekistan and Tajikistan; to the east and south by Pakistan; to the west by Iran; and in the extreme north-east by China and India
Area 647 497 sq km/249 934 sq mi
Capital Kābul

Chief towns Herat, Kandahar
Population 25 825 000 (1999e)
Time zone GMT +4.5
Currency 1 Afghani (Af) = 100 puls
Languages Dari, Pushtu
Religions Islam 99% (Sunni 74%, Shiite 25%), others 1%
Ethnic groups Pushtun 38%, Tajik 25%, Hazara 19%, Uzbek 6%, others 12%

Physical description

A mountainous country centred on the Hindu Kush system which reaches over 7 000m in the centre and north-east, making it the second highest range in the world; many secondary ranges; north-west of the Hindu Kush, heights decrease towards the Turkmenistan border; also north-west is the fertile valley of Herat; arid uplands lie to the south of the Hindu Kush descending into desert in the south-west; Afghanistan is landlocked and is over 500km/300mi from the sea.

Climate

Continental climate with winter severity increased by altitude; summers are warm everywhere except on the highest peaks; protected from summer monsoons by the southern mountains; rain mostly occurs during spring and autumn; annual rainfall averages 338mm; lower levels have a desert or semi-arid climate.

Government

The Taliban regime was overthrown in late 2001 after military action by the USA and its allies. In Dec 2001 a peace accord was signed in Bonn, appointing an interim power-sharing administration headed by Hamid Karzai. In Jun 2002 the traditional grand council, the Loya Jirga, confirmed Karzai's appointment as President; the transitional government will rule until elections in 2004.

Economy

Traditionally based on agriculture, especially wheat, fruit and vegetables, maize, barley, cotton, sugar-beet, sugar cane; sheep, cattle, goats; forest wood for fuel; food processing, textiles (especially carpets), leather goods, plastics, furniture, footwear, mechanical spares; natural gas production in the north, largely for export; illegally-produced opium; most sectors have been affected by civil war, especially sugar and textiles.

History

The nation first formed in 1747 under Ahmad Shah Durrani. In the 19c and early 20c Britain saw Afghanistan as a bridge between India and the Middle East, but failed to gain control during the Afghan Wars. The feudal monarchy survived until after World War II, when the constitution became more liberal under several Soviet-influenced five-year economic plans. In 1973 the king was deposed and a republic was formed. A new constitution was adopted in 1977, but a coup in 1978 installed a new government under the communist leader, Nur Muhammad Taraki; a further coup in 1979 led to invasion by Soviet forces, which was fiercely resisted by the Mujahidin. In 1989 the Soviet troops finally withdrew, and in 1992 Mujahidin groups forced the resignation of the communist government of Muhammad Najibullah and proclaimed the Islamic State of Afghanistan. Fighting between factions continued, until the rise in 1994 of the Taliban, who sought to replace the factionalism with Islamic law; this included repression of women and public floggings and executions. Within two years the Taliban had taken Kabul, executed Najibullah, and the civil war had resulted in 25 000 to 45 000 Afghan deaths. By 1998 the portion of the country under Taliban control was almost 90 per cent, but fierce resistance from the opposition Northern Alliance meant the civil war continued. In 2001 a US-led coalition began military action against the Taliban, believing them to harbour senior members of Al Qaeda responsible for the September 2001 terror attacks on the US. The Taliban regime was overthrown and peacekeepers sent in. A UN-brokered deal saw a power-sharing administration installed, led by Hamid Karzai, and rebuilding work began although political tensions and sporadic violence continued.

ALBANIA

Official name Republic of Albania
Local name Shqīpērī
Location A mountainous republic in the western part of the Balkan Peninsula, bounded to the west by the Adriatic Sea; to the north by Serbia and Montenegro; to the north-east by Macedonia; and to the south-east by Greece
Area 28 748 sq km/11 097 sq mi
Capital Tirana
Chief towns Shkodër, Durrës, Vlorë, Korçë, Elbasan
Population 3 365 000 (1999e)
Time zone GMT +1
Currency 1 Lek (Lk) = 100 qindarka
Language Albanian
Religions Islam 60% (Sunni), Christianity 12% (Orthodox 8%, RC 4%), none/unaffiliated 28%
Ethnic groups Albanian 95%, Greek 3%, others 2%

Physical description

A mountainous country, relatively inaccessible and untravelled; the northern Albanian Alps rise to 2 692m; rivers include the Drin, Shkumbin, Seman, Vijosë; there are many lakes throughout the country; half the population is concentrated in the western low-lying area, which occupies only one quarter of the country's territory.

Climate

A Mediterranean-type climate: hot and dry on the plains in summer (average July temperature 24°–25°C), with frequent thunderstorms; winters are mild, damp and cyclonic (average January temperature 8°–9°C); winters in the mountains are often severe, with snow cover lasting for several months; annual mountain precipitation exceeds 1 000mm.

Government

The first free elections were held in 1991 as the country began to move towards democratic reform and westernization.

Economy

Oil, mining, chemicals and natural gas; hydroelectric power plants on several rivers; agricultural product processing; textiles; oil products; cement; main crops are wheat, sugar-beet, maize, potatoes, fruit and oats; in the early 1990s the economy declined and severe food shortages led to violent rioting. All industry is nationalized; the economy is also committed to eliminating private farming through the progressive transformation of farm co-operatives into state farms; forest land occupies 47% of Albanian territory.

History

The history of the Albanians dates back to the 2c AD, when Ptolemy referred to a tribe, the Albanoi, in the region of modern Albania. The Albanian Ghegs and Tosks speak two forms of an Indo-European language now considered a dialect of Illyrian, the Albanians being recognized as descendants of the ancient Illyrians but with Slav, Greek, Vlach and Turkish blood. In the Middle Ages they were included within the empires of Byzantium, Samuel (of Macedonia) and Stephen I

Nemanja of Serbia, but from the 12c an independent Albanian enclave developed around Krujë. Their decentralized tribal way of life was little changed under Ottoman rule (1503–1913) and was only destroyed with the establishment of the communist regime (1945). After local uprisings, the Albanian national movement formally began with the League of Prizren (1878–81). The first general uprising resulted in independence in 1912, and in 1913 the first independent Albanian state was established. Its boundaries excluded many Albanians, many of whom still live in the Serbian province of Kosovo. Albania's independence was short-lived at first, as Italian forces occupied the country from 1914 until 1920; however, it became a republic in 1925, and a monarchy, under King Zog I, in 1928. During World War II Albania was occupied by Germany and Italy and it became a new republic in 1946. After being involved in a dispute with the USSR in 1961, it withdrew from the Warsaw Pact in 1968 but maintained close links with communist China until 1978. The Socialist People's Republic was instituted in 1976. The country gradually began to move towards democratic reform and westernization, and the first free elections were held in 1991. In the early 1990s the economy declined and severe food shortages led to violent rioting. The communists retained power in 1991 but were defeated the following year by the Democratic Party. There was further rioting in early 1997, when many Albanians lost their life savings in the collapse of investment schemes. An influx of refugees from the conflicts in the former Yugoslavia in the late 1990s was an additional economic burden.

ALGERIA

Official name Democratic and Popular Republic of Algeria
Local name Al-Jazā'ir (Arabic), Algérie (French)
Location A North African republic, bounded to the west by Morocco; to the south-west by Western Sahara, Mauritania and Mali; to the south-east by Niger; to the east by Libya; to the north-east by Tunisia; and to the north by the Mediterranean Sea
Area 2 460 500 sq km/949 753 sq mi
Capital Algiers

Chief towns Constantine, Oran, Skikda, Annaba, Mostaganem, Blida, Tlemcen
Population 31 133 000 (1999e)
Time zone GMT +1
Currency 1 Algerian Dinar (AD, DA) = 100 centimes
Language Arabic, Tamazight; French is also spoken
Religions Islam 99% (Sunni), others 1%
Ethnic groups Arab 74%, Berber 25%, European 1%

Physical description

From the Mediterranean coast, the mountains rise in a series of ridges and plateaux to the Atlas Saharien; 91% of the population is located on the narrow coastal plain; part of the Sahara Desert lies to the south of the Atlas Saharien; in the north-east of this region is a major depression, the Chott Melrhir, which extends east into Tunisia; the Hoggar Mountains in the far south rise to 2 918m at Mount Tahat.

Climate

Typical Mediterranean climate on the north coast; annual average rainfall of 400–800mm (mostly November–March); snow on the higher ground; Algiers, representative of the coastal region, has an annual rainfall of 760mm with average maximum daily temperatures of 15°–29°C; the rest of the country has an essentially rainless Saharan climate.

Government

A President is elected as head of state every five years by universal suffrage and he appoints a Cabinet; the President and a 430-member National Assembly share legislative power.

Economy

Large-scale nationalization after 1963; agriculture, mainly on the north coast (wheat, barley, oats, grapes, citrus fruits, vegetables); food processing, textiles, clothing; petroleum products account for c.30% of the national income; natural gas reserves are estimated to be the world's fourth largest; pioneer in the development of liquid natural gas; constructed with Italy the first trans-Mediterranean gas pipeline.

History

The indigenous peoples of Algeria (Berbers) have been driven back from the coast by many invaders, including the Phoenicians, Romans (Algeria became a province of the Roman Empire), Vandals, Arabs, Turks and French. Islam and Arabic were introduced by the Arabs in the 8–11c, and Islam (Sunni Muslim) is now the chief religion. The Turkish invasion took place in the 16c, and the French colonial campaign in the 19c resulted in control by 1902. During the 20c the National Liberation Front (FLN) engaged in guerrilla war with French forces in 1954–62, and Algeria gained independence in 1962. The first President of the republic, Ahmed Ben Bella, was replaced after a coup led by Houari Boumédienne in 1965, who governed by decree until 1976, when elections were held and a new constitution declared him President. He was succeeded in 1979 by Chadli Benjedid. In 1992 a state of emergency was declared as a result of clashes between government forces and the Islamic Salvation Front, and for the rest of the 1990s Algeria was wracked by a bloody civil war between its secular government and Islamic fundamentalist insurgents in which an estimated 75 000 people died. A 'civil concord' in 1999 restored stability although sporadic violence continued. Recent years have also seen increased recognition of the Berber community, and the Berber language Tamazight was officially recognized in 2001.

⮕ **American Samoa ▸ United States of America**

ANDORRA

Official name Principality of Andorra; the Valleys of Andorra

Local name Andorra

Location A small, mountainous, semi-independent, neutral state on the southern slopes of the central Pyrenees between France and Spain

Area 468 sq km/181 sq mi

Capital Andorra la Vella

Population 65 900 (1999e)

Time zone GMT +1

Currency 1 Euro (€) = 100 cents

Language Catalan; French and Spanish are also spoken

Religions Christianity 95% (RC 94%, Prot 1%), none/unaffiliated 5%

Ethnic groups Spanish 61%, Andorran 30%, French 6%, others 3%

Physical description

A mountainous country, reaching 2 946m at Coma Pedrosa, occupying two valleys (del Norte and del Orient) of the River Valira.

Climate

Winters are cold but dry and sunny; the lowest average monthly rainfall is 34mm in January; the midsummer months are slightly drier than spring and autumn.

Government

The Co-Princes of the Principality are the President of France and the Bishop of Urgel; the General Council of the Valleys appoints the Head of Government, who appoints four Councillors elected from the parishes.

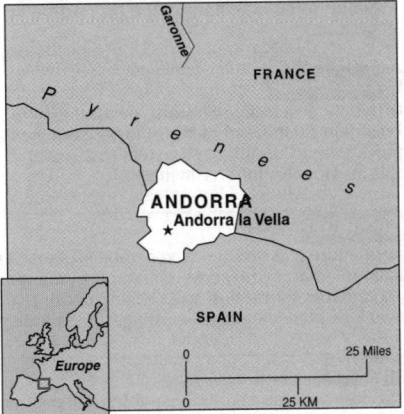

Economy

Hydroelectric power on the River Valira; no restriction on currency exchange, and no direct or value-added taxes; commerce; tobacco; potatoes; construction; forestry; in recent years, textiles, publishing, leather, mineral water, furniture; tourism; skiing at five mountain resorts.

History

One of the oldest states in Europe, it has been under the joint protection of France and Spain since 1278. In Jan 2002 the Euro replaced the French franc and Spanish peseta as the official currency.

Nations of the World

ANGOLA

Official name Republic of Angola
Local name Angola
Location A republic in south-west Africa, bounded to the south by Namibia; to the east by Zambia; and to the north by the Democratic Republic of Congo; with the separate province of Cabinda enclosed by the Congo
Area 1 245 790 sq km/480 875 sq mi
Capital Luanda
Chief towns Huambo, Benguela, Lobito, Namibe

(Moçâmedes), Cabinda, Malanje, Lubango
Population 11 178 000 (1999e)
Time zone GMT +1
Currency 1 New Kwanza (Kzrl) = 100 lwei
Language Portuguese; many Bantu languages are also spoken
Religions Christianity 81% (RC 69%, Prot 12%), traditional beliefs 19%
Ethnic groups Ovimbundu 37%, Mbundu 25%, Bakongo 13%, others 25%

Physical description

A narrow coastal plain, widening in the north towards the Congo Delta; high plateau inland with an average elevation of 1 200m; the highest point is Serro Môco (2 619m); numerous rivers rise in the plateau but few are navigable for any length.

Climate

Mostly a tropical plateau climate, with a single wet season in October–March and a long dry season; more temperate above 1 500m; Huambo is representative of the upland region with an average annual rainfall of 1 450mm and average daily temperatures of 24°–29°C; temperature and rainfall are much reduced on the coast, which is semi-desert as far north as Luanda (eg Namibe in the south has an average annual rainfall of 55mm; in the far north it is 600mm).

Government

Officially a democratic state, governed by a President (also head of state), who exercises power via a Council of Ministers (c.20) and a 220-member National Assembly.

Economy

Agriculture (cassava, corn, vegetables, plantains, bananas, coffee, cotton, sisal, timber, tobacco, palm oil, maize); reserves of diamonds, manganese, iron ore, gypsum, asphalt, limestone, salt, phosphates; extraction and refining of oil (mainly off the coast of Cabinda province), provides over 75% of recent export earnings; food processing; textiles; cement; paper; pulp.

History

The area became a Portuguese colony after exploration in 1483; an estimated 3 million slaves were sent to Brazil during the next 300 years. Boundaries were formally defined during the Congress of Berlin in 1884–5. Angola became an Overseas Province of Portugal in 1951 and gained independence in 1975. Shortly afterwards, civil war broke out between three internal factions: the Marxist MPLA (Popular Movement for the Liberation of Angola) government, UNITA (National Union for the Total Independence of Angola) and the FNLA (National Front for the Liberation of Angola). The FNLA and UNITA received arms from the USA in 1975–6, and in 1976 Cuban combat troops arrived to back up the MPLA. South African forces occupied an area along the Angola–Namibia frontier in 1975–6, and were active again in support of UNITA in 1981–4. Meanwhile, Angola backed the Namibian independence movement SWAPO (South West Africa Peoples' Organization), who launched attacks on Namibia from Angolan territory in the 1970s. Eventually an international agreement signed in Geneva in 1988 linked arrangements for the independence of Namibia with the withdrawal of Cuban troops and the cessation of South African support for UNITA. In 1991 a peace agreement between UNITA and the government was followed by multi-party elections, but the first results were not accepted by UNITA and fighting resumed. Another peace agreement was reached in 1994, though UNITA did not appear to comply with its terms, and in 1995 UN peace-keeping forces entered Angola. They were involved, among other things, in the task of starting to clear up millions of land mines laid during the civil war. However, fighting resumed in 1998 and the UN peacekeepers withdrew in 1999. In Feb 2002 the leader of UNITA, Jonas Savimbi, was killed and in April a new UNITA ceasefire was agreed. A Prime Minister was appointed for the first time since 1999 and many refugees began to return home.

⊃ **Anguilla ▶ United Kingdom**

ANTIGUA AND BARBUDA

Official name State of Antigua and Barbuda
Local name Antigua and Barbuda
Location An independent group of three tropical islands in the Leeward group of the Lesser Antilles in the eastern Caribbean Sea: Antigua, Barbuda and the uninhabited Redonda
Area 442 sq km/171 sq mi
Capital St John's
Chief town Codrington (on Barbuda)
Population 64 200 (1999e)

Time zone GMT −4
Currency 1 East Caribbean Dollar (EC$) = 100 cents
Language English
Religions Christianity 96% (Prot 87%, RC 9%), Rastafarianism 1%, others 2%, none/unaffiliated 1%
Ethnic groups African descent 92%, British 4%, others 4%

Physical description

The western part of Antigua rises to 470m at Boggy Peak; Barbuda is a flat, coral island reaching only 44m at its highest point, with a large lagoon on its western side.

Climate

Tropical, with temperatures ranging from 24°C in January, to 27°C in August–September, and an average annual rainfall of 1 000mm.

Government

The Queen is head of state, represented by a Governor-General; there is a bicameral Legislature consisting of a 17-member Senate and a 17-member House of Representatives elected for five year periods.

Economy

Rum; sugar (marked decline in 1960s, now recovering); cotton; tourism (40% of the national income).

History

Antigua was discovered by Columbus in 1493. It was colonized by the English in 1632 and ceded

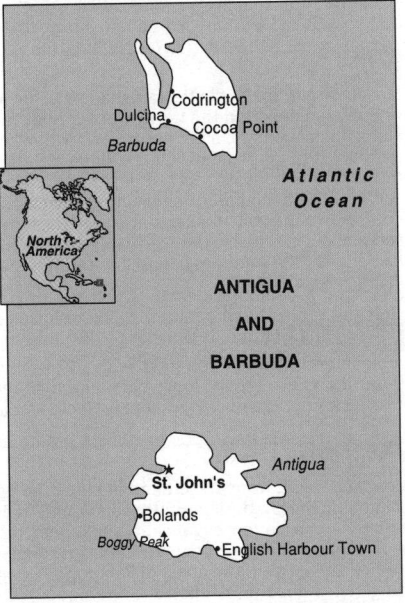

to England in 1667. Barbuda was colonized from Antigua in 1661. Administered as part of the Leeward Islands Federation from 1871 until 1956, it became an associated state of the UK in 1967. Full independence of Antigua and Barbuda was achieved in 1981. The head of state remains the British monarch, represented by the Governor-General. The Prime Minister on independence was Vere Cornwall Bird of the Antigua Labour Party, who held power until he was succeeded by his son, Lester Bird, in 1994.

ARGENTINA

Official name Argentine Republic
Local name Argentina
Location A republic in south-eastern South America, bounded to the east by the southern Atlantic Ocean; to the west by Chile; to the north by Bolivia and Paraguay; and to the north-east by Brazil and Uruguay
Area 3 761 274 sq km/1 451 852 sq mi

Capital Buenos Aires
Chief towns Córdoba, Rosario, Mendoza, La Plata, San Miguel de Tucumán
Population 36 738 000 (1999e)
Time zone GMT –3
Currency 1 Peso ($) = 100 centavos
Language Spanish

Physical description

The Andes stretch the entire length of Argentina (north to south), forming the boundary with Chile; the mountains extend far to the east in north Argentina, but their width decreases towards the south; high ranges, plateaux and rocky spurs are found in the north-west; the highest peak is Aconcagua (6 960m); a grassy, treeless plain (the *pampa*) is to the east; uneven, arid steppes lie to the south; the island of Tierra del Fuego is situated off the southern tip; north Argentina is drained by the Paraguay, Paraná and Uruguay rivers, which join in the River Plate estuary; several rivers flow to the Atlantic Ocean in the south; there are many lakes in the *pampa* and Patagonia regions, the largest being Lago Argentino (1 415 sq km/546 sq mi).

Climate

Most of Argentina lies in the rainshadow of the Andes; dry steppe or elevated desert in the north-west corner; moderately humid sub-tropical climate in the north-east, with average annual temperature 16°C and rainfall 500–1 000mm at Buenos Aires; the central *pampa* region and a strip along the foot of the mountains are semi-arid with temperatures ranging from tropical to moderately cool; between these two semi-arid areas lies the rainshadow; desert plateau extends to the coast; some rainfall prevents absolute barrenness; the southern part is directly influenced by strong prevailing westerlies.

Government

A bicameral National Congress, with a 254-member Chamber of Deputies, is elected for four years, and a 46-member Senate is elected for nine years; a President is elected for a six-year term.

Economy

Considerable European settlement since the opening up of the pampas in the 19c; agricultural produce, chiefly cereals and meat; also potatoes, cotton, sugar cane, sugar beet, tobacco, linseed oil, rice, soya, grapes, olives, peanuts; meat processing; cement; fertilizer; steel; plastics; paper; pulp; textiles; motor vehicles; oil and gas, chiefly off the coast of Patagonia; coal, gold, silver, copper, iron ore, beryllium, mica, tungsten, manganese, limestone, uranium.

Religions

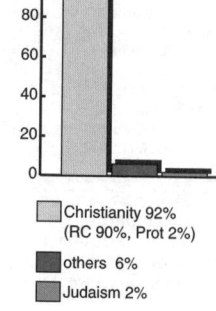

☐ Christianity 92% (RC 90%, Prot 2%)

■ others 6%

■ Judaism 2%

Ethnic groups

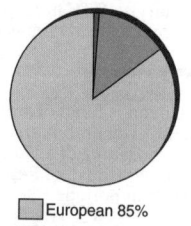

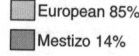

☐ European 85%

■ Mestizo 14%

■ others 1%

History

The majority of the population is of European origin and the remainder is of mestizo or South American Indian origin. Argentina was settled in the 16c by the Spanish. It declared its independence in 1816, and the United Provinces of the Río de la Plata were established. A federal constitution was agreed in 1853. Following a war with Paraguay in 1865–70, Argentina acquired the Gran Chaco plain, but an attempt to gain control of the Falkland Islands in 1982 resulted in defeat in the Falklands War with the UK. Following years of military rule, civilian rule was re-established in 1983, when Raúl Alfonsín became President; he was succeeded by Carlos Menem in 1989, who was himself succeeded in 1999 by Fernando de la Rúa. In the late 1990s Argentina faced an economic crisis, and widespread popular demonstrations in Dec 2001 led to the resignation of de la Rúa. After three interim presidents Eduardo Duhalde became President in 2002, but the devaluation of the peso and other measures failed to resolve the economic crisis and Argentina's financial difficulties increased when it defaulted on a World Bank loan in late 2002.

Nations of the World

ARMENIA

Official name Republic of Armenia
Local name Hayastani Hanrapetoutiun
Location A mountainous republic in southern Transcaucasia, bounded to the north by Georgia; to the east and south-west by Azerbaijan; to the south-east by Iran; and to the north-west by Turkey
Area 29 800 sq km/11 500 sq mi
Capital Yerevan

Chief towns Vanadzor, Gyumri
Population 3 409 000 (1999e)
Time zone GMT +4
Currency 1 Dram (Drm) = 100 louma
Language Armenian
Religions Christianity 94% (Orthodox), others 6%
Ethnic groups Armenian 93%, Azeri 3%, Russian 2%, others 2%

Physical description

Mountainous, rising to 4 090m at Mount Aragats in the west; the largest lake is the Sevan in the east; the chief river is the Araks.

Climate

Dry and cold in the summer, cold in the winter.

Government

A 190-member unicameral National Assembly, to be elected every four years, was introduced in 1995.

Economy

Seriously affected by the 1988 earthquake and conflict with Azerbaijan; building materials, chemicals, carpets, electrical engineering, foodstuffs, machine tools, textiles; hydroelectric power on the River Razdan; grains, cotton, tropical fruits, grapes, olives, livestock.

History

The Armenians are a Christian nation of Indo-European origin, speaking a language of that family with some Caucasian features. Their history goes back to the Roman period and includes years of relative independence; their highly developed ancient culture, particularly in fine art, architecture and sculpture, reached its zenith in the 14c. They are highly nationalistic, and their resentment of foreign domination during the 19c provoked their Russian and Turkish rulers. Those who were not retained under Turkish control were taken over by the Russians in 1828. During World War I, the Turks deported two-thirds of Armenians (1.75 million) to Syria and Palestine; 600 000 were either killed or died of starvation during the journey; later, many settled in Europe, the USA and the USSR. Galvanized by earlier Turkish massacres and encouraged by Lenin, Armenia declared its independence in 1918; however, it lost it again on Lenin's orders in 1920 for allegedly consorting with Soviet enemies. Armenia was proclaimed a Soviet Socialist Republic in 1920, and became a constituent republic of the USSR in 1936. At this time Soviet Armenia laid claim to Turkish Armenia. In 1988 there was a severe earthquake which harmed the country's economy, and further damage was done from 1991 by the dispute with neighbouring Azerbaijan over Nagorno-Karabakh, a mountainous autonomous region ruled by Azerbaijan since 1923 despite having a mainly Armenian population. With the disintegration of the USSR, Armenia declared its independence in 1991 as the Republic of Armenia and became a member of the CIS (Commonwealth of Independent States). The following year a state of emergency was declared as a result of the worsening economic situation, and the dispute with Azerbaijan escalated into full-scale war. A cease-fire agreement was reached in 1994 and Nagorno-Karabakh declared itself independent in 1996, but the conflict remained unresolved.

➔ **Aruba ▸ Netherlands, The**

AUSTRALIA

Nations of the World

Official name Commonwealth of Australia
Local name Australia
Location An independent country and the smallest continent in the world, entirely in the southern hemisphere
Area 7 692 300 sq km/2 969 228 sq mi
Capital Canberra

Chief towns Melbourne, Brisbane, Perth, Adelaide, Sydney
Population 18 784 000 (1999e)
Time zone GMT +8/10.5
Currency 1 Australian Dollar ($A) = 100 cents
Language English

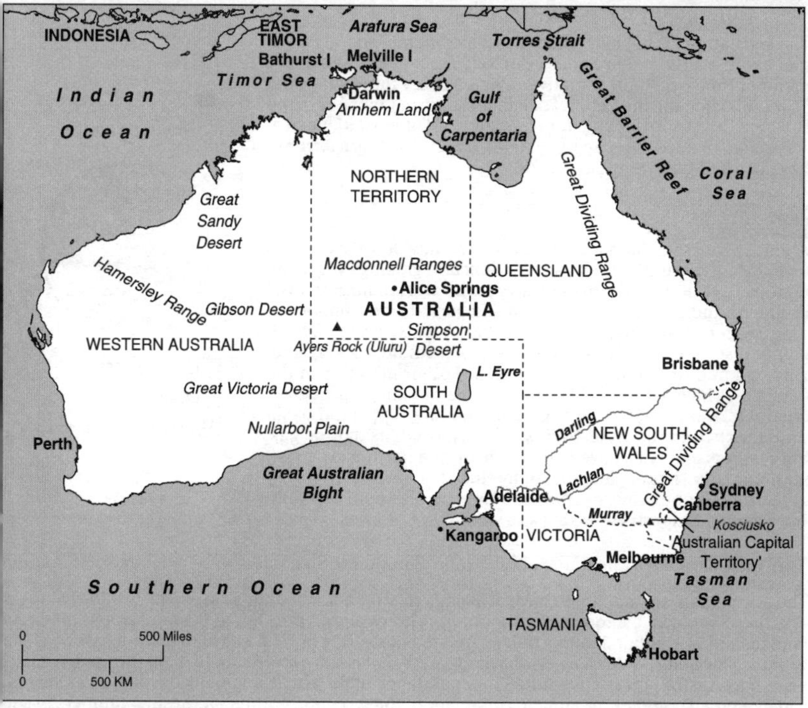

[Map of Australia showing states, territories, cities, and physical features including:
INDONESIA, EAST TIMOR, Arafura Sea, Torres Strait, Bathurst I, Melville I, Timor Sea, Darwin, Arnhem Land, Gulf of Carpentaria, Great Barrier Reef, Coral Sea, Indian Ocean, NORTHERN TERRITORY, Great Sandy Desert, Macdonnell Ranges, Alice Springs, QUEENSLAND, Great Dividing Range, Hamersley Range, Gibson Desert, AUSTRALIA, Simpson Desert, Ayers Rock (Uluru), WESTERN AUSTRALIA, Great Victoria Desert, SOUTH AUSTRALIA, L. Eyre, Brisbane, Darling, NEW SOUTH WALES, Perth, Nullarbor Plain, Great Australian Bight, Adelaide, Lachlan, Sydney, Canberra, Kosciusko, Murray, Kangaroo I, VICTORIA, Australian Capital Territory, Melbourne, Tasman Sea, Southern Ocean, TASMANIA, Hobart. Scale 500 Miles / 500 KM]

Physical description

Almost 40% of its land mass is north of the Tropic of Capricorn; the Australian continent consists largely of plains and plateaux, most of which average 600m above sea level; the West Australian Plateau occupies nearly half the whole area; in the centre are the MacDonnell Ranges: the highest points being Mount Liebig (1 524m) and Mount Zeil (1 510m); in the north-west the Kimberley Plateau rises to 936m at Mount Ord, and in the west the Hamersley Ranges rise to 1 226m at Mount Bruce; most of the plateau is dry and barren desert, notably the Gibson Desert in the west, the Great Sandy Desert in the north-west, the Great Victoria Desert in the south and the Simpson Desert in the central area; in the south is the Nullarbor Plain; the Eastern Highlands or Great Dividing Range lie parallel to the eastern seaboard, rising to 2 228m at Mount Kosciusko, in the Australian Alps; between the Western Plateau and the Eastern Highlands lies a broad lowland belt extending south into the Murray–Darling plains; off the north-east coast, stretching for over 1 900km/1 200mi, is the Great Barrier Reef; the island of Tasmania, a southern extension of the Eastern Highlands, rises to 1 617m at Mount Ossa, and is separated from the mainland by the Bass Strait; Australia's longest river is the Murray, its chief tributaries being the Darling, Murrumbidgee and Lachlan. Fertile land with a temperate climate and reliable rainfall is limited to the lowlands and valleys near the coast in the east and south-east, and to a small part of the south-west corner. The population is concentrated in these two regions.

Nations of the World

Climate

More than one third of Australia receives under 260mm average annual rainfall; less than one third receives over 500mm; half the country has a rainfall variability of more than 30%, with many areas experiencing prolonged drought; Darwin's average daily temperature is 26°–34°C in November and 19°–31°C in July; rainfall varies from 386mm in January to zero in July; Melbourne's average daily temperature is 6°–13°C in July and 14°–26°C in January–February, with a monthly rainfall averaging 48–66mm; in Tasmania, climatic conditions vary greatly between mountain and coast; there is much heavier rainfall in the west (over 2 500mm per annum in places) than in the east (500–700mm per annum).

Government

The legislature (as of 1980) comprises a bicameral Federal Parliament with a 64-member Senate elected for six years, and a 125-member House of Representatives elected every three years; the Prime Minister and the Cabinet of Ministers are responsible to the House; a Governor-General, representing the Queen (as Queen of Australia), presides over an Executive Council. Northern Territory has been self-governing since 1978.

Economy

About 26% of total land area is unused (mainly desert); c.67% is used for agricultural purposes, including arid grazing (44%) and non-arid grazing (17%), the country is the world's largest wool producer, and a top exporter of veal and beef; its most important crop is wheat; other major cereals are barley, oats, maize and sorghum; discoveries of petroleum reserves, bauxite, nickel, lead, zinc, copper, tin, uranium, iron ore, and other minerals in the early 1960s have turned Australia into a major mineral producer; commercial oil production began in 1964; the Gippsland basin produces two-thirds of Australia's oil and most of its natural gas, but major discoveries have been made off the north-west coast; manufacturing has expanded rapidly since 1945, especially in engineering, shipbuilding, car manufacture, metals, textiles, clothing, chemicals, food processing and wine.

Religions

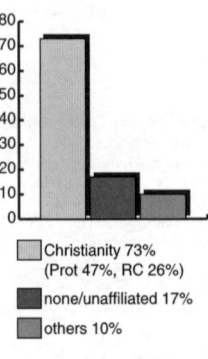

Christianity 73%
(Prot 47%, RC 26%)

none/unaffiliated 17%

others 10%

Ethnic groups

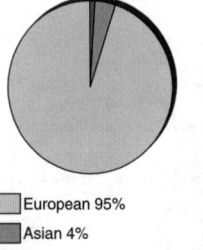

European 95%

Asian 4%

Aboriginal and others 1%

History

The Aboriginals are thought to have arrived in Australia from South-East Asia c.40 000 years ago. The first European visitors were the Dutch, who explored the Gulf of Carpentaria in 1606 and landed in 1642. Captain James Cook arrived in Botany Bay in 1770, and claimed the east coast for Britain. New South Wales was established as a penal colony in 1788. In 1829 all the territory now known as Australia was constituted a dependency of Britain. It originally developed as several widely-spread colonies, relating to Britain more than to one another. Increasing numbers of settlers were attracted to Australia, especially after the introduction of Spanish Merino sheep. Gold was discovered in New South Wales and Victoria (1851), and in Western Australia (1892). Transportation of convicts to eastern Australia ended in 1840, but continued until 1853 in Tasmania and 1868 in Western Australia. During this period, the colonies drafted their own constitutions and set up governments: New South Wales (1855), Tasmania and Victoria (1856), South Australia (1857), Queensland (1860) and Western Australia (1890). In 1901 a federal Commonwealth of Australia was established by agreement between the colonies, with the new city of Canberra chosen as the site for its capital. A policy of preventing immigration by non-whites stayed in force from the end of the 19c until 1974. The growing movement for independence in recent years culminated with the pledge of Paul Keating in 1993 to make Australia a republic by 2001, subject to a referendum, to which Queen Elizabeth II agreed. In 1996 Keating's Labor Party lost power, but the Liberal–National Party coalition led by John Howard continued the movement; in Feb 1998 a constitutional convention voted in favour of adopting a republican system of government, and the proposal was put to the Australian people in Nov 1999. Opposed by the reigning Prime Minister, it failed not so much because the Australians doubted their capacity to elect their head of state as because their politicians, anxious to preserve the existing Westminster-type political system, offered them no such option. Republican advocates were as keen as other politicians to insist that a President should be a nominee of the politicians, lest the President acquire a popular mandate.

States and territories

Name	Area		State capital
	sq km	sq mi	
Australian Capital Territory	2 432	939	Canberra
New South Wales	801 427	309 431	Sydney
Northern Territory	1 346 200	519 768	Darwin
Queensland	1 732 700	668 995	Brisbane
South Australia	984 376	380 070	Adelaide
Tasmania	68 331	26 383	Hobart
Victoria	227 600	87 876	Melbourne
Western Australia	2 525 500	975 096	Perth

AUSTRIA

Official name Republic of Austria
Local name Österreich
Location A mountainous republic in central Europe, bounded to the north by Germany and the Czech and Slovak Republics; to the south by Italy and Slovenia; to the west by Switzerland and Liechtenstein; and to the east by Hungary
Area 83 854 sq km/32 368 sq mi
Capital Vienna

Chief towns Graz, Linz, Salzburg, Innsbruck, Klagenfurt
Population 8 139 000 (1999e)
Time zone GMT +1
Currency 1 Euro (€) = 100 cents
Language German
Religions Christianity 84% (RC 77%, Prot 7%), Islam 2%, none/unaffiliated 8%, others 6%
Ethnic groups Austrian 98%, others 2%

Physical description

Situated at the eastern end of the Alps, the country is almost entirely mountainous; the ranges of the Ötztal, Zillertal, Hohe Tauern and Niedere Tauern stretch eastwards from the main Alpine massif; the highest point is Gross-glockner, at 3 797m; chief passes into Italy are the Brenner and Plöcken; most of the country is in the drainage basin of the River Danube; the Neusiedler See on the Hungarian border is the largest lake in Austria.

Climate

There are three climatic regions: the Alps (often sunny in winter but cloudy in summer); the Danube valley and the Vienna basin (the driest region); and the south-east, a region of heavy thunderstorms, with often severe winters but warmer summers than north of the Alps. In general, most rain falls in the summer months; winters are cold; there is a warm, dry wind (the Föhn) in some north-to-south valleys, especially in autumn and spring, which can be responsible for fires and snow-melt leading to avalanches.

Government

The Assembly includes a National Council elected for four years (183 deputies), and a Council (63 members); a President holds office for six years, and appoints a Chancellor; each *Land* is adminis-tered by its own government headed by a Governor elected by the Provincial Parliament.

Economy

The principal agricultural areas along the River Danube and to the north of the Alps produce crops, cattle, orchards and vineyards; there is forestry on the lower mountain slopes; iron and steel are the main metal and mineral resources, which also include lignite, lead and zinc ores, graphite, talc, kaolin, clay and salt; other natural resources include oil (and petrochemicals), nat-ural gas and hydroelectric power; diverse manufacturing industry; tourism.

History

Austria was part of the Roman Empire until the 5c, then was occupied by Germanic tribes and in the late 8c became a frontier area of Charlemagne's empire. It became a duchy and passed to the Habsburg family (1282), who made it the foundation of their empire; the head of the Habsburg house was almost continually the Holy Roman Emperor, making Austria the leading German state. Habsburg defeats in the 19c (notably the Austro-Prussian War) and Hungarian nationalism led to the Dual Monarchy of Austria-Hungary. The assassination of Archduke Franz Ferdinand by Serbian nationalists triggered World War I. Following the collapse of Austria-Hungary at the end of the war, those German-speaking lands of the Habsburg Empire not annexed by other successor states constituted themselves on 12 Nov 1918 as 'German Austria', renamed Austria on the insistence of the victor powers. Between the wars the republic led an uneasy existence, with most of public opinion and most politicians seeking union with Germany. Union with Hitler's Germany, which occurred when Austria was annexed by the German Reich in Mar 1938 (Anschluss), under the name *Ostmark*, was more controversial. After World War II, Austria was reconstituted as a distinct territory by the Allies and in 1955 became an independent, neutral, democratic state. Austria joined the EC in 1995. The inclusion of the far right Freedom Party in a coalition government with the centre right People's Party in 2000 led to the imposition of EU sanctions for seven months. The schilling was replaced by the Euro in Jan 2002.

AZERBAIJAN

Official name Republic of Azerbaijan
Local name Azarbaijan
Location A republic in eastern Transcaucasia, bounded to the east by the Caspian Sea and to the south by Iran; Armenia splits the country in the south-west and forms the western boundary; Georgia and Russia lie to the north
Area 86 600 sq km/33 428 sq mi
Capital Baku

Chief towns Kirovabad, Sumgait
Population 7 908 000 (1999e)
Time zone GMT +4
Currency 1 Manat = 100 gopik
Language Azeri
Religions Islam 93% (Shiite), Christianity 5% (Orthodox), others 2%
Ethnic groups Azerbaijani 83%, Russian 6%, Armenian 6%, Dagestani 3%, others 2%

Physical description

Crossed by the Greater Caucasus in the north and the Lesser Caucasus in the south-west; they are separated by the plain of River Kura; the highest peak is Mount Bazar-Dyuzi (4 480m) in the north-east; forests cover 10.5% of the country's total area.

Climate

Continental; hot in summer, cold in winter.

Government

A 125-member unicameral National Assembly (*Milli Majlis*) was introduced in 1995.

Economy

Oil extraction and refining; iron; steel; aluminium; copper; chemicals; cement; foodstuffs; textiles; carpets; fishing; timber; salt extraction; grain; cotton; rice; grapes; fruit; vegetables; tobacco; silk.

History

The Azeris have a long history, mainly of subjection to the neighbouring empires. A Turkish people converted to Islam, they came under Tsarist Russian rule in 1813. The development of the oil industry in and around Baku produced leaders who, encouraged by Lenin, declared independence in 1918. However, in 1920 they were reconquered on his instructions for allegedly siding with Soviet enemies, and Azerbaijan was proclaimed a Soviet Socialist Republic; it became a constituent republic of the USSR in 1936. Between Dec 1988 and Jan 1990 riots promoted by the nationalist Azerbaijan Popular Front culminated in an anti-Armenian pogrom in the capital, and Soviet troops mounted a violent assault on the city to restore order. Before emerging as an independent republic in 1991 following the disintegration of the USSR, Azerbaijan became locked in a struggle with

Armenia over the autonomous region that Stalin had set up for the latter's co-nationals in Nagorno-Karabakh. This degenerated into full-scale war in 1992. A cease-fire was announced in 1994 and Nagorno-Karabakh declared itself independent in 1996, but the conflict remained unresolved. Azerbaijan joined the CIS (Commonwealth of Independent States) in 1991.

⟳ **Azores ▸ Portugal**

THE BAHAMAS

Official name Commonwealth of the Bahamas
Local name Bahamas
Location An independent archipelago of c.700 low-lying islands and over 2 000 cays, forming a chain extending c.500mi/800km south-east from the coast of Florida
Area 13 934 sq km/5 379 sq mi
Capital Nassau
Chief town Freeport

Population 283 700 (1999e)
Time zone GMT –5
Currency 1 Bahamian Dollar (BA$, B$) = 100 cents
Language English
Religions Christianity 95% (Prot and others 74%, RC 21%), none/unaffiliated 3%, others 2%
Ethnic groups black 85%, white 15%

Physical description

The coralline limestone islands of the Bahamas comprise the two oceanic banks of Little Bahama and Great Bahama; the highest point is only 120m above sea level.

Climate

Subtropical, with average temperatures of 21°C in winter and 27°C in summer; the average annual rainfall is 750–1500mm; hurricanes are frequent in June–November.

Government

A bicameral assembly, consisting of a House of Assembly with 49 elected members and a Senate with 16 nominated members; the head of state, the British monarch, is represented by a Governor-General.

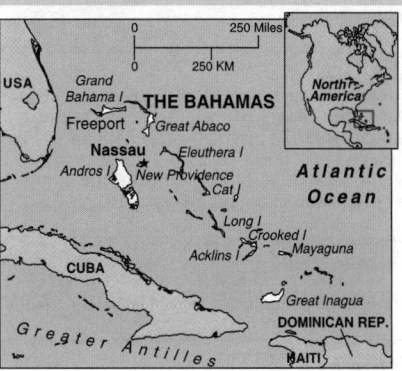

Economy

Tourism is the mainstay of the economy, especially at New Providence (Nassau and Paradise Island) and Grand Bahama; important financial centre (status as a tax haven); oil refining; fishing; rum and liqueur distilling; cement; pharmaceuticals; steel pipes; fruit, vegetables.

History

The Bahamas were discovered by Columbus in 1492, but the first permanent European settlement was not until 1647, by English and Bermudan religious refugees. The Bahamas became a British Crown Colony in 1717. A notorious rendezvous for buccaneers and pirates, they gained independence in 1973. The head of state remains the British Monarch, represented by a Governor-General; the Prime Minister on independence was Sir Lynden Pindling, who was succeeded in 1992 by Hubert Ingraham, who was himself succeeded in 2002 by Perry Christie.

Nations of the World

Nations of the World

BAHRAIN

Official name Kingdom of Bahrain
Local name Mamlakat Al-Bahrayn
Location A group of 35 islands comprising a monarchy in the Arabian Gulf, midway between the Qatar Peninsula and mainland Saudi Arabia; a causeway (25km/16mi in length) connects Bahrain to Saudi Arabia
Area 678 sq km/262 sq mi
Capital Manama

Chief town Al Muharraq
Population 629 100 (1999e)
Time zone GMT +3
Currency 1 Bahrain Dinar (BD) = 1 000 fils
Language Arabic
Religions Islam 95% (Shiite 73%, Sunni 22%), others 5%
Ethnic groups Bahraini 63%, Asian 13%, other Arab 10%, Iranian 8%, others 6%

Physical description

The island of Bahrain is c.48km/30mi long and 13–16km/8–10mi wide, comprising a total area of 562 sq km/217 sq mi; the highest point is Jabal Dukhan (135m); largely bare and infertile, though helped by many major drainage schemes since 1973.

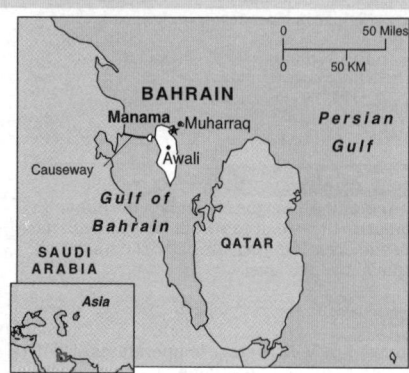

Climate

Cool north/north-east winds, with a little rain in December–March (the average temperature in January is 19°C); rest of the year dominated by either a moist north-east wind (the *Shamal*) or the hot, sand-bearing *Qaws* from the south; average summer temperature is 36°C.

Government

A constitutional monarchy governed by the king, who appoints a Council of Ministers headed by a Prime Minister. Reforms in 2001 led to the additional creation of an elected Parliament.

Economy

Oil (on land and offshore), natural gas, lime, gypsum; oil refining, aluminium smelting, ship repairing; a major centre for oil trading, banking and commerce.

History

Bahrain was a flourishing trade centre in 2000–1800BC. It was ruled by Iran from 1602 until the Iranian rulers were ousted in 1783 by the al-Khalifa family, who still rule to this day. Political control of Bahrain was held by Britain from 1820 to 1971, and oil was discovered during this time, in 1932. In 1971 Bahrain gained independence and Isa Bin Salman became Emir. He dissolved the National Assembly in 1975 as a result of disputes between Sunni and Shiite Muslim communities. On his death in 1999 he was succeeded by his son, Hamad Bin Isa. Following a referendum on political reform in 2001, the country became a constitutional monarchy and the Emir adopted the title of King. Elections to a new legislative assembly were held in 2002 and an independent justiciary is to be created.

➔ **Balearic Islands ▸ Spain**

BANGLADESH

Official name People's Republic of Bangladesh
Local name Gana Prajatantri Bangladesh
Location An Asian republic lying between the foothills of the Himalayas and the Indian Ocean, bounded to the west, north-west and east by India; to the south-east by Myanmar; and to the south by the Bay of Bengal
Area 143 998 sq km/55 583 sq mi
Capital Dacca

Chief towns Chittagong, Khulna, Narayanganj
Population 127 118 000 (1999e)
Time zone GMT +6
Currency 1 Taka (TK) = 100 poisha
Language Bengali (Bangla); English is the second language
Religions Islam 87% (mostly Sunni), Hinduism 12%, others 1%
Ethnic groups Bengali 98%, others 2%

Physical description

Mainly a vast, low-lying alluvial plain, cut by a network of rivers, canals, swamps and marshes; main rivers are the Ganges (Padma), Brahmaputra (Jamuna) and Meghna, joining in the south to form the largest delta in the world; subject to frequent flooding; in the east, fertile valleys and peaks of Chittagong Hill Tracts rise to c.1 000m; lush vegetation, with bamboo and palm forests in the east, mixed monsoon forest in the Madhuper Jungle, vast areas of the southern delta are covered in mangroves and hardwood forest.

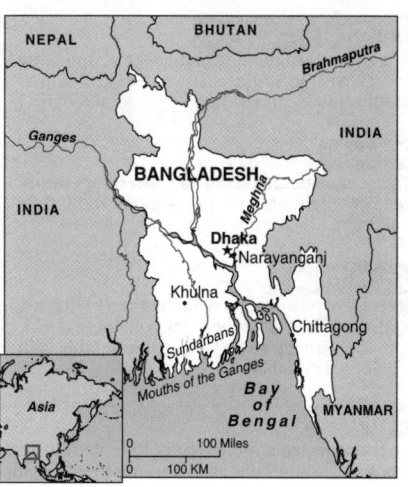

Climate

Tropical monsoon climate; a hot season in March–June with heavy thunderstorms; very humid, with higher temperatures inland; the main rainy season is June–September; cyclones in the Bay of Bengal cause sea surges and widespread inundation of coastal areas.

Government

Parliament has one 300-member chamber, with 30 seats reserved for women; members are elected every five years.

Economy

85% of the working population is employed in agriculture, especially rice; tea, tobacco, sugar; supplies 80% of the world's jute; jute mills, paper, aluminium, textiles, glass; shipbuilding; fishing; natural gas; coal; peat; limestone.

History

Bangladesh formed part of the State of Bengal until Muslim East Bengal was created in 1905, separate from Hindu West Bengal. Reunited in 1911, East and West Bengal were again partitioned in 1947, with West Bengal remaining in India and East Bengal forming East Pakistan. Disparity in investment and development between East and West Pakistan (separated by over 1 000mi/1 600km), coupled with language differences, caused East Pakistan to seek autonomy. The suspension of democracy following a sweeping electoral victory by the Awami League in East Pakistan in 1970, the devastation of this province of Pakistan by a cyclone in the same year (it is one of the world's most densely populated areas), and the Dacca government's ineffectual response to the disaster — which claimed 220 000 lives and countless homes and crops — triggered fighting, which developed into a full-scale border war in 1971. Pakistan surrendered the territory only months later, following a popular uprising and military intervention by India, which had accepted huge numbers of Bangladeshi refugees; thus the independent republic of Bangladesh was created. Political unrest led to the suspension of the constitution in 1975, and the assassination of the first President. There were further coups in 1975, when the Awami League was overthrown and disbanded, as well as in 1977 and 1982. The constitution was restored in 1986. The Awami League later regrouped and rose to become a major political force, and in 1996, led by Sheikh Hasina Wazed, it defeated the Bangladesh Nationalist Party of Khaleda Zia to become the country's ruling party. Sheikh Hasina completed her term of office in 2001, the first elected prime minister to do so, and subsequent elections returned Khaleda Zia to power.

BARBADOS

Official name Barbados
Local name Barbados
Location An independent state and the most easterly of the Caribbean Islands, situated in the Atlantic Ocean
Area 430 sq km/166 sq mi
Capital Bridgetown
Chief town Speightstown

Population 259 200 (1999e)
Time zone GMT −4
Currency 1 Barbados Dollar (BD$) = 100 cents
Language English
Religions Christianity 71% (Prot and others 67%, RC 4%), none/unaffiliated 17%, others 12%
Ethnic groups black 80%, white 4%, others 16%

Physical description

A small, triangular island, 32km/20mi long (north-west to south-east); it rises to 340m at Mount Hillaby and is ringed by a coral reef.

Climate

Tropical, with an average annual temperature of 27°C and an average annual rainfall of 1420mm.

Government

Executive power rests with the Prime Minister, appointed by a Governor-General; there is a 21-member Senate, and a House of Assembly with 27 elected members.

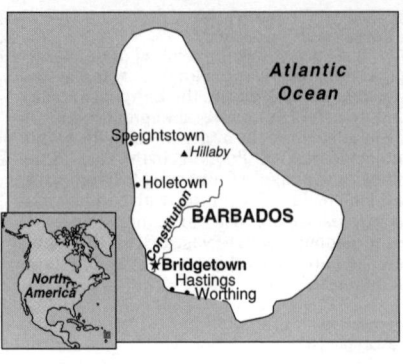

Economy

Sugar cane; rum; molasses; cotton; bananas; vegetables; natural gas; garments, electronic and electrical equipment; medical supplies; tourism.

History

It was colonized by the English in 1627 and attained self-government in 1961, becoming an independent sovereign state within the Commonwealth of Nations in 1966.

BELARUS

Official name Republic of Belarus
Local name Belarus
Location A republic in eastern Europe, bounded to the west by Poland; to the north-west by Lithuania; to the north by Latvia; to the east by Russia; and to the south by the Ukraine
Area 207 600 sq km/80 134 sq mi
Capital Minsk
Chief towns Gomel , Vitebsk, Mogilev, Bobruysk, Grodno, Brest

Population 10 402 000 (1999e)
Time zone GMT +2
Currency 1 Rouble (BR) = 100 kopeks
Languages Belarusian, Russian
Religions Christianity 72% (Orthodox 60%, RC 8%, Prot 4%), others 28% (including Islam and Judaism)
Ethnic groups Belarusian 78%, Russian 13%, Polish 4%, Ukrainian 3%, others 2%

Physical description

It is largely flat, with low hills in the north-west rising to 345m; rivers include the Dnieper, Zapadnaya Dvina and Neman; there are c.11 000 lakes; a third of the country is covered by forests.

Climate

Mild winters and cool summers.

Government

A bicameral Parliament (*Natsionalnoye Sobranie*) consisting of a 64-member Council of the Republic and a 100-member Chamber of Representatives.

Economy

Machine tools, vehicles, agricultural machinery, glass, foodstuffs, fertilizers, textiles, electronics, artificial silk and leather; oil extraction and refining, salt extraction; farm land covers 46% of the land area; it is an important flax-growing area, and other agricultural activities include meat and dairy production.

History

The Belorussians were one of the original Slav tribes, like the Russians themselves. They remained slightly distinct because they lived in the exposed western border area and were subject to long periods of foreign, particularly Polish, rule. Under Tsarist control from 1795, they eventually developed a national movement that declared independence in 1917. However, a feeble Belorussia had a troubled existence; it declared a Belorussian Soviet Socialist Republic in 1919 and was incorporated into the USSR in 1921. In 1945 its territory was expanded at the expense of Poland and, for Soviet political reasons, it was given separate membership of the UN. Yet its sense of national identity remained comparatively undeveloped until it achieved independence in 1991 on the disintegration of the Soviet Union; also that year it became a founding member of the CIS (Commonwealth of Independent States). It has since become more commonly known as Belarus, and in 1997 united with Russia as an 'integrated political and economic community'. In 2000 plans were announced for a single currency, although in 2002 the authoritarian President, Alexander Lukashenko, dismissed proposals for full union with Russia under a single government.

BELGIUM

Official name Kingdom of Belgium
Local name Belgique (French), België (Flemish)
Location A kingdom in north-western Europe, bounded to the north by the Netherlands; to the south by France; to the east by Germany and Luxembourg; and to the west by the North Sea
Area 32 545 sq km/12 562 sq mi
Capital Brussels
Chief towns Antwerp, Ghent, Charleroi, Liège, Bruges, Namur, Mons

Population 10 182 000 (1999e)
Time zone GMT +1
Currency 1 Euro (€) = 100 cents
Languages Flemish (Dutch), French, German (mainly on the eastern border); Brussels is officially a bilingual city
Religions Christianity 85% (RC 75%, Prot 10%), Islam 2%, none/unaffiliated 10%, others 3%
Ethnic groups Fleming 55%, Walloon 33%, Italian 2%, Moroccan 1%, others 9%

Physical description

Mostly low-lying, with some hills in the southeast region (Ardennes); there are large areas of fertile soil which have been intensively cultivated for many centuries; the main river systems, the Sambre–Meuse and the Scheldt, drain across the Dutch border and are linked by a complex network of canals; Belgium has a low-lying dune-fringed coastline of 64km/40mi along the North Sea.

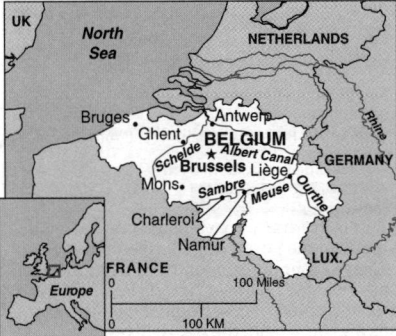

Climate

Cool and temperate with strong maritime influences.

Government

A hereditary and constitutional monarchy, with legislative power vested in a monarch, a Senate and a Chamber of Representatives.

Economy

One of the earliest countries in Europe to industrialize, using the rich coalfields of the Ardennes; Flanders has had a famous textile industry since the Middle Ages; Belgium is a long-standing centre for European trade; its important iron and steel industry, dependent on raw materials from Luxembourg and Germany, has led to many related industries, including metallurgical and engineering products, processed food and beverages, chemicals, textiles, glass and petroleum; there is trade in gemstones (especially diamonds); agriculture is mainly livestock, also wheat, potatoes, sugar-beet and flax; in 1948 there was full economic union between Belgium, Netherlands and Luxembourg (Benelux Economic Union); a founder-member of the EEC; Brussels is the headquarters of several major international organizations.

History

A line drawn east to west just to the south of Brussels divides the population by race and language into two approximately equal parts; north of the line the inhabitants are Flemings of Teutonic stock who speak *Flemish*, while south of the line they are French-speaking Latins known as *Walloons*. Belgium was part of the Roman Empire until the 2c AD, and after being invaded by Germanic tribes it became part of the Frankish Empire. In the early Middle Ages, some semi-independent provinces and cities grew up and from 1385 were absorbed by the House of Burgundy. They were known as the Spanish Netherlands, and were ruled by the Habsburgs from 1477 until the Peace of Utrecht (1713); the Spanish provinces were then transferred to Austria as the Austrian Netherlands. The country was conquered by the French in 1794 and formed part of the First French Republic and Empire until in 1815 it united with the northern (Dutch) provinces under King William I of the Netherlands. The southern (Belgian) provinces were unhappy with the union because of William's religious, linguistic and economic policies. The Belgian Revolution began with riots in Brussels on 25 Aug 1830. A provisional government, called a National Convention, declared the independence of Belgium and drafted a new constitution (7 Feb 1831), which made Belgium a constitutional monarchy with Leopold of Saxe-Coburg as its first king (Leopold I). The Great Powers recognized Belgian independence at the Conference of London (20 Jan 1831). However, William I refused to cooperate; as a result an armed standoff dragged on for most of the 1830s. Finally in Apr 1839 the Dutch government capitulated and signed a treaty which completed the independence of Belgium. During the 20c, Belgium was occupied by Germany in both World Wars, and political tension between Walloons and Flemings caused the collapse of several governments. Belgium was a founder-member of the EEC in 1958. In 1980 Wallonia and Flanders were given regional 'subgovernments', and in 1989 a new federal constitution divided Belgium into three autonomous regions: the Walloon Region (Wallonia), the Flemish Region (Flanders) and the bilingual Brussels-Capital Region. The political federalization of Belgium was completed by constitutional amendment in 1993. The Belgian franc was replaced by the Euro in Jan 2002.

BELIZE

Official name Belize
Local name Belize
Location An independent state in Central America, bounded to the north by Mexico; to the west and south by Guatemala; and to the east by the Caribbean Sea
Area 22 963 sq km/8 864 sq mi
Capital Belmopan
Chief towns Belize City, Dangriga, Punta Gorda, San Ignacio

Population 235 800 (1999e)
Time zone GMT −6
Currency 1 Belize Dollar (BZ$) = 100 cents
Language English; Spanish and local Maya languages are also spoken
Religions Christianity 92% (RC 62%, Prot 30%), others 6%, none/unaffiliated 2%
Ethnic groups Mestizo 44%, Creole 30%, Maya 11%, Garifuna 7%, others 8%

Physical description

The country has an extensive coastal plain, swampy in the north, more fertile in the south; the Maya Mountains extend almost to the east coast, rising to 1 120m at Victoria Peak; they are flanked by pine ridges, tropical forests, savannahs and farm land; the Belize River flows west to east; inner coastal waters are protected by the world's second longest barrier reef.

Climate

Generally subtropical but tempered by trade winds; coastal temperatures vary between 10°C and 36°C, with a greater range in the mountains; there is variable rainfall with an average of 1 295mm in the north and 4 445mm in the south; dry season in February–May; hurricanes have caused severe damage.

Government

A Governor-General represents the British Monarchy and appoints a Prime Minister; a bicameral National Assembly, with an eight-member Senate and a 28-member House of Representatives.

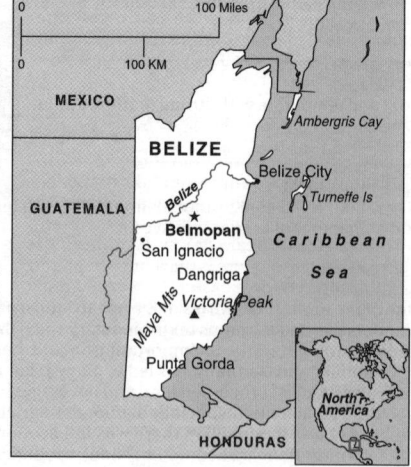

Economy

Traditionally based on timber and forest products, more recently on agriculture, especially sugar, citrus fruit, cocoa, rice, tobacco, bananas, beef; fishing; boatbuilding; food processing; textiles; furniture; batteries; cigarettes.

History

There is evidence of early Maya settlement in Belize, and its coast was colonized in the 17c by shipwrecked British sailors and disbanded soldiers from Jamaica, who defended the territory against the Spanish. Created a British colony in 1862, it was administered from Jamaica, but the tie with Jamaica was severed in 1884. A ministerial system of government was introduced in 1961, and in 1964 full internal self-government was achieved. The country changed its name from British Honduras to Belize in 1973 and gained full independence in 1981; the People's United Party continued in government under Prime Minister George Price. Guatemalan claims over Belize territory led to a British military presence, until in the early 1990s Guatemala established diplomatic relations with Belize. Belize joined the Organization of American States (OAS) in 1991. Almost all of the British presence was withdrawn in 1993. The British Monarch remains head of state, represented by a Governor-General. Talks in 2002 led to hopes of a final resolution of the border dispute with Guatemala.

BENIN

Official name Republic of Benin
Local name Bénin
Location A Republic in West Africa, bounded to the north by Niger; to the east by Nigeria; to the south by the Bight of Benin; to the west by Togo; and to the north-west by Burkina Faso
Area 112 622 sq km/43 472 sq mi
Capital Porto Novo
Chief towns Ouidah, Abomey, Kandi, Parakou, Natitingou

Population 6 306 000 (1999e)
Time zone GMT +1
Currency 1 CFA Franc (CFAFr) = 100 centimes
Language French; several local languages are also spoken
Religions traditional beliefs 61%, Christianity 22% (RC 19%, Prot 3%), Islam 17%
Ethnic groups Fon 39%, Bariba 21%, Yoruba 10%, others 30%

Physical description

Rises from a 100km/62mile-long sandy coast with lagoons, to low-lying plains, then to a savannah plateau at c.400m; the Atakora Mountains rise to over 500m in the north-west; the Alibori River valley lies in the north-east and joins the River Niger valley; several rivers flow south to the Gulf of Guinea.

Climate

Tropical climate, divided into three zones; in the south, there is rain throughout the year, especially during the 'Guinea Monsoon' (May–October); in the central area there are two rainy seasons (peaks in May–June and October); in the north, there is one (July–September); the northern dry season (October–April) is hot, has low humidity, and is subject to the dry *harmattan* wind from the north-east.

Government

A 83-member unicameral National Assembly is elected every four years; members cannot renew their appointments.

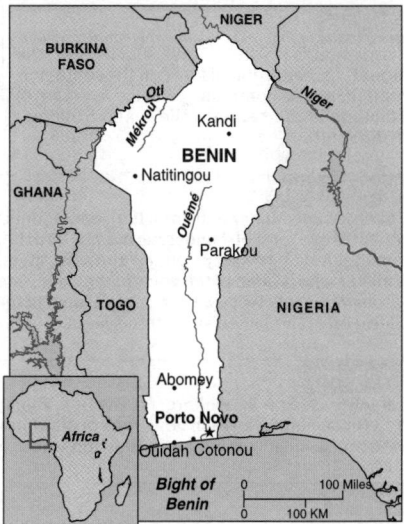

Economy

Cotton, palm products, cocoa, coffee, crude oil.

History

As the Kingdom of Dahomey, it was based on its capital at Abomey, and in the late 17c and early 18c extended its authority from the coast to the interior, to the west of the Yoruba states. In the 1720s the cavalry of the Oyo Kingdom of the Yoruba devastated Dahomey, but when the Oyo Empire collapsed in the early 19c, Dahomey regained its power. It became famous for its trade in palm oil and slaves, and was influenced by the neighbouring Yoruba. The state was annexed by the French in 1883 and consituted a territory of French West Africa in 1904, but regained its independence in 1960. In 1972 it was declared a Marxist–Leninist state under the leadership of President Mathieu Kérékou, who renamed it Benin in 1975. The country gradually gained stability and moved towards democratic government. In the first free elections (1991) Kérékou was defeated by his Prime Minister Nicéphore Soglo, but he returned to power in 1996 and was re-elected in 2001.

⮱ **Bermuda ▸ United Kingdom**

BHUTAN

Official name Kingdom of Bhutan
Local name Druk-Yul
Location A small state in the eastern Himalayas, bounded to the north by China and to the south by India
Area 46 600 sq km/18 000 sq mi
Capital Thimbu/Thimphu
Chief Town Phuntsholing

Population 1 952 000 (1999e)
Time zone GMT +5.5
Currency 1 Ngultrum (Nu) = 100 chetrum
Language Dzongkha
Religions Buddhism 73%, Hinduism 22%, Islam 5%
Ethnic groups Bhote 50%, Nepalese 35%, others 15%

Physical description

High peaks of the east Himalayas, reaching over 7 000m in the north; forested mountain ridges with fertile valleys descend to low foothills in the south; many rivers flow to meet the River Brahmaputra.

Climate

Permanent snowfields and glaciers in the mountains; subtropical forest in the south; torrential rain is common, with an average of 1 000mm in the central valleys and 5 000mm in the south.

Government

Governed by a Maharajah, from 1907, now addressed as King of Bhutan; an absolute monarchy was replaced by a form of democratic monarchy in 1969; the King is the head of state, advised by a nine-member Royal Advisory Council and a six-member Council of Ministers which is led by a Prime Minister who is head of the government; a 151-member unicameral legislative National Assembly (*Tsongdu*) meets twice a year, comprising village elders, monastic representatives and administrative officials elected every three years.

Economy

Largely based on agriculture, mainly rice, wheat, maize, mountain barley, potatoes, vegetables, fruit (especially oranges); large area of plantation forest; hydroelectric power; local handicrafts; food processing; cement processing; plywood; postage stamps; tourism.

History

British involvement dates from 1774 with the signing of a treaty of cooperation between Bhutan and the East India Company; the southern part of the country was annexed by Britain in 1865. In 1910 Britain agreed not to interfere in internal affairs, transferring the supervision of Bhutan's external affairs to British India, and in 1949 Bhutan signed a similar treaty with India. In 1990 large numbers of ethnic Nepalese moved to Nepal and India following the introduction of strict cultural laws. Bhutan has been governed since 1907 by a Maharajah, who is now addressed as King of Bhutan. The absolute monarchy was replaced in 1969 by a form of democratic monarchy, with the King as the head of the government, and further reforms took place in 1998. The King's authority was reduced, the National Assembly gained powers and the leader of the Council of Ministers became the head of government. A written constitution is under discussion with further reforms predicted.

BOLIVIA

Official name Republic of Bolivia
Local name Bolivia
Location A landlocked republic in western central South America, bounded to the north and east by Brazil; to the west by Peru; to the south-west by Chile; to the south by Argentina; and to the south-east by Paraguay
Area 1 098 580 sq km/424 052 sq mi
Capital La Paz/Sucre
Chief towns Cochabamba, El Alto, Oruro, Potosí, Santa Cruz, Sucre

Population 7 983 000 (1999e)
Time zone GMT −4
Currency 1 Boliviano ($b) = 100 centavos
Languages Spanish, Quechua, Ayamará
Religions Christianity 97% (RC 92%, Prot 5%), Baha'i 3%
Ethnic groups Mestizo 30%, Quechua 30%, Aymará 25%, European 10%, others 5%

Physical description

A landlocked country, bounded to the west by the Cordillera Occidental of the Andes, rising to 6 542m at Sajama; separated from the Cordillera Real to the east by the flat, 400km/250mile-long Altiplano Plateau which lies at 3 600m above sea level; major lakes in this region are Titicaca and Poopó; several rivers flow from the Andes towards the Brazilian frontier.

Climate

Varies, according to altitude; humid and tropical in the lowlands, cold and semi-arid in the mountains.

Government

A bicameral Congress, with a 27-member Senate and a 130-member Chamber of Deputies elected for four years; an elected President appoints a Cabinet of 18 Ministers.

Economy

Largely dependent on minerals for foreign exchange; silver largely exhausted, but replaced by tin (one fifth of world supply), tungsten, antimony, lead, gold; oil and natural gas, pipelines to Argentina and Chile; sugar cane, rice, cotton, potatoes, cereals; livestock; illegally-produced cocaine.

History

Bolivia formed part of the Inca Empire in the 15c, and there is evidence of earlier civilization. It was conquered by the Spanish in the 16c, and achieved independence after the war of liberation in 1825. Much territory was lost after wars with neighbouring countries, with the Chaco War (1932–5) in particular having a devastating effect. In 1952 the *Movimiento Nacionalista Revolucionario* (National Revolutionary Movement), an alliance of mineworkers and peasants led by Víctor Paz Estenssoro, overthrew the military dictatorship and came to power. It brought about some far-reaching social reforms during the 1950s, including universal suffrage, the nationalization of the tin mines, and the improvement in status of the South American Indians. However, Bolivia's instability continued, as evidenced by several more changes of government and military coups during the 20c. US-backed attempts to eradicate the production of coca have created further popular disquiet.

Nations of the World

BOSNIA-HERZEGOVINA

Official name Republic of Bosnia-Herzegovina
Local name Bosnia-Herzegovina
Location A republic in central Europe, formerly one of the six republics established in 1945 within the Socialist Federal People's Republic of Yugoslavia; bounded by the west and north by Croatia; and to the south and east by Serbia and Montenegro
Area 51 129 sq km/19 736 sq mi
Capital Sarajevo

Chief towns Banja Luka, Zenica, Tuzla, Mostar
Population 3 482 000 (1999e)
Time zone GMT +1
Currency 1 Dinar (D, din) = 100 paras
Languages Bosnian, Serbian, Croatian
Religions Christianity 50% (Orthodox 31%, RC 15%, Prot 4%), Islam 40%, others 9%, none/unaffiliated 1%
Ethnic groups Bosniak 40%, Serb 31%, Croat 19%

Physical description

The region is mountainous and includes part of the Dinaric Alps; it is noted for its limestone gorges.

Climate

Continental, with hot summers and cold winters.

Government

A collective presidency and bicameral National Assembly, consisting of a 15-member House of Peoples and a 42-member House of Representatives. The Bosniac-Croat Federation has a 140-member House of Representatives, and the Republika Srpska an 83-member National Assembly.

Economy

Agricultural trade; mostly dependent on UN aid.

History

In Mar 1992, under President Alija Izetbegović, it followed the republics of Slovenia and Croatia in declaring its independence from Yugoslavia. Civil war broke out among die-hard communist and nationalist elements from the Yugoslav National Army and extreme nationalist paramilitary groups, gradually and brutally engulfing the civilian population until all civil order dissolved. A three-sided civil war raged between the Muslims loyal to the government, and the Serbs and Croats who proclaimed themselves independent and began fighting for territory. By the end of 1992 the Serbs had besieged Sarajevo and were carrying out a brutal policy of ethnic cleansing, which UN peace-keeping forces attempted to stop. An alliance made in 1994 between Bosnian Muslims and Bosnian Croats enabled the recapture of territory during 1995, and NATO air-strikes helped to end the Sarajevo siege. The signing of the Dayton Peace Accord in Dec 1995 brought relative, if rather tense, peace. It acknowledged a Bosnian state which was to be divided into separate administrations along ethnic and geographic lines into a Bosnian Serb Republic in the north and east, and a Bosnian Croat Federation in the west. A central government for the republic as a whole is led by a rotating presidency of a Bosnian Muslim, a Croat and a Serb. NATO-led UN peace-keeping and stabilizing forces were mandated to remain after 2000. The Hague war crimes tribunal has convicted a number of people for the atrocities committed between 1992 and 1995, and former Serb president Slobodan Milosevic is to be tried for genocide committed in the country.

BOTSWANA

Official name Republic of Botswana
Local name Botswana
Location A landlocked republic in southern Africa, bounded to the south by the Republic of South Africa; to the west and north by Namibia; and to the east by Zimbabwe
Area 582 096 sq km/224 689 sq mi
Capital Gaborone
Chief towns Francistown, Lobatse, Selebi-Phikwe, Orapa, Jwaneng
Population 1 464 000 (1999e)
Time zone GMT +2
Currency 1 Pula (P, Pu) = 100 thebe
Languages English, Setswana
Religions traditional beliefs 50%, Christianity 50%
Ethnic groups Tswana 80%, Shona 12%, San 3%, others 5%

Physical description

Landlocked, undulating, sand-filled plateau with an average elevation of c.1 000m; most people live in the fertile east, bordered by the River Limpopo; to the west the environment changes progressively through dry scrubland and savannah to the sand-covered Kalahari Desert; varied fauna and flora in the rich Okavango River delta in the north-west; deciduous forest in the extreme north and north-west.

Climate

Largely sub-tropical, increasingly arid in the south and west; rainfall in the north and east falls almost totally in summer (October–April) with an annual average of 450mm; average maximum daily temperatures range between 23°C and 32°C; annual rainfall is erratic in the Kalahari Desert, decreasing south and west to below 200mm.

Government

Governed by a legislative National Assembly of 34 elected, and four other members; the President appoints a Cabinet of c.15 members; there is also a House of Chiefs consisting of 15 members.

Economy

Mainly subsistence farming, especially livestock; continual problems of drought and disease; some crops, especially sorghum, as well as maize, millet, beans; cotton, groundnuts, sunflower seeds; main minerals, nickel (second largest African producer), diamonds, cobalt; also coal, brine, asbestos, talc, manganese, gypsum, gold, chromium, silver, platinum; livestock processing and products; tourism, especially wildlife observation.

History

It was visited by missionaries in the 19c and came under British protection in 1885. The southern part became a British Crown Colony, then part of Cape Colony in 1895, while the northern part became the Bechuanaland Protectorate. In 1964 it achieved self-government, and in 1966 it gained independence and changed its name under the leadership of President Seretse Khama, who was succeeded in 1980 by Ketumile Masire. Masire was replaced by Festus Mogae in 1998.

Nations of the World

BRAZIL

Official name Federative Republic of Brazil
Local name Brasil
Location A republic in eastern and central South America, bounded to the north by French Guiana, Suriname, Guyana and Venezuela; to the north-west by Colombia; to the west by Peru, Bolivia and Paraguay; to the south-west by Argentina; to the south by Uruguay; and to the east by the Atlantic Ocean

Area 8 511 965 sq km/3 285 618 sq mi
Capital Brasilia
Chief towns São Paulo, Rio de Janeiro, Belo Horizonte, Recife, Salvador
Population 171 853 000 (1999e)
Time zone GMT −1/4
Currency 1 Real (R$) = 100 centavos
Language Portuguese

Physical description

The low-lying Amazon basin in the north, once an inland sea, is now drained by rivers that carry one fifth of the Earth's running water; where the forest canopy has been cleared, soils are susceptible to erosion; the Brazilian Plateau lies to the centre and south with an average height of 600–900m; vegetation changes from thorny scrub forest in the north to wooded savannah (*campo cerrado*) in the interior; the Brazilian Highlands in the north rise to 2 890m at Pico da Bandeira; the country's highest peak, Pico da Neblina (3 014m), lies in the Guiana Highlands to the south; there are eight river systems, notably the Amazon in the north, the São Francisco in the centre, and the Paraguay, Paraná and Uruguay in the south; on the Atlantic coast a thin strip of land, c.100km/ 62miles wide, contains 30% of the population.

Climate

Almost entirely tropical; the Equator passes through the northern region, and the Tropic of Capricorn through the south-eastern; in the Amazon basin the annual rainfall is 1 500–2 000mm, with no dry season; the average midday temperatures are 27°–32°C; there are more distinct wet and dry seasons on the Brazilian Plateau; the dry region in the north-east is susceptible to long droughts, with daily temperatures 21°–36°C, and monthly rainfall as little as 3mm in August, rising to 185mm in March; on the narrow coastal strip, the climate is hot and tropical, with rainfall varying greatly north to south; the southern states lie outside the tropics, with a seasonal, temperate climate.

Government

The bicameral National Congress made up of 69 Senators (three from each state) is elected for eight years, and 479 Deputies are elected for four years by proportional representation; State Governors with limited powers are elected every four years.

Economy

One of the world's largest farming countries; the world's largest exporter of coffee, and the second largest exporter of cocoa and soya beans; beef, sugar cane, cotton, butter, maize, oranges; iron ore (reserves possibly the world's largest), manganese, bauxite, nickel, uranium, gold, gemstones; steel, chemicals, petrochemicals, machinery, motor vehicles, textiles, consumer goods, cement, lumber; shipping; fishing; tourism; offshore oil production has increased since the 1960s; large investments in hydroelectricity, cane alcohol, coal and nuclear power; an important hydroelectric scheme at the Itaipu Dam on the River Paraná; the country is a world leader in the development of alcohol fuel; timber reserves are the third largest in the world but continuing destruction of the Amazon rainforest is causing much concern worldwide; a road network is being extended through the rainforest.

Religions

Christianity 94%
(RC 87%, Prot 7%)

none 3%

others 3%

Ethnic groups

white 55%

mixed 22%

black 12%

others 11%

History

It was claimed for the Portuguese after a fortuitous landfall by Pedro Cabral in 1500, and the first settlement was at Salvador da Bahia. There were 13 feudal grants, which were replaced in 1572 by a viceroyalty. The country was divided into north and south, with capitals at Salvador and Rio de Janeiro. During the Napoleonic Wars, the Portuguese court transferred to Brazil. Brazilian independence was declared in 1822, and a monarchy was established. In 1889 there was a coup, which was followed in 1891 by the declaration of a republic. Large numbers of European immigrants arrived in the early 20c; the revolution, headed by Getúlio Vargas, established a dictatorship in 1930–45, but a liberal republic was restored in 1946. Another coup in 1964 led to a military-backed presidential regime, and a military junta was established in 1969. Under President Figueiredo (1979–85) the military government began a process of liberalization, allowing the return of political exiles to stand for state and federal offices, and in 1985 elections ending military rule took place. A new constitution was approved under Figueiredo's successor José Sarney (1985–9). Subsequent governments and leaders have faced a particularly difficult economic situation. 2002 saw the election of Luiz Inacio Lula da Silva, Brazil's first left wing president for 40 years.

⊋ **British Antarctic Territory ▶ United Kingdom**

⊋ **British Indian Ocean Territory ▶ United Kingdom**

⊋ **British Virgin Islands ▶ United Kingdom**

Nations of the World

BRUNEI

Official name State of Brunei, Abode of Peace
Local name Brunei
Location A state on the north-west coast of Borneo, south-eastern Asia, bounded by the South China Sea in the north-west, and on all other sides by Malaysia's Sarawak state
Area 5 765 sq km/2 225 sq mi
Capital Bandar Seri Begawan
Chief towns Kuala Belait, Seria

Population 323 000 (1999e)
Time zone GMT +8
Currency 1 Brunei Dollar (B$) = 100 sen
Language Malay; English is widely spoken
Religions Islam 65%, Buddhism 12%, traditional beliefs and others 15%, Christianity 8%
Ethnic groups Malay 64%, Chinese 20%, others 16%

Physical description

Swampy coastal plain rising through foothills to a mountainous region on the Sarawak border; equatorial rainforest covers 75% of the land area. The Limbang River Valley in Sarawak divides the state into two sections.

Climate

Tropical climate, with high temperatures and humidity, and no marked seasons; average daily temperature ranges between 24°C and 30°C; annual average rainfall is 2 540mm on the coast, doubling in the interior.

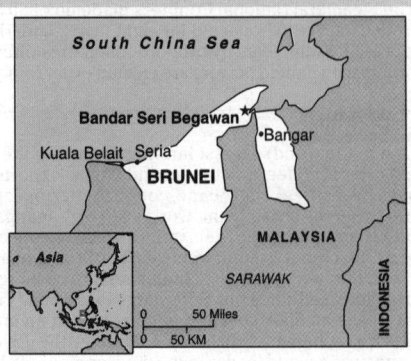

Government

A constitutional monarchy with the Sultan as head of state, advised by a Privy Council and a Council of Ministers.

Economy

Largely dependent on oil (discovered in 1929) and gas resources; main crops are rice, bananas, peppers; some rubber and timber.

History

Formerly a powerful Muslim Sultanate, it came under British protection in 1888, achieved internal self-government in 1971, and gained independence in 1984. It is a constitutional monarchy with a Sultan (Muda Hassanal Bolkiah Mu'izzadin Waddaulah, from 1967) as head of state.

BULGARIA

Official name Republic of Bulgaria
Local name Bălgarija
Location A republic in the east of the Balkan Peninsula, south-eastern Europe, bounded to the north by Romania; to the west by Serbia and Montenegro and Macedonia; to the south-east by Turkey; to the south by Greece; and to the east by the Black Sea
Area 110 912 sq km/42 812 sq mi
Capital Sofia
Chief towns Plovdiv, Varna, Ruse, Burgas, Stara Zagora, Pleven

Population 8 195 000 (1999e)
Time zone GMT +2
Currency 1 Lev (Lv) = 100 stotinki
Language Bulgarian
Religions Christianity 80% (Orthodox), Islam 13%, Judaism 1%, none/unaffiliated 5%, others 1%
Ethnic groups Bulgarian 85%, Turk 9%, others 6%

Physical description

Central Bulgaria is traversed west to east by the Balkan Mountains, rising to over 2 000m; the Rhodope Mountains in the south-west rise to nearly 3 000m just south of Sofia; the Bulgarian lowlands stretch south from the River Danube with an average width of 100km/60mi; rivers flow north to the Danube or south to the Aegean; they include the Maritsa, Iskur, Yantra and Struma.

Climate

Largely continental, with hot summers and cold winters, but to the south the climate is increasingly Mediterranean; winters are slightly warmer on the Black Sea coast.

Government

A President is head of state; a unicameral 250-member National Assembly is elected for up to five years; a Prime Minister is head of government.

Economy

Mainly agricultural produce, especially grain, fruits, vegetables, rice, tobacco, sheep, hogs, poultry, cheese, sunflower seeds, unginned cotton, attar of roses, wine; manufacturing industries include food processing, machine building, chemicals, metal products, electronics, textiles; there are natural reserves of coal, iron ore, offshore oil (Black Sea) and natural gas; tourism.

History

In the 7c Bulgars crossed the Danube and gradually merged in with the Slavonic population and established the Kingdom of Bulgaria, which was continually at war with the Byzantine Empire until it was destroyed by the Turks in the 14c. It was under Turkish rule until 1878 but full independence was only achieved in 1908. Bulgaria was a kingdom from 1908 to 1946, after which it was proclaimed a Socialist People's Republic. It was aligned with Germany in the World Wars and in 1944 was occupied by the USSR. In the early 1990s a multi-party government introduced political and economic reforms. In 2001 the former king, Simeon Saxe-Coburg Gotha (Simeon II), was elected Prime Minister. Bulgaria was invited to join NATO in 2002.

BURKINA FASO

Official name Burkina Faso
Local name Burkina Faso
Location A landlocked republic in West Africa, bounded to the north by Mali; to the east by Niger; to the south-east by Benin; to the south by Togo and Ghana; and to the south-west by Côte d'Ivoire
Area 274 540 sq km/105 972 sq mi
Capital Ouagadougou
Chief towns Bobo-Dioulasso, Koudougou, Ouahigouya, Tenkodogo
Population 11 576 000 (1999e)
Time zone GMT
Currency 1 CFA Franc (CFAFr) = 100 centimes
Language French; many local languages are also spoken
Religions traditional beliefs 45%, Islam 44%, Christianity 11% (RC 10%, others 1%)
Ethnic groups Mossi 45%, Mande 10%, Fulani 9%, Bobo 7%, others 29%

Physical description

Low-lying plateau, falling away to the south; many rivers (tributaries of the Volta or Niger) are unnavigable in the dry season; wooded savannahs in the south; semi-desert in the north.

Climate

Tropical climate, with an average temperature of 27°C in the dry season (December–May); rainy season (June–October), with violent storms (August); the *harmattan* wind blows from the north-east (December–March); rainfall decreases from south to north.

Government

Governed by a President elected for seven years and a 107-member National Assembly elected for five years under a multiparty constitution.

Nations of the World

Economy

An agricultural country, largely at subsistence level and subject to drought conditions (especially in 1973–4); mainly sorghum, millet, maize, rice, cotton, groundnuts, sesame, sugar cane, livestock; reserves of titanium, limestone, iron ore, vanadium, manganese, zinc, nickel, copper, phosphate, gold; processed foods; cigarettes; shoes; bicycles.

History

It was part of the Mossi Empire in the 18–19c before becoming a French protectorate in 1898. At first it was part of French Sudan (now Mali), then in 1919 it was made into Upper Volta. This was abolished in 1932, with most land joined to the Côte d'Ivoire. In 1947 its original borders were reconstituted, and in 1958 it gained autonomy within the French community, followed by independence as Upper Volta in 1960. It was renamed Burkina Faso in 1984. In the three decades following independence there were several military coups, the last by Blaise Compaoré in 1987; military rule ended in 1991 with multi-party elections which were won by Compaoré and the Popular Front.

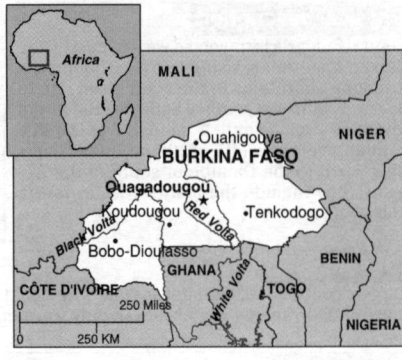

➲ **Burma ▶ Myanmar**

BURUNDI

Official name Republic of Burundi
Local name Burundi
Location A small landlocked republic in central Africa, bounded to the north by Rwanda; to the east and south by Tanzania; to the south-west by Lake Tanganyika; and to the west by the Democratic Republic of the Congo
Area 27 834 sq km/10 744 sq mi
Capital Bujumbura
Chief towns Bubanza, Ngozi, Muyinga, Muramvya, Gitega, Bururi, Rutana
Population 5 736 000 (1999e)
Time zone GMT +2
Currency 1 Burundi Franc (BuFr, FBu) = 100 centimes
Languages French, Kirundi
Religions Christianity 70%, traditional beliefs 29%, Islam 1%
Ethnic groups Hutu 85%, Tutsi 14%, others 1%

Physical description

Lies across the Nile–Congo watershed; bounded to the west by a narrow plain of the River Ruizi in the north-west and Lake Tanganyika in the west; the River Akanyaru forms the northern border with Rwanda; the average height of the interior plateau is c. 1500m, sloping east towards Tanzania; the highest point is at Mount Karonje (2 685m).

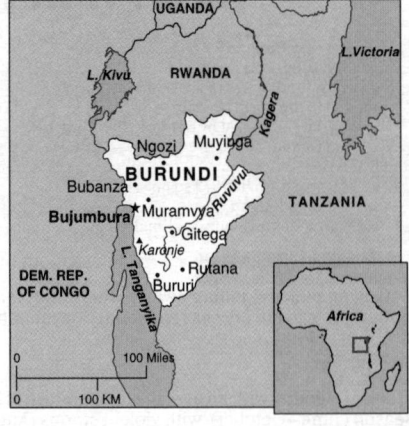

Climate

Equatorial climate, varying with altitude and season; moderately wet, except during the dry season (June–Sept); the average annual rainfall at Bujumbura is 850mm.

Government

A Transitional National Assembly was introduced in 1998, enlarging the unicameral Assembly to 117 members.

Economy

A very poor country, relying mainly on agriculture: main subsistence crops include manioc, yams, corn, haricot beans; cash crops include coffee, cotton, tea; light consumer goods (eg shoes, soap, beverages, blankets); reserve of rare-earth metals, peat, nickel, tungsten, columbium, tantalum, phosphate.

History

From the 16c the country was ruled by Tutsi kings who dominated a Hutu population. Germany annexed the area in 1890, and included it in German East Africa. After World War I it became a League of Nations mandated territory, being administered by the Belgians from 1919. In 1946 it joined with Rwanda to become the UN Trust Territory of Ruanda–Urundi, but broke this union on gaining independence in 1962; it became a full republic in 1966. Civil war broke out in 1972 and there were military coups in 1976 and 1987. A multi-party constitution was adopted in 1992 which the following year saw the end of Tutsi dominance with the appointment of a Hutu head of state and a Hutu majority in the National Assembly. Soon after the election, however, the Tutsi-dominated army staged a couple of coups in close succession, which sparked off fierce ethnic conflict and led to the loss of hundreds of thousands of lives during the ensuing years. In 1996 the incumbent Hutu President was ousted by another coup and Pierre Buyoya, a Tutsi, became head of the military junta. A transitional power-sharing government (from 2001) and ongoing peace talks have so far failed to resolve the civil war.

CAMBODIA

Official name State of Cambodia
Local name Preah Reach Ana Pak Kampuchea
Location A republic in southern Indochina, South-East Asia, bounded to the north-west by Thailand; to the north by Laos; to the east by Vietnam; and to the south and south-west by the Gulf of Thailand
Area 181 035 sq km/69 880 sq mi
Capital Phnom Penh

Chief towns Battambang, Kompong Som, Kompong Cham
Population 11 627 000 (1999e)
Time zone GMT +9
Currency 1 Riel (CRI) = 100 sen
Language Khmer; French is also widely spoken
Religions Buddhism 95%, Islam 2%, others 3%
Ethnic groups Khmer 93%, Chinese 3%, Vietnamese 2%, others 2%

Physical description

Occupies an area surrounding the Tonlé Sap (lake), a freshwater depression on the Cambodian Plain, which is crossed by the floodplain of the Mekong River in the east; the highest land lies in the south-west, where the Cardamom Mountains run for 160km/100mi across the Thailand border, rising to 1 813m at Phnom Aural.

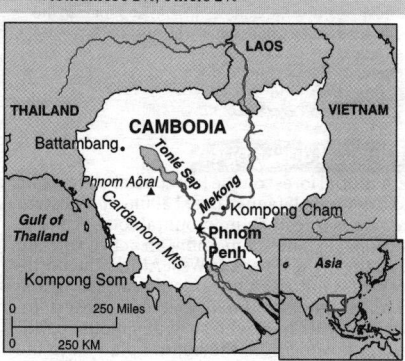

Climate

Tropical monsoon climate, with a wet season in May–September; heavy rainfall in the south-western mountains; high temperatures in the lowland region throughout the year; the average monthly rainfall at Phnom Penh is 257mm in October, 7mm in January.

Government

A pluralistic political system and a limited monarchy.

Economy

Most of the population are employed in subsistence agriculture, especially rice and corn; rubber; pepper; forestry; rice milling; fish processing; phosphates; gemstones; motor-assembly; cigarettes; industrial development disrupted by civil war.

History

Originally part of the Kingdom of Funan, it was taken over by the Khmers in the 6c. From the 15c it was in dispute with the Vietnamese and the Thais. In 1863 it was established as a French protectorate, and it became part of Indochina in 1887. It gained independence from France in 1953, with Prince Sihanouk as Prime Minister. In 1970 Sihanouk was deposed, a right-wing government was formed, and the country was renamed the Khmer Republic. Fighting throughout the country involved troops from North and South Vietnam and the USA. In 1975 Phnom Penh surrendered to the Khmer Rouge, a communist guerrilla force which opposed the government, and the following year the republic of Democratic Kampuchea was proclaimed. An attempt to reform the economy on cooperative lines and the introduction of an extreme and brutal regime by Pol Pot in 1975–8 caused the deaths of an estimated 2.5 million people. There was further fighting in 1977–8, and Phnom Penh was captured by the Vietnamese in 1979, causing the Khmer Rouge to flee. The Vietnamese immediately established a government in Cambodia which was led by Heng Samrin, but the fighting with the Khmer Rouge guerrillas did not stop. In 1983 an anti-Vietnamese government-in-exile (the Coalition Government of Democratic Kampuchea) was recognized by the UN. Unrest continued until 1987. A peace conference in Paris in 1988–9 between the Phnom Penh regime, the opposition coalition led by Prince Sihanouk, and the Khmer Rouge ended with no agreement. In 1989 the name of Cambodia was restored and Vietnamese troops completed their withdrawal. A UN peace plan was agreed in 1991, and in 1992 a UN Transitional Authority in Cambodia was planned. The Khmer Rouge refused to comply, and UN trade sanctions were imposed in 1993. Also in 1993 a new constitution was adopted and multi-party elections took place. In the new democratic monarchy, Prince Sihanouk became king, his son Prince Norodom Ranariddh was appointed Prime Minister, and Hun Sen became second Prime Minister. The Khmer Rouge continued to launch attacks until 1996, when internal divisions caused it to weaken. Meanwhile the ruling coalition suffered divisions; in 1997 Hun Sen and his armed supporters ousted Prince Ranariddh, but the political situation remained deeply unstable. Pol Pot died in Apr 1998. In Apr 1999 Cambodia was admitted to the Association of South-East Asian Nations.

CAMEROON

Official name Republic of Cameroon

Local name Cameroon

Location A republic in West Africa, bounded to the south-west by Equatorial Guinea; to the south by Gabon; to the south-east by the Congo; to the east by the Central African Republic; to the north-east by Chad; and to the north-west by Nigeria

Area 475 439 sq km/183 519 sq mi

Capital Yaoundé

Chief town Douala

Population 15 456 000 (1999e)

Time zone GMT +1

Currency 1 CFA Franc (CFAFr) = 100 centimes

Languages French, English; many local languages are also spoken

Religions Christianity 53% (RC 35%, Prot 18%), traditional beliefs 25%, Islam 22%

Ethnic groups Fang 21%, Bamileke and Bamum 19%, Douala, Luanda and Bassa 15%, Fulani 10%, others 35%

Physical description

Equatorial forest on the low coastal plain rising to a central plateau of over 1300m; the western region is forested and mountainous, rising to 4070m at Mount Cameroon, an active volcano and the highest peak in West Africa; the north-central land rises towards the Massif d'Adamaoua; low savannah and semi-desert towards Lake Chad, with several national parks; rivers flowing from the central plateau to the Gulf of Guinea include the River Sanaga.

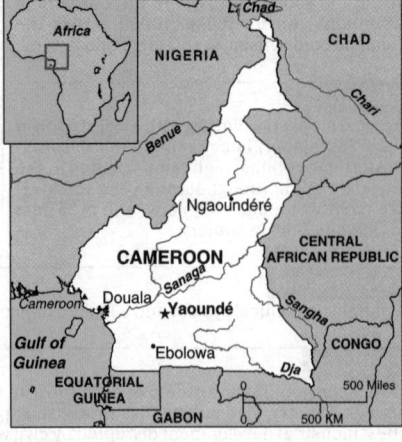

Climate

The north has a wet season in April–September, with the remainder of the year being dry; annual rainfall in the north is 1000–1750mm; the northern plains are semi-arid; the equatorial south experiences rain throughout the year, with two wet seasons and two dry seasons; Yaoundé, representative of the south, has an average annual rainfall of 4030mm and maximum daily temperatures ranging between 27°C and 30°C; a small part of Mount Cameroon receives over 10 000mm of rain per annum.

Government

Governed by an Executive President, Cabinet, and a 180-member National Assembly elected for five years.

Nations of the World

Economy

Agriculture employs c.80% of the workforce; the world's fifth largest cocoa producer; coffee, cotton, rubber, bananas, timber; light manufacturing; assembly; domestic processing; aluminium; crude oil; fertilizers; cement; gold; bauxite; natural gas; tin; tourism, especially to national parks and reserves.

History

The country was first explored by the Portuguese navigator Fernando Po, and later by traders from Spain, the Netherlands and Britain. It became a German protectorate, Kamerun, in 1884, and after World War I was divided into French and British Cameroon in 1919, which was confirmed by the League of Nations mandate in 1922. The UN turned mandates into trusteeships in 1946. French Cameroon acquired independence as the Republic of Cameroon in 1960, while the northern sector of British Cameroon voted to become part of Nigeria, and the southern sector part of Cameroon; the Federal Republic of Cameroon was established, with separate parliaments, in 1961. The federal system was abolished in 1972, and the country's name was changed to the United Republic of Cameroon; the word 'United' was dropped from the name after a constitutional amendment in 1984. From 1972 to 1992 it was ruled by one party, the Cameroon People's Democratic Movement, with Paul Biya as President from 1982. Multi-party elections in 1992 resulted in Biya's re-election, and he won again in disputed elections in 1997. Cameroon joined the Commonwealth of Nations in 1995, the first country to do so that has never been fully under British rule at any point in its history.

CANADA

Official name Canada
Local name Canada
Location An independent country in North America, bounded to the south by the USA; to the west by the Pacific Ocean; to the north-west by Alaska; to the north by the Arctic Ocean and Baffin Bay; to the north-east by the Davis Strait; and to the east by the Labrador Sea and the Atlantic Ocean

Area 9 970 610 sq km/3 848 655 sq mi
Capital Ottawa
Chief towns Calgary, Edmonton, Montreal, Quebec, Toronto, Vancouver, Victoria, Winnipeg.
Population 31 006 000 (1999e)
Time zone −3.5/8
Currency 1 Canadian Dollar (C$, Can$) = 100 cents
Languages English, French

Physical description

Dominated in the north-east by the pre-Cambrian Canadian Shield; the mountains of Nova Scotia and New Brunswick rise in the east; the fertile St Lawrence lowlands are in south Quebec and Ontario; there is flat prairie country south and west of the Shield, stretching to the Western Cordillera, which includes the Rocky, Cassiar and Mackenzie Mountains; the Coast Mountains flank a rugged, heavily-indented coastline, rising to 5 950m at Mount Logan, the highest peak in Canada; major rivers include the Yukon and Mackenzie in the west, North Saskatchewan, South Saskatchewan, Saskatchewan and Athabasca in the centre, and Ottawa and St Lawrence in the east; the Great Lakes occupy the south-east of Ontario.

Religions

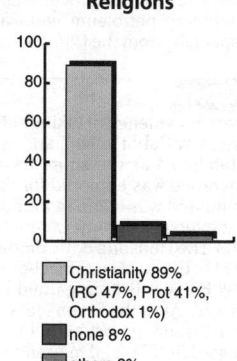

Christianity 89%
(RC 47%, Prot 41%,
Orthodox 1%)

none 8%

others 3%

Climate

The north coast is permanently ice-bound or obstructed by ice floes, except for Hudson Bay (frozen for c.9 months each year); cold air from the Arctic sweeps south and east in winter and spring; mild winters and warm summers on the west coast and some inland valleys of British Columbia; winter temperatures on the Atlantic shores are warmer than those of the interior, but summer temperatures are lower; much of the southern interior has warm summers and long, cold winters.

Government

A bicameral Federal Parliament includes a Senate of 104 nominated members and a House of Commons of 301 elected members; provinces administer and legislate on education, property laws, civil rights, health and local affairs; the British monarch is head of state, represented by a Governor-General, usually appointed for a five-year term.

Nations of the World

Economy

Traditionally based on natural resources and agriculture; the world's second largest exporter of wheat; forest covers 44% of the land area; widespread minerals (world's largest producer of asbestos, zinc, silver and nickel; second largest producer of potash, gypsum, molybdenum and sulphur); hydroelectricity, oil (especially Alberta), natural gas; major industrial development in recent decades involves food processing, vehicles and parts, chemicals and machinery; petroleum, metal and metal products; fishing; tourism (especially from the USA); increasing shift to service sector.

History

There is evidence of Viking settlement in c.1000. The country was visited by Cabot in 1497, and in 1528 St John's, Newfoundland, was established as the shore base for the English fisheries. The St Lawrence was explored for France by Cartier in 1534, and Newfoundland was claimed for England in 1583, making it England's first overseas colony. Champlain founded the city of Quebec in 1608. The Hudson's Bay Company was founded in 1670, and in the late 17c there was conflict between the British and the colonists of New France. Britain gained large areas from the 1713 Treaty of Utrecht. After the Seven Years' War, during which Wolfe captured Quebec (1759), the Treaty of Paris gave Britain almost all of France's possessions in North America. The province of Quebec was created in 1774, and migration of loyalists from the USA after the American Revolution led to the division of Quebec into Upper and Lower Canada, reunited as Canada in 1841. The Dominion of Canada was created in 1867 by a confederation of Quebec, Ontario, Nova Scotia and New Brunswick. Rupert's Land and Northwest Territories were bought from the Hudson's Bay Company in 1869–70, and were later joined by Manitoba (1870), British Columbia (1871, after promise of a transcontinental railroad), Prince Edward Island (1873), Yukon (1898, following the Klondike Gold Rush), Alberta and Saskatchewan (1905) and Newfoundland (1949). In 1982 the Canada Act gave Canada full responsibility for its constitution. There has been recurring political tension in recent decades arising from the French-Canadian separatist movement in Quebec, and from the desire for autonomy of the Native American and Inuit populations; a 1992 referendum approved the creation of the vast autonomous territory of Nunavut for the Inuit people, and this was implemented on 1 Apr 1999. Canada joined the Organization of American States (OAS) in 1990.

*Percentages add to more than 100% as some people identify with more than one ethnicity.

Ethnic groups*

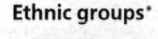
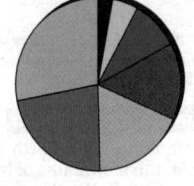
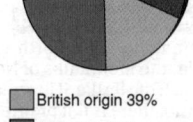
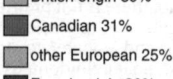

British origin 39%
Canadian 31%
other European 25%
French origin 20%
Irish origin 13%
others 7%
Amerindian 4%

Provinces

Name	Area sq km	Area sq mi	Provincial capital
Alberta	661 848	255 472	Edmonton
British Columbia	944 735	364 667	Victoria
Manitoba	647 797	250 050	Winnipeg
New Brunswick	72 908	28 142	Fredericton
Newfoundland and Labrador	405 212	156 412	St John's
Northwest Territories	1 346 106	519 597	Yellowknife
Nova Scotia	55 284	21 340	Halifax
Nunavut	2 093 190	807 971	Iqaluit
Ontario	1 076 395	415 488	Toronto
Prince Edward Island	5 660	2 185	Charlottetown
Quebec	1 542 056	595 234	Quebec City
Saskatchewan	651 036	251 300	Regina
Yukon Territory	482 443	186 223	Whitehorse

⊃ **Canary Islands ▸ Spain**

CAPE VERDE

Official name Republic of Cape Verde
Local name Cabo Verde
Location An island group in the Atlantic Ocean which lies off the west coast of Africa
Area 4 033 sq km / 1 557 sq mi
Capital Praia
Chief town Mindelo
Population 405 700 (1999e)

Time zone GMT −1
Currency 1 Escudo Caboverdiano (CVEsc) = 100 centavos
Language Portuguese; Creole is widely spoken
Religions Christianity 98% (RC), others 1%, none/unaffiliated 1%
Ethnic groups Mestico 61%, African 29%, European 1%, others 9%

Physical description

The islands are of volcanic origin, mostly mountainous; the highest peak is Cano at 2 829m, an active volcano on Fogo Island; the coastal plains are semi-desert; savannah or thin forest lies on the mountains; there are fine, sandy beaches on most islands.

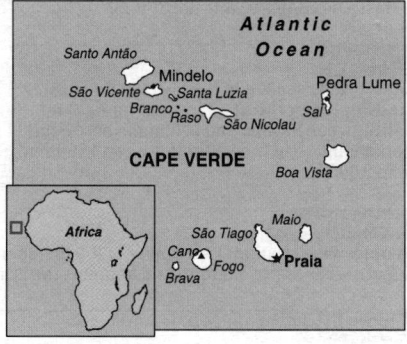

Climate

Located at the northern limit of the tropical rain belt; low and unreliable rainfall mainly in August and September; cooler and damper in the uplands; severe drought can occur; the tropical heat is subject to only a small temperature range throughout the year.

Government

Governed by a President, Council of Ministers, and unicameral People's National Assembly of 79 members, elected for five years.

Economy

Formerly an important victualling point for transatlantic shipping; the economy has suffered because of drought; substantial emigration in the early 1970s, with 80% unemployment by 1976; c.70% of the workforce are farmers occupying irrigated inland valleys; maize, beans, potatoes,

Nations of the World

cane sugar, bananas, yams, coffee; livestock; increase in fishing since 1975; mining of salt, lime-stone, volcanic silica ash (*pozzolana*).

History

It was colonized by the Portuguese in the 15c and was used as a penal colony. Administered with Portuguese Guinea until 1879, it became an overseas province of Portugal in 1951. It gained full independence in 1975 as a result of the campaign by the African Party for the Independence of Cape Verde and Guinea-Bissau, which remained the only legal party (dropping Guinea-Bissau from its name in 1980) until multi-party elections took place in 1991. That year the new Movement for Democracy Party came to power, with Antonio Mascarenhas Monteiro as President. The African Party for the Independence of Cape Verde returned to power in 2001 when Pedro Pires was elected President.

⮑ **Cayman Islands ▸ United Kingdom**

CENTRAL AFRICAN REPUBLIC

Official name Central African Republic
Local name République Centrafricaine
Location A republic in central Africa, bounded to the north by Chad; to the north-east by Sudan; to the south by the Democratic Republic of the Congo and Congo; and to the west by Cameroon
Area 626 780 sq km/241 937 sq mi
Capital Bangui
Chief towns Berbérati, Bouar, Bossangoa

Population 3 445 000 (1999e)
Time zone GMT +1
Currency 1 CFA Franc (CFAFr) = 100 centimes
Language French; Sango is also widely spoken
Religions Christianity 50% (Prot 25%, RC 25%), traditional beliefs 22%, Islam 14%, none/ unaffiliated 13%, others 1%
Ethnic groups Baya 34%, Banda 27%, Mandjia 21%, Sara 10%, others 8%

Physical description

On a plateau forming the watershed between the Chad and Congo river basins; most northern rivers drain towards Lake Chad, and southbound rivers flow towards the River Ubangi; the highest ground is found in the north-east (Massif des Bongos) and north-west.

Climate

Single rainy season in the north between May and September with an average annual rainfall between 875mm and 1000mm; more equatorial climate in the south, between 1500mm and 2000mm.

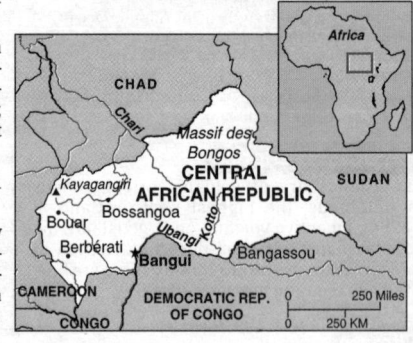

Government

A unicameral National Assembly of 109 members serves for a maximum of five years. The President serves a six-year term and appoints the Prime Minister.

Economy

c.85% of the working population is engaged in subsistence agriculture, growing cassava, groundnuts, cotton, maize, coffee, millet, sorghum, tobacco, rice, sesame seed, plantain, bananas, yams; timber, diamonds, uranium; sawmilling, brewing, diamond splitting, leather and tobacco processing.

History

For a time part of French Equatorial Africa (known as Ubangi Shari), it became an autonomous republic within the French community in 1958 and gained independence in 1960. A monarchy known as the Central African Empire was established under Bokassa I in 1976. Bokassa was forced to flee in 1979 (he returned in 1986 for trial and was found guilty of murder and other crimes in

1987). The country reverted to a republic and David Dacko became President until he was ousted by a military coup in 1981, led by André-Dieudonné Kolingba. Civilian rule returned under Kolingba in 1986, and in 1992 the constitution was amended to allow for opposition parties and to reduce the powers of the President. Elections the following year brought in a coalition government and Ange-Félix Patasse as President. The political situation remained unstable, with several coup attempts in recent years, culminating in a successful coup in Mar 2003 which deposed Patasse and installed General François Bozize as President.

CHAD

Official name Republic of Chad
Local name Tchad
Location A republic in north central Africa, bounded to the north by Libya; to the east by Sudan; to the south by Central African Republic; and to the west by Cameroon, Nigeria and Niger
Area 1 284 640 sq km/495 871 sq mi
Capital N'Djamena
Chief towns Moundou, Sarh, Abéché

Population 7 557 000 (1999e)
Time zone GMT +1
Currency 1 CFA Franc (CFAFr) = 100 centimes
Languages French, Arabic; many local languages are also spoken
Religions Islam 50%, Christianity 25% (RC 20%, Prot 5%), traditional beliefs 25%
Ethnic groups Arab 26%, Sara 25%, Teda 18%, others 31%

Physical description

Occupies a landlocked and mostly arid, semi-desert plateau at the edge of the Sahara Desert with an average altitude of 200–500m; the Logone and Chari rivers drain into Lake Chad in the south-west; isolated massifs along the Sudan frontier rise to 1 500m; the Tibesti Mountains in the north rise to 3 415m at Emi Koussi; vegetation is generally desert scrub or steppe; most people live in the tropical south.

Climate

Moderately wet in the south between May and October, but dry for the rest of the year; the hot and arid north is almost rainless; the central plain is hot and dry, with a brief rainy season during June–September.

Government

A unicameral National Assembly of 125 members, and a President elected for five years.

Economy

Severely damaged in recent years by drought, locusts and civil war; export of cotton, kaolin, animal products; agriculture mainly cassava, groundnuts, millet, sorghum, rice, yams, sweet potatoes, dates; livestock, fishing; oil exploration, with refining facilities; uranium, gold, bauxite; salt is mined around Lake Chad.

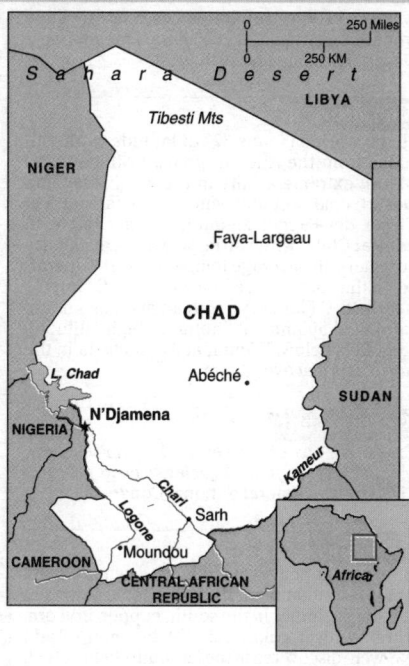

History

It was part of French Equatorial Africa in the 19c, and became a French colony in 1920. In 1960 it gained full independence. In 1982 rebel forces took the capital, forming a new government under Hissène Habré; fighting continued between Libyan-supported rebels and the French-supported government until a cease-fire was agreed in 1987, when Libya withdrew and Habré was appointed President. In 1990 he was deposed in another Libyan-backed coup, this time led by Idriss Déby. The country gradually underwent a process of democratization and a new constitution was approved in 1996. In 1998 a rebellion by the Movement for Democracy and Justice in Chad led to civil war, and sporadic violence continues despite a peace deal in 2002.

⊕ **Channel Islands ▸ United Kingdom**

CHILE

Official name Republic of Chile
Local name Chile
Location A republic in south-western South America, bounded to the west by the Pacific Ocean; to the east by Argentina; to the north-east by Bolivia; and to the north-west by Peru
Area 756 626 sq km/292 058 sq mi
Capital Santiago
Chief towns Valparaíso, Concepción, Talcahuano, Antofagasta, Viña del Mar
Population 14 974 000 (1999e)
Time zone GMT −4
Currency 1 Chilean Peso (Ch$) = 100 centavos
Language Spanish
Religions Christianity 88% (RC 80%, Prot 8%), others 1%, none/unaffiliated 11%
Ethnic groups Mestizo 94%, Amerindian 6%

Physical description

A narrow coastal belt, backed by the Andean mountain ridges rising in the north to 6 723m at Llullaillaco; the mountains are lower in the centre and south; they are ice-capped and separated by sea channels in the far south; a fertile, central, Andean valley, 40–60km/25–40mi wide at 1 200m, separates the coastal range from the main inland cordilleras; the Atacama Desert lies in the far north-west.

Climate

Highly varied (spans 37° of latitude, with altitudes from the Andean peaks to the coastal plain); extreme aridity in the North Atacama Desert; cold, wet and windy in the far south at Tierra del Fuego; Mediterranean climate in central Chile, with warm, wet winters and dry summers; the average temperature at Valparaíso on the coast varies from below 12°C (July) to nearly 18°C (January), with an average annual rainfall of 505mm; at Santiago (high altitude), rainfall is below 375mm; at Antofagasta in the north, it is just over 12mm.

Government

Executive power is exercised by a President, elected for four years; legislative power is exercised by a bicameral National Congress.

Economy

Based on agriculture and mining; wheat, corn, potatoes, sugar beet, fruit, livestock; fishing in the north, timber in the south; copper, iron ore, nitrates, silver, gold, coal, molybdenum; oil and gas were discovered in the far south (1945); steel, wood pulp, cellulose, mineral processing.

History

Originally occupied by South American Indians, the arrival of the Spanish in the 16c made Chile part of the Viceroyalty of Peru. In 1810 it declared its independence from Spain, which resulted in war until the Spanish were defeated in 1818. The first President was General Bernardo O'Higgins. Border disputes with Bolivia, Peru and Argentina brought a Chilean victory in the War of the Pacific (1879–84). In the late 1920s economic unrest led to a military dictatorship until 1931. The Marxist coalition government of President Allende was ousted in 1973 and replaced by a military junta led by General Pinochet, who banned all political activity, resulting in considerable political opposition, both at home (led by Eduardo Frei Montalva) and abroad. A constitution providing for an eventual return to democracy came into effect in 1981, and after 1988 there were limited political reforms. Free elections were held in late 1989, and in 1990 the National Congress was restored and Pinochet's rule ended. In 2000 he faced charges relating to human rights abuses during his time in office, but in 2002 all charges were dropped as he was ruled mentally unfit to stand trial.

CHINA

Official name People's Republic of China

Local name Zhonghua

Location A socialist state in central and eastern Asia, which also claims the island of Taiwan. The country is bounded to the north-west by Kyrgyzstan and Kazakhstan; to the north by Mongolia; to the north-east by Russia; to the east by North Korea, the Bo Hai Gulf, the Yellow Sea and the East China Sea; to the south by the South China Sea, the Gulf of Tongking, Vietnam, Laos, Myanmar (formerly Burma), India, Bhutan and Nepal; and to the west by India, Pakistan, Afghanistan and Tajikistan

Area 9 597 000 sq km/3 704 000 sq mi

Capital Beijing

Chief towns Shanghai, Tianjin, Shenyang, Wuhan, Guangzhou

Population 1 246 872 000 (1999e)

Time zone GMT +8

Currency 1 Renminbi Yuan (RMBY, $, Y) = 10 jiao = 100 fen

Languages standard Chinese (Putonghua) or Mandarin, also Yue (Cantonese), Wu, Minbei, Minnan, Xiang, Gan, Hakka; minority languages

Religions Chinese folk religion 20%, Buddhism 6%, Islam 2%, others 13%, none/unaffiliated 59%

Ethnic groups Han 92%, others 8%

Physical description

Over two thirds of the country is upland hill, mountain and plateau; the highest mountains are in the west, where the Tibetan Plateau rises to an average altitude of 4 000m ('the roof of the world'); the land descends to the desert or semi-desert of Sinkiang and Inner Mongolia north and east of the Tibetan Plateau; the broad and fertile plains of Manchuria lie in the north-east, separated from North Korea by the densely forested Changpai Shan uplands; further east and south, the prosperous Sichuan Basin is drained by the Yangtze River; the southern plains and east coast, with rich, fertile soils, are heavily populated.

Climate

Varied, with seven zones: (1) north-east China has cold winters, with strong north winds and warm, humid summers, but unreliable rainfall; in Manchuria, the rivers are frozen for four to six months each year, and snow lies for 100–150 days; (2) central China has warm and humid summers, sometimes typhoons or tropical cyclones on the coast; (3) south China, partly within the tropics, is the wettest area in summer; frequent typhoons (especially during July–October); (4) south-west China has summer temperatures moderated by altitude, winters are mild with little rain; summers are wet on the mountains; (5) Tibet autonomous region, a high plateau surrounded by mountains, has severe winters with frequent light snow and hard frost, summers are warm, but nights are cold; (6) Xinjiang and the western interior has an arid desert climate, cold winters, and well distributed rainfall throughout the year; (7) Inner Mongolia has an extreme continental-type climate, with cold winters and warm summers, and strong winds in winter and spring.

Government

Governed by an elected National People's Congress of 2 978 deputies; State Council of over 45 ministers, led by a Prime Minister. A President is head of state.

Economy

Since 1949, largely based on heavy industry, producing iron and steel, coal, machinery, armaments, textiles, petroleum; more recently, light industries (eg household goods, consumables); special economic zones set up to attract foreign investment; rich mineral deposits, especially coal, tungsten, iron, tin, phosphate, aluminium, copper, lead, zinc, antimony, manganese, sulphur, bauxite, salt, asbestos; the largest oil-producing country in the Far East; major subsistence crops include rice, grain, beans, potatoes, tea, sugar, cotton, oil-seed.

History

Chinese civilization is believed to date from the Xia Dynasty of c.2200–1767 BC; the Shang Dynasty (c.1766–1122 BC) saw the introduction of bronze, and was presided over by a chariot-riding warrior

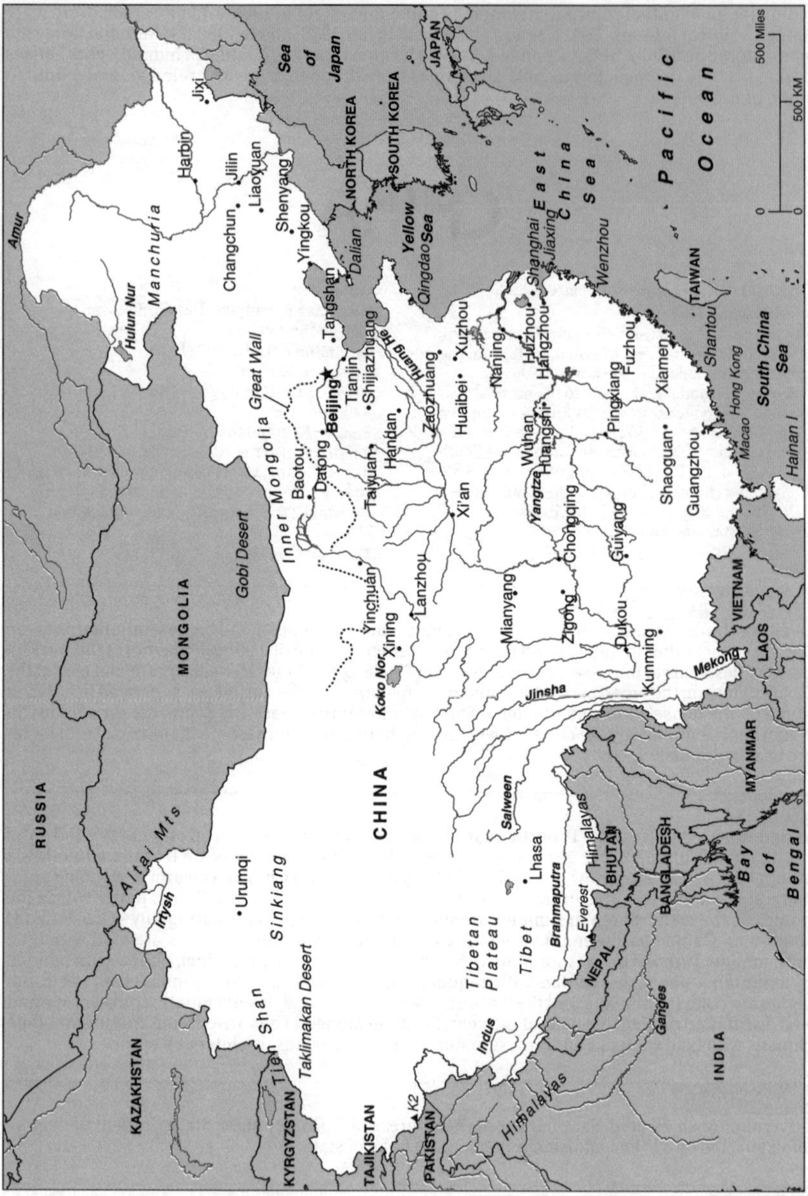

aristocracy; the Western Zhou Dynasty ruled over a prosperous feudal agricultural society (c.1066–771BC); the Eastern Zhou Dynasty (770–256BC) was the era of Confucius and Lao Zi (Lao-tzu); the Qin Dynasty (221–206BC) unified the warring states and provided a system of centralized control; there was expansion west during the Western and Eastern Han dynasties (206BC–AD220). From the 4c, a series of northern dynasties was set up by invaders, with several dynasties in the south; these were gradually reunited during the Sui (581–618) and Tang (618–907) dynasties. After a period of partition into Five Dynasties (907–60) there emerged the Song Dynasty (960–1279), remembered for literature, philosophy and inventions (eg movable type, gunpowder); Genghis Khan established the Mongol Yuan Dynasty (1279–1368). There followed visits by Europeans, such as Marco Polo, in the 13–14c, and the Ming Dynasty (1368–1644) increased contacts with the West. It was overthrown by Manchus, who ruled until 1911, and enlarged the empire to include Manchuria, Mongolia, Tibet, Taiwan and parts of Turkestan. Opposition to foreign penetration led to the Opium Wars (1839–42, 1858–60), in which defeat compelled China to open ports to foreign trade. The Sino-Japanese War (1895) gave control of Taiwan and Korea to Japan. The Boxer Rising (1898–1900) was a massive protest against foreign influence; the Republic of China was founded by Sun Yat-sen (1912) after the fall of the Qing Dynasty, but was followed by chaos and an era of regional warlords. Unification came under Jiang Jieshi (Chiang Kai-shek), who made Nanjing the capital in 1928. Conflict between nationalists and communists led to the Long March (1934–5), with communists moving to north-west China under Mao Zedong (Mao Tse-tung). The deeply corrupt nationalist regime was defeated in 1950 and withdrew to Taiwan. The People's Republic of China was proclaimed in 1949, with its capital at Beijing (Peking). The first Five-Year Plan (1953–7) was a period of nationalization and collectivization; the Great Leap Forward (1958–9) emphasized local authority and the establishment of rural communes; the Cultural Revolution was initiated by Mao Zedong in 1966; many policies were reversed after Mao's death in 1976, and there was a drive towards rapid industrialization and wider trade relations with the West. The killing of student-led pro-democracy protesters in Tiananmen Square, Beijing, in 1989 provoked international outrage and the introduction of economic sanctions, but these had no effect and were relaxed after 1990. Gradual steps towards a controlled market economy continued throughout the 1990s. In 1997 China entered a new era with the death of Deng Xiaoping, who was succeeded as leader by Jiang Zemin, and the handover in July of former British Crown Colony Hong Kong. It is a one-party communist state governed nominally by an elected National People's Congress of 2 978 deputies and in practice by a self-perpetuating State Council of over 45 ministers, led by a Prime Minister. Jiang Zemin was succeeded as President in Mar 2003 by Hu Jintao.

❖ Hong Kong

Area 16 sq km/6 sq mi	**Population** 437 300 (1999e)

History

Britain first occupied Hong Kong during the first Opium War in 1841, and it was officially ceded to Britain by China the following year in one of the terms of the Treaty of Nanjing: in addition to paying an indemnity, opening five treaty ports to foreign trade, and abolishing the Cohong, China was compelled to cede the island of Hong Kong 'in perpetuity' to Britain. Under British rule, Hong Kong became a free-trade entrepot, attracting migrants from the nearby province of Guangdong. The Kowloon Peninsula on the adjoining mainland was added to Britain's colony of Hong Kong in 1860, following the second of the Opium Wars (1856–60). Hong Kong was occupied by the Japanese in World War II, but re-occupied by the British in 1945. The New Territories had been leased to Britain for 99 years in 1898, and, under the Sino-British Declaration initialled in 1984 by which Britain agreed to cede the whole of Hong Kong at the end of the lease, the region was restored to China in July 1997. Tung Chee-Hwa was appointed the first chief executive of the new Hong Kong Special Administrative Region and pledged to abide by the 'one country, two systems' plan which was also outlined in the 1984 declaration to preserve the existing way of life.

❖ Macao

Area 1 067 sq km/412 sq mi	**Population** 6 847 000 (1999e)

History

Macao was used as a base for Catholic missionaries in the 17c and 18c as well as being a port of call for British traders on their way to Canton in the early 19c. Until the 19c, Macao was a flourishing trade centre, but the silting of its harbour and increasing competition from Hong Kong led to its decline. With the overthrow of the Salazar dictatorship in Portugal in 1975 and the new government's commitment to decolonization, China exercised more influence in the colony. In 1987 it was agreed that Macao be formally returned to Chinese control in 1999 under the same arrangements applying to the British return of Hong Kong to China in 1997 (ie that the capitalist system should remain in place).

COLOMBIA

Official name Republic of Colombia
Local name Colombia
Location A republic in the north-west of South America. It is bounded to the north by Panama and the Caribbean Sea; to the west by the Pacific Ocean; to the east by Venezuela; to the south-east by Brazil; and to the south by Ecuador and Peru
Area 1 140 105 sq km/440 080 sq mi
Capital Bogotá

Chief towns Medellín, Cali, Barranquilla
Population 39 309 000 (1999e)
Time zone GMT –5
Currency 1 Colombian Peso (Col$) = 100 centavos
Language Spanish
Religions Christianity 95% (RC), others 5%
Ethnic groups Mestizo 58%, white 20%, Mulatto 14%, black 4%, mixed black and Amerindian 3%, Amerindian 1%

Physical description

Caribbean and Pacific coastlines, with several island possessions; on the mainland, the Andes run north to south, branching into three ranges dividing narrow, coastal plains from the forested lowlands of the Amazon basin; the Cordillera Central, separated from the Cordillera Occidental in the west by the River Cauca, rises up to 5 750m at Huila, the highest peak; the Cordillera Oriental in the east surrounds large areas of plateau; rivers flow to the Pacific Ocean, Caribbean Sea and Amazon.

Climate

Hot and humid coastal plains in the north-west and west, annual rainfall is over 2 500mm; drier period on the Caribbean coast (December–April); the annual rainfall of the Andes is 1 000–2 500mm, falling evenly throughout the year; hot and humid tropical lowlands in the east, with annual rainfall of 2 000–2 500mm.

Government

A new constitution in 1991; governed by a bicameral Congress (a 100-member Senate and a Chamber of Representatives with 160 members elected for four years); a President, elected for a four-year term, appoints a Cabinet and is advised by a Council of State.

Economy

Virtually self-sufficient in food; major crops include coffee, bananas, cotton, sugar, maize, rice, beans, wheat, potatoes, cut flowers; textiles, leather, chemicals, consumer goods; gold, silver, platinum, emeralds, nickel, coal, oil, natural gas; development of the interior is hampered by a lack of good communications. There is widespread illegal cocaine trafficking, which the government has been attempting to eradicate with help from the USA since mid-1989.

History

From the early 16c the country was conquered by the Spanish, who dominated the Amerindian peoples. Governed by Spain within the Viceroyalty of Peru, it later became the Viceroyalty of New Granada. After the campaigns of Simón Bolivar, it gained independence in 1819, and formed a union with Ecuador, Venezuela and Panama as Gran Colombia; the union ended with the secession of Venezuela in 1829, and Ecuador in 1830, leaving New Granada to adopt the name Colombia. Colombia suffered civil war (known as La Violencia) in the 1950s, and there was considerable political unrest in the 1980s and 1990s, when a new constitution was adopted in 1991 and a state of emergency was declared in 1992. Struggling against drug-related violence, rebel and paramilitary attacks and a soaring kidnapping rate, successive presidents have tried to secure a ceasefire in the civil war but peace talks have so far had little real impact.

COMMONWEALTH OF INDEPENDENT STATES (CIS)

A grouping of 12 independent states out of the 15 republics which formerly made up the Soviet Union. Formed in 1991 by Armenia, Azerbaijan, Belarus, Kazakhstan, Kyrgyzstan, Moldova, Russia, Tajikistan, Turkmenistan, Ukraine and Uzbekistan; Georgia joined in 1993.

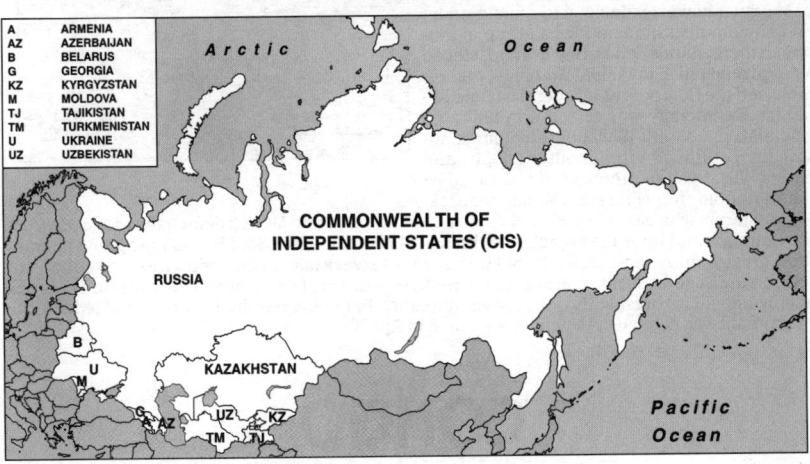

A	ARMENIA
AZ	AZERBAIJAN
B	BELARUS
G	GEORGIA
KZ	KYRGYZSTAN
M	MOLDOVA
TJ	TAJIKISTAN
TM	TURKMENISTAN
U	UKRAINE
UZ	UZBEKISTAN

➔ ▶Armenia, Azerbaijan, Belarus, Georgia, Kazakhstan, Kyrgyzstan, Moldova, Russia, Tajikistan, Turkmenistan, Ukraine, Uzbekistan

COMOROS

Official name Union of the Comoros

Local name Comores

Location A group of three volcanic islands (Grand Comore, Anjouan and Mohéli) at the northern end of the Mozambique Channel, between Mozambique and Madagascar

Area 1 862 sq km/719 sq mi

Capital Moroni

Population 562 700 (1999e)

Time zone GMT +3

Currency 1 Comorian Franc (KMF) = 100 centimes

Languages French, Arabic

Religions Islam 86% (Sunni), Christianity 14% (RC)

Ethnic groups Comorian 97%, others 3%

Physical description

The island interiors vary from steep mountains to low hills.

Climate

Tropical; May–October is the dry season and November–April is the hot, humid season; average temperatures are 20°C in July and 28°C in November.

Government

Governed by a President (elected for a six-year term) who is head of government as well as head of state, a Council of Ministers, and a 42-member unicameral Federal Assembly, elected every five years.

Nations of the World

Economy

Largely agricultural; vanilla, copra, cacao, sisal, coffee, cloves, vegetable oils, perfume.

History

Under French control from 1843 to 1912, it became a French Overseas Territory in 1947. Internal political autonomy was achieved in 1961, and unilateral independence was declared in 1975 by the Comorian President Ahmed Abdallah, who was deposed later that year. The island of Mayotte, however, decided to remain under French administration. In 1978 a group of European mercenaries, led by Bob Denard, staged a coup, reinstalled President Abdallah, and established the Comoros as a Federal Islamic Republic. Democracy was restored in 1984 and Abdallah ruled until 1989, but the political instability continued throughout the 1980s and early 1990s. Despite promises of increased island autonomy from President Muhammad Taki Abdoulkarim, who came to power in 1996, in 1997 Anjouan and Mohéli demanded to secede from the Comoros and return to French rule. President Majiddine Ben Said Massonde agreed to grant them greater autonomy in Apr 1999 but was deposed a week later in a bloodless army coup by Azali Assoumani. A new constitution in 2002 created a new Union of the Comoros, with the three islands having individual presidents and greater autonomy but being reunited in an overall federation. Assoumani was elected President of the Union in Apr 2002.

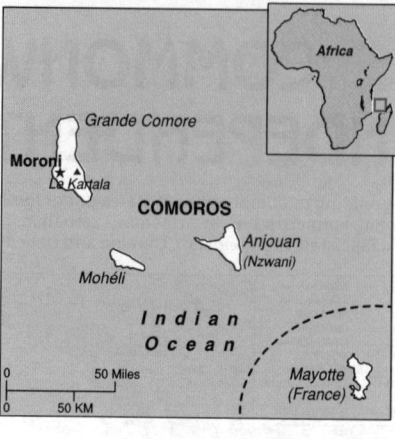

CONGO

Official name Republic of Congo	**Chief towns** Pointe-Noire (port), Loubomo, Nkayi
Local name Congo	**Population** 2 717 000 (1999e)
Location A west central African republic, bounded to the west by Gabon; to the north-west by Cameroon; to the north by the Central African Republic; to the east and south by the Democratic Republic of the Congo; and to the south-west by the Atlantic Ocean	**Time zone** GMT +1
	Currency 1 CFA Franc (CFAFr) = 100 centimes
	Languages French, Kikongo, Lingala
	Religions Christianity 50% (RC), traditional beliefs 48%, Islam 2%
Area 341 945 sq km/131 990 sq mi	**Ethnic groups** Kongo 49%, Sangha 20%, Teke 17%, Mbosi 11%, others 3%
Capital Brazzaville	

Physical description

A short Atlantic coastline fringing a broad mangrove plain that rises inland to a ridge of mountains reaching 900m; the inland mountain ridge is deeply cut by the River Congo flowing south-west to the coast; beyond this ridge, the Niari Valley rises up through terraced hills to reach 1 040m at Mont de la Lékéti on the Gabon frontier; mainly covered by dense grassland, mangrove and forest; several rivers flow east and south to meet the Oubangui and Congo rivers, which form the eastern and southern borders.

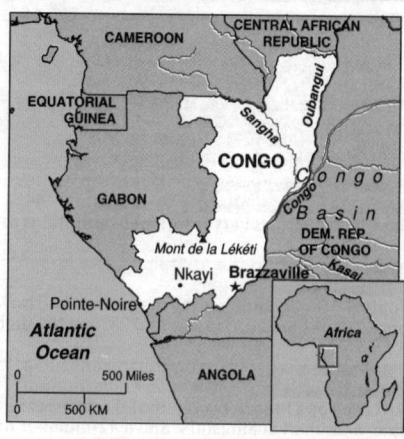

Climate

Hot, humid, equatorial climate; annual rainfall is 1 250–1 750mm, decreasing near the Atlantic coast and in the south; temperatures vary little, with average daily maximum temperatures at Brazzaville 28°–33°C; the dry season is June–September.

Government

A President appoints a Prime Minister and Cabinet; legislative power is held by a bicameral Parliament consisting of a National Assembly of 125 members and a Senate of 60 members.

Economy

Based on agriculture and forestry; the main cash crops are sugar cane, coffee, cocoa, palm oil, tobacco, groundnuts; the main subsistence crops are manioc, rice, yams, potatoes, maize, bananas; oil; timber; diamonds; lead; zinc; gold; potash; cement; oil refining; timber processing; brewing; sugar refining; soap.

History

It was discovered by the Portuguese in the 14c. The French established a colonial presence there in the 19c, and from 1908 to 1958 it was part of French Equatorial Africa, known as the 'Middle Congo'. It gained independence as the Republic of Congo in 1960, and in 1968 a military coup created the first Marxist state in Africa, renaming the country the People's Republic of the Congo. Marxism was renounced in 1990 and opposition parties were permitted. Elections took place in 1993 but the results were disputed and fighting between ethnic and political groups broke out. In 1997 President Pascal Lissouba was ousted by a military coup and replaced by former military leader and head of state (1979–92), Denis Sassou-Nguesso. Civil war ensued. Peace talks from 1999 led to a new constitution in 2001, but violence flared again after disputed elections in 2002 in which Sassou-Nguesso was re-elected.

Nations of the World

CONGO, DEMOCRATIC REPUBLIC OF

Official name Democratic Republic of Congo
Local name Congo
Location A central African republic, bounded to the west by the Congo and the Atlantic Ocean; to the south-west by Angola; to the south-east by Zambia; to the east by Tanzania, Burundi, Rwanda and Uganda; to the north-east by Sudan; and to the north and north-west by the Central African Republic
Area 2 343 950 sq km/904 765 sq mi
Capital Kinshasa

Chief towns Lubumbashi, Kisangani, Mbuji-Mayi, Kananga
Population 50 481 000 (1999e)
Time zone GMT +1/2
Currency 1 Congolese Franc = 100 centimes
Languages French, Kikongo, Lingala
Religions Christianity 60% (RC 45%, Prot 15%), traditional beliefs 30%, Islam 10%
Ethnic groups Bantu and Hamitic 44%, others 56%

Physical description

The land rises in the east from a low-lying basin to a densely-forested plateau, which is bounded to the east by volcanic mountains marking the western edge of the Great Rift Valley; the Ruwenzori Mountains in the northeast, on the Ugandan frontier rise to 5 110m in the Mount Stanley Massif; the Mitumbar Mountains lie further south; in the Rift Valley the chain of lakes includes Albert, Edward, Kivu and Tanganyika; a narrow strip of land follows the River Congo to the Atlantic Ocean and a short 43km/27mi coastline.

Climate

The country is crossed by the Equator and has a hot and humid climate; the average annual rainfall at Kisangani is 1700mm; the average maximum daily temperatures range between 28°C and 31°C.

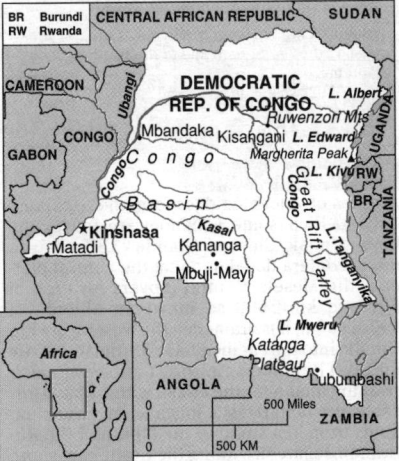

Nations of the World

Government

A one-party state, governed by a President, elected for seven years, a 27-member National Executive Council, and a National Legislative Council of 210 members, elected every five years; ultimate power lies with the Popular Movement of the Revolution, whose higher policy-making body is an 80-member Central Committee.

Economy

Nearly 80% of the population are involved in subsistence farming; livestock, maize, yams, cassava, rice, beans, fruit; cash crops include cotton, sugar, oil palm products, quinquina, coffee, tea, cocoa; extensive mineral reserves; world's biggest producer of cobalt, industrial diamonds, copper; other reserves include tin, manganese, zinc, columbium, tantalum, gold, silver, iron ore, rare-earth metals, offshore oil; cement; textiles; cotton; wood products; tobacco processing; vegetable oil; chemicals; major source of hydroelectricity.

History

The Bantu had settled most of the country by 1000AD, and the first Europeans to visit were the Portuguese, in 1482. There were expeditions by Henry Morton Stanley in 1874–7, and the country was claimed by King Leopold II of Belgium and recognized in 1895 at the Congress of Berlin as the Congo Free State. In 1908 it became a Belgian colony and was renamed the Belgian Congo. On gaining independence in 1960 it was renamed the Democratic Republic of the Congo, and the mineral-rich Katanga (later, Shaba) province claimed independence; this resulted in civil war which destroyed the new government of Patrice Lumumba. A UN peace-keeping force entered the country and remained until 1964. The following year President Mobutu Sese Seko seized power in a coup backed by the CIA. He renamed the country Zaire in 1971 and at first was credited with introducing a hitherto unknown degree of stability; however, his regime became increasingly corrupt and unpopular. Further conflict erupted in 1977–8, and there were power struggles in the early 1990s, with violent ethnic unrest in Shaba, Kivu and Kasai provinces in 1993. In addition, over 1 million refugees from the civil war in Rwanda entered Zaire in 1994. In 1996 Zaire was invaded by a rebel army led by Laurent Kabila, an ethnic Tutsi, who the following year succeeded in overthrowing the government and forcing Mobutu into exile. Kabila was installed as head of state and the country was renamed the Democratic Republic of the Congo, but civil war with extensive foreign intervention continued. Kabila was assassinated in 2001 and succeeded by his son Laurent. Talks throughout 2002 led to a peace deal in Dec, and the formation of a transitional power-sharing government, although sporadic violence continued and tensions remained high.

COSTA RICA

Official name Republic of Costa Rica
Local name Costa Rica
Location The second smallest republic in Central America, bounded to the west by the Pacific Ocean; to the north by Nicaragua; to the east by the Caribbean; and to the south-east by Panama
Area 51 022 sq km/19 694 sq mi
Capital San José
Chief towns Cartago, Heredia, Liberia, Puntarenas, Limón
Population 3 674 000 (1999e)
Time zone GMT –6
Currency 1 Costa Rican Colón (CR¢) = 100 céntimos
Language Spanish
Religions Christianity 85% (RC), others 15%
Ethnic groups white and Mestizo 95%, black and Mulatto 3%, Amerindian 1%, Chinese 1%

Physical description

A series of volcanic ridges form the backbone of Costa Rica (some volcanoes are active); the highest peak, Chirripó Grande (3 819m), is in the Cordillera de Talamanca; the central plateau, the Meseta Central, covers an area of 5 200 sq km/2 000 sq mi at an altitude of 800–1 400m; it is drained in the west by the Rio Grande into the Pacific and in the north-east by the River Reventazón into the Caribbean; much swampy land near the coast, with tropical forest as the land rises; a lowland savannah extends from just south of the mouth of the Río Grande de Tárcoles along the north-east shore of the Golfo de Nicoya towards Nicaragua.

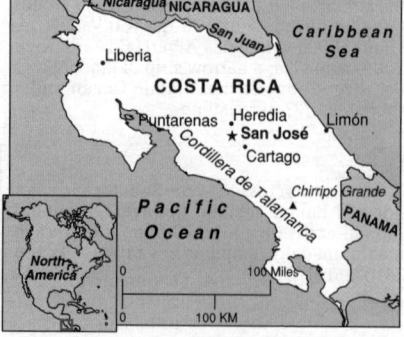

Climate

Tropical climate, with a small temperature range and abundant rainfall; more temperate in the central uplands; dry season is December–May; average annual rainfall is 3 300mm, with much local variation; the average annual temperature is 26°–28°C.

Government

Democratic republic governed by an Executive President and Legislative Assembly of 57 Deputies (elected for four years), and a 20-member Cabinet.

Economy

Primarily agriculture, mainly coffee (especially in Meseta Central), bananas, sugar, cattle; timber, fishing, gold, silver, bauxite; oil exploration in collaboration with Mexico; food processing, textiles, fertilizers, plastics, pharmaceuticals, electrical equipment.

History

Visited by Columbus in 1402, it was named Costa Rica ('rich coast') in the belief that vast gold treasures existed. It gained independence from Spain in 1821, and was a member of the Central American Federation in 1824–39. During the 20c there was political unrest, with civil war in 1948, following which the army was disbanded. Under President Arias Sánchez (1986–90), attempts were made to formulate a peace plan for Central America, to end the civil wars in neighbouring Nicaragua and in El Salvador, and the USA reduced its aid. During the 1990s there were outbreaks of industrial unrest and serious economic problems which remained unsolved.

CÔTE D'IVOIRE

Official name Republic of Côte d'Ivoire
Local name Côte d'Ivoire
Location A republic in West Africa, bounded to the south-west by Liberia; to the north-west by Guinea; to the north by Mali and Burkina Faso; to the east by Ghana; and to the south by the Gulf of Guinea
Area 320 633 sq km/123 764 sq mi
Capital Abidjan/Yamoussoukro
Chief towns Abidjan, Bouaké, Daloa, Man, Korhogo, Gagnoa
Population 15 818 000 (1999e)
Time zone GMT
Currency 1 CFA Franc (CFAFr) = 100 centimes
Language French; many local languages are also spoken
Religions Islam 45%, traditional beliefs 30%, Christianity 25%
Ethnic groups Akan 40%, Kru 17%, Voltaic 15%, Malinke 15%, Southern Mande 11%, others 2%

Physical description

Sandy beaches and lagoons, backed by a broad forest-covered coastal plain; the land rises towards savannah at 300–350m; the Mount Nimba massif in the north-west is 1 752m; rivers generally flow north to south.

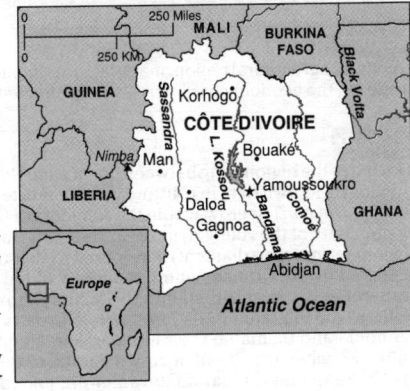

Climate

Tropical, varying with distance from the coast; rainfall decreases towards the north; the average annual rainfall at Abidjan is 2 100mm; average temperatures are 25°–27°C.

Government

Governed by a 175-member National Assembly and an Executive President (both elected for five-year terms), with a Council of Ministers.

Economy

Largely based on agriculture, which employs c.82% of the population; the world's largest cocoa producer and third-largest coffee producer; bananas, rice, pineapples, cotton, coconuts, palm oil, sugar, cassava, corn; livestock; fishing; food processing; timber; textiles; clothing; vehicle assembly; small shipyards; fertilizers; battery production; oil refining; cement.

History

It was explored by the Portuguese in the 15c and came under French influence from 1842. Declared a French protectorate in 1889 and a French colony in 1893, it became a territory within French West Africa in 1904. It gained independence as a one-party republic in 1960, with Felix Houphouët-Boigny as President. He introduced a multi-party system for the first time in 1990, when the elections were won by his Democratic Party of the Côte d'Ivoire (PDCI). He was succeeded on his death in 1993 by Henri Konan-Bédié, who ruled until overthrown in a 1999 coup by Robert Guëi. Guëi fled in 2000 after popular protests against rigged elections and Laurent Gbagbo became President. Political upheaval continued leading to civil war from 2002 between Gbagbo's government and rebel groups, but hopes of peace were raised in Mar 2003 with the creation of a power-sharing government.

CROATIA

Official name Republic of Croatia

Local name Hrvatska

Location A mountainous republic in eastern Europe, bounded to the south-west and west by the Adriatic Sea; to the north by Slovenia; to the north-east by Hungary; to the east by Serbia and Montenegro; and to the south-east by Bosnia-Herzegovina

Area 56 538 sq km/21 824 sq mi

Capital Zagreb

Chief towns Rijeka, Cakovec, Split, Zadar

Population 4 677 000 (1999e)

Time zone GMT +1

Currency 1 Kuna (HRK) = 100 lipa

Language Croatian

Religions Christianity 88% (RC 77%, Orthodox 11%), Islam 1%, others 11%

Ethnic groups Croat 78%, Serb 12%, Bosniak 1%, others 9%

Physical description

A mountainous republic, with islands on the Adriatic coast; the inland terrain includes fertile plains.

Climate

Continental; hot summers and cold winters.

Government

A directly elected President, and a bicameral Assembly consisting of a Chamber of Deputies and a Chamber of Districts.

Economy

Chiefly an agricultural region; manufactures include machinery and cement; there are supplies of crude oil; the economy has been severely affected by military conflict.

History

It includes the region lying between Bosnia and Hungary, called Slavonia, which was recorded as a kingdom in its own right in 1240 and was administered by the Hungarian King Béla IV as a *banovina* with its own *ban* (viceroy) within the Kingdom of Croatia in 1260. In the 13–14c Slavonia was ruled by members of the ruling dynasty in Hungary, but was returned to the Croatian ban in 1476. The Slavonian *sabor* (parliament) was joined to that of Croatia in the mid-16c but Slavonia was then occupied by the Ottomans until the Treaty of Karlowitz (1699), when it passed to the Habsburg Emperor and was absorbed into the Military Frontier. The Croatian people were originally Slav settlers who migrated (6–7c) from White Croatia in the Ukraine to the old Roman provinces of Pannonia and Dalmatia. Their independent kingdom, ruled by Croatian kings, existed from 910 until 1102, when the Croatian crown passed to the Hungarian Árpád Dynasty. From 1526 to 1918 the Croatian and Hungarian crowns were joined under the Habsburg Dynasty, but during the 15–16c the Croats became divided between three empires: the Croats in Croatia and Slavonia were subject to the Habsburgs; those in Dalmatia were subject to Venice; and those in Bosnia and Herzegovina to the Ottomans. In 1868 Croatia and Slavonia were made a joint crown land under Hungarian rule. Not until 1918 and the creation of the Kingdom of Serbs, Croats and Slovenes (later Yugoslavia) were the Croats all subject to one government. During occupation by the Axis powers in 1941–5, after the disintegration of Yugoslavia, part of Croatia and Bosnia-Herzegovina formed the Independent State of Croatia, a satellite state of the Axis powers. Benito

Mussolini chose Prince Aimone of Saxony, the Duke of Spoleto, to be King, but the Prince never took over his kingdom. The state was, instead, subject to the brutal regime of Ante Pavelić, the leader of the Ustaša fascist movement. In 1945 Croatia became one of the constituent republics of the Socialist Federal Republic of Yugoslavia. In 1991 the Croatian President Franjo Tudjman declared Croatia's independence from the Yugoslav Federation, which was followed by confrontation with the National Army and civil war; an official cease-fire was declared in 1992 but fighting restarted in 1993. From 1992 to 1995 Croatian forces were involved in the war in Bosnia-Herzegovina, where there is a large Croat population. Tudjman ruled until his death in 1999, and subsequent governments have attempted to restore stable democratic rule. Many key figures from the conflicts involving Croatia in the early 1990s have since been tried at the Hague war crimes tribunal.

CUBA

Official name Republic of Cuba
Local name Cuba
Location An island republic in the Caribbean Sea
Area 110 860 sq km/42 792 sq mi
Capital Havana
Chief towns Santiago de Cuba, Camagüey, Holguín, Santa Clara, Guantánamo

Population 11 096 000 (1999e)
Time zone GMT −5
Currency 1 Cuban Peso (Cub$) = 100 centavos
Language Spanish
Religions Christianity 43% (RC 40%, Prot 3%), traditional beliefs 2%, none/unaffiliated 55%
Ethnic groups white 66%, Mulatto 23%, black 11%

Physical description

An archipelago, comprising the island of Cuba, Isla de la Juventud, and c.1 600 islets and cays; the main island is 1 250km/777mi long, varying in width from 191km/119mi in the east to 31km/19mi in the west; heavily indented coastline; the south coast is generally low and marshy and the north coast is steep and rocky, with some fine harbours; the main ranges are the Sierra del Escambray in the centre, the Sierra de los Organos in the west, and the Sierra Maestra in the east; the highest peak is Pico Turquino (2 005m); the island is mostly flat, with wide, fertile valleys and plains.

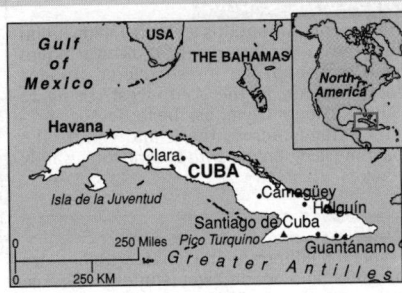

Climate

Subtropical, warm and humid; the average annual temperature is 25°C; the dry season is November–April; the average annual rainfall is 1 375mm; hurricanes usually occur between June and November.

Government

Governed by a 31-member State Council, appointed by a National Assembly of People's Power (510 deputies) following the proposal of the head of state.

Economy

After 1959, plantation estates were nationalized, and land plots distributed to peasants; the world's second largest sugar producer (accounting for 75% of export earnings); tobacco, rice, maize, coffee, citrus; dairy cattle; fishing; sugar milling; oil refining; food and tobacco processing; textiles; paper and wood products; metals, cement; the world's fifth largest producer of nickel; tourism; before Castro, over half of trade was with the USA; later with the markets of the former USSR.

History

It was visited by Columbus in 1492, and was a Spanish colony until 1898. Spain relinquished its rights over Cuba following a US-supported revolution led by José Martí. Cuba gained independence in 1902, with the USA retaining naval bases, and reserving the right of intervention in domestic affairs. The struggle against the dictatorship of General Batista led by Fidel Castro, unsuccessful in 1953, was finally successful in 1959, and a communist state was established. In 1961 an invasion by US-supported Cuban exiles was defeated at the Bay of Pigs, and in 1962 the discovery of the installation of Soviet missile bases in Cuba prompted a US naval blockade. The collapse of the Soviet Union in 1991 meant that Cuba lost the commercial, military and economic support that it had enjoyed since 1960, and Castro was forced to reduce public services and intro-

Nations of the World

duce food rationing. In 1992 agreement was reached for the withdrawal of Russian troops. After emigration was permitted (1980), many Cubans settled in Florida, leading to the need for an agreement between Cuba and the USA (1994) to regulate the flow of asylum seekers. For over 30 years the USA maintained a continually tightening economic and political blockade of Castro's Cuba, a blockade cemented by the Helms–Burton Act of 1996. However, by 2000 there were signs that relations between the two countries were improving.

CYPRUS

Official name Republic of Cyprus
Local name Kipros (Greek) Kibris (Turkish)
Location An island republic in the north-east Mediterranean Sea
Area 9 251 sq km/3 571 sq mi
Capital Nicosia
Chief towns Larnaca, Limassol, Kyrenia; Famagusta (the chief port prior to the 1974 Turkish invasion) is now under Turkish occupation, and declared closed by the Cyprus government.
Population 754 100 (1999e)
Time zone GMT +3
Currency 1 Cyprus Pound (C£) = 100 cents
Languages Greek, Turkish, with English widely spoken
Religions Christianity 78% (Orthodox), Islam 18%, others 4%
Ethnic groups Greek 78%, Turkish 18%, others 4%

Physical description

The Kyrenia Mountains extend 150km/90mi along the north coast, rising to 1 024m at Mount Kyparissovouno; the forest-covered Troödos Mountains are in the south-west, rising to 1 951m at Mount Olympus; the fertile Mesaoria plain extends across the island centre; the coastline is indented, with several long, sandy beaches.

Climate

A typical Mediterranean climate with hot, dry summers and warm, wet winters; average annual rainfall is 500mm, with great local variation; average daily temperatures (July–August) range from 22°C on the Troödos Mountains to 29°C on the central plain; winters are mild, with an average temperature of 4°C in higher parts of the mountains, and 10°C on the plain; there is snow on higher land in winter.

Government

Governed by a President (head of state), elected for a five-year term by the Greek community, and a House of Representatives of 80 elected members; Turkish members ceased to attend in 1983, when the Turkish community declared itself independent (as the 'Turkish Republic of Northern Cyprus', recognized only by Turkey).

Economy

The Greek Cypriot area has now largely recovered from the 1974 invasion, with light manufacturing a main growth sector; paper, paperboard products; chemicals; food and wine; clothing; footwear; cigarettes; petroleum refining; cement production; electricity generation; mineral exports include asbestos, clay, chrome and umber; tourism is also recovering and now accounts for c.15% of national income; the Turkish Cypriot economy is heavily dependent on agriculture, producing potatoes, citrus fruit, grapes, cereals, carobs, vegetables, olives and almonds; irrigation schemes aim to increase the area under cultivation.

History

Cyprus has a recorded history of 4 000 years, with its rulers including the Greeks, Ptolemies, Persians, Romans, Byzantines, Arabs, Franks, Venetians, Turks and British. Byzantine control of the island ended at the time of the Third Crusade when Richard I, the Lionheart, conquered Cyprus on his way to Palestine and established Guy of Lusignan as King of Cyprus. This marked the beginning of a long period in which aspiring Crusaders could look on Cyprus as a relatively safe haven. St Louis's Crusaders, for instance, wintered in Cyprus in 1248–9, and as late as 1365 Peter I of Lusignan, titular King of Jerusalem, was King of Cyprus. In the 15c, because the piracy out of the island had remained a constant threat to Muslim seaborne trade in the eastern Mediterranean, the Circassian Mamluk, Sultan al-Ashraf Barsbay, mounted an attack and established Mamluk influence. Later, when Cyprus became effectively a protectorate of the Venetian empire, it still paid tribute to the Mamluk Sultan. The last vestige of Frankish influence in the eastern Mediterranean, the island fell to the Ottoman Sultan, Selim II, in 1571 and remained under Ottoman control until occupied by the British in 1878. It became a British Crown Colony in 1925. Greek Cypriot demands for union with Greece (enosis) led in the 1950s to guerrilla warfare waged against the British administration by EOKA under Grivas and Makarios III, and a four-year state of emergency (1955–9). Cyprus achieved independence in 1960, with Britain retaining sovereignty over the military bases at Akrotiri and Dhekelia. There was Greek–Turkish fighting throughout the 1960s, with a UN peace-keeping force sent in 1964, and further terrorist activity in 1971. The 1974 Turkish invasion led to occupation of over one third of the island, with displacement of over 160 000 Greek Cypriots; the island was divided into two parts by the Attila Line, from the north-west coast above Pomos to Famagusta in the east, cutting through Nicosia where it is called the Green Line. Famagusta (the chief port prior to the 1974 Turkish invasion) remains under Turkish occupation, and has been declared closed by the Cyprus government. Turkish government members ceased to attend government in 1983, when the Turkish community declared itself independent (as the 'Turkish Republic of Northern Cyprus'). Peace talks on reunification in both 1990 and 1992 were inconclusive, but in 1993 Cyprus and Greece agreed upon a common defence policy, and Turkey affirmed its commitment to a political agreement with Cyprus. The situation remained unresolved throughout the 1990s however, and there were sporadic outbreaks of violence, despite the presence of UN peacekeepers along the border. UN-sponsored talks in 2002, aimed at creating a federal system for a reunified country, ended in failure in Mar 2003. Cyprus will join the EU in 2004.

CZECH REPUBLIC

Official name Czech Republic
Local name Česká Republika
Location A landlocked republic in eastern Europe, bounded to the west by Germany; to the north and east by Poland; to the south-east by Slovakia; and to the south by Austria
Area 78 864 sq km/30 441 sq mi
Capital Prague
Chief towns Brno, Plzen, Ostrava, Olomouc

Population 10 281 000 (1999e)
Time zone GMT +1
Currency 1 Koruna (Kčs) = 100 haléřu
Language Czech
Religions Christianity 48% (RC 40%, Prot 5%, Orthodox 3%), others 12%, none/unaffiliated 40%
Ethnic groups Czech 82%, Moravian 13%, Slovak 3%, others 2%

Physical description

Bohemia and West Moravia are separated from East Moravia and Slovakia by the River Morava valley; the western range of the Carpathians rise in the east; drained by the Morava, Moldau, Elbe and Oder rivers; there are many lakes; the land is richly wooded, chiefly with mixed and coniferous forests.

Climate

Continental, with warm, humid summers and cold, dry winters.

Government

A Prime Minister and the Council of Ministers exercise executive power; a President is elected by the bicameral Parliament which consists of a Chamber of Deputies and a Senate.

Economy

Iron, steel, chemicals, machinery, glass, vehicles, cement, armaments, wood, paper, beer; steel production around the Ostrava coalfields; agriculture produces sugar beet, potatoes, wheat, barley and maize; there are large dams and reservoirs on rivers for energy and water conservation; large quantity of mineral springs has led to the development of many health spas.

Nations of the World

History

It comprises the former provinces of Bohemia, Silesia and Moravia, and from 1918 to 1993 it formed part of Czechoslovakia. It became an independent republic in 1993 following the dissolution of Czechoslovakia in 1992, and Václav Havel, formerly President of Czechoslovakia, became President. In Mar 1999 the Czech Republic was admitted to NATO. Havel served until Feb 2003. In 2002 the Czech Republic was formally invited to join the EU.

DENMARK

Official name Kingdom of Denmark
Local name Danmark
Location A kingdom in northern Europe, it is the smallest of the Scandinavian countries and consists of most of the Jutland Peninsula, several islands in the Baltic Sea (the largest include Zealand, Fyn, Lolland, Falster and Bornholm), and some of the northern Frisian Islands in the North Sea
Area (excluding dependencies) 43 076 sq km/ 16 627 sq mi

Capital Copenhagen
Chief towns Århus, Odense, Ålborg, Esbjerg, Randers, Kolding
Population 5 357 000 (1999e)
Time zone GMT +1
Currency 1 Danish Krone (Dkr) = 100 øre
Language Danish
Religions Christianity 93% (Prot 92%, RC 1%), others 5%, none/unaffiliated 2%
Ethnic groups Danish 96%, Faroese and Inuit 1%, others 3%

Physical description

Uniformly low-lying; the highest point (Ejer Bavnehöj in east Jylland) is less than 200m; there are no large rivers and few lakes; the shoreline is indented by many lagoons and fjords, the largest of which is Lim Fjord (which cut off the northern extremity of Denmark in 1825).

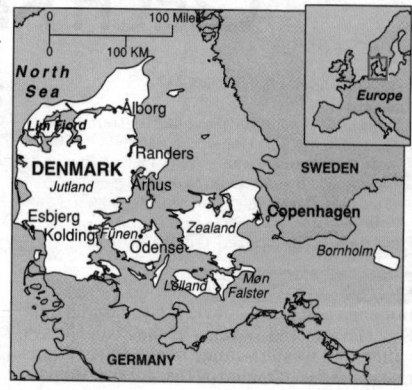

Climate

Much modified by the Gulf Stream, giving cold and cloudy winters, and warm, sunny summers; annual rainfall is usually below 675mm.

Government

A constitutional monarchy since 1849; a unicameral system was adopted in 1953; legislative power lies jointly with the monarch and the 179-member Diet (*Folketing*).

Economy

A lack of raw materials has resulted in development of processing industries such as foodstuffs, brewing, machinery, hardware, shipping, furniture, glass, porcelain, chemicals and pharmaceuticals; intensive agriculture (corn, horticulture, vegetables, pigs, cattle and poultry); forestry; windmill production.

History

It formed part of Viking kingdoms in the 8–10c and was the centre of the Danish Empire under Canute in the 11c. In 1389 it was joined with Sweden and Norway under one ruler; Sweden separated from the union in the 16c, as did Norway in 1814. Schleswig-Holstein was lost to Germany in 1864, but northern Schleswig was returned after a plebiscite in 1920. Denmark was occupied by Germany during World War II. Iceland became independent of Danish rule in 1944, and Greenland and the Faroes remain dependencies. Denmark joined the EC in 1973. Its monarch, Queen Margrethe II, acceded to the throne in 1972. A referendum in 2000 rejected a proposal to replace the krone with the Euro.

❖ Faroe Islands

Location The group of islands lying between the Shetland Islands and Iceland, and subject to the Danish crown

Area 1 399 sq km/540 sq mi

Capital Torshavn

Population 41 100 (1999e)

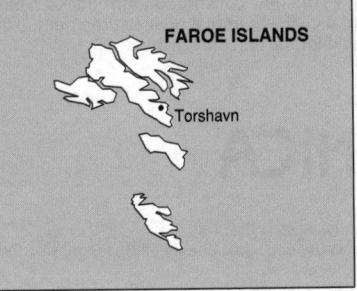

FAROE ISLANDS

Torshavn

❖ Greenland

Location The second-largest island in the world (after Australia), lying north-east of North America in the North Atlantic and Arctic oceans, and subject to the Danish crown

Area 2 175 600 sq km/839 780 sq mi

Capital Nuuk (Godthåb)

Population 59 800 (1999e)

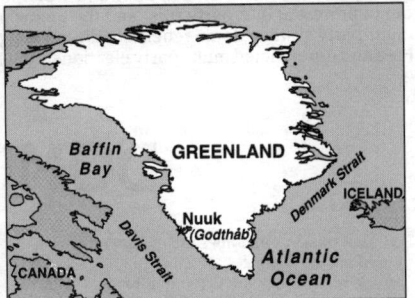

Baffin Bay GREENLAND

Nuuk (Godthåb)

CANADA Davis Strait Denmark Strait ICELAND

Atlantic Ocean

Nations of the World

DJIBOUTI

Official name Republic of Djibouti
Local name Djibouti
Location A republic in north-east Africa, bounded to the north-west, west and south by Ethiopia; to the south-east by Somalia; and to the north by Eritrea and the Gulf of Aden
Area 23 310 sq km/8 998 sq mi
Capital Djibouti
Chief towns Tadjoura, Dikhil, Obock, Ali-Sabieh

Population 447 400 (1999e)
Time zone GMT +3
Currency 1 Djibouti Franc (DF, DjFr) = 100 centimes
Languages Arabic, French
Religions Islam 94% (Sunni), Christianity 6% (RC 4%, Prot 2%)
Ethnic groups Issa 53%, Afar 36%, Arab 6%, others 5%

Physical description

A series of plateaux dropping down from mountains to flat low-lying rocky desert; 350km/220mi of fertile coastal strip around the Gulf of Tadjoura, which juts deep into the country; highest point, Moussa Ali, rising to 2 020m in the north.

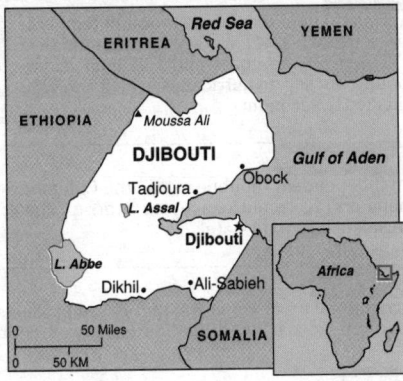

Red Sea YEMEN
ERITREA
ETHIOPIA Moussa Ali
DJIBOUTI Gulf of Aden
Tadjoura Obock
L. Assal
Djibouti
L. Abbe
Dikhil Ali-Sabieh Africa
0 50 Miles
0 50 KM SOMALIA

Climate

Semi-arid with a hot season (May–September); very high temperatures on coastal plains all year round, maximum average daily temperature dropping below 30°C for only three months (December–February); slightly lower humidity and temperatures in the interior highlands (over 600m); rainfall average 130mm annually at Djibouti.

Government

Governed by a President (elected for six years), a legislative Chamber of Deputies (elected for five years), an executive Prime Minister and a Council.

Economy

Crop-based agriculture is possible only with irrigation; date palms, fruit, vegetables; raising of livestock among the nomadic population; some fishing; a small industrial sector; tourism. The economy is based on the port of Djibouti, which is well situated to handle ships using the Suez Canal and Red Sea; it was badly affected by local wars, and by the closure of the Suez Canal between 1967 and 1975.

History

It was the object of French colonial interest in the mid-19c and became the capital of French Somaliland in 1892. Following World War II it became a French Overseas Territory, and from 1967 was called the French Territory of the Afars and the Issas. It gained independence in 1977 under the rule of President Hassan Gouled Aptidon and the Popular Rally for Progress Party. In 1991 fighting broke out in protest at one-party rule, and the following year a new constitution introduced a limited multi-party system. Some rebels continued to fight a civil war until a peace agreement in 2000. Free and unrestricted multi-party elections were held for the first time in 2003.

DOMINICA

Official name Commonwealth of Dominica
Local name Dominica
Location An independent republic located in the Windward Islands, in the east Caribbean Sea
Area 751 sq km/290 sq mi
Capital Roseau
Chief towns Portsmouth, Grand Bay
Population 64 900 (1999e)

Time zone GMT –4
Currency 1 East Caribbean Dollar (EC$) = 100 cents
Language English; French Creole is also spoken
Religions Christianity 93% (RC 77%, Prot 16%), others 7%
Ethnic groups African/mixed African-European 97%, Amerindian 2%, others 1%

Physical description

Roughly rectangular in shape, with a deeply-indented coastline; the island is c.50km/30mi long and 26km/16mi wide, rising to 1447m at Morne Diablotin; volcanic origin, with many fumaroles and sulphur springs; it has a central ridge, with lateral spurs and deep valleys, with several rivers; forestry covers 67% of the land area.

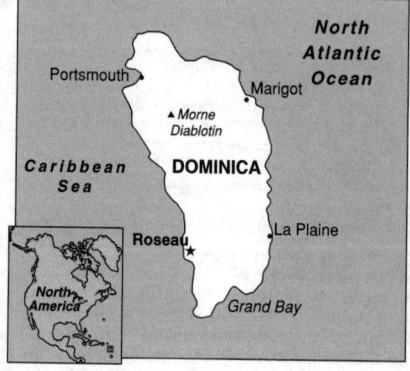

Climate

Warm and humid; average monthly temperatures are 26°–32°C; average annual rainfall is 1750mm on the coast and 6250mm in the mountains; severe hurricanes in 1979 and 1980 affected the economy.

Government

An independent republic within the Commonwealth, governed by a House of Assembly of 30 members (21 elected for a 5-year term); a Cabinet is presided over by a Prime Minister; an elected President is head of state.

Economy

Agricultural processing; coconut-based products; cigars; citrus fruits (notably limes), bananas, coconuts, cocoa; lime juice, lime oil, bay oil, copra, rum; pumice; water bottling; tourism.

History

It was discovered by Columbus in 1493, and there were attempts at colonization by the French and British in the 18c. It became a British Crown Colony in 1805. It was part of the Federation of the West Indies from 1958 to 1962, and gained independence in 1978.

DOMINICAN REPUBLIC

Official name Dominican Republic
Local name República Dominicana
Location A republic of the West Indies, comprising the eastern two-thirds of the island of Hispaniola, and bordering Haiti to the west
Area 48 442 sq km/18 699 sq mi
Capital Santo Domingo
Chief towns Santiago, La Vega, San Juan, San Francisco de Macorís, La Romana

Population 8 130 000 (1999e)
Time zone GMT −4
Currency 1 Dominican Republic Peso (RD$, DR$) = 100 centavos
Language Spanish
Religions Christianity 92% (RC), others 1%, none/unaffiliated 7%
Ethnic groups Mulatto 74%, white 16%, black 10%

Physical description

Crossed north-west to south-east by the Cordillera Central, a heavily-wooded range with many peaks over 3 000m; the Pico Duarte (3 175m) is the highest peak in the Caribbean; in the south-west, Lake Enriquillo lies in a broad valley cutting east to west; there is a wide coastal plain to the east.

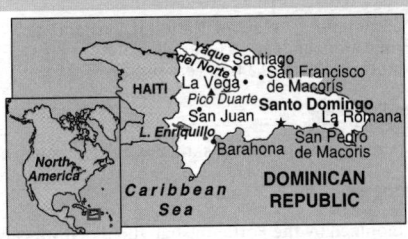

Climate

Tropical maritime with a rainy season from May to November; the average temperature at Santo Domingo ranges between 24°C (January) and 27°C (July); average annual rainfall is 1400mm; hurricanes may occur in June–November.

Government

Governed by a National Congress (30-member Senate, 120-member Chamber of Deputies); all members and the President are elected for four-year terms.

Economy

Mainly agriculture, especially sugar, cocoa; coffee, rice, cotton, tobacco, bananas, mangoes, tomatoes, oranges; sugar processing; bauxite, iron, nickel, gold; textiles; cement; tourism expanding, with resort complexes on the north coast.

History

It was discovered by Columbus in 1492 and became a Spanish colony in the 16–17c; the eastern province of Santo Domingo remained Spanish after the partition of Hispaniola in 1697. Taken over by Haiti on several occasions, it gained independence in 1844 under its modern name, but was reoccupied by Spain in 1861–5. A long dictatorship at the end of the 19c was followed by revolution and bankruptcy. Dictatorships, revolutions and military coups continued through the 20c, with right-wing parties holding power for most of the 1970s, 1980s and early 1990s. Joaquín Balaguer, who was President in 1966–78 and from 1986, was re-elected in 1994, but a political crisis arose amid allegations of fraud and corruption, and fresh elections were called. These resulted in the election in 1996 of Leonel Fernández, leader of the Liberation Party, who was in turn succeeded in 2000 by Hipólito Mejía of the Revolutionary Party.

EAST TIMOR

Official name Democratic Republic of East Timor
Local name República Democrática de Timor-Leste, Timor Lorosa'e
Location A republic in South-East Asia. It occupies the eastern half of the island of Timor and the enclave of Oecusse in the west of the island.
Area 14 874 sq km/5 743 sq mi
Capital Dili

Chief towns Baucau, Pante Macassar
Population 750 000 (2002e)
Time zone GMT +8
Currency 1 US dollar ($) = 100 cents
Language Portuguese, Tetum; English and Indonesian are also spoken
Religions Christianity 93% (RC 90%, Prot 3%), Islam 4%, others 3%
Ethnic Groups Malay, Papuan

Nations of the World

Physical description

Mountainous, with numerous rivers; the highest peak is Tatamailau (2 950m); East Timor also includes the smaller islands of Pulau Atauro and Jaco.

Climate

Hot and humid equatorial climate; dry season (June–September), rainy season (December–March); the average temperature is 27°C on the coast, falling inland and with altitude.

Government

A unicameral, elected National Parliament; Prime Minister leads a Council of State; a President is elected for a five-year term.

Economy

Mainly agrarian; coffee, sandalwood, coconuts, cloves; marble.

History

Colonized by the Portuguese in the 16c, it was given to Portugal in 1859. Colonial administration withdrew in 1975 and it declared itself independent as the Democratic Republic of East Timor. Violent civil war broke out and East Timor was annexed by Indonesia in 1976, but this annexation was not recognized by the UN. Resistance to Indonesian rule was met with strict repression. In 1999 a popular plebiscite reversed the annexation after a long nationalist struggle, and a UN Transitional Administration in East Timor (UNTAET) was created. East Timor became fully independent on 20 May 2002 with independence fighter Xanana Gusmao as the first President.

ECUADOR

Official name Republic of Ecuador
Local name Ecuador
Location A republic straddling the Equator in the north-west of South America. It is bounded to the north by Colombia; to the south and east by Peru; and to the west by the Pacific Ocean, and includes the Galápagos Islands
Area 270 699 sq km/104 490 sq mi
Capital Quito
Chief towns Guayaquil, Cuenca, Riobamba, Esmeraldas

Population 12 562 000 (1999e)
Time zone GMT –5
Currency 1 Sucre (Su, S/.) = 100 centavos
Language Spanish; Quechua is also spoken
Religions Christianity 96% (RC 94%, Prot 2%), others 4%
Ethnic groups Mestizo 50%, Amerindian 35%, white 10%, black 5%

Physical description

Coastal plain (*Costa*) in the west, descending from rolling hills in the north to a broad lowland basin averaging 100km/60mi in width before opening out into the Gulf of Guayaquil; Andean uplands (*Sierra*) in the central region, three main ranges rising to snow-capped peaks which include Cotopaxi (5 896m); forested alluvial plains of the *Oriente* in the east, dissected by rivers flowing from the Andes towards the Amazon; frequent serious earthquakes; the Galápagos Islands comprise six main volcanic islands, with a land area of c.7 812 sq km/3 015 sq mi.

Climate

Hot and humid coast, rain throughout the year (especially December–April); varies from

2 000mm in the north to 200mm in the south; central Andes temperatures are much reduced by altitude; Quito has warm days and chilly nights, with frequent heavy rain in the afternoon; hot and wet equatorial climate in the east.

Government

Unicameral National Congress consisting of a 71-member House of Deputies and four permanent committees of 28 members elected every four years; a President is elected for a four year term.

Economy

Agriculture employs c.50% of the workforce; beans, cereals, potatoes, livestock in the *Sierra*; bananas, coffee, cocoa, cane sugar, rice, cotton, vegetable oil in the *Costa*; fishing (especially shrimps), balsawood, food processing, textiles, petrochemicals, steel, cement, pharmaceuticals; oil piped from the *Oriente* to refineries at Esmeraldas.

History

Formerly part of the Inca Empire, it was taken by the Spanish in 1527 and included in the Viceroyalty of New Granada. On gaining independence in 1822, it joined with Panama, Colombia and Venezuela to form Gran Colombia, but left the union to become an independent republic in 1830. The country's political history is highly unstable (there were 22 presidents between 1925 and 1948, none completing a term in office). Following inconclusive election results and the implementation of reforms there was unrest in the early 1990s, coupled with sporadic disputes on the border with Peru. Political instability continues.

EGYPT

Official name Arab Republic of Egypt
Local name Jumhuriyat Misr Al-Arabiya
Location A republic in north-east Africa, bounded to the west by Libya; to the south by Sudan; to the east by the Red Sea; to the north-east by Israel; and to the north by the Mediterranean Sea
Area 1 001 449 sq km/386 559 sq mi
Capital Cairo
Chief towns Alexandria, Port Said, Aswan, Suez, El Gîza

Population 67 274 000 (1999e)
Time zone GMT +2
Currency 1 Egyptian Pound (£E, LE) = 100 piastres
Language Arabic
Religions Islam 94% (mostly Sunni), Christianity 6% (mostly Coptic)
Ethnic groups Eastern Hamitic 91%, others 9%

Physical description

The River Nile flows north from the Sudan, dammed south of Aswan, creating Lake Nasser; a huge delta lies to the north of Cairo, 250km/160mi across and 160km/100mi north to south; the narrow Eastern Desert, sparsely inhabited, lies between the Nile and the Red Sea; the broad Western Desert covers over two thirds of the country and contains seven major depressions, the largest and lowest of which is the Qattara Depression (133m below sea level); the Sinai Peninsula in the south is a desert region with mountains rising to 2 637m at Gebel Katherîna, Egypt's highest point; 90% of the population lives on the Nile floodplain (c.3% of the country's area).

Climate

Mainly desert, except for an 80km/50mile-wide Mediterranean coastal fringe, where annual rainfall is 100–200mm; very hot on the coast when the dust-laden *khamsin* wind blows north from the Sahara (March–June); Alexandria, representative of the coastal region, has an annual average rainfall of 180mm; elsewhere, rainfall is less than 50mm.

Nations of the World

Government

Governed by a People's Assembly of 454 members (including 10 presidential appointments) which elects a President every six years; the President appoints a Prime Minister and a Council; there is also a 210-member Consultative Council.

Economy

Agriculture on the floodplain of the River Nile accounts for about one third of the national income; the building of the Aswan High Dam extended irrigated cultivation; cotton, rice, fruit, vegetables; food processing, textiles, construction, light manufacturing, military equipment; oil, iron ore, aluminium, cement, gypsum, phosphates, manganese, tin, nitrates; a major tourist area (but tourism has been severely affected by terrorist activity since the 1990s).

History

The history of Egypt can be traced as far back as c.6000BC, to Neolithic cultures on the River Nile. A unified kingdom embracing lower and upper Egypt was first created in c.3100BC, ruled by Pharaoh dynasties; the pyramids at El Gîza were constructed during the Fourth Dynasty. Egyptian power was greatest during the New Empire period (1567–1085BC). It became a Persian province in the 6c BC and was conquered by Alexander the Great in the 4c BC. Ptolemaic Pharaohs ruled Egypt until 30BC. It was conquered by Arabs in AD672. From 1798 until 1801, it was occupied by France under Napoleon. The Suez Canal was constructed in 1869. A revolt in 1879 against the ruling Khedive was put down by British intervention in 1882. Egypt became a formal British protectorate in 1914, but declared its independence in 1922. It was used as a base for Allied forces during World War II. King Farouk was deposed by the army in 1952, and Egypt was declared a republic the following year. Nasser asserted his authority, negotiating the British withdrawal from the Suez base in 1955. In 1956 he nationalized the Suez Canal, and survived a joint Anglo-French and Israeli invasion. An attack on Israel, followed by Israeli invasion in 1967, resulted in the loss of the Sinai Peninsula and control of part of the Suez Canal (regained following negotiations in the 1970s). In 1981 President Sadat was assassinated, and relations with Arab nations were strained, but they improved again during the 1980s. During the 1990s there were violent attacks and clashes between Muslim and Coptic Christians. The Islamic fundamentalists (mainly the Islamic Group and al-Jihad organizations) grew increasingly violent in their campaign against the government, and by the end of the decade more than 60 foreign tourists as well as Egyptians were included among their victims. Sadat's successor, President Hosni Mubarak, followed a policy of moderation and reconciliation, playing an active role in the Middle East peace process to resolve the Arab–Israeli conflict in the 1990s, but has been unable to stem terrorism at home.

EL SALVADOR

Official name Republic of El Salvador
Local name El Salvador
Location The smallest of the Central American republics, bounded to the north and east by Honduras; to the west by Guatemala; and to the south by the Pacific Ocean
Area 21 476 sq km/8 290 sq mi
Capital San Salvador
Chief towns Santa Ana, San Miguel, Mejicanos

Population 5 839 000 (1999e)
Time zone GMT –6
Currency 1 Colón (¢ES) = 100 centavos
Language Spanish
Religions Christianity 97% (RC 77%, Prot 20%), others 3%
Ethnic groups Mestizo 91%, Amerindian 8%, white 1%

Physical description

Two volcanic ranges running east to west divide El Salvador into three geographical regions, ranging from a narrow coastal belt in the south through upland valleys and plateaux (average height, 600m) to mountains in the north (highest point, Santa Ana, is 2 381m); the River Lempa, dammed for hydroelectricity, flows south to the Pacific; many volcanic lakes; earthquakes are common.

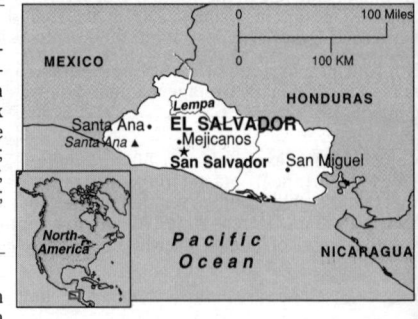

Climate

Varies greatly with altitude; hot and tropical on the coastal lowlands; single rainy season

(May–October); temperate uplands; average annual temperature at San Salvador is 23°C; average annual rainfall is 1775mm.

Government

Governed by a President elected for five years, and a 60-member elected National Assembly.

Economy

Largely based on agriculture; main crops coffee and cotton; sugar, maize, balsam (world's main source), food processing; textiles; shoes; furniture; chemicals; fertilizers; pharmaceuticals; cement; rubber goods; oil products.

History

Originally part of the Aztec kingdom, it was conquered by the Spanish in 1526, and achieved independence from Spain in 1821. A member of the Central American Federation until its dissolution in 1839, it became an independent republic in 1841. In the mid-20c it was ruled by dictatorships, suffered political unrest, and waged war with Honduras in 1965 and 1969. There was also considerable political unrest in the 1970s, with guerrilla activity directed against the US-supported government. Following the assassination of the Archbishop of San Salvador, Oscar Romero, in 1980, a civil war erupted in which 75 000 died and many became refugees. A peace agreement was signed in 1992 in which the left-wing guerrilla group Frente Farabundo Marti de Liberación Nacional (FMLN) was recognized as a political party; it won a few seats in the 1994 elections in which the right-wing Alianza Republicana Nacionalista (ARENA) under President Armando Calderón Sol came to power. Severe earthquakes in early 2001 caused widespread devastation.

⊕ England ▸ United Kingdom

EQUATORIAL GUINEA

Official name Republic of Equatorial Guinea
Local name Guinea Ecuatorial
Location A republic in western central Africa, comprising a mainland area (Río Muni) and several islands (notably Bioko and Annabón) in the Gulf of Guinea
Area 26 016 sq km/10 042 sq mi
Capital Malabo
Chief towns Bata and Evinayong on the mainland, Luba and Riaba on Bioko

Population 465 700 (1999e)
Time zone GMT +1
Currency 1 CFA Franc (CFAFr) = 100 centimes
Languages Spanish, French; pidgin English and Fang are also spoken
Religions Christianity 89% (RC), traditional beliefs 4%, Islam 1%, none/unaffiliated 6%
Ethnic groups Fang 82%, Bubi 11%, Ndowe 4%, others 3%

Physical description

The mainland rises sharply from a narrow coast of mangrove swamps towards the heavily-forested African plateau; deeply cut by several rivers; Bioko Island, about 160km/100mi northwest of the mainland, is of volcanic origin, rising to 3 007m at Pico de Basilé.

Climate

Hot and humid equatorial; average annual rainfall is c.2 000mm; average maximum daily temperature is 29°–32°C.

Government

A House of Representatives elected for five years and a smaller State Council.

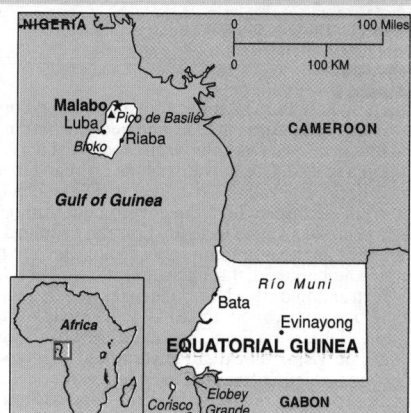

Economy

Largely based on agriculture; cocoa, coffee, timber, bananas, cassava, palm oil, sweet potatoes.

Nations of the World

History

Equatorial Guinea was first visited by Europeans in the 15c. The island of Fernando Po (Bioko) was claimed by Portugal in 1494 and held until 1788. Occupied by Britain from 1781 until 1843, the rights to the area were acquired by Spain in 1844. It gained independence in 1968 and was ruled by President Macias Nguema until a military coup in 1979 led by his nephew, Obiang Nguema, put an end to his repressive regime. A new constitution was approved in 1991 and multi-party democracy was legalized in 1992, although subsequent elections in 1993 and presidential elections in 1996 and 2002 that returned Nguema were condemned by observers for irregularities and fraud.

ERITREA

Official name Eritrea
Local name Eritrea
Location A country in north-east Africa, bounded to the north and north-west by the Sudan; to the west and south-west by Ethiopia; to the south by Djibouti; and to the east by the Red Sea
Area 93 679 sq km/36 160 sq mi
Capital Asmara

Chief towns Assab, Massawa, Keren, Tessenai
Population 3 985 000 (1999e)
Time zone GMT +3
Currency 1 Nakfa (Nfa) = 100 cents
Languages Arabic, Tigrinya
Religions Islam 50%, Christianity 50% (Coptic)
Ethnic groups Tigrinya 50%, Tigrean and Kunama 40%, Afar 4%, Saho 3%, others 3%

Physical description

Low-lying coastline stretching 1 000km/620mi along the Red Sea, rising to an inland plateau.

Climate

Hot and dry along the Red Sea desert coast; cooler and wetter in the central highlands; semi-arid in the western hills and lowlands.

Government

A President appoints the State Council which exercises executive power; legislative power is exercised by the National Assembly; at the end of a transition period (maximum four years) multiparty elections are planned.

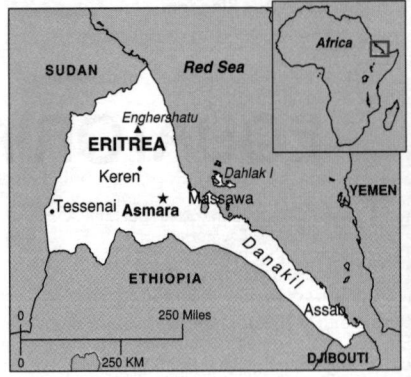

Economy

Fishing; minerals, oil, gas.

History

Taken by Italy in 1884, it became an Italian colony in 1890. It was used as a base for the Italian invasion of Abyssinia in 1935, and became part of Italian East Africa in 1936. It was then taken by the British in 1941, federated with Ethiopia at the request of the UN in 1952, and made a province of Ethiopia in 1962. This galvanized the Eritrean Liberation Front (ELF), which had been founded as the Eritrean Liberation Movement in 1958 (it changed its name in 1961), into action, and it waged guerrilla warfare against the government throughout the 1960s and 1970s. In 1970 a communist faction broke away to form the Eritrean People's Liberation Front (EPLF), which emerged during the 1980s as the dominant rebel group. Despite this division and much fighting between rebel groups, it managed, through support from the Eastern bloc and some Arab countries, to prevent its destruction both while Haile Selassie was Emperor and when Mengistu was President. When Soviet support waned, the EPLF joined with other Ethiopian rebel groups, including the Tigray People's Liberation Front, and overthrew the Dergue in 1991. The EPLF immediately formed a separate provisional Eritrean government. A referendum on independence was held in Apr 1993, following which Eritrean independence was declared and the EPLF prepared to become the ruling political party by renaming itself the People's Front for Democracy and Justice in 1994. In May 1998 Eritrea and Ethiopia began an armed struggle over border territory, a conflict that lasted two years.

ESTONIA

Official name Republic of Estonia
Local name Eesti Vabariik
Location A republic in eastern Europe, bounded to the west by the Baltic Sea; to the north by the Gulf of Finland; to the east by Russia; and to the south by Latvia
Area 45 100 sq km/17 409 sq mi
Capital Tallinn
Chief towns Tartu, Narva, Kohtla-Järve, Pärnu
Population 1 409 000 (1999e)

Time zone GMT +2
Currency 1 Kroon (KR) = 100 senti
Languages Estonian, Russian
Religions Christianity, predominantly Lutheran protestant, also Orthodox, Baptist, Methodist and Pentecostal; Judaism
Ethnic groups Estonian 65%, Russian 28%, Ukrainian 3%, Belarusian 2%, Finnish 1%, others 1%

Physical description

There are over 1 500 lakes in a fairly flat terrain; there are many islands on the coast, notably Saaremaa, Hiiumaa and Muhu; 36% of the area is forested.

Climate

Cool summers, wet winters

Government

A 101-member unicameral Parliament (*Riigiko-gu*) is elected once every four years; the President is elected by Parliament and serves a five-year term.

Economy

Shale oil; machines; metalworking; chemicals; food processing; cotton; fabrics; timber; dairy farming; pigs; fishing; the economy suffered as a result of the transfer to a free market system but began to stabilize in 1993.

History

Occupied by Vikings in the 9c, during its history it has been owned by Denmark, Sweden, Poland, Russia and the Teutonic Knights of Germany. For a time it was divided into two areas: northern Estonia and Livonia (southern Estonia and Latvia), but was ceded to Russia in its entirety by Sweden in the Treaty of Nystadt in 1721. It achieved independence in 1918, became a Soviet Socialist Republic in 1940, and was occupied by Germany during World War II. There was a resurgence of the nationalist movement in the 1980s and it declared its independence on the dissolution of the USSR in 1991. A new constitution was agreed the following year, and Lennart Meri was elected President. In 2002 Estonia was formally invited to join both the EU and NATO.

ETHIOPIA

Official name Federal Democratic Republic of Ethiopia
Local name Ityopiya
Location A landlocked republic in north-east Africa, bounded to the west and south-west by Sudan; to the south by Kenya; to the east and north-east by Somalia; and to the north by Djibouti and Eritrea
Area 1 128 497 sq km/435 600 sq mi
Capital Addis Ababa

Chief towns Dire Dawa, Harer
Population 59 680 000 (1999e)
Time zone GMT +3
Currency 1 Ethiopian Birr (EB) = 100 cents
Language Amharic
Religions Christianity 42% (Coptic), Islam 40%, traditional beliefs 14%, others 4%
Ethnic groups Oromo 40%, Amhara and Tigrean 32%, Sidamo 9%, Shankella 6%, Somali 6%, others 7%

Physical description

Dominated by a mountainous central plateau; split diagonally by the Great Rift Valley; the highest point is Ras Dashen Mount (4 620m); the plateau is crossed east to west by the Blue Nile, which has its source in Lake Tana; the north and east are relatively low-lying; in the north-east the Danakil Depression dips to 116m below sea level; the country is landlocked, having lost about 10% of its territory and all of its Red Sea coastline, since the former province of Eritrea separated from Ethiopia.

Climate

Tropical, moderated by higher altitudes; distinct wet season (April–September); temperatures warm, but rarely hot all year round; annual rainfall generally over 1 000mm; hot, semi-arid north-east and south-east lowlands receive less than 500mm annually; severe droughts in the 1980s caused widespread famine, deaths and resettlement, with massive amounts of foreign aid.

Government

A President and Prime Minister, a Council of Representatives and a Council of Ministers.

Economy

One of the world's poorest countries; over 80% of the population is employed in agriculture, especially subsistence farming; exports mainly coffee, also sugar, cotton, pulses, oil seeds; production severely affected by drought; small amounts of oil, gold, cement, salt; food processing, tobacco, textiles; distribution of foreign aid hindered by internal conflicts and poor local organization.

History

It is the oldest independent country in sub-Saharan Africa, and the first African country to be Christianized. Abyssinian independence was recognized by the League of Nations in 1923, but after the invasion of Italy in 1935 the country was annexed as Italian East Africa from 1936 to 1941, when Emperor Haile Selassie returned from exile. A military coup led to the establishment of the Marxist Provisional Military Administrative Council (PMAC) or Dergue, in 1974, and left-wing opposition was met by mass arrests and executions in 1977–8. In addition to conflict with Somalia over the Ogaden district during the 1970s and 1980s, there was internal division with separatist Eritrean and Tigrean forces, who secured victories over government troops in the early 1980s, while the country suffered severe famine. Eritrea secured independence in 1993. The PMAC dissolved in 1987, with the transfer of power to the People's Democratic Republic, but an attempted coup in 1989 was followed by the complete collapse of Mengistu's regime in 1991 and renewed famine in 1992. A transitional government ruled until a new federal system, the Federal Democratic Republic of Ethiopia, was established in 1995, under President Negasso Gidada. Relative stability and economic growth slowly returned, until a border dispute with Eritrea flared up in May 1998, ending two years later with the loss of thousands of lives.

FIJI

Official name Republic of Fiji
Local name Matanitu Ko Viti
Location A Melanesian island group of 844 islands and islets in the south-west Pacific Ocean (c.100 permanently inhabited), forming an independent republic
Area 18 333 sq km/7 076 sq mi
Capital Suva
Chief towns Lautoka, Ba, Labasa, Nadi, Nausori

Population 812 900 (1999e)
Time zone GMT +11
Currency 1 Fiji Dollar (F$) = 100 cents
Languages Fijian, Hindi
Religions Hinduism 38%, Christianity 46% (Prot 37%, mainly Methodist, RC 9%), Islam 8%, Sikhism 1%, others 7%
Ethnic groups Fijian 51%, Indian 44%, others 5%

Physical description

The larger islands are generally mountainous and rugged; extensive areas of flat land in the river deltas; there are fertile plains around the coastline; the highest peak, Tomaniivi (Mount Victoria) is on Viti Levu (1 324m); there are hot springs in isolated places; most smaller islands consist of limestone, with little vegetation; there is an extensive coral reef (Great Sea Reef) stretching for 500km/300mi along the western fringe; dense, tropical forest lies on the wet, windward side in the south-east; mainly treeless on the dry, leeward side.

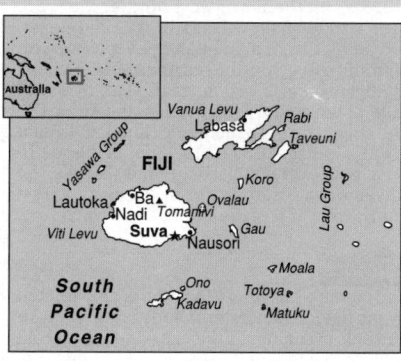

Climate

Winds are variable in the wet season between November and April, with tropical cyclonic storms likely; temperatures average 23°–27°C; the annual rainfall varies from 1 900mm to 3 050mm, the higher rainfall falling in the east and south-east; humidity on the windward slopes averages 74%.

Government

A bicameral Parliament of a nominated Senate of 34 members and an elected House of Representatives of 70 members.

Economy

Primarily agrarian, with sugar cane accounting for over two thirds of export earnings; copra, ginger, vegetables, fruit; livestock; tuna; timber; sugar-milling, processing of coconut-oil; gold-mining; light industry; major tourist area; important air staging post between North America and Oceania.

History

Fiji was visited by Tasman in 1643, and by Cook in 1774. It became a British colony in 1874, and gained independence within the Commonwealth of Nations in 1970. The 1987 election brought to power an Indian-dominated coalition, which led to military coups in May and Sep, and withdrawal of Fiji from the Commonwealth; a civilian government was restored in Dec. A new constitution upholding ethnic Melanesian political power was effected in 1990, but was attacked by opposition parties as racist. In 1997 the racist elements were taken out, and Fiji was readmitted to the Commonwealth. Three years later, Fiji was partially suspended from the Commonwealth following a failed coup and the imposition of martial law. Elections restored civilian government in 2001 and Fiji was again readmitted to the Commonwealth.

Nations of the World

Nations of the World

FINLAND

Official name Republic of Finland
Local name Suomen Tasavalta
Location A republic in northern Europe, bounded to the east by Russia; to the south by the Gulf of Finland; to the west by the Gulf of Bothnia and Sweden; and to the north by Norway
Area 338 145 sq km/130 524 sq mi
Capital Helsinki
Chief towns Tampere, Turku, Espoo, Vantaa

Population 5 158 000 (1999e)
Time zone GMT +2
Currency 1 Euro (€) = 100 cents
Languages Finnish (94%), Swedish (6%)
Religions Christianity 91% (Prot 89%, Orthodox 1%, RC 1%), none/unaffiliated 9%
Ethnic groups Finnish 93%, Swedish 6%, others 1%

Physical description

A low-lying glaciated plateau, with an average height of 150m; highest peak is Haltiatunturi (1 328m) on the north-west border; there are over 60 000 shallow lakes in the south-east, providing a system of inland navigation; with land still rising from the sea, the area is increasing by 7 sq km/2.7 sq mi each year; over one third of the country lies north of the Arctic Circle; chief rivers are the Tornio, Kemi and Oulu; the archipelago of Saaristomeri is in the south-west, with over 17 000 islands and skerries; the Ahvenanmaa islands are in the west; forest land covers 65% of the country, and water 10%.

Climate

The country's northern location is ameliorated by the Baltic Sea; western winds bring warm air currents in summer; Eurasian winds bring cold spells in winter and heatwaves in summer; annual precipitation in the south is 600–700mm, and 500–600mm in the north, with half of it falling as snow; during summer the sun stays above the horizon for over 70 days.

Government

Governed by a single-chamber House of Representatives (*Eduskunta*) of 200 elected members serving a four-year term, and a President elected for six years, assisted by a Council of State.

Economy

A traditional focus on forestry (mainly pine, spruce, and birch; paper is the chief timber product and farming; agriculture yields hay, barley, oats, spring and autumn wheat, rye, sugar beet, potatoes and spring oil-yielding plants; rapid economic growth since the 1950s, and a diversification of exports, such as metals, engineering, clothing, chemicals and food processing; copper and iron ore mining; wide use of hydroelectric power; tourism.

History

Finland was ruled by Sweden from 1157 until its cession to Russia in 1809. In the 19c it became an autonomous grand duchy of the Russian tsar, and a nationalist movement developed. It became an independent republic in 1917 and its parliamentary system was created in 1928. It was invaded by the Soviets in 1939 and 1940 in the Russo-Finnish War, and lost territory to the USSR after 1944. Finland has remained neutral since World War II. It joined the EC in 1995. The markka was replaced by the Euro in Jan 2002.

FRANCE

Nations of the World

Official name French Republic

Local name République Française

Location A republic in western Europe, bounded to the north and north-east by the English Channel, Belgium, Luxembourg and Germany; to the east by Switzerland, Italy and Monaco; to the south by the Mediterranean Sea, Spain and Andorra; and to the west by the Bay of Biscay

Area 551 000 sq km/213 000 sq mi

Capital Paris

Chief towns Marseilles, Lyons, Toulouse, Nice, Strasbourg

Population 58 978 000 (1999e)

Time zone GMT +1

Currency 1 Euro (€) = 100 cents

Language French

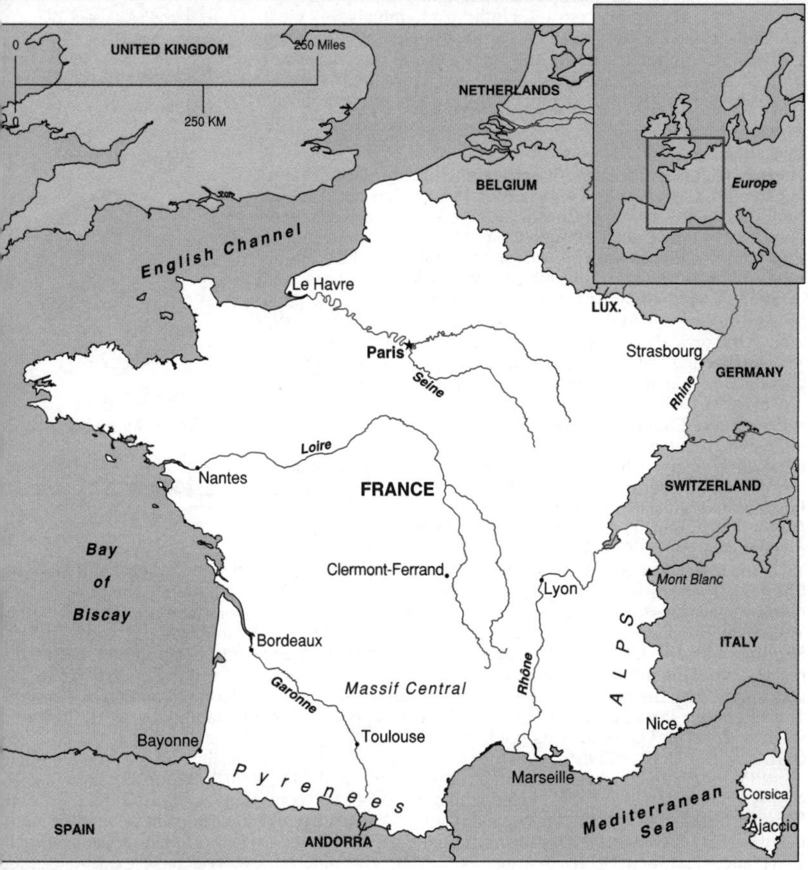

Physical description

A country of low and medium-sized hills and plateaux deeply cut by rivers; bounded to the south and east by large mountain ranges, notably (in the interior) the Armorican Massif, the Massif Central, the Cévennes, the Vosges and the Ardennes; in the east the Jura and the Alps (rising to 4 807 m at Mont Blanc); in the south the Pyrenees; chief rivers include the Loire, Rhône, Seine and Garonne; also includes the island of Corsica in the Mediterranean Sea.

Climate

The south has a Mediterranean climate, with warm, moist winters and hot, dry summers; in the north-west the climate is maritime, with an average annual rainfall of 573mm; the east has a continental climate with an average annual rainfall of 786mm.

Nations of the World

Government

Governed by a President, elected every seven years, who appoints a Prime Minister and presides over a Council of Ministers; the bicameral legislature consists of a National Assembly of 577 deputies elected every five years, and a 319-member Senate indirectly elected by an electoral college, triennially (a third at a time), for nine-year terms.

Economy

Western Europe's foremost producer of agricultural products, chiefly cereals, beef, sugar beet, potatoes, wine, grapes and dairy products; there are coalfields in northern France, Lorraine and the Massif Central; metal and chemical industries are based on reserves of iron ore, bauxite, potash, salt and sulphur; heavy industry (steel, machinery, textiles, clothing, chemicals, vehicles) is based around northern coalfields; other industry includes food processing, armaments and electronics; several nuclear power sites, providing 75 per cent of all electricity; hydroelectric power comes from the Alps; tourism and fishing are also important.

History

There is evidence of prehistoric settlement in France, as revealed in Paleolithic carvings and rock paintings (eg at Lascaux) and in Neolithic megaliths (eg at Carnac). Celtic-speaking Gauls were dominant by the 5c BC. The country was part of the Roman Empire from 125 BC to the 5c AD, and was invaded by several Germanic tribes in the 3–5c. The Franks inaugurated the Merovingian epoch in the 5c. Clovis I was the first Merovingian king to control large parts of Gaul; the last to hold significant power was Dagobert I (died 638), though the royal dynasty survived until Childeric III's deposition in 751. The Carolingian ruling dynasty ultimately replaced the Merovingians when Pepin III, the Short became King of the Franks in 751. The power of the Carolingian kings came to a peak in the 8c, with the succession of Charlemagne. A feudal monarchy was founded in 987 by Hugh Capet; this was the third Frankish royal dynasty (the Capetian Dynasty), which ruled France until 1328. The Plantagenets of England acquired several French territories in the 12c, but lands were gradually recovered during the Hundred Years' War (1337–1453), apart from Calais (regained in 1558). The Capetian dynasty was followed by the Valois and Bourbon dynasties, from 1328 and 1589 respectively. In the 16c there was ongoing rivalry between Francis I and Emperor Charles V, then the Wars of Religion took place from 1562 until 1598. In the 17c the power of the monarchy was restored, reaching its peak under Louis XIV. However, the French Revolution of 1789 dismantled the ancien régime in the name of liberty, equality and fraternity, and the First Republic was declared in 1792. The First Empire (1804–14) was ruled by Napoleon I, before the restoration of the monarchy for a period between 1814 and 1848. The Second Republic (1848–52) was followed by the Second Empire (1852–70), ruled by Louis Napoleon (Napoleon III), and the Third Republic lasted from 1870 to 1940. There was great political instability between the World Wars, with several governments holding office for short periods. The country was occupied by Germany from 1940 until 1944, with the pro-German government at Vichy and the Free French in London under the conservative and nationalist de Gaulle. The Fourth Republic began in 1946; shortly afterwards there was war in Indochina (1946–54), and conflict in Algeria (1954–62). The Fifth Republic began in 1958 under President de Gaulle. That same year, France became a founding member of the EEC. Presidents Pompidou and Giscard d'Estaing had policies not unlike de Gaulle's, but in 1981 France's first Socialist President for 35 years, François Mitterrand, was elected. He was succeeded in 1995 by the right-wing Jacques Chirac. The French franc was replaced by the Euro in Jan 2002.

Religions

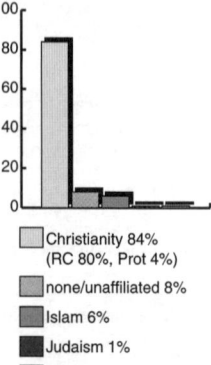

☐ Christianity 84% (RC 80%, Prot 4%)

☐ none/unaffiliated 8%

☐ Islam 6%

☐ Judaism 1%

☐ Buddhism 1%

Ethnic groups

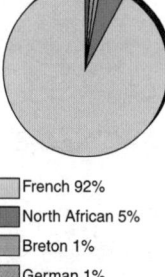

☐ French 92%

☐ North African 5%

☐ Breton 1%

☐ German 1%

☐ others 1%

Overseas departments

❖ French Guiana

Location Situated on the north-eastern coast of South America, it is bounded to the west by Suriname; to the east and south by Brazil; and to the north by the Atlantic Ocean
Area 90 909 sq km/35 091 sq mi
Capital Cayenne
Population 168 000 (1999e)

❖ Guadeloupe

Location A group of seven islands in the central Lesser Antilles, in the east Caribbean Sea

Area 1 779 sq km/687 sq mi

Capital Basse-Terre

Population 420 900 (1999e)

◆ Martinique

Location An island in the Windward group of the Lesser Antilles, east Caribbean Sea, between Dominica and St Lucia
Area 1 079 sq km/416 sq mi
Capital Fort-de-France
Population 411 500 (1999e)

◆ Réunion

Location An island in the Indian Ocean, to the east of Madagascar
Area 2 510 sq km/969 sq mi
Capital St Denis
Population 717 700 (1999e)

Overseas territories

◆ French Polynesia

Location An island grouping of five scattered archipelagoes in the south-east Pacific Ocean, between the Cook Is in the west and the Pitcairn Is in the east
Area 3 941 sq km/1 521 sq mi
Capital Papeete
Population 242 100 (1999e)

◆ New Caledonia

Location A group of islands in the south-west Pacific Ocean, 1 100 km/680 mi east of Australia
Area 18 575 sq km/7 170 sq mi
Capital Nouméa
Population 197 400 (1999e)

◆ French Southern and Antarctic Territories

Location A group of islands in the southern Indian Ocean, and Adélie Land in Antarctica
Area 507 781 sq km/196 003 sq mi
Population none

◆ Wallis and Futuna Islands

Location An island grouping in the south-central Pacific Ocean, lying north-east of Fiji
Area 274 sq km/106 sq mi
Capital Matu-Utu (on Uvéa)
Population 15 100 (1999e)

Territorial collectivities

Mayotte

Location A small island group of volcanic origin, east of the Comoros Is, in the west Indian Ocean
Area 374 sq km/144 sq mi
Capital Mamoudzou
Population 149 300 (1999e)

◆ St Pierre and Miquelon

Location Two islands in the North Atlantic Ocean, south of Newfoundland
Area 240 sq km/93 sq mi
Capital St Pierre
Population 6 970 (1999e)

GABON

Official name Gabonese Republic
Local name République Gabonaise
Location A republic in west equatorial Africa, bounded to the south, east and north-east by the Congo; to the north by Cameroon; to the north-west by Equatorial Guinea; and to the west by the Atlantic Ocean
Area 267 667 sq km/103 319 sq mi
Capital Libreville

Chief towns Lambaréné, Franceville, Port Gentil
Population 1 226 000 (1999e)
Time zone GMT +1
Currency 1 CFA Franc (CFAFr) = 100 centimes
Language French
Religions Christianity 95% (RC 65%, Prot and others 30%), traditional beliefs 4%, Islam 1%
Ethnic groups Fang 35%, Mpongwe 16%, Mbete 14%, Punu 11%, others 24%

Physical description

On the Equator for 880km/550mi west to east; lagoons and estuaries on the coast; land rises towards the African central plateau, cut by several rivers, notably the Ogooué.

Climate

Typical equatorial climate, hot, wet and humid; annual average rainfall is 1 250–2 000mm inland; rainfall at Libreville is 2 510mm with an average maximum daily temperature of 33°–37°C.

Government

A President elected for a five-year term holds executive power; he appoints a Prime Minister who, is head of government, appoints the Council of Ministers; a legislative National Assembly is elected for a five-year term.

Nations of the World

Economy

A small area of land is under cultivation but it employs 65% of the population; corn, coffee, cocoa, bananas, rice, yams, cassava; the major industry is timber extraction, notably of okoumé (world's largest producer); rapid economic growth since independence, largely because of offshore oil, natural gas and minerals; manganese, gold, uranium; timber and mineral processing, food processing, oil refining; completion of a road-building programme and the Trans-Gabon railway system have been a stimulus to the economy.

History

Gabon was visited by the Portuguese in the 15c and was under French control from the mid-19c. A slave ship was captured by the French and the liberated slaves formed the settlement of Libreville in 1849. The country was occupied by France in 1885, and became one of four territories of French West Africa in 1910. It gained independence in 1960 under President M'ba, and in 1991 a new constitution was introduced allowing a multi-party system. President Omar Bongo who has been in power since M'ba's death in 1967, retained his position on being re-elected in the multi-party presidential elections in 1993 and 1998, and his *Parti Démocratique Gabonais* ('Gabonese Democratic Party') remained the ruling party on being re-elected in 1996 and 2002.

THE GAMBIA

Official name Republic of the Gambia
Local name Gambia
Location A republic situated in west Africa, bounded on all sides by Senegal except for the Atlantic Ocean coastline in the west
Area 10 402 sq km/4 015 sq mi
Capital Banjul
Chief towns Serrekunda, Brikama, Bakau, Georgetown

Population 1 336 000 (1999e)
Time zone GMT
Currency 1 Dalasi (D) = 100 butut
Language English; Madinka, Fula and Wolof are also spoken
Religions Islam 95%, Christianity 4%, traditional beliefs 1%
Ethnic groups Mandinka 40%, Fulani 18%, Wolof 16%, Dyola 10%, Soninke 8%, others 8%

Physical description

The Gambia is a strip of land stretching 322km/200mi east to west along the River Gambia; flat country, not rising above 90m.

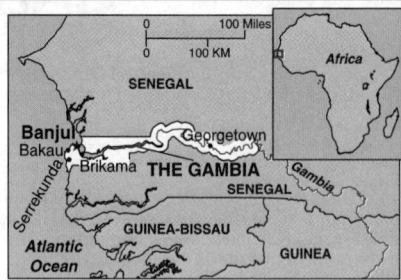

Climate

Tropical; the rainy season is from June to September with rainfall decreasing inland; there is high humidity in the wet season with high night temperatures; the average annual rainfall at Banjul is 1 295mm, average temperatures range from 23°C in January, to 27°C in July, rising inland to over 40°C.

Government

A House of Representatives is elected for a five-year term, a President (also elected for five years) and a Cabinet.

Economy

Chiefly agriculture, especially groundnuts; cotton, rice millet, sorghum, fruit, vegetables, livestock; groundnut processing; brewing; soft drinks; agricultural machinery assembly; metal working; clothing; fishing; tourism.

History

Visited by the Portuguese in 1455, it was settled by the English in the 17c and became an independent British Crown Colony in 1843. It joined the Commonwealth of Nations in 1965 and became a republic in 1970 under the presidency of Sir Dawda Kairaba Jawara. Between 1982 and 1989 the Gambia and Senegal joined to form the Confederation of Senegambia. In 1994 Jawara was ousted in a military coup, and Yahya Jammeh took his place. A new constitution in 1996 allowed opposition parties but it wasn't implemented in practice and Jammeh was re-elected unopposed. Multiparty elections were held in 2001, with Jammeh again re-elected.

GEORGIA

Official name Republic of Georgia

Local name Sakartvelos Respublica

Location A republic in eastern Europe, occupying central and western Transcaucasia. It is bounded to the south-east by Azerbaijan; to the south by Armenia; to the south-west by Turkey; to the west by the Black Sea; and to the north by Russia

Area 69 700 sq km/26 900 sq mi

Capital Tbilisi

Chief towns Kutaisi, Rustavi, Batumi, Sukhumi, Poti

Population 5 066 000 (1999e)

Time zone GMT +4

Currency 1 Lari (GEL) = 100 tetri

Languages Georgian, Russian

Religions Christianity 83% (Georgian Orthodox 65%, Russian Orthodox 10%, Armenian Orthodox 8%), Islam 11%, others 6%

Ethnic groups Georgian 70%, Armenian 8%, Russian 6%, Azeri 6%, Ossetian 3%, others 7%

Physical description

Contains the Greater Caucasus in the north and the Lesser Caucasus in the south; chief rivers are the Kura and Rioni; forest covers c.39% of the republic.

Climate

Subtropical, warm and humid in the west; continental in the east with hot summers and cold winters.

Government

The elected President serves a five-year term (subject to a maximum of two terms); a unicameral Supreme Council of 235 members is elected every four years.

Economy

Manganese; coal; iron and steel; oil refining; chemicals; machines; textiles; food processing; tea; fruit; the Kakhetia region is famed for its orchards and wines; economic instability as a result of internal conflicts.

History

Founded in the 4th century BC, it was later ruled by the Romans and then the Arabs. An independent empire in the 11th century later fell to Persia and Turkey. Part of the Russian empire from the early 19th century, it declared independence in 1918. It was proclaimed a Soviet Socialist Republic in 1921, and formed the Transcaucasian Republic with Armenia and Azerbaijan before becoming a constituent republic of the USSR in 1936. In 1989 independence riots were brutally suppressed, but nevertheless led to independence being declared in 1991. Immediately there was unrest between supporters of President Zviad Gamsakhurdia and the National Guard, resulting in the deposition of the President and the suspension of parliament, and renewed fighting between the government and provincial separatist movements. In 1992 a State Council took control and Eduard Shevardnadze became chairman; in Sep he was appointed President and set about restoring stability to the nation. In addition to the civil conflict, which continued throughout 1993, there was fighting by nationalists in the region of Abkhazia, to whom Shevardnadze agreed in 1994 to give a measure of autonomy, although tensions continued. Georgia joined the CIS (Commonwealth of Independent States) in 1993.

GERMANY

Official name Federal Republic of Germany
Local name Bundesrepublik Deutschland
Location It is bounded to the east by Poland and the Czech Republic; to the south-east by Austria; to the south-west by Switzerland; to the west by France, Luxembourg, Belgium and the Netherlands; and to the north by the North Sea, Denmark and the Baltic Sea
Area 357 868 sq km/138 137 sq mi

Capital Berlin
Chief towns Bonn, Hamburg, Munich, Cologne, Essen, Leipzig, Frankfurt (am Main)
Population 82 087 000 (1999e)
Time zone GMT +1
Currency 1 Euro (€) = 100 cents
Language German; Sorbian (a Slavic language) is spoken by a few

Physical description

The Baltic coastline is backed by a fertile low-lying plain, low hills, and many glacial lakes; the central uplands include the Rhenish Slate Mountains, the Black Forest, and the Odenwald and Spessart; the land rises in the south in several ranges, notably the Bavarian Alps (highest peak is the Zugspitze, 2 962m), also the Harz Mountains of the Thüringian Forest; major rivers include the Rhine (south to north), Elbe, Ems, Weser, Ruhr, Danube, Oder and Neisse; a complex canal system links the chief rivers.

Religions

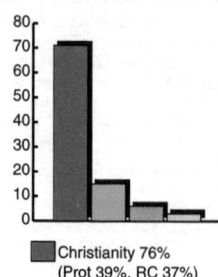

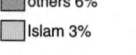

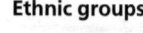

- Christianity 76% (Prot 39%, RC 37%)
- none/unaffiliated 15%
- others 6%
- Islam 3%

Climate

Winters are mild but stormy in the north-west; elsewhere, the climate is continental (more temperate in the east); the east and south have lower winter temperatures, with considerable snowfall and some freezing of canals; average winter temperature in the north is 2°C, and in the south it is –3°C; average summer temperature in the north is 16°C, and slightly higher in the south; the average annual rainfall on the plains is 600–700mm, increasing in parts of the Alps to 2 000mm.

Government

The system of government is built around states (*Länder*) with considerable powers; there is a two-chamber legislature; a President is elected for five years by members of the *Bundesrat* and *Land* parliaments; the Chancellor is elected by the *Bundestag* from the majority party; after political unification in 1990 the five former East German *Länder*, abolished after World War II, were re-established, with the unified Berlin forming a sixth *Land*.

Ethnic groups

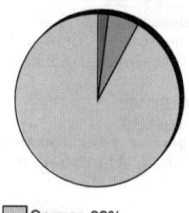

- German 92%
- others 6%
- Turkish 2%

Economy

A leading industrial nation, following major reconstruction after World War II; in the north and the centre there is substantial heavy industry, especially iron and steel (in the Ruhr Valley), coal mining, cement, metal products, chemicals, textiles, machinery, electrical goods, food processing, precision and optical equipment, and vehicles; coal, iron ore, zinc, lead and potash are mined; agriculture includes arable and livestock farming, fruit, wheat, barley, potatoes, sugar beet and forestry; the Rhine and Mosel valleys are major wine-producing areas; tourism is increasing, especially in the south.

History

A central European state formed by the political unification of West Germany and East Germany in 1990. It was the location of the union of the ancient Germanic tribes within the Frankish Empire of Charlemagne in the 8c and of an elective monarchy after 918 under Otto I, with the Holy Roman Empire divided into several hundred states. Many reforms and territorial changes took place during the Napoleonic era, and after the Congress of Vienna (1814–15) a German Confederation of 39 states under Austria was formed. Under Bismarck, Prussia succeeded Austria as the leading German power and excluded her from the North German Confederation. The union of Germany and foundation of the Second Reich (1871), with the King of Prussia as hereditary German Emperor,

gave rise, from around 1900, to an aggressive foreign policy which eventually led to World War I. After the German defeat, the Second Reich was replaced by the democratic Weimar Republic and, in 1933, political power passed to the Nazi Party. Hitler's acts of aggression as Chancellor and Leader (*Führer*) of the totalitarian Third Reich, eventually led to World War II and a second defeat for Germany, with the collapse of the German political regime. The area of Germany was subsequently reduced, and occupied by the UK, USA, France, USSR and Poland, whose zone is now recognized as sovereign Polish territory. This Western occupation softened with the creation of the Federal Republic of Germany (1949) out of the three western zones, and a socialist German Democratic Republic (East Germany) out of the Soviet-occupied zone. Western forces continued to occupy West Berlin, which became a province of West Germany, while East Germany was governed on the communist Soviet model, with the Socialist Unity Party (SED) guaranteed a pre-eminent role. Anti-Soviet demonstrations in East Germany were put down in 1953, and both republics were recognized as sovereign states the following year. In 1958 West Germany was a founder-member of the EEC. The flow of refugees from East to West Germany continued until 1961, but was largely stopped by the building of the Berlin Wall. East Germany was accorded diplomatic recognition and membership of the UN after signing a treaty with West Germany in 1973. In East Germany the movement for democratic reform, as well as mounting economic crisis, culminated (Nov 1989) in the opening of the Berlin Wall and other border crossings to the West, and a more open government policy. Free elections (Mar 1990) led first to economic union with West Germany (July) and then full political unification (Oct), in which West Germany's federal system of government, built around 10 states (*Länder*) with considerable powers, absorbed East Germany as five additional states. Germany is a leading industrial and trading nation, and a dominant force in the European Monetary System, but since 1991 has experienced increasing economic problems and outbreaks of racial violence by the far Right. Chancellor Helmut Kohl and the CDU (Christian Democratic Union) held power for 16 years from 1982, and were defeated in 1998 by the SPD (Social Democratic Party) led by Gerhard Schröder. The Deutsche Mark was replaced by the Euro in Jan 2002.

GHANA

Official name Republic of Ghana
Local name Ghana
Location A republic in West Africa, bounded to the west by the Côte d'Ivoire; to the north by Burkina Faso; to the east by Togo; and to the south by the Gulf of Guinea
Area 238 686 sq km/92 133 sq mi
Capital Accra
Chief towns Sekondi-Takoradi, Kumasi, Tamale

Population 18 888 000 (1999e)
Time zone GMT
Currency 1 Cedi (¢) = 100 pesewas
Language English; several African languages are also spoken
Religions Christianity 50% (Prot 32%, RC 18%), traditional beliefs 34%, Islam 10%, others 6%
Ethnic groups Akan 53%, Mossi 17%, Ewe 12%, Ga-Adangame 8%, Gurma 2%, others 8%

Physical description

Coastline of sand bars and lagoons; low-lying plains inland, leading to the Ashanti plateau in the west and the River Volta basin in the east, dammed to form Lake Volta; mountains rise in the east to 885m at Afadjado.

Climate

Tropical climate, including a warm, dry coastal belt in the south-east, a hot, humid south-west corner, and hot, dry savannah in the north; Kumasi has an average annual rainfall of 1400mm.

Government

The unicameral Parliament of 200 members is elected by popular vote every four years; the head of state is also elected for a four-year term but is renewable only once.

Economy

Mainly agricultural; commercial reserves of oil, diamonds, gold, manganese, bauxite, wood; cocoa (world's leading producer) provides two thirds of export revenue; tobacco, rubber, cotton, peppers, pineapples, avocados, ginger; mining, lumbering, aluminium, light manufacturing, fishing. There are 40 forts and castles built along the coast dating from the late 15c onwards that have been designated World Heritage monuments.

History

Ghana was discovered by Europeans in the 15c, and became the centre of the slave trade in the 18c. The modern state was created by the union of two former British territories, British Gold Coast (Crown Colony in 1874) and British Togoland in 1957, and the name was taken from the ancient Kingdom of Ghana. It became an independent republic within the Commonwealth of Nations in

1960, the first British colony in Africa to achieve independence. Kwame Nkrumah, who had led the nationalist movement and had been Prime Minister when Ghana became independent in 1957, became the first President, but was later deposed. Jerry Rawlings seized power from President Hilla Limann in a military coup in 1981 and became President in 1992, when a multi-party constitution was approved. John Kufuor became President in 2001.

⊅ **Gibraltar ▸ United Kingdom**

GREECE

Official name Hellenic Republic
Local name Elliniki Dimokratia
Location A republic in south-eastern Europe, occupying the southern part of the Balkan Peninsula and numerous islands in the Aegean and Ionian seas
Area 131 957 sq km/50 935 sq mi
Capital Athens
Chief towns Thessaloniki, Patras, Heraklion, Volos, Larisa, Piraieus
Population 10 707 000 (1999e)
Time zone GMT +2
Currency 1 Euro (€) = 100 cents
Language Greek
Religions Christianity 98% (Orthodox), Islam 1%, others 1%
Ethnic groups Greek 98%, others 2%

Physical description

The country consists of a large area of mainland including the Peloponnese in the south, linked to the rest of the mainland by the narrow Isthmus of Corinth; there are over 1400 islands, notably Crete, Euboea, Lesbos, Rhodes, Chios, Cephalonia, Corfu, Lemnos, Samos and Naxos; nearly 80% of the country is mountainous or hilly; main ranges are the Pindhos Mountains in the north, the Rhodope Mountains in the north-east, and the east coast range, which includes Mount Olympus (2 917m), the highest point in Greece; there are several rivers and small lakes.

Climate

Mediterranean on the coast and islands, with mild, rainy winters and hot, dry summers; rainfall occurs almost entirely in the winter months; average annual rainfall in Athens is 414mm.

Government

Governed by a Prime Minister, Cabinet and unicameral Parliament of 300 deputies, elected for four years; a President (head of state) is elected by Parliament for a five-year term; Mount Athos in Macedonia region is a self-governing community of 20 monasteries.

Economy

The service sector accounts for c.55% of the national income; agricultural sector is based on cereals, cotton, tobacco, fruit, figs, raisins, wine, olive oil and vegetables; ores and minerals include iron, magnesite, bauxite, lignite; there is little coal and some oil; manufacturing is based on the production of processed foods, textiles, metals, chemicals, electrical equipment, cement, glass, transport equipment and petroleum products; tourism is important, especially on the islands.

History

Greece has been inhabited since Palaeolithic times, and its prehistoric civilization culminated in the remarkable Minoan culture of Crete (3400–1100BC). The Dorians (a sub-group of Hellenic peoples) invaded from the north in the 12c BC, and Greek colonies were established along the north and south Mediterranean coasts and on the shores of the Black Sea. In the 8–6c BC the Greeks settled throughout the eastern Mediterranean, establishing colonies along the shores of Asia Minor and the adjoining islands. There were many city states on the mainland, notably Sparta and Athens. In the southern part of the Balkan Peninsula, a distinctive Greek culture has persisted unbroken since antiquity; the Slav and Avar invaders who arrived in waves in the 6c and later settled in the southern part of the Balkan Peninsula were Hellenized and assimilated into the original population. In the 5c BC Persian invasions were repelled at Marathon, Salamis, Plataea and Mycale, and Greek literature and art flourished. Conflict between Sparta and Athens (the Peloponnesian War, 431–404 BC) weakened the country, which was overwhelmed by the Macedonians (4c BC) under Philip II of Macedon, who unified the Greek city states under their hegemony. Military expeditions under his son, Alexander III, the Great, penetrated Asia and Africa. Macedonian power was broken by the Romans in 197 BC, and Greece and Crete then formed part of the Greek-speaking Byzantine Empire which stretched deep into Asia Minor and the Middle East. The Byzantine Age (330–1204) was a period of political and cultural hegemony for the Greeks in the Balkans and eastern Mediterranean. After the Sack of Constantinople (1204), the Balkan Greeks fell prey to the ambitions of the Franks and Venetians, and finally to the Turks who occupied Greece from 1460 to 1830. Crete was purchased by the Venetian Republic in 1210 and enjoyed an artistic renaissance, but after it too fell to the Ottomans (1669), it went into a long decline. The Greek national revival began in the late 18c, and led to the Greek War of Independence (1821–8) against the Turks. By the end of the war Greece, though ravaged, was a free state, and it gained formal recognition of its independence from the Ottoman Porte in 1832. During the war, the Cretans joined the insurgents but were quickly crushed and made subject to the Egyptian Viceroy, Ali Pasha. Once again under Ottoman control from 1840, Cretan demands for enosis grew apace with revolts (1858, 1866–9 and 1895), but these were handled cautiously by the Greek government lest it antagonize the Ottoman Porte. After a brief military campaign, Crete was declared independent under a High Commissioner appointed by the Great Powers (1898). The Cretan assembly declared its enosis in 1908, but not until the Treaties of London (1913) was it joined to the Kingdom of Greece. After gaining independence, Greek society was riddled with divisions, with the 19c seeing continuous arguments over the constitution and form of government. In the 20c the Greeks were at war from 1912 to 1922, and from 1940 to 1949: first the Balkan Wars, then World War I, both of which brought substantial territorial gains, and then the disastrous war against the Turks in Anatolia (1919–22) during which c.30 000 Christians were killed in Izmir (Smyrna) in Sep 1922, and over a million Greeks were forced to leave Asia Minor. The Greek Republic was established in 1924 and the monarchy restored in 1935. Meanwhile, Crete became a stronghold of support for its native son, Eleuthérios Venizélos, and rebelled against Metaxas (1938). During World War II, Greece and Crete were occupied by the Germans, and Greece was afterwards ravaged by the bloody Greek Civil War (1944–9). Following a tentative period of democracy, a military coup in 1967 led to the right-wing dictatorship of the Greek Colonels (1967–74). The monarchy was formally abolished and democracy restored in 1974, since when there has been relative peace and stability. Greece joined the EC in 1981. The drachma was replaced by the Euro in Jan 2002.

→ **Greenland ▶ Denmark**

GRENADA

Official name Grenada	**Population** 97 000 (1999e)
Local name Grenada	**Time zone** GMT –4
Location An independent constitutional monarchy of the West Indies and the most southerly of the Windward Islands, in the eastern Caribbean Sea	**Currency** 1 East Caribbean Dollar (EC$) = 100 cents
	Language English
Area 344 sq km/133 sq mi	**Religions** Christianity 90% (RC 52%, Prot 38%), others 10%
Capital St George's	**Ethnic groups** African descent 83%, mixed 13%, East Indian 3%, European 1%
Chief towns Gouyave, Victoria, Grenville	

Physical description

Comprises the main island of Grenada (34km/21mi long and 19km/12mi wide) and the South Grenadines (including Carriacou), an arc of small islands extending from Grenada north to St Vincent; Grenada is of volcanic origin, with a ridge of mountains along its entire length; the highest point is Mount St Catherine, which rises to 843m.

Climate

Subtropical; the average annual temperature is 23°C; the annual rainfall varies from 1 270mm on the coast to 5 000mm in the interior.

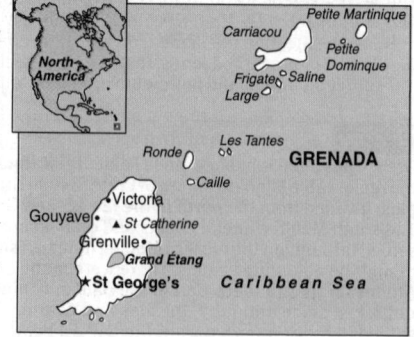

Government

The 1973 constitution of Grenada recognizes the British Monarch as head of state; a bicameral legislature comprises an appointed 13-member Senate and an elected 15-member House of Representatives; a Prime Minister heads a Cabinet of 15 ministers.

Economy

Based on agriculture, notably fruit, vegetables, cocoa, nutmegs, bananas, mace; diversification policy, introducing guavas, citrus fruits, avocados, plums, mangoes, cashew nuts; processing of agricultural products and their derivatives (sugar, rum, coconut oil, lime juice, honey).

History

It was discovered by Columbus in 1498, and named Concepción. Settled by the French in the mid-17c, it was ceded to Britain in 1763 by the Treaty of Paris, but retaken by France in 1779, and ceded again to Britain in 1783. It became a British Crown Colony in 1877 and gained independence in 1974 under Prime Minister Eric Gairy. A popular people's revolution was successfully mounted in 1979 by Maurice Bishop, who became Prime Minister but was killed during a further uprising in 1983. US troops invaded the island in Oct 1983 to restore stable government, which was maintained during the administration of Herbert Blaize (1984–9). In 1995 the New National Party led by Keith Mitchell defeated the National Democratic Congress government under Prime Minister Nicholas Brathwaite and came to power, later winning all 15 parliamentary seats in the 1999 elections.

⊃ **Guadeloupe ▸ France**

⊃ **Guam ▸ United States of America**

GUATEMALA

Official name Republic of Guatemala
Local name Guatemala
Location The northernmost of the central American republics, bounded to the north and west by Mexico; to the south-west by the Pacific Ocean; to the east by Belize and the Caribbean Sea; and to the south-east by Honduras and El Salvador
Area 108 889 sq km/42 031 sq mi
Capital Guatemala City
Chief towns Quezaltenango, Escuintla, Antigua, Mazatenango
Population 12 336 000 (1999e)
Time zone GMT −6
Currency 1 Quetzal (Q) = 100 centavos
Language Spanish; several Indian languages are also spoken
Religions Christianity 95% (RC 73%, Prot 22%), traditional beliefs (Mayan) 5%
Ethnic groups Amerindian 44%, Mestizo (Ladino) 40%, white 5%, black 2%, others 9%

Physical description

Over two thirds mountainous with large forested areas; from the narrow Pacific coastal plain, the highlands rise steeply to heights of between 2 500m and 3 000m; there are many volcanoes on the southern edge of the highlands; rivers flow to both the Pacific Ocean and the Caribbean Sea; the low undulating tableland of El Petén lies to the north.

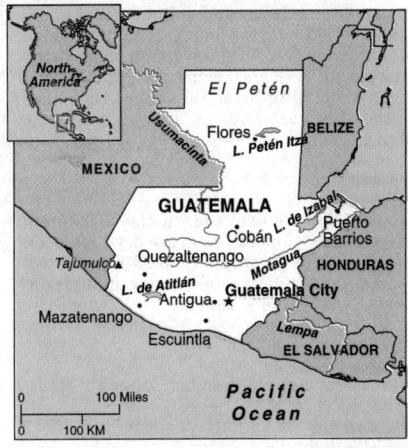

Climate

Humid and tropical on the lowlands and the Caribbean coast; rainy season from May to October; Guatemala City average temperatures are 17°C in January and 21°C in July; average annual rainfall is 1 316mm; much higher rainfall on exposed slopes; the area is subject to severe hurricanes and earthquakes.

Government

The 1985 Constitution provides for the election of a President (who appoints a Cabinet), and a National Assembly of 100 Deputies elected for five-year terms.

Economy

Agricultural products account for c.65% of exports, chiefly coffee, bananas, cotton, sugar; wheat, maize, beans on higher ground; cotton, sugar cane, rice, beans on the Pacific coastal plain; cattle raising and beef production; forestry; foodstuffs; chemicals; textiles; construction materials; tyres; pharmaceuticals; newer industries include the manufacture of electrical goods, plastic sheet and metal furniture; reserves of nickel, lead, silver, oil.

History

Mayan and Aztec civilizations flourished before the Spanish conquest of 1523–4, and Guatemala gained independence as part of the Central American Federation in 1821. The Federation was officially dissolved in 1840, following which the country has had a series of dictatorships broken by short periods of representative government. In 1985 civilian rule was restored. In 1996, after a 35-year civil war between left-wing Guatemalan National Revolutionary Unity guerrillas and the government, a peace agreement was finally reached, thus ending Latin America's longest civil war. Guatemala's long-standing dispute regarding its claim to Belize edged closer to resolution in 1991, when Guatemala recognized Belize's independence. Talks in 2002 led to hopes that the border dispute might finally be resolved.

➔ **Guiana, French ▸ France**

GUINEA

Official name Republic of Guinea
Local name République de Guinée
Location A republic in West Africa, bounded to the north-west by Guinea-Bissau; to the north by Senegal and Mali; to the east by Côte d'Ivoire; to the south by Liberia and Sierra Leone; and to the south-west by the Atlantic Ocean
Area 246 048 sq km/94 974 sq mi
Capital Conakry
Chief towns Kankan, Kindia, Labé

Population 7 539 000 (1999e)
Time zone GMT
Currency 1 Guinea Franc (GFr) = 100 centimes
Language French; several local languages are also spoken widely
Religions Islam 85%, Christianity 8%, traditional beliefs 7%
Ethnic groups Fulani 40%, Malinke 30%, Soussou 12%, Kissi 9%, others 9%

Physical description

The coast is characterized by mangrove forests, rising to a forested and widely cultivated narrow coastal plain; the Fouta Djallon massif beyond lies c.900m above the coastal plain; higher peaks near the Senegal frontier include Mount Tangue (1 537m); savannah plains in the east are cut by rivers flowing towards the upper basin of the River Niger; the Guinea Highlands in the south are forested and generally rise above 1 000m.

Climate

Tropical climate (wet season May–October); the average temperature in the dry season on the coast is 32°C, dropping to 23°C in the wet season; cooler inland; the average annual rainfall at Conakry is 4 923mm.

Government

A President and a 10-member Council of Ministers.

Economy

Largely agricultural country, growing rice, maize, yams, cassava, sugar cane, groundnuts, coffee, bananas, palm kernels, pineapples, timber; rich in minerals, with a third of the world's bauxite reserves; iron ore, diamonds, gold, uranium; independence brought a fall in production and a deterioration in the infrastructure as a result of the withdrawal of French expertise and investment.

History

Part of the Mali Empire in the 16c, it became a French protectorate in 1849 and was governed with Senegal as Rivières du Sud. It became a separate colony in 1893, and a constituent territory within French West Africa in 1904. It reverted to separate colonial status as an Overseas Territory in 1946, and became an independent republic in 1958, with Ahmed Sékou Touré as President. After Sékou Touré's death in 1984 a coup established a Military Committee for National Recovery and established Lansana Conté as President. In 1992 a multi-party system was introduced, and Conté was re-elected in 1993 and 1998. An influx of refugees from conflicts in neighbouring countries has created an additional economic burden, with rebel attacks also increasing tensions.

GUINEA-BISSAU

Official name Republic of Guinea-Bissau

Local name Republica da Guiné-Bissau

Location A republic in West Africa, bounded to the south-east by Guinea; to the north by Senegal; and to the south-west by the Atlantic Ocean

Area 36 260 sq km/14 000 sq mi

Capital Bissau

Chief towns Bafatá, Bolama, Mansôa

Population 1 235 000 (1999e)

Time zone GMT

Currency 1 CFA Franc (CFAFr) = 100 centimes

Languages Portuguese, Guinean Creole; many African languages are also spoken

Religions traditional beliefs 52%, Islam 42%, Christianity 6%

Ethnic groups Balante 26%, Fulani 24%, Malinke 13%, Mandyako 10%, Pepel 10%, others 17%

Physical description

An indented coast typified by islands and mangrove-lined estuaries, backed by forested coastal plains; chief rivers are the Cacheu, Geba and Corubal; a low-lying country with savannah-covered plateaux in the south and east, rising to 310m on the Guinea border; includes the heavily-forested Bijagos Archipelago.

Climate

Tropical climate with a wet season (June–October); average annual rainfall at Bissau is 1 950mm and the temperature range is 24°–27°C.

Government

A President is head of state; a National People's Assembly has 150 Representatives.

Economy

Based on agriculture, especially rice, maize, sorghum, cassava, beans, yams, peanuts, coconuts, palm oil, groundnuts, timber; cattle, sheep, shrimps, fish; construction, food processing, brewing, soft drinks; reserves of petroleum, bauxite, phosphate.

History

Discovered by the Portuguese in 1446, it became a Portuguese colony in 1879. After becoming an Overseas Territory of Portugal in 1952, it gained independence in 1973, with Luís de Almeida Cabral as President from 1974. He was deposed by a military coup led by João Vieira in 1980, and the constitution was changed in 1984 to make Vieira President. A multi-party system was introduced in 1991. The first multi-party elections were held in 1994; they were won by the ruling party and Vieira was re-elected. In May 1999 Vieira was ousted in a coup and civil war ensued until the election of Kumba Yalla in 2000.

GUYANA

Official name Co-operative Republic of Guyana
Local name Guyana
Location A republic on the northern coast of South America, bounded to the east by Suriname; to the west by Venezuela; to the south by Brazil; and to the north by the Atlantic Ocean
Area 214 969 sq km/82 978 sq mi
Capital Georgetown
Population 705 200 (1999e)

Time zone GMT –3.5
Currency 1 Guyana Dollar (G$) = 100 cents
Language English; Hindi, Urdu and local dialects are also spoken
Religions Christianity 55% (Prot 36%, RC 19%), Hinduism 35%, Islam 9%, others 1%
Ethnic groups East Indian 49%, black 32%, mixed 12%, Amerindian 6%, Chinese 1%

Physical description

Inland forest covers c.85% of the land area; grass-covered savannah in the hinterland; the coastal plain, below sea level at high tide, is protected by sea defences, dams and canals; main rivers are the Essequibo, Demerara and Berbice, with many rapids and waterfalls in the upper courses; the highest peak is Mount Roraima, rising to 2 875m in the Pakaraima Mountains to the west.

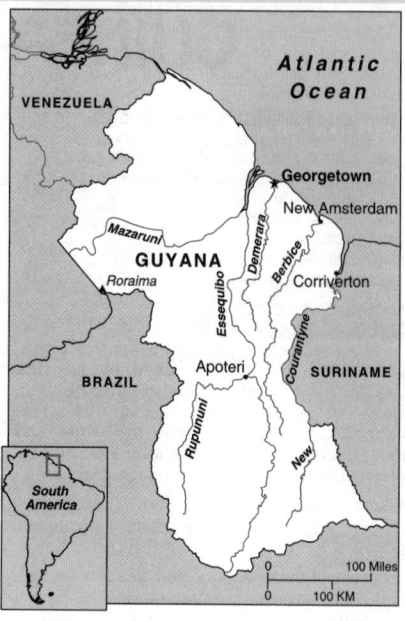

Climate

Equatorial climate in the lowlands, hot, wet, with constant high humidity; Georgetown, representative of the coastal lowland area, has minimum temperatures of 23°C, maximum 34°C and two seasons of high rainfall (May–July, November–January); lower temperatures and less rainfall on the high plateau inland.

Government

A President and a unicameral 65-member National Assembly, elected every five years.There is high unemployment, influenced by labour unrest, low productivity and a high foreign debt. The International Monetary Fund made Guyana ineligible for further credits due to lack of repayment in 1985.

Economy

Largely based on sugar, rice, bauxite; shrimps, livestock, cotton, molasses, timber, rum.

History

It was sighted by Columbus in 1498 and settled by the Dutch in the late 16c. Several areas were ceded to Britain in 1815, and the country formally came under British rule when they were consolidated as British Guiana in 1831. Following racial disturbances in 1962, Guyana gained independence in 1966 and became a republic in 1970, led by President Forbes Burnham. He was succeeded on his death in 1985 by Desmond Hoyte, whose People's National Congress Party was defeated in 1992 by the People's Progessive Party under Cheddi Jagan. Jagan was succeeded on his death in 1997 by Samuel Hinds; his widow, Janet Jagan, was President from 1997 to 1999, when she was succeeded by Bharrat Jagdeo.

HAITI

Official name Republic of Haiti
Local name République d'Haïti
Location A republic in the West Indies. It occupies the western third of the island of Hispaniola in the Caribbean Sea
Area 27 750 sq km/10 712 sq mi
Capital Port-au-Prince
Chief towns Port-de-Paix, Cap-Haïtien, Gonaïves, Les Cayes, Jacmel, Jérémie

Population 6 884 000 (1999e)
Time zone GMT −5
Currency 1 Gourde (G, Gde) = 100 centimes
Languages French, Creole
Religions Christianity 95% (RC 80%, Prot 15%), others 4%, none/unaffiliated 1%
Note: Around half the population practice voodoo
Ethnic groups Black 95%, Mulatto and white 5%

Physical description

Consists of two mountainous peninsulas (the Massif du Nord in the north and the Massif de la Hotte in the south), separated by a deep structural depression, the Plaine du Cul-de-Sac; to the east is the Massif de la Selle, with Haiti's highest peak, La Selle (2 680m); Haiti includes the islands of Gonâve off the west coast and Tortue off the north coast.

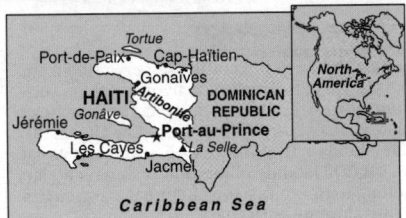

Climate

Tropical maritime; average monthly temperatures range from 24°C to 29°C; annual average rainfall for the north coast and mountains is 1 475–1 950mm, but only 500mm on the west side; the wet season is May–September; hurricanes are common.

Government

President elected by popular vote for a five-year term; Prime Minister appointed by the President; Cabinet chosen by the Prime Minister in consultation with the President.

Economy

Based on agriculture; large plantations grow coffee, sugar, sisal; rice, bananas, corn, sorghum, cocoa; sugar refining; textiles; flour milling; cement; bauxite; light assembly industries; lobster fishing; tourism.

History

Hispaniola was discovered by Columbus in 1492, and Haiti was created when the western third of the island was ceded to France in 1697. In 1791–1804 the Haitian Revolution, the only successful slave revolution in the New World, took place. It culminated in the independence of Haiti (1804). A white–coloured confrontation was superseded in Aug 1791 by a slave revolt led by Toussaint L'Ouverture, who expelled Maitland's British expeditionary force (1798), overcame the white and coloured armies by 1800 and, in 1801, sent an independence constitution to Paris. By then, France was under Napoleon's control and he despatched an army to crush the black Jacobins. Toussaint was captured by trickery but the 20 000-strong French force was decimated by yellow fever and withdrew (Nov 1803), leaving the African-born slave, Dessalines, to proclaim himself Emperor of an independent Haiti (1804). Haiti had an Emperor until 1859, when it became a republic. From 1822 to 1844 Haiti was united with Santo Domingo (Dominican Republic); from 1915 to 1934 it was under US occupation; and from 1957 to 1986 the Duvalier family had absolute power, their rule being enforced by a civilian militia known as the Tonton Macoute. Following a military coup in 1991 and the deposition of Jean-Bertrand Aristide, the UN imposed a trade embargo on Haiti which had a severe effect on the economy. Under military rule the Tonton Macoute were revived under the name *attachés*. Following US-led negotiations with the military leaders, Aristide was restored to power in 1994, but he was voted out of office in the elections the following year and René Préval became President in 1996. Aristide was re-elected in 2000, but attempted coups meant some political instability continued.

HONDURAS

Official name Republic of Honduras
Local name Honduras
Location A republic in Central America, bounded to the south-west by El Salvador; to the west by Guatemala; to the east and south-east by Nicaragua; to the north by the Caribbean Sea; and to the south by the Pacific Ocean
Area 112 088 sq km/43 266 sq mi
Capital Tegucigalpa
Chief towns San Pedro Sula, Choluteca, La Ceiba, El Progreso
Population 5 997 000 (1999e)
Time zone GMT –6
Currency 1 Lempira (L, La) = 100 centavos
Language Spanish; English is also spoken
Religions Christianity 97% (RC 94%, Prot 3%), others 3%
Ethnic groups Mestizo 90%, Amerindian 7%, black 2%, white 1%

Physical description

Coastal lands in the south are separated from the Caribbean coastlands by mountains running north-west to south-east; the southern plateau rises to 2 849m at Cerro Las Minas; the Bay Islands in the Caribbean Sea and a group of nearly 300 islands in the Gulf of Fonseca also belong to Honduras; the Laguna Caratasca lies in the extreme north-east.

Climate

Tropical climate in coastal areas, temperate in the centre and west; two wet seasons in upland areas (May–July, September–October); variable temperatures in the interior, 15°–24°C; on the coastal plains the average is c.30°C.

Government

An executive President and a National Assembly are elected for four-year periods.

Economy

Forestry (nearly half the land area), mining and cattle raising; bananas, coffee, beef, cotton, tobacco, sugar; gold, silver, lead, zinc; offshore oil exploration in the Caribbean; cement, textiles, wood products, cigars, light manufacturing, fishing. It is the least developed country in Central America, dependent largely on agriculture (providing one third of the national income).

History

The centre of Maya culture in the 4–9c, it was settled by the Spanish in the early 16c, and became a province of Guatemala. Honduras gained independence from Spain in 1821 and joined the Central American Federation. It became an independent sovereign state in 1838. There were several military coups in the 1960s and 1970s, and during the 1980s it was the base for rebels (Contras) fighting against the government of Nicaragua. Honduras became dependent on help from the USA, which supported the rebels. The Contra war ended in 1990, but internal unrest continued throughout the 1990s and raised concerns about human rights abuses. In Oct 1998 the economy was devastated by the impact of the unprecedented Hurricane Mitch and the country continues to suffer from poverty and violence.

⤳ **Hong Kong ▸ China**

HUNGARY

Official name Republic of Hungary

Local name Magyar Koztarsasag

Location A landlocked republic in the Danube basin, central Europe, bounded to the north by Slovakia; to the east by the Ukraine and Romania; to the south by Serbia and Montenegro; to the south-west by Croatia; and to the west by Slovenia and Austria

Area 93 030 sq km/35 910 sq mi

Capital Budapest

Chief towns Debrecen, Miskolc, Szeged, Pécs, Györ

Population 10 197 119 (2001)

Time zone GMT +1

Currency 1 Forint (Ft) = 100 fillér

Language Magyar (Hungarian)

Religions Christianity 79% (RC 58%, Prot 21%), Judaism 1%, others 2%, none/unaffiliated 18%

Ethnic groups Magyar 90%, Romany 4%, German 3%, Serb 2%, others 1%

Physical description

Drained by the River Danube (flowing north to south) and its tributaries; there is frequent flooding, especially in the Great Plains, east of the Danube; a low spur of the Alps crosses Hungary in the west, separating the Little Hungarian Plain from the Transdanubian downlands; the highest peak is Kékes (1 014m).

Climate

The landlocked position gives a fairly extreme continental climate with a marked difference between summer and winter; it is wettest in spring and early summer; winters are cold with snow lying for 30–40 days and the River Danube is sometimes frozen over for long periods; fog is frequent during settled winter weather.

Government

Governed by a 386-member unicameral legislature (National Assembly), elected every four years; this elects a President for a five-year term, and a Prime Minister.

Economy

Large-scale nationalization took place in 1946–9 as part of the centralized planning strategy of the new republic; greater independence was given to individual factories and farms from 1968; agriculture includes grain, potatoes, sugar beet; strong economic growth in recent years; main industries are mining, metallurgy, engineering, chemicals, textiles, motor manufacture and food processing.

History

The Magyars probably settled the Hungarian plain in the 9c and a kingdom was formed under St Stephen I in the 11c. This was conquered byTurks in 1526 and became part of the Habsburg Empire in the 17c. Austria and Hungary were reconstituted as the Dual Monarchy of Austria-Hungary in 1867. The year 1869 was declared the Hungarian Millennium to celebrate the 1 000th anniversary of the Magyars' original settlement. It was used by the Hungarian government within Austria-Hungary to celebrate undoubted political and economic achievements in the course of the previous half century. It was also used as an anti-Habsburg demonstration and marked an intensification of the attempt to Magyarize Hungary's subject nationalities. Protests were made by the Magyar poor, as well as by Slavs and Romanians. AfterWorldWar I Hungary became a republic, but a communist revolt introduced a new regime in 1919. A nominally monarchical constitution under a regent, Admiral Miklós Horthy, was restored in 1920, but after the failure of its policy of alliance with Germany in World War II, a new republic under communist government was formed in 1949. In 1956 there was a national insurrection known as the Hungarian Uprising, which followed the denunciation of Stalin at the 20th Congress of the Soviet Communist Party for his oppressive rule. Rioting students and workers pulled down statues of Stalin and demanded radical reform. When the new Prime Minister Imre Nagy announced plans for Hungary's withdrawal from the Warsaw Pact, among other things, Soviet troops and tanks crushed the uprising. Many were killed, thousands fled abroad, and Nagy was executed. Reform was set back for more than a decade. In 1989 pressure for political change was led from within the Communist Party; the same year Hungary was declared a democratic state and in 1990 multi-party elections were held. Since the elections of

1994, when the Hungarian Democratic Forum (MDF) were ousted by a Hungarian Socialist Party-led coalition under Prime Minister Gyula Horn, Hungary has experienced gradual economic growth. In 1999 Hungary was admitted to NATO, and in 2002 was formally invited to join the EU.

ICELAND

Official name Republic of Iceland
Local name Ísland
Location An island state lying between the northern Atlantic Ocean and the Arctic Ocean, south-east of Greenland and 550mi/900km west of Norway
Area 103 000 sq km/40 000 sq mi
Capital Reykjavik
Chief towns Akureyri, Húsavík, Akranes, Keflavík, Ísafjördur

Population 272 500 (1999e)
Time zone GMT
Currency 1 Króna (IKr, ISK) = 100 aurar
Language Icelandic
Religions Christianity 94% (Prot 93%, RC 1%), none/unaffiliated 6%
Ethnic groups Icelandic 94%, Danish 1%, others 5%

Physical description

A volcanic island of relatively recent geological origin, at the northern end of the mid-Atlantic Ridge, with several active volcanoes (eg Hekla); famous for its geysers, notably *Geysir* from which the term is derived; many towns are heated by subterranean hot water; there is a geothermal power station at Krafla; the coastline is heavily indented, with many long fjords; high ridges rise to 2 119m at Hvannadalshnúkur in the south-east; large snowfields and glaciers cover much of the land area.

Denmark Strait
Ísafjördur
Arctic Ocean
Breidafjördur — Gláma — Hunaflói
Húsavík
Akranes — Langjökull — Akureyri
Keflavík — ★ Reykjavík
ICELAND
Vatnajökull
Hvannadalshnúkur
Norwegian Sea
Europe
Atlantic Ocean
0   100 Miles
0   100KM

Climate

Changeable climate, with relatively mild winters; average daily temperatures are minimum −2°C (January), maximum 14°C (July–August); Reykjavík is generally ice-free throughout the year; summers are cool and cloudy; average monthly rainfall reaches 94mm (October).

Government

Governed by a 63-member Parliament, which includes a 21-member Upper House; a President appoints a Prime Minister and Cabinet.

Economy

Largely based on inshore and deep-water fishing (75% of the national income); stock farming, dairy farming, potatoes and greenhouse vegetables are important; there is also production of aluminium and diatomite; tourism.

History

It was settled by the Norse in the 9c, and in the 10c was the seat of the world's oldest parliament, the *Althing*. It united with Norway in 1262, and with Denmark in 1380. In 1918 Iceland became an independent kingdom with the same sovereign as Denmark, and since 1944 it has been an independent republic. The extension of the fishing limit around Iceland in 1958 and 1975 precipitated the 'Cod War' disputes with the UK. Subsequent attempts to restrict fishing in Icelandic waters were successful under the right-wing coalition government of Davíd Oddsson, and problems in the fishing industry led to a worsening economic situation in the early 1990s. Ólafur Ragnar Grimsson was elected to succeed Vigdís Finnbogadóttir as President in 1996.

INDIA

Official name Republic of India
Local name Bhārat (Hindi)
Location A federal republic in southern Asia, bounded to the north-west by Pakistan; to the north by China, Nepal and Bhutan; to the east by Myanmar and Bangladesh; to the south-east by the Bay of Bengal; and to the south-west by the Arabian Sea
Area 3 166 829 sq km/1 222 396 sq mi

Capital New Delhi
Chief towns * Ahmadabad, Bangalore, Chennai, Hyderabad, Jaipur, Kanpur, Kolkata, Lucknow, Mumbai, Nagpur, Poona.
Population 1 000 849 000 (1999e)
Time zone GMT +5.5
Currency 1 Indian Rupee (Re, Rs) = 100 paisa
Languages Hindi, English and 14 others

Physical description

The second largest state in Asia, bordered to the north by the Himalayas; folded mountain ridges and valleys lie to the north; the highest peaks are over 7 000m in the Karakoram Range and the Ladakh Plateau; the central river plains of the Ganges, Yamuna, Ghaghara and Brahmaputra are to the south; the best agricultural land is in the east; control measures are needed to prevent flooding; the Thar Desert north-west of Rajasthan is bordered by semi-desert areas; the Deccan Plateau in the southern peninsula, with hills and wide valleys, is bounded by the Western and Eastern Ghats; the coastal plains are important areas of rice cultivation.

Climate

Dominated by the Asiatic monsoon; rains come from the south-west (June–October); rainfall decreases (December–February) as winds blow in from the north, followed by drought until

Nations of the World

March or May; temperatures in the northern mountains vary greatly with altitude; rainfall decreases east to west on the northern plains, with desert conditions in the extreme west; temperatures vary with altitude on the Deccan Plateau, although towards the south of the plateau region the climate is tropical, even in the cool season; the west coast is subject to rain throughout the year, particularly in the south, where humidity is high; cyclones and storms on the south-east coast (especially October–December), with high temperatures and humidity during the monsoon season.

Government

A federal democratic republic within the Commonwealth since 1950; each of the 25 states is administered by a Governor appointed by the President for five years; each state has an Assembly (numbers range from 30 to 425 members); each of the seven union territories is administered by the President who is elected for a five-year term; the President, advised by a Council of Ministers, appoints a Prime Minister; Parliament comprises the President, an Upper House (*Rajya Sabha*) of no more than 250 members, and a 544-member House of the People (*Lok Sabha*).

Economy

Over two thirds of the work force is employed in agriculture; tea, rice, wheat, coffee, sugar cane, cotton, jute, oilseed, maize, pulses, milk; floods and drought cause major problems; fishing, forestry; considerable increase in industrial production since independence; iron, steel, aluminium; vehicles; oil products; cement; chemicals; fertilizers; paper; jute goods; textiles; sugar; coal, iron, mica, manganese, bauxite, limestone, chromite, barites, oil, natural gas.

History

The Indus civilization, which emerged in c.2500BC, was destroyed in 1500BC by the Aryans, who developed the Brahminic caste system. The Mauryan Emperor Asoka unified most of India, and established Buddhism as the state religion in the 3c BC. Hinduism spread in the 2c BC, and there were Muslim influences during the 7–8c, with a sultanate established at Delhi. Delhi was captured by Timur in 1398 and the Mughal Empire was established by Babur in 1526, and extended by Akbar and Aurangzeb. The Portuguese, French, Dutch and British had footholds in India in the 18c, which led to conflict between France and Britain in 1746–63. The development of British interests was represented by the British East India Company, and British power was established after the Indian Uprising (1857) was crushed. A movement for independence arose in the late 19c, and the Government of India Act in 1919 allowed the election of Indian ministers to share power with appointed British governors; a further Act in 1935 allowed the election of independent provincial governments. Passive resistance campaigns led by Mahatma Gandhi began in the 1920s, and independence was granted in 1948, on the basis of partition which established a Muslim state (Pakistan). Indian states were later reorganized on a linguistic basis. There was a Pakistan–India war over disputed territory in Kashmir and Jammu in 1948, and there has been sporadic Hindu–Muslim hostility, notably in 1978, as well as further India–Pakistan conflict in 1965 and 1971 (the Indo-Pakistan Wars). Separatist movements continue, especially that of the Sikhs' demand for an independent Sikh state in the Punjab. The suppression of the militant Sikh movement in 1984 led to the assassination of Indira Gandhi. Also that year a major gas leak in 1984 at the city of Bhopal caused c.2 500 deaths. Rajiv Gandhi, leader of the Congress (I) Party, was assassinated in 1991 during the general election. Torrential rainstorms in 1992 resulted in many people being killed in the southern states, and increasing tension generally resulted in inter-communal violence and the declaration in 1993 of a national state of emergency. P V Narasimha Rao, leader of the Congress (I) Party, came to power as Prime Minister in 1991. He and his party were heavily defeated in 1996 and a period of political instability followed in which there were several general elections and allegations of widespread corruption in public life. In 1999 fresh conflict erupted between India and Pakistan in the border region of Kashmir, bringing the two countries to the brink of war in 2002. Sporadic religious violence also continues. The country has also suffered from natural disasters: a cyclone in 1999 killed an estimated 10 000 people while a devastating earthquake in Gujarat in 2001 killed over 20 000 people.

* India has renamed several of its cities and states in recent years, reverting to pre-colonial names. Thus, Bombay is now known as Mumbai, Calcutta as Kolkata, and Madras as Chennai. Other such changes may follow.

Religions

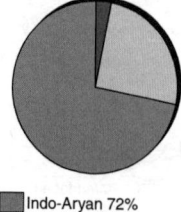

- ■ Hinduism 82%
- □ Islam 12% (Sunni)
- ■ Sikhism 2%
- □ Christianity 2%
- ■ Jainism 1%
- ■ Buddhism 1%

Ethnic groups

- ■ Indo-Aryan 72%
- □ Dravidian 25%
- ■ others 3%

INDONESIA

Official name Republic of Indonesia
Local name Republik Indonesia
Location A republic in South-East Asia
 comprising the world's largest island group
Area 1 906 240 sq km/735 809 sq mi
Capital Jakarta
Chief towns Jayapura, Bandung, Semarang,
Surabaya, Medan, Palembang
Population 231 328 000 (2002e)
Time zones GMT +7/9
Currency 1 Rupiah (Rp) = 100 sen
Language Bahasa Indonesia; English, Dutch and
 Javanese are also widely spoken

Physical description

Five main islands and 30 smaller archipelagos totalling 13 677 islands and islets, of which c.6 000 are inhabited; over 100 volcanic peaks on Java, of which 15 are active.

* The island of Irian Jaya was officially renamed Papua in 2002.

Climate

Hot and humid equatorial climate; dry season (June–September), rainy season (December–March), apart from the Moluccas (June–September); the average temperature is 27°C on island coasts, falling inland and with altitude.

Government

Governed by a President elected for a five-year term, advised by a Cabinet and several advisory agencies.

Economy

Mainly agrarian, notably rice; maize, cassava, sugar, sweet potatoes, bananas, coffee, tobacco, tea, rubber, coconuts, palm oil; fishing, timber; oil, natural gas and petroleum products from Borneo and Sumatra account for nearly 60% of national income; tin, nickel, bauxite, copper, manganese; small manufacturing industry, based on textiles, paper, cement, chemicals, fertilizers, motorcycles, household goods.

Religions

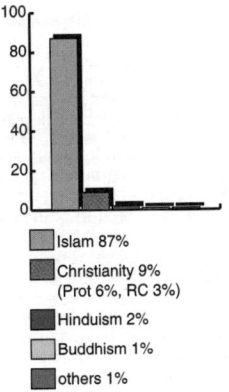

Islam 87%

Christianity 9%
(Prot 6%, RC 3%)

Hinduism 2%

Buddhism 1%

others 1%

History

It includes the island group of the Moluccas, also called the Spice Islands; Kalimantan, a group of four provinces in the Indonesian part of Borneo; Sumatra, which is the fifth-largest island in the world and was the centre of the Buddhist kingdom of Sri Vijaya in the 7–13c, and was discovered by Marco Polo in the 13c; and the western half of the mountainous island of Timor. Since the independence of Indonesia in 1945, all these places have developed separatist movements of varying in-

Nations of the World

tensity. The western part of Timor was colonized by the Dutch in the 17c, and given to Holland in 1859 as Dutch Timor, but as West Timor it was included in Indonesia at independence, and is administered as part of the province of Nusa Tenggara Timur. East Timor had been under Portuguese control, but in 1975 declared itself independent as the Democratic Republic of East Timor. Violent civil war broke out and East Timor was annexed by Indonesia in 1976, but this annexation was not recognized by the UN and was reversed by popular plebiscite in 1999 after a long nationalist struggle against Indonesian ascendancy. Indonesia was settled in early times by Hindus and Buddhists, whose power lasted until the 14c. Islam was introduced in the 14–15c. Portuguese settlers arrived in the early 16c, and in the early 17c the Dutch East India Company was established in 1602. Occupied by the Japanese in World War II, Indonesia declared its independence in 1945, under Dr Sukarno. The 1945 constitution established a 1 000-member People's Consultative Assembly. The federal system was replaced by unified control in 1950. The expulsion of Dutch citizens led to a breakdown of the economy, causing hardship and unrest. Sukarno's rule became increasingly authoritarian and was opposed by

Ethnic groups

- ☐ Javanese 45%
- ☐ others 25%
- ☐ Sudanese 14%
- ☐ Coastal Malays 8%
- ☐ Madurese 8%

the Communist Party; there was an unsuccessful military coup in 1965 but the ensuing disarray enabled General Suharto to purge the Communist Party, depose Sukarno (1967) and make himself President. Following his re-election in 1988, Suharto instituted a New Order policy to revolutionize the country's economy; however, his period in office was dogged by Islamic fundamentalist uprisings, ethnic violence, and by the long-running civil war in East Timor. Following an economic collapse and calls for political reform, the Suharto regime collapsed. On 21 May 1998 Suharto was replaced by his deputy, B J Habibie, but Habibie's cautious reforms proved incapable of placating an aroused public. The debacle in East Timor further damaged government prestige and in June 1999, in the first democratically held elections for 44 years, Habibie was succeeded by Abdurrahman Wahid, who appointed a new cabinet. Allegations of corruption persisted and Wahid was replaced by Megawati Sukarnoputri in 2001.

IRAN

Official name Islamic Republic of Iran
Local name Jomhoori-e-Islami-e-Iran
Location A republic in south-west Asia, bounded to the north by Armenia, Azerbaijan, Turkmenistan and the Caspian Sea; to the east by Afghanistan and Pakistan; to the south by the Gulf of Oman and the Arabian Gulf; to the south-west by Iraq; and to the north-west by Turkey
Area 1 648 000 sq km/636 128 sq mi
Capital Tehran
Chief towns Mashhad, Isfahan, Tabriz, Shiraz, Abadan
Population 65 180 000 (1999e)
Time zone GMT +3.5
Currency 1 Iranian Rial (Rls, RI) = 100 dinars
Language Farsi, with several minority languages spoken
Religions Islam 99% (Shiite 91%, Sunni 8%), others 1%
Ethnic groups Persian 51%, Azeri 24%, Gilaki and Mazandarani 8%, Kurdish 7%, others 10%

Physical description

Largely composed of a vast arid central plateau, average elevation of 1 200m, with many salt and sand basins; rimmed by mountain ranges that drop down to narrow coastal lowlands; bound to the north by the Elburz Mountains, rising to 5 670m at Mount Demavend; the Zagros Mountains in the west and south rise to 3 000–4 600m.

Climate

Mainly a desert climate, with annual rainfall below 300mm; average temperatures at Tehran are 2°C (January), 29°C (July), average annual rainfall is 246mm; the Caspian coastal strip is much wetter (800–2 000mm) than the interior and rain is more widely distributed throughout the year; hot and humid on the shores of the Arabian Gulf; frequent earthquakes.

Government

Governed by a President, elected for a four-year term, who appoints a Prime Minister and other ministers; the Ayatollah is the appointed religious leader with the authority to protect the constitution; there is a 270-member National Consultative Assembly.

Economy

The world's fourth largest oil producer, but production was severely disrupted by the 1978 revolution and the Iran–Iraq War; natural gas, iron ore, copper, manganese, chromite, coal, salt; textiles; sugar refining, food processing; petrochemicals, iron and steel; cement; fertilizers; machinery; traditional handicrafts (especially carpets); one third of the population are involved in agriculture and forestry; wheat, rice, tobacco, barley, sugar beet, cotton, dates, raisins, tea; sheep, goats; silkworms.

History

Iran was an early centre of civilization and its dynasties include the aggressive Sassanids (from 3c) and its first royal house, the Achaemenids (from 7c). It was ruled by the Arabs, Turks and Mongols until the Safavid Dynasty in the 16–18c and the Qajar Dynasty in the 19–20c. A military coup in 1921 led to independence in 1925 under Reza Shah Pahlavi, who abdicated and was succeeded as Shah by his son Muhammad Reza Shah Pahlavi in 1941. Protests against the Shah's regime in the 1970s led to a revolution in 1978. The Shah went into exile and an Islamic Republic was proclaimed under Ayatollah Khomeini in 1979. Following the ex-Shah's admission to the USA for medical treatment, the US Embassy in Tehran was seized for over a year in 1979–81, with the revolutionary government demanding his return to Iran. The Iran–Iraq War took place in 1980–8, claiming possibly one million Iranian lives. On Khomeini's death in 1989 the president, Sayed Ali Khamena, became Ayatollah, leading to a political struggle for presidential power out of which emerged Hashemi Rafsanjani. He remained President until 1997, when he was defeated by Sayed Ayatollah Muhammad Khatami. During the Gulf War Iran remained neutral, and gave refuge to c.1.5 million Kurdish and Shia people fleeing Iraq. During the 1990s relations between Iran and the West, particularly the USA, became strained due to its alleged abuses of human rights, its lack of cooperation during the Middle East peace process, its expansion of its military resources, and its rumoured involvement in both international terrorism and the development of nuclear weapons. There has been some liberalization under Khatami, especially since the Liberals won a parliamentary majority in 2000.

IRAQ

Official name Republic of Iraq	**Chief towns** Basra, Kirkuk, Mosul
Local name Jumhouriya al Iraquia	**Population** 22 427 000 (1999e)
Location A republic in south-west Asia, bounded to the east by Iran; to the north by Turkey; to the north-west by Syria; to the west by Jordan; to the south-west and south by Saudi Arabia; and to the south-east by Kuwait and the Arabian Gulf	**Time zone** GMT +3
	Currency 1 Iraqi Dinar (ID) = 1 000 fils
	Language Arabic
	Religions Islam 96% (Shiite 54%, Sunni 42%), Christianity 3%, others 1%
Area 434 925 sq km/167 881 sq mi	**Ethnic groups** Arab 77%, Kurdish 18%, Turkmen, Assyrian and others 5%
Capital Baghdad	

Physical description

Largely comprises the vast alluvial tract of the Tigris–Euphrates lowland (which is equal to ancient Mesopotamia); both rivers are separated in their upper courses by the plain of Al Jazirah, rising to 1547m; about 190km/118mi from the Arabian Gulf they join to form the navigable Shatt al-Arab; the lowland here has swamp vegetation; mountains in the north-east rise to over 3000m; desert in other areas.

Climate

Mainly arid; summers are very hot and dry; winters are often cold; average temperatures at Baghdad are 10°C in January and 35°C in July, with an average annual rainfall of 140mm; rainfall is highest in the north-east, where the average is 400–600mm.

Government

A President, elected from and by the Revolutionary Command Council, is head of state and appoints the Council of Ministers; legislative power rests with the National Assembly and the Revolutionary Command Council; the Kurdish regional assembly has various limited powers of legislation.

Economy

The world's second largest producer of oil, but production was severely disrupted during the Iran–Iraq War and the Gulf War with several oil installations destroyed; natural gas, oil refining, petrochemicals; cement; textiles; dates, cotton, rice, winter wheat, barley, lentils; sheep; cattle; major irrigation schemes under way; rich archaeological remains, especially along the Euphrates Valley; the economy has suffered from trade sanctions first imposed by the UN in 1990.

History

Iraq was part of the Ottoman Empire from the 16c until World War I. It was captured by British forces in 1916 and became a British-mandated territory in 1921. It gained independence under the Hashemite Dynasty in 1932, and the monarchy was replaced by military rule in 1958. Since the 1960s, Kurdish nationalists in the north-east have been fighting to establish a separate state. Saddam Hussein came to power as President in 1979. His invasion of Iran in 1980 led to the Iran–Iraq War, which lasted until 1988. The invasion of Kuwait in 1990 led to UN sanctions, the Gulf War in 1991, and Iraqi withdrawal. Tension in the area remained, and Iraqi attacks on Kurdish settlements and Shiite refugees continued. The UN sanctions were not lifted due to Iraq's refusal to cooperate with proposed UN inspections and monitoring of its arms programme. Iraqi–US relations deteriorated further in the late 1990s, and air-strikes by US and UK aircraft commenced in Dec 1998. Iraq's failure to comply with UN resolutions regarding weapons monitoring led to a further UN resolution in Nov 2002, after pressure from the USA. UN weapons inspectors returned to Iraq but political pressure on Saddam Hussein continued, backed by the threat of military action by the USA. The UN inspectors were withdrawn and war began in Mar 2003 as US and UK forces entered Iraq in order to force a regime change.

IRELAND

Official name Republic of Ireland

Local name Poblacht na hEireann

Location A republic occupying southern, central and north-western Ireland, separated from Great Britain by the Irish Sea and St George's Channel, and bounded to the north-east by Northern Ireland, part of the UK

Area 70 282 sq km/27 129 sq mi

Capital Dublin

Chief towns Cork, Limerick, Waterford, Galway, Drogheda, Dundalk, Sligo

Population 3 633 000 (1999e)

Time zone GMT

Currency 1 Euro (€) = 100 cents

Languages English, Irish Gaelic; the Gaelic-speaking areas, mostly in the west, are known as the *Gaeltacht*.

Physical description

The mountainous landscapes in the west are part of the Caledonian system of Scandinavia and Scotland, with quartzite peaks weathered into conical mountains such as Croagh Patrick (765m); a younger mountain system in the south, rising west towards Macgillycuddy's Reeks, creates a landscape of ridges and valleys; the lowlands in the east are drained by slow-moving rivers such as the Shannon, Liffey and Slaney; there are long east-to-west valleys in the south.

Climate

Mild and equable, with few extremes of temperature; rainfall is heaviest in the west, often over 3 000mm; it is drier in the east, the Dublin annual average being 785mm.

Government

A President (head of state) is elected for seven years; the National Parliament (*Oireachtas*) includes a House of Representatives (*Dáil Éireann*) of 166 elected members, and a 60-member Senate (*Seanad Éireann*); a Prime Minister is head of government.

Economy

Two thirds of the country is covered by improved agricultural land, sheep and cattle grazing on much of the remainder; mainly mixed pastoral farming with some arable cropping; forestry has been developed since the 1950s; fishing is important; manufacturing includes metals, food, drink, tobacco and textiles; there has been recent growth in light engineering, synthetic fibres, electronics, pharmaceuticals and plastics; hydroelectricity is generated on the main rivers; there are several peat-fired power stations, and the Kinsale natural gas field near Cork; tourism.

History

It was occupied by Goidelic-speaking Celts during the Iron Age, and a high kingship was established c.200AD, its capital being at Tara (Meath). Following conversion to Christianity by St Patrick in the 5c, Ireland became a centre of learning and missionary activity. The south-east was attacked by Vikings from c.800. Henry I of England declared himself Lord of Ireland in 1171, and Anglo-Norman expansion created a Lordship of Ireland which at one point dominated much of the island before being pushed back into Munster and Leinster by a Gaelic revival in 14–15c. Henry VIII took the title 'King of Ireland' in 1542, but direct Crown rule was confined to the area around Dublin known as the Pale, though the Anglo-Norman vassals of the Crown ruled over much more. Elizabethan conquest finally unified the island under English control, which was shaken by a Catholic rebellion during the War of the Three Kingdoms in the 1640s. Parliamentary forces under Oliver Cromwell reconquered Catholic Ireland in 1649–50. The Protestant communities in Ulster continued to survive this turmoil, as they did later on when supporters of the deposed Catholic King James VII and II were later defeated by William III at the Battle of the Boyne (1690). Following a century of suppression, the struggle for Irish freedom developed in the 18–19c, including such revolutionary movements as Wolfe Tone's United Irishmen (1796–8), and later Young Ireland (1848) and the Fenians (1866–7). The Act of Union, uniting Ireland and Britain, came into effect in 1801; the Catholic Relief Act (1829) was a sign of Catholic Emancipation and enabled Catholics to sit in Parliament; and Land Acts (1870–1903) attacked Irish poverty (prior to these acts, the Irish Famine in 1845–7 had drastically reduced the population). Two Home Rule Bills were introduced by Gladstone (1886, 1893), and a third Home Rule Bill was passed in 1914, but never came into effect because of World War I. In 1916 there was an armed rebellion against British rule (the Easter Rising), and in 1919 a republic was proclaimed by Sinn Féin. A partition proposed by Britain in 1920 was largely ignored by the Irish Republic. In 1921 a treaty gave Ireland dominion status as the Irish Free State, subject to the right of Northern Ireland to opt out; this right was exercised, and a frontier was agreed in 1925. The Irish constitution of 1937 renamed the country Éire and declared the country a sovereign, independent and democratic state with a directly elected President, a restored but weakened Senate, and a Dáil Éireann elected by proportional representation. All constitutional links between the Irish Republic and the UK were severed with the declaration of the republic in 1948. This came into effect in 1949 with the Republic of Ireland Act, which changed the relationship between Ireland and Britain. The republic retained special citizenship arrangements and trade preference with Britain, but left the Commonwealth of Nations. The Westminster parliament passed the Ireland Act (1949) which confirmed a special relationship for Irish citizens in the UK, but declared that Northern Ireland would remain part of the UK until its citizens declared otherwise. Since 1973 the Irish Republic has been a member of the EC. Since the 1990s Irish Prime Ministers Albert Reynolds (1992–4), John Bruton (1994–7) and Bertie Ahern (1997–) have been involved in the Northern Ireland peace process. The President of Ireland from 1990 was Mary Robinson. She was succeeded in 1997 by Mary McAleese. The Irish pound or punt was replaced by the Euro in Jan 2002.

⊃ **Isle of Man ▸ United Kingdom**

Religions

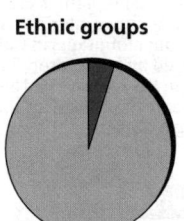

- Christianity 91% (RC 88%, Prot 3%)
- none/unaffiliated 5%
- others 4%

Ethnic groups

- Irish 95%
- others 5%

Nations of the World

ISRAEL

Official name State of Israel
Local name Medinat Israel
Location A democratic republic in the Middle East, with Tel Aviv-Jaffa as its capital, bounded to the north by Lebanon; to the north-east by Syria; to the east by Jordan; to the south-west by Egypt; and to the west by the Mediterranean Sea
Area 20 770 sq km/8 017 sq mi

Capital Tel Aviv-Jaffa
Chief towns Jerusalem, Haifa, Beersheba, Acre, Holon
Population 5 750 000 (1999e)
Time zone GMT +2
Currency 1 Shekel (IS) = 100 agora
Languages Hebrew, Arabic

Physical description

Extends 420km/260mi north to south; width varies from 20km/12mi to 116km/72mi; the narrow coastal plain is crossed by several rivers; mountainous interior, rising to 1 208m at Mount Meron; mountains in Galilee and Samaria, dissected by faults, dropping east to below sea level in the Jordan–Red Sea Rift Valley; the River Jordan forms part of the eastern border; the Negev Desert in the south occupies c.60% of the country's area.

Climate

Typically Mediterranean in the north and central area, with hot, dry summers and warm, wet winters; average temperatures at Tel Aviv-Jaffa are 14°C in January and 27°C in July; average annual rainfall is 550mm; rainfall is heavier inland, with occasional snow; low rainfall in Negev, decreasing in the south.

Government

A parliamentary democracy with a Prime Minister, a Cabinet and a unicameral 120-member Parliament (*Knesset*), elected for a four-year term; the President is elected for a maximum of two five-year terms.

Economy

Over 90% of exports are industrial products, including polished diamonds, transportation equipment, plastics, processed foods, textiles, chemicals, electronics, medical engineering, agricultural equipment, computers, alternative energy sources; major tourist area, primarily to the religious centres; copper, potash, phosphates; citrus fruits, melons, avocados, flowers, cotton, sugar beet, vegetables, olives, tobacco, bananas, beef and dairy products; a world leader in agro-technology, with areas of intensive cultivation; major irrigation schemes, including the 'National Water Carrier' project to transfer water from Lake Tiberias in the north to the Negev Desert in the south; the *kibbutz* system produces c.40% of food output, but in recent years has turned increasingly towards industry.

Religions

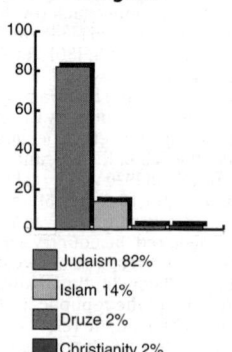

- Judaism 82%
- Islam 14%
- Druze 2%
- Christianity 2%

History

Zionists settled in Palestine in the 1880s when it was under Ottoman rule, and the British declared support for a Jewish 'national home' there in 1917. However, Zionist ambitions were never satisfied under the League of Nations mandate given to Britain (1918–47), although Jewish immigration in the 1930s and 1940s increased greatly due to Nazi persecution. The British evacuated Palestine after World War II, unable to control a new flood of Jewish immigration heavily supported by the USA. Tension between Arabs and Jews led the UN in 1947 to support the formation of two states in Palestine, one Jewish and the other Arab. When the Arab side rejected this, David Ben-Gurion announced the creation of the independent State of Israel on 14 May 1948. Military conflict with sur-

ounding countries ensued in which Israeli forces were victor-
ous. Further wars took place in 1956 (Suez Crisis) and 1967 (Six-
Day War), when Israel gained control of the Gaza Strip, the Sinai
Peninsula as far as the Suez Canal, the West Bank of the River Jordan including the eastern sector of Jerusalem, and the Golan
Heights in Syria; these areas have since been referred to as the
occupied territories'. Wars also broke out in 1973 (Yom Kippur
War) and in 1982 (Lebanon War), which forced the PLO to leave
Beirut in 1982–5. In contrast, a peace agreement between Israel
and Egypt's President, Anwar Sadat, was reached in 1979. During
the 1990s there were several attempts to launch peace talks to re-
olve the Israeli–Palestinian conflict. A declaration of principles
on Palestinian self-rule in the occupied territories was announced in 1993, Jericho and the Gaza Strip were given autonomous status in 1994–5, and Israel and Jordan signed a peace

Ethnic groups

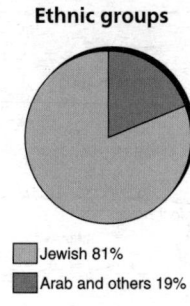

Jewish 81%
Arab and others 19%

Nations of the World

reaty in 1994. However, in 1996 there were recurrent suicide bombings in Israeli cities, an armed
truggle in south Lebanon, and more fighting between West Bank Palestinians and Israeli forces.
n 1997 Israeli troops were withdrawn from the West Bank town of Hebron, in accordance with the
erms of the 1993 Oslo peace agreement which required the handover of seven major West Bank
owns to Palestinian rule, but soon afterwards peace was under threat again when the government's policy of building Jewish settlements in Arab areas ignited violence, and there were further
bomb attacks by terrorist fundamentalists. In 1999 Netanyahu's Likud Party was defeated by the
Labour Party led by Ehud Barak. The following year, Barak ordered the withdrawal of troops from
outhern Lebanon and was involved in negotiations with Yasser Arafat in an attempt to resolve the
ssue of the administration of Jerusalem. Elections in Feb 2001 returned the right winger Ariel Sharon
as Prime Minister. Despite ongoing international efforts the conflict continues, marked by Palestinian
uicide bombings in Israel, and Israeli military incursions into Palestinian areas.

ITALY

Official name Italian Republic
Local name Repubblica Italiana
Location A republic in southern Europe,
comprising the boot-shaped peninsula
extending south into the Mediterranean Sea, as
well as Sicily, Sardinia and some smaller islands.
It is bounded to the north-west by France; to the
north by Switzerland and Austria; and to the
north-east by Slovenia
Area 301 225 sq km/116 273 sq mi

Capital Rome
Chief towns Milan, Turin, Genoa, Naples,
Bologna, Palermo, Florence, Venice
Population 56 735 000 (1999e)
Time zone GMT +1
Currency 1 Euro (€) = 100 cents
Language Italian; German is also spoken in the
Trentino-Alto Adige, French in Valle d'Aosta, and
Slovene in Trieste-Gorizia

Physical description

The Italian peninsula extends c.800km/500mi south-east from the Lombardy plains; the Apen-
ines rise to peaks above 2 000m; the Alps in the north form an arc from Nice in France to Fiume,
and the highest peaks along the Swiss–French frontier are at Mont Blanc (4 807m) and the Matter-
horn (4 477m); the broad, fertile Lombardo–Venetian plain is in the basin of the River Po; there are
everal lakes at the foot of the Alps, including Maggiore, Como and Garda; it is flat and marshy on
the Adriatic coast in the north; on the Riviera to the west, coastal mountains descend steeply to the
igurian Sea; chief rivers include the Po, Tiber, Arno, Volturno, Liri and Adige; the island of Sicily,
eparated from the mainland by the Strait of Messina, includes the limestone massifs of Monti
Nebrodi and the volcanic cone of Mount Etna (3 323m), one of three active volcanos in the coun-
ry: the others are Vesuvius (1 277m) and Stromboli (926m); Sardinia rises to 1 835m at Monti del
Gennargentu.

Climate

There is great variation with relief and latitude; rainfall on the River Po plain is well distributed
throughout the year with hot, sunny summers and short, cold winters; the higher areas of penin-
ular Italy are cold, wet, often snowy; coastal regions have a Mediterranean climate, with warm,
wet winters and hot, dry summers; the west coast is warmer than the Adriatic coast and receives
more rainfall; there are long hours of sunshine in the extreme south during summer.

Government

A democratic republic since 1946, when the monarchy was abolished; Parliament consists of a
630-member Chamber of Deputies and a 315-member Senate, both bodies elected for five years;
a President serves a seven-year term and appoints a Prime Minister.

Nations of the World

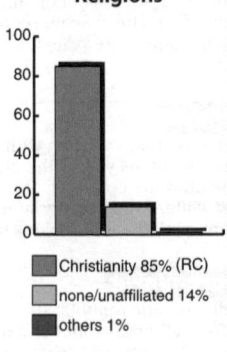

Europe

GERMANY
AUSTRIA
SWITZERLAND
LIECH.
A l p s
L. Maggiore
L. Como
D o l o m i t e s
Mont Blanc
Adige
L. Garda
SLOVENIA
Milan
ITALY
Po
Venice
CROATIA
Turin
A
Bologna
BOSNIA-
HERZEGOVINA
Genoa
San Marino
FRANCE
Arno
Florence
Adriatic Sea
Ligurian Sea
Elba
Corsica
(France)
n
n
Tiber
i
Sardinia
Rome
n
e
Volturno
s
Naples
Vesuvius
Cagliari
Tyrrhenian Sea
Stromboli
M e d i t e r r a n e a n   S e a
Palermo
Ionian Sea
Etna
Sicily
ALGERIA
TUNISIA
Pantelleria
0   100 Miles
0   100 KM

Economy

Industry is largely concentrated in the north while the poorer agricultural region is in the south; agriculture, wine, machine tools, vehicles, textiles, foodstuffs, chemicals, footwear, tourism.

History

In pre-Roman times, Italy, which was not a concept covering the racially-mixed Po Valley, was inhabited by Etruscans in the north, Latins in the centre of the country and Greeks in the south. Most regions were part of the Roman Empire by the 3c BC; barbarian tribes invaded in the 4c, and the last Roman emperor was deposed in AD476. Italy was later ruled by the Lombards and by the Franks under Charlemagne, who was crowned Emperor of the Romans in 800. It became part of the Holy Roman Empire under Otto I, the Great in 962, and conflict between popes and emperors continued throughout the Middle Ages. There were disputes between Guelfs and Ghibellines in the 12c. Italy was divided amongst five

Religions

- Christianity 85% (RC)
- none/unaffiliated 14%
- others 1%

main powers during the 14–15c (Kingdom of Naples, Duchy of Milan, republics of Florence and Venice, and the papacy). The country made a major contribution to European culture through the Renaissance. Four satellite republics were set up after a successful French invasion during the wars of the French Revolution, and Napoleon I was crowned King of Italy in 1805. The 19c saw the upurge of liberalism and nationalism (the Risorgimento); unification was achieved by 1870 under Victor Emmanuel II of Sardinia, aided by Cavour and Garibaldi; colonies were established in Eritrea (1870–89) and Somaliland (1889), but the attempt to secure a protectorate over Abyssinia was defeated at the Battle of Adowa 1896). During World War I, Italy fought alongside the Allies. The fascist movement brought Mussolini to power in 1922, and he led the Conquest of Abyssinia (1935–6) and occupation of Albania 1939). The alliance with Hitler in World War II led to the end of the Italian Empire. Political instability has resulted in over 45 governments in power since the formation of the democratic republic in 1946. Italy was a founding member of the EEC in 1958. Following corruption scandals in the early 1990s, a right-wing government was elected in 1994, causing fears in Europe about a resurgence of the extreme Right. However, in 1996 the elections were won by a left-wing coalition led by Prime Minister Romano Prodi, who in 1999 resigned to become President of the European Commission. In 2001 a new centre right coalition government was formed under Silvio Berlusconi. The lira was replaced by the Euro in Jan 2002.

Ethnic groups

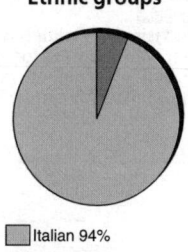

Italian 94%
others 6%

Nations of the World

JAMAICA

Official name Jamaica
Local name Jamaica
Location An island nation of the West Indies in the Caribbean Sea
Area 10 957 sq km/4 229 sq mi
Capital Kingston
Chief towns Montego Bay, Spanish Town
Population 2 652 000 (1999e)

Time zone GMT –5
Currency 1 Jamaican Dollar (J$) = 100 cents
Language English; Jamaican Creole is also spoken
Religions Christianity 61% (Prot 25%, Church of God 21%, RC 6%, others 9%), Rastafarianism 6%, others 15%, none/unaffiliated 18%
Ethnic groups black 90%, East Indian 2%, mixed 7%, others 1%

Physical description

The third-largest island in the Caribbean Sea with a maximum length of 234km/145mi and width varying from 35km/22mi to 82km/51mi; mountainous and rugged particularly in the east, where the Blue Mountains rise to 2 256m; over 100 small rivers, several of which are used for hydroelectric power.

Climate

Humid and tropical climate at sea level, more temperate at higher altitudes; coastal temperatures range from 21°C to 34°C, with an average annual rainfall of 1 980mm; virtually no rainfall on the south and south-west plains; the island lies within the hurricane belt.

Government

A Governor-General appoints a Prime Minister and a Cabinet; a bicameral Parliament consists of an elected 60-member House of Representatives and a nominated 21-member Senate.

Economy

Plantation agriculture still employs about a third of the workforce; sugar, bananas, citrus fruits, coffee, cocoa, ginger, coconuts, pimento; second-largest producer of bauxite in the world; alumina; gypsum; cement; fertilizer; textiles; foodstuffs; rum; chemical products; tourism is the biggest earner of foreign currency.

History

It was visited by Columbus in 1494 and settled by the Spanish in 1509. From 1640 West African slave labour was imported for work on the sugar plantations. Jamaica was occupied by the British in 1655. Self-government was introduced in 1944, and independence was achieved in 1962 under Prime Minister Alexander Bustamante. The British monarch remains chief of state.

JAPAN

Official name Japan
Local name Nihon
Location An island state off the east coast of Asia. It comprises the four large islands of Hokkaido, Honshu, Kyushu and Shikoku, and many small islands
Area 381 945 sq km/147 431 sq mi

Capital Tokyo
Chief towns Yokohama, Osaka, Nagoya, Sapporo, Kyoto, Kobe
Population 126 182 000 (1999e)
Time zone GMT +9
Currency 1 Yen (Y, ¥) = 100 sen
Language Japanese

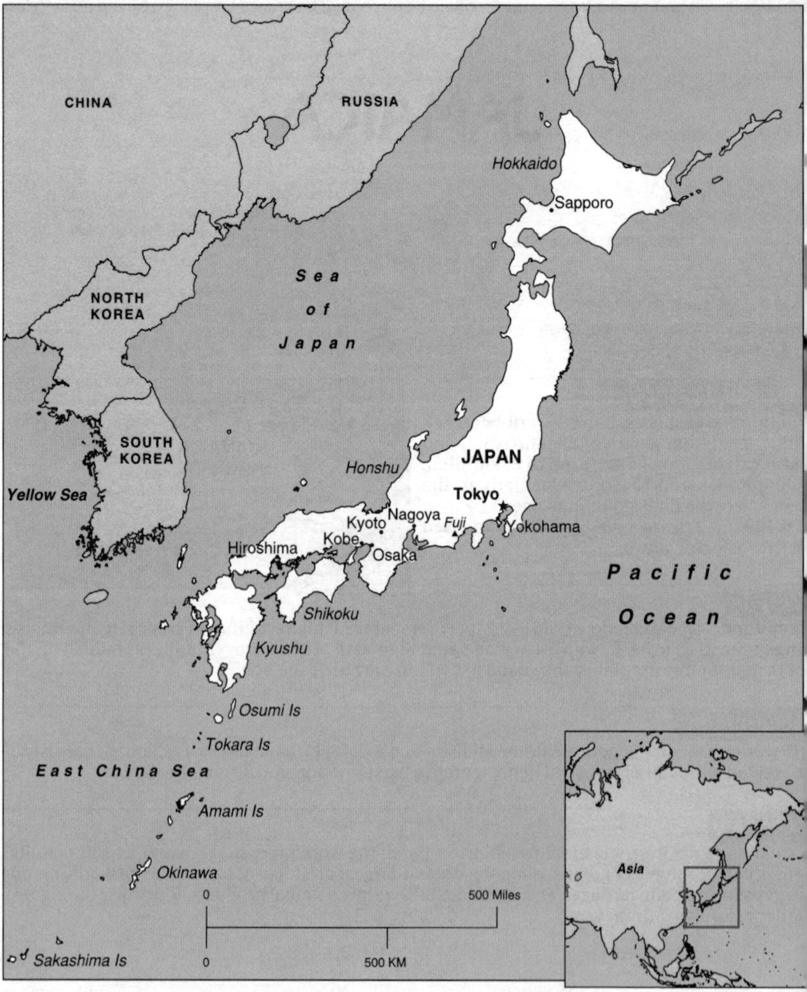

CHINA
RUSSIA
Hokkaido
Sapporo
NORTH KOREA
S e a
o f
J a p a n
SOUTH KOREA
Honshu
JAPAN
Tokyo
Yellow Sea
Kyoto Nagoya *Fuji* Yokohama
Hiroshima Kobe
Osaka
Pacific
Shikoku
Ocean
Kyushu
Osumi Is
Tokara Is
East China Sea
Amami Is
Okinawa
0   500 Miles
Asia
0   500 KM
Sakashima Is

Physical description

The islands consist mainly of steep mountains with many volcanoes; the northernmost island, Hokkaido, has a central range which runs north to south, rising to over 2 000m, falling to coastal uplands and plains; Honshu, the largest island, comprises parallel arcs of mountains bounded by narrow coastal plains and includes the sacred Mount Fuji, rising to 3 776m; the heavily populated Kanto plain lies in the east; the islands of Shikoku and Kyushu in the south-west consist of clusters of low cones and rolling hills, mostly at 1 000–2 000m high; to the south of this, the country tails off into the Ryukyu chain of volcanic islands, of which Okinawa is the largest; earthquakes occur frequently.

Climate

An oceanic climate, influenced by the Asian monsoon; there is heavy winter rainfall on the western coasts of north Honshu and in Hokkaido; in the north there are short, warm summers, and severe winters, with heavy snow; Akita in north Honshu has an average daily temperature of −5°–2°C in January, 19°–28°C in August, and rainfall in this area is a minimum of 104mm in February–March and a maximum of 211mm in September; there is variable winter weather throughout Japan, especially in the north and west; typhoons occur in summer and early autumn; there are mild and almost subtropical winters, with light rainfall, in south Honshu, Shikoku and Kyushu; the summer heat is often oppressive, especially in the cities.

Government

A constitutional monarchy with an Emperor as head of state, and a Prime Minister and Cabinet; bicameral Diet (*Kokkai*), with a 512-member House of Representatives (*Shugiin*) elected every four years and a 252-member House of Councillors (*Sangiin*) elected every six years.

Economy

Natural resources are limited, with less than 20% of the land under cultivation; there is intensive crop production, principally of rice; timber; fishing; metallurgy; engineering; electrical goods; electronics industries; vehicles; petrochemicals; ship-building; textiles; chemicals.

History

Originally occupied by the Ainu, in the 4c the country developed from individual communities into small states; by the 5c, the Yamato Dynasty was the most dominant. Its culture was strongly influenced by China (8–12c). It was united and ruled by shoguns from 1603 by the Tokugawa Dynasty of military dictators, who tamed the feudal lords. Contact with the West was severely restricted until the visit of the US Commodore, Matthew Perry in 1853. After the Meiji Restoration in 1868, successful wars were waged with China in 1894–5, and Russia in 1904–5. Japan annexed Korea in 1910, occupied Manchuria in 1931–2 and entered World War II with a surprise attack on the US fleet at Pearl Harbor, Hawaii, in 1941. It occupied British and Dutch possessions in South-East Asia 1941–2), and was pushed back during 1943–5. Atomic bombs were dropped on Hiroshima and Nagasaki in 1945. There was strong economic growth in the 1960s, which was severely affected by the international oil crisis in the 1970s. Investment in other countries led to increased economic success and a trade surplus with most trading partners, however Japan suffered in the global recession of the 1990s, and its huge banking sector was put in deep trouble. In 1993 a new coalition government was formed to replace that of the Liberal Democratic Party (LDP). Three coalitions ruled in turn during 1993–5, and in 1996 the LDP's Ryutaro Hashimoto became Prime Minister of a new coalition. Following a sharp downturn in the economy, he was replaced in 1998 by Keizo Obuchi. Obuchi died in 2000 and Yoshiro Mori was put in power, serving until his replacement in 2001 by Junichiro Koizumi.

Religions

- Shintoism and Buddhism 84%
- others 15%
- Christian 1%

Ethnic groups

- Japanese 99%
- others 1%

Nations of the World

Nations of the World

JORDAN

Official name Hashemite Kingdom of Jordan
Local name Al'Urdunn
Location A kingdom in the Middle East, bounded to the north by Syria; to the north-east by Iraq; to the east and south by Saudi Arabia; and to the west by Israel
Area 96 188 sq km/37 129 sq mi
Capital Amman

Chief towns Irbid, Zarqa, Salt, Karak, Aqaba
Population 4 561 000 (1999e)
Time zone GMT +2
Currency 1 Jordanian Dinar (JD) = 1 000 fils
Language Arabic
Religions Islam 94% (Sunni), Christianity 6%
Ethnic groups Arab 98%, others 2%

Physical description

Divided north to south by the Red Sea–Jordan rift valley, much of which lies below sea level; the lowest point is −400m at the Dead Sea; the main area of irrigated cultivation is at El Ghor in the north; the sides of the rift rise steeply through undulating hill country to heights above 1 000m; land levels out to the Syrian desert in the east, sandy in the south, hard and rocky further north; the highest point is Mount Ram (1 754m).

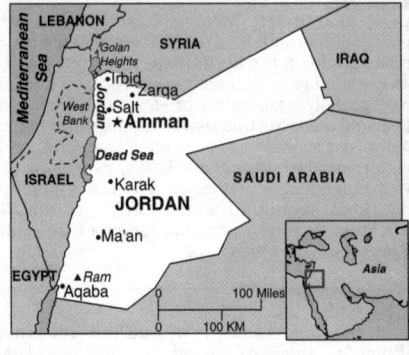

Climate

c.90% of Jordan is desert, annual rainfall is below 200mm; summers there are uniformly hot and sunny; typically Mediterranean climate elsewhere, with hot, dry summers and cool, wet winters; temperatures at Amman are 7°C (January), 25°C (July); average annual rainfall is 290mm.

Government

The monarch is head of state and of government; Parliament consists of a 30-member Senate and an elected 80-member House of Representatives.

Economy

Oil, cement, potash, phosphate (world's third largest exporter); light manufacturing; cereals, vegetables, citrus fruits, olives; major investment in Jordan valley agricultural development.

History

Jordan was part of the Roman Empire, and came under Arab control in the 7c. It was the centre of Crusader activity in the 11–12c, and part of the Turkish Empire from the 16c until World War I, after which the area was divided into Palestine (west of the River Jordan) and Transjordan (east of the River Jordan), both administered by Britain. Transjordan gained independence in 1946, and the British mandate over Palestine ended in 1948, with the newly created State of Israel fighting to control the West Bank area. An armistice in 1949 left Jordan in control of the West Bank, and the West and East Banks united within Jordan in 1951. However, Israel took control of the West Bank after the Six-Day War in 1967. Following attempts by the Jordanian army to expel Palestinian guerrillas from the West Bank in 1970–1, civil war erupted; an amnesty was declared in 1973, and claims to the West Bank were ceded to the PLO (Palestine Liberation Organization) in 1974. Legal and administrative links with the West Bank were cut in 1988, prompting the PLO to establish a government-in-exile, which as a result of the ongoing Middle East peace process was allowed a measure of self-rule in certain areas in 1994. A ban on political parties in Jordan was ended in 1991 and the first multi-party elections since 1956 took place in 1993. The monarch, who is head of state and of government, was King Hussein from 1952 to 1998. On his death he was succeeded by his son, Abdullah II.

KAZAKHSTAN

Official name Republic of Kazakhstan
Local name Kazak Respublikasy
Location A republic in western Asia, bounded to the north by Russia; to the south by Turkmenistan, Uzbekistan and Kyrgyzstan; to the east by China; and to the west by the Caspian Sea
Area 2 717 300 sq km/1 048 878 sq mi
Capital Astana
Chief towns Karaganda, Semipalatinsk, Chimkent, Petropavlovsk
Population 16 825 000 (1999e)
Time zone GMT +4/6
Currency 1 Tenge = 100 tiyn
Language Kazakh
Religions Islam 48%, Christianity 46% (Orthodox 44%, Prot 2%), others 6%
Ethnic groups Kazakh 46%, Russian 35%, Ukrainian 5%, German 4%, others 10%

Physical description

Steppeland in the north gives way to desert in the south; the lowest elevation is near the eastern shore of the Caspian Sea (132m below sea level); mountain ranges are situated in the east and south-east; the chief rivers are the Irtysh, Syrdarya, Ural, Emba and Ili; the largest lake is Lake Balkhash; the Aral Sea is located on the south border with Uzbekistan.

Climate

Continental; hot summers and cold winters.

Government

A President may appoint important ministerial positions but does not have the power to dissolve the government, and the government does not have power to impeach the President.

Economy

Coal, iron ore, bauxite, copper, nickel, oil; oil refining, metallurgy, heavy engineering, chemicals, leatherwork, footwear, food processing; cotton, fruit, grain, sheep.

History

Formerly the home of nomadic Kazakhs and ruled by Mongol khans, it was taken over by Tsarist Russia during the 19c. In the early 20c a nationalist movement was violently suppressed. The country became the Kazakh Autonomous Soviet Socialist Republic and joined the USSR in 1936. In 1991 it became an independent republic under President Nursultan Nazarbaev, leader of the the Socialist Party, the renamed former Communist Party, and became a founding member of the CIS (Commonwealth of Independent States).

KENYA

Official name Republic of Kenya
Local name Jamhuri ya Kenya
Location A republic in East Africa, bounded to the south by Tanzania; to the west by Uganda; to the north-west by Sudan; to the north by Ethiopia; to the north-east by Somalia; and to the east by the Indian Ocean
Area 564 162 sq km/217 766 sq mi
Capital Nairobi
Chief towns Mombasa, Kisumu, Nakuru, Malindi
Population 28 809 000 (1999e)
Time zone GMT +3
Currency 1 Kenyan shilling (Ksh) = 100 cents
Languages English and Swahili, with many tribal languages spoken
Religions Christianity 66% (Prot 38%, RC 28%), traditional beliefs 26%, Islam 7%, others 1%
Ethnic groups Kikuyu 22%, Luhya 14%, Luo 13%, Kalenjin 12%, Kamba 11%, others 28%

Physical description

Crossed by the Equator; the south-west plateau rising to 600–3 000m includes Mount Kenya (5 200m) and the Aberdare range; the Great Rift Valley in the west runs north to south; dry, arid semi-desert in the north, generally under 600m; Lake Turkana, the largest body of water, is situated in the north; the Chalbi Desert lies south-east of the lake; the coastal strip south of the River Tana is typified by coral reefs, mangrove swamps and small island groups.

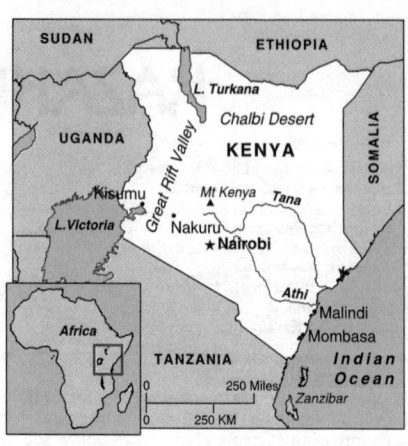

Climate

Tropical climate on the coast, with high temperatures and humidity; in Mombasa the average annual rainfall is 1 200mm, the average daily temperatures are 27°–31°C; annual rainfall decreases from 500mm in the south to 250mm in the far north; frost and snow lie in the high mountains.

Government

Governed by a President elected for a five-year term, with a unicameral National Assembly of 202 members.

Economy

Agriculture accounts for one third of the national income; coffee, tea, sisal, pyrethrum, cashew nuts, rice, wheat, maize, sugar cane; food processing, textiles; chemicals; cement; steel; paper; metal products; car assembly; oil refining; consumer goods; tobacco; rubber; reserves of soda ash, fluorspar, salt, diatomite, limestone, lead, gemstones, silver, gold. 14 national parks attract large numbers of tourists.

History

Anthropologists have found very early fossil hominids in the region. The coast was settled by Arabs in the 7c, and the country came under Portuguese control in the 16–17c, and under British control as an East African Protectorate in 1895. After it became a British colony in 1920, an independence movement led to the Mau Mau rebellion in 1952–60. Led by KANU (the Kenya African National Union), it gained independence in 1963 under Prime Minister Jomo Kenyatta, who became President when Kenya became a republic in 1964. He was succeeded on his death in 1978 by Daniel T arap Moi. In 1991 a multi-party system was legalized. Moi won the elections of 1992 and 1998 amid allegations of electoral fraud, and during the 1990s there were sporadic outbreaks of violent unrest fuelled by demands for constitutional change. Moi's long rule came to an end in Dec 2001, when KANU lost elections to opposition parties and the National Rainbow Coalition's Mwai Kibaki was elected President.

KIRIBATI

Official name Republic of Kiribati
Local name Kiribati
Location A group of 33 low-lying coral islands scattered over c. 3 million sq km/1.2 million sq mi of the central Pacific Ocean
Area 717 sq km/277 sq mi
Capital Bairiki (on Tarawa)

Population 85 500 (1999e)
Time zone GMT –12
Currency 1 Australian Dollar ($A) = 100 cents
Languages English, I-Kiribati
Religions Christianity 91% (RC 53%, Prot 38%), Baha'i 3%, others 6%
Ethnic groups Micronesian 98%, others 2%

Physical description

The islands seldom rise to more than 4m and usually consist of a reef enclosing a lagoon; Banaba, a solid coral outcrop with a fringing reef, rises to 87m.

Climate

Maritime equatorial climate in the central islands; the islands further north and south are tropical; the average annual temperature is 27°C; the average rainfall varies from 1 020mm near the Equator to 3 050mm in the extreme north and south; the rainy season is from November to April; some islands suffer from periodic drought.

Government

A sovereign and democratic republic, with a President and a 41-member (39 elected) House of Assembly.

Economy

Phosphates; copra, coconuts, bananas, pandanus, breadfruit, papaya; sea fishing.

History

The Gilbert and Ellice Is were proclaimed a British protectorate in 1892; annexed in 1915; the Ellice Is severed links with the Gilbert Is to form a separate dependency called Tuvalu in 1975; Gilbert achieved independence as Kiribati in 1979. In 1999, Kiribati joined the United Nations.

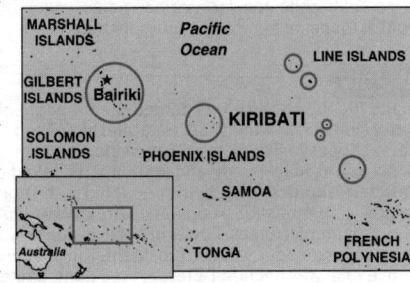

KOREA, NORTH

Official name Democratic People's Republic of Korea
Local name Chosōn Minjujuǔi In'min Konghwaguk
Location A socialist state in eastern Asia, in the northern half of the Korean Peninsula, bounded to the north by China; to the north-east by Russia; to the west by Korea Bay and the Yellow Sea; and to the east by the Sea of Japan
Area 122 098 sq km/47 130 sq mi

Capital Pyongyang
Chief towns Chongjin, Sinuiju, Wonsan, Kaesong
Population 21 386 000 (1999e)
Time zone GMT +9
Currency 1 Won (NKW) = 100 chon
Language Korean
Religions traditional beliefs 16%, Chondogyo 14%, Buddhism 2%, Christianity 1%, none/unaffiliated 67%
Ethnic groups Korean 100%

Physical description

Lies on a high plateau occupying the north part of a mountainous peninsula which projects south-east from China; many areas rise to over 2 000m; the plateau falls north-west to the Yalu River Valley; lower mountains and foothills in the south descend to narrow coastal plains in the east and wider coastal plains in the west.

Climate

Temperate, with warm summers and severely cold winters; rivers freeze for 3–4 months, and ice blocks harbours; daily temperatures at Pyongyang in the west range from −3°C to −13°C in January, and from 20°C to 29°C in July–August; average rainfall in Pyongyang ranges between a minumum of 11mm in February and a maximum of 237mm in July.

Government

Governed by a Supreme People's Assembly of 655 members, elected every four years; power lies in the hands of the Korean Workers' (Communist) Party, which elects a Central Committee, and whose leader was formerly the President. The Constitution was changed in 1998 to abolish the position of President, and the late Kim Il Sung was proclaimed 'Eternal President'. The Chairman of the National Defence Committee is now head of state.

Economy

Traditionally agricultural on low coastal zones in the east and west; extensive destruction during the Korean War, but rapid recovery with Soviet and Chinese aid; Western technology and increased military spending in the 1970s resulted in considerable overseas debts; machine building; chemicals; mining; metallurgy; textiles; food processing; coal, phosphates, iron, magnesium, tungsten, copper, lead, zinc; c.48% of the workforce is employed in agriculture, generally on

Nations of the World

large-scale collective farms; rice, maize, vegetables, wheat, barley, rape, sugar, millet, sorghum, beans, tobacco; livestock; timber; fishing.

History

In the 10c the country was named the Kingdom of Koryo by Wang Kon, founder of the Koryo Dynasty (918–1392) which had its capital at Kaesong (Songdo). It was an abbreviation of the ancient name, Koguryo. The Korean Peninsula was conquered by the Chinese in 1392. In 1895 it was formally annexed by Japan, and after Japan's defeat in World War II it was partitioned along the 38th parallel (latitude 38°N), being occupied in the north by communist Soviet troops and in the south by non-communist US troops. The Korean War (1950–3) was fought between these communist and non-communist forces. Power in North Korea lay in the hands of the Korean Workers' (Communist) Party, whose leader was the President. Kim Il Sung was President from 1972 until his death in 1994, and in 1998 was declared 'Eternal President'; since then, as the Chairman of the National Defence Committee, his son Kim Jong Il has held power. Reunification talks between North and South Korea in 1980 were broken off by North Korea, and there were further summit talks with South Korea in 1990 and, in conditions of near famine for the bulk of the population, in 1997–9. In 2000 Kim Jong Il met his South Korean counterpart, Kim Dae Jung, in the first meeting of North and South Korean leaders in over 50 years. Hopes of reconciliation faded in late 2002, as North Korea's decision to reactivate its nuclear programme led to rising tensions with South Korea, neighbouring states and the USA.

KOREA, SOUTH

Official name Republic of Korea
Local name Taehan-Min'guk
Location A republic in eastern Asia occupying the southern half of the Korean Peninsula, bounded to the west by the Yellow Sea; to the east by the Sea of Japan; to the south by the Korean Strait; and to the north by North Korea, from which it is separated by a demilitarized zone
Area 98 913 sq km/38 180 sq mi
Capital Seoul

Chief towns Inchon, Pusan, Taegu
Population 46 885 000 (1999e)
Time zone GMT +9
Currency 1 Won (W) = 100 jeon
Language Korean
Religions Christianity 51% (Prot 39%, RC 12%), Buddhism 47%, others 2%
Ethnic groups Korean 100%

Physical description

The Taebaek Sanmaek Range runs north to south along the east coast, reaching heights of over 900m; it descends through a series of ridges to broad, undulating coastal lowlands; c.3 000 islands off the west and south coasts; the largest is Cheju do, on which is situated Korea's highest peak, 1 950m.

Climate

Extreme continental climate, with cold winters and hot summers; typhoons possible in the wettest months (June–September); average daily temperatures at Seoul are −9°–0°C (January), 22°–31°C (August); rainfall minimum 20mm (February), maximum 376mm (July).

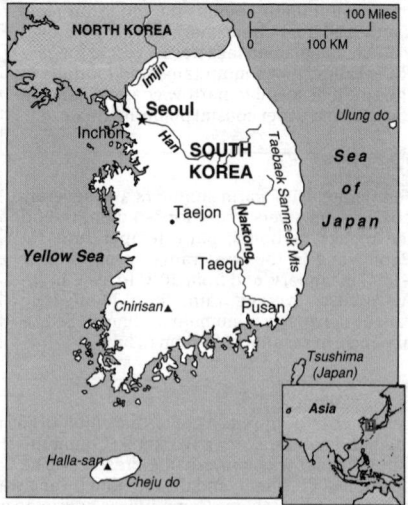

Government

Governed by a President, elected indirectly by a 5 000-member Electoral College for a single five-year term; the President leads and appoints a State Council; a 299-member National Assembly is elected for four years.

Economy

Light consumer goods, with a shift towards heavy industries; petrochemicals, textiles, electrical machinery, footwear, steel, ships, fish; one of the world's largest deposits of tungsten; only one fifth of Korea is suitable for cultivation; rice, barley, wheat, beans, grain, tobacco; cattle, pigs, poultry, fishing.

History

It was ruled by the ancient Choson Dynasty until the 1c BC, and split into three rival kingdoms. These were united in 668 by the Silla Dynasty, which was succeeded by the Koryo Dynasty in 935 and the Yi Dynasty in 1392–1910. Wang Kon, founder of the Koryo Dynasty (918–1392) which had its capital at Kaesong (Songdo), named the country the Kingdom of Koryo. It was an abbreviation of the ancient name, Koguryo. Independence was recognized by China in 1895. It was annexed by Japan in 1910, and on the defeat of Japan after World War II in 1945 the country was entered by Russia (from the north) and the USA (from the south) to enforce the Japanese surrender, dividing the country by the 38th parallel of latitude. In a bid to unite the country, North Korean forces invaded in 1950, sparking off the Korean War (1950–3). There was a military coup in 1961, led by Park Chung-hee, who formed a government but was assassinated in 1979. Reunification talks with North Korea took place in 1990 and 1997–9. By 2000 relations between South and North Korea had thawed, culminating in a summit meeting of South Korean President Kim Dae Jung and north Korea's Kim Jong Il, but tensions rose again in late 2002 over North Korea's nuclear programme and its opposition to the stationing of US troops in South Korea.

KUWAIT

Official name State of Kuwait
Local name Dawlat al-Kuwayt
Location An independent state at the head of the Arabian Gulf, bounded to the north and west by Iraq; to the south by Saudi Arabia; and to the east by the Arabian Gulf
Area 17 818 sq km/6 878 sq mi
Capital Kuwait City
Chief towns Shuwaikh, Mina al Ahmadi

Population 1 991 000 (1999e)
Time zone GMT +3
Currency 1 Kuwaiti Dinar (KD) = 1 000 fils
Language Arabic; English is also widely spoken
Religions Islam 85% (Sunni 45%, Shiite 40%), Hinduism 2%, others 13%
Ethnic groups Kuwaiti 47%, other Arab 36%, South Asian 8%, Iranian 4%, others 5%

Physical description

Consists of the mainland and nine offshore islands; the terrain is flat or gently undulating, rising in the south-west to 271m; the Wadi al Batin runs along the western border with Iraq; terrain is generally stony with a sparse vegetation.

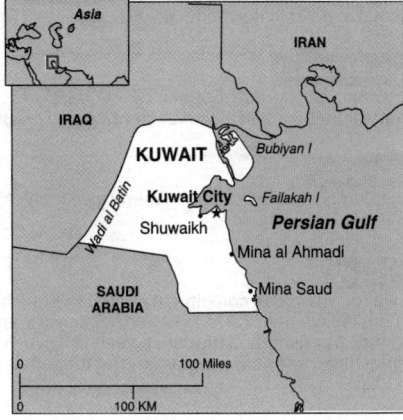

Climate

Hot, dry climate, with an average annual rainfall of 111mm; summer temperatures are very high, often above 45°C (July–August); winter daytime temperatures often exceed 20°C; humidity is generally high; sandstorms are common throughout the year.

Government

The Emir is head of state, governing through an appointed Prime Minister and Council of Ministers. The Emir also has the power to dissolve the 50-member National Assembly.

Economy

Traditionally pearl diving, seafaring, boatbuilding, fishing, nomadic herding; oil discovered in 1938 has made Kuwait a wealthy country but it has suffered economically from the effects of the Gulf War; petrochemicals, fertilizers, construction materials, asbestos, batteries; active programme of economic diversification, creating a post-oil high-technology state; agriculture gradually expanding; dates, citrus fruits, timber, livestock, poultry.

History

The port was founded in the 18c, and the state has been ruled since 1756 by the Sabah Family. Britain became responsible for Kuwait's foreign affairs in 1899. It became a British protectorate in 1914, and fully independent in 1961. The invasion and annexation by Iraq in Aug 1990 led to the

Nations of the World

Gulf War in Jan–Feb 1991, with severe damage to Kuwait City and the infrastructure of the country. The Kuwait government went into exile in Saudi Arabia until the country was liberated in 1991. Major post-war problems included large-scale refugee emigration, the burning of oil wells by Iraq (all capped by Nov 1991) and the pollution of Gulf waters by oil.

KYRGYZSTAN

Official name Republic of Kyrgyzstan
Local name Kyrgyz Respublikasy
Location A mountainous republic in north-east Middle Asia, bounded to the north by Kazakhstan; to the west by Uzbekistan; to the south and south-west by Tajikistan; and to the south-east and east by China.
Area 198 500 sq km/76 621 sq mi
Capital Bishkek
Chief towns Osh, Przhevalsk, Kyzyl-Kiya

Population 4 546 000 (1999e)
Time zone GMT +5
Currency 1 Som (Kgs) = 100 tyiyn
Languages Kyrgyz, Russian
Religions Islam 75%, Christianity 20% (Orthodox), others 5%
Ethnic groups Kyrgyz 55%, Russian 21%, Uzbek 13%, Ukrainian 3%, German 2%, Tatar 2%, others 4%

Physical description

The republic is largely occupied by the Tien Shan Mountains and the highest point is at Pik Pobedy (7439m); the chief river is the Naryn and Lake Issyk-Kul is the largest lake.

Climate

Varies according to location; sub-tropical in the south-west, dry in the north and west, continental to polar in the mountainous east.

Government

A bicameral Supreme Council (*Zhogorku Kenesh*) consists of a 70-member Assembly of People's Representatives and a 35-member Legislative Assembly.

Economy

Metallurgy; machines; coal; natural gas; textiles; food processing; gold; wheat, cotton, tobacco, animal husbandry.

History

It was proclaimed a constituent republic within the USSR in 1936, and in 1991 gained independence under President Askar Akayev and became a member of the CIS (Commonwealth of Independent States). A constitution introduced in 1993 advocated respect for the international and moral principles of law and human rights, and for the beliefs of Islam. The first multi-party elections were held in 1995.

LAOS

Official name Lao People's Democratic Republic
Local name Lao
Location A landlocked republic in South-East Asia, bounded to the east by Vietnam; to the south by Cambodia; to the west by Thailand and Myanmar; and to the north by China
Area 236 800 sq km/91 405 sq mi
Capital Vientiane
Chief towns Luang Prabang, Pakse, Savannakhét

Population 5 407 000 (1999e)
Time zone GMT +7
Currency 1 Kip (Kp) = 100 at
Language Lao
Religions Buddhism 76%, traditional beliefs 20%, Christianity 2% (Prot 1%, RC 1%), Islam 1%, Chinese folk religion 1%
Ethnic groups Lao Loum 68%, Lao Theung 22%, Lao Soung 9%, others 1%

Physical description

A landlocked country on the Indochinese Peninsula; dense jungle and rugged mountains in the east, rising to 2 751m; the Mekong River flows north west–SE, following much of the west frontier with Thailand.

Climate

Monsoonal with heavy rain in May–September; hot and dry February–April; average annual temperatures in Vientiane are 14°–34°C.

Government

Headed by a President and governed by a Prime Minister, who is also secretary-general of the Central Committee of the Lao People's Revolutionary Party.

Economy

Agricultural economy suffered severely in the Civil War; rice, coffee, tobacco, cotton, spices, opium; tin, iron ore, potash; forestry, rubber; cigarettes, matches, textiles, foodstuffs, energy.

Nations of the World

History

It was discovered by Europeans in the 17c, dominated by Thailand in the 19c, and became a French protectorate in 1893. Occupied by the Japanese in World War II, it gained independence from France in 1949. Civil war raged in 1953–75, between the Lao government, supported by the USA, and the communist-led Patriotic Front (Pathet Lao, now the Lao People's Revolutionary Party, LPRP), supported by North Vietnam. In 1975 the monarchy was abolished and a communist republic was established in 1975 with the Pathet Lao leader, Prince Souphanouvong, as President until he retired in 1986.

LATVIA

Official name Republic of Latvia
Local name Latvijas Republika
Location A republic in north-eastern Europe, bounded to the west by the Baltic Sea; to the north-west by the Gulf of Riga; to the north by Estonia; to the east by Russia; and to the south-east by Belarus and Lithuania
Area 63 700 sq km/24 600 sq mi
Capital Riga
Chief towns Daugavpils, Liepaja

Population 2 354 000 (1999e)
Time zone GMT +2
Currency 1 Lat (Ls) = 100 santims
Language Latvian
Religions Christianity, predominantly Lutheran Protestant, with Roman Catholic and Orthodox minorities
Ethnic groups Latvian 57%, Russian 31%, Belarusian 5%, Ukrainian 4%, others 3%

Physical description

A flat, glaciated area; the north-west coast is indented by the Gulf of Riga; the chief river is the Daugava; over 40% of Latvia is forested.

Climate

Moderate winters; cool, rainy summers.

Government

Parliament elects a President who, with Parliament's agreement, appoints a Prime Minister; the Prime Minister and Parliament exercise executive power within a democratic system.

Economy

Machines, metalworking, instruments, electrical engineering, electronics; chemicals; furniture; knitwear; food processing; fishing; cattle, pigs, oats, barley, rye, potatoes, flax.

History

Incorporated into Russia in 1721, it became an independent state in 1918, and was proclaimed a Soviet Socialist Republic in 1940. It was occupied by Germany during World War II. In the 1980s a new nationalist movement grew up, and in 1990 independence talks began with the USSR. Independence was declared in 1991 under President Anatolijs Gorbunovs, who was succeeded in 1993 by Guntis Ulmanis. In 1999 he was succeeded by Vaira Vike-Freiberga. The last Russian troops left Latvia in 1994, but tensions remain between the Russian and Latvian communities. In 2002 Latvia was formally invited to join NATO and the EU.

LEBANON

Official name Republic of Lebanon
Local name Al-Lubnān
Location A republic on the eastern coast of the Mediterranean Sea, south-west Asia, bounded to the north and east by Syria, and to the south by Israel
Area 10 452 sq km/4 034 sq mi
Capital Beirut
Chief towns Tripoli, Saida, Zahle

Population 3 563 000 (1999e)
Time zone GMT +2
Currency 1 Lebanese Pound/Livre (LL, LS) = 100 piastres
Language Arabic
Religions Islam 69%, Christianity 30%, Druze 1%
Ethnic groups Arab 95%, Armenian 4%, others 1%

Physical description

The narrow Mediterranean coastal plain rises gradually east to the Lebanon Mountains, which extend along most of the country; peaks include the Qornet es Saouda (3 087m); the arid eastern slopes fall abruptly to the fertile El Beqaa plateau (c.1 000m); the Anti-Lebanon range lies in the east; the River Litani flows south between the ranges.

Climate

Mediterranean, varying with altitude, with hot, dry summers and warm, moist winters; average rainfall at Beirut is 920mm and average temperatures are 13°–27°C. It is much cooler and drier in the Beqaa valley and irrigation is essential.

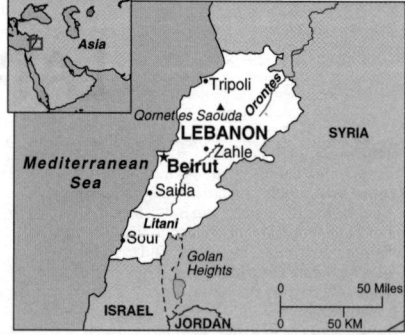

Government

The constitution provides for a Council of Ministers, a President (a Maronite Christian elected for a six-year term), a Prime Minister (a Sunni Muslim), a Cabinet, and a 128-member Parliament equally divided between Christians and Muslims; a timetable for militia disarmament was introduced in 1991.

Economy

The commercial and financial centre of the Middle East until the civil war, which severely damaged the economic infrastructure and reduced industrial and agricultural production; oil refinng; cement; textiles; chemicals; food processing; service industries; citrus fruits, apples, grapes, bananas, sugar beet, olives, wheat; the tourist industry has virtually collapsed; irrigation projects are under way to harness the waters of the Litani River.

History

From the 16c until after World War I, it was part of the Ottoman Empire. After the massacre of Roman Catholic Maronites by Muslim Druze in 1861, the Maronite area around Jabal Lubnan was granted special autonomous status. In 1920 the state of Greater Lebanon, based upon Maronite Christian Jabal Lubnan, was created under French mandate, and incorporated the Muslim coastal regions despite great opposition. Lebanon became a constitutional republic in 1926 and gained independence in 1941. Palestinian resistance units were established in Lebanon by the late 1960s, despite government opposition, and Palestinian raids into Israel were followed by Israeli reprisals. Several militia groups developed in the mid-1970s, notably the Shiite Muslim Afwaj al-Muqawama al-Lubnaniya (Amal) and the Muslim Lebanese National Movement (LNM). Palestinian firepower was used to back up the political struggle of the LNM against the Maronite Christian and Sunni Muslim establishment. Muslim and Christian differences grew more intense and from 1975 Lebanon was beset by civil disorder as rival political and religious factions sought to gain control. Palestinian commandos joined the predominantly leftist Muslim side, and the Syrian-dominated Arab Deterrent Force (ADF) was created to prevent Palestinian fighters gaining control. In 1976 Palestinian forces moved from Beirut to southern Lebanon, where the ADF was unable to deploy. West Beirut, also outside government control, became the scene of frequent conflict between opposing militia groups. Meanwhile, Christian militias, backed by Israel, sought to regain control in East Beirut and areas to the north. Following Palestinian terrorist attacks, Israel invaded southern Lebanon in 1978 and 1982, when the Israeli siege of Palestinian and Syrian forces in Beirut led to the withdrawal of Palestinian forces. The unilateral withdrawal of Israeli forces brought clashes between the Druze (backed by Syria) and the Christian Lebanese militia. A cease-fire was announced in late 1982 but was broken many times, and international efforts to achieve a political settlement were unsuccessful. In the mid-1980s rival groups began taking foreigners as hostages, who were gradually released in the early 1990s. Syrian troops entered Beirut in 1988 in an attempt to restore order but were attacked in 1989 by Lebanese troops under General Michel Aoun. The Arab League proposed a peace plan—the Ta'if Accord—which reduced the domination of Maronite Christians in government. A timetable for militia disarmament was introduced in 1991 and government elections took place in 1992, though they were boycotted by many Maronite Christian parties. The Amal and Hizbullah parties gained the most seats and Rafiq al-Hariri became Prime Minister and made plans to rebuild the economy. Clashes between Israeli troops, or the Israeli-backed South Lebanon army, and Hizbullah guerrillas continued in southern Lebanon throughout the 1990s, and despite the withdrawal of Israeli troops from the region in June 2000, border conflicts still persisted. The President of Lebanon has to be a Maronite Christian, the Prime Minister a Sunni Muslim, and the 108-member parliament is equally divided between Christians and Muslims.

LESOTHO

Official name Kingdom of Lesotho
Local name Lesotho
Location An African kingdom completely bounded by South Africa
Area 30 460 sq km/11 758 sq mi
Capital Maseru
Chief towns Mafeteng, Quthing
Population 2 129 000 (1999e)

Time zone GMT +3
Currency 1 Loti (plural Maloti) (M, LSM) = 100 lisente
Languages Sesotho, English; Zulu and Xhosa are also spoken
Religions Christianity 94% (RC 45%, Prot 41%, others 8%), traditional beliefs 6%
Ethnic groups Sotho 99%, others 1%

Physical description

230km/140mi east to west, 200km/120mi north to south; the Drakensberg Mountains lie in the north-east and east and include Lesotho's highest peak, Thabana-Ntlenyana (3 482m); the Mulati Mountains run south to west from the north-east border forming a steep escarpment; the population mainly lives west of the highlands at an altitude of 1 500–1 800m; serious soil erosion, especially in the west; the main rivers are the Orange and the Caledon.

Climate

Mild, dry winters; the warm summer season is October–April; the lowland summer maximum temperature is 32°C, the winter minimum is 7°C; annual average rainfall is 725mm.

Government

A hereditary monarchy dedicated to a multi-party democratic constitution; the monarchy lost effective power in 1990 in the transition to democracy.

Economy

Based on intensive agriculture and male contract labour working in South Africa; maize, sorghum, wheat, peas, beans, barley, cattle; diamonds; food processing; textiles; electrical consumer goods; carpets; pharmaceuticals; jewellery; crafts; tractor assembly; wool, mohair.

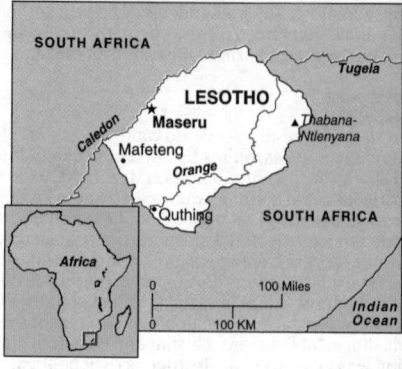

History

Lesotho was originally inhabited by hunting and gathering San (Bushmen). Bantu peoples arrived in the 16c, and the nation of the Basotho was organized in 1824 by Moshoeshoe I. After fighting both the Afrikaners and the British, Moshoeshoe put his country under British protection as Basutoland in 1868, and it was administered until 1880 from the Cape Colony. In 1884 it came under direct control of the British government as a British High Commission Territory. The Kingdom of Lesotho gained independence as a hereditary monarchy within the Commonwealth of Nations in 1966. The paramount chief serves as king, though the monarchy lost effective power in 1990 in the transition to democracy. King Moshoeshoe II, who had lost the throne to his eldest son Letsie III in 1990, but had regained it in 1995, died in 1996 and was again succeeded by Letsie III.

LIBERIA

Official name Republic of Liberia
Local name Liberia
Location A tropical republic in West Africa, bounded to the north-west by Sierra Leone; to the north by Guinea; to the east by the Côte d'Ivoire; and to the south by the Atlantic Ocean
Area 113 370 sq km/43 760 sq mi
Capital Monrovia
Chief towns Harper, Greenville, Buchanan, Robertsport

Population 2 924 000 (1999e)
Time zone GMT
Currency 1 Liberian Dollar (L$) = 100 cents
Language English; many local languages are also spoken
Religions Christianity 68%, Islam 14%, traditional beliefs 10%, others 8%
Ethnic groups Kpelle 19%, Bassa 16%, Grebo 8%, Gio 8%, Kru 6%, Mano 6%, others 37%

Physical description

Low coastal belt with lagoons, beaches, and mangrove marshes; a rolling plateau (500–800m) with grasslands and forest; land rises inland to mountains, reaching 1752m at Mount Nimba; rivers cut south-west down through the plateau.

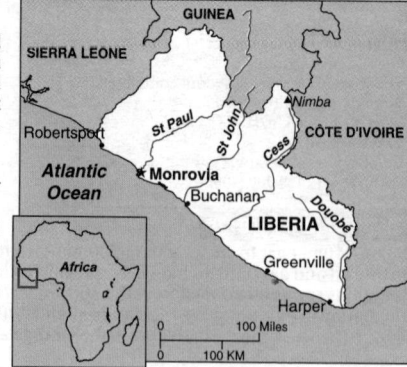

Climate

Equatorial climate, with high temperatures and abundant rainfall; rainfall declines from south to north; high humidity during the rainy season (April–September), especially on the coast; the average annual rainfall at Monrovia is 4150mm.

Government

The constitution introduced in 1986 provides for a bicameral National Assembly, comprising a 26-member Senate and a 64-member House of Representatives, both serving four-year terms.

Economy

...ased on minerals, especially iron ore; gold, diamonds, platinum group metals, barite, titanium, ...rconium, rare-earth metals, clay; two thirds of the population rely on subsistence agriculture; ...ubber, timber, palm oil, rice, cassava, coffee, cocoa, coconuts; the largest merchant fleet in the ...orld, including the registration of many foreign ships.

History

...lapped by the Portuguese in the 15c, it originated as a result of the activities of the philanthropic ...merican Colonization Society wishing to establish a homeland for former slaves. The country ...as first settled in 1822, and constituted as the Free and Independent Republic of Liberia in 1847. ...military coup and the assassination of the President in 1980 established a military government ...alled a People's Redemption Council, with a chairman (Samuel Doe) and a cabinet. Doe's National Democratic Party of Liberia formed the government in the mid-1980s under a new constitution, and Doe became President in 1986. Dissatisfaction with Doe's autocratic and corrupt rule ...esulted in civil war in 1990 and the intervention of an ECOWAS (Economic Community of West ...frican States) peace-keeping force. A cease-fire was agreed in 1990, and peace agreements were ...igned in 1993 and 1995, but the peace remained fragile and there were further outbreaks of fac...onal fighting, intensifying from 2001.

LIBYA

Official name Socialist People's Libyan Arab Jamahiriya
Local name Lībyā
Location A north African state, bounded to the north-west by Tunisia; to the west by Algeria; to the south-west by Niger; to the south by Chad; to the south-east by Sudan; to the east by Egypt; and to the north by the Mediterranean Sea
Area 1 758 610 sq km/678 823 sq mi

Capital Tripoli
Chief towns Misratah, Benghazi, Tobruk
Population 4 993 000 (1999e)
Time zone GMT +1
Currency 1 Libyan Dinar (LD) = 1 000 dirhams
Language Arabic
Religions Islam 97% (Sunni), others 3%
Ethnic groups Arab and Berber 94%, others 6%

Physical description

...ainly low-lying Saharan desert or semi-de...ert; the land rises in the south to over 2 000m ...n the Tibesti Massif; the highest point, Pic Bette ...2 286m), lies on the Chad frontier; surface ...ater is limited to infrequent oases.

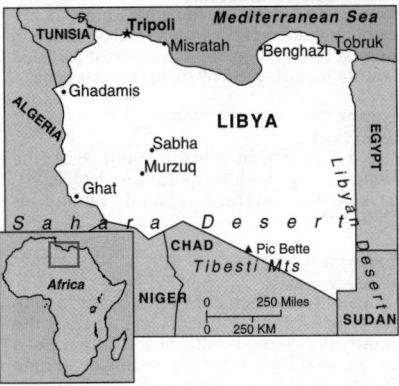

Climate

...lediterranean climate on the coast; Tripoli, re...resentative of the coastal region, has an aver...ge annual rainfall of 385mm with average ...naximum daily temperatures of 16°–30°C; an...ual rainfall in the desert seldom exceeds ...00mm; temperatures in the south are over ...0°C for three months of the year.

Government

...n principle, the State is governed by the masses, through People's Congresses. In practice, power ...ests in the hands of Colonel Gaddafi.

Economy

...Once a relatively poor country, with an agricultural economy based on barley, olives, fruit, dates, ...lmonds and tobacco; the economy was transformed by the discovery of oil and natural gas in ...959; natural gas liquefaction plant, iron ore, gypsum, sulphur; cement, petroleum processing, ...ron, steel, aluminium, food processing, textiles, crafts; cattle, sheep, goats, with nomadic farm...ng in the south.

Nations of the World

History

Controlled at various times by Phoenicians, Carthaginians, Greeks, Vandals and Byzantines, Liby
came under Arab domination during the 7c. It was under Turkish rule from the 16c until the Italian
gained control in 1911, and was named Libya by them in 1934. It suffered heavy fighting durin
World War II, then came under British and French control. It became the independent Kingdom
of Libya in 1951. A military coup established a republic under Muammar Gaddafi in 1969, and i
was governed by a Revolutionary Command Council. Foreign military installations were close
down in the early 1970s, and government policy since the revolution has been based on the promo
tion of Arab unity and the furtherance of Islam. Relations with other countries have been straine
by controversial activities, including the alleged organization of international terrorism: diplo
matic relations were severed by the UK after the murder of a policewoman in London in 1984
Tripoli and Benghazi were bombed by the US Air Force in response to alleged terrorist activity i
1986; two Libyan fighter planes were shot down by aircraft operating with the US Navy off the north
African coast in 1989; and sanctions were imposed by the UN Security Council against Libya in
1992 following its refusal to extradite for trial two men suspected of organizing the bombing of
PanAm aircraft over Lockerbie in 1988. On 5 Apr 1999 the suspects were handed over for trial unde
Scottish Law in the Netherlands, and sanctions were subsequently lifted.

LIECHTENSTEIN

Official name Principality of Liechtenstein
Local name Furstentum Liechtenstein
Location A small independent alpine principality
in central Europe, lying between the Austrian
state of Voralberg to the east and the Swiss
cantons of St Gallen and Graubünden to the west
Area 160 sq km/62 sq mi
Capital Vaduz
Population 32 100 (1999e)

Time zone GMT +1
Currency 1 Swiss Franc (SFr, SwF) = 100 centimes
= 100 rappen
Language German, spoken in the form of an
Alemannic dialect
Religions Christianity 88% (RC 80%, Prot 8%),
others 12%
Ethnic groups Liechtensteiner 62%, Swiss 17%,
Austrian 8%, German 5%, others 8%

Physical description

Bounded to the west by the River Rhine, its valley occupying c.40% of the country; much of
the rest of Liechtenstein consists of forested
mountains, rising to 2 599m in the Grauspitz.

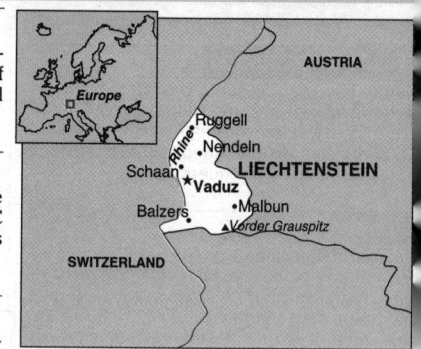

Climate

Mild, influenced by a warm south wind (the
Föhn); average high temperature of 20°–28°C
in summer; average annual rainfall is
1 050–1 200mm.

Government

A constitutional monarchy ruled by the hereditary princes of the House of Liechtenstein; the
country is governed jointly by the Prince, head
of state, and Parliament, consisting of a Prime
Minister, four Councillors, and a unicameral
Parliament (*Landtag*) of 25 members elected
for four years.

Economy

Agriculture includes vegetables, corn, wheat, potatoes, grapes and timber; the industrial sector
developing since the 1950s, is export-based, and centred on specialized and high-tech production; major industries are metalworking, engineering, chemicals, pharmaceuticals, textiles, ceramics and foodstuffs; revenue comes from international banking and finance, postage stamps and
tourism.

History

Originally the medieval counties of Vaduz and Schellenberg, this small territory came into the ands of the princes of Liechtenstein between 1699 and 1712. A principality of the Holy Roman mpire from 1719, Liechtenstein became a member of the Confederation of the Rhine in 1806 and f the German Confederation from 1815 to 1866. In 1862 it became a constitutional state and from 366 was fully independent. It is ruled by the hereditary princes of the House of Liechtenstein, urrently (since 1989) Prince Hans Adam II. Close economic and political ties have existed at different times with Austria and Switzerland.

LITHUANIA

Official name Republic of Lithuania
Local name Lietuva
Location A republic in north-eastern Europe, bounded to the south-west by Poland and to the west by the Baltic Sea
Area 65 200 sq km/25 167 sq mi
Capital Vilnius
Chief towns Kaunas, Klaipėda, Šiauliai
Population 3 585 000 (1999e)

Time zone GMT +2
Currency 1 Litas (Lt) = 100 centas
Language Lithuanian
Religions Christianity, predominantly Roman Catholic, with Lutheran Protestant, Baptist and Orthodox minorities; also Judaism and Islam.
Ethnic groups Lithuanian 81%, Russian 9%, Polish 7%, others 3%

Physical description

Glaciated plains cover much of the area; the chief river is the Neman.

Climate

Varies between maritime and continental; wet, with moderate winters and summers.

Government

A Prime Minister is appointed by a President and approved by a 141-member Parliament; the Prime Minister forms a Cabinet.

Economy

Electronics; electrical engineering; computer hardware; instruments; machine tools; shipbuilding; synthetic fibres; fertilizers; plastics; food processing; oil refining; agricultural activity centres on cattle, pigs and poultry.

History

t was united with Poland from 1385 to 1795. Intensive Russification led to revolts in 1905 and 1917. Occupied by Germany in both World Wars, it was proclaimed a republic in 1918 but annexed by the USSR in 1940. The growth of a nationalist movement in the 1980s led to a declaration of independence in 1990 under President Vytautas Landsbergis, who was succeeded in 1993 by Algirdas Brazauskas. Valdas Adamkus took office as President in 1998, and was succeeded by Rolandas Paksas in Jan 2003. In 2002 Lithuania was formally invited to join NATO and the EU.

LUXEMBOURG

Official name Grand Duchy of Luxembourg
Local name Lëtzeberg (Letz), Luxembourg (Fr), Luxemburg (Ger)
Location An independent constitutional monarchy in north-western Europe, bounded to the east by Germany; to the west by Belgium; and to the south by France
Area 2 586 sq km/998 sq mi
Capital Luxembourg
Chief towns Esch-sur-Alzette, Dudelange, Differdange

Population 429 100 (1999e)
Time zone GMT +1
Currency 1 Euro (€) = 100 cents
Languages French, German, Letzeburgish
Religions Christianity 99% (RC 97%, Prot 2%), Judaism 1%
Ethnic groups Luxembourger 72%, Portuguese 9%, Italian 5%, French 3%, Belgian 2%, German 2%, others 7%

Nations of the World

Physical description

Divided into the two natural regions of Ösling in the north (wooded, hilly land, of average height 450m) and the flatter, more fertile Gutland (average height 250m); water resources have been developed by canalization of the River Mosel, by hydroelectric dams on the River Our, and by reservoirs on the River Sûre.

Climate

It is drier and sunnier in the south, but winters can be severe; in the sheltered Mosel Valley, summers and autumns are warm enough for cultivation of vines.

Government

A hereditary monarchy with the Grand Duke or Grand Duchess as head of state; Parliament has a Chamber of Deputies with 64 members elected every five years and a State Council with 21 members appointed for life; the head of government is the Minister of State.

Economy

The city of Luxembourg is an important international centre; iron and steel (c.25% of the national income); food processing; chemicals; tyres; metal products; engineering; mixed farming; dairy farming; wine; forestry; tourism.

History

After being occupied by the Romans and then the Franks (in the 5c), Luxembourg came under the control of the House of Luxembourg in the 11c. The first Count of Luxembourg was created in 1060; the family, which owned lands in the area between the Maas and the Mosel from the 13c, took its name from the Castle of Lützelburg, and came to prominence when Henry VII was elected to the throne in 1308. Although they lost the throne after Henry's death, his son John gained control of Bohemia and the Luxemburgers' power grew comparable with that of the Habsburgs. Their most important representative was Emperor Charles IV, who elevated Luxembourg to a duchy in 1354. From 1346 until 1437 (when the dynasty died out in the male line with the death of Sigismund), all but one of the German kings came from the House of Luxembourg. The country of Luxembourg was controlled by various European powers (Burgundy 1443–77, Habsburgs 1477–1555, Spain 1555–1684, France 1684–97) before returning to Habsburg control after the War of the Spanish Succession, and being made a Grand Duchy and passed to the Netherlands following the Congress of Vienna in 1815. In 1830 much of Luxembourg joined the Belgians in the revolt against William I; this resulted in the division of the country, with the western, French-speaking region joining Belgium. The remaining Grand Duchy was granted political autonomy in 1838, and recognized as a neutral independent state in 1867. Occupied by Germany in both World Wars, it entered into economic union with Belgium in 1921, joined the Benelux economic union in 1948, and abandoned neutrality on joining NATO in 1949. The head of state is the Grand Duke or Grand Duchess, currently Grand Duke Henri, who succeeded in 2000 when his father, Grand Duke Jean, abdicated. Luxembourg was a founding member of the EEC in 1958. The Luxembourg franc was replaced by the Euro in Jan 2002.

➔ **Macao ▸ China**

MACEDONIA

Official name FormerYugoslav Republic of Macedonia
Local name Republika Makedonija
Location A republic in southern Europe, bounded to the west by Albania; to the south by Greece; to the east by Bulgaria; and to the north by Serbia and Montenegro
Area 25 713 sq km/9 925 sq mi
Capital Skopje

Chief towns Bitola, Gostivar, Tetovo, Kumanovo
Population 2 023 000 (1999e)
Time zone GMT +1
Currency 1 Denar (D, den) = 100 paras
Language Macedonian, Albanian
Religions Christianity 67% (Orthodox), Islam 30%, others 3%
Ethnic groups Macedonian 66%, Albanian 23%, Turkish 4%, others 7%

Physical description

Mountainous, covered with deep basins and valleys. The country is bisected by the River Vardar.

Climate

Cold winters and warm, dry summers.

Government

A 120-member unicameral National Assembly (*Sobranje*) is elected once every four years.

Economy

Market gardening; machinery; manufacturing.

History

The area of ancient Macedonia (consisting of the present region of Macedonia in northern Greece and the FormerYugoslav Republic of Macedonia) was inhabited by Macedonians who spoke a Slav language closer to Bulgarian than Serbo-Croat. Through the centuries, many tribes and nations settled in Macedonia and its ethnic composition is accordingly complex; the French *macédoine* is a synonym for 'medley' or 'mixture'. Slav tribes arrived in the 7c and mixed with the Greek and romanized Illyrians and Thracians, while the Byzantine rulers established settlements of Scythians and christianized Turks. In the 9c the Bulgars conquered Macedonia but the region returned to Byzantine rule until the Ottoman conquest (1355). Under the Turks, Sasi, Tartars, Cerkezi, Gypsies and Jews all settled and mixed with the local population. At the end of the 19c, a Macedonian nationalist movement emerged, its members insisting that the Macedonians were neither Bulgars nor Serbs, but a distinct Slav nation with its own language; this was a claim which the neighbouring Serbs, Bulgars and Greeks, nations all bent on territorial expansion, were determined to discount. After the Balkan Wars in 1913, Macedonia was divided between Greece and Serbia. It is the Serbian part that was given to Yugoslavia by the Treaty of Neuilly in 1919, an act confirmed by the treaties signed at the Paris Peace Conference in 1947, when the region was named the Republic of Macedonia within the Federal Republic of Yugoslavia. Despite claims to parts of it by Albania and Bulgaria, and deteriorating relations with Greece (which claims that its region called Macedonia is the only one entitled to the name), Macedonia formally seceded from Yugoslavia in 1991 and was admitted to the UN in 1993 as the FormerYugoslav Republic of Macedonia. UN and US peace-keeping forces arrived in 1992 and 1993 to maintain borders and prevent the conflict in Bosnia-Herzegovina spreading to Macedonia. There was ongoing tension and sporadic violence between ethnic Albanians and Macedonians throughout the 1990s. Kiro Gligorov was elected President in 1991 and, despite serious injury in an assassination attempt in 1995, remained in power. The UN force withdrew in 1998 as a result of a Chinese veto on its renewal, provoked by a Macedonian recognition of Taiwan. Violence intensified in 2001 with ethnic Albanian rebel groups demanding more rights. A peace deal in Aug led to improvements in the status of ethnic Albanians and Albanian became an official language in 2002.

MADAGASCAR

Official name Democratic Republic of Madagascar
Local name Republikan'i Madagasikara
Location An island republic in the Indian Ocean, separated from East Africa by the Mozambique Channel
Area 592 800 sq km/228 821 sq mi
Capital Antananarivo
Chief towns Toamasina, Mahajanga, Fianarantsoa, Antsiranana, Toliara
Population 14 873 000 (1999e)

Time zone GMT +3
Currency 1 Malagasy Franc (FMG, MgFr) = 100 centimes
Language Malagasy; French is also widely spoken
Religions Christianity 42% (RC 24%, Prot 18%), traditional beliefs 52%, Islam 6%
Ethnic groups Merina 26%, Betsimisaraka 16%, Betsileo 12%, Tsimihety 7%, Sakalava 7%, others 32%

Physical description

Dissected north to south by a ridge of mountains rising to 2 876m at Maromokotra; cliffs to the east drop down to a coastal plain through tropical forest; a terraced descent to the west through savannah to the coast which is heavily indented in the north.

Climate

Temperate climate in the highlands; the average annual rainfall is 1 000–1 500mm; tropical coastal region with an annual rainfall at Toamasina in the east of 3 500mm.

Government

Governed by a President, elected for seven years; a 150-member National People's Assembly is elected every five years, and a 90-member Senate every four years.

Economy

Chiefly agricultural; coffee, sugar, vanilla, cloves, rice, manioc, cotton, peanuts, sisal, tobacco, livestock; food processing, tanning, cement, soap, glassware, paper, textiles, oil products; graphite, chrome, coal, bauxite, ilmenite, semi-precious stones.

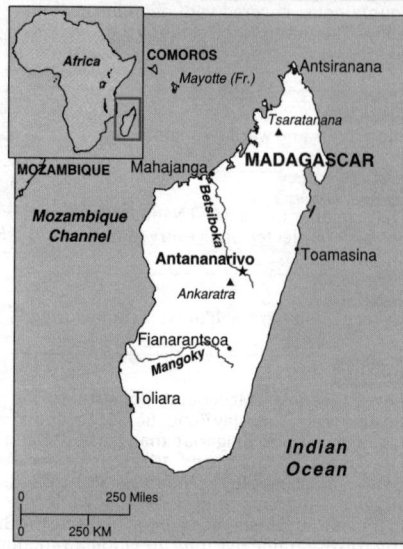

History

Madagascar was settled by Indonesians in the 1c AD and by African traders in the 8c. The French established trading posts in the late 18c and claimed the island as a protectorate in 1885. After becoming an autonomous overseas French territory (the Malagasy Republic) in 1958, it gained independence in 1960 and was named Madagascar again in 1975. Following anti-government riots, in 1992 a new constitution was approved which reduced the powers of the President, Didier Ratsiraka, who had held office since 1975. He was defeated in 1993 but returned to office in 1997 after winning the 1996 elections. Disputed elections in 2001 led to political confusion but Marc Ravalomanana emerged as the winner, and Ratsiraka then fled into exile.

⮩ **Madeira ► Portugal**

MALAWI

Official name Republic of Malawi
Local name Dziko la Malai
Location A republic in south-eastern Africa,
bounded to the south-west and south-east by
Mozambique; to the east by Lake Nyasa (Lake
Malawi); to the north by Tanzania; and to the west
by Zambia
Area 118 484 sq km/45 735 sq mi
Capital Lilongwe

Chief towns Blantyre, Zomba, Limbe, Salima
Population 10 000 000 (1999e)
Time zone GMT +2
Currency 1 Kwacha (MK) = 100 tambala
Languages English, Chichewa
Religions Christianity 70% (Prot 50%, RC 20%),
Islam 21%, traditional beliefs 9%
Ethnic groups Maravi 59%, Lomwe 20%, Yao 13%,
Ngoni 6%, others 2%

Physical description

Crossed north to south by the Great Rift Valley
in which lies Africa's third-largest lake, Lake
Nyasa (Lake Malawi); high plateaux on either
side (900–1200m); Shire highlands in the
south rise to nearly 3 000m at Mount Mulanje.

Climate

Tropical climate in the south, with high year-
round temperatures, 28°–37°C; average annual rainfall, 740mm; more moderate temperatures in centre; higher rainfall in the mountains
overlooking Lake Nyasa (1 500–2 000mm).

Government

A unicameral National Assembly consisting of
177 members is elected once every five years.

Economy

Based on agriculture, which employs 90% of
the population; tobacco, sugar, tea, cotton,
groundnuts, maize; textiles, matches, cigarettes, beer, spirits, shoes, cement.

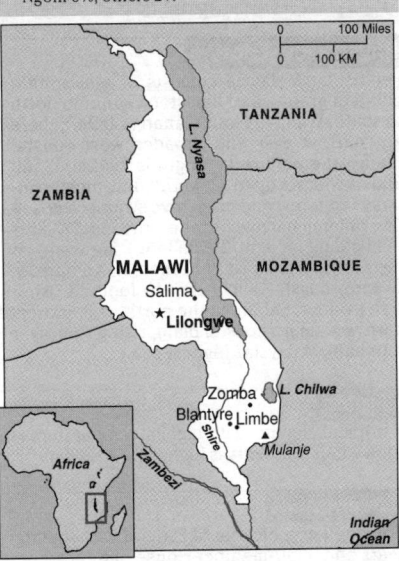

History

It was discovered by the Portuguese in the 17c, and European contact was established by David
Livingstone in 1859. Scottish church missions were established in the area, and it was claimed as
the British Nyasaland Districts Protectorate in 1891, and then called the British Central Africa Protectorate in 1893. It was established as the British colony of Nyasaland in 1907, and in the 1950s it
joined with Northern and Southern Rhodesia (now Zambia and Zimbabwe) to form the Federation
of Rhodesia and Nyasaland. After gaining independence in 1964, it became a republic in 1966
under President Hastings Banda. As a result of international pressure and growing unrest within
the country, a referendum was held in 1993 in which the population voted for a multi-party system.
Banda was voted out of office the following year and was replaced by Bakili Muluzi.

Nations of the World

MALAYSIA

Official name Federation of Malaysia

Local name Malaysia

Location An independent federation of states situated in South-East Asia

Area 329 749 sq km/127 283 sq mi

Capital Kuala Lumpur

Chief towns GeorgeTown, Ipoh, Malacca, Johor Baharu, Kuching, Kota Kinabalu

Population 21 376 000 (1999e)

Time zone GMT +8

Currency 1 Malaysian Dollar/Ringgit (M$) = 100 cents

Language Bahasa Malaysia (Malay); Chinese, English andTamil are also spoken

Religions Islam 53%, Buddhism 17%, Chinese folk religion 12%, Hinduism 7%, Christianity 6%, others 5%

Ethnic groups Malay and indigenous 58%, Chinese 26%, Indian 7%, others 9%

Physical description

Peninsular Malaysia consists of a mountain chain of granite and limestone running north to south, rising to MountTahan (2 189m); there are narrow east and broader west coastal plains; the peninsula length is 700km/435mi and its width is up to 320km/200mi; mostly tropical rainforest and mangrove swamp; a coastline of long, narrow beaches; the chief river is the Pahang (456km/283mi long). Sarawak, on the north-west coast of Borneo, has a narrow,

swampy coastal belt backed by foothills rising sharply towards mountain ranges on the Indonesian frontier; Sabah, in the north-east corner of Borneo, has a deeply indented coastline and a narrow western coastal plain, rising sharply into the Crocker Range, reaching 4 094m at Mount Kinabalu, Malaysia's highest peak.

Climate

A tropical climate, with highest temperatures in coastal areas; it is strongly influenced by monsoon winds; humidity is high.

Government

Governed by a bicameral Federal Parliament, consisting of a 69-member Senate elected for six years and a 180-member House of Representatives elected for five years; the head of state is a monarch elected for five years by sultans; a Prime Minister and a Cabinet advise.

Economy

The discovery of tin in the late 19c brought European investment; rubber trees introduced from Brazil; rice, palms, timber, fishing; iron ore, ilmenite, gold, bauxite, oil, natural gas; textiles, rubber and oil products, chemicals, electronic components, electrical goods, tourism.

History

Malaysia formed part of the Srivijaya Empire in the 9–14c and experienced Hindu and Muslim influences in the 14–15c. From the 16c, Portugal, the Netherlands and Britain vied for control. Singapore, Malacca and Penang were formally incorporated into the British Colony of the Straits Settlements in 1826. British protection which extended over Perak, Selangor, Negeri Sembilan and Pahang was constituted into the Federated Malay States in 1895, and protection treaties with several other states (Unfederated Malay States) were agreed in 1885–1930. The region was occupied by the Japanese in WorldWar II, after which Sarawak became a British colony, Singapore became a separate colony, the colony of North Borneo was formed, and the Malay Union was established, uniting the Malay states and the Straits Settlements of Malacca and Penang. In 1948 the British set up the Federation of Malaya. Growing resentment by the Chinese-dominated Malayan Communist Party (MCP) of Malay dominance within the Federation led to an insurrection led by the MCP against British rule. The insurrection and the campaign to crush it became known as the Malayan Emergency. Following growing MCP violence, including the murder of European estate managers, on 18 June 1948 the British administration declared a state of emergency throughout Malaya. In the early years of the insurrection, the MCP achieved a number of notable successes, including the assassination of the High Commissioner, Sir Henry Gurney, in Oct 1951. However, by the mid-1950s, through a combination of fierce military measures, substantial resettlement of the Chinese rural population (which had provided much of the MCP's support) and the introduction of political initiatives that clearly would soon take Malaya to independence, the insurrection was broken, although, officially, it did not end until 31 July 1960. Malaya gained independence in 1957 and the constitutional monarchy of the Federation of Malaysia came into existence in 1963. Two years later Singapore withdrew from the Federation.

MALDIVES

Official name Republic of Maldives
Local name Maldives Divehi Jumhuriya
Location A republic consisting of an island archipelago in the Indian Ocean
Area 300 sq km/120 sq mi
Capital Malé
Population 300 200 (1999e)

Time zone GMT +5.5
Currency 1 Rufiyaa (MRf, Rf) = 100 laaris
Language Dhivehi; English is spoken widely
Religions Islam 100% (Sunni)
Ethnic groups Sinhalese majority; Arab and African minorities

Physical description

Small, low-lying islands, with sandy beaches fringed with coconut palms.

Climate

Generally warm and humid; affected by southwest monsoons from April to October; the average annual rainfall is 2 100mm and the average daily temperature is 22°C.

Government

Governed by a President, elected every five years, a Ministers' Cabinet, and a Citizens' Cabinet of 40 members elected for five years plus 8 presidentially appointed members.

Economy

Breadfruit, banana, coconut, mango, cassava, sweet potato, millet; fishing; shipping; tourism.

History

A former dependency of Ceylon (now Sri Lanka), it was a British protectorate from 1887 until 1965, when it gained independence. Its sultanate was abolished in 1968 when it became a republic under President Ibrahim Nasir, who was succeeded in 1978 by Maumoon Abdul Gayoom. In recent years, the Maldivian authorities have expressed concern over the impact of global warming and rising sea levels, as 80% of the land is one metre or less above sea level.

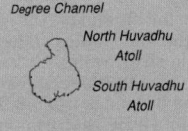

173

Nations of the World

MALI

Official name Republic of Mali
Local name Mali
Location A landlocked republic in West Africa, bounded to the north-east by Algeria; to the north-west by Mauritania; to the west by Senegal; to the south-west by Guinea; to the south by the Côte d'Ivoire; to the south-east by Burkina Faso; and to the east by Niger
Area 1 240 192 sq km/478 714 sq mi
Capital Bamako
Chief towns Ségou, Mopti, Sikasso, Kayes, Gao, Timbuktu
Population 10 429 000 (1999e)
Time zone GMT
Currency 1 CFA Franc (CFAFr) = 100 centimes
Language French; local languages are spoken widely
Religions Islam 85% (mostly Sunni), traditional beliefs 14%, Christianity 1%
Ethnic groups Bambara 34%, Fulani 17%, Senufo 12%, Soninke 8%, Songhai 7%, Tuareg 7%, Malinke 6%, others 9%

Physical description

A landlocked country on the fringe of the Sahara; the lower part of the Hoggar massif is located in the north; arid plains lie between 300m and 500m; there is featureless desert land in the north with sand dunes; mainly savannah land in the south; the main rivers are the Niger and Sénégal.

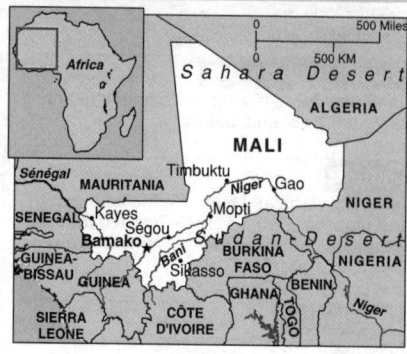

Climate

Hot, dry climate with rainfall increasing from north to south; in the south the rainfall season lasts for five months (June–October); the annual average rainfall is c.1 000mm in the south, decreasing to almost zero in the Saharan north.

Government

A 147-seat unicameral National Assembly is elected once every five years.

Economy

Mainly subsistence agriculture; sorghum, millet, rice, maize, cotton, groundnuts; crops severely affected by drought conditions; small amounts of marble, limestone, bauxite, nickel, manganese; fishing, livestock, food processing, textiles, leather, cement; some tourism.

History

Between the 13c and 15c the medieval Kingdom of Mali flourished in the Western Sudan, dominating the the trade routes of the Sahara with North Africa. The kingdom reached its peak in the 14c and declined in the 15c. Although it had a quasi-Islamic ruling group, it was dominated by Muslim merchants, and it became an important factor in the Islamicization of West Africa. Mali was governed by France from 1881 to 1895 and was a territory of French Sudan (part of French West Africa) until 1959, when it entered a partnership with Senegal as the Federation of Mali. It achieved independence as a separate nation in 1960. Its first President, Modibo Keita, was overthrown in 1968 in a military coup led by Moussa Traoré, who held power until his arrest in 1991 following pro-democracy rioting. In 1992 a new multi-party constitution was approved in a referendum and the elections were won by the Alliance for Democracy in Mali Party and President Alpha Oumar Konaré, who soon had to face the problem of rebellion against the government by Tuareg tribesmen (the Tuareg Unified Movements and Fronts of Azawad) in the north of the country. A peace agreement was signed in 1994. Konaré was replaced as President by Amadou Toumani Touré in 2002.

MALTA

Official name Republic of Malta
Local name Malta
Location An archipelago republic in the central Mediterranean Sea
Area 316 sq km/122 sq mi
Capital Valletta
Chief towns Sliema, Birkirkara, Qormi, Rabat, Victoria
Population 381 600 (1999e)

Time zone GMT +2
Currency 1 Maltese Lira (LM) = 100 cents = 1 000 mils
Languages English, Maltese; there are many Arabic words in the local vocabulary
Religions Christianity 98% (RC 97%, Prot 1%), others 1%, none/unaffiliated 1%
Ethnic groups Maltese 98%, British 2%

Physical description

The islands are generally low-lying, rising to 253m; there are no rivers or mountains; well-indented coastline.

Climate

Dry summers and mild winters; average annual rainfall is c.400mm; average daily winter temperature is 13°C.

Government

Governed by a President, Prime Minister, Cabinet, and a 65-member House of Representatives elected for five years.

Economy

Tourism and ship repair are the major industries; naval dockyards are now converted to commercial use; developing as a transshipment centre for the Mediterranean; exports include tobacco, canned foods, light engineering products, textiles, paints, detergents, and plastic and steel goods; main crops are potatoes, tomatoes, onions, wheat, barley, grapes, oranges and cut flowers; large numbers of cattle, sheep, goats and poultry.

History

Malta has at various times been controlled by Phoenicia, Greece, Carthage and Rome. It was conquered by Arabs in the 9c, and later by Spain, and under Emperor Charles V it was given to the Knights Hospitallers in 1530. Captured by the British during the Napoleonic Wars, and a Crown Colony from 1815, it was an important strategic base in both World Wars. In 1942 Malta was awarded the George Cross for its resistance to heavy air attacks. It achieved independence in 1964 and became a republic in 1974. In 2002 Malta was formally invited to join the EU.

➔ **Man, Isle of ▸ United Kingdom**

➔ **Mariana Islands, Northern ▸ United States of America**

MARSHALL ISLANDS

Official name Republic of the Marshall Islands
Local name Marshall Islands
Location An independent archipelago republic in the central Pacific Ocean
Area c.180 sq km/70 sq mi
Capital Majuro
Population 66 000 (1999e)

Time zone GMT +12
Currency 1 US Dollar ($, US$) = 100 cents
Languages Marshallese, English
Religions Christianity 97% (Prot 90%, RC 7%), others 3%
Ethnic groups Micronesian 97%, others 3%

Physical description

Low, coral limestone and sand islands, atolls and reefs, with few natural resources.

Climate

Hot and humid; the wet season is from May to November; occasional typhoons.

Government

Constitutional democracy in 'free association' with the USA; governed by a President, elected by a 33-member Parliament.

Economy

Farming; fishing; tropical agriculture.

History

Originally inhabited by Micronesians, it was explored by the Spanish in 1529 and became a German protectorate in 1886. After World War I it came under Japanese control, and after World War II it became a UN Trust Territory (1947–78), administered by the USA. Between 1946 and 1962 US nuclear weapon tests were held on the Bikini and Enewetak atolls. After the Marshall Islands became a self-governing republic in 1979, a compact of free association with the USA was signed in 1982, and came into force in 1986. By this the USA retains control of external security and defence and gives financial help while the republic retains its sovereignty in all other matters.

⊛ **Martinique ▸ France**

MAURITANIA

Official name Islamic Republic of Mauritania
Local name Mauritanie (French), Mūrītāniyā (Arabic)
Location A republic in north-west Africa, bounded to the south-west by Senegal; to the south and east by Mali; to the north-east by Algeria; to the north by Western Sahara; and to the west by the Atlantic Ocean
Area 1 029 920 sq km/397 549 sq mi

Capital Nouakchott
Chief towns Nouadhibou, Atar
Population 2 582 000 (1999e)
Time zone GMT
Currency 1 Ouguiya (U, UM) = 5 khoums
Language Arabic; French is also widely spoken
Religions Islam 99%, others 1%
Ethnic groups Arab and Berber 72%, Wolof 6%, Tukulor 5%, Soninke 3%, Fulani 1%, others 13%

Physical description

The Saharan zone in the north covers two thirds of the country with sand dunes, mountainous plateaux and occasional oases; the coastal zone has minimal rainfall and little vegetation; savannah grasslands lie in the Sahelian zone; the Sénégal River zone is the chief agricultural region; the highest point is Kediet Idjill (915m) in the north-west.

Climate

Dry and tropical with sparse rainfall; temperatures can rise to over 49°C in the Sahara.

Government

Governed by an executive President (six-year term), who appoints a Prime Minister, National Assembly and Senate.

Economy

Livestock, cereals, vegetables, dates; crop success is constantly under threat from drought; mining is based on vast iron ore reserves, also copper and gypsum; fish processing; gum arabic; textiles; cement; bricks; paints; industrial gas.

History

Discovered by the Portuguese in the 15c, it became a French protectorate within French West Africa in 1903 and a French colony in 1920. It gained independence in 1960. When the Spanish withdrew from Western Sahara in 1976, Mauritania and Morocco divided between them a large area in the south under the name of Tiris el Gharbia. However, after conflict with the Polisario Front guerrillas, Mauritania renounced all rights to the region in 1979, leaving Morocco to annex it. There were military coups in 1978 and 1984, and a new constitution was adopted in 1991 with the approval of multi-party elections. In 1989 violent disturbances broke out on the border with Senegal which resulted in the frontier being closed until diplomatic relations with Senegal were restored in 1992. During the 1990s there was ethnic tension and internal unrest by groups in opposition to the government.

MAURITIUS

Official name Republic of Mauritius
Local name Mauritius
Location A small island nation in the Indian Ocean
Area 1 865 sq km/720 sq mi
Capital Port Louis
Population 1 182 000 (1999e)
Time zone GMT +4

Currency 1 Mauritian Rupee (MR, MauRe) = 100 cents
Language English; French is also spoken
Religions Hinduism 52%, Christianity 28% (RC 26%, Prot 2%), Islam 17%, others 3%
Ethnic groups Indo-Mauritian 68%, Creole 27%, others 5%

Physical description

A volcanic island, with a central plateau reaching 550–730m in the south; it falls steeply to narrow coastlands in the south and southwest; the highest peak is Piton de la Petite Rivière Noire (826m); dry, lowland coast, with wooded savannah, mangrove swamp and bamboo in the east; surrounded by coral reefs enclosing lagoons and sandy beaches.

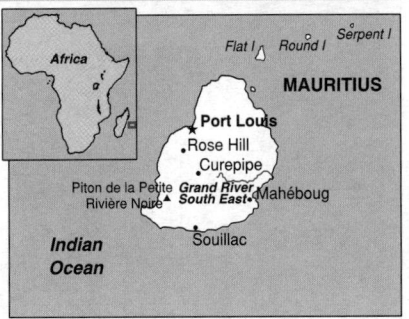

Climate

Tropical-maritime, with temperatures averaging between 22°C and 26°C; there is a wide variation in rainfall with most rain falling in the central plateau.

Government

A Prime Minister is appointed from the National Assembly by a President, who is head of state.

Economy

The sugar-cane industry employs over a quarter of the workforce; knitwear, clothing; diamond-cutting; watches; rum; fertilizer; tea; tobacco; potatoes; vegetables; fishing; tourism.

History

It was visited by Arabs in the 10c and discovered by the Portuguese in the 16c. The Dutch took possession in 1598–1710, followed by the French in 1710–1810, and the British in 1810. It was formally ceded to Britain by the Treaty of Paris in 1814, and governed jointly with the Seychelles as a single colony until 1903. It became an independent sovereign state within the Commonwealth of Nations in 1968 and an independent republic in 1992, and Cassam Uteem was elected to the largely ceremonial role of President. The Mauritian Socialist Party under Sir Anerood Jugnauth held power from 1982 to 1995, when they were defeated by an opposition alliance led by Navin Ramgoolam, but Jugnauth returned to power in the 2000 elections.

⊃ Mayotte ► France

MEXICO

Official name United Mexican States

Local name México

Location A federal republic in the south of North America, bounded to the north by the USA; to the west by the Gulf of California; to the west and south-west by the Pacific Ocean; to the south by Guatemala and Belize; and to the east by the Gulf of Mexico

Area 1 978 800 sq km/763 817 sq mi

Capital Mexico City

Chief towns Guadalajara, Léon, Monterrey, Ciudad Juárez

Population 100 294 000 (1999e)

Time zone GMT −6/8

Currency 1 Mexican Peso (Mex$) = 100 centavos

Language Spanish; American Indian languages are also spoken

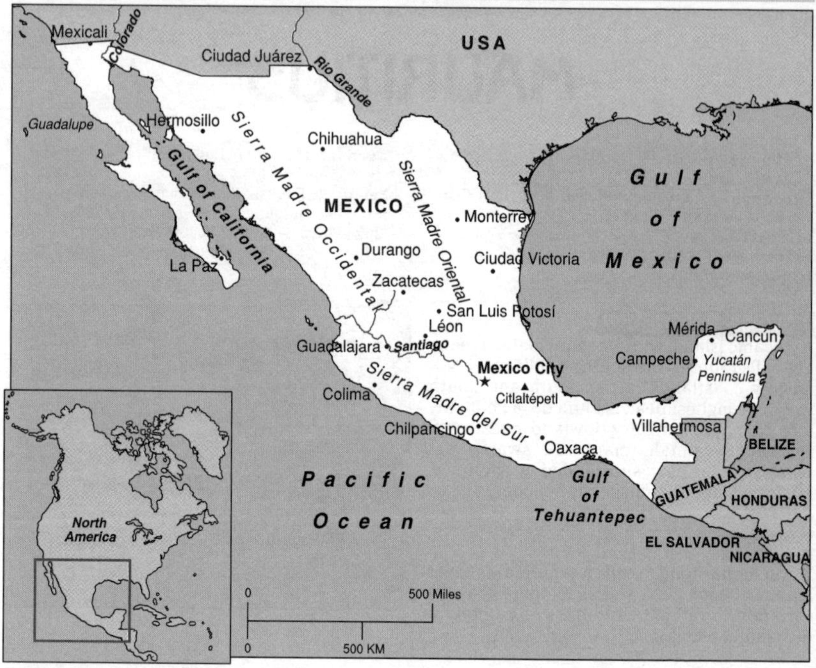

Physical description

Bisected by the Tropic of Cancer; situated at the south end of the North American Western Cordillera; narrow coastal plains border the Pacific Ocean and the Gulf of Mexico; land rises steeply to a central plateau, reaching a height of c.2 400m around Mexico City; the plateau is bounded by the Sierra Madre Occidental in the west and Sierra Madre Oriental in the east; volcanic peaks lie to the south, notably Citlaltépetl (5 699m); limestone lowlands of the Yucatán peninsula stretch into the Gulf of Mexico in the south-east; the country is subject to earthquakes which can be very severe.

Climate

Great climatic variation between the coastlands and mountains; desert or semi-desert conditions in the north-west; typically tropical climate on the east coast; generally wetter on the south coast; extreme temperature variations in the north, very cold in winter, very warm in summer.

Government

The country is governed by a President, elected for six years, a Cabinet, and a bicameral Congress with a 64-member Senate elected for six years and a 500-member Chamber of Deputies elected for three years.

Economy

Wide range of mineral exports; major discoveries of oil and natural gas in the 1970s (now world's fourth largest producer); fluorite and graphite (world's leading producer); gold, silver, lead, zinc, arsenic, cadmium, phosphates, sulphur, copper, antimony, iron, salt; sugar, maize, coffee, tobacco, fruit; large petrochemical industry; iron, steel, aluminium, vehicles, cement, food processing, textiles, clothing, crafts, cotton, cattle, machinery, fishing, tourism.

History

It was at the centre of Mesoamerican civilizations for over 2 500 years: the Gulf Coast Olmecs were based at La Venta; Zapotecs at Monte Albán near Oaxaca; Mixtecs at Mitla; Toltecs at Tula; Mayas in the Yucatán; and Aztecs at Tenochtitlán. The Spanish arrived in 1516, and in 1519 Cortés came ashore near Veracruz, destroying the powerful Aztec capital within two years and establishing the Viceroyalty of New Spain. The struggle for independence began in 1810 and Mexico became a federal republic in 1824. In all it lost nearly a third of its territory to the USA in 1836 and following the Mexican War (1846–8). There was civil war in 1858–61, and another Mexican War in 1862–7 during which French forces occupied Mexico City in 1863, declaring Archduke Maximilian of Austria to be Emperor of Mexico. The French withdrew and Maximilian was executed in 1867. The Mexican Revolution began in 1910 while Porfirio Díaz was President, largely fomented by his dictatorial regime, and did not end until 1920 and the establishment of a constitutional republic. Lázaro Cárdenas, President from 1934 to 1940, nationalized foreign-owned oil and railway companies, and carried out massive land reforms. After his presidency, however, the radicalism of the new one-party regime, dominated by the Institutional Revolutionary Party (PRI), increasingly became more rhetoric than reality. The second half of the 20c was rendered difficult due to economic problems, only partially relieved by mass emigration to the USA. Mexico became part of NAFTA in 1994, and in the same year Ernesto Zedillo Ponce de León became President. One of his first tasks as premier was to attempt to sort out the rebellion by the Zapatista National Liberation Army (EZLN) which had begun in Jan 1994 in the southern state of Chiapas, but violence in this area continued. In July 2000 the 71-year political stranglehold of the PRI came to an end when Vincente Fox Quesada of the PAN (National Action Party) was elected President.

Religions

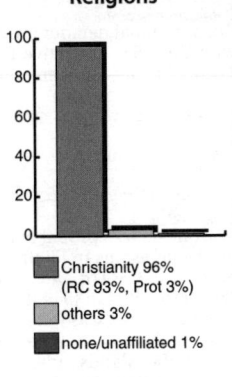

- Christianity 96% (RC 93%, Prot 3%)
- others 3%
- none/unaffiliated 1%

Ethnic groups

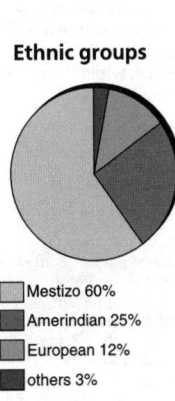

- Mestizo 60%
- Amerindian 25%
- European 12%
- others 3%

Nations of the World

MICRONESIA, FEDERATED STATES OF

Official name Federated States of Micronesia
Local name Micronesia
Location A republic consisting of a group of islands divided into four states in the western Pacific Ocean (Yap, Chuuk (formerly Truk), Pohnpei (formerly Ponape) and Kosrae)
Area 700 sq km/270 sq mi
Capital Palikir, on Ponape

Population 131 500 (1999e)
Time zone GMT +10/11
Currency 1 US Dollar (US$) = 100 cents
Language English
Religions Christianity 97% (RC 50%, Prot 47%), others 3%
Ethnic groups Trukese 42%, Pohnpeian 27%, others 31%

Physical description

Islands vary geologically, from low, coral atolls to high mountainous islands; Pohnpei, Kosrae and Truk have volcanic outcroppings.

Climate

Tropical; heavy rainfall all year round, especially in the eastern islands; subject to typhoons.

Nations of the World

Government

Constitutional democracy in 'free association' with the USA; executive President and Vice-President, and a unicameral legislature.

Economy

Fish; copra; tourism.

History

Micronesia was probably first settled by eastern Melanesians in 1500 BC. The Spanish colonized it in the 17c and sold it to Germany in 1898. From 1914 to 1944 it was occupied by the Japanese, then was taken by US forces and in 1947 became part of the UN Trust Territory of the Pacific Islands, administered by the USA. From 1965 there was a growing campaign for independence, and Micronesia became a self-governing federation in 1979. A compact of free association with the USA was signed in 1982, and came into force in 1986. By this the USA remained responsible for Micronesia's internal security and defence, while the federation retains its sovereignty in all other matters.

MOLDOVA

Official name Republic of Moldova
Local name Republica Moldovenească
Location A republic in eastern Europe, bounded to the west by Romania, and to the north, east and south by the Ukraine
Area 33 700 sq km/13 000 sq mi
Capital Chisinau
Chief towns Tiraspol, Bendery, Beltsy

Population 4 461 000 (1999e)
Time zone GMT +2
Currency 1 Leu (Mld) = 100 bani
Language Moldovan
Religions Christianity 98% (Orthodox), Judaism 2%
Ethnic groups Moldovan 65%, Ukrainian 14%, Russian 13%, Gagauzi 4%, Jewish 2%, others 2%

Physical description

The terrain consists of a hilly plain, reaching a height of 429m in the centre; chief rivers are the Dniester and Prut.

Climate

Moderate winters; warm summers.

Government

A 101-seat unicameral Parliament is elected every four years.

Economy

Wine; tobacco; food-canning; machines; electrical engineering; instruments; knitwear; textiles; fruit.

History

Between the 15c and 1812, Moldavia also included the region to the east called Bessarabia, the ownership of which was disputed between Russia and the Ottoman Turks. In 1812 Bessarabia, together with the eastern part of Moldavia, was ceded to Russia, and the two areas assumed the one name, Bessarabia. Although officially autonomous in 1812–28, Bessarabia thereafter came under Russian rule. Meanwhile the Danubian Principalities joined together to form the Principality of Romania in 1862. Following a nationalist movement, Bessarabia declared its independence from Russia in 1918 and united with Romania, but in 1940 Romania was forced to cede Bessarabia to the USSR, and it was incorporated with another small strip of land as the Moldavian Soviet Socialist Republic. Moldavia achieved independence from the USSR as the Republic of Moldova in 1991 and became a member of the CIS (Commonwealth of Independent States). Ethnic tension has grown in the country due partly to independence movements in the Dniestr and Gagauz regions, which have large Russian and Ukrainian populations, and also to a movement advocating unification with Romania. The Dniestr and Gagauz regions were granted autonomy in 1995. In 2001 the Communists won elections and Vladimir Voronin became President.

MONACO

Official name Principality of Monaco
Local name Monaco
Location A small principality on the Mediterranean Riviera, close to the Italian frontier with France
Area 1.9 sq km/0.75 sq mi
Capital Monaco
Chief town Monte Carlo

Population 32 100 (1999e)
Time zone GMT +1
Currency 1 Euro (€) = 100 cents
Language French
Religions Christianity 95% (RC 90%, Prot 5%), others 5%
Ethnic groups French 59%, Monagasque 17%, Italian 16%, others 8%

Physical description

Hilly, rugged and rocky; almost entirely urban.

Climate

Warm, dry summers and mild winters.

Government

Executive power is held by the Prince and a Council of Government; legislative authority is held by the Prince and a unicameral National Council; Monaco has close political ties with France.

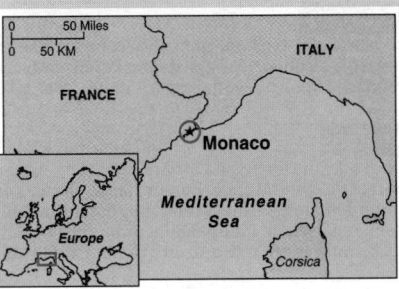

Economy

Chemicals; printing; textiles; precision instruments; plastics; postage stamps; tourism.

History

In 1297 the Grimaldi family won Monaco from the Genoese, who had held it since 1191, but they did not secure full possession until 1419. Though the Grimaldis were allies of France (except when they were under Spanish protection in 1524–1641), Monaco was formally annexed by France in 1793 during the French Revolutionary regime. It has been under French protection ever since, apart from a period under Sardinia in 1815–61. In Jan 2002 the French franc was replaced by the Euro as the official currency.

MONGOLIA

Official name State of Mongolia
Local name Mongol Ard Uls
Location A landlocked republic in eastern central Asia, bounded to the north by Russia and on other sides by China
Area 1 564 619 sq km/604 099 sq mi
Capital Ulan Bator
Chief towns Darhan, Erdenet

Population 2 617 000 (1999e)
Time zone GMT +8
Currency 1 Tugrik (Tug) = 100 möngö
Language Khalkha Mongolian
Religions Mainly Buddhism; accurate figures unavailable
Ethnic groups Mongol 90%, Kazakh 4%, Chinese 2%, Russian 2%, others 2%

Physical description

A landlocked, mountainous country with an average height of 1 580m; the highest point is Tavan-Bogdo-Uli at 4 373m; the high ground is mainly in the west, with folded mountains lying north-west to south-east to form the Mongolian Altai chain; the lower south-east section runs into the Gobi Desert; the largest lakes are found in the north-west; major rivers flow north and north-east; the lowland plains are mainly arid grasslands.

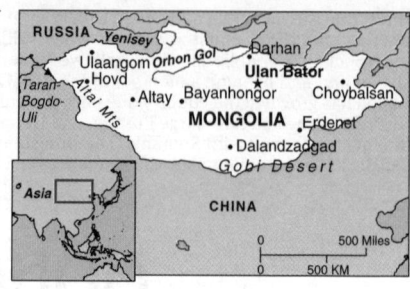

Climate

Continental, with hard and long-lasting frosts in winter; the average temperature at Ulan Bator is 27° in January and 9°–24°C in July; rainfall is generally low; arid desert conditions prevail in the south.

Government

A unicameral Great People's Hural (Parliament) elects a Prime Minister, who appoints a Cabinet.

Economy

Traditionally a pastoral, nomadic economy; a series of five-year plans aims to create an agricultural–industrial economy; c.70% of agricultural production is derived from cattle raising; foodstuffs; animal products; wool; hides; fluorspar; copper, coal, gold, tungsten, uranium, lead.

History

Originally the homeland of nomadic tribes, which united under Genghis Khan in the 13c to become part of the great Mongol Empire, Mongolia was assimilated into China, and divided into Inner and Outer Mongolia. Inner Mongolia remains an autonomous region of China, but Outer Mongolia declared itself an independent monarchy in 1911; the Mongolian People's Republic was formed in 1924, but was not recognized by China until 1946. A multi-party system was introduced in 1990.

⮑ **Montenegro ▸ Yugoslavia**

MOROCCO

Official name Kingdom of Morocco
Local name Mamlaka Al-Maghrebia
Location A kingdom in North Africa, bounded to the south-west by Western Sahara; to the south-east and east by Algeria; to the north-east by the Mediterranean Sea; and to the west by the Atlantic Ocean
Area 409 200 sq km/157 951 sq mi
Capital Rabat
Chief towns Casablanca, Fez, Marrakesh, Tangier, Meknès, Kenitra,Tétouan, Oujda, Agadir
Population 29 662 000 (1999e)
Time zone GMT
Currency 1 Dirham (DH) = 100 centimes
Language Arabic; French is also spoken
Religions Islam 99% (mostly Sunni), Christianity 1%
Ethnic groups Arab and Berber 99%, European 1%

Physical description

Dominated by a series of folded mountain ranges, rising in the Haut Atlas in the south to 4 165m at Mount Toubkal; the Atlas Mountains descend south-east to the north-west edge of the Sahara Desert; the broad coastal plain is bounded to the west by the Atlantic Ocean.

Climate

Mediterranean climate on the north coast; it is settled and hot in May–September; the average annual rainfall is 400–800mm, decreasing towards the Sahara, which is virtually rainless; Rabat, representative of the Atlantic coast, has average maximum daily temperatures of 17°–28°C; heavy winter snowfall in the High Atlas; the desert region experiences extreme heat in summer, with chilly winter nights.

Government

A 'constitutional' monarchy, but the Monarch appoints and presides over a Cabinet, which is led by a Prime Minister; there is a unicameral 306-member Chamber of Representatives, of which 206 are elected every six years, and the remainder are chosen by an electoral college.

Economy

Over half the population is engaged in agriculture; cereals (wheat and barley), citrus fruits, olives, vegetables, sugar beet, cotton, sunflowers; the largest known reserves of phosphate; coal, barite, cobalt, copper, manganese, antimony, zinc, iron ore, fluorspar, lead, silver; fishing; textiles; cement; soap; tobacco; chemicals; paper; timber products; vehicle assembly; crafts; tourism is centred on the four imperial cities and the warm Atlantic resorts.

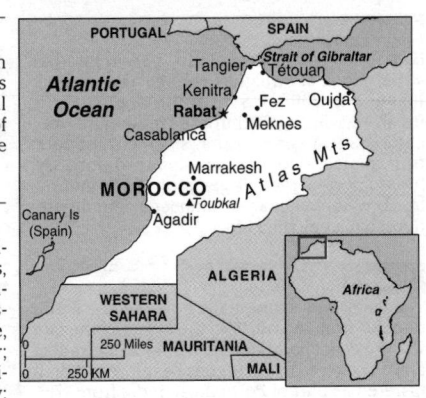

History

From the 12c BC the northern coast was occupied by Phoenicians, Carthaginians and Romans. Arabs invaded in the 7c AD, and Europeans began to establish an interest in the region in the 19c. The Treaty of Fez in 1912 established Spanish Morocco (capital, Tétouan) and French Morocco (capital, Rabat), and the international zone of Tangier was created in 1923; the protectorates gained independence in 1956, and Hassan II acceded as King of Morocco in 1961. Hassan died in 1999 and was succeeded by his son, Muhammad VI. In 1975 the former Spanish Sahara (Western Sahara) came under the joint control of Spain, Morocco and Mauritania; it became the responsibility of Morocco in 1979 but there is an independence movement in the region and Moroccan sovereignty is not recognized universally.

MOZAMBIQUE

Official name Republic of Mozambique
Local name Republica de Moçambique
Location A republic in south-eastern Africa, bounded to the south by Swaziland; to the south and south-west by South Africa; to the west by Zimbabwe; to the north-west by Zambia and Malawi; to the north by Tanzania; and to the east by the Mozambique Channel and the Indian Ocean
Area 789 800 sq km/304 863 sq mi

Capital Maputo
Chief towns Nampula, Beira, Pemba
Population 19 124 000 (1999e)
Time zone GMT +2
Currency 1 Metical (Mt, MZM) = 100 centavos
Language Portuguese; Swahili is widely spoken
Religions traditional beliefs 55%, Christianity 28% (RC 25%, others 3%), Islam 17%
Ethnic groups Makua 47%, Tsonga 23%, Malawi 12%, Shona 11%, Yao 4%, others 3%

Physical description

The main rivers are the Zambezi and Limpopo, providing irrigation and hydroelectricity; south of the Zambezi, the coast is low-lying, with sandy beaches and mangroves; low hills of volcanic origin are found inland; the Zimbabwe Plateau lies further north; the coast north of the Zambezi is more rugged and is backed by a narrower coastal plain; a savannah plateau inland has an average elevation of 800–1 000m; the highest peak, Mount Binga, is 2 436m.

Climate

Tropical, with relatively low rainfall in the coastal lowlands; average annual rainfall at Beira, representative of the central coast zone, is 1 520mm with maximum daily temperatures of 25°–32°C; in the drier areas of the interior lowlands, rainfall decreases to 500–750mm; Mozambique has one rainy season in December–March.

Government

A socialist one-party state from 1975 until 1990; a new constitution under a multiparty system was implemented in 1990; a President is head of state and a Legislative Assembly has 250 members.

Nations of the World

Economy

Badly affected by drought in 1981–4, internal strife, a lack of foreign exchange and extreme flooding in 2000; c.85% of the population is involved with agriculture; cashew nuts, tea, cotton, sugar cane, copra, sisal, groundnuts, fruit, maize, rice, cassava, tobacco; forestry, livestock; reserves of gemstones, diamonds, iron ore, copper, marble, alabaster, aluminium, fluorspar, coal, tin, gold.

History

The country was originally inhabited by Bantu peoples from the north in the 1–4c. By the late 15c the coast had been settled by Arab traders and discovered by Portuguese explorers. Administered as part of Portuguese India from 1751, Mozambique acquired separate colonial status as Portuguese East Africa in the late 19c, and became an overseas province of Portugal in 1951. An independence movement formed in 1962, the *Frente de Libertação de Moçambique* (Frelimo), which took up arms against colonial rule. Independence was gained in 1975 and Mozambique became a socialist one-party state. A brutal civil war erupted between the ruling party Frelimo and the opposition group Renamo until in 1992 a peace agreement was signed which made Renamo a legitimate political party. A new constitution under a multi-party system was implemented in 1990, and in 1994 the first multi-party elections were won by Frelimo. In 1986 Mozambique's first President, Samora Machel, was killed in an air crash and was succeeded by Joaquim Chissano. Despite an economic upturn in the late 1990s, which saw Mozambique transform itself from being one of the poorest countries in the world to achieving one of the highest growth rates in the world, extreme flooding in 2000 and 2001 plunged it back into economic devastation.

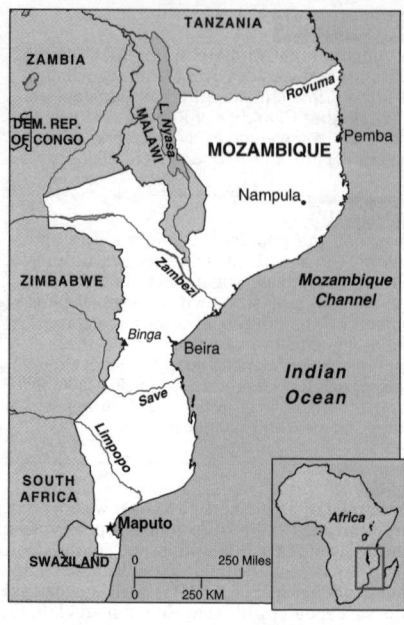

MYANMAR (BURMA)

Official name Union of Myanmar
Local name Myanmar
Location A republic in South-East Asia, bounded to the north and north-east by China; to the east by Laos and Thailand; to the north-west by India; to the west by Bangladesh; and to the south and west by the Bay of Bengal and the Andaman Sea
Area 678 576 sq km/261 930 sq mi
Capital Rangoon
Chief towns Mandalay, Henzada, Pegu, Myingyan

Population 48 081 000 (1999e)
Time zone GMT +6.5
Currency 1 Kyat (K) = 100 pyas
Language Burmese; several minority languages are also spoken
Religions Buddhism 89%, Christianity 6%, Islam 4%, Hindu 1%
Ethnic groups Burman 68%, Shan 9%, Karen 7%, Rakhine 4%, Chinese 3%, Mon 2%, Kachin 1%, others 6%

Physical description

Rimmed in the north, east and west by mountain ranges rising in the north to Hkakabo Razi (5 881m) and descending in a series of ridges and valleys; the principal rivers, the Irrawaddy, Salween and Sittang all run north to south; the Irrawaddy River delta extends over 240km/150mi of tidal forest.

Climate

Tropical monsoon climate, with a marked change between the cooler, dry season of November–April, which is dominated by the north-east monsoon, and the hotter, wet season of May–September, dominated by the south-west monsoon; coastal and higher mountains in the east and north have heavy annual rainfall (2 500–5 000mm); sheltered interior lowlands often as low as 1 000mm; lowland temperatures are high all year round (especially March to May); there is high humidity on the coast.

Government

A military council and a Cabinet head a State Peace and Development Council (formerly, the State Law and Order Restoration Council).

Economy

Largely dependent on agriculture (especially rice, beans, maize, sugar cane, pulses, oilseed) and forestry (teak and other hardwoods); agricultural processing; textiles; footwear; pharmaceuticals; fertilizers; wood and wood products; petroleum refining; zinc, lead, tin, copper, gypsum, limestone, chromium, asbestos, oil, coal.

History

The country was first unified in the 11c by King Anawrahta. Kublai Khan invaded in 1287. A second dynasty was established in 1486, but it was plagued by internal disunity and wars with Siam from the 16c. A new dynasty under King Alaunghpaya was founded in 1752. Burma was annexed to British India in 1886 following the Anglo-Burmese Wars of 1824–85. It separated from India in 1937 and was occupied by the Japanese in World War II. It gained independence as the Union of Burma under Prime Minister U Nu in 1948, who was overthrown in a military coup in 1962 led by U Ne Win in 1962. Ne Win became chairman of the revolutionary council and then state President when the country be-

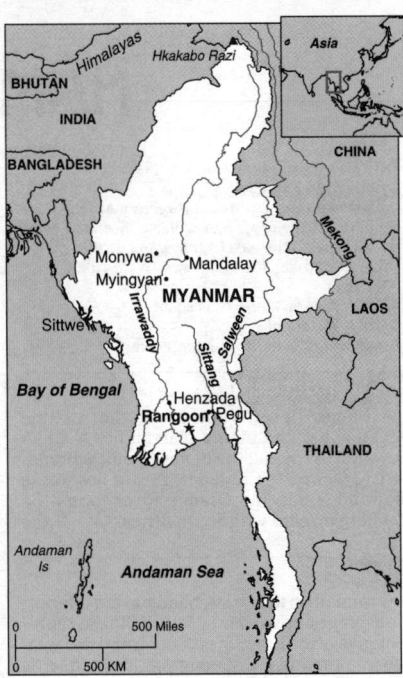

came a single-party socialist republic in 1974. In 1988 there was another military coup, this time led by General Saw Maung, who seized power, imposed martial law, and changed the country's name to Myanmar. He was replaced by his deputy, General Than Shwe, in 1992. The military government is opposed by the National League for Democracy (NLD) party, whose leader is Aung San Suu Kyi; numerous restrictions continue to be placed on the NLD's activities and on Aung San Suu Kyi herself. During the 1990s there was fighting between several different guerrilla groups as well as regular pro-democracy demonstrations and riots.

NAMIBIA

Official name Republic of Namibia
Local name Namibia
Location A republic in south-western Africa, bounded to the north by Angola; to the north-east by Zambia; to the east by Botswana; to the south by South Africa; and to the west by the Atlantic Ocean
Area 823 144 sq km/317 734 sq mi
Capital Windhoek
Chief towns Lüderitz, Keetmanshoop, Grootfontein
Population 1 648 000 (1999e)
Time zone GMT −2
Currency 1 Namibian Dollar (N$) = 100 cents
Language English
Religions Christianity 90%, traditional beliefs 10%
Ethnic groups Ovambo 50%, Kavango 9%, Damara 8%, Herero 8%, white 6%, Nama 5%, others 14%

Physical description

The Namib Desert runs along the Atlantic Ocean coast; the inland plateau has a mean elevation of 1 500m; the highest point is Brandberg (2 606m); the Kalahari Desert lies to the east and south; the Orange River forms the southern frontier with South Africa.

Climate

Low rainfall on the coast, higher in the interior; the average annual rainfall at Windhoek, representative of the interior, is 360mm and the average maximum daily temperature range is 20°–30°C.

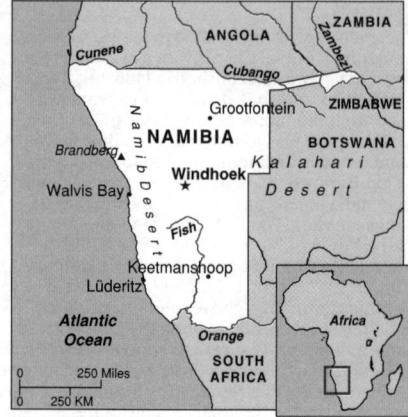

Government

Governed within a multiparty system by an Executive President, elected for a five-year term, assisted by a Cabinet headed by a Prime Minister; the legislative lower house of the bicameral parliament is an elected National Assembly, serving for up to five years; the National Council is the upper house representing regional leaders and serving for six years.

Economy

Agriculture employs c.60% of the population; livestock; subsistence farming in the north; major world producer of diamonds and uranium; copper, lead, zinc, arsenic, cadmium, salt, silver, tin, tungsten; fishing, food processing, brewing, plastics, furniture, textiles.

History

Pre-colonial Namibia was inhabited by Bantu tribes and San (Bushmen). It became the German protectorate of South West Africa in 1884, and from 1904 the Germans waged near-genocidal wars to crush the Herero and Nama peoples. Occupied by South African troops in 1914, it was mandated to South Africa by the League of Nations in 1920. South Africa continued to administer the area as South West Africa, but the UN challenged South African rule from 1966, changing the name to Namibia in 1968, and recognizing the South West Africa People's Organization (SWAPO) as representative of the Namibian people. After guerrilla war and the defeat of its forces in Mozambique, South Africa installed an interim administration in 1985, and Namibia gained full independence in 1990 under President Sam Nujoma. In 1994 the Walvis Bay area, a major port and South African enclave, was returned to Namibia. Nujoma was re-elected in 1994 and 1999.

NAURU

Official name Republic of Nauru
Local name Naeoro (Nauruan), Nauru (English)
Location An independent republic formed by a small, isolated island in the west-central Pacific Ocean, 42km/26mi to the south of the Equator and 4 000km/2 500mi north-east of Sydney, Australia
Area 21 sq km/8 sq mi
Capital There is no capital as such, but government offices are situated in Yaren District

Population 10 600 (1999e)
Time zone GMT + 11.5
Currency 1 Australian Dollar ($A) = 100 cents
Language Nauruan; English is also widely understood
Religions Christianity, predominantly Protestant, with a Roman Catholic minority; also Buddhism
Ethnic groups Nauruan 58%, other Pacific Islanders 26%, Chinese and Vietnamese 8%, European 8%

Physical description

The ground rises from sandy beaches to form a fertile coastal belt, c.100–300m wide, the only cultivable soil; a central plateau inland, which reaches 65m at its highest point, is composed largely of phosphate-bearing rocks.

Climate

Tropical, with average daily temperatures of 24°–34°C, and average humidity between 70 and 80 per cent; annual rainfall averages 1 524mm and falls mainly in the monsoon season from November to February, with marked yearly deviations.

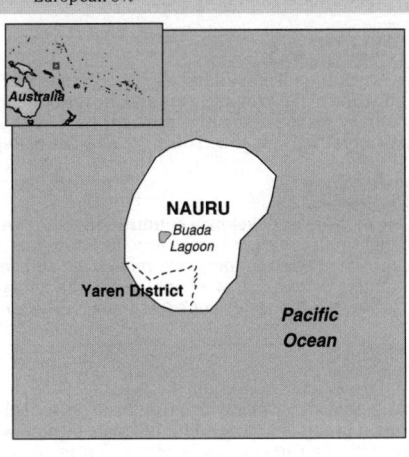

Government

A unicameral Parliament of 18 members, elected every three years; parliament elects the President, who appoints a Cabinet.

Economy

Based on phosphate mining, but reserves expected to run out soon, and over 60% of revenue from phosphate exports have been invested to provide future income; coconuts, some vegetables; tourism; tax haven.

History

Under German administration from the 1880s until 1914; after 1919, a League of Nations mandate was administered by Australia; there was a movement for independence by the 1960s; achieved self-government in 1966; gained full independence in 1968; joined the Commonwealth in 1999. In early 2003 a no-confidence vote in the President, René Harris, and his replacement by Bernard Dowiyogo led to political confusion; Dowiyogo died in Mar and Derog Gioura became Acting President.

NEPAL

Official name Kingdom of Nepal
Local name Nepal Adhirajya
Location A landlocked independent kingdom lying along the southern slopes of the Himalayas in central Asia, bounded to the north by the Tibet region of China, and to the east, south and west by India
Area 145 391 sq km/56 121 sq mi
Capital Kathmandu
Chief towns Patan, Bhadgaon

Population 24 303 000 (1999e)
Time zone GMT +5.5
Currency 1 Nepalese Rupee (NRp, NRs) = 100 paise/pice
Language Nepali
Religions Hinduism 90%, Buddhism 5%, Islam 3%, others 2%
Ethnic groups Nepali 59%, Bihari 20%, Tamang 3%, Tharu 3%, Newar 3%, others 12%

Nations of the World

Physical description

A landlocked country; it rises steeply from the Ganges Basin; high fertile valleys in the hill country at 1300m, such as the Vale of Kathmandu (a World Heritage site), are enclosed by ranges of folded mountains; the country is dominated by the glaciated peaks of the Himalayas, the highest of which is Mount Everest at 8 848m.

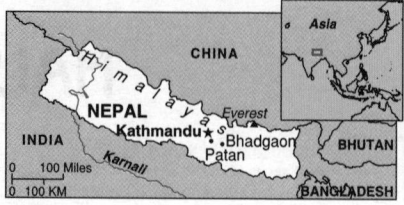

Climate

Varies from subtropical lowland, with hot, humid summers and mild winters, to an alpine climate over 3 300m, where peaks are permanently snow-covered; temperatures at Kathmandu vary from 40°C in May to 2°C in December; the monsoon season occurs during summer (June–September); average annual rainfall decreases from 1778mm in the east to 889mm in the west.

Government

A constitutional monarchy ruled by a hereditary King; a period of unrest in 1990 was followed by a reduction of the King's powers and the introduction of a new constitution with a multiparty parliamentary system; executive power is held by the King and a Council of Ministers and there is a bicameral legislature consisting of a House of Representatives and a National Council.

Economy

One of the least developed countries in Asia; agriculture employs 90% of the people; rice, wheat, millet, maize, barley, sugar cane; few minerals are exploited commercially, although there are deposits of coal, copper, iron, mica, zinc and cobalt; agricultural and forest-based goods, jute, handicrafts, carpets, medicinal herbs, ready-made garments, shoes, woollen goods; hydroelectric power is being developed; tourism has become increasingly important.

History

Nepal was ruled from about the 4c to the 10c by the Licchavi Dynasty, then from the 10c to 18c by the Malla Dynasty, under which Hinduism became the dominant religion. Modern Nepal was formed from a group of independent hill states which were united in the 18c. In 1769 the current ruling dynasty came to power following an invasion by Gurkhas, who moved the capital to Kathmandu. A parliamentary system was introduced in 1959, but was replaced in 1960 by a party-less system of *panchayats* (village councils). Nepal is a constitutional monarchy ruled by a hereditary King. In Jun 2001 the Crown Prince, Dipendra Bir Bikram, massacred his father King Birendra Bir Bikram (who had reigned since 1972) and eight other members of the Royal Family. He was briefly proclaimed king but died of his own injuries and was succeeded by Birendra's brother, Gyanendra. Recent years have also seen violent uprisings by Maoist republican rebels and a state of emergency was declared in Nov 2001, although a ceasefire was declared in Jan 2003.

THE NETHERLANDS

Official name Kingdom of the Netherlands
Local name Koninkrijk der Nederlanden
Location A maritime kingdom in north-western Europe, bounded to the west and north by the North Sea; to the east by Germany; and to the south by Belgium
Area 33 929 sq km/13 097 sq mi
Capital Amsterdam
Chief towns The Hague (seat of government), Rotterdam (largest city), Utrecht, Haarlem,

Eindhoven, Arnhem, Groningen
Population 15 808 000 (1999e)
Time zone GMT +1
Currency 1 Euro (€) = 100 cents
Language Dutch
Religions Christianity 63% (RC 36%, Prot 27%), Islam 3%, others 2%, none/unaffiliated 32%
Ethnic groups Dutch 94%, others 6%

Physical description

Generally low and flat, except in the south-east where hills rise to 321m; much of the coastal area lies below sea level, protected by coastal dunes and artificial dykes; without these, two fifths of the country would be submerged; around 27% of the land area is below sea level, an area inhabited by c.60% of the population; the country is largely a delta comprising silt from the mouths of the Rhine, Waal, Maas, Ijssel and Schelde rivers; the many canals connecting the rivers total 6 340km/3 940mi in length; land reclamation from the sea by polder dykes has been carried out for centuries; reclamation of the Zuiderzee (the remnant of which now forms the Ijsselmeer) began in 1920.

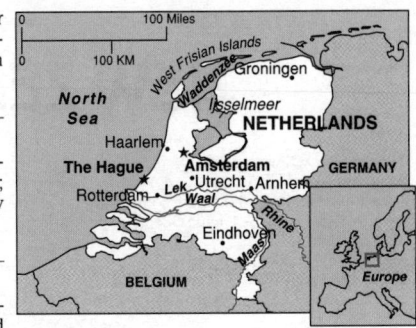

Climate
Cool, temperate, maritime; average temperatures are 1.7°C (January) and 17°C (July); annual rainfall, distributed fairly evenly throughout the year, exceeds 700mm.

Government
Under a constitutional monarchy there is a parliamentary democracy; the government is led by a Prime Minister, and the States-General (*Staten-Generaal*) consists of a 75-member Chamber and a 150-member Chamber, both elected for four years.

Economy
Rotterdam and the Europort are major European ports of transshipment, handling goods for EC member countries; Amsterdam is a world diamond centre; the Netherlands is the world's largest exporter of dairy produce; highly intensive agriculture includes animal husbandry, horticulture, potatoes, sugar beet and grains; major industries include engineering, chemicals, oil products, foodstuffs, electrical and high technology goods, and natural gas; fishing and tourism are also important.

History
The Netherlands was part of the Roman Empire until the 4c AD, and part of the Frankish Empire by the 8c before being incorporated into the Holy Roman Empire. The Netherlands passed to the Dukes of Burgundy in the 15c and then to Philip II, who succeeded to Spain and the Netherlands in 1555. Attempts to stamp out Protestantism led to rebellion in 1572. The seven northern provinces united against Spain in 1579. These United Provinces of the Netherlands achieved independence, which was finally recognized by Spain in 1648 at the end of the Eighty Years' War, and so founded the modern Dutch state. Between 1795 and 1813 it was overrun by the French, who established the Batavian Republic. Thereafter, it was united with Belgium as the Kingdom of the United Netherlands, until Belgium broke away to form a separate kingdom in 1830. Although the country was neutral in World War I, there was strong Dutch resistance to German occupation during World War II. The Netherlands joined with Belgium and Luxembourg to form the Benelux economic union in 1948. In the late 1940s there were conflicts over the independence of Dutch colonies in South-East Asia, particularly Indonesia. In 1958 the Netherlands was a founding member of the EEC. In 1980 Queen Beatrix acceded to the throne. The guilder was replaced by the Euro in Jan 2002.

Overseas territories

❖ Netherlands Antilles

Location A group of islands in the Caribbean Sea, comprising the southern group of Curaçao and Bonaire north of the Venezuelan coast, and the northern group of St Maarten, St Eustatins and Saba, lying east of Puerto Rico
Area 960 sq km/371 sq mi
Capital Willemstad
Population 207 800 (1999e)

❖ Aruba

Location An island in the Caribbean Sea, about 30km/19mi north of Venezuela, and 70km/44mi west of Curaçao
Area 193 sq km/75 sq mi
Capital Oranjestad
Population 68 700 (1999e)

⮑ New Caledonia ▸ France

Nations of the World

NEW ZEALAND

Official name New Zealand
Local name New Zealand
Location An independent state comprising a group of islands in the Pacific Ocean to the south-east of Australia
Area 268 812 sq km/103 761 sq mi
Capital Wellington
Chief towns Auckland, Christchurch, Dunedin, Hamilton

Population 3 662 000 (1999e)
Time zone GMT +12
Currency 1 New Zealand Dollar (NZ$) = 100 cents
Languages English, Maori
Religions Christianity 67% (Prot 52%, RC 15%), others 17%, none/unaffiliated 16%
Ethnic groups European 83%, Maori 15%, Pacific Islanders 6%, Asian 5%*

Physical description

The two principal islands, North and South, are separated by the Cook Strait; there is also Stewart Island, and several minor islands; from the northernmost point to the southernmost point the total length of the country is 1 770km/1 100mi; North Island is mountainous in the centre, with many hot springs; peaks rise to 2 797m at Mount Ruapehu; South Island is mountainous for its whole length, rising in the Southern Alps to 3 753m at Mount Cook; there are many glaciers and mountain lakes; the largest area of level lowland is the Canterbury Plain on the eastern side of South Island.

Climate

Highly changeable weather, with all months moderately wet; it is almost subtropical in the north and on the east coast, with mild winters and warm, humid summers; Auckland daily temperatures are 8°–13°C (July), 16°–23°C (January), average monthly rainfall 145mm (July), 79mm (December–January); the temperatures in South Island are generally lower.

Government

Governed by a Prime Minister, Cabinet and unicameral 120-member House of Representatives; elections take place every three years.

Economy

Based on farming, especially sheep and cattle; one of the world's major exporters of dairy produce; the third-largest exporter of wool; kiwi fruit; venison; mohair; textiles; timber; food processing; substantial coal and natural gas reserves; 80% of the country's electricity is supplied by hydroelectric power; tourism is a growing sector.

History

It is thought to have been settled by Polynesian explorers about 1 000 years ago. The first European sighting was made by Abel Tasman in 1642, and he named it Staten Landt. It later became known as Nieuw Zeeland, after the Dutch province. Captain Cook sighted it in 1769, and the first settlement was established in 1792. The country remained a dependency of New South Wales until 1841. Outbreaks of war in the 1840s and 1860s between immigrants and Maori, known as the Maori Wars, were disastrous for the Maori, much of whose land was taken. The country became the self-governing Dominion of New Zealand in 1907, and an active member of the Commonwealth of Nations. During the 1990s Maori activists demanded compensation for the land that the European settlers had taken from their people, and the government agreed either to pay compensation to certain tribes or to give them areas of land. The chief of state remains the British monarch, represented by a Governor-General.

* Percentages add to more than 100% as some people identify with more than one ethnicity.

NICARAGUA

Official name Republic of Nicaragua
Local name Nicaragua
Location The largest of the Central American republics, bounded to the north by Honduras; to the east by the Caribbean Sea; to the south by Costa Rica; and to the west by the Pacific Ocean
Area 148 000 sq km/57 128 sq mi
Capital Managua
Chief towns León, Granada, Masaya, Chinandega, Matagalpa, Corinto
Population 4 717 000 (1999e)
Time zone GMT −6
Currency 1 Córdoba Oro (C$) = 100 centavos
Language Spanish
Religions Christianity 100% (RC 95%, Prot 5%)
Ethnic groups Mestizo 70%, white 16%, black 9%, Amerindian 5%

Physical description

Mountainous western half with volcanic ranges rising to over 2 000m in the north-west; two large lakes, Lake Nicaragua and Lake Managua, lie in a broad structural depression extending north-west to south-east behind the coastal mountain range; rolling uplands and forested plains lie to the east; many short rivers flow into the Pacific Ocean and the lakes.

Climate

Tropical, with average annual temperatures ranging from 15°–35°C according to altitude; there is a rainy season from May–November when humidity is high; the average annual rainfall at Managua is 1 140mm; subject to devastating hurricanes.

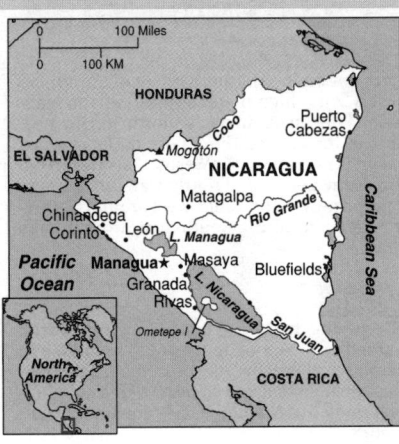

Government

A President with executive power and a unicameral National Assembly, both elected for a six-year period.

Economy

Agriculture accounts for over two thirds of total exports: cotton, coffee, sugar cane, rice, corn, beans, bananas, tobacco; livestock; shellfish; oil; natural gas; gold; silver; food processing; chemicals; metal products; textiles; beverages.

History

The Pacific coast was colonized by the Spaniards in the early 16c. Nicaragua gained independence from Spain in 1821 and left the Central American Federation in 1838. The plains of eastern Nicaragua, the Mosquito Coast, remained largely undeveloped and were under British protection until 1860. In the late 19c and early 20c the country was ruled by the dictatorial José Santos Zelaya, who was overthrown in 1907 by a coup supported by the USA. The USA continued to exert its influence until the 1930s, when another dictator, Anastasio Somoza (García) came to power in 1938; he ruled until his assassination in 1956. He was succeeded by first one son, Luis Somoza Debayle, and then another, Anastasio Somoza Debayle, the latter ruling from 1967 until the Sandinista National Liberation Front seized power in 1979 and established a socialist junta of national reconstruction. The former supporters of the Somoza government (the Contras), based in Honduras and supported by the USA until 1989, carried out guerrilla activities against the junta from 1979. Cease-fires and disarmament were agreed in 1990 and 1994, but unrest continued. In 1990 the National Opposition Union beat the Sandinista National Liberation Front in elections, and since 1996 the Liberals have been in power.

Nations of the World

NIGER

Official name Republic of Niger
Local name Niger
Location A landlocked republic in West Africa, bounded to the north-east by Libya; to the north-west by Algeria; to the west by Mali; to the south-west by Burkina Faso; to the south by Benin and Nigeria; and to the east by Chad
Area 1 186 408 sq km/457 953 sq mi
Capital Niamey
Chief towns Agadès, Diffa, Dosso, Maradi, Tahoua, Zinder
Population 9 962 000 (1999e)
Time zone GMT +1
Currency 1 CFA Franc (CFAFr) = 100 centimes
Language French; Hausa and Djerma are spoken widely
Religions Islam 80%, Christianity and traditional beliefs 20%
Ethnic groups Hausa 56%, Djerma and Songhai 22%, Fulani 9%, Tuareg 8%, others 5%

Physical description

Niger lies on the southern fringe of the Sahara Desert, on a high plateau; the Hamada Manguene Plateau lies in the far north; the Aïr Massif is in the centre; the Ténéré du Tafassasset Desert is in the east; the Western Talk Desert occupies the centre and north; water in quantity is found only in the south-west around the River Niger and in the south-east around Lake Chad.

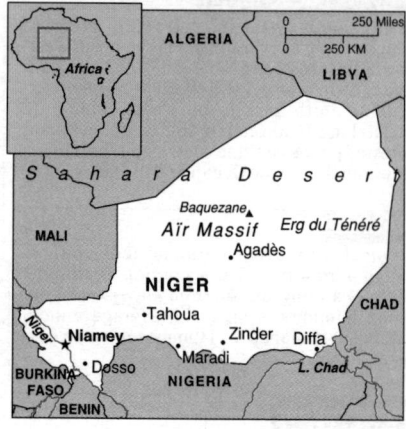

Climate

One of the hottest countries in the world; marked rainy season in the south from June to October; rainfall decreases in the north to almost negligible levels in desert areas; the annual rainfall at Niamey is 554mm; drought can occur.

Government

National Assembly elected for five year term; a President is head of state and appoints a Cabinet and Prime Minister.

Economy

Dominated by agriculture and mining; groundnuts; cotton; cowpeas; gum arabic; livestock; production was badly affected by severe drought conditions in the 1970s; uranium; tin; phosphates; coal; salt; natron; building materials; textiles; food processing.

History

Inhabited, according to archaeological evidence, during the Palaeolithic period, it was ruled by the Tuaregs from the 11c, the Zerma from the 17c, and the Hausa from the 14c, who ousted the Tuaregs in the 18c, but were themselves ousted by the Fulani. The first European occupiers were the French from 1883. Niger became a territory within French West Africa in 1904, and gained independence in 1960. There was a military coup in 1974 and political activity was not legalized again until 1989. Civil unrest in 1990 led to the approval of a multi-party constitution in 1992. Mahamane Ousmane was elected President the following year, remaining in power until he was ousted by a military coup in 1996. Pressure from France resulted in a presidential election, following which the military leader Ibrahim Baré Maïnassara came to power; he was assassinated in 1999, and Daouda Wanke became President. Constitution changes later in 1999 restored democracy and Tandja Mamadou was elected President. In the 1990s there was ethnic unrest caused by Tuareg rebels fighting government forces in the north, until a peace agreement was reached in 1995.

NIGERIA

Official name Federal Republic of Nigeria
Local name Nigeria
Location A republic in West Africa, bounded to the west by Benin; to the north by Niger; to the north-east by Chad; to the east by Cameroon; and to the south by the Gulf of Guinea and the Bight of Benin
Area 923 768 sq km/356 574 sq mi

Capital Abuja
Chief towns Lagos, Ibadan, Ogbomosho, Kano, Oshogbo, Ilorin, Abeokuta, Port Harcourt
Population 113 829 000 (1999e)
Time zone GMT +1
Currency 1 Naira (N, ₦) = 100 kobo
Language English; Hausa, Yoruba, Edo and Igbo are also spoken

Physical description

The coastal strip has a long, sandy shoreline with mangrove swamp, dominated by the River Niger delta; an undulating area of tropical rainforest and oil palm bush lie north of the coastal strip; the relatively dry central plateau is characterized by open woodland and savannah; the far north of the country is on the edge of the Sahara Desert and is largely a gently undulating savannah with tall grasses; there are numerous rivers in Nigeria, notably the Niger and Benue; the Gotel Mountains are on the south-eastern frontier and the highest point is at Mount Vogel (2 024m).

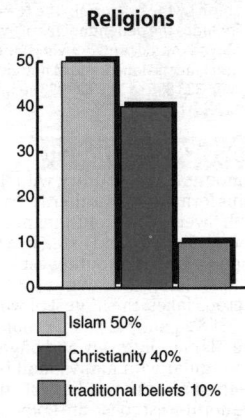

Climate

There are two rainy seasons in the coastal areas; the wettest part is the Niger delta and the mountainous south-eastern frontier, with an annual rainfall above 2 500mm, decreasing towards the west; Ibadan in the south-east has an average daily maximum temperature of 31°C and an average annual rainfall of 1 120mm; there is only one rainy season in the north; the dry season extends from October to April, when little rain falls.

Government

A bicameral National Assembly of a 109-seat Senate and a 360-seat House of Representatives, both serving seven-year terms, was introduced in 1999.

Economy

Based on agriculture until oil production began in the late 1950s; oil provides c.90% of exports; half the population is still engaged in agriculture; cocoa, rubber, palm oil, groundnuts, cotton, yams, cassava, rice, sugar cane, tobacco; livestock; fishing; forestry; natural gas, coal, tin, lead, zinc, lignite, iron ore, columbite (world's largest supplier), tantalite, limestone, marble; food; pulp and paper; textiles; rubber; sugar; beer; vehicles; pharmaceuticals.

Religions

- Islam 50%
- Christianity 40%
- traditional beliefs 10%

History

There are over 250 tribal groups, notably the Hausa and Fulani in the north, Yoruba in the south, and Igbo in the east. Nigeria was at the centre of the Nok culture in 500BC–AD200. Several African kingdoms developed throughout the area in the Middle Ages (eg the Hausa and Yoruba), and Muslim immigrants arrived in the 15–16c. European settlers arrived and participated in the gold and slave trades. A British colony was established at Lagos in 1861, and protectorates of North and South Nigeria were created in 1900. These were amalgamated as the Colony and Protectorate of Nigeria in 1914, which became a federation in 1954 and gained independence in 1960. Nigeria was declared a federal republic in 1963 under President Azikiwe. A military coup took place in 1966, and the Igbo people in the east formed the Republic of Biafra in 1967, resulting in the Biafran War and eventually the surrender of Biafra in 1970. There were further military coups in 1983 and 1985,

Nations of the World

after which military rule was broken only temporarily, in 1993. Later that year Sani Abacha took over as head of state. In 1995 political activity was legalized, but Nigeria was suspended from the Commonwealth of Nations following the execution of nine prodemocracy activists. In Feb 1999 Olusegun Obasanjo was elected President in a transition from military to civilian rule, and Nigeria was readmitted to the Commonwealth of Nations in May that year. In recent years there has been an increase in ethnic and religious tensions and violence.

🔁 **Northern Ireland ▸ United Kingdom**

🔁 **Northern Mariana Islands ▸ United States of America**

🔁 **North Korea ▸ Korea, North**

Ethnic groups

- Yoruba 21%
- Hausa 21%
- Igbo 19%
- Fulani 11%
- Ibibio 6%
- others 22%

NORWAY

Official name Kingdom of Norway
Local name Kongeriket Norge
Location A kingdom in north-west Europe, bounded to the north by the Arctic Ocean; to the east by Sweden, Finland and Russia; to the west by the North Sea and Norwegian Sea; and to the south by the Skagerrak. The Norwegian kingdom includes the dependencies of Svalbard and Jan Mayen (Arctic) and Bouvet Island, Peter I Island, and Queen Maud Land (Antarctica)
Area 323 895 sq km/125 023 sq mi
Capital Oslo

Chief towns Bergen, Trondheim, Stavanger, Kristiansand
Population 4 439 000 (1999e)
Time zone GMT +1
Currency 1 Norwegian Krone (NKr) = 100 øre
Language Norwegian, in the varieties of Bokmål and Nynorsk
Religions Christianity 89% (Prot 88%, RC 1%), others and none/unaffiliated 11%
Ethnic groups Norwegian 96%, Lapp 1%, others 3%

Physical description

A mountainous country, with the Kjölen Mountains forming the northern part of the boundary with Sweden, the Jotunheimen range in south-central Norway, and extensive plateau regions, especially in the south-west and centre; much of the interior rises above 1500m; there are numerous lakes, the largest of which is Lake Mjøsa (368 sq km/142 sq mi); major rivers include the Glåma, Dramselv and Lågen; the coastline is irregular with many small islands and long deep fjords; the two largest island groups, off the north-west coast, are Lofoten and Vesterålen.

Climate

An Arctic winter climate in the interior highlands, with snow, strong winds and severe frosts; comparatively mild winter conditions exist on the coast; rainfall is heavy on the west coast; average annual rainfall at Bergen is 1958mm; there are colder winters and warmer, drier summers in the southern lowlands.

Government

A hereditary monarchy with limited powers; government is led by a Prime Minister; Parliament (*Storting*) comprises an Upper House (*Lagting*) and a Lower House (*Odelsting*); members are elected every four years.

Economy

Based on the extraction and processing of raw materials (oil, natural gas), using plentiful hydro-electric power; major export manufactures are paper and paper products, industrial chemicals and basic metals; industries include shipbuilding, engineering, food processing, fishing and tourism; less than 3% of the land is under cultivation, producing barley, hay and oats; forest covers c.25% of the land.

History

A royal race from Sweden settled itself in southern Norway in the 7c, and the establishment of Norway as a united kingdom was achieved in the 11c by Olaf II, whose successor, Canute, brought Norway under Danish rule. It united with Sweden and Denmark in 1389, and Sweden was allowed to annex Norway in 1814 as a reward for its assistance against Napoleon I. Growing nationalism resulted in independence in 1905. Norway declared neutrality in both World Wars, but was occupied by Germany in 1940–4. Referendums in 1972 and 1994 have kept Norway out of the EC.

OMAN

Official name Sultanate of Oman
Local name Saltanat 'Uman
Location An independent state in the extreme south-eastern corner of the Arabian Peninsula. It is bounded to the north-west by the United Arab Emirates; to the north and west by Saudi Arabia; to the south-west by Yemen; to the north-east by the Gulf of Oman; and to the south-east and east by the Arabian Sea
Area 300 000 sq km/115 800 sq mi

Capital Muscat
Chief towns Matrah, Nazwa, Salalah
Population 2 447 000 (1999e)
Time zone GMT +4
Currency 1 Omani Rial (RO) = 1 000 baiza
Language Arabic
Religions Islam 86%, Hinduism 13%, others 1%
Ethnic groups Arab 74%, Pakistani 22%, others 4%

Physical description

The tip of the Musandam peninsula in the Strait of Hormuz is separated from the rest of the country by an 80km/50mi strip belonging to the United Arab Emirates; the Hajar range runs north-west to south-east parallel to the coast; several peaks in the Jabal Akhdar are over 3 000m; the alluvial plain of the Batinah lies east and north of the Hajar; a vast sand desert is to the north-east.

Climate

A desert climate with much regional variation; hot and humid coast from April to October with a maximum temperature of 47°C; hot and dry interior during this summer period; relatively temperate in mountains; light monsoon rains in the south from June to September.

Government

An independent state ruled by a Sultan who is both head of state and Premier.

Economy

Oil discovered in 1964 now provides over 90% of government revenue; natural gas is an important source of industrial power; attempts made to diversify the economy; copper smelting, date processing, banana packing, electric wire and cables, paper bags; c.70% of the population relies on agriculture; alfalfa, wheat, tobacco, fruit, vegetables, fishing.

History

Oman was a dominant maritime power of the western Indian Ocean in the 16c. It suffered internal dissension in 1913–20 between supporters of the Sultanate and members of the Ibadhi sect who

Nations of the World

wanted to be ruled exclusively by their religious leader. A separatist tribal revolt in 1964 led to a police coup that in 1970 installed a new sultan from the ruling family, Qaboos bin Said, who became both head of state and Premier. Successful moves were made in the 1990s towards the election of women to government, and Oman's first female government minister was appointed in Mar 2003.

PAKISTAN

Official name Islamic Republic of Pakistan
Local name Pākistān
Location An Asian state, bounded to the east by India; to the west by Afghanistan and Iran; and to the north by China
Area 803 943 sq km/310 322 sq mi
Capital Islamabad

Chief towns Karachi, Lahore, Faisalabad, Rawalpindi
Population 138 123 000 (1999e)
Time zone GMT +5
Currency 1 Pakistan Rupee (PRs, Rp) = 100 paisa
Language Urdu; English and several local languages are also spoken

Physical description

Largely centred on the alluvial floodplain of the River Indus; bounded to the north and west by mountains rising to 8 611m at K2; mostly flat plateau, low-lying plains, and arid desert to the south of the Karakoram range. The disputed area of Jammu and Kashmir lies to the north.

Climate

Dominated by the Asiatic monsoon; in the mountains and foothills of the north and west, the climate is cool with summer rain and winter snow; in the upland plateaux, summers are hot and winters are cool, with the possibility of some winter rain; in summer the Indus Valley is extremely hot and is fanned by dry winds, often carrying sand; throughout the country, the hottest season lasts from March to June, with the highest temperatures occurring in the south; the rainy season lasts from late June to early October and coincides with the south-western monsoon.

Religions

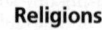

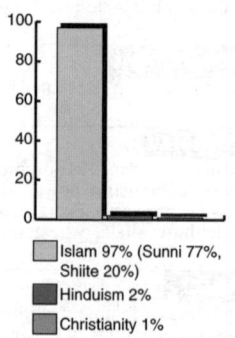

Islam 97% (Sunni 77%, Shiite 20%)
Hinduism 2%
Christianity 1%

Government

Governed by an elected President and a bicameral federal Parliament consisting of a 237-member National Assembly (*Majlis as-Shoora*) and an 87-member Senate.

Economy

Agriculture employs 55% of the labour force; concentrated on the floodplains of the five major rivers of Pakistan, and supported by an extensive irrigation network; wheat, maize, sugar cane, rice, cotton; cotton production is important, supporting major spinning, weaving, and processing industries; textiles; food processing; tobacco; engineering; cement; fertilizers; chemicals; natural gas; limestone; gypsum; iron ore; rock salt; uranium.

History

Pakistan's walled cities at Mohenjo-Daro, Harappa and Kalibangan are evidence of civilization in the Indus Valley over 4 000 years ago. Muslims ruled the region under the Mughal Empire from 1526 to 1761, and the British ruled most areas from the 1840s.

Pakistan was separated from India to form a state for the Muslim minority in 1947, consisting of West Pakistan (Baluchistan, North-West Frontier, West Punjab, Sind) and East Pakistan (East Bengal), which were physically separated by 1 000mi/1 600km. Conflict with India broke out over Jammu and Kashmir in 1949. The successful Indian occupation of most of the disputed territory was the cause of wars in 1965 and 1971. Pakistan was proclaimed an Islamic republic in 1956. Differences between East and West Pakistan developed into civil war in 1971, resulting in East Pakistan becoming an independent state (Bangladesh). A military coup led by General Zia ul-Haq took place in 1977, and former Prime Minister Zulfikar Ali Bhutto was executed in 1979, despite international appeals for clemency. In 1991 there was increased violence within the country, particularly in Sind, and during the 1990s there were several changes of government amid allegations of corruption. In 1999, 600 highly trained militia crossed the 1949 cease-fire line (called the Line of Control since 1972) into Kashmir, provoking retaliatory air strikes from India, re-opening the conflict over the region, and defying the Lahore Declaration (1999) in which the Indian and Pakistani prime ministers had promised that their countries would settle their differences by negotiation, despite the fact that their claims remained totally incompatible. When the democratically elected Premier Nawaz Sharif developed into an elected dictator, there was another military coup in 1999, led by General Pervez Musharraf, and Pakistan was suspended from the Commonwealth; Musharraf became President. He was elected to a five year term in Jan 2002 in a controversial referendum, and elections to the National Assembly took place in Oct. Meanwhile tensions with India over Kashmir continued to increase, bringing the two countries to the brink of war in 2002.

Ethnic groups

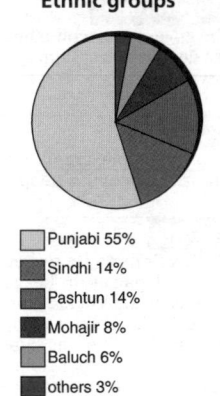

- Punjabi 55%
- Sindhi 14%
- Pashtun 14%
- Mohajir 8%
- Baluch 6%
- others 3%

Nations of the World

PALAU

Official name Republic of Palau	**Time zone** GMT + 10
Local name Palau	**Currency** 1 US Dollar ($, US$) = 100 cents
Location A group of c.350 small islands and islets in the west Pacific Ocean, 960km/600mi east of the Philippines	**Languages** Palauan, English
	Religions Christianity 66% (mostly RC), traditional beliefs (Modekngei) 34%
Area 494 sq km/191 sq mi	
Capital Koror	**Ethnic groups** A composite of Polynesian, Malayan and Melanesian peoples
Population 18 500 (1999e)	

Physical description

Varies from the high, mountainous main island of Babelthuap to low-lying coral islands often surrounded by coral reefs.

Climate

Warm all year, with high humidity; the average annual temperature is 27°C and the average annual rainfall is 3 810mm; typhoons are common.

Nations of the World

Government

The government combines elements of a modern democratic system and a system of hereditary chiefs.

Economy

Taro, pineapple, breadfruit, bananas, yams, citrus fruit, coconuts, pepper; fishing; tourism.

History

Held by Germany between 1899 and 1914; mandated to Japan by the League of Nations in 1920; invaded by USA in 1944; became a self-governing republic in 1981. A compact of 'free association' with the USA was signed in 1994, by which the USA takes responsibility for Palau's defence while Palau retains its sovereignty in all other matters.

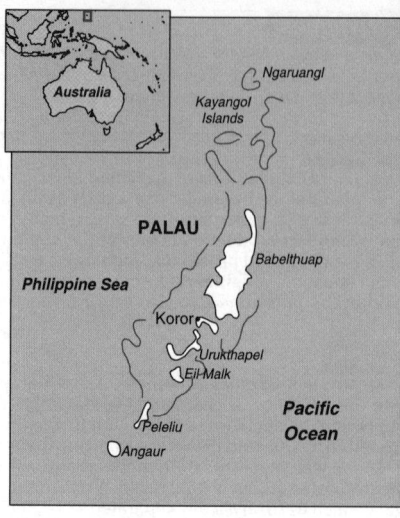

PANAMA

Official name Republic of Panama
Local name Panamá
Location A republic occupying the south-eastern end of the isthmus of Central America, bounded to the north by the Caribbean Sea; to the south by the Pacific Ocean; to the west by Costa Rica; and to the east by Colombia
Area 77 082 sq km/29 753 sq mi
Capital Panama City

Chief towns David, Colón, Santiago
Population 2 779 000 (1999e)
Time zone GMT -5
Currency 1 Balboa (B, Ba) = 100 centésimos
Language Spanish
Religions Christianity 89% (RC 84%, Prot 5%), Islam 5%, Baha'i 1%, others 5%
Ethnic groups Mestizo 62%, black 13%, white 12%, Mulatto 8%, Amerindian 5%

Physical description

Mostly mountainous; the Serranía de Tabasará in the west rises to over 2 000m; the Azuero peninsula lies to the south; lake-studded lowland cuts across the isthmus; dense tropical forests lie on the Caribbean coast.

Climate

Tropical, with a mean annual temperature of 32°C; the average annual rainfall at Colón, on the Caribbean coast, is 3 280mm, while in Panama City it is 1 780mm.

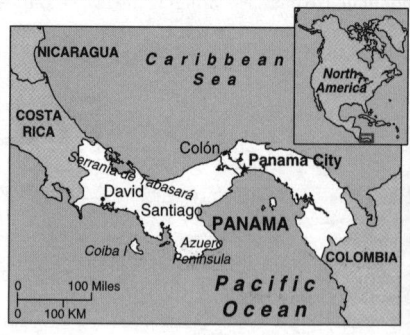

Government

Governed by a President, elected for five years, and a Cabinet, with a 67-member Legislative Assembly.

Economy

Centred mainly on the Panama Canal and the ports of Colón and Panama; Canal revenue accounts for four fifths of the country's wealth; great increase in the banking sector since 1970; attempts to diversify include oil refining, cigarettes, clothing, beverages, construction materials, paper products, shrimps, tourism; copper, gold, silver deposits; bananas, coffee, cacao, sugar cane.

History

It was visited by Columbus in 1502 and quickly gained strategic importance as a centre of Spanish trade movement, a vital link between the Caribbean and Pacific. It remained under Spanish colonial rule until 1821, when it gained its independence and joined the union known as Gran Colombia. The US-inspired revolution of 1903 led to a break from the Colombian union. Although Panama has an elected President and Legislative Assembly, the military arose as the ruling force, led by General Manuel Noriega until 1989, until the armed forces were abolished by a new constitution in 1991. In Dec 1989 US peace-keeping forces invaded Panama City after allegations of corruption and drugs trafficking against Noriega had led to strict US sanctions and heightened tensions in the area, and Noriega was deposed, tried and convicted for drugs offences in the USA. Mireya Moscoso was elected President in May 1999. Panama assumed sovereignty of the Panama Canal, previously administered by the USA, in 1999.

PAPUA NEW GUINEA

Official name Papua New Guinea
Local name Papua New Guinea
Location An independent island group in the south-west Pacific Ocean
Area 462 840 sq km/178 656 sq mi
Capital Port Moresby
Chief towns Lae, Madang, Rabaul
Population 4 705 000 (1999e)

Time zone GMT +10
Currency 1 Kina (K) = 100 toea
Language Pidgin English; approximately 750 other languages are spoken
Religions Christianity 66% (Prot and others 44%, RC 22%), traditional beliefs 34%
Ethnic groups Papuan 85%, Melanesian 1%, others 14%

Physical description

Complex system of mountains, with snow-covered peaks rising above 4 000m; the highest point is Mount Wilhelm (4 509m); large rivers flow to the south, north and east; mainly covered with tropical rainforest; vast mangrove swamps lie along the coast; the archipelago islands are mountainous, mostly volcanic, and fringed with coral reefs.

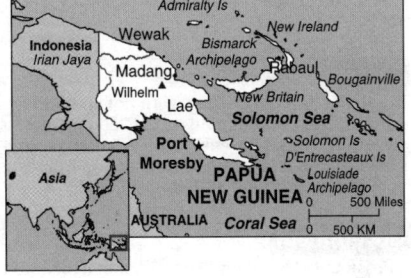

Climate

Typically monsoonal, with temperatures and humidity constantly high; the average temperature range is 22°–33°C; high rainfall, which averages 2 000–2 500mm.

Government

A Governor-General represents the British Crown; governed by a Prime Minister and Cabinet, with a unicameral 109-member national Parliament elected for five years.

Economy

Over two thirds of the workforce are engaged in farming, fishing and forestry; yams, sago, cassava, bananas, vegetables, copra, coffee, cocoa, timber, palm oil, rubber, tea, sugar, peanuts; copper, gold; hydroelectric power, natural gas; food processing; brewing; tourism.

History

Possibly inhabited by South-East Asians who came to Papua New Guinea via Indonesia many thousands of years ago, it was visited by the Portuguese and the Spanish in the 16c before being colonized by the British and Dutch in the late 18c. In 1884 Britain proclaimed a protectorate in the south-east, while Germany proclaimed the north-east quadrant to be a German protectorate. German New Guinea was established in the north-east in 1899. The German colony was overrun by Australia in World War I, and in 1920 Australia was mandated to govern the British and German areas. These were combined in 1949 as the UN Trust Territory of Papua and New Guinea, which gained independence within the Commonwealth of Nations in 1975. In 1989 fighting began between separatists and government forces on the island of Bougainville. A cease-fire was agreed in 1994 but fighting resumed when peace talks failed. In 1997 foreign troops were brought in by the government to quash the Bougainville Revolutionary Army, but this action resulted in mutiny by the army. A peace deal was signed in 1998, but talks to resolve the situation continued. Papua New Guinea has also suffered from natural disasters, such as a devastating tsunami in 1998, in addition to sporadic violence and political tensions.

PARAGUAY

Official name Republic of Paraguay
Local name Paraguay
Location A landlocked country in central South America, bounded to the north-west by Bolivia; to the north and east by Brazil; and to the south-west by Argentina
Area 406 750 sq km/157 000 sq mi
Capital Asunción
Chief towns Villarrica, Concepción

Population 5 434 000 (1999e)
Time zone GMT −3
Currency 1 Guaraní (Gs) = 100 céntimos
Language Spanish; Guaraní is also spoken
Religions Christianity 99% (RC 90%, Prot 9%, mostly Mennonite), others 1%
Ethnic groups Mestizo 92%, white 2%, Amerindian 2%, others 4%

Physical description

Divided into two regions by the River Paraguay, lying mostly at altitudes below 450m; bordered to the south and east by the River Paraná; the Gran Chaco in the west is mostly cattle country or scrub forest; more fertile land lies in the east; the Paraná Plateau at 300–600m is mainly wet, treeless savannah.

Climate

Tropical in the north-west, with hot summers, warm winters, and rainfall up to 1 250mm; temperate in the south-east, with rainfall up to 1 750mm; the temperature at Asunción ranges from 12°C in winter to 35°C in summer.

Government

A President elected for five years and a bicameral National Congress consisting of a Chamber of Deputies and a Senate; no one having held the office of President may be re-elected.

Economy

Agriculture employs 40% of the labour force; oilseed, cotton, wheat, manioc, sweet potato, tobacco, corn, rice, sugar cane; livestock rearing; meat packing; pulp; timber; textiles; fertilizers; cement; kaolin; glass.

History

Originally inhabited by Guarans, it was settled by the Spanish after 1537, and by Jesuit missionaries who arrived in 1609. It gained independence from Spain in 1811. During the disastrous War of the Triple Alliance (1864–70) against Brazil, Argentina and Uruguay, Paraguay lost over half of its population. In 1935 it regained territory disputed with Bolivia after the three-year Chaco War. Civil war broke out in 1947, and in 1954 General Alfredo Stroessner seized power, with US backing, and was appointed President, but he lost US support over time and was forced to stand down following a coup in 1989. The first multi-party elections were held in 1993.

PERU

Official name Republic of Peru
Local name Perú
Location A republic on the west coast of South America, bounded to the north by Ecuador; to the north-east by Colombia; to the east by Brazil and Bolivia; and to the south by Chile
Area 1 284 640 sq km/495 871 sq mi
Capital Lima
Chief towns Arequipa, Chiclayo, Cuzco, Trujillo

Population 26 625 000 (1999e)
Time zone GMT −5
Currency 1 New Sol (Pes) = 100 cénts
Languages Spanish, Quechua
Religions Christianity 98% (RC 93%, Prot 5%), others 2%
Ethnic groups Quechua 46%, Mestizo 34%, white 12%, Aymara 5%, others 3%

Physical description

Arid plains and foothills on the coast, with areas of desert and fertile river valleys; the central sierra, with an average altitude of 3 000m, contains 50% of the population; rivers cut through the plateau, forming deep canyons; the forested Andes and Amazon basin lie to the east; the major rivers flow to the Amazon.

Climate

Mild temperatures all year on the coast; dry, arid desert in the south; in the north, the coastal region has bursts of torrential rain every 10 years or so with rising sea temperatures and the cold current retreats south: this phenomenon is known as El Niño. Andean temperatures never rise above 23°C with a large daily temperature range and night frost in the dry season; in the Peruvian portion of the Amazon basin to the east, the climate is typically wet and tropical.

Government

A 120-member unicameral Congress was introduced in 1993; a President is elected for a five year term.

Economy

One of the world's leading producers of silver, zinc, lead, copper, gold, iron ore; 80% of Peru's oil is extracted from the Amazon forest; cotton, potatoes, sugar, rice, grapes, fruit, olives; sheep, cattle; steel, iron; vehicles; tyres; cement; wool; fishmeal, fish canning; fishing was severely affected by the adverse weather conditions of 1982–3 and by continuous overfishing; tourism, especially to ancient sites.

History

Peru had a highly developed Inca civilization in the 15c. The Spanish arrived in 1531, and the Viceroyalty of Peru was established. Gold and silver mines made Peru the principal source of Spanish power in South America. After declaring its independence in 1821, Peru entered into frequent border disputes during the 19c (eg the War of the Pacific in 1879–83). Clashes between Ecuador and Peru continued into the late 20c. There were also several military coups, and drug-related violence and terrorist activities resulted in large areas being declared under a state of emergency. In 1992–3 the constitution was suspended to allow President Alberto Fujimori absolute power to implement reform and deal with terrorism, and the government succeeded in capturing Abimael Guzmán, leader of the Sendero Luminoso (Shining Path) guerrilla movement. Fujimori resigned amidst controversy in 2000, and in 2001 Alejandro Toledo became Peru's first President of native Peruvian Indian descent.

PHILIPPINES

Official name Republic of the Philippines
Local name Pilipinas
Location A republic consisting of an archipelago of more than 7 100 islands and islets, situated to the north-east of Borneo and to the south of Taiwan
Area 299 679 sq km/115 676 sq mi
Capital Manila
Chief towns Quezon City, Basilan, Cebu, Bacolod, Davao, Iloilo

Population 79 346 000 (1999e)
Time zone GMT +8
Currency 1 Philippine Peso (PHP) = 100 centavos
Language Filipino; English and many local languages are also spoken
Religions Christianity 92% (RC 83%, Prot 9%), Islam 5%, others 3%
Ethnic groups Tagalog 30%, Cebuano 23%, Ilocano 9%, Ilongo 9%, Bicol 6%, Samar-Leyte 3%, others 20%

Physical description

Largely mountainous, with north to south ridges rising to over 2 500m; there are narrow coastal margins and broad interior plateaux; forests cover half the land area; some islands are ringed by coral reefs.

Climate

The lowlands have a warm and humid tropical climate throughout the year, with an average temperature of 27°C; average rainfall at Manila is 2 080mm; lying astride the typhoon belt, the Philippines are affected by c.15 cyclonic storms annually.

Government

The republic is governed by a President and a bicameral legislature, the Congress, comprising a Senate of 24 members elected for five years, and a House of Representatives with up to 250 members serving for three years.

Economy

Lumber, veneer, plywood; oil, copper, lead, iron, nickel, chromite, gold; rubber; textiles; oil products; food processing; electronics; vehicles; fishing; tourism; nearly half the workforce is employed in farming.

History

The Philippines was claimed for Spain by Magellan in 1521 but ceded to the USA after the Spanish–American War of 1898. It became a self-governing Commonwealth in 1935, was occupied by the Japanese during World War II, and achieved independence in 1946. During the period 1945–53 the communist-dominated Huk rebellion was suppressed. Then a Muslim separatist movement arose in the south, and following political unrest martial law was imposed (1972–81). The exiled political leader Benigno Aquino was assassinated on returning to Manila in 1983. A coup in 1985 ended the 20-year rule of President Ferdinand Marcos, and Aquino's widow, Cory Aquino, was elected to take over the presidency in 1986. She instituted a new constitution in 1987, but political unrest continued. Having survived six attempted military coups, she refused to stand for re-election and was succeeded in 1992 by Fidel Ramos; his successor in 1998, Joseph Estrada, resigned in 2001 amid impeachment proceedings and was succeeded by Gloria Arroyo. Violence by Muslim separatist groups continues.

⮞ Pitcairn Islands ▸ United Kingdom

POLAND

Official name Republic of Poland
Local name Rzeczpospolita Polska
Location A republic in central Europe, bounded to the north by Russia and the Baltic Sea; to the west by Germany; to the south-west by the Czech Republic; to the south by Slovakia; to the south-east by the Ukraine; and to the north-east by Belarus and Lithuania
Area 312 612 sq km/120 668 sq mi
Capital Warsaw

Chief towns Łódz, Kraków, Wrocław, Poznań, Gdańsk, Katowice, Lublin
Population 38 609 000 (1999e)
Time zone GMT +1
Currency 1 Złoty (Zl) = 100 groszy
Language Polish
Religions Christianity 96% (RC 93%, Orthodox 2%, Prot 1%), others 2%, none/unaffiliated 2%
Ethnic groups Polish 98%, German 1%, others 1%

Physical description

Mostly part of the great European plain, with the Carpathian and Sudetes Mountains in the south rising in the High Tatra to 2 499m at Mount Rysy; the Polish plateau to the north of the Tatra is cut by the Bug, San and Vistula rivers; Europe's richest coal basin lies in the west (Silesia); north of the plateau there are lowlands with many lakes; the Baltic coastal area is flat, with sandy heathland and numerous lagoons (coastline length is 491km/305mi); the main Polish rivers are the Vistula and Oder; rivers are often frozen in winter and liable to flood; forests cover one fifth of the land.

Climate

Continental climate, with severe winters and hot summers; rain falls chiefly in summer and seldom exceeds 650mm annually.

Government

A two-chamber legislature, comprising a 460-member Lower Assembly (the *Sejm*) and a 100-member Senate; a President is elected for a five year term, and appoints a Prime Minister to lead the government (a Council of Ministers).

Economy

Nearly 50% of the land is under cultivation, growing rye, wheat, barley, oats, potatoes and sugar beet; bacon, eggs, geese, turkeys, pork; major producer of coal; other deposits include lead, zinc, sulphur, potash and copper; major industries are shipbuilding, vehicles, machinery, electrical equipment, food processing and textiles.

History

Poland was inhabited from 2000 BC or earlier and became an independent kingdom in the 9c. The Poles under the Piast Dynasty emerged as the most powerful of a number of Slavic groups in 1025. Towards the end of Jagiełłon rule Poland formed a union with Lithuania (1569), at which point it stretched from the Baltic to the Black Sea. This Commonwealth was weakened by attacks from Russia, Brandenburg, Turkey and Sweden, and eventually in 1772, 1793 and 1795 Poland was partitioned between Prussia, Russia and Austria, and was deprived of its independent statehood; Russia gained the lion's share of its territories. Following the 1815 Congress of Vienna, Poland became a semi-independent state called the Congress Kingdom of Poland, and was incorporated into the Russian Empire under Alexander I. The Poles constantly struggled for national liberation, and there were uprisings in 1830, 1846–9 and 1863, which led to the kingdom being fully absorbed and subjected to a repressive campaign of Russification. However, the struggle continued and was eventually won at the end of World War I in 1918 when an independent Polish state emerged. Germany invaded Poland in 1939, precipitating World War II, and Poland was partitioned between Germany and the USSR in the same year. Throughout the war a major resistance movement developed, and a government in exile was set up. In 1944 a People's Democracy was established under Soviet influence, and by 1947 communists controlled the government. The late 1970s saw the rise of an independent trade union known from 1980 as Solidarity. Its leaders were detained in

Nations of the World

1981–3, and a state of martial law was imposed. The economic situation worsened, and there was continuing unrest in the 1980s. In 1989 multi-party politics were legalized and elections were held: the communist government lost support and Solidarity had major successes. Solidarity's leader Lech Wałesa became President of Poland in Dec 1990, but was defeated by the former communist Aleksander Kwasniewski in 1995. The transition to a market economy in the 1990s was accompanied by popular discontent, political difficulties and recession, but nevertheless a private sector developed within the economy. In 1997 another new constitution was adopted which eradicated all signs of the former communist system and a Solidarity-led government was formed. In Mar 1999 Poland joined NATO, and in 2002 it was formally invited to join the EU.

⊕ **Polynesia, French ▶ France**

PORTUGAL

Official name Republic of Portugal
Local name Portugal
Location A country in south-western Europe on the western side of the Iberian Peninsula, bounded to the north and east by Spain; and to the south and west by the Atlantic Ocean
Area 88 500 sq km/34 200 sq mi
Capital Lisbon

Chief towns Oporto, Setúbal, Coimbra
Population 9 918 000 (1999e)
Time zone GMT
Currency 1 Euro (€) = 100 cents
Language Portuguese
Religions Christianity 96% (RC 94%, Prot 2%), others 1%, none/unaffiliated 3%
Ethnic groups Portuguese 99%, others 1%

Physical description

There are several mountain ranges formed by the west spurs of the Spanish mountain system; the chief range is the Serra da Estrêla in the north, rising to 1991m; the four main rivers (the Douro, Minho, Tagus and Guadiana) are the lower courses of rivers beginning in Spain.

Climate

Basically a maritime climate, with increased variation between summer and winter temperatures inland; the west coast is relatively cool in summer; there is most rainfall in winter.

Government

Governed by a President, elected for five years, a Prime Minister and Council of Ministers, and a 250-member unicameral Assembly of the Republic, elected every four years.

Economy

There are several labour-intensive areas in the economy, such as textiles, leather, wood products, cork and ceramics; other exports include timber, wine, fish, chemicals and electrical machinery; steelworks, shipbuilding; mineral deposits (copper, wolfram, tin, iron ore, pyrites, zinc, lead, barium, titanium, uranium, sodium and calcium); agricultural products include wheat, maize, rice, rye, beans, potatoes, fruit, olive oil, meat and dairy produce; large forests of pine, oak, cork-oak, eucalyptus and chestnut cover about 20% of the country; tourism, especially in the south.

History

Portugal became a kingdom under Alphonso I in 1139. The Portuguese Empire began in the 15c, a time of major world exploration by the Portuguese. Portugal came under Spanish domination from 1580 to 1640, and was invaded by the French in 1807. The monarchy was overthrown and the First Republic established in 1910. A military coup took place in 1926, and in the early 1930s the country came under the Estado Novo regime of Dr Salazar, whose dictatorship of over 35 years (1932–68) was safeguarded by the feared PIDE. A military coup in 1974 was followed by 10 years of political unrest under 15 governments. Portugal joined the EC in 1986. The escudo was replaced by the Euro in Jan 2002.

❖ Azores

Location An island archipelago of volcanic origin in the North Atlantic ocean, lying 1400–1800km/ 870–1100mi to the west of the Cabo da Roca on mainland Portugal
Area 2300 sq km/900 sq mi
Chief town Ponta Delgada
Population 250 000 (1999e)

❖ Madeira

Location The main island in a Portuguese archipelago off the coast of North Africa, 990km/ 615mi south-west of Lisbon
Area 796 sq km/307 sq mi
Capital Funchal
Population 275 000 (1999e)

⟐ **Puerto Rico ▸ United States of America**

QATAR

Official name State of Qatar
Local name Dawlat Qatar
Location A low-lying state on the east coast of the Arabian Peninsula, comprising the Qatar Peninsula and numerous small offshore islands. It is bounded to the south by Saudi Arabia and the United Arab Emirates, and elsewhere by the Arabian Gulf
Area 11437 sq km/4 415 sq mi
Capital Doha

Chief towns Dukhan, Al Khawr, Umm Sai'd, Al Wakrah
Population 723 500 (1999e)
Time zone GMT +3
Currency 1 Qatar Riyal (QR) = 100 dirhams
Language Arabic
Religions Islam 95%, others 5%
Ethnic groups Arab 40%, Pakistani 18%, Indian 18%, Iranian 10%, others 14%

Physical description

The peninsula, 160km/100mi long and 55–80km/ 34–50mi wide, slopes gently from the Dukhan Heights (98m) to the east shore; barren terrain, mainly sand and gravel; coral reefs offshore.

Climate

Desert climate with average temperatures of 23°C in the winter and 35°C in the summer; high humidity; sparse annual rainfall not exceeding 75mm per annum.

Government

A hereditary monarchy, with an Emir who is both head of state and Prime Minister; a Council of Ministers is assisted by a 30-member nominated Consultative Council.

Economy

Based on oil; offshore gas reserves are thought to constitute an eighth of known world reserves; oil refineries, petrochemicals, liquefied natural gas; fertilizers; steel; cement; ship repairing; engineering; food processing; fishing; aubergines, lucerne, squash, hay, tomatoes.

History

Under the suzerainty of Bahrain for most of the 19c, Qatar was then ruled by the Turks before becoming a British protectorate after the Turkish withdrawal in 1916. It declared its independence in 1971. Qatar is a hereditary monarchy, with an Emir who until 1996 was both head of state and Prime Minister. Sheikh Khalifa bin Hamad al-Thani ruled from 1972 until 1995, when he was deposed by his son, Sheikh Ahmad bin Khalifa al-Thani. The latter's liberal reforms led to an attempted coup by Sheikh Khalifa in 1996, but democratic reforms have slowly continued.

⟐ **Réunion ▸ France**

⊛ Republic of China ▸ Taiwan

ROMANIA

Official name Romania
Local name România
Location A republic in south-eastern Europe, bounded to the south by Bulgaria; to the west by Serbia and Montenegro and Hungary; to the east by Moldova and the Black Sea; and to the north and east by the Ukraine.
Area 237 500 sq km/91 675 sq mi
Capital Bucharest
Chief towns Braşov, Constanţa, Iaşi, Timişoara,

Cluj-Napoca
Population 22 334 000 (1999e)
Time zone GMT +2
Currency 1 Leu (L, plural Lei) = 100 bani
Language Romanian
Religions Christianity 94% (Orthodox 82%, RC 6%, Prot 6%), Islam 1%, others 1%, none/unaffiliated 4%
Ethnic groups Romanian 89%, Magyar 9%, Romany 1%, others 1%

Physical description

The Carpathian Mountains separate Old Romania from Transylvania, and form the heart of the country; the Eastern Carpathians, between the northern frontier and the Prahova Valley, constitute an area of extensive forest cut by many passes; the higher Southern Carpathians are situated between the Prahova Valley and the Timis-Cerna gorges; the Western Carpathians lie between the River Danube and the River Somes; the highest peak is Negoiul (2 548m); the Romanian Plain in the south includes the Baragan Plain (to the east), the richest arable area, and the Oltenian Plain (to the west), crossed by many rivers; there are c.3 500 glacial ponds, lakes and coastal lagoons; over one quarter of the land is forested.

Climate

Continental, with cold, snowy winters and warm summers; the mildest area in winter is along the Black Sea coast; the plains of the north and east can suffer from drought; average annual rainfall is 1 000mm (in the mountains) and 400mm (in the Danube delta).

Government

A President is head of state and appoints a Prime Minister and Cabinet; there is a Senate and an Assembly of Deputies.

Economy

Since World War II there has been a gradual change from an agricultural to industrial economy; the state owned c.37% of the farmland, mainly organized as collectives and state farms; products included wheat, maize, sugar beet, fruit, potatoes, vines and meat from livestock; there are natural resources of oil, natural gas, salt, iron ore, copper; industries include iron and steel, metallurgy, engineering, chemicals, textiles, foodstuffs, electrical goods, electronics, machinery, rubber, timber and tourism; there were mounting economic difficulties in the 1980s and early 1990s.

History

The Romanian people are descended from the Dacians, Romans, Vlachs, Slavs and the other settlers in Moldavia and Wallachia (modern Romania) who speak Romanian. While the culture of the Slav settlers came to dominate elsewhere in the north Balkans, the Romanians' ancestors assimilated to the Latin culture of the earlier Romanized inhabitants. Under the Ottomans (15–19c), the Romanians began their movement for national independence in the 1820s, aspiring to the unification of Moldavia, Wallachia and Transylvania. In 1862 Moldavia and Wallachia merged to form the unitary Principality of Romania, and a monarchy was created in 1866. Romania joined the Allies in World War I, and united with Transylvania, Bessarabia and Bukovina in 1918. In 1920 Transylvania, with its mixed Romanian and Magyar population, was finally joined to the Kingdom of Romania by the Treaty of Trianon. Romania supported Germany in World War II and Soviet forces occupied the country in 1944. After the war it lost territories to Russia, Hungary and Bulgaria. The monarchy was abolished and a People's Republic declared in 1947 under the autocratic President Nicolae Ceausescu, leader of the Romanian Communist Party. Romania became a Socialist Republic in 1965. Becoming increasingly independent of the USSR from the 1960s, it formed relationships with China, and several Western countries. In 1989 violent repression of protest, resulting in the deaths of thousands of demonstrators, sparked a popular uprising and the overthrow of the Ceausescu regime and execution of the President and his wife. Ion Iliescu formed a National Salvation Front and was elected President of Romania. A provisional government led by previously imprisoned dissidents promised free elections in 1990, but unrest and demonstrations continued. In 1991 the country became a multi-party democracy. In 1996 Iliescu was defeated in the elections by Emil Constantinescu, but he returned to power after elections in 2000. In 2002 Romania was formally invited to join NATO.

RUSSIA

Official name The Russian Federation
Local name Rossiya
Location A republic occupying much of eastern Europe and northern Asia, bounded to the north by the Arctic Ocean; to the north-west by Norway, Finland, Estonia, Latvia, Belarus and the Ukraine; to the west by the Black Sea, Georgia and Azerbaijan; to the south-west by the Caspian Sea and Kazakhstan; to the south-east by China, Mongolia and North Korea; and to the east by the Sea of Okhotsk and the Bering Sea

Area 17 075 400 sq km/6 591 104 sq mi
Capital Moscow
Chief towns St Petersburg, Nizhniy Novgorod, Rostov-on-Don, Volgograd, Yekaterinburg, Novosibirsk, Chelyabinsk, Kazan, Samara, Omsk
Population 146 394 000 (1999e)
Time zone GMT +2/12
Currency 1 Rouble (R) = 100 kopeks
Language Russian

Physical description

Vast plains dominate the western half; the Ural Mountains separate the East European Plain in the west from the West Siberian Lowlands in the east; the Central Siberian Plateau lies east of the River Yenisei; further east lies the North Siberian Plain; the Caucasus, Tien Shan and Pamir ranges lie along the southern frontier; the Lena, Ob, Severnaya Dvina, Pechora, Yenisey, Indigirka and Kolyma rivers flow to the Arctic Ocean; the Amur, Amgun and rivers of the Kamchatka Peninsula flow to the Pacific Ocean; the Caspian Sea basin includes the Volga and Ural rivers; there are over 20 000 lakes, the largest being the Caspian Sea, Lake Taymyr and Lake Baikal.

Climate

There are several different climate regions; variable weather in the north and the centre, and winter temperatures are increasingly severe in the east and north; average temperature in Moscow is 9°C in January and 18°C in July; average annual rainfall is 630mm; Siberia has a continental climate, with very cold and prolonged winters, and short, often warm summers.

Nations of the World

Government

Under the constitution introduced in 1993, the President, who is the head of both state and government, holds office for no more than two consecutive terms of four years. Legislation is entrusted to the Federal Assembly, consisting of the 178-member Federation Council and the 450-member State *Duma*.

Economy

Oil, natural gas, coal, peat, gold, copper, platinum, zinc, tin, lead; wheat, fruit, vegetables, tobacco, cotton, sugar beet; metallurgy; machines; ships; vehicles; chemicals; textiles; timber.

History

Russia has been settled by many ethnic groups, initially the nomadic Slavs, Turks and Bulgars (3–7c AD). The Byzantine Christian Church had been established by the end of the 10c. Moscow was established as a centre of political power in the north during the 14c. The overlordship of the Mongol Golden Horde was challenged successfully from 1380. Ivan III, the Great proclaimed himself 'Sovereign of all Russia' in 1480, and Ivan IV, the Terrible doubled the size of the empire between 1533 and his death in 1584. Internal disorder amongst a feudal nobility and constant warfare with border countries (eg Poland and Sweden) retarded Russian development until Tsar Peter I, the Great. Under Catherine II, the Great, Russia became a great power, extending its territory into southern and eastern Asia. Defeat in the Russo-Japanese War (1904–5) precipitated a revolution which, although unsuccessful, brought Russia's first constitution and parliament. The Russian Revolution in 1917 ended the monarchy, and within the communist Union of Soviet Socialist Republics (formed in 1920), Russia was the dominant political force, covering 75 per cent of the Soviet area with 50 per cent of its population. With the disbandment of the Union in 1991, Russia became an independent republic and assumed the Soviet Union's permanent seat on the UN Security Council. It also became a founding member of the CIS (Commonwealth of Independent States). Relations with some former Soviet republics deteriorated in the early 1990s, and the process of transition to a market economy caused a severe economic crisis in 1993, followed by a national referendum to endorse President Boris Yeltsin's economic reforms, and increased presidential powers. In 1994 ethnic unrest in Chechnya, where Muslim Chechens declared an independent republic, resulted in the massacre and humiliation of Russian troops, who withdrew in Jan 1997. The loss of prestige by the Russian army was too great to be acceptable, and armed conflict resumed in 1999. Despite failing health during the 1990s, Yeltsin clung on to power and, even though the Communist Party won the parliamentary elections of 1995, was re-elected in 1996. He was succeeded in 2000 by Vladimir Putin, who established closer links with NATO in 2002.

Religions

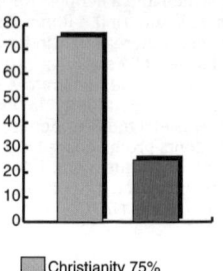

☐ Christianity 75% (Orthodox)

■ others, including Islam 25%

Ethnic groups

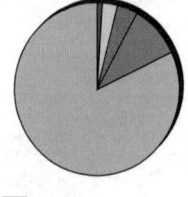

☐ Russian 82%
☐ others 10%
■ Tatar 4%
☐ Ukrainian 3%
■ Chuvash 1%

RWANDA

Official name Republic of Rwanda
Local name Rwanda
Location A landlocked republic in central Africa, bounded to the north by Uganda; to the east by Tanzania; to the south by Burundi; and to the west by the Democratic Republic of the Congo and Lake Kivu
Area 26 338 sq km/10 166 sq mi
Capital Kigali
Chief towns Butare, Ruhengeri

Population 8 155 000 (1999e)
Time zone GMT +2
Currency 1 Rwanda Franc (RF, RWFr) = 100 centimes
Languages English, French, Kinyarwanda; Swahili is widely used in commerce
Religions Christianity 74% (RC 65%, Prot 9%), Islam 1%, traditional beliefs and others 25%
Ethnic groups Hutu 90%, Tutsi 9%, others 1%

Physical description

The country is situated at a relatively high altitude, the highest point being Karisimbi (4 507m) in the Virunga range; the western third of the country drains into Lake Kivu and then the River Congo,

he remainder drains towards the River Nile;
here are many lakes.

Climate

A highland tropical climate; the two wet seasons run from October to December and March
o May, with the highest rainfall in the west, decreasing in the central uplands and to the north
and east; the average annual rainfall at Kigali is
1 000mm.

Government

National Development Council, a President
and a Council of Ministers.

Economy

Largely agricultural; coffee, tea, pyrethrum,
maize, beans; livestock; cassiterite; wolfram;
columbo-tantalite; beryl; amblygonite; reserves of methane; agricultural processing; beer; soft
drinks; soap; furniture; plastic goods; textiles; cigarettes.

History

In the 16c theTutsi tribe moved into the country and took over from the Hutu, forming a monarchy.
Rwanda became a German protectorate in 1899, and was mandated with Burundi to Belgium as the
Territory of Ruanda–Urundi in 1919. It became a UN Trust Territory administered by Belgium after
World War II. Unrest in 1959 led to a Hutu revolt and the overthrow of Tutsi rule, and in 1962 the union
with Burundi was broken as both nations gained independence. A military coup took place in
1973, and there was a gradual return to stability under the new Hutu President Habyarimana,
whose party, the National Revolutionary Movement for Development (MRND), was the only legal
party until 1991. The first multi-party elections took place in 1992. In 1990 the mainly Tutsi rebels
belonging to the *Front Patriotique Rwandaise* (FPR) invaded from bases in Uganda and were
fought back with the help of French and Belgian forces. The FPR boycotted the multi-party elections. A coalition government was formed in 1992 but the ethnic unrest continued unabated, and
was exacerbated by massacres of Tutsis by the Hutu-dominated army. There were moves towards a
peace agreement in 1993, but President Habyarimana, who had been negotiating the accord, was
killed in an air crash in 1994. The fighting between the Hutu and Tutsi peoples re-ignited, resulting
in the loss of many thousands of lives (often in large-scale massacres) and the flight of hundreds of
thousands of refugees to Burundi and Tanzania. Many of the Hutu exiles returned home in the late
1990s, but the violence continued, although recent years have seen moves toward peace and
reconciliation. The involvement of the Rwandan military in the civil war in the neighbouring
Democratic Republic of Congo caused great suffering and tension in the region until a peace deal
in 2002 led to the withdrawal of all Rwandan troops.

⊚ **St Helena ▸ United Kingdom**

ST KITTS AND NEVIS

Official name Federation of St Kitts and Nevis

Local name St Kitts and Nevis

Location An independent state in the North
Leeward Islands in the eastern Caribbean Sea. It
comprises the islands of St Kitts, Nevis and
Sombrero

Area 269 sq km/104 sq mi

Capital Basseterre

Population 42 800 (1999e)

Time zone GMT –4

Currency 1 East Caribbean Dollar (EC$) = 100
cents

Language English

Religions Christianity 78% (Prot 71%, RC 7%),
others 22%

Ethnic groups black 93%, mulatto 4%, white 1%,
others 2%

Physical description

St Kitts is 37km/23mi long and has an area of 168 sq km/65 sq mi; a mountain range rises to 1 156m
at Mount Misery; Nevis, 3km/2mi south-east, has an area of 93 sq km/36 sq mi and is dominated by
a central peak rising to 985m.

Nations of the World

Climate

Warm, with an average annual temperature of 26°C and an average annual rainfall of 1375mm; low humidity; subject to hurricanes.

Government

The British Monarch is represented by a Governor-General; governed by a Prime Minister and two legislative chambers, a 14-member National Assembly and an eight-member Nevis Island Assembly.

Economy

Sugar and its products supply 60% of total exports; copra; cotton; electrical appliances; footwear; garments; tourism.

History

Originally inhabited by Caribs, the islands were visited by Christopher Columbus in 1493, who named the larger one Saint Christopher. The name was shortened to St Kitts by English settlers when the island became the first British colony in the West Indies, in 1623. Control was disputed between France and Britain in the 17–18c, and the island was ceded to Britain in 1783. St Kitts and Nevis were united in 1882, along with Anguilla (which became a separate British dependency in 1980). They became a state in association with the UK in 1967 and gained independence within the Commonwealth of Nations in 1983. In 1997 the government of Nevis voted to secede from St Kitts and the issue went to a referendum. The referendum of 10 Aug 1998 failed to secure the two-thirds majority required to achieve independence.

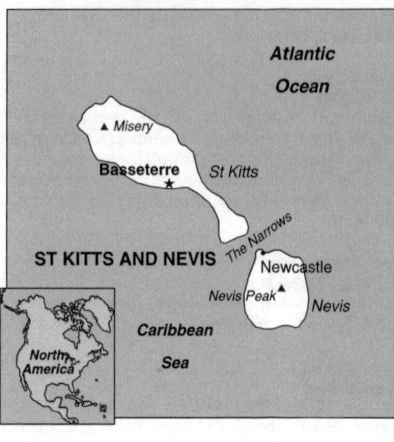

ST LUCIA

Official name St Lucia
Local name St Lucia
Location An independent constitutional monarchy and the second-largest of the Windward Islands, situated in the eastern Caribbean Sea
Area 616 sq km/238 sq mi
Capital Castries
Chief towns Vieux Fort, Soufrière

Population 154 000 (1999e)
Time zone GMT –4
Currency 1 East Caribbean Dollar (EC$) = 100 cents
Language English; French patois is also spoken
Religions Christianity 100% (RC 90%, Prot 10%)
Ethnic groups black 90%, mixed 6%, East Indian 3%, white 1%

Physical description

The island is 43km/27mi long and 23km/14mi wide; mountainous centre, rising to 950m at Mount Gimie; the twin volcanic peaks of Gros and Petit Piton rise steeply from the sea on the south-west coast of the island.

Climate

Tropical; annual temperatures range from 18°C to 34°C; the wet season is June–December; average annual rainfall is 1500mm on the north coast and 4000mm in the interior.

Government

The British Monarch is represented by a Governor-General; there is a 17-member House of Assembly, elected every five years, and an 11-member Senate.

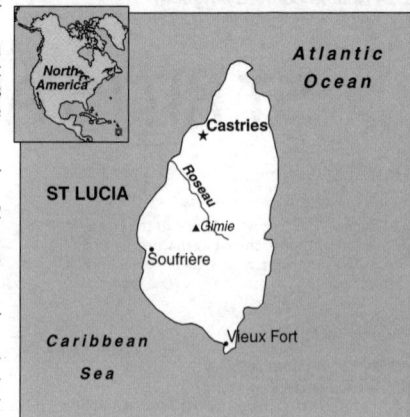

Economy

Tourism is the fastest-growing sector of the economy; bananas, cocoa, copra, citrus fruits, coconut oil; garments, textiles; electronic components; beverages; corrugated boxes; paper products; oil refining; transshipment.

History

Originally inhabited by Arawak Indians who were displaced by Caribs, it was reputedly discovered by Christopher Columbus in 1502. The British failed to settle it at first and it was eventually settled by the French, but ownership was disputed between Britain and France from 1659. It became a British Crown Colony in 1814, and gained independence within the Commonwealth of Nations in 1979.

⊛ **St Pierre and Miquelon ▸ France**

ST VINCENT AND THE GRENADINES

Official name St Vincent and the Grenadines
Local name St Vincent and the Grenadines
Location An island country in the Windward Islands, situated in the eastern Caribbean Sea
Area 390 sq km/150 sq mi
Capital Kingstown
Population 120 500 (1999e)

Time zone GMT −4
Currency 1 East Caribbean Dollar (EC$) = 100 cents
Language English
Religions Christianity 81% (Prot 62%, RC 19%), others 19%
Ethnic groups black 81%, mixed 15%, others 4%

Physical description

Comprises the island of St Vincent (length 29km/18mi; width 16km/10mi) and the northern Grenadine Islands; St Vincent is volcanic in origin; the highest peak is Soufrière, an active volcano rising to a height of 1 234m; the most recent eruption was in 1997.

Climate

Tropical, with an average annual temperature of 25°C, and an average annual rainfall of 1 500mm on the coast, 3 800mm in the interior.

Government

The British Monarch is represented by a Governor-General; a Prime Minister leads a 21-member House of Assembly, 15 of whom are elected.

Economy

Based on agriculture; bananas, arrowroot (world's largest producer), coconuts, nutmeg, mace, cocoa, sugar cane; food processing; cigarettes; textiles; beverages; furniture; tourism.

History

St Vincent was visited by Christopher Columbus in 1498. The first European settlement was by British settlers in 1762, who entered into conflict with the native Caribs, and the French, defeating both in 1762. Most of the Caribs were deported in 1797, and black Africans were imported as slave labour. St Vincent and the Grenadines was part of the Windward Islands Colony (1880–1958) and then joined the West Indies Federation in 1958–62. It was a British colony from 1871 to 1956, when colonial rule ended, and gained its independence in 1979 under Prime Minister Milton Cato, who was succeeded in 1984 by James Fitz-Allen Mitchell, who served until 2000. Popular protests that year led to early elections and Ralph Gonsalves became Prime Minister.

SAMOA

Official name Independent State of Samoa
Local name Samoa
Location An island nation in the south-west Pacific Ocean, 1 600mi/2 600km north-east of Auckland, New Zealand
Area 2 842 sq km/1 097 sq mi
Capital Apia

Population 230 000 (1999e)
Time zone GMT −11
Currency 1 Tala (S$) = 100 sene
Languages Samoan, English
Religions Christianity 100%
Ethnic groups Samoan 93%, mixed 6%, European 1%

Physical description

Formed from ranges of extinct volcanoes, rising to 1 829m on Savai'i; many dormant volcanoes (last activity was between 1905 and 1911); thick tropical vegetation; several coral reefs along the coast.

Pacific Ocean
Falealupo
Savai'i
Silisili
SAMOA
Apia
Falevai
Upolu
Lalomanu
Australia

Climate

Tropical; the rainy season is December–April; average annual temperatures are 22°–30°C; average annual rainfall is 2 775mm; hurricanes occur.

Government

Governed by a monarch as head of state, a Prime Minister, and a 47-member Legislative Assembly elected for three years.

Economy

Largely agricultural subsistence economy; taro; yams, breadfruit, pawpaws, coconuts, cocoa, bananas; tourism increasing; the internal transportation system depends largely on roads and ferries.

History

Inhabited since around 1000BC, Samoa was visited by the Dutch in 1772, and in 1889 was divided between Germany (which acquired Western Samoa) and the USA (which acquired Tutuila and adjacent small islands, now known as American Samoa). After 1914 Western Samoa was administered by New Zealand, from 1919 to 1946 under a League of Nations mandate, and then as a UN Trust Territory, until it gained independence in 1962. Malietoa Tanumafili II came to power in 1963. The legislative assembly voted to change the country's name to Samoa in 1997.

⊖ Samoa, American ▶ United States of America

SAN MARINO

Official name Republic of San Marino
Local name San Marino
Location A very small landlocked republic completely surrounded by central Italy, lying 12mi/20km from the Adriatic Sea
Area 61 sq km/24 sq mi
Capital San Marino
Chief towns Serravalle
Population 25 100 (1999e)

Time zone GMT +1
Currency 1 Euro (€) = 100 cents
Language Italian
Religions Christianity 93% (RC), others and none/unaffiliated 7%
Ethnic groups San Marinesi 88%, Italian 11%, others 1%

Physical description

Ruggedly mountainous, centred on the limestone ridges of Mount Titano and the valley of the River Ausa.

Climate

Temperate climate, with cool winters and warm summers (20°–30°C); rainfall is moderate, with an annual average of 880mm.

Government

Governed by an elected 60-member unicameral Parliament (the Great and General Council), led by two *capitani reggenti* elected every six months, and a 10-member Congress of State.

Economy

Mainly farming, livestock raising, light industry and tourism; manufacturing products include cotton, brick and pottery; the largest share of government revenue is from the sale of postage stamps.

History

Founded by a 4c Christian saint as a refuge against religious persecution, its independence was recognized by the pope in 1631, and in 1862 a treaty of friendship with the Kingdom of Italy preserved San Marino's independence. The San Marino lira was replaced by the Euro in Jan 2002 as the official currency.

SÃO TOMÉ AND PRÍNCIPE

Official name Democratic Republic of São Tomé
Local name São Tomé e Príncipe
Location An equatorial island republic in the Gulf of Guinea, off the coast of west Africa
Area 963 sq km/372 sq mi
Capital São Tomé
Chief town Santo António
Population 154 900 (1999e)

Time zone GMT +1
Currency 1 Dobra (Db) = 100 centavos
Language Portuguese
Religions Christianity 90% (RC 80%, Prot 5%, others 5%), others 10%
Ethnic groups black 90%, Portuguese and Creole 10%

Physical description

Volcanic islands, heavily forested; São Tomé lies c.440km/275mi off the coast of north Gabon, has an area of 845 sq km/326 sq mi and reaches a height of 2 024m; Príncipe, the smaller of the two islands, lies c.200km/125mi off the north coast of Gabon and has similar terrain.

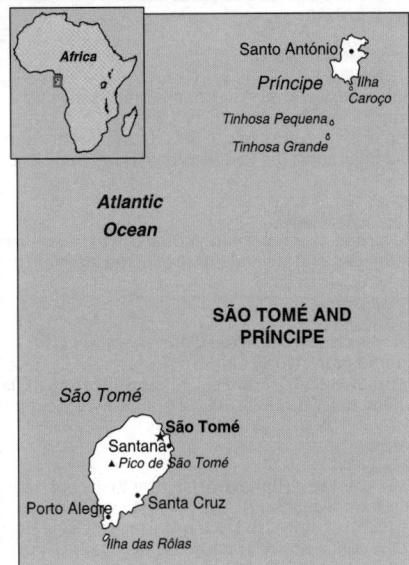

Climate

Tropical; the average annual temperature is 27°C on the coast, 20°C in the mountains; there is a rainy season from October to May; the annual average rainfall varies from 500mm to 1 000mm.

Government

Democratic republic, with a President and a 55-member National Assembly.

Economy

Based on agriculture, employing c.70% of the population; cocoa, copra, palm kernels, coffee; attempts to diversify the economy since 1985 have met with limited success.

History

It was discovered by the Portuguese between 1469 and 1472, and became a Portuguese colony in

1522. From 1641 to 1740 it was held by the Dutch, then was recovered by Portugal. It later became a port of call en route to the East Indies. Resistance to Portuguese rule led to riots in 1953, and the formation of an overseas liberation movement based in Gabon. It gained independence in 1975 and was a one-party state until a new constitution was introduced in the early 1990s, since when multiparty elections have been held. Príncipe was granted autonomy in 1995. Poor economic conditions have led to discontent in recent years.

SAUDI ARABIA

Official name Kingdom of Saudi Arabia
Local name Al-'Arabīyah as Sa'ūdīyah
Location An Arabic kingdom comprising about four-fifths of the Arabian Peninsula, bounded to the west by the Red Sea; to the north-west by Jordan; to the north by Iraq; to the north-east by Kuwait; to the east by the Arabian Gulf, Qatar and the United Arab Emirates; to the south-east and south by Oman; and to the south and south-west by Yemen
Area 2 331 000 sq km/899 766 sq mi

Capital Riyadh
Chief towns Jeddah, Mecca, Medina, Ta'if, Ad Dammam, Abha
Population 21 505 000 (1999e)
Time zone GMT +3
Currency 1 Saudi Arabian Riyal (SR, SRIs) = 20 qursh = 100 halala
Language Arabic
Religions Islam 99% (mostly Sunni), Christianity and others 1%
Ethnic groups Arab 90%, Afro-Asian 10%

Physical description

The Red Sea coastal plain is bounded to the east by mountains; the highlands in the south-west include Jabal Sawda, Saudi Arabia's highest peak (3 133m); the Arabian Peninsula slopes gently north and east towards the oil-rich Al Hasa plain on the Arabian Gulf; the interior comprises two extensive areas of sand desert, the Nafud in the north and the Great Sandy Desert in the south; the central Najd has some large oases; salt flats are numerous in the eastern lowlands; a large network of wadis drains north to east.

Climate

Hot and dry, with average temperatures varying from 21°C in the north, to 26°C in the south; day temperatures may rise to 50°C in the interior sand deserts; night frosts are common in the north and highlands; the Red Sea coast is hot and humid; average rainfall is low.

Government

Governed as an absolute monarchy based on Islamic law and Arab Bedouin tradition; a King is both head of state and Prime Minister, assisted by a Council of Ministers.

Economy

Oil was discovered in the 1930s; now the world's leading oil exporter; reserves account for about a quarter of the world's known supply; rapidly developing construction industry; natural gas; steel; petrochemicals; fertilizers; refined oil products; large areas opened up for cultivation in the 1980s; wheat, dairy produce, dates, grains, livestock; pilgrimage trade.

History

Famed as the birthplace of Islam with the holy cities of Mecca, Medina and Jedda, the modern state was founded by Saudi Arabia's first king, Ibn Saud, leader of the fundamentalist Wahhabi sect, who by 1932 had united the four tribal provinces of Hejaz in the north-west, Asir in the south-west, Najd in the centre and Al Hasa in the east. Saudi Arabia is governed as an absolute monarchy based on Islamic law and Arab Bedouin tradition, and has raised international concern over human rights abuses and public executions. King Fahd ibn Abd al-Aziz al-Saud became both head of state and Prime Minister in 1982. Since the discovery of oil in the 1930s, Saudi Arabia has become the world's leading oil exporter.

⊕ Scotland ▸ United Kingdom

SENEGAL

Nations of the World

Official name Republic of Senegal
Local name Sénégal
Location A country in West Africa, bounded to the north by Mauritania; to the east by Mali; to the south by Guinea and Guinea-Bissau; and to the west by the Atlantic Ocean
Area 196 840 sq km/75 980 sq mi
Capital Dakar
Chief towns Thiès, Kaolack, St Louis, Ziguinchor

Population 10 052 000 (1999e)
Time zone GMT
Currency 1 CFA Franc (CFAFr) = 100 centimes
Languages French, Wolof
Religions Islam 92% (Sunni), traditional beliefs 6%, Christianity 2% (RC)
Ethnic groups Wolof 43%, Fulani 24%, Serer 15%, Diola 4%, others 14%

Physical description

The most westerly country in Africa; the coast is characterized by dunes, mangrove forests and mudbanks; an extensive low-lying basin of savannah and semi-desert vegetation lies to the north; seasonal streams drain to the River Sénégal; the south rises to c.500m.

Climate

Tropical with a rainy season between June and September; high humidity levels and high night-time temperatures, especially on the coast; rainfall decreases from the south (1000–1500mm) to the north (300–350mm); the average annual rainfall at Dakar is 541mm and the average temperature ranges from 22°C to 28°C.

Government

Governed by a President (elected for a five-year term), Prime Minister, Cabinet and 120-member National Assembly.

Economy

Mainly agricultural, employing c.75% of the workforce; groundnuts, cotton, sugar, millet, sorghum, manioc, maize, rice, livestock; phosphate, titanium, zirconium, iron ore, gold, oil, natural gas, salt; fishing; timber; agricultural processing; textiles; chemicals; cement; footwear; shipbuilding and repairing; tourism.

History

Senegal was part of the Mali Empire in the 14–15c. The French established a fort at Saint-Louis in 1659, and it was incorporated as a territory within French West Africa in 1902. It became an autonomous state within the French community in 1958, and joined with French Sudan as the independent Federation of Mali in 1959, but withdrew in 1960 to become a separate independent republic. Its first President was Léopold Senghor, who was succeeded in 1981 by Abdou Diouf. From 1982 to 1989 Senegal joined with the Gambia to form the Confederation of Senegambia. In 1989 a violent dispute with neighbouring Mauritania began following the killing and expulsion of hundreds of Senegalese people living in Mauritania. Virtual war continued throughout 1990 and peace was restored in 1991–2. This was soon followed by a violent separatist uprising led by the Movement of Democratic Forces of Casamance in southern Senegal in 1993, which despite a cease-fire sporadically erupted again in the mid- to late 1990s. In 2000 the Senegalese Democratic Party's Abdoulaye Wade was elected President, ending 40 years of socialist rule, and he has made some progress towards a peace deal with the Casamance rebels.

⊕ Serbia and Montenegro ▸ Yugoslavia

Nations of the World

SEYCHELLES

Official name Republic of Seychelles
Local name Seychelles
Location An island group in the south-west Indian Ocean, north of Madagascar, comprising 115 islands
Area 453 sq km/175 sq mi
Capital Victoria
Population 79 200 (1999e)

Time zone GMT +4
Currency 1 Seychelles Rupee (SR) = 100 cents
Language Creole; French and English are spoken
Religions Christianity 98% (RC 90%, Prot 8%), others (including Hinduism) 2%
Ethnic groups Mulatto 94%, Malagasy 3%, Chinese 2%, English 1%

Physical description

The islands fall into two main groups; the first, a compact group of 41 granitic islands rising steeply from the sea, includes Mahé and its nearest neighbours; these islands are mountainous, rising to 906m on Mahé; the steep forest-clad slopes drop down to coastal lowlands with a vegetation of grass and dense scrub; the second is a group of low-lying coralline islands and atolls which are situated to the south-west.

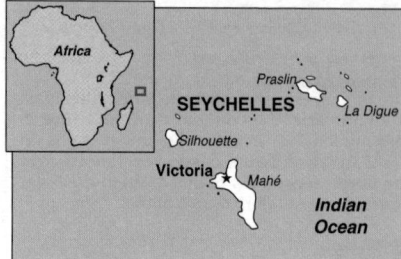

Climate

Tropical with a rainfall that varies with altitude and is higher on the southern sides of the islands; the wettest months are November to March; the Seychelles are rarely affected by tropical storms.

Government

Governed by a President, elected for a five-year term, a Council of Ministers and a 25-member unicameral National Assembly.

Economy

Fruit; vegetables; livestock; fishing; cinnamon; copra; from the 1970s, tourism expanded to become the most important industry by the 1990s; diversifying small industry; brewing; soap; plastics; furniture; cigarettes; soft drinks; steel fabricated goods.

History

The Seychelles was visited by Vasco da Gama in 1502, and colonized by the French in 1768. The population is largely descended from 18c French colonists and their freed African slaves. Captured by Britain in 1794, it was incorporated as a dependency of Mauritius in 1814 and became a separate British Crown Colony in 1903. It became an independent republic within the Commonwealth of Nations in 1976. Following a coup in 1977, when France-Albert René became President, it became a one-party state. Opposition parties have been permitted since 1991, however, and in 1993 the first multi-party elections were won by René's Seychelles People's Progressive Front. René was re-elected in 1998 and 2001.

SIERRA LEONE

Official name Republic of Sierra Leone
Local name Sierra Leone
Location A coastal republic in West Africa, bounded to the north by Guinea; to the south-east by Liberia; and to the south and south-west by the Atlantic Ocean
Area 72 325 sq km/27 917 sq mi
Capital Freetown
Chief towns Bo, Sefadu, Makeni, Kenema, Lunsar

Population 5 297 000 (1999e)
Time zone GMT
Currency 1 Leone (Le) = 100 cents
Languages English, Mende, Temnel; Krio is also widely spoken
Religions traditional beliefs 52%, Islam 39% (Sunni), Christianity 9%
Ethnic groups Mende 35%, Temne 32%, Limba 8%, Kuranko 4%, others 21%

Physical description

Length, 322km/200mi; width 290km/180mi; a low narrow coastal plain; the western half rises to an average height of 500m in the Loma Mountains; the highest point is Loma Mansa (1 948m); the Tingi Mountains in the south-east rise to 1 853m.

Climate

Equatorial, with a rainy season from May to October; the highest rainfall is on the coast; temperatures are uniformly high throughout the year, c.27°C; the average annual rainfall at Freetown is 3 436mm.

Government

A unicameral 80-seat House of Representatives (68 elected by popular vote, 12 by virtue of being paramount chiefs) is elected every five years.

Economy

Mining is the most important sector of the economy; diamonds represent c.60% of exports; bauxite, gold, titanium, iron ore, columbium, limestone, salt, aluminium, chromite; over 70% of the population is involved in subsistence agriculture, chiefly rice, coffee, cocoa, ginger, palm kernels, cassava, citrus fruits; food processing; soap; timber; furniture.

History

The area was visited by Portuguese navigators in the 15c and British slave traders in the 16c and 17c. In the 1780s coastal land was bought from local chiefs by English philanthropists who established settlements for freed slaves. Thus, Freetown was established. Sierra Leone became a British Crown Colony in 1808, and the hinterland was declared a British protectorate in 1896. The latter remained separate from the Freetown colony until 1951. The country gained independence in 1961 and became a republic in 1971 under the one-party state of President Siaka Stevens, who retired in 1985 and was succeeded by Joseph Saidu Momoh as President, whose rule was corrupt. Following the adoption of a new constitution in 1991 with provision for multi-party politics, there was a military coup in 1992 led by Captain Valentine Strasser; this resulted in the suspension of political activity and the dissolution of the new constitution until 1995. Despite the legalization of opposition parties, rebel forces grew in power and Strasser was ousted in 1996. Later that year Ahmad Tejan Kabbah was democratically elected as President. Despite the signing of a cease-fire with the rebels, he had to flee the country in 1997 after another coup, but was restored to power the following year with the help of a coalition of Nigerian-led West African forces. In July 1999 a peace accord was struck in an attempt to end the violence. UN troops faced some initial difficulties but complete disarmament of rebel forces was achieved in 2002. Kabbah was re-elected the same year, and progress began towards restoring stability to the country.

SINGAPORE

Official name Republic of Singapore

Local name Singapore

Location A republic at the southern tip of the Malay Peninsula, South-East Asia. It consists of the island of Singapore (linked to Malaysia by a causeway) and about 50 adjacent islets

Area 618 sq km/238 sq mi

Capital Singapore City

Population 3 532 000 (1999e)

Time zone GMT +8

Currency 1 Singapore Dollar (S$) = 1 Ringgit = 100 cents

Languages English, Chinese, Tamil; Malay is the national tongue

Religions Buddhism 28%, traditional beliefs 21%, Islam 16%, Taoism 13%, Hinduism 5%, none/unaffiliated 17%

Ethnic groups Chinese 76%, Malay 15%, Indian 7%, others 2%

Physical description

The highest point of low-lying Singapore Island is at Bukit Timah (177m); the island measures c.42km/26mi by 22km/14mi at its widest; an important deep-water harbour lies to the south-east.

Climate

Equatorial, with high humidity, an average annual rainfall of 2 438mm, and a daily temperature range from 21°C to 34°C.

Government

A Prime Minister, elected every four years, leads a single-chamber Parliament of 81 members, elected for four-year terms.

Economy

Major transshipment centre; oil refining, rubber, food processing, chemicals, electronics, ship repair, financial services, fishing.

History

Originally part of the Sumatran Sri Vijaya kingdom, in 1819 it was leased by the British East India Company, on the advice of Sir Stamford Raffles, from the Sultan of Johore. Singapore, Malacca and Penang were incorporated as the Straits Settlements in 1826; they became a British Crown Colony in 1867, and were occupied by the Japanese during World War II. Self-government was established in Singapore in 1959, led by Lee Kuan Yew who became Prime Minister, and it was part of the Federation of Malaya from 1963 until it withdrew and became an independent state in 1965. After a record 31 years' service, Lee Kuan Yew resigned as Prime Minister in 1990 and was succeeded by Goh Chok Tong.

SLOVAKIA

Official name Republic of Slovakia

Local name Slovenska Republika

Location A landlocked republic in eastern Europe, bounded to the north by Poland; to the east by the Ukraine; to the south by Hungary; to the south-west by Austria; and to the west by the Czech Republic

Area 49 035 sq km/18 927 sq mi

Capital Bratislava

Chief towns Košice, Banská Bystrica, Prešov

Population 5 396 000 (1999e)

Time zone GMT +1

Currency 1 Koruna (Kčs) = 100 haléru

Language Slovak

Religions Christianity 69% (RC 59%, Prot 6%, Orthodox 4%), none/unaffiliated 31%

Ethnic groups Slovak 86%, Magyar 11%, Romany 2%, others 1%

Physical description

Lowlands in the south; Tatra Mountains in the north rise to 2 655m at Gerlachovsky.

Climate

Continental; hot in summer, cold in winter.

Government

A President is elected for five years; a 150-member National Council; the Prime Minister and the Cabinet hold executive power.

Economy

Agriculture, especially cereals, wine and fruit.

History

It formed part of Great Moravia in the 9c, belonged to the Magyar Empire from the 10c, and from 1918 to 1993 formed part of Czechoslovakia. A Slovak national movement gradually grew up during the 19c and 20c, and was dependent on support from the US Slovaks through the Pittsburgh Agreement, and from Masaryk and Stefanik. Slovakia finally managed to break away from Hungarian rule when the Austro-Hungarian Empire collapsed after World War I. It became a province of Czechoslovakia in 1918, but many Slovaks (not only the nationalists) had genuine complaints the Czechs had established a centralized state in 1918, were less devoutly Catholic and were economically better off, and in 1939, on Hitler's instructions, a supposedly independent republic under German protection was carved out of Czechoslovakia. However, those who led the new republic (such as Tiso and Tuka) soon lost popularity as the Germans exploited the Slovak economy and expected Slovaks to fight in the hated Russian front. Resistance produced the Slovak Uprising in 1944. Although it was put down by the Germans, their presence and brutality simply recruited more volunteers to fight against them and Tiso. Little was done after 1945 to meet legitimate Slovak aspirations, but with the collapse of the communist regime in Czechoslovakia in 1990, nationalist demands intensified again. In Jan 1993 Slovakia finally gained its independence under President Michal Kovác. In 2002 the country was formally invited to join the EU and NATO.

SLOVENIA

Official name Slovenian Republic
Local name Republika Slovenija
Location A mountainous republic in central Europe, bounded to the north by Austria; to the west by Italy; to the south by Croatia; and to the east by Hungary
Area 20 251 sq km/7 817 sq mi
Capital Ljubljana
Chief towns Maribor, Kranj, Celje, Koper

Population 1 971 000 (1999e)
Time zone GMT +1
Currency 1 Tolar (SIT) = 100 stotin
Language Slovene
Religions Christianity 72% (RC, including Uniate, 71%, Prot 1%), Islam 1%, others 21%, none/unaffiliated 5%
Ethnic groups Slovene 91%, Croat 3%, Serb 2%, Bosniak 1%, others 3%

Physical description

The land is forested and mountainous, linked to Austria by a number of pass roads; it drops down towards the Adriatic coast; the chief rivers in the republic are the Sava and Drava.

Climate

Hot summers and cold winters in the plateaus and valleys in the east; mediterranean climate on the west coast.

Government

The Prime Minister and Cabinet of Ministers hold executive power; legislative power is held by a bicameral National Assembly consisting of a State Chamber and a State Council.

Economy

Maize, wheat, sugar beet, potatoes; livestock; timber; lignite; textiles; vehicles; steel; coal; lead; mercury.

History

Settled by Slovenians in the 6c, it was later controlled by Slavs and Franks, and was part of the Austro-Hungarian Empire until 1918 when it joined with Croatia, Montenegro, Serbia and Bosnia-Herzegovina to form the Kingdom of Serbs, Croats and Slovenes. This was renamed Yugoslavia in 1929 and became a people's republic in 1946. In July 1991, President Milan Kucan declared the Republic's independence from the Yugoslav Federation. The Yugoslav National Army invaded but, after the so-called

'Ten-Day War', Serbia's President, Slobodan Milosevic, acknowledged Slovenia's independence in the vain hope that he could arrest the secession of the Republics of Croatia and Bosnia. In 2002 Slovenia was formally invited to join the EU and NATO.

SOLOMON ISLANDS

Official name Solomon Islands
Local name Solomon Islands
Location An independent country consisting of an archipelago of several hundred islands in the south-west Pacific Ocean
Area 27 556 sq km/10 637 sq mi
Capital Honiara
Chief towns Gizo, Auki, Kirakira
Population 455 400 (1999e)

Time zone GMT +11

Currency 1 Solomon Islands Dollar (SI$) = 100 cents

Language English; pidgin English is also spoken

Religions Christianity 91% (Prot 62%, RC 19%, others 10%), others 9%

Ethnic groups Melanesian 93%, Polynesian 4%, Micronesian 2%, others 1%

Physical description

Comprises the six main islands of Choiseul, Guadalcanal, Malaita, New Georgia, Makira and Santa Isabel; the large islands have forested mountain ranges of mainly volcanic origin, deep, narrow valleys, and coastal belts lined with coconut palms; they are ringed by reefs; the highest point is Mount Makarakomburu (2 477m) on Guadalcanal, the largest island.

Climate

Equatorial; the average temperature is 27°C; high humidity; rainfall averages c.3 500mm per year.

Government

The British Monarch is represented by a Governor-General; the Prime Minister leads a Parliament of 38 members elected for four years.

Economy

Based on agriculture; forestry; livestock; fisheries; taro; rice; bananas; yams; copra; oil palm; fish processing, food processing; crafts.

History

Already inhabited since at least 1500BC, they were discovered by the Spanish in 1568. The southern Solomon Islands were placed under British protection in 1893, and the outer islands were added to the protectorate in 1899. The Battle of Guadalcanal and other fierce fighting in World War II took place here. The islands gained their independence within the Commonwealth of Nations in 1978. Tension between different ethnic groups on the island of Guadalcanal in the late 1990s led to rebel violence and an attempted coup, after which the Prime Minister Bartholomew Ulufa'alu was forced to resign. Peace talks resolved the immediate crisis but tensions continue.

Nations of the World

SOMALIA

Official name Somali Democratic Republic
Local name Somaliya
Location A north-east African republic, bounded to the north-west by Djibouti; to the west by Ethiopia; to the south-west by Kenya; to the east by the Indian Ocean; and to the north by the Gulf of Aden
Area 686 803 sq km/265 106 sq mi

Capital Mogadishu
Chief towns Hargeysa, Berbera, Kismayu
Population 7 141 000 (1999e)
Time zone GMT +3
Currency 1 Somali Shilling (SoSh) = 100 cents
Languages Somali, Arabic
Religions Islam 98% (Sunni), Christianity 2%
Ethnic groups Somalian 98%, Arab 2%

Physical description

Occupies the eastern Horn of Africa where a dry coastal plain broadens to the south and rises inland to a plateau at nearly 1000m; forested mountains on the Gulf of Aden coast rise to 2416m at Mount Shimbiris.

Climate

Considerable variation in climate; Berbera on the north coast has an annual average rainfall of 61mm and average maximum daily temperatures of 29°–42°C; more rainfall from April to September on the east coast; Mogadishu has an annual average rainfall of 490mm and average daily maximum temperatures of 28°–32°C; serious and persistent threat of drought.

Government

No functioning government from 1991 until 2000. Transitional national government created in 2000, comprising a National Assembly, elected President, Prime Minister and Cabinet.

Economy

A largely nomadic people (70%) raising cattle, sheep, goats, camels; cultivation close to rivers; bananas, sugar, spices, cotton, rice, citrus fruits, maize, sorghum, oilseeds, tobacco; textiles; cigarettes; food processing; fishing; some tin, gypsum, uranium, iron ore; difficult communications within the country are being helped by a major road-building programme.

History

The country was settled by Muslims in the 7–10c, and was the object of Italian, French and British interests after the opening of the Suez Canal in 1869. After World War II, the modern Somali Republic was formed by the amalgamation of the Italian and British protectorates. It gained its independence in 1960, since when there has been territorial conflict with Ethiopia (which has a large Somali population) and Kenya. A military coup took place in 1969 led by Muhammad Siad Barre, who established a dictatorship and renamed the country the Somali Democratic Republic. In 1988 civil war began with fighting between government forces and rebel groups, particularly the Somali National Movement (SNM), forcing Barre to flee in 1991. The SNM then declared the north-east region independent as the Somaliland Republic, which has not received international recognition but continues to function. With agriculture disrupted by the fighting as well as severe drought, the population of Somalia faced starvation: thousands ended up in refugee camps and a multinational UN force intervened to secure routes for relief convoys carrying food aid. During the early 1990s UN peace-keepers attempted unsuccessfully to secure a ceasefire and the UN troops were withdrawn in early 1995. Fighting continued in the late 1990s between rival clan-based factions in a land in which the State had effectively disintegrated. In 2000 Abd-al-Qassim Salat Hasan was sworn in as President, with a mandate to form the first national government in nine years. The new transitional government faces ongoing violence and tensions between different rebel factions in the country, although peace talks and a ceasefire in late 2002 raised hopes of a breakthrough.

SOUTH AFRICA

Official name Republic of South Africa
Local name South Africa
Location A republic in the south of the African continent, divided into the nine provinces of Eastern Cape, Free State, Gauteng, KwaZulu-Natal, Limpopo, Mpumalanga, Northern Cape, North West Province and Western Cape. It is bounded to the north-west by Namibia; to the north by Botswana; to the north-east by Zimbabwe, Mozambique and Swaziland; to the east and south-east by the Indian Ocean; and to the south-west and west by the southern Atlantic

Ocean; Lesotho is landlocked within its borders
Area 1 233 404 sq km/476 094 sq mi
Capital Pretoria/Cape Town
Chief towns Durban, Johannesburg, Port Elizabeth
Population 43 426 000 (1999e)
Time zone GMT +2
Currency 1 Rand (R) = 100 cents
Languages Afrikaans, English, IsiNdebele, IsiXosa, IsiZulu, Sepedi, Sosetho, SiSwati, Setswana, Tshivenda, Xitsonga

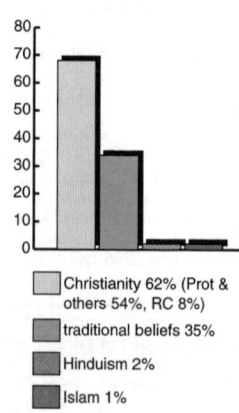

Physical description

Occupies the southern extremity of the African plateau, fringed by fold mountains and a lowland coastal margin to the west, east and south; the northern interior comprises the Kalahari Basin, scrub grassland and arid desert, at an altitude 650–1 250m; the peripheral highlands rise to over 1 200m; the Great Escarpment rises east to 3 482m at Thabana Ntlenyana; the Orange River flows west to meet the Atlantic; its chief tributaries are the Vaal and Caledon rivers.

Climate

Subtropical in the east, with lush vegetation; the average monthly rainfall at Durban is 28mm in July, 130mm in March, the annual average is 1 101mm; dry moistureless climate on the west coast; the annual average rainfall at Cape Town is 510mm, with minimum daily temperatures of 7°C in July, to an average maximum of 26°C in January–February; desert region further north, with an annual average rainfall of less than 30mm.

Religions

Christianity 62% (Prot & others 54%, RC 8%)
traditional beliefs 35%
Hinduism 2%
Islam 1%

Government

The Prime Minister and Cabinet of Ministers hold executive power; legislative power is held by a bicameral Parliament consisting of a National Assembly and a National Council of Provinces.

Economy

Industrial growth as a result of 19c gold and diamond discoveries; over half of the country's export income is from gold; grain; wool; sugar; tobacco; cotton; citrus fruit; dairy products; livestock; fishing; motor vehicles; machinery; chemicals; fertilizers; textiles; clothes; metal products; electronics; computers; tourism; uranium; metallic ores; asbestos.

History

South Africa was originally inhabited by Khoisan tribes, and many Bantu tribes arrived from the north after c.1000. The Portuguese reached the Cape of Good Hope in the late 15c, and it was settled by the Dutch in 1652. The British arrived in 1795 and annexed the Cape in 1814. In 1836 the Boers or Afrikaners undertook the Great Trek north-east across the Orange River to Natal, and the first Boer republic was founded in 1839. Natal was annexed by the British in 1846, but the Boer republics of Transvaal (founded 1852) and Orange Free State (1854) received recognition. The discovery of diamonds in 1866 and gold in 1886 led to rivalry between the British and the Boers, which resulted in the Boer Wars of 1880–1 and 1899–1902. In 1910 Transvaal, Natal, Orange Free State and Cape Province were united to form the Union of South Africa, a dominion of the British Empire; it became a sovereign state within the Commonwealth of Nations in 1931 and formed an independent republic in 1961. Botswana and Lesotho obtained independence in 1966; Swaziland gained independence in 1968; independence was granted by South Africa to Transkei in 1976, Bophuthatswana in 1977, Venda in 1979 and Ciskei in 1981, but was not recognized internationally. South African politics became dominated by the treatment of the non-white majority. Between 1948 and 1991 the apartheid policy resulted in the development of separate political institutions for different racial groups; for example Africans were considered permanent citizens of the 'homelands' to which each tribal group was assigned and were given no representation in the South African parliament. Continuing racial violence and strikes led to the declaration of a state of emergency in 1986. Several countries imposed economic and cultural sanctions (especially in the field of sport) in protest at the apartheid system. The progressive dismantling of apartheid by the government of F W de Klerk took place from 1990, but negotiations towards a non-racial democracy were marked by continuing violent clashes. In 1993 a new constitution gave the vote to all South African adults, and in 1994 free democratic elections resulted in the formation of an ANC-led multi-racial government, and Nelson Mandela became President. In the same year, South Africa rejoined the Commonwealth of Nations. Mandela was succeeded by Thabo Mbeki in May 1999.

⇨ **South Georgia ▸ United Kingdom**

⇨ **South Korea ▸ Korea, South**

⇨ **South Sandwich Islands ▸ United Kingdom**

Ethnic groups

- black 75%
- white 14%
- mixed 9%
- Asian 2%

Nations of the World

SPAIN

Official name Kingdom of Spain
Local name España
Location A country in south-western Europe, bounded in the north by France across the Pyrenees, and in the west by Portugal
Area 492 431 sq km/190 078 sq mi
Capital Madrid

Chief towns Barcelona, Valencia, Seville, Saragossa, Málaga
Population 39 168 000 (1999e)
Time zone GMT +1
Currency 1 Euro (€) = 100 cents
Language Spanish (Castilian); Catalan, Galician and Basque are also spoken in certain regions

Physical description

The country consists mainly of a furrowed central plateau (the Meseta, average height 700m) crossed by mountains; the Andalusian or Baetic Mountains in the south-east rise to 3 478m at

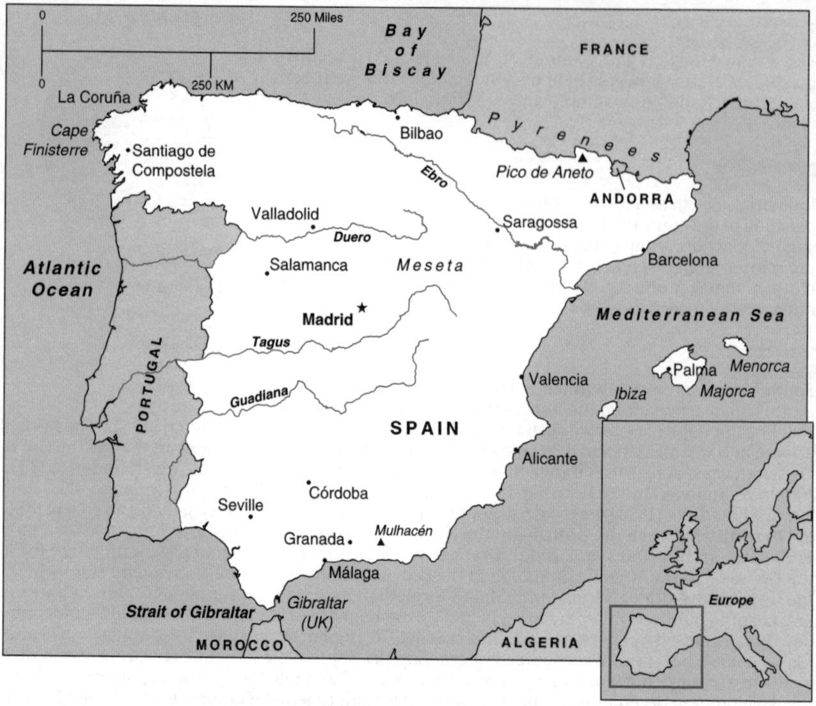

Nations of the World

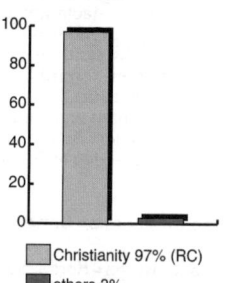

Mulhacén; the Pyrenees in the north rise to 3 404m at Pico de Aneto; rivers run east to west, notably the Tagus, Ebro, Guadiana, Miño, Duero, Guadalquivir, Segura and Júcar.

Religions

Climate

The Meseta has a continental climate, with hot summers, cold winters and low rainfall; there is high rainfall in the mountains, with deep winter snow; the south Mediterranean coast has the warmest winter temperatures on the European mainland.

☐ Christianity 97% (RC)
■ others 3%

Government

The country is governed by a bicameral Parliament (*Cortes*) comprising a 257-member Congress of Deputies elected for four years and a 208-member Senate; since 1978 there has been a move towards local government autonomy with the creation of 17 self-governing regions.

Ethnic groups

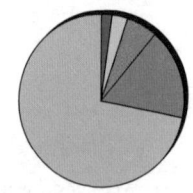

Economy

The traditionally agricultural economy has gradually been supplemented by varied industries; textiles, iron, steel, shipbuilding, electrical appliances, cars, cork, salt, wine, potash, forestry, fishing, tourism; coal, lignite, sulphur, zinc, lead, wolfram, copper.

☐ Castilian Spanish 72%
■ Catalan 17%
■ Galician 6%
☐ others 3%
■ Basque 2%

History

Early inhabitants included Iberians, Celts, Phoenicians, Greeks and Romans. From the 8c there was Muslim domination, and then Christian reconquest, which was completed by 1492. Spain assumed its modern form with the dynastic union of the crowns of Aragon and Castile, a union that was effective by 1579. In the 16c the Spanish exploration of the New World led to the growth of the Spanish Empire. There was a period of decline after the Revolt of the Netherlands in 1581 (leading to the Eighty Years' War). Significant set-backs included the defeat of the Spanish Armada in 1588, defeat by France, acknowledged in the Treaty of the Pyrenees (1659), the War of the Spanish Succession in 1702–13, Spain's involvement in the Peninsular War against Napoleon I in 1808–14, and the Spanish–American War in 1898 that led to the loss of Cuba, Puerto Rico and the remaining Pacific possessions. The dictatorship of Miguel Primo de Rivera (1923–30) was followed by the exile of the King and the establishment of the Second Republic in 1931. A military revolt headed by General Franco in 1936 led to the Spanish Civil War and a Fascist dictatorship. Prince Juan Carlos of Bourbon, nominated in 1969 to succeed Franco, acceded to the throne in 1975, and survived attempted military coups in 1978 and 1981. A democratic constitution was implemented in 1978 and Spain joined the EC in 1986. From the 1960s onwards, the Basque separatist movement, ETA, has carried out numerous terrorist attacks and kidnappings, but announced in Sep 1998 a cease-fire that lasted until Nov 1999. The peseta was replaced by the Euro in Jan 2002.

❖ Balearic Islands

Location A Spanish archipelago of five major islands and 11 islets in the West Mediterranean Sea, situated near the east coast of Spain
Area 5 014 sq km/1 935 sq mi
Capital Palma de Mallorca
Population 785 000 (1999e)

❖ Canary Islands

Location An island archipelago in the Atlantic Ocean, lying 100km/62mi off the north-west coast of Africa
Area 7 273 sq km/2 807 sq mi
Chief town Las Palmas
Population 1 605 000 (1999e)

SRI LANKA

Official name Democratic Socialist Republic of Sri Lanka
Local name Sri Lanka
Location An island state in the Indian Ocean situated off the south-east coast of India
Area 65 610 sq km/25 325 sq mi
Capital Colombo
Chief towns Jaffna, Kandy, Galle

Population 19 145 000 (1999e)
Time zone GMT +5.5
Currency 1 Sri Lankan Rupee (SLR, SLRs) = 100 cents
Languages Sinhala, Tamil
Religions Buddhism 69%, Hinduism 15%, Christianity 8%, Islam 8%
Ethnic groups Sinhalese 74%, Tamil 18%, Sri Lankan Moor 7%, others 1%

Physical description

A pear-shaped island, which measures 440km/273mi long and 220km/137mi wide; low-lying areas in the north and south, surrounding the south-central uplands; the highest peak is Pidurutalagala at 2 524m; the coastal plain is fringed by sandy beaches and lagoons; the northern region is generally arid in the dry season; nearly half the country is tropical monsoon forest or open woodland.

Climate

High temperatures and humidity in the northern plains; the average daily temperatures at Trincomalee are 24°–33°C; temperatures in the interior are reduced by altitude; the greatest rainfall is on the south-west coast and in the mountains.

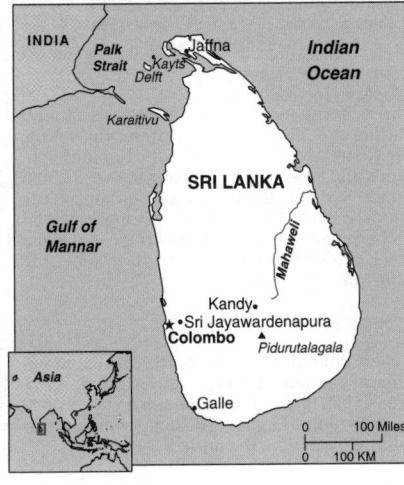

Government

Governed by a President, elected for a six-year term, and a 225-member National State Assembly, which sits for six years.

Economy

Agriculture employs 46% of the labour force; rice, rubber, tea, coconuts, spices, sugar cane; timber;

fishing; graphite, coal, precious and semi-precious stones; electricity produced largely by water power; textiles; chemicals; paper; rubber; tobacco; food processing; oil; wood; metal products.

History

The Sinhalese (from northern India) colonized part of the island in the 5c BC and dominated the northern plain until around AD1200, when they gradually moved south-westwards due to the many Tamil invasions from southern India. Buddhism spread amongst the Sinhalese from about 200BC. Some coastal areas of the country were conquered by the Portuguese in the 15c, then it was taken over by the Dutch in 1658. British occupation began in 1796, and the island became a British colony in 1802. The whole island was united for the first time in 1815, when it was named Ceylon. Tamil labourers were brought in from southern India during colonial rule, to work on coffee and tea plantations. Ceylon was given Dominion status within the Commonwealth of Nations in 1948, and became an independent republic as the Republic of Sri Lanka in 1972. Acute political tension exists between the Buddhist Sinhalese majority and the Hindu Tamil minority, who wish to establish an independent state in the Tamil majority areas in the north and east. In the early 1980s Tamil separatists began fighting government forces for control of these areas. The fighting between the LTTE Tamil guerrillas and government forces remained mainly in the Jaffna Peninsula at first, though sporadic terrorist attacks took place nearer the capital. The civil war continued, despite an attempt by India in 1987 to enforce a compromise based on a united but somewhat de-centralized Sri Lanka which would publicly acknowledge Indian regional hegemony, and various attempts at peace talks throughout the 1990s. A state of emergency was declared in 1996. In 1994 Chandrika Bandaranaike Kumaratunga, as leader of the nine-party People's Alliance, a coalition which includes the Sri Lanka Freedom Party (SLFP), was elected first Prime Minister and then President of Sri Lanka, thus ending the 17-year rule by the United National Party (UNP). A ceasefire between Tamil rebels and government forces was signed in 2002, and further peace talks led to hopes of a permanent resolution to the conflict.

THE SUDAN

Official name Democratic Republic of the Sudan
Local name As-Sūdān
Location A north-east African republic, bounded to the north by Egypt; to the north-west by Libya; to the west by Chad; to the south-west by the Central African Republic; to the south by the Democratic Republic of the Congo; to the south-east by Uganda and Kenya; to the east by Ethiopia; and to the north by the Red Sea
Area 2 504 530 sq km/966 749 sq mi

Capital Khartoum
Chief towns Port Sudan, Wad Medani, Omdurman
Population 34 476 000 (1999e)
Time zone GMT +2
Currency 1 Sudanese Dinar (SD) = 10 pounds
Language Arabic
Religions Islam 70% (mostly Sunni), traditional beliefs 23%, Christianity 7%
Ethnic groups Arab 50%, Dinka 13%, Nuba 8%, Beja 6%, Nuer 5%, Azande 3%, others 15%

Physical description

The largest country on the African continent, astride the middle reaches of the River Nile; the eastern edge is formed by the Nubian Highlands and an escarpment rising to over 2 000m on the Red Sea; the Imatong Mountains in the south rise to 3 187m at Kinyeti, the highest point in the Sudan; the Darfur Massif is located in the west; the White Nile flows north to meet the Blue Nile at Khartoum.

Climate

Desert conditions in the north, with minimal annual rainfall of 160mm at Port Sudan, increasing in the south to 1 000mm; in the hottest months (July–August), the temperature rarely falls below 24°C in the north.

Government

Transitional; the 15-member military junta gave way to a 400-member, unicameral National Assembly. The Assembly was dissolved in December 1999.

Economy

Dominated by agriculture, employing over 75% of the people; large-scale irrigation schemes, fed by dams; commercial farming in the north and livestock farming in the south; cotton, sugar, groundnuts, castor seeds, sorghum, wheat; gum arabic (80% of world supply); reserves of copper, lead, iron ore, chromite, manganese, gold, salt; food processing; sugar; textiles; soap; shoes; soft drinks; beer; paper products; cement; development hindered by a poor transport system.

History

Sudan was Christianized in the 6c, and came under Muslim influences from the 13c. Egyptian control of northern Sudan began in the early 19c when Mohammed Ahmed, a religious leader who announced himself the Mahdi (the 'expected one'), began to unify western and central areas of the country. In 1881 he initiated a revolution which led to the fall of Khartoum in 1885. A combined British–Egyptian offensive was mounted against the Mahdists, defeated them at the Battle of Omdurman in 1898, and led to a jointly administered condominium under a British governor. The Sudan gained its independence in 1956, and since then parts of the country have been almost constantly ravaged by civil war. After seizing power in 1969, General Nimeri managed to bring the civil war in the south to an end in 1972. However, fighting restarted in the 1980s and Nimeri was overthrown in 1985. Another coup, led by General Omar Hassan Ahmad al-Bashir in 1989, resulted in a strongly Islamic regime and the banning of all political parties until 1996, when Bashir and his supporters won the elections. The North–South rivalry (the Muslim Brotherhood's National Islamic Front (NIF) is based in the north, while the Sudan People's Liberation Army (SPLA) has its stronghold in the south) has contributed to years of instability, several coups, and severe food shortages, the last mentioned exacerbated by drought and by the influx of refugees from Ethiopia and Chad in the early 1990s. Peace talks in 2002 led to a ceasefire, although sporadic violence continued and progress toward a permanent resolution has been slow.

SURINAME

Official name Republic of Suriname
Local name Suriname
Location A republic in north-eastern South America, bounded to the west by Guyana; to the south by Brazil; to the east by French Guiana; and to the north by the Atlantic Ocean
Area 163 265 sq km/63 020 sq mi
Capital Paramaribo
Chief towns Brokopondo, Nieuw Amsterdam
Population 431 200 (1999e)

Time zone GMT –3.5
Currency 1 Suriname Guilder (SGld)/Florin (f) = 100 cents
Language Dutch
Religions Christianity 48% (Prot 25%, RC 23%), Hinduism 27%, Islam 21%, traditional beliefs 4%
Ethnic groups Hindustani 37%, Creole 31%, Javanese 15%, black 9%, Amerindian 3%, Chinese 3%, others 2%

Physical description

Diverse natural regions, ranging from coastal lowland through savannah to mountainous upland; the coastal strip is mostly covered by swamp; the highland interior in the south is overgrown with dense tropical forest.

Climate

Tropically hot and humid, with two rainy seasons in May–July and November–January; Paramaribo temperatures range from 22°–33°C; the average monthly rainfall is 310mm in the north and 67mm in the south.

Government

The 1987 constitution provides for a 51-member National Assembly elected for five years, and a President elected by the Assembly.

Economy

Lack of foreign exchange has hindered development of the economy, which is based on mining

Nations of the World

and agriculture; bauxite mining provides c.80% of export income; sugar cane, rice, citrus fruits, coffee, bananas, oil palms, cacao, fishing; vast timber resources.

History

Sighted by Columbus in 1498, Suriname was first settled by the British in 1651. It was taken by the states of Zeeland in 1667, captured by the British in 1799, and restored to the Netherlands in 1818. It became an independent republic in 1975, after which around 40 per cent of the population emigrated to the Netherlands. A military coup took place in 1980, civilian government was restored in 1988, but another coup was staged in 1990. The following year elections brought a coalition called the New Front for Democracy and Development to power, led by Ronald Venetiaan, who served until 1996 and again from 2000.

SWAZILAND

Official name Kingdom of Swaziland
Local name Umbouso we Swatini
Location A monarchy in south-east Africa, bounded to the north, west, south and south-east by South Africa, and to the north-east by Mozambique
Area 17 363 sq km/6 702 sq mi
Capital Mbabane
Population 985 300 (1999e)

Time zone GMT +2
Currency 1 Lilangeni (plural Emalangeni) (Li, E) = 100 cents
Languages English (government, business), Swazi
Religions Christianity 60%, traditional beliefs 40%
Ethnic groups Swazi 84%, Zulu 10%, European 4%, Tsonga 2%

Physical description

A small country, 192km/119mi north to south and 144km/89mi east to west; mountainous Highveld in the west; the highest point in Swaziland is Emblembe at 1 862m; the more populated Middleveld in the centre descends to 600–700m; the rolling, bush-covered Lowveld in the east is irrigated by river systems.

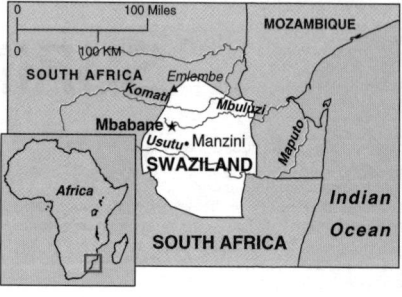

Climate

Humid, near temperate climate in the west, with an average annual rainfall of 1 000–2 280mm; subtropical and drier in the centre; tropical in the east, with relatively little rain (500–890mm, susceptible to drought); the average annual temperature is 16°C in the west and 22°C in the east.

Government

The monarch, who holds executive, legislative and judicial power, chooses a Cabinet and a Prime Minister; governed by a bicameral Parliament consisting of a 50-member National Assembly and a 20-member Senate.

Economy

Agriculture employs 70% of the population; maize, groundnuts, beans, sorghum, sweet potatoes, cotton, tobacco, pineapples, rice, sugar cane, citrus; several hydroelectric schemes; asbestos; iron ore; coal; wood products; sugar refining; canning; food and drink processing; textiles; cement; paper; chemicals; televisions.

History

The Swazi people probably arrived in the area in the 16c. Boundaries with the Transvaal were decided in the 19c, and independence was guaranteed in 1881 and again in 1884, when the country became a South African protectorate. The British agreed to the Transvaal administration of Swaziland in 1894 but, after the Second Boer War, Swaziland, though retaining its monarchy, came under British rule as a British High Commission territory in 1903. It gained independence in 1968 under King Sobhuza II. Mswati III acceded to the throne in 1986 and faced increasingly strong demands for the democratization of the constitution.

SWEDEN

Official name Kingdom of Sweden
Local name Konungariket Sverige
Location A constitutional monarchy in northern Europe, occupying the eastern side of the Scandinavian Peninsula, bounded to the east by Finland, the Gulf of Bothnia and the Baltic Sea; to the south-west by the Skagerrak and Kattegat; and to the west and north-west by Norway
Area 411 479 sq km/158 830 sq mi
Capital Stockholm
Chief towns Gothenburg, Malmö, Uppsala, Norrköping, Västerås, Örebro, Linköping
Population 8 911 000 (1999e)
Time zone GMT +1
Currency 1 Swedish Krona (Skr) = 100 øre
Language Swedish
Religions Christianity 93% (Prot 90%, RC 2%, others 1%), Islam 1%, others and none/unaffiliated 6%
Ethnic groups Swedish 91%, Finnish and Lapp 3%, others 6%

Nations of the World

Physical description

There is a large amount of inland water (9%), the chief lakes being Vänern, Vättern and Mlar; there are many coastal islands, notably Gotland and Öland; c.57% of the country is forested; the Kjölen Mountains in the west form much of the boundary with Norway; the highest peak is Kebnekaise (2 111m); several rivers flow south-east towards the Gulf of Bothnia; there are many waterfalls.

Climate

Typically continental, with a considerable range of temperature between summer and winter, except in the south-west, where winters are warmer; enclosed parts of the Baltic Sea often freeze in winter; the average number of days with a mean temperature below freezing increases from 71 in Malmö to 184 at Haparanda near the Arctic Circle.

Government

A representative and parliamentary democracy, with a monarch as head of state; governed by a Prime Minister and a single-chamber Parliament (*Riksdag*) of 349 elected members.

Economy

A gradual shift from the traditional emphasis on raw materials (timber and iron ore) to advanced technology; transportation equipment; electronics; electrical equipment; chemicals; engineering; steelmaking; non-ferrous metals; hydroelectricity provides 70% of the country's power; c.57% of Sweden is forested; wheat, barley, oats; hay; sugar beet, peas, grain; cattle; fishing; tourism.

History

Formed from the union of the kingdoms of the Goths and Svears in the 7c, it did not include the southern parts of the peninsula (Skne, Halland and Blekinge) which were part of Denmark until conquered in 1658. Sweden was united with Denmark and Norway under Danish leadership in the Kalmar Union (1397). This union ended in 1527, following a revolt led by Gustav I Vasa, founder of modern Sweden. The Swedish state also included Finland until all Finnish areas were finally lost to Russia in 1814. Norway was separated from Denmark in 1814 and united in personal union with Sweden as compensation for the loss of Finland, but that union was dissolved in 1905. Sweden has been a neutral country since 1814, but became a member of the EC in 1995.

SWITZERLAND

Official name Swiss Confederation
Local name Schweiz (German), Suisse (French), Svizzera (Italian)
Location A landlocked European republic, bounded to the east by Liechtenstein and Austria; to the south by Italy; to the west by France; and to the north by Germany
Area 41 228 sq km/15 914 sq mi
Capital Berne
Chief towns Zurich (largest city), Lucerne, St Gallen, Lausanne, Basle, Geneva
Population 7 275 000 (1999e)

Time zone GMT +1
Currency 1 Swiss Franc (SFr, SwF) = 100 centimes = 100 rappen
Languages German (65%), French (18%), Italian (12%) and Romansch (1%); many of the Swiss speak more than one of these
Religions Christianity 86% (RC 46%, Prot 40%), Islam 2%, others 3%, none/unaffiliated 9%
Ethnic groups German 65%, French 18%, Italian 10%, Yugoslav 3%, Spanish 2%, Romansch 1%, others 1%

Physical description

The Alps run roughly east to west in the south; the highest peak is Dufourspitze (4 634m); the average height of the Pre-Alps in the north-west is 2 000m; the Jura Mountains run south-west to north-west; the central plateau, at an average altitude of 580m, is fringed by large lakes; chief rivers are the Rhine, Rhône, Adige, Inn, and the tributaries of the Po; there are c.3 000 sq km/1 160 sq mi of glaciers, notably the Aletsch; major lakes include Constance, Zurich, Lucerne, Neuchâtel and Geneva.

Climate

A temperate climate, varying greatly with relief and altitude; there are warm summers, with considerable rainfall; winter temperatures average 0°C; average annual rainfall in the central plateau is c.1 000mm; average annual temperature is 79°C; the Föhn, a warm wind, is noticeable in the Alps during late winter and spring.

Government

Governed by a Parliament comprising a 46-member Council of States (*Ständerat*) and a 200-member National Council (*Nationalrat*), directly elected for four years; a President is elected yearly.

Economy

Increased specialization and development in high-technology products; machinery; precision instruments; watches; drugs; chemicals; textiles; dairy farming; wheat, potatoes, sugar beet, grapes, apples; an all-year tourist area; a major financial centre with the headquarters of many international organizations.

History

Part of the Holy Roman Empire in the 10c, the Swiss Confederation was created in 1291, when the cantons of Uri, Schwyz and Unterwalden formed a defensive league. The Confederation expanded during the 14c and was the centre of the Reformation in the 16c. Swiss independence and neutrality was recognized under the Treaty of Westphalia in 1648. The country was conquered by Napoleon I, who in 1798 instituted the Helvetian Republic. In 1815 it was organized as a confederation of 22 cantons, and in 1848 a federal constitution was adopted. Switzerland has been neutral for two centuries, and was neutral in both World Wars, but did join the UN in 2002.

SYRIA

Official name Syrian Arab Republic

Local name As-Sūrīyah

Location A republic in the Middle East, bounded to the west by the Mediterranean Sea and Lebanon; to the south-west by Israel and Jordan; to the east by Iraq; and to the north by Turkey

Area 185 180 sq km/71 479 sq mi

Capital Damascus

Chief towns Halab (Aleppo), Homs, Hama, Latakia

Population 17 214 000 (1999e)

Time zone GMT +2

Currency 1 Syrian pound (LS, S$) = 100 piastres

Language Arabic

Religions Islam 90% (Sunni 74%, others 16%), Christianity 10%

Ethnic groups Arab 90%, Kurdish 6%, Armenian and others 4%

Physical description

Behind a narrow Mediterranean coastal plain, the Jabal al Nusayriyah mountain range rises to c.1 500m; steep drop in the east to the Orontes River valley; the Anti-Lebanon range in the south-west rises to 2 814m at Mount Hermon; open steppe and desert to the east.

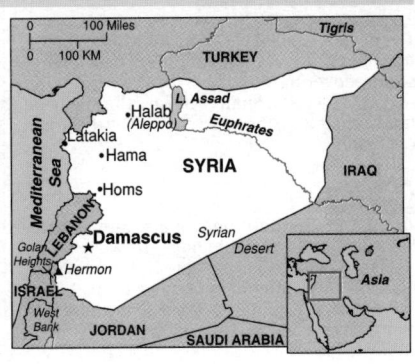

Climate

Coastal Mediterranean climate, with hot, dry summers and mild, wet winters; desert or semi-desert climate in 60% of country, with an annual rainfall below 200mm; the *khamsin* wind causes temperatures to rise to 43°–49°C; in Damascus the average annual rainfall is 225mm, and average temperatures range from 7°C in January to 27°C in July.

Government

Governed by a President, elected for a seven-year term; a 250-member People's Council is elected for a four-year term.

Economy

Since 1974 oil has been the most important source of export revenue; cotton; phosphate; textiles; beverages; tobacco; cement; oil refining; food processing; tourism; cotton, wheat, barley, rice, olives, millet, sugar-beet, fruit; cattle breeding, poultry; the Euphrates Dam Project, begun in 1978, supplies 97% of domestic electricity demand, and is intended to increase the area of arable land by 6 400 sq km/2 500 sq mi.

History

The country has been part of the Phoenician, Persian, Roman and Byzantine empires. It was conquered by Muslim Arabs in the 7c, when Damascus became the capital of the Umayyad Dynasty, and was subsequently ruled by foreign dynasties including the Egyptian Fatimids and Mamluks, before being conquered by Turks in the 11c. The scene of many battles during the Crusades in the Middle Ages, it was part of the Ottoman Empire in 1517 and enjoyed a brief period of independence in 1920, before being made a French mandate. Syria gained its independence in 1946. It merged with Egypt and Yemen to form the United Arab Republic in 1958, but re-established itself as an independent state under its present name in 1961. Syria suffered setbacks in the Six-Day War of 1967, when the Golan Heights region was seized by Israel, and in the Yom Kippur War of 1973. After the outbreak of civil war in Lebanon in 1975, Syrian troops were sent to restore order; Syrian soldiers were also part of the international coalition force which opposed Iraq in the Gulf War. Syria cautiously took part in the Middle East peace talks in 1992, which gave rise to hopes of a peace agreement being reached with Israel. President Hafez al-Asad seized power in a coup in 1970, formally taking office in 1971. On his death in 2000, he was succeeded by his son, Bashar.

Nations of the World

TAIWAN

Official name Republic of China
Local name T'aiwan
Location An island republic consisting of Taiwan Island and several smaller islands, lying c.80mi/130km off the south-east coast of China
Area 36 000 sq km/13 896 sq mi
Capital Taipei
Chief towns Chilung, Kaohsiung, Taichung

Population 22 113 000 (1999e)
Time zone GMT +8
Currency 1 New Taiwan Dollar (NT$) = 100 cents
Language Mandarin Chinese
Religions Chinese folk religion 45%, Buddhism 42%, Christianity 5%, Islam 1%, others 7%
Ethnic groups Taiwanese Chinese (including Hakka) 84%, mainland Chinese 14%, Ainu 2%

Physical description

The island is c.395km/245mi long, 100–145km/60–90mi wide; a mountain range runs north to south, covering two thirds of the island; the highest peak is Yu Shan (3 997m); the low-lying land is mainly on the west; crossed by the Tropic of Cancer.

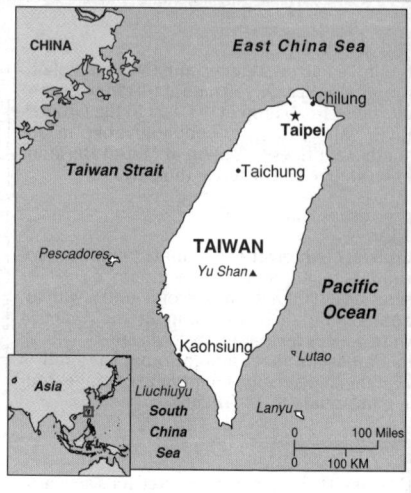

Climate

Tropical monsoon-type climate; annual rainfall is generally over 2 000mm; the wettest period is in summer (May–September), when it is also hot and humid; typhoons bring heavy rains between July and September; mild and short winters; the average daily temperature at Taipei is 12°–19°C in January, and 24°–33°C in July–August; the monthly rainfall is 71mm in December and 290mm in June.

Government

Governed by a President, who appoints a Premier; the National Assembly has 920 members; Parliament (*Yuan*) has 313 members.

Economy

Transition from agriculture to industry since the 1950s; high technology; textiles; footwear; electronics; plastics; cement; furniture; consumer goods; iron and steel; petrochemicals; machinery; plywood; canned food; small deposits of coal, natural gas, limestone, marble, asbestos; fish; sugar, bananas, pineapples, citrus fruits, vegetables, tea.

History

Taiwan was discovered by the Portuguese in 1590 and conquered by Manchus of the Qing Dynasty in the 17c. Ceded to Japan in 1895, it was returned to China in 1945. The Nationalist government (the Guomindang) was moved there after being defeated by the communists in China in 1949, and martial law was in force until replaced by National Security law in 1987. Demands for democratization in the late 1980s led to the first multi-party elections in 1992, which were won by the Guomindang. In 1991 Taiwan officially recognized the communist People's Republic of China for the first time in over 40 years, thus ending its state of war. Tensions between the two countries remain high. Lee Teng-hui became President on the death of Jiang Jing'guo in 1988, and won the first democratic presidential elections in 1996. In 2000 Chen Shui-bian became President, ending the Guomindang's fifty-year dominance.

TAJIKISTAN

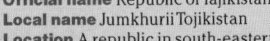

Official name Republic of Tajikistan
Local name Jumkhurii Tojikistan
Location A republic in south-eastern Middle Asia, bounded to the west and north by Uzbekistan; to the north by Kyrgyzstan; to the east by China; and to the south by Afghanistan
Area 143 100 sq km/55 200 sq mi
Capital Dushanbe
Chief towns Khudzand, Kulyab, Kurgan-Tyube

Population 6 103 000 (1999e)
Time zone GMT +5
Currency 1 Somoni (S) = 100 dirams
Languages Tajik, Uzbek, Russian
Religions Islam 85% (Sunni 80%, Shiite 5%), others 15%
Ethnic groups Tajik 66%, Uzbek 26%, Russian 3%, others 5%

Physical description

The Tien Shan, Gissar-Alai and Pamir ranges cover over 90% of the area; Communism Peak reaches 7 495m; the River Amudarya flows east to west along the southern border; the largest lake is Lake Kara-Kul.

Climate

Predominantly continental; hot summers and mild winters.

Government

A bicameral Supreme Assembly (*Majlisi Oli*) comprising a 63-member Assembly of Representatives and 33-member National Assembly; an elected President appoints a Council of Ministers and a Prime Minister.

Economy

Oil, natural gas, coal; lead, zinc; machinery, metalworking; chemicals; food processing; cotton; wheat, maize, vegetables, fruit; hot mineral springs and health resorts.

History

Inhabited by Tajiks, who originated in Iran, it was conquered by Arabs in the 7c and 8c, then by the khanate of Bukhara from the 15c to the 18c. The area was then conquered by the Afghans, but by 1868 had come completely under Russian control. It became a Soviet Socialist Republic in 1929, joined the USSR in 1936, and achieved full independence in 1991, the year it became a member of the CIS (Commonwealth of Independent States). Civil war between government forces and Muslim rebels began in 1992. A peace treaty was reached in 1994, but sporadic violence continued until another treaty was signed in 1997, and peaceful stability has yet to be achieved.

TANZANIA

Official name United Republic of Tanzania
Local name Tanzania
Location An East African republic, consisting of the mainland region of Tanganyika, and Zanzibar, just off the coast in the Indian Ocean, which includes Zanzibar Island, Pemba Island and some small islets
Area 939 652 sq km/362 706 sq mi
Capital Dodoma
Chief towns Dar es Salaam, Zanzibar, Mwanza,
Tanga, Arusha
Population 31 271 000 (1999e)
Time zone GMT +3
Currency 1 Tanzanian Shilling (Tsh) = 100 cents
Languages English, Swahili
Religions Christianity 35%, Islam 33%, traditional beliefs 30%, others 2%
Ethnic groups Nyamwezi and Sukuma 22%, Swahili 9%, Hehet and Bena 7%, Makonde 6%, Haya 6%, other tribes 50%

Physical description

The largest East African country, just south of the Equator; the coast is fringed by long sandy beaches protected by coral reefs; the coastal plain rises towards a central plateau with an average elevation of 1000m; high grasslands and mountain ranges lie to the centre and south; the Rift Valley branches around Lake Victoria in the north, where there are several high volcanic peaks, notably Mount Kilimanjaro (5895m); the extensive Serengeti plain lies to the west; the eastern branch of the Rift Valley runs through central Tanzania from north to east of Lake Victoria, containing several lakes; the western branch runs south down the west side of Lake Victoria, and includes Lake Tanganyika and Lake Rukwa.

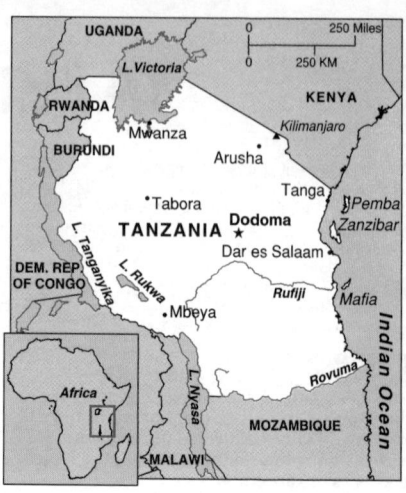

Climate

Hot, humid and tropical on the coast and offshore islands; the average temperatures are c.23°C during June–Sept and 27°C during December–March; average annual rainfall is over 1100mm; hot and dry on the central plateau, with an average annual rainfall of 250mm; semi-temperate at altitudes above 1500m; permanent snow on high peaks.

Government

Governed by a President, elected for a five-year term, a Cabinet, and a National Assembly of 243 members serving a five-year term; agreement in 1993 to a separate government for Tanganyika (mainland Tanzania).

Economy

Largely based on agriculture: rice, sorghum, coffee, sugar, cloves (most of the world's market), coconuts, tobacco, cotton; reserves of iron, coal, tin, gypsum, salt, phosphate, gold, diamonds, oil; food processing; cement; cigarettes; tourism centres on Mount Kilimanjaro, beaches and reefs, national parks and the five game reserves.

History

Inhabited by Caucasoid peoples and then in the 5c by Bantus from western Africa, it had early links with Arab, Indian and Persian traders. The Swahili culture developed in the 10–15c, and Portuguese explorers arrived in the 15c. The island of Zanzibar was the capital of the Omani empire in the 1840s. Exploration of the interior by German missionaries and British explorers took place in the mid-19c, and Zanzibar became a British protectorate in 1890. German East Africa was established in 1891 and by 1907 Germany controlled the whole country. After World War I Tanganyika (mainland Tanzania) became a British mandate (1919) and in 1961 it became the first East African country to gain independence and become a member of the Commonwealth of Nations; it became a republic in 1962. Zanzibar was given independence as a constitutional monarchy, with the Sultan as head of state; the Sultan was overthrown in 1964, and an Act of Union between Zanzibar and Tanganyika led to the United Republic of Tanzania. A multi-party system was approved in 1992 and an agreement was reached in 1993 to set up a separate government for Tanganyika. In the mid-1990s hundreds of thousands of refugees from war and ethnic violence in Rwanda and Burundi arrived in Tanzania, exacerbating mounting internal tensions.

THAILAND

Official name Kingdom of Thailand	**Capital** Bangkok
Local name Prathet Thai	**Chief towns** Chiang Mai, Nakhon Ratchasima
Location A kingdom in South-East Asia, bounded to the west by the Andaman Sea; to the west and north-west by Myanmar; to the north-east and east by Laos; to the east by Cambodia; and to the south by Malaysia	**Population** 60 609 000 (1999e)
	Time zone GMT +7
	Currency 1 Baht (B) = 100 satang
	Language Thai
	Religions Buddhism 95%, Islam 4%, others 1%
Area 513 115 sq km/198 062 sq mi	**Ethnic groups** Thai 75%, Chinese 14%, others 11%

Physical description

The central agricultural region is dominated by the floodplain of the Chao Phraya River; a north-eastern plateau rises above 300m and covers one third of the country; mountainous northern region rising to 2 595m at Doi Inthanon; a narrow, low-lying southern region separates the Andaman Sea from the Gulf of Thailand and is covered in tropical rainforest; mangrove-forested islands off the coast.

Climate

Equatorial climate in the south; tropical monsoon climate in the north and centre.

Government

The King is head of state, advised by a 12-member Privy Council; governed by a Prime Minister, a Cabinet, and a bicameral National Assembly consisting of a 347-member House of Representatives and a 264-member Senate.

Economy

Agriculture is the most important economic activity; rice, manioc, maize, bananas, pineapple, sugar cane; rubber, teak; textiles; electronics; cement; chemicals; food processing; tourism; tin (world's third-largest supplier), tungsten (world's second-largest supplier), manganese, antimony, lead, zinc, copper, natural gas.

Nations of the World

History

There is evidence that Thailand had Bronze Age communities in c.4000BC. By the 7c Buddhism had spread to the country from India. Today 95 per cent of the population are Theravada Buddhists, and the religion continues to enjoy royal patronage. Thailand's successful nationalist and reform movements have often had Buddhist leaders, and the work of the monastic order or *sangha* remains highly regarded in social terms. The Thai nation was founded in the 13c, and is the only country in south and south-east Asia to have escaped colonization by a European power. It was occupied by the Japanese during World War II, and had a military-controlled government for most of the time from 1945 until mass demonstrations in 1992 resulted in the fall of the military-controlled government and led to a reduction in the power of the military. King Bhumibol Adulyadej became head of state in 1946.

TOGO

Official name Republic of Togo
Local name Togo
Location A republic in West Africa, bounded to the west by Ghana; to the north by Burkina Faso; and to the east by Benin
Area 56 600 sq km/21 848 sq mi
Capital Lomé
Chief towns Sokodé, Kpalimé, Atakpamé
Population 5 081 000 (1999e)

Time zone GMT
Currency 1 CFA Franc (CFAFr) = 100 centimes
Language French; many local languages are also spoken
Religions traditional beliefs 55%, Christianity 30% (RC 23%, Prot 7%), Islam 15%
Ethnic groups Ewe-Adja 41%, Tem-Kabre 25%, Gurma 16%, others 18%

Physical description

Togo rises from the lagoon coast of the Gulf of Guinea, past low-lying plains to the Atakora Mountains, which run north-east to south-west across the north of the country; the highest peak is Pic Baumann (986m); flat plains lie to the north-west.

Climate

Tropical; rain throughout the year in the south; one rainy season in the north between July and

September; the average annual rainfall at Lomé on the coast is 875mm.

Government

Governed by a President, a Cabinet, and a 77-member National Assembly, elected for five years.

Economy

Largely agricultural: coffee, cocoa, cotton, cassava, maize, rice, timber; phosphates; bauxite; limestone; iron ore; marble; cement; steel; oil refining; food processing; crafts; textiles; beverages.

History

Formerly part of the Kingdom of Togoland, it was a German protectorate from 1884 to 1914. After World War I it was divided between France (French Togo) and Britain (part of British Gold Coast) by mandate of the League of Nations (1922). In 1946 the British and French governments placed their territories under UN trusteeships. French Togo became an autonomous republic within the French Union in 1956, while British Togoland voted to join the Gold Coast (Ghana) when Ghana gained independence in 1957. French Togo gained independence in 1960. Relations between Ghana and Togo gradually worsened, particulary in the 1990s when Ghana was accused of harbouring Togolese rebels. There were military coups in Togo in 1963 and 1967, the latter bringing General Gnassingbé Eyadéma to power. In 1979 a new constitution was adopted and Eyadéma proclaimed the third Togolese Republic, with himself as President. He was re-elected in 1986 and, having been forced by violent demonstrations to legalize other political parties, won the first multi-party presidential elections in 1993. Eyadéma was re-elected in 1998 and in 2002 the constitution was changed to let him stand again in 2003.

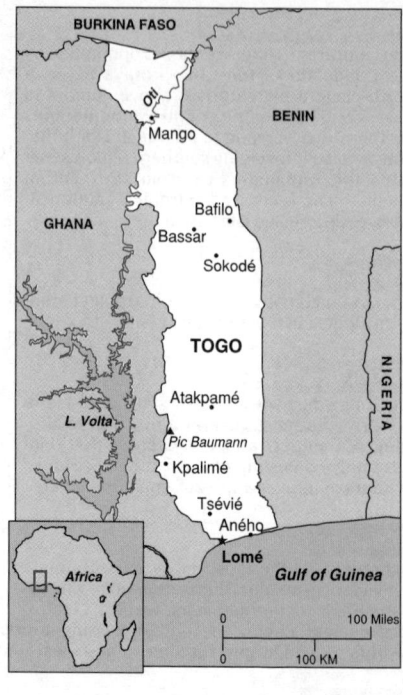

TONGA

Official name Kingdom of Tonga	**Time zone** GMT + 13
Local name Tonga	**Currency** 1 Pa'anga/Tongan Dollar (T$) = 100
Location An independent island group in the south-west Pacific Ocean	seniti
Area 646 sq km/249 sq mi	**Languages** English, Tongan
Capital Nuku'alofa	**Religions** Christianity 79% (Prot 63%, RC 16%), others 21%
Population 109 100 (1999e)	**Ethnic groups** Tongan 98%, others 2%

Physical description

Tonga consists of 169 islands, 36 of which are inhabited, divided into three main groups (coral formations of Ha'apai and Tongatapu-Eua, mountainous Vava'u); the largest island is Tongatapu, with two thirds of the population and an area of 260 sq km/100 sq mi; the western islands are mainly volcanic and some are still active; they rise to a height of 500–1 000m; the highest point is the extinct volcano of Kao (1 014m).

Climate

Semi-tropical; the average annual temperature at Tongatapu is 23°C and the average annual rainfall is 1 750mm; there are occasional hurricanes in the summer months.

Government

Governed by a Sovereign, Privy Council, and a unicameral Legislative Assembly of Cabinet Members, nobles and elected people's representatives.

Economy

Largely based on agriculture; copra, coconuts, bananas, watermelons, yams, taro, cassava, groundnuts, rice, maize, tobacco, sugar cane; tourism and cottage handicrafts are small but growing industries.

History

Inhabited from as early as 1000BC, the islands were visited by Captain James Cook in 1773 and named the Friendly Islands. They received missionaries and were established as a nation under King George Tupou I. Tonga became a British protectorate in 1899, under its own monarchy, and gained independence in 1970. Taufa'ahau Tupou IV acceded to the throne in 1965. Tonga's first political party was formed in 1994 and its pro-democracy movement gained momentum.

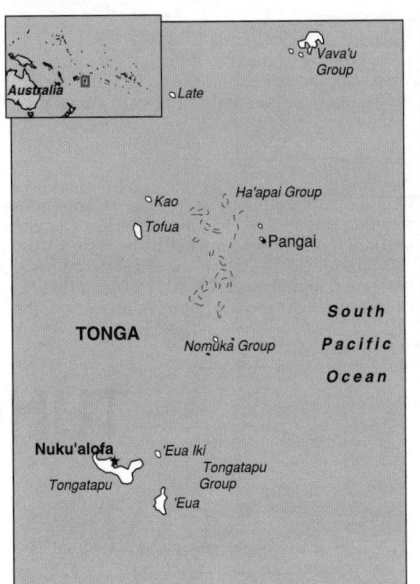

Nations of the World

TRINIDAD AND TOBAGO

Official name Republic of Trinidad and Tobago
Local name Trinidad and Tobago
Location A republic comprising the southernmost islands of the Lesser Antilles chain in the south-east Caribbean Sea, just off the South American mainland
Area 5 128 sq km/1 979 sq mi
Capital Port of Spain
Chief towns San Fernando, Arima, Scarborough
Population 1 102 000 (1999e)

Time zone GMT −4
Currency 1 Trinidad and Tobago Dollar (TT$) = 100 cents
Language English
Religions Christianity 60% (RC 32%, Prot 28%), Hinduism 24%, Islam 6%, others 5%, none/unaffiliated 5%
Ethnic groups black 40%, East Indian 40%, mixed 14%, others 6%

Physical description

The island of Trinidad is roughly rectangular in shape; separated from Venezuela in the south by the 11km/7mile-wide Gulf of Paria; crossed by three mountain ranges; the northern range includes El Cerro del Aripo (940m); the remainder of the land is low-lying, with large areas of mangrove swamps along the coasts; Pitch Lake in the south-west is the world's largest reservoir of natural asphalt; Tobago lies 30km/19mi north-east; the Main Ridge extends along most of the island, rising to 576m.

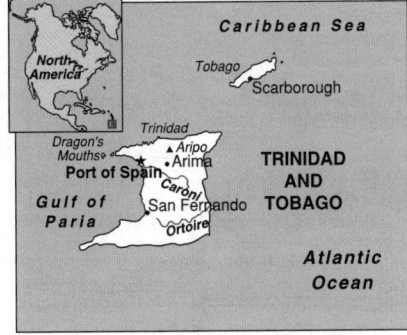

Climate

Tropical, with an annual average temperature of 29°C; the average rainfall is 1 270mm in the west, 3 048mm in the north-east.

Government

Governed by a President elected for a five-year term, and bicameral Parliament, comprising a 31-member Senate and a 36-member House of Representatives.

Nations of the World

Economy

Based on the oil and gas industry; an industrial complex on the west coast of Trinidad includes a steel mill, ammonia plants and facilities for producing methanol and urea; cement; oil refining; petrochemicals; asphalt; processing of sugar; cocoa; coffee; fruit; the main tourist centre is on Tobago.

History

Originally inhabited by Arawak and Carib Indians, the islands were visited by Columbus in 1498. Trinidad was settled by Spain in the 16c, raided by the Dutch and French in the 17c, when tobacco and sugar plantations worked by imported African slaves were established, and ceded to Britain in 1802 under the Treaty of Amiens. Tobago became a British colony in 1814. Trinidad and Tobago became a joint British Crown Colony in 1899, an independent member of the Commonwealth of Nations in 1962, and a republic in 1976 under the leadership of Eric Williams.

TUNISIA

Official name Republic of Tunisia
Local name Tunisiya
Location A north African republic, bounded to the west by Algeria; to the south-east by Libya; and to the north-east and north by the Mediterranean Sea
Area 164 150 sq km/63 362 sq mi
Capital Tunis
Chief towns Bizerta, Sousse, Sfax, Gabes

Population 9 514 000 (1999e)
Time zone GMT +1
Currency 1 Tunisian Dinar (TD, D) = 1 000 millimes
Language Arabic; French is also spoken
Religions Islam 98%, Christianity 1%, others 1%
Ethnic groups Arab and Berber 98%, European 1%, Jewish and others 1%

Physical description

The Atlas Mountains in the north-west rise to 1 544m at Chambi; the central depression runs west to east, containing several salty lakes; dry, sandy upland lies to the south.

Climate

Mediterranean climate on the coast, with hot, dry summers and wet winters; the daily maximum temperature is 14°–33°C; the average annual rainfall is 420mm at Tunis and over twice this level in the Atlas Mountains; further south, rainfall decreases and temperatures can be extreme.

Government

A 141-member National Assembly, elected every five years; a President, also elected for five years, appoints a Prime Minister and Cabinet.

Economy

Agriculture employs 50% of the population, but is of declining importance; the world's fourth-largest producer of olive oil; olives, wheat, barley, henna, almonds, cork, citrus fruits, dates, grapes, vegetables; livestock; fishing; sugar refining; oil refining; cement; tyres; textiles; carpets; food processing; paper; tourism; the world's fifth largest producer of phosphates; oil, iron ore, lead, zinc; reserves of gold, barite, fluorspar.

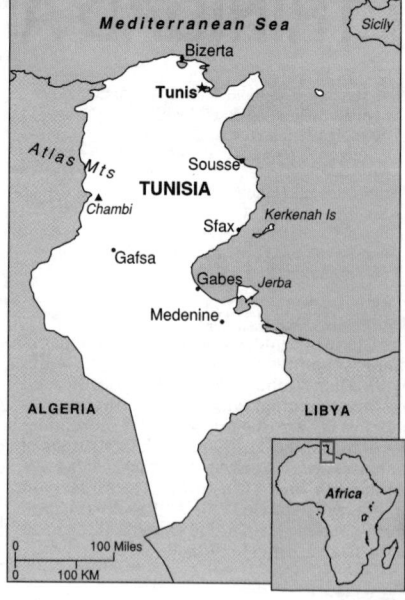

History

Ruled at various times by Phoenicians, Carthaginians, Romans, Byzantines, Arabs, Spanish and

Turks due to its situation at the hub of the Mediterranean, it became a French protectorate in 1883 and gained independence in 1956. That year the monarchy was abolished and in 1957 a republic was declared, led by President Habib Bourguiba. The government's refusal to meet demands for the legalization of other political parties in the 1970s led to serious unrest, and in 1987 Bourguiba was deposed by his Prime Minister, General Ben Ali, who introduced multi-party politics and was re-elected in 1994 and 1999.

TURKEY

Official name Republic of Turkey

Local name Türkiye

Location A republic lying partly in Europe and partly in Asia. The western area (Thrace) is bounded by the Aegean Sea and Greece, and to the north by Bulgaria and the Black Sea; the eastern area (Anatolia) is bounded by Georgia, Armenia, Azerbaijan and Iran, and to the south by Iraq, Syria and the Mediterranean Sea

Area 779 452 sq km/300 868 sq mi

Capital Ankara

Chief towns Istanbul, Izmir, Adana, Bursa, Gaziantep

Population 65 599 000 (1999e)

Time zone GMT +3

Currency 1 Turkish Lira (TL) = 100 kurus

Language Turkish

Religions Islam 99% (mostly Sunni), others 1%

Ethnic groups Turkish 80%, Kurdish 16%, Arab 2%, others 2%

Physical description

The Turkish Straits (the Dardanelles, Sea of Marmara and Bosporus) connect the Black Sea in the north-east and the Mediterranean Sea in the south-west; it is a mountainous country at an average height of 1 100m; ranges extend west to east along the north and south coasts of Anatolia; average altitude of the high central plateau is 1 000–2 000m; the Taurus Mountains cover the entire southern part of Anatolia; east Anatolia is the highest region, and the highest peak is Mount Ararat (5 165m); the alluvial

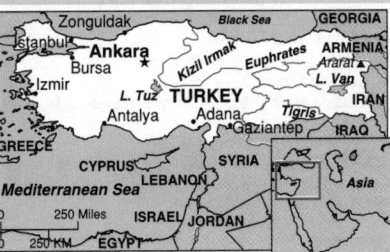

coastal plains are 2030 km/1219 mi wide; chief rivers include the Kizil Irmak, Sakarya and Seyhan; the River Tigris and the River Euphrates have their origins in Turkey.

Climate

A typically Mediterranean climate on the Aegean and Mediterranean coasts, with hot, dry summers and warm, wet winters; further east along the Black Sea coast, rainfall becomes heavy in summer and autumn; rainfall is low on the interior plateau, with cold winters and warm or hot summers and occasional thunderstorms.

Government

The constitution provides for a single-chamber, 450-member National Assembly; a President appointed by the Assembly holds office for seven years, appointing a Prime Minister and a Council of Ministers.

Economy

Agriculture employs over 60% of the workforce, the principal products being cotton, tobacco, cereals, figs, silk, olive oil, dried fruits, nuts, mohair, wool and hides; there is a wide range of important mineral resources, including chrome, coal, lignite, copper concentrate and sulphur; there is oil in eastern Turkey; manufacturing industries include food processing, textiles, iron and steel, cement, leather goods, glass, and ceramics; tourism is increasing; many Turks find work in Europe, especially Germany.

History

Modern Turkey developed out of the Ottoman Empire and includes the area known as Asia Minor. It was formerly part of the empire of Alexander I, and of the Byzantine Empire. In the 13c the Seljuk Sultanate was replaced by the Ottoman Sultanate in north-west Asia Minor. The Turkish invasion of Europe began with the Balkans in 1375, and in 1453 Constantinople fell to the Turks. The empire was at its peak in the 16c under Süleyman I, the Magnificent, but in the 17c the Turks were pressed back by Russian and Austrian armies. In the 19c Turkey was regarded by Britain as a bulwark against

Nations of the World

Russian expansion but, following alleged Armenian massacres, Britain abandoned its support of Turkey. The Young Turks seized power in 1908 and became embroiled in the Balkan Wars (1912–13). During World War I Turkey allied with Germany. Following the Young Turk Revolution, the Republic of Turkey was founded in 1923, led by Kemal Atatürk, who introduced a policy of westernization and economic development. Turkey was neutral throughout most of World War II, before siding with the Allies, and its neutralist policy was abandoned when it joined NATO in 1952. There were military coups in 1960 and 1980. Relations with Greece were strained, leading to an invasion of Cyprus in 1974; this in turn strained relations with the Allies and resulted in a four-year US trade embargo. Since the 1980s the south-east of Turkey has suffered fierce fighting between the separatist PKK (Kurdish Workers' Party), who want to establish an independent Kurdistan for Turkey's 12 million Kurds, and government forces. In 1993 Turkey's first woman Prime Minister, Tansu Çiller, took office; there have been several heads of government since Çiller departed in 1996. Turkey's desire to join the EU has led to several reforms in recent years.

TURKMENISTAN

Official name Republic of Turkmenistan
Local name Turkmenostan
Location A republic in south-west Middle Asia, bounded to the north by Kazakhstan and Uzbekistan; to the south by Iran and Afghanistan; and to the west by the Caspian Sea
Area 488 100 sq km/188 400 sq mi
Capital Ashkhabad
Chief towns Chardzhou, Mary, Türkmenbashi, Nebit-Dag

Population 4 366 000 (1999e)
Time zone GMT +3
Currency 1 Manat (TMM) = 100 tenesi
Languages Turkmen, Russian, Uzbek
Religions Islam 89% (mostly Sunni), Christianity 9% (Orthodox), others 2%
Ethnic groups Turkmen 77%, Uzbek 9%, Russian 7%, Kazakh 2%, others 5%

Physical description
Low-lying with hills in the south; mainly desert; the chief river is the Amudarya.

Climate
Continental, hot and arid in the large desert areas.

Government
The President is both head of state and government; the legislative body is the 50-member Assembly (*Majlis*).

Economy
Oil refining; chemicals; food processing; rugs; machinery; cotton; silk; Turkmenistan is noted for Turkoman horses and Karakul sheep.

History
About 80 per cent of the country is occupied by the Kara Kum Desert; the people live mainly around oases. Originally occupied by various tribes who were unified under the Russians in 1869, Turkmenistan was proclaimed a Soviet Socialist Republic in 1924. In 1991 it gained its independence under President Saparmurad Niyazov and became a member of the CIS (Commonwealth of Independent States). In 1999 Niyazov became 'president for life'.

➔ **Turks and Caicos Islands ▸ United Kingdom**

TUVALU

Official name Tuvalu
Local name Tuvalu
Location An independent island group in the south-west Pacific, 1 050km/650mi north of Fiji
Area 26 sq km/10 sq mi
Capital Fongafale (on Funafuti)

Population 10 600 (1999e)
Time zone GMT +12
Currency 1 Australian Dollar (A$) = 100 cents
Languages Tuvaluan, English
Religions Christianity 98%, Baha'i 1%, others 1%
Ethnic groups Polynesia 95%, others 5%

Physical description

Comprises nine low-lying coral atolls, running north-west to south-east in a chain 580km/360mi long.

Climate

Hot and humid; the average annual temperature is 30°C and the average annual rainfall is 3 535mm.

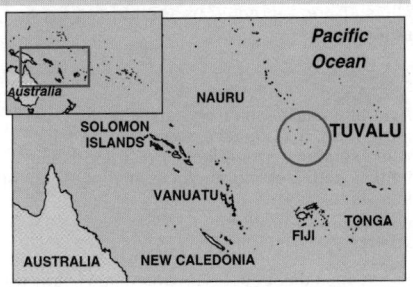

Government

The British Monarch is represented by a Governor-General; governed by a Prime Minister, Cabinet, and a unicameral 12-member Parliament.

Economy

Copra, tropical fruit; fishing; crafts; postage stamps.

History

Invaded by Samoans in the 16c; became a British protectorate as the Ellice Is in 1892; administered as a colony jointly with the Gilbert Is (now Kiribati) from 1915; separate constitutions, following the 1974 referendum; gained independence in 1978; became a member of the UN in 2000.

UGANDA

Official name Republic of Uganda
Local name Uganda
Location A landlocked East African republic, bounded to the south by Rwanda, Tanzania and Lake Victoria; to the east by Kenya; to the north by Sudan; and to the west by the Democratic Republic of the Congo
Area 238 461 sq km/92 029 sq mi
Capital Kampala
Chief towns Jinja, Mbale, Tororo, Soroti, Entebbe

Population 22 805 000 (1999e)
Time zone GMT +3
Currency 1 Uganda Shilling (USh) = 100 cents
Language English; Swahili and other languages are also spoken
Religions Christianity 66% (RC 33%, Prot 33%), traditional beliefs 18%, Islam 16%
Ethnic groups Ganda 19%, Banyoro 15%, Teso 9%, Banyan 8%, Basogo 8%, Bagisu 7%, Bachiga 7%, others 27%

Physical description

Landlocked country, mainly on a plateau with an elevation of between 900m and 1 000m; dry savannah or semi-desert north of Lake Kyoga; the population is concentrated in the fertile Lake Victoria basin; the Western Rift Valley runs along Uganda's frontier with the Democratic Republic of Congo; straddling the frontier is the Mount Stanley massif, including Margherita Peak (5 110m), the highest point in Uganda and the Democratic Republic of Congo; main lakes include Victoria (south-east), George (south-west), Edward (south-west), Albert (west), Kwania (central), Kyoga (central) and Bisina (formerly Lake Salisbury, in the east); the two main rivers are the upper reaches of the River Nile: the Victoria Nile and the Albert Nile.

Nations of the World

Climate

The highest rainfall is in the mountains to the west and south-west and along the shores of Lake Victoria, exceeding 1500mm per year; daily temperatures at Entebbe on the north shore of the lake are 24°–28°C; central and north-eastern areas receive less than 1000mm of rain annually.

Government

Parliament is part-elected and part-appointed by special interest groups; a Cabinet and Prime Minister are appointed by the elected President.

Economy

Agriculture is the main economic activity; coffee, cotton, tea, tobacco, sugar, maize, millet, yams, sorghum, groundnuts; livestock; fishing; textiles; fertilizers; food processing; plywood; brewing; tungsten; copper, tin, beryl, phosphate limestone.

History

Bantu-speaking peoples migrated into south-west Uganda c.500BC and by the 14c AD were organized into several kingdoms. Uganda was discovered by Arab traders in the 1830s, explored by John Hanning Speke in the 1860s and granted to the Imperial British East Africa Company in 1888. The Kingdom of Buganda became a British protectorate in 1893, and other territory was included by 1903. Uganda gained its independence in 1962 as a federation of the kingdoms of Ankole, Buganda, Bunyoro, Busoga and Toro, announced by Prime Minister Dr Milton Obote, who in 1966 deposed the President, King Mutesa II, and assumed all powers himself. In 1971 a coup was led by General Idi Amin Dada, who expelled all Asian residents who were not Ugandan citizens. Reacting to Amin's repressive regime, Tanzanian troops and Ugandan exiles marched on Kampala, overthrowing the government in 1979. Obote returned to power but failed to restore stability and another coup took place in 1985. The military government ruled until 1986 when it was overthrown by Yoweri Museveni, who became President and began the process of rebuilding the country but kept a ban on other political parties. The first free presidential elections took place in 1996, and Museveni was re-elected. He was again elected in 2001. Ugandan troops fought in the conflict in the Democratic Republic of Congo from 1997 to 2002, and fighting has also occurred with rebel groups within Uganda.

UKRAINE

Official name Ukraine
Local name Ukraina
Location A republic in eastern Europe, bounded to the south-west by Moldova and Romania; to the west by Hungary, Slovakia and Poland; to the north by Belarus; to the east by Russia; and to the south by the Black Sea
Area 603 700 sq km/233 028 sq mi
Capital Kiev
Chief towns Kharkov, Donetsk, Odessa, Dnepropetrovsk, Lvov, Zaporozhye, Krivoy Rog
Population 49 811 000 (1999e)
Time zone GMT +2
Currency 1 Hryvnia = 100 kopiykas
Languages Ukrainian, Russian
Religions Christianity 93% (Orthodox 76%, RC 14%, Prot 3%), Judaism 2%, others 5%
Ethnic groups Ukrainian 73%, Russian 22%, Jewish 1%, others 4%

Physical description

Generally a plain with high elevations in the west, south and south-east; the Ukrainian Carpathian Mountains in the west rise to 2 061m at Mount Goveria; the Crimean Peninsula separates the Black Sea from the Sea of Azov; the Crimean Mountains lie along the south coast of the peninsula; chief rivers are the Dnieper, Dniester, Severskiy Donets and Prut; there are many reservoirs and lakes.

Climate

Temperate, continental; cold winters and warm summers.

Government

A 450-seat unicameral Supreme Council (*Verkhovna Rada*) is elected once every four years.

Economy

Coal (from the large Donets coalfield), iron ore; manufacturing industries include metallurgy, machinery, fertilizers, fibres, synthetic resins, plastics, dyes, rubber products and food processing; natural gas, oil refining; a major grain-exporting republic; other agricultural products are wheat, sugar beet, sunflower, cotton, flax, tobacco, soya, hops, fruit and vegetables; tourism on the Crimean coast.

History

Inhabited by Scythians in ancient times, the country was then invaded by Goths, Huns and Khazars. Kiev became the centre of power, but it was overrun by the Golden Horde in the 14c. Ruled by Lithuania in the 14–15c, Ukraine came under Polish rule in the 16c, when many people fled and formed resistance movements (Cossacks). It gradually became part of Russia in the 17–18c. Ukraine declared its independence in 1918, but Kiev was occupied by Soviet troops and the country became a Soviet Socialist Republic in 1922. In 1986 the Chernobyl nuclear disaster occurred, leaving a huge area of the country permanently contaminated. On the disintegration of the USSR, Ukraine successfully declared its independence in 1991 under President Leonid Kravchuk and became a founding member of the CIS (Commonwealth of Independent States). This was soon followed by a dispute with Russia over control of the Black Sea fleet and the status of the largely Russian-populated Crimean peninsula, whose declaration of autonomy in 1992 was rejected by the Ukraine.

UNITED ARAB EMIRATES

Official name United Arab Emirates

Local name Ittihād al-imārāt al-'Arabīyah

Location A federation in the eastern central Arabian Peninsula comprising seven internally self-governing emirates. It is bounded to the north by the Arabian Gulf; to the east by Oman; and to the south and west by Saudi Arabia

Area 83 600 sq km/32 300 sq mi

Capital Abu Dhabi

Chief towns Dubai, Sharjah, Ras al Khaimah

Population 2 344 000 (1999e)

Time zone GMT +4

Currency 1 Dirham (DH) = 100 fils

Languages Arabic, English

Religions Islam 96%, others 4%

Ethnic groups Asian 52%, Emirian 18%, other Arab 24%, others 6%

Physical description

Located along the southern shore (Trucial Coast) of the Arabian Gulf; Al Fujairah has a coastline along the Gulf of Oman; salt marshes predominate on the coast; barren desert and gravel plain inland; the Hajar Mountains in Al Fujairah rise to over 1 000m.

Climate

Hot with limited rainfall; winter temperatures average 21°C, with high humidity (in excess of 70%); less humid in summer, with maximum temperatures rising to 45°C; sandstorms are common; the average annual rainfall in Abu Dhabi is 32mm.

Government

Governed by a Supreme Council comprising the hereditary rulers of the seven emirates.

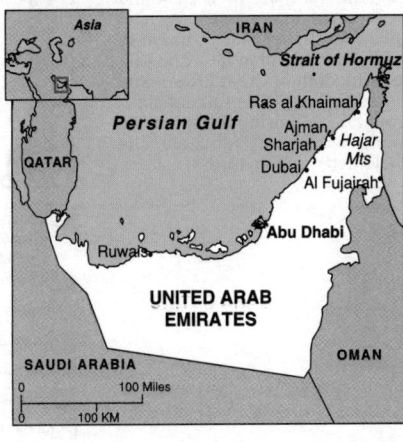

Nations of the World

Economy

An important commercial and trading centre; the economy is based on oil and gas with Abu Dhabi the major producer, followed by Dubai; iron and steel; petrochemicals; construction; ship repairing; fishing; light industry; tourism; saline water supplies have restricted agriculture to the oases and the irrigated valleys of the Hajar Mountains: vegetables, fruits, dates, dairy farming.

History

As early as the third millennium BC it was crossed by many Sumerian trade routes. It came under Muslim influence from the 6c and was visited by the Portuguese in the 16c. The British East India Company arrived in the 17c. Various peace treaties with Britain were signed from 1820 by the ruling sheikhs of what became known thereafter as the Trucial States — Abu Dhabi, Ajman, Dubai, Fujairah, Ras al Khaimah, Sharjah and Umm al Qaiwain on the Persian Gulf and Gulf of Oman — which accepted British protection in 1892. Abu Dhabi's huge oilfields were discovered in 1958. The new state formed by six emirates was established in 1971, when the special peace treaties ended and a Treaty of Friendship with Britain was signed; the emirate of Ras al Khaimah joined the following year.

UNITED KINGDOM

Official name United Kingdom of Great Britain and Northern Ireland
Local name United Kingdom
Location A kingdom in Western Europe, comprising England, Scotland, Wales and Northern Ireland
Area 244 755 sq km/94 475 sq mi
Capital London

Chief towns Belfast, Birmingham, Cardiff, Edinburgh, Glasgow, Liverpool, Manchester, Newcastle upon Tyne
Population 58 789 194 (2001)
Time zone GMT
Currency 1 Pound Sterling (£) = 100 pence
Language English; Welsh and Gaelic are spoken by minorities

Climate

Temperate maritime climate, moderated by prevailing south-west winds; generally wetter and warmer in the west.

Government

A kingdom with a monarch as head of state; governed by a bicameral Parliament comprising an elected 659-member House of Commons, and a House of Lords with hereditary peers, life peers, Anglican bishops and law lords; a Cabinet is appointed by the Prime Minister.

History

Wales was effectively joined to England in 1301, then Scotland was joined under one crown in 1603 (and by legislative union in 1707) and Ireland in 1801 (the United Kingdom of Great Britain and Ireland). The present name dates from 1922, following the establishment of the Irish Free State. The UK joined the EC in 1973.

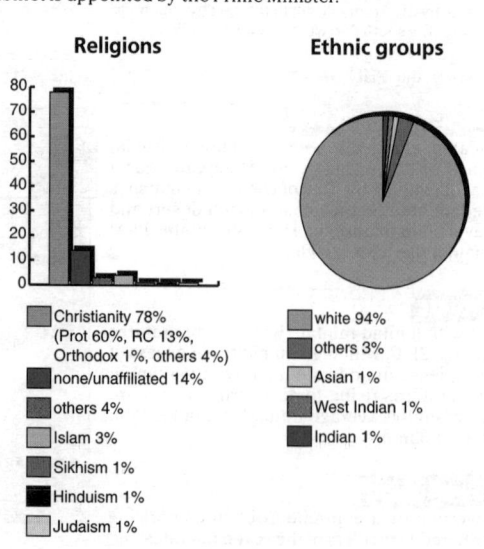

Religions

Christianity 78% (Prot 60%, RC 13%, Orthodox 1%, others 4%)
none/unaffiliated 14%
others 4%
Islam 3%
Sikhism 1%
Hinduism 1%
Judaism 1%

Ethnic groups

white 94%
others 3%
Asian 1%
West Indian 1%
Indian 1%

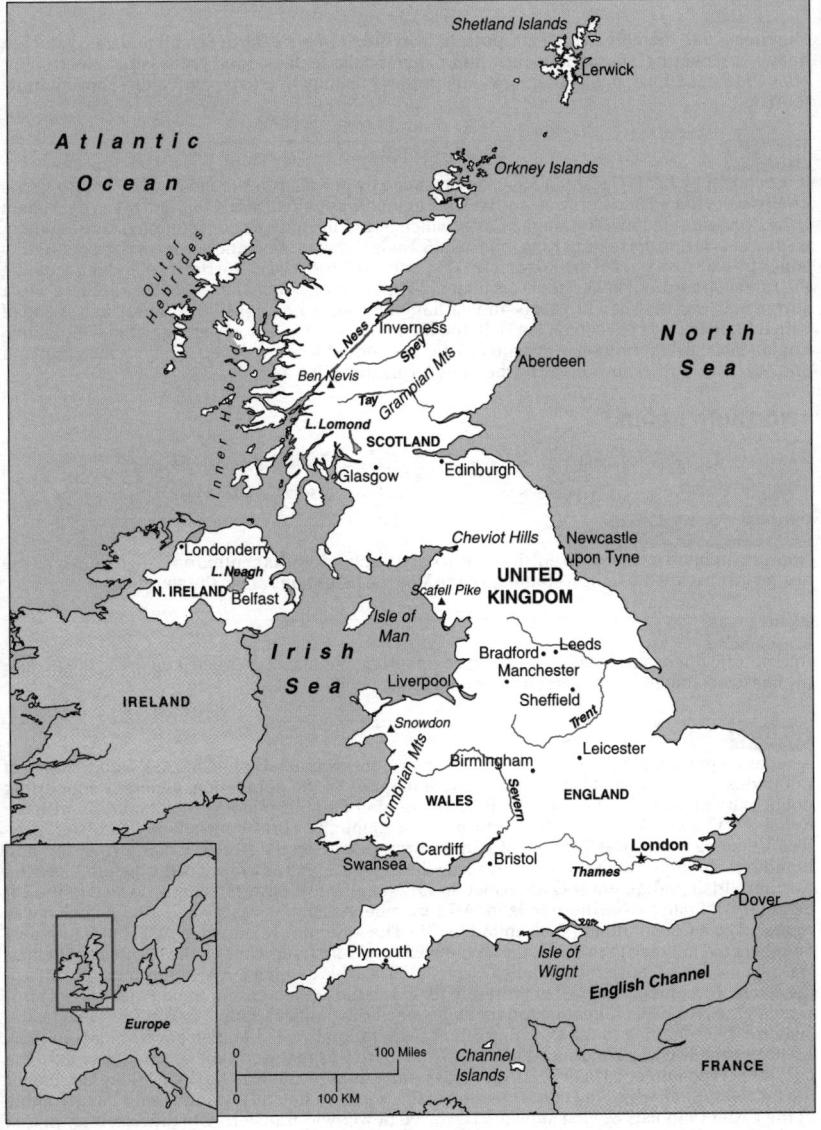

❖ England

Area 130 357 sq km/50 318 sq mi
Capital London

Chief towns Birmingham, Liverpool, Manchester, Newcastle upon Tyne
Population 49 138 831 (2001)

Physical description

Largely undulating lowland, rising in the south to the Mendips, Cotswolds, Chilterns and North Downs, in the north to the north–south ridge of the Pennines and in the north-west to the Cumbria Mountains; drained in the east by the Tyne, Tees, Humber, Ouse and Thames rivers, and in the west by the Eden, Ribble, Mersey and Severn rivers; the Lake District in the north-west includes Derwent Water, Ullswater, Windermere and Bassenthwaite.

Nations of the World

Economy

Minerals (coal, tin, china clay, salt, potash, lead ore, iron ore), North Sea oil and gas; vehicles, heavy engineering; petrochemicals, pharmaceuticals; textiles; food processing; electronics; telecommunications; publishing; brewing; pottery; fishing; livestock, agriculture, horticulture; tourism.

History

It was taken by Julius Caesar in 55BC, and invaded by Nordic tribes in the 5c, when many Celtic groups were forced into Cornwall and Wales. England was unified in 924–39, and taken by William I, the Conqueror in 1066. The Magna Carta, which began the nation's constitutional development, was signed during the reign of King John in 1215. Under Edward I England succeeded in conquering Wales by 1283. The Wars of the Roses from 1455 until 1485 resulted in the House of Tudor becoming the ruling family until 1603. There was major colonial expansion in the 16c. In the 17c there was a seven-year war between Royalists and Parliamentarians (the English Civil Wars), at the end of which Charles I was executed (1649). In the 18c the first Act of Union was signed in 1707, joining England in legislative union with Scotland; the second, which was signed in 1800, joined England and Scotland with Ireland, creating the United Kingdom (UK).

❖ Northern Ireland

Area 14 120 sq km/5 450 sq mi	**Chief towns** Londonderry, Armagh
Capital Belfast	**Population** 1 685 267 (2001)

Physical description

Northern Ireland occupies the north-eastern part of Ireland, and is centred on Lough Neagh; to the north and east are the Antrim Mountains; the Mourne Mountains are in the south-east.

Economy

Agriculture; linen; shipbuilding; textiles; engineering; chemicals; service industries; the economy has been affected by the sectarian troubles since 1969.

History

A separate parliament to the rest of Ireland (Stormont) was established in 1920, with a House of Commons and a Senate. There is a Protestant majority in the population, generally supporting political union with Great Britain; many of the Roman Catholic minority look for union with the Republic of Ireland. Violent conflict between the communities broke out in 1968 (the Ulster 'Troubles'), leading to the establishment of a British Army peace-keeping force. Sectarian murders and bombings continued both within and outside the province, and as a result of the disturbances the Northern Irish parliament was abolished in 1972. Legislative powers are now vested in the UK Secretary of State for Northern Ireland. A 78-member Assembly was formed in 1973, which was replaced by a Constitutional Convention in 1975. The Assembly reformed in 1982, but Nationalist members did not take their seats. Under the 1985 Anglo-Irish Agreement, the Republic of Ireland was given a consultative role in the government of Northern Ireland. All Northern Ireland MPs in the British Parliament resigned in protest in 1986, and the agreement continued to attract controversy in the late 1980s. Direct negotiations between the political parties took place in Belfast in 1991 and 1992, leading to the Downing Street Declaration by UK and Irish governments in 1993. An IRA cease-fire was announced in 1994–6, but there was renewed violence in 1996–7 until the cease-fire recommenced in 1997. Further cross-party talks resulted in the Good Friday Agreement the following year, which led to the creation of the Northern Ireland Assembly with David Trimble of the Ulster Unionists as First Minister. Devolved power was transferred to the Assembly in Dec 1999. Since then the peace process has made progress despite some setbacks and continuing negotiations. Devolved government was suspended in late 2002 leading to further talks.

❖ Scotland

Area 78 742 sq km/30 394 sq mi	**Chief towns** Glasgow, Dundee, Aberdeen
Capital Edinburgh	**Population** 5 062 011 (2001)

Physical description

Divided into the Southern Uplands (rising to 843m at Merrick), the Central Lowlands (the most densely populated area) and the Northern Highlands (divided by the fault line following the Great Glen, and rising to 1 344m at Ben Nevis); there are 787 islands, most of which lie off the heavily-indented west coast and only c.60 exceed 8 sq km/3 sq mi; there are several wide estuaries on the east coast, primarily the Firths of Forth, Tay and Moray; the interior has many freshwater lochs, the largest being Loch Lomond (70 sq km/27 sq mi) and the deepest Loch Morar (310m); the longest river is the River Tay (192km/119mi).

Economy

Industries are mainly in the central belt but heavy industry (such as shipbuilding, steel, vehicles) declined throughout the 1980s, with the closure of many coal pits; whisky; oil services on the east coast; electronics; textiles; agriculture and forestry; fishing and fish farming; tourism.

History

Roman attempts to limit incursions of northern tribes were marked by the building of the Antonine Wall (AD142), which extended from the Forth estuary to the Clyde, and Hadrian's Wall (AD122–8), which extended from the Solway Firth to the River Tyne and was the principal northern frontier of the Roman province of Britain. There were the beginnings of unification in the 9c, but wars were fought between England and Scotland during the Middle Ages until Scottish independence was restored by Robert Bruce, and recognized by England in 1328. The Stuarts succeeded to the throne in the 14c and united the crowns of Scotland and England in 1603; the parliaments were united under the Act of Union in 1707. There were unsuccessful Jacobite rebellions in 1715 and 1745. A proposal for devolution failed in a referendum in 1979, but another in 1997 gave it overwhelming approval. In addition to Scotland's separate legal and educational system, and other institutions which are distinct from those of England or Wales, a Scottish parliament with tax-raising powers was elected, officially opening on 1 July 1999.

❖ Wales

Area 20 761 sq km/8 014 sq mi	**Chief towns** Swansea, Wrexham
Capital Cardiff	**Population** 2 903 085 (2001)

Physical description

Rises in the north-west to 1 085m at Snowdon in the Snowdonia range; the Cambrian Mountains rise in the centre, and the Brecon Beacons in the south; drained by the Severn, Clwyd, Conwy, Dee, Dovey, Taff, Tawe, Teifi, Towy, Usk and Wye rivers.

Economy

Industrialized southern valleys and the coastal plain are based on local coal; tourism in north and north-west, with seaside resorts and mountains; important source of water for England; slate, lead, steel, engineering, oil refining; fishing, forestry, sheep, dairy products; much light industry in recent decades, following the Great Depression and reduction in coal and steel industries; Royal Mint at Llantrisant.

History

Celtic in origin, the original people of Wales, who had managed to resist the Romans, increased in number around the 4c when Anglo-Saxon invaders of Britain drove the Brythonic Celts into Wales, calling them *Waelisc*, 'foreign'. In the 8c Welsh territory was lost to Offa, King of Mercia, who built a frontier dyke from the Dee to the Wye, and in the 9c Rhodri Mawr united Wales against the Saxons, Norse and Danes. Edward I of England established authority over Wales, building several castles in the 12–13c, and his son was created the first Prince of Wales (1301). In the early 15c there was a Welsh revolt against Henry IV led by Owen Glendower. Wales was politically united with England at the Act of Union in 1535. It became the centre of Nonconformist religion in the 18c. A political nationalist movement developed, embodied in Plaid Cymru, which returned its first MP in 1966. A referendum in 1979 opposed devolution, but another in 1997 narrowly approved it, and the opening session of the Welsh Assembly was held in June 1999.

UK Islands

❖ Channel Islands

Location An island group of the British Isles in the English Channel, west of the Cotentin Peninsula of Normandy. A dependent territory of the British Crown, it has individual legislative assemblies and legal system and is divided into the Bailiwicks of Jersey and of Guernsey. Both English and Norman-French are spoken	**Area** 194 sq km/75 sq mi
	Capital St Helier (Jersey); St Peter Port (Guernsey)
	Population 149 907 (2001e)
	Time zone GMT
	Main islands Guernsey, Jersey, Alderney, Sark; other islands include Herm, Jethou, Brechou, the Caskets, the Minquiers and the Chauseys

Nations of the World

Government

A Bailliff presides over the Royal court and the Representative Assembly (the States).

Economy

Fruit, vegetables; flowers; dairy produce, Jersey and Guernsey cattle; tourism; used as a tax haven.

History

The islands were granted to the Dukes of Normandy in the 10c; the only part of Normandy remaining with England after 1204; occupied by Germany in World War II.

❖ Isle of Man

Location A British Crown Dependency in the Irish Sea, west of England and east of Northern Ireland **Area** 572 sq km/221 sq mi	**Capital** Douglas **Population** 76 315 (2001) **Time zone** GMT

Government

The island has its own Parliament, the bicameral Court of Tynwald, which consists of the elected House of Keys and the Legislative Council (composed of the Lieutenant-Governor, the President, the Lord Bishop of Sodor and Man, the Attorney-General and seven members elected by the House of Keys); Acts of the British Parliament do not generally apply to the Isle of Man.

Economy

Tourism; agriculture; light engineering; used as a tax haven.

History

Ruled by the Welsh from the 6c until the 9c, then by the Scandinavians, Scots and English; it was purchased by the British Government partly in 1765 and wholly in 1828. Manx survived as an everyday language until the 19c.

Dependent territories

❖ Anguilla

Location The most northerly of the Leeward Islands, East Caribbean Sea **Area** 155 sq km/60 sq mi	**Capital** The Valley **Population** 11 560 (2001) **Time zone** GMT −4

Government

A Governor is appointed by the British Sovereign; 11-member Legislative Assembly.

Economy

Peas, corn, sweet potatoes, salt; boatbuilding; fishing; tourism.

History

Colonized by English settlers from St Christopher in 1650; ultimately incorporated in the Colony of St Kitts–Nevis–Anguilla; separated in 1980.

❖ Bermuda

Location A group of c.150 low-lying, coral islands and islets situated in the West Atlantic Ocean c.900km/560mi east of Cape Hatteras, North Carolina	**Area** 53 sq km/20 sq mi **Capital** Hamilton **Population** 62 500 (1999e) **Time zone** GMT −4

Government

The British Monarch is represented by a Governor-General; governed by a Senate (11 members), a House of Assembly (40 members, elected for five years), and a 12-member Cabinet headed by a Prime Minister.

Economy

Mainly year-round tourism; increasingly an international company business centre; petroleum products; pharmaceuticals; aircraft supplies; boatbuilding, ship repair; vegetables; citrus and banana plantations; fish processing centre.

History

Discovered by Spanish mariner, Juan Bermudez, in the early 16c; colonized by English settlers in 1612; important naval station, and (until 1862) penal settlement; a new constitution providing internal self-government came into force in 1968; movement for independence caused tension in the 1970s, including the assassination of the Governor-General in 1973.

❖ British Antarctic Territory

Location A British colonial territory which includes the South Orkney Islands, the South Shetland Islands, the Antarctic Graham Land Peninsula, and the land mass extending to the South Pole
Area 5.7m sq km/2.2m sq mi

Government

Administered by a High Commissioner in the Falkland Islands.

Economy

The territory (which lies 20°–80° W and south of 60°S) is populated solely by scientists of the British Antarctic Survey; some tourism; postage stamps.

History

First sighted by explorers in the early 19c, it was part of the Falkland Islands Dependencies when the British Antarctic Survey arrived in 1943–4, and became the British Antarctic Territory in 1962.

❖ British Indian Ocean Territory

Location A British territory in the Indian Ocean, 1900km/1180mi north-east of Mauritius, consisting of the Chagos Archipelago
Area 60 sq km/23 sq mi

Government

It is administered by a High Commissioner, based in the Foreign and Commonwealth Office in London.

Economy

Construction projects and services in support of the military base on Diego Garcia.

History

Acquired by France in the 18c; annexed by Britain in 1814; dependency of Mauritius until 1965. The territory was established to meet UK and US defence requirements in the Indian Ocean. There is a UK–US naval support facility on Diego Garcia.

❖ British Virgin Islands

Location An island group at the north-western end of the Lesser Antilles chain in the east Caribbean Sea
Area 153 sq km/59 sq mi
Capital Road Town (on Tortola I)
Population 19 200 (1999e)
Time zone GMT –4

Government

A Governor represents the British Sovereign; there is a six-member Executive Council and a Legislative Council of 11 members.

Economy

Over 50% of national income is from tourism; construction; rum; paint; gravel and stone extraction; livestock; coconuts; sugar cane; fruit and vegetables; fish.

History

Tortola was colonized by British planters in 1666; a constitutional government was granted in 1774; became part of the Leeward Is in 1872; became a separate Crown Colony in 1956.

Nations of the World

❖ Cayman Islands

Location An island group in the West Caribbean Sea, comprising the islands of Grand Cayman, Cayman Brac and Little Cayman, c.240km/150mi south of Cuba	**Area** 260 sq km/100 sq mi **Capital** George Town **Population** 39 300 (1999e) **Time zone** GMT −5

Government

A Governor represents the British Sovereign, and presides over a 15-member Legislative Assembly.

Economy

Mainly tourism; international finance; property development; marked increase in cruise ship traffic; over 450 banks and trust companies established on the islands; oil transshipment; crafts, jewellery; cattle, poultry; vegetables; tropical fish; turtle products.

History

Discovered by Columbus in 1503; ceded to Britain in 1670; colonized by British settlers from Jamaica; became a British Colony in 1959.

❖ Falkland Islands

Location Situated in the South Atlantic Ocean, c.650km/400mi north-east of the Magellan Strait **Area** 12 200 sq km/4 700 sq mi	**Capital** Stanley **Population** 2 491 (2001) **Time zone** GMT −4

Government

External affairs and defence are the responsibility of the British government, which appoints civil and military commissioners; internal affairs are governed by executive and legislative councils.

Economy

Chiefly agricultural; oats; sheep; service industries to the continuing military presence in the islands.

History

Seen by several early navigators, including Capt John Strong in 1689–90, who named the islands; French settlement in 1764; a British base was established in 1765; the French yielded their settlement to the Spanish in 1767; occupied in the name of the Republic of Buenos Aires in 1820; Britain asserted possession in 1833; formal annexation in 1908 and 1917; Argentina's claims to sovereignty over the whole area resulted in invasion by Argentine military forces in April 1982; dispatch of British Task Force led to the return of the islands to British rule in June 1982.

❖ Gibraltar

Location The narrow peninsula rising steeply from the low-lying coast of south-west Spain at the eastern end of the Strait of Gibraltar, which is an important strategic point of control for the	western Mediterranean **Area** 5.9 sq km/2.3 sq mi **Population** 29 200 (1999e) **Time zone** GMT +1

Government

The British Monarch is represented by a Governor, and an 18-member House of Assembly.

Economy

Largely dependent on the presence of British forces; the Royal Naval Dockyard was converted to a commercial yard in 1985; transshipment trade and fuel supplies to shipping; tourism.

History

Settled by the Moors in 711, Gibraltar was taken by Spain in 1462, and ceded to Britain in 1713, becoming a British Crown Colony in 1830. As a Crown Colony, it played a key role in Allied naval operations during both World Wars. A proposal to end British rule was defeated by a referendum in 1967. The frontier with Spain was closed from 1969 until 1985, and Spain continues to claim sovereignty. Negotiations between the two countries to decide its future began in 2001, but an unofficial public referendum in Nov 2002 rejected the idea of joint sovereignty.

❖ Montserrat

Location A volcanic island in the Leeward Is,
Lesser Antilles, East Caribbean Sea
Area 106 sq km/41 sq mi

Capital Plymouth
Population 12 800 (1999e)
Time zone GMT –4

Government

The British Sovereign is represented by a Governor; there is a seven-member Executive Council and a 12-member Legislative Council.

Economy

Tourism is the mainstay of the economy, accounting for 25% of national income; cotton; peppers; market gardening; livestock; electronic assembly; crafts; rum distilling; postage stamps.

History

Visited by Columbus in 1493; colonized by English and Irish settlers in 1632; plantation economy based on slave labour; became a British Crown Colony in 1871; joined the Federation of the West Indies in 1958–62. The eruption of the Soufrière Hills volcano in 1997 led to the evacuation of many residents and made much of the island uninhabitable for years.

❖ Pitcairn Islands

Location An island group in the South-East
Pacific Ocean, east of French Polynesia,
comprising Pitcairn Island and the uninhabited
islands of Duce, Henderson and Oeno

Area 27 sq km/10 sq mi
Capital Adamstown
Population 49 (1999e)
Time zone GMT –8.5

Government

An island Magistrate presides over a ten-member Council.

Economy

Postage stamps; tropical and subtropical crops, crafts, forestry.

History

Visited by the British in 1767; occupied by nine mutineers from HMS *Bounty* in 1790; overpopulation led to emigration to Norfolk I in 1856 but some returned in 1864; control of the island was transferred to the Governor of Fiji in 1952; it is now a British Colony, governed by the High Commissioner in New Zealand.

❖ St Helena

Location A volcanic island in the South Atlantic
Ocean, lying 1 920km/1 200mi from the south-
west coast of Africa
Area 122 sq km/47 sq mi

Capital Jamestown
Population 7 100 (1999e)
Time zone GMT

Government

The British Sovereign is represented by a Governor; there is a 15-seat Legislative Council and a nine-seat Executive Council.

Economy

Fish processing; coffee; crafts.

History

Discovered by the Portuguese on St Helena's feast day in 1502; annexed by the Dutch in 1633; annexed by the East India Company in 1659; Napoleon was exiled here from 1815 until 1821; Ascension I and Tristan da Cunha were made dependencies in 1922.

Nations of the World

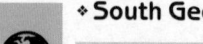

Nations of the World

❖ South Georgia

Location A barren, mountainous snow-covered island in the South Atlantic Ocean, about 500km/ 300mi east of the Falkland Is
Area c.3 750 sq km/1 450 sq mi

Government
It is a British Dependent Territory, administered from the Falkland Is.

Economy
Fishing in adjacent waters; postage stamps.

History
Research stations are maintained here and on the neighbouring Bird Is. Grytviken is the only village. The explorer, Ernest Shackleton, is buried on the island. Discovered by the London merchant De la Roche in 1675; Captain Cook landed in 1775; British annexation in 1908 and 1917; a sealing and whaling centre until 1965; invaded by Argentina and recaptured by Britain in 1982.

❖ South Sandwich Islands

Location A group of small, uninhabited islands in the South Atlantic Ocean, lying c.720km/450mi south-east of South Georgia.
Area 1 152 sq km/445 sq mi

Government
It is a British Dependent Territory, administered from the Falkland Is.

Economy
None.

History
Discovered by Captain Cook in 1775; annexed by Britain in 1908 and 1917.

❖ Turks and Caicos Islands

Location A British Colony comprising a pair of island groups which form the south-eastern archipelago of the Bahamas chain; they lie 920km/570mi south-east of Miami
Area 500 sq km/200 sq mi
Capital Cockburn Town (on Grand Turk)
Population 16 900 (1999e)
Time zone GMT –5

Government
The British Sovereign is represented by a Governor, who presides over an eight-member Council.

Economy
Corn, beans; fishing, fish-processing; tourism is a rapidly expanding industry.

History
Discovered by the Spanish in 1512; linked formally to the Bahamas in 1765; transferred to Jamaica in 1848; became a British Crown Colony in 1972; achieved internal self-government in 1976.

UNITED STATES OF AMERICA

Nations of the World

Official name United States of America
Local name United States of America
Location A federal republic in North America and the fourth-largest country in the world. It includes the detached states of Alaska and Hawaii. The mainland is bounded to the north by Canada; to the east by the Atlantic Ocean; to the south by the Gulf of Mexico; and to the west by the Pacific Ocean

Area 9 160 454 sq km/3 535 935 sq mi
Capital Washington, DC
Chief towns New York, Chicago, Los Angeles, Philadelphia, Detroit, Houston
Population 281 421 906 (2000)
Time zone GMT −5/10
Currency 1 US Dollar ($, US$) = 100 cents
Language English; there is a sizeable Spanish-speaking minority

Physical description

The East Atlantic coastal plain is backed by the Appalachian Mountains from the Great Lakes in the north to Alabama in the south; this series of parallel ranges includes the Allegheny, Blue Ridge and Catskill mountains; to the south the plain broadens out towards the Gulf of Mexico and into the Florida Peninsula; to the west, the Gulf Plains stretch north to meet the higher Great Plains from which they are separated by the Ozark Mountains; further west, the Rocky Mountains rise to over 4 500m; the highest point is Mount McKinley, Alaska, at 6 194m; the lowest point is in Death Valley (86m); drainage in the north is into the St Lawrence River or the Great Lakes; in the east, the Hudson, Delaware, Potomac, and other rivers flow east into the Atlantic Ocean; the central plains of the United States are drained by the great Red River−Missouri−Mississippi River System and by other rivers flowing into the Gulf of Mexico; in the west the main rivers are the Columbia and Colorado.

Religions

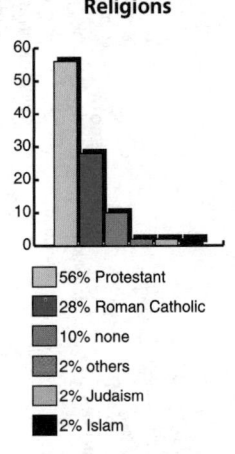

☐ 56% Protestant
■ 28% Roman Catholic
■ 10% none
■ 2% others
☐ 2% Judaism
■ 2% Islam

Climate

Varies from conditions in hot tropical deserts (in the south-west) to those typical of Arctic continental regions; most regions are affected by westerly depressions that can bring changeable weather; rainfall is heaviest in the Pacific north-west, lightest in the south-west; in the Great Plains, wide temperature variation is the result of cold air from the Arctic as well as warm tropical air from the Gulf of Mexico; on the west coast the influence of the Pacific Ocean results in a smaller range of temperatures between summer and winter; on the east coast there is a gradual increase in winter temperatures southwards; the states bordering the Gulf of Mexico are subject to hurricanes and tornadoes moving north-east from the Caribbean Sea.

Ethnic groups

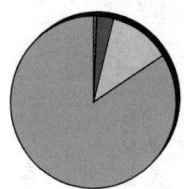

☐ white (including Hispanic) 84%
☐ black 12%
■ Asian 3%
■ Amerindian 1%

Government

The Congress consists of two bodies: a 435-member House of Representatives elected for two-year terms, and a 100-member Senate elected for six-year terms; a President, who is elected every four years by a College of State Representatives, appoints an Executive Cabinet responsible to Congress; the USA is divided into 50 federal states and the District of Columbia, each state having its own two-body legislature and Governor.

Economy

In the 20c the USA has become the chief industrial nation in the world, with vast mineral and agricultural resources, a highly diversified economy, and an advanced system of communications and transportation; increases in consumption in the 1980s led to an unfavourable balance of trade, and the need to reduce public spending.

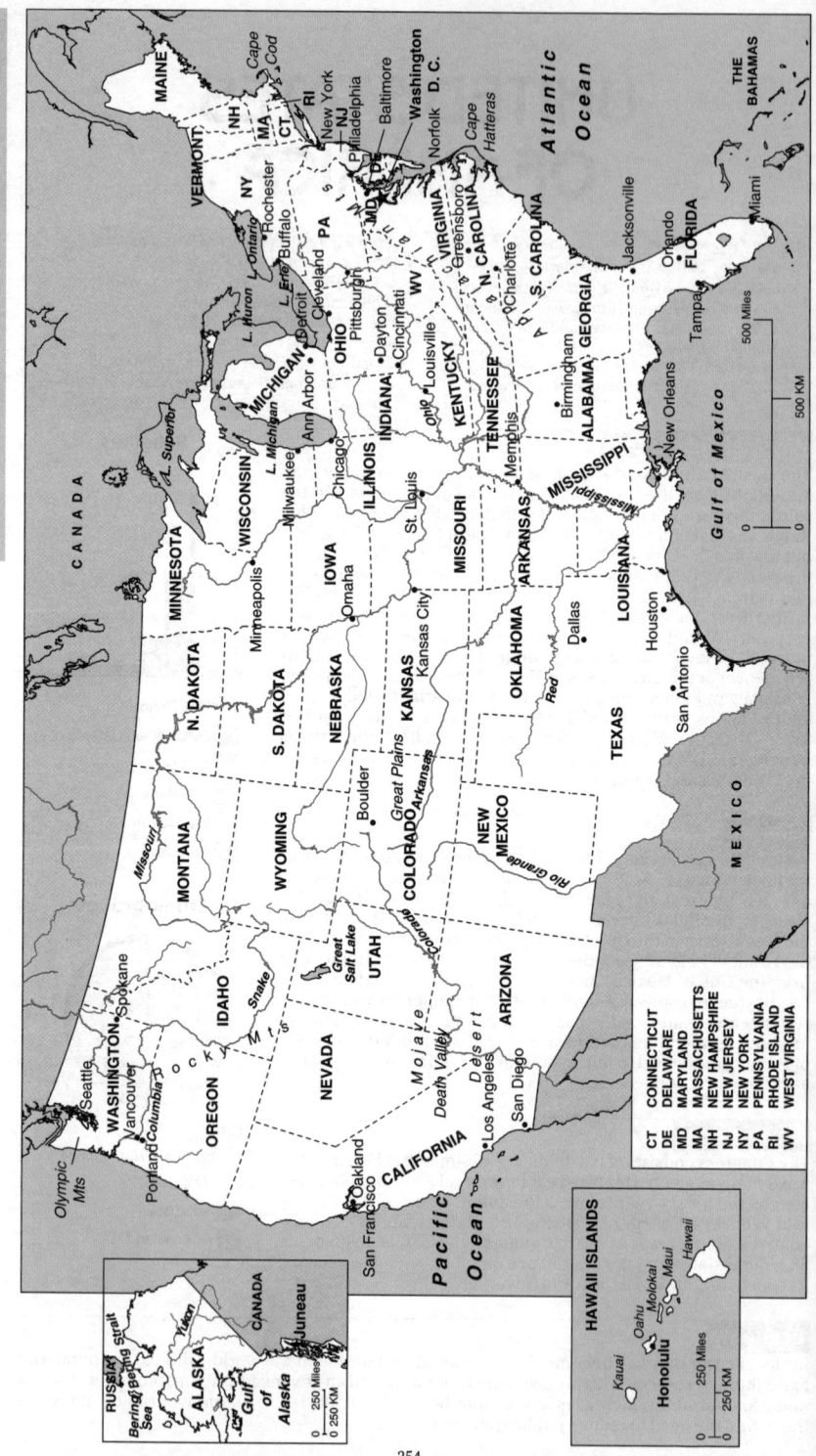

Nations of the World

History

The country was first settled by migrant groups from Asia over 25 000 years ago. These Native Americans remained undisturbed until the country was explored by the Norse (9c) and the Spanish (16c), who settled in Florida and Mexico. In the 17c, there were settlements by the British, French, Dutch, Germans and Swedish. Many black Africans were introduced as slaves to work on the plantations. In the following century, British control grew throughout the area. A revolt of the English-speaking colonies in the American Revolution (1775–83) led to the creation of the United States of America, which then lay between the Great Lakes, the Mississippi and Florida; the Declaration of Independence was made on 4 July 1776. Louisiana was sold to the USA by France in 1803 (the Louisiana Purchase) and the westward movement of settlers began. Florida was ceded by Spain in 1819, and further Spanish states joined the Union between 1821 and 1853. In 1860–1, 11 Southern states left the Union over the slavery issue, and formed the Confederacy; the Civil War (1861–5) ended in victory for the North, and the Southern states later rejoined the Union. As a result of the North's victory, slavery was abolished in 1865. In 1867 Alaska was purchased from Russia, and the Hawaiian Islands were annexed in 1898 (both admitted as states in 1959). The USA entered World War I on the side of the Allies in 1917. Native Americans were given the right to become US citizens in 1924. In 1929 the stockmarket on Wall Street crashed, resulting in the Great Depression. After the Japanese attack on Pearl Harbor in 1941, the USA entered World War II. The campaign for black civil rights developed in the 1960s, accompanied by much civil disturbance. From 1964 to 1975 the USA intervened in the Vietnam War, supporting non-communist South Vietnam. The USA led the space exploration programme of the 1960s and 1970s (in 1969 US astronaut Neil Armstrong was the first person on the moon). The Watergate scandal (1972–4) forced President Nixon to resign; there was further scandal in 1986 over arms sales to Iran to fund Contra rebels in Nicaragua. The Cold War between the USA and the USSR came to an end in 1990; since then US military force has been deployed in UN peace-keeping missions in countries such as Bosnia. In the 1991 Gulf War, US troops led the assault against Saddam Hussein following Iraq's invasion of Kuwait. In 1992 there was rioting in Los Angeles and other cities over racial issues. After Democratic President Bill Clinton came to power in 1993, the White House was dogged by various financial and sexual scandals, such as the Whitewater affair of 1994, and the Monica Lewinsky affair, which resulted in the President's impeachment and acquittal in 1999. After five weeks of court cases following the 2000 presidential election the Democrat Al Gore conceded and Republican George W Bush was sworn in as President in Jan 2001. On 11 Sep 2001 terrorists hijacked four aeroplanes, crashing one into the Pentagon and two into the World Trade Center in New York, leading to the collapse of both towers and the loss of thousands of lives. The fourth plane crashed in Pennsylvania. The Al Qaeda organization led by Osama bin Laden was blamed and the USA and its allies began military action in Afghanistan in late 2001 that overthrew the Taliban regime suspected of sheltering them. In 2002 the USA pushed for a UN resolution on Iraq, due to its non-compliance with UN resolutions on weapons inspections, and began a military build-up in the region. Military action against the Iraqi president Saddam Hussein began in Mar 2003.

States of the USA

Population: figures from the 2000 population census.

Abbreviations are given after each state name: the first is the most common abbreviation, the second is the ZIP (postal) code.

State	Entry to Union	Population	Area	Capital	Inhabitant	Nickname
Alabama (Ala; AL)	1819 (22nd)	4 447 100	131 443 sq km/ 50 750 sq mi	Montgomery	Alabamian	Camellia State, Heart of Dixie
Alaska (Alaska; AK)	1959 (49th)	626 932	1 477 268 sq km/ 570 373 sq mi	Juneau	Alaskan	Mainland State, The Last Frontier
Arizona (Ariz; AZ)	1912 (48th)	5 130 632	295 276 sq km/ 114 006 sq mi	Phoenix	Arizonan	Apache State, Grand Canyon State
Arkansas (Ark; AR)	1836 (25th)	2 673 400	137 754 sq km/ 53 187 sq mi	Little Rock	Arkansan	Bear State, Land of Opportunity
California (Calif; CA)	1850 (31st)	33 871 648	403 971 sq km/ 155 973 sq mi	Sacramento	Californian	Golden State
Colorado (Colo; CO)	1876 (38th)	4 301 261	268 658 sq km/ 103 729 sq mi	Denver	Coloradan	Centennial State
Connecticut (Conn; CT)	1788 (5th)	3 405 565	12 547 sq km/ 4 844 sq mi	Hartford	Nutmegger	Nutmeg State, Constitution State

Nations of the World

Nations of the World

State	Entry to Union	Population	Area	Capital	Inhabitant	Nickname
Delaware (Del; DE)	1787 (1st)	783 600	5 133 sq km/ 1 985 sq mi	Dover	Delawarean	Diamond State, First State
District of Columbia (DC; DC)		572 059	159 sq km/ 61 sq mi	Washington	Washington-ian	
Florida (Fla; FL)	1845 (27th)	15 982 378	139 697 sq km/ 53 937 sq mi	Tallahassee	Floridian	Everglade State, Sunshine State
Georgia (Ga; GA)	1788 (4th)	8 186 453	152 571 sq km/ 58 908 sq mi	Atlanta	Georgian	Empire State of the South, Peach State
Hawaii (Hawaii; HI)	1959 (50th)	1 211 537	16 636 sq km/ 6 423 sq mi	Honolulu	Hawaiian	Aloha State
Idaho (Idaho; ID)	1890 (43rd)	1 293 953	214 325 sq km/ 82 751 sq mi	Boise	Idahoan	Gem State
Illinois (Ill; IL)	1818 (21st)	12 419 293	144 123 sq km/ 55 646 sq mi	Springfield	Illinoisan	Prairie State, Land of Lincoln
Indiana (Ind; IN)	1816 (19th)	6 080 485	92 903 sq km/ 35 870 sq mi	Indianapolis	Hoosier	Hoosier State
Iowa (Iowa; IA)	1846 (29th)	2 926 324	144 716 sq km/ 55 875 sq mi	Des Moines	Iowan	Hawkeye State, Corn State
Kansas (Kans; KS)	1861 (34th)	2 688 418	211 922 sq km/ 81 823 sq mi	Topeka	Kansan	Sunflower State, Jayhawker State
Kentucky (Ky; KY)	1792 (15th)	4 041 769	102 907 sq km/ 39 732 sq mi	Frankfort	Kentuckian	Bluegrass State
Louisiana (La; LA)	1812 (18th)	4 468 976	112 836 sq km/ 43 566 sq mi	Baton Rouge	Louisianian	Pelican State, Sugar State, Creole State
Maine (Maine, ME)	1820 (23rd)	1 274 923	79 931 sq km/ 30 861 sq mi	Augusta	Downeaster	Pine Tree State
Maryland (Md; MD)	1788 (7th)	5 296 486	25 316 sq km/ 9 775 sq mi	Annapolis	Marylander	Old Line State, Free State
Massa-chusetts (Mass; MA)	1788 (6th)	6 349 097	20 300 sq km/ 7 838 sq mi	Boston	Bay Stater	Bay State, Old Colony
Michigan (Mich; MI)	1837 (26th)	9 938 444	150 544 sq km/ 58 125 sq mi	Lansing	Michigander	Wolverine State, Great Lake State
Minnesota (Minn; MN)	1858 (32nd)	4 919 479	206 207 sq km/ 79 617 sq mi	St Paul	Minnesotan	Gopher State, North Star State
Mississippi (Miss; MS)	1817 (20th)	2 844 658	123 510 sq km/ 47 687 sq mi	Jackson	Mississippian	Magnolia State
Missouri (Mo; MO)	1821 (24th)	5 595 211	178 446 sq km/ 68 898 sq mi	Jefferson City	Missourian	Bullion State, Show Me State
Montana (Mont; MT)	1889 (41st)	902 195	376 991 sq km/ 145 556 sq mi	Helena	Montanan	Treasure State, Big Sky Country
Nebraska (Nebr; NE)	1867 (37th)	1 711 263	199 113 sq km/ 76 878 sq mi	Lincoln	Nebraskan	Cornhusker State, Beef State
Nevada (Nev; NV)	1864 (36th)	1 998 257	273 349 sq km/ 105 540 sq mi	Carson City	Nevadan	Silver State, Sagebrush State

State	Entry to Union	Population	Area	Capital	Inhabitant	Nickname
New Hampshire (NH; NH)	1788 (9th)	1 235 786	23 292 sq km/ 8 993 sq mi	Concord	New Hampshirite	Granite State
New Jersey (NJ;NJ)	1787 (3rd)	8 414 350	19 210 sq km/ 7 417 sq mi	Trenton	New Jerseyite	Garden State
New Mexico (N Mex;NM)	1912 (47th)	1 819 046	314 334 sq km/ 121 364 sq mi	Santa Fe	New Mexican	Sunshine State, Land of Enchantment
New York (NY; NY)	1788 (11th)	18 976 457	122 310 sq km/ 47 224 sq mi	Albany	New Yorker	Empire State
North Carolina (NC;NC)	1789 (12th)	8 049 313	126 180 sq km/ 48 718 sq mi	Raleigh	North Carolinian	Old North State, Tar Heel State
North Dakota (N Dak; ND)	1889 (39th)	642 200	178 695 sq km/ 68 994 sq mi	Bismarck	North Dakotan	Flickertail State, Sioux State, Peace Garden State
Ohio (Ohio; OH)	1803 (17th)	11 353 140	106 067 sq km/ 40 952 sq mi	Columbus	Ohioan	Buckeye State
Oklahoma (Okla; OK)	1907 (46th)	3 450 654	177 877 sq km/ 68 678 sq mi	Oklahoma City	Oklahoman	Sooner State
Oregon (Oreg; OR)	1859 (33rd)	3 421 399	251 385 sq km/ 97 060 sq mi	Salem	Oregonian	Sunset State, Beaver State
Pennsylvania (Pa; PA)	1787 (2nd)	12 281 054	116 083 sq km/ 44 820 sq mi	Harrisburg	Pennsylvanian	Keystone State
Rhode Island (RI; RI)	1790 (13th)	1 048 319	2 707 sq km/ 1 045 sq mi	Providence	Rhode Islander	Little Rhody, Plantation State
South Carolina (SC; SC)	1788 (8th)	4 012 012	77 988 sq km/ 30 111 sq mi	Columbia	South Carolinian	Palmetto State
South Dakota (S Dak; SD)	1889 (40th)	754 844	196 576 sq km/ 75 898 sq mi	Pierre	South Dakotan	Sunshine State, Coyote State
Tennessee (Tenn; TN)	1796 (16th)	5 689 283	106 759 sq km/ 41 220 sq mi	Nashville	Tennessean	Volunteer State
Texas (Tex; TX)	1845 (28th)	20 851 820	678 358 sq km/ 261 914 sq mi	Austin	Texan	Lone Star State
Utah (Utah; UT)	1896 (45th)	2 233 169	212 816 sq km/ 82 168 sq mi	Salt Lake City	Utahn	Mormon State, Beehive State
Vermont (Vt; VT)	1791 (14th)	608 827	23 955 sq km/ 9 249 sq mi	Montpelier	Vermonter	Green Mountain State
Virginia (Va; VA)	1788 (10th)	7 078 515	102 558 sq km/ 39 598 sq mi	Richmond	Virginian	Old Dominion State, Mother of Presidents
Washington (Wash; WA)	1889 (42nd)	5 894 121	172 447 sq km/ 66 582 sq mi	Olympia	Washingtonian	Evergreen State, Chinook State
West Virginia (W Va; WV)	1863 (35th)	1 808 344	62 758 sq km/ 24 231 sq mi	Charleston	West Virginian	Panhandle State, Mountain State
Wisconsin (Wis; WI)	1848 (30th)	5 363 675	145 431 sq km/ 56 151 sq mi	Madison	Wisconsinite	Badger State, America's Dairyland
Wyoming (Wyo; WY)	1890 (44th)	493 782	251 501 sq km/ 97 105 sq mi	Cheyenne	Wyomingite	Equality State

Nations of the World

Nations of the World

Territories and departments

❖ American Samoa

Location A Territory of the USA in the South Pacific Ocean, some 3 500km/2 175mi north-east of New Zealand
Area 197 sq km/76 sq mi

Capital Pago Pago
Population 57 291 (2000)
Time zone GMT –11

Government

A bicameral legislature was established in 1948; the Governor is the administrative head of the executive branch; legislature (the *Fono*) comprises the Senate (18 members, chosen every four years by county councils according to Samoan custom) and the House of Representatives (20 members, plus one non-voting member, chosen every two years by popular vote).

Economy

Principal crops are taro, breadfruit, yams, bananas, coconuts; fish canning, tuna fishing, local inshore fishing; handicrafts.

History

The USA acquired rights to American Samoa in 1899, and the islands were ceded by their chiefs in 1900–25; it is now an unincorporated and unorganized Territory of the USA, administered by the Department of the Interior.

❖ Guam

Location A Territory of the USA and the largest and southernmost islands of the Mariana Islands, West Pacific Ocean
Area 541 sq km/209 sq mi

Capital Agaña
Population 154 805 (2000)
Time zone GMT +10

Government

Elected Governor and a unicameral legislature of 21 members.

Economy

Highly dependent on government activities; military installations cover 35% of the island; diversifying industrial and commercial projects; oil refining; dairy products; garments; printing; furniture; watches; copra; palm oil; processed fish; rapidly growing tourist industry.

History

Occupied by Japan from 1941 until 1944.

❖ Mariana Islands, Northern

Location An Overseas Territory of the USA comprising a group of 14 islands in the North-West Pacific Ocean, c.2 400km/1 500mi to the east of the Philippines
Area 471 sq km/182 sq mi
Capital Saipan
Population 69 221 (2000)
Time zone GMT +10

Government

A Governor serves a four-year term, with a bicameral legislature consisting of a nine-member Senate and an 18-member House of Representatives.

Economy

Sugar cane; coconuts; coffee; tourism.

History

From 1947 held by the USA under UN Mandate as part of the US Trust Territory of the Pacific Islands; became a self-governing commonwealth of the USA in 1978.

❖ Puerto Rico

Location The easternmost island of the Greater Antilles, situated between the Dominican Republic in the west and the US Virgin Islands in the east, c.1 600km/1 000miles south-east of Miami

Area 8 897 sq km/3 434 sq mi
Capital San Juan
Chief towns Ponce, Bayamón, Mayaguez
Population 3 808 610 (2000)
Time zone GMT −4

Government

Executive power is exercised by a Governor, elected for a four-year term; a bicameral Legislative Assembly consists of a 27-member Senate and 51-member House of Representatives, also elected every four years; a Resident Commissioner, who is a member of the US House of Representatives, is elected for four years.

Economy

Manufacturing is the most important sector of the economy; textiles; clothing; electrical and electronic equipment; food processing; petrochemicals; dairying, livestock; sugar, tobacco, coffee, pineapples, coconuts; tourism.

History

Originally occupied by Carib and Arawaks; discovered by Columbus in 1493; remained a Spanish colony until it was ceded to the USA in 1898; high levels of emigration to the USA in the 1940s–1950s; became a semi-autonomous commonwealth in association with the USA in 1952; US trade and investment important.

❖ US Virgin Islands

Location An Unincorporated Territory of the USA comprising a group of more than 50 islands in the south and west of the Virgin Islands group, Lesser Antilles, Caribbean Sea, 64km/40mi east of Puerto Rico. There are three main islands: St

Croix, St Thomas and St John
Area 342 sq km/132 sq mi
Capital Charlotte
Population 108 612 (2000)
Time zone GMT −4

Government

A Governor serves a four-year term, with an elected 15-member unicameral legislature.

Economy

The chief industry is tourism; St Croix industries include oil and alumina refining, clocks and watches, textiles, rum, fragrances, pharmaceuticals, vegetables, fruit, sorghum.

History

Denmark colonized St Thomas and St John in 1671, and bought St Croix from France in 1733; purchased by the USA in 1917.

URUGUAY

Official name Oriental Republic of Uruguay
Local name Uruguay
Location A republic in eastern South America, bounded to the east by the Atlantic Ocean; to the north by Brazil; and to the west by the River Uruguay and Argentina
Area 176 215 sq km/68 018 sq mi
Capital Montevideo
Chief towns Salto, Paysandú, Mercedes, Las

Piedras
Population 3 309 000 (1999e)
Time zone GMT −3
Currency 1 New Uruguayan Peso (NUr$, UrugN$) = 100 centésimos
Language Spanish
Religions Christianity 63% (RC 60%, Prot 3%), Judaism 2%, others/unaffiliated 35%
Ethnic groups white 90%, Mestizo 6%, black 4%

Physical description

Grass-covered plains of the south rise north to a high sandy plateau; the River Negro flows south to west to meet the River Uruguay on the Argentine frontier.

Nations of the World

Climate

Temperate with warm summers and mild winters; the average annual rainfall at Montevideo is 978mm with an average temperature of 16°C.

Government

A President is advised by a Council of Ministers, and a bicameral legislature consists of a 30-member Senate and a 99-member Chamber of Deputies, both elected for five years.

Economy

Traditionally based on livestock and agriculture; meat, wool, hides, maize, wheat, sorghum, rice, citrus fruit, potatoes, vegetable oils; fishing; food processing and packing; cement; chemicals; textiles; leather; steel; light engineering.

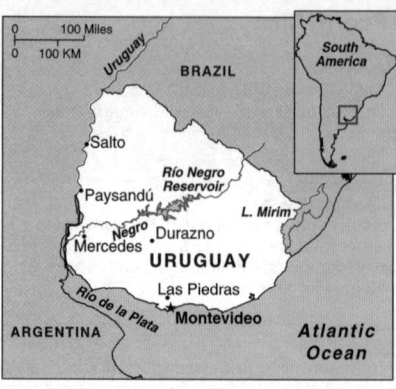

History

Originally occupied by various Indian tribes known collectively as the Charrúas people, it was discovered by the Spanish in 1515 and became part of the Spanish Viceroyalty of Río de la Plata in 1726. Between 1814 and 1825 it was a province of Brazil, and it gained independence in 1828. During the 19c there was a struggle for political control between the liberals (the 'redshirts', or *Colorados*), and the conservatives (the 'whites', or *Blancos*), which was resolved when the former took office for 86 years (1872–1958). There was unrest caused by the Marxist terrorist Tupamaros in the late 1960s and early 1970s, and military rule prevailed from 1971 until civilian rule was restored in 1985, with Julio María Sanguinetti as President until 1990. He returned to office in 1995, and was succeeded by Jorge Batlle Ibáñez in 1999.

UZBEKISTAN

Official name Republic of Uzbekistan
Local name Uzbekistan
Location A republic in central and northern Middle Asia, bounded to the south by Afghanistan; to the south-west by Turkmenistan; to the west and north-east by Kazakhstan; to the north-west by the Aral Sea; and to the east by Kyrgyzstan and Tajikistan
Area 447 400 sq km/172 696 sq mi
Capital Tashkent

Chief towns Samarkand, Andizhan, Namangan
Population 24 102 000 (1999e)
Time zone GMT +5
Currency 1 Sum = 100 tiyin
Language Uzbek
Religions Islam 88% (Sunni), Christianity 9% (Orthodox), others/unaffiliated 3%
Ethnic groups Uzbek 71%, Russian 8%, Tajik 5%, Kazakh 4%, others 12%

Physical description

Large area occupied by the Kyzyl-Kum desert; the chief rivers are the Amudarya and Syrdarya

Climate

Long, hot summers, mild winters.

Government

Executive power is largely vested in the presidency; the President is elected by popular vote; a 25–seat unicameral Assembly (*Oliy Majilis*) also serves a five-year term.

Economy

Coal, oil, oil refining; metallurgy; fertilizers; machinery; cotton, silk; food processing; intensive cultivation with the aid of irrigation.

History

In the 12–13c it was the centre of Genghis Khan's empire, and its cities of Samarkand and Tashkent grew rich from the silk caravan trade. It was divided into the khanates of Bukhara, Khiva and Kokand, which were subjected to attacks by Russia from the early 18c until they were annexed in 1876. The Uzbeks rebelled against Russian rule in 1918 but were suppressed and the country was proclaimed a Soviet Socialist Republic in 1924. It declared its independence from the USSR in 1991 under President Islam Karimov, and became a member of the CIS (Commonwealth of Independent States). Karimov was re-elected in 1995 and 2000 in elections criticized for irregularities.

VANUATU

Official name Republic of Vanuatu
Local name Vanuatu
Location An independent republic comprising an irregular Y-shaped island chain in the South-West Pacific Ocean, 400km/250mi north-east of New Caledonia
Area 14 763 sq km/5 698 sq mi
Capital Port-Vila (on Éfaté)

Population 189 000 (1999e)
Time zone GMT +11
Currency 1 Vatu (V, VT) = 100 centimes
Languages English, French; Bislama is the national language
Religions Christianity 77% (Prot 52%, RC 15%, others 10%), traditional beliefs 8%, others 15%
Ethnic groups Melanesian 95%, others 5%

Physical description

Mainly volcanic and rugged, with raised coral beaches fringed by reefs; the highest peak (on Espiritu Santo) rises to 1 888m; there are several active volcanoes; densely forested, with narrow strips of cultivated land on the coast.

Climate

Tropical, with a hot and rainy season in November–April when cyclones may occur; annual temperatures at Port-Vila are 16°–33°C, and the average annual rainfall is 2 310mm.

Government

Governed by a President, Prime Minister and Cabinet, and a representative 46-member Assembly.

Economy

Agriculture includes yams, breadfruit, taro, manioc, bananas, copra, cocoa, coffee; cattle, pigs; manganese; fish processing, foodstuffs; crafts; tourism is rapidly increasing, especially from cruise ships.

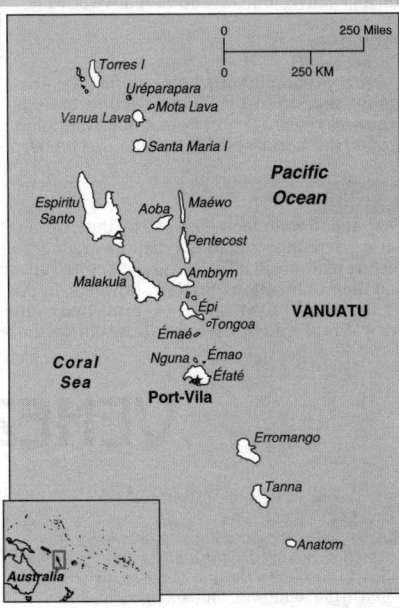

History

Visited by the Portuguese in 1606; under Anglo-French administration as the condominium of the New Hebrides in 1906; gained independence as the Republic of Vanuatu in 1980.

VATICAN

Official name Vatican City State
Local name Citta'del Vaticano
Location An independent papal sovereign state, and the smallest state in the world. Surrounded on all sides by Rome, Italy, it is a World Heritage Site and includes St Peter's, the Vatican Palace and Museum, several buildings in Rome, and the Pope's summer villa at Castel Gandolfo
Area 0.4 sq km/0.2 sq mi

Capital Vatican City
Population 870 (1999e)
Time zone GMT +1
Currency 1 Euro (€) = 100 cents
Language Latin; Italian is widely spoken
Religions Christianity 100% (RC)
Ethnic groups predominantly European, especially Italian

Climate

Mediterranean; hot summers and mild winters.

Government

The Supreme Pontiff of the Roman Catholic Church, the Pope, is Head of State, elected for life by the Sacred College of Cardinals and has full legislative, judicial and executive powers.

Economy

Unique, predominantly non-commercial economy; supported by financial contributions (known as *Peter's Pence*) from Roman Catholics around the world; some sales of tourist items, publications, stamps and museum fees.

History

The Vatican was created in 1929 by the Lateran Pacts signed by Pope Pius XI and Mussolini. These pacts or treaties ended the dispute arising from Italian occupation of the Papal States and the seizure of Rome in 1870, for the papacy had always refused to recognize the loss of the Papal States and their unification into Italy; however, in 1871 the Vatican papal state had been granted extra-territoriality. The Vatican is now protected by the 1954 La Haye Convention. In Jan 2002 the Italian lira was replaced by the Euro as the official currency.

VENEZUELA

Official name Republic of Venezuela
Local name Venezuela
Location The most northerly country in South America, bounded to the north by the Caribbean Sea; to the east by Guyana; to the south by Brazil; and to the south-west and west by Colombia
Area 912 050 sq km/352 051 sq mi
Capital Caracas
Chief towns Maracaibo, Ciudad Guayana,

Valencia, Barquisimeto
Population 23 203 000 (1999e)
Time zone GMT −4
Currency 1 Bolívar (Bs) = 100 centesimi
Language Spanish
Religions Christianity 94% (RC 92%, Prot 2%), others /unaffiliated 6%
Ethnic groups Mestizo 69%, white 21%, black 9%, Amerindian 1%

Physical description

The Guiana Highlands in the south-east cover over half the country; the Venezuelan Highlands lie in the west and along the coast, reaching heights of over 5 000m; there are lowlands around Lake Maracaibo and in the valley of the Orinoco River, which crosses the country south to north-east.

Climate

Generally hot and humid; one rainy season from April to October; annual temperatures at Caracas are 13°–27°C, monthly rainfall between 10mm and 109mm; annual rainfall on the coast increases from very low amounts around Lake Maracaibo to 1 000mm in the east; in the Guiana Highlands to the south-east, annual rainfall is c.1 500mm.

Government

Governed by an elected two-chamber National Congress, comprising a Senate and a 196-member Chamber of Deputies; a President is advised by a Council of Ministers.

Economy

Largely an agricultural country until the 1920s, when the development of oil from Maracaibo transformed the economy: over 90% of export revenue is now derived from oil; iron ore, natural gas, aluminium, gold, nickel, iron, copper, manganese; cement; steel; chemicals; food; shipbuilding; vehicles; 20% of the land is under cultivation: coffee, cocoa, maize, tobacco, sugar; dairy and beef cattle.

History

Originally inhabited by Caribs and Arawaks, it was seen by Columbus in 1498, and settled by the Spanish in 1520. There were frequent revolts against Spanish colonial rule, and in the early 19c an independence movement arose under Simón Bolívar; this led to the formal establishment of the state of Gran Colombia (Colombia, Ecuador and Venezuela) in 1821. Following the collapse of Gran Colombia in 1829, Venezuela became an independent republic in 1830 under President José Páez. Since the 1960s there has been relative political stability, with the two major parties, the Democratic Action and the Christian Democrats, each holding power in turn. President Carlos Andrés Pérez, who came to power in 1989 soon faced rioting in response to his austerity measures. He survived two attempted coups in 1992, but was removed from office charged with corruption in 1993 (and imprisoned in 1996). He was succeeded in 1994 by Rafael Caldera, who was himself succeeded by Hugo Chávez Frías in 1998, who introduced economic reforms that led to widespread popular protests. He resigned in Apr 2002 but returned to power days later after the transitional government collapsed, and popular unrest continues.

VIETNAM

Official name Socialist Republic of Vietnam
Local name Viêtnam
Location An independent socialist state in Indochina, bounded to the east by the South China Sea (including the Gulf of Tongking in the north); to the west by Laos and Cambodia; and to the north by China
Area 329 566 sq km/127 213 sq mi
Capital Hanoi
Chief towns Ho Chi Minh City (formerly Saigon), Haiphong, Da Nang, Nha Trang
Population 77 311 000 (1999e)
Time zone GMT +7
Currency 1 Dông (D) = 10 hào = 100 xu
Language Vietnamese
Religions Buddhism 55%, Christianity 7%, others 23%, none/unaffiliated 15%
Ethnic groups Vietnamese 86%, Chinese 3%, Thai 2%, others 9%

Physical description

Occupies a narrow strip along the coast of the Gulf of Tongking and the South China Sea; broader at the Mekong River Delta, in the south, and along the Red River Valley to the north; the highest peak is Fan si Pan at 3 143m; a limestone plateau in the south stretches west into Cambodia.

Climate

Tropical monsoon-type, dominated by south to south-east winds during May–September and north to north-east winds during October–April; the average annual rainfall is 1 000mm in the lowlands, 2 500mm in the uplands; high humidity in the rainy season; temperatures are high in the south, cooler in the north during October–April.

Government

Governed by a Prime Minister and a two-chamber legislature, comprising a 496-member National Assembly, elected every five years, and a 15-member Council of State, appointed by the Assembly.

Economy

Over 70% of the workforce is employed in agriculture: rice, maize, sorghum, beans, sugar, sweet potatoes, tea, coffee, rubber, tobacco, groundnuts; fishing; forestry; wood and rubber products; textiles; paper; fertilizers; glass; cement; food processing; light engineering; coal, tin; zinc; offshore oil; the Vietnam War brought depopulation of the countryside, and considerable destruction of forest and farmland; towns overcrowded with refugees have since contributed to the economic problems, as have natural disasters caused by typhoons and flooding.

History

Under the influence of China for many centuries, it was visited by the Portuguese in 1535. Dutch, French and English traders arrived in the 17c, with missionaries. In 1802 the regions of Tongking in the north, Annam in the centre, and Cochin-China in the south united as the Vietnamese Empire, which was conquered by the French in the 19c. French protectorates were established in Cochin-China in 1867, and in Annam and Tongking in 1884, and the French Indo-Chinese Union with Cambodia and Laos

was formed in 1887. Vietnam was occupied by the Japanese in World War II, and after the war the communist Viet Minh League under Ho Chi Minh was formed, but was not recognized by France. The Indo-China War took place in 1946–54, and resulted in the withdrawal of the French. In 1954 an armistice divided the country between the communist 'Democratic Republic' in the north and the 'State' of Vietnam in the south. Civil war in 1964–75 (the Vietnam War) led to US intervention on the side of South Vietnam from 1965 until US troops were withdrawn in 1973. Saigon in South Vietnam fell in 1975, and with the defeat of South Vietnam nearly 200 000 Vietnamese fled the country. The country was reunified as the Socialist Republic of Vietnam in 1976. Large numbers of refugees tried to find homes in the West in the late 1970s, and the Chinese invasion of Vietnam in 1979 greatly increased the number of boat people attempting to leave the country by sea. After the collapse of the USSR in 1991, Vietnam improved its relations with China and the USA. A new constitution was adopted by the ruling Communist Party in 1992 which approved many economic and political reforms. Full diplomatic relations with the USA were reinstated in 1995.

⮆ **Virgin Islands, British ▸ United Kingdom**

⮆ **Virgin Islands, United States ▸ United States of America**

⮆ **Wales ▸ United Kingdom**

⮆ **Wallis and Futuna ▸ France**

YEMEN

Official name Republic of Yemen
Local name Al-Yamaniya
Location A republic in the south of the Arabian Peninsula, bounded to the north by Saudi Arabia; to the west by the Red Sea; to the south by the Gulf of Aden; and to the east by Oman
Area 531 570 sq km/205 186 sq mi
Capital San'a

Chief towns Ta'iz
Population 16 942 000 (1999e)
Time zone GMT +3
Currency 1 Yemeni Riyal (YR, YRI) = 100 fils
Language Arabic
Religions Islam 97% (Shiite 56%, Sunni 41%), others 3%
Ethnic groups Arab 96%, others 4%

Physical description

A narrow desert plain bordering the Red Sea rises abruptly to mountains at 3 000–3 700m; a flat, narrow coastal plain in the south is backed by mountains rising to almost 2 500m; to the north, a plateau merges with the gravel plains and sand wastes of the Rub al Khali Basin.

Climate

Hot and humid on the coastal strip in the west, with an annual temperature of 29°C; milder in the highlands and winters can be cold; annual rainfall is higher in the north and west than in the east and south; hot all year round in the south, with maximum temperatures over 40°C in July and August; very high humidity in this area; average temperatures at Aden are 24°C in January, 32°C in July.

Government

Governed by a President, a 308-member House of Representatives, a Presidential Council and a Council of Ministers.

Economy

Based on agriculture: livestock, millet, sorghum, vegetables, wheat, barley, fruit, cotton, coffee; irrigation schemes are likely to increase the area under cultivation; Qat, a narcotic leaf, is a major export; textiles; cement; aluminium products; fishing; oil refining.

History

From c.750BC there were advanced civilizations in southern Arabia. It came under the control of the Muslim caliphate in the 7c AD, and was ruled by Egyptian caliphs from c.1000. Part of the Ottoman Empire from the 16c until 1918, it was then ruled by the Hamid al-Din Dynasty until the revolution in 1962, when the Yemen Arab Republic (North Yemen) was proclaimed by the army. Fighting between royalists and republicans continued until 1967, when the republican regime was recognized. Aden was under British occupation from 1839 (therefore avoiding Ottoman rule), and had formed part of the Federation of South Arabia in 1963. British troops withdrew in 1967, but the area was overrun by the National Liberation Front, and the People's Republic of Yemen (South Yemen) was formed from Aden and its neighbouring emirates. It was renamed the People's Democratic Republic of Yemen in 1970. During the 1970s South Yemen had border disputes with Oman and North Yemen, but in 1990 the Yemen Arabic Republic (North Yemen) and the People's Democratic Republic of Yemen (South Yemen) formally united as the Republic of Yemen. Ali Abdullah Saleh became the first President of the united country, and the first free, multi-party elections took place in 1993. There was another brief but violent civil war between the north and south of the country in 1994.

YUGOSLAVIA*

Official name Federal Republic of Yugoslavia*
Local name Jugoslavija*
Location A federal union in the Balkan Peninsula of south-eastern Europe, consisting of the republics of Serbia and Montenegro. It is bounded to the west by Bosnia-Herzegovina and Croatia; to the north by Hungary; to the north-east by Romania; to the east by Bulgaria; and to the south by Macedonia and Albania
Area 256 409 sq km/98 974 sq mi
Capital Belgrade

Chief towns Priština, Subotica
Population 11 206 900 (1999e)
Time zone GMT +2
Currency 1 New Dinar (D, Din) = 100 paras (Serbia), 1 Euro (€) = 100 cents (Montenegro)
Language Serbo-Croat
Religions Christianity 70% (Orthodox 65%, RC 4%, Prot 1%), Islam 19%, others 11%
Ethnic groups Serb 62%, Albanian 17%, Montenegrin 5%, Magyar 3%, others 13%

Physical description

Dominated in the north by the Danube, Tisza and Sava rivers, with fertile plains in the north-east; drained in the centre by the River Morava; ranges in the south are cut by deep river valleys; there are several great lakes in the south; highest point is Durmitor (2522m) in the south-west.

Climate

A Mediterranean climate on the Adriatic coast; a continental climate in the north and north-east; rain falls throughout the year; there is a colder upland climate, with winter snow.

Nations of the World

Nations of the World

Government

Each republic has a National Assembly and a President; a federal Parliament is led by a President and Council of Ministers.

Economy

The industrial base extended following World War II; machine tools; chemicals; textiles; food processing; wood and metal products; oil refining; increased agricultural output, especially wheat, maize, sugar beet, livestock; wine; forestry; fishing; civil war has severely affected the economic situation.

History

After World War I the Serbs of Montenegro and the Kingdom of Serbia were joined with the South Slavs of the former Habsburg Monarchy, the Croats, Slovenes and some Serbs, to become the Kingdom of Serbs, Croats and Slovenes, who were united under one monarch, Peter I, the King of Serbia and head of the Karageorgevic Dynasty. Formal unification was

proclaimed by the Regent Alexander I Karageorgevic (1 Dec 1918), who, later as King, renamed the kingdom the Kingdom of Yugoslavia (1929). The term 'Yugoslavs', literally the 'South Slavs', is the collective name for the inhabitants of Yugoslavia who are members of several different nations; while the Serbs, Croats, Slovenes, Bosnian Muslims and Macedonians are all South Slavs, Yugoslavia has many non-Slav inhabitants including the Hungarians in the Vojvodina and the Albanians in Kosovo. In the early 1940s there was civil war between Serbian royalists (Chetniks), Croatian nationalists and communists. Yugoslavia was occupied by Germany during World War II; in 1945 the Federal People's Republic (Croatia, Slovenia, Bosnia-Herzegovina, Macedonia, Montenegro and Serbia) was established under Tito. The resentment that had built up during the interwar years among different nations within Yugoslavia combined with long-standing national rivalries to erupt in a 'civil war' of brutal reprisals; the only semblance of 'Yugoslav' unity remained in the communist-led partisan army, which waged a brave and effective tactical campaign against the occupying Axis forces. After the war, Tito's version of communism promised to neutralize old national rivalries and to unite the nations of Yugoslavia in pursuit of a common future. While Yugoslavia was reorganized as a federation of six republics and two autonomous provinces, each of which was based around a core nation, the different national identities were strictly repressed. After Tito's death in 1980, however, nationalisms resurfaced and Yugoslavia fell into political and economic decline. At the end of the 1980s, political disagreement between the federal republics increased; in 1989 Slovenia declared its sovereignty and its strong opposition to the Communist Party. Despite the government's attempt to preserve Yugoslav unity by planning a multi-party system with direct elections, ethnic unrest in Serbia and Croatia placed further strains on the federal system. Croatia and Slovenia ceded from Yugoslavia in 1991, and Bosnia-Herzegovina in 1992. Macedonia declared its independence in 1992. Of the six republics that made up Yugoslavia as established in 1945, only Serbia and Montenegro remained as the Federal Republic of Yugoslavia, which was declared on 27 Apr 1992 and recognized by the UN in 2000. Slobodan Milosevic, previously President of Serbia, became President of Yugoslavia in 1997. In 1999 Serbian violence in suppressing secessionism in Kosovo and the ethnic cleansing of the province's Albanian population led to the bombing of Serbia by NATO in Mar–Jun. During the conflict, Milosevic was indicted by the UN war crimes tribunal for his part in the atrocities carried out in the province, and his trial at the Hague tribunal began in Feb 2002. Kosovo is now a UN-administered autonomous province within Serbia, with its own parliament and the Euro as its currency. Milosevic was defeated in elections in 2000 by Vojislav Kostunica. Serbian Prime Minister Zoran Djindjic was assasinated in Mar 2003.

* In Feb 2003 the Federal Republic of Yugoslavia was officially dissolved and superceded by Serbia and Montenegro (locally known as Srbija i Crna Gora), a loose union of the two republics. A joint Parliament will be responsible for defence and foreign affairs, while the individual parliaments of each republic will run domestic affairs separately. Referendums on total independence will be held in 2005. Svetozar Marovic was elected as Serbia and Montenegro's first president in Mar 2003.

ZAMBIA

Official name Republic of Zambia
Local name Zambia
Location A landlocked republic in southern Africa, bounded to the west by Angola; to the south by Namibia; to the south-east by Zimbabwe and Mozambique; to the east by Malawi; to the north-east by Tanzania; and to the north-west by the Democratic Republic of Congo
Area 752 613 sq km/290 509 sq mi
Capital Lusaka
Chief towns Ndola, Kitwe, Kabwe, Livingstone

Population 9 664 000 (1999e)
Time zone GMT +2
Currency 1 Kwacha (K) = 100 ngwee
Language English; local languages are also spoken
Religions Christianity 68% (Prot 35%, RC 27%, African Christian 6%), traditional beliefs 31%, Islam and Hinduism 1%
Ethnic groups Bemba 35%, Maravi 19%, Tonga 14%, others 32%

Physical description

Occupies a high plateau at an altitude of 1 000–1 400m; the highest point is 2 067m, south-east of Mbala; the Zambezi River rises in the north extremity of North-West Province.

Climate

Temperate climate on upland plateau; rainy season is October–March; at Lusaka the average rainfall is 840mm and the maximum average daily temperatures range between 23°C and 35°C; tropical climate in the lower river valleys.

Government

Governed by a 150-member National Assembly serving five-year terms, a President, Chairman of Cabinet and Council of Ministers; a multiparty system was introduced in 1991.

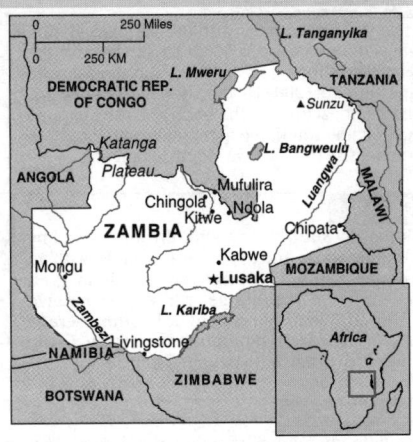

Economy

Based on copper and cobalt, which provide over half the national income; gold, lead, silver, zinc; maize, sugar, cassava, millet, sorghum, pulses, groundnuts, cotton, tobacco; cattle; manufacturing industries include copper wire, cement, fertilizer, explosives, vehicle assembly, sugar refining, food processing, textiles, glassware, tyres, bricks, brewing and oil refining.

History

Most ethnic groups at present in Zambia arrived there between the 16c and the 18c. Arab slave-traders arrived in the 19c, as did European settlers, following David Livingstone's discovery of the Victoria Falls in 1855. The country was administered by the British South Africa Company under Cecil Rhodes. Known as Barotseland, it was declared a British sphere of influence in 1888 and named Northern Rhodesia in 1911. It became a British protectorate in 1924. Massive copper deposits were discovered in late 1920s. Between 1953 and 1963 Northern Rhodesia joined with Southern Rhodesia (now Zimbabwe) and Nyasaland (now Malawi) as the Federation of Rhodesia and Nyasaland. Northern Rhodesia gained its independence in 1964 as the Republic of Zambia under President Kenneth Kaunda. The first multi-party elections since independence were held in 1991, bringing Frederick Chiluba to power as President. He survived coup attempts in 1993 and 1997. Kaunda was implicated in the latter and placed under house arrest until June 1998, when charges were dropped. Levy Mwanawasa became President in 2002.

Nations of the World

ZIMBABWE

Official name Republic of Zimbabwe
Local name Zimbabwe
Location A landlocked republic in southern Africa, bounded to the south by South Africa; to the south-west by Botswana; to the north-west by Zambia; and to the north-east, east and south-east by Mozambique
Area 391 090 sq km/150 961 sq mi
Capital Harare
Chief towns Bulawayo, Gweru, Mutare

Population 11 163 000 (1999e)
Time zone GMT +2
Currency 1 Zimbabwe Dollar (Z$) = 100 cents
Language English
Religions Christianity 45% (Prot 33%, RC 12%), traditional beliefs 40%, Islam 1%, others 14%
Ethnic groups Shona 71%, Ndebele 16%, other Bantu-speaking peoples 11%, white 1%, mixed and Asian 1%

Physical description

High plateau country with the 'Middleveld' ranging in altitude from 900m to 1 200m and the 'Highveld' running south-west to north-east, with an altitude of 1 200–1 500m; the relief dips towards the Zambezi River in the north and the Limpopo River in the south; the mountains on the eastern frontier rise to 2 592m at Mount Inyangani.

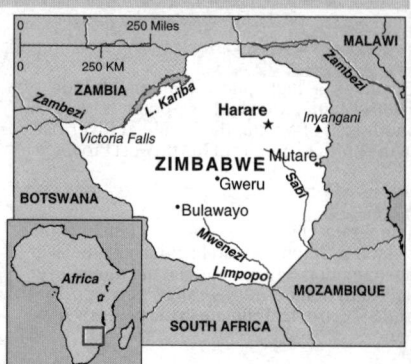

Climate

Generally subtropical, strongly influenced by altitude; warm and dry in the lowlands, with an annual rainfall of between 400mm and 600mm; the mountains in the east receive 1 500–2 000mm of rain annually; the average maximum daily temperatures at Harare, in the Highveld, range between 21°C and 29°C.

Government

A single-chamber Parliament, the House of Assembly, with 150 members (120 elected); an Executive President combines the posts of head of state and head of government.

Economy

Agriculture involves 70% of the population: maize, sorghum, millet, rice, cassava, vegetables, tobacco, coffee, cotton, tea, groundnuts, wheat, sugar cane; cattle, pigs, poultry, forestry; rich mineral resources include gold, asbestos, nickel, coal, copper, chrome ore, iron ore, tin, silver, cobalt; iron; steel; foodstuffs; drink; tobacco; clothing; footwear; wood; furniture; paper; tourism.

History

From the 12c to 16c the country was a medieval Bantu kingdom, with its capital at Great Zimbabwe. In the 19c it was taken over by the Ndebele people under King Mzilikazi and named the Kingdom of Matabeleland, which was often in dispute with the Shona people of Mashonaland to the north. It was visited by David Livingstone in the 1850s, and came under British influence in the 1880s when the British South Africa Company under Cecil Rhodes began its exploitation of the rich mineral resources of the area. The British South Africa Company invaded Mashonaland in 1890 and by 1900 controlled much of Central Africa. Its area was divided into Northern and Southern Rhodesia in 1911. Southern Rhodesia became a self-governing British colony in 1923, and in 1953 Northern and Southern Rhodesia formed a multi-racial federation with Nyasaland. Nyasaland and Northern Rhodesia gained their independence in 1963. Opposition to the independence of Southern Rhodesia under African rule resulted in a Unilateral Declaration of Independence (UDI) by the white-dominated government of Prime Minister Ian Smith in 1965. Economic sanctions and internal guerrilla activity forced the government to negotiate with the main African groups of the Patriotic Front. Power eventually transferred to the African majority, and the country gained its independence as Zimbabwe in 1980. Robert Mugabe became Prime Minister on independence, and President in 1987. In the early 1990s he and his government announced plans to redistribute land from white farmers to blacks, but in 1998 were forced by international pressure to abandon them. However, from 2000 this policy was implemented, often violently by squatters, despite protestations from the international community. Mugabe's tight grip on power has been contested in recent years by the opposition Movement for Democratic Change.

Social Structure

Major cities of the world

Cities are listed alphabetically followed by population figures, with year of estimate in brackets; those without 'e' indicate the year of census.

Abidjan Côte d'Ivoire	2 797 000 (1995e)	**Barranquilla** Colombia	1 064 255 (1995e)
Abu Dhabi United Arab Emirates	928 360 (1995)	**Basra** Iraq	663 000 (1996e)
Acapulco Mexico	597 000 (1996e)	**Beijing (Peking)** China	8 200 000 (1996e)
Accra Ghana	1 781 100 (1995e)	**Beirut** Lebanon	1 564 000 (1995e)
Adana Turkey	1 047 300 (1994e)	**Belém** Brazil	1 309 000 (1995e)
Addis Ababa Ethiopia	2 316 400 (1994e)	**Belfast** UK	227 391 (2001)
Adelaide Australia	1 081 000 (1995e)	**Belgorod** Russia	322 000 (1995e)
Aden Yemen	303 000 (1996e)	**Belgrade** Serbia and	
Agadir Morocco	1 370 000 (1994e)	Montenegro	1 301 000 (1996e)
Agra India	1 025 000 (1996e)	**Belo Horizonte** Brazil	2 628 000 (1995e)
Ahmadabad India	3 372 000 (1996e)	**Bengpu** China	523 000 (1996e)
Ahvaz Iran	731 500 (1996e)	**Benxi** China	891 000 (1996e)
Ajme India	497 000 (1996e)	**Berlin** Germany	3 472 009 (1995e)
Albuquerque USA	419 681 (1996e)	**Berne** Switzerland	128 422 (1995e)
Aleppo Syria	1 591 400 (1994e)	**Bhavnagar** India	499 000 (1996e)
Alexandria Egypt	3 382 000 (1994e)	**Bhilai Nagar** India	485 000 (1996e)
Algiers Algeria	3 208 000 (1995e)	**Bhopal** India	1 297 000 (1996e)
Aligarh India	595 000 (1996e)	**Bilbao** Spain	371 787 (1994e)
Allahabad India	993 000 (1996e)	**Birmingham** UK	977 091 (2001)
Alma-Ata Kazakhstan	1 150 500 (1995e)	**Bissau** Guinea-Bissau	236 000 (1996e)
Amagasaki Japan	488 574 (1995)	**Bochum** Germany	401 129 (1995e)
Amman Jordan	963 440 (1994)	**Bogota** Colombia	5 237 635 (1995e)
Amritsar India	885 000 (1996e)	**Bologna** Italy	394 969 (1994e)
Amsterdam Netherlands	722 245 (1995e)	**Bombay ▸ Mumbai**	
Ankara Turkey	2 782 000 (1994e)	**Bonn** Germany	239 072 (1995e)
Anshan China	1 546 000 (1996e)	**Boston** USA	558 394 (1996e)
Antananarivo Madagascar	1 052 835 (1994)	**Brasilia** Brazil	1 962 000 (1995e)
Antwerp Belgium	459 072 (1995e)	**Brasov** Romania	324 104 (1994e)
Anyang China	484 000 (1996e)	**Bratislava** Slovakia	450 776 (1995e)
Aracaju Brazil	451 000 (1996e)	**Brazzaville** Congo	998 000 (1996e)
Archangel Russia	374 000 (1995e)	**Bremen** Germany	549 182 (1995e)
Arequipa Peru	619 156 (1994e)	**Brisbane** Australia	1 489 100 (1995e)
Asahikawa Japan	360 569 (1995)	**Bristol** UK	380 615 (2001)
Ashkhabad Turkmenistan	518 000 (1994e)	**Brno** Czech Republic	389 576 (1995e)
Astrakhan Russia	486 000 (1995e)	**Brussels** Belgium	951 580 (1995e)
Asunción Paraguay	502 426 (1993)	**Bryansk** Russia	462 000 (1995e)
Athens Greece	824 000 (1996e)	**Bucaramanga** Colombia	351 737 (1995e)
Atlanta USA	401 907 (1996e)	**Bucharest** Romania	2 027 512 (1997e)
Auckland New Zealand	353 670 (1996)	**Budapest** Hungary	1 909 000 (1996)
Austin USA	541 278 (1996e)	**Buenos Aires** Argentina	2 988 006 (1995e)
Baghdad Iraq	4 478 000 (1995e)	**Buffalo** USA	310 548 (1996e)
Bakhtaran Iran	698 000 (1996e)	**Bulawayo** Zimbabwe	699 000 (1996e)
Baku Azerbaijan	1 087 000 (1994e)	**Bursa** Turkey	996 600 (1994e)
Baltimore USA	675 401 (1996e)	**Bydgoszcz** Poland	385 700 (1995e)
Bamako Mali	800 000 (1995e)	**Cairo** Egypt	6 849 000 (1994e)
Bandung Indonesia	1 921 000 (1995e)	**Calcutta ▸ Kolkata**	
Bangalore India	2 869 000 (1995e)	**Calgary** Canada	767 059 (1996)
Bangkok Thailand	5 584 228 (1994e)	**Cali** Colombia	1 718 871 (1995e)
Bangui Central African Republic	524 000 (1994e)	**Calicut** India	487 000 (1996e)
Banjarmasin Indonesia	514 500 (1996e)	**Callao** Peru	615 046 (1994)
Banjul The Gambia	42 407 (1994)	**Caloocan City** Philippines	642 670 (1994e)
Baoding China	577 800 (1996e)	**Campinas** Brazil	765 000 (1996e)
Baoji China	378 000 (1996e)	**Campo Grande** Brazil	401 000 (1996e)
Baotou China	1 110 000 (1996e)	**Campos** Brazil	379 900 (1996e)
Barcelona Spain	1 630 867 (1994e)	**Canberra** Australia	303 700 (1995e)
Barcelona Venezuela	237 000 (1996e)	**Canton (Guangzhou)** China	4 218 000 (1995e)
Bareilly India	726 000 (1996e)	**CapeTown** South Africa	1 013 000 (1996e)
Bari Italy	338 949 (1994e)	**Caracas** Venezuela	4 039 000 (1996e)
Barnaul Russia	596 000 (1995e)	**Cardiff** UK	305 340 (2001)
Barquisimeto Venezuela	648 000 (1996e)	**Cartagena** Colombia	745 689 (1995e)

Social Structure

Casablanca Morocco	2 943 000 (1994e)	Dukou China	470 000 (1996e)
Catania Italy	327 163 (1994e)	Duque de Caxias Brazil	723 000 (1996e)
Cebu City Philippines	688 196 (1994e)	Durban South Africa	833 000 (1996e)
Chandigarh India	663 000 (1996e)	Durgapur India	505 000 (1996e)
Changchun China	2 021 000 (1996e)	Dushanbe Tajikistan	524 000 (1994e)
Changsha China	1 477 000 (1996e)	Düsseldorf Germany	572 638 (1995e)
Changzhou China	557 000 (1996e)	Dzhambul Kazakhstan	310 600 (1995e)
Charlotte USA	441 297 (1996e)	Edinburgh UK	448 624 (2001)
Cheboksary Russia	450 000 (1995e)	Edmonton Canada	637 442 (1995)
Chelyabinsk Russia	1 086 000 (1995e)	El Giza Egypt	2 270 000 (1996e)
Chemnitz Germany	274 162 (1995e)	El Mahalla el-Koubra Egypt	423 000 (1996e)
Chengdu China	2 033 000 (1966e)	El Mansoura Egypt	398 000 (1996e)
Chennai (Madras) India	4 601 000 (1996e)	El Paso USA	599 865 (1996e)
Cherepovets Russia	320 000 (1995e)	Eskisehir Turkey	451 000 (1994e)
Chiba Japan	856 882 (1995)	Essen Germany	617 955 (1995e)
Chicago USA	2 721 547 (1996e)	Faisalabad Pakistan	1 875 000 (1995e)
Chiclayo Peru	430 000 (1996e)	Faridabad India	666 000 (1996e)
Chifeng China	393 000 (1996e)	Feira de Santana Brazil	403 000 (1996e)
Chihuahua Mexico	411 000 (1996e)	Fez Morocco	564 000 (1994e)
Chimkent Kazakhstan	397 600 (1995e)	Florence Italy	392 800 (1994e)
Chita Russia	322 000 (1995e)	Fortaleza Brazil	1 952 000 (1995)
Chittagong Bangladesh	1 995 000 (1996e)	Fort Worth USA	479 716 (1996e)
Chongjin Korea, North	601 000 (1996e)	Frankfurt am Main Germany	652 412 (1995e)
Chongju Korea, South	531 195 (1995)	Freetown Sierra Leone	581 000 (1996e)
Chongqing China	3 325 000 (1996e)	Fujisawa Japan	368 636 (1995)
Chonju Korea, South	563 406 (1995)	Fukuoka Japan	1 284 741 (1995)
Christchurch New Zealand	313 969 (1996)	Fukuyama Japan	374 510 (1995)
Chungho Taiwan	387 123 (1995e)	Funabashi Japan	540 814 (1995)
Cincinnati USA	345 816 (1996e)	Fushun China	1 413 000 (1996e)
Ciudad Guayana Venezuela	577 000 (1996e)	Fuxin China	755 000 (1996e)
Ciudad Juárez Mexico	673 000 (1996e)	Fuzhou China	1 005 000 (1996e)
Cleveland USA	498 246 (1996e)	Ganzhou China	434 000 (1996e)
Cluj-Napoca Romania	332 297 (1996e)	Gaziantep Turkey	716 000 (1994e)
Cochabamba Bolivia	448 756 (1994e)	Gdańsk Poland	463 100 (1995e)
Cochin India	708 000 (1996e)	Genoa Italy	659 754 (1994)
Coimbatore India	998 000 (1996e)	Georgetown Guyana	298 000 (1996e)
Cologne Germany	963 817 (1995e)	Gifu Japan	407 145 (1995)
Colombo Sri Lanka	754 000 (1996e)	Glasgow UK	577 869 (2001)
Columbus USA	657 053 (1996e)	Goiania Brazil	993 000 (1996e)
Conakry Guinea	1 508 000 (1995e)	Gomel Belarus	512 000 (1996e)
Constanta Romania	348 985 (1994e)	Gorakhpur India	607 000 (1996e)
Constantine Algeria	537 000 (1996e)	Gorky Russia	1 383 000 (1995e)
Contagem Brazil	480 000 (1996e)	Gorlovka Ukraine	322 000 (1996e)
Copenhagen Denmark	1 353 333 (1995)	Gothenburg Sweden	449 189 (1996e)
Córdoba Argentina	1 130 000 (1996e)	Grozny Russia	364 000 (1994e)
Coventry UK	300 844 (2001)	Guadalajara Mexico	1 807 000 (1995e)
Cracow Poland	746 000 (1995e)	Guarulhos Brazil	805 000 (1996e)
Cucuta Colombia	479 309 (1996e)	Guatemala City Guatemala	823 301 (1994e)
Culiacan Mexico	383 000 (1996e)	Guayaquil Ecuador	1 925 479 (1996e)
Curitiba Brazil	1 513 000 (1995e)	Guilin China	427 000 (1996e)
Dakar Senegal	785 071 (1994e)	Guiyang China	1 116 000 (1996e)
Dalian China	2 014 000 (1996e)	Gujranwala Pakistan	1 663 000 (1995e)
Dallas USA	1 053 292 (1996e)	Guntur India	579 000 (1996e)
Damascus Syria	1 549 932 (1994e)	Gwalior India	853 000 (1996e)
Da Nang Vietnam	415 000 (1996e)	Gwangju Korea, South	1 257 504 (1995)
Dandong China	586 000 (1996e)	Hachioji Japan	503 320 (1995)
Daqing China	726 000 (1996e)	The Hague Netherlands	442 105 (1995e)
Dar es Salaam Tanzania	1 630 000 (1995e)	Haiphong Vietnam	811 000 (1996e)
Datong China	901 000 (1996e)	Hakodate Japan	298 868 (1995)
Davao City Philippines	960 910 (1994e)	Hamamatsu Japan	561 568 (1995)
Delhi India	8 865 000 (1996e)	Hamburg Germany	1 705 872 (1995e)
Denver USA	497 840 (1996e)	Hamhumg Korea, North	771 000 (1996e)
Detroit USA	1 000 272 (1996e)	Hamilton Canada	318 947 (1994)
Dhaka Bangladesh	4 241 000 (1996e)	Handan China	925 000 (1996e)
Diyarbakir Turkey	448 300 (1994e)	Hangzhou China	1 237 000 (1996e)
Dnepropetrovsk Ukraine	1 147 000 (1996e)	Hanoi Vietnam	2 692 000 (1996e)
Doha Qatar	356 000 (1996e)	Hanover Germany	525 763 (1995e)
Donetsk Russia	1 088 000 (1996e)	Harare Zimbabwe	1 339 000 (1996e)
Dortmund Germany	600 918 (1995e)	Harbin China	2 917 000 (1996e)
Douala Cameroon	1 491 000 (1996e)	Havana Cuba	2 241 000 (1995e)
Dresden Germany	474 443 (1995e)	Hefei China	863 000 (1996e)
Dubai United Arab Emirates	679 000 (1996e)	Hegang China	581 000 (1996e)
Dublin Ireland	952 700 (1996)	Helsinki Finland	525 031 (1996)
Duisburg Germany	536 106 (1995e)	Hengyang China	550 000 (1996e)

City	Population
Hermosillo Mexico	336 000 (1996e)
Higashiosaka Japan	517 228 (1995)
Himeji Japan	470 986 (1995)
Hirakata Japan	400 130 (1995)
Hiroshima Japan	1 108 868 (1995)
Ho Chi Minh City Vietnam	4 675 000 (1996e)
Hohot China	739 000 (1996e)
Homs Syria	644 204 (1994e)
Hong Kong Hong Kong	6 218 000 (1996)
Honolulu USA	423 475 (1996e)
Houston USA	1 744 058 (1996e)
Howrah India	1 075 000 (1996e)
Huaibei China	412 000 (1996e)
Huainan China	761 000 (1996e)
Huangshi China	537 000 (1996e)
Hubli-Dharwar India	803 000 (1996e)
Hunjiang China	617 000 (1996e)
Hyderabad India	3 253 000 (1996e)
Hyderabad Pakistan	1 107 000 (1995e)
Iasi Romania	337 643 (1994e)
Ibadan Nigeria	1 365 000 (1996e)
Icel Turkey	493 000 (1996e)
Ichikawa Japan	440 527 (1995)
Inchon Korea, South	2 307 618 (1995)
Indianapolis USA	746 737 (1996e)
Indore India	1 307 000 (1996e)
Irkutsk Russia	585 000 (1995e)
Isfahan Iran	1 433 000 (1996e)
Istanbul Turkey	7 615 500 (1994e)
Ivanovo Russia	474 000 (1995e)
Iwaki Japan	360 497 (1995)
Izhevsk Russia	654 000 (1995e)
Jabalpur India	901 000 (1996e)
Jaboatoa Brazil	508 000 (1996e)
Jacksonville USA	679 792 (1996e)
Jaipur India	1 575 000 (1995e)
Jakarta Indonesia	9 367 000 (1995e)
Jalandhar India	644 000 (1996e)
Jamshedpur India	571 000 (1996e)
Jedda Saudi Arabia	1 947 000 (1995e)
Jerusalem Israel	591 400 (1996e)
Jiamusi China	561 000 (1996e)
Jiaozuo China	449 000 (1996e)
Jilin China	1 385 000 (1996e)
Jinan China	1 494 000 (1996e)
Jingdezhen China	390 000 (1996e)
Jinzhou China	797 000 (1996e)
Jixi China	801 000 (1996e)
Joao Pessoa Brazil	433 000 (1996e)
Jodhpur India	799 000 (1996e)
Johannesburg South Africa	1 725 000 (1995e)
Juiz de Fora Brazil	423 000 (1996e)
Kabul Afghanistan	700 000 (1994e)
Kaesong Korea, North	391 000 (1996e)
Kagoshima Japan	546 294 (1995)
Kaifeng China	584 000 (1996e)
Kalinin Russia	455 000 (1995e)
Kaliningrad Russia	419 000 (1995e)
Kaluga Russia	347 000 (1995e)
Kampala Uganda	952 000 (1996e)
Kanazawa Japan	453 977 (1995)
Kano Nigeria	657 300 (1995e)
Kanpur India	2 120 000 (1996e)
Kansas City USA	441 259 (1996e)
Kaohsiung Taiwan	1 426 518 (1996e)
Karachi Pakistan	9 863 000 (1995e)
Karaganda Kazakhstan	573 700 (1995e)
Karaj Iran	462 000 (1996e)
Kathmandu Nepal	535 000 (1994e)
Katowice Poland	355 100 (1995e)
Kaunas Lithuania	429 000 (1994e)
Kawaguchi Japan	448 801 (1995)
Kawasaki Japan	1 202 811 (1995)
Kayseri Turkey	454 000 (1994e)
Kazan Russia	1 085 000 (1995e)
Keelung Taiwan	370 049 (1996e)
Kemerovo Russia	503 000 (1995e)
Kenitra Morocco	234 000 (1994e)
Khabarovsk Russia	618 000 (1995e)
Kharkov Ukraine	1 555 000 (1996e)
Khartoum The Sudan	924 505 (1994)
Khartoum North The Sudan	879 105 (1994)
Kherson Ukraine	363 000 (1996e)
Khulna Bangladesh	812 000 (1996e)
Kiev Ukraine	2 630 000 (1996e)
Kigali Rwanda	419 000 (1996e)
Kingston Jamaica	538 100 (1995)
Kingston upon Hull UK	243 595 (2001)
Kinshasa Congo, Democratic Republic of	4 655 313 (1994e)
Kirkuk Iraq	667 000 (1996e)
Kirov Russia	464 000 (1995e)
Kishinyov Moldova	662 000 (1994e)
Kitakyushu Japan	1 019 562 (1995)
Kitchener Canada	184 600 (1996)
Kitwe Zambia	398 000 (1996e)
Kobe Japan	1 423 830 (1995)
Kochi Japan	322 077 (1995)
Kolhapur India	526 000 (1996e)
Kolkata (Calcutta) India	5 490 000 (1996e)
Komsomolosk Russia	309 000 (1995e)
Konya Turkey	576 000 (1994e)
Koriyama Japan	326 831 (1995)
Kota India	624 000 (1996e)
Krasnodar Russia	646 000 (1995e)
Krasnoyarsk Russia	869 000 (1995e)
Krivoy Rog Ukraine	720 000 (1996e)
Kuala Lumpur Malaysia	1 388 000 (1995e)
Kumamoto Japan	650 322 (1995)
Kumasi Ghana	441 000 (1996e)
Kunming China	1 728 000 (1996e)
Kurashiki Japan	422 824 (1995)
Kurgan Russia	363 000 (1996e)
Kursk Russia	442 000 (1995e)
Kuwait City Kuwait	31 241 (1994e)
Kuybyshev Russia	1 184 000 (1995e)
Kyoto Japan	1 463 601 (1995)
Lagos Nigeria	1 484 000 (1995e)
Lahore Pakistan	5 085 000 (1995e)
Lanzhou China	1 434 000 (1996e)
La Paz Bolivia	829 000 (1996e)
La Plata Argentina	688 000 (1996e)
Las Palmas Grand Canary	371 787 (1994e)
Leeds UK	715 404 (2001)
Leicester UK	279 923 (2001)
Leipzig Germany	481 121 (1995e)
Leon Mexico	681 000 (1996e)
Leshan China	405 000 (1996e)
Lianyungang China	396 000 (1996e)
Liaoyang China	573 000 (1996e)
Liaoyuan China	399 000 (1996e)
Libreville Gabon	362 386 (1994e)
Lima Peru	5 706 127 (1994e)
Lipetsk Russia	474 000 (1995e)
Lisbon Portugal	913 000 (1996e)
Liupanshui China	399 000 (1996e)
Liuzhou China	691 000 (1996e)
Liverpool UK	439 476 (2001)
Ljubljana Slovenia	276 119 (1996e)
Lodz Poland	828 500 (1995e)
Lomé Togo	431 000 (1996e)
London Canada	331 600 (1995)
London UK	7 172 036 (2001)
Londrina Brazil	391 000 (1996e)
Long Beach USA	421 904 (1996e)
Los Angeles USA	3 553 639 (1996e)
Luanda Angola	2 001 000 (1994e)
Lublin Poland	352 500 (1995e)

Social Structure

Lucknow India	1 723 000 (1996e)
Ludhiana India	1 233 000 (1996e)
Luoyang China	858 000 (1996e)
Lusaka Zambia	971 000 (1996e)
Luxembourg Luxembourg	76 446 (1995e)
Lyons France	436 000 (1996e)
Maceio Brazil	558 000 (1996e)
Machida Japan	360 408 (1995)
Madras ▸ Chennai	
Madrid Spain	3 041 101 (1994e)
Madurai India	1 146 000 (1996e)
Magnitogorsk Russia	427 000 (1995e)
Makassar Indonesia	929 000 (1996e)
Makeyevka Ukraine	409 000 (1996e)
Makhachkala Russia	339 000 (1995e)
Malaga Spain	531 443 (1994e)
Malang Indonesia	611 000 (1996e)
Managua Nicaragua	1 195 000 (1995e)
Manaus Brazil	933 000 (1996e)
Manchester UK	392 819 (2001)
Mandalay Myanmar (Burma)	698 000 (1996e)
Manila Philippines	1 894 667 (1994e)
Maputo Mozambique	1 231 000 (1996e)
Maracaibo Venezuela	1 346 000 (1995e)
Maracay Venezuela	991 000 (1996e)
Mar del Plata Argentina	540 000 (1996e)
Mariupol Ukraine	510 000 (1996)
Marrakesh Morocco	602 000 (1994e)
Marseilles France	846 000 (1996e)
Masan Korea, South	441 358 (1995)
Matsudo Japan	461 489 (1995)
Matsuyama Japan	460 870 (1995)
Mecca Saudi Arabia	701 000 (1996e)
Medan Indonesia	2 200 000 (1996e)
Medellin Colombia	1 621 356 (1995e)
Meerut India	933 000 (1996e)
Meknes Morocco	401 000 (1994e)
Melbourne Australia	3 218 100 (1995e)
Memphis USA	596 725 (1996e)
Mendoza Argentina	727 000 (1996e)
Meshed Iran	1 916 000 (1995e)
Mexicali Mexico	395 000 (1996e)
Mexico City Mexico	9 815 795 (1996e)
Miami USA	365 127 (1996e)
Milan Italy	1 334 171 (1994e)
Milwaukee USA	590 503 (1996e)
Minneapolis USA	358 785 (1996e)
Minsk Belarus	1 700 000 (1996e)
Mogadishu Somalia	742 000 (1996e)
Mogilyov Belarus	367 000 (1996e)
Mombasa Kenya	488 000 (1996e)
Monrovia Liberia	536 000 (1996e)
Monterrey Mexico	1 215 000 (1996e)
Montevideo Uruguay	1 378 707 (1996)
Montreal Canada	1 017 666 (1994)
Moradabad India	551 000 (1996e)
Moscow Russia	8 717 000 (1995e)
Mosul Iraq	640 000 (1996e)
Mudanjiang China	662 000 (1996e)
Multan Pakistan	1 257 000 (1995e)
Mumbai (Greater) (Bombay) India	9 925 891 (1996e)
Munich Germany	1 244 676 (1995e)
Murcia Spain	341 531 (1994e)
Murmansk Russia	407 000 (1995e)
Mysore India	597 000 (1996e)
Naberezhnye Chelny Russia	526 000 (1995e)
Nagano Japan	358 512 (1995)
Nagasaki Japan	438 724 (1995)
Nagoya Japan	2 152 258 (1995)
Nagpur India	1 756 000 (1995e)
Naha Japan	301 928 (1995)
Nairobi Kenya	1 697 000 (1995e)
Namangan Uzbekistan	341 000 (1994e)
Nanchang China	1 256 000 (1996e)

Nanjing China	2 394 000 (1996e)
Nanning China	771 000 (1996e)
Nantong China	380 000 (1996e)
Naples Italy	1 061 000 (1994e)
Nara Japan	359 234 (1995)
Nashville USA	511 263 (1996e)
Nassau The Bahamas	191 000 (1996e)
Natal Brazil	574 000 (1996e)
N'Djamena Chad	530 965 (1994e)
Ndola Zambia	479 000 (1996e)
Netzahualcóyotl Mexico	1 455 000 (1996e)
Newark USA	268 510 (1996e)
Newcastle Australia	466 000 (1995e)
New Delhi India	345 000 (1996e)
New Orleans USA	476 625 (1996e)
New York USA	7 380 906 (1996e)
Niamey Niger	439 000 (1996e)
Nice France	465 000 (1996e)
Nicosia Cyprus	186 400 (1994e)
Niigata Japan	494 785 (1995)
Nikolayev Ukraine	508 700 (1996e)
Ningbo China	634 000 (1996e)
Niš Serbia and Montenegro	689 000 (1996e)
Nishinomiya Japan	390 388 (1995)
Niteroi Brazil	485 000 (1996e)
Nizhny Tagil Russia	409 000 (1995e)
Nova Iguacu Brazil	1 426 000 (1996e)
Nouakchott Mauritania	755 000 (1995e)
Novokuznetsk Russia	572 000 (1995e)
Novosibirsk Russia	1 369 000 (1995e)
Nuremberg Germany	495 845 (1995e)
Oakland USA	367 230 (1996e)
Odessa Ukraine	1 046 000 (1996e)
Ogbomosho Nigeria	711 900 (1995e)
Oita Japan	426 981 (1995)
Okayama Japan	616 056 (1995)
Oklahoma City USA	469 852 (1996e)
Olinda Brazil	369 500 (1996e)
Omaha USA	364 253 (1996e)
Omdurman The Sudan	1 267 077 (1994)
Omiya Japan	433 768 (1995)
Omsk Russia	1 163 000 (1996e)
Oporto Portugal	394 000 (1996e)
Oran Algeria	696 000 (1996e)
Ordzhonikidze Russia	312 000 (1995e)
Orenburg Russia	532 000 (1995e)
Oryol Russia	348 000 (1995e)
Osaka Japan	2 602 352 (1995)
Osasco Brazil	677 000 (1996e)
Osijek Croatia	240 000 (1996e)
Oslo Norway	487 908 (1996e)
Ostrava Czech Republic	325 827 (1995e)
Ottawa Canada	313 971 (1994)
Oujda Morocco	331 000 (1994e)
Padang Indonesia	790 000 (1996e)
Palembang Indonesia	1 561 000 (1996e)
Palermo Italy	694 749 (1994e)
Palma Majorca	322 008 (1994e)
Panama City Panama	445 902 (1994e)
Panchiao Taiwan	539 115 (1995e)
Panshan China	339 000 (1996e)
Paris France	2 336 000 (1996e)
Patna India	1 141 000 (1996e)
Pavlodar Kazakhstan	340 700 (1995e)
Penza Russia	534 000 (1995e)
Perm Russia	1 032 000 (1995e)
Perth Australia	1 262 600 (1995e)
Peshawar Pakistan	1 676 000 (1995e)
Philadelphia USA	1 478 002 (1996e)
Phoenix USA	1 159 014 (1996e)
Pingdingshan China	502 000 (1996e)
Pingxiang China	506 000 (1996e)
Pittsburgh USA	350 363 (1996e)
Plovdiv Bulgaria	344 326 (1996e)

Poltava Ukraine	321 000 (1996e)
Pontianak Indonesia	419 000 (1996e)
Poona India	1 688 000 (1995e)
Port-au-Prince Haiti	846 247 (1995e)
Port Elizabeth (Nelson Mandela Metropole) South Africa	797 000 (1996e)
Portland USA	480 824 (1996e)
Port Louis Mauritius	144 776 (1994e)
Port Moresby Papua New Guinea	176 000 (1996e)
Porto Alegre Brazil	1 569 000 (1996e)
Port of Spain Trinidad	70 000 (1996e)
Port Said Egypt	460 000 (1994e)
Poznań Poland	582 300 (1995e)
Prague Czech Republic	1 213 299 (1995e)
Pretoria (Tshwane) South Africa	925 000 (1996e)
Puebla Mexico	991 000 (1996e)
Pusan Korea, South	3 813 814 (1995)
Pyongyang Korea, North	2 716 000 (1995e)
Qinhuangdao China	405 000 (1996e)
Qiqihar China	1 261 000 (1996e)
Qom Iran	624 000 (1996e)
Quebec Canada	175 039 (1994)
Quezon City Philippines	1 676 644 (1994e)
Quito Ecuador	1 444 363 (1996e)
Rabat Morocco	1 220 000 (1994e)
Raipur India	540 000 (1996e)
Rajkot India	666 000 (1996e)
Ranchi India	739 000 (1996e)
Rangoon Myanmar (Burma)	3 851 000 (1995e)
Rawalpindi Pakistan	1 290 000 (1995e)
Recife Brazil	1 496 000 (1995e)
Reykjavik Iceland	104 276 (1995e)
Ribeirao Preto Brazil	444 000 (1996e)
Riga Latvia	839 670 (1995e)
Rio de Janeiro Brazil	6 574 000 (1995e)
Riyadh Saudi Arabia	1 800 000 (1995e)
Rome Italy	2 687 881 (1994e)
Rosario Argentina	1 136 000 (1996e)
Rostov-na-Donu Russia	1 026 000 (1995e)
Rotterdam Netherlands	599 414 (1995e)
Sacramento USA	376 243 (1996e)
Safi Morocco	278 000 (1994)
Sagamihara Japan	570 594 (1995)
St Catharines-Niagara Canada	125 887 (1994)
St Louis USA	351 565 (1996e)
St Petersburg Russia	4 838 000 (1995e)
Sakai Japan	802 965 (1995)
Salem India	445 000 (1996e)
Salonika Greece	453 000 (1996e)
Salvador Brazil	2 203 000 (1995e)
Samarkand Uzbekistan	368 000 (1994e)
San'a Yemen	503 600 (1995e)
San Antonio USA	1 067 816 (1996e)
San Cristobal Venezuela	413 000 (1996e)
San Diego USA	1 171 121 (1996e)
San Francisco USA	735 315 (1996e)
San José USA	838 744 (1996e)
San Juan Puerto Rico	438 076 (1995e)
San Luis Potosí Mexico	412 000 (1996e)
San Miguel de Tucumán Argentina	551 000 (1996e)
San Pedro Sula Honduras	368 500 (1994e)
San Salvador El Salvador	439 000 (1996e)
Santa Cruz de la Sierra Bolivia	767 260 (1994e)
Santiago Chile	5 076 808 (1995e)
Santiago de Cuba Cuba	440 084 (1994e)
Santo André Brazil	734 000 (1996e)
Santo Domingo Dominican Republic	2 138 262 (1994e)
Santos Brazil	505 000 (1996e)
São Bernardo do Campo Brazil	613 000 (1996e)
São Gonçalo Brazil	777 000 (1996e)
São João de Meriti Brazil	513 000 (1996e)
São José dos Campos Brazil	389 000 (1996e)
São Luis Brazil	623 000 (1996e)
São Paulo Brazil	9 393 753 (1996)
Sapporo Japan	1 756 968 (1995)
Saragossa Spain	606 620 (1994e)
Sarajevo Bosnia-Herzegovina	250 000 (1995e)
Saransk Russia	320 000 (1995e)
Saratov Russia	895 000 (1995e)
Scarborough Canada	510 000 (1994)
Seattle USA	524 704 (1996e)
Semarang Indonesia	1 477 000 (1995e)
Semipalatinsk Kazakhstan	320 200 (1995e)
Sendai Japan	971 263 (1995)
Seoul Korea, South	10 229 262 (1995)
Shanchung Taiwan	382 880 (1995e)
Shanghai China	7 830 000 (1996e)
Shantou China	602 000 (1996e)
Shaoguan China	404 000 (1996e)
Sheffield UK	513 234 (2001)
Shenyang China	4 449 000 (1996e)
Shihezi China	376 000 (1996e)
Shijiazhuang China	1 333 000 (1996e)
Shiraz Iran	1 009 000 (1996e)
Shizuoka Japan	474 089 (1995)
Sholapur India	744 000 (1996e)
Shoubra el-Kheima Egypt	956 000 (1996e)
Shuangyashan China	467 000 (1996e)
Sialkot Pakistan	366 000 (1996e)
Sian (Xian) China	2 410 000 (1996e)
Simferopol Ukraine	348 000 (1996e)
Singapore Singapore	3 045 000 (1996e)
Sinuiju Korea, North	361 000 (1996e)
Skopje Macedonia	541 280 (1994e)
Smolensk Russia	355 000 (1995e)
Smyrna Turkey	1 959 000 (1995e)
Sochi Russia	355 000 (1995e)
Sofia Bulgaria	1 116 823 (1996e)
Songnam Korea, South	869 243 (1995)
Sorocaba Brazil	431 561 (1996e)
Srinagar India	742 000 (1996)
Stavropol Russia	342 000 (1995e)
Stockholm Sweden	711 119 (1996e)
Stuttgart Germany	588 482 (1995e)
Suita Japan	342 794 (1995)
Surabaya Indonesia	2 726 000 (1995e)
Surakarta Indonesia	588 000 (1996e)
Surat India	1 620 000 (1995e)
Suva Fiji	731 000 (1996e)
Suwon Korea, South	755 502 (1995)
Suzhou China	778 000 (1996e)
Sverdlovsk Russia	1 280 000 (1995e)
Sydney Australia	3 772 700 (1996e)
Szczecin Poland	419 600 (1995e)
Tabriz Iran	1 301 000 (1995e)
Taegu Korea, South	2 449 139 (1995)
Taejon Korea, South	1 272 143 (1995)
Taichung Taiwan	857 590 (1996e)
Tainan Taiwan	707 658 (1996e)
Taipei Taiwan	2 626 138 (1996e)
Taiyuan China	1 861 000 (1996e)
Takamatsu Japan	330 997 (1995)
Takatsuki Japan	362 259 (1995)
Tallinn Estonia	434 763 (1995e)
Tambov Russia	316 000 (1995e)
Tangier Morocco	307 700 (1994e)
Tangshan China	1 213 000 (1996e)
Tanta Egypt	396 000 (1996e)
Tashkent Uzbekistan	2 106 000 (1994e)
Tbilisi Georgia	1 295 000 (1995e)
Tegucigalpa Honduras	775 300 (1994e)
Tehran Iran	6 632 000 (1996e)
Tel Aviv Israel	355 900 (1996e)
Teresina Brazil	588 000 (1996e)
Tetouan Morocco	272 000 (1994e)
Thane India	956 000 (1996e)

Social Structure

Tianjin (Tientsin) China	5 479 000 (1996e)
Tijuana Mexico	479 000 (1996e)
Timisoara Romania	325 359 (1994e)
Tirana Albania	257 000 (1996e)
Tiruchchirapalli India	475 000 (1996e)
Tokyo Japan	7 966 195 (1995)
Toledo USA	317 606 (1996e)
Tolyatti Russia	702 000 (1995e)
Tomsk Russia	470 000 (1995e)
Tonghua China	378 000 (1996e)
Toronto Canada	590 838 (1994)
Toulouse France	385 500 (1996e)
Toyama Japan	341 038 (1995)
Toyohasi Japan	352 913 (1995)
Toyonaka Japan	325 303 (1995)
Toyota Japan	398 912 (1995)
Tripoli Libya	626 000 (1996e)
Trivandrum India	707 000 (1996e)
Trujillo Peru	509 312 (1994e)
Tucson USA	449 002 (1996e)
Tula Russia	532 000 (1995e)
Tulsa USA	378 491 (1996e)
Tunis Tunisia	674 100 (1994e)
Turin Italy	945 551 (1994e)
Tyumen Russia	494 000 (1995e)
Ufa Russia	1 094 000 (1995e)
Ulan Bator Mongolia	619 000 (1994e)
Ulan-Ude Russia	366 000 (1995e)
Ulsan Korea, South	967 394 (1995)
Ulyanovsk Russia	678 000 (1995e)
Urawa Japan	453 000 (1995)
Urumqi China	1 203 000 (1996e)
Ust-Kamenogorsk Kazakhstan	326 300 (1995e)
Utsunomiya Japan	435 446 (1995)
Vadodara India	1 357 000 (1996e)
Valencia Spain	764 293 (1994e)
Valencia Venezuela	1 466 000 (1996e)
Valladolid Spain	336 917 (1994e)
Vancouver Canada	508 814 (1994)
Varanasi India	1 217 000 (1996e)
Vargas Venezuela	395 000 (1996e)
Varna Bulgaria	301 421 (1996e)
Venice Italy	306 439 (1994e)
Veracruz Mexico	315 000 (1996e)
Victoria Seychelles	25 000 (1994e)
Vienna Austria	1 690 000 (1996e)
Vientiane Laos	457 000 (1996e)
Vijayawada India	881 000 (1996e)
Vilnius Lithuania	580 100 (1997e)
Vina del Mar Chile	322 220 (1995e)
Vinnitsa Ukraine	388 000 (1996e)
Virginia Beach USA	430 385 (1996e)

Visakhapatnam India	928 000 (1996e)
Vitebsk Belarus	365 000 (1996e)
Vladimir Russia	339 000 (1995e)
Vladivostok Russia	632 000 (1995e)
Volgograd Russia	1 003 000 (1995e)
Voronezh Russia	908 000 (1995e)
Voroshilovgrad Ukraine	487 000 (1996e)
Wakayama Japan	339 951 (1995)
Warangal India	549 000 (1996e)
Warsaw Poland	1 640 700 (1995e)
Washington USA	543 213 (1996e)
Weifang China	412 000 (1996e)
Wellington New Zealand	158 275 (1996)
Wenzhou China	475 900 (1996e)
Windhoek Namibia	184 000 (1996e)
Winnipeg Canada	641 700 (1994)
Wroclaw Poland	642 900 (1995e)
Wuhan China	4 015 000 (1996e)
Wuhu China	506 000 (1996e)
Wuppertal Germany	383 776 (1995e)
Wuxi China	927 000 (1996e)
Xiamen China	448 000 (1996e)
Xiangfan China	447 000 (1996e)
Xiangtan China	515 000 (1996e)
Xiangyang China	468 000 (1996e)
Xining China	639 000 (1996e)
Xinxiang China	549 000 (1996e)
Xuzhou China	932 000 (1996e)
Yakeshi China	464 000 (1996e)
Yangquan China	421 000 (1996e)
Yantai China	461 000 (1996e)
Yaoundé Cameroon	824 000 (1996e)
Yaroslavl Russia	629 000 (1995e)
Yerevan Armenia	1 226 000 (1994e)
Yichang (Ichang) China	417 000 (1996e)
Yichun (Ichun) China	951 000 (1996e)
Yinchuan China	392 000 (1996e)
Yingkou China	482 000 (1996e)
Yogyakarta Indonesia	583 000 (1996e)
Yokohama Japan	3 307 408 (1995)
Yukosuko Japan	432 202 (1995)
Zagreb Croatia	845 000 (1996e)
Zamboanga City Philippines	464 466 (1994e)
Zaporozhye Ukraine	882 000 (1996e)
Zarqa Jordan	344 524 (1994)
Zhangjiakou China	615 000 (1996e)
Zhengzhou China	1 333 000 (1996e)
Zhenjiang China	424 000 (1996e)
Zhuzhou China	465 000 (1996e)
Zibo China	992 000 (1996e)
Zigong China	469 000 (1996e)
Zürich Switzerland	342 872 (1995e)

Largest cities by population

■ **World**

Seoul Korea, South	10 229 262	**Jakarta** Indonesia	9 367 000
Mumbai (Bombay) India	9 925 891	**Delhi** India	8 865 000
Karachi Pakistan	9 863 000	**Moscow** Russia	8 717 000
Mexico City Mexico	9 815 795	**Beijing (Peking)** China	8 200 000
São Paulo Brazil	9 393 753	**Tokyo** Japan	7 966 195

■ **Europe**

Moscow Russia	8 717 000	**Madrid** Spain	3 041 101
Istanbul Turkey	7 615 500	**Rome** Italy	2 687 881
London UK	7 172 036	**Paris** France	2 336 000
St Petersburg Russia	4 838 000	**Bucharest** Romania	2 027 512
Berlin Germany	3 472 009	**Budapest** Hungary	1 909 000

■ USA

New York New York	7 380 906	**San Diego** California	1 171 121
Los Angeles California	3 553 639	**Phoenix** Arizona	1 159 014
Chicago Illinois	2 721 547	**San Antonio** Texas	1 067 816
Houston Texas	1 744 058	**Dallas** Texas	1 053 292
Philadelphia Pennsylvania	1 478 002	**Detroit** Michigan	1 000 272

World population estimates

Date (AD)	Millions	Date (AD)	Millions	Date (AD)	Millions
1	300	1900	1 650	2000	6 071
1000	310	1950	2 519	2010	6 830
1250	400	1960	3 021	2020	7 540
1500	500	1970	3 692	2030	8 130
1750	790	1980	4 435	2040	8 594
1800	980	1990	5 264	2050	8 918
1850	1 260				

The above are based on United Nations estimates and predictions published in 2002. In contrast to predictions made in the early 1990s (eg 11 000 000 000 world population by 2050), the totals are down, mainly due to government-sponsored birth-control schemes in China. By that year, China is expected to be overtaken by India as the world's most-populous nation (see below).

Population of the six most populous nations[1]

	1950		2050	
China	1st	555m	2nd	1 462m
India	2nd	358m	1st	1 572m
USA	3rd	158m	3rd	397m
USSR	4th	103m	—	—
Japan	5th	84m	16th	109m
Indonesia	6th	80m	5th	311m

[1] compared for 2050 against 1950 in medium-variant predictions.

Nations of the world A–Z

In the case of countries that do not use the Roman alphabet (such as the Arabic countries), there is variation in the spelling of names and currencies, depending on the system of transliteration used.

Where more than one language is shown within a country, the status of the languages may not be equal. Some languages have a 'semi-official' status, or are used for a restricted set of purposes, such as trade or tourism.

Population census estimates are for 1999.

English name	Official name (in English)	Capital (English name in parentheses)	Official language(s)	Currency	Population
Afghanistan	Islamic State of Afghanistan	Kābul	Dari, Pushtu	1 Afghani (Af) = 100 puls	25 825 000 inc. nomads
Albania	Republic of Albania	Tiranë (Tirana)	Albanian	1 Lek (Lk) = 100 qindarka	3 365 000
Algeria	Democratic and Popular Republic of Algeria	El Djazair (Algiers)	Arabic, Tamazight	1 Algerian Dinar (AD, DA) = 100 centimes	31 133 000
Andorra	Principality of Andorra; the Valleys of Andorra	Andorra la Vella	Catalan, French, Spanish	1 Euro (€) = 100 cents	65 900
Angola	Republic of Angola	Luanda	Portuguese	1 New Kwanza (Kzrl) = 100 lwei	11 178 000
Antigua and Barbuda	State of Antigua and Barbuda	St John's	English	1 East Caribbean Dollar (EC$) = 100 cents	64 200
Argentina	Argentine Republic	Buenos Aires	Spanish	1 Peso ($) = 10 000 australes	36 738 000
Armenia	Republic of Armenia	Yerevan	Armenian	1 Dram (Drm) =100 louma	3 409 000
Australia	Commonwealth of Australia	Canberra	English	1 Australian Dollar ($A) = 100 cents	18 784 000

Social Structure

Social Structure

English name	Official name (in English)	Capital (English name in parentheses)	Official language(s)	Currency	Population
Austria	Republic of Austria	Vienna	German	1 Euro (€) = 100 cents	8 139 000
Azerbaijan	Republic of Azerbaijan	Baku	Azeri	1 Manat =100 gopik	7 908 000
The Bahamas	Commonwealth of the Bahamas	Nassau	English	1 Bahamian Dollar (BA$, B$) = 100 cents	283 700
Bahrain	Kingdom of Bahrain	Al-Manāmah (Manama)	Arabic	1 Bahraini Dinar (BD) = 1 000 fils	629 100
Bangladesh	People's Republic of Bangladesh	Dhaka (Dacca)	Bengali	1 Taka (TK) = 100 poisha	127 118 000
Barbados	Barbados	Bridgetown	English	1 Barbados Dollar (BD$) = 100 cents	259 200
Belarus	Republic of Belarus	Minsk	Belarusian, Russian	1 Rouble (BR) =100 kopeks	10 402 000
Belgium	Kingdom of Belgium	Bruxelles (Brussels)	Flemish, French, German	1 Euro (€) = 100 cents	10 182 000
Belize	Belize	Belmopan	English	1 Belize Dollar (BZ$) = 100 cents	235 800
Benin	Republic of Benin	Porto Novo	French	1 CFA Franc (CFAFr) = 100 centimes	6 306 000
Bhutan	Kingdom of Bhutan	Thimbu/ Thimphu	Dzongkha	1 Ngultrum (Nu) = 100 chetrum	1 952 000
Bolivia	Republic of Bolivia	La Paz/Sucre	Spanish	1 Boliviano ($b) = 100 centavos	7 983 000
Bosnia-Herze-govina	Republic of Bosnia-Herzegovina	Sarajevo	Bosnian, Serbian, Croatian	1 Dinar (D, din) = 100 paras	3 482 000
Botswana	Republic of Botswana	Gaborone	English, Setswana	1 Pula (P, Pu) = 100 thebe	1 464 000
Brazil	Federative Republic of Brazil	Brasilia	Portuguese	1 Real (R$) = 100 centavos	171 853 000
Brunei	State of Brunei, Abode of Peace	Bandar Seri Begawan	Malay, English	1 Brunei Dollar (B$) = 100 sen	323 000
Bulgaria	Republic of Bulgaria	Sofija (Sofia)	Bulgarian	1 Lev (Lv) = 100 stotinki	8 195 000
Burkina Faso	Burkina Faso	Ouagadougou	French	1 CFA Franc (CFAFr) = 100 centimes	11 576 000
Burma ► Myanmar					
Burundi	Republic of Burundi	Bujumbura	French, Kirundi	1 Burundi Franc (BuFr, FBu) = 100 centimes	5 736 000
Cambodia	State of Cambodia	Phnum Pénh (Phnom Penh)	Khmer	1 Riel (CRI) = 100 sen	11 627 000
Cameroon	Republic of Cameroon	Yaoundé	English, French	1 CFA (Franc) (CFAFr) = 100 centimes	15 456 000
Canada	Canada	Ottawa	English, French	1 Canadian Dollar (C$, Can$) = 100 cents	31 006 000
Cape Verde	Republic of Cape Verde	Praia	Portuguese	1 Escudo Caboverdiano (CVEsc) = 100 centavos	405 700
Central African Republic	Central African Republic	Bangui	French, Sango	1 CFA Franc (CFAFr) = 100 centimes	3 445 000
Chad	Republic of Chad	N'Djamena	French, Arabic	1 CFA Franc (CFAFr) = 100 centimes	7 557 000
Chile	Republic of Chile	Santiago	Spanish	1 Chilean Peso (Ch$) = 100 centavos	14 974 000
China	People's Republic of China	Beijing (Peking)	Mandarin Chinese	1 Renminbi Yuan (RMBY, $, Y) = 10 jiao = 100 fen	1 246 872 000

English name	Official name (in English)	Capital (English name in parentheses)	Official language(s)	Currency	Population
Colombia	Republic of Colombia	Bogotá	Spanish	1 Colombian Peso (Col$) = 100 centavos	39 309 000
Comoros	Federal Islamic Republic of the Comoros	Moroni	French, Arabic	1 Comorian Franc (KMF) = 100 centimes	562 700
Congo	Republic of Congo	Brazzaville	French, Kikongo, Lingala	1 CFA Franc (CFAFr) = 100 centimes	2 717 000
Congo, Democratic Republic of	Democratic Republic of Congo	Kinshasa	French, Kikongo, Lingala	1 Congolese Franc = 100 centimes	50 481 000
Costa Rica	Republic of Costa Rica	San José	Spanish	1 Costa Rican Colón (CRℂ) = 100 céntimos	3 674 000
Côte d'Ivoire (Ivory Coast)	Republic of Côte d'Ivoire	Abidjan/ Yamoussoukro	French	1 CFA Franc (CFAFr) = 100 centimes	15 818 000
Croatia	Republic of Croatia	Zagreb	Croatian	1 Kuna (HRK) = 100 lipa	4 677 000
Cuba	Republic of Cuba	La Habana (Havana)	Spanish	1 Cuban Peso (Cub$) = 100 centavos	11 096 000
Cyprus	Republic of Cyprus	Levkosia (Nicosia)	Greek, Turkish	1 Cyprus Pound (C£) = 100 cents	754 100
Czech Republic	Czech Republic	Praha (Prague)	Czech	1 Koruna (Kčs) = 100 haléřu	10 281 000
Denmark	Kingdom of Denmark	København (Copenhagen)	Danish	1 Danish Krone (Dkr) = 100 øre	5 357 000
Djibouti	Republic of Djibouti	Djibouti	Arabic, French	1 Djibouti Franc (DF, DjFr) = 100 centimes	447 400
Dominica	Commonwealth of Dominica	Roseau	English, French Creole	1 East Caribbean Dollar (EC$) = 100 cents	64 900
Dominican Republic	Dominican Republic	Santo Domingo	Spanish	1 Dominican Republic Peso (RD$, DR$) = 100 centavos	8 130 000
East Timor	Democratic Republic of East Timor	Dili	Portuguese, Tetum	1 US dollar ($) = 100 cents	750 000 (2002e)
Ecuador	Republic of Ecuador	Quito	Spanish, Quechua	1 Sucre (Su, S/.) = 100 centavos	12 562 000
Egypt	Arab Republic of Egypt	Al-Qāhirah (Cairo)	Arabic	1 Egyptian Pound (£E, LE) = 100 piastres	62 274 000
El Salvador	Republic of El Salvador	San Salvador	Spanish	1 Colón (¢ES) = 100 centavos	5 839 000
Equatorial Guinea	Republic of Equatorial Guinea	Malabo	Spanish, French	1 CFA Franc (CFAFr) = 100 centimes	465 700
Eritrea	Eritrea	Asmara	Arabic, Tigrinya	1 Nakfa (Nfa) = 100 cents	3 985 000
Estonia	Republic of Estonia	Tallinn	Estonian, Russian	1 Kroon (KR) = 100 sents	1 409 000
Ethiopia	Federal Democratic Republic of Ethiopia	Adis Abeba (Addis Ababa)	Amharic	1 Ethiopian Birr (EB) = 100 cents	59 680 000

Federated States of Micronesia ▶ Micronesia

English name	Official name (in English)	Capital (English name in parentheses)	Official language(s)	Currency	Population
Fiji	Republic of Fiji	Suva	Fijian, Hindi	1 Fiji Dollar (F$) = 100 cents	812 900
Finland	Republic of Finland	Helsinki	Finnish, Swedish	1 Euro (€) = 100 cents	5 158 000
France	French Republic	Paris	French	1 Euro (€) = 100 cents	58 978 000
Gabon	Gabonese Republic	Libreville	French	1 CFA Franc (CFAFr) = 100 centimes	1 226 000
The Gambia	Republic of the Gambia	Banjul	English	1 Dalasi (D) = 100 butut	1 336 000

Social Structure

English name	Official name (in English)	Capital (English name in parentheses)	Official language(s)	Currency	Population
Georgia	Republic of Georgia	Tbilisi	Georgian, Russian	1 Lari (GEL) = 100 tetri	5 066 000
Germany	Federal Republic of Germany	Berlin	German	1 Euro (€) = 100 cents	82 087 000
Ghana	Republic of Ghana	Accra	English	1 Cedi (¢) = 100 pesewas	18 888 000
Greece	Hellenic Republic	Athínai (Athens)	Greek	1 Euro (€) = 100 cents	10 707 000
Grenada	Grenada	St George's	English	1 East Caribbean Dollar (EC$) = 100 cents	97 000
Guatemala	Republic of Guatemala	Guatemala City	Spanish	1 Quetzal (Q) = 100 centavos	12 336 000
Guinea	Republic of Guinea	Conakry	French	1 Guinea Franc (GFr) = 100 centimes	7 539 000
Guinea-Bissau	Republic of Guinea-Bissau	Bissau	Portuguese, Guinean Creole	1 CFA Franc (CFAFr) = 100 centimes	1 235 000
Guyana	Co-operative Republic of Guyana	Georgetown	English	1 Guyana Dollar (G$) = 100 cents	705 200
Haiti	Republic of Haiti	Port-au-Prince	French, Creole	1 Gourde (G, Gde) = 100 centimes	6 884 000
Holland ▸ Netherlands, The					
Honduras	Republic of Honduras	Tegucigalpa	Spanish	1 Lempira (L, La) = 100 centavos	5 997 000
Hungary	Republic of Hungary	Budapest	Magyar	1 Forint (Ft) = 100 fillér	10 197 119 (2001)
Iceland	Republic of Iceland	Reykjavik	Icelandic	1 Króna (IKr, ISK) = 100 aurar	272 500
India	Republic of India	New Delhi	Hindi, English	1 Indian Rupee (Re, Rs) = 100 paisa	1 000 849 000
Indonesia	Republic of Indonesia	Jakarta	Bahasa Indonesia	1 Rupiah (Rp) = 100 sen	231 328 000 (2002e)
Iran	Islamic Republic of Iran	Tehrān (Tehran)	Farsi	1 Iranian Rial (Rls, RI) = 100 dinars	65 180 000
Iraq	Republic of Iraq	Baghdād (Baghdad)	Arabic	1 Iraqi Dinar (ID) = 1 000 fils	22 427 000
Ireland	Republic of Ireland	Baile Átha Cliath (Dublin)	Irish Gaelic, English	1 Euro (€) = 100 cents	3 633 000
Israel	State of Israel	Tel Aviv-Jaffa	Hebrew, Arabic	1 Shekel (IS) = 100 agora	5 750 000
Italy	Italian Republic	Roma (Rome)	Italian	1 Euro (€) = 100 cents	56 735 000
Ivory Coast ▸ Côte d'Ivoire					
Jamaica	Jamaica	Kingston	English	1 Jamaican Dollar (J$) = 100 cents	2 652 000
Japan	Japan	Tōkyō (Tokyo)	Japanese	1 Yen (Y, ¥) = 100 sen	126 182 000
Jordan	Hashemite Kingdom of Jordan	'Ammān (Amman)	Arabic	1 Jordanian Dinar (JD) = 1 000 fils	4 561 000
Kazakhstan	Republic of Kazakhstan	Astanta	Kazakh	1 Tenge = 100 tiyn	16 825 000
Kenya	Republic of Kenya	Nairobi	Swahili, English	1 Kenyan shilling (Ksh) = 100 cents	28 809 000
Kiribati	Republic of Kiribati	Bairiki, on Tawara	English, I-Kiribati	1 Australian Dollar ($A) = 100 cents	85 500
Korea, North	Democratic People's Republic of Korea	P'yŏngyang (Pyongyang)	Korean	1 Won (NKW) = 100 chon	21 386 000
Korea, South	Republic of Korea	Sŏul (Seoul)	Korean	1 Won (W) = 100 jeon	46 885 000
Kuwait	State of Kuwait	Al-Kuwayt (Kuwait City)	Arabic	1 Kuwaiti Dinar (KD) = 1 000 fils	1 991 000
Kyrgyzstan	Republic of Kyrgyzstan	Bishkek	Kyrgyz, Russian	1 Som (Kgs) = 100 tiyyn	4 546 000

English name	Official name (in English)	Capital (English name in parentheses)	Official language(s)	Currency	Population
Laos	Lao People's Democratic Republic	Viangchan (Vientiane)	Lao	1 Kip (Kp) = 100 at	5 407 000
Latvia	Republic of Latvia	Riga	Latvian	1 Lat (Ls) = 100 santims	2 354 000
Lebanon	Republic of Lebanon	Bayrūt (Beirut)	Arabic	1 Lebanese Pound/ Livre (LL, L£) = 100 piastres	3 563 000
Lesotho	Kingdom of Lesotho	Maseru	English, Sesotho	1 Loti (*plural* Maloti) (M, LSM) = 100 lisente	2 129 000
Liberia	Republic of Liberia	Monrovia	English	1 Liberian Dollar (L$) = 100 cents	2 924 000
Libya	Socialist People's Libyan Arab Jamahiriya	Tarābulus (Tripoli)	Arabic	1 Libyan Dinar (LD) = 1 000 dirhams	4 993 000
Liechten- stein	Principality of Liechtenstein	Vaduz	German	1 Swiss Franc (SFr, SwF) = 100 centimes = 100 rappen	32 100
Lithuania	Republic of Lithuania	Vilnius	Lithuanian	1 Litas (Lt) = 100 centas	3 585 000
Luxembourg	Grand Duchy of Luxembourg	Luxembourg	French, German, Letzeburgish	1 Euro (€) = 100 cents	429 100
Macedonia	Former Yugoslav Republic of Macedonia	Skopje	Macedonian, Albanian	1 Denar (D, den) = 100 paras	2 023 000
Madagascar	Democratic Republic of Madagascar	Antananarivo	Malagasy, French	1 Malagasy Franc (FMG, MgFr) = 100 centimes	14 873 000
Malawi	Republic of Malawi	Lilongwe	Chichewa, English	1 Kwacha (MK) = 100 tambala	10 000 000
Malaysia	Malaysia	Kuala Lumpur	Bahasa Malaysia	1 Malaysian Dollar/ Ringgit (M$) = 100 cents	21 376 000
Maldives	Republic of Maldives	Malé	Dhivehi	1 Rufiyaa (MRf, Rf) = 100 laaris	300 200
Mali	Republic of Mali	Bamako	French	1 CFA Franc (CFAFr)= 100 centimes	10 429 000
Malta	Republic of Malta	Valletta	English, Maltese	1 Maltese Lira (LM) = 100 cents = 1 000 mils	381 600
Marshall Islands	Republic of the Marshall Islands	Majuro	Marshallese, English	1 US Dollar ($, US$) = 100 cents	66 000
Mauritania	Islamic Republic of Mauritania	Nouakchott	Arabic	1 Ouguiya (U, UM) = 5 khoums	2 582 000
Mauritius	Republic of Mauritius	Port Louis	English	1 Mauritian Rupee (MR, MauRe) = 100 cents	1 182 000
Mexico	United Mexican States	Ciudad de México (Mexico City)	Spanish	1 Mexican Peso (Mex $) = 100 centavos	100 294 000
Micronesia	Federated States of Micronesia	Palikir, on Ponape	English	1 US Dollar (US$) = 100 cents	131 500
Moldova	Republic of Moldova	Kishinev (Chisinau)	Moldovan	1 Leu (Mld) = 100 bani	4 461 000
Monaco	Principality of Monaco	Monaco	French	1 Euro (€) = 100 cents	32 100
Mongolia	State of Mongolia	Ulaanbaatar (Ulan Bator)	Khalka Mongolian	1 Tugrik (Tug) = 100 möngö	2 617 000
Morocco	Kingdom of Morocco	Rabat	Arabic	1 Dirham (DH) = 100 centimes	29 662 000
Mozambique	Republic of Mozambique	Maputo	Portuguese	1 Metical (Mt, MZM) = 100 centavos	19 124 000

Social Structure

English name	Official name (in English)	Capital (English name in parentheses)	Official language(s)	Currency	Population
Myanmar (Burma)	Union of Myanmar	Yangon (Rangoon)	Burmese	1 Kyat (K) = 100 pyas	48 081 000
Namibia	Republic of Namibia	Windhoek	English	1 Namibian Dollar (N$) = 100 cents	1 648 000
Nauru	Republic of Nauru	Yaren District	Nauruan, English	1 Australian Dollar ($A) = 100 cents	10 600
Nepal	Kingdom of Nepal	Kathmandu	Nepali	1 Nepalese Rupee (NRp, NRs) = 100 paise/pice	24 303 000
The Netherlands	Kingdom of the Netherlands	Amsterdam	Dutch	1 Euro (€) = 100 cents	15 808 000
New Zealand	New Zealand	Wellington	English, Maori	1 New Zealand Dollar (NZ$) = 100 cents	3 662 000
Nicaragua	Republic of Nicaragua	Managua	Spanish	1 Córdoba Oro (C$) = 100 centavos	4 717 000
Niger	Republic of Niger	Niamey	French	1 CFA Franc (CFAFr) = 100 centimes	9 962 000
Nigeria	Federal Republic of Nigeria	Abuja	English, Hausa	1 Naira (N, ₦) = 100 kobo	113 829 000
Norway	Kingdom of Norway	Oslo	Norwegian	1 Norwegian Krone (NKr) = 100 øre	4 439 000
Oman	Sultanate of Oman	Masqat (Muscat)	Arabic	1 Omani Rial (RO) = 1 000 baizas	2 447 000
Pakistan	Islamic Republic of Pakistan	Islāmābād (Islamabad)	Urdu	1 Pakistan Rupee (PRs, Rp) = 100 paisa	138 123 000
Palau	Republic of Palau	Koror	Palauan, English	1 US Dollar ($, US$) = 100 cents	18 500
Panama	Republic of Panama	Panamá (Panama City)	Spanish	1 Balboa (B, Ba) = 100 centésimos	2 779 000
Papua New Guinea	Papua New Guinea	Port Moresby	English, Tok Pïsin, Hiri Motu	1 Kina (K) = 100 toea	4 705 000
Paraguay	Republic of Paraguay	Asunción	Spanish	1 Guaraní (Gs) = 100 céntimos	5 434 000
Peru	Republic of Peru	Lima	Spanish, Quechua	1 New Sol (Pes) = 100 cénts	26 625 000
Philippines	Republic of the Philippines	Manila	Filipino, English	1 Philippine Peso (PHP) = 100 centavos	79 346 000
Poland	Republic of Poland	Warszawa (Warsaw)	Polish	1 Złoty (Zl) = 100 groszy	38 609 000
Portugal	Republic of Portugal	Lisboa (Lisbon)	Portuguese	1 Euro (€) = 100 cents	9 918 000
Qatar	State of Qatar	Ad-Dawhah (Doha)	Arabic	1 Qatar Riyal (QR) = 100 dirhams	723 500
Romania	Romania	Bucureşti (Bucharest)	Romanian	1 Leu (L, *plural* Lei) = 100 bani	22 334 000
Russia	The Russian Federation	Moskva (Moscow)	Russian	1 Rouble (R) = 100 kopeks	146 394 000
Rwanda	Republic of Rwanda	Kigali	Kinya-rwanda, French, English	1 Rwanda Franc (RF, RWFr) = 100 centimes	8 155 000
St Kitts and Nevis	Federation of St Kitts and Nevis	Basseterre	English	1 East Caribbean Dollar (EC$) = 100 cents	42 800
St Lucia	St Lucia	Castries	English	1 East Caribbean Dollar (EC$) = 100 cents	154 000
St Vincent and the Grenadines	St Vincent and the Grenadines	Kingstown	English	1 East Caribbean Dollar (EC$) = 100 cents	120 500
Samoa	Independent State of Samoa	Apia	Samoan, English	1 Tala (S$) = 100 sene	230 000
San Marino	Republic of San Marino	San Marino	Italian	1 San Marino Lira (SML) = 100 centesimi	25 100

English name	Official name (in English)	Capital (English name in parentheses)	Official language(s)	Currency	Population
São Tomé and Príncipe	Democratic Republic of São Tomé and Príncipe	São Tomé	Portuguese	1 Dobra (Db) = 100 centavos	154 900
Saudi Arabia	Kingdom of Saudi Arabia	Ar-Riyād (Riyadh)	Arabic	1 Saudi Arabian Riyal (SR, SRIs) = 20 qursh = 100 halala	21 505 000
Senegal	Republic of Senegal	Dakar	French, Wolof	1 CFA Franc (CFAFr) = 100 centimes	10 052 000
Serbia and Montenegro	Serbia and Montenegro	Beograd (Belgrade)	Serbo-Croat (Serbian)	1 New Dinar (D, Din) = 100 paras (Serbia), 1 Euro (€) = 100 cents (Montenegro)	11 206 900
Seychelles	Republic of Seychelles	Victoria	Creole English, French	1 Seychelles Rupee (SR) = 100 cents	79 200
Sierra Leone	Republic of Sierra Leone	Freetown	English, Mende, Temnel	1 Leone (Le) = 100 cents	5 297 000
Singapore	Republic of Singapore	Singapore City	Chinese, English, Malay, Tamil	1 Singapore Dollar (S$) = 1 Ringgit = 100 cents	3 532 000
Slovakia	Republic of Slovakia	Bratislava	Slovak	1 Koruna (Kčs) = 100 halierov	5 396 000
Slovenia	Slovenian Republic	Ljubljana	Slovene	1 Tolar (SIT) =100 stotin	1 971 000
Solomon Islands	Solomon Islands	Honiara	English	1 Solomon Islands Dollar (SI$) = 100 cents	455 400
Somalia	Somali Democratic Republic	Muqdisho (Mogadishu)	Arabic, Somali	1 Somali Shilling (SoSh) = 100 cents	7 141 000
South Africa	Republic of South Africa	Pretoria/ Cape Town	Afrikaans, English, IsiNdebele, IsiXosa, IsiZulu, Sepedi, Sosetho, SiSwati, Setswana, Tshivenda, Xitsonga	1 Rand (R) = 100 cents	43 426 000
Spain	Kingdom of Spain	Madrid	Spanish	1 Euro (€) = 100 cents	39 168 000
Sri Lanka	Democratic Socialist Republic of Sri Lanka	Colombo	Sinhala, Tamil	1 Sri Lankan Rupee (SLR, SLRs) = 100 cents	19 145 000
The Sudan	Democratic Republic of the Sudan	Al-Khartūm (Khartoum)	Arabic	1 Sudanese Dinar (SD) = 10 pounds	34 476 000
Suriname	Republic of Suriname	Paramaribo	Dutch	1 Suriname Guilder (SGld)/Florin (f) = 100 cents	431 200
Swaziland	Kingdom of Swaziland	Mbabane	Swazi, English	1 Lilangeni (*plural* Emalangeni) (Li, E) = 100 cents	985 300
Sweden	Kingdom of Sweden	Stockholm	Swedish	1 Swedish Krona (Skr) = 100 øre	8 911 000
Switzerland	Swiss Confederation	Bern (Berne)	French, German, Italian, Romansch	1 Swiss Franc (SFr, SwF) = 100 centimes = 100 rappen	7 275 000
Syria	Syrian Arab Republic	Dimashq (Damascus)	Arabic	1 Syrian pound (LS, S$) = 100 piastres	17 214 000
Taiwan	Republic of China	T'aipei (Taipei)	Mandarin Chinese	1 New Taiwan Dollar (NT$) = 100 cents	22 113 000
Tajikistan	Republic of Tajikistan	Dushanbe	Tajik, Uzbek, Russian	1 Somoni (S) = 100 dirams	6 103 000

Social Structure

English name	Official name (in English)	Capital (English name in parentheses)	Official language(s)	Currency	Population
Tanzania	United Republic of Tanzania	Dodoma	Swahili, English	1 Tanzanian Shilling (TSh) = 100 cents	31 271 000
Thailand	Kingdom of Thailand	Bangkok	Thai	1 Baht (B) = 100 satang	60 609 000
Togo	Republic of Togo	Lomé	French	1 CFA Franc (CFAFr) = 100 centimes	5 081 000
Tonga	Kingdom of Tonga	Nuku'alofa	English, Tongan	1 Pa'anga/Tongan Dollar (T$) = 100 seniti	109 100
Trinidad and Tobago	Republic of Trinidad and Tobago	Port of Spain	English	1 Trinidad and Tobago Dollar (TT$) = 100 cents	1 102 000
Tunisia	Republic of Tunisia	Tunis	Arabic, French	1 Tunisian Dinar (TD, D) = 1 000 millimes	9 514 000
Turkey	Republic of Turkey	Ankara	Turkish	1 Turkish Lira (TL) = 100 kurus	65 599 000
Turkmen-istan	Republic of Turkmenistan	Ashkhabad	Turkmen, Russian, Uzbek	1 Manat (TMM) = 100 tenesi	4 366 000
Tuvalu	Tuvalu	Fongafale (on Funafuti)	Tuvaluan, English	1 Australian Dollar (A$) = 100 cents	10 600
Uganda	Republic of Uganda	Kampala	English, Swahili	1 Uganda Shilling (USh) = 100 cents	22 805 000
Ukraine	Ukraine	Kiev	Ukrainian, Russian	1 Hryvnia = 100 kopiykas	49 811 000
United Arab Emirates	United Arab Emirates	Abū Zaby (Abu Dhabi)	Arabic, English	1 Dirham (DH) = 100 fils	2 344 000
United Kingdom	United Kingdom of Great Britain and Northern Ireland	London	English	1 Pound Sterling (£) = 100 pence	58 789 194 (2001)
United States of America	United States of America	Washington, DC	English	1 US Dollar ($, US$) = 100 cents	281 421 906 (2000)
Uruguay	Oriental Republic of Uruguay	Montevideo	Spanish	1 New Uruguayan Peso (NUr$, UrugN$) = 100 centésimos	3 309 000
Uzbekistan	Republic of Uzbekistan	Tashkent	Uzbek	1 Sum = 100 tiyin	24 102 000
Vanuatu	Republic of Vanuatu	Port-Vila	Bislama, English, French	1 Vatu (V, VT) = 100 centimes	189 000
Vatican City	Vatican City State	Vatican City	Italian	1 Euro (€) = 100 cents	870
Venezuela	Republic of Venezuela	Caracas	Spanish	1 Bolívar (Bs) = 100 centesimi	23 203 000
Vietnam	Socialist Republic of Vietnam	Ha-noi (Hanoi)	Vietnamese	1 Dông (D) = 10 hào = 100 xu	77 311 000
Western Samoa	▸ Samoa				
Yemen	Republic of Yemen	San'a	Arabic	1 Yemeni Riyal (YR, YRI) = 100 fils	16 942 000
Yugoslavia	▸ Serbia and Montenegro				
Zaire	▸ Congo, Democratic Republic of				
Zambia	Republic of Zambia	Lusaka	English	1 Kwacha (K) = 100 ngwee	9 664 000
Zimbabwe	Republic of Zimbabwe	Harare	English	1 Zimbabwe Dollar (Z$) = 100 cents	11 163 000

Counties of England

	Abbreviation[1]	Area sq km	sq mi	Population[2]	Persons per sq km
Metropolitan areas					
Greater Manchester	none	1 286	497	2 482 352	1 930
Merseyside	none	655	253	1 362 034	2 079
South Yorkshire	S Yorks	1 559	602	1 266 337	812
Tyne and Wear	none	540	208	1 075 979	1 992
West Midlands	W Midlands	899	347	2 555 596	2 843
West Yorkshire	W Yorks	2 034	785	2 079 217	1 022
Non-metropolitan counties					
Bedfordshire	Beds	1 192	460	381 571	320
Buckinghamshire	Bucks	1 568	605	479 028	306
Cambridgeshire	Cambs	3 056	1 180	552 655	181
Cheshire	Ches	2 081	803	673 777	324
Cornwall and Isles of Scilly	none	3 559	1 374	501 267	141
Cumbria	[Cumb]	6 824	2 635	487 607	71
Derbyshire	Derby	2 551	985	734 581	288
Devon	[Dev]	6 562	2 534	704 499	107
Dorset	[Dors]	2 542	981	390 986	154
Durham	Dur	2 232	862	493 470	221
East Sussex	[E Suss]	1 713	661	492 324	287
Essex	[Ess]	3 469	1 339	1 310 922	378
Gloucestershire	Glos	2 653	1 024	564 559	213
Hampshire	Hants	3 689	1 424	1 240 032	336
Hertfordshire	Herts	1 639	633	1 033 977	631
Kent	none	3 543	1 368	1 329 653	375
Lancashire	Lancs	2 897	1 119	1 134 976	392
Leicestershire	Leics	2 084	805	609 579	293
Lincolnshire	Lincs	5 921	2 286	646 646	109
London [3]	none	1 579	610	7 172 036	4 542
Norfolk	[Norf]	5 372	2 074	796 733	148
Northamptonshire	Northants	2 367	914	629 676	266
Northumberland	Northumb	5 026	1 941	307 186	61
North Yorkshire	N Yorks	8 038	3 103	569 660	70
Nottinghamshire	Notts	2 085	805	748 503	359
Oxfordshire	Oxon	2 606	1 006	605 492	232
Shropshire	[Shrops]	3 197	1 234	283 240	86
Somerset	Som	3 452	1 333	498 093	144
Staffordshire	Staffs	2 623	1 013	806 737	308
Suffolk	[Suff]	3 798	1 466	668 548	176
Surrey	[Sur]	1 677	647	1 059 015	631
Warwickshire	War	1 979	764	505 885	256
West Sussex	[W Suss]	1 988	768	753 612	379
Wiltshire	Wilts	3 246	1 253	432 973	133
Worcestershire	Worcs	1 761	680	542 107	308
Unitary authorities					
Bath and North East Somerset	none	351	136	169 045	482
Blackburn with Darwen	none	137	53	137 471	1 003
Blackpool	none	35	14	142 284	4 065
Bournemouth	none	46	18	163 441	3 553
Bracknell Forest	none	109	42	109 606	1 006
Brighton and Hove	none	82	32	247 820	3 022
Bristol, City of	none	110	42	380 615	3 460
Darlington	none	197	76	97 822	497
Derby	none	78	30	221 716	2 843
East Riding of Yorkshire	none	2 415	932	314 076	130
Halton	none	74	29	118 215	1 597
Hartlepool	none	94	36	88 629	943
Herefordshire, County of	[Herefs]	2 162	835	174 844	81
Isle of Wight	IOW	380	147	132 719	349
Kingston upon Hull, City of	none	71	27	243 595	3 431
Leicester	none	73	28	279 923	3 834
Luton	none	43	17	184 390	4 288
Medway	none	192	74	249 502	1 299
Middlesbrough	none	54	21	134 847	2 497
Milton Keynes	none	309	119	207 063	670
North East Lincolnshire	none	192	74	157 983	823
North Lincolnshire	none	833	322	152 839	183
North Somerset	N Som	373	144	188 556	506

Social Structure

	Abbreviation[1]	Area sq km	sq mi	Population[2]	Persons per sq km
Nottingham	none	75	29	266 995	3 560
Peterborough	none	344	133	156 060	454
Plymouth	none	80	31	240 718	3 009
Poole	none	65	25	138 299	2 127
Portsmouth	none	40	15	186 704	4 668
Reading	none	40	15	143 124	3 578
Redcar and Cleveland	none	245	95	139 141	568
Rutland	none	394	152	34 560	88
Slough	none	27	10	119 070	4 410
Southampton	none	50	19	217 478	4 350
South Gloucestershire	S Glos	497	192	245 644	494
Southend-on-Sea	none	42	16	160 256	3 816
Stockton-on-Tees	none	204	79	178 405	855
Stoke-on-Trent	none	93	36	240 643	2 586
Swindon	none	230	89	180 061	783
Telford and Wrekin	none	290	112	158 285	546
Thurrock	none	164	63	143 042	872
Torbay	none	63	24	129 702	2 059
Warrington	none	176	68	191 084	1 086
West Berkshire	W Berks	704	272	144 445	271
Windsor and Maidenhead	none	198	76	133 606	675
Wokingham	none	179	69	150 257	759
York	none	271	105	181 131	668
TOTAL		130 423	50 354	49 138 831	377

[1] Square brackets denote that the abbreviation is not generally regarded as established. Those without square brackets are generally accepted abbreviations.
[2] 2001 Census figures.
[3] London is divided into Inner London and Outer London, and comprises 32 boroughs and the City of London.
Note: Figures do not add exactly because of rounding. Total area includes inland, but not tidal, water.
Population data source: ONS, © Crown copyright 2002.

Council areas of Scotland

Unitary authority[1]	Admin centre	Area sq km	sq mi	Population[2]	Persons per sq km
Aberdeen City	Aberdeen	186	72	212 125	1 140
Aberdeenshire	Aberdeen	6 318	2 439	226 871	36
Angus	Forfar	2 181	842	108 400	50
Argyll and Bute	Lochgilphead	6 930	2 676	91 306	13
Clackmannanshire	Alloa	157	61	48 077	306
Dumfries and Galloway	Dumfries	6 439	2 486	147 765	23
Dundee City	Dundee	65	25	145 663	2 240
East Ayrshire	Kilmarnock	1 252	483	120 235	96
East Dunbartonshire	Kirkintilloch	172	66	108 243	629
East Lothian	Haddington	678	262	90 088	133
East Renfrewshire	Giffnock	173	67	89 311	516
Edinburgh, City of	Edinburgh	262	101	448 624	1 712
Eilean Siar[4]	Stornoway	3 134	1 210	26 502	8
Falkirk	Falkirk	299	115	145 191	486
Fife	Glenrothes	1 323	511	349 429	264
Glasgow City	Glasgow	175	68	577 869	3 302
Highland	Inverness	25 784	9 955	208 914	8
Inverclyde	Greenock	162	63	84 203	520
Midlothian	Dalkeith	356	137	80 941	227
Moray	Elgin	2 238	864	86 940	39
North Ayrshire	Irvine	884	341	135 817	154
North Lanarkshire	Motherwell	474	183	321 067	677
Orkney Islands	Kirkwall	992	383	19 245	19
Perth and Kinross	Perth	5 311	2 051	134 949	25
Renfrewshire	Paisley	261	101	172 867	662
Scottish Borders	Newton St Boswells	4 734	1 828	106 764	23
Shetland Islands	Lerwick	1 438	555	21 988	15
South Ayrshire	Ayr	1 202	464	112 097	93
South Lanarkshire	Hamilton	1 771	684	302 216	171
Stirling	Stirling	2 196	848	86 212	39
West Dunbartonshire	Dumbarton	162	63	93 378	576
West Lothian	Livingston	425	164	158 714	373
TOTAL[3]		78 133	30 168	5 062 011	65

[1] The counties of Scotland were replaced by 9 regional and 53 district councils in 1975; these in turn became 29 Unitary Authorities or Council Areas on 1 April 1996, the 3 island councils remaining as before.
[2] 2001 Census figures.
[3] Figures may not add exactly because of rounding. Total area includes inland, but not tidal, water.
[4] Formerly known as Western Isles.
Data obtained from the General Register Office for Scotland, © Crown copyright 2002.

Social Structure

Council areas of Wales

Unitary authority	Admin centre	Area sq km	sq mi	Population[1]	Persons per sq km
Anglesey, Isle of	Llangefni	719	277	66 828	93
Blaenau Gwent	Ebbw Vale	109	42	70 058	643
Bridgend	Bridgend	246	95	128 650	523
Caerphilly	Hengoed	279	108	169 521	608
Cardiff	Cardiff	139	54	305 340	2 197
Carmarthenshire	Carmarthen	2 398	926	173 635	72
Ceredigion	Aberaeron	1 797	694	75 384	42
Conwy	Conwy	1 130	436	109 597	97
Denbighshire	Ruthin	844	326	93 092	110
Flintshire	Mold	437	169	148 565	340
Gwynedd	Caernarfon	2 548	984	116 838	46
Merthyr Tydfil	Merthyr Tydfil	111	43	55 983	504
Monmouthshire	Cwmbran	851	328	84 879	98
Neath Port Talbot	Port Talbot	442	171	134 471	304
Newport	Newport	191	74	137 017	717
Pembrokeshire	Haverfordwest	1 590	614	112 901	71
Powys	Llandrindod Wells	5 204	2 009	126 344	24
Rhondda, Cynon, Taff	Clydach Vale	424	164	231 952	547
Swansea	Swansea	378	146	223 293	591
Torfaen	Pontypool	126	49	90 967	721
Vale of Glamorgan	Barry	337	130	119 293	354
Wrexham	Wrexham	499	193	128 477	257
TOTAL		20 799	8 032	2 903 085	140

[1] 2001 Census figures.
Population data source: ONS, © Crown copyright 2002.

UK islands

Name	Admin centre	Area sq km	sq mi	Population[1]	Persons per sq km
Isle of Man	Douglas	572	221	76 315	133
Jersey	St Helier	116	45	87 186	752
Guernsey	St Peter Port	63	24	59 807	949
Alderney (dependency of Guernsey)	St Anne's	8	3	2 294	287
Sark	—	4	2	620[2]	155

[1] 2001 Census figures.
[2] 2000 figure.
Data obtained from: States of Guernsey, Advisory and Finance Committee, © States of Guernsey 2002; Economic Affairs Division, Isle of Man Government Treasury, © Isle of Man Government 2002; Statistics Unit, States of Jersey Policy and Resources Department.

Districts of Northern Ireland

Name	Admin centre	Area sq km	sq mi	Population[1]	Persons per sq km
Antrim	Antrim	563	217	48 366	86
Ards	Newtownards	369	142	73 244	198
Armagh	Armagh	672	259	54 263	81
Ballymena	Ballymena	638	246	58 610	92
Ballymoney	Ballymoney	419	162	26 894	64
Banbridge	Banbridge	444	171	41 392	93
Belfast	—	140	54	277 391	1 981
Carrickfergus	Carrickfergus	87	34	37 659	432
Castlereagh	Belfast	85	33	66 488	782
Coleraine	Coleraine	485	187	56 315	116
Cookstown	Cookstown	623	240	32 581	52
Craigavon	Craigavon	382	147	80 671	211
Derry	—	382	147	105 066	275
Down	Downpatrick	646	249	63 828	99
Dungannon	Dungannon	779	301	47 735	61
Fermanagh	Enniskillen	1 876	715	57 527	31

Social Structure

Name	Admin centre	Area sq km	sq mi	Population[1]	Persons per sq km
Larne	Larne	338	131	30 832	91
Limavady	Limavady	587	227	32 422	55
Lisburn	Lisburn	444	171	108 694	245
Magherafelt	Magherafelt	573	221	39 780	69
Moyle	Ballycastle	495	191	15 933	32
Newry and Mourne	Newry	895	346	87 058	97
Newtownabbey	Newtownabbey	152	59	79 995	526
North Down	Bangor	73	28	76 323	1 045
Omagh	Omagh	1 129	436	47 952	42
Strabane	Strabane	870	336	38 248	44
TOTAL		14 146	5 450	1 685 267	119

[1] 2001 Census figures.
Population data source: Northern Ireland Statistics and Research Agency, © Crown Copyright 2002.

Europe — administrative divisions

■ **Albania**

Province	Area sq km	sq mi	Population (1993 est)
Berat	939	363	136 939
Bulquizë	469	181	43 363
Delvinë	348	134	29 926
Devoll	429	166	37 744
Dibrë	1 088	420	91 916
Durrës	433	167	162 846
Elbasan	1 372	530	215 240
Fier	785	303	208 646
Gjirokastër	1 752	439	60 547
Gramsh	695	268	42 087
Has	393	152	21 271
Kavajë	414	160	85 120
Kolonjë	805	311	25 089
Korçë	1 752	676	171 205
Krujë	333	129	59 997
Kucovë	84	32	40 035
Kukës	938	362	78 061
Kurbin	273	105	50 712
Lezhë	479	185	65 075
Librazhd	1 023	395	75 300
Lushnjë	712	275	136 865
Malesia e Madhe	555	214	43 924
Mallakastër	393	152	36 287
Mat	1 029	397	75 436
Mirditë	867	335	49 900
Peqin	109	42	29 831
Permet	930	359	36 979
Pogradec	725	280	72 203
Pukë	1 034	399	47 621
Sarandë	749	289	53 730
Shkodër	1 973	762	195 424
Skrapar	775	299	44 339
Tepelenë	817	315	42 365
Tiranë	1 238	478	384 010
Tropojë	1 043	403	44 761
Vlorë	1 609	621	171 131

■ **Austria**

State	Area sq km	sq mi	Population (1998 est)	Capital
Burgenland	3 966	1 531	277 600	Eisenstadt
Carinthia (Kärnten)	9 533	3 681	564 100	Klagenfurt
Lower Austria (Niederösterreich)	19 172	7 402	1 536 400	Sankt Pölten
Salzburg	7 154	2 762	514 000	Salzburg
Styria (Steiermark)	16 387	6 327	1 203 600	Graz
Tyrol (Tirol)	12 647	4 883	665 400	Innsbruck
Upper Austria (Oberösterreich)	11 980	4 626	1 375 300	Linz
Vienna (Wien)	415	160	1 599 500	—
Vorarlberg	2 601	1 004	346 900	Bregenz

■ **Belgium**

Province	Area sq km	sq mi	Population (1998 est)	Capital
Antwerp	2 867	1 107	1 637 857	Antwerp
E Flanders	2 982	1 151	1 357 576	Ghent
Flemish Brabant	2 106	813	1 007 882	Leuven
Hainaut	3 787	1 462	1 282 783	Mons
Liège	3 862	1 491	1 016 762	Liège
Limbourg	2 422	935	783 927	Hasselt
Luxembourg	4 441	1 715	243 790	Arlon
Namur	3 665	1 415	438 864	Namur
Walloon Brabant	1 091	421	344 508	Wavre
W Flanders	3 314	1 210	1 125 140	Bruges

■ **Bulgaria**

Province	Area sq km	sq mi	Population (1996 est)	Capital
Burgas	14 724	5 683	847 000	Burgas
Khaskovo	13 824	5 336	889 000	Khashkovo
Lovech	15 150	5 848	990 000	Lovech
Montana	10 606	4 098	616 000	Montana (formerly Mikhailovgrad)
Plovdiv	13 585	5 244	1 214 000	Plovdiv
Ruse	10 842	4 185	760 000	Ruse
Sofiya	19 021	7 342	967 000	Sofia (Sofiya)
Varna	11 928	4 604	901 000	Varna

■ **Cyprus**

District	Area sq km	sq mi	Population (1998 est)	Capital
Famagusta	1 979	764	34 300	Famagusta
Larnaca	1 126	435	110 900	Larnaca
Limassol	1 393	538	191 500	Limassol
Nicosia	2 717	1 049	269 200	Nicosia
Paphos	1 395	539	57 400	Paphos

■ **Czech Republic**

Region	Area sq km	sq mi	Population (1996 est)	Capital
C Bohemia (Středočeský)	11 013	4 251	1 106 738	Prague
E Bohemia (Východočeský)	11 240	4 339	1 235 641	Hradec Králové
N Bohemia (Severočeský)	7 799	3 010	1 178 208	Ústí nad Labem
N Moravia (Severomoravský)	11 067	4 273	1 972 336	Ostrava
Prague (city)	496	192	1 209 855	—
S Bohemia (Jihočeský)	11 345	4 380	700 831	České Budějovice
S Moravia (Jihomoravský)	15 028	5 802	2 057 239	Brno
W Bohemia (Západočeský)	10 875	4 199	860 469	Plzeň

■ **Denmark**

County	Area sq km	sq mi	Population (1998 est)	Capital
Århus (Aerhus)	4 561	1 761	631 586	Århus
Bornholm	588	227	44 786	Rønne
Copenhagen (København)	526	203	610 261	—
Frederiksborg	1 347	520	359 839	Hillerød
Fyn	3 486	1 346	471 873	Odense
N Jutland (Nordjylland)	6 173	2 383	493 114	Aalborg (Aelborg)
Ribe	3 131	1 209	223 818	Ribe
Ringkøbing	4 853	1 874	271 978	Ringkøbing
Roskilde	891	344	228 202	Roskilde
S Jutland (Sønderjylland)	3 938	1 520	253 836	Aebeurace
Storstrøm	3 398	1 312	258 295	Nykøbing Falster
Vejle	2 997	1 157	344 507	Vejle
Viborg	4 122	1 592	233 143	Viborg
W Zealand (Vestsjaelland)	2 984	1 152	258 295	Sorø

Social Structure

Social Structure

Finland

Province	Area sq km	sq mi	Population (1997 est)	Capital
Åland	1 527	590	25 392	Mariehamn
Eastern Finland	48 727	18 813	603 724	Mikkeli
Lapland	93 057	35 929	199 051	Rovaniemi
Oulu	56 868	21 957	452 942	Oulu
Southern Finland	30 229	11 671	2 037 147	Hämeenlinna
Western Finland	74 186	28 643	1 829 093	Turku

France

Region	Area sq km	sq mi	Population (1999 est)	Capital
Alsace	8 280	3 197	1 734 100	Strasbourg
Aquitaine	41 309	15 950	2 908 400	Bordeaux
Auvergne	26 013	10 044	1 308 900	Clermont-Ferrand
Brittany (Bretagne)	27 209	10 505	2 906 200	Rennes
Burgundy (Bourgogne)	31 582	12 194	1 610 100	Dijon
Centre	39 151	15 116	2 440 300	Orléans
Champagne-Ardenne	25 606	9 887	1 342 400	Reims
Corsica (Corse)	8 680	3 351	260 200	Ajaccio
Franche-Comté	16 202	6 256	1 117 100	Besançon
Ile de France	12 011	4 637	10 952 000	Paris
Languedoc-Roussillon	27 376	10 570	2 295 600	Montpellier
Limousin	16 942	6 541	710 900	Limoges
Lorraine	23 547	9 092	2 310 400	Nancy
Midi-Pyrénées	45 349	17 509	2 551 700	Toulouse
Nord-Pas-de-Calais	12 413	479	3 996 600	Lille
Normandy, Lower (Basse-Normandie)	17 589	6 791	1 422 200	Caen
Normandy, Upper (Haute-Normandie)	12 318	4 756	1 780 200	Rouen
Pays de la Loire	32 082	1 237	3 222 100	Nantes
Picardy (Picardie)	19 399	7 490	1 857 800	Amiens
Poitou-Charentes	25 809	9 965	1 640 100	Poitiers
Provence-Alpes-Côte d'Azur	31 400	12 124	4 506 200	Marseilles
Rhône-Alpes	43 698	16 872	5 645 400	Lyons

Germany

District	Area sq km	sq mi	Population (1995 est)	Capital
Baden-Württemberg	35 751	13 804	10 387 000	Stuttgart
Bavaria	70 546	27 239	12 056 000	Munich
Berlin	889	340	3 445 000	Berlin
Brandenburg	29 481	11 379	2 563 000	Potsdam
Bremen	404	156	676 000	Bremen
Hamburg	755	292	1 707 000	Hamburg
Hessen	21 114	8 152	6 031 000	Wiesbaden
Mecklenburg-Vorpommern	23 170	8 944	1 814 000	Schwerin
Niedersachsen	47 609	18 271	7 831 000	Hannover
Nordrhein-Westfalen	34 070	13 155	17 963 000	Düsseldorf
Rheinland-Pfalz	19 849	7 664	4 010 000	Mainz
Saarland	2 570	992	1 083 000	Saarbrücken
Sachsen	18 412	7 080	4 536 000	Dresden
Sachsen-Anhalt	20 445	7 894	2 714 000	Magdeburg
Schleswig-Holstein	15 739	6 077	2 750 000	Kiel
Thüringen	16 171	6 242	2 485 000	Erfurt

Greece

Region	Area sq km	sq mi	Population (1991 census)	Capital
Attica (Attikí)	3 808	1 470	3 523 407	Athens
C Greece (Stereá Ellás)	15 549	6 004	582 280	Lamia
C Macedonia (Kedrikí Makedhonía)	19 147	7 393	1 710 513	Thessaloniki
Crete (Kríti)	8 336	3 218	540 054	Heraklion
E Macedonia and Thrace (Anatolikí Makedhonía kaí Thráki)	14 157	5 466	570 496	Comotini
Epirus (Ípiros)	9 203	3 553	339 728	Ioannina
Ionian Is (Iónioi Nísoi)	2 307	891	193 734	Corfu
N Aegean (Vóreion Aiyaíon)	3 836	1 481	199 231	Mytilene
Peleponnese (Pelopónnisos)	15 490	5 981	607 428	Tripolis
S Aegean (Nótion Aiyaíon)	5 286	2 041	257 481	Hermoupolis
Thessaly (Thessalía)	14 037	5 420	734 846	Larissa
W Greece (Dhytikí Ellás)	11 350	4 382	707 687	Patras
W Macedonia (Dhytikí Makedhonía)	9 451	3 649	293 015	Kozani

■ **Hungary**

County	Area sq km	sq mi	Population (1995 est)	Capital
Baranya	4 487	1 732	415 000	Pécs
Bács-Kiskun	8 362	3 229	541 000	Kecskemét
Békés	5 632	2 175	405 000	Békéscsaba
Borsod-Abaúj-Zemplén	7 247	2 798	750 000	Miskolc
Budapest[1]	525	203	4 487 000	—
Csongrád	4 263	1 646	429 000	Szeged
Fejér	4 373	1 688	426 000	Székesfehérvár
Györ-Moson-Sopron	4 062	1 568	426 000	Györ
Hajdú-Bihar	6 211	2 398	550 000	Debrecen
Heves	3 637	1 404	330 000	Eger
Jász-Nagykún-Szolnok	5 607	2 165	423 000	Szolnok
Komárom-Esztergom	2 251	869	313 000	Tatabánya
Nógrád	2 544	982	224 000	Salgótarján
Pest	6 394	2 469	973 000	Budapest
Somogy	6 036	2 331	338 000	Kapsovár
Szabolcs-Szatmár-Bereg	5 938	2 293	573 000	Nyíregyháza
Tolna	3 704	1 430	250 000	Szekszárd
Vas	3 337	1 288	273 000	Szombathely
Vezprém	4 639	1 791	379 000	Veszprém
Zala	3 784	1 461	302 000	Zalaegerszeg

[1] Budapest has county status.

■ **Iceland**

Region	Area sq km	sq mi	Population (1991 est)	Capital
Austurland	21 991	8 491	11 189	Egilsstadir
Höfudborgarsvaedi	1 982[1]	765	172 257	Reykjavik
Nordurland eystra	22 368	8 636	27 293	Akureyri
Nordurland vestra	13 093	5 055	10 331	Saudárkrókur
Sudurland	25 214	9 735	16 247	Selfoss
Sudurnes	—[1]	—[1]	15 318	Keflavik
Vestfirdir	9 470	3 657	7 123	Ísafjördur
Vesturland	8 701	3 360	14 359	Borgarnes

[1] Höfudborgarsvaedi includes Sudurnes.

■ **Ireland**

County	Area sq km	sq mi	Population (1996 est)	Admin centre
Carlow	896	346	41 616	Carlow
Cavan	1 891	730	52 944	Cavan
Clare	3 188	1 231	94 006	Ennis
Cork	7 459	2 880	420 510	Cork
Donegal	4 830	1 865	129 994	Lifford
Dublin	922	356	1 058 264	Dublin
Galway	5 939	2 293	188 854	Galway
Kerry	4 701	1 815	126 130	Tralee
Kildare	1 694	654	134 992	Naas
Kilkenny	2 062	796	75 336	Kilkenny
Laoighis (Leix)	1 720	664	52 945	Portlaoise
Leitrim	1 526	589	25 057	Carrick
Limerick	2 686	1 037	165 042	Limerick
Longford	1 044	403	30 166	Longford
Louth	821	317	92 166	Dundalk
Mayo	5 398	2 084	111 524	Castlebar
Meath	2 339	903	109 732	Trim
Monaghan	1 290	498	51 313	Monaghan
Offaly	1 997	771	59 117	Tullamore
Roscommon	2 463	951	51 975	Roscommon
Sligo	1 795	693	55 821	Sligo
Tipperary	4 254	1 642	133 535	Clonmel
Waterford	1 839	710	94 680	Waterford
Westmeath	1 764	681	63 314	Mullingar
Wexford	2 352	908	104 371	Wexford
Wicklow	2 025	782	102 683	Wicklow

Social Structure

Social Structure

■ **Italy**

Region	Area sq km	sq mi	Population (1997 est)	Capital
Abruzzi	10 794	4 168	1 276 040	L'Aquila
Basilicata	9 992	3 858	610 330	Potenza
Calabria	15 080	5 823	2 070 992	Catanzaro
Campania	13 595	5 249	5 796 899	Naples (Napoli)
Emilia-Romagna	22 124	8 542	3 947 102	Bologna
Friuli-Venezia Giulia	7 844	3 029	1 184 654	Trieste
Lazio	17 227	6 649	5 242 709	Rome (Roma)
Liguria	5 418	2 092	1 641 835	Genoa (Genova)
Lombardy (Lombardia)	23 859	9 214	8 988 951	Milan (Milano)
Marche	9 693	3 743	1 450 879	Ancona
Molise	4 438	1 713	329 894	Campobasso
Piedmont (Piemonte)	25 399	9 807	4 291 441	Turin (Torino)
Puglia	19 357	7 473	4 090 068	Bari
Sardinia (Sardegna)	24 090	9 301	1 661 429	Cagliari
Sicily (Sicilia)	25 707	9 926	5 108 067	Palermo
Tuscany (Toscana)	22 992	8 877	3 527 303	Florence (Firenze)
Trentino-Alto Adige	13 607	5 252	924 281	Bozen (Bolzano)[1], Trent, Trient (Trento)[1]
Umbria	8 456	3 265	831 714	Perugia
Valle d'Aosta	3 262	1 259	119 610	Aosta
Veneto	18 365	7 090	4 469 156	Venice (Venezia)

[1] Joint regional capitals.

■ **Liechtenstein**

Commune	Area sq km	sq mi	Population (1998 est)
Balzers	19.6	7.6	4 118
Eschen	10.3	4.0	3 571
Gamprin	6.1	2.4	1 173
Mauren	7.5	2.9	3 114
Planken	5.3	2.0	347
Ruggell	7.4	2.9	1 693
Schaan	26.8	10.3	5 262
Schellenberg	3.5	1.4	955
Triesen	26.4	10.2	4 168
Triesenberg	29.8	11.5	2 508
Vaduz	17.3	6.7	5 106

■ **Luxembourg**

District/canton	Area sq km	sq mi	Population (1995 est)
Diekirch (district)	1 157	447	55 910
Clervaux	332	128	10 050
Diekirch	239	92	22 930
Redange	267	103	10 880
Vianden	54	21	2 710
Wiltz	265	102	9 340
Grevenmacher (district)	525	203	41 370
Echternach	186	72	11 300
Grevenmacher	211	82	17 610
Remich	128	49	12 460
Luxembourg (district)	904	349	277 620
Capellen	199	77	30 290
Esch	243	94	113 960
Luxembourg (city)	238	92	114 830
Mersch	224	86	18 540

■ **Malta**

Census region	Area sq km	sq mi	Population (1995 est)
Gozo and Comino	70	27	29 026
Inner Harbour	15	6	88 761
N Malta	78	30	44 852
Outer Harbour	32	12	112 882
SE Malta	53	20	50 650
W Malta	69	27	51 961

■ The Netherlands

Province	Area sq km	sq mi	Population (1998 est)	Capital
Drenthe	2 680	1 025	464 700	Assen
Flevoland	2 412	549	293 300	Lelijstad
Friesland	5 741	1 295	618 100	Leeuwarden
Gelderland	5 143	1 935	1 895 700	Arnhem
Groningen	2 967	906	558 000	Groningen
Limburg	2 196	838	1 137 900	Maastricht
N Brabant (Noord-Brabant)	5 016	1 910	2 319 300	's-Hertogenbosch
N Holland (Noord-Holland)	4 059	1 029	2 486 100	Haarlem
Overijssel	3 420	1 289	1 063 500	Zwolle
S Holland (Zuid-Holland)	3 446	1 123	3 359 000	The Hague
Utrecht	1 434	514	1 088 600	Utrecht
Zeeland	2 932	692	369 900	Middelburg

■ Norway

County	Area sq km	sq mi[1]	Population (1998 est)	Capital
Akershus	4 917	1 898	453 490	—
Aust-Agder	9 212	3 557	101 152	Arendal
Buskerud	14 927	5 763	232 967	Drammen
Finnmark	48 637	18 779	74 879	Vadsø
Hedmark	27 388	10 575	186 118	Hamar
Hordaland	15 634	6 036	428 823	Bergen
Møre og Romsdal	15 104	5 832	241 972	Molde
Nordland	38 327	14 798	239 280	Bodø
Nord-Trøndelag	22 463	8 673	126 785	Steinkjer
Oppland	25 260	9 753	182 162	Lillehammer
Oslo	454	175	499 693	Oslo
Østfold	4 183	1 615	243 585	Moss
Rogaland	9 141	3 529	364 341	Stavanger
Sogn og Fjordane	18 634	7 195	107 790	Leikanger
Sør-Trøndelag	18 831	7 271	259 177	Trondheim
Telemark	15 315	5 913	163 857	Skien
Troms	25 954	10 021	150 288	Tromsø
Vest-Agder	7 281	2 811	152 553	Kristiansand
Vestfold	2 216	856	208 687	Tønsberg

[1] Excludes Svalbard and Jay Mayen (63 080 sq km/24 360 sq mi).

■ Poland

Voivodships (Provinces)	Area sq km	sq mi	Population (1999 est)
Dolnoslaskie	19 948	7 700	2 985 000
Kujawsko-Pomorskie	17 970	6 936	2 098 000
Łódzkie	18 219	7 033	2 673 000
Lubelskie	25 115	9 694	2 242 000
Lubuskie	13 984	5 398	1 020 000
Malopolskie	15 144	5 846	3 207 000
Mazowieckie	35 597	13 740	5 065 000
Opolskie	9 412	3 633	1 091 000
Podkarpackie	17 926	6 919	2 117 000
Pomorskie	18 293	7 061	2 179 000
Slaskie	12 294	4 745	4 894 000
Swietokrzyskie	11 672	4 505	1 328 000
Warminsko-Mazurskie	24 203	9 342	1 460 000
Wielkopolskie	29 826	11 513	3 346 000
Zachodniopomorskie	22 902	8 840	1 730 000

■ Portugal

Region	Area sq km	sq mi	Population (1999 est)	Capital
Aveiro	2 808	1 084	689 100	Aveiro
Beja	10 225	3 948	153 150	Beja
Braga	2 695	1 041	796 160	Braga
Bragança	6 597	2 546	147 720	Bragança
Castelo Branco	6 616	2 553	199 890	Castelo Branco
Coimbra	3 971	1 532	420 410	Coimbra
Évora	7 393	2 854	166 330	Évora
Faro	4 986	1 924	349 740	Faro
Guarda	5 540	2 138	176 220	Guarda

Social Structure

291

Social Structure

Region	Area		Population	Capital
	sq km	sq mi	(1999 est)	
Leiria	3508	1354	435340	Leiria
Lisboa	2758	1064	2056100	Lisboa (Lisbon)
Portalegre	6065	2342	123070	Portalegre
Porto	2341	904	1714690	Porto
Santarém	6707	2588	437850	Santarém
Setúbal	5064	1955	744700	Setúbal
Viana do Castelo	2210	853	250690	Viano do Costelo
Vila Real	4305	1661	229550	Vila Real
Viseu	5007	1933	399320	Viseu
Autonomous regions				
The Azores	2247	868	246030	Ponta Delgada
Madeira	794	306	261530	Funchal

■ **Romania**

County	Area		Population	Capital
	sq km	sq mi	(1997 est)	
Alba	6242	2409	402097	Alba Iulia
Arad	7754	2993	476988	Arad
Argeş	6826	2634	676005	Piteşti
Bacău	6621	2555	746131	Bacău
Bihor	7544	2911	625596	Oradea
Bistriţa-Năsăud	5355	2067	326539	Bistriţa
Botoşani	4986	1924	460115	Botoşani
Brăila	4766	1840	388891	Brăila
Braşov	5363	2070	636434	Braşov
Buzău	6103	2355	508492	Buzău
Caraş-Severin	8520	3288	332884	Reşiţa
Călăraşi	5088	1964	360773	Călăraşi
Cluj	6674	2576	724355	Cluj-Napoca
Constanţa	7071	2729	746686	Constanţa
Covasna	3705	1431	231491	Sfîntu Gheorghe
Dîmboviţa	4054	1565	553986	Tîrgovişte
Dolj	7413	2862	749311	Craiova
Galaţi	4466	1721	641647	Galaţi
Giurgiu	3526	1361	298795	Giurgiu
Gorj	5602	2163	397714	Tîrgu Jiu
Harghita	6639	2562	343330	Miercurea-Ciuc
Hunedoara	7063	2726	543109	Deva
Ialomiţa	4453	1720	304740	Slobozia
Iaşi	5476	2113	823735	Iaşi
Maramureş	6304	2433	533672	Baia Mare
Mehedinţi	4933	1904	325344	Drobeta-Turnu-Severin
Mureş	6714	2592	602626	Tîrgu Mureş
Neamţ	5896	2276	583141	Piatra Neamţ
Olt	5498	2129	513961	Slatina
Prahova	4716	1819	864159	Ploieşti
Sălaj	3864	1492	259305	Zalău
Satu Mare	4418	1705	392054	Satu Mare
Sibiu	5432	2097	444701	Sibiu
Suceava	8555	3303	711568	Suceava
Teleorman	5790	2235	466010	Alexandria
Timiş	8697	3358	692870	Timişoara
Tulcea	8499	3280	265778	Tulcea
Vaslui	5318	2053	433356	Vaslui
Vâlcea	5765	2225	460840	Râmnicu Vâlcea
Vrancea	4857	1874	391762	Focşani
Municipality				
Bucharest	1821	703	2027512	Bucharest

■ **Slovakia**

Region	Area		Population	Capital
	sq km	sq mi	(1996 est)	
Bratislava (city)	367	142	450775	—
C Slovakia (Strědoslovenský)	17986	6944	1636003	Banská Bystrica
E Slovakia (Východoslovenský)	16191	6251	1544077	Košice
W Slovakia (Západoslovenský)	14492	5595	1725352	Bratislava

■ **Slovenia**
Has 148 municipalities, 11 of which are urban.

■ **Spain**

Province	Area sq km	sq mi	Population (1998 est)	Capital
Álava	3 047	1 176	284 595	Vitoria Gasteiz
Albacete	14 862	5 737	358 597	Albacete
Alicante	5 863	2 263	1 388 933	Alicante
Almería	8 774	3 387	505 448	Almería
Asturias	10 565	4 078	1 081 834	Oviedo
Ávila	8 048	3 106	167 132	Ávila
Badajoz	21 657	8 360	663 803	Badajoz
Beleares (Balearic Is)	5 014	1 935	796 483	Palma
Barcelona	7 733	2 985	4 666 271	Barcelona
Burgos	14 309	5 523	346 355	Burgos
Cáceres	19 945	7 699	405 616	Cáceres
Cádiz	7 385	2 850	1 107 484	Cádiz
Cantabria (Santander)	5 289	2 041	527 137	Santander
Castellón	6 679	2 579	461 712	Castellón
Ciudad Real	19 749	7 519	479 474	Ciudad Real
Córdoba	13 718	5 295	767 175	Córdoba
La Coruña	7 876	3 040	1 106 325	La Coruña
Cuenca	17 061	6 585	199 086	Cuenca
Girona (Gerona)	5 886	2 272	543 191	Girona
Granada	12 531	4 387	801 177	Granada
Guadalajara	12 190	4 705	159 331	Guadalajara
Guipúzcoa	1 997	771	676 439	San Sebastián
Huelva	10 885	4 202	453 958	Huelva
Huesca	15 613	6 027	204 956	Huesca
Jaén	13 498	5 210	645 792	Jáen
León	15 468	5 971	506 365	León
Lérida	12 028	4 642	357 903	Lérida
Lugo	9 803	3 784	367 751	Lugo
Madrid	7 995	3 086	5 091 336	Madrid
Málaga	7 276	2 808	1 240 580	Málaga
Murcia	11 317	4 368	1 115 068	Murcia
Navarra	10 421	4 022	530 819	Pamplona
Orense	7 278	2 809	344 170	Orense
Palencia	8 035	3 101	179 623	Palencia
Las Palmas	4 072	1 572	849 863	Las Palmas
Pontevedra	4 477	1 728	906 298	Vigo
La Rioja	5 034	1 943	263 644	Logrono
Salamanca	12 336	4 761	349 550	Salamanca
Santa Cruz de Tenerife	3 170	1 224	780 152	Santa Cruz de Tenerife
Segovia	6 949	2 682	146 755	Segovia
Sevilla	14 001	5 404	1 714 845	Sevilla
Soria	10 287	3 971	91 593	Soria
Tarragona	6 283	2 425	580 245	Tarragona
Teruel	14 785	5 707	136 840	Teruel
Toledo	15 368	5 932	519 664	Toledo
Valencia	10 763	4 154	2 172 796	Valencia
Valladolid	8 202	3 166	492 029	Valladolid
Vizcaya	2 217	856	1 137 594	Bilbao
Zamora	10 559	4 076	205 021	Zamora
Zaragoza	17 252	6 659	841 438	Zaragoza

■ **Sweden**

County	Area sq km	sq mi	Population (1998 est)	Capital
Blekinge	2 941	1 136	151 414	Karlskrona
Dalarna	28 194	10 886	282 898	Falun
Gävleborg	18 191	7 024	282 226	Gävle
Gotland	3 140	1 212	57 643	Visby
Halland	5 454	2 106	272 539	Halmstad
Jämtland	49 443	19 090	131 766	Östersund
Jönköping	9 944	3 839	328 059	Jönköping
Kalmar	11 170	4 313	238 104	Kalmar
Kronoberg	8 458	3 266	178 078	Växjö
Norrbotten	98 913	39 191	260 473	Lulece
Örebro	8 519	3 289	274 584	Örebro
Östergötland	10 562	4 078	412 411	Linköping
Skåne	10 025	3 870	1 120 426	Malmö
Södermanland	6 060	2 340	256 269	Nyköping
Stockholm	6 488	2 505	1 783 440	Stockholm

Social Structure

County	Area sq km	sq mi	Population (1998 est)	Capital
Uppsala	6 989	2 698	291 413	Uppsala
Värmland	17 584	6 789	278 313	Karlstad
Västerbotten	55 401	21 390	257 803	Umeå
Västernorrland	21 678	8 370	251 884	Härnösand
Västmanland	6 302	2 433	257 661	Västeraces
Västra Götalands	23 942	9 244	1 486 918	Gothenburg

■ **Switzerland**

Canton	Area sq km	sq mi	Population (1998 est)	Capital
Aargau	1 395	540	536 462	Aarau
Appenzell Ausser-Rhoden[1]	243	94	53 816	Herisau
Appenzell Inner-Rhoden[1]	172	66	14 873	Appenzell
Basle (Basel-Landschaft)[1]	428	165	256 761	Liestal
Basle (Basel-Stadt)[1]	37	14	190 505	Basel
Berne	5 932	2 290	941 144	Berne
Fribourg	1 591	614	232 086	Fribourg
Geneva (Genève)	245	94	398 910	Geneva
Glarus	684	264	38 698	Glarus
Graubünden (Fr: Grisons)	7 106	2 744	186 118	Chur (Coire)
Jura	837	323	68 995	Delémont
Lucerne (Luzern)	1 429	552	343 254	Lucerne
Neuenberg (Neuchâtel)	716	276	165 594	Neuchâtel
Nidwalden[1]	241	93	37 320	Stans
Obwalden[1]	480	186	31 989	Sarnen
St Gall (Sankt Gallen)	1 950	752	444 891	St Gall
Schaffhausen	298	115	73 725	Schaffhausen
Schwyz	851	328	126 479	Schwyz
Solothurn	791	305	243 450	Solothurn
Thurgau	863	333	226 479	Frauenfeld
Ticino	2 738	1 056	306 179	Bellinzona
Uri	1 057	408	35 612	Altdorf
Valais	5 213	2 015	274 458	Sion
Vaud	2 822	1 090	611 613	Lausanne
Zug	207	80	96 517	Zug
Zürich	1 661	641	1 187 609	Zürich

[1] Demicanton — functions as a full canton.

■ **Turkey**

Geographic region	Area sq km	sq mi	Population (1990 est)
Black Sea Coast (Karadeniz Kiyisi)	81 295	31 388	6 900 805
C Anatolia (Iç Anadolu)	236 347	91 254	13 154 473
E Anatolia (Doğu Anadolu)	176 311	68 074	6 909 594
Marmara and Aegean coasts (Marmara ve Ege kiyilari)	85 560	33 035	11 784 535
Mediterranean Coast (Akdeniz kiyisi)	59 395	22 933	5 497 536
SE Anatolia (Güneydoğu)	39 749	15 347	2 793 894
Thrace (Trakya)	23 764	9 175	6 021 591
W Anatolia (Bati Anadolu)	77 031	29 742	3 906 681

United Nations membership

Grouped according to year of entry.

1945 Argentina, Australia, Belgium, Byelorussian SSR (Belarus, 1991), Bolivia, Brazil, Canada, Chile, China (Taiwan to 1971), Colombia, Costa Rica, Cuba, Czechoslavakia (to 1993), Denmark, Dominican Republic, Ecuador, Egypt, El Salvador, Ethiopia, France, Greece, Guatemala, Haiti, Honduras, India, Iran, Iraq, Lebanon, Liberia, Luxembourg, Mexico, Netherlands, New Zealand, Nicaragua, Norway, Panama, Paraguay, Peru, Philippines, Poland, Saudi Arabia, South Africa, Syria, Turkey, Ukrainian SSR (Ukraine, 1991), USSR (Russia, 1991), UK, USA, Uruguay, Venezuela, Yugoslavia (to 1992)
1946 Afghanistan, Iceland, Sweden, Thailand
1947 Pakistan, Yemen (N, to 1990)
1948 Burma (Myanmar, 1989)
1949 Israel
1950 Indonesia
1955 Albania, Austria, Bulgaria, Kampuchea (Cambodia, 1989), Ceylon (Sri Lanka, 1970), Finland, Hungary, Ireland, Italy, Jordan, Laos, Libya, Nepal, Portugal, Romania, Spain
1956 Japan, Morocco, The Sudan, Tunisia
1957 Ghana, Malaya (Malaysia, 1963)
1958 Guinea
1960 Cameroon, Central African Republic, Chad, Congo, Côte d'Ivoire (Ivory Coast), Cyprus, Dahomey (Benin, 1975), Gabon, Madagascar, Mali, Niger, Nigeria, Senegal, Somalia, Togo, Upper Volta (Burkina Faso, 1984), Zaïre (Democratic Republic of Congo, 1997)
1961 Mauritania, Mongolia, Sierra Leone, Tanganyika (within Tanzania, 1964)
1962 Algeria, Burundi, Jamaica, Rwanda, Trinidad and Tobago, Uganda
1963 Kenya, Kuwait, Zanzibar (within Tanzania, 1964)
1964 Malawi, Malta, Zambia, Tanzania

1965 The Gambia, Maldives, Singapore
1966 Barbados, Botswana, Guyana, Lesotho, Yemen (S, to 1990)
1968 Equatorial Guinea, Mauritius, Swaziland
1970 Fiji
1971 Bahrain, Bhutan, China (People's Republic), Oman, Qatar, United Arab Emirates
1973 The Bahamas, German Democratic Republic (within GFR 1990), German Federal Republic
1974 Bangladesh, Grenada, Guinea-Bissau
1975 Cape Verde, Comoros, Mozambique, Papua New Guinea, São Tomé and Príncipe, Suriname
1976 Angola, Seychelles, Western Samoa (Samoa, 1997)
1977 Djibouti, Vietnam
1978 Dominica, Solomon Islands
1979 St Lucia
1980 St Vincent and the Grenadines, Zimbabwe
1981 Antigua and Barbuda, Belize, Vanuatu
1983 St Kitts and Nevis
1984 Brunei
1990 Liechtenstein, Namibia, Yemen (formerly N Yemen and S Yemen)
1991 Estonia, Federated States of Micronesia, Latvia, Lithuania, Marshall Islands, N Korea, S Korea
1992 Armenia, Azerbaijan, Bosnia-Herzegovina, Croatia, Georgia, Kazakhstan, Kyrgyzstan, Moldova, San Marino, Slovenia, Tajikistan, Turkmenistan, Uzbekistan
1993 Andorra, Czech Republic, Eritrea, Former Yugoslav Republic of Macedonia, Monaco, Slovakia
1994 Palau
1999 Kiribati, Nauru, Tonga
2000 Tuvalu, Yugoslavia
2002 Switzerland, East Timor

United Nations — specialized agencies

Abbreviated form	Full title	Area of concern
ILO	International Labour Organization	Social justice
FAO	Food and Agriculture Organization	Improvement of the production and distribution of agricultural products
UNESCO	United Nations Educational, Scientific and Cultural Organization	Stimulation of popular education and the spread of culture
ICAO	International Civil Aviation Organization	Encouragement of safety measures in international flight
IBRD	International Bank for Reconstruction and Development	Aid of development through investment
IMF	International Monetary Fund	Promotion of international monetary co-operation
UPU	Universal Postal Union	Uniting members within a single postal territory
WHO	World Health Organization	Promotion of the highest standards of health for all people
ITU	International Telecommunication Union	Allocation of frequencies and regulation of procedures
WMO	World Meteorological Organization	Standardization and utilization of meteorological observations
IFC	International Finance Corporation	Promotion of the international flow of private capital
IMO	International Maritime Organization	Co-ordination of safety at sea
IDA	International Development Association	Credit on special terms to provide assistance for less developed countries
WIPO	World Intellectual Property Organization	Protection of copyright, designs, inventions, etc
IFAD	International Fund for Agricultural Development	Increase of food production in developing countries by the generation of grants or loans

Social Structure

MIGA	Multilateral Investment Guarantee Agency	Promotion of foreign investment in economies of developing countries
ICSID	International Centre for Settlement of Investment Disputes	Settlement of investment disputes between governments and foreign investors
UNIDO	United Nations Industrial Development Organization	Assists developing countries in improving their economies and growth

Commonwealth membership

The Commonwealth is an informal association of sovereign states.
Member countries are grouped by year of entry.

1931	Australia, Canada, New Zealand, United Kingdom, South Africa (left 1961, rejoined 1994)
1947	India, Pakistan (left 1972, rejoined 1989; suspended 1999)
1948	Sri Lanka
1957	Ghana, Malaysia
1960	Nigeria (suspended 1995, readmitted 1999)
1961	Cyprus, Sierra Leone, Tanzania
1962	Jamaica, Trinidad and Tobago, Uganda
1963	Kenya
1964	Malawi, Malta, Zambia
1965	The Gambia, Singapore
1966	Barbados, Botswana, Guyana, Lesotho
1968	Mauritius, Nauru, Swaziland
1970	Tonga, Samoa (formerly Western Samoa), Fiji (left 1987, rejoined 1997; suspended 2000, readmitted 2001)
1972	Bangladesh
1973	The Bahamas
1974	Grenada
1975	Papua New Guinea
1976	Seychelles
1978	Dominica, Solomon Islands, Tuvalu
1979	Kiribati, St Lucia, St Vincent and the Grenadines
1980	Vanuatu, Zimbabwe (suspended 2002)
1981	Antigua and Barbuda, Belize
1982	Maldives
1983	St Kitts and Nevis
1984	Brunei
1990	Namibia
1995	Cameroon, Mozambique

The Republic of Ireland resigned from the Commonwealth in 1949.

European Union membership

Member countries are listed by year of entry.

1958	Belgium	1973	United Kingdom
1958	France	1981	Greece
1958	Germany	1986	Portugal
1958	Italy	1986	Spain
1958	Luxembourg	1995	Austria
1958	The Netherlands	1995	Finland
1973	Denmark	1995	Sweden
1973	Republic of Ireland		

Candidate countries: Bulgaria, Cyprus, Czech Republic, Estonia, Hungary, Latvia, Lithuania, Malta, Poland, Romania, Slovakia, Slovenia, Turkey.

European Community organizations

Abbreviation	Full title	Area of concern
—	European Court of Justice	Adjudication of disputes arising from application of the Treaties
CAP	Common Agricultural Policy	Aiming to ensure reasonable standards of living for farmers; its policies have led to surpluses in the past
EMS	European Monetary System	Assistance of trading relations between member countries; all members of the community are in the EMS except Denmark, Sweden and the UK
EIB	European Investment Bank	Financing of capital investment projects to assist development of the Community
ECSC	European Coal and Steel Community	Regulation of prices and trade in these commodities
EURATOM	European Atomic Energy Community	Creation of technical and industrial conditions to produce nuclear energy on a large scale

European Parliament political groupings

Seats held as at 31 March 2003.

Country	PES	EPP-ED	UEN	ELDR	EUL/ NGL	Green/ EFA	EDD	IND	Total
Austria	7	7				2		5	21
Belgium	5	5		5		7		3	25
Denmark	2	1	1	6	3		3		16
Finland	3	5		5	1	2			16
France	18	20	4	1	15	9	9	11	87
Germany	35	53			7	4			99
Greece	9	9			7				25
Ireland	1	5	6	1		2			15
Italy	16	35	10	8	6	2		10	87
Luxembourg	2	2		1		1			6
Netherlands	6	9		8	1	4	3		31
Portugal	12	9	2		2				25
Spain	24	28		2	4	4		1	63
Sweden	6	7		4	3	2			22
United Kingdom	29	37		11		6	3	1	87
Total	175	232	23	52	49	45	18	31	625*

PES = Party of European Socialists (including the British Labour Party, the French Socialist Party and the German Social Democratic Party)

EPP-ED = European People's Party (Christian Democrats) and European Democrats (including the British Conservative Party, the Ulster Unionist Party and the Swedish Moderate Party)

UEN = Union for Europe of the Nations (including the Irish Fianna Fáil and the Italian Alleanza Nazionale)

ELDR = European Liberal Democrat and Reform Party (including the British Liberal Democrats and the Luxembourg Democratic Party)

EUL/NGL = Confederal Group of the European United Left/Nordic Green Left (including the French Communist Party and the Dutch Socialist Party)

Greens/EFA = European Federation of Green Parties/European Free Alliance (including the Green parties, Scottish Nationalist Party and Plaid Cymru)

EDD = Group for a Europe of Democracies and Diversities (including the UK Independence Party)

IND = Independents

* There are 626 members in total; one seat vacant as at 31 March 2003.

Political definitions

Politics is the science of government: it studies and regulates the creation of legislation, as well as defining the role of the individual within society. Below are 50 concise definitions of the most widely used political terms.

Act of Parliament Bill passed through both houses of the UK Parliament.

Anarchism Rejection of the state and other forms of authority.

Authoritarianism Government not dependent on the consent of society.

Bill, parliamentary Draft of proposed new law for consideration by legislature.

Cabinet Group of senior ministers usually heading government departments.

Civil disobedience Strategy to achieve political goals by refusing to co-operate with a government or its agents.

Civil rights Rights guaranteed by a state to its citizens.

Coalition Arrangement between countries or political parties to pursue a common goal.

Communism Political ideology featuring common ownership of property, associated with the theories of Karl Marx (1818–83), published in his *Communist Manifesto* (1848).

Conservatism Political beliefs stressing adherence to established authority.

Constitution Principles that determine the way a country may be governed, usually in the form of a written document.

Democracy Rule by the people, usually with decision-making in the hands of popularly elected representatives.

Devolution Delegation of authority from central government to a subordinate elected institution.

Dictatorship Rule by a single person, or several people (eg military dictatorship), unelected and authoritarian in character.

Dissidents People who oppose a regime and may suffer discrimination.

Fascism Nationalistic and authoritarian movement associated with the 1930s.

Federalism Territorial political organization aiming to maintain national unity while permitting regional diversity.

Green Movement opposing ecological and environmental effects caused by technological and economic policies.

House of Commons Lower (and effectively ruling) chamber of UK Parliament.

House of Lords Non-elected house of UK Parliament, containing hereditary and life peers.

House of Representatives One of the two chambers of the US legislature.

Human rights Fundamental rights beyond those prescribed by law.

Social Structure

Social Structure

Ideology Set of beliefs and attitudes that support particular interests.

Imperialism Extension of state power through acquisition of other territories.

Left wing Political position occupied by those with radical and reforming tendencies towards social and political order.

Legislature Institution with power to pass laws.

Liberalism Doctrine that urges freedom of the individual, religion, trade and economics (*laissez faire*).

Nationalism Doctrine that views the nation as the principal unit of political organization.

Nationalization Taking an industry into state ownership.

Ombudsman Official who investigates complaints regarding government actions.

Pluralism Existence within a society of a variety of groups, limiting the power of any one group.

Pressure group Organization formed to support a particular political interest.

Privatization Transfer to private ownership of organizations owned by the state.

Privy Council Body advising the British monarch, appointed by the Crown.

Proletariat In socialist philosophy, term denoting working class.

Proportional representation Voting system ensuring that the representation of voters is in proportion to their numbers.

Racism Ideology alleging inferiority of racial or ethnic groups in terms of their biological or physical characteristics.

Radicalism Ideology arguing for substantial political and social change.

Referendum Device whereby the electorate can vote on a measure put before it by a government.

Right wing Political position of support for established institutions and opposition to socialist developments.

Sanction Penalty imposed by one state against another, such as denial of trade.

Sectarianism Excessive loyalty or attachment to a particular sect or party.

Senate One of the two chambers of a national or state legislature.

Separatism Demand for separation from territorial and political sovereignty of the state to which the separatists belong.

Socialism Doctrine favouring state intervention to create an egalitarian society.

Terrorism Violent behaviour to promote a particular political cause, often aimed at overthrow of the established order.

Totalitarianism System in which political opposition is suppressed and decision-making is highly centralized.

Trade union Association of people, usually in the same trade, joining together to improve pay and working conditions.

Tribunal Official body appointed to inquire into and give judgement on some matter of dispute.

Welfare state System whereby state is responsible for protecting and promoting citizens' welfare in areas such as health, employment, pensions and education.

Legislative systems of government

A bicameral political system is one in which there are two chambers in the legislature, whereas a unicameral system has only one chamber.

■ Bicameral

Africa
Algeria, Botswana, Burkina Faso, Comoros, Ethiopia, Gabon, Lesotho, Liberia, Madagascar, Morocco, Namibia, Nigeria, South Africa, Swaziland

Asia
India, Japan, Kyrgyzstan, Malaysia, Nepal, Pakistan, Philippines, Tajikistan, Thailand

Australasia
Australia, Fiji, Palau

Europe
Austria, Belarus, Belgium, Bosnia-Herzegovina, Czech Republic, France, Germany, Ireland, Italy, Kazakhstan, Netherlands, Poland, Romania, Russian Federation, Spain, Switzerland, Serbia and Montenegro, UK

Middle East
Egypt, Jordan, Oman

North America
Antigua and Barbuda, The Bahamas, Barbados, Belize, Canada, Dominican Republic, Grenada, Haiti, Jamaica, Mexico, Puerto Rico, St Lucia, Trinidad and Tobago, USA

South America
Argentina, Bolivia, Brazil, Chile, Colombia, Paraguay, Uruguay, Venezuela

■ Unicameral

Africa
Angola, Benin, Burundi, Cameroon, Cape Verde, Central African Republic, Chad, Congo, Côte d'Ivoire, Democratic Republic of Congo, Djibouti, Equatorial Guinea, Eritea, The Gambia, Ghana, Guinea, Guinea-Bissau, Kenya, Libya, Malawi, Mali, Mauritius, Mozambique, Niger, Rwanda, São Tomé and Príncipe, Senegal, Seychelles, Sierra Leone, Somalia, The Sudan, Tanzania, Togo, Tunisia, Uganda, Zambia, Zimbabwe

Asia
Bangladesh, Bhutan, Brunei, Cambodia, China, East Timor, Indonesia, Laos, Maldives, Mongolia, Myanmar (Burma), North Korea, Papua New Guinea, Singapore, South Korea, Sri Lanka, Turkmenistan, Uzbekistan, Vietnam

Australasia
Federated States of Micronesia, Kiribati, Marshall Islands, Nauru, New Zealand, Papua New Guinea, Samoa, Solomon Islands, Tonga, Tuvalu, Vanuatu

Europe
Albania, Andorra, Bulgaria, Cyprus, Denmark, Estonia, Finland, Georgia, Gibraltar, Greece, Greenland, Hungary, Iceland, Latvia, Liechtenstein, Lithuania, Luxembourg, Macedonia, Malta, Moldova, Monaco, Norway, Portugal, San Marino, Slovakia, Slovenia, Sweden, Ukraine

Middle East
Armenia, Azerbaijan, Bahrain, Iran, Iraq, Israel, Kuwait, Lebanon, Qatar, Saudi Arabia, Syria, Turkey, United Arab Emirates, Yemen

North America
Costa Rica, Cuba, Dominica, El Salvador, Guatemala, Honduras, Nicaragua, Panama, St Kitts and Nevis, St Vincent and the Grenadines

South America
Ecuador, Guyana, Peru, Suriname

Passage of a public bill to law in the UK

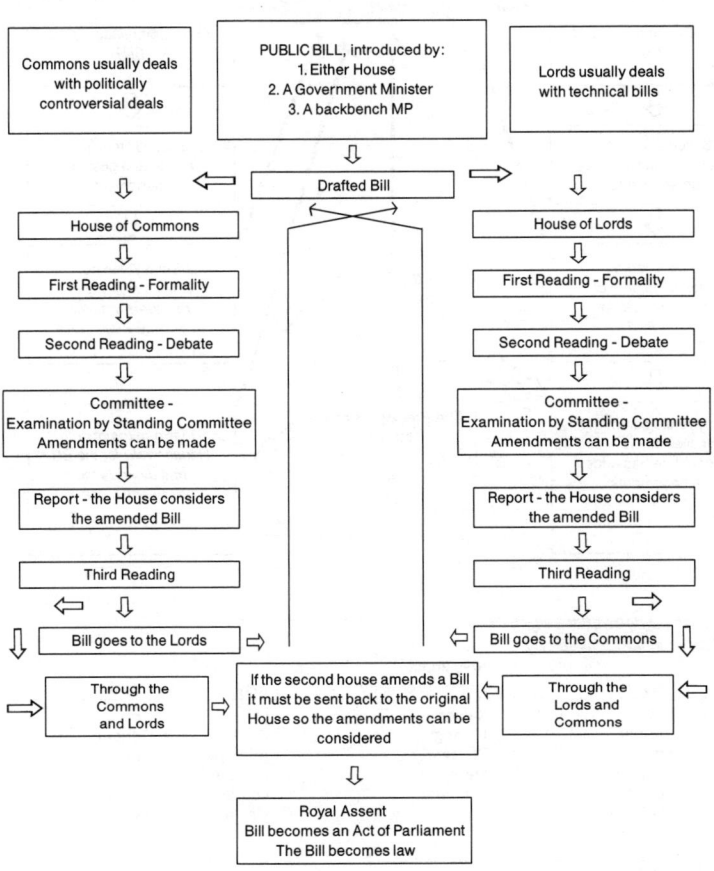

Social Structure

Social Structure

Passage of a public bill to law in the USA

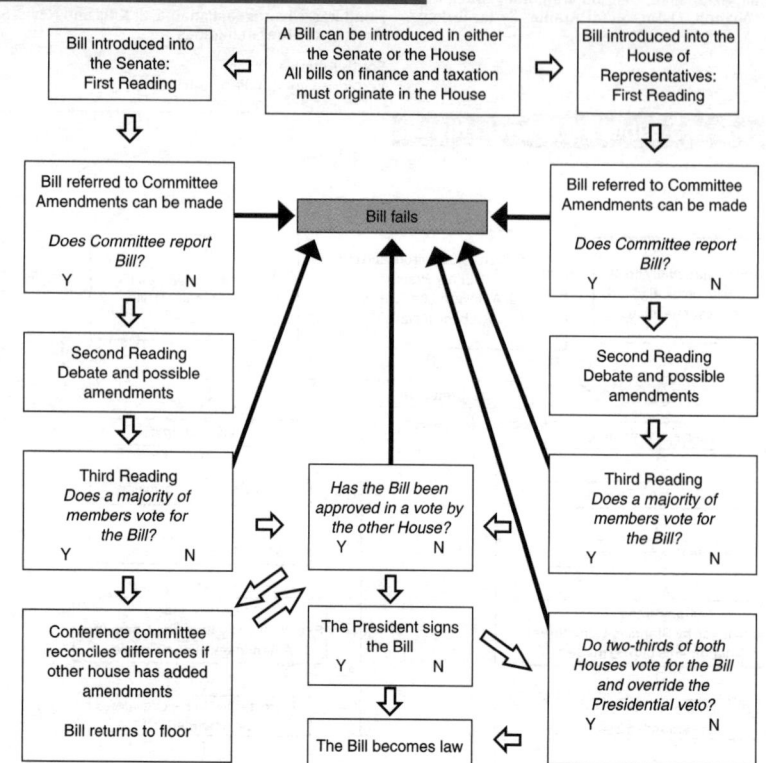

Ranks of the aristocracy

England	France	Holy Roman Empire (Germany)	Italy	Spain
king	roi	Kaiser	re	rey
prince	prince	Herzog	duca	duque
duke	duc	Pfalzgraf	principe	principe
marquess	marquis	Markgraf	marchese	marques
earl	comte	Landgraf	conde	conde
viscount	vicomte		visconte	vizconde
baron				

Military ranks

Army	Air Force	Navy
France		
Général d'Armée	Général d'Armée Aérienne	Amiral
Général de Corps d'Armée	Général de Corps Aérien	Vice-Amiral d'Escadre
Général de Division	Général de Division Aérienne	Vice-Amiral
Général de Brigade	Général de Brigade Aérienne	Contre-Amiral
Colonel	Colonel	Capitaine de Vaisseau
Lieutenant-Colonel	Lieutenant-Colonel	Capitaine de Frégate
Commandant	Commandant	Capitaine de Corvette
Capitaine	Capitaine	Lieutenant de Vaisseau
Lieutenant	Lieutenant	Enseigne de Vaisseau de 1ère classe
Sous-Lieutenant	Sous-Lieutenant	Enseigne de 2ème classe

Army	Air Force	Navy
Germany		
General	General	Admiral
Generalleutnant	Generalleutnant	Vizeadmiral
Generalmajor	Generalmajor	Konteradmiral
Brigadegeneral	Brigadegeneral	Flotillenadmiral
Oberst	Oberst	Kapitan zur See
Oberstleutnant	Oberstleutnant	Fregattenkapitän
Major	Major	Korvettenkapitän
Hauptmann	Hauptmann	Kapitänleutnant
Oberleutnant	Leutnant	Oberleutnant zur See
Leutnant	Oberfahnrich	Leutnant zur See
Russia		
Marshal of the Army of the Russian Federation	Marshal of the Air Force of the Russian Federation	Admiral of the Fleet of the Russian Federation
Army General	General of the Air Force	Admiral of the Fleet
Colonel-General	Colonel-General	Admiral
Lieutenant-General	Lieutenant-General	Vice-Admiral
Major-General	Major-General	Rear-Admiral
Colonel	Colonel	Captain 1st class
Lieutenant-Colonel	Lieutenant-Colonel	Captain 2nd class
Major	Major	Captain 3rd class
Captain	Captain	Captain-Lieutenant
Senior Lieutenant	Senior Lieutenant	Senior Lieutenant
Lieutenant	Lieutenant	Lieutenant
Junior Lieutenant	Junior Lieutenant	Junior Lieutenant
UK		
Field Marshal	Marshal of the Royal Air Force	Admiral of the Fleet
General	Air Chief Marshal	Admiral
Lieutenant-General	Air Marshal	Vice-Admiral
Major-General	Air Vice-Marshal	Rear-Admiral
Brigadier	Air Commodore	Commodore Admiral
Colonel	Group Captain	Captain RN
Lieutenant-Colonel	Wing Commander	Commander
Major	Squadron Leader	Lieutenant Commander
Captain	Flight Lieutenant	Lieutenant
Lieutenant	Flying Officer	Sub-Lieutenant
Second-Lieutenant	Pilot Officer	Midshipman
USA		
General of the Army	General of the Air Force	Fleet Admiral
General	General	Admiral
Lieutenant-General	Lieutenant-General	Vice-Admiral
Major-General	Major-General	Rear-Admiral
Brigadier-General	Brigadier-General	Commodore Admiral
Colonel	Colonel	Captain
Lieutenant-Colonel	Lieutenant-Colonel	Commander
Major	Major	Lieutenant-Commander
Captain	Captain	Lieutenant
First-Lieutenant	First-Lieutenant	Lieutenant Junior Grade
Second-Lieutenant	Second-Lieutenant	Ensign

Social Structure

Honours: Europe

■ **Denmark**

Order of Dannebrog Believed to have been founded in 1219 and one of the oldest orders in existence, revived in 1671, with six main classes: Grand Commanders, Knights Grand Cross, Commanders of the First Degree, Commanders, Knights of the First Degree and Knights, and an auxiliary class known as the Badge of Honour.

Order of the Elephant Founded in 1462 and revived by King Christian V in 1693; the premier order of Denmark.

■ **France**

Croix de Guerre Military award established in 1915 to commemorate individuals mentioned in despatches.

Légion d'Honneur Instituted by Napoleon in 1802 to reward distinguished military or civil service, and divided into five classes: Grands Croix, Grands Officiers, Commandeurs, Officiers and Chevaliers.

■ **Germany**

The Iron Cross Established by Frederick William in 1813 as an award for gallantry in action; various grades of award.

Order of Merit Instituted by the Federal German Republic in 1951, and divided into eight classes: Grand Cross (three grades), Large Merit Cross (three grades) and Merit Cross (two grades).

Social Structure

■ **Italy**

Ordine al Merito della Repubblica Italiana Established in 1952, with five classes of award: Grand Cross, Grand Officer, Commander, Officer and Member.

■ **Netherlands**

Huisorde van Oranje Established in 1905, awarded for outstanding services to the Royal House; corresponds to the Royal Victorian Order in the United Kingdom.

Militaire Willemsorde Founded by King William I in 1815; the highest military decoration open to members of the forces of all ranks and to civilians for acts of bravery and devotion to duty.

Nederlandsche Leeuw Founded by King William I in 1815, awarded to those of proven patriotism, outstanding zeal and devotion to civil duty, and to those with extraordinary ability in the arts and sciences; open to civilians, members of the military and foreigners; divided into three classes: Grand Cross, Commander and Knight, with an attached brotherhood whose members are nominated for acts of distinction, self-sacrifice and philanthropy.

Orde van Oranje Nassau Established in 1892; awarded to Netherlanders and foreigners for distinguished performance to the state or society; open to civilians or members of the forces; divided into five classes: Grand Cross, Grand Officer, Knight Commander, Officer and Knight.

Honours: UK

CBE ▸ **The Most Excellent Order of the British Empire**

The Distinguished Service Order (DSO) Established in 1886; bestowed as a reward for the distinguished service in action of commissioned officers in the Navy, Army and Royal Air Force; extended in 1942 to cover officers of the Merchant Navy.

The George Cross (GC) Instituted in 1940 as a reward for gallantry, and conferred upon those responsible for 'acts of the greatest heroism or of the most conspicuous courage in circumstances of extreme danger'.

The Imperial Service Order (ISO) Instituted in 1902 to reward members of the Civil Service; one class of membership; numbers limited to 1 700 in total, 1 100 belonging to the Home Civil Service, and 600 coming from the Overseas Civil Service.

MBE ▸ **The Most Excellent Order of the British Empire**

The Most Ancient and Most Noble Order of the Thistle (KT) An ancient order revived by King James II in 1687, and re-established by Queen Anne in 1703; limited to 16 knights.

The Most Distinguished Order of St Michael and St George Founded in 1818 by King George III; conferred upon British subjects for services abroad or in the British Commonwealth, with the motto 'Auspicium melioris aevi' (Token of a better age), and divided into three classes: Knight Grand Cross (GCMG), Knight Commander (KCMG) and Companion (CMG).

The Most Excellent Order of the British Empire An order of knighthood, the first to be granted to both sexes equally; instituted 1917; divided into military and civil divisions in 1918, with five classes: Knight or Dame Grand Cross (GBE), Knight or Dame Commander (KBE/DBE), Commander (CBE), Officer (OBE) and Member (MBE).

The Most Honourable Order of the Bath Founded in 1399, revived by King George in 1725; originally a military order, the civil branch was established in 1847; women became eligible in 1971; the order has three divisions: Knight or Dame Grand Cross (GCB), Knight or Dame Commander (KCB/DCB), and Companion (CB).

The Most Noble Order of the Garter (KG) Instituted in 1348 by Edward III; limited to 24 knights companion only, and with the motto 'Honi soit qui mal y pense' (Shame on him who thinks evil of it).

OBE ▸ **The Most Excellent Order of the British Empire**

The Order of Merit (OM) Instituted in 1902, with civil and military divisions, and limited to 24 in number.

The Order of the Companions of Honour Instituted in 1917 at the same time as the Most Excellent Order of the British Empire; it carries no title or precedence and consists of one class ranking immediately after the first class of the Order of the British Empire; membership is limited to 65 in number, excluding honorary members.

The Royal Red Cross Instituted by Queen Victoria in 1883; the first military order designed solely for women, and conferred upon members of the nursing services for their efforts in the field, and for others undertaking voluntary work on behalf of the sick or wounded or on behalf of the Red Cross.

The Royal Victorian Chain Founded in 1902 by King Edward VII, it confers no precedence on the holder, and is largely, although not exclusively, awarded to foreign monarchs.

The Royal Victorian Order Established by Queen Victoria in 1896, with no limit to the number of members; conferred for services to the sovereign or Royal Family; bestowed upon foreigners as well as British subjects; women became eligible in 1936.

The Victoria Cross (VC) Instituted by Queen Victoria in 1856 to reward conspicuous bravery, and the most highly coveted of British military decorations.

Honours: USA

The Bronze Star Established in 1944; awarded to members of the forces for acts of heroism or merit and for services beyond the call of duty, but not sufficiently outstanding to merit the Silver Star or Legion of Merit.

The Congressional Medal of Honor Instituted in 1861/1862, and first awarded during the American Civil War; conferred upon members of the forces showing exceptional gallantry and bravery in action.

The Distinguished Service Cross Instituted in 1918; confined to the army, and awarded to those showing extraordinary heroism in circumstances which do not justify the Congressional Medal of Honor.

The Legion of Merit Instituted in 1942; awarded to members of both the United States and foreign forces for distinguished service and meritorious conduct over a period of time.

The Purple Heart First instituted by George Washington in 1782 and reinstituted by Congress in 1932; awarded to those wounded in military action, and bears the inscription 'For Military Merit'.

The Medal for Merit Established by President Roosevelt in 1942 to award civilians of the United States or her allies for distinguished and meritorious service.

The Silver Star First authorised during World War I, it takes precedence over the Legion of Merit.

Charities (UK)

This table gives information on the top 25 UK charities by voluntary income (excluding legacies). Data is for 1998 or 1999.

Abbreviated name	Full name	Date founded	Voluntary income in £million
—	PPP Healthcare Medical Trust	1983	422
CAF	Charities Aid Foundation	1974	151
—	National Trust	1895	65.9
—	Diana, Princess of Wales Memorial Fund	1997	59.5
—	Oxfam	1942	54.5
—	Church of Scotland Unincorporated Boards	n/a	43.1
—	Salvation Army Trust	1865	42.7
—	ACTIONAID	1972	34.6
NSPCC	National Society for the Prevention of Cruelty to Children	1884	34
—	Macmillan Cancer Relief	1911	33.5
CRF	Imperial Cancer Research Fund	1902	30.7
—	United Bible Societies' Trust Association	1946	30.1
—	Save the Children Fund	1919	30
—	Royal British Legion	1921	29.8
—	Tear Fund	1968	29.5
—	Christian Aid	1949	29.3
—	Marie Curie Cancer Care	1948	28.4
RNLI	Royal National Lifeboat Institution	1824	25.2
—	British Red Cross Society	1870	24.7
RSPB	Royal Society for the Protection of Birds	1889	24.3
—	Salvation Army International Trust	1865	23.2
—	Help the Aged	1961	22.9
—	Ogden Charitable Trust	1999	22.5
DEC	Disasters Emergency Committee	1963	21.6
—	Cancer Research Campaign	1923	20.2

Data from *Dresdner RCM Top 3000 Charities 2000*, published by CaritasData Ltd.

Charities (USA)

This table gives information on a number of the top US charities by total income. Data is from 1998 or 1999 unless otherwise stated.

Abbreviated name	Full name	Date founded	Income in US$000
ALSAC-SJCRH	ALSAC-St Jude Children's Research Hospital	1957	274 123
ACS	American Cancer Society	1913	579 727
AHA	American Heart Association	1924	151 966
—	American National Red Cross	1881	2 057 829
AF	AmeriCares Foundation	1979	198 909
—	Arthritis Foundation	1948	61 447
BGEA	Billy Graham Evangelistic Association	1950	109 280
—	Boys Town/Father Flanagan's Boys' Home	1917	138 258
—	Campus Crusade for Christ	1951	189 400
CRS	Catholic Relief Services	1943	127 233
CTW	Children's Television Workshop	1969	158 154
CCF	Christian Children's Fund	1938	120 760
—	City of Hope	1913	100 834

Social Structure

Social Structure

Abbreviated name	Full name	Date founded	Income in US$000
CH	Covenant House	1969	58 553
LSA	Leukemia Society of America	1949	66 887
—	March of Dimes Birth Defects Foundation	1938	178 394
MDA	Muscular Dystrophy Association	1950	118 819[1]
NBA	National Benevolent Association of the Christian Church	1887	152 871
NJMRC	National Jewish Medical and Research Center	1899	92 286
NMSS	National Multiple Sclerosis Society	1946	59 203
NWF	National Wildlife Federation	1936	82 378
—	The Nature Conservancy	1951	493 767
PPHF	People-to-People Health Foundation	1958	93 936
—	Rotary Foundation of Rotary International	1917	152 542
SCF	Save the Children Federation	1932	111 556
—	Shriners Hospitals for Children	1922	562 807
UJA	United Jewish Appeal	1939	323 115
WV	World Vision	1950	188 423

[1] Data from 1995.

HISTORY

Prehistory to 5000BC

■ Primitive hominids (*Australopithecus*) appear in Africa c.4 000 000BC.

■ c.2 000 000BC, *Homo habilis* is found in Africa, hunting small game and using stones as tools, such as hand axes, to cut meat and pound bones for their marrow.

■ *Homo erectus* emerges in eastern and south-eastern Asia c.1 500 000BC, living beside rivers and lakes, and spreads to Europe by c.700 000BC. Fire is used for the first time to cook meat.

■ The earliest true human being, *Homo sapiens*, appears in Europe c.400 000BC.

■ Neanderthal man is living in caves in Europe c.120 000BC, using crude flint tools, looking after the sick and aged, and burying the dead.

■ From c.100 000BC Cro-Magnon man (*Homo sapiens sapiens*) begins to spread from Africa into Asia and China, and by 50 000BC Australia is reached. A wider range of stone tools is used as well as other materials such as wood and bone. Furs and leather are worn. Materials are traded over considerable distances. The woolly mammoth is hunted.

■ North America begins to be peopled c.30 000BC as human beings cross from Siberia to Alaska by a land bridge that is later cut by the Bering Strait. Giant bison and mammoths are hunted in the grasslands.

■ Southern African decorated stone tablets dating from c.27 000BC are the first examples of painting. Cave painting develops c.17 000BC with such fine examples as Lascaux in France and Altamira in Spain.

■ Female figurines with exaggerated sexual characteristics are carved in many parts of Europe.

■ By 20 000BC the last Ice Age is at its height. In Australia paintings are made on rocks.

■ Tools with stone blades are made c.15 000BC. Beads and pendants are worn.

■ The range of human weaponry expands, with knives, spears and bows in use c.12 000BC.

■ Farming begins c.10 000BC in various parts of the world, notably the Fertile Crescent in the Middle East.

■ Previously nomadic societies begin to make permanent settlements c.9000BC. Wild cereals are harvested, and dogs, goats and pigs are domesticated. Human occupation in the Americas extends to the southern extremes of South America.

■ c.8000BC villages built using mud bricks appear in Syria and Palestine. Jericho, the earliest walled town, is inhabited before 7500BC. Forest spreads in northern Europe as the ice sheet gradually retreats. Wild cattle and elk are hunted. Cattle are herded in the Sahara region. Pulses and cereals are cultivated.

■ Sheep and cattle are domesticated in the Near East c.7000BC. Linen is used to make textiles and pure copper is beaten for ornaments. In South America root crops are cultivated, while rice begins to be grown in China.

■ The first known pottery and woollen textiles are made in central Turkey c.6000BC. Lead is smelted. Farming spreads to south-eastern Europe, while oak forests extend into northern Europe. Cattle are used to pull ploughs in the Near East. Cereals begin to be cultivated in North Africa, while millet is grown in China, and wheat and barley in Pakistan.

History

History and politics	Religion and philosophy

5000BC–AD1

■ Successive civilizations arise in Mesopotamia, including the Sumerians and the empire of Akkad. The Sumerians invent the wheel and write in cuneiform script.
■ Farming spreads to Europe; olives and grapes are cultivated in the Mediterranean region, as is maize in Mexico and rice in India and China.
■ Egypt is united under one pharaoh and the first pyramids are built. Hieroglyphics are devised, the 365-day calendar is established, papyrus is first used, and the cat is domesticated.
■ In Greece, a civilization evolves from the Cycladic culture through the Minoan and Mycenean periods, trading with Egypt and building extensive palaces.

5000BC

c.5000BC Foundation of the city of Eridu in Mesopotamia. It is traditionally regarded as the first city.

5000BC Civilizations develop in Fayoum and Nubia.

4000BC Colonization of the Pacific islands.

3372BC First date in the Mayan calendar.

c.3100BC Building of Stonehenge, England, is begun.

3000BC

3000BC Towns are built on the Peruvian coast.

3000BC Lake Chad begins to dry up.

c.2400BC In Egyptian religion, Osiris is made both the god of fertility and the god of the dead. His son is Anubis.

c.2334BC Sargon of Akkad establishes the Akkadian Empire in southern Mesopotamia. He is one of the first great empire builders.

c.2300–1750BC Flourishing of Indus Valley civilization around the River Indus in Pakistan.

c.2150BC Collapse of Akkadian Empire in Mesopotamia.

2040BC End of First Intermediate Period in Egypt. Beginning of Middle Kingdom.

2000BC

2000BC First settlers arrive in New Guinea.

2000BC Migration of Bantu south from Central Africa.

1950BC End of empire of Ur, Sumeria.

1595BC Hittites conquer Babylon.

2000BC Birth of Abraham.

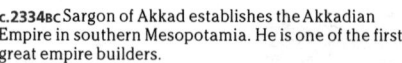
Abraham is traditionally regarded as the father of the three great monotheistic religions: Judaism, Christianity and Islam.

c.1500BC Start of the Vedic period of Hindu literature. The writings produced are known collectively as the *Veda.*

1300BC First settlers arrive in Fiji, Tonga and Samoa.

1500BC Stone temples are built in Mexico.

c.1270BC Israelites leave Egypt.

c.1200BC Legendary Trojan Wars between the Greeks and the Trojans.

1200–600BC Olmec civilization flourishes in Mexico.

1122BC End of Shang Dynasty in China, replaced by the Zhou Dynasty.

c.1100–612BC Assyrian Empire.

c.1290BC Moses leads the Hebrews out of Egypt, and after a long period in the wilderness receives the Ten Commandments at Mount Sinai.

Science and technology	Arts and culture

5000BC–AD1

- The Indus valley civilization arises in India, based on the city of Mohenjo-Daro. The Olmecs dominate Mexico, creating huge ceremonial earthworks and massive sculpures.
- The Greek city-state develops, with Athens and Sparta as the major powers. Colonies are set up throughout the Mediterranean. The first coins are struck. Alexander the Great conquers the Persian Empire.
- The city of Rome rises to power and extends its rule, its government evolving from republic to empire.
- China becomes united under a single emperor; the Great Wall is built.
- The Mayan culture arises in Guatemala and Mexico.

5000BC

5000BC Maize grown in Mexico.

c.4500BC Beginning of Neolithic period (new Stone Age) in Europe.

c.3700BC Bronze (an alloy of copper and tin) is invented in Egypt.

3500BC Potatoes grown in South America.

c.3500BC The wheel is invented in Mesopotamia.

3500BC Copper in use in Thailand.

c.3500BC In Ancient Egypt the later Gerzean or Naqada II culture begins, characterized by buff-coloured pottery decorated with scenes in purplish paint.

3200BC Sumerians invent cuneiform writing.

3000BC

3000BC Agriculture develops in Mexico.

3000BC Wheeled vehicles in use in the Middle and Near East.

c.2700BC Acupuncture is first developed in China.

c.2600BC Glassware is invented in Egypt.

c.2500BC Soap is invented in Sumer, Babylonia.

c.2300BC The earliest surviving maps are land surveys for the purposes of taxation in use by the Babylonians.

c.2300BC Beginning of Bronze Age in central Europe.

c.3000BC The earliest known form of pictograph writing is in use in Egypt.

c.3000BC The Sumerian predecessors of the Babylonians write poetry, of which fragments remain.

c.3000BC On Egyptian tomb walls, stylized pictures of the deceased and his servants are painted.

c.2600BC Work begins on the Great Pyramid of Khufu at Giza.

2000BC

c.1900BC Work begins on the Minoan palace complex at Knossos, Crete.

Knossos was noted for the sophistication of its art and architecture. It flourished c.1900–1400BC, and was dominated by the Minoan palace. It is associated in legend with Minos, the labyrinth of Theseus, and the Minotaur.

c.1340BC Egyptian pharaoh Tutankhamun is buried in a magnificent tomb at Thebes.

c.1323BC Hittites in Anatolia begin working iron.

1300BC The first canal across the isthmus of Suez is dug, linking the Nile delta with the Red Sea.

c.2000BC Part of the *Epic of Gilgamesh* is written down on clay tablets in Babylonia, the earliest known great poetic work.

c.2000BC Tales are recorded in Egypt.

c.1750BC Death of Amorite king of Babylon Hammurabi.

Hammurabi ruled from c.1792–c.1750BC, and is best known for his Code of Laws (a tablet inscribed with it is in the Louvre, Paris).

c.1550BC Fine pottery is made at Knossos, Crete, and the palace is decorated with frescoes.

History

History and politics	Religion and philosophy
1000BC	
c.962BC Solomon succeeds his father David as King of Israel. His reign is characterized by an elaborate building programme and expansion in trade and political contacts.	
c.900BC Etruscans settle in Italy.	**c.630BC** Birth of Persian religious leader and prophet Zoroaster (d.c.553BC).
850BC Chavín culture appears in Peru.	
800BC Development of India's caste system.	**c.600BC** The *Upanishads*, the last section of the Hindu scriptures (the *Veda*) are composed in Sanskrit.
814BC Carthage founded by the Phoenicians.	
753BC Foundation of Rome.	**600BC** Foundation of Taoism in China by philosopher and sage Lao-tzu.
750BC Kush conquer Egypt.	
721BC Assyrians conquer Israel.	**551BC** Birth of Chinese philosopher Confucius (d.479BC).
666BC Assyrians defeat Kush and conquer Egypt.	
550BC Foundation of Persian Achaemenid Empire by Cyrus II, the Great (c.600–529BC).	Confucius emerged as a great moral teacher who tried to replace the old religious observances with moral values as the basis of social and political order.
539BC Carthaginians defeated by the Greeks.	
525BC Persia conquers Egypt.	**c.540BC** Birth in India of Vardhama Mahavira, founder of Jainism.
510BC Last king of Rome deposed; foundation of the Roman Republic.	
500BC	
c.500BC Gallianazo and Salinar cultures flourish in Peru.	**c.500BC** Buddhism is founded in India by Prince Siddhartha Gautama (c.560–480BC), who became Buddha ('the enlightened') through meditation.
c.499BC Persian Empire at its height.	
490BC Athenians defeat the Persians with an overwhelming victory at the Battle of Marathon.	
	469BC Birth of Greek philosopher Socrates (d.399BC).
431–404BC Peloponnesian War between the Greek city-states of Athens and Sparta.	One of the three great figures in ancient philosophy, Socrates' pivotal influence was such that all earlier Greek philosophy is classified as 'pre-Socratic'.
400BC Nok culture in West Africa.	
	384BC Birth of Greek philosopher and scientist Aristotle (d.322BC).
332BC King of Macedonia, Alexander the Great (356–323BC), conquers Egypt.	**c.372BC** Chinese philosopher and sage Mencius born (d.c.289BC).
330BC Alexander the Great defeats Darius III (c.381–330BC), King of Persia, ending the Achaemenid Dynasty.	Mencius helped to develop and popularize the Confucian ideas and founded a school to promote their study.
323BC On the death of Alexander the Great, Ptolemy I (c.367–283BC) obtains Egypt, founding the Ptolemaic Dynasty.	**c.348BC** Death of Greek philosopher Plato (b.c.428BC).
321BC The extensive Mauryan Empire is founded in India by Chandra Gupta.	
312BC Macedonian general Seleucus I Nictator (c.358–281BC) founds the Seleucid Dynasty.	
c.300BC Rome rises to power.	**300BC** Greek philosopher and founder of Stoicism, Zeno of Citium (c.334–c.265BC), founds a school in the *Stoa poikile* ('painted porch'), from where the Stoics get their name.
264–146BC Punic Wars; a series of wars between Rome and Carthage.	**c.273–232BC** Mauryan emperor Aśoka organizes Buddhism as the state religion of India, whilst giving freedom to other religious sects.
221BC Shi Huangdi (c.259–210BC), Chinese emperor and founder of the Qin Dynasty, creates the first unified Chinese empire.	
218BC Carthaginian soldier Hannibal (247–182BC) crosses the Alps into Italy with an army including elephants.	
206BC In China Liu Bang (256–195BC) founds the Han Dynasty after a rebellion overthrows the Qin Dynasty.	

Science and technology	Arts and culture
	— 1000BC
c.1000BC Start of the Iron Age in south and central Europe.	**c.900BC** Greek epic poet Homer writing.
781BC Chinese astronomers observe a solar eclipse.	A major figure of Ancient Greek literature, Homer was regarded in Greek and Roman antiquity as the author of the *Iliad* (dealing with episodes in The Trojan War) and the *Odyssey* (dealing with Odysseus's adventures on his return from Troy).
c.700BC Lydians develop a system of coined money in south-west Asia Minor.	
600BC The massive Temple of Zeus in Sicily is built.	
585BC Greek natural philosopher and astronomer Thales (c.620–c.555BC), traditionally regarded as the founder of Greek philosophy, accurately predicts a solar eclipse.	**776BC** The traditional date of the first Olympic Games, held at Olympia in western Greece.
c.580BC Greek philosopher, mystic and mathematician Pythagoras born (d.c.500BC).	**c.700BC** Greek writer Hesiod writes his epic poems *Opera et dies* ('Works and Days') and *Theogonia* ('Theogony').
Pythagoras is associated with mathematical discoveries involving the chief musical intervals, the relations of numbers, the theorem of right-angled triangles which bears his name, and with more fundamental beliefs about the understanding and representation of the world of nature through numbers.	**c.610BC** Greek lyric poet Sappho of Lesbos born (d.c.580BC). It is from her that the four-line sapphic stanza takes its name and the term 'lesbian' has acquired its meaning.
c.575BC The Ishtar Gate, a huge and elaborate gateway into the city of Babylon, is built.	**c.534BC** Greek poet and reputed founder of Greek drama Thespis, wins the first prize for tragedy at a festival in Athens.
	— 500BC
c.500BC The Chinese begin to use single-gate locks on their canals.	
c.460BC Birth of Greek physician and 'father of medicine' Hippocrates (d. 377/359BC).	**c.496BC** Birth of Athenian tragedian Sophocles (d.405BC). One of the great figures of Greek drama, *Oedipus Tyrannus* is generally regarded as his masterpiece.
Skilled in diagnosis and prognosis, Hippocrates gathered together all the work of his predecessors which he believed to be sound, and laid the early foundations of scientific medicine. The Hippocratic oath has been seen as the foundation of Western medical ethics.	**431BC** Greek tragic dramatist Euripides (484/480–406BC) writes *Medea*.
447BC The Parthenon is built in Athens.	**c.430BC** Greek sculptor Phidias completes his *Statue of Zeus* at Olympia, one of the Seven Wonders of the World.
c.335BC Birth of Greek anatomist Herophilus (d.c.280BC). He founded the Alexandrian school of anatomy and was the first to dissect the human body to compare it with that of other animals.	**c.385BC** Greek comic dramatist Aristophanes dies (b.c.448BC). Of the 50 plays he wrote, 11 are extant.
c.300BC Greek mathematician Euclid writes his *Elements*, a treatise on geometry in 13 books. It is the earliest substantial mathematical treatise to have survived, and is probably better known than any other mathematical book.	**c.350BC** Greek sculptor Praxiteles completes his most celebrated work *Aphrodite of Cnidos*.
c.287BC Birth of Greek mathematician Archimedes (d.212BC).	**c.300BC** Greek historian and high priest of Heliopolis, Manetho, writes his history (in Greek) of the 30 dynasties of Egypt.
Archimedes is remembered as the inventor of the Archimedean screw (which is still used for raising water) and for the 'Archimedes' principle'. He also demonstrated the powers of levers in moving large weights. In mathematics Archimedes discovered the formulae for the areas and volumes of cylinders, spheres, parabolas, and other plane and solid figures.	**c.280BC** The *Colossus of Rhodes*, a giant statue of the sun-god Helios and one of the Seven Wonders of the World, is completed by Greek sculptor Chares of Lyndos.
c.250BC Greek mathematician, astronomer and geographer Erastosthenes (c.276–194BC) calculates the circumference of the Earth with considerable accuracy.	**224BC** Roman comic dramatist Plautus (c.250–184BC) begins to write.
221BC Construction of the Great Wall of China begins.	

History

History

200BC	History and politics	Religion and philosophy
		c.200BC The Old Testament is translated into Greek.
	185BC End of Mauryan Empire in India.	
	149–146BC The Third Punic War (between the Roman Republic and the Carthaginian Empire) results in the destruction of Carthage.	
		136BC Confucianism becomes the official state ideology in China, due largely to the influence of scholar and philosopher Dong Zhongshu (c.179–104BC).
	63BC Conquest of Jerusalem by Roman Pompey (106–48BC). Palestine becomes a province of Rome.	
	45BC Roman general and statesman Julius Caesar (100/102–44BC) defeats Pompey's legates in Spain and is appointed dictator.	
	30BC Egypt becomes a Roman province following the seizure of Alexandria. Suicides of Cleopatra (b.69BC) and Mark Antony (b.c.83BC).	
	27BC Foundation of Roman Empire with Augustus (63BC–AD14) as first emperor.	
		c.4BC Birth of Jesus Christ in Bethlehem.

AD1–299

■ The Roman Empire is at its height, including Britain as far north as the Antonine Wall (built c.143) in southern Scotland. The presence of its merchants is recorded at the Imperial Court in China (166). The prized status of Roman citizen is granted to all free inhabitants of the Empire (212).
■ Chinese civilization continues to advance with such innovations as a simple practical compass (271). Contact with other cultures increases: a Chinese ambassador visits Persia (97), and Chinese silks are brought by camel to Dimashq (Damascus) (220).

AD1		
	1 Bantu people begin to migrate to East Africa.	
	9 Plans to extend the Roman frontier from the Rhine to the Elbe are abandoned when three Roman legions are ambushed and annihilated by Germanic tribes in the Teutoburg Forest.	
	25 Chinese capital moves east from Changan to Luoyang. Start of Eastern Han Dynasty.	**c.30** Jesus Christ is crucified.
		c.40 Hellenistic Jewish philosopher Philo Judaeus (c.20BC–c.40AD) leads a deputation to the Emperor Caligula to plead on behalf of Jews who refuse to worship him.
	43 Romans invade Britain, led by Emperor Claudius I (10BC–AD54).	
		64 Fire destroys two-thirds of Rome. Christians are blamed and many are put to death.
	60 In England, Boudicca, Queen of the Iceni, leads an unsuccessful rebellion against Roman rule.	
	70 Jerusalem is destroyed by the Romans.	**68** The *Dead Sea Scrolls* are hidden in a cave near Qumran on the Dead Sea during the Roman invasion of the area.
	78 Height of Kushan Empire in northern India and Central Asia under King Kaniska.	**c.75** Buddhism is introduced to China.
	79 Mount Vesuvius in southern Italy erupts, burying Pompeii under ashes.	

100		
	100 Foundation of the city of Teotihuacán in Mexico.	
	117 Death of Roman emperor Trajan (b.c.53). His reign saw the Roman Empire at its greatest extent.	**c.120** Development of Gnosticism.
	122–8 Hadrian's Wall is built as the northern frontier of Roman Britain.	**c.125** Syrian Gnostic philosopher Basilides founds a sect in Alexandria. His disciples (Basilidians) are active into the 4c.

Science and technology	Arts and culture
	c.200BC Sculptors carve the reliefs on the stupa at Bharhut, India.
	166BC Roman comic dramatist Terence (c.195–159BC) writes his first play, *Andria* ('The Girl from Andros').
	150BC The *Venus de Milo*, a statue of Aphrodite, is carved in Greece.
129BC Greek astronomer and mathematician Hipparchos (c.180–125BC) completes his catalogue of 850 stars, giving their positions in celestial latitude and longitude. This work remained of prime importance until the 17c.	**90BC** Hydraulic organs are first played by Romans.
c.40BC Death of Greek physician Asclepiades (b.124BC). He advanced the doctrine that disease results from discord in the corpuscles of the body, and recommended good diet and exercise as a cure.	**27BC** Roman scholar and writer Marcus Terentius Varro dies (b.116BC). His works include the *Disciplinarum Libri IX*, an encyclopedia of the liberal arts.
	19BC Death of Roman poet Virgil (b.70BC). One of the greatest poets of antiquity, the *Aeneid* is unfinished at his death.

200BC

AD1–299

■ An anonymous text called *A Voyage around the Red Sea* (1c) describes nautical trading routes from the Red Sea to East Africa and as far east as the Ganges Delta.
■ In Africa, the Aksum civilization begins to dominate Ethiopia (50), and Bantu-speaking peoples migrate into the southern part of the continent (265).
■ The Mayan civilization develops in Central America around centres such as Tikal and Palenque (c.284).

AD1

c.30 Roman writer and physician Aulus Cornelius Celsus writes his *De Medicina*, giving accounts of symptoms and treatments of diseases, surgical methods and medical history.

c.62 Greek mathematician Hero of Alexandria invents the *aeolipile*, the earliest known steam engine.

78 Chinese scholar and inventor Chang Heng born (d.139). Among several other inventions, he is credited with the construction of the world's first seismograph.

82 The Colosseum in Rome is completed.

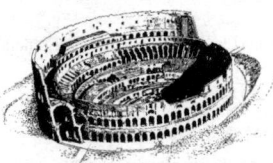

c.90 Death of Greek physician Pedanius Dioscorides (b.c.40). His *De materis medica* was the standard work on substances used in medicine for many centuries.

8 Roman poet Ovid (43BC–AD17) completes his *Metamorphoses*, a collection of mythological tales in 15 books.

> Later acclaimed as a master of the elegiac couplet, Ovid had his first literary success with a collection of love poems, the *Amores* ('Loves'), followed by *Heroides* ('Heroines'). The *Ars Amandi* or *Ars Amatoria* ('The Art of Love'), a handbook of seduction, appeared about 1BC, followed by the *Remedia Amoris* ('Cures for Love').

c.46 Greek historian, biographer and philosopher Plutarch born (d.c.120). His best-known work is *Parallel Lives*.

c.50 Translator of Aesop's fables into Latin verse Phaedrus dies (b.c.15BC). In addition to reproducing the fables of Aesop, he invented his own and also borrowed from other sources.

65 Roman philosopher, statesman and tragedian Seneca commits suicide after his implication in the conspiracy of Piso (b.c.4BC).

82 Chinese historian Ban Gu (32–92) completes his history of the Western Han Dynasty, initiating an unparalleled tradition of dynastic histories.

100

c.100 Greek physician Aretaeus writes his great work, discussing the causes, symptons and cures of diseases.

105 Paper is invented in China by Zai Lun (c.50–118); it is made from tree bark and rags.

118 The Pantheon in Rome is rebuilt by the emperor Hadrian (76–138).

c.114 Chinese historian and moralist Ban Zhao dies (b.45). She helped complete Ban Gu's history of the Western Han Dynasty, and her book of moral admonitions for women had a lasting influence on attitudes towards women in China.

120 Roman historian Tacitus dies (b.c.55). His major work is the 12-volume *Historiae* ('Histories').

History

130

History and politics	Religion and philosophy
138 Antoninus Pius (86–161) succeeds Hadrian (76–138) as Roman emperor. His reign is peaceful and happy.	**132** Jewish leader Simon Bar Kokhba (d.135) leads an unsuccessful rebellion against the Romans in Judea, precipitating the diaspora.
161 Marcus Aurelius (121–80) becomes Roman emperor on the death of Antoninus Pius.	
184 Start of Yellow Turban Rebellion in China, which weakens Han rule.	**c.178** Roman philosopher Celsus publishes his *True Discourse*, one of the first anti-Jewish and anti-Christian polemics.
192–7 Period of civil war in the Roman Empire following the death of the emperor Commodus.	
197–9 Roman emperor Lucius Septimius Severus (146–211) defeats the Parthians.	

200

c.200 Burial mounds are built by Native Americans in Ohio.	**c.205** Greek philosopher Plotinus born (d.270). His 54 works established the foundations of Neoplatonism as a philosophical system.
220 Collapse of Han Dynasty in China, followed by the Three Kingdoms Period.	
c.224 In Persia, Ardashir I (d.241) overthrows Ardavan, last of the Parthian kings, and founds the Sassanid Dynasty.	**c.224** Sassanid king Ardashir I makes Zoroastrianism the state religion of Persia.
c.240 Kushan Empire in northern India declines.	
250 Yamato dominates Japan.	**c.250** Death of Indian Buddhist monk-philosopher Nāgārjuna (b.c.150). He was the founder of the Madhyamika or Middle Path school of Buddhism.
260 Roman emperor Valerian (c.193–260) is defeated by the Persians at Edessa. He dies in captivity.	
280 Jin Dynasty completes the reunification of China, ending the Three Kingdoms Period.	
293 Roman emperor Diocletian (245–313) establishes the tetrarchy, with the Roman Empire ruled by two emperors, each assisted by a Caesar.	**285** Confucianism reaches Japan.

300–599

■ The Roman Empire declines in the face of barbarian incursions. Byzantium, rebuilt and renamed Constantinople, becomes the imperial capital (330), then the empire is split (395) between West (ruled from Milan) and East (ruled from Constantinople).
■ Christianity spreads throughout the Roman Empire, especially after the conversion of the Emperor Constantine (312).
■ Westward movement of Huns triggers migrations of other peoples such as the Ostrogoths and Vandals into Roman territory.

300

c.300 Rise of the Maya civilization in southern Mexico.	
c.300 The first settlers arrive in Tahiti.	
c.320 Founding of Gupta Dynasty in India by Chandra Gupta I.	**324** Christianity becomes the official religion of the Roman Empire.
	329 Palestinian hermit St Hilarion (c.291–371) founds the first monastery in Palestine.
330 Constantinople becomes the capital of the Roman Empire.	
	350 Christianity reaches Ethiopia.
350 Kingdom of Axum (Ethiopia) conquers the kingdom of Kush in Nubia.	
370 Europe is invaded by Huns from Asia.	
378 At the Battle of Adrianople, the Romans are defeated by the Visigoths.	
c.380 Expansion of the Gupta Empire in India under Chandra Gupta II.	**386** St Jerome (c.342–420) begins the first Latin translation of the Bible from the Hebrew (the Vulgate Bible).
395 The Roman Empire is formally split into two, the Eastern Empire (Byzantine Empire) and the Western Empire, on the death of Emperor Theodosius I (b.c.343).	**397** Numidian Christian St Augustine of Hippo (354–430) writes his *Confessions*.

Science and technology	Arts and culture
c.130 Egyptian astronomer and geographer Ptolemy (c.90–168) completes his *Almagest*, a 'great compendium of astronomy'. His Earth-centred view of the universe dominated cosmological thought until the work of Copernicus in the 16c.	**c.140** Roman lawyer and satirist Juvenal dies (b.c.55). Both Dryden and Dr Johnson would later be influenced by Juvenal's satires of Roman life and society.
c.150 Soranus of Ephesus, a Greek gynaecologist, produces *On Midwifery and the Diseases of Women.*	**180** Greek historian Arrian dies (b.c.95). His chief work is the *Anabasis Alexandrou*, a history of the campaigns of Alexander the Great.

130

200

Science and technology	Arts and culture
c.201 Greek physician Galen dies (b.c.130). Long venerated as the standard authority on medical matters, Galen studied the function of the bodily organs through experimentation and the dissection of animals. Galen was also the first to use the pulse as a diagnostic aid. **206** Work begins on the Baths of Caracella in Rome. **c.250** Greek mathematician Diophantus writes his *Arithmetica*, dealing with the solution of algebraic equations. In contrast to earlier Greek works it uses a rudimentary algebraic notation, instead of a purely geometric one.	**c.250** The earliest known Sanskrit dramatist Bhasa active. The author of plays on religious and legendary themes, his greatest work is *Svapnavasavadatta* ('The Dream of Vasavadatta'). **c.264** Palestinian theologian and scholar Eusebius of Caesarea born (d.340). His most important work, *Ecclesiastical History*, is a record of the chief events in the Christian Church down to 324. **c.290** One of the earliest Greek novelists Heliodorus writes *Aethiopica*, which describes the love of Theagenes and Chariclea.

300–599

- The Romans leave Britain (410), which is invaded and settled by Angles, Saxons and Jutes.
- The civilization of Teotihuacán dominates Mexico. The Mayan civilization is at its height c.600.
- The middle of the 4c sees the height of Buddhist sculpture, painting, and temple construction. Buddhism reaches Japan from Korea c.550.
- Chinese mathematicians are capable of solving linear equations and reducing fractions. In India, the decimal system is invented.
- Silkworms are brought from China to the Byzantine Empire c.540.

300

Science and technology	Arts and culture
c.326 Work begins on Old Saint Peter's Basilica, Rome, at the order of Emperor Constantine I (c.274–337). **c.340** Greek mathematician Pappus of Alexandria writes his mathematical *Collection*, covering a wide range of geometrical problems. **343** Chinese alchemist Ge Hong dies (b.c.280). Ge Hong's most famous book, *Bao-pu zi* ('He who holds to Simplicity'), contains accounts of methods of producing solutions of minerals in order to make immortality elixirs. He also describes the apparent production of gold from other metals. **c.375** The first metal stirrups are used on horses in China. Unlike earlier leather stirrups that were aids to mounting, metal stirrups were to help warriors fight from horseback.	**c.330** Roman historian Ammianus Marcellinus born (d.390). He wrote a history of the Roman Empire from AD98. **340** Roman poet Claudian born (d.410). The last of the great Latin poets, his works include the epic poem *The Rape of Proserpine*. **365** Chinese poet Tao Qian born (d.427). One of the great poets of China, Tao Qian employed a less artificial style than his contemporaries. He also wrote short stories. **c.380** Chandra Gupta II becomes head of the Gupta Empire. His reign sees peace and religious tolerance alongside the flourishing of Indian art, architecture and sculpture.

History

History and politics	Religion and philosophy
400	
c.400 Moche culture now well established in Peru.	**c.400** The Palestinian Talmud is completed.
c.400 Polynesians reach Easter Island.	
400 Hepthalites ('White Huns') invade Sassanian Empire (Persia).	**402** Chinese Buddhist monk Fa Xian makes a pilgrimage to India to find holy texts. He left a valuable account of Indian Buddhism.
410 Rome is sacked by the Visigoths led by Alaric I (c.390–461).	
429 Vandals found North African kingdom.	
434 Attila (c.406–53) becomes King of the Huns.	
c.450 Flourishing of Nazca people in Peru.	
451 Attila the Hun is defeated when he invades Gaul.	**451** Italian pope Leo I (c.390–461) summons the Council of Chalcedon.
455 Vandals sack Rome.	
476 Emperor Romulus Augustulus is overthrown by Germanic warrior Odoacer (433–93), ending the Western Roman Empire.	**c.475** Roman philosopher and politician Anicius Manlius Severinus Boethius born (d.524). His most famous work is *De Consolatione Philosophiae* ('The Consolation of Philosophy').
486 Clovis (465–511) overthrows the last Roman governor in Gaul.	
493 Theodoric the Great (c.455–526) assassinates Odoacer and becomes Ostrogoth king of Italy.	
500	
534 North African Vandal kingdom destroyed by the Byzantines under General Belisarius (505–65).	**515** Italian monk St Benedict of Nursia (c.480–c.547) composes his *Regula Monachorum*, which became the common rule of all Western monasticism.
534 Franks conquer Burgundian kingdom.	
535 North Africa becomes part of the Byzantine Empire.	
535 Byzantine emperor Justinian I (c.482–565) declares war on the Ostrogoths, reclaiming Italy for the Empire.	
540 End of Gupta Dynasty in northern and parts of central and western India after attacks by the Hepthalites ('White Huns').	**563** St Columba founds the monastery at Iona.
552 Juan-juan Empire destroyed by Nomadic Turks led by Bumin, who founds the Turk Empire with control over central Asia.	**570** Prophet Muhammad born (d.c.632) in Mecca.
558 Clotaire becomes King of all Franks.	**594** Buddhism becomes the official religion of Japan.
568 Lombards invade northern Italy and found a kingdom around the River Po.	**597** Italian prelate Augustine (d.604) is made Bishop of the English and establishes his church at Canterbury.
581 Yang Jian overthrows the Northern Zhou Dynasty, founding the Sui Dynasty and unifying China (by 589) after three centuries of division.	

600–899

■ China, united under the Tang Dynasty, sees a flowering of literature, especially the poetry of Li Bo and Du Fu.
■ The Islamic era begins with the Hegira of Muhammad, and Arab expansion carries the faith throughout North Africa, the Near East and into Spain.
■ The Muslim world sees the introduction of paper from China c.751, and there are great advances in mathematics, medicine and astronomy.

600	
613–19 Sassanid king of Persia Chosroes II (d.628) conquers Syria, Palestine, Egypt and parts of Asia Minor, almost defeating the Byzantine Empire.	
618 Tang Dynasty replaces Sui Dynasty in China, founded by frontier general Li Yuan (566–635).	**622** Muhammad's migration to Medina, the Hegira, marks the beginning of the Islamic calendar.
628–33 Byzantine emperor Heraclius (c.575–641) defeats the Persians and restores lost territories in the East.	
632 Muhammad dies and the caliphate is instituted.	**c.625** Irish monk St Adomnan born (d.704). An abbot at Iona, his *Vita Sancti Columbae* reveals a great deal about the religious community there.
634–42 Second caliph Omar (c.581–644) builds up an empire comprising Persia, Syria and all North Africa, conquering lands recently won by the Byzantines and ending the Sassanian Empire.	

Science and technology	Arts and culture
415 Greek philosopher Hypatia is murdered by a Christian mob (b.c.370).	**c.410** Latin Christian poet Marcus Aurelius Clemens Prudentius dies (b.348). He is the best known of the early Christian verse-makers.
Hypatia was the first notable female astronomer and mathematician, and head of the Neoplatonist school in Alexandria.	
432 The Santa Maria Maggiore basilica is built in Rome.	**438** The Theodosian Code, a law code by Byzantine emperor Theodosius II (401–50), is published. **c.450** India's greatest dramatist Kálidása writes his drama *Sákuntala*.
c.460 Work begins on the Buddhist cave temples at Yun-kang, China.	**c.480** North African scholar and writer Martianus Mineus Felix Capella writes his *Satiricon*, a kind of encyclopedia in verse and prose.
499 Indian astronomer and mathematician Aryabatha (476–c.550) completes his *Aryabhatiya*, a work summarizing mathematical knowledge in his time.	**c.480** Greek epic poet Musaeus writes *Hero and Leander*.
c.500 In North America the Inuit begin hunting whales and seals.	**c.500** Greek anthologist Johannes Stobaeus compiles an anthology from 500 Greek poets and prose-writers, which preserves fragments from many lost works.
510 Chinese develop block-book printing, in which a wooden block is carved with the characters of text, inked, and then used to produce multiple copies.	
525 Schythian scholar Dionysius Exiguus (d.556) fixes the dating of the Christian era in his *Cyclus Paschalis*.	
532–7 The church of Hagia Sophia is built in Constantinople under the direction of Justinian I, emperor of the Byzantine Empire.	**538** Frankish prelate and historian Gregory of Tours born (d.594). His *Historia Francorum* ('History of the Franks') is the chief authority for the history of Gaul in the 6c.
550 The astrolabe, a scientific instrument for showing the positions of the Sun and bright stars at any given time, is developed. It is used for astronomy and in navigation.	**565** Byzantine historian Procopius dies (b.c.499). His works include *Historiae* (on the Persian, Vandal and Gothic wars) and *Anecdota* or *Historia Arcana* ('Secret History').
	570 Roman–British historian and monk St Gildas dies (b.c.493). His famous treatise *De Excidio et Conquestu Britanniae* is the only extant history of the Celts.

400

500

600–899
- In the 790s the Vikings begin their raids in western Europe.
- Under Charlemagne, crowned Emperor of the West in 800, western Europe experiences a revival of scholarship.
- The Cyrillic alphabet is created (863) and spreads through eastern Europe.
- The infirmaries of abbeys and monasteries in western Europe become centres for the care of the ill.

600

607–10 A great canal system is built in China, connecting the Yellow and Yangtze rivers.	**c.600** Chinese artist Yen Liben born (d.673). One of the most important painters of the early Tang Dynasty, his extant works include 'Portraits of the Emperors'.
628 Indian astronomer and mathematician Brahmagupta (598–c.665) completes his *Brahma-sphuta-siddhanta* ('The Opening of the Universe').	
	636 Spanish prelate St Isidore of Seville dies (b.c.560). He is best known for his *Etymologiae*, a weighty encyclopedia of knowledge, and a standard reference work throughout the Middle Ages.

History

	History and politics	Religion and philosophy
640		**c.640** In China, Ch'an Buddhism develops.
		c.645 Buddhism is recognized in Tibet.
	650 All Polynesian islands are now colonized except New Zealand.	**c.650** The revelations of Muhammad are collected and written down as the *Koran*.
	661 Mu'Awiyah (c.602–80) becomes first Umayyad caliph. He extends the caliphate in North Africa and Afghanistan.	**661** Beginning of the major Sunni–Shiite division within Islam.
		664 Synod of Whitby chooses Roman Christianity over Celtic Christianity in England.
	668 The three rival kingdoms of Korea are united by the Silla Dynasty.	
	689 Frankish king Pepin II (d.714) defeats the Frisians, adding western Frisia to the Frankish kingdom.	
	690 Wu Zetian (d.705) becomes Emperor of China, the only woman ever to do so.	
700	**698** Carthage is destroyed by Arabs.	
	c.700 The Kingdom of Ghana expands due to trade across the Sahara.	**c.700** *Lindisfarne Gospels*, an illuminated manuscript of the Gospels, is created at Lindisfarne.
	711 Spain invaded by Muslims from North Africa, who defeat the Visigoths.	**718** Anglo-Saxon missionary Boniface (c.680–c.754) sets out to preach the gospel to all the tribes of Germany.
		726 Iconoclasm movement starts when Byzantine emperor Leo III (c.680–741) prohibits the use of icons in public worship.
	736 Frankish ruler Charles Martel (c.688–741) defeats Muslim invaders from Spain at Poitiers.	
	c.750 The Pala Dynasty, the ruling dynasty in Bihar and Bengal, India, is founded by Gopala.	**750** Death of Hindu philosopher and theologian Śankara (b.c.700).
	c.750 In Mexico the city of Teotihuacán is sacked by the invading Toltec.	Śankara was the most famous exponent of *Advaita* (the *Vedanta* school of Indian philosophy), and is the source of the main currents of modern Hindu thought.
	750 In India the Rashtrakuta Dynasty is founded, soon dominating the entire area of northern Maharashtra.	
	750 'Abbasid Dynasty founded, replacing Umayyad Dynasty.	
	751 Pepin III, the Short (c.715–68) becomes King of the Franks.	
	755 In Tang China the Rebellion of An Lushan, although crushed, leaves the dynasty weakened.	**c.754** Death of Greek theologian and hymn-writer of the Eastern Church, St John of Damascus. Among his works is an encyclopedia of Christian theology, the *Fount of Wisdom*.
	756 Islamic Empire starts to break up into separate countries.	
	771 Charlemagne (747–814) becomes sole King of the Franks.	
	773 Charlemagne defeats the Lombards in Italy.	
	793 Beginning of Viking raids on England.	
	794 Japanese capital moved from Nara to Heian (present-day Kyoto). Start of the Heian Era.	
800	**c.800** Rajput Dynasties begin to dominate northern India.	**c.800** Large and sophisticated Hindu temples are built in eastern India.
	800 Establishment of the Holy Roman Empire with the coronation of Charlemagne as emperor.	
	802 King Jayavarman II asserts Khmer independence and the Angkorean Dynasty is founded.	

Science and technology	Arts and culture	
		640

644 Earliest known reference to a windmill, in Persia.

673 In the Battle of Cyzicus, the Byzantines use 'Greek fire' (a highly inflammable liquid, which is set alight and shot towards the enemy), invented by the architect Callinicus.

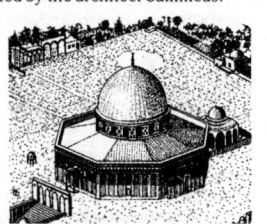

685–91 In Jerusalem the Dome of the Rock is built by Umayyad caliph 'Abd al-Malik (646/647–705).

658 Caedmon, an uneducated herdsman and the earliest English poet known by name, composes his 'Hymn of Creation'.

c.673 Anglo-Saxon monk and scholar Bede born (d.735). His greatest work, *Historia Ecclesiastica Gentis Anglorum* ('Ecclesiastical History of the English People'), was completed in 731. It is the single most valuable source for early English history.

699 Chinese painter and poet Wang Wei born (d.759). He linked painting with poetry in nature and mood, and may have pioneered monochrome ink painting.

700

700 Water wheels are used throughout Europe to drive mills.

705–15 Caliph al-Walid I (c.668–715) builds the Great Mosque of Damascus.

c.721 Arab alchemist Jabir ibn Hayyan born (d.c.815). He wrote a number of works on alchemy and metaphysics which were widely circulated in the Middle Ages.

725 Chinese inventor I-Hsing (682–727) produces a mechanical clock, the first Chinese clock to strike the hours and half-hours.

751 Knowledge of papermaking reaches Samarkand, Central Asia.

784–96 Offa, King of Mercia (d.796), builds the great earthwork known as Offa's Dyke to protect his frontiers against the Welsh.

787 Birth of Arab astronomer and astrologer Albumazar (d.885). In Baghdad he was the leading astrologer of his day, and he produced valuable work on the nature of tides.

793 A paper factory is established at Baghdad.

c.700 Anglo-Saxon poet and scholar Cynewulf born (d.c.800). The four poems attributed to him are contained in the *Exeter Book* and the *Vercelli Book*.

712 Chinese poet Du Fu born (d.770). He was one of the foremost lyricists in the Chinese language.

c.725 The Old English epic poem *Beowulf* is written.

> *Beowulf* was the earliest European epic poem to be written in a vernacular language. Surviving in the single late-10c 'Cotton manuscript' it describes the heroic life of Beowulf the dragon-slayer.

c.737 Alcuin born (d.804). A Northumbrian scholar and adviser to the Emperor Charlemagne, his works include poems, works on grammar, treatises, lives of saints, and over 200 letters.

754 Chinese emperor Xuan Zong (681–761) founds the Hanlin Academy.

c.760 Arab poet Abu Nuwas born (d.814). Considered one of the greatest poets of the 'Abbasid period, he was a favourite at the court in Baghdad and figures in the *Arabian Nights*.

762 Chinese poet Li Bo dies (b.701). He was regarded as the greatest poet in China, and wrote colourful verse on wine, women and nature.

800

c.800 First use of bow and arrow in Mississippi valley.

c.800 Arab mathematician al-Khwarizmi born (d.c.850). His writings in Latin translation were influential in transmitting Indian and Arab mathematics to medieval Europe.

804 Arab scholar Hunayn ibn Ishaq born (d.873). His translations of Greek writers such as Galen and Aristotle made Greek thought available to Arab philosophers and scientists.

c.800 Monks at Kells, Ireland, complete the *Book of Kells*, an illuminated manuscript of the Gospels.

807 Arab poet Abu Tammam born (d.c.850). He compiled a celebrated anthology of early Arab poetry, the *Hamasu*.

History

820

History and politics	Religion and philosophy
825 In England Egbert (d.839) ends Mercian dominance at the Battle of Ellendun.	**824** Chinese moralist Han Yu dies (b.768). He attacked Buddhism and promoted a revival of Confucian thought.
827 Muslim Aghlabids conquer Sicily.	
843 The Carolingian Empire is divided into three by the Treaty of Verdun.	**843** Period of iconoclasm in the Byzantine Church comes fully to an end with icons placed firmly within Orthodox belief.
843 Kenneth MacAlpin (d.858) becomes King of Picts and Scots.	
c.850 West African trading kingdom of Kanem established near Lake Chad.	**845** In China Emperor Wu-tsung begins persecution of Buddhists, destroying Buddhist temples and shrines.
866 Danes invade south-east England.	**c.865** *De Divisione Naturae*, an attempt to fuse Christian and neoplatonic doctrines, and to reconcile faith and reason, is written by Irish philosopher John Scotus Erigena (c.810–c.877).
867 Byzantine emperor Basil I (c.812–86) founds the Macedonian Dynasty.	
868 In a break from the 'Abbasid caliphate, the Tulunid Dynasty is founded in Egypt by Turk Ahmad ibn Tulun.	**867** Patriarch of Constantinople Photius (c.820–91) separates the Eastern Church from Rome.
882 Oleg (d.912) unites Novgorod and Kiev, founding the first Russian state.	
886 Anglo-Saxon king of Wessex Alfred the Great (849–99) formalizes the partition of England, with the Danelaw under Viking rule.	**c.870** Arab philosopher al-Kindi dies (b.c.800). He was one of the first to spread Greek thought into the Arab world, and was known as 'the philosopher of the Arabs'.
c.896 Magyar chieftain Árpád (d.c.907) occupies modern Hungary.	
896 Danish Vikings settle at the mouth of the Seine in France.	

900–999

- The Toltec state rises to power in Mexico, based on the city of Tula.
- The Vikings continue to explore, colonize and establish settlements, reaching Kiev and Constantinople in the east, and Greenland and North America in the west, and holding Normandy as a duchy under the French king.
- The Byzantine Empire undergoes a period of expansion through military successes, especially under Emperor Basil II.

900

History and politics	Religion and philosophy
c.900 Decline of Maya civilization in South America.	**c.909** Anglo-Saxon prelate St Dunstan born (d.988). He transformed Glastonbury into a centre of religious learning and re-established monasticism in England.
907 End of Tang Dynasty in China, followed by the Five Dynasties and Ten Kingdoms Period, a time of social and political turmoil.	
910 Arab Fatimid Dynasty established in North Africa.	
911 Rollo (c.860–c.932), Viking founder of the duchy of Normandy, arrives in France.	**923** Arab historian at-Tabari dies (b.839). He wrote a major commentary on the *Koran* and a history of the world from creation.
913 Koryo Dynasty founded by Wang Kon in Korea.	
937 Anglo-Saxon king Athelstan (c.895–939) defeats the Scots, Welsh and Vikings at the Battle of Brunanburh.	**935** Jewish philosopher Ben Joseph Sa'adia (882–942) writes *The Book of Beliefs and Opinions*.
945 Shiite Buyids take control of Baghdad, but allow the Sunni 'Abbasid caliph to retain his position.	

950

History and politics	Religion and philosophy
955 Otto I (912–73), Holy Roman Emperor, defeats the Hungarian Magyars at the Battle of Lechfield.	**c.950** Islamic philosopher Abu Nasr al-Farabi dies (b.878). Influenced by Plato's *Republic*, he published a utopian political philosophy, known under the title *The Perfect City*.
960 General Zhao Guangyin founds the Song Dynasty and begins to reunite China.	
969 Fatimids conquer Egypt and build a new capital at Cairo.	

Science and technology	Arts and culture
827 Ptolemy's *Almagest*, an encyclopedia of anatomy and mathematics, is translated into Arabic.	c.820 Frankish historian Einhard (c.770–840) writes his *Life of Charlemagne*, the greatest biographical work of the Middle Ages.
c.850 A medical school emerges at Salerno in southern Italy.	846 Chinese lyric poet Bo Juyi dies (b.772). His work was so admired that his poems were collected by imperial order and engraved on stone tablets.
	859 The Islamic university of Qarawiyin is founded in Fès, Morocco.
c.865 Persian physician and alchemist ar-Razi (Rhazes) born (d.923/932).	

820

Ar-Razi wrote many medical works, some of which were translated into Latin and had considerable influence in the Middle Ages. He successfully distinguished smallpox from measles, and was considered the greatest physician of the Arab world.

Science and technology	Arts and culture
868 The *Diamond Sutra* is the earliest datable printed document, produced in China using carved wooden blocks.	871–99 In England, under the reign of King Alfred, the *Anglo-Saxon Chronicle* is first assembled, an account of Anglo-Saxon and Norman England.
	c.880 Japanese poet Ono No Komachi dies (b.c.810). She is known in Japan as one of the 'Six Poetic Geniuses'.
	c.897 Japanese artist Kose Kanoaka dies (b.c.802). He was one of the first important secular artists in Japan.

900–999

- Buddhism spreads into Korea.
- In the Muslim world, the text of the Koran is finalized (935), and Cairo is founded as the capital of the Fatimid Dynasty. A caliphate is established at Córdoba in Spain.
- The Fujiwara family establishes its domination as regents of the Japanese emperors.
- The 990s see the rise of Dublin as the chief city of Ireland, and the first Irish coins are struck there.
- Venetian merchants are granted trading privileges in Constantinople.

900

918 First hospitals for the mentally ill are established in Baghdad and Cairo.	905 *Kokinshu*, an anthology of Japanese poetry, is completed.
929 Arab mathematician and astronomer al-Battani dies (b.c.858). He was the author of a collection of astronomical tables, 'On Stellar Motion', and improved upon Ptolemy's astronomical calculations.	915 Arab poet al-Mutanabbi born (d.965). One of the greatest Arab poets, his work was influential for centuries to come.
	c.935 German playwright Hrostwitha born (d.1000). A Benedictine nun, she wrote six comedies in Latin, the first known plays written by a woman.
c.940 Pope Sylvester II (Gerbert of Aurillac) born (d.1003). Skilled in chemistry, mathematics and philosophy, he wrote about the abacus and the astrolabe, and worked on celestial globes.	c.935 Persian poet Firdausi born (d.c.1020). His masterpiece *Shah Náma* ('Book of Kings') is based on actual events from the annals of Persia.

950

c.950 The first 'motte and bailey' castles are built between the Loire and Rhine rivers.

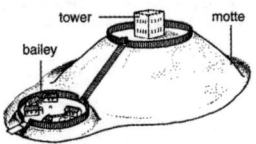

c.970 Japanese writer Murasaki Shikibu born (d.c.1015). Her *Genji Monogatari* ('The Tale of the Genji') is the first great work in Japanese and is regarded by many as the first novel.

970 University of al-Azhar founded in Cairo by the Fatimids.

History

	History and politics	Religion and philosophy
975		

977 Turkish Ghaznevid Dynasty founded in Afghanistan, western Iran and northern India.

985 Norwegian sailor Erik the Red founds Norse colonies on Greenland.

987 Hugh Capet (c.938–96) becomes King of France. The Capetian Dynasty he founded ruled France until 1328.

988 Vladimir I (c.956–1015), Grand Prince of Kiev, converts to Christianity, and adopts the Greek Orthodox rite from Byzantium as the official religion of Russia.

1000–1099

■ The expansion of the Vikings loses its impetus, and their power in Ireland is broken by Brian Boru at the Battle of Clontarf (1014). Their Norman descendants, however, aggressively acquire territory with the conquest of England and areas of the Mediterranean, especially in Italy.
■ The work of the Persian philosopher Avicenna epitomizes Eastern influence on European scholasticism and medicine.
■ The *Domesday Book* surveys and values all the lands in England.

1000

1000 New Zealand is settled by Polynesians.

1003 Icelandic explorer Leif Eriksson becomes one of the first Europeans to reach America.

1014 Rajendra I becomes ruler of the Cholas of southern India. He extended the kingdom to include Sri Lanka.
1014 Vikings defeated at the Battle of Clontarf, Ireland.

1017 Influential Tamil Brahmin philosopher Ramanuja born (d.1137). He prepared the way for the *bhakti* or devotional strain of Hinduism.

1028 Canute (c.995–1035), King of Denmark and England, conquers Norway.

1033 Birth of Italian theologian and philosopher St Anselm (d.1109). He is especially remembered for his ontological proof for the existence of God.

1040 Duncan I, King of Scots, overthrown and killed by Macbeth (b.c.1010).
1040 Ghaznavids defeated by Seljuk Turks.

1040 French Jewish scholar Rashi (Rabbi Shlomo Yitzhaqi) born (d.1105). His commentaries on the Bible were influential throughout the Middle Ages, and beyond.

1050

1054 East–West Schism divides the Orthodox Church of Byzantium and the Catholic Church of Rome.

1058 Muslim Almoravids invade Morocco, founding a new capital at Marrakesh (c.1070).
1060–71 Normans, under Roger I (1031–1101), take Calabria and Sicily from the Saracens.

1058 Islamic philosopher, theologian and jurist al-Ghazali born (d.1111). A prolific author, one of his major works was *The Revival of the Religious Sciences*.

1066 Harold II (b.c.1022) is defeated at the Battle of Hastings and the Norman Conquest of England is successful.

1071 Byzantine forces defeated by Seljuk Turks at Manzikart.

1075 Seljuks take Syria and Palestine.

1076 Almoravids sack the capital of western Sudanese Kingdom of Ghana, breaking its power.

1075 Investiture Controversy, a conflict between reforming popes and lay rulers over the leadership of Christian society (until 1122).

1086 *Domesday Book*, a survey of all lands in England, ordered by William the Conqueror (1027–87).

1086 Almoravids invade Spain from North Africa.

1094 El Cid (c.1043–99) defeats the Moors and takes Valencia.

1099 First Crusade (1095–9) captures Jerusalem.

Science and technology	Arts and culture	
		975

c.975 Arab numerals are first used in Europe.

968 Persian astronomer al-Sufi dies (b.903). He made some corrections to the work of Ptolemy and wrote the *Book of Fixed Stars*.

998 Muslim astronomer and mathematician Abu al-Wafa' dies (b.940). As well as his contributions to astronomy, he had an important influence on the development of trigonometry.

975 The *Exeter Book*, one of the most important collections of Old English poetry, is copied and later given to Exeter Cathedral.

990 Norweigan court poet Eyvindur, also known as Skáldaspillir ('the Plagiarist') dies.

1000–1099

- Coffee drinking becomes established in Persia and Arabia, and rice becomes the staple diet of China after being introduced from what is now Vietnam.
- The rise to dominance in Asia Minor of the Seljuk Turks, taking Baghdad and defeating the Byzantines at Manzikert, is seen by the Western Church as threatening pilgrimage routes to the Holy Land, leading Pope Urban II to preach the First Crusade.
- The feudal system becomes established throughout most of Europe.

1000

c.1000 Gunpowder used in Chinese warfare.

c.1000 Easter Island inhabitants start to carve huge stone statues.

1024 The first paper money is introduced in China.

1037 Persian philosopher and physician Avicenna (Ibn Sina) dies (b.980). His medical system was to be the standard in many medical schools up until the 17c.

c.1040 Arab mathematician Alhazen (Ibn al-Haytham) dies (b.c.965). His work on optics gave the first account of atmospheric refraction and reflection from curved surfaces, and the structure of the eye.

1048 Persian scientist al-Biruni dies (b.973). An outstanding scholar, he wrote on astronomy, mathematics, medicine, physics and history.

c.1020 Anglo-Saxon churchman and writer Ælfric ('the Grammarian') dies (b.c.955). He was the greatest vernacular prose writer of his time.

1036 Chinese painter, calligrapher, poet, philosopher and politician Su Dongpo born (d.1101).

c.1048 Persian poet, mathematician and astronomer Omar Khayyám born (d.c.1122). Initially famous for scientific achievements, he is now remembered for the poetry of *The Rubáiyát of Omar Khayyám*.

1050

c.1050 Chinese alchemist Pi Sheng invents the first movable type for use in printing. He created reusable type from a hardened mixture of clay and glue.

c.1072 Arab physician Avenzoar (Ibn Zohr) born (d.1162). He published influential medical works describing such conditions as kidney stones and pericarditis.

1095 Chinese administrator, engineer and scientist Shen Gua dies (b.1031).

Shen Gua's compilation of about 600 observations, *Brush Talks from Dream Brook*, is now one of the most important sources of information on early Chinese science and technology.

1077 The Bayeux Tapestry is completed.

The Bayeux Tapestry is an embroidered wall-hanging in coloured wool on linen, and narrates events leading up to the invasion of England by William of Normandy, and the Battle of Hastings in 1066.

c.1078 Byzantine politician and teacher of philosophy Michael Psellus dies (b.c.1018). His *Chronographia* recounts the reigns of Byzantine emperors from 976 onwards.

1088 First official university in Europe is founded at Bologna, Italy.

History

History and politics	Religion and philosophy

1100–1199

- In the Holy Land, the Knights Templar order is founded (c.1119). Saladin conquers the Crusader strongholds of Jerusalem and Acre (1187), provoking the Third Crusade, which recaptures Acre (1191).
- The formal knightly tournament develops in France and spreads to England.
- Playing cards appear in China (c.1120), while the game of draughts arises in Europe. Chess is introduced into England c.1150.
- Gothic architecture flourishes in Europe, notably in the construction of Chartres Cathedral.

1100

History and politics	Religion and philosophy
1106 Henry I (1068–1135), King of England, conquers Normandy from his brother, Robert Curthose (c.1054–1134), at the Battle of Tinchebrai.	**c.1100** Spanish–Jewish philosopher Abraham ibn Daud born (d.c.1180). He was the first to draw systematically on Aristotle.
1108 Louis VI, the Fat (1081–1137) crowned King of France.	
1113 Suryavarman II (d.c.1150) establishes sole rule over the Khmer Empire.	
1122 Jurchen nomads found Jin Dynasty in northern China.	**c.1119** Foundation of the religious and military order the Knights Templar to protect pilgrims to the Holy Land.
	1122 Concordat of Worms, an agreement which brings a temporary end to the Investiture Controversy.
1135 Stephen (c.1097–1154) takes the English throne, leading to civil war with Matilda, the Empress Maud (1102–67).	**1130** Philosopher Zhu Xi born (d. 1200). His commentaries on Confucian classics became accepted orthodoxy from the 14c.
1139 Alfonso I (1110–85) defeats the Moors at Ourique, and proclaims himself first king of Portugal, so securing Portuguese independence from León.	
1147 Almoravid Dynasty overthrown by Almohad Dynasty in north-west Africa.	**1142** French philosopher and scholar Peter Abelard dies (b.1079).
1147–9 Second Crusade ends after disastrous campaigns in Syria and Anatolia, and an unsuccessful siege at Damascus.	

1150

History and politics	Religion and philosophy
1154 Henry II (1113–89) crowned King of England, founding the Plantagenet Dynasty.	**1154** Pope Adrian IV (c.1100–59), originally Nicholas Breakspear, becomes the only Englishman to hold the office of pope.
1167 Establishment of the Lombard League in northern Italy against Emperor Frederick I, Barbarossa (c.1123–90).	
1168 In central Mexico the last Toltec king is driven from the capital Tula.	**c.1156** Carmelite order founded at Mount Carmel, Palestine.
1170 Thomas à Becket murdered in Canterbury Cathedral.	**1159** Divisions within the Roman Catholic Church lead to the election of a pope (Alexander III) and an antipope (Victor IV).
1171 Muslim sultan Saladin (1138–93) abolishes the Fatimid Dynasty in Egypt and founds the Ayyubid Dynasty.	
1180–5 Gempei War in Japan between rival Minamoto and Taira clans.	**1169–95** Islamic philosopher Ibn Rushd (known in Europe as Averröes) writes influential commentaries on the works of Aristotle.
1187 Saladin overwhelms Christian forces at Hattin and captures Jerusalem.	**1173** Thomas à Becket canonized.
1189 Richard I, the Lionheart (1157–99) becomes King of England.	**1177** Treaty of Venice restores single papacy.
1189–92 Third Crusade ends without recapture of Jerusalem but with successful close to the siege at Acre and the capture of Cyprus.	**1190** Jewish philosopher Moses Maimonides (1135–1204) completes his greatest work, *Guide to the Perplexed*.
1192 In Japan Minamoto Yoritomo (1147–99) takes the title shogun and institutes the shogunate.	
1192 Muslim victory at the Second Battle of Tarain gives Muhammad Ghuri (d.1206) control of all north India as far as Delhi.	**1191** Growth of Zen Buddhism in Japan due to introduction of Rinzai sect by the Buddhist monk Eisai (1141–1215).

Science and technology	Arts and culture

1100–1199

- In the Americas, the Toltec Empire of Mexico collapses after invasions by Chichimecs, who take its capital, Tula (1168), and Aztecs. The Inca Empire is dominant in the Andes region.
- Many of the great European universities are founded, including Oxford and Paris.
- The Cambodian Khmers are at the height of their power and greatly expand their capital at Angkor.
- In west Africa, Yoruba city-states begin to arise (c. 1150).
- The system of trial by jury is introduced in England in 1166.

1100

1101 Chinese astronomer and inventor Su Song dies (b.1020). He designed an elaborate water clock, housed in a tower some 10m in height, and probably accurate to within 100 seconds a day.

c.1113 Work starts on the temple of Angkor Wat in Cambodia, instigated by Suryavarman II.

c.1125 Adelard of Bath translates an Arabic version of Euclid's treatise on geometry, *Elements*, into Latin.

c.1130 First windmills in use in Europe (invented in 7c Persia).

c.1132 Work begins on the first church in the Gothic style, St Denis Abbey, Paris.

After the fall of the Roman Empire, the dominant architectural style to emerge was the Romanesque. This style was characterized by the use of round arches, clear plans and elevations and, typically, a two-tower façade. The Gothic style that followed was as a result of the development of the ribbed vault to support the roof, and flying buttresses that allowed the walls to be thinner. It was characterized by high-pointed arches.

c.1100 The Old French epic poem *La Chanson de Roland* ('The Song of Roland') is written. It is a masterpiece of *chansons de gestes* ('songs of deeds'), epic poems which centre on Charlemagne and the Crusades.

c.1136 *Historia Regum Britanniae* ('History of the Kings of Britain') written by Geoffrey of Monmouth.

Welsh chronicler and ecclesiastic Geoffrey of Monmouth studied at Oxford, was Archdeacon of Llandaff (c.1140), and was appointed Bishop of St Asaph (1152). His *Historia Regum Britanniae* traced the descent of British kings back to the Trojans, and he claimed to have based it on old Welsh chronicles which he alone had seen. It brought enduring romance by introducing the legends of King Arthur to European literature.

1148 Byzantine princess Anna Comnena dies (b.1083). She is known for her *Alexiad*, a life of her father (Alexius I Comnenus) which contains an account of the First Crusade.

1150

c.1150 Italian scholar Gerard of Cremona translates important medical works by Galen, Rhazes and Avicenna, increasing European medical knowledge.

1151 First European paper made at Xativa in Spain.

1163 Foundation stone of the Gothic cathedral Notre Dame de Paris is laid.

1174 Work begins on the bell tower at Pisa, Italy, later to become known as the Leaning Tower of Pisa.

c.1187 First record of a magnetic compass used as a navigational aid in Alexander Neckam's *De utensilibus*.

c.1150 Establishment of a university in Paris, France.

1155 Robert Wace (c.1115–83) completes his *Roman de Brut*, based on Geoffrey of Monmouth's *Historiae Regum Britanniae*.

c.1155–70 Anglo-Norman poet Thomas writes the earliest extant text of the legend of Tristan and Iseult.

c.1160 French poet and fable writer Marie de France writes the *Lais*, 14 romantic narratives based on Celtic material.

c.1167 Rapid development of the University of Oxford after Henry II bans English attendance at the University of Paris.

1176 First Eisteddfod held in Wales.

c.1183 Chrétien de Troyes, French poet and troubadour dies. His works include *Yvain et Lancelot*, *Érec et Énide* and *Cligès*.

Troubadours were poets composing lyrics on courtly love, who first appeared in Provence, and flourished from the 11c to the 13c. Most commonly the love is unfulfilled, and the hero of such romances will love the lady of his desire absolutely and ever increasingly, existing only to serve her. Such a relationship was based on the subject's dependence on his lord. The ideas of courtly love spread quickly through Europe and had a major effect on subsequent lyric poetry in that area.

History

History and politics	Religion and philosophy

1200–1299

■ Continuing Christian zeal to redeem the Holy Land is perverted into the Fourth Crusade's sack of Constantinople (1204), yet inspires the tragic Children's Crusade (1212); the French king Louis IX dies while crusading against Tunis (1270).
■ The Franciscan order of monks gains papal approval in 1209–10, as does the Dominican order in 1216.
■ England achieves a measure of internal peace with the signing of the Magna Carta (1215), but conflict with its neighbours includes the conquest of Wales (1277–82) and defeat in Scotland at Stirling Bridge by William Wallace (1297).

1200

1200 The Muslim Delhi Sultanate is founded in northern India.

1202–4 Fourth Crusade takes Zara then Constantinople.

1206 Temujin (c.1162–1227) establishes Mongol Empire, taking the title Genghis Khan ('Universal Ruler').

1211 Mongol armies enter China.

1215 Magna Carta ('Great Charter'), which began England's constitutional development, sealed at Runnymede by King John (1167–1216).

1216 King John dies and is succeeded by Henry III (1207–72).

1217–21 Fifth Crusade captures Damietta but fails in the Nile Delta.

1228–9 Sixth Crusade takes Jerusalem.

1229 The Berber Hafsid Dynasty replaces Almohads in Tunisia and eastern Algeria.

c.1235 Sundiata (d.1255) founds the Mali Empire in western Sudan.

1237–8 Mongols capture Moscow and Vladimir.

1240 Russian hero and saint Alexander Nevski (c.1220–63) defeats Swedish invaders in a battle on the River Neva.

1244 Jerusalem is lost to a joint Egyptian and Khwarazmian army.

c.1200 Indian philosopher Gangeśa founds the *Navya-nyaya* school of Hindu philosophy in Mithila, Bihar.

1209 Franciscan Order founded by St Francis of Assisi (1181–1226).

1209–28 A crusade in the south of France destroys the heretical Albigenses.

1225 Italian scholastic philosopher and theologian St Thomas Aquinas born (d.1274).

Thomas Aquinas's influence on the theological thought of succeeding ages was immense. His best-known writings are the *Summa contra Gentiles*, which deals chiefly with the principles of natural religion, and the *Summa Theologiae*, which includes the famous 'five ways' or proofs of the existence of God.

1250

1250 Saladin's Ayyubid Sultanate in Egypt is overthrown by the Mamluks.

1258 Hulagu (c.1217–65), grandson of Genghis Khan, captures Baghdad, and the Ilkhanid Dynasty rules in Iran and the central Islamic lands.

1260 Mongols defeated by Mamluks in the Battle of Ayn Julut. This effectively stops the Mongols westward advance.

1269 The Berber Marinid Dynasty replaces Almohad rule in Morocco.

1273 Rudolf I (1218–91) becomes King of Germany, founding the Habsburg Dynasty.

c.1274 William Wallace born (d.1305), Scottish knight and champion of the independence of Scotland.

1279 In China the Southern Song Dynasty is destroyed by the Mongols. Kublai Khan (1214–94), grandson of Genghis Khan, becomes Emperor of China.

c.1280 Creation of the Hanseatic League, an association formed to protect trading interests in northern Europe.

1281 Mongols are defeated when they attempt to invade Japan. When a typhoon struck the Mongol invaders, the Japanese saw it as a kamikaze ('divine wind').

1282 Sicilian Vespers; the massacre of the French in Sicily which began the Sicilian revolt against French rule.

1291 Creation of Swiss Confederation.

c.1297 Hindu Gujarat is conquered by the Delhi Sultanate.

1298 Edward I (1239–1307) defeats Wallace at Falkirk.

1250 Spanish Kabbalist Moses de León born (d.1305). He is the presumed author of *The Book of Splendour*, an influential work on Jewish mysticism.

1253 Death of Dogen (b.1200), founder of the Soto school of Japanese Zen Buddhism.

1263 Death of Japanese Buddhist Shinran (b.1173). Shinran founded the Pure Land school known as Jodo Shinshu ('True Pure Land').

c.1265 Scottish Franciscan philosopher and theologian John Duns Scotus born (d.1308). He rivalled Aquinas as the greatest theologian of the Middle Ages.

1273 Persian lyric poet and mystic Jalal ad-Din ar-Rumi dies (b.1207). In 1226 he founded a sect, and his disciples were later referred to in the West as the Whirling Dervishes.

1282 Death of Japanese Buddhist monk Nichiren (b.1222).

1290 Jews are expelled from England.

Science and technology	Arts and culture

1200–1299

■ In Asia the Mongols are united under Genghis Khan (1206), who extends his empire from China to the Black Sea. Under his descendants, the Mongols sack Baghdad (1258), ravage eastern Europe, and complete the conquest of China, with Kublai Khan becoming the first Yuan Emperor (1279–94).
■ By 1226 glass is being used in England to make bottles and windows.
■ Marco Polo leaves Europe (1271) and journeys to China, travelling across central Asia and through the Gobi Desert. His account of his travels sparks great western interest in the east.
■ The Mali Empire is established in West Africa and controls trade across the Sahara.

1200

c.1200 Emperor Lalibela has great churches hewn out of solid rock in Ethiopia.

c.1214 English philosopher and scientist Roger Bacon born (d.1292).

Bacon's views on the primacy of mathematical proof and on experimentalism have often seemed strikingly modern, and he published many works on mathematics, philosophy and logic, the importance of which was only recognized in later centuries.

c.1236 French Jewish astronomer Jacob ben Machir ibn Tibbon born (d.c.1312). In addition to important works of translation he also devised a quadrant which was used by mariners.

1238 Work begins on the Alhambra, the palace and fortress of the Moorish kings in Granada, Spain.

c.1200 German poet Gottfried von Strassburg writes his version of the legend of *Tristan and Isolde*.

c.1200 Chinese artist Xia Gui (fl.1180–1230) produces work for the Song Dynasty court. He was one of China's masters of landscape painting.

1209 Rioting in Oxford leads some scholars to move to Cambridge and development of the University of Cambridge begins.

1220 German poet Wolfram von Eschenbach dies (b.c.1170). It was from his epic *Parzifal* that Wagner derived the libretto of his opera *Parsifal*.

c.1235 French poet Guillaume de Lorris writes the first part (c.4 000 lines) of the dream-vision poem *Roman de la Rose*.

1241 Icelandic poet and historian Snorri Sturluson dies (b.1179). His main works were the *Prose Edda* and the *Heimskringla*, a series of sagas about Norwegian kings.

1250

c.1250 Italian mathematician Leonardo Fibonacci dies (b.c.1170).

Leonardo Fibonacci popularized the modern Arabic system of numerals, which originated in India. His major works were *Liber abaci* ('The Book of Calculation'), and *Liber quadratorum* ('The Book of Square Numbers'). He discovered the 'Fibonacci Sequence' of integers, and was the first outstanding mathematician of the Middle Ages.

c.1252 Completion of *Alfonsine Tables* in Spain. These astronomical tables were used to calculate eclipses and planetary positions for over two centuries.

c.1269 French scientist and soldier Petrus Peregrinus is the first to describe the properties of magnets in his *Epistola de magnete*. He also invented a compass with a graduated scale.

c.1270 Mondino dei Liucca born (d.1326). He published the first manual of anatomy at Bologna after carrying out his own dissections.

c.1280 Invention of spectacles by Alessandro della Spina and Salvino degli Armati in Italy.

1259 English chronicler Matthew Paris dies. His *Chronica Majora* established him as the finest chronicler of the 13c.

c.1260 Birth of Italian painter and founder of the Sienese school Duccio di Buoninsegna (d.c.1320).

1260 Italian sculptor Nicola Pisano (c.1225–c.1284) sculpts the panels of the pulpit in the Baptistry in Pisa.

1264 French encyclopedist Vincent de Beauvais dies (b.c. 1190). He gathered together the knowledge of the Middle Ages in his *Speculum Majus* ('Great Mirror').

c.1267 Italian painter and architect Giotto (di Bondone) born (d.1337). He was the most innovative artist of his time, and is generally regarded as the founder of the Florentine school.

c.1277 French poet and satirist Jean de Meung adds 18 000 lines to the *Roman de la Rose* — a work which was influential in the coming centuries.

c.1284 Catalan author Ramon Llull (c.1232–c.1316) writes his allegorical novel *Blanquerna*.

c.1292 Persian poet Sádi (Sheikh Muslih Addin) dies (b.c.1184). His most celebrated writing is the *Gulistan* ('Rose Garden'), a moral work in prose and verse.

History

History and politics	Religion and philosophy

1300–1399

- c.1300 the kingdom of Benin in West Africa is founded.
- c.1300 the Ottoman Turks begin their drive west to threaten the Byzantine Empire; by the century's end they control the Balkans.
- c.1325 the Aztecs found their capital Tenochtitlán. The Chimú state extends its rule in the central Andes of Peru.
- Gunpowder is introduced into Europe and the cannon makes its appearance on the battlefield.

1300

c.1300 Sultan Osman I (c.1259–c.1326) founds the Ottoman Empire in Turkey.

1305 William Wallace arrested and hanged by the English.

1307 Mansa Musa becomes ruler of the empire of Mali. He is best known for the splendour of his pilgrimage to Mecca.

1314 Under Robert Bruce (1274–1329) the Scots gain a decisive victory over Edward II's English forces at the Battle of Bannockburn.

c.1325 Aztecs found city of Tenochtitlán on Lake Texcoco in Mexico.

1331 The Byzantine town of Nicaea in Asia Minor falls to the Ottomans.

1336 The last great medieval Hindu state of Vijayanagar is founded in southern India.

1337 Edward III (1312–77) declares war on France. This begins a series of wars which became known as the Hundred Years' War.

1338 In Japan the Ashikaga Shogunate is founded.

1347–51 Black Death ravages Europe.

The Black Death originated in Asia and was spread from a Mongol invading army in the Crimea, then along trade routes to Europe by infected fleas living on rats. It has been suggested that in Europe the Black Death caused the demise of one third of the population, or 25 million people.

1309 Pope Clement V (c.1260–1314) moves the seat of the papacy from Rome to Avignon.

1327 German theologian and mystic Johannes Eckhart dies (b.c.1260). He taught mystic pantheism, which influenced later religious mysticism and speculative philosophy.

1332 Arab philosopher Ibn Khaldun born (d.1406). He wrote a monumental history of the Arabs, best known by its *Muqaddima*, or introduction.

c.1349 Influential English philosopher William of Ockham dies (b.c.1285). His best-known philosophical contributions are his successful defence of nominalism against realism, and the philosophical principle of 'Ockham's razor'.

1350

1355 Death of Stephen Dushan, King and Emperor of Serbia (b.c.1308). During his reign he extended Serbian rule into Macedonia, Bulgaria and Albania.

1361–3 Second outbreak of the Black Death in Europe.

1368 Ming Hongwu (1328–98) drives out the Mongols and founds the Ming Dynasty in China.

1369 Tatar Timur (1336–1405) ascends the throne of Samarkand.

c.1370 In Peru Nançen Pinco becomes ruler of the Chimú, and the Chimú state expands.

1381 Wat Tyler (d.1381) leads the Peasants' Revolt in south-east England, precipitated by the three oppressive poll taxes of 1377–81. It was quickly suppressed.

1385 Portugal gain independence from Spain after the Portuguese victory at the Battle of Aljubarrota.

1386–95 Timur subdues nearly all Persia, Mesopotamia, Georgia and the territory of the Golden Horde.

1389 Serbia falls to the Turks.

1392 Yi Song-gye (1335–92) founds the Yi Dynasty in Korea.

1397 The Kalmar Union sees Erik of Pomerania (c.1381–1459) crowned king of Denmark, Sweden and Norway.

1398 Timur invades India.

1378 The return of the papacy to Rome causes the Great Schism (until 1417), a period of deep crisis for the papal monarchy when there were two, and later three, rival popes.

1380 Death of Italian mystic St Catherine of Siena (b.1347). She wrote many devotional pieces, letters and poems; her *Dialogue* is the best known of her works.

1384 English religious reformer John Wycliffe dies (b.c.1329).

Wycliffe asserted the right of every man to examine the Bible for himself and promoted the first English translation of the Bible.

Science and technology	Arts and culture

1300–1399

- Italy experiences a cultural reflowering, with such works as Dante's *Divine Comedy* (c.1307–21), Boccaccio's *Decameron* (1348–58), Petrarch's *Canzoniere* (c.1351–3) and the paintings of Giotto.
- The Black Death appears in China c.1333, and spreads west, reaching Britain by 1348 and killing millions in Europe alone.
- In 1337 England embarks on war with France that is to last for more than a century.
- In China the Ming Dynasty (from 1368) sees a period of great craftsmanship in porcelain and bronze.

1300

c.1300 French scholastic philosopher Jean Buridan born (d.1358). He published works on mechanics, optics and logic.

c.1300 First use of the treadle in Europe.

c.1310 A Spanish alchemist and author, writing under the name Geber, begins to produce books on chemical and alchemical theory and practice.

It was through Geber's works that the discoveries of the early Arab chemists, along with many basic laboratory techniques, were relayed to Europe. His works continued to be influential until the 16c.

1311 Earliest dated portolan chart (a type of navigational chart used in Europe in the Middle Ages) produced by Petrus Vesconte in Genoa.

c.1320 First European use of cannon in warfare.

1348 Italian horologist Giovanni de' Dondi (1318–89) begins work on a complicated astronomical clock. In addition to the usual planetary motions it showed the feasts of the Church calculated in accordance with a perpetual calendar and was far ahead of its time.

1301 Chinese landscape painter, calligrapher and poet Ni Zan born (d.1374).

1304 Italian scholar and poet Petrarch born (d.1374). He was one of the earliest and greatest of modern lyric poets.

c.1307 Italian poet Dante Alighieri (1265–1321) begins his most celebrated work *Divina Commedia* ('Divine Comedy'), a poem which narrates a journey through Hell and Purgatory, and finally to Paradise. As well as providing a view of the highest culture and knowledge of the age, this work also established Italian as a literary language.

c.1337 Leading Chinese dramatist Wang Shifu dies (b.c.1250).

c.1345 English poet Geoffrey Chaucer born (d.1400).

The most influential English poet of the Middle Ages, Geoffrey Chaucer's first work as a poet was the *Book of the Duchess*, written in 1369. His greatest work, probably begun in the late 1380s and not completed, was *The Canterbury Tales*, recounting, with a prologue, the tales told by a group of pilgrims on their journey to Canterbury.

1350

1358 Italian writer Giovanni Boccaccio (1313–75) completes his greatest work, the *Decameron*, begun some 10 years before, with medieval subject matter and classical form.

c.1363 Japanese actor and playwright Zeami Motokiyo born (d.1443). Along with his father, he had great influence in shaping Noh theatre as it still exists today.

1368 French surgeon Guy de Chauliac dies (b.c.1300).

Born in Chauliac, Auvergne, Guy de Chauliac became the most famous surgeon of the Middle Ages. His *Chirurgia Magna* (1363) was translated into French over a century later and used as a manual by generations of doctors.

c.1370 Bohemian Hussite leader John Ziska born (d.1424).

During the Hussite wars, Ziska made the first important use of mobile field artillery, mounting his guns on wagons drawn by bullocks or horses so they could be used against enemy cavalry and infantry, as well as against fortifications.

1386 Work begins on Milan Cathedral, the third largest church in Europe.

1366 Italian artist Taddeo Gaddi dies (b.c.1300). His finest work is seen in the frescoes of Santa Croce, Florence.

c.1375 One of the greatest English poems of the period, *Sir Gawayne and the Green Knight*, is composed by an unknown author.

1378 Russian–Byzantine painter Theophanes the Greek (c.1335–c.1405) paints frescoes in the Church of Our Saviour of the Transfiguration in Novgorod.

1384 Flemish sculptor Claus Sluter (c.1305–1405) begins work on the tomb of Philip the Bold in Dijon.

1385 English poet William Langland (c.1332–c.1400) writes *The Vision of Piers Plowman*, a medieval alliterative poem on spiritual pilgrimage.

History

History and politics	Religion and philosophy

1400–1499

- The Chinese admiral and diplomat Zheng He leads a series of voyages west, reaching as far as east Africa (1405–33).
- The Portuguese capture of Ceuta in 1415 is the first step in their acquisition of an empire.
- c.1425 the first oil paintings are produced, in Italy.
- Partly through the inspiration of Joan of Arc, the French drive the English from all France, except Calais, by 1453, aided by the English internal conflict of the Wars of the Roses.
- The fall of Constantinople to the Ottoman Turks in 1453 marks the end of the Byzantine Empire.

1400

1401 The Welsh, led by Owen Glendower (c.1350–c.1416), rebel against Henry IV (c.1366–1413).

1402 Ottoman Turks are defeated by Timur at the Battle of Ankara.

1413 Thai armies sack Angkor Thom, the ancient capital of the Khmer Empire. The city is abandoned and not rediscovered until 1861.

1415 The French are defeated by Henry V (1387–1422) of England at the Battle of Agincourt.

1420 Ming Dynasty capital is moved from Nanjing to Beijing.

1431 French patriot and martyr St Joan of Arc (b.c.1412) is burnt at the stake, having halted the English ascendancy in France during the Hundred Years' War.

1434 Cosimo de' Medici (1389–1464) establishes the Medici principate in Florence.

c.1437 Montezuma I (c.1390–1464) becomes Aztec emperor of Mexico.

1448 First European fort built by Portuguese at Arguin in Mauritania.

1415 Bohemian religious reformer Jan Hus burnt at the stake for heresy (b.c.1369). The anger of his followers lead to the Hussite Wars; Hus's ideas were influential on the Protestant reformers of the 16c.

1417 Great Schism in the Catholic Church comes to an end with the election of Martin V (1368–1431) as pope at the Council of Constance.

1440 Indian mystic and poet Kabir born (d.1518).

> Kabir tried to unite Hindu and Muslim thought, and his preaching was a forerunner of Sikhism, which was established by his disciple Nanak.

1448 Russian Orthodox Church becomes autonomous.

1450

1453 End of the Hundred Years' War. Only Calais (lost in 1558) and the Channel Islands remain English territories.

1453 Byzantine Empire extinguished with the taking of Constantinople by the Ottoman Turks.

1454 Peace of Lodi ends conflicts between the warring states of Italy.

1455 Wars of the Roses begin. A series of civil wars in England named from the emblems of the two rival branches of the House of Plantagenet, York (white rose) and Lancaster (red rose).

c.1460 Songhai Empire rises to power in the former Mali Empire in West Africa.

1467 Onin War in Japan (until 1477); a struggle between rival daimyo (feudal lords) in a dispute over shogunal succession.

c.1470 In Peru the Inca conquer the Chimú.

1479 The crowns of Aragon and Castile are united, forming the basis of modern Spain.

1480 Ivan III of Moscow (1440–1505) defeats the Mongol Golden Horde.

1485 The end of the Wars of the Roses, when Henry VII (1457–1509), founder of the Tudor Dynasty, defeats Richard III (1452–85) at the Battle of Bosworth Field.

1488 Swabian League formed, a German alliance of towns, knights and princes to protect the Holy Roman Empire.

1492 Christians conquer Granada and end the last Muslim dynasty in Spain, the Nasrid.

1494 Start of the Italian Wars, a long series of conflicts which lasted until 1559.

1469 Guru Nanak born (d.1539), Indian religious leader and founder of Sikhism.

1471 German religious writer Thomas à Kempis dies (b.1379). Among his many writings was the influential devotional work *Imitatio Christi* ('The Imitation of Christ').

1472 Chinese Neo-Confucian philosopher Wang Yangming born (d.1529).

1478 The Spanish Inquisition, a tribunal for prosecuting heresy, is founded by papal bull.

1483 Martin Luther born (d.1546), German religious reformer and founder of the Reformation.

1492 Spaniard Rodrigo Borgia (1431–1503) becomes Pope Alexander VI.

c.1494 Birth of English translator of the Bible William Tyndale (d.1536).

Science and technology	Arts and culture

1400–1499

- c.1470 the Incas overthrow the Chimú state and dominate Peru; their crops include potatoes and cotton.
- A sea route to Asia from the Atlantic is opened when the Portuguese explorer Bartolomeu Dias rounds the Cape of Good Hope in 1488, and his compatriot Vasco da Gama follows this to make the first European sea voyage to India and back (1497–9).
- Christopher Columbus lands in the Caribbean Islands in 1492, and four years later establishes the first European settlement in the New World on Hispaniola. In 1497 John Cabot lands in Newfoundland.

1400

c.1403 In the field of printing, Koreans are the first to cast movable type in bronze.

1411 St Andrews University, the first university in Scotland, is founded.

1420 Tatar prince and astronomer Ulugh-Beg (1394–1449) founds an observatory at Samarkand. He went on to prepare new planetary tables and a new star catalogue.

1423 Austrian astronomer and mathematician Georg von Purbach born (d.1461). In astronomy his observational work resulted in the publication of a table of lunar eclipses, and in mathematics he is thought to have been the first to introduce sines into trigonometry.

1420 Japanese painter and priest Toyu Sesshu born (d.1506).

1424 French writer and courtier Alain Chartier (c.1390–c.1440) writes his much imitated poem, *La Belle dame sans merci*, ('The Beautiful Woman with No Mercy').

1432 Flemish painter Jan van Eyck (c.1389–1441) paints the famous altarpiece *The Adoration of the Holy Lamb*, at the church of Saint Bavon, Ghent.

1440 English mystic Margery Kempe dies (b.c.1373). Between 1432 and 1436 she dictated *The Book of Margery Kempe*, a remarkable early autobiography.

1436 Italian architect Leon Battista Alberti (1404–72) writes his *Della Pittura*, containing the first description of perspective construction.

1446 Italian architect Filippo Brunelleschi dies (b.1377). He is best known for the dome of Florence Cathedral.

1450

c.1450 German goldsmith Johannes Gutenberg (1400–68) invents a mould for casting movable type and the first printing press. In 1455 he produces his first printed work, the Gutenberg Bible. This is credited as being the first European book printed with movable type.

c.1450 Dutch painter Hieronymus Bosch born (d.1516). He is best known for his depictions of a bizarre, nightmarish world. His masterpiece is *The Garden of Earthly Delights*.

1452 Italian painter, sculptor, architect and engineer Leonardo da Vinci born (d.1519).

1466 Florentine sculptor Donatello dies (b.c.1386). His celebrated bronze statue of David is a key work of the Renaissance.

1472 German mathematician and astronomer Regiomontanus dies (b.1436). He worked on *Ephemerides*, which was used extensively by Christopher Columbus (1451–1506), and established the study of algebra and trigonometry in Germany.

1475 English printer and translator William Caxton (c.1422–1491), produces the first printed book in English, *The Recuyell of the Historyes of Troye*, at Bruges.

1476 Caxton sets up a printing press at Westminster.

1471 English writer Sir Thomas Malory dies. His masterpiece *Le Morte d'Arthur* is a prose romance of Arthurian legends.

1472 Italian architect Michelozzo di Bartolommeo dies (b.1396). He was court architect to Cosimo de' Medici.

1475 Italian sculptor, painter and poet Michelangelo born (d.1564). He is by far the most brilliant representative of the Italian Renaissance.

1483 Leonardo da Vinci designs flying machines and a parachute.

c.1482–4 Florentine painter Sandro Botticelli (1445–1510) paints *The Birth of Venus*.

1490–2 German geographer and navigator Martin Behaim (1440–1507) constructs the oldest extant terrestrial globe.

1494 German mineralogist and metallurgist Georgius Agricola born (d.1555). His *De Re Metallica* is a valuable record of mining, ore-smelting and metalworking in his lifetime.

1498 Leonardo da Vinci completes his fresco *The Last Supper*.

History

History

History and politics	Religion and philosophy

1500–1599

- The Portuguese send the first African slaves to the New World, to Brazil (1503). In 1511 they add Malacca to their growing empire.
- In 1518 smallpox breaks out in the Caribbean, one of many diseases introduced by Europeans.
- In 1519 the Portuguese navigator Ferdinand Magellan discovers a passage from the Atlantic to another ocean, which he names the Pacific, and crosses to the Philippines.
- Among the produce introduced to Europe from the New World are potatoes, tobacco, chocolate and quinine. In return, horses and cattle are introduced to the Americas.
- Protestantism comes into being in the Reformation.

1500

1501 Isma'il I (1487–1524) founds the Safavid Dynasty in Persia.

1502 Montezuma II (1466–1520) becomes the last Aztec emperor of Mexico.

1510 Portuguese conquer Goa.

1516–17 In Egypt the Mamluks are defeated by the Ottomans.

1520 Suleyman I, the Magnificent (1494–1566) becomes Ottoman Sultan.

1521 Hernán Cortés (1485–1547), Spanish conqueror of Mexico, takes the Aztec capital Tenochtitlán.

1523 Gustav I Vasa (1496–1560) breaks the Kalmar Union, establishing the state of Sweden and the Vasa Dynasty.

1526 Delhi Sultanate is destroyed by Babur (1483–1530) who becomes the first Mughal emperor of India.

1529 The first Ottoman siege of Vienna is unsuccessful.

1533 Francisco Pizarro (c.1478–1541), Spanish conqueror of Peru, takes the Inca capital of Cuzco.

1533 Ivan IV, the Terrible (1530–84) becomes Grand Prince of Moscow. He was the first prince to assume the title 'tsar'.

1540 Afghan chieftain Sher Shan (c.1486–1545) takes control of the Mughal Empire in India.

1550

1556 Akbar the Great (1542–1605) becomes Mughal emperor of India, defeating the Afghan threat and extending the empire's territories.

1557 China allows Portuguese settlement in Macao.

1558 Elizabeth I (1533–1603) becomes Queen of England.

1568 Start of the Eighty Years' War; uprisings and wars against Spanish Habsburg rule by 17 provinces in the Low Countries.

1568 Japanese warrior Oda Nobunaga (1534–82) begins the unification of Japan after two centuries of feudal warfare.

1571 Christian forces defeat the Ottomans in the Battle of Lepanto, a naval battle fought off the coast of Greece.

1578 Moroccans overcome Portuguese in north-west Africa.

1587 Elizabeth I has Mary Queen of Scots (1542–87) executed.

1583 Newfoundland claimed for England.

1588 The Spanish Armada, a fleet of 130 ships sent by Philip II of Spain (1527–98) to invade England, is defeated.

1590 Japanese soldier Hideyoshi Toyotomi (1536–98) unifies all Japan.

1591 Songhai Empire falls to invading Moroccan army.

1598 French Wars of Religion come to an end (began 1562) with the Edict of Nantes.

1517 Martin Luther draws up his list of 95 theses questioning the authority of the Church, and nails them to the door at Wittenberg Church. The Protestant Reformation begins.

1518 Swiss religious reformer Huldreich Zwingli (1484–1531) begins preaching in Zurich.

1534 The Act of Supremacy ends the pope's formal authority in England, and Henry VIII (1491–1547) is made head of the English Church.

1534 St Ignatius of Loyola founds the religious order of the Society of Jesus (Jesuits).

1545–63 The Council of Trent takes place, a series of councils of the Catholic Church to reform some doctrines and reaffirm others. It formed part of the Counter-Reformation.

1555 Catholicism and Lutheranism are allowed to coexist in Germany following the Peace of Augsburg treaty.

1559 *Index Librorum Prohibitorum* ('Index of Forbidden Books') drawn up by the Roman Catholic Church.

1564 French theologian and reformer John Calvin dies (b.1509). One of the most important reformers of the 16c, he systematized Protestant doctrine and organized its ecclesiastical discipline.

1574 Indian Hindi devotional poet Tulsīdās (1532–1623) begins his *Rāmacaritamānas* ('The Holy Lake of Rāma's Deeds'), a popular Eastern Hindi version of the Rāmāyana epic.

1577 Sikh Guru Ram Das (1534–81) founds Amritsar, later to become the centre of the Sikh religion.

Science and technology	Arts and culture

1500–1599

- Ottoman power is strengthened under Sultan Suleyman I, the Magnificent but his siege of Vienna fails (1529).
- The Inca Empire is conquered by Spain by 1535.
- The first mention in print of cricket being played in England is made in 1550.
- Sir Francis Drake is the first Englishman to circumnavigate the globe (1577–80); Sir Walter Raleigh attempts to found colonies in Virginia.
- Anglo-Spanish rivalry comes to a head with the launch, and defeat, of the Spanish Armada (1588).
- An early form of ballet emerges in France in the 1590s.

1500

c.1505 German locksmith Peter Henlein develops a mainspring as an alternative to weight-driven clocks, and pocket watches are made in Europe.

c.1510 French surgeon Ambroise Paré born (d.1590). Regarded by many as 'the father of modern surgery', he improved the treatment of gunshot wounds, and substituted ligature of the arteries for cauterization after amputation.

1512 Flemish geographer and cartographer Gerardus Mercator born (d.1594). To aid navigators, in 1569 he introduced a map projection (Mercator's map projection), which has been used for nautical charts ever since.

1518 English humanist and physician Thomas Linacre (c.1460–1524) founds the Royal College of Physicians.

1543 Theory of the Sun-centred universe is published by Polish astronomer Nicolaus Copernicus (1473–1543).

1543 Belgian anatomist Andreas Vesalius (1514–64) completes his greatest work, *De Humani Corporis Fabrica*. Based on the actual dissection of human cadavers, the book set a new level of clarity and accuracy in anatomy.

c.1500 German painter Lucas Cranach, the Elder (1472–1553) paints the *Crucifixion* at the Stadtkirche, Weimar.

1501–4 Michelangelo fashions his *David* out of a single colossal block of marble.

1504 Leonardo da Vinci begins the *Mona Lisa*.

1508–12 Michelangelo paints the frescoes on the ceiling of the Sistine Chapel.

1509 Dutch humanist and scholar Desiderius Erasmus (c.1466–1536) writes the famous *Encomium Moriae* ('In Praise of Folly').

1513 Italian statesman, writer and political philosopher Niccolò Machiavelli writes his masterpiece, *The Prince*.

1516 English politician and scholar Sir Thomas More writes *Utopia*.

1532 French satirist François Rabelais (1483/1494–1553) begins the series of books for which he is best known with *Pantagruel*.

1538 Venetian painter Titian (c.1488–1576), one of the greatest artists of the Renaissance, paints the *Venus of Urbino*.

1550

1562 Italian anatomist Gabriele Falloppius dies (b.1523). He particularly studied bones and the reproductive organs, and the Fallopian tube is named after him.

1570 Flemish geographer Abraham Ortelius (1527–98) produces *Theatrum Orbis Terrarum*, the first great atlas.

1576 Danish astronomer Tycho Brahe (1546–1601) establishes the Uraniborg Observatory. He is considered the greatest pre-telescope observer.

1587 Italian architect and engineer Antonio da Ponte (1512–c.1595) designs the Rialto Bridge in Venice.

1590 Italian astronomer, mathematician and natural philosopher Galileo Galilei (1564–1642) discovers that all bodies fall at the same rate.

1590 Dutch spectacle-maker Zacharias Janssen invents the compound microscope.

1593 Death of Chinese physician, naturalist and biologist Li Shizen (b.1518). His great work was the *Ben Cao Gang Mu* ('Great Pharmacopoeia') which he spent 30 years compiling.

1559 Japanese painter Kano Motonobu dies (b.1476). He achieved a synthesis of Kanga (ink painting in the Chinese style) with the lively colours of the Japanese style.

1564 William Shakespeare born (d.1616), playwright, poet and actor, and the greatest English dramatist.

From 1594 Shakespeare acted with the Lord Chamberlain's company of players, later 'the King's Men', the company for which he wrote many of his 37 plays. His prolific output brought him success in the fields of comedy, history and tragedy. Great popular success at the Globe was accompanied by acclaim at the court. His plays are still performed worldwide.

1578–80 English dramatist and novelist John Lyly (c.1554–1606) writes his hugely popular romance *Euphues*.

1590 The first three books of English poet Edmund Spenser's (c.1552–99) *The Faerie Queene* are published.

1593 English dramatist Christopher Marlowe is fatally stabbed in a tavern brawl (b.1564). His works include *Tamburlaine the Great*, *Dr Faustus*, and *The Jew of Malta*.

1596–8 Italian artist Caravaggio (1573–1610) paints *The Supper at Emmaus*.

1599 The Globe Theatre in London opens with Shakespeare's *Henry V*.

History

History and politics	Religion and philosophy

1600–1699

- In 1603 James VI of Scotland becomes James I of England, beginning the troubled Stuart era which sees civil war, execution of one king (Charles I) and deposition of another (James II).
- England's empire expands with its first permanent settlements in the Americas and India. Emigration to Massachusetts follows the landing of the Mayflower Pilgrims in 1620.
- The Dutch East India Company makes its base at Batavia (Jakarta) in 1619 and founds a colony at the Cape of Good Hope (1652). It is a Dutch ship from Macao that introduces tea to Europe c.1630, and it is in Amsterdam that the first weekly newspaper appears (1620).

1600

1600 In West Africa the Oyo Empire begins to flourish.

1600 In Japan, after the Battle of Sekigahara, Tokugawa Ieyasu (1543–1616) takes power, claiming the title shogun and establishing the Tokugawa Shogunate in 1603.

1605 The Gunpowder Plot, a conspiracy by Catholic gentry to blow up the English parliament, fails.

1607 Virginia becomes the first English colony in North America.

1608 French navigator and Governor of New France, Samuel de Champlain (c.1570–1635), founds Quebec.

1613 In Russia Mikhail Romanov (1596–1645) is elected tsar, founding the Romanov Dynasty.

1618 The start of the Thirty Years' War, a long and intermittent power struggle between the kings of France and the Habsburg rulers of the Holy Roman Empire and Spain.

1619 Dutch empire established in the East Indies.

1620 Pilgrim Fathers establish Plymouth colony in America.

1624 New Amsterdam (New York City) is founded by the Dutch.

1633 Japan bans foreign contact.

1642–8 English Civil Wars, between supporters of parliament and supporters of Charles I (1600–49), caused by parliamentary opposition to what it considered growing royal power.

1644 Manchus conquer China, overthrowing the Ming Dynasty and establishing the Qing Dynasty.

1648 The Peace of Westphalia ends the Thirty Years' War, and recognizes Dutch independence.

1649 Charles I of England is executed. The monarchy is abolished and Oliver Cromwell (1599–1658) establishes the Commonwealth.

c.1602 Whilst imprisoned for heresy, Italian philosopher Tommaso Campanella (1568–1639) writes his Utopian work, *City of the Sun*.

1604 Neo-Confucian Donglin Academy established near Shanghai.

1604 The principal Sikh scripture, the *Adi Granth*, is compiled by the fifth Sikh guru, Guru Arjan (1536–1606), and installed in the newly completed Golden Temple in Amritsar.

1611 The Authorized Version, or King James Bible is completed.

1624 English religious leader George Fox born (d.1691), founder of the Society of Friends, or 'Quakers'.

A Puritan by upbringing, at the age of 19 George Fox rebelled against the formalism of the established Church, and the State's control of it. He travelled around the country attracting many followers. In 1646 he had a divine revelation that inspired him to teach a gospel of brotherly love, and called his society the 'Friends of Truth'.

1648 Turkish Jewish mystic Sabbatai Zebi (1626–76) declares himself the Messiah and gains a large following.

1650

1652 Cape Town is founded by the Dutch East India Company.

1652–74 Anglo-Dutch Wars, three naval wars between England and the Dutch Republic, caused mainly by commercial and colonial rivalry.

1656 Mehmet Köprülü (d.1661) becomes Ottoman grand vizier. His work, and that of his successors, helped stabilize the Ottoman Empire.

1658 Aurangzeb (1618–1707) is the last and most magnificent of the Mughal emperors of India.

1659 The Treaty of the Pyrenees ends hostilities between France and Spain.

1650 French philosopher and mathematician René Descartes dies (b.1596).

Descartes is usually regarded as the father of modern philosophy. His works include the *Discours de la méthode* (1637), *Meditationes de prima Philosophiae* (1641), and *Principia Philosophiae* (1644). These set out the fundamental Cartesian doctrines, including the well-known proposition, *je pense, donc je suis* or *cogito ergo sum* ('I think, therefore I am').

1652 Russian religious leader and reformer Nikon (1606–81) becomes Patriarch of the Russian Church.

Science and technology	Arts and culture

1600–1699

- From 1642 the Dutch navigator Abel Janszoon Tasman discovers Tasmania, New Zealand, and explores the coast of Australia.
- While much of Europe is ravaged in the Thirty Years' War, Mogul power in India is at its height and Shah Jahan completes the Taj Mahal (1643).
- London suffers plague and fire but extensive rebuilding begins under the architect Christopher Wren.
- The French explorer Robert Cavelier de la Salle explores the Mississippi to its mouth (1682) and claims Louisiana for France.

History

1600

1600 English physician William Gilbert (1544–1603) publishes his *De Magnete*, in which he establishes the magnetic nature of the Earth.

1608 Dutch optician Hans Lippershey (c.1570–c.1619) invents the telescope.

1610 Galileo perfects the refraction telescope and uses it in the course of many astronomical revelations, including the mountains of the Moon and the existence of four of Jupiter's satellites.

1614 Scottish mathematician John Napier (1550–1617) describes his invention of logarithms in *Mirifici Logarithmorum Canonis Descriptio.*

1620 Dutch–British inventor Cornelis Jacobszoon Drebbel (c.1572–1633) successfully tests his invention of a rudimentary submarine in the River Thames.

1621 English mathematician William Oughtred (1575–c.1660) invents the earliest type of slide rule.

1628 English physician William Harvey (1578–1657) publishes his *Exercitatio Anatomica de Motu Cordis et Sanguinis*, in which the circulation of the blood is first described.

1632 Galileo defends the Copernican system of a Sun-centred universe in his *Dialogue on the Two Principal Systems of the World.*

c.1632 Work begins on the Taj Mahal mausoleum outside Agra in India.

1644 Italian physicist and mathematician Evangelista Torricelli (1608–47) gives the first description of a mercury barometer or 'Torricellian tube'.

1647 French mathematician Blaise Pascal (1623–62) patents an adding machine.

1605 Spanish writer Miguel de Cervantes (1547–1616) publishes the first part of *Don Quixote.*

1606 English dramatist Ben Jonson (1572–1637) writes *Volpone.*

1607 Italian composer Claudio Monteverdi (1567–1643) writes his first opera, *Orfeo.*

1612 American poet Anne Bradstreet is born (d.1672). Her most famous work is the volume of poems *The Tenth Muse lately sprung up in America.*

1614 Flemish painter Peter Paul Rubens (1577–1640) completes his triptych *Descent from the Cross.*

1623 Seven years after Shakespeare's death, two of his former fellow-actors, John Heminges and Henry Condell, collect and publish the 36 plays of the First Folio.

1623 English dramatist John Webster (c.1580–c.1625) writes *The Duchess of Malfi.*

1627 German composer Heinrich Schütz's *Dafne*, the first German opera, is produced in Torgau.

1631 English poet John Donne dies (b.c.1572).

1641 Sir Anthony Van Dyck dies (b.1599), Flemish painter and one of the great masters of portraiture of the 17c.

1642 Dutch painter Rembrandt (1606–69) produces his most famous work, *The Military Company of Captain Frans Banning Cocq* ('The Night Watch').

c.1644 Italian violin maker Antonio Stradivari born (d. 1737).

1650

1650 German engineer and physicist Otto von Guericke (1602–86) develops a primitive vacuum pump.

1654 The correspondence of French mathematicians Pierre de Fermat (1601–65) and Blaise Pascal (1623–62) lays the foundations of probability theory.

1656 English mathematician John Wallis (1616–1703) publishes *Arithmetica Infinitorum.* Wallis also introduced the symbol ∞ for infinity.

1657 Dutch physicist Christiaan Huygens (1629–93) invents the pendulum clock.

1650 Italian composer Giacomo Carissimi (1605–74) writes the oratorio *Jephthe.*

1650 Welsh religious poet Henry Vaughan (1622–95) prints his *Silex Scintillans* ('Sparkling Flint'), a volume of mystical and religious poems.

1652 French poet Georges de La Tour dies (b.1593).

1654 Dutch poet and dramatist Joost van den Vondel (1587–1679) writes *Lucifer*, a masterpiece of great religious drama.

1656 Spanish artist Diego de Silva y Velázquez (1599–1660) paints one of his masterpieces, *Las Meniñas* ('Maids of Honour').

History

1660

History and politics	Religion and philosophy
1660 In England the monarchy is restored, with Charles II (1630–85) of the House of Stuart taking the throne.	
1664 The English take control of the Dutch colony of New Amsterdam, renaming it New York.	**1677** Death of Dutch theologian and philosopher Benedict de Spinoza (b.1632). His *Ethics* is published posthumously.
1666 Great Fire of London.	
1670–71 In Russia Stenka Razin (c.1630–71) leads an unsuccessful Cossack and peasant revolt.	**1679** Death of English political philosopher Thomas Hobbes (b.1588). His major work was *Leviathan*.
1688 In England the Glorious Revolution sees James VII and II (1633–1701) flee, and William III (1650–1702) and Mary II (1662–94) established by parliament as joint monarchs.	**1685** In France the Edict of Nantes, which guaranteed at least limited religious toleration, is revoked.
1689 In Africa the Ashanti confederacy is founded by Osei Tutu (d.1712).	
1689 The Treaty of Nerchinsk settles border disputes between tsarist Russia and the Qing Dynasty.	
1689–97 King William's War; the first of the great wars between France and England for the control of North America.	
1690 William III's forces defeat those of James VII and II at the Battle of the Boyne, Ireland.	**1690** *Essay concerning Human Understanding* published by English empiricist philosopher John Locke (1632–1704).
1692 Salem Witch Trials in colonial Massachusetts.	
1692 In Scotland the Jacobite Macdonalds are killed at the Massacre of Glencoe.	**1697** French philosopher and critic Pierre Bayle (1647–1706) completes his *Dictionnaire historique et critique* ('Historical and Critical Dictionary').
1696 Peter I, the Great (1672–1725) becomes sole Tsar of Russia on the death of his half-brother Ivan.	**1699** Gobind Singh (1666–1708), last of the ten Sikh Gurus, institutes the Khalsa, a Sikh brotherhood marked by a new code of discipline, the 'Five Ks' and adoption of the name Singh for males and Kaur for females.

1700–1799

- England and Scotland are united in 1707, but Scottish resentment of this helps fuel the Jacobite rebellions of 1715 and 1745.
- The Danish navigator Vitas Bering is sent by Russia to explore Alaska (1728) and finds the strait that is now named after him.
- Britain wins the struggle with France for control of North America but is forced to grant independence to the colonies that become the United States.
- English navigator James Cook charts the coasts of Canada, Australia and New Zealand, explores the Pacific and discovers Hawaii.
- French explorer Louis de Bougainville carries out the first French voyage of circumnavigation, 1766–9, and charts many South Pacific islands.

1700

History and politics	Religion and philosophy
1700–21 Great Northern War between Sweden and the alliance of Russia, Denmark and Poland; Russia dominates the Baltic.	**1704** German philosopher and mathematician Gottfried Leibniz (1646–1716) completes his response to John Locke, the *New Essays on Human Understanding*.
1701 Elector Frederick III of Brandenburg (1657–1713) is crowned King Frederick I of Prussia.	
1701–13 War of the Spanish Succession; England, Holland and Austria declare war on France and Spain.	
1703 St Petersburg founded by Peter the Great.	
1704 Gibraltar taken from Spain by English forces.	
1707 Act of Union unites England and Scotland.	**1709** Irish Anglican Bishop and philosopher George Berkeley (1685–1753) publishes his *Essay towards a New Theory of Vision*.
1710 War of Mascates; Brazilian natives revolt against the Portuguese.	
1713 The Treaty of Utrecht ends the War of the Spanish Succession.	**1713** Jansenism is condemned by papal bull.
1715 Jacobite rebellion in Britain.	
1718 France founds New Orleans.	

Science and technology	Arts and culture

1662 Irish physicist and chemist Robert Boyle (1627–91) arrives at 'Boyle's law', which states that the pressure and volume of gas are inversely proportional.

1669 German chemist Hennig Brand discovers phosphorus.

1676 The Royal Greenwich Observatory is completed.

1679 French scientist Denis Papin (1647–c.1712) invents the 'steam digester' (a prototype pressure cooker).

1680 English astronomer Edmond Halley (1656–1742) correctly predicts the return of a comet (in 1758, 1835 and 1910) that had been observed in 1583 (Halley's comet).

1684 English scientist and mathematician Sir Isaac Newton (1642–1727) expounds his gravitation theory in *De Motu Corporum*.

1687 Isaac Newton publishes his greatest work, *Philosophiae Naturalis Principia Mathematica*, which includes his three laws of motion.

1689 English physician Thomas Sydenham dies (b.1624). His works, with their astute descriptions of diseases, were reprinted and translated throughout the 18c.

1694 Italian anatomist and microscopist Marcello Malpighi dies (b.1628). An early pioneer of histology, he conducted a remarkable series of microscopic studies.

1698 The first practical high-pressure steam engine for pumping water out of mines is invented in England by Thomas Savery (c.1650–1715).

1660 English Admiralty official Samuel Pepys (1633–73) begins his celebrated diary.

1665 English poet John Milton (1608–74) completes his most famous work, *Paradise Lost*.

1666 French playwright Molière (1622–73) produces his comic masterpiece *Le Misanthrope*.

1668 John Dryden (1631–1700) is appointed Poet Laureate.

1675 Dutch painter Jan Vermeer dies (b.1632).

1677 French dramatist and poet Jean Racine (1639–99) writes *Phèdre*.

1678 English writer John Bunyan (1628–88) completes the first part of *The Pilgrim's Progress*.

1678 English metaphysical poet Andrew Marvell dies (b.1621).

1688 Aphra Behn (1604–89), perhaps the first professional woman writer in England, publishes her novel *Oroonoko*.

1689 English composer Henry Purcell (1659–95) completes *Dido and Aeneas*, now regarded as the first great English opera.

1694 Japanese poet Matsuo Basho dies (b.1644). He is responsible for turning the 17-syllable haiku into a serious art form.

1700–1799

■ The British found Australia's first permanent European settlement, the penal colony of New South Wales (1788).
■ Revolution in France (1789) leads to war in Europe, and Napoleon Bonaparte comes to power as First Consul. The first income tax is introduced in Britain to help fund the war with France.
■ A metric system and a new calendar, as well as the guillotine, are among the innovations in Revolutionary France.
■ Europe sees a flowering in classical music, with composers such as Mozart and Beethoven producing their great works.

1701 English agriculturalist Jethro Tull (1674–1740) invents a seed-drill which plants seeds in rows.

1704 *Opticks* published by English scientist Sir Isaac Newton (1642–1727).

1709 English iron-master Abraham Darby (c.1678–1717) is the first to use coke successfully in the smelting of iron.

1712 English inventors Thomas Savery and Thomas Newcomen (1663–1729) construct a practical working engine widely used in collieries.

1714 German instrument maker Daniel Fahrenheit (1686–1736) invents an accurate mercury thermometer and devises the Fahrenheit temperature scale.

1700 American colonial merchant Samuel Sewall (1685–1759) writes his anti-slavery essay *The Selling of Joseph*.

c.1709 Italian harpsichord-maker Bartolommeo Cristofori (1655–1731) invents the pianoforte.

1712 English poet Alexander Pope (1688–1744) publishes his mock epic *The Rape of the Lock*.

1715 Italian composer Alessandro Scarlatti (1659–1725) writes his opera *Il Tigrane*.

1717 German-born English composer George Handel (1685–1759) composes his *Water Music*.

1719 *Robinson Crusoe* published by English writer Daniel Defoe (1660–1731).

History

History

1720

History and politics	Religion and philosophy
1720 The Bering Strait between Russia and Alaska is discovered by Vitus Bering (1681–1741), Danish navigator.	
1720 The South Sea Bubble financial crisis ruins many investors in Britain.	
1722 Safavid Dynasty overthrown by the Afghans.	**1726** The *Fifteen Sermons* of English moral philosopher Joseph Butler (1692–1752) are published.
1728 The Treaty of Liakhta is signed by China and Russia in an attempt to solve border disputes and increase trade.	**1730s** Wahhabite reformist religious movement within Islam begins to develop.
1736 Nadir Shah (1688–1747) becomes King of Persia.	
1736–96 Chinese empire under Qianlong (1711–99) expands to include Tibet, Mongolia, Turkestan, Annam, Burma and Nepal.	**1738** The Methodist Church is founded by John Wesley (1703–91) and his brother Charles (1707–88), as an evangelical movement within the Church of England.
1737 The town of Richmond, Virginia is founded by William Byrd (1674–1744).	
1740–8 War of the Austrian Succession.	**1739–40** *A Treatise of Human Nature* is published anonymously in London by Scottish philosopher David Hume (1711–76).
1741 Prussia conquers Silesia in the first Silesian War.	
	c.1740 High point of the First Great Awakening, a Christian revival movement in the American colonies, led by Jonathan Edwards (1703–58) and George Whitefield (1714–70).
1745 Jacobite rebellion in Britain.	
1746 Defeat at Culloden ends the Forty-Five Jacobite rebellion.	**1746** *Pensées philosophiques* published by French writer and philosopher Denis Diderot (1713–84).
1746 Chin-ch'uan rebellion in China.	

1750

History and politics	Religion and philosophy
1755 The Portuguese city of Lisbon is devastated by an earthquake.	**c.1750** Polish Jewish teacher and healer Baal-Shem-Tov (1699–1760) founds modern Hasidism.
1756–63 Seven Years' War; Austria, France, Russia, Sweden and Saxony oppose Prussia, Britain and Portugal.	
1757 British forces under Robert Clive (1725–74) defeat Siraj ud-Daula (c.1732–57), Nawab of Bengal.	
1759 British and Hanoverian forces defeat the French at Minden.	**1758** Swedish mystic and scientist Emmanuel Swedenborg (1688–1772) publishes *The New Jerusalem*.
1759 British general James Wolfe (1727–59) defeats the French on the Plains of Abraham near Quebec, winning Canada for Britain but dying in the battle.	
1761 Hyder Ali (1722–82) becomes ruler of Mysore, India.	**1762** French philosopher Jean Jacques Rousseau (1712–78) publishes *Du contrat social*, which greatly influences French revolutionary thought.
1761 The Afghans defeat the Marathas at Panipat, India.	
1768 Ali Bey (1728–73) becomes Sultan of Egypt and establishes independence from the Ottoman Empire.	**1764** The Jesuits are expelled from France (and from Spain in 1767).
1770 English navigator Captain James Cook (1728–79) lands at Botany Bay, Australia.	**1773** The Jesuits are suppressed by Pope Clement XIV (1705–74).
1772 Poland is partitioned between Russia, Austria and Prussia.	
1775–83 American Revolution.	**1776** A community of Christian revivalist Shakers is set up by Ann Lee (1736–84) near Albany, New York.
1776 The American Continental Congress adopts the Declaration of Independence, proclaiming separation from Britain.	
1776–86 Fulani Emirates founded.	**1781** German philosopher Immanuel Kant (1724–1804) produces his *Kritik der reinen Vernunft* ('Critique of Pure Reason').
1780 Joseph II (1741–90) becomes sole ruler of Austria on the death of his mother, Maria Theresa (b.1717), and introduces reforms.	
1783 American independence is established by the Peace of Paris.	**1783** Moses Mendelssohn (1729–86), an important figure in the Jewish Enlightenment, writes *Jerusalem*, which advocates Judaism as the religion of reason.

Science and technology	Arts and culture
	1720
	1721 Johann Sebastian Bach, German composer (1685–1750), finishes his *Brandenburg Concertos*.
1724 Dutch physician and botanist Hermann Boerhaave (1668–1738) writes his classic *Elementa Chemiae* ('Elements of Chemistry').	**1721** French philosopher Charles Montesquieu (1689–1755) completes his *Lettres persanes* ('Persian Letters').
1725 Italian historical philosopher Giambattista Vico (1668–1774) publishes his major work *Scienza Nuova* ('The New Science').	**1725** *The Four Seasons* completed by Venetian composer Antonio Vivaldi (1678–1741).
1730s Swedish naturalist Carolus Linnaeus (1707–78) publishes his system of classification for plants and animals.	**1726** Jonathan Swift (1667–1745), Anglo-Irish clergyman and satirist, publishes *Gulliver's Travels*.
1731 Invention of the quadrant, an instrument used in measuring angles in navigation, by English astonomer John Hadley (1682–1744).	**1731** *Manon Lescaut* published by French novelist Abbé Prévost (1697–1763).
1733 Mechanization of the textile industry is advanced by the invention of the flying-shuttle loom by English inventor John Kay (1704–64).	**1733** French composer and musical theorist Jean Philippe Rameau (1638–1764) completes his opera *Hippolyte et Aricie*.
	1738 Kirov Ballet founded in St Petersburg.
c.1740 English inventor Benjamin Huntsman (1704–76) develops a crucible process, improving steel production.	**1740** *Pamela*, an epistolary novel, is published by English novelist Samuel Richardson (1689–1761).
1742 Invention of the centigrade (Celsius) temperature scale by Swedish astronomer Anders Celsius (1701–44).	**1742** Handel completes his *Messiah*.
1749–67 French naturalist Georges Buffon (1707–88) produces his monumental *Histoire Naturelle*.	**1743–5** English painter and engraver William Hogarth (1697–1764) completes his moral narrative *Marriage á la mode* series.
	1749 English novelist Henry Fielding (1707–54) publishes *Tom Jones*.
	1750
1752 The Gregorian calendar is adopted in Britain.	**1751** The first volume of the *Encyclopédie*, a major reference work of the Enlightenment, is published in France.
1757 British naval officer John Campbell invents the sextant, allowing mariners to use the angle of a celestial object above the horizon to determine latitude and longitude at sea.	**1755** English writer Samuel Johnson (1709–84) publishes his *Dictionary of the English Language*.
	1759 French writer Voltaire (1694–1778) publishes his satirical novel *Candide*.
	1760 English painter Joshua Reynolds (1723–92) completes his portrait of Georgiana, Countess Spencer.
1764 British inventor James Hargreaves (1720–78) invents the spinning-jenny, which allows one person to spin several yarns at once.	**1761** Publication of *Fingal*, a supposed translation from an ancient work by the legendary Gaelic poet Ossian, but in fact largely the work of the Scottish poet James Macpherson (1736–96).
1765 Scottish engineer James Watt (1736–1819) improves the steam engine by adding a separate condenser.	**1762** German composer Christoph Gluck (1714–87) completes his opera *Orfeo ed Euridice*.
1766 English chemist Henry Cavendish (1731–1810) discovers hydrogen.	**1768** Italian painter Canaletto dies (b.1697).
1774 English clergyman and scientist Joseph Priestley (1733–1804) discovers oxygen.	**1770** English painter Thomas Gainsborough (1727–88) completes his *Blue Boy*.
c.1775 Start of the Industrial Revolution.	**1776** Bolshoi Ballet founded in Moscow.
	1778 The opera house La Scala opens in Milan.
The Industrial Revolution began in Britain with the mechanization of the cotton and woollen industries of Lancashire, central Scotland, and the West Riding of Yorkshire. The mechanization of heavier industries (iron and steel) was slower, but sustained the Industrial Revolution in its second phase from c.1830.	**1778** *Evelina* is published anonymously. It is English novelist Fanny Burney's (1752–1840) first and best novel.
1781 German-born British astronomer William Herschel (1738–1822) discovers Uranus.	*Evelina* describes the entry of a country girl into the gaieties of London life, and shows a natural style. As a portrayer of the domestic scene, Burney was a forerunner of Jane Austen, whom she influenced.
1783 French aeronautical inventors Joseph (1740–1810) and his brother Jacques (1745–99) Montgolfier conduct the world's first manned balloon flight.	

History

1785

History and politics	Religion and philosophy
1787 George Washington (1732–99) becomes the first President of the United States.	**1789** English philosopher Jeremy Bentham (1748–1832) publishes his *Introduction to the Principles of Morals and Legislation*.
1789 The French Revolution begins; fall of the Bastille.	**1790s** The Second Great Awakening takes place in the American colonies.
1793 Louis XVI (1754–93), King of France, is executed by revolutionary authorities.	**1792** English political writer Thomas Paine (1737–1809) publishes *The Rights of Man*.
1794 The Qajar Dynasty of Persian rulers is founded, retaining power until 1925.	**1795** The Methodist Church breaks away from the Church of England.
1798 Rising in Ireland by the United Irishmen fails.	
1799 Tipu Sultan (c. 1753–99), ruler of Mysore, is defeated and killed by British forces.	
1799 Napoleon Bonaparte (1769–1821) seizes power in France as First Consul.	

1800–1899

- White settlement in North America pushes steadily west, especially after the Lewis and Clark expedition (1804–6) opens up a route to the Pacific.
- Industrialization advances rapidly, first in Britain then in Europe, as does urbanization. Britain's first census is carried out in 1801. Among the century's innovations are the steamship, the railway, the telephone, the motor car, cinema and the bra.
- It is an age of political reforms, some achieved by peaceful political activity, others by revolutionary unrest, especially in the widespread European agitation in 1848. In this period, Britain alone sees four main Reform Acts.

1800

1803 With the Louisiana Purchase from France, the USA acquires full control of the Mississippi Valley.	
1804 Islamic religious leader Usman dan Fodio (1754–1817) launches the war that establishes the Fulani Empire in central Africa.	
1805 Battle of Trafalgar; Horatio Nelson (1758–1805) defeats the combined fleets of France and Spain but is mortally wounded.	**1807** German philosopher Georg Hegel (1770–1831) publishes his first great work *Phänomenologie des Geistes* ('The Phenomenology of Mind').
1806 The Holy Roman Empire comes to an end when Emperor Francis II (1768–1835) is forced to abdicate by Napoleon.	
1811 In Britain workers known as Luddites destroy newly introduced textile machinery.	Hegel was the last and perhaps the most important of the great German idealist philosophers. Although his philosophy can be difficult and obscure, it has been a great influence on later philosophies, including Marxism, Positivism and Existentialism.
1812 Napoleon invades Russia; his army suffers disastrous losses in a forced retreat.	
1813 Napoleon is defeated at Leipzig by the forces of Austria, Prussia, Russia and Sweden.	
1814 Napoleon is forced to abdicate and retire to Elba.	**1814** Pope Pius VII (1742–1823) formally re-establishes the Jesuits.
1815 Napoleon, having regained power, is finally defeated at Waterloo by Wellington (1769–1852) and Blücher (1742–1819), and exiled to St Helena.	**1819** German philosopher Arthur Schopenhauer (1788–1860) publishes *The World as Will and Idea*, emphasizing the primacy of the human will.
1818 Shaka (1787–1828) founds the Zulu Kingdom in southern Africa.	
1819 Singapore is acquired for the British East India Company by Sir Stamford Raffles (1781–1826).	

Science and technology	Arts and culture
1785 The power loom for spinning cotton is invented by English clergyman and inventor Edmund Cartwright (1743–1823).	**1786** Austrian composer Wolfgang Amadeus Mozart (1756–91) completes his opera *The Marriage of Figaro*.
	1786 Scottish poet Robert Burns (1759–96) publishes his *Poems, Chiefly in the Scottish Dialect*.
1793 US inventor Eli Whitney (1765–1825) invents the cotton gin, a machine that separates seeds from fibre.	**1789** English poet William Blake (1757–1827) publishes his *Songs of Innocence*. *Songs of Experience* follows in 1794.
1796 English physician Edward Jenner (1749–1823) makes the revolutionary discovery of vaccination, and successfully inoculates a child against smallpox.	**1798** *Lyrical Ballads*, the work of English poets William Wordsworth (1770–1850) and Samuel Taylor Coleridge (1772–1834), is published.
1798 In France US engineer Robert Fulton (1765–1815) constructs the first practical submarine.	**1799** Discovery at Rosetta (Raschid) in Egypt of the Rosetta Stone, a slab of basalt engraved with a trilingual inscription in Greek and Egyptian hieroglyphic and demotic, later to prove the key to the language of ancient Egypt.

1800–1899

- In South America former colonies of Spain and Portugal win their independence; in the North, the United States is torn by civil war.
- The British East India Company extends its power in India, but after the suppression of the Indian Mutiny rule passes to the British crown (1858). Queen Victoria becomes Empress of India.
- Turning its back on feudalism, Japan begins to modernize.
- Organized sport grows in popularity, especially in Britain, where the Football Association is founded in 1863.
- In 1887 Australia beat England in the first cricket Test match, in Melbourne.

Science and technology	Arts and culture
1800 Italian physicist Alessandro Volta (1745–1827) invents the electrochemical battery, the first source of continuous electricity.	**1800** Spanish painter Francisco Goya (1746–1828) paints his *Family of Charles IV*.
1801 Italian astronomer Giuseppe Piazzi (1746–1826) discovers the first minor planet (or asteroid), which he names Ceres.	**1802** German composer Ludwig van Beethoven (1770–1827) completes his 'Moonlight' sonata.
1806 The Beaufort Scale of wind speed is devised by British admiral Sir Francis Beaufort (1774–1857).	**1810** Scottish novelist and poet Sir Walter Scott (1771–1832) publishes *The Lady of the Lake*.
1807 The first commercial steamboat service is introduced in New York by engineer Robert Fulton (1765–1815).	**1810–14** Spanish artist Francisco Goya (1746–1828) creates the series of etchings *The Disasters of War*.
1807 Swedish chemist Jöns Jacob Berzelius (1779–1848) begins the work that leads him to draw up a table of atomic weights using oxygen as a base, devising the modern system of chemical symbols.	**1811** *Sense and Sensibility* is published by English novelist Jane Austen (1775–1817).
1809 Gas-powered street lighting is introduced in London.	**1812** Publication of the first volume of *Grimm's Fairy Tales* by German brothers Jacob (1785–1863) and Wilhelm (1786–1859) Grimm.
1812 French chef Nicolas Appert (1749–1841) opens the world's first commercial canning factory.	**1812** The first volume of *Childe Harold's Pilgrimage* by British poet George Gordon, Lord Byron (1788–1824), is published to instant acclaim.
1816 French physician René Lännec (1781–1826) invents the stethoscope.	**1816** Italian composer Gioacchino Rossini (1792–1868) produces his masterpiece, the comic opera *The Barber of Seville*.
	1818 English writer Mary Shelley (1797–1851) publishes her first and most impressive novel *Frankenstein, or the Modern Prometheus*.

History

	History and politics	Religion and philosophy
1820		

1821 The Greeks begin a war of independence against Turkey, realising their goal in 1832.

1822 Liberia is founded as a homeland for freed US slaves.

1823 Monroe Doctrine declares US hostility to further European colonization or political interference in the western hemisphere.

1825–8 Argentine – Brazilian War; fought to decide possession of the Banda Oriental territory.

1826 Ottoman Sultan Mahmud II (1785–1839) ends the power of the professional military corps of Janissaries by massacring them.

1828 Indian religious reformer Rammohun Roy (1774–1833) founds the Brahmo Samaj, a theistic movement which argues that reason should form the basis of Hinduism.

1827 The British and French fleets destroy a Turkish and Egyptian fleet at Navarino.

1829 Catholic Emancipation legislation in Britain allows Catholics to become MPs.

1830 The Church of Jesus Christ of the Latter-Day Saints (Mormons) is founded in the USA by Joseph Smith (1805–44).

1833 Slavery is abolished in the British Empire.

1833 Beginning of the Oxford Movement in the Church of England, aimed at reviving high doctrine and ceremony.

1836 Beginning of the Great Trek of the Boers from Cape Colony to escape British rule.

1836–42 First Anglo-Afghan War.

1843 Publication of *Either/Or* by Danish philosopher Søren Kierkegaard (1813–55), one of the founders of Existentialism.

1839–42 First of the Opium Wars, fought between Britain and China over the opium trade.

1840 Britain annexes New Zealand.

1844 The Muslim Babist sect is founded when Persian mystic Mirza Ali Muhammad (1819–50) declares himself the 'Bab' (gate) between man and God. Babism was the forerunner of the Baha'i faith.

1845–51 Irish famine, caused by the failure of the potato crop, leads to massive population loss through starvation and emigration.

1846–48 Mexican War between Mexico and the USA.

1848 A wave of revolutions sweeps central and western Europe. The Second Republic is established in France.

1848 The Christadelphians, a Christian sect, is founded in the USA by John Thomas (1805–71).

1850		

1850–64 The Taiping Rebellion against the Qing Dynasty in China costs millions of lives before it is crushed.

1852 President Louis-Napoleon of France (1808–73) dissolves the constitution of the Second Republic and assumes the title of Emperor Napoleon III.

1854 Britain and France join in the Crimean War on the side of Turkey against Russia.

1859 English utilitarian philosopher John Stuart Mill (1806–73) publishes *On Liberty.*

1856–7 Persia at war with Britain after taking Herat (Afghanistan).

1856–60 Second Opium War.

1862 English philosopher Herbert Spencer (1820–1903) publishes the first volume of his *System of Synthetic Philosophy.* An evolutionist, he supported Darwin and coined the phrase 'survival of the fittest'.

1857–8 The Indian Mutiny, an uprising against British rule in India, begins with a mutiny of Indian troops in British service. It leads to the transfer of government from the East India Company to the British Crown.

1861–5 US Civil War.

1863 Formation of the Seventh Day Adventist Church in the USA, led by Ellen Gould White (1827–1915).

1861 Emancipation of the Russian serfs.

1863 US President Lincoln (1809–65) abolishes slavery in the USA.

1863 Foundation of the Baha'i faith in Persia by Mirza Husayn Ali (1817–92).

1864 Geneva Convention founds the International Red Cross.

Science and technology	Arts and culture

1820

1821 English scientist Michael Faraday (1791–1867) invents the electric motor and generator.

1825 The first passenger steam railway comes into service, between Stockton and Darlington in north-east England.

1826 French scientist and pioneer of photography Joseph Niepce (1765–1833) produces the first photographic image, using a bitumen-coated pewter plate.

1827 Scottish botanist Robert Brown (1773–1858) first observes the movement of fine particles in a liquid, subsequently named 'Brownian movement'.

1831 English naturalist Charles Darwin (1809–82) begins the voyage of the *Beagle*, making many of the discoveries which later allow him to develop his idea of the origin of species.

1833 English mathematician Charles Babbage (1792–1871) initiates a major step in the development of the computer with his design for an 'analytical engine', intended to be programmable to carry out mathematical functions.

1837 Sir Charles Wheatstone (1802–75), English physicist, patents an electric telegraph.

1839 US inventor Charles Goodyear (1800–60) discovers the process of vulcanizing rubber.

1846 German astronomer Johann Galle (1812–1910) is the first person to observe the planet Neptune.

1848 The absolute (Kelvin) scale of temperature is devised by British physicist William (later Lord) Kelvin (1824–1907).

1820 Publication of *Lamia and Other Poems* by English poet John Keats (1795–1821), which contains his best-known work, including the great 'Odes'.

1821 English landscape painter John Constable (1776–1837) completes *The Haywain*.

1823 Beethoven completes his Symphony No 9.

1825 Russian poet and writer Alexander Pushkin (1799–1837) publishes *Boris Godunov*.

1828 US lexicographer Noah Webster (1758–1843) publishes *An American Dictionary of the English Language*.

1830 French composer Hector Berlioz (1803–69) completes his *Symphonie fantastique*.

1832 Japanese Ukiyo-e painter and wood engraver Ando Hiroshige (1797–1858) completes his *Fifty-three Stages of the Tokaido*.

1836 Serial publication begins of *The Pickwick Papers*, the first novel by Charles Dickens (1812–70).

Dickens is the most widely-known English writer after Shakespeare. His novels are a vivid portrayal of social life in Victorian England and they continue to find a receptive audience, not only in book form, but also as film and stage adaptations.

1848 Foundation of the Pre-Raphaelite Brotherhood, a group of English artists aiming to revolutionize Victorian art.

1850

1850 Invention of the bunsen burner, named after the German scientist Robert Bunsen (1811–99).

1850 German physiologist and physicist Hermann von Helmholtz (1821–94) invents an opthalmoscope.

1851 French physicist Jean Bernard Léon Foucault (1819–68) uses a freely-suspended pendulum to convincingly demonstrate the rotation of the Earth.

1855 English metallurgist Henry Bessemer (1813–98) patents his process for converting pig-iron into steel.

1859 Darwin publishes *The Origin of Species*.

1860 Florence Nightingale (1820–1910) establishes the first institution for the training of nurses.

1863 French chemist Louis Pasteur (1822–95) develops the technique of 'pasteurization'.

1863 The first underground railway is opened in London.

1851 The Great Exhibition in London celebrates British industry.

1851 US author Herman Melville (1819–91) publishes *Moby Dick*, considered one of the greatest US novels.

1852 US novelist Harriet Beecher Stowe (1811–96) publishes *Uncle Tom's Cabin*, an anti-slavery novel.

1853 Italian composer Giuseppe Verdi (1813–1901) completes his operas *Il Trovatore* and *La Traviata*.

1857 French novelist Gustave Flaubert (1821–80) publishes *Madame Bovary*, for which he is unsuccessfully prosecuted for immorality.

1858 German-born French composer Jacques Offenbach (1819–80) completes his *opera bouffe, Orpheus in the Underworld*.

1863 *Le Déjeuner sur l'herbe*, by French painter Edouard Manet (1832–83), causes a scandal with its provocative portrayal of a naked woman.

History

History and politics	Religion and philosophy
1867 The USA buys Alaska from Russia.	**1865** English religious leader William Booth (1829–1912) begins the Christian Mission in London's East End. It becomes the Salvation Army in 1878.
1868 The Meiji Restoration in Japan sees the overthrow of the last Shogun and the restoration of imperial rule.	
1868 The British Trades Union Congress is founded.	**1869–70** First Vatican Council called by Pope Pius IX (1792–1878); the doctrine of papal infallibility is declared.
1870–1 Franco-Prussian War; a crushing defeat for France leads to the fall of Napoleon III.	
1871 The King of Prussia becomes Emperor Wilhelm I (1797–1888) of the united Germany.	**1872** In the USA, the international Bible Students' Association (Jehovah's Witnesses) is founded by Charles Taze Russell (1852–1916).
1875 Britain buys the Suez Canal.	
1876 Queen Victoria of Great Britain and Ireland (1819–1901) is declared Empress of India.	
1879 Zulu Kingdom defeated by the British.	
1880–1 The First Boer War; it ends with the defeat of Britain at Majuba Hill.	**1882** In the Sudan Muhammad Ahmed (1843–85) claims to be the Islamic saviour the Mahdi.
1881 Tsar Alexander II of Russia (b.1818) is assassinated by revolutionary terrorists.	
1885 Foundation of the Indian National Congress, a political organization aimed at independence from Britain.	**1884** Death of Indian Hindu reformer Keshub Chunder Sen (b.1838).
1892 Scottish labour leader Keir Hardie (1856–1915) becomes the first Labour MP.	**1890** Death of English theologian, cardinal and leader of the Oxford Movement, John Henry Newman (b.1801).
1893 New Zealand is the first country to give women the right to vote.	
1894 French army captain Alfred Dreyfus (1859–1935) is wrongly convicted of passing military secrets to Germany, and his case becomes a national *cause célèbre*.	
1898 The USA gains Puerto Rico and the Philippines in the Spanish–American War.	
1899–1902 The Second Boer War.	

1900–2000

■ Early technological advances include the domestic refrigerator and powered flight.
■ The ever more powerful and efficient weapons produced by modern industry help kill millions in World War I. The newly developed aeroplane becomes militarily important. In Britain long-lasting effects of the wartime drive for efficiency are British Summer Time and the licensing laws.
■ Revolution in Russia leads to the first communist state (1917).
■ Inspired by the Suffragettes, British women win the right to vote in 1918, followed two years later by women in the United States. Many women go out to work for the first time during the two World Wars.
■ Unemployment and poverty characterize the worldwide depression of the 1930s.

History and politics	Religion and philosophy
1900 The Boxer Rising in China is put down by a combined force of foreign powers.	**1901** Pentecostalism, a Christian renewal movement, is established in Topeka, Kansas.
1901 Death of Queen Victoria of Great Britain after a reign of 64 years.	
1901 The Commonwealth of Australia is established, with Canberra as its capital.	**1902** US philosopher William James (1842–1910) publishes *The Varieties of Religious Experience*.
1904–5 Russo-Japanese War; Russia suffers naval and military disasters before eventual defeat.	
1905 An unsuccessful revolution in Russia results in the country's first constitution and parliament.	**1904** German sociologist Max Weber (1864–1920) publishes *The Protestant Ethic and the Spirit of Capitalism*.
1908 In Turkey the reformist Young Turks stage a revolution and depose the Sultan.	

Science and technology	Arts and culture

1866 A transatlantic telegraph cable is laid.

1866 Swedish chemist and industrialist Alfred Nobel (1833–96) invents dynamite.

1869 A transcontinental railway is established in the USA with the meeting of the Union and Pacific railroads.

1876 Scots-born US inventor Alexander Graham Bell (1847–1922) patents his telephone.

1878 Electric street lighting is introduced in London.

1882 The world's first hydroelectric plant comes into operation in Wisconsin, USA.

1883 The first fully automatic machine-gun, the Maxim gun, is invented by US-born British inventor Sir Hiram Maxim (1840–1916).

1884 German engineer Gottlieb Daimler (1834–1900) produces a petrol-burning internal-combustion engine.

1888 Scottish veterinarian and inventor John Dunlop (1840–1921) invents the pneumatic tyre.

1889 The Eiffel Tower, designed by French engineer Gustave Eiffel (1832–1923), is completed in Paris.

1895 German physicist Wilhelm Röntgen (1845–1923) discovers X-rays.

1897 German engineer Rudolf Diesel (1858–1913) demonstrates his compression-ignition engine.

1898 French physicists Marie (1867–1934) and Pierre (1859–1906) Curie isolate polonium and radium.

1865 Russian writer Leo Tolstoy (1828–1910) publishes the first part of his masterpiece, the novel *War and Peace*.

1869 First performance of the opera *Das Rheingold* by German composer Richard Wagner (1813–83).

1874 *Impression, soleil levant*, a painting by French artist Claude Monet (1840–1926), gives the name to the Impressionist school of painters.

1875 French composer Georges Bizet (1838–75) completes *Carmen* shortly before his death.

1876 US writer Mark Twain (1835–1910) publishes *Tom Sawyer*.

1879 Norweigan dramatist Henrik Ibsen (1828–1906) writes *A Doll's House*.

1884 The first part of the *Oxford English Dictionary* is published.

1886 The *Statue of Liberty*, designed by French sculptor Auguste Bartholdi (1834–1904), is unveiled.

1891 English author Thomas Hardy (1840–1928) publishes *Tess of the D'Urbervilles*.

1895 First performance of *The Importance of Being Earnest* by Irish writer Oscar Wilde (1854–1900).

1899 English composer Edward Elgar (1857–1934) completes his *Enigma Variations*.

1900–2000

- World War II sees the development of total war, with the mass bombing of enemy cities, and ends with the use of the most destructive weapon yet known, the atomic bomb.
- Humankind ventures into outer space.
- Popular culture comes into its own with the spread of radio and television broadcasting and the rise of pop music as a genre.
- With the introduction of the PC, computers increasingly dominate the workplace and daily life. Millions of people worldwide use the Internet for communication, entertainment and business.

1901 The first transatlantic wireless message is sent by Italian Guglielmo Marconi (1847–1937).

1901 Austrain-born US pathologist Karl Landsteiner (1868–1943) discovers the four major blood groups (A, O, B, AB).

1902 The Aswan Dam on the Nile is completed.

1903 The first powered flight of a heavier-than-air craft is carried out by Orville Wright (1871–1948) and his brother Wilbur (1867–1912) at Kitty Hawk, North Carolina.

1905 German-born US physicist Albert Einstein (1879–1955) publishes a paper on his special theory of relativity.

1908 US automobile engineer Henry Ford (1863–1947) begins production of the Model T.

1909 French aviator Louis Blériot (1872–1936) makes the first flight across the English Channel.

1900 First performance of the opera *Tosca* by Italian composer Giacomo Puccini (1858–1924).

1901 Russian composer Sergei Rachmaninov (1873–1943) composes his piano concerto *No2 in C Minor*.

1904 French sculptor Auguste Rodin (1840–1917) completes *Le Penseur* ('The Thinker').

1904 Russian writer Anton Chekhov (1860–1904) completes his play *The Cherry Orchard*.

1907 Spanish artist Pablo Picasso (1881–1973) completes *Les Demoiselles d'Avignon*, regarded as the first Cubist painting.

1908 English novelist E M Forster (1879–1970) publishes *A Room with a View*.

History

	History and politics	Religion and philosophy
1910		

1910 The Union of South Africa is established as a dominion of the British Empire.

1910–17 Revolution in Mexico.

1911 Revolution in China leads to the overthrow of the Qing Dynasty and the establishment of a republic.

1911 Birth of Indian cult leader Maharishi Mahesh Yogi.

> Maharishi Mahesh Yogi founded the science of creative intelligence and, as an exponent of the relaxation technique called transcendental meditation, he became one of the first Eastern gurus to attract a Western following.

1912–13 Balkan Wars; Turkey loses almost all of its territory in Europe.

1914 World War I begins.

1916 In Dublin Irish nationalists stage the Easter Rising.

1917 The USA enters World War I.

1917 The Russian Revolution overthrows the imperial regime and brings the first communist government to power.

1917 The Balfour Declaration by British Foreign Secretary Arthur Balfour (1848–1930) promises Zionists a national home in Palestine.

1918 World War I ends.

1912 Austrian social philosopher Rudolf Steiner (1861–1925) founds anthroposophy, a modern spiritual movement, in Switzerland.

1918 Formal foundation of the Native American Church, combining native religion with certain elements of Christianity.

1918 In Britain women over the age of 30 receive the right to vote.

1919 The League of Nations is established to preserve international peace.

1922 Fascist leader Benito Mussolini (1883–1945) comes to power in Italy.

1925 German politician Adolf Hitler (1889–1945) writes his political testament *Mein Kampf* while in prison.

1929 The New York Stock Exchange collapses, triggering the Depression.

1919 Swiss theologian Karl Barth (1886–1968) publishes his commentary of St Paul's Epistle to the Romans.

1922 Austrian-born British philosopher Ludwig Wittgenstein (1889–1951) publishes his *Tractatus Logico-philosophicus*.

1927 German philosopher Martin Heidegger (1889–1976) publishes *Being and Time*.

| 1930 | | |

1931 Japan invades Manchuria.

1932 The Kingdom of Saudi Arabia is established.

1933 Adolf Hitler (1889–1945) becomes Chancellor of Germany.

1933 US President Franklin D Roosevelt (1882–1945) begins to implement his New Deal programme for national recovery.

1934 Chinese communists under Mao Zedong (1893–1976) begin their 'Long March', withdrawing from south-eastern to north-western China.

1936–9 Spanish Civil War; it ends with the overthrow of the Republican government.

1939 World War II breaks out.

1940 The victory of the RAF over the Luftwaffe in the Battle of Britain causes Hitler to postpone plans to invade the UK.

1941 Germany invades Russia.

1941 A Japanese air attack on the US base at Pearl Harbor, Hawaii brings the USA into World War II.

1942 The British victory over the German Afrika Corps at El Alamein in Egypt is a turning point in the North African campaign.

1944 Landings in Normandy on D-Day (June 6) begin the Allied liberation of Europe.

1931 Tibetan Buddhist teacher and monk Geshe Kelsang Gyatso born. He is the founder of the New Kadampa Tradition of Buddhism.

1931 The Nation of Islam is founded in the USA by Wallace Ford Muhammad (b.c.1877), also known as Wali Farad.

1933 Death of Buddhist Anagarika Dharmapala (b.1864). He wrote and spoke as the champion of Buddhist reformism, and in his later years campaigned for the return of Buddhist sacred sites in North India into Buddhist hands.

1940 Foundation of the Taizé religious community by Swiss monk Roger Schutz-Marsauche (1915–).

1943 French writer and philosopher Jean-Paul Sartre (1905–80) publishes *Being and Nothingness*, one of the seminal texts of Existentialism.

Science and technology

1910–13 *Principia Mathematica* is produced by English philosophers and mathematicians Bertrand Russell (1872–1970) and Alfred Whitehead (1861–1947).

1914 The US Corps of Engineers completes the building of the Panama Canal.

1916 The British Army makes the first use of the military tank, in the Battle of the Somme.

1919 The first non-stop transatlantic flight is made by English aviators John Alcock (1892–1919) and Arthur Brown (1886–1948).

1920 US soldier John Brown (1860–1940) invents the 'Thompson' gun.

1924 A vaccine (BCG) against tuberculosis is introduced in France after being discovered by the bacteriologists Albert Calmette (1863–1933) and Camille Guérin (1872–1961).

1926 Scottish electrical engineer John Logie Baird (1888–1946) gives the first demonstration of a television image.

1927 *The Jazz Singer*, the first cinema film with a soundtrack ('talking picture'), is released by the US Warner Brothers company.

1927 US aviator Charles Lindbergh (1902–74) makes the first non-stop solo transatlantic flight.

1928 Penicillin is discovered by Scottish bacteriologist Alexander Fleming (1881–1955).

1929 US astronomer Edwin Hubble (1889–1953) announces his discovery that the universe is expanding.

1930 US astronomer Clyde Tombaugh (1906–97) discovers the planet Pluto.

1932 English physicist Jams Chadwick (1891–1974) discovers and names the neutron.

1935 US seismologist Charles Richter (1900–85) completes the Richter scale of earthquake measurement.

1935 The first practical radar system is developed by Scottish physicist Robert Watson-Watt (1892–1973).

1936 English mathematician Alan Turing (1912–54) makes an outstanding contribution to the development of computer science, outlining a theoretical 'universal' machine.

1937 British aeronautical engineer Frank Whittle (1907–96) invents the jet engine.
1937 Nylon is invented in the USA by industrial chemist Wallace Hume Carothers (1896–1937).

1938 US inventor Chester Carlson (1906–68) discovers the basic principles of 'xerography' (patented in 1940).

1942 Italian-born US physicist Enrico Fermi (1901–54) builds the world's first nuclear reactor.

1943 French naval officer and underwater explorer Jacques Cousteau (1910–97) invents the aqualung diving apparatus.

1944 The first jet fighter aircraft (the German Messerschmitt Me262) makes its appearance in combat.

Arts and culture

c.1910 Russian-born French artist Wassily Kandinsky (1866–1944) begins to produce the first abstract paintings.

1912 French novelist Marcel Proust (1871–1922) publishes the first volume of *À la recherche du temps perdu*.

1913 German writer Thomas Mann (1871–1950) publishes the novelette *Death in Venice*.

1914–16 English composer Gustav Holst (1874–1934) composes *The Planets*.

1915 Release of *The Birth of a Nation*, by US filmmaker D W Griffith (1875–1948).

1916 The Dada movement is founded in Zurich.

1920 Posthumous publication of *Poems* by Wilfred Owen (1893–1918), reflecting the horror of trench warfare in World War I.
1920 New Zealand author Katherine Mansfield (1888–1923) publishes *Bliss, and other stories*.

1922 *Ulysses* by Irish writer James Joyce (1882–1941) is published in Paris. It helps revolutionize the 20c novel, but because it is considered obscene, it is not published in Britain and the USA until 1936.

1924 US composer George Gershwin (1898–1937) completes his *Rhapsody in Blue*.

1925 Austrian writer Franz Kafka's (1883–1924) *The Trial* is published posthumously.
1925 US novelist F Scott Fitzgerald captures the spirit of the 1920s in *The Great Gatsby*.
1927 The British Broadcasting Corporation begins its radio service.

1930 English actor, playwright and composer Noël Coward (1899–1973) completes *Private Lives*.

1931 Surrealist Spanish artist Salvador Dalí (1904–89) paints *The Persistence of Memory*.

1932 *Brave New World*, a novel by English author Aldous Huxley (1894–1963), depicts a dystopian future in which people are scientifically bred.

1933 Spanish poet and playwright Frederico García Lorca (1898–1936) writes *Blood Wedding*.

1934 *Tropic of Cancer*, a novel by US author Henry Miller (1891–1980), is published in Paris but banned in Britain and the USA because of sexual explicitness.

1936 Russian composer Sergei Prokofiev (1891–1953) completes *Peter and the Wolf*.

1937 Picasso paints *Guernica*, a depiction of the destruction of that town by bombing in the Spanish Civil War.

1938 British sculptor Henry Moore (1898–1986) completes *Recumbent Figure*.

1940 *For Whom the Bell Tolls* is published by US writer Ernest Hemingway (1899–1961).

1941 Release of *Citizen Kane*, a US film directed by Orson Welles (1915–85), often acclaimed as the greatest film ever made.

1943 The musical *Oklahoma!* is written by US composers Oscar Hammerstein II (1895–1960) and Richard Rodgers (1902–79).

History

1945

History and politics	Religion and philosophy
1945 World War II ends; Germany surrenders (May); Japan also capitulates (August) after the USA drops atomic bombs on Hiroshima and Nagasaki.	**1945** Austrian-born British philosopher Karl Popper (1902–94) publishes *The Open Society and its Enemies.*
1947 The Truman Doctrine, announced by US President Truman (1884–1972), promises US aid to countries threatened by communist interference.	
1948 Israel proclaims its independence.	
1948 Assassination of Indian leader Mahatma Gandhi (b.1869).	**1948** Foundation of the World Council of Churches.
1949 NATO formed.	
1949 The Communists take power in China.	
1950–3 Korean War; United Nations forces defend South Korea against invasion by communist North Korea and China.	**1954** The Church of Scientology is founded, based on L Ron Hubbard's (1911–86) *Dianetics: The Modern Science of Mental Health.*
1953 Death of Soviet revolutionary and leader Joseph Stalin (b.1879).	
1954 French withdraw from Indochina.	**1954** South Korean religious leader Sun Myung Moon (1920–) founds the Unification Church.
1956 Suez Crisis; Egypt nationalizes the Suez Canal, prompting occupation of the canal zone by Britain and France, who are forced to withdraw by US and Russian pressure.	**1956** British philosopher A J Ayer (1910–89) publishes *The Problem of Knowledge.*
1957 Treaty of Rome establishes a European Economic Community comprising France, West Germany, Italy, Belgium, Netherlands and Luxembourg.	
1959 The Communists come to power in Cuba under Fidel Castro (1927–).	

1960

History and politics	Religion and philosophy
1961 The East German government builds a wall in Berlin to prevent its citizens moving from East to West.	**1962–5** The Second Vatican Council, called by Pope John XXIII (1881–1963), initiates far-reaching reforms in Catholicism.
1963 US President John F Kennedy is assassinated (b.1917).	
1964–75 Vietnam War between communist North Vietnam and non-communist South Vietnam; USA involved until 1973.	**1965** US black nationalist leader Malcolm X is killed by Black Muslim assassins (b.1925).
1966–76 The Cultural Revolution in China. Mao Zedong (1893–1976) encourages youth to persecute intellectuals.	**1966** The Catholic Church decides to publish no further editions of its index of prohibited books.
1967 In the Six-Day War, Israel quickly defeats an alliance of Egypt, Syria and Jordan.	**1966** The Hindu cult The International Society for Krishna Consciousness (Hare Krishna) is founded in the USA by A C Bhaktivedanta Swami Prabhupada (1896–1977).
1968 US civil rights leader Martin Luther King, Jr (b.1929) is assassinated.	**1967** French philosopher Jacques Derrida (1930–), founder of the deconstruction school of criticism, publishes *L'écriture et la différence.*
1968 Warsaw Pact troops invade Czechoslovakia to crush the liberalizing Dubček regime.	
1969 Northern Ireland enters a period of unrest and violence.	**1970** The complete New English Bible, in modern English, is published.
1971 Civil war in Pakistan sees Bangladesh declare independence.	**1971** Peruvian theologian Gustavo Gutiérrez (1928–) completes his seminal work *A Theology of Liberation.*
1973 US troops are withdrawn from Vietnam.	
1973 Yom Kippur War follows a surprise attack by Egypt and Syria on Israel.	**1978** Polish cardinal Karol Wojtyła (1920–) becomes Pope John Paul II, the first non-Italian pope since the 16c.
1973 Chilean Socialist President Salvador Allende (b.1908) is killed when his government is overthrown by the armed forces.	
1974 US President Richard Nixon (1913–94) resigns under threat of impeachment over the Watergate affair.	
1979 The Shah of Iran is deposed and an Islamic republic is set up under Ayatollah Khomeini (1900–89).	

Science and technology	Arts and culture
	1945 English author George Orwell (1903–50) publishes *Animal Farm*, a satire on totalitarianism.
1947 US test pilot Charles Chuck Yeager (1923–) makes the first supersonic flight, in the Bell X-1 rocket aircraft.	
1948 The transistor is invented in the USA, contributing greatly to the development of computers.	**1951** Publication of *Catcher in the Rye*, a novel by US writer J D Salinger (1919–).
	1952 US composer John Cage (1912–92) produces *4'33"* (silent throughout).
1952 The hydrogen bomb is tested by the USA.	**1953** Irish playwright Samuel Beckett (1906–89) writes his *Waiting for Godot*.
1953 The helical structure of DNA is discovered by English molecular biologist Francis Crick (1916–) and US biologist James Watson (1928–).	**1954–5** J R R Tolkien (1892–1973) publishes *The Lord of the Rings*.

1945

1960

1947 US test pilot Charles Chuck Yeager (1923–) makes the first supersonic flight, in the Bell X-1 rocket aircraft.

1948 The transistor is invented in the USA, contributing greatly to the development of computers.

1952 The hydrogen bomb is tested by the USA.

1953 The helical structure of DNA is discovered by English molecular biologist Francis Crick (1916–) and US biologist James Watson (1928–).

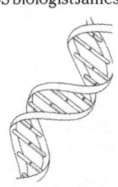

1954 Invention of the contraceptive pill.

1956 The first practical videotape recorder is demonstrated by US engineers Raymond Dolby (1933–) and Charles Ginsburg (1920–92).

1957 The Soviet Union launches the world's first artificial satellite, Sputnik 1.

1959 The Soviet space probe Luna 3 takes a photograph of the far side of the Moon.

1945 English author George Orwell (1903–50) publishes *Animal Farm*, a satire on totalitarianism.

1951 Publication of *Catcher in the Rye*, a novel by US writer J D Salinger (1919–).

1952 US composer John Cage (1912–92) produces *4'33"* (silent throughout).

1953 Irish playwright Samuel Beckett (1906–89) writes his *Waiting for Godot*.

1954–5 J R R Tolkien (1892–1973) publishes *The Lord of the Rings*.

1955 'Rock Around the Clock' by Bill Haley (1925–81) and the Comets is one of the first hit singles of the rock and roll era.

1956 Death of US artist Jackson Pollock (b.1912). He was the first exponent of tachism or action painting in the USA.

1956 First performance of *Look Back in Anger*, a play by English dramatist John Osborne (1929–94), which introduces the prototype of the 'angry young man' as hero.

1957 Publication of *On the Road*, a novel by US author Jack Kerouac (1922–69), which captures the discontent and restlessness of the 'Beat Generation'.

1959 Russian-born US novelist Vladimir Nabokov (1899–1977) publishes *Lolita*.

1960 US physicist Theodore Maiman (1927–) produces the first laser.

1961 Soviet airman Yuri Gagarin (1934–68) becomes the first human to travel in space.

1962 The US launch Telstar I, a communications satellite which relays the first transatlantic television signals.

1965 US physicists Arno Penzias (1933–) and Robert Wilson (1936–) discover microwave background radiation, a remnant of the Big Bang.

1966 The genetic code is elucidated by US biochemist Marshall Nirenberg (1927–) and others.

1967 The first successful heart transplant operation is carried out by South African surgeon Christiaan Barnard (1922–2001).

1969 US astronaut Neil Armstrong (1930–) becomes the first man to set foot on the Moon during the Apollo 11 mission.

1971 The introduction of the microprocessor is a great step forward in the development of computers.

1972 The pocket calculator is invented in the USA.

1975 First personal computer (Altair 8800) commercially available.

1976 The Anglo-French aircraft Concorde, the world's first supersonic airliner, enters regular service.

1978 The first 'test-tube baby' (ie conceived using *in-vitro* fertilization) is born, in the UK.

1960 Publication of *Rabbit, Run* by US novelist John Updike (1932–).

1961 US novelist Joseph Heller (1923–99) publishes *Catch-22*, creating both a bestseller and a new English expression.

1962 British pop group The Beatles (1960–70) have their first hit single 'Love Me Do'. They go on to inspire 'Beatlemania' and change the face of popular music.

1962 US artist Andy Warhol (c.1926–87) produces his multiple portrait of Marilyn Monroe, *Marilyn Diptych*.

1967 The Beatles release their album *Sergeant Pepper's Lonely Hearts Club Band*.

1973 US novelist Thomas Pynchon (1937–) publishes *Gravity's Rainbow*.

1973 Sydney Opera House opens.

1976 US composer Philip Glass (1937–) writes *Einstein on the Beach*.

1977 Millions mourn the death of 'The King', Elvis Presley (b.1935).

1977 Release of *Star Wars*, a science-fiction blockbuster film by US director George Lucas (1944–).

1979 Czech-born French novelist Milan Kundera (1929–) publishes *The Book of Laughter and Forgetting*.

History

	History and politics	**Religion and philosophy**
1980		

1980 Black majority rule comes into force in Zimbabwe.

1980–8 Millions of lives are lost in the Iran–Iraq War.

1982 Falklands War; Britain retakes the Falkland Islands after invasion by Argentina.

1984 Indian Prime Minister Indira Gandhi (b.1917) is assassinated by Sikh extremists.

1986 Chernobyl reactor disaster, Ukraine, USSR.

1988 Mikhail Gorbachev (1931–) becomes Soviet head of state and initiates a programme of reform and restructuring.

1989 The Chinese Army crushes mass anti-government protests in Beijing's Tiananmen Square.

1990 East and West Germany are reunited.

1989 The 14th Dalai Lama (Tenzin Gyatso, b.1935) receives the Nobel Prize for Peace in recognition of his commitment to the non-violent liberation of Tibet.

1991 In the Gulf War a US-led United Nations coalition expels Iraqi forces from Kuwait.
1991 USSR breaks up; civil war in Yugoslavia.

1992 Yugoslavia breaks up; Czechoslovakia splits in two.

1994 Nelson Mandela (1918–) is elected South Africa's first black President.
1994 World Trade Organization founded.

1994 The Church of England ordains women priests.

1995 South Pacific Forum condemns France for nuclear tests.

1997 Britain returns Hong Kong to China.

1995 Pope John Paul II participates in historic meetings aimed at discussing relations between the Orthodox and Roman Catholic churches.

1998 A tentative peace agreement is reached in Northern Ireland (Good Friday Agreement).

1999 Launch of the Euro, the single currency of the European Union.
1999 Inauguration of new Scottish Parliament and Welsh Assembly.
1999 NATO attacks Serbia over treatment of Albanians in Kosovo.

2000

2000 The leaders of North and South Korea have their first summit meeting in 50 years.
2000 Israel and Palestine pursue peace, but the administration of Jerusalem remains a stumbling block and violence ensues.

2001 World Trade Center, New York, destroyed in terrorist attack, killing thousands. The USA and its allies overthrow the Taliban regime in Afghanistan who were believed to be sheltering those responsible.

2002 The Euro becomes the official currency of 12 states in the European Union.
2002 East Timor gains its independence from Indonesia.
2002 India and Pakistan come to the brink of war over Kashmir.

2003 The USA and its allies declare war on Iraq.

Science and technology	Arts and culture
	1980

Science and technology	Arts and culture
1981 First use of the US space shuttle, a reusable crewed launch vehicle.	**1980** Italian novelist Umberto Eco (1932–) publishes *The Name of the Rose*.
1983 Compact discs first come on the market.	**1982** Chilean novelist Isabel Allende (1942–) publishes *House of the Spirits*, a bestselling novel in the 'magical realism' style, presenting surreal fantasy in a realistic way.
1984 The Apple Macintosh personal computer is introduced.	
1984 The technique of 'DNA fingerprinting' is developed by English molecular biologist Alec Jeffries (1950–).	**1982** US writer Alice Walker (1944–) publishes *The Color Purple*.
	1984 British writer J G Ballard (1930–) publishes *Empire of the Sun*.
1986 The Soviet space station Mir is launched as the first permanently manned space station.	**1987** US novelist Toni Morrison (1931–) publishes *Beloved*.
1987 Work begins on the Channel Tunnel between England and France (completed 1994).	**1988** British novelist Salman Rushdie (1947–) publishes *The Satanic Verses*.
1988 *A Brief History of Time*, an account of cosmology by English theoretical physicist Stephen Hawking (1942–), becomes a popular bestseller.	**1988** Australian novelist Peter Carey (1943–) publishes *Oscar and Lucinda*.
	1989 Japanese-born British novelist Kazuo Ishiguro (1954–) publishes *Remains of the Day*.
1990 Start of the Human Genome Project. **1990** The space shuttle Discovery launches the Hubble Space telescope; a problem with its primary mirror is soon apparent.	**1990** English composer Harrison Birtwhistle (1934–) completes the opera *Gawain*.
	**1992** Sri Lankan-born Canadian writer Michael Ondaatje (1943–) is joint winner of the Booker prize with his novel *The English Patient*. **1993** English sculptor Rachel Whiteread (1963–) completes *House*. **1993** Indian writer Vikram Seth (1952–) publishes his novel *A Suitable Boy*.
1993 British mathematician Andrew Wiles (1953–) announces his proof of Fermat's last theorem.	**1993** British artist Damien Hirst (1965–) causes a sensation with his *Mother and Child, Divided*. **1996** The new Globe Theatre opens in London.
1994 Creation of the World Wide Web.	
1997 The first successful cloning of an animal results in 'Dolly' the sheep, at the Roslin Institute, Scotland.	**1998** English poet Ted Hughes (1930–98) publishes *Birthday Letters*. **1999** Death of US-born British violin virtuoso Yehudi Menuhin (b.1916).
	2000
2000 Researchers in the USA and Britain, working on the Human Genome Project, publish the first draft of the human genome map. **2000** The International Space Station is manned with its first long-term crew.	**2000** In London, Bankside Power Station reopens as the Tate Modern gallery. **2000** British author J K Rowling (1965–) publishes the fourth Harry Potter book, *Harry Potter and the Goblet of Fire*. **2000** Northern Irish poet Seamus Heaney (1939–) publishes *Beowulf*.
2002 The first synthetic virus is created, following the genome sequence for polio.	**2002** German professor Gunther von Hagens causes controversy with his *Body Worlds* exhibition in London of cadavers.
2003 Scientists sequencing the human genome announce its completion.	

History

Journeys of exploration

Date	Name	Exploration
490BC	Hanno	Makes voyage round part of the coast of Africa
325BC	Alexander the Great	Leads fleet along the N Indian coast and up the Persian Gulf
84AD	Agricola	His fleet circumnavigates Britain
1003	Leif Ericsson	Voyages to N America and discovers 'Vinland' (possibly Nova Scotia)
1418	João Gonçalves Zarco	Discovers Madeira (dispatched by Henry the Navigator)
1434	Gil Eanes	Sails round Cape Bojadar (dispatched by Henry the Navigator)
1446	Dinís Dias	Discovers Cape Verde and the Senegal River (dispatched by Henry the Navigator)
1488	Bartolomeu Dias	Sails round the Cape of Storms (Cape of Good Hope)
1492	Christopher Columbus	Discovers the New World
1493	Christopher Columbus	Discovers Puerto Rico, Antigua and Jamaica
1497	John Cabot	Explores the coast of Newfoundland
1497	Vasco da Gama	Voyages round the Cape of Good Hope
1498	Vasco da Gama	Explores coast of Mozambique and discovers sea route to India
1498	Christopher Columbus	Discovers Trinidad and Venezuela
1499	Amerigo Vespucci	Discovers mouth of the River Amazon
1500	Pedro Alvares Cabral	Discovers Brazil
1500	Diogo Dias	Discovers Madagascar
1500	Gaspar Corte Real	Explores east coast of Greenland and Labrador
1501	Amerigo Vespucci	Explores S American coast
1502	Christopher Columbus	Explores Honduras and Panama
1513	Vasco Núñez de Balboa	Crosses the Panama Isthmus to discover the Pacific Ocean
1520	Ferdinand Magellan	Discovers the Straits of Magellan
1521	Ferdinand Magellan	Discovers the Philippines
1524	Giovanni da Verrazano	Discovers New York Bay and the Hudson River
1526	Sebastian Cabot	Explores the Rio de la Plata
1534	Jacques Cartier	Explores the Gulf of St Lawrence
1535	Jacques Cartier	Navigates the St Lawrence River
1536	Pedro de Mendoza	Founds Buenos Aires and explores Parana and Paraguay rivers
1539	Hernando de Soto	Explores Florida
1540	García López de Cárdenas	Discovers the Grand Canyon
1580	Francis Drake	Completes circumnavigation of the globe
1585	John Davis	Discovers Davis Strait on expedition to Greenland
1595	Walter Raleigh	Explores the Orinoco River
1610	Henry Hudson	Discovers Hudson's Bay
1616	William Baffin	Discovers Baffin Bay during search for the NW Passage
1617	Walter Raleigh	Begins expedition to Guiana
1642	Abel Janszoon Tasman	Discovers Tasmania and New Zealand
1678	Robert Cavelier de la Salle	Explores the Great Lakes of Canada
1692	Ijsbrand Iders	Explores the Gobi Desert
1736	Anders Celsius	Undertakes expedition to Lapland
1761	Carsten Niebuhr	Undertakes expedition to Arabia
1766	Louis de Bougainville	Voyage of discovery in Pacific, names Navigator Is
1769	James Cook	Names Society Is; charts coasts of New Zealand and E Australia
1770	James Cook	Lands at Botany Bay, Australia
1772	James Bruce	Explores Abyssinia and the confluence of the Blue Nile and White Nile
1774	James Cook	Discoveries and rediscoveries in the Pacific; discovers and names S Georgia and the S Sandwich Is
1778	James Cook	Discovers Hawaiian group; surveys coast of Bering Straits
1787	Horace Saussure	Makes first ascent of Mont Blanc
1790	George Vancouver	Explores the coast of NW America
1795	Mungo Park	Explores the course of the Niger
1818	John Ross	Attempts to discover NW Passage
1819	John Barrow	Enters Barrow Straits in the N Arctic
1823	Walter Oudney	Discovers Lake Chad in C Africa
1841	David Livingstone	Discovers Lake Ngami
1845	John Franklin	Attempts to discover NW Passage
1854	Richard Burton and John Speke	Explore interior of Somaliland
1855	David Livingstone	Discovers the Victoria Falls on the Zambesi River
1858	Richard Burton and John Speke	Discover Lake Tanganyika
1875	Henry Morton Stanley	Traces the Congo to the Atlantic
1888	Fridtjof Nansen	Crosses Greenland
1893	Fridtjof Nansen	Attempts to reach N Pole

Date	Name	Exploration
1905	Roald Amundsen	Sails through NW Passage
1909	Robert Edwin Peary	Reaches N Pole
1911	Roald Amundsen	Reaches S Pole
1912	Robert Falcon Scott	Reaches S Pole
1914	Ernest Shackleton	Leads expedition to the Antarctic
1953	Edmund Hillary and Tenzing Norgay	Make first ascent of Mt Everest
1961	Yuri Gagarin	Becomes first man in space
1969	Neil Armstrong and Buzz Aldrin	Make first landing on the moon

This table comprises mainly European explorers; 'discovers' is used to indicate the first recorded visit by a European.

Major battles and wars

Date	Event	Explanation
c.1200BC	Trojan Wars	Greeks v. Trojans
490–479BC	Persian Wars	Persia v. Greek city states
490BC	Battle of Marathon	Athens defeat of Persia
460–445BC	First Peloponnesian War	Sparta v. Athens
431–404BC	Second Peloponnesian War	Sparta, Corinth, Persia v. Athens
334–323BC	Conquests of Alexander the Great	v. Persia, Indian states
	Battle of Granicus (334BC)	
	Battle of Issus (333BC)	
	Battle of Gaugamela (331BC)	
306BC	Battle of Ipsus	'Battle of the Kings', warring 'successors' of Alexander the Great
264–241BC	First Punic War	Rome v. Carthage
218–202BC	Second Punic War	Rome v. Carthage
149–146BC	Third Punic War	Destruction of Carthage
112–106BC	Numidian War	Rome v. Juguertia, King of Numidia
73–71BC	Revolt of Spartacus	Slaves v. Rome
58–51BC	Gallic Wars of Caesar	Rome v. Celtic tribes of Gaul (ancient France)
55BC	Caesar's expedition to Britain	Rome v. British tribes
48BC	Battle of Pharsalus	Julius Caesar's defeat of Pompey
31BC	Battle of Actium	Octavian's defeat of Anthony and Cleopatra
70AD	Siege of Jerusalem	Rome v. Israel (destruction of the Temple)
84AD	Battle of Mons Graupius	Rome (Agricola) v. Scottish tribes
375–454	Hun raids on the Roman Empire	Attila v. tribes of Gaul and Italy
665	Battle of Basra	Arabs conquered by Muslims
771–814	Conquests of Charlemagne (Charles the Great)	v. Saxons, Lombards, Arabs (in Spain)
800–1016	Viking Raids	v. Britain, Normandy, Russia, Spain, Morocco, Italy
1066	Battle of Hastings and Norman Conquest of England	William (the Conqueror) v. Harold II (King of Anglo Saxons)
1089–94	El Cid's conquest of Valencia	v. the Moors
1095–1272	The Crusades	Christians v. Muslims
1190–1227	Conquests of Genghis Khan	v. Naimans, Uigurs, N China, Kara-Chitai empire, Kharezm empire
1211–1227	Genghis Khan's conquest of N China and development of the Mongol empire	
1206–1405	Mongol Conquests	v. China
1208–29	Albigensian Crusade	Inquisition v. Cathars
1220	Fall of Samarkand to Genghis Khan	
1282–1302	War of the Sicilian Vespers	Sicilian rebels v. French rulers
1297–1305	Revolt of William Wallace	Scots v. English
1314	Battle of Bannockburn	Scots (under Robert Bruce) v. English
1337–1453	Hundred Years' War	England v. France
	Battle of Sluys (1340)	English defeat of French
	Battle of Crécy (1346)	English defeat of French
	Battle of Poitiers (1356)	English defeat of French
	Battle of Agincourt (1415)	English defeat of French
1360–1405	Conquests of Tamerlane (Timur)	v. Mongols, Persia, Russia, India
1388	Battle of Otterburn (Chevy Chase)	Scots' defeat of English (under Sir Henry Percy, 'Hotspur')
1403	Battle of Shrewsbury	Glendower and Percies defeated by Henry V
1411	Battle of Harlaw	Highland v. Lowland Scots
1429	Siege of Orleans	Joan of Arc's defeat of English
1453	The Fall of Constantinople	Turkish conquest of Byzantine Empire
1455–85	Wars of the Roses	Series of civil wars in England (House of York v. House of Lancaster)
	Battle of St Albans (1455)	First battle of war: Yorkist victory

History

Date	Event	Explanation
	Battle of Bosworth Field (1485)	Lancastrian victory: death of Richard III, accession of Henry VII
1491–2	The Siege of Granada	Spanish defeat of Moors
1494–1559	Habsburg–Valois Wars	
1513	Battle of Flodden	English defeat of Scots
1542	Battle of Solway Moss	English defeat of Scots
1546–7	War of the Schmalkaldic League	France v. German Protestant Estates
1562	Massacre at Vassy	Huguenots killed by de Guise
1562–98	French Wars of Religion	Catholics v. Huguenots
1568–1648	Dutch Wars of Independence	Successful revolt of Netherlands v. Philip II of Spain
1571	Battle of Lepanto	Spanish and Italian defeat of Turkish navy
1572	St Bartholomew's Day Massacre	Slaughter of French Huguenots by Charles IX
1585–9	War of the Three Henries	Henry IV secures succession to French throne
1587	Sack of Cadiz by Drake	Defeat of Philip II's Spanish ships
1588	Defeat of the Spanish Armada	English defeat of Spanish navy
1592–9	Japanese invasion of Korea	
1596–1603	Tyrone's Rebellion in Ireland	Irish v. English
1605	Gunpowder Plot	Catholic conspiracy against James I and the English Parliament
1609–14	War of the Julich Succession	Protestant v. Catholic powers of Europe
1618–48	Thirty Years' War	French king v. Habsburg rulers
1620	Battle of the White Mountain (Prague)	Defeat of Bohemian Protestants
1628–31	War of the Mantuan Succession	France v. Spain
1639	First Bishops' War	Scotland v. England
1640	Second Bishops' War	Scots' defeat of English
1641–9	Great Irish Rebellion	Ireland v. England
1642–6	English Civil War	Royalist forces of Charles I v. Parliamentarians under Cromwell
	Battle of Marston Moor (1644)	Parliamentary defeat of Royalists
1688	The Glorious Revolution	William III and Mary II ascend English throne after flight of James II
1688–97	War of the League of Augsburg	European alliance's defeat of Louis XIV
1689	Battle of Killiecrankie	Highland Scots' defeat of government
1690	Battle of the Boyne	Defeat of James II's Catholic forces by Protestant William III
1692	The Glencoe Massacre	Slaughter of McDonalds by Campbells (anti-Jacobite forces)
1701–14	War of the Spanish Succession	Grand Alliance v. Louis XIV of France
1702–13	Queen Anne's War	Britain v. France
1704	Battle of Blenheim	Allied troops' defeat of Louis XIV
1715–16	Jacobite Rebellion	Led by Earl of Mar v. Hanoverians
	Battle of Sherrifmuir (1715)	Hanoverians v. Jacobites, indecisive battle
1739–43	War of Jenkins' Ear	Britain v. Spain
1740–48	War of the Austrian Succession	Prussia v. Austria
1745–6	Jacobite Rebellion	Led by Charles Edward Stuart (Bonnie Prince Charlie)
	Battle of Prestonpans (1745)	Jacobite defeat of Hanoverians
	Battle of Culloden (1746)	Jacobite Highlanders crushed by Hanoverian forces
1756–63	Seven Years' War	Austria, France, Russia, Sweden and Saxony v. Prussia, Britain and Portugal
1759	Battle of Quebec	British defeat of French
1763–6	Pontiac's War	Unsuccessful uprising of Native Americans v. British colonists
1775–83	US War of Independence	American settlers v. British government forces
	Battle of Bunker Hill (1775)	First battle of war; heavy British losses
	Battle of Stillwater or Saratoga (1777)	American defeat of British
	Battle of Yorktown (1781)	American defeat of British, decisive campaign of war
1789–92	French Revolution	Popular movement overthrowing *ancien régime* to establish new constitution
1792–1802	French Revolutionary Wars	French campaigns v. various neighbouring states
1792	Battle of Valmy	French defeat of Prussians
1798	Battle of Aboukir Bay or the Nile	Napoleon's French fleet destroyed by Nelson
1800–15	Napoleonic Wars	Fought to preserve new French constitution and influence under Napoleon Bonaparte
	Battle of Austerlitz (1805)	French defeat of Austro-Russian army
	Battle of Trafalgar (1805)	British defeat of Napoleonic fleet
1808–14	Peninsular War	France v. Britain

Date	Event	Explanation
	Battle of Corunna (1809)	British commander Sir John Moore killed by French
1812	Napoleon's retreat from Moscow	
1814–16	Gurkha War	Gurkhas v. British in India
1815	Battle of Waterloo	Napoleon defeated by Allied forces under Duke of Wellington
1821–32	Greek War of Independence	Greek rebellion v. Turkish rule
1836	Texan War of Independence, Battle of the Alamo	Americans v. Mexican rule
1838–9	Boer–Zulu War	
1839–42	First Opium War in China	British defeat of China
1843–51	Siege of Montevideo	Combined Argentine–Uruguayan army v. Montevideo with French and British support
1844–7	First Maori War	Maoris v. British settlers in New Zealand
1846–7	Mexican War	USA v. Mexico
1853–6	Crimean War	Britain v. Russia
	Battle of Balaclava (1856)	Unsuccessful Russian attack on British base; heavy British losses
1856–60	Second Opium War in China	British defeat of China
1857–8	Mormon Utah War	Mormons v. Federal Government of USA
1859	John Brown's raid on Harper Ferry	Abolitionist attack on Federal arsenal
1859–61	Italian War of Unification	Austria v. Italy and France
	Battle of Solferino (1859)	French defeat of Austria
1860–72	Second Maori War	Maoris v. British settlers in New Zealand
1861–5	American Civil War	North (Union states) v. South (Confederate)
	Battle of Shiloh (1862)	Heavy losses to both sides
	Battle of Gettysburg (1863)	Unionist defeat of Confederates
	Battles of Petersburg (1864)	Successful Unionist campaign v. Confederates
1866	Seven Weeks' War	Prussia and Italy's defeat of Austria and allies
1876	Battle of Little Bighorn (Custer's Last Stand)	Defeat of US cavalry under General Custer by Sioux and Cheyenne
1879	Zulu War	British defeat of Zulus
1879–84	War of the Pacific	Chile v. Peru and Bolivia
1880–1	First Boer War	Boers' defeat of British
1885	Fall of Khartoum	Mahdi defeat of Egyptians; death of British General Gordon
1890	Massacre of Wounded Knee	US defeat of Sioux
1899–1901	Boxer Uprising in China	Unsuccessful anti-foreign uprising
1899–1902	Great Boer War	Boers v. British
	Battle of Ladysmith (1900)	Sieges of the British by the Boers
	Battle of Mafeking (1900)	
1911–12	Chinese Revolution	Overthrow of Manchu dynasty
1914–18	World War I	Triple Entente (Britain, France and Russia) v. Triple Alliance (Germany, Austria–Hungary and Italy)
	Battles of Liège, Marne, Ypres and Tannenberg (1914)	Allied v. German forces
	Dardanelles and Gallipoli Campaigns (1915)	Unsuccessful Allied operations
	Battles of Loos and Ypres (1915)	Britain v. Germany
	Battle of Jutland (1916)	British fleet v. German fleet
	Battle of Verdun (1916)	France v. Germany
	Battle of Passchendaele (1917)	Third battle of Ypres, Britain v. Germany
	Battles of Amiens, Antwerp and the Second Battle of the Somme (1918)	Allied v. German forces
1916	Easter Rebellion in Dublin	Unsuccessful revolt by Irish nationalists v. British rule
1917	Russian Revolution	Overthrow of monarchy and beginning of Communism
1918	Hungarian Revolution	Communist revolt
1932–7	Communist rebellion in China	
1935–6	Italian invasion of Ethiopia	Mussolini's troops v. Ethiopia under Haile Selassie
1936–9	Spanish Civil War	Republicans v. Nationalists
	Battle of Ebro River (1938)	Nationalist defeat of Republicans
1939–45	World War II	Allied forces (Britain, France, USA, USSR) v. Germany, Japan, Italy
	Battle of Britain, Battle of Flanders, Evacuation of Dunkirk, Fall of France (1940)	Allied forces v. Germany
	Babi Yar Massacre (1941)	German slaughter of Jews
	Bombing of Pearl Harbor (1941)	Japanese attack on US naval base
	Battle of Stalingrad and Moscow (1941–2)	Soviet defeat of Germany

History

Date	Event	Explanation
	Battle of Tobruk (1941–2)	Allied v. German forces
	Battle of Midway Island (1942)	US defeat of Japanese air force
	Battle of El Alamein (1942)	British defeat of Rommel's Afrika Corps
	Battle of Singapore (1942)	Japanese siege and occupation
	Battle of Salerno, Invasion of Sicily (1943)	Allied defeat of Germany and Italy
	Burma Campaigns (1943–5)	British–Indian forces v. Japan
	D-Day allied invasion of Normandy (1944)	Allied defeat of Germany
	Battles of Anzio, Arnhem and Monte Cassino (1944)	Allied forces v. Germany
	Battle of the Bulge in the Ardennes (1944–5)	Eventual Allied defeat of Germany
	Battle of Iwo Jima (1945)	Allied capture of Japanese air-base
	Battle of the Rhine (1945)	Allied defeat of Germany
1945–9	Chinese Civil War	Communist v. non-communist forces
1946–54	French War of Indochina	Nationalist revolt v. France
1947–8	Indian Civil War	Pakistan v. India
1950–3	Korean War	Communist v. non-communist forces
1952–6	Mau-Mau uprisings in Kenya	Kikuyu revolt v. white settlers
1956	Suez War	Israel, Britain and France v. Egypt
1956–1975	Vietnam War	North Vietnam (communist) v. South Vietnam (non-communist) and US forces
1960–8	Civil War in the Congo	Military coup created first Marxist state in Africa, 1968
1961	Bay of Pigs Invasion	Cuban defeat of exiles supported by USA
1962–74	Mozambique War of Independence	Nationalist revolt against Portuguese rule
1967	Six-Day War	Israel v. Arab states
1967–70	Nigerian–Biafran War	Nigerian defeat of Biafra
1968	Soviet invasion of Czechoslovakia	Defeat of attempt at liberalization from communism
1968	Tet offensive in Vietnam	Viet Cong v. South Vietnam and USA
1970–1	Jordanian Civil War	Jordan v. Palestinian guerillas
1970–5	Cambodian War	Cambodia, South Vietnam and USA v. North Vietnam, Viet Cong and Khmer Rouge
1971	Civil War in Pakistan	East v. West Pakistan
1971	My Lai massacre	Slaughter of Vietnamese villagers by US troops
1973	Chilean Revolution	Marxist government overthrown in military coup
1974	Turkish invasion of Cyprus	Turkey v. Greek Cypriots
1975–2002	Angolan Civil War	Internal fighting after independence
1978–9	Ugandan Civil War	Ugandan exiles and Tanzanian defeat of Idi Amin Dada's regime
1978	Lebanese Civil War	Israeli invasion of S Lebanon
1979–1992	Soviet invasion of Afghanistan	Afghan resistance to Soviet invasion and to the Soviet-backed government remaining after their withdrawal in 1988
1979	Iranian Islamic Revolution	Republic established under Ayatollah Khomeini
1980–8	Iran–Iraq Gulf War	
1982	Falklands War	British defeat of Argentina
1982–90	Nicaraguan Civil War	Contras (supported by USA) v. Sandinistas (socialist junta)
1983	Invasion of Grenada	US troops on peace-restoring mission
1983–2002	Civil War in Sri Lanka	Tamil rebels v. Sinhalese government
1986	Civil War in Haiti	Military coup and new constitution
1990–6	Civil War in Rwanda	Tutsi v. Hutu groups
1991	Gulf War	Iraqi invasion of Kuwait in 1990 resulted in the defeat of Iraq by US-led allies (29 countries, including UK)
1991–5	Civil War in Yugoslavia	Declaration of independence from Yugoslavia by Slovenia, Macedonia and Croatia, joined by Bosnia-Herzegovina in 1992, developed into civil war between Croats, Bosnians (mainly Slavic Muslims) and Serbs
1992–2001	Afghan Civil War	Disputes between Islamic factions, and opposition to the Taliban regime
1996–2002	Civil War in the Democratic Republic of Congo (formerly Zaïre)	Tutsi rebels invade and stage a coup; civil war continued with military intervention from neighbouring foreign armies
1997–1999	Civil War in Sierra Leone	Military coup led by Major Johnny Paul Koroma and subsequent violence by Revolutionary United Front

Date	Event	Explanation
1999	Nato air-strikes on Serbia	Nato attacked Serbian military resources following the ethnic cleansing of Kosovo Albanians from their homes
2001	US and allied strikes on Afghanistan	US-led coalition overthrew the Taliban regime thought to be sheltering Al Qaeda terrorists
2003	War in Iraq led by USA and UK	US-led war in Iraq aimed at overthrow of President Saddam Hussein

The Main Crusades to the East

Name	Background	Leader(s)	Events
First Crusade (1096–9)	Proclaimed by Pope Urban II to safeguard pilgrim routes to the Holy Sepulchre	Bohemond I Godfrey of Bouillon Raymond, Count of Toulouse Robert, Count of Flanders Robert Curthose, Duke of Normandy Stephen, Count of Blois	Turks vanquished at Battle of Dorylaeum (Jul 1097); capture of Antioch in Syria (Jun 1098), Jerusalem (Jul 1099). Godfrey of Bouillon became ruler of the new Latin kingdom of Jerusalem. Three other crusader states were founded: Antioch, Edessa, Tripoli.
Second Crusade (1147–8)	Proclaimed by Eugenius III to aid the crusader states after the Muslim reconquest of Edessa (1144)	Conrad III of Germany Louis VII of France	German army heavily defeated by Turks near Dorylaeum (Oct 1147), and the French defeated at Laodicea (Jan 1148). The crusaders' military reputation was destroyed.
Third Crusade (1189–92)	Proclaimed by Gregory VIII after Saladin's defeat of the Latins at the Battle of Hattin (Jul 1187) and his conquest of Jerusalem (Oct 1187)	Frederick I Barbarossa Philip II Augustus of France Richard I of England	Cyprus conquered from Greeks (May 1191), and established as new crusader kingdom (survived until 1489); capture of Acre in Palestine (Jul 1191); Saladin defeated near Arsuf (Sep 1191). Most cities and castles of the Holy Land remained in Muslim hands.
Fourth Crusade (1202–4)	Proclaimed by Innocent III to recover the Holy Places	Boniface of Montferrat	Despite papal objections, crusade diverted from Egypt or Palestine (1) to Zara, a Christian town in Dalmatia, conquered for Venetians (Nov 1202); (2) to Byzantium (sack of Constantinople), Apr 1204, and foundation of Latin Empire of Constantinople.
Fifth Crusade (1217–21)	Proclaimed by Innocent III when a six-year truce between the kingdom of Jerusalem and Egypt expired	Andrew II of Hungary John of Brienne, King of Jerusalem Leopold, Duke of Austria	Three indecisive expeditions against Muslims in Palestine (1217); capture of Damietta in Egypt after protracted siege (May 1218– Nov 1219), but crusaders forced to relinquish Damietta (Aug 1221) and withdraw.
Sixth Crusade (1228–9)	Emperor Frederick II first took the Cross in 1215. Excommunicated by Gregory IX for delaying his departure, he finally arrived at Acre in Sep 1228	Frederick II	Negotiations with Egyptians secured Jerusalem and other places, including Bethlehem and Nazareth (Feb 1229); Frederick crowned King of Jerusalem in Church of Holy Sepulchre (Mar 1229). Jerusalem was held until recaptured by the Khorezmian Turks in 1244.

History

History

Name	Background	Leader(s)	Events
Seventh Crusade (1248–54)	Proclaimed by Innocent IV after the fall of Jerusalem and defeat of the Latin army near Gaza by the Egyptians and Khorezmians (1244)	Louis IX of France	Capture of Damietta (Jun 1249); defeat at Mansurah (Feb 1250); surrender of crusaders during attempted withdrawal; Damietta relinquished and large ransoms paid (May 1250).
Eighth Crusade (1270–2)	Proclaimed after the Mameluk conquest of Arsuf, Caesarea, Haifa (1265), Antioch and Joppa (1268)	Charles of Anjou, King of Naples-Sicily Edward of England (later Edward I) Louis IX of France	Attacked Tunisia in N Africa (Jul 1270); Louis died in Aug; Charles concluded treaty with Tunis and withdrew; Edward negotiated 11-years' truce with Mameluks in Palestine. By 1291 the Latins had been driven from the Holy Land.

Seven Wonders of the World

Originally compiled by Antipater of Sidon, a Greek poet, c.100BC.

Pyramids of Egypt
Oldest and only surviving 'wonder'. Built c. 2000BC as royal tombs, about 80 are still standing. The largest, the Great Pyramid of Cheops, at el-Gizeh, was 147m (481ft) high.

Hanging Gardens of Babylon
Terraced gardens adjoining Nebuchadnezzar's palace said to rise from 23–91m (75–300ft). Supposedly built by the king about 600BC to please his wife, a princess from the mountains, but they are also associated with the Assyrian Queen Semiramis.

Statue of Zeus at Olympia
Carved by Phidias, the 12m (40ft) statue marked the site of the original Olympic Games c. 400BC. It was constructed of ivory and gold, and showed Zeus (Jupiter) on his throne.

Temple of Artemis (Diana) at Ephesus
Constructed of Parian marble and more than 122m (400ft) long with over 100 columns 18m (60ft) high, it was begun about 350BC and took some 120 years to build. Destroyed by the Goths in AD262.

Mausoleum at Halicarnassus
Erected by Queen Artemisia in memory of her husband King Mausolus of Caria (in Asia Minor), who died 353BC. It stood 43m (140ft) high. All that remains are a few pieces in the British Museum and the word 'mausoleum' in the English language.

Colossus of Rhodes
Gigantic bronze statue of sun-god Helios (or Apollo); stood about 36m (117ft) high, dominating the harbour entrance at Rhodes. The sculptor Chares supposedly laboured for 12 years before he completed it in 280BC. It was destroyed by an earthquake in 224BC.

Pharos of Alexandria
Marble lighthouse and watchtower built about 270BC on the island of Pharos in Alexandria's harbour. Possibly standing 122m (400ft) high, it was destroyed by an earthquake in 1375.

Monarchs

Austria

Regnal dates Name

■ *Habsburg Dynasty*

1440–93	Frederick III
1493–1519	Maximilian I
1519–58	Karl V
1558–64	Ferdinand I
1564–76	Maximilian II
1576–1612	Rudolf II
1612–19	Matthias
1619–37	Ferdinand II
1637–57	Ferdinand III
1658–1705	Leopold I
1705–11	Josef I
1711–40	Karl VI
1740–2	*Interregnum*
1742–5	Karl VII
1745–65	Franz I
1765–90	Josef II
1790–2	Leopold II
1792–1835	Franz II
1835–48	Ferdinand I
1848–1916	Franz Josef
1916–18	Karl I

Belgium

Belgium became an independent kingdom in 1831. A national congress elected Prince Leopold of Saxe-Coburg as king.

Regnal dates Name

1831–65	Leopold I
1865–1909	Leopold II
1909–34	Albert I
1934–51	Leopold III
1951–93	Baudouin
1993–	Albert II

Denmark

Regnal dates Name

1448–81	Kristian I
1481–1513	Johan
1513–23	Kristian II
1523–34	Frederik I
1534–59	Kristian III
1559–88	Frederik II
1588–1648	Kristian IV
1648–70	Frederik III
1670–99	Kristian V
1699–1730	Frederik IV
1730–46	Kristian VI
1746–66	Frederik V
1766–1808	Kristian VII
1808–39	Frederik VI
1839–48	Kristian VIII
1848–63	Frederik VII
1863–1906	Kristian IX
1906–12	Frederik VIII
1912–47	Kristian X

History

| 1947–72 | Frederik IX |
| 1972– | Margrethe II |

England

Regnal dates Name

■ *West Saxon Kings*

802–39	Egbert
839–58	Æthelwulf
858–60	Æthelbald
860–5	Æthelbert
866–71	Æthelred
871–99	Alfred
899–924	Edward (the Elder)
924–39	Athelstan
939–46	Edmund
946–55	Edred
955–9	Edwy
959–75	Edgar
975–8	Edward (the Martyr)
978–1016	Æthelred (the Unready)
1016	Edmund (Ironside)

■ *Danish Kings*

1016–35	Knut (Canute)
1035–7	Harold *Regent*
1037–40	Harold I (Harefoot)
1040–2	Hardaknut
1042–66	Edward (the Confessor)
1066	Harold II

■ *House of Normandy*

1066–87	William I (the Conqueror)
1087–1100	William II (Rufus)
1100–35	Henry I

■ *House of Blois*

| 1135–54 | Stephen |

■ *House of Plantagenet*

1154–89	Henry II
1189–99	Richard I (Cœur de Lion)
1199–1216	John
1216–72	Henry III
1272–1307	Edward I
1307–27	Edward II
1327–77	Edward III
1377–99	Richard II

■ *House of Lancaster*

1399–1413	Henry IV
1413–22	Henry V
1422–61	Henry VI

■ *House of York*

| 1461–70 | Edward IV |

■ *House of Lancaster*

| 1470–1 | Henry VI |

■ *House of York*

1471–83	Edward IV
1483	Edward V
1483–5	Richard III

■ *House of Tudor*

1485–1509	Henry VII
1509–47	Henry VIII
1547–53	Edward VI
1553–8	Mary I
1558–1603	Elizabeth I

Finland

Finland was under Swedish control from the 13c until it was ceded to Russia in 1809 by the treaty of Friedrichsham. Russian rulers then assumed the title of Grand Duke of Finland. In 1917 it became an independent monarchy. However in November 1918, after initially accepting the throne the previous month, Landgrave Frederick Charles of Hesse, the brother-in-law of the German Emperor William II, withdrew his acceptance because of the Armistice and the ensuing abdication of William II. The previous regent remained in power until a Republic was declared in July 1919.

Regnal dates Name

1918	Dr Pehr Evind Svinhufvud *Regent*
1918	Landgrave Frederick Charles of Hesse (withdrew acceptance)
1918–19	Dr Pehr Evind Svinhufvud

France

France became a republic in 1793, and an empire in 1804 under Napoleon Bonaparte. The monarchy was restored in 1814 and then once more dissolved in 1848.

Regnal dates Name

987–996	Hugh Capet
996–1031	Robert II
1031–60	Henry I
1060–1108	Philip I
1108–37	Louis VI
1137–80	Louis VII
1180–1223	Philip II Augustus
1223–6	Louis VIII
1226–70	Louis IX
1270–85	Philip III
1285–1314	Philip IV
1314–16	Louis X
1316	John I
1316–22	Philip V
1322–8	Charles IV
1328–50	Philip VI
1350–64	John II
1364–80	Charles V
1380–1422	Charles VI
1422–61	Charles VII
1461–83	Louis XI
1483–98	Charles VIII
1498–1515	Louis XII
1515–47	Francis I
1547–59	Henry II
1559–60	Francis II
1560–74	Charles IX
1574–89	Henry III
1589–1610	Henry IV (of Navarre)
1610–43	Louis XIII
1643–1715	Louis XIV
1715–74	Louis XV
1774–92	Louis XVI
1814–24	Louis XVIII
1824–30	Charles X
1830–48	Louis-Philippe

Germany

Modern Germany was united under Prussia in 1871; it became a republic (1919) after World War I and the abdication of William II in 1918.

Regnal dates Name

1871–88	Wilhelm I
1888	Friedrich
1888–1918	Wilhelm II

Greece

In 1832 the Greek National Assembly elected Otto of Bavaria as King of modern Greece. In 1917 Constantine I abdicated the throne in favour of his son Alexander. In 1920 a plebiscite voted for his return. In 1922 he again abdicated. In 1923 the monarchy was deposed and a republic was proclaimed in 1924. In 1935 a plebiscite restored the monarchy until in 1967 a military junta staged a coup. The monarchy was formally abolished in 1973; Greece became a republic again in 1975.

Regnal dates Name

1832–62	Otto of Bavaria
1863–1913	George I (of Denmark)
1913–17	Constantine I
1917–20	Alexander
1920–2	Constantine I
1922–3	George II
1935–47	George II
1947–64	Paul
1964–7	Constantine II

Italy

Modern Italy became a united kingdom in 1861; it voted by referendum to become a republic in 1946.

Regnal dates Name

1861–78	Victor-Emmanuel II
1878–1900	Humbert I
1900–46	Victor-Emmanuel III
1946	Humbert II

History

Luxembourg

The Duchy of Luxembourg formally separated from the Netherlands in 1890.

Regnal dates	Name
1890–1905	Adolf of Nassau
1905–12	William
1912–19	Marie Adélaïde
1919–64	Charlotte
1964–2000	Jean
2000–	Henri

The Netherlands

Regnal dates	Name
1572–84	William the Silent
1584–1625	Maurice
1625–47	Frederick Henry
1647–50	William II
1672–1702	William III
1747–51	William IV
1751–95	William V
1806–10	Louis Bonaparte
1813–40	William I
1840–9	William II
1849–90	William III
1890–1948	Wilhelmina
1948–80	Juliana
1980–	Beatrix

Portugal

From 1383 to 1385 the Portuguese throne was the subject of a dispute between John of Castile and John of Aviz. In 1826 Peter IV (I of Brazil) renounced his right to the Portuguese throne in order to remain in Brazil. His abdication was contingent upon his successor and daughter, Maria II, marrying her uncle, Miguel. In 1828 Miguel usurped the throne on his own behalf. In 1834 Miguel was deposed and Maria II was restored to the throne. In 1910 Manuel II was deposed and Portugal became a republic.

Regnal dates	Name
1095–1112	Henry of Burgundy
1112–85	Alfonso I
1185–1211	Sancho I
1211–23	Alfonso II
1223–45	Sancho II
1245–79	Alfonso III
1279–1325	Diniz
1325–57	Alfonso IV
1357–67	Peter I
1367–83	Ferdinand
1385–1433	John I of Aviz
1433–8	Edward
1438–81	Alfonso V
1481–95	John II
1495–1521	Manuel I
1521–57	John III
1557–78	Sebastian
1578–80	Henry
1580–98	Philip I (II of Spain)
1598–1621	Philip II (III of Spain)
1621–40	Philip III (IV of Spain)
1640–56	John IV of Braganza
1656–83	Alfonso VI
1683–1706	Peter II
1706–50	John V
1750–77	Joseph
1777–1816	Maria I
1777–86	Peter III (King Consort)
1816–26	John VI
1826	Peter IV (I of Brazil)
1826–8	Maria II
1828–34	Miguel
1834–53	Maria II
1853–61	Peter V
1861–89	Luis
1889–1908	Charles
1908–10	Manuel II

Russia

In 1610 Vasili Shuisky was deposed as Tsar and the throne remained vacant until the election of Michael Romanov in 1613. In 1682 a condition of the succession was that the two step-brothers, Ivan V and Peter I (the Great) should jointly be proclaimed as Tsars. In 1917 the empire was overthrown and Tsar Nicholas II was forced to abdicate.

Regnal dates	Name
1283–1303	Daniel
1303–25	Yuri
1325–41	Ivan I
1341–53	Semeon
1353–9	Ivan II
1359–89	Dimitri Donskoy
1389–1425	Vasili I
1425–62	Vasili II
1462–1505	Ivan III (the Great)
1505–33	Vasili III
1533–84	Ivan IV (the Terrible)
1584–98	Feodor I
1598–1605	Boris Godunov
1605	Feodor II
1605–6	Dimitri II
1606–10	Vasili IV Shuisky
1613–45	Michael Romanov
1645–76	Alexei
1676–82	Feodor III
1682–96	Ivan V
1682–1725	Peter I (the Great)
1725–7	Catherine I
1727–30	Peter II
1730–40	Anne
1740–1	Ivan VI
1741–62	Elizabeth
1762	Peter III
1762–96	Catherine II (the Great)
1796–1801	Paul
1801–25	Alexander I
1825–55	Nicholas I
1855–81	Alexander II
1881–94	Alexander III
1894–1917	Nicholas II

Scotland

Regnal dates	Name
1005–34	Malcolm II
1034–40	Duncan I
1040–57	Macbeth
1057–8	Lulach
1058–93	Malcolm III
1093–4	Donald Bane Deposed 1094, Restored 1094–7
1094	Duncan II
1097–1107	Edgar
1107–24	Alexander I
1124–53	David I
1153–65	Malcolm IV
1165–1214	William I
1214–49	Alexander II
1249–86	Alexander III
1286–90	Margaret
1290–2	(Interregnum)
1292–96	John Balliol
1296–1306	(Interregnum)
1306–29	Robert I (the Bruce)
1329–71	David II
1371–90	Robert II
1390–1406	Robert III
1406–37	James I
1437–60	James II
1460–88	James III
1488–1513	James IV
1513–42	James V
1542–67	Mary Queen of Scots
1567–1625	James VI[1]

[1] In 1603, James VI succeeded Elizabeth I to the English throne (Union of the Crowns) and united the thrones of Scotland and England.

Spain

Philip V abdicated in favour of Luis in 1724, but returned to the throne in the same year following Luis' death. After the French invasion of Spain in 1808, Napoleon set up Joseph Bonaparte as king. In 1814 Ferdinand was restored to the crown. In 1868 a revolution deposed Isabella II. In 1870 Amadeus of Savoy was elected as king. In 1873 he resigned the throne and a temporary republic was formed. In 1874 Alfonso XII restored the Bourbon dynasty to the throne. In 1931 Alfonso XIII was deposed and a republican constitution was proclaimed. From 1939 Franco ruled Spain under a dictatorship until his death in 1975 and the restoration of King Juan Carlos.

Regnal dates	Name
1516–56	Charles I (Emperor Charles V)
1556–98	Philip II
1598–1621	Philip III
1621–65	Philip IV
1665–1700	Charles II
1700–24	Philip V
1724	Luis
1724–46	Philip V
1746–59	Ferdinand VI
1759–88	Charles III
1788–1808	Charles IV
1808	Ferdinand VII
1808–14	Joseph Bonaparte
1814–33	Ferdinand VII
1833–68	Isabella II
1870–3	Amadeus of Savoy
1874–85	Alfonso XII
1886–1931	Alfonso XIII
1975–	Juan Carlos

Sweden

Regnal dates	Name
■ *Vasa*	
1523–60	Gustav I
1560–8	Erik XIV
1568–92	Johan III
1592–9	Sigismund
1599–1611	Karl IX
1611–32	Gustav II Adolf
1632–54	Kristina
■ *Zweibrucken*	
1654–60	Karl X Gustav
1660–97	Karl XI
1697–18	Karl XII
1718–20	Ulrika Eleonora

■ *Hesse*	
1720–51	Fredrik
■ *Oldenburg-Holstein-Gottorp*	
1751–71	Adolf Fredrik
1771–92	Gustav III
1792–1809	Gustav IV Adolf
1809–18	Karl XIII
■ *Bernadotte*	
1818–44	Karl XIV Johan
1844–59	Oskar I
1859–72	Karl XV
1872–1907	Oskar II
1907–50	Gustav V
1950–73	Gustav VI Adolf
1973–	Karl XVI Gustav

United Kingdom

Regnal dates	Name
■ *House of Stuart*	
1603–25	James I (VI of Scotland)
1625–49	Charles I
■ *Commonwealth and Protectorate*	
1649–53	*Council of State*
1653–8	Oliver Cromwell *Lord Protector*
1658–9	Richard Cromwell *Lord Protector*
■ *House of Stuart (restored)*	
1660–85	Charles II
1685–8	James II
1689–94	William III (*jointly with* Mary II)

1694–1702	William III (*alone*)
1702–14	Anne
■ *House of Hanover*	
1714–27	George I
1727–60	George II
1760–1820	George III
1820–30	George IV
1830–7	William IV
1837–1901	Victoria
■ *House of Saxe-Coburg*	
1901–10	Edward VII
■ *House of Windsor*	
1910–36	George V
1936	Edward VIII
1936–52	George VI
1952–	Elizabeth II

Roman kings

The founding of Rome by Romulus is a Roman literary tradition.

Regnal dates	Name
753–715BC	Romulus
715–673BC	Numa Pompilius
673–642BC	Tullus Hostilius
642–616BC	Ancus Marcius
616–578BC	Tarquinius Priscus
578–534BC	Servius Tullius
534–509BC	Tarquinius Superbus

Roman emperors

Dates overlap where there are periods of joint rule (eg Marcus Aurelius and Lucius Verus) and where the government of the empire divides between east and west.

Regnal dates	Name
27BC – 14AD	Augustus (Caesar Augustus)
14–37	Tiberius
37–41	Caligula (Gaius Caesar)
41–54	Claudius
54–68	Nero
68–69	Galba
69	Otho
69	Vitellius
69–79	Vespasian
79–81	Titus
81–96	Domitian
96–98	Nerva
98–117	Trajan
117–138	Hadrian
138–161	Antoninus Pius
161–180	Marcus Aurelius
161–169	Lucius Verus
176–192	Commodus
193	Pertinax
193	Didius Julianus
193–211	Septemius Severus
198–217	Caracalla
209–212	Geta

Regnal dates	Name
217–218	Macrinus
218–222	Elagabalus
222–235	Alexander Severus
235–238	Maximin
238	Gordian I
238	Gordian II
238	Maximus
238	Balbinus
238–244	Gordian III
244–249	Philip
249–251	Decius
251	Hostilian
251–253	Gallus
253	Aemilian
253–260	Valerian
253–268	Gallienus
268–269	Claudius II (the Goth)
269–270	Quintillus
270–275	Aurelian
275–276	Tacitus
276	Florian
276–282	Probus
282–283	Carus
283–285	Carinus

Regnal dates	Name
283–284	Numerian
284–305	Diocletian – (East)
286–305	Maximian – (West)
305–311	Galerius – (East)
305–306	Constantius I
306–307	Severus – (West)
306–312	Maxentius – (West)
306–337	Constantine I
308–324	Licinius – (East)
337–340	Constantine II
337–350	Constans I
337–361	Constantius II
350–351	Magnentius
360–363	Julian
364–375	Valentinian I – (West)
364–378	Valens – (East)
365–366	Procopius – (East)
375–383	Gratian – (West)
375–392	Valentinian II – (West)
379–395	Theodosius I

History

History

Regnal dates	Name	Regnal dates	Name	Regnal dates	Name
395–408	Arcadius – (East)	455	Petronius Maximus – (West)	472–473	Olybrius – (West)
395–423	Honorius – (West)	455–456	Avitus – (West)	474–480	Julius Nepos – (West)
408–450	Theodosius II – (East)	457–474	Leo I – (East)	474	Leo II – (East)
421–423	Constantius III – (West)	457–461	Majorian – (West)	474–491	Zeno – (East)
423–455	Valentinian III – (West)	461–467	Libius Severus – (West)	475–476	Romulus Augustus – (West)
450–457	Marcian – (East)	467–472	Anthemius – (West)		

Emperors of the Holy Roman Empire

Regnal dates	Name	Regnal dates	Name	Regnal dates	Name
800–814	Charlemagne (Charles I)	1056–1106	Henry IV	1314–46	Louis IV
814–840	Louis I (the Pious)	1077–80	Rudolf[2]	1346–78	Charles IV
840–843	*Civil War*	1081–93	Hermann[2]	1378–1400	Wenceslas
843–855	Lothair	1093–1101	Conrad[2]	1400–10	Rupert
855–875	Louis II	1106–25	Henry V	1410–37	Sigismund
875–877	Charles II (the Bald)	1125–37	Lothair II	1438–9	Albert II
877–881	*Interregnum*	1138–52	Conrad III	1440–93	Frederick III
881–887	Charles III (the Fat)	1152–90	Frederick I (Barbarossa)	1493–1519	Maximilian I
887–891	*Interregnum*	1190–7	Henry VI	1519–56	Charles V
891–894	Guido of Spoleto	1198–1208	Philip[2]	1556–64	Ferdinand I
892–898	Lambert of Spoleto[1]	1198–1214	Otto IV	1564–76	Maximilian II
896–899	Arnulf[2]	1215–50	Frederick II	1576–1612	Rudolf II
901–905	Louis III	1246–7	Henry Raspe[2]	1612–19	Matthias
911–918	Conrad I[2]	1247–56	William of Holland[2]	1619–37	Ferdinand II
905–924	Berengar	1250–4	Conrad IV	1637–57	Ferdinand III
919–936	Henry I	1254–73	*Great Interregnum*	1658–1705	Leopold I
936–973	Otto I (the Great)	1257–72	Richard[2]	1705–11	Joseph I
973–983	Otto II	1257–75	Alfonso (Alfonso X of Castile)[2]	1711–40	Charles VI
983–1002	Otto III			1740–42	*Interregnum*
1002–24	Henry II (the Saint)	1273–91	Rudolf I	1742–5	Charles VII
1024–39	Conrad II	1292–8	Adolf	1745–65	Francis I
1039–56	Henry III (the Black)	1298–1308	Albert I	1765–90	Joseph II
		1308–13	Henry VII	1790–2	Leopold II
		1314–26	Frederick (III)[3]	1792–1806	Francis II

[1] Co-emperor [2] Rival [3] Co-regent

Popes

Antipopes (who claimed to be pope in opposition to those canonically chosen) are given in square brackets.

until c.64	Peter	257–8	Sixtus II	461–8	Hilarus
c.64–c.76	Linus	259–68	Dionysius	468–83	Simplicius
c.76–c.90	Anacletus	269–74	Felix I	483–92	Felix III (II)
c.90–c.99	Clement I	275–83	Eutychianus	492–6	Gelasius I
c.99–c.105	Evaristus	283–96	Caius	496–8	Anastasius II
c.105–c.117	Alexander I	296–304	Marcellinus	498–514	Symmachus
c.117–c.127	Sixtus I	308–9	Marcellus I	[498, 501–5	Laurentius]
c.127–c.137	Telesphorus	310	Eusebius	514–23	Hormisdas
c.137–c.140	Hyginus	311–14	Miltiades	523–6	John I
c.140–c.154	Pius I	314–35	Sylvester I	526–30	Felix IV (III)
c.154–c.166	Anicetus	336	Mark	530–2	Boniface II
c.166–c.175	Soter	337–52	Julius I	[530	Dioscorus]
175–89	Eleutherius	352–66	Liberius	533–5	John II
189–98	Victor I	[355–65	Felix II]	535–6	Agapetus I
198–217	Zephyrinus	366–84	Damasus I	536–7	Silverius
217–22	Callistus I	[366–7	Ursinus]	537–55	Vigilius
[217–c.235	Hippolytus]	384–99	Siricius	556–61	Pelagius I
222–30	Urban I	399–401	Anastasius I	561–74	John III
230–5	Pontian	402–17	Innocent I	575–9	Benedict I
235–6	Anterus	417–18	Zosimus	579–90	Pelagius II
236–50	Fabian	418–22	Boniface I	590–604	Gregory I
251–3	Cornelius	[418–19	Eulalius]	604–6	Sabinianus
[251–c.258	Novatian]	422–32	Celestine I	607	Boniface III
253–4	Lucius I	432–40	Sixtus III	608–15	Boniface IV
254–7	Stephen I	440–61	Leo I	615–18	Deusdedit *or*

	Adeodatus I	936–9	Leo VII	1216–27	Honorius III
619–25	Boniface V	939–42	Stephen IX	1227–41	Gregory IX
625–38	Honorius I	942–6	Marinus II	1241	Celestine IV
640	Severinus	946–55	Agapetus II	1243–54	Innocent IV
640–2	John IV	955–64	John XII	1254–61	Alexander IV
642–9	Theodore I	[963–5	Leo VIII]	1261–4	Urban IV
649–55	Martin I	964–6	Benedict V	1265–8	Clement IV
654–7	Eugenius 1[1]	965–72	John XIII	1271–6	Gregory X
657–72	Vitalian	973–4	Benedict VI	1276	Innocent V
672–6	Adeodatus II	[974, 984–5	Boniface VII]	1276	Hadrian V
676–8	Donus	974–83	Benedict VII	1276–7	John XXI[3]
678–81	Agatho	983–4	John XIV	1277–80	Nicholas III
682–3	Leo II	985–96	John XV	1281–5	Martin IV
684–5	Benedict II	996–9	Gregory V	1285–7	Honorius IV
685–6	John V	[997–8	John XVI]	1288–92	Nicholas IV
686–7	Cono	999–1003	Sylvester II	1294	Celestine V
[687	Theodore]	1003	John XVII	1294–1303	Boniface VIII
[687–92	Paschal]	1004–9	John XVIII	1303–4	Benedict XI
687–701	Sergius I	1009–12	Sergius IV	1305–14	Clement V
701–5	John VI	1012–24	Benedict VIII	1316–34	John XXII
705–7	John VII	[1012	Gregory]	[1328–30	Nicholas V]
708	Sisinnius	1024–32	John XIX	1334–42	Benedict XII
708–15	Constantine	1032–44	Benedict IX	1342–52	Clement VI
715–31	Gregory II	1045	Sylvester III	1352–62	Innocent VI
731–41	Gregory III	1045	Benedict IX	1362–70	Urban V
741–52	Zacharias		(second reign)	1370–8	Gregory XI
752	Stephen II (not	1045–6	Gregory VI	1378–89	Urban VI
	consecrated)	1046–7	Clement II	[1378–94	Clement VII]
752–7	Stephen II (III)	1047–8	Benedict IX	1389–1404	Boniface IX
757–67	Paul I		(third reign)	[1394–1423	Benedict XIII]
[767–9	Constantine II]	1048	Damasus II	1404–6	Innocent VII
[768	Philip]	1048–54	Leo IX	1406–15	Gregory XII
768–72	Stephen III (IV)	1055–7	Victor II	[1409–10	Alexander V]
772–95	Hadrian I	1057–8	Stephen IX (X)	[1410–15	John XXIII]
795–816	Leo III	[1058–9	Benedict X]	1417–31	Martin V
816–17	Stephen IV (V)	1059–61	Nicholas II	[1423–9	Clement VIII]
817–24	Paschal I	1061–73	Alexander II	[1425–30	Benedict XIV]
824–7	Eugenius II	[1061–72	Honorius II]	1431–47	Eugenius IV
827	Valentine	1073–85	Gregory VII	[1439–49	Felix V]
827–44	Gregory IV	[1080,		1447–55	Nicholas V
[844	John]	1084–1100	Clement VII]	1455–8	Callistus III
844–7	Sergius II	1086–7	Victor III	1458–64	Pius II
847–55	Leo IV	1088–99	Urban II	1464–71	Paul II
855–8	Benedict III	1099–1118	Paschal II	1471–84	Sixtus IV
[855	Anastasius	[1100–2	Theodoric]	1484–92	Innocent VIII
	Biblioth-	[1102	Albert]	1492–1503	Alexander VI
	ecarius]	[1105–11	Sylvester IV]	1503	Pius III
858–67	Nicholas I	1118–19	Gelasius II	1503–13	Julius II
867–72	Hadrian II	[1118–21	Gregory VIII]	1513–21	Leo X
872–82	John VIII	1119–24	Callistus II	1522–3	Hadrian VI
882–4	Marinus I	1124–30	Honorius II	1523–34	Clement VII
884–5	Hadrian III	[1124	Celestine II]	1534–49	Paul III
885–91	Stephen V (VI)	1130–43	Innocent II	1550–5	Julius III
891–6	Formosus	[1130–8	Anacletus II]	1555	Marcellus II
896	Boniface VI	[1138	Victor IV][2]	1555–9	Paul IV
896–7	Stephen VI	1143–4	Celestine II	1559–65	Pius IV
	(VII)	1144–5	Lucius II	1566–72	Pius V
897	Romanus	1145–53	Eugenius III	1572–85	Gregory XIII
897	Theodore II	1153–4	Anastasius IV	1585–90	Sixtus V
898–900	John IX	1154–9	Hadrian IV	1590	Urban VII
900–3	Benedict IV	1159–81	Alexander III	1590–1	Gregory XIV
903	Leo V	[1159–64	Victor IV][2]	1591	Innocent IX
[903–4	Christopher]	[1164–8	Paschal III]	1592–1605	Clement VIII
904–11	Sergius III	[1168–78	Callistus III]	1605	Leo XI
911–13	Anastasius III	[1179–80	Innocent III]	1605–21	Paul V
913–14	Lando	1181–5	Lucius III	1621–3	Gregory XV
914–28	John X	1185–7	Urban III	1623–44	Urban VIII
928	Leo VI	1187	Gregory VIII	1644–55	Innocent X
928–31	Stephen VII	1187–91	Clement III	1655–67	Alexander VII
	(VIII)	1191–8	Celestine III	1667–9	Clement IX
931–5	John XI	1198–1216	Innocent III	1670–6	Clement X

History

1676–89	Innocent XI	1769–74	Clement XIV	1914–22	Benedict XV
1689–91	Alexander VIII	1775–99	Pius VI	1922–39	Pius XI
1691–1700	Innocent XII	1800–23	Pius VII	1939–58	Pius XII
1700–21	Clement XI	1823–9	Leo XII	1958–63	John XXIII
1721–4	Innocent XIII	1829–30	Pius VIII	1963–78	Paul VI
1724–30	Benedict XIII	1831–46	Gregory XVI	1978	John Paul I
1730–40	Clement XII	1846–78	Pius IX	1978–	John Paul II
1740–58	Benedict XIV	1878–1903	Leo XIII		
1758–69	Clement XIII	1903–14	Pius X		

[1] Elected during the banishment of Martin I.   [2] Different individuals.   [3] There was no John XX.

Japanese emperors

The first 14 emperors (to Chuai) are regarded as legendary, and the regnal dates for the 15th to the 28th emperor (Senka), taken from the early Japanese chronicle, 'Nihon shoki', are not considered to be authentic.

Regnal dates	Name	Regnal dates	Name	Regnal dates	Name
660–585BC	Jimmu	724–749	Shomu	1287–98	Fushimi
581–549BC	Suizei	749–758	Koken	1298–1301	Go-Fushimi
549–511BC	Annei		(Empress)	1301–8	Go-Nijo
510–477BC	Itoku	758–764	Junnin	1308–18	Hanazono
475–393BC	Kosho	764–770	Shotoku	1318–39	Go-Daigo
392–291BC	Koan		(Empress)	1339–68	Go-Murakami
290–215BC	Korei	770–781	Konin	1368–83	Chokei
214–158BC	Kogen	781–806	Kammu	1383–92	Go-Kameyama
158–98BC	Kaika	806–809	Heizei		
97–30BC	Sujin	809–823	Saga	■ *Northern Court*	
29BC – 70AD	Suinin	823–833	Junna	1331–3	Kogon
71 – 130	Keiko	833–850	Nimmyo	1336–48	Komyo
131–190	Seimu	850–858	Montoku	1348–51	Suko
192–200	Chuai	858–876	Seiwa	1352–71	Go-Kogon
270–310	Ojin	876–884	Yozei	1371–82	Go-Enyu
313–399	Nintoku	884–887	Koko	1382–1412	Go-Komatsu
400–405	Richu	887–897	Uda	1412–28	Shoko
406–410	Hanzei	897–930	Daigo	1428–64	Go-Hanazono
412–453	Ingyo	930–946	Suzaku	1464–1500	Go-Tsuchimikado
453–456	Anko	946–967	Murakami		
456–479	Yuryaku	967–969	Reizei	1500–26	Go-Kashiwabara
480–484	Seinei	969–984	En-yu		
485–487	Kenzo	984–986	Kazan	1526–57	Go-Nara
488–498	Ninken	986–1011	Ichijo	1557–86	Ogimachi
498–506	Buretsu	1011–16	Sanjo	1586–1611	Go-Yozei
507–531	Keitai	1016–36	Go-Ichijo	1611–29	Go-Mizuno-o
531–535	Ankan	1036–45	Go-Suzaku	1629–43	Meisho
535–539	Senka	1045–68	Go-Reizei		(Empress)
539–571	Kimmei	1068–72	Go-Sanyo	1643–54	Go-Komyo
572–585	Bidatsu	1072–86	Shirakawa	1654–63	Go-Sai
585–587	Yomei	1086–1107	Horikawa	1663–87	Reigen
587–592	Sushun	1107–23	Toba	1687–1709	Higashiyama
592–628	Suiko	1123–41	Sutoku	1709–35	Nakamikado
	(Empress)	1141–55	Konoe	1735–47	Sakuramachi
629–641	Jomei	1155–8	Go-Shirakawa	1747–62	Momozono
642–645	Kogyoku	1158–65	Nijo	1762–70	Go-Sakuramachi
	(Empress)	1165–8	Rokujo		
645–654	Kotuko	1168–80	Takakura	1770–9	Go-Momozono
655–661	Saimei	1180–3	Antoku	1779–1817	Kokaku
	(Empress)	1183–98	Go-Toba	1817–46	Ninko
662–671	Tenji	1198–1210	Tsuchimikado	1846–66	Komei
671–672	Kobun	1210–21	Juntoku	1867–1912	Meiji
673–686	Temmu	1221	Chukyo	1912–26	Taisho
686–697	Jito (Empress)	1221–32	Go-Horikawa	1926–89	Hirohito
697–707	Mommu	1232–42	Shijo	1989–	Akihito
707–715	Gemmei	1242–6	Go-Saga		
	(Empress)	1246–59	Go-Fukakusa		
715–724	Gensho	1259–74	Kameyama		
	(Empress)	1274–87	Go-Uda		

Ancient Egyptian dynasties

Date BC	Dynasty	Period
c.3100–2890	I	**Early Dynastic Period**
c.2890–2686	II	(First use of stone in building.)
c.2686–2613	III	**Old Kingdom**
c.2613–2494	IV	(The age of the great
c.2494–2345	V	pyramid builders. Longest
c.2345–2181	VI	reign in history: Pepi II, 90 years.)
c.2181–2173	VII	**First Intermediate Period**
c.2173–2160	VIII	(Social order upset; few
c.2160–2130	IX	monuments built.)
c.2130–2040	X	
c.2133–1991	XI	
1991–1786	XII	**Middle Kingdom**
1786–1633	XIII	(Golden age of art and craftsmanship.)
1786–c.1603	XIV	**Second Intermediate Period**
1674–1567	XV	(Country divided into principalities.)
c.1684–1567	XVI	
c.1660–1567	XVII	
1567–1320	XVIII	**New Kingdom**
1320–1200	XIX	(Began with colonial
1200–1085	XX	expansion, ended in divided rule.)
1085–945	XXI	**Third Intermediate Period**
945–745	XXII	(Revival of prosperity and
745–718	XXIII	restoration of cults.)
718–715	XXIV	
715–668	XXV	
664–525	XXVI	**Late Period**
525–404	XXVII	(Completion of Nile – Red
404–399	XXVIII	Sea canal. Alexander the
399–380	XXIX	Great reached Alexandria
380–343	XXX	in 332BC.)
343–332	XXXI	

Chinese dynasties

Regnal dates	Name
c.22c–18c BC	Hsia
c.18c–12c BC	Shang or Yin
c.1111–256BC	Chou
c.1111–770BC	Western Chou
770–256BC	Eastern Chou
770–476BC	Ch'un Ch'iu Period
475–221BC	Warring States Period
221–206BC	Ch'in
206BC–220AD	Han
206BC–9AD	Western Han
9–23	Hsin Interregnum
25–220	Eastern Han
220–265	Three Kingdoms Period
265–420	Chin
265–317	Western Chin
317–420	Eastern Chin
420–589	Northern and Southern Dynasties
581–618	Sui
618–907	Tang
907–960	Five Dynasties and Ten Kingdoms Period
960–1279	Sung
960–1127	Northern Sung
1127–1279	Southern Sung
1115–1234	Chin (Jurchen Tartars)
1279–1368	Yuan (Mongol)
1368–1644	Ming
1644–1912	Ch'ing or Qing (Manchu)

Mughal emperors

The 2nd Mughal emperor, Humayun, lost his throne in 1540, became a fugitive, and did not regain his title until 1555.

Regnal dates	Name
1526–30	Babur
1530–56	Humayun
1556–1605	Akbar
1605–27	Jahangir
1627–58	Shah Jahan
1658–1707	Aurangzeb (Alamgir)
1707–12	Bahadur Shah I (or Shah Alam I)
1712–13	Jahandar Shah
1713–19	Farruksiyar
1719	Rafid-ud-Darajat
1719	Rafi-ud-Daulat
1719	Nekusiyar
1719	Ibrahim
1719–48	Muhammad Shah
1748–54	Ahmad Shah
1754–9	Alamgir II
1759–1806	Shah Alam II
1806–37	Akbar II
1837–57	Bahadur Shah II

History

Political leaders 1900–2002

Countries and organizations are listed alphabetically, with former or alternative names given in parentheses. Rulers are named chronologically since 1900 or (for new nations) since independence. For some major English-speaking nations, relevant details are also given of pre-20c rulers, along with a note of any political affiliation. The list does not distinguish successive terms of office by a single ruler. Listings complete to December 2002.

There is no universally agreed way of transliterating proper names in non-Roman alphabets; variations from the spellings given are therefore to be expected, especially in the case of Arabic rulers. Minor variations in the titles adopted by Chiefs of State, or in the name of an administration, are not given; these occur most notably in countries under military rule.

Afghanistan

■ Afghan Empire

Monarch

1881–1901	Abdur Rahman Khan
1901–19	Habibullah Khan
1919–29	Amanullah Khan
1929	Habibullah Ghazi
1929–33	Nadir Shah
1933–73	Zahir Shah

■ Republic of Afghanistan

Prime Minister

1973–8	Mohammad Daoud Khan

■ Democratic Republic of Afghanistan

Revolutionary Council — President

1978–9	Nour Mohammad Taraki
1979	Hafizullah Amin

Soviet Invasion

1979–86	Babrak Karmal
1986–7	Haji Mohammad Chamkani *Acting President*
1987–92	Mohammad Najibullah
1992	Sebghatullah Mojaddedi *Acting President*

General Secretary

1978–86	*As President*
1986–92	Mohammad Najibullah

Prime Minister

1929–46	Sardar Mohammad Hashim Khan
1946–53	Shah Mahmoud Khan Ghazi
1953–63	Mohammad Daoud
1963–5	Mohammad Yousef
1965–7	Mohammad Hashim Maiwandwal
1967–71	Nour Ahmad Etemadi
1972–3	Mohammad Mousa Shafiq
1973–9	*As President*
1979–81	Babrak Karmal
1981–8	Sultan Ali Keshtmand

■ Republic of Afghanistan (from 1987)

1988–9	Mohammad Hasan Sharq
1989–90	Sultan Ali Keshtmand
1990–2	Fazal Haq Khaliqyar
1992–3	Abdul Sabour Fareed
1993–6	Gulbuddin Hekmatyar

■ Islamic State of Afghanistan

President

1992–2001	Burhanuddin Rabbani*

Chairman Interim Government

2001–2	Hamid Karzai

President

2002–	Hamid Karzai

*ousted by the Taliban in 1996, but remained titular head of state; Taliban de facto rulers 1996–2001.

Albania

Monarch

1928–39	Zog I (Ahmed Zogu)
1939–44	*Italian rule*

■ People's Socialist Republic (from 1946)

President

1944–85	Enver Hoxha
1985–92	Ramiz Alia

■ Republic of Albania (from 1991)

1992–7	Sali Berisha
1997–2002	Rexhep Mejdani
2002–	Alfred Moisiu

Prime Minister

1914	Turhan Pashë Permëti
1914	Esad Toptani
1914–18	Abdullah Rushdi
1918–20	Turhan Pashë Permëti
1920	Sulejman Deluina
1920–1	Iljaz Bej Vrioni
1921	Pandeli Evangeli
1921	Xhafer Ypi
1921–2	Omer Vrioni
1922–4	Ahmed Zogu
1924	Iljaz Bej Vrioni
1924–5	Fan Noli
1925–8	Ahmed Zogu
1928–30	Koço Kota
1930–5	Pandeli Evangeli
1935–6	Mehdi Frashëri
1936–9	Koço Kota
1939–41	Shefqet Verlaci
1941–3	Mustafa Merlika-Kruja
1943	Eqrem Libohova
1943	Maliq Bushati
1943	Eqrem Libohova
1943	*Provisional Executive Committee* (Ibrahim Biçakçlu)
1943	*Council of Regents* (Mehdi Frashëri)
1943–4	Rexhep Mitrovica
1944	Fiori Dine
1944–54	Enver Hoxha
1954–81	Mehmed Shehu
1981–91	Adil Carcani
1991	Ylli Buffi
1991	Fatos Nano

1991–2	Vilson Ahmeti
1992–7	Aleksander Meksi
1997	Bashkim Fino
1997–8	Fatos Nano
1998–9	Pandeli Majko
1999–2002	Ilir Meta
2002	Pandeli Majko
2002–	Fatos Nano

Algeria

President

1962–5	Ahmed Ben Bella
1965–78	Houari Boumédienne
1979–92	Chandli Benjedid
1992	*High Commission of State: Chair*
	Mohamed Boudiaf
1992–4	Ali Kafi
1994–9	Liamine Zeroual
1999–	Abdelaziz Bouteflika

Prime Minister

1962–3	Ahmed Ben Bella
1963–79	*No Prime Minister*
1979–84	Mohamed Ben Ahmed Abdelghani
1984–8	Abdelhamid Brahimi
1988–9	Kasdi Merbah
1989–91	Mouloud Hamrouche
1991–2	Sid Ahmed Ghozali
1992–3	Belaid Abdessalam
1993–4	Redha Malek
1994–5	Mokdad Sifi
1995–8	Ahmed Ouyahia
1998–9	Ismail Hamdani
1999–2000	Ahmed Benbitour
2000–	Ali Benflis

Andorra

There are two heads of state, called Co-Princes: the President of France (see pp378–9) and the Bishop of Urgell, Spain (Joan Martí Alanis since 1971).

President of the Executive Council

1982–4	Óscar Ribas Reig
1984–90	Josep Pintat Solens
1990–4	Óscar Ribas Reig
1994–	Marc Forné Molné

Angola

President

1975–9	Antonio Agostinho Neto
1979–	José Eduardo dos Santos

Prime Minister

1975–8	Lopo do Nasciemento
1978–91	*No Prime Minister*
1991–2	Fernando José de frança van Dúnem
1992–6	Marcolino José Carlos Moco
1996–97	Fernando José de frança van Dúnem
1999–2002	*No Prime Minister*
2002–	Fernando da Piedade Dias dos Santos

Antigua and Barbuda

Prime Minister

1981–94	Vere Cornwall Bird
1994–	Lester Bird

Argentina

President

1898–1904	Julio Argentino Roca
1904–6	Manuel Quintana
1906–10	José Figueroa Alcorta
1910–14	Roque Sáenz Peña
1914–16	Victorino de la Plaza
1916–22	Hipólito Yrigoyen
1922–8	Marcelo T de Alvear
1928–30	Hipólito Yrigoyen
1930–2	José Félix Uriburu
1932–8	Augustin Pedro Justo
1938–40	Roberto M Ortiz
1940–3	Ramón S Castillo
1943–4	Pedro P Ramírez
1944–6	Edelmiro J Farrell
1946–55	Juan Perón
1955–8	Eduardo Lonardi
1958–62	Arturo Frondizi
1962–3	José María Guido
1963–6	Arturo Illia
1966–70	Juan Carlos Onganía
1970–1	Roberto Marcelo Levingston
1971–3	Alejandro Agustin Lanusse
1973	Héctor J Cámpora
1973–4	Juan Perón
1974–6	Martínez de Perón
1976–81	*Military Junta* (Jorge Rafaél Videla)
1981	*Military Junta* (Roberto Eduardo Viola)
1981–2	*Military Junta* (Leopoldo Galtieri)
1982–3	Reynaldo Bignone
1983–8	Raúl Alfonsín
1988–99	Carlos Saúl Menem
1999–2001	Fernando de la Rúa
2001	*Three Interim Presidents*
2002–	Eduardo Duhalde

Armenia

President

1991–8	Levon Ter-Petrossian
1998–	Robert Kocharyan

Prime Minister

1991–2	Gagik Haroutunian
1992–3	Khosrov Haroutunian
1993–6	Hrand Bagratian
1996–7	Armen Sarkissian
1997–8	Robert Kocharyan
1998–9	Armen Darbinian
1999	Vazgen Sarkissian
1999–2000	Aram Sarkissian
2000–	Andranik Markarian

Australia

Chief of State: British monarch, represented by Governor General

Prime Minister

1901–3	Edmund Barton *Prot*
1903–4	Alfred Deakin *Prot*
1904	John Christian Watson *Lab*
1904–5	George Houston Reid *Free*
1905–8	Alfred Deakin *Prot*
1908–9	Andrew Fisher *Lab*
1909–10	Alfred Deakin *Fusion*
1910–13	Andrew Fisher *Lab*
1913–14	Joseph Cook *Lib*

History

History

1914–15	Andrew Fisher *Lab*
1915–17	William Morris Hughes *Nat Lab*
1917–23	William Morris Hughes *Nat*
1923–9	Stanley Melbourne Bruce *Nat*
1929–32	James Henry Scullin *Lab*
1932–9	Joseph Aloysius Lyons *Un*
1939	Earle Christmas Page *Co*
1939–41	Robert Gordon Menzies *Un*
1941	Arthur William Fadden *Co*
1941–5	John Joseph Curtin *Lab*
1945	Francis Michael Forde *Lab*
1945–9	Joseph Benedict Chifley *Lab*
1949–66	Robert Gordon Menzies *Lib*
1966–7	Harold Edward Holt *Lib*
1967–8	John McEwen *Co*
1968–71	John Grey Gorton *Lib*
1971–2	William McMahon *Lib*
1972–5	Edward Gough Whitlam *Lab*
1975–83	John Malcolm Fraser *Lib*
1983–91	Robert James Lee Hawke *Lab*
1991–6	Paul Keating *Lab*
1996–	John Howard *Lib*

Co = Country
Con = Conservative
Free = Free Trade
Lab = Labor
Lib = Liberal
Nat = Nationalist
Nat Lab = National Labor
Prot = Protectionist
Un = United

Austria

President

1918–20	Karl Sätz
1920–8	Michael Hainisch
1928–38	Wilhelm Miklas
1938–45	*German rule*
1945–50	Karl Renner
1950–7	Theodor Körner
1957–65	Adolf Schärf
1965–74	Franz Jonas
1974–86	Rudolf Kirchsläger
1986–92	Kurt Waldheim
1992–	Thomas Klestil

Chancellor

1918–20	Karl Renner
1920–1	Michael Mayr
1921–2	Johann Schober
1922	Walter Breisky
1922	Johann Schober
1922–4	Ignaz Seipel
1924–6	Rudolph Ramek
1926–9	Ignaz Seipel
1929–30	Ernst Streeruwitz
1930	Johann Schober
1930	Carl Vaugoin
1930–1	Otto Ender
1931–2	Karl Buresch
1932–4	Engelbert Dollfuss
1934–8	Kurt von Schuschnigg
1938–45	*German rule*
1945	Karl Renner
1945–53	Leopold Figl
1953–61	Julius Raab
1961–4	Alfons Gorbach
1964–70	Josef Klaus
1970–83	Bruno Kreisky
1983–6	Fred Sinowatz
1986–97	Franz Vranitzky

1997–2000	Viktor Klima
2000–	Wolfgang Schüssel

Azerbaijan

President

1991–2	Ayaz Mutalibov
1992	Yakub Mamedov *Acting President*
1992–3	Abul Faz Elchibey
1993–	Heidar Aliyev

Prime Minister

1991–2	Hassan Hasanov
1992	Feirus Mustafayev *Acting Prime Minister*
1992–3	Rakhim Guseinov
1993	Ali Masimov *Acting Prime Minister*
1993	Panakh Guseinov
1993–4	Surat Guseinov
1994–6	Fuad Kuliyev
1996–	Artur Rasizade

The Bahamas

Chief of State: British monarch, represented by Governor General

Prime Minister

1973–92	Lynden O Pindling
1992–2002	Hubert A Ingraham
2002–	Perry Christie

Bahrain

Emir

1971–99	Isa Bin Salman Al-Khalifa
1999–2002	Hamad Bin Isa Al-Khalifa

King

2002–	Hamad Bin Isa Al-Khalifa

Prime Minister

1971–	Khalifa Bin Salman Al-Khalifa

Bangladesh

President

1971–2	Sayed Nazrul Islam *Acting President*
1972	Mujibur Rahman
1972–3	Abu Saeed Chowdhury
1974–5	Mohammadullah
1975	Mujibur Rahman
1975	Khondaker Mushtaq Ahmad
1975–7	Abu Saadat Mohammad Sayem
1977–81	Zia Ur-Rahman
1981–2	Abdus Sattar
1982–3	Abdul Fazal Mohammad Ahsanuddin Chowdhury
1983–90	Hossain Mohammad Ershad
1990–1	Shehabuddin Ahmed *Acting President*
1991–6	Abdur Rahman Biswas
1996–2001	Shehabuddin Ahmed
2001–2	A Q M Badruddoza Chowdhury
2002–	Iajuddin Ahmed

Prime Minister

1971–2	Tajuddin Ahmed
1972–5	Mujibur Rahman
1975	Mohammad Monsur Ali
1975–9	*Martial Law*

1979–82	Mohammad Azizur Rahman
1982–4	*Martial Law*
1984–5	Ataur Rahman Khan
1986–8	Mizanur Rahman Chowdhury
1988–90	Kazi Zafar Ahmed
1991–6	Khaleda Zia
1996	Mohammad Habibur Rahman
1996–2001	Sheikh Hasina Wajed
2001–	Khaleda Zia

Barbados

Prime Minister

1966–76	Errol Walton Barrow
1976–85	JMG (Tom) Adams
1985–6	H Bernard St John
1986–7	Errol Walton Barrow
1987–94	L Erskine Sandiford
1994–	Owen Arthur

Belarus

Chair of Supreme Soviet

1991–4	Stanislav Shushkevich
1994–6	Mecheslav Grib

President

1994–	Alexander Lukashenko

Prime Minister

1990–4	Vyacheslav Kebich
1994–6	Mikhail Chigir
1996–2000	Sergei Ling
2000–1	Uladzimir Yarmoshyn
2001–	Gennady Vasilyevich Novitsky

Belgium

Monarch

1865–1909	Leopold II
1909–34	Albert I
1934–50	Leopold III
1950–93	Baudouin I
1993–	Albert II

Prime Minister

1899–1907	Paul de Smet de Nayer
1907–8	Jules de Trooz
1908–11	Frans Schollaert
1911–18	Charles de Broqueville
1918	Gerhard Cooreman
1918–20	Léon Delacroix
1920–1	Henri Carton de Wiart
1921–5	Georges Theunis
1925	Alois van de Vyvere
1925–6	Prosper Poullet
1926–31	Henri Jaspar
1931–2	Jules Renkin
1932–4	Charles de Broqueville
1934–5	Georges Theunis
1935–7	Paul van Zeeland
1937–8	Paul Émile Janson
1938–9	Paul Spaak
1939–45	Hubert Pierlot
1945–6	Achille van Acker
1946	Paul Spaak
1946	Achille van Acker
1946–7	Camille Huysmans
1947–9	Paul Spaak
1949–50	Gaston Eyskens
1950	Jean Pierre Duvieusart
1950–2	Joseph Pholien

1952–4	Jean van Houtte
1954–8	Achille van Acker
1958–61	Gaston Eyskens
1961–5	Théodore Lefèvre
1965–6	Pierre Harmel
1966–8	Paul Vanden Boeynants
1968–72	Gaston Eyskens
1973–4	Edmond Leburton
1974–8	Léo Tindemans
1978	Paul Vanden Boeynants
1979–81	Wilfried Martens
1981	Marc Eyskens
1981–91	Wilfried Martens
1992–9	Jean-Luc Dehaene
1999–	Guy Verhofstadt

Belize

Chief of State: British Monarch, represented by Governor General

Prime Minister

1981–4	George Cadle Price
1985–9	Manuel Esquivel
1989–93	George Cadle Price
1993–8	Manuel Esquivel
1998–	Said Musa

Benin

President

■ Dahomey

1960–3	Hubert Coutoucou Maga
1963–4	Christophe Soglo
1964–5	Sourou Migan Apithy
1965	Justin Tométin Ahomadegbé
1965	Tairou Congacou
1965–7	Christophe Soglo
1967–8	Alphonse Amadou Alley
1968–9	Émile Derlin Zinsou
1969–70	*Presidential Committee* (Maurice Kouandete)
1970–2	*Presidential Committee* (Hubert Coutoucou Maga)
1972–5	Mathieu Kérékou

■ People's Republic of Benin

1975–90	Mathieu (*from 1980* Ahmed) Kérékou

■ Republic of Benin

1990–1	Ahmed Kérékou
1991–6	Nicéphore Soglo
1996–	Ahmed Kérékou

Prime Minister

1958–9	Sourou Migan Apithy
1959–60	Hubert Coutoucou Maga
1960–4	*As President*
1964–5	Justin Tométin Ahomadegbé
1965–7	*As President*
1967–8	Maurice Kouandete
1968–96	*As President*
1996–8	Adrien Houngbedji

Bhutan

Monarch (Druk Gyalpo)

1907–26	Uggyen Wangchuk
1926–52	Jigme Wangchuk
1952–72	Jigme Dorji Wangchuk
1972–	Jigme Singye Wangchuk

History

History

Prime Minister

1952–64	Jigme Palden Dorji
1964	Lhendup Dorji *Acting Prime Minister*
1964–98	*No Prime Minister*
1998–99	Lyonpo Jigme Thinley
1999–2000	Lyonpo Sangay Ngedup
2000–1	Lyonpo Yeshey Zimba
2001–2	Lyonpo Khandu Wangchuk
2002–	Lyonpo Kinzang Dorji

Bolivia

President

1899–1904	José Manuel Pando
1904–9	Ismael Montes
1909–13	Heliodoro Villazón
1913–17	Ismael Montes
1917–20	José N Gutiérrez Guerra
1920–5	Bautista Saavedra
1925–6	José Cabina Villanueva
1926–30	Hernando Siles
1930	Roberto Hinojusa *President of Revolutionaries*
1930–1	Carlos Blanco Galindo
1931–4	Daniel Salamanca
1934–6	José Luis Tejado Sorzano
1936–7	David Toro
1937–9	Germán Busch
1939	Carlos Quintanilla
1940–3	Enrique Peñaranda y del Castillo
1943–6	Gualberto Villaroel
1946	Nestor Guillen
1946–7	Tomas Monje Gutiérrez
1947–9	Enrique Hertzog
1949	Mamerto Urriolagoitía
1951–2	Hugo Ballivián
1952	Hernán Siles Suazo
1952–6	Víctor Paz Estenssoro
1956–60	Hernán Siles Suazo
1960–4	Víctor Paz Estenssoro
1964–5	René Barrientos Ortuño
1965–6	René Barrientos Ortuño *and* Alfredo Ovando Candía
1966	Alfredo Ovando Candía
1966–9	René Barrientos Ortuño
1969	Luis Adolfo Siles Salinas
1969–70	Alfredo Ovando Candía
1970	Rogelio Mirando
1970–1	Juan José Torres Gonzales
1971–8	Hugo Banzer Suárez
1978	Juan Pereda Asbún
1978–9	*Military Junta* (David Padilla Arericiba)
1979	Walter Guevara Arze
1979–80	Lydia Gueiler Tejada
1980–1	*Military Junta* (Luis García Meza)
1981–2	*Military Junta* (Celso Torrelio Villa)
1982	Guido Vildoso Calderón
1982–5	Hernán Siles Suazo
1985–9	Víctor Paz Estenssoro
1989–93	Jaime Paz Zamora
1993–97	Gonzalo Sánchez de Lozada
1997–2001	Hugo Bánzer Suárez
2001–2	Jorge Quiroga Ramírez
2002–	Gonzalo Sánchez de Lozada

Bosnia-Herzegovina

President

▪ Republic

1990–8	Alija Izetbegovic
1998–9	Zivko Radišic
1999–2000	Ante Jelavic
2000	Alija Izetbegovic
2000–1	Zivko Radišic
2001–2	Jozo Krizanovic
2002	Beriz Belkic
2002–	Mirko Sarovic

▪ Federation

1994–7	Kresimir Zubak
1997	Vladimir Šoljic
1997–8	Ejup Ganic
1999–2000	Ivo Andric-Luzanski
2000–1	Ejup Ganic
2001–2	Karlo Filipovic
2002–	Safet Halilovic

▪ Republika Srpska

1992–6	Radovan Karadzic
1996–8	Biljana Plavšic
1998–9	Nikola Poplašen
2000–2	Mirko Šarovic
2002–	Dragan Cavic

Prime Minister

▪ Republic

1990–2	Jure Pelivan
1992–3	Mile Akmadzic
1993–6	Haris Silajdžic
1996–7	Hasan Muratovic
1997–9	Boro Bosic *co-PM*
1997–2000	Haris Silajdžic *co-PM*
1999–2000	Svetozar Mihajlovic *co-PM*
2000	Spasoje Tusevljak
2000–1	Martin Raguz
2001	Bozidar Matic
2001–2	Zlatko Lagumdzija
2002–	Adnan Terzic

▪ Federation

1994–6	Haris Silajdžic
1996	Izudin Kapetanovic
1996–2001	Edhem Bicakcić
2001	Dragan Cavic *Acting Prime Minister*
2001–	Alija Behmen

▪ Republika Srpska

1992–3	Branko Djeric
1993–4	Vladimir Lukic
1994–5	Dusan Kozic
1995–6	Rajko Kasagic
1996–8	Gojko Klickovic
1998–2001	Milorad Dodik
2001–	Mladen Ivanic

Botswana

President

1966–80	Seretse Khama
1980–98	Ketumile Masire
1998–	Festus Mogae

Brazil

President

1898–1902	Manuel Ferraz de Campos Sales
1902–6	Francisco de Paula Rodrigues Alves
1906–9	Alfonso Pena
1909–10	Nilo Peçanha
1910–14	Hermes Rodrigues da Fonseca
1914–18	Venceslau Brás Pereira Gomes
1918–19	Francisco de Paula Rodrigues Alves
1919–22	Epitácio Pessoa
1922–6	Artur da Silva Bernardes
1926–30	Washington Luís Pereira de Sousa

1930–45	Getúlio Dorneles Vargas
1945–51	Eurico Gaspar Dutra
1951–54	Getúlio Dorneles Vargas
1954–5	João Café Filho
1955	Carlos Coimbra da Luz
1955–6	Nereu de Oliveira Ramos
1956–61	Juscelino Kubitschek de Oliveira
1961	Jânio da Silva Quadros
1961–3	João Belchior Marques Goulart
1963	Pascoal Ranieri Mazilli
1963–4	João Belchior Marques Goulart
1964	Pascoal Ranieri Mazilli
1964–7	Humberto de Alencar Castelo Branco
1967–9	Artur da Costa e Silva
1969–74	Emílio Garrastazu Médici
1974–9	Ernesto Geisel
1979–85	João Baptista de Oliveira Figueiredo
1985–90	José Sarney
1990–2	Fernando Collor de Mello
1992–4	Itamar Franco
1994–2002	Fernando Henrique Cardoso
2002–	Luiz Inacio Lula da Silva

Brunei

Monarch (Sultan)

1967–	Muda Hassanal Bolkiah Mu'izzadin Waddaulah

Bulgaria

Monarch

1887–1908	Ferdinand *Prince*
1908–18	Ferdinand I
1918–43	Boris III
1943–6	Simeon II

■ Republic of Bulgaria

President

1946–7	Vasil Kolarov
1947–50	Mincho Naichev
1950–8	Georgi Damianov
1958–64	Dimitro Ganev
1964–71	Georgi Traikov
1971–89	Todor Zhivkov
1989–90	Petar Mladenov

■ New Republic

1990–7	Zhelyu Zhelev
1997–2002	Petar Stoyanov
2002–	Georgi Parvanov

Premier

1946–9	Georgi Dimitrov
1949–50	Vasil Kolarov
1950–6	Vulko Chervenkov
1956–62	Anton Yugov
1962–71	Todor Zhivkov
1971–81	Stanko Todorov
1981–6	Grisha Filipov
1986–90	Georgy Atanasov
1990	Andrei Lukanov
1990–1	Dimitur Popov

First Secretary

1946–53	Vulko Chervenkov
1953–89	Todor Zhivkov
1989–90	Petar Mladenov
1990	Alexander Lilov

Prime Minister

1991–2	Filip Dimitrov

1992–4	Lyuben Berov
1994–5	Renate Indzhova *Acting Prime Minister*
1995–7	Zhan Videnov
1997	Stefan Sofiyanski *Acting Prime Minister*
1997–2001	Ivan Kostov
2001–	Simeon Saxe-Coburg Gotha (Simeon II)

Burkina Faso

President

■ Upper Volta

1960–6	Maurice Yaméogo
1966–80	Sangoulé Lamizana
1980	Saye Zerbo

People's Salvation Council

1982–3	Jean-Baptiste Ouedraogo *Chairman*

National Revolutionary Council

1983–4	Thomas Sankara *Chairman*

■ Burkina Faso

1984–7	Thomas Sankara *Chairman*
1987–	Blaise Compaoré

Prime Minister

1992–4	Youssouf Ouedraogo
1994–6	Roch Christian Kaboré
1996–2000	Kadré Désiré Ouedraogo
2000–	Paramanga Ernest Yonli

Burma ▸ Myanmar, Union of

Burundi

Monarch

1962–6	Mwambutsa IV
1966	Ntare V

■ Republic of Burundi

President

1966–77	Michel Micombero
1977–87	Jean-Baptiste Bagaza
1987–93	*Military Junta* (Pierre Buyoya)
1993	Melchior Ndadaye
1994	Cyprien Ntaryamira
1994–6	Sylvestre Ntibantunganya
1996–	Pierre Buyoya

Prime Minister

1961	Joseph Cimpaye
1961	Louis Rwagasore
1962–3	André Muhirwa
1963–4	Pierre Ngendandumwe
1964–5	Albin Nyamoya
1965	Pierre Ngendandumwe
1965	Pie Masumbuko *Acting Prime Minister*
1965	Joseph Bamina
1965–6	Léopold Biha
1966–76	Michel Micombero
1976–8	Edouard Nzambimana
1978–87	*No Prime Minister*
1987–8	Pierre Buyoya
1988–93	Adrien Sibomana
1993–4	Sylvie Kinigi
1994–5	Anatole Kanyenkiko
1995–6	Antoine Nduwayo
1996–8	Pascal-Firmin Ndimira
1998–	*No Prime Minister*

History

History

Cambodia

Monarch

1941–55	Norodom Sihanouk II
1955–60	Norodom Suramarit

Chief of State

1960–70	Prince Norodom Sihanouk

■ Khmer Republic (from 1970)

1970–2	Cheng Heng *Acting Chief of State*
1972–5	Lon Nol
1975–6	Prince Norodom Sihanouk
1976–81	Khieu Samphan
1981–91	Heng Samrin

■ Government in exile (until 1991)

President

1970–5	Prince Norodom Sihanouk
1982–93	Prince Norodom Sihanouk

Monarch

1993–	King Norodom Sihanouk

Prime Minister

1945–6	Son Ngoc Thanh
1946–8	Prince Monireth
1948–9	Son Ngoc Thanh
1949–51	Prince Monipong
1951	Son Ngoc Thanh
1951–2	Huy Kanthoul
1952–3	Norodom Sihanouk II
1953	Samdech Penn Nouth
1953–4	Chan Nak
1954–5	Leng Ngeth
1955–6	Prince Norodom Sihanouk
1956	Oum Chheang Sun
1956	Prince Norodom Sihanouk
1956	Khim Tit
1956	Prince Norodom Sihanouk
1956	Sam Yun
1956–7	Prince Norodom Sihanouk
1957–8	Sim Var
1958	Ek Yi Oun
1958	Samdech Penn Nouth *Acting Prime Minister*
1958	Sim Var
1958–60	Prince Norodom Sihanouk
1960–1	Pho Proung
1961	Samdech Penn Nouth
1961–3	Prince Norodom Sihanouk
1963–6	Prince Norodom Kantol
1966–7	Lon Nol
1967–8	Prince Norodom Sihanouk
1968–9	Samdech Penn Nouth
1969–72	Lon Nol

■ Khmer Republic (from 1970)

1972	Sisovath Sivik Matak
1972	Son Ngoc Thanh
1972–3	Hang Thun Hak
1973	In Tam
1973–5	Long Boret
1975–6	Samdech Penn Nouth
1976–9	Pol Pot
1979–81	Khieu Samphan
1981–5	Chan Si
1985–93	Hun Sen

Government in exile (until 1991)

1970–3	Samdech Penn Nouth
1982–91	Son Sann
1993–7	Norodom Ranariddh *First Prime Minister*
	Hun Sen *Second Prime Minister*
1997	Ung Huot *First Prime Minister*
	Hun Sen *Second Prime Minister*
1998–	Hun Sen

Cameroon

President

1960–82	Ahmadun Ahidjo
1982–	Paul Biya

Prime Minister

1960	Ahmadou Ahidjo
1960–1	Charles Assalé
1961–75	*No Prime Minister*
1975–82	Paul Biya
1982–3	Bello Bouba Maigari
1983–4	Luc Ayang
1991–2	Sadou Hayatou
1992–6	Simon Achidi Achu
1996–	Peter Mafany Musonge

Canada

Chief of State: British monarch, represented by Governor General

Prime Minister

1867–73	John A Macdonald *Con*
1873–8	Alexander Mackenzie *Lib*
1878–91	John A Macdonald *Con*
1891–2	John J C Abbot *Con*
1892–4	John S D Thompson *Con*
1894–6	Mackenzie Bowell *Con*
1896	Charles Tupper *Con*
1896–1911	Wilfrid Laurier *Lib*
1911–20	Robert Borden *Con/Un*
1920–1	Arthur Meighen *Un/Con*
1921–6	William Lyon Mackenzie King *Lib*
1926	Arthur Meighen *Con*
1926–30	William Lyon Mackenzie King *Lib*
1930–5	Richard Bedford Bennett *Con*
1935–48	William Lyon Mackenzie King *Lib*
1948–57	Louis St Laurent *Lib*
1957–63	John George Diefenbaker *Con*
1963–8	Lester Bowles Pearson *Lib*
1968–79	Pierre Elliott Trudeau *Lib*
1979–80	Joseph Clark *Con*
1980–4	Pierre Elliott Trudeau *Lib*
1984	John Turner *Lib*
1984–93	Brian Mulroney *Con*
1993	Kim Campbell *Con*
1993–	Jean Chrétien *Lib*

Con = Conservative   *Un* = Unionist
Lib = Liberal

Cape Verde

President

1975–91	Arístides Pereira
1991–2001	Antonio Mascarenhas Monteiro
2001–	Pedro Pires

Prime Minister

1975–91	Pedro Pires

1991–2000	Carlos Wahnon Veiga
2000–1	António Gualberto do Rosário
2001–	José Maria Neves

Central African Republic

President

1960–6	David Dacko
1966–79	Jean-Bédel Bokassa (*from 1977,* Emperor Bokassa I)
1979–81	David Dacko
1981–93	André Kolingba
1993–	Ange-Félix Patasse

Prime Minister

1991–2	Edouard Frank
1992–3	Thimothée Malendoma
1993	Enoch Derant Lakoué
1993–5	Jean-Luc Mandaba
1995–6	Gabriel Koyambounou
1996–7	Jean-Paul Ngoupandé
1997–9	Michel Gbezera-Bria
1999–2001	Anicet Georges Dologuélé
2001–	Martin Ziguélé

Chad

President

1960–75	François Tombalbaye
1975–9	*Supreme Military Council* (Félix Malloum)
1979	Goukouni Oueddi
1979	Mohammed Shawwa
1979–82	Goukouni Oueddi
1982–90	Hissène Habré
1990–	Idriss Déby

Prime Minister

1991–2	Jean Alingue Bawoyeu
1992–3	Joseph Yodemane
1993	Fidèle Moungar
1993–5	Delwa Kassire Koumakoye
1995–7	Koibla Djimasta
1997–9	Nassour Ouaidou Guelendouksia
1999–2002	Negoum Yamassoum
2002–	Haroun Kabadi

Chile

President

1900–1	Federico Errázuriz Echaurren
1901	Aníbal Zañartu *Vice President*
1901–3	Germán Riesco
1903	Ramón Barros Luco *Vice President*
1903–6	Germán Riesco
1906–10	Pedro Montt
1910	Ismael Tocornal *Vice President*
1910	Elías Fernández Albano *Vice President*
1910	Emiliano Figueroa Larraín *Vice President*
1910–15	Ramón Barros Luco
1915–20	Juan Luis Sanfuentes
1920–4	Arturo Alessandri
1924–5	*Military Juntas*
1925	Arturo Alessandri
1925	Luis Barros Borgoño *Vice President*
1925–7	Emiliano Figueroa
1927–31	Carlos Ibáñez
1931	Pedro Opaso Letelier *Vice President*
1931	Juan Esteban Montero *Vice President*
1931	Manuel Trucco Franzani *Vice President*

1931–2	Juan Estaban Montero
1932	*Military Juntas*
1932	Carlos G Dávila *Provisional President*
1932	Bartolomé Blanche *Provisional President*
1932	Abraham Oyanedel *Vice President*
1932–8	Arturo Alessandri Palma
1938–41	Pedro Aguirre Cerda
1941–2	Jerónimo Méndez Arancibia *Vice President*
1942–6	Juan Antonio Ríos Morales
1946–52	Gabriel González Videla
1952–8	Carlos Ibáñez del Campo
1958–64	Jorge Alessandri Rodríguez
1964–70	Eduardo Frei Montalva
1970–3	Salvador Allende Gossens
1973–90	Augusto Pinochet Ugarte
1990–3	Patricio Aylwin Azócar
1993–9	Eduardo Frei Ruíz-Tagle
2000–	Ricardo Lagos Escobar

China

▪ Qing (Ch'ing) dynasty

Emperor

| 1875–1908 | Guangxu (Kuang-hsü) |
| 1908–12 | Xuantong (Hsüan-t'ung) |

Prime Minister

1901–3	Ronglu (Jung-lu)
1903–11	Prince Qing (Ch'ing)
1912	Lu Zhengxiang (Lu Cheng-hsiang)
1912	Yuan Shikai (Yüan Shih-k'ai)

▪ Republic of China

President

1912	Sun Yat-sen (Sun Yixian) *Provisional*
1912–16	Yuan Shikai (Yüan Shih-k'ai)
1916–17	Li Yuanhong (Li Yüan-hung)
1917–18	Feng Guozhang (Feng Kuo-chang)
1918–22	Xu Shichang (Hsü Shih-ch'ang)
1921–5	Sun Yat-sen *Canton Administration*
1922–3	Li Yuanhong
1923–4	Cao Kun (Ts'ao K'un)
1924–6	Duan Qirui (Tuan Ch'i-jui)
1926–7	*Civil Disorder*
1927–8	Zhang Zuolin (Chang Tso-lin)
1928–31	Chiang K'ai-shek (Jiang Jieshi)
1931–2	Cheng Minxu (Ch'eng Ming-hsü) *Acting President*
1932–43	Lin Sen (Lin Sen)
1940–4	Wang Jingwei (Wang Ching-wei) *In Japanese-occupied territory*
1943–9	Chiang K'ai-shek
1945–9	*Civil War*
1949	Li Zongren (Li Tsung-jen)

Premier

1912	Tang Shaoyi (T'ang Shao-i)
1912–13	Zhao Bingjun (Chao Ping-chün)
1912–13	Xiong Xiling (Hsiung Hsi-ling)
1914	Sun Baoyi (Sun Pao-chi)
1915–16	*no Premier*
1916–17	Duan Qirui (Tuan Ch'i-jui)
1917–18	Wang Shizhen (Wang Shih-chen)
1918	Duan Qirui
1918–19	Qian Nengxun (Ch'ien Neng-hsün)
1919	Gong Xinzhan (Kung Hsin-chan)
1919–20	Jin Yunpeng (Chin Yün-p'eng)
1920	Sa Zhenbing (Sa Chen-ping)
1920–1	Jun Yunpeng

History

1921–2	Liang Shiyi (Liang Shih-i)
1922	Zhou Ziqi (Chow Tzu-ch'i) *Acting Premier*
1922	Yan Huiqing (Yen Hui-ch'ing)
1922	Wang Chonghui (Wang Ch'ung-hui)
1922–3	Wang Daxie (Wang Ta-hsieh)
1923	Zhang Shaozeng (Chang Shao-ts'eng)
1923–4	Gao Lingwei (Kao Ling-wei)
1924	Sun Baoyi (Sun Pao-ch'i)
1924	Gu Weijun (Ku Wei-chün) *Acting Premier*
1924	Yan Huiqing
1924–5	Huang Fu (Huang Fu) *Acting Premier*
1925	Duan Qirui
1925–6	Xu Shiying (Hsü Shih-ying)
1926	Jia Deyao (Chia Te-yao)
1926	Hu Weide (Hu Wei-te)
1926	Yan Huiqing
1926	Du Xigui (Tu Hsi-kuei)
1926–7	Gu Weijun
1927	*Civil Disorder*

President of the Executive Council

1928–30	Tan Yankai (T'an Yen-k'ai)
1930	T V Soong (Sung Tzu-wen) *Acting Premier*
1930	Wang Jingwei (Wang Ching-wei)
1930–1	Chiang K'ai-shek
1931–2	Sun Fo (Sun Fo)
1932–5	Wang Jingwei
1935–7	Chiang K'ai-shek
1937–8	Wang Chonghui (Wang Ch'ung-hui) *Acting Premier*
1938–9	Kong Xiangxi (K'ung Hsiang-hsi)
1939–44	Chiang K'ai-shek
1944–7	T V Soong
1945–9	*Civil War*
1948	Wang Wenhao (Wong Wen-hao)
1948–9	Sun Fo
1949	He Yingqin (Ho Ying-ch'in)
1949	Yan Xishan (Yen Hsi-shan)

■ **People's Republic of China**

President

1949–59	Mao Zedong (Mao Tse-tung)
1959–68	Liu Shaoqi (Liu Shao-ch'i)
1968–75	Dong Biwu (Tung Pi-wu)
1975–6	Zhu De (Chu Te)
1976–8	Sung Qingling (Sung Ch'ing-ling)
1978–83	Ye Jianying (Yeh Chien-ying)
1983–8	Li Xiannian (Li Hsien-nien)
1988–93	Yang Shangkun (Yang Shang-k'un)
1993–	Jiang Zemin (Chiang Tse-min)

Prime Minister

1949–76	Zhou Enlai (Chou En-lai)
1976–80	Hua Guofeng (Huo Kuo-feng)
1980–7	Zhao Ziyang (Chao Tzu-yang)
1987–98	Li Peng (Li P'eng)
1998–	Zhu Rongji

Communist Party

Chairman

1935–76	Mao Zedong
1976–81	Hua Guofeng
1981–2	Hu Yaobang (Hu Yao-pang)

General Secretary

| 1982–7 | Hu Yaobang |

1987–9	Zhao Ziyang
1989–2002	Jiang Zemin
2002–	Hu Jintao

CIS (Commonwealth of Independent States) ► Armenia, Azerbaijan, Belarus, Georgia, Kazakhstan, Kyrgyzstan, Moldova, Russia, Tajikistan, Turkmenistan, Ukraine, Uzbekistan

Colombia

President

1900–4	José Manuel Marroquín *Vice President*
1904–9	Rafael Reyes
1909–10	Ramón González Valencia
1910–14	Carlos E Restrepo
1914–18	José Vicente Concha
1918–21	Marco Fidel Suárez
1921–2	Jorge Holguín *President Designate*
1922–6	Pedro Nel Ospina
1926–30	Miguel Abadía Méndez
1930–4	Enrique Olaya Herrera
1934–8	Alfonso López
1938–42	Eduardo Santos
1942–5	Alfonso López
1945–6	Alberto Lleras Camargo *President Designate*
1946–50	Mariano Ospina Pérez
1950–3	Laureano Gómez
1953–7	Gustavo Rojas Pinilla
1957	*Military Junta*
1958–62	Alberto Lleras Camargo
1962–6	Guillermo León Valencia
1966–70	Carlos Lleras Restrepo
1970–4	Misael Pastrana Borrero
1974–8	Alfonso López Michelsen
1978–82	Julio César Turbay Ayala
1982–6	Belisario Betancur
1986–90	Virgilio Barco Vargas
1990–4	César Gaviria Trujillo
1994–8	Ernesto Samper Pizano
1998–2002	Andrés Pastrana Arango
2002–	Alvaro Uribe Velez

Commonwealth

Secretary-General

1965–75	Arnold Smith
1975–90	Shridath S Ramphal
1990–2000	Emeka Anyaoku
2000–	Donald C McKinnon

Comoros, Union of the

President

1976–78	Ali Soilih
1978–89	Ahmed Abdallah Abderemane
1989–96	Said Mohammed Djohar
1996–8	Mohammed Taki Abdoulkarim
1998–9	Tadjiddine Ben Said Massounde *Interim President*
1999–2002	Azali Assoumani
2002	Hamada Madi Bolero *Interim President*
2002–	Azali Assoumani

Prime Minister

1976–8	Abdallah Mohammed
1978–82	Salim Ben Ali
1982–4	Ali Mroudjae
1984–92	*No Prime Minister*

1992	Mohammed Taki Abdoulkarim
1993	Ibrahim Abdermane Halidi
1993	Said Ali Mohammed
1993–4	Ahmed Ben Cheikh Attoumane
1994	Mohammed Abdou Madi
1994–5	Halifa Houmadi
1995–6	Caambi el-Yachourtu
1996	Tadjiddine Ben Said Massounde
1996–7	Ahmed Abdou
1997–8	Nourdine Bourhane
1998–9	Abbas Djoussouf
1999–2000	Bianrifi Tarmidi
2000–	Hamada Madi Bolero

Congo

President

1960–3	Abbé Fulbert Youlou
1963–8	Alphonse Massemba-Debat
1968	Marien Ngouabi
1968	Alphonse Massemba-Debat
1968–9	Alfred Raoul
1969–77	Marien Ngouabi
1977–9	Joachim Yhomby Opango
1979–92	Denis Sassou-Nguesso
1992–7	Pascal Lissouba
1997–	Denis Sassou-Nguesso

Prime Minister

1958	Jacques Opangault
1958–60	Fulbert Youlou
1960–3	*No Prime Minister*
1963–6	Pascal Lissouba
1966–8	Ambroise Noumazalaye
1968–9	Alfred Raoul
1969–73	*No Prime Minister*
1973–5	Henri Lopès
1975–84	Louis Sylvain Goma
1984–9	Ange-Édouard Poungui
1989–90	Alphonse Poaty-Souchlaty
1990–1	Pierre Moussa *Acting Prime Minister*
1991	Louis Sylvain Goma
1991–2	André Milongo
1992	Stéphane Maurice Bongho-Nouarra
1992–3	Claude Antoine Dacosta
1993–6	Joachim Yhombi-Opango
1996–7	Charles David Ganao
1997	Bernard Kolelas

Congo, Democratic Republic of

President

1960–5	Joseph Kasavubu
1965–97	Mobutu Sese Seko (*formerly* Joseph Mobutu)

■ Democratic Republic of Congo

1997–2001	Laurent Kabila
2001–	Joseph Kabila

Prime Minister

1960	Patrice Lumumba
1960	Joseph Ileo
1960–1	*College of Commissioners*
1961	Joseph Ileo
1961–4	Cyrille Adoula
1964–5	Moïse Tshombe
1965	Evariste Kimba
1965–6	Mulamba Nyungu wa Kadima
1966–77	*As President*
1977–80	Mpinga Kasenga

1980	Bo-Boliko Lokonga Monse Mihambu
1980–1	Nguza Karl I Bond
1981–3	Nsinga Udjuu
1983–6	Léon Kengo Wa Dondo
1986–8	*No Prime Minister*
1988	Sambura Pida Nbagui
1988–90	Léon Kengo Wa Dondo
1990–1	Lunda Bululu
1991	Mulumba Lukeji
1991	Etienne Tshisekedi
1991	Bernardin Mungul Diaka
1991–2	Karl I Bond
1992–3	Etienne Tshisekedi
1993–4	Faustin Birindwa
1994–7	Léon Kengo Wa Dondo
1997	Etienne Tshisekedi
1997	Likulia Bolongo

Costa Rica

President

1894–1902	Rafael Yglesias y Castro
1902–6	Ascención Esquivel Ibarra
1906–10	Cleto González Víquez
1910–12	Ricardo Jiménez Oreamuno
1912–14	Cleto González Víquez
1914–17	Alfredo González Flores
1917–19	Federico Tinoco Granados
1919	Julio Acosta García
1919–20	Juan Bautista Quiros
1920–4	Julio Acosta García
1924–8	Ricardo Jiménez Oreamuno
1928–32	Cleto González Víquez
1932–6	Ricardo Jiménez Oreamuno
1936–40	León Cortés Castro
1940–4	Rafael Ángel Calderón Guardia
1944–8	Teodoro Picado Michalski
1948	Santos Léon Herrera
1948–9	*Civil Junta* (José Figueres Ferrer)
1949–52	Otilio Ulate Blanco
1952–3	Alberto Oreamuno Flores
1953–8	José Figueres Ferrer
1958–62	Mario Echandi Jiménez
1962–6	Francisco José Orlich Bolmarcich
1966–70	José Joaquín Trejos Fernández
1970–4	José Figueres Ferrer
1974–8	Daniel Oduber Quirós
1978–82	Rodrigo Carazo Odio
1982–6	Luis Alberto Monge Álvarez
1986–90	Oscar Arias Sánchez
1990–4	Rafael Angel Calderón Fournier
1994–8	José Maria Figueres Olsen
1998–2002	Miguel Angel Rodríguez Echevarría
2002–	Abel Pacheca de la Espriella

Côte d'Ivoire

President

1960–93	Félix Houphouët-Boigny
1993–9	Henri Konan-Bédié
1999–2000	Robert Guëi
2000–	Laurent Gbagbo

Prime Minister

1958–9	Auguste Denise
1959–60	Félix Houphouët-Boigny
1960–90	*No Prime Minister*
1990–3	Alassane Dramane Ouattara
1993–9	Daniel Kablan Duncan
1999	Robert Guëi
2000	Seydou Diarra
2000–	Pascal Affi N'Guessan

History

History

Croatia

President

1992–9	Franjo Tudjman
1999–2000	Vlatko Pavletic *Acting President*
2000	Zlatko Tomcic *Acting President*
2000–	Stjepan Mesic

Prime Minister

1990	Stjepan Mesic
1990–1	Josip Manolic
1991–2	Franjo Greguric
1992–3	Hrvoje Šarinic
1993–5	Nikica Valentic
1995–2000	Zlatko Mateša
2000–	Ivica Racan

Cuba

President

1902–6	Tomas Estrada Palma
1906–9	*US rule*
1909–13	José Miguel Gómez
1913–21	Mario García Menocal
1921–5	Alfredo Zayas y Alfonso
1925–33	Gerardo Machado y Morales
1933	Carlos Manuel de Céspedes
1933–4	Ramón Grau San Martín
1934–5	Carlos Mendieta
1935–6	José A Barnet y Vinagres
1936	Miguel Mariano Gómez y Arias
1936–40	Federico Laredo Bru
1940–4	Fulgencio Batista
1944–8	Ramón Grau San Martín
1948–52	Carlos Prío Socarrás
1952–9	Fulgencio Batista
1959	Manuel Urrutia
1959–76	Osvaldo Dorticós Torrado
1959–76	Fidel Castro Ruz *Prime Minister and First Secretary*
1976–	Fidel Castro Ruz *President*

Cyprus

President

1960–77	Archbishop Makarios III
1977–88	Spyros Kyprianou
1988–93	Georgios Vassiliou
1993–	Glafcos Clerides

Czechoslovakia

In 1993 Czechoslovakia divided into two separate states, the Czech Republic (see below) and Slovakia, or the Slovak Republic (see p399).

President

1918–35	Tomáš Garrigue Masaryk
1935–8	Edvard Beneš
1938–9	Emil Hácha

German Occupation

1938–45	Edvard Beneš *President in Exile*
1939–45	Emil Hácha *State President*
1939–45	Jozef Tiso *Slovak Republic President*

Post-war

1945–8	Edvard Beneš
1948–53	Klement Gottwald
1953–7	Antonín Zápotocký
1957–68	Antonín Novotný
1968–75	Ludvík Svoboda
1975–89	Gustáv Husák
1989–93	Václav Havel

Prime Minister

1918–19	Karel Kramář
1919–20	Vlastimil Tusar
1920–1	Jan Černý
1921–2	Edvard Beneš
1922–6	Antonín Švehla
1926	Jan Černý
1926–9	Antonín Švehla
1929–32	František Udržal
1932–5	Jan Malypetr
1935–8	Milan Hodža
1938	Jan Syrový
1938–9	Rudolf Beran
1940–5	Jan Šrámek *in exile*
1945–6	Zdeněk Fierlinger
1946–8	Klement Gottwald
1948–53	Antonín Zápotocký
1953–63	Viliám Široký
1963–8	Josef Lenárt
1968–70	Oldřich Černik
1970–88	Lubomír Štrougal
1988–9	Ladislav Adamec
1989–92	Marian Calfa
1992	Jan Strasky

First Secretary

1948–52	Rudolf Slánsky
1953–68	Antonín Novotný
1968–9	Alexander Dubček
1969–87	Gustáv Husák
1987–9	Miloš Jakeš
1989	Karel Urbánek
1989–93	Ladislav Adamec

■ **Czech Republic**

President

1993–	Václav Havel

Prime Minister

1993–7	Václav Klaus
1997–8	Josef Tosovsky
1998–2002	Miloš Zeman
2002–	Vladimir Spidla

Denmark

Monarch

1863–1906	Kristian IX
1906–12	Frederik VIII
1912–47	Kristian X
1947–72	Frederik IX
1972–	Margrethe II

Prime Minister

1900–1	H Sehested
1901–5	J H Deuntzer
1905–8	J C Christensen
1908–9	N Neergaard
1909	L Holstein-Ledreborg
1909–10	C Th Zahle
1910–13	Klaus Berntsen
1913–20	C Th Zahle
1920	Otto Liebe

History

1920	M P FrIls
1920–4	N Neergaard
1924–6	Thorvald Stauning
1926–9	Th Madsen-Mygdal
1929–42	Thorvald Stauning
1942	Wilhelm Buhl
1942–3	Erik Scavenius
1943–5	*No government*
1945	Wilhelm Buhl
1945–7	Knud Kristensen
1947–50	Hans Hedtoft
1950–3	Erik Eriksen
1953–5	Hans Hedtoft
1955–60	Hans Christian Hansen
1960–2	Viggo Kampmann
1962–8	Jens Otto Krag
1968–71	Hilmar Baunsgaard
1971–2	Jens Otto Krag
1972–3	Anker Jorgensen
1973–5	Poul Hartling
1975–82	Anker Jorgensen
1982–93	Poul Schlüter
1993–2001	Poul Nyrup Rasmussen
2001–	Anders Fogh Rasmussen

Djibouti

President

1977–99	Hassan Gouled Aptidon
1999–	Ismael Omar Guelleh

Prime Minister

1977–8	Abdallah Mohammed Kamil
1978–2001	Barkat Gourad Hamadou
2001–	Dileita Mohamed Dileita

Dominica

President

1977	Louis Cods-Lartigue *Interim President*
1978–9	Frederick E Degazon
1979–80	Lenner Armour *Acting President*
1980–4	Aurelius Marie
1984–93	Clarence Augustus Seignoret
1993–8	Crispin Anselm Sorhaindo
1998–	Vernon Shaw

Prime Minister

1978–9	Patrick Roland John
1979–80	Oliver Seraphine
1980–95	Mary Eugenia Charles
1995–2000	Edison James
2000	Rosie Douglas
2000–	Pierre Charles

Dominican Republic

President

1899–1902	Juan Isidro Jiménez
1902–3	Horacio Vásquez
1903	Alejandro Wos y Gil
1903–4	Juan Isidro Jiménez
1904–6	Carlos Morales
1906–11	Ramon Cáceres
1911–12	Eladio Victoria
1912–13	Adolfo Nouel y Bobadilla
1913–14	José Bordas y Valdés
1914	Ramon Báez
1914–16	Juan Isidro Jiménez
1916–22	*US occupation* (Francisco Henríquez y Carrajal)
1922–4	*US occupation* (Juan Batista Vicini Burgos)

1924–30	Horacio Vásquez
1930	Rafael Estrella Urena
1930–8	Rafael Leónidas Trujillo y Molina
1938–40	Jacinto Bienvenudo Peynado
1940–2	Manuel de Jesus Troncoso de la Concha
1942–52	Rafael Leónidas Trujillo y Molina
1952–60	Hector Bienvenido Trujillo
1960–2	Joaquín Videla Balaguer
1962	Rafael Bonnelly
1962	*Military Junta* (Huberto Bogaert)
1962–3	Rafael Bonnelly
1963	Juan Bosch Gavino
1963	*Military Junta* (Emilio de los Santos)
1963–5	Donald Reid Cabral
1965	*Civil War*
1965	Elias Wessin y Wessin
1965	Antonio Imbert Barreras
1965	Francisco Caamaño Deñó
1965–6	Héctor Garcia Godoy Cáceres
1966–78	Joaquín Videla Balaguer
1978–82	Antonio Guzmán Fernández
1982–6	Salvador Jorge Blanco
1986–96	Joaquín Videla Balaguer
1996–2000	Leonel Fernández Reyna
2000–	Hipólito Mejía

East Timor

President

2002–	Xanana Gusmao

Ecuador

President

1895–1901	Eloy Alfaro
1901–5	Leónides Plaza Gutiérrez
1905–6	Lizardo García
1906–11	Eloy Alfaro
1911	Emilio Estrada
1911–12	Carlos Freile Zaldumbide
1912–16	Leónides Plaza Gutiérrez
1916–20	Alfredo Baquerizo Moreno
1920–4	José Luis Tamayo
1924–5	Gonzálo S de Córdova
1925–6	*Military Juntas*
1926–31	Isidro Ayora
1931	Luis A Larrea Alba
1932–3	Juan de Dios Martínez Mera
1933–4	Abelardo Montalvo
1934–5	José María Velasco Ibarra
1935	Antonio Pons
1935–7	Federico Páez
1937–8	Alberto Enriquez Gallo
1938	Manuel María Borrero
1938–9	Aurelio Mosquera Narváez
1939–40	Julio Enrique Moreno
1940–4	Carlos Alberto Arroya del Río
1944–7	José María Velasco Ibarra
1947	Carlos Mancheno
1947–8	Carlos Julio Arosemena Tola
1948–52	Galo Plaza Lasso
1952–6	José María Velasco Ibarra
1956–60	Camilo Ponce Enríquez
1960–1	José María Velasco Ibarra
1961–3	Carlos Julio Arosemena Monroy
1963–6	*Military Junta*
1966	Clemente Yerovi Indaburu
1966–8	Otto Arosemena Gómez
1968–72	José María Velasco Ibarra
1972–6	Guillermo Rodríguez Lara
1976–9	*Military Junta*

History

1979–81	Jaime Roldós Aguilera
1981–4	Oswaldo Hurtado Larrea
1984–8	León Febres Cordero
1988–92	Rodrigo Borja Cevallos
1992–6	Sixto Durán Ballén
1996–7	Abdalá Bucaram Ortiz
1997	Rosalia Arteaga *Acting President*
1997–8	Fabián Alarcón Rivero
1998–2000	Jamil Mahuad Witt
2000–	Gustavo Noboa Bejerano

Egypt

Khedive

| 1895–1914 | Abbas Helmi II |

Sultan

| 1914–17 | Hussein Kamel |
| 1917–22 | Ahmed Fouad |

▪ Kingdom of Egypt

Monarch

1922–36	Fouad I
1936–7	Farouk *Trusteeship*
1937–52	Farouk I

▪ Republic of Egypt

President

1953–4	Mohammed Najib
1954–70	Gamal Abdel Nasser
1970–81	Mohammed Anwar El-Sadat
1981–	Mohammed Hosni Mubarak

Prime Minister

1895–1908	Mustafa Fahmy
1908–10	Butros Ghali
1910–14	Mohammed Said
1914–19	Hussein Rushdi
1919	Mohammed Said
1919–20	Yousuf Wahba
1920–1	Mohammed Tewfiq Nazim
1921	Adli Yegen
1922	Abdel Khaliq Tharwat
1922–3	Mohammed Tewfiq Nazim
1923–4	Yehia Ibrahim
1924	Saad Zaghloul
1924–6	Ahmed Zaywan
1926–7	Adli Yegen
1927–8	Abdel Khaliq Tharwat
1928	Mustafa An-Nahass
1928–9	Mohammed Mahmoud
1929–30	Adli Yegen
1930	Mustafa An-Nahass
1930–3	Ismail Sidqi
1933–4	Abdel Fattah Yahya
1934–6	Mohammed Tewfiq Nazim
1936	Ali Maher
1936–7	Mustafa An-Nahass
1937–9	Mohammed Mahmoud
1939–40	Ali Maher
1940	Hassan Sabri
1940–2	Hussein Sirry
1942–4	Mustafa An-Nahass
1944–5	Ahmed Maher
1945–6	Mahmoud Fahmy El-Nuqrashi
1946	Ismail Sidqi
1946–8	Mahmoud Fahmy El-Nuqrashi
1948–9	Ibrahim Abdel Hadi
1949–50	Hussein Sirry
1950–2	Mustafa An-Nahass

1952	Ali Maher
1952	Najib El-Hilali
1952	Hussein Sirry
1952	Najib El-Hilali
1952	Ali Maher
1952–4	Mohammed Najib
1954	Gamal Abdel Nasser
1954	Mohammed Najib
1954–62	Gamal Abdel Nasser
1958–61	*United Arab Republic*
1962–5	Ali Sabri
1965–6	Zakariya Mohyi Ed-Din
1966–7	Mohammed Sidqi Soliman
1967–70	Gamal Abdel Nasser
1970–2	Mahmoud Fawzi
1972–3	Aziz Sidki
1973–4	Mohammed Anwar El-Sadat
1974–5	Abdel Aziz Hijazy
1975–8	Mamdouh Salem
1978–80	Mustafa Khalil
1980–1	Mohammed Anwar El-Sadat
1981–2	Mohammed Hosni Mubarak
1982–4	Fouad Monyi Ed-Din
1984	Kamal Hassan Ali
1985–6	Ali Lotfi
1986–96	Atif Sidqi
1996–1999	Ahmed Kamal Al-Ganzouri
1999–	Atef Muhammed Ebeid

El Salvador

President

1899–1903	Tomás Regalado
1903–7	Pedro José Escalon
1907–11	Fernando Figueroa
1911–13	Manuel Enrique Araujo
1913–14	Carlos Meléndez *President Designate*
1914–15	Alfonso Quiñónez Molina *President Designate*
1915–18	Carlos Meléndez
1918–19	Alfonso Quiñónez Molina *Vice President*
1919–23	Jorge Meléndez
1923–7	Alfonso Quiñónez Molina
1927–31	Pio Romero Bosque
1931	Arturo Araujo
1931	*Military Administration*
1931–4	Maximiliano H Martinez *Vice President*
1934–5	Andrés I Menéndez *Provisional President*
1935–44	Maximiliano H Martinez
1944	Andrés I Menéndez *Vice President*
1944–5	Osmin Aguirre y Salinas *Provisional President*
1945–8	Salvador Castaneda Castro
1948–50	*Revolutionary Council*
1950–6	Oscar Osorio
1956–60	José María Lemus
1960–1	*Military Junta*
1961–2	*Civil-Military Administration*
1962	Rodolfo Eusebio Cordón *Provisional President*
1962–7	Julio Adalberto Rivera
1967–72	Fidel Sánchez Hernández
1972–7	Arturo Armando Molina
1977–9	Carlos Humberto Romero
1979–82	*Military Juntas*
1982–4	*Government of National Unanimity* (Alvaro Magaña)
1984–9	José Napoleón Duarte
1989–94	Alfredo Cristiani
1994–9	Armando Calderón Sol
1999–	Francisco Flores

Equatorial Guinea

President

1968–79	Francisco Macias Nguema
1979–	Teodoro Obiang Nguema Mbasogo

Prime Minister

1963–8	Bonifacio Ondó Edu
1968–82	*No Prime Minister*
1982–92	Cristino Seriche Bioko
1992–6	Silestre Siale Bileka
1996–2001	Ángel Serafín Seriche Dougan
2001–	Candido Muatetema Rivas

Eritrea

President

1993–	Issaias Afewerki

Estonia

President

1990–2	Arnold Rüütel
1992–2001	Lennart Meri
2001–	Arnold Rüütel

Prime Minister

1990–2	Edgar Savisaar
1992	Tiit Vähi
1992–4	Mart Laar
1994–5	Andres Tarand
1995–7	Tiit Vähi
1997–9	Mart Siimann
1999–2002	Mart Laar
2002–	Siim Kallas

Ethiopia

Monarch

1889–1911	Menelik II
1911–16	Lij Iyasu (Joshua)
1916–28	Zawditu
1928–74	Haile Selassie *Emperor from 1930*

Provisional Military Administrative Council

Chairman

1974–7	Teferi Benti
1977–87	Mengistu Haile Mariam

■ **People's Democratic Republic**

President

1987–91	Mengistu Haile Mariam
1991	Tesfaye Gebre Kidan *Acting President*
1991–5	Meles Zenawi

Prime Minister

1987–9	Fikre Selassie Wogderess
1989–91	Haile Yimenu *Acting Prime Minister*
1991	Tesfaye Dinka *Acting Prime Minister*
1991–5	Tamirat Layne *Acting Prime Minister*

■ **Federal Democratic Republic**

President

1995–2001	Negasso Gidada
2001–	Girma Wolde-Giorgis

Prime Minister

1995–	Meles Zenawi

European Union (EU) Commission

President

1967–70	Jean Rey
1970–2	Franco M Malfatti
1972–3	Sicco L Mansholt
1973–7	Francois-Xavier Ortoli
1977–81	Roy Jenkins
1981–5	Gaston Thorn
1985–95	Jacques Delors
1995–9	Jacques Santer
1999–	Romano Prodi

Fiji

Chief of State until 1987: British monarch, represented by Governor General

Prime Minister

1970–87	Kamisese Mara
1987	Timoci Bavadra

Interim Administration

Governor General

1987	Penaia Ganilau
1987	*Military Administration* (Sitiveni Rabuka)

■ **Republic**

Chairman

1987	Sitiveni Rabuka

President

1987–94	Penaia Ganilau
1994–2000	Kamisese Mara
2000	*Interim Military Government* (Frank Bainimarama)
2000–	Ratu Josefa Iloilovatu Uluivuda (*Acting President until 2001*)

Prime Minister

1987–92	Kamisese Mara
1992–9	Sitiveni Rabuka
1999–2000	Mahendra Chaudhry
2000	Ratu Tevita Momoedonu *Acting Prime Minister*
2000	Ratu Epeli Nailatika *Interim Prime Minister*
2000–1	Laisenia Qarase
2001	Ratu Tevita Momoedonu
2001–	Laisenia Qarase

Finland

President

1919–25	Kaarlo Juho Ståhlberg
1925–31	Lauri Kristian Relander
1931–7	Pehr Evind Svinhufvud
1937–40	Kyösti Kallio
1940–4	Risto Ryti
1944–6	Carl Gustaf Mannerheim
1946–56	Juho Kusti Paasikivi
1956–81	Urho Kekkonen
1982–94	Mauno Koivisto
1994–2000	Martti Ahtisaari
2000–	Tarja Halonen

Prime Minister

1917–18	Pehr Evind Svinhufvud

History

History

1918	Juho Kusti Paasikivi
1918–19	Lauri Johannes Ingman
1919	Kaarlo Castrén
1919–20	Juho Vennola
1920–1	Rafael Erich
1921–2	Juho Vennola
1922	Aino Kaarlo Cajander
1922–4	Kyösti Kallio
1924	Aino Kaarlo Cajander
1924–5	Lauri Johannes Ingman
1925	Antti Agaton Tulenheimo
1925–6	Kyösti Kallio
1926–7	Väinö Tanner
1927–8	Juho Emil Sunila
1928–9	Oskari Mantere
1929–30	Kyösti Kallio
1930–1	Pehr Evind Svinhufvud
1931–2	Juhu Emil Sunila
1932–6	Toivo Kivimäki
1936–7	Kyösti Kallio
1937–9	Aino Kaarlo Cajander
1939–41	Risto Ryti
1941–3	Johann Rangell
1943–4	Edwin Linkomies
1944	Andreas Hackzell
1944	Urho Jonas Castrén
1944–5	Juho Kusti Paasikivi
1946–8	Mauno Pekkala
1948–50	Karl August Fagerholm
1950–3	Urho Kekkonen
1953–4	Sakari Tuomioja
1954	Ralf Törngren
1954–6	Urho Kekkonen
1956–7	Karl August Fagerholm
1957	Väinö Johannes Sukselainen
1957–8	Rainer von Fieandt
1958	Reino Ilsakki Kuuskoski
1958–9	Karl August Fagerholm
1959–61	Väinö Johannes Sukselainen
1961–2	Martti Miettunen
1962–3	Ahti Karjalainen
1963–4	Reino Ragnar Lehto
1964–6	Johannes Virolainen
1966–8	Rafael Paasio
1968–70	Mauno Koivisto
1970	Teuvo Ensio Aura
1970–1	Ahti Karjalainen
1971–2	Teuvo Ensio Aura
1972	Rafael Paasio
1972–5	Kalevi Sorsa
1975	Keijo Antero Liinamaa
1975–7	Martti Miettunen
1977–9	Kalevi Sorsa
1979–82	Mauno Koivisto
1982–7	Kalevi Sorsa
1987–91	Harri Holkeri
1991–5	Esko Aho
1995–	Paavo Lipponen

France

President

■ **Third Republic**

1899–1906	Emile Loubet
1906–13	Armand Fallières
1913–20	Raymond Poincaré
1920	Paul Deschanel
1920–4	Alexandre Millerand
1924–31	Gaston Doumergue
1931–2	Paul Doumer
1932–40	Albert Lebrun

■ **Fourth Republic**

1947–54	Vincent Auriol
1954–8	René Coty

■ **Fifth Republic**

1958–69	Charles de Gaulle
1969–74	Georges Pompidou
1974–81	Valéry Giscard d'Estaing
1981–95	François Mitterrand
1995–	Jacques Chirac

Prime Minister

■ **Third Republic**

1899–1902	Pierre Waldeck-Rousseau
1902–5	Emile Combes
1905–6	Maurice Rouvier
1906	Jean Sarrien
1906–9	Georges Clemenceau
1909–11	Aristide Briand
1911	Ernest Monis
1911–12	Joseph Caillaux
1912–13	Raymond Poincaré
1913	Aristide Briand
1913	Jean Louis Barthou
1913–14	Gaston Doumergue
1914	Alexandre Ribot
1914–15	René Viviani
1915–17	Aristide Briand
1917	Alexandre Ribot
1917	Paul Painlevé
1917–20	Georges Clemenceau
1920	Alexandre Millerand
1920–1	Georges Leygues
1921–2	Aristide Briand
1922–4	Raymond Poincaré
1924	Frédéric François-Marsal
1924–5	Édouard Herriot
1925	Paul Painlevé
1925–6	Aristide Briand
1926	Édouard Herriot
1926–9	Raymond Poincaré
1929	Aristide Briand
1929–30	André Tardieu
1930	Camille Chautemps
1930	André Tardieu
1930–1	Théodore Steeg
1931–2	Pierre Laval
1932	André Tardieu
1932	Édouard Herriot
1932–3	Joseph Paul-Boncour
1933	Édouard Daladier
1933	Albert Sarrault
1933–4	Camille Chautemps
1934	Édouard Daladier
1934	Gaston Doumergue
1934–5	Pierre-Étienne Flandin
1935	Fernand Bouisson
1935–6	Pierre Laval
1936	Albert Sarrault
1936–7	Léon Blum
1937–8	Camille Chautemps
1938	Léon Blum
1938–40	Édouard Daladier
1940	Paul Reynaud
1940	Philippe Pétain

■ **Vichy Government**

1940–4	Philippe Pétain

History

■ Provisional Government of the French Republic

1944–6	Charles de Gaulle
1946	Félix Gouin
1946	Georges Bidault

■ Fourth Republic

1946–7	Léon Blum
1947	Paul Ramadier
1947–8	Robert Schuman
1948	André Marie
1948	Robert Schuman
1948–9	Henri Queuille
1949–50	Georges Bidault
1950	Henri Queuille
1950–1	René Pleven
1951	Henri Queuille
1951–2	René Pleven
1952	Edgar Faure
1952–3	Antoine Pinay
1953	René Mayer
1953–4	Joseph Laniel
1954–5	Pierre Mendès-France
1955–6	Edgar Faure
1956–7	Guy Mollet
1957	Maurice Bourgès-Maunoury
1957–8	Félix Gaillard
1958	Pierre Pfimlin
1958–9	Charles de Gaulle

■ Fifth Republic

1959–62	Michel Debré
1962–8	Georges Pompidou
1968–9	Maurice Couve de Murville
1969–72	Jacques Chaban Delmas
1972–4	Pierre Mesmer
1974–6	Jacques Chirac
1976–81	Raymond Barre
1981–4	Pierre Mauroy
1984–6	Laurent Fabius
1986–8	Jacques Chirac
1988–91	Michel Rocard
1991–2	Édith Cresson
1992–3	Pierre Bérégovoy
1993–5	Édouard Balladur
1995–7	Alain Juppé
1997–2002	Lionel Jospin
2002–	Jean-Pierre Raffarin

Gabon

President

1960–7	Léon M'ba
1967–	Omar (Bernard-Albert, *to 1973*) Bongo

Prime Minister

1960–75	*As President*
1975–90	Léon Mébiame (Mébiane)
1991–3	Casimir Oyé M'ba
1993–8	Paulin Obame-Nguema
1999–	Jean-François Ntoutoume-Emane

The Gambia

President

1965–94	Dawda Kairaba Jawara
1994–	Yahya Jammeh

Georgia

President

1991–2	Zviad Gamsakhurdia
1992	*Military Council*
1992–	Eduard Shevardnaze

Prime Minister

1990–1	Tengiz Sigua
1991	Murman Omanidze *Acting Prime Minister*
1991–2	Bessarion Gugushvili
1992–3	Tengiz Sigua
1993	Eduard Shevardnadze *Acting Prime Minister*
1993–5	Otar Patsatsia
1995–8	Niko Lekishvili
1998–2000	Vazha Lordkipanidze
2000–1	Giorgi Arsenishvili
2001–	Avtandil Djorbenadze

Germany

■ German Empire

Emperor

1888–1918	Wilhelm II

Chancellor

1909–17	Theobald von Bethmann Hollweg
1917	Georg Michaelis
1917–18	Georg Graf von Hertling
1918	Prince Max von Baden
1918	Friedrich Ebert

■ German Republic

President

1919–25	Friedrich Ebert
1925–34	Paul von Hindenburg

Reich Chancellor

1919	Philipp Scheidemann
1919–20	Gustav Bauer
1920	Hermann Müller
1920–1	Konstantin Fehrenbach
1921–2	Karl Joseph Wirth
1922–3	Wilhelm Cuno
1923	Gustav Stresemann
1923–4	Wilhelm Marx
1925–6	Hans Luther
1926–8	Wilhelm Marx
1928–30	Hermann Müller
1930–2	Heinrich Brüning
1932	Franz von Papen
1932–3	Kurt von Sleicher
1933	Adolf Hitler

Chancellor and Führer

1933–45	Adolf Hitler (*Führer from 1934*)
1945	Karl Dönitz

■ German Democratic Republic (East Germany)

President

1949–60	Wilhelm Pieck

Chairman of the Council of State

1960–73	Walter Ernst Karl Ulbricht
1973–6	Willi Stoph

History

1976–89	Erich Honecker
1989	Egon Krenz
1989–90	Gregor Gysi *General Secretary as Chairman*

Premier

1949–64	Otto Grotewohl
1964–73	Willi Stoph
1973–6	Horst Sindermann
1976–89	Willi Stoph
1989–90	Hans Modrow
1990	Lothar de Maizière

▪ German Federal Republic (West Germany)

President

1949–59	Theodor Heuss
1959–69	Heinrich Lübke
1969–74	Gustav Heinemann
1974–9	Walter Scheel
1979–84	Karl Carstens
1984–90	Richard von Weizsäcker

Chancellor

1949–63	Konrad Adenauer
1963–6	Ludwig Erhard
1966–9	Kurt Georg Kiesinger
1969–74	Willy Brandt
1974–82	Helmut Schmidt
1982–90	Helmut Kohl

▪ Germany

President

1990–4	Richard von Weizsäcker
1994–9	Roman Herzog
1999–	Johannes Rau

Chancellor

1990–8	Helmut Kohl
1998–	Gerhard Schröder

Ghana

President

1960–6	Kwame Nkrumah

National Liberation Council

Chairman

1966–9	Joseph Arthur Ankrah
1969	Akwasi Amankwa Afrifa
1969–70	*Presidential Committee*

President

1970–2	Edward Akufo-Addo

Chairman

1972–8	*National Redemption Council* (Ignatius Kuti Acheampong)
1978–9	*Supreme Military Council* (Fred W Akuffo)
1979	*Armed Forces Revolutionary Council* (Jerry John Rawlings)

President

1979–81	Hilla Limann

Provisional National Defence Council

Chairman

1981–2001	Jerry John Rawlings (*President from 1992*)

President

2001–	John Agyekum Kufuor

Prime Minister

1960–9	*As President*
1969–72	Kufi Abrefa Busia
1972–8	*As President*
1978–	*No Prime Minister*

Greece

Monarch

1863–1913	George I
1913–17	Constantine I
1917–20	Alexander
1920–2	Constantine I
1922–3	George II
1923–4	Paul Koundouriotis *Regent*

▪ Republic

President

1924–6	Paul Koundouriotis
1926	Theodore Pangalos
1926–9	Paul Koundouriotis
1929–35	Alexander T Zaïmis

Monarch

1935	George Kondylis *Regent*
1935–47	George II
1947–64	Paul
1964–7	Constantine II
1967–73	*Military Junta*
1973	George Papadopoulos *Regent*

▪ New Republic

President

1973	George Papadopoulos
1973–4	Phaedon Gizikis
1974–5	Michael Stasinopoulos
1975–80	Constantine Tsatsos
1980–5	Constantine Karamanlis
1985–90	Christos Sartzetakis
1990–5	Constantine Karamanlis
1995–	Constantine Stephanopoulos

Prime Minister

1899–1901	George Theotokis
1901–2	Alexander T Zaïmis
1902–3	Theodore Deligiannis
1903	George Theotokis
1903	Demetrius G Rallis
1903–4	George Theotokis
1904–5	Theodore Deligiannis
1905	Demetrius G Rallis
1905–9	George Theotokis
1909	Demetrius G Rallis
1909–10	Kyriakoulis P Mavromichalis
1910	Stephen N Dragoumis
1910–15	Eleftherios K Venizelos
1915	Demetrius P Gounaris
1915	Eleftherios K Venizelos
1915	Alexander T Zaïmis
1915–16	Stephen Skouloudis
1916	Alexander T Zaïmis
1916	Nicholas P Kalogeropoulos
1916–17	Spyridon Lambros

1917	Alexander T Zaïmis
1917–20	Eleftherios K Venizelos
1920–1	Demetrius G Rallis
1921	Nicholas P Kalogeropoulos
1921–2	Demetrius P Gounaris
1922	Nicholas Stratos
1922	Peter E Protopapadakis
1922	Nicholas Triandaphyllakos
1922	Sortirios Krokidas
1922	Alexander T Zaïmis
1922–3	Stylianos Gonatas
1924	Eleftherios K Venizelos
1924	George Kaphandaris
1924	Alexander Papanastasiou
1924	Themistocles Sophoulis
1924–5	Andreas Michalakopoulos
1925–6	Alexander N Chatzikyriakos
1926	Theodore Pangalos
1926	Athanasius Eftaxias
1926	George Kondylis
1926–8	Alexander T Zaïmis
1928–32	Eleftherios K Venizelos
1932	Alexander Papanastasiou
1932	Eleftherios K Venizelos
1932–3	Panagiotis Tsaldaris
1933	Eleftherios K Venizelos
1933	Nicholas Plastiras
1933	Alexander Othonaos
1933–5	Panagiotis Tsaldaris
1935	George Kondylis
1935–6	Constantine Demertzis
1936–41	John Metaxas
1941	Alexander Koryzis
1941	*Chairman of Ministers* George II
1941	*German Occupation* (Emmanuel Tsouderos)
1941–2	George Tsolakoglou
1942–3	Constantine Logothetopoulos
1943–4	John Rallis

Government in exile

1941–4	Emmanuel Tsouderos
1944	Sophocles Venizelos
1944–5	George Papandreou

Post-war

1945	Nicholas Plastiras
1945	Peter Voulgaris
1945	Damaskinos, Archbishop of Athens
1945	Panagiotis Kanellopoulos
1945–6	Themistocles Sophoulis
1946	Panagiotis Politzas
1946–7	Constantine Tsaldaris
1947	Demetrius Maximos
1947	Constantine Tsaldaris
1947–9	Themistocles Sophoulis
1949–50	Alexander Diomedes
1950	John Theotokis
1950	Sophocles Venizelos
1950	Nicholas Plastiras
1950–1	Sophocles Venizelos
1951	Nicholas Plastiras
1952	Demetrius Kiusopoulos
1952–5	Alexander Papagos
1955	Stephen C Stefanopoulos
1955–8	Constantine Karamanlis
1958	Constantine Georgakopoulos
1958–61	Constantine Karamanlis
1961	Constantine Dovas
1961–3	Constantine Karamanlis
1963	Panagiotis Pipinellis
1963	Stylianos Mavromichalis
1963	George Papandreou

1963–4	John Parskevopoulos
1964–5	George Papandreou
1965	George Athanasiadis-Novas
1965	Elias Tsirimokos
1965–6	Stephen C Stefanopoulos
1966–7	John Paraskevopoulos
1967	Panagiotis Kanellopoulos
1967–74	*Military Junta*
1967	Constantine Kollias
1967–73	George Papadopoulos
1973	Spyridon Markezinis
1973–4	Adamantios Androutsopoulos
1974–80	Constantine Karamanlis
1980–1	George Rallis
1981–9	Andreas Papandreou
1989	Tzannis Tzannetakis
1989–90	Xenofon Zolotas
1990–3	Constantine Mitsotakis
1993–6	Andreous Papandreou
1996–	Kostas Simitis

Grenada

Chief of State: British monarch, represented by Governor General

Prime Minister

1974–9	Eric M Gairy
1979–83	Maurice Bishop
1983–4	Nicholas Brathwaite *Chairman of Interim Council*
1984–9	Herbert A Blaize
1989–90	Ben Jones
1990–5	Nicholas Brathwaite
1995–	Keith Mitchell

Guatemala

President

1898–1920	Manuel Estrada Cabrera
1920–2	Carlos Herrera y Luna
1922–6	José María Orellana
1926–30	Lázaro Chacón
1930	Baudillo Palma
1930–1	Manuel María Orellana
1931	José María Reyna Andrade
1931–44	Jorge Ubico Castañeda
1944	Federico Ponce Vaidez
1944–5	Jacobo Arbenz Guzmán
1945–51	Juan José Arévalo
1951–4	Jacobo Arbenz Guzmán
1954	*Military Junta* (Carlos Díaz)
1954	Elfego J Monzón
1954–7	Carlos Castillo Armas
1957	*Military Junta* (Oscar Mendoza Azurdia)
1957	Luis Arturo González López
1957–8	*Military Junta* (Guillermo Flores Avendaño)
1958–63	Miguel Ydígoras Fuentes
1963–6	*Military Junta* (Enrique Peralta Azurdia)
1966–70	Julio César Méndez Montenegro
1970–4	Carlos Araña Osorio
1974–8	Kyell Eugenio Laugerua García
1978–82	Romeo Lucas García
1982	Angel Aníbal Guevara
1982–3	Efraín Rios Montt
1983–6	Oscar Humberto Mejía Victores
1986–91	Marco Vinicio Cerezo Arévalo
1991–3	Jorge Serrano Elias
1993–6	Ramiro de León Carpio

History

| 1996–2000 | Álvaro Arzú Irigoyen |
| 2000– | Alfonso Portillo Cabrera |

Guinea

President

| 1961–84 | Ahmed Sékou Touré |
| 1984– | Lansana Conté |

Prime Minister

1958–72	Ahmed Sékou Touré
1972–84	Louis Lansana Beavogui
1984–5	Diarra Traore
1985–96	*No Prime Minister*
1996–9	Sidia Toure
1999–	Lamine Sidime

Guinea-Bissau

President

1974–80	Luis de Almeida Cabral
1980–4	*Revolutionary Council* (João Bernardo Vieira)
1984–99	João Bernardo Vieira
1999–2000	Malai Bacai Sanhá *Interim President*
2000–	Kumba Yalla

Prime Minister

1992–4	Carlos Correia
1994–7	Manuel Saturnino da Costa
1997–8	Carlos Correia
1998–2000	Francisco Fadul
2000–1	Caetano N'Tchama
2001	Faustino Imbali
2001–2	Alamara Nhassé
2002–	Mário Pires

Guyana

President

1970	Edward A Luckhoo
1970–80	Arthur Chung
1980–5	Linden Forbes Sampson Burnham
1985–92	Hugh Desmond Hoyte
1992–7	Cheddi Bharrat Jagan
1997	Samuel Hinds
1997–9	Janet Jagan
1999–	Bharrat Jagdeo

Prime Minister

1966–85	Linden Forbes Sampson Burnham
1985–92	Hamilton Green
1992–7	Samuel Hinds
1997	Janet Jagan
1997–	Samuel Hinds

Haiti

President

1896–1902	P A Tirésias Simon Lam
1902	Boisrond Canal
1902–8	Alexis Nord
1908–11	Antoine Simon
1911–12	Michel Cincinnatus Leconte
1912–13	Tancrède Auguste
1913–14	Michael Oreste
1914	Oreste Zamor
1914–15	Joseph Davilmare Théodore
1915	Jean Velbrun-Guillaume
1915–22	Philippe Sudre Dartiguenave
1922–30	Joseph Louis Bornó

1930	Étienne Roy
1930–41	Sténio Joseph Vincent
1941–6	Élie Lescot
1946	*Military Junta* (Frank Lavaud)
1946–50	Dumarsais Estimé
1950	*Military Junta* (Frank Lavaud)
1950–6	Paul E Magloire
1956–7	François Sylvain
1957	*Military Junta*
1957	Léon Cantave
1957	Daniel Fignolé
1957	Antoine Kebreau
1957–71	François Duvalier ('Papa Doc')
1971–86	Jean-Claude Duvalier ('Baby Doc')
1986–8	Henri Namphy
1988	Leslie Manigat
1988	Henri Namphy
1988–90	Prosper Avril
1990–1	Ertha Pascal-Trouillot
1991	Jean-Bertrand Aristide
1991	Raoul Cédras
1991–2	Joseph Nérette
1992–3	Marc-Louis Bazin
1993–4	Jean-Bertrand Aristide
1994	Émile Jonassaint
1994–6	Jean-Bertrand Aristide
1996–2000	René Préval
2000–	Jean-Bertrand Aristide

Prime Minister

1988	Martial Célestin
1988–91	*No Prime Minister*
1991	René Préval
1991–2	Jean-Jacques Honorat *Interim Prime Minister*
1992–3	Marc Bazin
1993–4	Robert Malval
1994–5	Smarck Michel
1995–6	Claudette Werleigh
1996–7	Rosny Smarth
1998–2001	Jacques-Édouard Alexis
2001–2	Jean-Marie Cherestal
2002–	Yvon Neptune

Honduras

President

1900–3	Terencio Sierra
1903	Juan Angel Arias
1903–7	Manuel Bonilla Chirinos
1907–11	Miguel R Dávila
1912–15	Manuel Bonilla Chirinos
1915–20	Francisco Bertrand
1920–4	Rafael López Gutiérrez
1924–5	Vicente Tosta Carrasco
1925–8	Miguel Paz Barahona
1929–32	Vicente Mejía Clindres
1932–49	Tiburcio Carías Andino
1949–54	Juan Manuel Gálvez

Head of State

| 1954–6 | Julio Lozano Diaz |
| 1956–7 | *Military Junta* |

President

| 1958–63 | José Ramón Villeda Morales |

Head of State

| 1963–5 | Oswaldo López Arellano |

President

| 1965–71 | Oswaldo López Arellano |

1971–2	Ramón Ernesto Cruz

Head of State

1972–5	Oswaldo López Arellano
1975–8	Juan Alberto Melgar Castro
1978–82	Policarpo Paz García

President

1982–6	Roberto Suazo Córdova
1986–9	José Azcona Hoyo
1989–93	Rafael Leonardo Callejas
1993–7	Carlos Roberto Reina
1997–2002	Carlos Roberto Flores Facussé
2002–	Ricardo Maduro

Hungary

Monarch

1900–16	Franz Josef I
1916–18	Charles IV

President

1919	Mihály Károlyi
1919	*Revolutionary Governing Council* (Sándor Garbai)
1920–44	Miklós Horthy *Regent*
1944–5	*Provisional National Assembly*
1946–8	Zoltán Tildy
1948–50	Árpád Szakasits
1950–2	Sándor Rónai
1952–67	István Dobi
1967–87	Pál Losonczi
1987–8	Károly Németh
1988–9	Brunó Ferenc Straub
1989–90	Mátyás Szűrös
1990–2000	Árpád Göncz
2000–	Ferenc Madl

Premier

1899–1903	Kálmán Széll
1903	Károly Khuen-Héderváry
1903–5	István Tisza
1905–6	Géza Fejérváry
1906–10	Sándor Wekerle
1910–12	Károly Khuen-Héderváry
1912–13	Lázló Lukács
1913–17	István Tisza
1917	Móric Esterházy
1917–18	Sándor Wekerle
1918–19	Mihály Károlyi
1919	Dénes Berinkey
1919	*Revolutionary Governing Council*
1919	Gyula Peidl
1919	István Friedrich
1919–20	Károly Huszár
1920	Sándor Simonyi-Semadam
1920–1	Pál Teleki
1921–31	István Bethlen
1931–2	Gyula Károlyi
1932–6	Gyula Gömbös
1936–8	Kálman Darányi
1938–9	Béla Imrédy
1939–41	Pál Teleki
1941–2	Lázló Bárdossy
1942–4	Miklós Kállay
1944	Döme Sztójay
1944	Géza Lakatos
1944	Ferenc Szálasi
1944–5	*Provisional National Assembly* (Béla Dálnoki Miklós)
1945–6	Zoltán Tildy
1946–7	Ferenc Nagy

1947–8	Lajos Dinnyés
1948–52	István Dobi
1952–3	Mátyás Rákosi
1953–5	Imre Nagy
1955–6	András Hegedüs
1956	Imre Nagy
1956–8	János Kádár
1958–61	Ferenc Münnich
1961–5	János Kádár
1965–7	Gyula Kállai
1967–75	Jenö Fock
1975–87	György Lázár
1987–8	Károly Grosz
1988–90	Miklás Németh
1990–3	József Antall
1993–4	Péter Boross
1994–8	Gyula Horn
1998–2002	Viktor Orban
2002–	Peter Medgyessy

First Secretary

1949–56	Mátyás Rákosi
1956	Ernö Gerö
1956–88	János Kádár
1988–90	Károly Grosz

Iceland

President

1944–52	Sveinn Björnsson
1952–68	Ásgeir Ásgeirsson
1968–80	Kristján Eldjárn
1980–96	Vigdís Finnbogadóttir
1996–	Ólafur Ragnar Grimsson

Prime Minister

1900–1	C Goos
1901–4	P A Alberti
1904–9	Hannes Hafstein
1909–11	Björn Jónsson
1911–12	Kristján Jónsson
1912–14	Hannes Hafstein
1914–15	Sigurdur Eggerz
1915–17	Einar Arnórsson
1917–22	Jón Magnússon
1922–4	Sigurdur Eggerz
1924–6	Jón Magnússon
1926–7	John Þorláksson
1927–32	Tryggvi Þórhallsson
1932–4	Ásgeir Ásgeirsson
1934–42	Hermann Jónasson
1942	Ólafur Thors
1942–4	Björn Þórðarsson
1944–7	Ólafur Thors
1947–9	Stefán Jóhann Stefánsson
1949–50	Ólafur Thors
1950–3	Steingrímur Steinþórsson
1953–6	Ólafur Thors
1956–8	Hermann Jónasson
1958–9	Emil Jónsson
1959–61	Ólafur Thors
1961	Bjarni Benediktsson
1961–3	Ólafur Thors
1963–70	Bjarni Benediktsson
1970–1	Jóhann Hafstein
1971–4	Ólafur Jóhannesson
1974–8	Geir Hallgrímsson
1978–9	Ólafur Jóhannesson
1979	Benedikt Gröndal
1980–3	Gunnar Thoroddsen
1983–7	Steingrímur Hermannsson
1987–8	Thorsteinn Pálsson

History (side tab)

History

1988–91	Steingrímur Hermannsson
1991–	Davíd Oddsson

India

President

1950–62	Rajendra Prasad
1962–7	Sarvepalli Radhakrishnan
1967–9	Zakir Husain
1969	Varahagiri Venkatagiri *Acting President*
1969	Mohammed Hidayatullah *Acting President*
1969–74	Varahagiri Venkatagiri
1974–7	Fakhruddin Ali Ahmed
1977	B D Jatti *Acting President*
1977–82	Neelam Sanjiva Reddy
1982–7	Giani Zail Singh
1987–92	Ramaswami Venkataraman
1992–7	Shankar Dayal Sharma
1997–2002	Kocheril Raman Narayanan
2002–	A P J Abdul Kalam

Prime Minister

1947–64	Jawaharlal Nehru
1964	Gulzari Lal Nanda *Acting Prime Minister*
1964–6	Lal Bahadur Shastri
1966	Gulzari Lal Nanda *Acting Prime Minister*
1966–77	Indira Gandhi
1977–9	Morarji Desai
1979–80	Charan Singh
1980–4	Indira Gandhi
1984–9	Rajiv Gandhi
1989–90	Vishwanath Pratap Singh
1990–1	Chandra Shekhar
1991–6	P V Narasimha Rao
1996	Atal Behari Vajpayee
1996–7	H D Deve Gowda
1997	Inder Kumar Gujral
1998–	Atal Behari Vajpayee

Indonesia

President

1945–9	Ahmed Sukarno

■ Republic

1949–66	Ahmed Sukarno
1966–98	T N J Suharto
1998–9	B J Habibie
1999–2001	Abdurrahman Wahid
2001–	Megawati Sukarnoputri

Prime Minister

1945	R A A Wiranatakusumah
1945–7	Sutan Sjahrir
1947–8	Amir Sjarifuddin
1948	Mohammed Hatta
1948–9	Sjarifuddin Prawiraranegara
1949	Susanto Tirtoprodjo
1949	Mohammed Hatta
1950	Dr Halim
1950–1	Mohammed Natsir
1951–2	Sukiman Wirjosandjojo
1952–3	Dr Wilopo
1953–5	Ali Sastroamidjojo
1955–6	Burhanuddin Harahap
1956–7	Ali Sastroamidjojo
1957–9	Raden Haji Djuanda Kurtawidjaja
1959–63	Ahmed Sukarno

1963–6	S E Subandrio
1966–	*No Prime Minister*

Iran

Shah

1896–1907	Muzaffar Ad-Din
1907–9	Mohammed Ali
1909–25	Ahmad Mirza
1925–41	Mohammed Reza Khan
1941–79	Mohammed Reza Pahlavi

■ Islamic Republic

Leader of the Islamic Revolution

1979–89	Ruhollah Khomeini
1989–	Sayed Ali Khamenei

President

1980–1	Abolhassan Bani-Sadr
1981	Mohammed Ali Rajai
1981–9	Sayed Ali Khamenei
1989–97	Ali Akbar Hashemi Rafsanjani
1997–	Sayed Ayatollah Mohammad Khatami

Prime Minister

1979	Shahpur Bakhtiar
1979–80	Mehdi Bazargan
1980–1	Mohammed Ali Rajai
1981	Mohammed Javad Bahonar
1981	Mohammed Reza Mahdavi-Kani
1981–9	Mir Hossein Moussavi

Iraq

Monarch

1921–33	Faisal I
1933–9	Ghazi I
1939–58	Faisal II (*Regent* 1939–53, Abdul Illah)

■ Republic

Commander of the National Forces

1958–63	Abdul Karim Qassem

Head of Council of State

1958–63	Mohammed Najib Ar-Rubai

President

1963–6	Abd as-Salam Arif
1966–8	Abd ar-Rahman Arif
1968–79	Ahmad Hassan Al-Bakr
1979–	Saddam Hussein

Prime Minister

1958–63	Abdul Karim Qassem
1963	Ahmad Hassan al-Bakr
1963–5	Tahir Yahya
1965	Arif Abd ar-Razzaq
1965–6	Abd ar-Rahman al-Bazzaz
1966–7	Naji Talib
1967	Abd ar-Rahman Arif
1967–8	Tahir Yahya
1968	Abd ar-Razzaq an-Naif
1968–79	Ahmad Hassan al-Bakr
1979–91	Saddam Hussein
1991	Sadun Hammadi
1991–3	Mohammed Hamzah az-Zubaydi
1993–4	Ahmad Hussein Khudayir as-Samarrai
1994–	Saddam Hussein

Ireland

Governor General

1922–7	Timothy Michael Healy
1927–32	James McNeill
1932–6	Donald Buckley

President

1938–45	Douglas Hyde
1945–59	Sean Thomas O'Kelly
1959–73	Éamon de Valera
1973–4	Erskine H Childers
1974–6	Carroll Daly
1976–90	Patrick J Hillery
1990–7	Mary Robinson
1997–	Mary McAleese

Prime Minister

1919–21	Éamon de Valera
1922	Arthur Griffiths
1922–32	William Cosgrave
1932–48	Éamon de Valera
1948–51	John Aloysius Costello
1951–4	Éamon de Valera
1954–7	John Aloysius Costello
1957–9	Éamon de Valera
1959–66	Sean Lemass
1966–73	John Lynch
1973–7	Liam Cosgrave
1977–9	John Lynch
1979–82	Charles Haughey
1982–7	Garrett Fitzgerald
1987–92	Charles Haughey
1992–4	Albert Reynolds
1994–7	John Bruton
1997–	Bertie Ahern

Israel

President

1948–52	Chaim Weizmann
1952–63	Itzhak Ben-Zvi
1963–73	Zalman Shazar
1973–8	Ephraim Katzair
1978–83	Yitzhak Navon
1983–93	Chaim Herzog
1993–2000	Ezer Weizman
2000–	Moshe Katsav

Prime Minister

1948–53	David Ben-Gurion
1954–5	Moshe Sharett
1955–63	David Ben-Gurion
1963–9	Levi Eshkol
1969–74	Golda Meir
1974–7	Yitzhak Rabin
1977–83	Menachem Begin
1983–4	Yitzhak Shamir
1984–8	Shimon Peres
1988–92	Yitzhak Shamir
1992–5	Yitzhak Rabin
1995–6	Shimon Peres *Acting Prime Minister*
1996–9	Binyamin Netanyahu
1999–2001	Ehud Barak
2001–	Ariel Sharon

Italy

■ **Kingdom of Italy**

Monarch

1900–46	Victor Emmanuel III

■ **Italian Republic**

President

1946–8	Enrico de Nicola
1948–55	Luigi Einaudi
1955–62	Giovanni Gronchi
1962–4	Antonio Segni
1964–71	Giuseppe Saragat
1971–8	Giovanni Leone
1978–85	Alessandro Pertini
1985–92	Francesco Cossiga
1992–9	Oscar Luigi Scalfaro
1999–	Carlo Azeglio Ciampi

■ **Kingdom of Italy**

Prime Minister

1900–1	Giuseppe Saracco
1901–3	Giuseppe Zanardelli
1903–5	Giovanni Giolitti
1905–6	Alessandro Fortis
1906	Sydney Sonnino
1906–9	Giovanni Giolitti
1909–10	Sydney Sonnino
1910–11	Luigi Luzzatti
1911–14	Giovanni Giolitti
1914–16	Antonio Salandra
1916–17	Paolo Boselli
1917–19	Vittorio Emmanuele Orlando
1919–20	Francesco Saverio Nitti
1920–1	Giovanni Giolitti
1921–2	Ivanoe Bonomi
1922	Luigi Facta
1922–43	Benito Mussolini
1943–4	Pietro Badoglio
1944–5	Ivanoe Bonomi
1945	Ferrucio Parri
1945	Alcide de Gasperi

■ **Italian Republic**

1946–53	Alcide de Gasperi
1953–4	Giuseppe Pella
1954	Amintore Fanfani
1954–5	Mario Scelba
1955–7	Antonio Segni
1957–8	Adone Zoli
1958–9	Amintore Fanfani
1959–60	Antonio Segni
1960	Fernando Tambroni
1960–3	Amintore Fanfani
1963	Giovanni Leone
1963–8	Aldo Moro
1968	Giovanni Leone
1968–70	Mariano Rumor
1970–2	Emilio Colombo
1972–4	Giulio Andreotti
1974–6	Aldo Moro
1976–8	Giulio Andreotti
1979–80	Francisco Cossiga
1980–1	Arnaldo Forlani
1981–2	Giovanni Spadolini
1982–3	Amintore Fanfani
1983–7	Bettino Craxi
1987	Amintore Fanfani
1987–8	Giovanni Goria

History

History

1988–9	Ciriaco de Mita
1989–92	Giulio Andreotti
1992–3	Giuliano Amato
1993–4	Carlo Azeglio Ciampi
1994	Silvio Berlusconi
1995–6	Lamberto Dini
1996–8	Romano Prodi
1998–2000	Massimo D'Alema
2000–1	Giuliano Amato
2001–	Silvio Berlusconi

Jamaica

Chief of State: British monarch, represented by Governor General

Prime Minister

1962–7	William Alexander Bustamante
1967	Donald Burns Sangster
1967–72	Hugh Lawson Shearer
1972–80	Michael Norman Manley
1980–9	Edward Phillip George Seaga
1989–92	Michael Norman Manley
1992–	Percival James Patterson

Japan

Chief of State (Emperor)

1867–1912	Mutsuhito (Meiji Era)
1912–26	Yoshihito (Taisho Era)
1926–89	Hirohito (Showa Era)
1989–	Akihito (Heisei Era)

Prime Minister

1900–1	Hirobumi Ito
1901–6	Taro Katsura
1906–8	Kimmochi Saionji
1908–11	Taro Katsura
1911–12	Kimmochi Saionji
1912–13	Taro Katsura
1913–14	Gonnohyoe Yamamoto
1914–16	Shigenobu Okuma
1916–18	Masatake Terauchi
1918–21	Takashi Hara
1921–2	Korekiyo Takahashi
1922–3	Tomosaburo Kato
1923–4	Gonnohyoe Yamamoto
1924	Keigo Kiyoura
1924–6	Takaaki Kato
1926–7	Reijiro Wakatsuki
1927–9	Giichi Tanaka
1929–31	Osachi Hamaguchi
1931	Reijiro Wakatsuki
1931–2	Tsuyoshi Inukai
1932–4	Makoto Saito
1934–6	Keisuke Okada
1936–7	Koki Hirota
1937	Senjuro Hayashi
1937–9	Fumimaro Konoe
1939	Kiichiro Hiranuma
1939–40	Nobuyuki Abe
1940	Mitsumasa Yonai
1940–1	Fumimaro Konoe
1941–4	Hideki Tojo
1944–5	Kuniaki Koiso
1945	Kantaro Suzuki
1945	Naruhiko Higashikuni
1945–6	Kijuro Shidehara
1946–7	Shigeru Yoshida
1947–8	Tetsu Katayama
1948	Hitoshi Ashida

1948–54	Shigeru Yoshida
1954–6	Ichiro Hatoyama
1956–7	Tanzan Ishibashi
1957–60	Nobusuke Kishi
1960–4	Hayato Ikeda
1964–72	Eisaku Sato
1972–4	Kakuei Tanaka
1974–6	Takeo Miki
1976–8	Takeo Fukuda
1978–80	Masayoshi Ohira
1980–2	Zenko Suzuki
1982–7	Yasuhiro Nakasone
1987–9	Noburu Takeshita
1989	Sasuke Uno
1989–91	Toshiki Kaifu
1991–93	Kiichi Miyazawa
1993	Morihiro Hosokawa
1994	Tsutoma Hata
1994–6	Tomiichi Murayama
1996–8	Ryutaro Hashimoto
1998–2000	Keizo Obuchi
2000	Mikio Aoki *Acting Prime Minister*
2000–1	Yoshiro Mori
2001–	Junichiro Koizumi

Jordan

Monarch

1921–51	Abdullah ibn Hussein I
1951–2	Talal I
1952–99	Hussein ibn Talal
1999–	Abdullah ibn Hussein II

Prime Minister

1921	Rashid Tali
1921	Muzhir Ar-Raslan
1921–3	Rida Ar-Riqabi
1923	Muzhir Ar-Raslan
1923–4	Hassan Khalid
1924–33	Rida Ar-Riqabi
1933–8	Ibrahim Hashim
1939–45	Taufiq Abul-Huda
1945–8	Ibrahim Hashim
1948–50	Taufiq Abul-Huda
1950	Said Al-Mufti
1950–1	Samir Ar-Rifai
1951–3	Taufiq Abul-Huda
1953–4	Fauzi Al-Mulqi
1954–5	Taufiq Abul-Huda
1955	Said Al-Mufti
1955	Hazza Al-Majali
1955–6	Ibrahim Hashim
1956	Samir Ar-Rifai
1956	Said Al-Mufti
1956	Ibrahim Hashim
1956–7	Suleiman Nabulsi
1957	Hussein Fakhri Al-Khalidi
1957–8	Ibrahim Hashim
1958	Nuri Pasha Al-Said
1958–9	Samir Ar-Rifai
1959–60	Hazza Al-Majali
1960–2	Bahjat Talhuni
1962–3	Wasfi At-Tall
1963	Samir Ar-Rifai
1963–4	Sharif Hussein Bin Nasir
1964	Bahjat Talhuni
1965–7	Wasfi At-Tall
1967	Sharif Hussein Bin Nasir
1967	Saad Jumaa
1967–9	Bahjat Talhuni
1969	Abdul Munem Rifai
1969–70	Bahjat Talhuni

1970	Abdul Munem Rifai
1970	*Military Junta* (Mohammed Daud)
1970	Mohamed Ahmed Tugan
1970–1	Wasfi At-Tall
1971–3	Ahmad Lozi
1973–6	Zeid Rifai
1976–9	Mudar Badran
1979–80	Sharif Abdul Hamid Sharaf
1980	Kassem Rimawi
1980–4	Mudar Badran
1984–5	Ahmad Ubayat
1985–9	Zeid Ar-Rifai
1989	Sharif Zaid ibn Shaker
1989–91	Mudar Badran
1991	Taher Al-Masri
1991–3	Sharif Zaid ibn Shaker
1993–5	Abdel Salam Al-Majali
1995–7	Abdul Karim Kabariti
1997–8	Abdel Salam Al-Majali
1998–9	Fayez Tarawneh
1999–2000	Abdul Raouf Rawabdeh
2000–	Ali Abu al-Ragheb

Kazakhstan

President

1991–	Nursultan Nazarbayev

Prime Minister

1991–4	Sergei Tereshchenko
1994–7	Akezhan Kazhageldin
1997–9	Nurlan Balgimbayev
1999–2002	Kasymzhomart Tokaev
2002–	Imangali Tasmagambetov

Kenya

President

1963–78	Mzee Jomo Kenyatta
1978–2002	Daniel arap Moi
2002–	Mwai Kibaki

Kiribati

President

1979–91	Ieremia T Tabai
1991–4	Teatao Teannaki
1994–	Teburoro Tito

Korea, Democratic People's Republic of (North Korea)

President

1948–57	Kim Doo-bong
1957–72	Choi Yong-kun
1972–94	Kim Il Sung
1994–7	*position vacant*
1998–	Kim Il Sung (deceased) *Eternal President*

Chairman of National Defence Commission
1993–	Kim Jong Il

Prime Minister

1948–76	Kim Il Sung
1976–7	Park Sung-chul
1977–84	Li Jong-ok
1984–6	Kang Song-san
1986–8	Yi Kun-mo
1988–92	Yon Hyong-muk
1992–7	Kang Song-san
1997–	Hong Song-nam

Korea, Republic of (South Korea)

President

1948–60	Syngman Rhee
1960	Ho Chong *Acting President*
1960	Kwak Sang-hun *Acting President*
1960	Ho Chong *Acting President*
1960–3	Yun Po-sun
1963–79	Park Chung-hee
1979–80	Choi Kyu-hah
1980	Park Choong-hoon *Acting President*
1980–8	Chun Doo-hwan
1988–92	Roh Tae-woo
1993–7	Kim Young-sam
1997–	Kim Dae-jung

Prime Minister

1948–50	Lee Pom-sok
1950	Shin Song-mo *Acting Prime Minister*
1950–1	John M Chang
1951–2	Ho Chong *Acting Prime Minister*
1952	Lee Yun-yong *Acting Prime Minister*
1952	Chang Taek-sang
1952–4	Paik Too-chin
1954–6	Pyon Yong-tae
1956–60	Syngman Rhee
1960	Ho Chong
1960–1	John M Chang
1961	Chang To-yong
1961–2	Song Yo-chan
1962–3	Kim Hyun-chul
1963–4	Choe Tu-son
1964–70	Chung Il-kwon
1970–1	Paik Too-chin
1971–5	Kim Jong-pil
1975–9	Choi Kyu-hah
1979–80	Shin Hyun-hwak
1980	Park Choong-hoon *Acting Prime Minister*
1980–2	Nam Duck-woo
1982	Yoo Chang-soon
1982–3	Kim Sang-hyup
1983–5	Chin Lee-chong
1985–8	Lho Shin-yong
1988	Lee Hyun-jae
1988–90	Kang Young-hoon
1990–1	Ro Jai-bong
1991–2	Chung Won-shik
1992–3	Hyun Soong-jong
1993	Hwang In-sung
1993–4	Lee Hoi-chang
1994	Lee Yung-duck
1994–5	Yi Hong-ku
1995–7	Lee Soo-sung
1997–8	Koh Kun
1998–2000	Kim Jong-pil
2000	Park Tae-joon
2000	Lee Hun-jai *Acting Prime Minister*
2000–2	Lee Han-dong
2002–	Kim Suk-soo

Kuwait

Emir

Family name: al-Sabah

1896–1915	Mubarak
1915–17	Jaber II
1917–21	Salem Al-Mubarak
1921–50	Ahmed Al-Jaber
1950–65	Abdallah Al-Salem
1965–77	Sabah Al-Salem
1978–	Jaber Al-Ahmed Al-Jaber

History

History

Prime Minister

1962–3	Abdallah Al-Salem
1963–5	Sabah Al-Salem
1965–78	Jaber Al-Ahmed Al-Jaber
1978–	Saad Al-Abdallah Al-Salem

Kyrgyzstan

President

1991–	Askar Akayev

Prime Minister

1991	Nasirdin Isanov
1991–2	Andrey Andreyevich Yordan *Acting Prime Minister*
1992–3	Tursunbek Chyngyshev
1993–8	Apas Jumagulov
1998	Kubanychbek Djumaliyev
1998	Boris Silayev *Acting Prime Minister*
1998–9	Jumabek Ibraimov
1999	Boris Silayev *Acting Prime Minister*
1999–2000	Amangeldy Muraliyev
2000–2	Kurmanbek Bakiyev
2002–	Nikolai Tanayev

Laos

Monarch

1904–59	Sisavang Vong
1959–75	Savang Vatthana

■ **Lao People's Democratic Republic**

President

1975–87	Souphanouvong
1987–91	Phoumi Vongvichit
1991–2	Kaysone Phomvihane
1992–8	Nouhak Phoumsavan
1998–	Khamtai Siphandon

Prime Minister

1951–4	Souvanna Phouma
1954–5	Katay Don Sasorith
1956–8	Souvanna Phouma
1958–9	Phoui Sahanikone
1959–60	Sunthone Patthamavong
1960	Kou Abhay
1960	Somsanith
1960	Souvana Phouma
1960	Sunthone Patthamavong
1960	Quinim Pholsena
1960–2	Boun Oum Na Champassac
1962–75	Souvanna Phouma
1975–91	Kaysone Phomvihane
1991–8	Khamtai Siphandon
1998–2001	Sisavath Keobounphan
2001–	Boungnang Vorachit

Latvia

President

1990–3	Anatolijs Gorbunovs
1993–9	Guntis Ulmanis
1999–	Vaira Vike-Freiberga

Prime Minister

1990–3	Ivars Godmanis
1993–4	Valdis Birkavs
1994–5	Maris Gailis
1995–7	Andris Skele
1997–8	Guntars Krasts
1998–9	Vilis Kristopans

1999–2000	Andris Skele
2000–2	Andris Berzins
2002–	Einars Repse

Lebanon

President

1943–52	Bishara Al-Khoury
1952–8	Camille Shamoun
1958–64	Fouad Shehab
1964–70	Charle Hilo
1970–6	Suleiman Frenjieh
1976–82	Elias Sarkis
1982	Bashir Gemayel
1982–8	Amin Gemayel
1988–9	*No President*
1989	Rene Muawad
1989–98	Elias Hrawi
1998–	Emile Lahoud

Prime Minister

1943	Riad Solh
1943–4	Henry Pharaon
1944–5	Riad Solh
1945	Abdul Hamid Karame
1945–6	Sami Solh
1946	Saadi Munla
1946–51	Riad Solh
1951	Hussein Oweini
1951–2	Abdullah Yafi
1952	Sami Solh
1952	Nazem Accari
1952	Saeb Salam
1952	Fouad Chehab
1952–3	Khaled Chehab
1953	Saeb Salam
1953–5	Abdullah Yafi
1955	Sami Solh
1955–6	Rashid Karami
1956	Abdullah Yafi
1956–8	Sami Solh
1958–60	Rashid Karami
1960	Ahmad Daouq
1960–1	Saeb Salam
1961–4	Rashid Karami
1964–5	Hussein Oweini
1965–6	Rashid Karami
1966	Abdullah Yafi
1966–8	Rashid Karami
1968–9	Abdullah Yafi
1969–70	Rashid Karami
1970–3	Saeb Salam
1973	Amin al-Hafez
1973–4	Takieddine Solh
1974–5	Rashid Solh
1975	Noureddin Rifai
1975–6	Rashid Karami
1976–80	Selim al-Hoss
1980	Takieddine Solh
1980–4	Chafiq al-Wazan
1984–8	Rashid Karami
1988–90	Michel Aoun/Selim al-Hoss
1990–2	Umar Karami
1992–8	Rafiq al-Hariri
1998–2000	Selim al-Hoss
2000–	Rafiq al-Hariri

Lesotho

Monarch

1966–90	Moshoeshoe II
1991–4	Letsie III

1995–6   Moshoeshoe II
1996–   Letsie III

Prime Minister

1966–86   Leabua Jonathan

Chairman of Military Council

1986–91   Justin Metsing Lekhanya
1991–3   Elias Tutsoane Ramaema

Prime Minister

1993–8   Ntsu Mokhehle
1998–   Bethuel Pakalitha Mosisili

Liberia

President

1900–4   Garretson Wilmot Gibson
1904–12   Arthur Barclay
1912–20   Daniel Edward Howard
1920–30   Charles Dunbar Burgess King
1930–43   Edwin J Barclay
1943–71   William V S Tubman
1971–80   William Richard Tolbert

People's Redemption Council

Chairman

1980–6   Samuel K Doe

President

1986–90   Samuel K Doe
1991–4   Amos Sawyer *Interim President*

Council of State

Chairman

1994–5   David Kpormakor
1995–6   Wilton Sankawulo
1996–7   Ruth Perry

President

1997–   Charles Taylor

Libya

Monarch

1951–69   Mohammed Idris Al-Mahdi Al-Senussi

Revolutionary Command Council

Chairman

1969–77   Muammar Al-Gaddafi (Qaddafi)

General Secretariat

Secretary General

1977–9   Muammar Al-Gaddafi
1979–84   Abdul Ati Al-Ubaidi
1984–6   Mohammed Az-Zaruq Rajab
1986–90   Omar Al-Muntasir
1990–4   Abu Zayd 'Umar Durda
1994–   Zanati Mohammed Al-Zanati

Leader of the Revolution

1969–   Muammar Al-Gaddafi

Liechtenstein

Prince

1858–1929   Johann II
1929–38   Franz von Paula
1938–89   Franz Josef II
1989–   Hans Adam II

Prime Minister

1928–45   Franz Josef Hoop
1945–62   Alexander Friek
1962–70   Gérard Batliner
1970–4   Alfred J Hilbe
1974–8   Walter Kieber
1978–93   Hans Brunhart
1993   Markus Büchel
1994–2001   Mario Frick
2001–   Otmar Hasler

Lithuania

President

1990–3   Vytautas Landsbergis
1993–8   Algirdas Brazauskas
1998–   Valdas Adamkus

Prime Minister

1990–1   Kazimiera Prunskienė
1991   Albertas Simenas
1991–2   Gediminas Vagnorius
1992   Aleksandras Abisala
1992–3   Bronislovas Lubys
1993–6   Adolfas Slezevicius
1996   Laurynas Stankevicius
1996–9   Gediminas Vagnorius
1999   Irena Degutienė *Acting Prime Minister*
1999   Rolandas Paksas
1999   Irena Degutienė *Acting Prime Minister*
1999–2000   Andrius Kubilius
2000–1   Rolandas Paksas
2001–   Algirdas Brazauskas

Luxembourg

Grand Dukes and Duchesses

1890–1905   Adolf
1905–12   William IV
1912–19   Marie Adelaide
1919–64   Charlotte (*in exile 1940–4*)
1964–2000   Jean
2000–   Henri

Prime Minister

1889–1915   Paul Eyschen
1915   Mathias Mongenast
1915–16   Hubert Loutsch
1916–17   Victor Thorn
1917–18   Léon Kaufmann
1918–25   Emil Reuter
1925–6   Pierre Prum
1926–37   Joseph Bech
1937–53   Pierre Dupong (*in exile 1940–4*)
1953–8   Joseph Bech
1958   Pierre Frieden
1959–69   Pierre Werner
1969–79   Gaston Thorn
1979–84   Pierre Werner
1984–95   Jacques Santer
1995–   Jean-Claude Juncker

History

History

Macedonia, Former Yugoslav Republic of

President

1991–5	Kiro Gligorov
1995–8	Stojan Andov *Acting President*
1998–9	Kiro Gligorov
1999–	Boris Trajkovski

Prime Minister

1991–2	Branko Crvenkovski
1992–6	Petar Gosev
1996–8	Branko Crvenkovski
1998–2002	Ljubco Georgievski
2002–	Branko Crvenkovski

Madagascar

President

1960–72	Philibert Tsiranana
1972–5	Gabriel Ramanantsoa
1975	Richard Ratsimandrava
1975	Gilles Andriamahazo
1975–93	Didier Ratsiraka
1993–7	Albert Zafy
1997–2002	Didier Ratsiraka
2002–	Marc Ravalomanana

Prime Minister

1960–75	*As President*
1975–6	Joël Rakotomala
1976–7	Justin Rakotoriaina
1977–88	Désiré Rakotoarijaona
1988–91	Victor Ramahatra
1991–3	Guy Willy Razanamasy
1993–5	Francisque Ravony
1995–6	Emmanuel Rakotovahiny
1996–7	Norbert Ratsirahonana
1997–8	Paskal Rakotmavo
1998–2002	Tantely Andrianarivo
2002–	Jacques Sylla

Malawi

President

1966–94	Hastings Kamuzu Banda
1994–	Bakili Muluzi

Malaysia

Chief of State (Yang di-Pertuan Agong)

1957–63	Abdul Rahman
1963–5	Syed Putra Jamalullah
1965–70	Ismail Nasiruddin Shah
1970–5	Abdul Halim Muadzam Shah
1975–9	Yahya Petra Ibrahim
1979–84	Haji Ahmad Shah Al-Mustain Billah
1984–9	Mahmood Iskandar Shah
1989–94	Azlan Muhibuddin Shah
1994–9	Jaafar Ibni Abdul Rahman
1999–2001	Salehuddin Abdul Aziz Shah
2001	Mizal Zainal Abidin *Acting Chief of State*
2001–	Syed Sirajuddin Syed Putra Jamalullail

Prime Minister

■ **Malaya**

1957–63	Abdul Rahman Putra Al-Haj

■ **Malaysia**

1963–70	Abdul Rahman Putra Al-Haj
1970–6	Abdul Razak bin Hussein
1976–9	Haji Hussein bin Onn

1979–97	Mahathir bin Mohamad
1997	Anwar Ibrahim *Acting Prime Minister*
1997–	Mahathir bin Mohamad

Maldives

Monarch (Sultan)

1954–68	Mohammed Farid Didi

■ **Republic**

President

1968–78	Ibrahim Nasir
1978–	Maumoon Abdul Gayoom

Mali

President

1960–8	Modibo Keita
1969–91	Moussa Traoré
1991–2	Amadou Toumani Touré
1992–2002	Alpha Oumar Konaré
2002–	Amadou Toumani Touré

Prime Minister

1986–88	Mamadou Dembelé
1988–91	*No Prime Minister*
1991–2	Soumana Sacko
1992–3	Younoussi Touré
1993–4	Abdoulaye Sekou Sow
1994–2000	Ibrahim Boubacar Keita
2000–2	Mande Sidibe
2002–	Ahmed Mohamed ag Hamani

Malta

President

1974–6	Anthony Mamo
1976–81	Anton Buttigieg
1982–7	Agatha Barbara
1987–9	Paul Xuereb *Acting President*
1989–94	Vincent Tabone
1994–9	Ugo Mifsud Bonnici
1999–	Guido de Marco

Prime Minister

1962–71	G Borg Olivier
1971–84	Dom Mintoff
1984–7	Carmelo Mifsud Bonnici
1987–96	Edward Fenech Adami
1996–8	Alfred Sant
1998–	Edward Fenech Adami

Marshall Islands

President

1979–96	Amata Kabua
1996–7	Kunio Lemari *Acting President*
1997–2000	Imata Kabua
2000–	Kessai Note

Mauritania

President

1961–78	Mokhtar Ould Daddah
1979	Mustapha Ould Mohammed Salek
1979–80	Mohammed Mahmoud Ould Ahmed Louly

1980–4 Mohammed Khouna Ould Haydallah
1984– Maaouya Ould Sidi Ahmed Taya

Prime Minister

1992–6 Sidi Mohammed Ould Boubaker
1996–7 Cheikh el Avia Ould Mohammed
Khouna
1997–8 Mohammed Lemine Ould Guig
1998– Cheikh el Avia Ould Mohammed
Khouna

Mauritius

Chief of State until 1992: British monarch, represented by Governor General

Prime Minister

1968–82 Seewoosagur Ramgoolam
1982–95 Anerood Jugnauth
1995–2000 Navin Ramgoolam
2000– Anerood Jugnauth

■ Republic

President

1992 Veerasamy Ringadoo
1992–2002 Cassam Uteem
2002 Angidi Chettiar
2002 Arianga Pillay *Interim President*
2002– Karl Offmann

Mexico

President

1876–1911 Porfirio Diaz
1911 Francisco León de la Barra
1911–13 Francisco I Madero
1913–14 Victoriano Huerta
1914 Francisco Carvajal
1914 Venustiano Carranza
1914–15 Eulalio Gutiérrez *Provisional President*
1915 Roque González Garza *Provisional President*
1915 Francisco Lagos Chazaro *Provisional President*
1917–20 Venustiano Carranza
1920 Adolfo de la Huerta
1920–4 Alvaro Obregón
1924–8 Plutarco Elías Calles
1928–30 Emilio Portes Gil
1930–2 Pascual Ortíz Rubio
1932–4 Abelardo L Rodríguez
1934–40 Lazaro Cardenas
1940–6 Manuel Avila Camacho
1946–52 Miguel Alemán
1952–8 Adolfo Ruiz Cortines
1958–64 Adolfo López Mateos
1964–70 Gustavo Díaz Ordaz
1970–6 Luis Echeverría
1976–82 José López Portillo
1982–8 Miguel de la Madrid Hurtado
1988–94 Carlos Salinas de Gortari
1994–2000 Ernesto Zedillo Ponce de León
2000– Vincente Fox Quesada

Micronesia, Federated States of

President

1991–7 Bailey Olter (Pohnpei)
1997–9 Jacob Nena (Kosrae)
1999– Leo Falcam (Pohnpei)

Moldova

President

1991–6 Mircea Snegur
1996–2001 Petru Lucinschi
2001– Vladimir Voronin

Prime Minister

1991–2 Valery Muravsky
1992–7 Andrei Sangheli
1997–9 Ion Ciubuc
1999 Ion Sturza
1999–2001 Dumitru Barghis
2001– Vasile Tarlev

Monaco

Head of State

1889–1922 Albert
1922–49 Louis II
1949– Rainier III

Mongolia

Prime Minister

1924–8 Tserendorji
1928–32 Amor
1932–6 Gendun
1936–8 Amor
1939–52 Korloghiin Choibalsan
1952–74 Yumsjhagiin Tsedenbal

Chairman of the Praesidium

1948–53 Gonchighlin Bumatsende
1954–72 Jamsarangiin Sambu
1972–4 Sonomyn Luvsan
1974–84 Yumsjhagiin Tsedenbal
1984–90 Jambyn Batmunkh

President

1990–7 Punsalmaagiyn Ochirbat
1997– Natsagiyn Bagabandi

Premier

1974–84 Jambyn Batmunkh
1984–90 Dumaagiyn Sodnom
1990–2 Dashiyn Byambasuren
1992–6 Puntsagiyn Jasray
1996–8 Mendsaihany Enkhsahan
1998 Tsahiagiyin Elbegdorj
1998–9 Janlaviyn Narantsatsralt
1999–2000 Rinchinnyamiyn Amarjagal
2000– Nambaryn Enkhbayar

Montenegro ▸ Yugoslavia

Morocco

Monarch

1927–61 Mohammed V
1961–99 Hassan II
1999– Mohammed VI

Prime Minister

1955–8 Si Mohammed Bekkai
1958 Ahmad Balfrej
1958–60 Abdullah Ibrahim
1960–3 *As Monarch*

History

1963–5	Ahmad Bahnini
1965–7	*As Monarch*
1967–9	Moulay Ahmed Laraki
1969–71	Mohammed Ben Hima
1971–2	Mohammed Karim Lamrani
1972–9	Ahmed Othman
1979–83	Maati Bouabid
1983–6	Mohammed Karim Lamrani
1986–92	Izz Id-Dien Laraki
1992–4	Mohammed Karim Lamrani
1994–8	Abdellatif Filali
1998–2002	Abderrahmane el-Yousifi
2002–	Driss Jettou

Mozambique

President

| 1975–86 | Samora Moïses Machel |
| 1986– | Joaquim Alberto Chissano |

Prime Minister

| 1986–94 | Mario de Graça Machungo |
| 1994– | Pascoal Mocumbi |

Myanmar, Union of (Burma)

The Socialist Republic of the Union of Burma offically became the Union of Myanmar in 1989, following the military coup of 1988, but it is still often referred to as Burma.

President

1948–52	Sao Shwe Thaik
1952–7	Agga Maha Thiri Thudhamma Ba U
1957–62	U Wing Maung
1962	Sama Duwa Sinwa Nawng

Revolutionary Council

| 1962–74 | Ne Win |

State Council

1974–81	Ne Win
1981–8	U San Yu
1988	U Sein Lwin
1988	Maung Maung
1988–92	Saw Maung
1992	Than Shwe

Prime Minister

1947–56	Thakin Nu
1956–7	U Ba Swe
1957–8	U Nu
1958–60	Ne Win
1960–2	U Nu
1962–74	Ne Win
1974–7	U Sein Win
1977–8	U Maung Maung Ka
1988	U Tun Tin
1988–92	Saw Maung
1992–	Than Shwe

Namibia

President

| 1990– | Sam Daniel Nujoma |

Prime Minister

| 1990–2002 | Hage Geingob |
| 2002– | Theo-Ben Gurirab |

Nauru

President

1968–86	Hammer de Roburt
1986	Kennan Adeang
1986–9	Hammer de Roburt
1989	Kenas Aroi
1989–95	Bernard Dowiyogo
1995–6	Lagumot Harris
1996	Bernard Dowiyogo
1996–7	Kennan Adeang
1997–8	Kinza Clodumar
1998–9	Bernard Dowiyogo
1999–2000	Rene Harris
2000–1	Bernard Dowiyogo
2001–	Rene Harris

Nepal

Monarch

1881–1911	Prithvi Bir Bikram Shah
1911–50	Tribhuvan Bir Bikram Shah
1950–2	Bir Bikram
1952–5	Tribhuvan Bir Bikram Shah
1956–72	Mahendra Bir Bikram Shah
1972–2001	Birendra Bir Bikram Shah Dev
2001	Dipendra Bir Bikram Shah Dev
2001–	Gyanendra Bir Bikram Shah Dev

Prime Minister

1901–29	Chandra Sham Sher Jang Bahadur Rana
1929–31	Bhim Cham Sham Sher Jang Bahadur Rana
1931–45	Juddha Sham Sher Rana
1945–8	Padma Sham Sher Jang Bahadur Rana
1948–51	Mohan Sham Sher Jang Bahadur Rana
1951–2	Matrika Prasad Koirala
1952–3	Tribhuvan Bir Bikram Shah
1953–5	Matrika Prasad Koirala
1955–6	Mahendra Bir Bikram Shah
1956–7	Tanka Prasad Acharya
1957–9	*King also Prime Minister*
1959–60	Sri Bishawa Prasad Koirala
1960–3	*No Prime Minister*
1963–5	Tulsi Giri
1965–9	Surya Bahadur Thapa
1969–70	Kirti Nidhi Bista
1970–1	*King also Prime Minister*
1971–3	Kirti Nidhi Bista
1973–5	Nagendra Prasad Rijal
1975–7	Tulsi Giri
1977–9	Kirti Nidhi Bista
1979–83	Surya Bahadur Thapa
1983–6	Lokendra Bahadur Chand
1986–91	Marich Man Singh Shrestha
1991–4	Girija Prasad Koirala
1994–5	Man Mohan Adhikari
1995–7	Sher Bahadur Deuba
1997	Lokendra Bahadur Chand
1997	Surya Bahadur Thapa
1998–9	Girija Prasad Koirala
1999–2000	Krishna Prasad Bhattari
2000–1	Girija Prasad Koirala
2001–2	Sher Bahadur Deuba
2002–	Lokendra Bahadur Chand

The Netherlands

Monarch

| 1890–1948 | Wilhelmina |

1948–80	Juliana
1980–	Beatrix

Prime Minister

1897–1901	Nicholas G Pierson
1901–5	Abraham Kuyper
1905–8	Theodoor H de Meester
1908–13	Theodorus Heemskerk
1913–18	Pieter W A Cort van der Linden
1918–25	Charles J M Ruys de Beerenbrouck
1925–6	Hendrikus Colijn
1926	Dirk J de Geer
1926–33	Charles J M Ruys de Beerenbrouck
1933–9	Hendrikus Colijn
1939–40	Dirk J de Geer
1940–5	Pieter S Gerbrandy (*in exile*)
1945–6	Willem Schemerhorn/Willem Drees
1946–8	Louis J M Beel
1948–51	Willem Drees/Josephus R H van Schaik
1951–8	Willem Drees
1958–9	Louis J M Beel
1959–63	Jan E de Quay
1963–5	Victor G M Marijnen
1965–6	Joseph M L T Cals
1966–7	Jelle Zijlstra
1967–71	Petrus J S de Jong
1971–3	Barend W Biesheuvel
1973–7	Joop M Den Uyl
1977–82	Andreas A M van Agt
1982–94	Ruud F M Lubbers
1994–2002	Wim Kok
2002–	Jan Peter Balkenende

New Zealand

Chief of State: British monarch, represented by Governor General

Prime Minister

1893–1906	Richard John Seddon *Lib*
1906	William Hall-Jones *Lib*
1906–12	Joseph George Ward *Lib/Nat*
1912	Thomas Mackenzie *Nat*
1912–25	William Ferguson Massey *Ref*
1925	Francis Henry Dillon Bell *Ref*
1925–8	Joseph Gordon Coates *Ref*
1928–30	Joseph George Ward *Lib/Nat*
1930–5	George William Forbes *Un*
1935–40	Michael Joseph Savage *Lab*
1940–9	Peter Fraser *Lab*
1949–57	Sidney George Holland *Nat*
1957	Keith Jacka Holyoake *Nat*
1957–60	Walter Nash *Lab*
1960–72	Keith Jacka Holyoake *Nat*
1972	John Ross Marshall *Nat*
1972–4	Norman Eric Kirk *Lab*
1974–5	Wallace Edward Rowling *Lab*
1975–84	Robert David Muldoon *Nat*
1984–89	David Russell Lange *Lab*
1989–90	Geoffrey Palmer *Lab*
1990	Mike Moore *Lab*
1990–7	James Bolger *Nat*
1997–9	Jenny Shipley *Nat*
1999–	Helen Clark *Lab*

Lab = Labor
Lib = Liberal
Nat = National
Ref = Reform
Un = United

Nicaragua

President

1893–1909	José Santos Zelaya
1909–10	José Madriz
1910–11	José Dolores Estrada
1911	Juan José Estrada
1911–17	Adolfo Díaz
1912	Luis Mena *rival President*
1917–21	Emiliano Chamorro Vargas
1921–3	Riego Manuel Chamorro
1923–4	Martínez Bartolo
1925–6	Carlos Solórzano
1926	Emiliano Chamorro Vargas
1926–8	Adolfo Díaz
1926	Juan Bautista Sacasa *rival President*
1928–32	José Marcia Moncada
1933–6	Juan Bautista Sacasa
1936	Carlos Brenes Jarquin
1937–47	Anastasio Somoza García
1947	Leonardo Argüello
1947	Benjamin Lascayo Sacasa
1947–50	Victor Manuel Román y Reyes
1950–6	Anastasio Somoza García
1956–63	Luis Somoza Debayle
1963–6	René Schick Gutiérrez
1966–7	Lorenzo Guerrero Gutiérrez
1967–72	Anastasio Somoza Debayle
1972–4	*Triumvirate*
1974–9	Anastasio Somoza Debayle
1979–84	*Government Junta of National Reconstruction*
1984–90	Daniel Ortega Saavedra
1990–7	Violeta Barrios de Chamorro
1997–2001	Arnoldo Alemán Lacayo
2001–	Enrique Bolaños

Niger

President

1960–74	Hamani Diori
1974–87	Seyni Kountché
1987–91	Ali Saibou
1993–6	Mahamane Ousmane
1996–9	Ibrahim Baré Maïnassara
1999	Daouda Malam Wanke
1999–	Tandja Mamadou

Prime Minister

1957–8	Djibo Bakary
1958–60	Hamani Diori
1960–83	*No Prime Minister*
1983	Mamane Oumarou
1983–8	Ahmid Algabid
1988–9	Mamane Oumarou
1990–1	Aliou Mahamidou
1991–3	Amadou Cheiffou
1993–4	Mahamadou Issoufou
1994–5	Abdoulaye Souley
1995	Amadou Boubacar Cissé
1995–6	Hama Amadou
1996	Boukary Adji
1996–7	Amadou Boubacar Cissé
1997–2000	Ibrahim Assane Mayaki
2000–	Hama Amadou

History

History

Nigeria

President

1960–6	Nnamdi Azikiwe

Prime Minister

1960–6	Abubakar Tafawa Balewa

Military Government

1966	J T U Aguiyi-Ironsi
1966–75	Yakubu Gowon
1975–6	Murtala R Mohamed
1976–9	Olusegun Obasanjo

President

1979–83	Alhaji Shehu Shagari

Military Government

1983–4	Mohammadu Buhari
1985–93	Ibrahim B Babangida
1993	Ernest Shonekan *Interim President*
1993–8	Sani Abacha
1998–9	Abdulsalami Abubakar
1999–	Olusegun Obasanjo

North Korea ▸ Korea, Democratic People's Republic of

Norway

Monarch

1872–1905	Oscar II *union with Sweden*
1905–57	Haakon VII
1957–91	Olav V
1991–	Harald V

Prime Minister

1898–1902	Johannes Steen
1902–3	Otto Albert Blehr
1903–5	George Francis Hagerup
1905–7	Christian Michelsen
1907–8	Jørgen Løvland
1908–10	Gunnar Knudsen
1910–12	Wollert Konow
1912–13	Jens Bratlie
1913–20	Gunnar Knudsen
1920–1	Otto Bahr Halvorsen
1921–3	Otto Albert Blehr
1923	Otto Bahr Halvorsen
1923–4	Abraham Berge
1924–6	Johan Ludwig Mowinckel
1926–8	Ivar Lykke
1928	Christopher Hornsrud
1928–31	Johan Ludwig Mowinckel
1931–2	Peder L Kolstad
1932–3	Jens Hundseid
1933–5	Johan Ludwig Mowinckel
1935–45	Johan Nygaardsvold
1945–51	Einar Gerhardsen
1951–5	Oscar Torp
1955–63	Einar Gerhardsen
1963	John Lyng
1963–5	Einar Gerhardsen
1965–71	Per Borten
1971–2	Trygve Bratteli
1972–3	Lars Korvald
1973–6	Trygve Bratteli
1976–81	Odvar Nordli
1981	Gro Harlem Brundtland
1981–6	Kåre Willoch

1986–9	Gro Harlem Brundtland
1989–90	Jan P Syse
1990–6	Gro Harlem Brundtland
1996–7	Thorbjørn Jagland
1997–2000	Kjell Magne Bondevik
2000–1	Jens Stoltenberg
2001–	Kjell Magne Bondevik

Oman

Sultan

1888–1913	Faisal Bin Turki
1913–32	Taimur Bin Faisal
1932–70	Said Bin Taimur
1970–	Qaboos Bin Said

Prime Minister

1970–2	Tariq Bin Taimur
1972–	Qaboos Bin Said

Pakistan

President

1956–8	Iskander Mirza
1958–69	Mohammad Ayoub Khan
1969–71	Agha Mohammad Yahya Khan
1971–3	Zulfikar Ali Bhutto
1973–8	Fazal Elahi Chawdry
1978–88	Mohammad Zia Ul-Haq
1988–93	Ghulam Ishaq Khan
1993–7	Farooq Ahmad Khan Leghari
1997	Wasim Sajjad *Acting President*
1998–2001	Muhammed Rafiq Tarar
2001–	Pervez Musharraf

Prime Minister

1947–51	Liaqat Ali Khan
1951–3	Khawaja Nazimuddin
1953–5	Mohammad Ali
1955–6	Chawdry Mohammad Ali
1956–7	Hussein Shahid Suhrawardi
1957	Ismail Chundrigar
1957–8	Malik Feroz Khan Noon
1958	Mohammad Ayoub Khan
1958–73	*No Prime Minister*
1973–7	Zulfikar Ali Bhutto
1977–85	*No Prime Minister*
1985–8	Mohammad Khan Junejo
1988	Mohammad Aslam Khan Khattak
1988–90	Benazir Bhutto
1990	Ghulam Mustafa Jatoi
1990–3	Mian Mohammad Nawaz Sharif
1993–6	Benazir Bhutto
1996–7	Meraj Khalid *Acting Prime Minister*
1997–9	Mian Mohammad Nawaz Sharif
1999–2002	*No Prime Minister*
2002–	Mir Zafarullah Jamali

Palau

President

1981–5	Haruo Remeliik
1985	Thomas Remengesau *Acting President*
1985	Alfonso Oiterong
1985–8	Lazarus Salii
1988–9	Thomas Remengesau
1989–93	Ngiratkel Etpison
1993–2000	Kuniwo Nakamura
2001–	Tommy Remengesau

Panama

President

1904–8	Manuel Amador Guerrero
1908–10	José Domingo de Obaldia
1910	Federico Boyd
1910	Carlos Antonio Mendoza
1910–12	Pablo Arosemena
1912	Rodolfo Chiari
1912–16	Belisario Porras
1916–18	Ramón Maximiliano Valdés
1918	Pedro Antonio Diaz
1918	Cirilo Luis Urriola
1918–20	Belisario Porras
1920	Ernesto T Lefevre
1920–4	Belisario Porras
1924–8	Rodolfo Chiari
1928	Tomás Gabriel Duque
1928–31	Florencio Harmodio Arosemena
1931	Harmodio Arias
1931–2	Ricardo Joaquín Alfaro
1932–6	Harmodio Arias
1936–9	Juan Demóstenes Arosemena
1939	Ezequiel Fernández Jaén
1939–40	Augusto Samuel Boyd
1940–1	Arnulfo Arias Madrid
1941	Ernesto Jaén Guardia
1941	José Pezet
1941–5	Ricardo Adolfo de la Guardia
1945–8	Enrique Adolfo Jiménez Brin
1948–9	Domingo Diaz Arosemena
1949	Daniel Chanis
1949	Roberto Francisco Chiari
1949–51	Arnulfo Arias Madrid
1951–2	Alcibiades Arosemena
1952–5	José Antonio Remón
1955	José Ramón Guizado
1955–6	Ricardo Manuel Arias Espinosa
1956–60	Ernesto de la Guardia
1960–4	Roberto Francisco Chiari
1964–8	Marco A Robles
1968	Arnulfo Arias Madrid
1968	*Military Junta*
1968–9	Omar Torrijos Herrera
1969–78	Demetrio Basilio Lakas
1978–82	Aristides Royo
1982–4	Ricardo de la Esoriella
1984	Jorge Enrique Illueca Sibauste
1984–5	Nicolás Ardito Barletta
1985–8	Eric Arturo Delvalle
1988–9	Manuel Solís Palma
1989–94	Guillermo Endara Galimany
1994–9	Ernesto Pérez Balladares
1999–	Mireya Moscoso Rodriguez

Papua New Guinea

Prime Minister

1975–80	Michael T Somare
1980–2	Julius Chan
1982–5	Michael T Somare
1985–8	Paias Wingti
1988–92	Rabbie Namaliu
1992–4	Paias Wingti
1994–7	Julius Chan
1997	John Giheno *Acting Prime Minister*
1997	Julius Chan
1997–9	Bill Skate
1999–2002	Sir Mekere Morauta
2002–	Michael T Somare

Paraguay

President

1898–1902	Emilio Aceval
1902	Héctor Carvallo
1902–4	Juan Antonio Escurra
1904–5	Juan Gaona
1905–6	Cecilio Baez
1906–8	Benigno Ferreira
1908–10	Emiliano González Navero
1910–11	Manuel Gondra
1911	Albino Jara
1911	Liberato Marcial Rojas
1912	Pedro Peña
1912	Emiliano González Navero
1912–16	Eduardo Schaerer
1916–19	Manuel Franco
1919–20	José P Montero
1920–1	Manuel Gondra
1921	Félix Paiva
1921–3	Eusebio Ayala
1923–4	Eligio Ayala
1924	Luis Alberto Riart
1924–8	Eligio Ayala
1928–31	José Particio Guggiari
1931–2	Emiliano González Navero
1932	José Particio Guggiari
1932–6	Eusebio Ayala
1936–7	Rafael Franco
1937–9	Félix Paiva
1939–40	José Félix Estigarribia
1940–8	Higino Moríñigo
1948	Juan Manuel Frutos
1948–9	Juan Natalicio González
1949	Raimundo Rolón
1949	Felipe Molas López
1949–54	Federico Chaves
1954	Tomás Romero Pareira
1954–89	Alfredo Stroessner
1989–93	Andrés Rodríguez
1993–8	Juan Carlos Wasmosy
1998–9	Raúl Cubas Grau
1999–	Luis González Mácchi

Peru

President

1899–1903	Eduardo López de Romaña
1903–4	Manuel Candamo
1904	Serapio Calderón
1904–8	José Pardo y Barreda
1908–12	Augusto B Leguía
1912–14	Guillermo Billinghurst
1914–15	Oscar R Benavides
1915–19	José Pardo y Barreda
1919–30	Augusto B Leguía
1930	Manuel Ponce
1930–1	Luis M Sánchez Cerro
1931	Leoncio Elías
1931	Gustavo A Jiménez
1931	David Samanez Ocampo
1931–3	Luis M Sánchez Cerro
1933–9	Oscar R Benavides
1939–45	Manuel Prado
1945–8	José Luis Bustamante y Rivero
1948–56	Manuel A Odría
1956–62	Manuel Prado
1962–3	*Military Junta*
1963–8	Fernando Belaúnde Terry
1968–75	*Military Junta* (Juan Velasco Alvarado)

History

History

1975–80	*Military Junta* (Francisco Morales Bermúdez)
1980–5	Fernando Belaúnde Terry
1985–90	Alan García Pérez
1990–2000	Alberto Keinya Fujimori
2000–1	Valentín Paniagua *Interim President*
2001–	Alejandro Toledo Manrique

Prime Minister

1900	Enrique Coronel Zegarra y Cortés
1900–1	Domingo M Almenara Butler
1901–2	Cesáreo Chacaltana Reyes
1902	Cesáreo Octavio Deustua Escarza
1902–3	Eugenio Larrabure y Unanue
1903–4	José Pardo y Barreda
1904	Alberto Elmore Fernández de Córdoba
1904–7	Augusto B Leguía y Salcedo
1907	Agustín Tovar
1907–8	Carlos A Washburn Salas
1908–9	Eulogio Romero Salcedo
1909–10	Rafael Fernández de Villanueva Cortez
1910	Javier Prado y Ugarteche
1910	Germán Schreiber Waddington
1910	José Salvador Cavero
1910–11	Enrique C Basadre Stevenson
1911–12	Agustín G Ganoza Cavero
1912	Elías Malpartida
1912–13	Enrique Varela
1913	Federico Luna y Peralta
1913	Aurelio Sousa Matute
1913–14	Enrique Varela
1914	Pedro E Muñiz
1914	Manuel Melitón Carvajal
1914	Aurelio Sousa Matute
1914–15	Germán Schreiber Waddington
1915	Carlos Isaac Abrill
1915–17	Enrique de la Riva-Agüero y Looz Corswaren
1917–18	Francisco Tudela y Varela
1918–19	Germán Arenas y Loayza
1919	Juan Manuel Zuloaga
1919–22	Germán Leguía y Martínez Jakeway
1922–4	Julio Enrique Ego Aguirre
1924–6	Alejandrino Maguiña
1926–9	Pedro José Rada y Gamio
1929–30	Benjamín Huamán de los Heros
1930–1	Fernando Sarmiento
1931–2	Germán Arenas y Loayza
1932	Francisco R Lanatta
1932	Luis A Flores
1932	Ricardo Rivadeneira
1932–3	José Matías Manzanilla Barrientos
1933	Jorge Prado y Ugarteche
1933–4	José de la Riva-Agüero y Osma
1934–5	Carlos Arenas y Loayza
1935–6	Manuel Esteban Rodríguez
1936–9	Ernesto Montagne Markholz
1939	Alberto Rey de Castro y Romaña
1939–44	Alfredo Solf y Muro
1944–5	Manuel Cisneros Sánchez
1945–6	Rafael Belaúnde y Diez Canseco
1946–7	Julio Ernesto Portugal Escobedo
1947	José Alcamora
1948	Roque Augusto Saldías Maninat
1948	Armando Revoredo Iglesias
1948–54	*No Prime Minister*
1954–6	Roque Augusto Saldías Maninat
1956–7	Manuel Cisneros Sánchez
1958–9	Luis Gallo Porras
1959–61	Pedro Gerardo Beltrán Espantos
1961–2	Carlos Moreyra y Paz Soldán
1962–3	Nicolás Lindley López
1963	Julio Óscar Trelles Montes
1963–5	Fernando Schwalb López Aldana

1965–7	Daniel Becerra de la Flor
1967	Edgardo Seoane Corrales
1967–8	Raúl Ferrero Rebagliati
1968	Oswaldo Hercelles García
1968	Miguel Mujica Gallo
1968–73	Ernesto Montagne Sánchez
1973–5	Edgardo Mercado Jarrín
1975	Francisco Morales Bermúdez
1975–6	Óscar Vargas Prieto
1976	Jorge Fernández Maldonado Solari
1976–8	Guillermo Arbulú Galliani
1978–9	Óscar Molina Pallochia
1979–80	Pedro Richter Prada
1980–3	Manuel Ulloa Elías
1983–4	Fernando Schwalb López Aldana
1984	Sandro Mariátegui Chiappe
1984–5	Luis Pércovich Roca
1985–7	Luis Alva Castro
1987–8	Guillermo Larco Cox
1988–9	Armando Villanueva del Campo
1989	Luis Alberto Sánchez
1989–90	Guillermo Larco Cox
1990–1	Juan Carlos Hurtado Miller
1991	Carlos Torres y Torres Lara
1991–2	Alfonso de los Heros
1992–3	Óscar de la Puente Raygada
1993–4	Alfonso Bustamante y Bustamante
1994–5	Efraín Goldenberg Schreiber
1995–6	Dante Córdova Blanco
1996–8	Alberto Pandolfi
1998	Javier Valle Riestra
1998–9	Alberto Pandolfi
1999	Víctor Joy Way
1999–2000	Alberto Bustamante Belaúnde
2000	Federico Salas Guevara
2001	Javier Perez de Cuellar
2001–2	Roberto Daniño Zapata
2002–	Luis Solari

Philippines

President

■ Commonwealth

1935–44	Manuel L Quezon

Japanese Occupation

1943–4	José P Laurel

■ Commonwealth

1944–6	Sergio Osmeña

■ First Republic

1946–8	Manuel A Roxas
1948–53	Elpidio Quirino
1953–7	Ramon Magsaysay
1957–61	Carlos P Garcia
1961–5	Diosdado Macapagal
1965–72	Ferdinand E Marcos

Martial Law

1972–81	Ferdinand E Marcos

■ New Republic

1981–6	Ferdinand E Marcos
1986–92	Corazon C Aquino
1992–8	Fidel V Ramos
1998–2001	Joseph Estrada
2001–	Gloria Macapagal-Arroyo

Poland

■ Republic of Poland

President

1945–7	Bolesław Bierut *Acting President*
1947–52	Bolesław Bierut
1952–64	Aleksander Zawadzki
1964–8	Edward Ochab
1968–70	Marian Spychalski
1970–2	Józef Cyrankiewicz
1972–85	Henryk Jabłonski
1985–90	Wojciech Jaruzelski
1990–5	Lech Wałesa
1995–	Aleksander Kwaśniewski

Prime Minister

1947–52	Józef Cyrankiewicz
1952–4	Bolesław Bierut
1954–70	Józef Cyrankiewicz
1970–80	Piotr Jecoszewicz
1980	Edward Babiuch
1980–1	Józef Pinkowski
1981–5	Wojciech Jaruzelski
1985–8	Zbigniew Messner
1988–9	Mieczyslaw Rakowski
1989	Czeslaw Kiszczak
1989–90	Tadeusz Mazowiecki
1991	Jan Krzysztof Bielecki
1991–2	Jan Olszewski
1992	Waldemar Pawlak
1992–3	Hanna Suchocka
1993–5	Waldemar Pawlak
1995–6	Józef Oleksy
1996–7	Wlodzimierz Cimoszewicz
1997–2001	Jerzy Buzek
2001–	Leszek Miller

First Secretary

1945–8	Władysław Gomułka
1948–56	Bolesław Bierut
1956	Edward Ochab
1956–70	Władysław Gomułka
1970–80	Edward Gierek
1980–1	Stanisław Kania
1981–9	Wojciech Jaruzelski
1989	Mieczyslaw Rakowski

Portugal

President

■ First Republic

1910–11	Teófilo Braga
1911–15	Manuel José de Arriaga
1915	Teófilo Braga
1915–17	Bernardino Machado
1917–18	Sidónio Pais
1918–19	João do Canto e Castro
1919–23	António José de Almeida
1923–5	Manuel Teixeira Gomes
1925–6	Bernardino Machado

■ New State

1926	*Military Junta* (José Mendes Cabeçadas)
1926	*Military Junta* (Manuel de Oliveira Gomes da Costa)
1926–51	António Oscar Fragoso Carmona
1951–8	Francisco Craveiro Lopes
1958–74	Américo de Deus Tomás

■ Second Republic

1974	*Military Junta* (António Spínola)
1974–6	*Military Junta* (Francisco da Costa Gomes)

■ Third Republic

1976–86	António dos Santos Ramalho Eanes
1986–96	Mário Soares
1996–	Jorge Sampaio

Prime Minister

1932–68	António de Oliveira Salazar
1968–74	Marcelo Caetano
1974	Adelino da Palma Carlos
1974–5	Vasco Gonçalves
1975–6	José Pinheiro de Azevedo
1976–8	Mário Soares
1978	Alfredo Nobre da Costa
1978–9	Carlos Alberto de Mota Pinto
1979	Maria de Lurdes Pintasilgo
1980–1	Francisco de Sá Carneiro
1981–3	Francisco Pinto Balsemão
1983–5	Mário Soares
1985–95	Aníbal Cavaço Silva
1995–2001	António Guterres
2002–	José Manuel Durão Barroso

Qatar

Emir

Family name: al-Thani

1971–2	Ahmad Bin Ali
1972–95	Khalifah Bin Hamad
1995–	Ahmad Bin Khalifa

Prime Minister

1971–95	Khalifa Bin Ahmad
1995–6	Ahmad Bin Khalifa
1996–	Abdulla Bin Khalifa

Romania

Monarch

1881–1914	Carol I
1914–27	Ferdinand I
1927–30	Michael *Prince*
1930–40	Carol II
1940–7	Michael I

■ Republic

President

1947–8	Mihai Sadoveanu *Interim*
1948–52	Constantin I Parhon
1952–8	Petru Groza
1958–61	Ion Georghe Maurer
1961–5	Georghe Gheorghiu-Dej
1965–7	Chivu Stoica
1967–89	Nicolae Ceauşescu
1989–96	Ion Iliescu
1996–2000	Emil Constantinescu
2000–	Ion Iliescu

General Secretary

1955–65	Georghe Gheorghiu-Dej
1965–89	Nicolae Ceauşescu

Prime Minister

1900–1	Petre P Carp
1901–6	Dimitrie A Sturdza

History

History

1906–7	Gheorge Grigore Cantacuzino
1907–9	Dimitrie A Sturdza
1909	Ionel Brătianu
1909–10	Mihai Pherekyde
1910–11	Ionel Brătianu
1911–12	Petre P Carp
1912–14	Titu Maiorescu
1914–18	Ionel Brătianu
1918	Alexandru Averescu
1918	Alexandru Marghiloman
1918	Constantin Coandă
1918	Ionel Brătianu
1919	Artur Văitoianu
1919–20	Alexandru Vaida-Voevod
1920–1	Alexandru Averescu
1921–2	Take Ionescu
1922–6	Ionel Brătianu
1926–7	Alexandru Averescu
1927	Ionel Brătianu
1927–8	Vintila I C Brătianu
1928–30	Juliu Maniu
1930	Gheorghe C Mironescu
1930	Juliu Maniu
1930–1	Gheorghe C Mironescu
1931–2	Nicolae Iorga
1932	Alexandru Vaida-Voevod
1932–3	Juliu Maniu
1933	Alexandru Vaida-Voevod
1933	Ion G Duca
1933–4	Constantin Angelescu
1934–7	Gheorghe Tătărescu
1937	Octavian Goga
1937–9	Miron Cristea
1939	Armand Călinescu
1939	Gheorghe Argeşanu
1939	Constantine Argetoianu
1939–40	Gheorghe Tătărescu
1940	Ion Gigurtu
1940–4	Ion Antonescu
1944	Constantin Savbnătescu
1944–5	Nicolae Rădescu
1945–52	Petru Groza
1952–5	Gheorghe Gheorghiu-Dej
1955–61	Chivu Stoica
1961–74	Ion Gheorghe Maurer
1974–80	Manea Mănescu
1980–3	Ilie Verdet
1983–9	Constantin Dăscălescu
1989–91	Petre Roman
1991–2	Theodor Stolojan
1992–6	Nicolae Vacaroiu
1996–8	Victor Ciorbea
1998	Gavril Dejeu *Interim Prime Minister*
1998–9	Radu Vasile
1999	Alexandru Athanesiu *Interim Prime Minister*
1999–2000	Mugur Isarescu
2000–	Adrian Nastase

Russia

President

1991–9	Boris Yeltsin
2000–	Vladimir Putin

Prime Minister

1991–2	Boris Yeltsin
1992	Yegor Gaidar *Acting Prime Minister*
1992–8	Viktor Chernomyrdin
1998	Sergei Kiriyenko
1998	Viktor Chernomyrdin *Acting Prime Minister*
1998–9	Yevgeny Primakov

1999	Sergei Stepashin
1999–2000	Vladimir Putin
2000–	Mikhail Kasyanov

Rwanda

President

1962–73	Grégoire Kayibanda
1973–94	Juvénal Habyarimana
1994	Theodore Sindikubgabo *Interim President*
1994–2000	Pasteur Bizimungu
2000–	Paul Kagame

Prime Minister

1991–2	Sylvestre Nsanzimana
1992–4	Dismas Nsengiyaremye
1994	Jean Kambanda *Acting Prime Minister*
1994–5	Faustin Twagiramungu
1995–2000	Pierre-Célestin Rwigyema
2000–	Bernard Makuza

St Kitts and Nevis

Chief of State: British monarch, represented by Governor General

Prime Minister

1983–95	Kennedy A Simmonds
1995–	Denzil Douglas

St Lucia

Chief of State: British monarch, represented by Governor General

Prime Minister

1979	John Compton
1979–81	Allan Louisy
1981–3	Winston Francis Cenac
1983–96	John Compton
1996–7	Vaughan Lewis
1997–	Kenny Anthony

St Vincent and the Grenadines

Chief of State: British monarch, represented by Governor General

Prime Minister

1979–84	Milton Cato
1984–2000	James Fitz-Allen Mitchell
2000–1	Arnhim Eustace
2001–	Ralph Gonsalves

Samoa

President

1962–3	Tupua Tamesehe Mea'ole *and* Malietoa Tanumalfi II *Joint Presidents*
1963–	Malietoa Tanumafili II

Prime Minister

1962–1970	Fiame Mata'afa Faumuina Mulinu'u II
1970–6	Tupua Tamasese Leolofi IV
1976–82	Tupuola Taisi Efi
1982	Va'ai Kolone
1982	Tupuola Taisi Efi

1982–6	Tofilau Eti Alesana
1986–8	Va'ai Kolone
1988–98	Tofilau Eti Alesana
1998–	Tuilaepa Sailele Malielegaoi

San Marino

Regent

2 regents appointed every 6 months

SãoTomé and Príncipe

President

1975–91	Manuel Pinto da Costa
1991–2001	Miguel Trovoada
2001–	Fradrique de Menezes

Prime Minister

1974–5	Leonel Maria d'Alva
1975–8	Miguel Trovoada
1978–88	*No Prime Minister*
1988–91	Celestino Rocha da Costa
1991–2	Daniel Lima dos Santos Daio
1992–4	Norberto José d'Alva Costa Alegre
1994	Evaristo Carvalho
1994–5	Carlos da Graça
1995–6	Armindo Vaz d'Almeida
1996–9	Raul Bragança
1999–2002	Guilherme Posser da Costa
2002	Gabriel Costa
2002–	Maria das Neves

Saudi Arabia

Monarch

Family name: al-Saud

1932–53	Abdulaziz Bin Abdur-Rahman
1953–64	Saud Bin Abdulaziz
1964–75	Faisal Bin Abdulaziz
1975–82	Khalid Bin Abdulaziz
1982–96	Fahd Bin Abdulaziz
1996	Abdullah Bin Abdulaziz *Acting Monarch*
1996–	Fahd Bin Abdulaziz

Senegal

President

1960–80	Léopold Sédar Senghor
1981–2000	Abdou Diouf
2000–	Abdoulaye Wade

Prime Minister

1958–62	Mamadou Dia
1962–70	*No Prime Minister*
1970–80	Abdou Diouf
1981–3	Habib Thiam
1983	Moustapha Niasse *Interim Prime Minister*
1983–91	*No Prime Minister*
1991–8	Habib Thiam
1998–2000	Mamadou Lamine Loum
2000–1	Moustapha Niasse
2001–2	Madior Boye
2002–	Idrissa Seck

Serbia and Montenegro ▶ Yugoslavia

Seychelles

President

| 1976–7 | James R Mancham |
| 1977– | France-Albert René |

Sierra Leone

President

1971	Christopher Okero Cole
1971–85	Siaka Stevens
1985–92	Joseph Saidu Momoh
1992–6	Valentine Strasser
1996–7	Ahmad Tejan Kabbah
1997	*Military coup*
1997	Johnny Paul Koroma
1998–	Ahmad Tejan Kabbah

Prime Minister

■ **Commonwealth**

1961–4	Milton Margai
1964–7	Albert Michael Margai
1967	Siaka Stevens
1967	David Lansana
1967	Ambrose Genda
1967–8	*National Reformation Council* (Andrew Saxon-Smith)
1968	John Bangura
1968–71	Siaka Stevens

■ **Republic**

1971–5	Sorie Ibrahim Koroma
1975–8	Christian Alusine Kamara Taylor
1978–	*No Prime Minister*

Singapore

President (Yang di-Pertuan Negara)

1959–70	Yusof bin Ishak
1970–81	Benjamin Henry Sheares
1981–5	Chengara Veetil Devan Nair
1985–93	Wee Kim Wee
1993–9	Ong Teng Cheong
1999–	Sellapan Ramanathan Nathan

Prime Minister

| 1959–90 | Lee Kuan Yew |
| 1990– | Goh Chok Tong |

Slovakia

President

1993–8	Michal Kováč
1998–9	*No President*
1999–	Rudolf Schuster

Prime Minister

1993–4	Vladimír Mečiar
1994	Jozef Moravčik
1994–8	Vladimír Mečiar
1998–	Mikuláš Dzurinda

History

History

Slovenia

President

| 1991–2002 | Milan Kučan |
| 2002– | Janez Drnovsek |

Prime Minister

1990–2	Lojze Peterle
1992–2000	Janez Drnovšek
2000	Andrej Bajuk
2000–2	Janez Drnovsek
2002–	Anton Rop

Solomon Islands

Chief of State: British monarch, represented by Governor General

Prime Minister

1978–82	Peter Kenilorea
1982–4	Solomon Mamaloni
1984–6	Peter Kenilorea
1986–9	Ezekiel Alebua
1989–93	Solomon Mamaloni
1993–4	Francis Billy Hilly
1994–7	Solomon Mamaloni
1997–2000	Bartholomew Ulufa'alu
2000–1	Manasseh Sogavare
2001–	Allan Kemakeza

Somalia

President

| 1961–7 | Aden Abdallah Osman |
| 1967–9 | Abdirashid Ali Shermarke |

Supreme Revolutionary Council

| 1969–80 | Mohammed Siad Barre |

▪ Republic

1980–91	Mohammed Siad Barre
1991–2000	*Civil War*
2000	Abdullahi Derow Isaq *Acting President*
2000–	Abd-al-Qassim Salat Hasan

Prime Minister

1960	Mohammed Haji Ibrahim Egal
1960–4	Abdirashid Ali Shermarke
1964–7	Abdirizak Haji Hussein
1967–9	Mohammed Haji Ibrahim Egal
1969–70	Mohammed Siyad Barrah
1987–90	Mohammed Ali Samater
1990–1	Mohammed Hawadie Madar
1991	Umar Arteh Ghalib
1991–2000	*Civil War*
2000–1	Ali Khalif Galaid
2001–	Hassan Abshir Farah

South Africa

Governor General

1910–14	Herbert, Viscount Gladstone
1914–20	Sydney, Earl Buxton
1920–4	Arthur, Duke of Connaught
1924–31	Alexander, Earl of Athlone
1931–7	George Herbert Hyde Villiers
1937–43	Patrick Duncan
1943–5	Nicolaas Jacobus de Wet

1945–51	Gideon Brand Van Zyl
1951–9	Ernest George Jansen
1959	Lucas Cornelius Steyn
1959–61	Charles Robberts Swart

▪ Republic

President

1961–7	Charles Robberts Swart
1967	Theophilus Ebenhaezer Dönges
1967–8	Jozua François Nandé
1968–75	Jacobus Johannes Fouché
1975–8	Nicolaas Diederichs
1978–9	Balthazar Johannes Vorster
1979–84	Marais Viljoen
1984–89	Pieter Willem Botha
1989–94	Frederick Willem de Klerk
1994–9	Nelson Rolihlahla Mandela
1999–	Thabo Mbeki

Prime Minister

1910–19	Louis Botha *SAf*
1919–24	Jan Christiaan Smuts *SAf*
1924–39	James Barry Munnick Hertzog *Nat*
1939–48	Jan Christiaan Smuts *Un*
1948–54	Daniel François Malan *Nat*
1954–8	Johannes Gerardus Strijdom *Nat*
1958–66	Hendrik Frensch Verwoerd *Nat*
1966–78	Balthazar Johannes Vorster *Nat*
1978–84	Pieter Willem Botha *Nat*
1984–	*No Prime Minister*

Nat = National
SAf = South African Party
Un = United

South Korea ▸ Korea, Republic of

Spain

Monarch

| 1886–1931 | Alfonso XIII |

▪ Second Republic

President

| 1931–6 | Niceto Alcalá Zamora y Torres |
| 1936 | Diego Martínez Barrio *Acting President* |

Civil War

| 1936–9 | Manuel Azaña y Díez |
| 1936–9 | Miguel Cabanellas Ferrer |

▪ Nationalist Government

Chief of State

| 1936–75 | Francisco Franco Bahamonde |

Monarch

| 1975– | Juan Carlos I |

Prime Minister

1900–1	Marcelo de Azcárraga y Palmero
1901–2	Práxedes Mateo Sagasta
1902–3	Francisco Silvela y Le-Vielleuze
1903	Raimundo Fernández Villaverde
1903–4	Antonio Maura y Montaner
1904–5	Marcelo de Azcárraga y Palmero
1905	Raimundo Fernández Villaverde
1905	Eugenio Montero Ríos
1905–6	Segismundo Moret y Prendergast

1906	José López Domínguez
1906	Segismundo Moret y Prendergast
1906–7	Antonio Aguilar y Correa
1907–9	Antonio Maura y Montaner
1909–10	Segismundo Moret y Prendergast
1910–12	José Canalejas y Méndez
1912	Álvaro Figueroa y Torres
1912–13	Manuel García Prieto
1913–15	Eduardo Dato y Iradier
1915–17	Álvaro Figueroa y Torres
1917	Manuel García Prieto
1917	Eduardo Dato y Iradier
1917–18	Manuel García Prieto
1918	Antonio Maura y Montaner
1918	Manuel García Prieto
1918–19	Álvaro Figueroa y Torres
1919	Antonio Maura y Montaner
1919	Joaquín Sánchez de Toca
1919–20	Manuel Allendesalazar
1920–1	Eduardo Dato y Iradier
1921	Gabino Bugallal Araujo *Acting Prime Minister*
1921	Manuel Allendesalazar
1921–2	Antonio Maura y Montaner
1922	José Sánchez Guerra y Martínez
1922–3	Manuel García Prieto
1923–30	Miguel Primo de Rivera y Oraneja
1930–1	Dámaso Berenguer y Fusté
1931	Juan Bautista Aznar-Cabañas
1931	Niceto Alcalá Zamora y Torres
1931–3	Manuel Azaña y Díez
1933	Alejandro Lerroux y García
1933	Diego Martínez Barrio
1933–4	Alejandro Lerroux y García
1934	Ricardo Samper Ibáñez
1934–5	Alejandro Lerroux y García
1935	Joaquín Chapaprieta y Terragosa
1935–6	Manuel Portela Valladares
1936	Manuel Azaña y Díez
1936	Santiago Casares Quiroga
1936	Diego Martínez Barrio
1936	José Giral y Pereyra
1936–7	Francisco Largo Caballero
1937–9	Juan Negrín

Chairman of the Council of Ministers

1939–73	Francisco Franco Bahamonde

Prime Minister

1973	Torcuato Fernández Miranda y Hevía *Acting Prime Minister*
1973–6	Carlos Arias Navarro
1976–81	Adolfo Suárez
1981–2	Calvo Sotelo
1982–96	Felipe González
1996–	José María Aznar

Sri Lanka

President

1972–8	William Gopallawa
1978–89	Junius Richard Jayawardene
1989–93	Ranasinghe Premadasa
1994–	Chandrika Bandaranaike Kumaratunga

Prime Minister

■ Ceylon

1947–52	Don Stephen Senanayake
1952–3	Dudley Shelton Senanayake
1953–6	John Lionel Kotelawala
1956–9	Solomon West Ridgeway Dias Bandaranaike

1960	Dudley Shelton Senanayake
1960–5	Sirimavo Ratwatte Dias Bandaranaike
1965–70	Dudley Shelton Senanayake

■ Sri Lanka

1970–7	Sirimavo Ratwatte Dias Bandaranaike
1977–89	Ranasinghe Premadasa
1989–93	Dingiri Banda Wijetunge
1993–4	Ranil Wickremasingh
1994	Chandrika Bandaranaike Kumaratunga
1994–2000	Sirimavo Ratwatte Dias Bandaranaike
2000–1	Ratnasiri Wickremanayake
2001–	Ranil Wickremasinghe

The Sudan

Chief of State

1956–8	*Council of State*
1958–64	Ibrahim Abboud
1964–5	*Council of Sovereignty*
1965–9	Ismail Al-Azhari
1969–85	Jaafar Mohammed Nimeiri *President from 1971*
1993–	Omar Hassan Ahmed Al-Bashir *President*

Transitional Military Council

Chairman

1985–6	Abd Al-Rahman Siwar Al-Dahab

Supreme Council

Chairman

1986–9	Ahmad Al-Mirghani

Revolutionary Command Council

Chairman

1989–93	Omar Hassan Ahmed Al-Bashir

Prime Minister

1955–6	Ismail Al-Azhari
1956–8	Abdullah Khalil
1958–64	*As President*
1964–5	Serr Al-Khatim Al-Khalifa
1965–6	Mohammed Ahmed Mahjoub
1966–7	Sadiq Al-Mahdi
1967–9	Mohammed Ahmed Mahjoub
1969	Babiker Awadalla
1969–76	*As President*
1976–7	Rashid Al-Tahir Bakr
1977–85	*As President*
1985–6	*Transitional Military Council* (Al-Jazuli Dafallah)
1986–9	Sadiq Al-Mahdi *Military Council, Prime Minister*
1989–	*No Prime Minister*

Suriname

President

1975–80	J H E Ferrier
1980–2	Henk Chin-a-Sen
1982–8	L F Ramdat-Musier *Acting President*
1988–90	Ramsewak Shankar
1990–1	Johan Kraag
1991–6	Ronald Venetiaan
1996–2000	Jules Wijdenbosch
2000–	Ronald Venetiaan

History

History

National Military Council

Chairman

1980–7	Desi Bouterse
1987	Iwan Granoogst *Acting Premier*

Prime Minister

1975–80	Henk Arron
1980	Henk Chin-a-Sen
1980–2	*No Prime Minister*
1982–3	Henry Weyhorst
1983–4	Errol Alibux
1984–6	Wim Udenhout
1986–7	Pretaapnarain Radhakishun
1987–8	Jules Wijdenbosch
1988–90	Henk Arron
1990–1	Jules Wijdenbosch
1991–6	Jules Ajodhia

Vice President/Chairman of the Council of Ministers

1996–2000	Pretaapnarain Radhakishun
2000–	Jules Ajodhia

Swaziland

Monarch

1967–82	Sobhuza II *Chief since 1921*
1983	Dzeliwe *Queen Regent*
1983–6	Ntombi *Queen Regent*
1986–	Mswati III

Prime Minister

1967–78	Prince Makhosini
1978–9	Prince Maphevu Dlamini
1979–83	Prince Mbandla Dlamini
1983–6	Prince Bhekimpi Dlamini
1986–9	Sotsha Dlamini
1989–93	Obed Dlamini *Acting Prime Minister*
1993–6	Jameson Mbilini Dlamini
1996–	Barnabus S Dlamini

Sweden

Monarch

1872–1907	Oskar II
1907–50	Gustav V
1950–73	Gustav VI Adolf
1973–	Carl XVI Gustaf

Prime Minister

1900–2	Fredrik von Otter
1902–5	Erik Gustaf Boström
1905	Johan Ramstedt
1905	Christian Lundeberg
1905–6	Karl Staaf
1906–11	Arvid Lindman
1911–14	Karl Staaf
1914–17	Hjalmar Hammarskjöld
1917	Carl Swartz
1917–20	Nils Edén
1920	Hjalmar Branting
1920–1	Louis de Geer
1921	Oscar von Sydow
1921–3	Hjalmar Branting
1923–4	Ernst Trygger
1924–5	Hjalmar Branting
1925–6	Rickard Sandler
1926–8	Carl Gustaf Ekman
1928–30	Arvid Lindman
1930–2	Carl Gustaf Ekman
1932	Felix Hamrin
1932–6	Per Albin Hansson
1936	Axel Pehrsson-Branstorp
1936–46	Per Albin Hansson
1946–69	Tage Erlander
1969–76	Olof Palme
1976–8	Thorbjörn Fälldin
1978–9	Ola Ullsten
1979–82	Thorbjörn Fälldin
1982–6	Olof Palme
1986–91	Ingvar Carlsson
1991–4	Carl Bildt
1994–6	Ingvar Carlsson
1996–	Göran Persson

Switzerland

President

1900	Walter Hauser
1901	Ernst Brenner
1902	Joseph Zemp
1903	Adolf Deucher
1904	Robert Comtesse
1905	Marc-Emile Ruchet
1906	Ludwig Forrer
1907	Eduard Müller
1908	Ernst Brenner
1909	Adolf Deucher
1910	Robert Comtesse
1911	Marc-Emile Ruchet
1912	Ludwig Forrer
1913	Eduard Müller
1914	Arthur Hoffmann
1915	Giuseppe Motta
1916	Camille Decoppet
1917	Edmund Schulthess
1918	Felix Calonder
1919	Gustave Ador
1920	Giuseppe Motta
1921	Edmund Schulthess
1922	Robert Haab
1923	Karl Scheurer
1924	Ernest Chuard
1925	Jean-Marie Musy
1926	Heinrich Häberlin
1927	Giuseppe Motta
1928	Edmund Schulthess
1929	Robert Haab
1930	Jean-Marie Musy
1931	Heinrich Häberlin
1932	Giuseppe Motta
1933	Edmund Schulthess
1934	Marcel Pilet-Golaz
1935	Rudolf Minger
1936	Albert Meyer
1937	Giuseppe Motta
1938	Johannes Baumann
1939	Philipp Etter
1940	Marcel Pilet-Golaz
1941	Ernst Wetter
1942	Philipp Etter
1943	Enrico Celio
1944	Walter Stampfli
1945	Eduard von Steiger
1946	Karl Kobelt
1947	Philipp Etter
1948	Enrico Celio
1949	Ernst Nobs
1950	Max Petitpierre
1951	Eduard von Steiger
1952	Karl Kobelt
1953	Philipp Etter

1954	Rodolphe Rubattel
1955	Max Petitpierre
1956	Markus Feldmann
1957	Hans Streuli
1958	Thomas Holenstein
1959	Paul Chaudet
1960	Max Petitpierre
1961	Friedrich Wahlen
1962	Paul Chaudet
1963	Willy Spühler
1964	Ludwig von Moos
1965	Hans Peter Tschudi
1966	Hans Schaffner
1967	Roger Bonvin
1968	Willy Spühler
1969	Ludwig von Moos
1970	Hans Peter Tschudi
1971	Rudolf Gnägi
1972	Nello Celio
1973	Roger Bonvin
1974	Ernst Brugger
1975	Pierre Graber
1976	Rudolf Gnägi
1977	Kurt Furgler
1978	Willi Ritschard
1979	Hans Hürlimann
1980	Georges-André Chevallaz
1981	Kurt Furgler
1982	Fritz Honegger
1983	Pierre Aubert
1984	Leon Schlumpf
1985	Kurt Furgler
1986	Alphons Egli
1987	Pierre Aubert
1988	Otto Stich
1989	Jean-Pascal Delamuraz
1990	Arnold Koller
1991	Flavio Cotti
1992	René Felber
1993	Adolf Ogi
1994	Otto Stich
1995	Kaspar Villiger
1996	Jean-Pascal Delamuraz
1997	Arnold Koller
1998	Flavio Cotti
1999	Ruth Dreifuss
2000	Adolf Ogi
2001	Moritz Leuenberger
2002	Kaspar Villinger

Syria

President

1943–9	Shukri Al-Quwwatli
1949	Husni Az-Zaim
1949–51	Hashim Al-Atassi
1951–4	Adib Shishaqli
1954–5	Hashim Al-Atassi
1955–8	Shukri Al-Quwwatli
1958–61	*Part of United Arab Republic*
1961–3	Nazim Al-Qudsi
1963	Luai Al-Atassi
1963–6	Amin Al-Hafiz
1966–70	Nureddin Al-Atassi
1970–1	Ahmad Al-Khatib
1971–2000	Hafez Al-Assad
2000–	Bashar Al-Assad

Prime Minister

1946–8	Jamil Mardam Bey
1948–9	Khalid Al-Azm

1949	Husni Az-Zaim
1949	Muhsi Al-Barazi
1949	Hashim Al-Atassi
1949	Nazim Al-Qudsi
1949–50	Khalid Al-Azm
1950–1	Nazim Al-Qudsi
1951	Khalid Al-Azm
1951	Hassan Al-Hakim
1951	Maruf Ad-Dawalibi
1951–3	Fauzi As-Salu
1953–4	Adib Shishaqli
1954	Shewqet Shuqair
1954	Sabri Al-Asali
1954	Said Al-Ghazzi
1954–5	Faris Al-Khuri
1955	Sabri Al-Asali
1955–6	Said Al-Ghazzi
1956–8	Sabri Al-Asali
1958–61	*Part of United Arab Republic*
1961	Abd Al-Hamid As-Sarraj
1961	Mamun Kuzbari
1961	Izzat An-Nuss
1961–2	Maruf Ad-Dawalibi
1962	Bashir Azmah
1962–3	Khalid Al-Azm
1963	Salah Ad-Din Al-Bitaar
1963	Sami Al-Jundi
1963	Salah Ad-Din Al-Bitaar
1963–4	Amin Al-Hafez
1964	Salah Ad-Din Al-Bitaar
1964–5	Amin Al-Hafez
1965	Yousif Zeayen
1966	Salah Ad-Din Al-Bitaar
1966–8	Yousif Zeayen
1968–70	Nureddin Al-Atassi *Acting Prime Minister*
1970–1	Hafez Al-Assad
1971–2	Abdel Rahman Khleifawi
1972–6	Mahmoud Bin Saleh Al-Ayoubi
1976–8	Abdul Rahman Khleifawi
1978–80	Mohammed Ali Al-Halabi
1980–7	Abdel Rauof Al-Kasm
1987–2000	Mahmoud Al-Zubi
2000–	Muhammad Mustafa Mero

Taiwan (Republic of China)

President

1950–75	Chiang Kai-shek
1975–8	Yen Chia-kan
1978–87	Chiang Ching-kuo
1987–2000	Lee Teng-hui
2000–	Chen Shui-bian

President of Executive Council

1950–4	Ch'eng Ch'eng
1954–8	O K Yui
1958–63	Ch'eng Ch'eng
1963–72	Yen Chia-ken
1972–8	Chiang Ching-kuo
1978–84	Sun Yun-suan
1984–9	Yu Kuo-hwa
1989–90	Lee Huan
1990–3	Hau Pei-tsun
1993–6	Lien Chan

Prime Minister

1996–7	Lien Chan
1997–2000	Vincent Siew
2000	Tang Fei
2000–2	Chang Chun-hsiung
2002–	Yu Shyi-kun

History

History

Tajikistan

President

1991–2	Rakhman Nabiev
1992	Akbarsho Iskandrov *Acting President*
1992–	Imamoli Rakhmanov

Prime Minister

1991–2	Akbar Mirzoyev
1992–3	Abdumalik Abdullojanov
1993–4	Abduljalil Samadov *Acting Prime Minister*
1994–6	Jamshed Karimov
1996–9	Yahya Azimov
1999–	Akil Akilov

Tanzania

President

1964–85	Julius Kambarage Nyerere
1985–95	Ali Hassan Mwinyi
1995–	Benjamin William Mkapa

Prime Minister

1964–72	Rashid M Kawawa *Vice President*
1972–7	Rashid M Kawawa
1977–80	Edward M Sokoine
1980–3	Cleopa D Msuya
1983–4	Edward M Sokoine
1984–5	Salim A Salim
1985–90	Joseph S Warioba
1990–4	John Malecela
1994–5	Cleopa Msuya
1995–	Frederick Tulway Sumaye

Thailand

Monarch

1868–1910	Chulalongkorn, Rama V
1910–25	Rama VI
1925–35	Rama VII
1935–9	Rama VIII (Ananda Mahidol)
1939–46	Nai Pridi Phanomyong *Regent*
1946	Rama IX
1946–50	Rangsit of Chainat *Regent*
1950–	Bhumibol Adulyadej

Prime Minister

1932–3	Phraya Manopakom
1933–8	Phraya Phahon Phonphahuyasena
1938–44	Luang Phibun Songgram
1945	Thawi Bunyaket
1945–6	Mom Rachawongse Seni Pramoj
1946	Nai Khuang Aphaiwong
1946	Nai Pridi Phanomyong
1946–7	Luang Thamrong Nawasawat
1947–8	Nai Khuang Aphaiwong
1948–57	Luang Phibun Songgram
1957	Sarit Thanarat
1957	Nai Pote Sarasin
1957–8	Thanom Kittikatchom
1958–63	Sarit Thanarat
1963–73	Thanom Kittikatchom
1973–5	Sanya Dharmasaki
1975–6	Mom Rachawongse Kukrit Pramoj
1976	Seni Pramoj
1976–7	Thanin Kraivichien
1977–80	Kriangsak Chammanard
1980–7	Prem Tinsulanonda
1987–91	Chatichai Choonhaven
1991–2	Anand Panyarachun
1992	Suchinda Kraprayoon
1992	Anand Panyarachun
1992–5	Chuan Leekpai
1995–6	Banharn Silpa-Archa
1996–7	Chavalit Yongchaiyudh
1997–2001	Chuan Leekpai
2001–	Thaksin Shinawatra

Togo

President

1960–3	Sylvanus Olympio
1963–7	Nicolas Grunitzky
1967–	Gnassingbé Eyadéma

Prime Minister

1991–4	Joseph Koukou Koffigoh
1994–6	Edem Kodjo
1996–9	Kwassi Klutse
1999–2000	Eugene Koffi Adoboli
2000–2	Messan Agbeyome Kodjo
2002–	Koffi Sama

Tonga

Monarch

1893–1918	George Tupou II
1918–65	Salote Tupou III
1965–	Taufa'ahau Tupou IV

Prime Minister

1970–91	Fatafehi Tu'ipelehake
1991–2000	Baron Vaea
2000–	Prince 'Ulukalala Lavaka Ata

Trinidad and Tobago

President

1976–87	Ellis Emmanuel Clarke
1987–97	Noor Mohammed Hassanali
1997–	Arthur Robinson

Premier

1956–62	Eric Williams

Prime Minister

1962–81	Eric Williams
1981–6	George Chambers
1986–91	Raymond Robinson
1991–5	Patrick Manning
1995–2001	Basdeo Panday
2001–	Patrick Manning

Tunisia

Bey

1943–57	Muhammad VIII

President

1957–87	Habib Bourguiba
1987–	Zine Al-Abidine Bin Ali

Prime Minister

1956–7	Habib Bourguiba
1957–69	*No Prime Minister*
1969–70	Bahi Ladgham

1970–80	Hadi Nouira
1980–6	Mohammed Mezali
1986–7	Rashid Sfar
1987	Zine Al-Abidine Bin Ali
1987–9	Hadi Baccouche
1989–99	Hamed Karoui
1999–	Mohammed Ghannouchi

Turkey

Sultan of the Ottoman Empire

1876–1909	Abdülhamit
1909–18	Mehmet Reşat
1918–22	Mehmet Vahideddin

■ **Turkish Republic**

President

1923–38	Mustafa Kemal Atatürk
1938–50	İsmet İnönü
1950–60	Celal Bayar
1961–6	Cemal Gürsel
1966–73	Cevdet Sunay
1973–80	Fahri S Korutürk
1980	Ihsan Çaglayangil *Acting President*
1982–9	Kenan Evren
1989–93	Turgut Özal
1993–2000	Süleyman Demirel
2000–	Ahmet Necdet Sezer

Prime Minister

1923–4	İsmet İnönü
1924–5	Ali Fethi Okyar
1925–37	İsmet İnönü
1937–9	Celal Bayar
1939–42	Dr Refik Saydam
1942–6	Şükrü Saracoğlu
1946–7	Recep Peker
1947–9	Hasan Saka
1949–50	Şemşettin Günaltay
1950–60	Adnan Menderes
1960–1	Cemal Gürsel
1961–5	İsmet İnönü
1965	S Hayri Ürgüplü
1965–71	Süleyman Demirel
1971–2	Nihat Erim
1972–3	Ferit Melen
1973–4	Naim Talu
1974	Bülent Ecevit
1974–5	Sadi Irmak
1975–7	Süleyman Demirel
1977	Bülent Ecevit
1977–8	Süleyman Demirel
1978–9	Bülent Ecevit
1979–80	Süleyman Demirel
1980–3	Bülent Ülüsü
1983–9	Turgut Özal
1989–91	Yildrim Akbulut
1991	Mesut Yilmaz
1991–3	Süleyman Demirel
1993–6	Tansu Çiller
1996	Mesut Yilmaz
1996–7	Necmettin Erbakan
1997–8	Mesut Yilmaz
1999–2002	Bülent Ecevit
2002–	Abdullah Gül

Turkmenistan

President

1991–	Saparmurad Niyazov

Prime Minister

1991–2	Khan Akhmedov
1992–	*As President*

Tuvalu

Chief of State: British monarch, represented by Governor General

Prime Minister

1978–81	Toalipi Lauti
1981–9	Tomasi Puapua
1989–93	Bikenibeu Paeniu
1993–6	Kamuta Lataasi
1996–9	Bikenibeu Paeniu
1999–2000	Ionatana Ionatana
2000–1	Lagitupu Tuilimu *Acting Prime Minister*
2001	Faimalaga Luka
2001–2	Koloa Talake
2002–	Saufatu Sopoanga

Uganda

President

1962–6	Edward Muteesa II
1967–71	Apollo Milton Obote
1971–9	Idi Amin
1979	Yusuf Kironde Lule
1979–80	Godfrey Lukongwa Binaisa
1981–5	Apollo Milton Obote
1985–6	*Military Council* (Tito Okello Lutwa)
1986–	Yoweri Kaguta Museveni

Prime Minister

1962–71	Apollo Milton Obote
1971–81	*No Prime Minister*
1981–5	Eric Otema Alimadi
1985	Paulo Muwanga
1985–6	Abraham N Waliggo
1986–91	Samson B Kisekka
1991–4	George Cosmas Adyebo
1994–9	Kintu Musoke
1999–	Apollo Nsimbabi

Ukraine

President

1991–4	Leonid Kravchuk
1994–	Leonid Kuchma

Prime Minister

1990–2	Vitold Fokin
1992	Valentin Symonenko
1992–3	Leonid Kuchma
1993–4	Yukhim Zvyahilski *Acting Prime Minister*
1994–5	Vitalii Masol
1995–6	Yevhenii Marchuk
1996–7	Pavlo Lazarenko
1997	Vasyl Durdynets *Acting Prime Minister*
1997–9	Valery Pustovoytenko
1999–2001	Viktor Yushchenko
2001–2	Anatoli Kinakh
2002–	Viktor Yanukovich

United Arab Emirates

President

1971–	Zayed Bin Sultan al-Nahayan

Prime Minister

1971–9	Maktoum Bin Rashid al-Maktoum

History

History

| 1979–91 | Rashid Bin Said al-Maktoum |
| 1991– | Maktoum Bin Rashid al-Maktoum |

▪ Abu Dhabi

Tribe: al Bu Falah *or* al Nahyan (Bani Yas)

Family name: al-Nahyan

Shaikh

1855–1909	Zayed
1909–12	Tahnoun
1912–22	Hamdan
1922–6	Sultan
1926–8	Saqr
1928–66	Shakhbout
1966–	Zayed

▪ Ajman

Tribe: al Bu Kharayban (Naim)

Family name: al-Nuaimi

Shaikh

1900–10	Abdel-Aziz
1910–28	Humaid
1928–81	Rashid
1981–	Humaid

▪ Dubai

Tribe: al Bu Flasah (Bani Yas)

Family name: al-Maktoum

Shaikh

1894–1906	Maktoum
1906–12	Butti
1912–58	Said
1958–90	Rashid
1990–	Maktoum

▪ Fujairah

Tribe: Sharqiyyin

Family name: al-Sharqi

Shaikh

| 1952–75 | Mohammed |
| 1975– | Hamad |

▪ Ras al-Khaimah

Tribe: Huwalah

Family name: al-Qasimi

Shaikh

| 1921–48 | Sultan |
| 1948– | Saqr |

▪ Sharjah

Tribe: Huwalah

Family name: al-Qasimi

Shaikh

1883–1914	Saqr
1914–24	Khaled
1924–51	Sultan
1951–65	Saqr
1965–72	Khaled
1972–87	Sultan

| 1987 | Abdel-Aziz |
| 1987– | Sultan |

▪ Umm al-Qaiwain

Tribe: al-Ali

Family name: al-Mualla

Shaikh

1873–1904	Ahmad
1904–22	Rashid
1922–3	Abdullah
1923–9	Hamad
1929–81	Ahmad
1981–	Rashid

United Kingdom

For list of previous monarchs see pp357, 358, 359

Monarch

House of Hanover

1714–27	George I
1727–60	George II
1760–1820	George III
1820–30	George IV
1830–7	William IV
1837–1901	Victoria

House of Saxe-Coburg

| 1901–10 | Edward VII |

House of Windsor

1910–36	George V
1936	Edward VIII
1936–52	George VI
1952–	Elizabeth II

Prime Minister

1721–42	Robert Walpole *Whig*
1742–3	Earl of Wilmington (Spencer Compton) *Whig*
1743–54	Henry Pelham *Whig*
1754–6	Duke of Newcastle (Thomas Pelham-Holles) *Whig*
1756–7	Duke of Devonshire (William Cavendish) *Whig*
1757–62	Duke of Newcastle *Whig*
1762–3	Earl of Bute (John Stuart) *Tory*
1763–5	George Grenville *Whig*
1765–6	Marquess of Rockingham (Charles Watson Wentworth) *Whig*
1766–70	Duke of Grafton (Augustus Henry Fitzroy) *Whig*
1770–82	Lord North (Frederick North) *Tory*
1782	Marquess of Rockingham *Whig*
1782–3	Earl of Shelburne (William Petty-Fitzmaurice) *Whig*
1783	Duke of Portland (William Henry Cavendish) *Coal*
1783–1801	William Pitt *Tory*
1801–4	Henry Addington *Tory*
1804–6	William Pitt *Tory*
1806–7	Lord Grenville (William Wyndham) *Whig*
1807–9	Duke of Portland *Tory*
1809–12	Spencer Perceval *Tory*
1812–27	Earl of Liverpool (Robert Banks Jenkinson) *Tory*
1827	George Canning *Tory*

1827–8	Viscount Goderich (Frederick John Robinson) *Tory*
1828–30	Duke of Wellington (Arthur Wellesley) *Tory*
1830–4	Earl Grey (Charles Grey) *Whig*
1834	Viscount Melbourne (William Lamb) *Whig*
1834–5	Robert Peel *Con*
1835–41	Viscount Melbourne *Whig*
1841–6	Robert Peel *Con*
1846–52	Lord John Russell *Lib*
1852	Earl of Derby (Edward George Smith Stanley) *Con*
1852–5	Lord Aberdeen (George Hamilton-Gordon) *Peelite*
1855–8	Viscount Palmerston (Henry John Temple) *Lib*
1858–9	Earl of Derby *Con*
1859–65	Viscount Palmerston *Lib*
1865–6	Lord John Russell *Lib*
1866–8	Earl of Derby *Con*
1868	Benjamin Disraeli *Con*
1868–74	William Ewart Gladstone *Lib*
1874–80	Benjamin Disraeli *Con*
1880–5	William Ewart Gladstone *Lib*
1885–6	Marquess of Salisbury (Robert Gascoyne-Cecil) *Con*
1886	William Ewart Gladstone *Lib*
1886–92	Marquess of Salisbury *Con*
1892–4	William Ewart Gladstone *Lib*
1894–5	Earl of Rosebery (Archibald Philip Primrose) *Lib*
1895–1902	Marquess of Salisbury *Con*
1902–5	Arthur James Balfour *Con*
1905–8	Henry Campbell-Bannerman *Lib*
1908–15	Herbert Henry Asquith *Lib*
1915–16	Herbert Henry Asquith *Coal*
1916–22	David Lloyd George *Coal*
1922–3	Andrew Bonar Law *Con*
1923–4	Stanley Baldwin *Con*
1924	James Ramsay MacDonald *Lab*
1924–9	Stanley Baldwin *Con*
1929–31	James Ramsay MacDonald *Lab*
1931–5	James Ramsay MacDonald *Nat*
1935–7	Stanley Baldwin *Nat*
1937–40	Arthur Neville Chamberlain *Nat*
1940–5	Winston Churchill *Coal*
1945–51	Clement Attlee *Lab*
1951–5	Winston Churchill *Con*
1955–7	Anthony Eden *Con*
1957–63	Harold Macmillan *Con*
1963–4	Alec Douglas-Home *Con*
1964–70	Harold Wilson *Lab*
1970–4	Edward Heath *Con*
1974–6	Harold Wilson *Lab*
1976–9	James Callaghan *Lab*
1979–90	Margaret Thatcher *Con*
1990–7	John Major *Con*
1997–	Tony Blair *Lab*

Coal = Coalition
Con = Conservative
Lab = Labour
Lib = Liberal
Nat = Nationalist

United Nations

Secretary-General

1946–53	Trygve Lie *Norway*
1953–61	Dag Hammarskjöld *Sweden*
1962–71	U Thant *Burma*
1972–81	Kurt Waldheim *Austria*
1982–91	Javier Pérez de Cuéllar *Peru*
1992–6	Boutros Boutros-Ghali *Egypt*
1997–	Kofi Annan *Ghana*

United States of America

President

Vice President in parentheses

1789–97	George Washington (1st) (John Adams)
1797–1801	John Adams (2nd) *Fed* (Thomas Jefferson)
1801–9	Thomas Jefferson (3rd) *Dem-Rep* (Aaron Burr, 1801–5) (George Clinton, 1805–9)
1809–17	James Madison (4th) *Dem-Rep* (George Clinton, 1809–12) no Vice President *1812–13* (Elbridge Gerry, 1813–14) *no Vice President 1814–17*
1817–25	James Monroe (5th) *Dem-Rep* (Daniel D Tompkins)
1825–9	John Quincy Adams (6th) *Dem-Rep* (John C Calhoun)
1829–37	Andrew Jackson (7th) *Dem* (John C Calhoun, 1829–32) *no Vice President 1832–3* (Martin van Buren, 1833–7)
1837–41	Martin van Buren (8th) *Dem* (Richard M Johnson)
1841	William Henry Harrison (9th) *Whig* (John Tyler)
1841–5	John Tyler (10th) *Whig no Vice President*
1845–9	James Knox Polk (11th) *Dem* (George M Dallas)
1849–50	Zachary Taylor (12th) *Whig* (Millard Fillmore)
1850–3	Millard Fillmore (13th) *Whig no Vice President*
1853–7	Franklin Pierce (14th) *Dem* (William R King, 1853) *no Vice President 1853–7*
1857–61	James Buchanan (15th) *Dem* (John C Breckinridge)
1861–5	Abraham Lincoln (16th) *Rep* (Hannibal Hamlin, 1861–5) (Andrew Johnson, 1865)
1865–9	Andrew Johnson (17th) *Dem-Nat no Vice President*
1869–77	Ulysses Simpson Grant (18th) *Rep* (Schuyler Colfax, 1869–73) (Henry Wilson, 1873–5) *no Vice President 1875–7*
1877–81	Rutherford Birchard Hayes (19th) *Rep* (William A Wheeler)
1881	James Abram Garfield (20th) *Rep* (Chester A Arthur)
1881–5	Chester Alan Arthur (21st) *Rep no Vice President*
1885–9	Grover Cleveland (22nd) *Dem* (Thomas A Hendricks, 1885) *no Vice President 1885–9*
1889–93	Benjamin Harrison (23rd) *Rep* (Levi P Morton)
1893–7	Grover Cleveland (24th) *Dem* (Adlai E Stevenson)
1897–1901	William McKinley (25th) *Rep* (Garrat A Hobart, 1897–9) *no Vice President 1899–1901* (Theodore Roosevelt, 1901)
1901–9	Theodore Roosevelt (26th) *Rep no Vice President 1901–5* (Charles W Fairbanks, 1905–9)

History

History

1909–13	William Howard Taft (27th) *Rep* (James S Sherman, 1909–12) *no Vice President 1912–13*
1913–21	Woodrow Wilson (28th) *Dem* (Thomas R Marshall)
1921–3	Warren Gamaliel Harding (29th) *Rep* (Calvin Coolidge)
1923–9	Calvin Coolidge (30th) *Rep no Vice President 1923–5* (Charles G Dawes, 1925–9)
1929–33	Herbert Clark Hoover (31st) *Rep* (Charles Curtis)
1933–45	Franklin Delano Roosevelt (32nd) *Dem* (John N Garner, 1933–41) (Henry A Wallace, 1941–5) (Harry S Truman, 1945)
1945–53	Harry S Truman (33rd) *Dem no Vice President 1945–9* (Alben W Barkley, 1949–53)
1953–61	Dwight David Eisenhower (34th) *Rep* (Richard M Nixon)
1961–3	John Fitzgerald Kennedy (35th) *Dem* (Lyndon B Johnson)
1963–9	Lyndon Baines Johnson (36th) *Dem no Vice President 1963–5* (Hubert H Humphrey, 1965–9)
1969–74	Richard Milhous Nixon (37th) *Rep* (Spiro T Agnew, 1969–73) *no Vice President 1973, Oct–Dec* (Gerald R Ford, 1973–4)
1974–7	Gerald Rudolph Ford (38th) *Rep no Vice President 1974, Aug–Dec* (Nelson A Rockefeller, 1974–7)
1977–81	Jimmy Carter (39th) *Dem* (Walter F Mondale)
1981–9	Ronald Wilson Reagan (40th) *Rep* (George H W Bush)
1989–93	George Herbert Walker Bush (41st) *Rep* (J Danforth Quayle)
1993–2001	William Jefferson Blythe IV Clinton (42nd) *Dem* (Albert Gore)
2001–	George Walker Bush (43rd) *Rep* (Richard B Cheney)

Dem = Democrat
Fed = Federalist
Nat = National Union
Rep = Republican

Uruguay

President

1899–1903	Juan Lindolfo Cuestas
1903–7	José Batlle y Ordóñez
1907–11	Claudio Williman
1911–15	José Batlle y Ordóñez
1915–19	Feliciano Viera
1919–23	Baltasar Brum
1923–7	José Serrato
1927–31	Juan Capisteguy
1931–8	Gabriel Terra
1938–43	Alfredo Baldomir
1943–7	Juan José de Amézaga
1947	Tomás Berreta
1947–51	Luis Batlle Berres
1951–5	Andrés Martínez Trueba

National Government Council (1955–67)

1955–6	Luis Batlle Berres
1956–7	Alberto F Zubiría
1957–8	Alberto Lezama
1958–9	Carlos L Fischer

1959–60	Martín R Etchegoyen
1960–1	Benito Nardone
1961–2	Eduardo Victor Haedo
1962–3	Faustino Harrison
1963–4	Daniel Fernández Crespo
1964–5	Luis Giannattasio
1965–6	Washington Beltrán
1966–7	Alberto Heber Usher
1967	Oscar Daniel Gestido
1967–72	Jorge Pacheco Areco
1972–6	Juan María Bordaberry Arocena
1976–81	Aparicio Méndez
1981–4	Gregorio Conrado Álvarez Armelino
1984–90	Julio María Sanguinetti Cairolo
1990–4	Luis Alberto Lacalle Herrera
1994–9	Julio María Sanguinetti
1999–	Jorge Batlle Ibáñez

USSR (Union of Soviet Socialist Republics)

No longer in existence, but included for reference.

President

1917	Leo Borisovich Kamenev
1917–19	Yakov Mikhailovich Sverlov
1919–46	Mikhail Ivanovich Kalinin
1946–53	Nikolai Shvernik
1953–60	Klimentiy Voroshilov
1960–4	Leonid Brezhnev
1964–5	Anastas Mikoyan
1965–77	Nikolai Podgorny
1977–82	Leonid Brezhnev
1982–3	Vasily Kuznetsov *Acting President*
1983–4	Yuri Andropov
1984	Vasily Kuznetsov *Acting President*
1984–5	Konstantin Chernenko
1985	Vasily Kuznetsov *Acting President*
1985–8	Andrei Gromyko
1988–90	Mikhail Gorbachev

Executive President

1990–91	Mikhail Gorbachev
1991	Gennady Yanayev *Acting President*
1991	Mikhail Gorbachev

Chairman (Prime Minister)

Council of Ministers

1917	Georgy Evgenyevich Lvov
1917	Aleksandr Fyodorovich Kerensky

Council of People's Commissars

1917–24	Vladimir Ilyich Lenin
1924–30	Aleksei Ivanovich Rykov
1930–41	Vyacheslav Mikhailovich Molotov
1941–53	Josef Stalin

Council of Ministers

1953–5	Georgiy Malenkov
1955–8	Nikolai Bulganin
1958–64	Nikita Khrushchev
1964–80	Alexei Kosygin
1980–5	Nikolai Tikhonov
1985–90	Nikolai Ryzhkov
1990–1	Yuri Maslyukov *Acting Chairman*
1991	Valentin Pavlov
1991	Ivan Silayev *Acting*

General Secretary

1922–53	Josef Stalin
1953	Georgiy Malenkov
1953–64	Nikita Khrushchev
1964–82	Leonid Brezhnev

1982–4	Yuri Andropov
1984–5	Konstantin Chernenko
1985–91	Mikhail Gorbachev

See separate entries for former constituent states of USSR from 1990/91.

Uzbekistan

President

1991–	Islam Karimov

Prime Minister

1991–5	Abdulhashim Mutalov
1995–	Otkir Sultonov

Vanuatu

President

1980–9	George Sokomanu (*formerly* Kalkoa)
1989–94	Fred Timakata
1994–9	Jean-Marie Leye
1999–	John Bani

Prime Minister

1980–91	Walter Lini
1991	Donald Kalpokas
1991–5	Maxime Carlot Korman
1995–6	Serge Vohor
1996	Maxime Carlot Korman
1996–8	Serge Vohor
1998–9	Donald Kalpokas
1999–2001	Barak Sopé
2001–	Edward Natapei

Venezuela

President

1899–1908	Cipriano Castro
1908–36	Juan Vicente Gomez
1936–41	Eleazar Lopez Contreras
1941–5	Isaias Medina Angarita
1945–7	*Military Junta* (Rómulo Betancourt)
1947–8	Romulo Gallegos
1948–50	*Military Junta* (Carlos Delgado Chalbaud)
1950–9	*Military Junta* (Marcos Pérez Jiménez)
1959–64	Rómulo Betancourt
1964–9	Raul Leoni
1969–74	Rafael Caldera Rodriguez
1974–9	Carlos Andres Pérez
1979–84	Luis Herrera Campins
1984–9	Jaime Lusinchi
1989–93	Carlos Andres Pérez
1994–8	Rafael Caldera Rodríguez
1998–2002	Hugo Chávez Frías
2002	Pedro Carmona *Head of Transitional Government*
2002–	Hugo Chávez Frías

Vietnam

President

■ Democratic Republic of Vietnam

1945–69	Ho Chi Minh
1969–76	Ton Duc Thang

■ State of Vietnam

1949–55	Bao Dai

■ Republic of Vietnam

1955–63	Ngo Dinh Diem
1963–4	Duong Van Minh
1964	Nguyen Khanh
1964–5	Phan Khac Suu
1965–75	Nguyen Van Thieu
1975	Tran Van Huong
1975	Duong Van Minh
1975–6	*Provisional Revolutionary Government* (Huynh Tan Phat)

■ Socialist Republic of Vietnam

1976–80	Ton Duc Thang
1980–1	Nguyen Hun Tho *Acting President*
1981–7	Truongh Chinh
1987–92	Vo Chi Cong
1992–7	Le Duc Anh
1997–	Tran Duc Luong

Prime Minister

■ Democratic Republic of Vietnam

1955–76	Pham Van Dong

■ State of Vietnam

1949–50	Nguyen Van Xuan
1950	Nguyen Phan Long
1950–2	Tran Van Huu
1952	Tran Van Huong
1952–3	Nguyen Van Tam
1953–4	Buu Loc
1954–5	Ngo Dinh Diem

■ Republic of Vietnam

1955–63	Ngo Dinh Diem
1963–4	Nguyen Ngoc Tho
1964	Nguyen Khan
1964–5	Tran Van Huong
1965	Phan Huy Quat
1965–7	Nguyen Cao Ky
1967–8	Nguyen Van Loc
1968–9	Tran Van Huong
1969–75	Tran Thien Khiem
1975	Nguyen Ba Can
1975–6	Vu Van Mau

■ Socialist Republic of Vietnam

Premier

1976–87	Pham Van Dong
1987–8	Pham Hung
1988	Vo Van Kiet *Acting Premier*
1988–91	Do Muoi
1991–7	Vo Van Kiet
1997–	Phan Van Khai

General Secretary

1960–80	Le Duan
1986	Truong Chinh
1986–92	Nguyen Van Linh

Western Samoa ► Samoa

History

Yemen

■ Yemen Arab Republic (North Yemen)

Monarch (Imam)

1918–48	Yahya Mohammed Bin Mohammed
1948–62	Ahmed Bin Yahya
1962–70	Mohammed Bin Ahmed
1962	*Civil War*

President

1962–7	Abdullah Al-Sallal
1967–74	Abdur Rahman Al-Iriani
1974–7	*Military Command Council* (Ibrahim Al-Hamadi)
1977–8	Ahmed Bin Hussein Al-Ghashmi
1978–90	Ali Abdullah Saleh

Prime Minister

1964	Hamud Al-Jaifi
1965	Hassan Al-Amri
1965	Ahmed Mohammed Numan
1965	*As President*
1965–6	Hassan Al-Amri
1966–7	*As President*
1967	Muhsin Al-Aini
1967–9	Hassan Al-Amri
1969–70	Abd Allah Kurshumi
1970–1	Muhsin Al-Aini
1971	Abdel Salam Sabra *Acting Prime Minister*
1971	Ahmed Mohammed Numan
1971	Hassan Al-Amri
1971–2	Muhsin Al-Aini
1972–4	Qadi Abdullah Al-Hijri
1974	Hassan Makki
1974–5	Muhsin Al-Aini
1975	Abdel Latif Deifallah *Acting Prime Minister*
1975–90	Abdel-Aziz Abdel-Ghani

■ People's Democratic Republic of Yemen (South Yemen)

President

1967–9	Qahtan Mohammed Al-Shaabi
1969–78	Salim Ali Rubai
1978	Ali Nasir Mohammed Husani
1978–80	Abdel Fattah Ismail
1980–6	Ali Nasir Mohammed Husani
1986–90	Haidar Abu Bakr Al-Attas

Prime Minister

1969	Faisal Abd Al-Latif Al-Shaabi
1969–71	Mohammed Ali Haithem
1971–85	Ali Nasir Mohammed Husani
1985–6	Haidar Abu Bakr Al-Attas
1986–90	Yasin Said Numan

■ Republic of Yemen

President

1990–	Ali Abdullah Saleh

Prime Minister

1990–3	Haidar Abu Bakr Al-Attas
1993–7	Abdel-Aziz Abdel-Ghani
1997	Farag Said Ben Ghanem
1998–2001	Abdul Ali Al-Karim Al-Iryani
2001–	Abd al-Qadir Abd al-Rahman Bajammal

Yugoslavia

Monarch

1921–34	Aleksandar II
1934–45	Petar II (*in exile from 1941*)

■ Republic

National Assembly

Chairman

1945–53	Ivan Ribar

President

1953–80	Josip Broz Tito

Collective Presidency

1980	Lazar Koliševski
1980–1	Cvijetin Mijatović
1981–2	Serghei Kraigher
1982–3	Petar Stambolić
1983–4	Mika Spiljak
1984–5	Veselin Đuranović
1985–6	Radovan Vlajković
1986–7	Sinan Hasani
1987–8	Lazar Mojsov
1988–9	Raif Dizdarević
1989–90	Janez Drnovsek
1990–1	Borisav Jovic
1991	Stipe Mesic

Prime Minister

1929–32	Pear Živkovic
1932	Vojislav Marinković
1932–4	Milan Srškić
1934	Nikola Uzunović
1934–5	Bogoljub Jevtić
1935–9	Milan Stojadinović
1939–41	Dragiša Cvetković
1941	Dušan Simović

Government in exile

1942	Slobodan Jovanović
1943	Miloš Trifunović
1943–4	Božidar Purić
1944–5	Ivan Šubašić
1945	Drago Marušić

Home government

1941–4	Milan Nedić
1943–63	Josip Broz Tito
1963–7	Petar Stambolić
1967–9	Mika Špiljak
1969–71	Mitja Ribičič
1971–7	Džemal Bijedić
1977–82	Veselin Đuranović
1982–6	Milka Planinc
1986–9	Branko Mikulić
1989–91	Ante Marković

Communist Party

First Secretary

1937–52	Josip Broz Tito

League of Communists

1952–80	Josip Broz Tito

League of Communists Central Committee

President

1979–80	Stevan Doronjski *Acting President*

1980–1	Lazar Mojsov
1981–2	Dušan Dragosavac
1982–3	Mitja Ribičič
1983–4	Dragoslav Marković
1984–5	Ali Sukrija
1985–6	Vidoje Žarkovic
1986–7	Milanko Renovica
1987–8	Boško Krunić
1988–9	Stipe Suvar
1989–90	Milan Pancevski
1990	Miomir Grbović

■ Federal Republic of Yugoslavia

President

1992–3	Dobrica Cosic
1993–7	Zoran Lilic
1997–2000	Slobodan Milosevic
2000–	Vojislav Kostunica

Prime Minister

1992–3	Milan Panic
1993–8	Radoje Kontic
1998–2000	Momir Bulatovic
2000–1	Zoran Zizic
2001–	Dragisa Pesic

■ Serbia

President

1992–7	Slobodan Milosevic
1997	Vojislav Šešelj
1997–2002	Milan Milutinovic

■ Montenegro

President

1993–7	Momir Bulatovic
1997–2002	Milo Djukanović

Civil War broke out in 1991. Four of Yugoslavia's six republics declared their independence. Serbia and Montenegro remained part of the Federal Republic of Yugoslavia (declared 1992), which was renamed Serbia and Montenegro in 2003.

► **Bosnia-Herzegovina, Croatia, Macedonia, Slovenia.**

Zaïre ► Congo, Democratic Republic of

Zambia

President

1964–91	Kenneth Kaunda
1991–2002	Frederick Chiluba
2002–	Levy Mwanawasa

Prime Minister

1964–73	Kenneth Kaunda
1973–5	Mainza Chona
1975–7	Elijah Mudenda
1977–8	Mainza Chona
1978–81	Daniel Lisulu
1981–5	Nalumino Mundia
1985–9	Kebby Musokotwane
1989–91	Malimba Masheke
1991–	*No Prime Minister*

Zimbabwe

President

1980–7	Canaan Sodindo Banana
1987–	Robert Gabriel Mugabe

Prime Minister

1980–7	Robert Gabriel Mugabe

History

TIME

Perpetual calendar 1801–2040

The calendar for each year is given under the corresponding letter below.

1801	I	1849	C	1897	K	1945	C	1993	K
1802	K	1850	E	1898	M	1946	E	1994	M
1803	M	1851	G	1899	A	1947	G	1995	A
1804	B	1852	J	1900	C	1948	J	1996	D
1805	E	1853	M	1901	E	1949	M	1997	G
1806	G	1854	A	1902	G	1950	A	1998	I
1807	I	1855	C	1903	I	1951	C	1999	K
1808	L	1856	F	1904	L	1952	F	2000	N
1809	A	1857	I	1905	A	1953	I	2001	C
1810	C	1858	K	1906	C	1954	K	2002	E
1811	E	1859	M	1907	E	1955	M	2003	G
1812	H	1860	B	1908	H	1956	B	2004	J
1813	K	1861	E	1909	K	1957	E	2005	M
1814	M	1862	G	1910	M	1958	G	2006	A
1815	A	1863	I	1911	A	1959	I	2007	C
1816	D	1864	L	1912	D	1960	L	2008	F
1817	G	1865	A	1913	G	1961	A	2009	I
1818	I	1866	C	1914	I	1962	C	2010	K
1819	K	1867	E	1915	K	1963	E	2011	M
1820	N	1868	H	1916	N	1964	H	2012	B
1821	C	1869	K	1917	C	1965	K	2013	E
1822	E	1870	M	1918	E	1966	M	2014	G
1823	G	1871	A	1919	G	1967	A	2015	I
1824	J	1872	D	1920	J	1968	D	2016	L
1825	M	1873	G	1921	M	1969	G	2017	A
1826	A	1874	I	1922	A	1970	I	2018	C
1827	C	1875	K	1923	C	1971	K	2019	E
1828	F	1876	N	1924	F	1972	N	2020	H
1829	I	1877	C	1925	I	1973	C	2021	K
1830	K	1878	E	1926	K	1974	E	2022	M
1831	M	1879	G	1927	M	1975	G	2023	A
1832	B	1880	J	1928	B	1976	J	2024	D
1833	E	1881	M	1929	E	1977	M	2025	G
1834	G	1882	A	1930	G	1978	A	2026	I
1835	I	1883	C	1931	I	1979	C	2027	K
1836	L	1884	F	1932	L	1980	F	2028	N
1837	A	1885	I	1933	A	1981	I	2029	C
1838	C	1886	K	1934	C	1982	K	2030	E
1839	E	1887	M	1935	E	1983	M	2031	G
1840	H	1888	B	1936	H	1984	B	2032	J
1841	K	1889	E	1937	K	1985	E	2033	M
1842	M	1890	G	1938	M	1986	G	2034	A
1843	A	1891	I	1939	A	1987	I	2035	C
1844	D	1892	L	1940	D	1988	L	2036	F
1845	G	1893	A	1941	G	1989	A	2037	I
1846	I	1894	C	1942	I	1990	C	2038	K
1847	K	1895	E	1943	K	1991	E	2039	M
1848	N	1896	H	1944	N	1992	H	2040	B

Time

A

JANUARY	FEBRUARY	MARCH	APRIL	MAY	JUNE
S M T W T F S	S M T W T F S	S M T W T F S	S M T W T F S	S M T W T F S	S M T W T F S
1 2 3 4 5 6 7	1 2 3 4	1 2 3 4	1	1 2 3 4 5 6	1 2 3
8 9 10 11 12 13 14	5 6 7 8 9 10 11	5 6 7 8 9 10 11	2 3 4 5 6 7 8	7 8 9 10 11 12 13	4 5 6 7 8 9 10
15 16 17 18 19 20 21	12 13 14 15 16 17 18	12 13 14 15 16 17 18	9 10 11 12 13 14 15	14 15 16 17 18 19 20	11 12 13 14 15 16 17
22 23 24 25 26 27 28	19 20 21 22 23 24 25	19 20 21 22 23 24 25	16 17 18 19 20 21 22	21 22 23 24 25 26 27	18 19 20 21 22 23 24
29 30 31	26 27 28	26 27 28 29 30 31	23 24 25 26 27 28 29	28 29 30 31	25 26 27 28 29 30
			30		

JULY	AUGUST	SEPTEMBER	OCTOBER	NOVEMBER	DECEMBER
S M T W T F S	S M T W T F S	S M T W T F S	S M T W T F S	S M T W T F S	S M T W T F S
1	1 2 3 4 5	1 2	1 2 3 4 5 6 7	1 2 3 4	1 2
2 3 4 5 6 7 8	6 7 8 9 10 11 12	3 4 5 6 7 8 9	8 9 10 11 12 13 14	5 6 7 8 9 10 11	3 4 5 6 7 8 9
9 10 11 12 13 14 15	13 14 15 16 17 18 19	10 11 12 13 14 15 16	15 16 17 18 19 20 21	12 13 14 15 16 17 18	10 11 12 13 14 15 16
16 17 18 19 20 21 22	20 21 22 23 24 25 26	17 18 19 20 21 22 23	22 23 24 25 26 27 28	19 20 21 22 23 24 25	17 18 19 20 21 22 23
23 24 25 26 27 28 29	27 28 29 30 31	24 25 26 27 28 29 30	29 30 31	26 27 28 29 30	24 25 26 27 28 29 30
30 31					31

B (leap year)

JANUARY	FEBRUARY	MARCH	APRIL	MAY	JUNE
S M T W T F S	S M T W T F S	S M T W T F S	S M T W T F S	S M T W T F S	S M T W T F S
1 2 3 4 5 6 7	1 2 3 4	1 2 3	1 2 3 4 5 6 7	1 2 3 4 5	1 2
8 9 10 11 12 13 14	5 6 7 8 9 10 11	4 5 6 7 8 9 10	8 9 10 11 12 13 14	6 7 8 9 10 11 12	3 4 5 6 7 8 9
15 16 17 18 19 20 21	12 13 14 15 16 17 18	11 12 13 14 15 16 17	15 16 17 18 19 20 21	13 14 15 16 17 18 19	10 11 12 13 14 15 16
22 23 24 25 26 27 28	19 20 21 22 23 24 25	18 19 20 21 22 23 24	22 23 24 25 26 27 28	20 21 22 23 24 25 26	17 18 19 20 21 22 23
29 30 31	26 27 28 29	25 26 27 28 29 30 31	29 30	27 28 29 30 31	24 25 26 27 28 29 30

JULY	AUGUST	SEPTEMBER	OCTOBER	NOVEMBER	DECEMBER
S M T W T F S	S M T W T F S	S M T W T F S	S M T W T F S	S M T W T F S	S M T W T F S
1 2 3 4 5 6 7	1 2 3 4	1	1 2 3 4 5 6	1 2 3	1
8 9 10 11 12 13 14	5 6 7 8 9 10 11	2 3 4 5 6 7 8	7 8 9 10 11 12 13	4 5 6 7 8 9 10	2 3 4 5 6 7 8
15 16 17 18 19 20 21	12 13 14 15 16 17 18	9 10 11 12 13 14 15	14 15 16 17 18 19 20	11 12 13 14 15 16 17	9 10 11 12 13 14 15
22 23 24 25 26 27 28	19 20 21 22 23 24 25	16 17 18 19 20 21 22	21 22 23 24 25 26 27	18 19 20 21 22 23 24	16 17 18 19 20 21 22
29 30 31	26 27 28 29 30 31	23 24 25 26 27 28 29	28 29 30 31	25 26 27 28 29 30	23 24 25 26 27 28 29
		30			30 31

C

JANUARY	FEBRUARY	MARCH	APRIL	MAY	JUNE
S M T W T F S	S M T W T F S	S M T W T F S	S M T W T F S	S M T W T F S	S M T W T F S
1 2 3 4 5 6	1 2 3	1 2 3	1 2 3 4 5 6 7	1 2 3 4 5	1 2
7 8 9 10 11 12 13	4 5 6 7 8 9 10	4 5 6 7 8 9 10	8 9 10 11 12 13 14	6 7 8 9 10 11 12	3 4 5 6 7 8 9
14 15 16 17 18 19 20	11 12 13 14 15 16 17	11 12 13 14 15 16 17	15 16 17 18 19 20 21	13 14 15 16 17 18 19	10 11 12 13 14 15 16
21 22 23 24 25 26 27	18 19 20 21 22 23 24	18 19 20 21 22 23 24	22 23 24 25 26 27 28	20 21 22 23 24 25 26	17 18 19 20 21 22 23
28 29 30 31	25 26 27 28	25 26 27 28 29 30 31	29 30	27 28 29 30 31	24 25 26 27 28 29 30

JULY	AUGUST	SEPTEMBER	OCTOBER	NOVEMBER	DECEMBER
S M T W T F S	S M T W T F S	S M T W T F S	S M T W T F S	S M T W T F S	S M T W T F S
1 2 3 4 5 6 7	1 2 3 4	1	1 2 3 4 5 6	1 2 3	1
8 9 10 11 12 13 14	5 6 7 8 9 10 11	2 3 4 5 6 7 8	7 8 9 10 11 12 13	4 5 6 7 8 9 10	2 3 4 5 6 7 8
15 16 17 18 19 20 21	12 13 14 15 16 17 18	9 10 11 12 13 14 15	14 15 16 17 18 19 20	11 12 13 14 15 16 17	9 10 11 12 13 14 15
22 23 24 25 26 27 28	19 20 21 22 23 24 25	16 17 18 19 20 21 22	21 22 23 24 25 26 27	18 19 20 21 22 23 24	16 17 18 19 20 21 22
29 30 31	26 27 28 29 30 31	23 24 25 26 27 28 29	28 29 30 31	25 26 27 28 29 30	23 24 25 26 27 28 29
		30			30 31

D (leap year)

JANUARY	FEBRUARY	MARCH	APRIL	MAY	JUNE
S M T W T F S	S M T W T F S	S M T W T F S	S M T W T F S	S M T W T F S	S M T W T F S
1 2 3 4 5 6	1 2 3	1 2	1 2 3 4 5 6	1 2 3 4	1
7 8 9 10 11 12 13	4 5 6 7 8 9 10	3 4 5 6 7 8 9	7 8 9 10 11 12 13	5 6 7 8 9 10 11	2 3 4 5 6 7 8
14 15 16 17 18 19 20	11 12 13 14 15 16 17	10 11 12 13 14 15 16	14 15 16 17 18 19 20	12 13 14 15 16 17 18	9 10 11 12 13 14 15
21 22 23 24 25 26 27	18 19 20 21 22 23 24	17 18 19 20 21 22 23	21 22 23 24 25 26 27	19 20 21 22 23 24 25	16 17 18 19 20 21 22
28 29 30 31	25 26 27 28 29	24 25 26 27 28 29 30	28 29 30	26 27 28 29 30 31	23 24 25 26 27 28 29
		31			

JULY	AUGUST	SEPTEMBER	OCTOBER	NOVEMBER	DECEMBER
S M T W T F S	S M T W T F S	S M T W T F S	S M T W T F S	S M T W T F S	S M T W T F S
1 2 3 4 5 6	1 2 3	1 2 3 4 5 6 7	1 2 3 4 5	1 2	1 2 3 4 5 6 7
7 8 9 10 11 12 13	4 5 6 7 8 9 10	8 9 10 11 12 13 14	6 7 8 9 10 11 12	3 4 5 6 7 8 9	8 9 10 11 12 13 14
14 15 16 17 18 19 20	11 12 13 14 15 16 17	15 16 17 18 19 20 21	13 14 15 16 17 18 19	10 11 12 13 14 15 16	15 16 17 18 19 20 21
21 22 23 24 25 26 27	18 19 20 21 22 23 24	22 23 24 25 26 27 28	20 21 22 23 24 25 26	17 18 19 20 21 22 23	22 23 24 25 26 27 28
28 29 30 31	25 26 27 28 29 30 31	29 30	27 28 29 30 31	24 25 26 27 28 29 30	29 30 31

Time

E

JANUARY
```
S  M  T  W  T  F  S
      1  2  3  4  5
6  7  8  9 10 11 12
13 14 15 16 17 18 19
20 21 22 23 24 25 26
27 28 29 30 31
```

FEBRUARY
```
S  M  T  W  T  F  S
            1  2
3  4  5  6  7  8  9
10 11 12 13 14 15 16
17 18 19 20 21 22 23
24 25 26 27 28
```

MARCH
```
S  M  T  W  T  F  S
            1  2
3  4  5  6  7  8  9
10 11 12 13 14 15 16
17 18 19 20 21 22 23
24 25 26 27 28 29 30
```

APRIL
```
S  M  T  W  T  F  S
   1  2  3  4  5  6
7  8  9 10 11 12 13
14 15 16 17 18 19 20
21 22 23 24 25 26 27
28 29 30
```

MAY
```
S  M  T  W  T  F  S
         1  2  3  4
5  6  7  8  9 10 11
12 13 14 15 16 17 18
19 20 21 22 23 24 25
26 27 28 29 30 31
```

JUNE
```
S  M  T  W  T  F  S
                  1
2  3  4  5  6  7  8
9 10 11 12 13 14 15
16 17 18 19 20 21 22
23 24 25 26 27 28 29
30
```

JULY
```
S  M  T  W  T  F  S
      1  2  3  4  5  6
7  8  9 10 11 12 13
14 15 16 17 18 19 20
21 22 23 24 25 26 27
28 29 30 31
```

AUGUST
```
S  M  T  W  T  F  S
               1  2  3
4  5  6  7  8  9 10
11 12 13 14 15 16 17
18 19 20 21 22 23 24
25 26 27 28 29 30 31
```

SEPTEMBER
```
S  M  T  W  T  F  S
1  2  3  4  5  6  7
8  9 10 11 12 13 14
15 16 17 18 19 20 21
22 23 24 25 26 27 28
29 30
```

OCTOBER
```
S  M  T  W  T  F  S
         1  2  3  4  5
6  7  8  9 10 11 12
13 14 15 16 17 18 19
20 21 22 23 24 25 26
27 28 29 30 31
```

NOVEMBER
```
S  M  T  W  T  F  S
               1  2
3  4  5  6  7  8  9
10 11 12 13 14 15 16
17 18 19 20 21 22 23
24 25 26 27 28 29 30
```

DECEMBER
```
S  M  T  W  T  F  S
1  2  3  4  5  6  7
8  9 10 11 12 13 14
15 16 17 18 19 20 21
22 23 24 25 26 27 28
29 30 31
```

F (leap year)

JANUARY
```
S  M  T  W  T  F  S
      1  2  3  4  5
6  7  8  9 10 11 12
13 14 15 16 17 18 19
20 21 22 23 24 25 26
27 28 29 30 31
```

FEBRUARY
```
S  M  T  W  T  F  S
            1  2
3  4  5  6  7  8  9
10 11 12 13 14 15 16
17 18 19 20 21 22 23
24 25 26 27 28 29
```

MARCH
```
S  M  T  W  T  F  S
                  1
2  3  4  5  6  7  8
9 10 11 12 13 14 15
16 17 18 19 20 21 22
23 24 25 26 27 28 29
30 31
```

APRIL
```
S  M  T  W  T  F  S
      1  2  3  4  5
6  7  8  9 10 11 12
13 14 15 16 17 18 19
20 21 22 23 24 25 26
27 28 29 30
```

MAY
```
S  M  T  W  T  F  S
            1  2  3
4  5  6  7  8  9 10
11 12 13 14 15 16 17
18 19 20 21 22 23 24
25 26 27 28 29 30 31
```

JUNE
```
S  M  T  W  T  F  S
1  2  3  4  5  6  7
8  9 10 11 12 13 14
15 16 17 18 19 20 21
22 23 24 25 26 27 28
29 30
```

JULY
```
S  M  T  W  T  F  S
      1  2  3  4  5
6  7  8  9 10 11 12
13 14 15 16 17 18 19
20 21 22 23 24 25 26
27 28 29 30 31
```

AUGUST
```
S  M  T  W  T  F  S
            1  2
3  4  5  6  7  8  9
10 11 12 13 14 15 16
17 18 19 20 21 22 23
24 25 26 27 28 29 30
31
```

SEPTEMBER
```
S  M  T  W  T  F  S
      1  2  3  4  5  6
7  8  9 10 11 12 13
14 15 16 17 18 19 20
21 22 23 24 25 26 27
28 29 30
```

OCTOBER
```
S  M  T  W  T  F  S
            1  2  3  4
5  6  7  8  9 10 11
12 13 14 15 16 17 18
19 20 21 22 23 24 25
26 27 28 29 30 31
```

NOVEMBER
```
S  M  T  W  T  F  S
                  1
2  3  4  5  6  7  8
9 10 11 12 13 14 15
16 17 18 19 20 21 22
23 24 25 26 27 28 29
30
```

DECEMBER
```
S  M  T  W  T  F  S
      1  2  3  4  5  6
7  8  9 10 11 12 13
14 15 16 17 18 19 20
21 22 23 24 25 26 27
28 29 30 31
```

G

JANUARY
```
S  M  T  W  T  F  S
            1  2  3  4
5  6  7  8  9 10 11
12 13 14 15 16 17 18
19 20 21 22 23 24 25
26 27 28 29 30 31
```

FEBRUARY
```
S  M  T  W  T  F  S
                  1
2  3  4  5  6  7  8
9 10 11 12 13 14 15
16 17 18 19 20 21 22
23 24 25 26 27 28
```

MARCH
```
S  M  T  W  T  F  S
                  1
2  3  4  5  6  7  8
9 10 11 12 13 14 15
16 17 18 19 20 21 22
23 24 25 26 27 28 29
30 31
```

APRIL
```
S  M  T  W  T  F  S
      1  2  3  4  5
6  7  8  9 10 11 12
13 14 15 16 17 18 19
20 21 22 23 24 25 26
27 28 29 30
```

MAY
```
S  M  T  W  T  F  S
               1  2  3
4  5  6  7  8  9 10
11 12 13 14 15 16 17
18 19 20 21 22 23 24
25 26 27 28 29 30 31
```

JUNE
```
S  M  T  W  T  F  S
1  2  3  4  5  6  7
8  9 10 11 12 13 14
15 16 17 18 19 20 21
22 23 24 25 26 27 28
29 30
```

JULY
```
S  M  T  W  T  F  S
   1  2  3  4  5  6
6  7  8  9 10 11 12
13 14 15 16 17 18 19
20 21 22 23 24 25 26
27 28 29 30 31
```

AUGUST
```
S  M  T  W  T  F  S
               1  2
3  4  5  6  7  8  9
10 11 12 13 14 15 16
17 18 19 20 21 22 23
24 25 26 27 28 29 30
31
```

SEPTEMBER
```
S  M  T  W  T  F  S
   1  2  3  4  5  6
7  8  9 10 11 12 13
14 15 16 17 18 19 20
21 22 23 24 25 26 27
28 29 30
```

OCTOBER
```
S  M  T  W  T  F  S
         1  2  3  4
5  6  7  8  9 10 11
12 13 14 15 16 17 18
19 20 21 22 23 24 25
26 27 28 29 30 31
```

NOVEMBER
```
S  M  T  W  T  F  S
                  1
2  3  4  5  6  7  8
9 10 11 12 13 14 15
16 17 18 19 20 21 22
23 24 25 26 27 28 29
30
```

DECEMBER
```
S  M  T  W  T  F  S
      1  2  3  4  5  6
7  8  9 10 11 12 13
14 15 16 17 18 19 20
21 22 23 24 25 26 27
28 29 30 31
```

H (leap year)

JANUARY
```
S  M  T  W  T  F  S
            1  2  3  4
5  6  7  8  9 10 11
12 13 14 15 16 17 18
19 20 21 22 23 24 25
26 27 28 29 30 31
```

FEBRUARY
```
S  M  T  W  T  F  S
1  2  3  4  5  6  7
2  3  4  5  6  7  8
9 10 11 12 13 14 15
16 17 18 19 20 21 22
23 24 25 26 27 28 29
```

MARCH
```
S  M  T  W  T  F  S
1  2  3  4  5  6  7
8  9 10 11 12 13 14
15 16 17 18 19 20 21
22 23 24 25 26 27 28
29 30 31
```

APRIL
```
S  M  T  W  T  F  S
            1  2  3  4
5  6  7  8  9 10 11
12 13 14 15 16 17 18
19 20 21 22 23 24 25
26 27 28 29 30
```

MAY
```
S  M  T  W  T  F  S
                  1  2
3  4  5  6  7  8  9
10 11 12 13 14 15 16
17 18 19 20 21 22 23
24 25 26 27 28 29 30
31
```

JUNE
```
S  M  T  W  T  F  S
         1  2  3  4
7  8  9 10 11 12 13
14 15 16 17 18 19 20
21 22 23 24 25 26 27
28 29 30
```

JULY
```
S  M  T  W  T  F  S
      1  2  3  4
5  6  7  8  9 10 11
12 13 14 15 16 17 18
19 20 21 22 23 24 25
26 27 28 29 30 31
```

AUGUST
```
S  M  T  W  T  F  S
                  1
2  3  4  5  6  7  8
9 10 11 12 13 14 15
16 17 18 19 20 21 22
23 24 25 26 27 28 29
30 31
```

SEPTEMBER
```
S  M  T  W  T  F  S
      1  2  3  4  5  6
6  7  8  9 10 11 12
13 14 15 16 17 18 19
20 21 22 23 24 25 26
27 28 29 30
```

OCTOBER
```
S  M  T  W  T  F  S
            1  2  3
4  5  6  7  8  9 10
11 12 13 14 15 16 17
18 19 20 21 22 23 24
25 26 27 28 29 30 31
```

NOVEMBER
```
S  M  T  W  T  F  S
1  2  3  4  5  6  7
8  9 10 11 12 13 14
15 16 17 18 19 20 21
22 23 24 25 26 27 28
29 30
```

DECEMBER
```
S  M  T  W  T  F  S
      1  2  3  4  5
6  7  8  9 10 11 12
13 14 15 16 17 18 19
20 21 22 23 24 25 26
27 28 29 30 31
```

Time

I

JANUARY
```
S  M  T  W  T  F  S
         1  2  3
4  5  6  7  8  9 10
11 12 13 14 15 16 17
18 19 20 21 22 23 24
25 26 27 28 29 30 31
```

FEBRUARY
```
S  M  T  W  T  F  S
1  2  3  4  5  6  7
8  9 10 11 12 13 14
15 16 17 18 19 20 21
22 23 24 25 26 27 28
```

MARCH
```
S  M  T  W  T  F  S
1  2  3  4  5  6  7
8  9 10 11 12 13 14
15 16 17 18 19 20 21
22 23 24 25 26 27 28
29 30 31
```

APRIL
```
S  M  T  W  T  F  S
            1  2  3  4
5  6  7  8  9 10 11
12 13 14 15 16 17 18
19 20 21 22 23 24 25
26 27 28 29 30
```

MAY
```
S  M  T  W  T  F  S
               1  2
3  4  5  6  7  8  9
10 11 12 13 14 15 16
17 18 19 20 21 22 23
24 25 26 27 28 29 30
31
```

JUNE
```
S  M  T  W  T  F  S
1  2  3  4  5  6
7  8  9 10 11 12 13
14 15 16 17 18 19 20
21 22 23 24 25 26 27
28 29 30
```

JULY
```
S  M  T  W  T  F  S
         1  2  3  4
5  6  7  8  9 10 11
12 13 14 15 16 17 18
19 20 21 22 23 24 25
26 27 28 29 30 31
```

AUGUST
```
S  M  T  W  T  F  S
                  1
2  3  4  5  6  7  8
9 10 11 12 13 14 15
16 17 18 19 20 21 22
23 24 25 26 27 28 29
30 31
```

SEPTEMBER
```
S  M  T  W  T  F  S
      1  2  3  4  5
6  7  8  9 10 11 12
13 14 15 16 17 18 19
20 21 22 23 24 25 26
27 28 29 30
```

OCTOBER
```
S  M  T  W  T  F  S
            1  2  3
4  5  6  7  8  9 10
11 12 13 14 15 16 17
18 19 20 21 22 23 24
25 26 27 28 29 30 31
```

NOVEMBER
```
S  M  T  W  T  F  S
1  2  3  4  5  6  7
8  9 10 11 12 13 14
15 16 17 18 19 20 21
22 23 24 25 26 27 28
29 30
```

DECEMBER
```
S  M  T  W  T  F  S
            1  2  3  4  5
6  7  8  9 10 11 12
13 14 15 16 17 18 19
20 21 22 23 24 25 26
27 28 29 30 31
```

J (leap year)

JANUARY
```
S  M  T  W  T  F  S
            1  2  3
4  5  6  7  8  9 10
11 12 13 14 15 16 17
18 19 20 21 22 23 24
25 26 27 28 29 30 31
```

FEBRUARY
```
S  M  T  W  T  F  S
1  2  3  4  5  6  7
8  9 10 11 12 13 14
15 16 17 18 19 20 21
22 23 24 25 26 27 28
29
```

MARCH
```
S  M  T  W  T  F  S
   1  2  3  4  5  6
7  8  9 10 11 12 13
14 15 16 17 18 19 20
21 22 23 24 25 26 27
28 29 30 31
```

APRIL
```
S  M  T  W  T  F  S
            1  2  3
4  5  6  7  8  9 10
11 12 13 14 15 16 17
18 19 20 21 22 23 24
25 26 27 28 29 30
```

MAY
```
S  M  T  W  T  F  S
                  1
2  3  4  5  6  7  8
9 10 11 12 13 14 15
16 17 18 19 20 21 22
23 24 25 26 27 28 29
30 31
```

JUNE
```
S  M  T  W  T  F  S
      1  2  3  4  5
6  7  8  9 10 11 12
13 14 15 16 17 18 19
20 21 22 23 24 25 26
27 28 29 30
```

JULY
```
S  M  T  W  T  F  S
            1  2  3
4  5  6  7  8  9 10
11 12 13 14 15 16 17
18 19 20 21 22 23 24
25 26 27 28 29 30 31
```

AUGUST
```
S  M  T  W  T  F  S
1  2  3  4  5  6  7
8  9 10 11 12 13 14
15 16 17 18 19 20 21
22 23 24 25 26 27 28
29 30 31
```

SEPTEMBER
```
S  M  T  W  T  F  S
         1  2  3  4
5  6  7  8  9 10 11
12 13 14 15 16 17 18
19 20 21 22 23 24 25
26 27 28 29 30
```

OCTOBER
```
S  M  T  W  T  F  S
               1  2
3  4  5  6  7  8  9
10 11 12 13 14 15 16
17 18 19 20 21 22 23
24 25 26 27 28 29 30
31
```

NOVEMBER
```
S  M  T  W  T  F  S
1  2  3  4  5  6
7  8  9 10 11 12 13
14 15 16 17 18 19 20
21 22 23 24 25 26 27
28 29 30
```

DECEMBER
```
S  M  T  W  T  F  S
         1  2  3  4
5  6  7  8  9 10 11
12 13 14 15 16 17 18
19 20 21 22 23 24 25
26 27 28 29 30 31
```

K

JANUARY
```
S  M  T  W  T  F  S
                  1  2
3  4  5  6  7  8  9
10 11 12 13 14 15 16
17 18 19 20 21 22 23
24 25 26 27 28 29 30
31
```

FEBRUARY
```
S  M  T  W  T  F  S
      1  2  3  4  5  6
7  8  9 10 11 12 13
14 15 16 17 18 19 20
21 22 23 24 25 26 27
28
```

MARCH
```
S  M  T  W  T  F  S
      1  2  3  4  5  6
7  8  9 10 11 12 13
14 15 16 17 18 19 20
21 22 23 24 25 26 27
28 29 30 31
```

APRIL
```
S  M  T  W  T  F  S
            1  2  3
4  5  6  7  8  9 10
11 12 13 14 15 16 17
18 19 20 21 22 23 24
25 26 27 28 29 30
```

MAY
```
S  M  T  W  T  F  S
                  1
2  3  4  5  6  7  8
9 10 11 12 13 14 15
16 17 18 19 20 21 22
23 24 25 26 27 28 29
30 31
```

JUNE
```
S  M  T  W  T  F  S
      1  2  3  4  5
6  7  8  9 10 11 12
13 14 15 16 17 18 19
20 21 22 23 24 25 26
27 28 29 30
```

JULY
```
S  M  T  W  T  F  S
            1  2  3
4  5  6  7  8  9 10
11 12 13 14 15 16 17
18 19 20 21 22 23 24
25 26 27 28 29 30 31
```

AUGUST
```
S  M  T  W  T  F  S
1  2  3  4  5  6  7
8  9 10 11 12 13 14
15 16 17 18 19 20 21
22 23 24 25 26 27 28
29 30 31
```

SEPTEMBER
```
S  M  T  W  T  F  S
         1  2  3  4
5  6  7  8  9 10 11
12 13 14 15 16 17 18
19 20 21 22 23 24 25
26 27 28 29 30
```

OCTOBER
```
S  M  T  W  T  F  S
               1  2
3  4  5  6  7  8  9
10 11 12 13 14 15 16
17 18 19 20 21 22 23
24 25 26 27 28 29 30
31
```

NOVEMBER
```
S  M  T  W  T  F  S
1  2  3  4  5  6
7  8  9 10 11 12 13
14 15 16 17 18 19 20
21 22 23 24 25 26 27
28 29 30
```

DECEMBER
```
S  M  T  W  T  F  S
         1  2  3  4
5  6  7  8  9 10 11
12 13 14 15 16 17 18
19 20 21 22 23 24 25
26 27 28 29 30 31
```

L (leap year)

JANUARY
```
S  M  T  W  T  F  S
                  1  2
3  4  5  6  7  8  9
10 11 12 13 14 15 16
17 18 19 20 21 22 23
24 25 26 27 28 29 30
31
```

FEBRUARY
```
S  M  T  W  T  F  S
      1  2  3  4  5  6
7  8  9 10 11 12 13
14 15 16 17 18 19 20
21 22 23 24 25 26 27
28 29
```

MARCH
```
S  M  T  W  T  F  S
         1  2  3  4  5
6  7  8  9 10 11 12
13 14 15 16 17 18 19
20 21 22 23 24 25 26
27 28 29 30 31
```

APRIL
```
S  M  T  W  T  F  S
               1  2
3  4  5  6  7  8  9
10 11 12 13 14 15 16
17 18 19 20 21 22 23
24 25 26 27 28 29 30
```

MAY
```
S  M  T  W  T  F  S
1  2  3  4  5  6  7
8  9 10 11 12 13 14
15 16 17 18 19 20 21
22 23 24 25 26 27 28
29 30 31
```

JUNE
```
S  M  T  W  T  F  S
         1  2  3  4
5  6  7  8  9 10 11
12 13 14 15 16 17 18
19 20 21 22 23 24 25
26 27 28 29 30
```

JULY
```
S  M  T  W  T  F  S
               1  2
3  4  5  6  7  8  9
10 11 12 13 14 15 16
17 18 19 20 21 22 23
24 25 26 27 28 29 30
31
```

AUGUST
```
S  M  T  W  T  F  S
      1  2  3  4  5  6
7  8  9 10 11 12 13
14 15 16 17 18 19 20
21 22 23 24 25 26 27
28 29 30 31
```

SEPTEMBER
```
S  M  T  W  T  F  S
            1  2  3
4  5  6  7  8  9 10
11 12 13 14 15 16 17
18 19 20 21 22 23 24
25 26 27 28 29 30
```

OCTOBER
```
S  M  T  W  T  F  S
                  1
2  3  4  5  6  7  8
9 10 11 12 13 14 15
16 17 18 19 20 21 22
23 24 25 26 27 28 29
30 31
```

NOVEMBER
```
S  M  T  W  T  F  S
      1  2  3  4  5
6  7  8  9 10 11 12
13 14 15 16 17 18 19
20 21 22 23 24 25 26
27 28 29 30
```

DECEMBER
```
S  M  T  W  T  F  S
            1  2  3
4  5  6  7  8  9 10
11 12 13 14 15 16 17
18 19 20 21 22 23 24
25 26 27 28 29 30 31
```

Time

M

JANUARY	FEBRUARY	MARCH	APRIL	MAY	JUNE
S M T W T F S	S M T W T F S	S M T W T F S	S M T W T F S	S M T W T F S	S M T W T F S
1	1 2 3 4 5	1 2 3 4 5	1 2	1 2 3 4 5 6 7	1 2 3 4
2 3 4 5 6 7 8	6 7 8 9 10 11 12	6 7 8 9 10 11 12	3 4 5 6 7 8 9	8 9 10 11 12 13 14	5 6 7 8 9 10 11
9 10 11 12 13 14 15	13 14 15 16 17 18 19	13 14 15 16 17 18 19	10 11 12 13 14 15 16	15 16 17 18 19 20 21	12 13 14 15 16 17 18
16 17 18 19 20 21 22	20 21 22 23 24 25 26	20 21 22 23 24 25 26	17 18 19 20 21 22 23	22 23 24 25 26 27 28	19 20 21 22 23 24 25
23 24 25 26 27 28 29	27 28	27 28 29 30 31	24 25 26 27 28 29 30	29 30 31	26 27 28 29 30
30 31					

JULY	AUGUST	SEPTEMBER	OCTOBER	NOVEMBER	DECEMBER
S M T W T F S	S M T W T F S	S M T W T F S	S M T W T F S	S M T W T F S	S M T W T F S
1 2	1 2 3 4 5 6	1 2 3	1 2 3 4 5 6 7	1 2 3 4 5	1 2 3
3 4 5 6 7 8 9	7 8 9 10 11 12 13	4 5 6 7 8 9 10	8 9 10 11 12 13 14	6 7 8 9 10 11 12	4 5 6 7 8 9 10
10 11 12 13 14 15 16	14 15 16 17 18 19 20	11 12 13 14 15 16 17	15 16 17 18 19 20 21	13 14 15 16 17 18 19	11 12 13 14 15 16 17
17 18 19 20 21 22 23	21 22 23 24 25 26 27	18 19 20 21 22 23 24	22 23 24 25 26 27 28	20 21 22 23 24 25 26	18 19 20 21 22 23 24
24 25 26 27 28 29 30	28 29 30 31	25 26 27 28 29 30	29 30 31	27 28 29 30	25 26 27 28 29 30 31
31					

N (leap year)

JANUARY	FEBRUARY	MARCH	APRIL	MAY	JUNE
S M T W T F S	S M T W T F S	S M T W T F S	S M T W T F S	S M T W T F S	S M T W T F S
1	1 2 3 4 5	1 2 3 4	1	1 2 3 4 5 6	1 2 3
2 3 4 5 6 7 8	6 7 8 9 10 11 12	5 6 7 8 9 10 11	2 3 4 5 6 7 8	7 8 9 10 11 12 13	4 5 6 7 8 9 10
9 10 11 12 13 14 15	13 14 15 16 17 18 19	12 13 14 15 16 17 18	9 10 11 12 13 14 15	14 15 16 17 18 19 20	11 12 13 14 15 16 17
16 17 18 19 20 21 22	20 21 22 23 24 25 26	19 20 21 22 23 24 25	16 17 18 19 20 21 22	21 22 23 24 25 26 27	18 19 20 21 22 23 24
23 24 25 26 27 28 29	27 28 29	26 27 28 29 30 31	23 24 25 26 27 28 29	28 29 30 31	25 26 27 28 29 30
30 31			30		

JULY	AUGUST	SEPTEMBER	OCTOBER	NOVEMBER	DECEMBER
S M T W T F S	S M T W T F S	S M T W T F S	S M T W T F S	S M T W T F S	S M T W T F S
1	1 2 3 4 5	1 2	1 2 3 4 5 6 7	1 2 3 4	1 2
2 3 4 5 6 7 8	6 7 8 9 10 11 12	3 4 5 6 7 8 9	8 9 10 11 12 13 14	5 6 7 8 9 10 11	3 4 5 6 7 8 9
9 10 11 12 13 14 15	13 14 15 16 17 18 19	10 11 12 13 14 15 16	15 16 17 18 19 20 21	12 13 14 15 16 17 18	10 11 12 13 14 15 16
16 17 18 19 20 21 22	20 21 22 23 24 25 26	17 18 19 20 21 22 23	22 23 24 25 26 27 28	19 20 21 22 23 24 25	17 18 19 20 21 22 23
23 24 25 26 27 28 29	27 28 29 30 31	24 25 26 27 28 29 30	29 30 31	26 27 28 29 30	24 25 26 27 28 29 30
30 31					31

International time differences

The time zones of the world are conventionally measured from longitude 0° at Greenwich Observatory (Greenwich Mean Time, GMT).

Each 15° of longitude east of this point is one hour ahead of GMT (eg when it is 2pm in London it is 3pm or later in time zones to the east). Hours ahead of GMT are shown by a plus sign, eg +3, +4/8.

Each 15° west of this point is one hour behind GMT (eg 2pm in London would be 1pm or earlier in time zones to the west). Hours behind GMT are shown by a minus sign, eg –3, –4/8.

Some countries adopt time zones that vary from standard time. Also, during the summer, several countries adopt Daylight SavingTime (or SummerTime), which is one hour ahead of the times shown below.

Afghanistan	+4½	Djibouti	+3	Latvia	+2	St Vincent and the	
Albania	+1	Dominica	–4	Lebanon	+2	Grenadines	–4
Algeria	+1	Dominican		Lesotho	+2	Samoa	–11
Andorra	+1	Republic	–4	Liberia	0	San Marino	+1
Angola	+1	EastTimor	+8	Libya	+1	SãoTomé and	
Antigua and		Ecuador	–5	Liechtenstein	+1	Príncipe	0
Barbuda	–4	Egypt	+2	Lithuania	+2	Saudi Arabia	+3
Argentina	–3	El Salvador	–6	Luxembourg	+1	Senegal	0
Armenia	+4	Equatorial		Macedonia	+1	Serbia and	
Australia	+8/10½	Guinea	+1	Madagascar	+3	Montenegro	+1
Austria	+1	Eritrea	+3	Malawi	+2	Seychelles	+4
Azerbaijan	+4	Estonia	+2	Malaysia	+8	Sierra Leone	0
Bahamas,The	–5	Ethiopia	+3	Maldives	+5	Singapore	+8
Bahrain	+3	Falkland Is	–4	Mali	0	Slovakia	+1
Bangladesh	+6	Fiji	+12	Malta	+1	Slovenia	+1
Barbados	–4	Finland	+2	Marshall Is	+12	Solomon Is	+11
Belarus	+2	France	+1	Mauritania	0	Somalia	+3
Belgium	+1	Gabon	+1	Mauritius	+4	South Africa	+2
Belize	–6	Gambia,The	0	Mexico	–6/8	Spain	+1
Benin	+1	Georgia	+4	Micronesia,		Sri Lanka	+5½
Bermuda	–4	Germany	+1	Federated		Sudan,The	+2
Bhutan	+6	Ghana	0	States of	+10/11	Suriname	–3
Bolivia	–4	Gibraltar	+1	Moldova	+2	Swaziland	+2
Bosnia-		Greece	+2	Monaco	+1	Sweden	+1
Herzegovina	+1	Greenland	–3	Mongolia	+8	Switzerland	+1
Botswana	+2	Grenada	–4	Morocco	0	Syria	+2
Brazil	–2/5	Guatemala	–6	Mozambique	+2	Taiwan	+8
Brunei	+8	Guinea	0	Myanmar (Burma)	+6½	Tajikistan	+5
Bulgaria	+2	Guinea-Bissau	0	Namibia	+1	Tanzania	+3
Burkina Faso	0	Guyana	–4	Nauru	+12	Thailand	+7
Burundi	+2	Haiti	–5	Nepal	+5¾	Togo	0
Cambodia	+7	Honduras	–6	Netherlands	+1	Tonga	+13
Cameroon	+1	Hong Kong	+8	New Zealand	+12	Trinidad and	
Canada	–3½/8	Hungary	+1	Nicaragua	–6	Tobago	–4
CapeVerde	–1	Iceland	0	Niger	+1	Tunisia	+1
Central African		India	+5½	Nigeria	+1	Turkey	+2
Republic	+1	Indonesia	+7/9	Norway	+1	Turkmenistan	+5
Chad	+1	Iran	+3½	Oman	+4	Tuvalu	+12
Chile	–4	Iraq	+3	Pakistan	+5	Uganda	+3
China	+8	Ireland	0	Panama	–5	Ukraine	+2
Colombia	–5	Israel	+2	Papua New		United Arab	
Comoros	+3	Italy	+1	Guinea	+10	Emirates	+4
Congo	+1	Jamaica	–5	Paraguay	–4	UK	0
Congo,		Japan	+9	Peru	–5	Uruguay	–3
Democratic		Jordan	+2	Philippines	+8	USA	–5/10
Republic of	+1/2	Kazakhstan	+4/6	Poland	+1	Uzbekistan	+5
Costa Rica	–6	Kenya	+3	Portugal	0	Vanuatu	+11
Côte d'Ivoire	0	Kiribati	+12	Qatar	+3	Vatican City	+1
Croatia	+1	Korea, North	+9	Romania	+2	Venezuela	–4
Cuba	–5	Korea, South	+9	Russia	+2/12	Vietnam	+7
Cyprus	+2	Kuwait	+3	Rwanda	+2	Yemen	+3
Czech Republic	+1	Kyrgyzstan	+5	St Kitts and Nevis	–4	Zambia	+2
Denmark	+1	Laos	+7	St Lucia	–4	Zimbabwe	+2

Time

Year equivalents

Jewish[1] (AM)

5756	(25 Sep 1995–13 Sep 1996)
5757	(14 Sep 1996–1 Oct 1997)
5758	(2 Oct 1997–20 Sep 1998)
5759	(21 Sep 1998–10 Sep 1999)
5760	(11 Sep 1999–29 Sep 2000)
5761	(30 Sep 2000–17 Sep 2001)
5762	(18 Sep 2001–6 Sep 2002)
5763	(7 Sep 2002–26 Sep 2003)
5764	(27 Sep 2003–15 Sep 2004)
5765	(16 Sep 2004–3 Oct 2005)
5766	(4 Oct 2005–22 Sep 2006)
5767	(23 Sep 2006–12 Sep 2007)
5768	(13 Sep 2007–29 Sep 2008)
5769	(30 Sep 2008–18 Sep 2009)
5770	(19 Sep 2009–8 Sep 2010)
5771	(9 Sep 2010–28 Sep 2011)
5772	(29 Sep 2011–16 Sep 2012)
5773	(17 Sep 2012–4 Sep 2013)
5774	(5 Sep 2013–24 Sep 2014)
5775	(25 Sep 2014–13 Sep 2015)
5776	(14 Sep 2015–2 Oct 2016)
5777	(3 Oct 2016–20 Sep 2017)
5778	(21 Sep 2017–9 Sep 2018)
5779	(10 Sep 2018–29 Sep 2019)
5780	(30 Sep 2019–18 Sep 2020)

Islamic[2] (H)

1416	(31 May 1995–18 May 1996)
1417	(19 May 1996–8 May 1997)
1418	(9 May 1997–27 Apr 1998)
1419	(28 Apr 1998–16 Apr 1999)
1420	(17 Apr 1999–5 Apr 2000)
1421	(6 Apr 2000–25 Mar 2001)
1422	(26 Mar 2001–14 Mar 2002)
1423	(15 Mar 2002–3 Mar 2003)
1424	(4 Mar 2003–21 Feb 2004)
1425	(22 Feb 2004–9 Feb 2005)
1426	(10 Feb 2005–30 Jan 2006)
1427	(31 Jan 2006–20 Jan 2007)
1428	(21 Jan 2007–9 Jan 2008)
1429	(10 Jan 2008–28 Dec 2008)
1430	(29 Dec 2008–17 Dec 2009)
1431	(18 Dec 2009–6 Dec 2010)
1432	(7 Dec 2010–26 Nov 2011)
1433	(27 Nov 2011–14 Nov 2012)
1434	(15 Nov 2012–4 Nov 2013)
1435	(5 Nov 2013–24 Oct 2014)
1436	(25 Oct 2014–13 Oct 2015)
1437	(14 Oct 2015–1 Oct 2016)
1438	(2 Oct 2016–21 Sep 2017)
1439	(22 Sep 2017–10 Sep 2018)
1440	(11 Sep 2018–31 Aug 2019)
1441	(1 Sep 2019–19 Aug 2020)

Hindu[3] (SE)

1917	(22 Mar 1995–20 Mar 1996)
1918	(21 Mar 1996–21 Mar 1997)
1919	(22 Mar 1997–21 Mar 1998)
1920	(22 Mar 1998–21 Mar 1999)
1921	(22 Mar 1999–20 Mar 2000)
1922	(21 Mar 2000–21 Mar 2001)
1923	(22 Mar 2001–21 Mar 2002)
1924	(22 Mar 2002–21 Mar 2003)
1925	(22 Mar 2003–20 Mar 2004)
1926	(21 Mar 2004–21 Mar 2005)
1927	(22 Mar 2005–21 Mar 2006)
1928	(22 Mar 2006–21 Mar 2007)
1929	(22 Mar 2007–20 Mar 2008)
1930	(21 Mar 2008–21 Mar 2009)
1931	(22 Mar 2009–21 Mar 2010)
1932	(22 Mar 2010–21 Mar 2011)
1933	(22 Mar 2011–20 Mar 2012)
1934	(21 Mar 2012–21 Mar 2013)
1935	(22 Mar 2013–21 Mar 2014)
1936	(22 Mar 2014–21 Mar 2015)
1937	(22 Mar 2015–20 Mar 2016)
1938	(21 Mar 2016–21 Mar 2017)
1939	(22 Mar 2017–21 Mar 2018)
1940	(22 Mar 2018–21 Mar 2019)
1941	(22 Mar 2019–20 Mar 2020)

Hindu[4] (VE)

2052	(14 Mar 1995–13 Mar 1996)
2053	(14 Mar 1996–13 Mar 1997)
2054	(14 Mar 1997–13 Mar 1998)
2055	(14 Mar 1998–13 Mar 1999)
2056	(14 Mar 1999–13 Mar 2000)
2057	(14 Mar 2000–13 Mar 2001)
2058	(14 Mar 2001–13 Mar 2002)
2059	(14 Mar 2002–13 Mar 2003)
2060	(14 Mar 2003–13 Mar 2004)
2061	(14 Mar 2004–13 Mar 2005)
2062	(14 Mar 2005–13 Mar 2006)
2063	(14 Mar 2006–13 Mar 2007)
2064	(14 Mar 2007–13 Mar 2008)
2065	(14 Mar 2008–13 Mar 2009)
2066	(14 Mar 2009–13 Mar 2010)
2067	(14 Mar 2010–13 Mar 2011)
2068	(14 Mar 2011–13 Mar 2012)
2069	(14 Mar 2012–13 Mar 2013)
2070	(14 Mar 2013–13 Mar 2014)
2071	(14 Mar 2014–13 Mar 2015)
2072	(14 Mar 2015–13 Mar 2016)
2073	(14 Mar 2016–13 Mar 2017)
2074	(14 Mar 2017–13 Mar 2018)
2075	(14 Mar 2018–13 Mar 2019)
2076	(14 Mar 2019–13 Mar 2020)

Gregorian equivalents are given in parentheses and are AD (= Anno Domini).

[1] Calculated from 3761BC, said to be the year of the creation of the world. AM = Anno Mundi.

[2] Calculated from AD622, the year in which the Prophet went from Mecca to Medina. H = Hegira.

[3] Calculated from AD78, the beginning of the Saka era (SE), used alongside Gregorian dates in Government of India publications since 22 Mar 1957.

[4] Calculated from 58BC, the beginning of the Vikrama era (VE). Other important Hindu eras include: Kalacuri era (AD248), Gupta era (AD320) and Harsa era (AD606).

The seasons

N Hemisphere	S Hemisphere	Duration
Spring	Autumn	From vernal/autumnal equinox (c.21 Mar) to summer/winter solstice (c.21 Jun)
Summer	Winter	From summer/winter solstice (c.21 Jun) to autumnal/spring equinox (c.23 Sep)
Autumn	Spring	From autumnal/spring equinox (c.23 Sep) to winter/summer solstice (c.21 Dec)
Winter	Summer	From winter/summer solstice (c.21 Dec) to vernal/autumnal equinox (c.21 Mar)

Months (Associations of gems and flowers)

In many Western countries, the months are traditionally associated with gemstones and flowers. There is considerable variation between countries. The following combinations are widely recognized in North America and the UK.

Month	Gemstone	Flower
January	Garnet	Carnation, Snowdrop
February	Amethyst	Primrose, Violet
March	Aquamarine, Bloodstone	Jonquil, Violet
April	Diamond	Daisy, Sweet Pea
May	Emerald	Hawthorn, Lily of the Valley
June	Alexandrite, Moonstone, Pearl	Honeysuckle, Rose
July	Ruby	Larkspur, Water Lily
August	Peridot, Sardonyx	Gladiolus, Poppy
September	Sapphire	Aster, Morning Glory
October	Opal, Tourmaline	Calendula, Cosmos
November	Topaz	Chrysanthemum
December	Turquoise, Zircon	Holly, Narcissus, Poinsettia

Wedding anniversaries

In many Western countries, different wedding anniversaries have become associated with gifts of different materials. There is some variation between countries.

1st	Cotton, Paper	6th	Sugar	11th	Steel	20th	China	45th	Sapphire
2nd	Paper, Cotton	7th	Copper, Wool	12th	Silk, Linen	25th	Silver	50th	Gold
3rd	Leather	8th	Bronze, Pottery	13th	Lace	30th	Pearl	55th	Emerald
4th	Fruit, Flowers	9th	Pottery, Willow	14th	Ivory	35th	Coral	60th	Diamond
5th	Wood	10th	Tin	15th	Crystal	40th	Ruby	70th	Platinum

Chinese animal years and times 1960–2019

Chinese	English	Years					Time of day (hours)
Shu	Rat	1960	1972	1984	1996	2008	2300–0100
Niu	Ox	1961	1973	1985	1997	2009	0100–0300
Hu	Tiger	1962	1974	1986	1998	2010	0300–0500
Tu	Hare	1963	1975	1987	1999	2011	0500–0700
Long	Dragon	1964	1976	1988	2000	2012	0700–0900
She	Serpent	1965	1977	1989	2001	2013	0900–1100
Ma	Horse	1966	1978	1990	2002	2014	1100–1300
Yang	Sheep	1967	1979	1991	2003	2015	1300–1500
Hou	Monkey	1968	1980	1992	2004	2016	1500–1700
Ji	Cock	1969	1981	1993	2005	2017	1700–1900
Gou	Dog	1970	1982	1994	2006	2018	1900–2100
Zhu	Boar	1971	1983	1995	2007	2019	2100–2300

Time

Time

National holidays

The first part of each listing gives the holidays that occur on fixed dates (though it should be noted that holidays often vary according to local circumstances and the day of the week on which they fall). Most dates are accompanied by an indication of the purpose of the day, eg Independence = Independence Day; dates which have no gloss are either fixed dates within the Christian calendar (for which see below) or bank holidays.

The second part of the listing gives holidays that vary, usually depending on religious factors. The most common of these are given in abbreviated form (see list below).

A number in brackets such as (Independence) (2) refers to the number of days devoted to the holiday. The listings do not include holidays that affect only certain parts of a country, half-day holidays, or Sundays.

National holidays are subject to change.

The following abbreviations are used for variable religious feast-days:

A	Ascension Thursday
Ad	Id-ul-Adha (also found with other spellings — especially Eid-ul-Adha; various names relating to this occasion are used in different countries, such as Tabaski, Id el-Kebir, Hari Raja Haji)
Ar	Arafa
As	Ashora (found with various spellings)
C	Carnival (immediately before Christian Lent, unless specified)
CC	Corpus Christi
D	Diwali, Deepavali
EM	Easter Monday
ER	End of Ramadan (known generally as Id/Eid-ul-Fitr, but various names relating to this occasion are used in different countries, such as Karite, Hari Raja Puasa)
ES	Easter Sunday
GF	Good Friday
HS	Holy Saturday
HT	Holy Thursday
NY	New Year
PB	Prophet's Birthday (known generally as Maul-id-al-Nabi in various forms and spellings)
R	First day of Ramadan
WM	Whit Monday

The following fixed dates are shown without gloss:

Jan 1	New Year's Day	Nov 1	All Saints' Day
Jan 6	Epiphany	Nov 2	All Souls' Day
Mar 21	Novrus (Persian New Year; various spellings)	Dec 8	Immaculate Conception
		Dec 24	Christmas Eve
May 1	Labour Day (often known by a different name, such as Workers' Day)	Dec 25	Christmas Day
		Dec 26	Boxing Day/St Stephen's Day
Aug 15	Assumption of Our Lady	Dec 31	New Year's Eve

Afghanistan Mar 21, Apr 28 (Victory of the Muslim Nation), May 1, 4 (Remembrance for Martyrs and Disabled), Aug 19 (Independence); Ad (3), Ar, As, ER (3), NY (Hindu), PB, R

Albania Jan 1, Mar 21, May 1, Nov 28 (Independence), 29 (Liberation), Dec 25; Ad, ER, ES, NY (Albanian), Orthodox Easter (Apr/May)

Algeria Jan 1, May 1, Jun 19 (Revolutionary Readjustment), Jul 5 (Independence), Nov 1 (Revolution); Ad (2), As, ER (2), NY (Muslim), PB

Andorra Jan 1, 6, Mar 14 (Constitution), May 1, Jun 24 (People's Festival), Aug 15, Sep 8 (Our Lady of Meritxell), Nov 1, Dec 8, 21 (St Thomas), 25, 26; EM, GF, WM

Angola Jan 1, 4 (Martyrs of the Colonial Repression), Feb 4 (Beginning of the Armed Struggle), Mar 8 (Women), May 1, Jun 1 (Children), Sep 17 (Nation's Founder/National Hero), Nov 2, 11 (Independence), Dec 25

Antigua and Barbuda Jan 1, Nov 1 (Independence), Dec 25, 26; EM, GF, WM, Labour (1st Mon in May), Emancipation (1st Mon in Aug) (2)

Argentina Jan 1, Apr 2 (Malvinas), May 1, 25 (National), Jun 20 (Flag), Jul 9 (Independence), Aug 17 (Death of General San Martín), Oct 12 (Americas Discovery), Dec 8, 25; GF, HT

Armenia Jan 1, 6 (Armenian Christmas), Apr 24 (Day of Remembrance of the Victims of the Genocide), May 28 (Declaration of the First Armenian Republic, 1918), Sep 21 (Independence), Dec 7 (Day of Remembrance of the Victims of the Earthquake); EM, ES, GF, HS

Australia Jan 1, 26 (Australia), Apr 25 (Anzac), Dec 25, 26; Queen's Birthday (Jun, *except Western Australia*, Sept/Oct), EM, GF, HS; *additional days vary between states*

Austria Jan 1, 6, May 1, Aug 15, Oct 26 (National), Nov 1, Dec 8, 25, 26; A, CC, EM, WM

Azerbaijan Jan 1, 20 (Martyrs), 8 Mar (Women), May 9 (Victory), 28 (Republic), June 15 (National Salvation), 26 (Army and Navy), Oct 18 (Independence), Nov 12 (Constitution), 17 (National Revival), Dec 31 (Azerbaijani Solidarity Worldwide); Ad, ER, NY (Muslim) (2)

Bahamas,The Jan 1, Jul 10 (Independence), Oct 12 (Discovery), Dec 25, 26; EM, GF, WM; Labour (1st Mon in Jun), Emancipation (1st Fri in Aug)

Bahrain Jan 1, Dec 16 (National); Ad (3), As, ER (3), NY (Muslim), PB

Bangladesh Feb 21 (Shaheed Dibash/International Mother Language), Mar 26 (Independence/National), May 1, Nov 7 (National Revolution and Solidarity), Dec 16 (Victory), 25; Ad (3), As, Buddha Purnima (Apr/May), Durgapuja (Jijaya Dashami), ER (3), Jamatul Wida, Janmashtami, NY (Bengali), PB, Shab-e-Barat, Shab-e-Qadr

Barbados Jan 1, 21 (Errol Barrow), Apr 28 (National Heroes), May 1, Aug 1 (Emancipation), Dec 1 (Independence), Dec 25, 26; EM, GF, WM, Kadooment (Aug)

Belarus Jan 1, 7 (Orthodox Christmas), Mar 8 (Women), May 1, 6 (Memorial/Radounitsa), 9 (Victory), Jul 3 (Independence), Nov 7(October Revolution), Dec 25; ES, Orthodox Easter Sunday

Belgium Jan 1, May 1, Jul 21 (Independence), Aug 15, Nov 1, 11 (Armistice), Dec 25; A, EM, ES, WM; *also community holidays* (Jul 11 Flemish, Sep 27 French, Nov 15 German)

Belize Jan 1, Mar 9 (Baron Bliss), May 1, 24 (Commonwealth), Sep 10 (St George's Caye), 21 (Independence), Oct 12 (Columbus), Nov 19 (Garifuna Settlement), Dec 25, 26; EM, GF, HS

Benin Jan 1, 10 (Traditional religions), May 1, Aug 1 (National), 15, Nov 1, Dec 25; A, Ad, EM, WM

Bhutan May 2 (Birthday of Jigme Dorji Wangchuk), Jun 2 (Coronation of Fourth Hereditary King), Jul 21 (First Sermon of Lord Buddha, Death of Jigme Dorji Wangchuk), Nov 11–13 (Birthday of HM Jigme Singye Wangchuk), Dec 17 (National)

Bolivia Jan 1, May 1, Aug 6 (Independence), Nov 2, Dec 25; C, CC, GF

Bosnia-Herzegovina Jan 9 (Republic), Mar 1 (Independence), May 1, Nov 25 (Republic)

Botswana Jan 1, 2, May 1, Jul1 (Sir Seretse Khama), Sep 30 (Botswana), Dec 25, 26; A, EM, GF, HS, President's Day (Jul); Jul, Oct Public Holidays

Brazil Jan 1, Apr 21 (Tiradentes), May 1, Sep 7 (Independence), Oct 12 (Our Lady of Aparecida), Nov 2, 15 (Proclamation of the Republic), Dec 25; C (5), CC, GF; *much local variation*

Brunei Jan 1, Feb 23 (National), May 31 (Royal Brunei Armed Forces), Jul 15 (Sultan's Birthday), Dec 25; Ad, ER (2), Isra' Me'raj, NY (Chinese), NY (Muslim), PB, R, Revelation of the Koran

Bulgaria Jan 1, Mar 3 (National), May 1, 24 (Slavonic Script and Bulgarian Culture), Sep 6 (Unification), 22 (Independence), Dec 24, 25, 26; Orthodox Easter (Apr/May)

Burkina Faso Jan 1, 3 (1966 Revolution), Mar 8 (Women), May 1, Aug 5 (Independence), 15, Nov 1, Dec 11 (National), 25; A, Ad, EM, ER, PB

Burma ▶ **Myanmar**

Burundi Jan 1, May 1, Jul 1 (Independence), Aug 15, Sep 18 (Victory of Uprona), Nov 1, Dec 25; A

Cambodia Jan 1, 7 (Victory over Genocide), Mar 8 (Women), Apr 3 (Culture), May 1, Jun 1 (Children), 18 (Queen's Birthday), Sep 24 (Constitution and Coronation), Oct 23 (Paris Peace Agreement), 30 (King's Birthday) (3), Nov 9 (Independence), Dec 10 (Human Rights); Cambodian New Year (Apr) (3), Pchum Ben (Sep) (3), Royal Ploughing Ceremony (May), Visakha Bochea (May), Water/Moon Festival (Nov) (3)

Cameroon Jan 1, Feb 11 (Youth), May 1, 20 (National), Aug 15, Dec 25; A, Ad, ER, GF

Canada Jan 1, Jul 1 (Canada), Nov 11 (Remembrance), Dec 25, 26; EM, GF, Labour (1st Mon in Sep), Thanksgiving (2nd Mon in Oct), Victoria (Mon preceding May 25)

Cape Verde Jan 1, 13 (Democracy and Freedom), 20 (National Heroes), May 1, Jul 5 (Independence), Aug 15, Sep 12 (National), Nov 1, Dec 25; ES, GF, Ash Wednesday

Central African Republic Jan 1, Mar 29 (Death of President Boganda), May 1, Jun 1 (Mothers), Aug 13 (Independence), 15, Sep 1 (Arrival of the Military Committee for National Recovery), Nov 1, Dec 1 (Republic), 25; A, EM, WM

Chad Jan 1, May 1, 25 (OAU Foundation), Aug 11 (Independence), Nov 1, 28 (Republic), Dec 25; Ad, EM, ES, ER

Chile Jan 1, May 1, 21 (Navy), Aug 15, Sep 18 (Independence), 19 (Armed Forces), Oct 12 (Americas), Dec 8, 25, 26; CC, GF, EM, Aug public holiday, May public holiday

China Jan 1, May 1, Oct 1 (National) (2); Spring Festival (4) (Jan/Feb)

Colombia Jan 1, 6, Mar 19 (St Joseph), May 1, Jun 29 (Sts Peter and Paul), Jul 20 (Independence), Aug 7 (Battle of Boyacá), 15, Oct 12 (Columbus), Nov 1, 11 (Independence of Cartagena), Dec 8, 25; A, CC, GF, HT, Sacred Heart (Jun)

Comoros May 9 (Islamic New Year), 18 (Ashoura), Jul 6 (Independence), 18 (Mouloud/Prophet's Birthday), Nov 17 (President Abdallah's Assassination), 28 (Leilat al-Meiraj/Ascension of the Prophet); Ad, ER, R

Congo Jan 1, Mar 18 (Day of the Supreme Sacrifice), May 1, Jul 31 (Revolution), Aug 13–15 (The Three Glorious Days), Nov 1 (Day of the Dead), Dec 25 (Children), 31 (Foundation of the Party and People's Republic)

Congo, Democratic Republic of Jan 1, 4 (Martyrs of Independence), May 1, 20 (Mouvement Populaire de la Révolution), Jun 24 (Anniversary of Currency, Promulgation of the 1967 Constitution, and Day of the Fishermen), 30 (Independence), Dec 25

Costa Rica Jan 1, Mar 19 (St Joseph), Apr 11 (Battle of Rivas), May 1, Aug 15 (Mothers), 31 (International Black People), Sep 15 (Independence), Oct 12 (Culture), Nov 2, Dec 24, 25, 31; Holy Week

Côte d'Ivoire Jan 1, May 1, Aug 15, Nov 1, Dec 7 (Independence), 24, 25, 31; A, Ad, EM, ER, GF, WM

Croatia Jan 1, May 1, 30 (National), Jun 22 (Antifascism), Aug 5 (National Thanksgiving), 15, Nov 1, Dec 25, 26; EM, GF

Time

Cuba Jan 1 (Day of Liberation), May 1, Jul 25 (National Rebellion) (2), Oct 10 (Beginning of the Independence Wars)

Cyprus Jan 1, 6, Mar 25 (Greek National), Apr 1 (Greek Cypriot National), May 1, Aug 15, Oct 1 (Independence), 28 (Greek National Ochi), Dec 24, 25, 26; ES, Green Monday, Kataklysmos, Orthodox Easter (Apr/May) (3)

Czech Republic Jan 1, May 1, 8 (Liberation), Jul 5 (Sts Cyril and Methodius), 6 (Martyrdom of Jan Hus), Sep 28 (Statehood), Oct 28 (Independence), Nov 17 (Fight for Freedom and Democracy), Dec 24, 25, 26; EM

Denmark Jan 1, Jun 5 (Constitution), Dec 25, 26; A, EM, GF, HT, WM, General Prayer (Apr/May)

Djibouti Jan 1, May 1, Jun 27 (Independence) (2), Dec 25; Ad (2), ER (2), NY (Muslim), PB, Al-Isra Wal-Mira'age (Mar/Apr)

Dominica Jan 1, May 1, Nov 3 (Independence), 4 (Community Service), Dec 25, 26; C (2), EM, GF, WM, August Monday

Dominican Republic Jan 1, 6, 21 (Our Lady of Altagracia), 26 (Duarte), Feb 27 (Independence), May 1, Aug 16 (Restoration of the Republic), Sep 24 (Our Lady of Mercy), Dec 25; CC, GF

East Timor Jan 1, May 1, 20 (Independence), Aug 15, 30 (Constitution), Sep 20 (Liberation), Nov 1, 12 (Santa Cruz), Dec 8, 25; GF

Ecuador Jan 1, May 1, 24 (Battle of Pichincha), Aug 10 (Independence), Oct 9 (Independence of Guayaquil), Nov 2, 3 (Independence of Cuenca), Dec 25; GF

Egypt Apr 25 (Sinai Liberation), May 1, 23 (Revolution), Oct 6 (Armed Forces); Ad (2), Ar, ER (2), NY (Muslim), PB, Sham El Nessim (Apr/May)

Eire ► Ireland, Republic of

El Salvador Jan 1, May 1, 10 (Mothers), Aug 6 (El Salvador del Mundo) (2), Sep 15 (Independence), Nov 2, Dec 25, 31; GF, HT; *some local variation; public and private sector holidays may differ*

England and Wales Jan 1, Dec 25, 26; EM, GF, Early May, Spring (May) and Summer (Aug) Bank Holidays

Equatorial Guinea Jan 1, May 1, Jun 5 (President's Birthday), Aug 3 (Armed Forces), Oct 12 (Independence), Dec 10 (Human Rights), 25; CC, GF, Constitution (Aug)

Eritrea Jan 1, 7 (Eritrean Christmas), 19 (Eritrean Epiphany), May 24 (Freedom), Jun 20 (Martyrs), Sep 1 (Start of the Armed Struggle), 11 (Eritrean Orthodox Church NY), 27 (Feast of the Cross); Eritrean Easter (Mar/Apr) (2), Eritrean Whit Sunday (Mar/Apr)

Estonia Jan 1, Feb 24 (Independence), May 1 (Spring), Jun 23 (Victory), 24 (St John/Midsummer), Aug 20 (Restoration of Independence), Dec 25, 26; GF, ES, Whit Sunday

Ethiopia Jan 7 (Ethiopian Christmas), 19 (Ethiopian Epiphany), Feb 18 (President), Mar 2 (Victory of Adwa), May 1, 28 (Downfall of the Dergue), Sep 27 (Finding of the True Cross); Ad, ER, NY (Ethiopian) (Sep), PB, Ethiopian Good Friday and Easter Sunday

Fiji Jan 1, Dec 25, 26; D, EM, GF, HS, PB, Queen's Birthday (Jun), National Youth (Apr/May), Ratu Sir Lala Sukuna (1st Mon in Jun), Fiji (Oct)

Finland Jan 1, 6, May 1, Nov 1, Dec 6 (Independence), 24, 25, 26; A, EM, ES, GF, Midsummer Day (Jun), Whitsun (May/Jun)

France Jan 1, May 1, 8 (Victory), Jul 14 (Bastille), Aug 15, Nov 1, 11 (Armistice), Dec 25; A, EM, WM

Gabon Jan 1, May 1, Aug 15, 16 (Independence) (2), Nov 1, Dec 25; Ad, EM, ER, WM

Gambia, The Jan 1, Feb 18 (Independence), May 1, Aug 15 (St Mary), Dec 25; Ad, As, ER (2), GF, PB

Georgia Jan 1, 7 (Orthodox Christmas), 19 (Orthodox Epiphany), Mar 3 (Mothers), Apr 9 (National), May 9 (National), 26 (Independence), Aug 28 (St Mary), Oct 14 (Mtskhetoba), Nov 23 (St Georgi); ES, EM

Germany Jan 1, May 1, Oct 3 (Unity), Dec 25, 26; A, EM, GF, WM; *much regional variation*

Ghana Jan 1, Mar 6 (Independence), May 1, Jun 4 (Revolution), Jul 1 (Republic), Dec 1 (National Farmers), 25, 26; EM, GF

Greece Jan 1, 6, Mar 25 (Independence), May 1, Aug 15, Oct 28 (Ochi), Dec 25, 26; GF, EM, ES, WM, Whit Sunday, Shrove Monday

Grenada Jan 1, 2, Feb 7 (Independence), May 1, Aug 3 (Emancipation) (2), Oct 25 (Thanksgiving), Dec 25, 26; CC, EM, GF, WM

Guatemala Jan 1, May 1, 10 (Mothers), Jun 30 (Army), Sep 15 (Independence), Oct 20 (Revolution), Nov 1, Dec 25, 31; GF, HT, Assumption (*date varies locally*)

Guinea Jan 1, Apr 3 (Second Republic), May 1, Aug 15, Oct 2 (Independence), Dec 25; Ad, ER, PB

Guinea-Bissau Jan 1, 20 (National Heroes), Feb 8 (BNG Anniversary and Monetary Reform), Mar 8 (Women), May 1, Aug 3 (Martyrs of Colonialism), Sep 12 (National), 24 (Establishment of the Republic), Nov 14 (Readjustment), Dec 25

Guyana Jan 1, Feb 23 (Republic), May 1, 26 (Independence), Aug 1 (Freedom), Dec 25, 26; Ad, D, EM, GF, PB, Phagwah (May), Caribbean (Jul)

Haiti Jan 1 (Independence), 2 (Ancestors), Apr 14 (Americas), May 1, 18 (Flag/University), Aug 15, Oct 17 (Death of Dessalines), 24 (United Nations), Nov 1, 2, 18 (Battle of Vertières), Dec 25; A, C, CC, GF

Honduras Jan 1, May 1, Sep 15 (Independence), Oct 3 (Soldiers), 12 (Americas), 21 (Armed Forces), Dec 25; GF, HT

Hungary Jan 1, Mar 15 (Independence), May 1, Aug 20 (National/St Stephen), Oct 23 (Republic), Nov 1, Dec 25, 26; EM, WM

Iceland Jan 1, May 1, Jun 17 (National), Dec 25, 26; A, EM, ES, GF, HT, WM, Whit Sunday, First Day of Summer (Apr), August Holiday Monday

India Jan 1 (*some states*), 26 (Republic), May 1 (*some states*), Jun 30, Aug 15 (Independence), Oct 2 (Mahatma Ghandi's Birthday), Dec 25, 31; NY (Parsi, Aug, *some states*)

Indonesia Jan 1, Aug 17 (Independence), Dec 25; A, Ad, ER (2), GF, NY (Chinese), NY (Muslim), NY (Balinese Hindu), PB, Ascension of the Prophet, Waisak (May)

Iran Feb 11 (Islamic Revolution), Mar 19 (Nationalization of Oil), 21, 31 (Islamic Republic), Apr 2 (13th Day of New Year), Jun 3 (Death of Imam Khomeini), 4 (Uprising); Ad, As, ER, PB, Eid Ghadir Khom, Tasooah, Arbaeen, Death of the Prophet, Martyrdom of Imam Reza, Birthday of Imam Ali, Ascension of the Prophet, Birthday of Imam Hussein, Birthday of the 12th living Imam, Martyrdom of Imam Ali, Death of Hadrath Zahra

Iraq Jan 1, 6 (Army), Feb 8 (8th February Revolution), Mar 21, May 1, Jul 14 (14th July Revolution), 17 (17th July Revolution); Ad (4), As, ER (3), NY (Muslim), PB

Ireland Jan 1, Mar 17 (St Patrick), Dec 25, 26; EM, 1st Mon in May, 1st Mon in Jun, 1st Mon in Aug, last Mon in Oct public holidays

Ireland, Northern ► Northern Ireland

Israel Jan 18 (Tu B'Shvat), Apr 29 (Martyrs and Heroes of the Holocaust), May 6 (Memorial for the Fallen in Wars), 7 (Independence), 20 (Lag Ba'omer), 30 (Jerusalem); NY (Jewish) (Sep/Oct) (2), Purim (Mar), Passover (Apr), Pentecost (Jun), Tisha B'Av (Aug), Day of Atonement (Oct), Feast of Tabernacles (Oct), Chanuka (Dec)

Italy Jan 1, 6, Apr 25 (Liberation), May 1, Jun 2 (National), Aug 15, Nov 1, Dec 8, 25, 26; EM; *much local variation*

Jamaica Jan 1, May 23 (Labour), Aug 1 (Emancipation), 6 (Independence), Oct 21 (National Heroes), Dec 25, 26; Ash Wednesday, EM, GF

Japan Jan 1, Feb 11 (National Foundation), Apr 29 (Greenery), May 3 (Constitution Memorial), 5 (Children), Sep 15 (Respect for the Aged), Nov 3 (Culture), 23 (Labour Thanksgiving), Dec 23 (Emperor's Birthday); Autumnal Equinox, Coming-of-Age (2nd Mon in Jan), Marine Day (Jul), Sports (2nd Mon in Oct), Vernal Equinox

Jordan Jan 1, May 1, 25 (Independence), Jun 9 (Accession of King Abdullah),10 (Great Arab Revolt), Nov 14 (late King Hussein's Birthday); Ad (4), R, ER (3), NY (Muslim), PB, Al-Isra' wal mi'raj

Kazakhstan Jan 1, Mar 8 (Women), 21, May 1, 9 (Victory), Aug 30 (Constitution), Oct 25 (State Sovereignty), Dec 16 (Independence), 31

Kenya Jan 1, May 1, Jun 1 (Madaraka), Oct 10 (Moi), 20 (Kenyatta) (2), Dec 12 (Jamhuri), 25, 26; EM, ER, GF

Kiribati Jan 1, Mar 8 (Women), Apr 17 (National Health), Jul 11 (Gospel), 12 (Independence) (3), Aug 6 (Youth), Dec 10 (Human Rights), 25, 26; GF, HS, EM, ES; *length of holidays varies locally*

Korea, Democratic People's Republic of (North Korea) Jan 1, Feb 16 (Kim Jong Il's Birthday), Mar 8 (Women), Apr 15 (Kim Il Sung's Birthday), Apr 25 (Army Foundation), May 1, Jul 27 (Fatherland Liberation War Victory), Aug 15 (Liberation), Sep 9 (Foundation of the Republic), Oct 10 (Foundation of the Workers' Party), Dec 27 (Constitution)

Korea, Republic of (South Korea) Jan 1–3, Mar 1 (Independence Movement), 10 (Labour), Apr 5 (Arbor), May 5 (Children), Jun 6 (Memorial), Jul 17 (Constitution), Aug 15 (Liberation), Oct 1 (Armed Forces), 3 (National Foundation), 9 (Korean Alphabet), Dec 25; NY (Chinese, Jan/Feb), Lord Buddha's Birthday (May), Moon Festival (Sep/Oct)

Kuwait Jan 1, Feb 25 (National), 26 (Liberation); Ad (4), ER (3), NY (Muslim), PB, Ascension of the Prophet

Kyrgyzstan Jan 1, 7 (Russian Orthodox Christmas), Mar 8 (Women), 21, May 1, 5 (Constitution), 9 (Victory), Aug 31 (Independence); Ad, ER, Navroos

Laos Jan 1, 20 (Foundation of the Lao People's Revolutionary Army), Mar 8 (Women), 22 (Foundation of the Lao People's Revolutionary Army), May 1, Jun 1 (Children), Aug 23 (Declaration of Power), Oct 7 (Teachers), 12 (Independence), Dec 2 (National Foundation); New Year/Water Festival (3) (Apr), Boat Racing Festival (Oct), That Luang Festival (Nov), Makhabouxa (Feb), Visakhabouxa (May), Hokhaopadabdine (Aug), Hokhaosalak (Sep), Buddhist days (2)

Latvia Jan 1, May 1 (Convocation of the Constituent Assembly), Jun 23 (Ligo), 24 (Jani/Summer Solstice), Nov 18 (Proclamation of the Republic), Dec 25, 26, 31; EM, ES, GF, Mothers (2nd Sun in May)

Lebanon Jan 1, Feb 9 (St Maron), May 1, 6 (Martyrs), 25 (Resistance and Liberation), Aug 15, Nov 1, 22 (Independence), Dec 25; Ad (3), As, EM, GF, ER (3), NY (Muslim), PB

Lesotho Jan 1, Mar 11 (Moshoeshoe), Apr 4 (Heroes), May 1, Jul 17 (King's Birthday), Oct 4 (Independence), Dec 25, 26; A, EM, GF

Liberia Jan 1, Feb 11 (Armed Forces), Mar 15 (J J Roberts), Apr 12 (Redemption), May 14 (National Unification), Jul 26 (Independence), Aug 24 (National Flag), Nov 29 (President Tubman's Birthday), Dec 25; Decoration (Mar), National Fast and Prayer (Apr), Thanksgiving (Nov)

Libya Mar 2 (Declaration of Establishment of Authority of People), 8 (National), 28 (Evacuation of British Troops), Jun 11 (Evacuation of US Troops), Jul 23 (National), Sep 1 (National), Oct 7 (Evacuation of Italian Fascists); Ad (4), ER (3), PB

Liechtenstein Jan 1, 2 (Berchtold), 6, Feb 2 (Candlemas), Mar 19 (St Joseph), May 1, Aug 15, Sep 8 (Nativity of Our Lady), Nov 1, Dec 8, 24, 25, 26, 31; A, C, CC, EM, ES, GF, WM, Whit Sunday

Lithuania Jan 1, Feb 16 (Independence), Mar 11 (Restoration of Statehood), Jul 6 (Coronation of Mindaugas/Statehood), Aug 15, Nov 1, Dec 25, 26; ES; Mothers Day (1st Sun in May)

Luxembourg Jan 1, May 1, Jun 23 (National), Aug 15, Nov 1, 2, Dec 25, 26, 31; A, EM, WM, Shrove Monday

Macedonia Jan 1, 6 (Orthodox Christmas) (2), Mar 8 (Women), May 1, 24 (Sts Cyril and Methodius), Aug 2 (St Elijah's Uprising), Sep 8 (Independence), Dec 25, 26; Ad, EM, ER, Old NY

Madagascar Jan 1, Mar 29 (Memorial), May 1, Jun 26 (Independence), Aug 15, Nov 1, Dec 25, 30 (National); A, EM, GF, WM

423

Time

Malawi Jan 1, 15 (Chilembwe), Mar 3 (Martyrs), May 1, Jun 14 (Freedom), Jul 6 (Independence), Dec 25, 26; EM, ER, GF, Mothers (2nd Mon in Oct)

Malaysia Jan 1 (*most states*), May 1, Jun 7 (Head of State's Birthday), Aug 31 (National), Dec 25; Ad (2), D (*most states*), ER (2), NY (Chinese) (Jan/Feb), NY (Muslim), PB, Wesak; *several local festivals*

Maldives Jan 1, May 3 (National), Jul 26 (Independence) (2), Nov 3 (Victory), 11 (Republic); Ad (4), Ar, ER (3), NY (Muslim), PB, R, Day the Maldives Embraced Islam

Mali Jan 1, 20 (Memorial), Mar 26 (Martyrs), May 1, 25 (African Unity), Sep 22 (National), Dec 25; Ad, ER, PB, R

Malta Jan 1, Feb 10 (St Paul's Shipwreck), Mar 19 (St Joseph), 31 (Freedom), May 1, Jun 7 (Sette Giugno), 29 (Sts Peter and Paul), Aug 15, Sep 8 (Our Lady of the Victories), 21 (Independence), Dec 8, 13 (Republic), 25; GF

Marshall Islands Jan 1, Mar 1 (Nuclear Victims), May 1 (Constitution), Nov 17 (President), Dec 25; Fishermen (1st Fri in Jul), Workers (1st Fri in Sep), Customs (last Fri in Sep), Thanksgiving (3rd Thur in Nov), Gospel (1st Fri in Dec)

Mauritania Jan 1, May 1, 25 (Celebration of the African Union), Nov 28 (National); Ad, ER, NY (Muslim), PB

Mauritius Jan 1, 2, Feb 1 (Abolition of Slavery), Mar 12 (National), May 1, Nov 1, 2 (Arrival of Indentured Labourers), Dec 25; D, Chinese Spring Festival (Jan/Feb), ER, Ganesh Chathurti (Aug/Sep), Maha Shivaratree (Feb/Mar), Ougadi (Mar/Apr), Thaipoosam Cavadee (Jan/Feb)

Mexico Jan 1, Feb 5 (Constitution), Mar 21 (Birthday of Benito Juárez), May 1, 5 (Puebla Battle), Sep 1 (Presidential Report), 16 (Independence), Oct 12 (Columbus), Nov 2, 20 (Mexican Revolution), Dec 12 (Our Lady of Guadaloupe), 25, 31; HT, GF

Micronesia, Federated States of Jan 1, May 10 (Proclamation of the Federated States of Micronesia), Oct 24 (United Nations Day), Nov 4 (National Day), Dec 25; *additional days vary between states*

Moldova Jan 1, 7 (Orthodox Christmas) (2), Mar 8 (Women), May 1, 9 (Victory), Aug 27 (Independence), 31 (Limba Noastra/Our Language); EM, ES; 1st Mon after Easter

Monaco Jan 1, 27 (St Devote), May 1, Aug 15, Nov 1, 19 (National), Dec 8, 25; A, CC, EM, WM

Mongolia Jan 1, 2, Mar 8 (Women), May 1, Jul 10 (People's Revolution) (3), Nov 7 (October Revolution)

Morocco Jan 1, 11 (Independence Manifest), May 1, Jul 30 (Feast of the Throne), Aug 14 (Qued-ed-Dahab Allegiance), Aug 21 (King and People), Nov 6 (Green March), 18 (Independence); Ad, ER, NY (Muslim), PB

Mozambique Jan 1, Feb 3 (Heroes), Apr 7 (Mozambican Women), May 1, Jun 25 (Independence), Sep 7 (Victory), 25 (Armed Forces), Oct 4 (Peace and Reconciliation), Dec 25 (Christmas/Family)

Myanmar (Burma) Jan 4 (Independence), Feb 12 (Union), Mar 2 (Peasants), 27 (Armed Forces), May 1, Jul 19 (Martyrs), Dec 25; Ad, D, 4 Full Moon days, National (Nov), NY (Burmese), NY (Kayin), Tazaungdaing Festival (Nov), Thingyan (Apr) (3–5)

Namibia Jan 1, Mar 21 (Independence), May 1, 4 (Cassinga), Aug 26 (Heroes), Dec 10 (Human Rights), Dec 25, 26 (Family); A, GF, EM

Nauru Jan 1, 31 (Independence), Feb 1, May 17 (Constitution), Oct 26 (Angam), Dec 25, 26; GF, EM (2)

Nepal Feb 19 (Democracy), Jul 8 (King's Birthday), Nov 8 (Constitution); NY (Nepalese) (Apr), Vijaya Dashami (Oct), Bhai Tika (Nov)

Netherlands Jan 1, Apr 30 (Queen), May 5 (Liberation), Dec 25, 26; A, EM, GF, WM

New Zealand Jan 1, 2, Feb 6 (Waitangi), Apr 25 (Anzac), Dec 25, 26; EM, GF, Queen's Birthday (Jun), Labour (Oct)

Nicaragua Jan 1, May 1, Jul 19 (Sandinista Revolution), Sep 14 (Battle of San Jacinto), 15 (Independence), Dec 8, 25; GF, HT

Niger Jan 1, Apr 24 (Concord), May 1, Aug 3 (Independence), Dec 18 (Republic), 25; Ad, EM, ER, PB, Leilat-ul-kadr

Nigeria Jan 1, May 1, 29 (Democracy), Oct 1 (National), Dec 25, 26; Ad, EM, ER, GF

Northern Ireland Jan 1, Mar 17 (St Patrick), Dec 25, 26; GF, EM, Early May, Spring (May) Bank Holiday, Battle of the Boyne/Orangemen (Jul), Summer Bank Holiday (Aug)

Norway Jan 1, May 1, 17 (Constitution), Dec 25, 26; A, EM, GF, HT, WM

Oman Nov 18 (National) (2), Dec 31; Ad (5), ER (4), NY (Muslim), PB, Lailat al-Miraj (Mar/Apr)

Pakistan Jan 1, Feb 5 (Kashmir), Mar 23 (Pakistan), May 1, Jul 1, Aug 14 (Independence), Nov 9 (Iqbal), Dec 25 (Christmas/Birthday of Quaid-e-Azam); Ad (2), As (2), ER (3), PB, R; *additional religious optional holidays*

Palau Jan 1, Mar 15 (Youth), May 5 (Senior Citizens), Jun 1 (President), Jul 9 (Constitution), Oct 1 (Independence), 24 (United Nations), Dec 25; Labour (1st Mon in Sep), Thanksgiving (last Thurs in Nov)

Panama Jan 1, 9 (Martyrs), May 1, Nov 3 (Independence), 10 (First Call of Independence), 28 (Independence from Spain), Dec 8 (Mothers), 25; C, GF; *some local variation*

Papua New Guinea Jan 1, Jul 23 (Remembrance), Sep 16 (Independence), Dec 25, 26; EM, ES, GF, HS, Queen's Birthday (Jun)

Paraguay Jan 1, Mar 1 (Battle of Cerro Corá), May 1, 15 (Independence), Jun 12 (Chaco Peace), Aug 15 (Foundation of Asuncion), Dec 8, 25; GF, HT

Peru Jan 1, May 1, Jun 24 (Peasants), 29 (Sts Peter and Paul), Jul 28 (Independence) (2), Aug 30 (St Rose of Lima), Oct 8 (Battle of Angamos), Nov 1, Dec 8, 25; GF, HT

Philippines Jan 1, Apr 9 (Araw Ng Kagitingan), May 1, Jun 12 (Independence), Aug 30 (National Heroes), Nov 1, 2, 30 (Bonifacio), Dec 25, 30 (Rizal), 31; GF, HT

Poland Jan 1, May 1, 3 (National), Aug 15, Nov 1, 11 (Independence), Dec 25, 26; CC, EM

Portugal Jan 1, Apr 25 (Liberty), May 1, Jun 10 (Camões-Portugal), Aug 15, Oct 5 (Republic), Nov 1, Dec 1 (Independence), Dec 8, 24, 25; C, CC, GF

Qatar Sep 3 (Independence), Dec 31; Ad (4), ER (4)

Romania Jan 1, 2, May 1, Dec 1 (National), 25, 26; Orthodox Easter (Apr/May) (2); *other major religions each have 2 days for festivals*

Russia Jan 1, 2, 7 (Russian Orthodox Christmas), Feb 23 (Soldiers), Mar 8 (Women), May 1 (Spring and Labour) (2), 9 (Victory), Jun 12 (Independence), Aug 22 (Flag), Nov 7 (Accord and Conciliation), Dec 12 (Constitution); Russian Orthodox Easter (Apr/May)

Rwanda Jan 1, 28 (Democracy), May 1, Jul 1 (Independence), 5 (Peace), Aug 1 (Harvest), 15, Sep 25 (Referendum), Oct 26 (Armed Forces), Nov 1, Dec 25; A, EM, WM

St Kitts and Nevis Jan 1, 2, Sep 19 (Independence), Dec 25, 26; EM, GF, WM, Labour (May), August Monday

St Lucia Jan 1, 2, Feb 22 (Independence), May 1, Dec 13 (National), Dec 25, 26; Emancipation (Aug)

St Vincent and the Grenadines Jan 1, Mar 14 (National Heroes), May 1, Oct 27 (Independence), Dec 25, 26; C (Jul), EM, GF, WM, Caricom (Jul), Emancipation (Aug)

Samoa Jan 1, May 12 (Anzac), Jun 1 (Mothers of Samoa), Aug 4 (Labour), Oct 12 (White Sunday) (2), Nov 7 (Arbor), Dec 25, 26; EM, GF

San Marino Jan 1, 6, Feb 5 (Liberation and St Agatha), Mar 25 (Arengo), Apr 1 (Captains Regents' Ceremony), May 1, Jul 28 (Fall of Fascism), Aug 15, Sep 3 (San Marino and Republic), Oct 1 (Investiture of the New Captains Regent), Nov 1, 2 (Commemoration of the Dead), Dec 8, 25, 26

São Tomé and Príncipe Jan 1, Feb 3 (Liberty Heroes), May 1, Jul 12 (National Independence), Sep 6 (Armed Forces), 30 (Agricultural Reform), Dec 21 (Power of the People), 25 (Family)

Saudi Arabia Sep 23 (National); Ad (4), ER (3)

Scotland Jan 1, 2, Dec 25, 26; GF, Early May, Spring (May) and Summer (Aug) Bank Holidays

Senegal Jan 1, Feb 1 (Senegambia), Apr 4 (National), May 1, Aug 15, Nov 1, Dec 25; Ad, EM, ER, NY (Muslim), PB, WM

Serbia and Montenegro (Yugoslavia) Jan 1, 2, 7 (Orthodox Christmas), Feb 15 (National) (Serbia), Apr 27 (Constitution), May 1 (2), 9 (Victory), Jul 13 (Uprising) (Montenegro); Orthodox Easter (Apr/May) (4)

Seychelles Jan 1, 2, May 1, Jun 5 (Liberation), 18 (National), 29 (Independence), Aug 15, Nov 1, Dec 8, 25; CC, GF, HS

Sierra Leone Jan 1, Apr 19 (Republic), Apr 27 (Independence), Dec 25, 26; Ad, EM, ER, GF, PB

Singapore Jan 1, May 1, Aug 9 (National), Dec 25; Ad, D, ER, GF, NY (Chinese, Jan/Feb) (2), Vesak

Slovakia Jan 1 (New Year/Establishment of Republic), 6, May 1, 8 (Triumph over Fascism), Jul 5 (Sts Cyril and Methodius), Aug 29 (Slovak National Uprising), Sep 1 (Constitution), 15 (Our Lady of the Seven Sorrows), Nov 1, Dec 24, 25, 26; GF, EM

Slovenia Jan 1, 2, Feb 8 (Culture), Apr 27 (National Resistance), May 1 (2), Jun 25 (National), Aug 15, Oct 31 (Reformation), Nov 1, Dec 25, 26 (Independence); EM

Solomon Islands Jan 1, Jul 7 (Independence), Dec 25, 26; EM, GF, HS, WM, Queen's Birthday (Jun)

Somalia Jan 1, May 1, Jun 26 (Independence), Jul 1 (Union), Oct 21 (Revolution) (2); Ad (2), ER (2), PB

South Africa Jan 1, Mar 21 (Human Rights), Apr 27 (Freedom Day), May 1, Jun 16 (Youth), Aug 9 (Women), Sep 24 (Heritage), Dec 16 (Reconciliation), 25, 26; GF, EM (Family)

Spain Jan 1, 6, May 1, Aug 15, Nov 1, Dec 6 (Constitution), 8, 25; GF, HT (*most areas*); *much regional variation*

Sri Lanka Jan 15 (Tamil Thai Pongal), Feb 4 (National), May 1, Dec 25; Ad, D, ER, GF, NY (Sinhala/Tamil) (Apr) (2), PB, Mahasivarathri (Feb/Mar), Full Moon (*monthly*), day following Vesak Full Moon (May)

Sudan, The Jan 1 (Independence), Mar 3 (Unity), Apr 6 (Revolution), Dec 25; Ad (5), ER (5), NY (Muslim), PB, Sham al-Naseem (Apr/May)

Suriname Jan 1, May 1, Jul 1 (Freedom), Nov 25 (Independence), Dec 25, 26; EM, ER, GF, Holi Phagwa (Mar)

Swaziland Jan 1, Apr 19 (King's Birthday), 25 (National Flag), May 1, Sep 6 (Somhlolo), Dec 25, 26; A, EM, GF, Incwala (Dec/Jan), Umhlanga/Reed Dance (Aug/Sep), July public holiday

Sweden Jan 1, 6, May 1, Nov 1, Dec 25, 26; A, EM, GF, WM, Midsummer (Jun)

Switzerland Jan 1, Aug 1 (National), Dec 25, 26; A, EM, GF, WM; *other canton and local holidays*

Syria Jan 1, Mar 8 (Revolution), Apr 17 (Evacuation), May 1, 6 (Martyrs), Jul 23 (Egyptian Revolution), Sep 1 (Libyan Unity), Oct 6 (Liberation), Dec 25; Ad (3), ER (4), ES, NY (Muslim), PB

Taiwan Jan 1 (Foundation of the Republic of China), Feb 28 (Peace Memorial), Apr 5 (National Tomb Sweeping), May 1, Oct 10 (National); NY (Chinese) (Jan/Feb) (3), Dragon Boat Festival (Jun), Mid-Autumn Festival (Sep/Oct)

Tajikistan Jan 1, Mar 8 (Women), 21, May 9 (Victory), Sep 9 (Independence), Oct 14 (Formation of the Tajik Republic); ER

Tanzania Jan 1, 12 (Zanzibar Revolution), Apr 26 (Union), May 1, Jul 7 (Industrial), Aug 8 (Farmers), Dec 9 (Independence/Republic), 25, 26; Ad, EM, ER (2), GF, PB

Thailand Jan 1, Apr 6 (Chakri), 13 (Songkran) (3), May 1, 5 (Coronation), Aug 12 (Queen's Birthday), Oct 23 (Chulalongkorn Memorial), Dec 5 (King's Birthday), 10 (Constitution), 31; Buddhist Lent (Jul), Makha Bucha (Feb), Visakha Bucha (May)

Togo Jan 1, 13 (National Liberation), 24 (Economic Liberation), Feb 2 (Triumphant Return), Apr 24 (Victory), 27 (Independence), May 1, Jun 1 (Trees), 21 (Pya Martyrs), Aug 15, 30 (Historical Address of Kpalimé), Sep 23 (Anniversary of Terrorist Aggression), Nov 1, 30 (Creation of the RPT), Dec 25; A, Ad, EM, WM

Tonga Jan 1, Apr 25 (Anzac), May 4 (Birthday of Crown Prince Tupouto'a), Jun 4 (Emancipation), Jul 4 (King's Birthday), Nov 4 (Constitution), Dec 4 (King Tupou I), 25, 26; EM, GF

Time

Trinidad and Tobago Jan 1, Mar 30 (Spiritual Baptist Liberation Shouter), May 30 (Indian Arrival), Jun 19 (Labour), Aug 1 (Emancipation), 31 (Independence), Dec 25, 26; CC, D, EM, ER, GF

Tunisia Jan 1, 18 (Revolution), Mar 20 (Independence), Apr 9 (Martyrs), May 1, Jun 1 (Victory), 2 (Youth), Jul 25 (Republic), Aug 13 (Women), Sep 3 (3 Sep 1934), Oct 15 (Evacuation), Nov 7 (Election of President); Ad (2), ER (2), NY (Muslim), PB

Turkey Jan 1, Apr 23 (National Sovereignty and Children), May 19 (Atatürk Commemoration/Youth and Sports), Aug 30 (Victory), Oct 29 (Republic); Ad (4), ER (3)

Turkmenistan Jan 1, 12 (Remembrance/Anniversary of the Battle of Geok-Tepe), Feb 19 (President's Birthday), Mar 8 (Women), 21, May 9 (Victory); Ad, Day of Revival and Unity (May), Independence (Oct)

Tuvalu Jan 1, May 13 (Gospel), Jun 14 (Queen's Birthday), Aug 5 (Children), Oct 1 (Independence), Dec 25, 26; EM, GF; Commonwealth Day (2nd Mon in Mar)

Uganda Jan 1, 26 (NRM Anniversary), Mar 8 (Women), May 1, Jun 3 (Martyrs), 9 (Heroes), Oct 9 (Independence), Dec 25, 26; Ad, EM, ER, GF

UK ▶ England and Wales; Northern Ireland; Scotland

Ukraine Jan 1, 7 (Eastern Orthodox Christmas), Mar 8 (Women), May 1 (2), 9 (Victory), Jun 28 (Constitution), Aug 24 (Independence); Orthodox Easter (Apr/May) (2)

United Arab Emirates Jan 1, Aug 6 (Accession of Ruler), Dec 2 (National); Ad (4), Ascension of the Prophet, ER (3), NY (Muslim), PB, R

Uruguay Jan 6 (Children), May 1, Jun 19 (Artigas's Birthday), Jul 18 (Constitution), Oct 12 (Americas), Dec 25; C (2), GF, HT

USA Jan 1, Jul 4 (Independence), Nov 11 (Veterans), Dec 25; Martin Luther King's Birthday (3rd Mon in Jan), Washington's Birthday (3rd Mon in Feb), Memorial (last Mon in May), Labor (1st Mon in Sep), Columbus (2nd Mon in Oct), Thanksgiving (4th Thurs in Nov); *additional days vary between states*

Uzbekistan Jan 1, Mar 8 (Women), 21, May 9 (Memory and Respect), Sep 1 (Independence), Oct 1 (Teachers), Dec 8 (Constitution); Ad, ER

Vanuatu Jan 1, Feb 21 (Memory of the Father of Independence), Mar 5 (Custom Chiefs), May 1, Jul 24 (Children), 30 (Independence), Aug 15, Oct 5 (Constitution), Nov 29 (Unity), Dec 25, 26; A, EM, ES, GF

Venezuela Jan 1, Apr 19 (Independence), May 1, Jun 24 (Battle of Carabobo), Jul 5 (National), 24 (Bolívar's Birthday), Oct 12 (Discovery), Dec 17 (Liberator's Death), 25; C (2), GF, HT

Vietnam Jan 1, Apr 30 (Saigon Liberation), May 1, Sep 2 (National); NY (Vietnamese) (4)

Western Samoa ▶ Samoa

Yemen May 1, 22 (National), Sep 26 (Revolution), Oct 14 (Revolution), Nov 30 (Independence); Ad (5), ER (5), NY (Muslim)

Yugoslavia ▶ Serbia and Montenegro

Zaïre ▶ Congo, Democratic Republic of

Zambia Jan 1, May 1, 25 (Africa Freedom), Oct 24 (Independence), Dec 25; EM, GF, HS, Youth (2nd Mon in Mar), Heroes (1st Mon in Jul), Unity (1st Tues in Jul), Farmers (1st Mon in Aug)

Zimbabwe Jan 1, Apr 18 (Independence), May 1, 25 (Africa), Aug 11 (Heroes), 12 (Defence Forces), Dec 22 (Unity), 25, 26; EM, ES, GF, HS

NATURAL HISTORY

Cereals

English name	Species	Area of origin
barley	*Hordeum vulgare*	Middle East
maize (or corn, sweet corn, Indian corn)	*Zea mays*	C America
millet, bulrush	*Pennisetum americanum*	tropics, warm temperate regions
millet, common	*Panicum miliaceum*	tropics, warm temperate regions
millet, foxtail (or Italian millet)	*Setaria italica*	tropics, warm temperate regions
oats	*Avena sativa*	Mediterranean basin
rice	*Oryza sativa*	Asia
rye	*Secale cereale*	Mediterranean, SW Asia
sorghum (or Kaffir corn)	*Sorghum bicolor*	Africa, Asia
wheat	Genus *Triticum*, 20 species	Mediterranean, W Asia

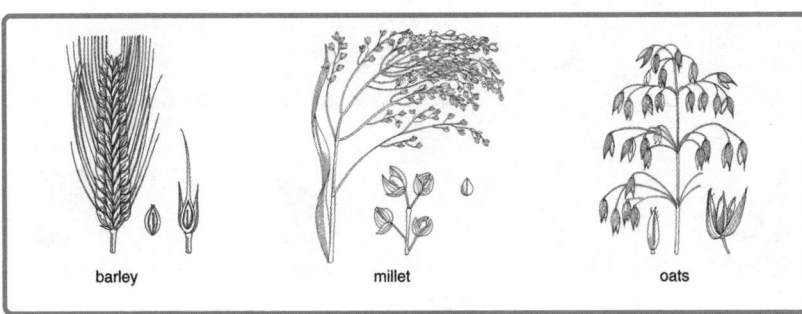

barley   millet   oats

Edible fruits (Temperate and Mediterranean)

English name	Species	Colour	Area of origin
apple	*Malus pumila*	green, yellow, red	temperate regions
apricot	*Prunus armeniaca*	yellow, orange	Asia
bilberry	*Vaccinium myrtillus*	blue, black	Europe, N Asia
blackberry (or bramble)	*Rubus fruticosus*	purple, black	N hemisphere
blackcurrant	*Ribes nigrum*	black	Europe, Asia, Africa
blueberry	*Vaccinium corymbosum*	blue, purple, black	America, Europe
Cape gooseberry ► physalis			
cherry (sour)	*Prunus cerasus*	red	temperate regions
cherry (sweet)	*Prunus avium*	purple, red	temperate regions
clementine	*Citrus reticulata*	orange	W Mediterranean
cranberry	*Vaccinium oxycoccus*	red	N America
damson	*Prunus damascena*	purple	temperate regions
date	*Phoenix dactylifera*	yellow, red, brown	Persian Gulf
date-plum ► persimmon			
fig	*Ficus carica*	white, black, purple, green	W Asia
gooseberry	*Ribes grossularia*	green, red	Europe
grape	*Vitis vinifera*	green, purple, black	Asia
grapefruit	*Citrus × paradisi*	yellow	W Indies
greengage	*Prunus italica*	green	temperate regions
kiwi fruit	*Actinidia chinensis*	brown skin, green flesh	China
kumquat	*Fortunella margarita*	orange	China
lemon	*Citrus limon*	yellow	India, S Asia
lime	*Citrus aurantifolia*	green	SE Asia
loganberry	*Rubus loganobaccus*	red	America
loquat	*Eriobotrya japonica*	yellow	China, Japan
lychee	*Litchi chinensis*	reddish-brown skin, white flesh	China
mandarin (or tangerine)	*Citrus reticulata*	orange	China
medlar	*Mespilus germanica*	russet brown	SE Europe, Asia

Natural History

English name	Species	Colour	Area of origin
melon	*Cucumis melo*	green, yellow	Egypt
minneola ▸ tangelo			
mulberry	*Morus nigra*	purple, red	W Asia
nectarine	*Prunus persica nectarina*	orange, red	China
orange	*Citrus sinensis*	orange	China
peach	*Prunus persica* var. nectarina	yellow, red	China
pear	*Pyrus communis*	yellow	Middle East, E Europe
persimmon (or date-plum)	*Diospyros kaki*	yellow, orange	E Asia
physalis (or Cape gooseberry)	*Physalis alkekengi*	yellow	S America
plum	*Prunus domestica*	red, yellow, purple, orange	temperate regions
pomegranate	*Punica granatum*	red, yellow	Persia
pomelo	*Citrus maxima*	yellow	Malaysia
quince	*Cydonia oblonga*	golden	Iran
raspberry	*Rubus idaeus*	red, crimson	N hemisphere
redcurrant	*Ribes rubrum*	red	Europe, Asia, Africa
rhubarb	*Rheum rhaponticum*	red, green, pink	Asia
satsuma	*Citrus reticulata*	orange	Japan
strawberry	*Fragaria ananassa*	red	Europe, Asia
tangelo (or minneola, or ugli)	*Citrus × tangelo*	orange, yellow	N America
tangerine ▸ mandarin			
ugli ▸ tangelo			
water melon	*Citrullus vulgaris*	green, yellow	Africa
white currant	*Ribes rubrum* cv.	white	W Europe

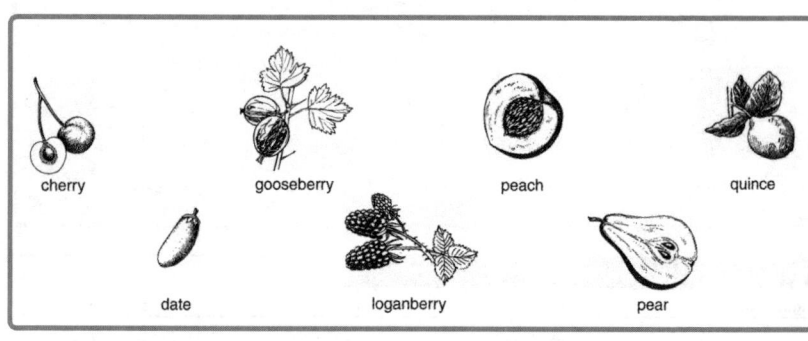

cherry gooseberry peach quince

date loganberry pear

Edible fruits (Tropical)

English name	Species	Colour	Area of origin
acerola	*Malpighia glabra*	yellow, red	America
avocado	*Persea americana*	green, purple	C America
banana	*Musa acuminita*	yellow	India, S Asia
breadfruit	*Artocarpus altilis*	greenish brown, yellow	Malaysia
carambola	*Averrhoa carambola*	yellow, green	S China
cherimoya	*Annona cherimola*	green skin, white flesh	Peru

papaya pineapple soursop

English name	Species	Colour	Area of origin
guava	*Psidium guajava*	green, yellow	S America
mango	*Mangifera indica*	green, yellow, orange, red, purple	S Asia
papaya (or pawpaw)	*Carica papaya*	green, yellow, orange	tropics
passion fruit	*Passiflora edulis*	purple, yellow, brown	S America
pineapple	*Ananas comosus*	green, yellow	S America
sapodilla plum	*Manilkara zapota*	brown	C America
soursop	*Anona muricata*	green	America
tamarind	*Tamarindus indica*	brown	Africa, S Asia

Herbs

Herbs may be used for medicinal, cosmetic or culinary purposes. Any part of those marked * may be poisonous when ingested.

English name	Species	Origin	Part of plant used
aconite* (or monkshood or winter aconite)	*Aconitum napellus*	Europe, NW Asia	tuber
agrimony	*Agrimonia eupatoria*	Europe	flowers
alecost (or costmary)	*Balsimata major*	E Mediterranean	leaves, flowers
aloe	*Aloe vera*	Africa	leaves
aniseed	*Pimpinella anisum*	Asia	fruits (seed heads)
basil	*Ocimum basilicum*	tropics	leaves, flowering shoots
borage	*Borago officinalis*	Mediterranean	leaves, flowers
celandine	*Chelidonium majus*	Europe	buds
celery	*Apium graveolens*	Europe	roots, stems, leaves
chamomile	*Anthemis nobilis*	Europe, Asia	flowers
chervil	*Anthriscus cerefolium*	Europe, Asia	leaves
chicory	*Cichorium intybus*	Europe	leaves, roots
chives	*Allium schoenoprasum*	Europe, America	leaves
coriander	*Coriandrum sativum*	N Africa, W Asia	leaves, fruits
dandelion	*Taraxacum officinalis*	Europe	leaves, roots
deadly nightshade*	*Atropa belladonna*	Europe, Asia	root
dill	*Anethum graveolens*	S Europe	leaves, fruits (seeds)
elderberry	*Sambucus nigra*	Europe	flowers, fruits
epazote	*Chenopodium ambrosioides*	C and S America	leaves
fennel, Florentine	*Foeniculum vulgare* var. *azoricum*	Mediterranean	leaves, stems, fruits (seeds)
feverfew	*Tanacetum parthenium*	SE Europe, W Asia	leaves, flowers
foxglove*	*Digitalis purpurea*	Europe	leaves
garlic	*Allium sativum*	Asia	bulbs
gentian	*Gentiana lutea*	Europe	rhizomes, roots
ginseng	*Panax pseudo-ginseng*	China	roots
guaiacum	*Guaiacum officinale*	Caribbean	leaves
heartsease (or wild pansy)	*Viola tricolor*	Europe	flowers
hemlock*	*Conium maculatum*	Europe	all parts
hemp (or ganja or cannabis or marijuana)	*Cannabis sativa*	Asia	leaves, flowers
henbane	*Hyoscyamus niger*	Europe, W Asia, N Africa	leaves, fruits (seeds)
henna	*Lawsonia inermis*	Asia, Africa	leaves
horseradish	*Armoracia rusticana*	SE Europe, W Asia	roots, flowering shoots, leaves
hyssop	*Hyssopus officinalis*	S Europe	leaves, flowers
juniper	*Juniperus communis*	Mediterranean	fruits (berries), wood
lavender	*Lavandula vera*	Mediterranean	flowers, stems
leek	*Allium porrum*	Europe	stem, leaves
lemon	*Citrus limon*	Asia	fruits
lemon balm	*Melissa officinalis*	S Europe	leaves
lily of the valley	*Convallaria majalis*	Europe, N America	leaves, flowers
lime	*Tilia cordata*	Europe	flowers
liquorice	*Glycyrrhiza glabra*	Europe	roots
lovage	*Levisticum officinale*	W Asia	leaves, shoots, stems, roots
mandrake	*Mandragora officinarum*	Himalayas, SE Europe, W Asia	roots
marjoram	*Oreganum majorana*	Africa, Mediterranean, Asia	leaves, shoots, stems
marsh mallow	*Althaea officinalis*	Europe, Asia	leaves, roots
maté	*Ilex paraguariensis*	S America	leaves
milfoil ▶ yarrow			
monkshood ▶ aconite			
mugwort	*Artemesia vulgaris*	Europe, Asia	leaves

Natural History

Natural History

English name	Species	Origin	Part of plant used
myrrh	*Commiphora myrrha*	Arabia, Africa	resin
myrtle	*Myrtus communis*	Asia, Mediterranean	leaves, flower heads, fruits (berries)
nasturtium	*Tropaeolom majus*	Peru	leaves, flowers, fruits
onion	*Allium cepa*	Asia	bulbs
oregano	*Origanum vulgare*	Mediterranean	leaves, shoots, stems
parsley	*Petroselinum crispum*	Mediterranean	leaves, stems
peony	*Paeonia officinalis*	Europe, Asia, N America	roots, seeds
peppermint	*Mentha × piperita*	Europe	leaves
poppy, opium*	*Papaver somniferum*	Asia	fruits, seeds
purslane	*Portulaca oleracea*	Europe	leaves
rosemary	*Rosmarinus officinalis*	Mediterranean	leaves
rue	*Ruta graveolens*	Mediterranean	leaves, stems, flowers
saffron	*Crocus sativus*	Asia Minor	flowers
sage	*Salvia officinalis*	N Mediterranean	leaves
sorrel	*Rumex acetosa*	Europe	leaves
spearmint	*Mentha spicata*	Europe	leaves
tansy	*Tanacetum vulgare*	Asia	leaves, flowers
tarragon, French	*Artemesia dracunculus*	Asia, E Europe	leaves, stems
thyme	*Thymus vulgaris*	Mediterranean	leaves, stems, flowers
valerian	*Valeriana officinalis*	Europe, Asia	rhizomes, roots
vervain	*Verbena officinalis*	Europe, Asia, N Africa	leaves, flowers
watercress	*Nasturtium officinale*	Europe, Asia	leaves, shoots, stems
witch hazel	*Hamamelis virginiana*	N America, E Asia	leaves, shoots, bark
wormwood	*Artemesia absinthium*	Europe	leaves, flowering shoots
yarrow (or milfoil)	*Achillea millefolium*	Europe, W Asia	flower heads, leaves

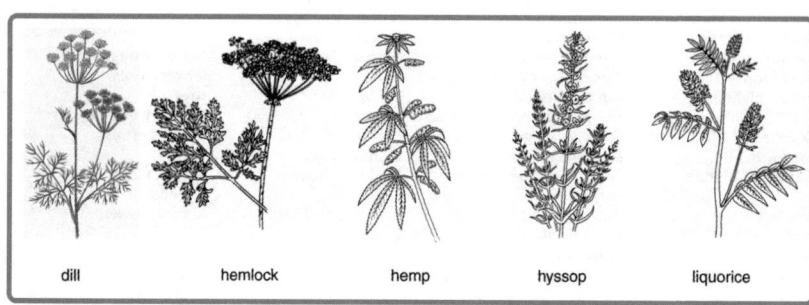

dill   hemlock   hemp   hyssop   liquorice

Spices

English name	Species	Origin	Part of plant used
allspice	*Pimenta dioica*	America, W Indies	fruits
annatto	*Bixa orellana*	S America, W Indies	seeds
asafoetida	*Ferula assa-foetida*	W Asia	sap
bay	*Laurus nobilis*	Mediterranean, Asia Minor	leaves
caper	*Capparis spinosa*	Europe	flower buds
caraway	*Carum carvi*	Europe, Asia	seeds
cardamom	*Elettaria cardamomum*	SE Asia	seeds

cumin   vanilla

English name	Species	Origin	Part of plant used
cayenne	*Capsicum annuum*	America, Africa	fruit pods
chilli pepper	*Capsicum frutescens*	America	fruit pods
cinnamon	*Cinnamomum zeylanicum*	India	bark
cloves	*Eugenia caryophyllus*	Moluccas	buds
cocoa	*Theobroma cacoa*	S America	seeds (beans)
coconut	*Cocus nucifera*	Polynesia	fruits
coriander	*Coriandrum sativum*	S Europe	fruits
cumin	*Cuminum cyminum*	Mediterranean	fruits (seed heads)
curry leaf	*Murraya koenigi*	India	leaves
fennel	*Foeniculum vulgare*	S Europe	fruits
fenugreek	*Trigonella foenum-graecum*	India, S Europe	seeds
ginger	*Zingiber officinale*	SE Asia	rhizomes
horseradish	*Armoracia rusticana*	E Europe	roots
mace	*Myristica fragrans*	Moluccas	seeds
mustard, black	*Brassica nigra*	Europe, Africa, Asia, America	seeds
mustard, white	*Sinapis alba*	Europe, Asia	seeds
nutmeg	*Myristica fragrans*	Indonesia	seeds
paprika	*Capsicum annuum*	S America	fruit pods
pepper	*Piper nigrum*	India	seeds
sandalwood	*Santalum album*	India, Indonesia, Australia	heartwood, roots
sassafras	*Sassafras albidum*	N America	root bark
sesame	*Sesamum indicum*	tropics	seeds
soya	*Glycine max*	China	fruit (beans)
tamarind	*Tamarindus indica*	Africa	fruits
turmeric	*Curcuma longa*	SE Asia	rhizomes
vanilla	*Vanilla planifolia*	C America	fruit pods

Vegetables

English name	Species	Part eaten	Colour	Area of origin
artichoke, Chinese	*Stachys affinis*	tuber	white	China
artichoke, globe	*Cynara scolymus*	buds	green, purple	Mediterranean
artichoke, Jerusalem	*Helianthus tuberosus*	tuber	white	N America
asparagus	*Asparagus officinalis*	young shoots	green, white	Europe, Asia
aubergine (or eggplant)	*Solanum melongena*	fruit	purple, white	Asia, Africa
avocado	*Persea americana*	fruit	green, purple	C America
bean sprout	*Vigna radiata*	shoots	white, pale brown	China
bean, blackeyed	*Vigna unguiculata*	seeds	white/black	India, Iran
bean, borlotti (or Boston bean or pinto bean)	*Phaseolus vulgaris*	seeds	pink/brown	America
bean, broad	*Vicia faba*	seeds and pods	white	Africa, Europe
bean, flageolet	*Phaseolus vulgaris*	seeds	white, pale green	America
bean, French	*Phaseolus vulgaris*	pods	green	America
bean, haricot	*Phaseolus vulgaris*	seeds	white	America
bean, kidney	*Phaseolus vulgaris*	seeds	red	America
beans, runner	*Phaseolus coccineus*	pods	green	America
bean, soya	*Glycine max*	seeds	green	E Asia
beetroot	*Beta vulgaris*	root	white, dark red	Mediterranean
broccoli	*Brassica oleracea*	buds and leaves	green, purple	Europe
Brussels sprout	*Brassica oleracea* (gemmifera)	buds	green	N Europe
cabbage	*Brassica oleracea*	leaves	green, red, white	Europe, W Asia
cardoon	*Cynara cardunculus*	inner stalks and flower heads	white, green	Mediterranean
carrot	*Daucus carota*	root	orange	Asia
cauliflower	*Brassica oleracea* (Botrytis)	flower buds	white, green	Middle East
celeriac	*Apium graveolens* var. *rapaceum*	root	white	Mediterranean
celery	*Apium graveolens* var. *dulce*	stalks	white, green	Europe, N Africa, America
chayote (or chocho)	*Sechium edule*	fruit	white, green	America
chick-pea	*Cicer arietinum*	seeds	beige, golden, dark brown	W Asia
chicory	*Cichorium intybus*	leaves	red, green	Europe, W Asia
chinese leaf	*Brassica pekinensis*	leaf stalks	white, green	E Asia, China
chives	*Allium schoenoprasum*	leaves	green, white	Europe, N America
courgette (or zucchini)	*Cucurbita pepo*	fruit	green	S America, Africa
cucumber	*Cucumus sativus*	fruit	green	S Asia
eggplant ▸ aubergine				

431

Natural History

English name	Species	Part eaten	Colour	Area of origin
endive	*Cichorium endivia*	leaves	yellow, green	S Europe, E Indies, Africa
fennel, Florentine	*Foeniculum vulgare* var. *dulce*	leaf stalks	white, green	Europe
kale (or borecole)	*Brassica oleracea* (Acephala)	leaves	green	Europe
kohlrabi	*Brassica oleracea* (Gongylodes)	stems	white	Europe
laver	*Porphyra leucosticta, P. umbilicalis*	leaves and stems	purple-pink	Europe
leek	*Allium porrum*	leaves and stems	green, white	Europe, N Africa
lentil	*Lens culinaris*	seeds	white, green, pink, red	S Asia
lettuce	*Lactuca sativa*	leaves	green, white	Middle East
marrow	*Cucurbita pepo*	fruit	green	America
mooli	*Raphanus sativus*	root	white	E Africa
mushroom	*Agaricus campestris*	fruiting body	brown, white	worldwide
okra	*Abelmoschus esculentus*	pods and seeds	green, white	Africa
onion	*Allium cepa*	bulb	white, pink	C Asia
parsnip	*Pastinaca sativa*	root	white, yellow	Europe
pea	*Pisum sativum*	pods and seeds	green	Asia, Europe
pepper	*Capsicum annuum*	fruit	red, green, yellow	S America
potato	*Solanum tuberosum*	tuber	white	S America
pumpkin	*Cucurbita pepo*	fruit	yellow, orange	S America
radish	*Raphanus sativus*	root	red, white	China, Japan
salsify	*Tragopogon porrifolius*	root	white	S Europe
sorrel	*Rumex acetosa*	leaves	green	Europe
spinach	*Spinacea oleracea*	leaves	green	Asia
squash, winter	*Cucurbita maxima*	fruit	green, yellow, orange	America
squash, summer	*Cucurbita pepo*	fruit	yellow, orange, green	America
swede	*Brassica napus* (Napobrassica)	root	yellow, white	Europe
sweet potato	*Ipomoea batatas*	tuber	white, yellow, red to purple	C America
swiss chard	*Beta vulgaris* subsp. *cicla*	leaves and stems	green, white	Europe
tomato	*Lycopersicon esculentum*	fruit	red	S America
turnip	*Brassica rapa*	root	white	Middle East
watercress	*Nasturtium officinale*	leaves and stems	green	Europe, Asia
yam	Genus *Dioscorea*, 60 species	tuber	white, orange	tropics

zucchini ► courgette

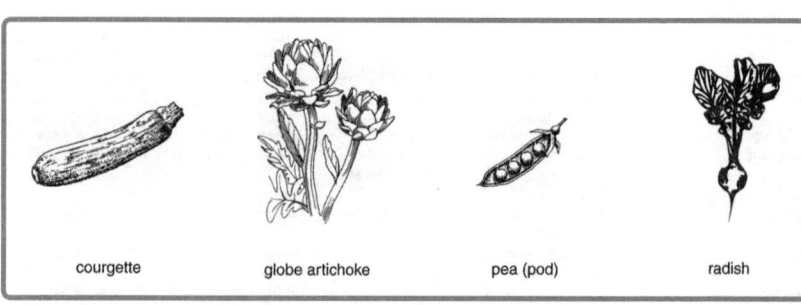

| courgette | globe artichoke | pea (pod) | radish |

Flowers (Bulbs, corms, rhizomes and tubers)

English name	Genus/Family	Colour	Country/Continent of origin
acidanthera	*Acidanthera*	white	NE Africa
African lily (or lily-of-the-Nile)	*Agapanthus*	white, purple	S Africa
agapanthus	*Agapanthus*	blue, white	S Africa
allium	*Allium*	blue, lilac, white, rose	Asia, Europe
amaryllis (or belladonna lily)	*Amaryllis*	rose-pink	S Africa, tropical America

English name	Genus/Family	Colour	Country/Continent of origin
anemone	*Anemone*	white, lilac, blue	Mediterranean, Asia, Europe
belladonna lily ► amaryllis			
bluebell	*Hyacinthoides*	blue	Europe
camassia	*Camassia*	white, cream, blue, purple	N America
chionodoxa (or glory of the snow)	*Chionodoxa*	blue, white, pink	Greece, Turkey
crinum	*Crinum*	rose-pink, white	S Africa
crocosmia	*Crocosmia*	orange	S Africa
crocus	*Crocus*	purple, rose, yellow, pink, orange	Mediterranean, Asia, Africa
crown imperial	*Fritillaria*	orange	N India
curtonus	*Curtonus*	orange	S Africa
cyclamen	*Cyclamen*	white, pink, red	Asia, Mediterranean
daffodil (or narcissus)	*Narcissus*	white, yellow, orange	Mediterranean, Europe
dog's tooth violet ► erythronium			
erythronium (or dog's tooth violet)	*Erythronium*	purple, pink, white, yellow	Europe, Asia
fritillaria	*Fritillaria*	red, yellow	Europe, Asia, N America
galtonia	*Galtonia*	white	S Africa
gladiolus	*Gladiolus*	purple, yellow	Europe, Asia
glory of the snow ► chionodoxa			
harebell	*Campanula*	blue	N temperate regions
hippeastrum	*Hippeastrum*	pink, white, red	tropical America
hyacinth	*Hyacinthus*	blue, white, red	S Europe, Asia
hyacinth, grape	*Muscari*	blue	Europe, Mediterranean
hyacinth, wild	*Scilla*	blue, purple, pink, white	Asia, S Europe
iris	*Iris*	purple, white, yellow	N temperate regions
lthuriel's spear	*Brodiaea*	white, pink, blue	N America
lapeirousia	*Lapeirousia*	red	S Africa
lily	*Lilium*	white, pink, crimson, yellow, orange, red	China, Europe, America
lily-of-the-Nile ► African lily			
lily-of-the-valley	*Convallaria*	white	Europe, Asia, America
naked ladies	*Colchicum*	white, pink, purple	Asia, Europe
nerine	*Nerine*	pink, salmon	S Africa
ornithogalum	*Ornithogalum*	white, yellow	S Africa
peacock (or tiger flower)	*Tigridia*	white, orange, red, yellow	Asia
rouge, giant	*Tigridia*	white, yellow, red, lilac	Mexico
snake's head	*Fritillaria*	purple, white	Europe
snowdrop	*Galanthus*	white	Europe
snowflake	*Leucojum*	white, green	S Europe
solfaterre	*Crocosmia × crocosmiflora*	orange, red	S Africa
Solomon's seal	*Polygonatum*	white	Europe, Asia
squill	*Scilla*	blue, purple	Europe, Asia, S Africa
sternbergia	*Sternbergia*	yellow	Europe
striped squill	*Puschkinia*	bluish-white	Asia
tiger flower ► peacock			
tiger lily	*Lilium*	orange	Asia
tulip	*Tulipa*	orange, red, pink, white, crimson, lilac	Europe, Asia
wand flower	*Dierama*	white, pink, mauve, purple	S Africa
winter aconite	*Eranthis*	yellow	Greece, Turkey

cyclamen

gladiolus

lily

Flowers (Herbaceous)

English name	Genus/Family	Colour	Country/Continent of origin
acanthus	*Acanthus*	white, rose, purple	Europe
African violet	*Saintpaulia*	violet, white, pink	Africa
alum root	*Heuchera*	rose, pink, red	N America
alyssum	*Alyssum*	white, yellow, pink	S Europe
anchusa	*Anchusa*	blue	Asia, S Europe
anemone	*Hepatica*	white, red-pink, blue	Europe, Caucasus
asphodel	*Asphodelus*	white, yellow	S Europe
aster	*Aster*	white, blue, purple, pink	Europe, Asia, N America
astilbe	*Astilbe*	white, pink, red	Asia
aubrietia	*Aubrieta*	purple	SE Europe
begonia	*Begonia*	pink	S America, the Pacific
bellflower	*Campanula*	blue, white	N temperate regions
bergamot	*Monarda*	white, pink, red, purple	N America
bistort	*Polygonum*	rose-pink	Japan, Himalayas
bleeding heart	*Dicentra*	pink, white, red	China, Japan, N America
bugbane	*Cimicifuga*	white	N America, Japan
busy lizzie	*Impatiens*	crimson, pink, white	tropics
buttercup	*Ranunculus*	yellow	temperate regions
carnation	*Dianthus*	white, pink, red	temperate regions
catmint	*Nepeta*	blue, mauve	Europe, Asia
celandine, giant	*Ranunculus*	white, copper-orange	Europe
Christmas rose	*Helleborus*	white, pink	Europe
chrysanthemum	*Chrysanthemum*	yellow, white	China
cinquefoil	*Potentilla*	orange, red, yellow	Europe, Asia
columbine (or granny's bonnet)	*Aquilegia*	purple, dark blue, pink, yellow	Europe
Cupid's dart	*Catananche*	blue, white	Europe
dahlia	*Dahlia*	red, yellow, white	Mexico
daisy	*Bellis*	white, yellow, pink	Europe
delphinium	*Delphinium*	white, mauve, pink, blue	Europe, N America
echinacea	*Echinacea*	rose-red, purple	N America
edelweiss	*Leontopodium*	yellow, white	Europe, Asia
evening primrose	*Oenothera*	yellow	N America
everlasting flower (or immortelle)	*Helichrysum bracteatum*	yellow	Australia
everlasting flower, pearly	*Anaphalis*	white	N America, Himalayas
fleabane	*Erigeron*	white, pink, blue, violet	Australia
forget-me-not	*Myosotis*	blue	Europe
foxglove	*Digitalis*	white, yellow, pink, red	Europe, Asia
fraxinella	*Dictamnus*	white, mauve	Europe, Asia
gentian	*Gentiana*	blue, yellow, white, red	temperate regions
geranium	*Pelargonium*	scarlet, pink, white	temperate regions, subtropics
geum	*Geum*	orange, red, yellow	S Europe, N America
goat's beard	*Aruncus*	white	N Europe
golden rod	*Solidago*	yellow	Europe
granny's bonnet ▸ columbine			
gypsophila	*Gypsophila*	white, pink	Europe, Asia
Hattie's pincushion (or the melancholy gentleman)	*Astrantia*	white, pink	Europe
heliopsis	*Heliopsis*	orange-yellow	N America
hellebore	*Helleborus*	plum-purple, white	Asia, Greece
herb Christopher	*Actaea*	white	N America
hollyhock	*Alcaea*	white, yellow, pink, red, maroon	Europe, China
hosta	*Hosta*	violet, white	China, Japan
immortelle ▸ everlasting flower			
kaffir lily	*Schizostylis*	red, pink	S Africa
kirengeshoma	*Kirengeshoma*	yellow	Japan
liatris	*Liatris*	heather-purple	N America
lobelia	*Lobelia*	white, red, blue, purple	Africa, N America, Australia
loosestrife	*Lysimachia*	rose-pink, purple	Europe
lotus	*Lotus*	yellow, pink, white	Asia, America
lupin	*Lupinus*	blue, yellow, pink, red	N America
marigold, African (or French marigold)	*Tagetes*	yellow, orange	Mexico
marigold, pot	*Calendula*	orange, apricot, cream	unknown
meadow rue	*Thalictrum*	yellow-white	Europe, Asia
mullein	*Verbascum*	yellow, white, pink, purple	Europe, Asia
nasturtium	*Tropaeolum*	yellow, red, orange	S America, Mexico

English name	Genus/Family	Colour	Country/Continent of origin
orchid	*Orchidaea*	red, purple, white, violet, green, brown, yellow, pink	tropics
ox-eye	*Buphthalmum*	yellow	Europe
pansy	*Viola*	white, yellow	temperate regions
peony	*Paeonia*	white, yellow, pink, red	Asia, Europe
Peruvian lily	*Alstroemeria*	cream, pink, yellow, orange, red	S America
petunia	*Petunia*	blue, violet, purple, white, pink	S America
phlox	*Phlox*	blue, white, purple, red	America
poppy	*Papaver*	red, orange, white, yellow, lilac	N temperate regions
primrose	*Primula*	yellow	N temperate regions
primula	*Primula*	white, pink, yellow, blue, purple	N temperate regions
red-hot poker	*Kniphofia*	white, yellow, orange, red	S Africa
salvia	*Salvia*	red, yellow, blue	S America, Europe, Asia
sea holly	*Eryngium*	blue, green-grey, white	Europe, S America
sidalcea	*Sidalcea*	lilac, pink, rose	N America
snapdragon	*Antirrhinum*	white, yellow, pink, red, maroon	Europe, Asia, S America
speedwell	*Veronica*	blue, white	Europe, Asia
spiderwort	*Tradescantia*	white, blue, pink, red, purple	N America
stokesia	*Stokesia*	white, blue, purple	N America
sunflower	*Helianthus*	yellow	N America
sweet pea	*Lathyrus*	purple, pink, white, red	Mediterranean
sweet william	*Dianthus*	white, pink, red, purple	S Europe
thistle, globe	*Echinops*	blue, white-grey	Europe, Asia
thistle, Scotch (or cotton thistle)	*Onopordum*	purple	Europe
violet	*Viola*	mauve, blue	N temperate regions
water chestnut	*Trapa*	white, lilac	Asia
water lily	*Nymphaea*	white, blue, red, yellow	worldwide
wolfsbane	*Aconitum*	blue, white, rose, yellow	Europe, Asia
yarrow	*Achillea*	white, cream	Europe, W Asia

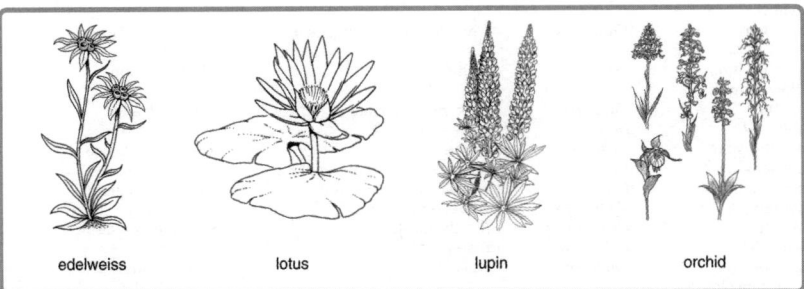

edelweiss   lotus   lupin   orchid

Flowers (Shrubs)

English name	Genus/Family	Colour	Country/Continent of origin
abelia	*Abelia*	white, rose-purple	Asia, China, Mexico
abutilon	*Abutilon*	lavender-blue	S America
acacia (or mimosa or wattle)	*Acacia*	yellow	Australia, tropical Africa, tropical America
almond, dwarf	*Prunus*	white, crimson, rose-pink	Asia, Europe
ampelopsis	*Ampelopsis*	green (blue-black fruit)	Far East
anthyllis	*Anthyllis*	yellow	Europe
azalea	*Rhododendron*	pink, purple, white, yellow, crimson	N hemisphere
berberis	*Berberis*	yellow, orange	Asia, America, Europe
bottle brush	*Callistemon*	red	Australia
bougainvillea	*Bougainvillea*	lilac, pink, purple, red, orange, white	S America
broom	*Cytisus*	yellow	Europe
buckthorn	*Rhamnus*	red, black	N hemisphere

Natural History

English name	Genus/Family	Colour	Country/Continent of origin
buddleia	*Buddleja*	purple, yellow, white	China, S America
cactus	*Cactaceae*	red, purple, orange, yellow, white	America
calico bush (or mountain laurel)	*Kalmia*	white, pink	China
camellia	*Camellia*	white, pink, red	Asia
caryopteris	*Caryopteris*	blue, violet	Asia
ceanothus	*Ceanothus*	pink, blue, purple	N America
ceratostigma	*Ceratostigma*	purple-blue	China
Chinese lantern	*Physalis*	orange, red	Japan
cistus	*Cistus*	white, pink	Europe
clematis	*Clematis*	white, purple, violet, blue, pink, yellow	N temperate regions
clerodendron	*Clerodendron*	white, purple-red	China
colquhounia	*Colquhounia*	scarlet, yellow	Himalayas
cornelian cherry	*Cornus*	yellow	Europe
coronilla	*Coronilla*	yellow	S Europe
corylopsis	*Corylopsis*	yellow	China, Japan
cotoneaster	*Cotoneaster*	white (red fruit)	Asia
currant, flowering	*Ribes*	red, white, pink	N America
desfontainia	*Desfontainia*	scarlet-gold	S America
deutzia	*Deutzia*	white, pink	Asia
diplera	*Diplera*	pale pink	China
dogwood	*Cornus*	white	Europe, SW Asia
embothrium	*Embothrium*	scarlet	S America
escallonia	*Escallonia*	white, pink	S America
euchryphia	*Euchryphia*	white	Chile, Australasia
euryops	*Euryops*	yellow	S Africa
fabiana	*Fabiana*	white, mauve	S America
firethorn	*Pyracantha*	white (red, orange, yellow fruits)	China
forsythia	*Forsythia*	yellow	China
frangipani	*Plumeria*	white, pink, yellow	tropical America
fuchsia	*Fuchsia*	red, pink, white	C and S America, New Zealand
gardenia	*Gardenia*	white	tropics
garland flower	*Daphne*	pink, crimson, white, purple	Europe, Asia
garrya	*Garrya*	green	California and Oregon
gorse (or furze or whin)	*Ulex*	yellow	Europe, Britain
hawthorn	*Crataegus*	white (orange-red berries)	N America, Europe, N Africa
heath, winter-flowering	*Erica*	white, pink, red	Africa, Europe
heather	*Calluna*	pink, purple, white	Europe, W Asia
hebe	*Hebe*	blue-white	New Zealand
helichrysum	*Helichrysum*	yellow	Australia, S Africa
hibiscus	*Hibiscus*	pink, mauve, purple, white, red	China, India
honeysuckle	*Lonicera*	white, yellow, pink, red	temperate regions
hydrangea	*Hydrangea*	white, pink, blue	Asia, America
hyssop	*Hyssopus*	bluish-purple	S Europe, W Asia
indigofera	*Indigofera*	rose-purple	Himalayas
ipomoea (or morning glory)	*Ipomoea*	white, red, blue	tropical America
japonica	*Chaenomeles*	white, pink, orange, red, yellow	N Asia
jasmine	*Jasminum*	white, yellow, red	Asia
Jerusalem sage	*Phlomis*	yellow	Europe
kerria	*Kerria*	yellow	China
kolkwitzia	*Kolkwitzia*	pink	China
laburnum	*Laburnum*	yellow	Europe, Asia
lavender	*Lavandula*	purple	Europe
leptospermum	*Leptospermum*	red, white	Australasia
lespedeza	*Lespedeza*	rose-purple	China, Japan
leycesteria	*Leycesteria*	claret	Himalayas
lilac (or syringa)	*Syringa*	purple, pink, white	Balkans
lion's tail	*Leonotis*	red	S Africa
magnolia	*Magnolia*	yellow, white, rose, purple	China, Japan
mahonia	*Mahonia*	yellow	Japan
malus	*Malus*	white, pink, red	N America, Asia
menziesa	*Menziesa*	wine-red	Japan
mimosa ► acacia			
mimulus	*Mimulus*	cream, orange, red	N America
mock orange	*Philadelphus*	white	Europe, Asia, N America
moltkia	*Moltkia*	violet-blue	Greece

English name	Genus/Family	Colour	Country/Continent of origin
morning glory ▸ ipomoea			
mother-of-pearl	*Symphoricarpus*	pink, white, red fruit	N America
mountain ash ▸ rowan			
myrtle	*Myrtus*	pink, white	Europe
oleander	*Nerium*	white, pink, purple, red	Mediterranean
olearia	*Olearia*	white, yellow	New Zealand
oleaster	*Elaeagnus*	yellow	Europe, Asia, N America
osmanthus	*Osmanthus*	white	China
pearl bush	*Exochorda*	white	China
peony	*Paeonia*	pink, red, white, yellow	Europe, Asia, N America
pieris	*Pieris*	white	China
poinsettia	*Euphorbia*	scarlet	Mexico
potentilla	*Potentilla*	yellow, red, orange	Asia
rhododendron	*Rhododendron*	red, purple, pink, white	S Asia
rhus	*Rhus*	foliage grey, purple, red	Europe, N America
ribbon woods	*Hoheria*	white	New Zealand
robinia	*Robinia*	rose-pink	N America
rock rose (or sun rose)	*Helianthemum*	white, yellow, pink, orange, red	Europe
rose	*Rosa*	pink, red, white, cream, yellow	N temperate regions
rosemary	*Rosmarinus*	violet	Europe, Asia
rowan (or mountain ash)	*Sorbus*	white (red, yellow berries)	Europe, Asia
sage, common	*Salvia*	green, white, yellow, reddish purple	S Europe
St John's wort	*Hypericum*	yellow	Europe, Asia
sea buckthorn	*Hippophae*	silver, orange	SW Europe
senecio	*Senecio*	yellow	New Zealand
skimmia	*Skimmia*	white	Japan, China
snowberry	*Symphoricarpos*	pink, white	N America
spiraea	*Spiraea*	white, pink, crimson	China, Japan
stachyurus	*Stachyurus*	pale yellow	China
staphylea	*Staphylea*	rose-pink	Europe, Asia
sun rose ▸ rock rose			
syringa ▸ lilac			
tamarisk	*Tamarix*	pink, white	Europe
thyme	*Thymus*	purple, white, pink	Europe
veronica	*Veronica*	white, pink, lilac, purple	New Zealand
viburnum	*Viburnum*	white, pink	Europe, Asia, Africa
Virginia creeper	*Parthenocissus*	foliage orange, red (blue-black fruits)	N America
wattle ▸ acacia			
weigela	*Weigela*	pink, red	N China
winter sweet	*Chimonanthus*	yellow	China
wisteria	*Wisteria*	mauve, white, pink	China, Japan
witch-hazel	*Hamamelis*	red, yellow	China, Japan

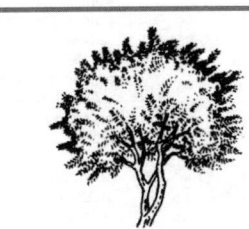

acacia

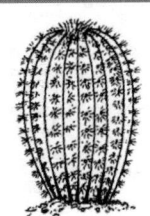

cactus

Fungi

English name	Species	Colour	Edibility
base toadstool (or ugly toadstool)	*Lactarius necator*	green, brown	poisonous
beautiful clavaria	*Ramaria formosa*	yellow, ochre, red, purple	poisonous
beefsteak fungus	*Fistulina hepatica*	red	edible
blusher	*Amanita fubescens*	red, brown	poisonous (raw) or edible (cooked)

Natural History

English name	Species	Colour	Edibility
brain mushroom	*Gyromitra esculenta*	chestnut, dark brown	poisonous
buckler agaric	*Entoloma clypeatum*	grey, brown	edible
Caesar's mushroom	*Amanita Caesarea*	red, yellow	edible
chanterelle	*Cantharellus cibarius*	yellow, ochre	excellent
clean mycena	*Mycena pura*	purple	poisonous
clouded agaric	*Lepista nebularis*	grey, brown	poisonous
common earthball	*Scleroderma aurantium*	ochre, yellow, brown	poisonous
common grisette	*Amanita vaginata*	grey, yellow	edible
common morel	*Morchella esculenta*	light brown, black	edible
common puffball	*Lycoperdon perlatum*	white, cream, brown	edible
common stinkhorn	*Phallus impudicus*	white, green	inedible
death cap	*Amanita phalloides*	grey, green, yellow, brown	deadly
deceiver, common laccaria	*Laccaria laccata*	purple, pink, orange	edible
destroying angel	*Amanita virosa*	white, brown	deadly
dingy agaric	*Tricholoma portentosum*	grey, black, yellow, lilac	edible
dryad's saddle	*Polyporus squamosus*	yellow, brown	edible
fairies bonnets	*Coprinus disseminatus*	grey, purple	worthless
fairy ring champignon	*Marasmius oreades*	beige, ochre, red, brown	edible
field mushroom	*Agaricus campestris*	white, brown	excellent
firwood agaric	*Tricholoma auratum*	green, yellow, brown	edible
fly agaric	*Amanita muscaria*	red, orange, white	poisonous
garlic marosmius	*Marosmius scorodonius*	red, brown	edible
gypsy mushroom	*Rozites caperata*	yellow, ochre	edible
hedgehog mushroom	*Hydnum repandum*	white, beige, yellow	edible
honey fungus	*Armillaria mellea*	honey, brown, red	inedible
horn of plenty (or trumpet of the dead)	*Craterellus cornucopiodes*	brown, black	very good
horse mushroom	*Agaricus arvensis*	white, yellow, ochre	very good
Jew's ear fungus	*Auricularia auricula judae*	yellow, brown	worthless
larch boletus	*Suillus grevillei*	yellow	edible
liberty cap (or 'magic mushroom')	*Psilocybe semilanceata*	brown	poisonous
lurid boletus	*Boletus luridus*	olive, brown, yellow	poisonous (raw) or edible (cooked)
morel	*Morchella*	brown	good
naked mushroom	*Lepista nuda*	purple, brown	edible
old man of the woods	*Strobilomyces floccopus*	brown, black	edible
orange-peel fungus	*Aleuria aurantia*	orange, red	edible
oyster mushroom	*Pleurotus ostreatus*	brown, black, grey, blue, purple	edible
panther cap (or false blusher)	*Amanita pantherina*	brown, ochre, grey, white	poisonous
parasol mushroom	*Macrolepiota procera*	beige, ochre, brown	excellent
penny-bun fungus	*Boletus edulis*	chestnut brown	excellent
périgord truffle	*Tuber melanosporum*	black, red-brown	excellent
Piedmont truffle	*Tuber magnatum*	white	edible
purple blewit	*Tricholomopsis rutilans*	yellow, red	edible
saffron milk cap	*Lactorius delicioses*	orange, red	poisonous (raw) or edible (cooked)
St George's mushroom	*Calocybe gambosa*	white, cream	edible
Satan's boletus	*Boletus satanus*	grey	poisonous (raw) or edible (cooked)
scarlet-stemmed boletus	*Boletus calopus*	grey, brown	poisonous
shaggy ink cap (or lawyer's wig)	*Coprinus comatus*	white, ochre	edible
sickener (or emetic russula)	*Russula emetica*	pink, red	poisonous
stinkhorn	*Phallus impudicus*	olive, green	inedible
stinking russula	*Russula foetens*	ochre, brown	poisonous
stout agaric	*Amanita spissa*	grey, brown	edible
strong scented garlic	*Tricholoma saponaceum*	grey, green, brown	poisonous
sulphur tuft (or clustered woodlover)	*Hypholoma fasciculare*	yellow, red, brown	poisonous
summer truffle	*Tuber aestivum*	dark brown	very good
white truffle	*Tuber magnatum*	cream, pale brown	excellent
winter fungus (or velvet shank)	*Flammulina velutipes*	yellow, brown, ochre	edible
wood agaric	*Collybia dryophila*	yellow, brown, rust	edible
wood mushroom	*Agaricus sylvaticus*	grey, red, brown	edible
woolly milk-cap (or griping toadstool)	*Lactarius torminosus*	pink, brown	poisonous
yellow stainer	*Agaricus xanthodermus*	white, yellow, grey	poisonous

English name	Species	Colour	Edibility
yellow-brown boletus (or slippery jack)	*Suillus luteus*	yellow, brown	edible

chanterelle

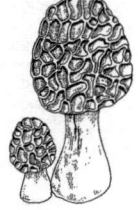
morel

puffball, common

stinkhorn

Trees (Europe and N America)

English name	Species	Deciduous/Evergreen	Continent of origin
alder, common	*Alnus glutinosa*	deciduous	Europe
almond	*Prunus dulcis*	deciduous	W Asia, N Africa
apple	*Malus pumila*	deciduous	Europe, W Africa
apple, crab	*Malus sylvestris*	deciduous	Europe, Asia
ash, common	*Fraxinus exzcelsior*	deciduous	Europe
aspen	*Populus tremula*	deciduous	Europe
bean tree, Red Indian	*Catalpa bignonioides*	deciduous	America, E Asia
beech, common	*Fagus sylvatica*	deciduous	Europe
beech, copper	*Fagus purpurea* ('Atropunicea')	deciduous	Europe
beech, noble	*Nothofagus obliqua*	deciduous	S America
birch, silver	*Betula pendula*	deciduous	Europe, America, Asia
box	*Buxus sempervirens*	evergreen	Europe, N Africa
Brazil nut	*Bertholletia excelsa*	evergreen	S America
camellia, deciduous	*Stewartia pseudo-camellia*	deciduous	Asia
castor-oil tree, prickly	*Eleutherococcus pictus*	deciduous	tropics
cedar of Lebanon	*Cedrus libani*	evergreen	Asia
cedar, smooth Tasmanian	*Athrotaxis cupressoides*	evergreen	Australia
cedar, white	*Thuja occidentalis*	evergreen	America
cherry, morello (or sour cherry)	*Prunus cerasus*	deciduous	Europe, Asia
cherry, wild (or gean)	*Prunus avium*	deciduous	Europe
chestnut, horse	*Aesculus hippocastanum*	deciduous	Asia, SW Europe
chestnut, sweet (or Spanish chestnut)	*Castanea sativa*	deciduous	Europe, Africa, Asia
cypress, Lawson	*Chamaecyparis lawsoniana*	evergreen	America
deodar	*Cedrus deodara*	evergreen	Asia
dogwood, common	*Cornus sanguinea*	deciduous	Europe
elm, Dutch	*Ulmus × hollandica*	deciduous	Europe
elm, English	*Ulmus procera*	deciduous	Europe
elm, wych	*Ulmus glabra*	deciduous	Europe
fig	*Ficus carica*	evergreen	Asia
fir, Douglas	*Pseudotsuga menziesii*	evergreen	America
fir, red	*Abies magnifica*	evergreen	America
ginkgo	*Ginkgo biloba*	deciduous	Asia
grapefruit	*Citrus × paradisi*	evergreen	Asia
gum, blue	*Eucalyptus globulus*	evergreen	Australia
gum, cider	*Eucalyptus gunnii*	evergreen	Australia
gum, snow	*Eucalyptus panciflora*	evergreen	Australia
gutta-percha tree	*Eucommia ulmoides*	deciduous	China
hawthorn	*Crataegus monogyna*	deciduous	Europe
hazel, common	*Corylus avellana*	deciduous	Europe, W Asia, N Africa
hemlock, Western	*Tsuga heterophylla*	evergreen	America
holly	*Ilex aquifolium*	evergreen	Europe, N Africa, W Asia
hornbeam	*Carpinus betulus*	deciduous	Europe, Asia
Joshua-tree	*Yucca brevifolia*	evergreen	America
Judas-tree	*Cercis siliquastrum*	deciduous	S Europe, Asia
juniper, common	*Juniperus communis*	evergreen	Europe, Asia
laburnum, common	*Laburnum anagyroides*	deciduous	Europe
larch, European	*Larix decidua*	deciduous	Europe

Natural History

English name	Species	Deciduous/ Evergreen	Continent of origin
larch, golden	*Pseudolarix kaempferi*	deciduous	E Asia
leatherwood	*Eucryphia lucida*	evergreen	Australia
lemon	*Citrus limon*	evergreen	Asia
lime	*Citrus aurantiifolia*	evergreen	Asia
lime, small-leafed	*Tilia cordata*	deciduous	Europe
locust tree	*Robinia pseudoacacia*	deciduous	America
magnolia (or white laurel)	*Magnolia virginiana*	evergreen	America
maple, field (or common maple)	*Acer campestre*	deciduous	Europe
maple, sugar	*Acer saccharum*	deciduous	America
medlar	*Mespilus germanica*	deciduous	Europe
mimosa	*Acacia dealbata*	deciduous	Australia, Europe
mockernut	*Carya tomentosa*	deciduous	America
monkey puzzle	*Araucaria araucana*	evergreen	S America
mountain ash ▸ rowan			
mulberry, common	*Morus nigra*	deciduous	Asia
mulberry, white	*Morus alba*	deciduous	Asia
myrtle, orange bark	*Myrtus apiculata*	evergreen	S America
nutmeg, California	*Torreya californica*	evergreen	America
oak, California live	*Quercus agrifolia*	deciduous	America
oak, cork	*Quercus suber*	evergreen	S Europe, N Africa
oak, English (or common oak)	*Quercus robur*	deciduous	Europe, Asia, Africa
oak, red	*Quercus rubra*	deciduous	America
olive	*Olea europaea*	evergreen	S Europe
orange, sweet	*Citrus sinensis*	evergreen	Asia
pagoda-tree	*Sophora japonica*	deciduous	China, Japan
pear	*Pyrus communis*	deciduous	Europe, W Asia
pine, Austrian	*Pinus nigra* subsp. *nigra*	evergreen	Europe, Asia
pine, Corsican	*Pinus nigra* subsp. *laricio*	evergreen	Europe
pine, Monterey	*Pinus radiata*	evergreen	America
pine, Scots	*Pinus sylvestris*	evergreen	Europe
plane, London	*Platanus × hispanica*	deciduous	Europe
plane, Oriental	*Platanus orientalis*	deciduous	SE Europe, Asia
plum	*Prunus domestica*	deciduous	Europe, Asia
poplar, balsam	*Populus balsamifera*	deciduous	America, Asia
poplar, black	*Populus nigra*	deciduous	Europe, Asia
poplar, Lombardy	*Populus nigra* 'Italica'	deciduous	Europe
poplar, white	*Populus alba*	deciduous	Europe
quince	*Cydonia oblonga*	deciduous	Asia
raoul	*Nothofagus procera*	deciduous	S America
rowan (or mountain ash)	*Sorbus aucuparia*	deciduous	Europe
sassafras, American	*Sassafras albidum*	deciduous	America
service tree, true	*Sorbus domestica*	deciduous	Europe
silver fir, common	*Abies alba*	evergreen	Europe
spruce, Norway	*Picea abies*	evergreen	Europe
spruce, sitka	*Picea sitchensis*	evergreen	America, Europe
strawberry tree	*Arbutus unedo*	evergreen	Europe
sycamore ('plane')	*Acer pseudoplatanus*	deciduous	Europe, W Asia
tamarack	*Larix laricina*	deciduous	N America
tree of heaven	*Ailanthus altissima*	deciduous	China
tulip tree	*Liriodendron tulipfera*	deciduous	America
walnut, black	*Juglans nigra*	deciduous	America
walnut, common	*Juglans regia*	deciduous	Europe, Asia
whitebeam	*Sorbus aria*	deciduous	Europe
willow, pussy (or goat willow or sallow willow)	*Salix caprea*	deciduous	Europe, Asia
willow, weeping	*Salix babylonica*	deciduous	Asia
willow, white	*Salix alba*	deciduous	Europe
yew, common	*Taxus baccata*	evergreen	N temperate regions

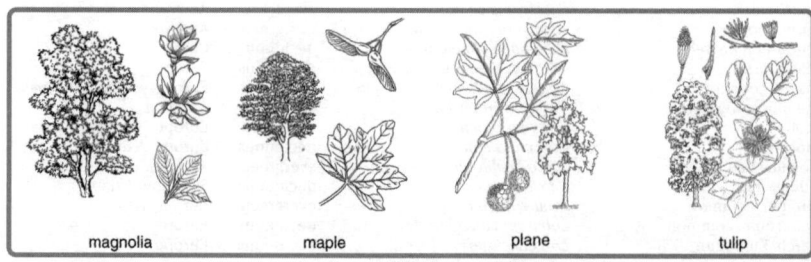

magnolia   maple   plane   tulip

Trees (Tropical)

Name	Species	Deciduous/ Evergreen	Continent of origin
African tulip tree	*Spathodea campanulata*	evergreen	Africa
almond, tropical	*Terminalia catappa*	deciduous	Asia
angel's trumpet	*Brugmansia × candida*	deciduous	S America
autograph tree	*Clusia rosea*	evergreen	Asia
avocado	*Persea americana*	evergreen	America
bamboo	*Schizostachyum glauchifolium*	deciduous	America
banana	*Musa × paradisiaca*	plant dies after fruiting	Asia
banyan	*Ficus benghalensis*	evergreen	Asia
baobab (or dead rat's tree)	*Adansonia digitata*	deciduous	Africa
beach heliotrope	*Argusia argentea*	evergreen	S America
bo tree	*Ficus religiosa*	deciduous	Asia
bombax	*Bombax ceiba*	deciduous	Asia
bottle brush	*Callistemon citrinus*	evergreen	Australia
breadfruit	*Artocarpus altilis*	evergreen	Asia
brownea	*Brownea macrophylla*	evergreen	C America
calabash	*Crescentia cujete*	evergreen	America
candlenut	*Aleurites moluccana*	evergreen	Asia
cannonball	*Courouptia guianensis*	evergreen	S America
chinaberry (or bead tree)	*Melia azedarach*	deciduous	Asia
Christmas-berry	*Schinus terebinthifolius*	evergreen	America
coconut palm	*Cocus nucifera*	evergreen	Asia
coffee tree	*Coffea liberica*	evergreen	Africa
Cook pine	*Araucaria columnaris*	evergreen	America
coral tree	*Erythrina coralloides*	deciduous	C America
coral shower	*Cassia grandis*	deciduous	Asia
cotton, wild	*Cochlospermum vitifolium*	deciduous	C and S America
crape myrtle	*Lagerstroemia indica*	deciduous	Asia
date palm	*Phoenix dactylifera*	evergreen	Asia and Africa
dragon tree	*Dracaena draco*	evergreen	Africa (Canary Is)
durian	*Durio zibethinus*	evergreen	Asia
ebony	*Diospyros ebenum*	evergreen	Asia
elephant's ear	*Enderolobium cyclocarpum*	deciduous	S America
flame tree	*Delonix regia*	deciduous	Africa (Madagascar)
gold tree	*Cybistax donnell-smithii*	deciduous	Asia
golden rain	*Koelreuteria paniculata*	deciduous	Asia
golden shower	*Cassia fistula*	deciduous	Asia
guava	*Psidium guajava*	evergreen	S America
ironwood (or casuarina)	*Casuarina equisetifolia*	deciduous	Australia and Asia
jacaranda	*Jacaranda mimosifolia*	deciduous	S America
jackfruit (or jack)	*Artocarpus heterophyllus*	evergreen	Asia
kapok tree	*Ceiba pentandra*	deciduous	Old and New World tropics
koa	*Acacia koa*	evergreen	Oceania (Hawaii)
lipstick tree	*Bixa orellanna*	evergreen	America
lychee	*Litchi chinensis*	evergreen	China
macadamia nut	*Macadamia integrifolia*	evergreen	Australia
mahogany	*Swietenia mahogoni*	evergreen	S America
mango	*Mangifera indica*	evergreen	Asia
mesquite	*Prosopis pallida*	evergreen	America
monkeypod (or rain tree)	*Albizia saman*	evergreen	S America
Norfolk island pine	*Araucaria heterophylla*	evergreen	Oceania (Norfolk I)
octopus tree	*Schefflera actinophylla*	evergreen	Australia
ohi'a lehua	*Metrosideros collina*	evergreen	Oceania (Hawaii)
pandanus (or screw pine)	*Pandanus tectorius*	evergreen	Oceania
paperbark tree	*Melaleuca quinquenervia*	evergreen	Australia
powderpuff	*Calliandra haematocephala*	evergreen	S America
royal palm	*Roystonea regia*	evergreen	America (Cuba)
sandalwood	*Santalum album*	deciduous	Asia
sand-box tree	*Hura crepitans*	deciduous	Americas
sausage tree	*Kigelia pinnata*	evergreen	Africa
scrambled egg tree	*Cassia glauca*	evergreen	Americas
Surinam cherry	*Eugenia uniflora*	evergreen	S America
teak tree	*Tectona grandis*	evergreen	Asia
tiger's claw	*Erythrina variegata*	deciduous	Asia
yellow oleander	*Thevetia peruviana*	evergreen	Americas (W Indies)

Natural History

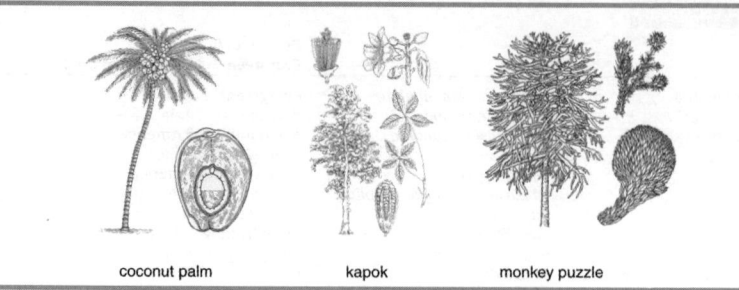

| coconut palm | kapok | monkey puzzle |

Fish—Record holders

Fastest	Over short distances, the sailfish can reach a speed of 110kph/68mph; however marlins are the fastest over longer distances, and can reach a burst speed of 68–80kph/40–50mph.
Largest	The whale shark (*Rhincodon typus*) is said to reach over 18m/59ft, with the largest on record being 12.65m/41ft 6in, weighing an estimated 21.5 tonnes.
Smallest	The dwarf pygmy goby (*Pandaka pygmaea*), found in the streams and rivers of Luzon in the Philippines, measures 7.5–9.9mm and weighs 4–5mg.
Smallest in British waters	Guillet's goby (*Lebetus guilleti*) reaches a maximum length of 24mm.
Most widespread	The distribution of the bristlemouths of genus *Cyclothone* is worldwide excluding the Arctic.
Most restricted	The devil's hole pupfish (*Cyprinodon diabolis*) inhabits only a small area of water above a rock shelf in a spring-fed pool in Ash Meadows, Nevada, USA.
Deepest dweller	In 1970 a brotulid *Bassogigas profundissimus* was recovered from a depth of 8 299m/27 230ft, making it the deepest living vertebrate.
Largest fish ever caught on a rod	In 1959 a great white shark measuring 5.13m/16ft 10in and weighing 1 208kg/2 664 lb was caught off S Australia.
Largest freshwater fish found in Britain and Ireland	Reportedly, in 1815 a pike (*Esox lucius*) was taken from the River Shannon in Ireland weighing 41.7kg/92 lb; however there is evidence of a pike weighing 32.7kg/72 lb having been caught on Loch Ken, Scotland, in 1774.
Largest saltwater fish caught by anglers in the UK	In 1933 a tunny weighing 385.989kg/851 lb was caught near Whitby, Yorkshire.
Longest-lived species	Some specimens of the sturgeon are thought to be over 80 years old.
Shortest-lived species	Tooth carp of the suborder *Cyprinodontidae* live for only 8 months in the wild.
Greatest distance covered by a migrating fish	A bluefin tuna was tagged in 1958 off California and caught in 1963 in Japan; it had covered a distance of 9 335km/5 800mi.

Birds—Record holders

Highest flier	Ruppell's griffon, a vulture, has been measured at 11 275m (about 7mi) above sea level.
Furthest migrator	The arctic tern travels up to 36 000km/22 400mi each year, flying from the Arctic to the Antarctic and back again.
Fastest flier	The peregrine falcon can dive through the air at speeds up to 185kph/115mph. The fastest bird in level flight is the eider duck, which can reach 80kph/50mph.
Fastest animal on two legs	The ostrich can maintain a speed of 50kph/31mph for 15 minutes or more, and it may reach 65–70kph/40–43mph in short bursts, eg when escaping from predators.
Smallest	The bee hummingbird of Cuba is under 6cm/2.4in long and weighs 3g/0.1oz.
Greatest wingspan	The wandering albatross can reach 3.65m/12ft.
Heaviest flying bird	The great bustard and the kori bustard both weigh up to 18kg/40 lb, with swans not far behind at about 16kg/35 lb.
Deepest diver	The emperor penguin can reach a depth of 265m/870ft. The great northern diver or loon can dive to about 80m/262ft — deeper than any other flying bird.
Most abundant	Africa's red-billed quelea is the most numerous wild bird, with an estimated population of about 1 500 million. The domestic chicken is the most abundant of all birds, numbering over 4 000 million.
Most feathers	The greatest number of feathers counted on a bird was 25 216, on a swan.

Mammals—Record holders

Largest	The blue whale, up to 30m/98ft long and weighing up to 150 tonnes, is the largest known mammal. The largest existing land mammal is the male African elephant, standing up to 3.3m/11ft at the shoulder and weighing up to 7 tonnes.
Tallest	The giraffe stands up to 5.5m/18ft high.
Smallest	The pygmy white-toothed shrew, also called the Etruscan shrew, has a body about 5cm/2in long and weighs up to 2.5g/0.1oz. Some bats weigh even less.
Fastest on land	The cheetah can reach 100kph/62mph, but only in short bursts. The pronghorn can maintain speeds of 50kph/31mph for several kilometres.
Most prolific breeder	A North American meadow mouse produced 17 litters in a single year (4–9 babies per litter).
Most widespread	Humans are the most widely distributed mammals, closely followed by the house mouse, which has accompanied humans to all parts of the world.

Collective names for animals, fish and birds

Animal	Collective name	Animal	Collective name
ants	colony, nest, swarm	larks	bevy, exaltation
apes	shrewdness	leopards	leap
asses	pace	lions	pride
baboons	troop	locusts	plague, swarm
badgers	cete	magpies	tiding, tittering
bears	sleuth, sloth	moles	labour
bees	colony, erst, grist, hive, nest, swarm	monkeys	troop
birds	flight, flock, volery	mules	span
buffalo	gang, herd, obstinacy	nightingales	watch
caterpillars	army	otters	romp
cats	clowder, pounce	owls	parliament, stare
cattle	drove, herd	oxen	drove, herd, yoke
chickens	brood, clutch	oysters	bed
clams	bed	parrots	company, pandemonium
cockroaches	intrusion	partridges	covey
cranes	sedge, siege	peacocks	muster, ostentation
crocodiles	bask	penguins	colony, muster, parcel
crows	murder	pheasants	bevy, bouquet, nest, nid, nide, nye
deer	herd	pigs	litter
dogs	kennel, pack	plovers	congregation, wing
dolphins	school	ponies	string
doves	dole	porcupines	prickle
ducks	brace, flock, paddling, safe, team	porpoises	school, turmoil
eagles	convocation	quail	bevy, covey
elephants	herd, parade	rabbits	bury
elk	gang	rats	colony
ferrets	busyness	ravens	unkindness
fish	draught, school, shoal	rhinoceros	crash
flamingos	stand	rooks	building, parliament, rookery
flies	busyness, swarm	seals	herd, pod, rookery
foxes	leash, skulk	sharks	shiver
frogs	army	sheep	drove, flock, trip
geese	flock, gaggle, skein	sparrows	host
giraffes	tower	squirrels	dray, scurry
gnats	cloud, horde	starlings	murmuration
goats	herd, tribe, trip	storks	mustering
goldfinches	charm, chirm	swans	bevy, wedge
gorillas	band	swine	drift, sounder
grouse	pack	teal	spring
hares	down, husk, mute	tigers	ambush, streak
hawks	cast	toads	knot
hens	brood	trout	hover
herons	siege	turkeys	rafter
hippopotami	bloat	turtle	bale, dole, turn
hogs	drift	vipers	nest
horses	drove, herd, stable, team	whales	gam, herd, pod, school
hounds	cry, mute, pack	wolves	pack, rout, route
hyenas	cackle	woodcocks	fall
jellyfish	smack	woodpeckers	descent
kangaroos	herd, mob, troop	zebras	zeal
kittens	kindle, litter		

Natural History

Natural History

Mammals

Mammals are the group of animals to which humans belong. They are characterized by the presence of mammary glands in the female which produce milk on which the young can be nourished. They are divided into monotremes or egg-laying mammals; marsupials in which the young are born at an early stage of development and then grow outside the mother's womb, often in a pouch; placental mammals in which the young are nourished in the womb by the mother's blood and are born at a late stage of development. A crucial aspect of mammals is the fact that their hair and skin glands allow them to regulate their temperatures from within, ie they are endothermic (warm-blooded). This confers on them a greater adaptability to more varied environments than that of reptiles. There are over 4 000 species of mammals, most of which are terrestrial, the exceptions being species of bat which have developed the ability to fly, and the whale which leads an aquatic existence.

Name	Family/Species	Size (cm)[1]	Distribution	Food	Special features
■ Monotremes					
echidna, long-beaked	Species *Zaglossus bruijni*	45–90	New Guinea	earthworms	prominent beak; short spines scattered among fur
echidna, short-beaked	Species *Tachyglossidae aculeatus*	30–45	Australia, Tasmania and New Guinea	ants, termites	fur covered in protective spines; known to live up to 50 years in captivity
platypus	Family *Ornithorhynchidae*	45–60	E Australia and Tasmania	invertebrates, larvae	noted for its duck-like snout
■ Marsupials					
bandicoot	Family *Peramelidae*	15–56	Australia and New Guinea	insectivorous and omnivorous	highest reproductive rate of all marsupials
kangaroo	Family *Macropodidae*	to 165	Australia and New Guinea	grasses, plants	most popularly known of Australian mammals, noted for its bounding motion and prominent female pouch; includes all species of wallaby
kangaroo, rat	Family *Macropodidae*	28.4–30	Australia and New Guinea	grasses, plants	rabbit-sized version of its larger namesake
koala	Family *Phascolarctidae*	78	E Australia	eucalyptus leaves	marsupial with popular reputation; intensive management has significantly revived population numbers which at one time seemed threatened with extinction
mole, marsupial	Family *Notoryctidae*	13–15	Australia	insects, larvae	only Australian mammal that has specialized in burrowing
oppossum	Family *Didelphidae*	7–55	C and S America	earthworms, fruit, insects, small vertebrates, crustaceans, fish, frogs, reptiles	generally known for its dreadful smell
possum, brushtail	Family *Phalangeridae*	34–70	Australia, New Guinea, Solomon Is and New Zealand	leaves, fruit, bark, eggs, invertebrates	the most commonly encountered of all Australian mammals
wallaby ► kangaroo					
wombat	Family *Vombatidae*	870–115	SE Australia and Tasmania	grasses	poor eyesight compensated by keen senses of smell and hearing
■ Placental mammals					
aardvark	Family *Orycteropodidae*	105–130	Africa S of the Sahara	ants, termites	secretive, nocturnal creature; characterized by its long, tubular snout
anteater	Family *Myrmecophagidae*	16–22	C and S America	ants and sometimes termites	noted, particularly the giant anteater, for its elongated snout
antelope, dwarf	Tribe *Neotragini*	45–55	Africa	leaves, grass, fruit, buds	unusual among hoofed mammals in that the female is larger than the male

Name	Family/Species	Size (cm)[1]	Distribution	Food	Special features
armadillo	Family *Dasypodidae*	12.5–100	southern N America, C and S America	vertebrates, insects, fungi, tubers, fruit, carrion,	noted, particularly the giant armadillo, for its protective suit of armour
ass	Subgenus *Asinus*	200–210	Africa and Asia	grass, leaves	renowned as a beast of burden
baboon and mandrill	Genus *Papio*	56–80	Africa	fruit, plants, insects, small mammals	able to walk over long distances
badger	Family *Mustelidae*	50–100	Africa, Europe, Asia and N America	vertebrates, invertebrates, fruit, roots, earthworms	mainly nocturnal; European species characterized by its distinctive black and white markings
bat	Order *Chiroptera*	15–200 (wingspan)	worldwide except for the Arctic and Antarctic	insects, vertebrates, fish, fruit	the only vertebrate, except for birds, capable of sustained flight; noted for its powers of echo location and tendency to cluster in large numbers
bear, black	Species *Ursus americanus*	1.3–1.8m	N America	omnivorous	smaller and more secretive than the brown or grizzly bear, its greater ability to adapt has helped it to survive in greater numbers
bear, grizzly (or brown bear)	Species *Ursus arctos*	200–280	NW America and former USSR	omnivorous	noted for its size (up to half a ton); much reduced population due to hunting, loss of natural habitat
beaver	Genus *Castor*	80–120	N America, Asia and Europe	plants, wood	renowned for its industry and ability to construct dams and lodges in streams and ponds
beaver, mountain	Family *Aplondontidae*	30–41	Pacific Coast of Canada and USA	leaves, plant materials	land-dwelling and burrowing animal; causes great damage to forest areas
bison, American	Species *Bison bison*	to 380	N America	grazing fodder	once numbered in millions in the prairies of N America, now survives only in parks and refuges
bison, European	Species *Bison bonasus*	to 290	former USSR	grazing fodder	became extinct in the wild in 1919, but has now been re-established in parts of the former USSR
boar	Family *Suidae*	58–210	Europe, Africa and Asia	plants, larvae, frogs, mice, earthworms	wild pig; characteristically ugly appearance; intelligent and highly adaptable; includes species of warthog
buffalo, wild water	Species *Bubalus arnee*	240–280	SE Asia	grazing fodder	adept at moving through the muddy areas which they inhabit
bush baby	Subfamily *Galaginae*	12–32	Africa and S Asia	insects, fruit, gum	highly agile, arboreal creature
bushbuck	Species *Tragelaphus scriptus*	110–145	Africa S of the Sahara	grazing fodder	occupies habitats with dense cover; dark brown or chestnut coat with white markings
camel	Species *Camelus bactrianus*	190–230 (height of hump)	Mongolia	plants, vegetation	two humps
capybara	Family *Hydrochoeridae*	106–134	S America	grass	largest living rodent, lives in groups by the edge of water; traditionally hunted for its meat and skin
cat	Family *Felidae*	20–400	worldwide	carnivorous	acute sense of vision and smell

Natural History

Name	Family/Species	Size (cm)[1]	Distribution	Food	Special features
cattle	Family *Bovidae*	180–200	worldwide	grass	agricultural animal existing in both long-horned and polled or hornless breeds
chamois	Species *Rupicapra rupicapra*	125–135	Europe and Asia	grass, leaves, lichen	has adapted to alpine and subalpine conditions and to life on snowy mountains; part of its defence mechanism in fighting is its evasive running and dodging movement
cheetah	Family *Felidae*	112–135	Africa	hoofed animals up to 40kg, such as gazelles, impala, wildebeest calves	the fastest of all land animals, reaching speeds of 100kph/62mph
chimpanzee	Genus *Pan*	70–85	W and C Africa	fruit, leaves, seeds, insects, small mammals	most intelligent of the great apes; recent studies suggest that adults teach their offspring how to use tools
chinchilla	Family *Chinchillidae*	25	S America	grazing fodder	widely hunted as food and for its valuable fur
civet	Family *Viverridae*	33–84	Africa and Asia	fruit, small mammals, birds, rodents, insects, small reptiles	cat-like carnivore; nocturnal hunter; economic source of civet oil
colugo	Genus *Cynocephalus*	33–42	SE Asia	leaves, shoots, buds, flowers	also known as flying lemur, a reference to the membrane which stretches from its neck to the tips of its fingers, toes and tail, allowing it to glide from tree to tree
coyote	Species *Canis latrans*	70–97	N America	squirrels, rabbits, mice, antelope, deer, mountain sheep	makes unique howling sound; regarded as agricultural pest for its attacks on farm animals, but also kills agricultural vermin
coypu	Species *Myocastor coypu*	50	S America	freshwater plants	highly aquatic rodent; burrows into banks; beaver-like qualities
deer	Family *Cervidae*	41–152	N and S America, Europe and Asia	grass, shoots, twigs, leaves, flowers, fruit	distinguished in the male by the presence of antlers most characteristically used to attack other males during the rutting period; species include red deer, reindeer, waipiti, and the moose or elk
dingo	Species *Canis dingo*	150	Australasia	rabbits, lizards, grasshoppers, wild pigs, kangaroos	history of the dingo in Australia dates back 8 000 years; descendant of the wolf; lives in packs
dog	Species *Canis familiaris*	20–75	worldwide	carnivorous	first animal to be domesticated; c.400 domestic breeds
dolphin	Family *Delphinidae*	120–400	worldwide	fish, squid	renowned for grace, agility, intelligence; highly developed social organization and communication systems
dolphin, river	Family *Platanistidae*	210–260	SE Asia and S America	fish, shrimp, squid, octopus	virtually blind, but with highly sensitive system of echo location
dormouse	Family *Gliridae*	6–19	Europe, Africa, Turkey, Asia and Japan	omnivorous	halfway between mouse and squirrel both in form and behaviour

Natural History

Name	Family/Species	Size (cm)[1]	Distribution	Food	Special features
dromedary	Species *Camelus dromedarius*	190–230 (height of hump)	SW Asia, N Africa and Australia	plants, vegetation	domesticated camel with one hump; important as a beast of burden, and source of wool and milk
duiker	Subfamily *Cephalophinae*	55–72	Africa S of the Sahara	leaves, fruit, shoots, buds, seeds, bark, small birds, rodents	named after its habit of diving into cover when disturbed
eland	Genus *Taurotragus*	250–350	Africa	grazing fodder	elegant and highly mobile spiral horned antelope; experiments in the agricultural domestication of the common eland have taken place in Africa
elephant, African	Species *Loxodonta africana*	600–750	Africa S of the Sahara	grass, plants, leaves, twigs, flowers, fruit	largest living mammal, with distinctive trunk and large tusks and ears; drastically reduced population
fox	Family *Canidae*	24–100	N and S America, Europe, Asia and Africa	rodents, birds, invertebrates, fruit, fish, rabbits, hares, earthworms	justified reputation for cunning, intelligence and resourcefulness
gazelle	Genus *Gazella*	122–166	Africa	leaves, grass, fruit	birth peaks adapted to coincide with abundance of feeding vegetation during the spring and early rains
gerbil	Subfamily *Gerbillinae*	6–7.5	Africa and Asia	seeds, fruits, leaves, stems, roots, bulbs, insects, snails	defence mechanisms include colour of skin closely allied to the environment for hiding purposes, wide field of vision, and the ability to hear low frequency sounds such as the beating of owls' wings; domesticated form is the Mongolian gerbil often kept as a pet
gerenuk	Genus *Litocranius*	140–160	Africa	leaves, shoots, flowers, fruit	graceful, delicate creature; rises on hind legs in order to extend its reach when feeding on the leaves of tall shrubs and bushes
gibbon	Family *Hylobatidae*	45–65	SE Asia	fruit, leaves, invertebrates	renowned for spectacular ablility to move among trees using swinging movements of arms; loud and sophisticated voice
giraffe	Species *Giraffa camelopardalis*	380–470	Africa S of the Sahara	leaves, shoots, herbs, flowers, fruit, seed	distinguished by its mottled coat and the length of its neck which allows it to feed on foliage which is out of the reach of smaller mammals
gnu	Genus *Connochaetes*	194–209	Africa	grazing fodder	characterized by massive head and mane, bearded throat, tail which reaches almost to the ground
goat, mountain	Species *Oreamnos americanus*	to 175	N America	grazing fodder	large, ponderous rock climber, adapted to living in snowy mountains of N America

Natural History

Name	Family/Species	Size (cm)[1]	Distribution	Food	Special features
goat, wild	Species *Capra aegagrus*	130–140	S Europe, Middle East and Asia	grazing fodder	subspecies includes domestic goat
gopher	Family *Geomyidae*	12–22.5	N America	plant materials	highly adapted to its burrowing and subterranean existence
gorilla	Genus *Gorilla*	150–170	C Africa	leaves and stems	largest living primate; the most intelligent of land animals (after humans); unjustified reputation for ferocity, perhaps based on its size, and habit of beating its chest in a show of aggression
guinea pig	Genus *Cavia*	28	S America	herbs, grasses	tailless rodent; domesticated form is the *Cavia porcellus*
hamster	Subfamily *Cricetinae*	5.3–10.2	Europe, Middle East, former USSR and China	mainly seeds, shoots, root vegetables	familiar western pet, but aggressive towards own species in the wild
hare	Genus *Lepus*	40–76	N and S America, Africa, Europe, Asia and Arctic	grass, herbs, plants, bark, twigs	well-developed ability to run from predators; species include jack-rabbits and the Arctic hare
hare, Patagonian	Genus *Dolichotis*	45	S America	grasses, herbs	unusual characteristic in a mammal of being strictly monogamous
hartebeest	Genus *Alcelaphus*	195–200	Africa	grass, vegetation	distinctive long face, sloping back
hedgehog	Subfamily *Erinaceinae*	10–15	Europe, Asia and Africa	earthworms, beetles, slugs, earwigs, caterpillars	ability to curl up and use prickly, spined back as protection
hippopotamus	Family *Hippopotamidae*	150–345	Africa	terrestrial vegetation	large, heavy and barrel-shaped with short stumpy legs; wallows in water
horse	Subgenus *Equus*	200–210	worldwide in domesticated form; Asia, N and S America and Australia in the wild	grass, leaves	historically useful as a beast of burden and means of transport, and for agricultural, military and recreational purposes
hyena	Family *Hyaeninae*	85–140	Africa and Asia	carrion, mammals, insects, small vertebrates, eggs, fruit, vegetables	scavenger and hunter, with highly developed systems of communication; family includes the aardwolf
ibex	Species *Capra ibex*	85–143	C Europe, Asia and Africa	grazing fodder	large horned creature saved from extinction in C Europe
impala	Genus *Aepyceros*	128–142	Africa	grass, leaves, flowers, fruit, seeds	attractive, graceful creature with fawn and mahogany coat; females and young gather in large herds; male has lyre-shaped horns
jackal	Genus *Canis*	65–106	Africa, SE Europe and Asia	fruit, invertebrates, reptiles, birds, small mammals, carrion	unfair reputation as cowardly scavenger
jaguar	Species *Panthera onca*	112–185	C and S America	deer, monkeys, sloths, birds, turtles, frogs, fish, small rodents	largest cat to be found in the Americas
jerboa	Family *Dipodidae*	4–26	N Africa, Turkey, Middle East and C Asia	seeds, vegetation, insects	long hind legs allow movement by hopping and jumping

Name	Family/Species	Size (cm)[1]	Distribution	Food	Special features
lemming	Tribe *Lemmini*	10–11	N America and Eurasia	plants, bulbs, roots, mosses	Norway lemming is noted for its mass migration which sometimes results in drowning
lemur	Family *Lemuridae*	12–70	Madagascar Africa	flowers, leaves, bamboo shoots	mainly nocturnal and arboreal
lemur, flying ▸ colugo					
leopard	Species *Panthera pardus*	100–190	Africa and Asia	mainly small mammals, birds	opportunistic, nocturnal hunter; adept at climbing trees
lion	Species *Panthera leo*	240–300	Africa and Asia	meat of animals which weigh 50–500 kg	known as the 'King of Beasts'; the most socially organized of the cat family
llama	Species *Lama glama*	230–400	S America	plants and vegetation	S American beast of burden
lynx	Species *Felis lynx*	67–110	Europe and N America	rodents, small hoofed mammals	lives in cold northern latitudes; well adapted to travelling through deep snow
macaque	Genus *Macaca*	38–70	Asia and N Africa	mainly fruit, insects, leaves, crops, small animals	heavily built and partly terrestrial genus of monkey; includes the Rhesus monkey adapted to life in the Himalayas, and the Barbary apes imported into Gibraltar in the 18c
marmoset	Family *Callitrichidae*	17.5–40	S America	fruit, flowers, nectar, gum, frogs, snails, lizards, spiders, insects	small, colourful, squirrel-like monkeys; includes species of tamarins
marten	Genus *Martes*	30–75	N America, Europe and Asia	mice, squirrels, rabbits, grouse, fruit, nuts	one species, the fisher, unique for its ability to penetrate the quilled defences of the porcupine
mole	Family *Talpidae*	2.4–7.5	Europe, Asia and N America	earthworms, insect larvae, slugs	almost exclusively subterranean existence
mongoose	Family *Viverridae*	24–58	Africa, S Asia and SW Europe	vertebrates, insects, fruit, snakes	some species live in social groups; often seen in the tripod position, ie standing up on hind legs and tail
monkey, capuchin	Family *Cebidae*	25–63	S America	insects, fruit, leaves, seeds, other small mammals	mainly lives in social groupings for the purposes of defence, foraging for food, and rearing young
mouse ▸ rat					
narwhal	Species *Monodon monoceros*	400–500	former USSR, N America and Greenland	shrimp, cod, flounder	distinctive single tusk in the male can reach lengths of up to 3m
okapi	Species *Okapia johnstoni*	190–200	C Africa	mainly leaves and shoots	secretive and elusive creature; strange-looking mixture of giraffe and zebra
orang-utan	Species *Pongo pygmaeus*	150	forests of N Sumatra and Borneo	fruit, leaves, insects	sparse covering of long red-brown hair; adults have large naked fatty folds around face; life span of 35 years in the wild; much diminished population
otter	Subfamily *Lutrinae*	40–123	N and S America, Europe, Asia and Africa	frogs, crabs, fish, aquatic birds	only truly amphibious members of the general weasel family; greatly reduced population due to persecution, loss of natural habitat

Natural History

Natural History

Name	Family/Species	Size (cm)[1]	Distribution	Food	Special features
panda, giant	Species *Ailuropoda melanoleuca*	130–150	China	bamboo	rare; poor breeder; the success rate of breeding in captivity has been extremely low
polar bear	Species *Ursus maritimus*	250–300	N polar regions	mainly seals, carcasses of large marine animals	unique for its large size, white coat and adaptation to aquatic living
porcupine (New World)	Family *Erethizontidae*	30–86	N and S America	bark, roots, shoots, leaves, berries, seeds, nuts, flowers	arboreal version of Old World porcupine; excellent climber
porcupine (Old World)	Family *Hystricidae*	37–47	Africa and Asia	roots, bulbs, fruit, berries	heavily quilled and spiny body
porpoise	Family *Phocoenidae*	120–150	N temperate zone, W Indo-Pacific, temperate and sub-antarctic waters of S America and Auckland Islands	fish, squid, crustaceans	large range of sounds for the purpose of echo location
puma	Species *Felis concolor*	105–196	N and S America	deer, rodents	wide-ranging hunter; includes subspecies cougar
rabbit, European	Genus *Oryctolagus*	38–58	Europe, Africa, Australia, New Zealand and S America	grass, herbs, roots, plants, bark	burrowing creature; opportunistic animal in widespread environment; noted for its breeding capacity; domesticated rabbits descended from this genus
racoon	Genus *Procyon*	55	N, S and C America	frogs, fish, birds, eggs, fruit, nuts, small rodents, insects, corn	black masked face; distinctive ringed tail; reputation for mischief
rat (New World)	Subfamily *Hesperomyinae*	5–8	N and S America	seeds, grain, plants, nuts, fruit, fungi, insects, crustaceans, fish	numerous species adapted to living in all possible forms of habitat
rat (Old World)	Subfamily *Murinae*	4.5–8.2	Europe, Asia, Africa and Australia	omnivorous	large number of species; one of the most successful mammals at adapting to any form of environment
reedbuck	Genus *Redunca*	110–176	Africa	grass, leaves, crops	graceful, elegant animal; distinctive whistling sounds, leaping movements
rhinoceros	Family *Rhinocerotidae*	250–400	Africa and tropical Asia	plant foliage	name derives from horn growing from snout; use of the horn for commercial purposes has brought the animal to the verge of extinction
seal	Family *Phocidae*	117–490	mainly polar, subpolar and temperate seas	fish, squid, crustaceans	graceful swimmer and diver; some species have been the object of controversial culling procedures
sheep, American bighorn	Species *Ovis canadensis*	168–186	N America	grazing fodder	large horns and body similar to an ibex; clings to the vicinity of cliffs
sheep, barbary	Genus *Ammotragus*	155–165	N Africa	grazing fodder	large head and horns up to 84cm in length

Name	Family/Species	Size (cm)[1]	Distribution	Food	Special features
sheep, blue	Genus *Pseudois*	91 (shoulder height)	Asia	grazing fodder	blue coat; curved horns
shrew	Family *Soricidae*	3.5–4.8	Europe, Asia, Africa, N America and northern S America	insects, earthworms	generally poor eyesight compensated for by acute sense of smell and hearing
shrew, elephant-	Order *Macroscelidea*	10.4–29.4	Africa	invertebrates, plants, fruit, seeds	distinctive creature with beady eyes, long pointed snout and short legs
skunk	Subfamily *Mephitinae*	40–68	N and S America	insects, small mammals, eggs, fruit	evil-smelling defence mechanism; major carrier of rabies
sloth, three-toed	Family *Bradypodidae*	56–60	S America	leaves	smaller version of the two-toed sloth; slightly more active both by day and night
sloth, two-toed	Family *Megalonychidae*	58–70	S America	leaves	arboreal, nocturnal creature noted for the slowness of its movement
springbuck	Genus *Antidorcas*	96–115	S Africa	mainly grass	gregarious creature which migrates in herds of tens of thousands
springhare	Family *Pedetidae*	36–43	S Africa	grass and soil	burrowing creature like a miniature kangaroo; moves usually by hopping; hunted by humans as a source of food and for its skin
squirrel	Family *Sciuridae*	6.6–10	N and S America, Europe, Africa and Asia	nuts, seeds, plants, insects	large number of species living in a variety of environments and including arboreal, burrowing and flying creatures; species include the marmot and chipmunk; grey squirrel noted for its ability to strip bark and damage young trees
tapir	Genus *Tapirus*	180–250	C and S America and SE Asia	grass, leaves, vegetation, buds, fruit, shoots	strange-looking, nocturnal mammal with distinctive snout; all species exist in vastly reduced numbers
tarsier	Genus *Tarsius*	11–14	islands of SE Asia	insects, lizards, bats, birds, snakes	proportionally large eyes; extraordinary ability to rotate neck
tiger	Species *Panthera tigris*	220–360	India, Manchuria, China and Indonesia	hoofed animals, eg deer and wild pigs	solitary hunters, stalk for prey
vole	Tribe *Microtini*	10–11	N America, Europe, Asia and the Arctic	grasses, seeds, aquatic plants, insects	population fluctuates in regular patterns or cycles
walrus	Species *Odobenus rosmarus*	250–320	Arctic seas	marine molluscs and invertebrates	characterized by its thick folds of skin, twin tusks
waterbuck	Species *Kobus ellipsiprymnus*	177–235	Africa	grasses, reeds, rushes, aquatic vegetation	shaggy coat and heavy gait; gives off an oily, detectable secretion on its coat
weasel	Subfamily *Mustelinae*	15–55	Arctic, N and S America, Europe, Asia and Africa	rodents, rabbits, birds, insects, lizards, frogs	certain species have been exploited for their fur, eg mink, ermine; includes species of ferret and polecat
whale, beaked	Family *Ziphiidae*	400–1 280	worldwide	mainly squid	named after its distinctive, protuberant, dolphin-like beak

Natural History

Name	Family/Species	Size (cm)[1]	Distribution	Food	Special features
whale, blue	Species *Balaenoptera musculus*	to 3 000	Arctic and subtropics	krill	largest living animal
whale, grey	Species *Eschrichtius robustus*	1 190–1 520	N Pacific	fish, crustaceans, ocean floor molluscs	long migration to breed, from the Arctic to the subtropics; one of the most heavily barnacled of the whale species
whale, humpback	Species *Megaptera novaeangliae*	1 600	worldwide	mainly fish, krill	highly acrobatic, with wide range of sounds; migrates between Arctic and mid-Pacific
whale, killer	Species *Orcinus orca*	900–1 000	worldwide in cool coastal waters	fish, squid, birds, and other marine mammals	toothed whale; dorsal fin narrow and vertical; co-operative and highly co-ordinated hunter, with triangular fins and distinctive white and black colouring; not generally a threat to humans
whale, long-finned pilot	Species *Globicephala melaena*	600	temperate waters of the N Atlantic	cuttlefish, squid	best known for mysterious mass strandings on beaches
whale, sperm	Species *Physeter catodon*	to 2 070	widespread in temperate and tropical waters	mainly squid	largest of the toothed whales; prodigious deep sea diver
whale, white	Species *Delphinaptems leucas*	300–500	N Russia, N America and Greenland	crustaceans, worms, molluscs	distinctive white skin; wide range of bodily, facial and vocal expressions
wild cat	Species *Felis silvestris*	50–80	Europe, India and Africa	small mammals, birds	domestic cat may be descended from the African wild cat
wolf, grey	Species *Canis lupus*	100–150	N America, Europe, Asia and Middle East	moose, deer, caribou	noted for hunting in packs
wolverine	Species *Gulo gulo*	to 83	Arctic and subarctic regions	small mammals, deer, caribou, birds, plants, carrion	heavily built; long, dark coat of fur; adapted for hunting in soft, deep snow
zebra	Subgenus *Hippotigris*	215–230	Africa	grass, leaves	famous for black and white stripes

[1] To convert cm to inches, multiply by 0.3937; generally, size denotes length from head to tip of tail.

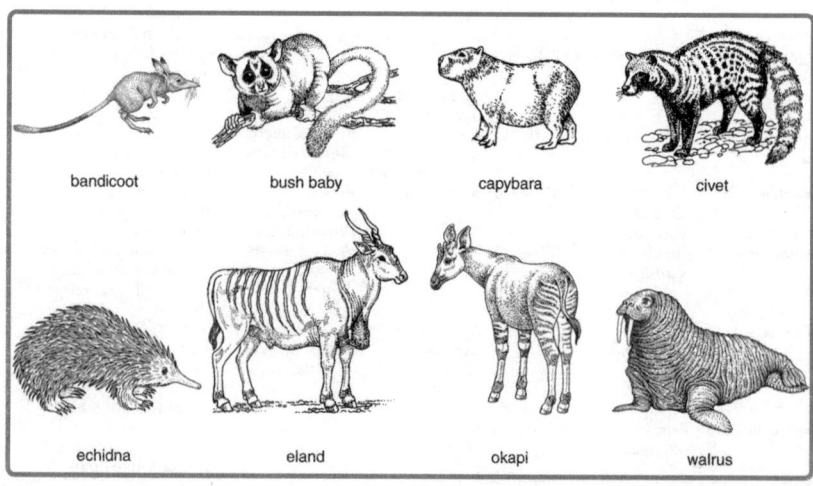

bandicoot   bush baby   capybara   civet

echidna   eland   okapi   walrus

Length of pregnancy in some mammals

Animal	Gestation period*	Animal	Gestation period*
camel	406	kangaroo	40
cat	62	lion	108
chimpanzee	237	mink	50
cow	280	monkey, rhesus	164
dog	62	mouse	21
dolphin	276	opossum	13
elephant, African	640	orang-utan	246–275
ferret	42	pig	113
fox	52	rabbit	32
giraffe	395–425	rat	21
goat	151	reindeer	215–245
guinea pig	68	seal, northern fur	350
hamster	16	sheep	148
hedgehog	35–40	skunk	62
horse	337	squirrel, grey	44
human	266	tiger	105–109
hyena	110	whale	365

*average number of days

Birds

Birds are warm-blooded, egg-laying, and, in the case of adults, feathered vertebrates of the class Aves; there are approximately 8 600 species classified into 29 Orders and 181 Families. Birds are constructed for flight. The body is streamlined to reduce air resistance, the fore-limbs are modified as feathered wings, and the skeletal structure, heart and wing muscles, centre of gravity, and lung capacity are all designed for the act of flying. Two exceptions to this are the ratites or flightless birds which have become too large to be capable of sustained flight, eg the ostrich, kiwi and emu, and the penguin which has evolved into a highly aquatic creature. Birds are thought to have evolved from reptiles, their closest living relative being the crocodile.

Name	Family/Species	Size (cm)[1]	Distribution	Food	Special features
■ Flightless birds					
cassowary	*Casauriidae*	150	Australia and New Guinea	fruit, plants, insects	claws capable of inflicting fatal wounds on humans
emu	*Dromaiidae*	160–190	Australia	plants, fruit, flowers, insects	highly mobile, nomadic population
kiwi	*Apterygidae*	35–55	New Zealand	earthworms, insects, seeds, berries	smallest of the Ratitae order; nocturnal
ostrich	*Struthonidae*	275	dry areas of Africa	mainly leaves, flowers, seeds of plants	fastest animal on two legs
rhea	*Rheidae*	100–150	grasslands of S America	leaves, roots, seeds, insects, small vertebrates	lives in flocks
tinamou	*Tinamidae*	15–49	C and S America	seeds, fruit, insects, small animals	sustains flight over short distances

cassowary   emu   kiwi

■ Birds of prey					
buzzard	*Accipitridae*	80	worldwide except Australasia and Malaysia	small mammals	spends much time perching; kills prey on ground

Natural History

Natural History

Name	Family/Species	Size (cm)[1]	Distribution	Food	Special features
condor	*Cathartidae*	60–100	the Americas	carrion	Andean condor has largest wingspan of any living bird (up to 3m)
eagle, bald	*Accipitridae*	80–100	N America	fish, birds, mammals	name refers to white plumage on head and neck; national symbol of USA
eagle, golden	*Accipitridae*	80–100	N hemisphere	rabbits, hares, carrion	kills with talons; most numerous large eagle
eagle, harpy	*Accipitridae*	90	C America to Argentina	some birds, tree-dwelling mammals	the world's largest eagle; black, white and grey; large feet
eagle, sea	*Accipitridae*	70–120	coastline worldwide	fish	breeds on sea cliffs
falcon	*Falconidae*	15–60	worldwide	birds, carrion, large insects, small mammals	remarkable powers of flight and sight
harrier	*Accipitridae*	50	worldwide	small mammals, birds	hunts by flying low in regular search pattern
kite	*Accipitridae*	52–58	worldwide	insects, snails, small vertebrates, carrion	most varied and diverse group of hawks
osprey	*Pandionidae*	55–58	worldwide	fish	feet specially adapted for catching fish
owl	*Strigidae*	12–73	worldwide	mainly small mammals	acute sight and hearing; swallows prey whole; nocturnal
owl, barn	*Tytonidae*	30–45	worldwide	small vertebrates	feathered legs; nests high above ground
secretary bird	*Sagittaridae*	100	Africa	rodents, reptiles, large beetles, grasshoppers	walks up to 30km/20mi per day
sparrowhawk	*Accipitridae*	to 27 (male), to 38 (female)	Eurasia, NW Africa, C and S America	small birds	long tail, small round wings
vulture (New World)	*Cathartidae*	60–100	the Americas	carrion, carcasses	lives in colonies; locates food mainly by sight; head often lacking long feathers
vulture (Old World)	*Accipitridae*	150–270 (wingspan)	worldwide except the Americas	carrion	no sense of smell

barn owl   condor   peregrine falcon   secretary bird

■ **Songbirds**

accentor	*Prunellidae*	14–18	Palaearctic	insects, seeds	complex social organization and mating systems
bird of paradise	*Paradisaeidae*	12.5–100	New Guinea, Moluccas and Eastern Australia	frogs, nestling birds, insects, fruit, plants	brilliantly ornate plumage; elaborate courtship displays
bowerbird	*Ptilinorhynchidae*	25–37	Australia and New Guinea	mainly fruit, vegetable matter	male builds bowers to attract female for mating

Name	Family/Species	Size (cm)[1]	Distribution	Food	Special features
bulbul	*Pycnonotidae*	13–23	Africa, Madagascar, S Asia and the Philippines	fruits, berries, insects	several species renowned for powerful, beautiful singing voice
bunting	*Emberizidae*	15–20	worldwide	seeds, crustaceans, insects	large family including species of sparrow, finch, and cardinals
butcherbird	*Cracticidae*	26–58	Australia, New Guinea and New Zealand	large insects, crustaceans, reptiles, small mammals, young birds	highly aggressive; sings loudly at dawn, thus has alternative name of 'bushman's clock'
chaffinch	*Fringillidae*	11–19	Europe, N and S America, Africa and Asia	seeds	strong bill; melodious singing voice
cowbird	*Icteridae*	17–54	N and S America	fruit, seeds, crustaceans, insects	forages for food using distinctive gaping movements of the bill
crow	*Corvidae*	20–66	worldwide, except New Zealand	omnivorous	adaptable, intelligent; with complex social systems
dipper	*Cinclidae*	17–20	Europe, S Asia and W regions of N and S America	water insects, molluscs, crustaceans, worms, tadpoles, small fish	strong legs and toes allow mobility to walk under water
drongo	*Dicruridae*	18–38	S Asia and Africa	insects, lizards, small birds	pugnacious
flowerpecker	*Dicaeidae*	8–20	SE Asia and Australasia	berries, nectar, insects	short tongue specially adapted for feeding on nectar
flycatcher (Old World)	*Muscicapidae*	9–27	worldwide except N and S America	insects	tropical species brightly coloured; feeds on the wing
flycatcher, silky	*Ptilogonidae*	to 14	N and S America	insects	feeds on the wing
honeycreeper, Hawaiian	*Drepanididae*	10–20	Hawaiian Is	nectar, fruit, seeds, insects	widely varying bills between species adapted to different environments
honeyeater	*Meliphagidae*	10–32	Australasia, Pacific Is, Hawaii and S Africa	nectar, insects, fruits, berries	brush tongue adapted for nectar feeding
lark	*Alaudidae*	11–19	worldwide	seeds, flowers, leaves, insects	ground-dwelling; elaborate singing displays
leafbird	*Irenidae*	12–24	S Asia	insects, fruit	forest dwellers; ability to mimic sounds of other birds
magpie-lark	*Grallinidae*	19–50	Australasia and New Guinea	insects, tadpoles, seeds, fruit	adaptation to urban surroundings makes it amongst the best-known birds in Australia
mockingbird	*Mimidae*	20–33	N and S America	invertebrates, fruit	great ability to mimic sounds
nuthatch	*Sittidae*	14–20	worldwide except S America and New Zealand	insects, invertebrates, seeds, nuts	name reflects ability of the European species to break open nuts
oriole	*Oriolidae*	18–30	Europe, Asia, Philippines, Malaysia, New Guinea and Australia	insects, fruit	melodious singing voice
palmchat	*Dulidae*	18	Hispaniola and W Indies	berries, flowers and plants	communal nesting with individual compartments for each nesting pair

Natural History

Name	Family/Species	Size (cm)[1]	Distribution	Food	Special features
robin	*Turdinae*	13	worldwide except New Zealand	worms, snails, fruit, insects	territorial, uses song to deter intruders
shrike	*Laniidae*	15–35	Africa, N America, Asia and New Guinea	mainly insects	noted for its sharply hooked bill
shrike, cuckoo-	*Campephagidae*	14–40	Africa, S Asia	mainly insects, caterpillars	peculiar courtship display; family includes colourful minivets
shrike, vanga	*Vangidae*	12–30	Madagascar	insects, frogs, small reptiles	dwindling numbers of population; some endangered species
sparrow	*Ploceidae*	10–20	African tropics in origin, now worldwide	seeds, insects, bread, household scraps	some species renowned for having adapted to an urban environment
starling	*Sturnidae*	16–45	Europe, Asia and Africa	fruit, insects, pollen, nectar, seeds	gregarious; nests in colonies, roosts communally
sunbird	*Nectariniidae*	8–16	Africa, SE Asia and Australasia	insects, nectar	named for its bright plumage
swallow	*Hirundinidae*	12–23	worldwide	insects	noted for strong and agile flight
thrush	*Turdinae*	12–26	worldwide, except New Zealand	worms, snails, fruit	loud and varied singing voice
tit	*Paridae*	11–14	N America, Europe, Asia and Africa	insects, seeds, vegetable matter, nuts	nests in holes, wide range of singing voice
tree-creeper	*Certhiidae*	12–15	N hemisphere and S Africa	insects, seeds	forages on trees for food
tree-creeper, Australian	*Climacteridae*	15	Australia and New Guinea	mainly ants	forages for food on the trunks and limbs of trees
vireo	*Vireonidae*	10–17	N and S America	insects, fruit	distinctive thick and slightly hooked bill
wagtail	*Motacillidae*	14–17	worldwide, although rare in Australia	insects, seeds	spectacular song in flight
warbler, American	*Parulidae*	10–16	N and S America	insects, berries, vegetable matter	well developed and often complex songs
wattle-bird	*Callaeidae*	25–53	New Zealand	insects, fruit, invertebrates	distinctive fleshy fold of skin at base of bill
waxbill	*Estrildidae*	9–13.5	Africa, SE Asia and Australasia	mainly seeds, grain	several species drink by sucking, in the manner of pigeons and doves
waxwing	*Bombycillidae*	18	W hemisphere	fruit, berries, insects	wax-like, red tips on secondary flight feathers
white-eye	*Zosteropidae*	12	Africa, SE Asia and Australasia	insects, spiders, nectar, fruit	distinctive ring of tiny white feathers formed round the eyes
wood-swallow	*Artamidae*	15–20	tropical Asia and Australasia	insects	tends to huddle together in small groups on branches of trees; elegant flyer and glider; highly aggressive towards other birds
wren	*Troglodytidae*	8–15	N and S America, Europe and Asia	invertebrates	nests play ceremonial role in courtship

bird of paradise   chaffinch   tree-creeper   waxwing

Name	Family/Species	Size (cm)[1]	Distribution	Food	Special features
■ **Waterfowl**					
diver ▸ loon					
duck	*Anatidae*	wide range	worldwide	vegetation	gregarious; migratory
flamingo	*Phoenicopterides*	90–180	tropics, N America, S Europe	minute organisms	red/pink colour of plumage caused by diet
goose	*Anatidae*	wide range	N hemisphere	grass, underwater plants	migratory
great northern diver ▸ loon					
grebe	*Podicipedidae*	22–60	worldwide	insects, crustaceans, fish	highly aquatic, adapted for swimming and diving under water
hammerhead	*Scopidae*	56	Africa S of the Sahara, Madagascar, and S Arabia	mainly frogs and tadpoles, also small fish, shrimps, insects	builds a remarkably elaborate nest with entrance tunnel and internal chamber
heron	*Ardeidae*	30–140	worldwide	carnivorous; aquatic prey	mainly a wading bird
ibis	*Threskiornithidae*	50–100	warmer regions of all continents	crustaceans, insects, larvae, small fish, frogs, small reptiles	family also includes species of spoonhill named for shape of bill
loon or diver	*Gaviidae*	66–95	high latitudes of the N hemisphere, migrating to temperate zones	mainly fish	highly territorial and aggressive; loud warning calls; also known as diver; includes great northern diver which can dive deeper than any other flying bird
screamer	*Anhimidae*	69–90	warmer parts of S America	herbivorous	highly vocal, trumpet-like alarm calls give it its name
shoebill	*Balaenicipitidae*	120	E Africa	fish, aquatic prey	also known as the whale-headed stork because it has a large head on a short neck
stork	*Ciconiidae*	60–120	S America, Asia, Africa and Australia	fish, insects, frogs, snakes, mice, lizards	known for its long bill and long neck
swan	*Anatidae*	100–160	worldwide, freshwater, sheltered shores and estuaries	underwater plants	very long neck

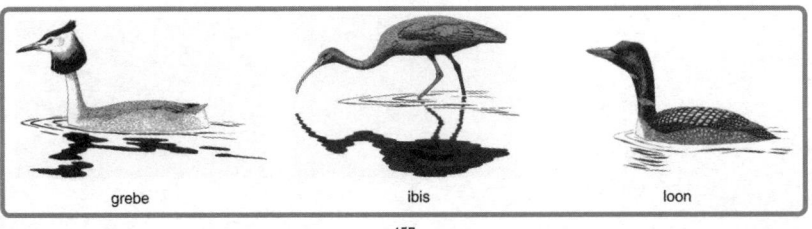

grebe   ibis   loon

Natural History

Name	Family/Species	Size (cm)[1]	Distribution	Food	Special features
■ Shorebirds					
auk	*Alcidae*	16–76	cold waters of the N hemisphere	fish, plankton	same family as the extinct and flightless great auk; species include varieties of puffin and guillemot
avocet	*Recurvirostridae*	29–48	worldwide, except high latitudes	insects, larvae	particularly graceful walk; long slender legs give rise to alternative name of stilt
courser	*Glareolidae*	15–25	Africa, S Europe, Asia and Australia	insects	inhabits dry, flat savanna, grassland and the shores of large rivers
curlew, stone-	*Burhinidae*	36–52	Africa, Europe, Asia, Australia and parts of S America	eggs, insects, worms, molluscs, crustaceans, small vertebrates, amphibians	leg joints give alternative name of thickknee
gull	*Laridae*	31–76	worldwide, scarce in the tropics	fish, marine invertebrates	highly gregarious with elaborate systems of communication
jacana	*Jacanidae*	17–53	tropics	insects, frogs, fish, invertebrates	ability to walk on floating vegetation gives alternative name of lily trotter
oystercatcher	*Haematopididae*	40–45	tropical and temperate coastlines, except tropical Africa and S Asia	shellfish, worms, insects	powerful bill for breaking shells; despite the name, they do not eat oysters
phalarope	*Phalaropidae*	19–25	high latitudes of the N hemisphere	insects, crabs, shrimps	wading bird which also regularly swims
plover	*Charadriidae*	15–40	worldwide	shellfish, insects	swift runner; strong flier
plover, crab	*Dromadidae*	38	coasts of E Africa, India, Persian Gulf, Sri Lanka and Madagascar	crabs	single species with mainly white and black plumage
sandpiper	*Scolopacidae*	12–60	worldwide	invertebrates, insects, berries	spectacular flight patterns
seedsnipe	*Thinocoridae*	17–28	W coast of S America	seeds, leaves	named after its diet
sheathbill	*Chionididae*	35–43	sub-Antarctic and E coast of S America	plankton, algae, carcasses, offal	scavenger of a communal and quarrelsome nature
skimmer	*Rhynchopidae*	37–51	tropics and subtropics of N and S America, Africa, and S Asia	fish, shrimps	uniquely shaped bill aids capture of prey in shallow waters
skua	*Stercorariidae*	43–61	mainly high latitudes of the N hemisphere	fish, small seabirds, insects, eggs	known for chasing other seabirds until they disgorge their food
snipe, painted	*Rostratulidae*	19–24	S America, Africa, S Asia and Australia	molluscs, earthworms, seeds	spectacular female plumage; distinctive running action with lowered head

stilt ▶ avocet

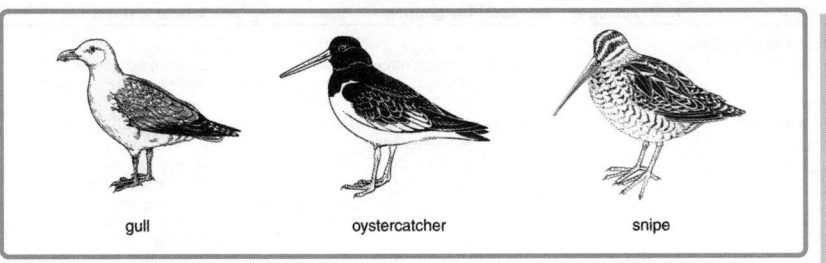

gull   oystercatcher   snipe

Name	Family/Species	Size (cm)[1]	Distribution	Food	Special features
■ **Seabirds**					
albatross	*Diomedidae*	70–140	S hemisphere	fish	noted for its size and power of flight
cormorant (or shag)	*Phalacrocoracidae*	50–100	worldwide	fish, crustaceans	marine equivalent of falcons, used in fishing
darter	*Anhingidae*	80–100	tropical, subtropical, temperate regions	fish, insects	distinctive swimming action occasions name of snake-bird
frigatebird	*Fregatidae*	70–110	tropical oceans	fish, young birds	enormous wings; adept at flying; forces other birds to disgorge their food
fulmar	*Procellariidae*	to 60	N and S oceans	fish	comes to land only to breed; can eject foul-smelling vomit to deter predators
gannet	*Sulidae*	up to 90	worldwide	fish, squid	complex behaviour during mating
guillemot	*Alcidae*	38–42	N hemisphere	fish, crustaceans, worms	eggs shaped so they do not roll off cliff ledge
pelican	*Pelecanidae*	140–180	tropics and subtropics	fish, crustaceans	known for its long bill
penguin	*Spheniscidae*	40–115	S hemisphere	fish, crustaceans, squid	flightless: wings modified as flippers; feathers waterproof; highly social
petrel, diving	*Pelecanoididae*	16–25	S hemisphere	fish	great resemblance to the auk
petrel, storm-	*Hydrobatidae*	12–25	high latitudes of N and S hemispheres	fish, other marine organisms	considerable powers of migration
puffin	*Alcidae*	28–32	N hemisphere	fish and crustaceans	nests in burrows in very large colonies
shag ► cormorant					
shearwater	*Procellariidae*	28–91	subantarctic and sub-tropical zones	fish, plankton	many species known for long migrations
tropicbird	*Phaethontidae*	25–45	tropical seas	small fish and squid	elongated central tail feathers produce distinctive flight pattern

darter   gannet   puffin   shearwater

Natural History

Name	Family/Species	Size (cm)[1]	Distribution	Food	Special features
■ Arboreal birds					
barbet	*Capitonidae*	9–32	tropics, except Australasia	mainly fruits, berries, buds, insects	nests in holes made in rotten timber or sand banks
bee-eater	*Meropidae*	15–38	Africa, Asia and Australia	insects	colourful plumage
cuckoo	*Cuculidae*	15–90	worldwide	insects, especially caterpillars	some species lay eggs in the nests of other birds and rely on foster parents to feed the young
cuckoo-roller	*Leptosomatidae*	38–43	Madagascar and Comoros Is	large insects, chameleons	diminishing population due to destruction of natural habitat
honeyguide	*Indicatoridae*	10–20	Africa and S Asia	insects, beeswax	named for peculiar habit of eating the wax of honeycombs
hoopoe	*Upupidae*	31	Africa, SE Asia and S Europe	mainly small insects	named after its distinctive 'hoo hoo' call
hornbill	*Bucerotidae*	38–126	tropics of Africa and Australasia	fruit, insects, small animals	noted for its long, heavy bill
jacamar	*Galbulidae*	13–30	tropical America	insects	long, slender bill; attractive, green, metallic plumage
kingfisher	*Alcedinidae*	10–46	worldwide	insects, shrimps, frogs, lizards, crabs, snails, worms	colourful plumage, strong bill; characteristic diving movements to catch prey
motmot	*Momotidae*	20–50	tropical America	insects, frogs, small reptiles, fruit	typically attractive, with distinctive long tail feathers
mousebird	*Coliidae*	30–35	Africa S of the Sahara	leaves, fruit, seeds, nectar	distinguished by its crest and long tail
parrot	*Psittacidae*	10–100	mainly tropics of S hemi-shere	seeds, nuts, berries, fruit, insects	mainly sedentary; unmelodic voice, not known to mimic sounds outside captivity
pigeon	*Columbidae*	17–90	worldwide, except high latitudes	seeds, flowers, fruit, berries, leaves, small snails	large family including species of dove, known for its distinctive cooing sound
puffbird	*Bucconidae*	14–32	tropical America	insects, lizards	named after its stout, puffy appearance
roller	*Coraciidae*	27–38	Africa, Europe, Asia, Australia	insects, frogs, fruit	named after its courtship display of diving from great heights in a rolling motion
sandgrouse	*Pteroclididae*	25–48	Africa, S Europe and S Asia	seeds, berries, insects	mainly terrestrial birds
tody	*Todidae*	10–12	Greater Antilles	mainly insects, seeds	captures its insect prey from the underside of leaves and twigs
toucan	*Ramphastidae*	34–66	S America	seeds, berries, fruits, insects, small animals	known for its bright plumage and immense bill
trogon	*Trogonidae*	25–35	tropics, except Australasia	mainly insects, fruit	colourful, attractive plumage
turaco	*Musophagidae*	35–76	Africa S of the Sahara	mainly fruit	noted for its loud and resounding call
woodhoopoe	*Phoeniculidae*	21–43	Africa S of the Sahara	insects, fruit	long graduated tail; strongly hooked bill; some species also called scimitar bill
woodpecker	*Picidae*	10–58	worldwide, except Australasia and Antarctica	insects, fruit, nuts	named after its manner of excavating wood and tree bark for food

| | barbet | cuckoo | hornbill | woodpecker |

Name	Family/Species	Size (cm)[1]	Distribution	Food	Special features
■ Aerial feeders					
frogmouth	*Podargidae*	23–53	SE Asia and Australasia	beetles, scorpions, centipedes, frogs, snails, mice, small birds, fruit	distinctively shaped bill with extremely wide gape
hummingbird	*Trochilidae*	6–22	N and S America	nectar, insects	the humming sound is made by the wings when hovering
nightjar	*Caprimulgidae*	19–29	worldwide	mainly insects	nocturnal
nightjar, owlet-	*Aegothelidae*	23–44	Australasia	insects, small vertebrates	perches in upright owl-like way
oilbird	*Steatornithidae*	53	tropical S America	fruit	the only nocturnal, fruit-eating bird
potoo	*Nyctibiidae*	23–51	tropical C and S America	insects	nocturnal bird, also known as 'tree-nighthawk'
swift	*Apodidae*	10–25	worldwide	insects	lands only on near-vertical surfaces; spends most of life flying
swift, crested	*Hemiprocnidae*	17–33	SE Asia and New Guinea	insects	named after the prominent crest on its head
■ Passerines[2]					
antbird	*Formicariidae*	8–36	parts of S America and W Indies	small insects, spiders, lizards, frogs	named after the habit some species have of following armies of ants to prey
bellbird	*Cotingidae*	9–45	C and S America	fruit	long, metallic sounding display call
broadbill	*Eurylaimidae*	13–28	tropical Africa and Asia, and the Philippines	mainly insects	noted for its colourful broad bill
false sunbird	*Philepittidae*	15	Madagascar	fruit	noted for the bright blue and emerald wattle which develops around the eyes of the male during breeding season
flycatcher (New World)	*Tyrannidae*	9–27	N and S America	insects	feeds on wing
flycatcher, tyrant	*Tyrannidae*	5–14	N and S America, W Indies and Galapagos Is	insects, fish, fruit	many species known for spectacular aerial courtship display
gnateater	*Conopophagidae*	14	parts of S America	insects	long thin legs; short tail
lyrebird	*Menuridae*	80–90	SE Australia	invertebrates	named after its extravagant tail which resembles a Greek lyre
manakin	*Pipridae*	9–15	C and S America	fruit, insects	highly elaborate courtship display

Natural History

Name	Family/Species	Size (cm)[1]	Distribution	Food	Special features
ovenbird	*Furnariidae*	to 25	S America	mainly insects	one species, the true ovenbird, builds substantial nests like mud-ovens
pitta	*Pittidae*	15–28	Africa, SE Asia Asia and Australasia	mainly insects, spiders, worms, snails	long legs; short tail; colourful plumage
plantcutter	*Phytotomidae*	18–19	western S America	buds, shoots, leaves, fruit	bill is ideally adapted for feeding on fruit and plants; regarded as a horticultural and agricultural pest
scrub-bird	*Atrichornithidae*	16–21	E and SW Australia	insects, small lizards, frogs	small terrestrial bird; long graduated tail
tapaculo	*Rhinocryptidae*	8–25	S and C America	insects, larvae, spiders	distinctive moveable flap covers the nostril
woodcreeper	*Dendrocolaptidae*	20–37	S America and W Indies	insects, frogs, lizards	stiff tail feathers used as support in climbing trees, foraging for food
wren, New Zealand	*Xenicidae*	8–10	New Zealand	insects	bird family thought to have colonized the islands in the Tertiary Period[3]

hummingbird

swift

■ **Game-birds and cranes**

bustard	*Otitidae*	37–132	Africa, S Europe, Asia and Australia	plants, leaves, seeds, berries, insects, small reptiles and mammals, birds' eggs, nestlings	characterized by its frequent pauses during walking to observe its surroundings
coot	*Rallidae*	14–51	worldwide	small animals, vegetable food	conspicuous for its loud harsh vocal strains at night
crane	*Gruidae*	80–150	worldwide, except S America and Antarctica	omnivorous	characterized by its long legs
currasow	*Cracidae*	75–112	Southern N America and S America	leaves, insects, frogs	noted for agility in running along branches before taking flight
finfoot	*Heliornithidae*	30–62	tropics of America, and SE Asia	mainly insects	long, slender neck; agile on land and in water
grouse	*Tetraonidae*	30–90	N hemisphere	leaves, buds, berries, fruit, insects	many species threatened by hunting and use of pesticides
guinea fowl	*Numididae*	45–60	Africa	mainly insects, bulbs	virtually unfeathered head and neck; often domesticated
hoatzin	*Opisthocomidae*	60	tropical S America	leaves, fruit and flowers of the white mangrove, fish, crabs	musky odour; top-heavy; retarded flight; unique digestive system

Name	Family/Species	Size (cm)[1]	Distribution	Food	Special features
kagu	*Rhynochetidae*	56	New Caledonia	earthworms	sole species; forest dwelling
limpkin	*Aramidae*	60–70	C and S America	large snails	sole species; noted for its wailing voice
mesite	*Mesoenatidae*	25–27	Madagascar	fruit, insects	highly terrestrial, sedentary; endemic to Madagascar
pheasant	*Phasianidae*	40–235	worldwide	seeds, shoots, berries, insects	elaborate courtship display
plains wanderer	*Pedionomidae*	16	SE Australia	insects, seeds, vegetable substances	male incubates the eggs and raises the young
quail, button	*Turnicidae*	11–19	Africa, S Asia and Australia	insects, seeds, plants	secretive; terrestrial; only three toes, hind toe absent
seriema	*Cariamidae*	75–90	S America	omnivorous, especially small snakes	heavily feathered head and crest
sunbittern	*Eurypygidae*	46	forest swamps of C and S America	insects, crustacea, minnows	complex markings
trumpeter	*Psophiidae*	43–53	tropical S America	berries, fruit, insects	named after its trumpeting call of warning or alarm
turkey	*Meleagrididae*	90–110	N America	fruit, seeds, vegetation, invertebrates	characterized by male's distinctive strutting displays during breeding

bustard   crane   quail

[1] To convert cm to inches, multiply by 0.3937.
[2] Any bird of the worldwide order *Passeriformes* ('perching birds'), which comprises more than half the living species of birds; landbirds.
[3] See Geological time scale p.35

Amphibians

Amphibians are a class of cold-blooded vertebrates including frogs, toads, newts and salamanders. There are approximately 4 000 species. They have a moist, thin skin without scales, and the adults live partly or entirely on land, but can usually only survive in damp habitats. They return to water to lay their eggs, which hatch to form fish-like larvae or tadpoles that breathe by means of gills, but gradually develop lungs as they approach adulthood.

Name	Size (cm)[1]	Distribution	Special features
common spadefoot	to 8	C Europe	toad with a pale-coloured tubercle (the spade) on its hind foot
frog, arrow-poison	0.85–1.24	C and S America	smallest known amphibian; skin highly poisonous
frog, common	to 10	Europe except Mediterranean region and most of Iberia	most widespread European frog
frog, edible	to 12	S and C Europe	often heavily spotted; whitish vocal sacs
frog, goliath	to 81.5	Africa	world's largest frog
frog, leopard	5–13	N America	usually has light-edged dark spots on body
frog, marsh	to 15	SW and E Europe and SE England	extremely aquatic
frog, painted	to 7	Iberia and SW France	usually smooth and yellow-brown, grey or reddish with dark spots

Natural History

Name	Size (cm)[1]	Distribution	Special features
frog, parsley	to 5	W Europe	slender bodied, with a whitish underside
hellbender	to 63	America	salamander with wrinkled folds of flesh on body
mudpuppy	18–43	N America	salamander with bright red external gills
natterjack	to 10	SW and C Europe	toad with bright yellow stripe along its back
newt, alpine	to 12	C Europe	dark mottled back and a uniformly orange belly and bluish spotted sides
newt, Bosca's	7–10	Iberian peninsula	similiar to smooth newt without a dorsal crest
newt, marbled	to 15	Iberia and W France	bright yellow or orange stripe on velvety green and black mottled back
newt, palmate	to 9	W Europe	palmate (webbed feet); short filament at end of breeding male's tail
newt, smooth	to 11	Europe	breeding male develops a wavy crest
newt, warty (great crested newt)	to 17	Europe except Iberia and Ireland	bright red, orange or yellow spotted belly and warty skin
salamander, alpine	to 15	C Europe	large glands on back of head
salamander, fire	to 25	C and S Europe	large glands on sides of head contain venomous secretion
salamander, giant Chinese	114 (average)	China	world's largest amphibian
salamander, goldstriped	15–16	Iberian peninsula	thin with shiny skin
salamander, spectacled	to 11	W Italy	only European salamander with four toes on hind feet
toad, common	to 15	Europe except N Scandinavia, Ireland and some Mediterranean islands	largest European toad; usually brownish or greyish with warty skin
toad, green	to 10	E Europe	distinctive colouring: grey or greenish with darker marbled markings
toad, marine	to 23.8	S America	world's largest toad
toad, midwife	to 5	W Europe	male carries strings of eggs wrapped around hind legs
toad, surinam	to 20	S America	female incubates eggs on her back
toad, yellow-bellied	to 5	C and S Europe	usually bright yellow or orange, black-blotched belly
treefrog, common	to 5	C and S Europe	usually bright green; often found in trees high above ground

[1] To convert cm to inches, multiply by 0.3937

arrow-poison frog   fire salamander   midwife toad

Reptiles

Reptiles are egg-laying vertebrates of the class Reptilia, having evolved from primitive amphibians; there are 6 547 species divided into Squamata (lizards and snakes), Chelonia (tortoises and turtles), Crocodylia (crocodiles and alligators) and Rhynococephalia (the tuatara).

Most reptiles live on the land, breathe with lungs, and have horny or plated skins. Reptiles require the rays of the sun to maintain their body temperature, ie they are cold-blooded or ectothermic. This confines them to warm, tropical and subtropical regions, but does allow some species to exist in particularly hot desert environments in which mammals and birds would find it impossible to sustain life. Extinct species of reptile include the dinosaur and pterodactyl.

Name	Family	Size (cm)[1]	Distribution	Food	Special features
alligator	*Alligatoridae*	200–550	S USA, C and S America and E China	fish, birds, mammals, amphibians, reptiles	able to inflict fatalities on humans but attacks rare; only the American alligator is currently free from being an endangered species, noted for its longevity in protected environments
anguid	*Anguidae*	6–30	N and S America, Europe, Asia and NW Africa	small lizards, mice, birds' eggs, tadpoles, earthworms, spiders, scorpions, grasshoppers, moths, wasps, larvae	distinctive bony-plated scales which reach round the underside giving the creature a rigid appearance
boa	*Boidae*	200–400	Western N America, S America, Africa, Madagascar, Asia, Fiji, Solomon Is and New Guinea	birds, mammals	famous constricting snake, includes within its family species of anaconda
chameleon	*Chamaeleontidae*	2–28	Africa outwith the Sahara, Madagascar, Middle East, S Spain, S Arabian peninsula, Sri Lanka, Crete, India and Pakistan	insects, spiders, scorpions, small birds, mammals	noted for its ability to change colour and blend into its environment
crocodile	*Crocodylidae*	150–750	pantropical and some temperate regions of Africa	vertebrates	distinguished from the alligator by the visible fourth tooth in the lower jaw; famous for its huge jaws, fierce appearance, and violent hunting and ambush techniques when capturing prey; populations have been decimated by the demand for luxury leather and several species are endangered
gecko	*Gekkonidae*	1.5–24	N and S America, Africa, S Europe, Asia and Australia	mainly insects	noted for its vocalization and ability to climb; able to shed its tail as a defence mechanism against predators
iguana	*Iguanidae*	to 200	C and S America, Madagascar, Fiji and Tonga	mainly insects	terrestrial and tree-dwelling lizard; active by day, able to survive in exceptionally high temperatures
lizard, beaded	*Helodermatidae*	33–45	SW USA, W Mexico to Guatemala	small mammals, birds, lizards, frogs, birds, eggs insects, earth-worms, carrion	possesses a mildly venomous bite
lizard, blind	*Dibamidae*	12–16.5	SE Asia	insects	so-named because the eyes are concealed within the skin
lizard, Bornean earless	*Lanthanotidae*	to 20	Borneo	fish, earthworms, birds' eggs	lacks an external ear opening; partly aquatic and a good swimmer; capable of short, rapid movements on land

Natural History

Natural History

Name	Family	Size (cm)[1]	Distribution	Food	Special features
lizard, chisel-tooth	*Agamidae*	4–35	Africa, Asia and Australia	insects, fruit, plants, eggs	named after its distinctive teeth; family includes the flying dragon which is able to glide from perch to perch
lizard, girdle-tailed	*Cordylidae*	5–27.5	Africa S of the Sahara, Madagascar	mainly insectivorous and carnivorous	terrestrial; active by day; adapted to arid environments
lizard, monitor	*Varanidae*	12–150	Africa, S Asia, Indo-Australian archipelago, Philippines, New Guinea and Australia	carrion, large snails, grasshoppers, beetles, scorpions, crocodiles' and birds' eggs, fish, lizards, snakes, birds, shrews, squirrels	consumes its prey whole in the manner of snakes; includes the Komodo dragon, the largest living lizard, which has a prodigious appetite and is capable of killing pigs and small deer
lizard, night	*Xantisiidae*	3.5–12	C America	mainly insects	most species active by night, secretive by day
lizard, snake	*Pygopodidae*	6.5–31	New Guinea and Australia	mainly insects	snake-like appearance; broad but highly extensible tongue
lizard, wall and sand	*Lacertidae*	4–22	Europe, Africa, Asia and Indo-Australian archipelago	mainly insects, snails, worms	highly conspicuous lizard living in open and sandy environments; terrestrial, active by day
lizard, worm	*Amphisbaenidae*	15–35	subtropical regions of N and S America, Africa, Middle East, Asia and Europe	mainly insects, snails, worms	worm-like, burrowing reptile; some of the species have the rare ability to move backwards and forwards
pipesnake	*Aniliidae*	<100	S America, SE Asia	snakes, eels	tail has brilliantly coloured red underside; burrows in swampy regions and feeds on other snakes
python	*Pythonidae*	100–1 000	tropical and subtropical Africa, SE Asia, Australia, Mexico and C America	birds, mammals	capable of killing humans, especially children, by constriction
skink	*Scincidae*	2.8–35	tropical and temperate regions	crabs, insects, seeds	family of terrestrial, tree-dwelling or burrowing species, including highly adept swimmers and those able to swim through sand
snake, dawn blind	*Anomalepidae*	11–30	C and S America	ants, termites	short tail, indistinct head, one or two teeth in the lower jaw
snake, front fanged	*Elapidae*	38–560	worldwide in warm regions	frogs, snakes, eels, rodents, lizards, and other vertebrates	highly venomous family with short fangs; responsible for numerous human fatalities; includes the mamba, the adder and the cobra with its famous broad, hooded head
snake, harmless	*Colubridae*	13–350	worldwide	wide variety of vertebrates	large family which includes terrestrial, burrowing, arboreal and aquatic species; called harmless because of the inability of most species to inject or produce venomous saliva

Name	Family	Size (cm)[1]	Distribution	Food	Special features
snake, shieldtail	*Uropeltidae*	20–50	S India and Sri Lanka	earthworms and insects	small burrowing snake, with tiny eyes, so-called because the tail ends abruptly and forms a rough cylindrical shield
snake, thread	*Leptotyphlopidae*	15–90	C and S America, Africa and Asia	ants and termites	small and exceptionally slender burrowing snake
snake, typical blind	*Typhlopidae*	15–90	C and S America, Africa S of the Sahara, SE Europe, S Asia, Taiwan and Australia	ants, termites, larvae	burrowing snake with tiny, concealed eyes and no teeth on lower jaw
tortoise	*Testudinidae*	10–140	S Europe, Africa, Asia, C and S America	mainly herbivorous	includes smallest species of turtle, the Speckled Cape tortoise (10cm) and one of the longest-lived turtles, the spur-thighed tortoise with a possible life span of over a century
tuatara	*Sphenodontidae*	45–61	islands off New Zealand	ground insects, geckos, skinks, birds' eggs	lizard-like reptile with a third eye in the top of its head
turtle, Afro-American side-necked	*Pelomedusidae*	12–90	S America, Africa, Madagascar, Seychelles and Mauritius	herbivorous and omnivorous species	seabed-dweller that rarely requires to come to the surface
turtle, American mud and musk	*Kinosternidae*	11–27	N and S America	molluscs, insects, crustaceans, fish, plants	lives permanently or semi-permanently in freshwater; glands produce distinctive and evil smelling secretion
turtle, Austro-American side-necked	*Chelidae*	14–48	S America, Australia and New Guinea	omnivorous and carnivorous species	family includes the peculiar looking matamata, the most adept of the ambush-feeders at the gape and suck technique of capturing prey
turtle, big-headed	*Platyssternidae*	20	SE Asia	small invertebrates	distinctive large head which cannot be retracted; active at night; exceptionally good climber
turtle, Central American river	*Dermatemydidae*	to 65	Vera Cruz, Mexico, Honduras	fish, insects, fruit, leaves, plants	freshwater creature with well-developed shell
turtle, Mexican musk	*Staurotypidae*	to 38	Mexico to Honduras	worms, fish, newts	freshwater creature dwelling in marshes and swamps
turtle, pig-nosed softshell	*Carettochelyidae*	55 or over	New Guinea and N Australia	crustaceans, insects, molluscs, fish, aquatic plants, fruit	specialized swimmer named for its plateless skin and fleshy, pig-like snout
turtle, pond and river	*Emydidae*	11.4–80	N and C America, S Europe, N Africa, Asia and Argentina	insects, molluscs, vertebrates, plants	family ranges from tiny bog turtle (11.4cm) to the largest of the river turtles, the Malaysian giant turtle; includes box turtle with possible life span of over a century, also species of terrapin
turtle, sea	*Cheloniidae*	75–213	pantropical, and some subtropical and temperate regions	sponges, jellyfish, mussels, crabs, sea urchins, fish	rapid movement through water contrasts with characteristically slow movements of turtles on land

Natural History

Name	Family	Size (cm)[1]	Distribution	Food	Special features
turtle, snapping	*Chelydridae*	47–66	N and C America	carrion, insects, fish, turtles, molluscs, plant food	large-headed, aggressive sea-bed dweller; includes other turtles in its diet; ambush feeder with rapid snapping movements; alligator snapping turtle has unique worm-like projection on the tongue which fills with blood, turns red, and acts as lure to catch fish
turtle, softshell	*Trionychidae*	30–115	N America, Africa, Asia and Indo-Australian archipelago	insects, crustaceans, fish	named after its leathered, plateless skin; noted for its prominent, pointed snout
viper	*Viperidae*	25–365	N and S America, Africa, Europe and Asia	vertebrates	famous, venomous family of snakes, including the rattlesnake which vibrates its tail when disturbed, and the sidewinder with its distinctive sideways movements
whiptail and racerunner	*Teiidae*	37–45	N and S Asia	small mammals, birds, fish, frogs, tadpoles, lizards, insects, snails, plants	captured and eaten by South American Indians, the fat and flesh also being used in traditional medicines
xenosaur	*Xenosauridae*	10–15	Mexico, Guatemala and S China	insects, tadpoles, fish	terrestrial, sedentary and secretive

[1] To convert cm to inches, multiply by 0.3937.

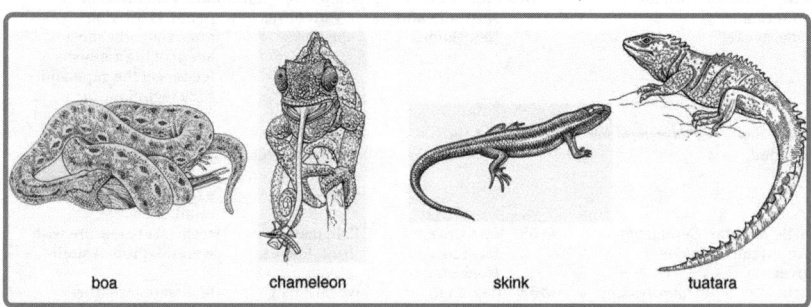

boa   chameleon   skink   tuatara

Fish

Name	Family	Size (cm)[1]	Habitat	Distribution	Special features
albacore	*Scombridae*	to 130	open waters	tropical, warm temperate	tuna fish with large pectoral fins; prized food and sport fish
anchovy	*Engraulidae*	9–12	surface ocean	temperate	important food fish in S Europe, Black Sea, Peru
angler fish	*Chaunacidae*	5–8	deep ocean	tropical, temperate	large jaws; fishing lure at tip of modified dorsal ray
barracuda	*Sphyraenidae*	30–240	surface ocean	tropical, warm temperate	carnivorous; voracious; large teeth
blenny	*Blenniidae*	20–49	sea bed	temperate, tropical	devoid of scales
bonito	*Scombridae*	to 90	open sea surface water	temperate, warm	commercially important; member of tuna family; food fish; sport fish
bream	*Cyprinidae*	41–80	freshwater lakes, rivers	temperate (N Europe)	deep-bodied; food fish
brill	*Scophthalmidae*	to 70	sea bed	temperate	flat fish; eyes on left side; food fish

Name	Family	Size (cm)[1]	Habitat	Distribution	Special features
butterfly fish	*Chaetodontidae*	to 15	reefs	tropical	deep, compressed body; brightly coloured
carp	*Cyprinidae*	51–61	beds of freshwater lakes, rivers	temperate	important food fish; used in aquaculture
catfish	*Ictaluridae*	90–135	sea bed	temperate (N America)	females lay eggs in nest scooped out in mud; important food fish
chub	*Cyprinidae*	30–60	lakes, rivers	temperate (Europe)	popular sport fish
cod	*Gadidae*	to 120	ocean shelf	temperate, N hemisphere	common cod very important food fish
conger eel	*Congridae*	274	sea bed, deep inshore pools	temperate	rounded cylindrical body; upper jaw longer than lower
dab	*Pleuronectidae*	20–40	shallow sea bed	temperate (Europe)	flat fish; eyes on right side; food fish
dace	*Cyprinidae*	15–30	freshwater lakes, rivers	temperate (Europe, former USSR)	sport fish
damsel fish	*Pomacentridae*	5–15	reefs, rocky shores	tropical, temperate	brightly coloured
dogfish	*Scyliorhinidae*	60–100	sea bed	temperate (Europe)	skin very rough; food fish (sold as rock salmon)
dolphin fish (dorado)	*Corypaenidae*	to 200	surface	tropical, warm temperate	predatory; prized sport fish; food fish
dory	*Zeidae*	30–60	mainly shallow ocean	temperate	deep-bodied; food fish
eagle ray	*Myliobatidae*	to 200	mainly inshore sea bed	tropical, temperate	pectoral fins form 'wings'; young born live
eel	*Anguillidae*	to 50 (male), to 100 (female)	rivers, mid-ocean	temperate	elongate cylindrical body form; adults live in rivers but spawn in sea; important food fish
electric eel	*Electrophoridae*	to 240	shallow streams	Orinoco, Amazon basins (S America)	produces powerful electric shocks to stun prey and as defence
electric ray (or torpedo ray)	*Torpenidae*	to 180	sea bed	tropical, temperate	produces strong electric shocks to stun prey
file fish	*Monacanthidae*	5–13	reefs, shallow water	tropical, warm temperate	rough skin; food fish
flounder	*Pleuronectidae*	to 51	shallow sea bed, saline estuaries, lakes	temperate (Europe)	flat fish (eyes may be on fright or left side); locally important food fish
flying fish	*Exocoetidae*	25–50	surface ocean	tropical, warm temperate	enlarged pelvic and pectoral fins give ability to jump and glide above water surface
goat fish ► red mullet					
goby	*Gobiidae*	1–27	shallow sea bed, rocky pools	tropical, temperate	pelvic fins joined to form single sucker-like fin
goldfish	*Cyprinidae*	to 30	freshwater ponds, rivers	temperate	popular ornamental fish
grenadier ► rat-tail					
grey mullet	*Mugilidae*	to 75	coastal sea bed; occasionally tropical freshwaters	tropical, temperate	food fish
grouper	*Serranidae*	5–370	deep sea	tropical, warm temperate	common around reefs, wrecks; prized sport and food fish
gurnard (or sea robin)	*Triglidae*	to 75	sea bed	tropical, warm temperate	bony plates on head; many produce audible sounds
hake	*Merlucciidae*	to 180	continental shelf waters	temperate	large head and jaws; food fish
halibut	*Pleuronectidae*	to 250	sea bed	temperate (Atlantic)	flat fish; eyes on right side; prized food fish
herring	*Clupeidae*	to 40	surface ocean	temperate (N Atlantic, Arctic)	important food fish
lamprey	*Petromyzonidae*	to 91	streams, rivers; parasitic in open sea	temperate (N Atlantic)	primitive jawless fish; mouth sucker-like; food fish

Natural History

Name	Family	Size (cm)[1]	Habitat	Distribution	Special features
lantern fish	*Myctophidae*	2–15	deep sea, but many migrate to surface at night	tropical, temperate	body has numerous light organs
lemon sole	*Pleuronectidae*	to 66	sea bed	temperate	flat fish; specialized feeder on polychaete worms; food fish
loach	*Cobitidae*	to 15	freshwater lakes, rivers	temperate (Europe, Asia)	popular aquarium fish
mackerel	*Scombridae*	to 66	surface ocean	temperate (N Atlantic)	seasonal migrations; important food fish
manta ray (or devil ray)	*Mobulidae*	120–900 (width)	surface ocean	tropical	fleshy 'horns' at side of head; young born, not hatched
minnow	*Cyprinidae*	to 12	fast flowing freshwater lakes, rivers	temperate (N Europe, Asia)	locally abundant
monkfish	*Squatinidae*	to 180	sea bed	temperate (N Atlantic, Mediterranean)	pectoral fins very broad, tail slender, intermediate in shape between shark and ray; food fish
moorish idol	*Zanclidae*	to 22	reefs	tropical (Indo-Pacific)	body deep, tall dorsal and anal fins; bold black/white stripes with some yellow
moray eel	*Muraenidae*	to 130	rocky shores	temperate, tropical	pointed snout; long, sharp teeth; aggressive
parrot fish	*Scaridae*	25–190	reefs	tropical	jaw teeth fused to form parrot-like beak for scraping algal growth from reefs, and for breaking coral
perch	*Percidae*	30–50	freshwater lakes, rivers, Baltic Sea	temperate	food fish; sport fish
pike	*Escocidae*	to 130	freshwater lakes, rivers	temperate	snout pointed; jaws large; predatory; prized by anglers
pilchard (or sardine)	*Clupeidae*	to 25	surface	temperate (N Atlantic, Mediterranean)	important food fish, often canned
pipefish	*Syngnathidae*	15–160	shallow seas	tropical, warm temperate	slender segmented body; males of some species carry eggs in brood pouch
plaice	*Pleuronectidae*	50–90	shallow sea bed	temperate (Europe)	flatfish; eyes on right side; important food fish
puffer	*Tetraodontidae*	3–25	inshore shallow seas, reefs	tropical, warm temperate	body often spiny; some organs and tissues very poisonous, but a food delicacy in Japan
rat-tail (or grenadier)	*Macrouridae*	40–110	close to deep-sea bed	temperate, tropical	large head, tapering body; some species make sounds by resonating swim bladder
ray	*Rajidae*	39–113	sea bed	temperate	skate and ray family; front part of body flattened with large pectoral fins
red mullet (or goat fish)	*Mullidae*	to 40	sea bed	tropical, temperate	food fish
remora	*Echeneidae*	12–46	open sea	tropical, warm temperate	large sucking disc on head, with which it attaches itself to other fish, especially sharks
roach	*Cyprinidae*	35–53	freshwater lakes, rivers	temperate (Europe, former USSR)	popular sport fish
sailfish	*Istiophoridae*	to 360	open ocean surface	tropical, warm temperate	long tall dorsal fin; prized sport fish
salmon	*Salmonidae*	to 150	surface ocean; rivers	temperate	swims upriver to breed; prized sport and food fish
sandeel	*Ammodytidae*	to 20	inshore sea bed	temperate (N hemisphere)	very important food for seabirds

Name	Family	Size (cm)[1]	Habitat	Distribution	Special features
sardine ▸ pilchard					
scorpion-fish	*Scorpaenidae*	to 50	shallow sea bed, reefs	tropical, temperate	distinctive fin and body spines; venom glands
sea bass	*Percichthyidae*	60–100	inshore waters; reefs	tropical, temperate	food fish; popular sport fish
sea robin ▸ gurnard					
sea-bream	*Sparidae*	35–51	close to sea bed	tropical, temperate	food fish; sport fish
seahorse	*Syngnathidae*	to 15	surface ocean	tropical, warm temperate	snout extended to form horse-like head; swims upright
shark, basking	*Cetorhinidae*	870–1 350	surface ocean	tropical, temperate	feeds on plankton; second largest living fish
shark, great white	*Isuridae*	to 630	surface ocean	tropical	fierce; voracious; young born, not hatched
shark, hammerhead	*Sphyrnidae*	360–600	mainly surface ocean	tropical, warm temperate	head flattened into hammer shape; voracious; young born, not hatched
shark, tiger	*Galeorhinidae*	360–600	surface ocean	tropical, warm temperate	vertical stripes on body; fierce
shark, whale	*Rhinco-dontidae*	1 020–1 800	surface ocean	tropical	largest living fish; feeds on plankton
skate	*Rajidae*	200–285	mid-ocean, sea bed	temperate	food fish
smelt	*Osmeridae*	20–30	freshwater lakes, rivers; inshore seas	temperate	related to salmon and trout; food fish
sole	*Soleidae*	30–60	sea bed	tropical, temperate	flat fish; eyes on right side; food fish
sprat	*Clupeidae*	13–16	surface–mid-ocean	temperate	food fish; called whitebait when small
squirrel fish	*Holocentridae*	12–30	reefs	tropical	brightly coloured; nocturnal
stickleback	*Gasterosteidae*	5–10	freshwater lakes, rivers; inshore seas	temperate (N hemisphere)	male builds nest, guards eggs
sting ray	*Dasyatidae*	106–140	sea bed; tropical freshwaters	tropical, temperate	tail whip-like, armed with poison spine(s)
sturgeon	*Acipenseridae*	100–500	shallow sea bed; rivers	temperate (N hemisphere)	primitive fish; eggs prized as caviar
sunfish	*Molidae*	to 400	surface–mid-open ocean	tropical, warm temperate	tail fin absent; body almost circular
surgeon fish (or tang)	*Acanthuridae*	20–45	reefs	tropical, subtropical	brightly coloured; sharp spine on sides of tail can be erected for defence
swordfish	*Xiphiidae*	200–500	surface–mid-open ocean	tropical, temperate	upper jaw extended to form flat 'sword'; food and sport fish
tang ▸ surgeon fish					
trigger fish	*Balistidae*	10–60	sea bed outside reefs	tropical	colourful; dorsal spine can be erected to wedge fish in crevice as defence; food fish, but can be poisonous
trout	*Salmonidae*	23–140	surface ocean; freshwater lakes, rivers	temperate	brown trout confined to fresh water; sea trout migratory; prized food fish
tuna, skipjack	*Scombridae*	to 100	mid-ocean	tropical, temperate	fast swimmer; important food fish
tuna, yellow fin	*Scombridae*	to 200	surface ocean	tropical, warm temperate	elongated body, long dorsal and anal fins; important food fish
turbot	*Scophtha-lamidae*	50–100	shallow sea bed	temperate (N Atlantic)	flat fish; eyes on left side of body; prized food fish
wrasse	*Labridae*	7–210	reefs, rocky coasts	tropical, warm temperate	brightly coloured

Natural History

Natural History

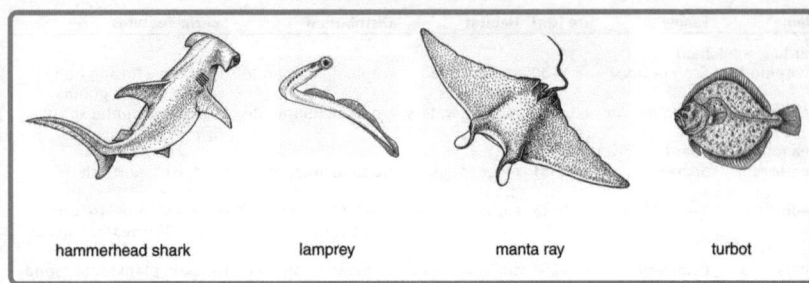

hammerhead shark   lamprey   manta ray   turbot

Invertebrates

For molluscs, lengths given are normally maximum shell lengths, but (b) indicates body length; for spiders, lengths are body lengths, although legs may be much longer; for insects, sizes given are normally body lengths, but (w) indicates wingspan.

Name	Species	Length	Range and habitat	Notable features
MOLLUSCS: Phylum Mollusca				
■ **Slugs and snails/Gastropoda (c.50 000 species)**				
abalone	*Haliotis* (several species)	<30cm	warm seas worldwide	feeds on seaweeds; mainly in coastal waters; collected for food and for the pearly shells
conch	*Strombus* (several species)	<33cm	tropical seas	feeds on seaweeds; shells with a broad 'wing', often used as trumpets
cone shell	*Conus* (c.600 species)	<23cm	warm seas worldwide	feeds on fish and molluscs, killed by poison darts; some species dangerous to humans; beautiful shells much sought by collectors
cowrie	(c.150 species in several genera)	<10cm	warm seas worldwide	feeds on sea anemones and other small creatures; shiny, china-like shells were once used as money
limpet, common	*Patella vulgata*	<5.5cm	worldwide	feeds on seaweeds in intertidal zone; conical shell pulled tightly down on rocks when tide is out
limpet, slipper	*Crepidula fornicata*	<6cm	originally N America, now common on coasts of Europe	strains food particles from the water; slipper-like shells cling together in chains; a serious pest in oyster and mussel farms, settling on the shells and cutting off their food supplies
periwinkle, common	*Littorina littorea*	<2.5cm	N Atlantic and adjacent seas; rocky shores	feeds on seaweeds; thick, dull brown shell; the fishmonger's winkle
sea butterfly	(c.100 species in several genera)	<5cm	oceans worldwide; most common in warm waters	carnivorous, eating a variety of small marine creatures; with or without shells, they swim by flapping wing-like extensions of the foot
slug, great grey	*Limax maximus*	<20cm (b)	Europe	mainly feeds on fungi and rotting matter; mottled grey and brown; common in gardens; mates in mid-air, hanging from a rope of slime
snail, giant African	*Achatina fulica*	<15cm	originally Africa, now tropical Asia and Pacific	vegetarian; a serious agricultural pest; lays hard-shelled eggs as big as those of a thrush
snail, great ramshorn	*Planorbarius corneus*	<3cm	Europe; still and slow-moving freshwater	vegetarian, often browsing on algae; shell forms a flat spiral; body has bright red blood
snail, roman	*Helix pomatia*	<5cm	C and S Europe; lime soils	vegetarian; often a pest, but cultivated for food in some areas
whelk	*Buccinum undatum*	<12cm	N Atlantic and neighbouring seas	carnivorous, feeding on living and dead animals; large numbers are collected for human consumption

Name	Species	Length	Range and habitat	Notable features

■ Bivalves/Lamellibranchia (c.8 000 species)

Name	Species	Length	Range and habitat	Notable features
cockle, common	*Cardium edule*	<5cm	European coasts	burrows in sand and mud near low-tide level; important food for fish and wading birds
mussel, common	*Mytilus edulis*	<11cm	coasts of Europe and eastern North America	bluish shell clings to rocks with tough threads; farmed on a large scale for human consumption, especially in S Europe
oyster	*Ostrea edulis*	<15cm	coasts of Europe and Africa	cements trough-shaped lower valve to stones, with flat upper valve sitting on it like a lid; large numbers farmed for human consumption
piddock	*Pholas dactylus*	<12cm	coasts of Europe and eastern North America	uses rasp-like shell to bore into soft rocks and wood, making an inescapable tomb; sucks in water and food through long siphons
razor-shell, pod	*Ensis siliqua*	<20cm	European coasts	long, straight shell, shaped like a cut-throat razor, is open at both ends; burrows in sand
scallop, great	*Pecten maximus*	<15cm	European coasts; usually below tide level	strongly ribbed, eared shells with one valve flatter than the other; lives freely on seabed and swims by opening and closing its valves

■ Squids and octopuses/Cephalopoda (c.750 species)

Name	Species	Length	Range and habitat	Notable features
cuttlefish, common	*Sepia officinalis*	<30cm	coastal waters of Atlantic and neighbouring seas	eats shrimps and other crustaceans, caught with tentacles; lives on seabed; flat, oval body can change colour; cuttle-bone is the internal shell
octopus, blue-ringed	*Hapalochlaena maculosa*	10cm (span)	Australian coasts	the most dangerous species, despite its size; the only octopus whose venom is known to have killed people
octopus, common	*Octopus vulgaris*	<3m (span)	Atlantic and Mediterranean coastal waters	eats small fish and crustaceans, killed by a poisonous bite; not dangerous to people
squid, common	*Loligo vulgaris*	<50cm	Atlantic and Mediterranean coastal waters	eats fish, crustaceans and smaller squids; cylindrical body with a triangular fin at the rear; deep pink in life, fading to grey after death
squid, giant	*Architeuthis princeps*	<15m	oceans worldwide	largest invertebrate, although tentacles account for over half its length; eats fish, seals and small whales; main food of the sperm whale

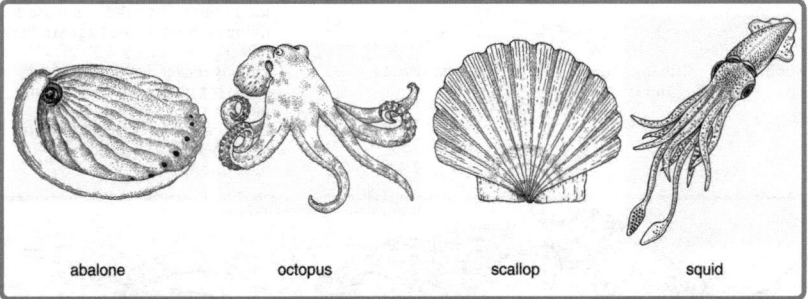

| abalone | octopus | scallop | squid |

CRUSTACEANS: Phylum Arthropoda

■ Crustacea (c.30 000 species)

Name	Species	Length	Range and habitat	Notable features
barnacle, acorn	*Semibalanus balanoides*	<1.5cm (diam.)	worldwide	cemented to intertidal rocks; the shell opens when the tide is in and the animal combs food particles from the water with its legs

Natural History

Name	Species	Length	Range and habitat	Notable features
crab, edible	*Cancer pagurus*	<20cm	eastern N Atlantic and neighbouring seas	scavenger; inhabits rocky coasts to depths of about 50m; widely caught for human consumption
crab, fiddler	*Uca* (many species)	<3cm	tropical seashores and mangrove swamps	scavengers; male has one big, colourful claw, often much bigger than the rest of his body
crab, hermit	(several species and genera)	<15cm	worldwide; mainly in coastal waters	scavengers; elongated, soft-bodied crabs use empty seashells as portable homes
crab, robber	*Birgus latro*	<45cm	islands and coasts of Indian and Pacific oceans	related to hermit crab, but does not live in discarded shells; terrestrial scavenger, feeds mainly on carrion; often climbs trees
crayfish, noble	*Astacus astacus*	<15cm	Europe	inhabits shallow, well aerated streams, feeding on other animals, living or dead; reared in large numbers for human consumption, especially in France
krill	*Euphausia superba*	<5cm	mainly the southern oceans	planktonic shrimp-like animal; the main food of the whalebone whales and many other animals in the southern oceans
lobster, common	*Homarus vulgaris*	<70cm	European coasts	scavenger; lives on rocky coasts down to depths of about 30m; bluish black in life; now rare in many places through overfishing
lobster, Norway	*Nephrops norvegicus*	<25cm	European seas	a spiny scavenger; lives on sandy and muddy seabeds at depths of 30–200m; marketed as scampi
lobster, spiny	*Palinurus vulgaris*	<45cm	Mediterranean and Atlantic; rocky coasts	very spiny, with stout antennae much longer than the body; no pincers; feeds on molluscs; a popular food in S Europe; also known as crayfish
prawn, common	*Palaemon serratus*	<10cm	European coasts; usually stony or rocky shores	scavenger; almost transparent in life; differs from shrimps in its serrated rostrum
shrimp, common	*Crangon crangon*	<7cm	coasts of Europe and eastern North America	eats other small animals, living or dead; common on sand and mud, and much used for human consumption; front legs stout and clawed
water flea	*Daphnia* (many species)	<0.5cm	worldwide; freshwater	reddish brown or greenish, abundant in muddy ponds and other freshwater; swims by waving long antennae; a major food of small fish and much used, living or dried, to feed aquarium fish
woodlouse	(many genera and species)	<2.5cm	worldwide	scavengers; feed mainly on decaying plant material; the only major group of terrestrial crustaceans, but still confined to damp places; also called sow-bugs and slaters

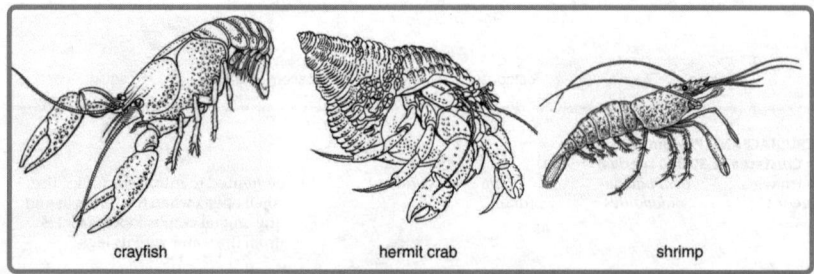

crayfish   hermit crab   shrimp

Natural History

Name	Species	Length	Range and habitat	Notable features
■ SPIDERS: Phylum Arthropoda				
■ Arachnida (c.40 000 species)				
bird-eating spider	(c.800 species in several genera)	<10cm	warmer parts of the Americas and southern Africa	stout-bodied, hairy hunting spiders, often in trees, where they sometimes capture nestling birds; venom not dangerous to people, although the hairs may cause a painful rash; often called tarantulas
black widow	*Latrodectus mactans*	<1.6cm	most warm parts of the world, including S Europe	black with red markings beneath; a dangerous spider that has caused many human deaths, but bites are now quickly cured with antivenin; female sometimes eats the smaller male after mating
bolas spider	(several species and genera)	<1.5cm	North and South America, Africa and Australasia	catch moths by whirling a single thread of silk with a blob of sticky gum on the end
crab spider	(c.3 000 species in numerous genera)	<2cm	worldwide	mostly squat, crab-like spiders that lie in wait for prey — often in flowers — and grab it with their long front legs
funnel-web spider	*Atrax* (3 species)	<5cm	Australia	among the deadliest spiders, although antivenins are now available for treating bites; inhabit tubular webs in the ground or among rocks
garden spider	*Araneus diadematus*	<1.2cm	N hemisphere	black to ginger, with a white cross on the back; makes orb-webs up to 50cm across on fences and vegetation; not only in gardens
gladiator spider	*Dinopis* (several species)	<2.5cm	warm regions and some cooler parts of North America and Australia	slender spiders with enormous eyes; make sticky webs which they throw at passing prey, usually at night
house spider	*Tegenaria* (c.90 species)	<2cm	mostly N hemisphere	long-legged, fast-running spiders often seen running over floors at night; make scruffy triangular webs in neglected corners; harmless
jumping spider	(c.4 000 species in many genera)	<1.5cm	worldwide	large-eyed, day-active spiders that leap onto their prey; often brilliantly coloured
money spider	(many species and genera)	<0.6cm	worldwide, but most common in cooler areas of N hemisphere	believed to bring wealth or good fortune, perhaps because of the silvery appearance of their little hammock-like webs which cover grassland and glisten with dew on autumn mornings
orb-web spider	(c.2 500 species in many genera)	<3cm	worldwide	the makers of the familiar wheel-shaped webs, up to a metre or more in diameter; mostly brown, but some are very colourful; not dangerous
raft spider	*Dolomedes* (c.100 species)	<2.5cm	worldwide	hunting spiders that lurk at the edge of pools or on floating objects, picking up vibrations of prey (insects and small fish) and streaking after them
spitting spider	*Scytodes thoracica*	<0.6cm	worldwide; normally only in buildings	catches small insects by spitting strands of sticky, venom-coated gum at them
tarantula	*Lycosa narbonensis*	<3cm	S Europe	a wolf spider whose bite was believed to be curable only by performing a frantic dance — the tarantella; although painful, the bite is not really dangerous; the name is now often applied to the hairy bird-eating spiders

Natural History

Name	Species	Length	Range and habitat	Notable features
trapdoor spider	(c.700 species in several genera)	<3cm	most warm parts of the world, including S Europe	live in burrows closed by hinged lids of silk and debris; spiders lie in wait under the lid and grab passing prey
water spider	*Argyroneta aquatica*	<1.5cm	Eurasia; in ponds and slow-moving streams	the world's only truly aquatic spider, living in an air-filled, thimble-shaped web fixed to water plants; darts out to catch passing prey
wolf spider	(c.2 500 species in many genera)	<3cm	worldwide, but most common in cooler parts of N hemisphere	large-eyed hunting spiders, mostly ground-living; some chase their prey at speed; generally harmless but some of the larger species have dangerous bites
zebra spider	*Salticus scenicus*	<0.6cm	N hemisphere; often in and around houses	black and white jumping spider, commonly hunting on rocks and walls, especially those covered with lichen

black widow

house spider

orb-web spider

zebra spider

■ **INSECTS: Phylum Arthropoda**

■ **Bristletails/Thysanura (c.600 species)**

silverfish	*Lespisma saccharina*	10mm	worldwide	wingless scavenger of starchy foods in houses

■ **Mayflies/Ephemeroptera (c.2 500 species)**

mayfly	*Hexagenia bilineata*	16mm	worldwide	flimsy insects with 2 or 3 long 'tails'; they grow up in water and have a very short adult life, often only a few hours

■ **Dragonflies/Odonata (c.5 000 species)**

dragonfly	(many species)	<20–130mm	worldwide	long-bodied insects, with gauzy wings spanning up to 150mm; most fly rapidly and catch insects in mid-air; they grow up in water

■ **Crickets and grasshoppers/Orthoptera (c.17 000 species)**

cricket, bush	(thousands of species)	<150mm	worldwide, apart from coldest areas	omnivorous or insect-eating; like grasshoppers but with very long antennae; several N American species are called katydids
cricket, house	*Acheta domesticus*	<20mm	worldwide	scavenger in houses and rubbish dumps
locust, desert	*Schistocerca gregaria*	85mm	Africa and S Asia	herbivorous; swarms periodically destroy crops in Africa
locust, migratory	*Locusta migratoria*	<50mm	Africa and S Europe	herbivorous; swarm in Africa, but solitary in Europe

■ **Stick insects and leaf insects/Phasmida (c.2 500 species, mostly tropical)**

insect, leaf	(c.50 species)	<90mm	SE Asia	very flat, leaf-like, green or brown herbivores
insect, stick	(over 2 400 species)	<350mm	warm areas, including S Europe	herbivorous; stick-like green or brown bodies with or without wings; often kept as pets

■ **Earwigs/Dermaptera (c.1 300 species)**

earwig	(many species)	<30mm	originally Africa, now worldwide	slender, brownish insects, with or without wings and always with prominent pincers at the rear; most are omnivorous scavengers

Name	Species	Length	Range and habitat	Notable features
■ Cockroaches and mantids/Dictyoptera (c.5 500 species)				
American cockroach	*Periplaneta americana*	40mm	worldwide	scavenger, living outside (if warm) or in buildings; chestnut brown
praying mantis	(c.2 000 species)	<75mm	all warm areas	catch other insects with spiky front legs
■ Termites/Isoptera (over 2 000 species)				
termites	(many species)	<22mm	mostly tropical	small and ant-like, with or without wings; colonies in mounds of earth, in dead wood or underground; many are timber pests
■ Bugs/Hemiptera (c.70 000 species)				
aphid	(numerous species)	<5mm	worldwide	sap-sucking insects, with or without wings; many, including trackfly and greenfly, are serious pests
bedbug	*Cimex lectularius*	5mm	worldwide	bloodsucking; hides by day and feeds at night, often attacking people in their beds
cicada	(numerous species)	<40mm (w)	worldwide, mainly in warm climates	sap-sucking; males make loud, shrill sounds; young stages live underground on roots; one American species takes 17 years to mature
froghopper	*Philaenus spumarius*	6mm	N hemisphere	sap-sucker; young stages live in froth, often called cuckoo-spit
pondskater	*Gerris lacustris*	10mm	N hemisphere	skims across the surface of still water and catches other insects
■ Thrips/Thysanoptera (over 3 000 species)				
thrips	(many species)	2.5mm	worldwide	tiny winged or wingless herbivorous insects, many of which grow up in crops and cause much damage; they fly in huge numbers in sultry weather in summer and are often called thunder-bugs
■ Lacewings/Neuroptera (over 6 000 species)				
antlion	*Myrmeleon formicarius*	90mm (w)	Eurasia	larvae make small pits in sandy soil and feed on ants and other insects that fall into them
green lacewing	(several genera and many species)	<50mm	worldwide	predators of aphids and other small insects in a wide range of habitats; delicate green wings
■ Scorpion flies/Mecoptera (c.400 species)				
scorpion fly	*Panorpa*	20mm	worldwide	scavenging insects in which the male abdomen is usually turned up like a scorpion's tail, although they are quite harmless

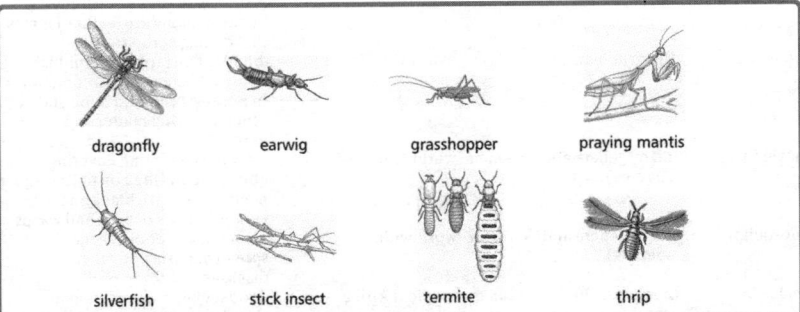

dragonfly   earwig   grasshopper   praying mantis

silverfish   stick insect   termite   thrip

Name	Species	Length	Range and habitat	Notable features
■ Butterflies and moths/Lepidoptera (c.150 000 species)				
■ Butterflies (c.18 000 species)				
birdwing butterfly	(several genera and species)	<300mm (w)	SE Asia and N Australia, tropical forests	they include the world's largest butterflies; many are becoming rare through collecting and loss of habitat

Natural History

Name	Species	Length	Range and habitat	Notable features
cabbage white butterfly	*Pieris brassicae*	<70mm (w)	Eurasia, N Africa, flowery places	caterpillar is a serious pest of cabbages and other brassicas
fritillary butterfly	(many genera and species)	<80mm (w)	mostly N hemisphere	mostly orange with black spots above and silvery spots below; live in woods and open spaces including arctic tundra
monarch butterfly	*Danaus plexippus*	<100mm (w)	mostly Pacific area and North America	orange with black markings; a great migrant; it hibernates in huge swarms in Mexico and southern USA; a rare visitor to Europe
skipper butterfly	(many genera and species)	<80mm (w)	worldwide	mostly small brown or orange grassland insects with darting flight
swallowtail butterfly	(many genera and species)	<120mm (w)	worldwide, but mostly tropical	large, usually colourful and with prominent 'tails' on hindwings; many becoming rare through collecting and loss of habitat

■ **Moths (c. 132 000 species)**

Name	Species	Length	Range and habitat	Notable features
burnet moth	*Zygaena* (many species)	<40mm (w)	Eurasia and N Africa	slow, night- and day-flying moths, protected by foul-tasting body fluids and gaudy black and red colours
clothes moth	(several species)	<15mm (w)	worldwide	small, often rather shiny moths whose caterpillars damage woollen fabrics; live mainly in buildings
death's head hawkmoth	*Acherontia atropos*	<135mm (w)	Africa and Eurasia	sturdy moth with a skull-like pattern on its thorax; larvae on potato and related plants
hummingbird hawkmoth	*Macroglossum stellatarum*	<60mm (w)	Eurasia	day-flying, producing loud hum as it hovers in front of flowers to feed; larvae on bedstraws
pine processionary moth	*Thaumetopoea pityocampa*	<40mm (w)	S and C Europe	greyish moth whose larvae live in silken tents on pine trees and go out to feed in long processions at night; a serious forest pest
silk moth	*Bombyx mori*	<60mm (w)	native of China; now unknown in the wild	cream-coloured moth bred for the fine silk obtained from its cocoon — over 1km from a single cocoon; larvae eat mulberry leaves; all cultured moths flightless
tiger moth	(many genera and species)	<100mm (w)	worldwide	mostly brightly coloured and hairy, with evil-tasting body fluids

■ **True flies/Diptera (c.90 000 species, a few without wings)**

Name	Species	Length	Range and habitat	Notable features
crane fly (or leather-jacket)	(many genera and species)	<35mm (w)	worldwide	slender, long-legged flies, often resting with wings outstretched; larvae of many are leather-jackets that damage crop roots
house fly	*Musca domestica*	7mm	worldwide	abundant on farms and rubbish dumps; becoming less common in houses; breeds in dung and other decaying matter and carries germs
hover fly	(many genera and species)	<40mm	worldwide	many have amazing hovering ability; adults feed on pollen and nectar; many are black and yellow mimics of bees and wasps
mosquito	(many genera and species)	<15mm	worldwide	females are bloodsuckers; spread malaria and other diseases
tsetse fly	*Glossina* (c.20 species)	10mm	tropical Africa	bloodsuckers; spread human sleeping sickness, cattle diseases

Name	Species	Length	Range and habitat	Notable features
■ Fleas/Siphonaptera (c.1 800 species)				
European flea	(many species)	3mm	worldwide	wingless, bloodsucking parasites feeding on birds and mammals; long hind legs enable them to jump many times their own lengths; the maggot-like larvae are not parasitic
■ Bees, wasps and ants/Hymenoptera (over 120 000 species)				
ant, army	(several genera and species)	<40mm	tropics	live in mobile colonies, some of over a million ants; kill any animal unable to get out of their way; workers much smaller than the 40mm-long queen; African species often called driver ants
ant, honeypot	(several genera and species)	20mm	deserts across the world	some workers gorge themselves with sugar-rich food and become living honeypots from which other ants can feed
bee, bumble	*Bombus* (many species)	<35mm	worldwide, except Australia	plump, hairy bees living in annual colonies; only mated queen survives winter to start new colonies in spring
bee, honey	*Apis mellifera*	<20mm	worldwide (probably native of SE Asia)	less hairy than bumble bee; lives in permanent colonies, sometimes in hollow trees but mostly in artificial hives; stores honey for winter
hornet, European	*Vespa crabro*	<35mm	Eurasia and now America	large brown and yellow wasp; nests in hollow trees and feeds young on other insects
ichneumon	(thousands of genera and species)	<50mm	worldwide	parasites, mostly laying their eggs in young stages of other insects; the young grow inside their hosts and gradually kill them
sawfly	(numerous families)	<50mm	worldwide	named after the saw-like ovipositor of most females, used to cut slits in plants before laying eggs there; larvae all vegetarians
weaver, ant	*Oecophylla* (several species)	10mm	Old World tropics	nest made from leaves, joined by sticky silk produced by the grubs
■ Beetles/Coleopteria (over 350 000 species; front wings usually form casing over body)				
sexton beetle	*Nicrophorus* (several species)	<25mm	worldwide	often orange and black; beetles work in pairs to bury small dead animals, near which they then lay their eggs
click beetle (or wireworm)	(many genera and species)	<40mm	worldwide	bullet-shaped beetles which flick into the air to turn over, making a loud click; larvae, called wireworms, damage crop roots
Colorado beetle	*Leptinotarsa decemlineata*	10mm	N America and now Europe	black and yellow adults and pink grubs both seriously damage potato crops
deathwatch beetle	*Xestobium rufovillosum*	7mm	N hemisphere	tunnelling larvae do immense damage to old building timbers; adults tap wood as mating call; also found in dead trees
devil's coach-horse	*Staphylinus olens*	25mm	Eurasia	slender black beetle with short front wings; lives in gardens and often enters houses; also called cocktail because it raises its rear end
glow-worm	*Lampyris noctiluca*	15mm	Europe	wingless female glows with greenish light to attract males flying overhead; feeds on snails
furniture beetle (or woodworm)	*Anobium punctatum*	5mm	worldwide	larvae, known as woodworm, tunnel in dead wood and cause much damage to furniture and building timbers
goliath beetle	*Goliathus* (several species)	<150mm	Africa	world's heaviest beetles, up to 100g; fly well and feed on fruit

Natural History

Name	Species	Length	Range and habitat	Notable features
grain weevil	*Sitophilus granarius*	3mm	worldwide	a serious pest, breeding in and destroying all kinds of stored grain
ladybird	(c.3 500 species in many genera)	10mm	worldwide	aphid-eating habits make them friends of gardeners; most are red or yellow, with various spot patterns
scarab beetle	*Scarabaeus* (many species)	<30mm	most warm parts of the world	dung-feeding — some form the dung into balls and roll it around before burying it; known as tumblebugs in N America; introduced into Australia to deal with sheep and cattle dung
stag beetle	*Lucanus cervus*	50mm	Eurasia	males have huge antler-like jaws, with which they wrestle rivals
woodworm ▸ furniture beetle				

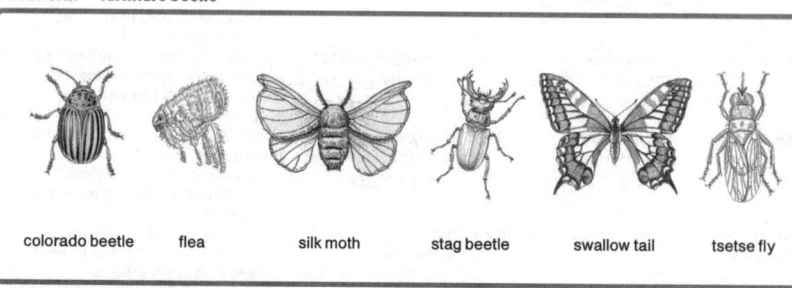

| colorado beetle | flea | silk moth | stag beetle | swallow tail | tsetse fly |

Endangered species (Mammals, birds, reptiles)

Species are classified as endangered when they are in danger of extinction through drastic depletion of their numbers or habitats. Although the majority of endangered species are included in this list, there is space for only a few of the endangered subspecies. Many more species may actually be endangered, but there is not enough information known about them to determine whether they are endangered, vulnerable or just rare. (A few examples of these are included below, coded[2].) Also included in this list are taxa that may be extinct now, but have definitely been seen in the wild in the past 50 years.

Name	Species	Location	Cause of endangerment
■ Mammals			
addax	*Addax nasomaculatus*	Chad; Mali; Mauritania; Niger	
anoa, lowland	*Bubalus depressicornis (Anoa depressicornis)*	Sulawesi, Indonesia	hunting; destruction of habitat
anoa, mountain	*Bubalus quarlesi (Anoa quarlesi)*	Sulawesi and Buton, Indonesia	hunting; destruction of habitat
antelope, giant sable	*Hippotragus niger variani*	Angola	human settlement; destruction of habitat
armadillo, Brazilian three-banded	*Tolypeutes tricinctus*	Brazil	
ass, African wild	*Equus africanus (Equus asinus)*	Ethiopia; Somalia	hunting for the medical properties of its meat and fat; poaching; human disturbance in the form of tourism; droughts; competition for pasture and water from domestic livestock
aye-aye	*Daubentonia madagascariensis*	Madagascar	primate threatened by loss of forest habitat
bandicoot, giant	*Peroryctes broadbenti*	Papua New Guinea	
bandicoot, golden	*Isoodon auratus*	Australia	
bandicoot, western barred	*Perameles bougainville*	Australia	
bat, Bulmer's fruit	*Aproteles bulmerae*	Papua New Guinea	
bat, cusp-toothed fruit	*Pteralopex atrata*	Solomon Is	
bat, golden-capped fruit	*Acerodon jubatus*	Philippines	
bat, gray	*Myotis grisescens*	SE USA	disturbance of habitat by caving, vandalism
bat, Philippines tube-nosed fruit	*Nyctimene rabori*	Philippines	

Name	Species	Location	Cause of endangerment
bat, Seychelles sheath-tailed	*Coleura seychellensis*	Seychelles	
bat (a species of)	*Pteralopex acrodonta*	Fiji	
bat (a species of)	*Pteralopex anceps*	Papua New Guinea	
bat (a species of)	*Pteralopex pulchra*	Solomon Is	
bear, Baluchistan	*Selenarctos thibetanus gedrosianus* (*Ursus thibetanus gedrosianus*)	Iran; Pakistan	human persecution; hunting because of its damage to crops and the threat posed by it to domestic stock
bettong, northern	*Bettongia tropica*	Australia	
boodie	*Bettongia lesueur*	Australia	
buffalo, wild water	*Bubalus arnee*	Bhutan; India; Nepal; Thailand	
cat, Iriomote	*Prionailurus bengalensis iriomotensis* (*Prionailurus iriomotensis*)	Iriomote I, Japan	loss of natural habitat to agriculture
cat, Pakistan sand	*Felis margarita scheffeli*	Pakistan	animal trade
cheetah, Asiatic	*Acinonyx jubatus venaticus*	Iran	fur trade; decline in population of its natural prey, the gazelle
chuditch	*Dasyurus geoffroii*	Australia	
civet, Malabar large spotted	*Viverra megaspila civettina*	S India	possibly already extinct due to persecution, loss of habitat to agriculture
cougar, Florida	*Puma concolor coryi* (*Felis concolor coryi*)	SE USA	loss of habitat; hunting; decreased prey on which to feed
deer, Argentinian pampas	*Ozotoceros bezoarticus celer*	Argentina	hunting; disease; loss of habitat to agriculture, domestic livestock
deer, Calamian hog	*Axis calamianensis*	Calamian Is, Philippines	
deer, Key	*Odocoileus virginianus clavium*	Washington and Oregon, USA	loss of habitat to agriculture
deer, Kuhl's hog or Bawean	*Axis kuhlii*	Bawean I, Indonesia	
deer, Manipur brow-antlered	*Cervus eldii eldii*	India	hunting; loss of habitat to domestic stock grazing, cultivation, logging, burning
deer, Père David's	*Elaphurus davidianus*	China	
deer, Persian fallow	*Dama mesopotamica*	Iran	hunting; loss of forest habitat to irrigation, agriculture, grazing of domestic livestock
deer, Siberian musk	*Moschus moschiferus* (*Moschus sibiricus*)	China; Korea; Mongolia; Russia	
deer, swamp	*Cervus duvauceli*	India; Nepal	poaching, human disturbance; competition for grazing from domestic livestock
deer, Thailand brow-antlered	*Cervus eldi siamensis*	Thailand; Laos; Cambodia; Vietnam	hunting; loss or destruction of habitat by the effects of war, agriculture, land development, shifting cultivation, forest clearance
deer, Visayan spotted	*Cervus alfredi*	Visayan Is, Philippines	
deer, Yarkand	*Cervus elaphus yarkandensis*	China	poaching; human disturbance; deterioration of habitat caused by domestic livestock, particularly grazing sheep
dibbler	*Parantechinus apicalis* (*Antechinus apicalis*)	Australia	
dog, wild	*Lycaon pictus*	Africa, south of the Sahara	human hunting, persecution
dog, Mexican prairie	*Cynomys mexicanus*	Mexico	
dolphin, Indus River	*Platanista minor* (*Platanista indi*)	Indus River, Pakistan	withdrawal of water for irrigation; illegal exploitation by fishermen
dolphin, Yangtse River (or baiji)	*Lipotes vexillifer*	Chiang Jiang River, China	
drill	*Mandrillus leucophaeus* (*Papio leucophaeus*)	Cameroon; Equatorial Guinea; Nigeria	hunting; loss of habitat due to clearance of forest, cultivation of land
duiker, Jentink's	*Cephalophus jentinki*	Liberia; Sierra Leone; Côte d'Ivoire	destruction of natural habitat; almost extinct
dunnart, Julia creek	*Sminthopsis douglasi*	Australia	
echidna, long-beaked	*Zaglossus bruijni*	Indonesia; Papua New Guinea	
elephant, Indian	*Elephas maximus*	Asia	severe loss of natural habitat

Natural History

Name	Species	Location	Cause of endangerment
ferret, black-footed	Mustela nigripes	USA	poisoning; loss of grassland habitat
flying fox, Chuuk	Pteropus insularis	Federated States of Micronesia	
flying fox, Comoro black	Pteropus livingstonei	Comoros	
flying fox, Guam[1]	Pteropus tokudae	Guam, Mariana Is, USA	hunting; loss of forest areas
flying fox, Mortlock Island	Pteropus phaecephalus	Federated States of Micronesia	
flying fox, Pemba	Pteropus voeltzkowi	Tanzania	
flying fox, Pohnpei	Pteropus molossinus	Federated States of Micronesia	
flying fox, Rodrigues	Pteropus rodricensis	Rodrigues I, Mauritius	almost total loss of natural habitat
flying fox, Ryuku	Pteropus dasymallus	Japan; Taiwan	
fox, Simien (or Ethiopian wolf)	Canis simensis	Ethiopia	hunting; loss of habitat; decreasing availability of rodents as food
gazelle, Arabian sand	Gazella subgutturosa marica	Jordan and Arabian peninsula	hunting; deterioration of habitat due to overgrazing
gazelle, Cuvier's	Gazella cuvieri	Algeria; Morocco; Tunisia	hunting; loss of habitat to overgrazing by livestock, forest plantation
gazelle, dama	Gazella dama	Burkina Faso; Chad; Mali; Niger; The Sudan	
gazelle, slender-horned	Gazella leptoceros	Algeria; Chad; Egypt; Libya; Mali; Niger; The Sudan; Tunisia	hunting; deterioration of habitat
genet, crested	Genetta cristata	Cameroon; Nigeria	
gibbon, black	Hylobates concolor	Cambodia; China; Laos; Vietnam	
gibbon, hoolock	Hylobates hoolock	Bangladesh; China; India; Myanmar (Burma)	
gibbon, Mentawai	Hylobates klossi	Indonesia	
gibbon, pileated	Hylobates pileatus	Cambodia; Laos; Thailand	loss of forest habitat
gibbon, silvery	Hylobates moloch	Indonesia	destruction of forest habitat for timber, human settlement
glider, Mahogany	Petaurus gracilis	Australia	
guenon, Preuss's	Cercopithecus preussi	Cameroon; Equatorial Guinea	
guenon, red-bellied	Cercopithecus erythrogaster	Nigeria; Togo	
guenon, sun-tailed	Cercopithecus solatus	Gabon	
guenon, white-throated	Cercopithecus sclateri	Nigeria	
hare, hispid	Caprolagus hispidus	Bangladesh; India; Nepal	loss of habitat due to human settlement; cultivation; forestry; burning of thatchlands; also illegally hunted for food
hartebeest, Swayne's	Alcelaphus buselaphus swaynei	Ethiopia	hunting; destruction of habitat
hartebeest, Tora	Alcelaphus buselaphus tora	Ethiopia; The Sudan; Egypt	hunting; loss of habitat; disease
hirola	Damaliscus hunteri	Kenya; Somalia	
hog, pygmy	Sus salvanius	N India	destruction of thatchland habitat by settlement, forestry, fires; also hunted for its meat
horse, Przewalski's[1]	Equus ferus przewalskii	China; Mongolia	severe competition for natural pasture and water from domestic livestock; possibly already extinct in the wild
huemul, South Andean	Hippocamelus bisulcus	Argentina; Chile	
hutia, Cabrera's	Capromys angelcabrerai (Mesocapromys angelcabrerai)	Cuba	
hutia, dwarf	Capromys nanus (Mesocapromys nanus)	Cuba	
hutia, Garrido's	Capromys garridoi (Mysateles garridoi)	Cuba	

Name	Species	Location	Cause of endangerment
hutia, large-eared	*Capromys auritus* (*Mesocapromys auritus*)	Cuba	
hutia, little earth	*Capromys sanfelipensis* (*Mesocapromys sanfelipensis*)	Cuba	
hyena, Barbary	*Hyaena hyaena barbara*	N Africa	loss of habitat due to human settlement, agriculture
ibex, Pyrenean	*Capra pyrenaica pyrenaica*	Spain	hunting; now virtually extinct
ibex, Walia	*Capra walia*	Ethiopia	destruction of habitat by agriculture, livestock
impala, black-faced	*Aepyceros melampus petersi*	Angola; Namibia	hunting; low reproductive rate
indri	*Indri indri*	Madagascar	primate threatened by widespread destruction of forests
kangaroo rat, Morro Bay	*Dipodomys heermanni morroensis*	California, USA	loss or change of natural habitat; urban development; predation by domestic cats
kangaroo rat, Stephens'	*Dipodomys stephensi*	USA	
kangaroo rat, San Quintin	*Dipodomys elator*	Mexico	
kangaroo, Goodfellow's tree	*Dendrolagus goodfellowi*	Papua New Guinea	
kangaroo, Scott's tree	*Dendrolagus scottae*	Papua New Guinea	
kouprey	*Bos sauveli* (*Novibos sauveli*)	Cambodia; Laos; Thailand; Vietnam	hunting for meat, horns; effects of warfare; low reproductive rate
kowari	*Dasycercus byrnei*	Australia	
lemur, broad-nosed gentle	*Hapalemur sinus*	Madagascar	
lemur, crowned	*Eulemur coronatus*	Madagascar	
lemur, golden bamboo	*Hapalemur aureus*	Madagascar	
lemur, mongoose	*Eulemur mongoz* (*Lemur mongoz*)	Comoros; Madagascar	
lemur, ruffed	*Varecia variegata*	Madagascar	
lemur, hairy-eared dwarf	*Allocebus trichotis* (*Cheirogaleus trichotis*)	Madagascar	
leopard, Amur	*Panthera pardus orientalis*	China; North Korea; Russia	human persecution; depletion of natural prey
leopard, S Arabian	*Panthera pardus nimr*	Oman; Saudi Arabia; Yemen	persecution by shepherds protecting their flocks
leopard, snow	*Uncia uncia* (*Panthera uncia*)	Afghanistan; Bhutan; China; India; Nepal; Russia	hunting for fur and because of the threat it poses to domestic livestock; loss of natural prey
leopard, Sri Lankan	*Panthera pardus kotiya*	Sri Lanka	human persecution; depletion of natural prey
lion, Asiatic	*Panthera leo persica*	India	loss of natural habitat and prey
lynx, Spanish	*Lynx pardinus* (*Felis pardinus*)	Portugal; Spain	loss of habitat due to reforestation; the effects of myxomatosis on its main prey, the rabbit; incidental killing, trapping
macaque, lion-tailed	*Macaca silenus*	S India	loss of habitat; hunting for meat; animal trade
mala	*Lagorchestes hirsutus*	Australia	
mangabey, Tana River	*Cercocebus galeritus galeritus*	Kenya; Tanzania	primate threatened by loss of habitat due to agriculture
markhor	*Capra falconeri*	Afghanistan; Pakistan; India	hunting; loss of habitat to stock grazing
marmoset, buffy-headed	*Callithrix flaviceps*	SE Brazil	destruction of natural habitat
marmoset, buffy-tufted ear	*Callithrix aurita*	Brazil	
marmot, Vancouver Island	*Marmota vancouverensis*	Vancouver I, Canada	collection; exploitation; loss of habitat due to logging
mink, European	*Mustela lutreola*	Belarus; Estonia; France; Georgia; Russia; Spain	
mongoose, Liberian	*Liberiictis kuhni*	Liberia; Côte d'Ivoire; Guinea	

Natural History

Name	Species	Location	Cause of endangerment
monkey, C American (or red-backed squirrel monkey)	*Saimiri oerstedii*	Panama; Costa Rica	animal exportation; loss of forest habitat
monkey, Douc	*Pygaturix nemaeus*	Cambodia; China; Laos	
monkey, François's leaf	*Trachypithecus francoisi*	China; Laos; Vietnam	
monkey, grizzled leaf	*Presbytis comata (Presbytis aygula)*	Indonesia	
monkey, Ka'apor capuchin	*Cebus kaapori*	Brazil	
monkey, mentawai leaf	*Presbytis potenziani*	Indonesia	
monkey, pig-tailed snub-nosed	*Nasalis concolor (Simias concolor)*	Indonesia	
monkey, tonkin snub-nosed	*Pygathrix avunculus (Rhinopithecus avunculus)*	Vietnam	
monkey, woolly spider (or muriqui monkey)	*Brachyteles arachnoides*	São Paulo state, Brazil	hunting; clearance of forest habitat for fuel, agriculture, human settlement
monkey, yellow-tailed woolly	*Lagothrix flavicauda*	Peru	hunting for its skin, meat; destruction of its habitat for human settlement
mouse, saltmarsh harvest	*Reithrodontomys raviventris*	California, USA	water pollution; loss of habitat due to urban, industrial development
muntjac, Fea's	*Muntiacus feae*	China; Myanmar (Burma)	hunting for the meat of this small deer which is highly valued
numbat	*Myrmecobius fasciatus*	Australia	
nyala, mountain	*Tragelaphus buxtoni*	Ethiopia	
orang-utan	*Pongo pygmaeus*	Indonesia; Malaysia	animal trade; felling of forests by timber industry
oryx, Arabian	*Oryx leucoryx*	Oman	hunting for its meat, skin, medical uses
oryx, scimitar-horned	*Oryx dammah (Oryx tao)*	Chad	
otter-civet	*Cynogale bennettii*	Brunei; Indonesia; Malaysia; Thailand	
ox, Vu Quang	*Pseudoryx nghetinhensis*	Vietnam	
pacarana	*Dinomys branickii*	Bolivia; Brazil; Colombia; Ecuador; Peru; Venezuela	
peccary, Chacoan	*Catagonus wagneri*	Argentina; Bolivia; Paraguay	
phascogale, red-tailed	*Phascogale calura*	Australia	
pig, Visayan warty	*Sus cebifrons*	Philippines	
possum, Fergusson Island striped	*Dactilopsila tatei*	Papua New Guinea	
possum, Leadbetter's	*Gymnbelideus leadbeateri*	Victoria, Australia	felling of forest areas has led to loss of habitat
possum, Mountain pygmy	*Burramys parvus*	Australia	
potoroo, long-footed	*Potorus longipes*	Australia	
pronghorn, Baja Californian	*Antilocapra americana peninsularis*	Mexico	hunting; competition for fodder from domestic livestock
pronghorn, Sonoran	*Antilocapra americana sonoriensis*	Mexico; Arizona, USA	destruction of habitat; competition for food and water from livestock; hunting
rabbit, Amami	*Pentalagus furnessi*	Ryukyu I, Japan	loss of habitat; predation by wild dogs
rabbit, Omilteme	*Sylvilagus insonus*	Mexico	
rabbit, riverine	*Bunologus monticularis*	South Africa	
rabbit, Sumatran	*Nesolagus netscheri*	Indonesia	
rabbit, Tehuant-epec jack-	*Lepus flavigularis*	Mexico	
rabbit, Tres Marias	*Sylvilagus graysoni*	Tres Marias Is, Mexico	
rabbit, volcano	*Romerolagus diazi*	Mexico	loss of habitat; wanton destruction by shooting
rat, Anthony's wood	*Neotoma anthonyi*	Todos Santos I, Mexico	
rat, Bunker's wood	*Neotoma bunkeri*	Mexico	

Natural History

Name	Species	Location	Cause of endangerment
rat, central rock	*Zyzomys pedunculatus*	Australia	
rat, Poncelet's giant	*Solomys ponceleti*	Papua New Guinea	
rat, San Martin Island wood	*Neotoma martinensis*	San Martin I, Mexico	
rat (a species of)	*Phaenomys ferrugineus*	Brazil	
rat (a species of)	*Rhagomys rufescens*	Brazil	
rat (a species of)	*Juscelinomys candango*	Brazil	
rhinoceros, black	*Diceros bicornis*	Africa	
rhinoceros, great Indian	*Rhinoceros unicornis*	Bhutan; India; Nepal	hunting; poaching for rhino horn; loss of habitat to agriculture, stock grazing
rhinoceros, Javan	*Rhinoceros sondaicus*	Cambodia; Java; Laos; Vietnam	hunting for rhino horn, medical properties of rhino blood; loss of habitat to human settlement
rhinoceros, northern white	*Ceratotherium simum cottoni*	Congo, Democratic Republic of	hunting for the supposed aphrodisiac qualities of the rhino horn; disturbance by military operations
rhinoceros, Sumatran	*Dicerorhincus sumatrensis (Didermocerus sumatrensis)*	SE Asia	hunting for the aphrodisiac and medical qualities of the horn and other parts of the carcass which fetches high prices; loss of forest habitat to timber exploitation, human settlement
seal, Hawaiian monk	*Monachus schauinslandi*	Hawaiian Is, USA	initial decline in population due to 19c seal fishermen; present population threatened by attacks by sharks; human disturbance of breeding grounds leading to low rates of reproduction, high rates of juvenile mortality
seal, Mediterranean monk	*Monachus monachus*	N Africa; Lebanon; Cyprus; Turkey; Albania	persecution by fishermen; human disturbance; marine pollution
serow, Sumatran	*Capricornis sumatraensis sumatraensis*	Sumatra; Malaysia	hunting; destruction of habitat
sheep, dwarf blue	*Pseudois schaeferi*	China	
shrew, nimba otter	*Micropotamogale lamottei*	Côte d'Ivoire; Guinea; Liberia	
sifaka, diademed	*Propithecus diadema*	Madagascar	
sifaka, golden-crowned	*Propithecus tattersalli*	Madagascar	
sika, Formosan[1]	*Cervus nippon taiouanus*	Taiwan	hunting for meat, antlers; the medical properties of the carcass; loss of habitat to agriculture; probably already extinct in the wild
sika, N China	*Cervus nippon mandarinus*	China	hunting; loss of habitat; possibly already extinct in the wild
sika, Ryukyu	*Cervus nippon keramae*	Ryukyu Is, Japan	drought; low qualities of feeding vegetation; competition with goats for grazing fodder
sika, Shansi[1]	*Cervus nippon grassianus*	China	hunting for the antler trade; clearance of forest habitat for agriculture
sika, S China	*Cervus nippon pseudaxis (Cervus nippon kopschi)*	China; Vietnam	hunting for the antler trade; trapping; loss of habitat
sloth, maned	*Bradypus torquatus*	Brazil	loss of forest habitat
solenodon, Cuban	*Solenodon cubanus*	Cuba	
solenodon, Haitian	*Solenodon paradoxus*	Dominican Republic; Haiti	land development; deforestation
squirrel, Delmarva fox	*Sciurus niger cinereus*	Maryland, USA	loss of habitat due to logging
tamaraw	*Bubalus mindorensis*	Philippines	hunting; loss of forest habitat
tamarin, cotton-top	*Saguinus oedipus oedipus*	NW Colombia	animal trade; loss of habitat to agriculture
tamarin, black-faced lion	*Leontopithecus caissara*	Brazil	
tamarin, golden-headed lion	*Leontopithecus rosalia chrysomelas*	E Brazil	loss of Atlantic rainforest
tamarin, golden lion	*Leontopithecus rosalia*	Brazil	loss of forest habitat to agriculture, urban development

Natural History

Name	Species	Location	Cause of endangerment
tamarin, golden-rumped lion	*Leontopithecus rosalia chrysopygus*	São Paulo area of Brazil	loss of forest habitat; possibly careless use of defoliants by farmers
tamarin, white-footed	*Saguinus leucopus*	Colombia	
tapir, Malayan	*Tapirus indicus*	Indonesia; Myanmar (Burma); Thailand; Vietnam; Malaysia	human disturbance; loss of forest habitat to logging, oil exploration, human settlement, mining, agriculture
tapir, mountain	*Tapirus pinchaque* (*Tapirus roulini*)	S America	human disturbance; competition for natural habitat with livestock
tiger	*Panthera tigris*	Eurasia	loss of habitat and prey; hunting for sport; because of the threat posed by it to both humans and domestic livestock
uakari, bald	*Cacajao calvus*	Brazil; Peru	primate threatened by hunting; animal trade
uakari, black	*Cacajao melanocephalus*	Brazil; Colombia; Venezuela	
vaquita	*Phocoena sinus*	Mexico	
wallaby, Alpine	*Thylogale calabyi*	Papua New Guinea	
wallaby, banded hare	*Logostrophus fasciatus*	Australia	
wallaby, bridle nailtail	*Onychogalea fraenata*	Queensland, Australia	loss of natural habitat to settlement; introduction of livestock; predation from foxes
wallaby, prosperine rock	*Petrogale persephone*	Australia	
weasel, Colombian	*Mustela felipei*	Colombia; Ecuador	
whale, blue	*Balaenoptera musculus*	Atlantic, Pacific and Indian Oceans	whaling
whale, northern right	*Eubalaena glacialis* (*Baleana glacialus*)	Northern temperate and sub-polar waters (North Atlantic and North Pacific)	whaling
wolf, Ethiopian ▸ fox, Simien			
wolf, red	*Canis rufus* (*Canis niger*)	Texas and Louisiana, USA	loss of habitat; hunting; trapping; hybridization with coyotes
wombat, northern hairy-nosed	*Lasiorhinus krefftii*	Australia	
woylie	*Bettongia penicillata*	Australia	
yak, wild	*Bos mutus* (*Bos grunniens*)	Tibet; Kashmir; W China	hunting
zebra, Grevy's	*Equus grevyi*	Ethiopia; Kenya	hunted because of its attractive, highly-prized skin

▪ Birds

Name	Species	Location	Cause of endangerment
adjutant, greater	*Leptoptilos dubius*	India	
'akialoa, Kauai	*Hemignathus obscurus*	Kauai, Hawaiian Is, USA	disease; overgrazing of forest habitat by livestock; competition with imported birds; predation by rats
'akiapola'au	*Hemignathus wilsoni*	Hawaiian Is, USA	deterioration of forest habitat; disease; competition with imported birds; predation by rats
albatross, Amsterdam Island	*Diomedea amsterdamensis*	Amsterdam I, French Southern and Antarctic Territories	
albatross, short-tailed	*Diomedea albatrus*	Japan	loss of habitat; exploitation for feathers; low rate of reproduction
alethe, Cholo	*Alethe choloensis*	Malawi; Mozambique	
antbird, grey-headed	*Myrmeciza griseiceps*	Ecuador; Peru	
antpitta, brown-banded[1]	*Grallaria milleri*	Colombia	
antpitta, moustached[1]	*Grallaria alleni*	Colombia	
antpitta, Tachira	*Grallaria chthonia*	Venezuela	
antwren, Alagoas	*Myrmotherula snowi* (*Terenura sicki*)	Brazil	destruction of tropical forest habitat
antwren, ash-throated	*Herpsilochmus parkeri*	Peru	
antwren, black-hooded	*Formicivora erythronotos*	Brazil	

Name	Species	Location	Cause of endangerment
antwren, Restinga	*Formicivora littoralis*	Brazil	
attila, ochraceous	*Attila torridus*	Colombia; Ecuador; Peru	
becard, slaty	*Pachyramphus spodiurus*	Ecuador; Peru	
blackbird, Forbes's	*Curaeus forbesi*	Brazil	
blackbird, yellow-shouldered	*Agelaius xanthomus*	Puerto Rico	
booby, Abbott's	*Papasula abbotti* (*Sula abbotti*)	Christmas I and Cocos Is, Australia; Indonesia	
bushbird, recurve-billed	*Clytoctantes alixii*	Colombia; Venezuela	
calyptura, kinglet[1]	*Calyptura cristata*	Brazil	
cockatoo, Philippine	*Cacatua haematuropygia*	Philippines	
cockatoo, salmon-crested	*Cacatua moluccensis*	Indonesia	
cockatoo, Tanimbar	*Cacatua goffini*	Tanimbar Is, Indonesia	
cockatoo, white	*Cacatua alba*	Indonesia	
condor, California	*Gymnogyps californianus*	California, USA	low reproductive potential; shooting, trapping, poisoning, egg-collecting; extinction appears inevitable
coquette, short-crested	*Lophornis brachylopha*	Mexico	
coucal, green-billed	*Centropus chlororhynchus*	Sri Lanka	
crane, whooping	*Grus americana*	Canada	pollution; destruction, disturbance of wetland habitat
creeper, oahu	*Paroreomyza maculata*	Hawaiian Is, USA	disease to which Hawaiian honeycreepers have limited immunity; destruction of rainforest habitat by grazing livestock; competition from imported birds; predation by mammals
crow, Hawaiian	*Corvus hawaiiensis*	Hawaiian Is, USA	disease; loss of habitat to wild pigs, cattle, goats; predation by black rats
crow, Mariana	*Corvus kubaryi*	Guam, Mariana Is, USA	
curassow, Alagoas	*Mitu mitu*	Brazil	seriously threatened with extinction by hunting; loss of rainforest habitat
curassow, blue-knobbed	*Crax alberti*	Colombia	
curassow, helmeted	*Pauxi pauxi*	Colombia; Venezuela	
curlew, Eskimo[1]	*Numenius borealis*	Arctic tundra: Canada, Alaska; S America	shooting; loss of prairie habitat to agriculture; climatic changes possibly altering migratory and reproductive processes
dove, blue-eyed ground	*Columbina cyanopis*	Brazil	
dove, Grenada	*Leptotila wellsi*	Grenada	
dove, ochre-bellied	*Leptotila ochraceiventris*	Ecuador; Peru	
dove, purple-winged ground[1]	*Claravis godefrida*	Argentina; Brazil; Paraguay	
dove, Socorro	*Zenaida graysoni*	Revillagigedo Is, Mexico	
eagle, Adalbert's	*Aquila adalberti*	Portugal; Spain	poisoning and contamination by pesticides; shooting; loss of habitat to forest clearance, overgrazing
eagle, Great Philippine	*Pithecophaga jefferyi*	Philippines	shooting; animal trade; destruction of forest habitat
eagle, Madagascar fish	*Haliaeetus vociferoides*	Madagascar	hunting; human persecution
eagle, Madagascar serpent	*Eutriorchis astur*	Madagascar	clearing of forest habitat
emerald, Honduran	*Amazilia luciae*	Honduras	
finch, Cochabamba mountain-	*Poospiza garleppi*	Bolivia	
finch, Laysan	*Telespiza cantans*	Hawaiian Is, USA	
finch, Nihoa	*Telespiza ultima*	Hawaiian Is, USA	
finch, pale-headed brush-[1]	*Atlapetes pallidiceps*	Ecuador	
finch, rufous-breasted warbling-	*Poospiza rubecula*	Peru	

Natural History

Name	Species	Location	Cause of endangerment
fire-eye, fringe-backed	*Pyriglena atra*	Brazil	loss of tropical forest habitat to human settlement; industrial, agricultural development
florican, Bengal	*Eupodotis bengalensis* (*Houbaropsis bengalensis*)	India; Nepal; Vietnam	
florican, lesser	*Eupodotis indica* (*Sypheotides indica*)	India; Nepal	
flycatcher, Guam	*Myiagra freycineti*	Guam, Mariana Is, USA	
flycatcher, Tahiti monarch	*Pomarea nigra*	Tahiti	causes of decline are unknown
fody, Mauritius	*Foudia rubra*	Mauritius	destruction of montane evergreen forest habitat; competition from other species of fody; predation of nests by macaque monkeys, black rats
fody, Yellow	*Foudia flavicans*	Rodrigues I, Mauritius	destruction of forest habitat; competition from other species of fody
foliage-gleaner, Alagoas	*Philydor novaesi*	Brazil	
foliage-gleaner, rufous-necked	*Automolus ruficollis*	Ecuador; Peru	
francolin, ochre-breasted	*Francolinus ochropectus*	Djibouti	
grebe, Alaotra	*Tachybaptus rufolavatus*	Madagascar	
grebe, Colombian[1]	*Podiceps andinus*	Colombia	competition for food from trout; possible contamination by pesticides
grebe, Puna	*Podiceps taczanowskii*	Peru	pollution of lake habitat by copper mining
guan, Trinidad piping	*Pipile pipile*	Trinidad	hunting; loss of forest habitat; may already be extinct
guan, white-winged	*Penelope albipennis*	Peru	hunting; loss of forest habitat to charcoal burning
guineafowl, white-breasted	*Agelastes meleagrides*	Côte d'Ivoire; Liberia; Sierra Leone	
hawk, grey-backed	*Leucopternis occidentalis*	Ecuador; Peru	
heron, white-bellied	*Ardea insignis* (*Ardea imperialis*)	Bangladesh; Bhutan; India; Myanmar (Burma)	
heron, white-eared night	*Gorsachius magnificus*	China	
honeyeater, Tagula[2]	*Meliphaga vicina*	Tagula I, Papua New Guinea	alteration of habitat; destruction of habitat by fire; competition with other species
ibis, crested	*Nipponia nippon*	Sado I, Japan	hunting; loss of forest habitat
ibis, Waldrapp	*Geronticus eremita*	Morocco	hunting; nest disturbance; poaching for eggs; animal, zoo trade; reproductive failure due to pesticide contamination
jacamar, three-toed	*Jacamaralcyon tridactyla*	Brazil	
jay, dwarf	*Cyanolyca nana*	Mexico	
junco, Guadalupe	*Junco insularis*	Guadalupe I, Mexico	
kagu	*Rhynochetos jubatus*	New Caledonia	trapping; animal trade; destruction of forest habitat by nickel mining; predation by dogs, cats, pigs, rats
kakapo	*Strigops habroptilus*	New Zealand	human disturbance; loss of forest habitat; competition for food; predation by rats, stoats
kamao	*Myadestes myadestinus*	Hawaiian Is, USA	
kestrel, Mauritius	*Falco punctatus*	Mauritius	destruction of forest habitat; hunting; predation of nests by macaque monkeys
kokako	*Callaeas cinerea*	New Zealand	
lark, Raso	*Alauda razae*	Raso I, Cape Verde	
macaw, blue-throated	*Ara glaucogularis*	Bolivia	
macaw, glaucous[1]	*Anodorhynchus glaucus*	S America	possibly already extinct

Name	Species	Location	Cause of endangerment
macaw, Lear's or indigo	*Anodorhynchus leari*	S America	rare bird in great demand among aviculturists who threaten its continued existence in the wild
macaw, little blue	*Cyanopsitta spixii*	Brazil	
malimbe, Ibadan	*Malimbus ibadanensis*	Nigeria	
merganser, Brazilian	*Mergus octosetaceus*	Argentina; Brazil; Paraguay	
mockingbird, Charles	*Nesomimus trifasciatus*	Galapagos Is, Ecuador	
mockingbird, Socorro	*Mimodes graysoni*	Socorro I, Mexico	
monal, Chinese	*Lophophorus lhuysii*	W China	hunting
myna, Bali (or Rothschild's starling)	*Leucopsar rothschildi*	Bali, Indonesia	loss of forest habitat to human settlement; competition from other starlings; trapping for the cagebird trade
nightjar, white-winged	*Caprimulgus candicans*	Brazil	
nukupu'u	*Hemignathus lucidus*	Hawaiian Is, USA	disease; predation by rats; competition from other birds
olomao	*Myadestes lanaiensis*	Hawaiian Is, USA	
oo, bishop's	*Moho bishopi*	Hawaiian Is, USA	
oo, kauai	*Moho braccatus*	Hawaiian Is, USA	
oriole, Martinique	*Icterus bonana*	Martinique	
'o'u	*Psittirostra psittacea*	Hawaiian Is, USA	loss of forest habitat due to overgrazing by livestock; competition with imported birds; disease; predation
owl, Madagascar red[2]	*Tyto soumagnei*	Madagascar	loss of humid forest habitat
owl, Sokeke scops-	*Otus ireneae*	Kenya	over-collecting; destruction of evergreen forest habitat by felling, banana cultivation
oystercatcher, Chatham Islands	*Haematopus unicolor chathamensis*	Chatham Is, New Zealand	destruction of vegetation by grazing sheep
palila	*Loxioides bailleui*	Hawaiian Is, USA	
parakeet, Mauritius	*Psittacula echo*	Mauritius	loss of evergreen forest habitat; competition for nest sites; nest predation by macaque monkeys, rats
parrot, ground	*Pezoporus wallicus*	SW Australia	clearing, burning, draining of grassland and wetland habitat
parrot, Imperial	*Amazona imperialis*	Dominica	hunting for meat, sport
parrot, indigo-winged	*Hapalopsittaca fuertesi*	Colombia	
parrot, Paradise[1]	*Psephotus pulcherrimus*	Australia	drought; expansion of livestock grazing; last confirmed sighting was in 1927, but there have been more recent unconfirmed sightings
parrot, Puerto Rican	*Amazona vittata*	Puerto Rico	clearance of lowland forest habitat; predation of nests by rats
parrot, red-faced	*Hapalopsittaca pyrrhops*	Ecuador; Peru	
parrot, red-tailed	*Amazona brasiliensis*	SE Brazil	animal trade; loss of forest habitat
parrot, St Lucia	*Amazona versicolor*	St Lucia, W Indies	hunting; loss of forest habitat to agriculture
parrot, yellow-eared	*Ognorhynchus icterotis*	Colombia; Ecuador	
partridge, bearded wood-	*Dendrortyx barbatus*	Mexico	
partridge, Hainan	*Arborophila ardens*	China	
partridge, Sichuan	*Arborophila rufipectus*	China	
petrel, Bermuda	*Pterodroma cahow*	Bermuda	human persecution; disturbance, predation by rats, wild pigs; competition for nesting sites with tropical birds
petrel, black	*Procellaria parkinsoni*	New Zealand	predation on breeding adults and fledglings by cats
petrel, Chatham Islands	*Pterodroma axillaris*	Chatham Is, New Zealand	competition from other subspecies
petrel, Galapagos	*Pterodroma phaeopygia*	Galapagos Is, Ecuador	destruction of habitat due to agriculture; predation by dogs, pigs, black rats

Natural History

Name	Species	Location	Cause of endangerment
petrel, Guadalupe storm-	*Oceanodroma macrodactyla*	Guadalupe I, Mexico	
petrel, Hawaiian dark-rumped	*Pterodroma phaeopygia sandwichensis*	Hawaiian Is, USA	predation by black rats, cats, mongooses
petrel, Madeira	*Pterodroma madeira*	Madeira	
petrel, magenta	*Pterodroma magentae*	New Zealand	predation by cats, rats; deterioration of forest habitat due to overgrazing of livestock, presence of other herbivores
petrel, Mascarene	*Pterodroma aterrima (Pseudobulweria aterrima)*	Réunion	
pheasant, brown-eared	*Crossoptilon mantchuricum*	N China	human persecution; loss of forest habitat
pheasant, cheer	*Catreus wallichii*	India; Nepal; Pakistan	hunting; destruction of forest habitat
pheasant, Elliot's	*Syrmaticus ellioti*	E China	hunting; destruction of forest habitat
pigeon, Marquesan imperial-	*Ducula galeata*	Nukuhiva, French Polynesia	hunting for its meat; loss of habitat to human disturbance, grazing of cattle, pigs, goats
pigeon, pink	*Columba mayeri (Nesoenas mayeri)*	Mauritius	predation of nests by macaque monkeys, black rats; hunting; loss of forest habitat
pigeon, plain[2]	*Columba inornata wetmorei*	Puerto Rico	human persecution; plundering of nests; loss of forest habitat to housing development
pitta, Gurney's	*Pitta gurneyi*	Thailand	
pitta, Schneider's	*Pitta schneideri*	Indonesia	
plantcutter, Peruvian	*Phytotoma raimondii*	Peru	
plover, shore	*Charadrius novaeseelandiae (Thinornis novaeseelandiae)*	Chatham Is, New Zealand	animal trade; destruction of vegetation by grazing sheep
pochard, Madagascar	*Aytha innotata*	Madagascar	
poorwill, Jamaican[1]	*Siphonorhis americanus*	Jamaica	
puaiohi	*Myadestes palmeri*	Hawaiian Is, USA	
puffleg, black-breasted	*Eriocnemis nigrivestis*	Ecuador	
puffleg, turquoise-throated[1]	*Eriocnemis godini*	Colombia; Ecuador	
rail, Austral[1]	*Rallus antarcticus*	Argentina; Chile	
rail, bar-winged	*Nesoclopeus poecilopterus*	Fiji	predation by mongooses, cats, rats
rail, junin	*Laterallus tuerosi*	Peru	
rail, Lord Howe	*Gallirallus sylvestris (Tricholimnas sylvestris)*	Lord Howe I, Australia	damage to vegetation by wild goats, pigs; predation of eggs by rats
rail, plain-flanked	*Rallus wetmorei*	Venezuela	
recurvebill, Bolivian	*Simoxenops striatus*	Bolivia	
redstart, yellow-faced	*Myiobarus pariae*	Venezuela	
robin, Chatham	*Petroica traversi*	Chatham Is, New Zealand	destruction and deterioration of scrub forest habitat by human disturbance, climatic conditions; nesting of petrels
robin, Seychelles magpie	*Copsychus sechellarum*	Seychelles	predation by cats; competition for nest sites; decreased availability of food
scrub-bird, noisy	*Atrichornis clamosus*	SW Australia	clearance of eucalyptus forest habitat; drought; predation by cats
seedeater, hooded[1]	*Sporophila melanops*	Brazil	
seedeater, Narosky's	*Sporophila zelichi*	Argentina	
seedeater, Tumaco[1]	*Sporophila insulata*	Tumaco I, Colombia	
shama, black	*Copsychus cebuensis*	Philippines	
shelduck, crested	*Tadorna cristata*	China; North Korea; Russia	
siskin, red	*Carduelis cucullata*	Colombia; Venezuela	trapping for the cagebird trade
spinetail, blackish-headed	*Synallaxis tithys*	Ecuador; Peru	
spoonbill, black-faced	*Platalea minor*	China; North Korea	
starling, Rarotonga	*Aplonis cinerascens*	Cook Is	

Name	Species	Location	Cause of endangerment
starling, Rothschild's ▶ myna, Bali			
stilt, black	*Himantopus novasealandiae*	New Zealand	loss of breeding and feeding habitat
stork, Oriental	*Ciconia boyciana*	China, Russia	shooting; contamination by mercury causing mortality or reproductive failure; loss of wetland habitat to agriculture; extinct in Europe
sunbird, Prigogine's double-collared	*Nectarinia prigoginei*	Congo, Democratic Republic of	
takahe	*Porphyrio mantelli (Notornis mantelli)*	South I, New Zealand	
tanager, cherry-throated[1]	*Nemosia rourei*	SE Brazil	unrecorded for over a century, probably already extinct
tanager, cone-billed[1]	*Conothraupis mesoleuca*	Brazil	
tapaculo, chestnut-sided	*Scytalopus psychopompus*	Brazil	
thicketbird, long-legged	*Trichocichla rufa*	Fiji	predation by cats, rats, mongooses
thrasher, white-breasted	*Ramphocinclus brachyurus*	Martinique	hunting; predation by rats, mongooses
tinamou, Kalinowski's[1]	*Nothoprocta kalinowskii*	Peru	hunting; loss of forest habitat
tit-spinetail, white-browed	*Leptasthenura xenothorax*	Peru	
tit-tyrant, ash-breasted	*Anairetes alpinus*	Bolivia; Peru	
tragopan, Cabot's	*Tragopan caboti*	SE China	loss of forest habitat to agricultural cultivation
tragopan, western	*Tragopan melano-cephalus*	India; Pakistan	hunting; trapping; disturbance by humans, goats; destruction of forest habitat
turaco, Bannerman's	*Tauraco bannermani*	Cameroon	
tyrannulet, Alagoas	*Phylloscartes ceciliae*	Brazil	
vireo, black-capped	*Vireo atricapillus*	Mexico; USA	
warbler, Aldabra bush-	*Nesillas aldabrana*	Seychelles	
warbler, Bachman's[1]	*Vermivora bachmanii*	USA	destruction of deciduous swampland forest habitat for timber, agriculture, sugar cane plantation; now N America's rarest songbird
warbler, Kirtland's	*Dendroica kirtlandii*	USA	loss of forest habitat; reduced breeding due to invasion by cowbirds who have parasitized nests
warbler, Nauru reed-	*Acrocephalus rehsei*	Nauru	
warbler, Rodrigues brush-	*Bebrornis rodericanus (Acrocephalus rodericamus)*	Rodrigues I, Mauritius	human disturbance; clearance of thicket habitat
warbler, Semper's[1]	*Leucopeza semperi*	St Lucia, West Indies	predation by mongooses
wattle-eye, banded	*Platysteira laticincta*	Cameroon	
weaver, Clarke's	*Ploceus golandi*	Kenya	
white-eye, Seychelles grey	*Zosterops modestus*	Seychelles	
white-eye, Truk	*Rukia ruki*	Caroline Is, Federated States of Micronesia	occupies limited and unprotected range of mountain forest habitat
white-eye, white-chested	*Zosterops albogularis*	Norfolk I	almost complete destruction of rainforest habitat
woodpecker, American ivory-billed[1]	*Campephilus principalis*	Cuba; SE USA	bird collection; clearance of swampland habitat; human disturbance
woodpecker, Imperial[1]	*Campephilus imperialis*	Mexico	shooting; loss of forest habitat due to logging
woodpecker, ivory-billed[1]	*Campephilus principalis*	Cuba; USA	shooting; loss of pine forest habitat to timber trade, sugar cane plantation
woodpecker, Okinawa	*Sapheopipo noguchii*	Okinawa, Japan	loss of woodland habitat to woodcutting, fires
woodpecker, red-cockaded	*Picoides borealis*	USA	

Natural History

Name	Species	Location	Cause of endangerment
woodstar, Chilean[2]	*Eulidua yarrellii*	Chile	reasons for decline in population are unknown
woodstar, Esmeraldas	*Acestrura berlepschi*	Ecuador	
woodstar, little	*Acestrura bombus*	Ecuador; Peru	
wren, New Zealand bush	*Xenicus longipes*	New Zealand	predation by black rats
▪ **Reptiles**			
alligator, Chinese	*Alligator sinensis*	E China	exploitation for meat, leather; extermination as vermin
anole, giant or Culebra Island giant[1]	*Anolis roosevelti*	Puerto Rico	loss of habitat, probably already extinct
blue tongue, pygmy	*Tiliqua adelaidensis*	Australia	
boa, Round Island[1]	*Bolyeria multocarinata*	Round I, near Mauritius	deterioration of palm forest habitat, possibly already extinct
boa, Round Island keel-scaled	*Casarea dussumieri*	Round I, near Mauritius	deterioration of palm forest habitat
chamaeleon, Smith's dwarf	*Bradypodion taeniabronchum*	South Africa	
cobra, C Asian or Oxus[2]	*Naja oxiana*	C Asia (Afghanistan)	loss of natural habitat
crocodile, Cuban	*Crocodylus rhombifer*	Cuba	exploitation for skins; loss of habitat; hybridization
crocodile, Mindoro or Philippines	*Crocodylus mindorensis*	Philippines	
crocodile, Orinoco	*Crocodylus intermedius*	Colombia; Venezuela	hunting; exploitation for skins
crocodile, Siamese	*Crocodylus siamensis*	Cambodia; Indonesia; Malaysia; Thailand	hunting; exploitation for skins
gecko, Monito	*Sphaerodactylus micropithecus*	Puerto Rico	
gecko, Round Island day	*Phelsuma guentheri*	Mauritius	
gharial	*Gavialis gangeticus*	Bangladesh; India; Pakistan; Nepal	hunting for its skin; human disturbance; loss of habitat to cultivation
gharial, false	*Tomistoma schlegelii*	Malay Peninsula; Sumatra; Borneo	trapping, hunting for its hide
iguana, Acklin's ground[2]	*Cyclura rileyi*	The Bahamas	hunting; poaching; zoo trade
iguana, Anegada ground	*Cyclura pinguis*	Virgin Is, USA	loss of habitat; human disturbance; predation by pets, wild animals
iguana, Jamaica ground	*Cyclura collei (Cychera lophoma)*	Jamaica	
lerista, Allan's	*Lerista allanae*	Australia	
lizard, black or Californian legless[2]	*Anniella pulchra niger*	California, USA	loss of habitat
lizard, blunt-nosed (or San Joaquin leopard lizard)	*Gambelia silus (Crotaphytus wislizenii silus)*	USA; Mexico	destruction of habitat by agriculture
lizard, Hierro giant	*Gallotia simonyi*	Hierro, Canary Is	human disturbance; loss of habitat
lizard, St Croix ground	*Ameiva polops*	Virgin Is, USA	loss of habitat; predation by the mongoose
lizard (a species of)	*Liolaemus gravenhorstii*	Chile	
racer, Antiguan	*Alsophis antiguae*	Antigua and Barbuda	
racer, black	*Alsophis ater*	Jamaica	
skink, Blue Mountain water	*Eulamprus leuraensis*	Australia	
skink, Chevron	*Leiolopisma bomalonotum*	New Zealand	
skink, Lancelin Island	*Ctenotus lancelini*	Australia	
snake, black striped	*Simoselaps calonotus*	Australia	
snake, Kikuzato's brook	*Opisthotropis kikuzatoi (Liopeltis kikuzatoi)*	Japan	
snake, San Francisco garter	*Thamnophis sirtalis tetrataenia*	California, USA	collecting as specimens; loss of habitat to drainage, housing developments
snake (a species of)	*Liophis cursor*	Martinique	

Name	Species	Location	Cause of endangerment
snake (a species of)	*Liophis ornatus*	St Lucia, West Indies	
terrapin, Batagur	*Batagur baska*	Bangladesh; India; Indonesia; Malaysia	water pollution; damage to nesting areas by commercial sand removal, tin mining, flooding, silt deposits
terrapin, painted	*Callagur borneoensis*	Indonesia; Malaysia; Thailand	
tortoise, Bolson	*Gopherus flavomarginatus*	Mexico	
tortoise, Madagascar	*Geochelone yniphora*	Madagascar	
tuatara, Brother's Island	*Sphendon guntheri*	New Zealand	
turtle, green	*Chelonia mydas*	warm waters, especially Indian Ocean; Australia; Indonesia	exploitation of turtle meat, hides, eggs, shells; killing of turtles in the trawling nets of fishermen; human disturbance; loss of natural habitat; international trade in turtles
turtle, hawksbill	*Eretmochelys imbricata*	tropical and subtropical seas: Atlantic, Indian and Pacific Oceans, Gulf of Mexico and Caribbean	exploitation for tortoiseshell, skin, stuffed turtles as souvenirs
turtle, Kemp's Ridley	*Lepidochelys kempii*	Gulf of Mexico; USA	exploitation of turtles for eggs; leather; killing of turtles by trawlers fishing for shrimps
turtle, leatherback	*Dermochelys coriacea*	tropical and subtropical seas: Atlantic, Indian and Pacific Oceans; some temperate regions	exploitation for eggs which are considered a delicacy
turtle, Olive Ridley	*Lepidochelys olivacea*	tropical and subtropical seas: Atlantic, Indian and Pacific Oceans; India; Costa Rica; Mexico	exploitation for eggs, skin, oil
turtle, S American river	*Podocnemis expansa*	northern S America (Bolivia, Brazil)	exploitation for meat, eggs, oil; animal trade
turtle, western swamp	*Pseudemydura umbrina*	near Perth, W Australia	drainage and clearance of habitat for agriculture; disruption by wildfires; predation by foxes, wild dogs
viper, Cyclades blunt-nosed	*Vipera schweizeri* (*Macrovipera schweizeri*)	Greece	
viper, Latifi's	*Vipera latifii*	Lar Valley, Iran	loss of habitat to hydroelectric plant
woma	*Aspidites ramsayi*	Australia	
common name not known	*Aprasia aurita*	Australia	
common name not known	*Abronia montecristoi*	El Salvador	
common name not known	*Diploglossus anelpistus*	Dominican Republic	

[1] Denotes species is certainly endangered and probably extinct.

[2] Denotes there is not enough information available to enable placing of species in rare, vulnerable or endangered category.

Natural History

HUMAN BODY, HEALTH AND NUTRITION

DNA

DNA, or deoxyribonucleic acid, is the nucleic acid containing the sugar deoxyribose, that forms the material of which the chromosomes and genes of humans are composed. It contains coded instructions for the transmission of genetic information from one generation to the next, and for the manufacture of all the proteins that are required for growth and development of a whole new organism.

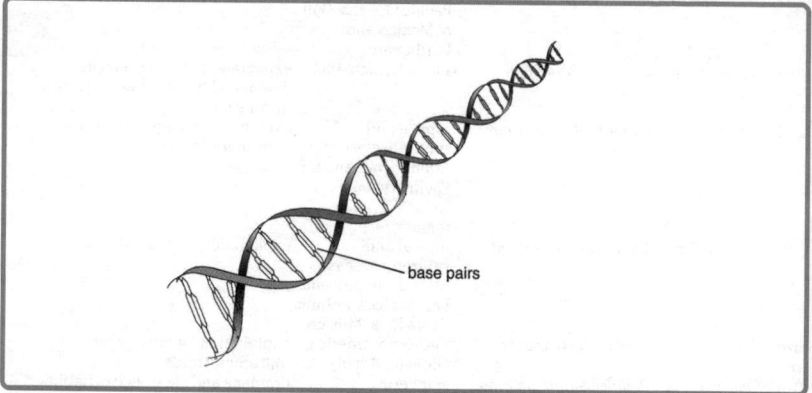

base pairs

The chromosomes

A chromosome is a rod-like portion of the chromatin of a cell nucleus, performing an important part in mitotic cell division, and in the transmission of hereditary characteristics. Normally constant in number for any species, there are 22 pairs of chromosomes and two sex chromosomes in the human.

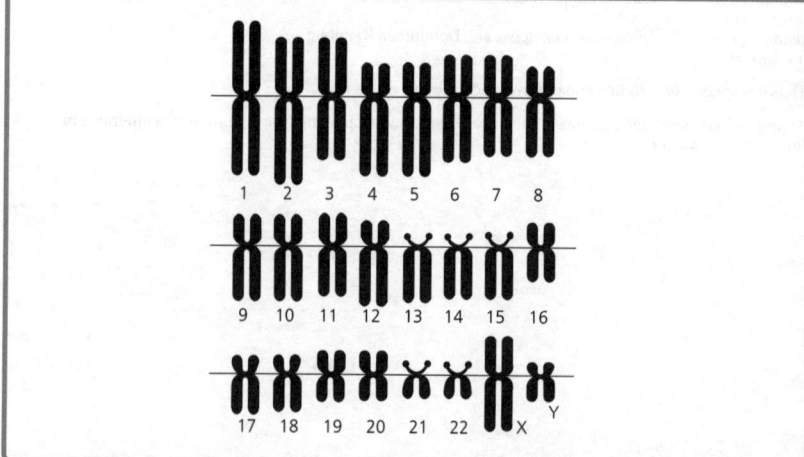

The skeleton

Human beings have an internal skeleton or endoskeleton made of bone or cartilage. It supports the tissues and organs of the body, and protects soft internal organs such as the lungs. The muscles are attached to the bones of the skeleton by means of tendons, and when they contract they pull against the bones, causing them to move. The point of articulation or contact between two or more bones of the skeleton is known as a joint, different types of joint allowing varying degrees of movement. In total, the adult human skeleton has 206 bones.

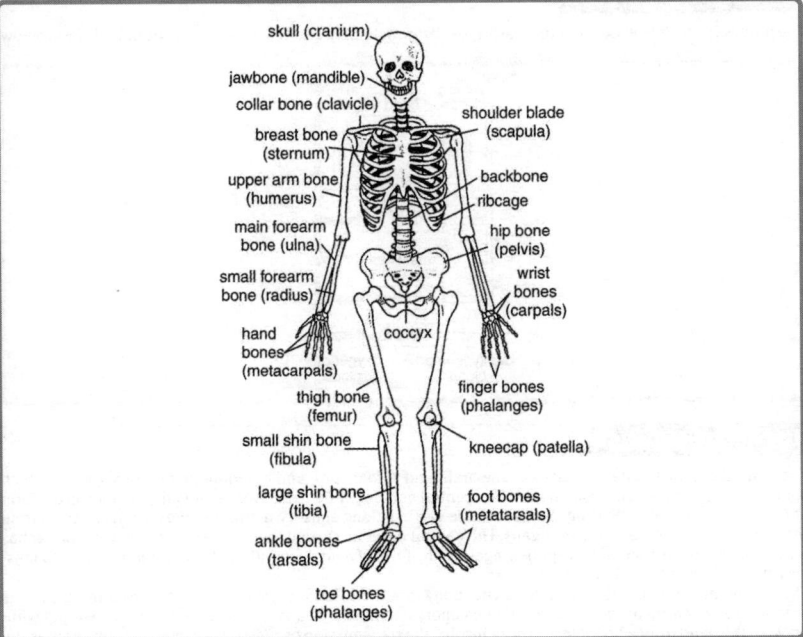

The muscles

Muscles consist of bundles of small fibres, each of which is in turn composed of many protein myofibrils, which lengthen or shorten as their filaments slide past each other. This movement, which occurs in response to a stimulus from the nervous system, or a hormonal signal, causes contraction of the whole muscle.

Voluntary muscle, which is under conscious control, produces voluntary movements by pulling against the bones of the skeleton, to which it is attached by means of tendons, so that contractions of such muscles cause the bones to move. Movement of a limb requires the combined action of a pair of muscles which can pull in opposite directions and are said to be antagonistic. For example, when the biceps muscle at the front of

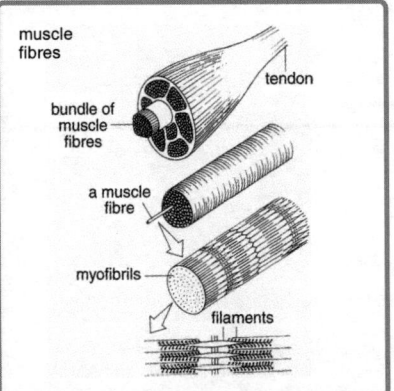

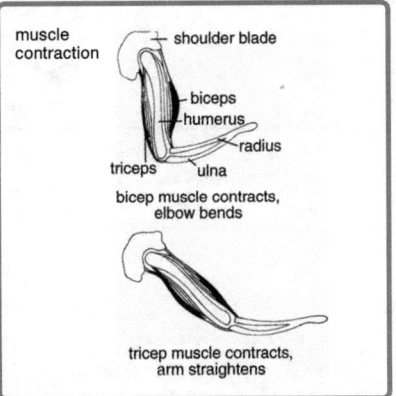

bicep muscle contracts, elbow bends

tricep muscle contracts, arm straightens

Human Body, Health and Nutrition

the upper arm contracts, and the triceps muscle at the back of the arm relaxes, the arm bends at the elbow. When the triceps contracts and the biceps relaxes, the arm is straightened again.

Involuntary muscle (also called smooth muscle) maintains the movements of the internal body systems, and forms part of many internal organs, such as the intestines and uterus. Cardiac muscle, found only in the heart, does not become fatigued, and continues to contract rhythmically even when it is disconnected from the nervous system.

The circulatory system

The process by which blood is continuously moved throughout the body is shown in diagrammatic form below.

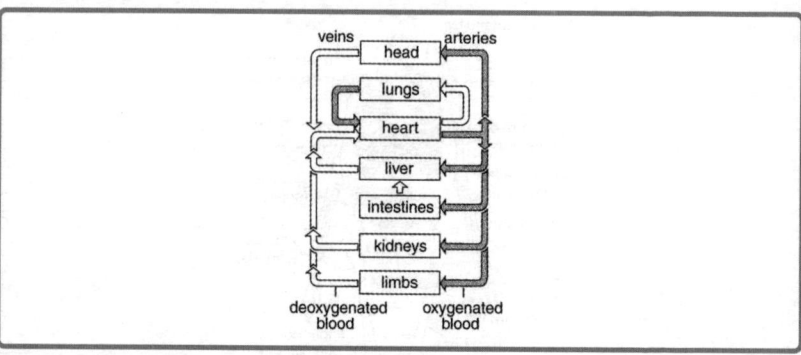

The nervous system

The central nervous system consists of the brain and spinal cord, and a peripheral nervous system, which comprises the rest of the nervous system. The central nervous system receives sensory information in the form of nerve impulses (electrical signals). These are carried along sensory neurones (sensory nerve cells) from sensory receptor cells and sense organs. The central nervous system then processes the information it has received, and relays a suitable response, again in the form of a nerve impulse, along motor neurones to muscles or glands (often referred to as effectors).

The autonomic nervous system controls vital body functions that are not under conscious control, such as breathing and heartbeat. Nerves of another category operate by means of reflexes (eg to produce rapid withdrawl of the hand from a hot object). These involve the transmission of sensory information only as far as the spinal cord, which then sends a response directly to the muscles, without the need for processing of information in the brain.

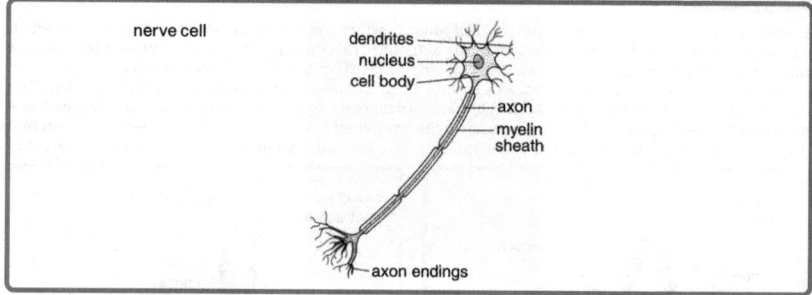

The lymphatic system

Lymph is a colourless fluid, derived from blood, that bathes all the tissues, cleansing them of cellular debris and bacteria. It contains lymphocytes and antibodies which prevent the spread of infection. The network of vessels that carries lymph throughout the body is known as the lymphatic system.

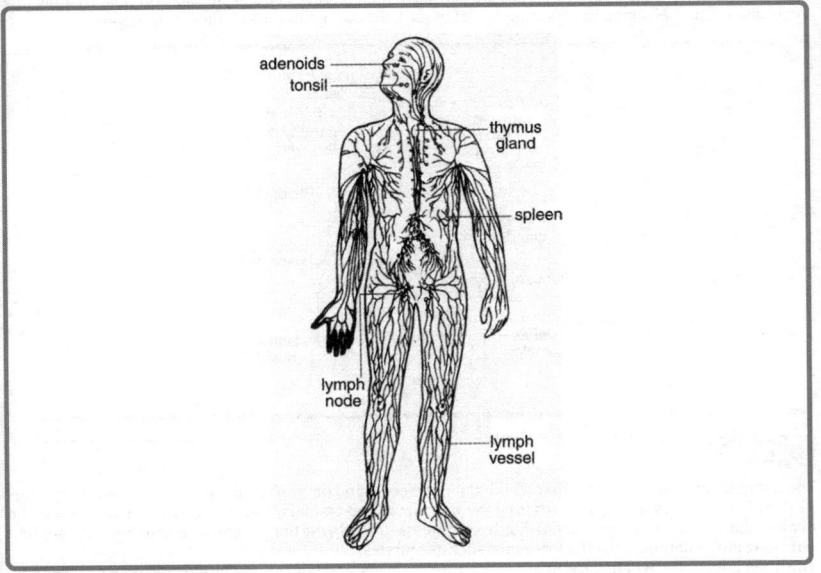

The digestive system

The body uses the food we eat to provide energy for growth and repair, however the body cannot use the food until it has been processed by the digestive system. The processing is carried out along the alimentary canal, a tubular organ that extends from the mouth, where the food is ingested, to the anus, where waste material is eliminated. The alimentary canal consists of the mouth cavity, pharynx, oesophagus, stomach, duodenum, small intestine, large intestine and rectum. Specialised regions such as the small intestine secrete different enzymes and absorb the products of digestion.

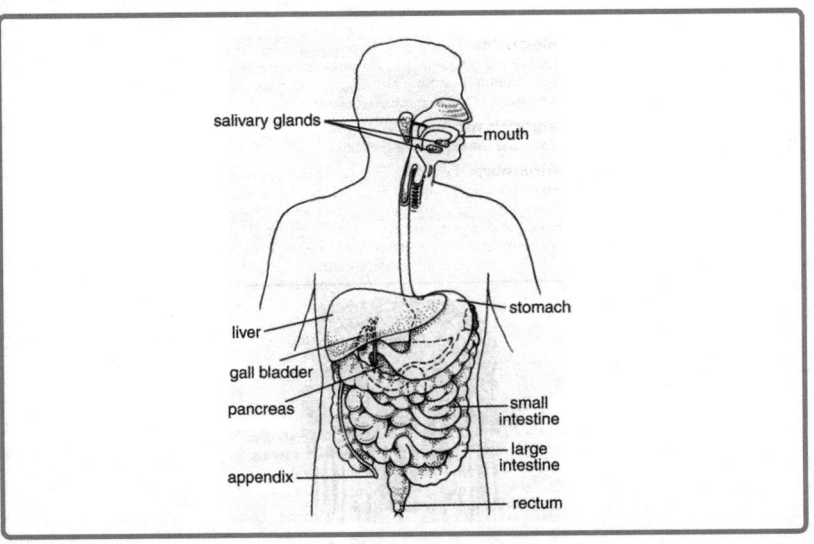

Human Body, Health and Nutrition

The glands

The hormonal, or endocrine, system works in tandem with the nervous system to control body activities. The hormonal communications system that exerts this control consists of a network of endocrine glands. These glands release 20 different hormones, or chemical messengers, each of which affects particular glands or tissues in other parts of the body. Hormones are carried to their target tissues by the bloodstream. By attaching themselves to the cells' membranes in the target tissues, the hormones pass on their instructions.

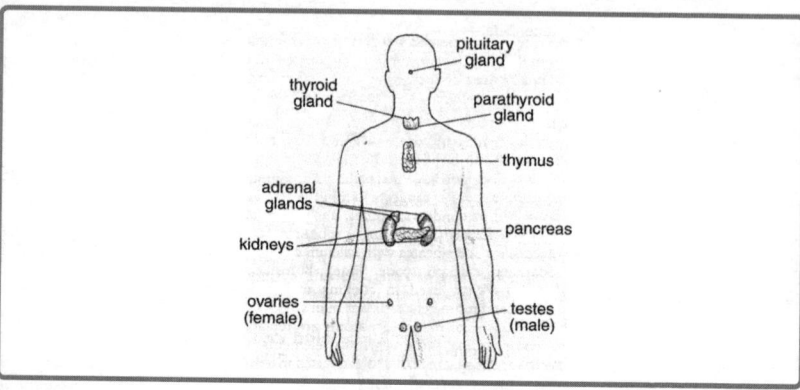

The brain

The human brain contains more than 10 billion nerve cells, and on average weighs about 1400g. It receives sensory information via spinal nerves from the spinal cord and cranial nerves from sense organs such as the eye and the ear. When this information has been processed within the brain, appropriate instructions are sent out along motor neurones to effector organs such as muscles.

The brain is enclosed within three membranes, the meninges, and is protected by the rigid bones of the skull. The forebrain consists of the cerebral hemispheres, the thalamus and the hypothalamus. The outermost layer of the cerebral hemispheres, which are deeply folded and cover most of the surface of the human brain, is known as the cerebral cortex. It is involved in the integration of all sensory input to the brain, including memory and learning, enabling behaviour to be based on past experience. The midbrain connects the forebrain to the hindbrain, which comprises the cerebellum, the medulla oblongata and the pons. The cerebellum coordinates complex muscular processes such as maintaining posture, and the medulla oblongata contains centres that regulate breathing, heartbeat and blood pressure.

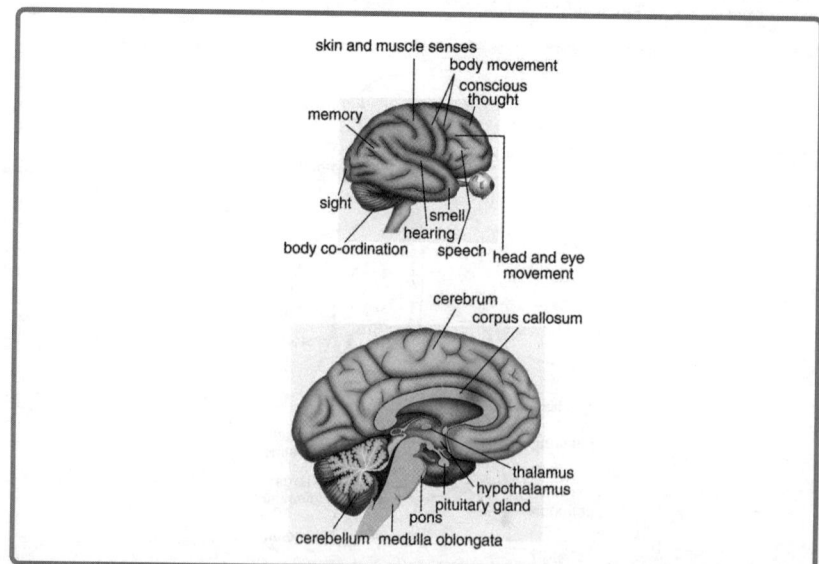

The heart

The heart is divided into four chambers, namely the right and left atria (sometimes called auricles), and the right and left ventricles. Blood that has been oxygenated in the lungs enters the left atrium of the heart and passes to the left ventricle, contraction of which passes oxygenated blood into the aorta, a major blood vessel that leads to the arteries and thence to all the tissues of the body. Deoxygenated blood from the body tissues is returned to the heart via the veins, which lead into the superior vena cava and inferior vena cava, two major blood vessels. These convey the blood to the right atrium of the heart, and from there to the right ventricle, which pumps blood on to the lungs, where it is oxygenated and then returned to the heart so that the cycle can begin again. The presence of several valves within the heart ensures that the blood can only flow in one direction.

The muscular contractions of the heart are self-sustaining, because it consists of a special type of muscle, known as cardiac muscle, which does not become fatigued, and continues to contract rhythmically even when it is disconnected from the nervous system. The average rate of contraction, measured as the pulse rate, is about 72 beats per minute in men and about 80 beats per minute in women.

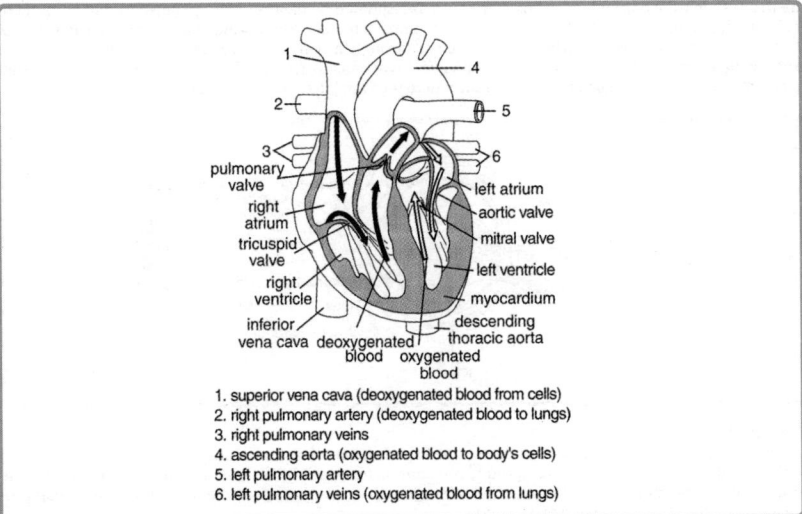

1. superior vena cava (deoxygenated blood from cells)
2. right pulmonary artery (deoxygenated blood to lungs)
3. right pulmonary veins
4. ascending aorta (oxygenated blood to body's cells)
5. left pulmonary artery
6. left pulmonary veins (oxygenated blood from lungs)

The lungs

The lungs are large spongy respiratory organs which remove carbon dioxide from the blood and replace it with oxygen. The surface area of the lungs is greatly increased by the presence of millions of tiny air sacs, known as alveoli. In humans, the total surface area of the alveoli is about $70m^2$. Air containing oxygen is drawn into the lungs through the trachea (windpipe), which divides at its lower end to form two bronchi, which in turn divide into many fine tubes known as bronchioles. Each bronchiole terminates in a cluster of alveoli, which are lined with a thin moist membrane richly supplied with capillaries (very small blood vessels). Oxygen from the air on

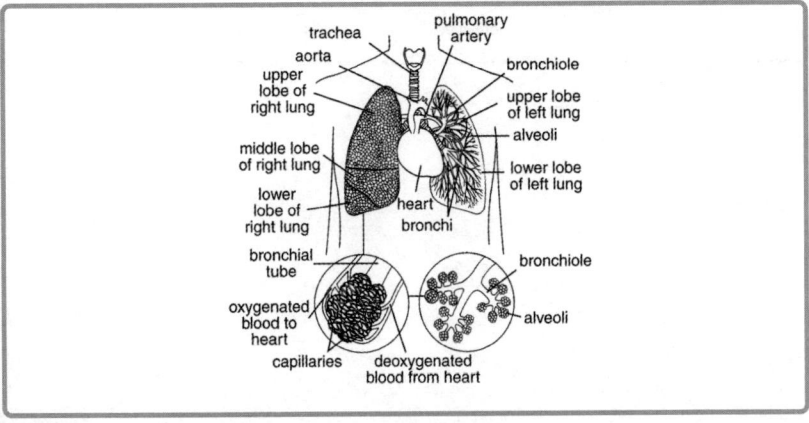

one side of the membrane passes through the thin walls of the alveoli into the capillaries, while carbon dioxide passes out of the capillaries into the lungs in the same way. Air is forced in and out of the lungs as a result of movements of the diaphragm (a sheet of muscle that separates the thorax from the abdomen). During inhalation the diaphragm is lowered, and the lungs expand to fill with air. During exhalation, the diaphragm is raised, and air is forcibly expelled from the lungs.

The eye

The eye is surrounded by a white fibrous outer layer (the sclera), which is modified at the front of the eye to form the transparent cornea. The sclera is lined by a vascular layer or choroid, which is in turn lined at the back of the eye by the retina, which contains millions of light-sensitive cells of two types. These are the rods (which function at low light levels, and are responsible for black and white vision), and the cones (which are responsible for colour vision).

Light enters the eye through the cornea, and passes through a watery medium (the aqueous humour) and then through the pupil, a small circular aperture in the iris. The iris is an adjustable ring of muscle that forms the coloured part of the eye, and controls the size of the pupil and thus the amount of light entering the eye. Behind the iris lies the transparent lens, whose curvature is regulated by means of ciliary muscles that contract to make it thin, for viewing distant objects, or relax to make it thicker, for viewing nearby objects. The shape of the lens is adjusted in this way so that light is directed through the jelly-like vitreous humour lying between the lens and the retina, and is focused onto the retina. The light-sensitive rods and cones of the latter then transmit nerve impulses via the optic nerve to the brain, where they are interpreted as vision.

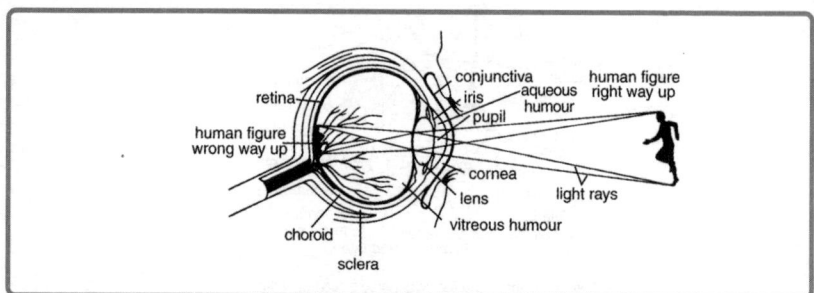

■ Astigmatism

In the normal eye, light travels through the lens to a single focal point, producing clear, undistorted vision. In the astigmatic eye, a defect in the lens produces distortion because not all light rays from it are brought to the same focus on the retina. It can be corrected by surgery or by wearing spectacles or contact lenses that produce exactly the opposite degree of distortion.

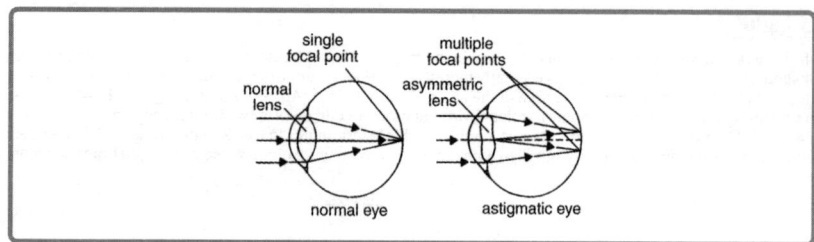

The ear

The ear consists of three parts. The outer ear transmits sound waves from outside the ear to the tympanic membrane (eardrum), and consists of a pinna (commonly referred to as the 'ear') that projects from the head and is made of a thin layer of cartilage covered with skin. It funnels sound into a channel that leads to the tympanic membrane. In some mammals, eg dogs, the pinna can be moved independently in order to detect the direction of sounds.

The middle ear is an air-filled cavity containing three small bones or ossicles, known as the malleus (hammer), incus (anvil) and stapes (stirrup). The Eustachian tube links the middle ear to the pharynx at the back of the throat, ensuring that the air pressure remains the same on both sides of the tympanic membrane. The ossicles transmit vibrations from the tympanic membrane to the fenestra ovalis (oval window), the upper of two membrane-covered openings that separate the middle ear from the fluid-filled inner ear. Vibrations from the fenestra ovalis are finally transmitted to the spiral-shaped cochlea in the inner ear. The cochlea is filled with fluid and lined with sensory cells (hair cells) that detect vibrations as movements of fluid, and relay them as nerve impulses via the auditory nerve to the brain, where they are interpreted as the tone and pitch of the original sound.

The inner ear also contains three fluid-filled semicircular tubes, known as semicircular canals, which can detect movements of the head and are concerned with the maintenance of balance.

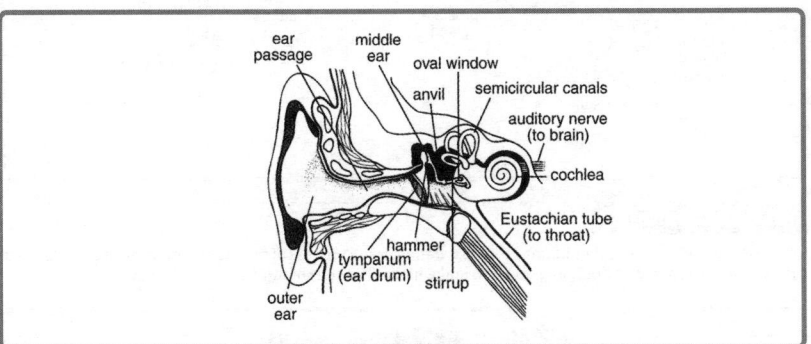

The skin

The skin consists of a thin outer layer (the epidermis), which is continually being renewed as dead cells are shed from its surface, and a thicker underlying layer (the dermis), which is composed of a network of collagen and elastic fibres containing blood and lymph vessels, sensory nerve endings, hair follicles, sweat and sebaceous glands, and smooth muscle.

The skin is an important sense organ, sensitive to touch, pressure, changes in temperature, and painful stimuli. It prevents fluid loss and dehydration, and protects the body from invasion by micro-organisms and parasites. In humans and other warm-blooded animals it has an important role in temperature regulation, heat loss being achieved by sweating and by dilation of the skin capillaries. In order to conserve heat, the skin capillaries contract and the hairs on the surface are raised, trapping a layer of warm air next to the skin.

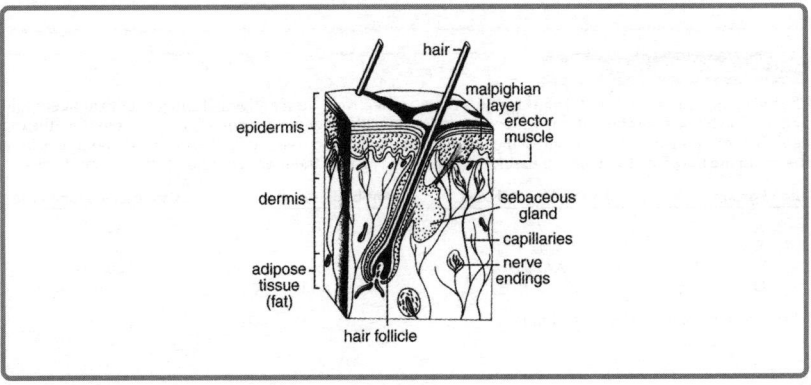

Human Body, Health and Nutrition

Human Body, Health and Nutrition

The reproductive organs

The male reproductive system is closely associated with the urinary system. The bladder stores urine, releasing it to the outside along the urethra, the tube inside the penis which also carries sperm during ejaculation. Sperm are made inside the testis and stored in coiled tubes called the epididymis until, during ejaculation, they are carried to the penis along the sperm duct or vas deferens. The prostate gland, which is located where the sperm ducts and urethra join, releases semen, the milky medium in which sperm are ejaculated from the penis.

Within the female reproductive system, a single sex cell, or ovum, is released each month from one of the ovaries. It travels along the Fallopian tube to the uterus. The neck of the uterus, or cervix, forms a narrow opening between the uterus and the vagina.

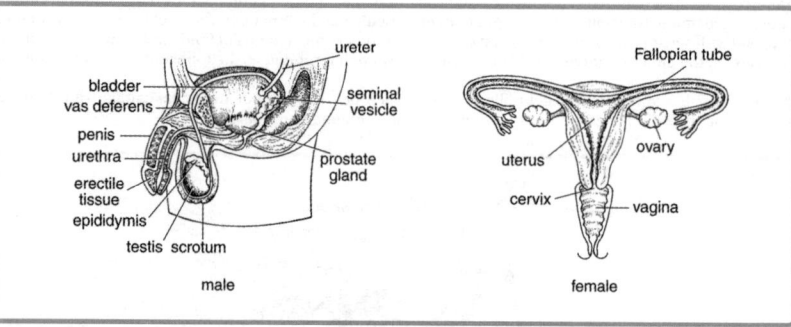

male

female

Artificial respiration

Artificial respiration, or cardio-pulmonary resuscitation, is the process of forcing air into and out of the lungs of a person who has stopped breathing, to try to make him or her start breathing naturally again.

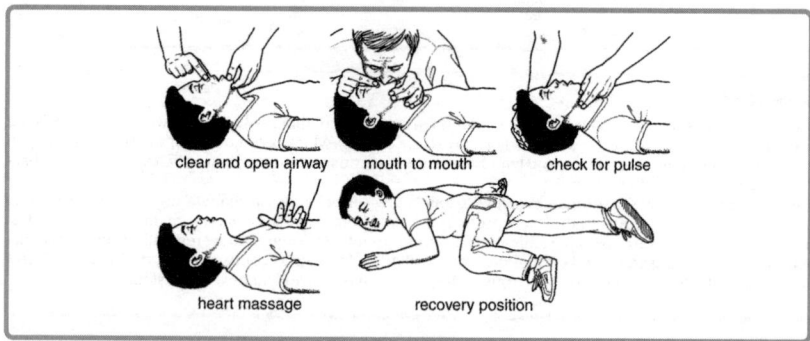

clear and open airway mouth to mouth check for pulse

heart massage recovery position

ABO blood group system

The red blood cells of the A, B, AB and O groups carry, respectively, the A antigen, B antigen, both antigens and neither. The blood contains natural antibodies against the blood group antigen which is absent from the red cells. Before a transfusion, the blood of the recipient and donor is cross-matched to ensure that red cells from the donor are not given to a person possessing antibodies against them, with possible fatal consequences.

Blood group	Antigens on red cells	Antibodies in plasma	Can receive blood type
A	A	B	A and O
B	B	A	B and O
AB[1]	A and B	none	A, B, AB, O
O[2]	none	A and B	O

[1] Universal recipient [2] Universal donor

Main types of vitamin

Vit-amin	Chemical name	Deficiency symptoms	Source
■ Fat soluble vitamins			
A	retinol (carotene)	night blindness; rough skin; impaired bone growth	milk, butter, cheese, egg yolk, liver, fatty fish, dark green vegetables, yellow/red fruits and vegetables, especially carrots
D	cholecalciferol	rickets; osteomalacia	egg yolk, liver, fatty fish; made on skin in sunlight
E	tocopherols	multiple diseases produced in laboratory animals; in humans, multiple symptoms follow impaired fat absorption	vegetable oils
K	phytomenadione	haemorrhagic problems	green leafy vegetables, beef, liver
■ Water soluble vitamins			
B_1	thiamin	beri-beri, Korsakov's syndrome	germ and bran of seeds, grains, yeast
B_2	riboflavin	skin disorders; failure to thrive	liver, milk, cheese, eggs, green leafy vegetables, pulses, yeast
B_6	pyridoxine	dermatitis; neurological disorders	liver, meats, fruits, cereals, leafy vegetables
	pantothenic acid	dermatitis; neurological disorders	widespread in plants and animals; destroyed in heavily-processed food
	biotin	dermatitis	liver, kidney, yeast extract; made by micro-organisms in large intestine
B_{12}	cyanocobalamin	anaemia; neurological disturbance	liver, kidney, milk; none found in plants
	folic acid	anaemia	liver, green leafy vegetables, peanuts; cooking and processing can cause serious losses in food
C	ascorbic acid	scurvy	blackcurrants, citrus fruits, other fruits, green leafy vegetables, potatoes; losses occur during storage and cooking

Main trace minerals

Mineral	Deficiency symptoms	Source
calcium	rickets in children; osteoporosis in adults	milk, butter, cheese, sardines, green leafy vegetables, citrus fruits
chromium	adult-onset diabetes	brewer's yeast, black pepper, liver, whole-meal bread, beer
copper	anaemia; Menkes' syndrome	green vegetables, fish, oysters, liver
fluorine	tooth decay; possibly osteoporosis	fluoridated drinking water, seafood, tea
iodine	goitre; cretinism in new-born children	seafood, salt water fish, seaweed, iodized salt, table salt
iron	anaemia	liver, kidney, green leafy vegetables, egg yolk, dried fruit, potatoes, molasses
magnesium	irregular heart beat; muscular weakness; insomnia	green leafy vegetables (eaten raw), nuts, whole grains
manganese	not known in humans	legumes, cereal grains, green leafy vegetables, tea
molybdenum	not known in humans	legumes, cereal grains, liver, kidney, some dark green vegetables
phosphorus	muscular weakness; bone pain; loss of appetite	meat, poultry, fish, eggs, dried beans and peas, milk products
potassium	irregular heart beat; muscular weakness; fatigue; kidney and lung failure	fresh vegetables, meat, orange juice, bananas, bran
selenium	not known in humans	seafood, cereals, meat, egg yolk, garlic
sodium	impaired acid-base balance in body fluids (very rare)	table salt, other naturally occurring salts
zinc	impaired wound healing; loss of appetite; impaired sexual development	meat, whole grains, legumes, oysters, milk

Human Body, Health and Nutrition

Human Body, Health and Nutrition

Composition of selected foods

Approximate values given are for 100g of the food named.

Food	Kilocalories[1]	Protein (g)	Carbohyd-rates (g)	Fat (g)	Fibre (g)
almonds	564	19	20	54	15
apples	38	trace	15	trace	2
apricots, dried	182	5	67	1	24
apricots, raw	25	1	13	trace	2
asparagus, cooked	18	2	4	trace	1
aubergine (or eggplant), cooked	14	1	4	trace	2
avocados	221	2	6	16	2
bacon, back, grilled	271	15	2	24	0
bacon, streaky, grilled	308	16	2	27	0
bananas	85	1	22	trace	2
beans, broad, cooked	46	4	66	1	4
beans, dried white, cooked	118	8	21	7	25
beans, green, cooked	25	2	5	trace	4
beef, rump steak, grilled	218	30	0	12	0
beetroot, cooked	43	1	7	trace	2
biscuits, chocolate digestive	506	6	64	25	4
biscuits, digestive	486	7	62	23	5
blackberries, raw	29	1	13	1	7
blackcurrants	29	2	14	trace	9
brazil nuts, raw	618	14	11	67	9
bread, white	232	10	58	2	3
bread, wholemeal	216	10	55	3	9
broccoli, cooked	26	3	5	trace	4
brussel sprouts, cooked	18	4	6	trace	3
butter, salted	740	1	trace	82	0
cabbage, cooked	11	2	trace	trace	2
cabbage, raw	25	2	5	trace	3
carrots, cooked	20	1	5	trace	3
carrots, raw	25	1	6	trace	3
cauliflower, cooked	22	2	4	trace	2
celery, raw	36	1	2	trace	2
cheese, Brie	314	19	2	23	0
cheese, Cheddar	414	25	2	32	0
cheese, cottage	96	17	2	4	0
cheese, Edam	314	30	trace	23	0
cherries, raw	70	1	17	trace	1
chick peas, dry	320	20	50	6	15
chicken, meat only, roast	142	19	0	4	0
chocolate bar, plain	510	4	63	29	0
cod, cooked	94	19	0	1	0
corn (on the cob)	91	3	21	1	5
courgettes, cooked	14	1	3	trace	1
crab, cooked	129	18	1	5	0
cream, double	446	2	3	48	0
crisps	517	6	40	37	11
cucumber, raw	15	1	3	trace	trace
dates	214	2	73	1	7
egg, boiled	163	13	1	12	0
eggplant ▸ aubergine					
figs, dried	214	4	69	1	19
flour, white	350	9	80	1	4
flour, wholemeal	318	13	56	2	10
grapefruit	41	1	11	trace	trace
grapes, raw	69	1	16	1	1
haddock, cooked	96	19	0	1	0
ham, lean	168	22	0	5	0
honey	289	trace	82	0	0
jam	261	1	79	trace	1
lamb chop, boned, grilled	353	24	0	29	0
leeks, cooked	25	1	7	0	4
lentils, cooked	106	8	19	trace	4
lettuce, raw	12	1	3	trace	1
liver, cooked	254	20	6	13	0
lobster, cooked	119	20	trace	3	0
mackerel, cooked	188	25	0	11	0
margarine	730	trace	1	80	0
melon, honeydew	21	1	5	trace	1

Food	Kilocalories[1]	Protein (g)	Carbohyd-rates (g)	Fat (g)	Fibre (g)
melon, water	21	trace	5	trace	1
milk, cow's, skimmed	36	4	5	trace	0
milk, cow's, whole	65	4	5	4	0
mushrooms, raw	14	3	4	trace	2
mussels, cooked	86	17	0	1	0
nectarines	64	1	17	trace	2
oatmeal, cooked	399	2	10	1	7
oats, porridge	377	10	70	7	7
oil, vegetable	900	0	0	100	0
onions, raw	38	2	9	trace	1
orange juice	45	1	10	trace	0
oranges, peeled, raw	49	1	12	trace	2
parsnip, cooked	50	1	17	trace	4
pasta, dry	353	12	71	2	4
peaches, raw	38	1	8	trace	1
peanuts, fresh	571	26	19	48	8
pears, raw	61	1	15	trace	2
peas, fresh, cooked	54	5	4	trace	5
pepper, green, raw	14	1	5	trace	1
pepper, red, raw	20	1	7	trace	1
pineapple, raw	46	trace	14	trace	1
pork chop, boned, grilled	328	28	0	24	0
potatoes, baked in skin	86	3	21	trace	2
potatoes, boiled in skin	75	2	17	trace	2
prawns, cooked	107	18	0	1	0
prunes	136	1	77	trace	14
raisins	246	3	77	trace	7
raspberries, raw	25	1	14	1	7
rice, brown, cooked	129	3	26	1	1
rice, white, cooked	121	3	33	trace	1
salmon, cooked	196	20	0	13	0
spinach, cooked	23	3	4	trace	6
strawberries, raw	37	1	8	1	2
sugar	394	0	100	0	0
swede, cooked	18	1	4	trace	3
tomatoes, raw	14	1	5	trace	1
tuna, canned in brine	118	28	0	1	0
turkey, meat only, roast	140	36	0	3	0
turnip, cooked	14	1	5	trace	2
walnuts	525	15	16	64	5
yogurt, skimmed milk	50	3	5	2	0
yogurt, whole milk	62	3	5	3	0

[1] To convert kilocalories into kilojoules multiply by 4.184.

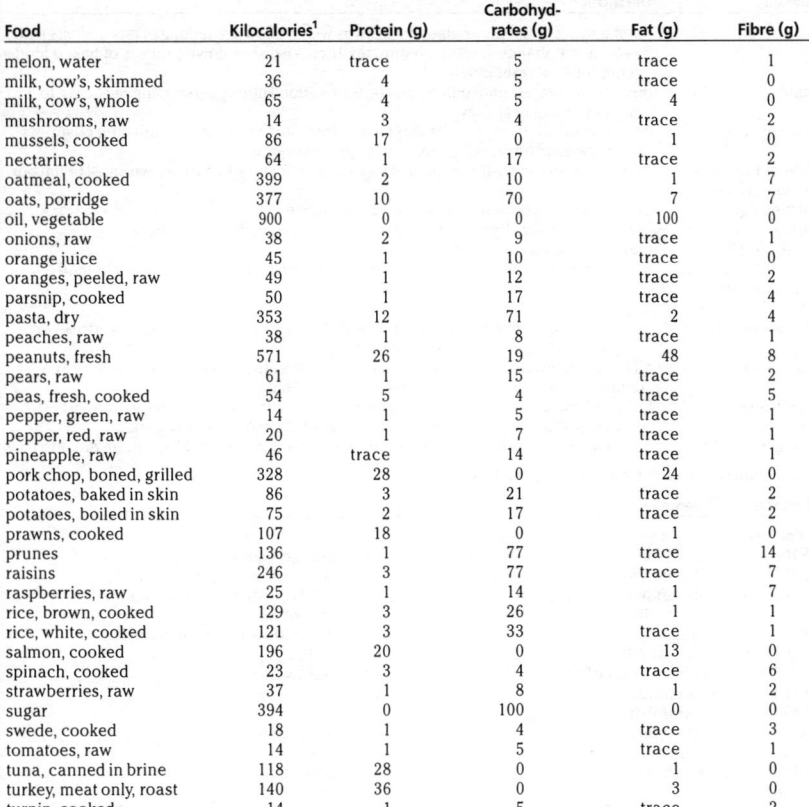

Human Body, Health and Nutrition

E numbers

Glossary	Description
acidifiers	impart a sharp flavour; control acidity, eg for setting jams
anti-caking agents	prevent particles sticking together to enable the product to flow freely, eg in salt and icing sugar
anti-foaming agents	prevent excessive froth and scum formation during boiling
antioxidants	prevent or inhibit the harmful effects of oxidation in fat and oils, thus preventing fatty foods from turning rancid; also used to prevent discolouration due to oxidation eg in cut fruits
azo dyes	have a particular chemical structure and may be responsible for allergic reactions eg attacks of asthma and eczema, nettle rash, watering eyes and nose, blurred vision and hyperactivity in children; include E102, E107, E110, E122, E123, E124, E128, E151, 154, 155, E181
bases	added to reduce acidity or increase alkalinity; also react with acids to make carbon dioxide for aeration
bleaching agents	artificially bleach and whiten flour
buffers	maintain the acid–alkali balance at a constant level
bulking agents	add to the bulk of foods without increasing their energy value, eg in slimming products
chelating agents	combine chemically with toxic substances such as trace metals, rendering them harmless
coal tar dyes	dyes formerly made from coal, now made industrially; may have same configuration as **azo dyes**; include those additives listed under azo dyes above plus E104, E127, E131, E132, 133
colours	make food, particularly processed food, look more attractive and 'realistic'

Human Body, Health and Nutrition

Glossary	Description
emulsifiers	plant gums, chemicals or plant derivatives which allow the mixing of fats and oils with water and enhance smooth creamy textures; also slow down process of baked foods going stale (▸ **stabilizers**)
emulsifying salts	mixture of citrates, phosphates and tartrates added during processing of cheese to prevent it turning stringy
firming agents	calcium and magnesium salts that ensure fruits and vegetables retain their crispness and firmness and do not go soft during processing
flavour modifiers or enhancers	reduce or enhance taste or smell of a food without imparting their own smell or flavour
glazing agents	provide a protective coating or shiny appearance
humectants	prevent food from drying out by absorbing water from the atmosphere
plasticizers	make a substance more flexible
preservatives, antibacterial, antimicrobial etc	inhibit growth of bacteria, fungi and viruses which cause food poisoning or food decay, thus increasing storage time
release agents	used to coat machinery or food to prevent sticking during manufacture, and also to enable food to slip easily out of packaging
sequestrants	attach themselves to trace metals eg iron or copper to prevent them speeding up oxidation and thus causing the deterioration of food
stabilizers	like **emulsifiers**, they prevent mixtures from separating out and enhance smooth creamy textures; they also delay the process of baked foods going stale
thickeners	increase the viscosity of a food; usually of plant origin (except 551, silicon dioxide)

A selection of common E numbers is given below.

Number		Name	Function
■ **Colours**			
E100		Curcumin	orange-yellow
E101		Riboflavin	yellow/orange-yellow
101	(a)	Riboflavin-5' - phosphate	yellow/orange-yellow; vitamin B_2
E102		Tartrazine	yellow
E104		Quinoline yellow	dull yellow/greenish yellow
107		Yellow 2G	yellow
E110		Sunset Yellow FCF	yellow
E120		Cochineal	red
E122		Carmoisine	red
E123		Amaranth	purplish red
E124		Poncean 4R	red
E127		Erythrosine	pink/red
128		Red 2G	red
129		Allura red AC	red (prohibited throughout EC)
E131		Patent blue V	dark bluish-violet; diagnostic agent
E132		Indigo carmine	blue; diagnostic agent
133		Brilliant blue FCF	blue/green
E140		Chlorophyll	olive/dark green
E141		copper complexes of Chlorophyll and Chlorophyllins	olive green/green
E142		Green S	green
E150		Caramel colour	brown/black
E151		Black PN	black
E153		Carbon black	black
154		Brown FK	brown
155		Brown HT	brown
E160	(a)	Alpha-carotene, beta-carotene, gamma-carotene	orange-yellow; becomes vitamin A in the body
E160	(b)	Annatto, Bixin, Norbixin	yellow/peach/red
E160	(c)	Capsanthin	red/orange
E160	(d)	Lycopene	red
E160	(e)	beta-apo-8'-carotenal	orange/yellowish-red
E160	(f)	Ethyl ester of beta-apo-8'-carotenoic acid	orange/yellow
E161	(a)	Xanthophylls Flavoxanthin	yellow
E161	(b)	Xanthophylls Lutein	yellow/reddish
E161	(c)	Xanthophylls Cryptoxanthin	yellow
E161	(d)	Xanthophylls Rubixanthin	yellow
E161	(e)	Xanthophylls Violoxanthin	yellow
E161	(f)	Xanthophylls Rhodoxanthin	yellow
E161	(g)	Xanthophylls Canthaxanthin	orange
E162		Beetroot red	purplish-red
E163		Anthocyanins	red/blue/violet
E170		Calcium carbonate	white surface food colour; also alkali for deacidification of wine; firming agent; releasing agent; calcium supplement
E171		Titanium dioxide	white; increases opacity

Number	Name	Function
E172	Iron oxides, iron hydroxides	yellow/red/orange/brown/black
E173	Aluminium	metallic surface colour
E174	Silver	metallic surface colour
E175	Gold	metallic surface colour
E180	Pigment Rubine	reddish

■ Preservatives

Number	Name	Function
E200	Sorbic acid	active against yeast and moulds (in a slightly acid medium)
E201	Sodium sorbate	
E202	Potassium sorbate	antifungal and antibacterial
E203	Calcium sorbate	antifungal and antibacterial
E210	Benzoic acid	antifungal and antibacterial (in an acid medium)
E211	Sodium benzoate	antifungal and antibacterial (in a slightly acid medium)
E212	Potassium benzoate	antifungal and antibacterial
E213	Calcium benzoate	antifungal and antibacterial
E214	Ethyl 4-hydroxybenzoate	antifungal and antibacterial
E215	Ethyl 4-hydroxybenzoate, sodium salt	antifungal and antibacterial
E216	Propyl 4-hydroxybenzoate	antimicrobial
E217	Propyl 4-hydroxybenzoate, sodium salt	antimicrobial
E218	Methyl 4-hydroxybenzoate	antimicrobial
E219	Methyl 4-hydroxybenzoate, sodium salt	active against fungi and yeasts, less active against bacteria
E220	Sulphur dioxide	also bleaching agent; improving agent; stabilizer; antioxidant; used in beer and wine making
E221	Sodium sulphite	antimicrobial; also sterilizer; prevents discolouration
E222	Sodium hydrogen sulphite	preservative for alcoholic beverages
E223	Sodium metabisulphite	antimicrobial; also antioxidant; bleaching agent
E224	Potassium metabisulphite	antimicrobial; also antibrowning agent
E226	Calcium sulphite	also firming agent; disinfectant
E227	Calcium hydrogen sulphite	also firming agent; used in washing beer casks and to prevent secondary fermentation
E230	Biphenyl	fungistatic agent; acts against *Penicillium*
E231	2-Hydroxybiphenyl	antibacterial and antifungal
E232	Sodium biphenyl-2-yl oxide	antifungal (alternative to E231)
E233	2 (Thiazol-4-yl) benzimidazole	fungicide; treatment of nematode worms in man
234	Nisin	
E236	Formic acid	antibacterial; also flavour adjunct (prohibited in UK)
E237	Sodium formate	(prohibited in UK)
E238	Calcium formate	(prohibited in UK)
E239	Hexamine	antimicrobial
E249	Potassium nitrate	also curing agent; prevents growth of *Clostridium botulinum* (the bacterium responsible for botulism)
E250	Sodium nitrite	prevents growth of *Clostridium botulinum*; also used in curing salt; red meat colour
E251	Sodium nitrate	also used in curing salt; colour fixative
E252	Potassium nitrate	also used in curing salt; colour fixative
E260	Acetic acid	antibacterial; also food acidity stabilizer; colour diluent; flavouring agent
E261	Potassium acetate	preservative of natural colour; also neutralizing agent; acidity regulator
E262	Sodium hydrogen diacetate	antimicrobial; also acidity regulator; sequestrant
262	Sodium acetate	buffer
E263	Calcium acetate	antimould agent; anti-rope (development of sticky yellow patches in bread) agent; sequestrant; firming agent; stabilizer; buffer
E270	Lactic acid	also increases antioxidant effect of other substances; acid and flavouring
E280	Propionic acid	antifungal
E281	Sodium propionate	antimicrobial
E282	Calcium propionate	antimicrobial

Human Body, Health and Nutrition

Human Body, Health and Nutrition

Number	Name	Function
E283	Potassium propionate	antimould (especially against 'rope' micro-organisms in bread)
E290	Carbon dioxide	also coolant; freezant (liquid form); packaging gas; aerator
296	Malic acid	also acid; flavouring
297	Fumaric acid	also acidifier, raising agent; antioxidant

■ **Antioxidants**

Number	Name	Function
E300	L-Ascorbic acid	also Vitamin C; antibrowning agent; flour improving agent; meat colour preservative
E301	Sodium L-ascorbate	also Vitamin C; colour preservative
E302	Calcium L-ascorbate	also Vitamin C; meat colour preservative
E304	6-0-Palmitoyl-L-ascorbic acid	same function as Vitamin C; also colour preservative; antibrowning agent
E306	Extracts of natural origin rich in tocopherols	also Vitamin E
E307	Synthetic alpha-tocopherol	also Vitamin E
E308	Synthetic gamma-tocopherol	also Vitamin E
E309	Synthetic delta-tocopherol	also Vitamin E
E310	Propyl gallate	antioxidant in oils and fats
E311	Octyl gallate	
E312	Dodecyl gallate	
E320	Butylated hydroxyanisole	
E321	Butylated hydroxytoluene	

■ **Emulsifiers, stabilizers and others**

Number	Name	Function
E322	Lecithins	emulsifier
E325	Sodium lactate	humectant; glycerol substitute; increases antioxidant effect of other substances; bodying agent
E326	Potassium lactate	increases antioxidant effect of other substances; buffer
E327	Calcium lactate	antioxidant; buffer; firming agent; fruit and vegetable colour preservative; powdered and condensed milk improver; yeast food; dough conditioner
E330	Citric acid	enhances effects of antioxidants; fruit colour preservative; retains Vitamin C; acidity stabilizer; sequestrant; flavouring; setting agent
E331 (a)	Sodium dihydrogen citrate	enhances effects of antioxidants; acidity-controlling and carbonation-retaining buffer; emulsifying salt; sequestrant; prevents curds forming and cream clotting in aerosols
E331 (b)	*di* Sodium citrate	antioxidant; enhances effects of anti-oxidants; buffer; emulsifying salt
E331 (c)	*tri* Sodium citrate	antioxidant; buffer; emulsifying salt; sequestrant; stabilizer; used with polyphosphates and flavours to inject into chickens before freezing
E332	Potassium dihydrogen citrate	buffer; emulsifying salt; yeast food
E332	*tri* Potassium citrate	antioxidant; buffer in confectionery and artifically sweetened jellies and preserves; emulsifying salt; sequestrant
E333	*mono, di* and *tri* Calcium citrate	buffers to neutralize acids in jams, jellies and confectionery; firming agents; emulsifying salts; sequestrants; flour improvers
E334	L-(+)-Tartaric acid	antioxidant; enhances effects of anti-oxidants; acidity adjuster; sequestrant; food colour diluent; flavouring; acid
E335	*mono* Sodium L-(+)-tartrate and *di* Sodium L-(+)-tartrate	antioxidant; enhances effects of antioxidants; buffer; emulsifying salt; sequestrant
E336	*mono* Potassium L-(+)-tartrate (cream of tartar)	acid; buffer; emulsifying salt; raising agent for flour, used with sodium bicarbonate; inverting agent for sugar
E336	*di* Potassium L-(+)-tartrate	antioxidant; enhances effects of anti-oxidants; buffer; emulsifying salt

Number		Name	Function
E337		Potassium sodium L-(+)-tartrate	buffer for confectionery and preserves; emulsifying salt; stabilizer; enhances effects of antioxidants
E338		Orthophosphoric acid	enhances effects of antioxidants; acidulant; flavouring agent; acidifier in cheese and beer production; sequestrant
E339		Sodium dihydrogen orthophosphate	texture improver; speeds brine penetration; enhances effects of anti-oxidants; buffer; nutrient; gelling agent; stabilizer; sugar clarifying agent
E340	(a)	Potassium dihydrogen orthophosphate	buffer; sequestrant; emulsifying salt; enhances effects of antioxidants
E340	(b)	di Potassium hydrogen orthophosphate	buffer; emulsifying salt; enhances effects of antioxidants; yeast food; sequestrant
E340	(c)	tri Potassium orthophosphate	emulsifying salt; enhances effects of anti-oxidants; buffer; sequestrant
E341	(a)	Calcium tetrahydrogen diorthophosphate	bakery improving agent; firming agent; sequestrant; yeast food; aerator-acidulant; enhances effects of anti-oxidants; texturizer
E341	(b)	Calcium hydrogen orthophosphate	firming agent; yeast food; nutrient min-eral supplement; enhances effects of antioxidants; animal feed supple-ment; abrasive in toothpaste; dough conditioner
E341	(c)	tri Calcium di orthophosphate	anti-caking agent; nutrient yeast food; vegetable extract diluent; clarifying agent
350		Sodium malate	buffer; seasoning agent
350		Sodium hydrogen malate	buffer
351		Potassium malate	buffer
352		Calcium malate	buffer; firming agent; seasoning agent
352		Calcium hydrogen malate	firming agent
353		Metatartaric acid	sequestrant (wine)
355		Adipic acid	acid buffer; neutralizing agent; flavour-ing agent; raising agent in baking powders
363		Succinic acid	acid; buffer; neutralizing agent
370		1,4-Heptonolactone	acid; sequestrant
375		Nicotinic acid	B vitamin; colour protector
380		tri Ammonium citrate	buffer; emulsifying salt; softening agent
381		Ammonium ferric citrate	dietary iron supplement; raises red blood cell level
381		Ammonium ferric citrate, green	dietary iron supplement
385		Calcium disodium ethylenediamine-NNN'N' tetra-acetate (EDTA)	chelating agent; antioxidant
E400		Alginic acid	alginate production
E401		Sodium alginate	stabilizer; suspending agent; thickening agent; gelling agent (with a source of calcium); copper fining agent in brewing
E402		Potassium alginate	emulsifier; stabilizer; boiled water additive; gelling agent
E403		Ammonium alginate	emulsifier; stabilizer; colour diluent; thickener
E404		Calcium alginate	emulsifier; stabilizer; thickener; gelling agent
E405		Propane-1,2-diol alginate	emulsifier; stabilizer; thickener; solvent; foam stabilizing agent
E406		Agar	thickener; stabilizer; gelling agent; humectant; copper fining agent in brewing
E407		Carrageenan	stabilizer; thickener; suspending and gelling agent; texture modifier
E410		Locust gum or Carob bean gum	gelling agent; stabilizer; emulsifier; thickening agent; texture modifier
E412		Guar gum	thickening agent; emulsion stabilizer; suspending agent; dietary bulking agent; helps diabetics control blood sugar levels

Number	Name	Function
E413	Tragacanth	emulsifier; stabilizer; thickener; prevents crystallization of sugar; converts royal icing to a paste
E414	Gum arabic	fretards sugar crystallization; thickener; converts royal icing to a paste; emulsifier; stabilizer; glazing agent; copper fining agent in brewing
E415	Xanthan gum	stabilizer; thickener; emulsifier; 'pseudo-plasticizer' to improve pouring; gelling agent (with guar gum)
416	Karaya gum	stabilizer; emulsifier; thickener; binding agent in meat products; prevents formation of ice crystals; filling agent; citrus and spice flavouring agent
E420	Sorbitol syrup	sweetening agent; glycerol substitute; retards crystallization; masks taste of saccharin; texturizing agent; humectant; stabilizer
E421	Mannitol	texturizing agent; dietary supplement; humectant; sweetener; anti-caking agent; anti-sticking agent
E422	Glycerol	solvent; humectant; sweetener; bodying agent (with gelatins and gums); plasticizer
430	Polyoxyethylene (8) stearate	emulsifier; stabilizer
431	Polyoxyethylene (40) stearate	emulsifier; makes bread 'feel fresh'
432	Polyoxyethylene (20) sorbitan monolaurate	emulsifier; stabilizer; dispersing agent
433	Polyoxyethylene (20) sorbitan mono-oleate	emulsifier; de-foamer; preserves moistness; prevents oil leaking from artificial whipped cream; solubility improver
434	Polyoxyethylene (20) sorbitan monopalmitate	emulsifier; stabilizer; dispersing agent (flavours); defoaming agent; wetting agent
435	Polyoxyethylene (20) sorbitan monostearate	emulsifier; stabilizer; prevents leakage of oils; preserves moistness; wetting and dispersing agent; prevents greasy taste; foaming agent
436	Polyoxyethylene (20) sorbitan tristearate	emulsifier; prevents leakage of oils and water; preserves moistness; wetting and solution agent; defoaming agent; flavour dispersing agent
E440 (a)	Pectin	emulsifying and gelling agent in acid media; bodying agent; syrups; stabilizer
E440 (b)	Amidated pectin	emulsifier; stabilizer; gelling agent; thickener
442	Ammonium phosphatides	stabilizer; emulsifier
E450 (a)	*di* Sodium dihydrogen diphosphate	buffer; sequestrant; emulsifier; raising agent (with sodium bicarbonate); colour improver; chelating agent
E450 (a)	*tri* Sodium diphosphate	buffer; sequestrant; emulsifier; colour improver; chelating agent
E450 (a)	*tetra* Sodium diphosphate	buffer; emulsifying salt; sequestrant; gelling agent; stabilizer; hydration aid
E450 (a)	*tetra* Potassium diphosphate	emulsifying salt; buffer; sequestrant; stabilizer
E450 (b)	*penta* Sodium triphosphate	emulsifying salt; texturizer; buffer; sequestrant; stabilizer; water-binding agent; protein solubilization agent
E450 (b)	*penta* Potassium triphosphate	emulsifying salt; texturizer; buffer; sequestrant; stabilizer
E450 (c)	Sodium polyphosphates	emulsifying salts; sequestrants; stabilizers; texturizers
E450 (c)	Potassium polyphosphates	emulsifying salts; stabilizers; sequestrants
E460	Microcrystalline cellulose	bulking agent; binder; anti-caking agent; dietary fibre; hydration aid; emulsion stabilizer; heat stabilizer; alternative ingredient; tablet binder and disintegrant; quickdrying carrier and dispersant; cellulose component; texture modifier

Number	Name	Function
E460	Alpha-cellulose	bulking aid; anti-caking agent; binder; dispersant; thickening agent; filter aid; assists isinglass finings in brewing
E461	Methylcellulose	emulsifier; stabilizer; thickener; bulking agent; binding agent; film former; water-soluble gum substitute; useful in sugar- and gluten-free diets; fat barrier
E463	Hydroxypropylcellulose	stabilizer; emulsifier; thickener; suspending agent
E464	Hydroxypropylmethylcellulose	gelling or suspending agent; emulsifier; stabilizer and thickening agent; fat barrier
E465	Ethylmethylcellulose	emulsifier; foam stabilizer; thickener; suspending agent
E466	Carboxymethylcellulose, sodium salt	thickening agent; texture modifier; stabilizer; moisture migration controller; gelling agent; bulking agent; prevents crystal growth and syneresis (drawing together of particles in a gel); decreases fat absorption; foam stabilizer
E470	Sodium, potassium and calcium salts of fatty acids	emulsifiers; stabilizers; anti-caking agents
E471	Mono- and di-glycerides of fatty acids	retains foaming power of egg protein in presence of fat (in cakes); emulsifier; stabilizer; thickening agent
E472 (a)	Acetic acid esters of mono- and di-glycerides of fatty acids	emulsifiers; stabilizers; coating agents; texture modifiers; solvents; lubricants
E472 (b)	Lactic acid esters of mono- and di-glycerides of fatty acids	emulsifiers; stabilizers
E472 (c)	Citric acid esters of mono- and di-glycerides of fatty acids	emulsifiers; stabilizers
E472 (d)	Tartaric acid esters of mono- and di-glycerides of fatty acids	emulsifiers; stabilizers
E472 (e)	Mono- and di-acetyltartaric acid esters of mono- and di-glycerides of fatty acids	emulsifiers; stabilizers
E473	Sucrose esters of fatty acids	emulsifiers; stabilizers
E474	Sucroglycerides	emulsifiers; stabilizers
E475	Polyglycerol esters of fatty acids	emulsifiers; stabilizers
476	Polyglycerol esters of polycondensed fatty acids of castor oil	emulsifiers; stabilizers; improves chocolate fluidity (with lecithin) for coating
E477	Propane-1,2-diol esters of fatty acids	emulsifiers; stabilizers
478	Lactylated fatty acid esters of glycerol and propane-1,2-diol	emulsifiers; stabilizers; whipping agents; plasticizers; surface-active agents
E481	Sodium stearoyl-2-lactylate	emulsifier; stabilizer
E482	Calcium stearoyl-2-lactylate	emulsifier; stabilizer; whipping aid
E483	Stearyl tartrate	emulsifier; stabilizer; flour improver
491	Sorbitan monostearate	emulsifier; stabilizer; glazing agent
492	Sorbitan tristearate	emulsifier; stabilizer
493	Sorbitan monolaurate	emulsifier; stabilizer; anti-foaming agent
494	Sorbitan mono-oleate	emulsifier; stabilizer
495	Sorbitan monopalmitate	oil-soluble emulsifier; stabilizer
500	Sodium carbonate	base; removal of testinic acid in brewing
500	Sodium hydrogen carbonate	base; aerating agent; diluent
500	Sodium sesquicarbonate	base
501	Potassium carbonate and potassium hydrogen carbonate	base alkali
503	Ammonium carbonate	buffer; neutralizing agent; raising agent
503	Ammonium hydrogen carbonate	alkali; buffer; aerating agent; raising agent
504	Magnesium carbonate	alkali; anti-caking agent; acidity regulator; anti-bleaching agent
507	Hydrochloric acid	acid; for consistent quality in beer
508	Potassium chloride	gelling agent; salt substitute; dietary supplement
509	Calcium chloride	sequestrant; firming agent; for consistent quality in beer
510	Ammonium chloride	yeast food; flavour
513	Sulphuric acid	acid; for consistent quality in beer
514	Sodium sulphate	diluent; for consistent quality in beer
515	Potassium sulphate	salt substitute

Human Body, Health and Nutrition

Number	Name	Function
516	Calcium sulphate	firming agent; sequestrant; nutrient; yeast food; inert excipient; for consistent quality in beer
518	Magnesium sulphate	dietary supplement; firming agent; used in beer-making
524	Sodium hydroxide	alkali; soap making
525	Potassium hydroxide	base; oxidizing agent (black olives)
526	Calcium hydroxide	firming agent; neutralizing agent; removes testinic acid and ensures consistent quality in beer making
527	Ammonium hydroxide	food colouring diluent and solvent; alkali
528	Magnesium hydroxide	alkali
529	Calcium oxide	alkali; nutrient
530	Magnesium oxide	anti-caking agent; alkali
535	Sodium ferrocyanide	anti-caking agent; crystal modifier
536	Potassium ferrocyanide	anti-caking agent; metals removal in wine making ('blue finings')
540	*di* Calcium diphosphate	neutralizing agent; dietary supplement; buffering agent; yeast food; mineral supplement (little used in UK)
541	Sodium aluminium phosphate	aerator acidulant (raising agent)
541	Sodium aluminium phosphate, basic	emulsifying salt
542	Edible bone phosphate	anti-caking agent; mineral supplement; tablet filler
544	Calcium polyphosphates	emulsifying salts; mineral supplements; calcium source; firming agents (not used in UK)
545	Ammonium polyphosphates	emulsifiers; emulsifying salts; sequestrants; yeast foods; stabilizers

■ Anti-caking agents

551	Silicon dioxide	also suspending agent; thickener; stabilizer; assists isinglass finings in clearing beer
552	Calcium silicate	also antacid (pharmacology); glazing, polishing and release agent (sweets); dusting agent (chewing gum); coating agent (rice); suspending agent
553 (a)	Magnesium silicate, synthetic and magnesium trisilicate	also tablet excipient; antacid (pharmacology); glazing, polishing and release agent (sweets); dusting agent (chewing gum); coating agent (rice)
553 (b)	Talc	also release agent; chewing gum component; filtering aid; dusting powder
554	Aluminium sodium silicate	
556	Aluminium calcium silicate	
558	Bentonite	also clarifying agent; filtration aid; emulsifier; suspending agent
559	Kaolin, heavy, and Kaolin, light	also clarifying agent
570	Stearic acid	
572	Magnesium stearate	also emulsifier; release agent
575	D-Glucono-1,5-lactone	also acid; sequestrant; prevents formation of milkstone (magnesium, calcium phosphate deposits) and beerstone
576	Sodium gluconate	also sequestrant; dietary supplement
577	Potassium gluconate	also sequestrant
578	Calcium gluconate	also buffer; firming agent; sequestrant

■ Flavour enhancers

620	L-Glutamic acid	also salt substitute
621	*mono* Sodium glutamate	
622	Potassium hydrogen L-glutamate	also salt substitute
623	Calcium dihydrogen di-L-glutamate	also salt substitute
627	Guanosine 5'-(*di* Sodium phosphate)	
631	Inosine 5'-(*di* Sodium phosphate)	
635	Sodium 5'-ribonucleotide	
636	Maltol	'freshly baked' flavour
637	Ethyl maltol	sweet flavour
900	Dimethylpolysiloxane	also water repellent; anti-foaming agent; chewing gum base; anti-caking agent; used in beer making

Number	Name	Function
■ Glazing agents		
901	Beeswax, white, and beeswax, yellow	also release agent; fruit and honey flavourings
903	Carnauba wax	also enhances hardness and lustre of other waxes; used in cosmetics
904	Shellac	
905	Mineral hydrocarbons	also sealing agent; chewing gum ingredient; defoaming agent; coating for fresh fruit and vegetables; lubricant and binder for capsules and tablets; lubricant in food-processing equipment and meat-packing plants
907	Refined microcrystalline wax	also chewing gum ingredient; polishing and release agent; stiffening agent; tablet coating
■ Improving agents		
920	L-cysteine hydrochloride and L-cysteine hydrochloride monohydrate	also flavouring (chicken); used in shampoo
924	Potassium bromate	also flour-maturing agent; used in beer making
925	Chlorine	also flour bleaching; drinking water
926	Chlorine dioxide	also bleaching agent; oxidizing agent; water purifying agent; taste and odour control of water; bactericide and antiseptic
927	Azo dicarbonamide	also flour maturing agent

Infectious diseases and infections

Name	Cause	Transmission	Incubation	Symptoms
AIDS (Acquired Immune Deficiency Syndrome)	human immuno-deficiency virus (HIV)	sexual intercourse, sharing of syringes, blood transfusion	several years	fever, lethargy, weight loss, diarrhoea, lymph node enlargement, viral and fungal infections
amoebiasis	*Entamoeba histolytica*	organism in contaminated food	up to several years	fever, diarrhoea, exhaustion, rectal bleeding
anthrax	*Bacillus antracis* bacterium	animal hair	1–3 days	small red pimple on hand or face enlarges and discharges pus
appendicitis	usually *E. coli* organism	not transmitted	sudden onset	abdominal pain which moves from left to right after a few hours, nausea
bilharziasis (schistosomiasis)	*Schistosoma haematobium*, (also called Bilharzia) *S. mansoni* or *S. japonicum*	certain snails living in calm water	varies with lifespan of parasite	fever, muscle aches, abdominal pain, headaches
bronchiolitis (babies only)	respiratory syncytical virus (RSV)	droplet infection	1–3 days	blocked or runny nose, irritability
brucellosis	*Brucella abortus* or *B. meliteusis* bacteria	cattle or goats	3–6 days	fever, drenching sweats, weight loss, muscle and joint pains, confusion and poor memory
bubonic plague	*Yersinia pestis* bacterium	fleas	3–6 days	fever, muscle aches, headaches, exhaustion, enlarged lymph glands ('buboes')
chicken pox (varicella)	*varicella-zoster* virus	droplet infection	14–21 days	blister-like eruptions, lethargy, headaches, sore throat
cholera	*Vibrio cholerae*	contaminated water	a few hours to 5 days	severe diarrhoea, vomiting
common cold (coryza)	Rhinoviruses	droplet infection	1–3 days	blocked or runny nose, sneezing, sore throat, runny eyes

Name	Cause	Transmission	Incubation	Symptoms
conjunctivitis	virus, bacterium or allergy	variable	variable	if viral, water discharge from eyes; if bacterial, sticky yellow discharge from eyes
dengue fever (break-bone fever)	B group of arbo-viruses	mosquito	5–6 days	fever, severe muscle cramps, enlarged lymph nodes
diphtheria	*Corynebacterium diphtheriae*	droplet infection	4–6 days	grey exudate across throat; swelling of throat tissues may lead to asphyxiation; toxin secreted by bacteria may seriously damage heart
dysentery	*Shigella* genus of bacteria	contaminated food or water	variable; can cause death within 48 hours	diarrhoea, with or without bleeding
gastro-enteritis	bacteria, viruses and food poisoning	droplet infection of food	variable	varies from nausea to severe fever, vomiting and diarrhoea
German measles (rubella)	togavirus	droplet infection	18 days	1–2 days catarrh and sore throat, then red rash, enlargement of lymph nodes
glandular fever (infectious mononucleosis)	Epstein-Barr virus	saliva of infected person	1–6 weeks	sore throat, fever, enlargement of tonsils and lymph nodes, lethargy, depression
gonorrhoea	*Neisseria gonorrhoeae* bacterium	usually sexually transmitted	2–10 days	in men, burning sensation on urination and discharge from urethra; in women (if any), vaginal discharge
hepatitis	hepatitis A, B or C virus	contaminated food or water (type A); sexual relations, sharing syringes, transfusion (type B)	3–6 weeks (type A); up to a few weeks (type B)	often no symptoms, otherwise similar to 'flu; loss of appetite, tenderness below right ribs, jaundice
influenza ('flu)	influenza A, B or C virus	droplet infection	1–3 days	fever, sweating, muscle aches
kala-azar (leishmaniasis)	parasites, Genus leishmania	sandfly	usually 1–2 months, can be up to 10 years	lymph gland, spleen and liver enlarge-ment
laryngitis	same viruses that cause colds and 'flu, ie adeno and rhinoviruses	droplet infection	1–3 days	sore throat, coughing, hoarseness
lassa fever	arenavirus	urine	3 weeks	fever, sore throat, muscle aches and pains, haemorrhage into the skin
Legionnaire's disease	*Legionella pneumophila* bacterium	water droplets in infected hum-idifiers, cooling towers; stagnant water in cisterns and shower heads	1–3 days	'flu and pneumonia-like symptoms, fever, diarrhoea, mental confusion
leprosy	*Mycobacterium leprae* bacterium	droplet infection; minimally contagious	variable	insensitive white patches on skin, nodules, thickening of and damage to nerves
malaria	*Plasmodium falci-parium, P. vivax, P. ovale, P. malariae*	anopheles mosquito	several weeks for *P. falciparium*, to several months for *P. vivax*	severe swinging fever, cold sweats, shivers

Name	Cause	Transmission	Incubation	Symptoms
Marburg (or green monkey) disease	unclassified virus	monkeys, body fluids	5–9 days	fever, diarrhoea; affects brain, kidneys and lungs
measles	paramyxovirus	droplet infection	14 days	fever, severe cold symptoms, bloody red rash
meningitis	various bacteria, viruses or fungi eg *Cryptococcus*	droplet infection	variable	severe headache, stiffness in neck muscles, dislike of the light, nausea, vomiting, confusion
mumps	paramyxovirus	droplet infection	18 days	lethargy, fever, pain at the angle of the jaw, swelling of parotid gland(s)
orchitis	bacterium or virus; if bacterial, urinary infection due to eg gonorrhoea; if viral, due to eg mumps	see cause	variable	painful red and swollen testes, fever, nausea
osteomyelitis	usually staphylococci organisms	infection spreads from eg boil or impetigo	1–10 days	abrupt onset of fever, and pain at site of infected bone (usually tibia
parotitis	bacterium or virus	common in mumps (viral), may follow severe febrile illness or abdominal operation	1–10 days	inflammation of one or both parotid glands
pericarditis	bacterium or virus eg *Coxsackie B*	infection follows a chest disease or heart attack	variable	inflamed pericardium (fibrous bag which encloses the heart); tight chest pain
peritonitis	usually *E. coli* organism; sometimes chemical irritation	usually appendicitis; perforation of the gut allows escape of barrel contents into peritoneal cavity	1–10 days	severe abdominal pain, vomiting, rigidity, shock
pharyngitis	bacteria or virus	droplet infection	3–5 days	sore throat, fever, pain on swallowing, enlarged neck glands
pneumonia	*Streptococcus pneumoniae* bacterium, *Legionella pneumophila* etc	droplet infection	1–3 weeks	cough, fever, chest pain
poliomyelitis	three types of polio virus	droplet infection and hand to mouth infection from faeces	7–14 days	affects spinal cord and brain; headache, fever, neck and muscle stiffness; may result in meningitis or paralysis
proctitis	fungal infection possible	contact	variable	inflammation of the rectum and anus resulting from thrush, piles or fissures; pain on defecation
psittacosis	*Chlamydis psittaci*	infected birds (eg parrots)	1–2 weeks	headache, chest pain, fever, nausea
puerperal fever	infection within uterine cavity or vagina	follows childbirth	1–10 days	fever; often fatal in past, now rare
pylitis	bacteria	kidney infection	1–10 days	fever, rigor, loin pain, burning on passing urine

Human Body, Health and Nutrition

Name	Cause	Transmission	Incubation	Symptoms
rabies	virus	bite or lick by infected animal	2–6 weeks	headache, sickness, excitability, fear of drinking water, convulsions, coma and death
river blindness (or onchocerciasis)	*Onchocerca volvulus* worm	bites of infected flies of genus *Simulium*	worms mature in 2–4 months, may live 12 years	worms inhabit skin, causing nodules and sometimes blindness
salpingitis	infection of the Fallopian tubes	usually gonorrhoea	variable	abdominal pain, fever, irregular periods, vaginal discharge
SARS (Severe Acute Respiratory Syndrome)	coronavirus	droplet infection; possibly also direct contact	2–10 days	fever, cough, breathing difficulty
scarlet fever	*haemolytic streptococcus*	droplet infection or streptococci-infected milk or ice cream	2–4 days	sudden onset; headache, sore throat, fever, vomiting, red skin rash
shingles	*Herpes zoster* virus (also causes chicken pox)	dormant virus in body becomes active following a minor infection	variable	pain, numbness, blisters
sinusitis	virus or bacteria	droplet infection; common with a cold	1–3 days	fever, sinus pain, nasal discharge
sleeping sickness (or African trypanosomiasis)	1. *Trypanosoma brucei gambieuse* or 2. *Tb. rhodesieuse*	bites by infected tsetse fly	1. weeks–months; 2. 7–14 days	fever, lymph node enlargement, headache, behavioural change, drowsiness, coma, sometimes death
smallpox	variole major or minor virus	now eradicated worldwide	12 days	fever, rash followed by pustules on face and extremities
syphilis	*Treponema pallidum*	sexually transmitted: organism enters bloodstream through a mucous membrane, usually genital	ulcer after 2–6 weeks, skin rash after weeks or months	late syphilis damages brain, heart and main blood vessels, and unborn babies
tetanus	*Clostridium tetani*	bacteria from soil infect wounds	2 days–4 weeks	muscular spasms cause lockjaw and affect breathing; potentially fatal
thrush	*Candida albicans* yeast	the yeast is present on skin of most people and multiplies when resistance to infection is low; during pregnancy or when taking contraceptive pill	variable	white spots on tongue and cheeks; irritant vaginal discharge; rash in genital area or between folds of skin
tonsillitis	usually same viruses responsible for colds; sometimes bacterial (streptococci)	droplet infection	1–3 days	red inflamed tonsils, sore throat
trachoma	*Chlamydia trachomatis* organism	poor hygiene: organism infects eye	5 days	conjunctivitis, swelling and scarring in cornea, often leading to blindness
tuberculosis	*Myobacterium tuberculosis* bacterium	inhalation of bacterium from person with active tuberculosis pneumonia or from infected milk	up to several years	cough with bloodstained sputum, weight loss, chest pain

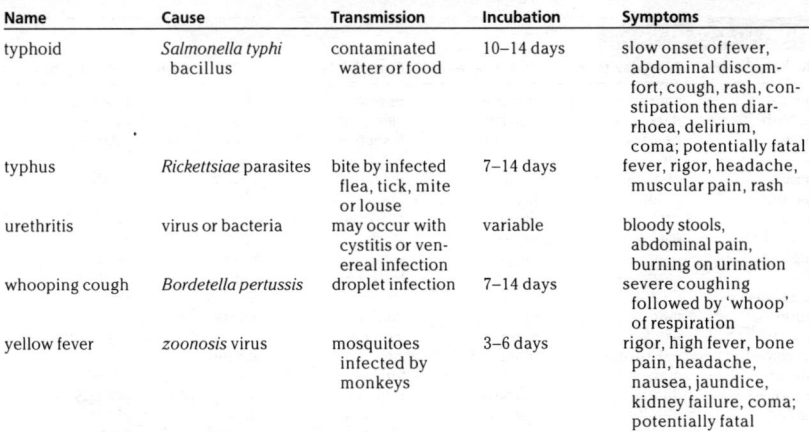

Name	Cause	Transmission	Incubation	Symptoms
typhoid	*Salmonella typhi* bacillus	contaminated water or food	10–14 days	slow onset of fever, abdominal discomfort, cough, rash, constipation then diarrhoea, delirium, coma; potentially fatal
typhus	*Rickettsiae* parasites	bite by infected flea, tick, mite or louse	7–14 days	fever, rigor, headache, muscular pain, rash
urethritis	virus or bacteria	may occur with cystitis or venereal infection	variable	bloody stools, abdominal pain, burning on urination
whooping cough	*Bordetella pertussis*	droplet infection	7–14 days	severe coughing followed by 'whoop' of respiration
yellow fever	*zoonosis* virus	mosquitoes infected by monkeys	3–6 days	rigor, high fever, bone pain, headache, nausea, jaundice, kidney failure, coma; potentially fatal

Major causes of death

Death from respiratory ailments, infectious diseases and injuries (other than traffic accidents) tends to be lower in the developed world due to preventative medicine, safer living conditions and powerful modern drugs; however, people in the developed world are the most likely to die from cancer or heart disease.

The table below shows the standardized death rate per 100 000 of the population in various countries from the selected causes listed. AIDS is not included in these statistics.

Country	Infectious and parasitic diseases	Malignant neoplasms (Cancer)	Diseases of the circulatory system	Diseases of the respiratory system (Heart disease)	Motor vehicle accidents	Homicide
Argentina	24.1	119.0	267.8	44.2	10.1	4.0
Australia	3.8	126.2	168.3	32.0	10.0	1.7
The Bahamas	14.7	112.9	211.0	56.7	5.8	13.3
Canada	3.7	126.1	142.1	32.6	9.8	1.5
Chile	14.9	120.3	154.8	62.8	12.1	2.8
Cuba	11.9	108.4	221.6	47.0	16.7	6.8
Estonia	11.6	140.5	416.6	29.8	22.7	19.8
Finland	4.3	107.2	211.3	32.2	6.9	2.7
France	5.7	130.8	107.9	23.2	12.9	1.1
Germany	3.7	130.8	202.6	26.5	10.7	1.1
Israel	7.3	114.6	183.7	18.3	10.2	1.4
Italy	2.0	133.7	166.0	22.1	12.4	1.5
Latvia	18.0	137.0	471.7	36.1	27.7	16.0
Mauritius	16.4	68.8	346.2	75.1	17.6	1.2
Mexico	27.6	81.2	174.7	67.6	16.2	17.7
The Netherlands	4.3	136.7	160.9	35.8	6.9	1.1
Poland	5.9	149.0	323.6	23.3	16.7	2.5
Russia	19.6	142.5	501.2	56.5	20.4	26.6
Singapore	12.3	130.8	186.6	94.7	7.6	1.5
Spain	5.8	120.8	143.8	33.8	12.4	0.8
Sweden	3.5	106.6	172.8	25.5	4.9	1.0
Trinidad and Tobago	12.4	102.5	308.9	51.6	10.4	11.4
UK	3.9	137.1	192.6	63.7	5.6	1.0
USA	7.9	130.8	187.5	41.6	14.9	9.4
Venezuela	41.0	95.8	248.7	48.1	24.0	15.1

Source: *World Health Statistics Annual 1996* (WHO, 1998)

Human Body, Health and Nutrition

Human Body, Health and Nutrition

An A to Z of phobias

Technical term	Everyday term	Technical term	Everyday term	Technical term	Everyday term
acero-	sourness	eisoptro-	mirrors	neo-	newness
achluo-	darkness	electro-	electricity	nepho-	clouds
acro-	heights	entomo-	insects	noso- (patho-)	disease
aero-	air	eoso-	dawn	ocho-	vehicles
agora-	open spaces	eremo-	solitude	odonto-	teeth
aichuro-	points	erete-	pins	oiko-	home
ailuro-	cats	ereuthro-	blushing	olfacto-	smell
akoustico-	sound	ergasio-	work	ommato-	eyes
algo-	pain	geno-	sex	oneiro-	dreams
amaka-	carriages	geuma-	taste	ophidio-	snakes
amatho-	dust	grapho-	writing	ornitho-	birds
andro-	men	gymno-	nudity	ourano-	heaven
anemo-	wind	gyno-	women	pan- (panto-)	everything
angino-	narrowness	hamartio-	sin	partheno-	girls
anthropo-	man	haphe-	touch	patroio-	heredity
antlo-	flood	harpaxo-	robbers	penia-	poverty
apeiro-	infinity	hedono-	pleasure	phasmo-	ghosts
arachno-	spiders	haemato-	blood	phobo-	fears
astheno-	weakness	helmintho-	worms	photo-	light
astra-	lightning	hodo-	travel	pnigero-	smothering
ate-	ruin	homichlo-	fog	poine-	punishment
aulo-	flute	horme-	shock	poly-	many things
aurora-	Northern Lights	hydro-	water	poto-	drink
bacilli-	microbes	hypegia-	responsibility	pterono-	feathers
baro-	gravity	hypno-	sleep	pyro-	fire
baso-	walking	ideo-	ideas	rypo-	soiling
batracho-	reptiles	kakorraphia-	failure	Satano-	Satan
belone-	needles	katagelo-	ridicule	sela-	flashes
bronto-		keno-	void	sidero-	stars
(tonitro-,		kineso-	motion	sito-	food
kerauno-)	thunder	klepto-	stealing	sperma-	
cheima-	cold	kopo-	fatigue	(spermato-)	germs
chiono-	snow	kristallo-	ice	stasi-	standing
chrometo-	money	lalio-	stuttering	stygio- (hade-)	hell
chrono-	duration	linono-	string	syphilo-	syphilis
chrystallo-	crystals	logo-	words	thaaso-	sitting
claustro-	closed spaces	lysso- (mania-)	insanity	thalasso-	sea
cnido-	stings	mastigo-	flogging	thanato-	death
cometo-	comets	mechano-	machinery	theo-	God
cromo-	colour	metallo-	metals	thermo-	heat
cyno-	dogs	meteoro-	meteors	toxi-	poison
demo-	crowds	miso-	contamination	tremo-	trembling
demono-	demons	mono-	one thing	triskaideka-	thirteen
dermato-	skin	musico-	music	zelo-	jealousy
dike-	injustice	muso-	mice	zoo-	animals
dora-	fur	necro-	corpses	xeno-	strangers
		nelo-	glass		

Everyday term	Technical term	Everyday term	Technical term	Everyday term	Technical term
air	aero-	demons	demono-	fog	homichlo-
animals	zoo-	disease	noso- (patho-)	food	sito-
birds	ornitho-	dogs	cyno-	fur	dora-
blood	haemato-	dreams	oneiro-	germs	sperma-
blushing	ereutho-	drink	poto-		(spermato-)
carriages	amaka-	duration	chrono-	ghosts	phasmo-
cats	ailuro-	dust	amatho-	girls	partheno-
closed spaces	claustro-	electricity	electro-	glass	nelo-
clouds	nepho-	everything	pan- (panto-)	God	theo-
cold	cheima-	eyes	ommato-	gravity	baro-
colour	cromo-	failure	kakorraphia-	heat	thermo-
comets	cometo-	fatigue	kopo-	heaven	ourano-
contamination	miso-	fears	phobo-	heights	acro-
corpses	necro-	feathers	pterono-	hell	stygio- (hade-)
crowds	demo-	fire	pyro-	heredity	patroio-
crystals	chrystallo-	flashes	sela-	home	oiko-
darkness	achluo-	flogging	mastigo-	ice	kristallo-
dawn	eoso-	flood	antlo-	ideas	ideo-
death	thanato-	flute	aulo-	infinity	apeiro-

Everyday term	Technical term	Everyday term	Technical term	Everyday term	Technical term
injustice	dike-	points	aichuro-	stealing	klepto-
insanity	lysso- (mania-)	poison	toxi-	stings	cnido-
insects	entomo-	poverty	penia-	strangers	xeno-
jealousy	zelo-	punishment	poine-	string	linono-
light	photo-	reptiles	batracho-	stuttering	lalio-
lightning	astra-	responsibility	hypegia-	syphilis	syphilo-
machinery	mechano-	ridicule	katagelo-	taste	geuma-
man	anthropo-	robbers	harpaxo-	teeth	odonto-
many things	poly-	ruin	ate-	thirteen	triskaideka-
men	andro-	Satan	Satano-	thunder	bronto-
metals	metallo-	sea	thalasso-		(tonitro-,
meteors	meteoro-	sex	geno-		kerauno-)
mice	muso-	shock	horme-	touch	haphe-
microbes	bacilli-	sin	hamartio-	travel	hodo-
mirrors	eisoptro-	sitting	thaaso-	trembling	tremo-
money	chrometo-	skin	dermato-	vehicles	ocho-
motion	kineso-	sleep	hypno-	void	keno-
music	musico-	smell	olfacto-	walking	baso-
narrowness	angino-	smothering	pnigero-	water	hydro-
needles	belone-	snakes	ophidio-	weakness	astheno-
newness	neo-	snow	chiono-	wind	anemo-
Northern Lights	aurora-	soiling	rypo-	women	gyno-
nudity	gymno-	solitude	eremo-	words	logo-
one thing	mono-	sound	akoustico-	work	ergasio-
open spaces	agora-	sourness	acero-	worms	helmintho-
pain	algo-	spiders	arachno-	writing	grapho-
pins	erete-	standing	stasi-		
pleasure	hedono-	stars	sidero-		

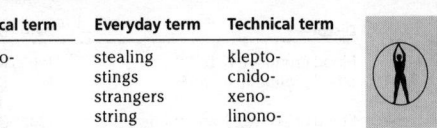

Important discoveries in medicine

Discovery	Date	Discoverer(s)	Nationality
adrenal gland, function of	1856	Vulpian (b.1826)[1]	French
adrenaline	1901	Jokichi Takamine (1854–1922) based on work by Edward Sharpey-Schafer (1850–1935) and Oliver	Japanese UK
AIDS (Aquired Immune Deficiency Syndrome)	1981	scientists in Los Angeles	—
allergenic nature of hay fever	1906	Clemens Peter von Pirquet (b.1874)	Austrian
allergy recognized in skin's reaction to tuberculin	1906	Clemens Peter von Pirquet (b.1874)	Austrian
anaesthetic, epidural	1885	James Leonard Corning (1855–1923)	US
anaesthetic, general	c.1840	priority claimed by Crawford Long (1815–78) Gardner Cotton (1814–98) Horace Wells (1815–48) Charles Jackson (1805–80)	all US
anaesthetic, local (mandrake leaves and polenta)	described in *Natural History*	Pliny the Elder (23–79AD)	Roman
anaphylaxis	1902	Charles Robert Richet (1850–1935) Pierre Portier	French French
androsterone	1931	Adolf Friedrich Johann Butenandt (1903–95)	German
anthrax bacillus	1850	Casimir Joseph Davaine (1812–82)	French
anthrax bacillus	1876	Louis Pasteur (1822–95) Robert Koch (1843–1910)	French German
anthrax, serum against	1895	Achille Sclavo (b.1861) E Marchoux	Italian French
antihistamine	1937	Bonet Hans Staub (b.1890)	Swiss
antipyretic agent (lowers temperature)	4–5c BC	Hippocrates (c.460–c.377 or 359BC)	Greek
antisepsis	1865	Joseph Lister (1827–1912)	UK
asepsis by boiling and by dry heat autoclave	1883	Octave Terrillon Louis-Félix Terrier (b.1837)	French French
atropine (isolated)	1819	Rudolph Brondes	—
bacillus ▸ diphtheria, gangrene, tuberculosis, typhus bacillus	1673	Anton van Leeuwenhoek (1632–1723)	Dutch
benzoadiazepines (tranquillizers) ('the time pill')	1986	Fred W Turck Susan Losee Olsen	US US
blood circulation	1628	William Harvey (1578–1677)	UK

Human Body, Health and Nutrition

Discovery	Date	Discoverer(s)	Nationality
blood groups A, O, B, AB	1901	Karl Landsteiner (1868–1943)	Austrian–US
blood groups M, N and P	1927	Karl Landsteiner (1868–1943)	Austrian–US
		Philip Levine	US
blood pressure greater than atmospheric pressure	1733	Stephen Hales (1677–1761)	UK
brain, electric activity in the (▸ EEG)	1875	Richard Caton	UK
cellular division	1855	Rudolph Virchow (1821–1902)	German
chloroform, anaesthetic properties of	1847	James Young Simpson (1811–70)	UK
cholera vibrion	1883	Robert Koch (1843–1910)	German
chromosome X, heredity linked to sex	1909	Thomas Hunt Morgan (1866–1945)	US
chromosomes	1888	Thomas Hunt Morgan (1866–1945)	US
chromosomes (48) in man	—	Herbert McLean Evans (1882–1971)	US
circadian rhythm of 25 hours	1972	Michel Siffre	—
coagulation, role of fibrin in	1771	William Henson	UK
coagulation (formation of fibrin following dissolution of fibrinogen under influence of thrombin)	1876	Olaf Hammarsten (b.1841)	Swedish
cochlea or inner ear, stimulation mechanism of	1961	Georg von Békésy (1899–1972)	Hungarian–US
corpuscles, red	1675 or 1684	Anton van Leeuwenhoek (1632–1723)	Dutch
cortisone (adrenal cortex hormone) (isolated)	1934	Edward Calvin Kendall (1886–1972)	US
cyclosporin-A, immunosuppressive properties of	1972	J-F Borel	Swiss
digestive system	—	Claude Bernard (1813–78)	French
diphtheria bacillus	1882	Theodor Albrecht Edwin Klebs (b.1834)	Swiss–US
diphtheria, serum against	1892	Emil Adolf von Behring (1854–1917)	German
		Shibasaburo Kitasato (1852–1931)	Japanese
		Pierre Émile Roux (1853–1933)	French
disinfection of wounds, chemical	1825	Antoine Labarraque	French
DNA, structure of	1953, 1961	Francis Harry Crompton Crick (1916–)	UK
		James D Watson (1928–)	US
Down's Syndrome, cause of ('the extra chromosome')	1958	Turpin	French
		Gautier	French
		Lejeune	French
electro-encephalogram (EEG) (spontaneous activity of the brain)	1929	Hans Berger (1873–1941)	German
endorphins	1975	John Hughes	US
		Roger Guillemin (1924–)	French–US
enzymes	1833	Anselme Payen	French
		Jean-François Persoz	French
enzymes, restriction	1970	Hamilton Smith	US
estrogen produced by ovarian follicle	1924	Courrier	French
estrone	1929	Edward Adelbert Doisy (1893–1986)	US
		Adolf Friedrich Johann Butenandt (1903–95)	German
ether first used as anaesthetic	1846	William Thomas Morton (1819–68)	US
fertilization	1875	Oskar Hertwig	German
gangrene, gas bacillus of	1878	Louis Pasteur (1822–95)	French
genes, chemical regulation by	1952	Jacques Monod (1910–76)	French
		Edwin Joseph Cohn (1892–1953)	US
gonococcus	1879	Albert Ludwig Siegmund Neisser (1855–1916)	German
heparin (anticoagulant secreted by liver cells)	1916	Jay McLean	US
hepatitis-C virus	1989	Dr Qui-Lim-Choo's research team of the Chiron Corporation	US
heredity	1865	Gregor Johann Mendel (1822–84)	Austrian
HIV virus (isolated)	1983	Luc Montaigner and others	French
HLA (human leucocyte locus A) system (responsible for transplant rejection)	1950–77	Jean Dausset (1916–)	French
hormone ▸ adrenaline, cortisone, inhibin, insulin, progesterone, testosterone			
inhibin	1985	Roger Guillemin (1924–)	French–US
insulin (isolated)	1921	Frederick Grant Banting (1891–1941)	Canadian
		Charles Herbert Best (1899–1978)	Canadian
		John James McLeod (1876–1935)	Canadian
insulin	1921	Nicolas Paulesco	Romanian
interferon	1957	Alick Isaacs (1921–67)	UK
		J Lindemann	Swiss

Discovery	Date	Discoverer(s)	Nationality
interleukin 2	1985	Steven Rosenberg	US
interleukin 3	1986	Steven Clark	US
		Yu Chang Yang	US
leprosy bacillus	1869	Gerhard Henrik Armauer Hansen (1841–1912)	Norwegian
malaria, plasmodium protozoan as agent of	1880	Charles-Louis-Alphonse Laveran (1845–1922)	French
microbes	1762	M A Plenciz (1705–86)	Austrian
morphine	1805	Friedrich Serturner	German
mosquitoes in infectious diseases, role of	1895	Ronald Ross (1857–1932)	UK
mosquitoes, transmission of filariae by	1883	Patrick Manson (1844–1922)	UK
nervous reaction, chemical transmission of	1936	Otto Loewi (1873–1961)	German–US
		Henry Hallet Dale (1875–1968)	UK
nitrous oxide (laughing gas)	1776	Joseph Priestley (1733–1804)	UK
nitrous oxide, analgesic and laughter-provoking effect of	1799	Humphry Davy (1778–1829)	UK
nucleic acid	1869	Johann Friedrich Miescher (1844–95)	Swiss
oncogenes	1981	Robert Weinberg	US
		Geoffrey Cooper	US
		Michael Wigler	US
ovulation, substances acting against	1921	Haberlandt	German
penicillin	1928	Alexander Fleming (1881–1955)	UK
phagocytes (cells which devour infective organisms)	1882–6	Ilya Ilich Mechnikov (1845–1916)	Russian
phenol, disinfectant properties of	1865	Joseph Lister (1827–1912)	UK
Phenytoin (for treatment of epilepsy)	1939	—	—
pituitary, secretion of growth hormone	1921	Herbert McLean Evans (1882–1971)	US
prion (proteinaceous infectious particles)	1982	Stanley Prusiner	US
progesterone	1929	George Washington Corner (b.1889)	US
		Edgar Allen (1892–1943)	US
protozoa (unicellular organisms)	1675	Anton van Leeuwenhoek (1632–1723)	Dutch
quinoline (later discovered to be antimicrobial agent)	1834	Friedlieb Ferdinand Runge (1795–1867)	German
rabies vaccination	1885	Louis Pasteur (1822–95)	French
relapsing fever, spirochaete of	1873	Obermeier	German
respiration, use of oxygen in	1770–80	Antoine Lavoisier (1743–94)	French
rhesus factor	1939–40	Karl Landsteiner (1868–1943)	Austrian–US
		Philip Levine	US
scurvy, lemon juice treatment of	c.1740	James Lind (1716–94)	UK
skin culture	1950	Howard Green	US
sleeping sickness, transmission by tsetse flies	1895	David Bruce (1855–1931)	UK
smallpox vaccination	1796	Edward Jenner (1749–1823)	UK
smallpox inoculation, introduction of	1718	Lady Mary Wortley Montagu (1689–1762)	UK
spermatozoa	1677	Anton van Leeuwenhoek (1632–1723)	Dutch
Staphylococcus and Streptococcus	1880	Louis Pasteur (1822–95)	French
streptomycin (antibiotic against tuberculosis)	1943	Selman Abraham Walksman (1888–1973)	US
sulphonamides (first antibiotics)	1935	Gerhard (Johannes Paul) Domagk (1895–1964)	German
T-lymphocytes	1966	J David	US
		V Blum	US
testosterone (isolated)	1929	—	—
testosterone (synthesized)	1935	Leopold Stephen Ružička (1887–1976)	Swiss
tetanus, serum against	1890	Emil von Behring (1854–1917)	German
		Shibasaburo Kitasato (1852–1931)	Japanese
		Pierre-Paul-Émile Roux (1853–1933)	French
thyroxine (thyroid hormone) (isolated)	1914	Edward Calvin Kendall (1886–1972)	US
tomography	1915	André Bocage	French
tuberculosis bacillus	1882	Robert Koch (1843–1910)	German
tubocarine (muscle relaxant)	1935	Harold King	
Tumor Necrosis Factor (TNF)	1975	Carswell	US
typhus bacillus	1880	Karl Joseph Eberth (1835–1926)	German
vaccination	c.10c	—	Turkey and China
vaccination ▸ rabies, smallpox	1892	Dmitry Ivanovsky	Russian
viruses, cultivation of (on chicken embryos)	1986	Goodpasture	US

Human Body, Health and Nutrition

Discovery	Date	Discoverer(s)	Nationality
vitamin A	1913	Elmer Verner McCollum (b.1870)	US
		M Davis	US
		Thomas Burr Osborne (b.1859)	US
		L B Mendel	US
vitamin B (niacin) (isolated)	1913	Casimir Funk (1884–1967)	Polish–US
vitamin B_1 (thiamin)	1897	Christiaan Eijkman (1858–1930)	Dutch
vitamin B_2 (riboflavin)	1933	R Kühn	German
		P György	German
		T Wagner-Jauregg	German
vitamin B_3	1937	Madden	UK
		Strong	UK
		Woolley	UK
		Elvehjem	UK
vitamin B_5	1933	Williams	US
vitamin B_6	1936	T W Birch	US
		P Gyorgy	German
vitamin B_9	1938	Day	UK
vitamin B_{12}	1927	Minot	UK
		Murphy	UK
vitamin B_{12} (isolated)	1948	E L Smith	UK
		L F J Parke	UK
	same date	E L Rickes	US
	in US	N G Brink	US
		F R Koniuszy	US
		T R Wood	US
		K Folkers	US
vitamin C (isolated but not recognized as a vitamin)	1928	Albert von Nagyrapolt Szent Györgyi (1893–1986)	Hungarian–US
vitamin C (isolated)	1932	Glen King	US
vitamin D (role in prevention of rickets)[2]	1918	E Mellenby	UK
vitamin D (isolated)	1924	Steenbock	German
		Hass	German
		Weinstock	German
vitamin E	1923	Herbert McLean Evans (1882–1971)	US
		K S Bishop	US
vitamin K_1	1934	K Dam	Danish
		Schönheyder	Danish
vitamins, necessity of	1906	Sir Frederick Gowland Hopkins (1861–1947)	UK
X-rays	1892	Heinrich Hertz (1857–94)	German
X-rays, properties of	1895	Wilhelm Konrad von Röntgen (1845–1923)	German
yellow fever, transmission by *stegmyia* mosquito	1881	Ronald Ross (1857–1932)	UK
		Carlos Juan Finlay (1833–1915)	Cuban

[1] Vulpian = Edmé Félix Alfred Vulpian. [2] Not known as Vitamin D at this time.

Complementary medicine

Complementary medicine is the treatment of diseases and disorders using procedures other than those traditionally practised in orthodox medicine. The term 'alternative medicine' is also used. The main types are explained below.

acupressure Ancient Chinese and Japanese healing massage using fingertip pressure on pain-relieving points around the body. These pressure points (acupoints) lie along the meridians (invisible body channels) used in **acupuncture**. Acupressure balances the flow of Qi (or Chi), the energy flowing through the meridians.

acupuncture A traditional Chinese method of healing in which symptoms are relieved by the insertion of special needles into one or more of 2 000 specific points (acupoints) that lie along invisible channels called meridians. This ancient therapy is believed to control the flow of Qi (or Chi), the energy flowing along the meridians. Used in the treatment of arthritis, allergy, back pain and many other disorders.

Alexander technique A system of body awareness which involves retraining the body's movements, positions and posture during all activities, including sitting or reading. The method, which must be learned from qualified teachers, is believed to encourage good mental and physical health, and resistance to stress, by promoting harmony between mind and body. Named after Australian-born physiotherapist F M Alexander (d.1955).

aromatherapy Use of concentrated plant oils — such as bergamot, eucalyptus or rosemary — to treat conditions including stress, headache and arthritis. Extracts, or essential oils, are generally massaged into the skin by aromatherapists, but can also be inhaled or added to baths.

art therapy Use of drawing and painting to encourage patients to explore and resolve deep-seated fears and emotions that they find difficult to express in words. Used to treat addiction, alcoholism, anorexia and other conditions.

aura therapy An aura is said to be a magnetic field surrounding the body, visible to aura practitioners as lines of light. Aura therapy involves analysis of the aura, which is said to be indicative of a person's health, and balancing or recharging it to treat health problems.

autogenics Relaxation therapy used to reduce and control stress and fatigue by facilitating voluntary control of bodily tension. It is based on six taught mental exercises, which are repeated, sitting or lying down, twice or three times a day.

autosuggestion Form of self-**hypnotherapy** which empties the mind by the repetition of positive phrases or ideas to oneself in order to enhance well-being, relieve pain, and change attitudes or habits like addictions and phobias.

Bach remedies or **Bach flower healing** Use of wild flower preparations — chosen according to an individual's particular personality and emotional state — to treat physical and psychological disorders. Named after British physician Edward Bach (1880–1936).

biochemic tissue salts Use of 12 mineral salts to cure disorders by restoring the natural salt balance within the body.

chiropractic Manipulation of the spine and other joints to relieve musculo-skeletal complaints, especially back and neck pain.

cranial osteopathy Gentle manipulation of the bones of the skull and face to correct pressure changes to the brain and nerves in order to treat conditions such as migraine and neuralgia.

craniosacral therapy (CST) Gentle manipulation of the skull and face in order to release tensions and imbalances which are said to arise in the bones and membranes of the skull. Used to treat a wide range of physical and psychological symptoms.

crystal healing Selection and use of crystals that are said to promote healing and wellbeing in humans.

dance movement therapy Use of body movement to express deep feelings too difficult to explain in words. Used to treat depression and anxiety as well as more serious mental illnesses.

Feldenkrais method Technique of teaching people how to improve the way they move by learning how they are moving. The aim is to move with maximum efficiency and minimum movement. Believed to reduce risk of injury in eg dancers or athletes.

herbal medicine or **herbalism** Use of herbs to treat ailments, a practice that dates back thousands of years.

homeopathy Treatment of an illness using dilute doses of substances that produce symptoms similar to those of the illness itself (treating like with like). The aim is to restore the body's natural balance by boosting its healing powers.

hydrotherapy Use of water to stimulate the body's ability to heal itself, based on the fact that water is essential for life. Treatment includes hot and cold baths, and the steam baths found at spas and health farms. Used also to treat disability by developing movement in water.

hypnotherapy Use of suggestion under hypnosis to treat conditions including stress, phobias, and addiction to tobacco and alcohol.

iridology Diagnosis of disorders achieved by studying the patterns on the irises of the eyes. Iridologists believe that each section of the iris indicates the condition of a specific part of the body.

kinesiology Monitoring of muscle strength and tone, using gentle finger pressure, to indicate how the whole body is working. Based on the belief that muscle groups are linked to particular body organs. If imbalances are found, gentle massage is applied to

pressure points to restore normal energy flow to muscles and their organs.

macrobiotics Dietary regime based on Chinese philosophy of yin (flexible and cool) and yang (strong and hot), balancing the two elements to complement an individual's nature and lifestyle. Believed to improve health and resistance to disease. In common usage, the term macrobiotics often refers to the devising and following of diets using whole grains and organically-grown fruit and vegetables, which are thought to prolong life.

massage Ancient therapy whereby one person uses hands and fingers to stroke, press and knead the body of another person who is lying horizontally. It is used to relax mind and body, and reduce tension, as well as treating disorders such as back pain.

meditation Achieving a tranquil mental state, without the use of drugs, to reduce tension, decrease blood pressure and regain confidence when stressed. This technique enables individuals to calm their bodies by controlling their thoughts. The meditative state is reached by focusing on a neutral thought or silently repeating a mantra while breathing in a controlled way.

moxibustion A form of **acupuncture**. A piece of burning moxa (a pithy material, eg sunflower pith or cotton wool) is placed on the head of an inserted acupuncture needle to heat it. Alternatively, the burning moxa is held above the acupuncture point to warm the skin. Both methods are used to relieve pain after operations, and for arthritis.

naturopathy Using natural cures to seek the underlying cause of illnesses rather than merely alleviating the symptoms. Naturopaths treat patients as whole individuals, taking into account their emotions and lifestyles. Evidently effective against stress and anxiety, as well as degenerative diseases such as emphysema and arthritis.

negative ion therapy Treatment whereby the body is exposed to harmless ions; claimed to effect various cures.

osteopathy Diagnosis and treatment of disorders of the bones, joints, muscles, tendons and nerves. Commonly used to treat back and neck problems, tension headaches and sports injuries. Based on the concept that the musculo-skeletal system plays a key role in the body's health. Osteopaths assess the damage, then manipulate the affected area.

reflexology Treatment of disorders by massaging the feet. Reflexologists relate different zones of the feet to different organs or parts of the body by way of meridians or energy channels. By massaging a particular foot region, they treat a particular organ or part of the body by releasing blocks in the meridians.

Rolfing Massaging of muscles and connective tissues in order to improve body posture and thereby improve the health and physical wellbeing of the whole body. Named after US physiotherapist Dr Ida Rolf (1897–1979).

shiatsu or **shiatzu** Ancient Japanese massage using the fingers or palms of the hand which, like **acupressure**, involves the application of pressure to points lying along the body's meridians in order to control the energy flow (Qi). Used in the treatment of many conditions including migraine, back pain, stress and digestive problems.

t'ai chi ch'uan Technique whereby people focus on their body and emotions by performing slow, circular, dance-like movements. T'ai chi is believed to remedy imbalances in the movement of the body's natural energy, Qi, so improving a person's wellbeing. It is also used as a system of exercise and self-defence.

Human Body, Health and Nutrition

Human Body, Health and Nutrition

thalassotherapy Treatment to detoxify and relax the body, involving the application of mud and seaweed compresses, seawater baths and massage.

yoga System of physical, mental and spiritual training designed to make the body more relaxed and more flexible. It involves adopting a series of postures while maintaining an inner calm of concentrated awareness. Yoga is used to help pain, especially back pain, stress and many other conditions.

Commonly prescribed drugs

This list includes drugs that are commonly prescribed in the UK, the USA and other countries of the developed world. They are grouped according to their usage, and listed by their generic names, not by brand names.

Anabolic steroids Used to help muscle repair following injury. Abused by body builders and athletes to improve their physique.
◇ Nandrolene; Stanozolol.

Analgesic drugs Pain-relieving drugs. Non-opioid analgesics are used for mild pain; opioid analgesics for severe pain.
◇ **Non-opioid analgesics** Aspirin; Paracetamol; Benorylate; Nefopam; Sodium salicylate.
◇ **Opioid analgesics** Buprenorphine; Dihydrocodeine; Codeine; Morphine; Dextropropoxyphene; Pentazocine; Diamorphine; Pethidine.

Antacid drugs Neutralize stomach acids, relieving heartburn, peptic ulcers and other gastric complaints.
◇ Aluminium hydroxide; Magnesium carbonate; Magnesium trisilicate; Sodium bicarbonate.

Anthelminthic drugs Kill parasitic worms such as tapeworms, threadworms and roundworms.
◇ Bephenium; Piperazine; Mebendazole; Pyrantel; Niclosamide; Thiabendazole.

Antibacterial drugs (antibiotics) Used to treat bacterial infections.
◇ Amocycillin; Gentamicin; Ampicillin; Minocycline; Cefaclor; Cephradine; Oxytetracycline; Cephalexin; Phenoxymethyl penicillin; Doxycycline; Benzylpenicillin; Erythromycin; Streptomycin; Flucloxacillin; Tetracycline.

Anticancer drugs Used to treat certain cancers. Some are cytotoxic, which means they kill cancer cells; others (marked *) are similar to sex hormones or hormone antagonists and, although not curative, may provide palliation of symptoms.
◇ Aminoglutethimide*; Lomustine; Chlorambucil; Medroxy-Cyclophosphamide; Progesterone*; Doxorubicin; Megestrol*; Ethinyloestradiol*; Methotrexate; Etoposide; Procarbazine; Fluorouracil; Stilboestrol*; Tamoxifen*.

Anticoagulant drugs Used both to prevent and to treat strokes or heart attacks by stopping the abnormal formation of blood clots.
◇ Heparin; Warfarin; Phenindione.

Antidepressant drugs ▸ **Psychotherapeutic drugs** see p526

Antidiarrhoeal drugs Used to make faeces more bulky, or to slow down gut mobility.
◇ Codeine; Kaolin; Co-phenotrope; Loperamide.

Antiemetic drugs Used to treat vomiting and nausea.
◇ Chlorpromazine; Metoclopramide; Cinnarizine; Prochlorperazine; Dimenhydrinate; Promethazine; Hyoscine; Thiethylperazine.

Antifungal drugs Used to treat fungal infections including thrush, ringworm and athlete's foot.
◇ Amphotericin B; Ketoconazole; Clotrimazole; Miconazole; Econazole; Nystatin; Flucytosine; Tolnaftate; Griseofulvin.

Antihistamine drugs Used to treat allergic reactions such as hay fever and urticaria.
◇ Astemizole; Promethazine; Azatadine; Terfenadine; Chlorpheniramine; Trimeprazine; Triprolidine.

Antihypertensive drugs Used to treat high blood pressure to reduce the risk of heart failure or stroke.
◇ Atenolol;   Hydrochlorothiazide;   Captopril; Methyldopa; Clonidine; Minoxidil; Chlorthalidone; Nifedipine; Cyclopenthiazide; Oxprenolol; Diltiazem; Prazosin; Enalapril; Propanolol; Hydralazine; Verapamil.

Antimuscarinic drugs Block the transmission of impulses along parts of the nervous system. Used to treat asthma, irritable bowel syndrome, Parkinson's disease and other conditions.
◇ Atropine; Hyoscine; Ipratropium; Benzhexol; Orphenadrine; Dicyclomine.

Antirheumatic drugs Used to treat rheumatoid arthritis.
◇ Azathioprine; Gold; Chlorambucil; Penicillamine; Chloroquine; Prednisolone; Dexamethasone.

Antispasmodic drugs Used to control spasms in the wall of the bladder (causing irritable bladder) or intestine (causing irritable bowel syndrome).
◇ Dicyclomine; Peppermint oil; Hyoscine.

Antiviral drugs Used to treat infections caused by viruses.
◇ Acyclovir; Inosine pranobex; Amantadine; Zidovudine; Idoxuridine.

Beta-blocker drugs Used to reduce heart rate in treating anxiety, high blood pressure and angina.
◇ Acebutolol; Oxprenolol; Atenolol; Pindolol; Metoprolol; Propanolol; Nadolol.

Bronchodilator drugs Widen the airways to the lungs. Used to treat asthma and bronchitis.
◇ Aminophylline; Rimiterol; Fenoterol; Salbutamol; Terbutaline; Pirbuterol; Theophylline; Reproterol.

Calcium channel blocker drugs Used to treat irregular heartbeat, high blood pressure and angina by reducing the workload of the heart.
◇ Diltiazem; Verapamil; Nifedipine.

Cholesterol-lowering drugs Used to lower levels of cholesterol in the blood in patients with heart disease; most common are those in the statin group.
◇ Atorvastatin, Fluvastatin, Lovastatin, Pravastatin, Simvastatin.

Corticosteroid drugs Wide-ranging uses include the treatment of rheumatoid arthritis, eczema and asthma, and Crohn's disease.
◇ Beclomethasone; Fludrocortisone; Betamethasone; Hydrocortisone; Cortisone; Prednisolone; Dexamethasone; Prednisone.

Diuretic drugs Used to treat high blood pressure and oedema (fluid retention) by increasing the amount of water lost from the body in urine.
◇ Amiloride; Cyclopenthiazide; Bendrofluazide; Frusemide; Bumetanide; Spironolactone; Chlorothiazide; Triamterene; Chlorthalidone.

Hypoglycaemic drugs (oral) Used to lower levels of glucose in the blood to normal levels in patients with one form of diabetes (type 2).
◇ Chlorpropamide; Glipizide; Glibenclamide; Tolazamide; Gliclazide; Tolbutamide.

Immunosuppressant drugs Used to suppress activity of the immune system so that it does not cause the rejection of a recently transplanted organ.
◇ Antilymphocyte Immunoglobulin; Cyclosporin; Methotrexate; Azathioprine; Prednisolone; Chlorambucil; Cyclophosphamide.

NSAID (non-steroidal anti-inflammatory drugs) Used to relieve pain and inflammation of joints in patients suffering from arthritis.
◇ Diclofenac; Indomethacin; Diflunisal; Ketoprofen; Fenbufen; Mefenamic acid; Fenoprofen; Naproxen; Flurbiprofen; Prioxicam; Ibuprofen.

Oral contraceptive drugs Used by women to prevent conception by stopping the release of eggs from the ovaries or thickening the mucus to block entry of sperm into the uterus.
◇ Ethinyloestradiol; Mestranol; Gestodene; Norethisterone; Levonorgestrel.

Thrombolytic drugs Used to dissolve blood clots in cases of heart attack or stroke.
◇ Anistreplase; Streptokinase.

Common illegal drugs

Type	Name	How taken	Major effects	Hazards associated with abuse
Depressants	Barbiturates — 'downers': amytal, nembutal, seconal	Taken orally or injected	Euphoria, tiredness, reduction in anxiety, slurred speech, slowed breathing and heart rate, confusion.	Dependence, tolerance; combination with alcohol may cause death.
Narcotic analgesics	Heroin	Sniffed, smoked or injected	Euphoria, reduction in pain, slurred speech, tiredness, loss of self-control, mood swings.	Dependence, tolerance; risk of overdose, or poisoning if heroin is impure; risk of HIV or hepatitis from needle sharing.
Psychedelics/ hallucinogens	Cannabis	Smoked or taken in food or tea	Euphoria, altered perception of time and sensory phenomena, hunger.	Long-term use may cause paranoia and anxiety in vulnerable users.
	Lysergic acid diethylamide (LSD)	Taken orally	Distortion of auditory and visual imagery, hallucinations, increased/distorted feelings of sensory awareness, unpredictable behaviour.	Paranoia, flashbacks — recurrence of hallucinatory events without taking drug; possible long-term psychological damage.
Solvents	Various adhesives, cleaning fluid	Sniffed	Confusion, feeling of well-being, giddiness.	Brain, liver and kidney damage; may cause heart failure and sometimes death.
Stimulants	Amphetamines — 'uppers': benzedrine, dexedrine, methedrine	Taken orally, sniffed, injected or smoked	Feeling of self-confidence, hyperactivity, excitement, restlessness, racing pulse; often followed by depression.	Dependence, tolerance, paranoia, violent behaviour, weight loss, hallucinations; death from overdose.
	Cocaine	Sniffed, smoked or injected	Temporary feeling of euphoria and self-confidence, appetite loss, increased heart rate; often followed by anxiety, agitation, depression.	Long-term use may cause mental impairment, hallucinations, damage to nasal passages; risk of seizures or death from overdose.
	Crack cocaine	Smoked	Intense feelings of power and euphoria last for five minutes, followed by a 'crash' and a deep craving for another crack 'hit'.	Paranoia, violent behaviour, suicidal feelings, loss of sex drive, possible death from heart attack.
	MDMA — 'Ecstasy'	Taken orally	Mood elevation, increased energy, euphoria.	Severe dehydration, slight possibility of sudden death.

Human Body, Health and Nutrition

Human Body, Health and Nutrition

Psychotherapeutic drugs

These are used in the treatment of mental disorders, and can be very effective in the alleviation of both long- and short-term symptoms, though some carry risk of dependence.

Drug class	Reasons for use	Drug names	How they work	Possible risks
Antianxiety drugs	To reduce feelings of tension, nervousness and anxiety if they interfere with a person's ability to cope with everyday life.	**Benzodiazepines:** Alprazolam, Chlordiazepoxide, Diazepam, Oxazepam	Depress action of the central nervous system, promoting drowsiness and relaxation.	Drug dependence and severe withdrawal symptoms; dizziness; drowsiness; impaired concentration.
		Beta-blockers: Nadolol, Oxprenolol, Pindolol, Propranolol	Block nerve endings, stopping release of neurotransmitters, so reducing tremor, palpitations and sweating.	Breathing difficulties, cold hands and feet, tiredness, reduced capacity for strenuous exercise.
Antidepressant drugs	To treat serious depression by stimulating the nervous system to elevate the mood of the depressed individual.	**Selective serotonin re-uptake inhibitors (SSRIs):** Fluroxetine (Prozac), Paroxetine (Seroxat), Fluro-amine (Faverin)	Elevate level of the neurotransmitter serotonin, so stimulating brain cell activity; also used in the treatment of the eating disorder bulimia nervosa.	Nausea, nervousness, weight loss (rarely), insomnia, headache; known as the 'cleanest' of the anti-depressants, SSRIs are favoured for having relatively few side effects.
		Tricyclics: Amitriptyline, Clomipramine, Dothiepin, Imipramine, Mianserin, Trazodone	Both tricyclics and MAOIs elevate the levels of two neurotransmitters — serotonin and noradrenalin — in the brain, so stimulating brain cell activity.	Weight gain, blurred vision, dry mouth, dizziness, drowsi-ness, constipation; overdose may cause coma or even death.
		Monoamine oxidase inhibitors (MAOIs): Isocarboxazid, Phenelzine, Tranylcypromine		MAOIs can cause dangerously high blood pressure if taken with food containing tyramine: red wine, beer, cheese, pickles.
Antipsychotic drugs (major tranquillizers)	To treat abnormal behaviour shown by patients with psychotic disorders involving loss of contact with reality, particularly schizophrenia.	**Phenothiazines:** Chlorpromazine, Fluophenazine, Perphenazine, Thioridazine, Trifluoperazine **Butyrophenones:** Haloperidol	Antipsychotic drugs block the action of the neurotransmitter dopamine, so inhibiting nerve activity in the brain.	Blurred vision, dry mouth, urine retention, drowsi-ness, lethargy, jerky movements of the mouth and face, involuntary movements of the limbs.
Other drugs		**Lithium**	Used to treat manic depression; acts on brain neuro-transmitters to reduce extreme mood swings.	Dry mouth; overdose may cause blurred vision, twitching, vomiting.

Immunization schedule for children up to age 18

Age	Vaccine	How given
2 months	Diphtheria, whooping cough (pertussis), tetanus	Combined DPT injection
	Polio	By mouth
4 months	Diphtheria, whooping cough (pertussis), tetanus	Combined DPT injection
	Polio	By mouth
6 months	Diphtheria, whooping cough (pertussis), tetanus	Combined DPT injection
	Polio	By mouth
1–2 years	Measles, mumps, rubella (German measles)	Combined MMR injection
4–5 years	Diphtheria and tetanus boosters	Combined injection
	Polio booster	By mouth
10–13 years	BCG (tuberculosis)	Injection
13–14 years	German measles (for girls who did not have the MMR injection at 12–24 months)	Injection
16–18 years	Tetanus booster	Injection
	Polio booster	By mouth

Immunization for foreign travel

Immunization is recommended for travellers of all ages who are visiting countries where there is a chance of contracting serious or potentially fatal diseases. Travellers should check which immunizations are required for their destinations, and whether they require immunization certificates.

Disease	Area where immunization needed	Effective for	Level of protection[1]
Cholera	Immunization no longer required by WHO but some countries still require evidence of vaccination. Check with embassy prior to travel.	6 months	M
Hepatitis A	Countries with poor hygiene and sanitation.	1 or 10 years	M
Meningococcal meningitis	For areas recommended by your doctor.	3–5 years	H
Polio	For all areas, if no recent booster received.	10 years	H
Rabies	Vaccine not recommended as routine.	1–3 years	H
Tetanus	For all areas, if no recent booster received.	10 years	H
Tuberculosis	For areas recommended by your doctor.	over 15 years	H
Typhoid fever	Countries with poor hygiene and sanitation.	10 years	M
Yellow fever	Some African and South American countries.	10 years	H

[1] M = provides moderate level of protection; H = provides high level of protection.

Measuring your Body Mass Index

Body Mass Index (BMI) gives an accurate measure of obesity. In order to determine your BMI, find out your height in metres and weight in kilograms. To convert height in inches to metres, multiply the number of inches by 0.0254; to convert weight in pounds to kilos, multiply the number of pounds by 0.4536.

$$BMI = \frac{weight\ (kg)}{height\ (m) \times height\ (m)}$$

BMI values:
Less than 18 – underweight   25 to 30 – overweight
18 to 25 – in the ideal weight range   Over 30 – obese; endangering health

Human Body, Health and Nutrition

Human Body, Health and Nutrition

Optimum weight according to height

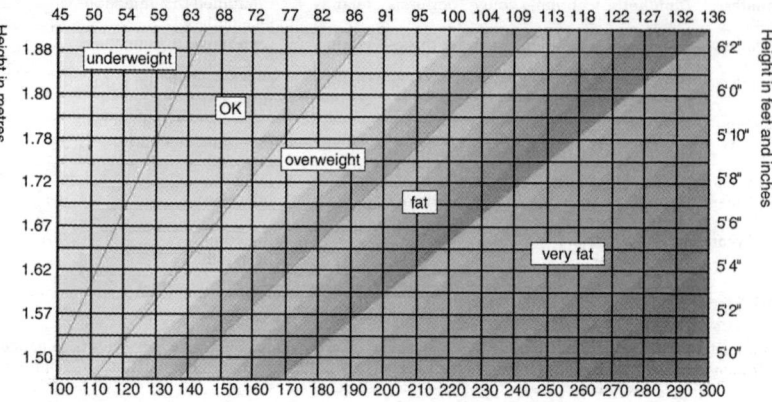

Weight in kilograms

Weight in pounds

Energy expenditure

During exercise, the amount of energy consumed depends on the age, sex, size and fitness of the individual, and how vigorous the exercise is. This table shows the approximate energy used up by a person of average size and fitness carrying out certain activities over a one-hour period.

| | Energy used per hour | |
Activity	kcals[1]	kJ[1]
Badminton	340	1 428
Climbing stairs	620	2 604
Cycling	660	2 772
Football	540	2 268
Gardening, heavy	420	1 764
Gardening, light	270	1 134
Golf	270	1 134
Gymnastics	420	1 764
Hockey	540	2 268
Housework	270	1 134
Jogging	630	2 646
Rugby	540	2 268
Squash	600	2 520
Standing	120	504
Staying in bed	60	252
Swimming	720	3 024
Tennis	480	2 016
Walking, brisk	300	1 260
Walking, easy	180	756

[1] kcals = kilocalories; kJ = kilojoules.

Average daily energy requirements

CHILDREN	Energy used per day	
Age	kcals[1]	kJ[1]
0–3 months	550	2 300
3–6 months	760	3 200
6–9 months	905	3 800
9–12 months	1 000	4 200
8 years	2 095	8 800
15 years (female)	2 285	9 600
15 years (male)	3 000	12 600

ADULT FEMALES	Energy used per day	
Age	kcals[1]	kJ[1]
18–55 years		
Inactive	1 900	7 980
Active	2 150	9 030
Very active	2 500	10 500
Pregnant	2 380	10 000
Breastfeeding	2 690	11 300
Over 56 years		
Inactive	1 700	7 140
Active	2 000	8 400

ADULT MALES	Energy used per day	
Age	kcals[1]	kJ[1]
18–35 years		
Inactive	2 500	10 500
Active	3 000	12 600
Very active	3 500	14 700
36–55 years		
Inactive	2 400	10 080
Active	2 800	11 760
Very active	3 400	14 280
Over 56 years		
Inactive	2 200	9 240
Active	2 500	10 500

[1] kcals = kilocalories; kJ = kilojoules.

Human Body, Health and Nutrition

Dietary recommendations

■ **Dietary recommendations to protect the heart**
Eat less fat, especially saturated fats.
Avoid sugary and processed foods.
Avoid obesity.
Eat plenty of fibre-rich foods.
Cut down on salt — too much salt can increase your blood pressure.

■ **Dietary recommendations to reduce cancer risks**
Eat foods rich in fibre daily: these help to prevent bowel and colon cancers.
Eat fresh fruit and vegetables daily: these are rich in fibre and vitamins.
Eat less fat. There seems to be a close correlation between fat consumption and breast cancer.
Consume alcohol only in moderation. Excessive alcohol intake has been linked to cancers of the bowel, liver, mouth, oesophagus, stomach and throat, especially in smokers.
Eat fewer smoked and salted foods. High consumption of salt-cured meat and fish and nitrate-cured meat has been linked to throat and stomach cancers. There is also a link between eating pickled foods and stomach cancer.
Keep body weight at recommended level.

■ **Dietary recommendations to lose weight**
To be healthy, a diet designed to reduce body weight needs to be in tune with the body's physiology. An effective diet should promote the loss of fatty, or adipose, tissue from the body so that its overall fat content is reduced. To do this successfully, the dieter should eat a well-balanced, high-carbohydrate, high-fibre, low-fat diet with an energy content of between 1 200 and 1 500 calories per day, combining this with regular exercise. Foods that can be consumed in this kind of low-calorie diet are shown (*below*) as Type A and Type B foods; Type C foods should be avoided, and fat-containing Type B foods, such as meat, should be eaten in moderation.

■ **Dieting tips**
Reduce alcohol intake to a minimum.
Avoid convenience foods because many contain 'hidden' fats and sugar.
Exercise at least three times a week.

Remove fat from meat, and fatty skin from poultry.

Avoid frying food — bake, grill, microwave or steam instead.

Avoid mayonnaise and rich sauces.

If you overeat, work out why you do it (eg through boredom or depression) and find other ways of relieving these feelings.

Plan meals for the next day the night before, or early in the morning, to avoid impulse eating of high-calorie foods.

Use a smaller plate to make smaller helpings look larger than they really are.

Eat regularly. Do not miss meals but try to eat 3–5 small meals each day.

Avoid second helpings.

Avoid between-meal snacks, except for raw fruit and vegetables if very hungry.

Eat at a table rather than eg in front of the television, which may encourage you to eat more and faster.

Take more time when eating — chew well.

Type A foods	Type B foods	Type C foods
Vegetarian foods	**Vegetarian foods**	**Meat, fish and dairy foods**
Cereals (unsweetened)	Dried fruit	Bacon
Fruits — all except avocados	Margarine, polyunsaturated	Beef, fatty cuts
Vegetables — all, including potatoes	Nuts, except peanuts	Butter
Vegetable protein, eg tofu	Pasta, especially wholewheat	Cheeses, apart from low-fat
Wholemeal bread	Pulses, such as beans and lentils	Duck
	Rice, especially wholegrain	Fish, fried
Meat, fish and dairy foods	Vegetable oils	Ice cream
Chicken and other poultry (not duck)		Lamb, fatty cuts
with skin removed	**Meat, fish and dairy foods**	Mayonnaise
Cod, haddock and other non-oily fish	Beef, lean cuts	Milk, full cream
Mussels and other shellfish	Eggs	Pâté
Salmon (if tinned, in brine or water)	Lamb, lean cuts	Pork, fatty cuts
Tuna (if tinned, in brine or water)	Oily fish such as herring or mackerel	Salami
Yoghurt (plain, low fat)	Pork, lean cuts	Sausages
	Sardines (if tinned, in brine)	
		Convenience foods
		Biscuits
		Burgers
		Cakes
		Chips
		Chocolate
		Crisps

Culinary terms of foreign origin

aïoli a garlic-flavoured mayonnaise. [French; from Provençal *ai*, garlic]

à la carte said of a meal in a restaurant, with each dish priced and ordered separately. [French, = from the menu]

à la mode said of beef, larded and stewed with vegetables; said of desserts, served with ice cream (North American). [French, = in fashion]

al dente said of pasta and vegetables, cooked so as to remain firm when bitten. [Italian, = to the tooth]

antipasto (*plural* **antipasti**, **antipastos**) food served at the beginning of a meal to sharpen the appetite. [Italian]

aperitif an alcoholic drink taken before a meal to stimulate the appetite. [from French *apéritif*; from Latin *aperire*, to open]

aqua vitae a strong alcoholic drink, especially brandy. [Latin, = water of life]

au gratin covered with breadcrumbs and/or grated cheese, cooked in the oven and/or browned under the grill, so that a crisp, golden topping is formed. [French, = literally 'with the burnt scrapings'; from *gratter*, to scrape]

au naturel cooked plainly, or uncooked; served without dressing. [French, = in the natural state]

bain-marie a vessel of hot or boiling water in which a container of food can be cooked gently or kept warm. [French, = bath of Mary; from Latin *balneum Mariae*; origin uncertain, perhaps from Mary, or Miriam, sister of Moses, who reputedly wrote a book on alchemy]

baklava or **baclava** a rich cake of Middle Eastern origin made of layers of flaky pastry with a filling of honey, nuts and spices. [Turkish]

balti 1 a style of Indian cooking originating in Britain, in which food is both cooked and served in a pan resembling a wok. **2** the pan in which this is cooked. [Hindi, = bucket]

béarnaise (sauce) a rich sauce made from egg yolks, butter, shallots, tarragon, chervil and wine vinegar. [French; after *Bearn*, a region in SW France]

béchamel (sauce) a white sauce flavoured with onion and herbs and sometimes enriched with cream. [French; named after the Marquis de Béchamel (d.1703), a French courtier who attended Louis XIV]

bhaji an Indian appetizer of vegetables, chickpea flour, and spices, formed into a ball and deep-fried. [Hindi]

biriani or **biryani** (*plural* **birianis** or **biryanis**) a type of spicy Indian dish consisting mainly of rice, with meat or fish and vegetables, etc. [Urdu]

bisque a thick rich soup, usually made from shellfish, cream, and wine. [French]

blanch 1 to prepare (vegetables or meat) for cooking or freezing by boiling in water for a short time. **2** to remove the skins (from almonds, etc) by soaking them in boiling water. [from Old French *blanchir*]

blancmange a cold sweet jelly-like pudding made with milk. [from Old French *blanc*, white + *manger*, food]

blanquette a dish made with white meat such as chicken or veal, cooked in a white sauce. [from French *blanquette* (related to English blanket); from Old French *blankete*; from *blanc*, white]

Bolognese said especially of pasta, served with a tomato and meat sauce, usually also containing mushrooms, garlic, etc. [named after Bologna in N Italy]

bombe a dessert, usually ice cream, frozen in a round or melon-shaped mould. [French, = bomb]

bonne femme said of a dish, eg sole bonne femme, cooked simply and garnished with fresh vegetables and herbs. [from French *à la bonne femme*, in the manner of a good wife]

bouillabaisse a thick spicy fish soup from Provence. [French]

bouillon a thin clear soup made by boiling meat and vegetables in water, often used as a basis for thicker soups. [French; from *bouillir*, to boil]

bouquet garni a bunch or small packet of mixed herbs used to add flavour to food, usually removed before serving. [from French *bouquet* + *garnir*, to garnish]

bourguignon said of meat dishes, stewed with onion, mushrooms and Burgundy wine. [French, = Burgundian]

braise to cook (meat, etc) slowly with a small amount of liquid in a closed dish. [from French *braiser*, from *braise*, live coals]

brochette a small metal or wooden skewer for holding food together or steady while it is being cooked. [French; a diminutive of *broche*, brooch or needle]

brioche a type of bread-like cake made with a yeast dough, eggs, and butter. [French]

brûlé usually said of a dessert, having brown sugar on top and cooked so that the sugar melts. [French, = burnt]

cacciatore or **cacciatora** said of meat, especially chicken or veal, cooked with tomatoes, mushrooms, onions and herbs. [Italian, = hunter]

calamari *plural noun* squid. [Italian, plural of *calamaro*, squid]

calzone a folded round of pizza dough stuffed with a savoury filling. [Italian, = trouser leg]

canapé a type of food served at parties, etc consisting of a small piece of bread or toast spread or topped with something savoury. [French, = sofa]

cannelloni a kind of pasta in the form of large tubes, served with a filling of meat, cheese, etc. [Italian; from *cannello*, tube]

cappuccino (*plural* **cappuccinos**) coffee with frothy milk and usually chocolate powder on top. [Italian]

ceviche (Mexican cookery) raw fish marinated in lime juice and served as an hors d'oeuvre. [American Spanish]

chapati or **chapatti** in Indian cooking, a thin flat portion of unleavened bread. [from Hindi *capati*]

chasseur said of a sauce or food cooked in a sauce containing mushrooms, shallots, white wine and herbs. [French, = hunter]

Chateaubriand or **chateaubriand** a thick steak cut from grilled fillet of beef, usually served with fried potatoes and mushrooms. [named after François René, Vicomte de Chateaubriand (1768–1848), French author and statesman]

chiffon a light frothy mixture, made with beaten whites of eggs. [French, = rag]

choux pastry a very light pastry made with eggs. [from French *pâte choux*, cabbage pastry]

ciabatta Italian bread with a sponge-like texture, made with olive oil. [Italian, = slipper]

consommé thin clear soup made from meat stock. [French; from *consommer*, to eat, consume]

cordon bleu *noun* (*plural* **cordons bleus**) a cook of the highest standard; *adjective* said of a cook or cookery, being of the highest standard. [French, = blue ribbon]

coupe a dessert made with fruit and ice cream. [French, = glass, cup]

couscous a N African dish of crushed wheat steamed and served eg with meat. [French; from Arabic *kuskus*]

crème **1** cream, or a creamy food. **2** a liqueur. [French, = cream]

crème fraîche cream thickened with a culture of bacteria, used in cooking. [French, = fresh cream]

crêpe or **crepe** a thin pancake. [French; from Latin *crispus*, crisp]

croissant a crescent-shaped bread roll, made with a high proportion of fat, and flaky in consistency. [French, = crescent]

croquante a crisp pie or tart; a crisp cake containing almonds. [French]

croquette a ball or roll of eg minced meat, fish, or potato, coated in breadcrumbs and fried. [French; from *croquer*, to crunch]

croûte a thick slice of fried bread for serving entrées (▸ **en croute**). [French, = crust]

croûton a small cube of fried or toasted bread, served in soup, salads etc. [French; a diminutive of *croûte*, crust]

dal or **dahl** or **dhal** **1** any of various edible dried split pea-like seeds. **2** a cooked dish made of any of these seeds. [from Hindi *dal*, to split]

doner kebab thin slices cut from a block of minced and seasoned lamb grilled on a spit, eaten on unleavened bread. [from Turkish *döner*, rotating]

enchilada (*plural* **enchiladas**) a Mexican dish consisting of a flour tortilla with a meat filling, served with a chilli-flavoured sauce. [from Spanish *enchilar*, to season with chilli]

en croûte wrapped in pastry and baked. [from French *croûte*, crust]

entrecôte a boneless steak cut from between two ribs. [French; from *entre*, between + *côte*, rib]

entrée **1** a small dish served after the fish course and before the main course at a formal dinner. **2** (chiefly USA) a main course. [French, = entrance]

escalope a thin slice of boneless meat, especially veal. [French]

espresso (*plural* **espressos**) **1** coffee made by forcing steam or boiling water through ground coffee beans. **2** the machine for making it. [Italian, = pressed out]

farce stuffing or force-meat. [French]

farci stuffed. [from French *farce*, stuffing; from Latin *farcire*, to stuff]

fettuccine pasta in the form of flat wide ribbons. [Italian, a diminutive (plural) of *fettuccia*, tape]

fines herbes *plural noun* a mixture of herbs for use in cooking. [French, = fine herbs]

flambé *adjective* said of food, soaked in brandy and set alight before serving; *verb* (**flambéed**, **flambéing**) to serve (food) in this way. [from French *flamber*, to expose to flame]

florentine *adjective* containing or served with spinach, eg eggs florentine; *noun* a biscuit on a chocolate base covered on one side with preserved fruit and nuts. [from Latin *Florentinus*, from *Florentia* (Florence)]

focaccia a flat round of Italian bread topped with olive oil and herbs or spices. [Italian, = cake]

fondue **1** a Swiss dish of hot cheese sauce into which bits of bread are dipped. **2** a steak dish (also called **fondue bourguignonne**), the pieces of meat being cooked at the table by dipping them briefly into hot oil or stock. [French; from *fondre*, to melt]

frankfurter a type of spicy smoked sausage. [from German *Frankfurter Wurst*, Frankfurt sausage]

fricassee a cooked dish usually of pieces of meat or chicken served in a sauce. [from Old French *fricasser*, to cook chopped food in its own juice]

fromage frais a creamy low-fat cheese with the consistency of whipped cream. [French, = fresh cheese]

Human Body, Health and Nutrition

Human Body, Health and Nutrition

fusilli pasta shaped into short thick spirals. [Italian]

galantine a dish of boneless cooked white meat or fish served cold in jelly. [Old French]

garam masala a mixture of ground spices used to make curry. [Hindi, = hot mixture]

garni trimmed, garnished. [French; from *garnir*, to garnish]

gateau or **gâteau** (*plural* **gateaux, gateaus, gâteaux**) a large rich cake, especially filled with cream and decorated with fruit, nuts, etc. [French]

ghee butter made from cow's or buffalo's milk, purified by heating, used in Indian cooking. [from Hindi *ghi*]

glacé *adjective* 1 coated with a sugary glaze; candied: eg glacé cherries. 2 said of icing on cakes etc, made with icing sugar and liquid. 3 said of drinks etc, frozen or served with ice, eg mousse glacée; *verb* (**glacéed, glacéing**) 1 to crystallize fruit etc. 2 to ice cakes etc with glacé icing. [French]

gnocchi an Italian dish of small dumplings made with flour, cooked potato, or semolina, poached and served with various sauces. [Italian, = lumps]

gougère a kind of choux pastry that has grated cheese added to it before baking. [French]

goujons small strips of fish or chicken coated in seasoned flour, egg and breadcrumbs, and deep-fried. [from French *goujon*, gudgeon (the fish)]

gratin the golden brown crust covering a gratinated food or dish; ► **au gratin.**

gratinate to cook with a topping of buttered breadcrumbs and/or cheese browned until crisp; to cook au gratin; ► **au gratin.** [from French *gratiner*, to cook au gratin]

gratiné cooked or served au gratin; ► **au gratin.** [from French *gratiner*, to cook au gratin]

gremolata a colourful, flavoursome garnish, made of chopped parsley, lemon or orange peel, garlic, etc. [Italian]

haute cuisine cookery (especially French) of a very high standard. [French, = high cooking]

hors d'oeuvre a savoury appetiser served at the beginning of a meal. [French, = out of the work]

hummus or **hommous** or **houmus** a Middle Eastern hors d'oeuvre or dip consisting of pureed cooked chickpeas and tahini paste, flavoured with lemon juice and garlic. [from Turkish *humus*]

jardinière an accompaniment of mixed vegetables for a meat dish. [from French *jardinière*, feminine of *jardinier*, gardener]

jus juice; gravy. [French]

kofta (*plural* **koftas**) (Indian cookery) minced and seasoned meat or vegetables, shaped into balls and fried. [Hindi, = pounded meat]

lasagne pasta in the form of thin flat sheets, often cooked in layers with a mixture of meat and tomatoes, and a cheese sauce. [Italian]

lyonnaise made with sautéed sliced potatoes and onions or potatoes in an onion sauce. [named after Lyon, France]

macaroni (*plural* **macaronis, macaronies**) pasta in the form of short tubes. [from Italian *maccaroni*]

mascarpone a soft Italian cream cheese. [Italian]

mayonnaise a cold creamy sauce made of egg yolk, oil, vinegar or lemon juice, and seasoning. [French]

meringue a crisp cooked mixture of sugar and egg whites, or a cake made from this. [French]

mesclun a mixed green salad of young leaves and shoots of rocket, chicory, fennel, etc. [French; from Niçois *mesclumo*, mixture]

minestrone thick soup containing vegetables and pasta. [Italian; from *minestrare*, to serve]

moussaka a dish made with minced meat, aubergines, onions, tomatoes, etc, covered with a cheese sauce and baked, traditionally eaten in Greece, Turkey and the Balkans. [Greek]

mousse 1 a dessert made from a whipped mixture of cream, eggs and flavouring, eaten cold. 2 a similar meat or fish dish. [French, = froth]

mozzarella a soft white Italian cheese, especially used as a topping for pizza. [Italian]

muesli a mixture of crushed grain, nuts and dried fruit, eaten with milk, especially for breakfast. [Swiss German]

mulligatawny a thick curry-flavoured meat soup, originally made in E India. [from Tamil *milagu-tannir*, pepper-water]

nan a slightly leavened Indian bread, similar to pitta bread. [Hindi]

navarin a stew of lamb or mutton with root vegetables such as turnip. [French]

nougat a chewy sweet containing nuts, etc. [French; from Latin *nux*, nut]

nouvelle cuisine a simple style of cookery characterized by much use of fresh produce and elegant presentation. [French, = new cookery]

omelette (*especially USA* **omelet**) a dish of beaten eggs fried in a pan, often folded round a savoury or sweet filling such as cheese or jam. [from Old French *alemette*; from *lemelle*, knife-blade]

paella a Spanish dish of rice, fish, or chicken, vegetables and saffron. [Catalan; from Latin *patella*, pan]

pakora an Indian dish of chopped spiced vegetables formed into balls, coated in batter, and deep-fried. [Hindi]

papillote 1 frilled paper used to decorate the bones of chops, etc. 2 oiled or greased paper in which meat is cooked and served. [French, apparently from *papillon*, butterfly]

Parmesan a hard dry Italian cheese, especially served grated with pasta dishes. [from Italian *Parmegiano*, from Parma]

passata an Italian sauce of puréed and sieved tomatoes. [Italian, = passed (ie through a sieve)]

pasta 1 a dough made with flour, water, and eggs shaped in a variety of forms such as spaghetti, macaroni, lasagne, etc. 2 a cooked dish of this, usually with a sauce. [Italian; from Latin *pasta*, paste, dough; from Greek *pasta*, barley porridge]

pâté a spread made from ground or chopped meat, fish or vegetables blended with herbs, spices, etc. [French; formerly meaning pie or pasty]

patisserie a shop selling fancy cakes, sweet pastries, etc. [from French *pâtisserie*; from Latin *pasta*, dough]

pesto an Italian sauce originating in Liguria and made from fresh basil leaves, pine kernels, olive oil, garlic and Parmesan cheese. [Italian; from *pestare*, to crush, pound]

petit four (*plural* **petits fours**) a small sweet biscuit, usually decorated with icing. [French, = little oven]

pilaf or **pilaff** or **pilau** an oriental dish of spiced rice with chicken, fish, etc. [from Turkish *pilaw*]

pizza a circle of dough spread with cheese, tomatoes, etc and baked, made originally in Italy. [Italian]

polenta an Italian dish of cooked ground maize. [Italian; from Latin *polenta*, hulled and crushed grain]

poppadum or **poppadom** a paper-thin pancake grilled till crisp for serving with Indian dishes. [Tamil]

praline a sweet consisting of nuts in caramelized sugar. [named after Marshal Duplessis-Praslin (1598–1675), a French soldier whose cook invented it]

pretzel a salted and glazed biscuit in the shape of a knot. [German]

profiterole a small sweet or savoury confection of choux pastry. [French; said to be a diminutive from *profiter*, to profit]

prosciutto finely cured uncooked ham, often

smoked. [Italian = pre-dried]

provençale a style of cookery that traditionally uses olive oil, tomatoes, onion, garlic and white wine, eg eggs à la provençale, and, in meat dishes, requires slow-cooking. [named after the area of Provence, SE France]

pumpernickel a dark heavy coarse rye bread, eaten especially in Germany. [German, = lout, perhaps literally 'stink-devil' or 'fart-devil']

purée *noun* a quantity of fruit or vegetables reduced to a pulp by liquidising or rubbing through a sieve; *verb* (**purées, puréed**) to reduce to a purée. [from French *purer*, to strain]

puri a small cake of unleavened Indian bread, deep-fried and served hot. [Hindi]

quenelle a dumpling of fish, chicken, veal, etc. [French]

quesadilla (Mexican cookery) a tortilla filled with cheese, chillis, etc, folded and fried or grilled. [Mexican Spanish; diminutive of *quesada*; from *quese*, cheese]

quiche a tart with a savoury filling usually made with eggs. [French; from German *Kuchen*, cake]

ragout a highly seasoned stew of meat and vegetables. [from French *ragoût*]

ramekin 1 a small baking dish for a single serving of food. **2** an individual serving of food, especially of a savoury dish containing cheese and eggs, served in a ramekin. [from French *ramequin*]

ratafia 1 a flavouring essence made with the essential oil of almonds. **2** a cordial or liqueur flavoured with fruit kernels and almonds. **3** an almond-flavoured biscuit or small cake. [French; probably from Creole or *tafia*, a type of rum]

ratatouille a southern French stew made with tomatoes, peppers, courgettes, aubergines, onions, and garlic. [French]

ravioli *plural noun* small, square pasta cases with a savoury filling of meat, cheese, etc. [Italian]

risotto (*plural* **risottos**) an Italian dish of rice cooked in a meat or seafood stock with onions, tomatoes, cheese, etc. [from Italian *riso*, rice]

roti (*plural* **rotis**) **1** a cake of unleavened bread, traditionally made in parts of India and the Caribbean. **2** a kind of sandwich made of this wrapped around curried vegetables, seafood, or chicken. [Hindi, = bread]

roulade meat, cake or soufflé mixture served rolled up, usually with a filling. [French]

roux (*plural* **roux**) a cooked mixture of flour and fat, used to thicken sauces. [from French *beurre roux*, brown butter]

rugelach or **ruggelach** *plural noun* (Jewish cookery) small crescent-shaped pastries filled with fruit, nuts, cheese, etc. [from Yiddish *rugelekh*, plural of *rugele*]

salami (*plural* **salamis**) a highly seasoned type of sausage, usually served sliced. [Italian]

salsa (Mexican cookery) a spicy sauce made with tomatoes, onions, chillies and oil. [Spanish and Italian *salsa*, sauce]

salsa verde Italian green sauce, made with anchovies, garlic, capers, oil and herbs. [Spanish and Italian *salsa*, sauce]

samosa a small deep-fried triangular spicy meat or vegetable pasty of Indian origin. [Hindi]

sauerkraut shredded cabbage pickled in salt water, a popular German dish. [from German *sauerkraut*, sour cabbage]

sauté *verb* (**sautés, sautéed** *or* **sautéed, sautéing** *or* **sautéing**) to fry gently for a short time; *adjective* fried in this way: eg sauté potatoes. [French, = tossed; from *sauter*, to jump]

schnapps in N Europe, any strong dry alcoholic spirit, especially Dutch gin distilled from potatoes. [German, = dram of liquor]

schnitzel a veal cutlet. [German]

sorbet a dish of sweetened fruit juice, frozen and served as a kind of ice cream; a water ice. [French; from Arabic *sharbah*, drink]

soufflé a light sweet or savoury baked dish, a frothy mass of whipped egg whites with other ingredients mixed in. [French; from *souffler*, to puff up]

spaghetti pasta in the form of long thin string-like strands. [Italian; from *spago*, cord]

stroganoff a dish, also called **beef stroganoff**, that is traditionally made with strips of sautéed fillet steak, onions and mushrooms, cooked in a lightly spiced, creamy white wine sauce and served with pilaf rice; there are many variations on this, including one that uses only vegetables. [named after Count Paul Stroganov, a 19c Russian diplomat]

strudel a baked roll of thin pastry with a filling of fruit, especially apple. [German, = whirlpool, ie from the rolling]

table d'hôte (*plural* **tables d'hôte**) a meal with a set number of choices and a set number of courses offered for a fixed price, especially to residents in a hotel. [French, = host's table]

tagliatelle pasta made in the form of long narrow ribbons. [Italian]

tandoori food cooked on a spit over charcoal in a clay oven. [from Hindi *tandoor*, clay oven]

tapas light savoury snacks or appetizers, especially those based on Spanish foods and cooking techniques and served with drinks. [from Spanish *tapa*, cover or lid]

thermidor *postpositive adjective* (eg lobster thermidor) denoting a method of preparation, the flesh being mixed with a cream sauce seasoned with mustard, and served in the shell. [from Greek *therme*, heat, and *doron* gift; Thermidor was the eleventh month of the French Revolutionary calendar, 19 July–17 August]

tikka in Indian cookery, meat that is marinated in yoghurt and spices and cooked in a clay oven. [Hindi]

timbale a dish of meat or fish, etc cooked in a cup-shaped mould or shell. [from French *timbale*; from Spanish *atabal*; from Arabic *at-tabl*, the drum]

tortilla (*plural* **tortillas**) a thin round flat Mexican maize cake cooked on a griddle and usually eaten hot, with a filling or topping of meat or cheese. [Spanish; a diminutive of *torta*, cake]

tournedos (*plural* **tournedos**) a small round thick fillet of beef. [French]

vacherin a dessert made with meringue and whipped cream, usually with ice cream, fruit, nuts, etc. [French]

velouté a smooth white sauce made with stock [French, = velvety]

vermicelli 1 pasta in very thin strands, thinner than spaghetti. **2** tiny splinters of chocolate used for desserts and cake decoration. [Italian, = little worms]

vinaigrette a salad dressing made by mixing oil, vinegar and seasonings, especially mustard. [French; from *vinaigre*, vinegar]

vol-au-vent a small round puff-pastry case with a savoury filling. [French, = flight in the wind]

wurst any of various types of large German sausage. [German, = something rolled; related to Latin *vertere*, to turn]

yakitori a Japanese dish of boneless pieces of chicken grilled on skewers and basted with a thick sweet sauce of sake, mirin and soy sauce. [Japanese; from *yaki*, grill + *tori*, bird]

zabaglione a dessert made from egg yolks, sugar and wine whipped together.

Human Body, Health and Nutrition

Chefs, restaurateurs and cookery writers

Beard, James (1903–85) US chef and cookery writer, born Portland, Oregon. An influential teacher, he wrote many books including *The James Beard Cookbook* (1959) and *James Beard's American Cookery* (1972).

Beeton, Mrs Isabella Mary, née **Mayson** (1836–65) English cookery writer. Her *Book of Household Management* first appeared in a magazine owned by her husband, Samuel Beeton, in 1859–60. It made her a household name.

Blanc, Raymond René (1949–) French chef and restaurateur, born near Besançon. He began to cook in 1975 in England and opened Les Quat' Saisons in Oxford in 1977, and Le Manoir aux Quat' Saisons in 1984. Books include *Blanc Mange* (1994) and *Blanc Vite* (1999).

Bocuse, Paul (1926–) French restaurateur and cookery writer, born Collonges-au-Mont-d'Or. He took over the family business, Restaurant Bocuse or L'Auberge du Pont de Collonges, and runs the French Pavilion at Disneyworld, Orlando. Books include *La Bonne chère* (1995).

Brown, David (1951–) and **Hilary** (1952–) Scottish husband and wife team of restaurateurs, both born Glasgow. In 1975 they opened La Potinière in Gullane, East Lothian, where she was the chef. It received a Michelin star in 1990, but closed in 2002.

Carluccio, Antonio Mario Gaetano (1937–) Italian restaurateur, cookery writer and broadcaster, born Vietri sul Mare. He became restaurateur at Neal Street Restaurant in 1981 (proprietor since 1989). His books include *An Invitation to Italian Cooking* (1986), *A Passion for Pasta* (1993), *Antonio Carluccio's Italian Feast* (1996, also television series) and *Complete Italian Food* (1997).

Child, Julia, née **McWilliams** (1912–) US cookery writer and broadcaster, born Pasadena, California. She co-founded a cooking school in Paris in 1951, co-wrote *Mastering the Art of French Cooking* in 1961, among other books, and hosted the television series *The French Chef* (1963–76).

Claiborne, Craig (1920–2000) US food critic and cookery writer, born Sunflower, Missouri. He was food editor of the *New York Times* (1957–88). Books included the *New York Times Cook Book* (1961) and *Craig Claiborne's Memorable Meals* (1985).

David, Elizabeth (1913–92) English cookery writer, born Sussex. She drew from her time spent abroad to write such influential books as *French Provincial Cooking* (1960).

Delmonico, Lorenzo (1813–81) US restaurateur, born Marengo, Switzerland. After arriving in New York with his uncles in 1832, he opened Delmonico's c.1834. He started a new restaurant culture by introducing European standards and foods (eg fresh salads, vegetables) and longer opening hours.

Diat, Louis Felix (1885–1957) US restaurateur, born Montmarault, France. Known as 'Monsieur Louis', he was chef at the New York Ritz-Carlton hotel's famous restaurant (1910–51) and championed French cooking there and through his books, eg *Cooking à la Ritz* (1941). He created vichysoisse.

Dimbleby, Josceline Rose (1943–) English cookery writer; wrote for Sainsbury's from 1978 and was cookery editor for the *Sunday Telegraph* from 1982. Books include *A Taste of Dreams* (1976), *Salads for all Seasons* (1981) and *Josceline Dimbleby's Complete Cookbook* (1997).

Eriksen, Gunn (1956–) Scottish chef and restaurateur, born Grimstad, Norway. In 1980 she joined Fred Brown, owner of the Altnaharrie Inn across Loch Broom from Ullapool, and began to develop her now renowned characteristic cooking style.

Escoffier, Auguste (c.1847–1935) French chef, born Villeneuve-Loubet. He used his culinary skills in the Franco-Prussian War and at the Grand Hotel in Monte Carlo before going to the London Savoy and then to the Carlton. He invented the *bombe Nero* and *pêche melba*.

Farmer, Fannie Merritt (1857–1915) US cookery expert, born Boston. She was a director of the Boston Cooking School and edited its bestselling cook book (now called 'Fannie Farmer's') in 1896 before founding Miss Farmer's School of Cookery — the first to cater for housewives and nurses rather than servants and teachers.

Fisher, F(rances) K(ennedy), née **Kennedy** (1908–92) US cookery writer, born Albion, Michigan. Her books, which are like collections of culinary essays celebrating US regional food, include *How to Cook a Wolf* (1942) and *The Art of Eating* (1976).

Floyd, Keith (1943–) English cookery writer and broadcaster, born Somerset. He is known for the flamboyant style of his television programmes and for his many *Floyd on ...* books, eg *Floyd on France*, *Floyd on Fish*.

Franey, Pierre (1921–96) US chef and restaurateur, born Tonnerre, France. He was chef at Le Pavillon in New York, collaborated on books and articles with **Craig Claiborne**, and published his own articles written for the *New York Times*.

Gray, Rose (1939–) British chef and restaurateur. In 1987 she and Ruth Rogers opened the successful Italian-cooking based River Café in Hammersmith, London. *The River Café Cook Book* and other titles followed.

Grigson, (Heather) Jane, née **McIntyre** (1928–90) English cookery writer. She was correspondent for the *Observer* and wrote the cookery classics *English Food* (1974), *Jane Grigson's Vegetable Book* (1978) and *Jane Grigson's Fruit Book* (1982), all influenced by her country lifestyle.

Grigson, Sophie (Hester Sophia Frances) (1959–) English cookery writer and broadcaster, and cookery correspondent for several newspapers. Television series and related books include *Eat your Greens* (1993), *Travels à la Carte* (1994), *Taste of the Times* (1997) and the *Complete Sophie Grigson Cookbook* (2001).

Grossman, Loyd Daniel Gilman (1950–) US chef, broadcaster and cookery writer. Books include *The World on a Plate* (1997).

Guérard, Michel Etienne (1933–) French chef, restaurateur and cookery writer, born Vétheuil. His restaurant Les Prés d'Eugénie in Eugénie les Bains has three Michelin stars. Books include *Minceur Exquise* (1989).

Harvey, Frederick Henry (1835–1901) US restaurateur, born London, England. Starting in 1876 at the railroad depot in Kansas, he created a chain of restaurants along the Atchison, Topeka and Santa Fe railroad; these became known for their good food, fresh linens, and their trained waitresses or 'Harvey Girls'.

Heathcote, Paul (1960–) English chef and restaurateur, born Bolton. His first restaurant was Paul Heathcote's Longridge Restaurant; others include Heathcote's Brasserie in Preston and Simply Heathcote's in Manchester.

Hom, Ken(neth) (1949–) US chef, cookery writer and broadcaster. He has earned renown as a food consultant and for popularizing Chinese cooking. His books and television series include *Hot Wok* (1996).

Jaffrey, Madhur (1933–) US cookery writer, broadcaster and actress, born Delhi, India. She began publishing the recipes sent to her by her mother in India. Books include *Flavours of India* (1995).

Johnstone, (Christian) Isobel, pseudonym **Margaret Dods** (1781–1857) Scottish cookery writer and novelist, born Fife. She had a huge success in 1826 with 'Meg Dods' Cookery', properly *The Cook and Housewife's Manual* by Mistress Margaret Dods.

Kerr, Graham Victor (1934–) New Zealand cookery writer and broadcaster, born in London, England. He became known for his widely-screened television show *The Galloping Gourmet*, and for such books as the *Graham Kerr Cookbook* (1966) and *Galloping Gourmets* (1969).

Ladenis, Nico (Nicholas Peter) (1934–) Kenyan chef and restaurateur. He and his wife opened the Chez Nico restaurant, specializing in French cuisine, in 1971; current ventures include Incognico and Deca, both in London. Books include *My Gastronomy* (1987) and *Nico* (1996).

Lawson, Nigella (1960–) English cookery writer and broadcaster. She wrote the bestsellers *How to Eat* (1998), *How to Be a Domestic Goddess* (2000) and *Nigella Bites* (2001), and presented the television series of the latter.

Leith, Prue (Prudence Margaret) (1940–) English chef, restaurateur and cookery writer. She started Leith's restaurant in 1969 (one Michelin star) and Leith's School of Food and Wine in 1975. Books include *Leith's Cookery Bible* (1991).

Little, (Robert) Alastair (1950–) English chef and restaurateur, born Colne, Lancashire. He opened the London restaurant Alastair Little in 1985, and became food columnist for the *Daily Mail* in 1993. Books include *Keep it Simple* (1993) and *Alastair Little's Italian Kitchen* (1996).

Mosimann, Anton (1947–) Swiss chef, restaurateur, cookery writer and broadcaster. His first position as chef in the UK was at the Dorchester Hotel, London. He opened the restaurant Mosimann's in 1988. His television series and related books include *Anton Mosimann Naturally* (1991–2); other books include *Mosimann's World* (1996).

Nairn, Nick (1959–) Scottish chef and broadcaster. He and his wife opened the Braeval restaurant in 1986. Nairn's Restaurant opened in 1997 and he also runs a cooking school in Aberfoyle, Perthshire. Television appearances include *Ready Steady Cook* and *Nick Nairn's Wild Harvest*.

Novelli, Jean-Christophe (1961–) French chef and restaurateur, born Arras. He worked in the UK with Keith Floyd and later opened his own restaurant, Maison Novelli, in 1996. He has received a Michelin star at four of his various ventures but now cooks at L'Auberge du Lac in Hertfordshire.

Oliver, Jamie (1975–) English chef, cookery writer and broadcaster. He wrote the bestseller, *The Naked Chef* (1999) after his successful TV series of the same name, following it up with *The Return of the Naked Chef* (2000) and *Happy Days with the Naked Chef* (2001).

Prudhomme, Paul (1940–) US chef, restaurateur, cookery writer and broadcaster, born Opelousa, Louisiana. In 1979 he opened K-Paul's Louisiana Kitchen in New Orleans which is known for its cajun and creole cooking. He often appears on television and his books include *Chef Paul Prudhomme's Louisiana Tastes* (2000).

Ramsay, Gordon (1967–) Scottish chef and restaurateur, born Renfrewshire. He trained under Marco Pierre White, the Roux brothers, Guy Savoy and Joël Robuchon, and now runs Restaurant Gordon Ramsay in London, which has three Michelin stars. He also co-owns Pétrus and runs Gordon Ramsay at Claridges, both of which have one Michelin star.

Rhodes, Gary (1960–) English chef, restaurateur and broadcaster. He worked at the Castle Hotel, Taunton, and the Greenhouse in Mayfair, London, before launching his own restaurants, eg City Rhodes. Books include *Fabulous Foods* (1997).

Robuchon, Joël (1945–) French chef and restaurateur, born Poitiers. He ran the Restaurant Jamin in Paris (1981–94) and Restaurant Joël Robuchon (1994–6) before retiring in 1996. Books include *Simply French* (1991).

Rombauer, Irma, née **Louisa von Starkloff** (1877–1962) US cookery writer, born St Louis, Missouri. She wrote the perpetual bestseller, *The Joy of Cooking* (illustrated and revised in later editions by her daughter Marion Rombauer Becker, 1903–76). An encyclopedic collection of classic American and European recipes, culinary techniques and food preparation instructions, it has sold around 8 million copies, and has had an immeasurable influence on American cuisine.

Roux, Albert Henri (1935–) and **Michel André** (1941–) French chefs and restaurateurs, born Semur-en-Brionnais. They opened Le Gavroche in London in 1967, which is now run by Albert; Michel runs the Waterside Inn in Bray, Berkshire. The Waterside Inn has three Michelin stars. Their television appearances include *At Home with the Roux Brothers* (1988), and books include *Desserts: A Lifelong Passion* (1994).

Sardi, (Melchior Pio Vi) Vincent (1885–1969) US restaurateur, born in San Marzano Oliveto, Italy. From c.1907 he lived in New York City, where Sardi's, his restaurant in the theatre district, became a favourite haunt of many theatre-goers.

Savoy, Guy (1953–) French chef and restaurateur, born Nevers. His restaurants in Paris include the Restaurant Guy Savoy which has three Michelin stars. Books include *La Gourmandise apprivoisée* (1987, 'Tamed Greed').

Smith, Delia (1941–) English cookery writer and broadcaster, born Woking, Surrey. She followed her first of many books, *How to Cheat at Cooking* (1973), with several television series and bestsellers, eg *Delia Smith's Summer Collection* (1993) and *Delia Smith's Winter Collection* (1995).

Soyer, Alexis (1809–58) French chef, born Meaux. The most famous of his time, he was chef in the Reform Club in London (1837–50). He wrote *Culinary Campaign in the Crimea* (1857) after trying to reform the food supply system in the Crimea by introducing the 'Soyer stove'.

Spry, Constance (1886–1960) English flower arranger and cookery writer, born Derby. She ran flower shops and cookery schools, held advisory positions and wrote *The Constance Spry Cookbook* (1956).

Stein, Rick (c.1948–) English chef and restaurateur, born Churchill, near Chipping Norton. Specializing in seafood, he runs the Seafood Restaurant in Padstow, Cornwall, which he and his wife opened in 1975. He became known through the television series *Taste of the Sea* (1995) and *Fruits of the Sea* (1997) and has written many other seafood cookery books.

Two Fat Ladies Clarissa Dickson Wright (1946–) and Jennifer Paterson (1928–99). Both professional cooks (Paterson also wrote for *The Spectator* and *The Oldie*), they came to fame with the television series *Two Fat Ladies* and related publications, eg *Two Fat Ladies Ride Again* (1997).

White, Marco Pierre (1961–) English chef and restaurateur, born Leeds. He learned from Albert Roux,

Nico Ladenis and Raymond Blanc, and opened his first (of several) restaurants, Harveys, in 1987. Publications include *Canteen Cuisine* (1995), and *The Mirabelle Cookbook* (1999).

Wilson, David (1938–) Scottish chef and restaurateur, born Bishopbriggs, near Glasgow. In 1972 he and his wife took over the Peat Inn in Fife, which gained international renown and a Michelin rosette (1987).

Worrall Thompson, Antony (1952–) English chef, restaurateur and cookery writer. His London restaurants have included Ménage à Trois, 190 Queensgate, Dell'ugo and Notting Grill. He has also appeared on television in *Ready Steady Cook* and *The Food and Drink Programme*.

Varieties of wines and grapes

Wines are often named after the grape from which they are made, or the region or château in which they are produced.

Alsace mainly dry, white wine produced in the Alsace region of NE France; the wines are named after the grapes, eg Riesling, Gewürztraminer, Sylvaner, Pinot Blanc and Pinot Gris.

Anjou Blanc a dry white wine produced in the western Loire region of France and made from blends of such grape varieties as Chenin Blanc, Chardonnay and Sauvignon.

Asti Spumante a sweet, aromatic sparkling wine made from the Muscat grape and named after the town of Asti in Piedmont, Italy.

Auslese an expensive full-flavoured, sweet wine made in Germany from exceptionally high-quality mature grapes, particularly the Riesling grape.

Beaujolais a large area in southern Burgundy, France, famous for light, fruity red wines made from the Gamay grape.

Beaujolais Nouveau a young red wine from the Beaujolais area, available in late November.

Beaune French town in the centre of Burgundy with its own vineyard sites which are known for their soft, fragrant red wines.

Bordeaux French city and seaport in the centre of the famous wine-producing region of Bordeaux in SW France where red wines (known as claret) and white wines are produced. The finest wines come from the areas Médoc, Graves, St-Émilion and Pomerol.

Burgundy 1 famous wine-producing region in France, divided into five districts: Chablis, Côte d'Or, Chalonnais, Mâconnais and Beaujolais. **2** a French wine made in the Burgundy region; most are red, some are white, all are dry. Burgundy's vineyards are divided into the Grands crus, Premier crus, and the remainder which are named after communes. **3** any similar red wine.

Cabernet Sauvignon 1 a red-wine grape which is the basis of most Bordeaux wine; an adaptable variety originally from Bordeaux, it is now grown throughout the world. **2** the wine produced from this grape.

Carignan a red-wine grape used to make table wine and dessert wine; grown in the Midi, N and C America, N Africa and Australia.

Chablis a dry white wine made from the Chardonnay grape in the Burgundy region of central France, named after the small French town near to where it is made.

Chardonnay 1 a white grape variety used in Burgundy and Champagne; originally from Burgundy, it is now also grown in California, Australia, New Zealand, etc. **2** a dry white wine made from this grape.

Chateauneuf-du-Pape a district of the Rhône region of France known especially for its expensive red wine; the wine is blended, using mainly Grenache, Syrah and Cinsault grapes.

Chenin Blanc a white-wine grape widely grown in the Loire Valley in France, and in South Africa (called Steen) and California; it is used to make Vouvray and Saumur wines.

Chianti a dry, usually red, blended Italian wine made in Tuscany.

Cinsault a red-wine grape grown especially in the Rhône valley and, being low in tannin, is used in blended wines eg Chateauneuf-du-Pape.

Colombard a white-wine grape, used especially in South Africa.

Corbières a district of the Languedoc-Roussillon area where red, white and rosé wines are made.

Côtes du Rhône the appellation for the lesser red, white and rosé wines produced in the Rhône valley.

Dão a mountain district in northern Portugal where mainly red wine is produced.

Fitou a red wine produced from the Carignan grape in the Languedoc-Roussillon area of France.

Frascati a full-bodied, fragrant white wine made in the town of Frascati, S Italy.

Gamay a red-wine grape used widely in France and elsewhere; used in Beaujolais, and in Anjou as a base for rosé wines.

Gewürztraminer a spicy variety of white grape grown especially in the Alsace region which is used to make a medium-dry aromatic wine.

Grenache a fruity grape used for making strong, sweet wines; grown in Europe (especially Spain), N Africa, Australia, C and N America; used in rosé wines and in blended wines eg Chateauneuf-du-Pape.

Graves a large area within the Bordeaux region in France which produces red and white wines.

Lambrusco a red or white-wine grape; used to make a light, sweet sparkling red wine of the same name in northern Italy.

Liebfraumilch a white blended wine from the Rhine region of Germany; by law it is made with Riesling, Sylvaner or Müller-Thurgau grapes from the regions of Rheinhessen, Nahe, Rheinpfalz or Rheingau.

Mâcon a town in southern Burgundy where white and red wine is produced.

Madeira a fortified wine made on the N Atlantic island of Madeira.

Malaga a dark dessert wine from Andalucia, Spain, made from grapes that are partially sun-dried before use.

Marsala a brown, fortified wine made in the town of Marsala, Sicily.

Médoc the premier area of Bordeaux in France known for its fine red wines; many famous châteaux are situated here, eg Château Mouton-Rothschild.

Merlot 1 an important variety of black grape often used in blends with Cabernet Sauvignon and in many soft fruity wines for drinking young. **2** a red wine that is produced in France, Italy and the USA from, or mainly from, this variety of grape.

Minervois a well-rated district in the Languedoc-Roussillon area which produces well-balanced, robust red wines made from Carignan, Cinsault and Grenache grapes.

Moselle or **Mosel** the region around the Moselle river which runs through NE France, Luxembourg and Germany; it is known for its light, crisp, perfumed dry white wine made mainly from the Riesling grape.

Müller-Thurgau a white-wine grape widely used in Germany, as well as in California, England and New Zealand; similar to the Muscat grape in flavour.

Muscadet 1 a white-wine grape successfully grown in the Loire valley in France. **2** a dry white wine, the best-known of those made in the Loire eg Muscadet de Sèvre-et-Maine.

Muscat or **Muscadelle** or **Moscatello** names of a large family of white and red grapes; they have a musky smell, and are dried for raisins as well as used to make scented, grapey wines; most wines from the Muscat grape are sweet, except that made in Alsace.

Niersteiner a well-known German wine made from the Riesling grape in the Nierstein district of the Rheinhessen region in Germany.

Pinot an important variety of black and white grape grown throughout the world. Pinot Noir is the traditional grape of Burgundy and is used in making champagne; as it is difficult to grow elsewhere, it is an irresistible challenge to wine-makers.

Pinotage a red-wine grape used especially in South Africa.

Pomerol a district of Bordeaux which produces red and white vines, including the high-quality red wine Château Petrus.

Riesling a white-wine grape grown most successfully in Germany, but also in Alsace, Austria and elsewhere; it is used to make wine ranging from dry to very sweet.

Rioja a small wine-making area in NE Spain, which produces mainly dry red wine.

St-Émilion a fine, fruity red wine made particularly from the Merlot grape in the St-Émilion area of Bordeaux.

Sancerre a district in the Loire Valley known especially for its pale, dry white wines, and for its rosés, which are made from the Pinot Noir grape.

Saumur a district of Anjou in NW France where both still and sparkling wines are made.

Sauternes an appellation used by five communes (Sauternes, Barsac, Bommes, Fargues and Preignac) in the Graves district of Bordeaux which produce sweet white wine, mainly from the Sémillon grape.

Sauvignon Blanc a white-wine grape used in Bordeaux and Sancerre; makes excellent wine in New Zealand and California.

Sémillon a white grape used in Bordeaux whites, especially the Sauternes district where is it harvested half rotten and therefore with a high concentration of sugar; it is also successful in Australia's Hunter Valley region.

Soave a light, dry, flowery white wine made near the village of Soave, NE Italy.

Spätlese a German term for wine made from grapes that have been harvested late, resulting in a wine with more body and sweetness than other German white wines.

Sylvaner a German white-wine grape used to make fruity wines and grown in Europe, N and S America and Australia.

Syrah a red-wine grape, the foremost grape of the hot Rhône valley; particularly at home in Australia, where it is known as Shiraz.

Tarragona a wine region in Spain, where much red and white table wine, and the sweet, red fortified wine Tarragona are produced.

Valpolicella a light, fragrant red wine made near the village of Valpolicella in the Veneto region of NE Italy.

Vouvray a usually sweet, but always fresh and fruity, white wine produced from the Chenin Blanc grape in Touraine, in the Loire Valley.

Zinfandel a red-wine grape used widely in California for making dry red wine.

Terms relating to wine-making and wine-tasting

acetic tasting or smelling of vinegar, due to the presence of acetic acid; caused by oxidization or by faulty fermentation or bottling.

acidity the taste caused by the natural organic acids in wine, which in the correct proportions make a wine well-balanced.

aftertaste the taste that remains in the mouth or comes into it after tasting wine.

appellation contrôlée and **appellation d'origine contrôlée** (French; abbreviation AC or AOC) **1** the system which within France designates and controls the names especially of wine, but also of cognac, armagnac, calvados and some foods, guaranteeing the authenticity of the producing region and the methods of production, and which outside France protects the generic names from misappropriation. **2** the highest designation of French wine awarded under this system.

argol the harmless crystalline potassium deposit that is left on the sides of wine vats during fermentation. Also called tartrate.

balance a noun describing a wine's combination of alcoholic strength, acidity, residual sugar and tannins.

big amply flavoured, often with a high alcohol content.

body the 'weight' of a wine on the palate, or the sensation of fullness it imparts due to its density or viscosity. Wines range from being light-bodied to full-bodied.

bouquet the delicate smell of wine. [French; a diminutive of *bois*, a wood]

breathe to develop flavour when exposed to the air.

brut said especially of champagne: very dry.

Buck's fizz or **buck's fizz** a drink consisting of champagne, or sparkling white wine, and orange juice. [named after Buck's Club, London]

chambré said of wine: at room temperature.

character having positive, distinctive characteristics.

château used in names of wines, especially from the Bordeaux area: a vineyard estate around a castle or house.

claret a French red wine, especially from the Bordeaux area.

clarity the quality of being clear and pure; the clarity of a wine is an indication of both its condition (faulty wine often appears cloudy), and of how much clarification (the removal of suspended material, the lees) has been carried out.

clean pure-tasting and pure-smelling; a term usually applied to white wine.

coarse rough or crude; lacking refinement.

common plain and of no distinctive character, though not necessarily low quality.

corked said of wine: spoiled as a result of having a faulty cork, which has affected the taste of the wine.

crisp with a dry, refreshing taste; usually said of white wines with a pleasantly high level of acidity.

cru specialist term for a high-quality vineyard; often translated in English as 'growth'; eg grand cru, premier cru.

decant to pour (wine, etc) from one bottle or container to another, leaving any sediment behind.

decanter an ornamental bottle with a stopper, used for decanted wine, sherry, whisky, etc.

demijohn a large bottle with a short narrow neck and one or two small handles, used for storing eg wine.

DOC *abbreviation* said of wine: *Denominazione di Origine Controllata* (Italian), the Italian equivalent of appellation contrôlée. Compare DOCG.

DOCG *abbreviation* said of wine: *Denominazione di Origine Controllata Garantita* (Italian), a designation

Human Body, Health and Nutrition

Human Body, Health and Nutrition

of wines, guaranteeing quality, strength, etc. Compare DOC.

dry said of wine, etc: not sweet.

earthy with a flavour and bouquet enhanced by characteristics of the soil in which the vine was grown (usually applicable only to grapes grown in a hot climate).

en primeur said of tasting, buying or investing in wine: when the wine is new.

fat full-bodied and viscous, but unbalanced due to insufficient acidity.

fine an ill-defined term, usually referring to the superior wines of the classic regions of Europe, eg Bordeaux and Burgundy.

finesse refinement; having the best possible characteristics a wine can have.

finish aftertaste.

flabby lacking in acidity; like a fat wine, well flavoured but with little 'bite'.

flinty usually said of highly rated white wines: having a dry, clean, hard taste reminiscent of gun flint, eg Pouilly Blanc Fumé.

flowery containing the scent of flowers in the bouquet.

fortify to add extra alcohol to (wine) in the course of production, in order to produce sherry, port, etc.

fresh refreshing.

frizzante an Italian term for semi-sparkling.

fruity smelling strongly of fruit, eg blackberries, blackcurrants, gooseberries or raspberries as well as grapes.

full or **full-bodied** having a rich flavour or quality.

generous rich, invigorating.

glühwein or **Glühwein** mulled wine, especially as prepared in Germany, Austria, etc.

grand cru produced by a famous vineyard or group of vineyards.

grapey having a strong flavour of grapes, eg wine made from the Muscat grape.

grappa a brandy (originally from Italy) distilled from what is left after the grapes have been pressed for wine-making.

green too acid, usually due to having been made from unripe grapes.

hanepoot a kind of grape for eating and wine-making.

hard with an unpleasant excess of tannin and lack of fruit; hard wines usually improve with time.

hearty usually said of red wines, eg from the Rhône valley: with a generous, warm flavour.

heavy too alcoholic; or full-bodied but lacking in finesse.

hock a white wine, originally only the one made in Hochheim, on the River Main, in Germany, but now applied to all white wines from the Rhine valley.

honest ordinary and undistinguished; unremarkable, eg an honest wine.

hot too alcoholic.

lay down to store (wine) in a cellar.

lees the sediment that settles at the bottom of liquids and alcoholic drinks, especially wine.

legs ▶ **tears**

length persistence of flavour on the palate; length is an indicator of quality.

light pleasantly slender in body and low in alcohol.

lively said of white wine: young and fresh, often with a slight natural sparkle.

long with an impressively enduring aftertaste, usually indicating high quality.

maceration in the making of red wine, the process in which the tannins etc are dissolved from the skins, seeds and stem fragments of the grapes to be added to the juice or new wine.

madeirized said of white wines: tinged with brown because of old age.

magnum a champagne or wine bottle that holds approximately 1.5 litres, ie twice the normal amount.

malic acid (formula $H_6 C_4 O_5$) an acid found in unripe fruits, and occurring in wines.

malmsey a strong sweet wine originally from Greece but now usually from Spain, Madeira, etc.

marc 1 the leftover skins and stems of grapes used in winemaking. **2** a kind of brandy made from these.

mature having a fully developed flavour.

medium neither dry nor sweet.

mellow fully flavoured with age; well matured.

mirin a sweet rice wine used in Japanese cookery.

mull to spice, sweeten and warm, eg mulled wine.

muscatel a rich sweet white wine made from Muscat grapes.

must the juice of grapes or other fruit before it is completely fermented to become wine.

noble rot on white grapes: a rot caused by the fungus *Botrytis cinerea*, which aids the production of sweet white wine.

nose a scent or aroma, especially a wine's bouquet.

nutty usually said of sherries or red wines: having a flavour reminiscent of nuts, eg walnuts or hazelnuts, which usually indicates good quality.

oenology the study or knowledge of wine (*adjective* **oenological**, *noun* **oenologist**).

oenophile a lover or connoisseur of wine; an oenologist.

oxidation a fault caused by exposure to oxygen, making any wine smell bad and making white wine darker.

palate an ability to discriminate between wines, different qualities of wine, etc.

pétillant lightly sparkling; a French term for a wine sparkling more than when *perlant* but not as much as when *mousseux*.

pipe 1 a cask or butt of varying capacity, but usually about 105 gallons in Britain (equal to 126 US gallons or 477 litres), used for wine or oil. **2** a measure of this amount.

piquant usually said of white wine: with an agreeably sharp flavour caused by high levels of acidity, eg wine from some areas of the Rhine, Loire and Mosel.

plonk *colloq* cheap, undistinguished wine.

port a sweet dark-red or tawny fortified wine. [from Oporto, the city in Portugal from where it was originally exported]

prädikat 1 in Germany: a distinction awarded to a wine, based on the ripeness of the grapes used to produce it. **2** a wine that qualifies for this award.

race said of wine: the special flavour by which its origin may be recognized.

rack to draw off (wine or beer) from its sediment.

racy said of wine: with a distinctive flavour imparted by the soil.

rape the refuse of grapes left after wine-making and used in making vinegar.

red biddy *colloq* a cheap alcoholic drink made from red wine and methylated spirits.

remuage in wine-making, the process of turning the bottles so that the sediment collects at the cork end for removal.

retsina a Greek white or rosé wine flavoured with pine resin.

Rhenish Rhine wine.

Rhine wine an imprecise term for any wine made from grapes grown in the valley of the River Rhine.

ripe said of the flavour or taste of wine: rich or strong.

robust said of wine: with a full, rich quality.

rosé a light-pink wine properly made by removing the skins of red grapes after fermentation has begun; it is sometimes also made by mixing red and white wines.

rouge *in full* vin rouge, French red wine.

sack a dry white wine from Spain, Portugal and the Canary Islands.

sangria a Spanish drink of red wine, fruit juice, sugar and spices.

sec 1 said of wine: dry. **2** said of champagne: medium sweet.

Sekt a German term for sparkling wines.

severe very sharp, almost astringent; this sourness is usually due to the wine being too acid and/or immature.

sharp sour-tasting, but not as sour as a severe wine; sharpness may be intentional, or a fault caused by immaturity or by the use of unripe grapes.

sherry 1 a fortified wine ranging in colour from pale gold to dark brown. **2** *loosely* a similar type of wine produced elsewhere. [from Jerez de la Frontera, the S Spanish town where it is produced].

short opposite of long; with little or no aftertaste.

smooth pleasantly textured with a mellow flavour.

soft a term describing the impact of the wine on the palate.

spicy with a flavour of spices and herbs, eg wines made from the Gewürztraminer grape.

spritzer a drink of white wine and soda water.

spritzig 1 a slightly sparkling, usually German, wine. **2** in wine-tasting: the slight prickle on the tongue that is effected by this kind of wine.

spumante an Italian term for fully sparkling, usually sweet wine, eg Asti Spumante.

stalky with an unpleasant taste of damp twigs; a fault caused by leaving the grape stalks in contact with the grapes for too long.

stum *noun* partly fermented grape juice that is added to a wine which has lost its strength, flavour, sharpness, etc in order to perk it up; *verb* to add stum to (a wine) and so restart the fermentation process.

sulphurous acid or (*USA*) **sulfurous acid** (formula H_2SO_3) a colourless weakly acidic solution of sulphur dioxide in water that acts as a preservative in wine-making. A sulphury wine contains too much sulphur, but usually improves an hour or two after opening.

supple usually said of red wine: a term evoking pliability in describing the impact on the palate.

sweet said of wine: having some taste of sugar or fruit; not dry.

tannin any of several substances in the pips, skins and stalks of the grapes which give a distinctive flavour to red wine. The tannin should mellow as the wine matures; if not, the wine tastes hard and disagreeable and is described as tannic.

tart very sharp.

tartar a deposit that forms a hard brownish-red crust on the insides of wine casks during fermentation.

tears (rhymes with 'ears') a noun used to describe the droplets that cling to the glass just above the surface of a glass of wine; a wine high in alcohol.

temperature an ideal tasting temperature for both red and white wines is $15°-20°C/59°-68°F$.

thin insipid and watery.

tierce a former measure of wine, equal to one-third of a pipe, ie approx. 35 British or 42 US gallons (159 litres).

tun *noun* a large cask or liquid measure equivalent to 252 British or 303 US gallons (1 146 litres) of wine; *verb* to put or store (liquid, eg ale, beer or wine) in a tun.

ullage 1 the amount of wine, etc by which a container falls short of being full. **2** the quantity of liquid lost from a container through leakage, evaporation, etc. **3** *slang* the dregs remaining in a glass, etc.

vault a wine cellar.

VDQS *abbreviation*: *vins délimités de qualité supérieure* (French); wines of superior quality from approved vineyards, the interim wine quality designation between vin de pays and appellation contrôlée.

velvety said of the feel of the wine, not the flavour: very soft and smooth.

vermouth an alcoholic drink consisting of wine flavoured with aromatic herbs, originally wormwood.

vin de pays country or local wine.

vin ordinaire inexpensive table wine for everyday use.

vine any of various woody climbing plants that produce grapes.

vineyard a plantation of grape-bearing vines, especially for wine-making.

vinho verde a light, sharp young Portuguese wine.

viniculture the cultivation of grapes for wine-making.

vino *slang* wine, especially of poor quality.

vinosity a wine-like character; the characteristic qualities of a particular wine; an acceptable standard, with good, balanced characteristics.

vinous 1 belonging or relating to, or resembling, wine. **2** caused by or indicative of an excess of wine, eg a vinous complexion.

vintage said of wine: good quality and from a specified year.

vintner *formal* a wine-merchant.

viticulture the cultivation of grapes for making wine; viniculture.

weighty usually said of full-bodied red wine: with great depth and character.

well-balanced having good balance.

white said of wine: made from white grapes or from skinned black grapes.

wine cellar 1 a cellar in which to store wines. **2** the stock of wine stored there.

wine cooler a receptacle for cooling wine in bottles, ready for serving.

wine glass 1 a drinking-glass typically consisting of a small bowl on a stem, with a wide base flaring out from the stem. **2** the capacity of this; a wineglassful.

wine list a list of the wines available, eg in a restaurant.

wine tasting 1 the sampling of a variety of wines. **2** a gathering specifically for this.

wine vault 1 a vaulted wine cellar. **2** a place where wine is tasted or drunk.

winepress in the manufacture of wine: a machine in which grapes are pressed to extract the juice.

winery *chiefly USA* a place where wine is prepared and stored.

wineskin *historical* the skin of a goat or sheep sewn up and used for holding wine.

wino *slang* someone, especially a down-and-out, addicted to cheap wine; an alcoholic.

winy or **winey** having a wine-like flavour.

woody with a flavour of wood; if overpowering, this may be a fault caused by the wine being left too long in the cask, or a problem with the cask.

yeasty with a smell of yeast, suggesting a second fermentation has happened or is about to happen.

Human Body, Health and Nutrition

Human Body, Health and Nutrition

Wine bottle sizes

Name	Capacity	
wine bottle	75cl	($26\frac{2}{3}$ fl oz) (standard size)
magnum	1.5 l	(2 standard bottles)
flagon	1.13 l or 2 pints	
methuselah	6 l	(8 standard bottles)
rehoboam	4.5 l	(6 standard bottles)

Name	Capacity	
jeroboam	3 l	(4 standard bottles)
salmanazar	9 l	(12 standard bottles)
balthazar	12 l	(16 standard bottles)
nebuchadnezzar	15 l	(20 standard bottles)

Some types of cheese

Cheese	Type and characteristics
■ England	
Cheddar	hard;cow's milk; white to yellow
Cheshire	hard; cow's milk; white to palest yellow
Lancashire	hard; cow's milk; white; crumbly
Leicester	hard; cow's milk; orange; crumbly
Stilton	semihard; cow's milk; mould-ripened; blue-veined
■ France	
Brie	soft; cow's milk; downy rind
Camembert	soft; cow's milk; downy rind
Pont l'Évêque	soft; cow's milk; washed rind
Port Salut	semisoft; cow's milk; yellow
Reblochon	soft; cow's milk; pressed
Roquefort	semihard; ewe's milk; blue-veined
Saint Paulin	semisoft; cow's milk; yellow
Vacherin	soft; cow's milk; soft interior with hard rind
■ Germany	
Münster	semisoft; cow's milk; bacteria-ripened
Tilsit	semihard; cow's milk; bacteria-ripened
■ Greece	
Feta	soft; ewe's or goat's milk; salty

Cheese	Type and characteristics
■ Italy	
Dolcelatte	semisoft; cow's milk; mould-ripened; blue/green-veined
Gorgonzola	semihard; cow's milk; mould-ripened; blue/green-veined
Parmesan	very hard; cow's milk; bacteria-ripened; long cure
Romano	very hard; cow's, ewe's or goat's milk; bacteria-ripened
■ Netherlands	
Edam	semihard; skimmed cow's milk; mild; red wax rind
Gouda	semihard; cow's milk; mild; yellow wax rind
■ Spain	
Manchego	semisoft–hard; ewe's milk; mild or sharp depending on length of cure
■ Switzerland	
Emmenthal	hard; cow's milk; creamy; large holes
Gruyère	hard; cow's milk; small holes
Sapsago	very hard; soured cow's milk; light green (clover mixed with the curd)

COMMUNICATION

Languages: number of speakers

■ Language families

Estimates of the numbers of speakers in the main language families of the world in the early 1980s. The list includes Japanese and Korean, which are not clearly related to any other languages.

Main language families		Main language families	
Indo-European	2 000 000 000	Nilo-Saharan	30 000 000
Sino-Tibetan	1 040 000 000	Amerindian (North, Central,	
Niger-Congo	260 000 000	South America)	25 000 000
Afro-Asiatic	230 000 000	Uralic	23 000 000
Austronesian	200 000 000	Miao-Yao	7 000 000
Dravidian	140 000 000	Caucasian	6 000 000
Japanese	120 000 000	Indo-Pacific	3 000 000
Altaic	90 000 000	Khoisan	50 000
Austro-Asiatic	60 000 000	Australian aborigine	50 000
Korean	60 000 000	Palaeosiberian	25 000
Tai	50 000 000		

■ Specific languages

The first column gives estimates (in millions) for mother-tongue speakers of the 20 most widely used languages. The second column gives estimates of the total population of all countries where the language has official or semi-official status; these totals are often over-estimates, as only a minority of people in countries where a second language is recognized may actually be fluent in it.

Mother-tongue speakers		Official language populations	
1 Chinese	1 000	1 English	1 400
2 English	350	2 Chinese	1 000
3 Spanish	250	3 Hindi	700
4 Hindi	200	4 Spanish	280
5 Arabic	150	5 Russian	270
6 Bengali	150	6 French	220
7 Russian	150	7 Arabic	170
8 Portuguese	135	8 Portuguese	160
9 Japanese	120	9 Malay	160
10 German	100	10 Bengali	150
11 French	70	11 Japanese	120
12 Panjabi	70	12 German	100
13 Javanese	65	13 Urdu	85
14 Bihari	65	14 Italian	60
15 Italian	60	15 Korean	60
16 Korean	60	16 Vietnamese	60
17 Telugu	55	17 Persian	55
18 Tamil	55	18 Tagalog	50
19 Marathi	50	19 Thai	50
20 Vietnamese	50	20 Turkish	50

Communication

Speakers of English

The first column gives figures for countries where English is used as a mother-tongue or first language; for countries where no figure is given, English is not the first language of a significant number of people. (A question-mark indicates that no agreed estimates are available.) The second column gives total population figures (mainly 1996 estimates) for countries where English has official or semi-official status as a medium of communication. These totals are likely to bear little correlation with the real use of English in the area.

Country	First language speakers of English	Country population	Country	First language speakers of English	Country population
Anguilla		1 650	Nauru	800	10 600
Antigua and Barbuda	61 400	64 400	Nepal	?	20 892 000
Australia	17 700 000	18 287 000	New Zealand	3 290 000	3 619 000
The Bahamas	230 000	280 000	Nigeria	?	103 912 000
Bangladesh	3 200 000	123 100 000	Pakistan	?	133 500 000
Barbados	265 000	265 000	Papua New Guinea	70 000	4 400 000
Belize	111 000	219 000	Philippines		71 750 000
Bermuda	61 000	61 400	Samoa	1 000	214 000
Bhutan	?	1 622 000	St Kitts and Nevis	39 400	39 400
Botswana	590 000	1 478 000	St Lucia	29 000	144 000
Brunei	10 000	290 000	St Vincent and the		
Cameroon	2 720 000	13 609 000	Grenadines	100 000+	113 000
Canada	18 112 000	29 784 000	Seychelles	2 000	76 100
Dominica	?	73 800	Sierra Leone	700 000	4 617 000
Fiji	160 000	802 000	Singapore	1 139 000	3 045 000
Ghana	?	16 904 000	Solomon Islands		396 000
Gibraltar	24 000	27 100	South Africa	3 800 000	41 734 000
Grenada	97 900	97 900	Sri Lanka	10 000	18 318 000
Guyana	700 000+	825 000	Suriname		436 000
India	330 000	952 969 000	Swaziland		934 000
Ireland	3 599 000	3 599 000	Tanzania	900 000	29 165 000
Jamaica	2 505 000	2 505 000	Tonga		101 000
Kenya		29 137 000	Trinidad and Tobago	1 262 000	1 262 000
Kiribati		81 800	Tuvalu		9 500
Lesotho		2 017 000	Uganda	190 000	20 158 000
Liberia	570 000	2 110 000	UK	57 190 000	58 784 000
Malawi	540 000	9 453 000	USA	228 700 000	265 455 000
Malaysia	100 000	20 359 000	US territories in		
Malta	8 000	373 000	Pacific	?	196 300
Mauritius	2 000	1 141 000	Vanuatu	60 000	172 000
Montserrat	12 000	12 000	Zambia	300 000	9 715 000
Namibia	13 000	1 709 000	Zimbabwe	260 000	11 515 000
			Other British territories	?	106 167
			TOTALS	349 764 500	2 038 046 117

Foreign words and phrases

ab initio (Lat) 'from the beginning'.

à bon marché (Fr) 'good market'; at a good bargain, cheap.

ab ovo (Lat) 'from the egg'; from the beginning.

absit omen (Lat) a superstitious formula; may there be no ill omen (as in a reference just made).

a cappella (Ital) 'in the style of the chapel'; sung without instrumental accompaniment.

Achtung (Ger) 'Look out! Take care!'.

acushla (Ir) term of endearment; darling.

addendum *plural* **addenda** (Lat) 'that which is to be added'; supplementary material for a book.

à deux (Fr) 'for two'; often denotes a dinner or conversation of a romantic nature.

ad hoc (Lat) 'towards this'; for this special purpose.

ad hominem (Lat) 'to the man'; appealing not to logic or reason but to personal preferences or feelings.

ad infinitum (Lat) 'to infinity'; denotes endless repetition.

ad litem (Lat) 'for the lawsuit'; used of a guardian appointed to act in court (eg because of insanity or insufficient years of the litigant).

ad nauseam (Lat) 'to the point of sickness'; disgustingly endless or repetitive.

ad referendum (Lat) 'for reference'; to be further considered.

ad valorem (Lat) 'to value'; 'according to what it is worth'; often used of taxes etc.

advocatus diaboli (Lat) 'devil's advocate'; person opposing an argument in order to expose any flaws in it.

affaire (Fr) liaison, intrigue; an incident arousing speculation and scandal.

afflatus (Lat) 'blowing or breathing'; inspiration (often divine).

aficionado (Span) 'amateur'; an ardent follower; a 'fan'.

a fortiori (Lat) 'from the stronger' (argument); denotes the validity and stronger reason of a proposition.

agent provocateur (Fr) 'provocative agent'; someone who incites others, by pretended sympathy, to commit crimes.

aggiornamento (Ital) 'modernization'; reform (often political).

aide-de-camp (Fr) 'assistant on the field'; an officer who acts as a confidential personal assistant for an officer of higher rank.

aide-mémoire (Fr) 'help-memory'; a reminder; memorandum-book; a written summary of a diplomatic agreement.

à la carte (Fr) 'from the menu'; each dish individually priced.

à la mode (Fr) 'in fashion, fashionable'; also in cooking, of meat braised and stewed with vegetables; with ice-cream (American English).

al dente (Ital) 'to the tooth'; culinary term denoting (usually) pasta fully cooked but still firm.

al fresco (Ital) 'fresh'; painting on fresh or moist plaster; in the fresh, cool or open air.

alma mater (Lat) 'bountiful mother'; one's former school, college, or university; official college or university song (American English).

aloha (Hawaiian) 'love'; a salutation, 'hello' or 'goodbye'.

alumnus *plural* **alumni** (Lat) 'pupil' or 'foster son'; a former pupil or student.

ambiance (Fr) surroundings, atmosphere.

amende honorable (Fr) a public apology satisfying the honour of the injured party.

amour-propre (Fr) 'own love, self-love'; legitimate self-esteem, sometimes exaggerated; vanity, conceit.

ancien régime (Fr) 'old regime'; a superseded and outdated political system or ruling elite.

angst (Ger) 'anxiety'; an unsettling feeling produced by awareness of the uncertainties and paradoxes inherent in the state of being human.

anno Domini (Lat) 'in the year of the Lord'; used in giving dates of the Christian era, counting forward from the year of Christ's birth.

annus mirabilis (Lat) 'year of wonders'; a remarkably successful or auspicious year.

Anschluss (Ger) 'joining together'; union, especially the political union of Germany and Austria in 1938.

ante-bellum (Lat) 'before the war'; denotes a period before a specific war, especially the American Civil War.

ante meridiem (Lat) 'before midday'; between midnight and noon, abbreviated to am.

à point (Fr) 'into the right condition'; to a nicety, a culinary term.

a posteriori (Lat) 'from the later'; applied to reasoning from experience, from effect to cause; inductive reasoning.

apparatchik (Russ) a Communist spy or agent; (humorous) any bureaucratic hack.

appellation contrôlée (Fr) 'certified name'; used in the labelling of French wines, a guarantee of specified conditions of origin, strength, etc.

après-ski (Fr) 'after-ski'; pertaining to the evening's amusements after skiing.

a priori (Lat) 'from the previous'; denotes argument from the cause to the effect; deductive reasoning.

atelier (Fr) a workshop; an artist's studio.

au contraire (Fr) 'on the contrary'.

au fait (Fr) 'to the point'; highly skilled; knowledgeable or familiar with something.

au fond (Fr) 'at the bottom'; fundamentally.

au naturel (Fr) 'in the natural state'; naked; also as a culinary term: cooked plainly, raw, or without dressing.

au pair (Fr) 'on an equal basis'; originally an arrangement of mutual service without payment; now used of a girl (usually foreign) who performes domestic duties for board, lodging and pocket money.

auto-da-fé (Port) 'act of the faith'; the public declaration or carrying out of a sentence imposed on heretics in Spain and Portugal by the Inquisition, eg burning at the stake.

avant-garde (Fr) 'front guard'; applied to those in the forefront of an artistic movement.

ave atque vale (Lat) hail and farewell.

babushka (Russ) 'grandmother'; granny; a triangular headscarf worn under the chin.

bain-marie (Fr) 'bath of Mary'; a water-bath; a vessel of boiling water in which another is placed for slow and gentle cooking, or for keeping food warm.

baksheesh (Persian) a gift or present of money, particularly in the East (India, Turkey, Egypt, etc).

bal costumé (Fr) a fancy-dress ball.

banzai (Jap) a Japanese battle cry, salute to the emperor, or exclamation of joy.

barrio (Span) 'district, suburb'; a community (usually poor) of Spanish-speaking immigrants (esp American English).

batik (Javanese) 'painted'; method of producing patterns on fabric by drawing with wax before dyeing.

beau geste (Fr) 'beautiful gesture'; a magnanimous action.

belle époque (Fr) 'fine period'; the time of gracious living for the well-to-do immediately preceding World War I.

bête noire (Fr) 'black beast'; a bugbear; something one especially dislikes.

Bildungsroman (Ger) 'educational novel'; a novel concerning its hero's early spiritual and emotional development and education.

blasé (Fr) 'cloyed'; dulled to enjoyment.

blitzkrieg (Ger) 'lightning war'; a sudden overwhelming attack by ground and air forces; a burst of intense activity.

bodega (Span) a wine shop that usually sells food as well; a building for wine storage.

bona fides (Lat) 'good faith'; genuineness.

bonne-bouche (Fr) 'good mouth'; a delicious morsel eaten at the end of a meal.

bonsai (Jap) art of growing miniature trees in pots; a dwarf tree grown by this method.

bon vivant (Fr) 'good living (person)'; one who lives well, particularly enjoying good food and wine; a jovial companion.

bon voyage (Fr) have a safe and pleasant journey.

bourgeois (Fr) 'citizen'; a member of the middle class; a merchant; conventional, conservative.

camera obscura (Lat) 'dark room'; a light-free chamber in which an image of outside objects is thrown upon a screen.

canard (Fr) 'duck'; a false rumour; a second wing fitted as a horizontal stabilizer near the nose of an aircraft.

carpe diem (Lat) 'seize the day'; enjoy the pleasures of the present moment while they last.

carte blanche (Fr) 'blank sheet of paper'; freedom of action.

casus belli (Lat) 'occasion of war'; whatever sparks off or justifies a war or quarrel.

cause célèbre (Fr) a very notable or famous trial; a notorious controversy.

caveat emptor (Lat) 'let the buyer beware'; warns the buyer to examine carefully the article about to be purchased.

c'est la vie (Fr) 'that's life'; denotes fatalistic resignation.

chacun à son goût (Fr) 'each to his own taste'; implies surprise at another's choice.

chambré (Fr) 'put into a room'; (of red wine) at room temperature.

chargé-d'affaires (Fr) a diplomatic agent of lesser rank; an ambassador's deputy.

chef d'oeuvre (Fr) a masterpiece; the best piece of work by a particular artist, writer, etc.

chicano (Span) *mejicano* 'Mexican'; or an American of Mexican descent.

chutzpah (Yiddish) 'effrontery'; nerve to do or say outrageous things.

Communication

Communication

cinéma vérité (Fr) 'cinema truth'; realism in films usually sought by photographic scenes of real life.

cinquecento (Ital) 'five hundred'; of the Italian art and literature of the 16c Renaissance period.

circa (Lat) 'surrounding'; of dates and numbers: approximately.

cliché (Fr) 'stereotype printing block'; the impression made by a die in any soft metal; a hackneyed phrase or concept.

cognoscente *plural* **cognoscenti** (Ital) 'one who knows'; one who professes critical knowledge of art, music, etc; a connoisseur.

coitus interruptus (Lat) 'interrupted intercourse'; coitus intentionally interrupted by withdrawal before semen is ejaculated; anticlimax when something ends prematurely.

comme il faut (Fr) 'as it is necessary'; correct; genteel.

compos mentis (Lat) 'having control of one's mind'; sane.

contra mundum (Lat) 'against the world'; denotes defiant perseverance despite universal criticism.

cordon bleu (Fr) 'blue ribbon'; denotes food cooked to a very high standard; a dish made with ham and cheese and a white sauce.

coup de foudre (Fr) 'flash of lightning'; a sudden and astonishing happening; love at first sight.

coup de grâce (Fr) 'blow of mercy'; a finishing blow to end pain; a decisive action which ends a troubled enterprise.

coup d'état (Fr) 'blow of state'; a violent overthrow of a government or subversive stroke of state policy.

coupé (Fr) 'cut'; (usually) two-door motor-car with sloping roof.

crème de la crème (Fr) 'cream of the cream'; the very best.

cuisine minceur (Fr) 'slenderness cooking'; a style of cooking characterized by imaginative use of light, simple, low-fat ingredients.

cul-de-sac (Fr) 'bottom of the bag'; a road closed at one end.

cum grano salis (Lat) with a grain (pinch) of salt.

curriculum vitae (Lat) 'course of life'; denotes a summary of someone's educational qualifications and work experience for presenting to a prospective employer.

décolleté (Fr) 'with bared neck and shoulders'; with neck uncovered; (of dress) low cut.

de facto (Lat) 'from the fact'; in fact; actually; irrespective of what is legally recognized.

de gustibus non est disputandum (Lat) (often in English shortened for convenience to *de gustibus*) 'there is no disputing about tastes'; there is no sense in challenging people's preferences.

déjà vu (Fr) 'already seen'; in any of the arts: unoriginal material; an illusion of having experienced something before; something seen so often it has become tedious.

de jure (Lat) 'according to law'; denotes the legal or theoretical position, which may not correspond with reality.

delirium tremens (Lat) 'trembling delirium'; psychotic condition caused by alcoholism, involving anxiety, shaking, hallucinations, etc.

Deo volente (Lat) 'God willing'; a sort of good-luck talisman.

de rigueur (Fr) 'of strictness'; compulsory; required by strict etiquette.

derrière (Fr) 'behind'; the buttocks.

déshabillé (Fr) 'undressed'; state of being only partially dressed, or of being casually dressed.

de trop (Fr) 'of too much'; superfluous; in the way.

deus ex machina (Lat) 'a god from a machine'; a contrived solution to a difficulty in a plot.

distingué (Fr) 'distinguished'; having an aristocratic or refined demeanour; striking.

dolce far niente (Ital) 'sweet doing nothing'; denotes the pleasure of idleness.

doppelgänger (Ger) 'double goer'; a ghostly duplicate of a living person; a wraith; someone who looks exactly like someone else.

double entendre (Fr) 'double meaning'; ambiguity (normally with indecent connotations).

doyen (Fr) 'dean'; most distinguished member or representative by virtue of seniority, experience, and often also excellence.

droit du seigneur (Fr) 'the lord's right'; originally the alleged right of a feudal superior to take the virginity of a vassal's bride; any excessive claim imposed on a subordinate.

Dummkopf (Ger) 'dumb-head'; blockhead; idiot.

echt (Ger) 'real, genuine'; denotes authenticity, typicality.

Eheu fugaces (Lat); opening of a quotation (Horace *Odes* II, XIV, 1–2) 'Alas! the fleeting years slip away'; bemoans the brevity of human existence.

élan (Fr) 'dash, rush, bound'; flair; flamboyance.

El Dorado (Span) 'the gilded man'; the golden land (or city) imagined by the Spanish conquerors of America; any place which offers the opportunity of acquiring fabulous wealth.

embarras de richesse (Fr) 'embarrassment of wealth'; a perplexing amount of wealth or an abundance of any kind.

embonpoint (Fr) *en bon point* 'in fine form'; well-fed; stout; plump.

emeritus (Lat) 'having served one's time'; eg of a retired professor, honourably discharged from a public duty; holding a position on an honorary basis only.

éminence grise (Fr) 'grey eminence'; someone exerting power through their influence over a superior.

enfant terrible (Fr) 'terrible child'; a precocious child whose sayings embarrass its parents; a person whose behaviour is indiscreet, embarrassing to his associates.

ennui (Fr) 'boredom'; world-weary listlessness.

en passant (Fr) 'in passing'; by the way; incidentally; applied in chess to the taking of a pawn that has just moved two squares as if it had moved only one.

en route (Fr) 'on the way, on the road'; let us go.

entente (Fr) 'understanding'; a friendly agreement between nations.

épater le bourgeois (Fr) 'shock the middle class'; to disconcert the prim and proper; commonly used of artistic productions which defy convention.

erratum *plural* **errata** (Lat) an error in writing or printing.

ersatz (Ger) 'replacement, substitute'; connotes a second-rate substitute; a supplementary reserve from which waste can be made good.

et al (Lat) *et alii* 'and other things'; used to avoid giving a complete and possibly over-lengthy list of all items eg of authors.

Et tu, Brute? (Lat) 'You too, Brutus?' (Caesar's alleged exclamation when he saw Brutus among his assassins); denotes surprise and dismay that a supposed friend has joined in a conspiracy against one.

eureka (Gr) *heureka* 'I have found!'; cry of triumph at a discovery.

ex cathedra (Lat) 'from the seat'; from the chair of office; authoritatively; judicially.

ex gratia (Lat) 'from favour'; of a payment; one that is made as a favour, without any legal obligation and without admitting legal liability.

ex officio (Lat) 'from office, by virtue of office'; used as a reason for membership of a body.

ex parte (Lat) 'from (one) part, from (one) side'; on behalf of one side only in legal proceedings; partial; prejudiced.

fait accompli (Fr) 'accomplished fact'; already done or settled, and therefore irreversible.

fata Morgana (Ital) a striking kind of mirage, attributed to witchcraft.

fatwa (Arabic) 'the statement of a formal legal opinion'; a formal legal opinion delivered by an Islamic religious leader.

faute de mieux (Fr) 'for lack of anything better'.

faux ami (Fr) 'false friend'; a word in a foreign language that does not mean what it appears to.

faux-naïf (Fr) 'falsely naive'; seeming or pretending to be unsophisticated, innocent, etc.

faux pas (Fr) 'false step'; a social blunder.

femme fatale (Fr) 'fatal woman'; an irresistibly attractive woman who brings difficulties or disasters on men; a siren.

fidus Achates (Lat) 'the faithful Achates' (Aeneas' friend); a loyal follower.

film noir (Fr) 'black film'; a bleak and pessimistic film.

fin de siècle (Fr) 'end of the century'; of the end of the 19c in Western culture or of an era; decadent.

floruit (Lat) 'he or she flourished'; denotes a period during which a person lived.

fons et origo (Lat) 'the source and origin'.

force de frappe (Fr) 'strike force'; equivalent of the 'independent nuclear deterrent'.

force majeure (Fr) 'superior force'; an unforeseeable or uncontrollable course of events, excusing one from fulfilling a contract; a legal term.

Führer (Ger) 'leader, guide'; an insulting term for anyone bossily asserting authority.

Gastarbeiter (Ger) 'guest-worker'; an immigrant worker, especially one who does menial work.

Gauleiter (Ger) 'district leader'; a chief official of a district under the Nazi régime; an overbearing wielder of petty authority.

gemütlich (Ger) amiable; comfortable; cosy.

gestalt (Ger) 'form, shape'; original whole or unit, more than the sum of its parts.

Gesundheit (Ger) 'health', 'your health'; said to someone who has just sneezed.

glasnost (Russ) 'publicity'; the policy of openness and forthrightness followed by the Soviet government, initiated by Mikhail Gorbachev.

Gnothi seauton (Gr) 'Know thyself'.

Götterdämmerung (Ger) 'twilight of the gods'; the downfall of any once powerful system.

goy *plural* **goys** *or* **goyim** (Hebrew) non-Jewish, a gentile.

grand mal (Fr) 'large illness'; a violently convulsive form of epilepsy.

grand prix (Fr) 'great prize'; any of several international motor races; any competition of similar importance in other sports.

gran turismo (Ital) 'great touring, touring on a grand scale'; a motor car designed for high speed touring in luxury (abbreviation GT).

gratis (Lat) *gratiis* 'kindness, favour'; free of charge.

gravitas (Lat) 'weight'; seriousness; weight of demeanour; avoidance of unseemly frivolity.

gringo (Mexican-Spanish) 'foreigner'.

guru (Hindi) a spiritual leader; a revered instructor or mentor.

habeas corpus (Lat) 'you should have the body'; a writ to a jailer to produce a prisoner in person, and to state the reasons for detention; maintains the right of the subject to protection from unlawful imprisonment.

haiku (Jap) 'amusement poem'; a Japanese poem consisting of only three lines, containing respectively five, seven, and five syllables.

hajj (Arabic) 'pilgrimage'; the Muslim pilgrimage to Mecca.

haka (Maori) a Maori ceremonial war dance; a similar dance performed by New Zealanders eg before a rugby game.

halal (Arabic) 'lawful'; meat from an animal killed in strict accordance with Islamic law.

haute couture (Fr) 'higher tailoring'; fashionable, expensive dress designing and tailoring.

haut monde (Fr) 'high world'; high society; fashionable society; composed of the aristocracy and the wealthy.

hic jacet (Lat) 'here lies'; the first words of an epitaph; memorial inscription.

hoi polloi (Gr) 'the many'; the rabble; the vulgar.

hombre (Span) 'man'.

honoris causa (Lat) 'for the sake of honour'; a token of respect; used to designate honorary university degrees.

hors concours (Fr) 'out of the competition'; not entered for a contest; unequalled.

ibidem (Lat) 'in the same place'; used in footnotes to indicate that the same book (or chapter) has been cited previously.

id (Lat) 'it'; the sum total of the primitive instinctive forces in an individual.

idée fixe (Fr) 'a fixed idea'; an obsession.

idem (Lat) 'the same'.

ikebana (Jap) 'living flowers'; the Japanese art of flower arrangement.

in absentia (Lat) 'in absence'; used for occasions, such as the receiving of a degree award, when the recipient would normally be present.

in camera (Lat) 'in the room'; in a private room; in secret.

incommunicado (Span) 'unable to communicate'; deprived of the right to communicate with others.

in extremis (Lat) 'in the last'; at the point of death; in desperate circumstances.

in flagrante delicto (Lat) 'with the crime blazing'; in the very act of committing the crime.

infra dig (Lat) 'below dignity'; below one's dignity.

in loco parentis (Lat) 'in place of a parent'.

in Shallah (Arabic) 'if God wills'; ► **Deo volente**

inter alia (Lat) 'among other things'; used to show that a few examples have been chosen from many possibilities.

in vitro (Lat) 'in glass'; in the test tube.

ipso facto (Lat) 'by the fact itself'; thereby.

je ne sais quoi (Fr) 'I do not know what'; an indefinable something.

jihad (Arabic) 'struggle'; a holy war undertaken by Muslims against unbelievers.

Jugendstil (Ger) 'youth style'; the German term for art nouveau.

kamikaze (Jap) 'divine wind'; Japanese pilots making a suicide attack; any reckless, potentially self-destructive act.

kanaka (Hawaiian) 'man'; used by Europeans (and Australians) to mean South Sea islander.

karaoke (Jap) 'empty orchestra'; in bars, clubs, etc members of the public sing a solo to a recorded backing.

karma (Sanskrit) 'act'; the concept that the actions in a life determine the future condition of an individual.

kibbutz (Hebrew) a Jewish communal agricultural settlement in Israel.

kitsch (Ger) 'rubbish'; work in any of the arts that is pretentious and inferior or in bad taste.

kvetch (Yiddish) 'complain, whine (incessantly)'.

la dolce vita (Ital) 'the sweet life'; the name of a film made by Federico Fellini in 1960 showing a life of wealth, pleasure and self-indulgence.

laissez-faire (Fr) 'let do'; a general principle of non-interference.

Lebensraum (Ger) 'life space'; room to live; used by Hitler to justify his acquisition of land for Germany.

Communication

leitmotiv (Ger) 'leading motive'; a recurrent theme.

lèse-majesté (Fr) 'injured majesty'; offence against the sovereign power; treason.

lingua franca (Ital) 'Frankish language'; originally a mixed Italian trading language used in the Levant, subsequently any language chosen as a means of communication among speakers of different languages.

locum tenens (Lat) 'place holder'; a deputy or substitute, especially for a doctor or a clergyman.

macho (Mexican-Spanish) 'male'; originally a positive term denoting masculinity or virility, it has come in English to describe an ostentatious virility.

magnum opus (Lat) 'great work'; a person's greatest achievement, especially a literary work.

maharishi (Sanskrit) a Hindu sage or spiritual leader; a guru.

mañana (Span) 'tomorrow'; an unspecified time in the future.

mea culpa (Lat) 'through my fault'; originally part of the Latin mass; an admission of fault and an expression of repentance.

memento mori (Lat) 'remember that you must die'; an object, such as a skull, or anything to remind one of mortality.

ménage à trois (Fr) 'household of three'; a household comprising a husband and wife and the lover of one of them.

mens sana in corpore sano (Lat) 'a sound mind in a sound body' (Juvenal *Satires* X, 356); the guiding rule of the 19c English educational system.

mirabile dictu (Lat) 'wonderful to tell'; an expression of (sometimes ironic) amazement.

modus operandi (Lat) 'mode of working'; the characteristic methods employed by a particular criminal.

modus vivendi (Lat) 'mode of living'; an arrangement or compromise by means of which those who differ may get on together for a time.

mot juste (Fr) 'exact word'; the word which fits the context exactly.

multum in parvo (Lat) 'much in little'; a large amount in a small space.

mutatis mutandis (Lat) 'with the necessary changes made'.

négociant (Fr) 'merchant, trader'; often used for *négociant en vins* 'wine merchant'.

ne plus ultra (Lat) 'not more beyond'; extreme perfection.

netsuke (Jap) a small Japanese carved ornament used to fasten small objects, eg a purse, tobacco pouch, or medicine box, to the sash of a kimono. They are now collectors' pieces.

noblesse oblige (Fr) 'nobility obliges'; rank imposes obligations.

non sequitur (Lat) 'it does not follow'; a conclusion that does not follow logically from the premise; a remark that has no relation to what has gone before.

nostalgie de la boue (Fr) 'hankering for mud'; a craving for a debased physical life without civilized refinements.

nota bene (Lat) 'observe well, note well'; often abbreviated NB.

nouveau riche (Fr) 'new rich'; one who has only lately acquired wealth (without acquiring good taste).

nouvelle cuisine (Fr) 'new cooking'; a style of simple French cookery that aims to produce dishes that are light and healthy, utilizing fresh fruit and vegetables, and avoiding butter and cream.

nouvelle vague (Fr) 'new wave'; a movement in the French cinema aiming at imaginative quality films.

obiter dictum (Lat) 'something said in passing'; originally a legal term for something said by a trial judge that was incidental to the case in question.

origami (Jap) 'paper-folding'; Japanese art of folding paper to make shapes suggesting birds, boats, etc.

O tempora! O mores! (Lat) 'O the times! O the manners' (Cicero *In Catilinam*); a condemnation of present times, as contrasted with a past which is seen as golden.

outré (Fr) 'gone to excess'; beyond what is customary or proper; eccentric.

pace (Lat) 'peace'; by your leave (indicating polite disagreement).

panem et circenses (Lat) 'bread and circuses', or 'food and the big match' (Juvenal *Satires* X, 80); amusements which divert the populace from unpleasant realities.

passim (Lat) 'everywhere, throughout'; dispersed through a book.

per capita (Lat) 'by heads'; per head of the population in statistical contexts.

perestroika (Russ) 'reconstruction'; restructuring of an organization.

persona non grata (Lat) one who is not welcome or favoured (originally a term in diplomacy).

pied à terre (Fr) 'foot to the ground'; a flat, small house etc kept for temporary or occasional accommodation.

plus ça change (Fr) abbreviated form of **plus ça change, plus c'est la même chose** 'the more things change, the more they stay the same'; a comment on the unchanging nature of the world.

post meridiem (Lat) 'after midday, after noon'; abbreviated to pm.

post mortem (Lat) 'after death'; an examination of a body in order to determine the cause of death; an after-the-event discussion.

poule de luxe (Fr) 'luxurious hen'; a sexually attractive promiscuous young woman; a prostitute.

pour encourager les autres (Fr) 'to encourage the others' (Voltaire *Candide*, on the execution of Admiral Byng); exemplary punishment.

premier cru (Fr) 'first growth'; wine of the highest quality in a system of classification.

prêt-à-porter (Fr) 'ready to wear'; refers to 'designer' clothes that are made in standard sizes as opposed to made-to-measure clothes.

prima donna (Ital) 'first lady'; leading female singer in an opera; a person who is temperamental and hard to please.

prima facie (Lat) 'at first sight'; a legal term for evidence that is assumed to be true unless disproved by other evidence.

primus inter pares (Lat) 'first among equals'.

prix fixe (Fr) 'fixed price'; used of a meal in a restaurant offered at a set price for a restricted choice. Compare **table d'hôte**.

pro bono publico (Lat) 'for the public good'; something done for no fee.

quid pro quo (Lat) 'something for something'; something given or taken as equivalent to another, often as retaliation.

quod erat demonstrandum (Lat) 'which was to be shown'; often used in its abbreviated form **qed**.

raison d'être (Fr) 'reason for existence'.

rara avis (Lat) 'rare bird' (Juvenal *Satires* VI, 165); something or someone remarkable and unusual.

realpolitik (Ger) 'politics of realism'; practical politics based on the realities and necessities of life, rather than moral or ethical ideas.

recherché (Fr) 'sought out'; carefully chosen; particularly choice; rare or exotic.

reculer pour mieux sauter (Fr) 'move backwards in order to jump better'; a strategic withdrawal to wait for a better opportunity.

reductio ad absurdum (Lat) 'reduction to absurdity'; originally used in logic to mean the proof of a proposition by proving the falsity of its contradictory; the application of a principle so strictly that it is carried to absurd lengths.

répondez, s'il vous plaît (Fr) 'reply, please'; in English mainly in its abbreviated form, **RSVP**, on invitations.

revenons à nos moutons (Fr) 'let us return to our sheep'; let us get back to our subject.

rijsttafel (Dutch) 'rice table'; an Indonesian rice dish served with a variety of foods.

risqué (Fr) 'risky, hazardous'; audaciously bordering on the unseemly.

Rus in urbe (Lat) 'The country in the town' (Martial *Epigrams* XII, 57); the idea of country charm in the centre of a city.

Salus populi suprema est lex (Lat) 'Let the welfare of the people be the chief law' (Cicero *De Legibus* III, 3).

samizdat (Russ) 'self-publisher'; the secret printing and distribution of banned literature in the former USSR and other Eastern European countries previously under Communist rule.

sanctum sanctorum (Lat) 'holy of holies'; the innermost chamber of the temple, where the Ark of the Covenant was kept; any private room reserved for personal use.

sangfroid (Fr) 'cold blood'; self possession; coolness under stress.

savoir faire (Fr) 'knowing what to do'; knowing what to do and how to do it in any situation.

schadenfreude (Ger) 'hurt joy'; pleasure in others' misfortunes.

schlimazel (Yiddish) 'bad luck'; a persistently unlucky person.

schlock (Yiddish) 'broken or damaged goods'; inferior; shoddy.

schmaltz (Yiddish) 'melted fat, grease'; showy sentimentality, particularly in writing, music, art, etc

schmuck (Yiddish) 'penis'; a (male) stupid person.

shogun (Jap) 'leader of the army'; ruler of feudal Japan.

sic (Lat) 'so, thus'; used in brackets within printed matter to show that the original is faithfully reproduced even if incorrect.

sic transit gloria mundi (Lat) 'so passes away earthly glory'.

sine die (Lat) 'without a day'; the adjournment of a meeting (often in court), indicating that no day has been fixed for its resumption; an indefinite adjournment.

sine qua non (Lat) 'without which not'; an indispensable condition.

sotto voce (Ital) 'below the voice'; in an undertone; aside.

status quo (Lat) 'the state in which'; the existing condition.

sub judice (Lat) 'under a judge'; under consideration by a judge or a court of law.

subpoena (Lat) 'under penalty'; a writ commanding attendance in court.

sub rosa (Lat) 'under the rose'; in secret; privately.

succès de scandale (Fr) 'success of scandal'; the success of a book, film, etc due not to merit but to its connection with, or reference to, a scandal.

summa cum laude (Lat) 'with the highest praise'; with great distinction; the highest class of degree award that can be gained by a US college student.

summum bonum (Lat) 'the chief good'.

table d'hôte (Fr) 'host's table'; a set meal at a fixed price. Compare **prix fixe**.

tabula rasa (Lat) 'scraped table'; a cleaned tablet; a mind not yet influenced by outside impressions and experience.

t'ai chi (Chin) 'great art of boxing'; a system of exercise and self-defence in which good use of balance and co-ordination allows effort to be minimized.

tempus fugit (Lat) 'time flies'; delay cannot be tolerated.

terra incognita (Lat) 'unknown land'; an unknown land (so marked on early maps); an area of study about which very little is known.

touché (Fr) 'touched'; claiming or acknowledging a hit made in fencing; claiming or acknowledging a point scored in an argument.

tour de force (Fr) 'turning movement'; feat of strength or skill.

trompe l'oeil (Fr) 'deceives the eye'; an appearance of reality achieved by the use of perspective and detail in painting, architecture, etc.

tsunami (Jap) 'wave in harbour'; a wave generated by movement of the earth's surface underwater; commonly (and erroneously) called a 'tidal wave'.

Übermensch (Ger) 'over-person'; superman.

ultra vires (Lat) 'beyond strength, beyond powers'; beyond one's power or authority.

urbi et orbi (Lat) 'to the city and the world'; used of the Pope's pronouncements; to everyone.

vade-mecum (Lat) 'go with me'; a handbook; pocket companion.

vin du pays (Fr) 'wine of the country'; a locally produced wine for everyday consumption.

vis-à-vis (Fr) 'face to face'; one who faces or is opposite another; in relation to.

viva voce (Lat) 'with the living voice'; in speech, orally; an oral examination, particularly at a university (commonly 'viva' alone).

volte-face (Fr) 'turn-face'; a sudden and complete change in opinion or in views expressed.

vox populi (Lat); 'voice of the people'; public or popular opinion.

Weltschmerz (Ger) 'world pain'; sympathy with universal misery; thoroughgoing pessimism.

wunderkind (Ger) 'wonder-child'; a 'child prodigy'; one who shows great talent and/or achieves great success at an early (or comparatively early) age.

zeitgeist (Ger) 'time-spirit'; the spirit of the age.

Communication

Communication

Differences between British and US English

There are many differences of meaning, pronunciation, spelling and syntax between British and US English. Some of the commoner differences in meaning in typical usage are listed below. The increasing influence of US usage on British English is having the effect of blurring distinctions. It should also be remembered that practice differs widely within the USA; and it is becoming increasingly difficult to establish linguistic boundaries between the language used in the USA and the language used in Canada.

There are also a number of general spelling differences between British and US English. Others are less distinct, because both varieties permit variants of form and inflections (for example, the forms **acknowledgement** and **acknowledgment** are found in both US and British English).

	British		US		British		US
-ae-	as in anaesthetic	-e-	as in anesthetic	-ogue	as in catalogue	-og	as in catalog
-oe-	as in oestrogen	-e-	as in estrogen	-ou-	as in mould	-o-	as in mold
-ence	as in defence, licence (noun)	-ense	as in defense, license (noun)	-l-	as in instil, instalment, skilful	-ll-	as in instill, installment, skillful
-re	as in centre	-er	as in center				
-our	as in flavour	-or	as in flavor	-ll-	as in traveller	-l-	as in traveler

British	US	British	US
Aeroplane	airplane	lorry	truck
aluminium	aluminum	loud-hailer	bull-horn
anticlockwise	counterclockwise	main road	highway
aubergine	eggplant	murder	homicide
autumn	fall	motorway	expressway
back garden	yard	number plate	licence plate
banknote	bill	(of a vehicle)	(of a vehicle)
bath	tub	nappy	diaper
biscuit (savoury)	cracker	pavement	sidewalk
biscuit (sweet)	cookie	pedestrian crossing	crosswalk
bonnet (of a car)	hood (of a car)	petrol	gasoline (gas)
braces	suspenders	pig	hog
brooch	pin	plot (of ground)	lot
bumper (of a car)	fender (of a car)	potato chips	french fries
camp-bed	cot	pram	baby carriage
caretaker	janitor	queue	line
chemist's shop	drugstore	railway	railroad
cheque	check	return ticket	round-trip ticket
cinema (building)	movie theater	reverse charge	collect call
city centre	downtown	(telephone call)	
coffin	casket	rise (in salary)	raise
cornflour	cornstarch	roundabout (traffic)	rotary
cotton reel	spool	rowing-boat	rowboat
courgette	zucchini	rubber	eraser
crisps	potato chips	rubbish	trash
cupboard	closet	scone	biscuit
current account (bank)	checking account	season ticket	commutation ticket
curriculum vitae	résumé	shoelace	shoestring
curtains	drapes	shop assistant	clerk
draughts (game)	checkers	silencer (car)	muffler (car)
drawing pin	thumb tack	spring onions	green onions
driving licence	driver's license	sweets	candy
dual carriageway	divided highway	tap	faucet
dustbin	garbage can	tart	pie
engine driver	engineer	terraced house	row house
estate agent	realtor	tights	pantihose
first floor	second floor	timber	lumber
flag day	tag day	traffic jam	gridlock
flat	apartment	tram	streetcar
frying pan	skillet	trolley (at supermarket, etc)	cart
grill	broil	trousers	pants
ground floor	first floor	turn-up (trousers)	cuff (pants)
handbag	purse, pocketbook	tyre	tire
hoarding	billboard	underground	subway
icing	frosting	undertaker	mortician
insect	bug	verandah	porch
ironmonger	hardware store	vest	undershirt
kerb	curb	waistcoat	vest
knickers	underpants	wallet	billfold
lavatory	washroom	windscreen	windshield
lawyer	attorney	zip	zipper
lift	elevator		

US	British	US	British
airplane	aeroplane	hardware store	ironmonger
aluminum	aluminium	highway	main road
apartment	flat	hog	pig
attorney	lawyer	homicide	murder
baby carriage	pram	hood (of a car)	bonnet (of a car)
bill	banknote	janitor	caretaker
billboard	hoarding	licence plate	number plate
billfold	wallet	(of a vehicle)	(of a vehicle)
biscuit	scone	line	queue
broil	grill	lot	plot (of ground)
bug	insect	lumber	timber
bull-horn	loud-hailer	mortician	undertaker
candy	sweets	movie theater	cinema
cart (at supermarket, etc)	trolley	muffler (car)	silencer (car)
casket	coffin	pantihose	tights
check	cheque	pants	trousers
checkers	draughts	pie	tart
checking	current	pin	brooch
account	account	pocketbook	handbag, purse
clerk	shop assistant	porch	verandah
closet	cupboard	potato chips	crisps
collect call (telephone)	reverse charge call	purse	handbag
commutation ticket	season ticket	railroad	railway
cookie	biscuit (sweet)	raise (in salary)	rise
cornstarch	cornflour	realtor	estate agent
cot	camp-bed	résumé	curriculum vitae
counterclockwise	anticlockwise	rotary (in traffic)	roundabout
cracker	biscuit (savoury)	round-trip ticket	return ticket
crosswalk	pedestrian crossing	row house	terraced house
cuff (pants)	turn-up (trousers)	second floor	first floor
curb	kerb	sidewalk	pavement
diaper	nappy	skillet	frying pan
divided highway	dual carriageway	spool	cotton reel
downtown	city centre	streetcar	tram
drapes	curtains	string	shoelace
drugstore	chemist's shop	subway	underground
eggplant	aubergine	suspenders	braces
elevator	lift	tag day	flag day
engineer	engine driver	thumb tack	drawing pin
eraser	rubber	tire	tyre
expressway	motorway	trash	rubbish
fall	autumn	truck	lorry
faucet	tap	tub	bath
fender (of a car)	bumper (of a car)	underpants	knickers
first floor	ground floor	undershirt	vest
french fries	potato chips	vest	waistcoat
frosting	icing	washroom	lavatory
garbage can	dustbin	windshield	windscreen
gasoline (gas)	petrol	yard	back garden
green onions	spring onions	zipper	zip
gridlock	traffic jam	zucchini	courgette

Proverbs

The date is the first known occurrence in print in English in a recognizable form. In many cases related sentiments are attested earlier, often in Greek and Latin. A number of other proverbs are derived from medieval French sources.
Some of the uses are not in the precise form given here. Proverbs often appear in many forms.

Proverb/Date/Notable uses	Proverb/Date/Notable uses

absence makes the heart grow fonder   19c
actions speak louder than words   17c
all's well that ends well   14c
an *apple* a day keeps the doctor away   19c
don't throw the *baby* out with the bathwater
   19c   *Thomas Carlyle*
beauty is in the eye of the beholder   18c   *Hume*
beauty is only skin deep   17c
beggars can't be choosers   16c
the early *bird* catches the worm   17c
a *bird* in the hand is worth two in the bush   15c

birds of a feather flock together   16c   *Bible: Ecclesiasticus 27*
once *bitten*, twice shy   19c
when the *blind* lead the blind, both shall fall into the
   ditch   9c   *Bible: Matthew 15*
You can't get *blood* from a stone   17c
blood is thicker than water   19c
brevity is the soul of wit   17c   *Shakespeare, Hamlet*
you can't make *bricks* without straw   17c   *Bible: Exodus 5*
don't cross your *bridges* until you come to them   19c

549

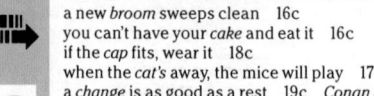

Communication

Proverb/Date/Notable uses	Proverb/Date/Notable uses

a new *broom* sweeps clean 16c

you can't have your *cake* and eat it 16c

if the *cap* fits, wear it 18c

when the *cat's* away, the mice will play 17c

a *change* is as good as a rest 19c *Conan Doyle*

charity begins at home 14c *John Wycliffe*

don't count your *chickens* before they are hatched 16c

clothes make the man 15c

every *cloud* has a silver lining 19c

cut your *coat* according to your cloth 16c

too many *cooks* spoil the broth 16c

curiosity killed the cat 20c

there's none so *deaf* as those that will not hear 16c

needs must when the *devil* drives 15c *Shakespeare, All's Well that Ends Well*

the *devil* finds work for idle hands to do 14c *Chaucer*

the *devil* looks after his own 17c

better the *devil* you know than the devil you don't 16c

discretion is the better part of valour 16c *Shakespeare, Henry IV Pt. 1*

give a *dog* a bad name and hang him 18c

you can't teach an old *dog* new tricks 16c

let sleeping *dogs* lie 14c *Chaucer*

barking *dogs* seldom bite 16c

to *err* is human, to forgive divine 16c

the *exception* proves the rule 17c

familiarity breeds contempt 14c

there are as good *fish* in the sea as ever came out of it 16c

a *fool* and his money are soon parted 16c

there's no *fool* like an old fool 16c

fools rush in where angels fear to tread 18c *Pope*

forewarned is forearmed 15c

those who live in *glass* houses shouldn't throw stones 17c *Chaucer*

all that *glitters* is not gold 13c *Shakespeare, Merchant of Venice, as 'all that glisters...'*

don't teach your *grandmother* to suck eggs 18c

the *grass* is always greener on the other side of the fence 20c

old *habits* die hard 18c *Benjamin Franklin*

many *hands* make light work 14c

first you catch your *hare* 19c *Thackeray*

more *haste* less speed 14c

he who *hesitates* is lost 18c

there is *honour* among thieves 17c

never look a gift *horse* in the mouth 16c

you may take a *horse* to water but you can't make him drink 12c

hunger is the best sauce 16c

where *ignorance* is bliss, 'tis folly to be wise 18c *Thomas Gray*

strike while the *iron* is hot 14c *Chaucer*

a little *knowledge* is a dangerous thing 18c *Pope*

better *late* than never 14c

he who *laughs* last, laughs longest 20c

least said, soonest mended 15c

a *leopard* doesn't change its spots 16c *Bible: Jeremiah 13.23*

many a *little* makes a mickle 13c

half a *loaf* is better than no bread 16c

look before you leap 14c

one man's *meat* is another man's poison 16c

it's no use crying over spilt *milk* 17c

a *miss* is as good as a mile 17c

if the *mountain* won't come to Mahomet, Mahomet must go to the mountain 17c *Bacon*

necessity is the mother of invention 16c

no *news* is good *news* 17c *James I*

don't cut off your *nose* to spite your face 16c

nothing ventured, nothing gained 17c

great *oaks* from little acorns grow 14c *Chaucer*

you can't make an *omelette* without breaking eggs 19c

out of sight, out of mind 13c

the *pen* is mightier than the sword 16c

take care of the *pence* and the pounds will take care of themselves 18c

in for a *penny*, in for a pound 17c

he that pays the *piper* calls the tune 19c

little *pitchers* have large ears 16c

there's no *place* like home 16c

a watched *pot* never boils 19c *Mrs Gaskell*

practice makes perfect 16c

prevention is better than cure 17c

pride goes before a fall 14c

procrastination is the thief of time 18c *Bible: Proverbs 16*

the *proof* of the pudding is in the eating 14c

you can't make a silk *purse* out of a sow's ear 16c

it never *rains* but it pours 18c

the *road* to hell is paved with good intentions 16c

spare the *rod* and spoil the child 11c *Bible: Proverbs 13*

Rome was not built in a day 16c

when in *Rome*, do as the Romans do 15c

better *safe* than sorry 19c

there is *safety* in numbers 17c *Bible: Proverbs 11, and John Bunyan*

what's *sauce* for the goose is sauce for the gander 17c

as well be hanged for a *sheep* as a lamb 17c

there's no *smoke* without fire 14c

speech is silver, but silence is golden 19c *Thomas Carlyle*

it's no use shutting the *stable* door after the horse has bolted 14c

a *stitch* in time saves nine 18c

a rolling *stone* gathers no moss 14c

it's the last *straw* that breaks the camel's back 17c

little *strokes* fell great oaks 15c

one *swallow* doesn't make a summer 16c

what you lose on the *swings* you gain on the roundabouts 20c

you can have too much of a good *thing* 15c

little *things* please little minds 16c

time and tide wait for no man 14c *Chaucer, in Latin*

don't put off till *tomorrow* what you can do today 14c *Chaucer*

it's better to *travel* hopefully than to arrive 19c *R L Stevenson*

the *tree* is known by its fruit 16c *Bible: Matthew 12*

trouble shared is trouble halved 20c *Dorothy L Sayers*

there's many a good *tune* played on an old fiddle 20c *Samuel Butler*

one good *turn* deserves another 15c

variety is the spice of life 18c

all things come to those who *wait* 16c

waste not, want not 18c

still *waters* run deep 15c

where there's a *will*, there's a way 17c

it's an ill *wind* that blows nobody any good 16c *Shakespeare, Henry VI, Pt 3*

it's easy to be *wise* after the event 17c *Ben Jonson*

the *wish* is father to the thought 16c *Shakespeare*

fine *words* butter no parsnips 17c

all *work* and no play makes Jack a dull boy 17c

a bad *workman* blames his tools 17c

Common abbreviations

See also **Computer languages** p567 and **Abbreviations and acronyms used in e-mail** p568

Communication

AA	Alcoholics Anonymous	ASL	American Sign Language
AA	Automobile Association	ASLEF	Associated Society of Locomotive
AAA	Amateur Athletics Association		Engineers and Firemen
AAA	American Automobile Association	ASLIB	Association of Special Libraries and
ABA	Amateur Boxing Association		Information Bureaux
ABA	American Booksellers Association	ASM	air-to-surface missile
ABC	American Broadcasting Corporation	ASPCA	American Society for the Prevention of
ABC	Australian Broadcasting Corporation		Cruelty to Animals
ABM	antiballistic missile	ASSR	Autonomous Soviet Socialist Republic
ABTA	Association of British Travel Agents	ASTMS	Association of Scientific, Technical, and
AC/ac	alternating current		Managerial Staffs
ACAS	Advisory, Conciliation, and Arbitration	ATP	adenosine triphosphate
	Service	ATS	Auxiliary Territorial Service
ACLU	American Civil Liberties Union	ATV	Associated Television
ACT	Australian Capital Territory	AU	astronomical unit
ACTH	adrenocorticotrophic hormone	AV	audio-visual
ACTU	Australian Council of Trade Unions	AVC	Additional Voluntary Contribution
AD	anno Domini (in the year of Our Lord)	AWACS	Airborne Warning and Control System
A-D	analog-to-digital (in computing)	AWU	Australian Workers' Union
ADH	antidiuretic hormone	BAFTA	British Academy of Film and Television
ADP	adenosine diphosphate		Arts
AEA	Atomic Energy Authority (UK)	BALPA	British Airline Pilots' Association
AEC	Atomic Energy Commission (USA)	B&W	black and white
AFC	American Football Conference	BASIC	(English) British American Scientific
AFL/CIO	American Federation of Labor/		International Commercial
	Congress of Industrial Organizations	BBC	British Broadcasting Corporation
AFV	armoured fighting vehicle	BC	before Christ
AGM	annual general meeting	BCD	binary coded decimal
AGR	advanced gas-cooled reactor	BCE	Before the Common Era
AH	anno Hegirae (in the year of Hegira)	BCG	bacille (bacillus) Calmette-Guérin
AHF	anti-haemophilic factor	BCS	Bardeen, Cooper & Schrieffer (theory)
AI	artificial intelligence	BEF	British Expeditionary Force
AID	artificial insemination by donor	BEV	Black English Vernacular
AIDS	Acquired Immune Deficiency	BIA	Bureau of Indian Affairs
	Syndrome	BIS	Bank for International Settlements
AIF	Australian Imperial Force	BLAISE	British Library Automated Information
AIH	artificial insemination by husband		Service
ALCM	air-launched cruise missile	BMA	British Medical Association
ALP	Australian Labor Party	BOSS	Bureau of State Security (South Africa)
ALU	arithmetic and logic unit	BP	blood pressure
AM	amplitude modulation	BSE	bovine spongiform encephalopathy
am	ante meridiem (before noon)	BSI	British Standards Institution
AMA	American Medical Association	BST	British Summer Time
amu	atomic mass unit	btu	British thermal unit
ANC	African National Congress	BUF	British Union of Fascists
ANS	autonomic nervous system	BUPA	British United Provident Association
ANSI	American National Standards Institute	CAA	Civil Aviation Authority
ANZAC	Australian and New Zealand Army	CAB	Citizen's Advice Bureau
	Corps	CACM	Central American Common Market
ANZUS	Australia, New Zealand and the United	CAD	computer aided design
	States	CAI	computer aided instruction
AOB	any other business	CAL	computer aided learning
AONB	Area of Outstanding Natural Beauty	CAM	computer aided manufacture
APEX	Association of Professional, Executive,	CAP	Common Agricultural Policy
	Clerical, and Computer Staff	CARICOM	Caribbean Community
APR	annual percentage rate	CARIFTA	Caribbean Free Trade Area
APRA	Alianza Popular Revolutionaria	CATV	cable television
	Americana (American Popular	CB	citizen's band (radio)
	Revolutionary Alliance)	CBE	Commander of the (Order of the) British
AR	aspect ratio		Empire
ARCIC	Anglican Roman Catholic International	CBI	Confederation of British Industry
	Commission	CCD	charge-coupled device
A/S	Advanced/Supplementary	CCK	cholecystokinin-pancreozymin
ASA	American Standards Association	CCR	camera cassette recorder
ASCII	American Standards Code for	CCTV	closed circuit television
	Information Interchange	CD	Civil Defence
ASDIC	Admiralty Submarine Detection	CD-ROM	compact disc read-only memory
	Investigation Committee	CDU	Christian Democratic Union
ASEAN	Association of South-East Asian	CE	Common Era
	Nations	CENTO	Central Treaty Organization

Communication

CERN	Organisation Européene pour la Recherche Nucléaire (formerly, Conseil Européen pour la Recherche Nucléaire)	**DSO**	Distinguished Service Order
		DST	daylight saving time
		DTP	desk top publishing
CFC	chlorofluorocarbon	**DVD**	digital versatile/video disk
CGS	centimetre-gram-second	**EAC**	European Atomic Commission
CGT	capital gains tax	**EA-ROM**	electrically alterable read-only memory
CGT	Confédération Générale du Travail	**EBCDIC**	Extended Binary-Coded Decimal Interchange Code
CH	Companion of Honour		
CHAPS	Clearing House Automated Clearance System	**EBU**	European Boxing Union
		EBU	European Broadcasting Union
CHIPS	Clearing House Interbank Payments System	**EC**	European Community
		ECA	European Commission on Agriculture
CIA	Central Intelligence Agency	**ECF**	extracellular fluid
CID	Criminal Investigation Department	**ECG**	electrocardiograph
CIO	Congress of Industrial Organizations	**ECM**	European Common Market
CIS	Commonwealth of Independent States	**ECO**	European Coal Organization
CJD	Creutzfeldt-Jakob disease	**ECOSOC**	Economic and Social Council (of the United Nations)
CM	Congregation of the Mission		
CMG	Companion of (the Order of) St Michael and St George	**ECOWAS**	Economic Community of West African States
CNAA	Council for National Academic Awards	**ECSC**	European Coal and Steel Community
CND	Campaign for Nuclear Disarmament	**ECT**	electroconvulsive therapy
CNES	Centre National d'Espace	**ECTG**	European Channel Tunnel Group
CNN	Cable News Network	**ECU**	European Currency Unit
CNS	central nervous system	**EDC**	European Defence Community
COMECON	Council for Mutual Economic Assistance	**EDF**	European Development Fund
		EDVAC	Electronic Discrete Variable Automatic Computer
CORE	Congress of Racial Equality		
CP	Congregation of the Passion	**EEC**	European Economic Community
CPI	Consumer Price Index	**EEG**	electroencephalography
CP/M	control program monitor	**EEOC**	Equal Employment Opportunity Commission
CPR	cardio-pulmonary resuscitation		
CPU	central processing unit	**EE-ROM**	electrically erasable read-only memory
CRO	cathode-ray oscilloscope	**EFA**	European Fighter Aircraft
CRT	cathode-ray tube	**EFC**	European Forestry Commission
CSE	Certificate of Secondary Education	**EFTA**	European Free Trade Association
CSF	cerebrospinal fluid	**EGF**	epidermal growth factor
CSIRO	Commonwealth Scientific and Industrial Research Organization	**EI**	Exposure Index
		ELDO	European Launcher Development Organization
CSO	colour separation overlay		
CTT	capital transfer tax	**ELF**	Eritrea Liberation Front
CV	cultivar (*culti*vated *va*riety)	**emf**	electromotive force
CV	curriculum vitae	**EMS**	European Monetary System
CVO	Commander of the Royal Victorian Order	**EMS**	Emergency Medical Service
		emu	electromagnetic units
CVS	chorionic villus sampling	**EMU**	Economic Monetary Union
CWA	County Women's Association	**EMU**	European and Monetary Union
CWS	Co-operative Wholesale Society	**ENIAC**	Electronic Numeral Indicator and Calculator
D-A	digital-to-analog (in computing)		
DALR	dry adiabatic lapse rate	**EOKA**	Ethniki Organosis Kipriakou Agonos (National Organization of Cypriot Struggle)
D&C	dilatation and curettage		
DBE	Dame Commander of the (Order of the) British Empire		
		EP	European Parliament
DBMS	database management system	**EPA**	Environmental Protection Agency
DBS	direct broadcasting from satellite	**EPR**	Einstein-Podolsky-Rosen (paradox)
DC/dc	direct current	**EPR**	electron paramagnetic resonance
DCF	discounted cash flow	**EP-ROM**	electronically programmable read-only memory
DCMG	Dame Commander of (the Order of) St Michael and St George		
		ERNIE	Electronic Random Number Indicator Equipment
DCVO	Dame Commander of the Royal Victorian Order		
		ERW	enhanced radiation weapon
DDT	dichloro-diphenyl-trichloroethane	**ESA**	Environmentally Sensitive Area
DES	Department of Education and Science	**ESA**	European Space Agency
DES	diethylstilboestrol	**ESC**	electronic stills camera
DFC	Distinguished Flying Cross	**ESCU**	European Space Operations Centre
DHA	District Health Authority	**ESO**	European Southern Observatory
DIA	Defense Intelligence Agency	**ESP**	extra-sensory perception
DLP	Democratic Labor Party (Australia)	**ESRO**	European Space Research Organization
DMSO	dimethyl sulphoxide		
DNA	deoxyribonucleic acid	**ESTEC**	European Space Research and Technology Centre
DOS	Disk Operating System		
DPP	Director of Public Prosecutions	**ETU**	Electricians Trade Union
DSN	Deep Space Network	**EUFA**	European Union Football Associations
		EURATOM	European Atomic Energy Community

FA	Football Association
FAA	Federal Aviation Administration
FAO	Food and Agriculture Organization
FBI	Federal Bureau of Investigation
FCA	Farm Credit Administration
FCC	Federal Communications Commission
FDIC	Federal Deposit Insurance Corporation
FIFA	Fédération Internationale de Football Association (International Association Football Federation)
FIMBRA	Financial Intermediaries, Managers and Brokers Regulatory Association
FLN	Front de Liberation Nationale
FM/fm	frequency modulation
FORTRAN	Formula Translation
FPS	foot-pound-second
FRELIMO	Frente de Libertação de Moçambique
FSB	Federal'naya Sluzhba Bezopasnosti (Federal Security Service)
FSH	follicle-stimulating hormone
FTC	Federal Trade Commission
GAR	Grand Army of the Republic
GATT	General Agreement on Tariffs and Trade
GBE	Knight/Dame Grand Cross of the (Order of the) British Empire
GBH	grievous bodily harm
GC	George Cross
GCC	Gulf Co-operation Council
GCE	General Certificate of Education
GCHQ	Government Communications Headquarters
GCMG	Knight/Dame Grand Cross of (the Order of) St Michael and St George
GCSE	General Certificate of Secondary Education
GCVO	Knight/Dame Grand Cross of the Royal Victorian Order
GDI	gross domestic income
GDP	gross domestic product
GEO	geosynchronous Earth orbit
GESP	generalized extra-sensory perception
GH	growth hormone
GLC	gas-liquid chromatography
GLCM	ground-launched cruise missile
GM	George Medal
GMC	General Medical Council
GMT	Greenwich Mean Time
GNP	gross national product
GnRH	gonadotrophin-releasing hormone
GP	General Practitioner
GPSS	General Purpose System Simulator
GUTS	grand unified theories
HCG	human chorionic gonadotrophin
HE	His/Her Excellency
HEP	hydro-electric power
HF	high frequency
HGV	heavy goods vehicle
HIH	His/Her Imperial Highness
HIM	His/Her Imperial Majesty
HLA	human leucocyte antigen
HM	His/Her Majesty
HMG	His/Her Majesty's Government
HMI	His/Her Majesty's Inspectorate
HMO	Health Maintenance Organization
HMS	His/Her Majesty's Ship/Service
HMSO	His/Her Majesty's Stationery Office
HNC	Higher National Certificate
HND	Higher National Diploma
hp	horsepower
HQ	headquarters
HR	House of Representatives
HRH	His/Her Royal Highness
IAEA	International Atomic Energy Agency
IBRD	International Bank for Reconstruction and Development
IC	integrated circuit
ICAO	International Civil Aviation Organization
ICFTU	International Confederation of Free Trade Unions
ICI	Imperial Chemical Industries
ICSID	International Centre for Settlement of Investment Disputes
IDA	International Development Agency
IFAD	International Fund for Agricultural Development
IFC	International Finance Corporation
ILO	International Labour Organization
IMF	International Monetary Fund
IMO	International Maritime Organization
IMRO	Investment Management Regulatory Organization
INLA	Irish National Liberation Army
INRI	Iesus Nazarenus Rex Iudeorum (Jesus of Nazareth, King of the Jews)
IPA	International Phonetic Alphabet
IQ	intelligence quotient
IR	infrared
IRA	Irish Republican Army
IRB	Irish Republican Brotherhood
IRBM	intermediate-range ballistic missile
ISBN	International Standard Book Number
ISO	International Organization for Standardization
ISSN	International Standard Serial Number
ITA	Initial Teaching Alphabet
ITAR-Tass	Informatsionnoe telegrafnoye agentstvo Rossi (Information and Telegraphic Agency of Russia) (previously **TASS**)
ITC	Independent Television Commission
ITCZ	intertropical convergence zone
ITN	Independent Television News
ITO	International Trade Organization
ITT	International Telephone and Telegraph Corporation
ITU	International Telecommunication Union
ITV	Independent Television
IUCN	International Union for the Conservation of Nature and Natural Resources
IUD	intra-uterine device
IUPAC	International Union of Pure and Applied Chemistry
IUPAP	International Union of Pure and Applied Physics
IVF	in vitro fertilization
IVR	International Vehicle Registration
IWW	Industrial Workers of the World
JP	Justice of the Peace
JET	Joint European Torus
KADU	Kenya African Democratic Union
KANU	Kenya African National Union
KB	Knight Bachelor; Knight of the Bath
KBE	Knight Commander of the (Order of the) British Empire
KC	King's Counsel
KCB	Knight Commander of the Bath
KCMG	Knight Commander of (the Order of) St Michael and St George
KCVO	Knight Commander of the Royal Victorian Order
KG	Knight of the (Order of the) Garter
KGB	Komitet Gosudarstvennoye Bezhopaznosti (Committee of State Security) (now **FSB**)
KKK	Ku Klux Klan

Communication

KMT	Kuomintang	**NKVD**	Narodnyi Komissariat Vnutrennikh Del
kpc	kiloparsec		(People's Commissariat of Internal
KT	Knight of the Thistle		Affairs)
LAFTA	Latin-American Free Trade Association	**NLRB**	National Labor Relations Board
LAN	local area network	**NMR**	nuclear magnetic resonance
LAUTRO	Life Assurance and Unit Trust	**NOW**	National Organization for Women
	Regulatory Organization	**NPT**	Non-Proliferation Treaty
LCD	liquid crystal display	**NRA**	National Recovery Administration
LDC	less developed country	**NRAO**	National Radio Astronomy Observatory
LEA	Local Education Authority	**NSF**	National Science Foundation
LED	light-emitting diode	**NSPCC**	National Society for the Prevention of
LEO	low Earth orbit		Cruelty to Children
LFA	Less Favoured Area	**NTSC**	National Television System Commission
LH	luteinizing hormone	**NUM**	National Union of Mineworkers
LHRH	luteinizing-hormone-releasing hormone	**NUT**	National Union of Teachers
LIFFE	London International Financial Futures	**NVC**	non-verbal communication
	Exchange	**OAPEC**	Organization of Arab Petroleum
LISP	List Processing		Exporting Countries
LMS	London Missionary Society	**OAS**	Organisation de l'Armée Secrète (Secret
LPG	liquefied petroleum gas		Army Organization)
LSD	lysergic acid diethylamide	**OAS**	Organization of American States
LSI	large-scale integration	**OAU**	Organization of African Unity
LVO	Lieutenant of the Royal Victorian Order	**OB**	Order of the Bath
MAC	Multiplexed Analog Component	**OB**	outside broadcast
MAO	monoamine oxidase	**OBE**	Officer of the (Order of the) British
MATV	Master Antenna Television		Empire
MBE	Member of the (Order of the) British	**OCarm**	Order of the Brothers of the Blessed
	Empire		Virgin Mary of Mount Carmel
MC	Master of Ceremonies	**OCart**	Order of Carthusians
MCA	Monetary Compensation Amount	**OCR**	optical character recognition/reader
MCC	Marylebone Cricket Club	**OCSO**	Order of the Reformed Cistercians of the
MDMA	methylenedioxymethamphetamine		Strict Observance
ME	myalgic encephalomyelitis	**OD**	ordnance datum
MH	Medal of Honor	**ODC**	Order of Discalced Carmelites
MHD	magnetohydrodynamics	**ODECA**	Organización de Estados Centro-
MICR	magnetic ink character recognition		americanos (Organization of Central
MIGA	Multilateral Investment Guarantee		American States)
	Agency	**OECD**	Organization for Economic Co-
Mired	micro reciprocal degrees		operation and Development
MIRV	multiple independently targetted re-	**OEEC**	Organization for European Economic
	entry vehicle		Co-operation
MKSA	metre-kilogram-second-ampere	**OEM**	Original Equipment Manufacturer
MLR	minimum lending rate	**OFM**	Order of Friars Minor
mmf	magnetomotive force	**OFMCap**	Order of Friars Minor Capuchin
MMI	man-machine interaction	**OFMConv**	Order of Friars Minor Conventual
MOH	Medal of Honor	**OGPU**	Otdelenie Gosurdarstvenni
mpc	megaparsec		Politcheskoi Upravi (Special
MPS	marginal propensity to save		Government Political Administration)
MPTP	methylphenyltetrahydropyridine	**OM**	Order of Merit
MRA	Moral Rearmament	**OMCap**	Order of Friars Minor of St Francis
MS	multiple sclerosis; manuscript		Capuccinorum
MSC	Manpower Services Commission	**OOBE**	out-of-the-body experience
MSG	monosodium glutamate	**OP**	Order of Preachers
MSH	melanocyte-stimulating hormone	**OPEC**	Organization of Petroleum Exporting
MVD	Ministerstvo Vnutrennikh Del (Ministry		Countries
	for Internal Affairs)	**OSA**	Order of the Hermit Friars of St
MVO	Member of the Royal Victorian Order		Augustine
NAACP	National Association for the	**OSB**	Order of St Benedict
	Advancement of Colored People	**OSFC**	Order of Friars Minor of St Francis
NANC	non-adrenergic, non-cholinergic		Capuccinorum
NASA	National Aeronautics and Space	**OTC**	over-the-counter (stocks and shares,
	Administration		drugs)
NASDA	National Space Development Agency	**OTEC**	ocean thermal energy conversion
NATO	North Atlantic Treaty Organization	**OU**	Open University
NDE	near-death experience	**OXFAM**	Oxford Committee for Famine Relief
NEDO	National Economic Development Office	**PA**	personal assistant
NEP	New Economic Policy	**PAC**	Pan-African Congress
NF	National Front	**PAC**	political action committee
NFC	National Football Conference	**PAL**	phase alternation line
NGC	New General Catalogue	**PAYE**	pay as you earn
NGF	nerve growth factor	**pc**	parsec
NHL	National Hockey League	**PC**	personal computer
NHS	National Health Service	**PC**	Poor Clares
NIH	National Institutes of Health	**PCP**	phenylcyclohexylpiperidine

PDGF	platelet-derived growth factor	**SALT**	Strategic Arms Limitation Talks
PDR	precision depth recorder	**SAS**	Special Air Service
PEN	International Association of Poets, Playwrights, Editors, Essayists, and Novelists	**SAT**	scholastic aptitude test
		SBR	styrene butadiene rubber
		SCID	severe combined immuno-deficiency
PEP	personal equity plan	**SCLC**	Southern Christian Leadership Conference
PEP	Political and Economic Planning		
PF	Patriotic Front	**SDI**	selective dissemination of information
PGA	Professional Golfers' Association	**SDI**	strategic defense initiative
PH	Purple Heart	**SDP**	Social Democratic Party
PIN	personal identification number	**SDR**	special drawing rights
PK	psychokinesis	**SDS**	Students for a Democratic Society
PKU	phenylketonuria	**SDU**	Social Democratic Union
PLA	People's Liberation Army	**SEAQ**	Stock Exchange Automated Quotations
plc	public limited company	**SEATO**	South East Asia Treaty Organization
PLO	Palestine Liberation Organization	**SEC**	Securities and Exchange Commission
pm	post meridiem (after noon)	**SECAM**	Séquence Electronique Couleur avec Mémoire (Electronic Colour Sequence with Memory)
PM of F	Presidential Medal of Freedom		
PNLM	Palestine National Liberation Movement		
		SERPS	State Earnings Related Pension Scheme
POW	prisoner of war	**SHAEF**	Supreme Headquarters Allied Expeditionary Force
PPI	plan position indicator		
PR	proportional representation	**SHAPE**	Supreme Headquarters Allied Powers, Europe
PRO	Public Record Office		
PRO	public relations officer	**SHF**	super high frequency
PSBR	public sector borrowing requirement	**SI**	Système International (International System)
PTA	parent-teacher association		
PTO	please turn over	**SIB**	Securities and Investments Board
PTFE	polytetrafluoroethylene	**SIOP**	Single Integrated Operation Plan
PVA	polyvinyl acetate	**SJ**	Society of Jesus
PVC	polyvinyl chloride	**SLBN**	submarine-launched ballistic missile
PWA	Public Works Administration	**SLCM**	sea-launched cruise missile
PWR	pressurized-water reactor	**SLDP**	Social and Liberal Democratic Party
PYO	pick-your-own	**SLE**	systemic lupus erythematosus
QC	Queen's Counsel	**SLR**	single lens reflex
QCD	quantum chromodynamics	**SNCC**	Student Non-Violent Co-ordinating Committee
QED	quantum electrodynamics		
RA	Royal Academy	**SNP**	Scottish National Party
R&A	Royal & Ancient Golf Club of St Andrews	**SOCist**	Cistercians of Common Observance
RAAF	Royal Australian Air Force	**SOE**	Special Operations Executive
RADA	Royal Academy of Dramatic Art	**SONAR**	sound navigation and ranging
RAF	Royal Air Force	**SP**	starting price
RAM	random access memory	**SQUID**	superconducting quantum interference device
RAM	Royal Academy of Music		
RAN	Royal Australian Navy	**SR**	Socialist Revolutionaries
RDA	recommended daily allowance	**SRO**	self-regulatory organization
REM	rapid eye movement	**SS**	Schutzstaffel (Protective Squad)
RHA	Regional Health Authority	**SSR**	Soviet Socialist Republic
RISC	reduced interaction set computer	**SSSI**	Site of Special Scientific Interest
RKKA	Rabochekrest'yanshi Krasny (Red Army of Workers and Peasants)	**START**	Strategic Arms Reduction Talks
		STD	subscriber trunk dialling
RM	Royal Marines	**STD**	sexually transmitted disease
rms	root-mean-square	**STOL**	short take-off and landing
RN	Royal Navy	**SWAPO**	South West Africa People's Organization
RNA	ribonucleic acid	**SWS**	slow wave sleep
RNLI	Royal National Lifeboat Institution	**TAB**	Totalisator Agency Board
ROM	read-only memory	**TARDIS**	Time and Relative Dimensions in Space
RP	received pronunciation	**TASS**	Telegrafnoye Agentsvo Sovietskovo Soyuza (Telegraph Agency of the Soviet Union) (now **ITAR-Tass**)
RPI	retail price index		
RPM	resale price maintenance		
rpm	revolutions per minute	**TB**	tuberculosis
RRP	recommended retail price	**TCDD**	tetrachlorodibenzo-p-dioxin
RS	Royal Society	**TEFL**	Teaching English as a Foreign Language
RSI	repetitive strain injury		
RSPB	Royal Society for the Protection of Birds	**TESL**	Teaching English as a Second Language
RSPCA	Royal Society for the Prevention of Cruelty to Animals	**TESOL**	Teaching English to Speakers of Other Languages
RSVP	répondez s'il vous plaît (please reply)	**TGWU**	Transport and General Workers Union
RTG	radio-isotope thermo-electric generator	**TNT**	trinitrotoluene
		TSB	Trustee Savings Bank
RVO	Royal Victorian Order	**TT**	Tourist Trophy
SA	Sturm Abteilung (Storm Troopers)	**TTL**	through the lens
sae	stamped addressed envelope	**TUC**	Trades Union Congress
SALR	saturated adiabatic lapse rate	**TV**	television

Communication

Communication

TVA	Tennessee Valley Authority		USSR	Union of Soviet Socialist Republics
UAE	United Arab Emirates		UV	ultraviolet
UAP	United Australia Party		VA	Veterans Administration
UCAR	Union of Central African Republics		VAT	value-added tax
UCCA	Universities' Central Council on Admissions		VC	Victoria Cross
			VCR	video cassette recorder
UDA	Ulster Defence Association		VD	venereal disease
UDI	Unilateral Declaration of Independence		VDU	visual display unit
UEFA	Union of European Football Associations		VHF	very high frequency
			VHS	Video Home Service
UFO	unidentified flying object		VIP	vasoactive intestinal polypeptide
UHF	ultra high frequency		VIP	very important person
UHT	ultra high temperature		VLF	very low frequency
UK	United Kingdom		VLSI	very large scale interpretation
UN	United Nations		VOA	Voice of America
UNCTAD	United Nations Conference on Trade and Development		VSEPR	valence shell electron pair repulsion
			VSO	Voluntary Service Overseas
UNDC	United Nations Disarmament Commission		VTOL	vertical take-off and landing
			VTR	video tape recorder
UNDP	United Nations Development Programme		WAAC	Women's Auxiliary Army Corps
			WAAF	Women's Auxiliary Air Force
UNEP	United Nations Environment Programme		WAC	Women's Army Corps
			WAP	wireless application protocol
UNESCO	United Nations Educational, Scientific, and Cultural Organization		WASP	White Anglo-Saxon Protestant
			WBA	World Boxing Association
UNFAO	United Nations Food and Agriculture Organization		WBC	World Boxing Council
			WCC	World Council of Churches
UNGA	United Nations General Assembly		WEA	Workers' Educational Association
UNHCR	United Nations High Commission for Refugees		WFTU	World Federation of Trade Unions
			WHO	World Health Organization
UNHRC	United Nations Human Rights Commission		WI	(National Federation of) Women's Institutes
UNICEF	United Nations Children's Fund (formerly United Nations International Children's Emergency Fund)		WIPO	World Intellectual Property Organization
			WMO	World Meteorological Organization
UNIDO	United Nations Industrial Development Organization		WPA	Work Projects Administration
			WRAC	Women's Royal Army Corps
UNO	United Nations Organization		WRAF	Women's Royal Air Force
UNRWA	United Nations Relief and Works Agency for Palestine Refugees in the Near East		WRNS	Women's Royal Naval Service
			WRVS	Women's Royal Voluntary Service
UNSC	United Nations Security Council		WVS	Women's Voluntary Service
UNSG	United Nations Secretary General		WWF	World Wide Fund for Nature (formerly World Wildlife Fund)
UNTT	United Nations Trust Territory			
UPU	Universal Postal Union		YHA	Youth Hostels Association
USA	United States of America		YMCA	Young Men's Christian Association
USAF	United States Air Force		YMHA	Young Men's Hebrew Association
USCG	United States Coast Guard		YWCA	Young Women's Christian Association
USIS	United States Information Service		YWHA	Young Women's Hebrew Association

Alphabets

There is no agreement over the use of a single transliteration system in the case of Hebrew. The equivalents given below are widely used, but several other possibilities can be found.

Hebrew

Letter	Name	Transliteration
א	'aleph	'
ב	beth	b
ג	gimel	g
ד	daleth	d
ה	he	h
ו	waw	w
ז	zayin	z
ח	heth	h
ט	teth	t
י	yodh	y, j
כ ך	kaph	k
ל	lamedh	l
מ ם	mem	m
נ ן	nun	n
ס	samekh	s
ע	ayin	'
פ ף	pe	p, f
צ ץ	saddhe	s
ק	qoph	q
ר	resh	r
ש	shin	sh, ś
ש	sin	s
ת	taw	t

Greek

Letter	Name	Transliteration
A α	alpha	a
B β	beta	b
Γ γ	gamma	g
Δ δ	delta	d
E ε	epsilon	e
Z ζ	zeta	z
H η	eta	e, ē
Θ θ	theta	th
I ι	iota	i
K κ	kappa	k
Λ λ	lambda	l
M μ	mu	m
N ν	nu	n
Ξ ξ	xi	x
O o	omicron	o
Π π	pi	p
P ϱ	rho	r
Σ σ, ς	sigma	s
T τ	tau	t
Y υ	upsilon	y
Φ φ	phi	ph
X χ	chi	ch, kh
Ψ ψ	psi	ps
Ω ω	omega	o, ō

Nato Alphabet

Letter	Code name	Pronunciation
A	Alpha	AL-FAH
B	Bravo	BRAH-VOH
C	Charlie	CHAR-LEE
D	Delta	DELL-TAH
E	Echo	ECK-OH
F	Foxtrot	FOKS-TROT
G	Golf	GOLF
H	Hotel	HOH-TELL
I	India	IN-DEE-AH
J	Juliet	JEW-LEE-ETT
K	Kilo	KEY-LOH
L	Lima	LEE-MAH
M	Mike	MIKE
N	November	NO-VEM-BER
O	Oscar	OSS-CAH
P	Papa	PAH-PAH
Q	Quebec	KEY-BECK
R	Romeo	ROW-ME-OH
S	Sierra	SEE-AIR-RAH
T	Tango	TAN-GO
U	Uniform	YOU-NEE-FORM
V	Victor	VIK-TAH
W	Whiskey	WISS-KEY
X	Xray	ECKS-RAY
Y	Yankee	YANG-KEY
Z	Zulu	ZOO-LOO

Morse & Braille

Letters	Morse	Braille
A	.-	⠁
B	-...	⠃
C	-.-.	⠉
D	-..	⠙
E	.	⠑
F	..-.	⠋
G	--.	⠛
H	....	⠓
I	..	⠊
J	.---	⠚
K	-.-	⠅
L	.-..	⠇
M	--	⠍
N	-.	⠝
O	---	⠕
P	.--.	⠏
Q	--.-	⠟
R	.-.	⠗
S	...	⠎
T	-	⠞
U	..-	⠥
V	...-	⠧
W	.--	⠺
X	-..-	⠭
Y	-.--	⠽
Z	--..	⠵

Communication

Communication

Arabic

Letter	Name	Usual transliteration		Letter	Name	Usual transliteration
ا	'alif	'		ض	dad	d
ب	ba	b		ط	ta	t
ت	ta	t		ظ	za	z
ث	tha	th		ع	'ain	'
ج	jim	j		غ	ghain	gh
ح	ha	h		ف	fa	f
خ	kha	kh		ق	qaf	q
د	dal	d		ك	kaf	k
ذ	dha	th		ل	lam	l
ر	ra	r		م	mim	m
ز	za	z		ن	nun	n
س	sin	s		ه	ha	h
ش	shin	sh		و	waw	w
ص	sad	s		ي	ya	y

Cyrillic

Letter		Usual transliteration		Letter		Usual transliteration
А	а	a		П	п	p
Б	б	b		Р	р	r
В	в	v		С	с	s
Г	г	g		Т	т	t
Д	д	d		У	у	u
Е	е	e		Ф	ф	f
Ё	ё	ё		Х	х	h, kh, ch
Ж	ж	ž, zh		Ц	ц	c, ts
З	з	z		Ч	ч	č, ch
И	и	i		Ш	ш	š, sh
Й	й	j		Щ	щ	šč, shch
К	к	k		Ы	ы	y
Л	л	l		Ь	ь	'
М	м	m		Ъ	ъ	"
Н	н	n		Э	э	ė
О	о	o		Ю	ю	ju, yu
				Я	я	ja, ya

Runic

The runic alphabet, known as the *futhark*, was made up of 24 basic symbols, although there was considerable regional variation in the overall number of symbols and symbols shapes used. Around 4 000 runic inscriptions and a few manuscripts survive, principally made by the early Scandinavians and Anglo-Saxons.

ᚡ	f	ᚷ	g	ᛁ	ï	ᛗ	e
ᚢ	u	ᚹ	w	ᛢ	p	ᛗ	m
ᚦ	þ	ᚺ	h	ᚤ	x	ᛚ	l
ᛟ	o	ᚾ	n	ᚻ	s	ᚼ	ng
ᚱ	r	ᛁ	i	ᛏ	t	ᛟ	œ
ᚴ	k	ᛈ	j	ᛒ	b	ᛗ	d

British sign language: fingerspelling

US sign language: fingerspelling

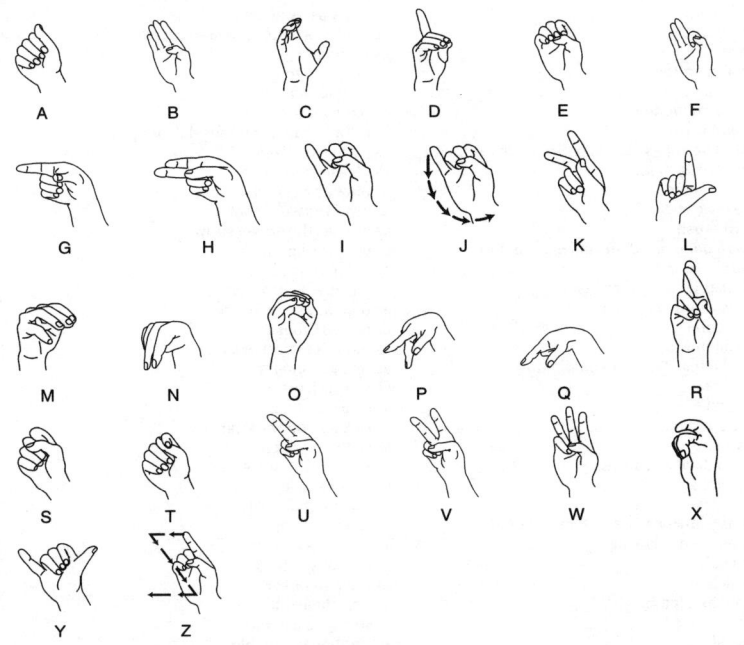

Communication

Semaphore

Semaphore was widely used in visual telegraphy, especially at sea, before the advent of electricity. Old-style railway signals are a simple form of semaphore, with a single arm having two positions to indicate 'stop' and 'go'.

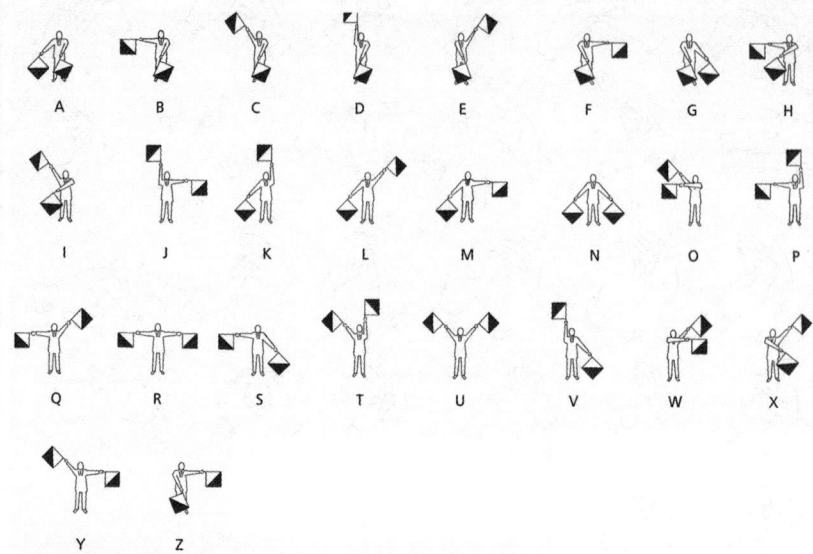

Some common similes

as bald as a coot
as black as ink *or* pitch
as blind as a bat
as blue as the sky
as bold as brass
as bright as a button
as brown as a berry
as calm as a millpond
as clean as a whistle
as clear as a bell *or* as crystal *or* (*ironically*) as mud
as cold as charity *or* ice
as cool as a cucumber
as cross as two sticks
as daft as a brush
as dead as a dodo *or* a door-nail *or* as mutton
as deaf as a post
as different as chalk and cheese
as drunk as a lord *or* a piper
as dry as a bone
as dull as ditchwater
as easy as falling off a log *or* as winking
as fair as a rose
as fit as a fiddle
as flat as a pancake
as free as a bird
as fresh as a daisy *or* as paint
as good as gold
as green as grass
as happy as a lark *or* as a sandboy *or* as Larry
as happy as the day is long
as hard as nails
as high as a kite
as innocent as a lamb
as keen as mustard
as large as life
as light as a feather
as light as down

as like as two peas in a pod *or* (*ironically*) chalk and cheese
as lively as a cricket
as mad as a hatter *or* a March hare
as merry as a grig
as near as a touch
as neat as ninepence
as often as not
as old as Adam *or* Methuselah *or* the hills
as plain as a pikestaff
as pleased as Punch
as poor as a church mouse
as proud as a peacock
as pure as the driven snow
as quick as lightning
as quiet as a mouse
as red as a beetroot
as regular as clockwork
as rich as Croesus
as right as a trivet *or* as rain
as ripe as a cherry
as safe as houses
as sharp as a razor
as sick as a dog *or* a parrot
as silent as the grave
as slippery as an eel
as sober as a judge
as soft as a baby's bottom
as sound as a bell
as sound as a roach
as steady as a rock
as stiff as a poker
as straight as a die
as strong as a horse
as stubborn as a mule
as sure as a gun *or* as eggs is eggs
as thick as a plank

as thick (=conspiratorial) as thieves
as thick (=stupid) as two short planks
as thin as a rake
as tough as leather *or* old boots
as ugly as sin

as warm as toast
as weak as a kitten
as wet as a drowned rat
as white as a sheet *or* as snow
as wise as an owl

-isms

Most of the words included here denote beliefs and practices. Some, however, denote aspects of discrimination; these include **ageism** and **sexism**.

ageism discrimination on the grounds of age

agnosticism belief in the impossibility of knowing God Greek *agnostos* unknown, unknowable

alcoholism addiction to alcohol

altruism unselfish concern for the welfare of others Latin *alteri huic* to this other

atavism reversion to an earlier type Latin *atavus* ancestor

atheism belief that God does not exist Greek *atheos* without god

barbarism state of being coarse or uncivilized Greek *barbaros* foreign, stammering

behaviourism basis of psychology in behaviour of people and animals

cannibalism practice of eating human flesh Spanish *Canibal* Carib

capitalism economic system based on the private ownership of wealth and resources

communism political and economic system based on collective ownership of wealth and resources

conservatism inclination to preserve the status quo

consumerism economic policy of encouraging spending and consuming

Cubism artistic movement using geometrical shapes to represent objects

cynicism belief in the worst in others Greek *kynikos* dog-like

defeatism belief in the inevitability of defeat

dogmatism tendency to present statements of opinion as if unquestionable Greek *dogma* opinion

dynamism state of having limitless energy and enthusiasm

egoism principle that self-interest is the basis of morality Latin *ego* I

elitism belief in the natural superiority of some people Latin *eligere* to elect

empiricism theory that knowledge can only be gained through experiment and observation Greek *empeiria* experience

environmentalism concern to protect the natural environment

escapism tendency to escape from unpleasant reality into fantasy

evangelism practice of trying to persuade someone to adopt a particular belief or cause Greek *evangelion* good news

exhibitionism tendency to behave so as to attract attention to oneself

existentialism philosophy emphasizing freedom of choice and personal responsibility for one's actions

Expressionism artistic movement emphasizing expression of emotions over representation of external reality

extremism adherence to fanatical or extreme opinions

fanaticism excessive enthusiasm for something Latin *fanaticus* filled with a god, frenzied

favouritism practice of giving unfair preference to a person or group

feminism advocacy of equal rights and opportunities for women

feudalism social system based on tenants' allegiance to a lord

functionalism theory that the intended use of something should determine its design

hedonism belief in the importance of pleasure above all else Greek *hedone* pleasure

heroism quality of showing great courage in one's actions

holism theory that any complex being or system is more than the sum of its parts Greek *holos* whole

humanism philosophy emphasizing human responsibility for moral behaviour

hypnotism practice of inducing a hypnotic state in others Greek *hypnos* sleep

idealism practice of living according to ideals

imperialism principle of extending control over other nations' territory Latin *imperium* sovereignty

Impressionism artistic movement emphasizing artists' impressions of nature

individualism belief in individual freedom and self-reliance

liberalism belief in tolerance of different opinions or attitudes

magnetism state of possessing magnetic attraction

mannerism excessive use of an individual artistic style

Marxism philosophy that political change is brought about by struggle between social classes

masochism derivation of pleasure from one's own pain or suffering named after Sacher-Masoch

materialism excessive interest in material possessions and financial success

monarchism support of the institution of monarchy

monetarism economic theory emphasizing the control of a country's money supply

mysticism practice of gaining direct communication with a deity through prayer and meditation Greek *mystes* initiate

narcissism excessive admiration for oneself or one's appearance

nationalism advocacy of national unity or independence

naturalism realistic and non-idealistic representation of objects

nihilism rejection of moral and religious principles Latin *nihil* nothing

objectivism tendency to emphasize what is objective

opportunism practice of taking advantage of opportunities regardless of principles

optimism tendency to expect the best possible outcome Latin *optimus* best

pacifism belief that violence and war are unjustified Latin *pax* peace, and *facere* to make

paganism belief in a religion which worships many gods Latin *paganus* peasant, civilian

pantheism doctrine that equates all natural forces and matter with god Greek *pas* all, *theos* god

parochialism practice of being narrow or provincial in outlook Latin *parochia* parish

paternalism practice of benevolent but over-protective management or government Latin *pater* father

patriotism devotion to one's country Greek *patriotes* compatriot

pessimism tendency to expect the worst possible

Communication

Communication

outcome Latin *pessimus* worst

plagiarism practice of stealing an idea from another's work and presenting it as one's own Latin *plagiarius* kidnapper

pluralism co-existence of several ethnic and religious groups in a society Latin *plus* more

Pointillism artistic movement using small dabs of unmixed colour to suggest shapes French *pointille* dot

polytheism belief in more than one god Greek *polys* many, *theos* god

pragmatism a practical, matter-of-fact approach to dealing with problems Greek *pragma* deed

professionalism practice of showing professional competence and conduct

racism *or* **racialism** discrimination on the grounds of ethnic origin

realism tendency to present things as they really are

regionalism devotion to or advocacy of one's own region

sadism derivation of pleasure from inflicting pain on others named after Marquis de Sade

Satanism belief in and worship of the devil

scepticism tendency to question widely-accepted beliefs Greek *skeptikos* thoughtful

sexism discrimination on the grounds of sex

socialism doctrine that a country's wealth belongs to the people as a whole

spiritualism practice of communicating with the spirits of the dead through a medium

stoicism tendency to accept misfortune or suffering without complaint Greek *Stoa Poikile* Painted Porch (where Zeno taught)

Surrealism artistic movement emphasizing use of images from the unconscious

symbolism use of symbols to express ideas or emotions

terrorism practice of using violence to achieve political ends

Thatcherism political system based on privatization and monetarism advocated by Margaret Thatcher

tokenism practice of doing something once or with minimum effort to appear to comply with a law or principle

tourism practice of travelling to and visiting places for pleasure and relaxation

vandalism practice of inflicting indiscriminate damage on others' property

vegetarianism practice of not eating meat or animal products

ventriloquism practice of making one's voice appear to come from another source Latin *ventri* belly, *loqui* to speak

voyeurism practice of watching private actions of others for pleasure or sexual gratification

Typefaces

The typefaces shown are modern versions of the main groups under which most typefaces may be classified. The dates indicating the introduction of each group are approximate.

Gothic

𝔄𝔅ℭ𝔇𝔈𝔉𝔊ℌ𝔍𝔍𝔎𝔏𝔐𝔑𝔒𝔓𝔔ℜ𝔖𝔗𝔘𝔙𝔚𝔛𝔜𝔷
abcdefghijklmnopqrstuvwxyz

Old English Text (c.1450)

Sans Serif

ABCDEFGHIJKLMNOPQRSTUVWXYZ
abcdefghijklmnopqrstuvwxyz

Univers (c.1816)

Venetian

ABCDEFGHIJKLMNOPQRSTUVWXYZ
abcdefghijklmnopqrstuvwxyz

Centaur (c.1470)

Egyptian

ABCDEFGHIJKLMNOPQRSTUVWXYZ
abcdefghijklmnopqrstuvwxyz

Rockwell (c.1830)

Old Face

ABCDEFGHIJKLMNOPQRSTUVWXYZ
abcdefghijklmnopqrstuvwxyz

Caslon Old Face (c.1495)

Old Style

ABCDEFGHIJKLMNOPQRSTUVWXYZ
abcdefghijklmnopqrstuvwxyz

Goudy Old Style (c.1850)

Transitional

ABCDEFGHIJKLMNOPQRSTUVWXYZ
abcdefghijklmnopqrstuvwxyz

Baskerville (c.1761)

Newspaper

ABCDEFGHIJKLMNOPQRSTUVWXYZ
abcdefghijklmnopqrstuvwxyz

Century Bold & Century Roman (c.1890)

Modern

ABCDEFGHIJKLMNOPQRSTUVWXYZ
abcdefghijklmnopqrstuvwxyz

Bodoni (c.1765)

Contemporary

ABCDEFGHIJKLMNOPQRSTUVWXYZ
abcdefghijklmnopqrstuvwxyz

Times New Roman (c.1932)

First name meanings in the UK and USA

The meanings of the most popular first names in the UK and USA are given below, along with a few other well-known names.

Name	Original meaning
Aaron	high mountain (*Hebrew*)
Adam	redness (*Hebrew*)
Alan	harmony (*Celtic*)
Albert	nobly bright (*Germanic*)
Alexander	defender of men (*Greek*)
Alexis	helper (*Greek*)
Alison	*French diminutive of* Alice; *of noble kind*
Amanda	fit to be loved (*Latin*)
Amy	loved (*French*)
Andrea	*female form of* Andrew
Andrew	manly (*Greek*)
Angela	messenger, angel (*Greek*)
Ann(e)	*English forms of* Hannah
Anthony	*Roman family name*
April	name of the month
Arthur	?bear, stone (*Celtic*)
Ashley	*Germanic place name*; ashwood
Austin	*English form of* Augustus; *venerated*
Barbara	strange, foreign (*Greek*)
Barry	spear, javelin (*Celtic*)
Beatrice	bringer of joy (*Latin*)
Benjamin	son of my right hand (*Hebrew*)
Bernard	bear + brave (*Germanic*)
Beth	*pet form of* Elizabeth
Betty	*pet form of* Elizabeth
Bill/Billy	*pet form of* William
Bob	*pet form of* Robert
Brandi	*variant of* Brandy, *from the common noun*
Brandon	*place name*; broom-covered hill (*Germanic*)
Brian	?hill (?*Celtic*)
Candice	*meaning unknown*
Carl	man, husbandman (*Germanic*)
Carol(e)	*forms of* Caroline, *Italian female form of* Charles
Catherine	pure (*Greek*)
Charles	man, husbandman (*Germanic*)
Christine	*French form of* Christina, *ultimately from* Christian; *anointed*
Christopher	carrier of Christ (*Greek*)
Claire	bright, shining (*Latin*)
Colin	*form of* Nicholas
Craig	rock (*Celtic*)
Crystal	*female use of the common noun*
Daniel	God is my judge (*Hebrew*)
Danielle	*female form of* Daniel
Darren	*Irish surname*
Darryl	*surname; uncertain origin*
David	beloved, friend (*Hebrew*)
Dawn	*female use of the common noun*
Dean	*surname*; valley *or* leader
Deborah	bee (*Hebrew*)
Dennis	of Dionysus (*Greek*), *the god of wine*
Derek	*form of* Theodoric; *ruler of the people* (*Germanic*)
Diane	*French form of* Diana; divine (*Latin*)
Donald	world mighty (*Gaelic*)
Donna	lady (*Latin*)
Doreen	*from* Dora, *a short form of* Dorothy; gift of God
Doris	woman from Doris (*Greek*)
Dorothy	gift of God (*Greek*)
Ebony	*female use of the common noun*
Edward	property guardian (*Germanic*)
Eileen	*Irish form of* ?Helen
Elizabeth	oath/perfection of God (*Hebrew*)
Emily	*Roman family name*

Name	Original meaning
Emma	all-embracing (*Germanic*)
Eric	ruler of all (*Norse*)
Erica	*female form of* Eric
Eugenie	*French form of* Eugene; well-born (*Greek*)
Frank	*pet form of* Francis; Frenchman
Frederick	peaceful ruler (*Germanic*)
Gail	*pet form of* Abigail; father rejoices (*Hebrew*)
Gareth	gentle (*Welsh*)
Gary	*US place name*
Gavin	*Scottish form of* Gawain; hawk + white (*Welsh*)
Gemma	gem (*Italian*)
Geoffrey	?peace (*Germanic*)
George	husbandman, farmer (*Greek*)
Graham	*Germanic place name*
Hannah	grace, favour (*Hebrew*)
Harold	army power/ruler (*Germanic*)
Harry	*pet form of* Henry; home ruler (*Germanic*)
Hayley	*English place name*; hay-meadow
Heather	*plant name*
Helen	bright/shining one (*Greek*)
Ian	*modern Scottish form of* John
Irene	peace (*Greek*)
Jacob	he seized the heel (*Hebrew*)
Jacqueline	*French female form of* Jacques (James)
James	*Latin form of* Jacob
Jane	*from Latin* Johanna, *female form of* John
Janet	*diminutive form of* Jane
Jasmine	flower name (*Persian*)
Jason	*form of* Joshua; Jehovah is salvation (*Hebrew*)
Jeffrey	*US spelling of* Geoffrey
Jean	*French form of* Johanna, *from* John
Jennifer	fair/white + yielding/smooth (*Celtic*)
Jeremy	*English form of* Jeremiah; Jehovah exalts (*Hebrew*)
Jessica	he beholds (*Hebrew*)
Joan	*contracted form of* Johanna, *from* John
Joanne	*French form of* Johanna, *from* John
John	Jehovah has been gracious (*Hebrew*)
Jonathan	Jehovah's gift (*Hebrew*)
Jordan	flowing down (*Hebrew*)
Joseph	Jehovah adds (*Hebrew*)
Joshua	Jehovah is gracious (*Hebrew*)
Joyce	?joyful (?*Latin*)
Julie	*French female form of Latin* Julius; descended from Jove
Karen	*Danish form of* Katarina (Catherine)
Katherine	*US spelling of* Catherine
Kathleen	*English form of Irish* Caitlin (*from* Catherine)
Kelly	*Irish surname*; warlike one
Kenneth	*English form of Gaelic*; fair one *or* fire-sprung
Kerry	*Irish place name*
Kevin	handsome at birth (*Irish*)
Kimberly	*South African place name*
Lakisha	La +?Aisha; woman (*Arabic*)
Latoya	La + *form of* Tonya (Antonia)
Laura	bay, laurel (*Latin*)
Lauren	*diminutive of* Laura
Lee	*Germanic place name*; wood, clearing
Leslie	*Scottish place name*
Lilian	lily (*Italian*)
Linda	serpent (symbol of wisdom) (*Germanic*)

Communication

Name	Original meaning	Name	Original meaning
Lindsay	*Scottish place name*	Ronald	counsel + power (*Germanic*)
Lisa	*pet form of* Elizabeth	Ruth	?vision of beauty (*Hebrew*)
Margaret	pearl (*Greek*)	Ryan	*Irish surname*
Marjorie	*from* Marguerite, *French form of* Margaret	Sally	*pet form of* Sarah
Mark	*English form of* Marcus, *from* Mars, *god of war*	Samantha	*female form of* Samuel; heard/name of God (*Hebrew*)
Martin	*from* Mars, *god of war* (*Latin*)	Sandra	*pet form of* Alexandra
Mary	*Greek form of* Miriam (*Hebrew*); *unknown meaning*	Sarah	princess (*Hebrew*)
		Scott	*surname*; from Scotland
Matthew	gift of the Lord (*Hebrew*)	Sharon	the plain (*Hebrew*)
Megan	*pet form of* Margaret	Shaun	*English spelling of Irish* Sean, *from* John
Melissa	bee (*Greek*)	Shirley	bright clearing (*Germanic*)
Michael	like the Lord (*Hebrew*)	Simon	*form of* Simeon; listening attentively (*Hebrew*)
Michelle	*English spelling of French* Michèle, *from* Michael	Stephanie	*French female form of* Stephen
Morgan	?sea + ?circle (*Welsh*)	Stephen	crown (*Greek*)
Nancy	*pet form of* Ann	Stuart	steward (*Germanic*)
Natalie	birthday of the Lord (*Latin*)	Susan	*short form of* Susannah; lily (*Hebrew*)
Neil	champion (*Irish*)	Teresa	woman of Theresia (*Greek*)
Nicholas	victory people (*Greek*)	Thomas	twin (*Hebrew*)
Nicola	*Italian female form of* Nicholas	Tiffany	manifestation of God (*Greek*)
Nicole	*French female form of* Nicholas	Timothy	honouring God (*Greek*)
Pamela	?all honey (*Greek*)	Trac(e)y	?*pet form of* Teresa
Patricia	noble (*Latin*)	Vera	faith (*Slavic*)
Paul	small (*Latin*)	Victoria	victory (*Latin*)
Pauline	*French female form of* Paul	Vincent	conquer (*Latin*)
Peter	stone, rock (*Greek*)	Virginia	maiden (*Latin*)
Philip	fond of horses (*Greek*)	Walter	ruling people (*Germanic*)
Rachel	ewe (*Hebrew*)	Wayne	*surname*; wagon-maker
Rebecca	?noose (*Hebrew*)	William	will + helmet (*Germanic*)
Richard	strong ruler (*Germanic*)	Zachary	Jehovah has remembered (*Hebrew*)
Robert	fame bright (*Germanic*)	Zoë	life (*Greek*)

Forms of address

In the fomulae given below, *F* stands for forename and *S* for surname.

- Very formal ceremonial styles for closing letters are now seldom used: 'Yours faithfully' is assumed below, unless otherwise indicated.
- Forms of spoken address are given only where a special style is followed.
- Holders of courtesy titles are addressed according to their rank, but without 'The', 'The Right Hon.', or 'The Most Hon.'.
- Ranks in the armed forces, and ecclesiastical and ambassadorial ranks, precede titles in the peerage, eg 'Colonel the Earl of ——' or 'The Rev the Marquess of ——'.
- Although the correct forms of address are given below for members of the Royal Family, it is more normal practice for letters to be addressed to their private secretary, equerry, or lady-in-waiting.
- More detailed information about forms of address is to be found in Debrett's *Correct Form* and Black's *Titles and Forms of Address*.

Ambassadors (foreign)
Address on envelope: 'His/Her Excellency the Ambassador of ——' or 'His/Her Excellency the —— Ambassador'. (The wife of an ambassador is not entitled to the style 'Her Excellency'.) *Begin*: 'Your Excellency'. (Within the letter, refer to 'Your Excellency' once, thereafter as 'you'.) *Close*: 'I have the honour to be, Sir/Madam (or according to rank), Your Excellency's obedient servant'. *Spoken address*: 'Your Excellency' at least once, and then 'Sir' or 'Madam' by name.

Archbishop (Anglican communion)
Address on envelope: 'The Most Reverend the Lord Archbishop of ——'. (The Archbishops of Canterbury and York are Privy Counsellors, and should be addressed as 'The Most Reverend and Right Hon. the Lord Archbishop of ——'.) *Begin*: 'Dear Archbishop' or 'My Lord Archbishop'. *Spoken address*: 'Your Grace'. *Begin an official speech*: 'My Lord Archbishop'.

Archbishop (Roman Catholic)
Address on envelope: 'His Grace the Archbishop of ——'. *Begin*: 'My Lord Archbishop'. *Close*: 'I remain, Your Grace, Yours faithfully' or 'Yours faithfully'. *Spoken address*: 'Your Grace'.

Archdeacon
Address on envelope: 'The Venerable the Archdeacon of ——'. *Begin*: 'Dear Archdeacon' or 'Venerable Sir'. *Spoken address*: 'Archdeacon'. *Begin an official speech*: 'Venerable Sir'.

Baron
Address on envelope: 'The Right Hon. the Lord ——'. *Begin*: 'My Lord'. *Spoken address*: 'My Lord'.

Baron's wife (Baroness)
Address on envelope: 'The Right Hon. the Lady [*S*——]'. *Begin*: 'Dear Lady'. *Spoken address*: 'Madam'.

Baroness (in her own right)
Address on envelope: either as for Baron's wife, or 'The Right Hon. the Baroness [S——]'. Otherwise, as for Baron's wife.

Baronet
Address on envelope: 'Sir [F——S——], Bt'. *Begin*: 'Dear Sir'. *Spoken address*: 'Sir [F——]'.

Baronet's wife
Address on envelope: 'Lady [S——]'. If she has the title 'Lady' by courtesy, 'Lady [F——S——]'. If she has the courtesy style 'The Hon.', this precedes 'Lady'. *Begin*: 'Dear Madam'. *Spoken address*: 'Madam'.

Bishop (Anglican communion)
Address on envelope: 'The Right Reverend the Lord Bishop of ——'. (The Bishop of London is a Privy Counsellor, so is addressed as 'The Right Rev and Right Hon. the Lord Bishop of London'. The Bishop of Meath is styled 'The Most Reverend'.) *Begin*: 'Dear Bishop' or 'My Lord'. *Spoken address*: 'Bishop'. *Begin an official speech*: 'My Lord'.

Bishop (Episcopal Church in Scotland)
Address on envelope: 'The Right Reverend [F——S——], Bishop of ——'. Otherwise as for a bishop of the Anglican communion. The bishop who holds the position of Primus is addressed as 'The Most Reverend the Primus'. *Begin*: 'Dear Primus'. *Spoken address*: 'Primus'.

Bishop (Roman Catholic)
Address on envelope: 'His Lordship the Bishop of ——' or 'The Right Reverend [F——S——], Bishop of ——'. In Ireland, 'The Most Reverend' is used instead of 'The Right Reverend'. If an auxiliary bishop, address as 'The Right Reverend [F——S——], Auxiliary Bishop of ——'. *Begin*: 'My Lord' or (more rarely) 'My Lord Bishop'. *Close*: 'I remain, My Lord' or (more rarely), 'My Lord Bishop, Yours faithfully', or simply 'Yours faithfully'. *Spoken address*: 'My Lord' or (more rarely) 'My Lord Bishop'.

Cabinet Minister ► Secretary of State

Canon (Anglican communion)
Address on envelope: 'The Reverend Canon [F——S——]'. *Begin*: 'Dear Canon' or 'Dear Canon [S——]'. *Spoken address*: 'Canon' or 'Canon [S——]'.

Canon (Roman Catholic)
Address on envelope: 'The Very Reverend Canon [F——S——]'. *Begin*: 'Very Reverend Sir'. *Spoken address*: 'Canon [S——]'.

Cardinal
Address on envelope: 'His eminence Cardinal [S——]'. If an archbishop, 'His Eminence the Cardinal Archbishop of ——'. *Begin*: 'Your Eminence' or (more rarely) 'My Lord Cardinal'. *Close*: 'I remain, Your Eminence (or 'My Lord Cardinal'), Yours faithfully'. *Spoken*: 'Your Eminence'.

Clergy (Anglican communion)
Address on envelope: 'The Reverend [F——S——]'. *Begin*: 'Dear Sir/Madam' or 'Dear Mr/Mrs [S——]'.

Clergy (Roman Catholic)
Address on envelope: 'The Reverend [F——S——]'. If a member of a religious order, the initials of the order should be added after the name. *Begin*: 'Dear Reverend Father'.

Clergy (Other churches)
Address on envelope: 'The Reverend [F——S——]'. *Begin*: 'Dear Sir/Madam' or 'Dear Mr/Mrs [S——]'.

Countess
Address on envelope: 'The Right Hon. the Countess of ——'. *Begin*: 'Dear Madam'. *Spoken address*: 'Madam'.

Dean (Anglican)
Address on envelope: 'The Very Reverend the Dean of ——'. *Begin* 'Dear Dean' or 'Very Reverend Sir/Madam'. *Spoken address*: 'Dean'. *Begin an official speech*: 'Very Reverend Sir/Madam'.

Doctor
Physicians, anaesthetists, pathologists and radiologists are addressed as 'Doctor'. Surgeons, whether they hold the degree of Doctor of Medicine or not, are known as 'Mr/Mrs'. In England and Wales, obstetricians and gynaecologists are addressed as 'Mr/Mrs', but in Scotland, Ireland and elsewhere as 'Doctor'. In addressing a letter to the holder of a doctorate, the initials DD, MD, etc are placed after the ordinary form of address, eg 'The Rev John Smith DD', the 'Rev Dr Smith' and 'Dr John Brown' are also used.

Dowager
Address on envelope: On the marriage of a peer or baronet, the widow of the previous holder of the title becomes 'Dowager' and is addressed 'The Right Hon. the Dowager Countess of ——', 'The Right Hon. the Dowager Lady ——', etc. If there is already a Dowager still living, she retains this title, the later widow being addressed 'The Most Hon. [F——], Marchioness of ——', 'The Right Hon. [F——], Lady ——', etc. However, many Dowagers prefer the style which includes their Christian names to that including the title Dowager. *Begin*, etc as for a peer's wife.

Duchess
Address on envelope: 'Her Grace the Duchess of ——'. *Begin*: 'Dear Madam'. *Spoken address*: 'Your Grace'. (For Royal Duchess ► **Princess**.)

Duke
Address on envelope: 'His Grace the Duke of ——'. *Begin*: 'My Lord Duke'. *Spoken address*: 'Your Grace'. (For Royal Duke ► **Prince**.)

Earl
Address on envelope: 'The Right Hon. the Earl of ——'. *Begin*: 'My Lord'. *Spoken address*: 'My Lord'. (For Earl's wife ► **Countess**.)

Governor of a colony or **Governor-General**
Address on envelope: 'His Excellency [ordinary designation], Governor(-General) of ——'. (The Governor-General of Canada has the rank of 'Right Honourable', which he retains for life.) The wife of a Governor-General is

Communication

styled 'Her Excellency' within the country her husband administers. *Begin*: according to rank. *Close*: 'I have the honour to be, Sir (or 'My Lord', if a peer), Your Excellency's obedient servant'. *Spoken address*: 'Your Excellency'.

Judge, High Court
Address on envelope: if a man, 'The Hon. Mr Justice [S——]'; if a woman, 'The Hon. Mrs Justice [S——]'. *Begin*: 'Dear Sir/Madam'; if on judicial matters, 'My Lord/Lady'. *Spoken address*: 'Sir/Madam'; only on the bench or when dealing with judicial matters should a High Court Judge be addressed as 'My Lord/Lady' or referred to as 'Your Lordship/Ladyship'.

Judge, Circuit
Address on envelope: 'His/Her Honour Judge [S——]'. If a Knight, 'His Honour Judge Sir [F——S——]'. *Begin*: 'Dear Sir/Madam'. *Spoken address*: 'Sir/Madam'; address as 'Your Honour' only when on the bench or dealing with judicial matters.

Justice of the Peace (England and Wales)
When on the bench, refer to and address as 'Your Worship'; otherwise according to rank. The letters 'JP' may be added after the person's name in addressing a letter, if desired.

Knight Bachelor
As Baronet, except that 'Bt' is omitted. Knight of the Bath, of St Michael and St George, etc. *Address on envelope*: 'Sir [F——S——]', with the initials 'GCB', 'KCB', etc added. *Begin*: 'Dear Sir'.

Knight's wife
As Baronet's wife, or according to rank.

Lady Mayoress
Address on envelope: 'The Lady Mayoress of ——'. *Begin*: 'My Lady Mayoress'. *Spoken address*: '(My) Lady Mayoress'.

Lord Mayor
Address on envelope: The Lord Mayors of London, York, Belfast, Cardiff, Dublin and also Melbourne, Sydney, Adelaide, Perth, Brisbane and Hobart are styled 'The Right Hon. the Lord Mayor of ——'. Other Lord Mayors are styled 'The Right Worshipful the Lord Mayor of ——'. *Begin*: 'My Lord Mayor', even if the holder of the office is a woman. *Spoken address*: '(My) Lord Mayor'.

Marchioness
Address on envelope: 'The Most Hon. the Marchioness of ——'. *Begin*: 'Dear Madam'. *Spoken address*: 'Madam'.

Marquess
Address on envelope: 'The Most Hon. the Marquess of ——'. *Begin*: 'My Lord'. *Spoken address*: 'My Lord'.

Mayor
Address on envelope: 'The Worshipful the Mayor of ——'; in the case of cities and certain towns, 'The Right Worshipful'. *Begin*: 'Mr Mayor'. *Spoken address*: 'Mr Mayor'.

Mayoress
Address on envelope: 'The Mayoress of ——'. *Begin*: 'Madam Mayoress' is traditional, but some now prefer 'Madam Mayor'. *Spoken address*: 'Mayoress' (or 'Madam Mayor').

Member of Parliament
Address on envelope: Add 'MP' to the usual form of address. *Begin*: according to rank.

Monsignor
Address on envelope: 'The Reverend Monsignor [F——S——]'. If a canon, 'The Very Reverend Monsignor (Canon) [F——S——]'. *Begin*: 'Reverend Sir'. *Spoken address*: 'Monsignor [S——]'.

Officers in the Armed Forces
Address on envelope: The professional rank is prefixed to any other rank, eg 'Admiral the Right Hon. the Earl of ——', 'Lieut.-Col. Sir [F——S——], KCB'. Officers below the rank of Rear-Admiral, and Marshal of the Royal Air Force, are entitled to 'RN' (or 'Royal Navy') and 'RAF' respecively after their name. Army officers of the rank of Colonel or below may follow their name with the name of their regiment or corps (which may be abbreviated). Officers in the women's services add 'WRNS', 'WRAF', 'WRAC'. *Begin*: according to social rank.

Officers (retired and former)
Address on envelope: Officers above the rank of Lieutenant (in the Royal Navy), Captain (in the Army) and Flight Lieutenant (in the Royal Air Force) may continue to use and be addressed by their armed forces rank after being placed on the retired list. The word 'retired' (or in an abbreviated form) should not normally be placed after the person's name. Former officers in the women's services do not normally continue to use their ranks.

Pope
Address on envelope: 'His Holiness, the Pope'. *Begin*: 'Your Holiness' or 'Most Holy Father'. *Close*: if a Roman Catholic, 'I have the honour to be your Holiness's most devoted and obedient child' (or 'most humble child'); if not Roman Catholic, 'I have the honour to be (or 'remain') Your Holiness's obedient servant'. *Spoken address*: 'Your Holiness'.

Prime Minister
Address on envelope: according to rank. The Prime Minister is a Privy Counsellor (see separate entry) and the letter should be addressed accordingly. *Begin*, etc according to rank.

Prince
Address on envelope: If a Duke, 'His Royal Highness the Duke of ——'; if not a Duke, 'His Royal Highness the Prince [F——]', if a child of the sovereign; otherwise 'His Royal Highness Prince [F——] of [Kent or Gloucester]'. *Begin*: 'Sir'. Refer to as 'Your Royal Highness'. *Close*: 'I have the honour to remain (or 'be'), Sir, Your Royal Highness's most humble and obedient servant'. *Spoken address*: 'Your Royal Highness' once, thereafter 'Sir'.

Princess
Address on envelope: If a Duchess, 'Her Royal Highness the Duchess of ——'; if not a Duchess, the daughter of a sovereign is addressed as 'Her Royal Highness the Princess [F——]', followed by any title she holds by marriage. 'The' is omitted in addressing a princess who is not the daughter of a sovereign. A Princess by marriage is

addressed 'HRH Princess [husband's F——] of ——'. *Begin*: 'Madam'. Refer to as 'Your Royal Highness'. *Close*: as for Prince, substituting 'Madam' for 'Sir'. *Spoken address*: 'Your Royal Highness' once, thereafter 'Ma'am'.

Privy Counsellor
Address on envelope: If a peer, 'The Right Hon. the Earl of ——, PC'; if not a peer, 'The Right Hon. [F——S——]', without the 'PC'. *Begin*, etc according to rank.

Professor
Address on envelope: 'Professor [F——S——]'; the styles 'Professor Lord [S——]' and 'Professor Sir [F——S——]' are often used, but are deprecated by some people. If the professor is in holy orders, 'The Reverend Professor'. *Begin*: 'Dear Sir/Madam', or according to rank. *Spoken address*: according to rank.

Queen
Address on envelope: 'Her Majesty the Queen'. *Begin*: 'Madam, with my humble duty'. Refer to as 'Your Majesty'. *Close*: 'I have the honour to remain (or 'be'), Madam, Your Majesty's most humble and obedient servant'. *Spoken address*: 'Your Majesty' once, thereafter 'Ma'am'. *Begin an official speech*: 'May it please Your Majesty'.

Rabbi
Address on envelope: 'Rabbi [initial and S——]' or, if a doctor, 'Rabbi Doctor [initial and S——]'. *Begin*: 'Dear Sir'. *Spoken address*: 'Rabbi [S——]' or '[Doctor S——]'.

Secretary of State
Address on envelope: 'The Right Hon. [F——S——], MP, Secretary of State for ——', or 'The Secretary of State for ——'. Otherwise according to rank.

Viscount
Address on envelope: 'The Right Hon. the Viscount ——'. *Begin*: 'My Lord'. *Spoken address*: 'My Lord'.

Viscountess
Address on envelope: 'The Right Hon. the Viscountess ——'. *Begin*: 'Dear Madam'. *Spoken address*: 'Madam'.

Computer languages

Name	Full name	Main use
Ada	—	Complex on-line real-time monitoring and control (eg military applications)
AED	Algol Extended for Design	Computer-aided design
ALGOL	Algorithmic Language	Concise expression of mathematical and logical processes and the control of these processes
APL	A Programming Language	Educational; mathematical problems particularly those concerned with multidimensional arrays
APT	Automatically Programmed Tools	Operate machine tools using numeric codes
BASIC	Beginners All-purpose Symbolic Instruction Code	Education, games
BCPL	B Combined Programming Language	Mathematical, scientific, systems programming
C	—	Operating systems (eg UNIX), business, scientific, games
C++	—	Operating systems, business, scientific, games
CHILL	—	Real-time language used for programming computer-based telecommunication systems and computer-controlled telephone exchanges
COBOL	Common Business Oriented Language	Business data processing
COGO	Co-ordinate Geometry	Solving coordinate geometry problems in civil engineering
COMAL	Common Algorithmic Language	Education
CORAL	Computer On-line Real-time Application Language	Military applications
FORTH	—	Astronomy, robotics, control applications
FORTRAN	Formula Translation	Mathematical, engineering, scientific
GPSS	General Purpose Systems Simulation	Simulation programs
HTML	Hypertext Mark-up Language	Web page construction
JAVA	—	Internet applications
LISP	List Processing	Linguistics, Artificial Intelligence, manipulation of mathematical and arithmetic logic
LOGO	—	Education, turtle graphics
ML	Meta Language	Dynamic programming
MO2	—	Parallel computations (derivative of Pascal)
OCCAM	—	Artificial Intelligence applications
Pascal	—	Education
PL1	Programming Language 1	Educational; commercial and scientific work
PL/M	Programming Language for Microcomputers	Educational; commercial and scientific work
PROLOG	Programming in Logic	Artificial Intelligence, expert systems
SGML	Standard Generalized Mark-up Language	Print applications
SIMULA	Simulation Language	Simulation programs
Smalltalk		Object-orientated language
SNOBOL	String Oriented Symbolic Language	Manipulation of textual data

Communication

Name	Full name	Main use
SQL	Structured Query Language	Database querying
XML	Extensible Mark-up Language	Web pages with multimedia content

Communication

Emoticons

Emoticons are combinations of keyboard characters that denote personal feelings or expressions, and are used particularly in e-mail. The following are some of the most commonly found examples:

:)	smile
:-)	another smile
:o)	another smile
;)	wink
: *	kiss
:-) x (-:	another kiss
:-I	grim
: (	unhappy
`:)	raising an eyebrow
: - o	shouting
: - b...	drooling
: - P	sticking out tongue
8 -)	wearing glasses
: o #)	man with a moustache
{}	hug
{*}	hug and a kiss
(_)? [_]?	tea or coffee
>^..^<	cat
< :3) ~	mouse
< ><	small fish
< (((><	large fish

Abbreviations and acronyms used in e-mail

AFK	Away from keyboard	IWALU	I will always love you
ATK	At the keyboard	JTLYK	Just to let you know
BAK	Back at keyboard	KIT	Keep in touch
BBL	Be back later	L8R	Later
BBS	Be back soon	LOL	Laughing out loud
BFN or B4N	Bye for now	LTNS	Long time no see
BRB	Be right back	NOMDB	Not over my dead body
BRT	Be right there	OIC	Oh, I see
BTW	By the way	OOO	Out of order
CYA	See ya	OTOH	On the other hand
CYAL8R	See you all later	POS	Parents over shoulder
DLTBBB	Don't let the bed bugs bite	ROE	Raising one eyebrow
F2F	Face to face	ROTFL	Rolling on the floor laughing
FCOL	For crying out loud	SI	Sarcasm intended
FYI	For your information	SWL	Screaming with laughter
FWIW	For what it's worth	SYS	See you soon
GFN	Gone for now	TAFN	That's all for now
GMTA	Great minds think alike	TRDF	Tears rolling down my face
GTGN	Got to go now	TTFN	Ta-ta for now
GTSY	Great to see you	TTYL	Talk to you later
HHOK	Ha, ha, only kidding	TTYT	Talk to you tomorrow
IASA	I am so annoyed	WB	Welcome back
IC	I see	WI	With irony
IMHO	In my humble opinion	WTG	Way to go
IMO	In my opinion	YR	Yeah, right

News agencies

Press name	Full name	Date founded	Location
AAP	Australian Associated Press	1935	Sydney
AASA	Agence Arabe Syrienne d'Information	1966	Damascus
ADN	Allgemeiner Deutscher Nachrichtendienst	1946	Berlin
AE	Agence Europe	1952	Brussels
AFP	Agence France-Presse	1944	Paris
AIO	Agencia Informativa Orbe de Chile	1952	Santiago
AIP	Agence Ivoirienne de Presse	1961	Abidjan
ALD	Agencia Los Diarios	1910	Buenos Aires
ALI	Agencia Lusa de Informacao	1987	Lisbon
AM	Agencia Meridional	1931	Rio de Janeiro
ANA	Athenagence	1896	Athens
ANP	Algemeen Nederlands Persbureau	1934	The Hague
ANSA	Agenzia Nazionale Stampa Associate	1945	Rome
ANTARA	Indonesian National News Agency	1937	Jakarta
AN	Agencia Nacional	1946	Brasilia
APA	Austria Presse-Agentur	1946	Vienna
APP	Agence Parisienne de Presse	1949	Paris
APP	Associated Press of Pakistan	1948	Islamabad
APS	Agence de Presse Senegalaise	1959	Dakar
APS	Algeria Presse Service	1962	Algiers
AP	Associated Press	1848	New York
ATA	Albanian Telegraphic Agency	1945	Tirana
AUP	Australian United Press	1928	Melbourne
BELGA	Agence Belga	1920	Brussels
BERNAMA	Malaysia National News Agency	1967	Kuala Lumpur
BOPA	Botswana Press Agency	1981	Gaborone
BTA	Bulgarska Telegrafitscheka Agentzia	1898	Sofia
CANA	Caribbean News Agency	1976	Bridgetown
CIP	Centre d'Information de Presse	1946	Brussels
CNA	Central News Agency	1924	Taipei
CNA	Cyprus News Agency	1976	Nicosia
CNS	China News Service	1952	Beijing
COLPRENSA	Colprensa	1980	Bogota
CP	Canadian Press	1917	Toronto
CTK	Ceskoslovenska Tiskova Kancelar	1918	Prague
DPA	Deutsche Presse-Agentur	1949	Hamburg
EFE	Agencia EFE	1939	Madrid
ENA	Eastern News Agency	1970	Dhaka
EXTEL	Exchange and Telegraph Company	1872	London
FIDES	Agenzia Internazionale Fides	1926	Vatican City
GNA	Agence Guinéenne de Presse	1981	Conakry
GNA	Ghana News Agency	1957	Accra
GNA	Guyana News Agency	1981	Georgetown
HHA	Hurriyet Haber Ajasi	1963	Istanbul
IC	Inforpress Centroamericana	1972	Guatemala
INA	Iraqi News Agency	1959	Baghdad
IPS	Inter Press Service	1964	Rome
IRNA	Islamic Republic News Agency	1936	Tehran
ITAR-Tass	Information and Telegraphic Agency of Russia	1992/1904	Moscow
JAMPRESS	Jampress	1984	Kingston
JANA	Jamahiriya News Agency	—	Tripoli
JIJI	Jiji Tsushin-Sha	1945	Tokyo
JTA	Jewish Telegraphic Agency	1919	Jerusalem
KCNA	Korean Central News Agency	1946	Pyongyang
KNA	Kenya News Agency	1963	Nairobi
KPL	Khao San Pathet Lao	1968	Vientiane
KUNA	Kuwait News Agency	1976	Kuwait City
KYODO	Kyodo Tsushin	1945	Tokyo
LAI	Logos Agencia de Informacion	1929	Madrid
MENA	Middle East News Agency	1955	Cairo
MTI	Magyar Tavariti Iroda	1880	Budapest
NAB	News Agency of Burma	1963	Rangoon
NAEWOE	Naewoe Press	1974	Seoul
NAN	News Agency of Nigeria	1978	Lagos
NA	Noticias Argentinas	1973	Buenos Aires
NOTIMEX	Noticias Mexicanas	1968	Mexico City
NOVOSTI	Agentstvo Pechati Novosti	1961	Moscow

Communication

Communication

Press name	Full name	Date founded	Location
NPS	Norsk Presse Service	1960	Oslo
NTB	Norsk Telegrambyra	1867	Oslo
NZPA	New Zealand Press Agency	1879	Wellington
OPA	Orbis Press Agency	1977	Prague
OTTFNB	Oy Suomen Tietoimisto Notisbyran Ab	1887	Helsinki
PANA	Pan-African News Agency	1979	Dakar
PAP	Polska Agencja Prasowa	1944	Warsaw
PA	Press Association	1868	London
PETRA	Jordan News Agency	1965	Amman
PNA	Philippines News Agency	1973	Manila
PPI	Pakistan Press International	1959	Karachi
PRELA	Prensa Latina	1959	Havana
PS	Presse Services	1929	Paris
PTI	Press Trust of India	1949	Bombay (now Mumbai)
RB	Ritzaus Bureau	1866	Copenhagen
REUTERS	Reuters	1851	London
ROMPRESS	Romanian News Agency	1949	Bucharest
SAPA	South African Press Association	1938	Johannesburg
SDA	Schweizerische Depeschenagentur	1894	Berne
SIP	Svensk-Internationella Pressbyran	1927	Stockholm
SLENA	Sierre Leone News Agency	1980	Freetown
SOFIAPRES	Sofia Press Agency	1967	Sofia
SOPAC-NEWS	South Pacific News Service	1948	Wellington
SPA	Saudi Press Agency	1970	Riyadh
TANJUG	Novinska Agencija Tanjug	1943	Belgrade
TAP	Tunis Afrique Presse	1961	Tunis
TT	Tidningarnes Telegrambyra	1921	Stockholm
UNI	United News of India	1961	New Delhi
UPI	United Press International	1958	New York
UPP	United Press of Pakistan	1949	Karachi
XINHUA	Xinhua	1937	Beijing
YONHAP	Yonhap (United) Press Agency	1980	Seoul
ZIANA	Zimbabwe Inter-Africa News Agency	1981	Harare

National newspapers — Europe

Name	Location	Circulation[1]	Date founded
ABC	Madrid	350 000	1905
Algemeen Dagblad	Rotterdam	415 800	1946
Apogevmatini	Athens	67 300	1956
Avriani	Athens	115 000	1980
B.T.	Copenhagen	175 600	1916
Berliner Zeitung	Berlin	230 600	1877
Berlingske Tidende	Copenhagen	155 400	1749
Bild am Sonntag (s)	Hamburg	2 639 000	1956
Bild Zeitung	Hamburg	4 643 900	1952
Blick	Zürich	335 100	1959
Correio do Manha	Lisbon	90 000	1979
Corriere della Sera	Milan	720 200	1876
Dagbladet	Oslo	228 000	1869
De Standaard/Het Nieuwsblad/De Gentenaar	Brussels	331 000	n/a
De Telegraaf	Amsterdam	743 000	1893
De Volkskrant	Amsterdam	361 200	1919
Diario de Noticias	Lisbon	41 900	1864
Diario Popular	Lisbon	29 200	1942
Die Welt	Bonn	214 700	1946
Die Zeit (weekly)	Hamburg	494 100	1946
Ekstra Bladet	Copenhagen	190 600	1904
El Pais	Madrid	412 300	1976
El Periodico	Barcelona	215 600	1978
Ethnos	Athens	58 800	1981
Evening Herald	Dublin	99 200	1891
Evening Press	Dublin	52 600	1954
Expressen	Stockholm	566 600	1944
France-Dimanche (s)	Paris	721 000	n/a
France-Soir	Paris	424 000	1944
Frankfurter Allgemeine Zeitung	Frankfurt	360 000	1949
Gazeta Wyborcza	Warsaw	500 000	n/a
Gazet Van Antwerpen	Antwerp	170 000	1891

Name	Location	Circulation[1]	Date founded
Helsingin Sanomat	Helsinki	463 500	1889
Het Laatste Nieuws	Brussels	306 800	1888
Il Giornale	Milan	238 800	1974
Il Giorno	Milan	255 400	1965
Il Messaggero	Rome	426 100	1878
Il Sole 24 Ore	Milan	340 000	1865
International Herald Tribune	Paris	190 700	1887
Irish Independent	Dublin	147 100	1905
Irish Times	Dublin	95 300	1859
La Libre Belgique	Brussels	82 800	1884
La Dernière Heure	Brussels	93 400	1906
La Lanterne	Brussels	132 800	1944
La Repubblica	Rome	620 000	1976
La Stampa	Turin	420 600	1867
La Vanguardia	Barcelona	208 000	1881
La Voix du Nord	Lille	400 000	1944
Le Figaro	Paris	424 000	1828
Le Monde	Paris	379 100	1944
Le Parisien Libère	Paris	339 300	1944
Les Echos	Paris	121 000	1908
Le Soir	Brussels	148 900	1887
L'Humanité	Paris	117 000	1904
L'Humanité Dimanche (s)	Paris	360 000	1946
Libération	Paris	171 100	1973
Luxemburger Wort/La Voix du Luxembourg	Luxembourg	82 800	1848
Népszabadság	Budapest	320 000	1942
Neue Kronenzeitung	Vienna	1 047 800	n/a
Ouest France	Rennes	790 000	1944
Politiken	Copenhagen	150 300	1884
Rude Pravo	Prague	400 000	1920
Süddeutsche Zeitung	Munich	405 400	1945
Sunday Independent (s)	Dublin	276 200	1905
Sunday Press (s)	Dublin	154 100	1949
Sunday World (s)	Dublin	232 100	1973
Täglich Alles	Vienna	542 000	1992
Ta Nea	Athens	135 000	1944
Vers L'Avenir	Namur	119 600	1918
Welt am Sonntag (s)	Hamburg	394 400	n/a
Ya	Madrid	380 000	1935

(s) published on Sundays only

[1] 1997 figures (rounded to nearest 100).

National newspapers — UK

Name	Location	Circulation[1]	Date founded
Daily Express	London	947 000	1900
Daily Mail	London	2 467 000	1896
Daily Mirror	London	2 042 000	1903
Daily Record	Glasgow	518 000	1895
Daily Star	London	843 000	1978
Daily Star Sunday(s)	London	464 000	2002
Daily Telegraph	London	928 000	1855
Financial Times	London	452 000	1880
The Guardian	London	409 000	1821
The Independent on Sunday (s)	London	221 000	1990
The Independent	London	222 000	1986
The Mail on Sunday (s)	London	2 385 000	1982
News of the World (s)	London	3 929 000	1843
Observer (s)	London	474 000	1791
The People (s)	London	1 142 000	1881
Scotland on Sunday (s)	Edinburgh	87 000	1988
Sunday Mail (s)	Glasgow	633 000	1914
Sunday Sport (s)	Manchester	187 000	1986
The Business (s)	London	90 000	1997
The Scotsman	Edinburgh	74 000	1817
The Sun	London	3 516 000	1964
The Sunday Express (s)	London	947 000	1918
The Sunday Mirror (s)	London	1 692 000	1963
The Sunday Telegraph (s)	London	742 000	1961

Communication

| The SundayTimes (s) | London | 1 422 000 | 1822 |
| TheTimes | London | 671 000 | 1785 |

(s) published on Sundays only

[1] February 2003 figures (rounded to nearest 1000).

Major newspapers — USA

Includes national newspapers and local newspapers having an all-day, morning, or evening circulation of 250 000 or more.

Name	Location	Circulation[1]	Date founded
Arizona Republic	Phoenix, Ariz	482 300	1890
Atlanta Constitution	Atlanta, Ga	433 100	1868
Baltimore Sun	Baltimore, Md	328 300	1837
Boston Globe	Boston, Mass	477 100	1872
Boston Herald	Boston, Mass	265 700	1892
Buffalo News	Buffalo, NY	316 300	1880
Chicago Sun-Times	Chicago, Ill	482 200	1948
ChicagoTribune	Chicago, Ill	674 600	1847
Cleveland Plain Dealer	Cleveland, Ohio	379 000	1842
Columbus Dispatch	Columbus, Ohio	252 700	1871
Dallas Morning News	Dallas, Texas	496 200	1885
Denver Post	Denver, Colo	413 700	1892
Denver Rocky Mountain News	Denver, Colo	446 500	1859
Detroit Free Press	Detroit, Mich	603 400	1831
Detroit News	Detroit, Mich	361 200	1873
ForthWorth Star-Telegram	Fort Worth, Texas	267 700	1906
Houston Chronicle	Houston, Texas	553 500	1901
Indianapolis Star	Indianapolis, Ind	267 600	1903
Kansas City Star	Kansas City, Mo	275 700	1880
Los AngelesTimes	Los Angeles, Cal	1 153 700	1881
Miami Herald	Miami, Fla	443 600	1910
Milwaukee Sentinel	Milwaukee, Wisc	279 200	1837
Minneapolis StarTribune	Minneapolis, Minn	406 400	1867
New OrleansTimes-Picayune	New Orleans, La	276 800	1837
NewYork Daily News	NewYork, NY	730 500	1919
NewYork Post	NewYork, NY	436 500	1801
NewYorkTimes[2]	NewYork, NY	1 149 600	1851
Newark Star-Ledger	Newark, NJ	406 600	1832
Newsday	Melville, NY	575 600	1940
Orange County Register	Santa Ana, Cal	368 500	1905
Orlando Sentinel	Orlando, Fla	269 500	1876
Philadelphia Inquirer	Washington, DC	404 900	1829
Portland Oregonian	Portland, Ore	358 800	1850
Sacramento Bee	Sacramento, Cal	296 600	1857
San Diego Union	San Diego, Cal	381 300	1868
San Francisco Chronicle	San Francisco, Cal	566 600	1865
San Jose Mercury News	San Jose, Cal	289 500	1851
SeattleTimes	Seattle, Wash	403 900	1886
St Louis Post-Dispatch	St Louis, Mo	309 000	1878
St PetersburgTimes	St Petersburg, Fla	343 700	1884
Sun-Sentinel	Fort Lauderdale, Fla	275 000	1910
TampaTribune	Tampa, Fla	261 500	1893
USAToday[2]	Arlington, Va	1 757 700	1982
Wall Street Journal[2]	NewYork, NY	1 812 600	1889
Washington Post	Washington, DC	812 600	1877

[1] March 2000 figures (rounded to nearest 100).

[2] National newspapers.

Symbols in general use

&,	ampersand (*and*)
&c.	et cetera
@	at; per (in costs)
×	by (measuring dimensions, eg 3 x 4)
£	pound
$	dollar (also peso, escudo, etc in certain countries)
¢	cent (also centavo, etc in certain countries)
©	copyright
®	registered
¶	new paragraph
§	new section
"	ditto
*	born (in genealogy)
†	died
*	hypothetical or unacceptable form (in linguistics)
☠	poison; danger
♂,□	male
♀,○	female
✠	bishop's name follows
☏	telephone number follows

⌒	this way
✂ ✂···	cut here

In astronomy

●	new moon
☽	moon, first quarter
○	full moon
☾	moon, last quarter

In meteorology

▲▲▲	cold front
⌒⌒⌒	warm front
⌒▼▲▼	stationary front
▲⌒▲⌒	occluded front

In cards

♥	hearts
♦	diamonds
♠	spades
♣	clubs

Clothes care symbols

⊠	Do not iron
⟁	Can be ironed with *cool* iron (up to 110°C)
⟁	Can be ironed with *warm* iron (up to 150°C)
⟁	Can be ironed with *hot* iron (up to 200°C)
⊠	Hand wash only
⬜60	Can be washed in a washing machine. The number shows the most effective washing temperature (in °C)
⬜60	Reduced (medium) washing conditions
⬜60	Much reduced (minimum) washing conditions (for wool products)
⊠	Do not wash
◉	Can be tumble dried (one dot within the circle means a low temperature setting; two dots for higher temperatures)

⊠	Do not tumble dry
⊗	Do not dry clean
Ⓐ	Dry cleanable (letter indicates which solvents can be used) A: all solvents Dry cleanable
Ⓕ	F: white spirit and solvent 11 can be used Dry cleanable
Ⓟ	P: perchloroethylene (tetrachloroethylene), white spirit, solvent 113 and solvent 11 can be used
Ⓟ	Dry cleanable, if special care taken
△Cl	Chlorine bleach may be used with care
⧄	Do not use chlorine bleach

Road signs

UK road signs
■ *Instruction signs*

Entry to
20 mph zone

End of
20 mph zone

School
crossing patrol

Maximum
speed

National speed
limit applies

Give way to traffic
on major road

No vehicles except
bicycles being pushed

No entry for
vehicular traffic

Give priority to vehicles
from opposite direction

No overtaking

No motor vehicles

No buses
(over 8 passenger seats)

No cycling

No towed caravans

No vehicle or
combination of
vehicles over length
shown

No vehicles over
height shown

No vehicles over
width shown

No vehicles over
maximum gross
weight shown
(in tonnes)

No waiting

No stopping
(Clearway)

Parking restricted to
permit holders

No stopping during
period indicated
except for buses

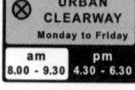

No stopping during
times shown except for
as long as necessary
to set down or pick up
passengers

■ *Warning signs*

Distance to 'STOP' line ahead

Distance to 'GIVE WAY' line ahead

Sharp deviation of route to left (or right if chevrons reversed)

Plate below some signs

Double bend first to left (symbol may be reversed)

Crossroads

Junction on bend ahead

T-junction

Staggered junction

Bend to right (or left if symbol reversed)

The priority through route is indicated by the broader line.

Roundabout

Uneven road

Dual carriageway ends

Road narrows on right (left if symbol reversed)

Road narrows on both sides

Two-way traffic crosses one-way road

Two-way traffic straight ahead

Traffic signals

Traffic signals not in use

Slippery road

Steep hill downwards

Steep hill upwards

Communication

Communication

US road signs
■ *Instruction signs*

Stop

Do not enter

Yield

Wrong way

No left turn

No U-turn

No parking any time

■ *Warning signs*

Crossroads

Road enters
from right

Two-way traffic

Divided highway

Bump

Stop ahead

Slippery when wet

Stop ahead

■ *Information signs*

Hospital

Telephone

Information

Camping

Communication

European road signs

■ *Austria*

Diversion

Tram turns at
yellow or red

Federal road
with priority

Federal road
without priority

U-turn
compulsory

Street lights
not on all night

Buses only

■ *Belgium*

You may pass
to the right or left

No parking from
1st to 15th of month

No parking from
16th to end of month

Difficult section of road

■ *Denmark*

Sight-seeing

Pass either side

Traffic merges

Compulsory
slow lane

Recommended
speed in a bend

■ *France*

Keep well over
to the right

Diversion or
relief route

Give way
to traffic

Traffic on the
roundabout has priority

"Priority road"
sign

"End of priority"
sign

Itinéraire Bis (Bison Futé)
Alternative (Holiday) routes

■ *Germany*

Diversion

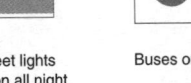

Tram or
bus stop

Autobahn number

Road number

Recommended
speed limit

Emergency diversion
for motorway traffic

■ *Italy*

Track for
motorcycles

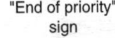

Snow chains
mandatory

Alternate
one-way
priority

Communication

■ *Netherlands*

Cycle track

Danger–trams crossing

2 hrs maximum (disc obligatory)

Built-up area

End of Built-up area

Parking prohibited

Stopping prohibited

■ *Norway*

Tunnel

Parking prohibited (upper panel) Allowed (lower)

Parking 2 hrs from 08.00–18.00 hrs (16.00 hrs Sat.)

Parking 2 hrs from 08.00–17.00 hrs

■ *Spain*

Recommended maximum speed

Turning permitted

Tourist accommodation

Compulsory lane for motorcycles

■ *Sweden*

Tunnel

Slow lane

Meeting point (narrow roads)

■ *Switzerland*

Postal vehicles have priority

Parking disc compulsory

Motorway

Semi-motorway

Tunnel (lights compulsory)

Flashing red light (level crossing)

Alternately flashing lights (level crossing)

Car index marks — UK

Prior to September 2001:

AA	Bournemouth	CN	Newcastle upon Tyne	FC	Oxford
AB	Worcester	CO	Exeter	FD	Dudley
AC	Coventry	CP	Leeds	FE	Lincoln
AD	Gloucester	CR	Portsmouth	FF	Bangor
AE	Bristol	CS	Glasgow	FG	Brighton
AF	Truro	CT	Lincoln	FH	Gloucester
AG	Beverley	CU	Newcastle upon Tyne	FJ	Exeter
AH	Norwich	CV	Truro	FK	Dudley
AJ	Middlesbrough	CW	Preston	FL	Peterborough
AK	Sheffield	CX	Leeds	FM	Chester
AL	Nottingham	CY	Swansea	FN	Maidstone
AM	Swindon	CZ	Belfast	FO	Gloucester
AN	Reading	DA	Birmingham	FP	Leicester
AO	Carlisle	DB	Manchester	FR	Preston
AP	Brighton	DC	Middlesbrough	FS	Edinburgh
AR	Chelmsford	DD	Gloucester	FT	Newcastle upon Tyne
AS	Inverness	DE	Swansea	FU	Lincoln
AT	Beverley	DF–DG	Gloucester	FV	Preston
AU	Nottingham	DH	Dudley	FW	Lincoln
AV	Peterborough	DJ	Liverpool	FX	Bournemouth
AW	Shrewsbury	DK	Manchester	FY	Liverpool
AX	Cardiff	DL	Portsmouth	FZ	Belfast
AY	Leicester	DM	Chester	GA–GB	Glasgow
AZ	Belfast	DN	Leeds	GC	Wimbledon
BA	Manchester	DO	Lincoln	GD–GE	Glasgow
BB	Newcastle upon Tyne	DP	Reading	GF	Wimbledon
BC	Leicester	DR	Exeter	GG	Glasgow
BD	Northampton	DS	Glasgow	GH	Wimbledon
BE	Lincoln	DT	Sheffield	GJ–GK	Wimbledon
BF	Stoke-on-Trent	DU	Coventry	GL	Truro
BG	Liverpool	DV	Exeter	GM	Reading
BH	Luton	DW	Cardiff	GN–GP	Wimbledon
BJ	Ipswich	DX	Ipswich	GR	Newcastle upon Tyne
BK	Portsmouth	DY	Brighton	GS	Luton
BL	Reading	DZ	Ballymena	GT	Wimbledon
BM	Luton	EA	Dudley	GU	Sidcup
BN	Manchester	EB	Peterborough	GV	Ipswich
BO	Cardiff	EC	Preston	GW–GY	Sidcup
BP	Portsmouth	ED	Liverpool	GZ	Belfast
BR	Newcastle upon Tyne	EE	Lincoln	HA	Dudley
BS	Inverness	EF	Middlesbrough	HB	Cardiff
BT	Leeds	EG	Peterborough	HC	Brighton
BU	Manchester	EH	Stoke-on-Trent	HD	Leeds
BV	Preston	EJ	Swansea	HE	Sheffield
BW	Oxford	EK	Liverpool	HF	Liverpool
BX	Swansea	EL	Bournemouth	HG	Preston
BY	Stanmore	EM	Liverpool	HH	Carlisle
BZ	Downpatrick	EN	Manchester	HJ–HK	Chelmsford
CA	Chester	EO	Preston	HL	Sheffield
CB	Manchester	EP	Swansea	HM	Wimbledon
CC	Bangor	ER	Peterborough	HN	Middlesbrough
CD	Brighton	ES	Dundee	HO	Bournemouth
CE	Peterborough	ET	Sheffield	HP	Coventry
CF	Reading	EU	Bristol	HR	Swindon
CG	Bournemouth	EV	Chelmsford	HS	Glasgow
CH	Nottingham	EW	Peterborough	HT–HU	Bristol
CJ	Gloucester	EX	Norwich	HV	Wimbledon
CK	Preston	EY	Bangor	HW	Bristol
CL	Norwich	EZ	Belfast	HX	Wimbledon
CM	Liverpool	FA	Stoke-on-Trent	HY	Bristol
		FB	Bristol	HZ	Omagh
				IA	Ballymena

Communication

IB	Armagh	NA–NF	Manchester	RV	Portsmouth
IJ	Downpatrick	NG	Norwich	RW	Coventry
IL	Enniskillen	NH	Northampton	RX	Reading
IW	Coleraine	NJ	Brighton	RY	Leicester
JA	Manchester	NK	Luton	RZ	Ballymena
JB	Reading	NL	Newcastle upon Tyne	SA	Aberdeen
JC	Bangor	NM	Luton	SB	Glasgow
JD	Wimbledon	NN	Nottingham	SC	Edinburgh
JE	Peterborough	NO	Chelmsford	SCY	Truro (Isles of Scilly)
JF	Leicester	NP	Worcester	SD	Glasgow
JG	Maidstone	NR	Leicester	SE	Aberdeen
JH	Reading	NS	Glasgow	SF–SH	Edinburgh
JI	Omagh	NT	Shrewsbury	SJ	Glasgow
JJ	Maidstone	NU	Nottingham	SK	Inverness
JK	Brighton	NV	Northampton	SL	Dundee
JL	Lincoln	NW	Leeds	SM	Carlisle
JM	Reading	NX	Dudley	SN	Dundee
JN	Chelmsford	NY	Cardiff	SO	Aberdeen
JO	Oxford	NZ	Coleraine	SP	Dundee
JP	Liverpool	OA–OC	Birmingham	SR	Dundee
JR	Newcastle upon Tyne	OD	Exeter	SS	Aberdeen
JS	Inverness	OE–OH	Birmingham	ST	Inverness
JT	Bournemouth	OI	Belfast	SU	Glasgow
JU	Leicester	OJ–ON	Birmingham	SV	*spare*
JV	Lincoln	OO	Chelmsford	SW	Carlisle
JW	Birmingham	OP	Birmingham	SX	Edinburgh
JX	Leeds	OR	Portsmouth	SY	*spare*
JY	Exeter	OS	Glasgow	SZ	Downpatrick
JZ	Downpatrick	OT	Portsmouth	TA	Exeter
KA–KD	Liverpool	OU	Bristol	TB	Liverpool
KE	Maidstone	OV	Birmingham	TC	Bristol
KF	Liverpool	OW	Portsmouth	TD–TE	Manchester
KG	Cardiff	OX	Birmingham	TF	Reading
KH	Beverley	OY	Stanmore	TG	Cardiff
KJ–KP	Maidstone	OZ	Belfast	TH	Swansea
KR	Maidstone	PA–PF	Wimbledon	TJ	Liverpool
KS	Edinburgh	PG–PH	Guildford	TK	Exeter
KT	Maidstone	PJ–PM	Guildford	TL	Lincoln
KU	Sheffield	PN	Brighton	TM	Luton
KV	Coventry	PO	Portsmouth	TN	Newcastle upon Tyne
KW	Sheffield	PP	Luton	TO	Nottingham
KX	Luton	PR	Bournemouth	TP	Portsmouth
KY	Sheffield	PS	Aberdeen	TR	Portsmouth
KZ	Ballymena	PT	Newcastle upon Tyne	TS	Dundee
LA–LF	Stanmore	PU	Chelmsford	TT	Exeter
LG	Chester	PV	Ipswich	TU	Chester
LH	Stanmore	PW	Norwich	TV	Nottingham
LJ	Bournemouth	PX	Portsmouth	TW	Chelmsford
LK–LP	Stanmore	PY	Middlesbrough	TX	Cardiff
LR	Stanmore	PZ	Belfast	TY	Newcastle upon Tyne
LS	Edinburgh	QA–QH	Wimbledon	TZ	Belfast
LT–LU	Stanmore	QJ–QN	Wimbledon	UA–UB	Leeds
LV	Liverpool	QP–QY	Wimbledon	UC	Wimbledon
LW–LY	Stanmore	RA–RC	Nottingham	UD	Oxford
LZ	Armagh	RD	Reading	UE	Dudley
MA–MB	Chester	RE–RF	Stoke-on-Trent	UF	Brighton
MC–MH	Chelmsford	RG	Newcastle upon Tyne	UG	Leeds
MJ	Luton	RH	Beverley	UH	Cardiff
MK–MM	Chelmsford	RJ	Manchester	UI	Londonderry
MN	*(not used)*	RK	Stanmore	UJ	Shrewsbury
MO	Reading	RL	Truro	UK	Birmingham
MP	Chelmsford	RM	Carlisle	UL	Wimbledon
MR	Swindon	RN	Preston	UM	Leeds
MS	Edinburgh	RO	Luton	UN–UO	Exeter
MT–MU	Chelmsford	RP	Northampton	UP	Newcastle upon Tyne
MV	Sidcup	RR	Nottingham	UR	Luton
MW	Swindon	RS	Aberdeen	US	Glasgow
MX–MY	Sidcup	RT	Ipswich	UT	Leicester
		RU	Bournemouth	UU–UW	Wimbledon

UX	Shrewsbury	VT	Stoke-on-Trent	WS	Bristol
UY	Worcester	VU	Manchester	WT–WU	Leeds
UZ	Belfast	VV	Northampton	WV	Brighton
VA	Peterborough	VW–VX	Chelmsford	WW–WY	Leeds
VB	Maidstone	VY	Leeds	WZ	Belfast
VC	Coventry	VZ	Omagh	XI	Belfast
VD	*series withdrawn*	WA–WB	Sheffield	XZ	Belfast
VE	Peterborough	WC	Chelmsford	YA–YD	Taunton
VF–VG	Norwich	WD	Dudley	YE–YF	Wimbledon
VH	Leeds	WE–WG	Sheffield	YG	Leeds
VJ	Gloucester	WH	Manchester	YH	Wimbledon
VK	Newcastle upon Tyne	WJ	Sheffield	YJ	Brighton
VL	Lincoln	WK	Coventry	YK–YP	Wimbledon
VM	Manchester	WL	Oxford	YR	Wimbledon
VN	Middlesbrough	WM	Liverpool	YS	Glasgow
VO	Nottingham	WN	Swansea	YT–YY	Wimbledon
VP	Birmingham	WO	Cardiff	YZ	Coleraine
VR	Manchester	WP	Worcester		
VS	Luton	WR	Leeds		

Since September 2001:

AA–AN	Peterborough	GP–GY	Brighton	PA–PT	Preston
AO–AU	Norwich	HA–HJ	Bournemouth	PU–PY	Carlisle
AV–AY	Ipswich	HK–HV	Portsmouth	RA–RY	Reading
BA–BY	Birmingham	HW	Isle of Wight	SA–SJ	Glasgow
CA–CO	Cardiff	HX–HY	Portsmouth	SK–SO	Edinburgh
CP–CV	Swansea	KA–KL	Luton	SP–ST	Dundee
CW–CY	Bangor	KM–KY	Northampton	SU–SW	Aberdeen
DA–DK	Chester	LA–LJ	Wimbledon	SX–SY	Inverness
DL–DY	Shrewsbury	LK–LT	Stanmore	VA–VY	Worcester
EA–EY	Essex	LU–LY	Sidcup	WA–WJ	Exeter
FA–FN	Nottingham	MA–MY	Manchester	WK–WL	Truro
FP	Nottingham	NA–NE	Newcastle	WM–WY	Bristol
FR–FY	Lincoln	NG–NO	Newcastle	YA–YK	Leeds
GA–GO	Maidstone	NP–NY	Stockton	YL–YU	Sheffield
		OA–OY	Oxford	YV–YY	Beverley

Note that I and Q are not used in the new format.

Car index marks — International

A	Austria	CY	Cyprus*	GCA	Guatemala
AFG	Afghanistan	CZ	Czech Republic	GE	Georgia
AL	Albania	D	Germany	GH	Ghana
AN	Angola	DK	Denmark	GR	Greece
AND	Andorra	DOM	Dominican Republic	GUY	Guyana*
AUS	Australia*	DY	Benin	H	Hungary
AZ	Azerbaijan	DZ	Algeria	HK	Hong Kong*
B	Belgium	E	Spain	HKJ	Jordan
BD	Bangladesh*	EAK	Kenya*	HN	Honduras
BDS	Barbados*	EAT	Tanzania*	HR	Croatia
BF	Burkina Faso	EAU	Uganda*	I	Italy
BG	Bulgaria	EC	Ecuador	IL	Israel
BH	Belize	ES	El Salvador	IND	India*
BIH	Bosnia-Herzegovina	EST	Estonia	IR	Iran
BOL	Bolivia	ET	Egypt	IRL	Ireland*
BR	Brazil	ETH	Ethiopia	IRQ	Iraq
BRN	Bahrain	F	France	IS	Iceland
BRU	Brunei*	FIN	Finland	J	Japan*
BS	The Bahamas*	FJI	Fiji*	JA	Jamaica*
BY	Belarus	FL	Liechtenstein	K	Cambodia
C	Cuba	FO	Faroe Is	KS	Kyrgyzstan
CAM	Cameroon	G	Gabon	KWT	Kuwait
CDN	Canada	GB	UK*	KZ	Kazakhstan
CH	Switzerland	GBA	Alderney*	L	Luxembourg
CI	Côte d'Ivoire	GBG	Guernsey*	LAO	Laos
CL	Sri Lanka*	GBJ	Jersey*	LAR	Libya
CO	Colombia	GBM	Isle of Man*	LB	Liberia
CR	Costa Rica	GBZ	Gibraltar	LS	Lesotho*

Communication

UK AIRPORTS

Communication

LT	Lithuania	RCA	Central African Republic	SYR	Syria
LV	Latvia			T	Thailand*
M	Malta*	RCB	Congo	TCH	Chad
MA	Morocco	RCH	Chile	TG	Togo
MAL	Malaysia*	RG	Guinea	TJ	Tajikistan
MC	Monaco	RH	Haiti	TM	Turkmenistan
MD	Moldova	RI	Indonesia*	TN	Tunisia
MEX	Mexico	RIM	Mauritania	TR	Turkey
MGL	Mongolia	RL	Lebanon	TT	Trinidad and Tobago*
MK	Macedonia	RM	Madagascar	UA	Ukraine
MOC	Mozambique*	RMM	Mali	UAE	United Arab Emirates
MS	Mauritius*	RN	Niger	USA	USA
MW	Malawi*	RO	Romania	UZ	Uzbekistan
MYA	Myanmar (Burma)	ROK	Korea, Republic of	V	Vatican City
N	Norway	ROU	Uruguay	VN	Vietnam
NA	Netherlands Antilles	RP	Philippines	WAG	The Gambia
NAM	Namibia*	RSM	San Marino	WAL	Sierra Leone
NAU	Nauru*	RU	Burundi	WD	Dominica*
NEP	Nepal*	RUS	Russia	WG	Grenada*
NGR	Nigeria	RWA	Rwanda	WL	St Lucia*
NIC	Nicaragua	S	Sweden	WS	Samoa
NL	Netherlands	SA	Saudi Arabia	WV	St Vincent and the Grenadines*
NZ	New Zealand*	SCN	St Kitts and Nevis*		
P	Portugal	SD	Swaziland*	YAR	Yemen
PA	Panama	SGP	Singapore*	YU	Serbia and Montenegro
PE	Peru	SK	Slovakia		
PK	Pakistan*	SLO	Slovenia	YV	Venezuela
PL	Poland	SME	Suriname*	Z	Zambia*
PNG	Papua New Guinea*	SN	Senegal	ZA	South Africa*
PY	Paraguay	SO	Somalia	ZRE	Congo, Democratic Republic of
Q	Qatar	ST	São Tomé and Príncipe		
RA	Argentina	SUD	Sudan	ZW	Zimbabwe*
RB	Botswana*	SY	Seychelles*		
RC	Taiwan				

*In countries so marked, the rule of the road is to drive on the left; in others, vehicles drive on the right.

UK airports

Alderney	Channel Is	London City	
Baltasound	Unst, Shetlands	Luton	Bedfordshire
Belfast City		Lydd	Kent
Belfast International		Manchester	
Benbecula	Hebrides	Newcastle	
Biggin Hill	Kent	North Bay	Barra, Hebrides
Blackpool	Lancashire	Norwich	Norfolk
Bournemouth	Dorset	Penzance	Cornwall
Bristol	Avon	Plymouth (Roborough)	Devon
Cambridge		Prestwick	Ayrshire
Cardiff		Ronaldsway	Isle of Man
Coventry	West Midlands	Saint Mary's	Scilly Isles
Dundee		Sandown	Isle of Wight
Dyce	Aberdeen	Scatsta	Shetlands
East Midlands	Derbyshire	Southampton	Hampshire
Exeter	Devon	Southend	Essex
Fair Isle	Shetlands	Stansted	London
Gatwick	London	Stornoway	Hebrides
Glenegedale	Islay	Sumburgh	Shetlands
Glasgow		Swansea	
Grimsetter	Orkney	Teeside	Cleveland
Guernsey	Channel Is	Tingwall	Lerwick, Shetlands
Heathrow	London	Tiree	Hebrides
Humberside		Tresco	Scilly Isles
Inverness		Turnhouse	Edinburgh
Jersey	Channel Is	West Midlands	Birmingham
Kirkwall	Orkney	Westray	Orkney
Leeds-Bradford		Wick	Caithness
Liverpool			

International airports

Abadan International	Iran	Agno	Lugano, Switzerland
Abu Dhabi	United Arab Emirates	Ain el Bay	Constantine, Algeria
Adana	Turkey	Albany County	New York, USA
Adelaide	Australia	Alborg	Norresundbyr,

582

Roedslet	Denmark	Cancun	Mexico
Albuquerque	New Mexico, USA	Cannon International	Reno, Nevada, USA
Alexandria	Egypt	Canton	Akron, Ohio, USA
Alfonso Bonilla Aragon	Cali, Colombia	Capodichino	Naples, Italy
Alicante	Spain	Carrasco	Montevideo, Uruguay
Alma Ata	Kazakhstan	Carthage	Tunis, Tunisia
Almeria	Spain	Cebu	Philippines
Amarillo	Texas, USA	Chiang Kai Shek	Taipei, Taiwan
Amborovy	Majunga, Madagascar	Changi	Singapore
Amilcar Cabral		Charleroi (Gossilies)	Belgium
International	Sal I, Cape Verde	Charles de Gaulle	Paris, France
Aminu International	Kano, Nigeria	Charleston	South Carolina, USA
Anchorage	Alaska, USA	Charleston	West Virginia, USA
Archangel	Russia	Charlotte	North Carolina, USA
Arlanda	Stockholm, Sweden	Château Bougon	Nantes, France
Arnos Vale	St Vincent	Chhatrapati Shivaji	
Arrecife	Lanzarote, Canary Is	International	Mumbai (Bombay), India
Arturo Marino Benitez	Santiago, Chile	Christchurch	New Zealand
Ashkabad	Turkmenistan	Ciampino	Rome, Italy
Asmara International	Eritrea	Cologne-Bonn	Cologne, Germany
Asturias	Spain	Columbus	Ohio, USA
Atatürk	Istanbul, Turkey	Congonhas	São Paulo, Brazil
Auckland	New Zealand	Copenhagen	
Augusto C Sandino	Managua, Nicaragua	International	Kastrup, Denmark
Baghdad International	Iraq	Cork	Ireland
Bahrain International	Bahrain	Costa Smeralda	Olbia, Sardinia
Bali International /		Côte d'Azure	Nice, France
Ngurah Rai	Denpasar, Indonesia	Cotonou	Benin
Balice	Kracow, Poland	Cristoforo Colombo	Genoa, Italy
Bandar Seri Begawan	Brunei	Crown Point	Scarborough, Tobago
Baneasa	Bucharest, Romania	Cuscatlan	Comalapa, El Salvador
Bangkok International	Thailand	D F Malan	Cape Town, South Africa
Barajas	Madrid, Spain	Dalaman	Turkey
Barcelona	Spain	Dallas / Fort Worth	Dallas, Texas, USA
Basle-Mulhouse	Basle, Switzerland	Damascus	Syria
Beijing (Peking)	China	Dar es Salaam	Tanzania
Beira	Mozambique	Darwin	Australia
Beirut International	Khaldeh, Lebanon	Des Moines	Iowa, USA
Belfast International	UK	Detroit-Wayne County	Detroit, Michigan, USA
Belgrade	Serbia and Montenegro	Deurne	Antwerp, Belgium
Belize City International	Belize	Dhahran International	Al Khobar, Saudi Arabia
Ben Gurion	Tel Aviv, Israel	Djibouti	Djibouti
Benina	Benghazi, Libya	Doha	Qatar
Benito Juarez	Mexico City, Mexico	Dois de Julho	
Berlin-Schonefeld	Berlin, Germany	International	Salvador, Brazil
Berline-Tegel	Berlin, Germany	Domodedovo	Moscow, Russia
Berne	Switzerland	Don Miguel Hidalgo y	
Billund	Denmark	Castilla	Guadalajara, Mexico
Birmingham	Alabama, USA	Dorval International	Montreal, Canada
Bishkek-Manas	Manas, Kyrgyzstan	Douala	Cameroon
Blackburne/Plymouth	Montserrat	Dresden	Germany
Blagnac	Toulouse, France	Dubai	United Arab Emirates
Bole	Addis Ababa, Ethiopia	Dublin	Ireland
Borispol	Kiev, Ukraine	Dubrovnik	Croatia
Boukhalef	Tangier, Morocco	Dulles International	Washington DC, USA
Boulogne	France	Dusseldorf	Germany
Bourgas	Bulgaria	Ecterdingen	Stuttgart, Germany
Bradley International	Hartford, Connecticut, USA	Edmonton International	Canada
		Eduardo Gomes	Manaus, Brazil
Brasilia International	Brazil	Eindhoven	Netherlands
Bremen	Germany	El Alto	La Paz, Bolivia
Brisbane	Australia	El Dorado	Bogata, Colombia
Brnik	Ljubljana, Slovenia	El Paso	Texas, USA
Bromma	Stockholm, Sweden	Elat	Israel
Brussels National	Belgium	Elmas	Cagliari, Italy
Buffalo	New York, USA	Entebbe	Uganda
Bujumbura	Burundi	Entzheim	Strasbourg, France
Bulawayo	Zimbabwe	Eppley Airfield	Omaha, Nebraska, USA
Butmir	Sarajevo, Bosnia-Herzegovina	Erie	Pennsylvania, USA
		Ernesto Cortissoz	Barranquilla, Colombia
Cairns	Queensland, Australia	Esbjerg	Denmark
Cairo International	Egypt	Esenboga	Ankara, Turkey
Calabar	Nigeria	Faleolo	Apia, Samoa
Calgary International	Canada	Faro	Portugal

Communication

Ferihegy	Budapest, Hungary
Findel	Luxembourg
Fiumicino (Leonardo da Vinci)	Rome, Italy
Flesland	Bergen, Norway
Fontanarossa	Catania, Sicily
Fornebu	Oslo, Norway
Fort de France	Lamentin, Martinique
Fort Lauderdale	Florida, USA
Fort Myers	Florida, USA
Frankfurt am Main	Germany
Freeport International	The Bahamas
Frejorgues	Montpellier, France
Fuenterrabia	San Sebastian, Spain
Fuerteventura	Canary Is
Fuhlsbuttel	Hamburg, Germany
G Marconi	Bologna, Italy
Galileo Galilei	Pisa, Italy
Gatwick	London, UK
Gaza International	Gaza, Israel
G'Bessia	Conakry, Guinea
General Abelard L Rodriguez	Tijuana, Mexico
General Juan N Alvarez	Acapulco, Mexico
General Manuel Marquez de Leon	La Paz, Mexico
General Mariano Escobedo	Monterrey, Mexico
General Mitchell	Milwaukee, Wisconsin, USA
General Rafael Buelna	Mazatlan, Mexico
Geneva	Switzerland
Gerona/Costa Brava	Gerona, Spain
Gillot	St Denis, Réunion
Golden Rock	St Kitts
Goleniow	Szczecin, Poland
Glasgow	UK
Granada	Spain
Grantley Adams International	Bridgetown, Barbados
Greater Cincinnati	Ohio, USA
Greater Pittsburgh	Pennsylvania, USA
Guam	Guam
Guararapes International	Recife, Brazil
Guarulhos International	São Paulo, Brazil
Halifax	Canada
Halim Perdanakusama	Jakarta, Indonesia
Hamilton Kindley Field	Hamilton, Bermuda
Hancock Field	Syracuse, New York State, USA
Hannover-Langenhagen	Hannover, Germany
Hanoi	Vietnam
Harare	Zimbabwe
Harrisburg	Pennsylvania, USA
Hartsfield	Atlanta, Georgia, USA
Hassan	Laayoune, Morocco
Hato	Curaçao, Netherlands Antilles
Hahaya International	Moroni, Comoros
Hanedi	Tokyo, Japan
Heathrow	London, UK
Hellenikon	Athens, Greece
Henderson Field	Honiari, Solomon Is
Heraklion	Crete, Greece
Hewanorra International	St Lucia
Ho Chi Minh City	Vietnam
Hong Kong International	Hong Kong
Hongqiao	Shanghai, China
Honolulu	Hawaii, USA
Hopkins	Cleveland, Ohio, USA
Houari Boumedienne International	Dar-el-Beida, Algeria
Houston	Texas, USA
Ibiza	Balearic Is, Spain
Indianapolis	Indiana, USA
Indira Ghandi International	Delhi, India
Inezgane	Agadir, Morocco
Islamabad	Pakistan
Isle Verde	San Juan, Puerto Rico
Izmir	Turkey
Itazuke	Fukuoka, Japan
Ivanka	Bratislava, Slovakia
Ivato	Antananarivo, Madagascar
J F Kennedy	New York, USA
Jackson Field	Port Moresby, Papua New Guinea
Jacksonville	Florida, USA
James M Cox	Dayton, Ohio, USA
Johannesburg International	South Africa
Jomo Kenyatta	Nairobi, Kenya
Jorge Chavez International	Lima, Peru
Jose Marti International	Havana, Cuba
Juan Santa Maria International	Alajuela, Costa Rica
Kagoshima	Japan
Kalmar	Sweden
Kamazu	Lilongwe, Malawi
Kansas City	Missouri, USA
Kaohsiung	Taiwan
Karachi	Pakistan
Karpathos	Karpathos, Greece
Katunayake	Colombo, Sri Lanka
Keflavik	Reykjavik, Iceland
Kent County	Grand Rapids, Michigan, USA
Kerkyra	Corfu, Greece
Key West	Florida, USA
Khartoum	The Sudan
Khoramaksar	Aden, Yemen
Khwaja Rawash	Kabul, Afghanistan
Kigali	Rwanda
Kimpo International	Seoul, Korea, Republic of (South Korea)
King Abdul Aziz	Jeddah, Saudi Arabia
King Khaled	Riyadh, Saudi Arabia
Kingsford Smith	Sydney, Australia
Kjevik	Kristiansand, Norway
Klagenfurt	Austria
Komaki	Nagoya, Japan
Kos	Greece
Košice	Slovakia
Kota Kinabulu	Sabah, Malaysia
Kotoka	Accra, Ghana
Kranebitten	Innsbruck, Austria
Kuching	Sarawak, Malaysia
Kungsangen	Norrköping, Sweden
Kuwait International	Kuwait
La Aurora	Guatemala City, Guatemala
La Coruña	Spain
La Guardia	New York, USA
La Mesa	San Pedro Sula, Honduras
La Parra	Jerez de la Frontera, Spain
Lahore	Pakistan
Landvetter	Gothenburg, Sweden
Larnaca International	Cyprus
Las Americas International	Santo Domingo, Dominican Republic
Las Palmas	Gran Canaria, Canary Is
Le Raizet	Point-à-Pitre, Guadeloupe
Leipzig	Germany
Les Angades	Oujda, Morocco
Lesquin	Lille, France

584

Lester B Pearson	
International	Toronto, Canada
Libreville	Gabon
Lic Gustavo Diaz Ordaz	Puerto Vallarta, Mexico
Lic Manuel Crecencio	
Rejon	Merida, Mexico
Liège (Bierset)	Belgium
Liepaja International	Latvia
Linate	Milan, Italy
Lincoln	Nebraska, USA
Lindbergh International	San Diego, USA
Linz	Austria
Lisbon	Portugal
Little Rock	Arkansas, USA
Llabanère	Perpignan, France
Logan International	Boston, Massachusetts,
	USA
Lomé	Togo
London City	UK
Long Beach	California, USA
Los Angeles	California, USA
Loshitsa	Minsk, Belarus
Louis Botha	Durban, South Africa
Louisville	Kentucky, USA
Luanda	Angola
Luano	Lubumashi, Congo,
	Democratic Republic of
Lubbock	Texas, USA
Luis Munoz Marin	
International	San Juan, Puerto Rico
Lungi	Freetown, Sierra Leone
Luqa	Malta
Lusaka	Zambia
Luxor	Egypt
Maastricht	Netherlands
McCarran International	Las Vegas, Nevada, USA
McCoy International	Orlando, Florida, USA
Mactan International	Cebu, Philippines
Mahon	Menorca
Mais Gate	Port-au-Prince, Haiti
Malaga	Spain
Male	Maldives
Malpensa	Milan, Italy
Managua	Nicaragua
Manchester	New Hampshire, USA
Manchester	UK
Maputo	Mozambique
Marco Polo	Venice, Italy
Mariscal Sucre	Quito, Ecuador
Maseru	Lesotho
Matsapha	Manzini, Swaziland
Maupertus	Cherbourg, France
Maxglan	Salzburg, Austria
Maya Maya	Brazzaville, Congo
Medina	Saudi Arabia
Mehrabad International	Tehran, Iran
Melita	Djerba, Tunisia
Memphis	Tennessee, USA
Menara	Marrakesh, Morocco
Merignac	Bordeaux, France
Miami	Florida, USA
Midway	Chicago, Illinois, USA
Ministro Pistarini	Buenos Aires, Argentina
Minneapolis/St Paul	Minneapolis, USA
Mirabel	Montreal, Canada
Mogadishu	Somalia
Mohamed V	Casablanca, Morocco
Moi International	Mombasa, Kenya
Monroe County	Rochester, New York
	State, USA
Morelos	Mexico City, Mexico
Münster/Osnabrück	Germany
Murmansk	Russia
Murtala Muhammed	Lagos, Nigeria

Nadi International	Fiji
Nagasaki	Japan
Narita	Tokyo, Japan
Narssarsuaq	Greenland
Nashville	Tennessee, USA
Nassau International	The Bahamas
Nauru	Nauru
N'Djamena	Chad
N'Djili	Kinshasa, Congo,
	Democratic Republic of
Nejrab	Aleppo, Syria
Netaji Subhash Chandra	
Bose International	Kolkata (Calcutta), India
Newcastle	UK
New Orleans	Louisiana, USA
Newark	New York, USA
Niamey	Niger
Ninoy Aquino	
International	Manila, Philippines
Niš	Serbia and Montenegro
Norfolk International	Virginia, USA
Norman Manley	
International	Kingston, Jamaica
North Front	Gibraltar
Nouadhibou	Mauritania
Nouakchott	Mauritania
Novo-Alexeyevka	Tblisi, Georgia
Nuremberg	Germany
Oakland International	California, USA
Octeville	Le Havre, France
Odense	Denmark
O'Hare	Chicago, Illinois, USA
Okecie	Warsaw, Poland
Okinawa	Naha, Japan
Oran	Algeria
Orebro	Sweden
Orlando	Florida, USA
Orly	Paris, France
Osaka	Japan
Osvaldo Veira	Bissau, Guinea-Bissau
Otopeni	Bucharest, Romania
Ouagadougou	Burkina Faso
Owen Roberts	Grand Cayman, West
	Indies
Pago Pago	Samoa
Palese	Bari, Italy
Palma	Majorca
Pamplona	Spain
Panama City	Panama
Paphos	Cyprus
Papola Casale	Brindisi, Italy
Paradisi	Rhodes, Greece
Patenga	Chittagong, Bangladesh
Penang	Malaysia
Peninsula	Monterey, California, USA
Peretola	Florence, Italy
Perth	Australia
Peshawar	Pakistan
Peterson Field	Colorado Springs,
	Colorado, USA
Philadelphia	Pennsylvania, USA
Piarco	Port of Spain, Trinidad
Pleso	Zagreb, Croatia
Pochentong	Phnom Penh, Cambodia
Point Salines	Grenada
Pointe Noire	Congo
Polonia	Medan, Indonesia
Ponta Delgado	São Miguel, Azores
Poprad Tatry	Poprad, Slovakia
Port Bouet	Abidjan, Côte d'Ivoire
Port Harcourt	Nigeria
Portland	Maine, USA
Portland	Oregon, USA
Port Sudan	The Sudan

Communication

Porto Pedra Rubras	Oporto, Portugal
Praia	Cape Verde
Prestwick	UK
Provence	Marseille, France
Pula	Croatia
Pulkovo	St Petersburg, Russia
Punta Arenas International	Chile
Punta Raisi	Palermo, Sicily
Queen Alia	Amman, Jordan
Queen Beatrix	Aruba, Netherlands Antilles
Raleigh/Durham	North Carolina, USA
Ras al Khaimah	United Arab Emirates
Rabiechowo	Gdansk, Poland
Regina	Canada
Reina Sofia	Tenerife, Canary Is
Rejon	Merida, Mexico
Richmond	Virginia, USA
Riem	Munich, Germany
Rio de Janeiro International	Brazil
Riyadh International	Saudi Arabia
Roberts International	Monrovia, Liberia
Rochambeau	Cayenne, French Guiana
Robert Mueller Municipal Airport	Austin, Texas, USA
Ronchi dei Legionari	Trieste, Italy
Rotterdam	Netherlands
Ruzyne	Prague, Czech Republic
Saab	Linköping, Sweden
Saint Eufemia	Lamezia Terma, Italy
Saint Louis	Missouri, USA
Saint Thomas	Virgin Is
Sainte Foy	Quebec, Canada
Sale	Rabat, Morocco
Salgado Filho International	Pôrto Alegre, Brazil
Salt Lake City	Utah, USA
San Antonio	Texas, USA
San Diego	California, USA
San Francisco	California, USA
San Giusto	Pisa, Italy
San Javier	Murcia, Spain
San José	California, USA
San Pablo	Seville, Spain
San Salvador	El Salvador
Sanaa International	Yemen
Sangster International	Montego Bay, Jamaica
Santa Caterina	Funchal, Madeira
Santa Cruz	La Palma, Canary Is
Santa Isabel	Malabo, Guinea
Santander	Spain
Santiago	Spain
Santos Dumont	Rio de Janeiro, Brazil
São Tomé	São Tomé and Príncipe
Satolas	Lyon, France
Schipol	Amsterdam, Netherlands
Schwechat	Vienna, Austria
Seeb	Muscat, Oman
Senou	Bamako, Mali
Seychelles International	Mahe, Seychelles
Sfax	Tunisia
Shannon	Ireland
Sharjah	United Arab Emirates
Sheremetyevo	Moscow, Russia
Silvio Pettirossi	Asunción, Paraguay
Simon Bolivar	Caracas, Venezuela
Simon Bolivar	Guayaquil, Ecuador
Sir Seewoosagur Ramgoolam	Plaisance, Mauritius
Sir Seretse Khama	Gaborone, Botswana
Skanes	Monastir, Morocco
Skopje	Macedonia

Sky Harbour	Phoenix, Arizona, USA
Sliac	Slovakia
Snilow	Lwow, Ukraine
Sofia International	Bulgaria
Sola	Stavanger, Norway
Sondica	Bilbao, Spain
Søndre Strømfjord	Greenland
Spilve	Riga, Latvia
Split	Croatia
Spokane	Washington, USA
Stansted	UK
Stapleton International	Denver, Colorado, USA
Sturup	Malmö, Sweden
Subang International	Kuala Lumpur, Malaysia
Sunan	Pyongyang, Korea, Democratic People's Republic of (North Korea)
Tacoma	Seattle, USA
Tallahassee	Florida, USA
Tamatve	Madagascar
Tampa	Florida, USA
Tarbes-Ossun-Lourdes	Jullian, France
Tegucigalpa	Toncontin, Honduras
Thalerhof	Graz, Austria
Theodore Francis	Providence, Rhode I, USA
Thessalonika	Greece
Timehri International	Georgetown, Guyana
Timişoara	Romania
Tirana	Albania
Tito Menniti	Reggio Calabria, Italy
Tontouta	Noumea, New Caledonia
Townsville	Australia
Tribhuyan	Kathmandu, Nepal
Tripoli	Libya
Trivandrum	India
Truax Field	Madison, Wisconsin, USA
Tucson	Arizona, USA
Tullamarine	Melbourne, Australia
Turin	Italy
Turku	Finland
Turnhouse	Edinburgh, UK
Ulemiste	Tallinn, Estonia
Unokovo	Moscow, Russia
Uplands	Ottawa, Canada
V C Bird International	Antigua
Vaasa	Finland
Vagar	Faroe Is
Valencia	Spain
Vancouver International	Canada
Vantaa	Helsinki, Finland
Varna International	Bulgaria
Verona	Italy
Victoria	British Columbia, Canada
Vigie	St Lucia
Vigo	Spain
Vilnius	Lithuania
Vilo de Porto	Santa Maria, Azores
Viracopos	São Paulo, Brazil
Vitoria	Spain
Washington International	Baltimore, Maryland, USA
Wattay	Vientiane, Laos
Wellington	New Zealand
Wichita	Kansas, USA
Will Rogers	Oklahoma City, Oklahoma, USA
Winnipeg International	Manitoba, Canada
Yangon	Myanmar (Burma)
Yoff	Dakar, Senegal
Yundum	Banjul, The Gambia
Zakynthos	Greece
Zia International	Dhaka, Bangladesh
Zürich	Switzerland

Airline designators

Code	Airline	Country
AA	American Airlines	USA
AC	Air Canada	Canada
AF	Air France	France
AH	Air Algerie	Algeria
AI	Air India	India
AJ	Air Belgium	Belgium
AM	Aeromexico	Mexico
AN	Ansett Australia	Australia
AQ	Aloha Airlines	Hawaii
AR	Aerolineas Argentinas	Argentina
AS	Alaska Airlines	USA
AT	Royal Air Maroc	Morocco
AV	Avianca	Colombia
AY	Finnair	Finland
AZ	Alitalia	Italy
BA	British Airways	UK
BD	British Midland	UK
BG	Biman Bangladesh Airlines	Bangladesh
BH	Transtate Airlines	Australia
BI	Royal Brunei Airlines	Brunei
BL	Pacific Airlines	Vietnam
BO	Bouraq Indonesia Airlines	Indonesia
BP	Air Botswana	Botswana
BT	Air Baltic	Latvia
BU	Braathens SAFE	Norway
BW	BWIA International Trinidad and Tobago Airways	Trinidad
BY	Britannia Airways	UK
CA	Air China	China
CB	ScotAirways	UK
CI	China Airlines	Taiwan
CJ	China North Airlines	Taiwan
CK	China Airlines Cargo	China
CM	COPA (Compania Panamena de Aviación)	Panama
CO	Continental Airlines	USA
CP	Canadian Airlines International	Canada
CS	Micronesia Continental	Mariana Is
CT	Air Sofia	Bulgaria
CU	Cubana	Cuba
CW	Air Marshall Islands	Marshall Is
CX	Cathay Pacific Airways	Hong Kong
CY	Cyprus Airways	Cyprus
CZ	China Southern Airlines	China
DA	Air Georgia	Georgia
DI	Deutsche BA	Germany
DL	Delta Air Lines	USA
DT	TAAG-Angola Airlines	Angola
DX	Danish Air Transport	Denmark
EI	Aer Lingus	Ireland
EK	Emirates	United Arab Emirates
ET	Ethiopian Airlines	Ethiopia
EU	Ecuatoriana	Ecuador
EW	Eastwest Airlines	Australia
FE	Royal Khmer Airlines	Cambodia
FF	Tower Air	USA
FG	Ariana Afghan Airlines	Afghanistan
FM	Shanghai Airlines	China
FI	Icelandair	Iceland
FJ	Air Pacific	Fiji
FQ	Air Aruba	Netherlands Antilles
FR	Ryanair	Ireland
FU	Air Littoral	France
GA	Garuda Indonesia	Indonesia
GF	Gulf Air	Bahrain
GH	Ghana Airways	Ghana
GL	Gronlandsfly	Greenland
GM	Air Slovakia	Slovakia
GN	Air Gabon	Gabon
GR	Aurigny Air Services	Channel Is
GT	GB Airways	Gibraltar
GV	Riga Airlines	Latvia
GY	Guyana Airways	Guyana
HA	Hawaiian Airlines	USA
HM	Air Seychelles	Seychelles
HP	America West Airlines	USA
HV	Transavia Airlines	Netherlands
HY	Uzbekistan Airlines	Uzbekistan
IB	Iberia	Spain
IC	Indian Airlines	India
IE	Solomon Airlines	Solomon Is
IF	Great China Airlines	China
IL	Istanbul Airways	Turkey
IN	Macedonian Airlines	Macedonia
IP	Airlines of Tasmania	Australia
IR	Iran Air	Iran
IV	Fujian Airlines	China
IY	Yemenia Airways	Yemen
JA	Air Bosna	Bosnia-Herzegovina
JE	Manx Airlines	Isle of Man
JG	Air Greece	Greece
JL	Japan Airlines	Japan
JM	Air Jamaica	Jamaica
JP	Adria Airways	Slovenia
JQ	Air Jamaica Express	Jamaica
JS	Air Koryo	Korea, Democratic People's Republic of (North Korea)
JU	JAT (Jugoslovenski Aerotransport)	Serbia and Montenegro
JY	European Airways	Channel Is
KA	Dragonair	Hong Kong
KE	Korean Air Lines	Korea, Republic of (South Korea)
KL	KLM	Netherlands
KM	Air Malta	Malta
KP	Kiwi International Airlines	USA
KQ	Kenya Airways	Kenya
KT	Kampuchea Airlines	Cambodia
KU	Kuwait Airways	Kuwait
KV	Kavminvodyaria	Russia
KX	Cayman Airways	Cayman Is
KZ	Nippon Cargo Airlines	Japan
LA	LAN-Chile	Chile
LG	Luxair	Luxembourg
LH	Lufthansa	Germany
LJ	Sierra National Airlines	Sierra Leone
LM	ALM (Antillean Airlines)	Netherlands Antilles
LN	Jamahiriya Libyan Arab Airlines	Libya
LO	LOT-Polish Airlines	Poland
LR	LACSA	Costa Rica
LT	LTU International Airways	Germany
LU	Theron Airways	South Africa
LV	Albanian Airlines	Albania
LX	Swiss International Airlines	Switzerland
LY	El Al Israel Airlines	Israel
LZ	Balkan-Bulgarian Airlines	Bulgaria
MA	Malev	Hungary
MD	Air Madagascar	Madagascar
MH	Malaysian Airlines	Malaysia
MK	Air Mauritius	Mauritius

Communication

Code	Airline	Country
MN	Commercial Airways	South Africa
MR	Air Mauritanie	Mauritania
MS	Egyptair	Egypt
MX	Mexicana	Mexico
NF	Air Vanuatu	Vanuatu
NG	Lauda Air	Austria
NH	All Nippon Airways	Japan
NM	Mount Cook Airlines	New Zealand
NU	Japan Transocean Air	Japan
NV	Northwest Territorial Airways	Canada
NW	Northwest Airlines	USA
NY	Air Iceland	Iceland
NZ	Air New Zealand	New Zealand
OA	Olympic Airways	Greece
OG	Go	UK
OK	Czech Airlines	Czech Republic
OM	MIAT-Mongolian Airlines	Mongolia
ON	Air Nauru	Australia
OO	Skywest Airlines	Australia
OS	Austrian Airlines	Austria
OU	Croatia Airlines	Croatia
OV	Estonian Air	Estonia
PC	Fiji Air	Fiji
PE	Air Europe	Italy
PF	Palestinian Airlines	Israel
PG	Bangkok Airways	Thailand
PH	Polynesian Airlines	Samoa
PK	Pakistan International Airlines	Pakistan
PL	Aeroperu	Peru
PR	Philippine Airlines	Philippines
PS	Ukraine International Airlines	Ukraine
PU	Pluna (Primeras Lineas Uruguayas de Navegación Aerea)	Uruguay
PX	Air Niugini	Papua New Guinea
PY	Surinam Airways	Suriname
PZ	TAM (Transportes Aereos del Mercosur)	Paraguay
QF	Qantas Airways	Australia
QL	Air Lesotho	Lesotho
QM	Air Malawi	Malawi
QR	Qatar Airways	Qatar
QS	Tatra Air	Slovakia
QU	Uganda Airlines	Uganda
QV	Lao Aviation	Laos
QW	Turks and Caicos Airways	Turks and Caicos
QX	Horizon Air	USA
QZ	Zambia Airways	Zambia
RA	Royal Nepal Airlines	Nepal
RB	Syrian Arab Airlines	Syria
RG	Varig	Brazil
RJ	Royal Jordanian	Jordan
RK	Air Afrique	Côte d'Ivoire
RM	Air Moldova	Moldova
RO	Tarom	Romania
RR	Royal Air Force	UK
SA	South African Airways	South Africa
SB	Air Caledonie International	New Caledonia
SD	Sudan Airways	The Sudan
SK	SAS (Scandinavian Airlines)	Sweden
SN	SN Brussels Airlines	Belgium
SQ	Singapore Airlines	Singapore

Code	Airline	Country
SU	Aeroflot	Russia
SV	Saudia	Saudi Arabia
SW	Air Namibia	Namibia
TC	AirTanzania	Tanzania
TE	Lithuanian Airlines	Lithuania
TG	Thai Airways International	Thailand
TI	Angkor Airlines	Cambodia
TK	Turkish Airlines	Turkey
TM	LAM (Linhas Aereas de Moçambique)	Mozambique
TN	Air Tahiti Nui	Tahiti
TP	TAP Air Portugal	Portugal
TR	Transbrasil SA Linhas Aereas	Brazil
TU	Tunis Air	Tunisia
TT	Air Lithuania	Lithuania
TV	Virgin Express	Belgium
TW	TWA (Trans World Airlines)	USA
UA	United Airlines	USA
UB	Myanmar Airlines	Myanmar (Burma)
UC	Ladeco	Chile
UF	Turkestan Airlines	Kazakhstan
UK	KLM UK	UK
UL	Sri Lankan Airlines	Sri Lanka
UM	Air Zimbabwe	Zimbabwe
UN	Transaero Airlines	Russia
UP	Bahamasair	The Bahamas
US	USAir	USA
UY	Cameroon Airlines	Cameroon
VE	Avensa	Venezuela
VN	Vietnam Airlines	Vietnam
VO	Tyrolean Airways	Austria
VP	VASP (Viacão Aèrea São Paulo)	Brazil
VR	Transportes Aereos de Cabo Verde	Cape Verde
VS	Virgin Atlantic Airways	UK
VT	Air Tahiti	Tahiti
VV	Aeorosvit Airlines	Ukraine
VX	Aces (Aerolineas Centrales de Colombia)	Colombia
WH	China Northwest Airlines	China
WJ	Labrador Airways	Canada
WM	Windward Islands Airways	Canada
WN	Southwest Airlines	USA
WR	Royal Tongan Airlines	Tonga
WT	Nigeria Airways	Nigeria
WX	Cityjet	Ireland
WY	Oman Aviation Services	Oman
YJ	National Airlines	South Africa
YK	Cyprus Turkish Airlines	Cyprus
YN	Air Creebec	Canada
YP	Aero Lloyd	Germany
YU	Dominair	Dominican Republic
YZ	Transportes Aereos Da Guiné-Bissau	Guinea-Bissau
ZB	Monarch Airlines	UK
ZC	Royal Swazi National Airways	Swaziland
ZP	Air St Thomas	Virgin Is
ZQ	Ansett New Zealand	New Zealand
ZX	Air BC	Canada
2J	Air Burkina	Burkina Faso
3D	Denim Air	Netherlands

Air distances

Air distances between some major cities, given in statute miles. To convert to kilometres, multiply number given by 1.6093.

* Shortest route

	Amsterdam	Anchorage	Beijing	Buenos Aires	Cairo	Chicago	Delhi	Hong Kong	Honolulu	Istanbul	Johannesburg	Lagos	London	Los Angeles	Mexico City	Montreal	Moscow	Nairobi	Paris	Perth	Rome	Santiago	Sydney	Tokyo
Anchorage	4475																							
Beijing	6566	4756																						
Buenos Aires	7153	8329	12000																					
Cairo	2042	6059	5685	7468																				
Chicago	4109	28	7599	5587	6135																			
Delhi	3985	8925	2368	8340	2753	8119																		
Hong Kong	5926	5063	1235	3124	5098	7827	2345																	
Honolulu	8368	2780	6778	8693	9439	4246	7888	5543																
Istanbul	1373	6024	4763	7783	764	5502	2833	5998	9547															
Johannesburg	5606	1042	10108	5725	4012	8705	6765	6728	12892	4776														
Lagos	3161	7587	8030	4832	2443	7065	5196	7541	10367	3207	2854													
London	217	4472	5054	6885	2187	3956	4169	5979	7252	1552	5640	3115												
Los Angeles	5559	2333	6349	6140	7589	1746	8717	7231	2553	6994	10443	7716	5442											
Mexico City	5724	3751	7912	4592	7730	1687	9806	8794	4116	7255	10070	7343	5703	1563										
Montreal	3422	3100	7557	5640	5431	737	7421	8564	4923	4795	8322	5595	3252	2482	2307									
Moscow	1338	4291	3604	8382	1790	5500	2698	4839	8802	1089	6280	4462	1550	6992	6700	4393								
Nairobi	4148	8714	8888	7427	2203	8177	4956	7301	11498	2967	1809	2377	4246	9688	9949	7498	3951							
Paris	261	4683	5108	6892	1995	4140	4089	5987	7463	1394	5422	2922	220	5633	5714	3434	1540	4931						
Perth	9118	8368	4987	9734	7766	11281	5013	3752	7115	7846	5564	10209	9246	9535	11098	12402	8355	7373	12587					
Rome	809	5258	5306	6931	1329	4828	3679	5773	8150	852	4802	2497	898	6340	6601	5431	1478	3349	688	8309				
Santiago	7714	7919	13822	710	8029	5328	12715	3733	8147	10109	5738	6042	8568	5594	4168	5551	10118	7547	461	15129	7548			
Sydney	1039	8522	5689	7760	9196	9324	6495	4586	5078	9883	7601	11700	10565	7498	9061	9980	9425	9410	10150	2037	10149	13092		
Tokyo	6006*	3443	1313	13100	6362	6286	3656	1807	3831	5757	8535	9130*	6218	5451	7014	6913	4668	8565	6208*	4925	6145	11049	4640	
Washington	3854	3430	7930	6097	5859	590	7841	8385	4822	5347	8199	5472	3672	2294	1871	493	4884	7918	3843	11829	4495	5061	9792	6763

Flying times

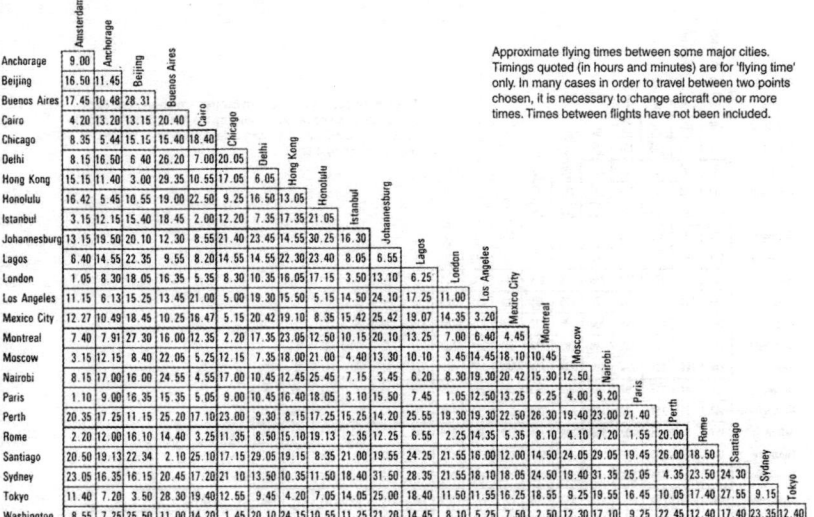

Approximate flying times between some major cities. Timings quoted (in hours and minutes) are for 'flying time' only. In many cases in order to travel between two points chosen, it is necessary to change aircraft one or more times. Times between flights have not been included.

	Amsterdam	Anchorage	Beijing	Buenos Aires	Cairo	Chicago	Delhi	Hong Kong	Honolulu	Istanbul	Johannesburg	Lagos	London	Los Angeles	Mexico City	Montreal	Moscow	Nairobi	Paris	Perth	Rome	Santiago	Sydney	Tokyo
Anchorage	9.00																							
Beijing	16.50	11.45																						
Buenos Aires	17.45	10.48	28.31																					
Cairo	4.20	13.20	13.15	20.40																				
Chicago	8.35	5.44	15.15	15.40	18.40																			
Delhi	8.15	16.50	6.40	26.20	7.00	20.05																		
Hong Kong	15.15	11.40	3.00	29.35	10.55	17.05	6.05																	
Honolulu	16.42	5.45	10.55	19.00	22.50	9.25	16.50	13.05																
Istanbul	3.15	12.15	15.40	18.45	2.00	12.20	7.35	17.35	21.05															
Johannesburg	13.15	19.50	20.10	12.30	8.55	21.40	23.45	14.55	30.25	16.30														
Lagos	6.40	14.55	22.35	9.55	8.20	14.55	14.55	22.30	23.40	8.05	6.55													
London	1.05	8.30	18.05	16.35	5.35	8.30	10.35	16.05	17.15	3.50	13.10	6.25												
Los Angeles	11.15	6.13	15.25	13.45	21.00	5.00	19.30	15.50	5.15	14.50	24.10	17.25	11.00											
Mexico City	12.27	10.49	18.45	10.25	16.47	5.15	20.42	19.10	8.35	15.42	25.42	19.07	14.35	3.20										
Montreal	7.40	7.91	27.30	16.00	12.35	2.20	17.35	23.05	12.50	10.15	20.10	13.25	7.00	6.40	4.45									
Moscow	3.15	12.15	8.40	22.05	5.25	12.15	7.35	18.00	21.00	4.40	13.30	10.10	3.45	14.45	18.10	10.45								
Nairobi	8.15	17.00	16.00	24.55	4.55	17.00	10.45	12.45	25.45	7.15	3.45	6.20	8.30	19.30	20.42	15.30	12.50							
Paris	1.10	9.00	16.35	15.35	5.05	9.00	10.45	16.40	18.05	3.10	15.50	7.45	1.05	12.50	13.25	6.25	4.00	9.20						
Perth	20.35	17.25	11.15	25.20	17.10	23.00	9.30	8.15	17.25	15.25	14.20	25.55	19.30	19.30	22.50	26.30	19.40	23.00	21.40					
Rome	2.20	12.00	18.10	14.40	3.25	11.35	8.50	15.10	19.13	2.35	12.25	6.55	2.25	14.35	5.35	8.10	4.10	7.20	1.55	20.00				
Santiago	20.50	19.13	22.34	2.10	25.10	17.15	29.05	19.15	8.35	21.00	19.55	24.25	21.55	16.00	12.00	14.50	24.05	29.05	19.45	26.00	18.50			
Sydney	23.05	16.35	16.15	20.45	17.20	21.10	13.50	10.35	11.50	18.40	31.50	28.35	21.55	18.10	18.05	24.50	19.40	31.35	25.05	4.35	23.50	24.30		
Tokyo	11.40	7.20	3.50	28.30	19.40	12.55	9.45	4.20	7.05	14.05	25.00	18.40	11.50	11.55	16.25	18.55	9.25	19.55	16.45	10.05	17.40	27.55	9.15	
Washington	8.55	7.25	25.50	11.00	14.20	1.45	20.10	24.15	10.55	11.25	21.20	14.45	8.10	5.25	7.50	2.50	12.30	17.10	9.25	22.45	12.40	17.40	23.35	12.40

Communication

Communication

European road distances

Road distances between some cities, given in kilometres. To convert to statute miles, multiply number given by 0.6214.

	Athens	Barcelona	Brussels	Calais	Cherbourg	Cologne	Copenhagen	Geneva	Gibraltar	Hamburg	Hook of Holland	Lisbon	Lyons	Madrid	Marseilles	Milan	Munich	Paris	Rome	Stockholm
Barcelona	3313																			
Brussels	2963	1318																		
Calais	3175	1326	204																	
Cherbourg	3339	1294	583	460																
Cologne	2762	1498	206	409	785															
Copenhagen	3276	2218	966	1136	1545	760														
Geneva	2610	803	677	747	853	1662	1418													
Gibraltar	4485	1172	2256	2224	2047	2436	3196	1975												
Hamburg	2977	2018	597	714	1115	460	460	1118	2897											
Hook of Holland	3030	1490	172	330	731	269	269	895	2428	550										
Lisbon	4532	1304	2084	2052	1827	2290	2971	1936	676	2671	2280									
Lyons	2753	645	690	739	789	714	1458	158	1817	1159	863	1778								
Madrid	3949	636	1558	1550	1347	1764	2498	1439	698	2198	1730	668	1281							
Marseilles	2865	521	1011	1059	1101	1035	1778	425	1693	1479	1183	1762	320	1157						
Milan	2282	1014	925	1077	1209	911	1537	328	2185	1238	1098	2250	328	1724	618					
Munich	2179	1365	747	977	1160	583	1104	591	2565	805	851	2507	724	2010	1109	331				
Paris	3000	1033	285	280	340	465	1176	513	1971	877	457	1799	471	1273	792	856	821			
Rome	817	1460	1511	1662	1794	1497	2050	995	2631	1751	1683	2700	1048	2097	1011	586	946	1476		
Stockholm	3927	2868	1616	1786	2196	1403	650	2068	3886	949	1500	3231	2108	3188	2428	2187	1754	1827	2707	
Vienna	1991	1802	1175	1381	1588	937	1455	1019	2974	1155	1205	2935	1157	2409	1363	898	428	1249	1209	2105

UK road distances

Road distances between British centres are given in statute miles, using routes recommended by the Automobile Association based on the quickest travelling time. To convert to kilometres, multiply number given by 1.6093.

	Aberdeen	Birmingham	Bristol	Cambridge	Cardiff	Dover	Edinburgh	Exeter	Glasgow	Holyhead	Hull	Leeds	Liverpool	Manchester	Newcastle	Norwich	Nottingham	Oxford	Penzance	Plymouth	Shrewsbury	Southampton	Stranraer	York
Birmingham	430																							
Bristol	511	85																						
Cambridge	468	101	156																					
Cardiff	532	107	45	191																				
Dover	591	202	198	121	234																			
Edinburgh	130	293	373	337	395	457																		
Exeter	584	157	81	233	119	248	446																	
Glasgow	149	291	372	349	393	490	45	444																
Holyhead	457	151	232	246	209	347	325	305	319															
Hull	361	136	227	157	246	278	229	297	245	215														
Leeds	336	115	216	143	236	265	205	288	215	163	59													
Liverpool	361	98	178	195	200	295	222	250	220	104	126	72												
Manchester	354	88	167	153	188	283	218	239	214	123	97	43	34											
Newcastle	239	198	291	224	311	348	107	361	150	260	121	91	170	141										
Norwich	501	161	217	62	252	167	365	295	379	309	153	173	232	183	258									
Nottingham	402	59	151	82	170	202	268	222	281	174	92	73	107	71	156	123								
Oxford	497	63	74	82	109	148	361	152	354	218	188	171	164	153	253	144	104							
Penzance	696	272	195	346	232	362	561	112	559	419	411	401	386	355	477	407	336	265						
Plymouth	624	199	125	275	164	290	488	45	486	347	341	328	294	281	410	336	265	193	78					
Shrewsbury	412	48	128	142	110	243	276	201	272	104	164	116	64	69	216	205	85	113	315	242				
Southampton	571	128	75	133	123	155	437	114	436	296	253	235	241	227	319	192	171	67	227	155	190			
Stranraer	241	307	386	361	406	503	130	457	88	332	259	232	234	226	164	393	295	371	572	502	287	447		
York	325	128	221	153	241	274	191	291	208	190	38	24	100	71	83	185	86	185	406	340	144	252	228	
London	543	118	119	60	155	77	405	170	402	263	215	196	210	199	280	115	128	56	283	215	162	76	419	209

International E-road network ('Euroroutes')

Reference and intermediate roads (class A roads) have two-digit numbers; branch, link, and connecting roads (class B roads, not listed here), have three-digit numbers.

North–South orientated reference roads have two-digit odd numbers ending in the figure 5, and increasing from west to east. East–West orientated roads have two-digit even numbers ending in the figure 0, and increasing from north to south.

Intermediate roads have two-digit odd numbers (for N–S roads) or two-digit even numbers (for E–W roads) falling within the numbers of the reference roads between which they are located.

Only a selection of the towns and cities linked by E-roads are given here.

[...] indicates a sea crossing.

Communication

▪ West–East orientation

Reference roads

E10	Narvik — Kiruna — Luleå
E20	Shannon — Dublin ... Liverpool — Hull ... Esbjerg — Nyborg ... Korsør-Køge — Copenhagen ... Malmö — Stockholm ... Tallinn — St Petersburg
E30	Cork — Rosslare ... Fishguard — London — Felixstowe ... Hook of Holland — Utrecht — Hannover — Berlin — Warsaw — Smolensk — Moscow
E40	Calais — Brussels — Aachen — Cologne — Dresden — Krakow — Kiev — Rostov na Donu — Leninogorsk
E50	Brest — Paris — Metz — Nuremberg — Prague — Mukačevo
E60	Brest — Tours — Besançon — Basle — Innsbruck — Vienna — Budapest — Bucharest — Constanţa — Irkeshtam
E70	La Coruña — Bilbao — Bordeaux — Lyons — Torino — Verona — Trieste — Zagreb — Belgrade — Bucharest — Varna
E80	Lisbon — Coimbra — Salamanca — Pau — Toulouse — Nice — Genoa — Rome — Pescara ... Dubrovnik — Sofia — Istanbul — Erzincan — Iran
E90	Lisbon — Madrid — Barcelona ... Mazara del Vallo — Messina ... Reggio di Calabria — Brindisi ... Igoumenitsa — Thessaloniki — Gelibolu ... Lapseki — Ankara — Iraq

Intermediate roads

E06	Olderfjord — Kirkenes	E48	Schweinfurt — Prague
E12	Mo i Rana — Umeå ... Vaasa — Helsinki	E52	Strasbourg — Salzburg
E14	Trondheim — Sundsvall	E54	Paris — Basle — Munich
E16	Londonderry — Belfast ... Glasgow — Edinburgh	E56	Nuremberg — Sattledt
		E58	Vienna — Bratislava
E18	Craigavon — Larne ... Stranraer — Newcastle ... Stavanger — Oslo — Stockholm — Kappelskär ... Mariehamn ... Turku — Helsinki — St Petersburg	E62	Nantes — Geneva — Tortona
		E64	Turin — Brescia
		E66	Fortezza — Székesfehérvár
E22	Holyhead — Manchester — Immingham ... Amsterdam — Hamburg — Sassnitz ... Trelleborg — Norrköping	E68	Szeged — Braşov
		E72	Bordeaux — Toulouse
		E74	Nice — Alessandria
E24	Birmingham — Ipswich	E76	Migliarino — Florence
E26	Hamburg — Berlin	E78	Grosseto — Fano
E28	Berlin — Gdańsk	E82	Porto — Tordesillas
E32	Colchester — Harwich	E84	Keşan — Silivri
E34	Antwerp — Bad Oeynhausen	E86	Krystalopigi — Yefira
E36	Berlin — Legnica	E88	Ankara — Refahiye
E42	Dunkirk — Aschaffenburg	E92	Igoumenitsa — Volos
E44	Le Havre — Luxembourg — Giessen	E94	Corinth — Athens
E46	Cherbourg — Liège	E96	Izmir — Sivrihisar
		E98	Topbogazi — Syria

▪ North–South orientation

Reference roads

E05	Greenock — Birmingham — Southampton ... Le Havre — Paris — Bordeaux — Madrid — Algeciras
E15	Inverness — Edinburgh — London — Dover ... Calais — Paris — Lyons — Barcelona — Algeciras
E25	Hook of Holland — Luxembourg — Strasbourg — Basle — Geneva — Turin — Genoa
E35	Amsterdam — Cologne — Basle — Milan — Rome
E45	Gothenburg ... Frederikshavn — Hamburg — Munich — Innsbruck — Bologna — Rome — Naples — Villa S Giovanni ... Messina — Gela
E55	Kemi-Tornio — Stockholm — Helsingborg ... Heslingør — Copenhagen — Gedser ... Rostock — Berlin — Prague — Salzburg — Rimini — Brindisi ... Igoumenitsa — Kalamata
E65	Malmö — Ystad ... Świnoujście — Prague — Zagreb — Dubrovnik — Bitolj — Antirrion ... Rion — Kalamata ... Kissamos — Chania
E75	Karasjok — Helsinki ... Gdańsk — Budapest — Belgrade — Athens ... Chania — Sitia
E85	Černovcy — Bucharest — Alexandropouli
E95	St Petersburg — Moscow — Yalta

Communication

Intermediate roads

E01	Larne — Dublin — Rosslare ... La Coruña — Lisbon — Seville	E51	Berlin — Nuremberg
E03	Cherbourg — La Rochelle	E53	Plzeň — Munich
E07	Pau — Zaragoza	E57	Sattledt — Ljubljana
E09	Orléans — Barcelona	E59	Prague — Zagreb
E11	Vierzon — Montpellier	E61	Klagenfurt — Rijeka
E13	Doncaster — London	E63	Sodankylä — Naantali ... Stockholm — Gothenburg
E17	Antwerp — Beaune	E67	Warsaw — Prague
E19	Amsterdam — Brussels — Paris	E69	Tromsø — Tornio
E21	Metz — Geneva	E71	Košice — Budapest — Split
E23	Metz — Lausanne	E73	Budapest — Metković
E27	Belfort — Aosta	E77	Gdańsk — Budapest
E29	Cologne — Sarreguemines	E79	Oradea — Calafat ... Vidín — Thessaloniki
E31	Rotterdam — Ludwigshafen	E81	Halmeu — Piteśti
E33	Parma — La Spezie	E83	Bjala — Sofia
E37	Bremen — Cologne	E87	Tulcea — Eceabat ... Çanakkale — Antalya
E39	Kristiansand — Aalborg	E89	Gerede — Ankara
E41	Dortmund — Altdorf	E91	Toprakkale — Syria
E43	Würzburg — Bellinzona	E93	Orel — Odessa
E47	Nordkap — Oslo — Copenhagen — Rødby ... Puttgarden — Lübeck	E97	Trabzon — Aşkale
E49	Magdeburg — Vienna	E99	Doğubeyazit — Ş Urfa

Deepwater ports of the world

Aalborg	Denmark	**Basrah**	Iraq	**Catania**	Sicily
Aarhus	Denmark	**Batumi**	Georgia	**Cayenne**	French Guiana
Abadan	Iran	**Beira**	Mozambique	**Cebu**	Philippines
Aberdeen	UK	**Beirut**	Lebanon	**Charleston**	USA
Abidjan	Côte d'Ivoire	**Belem**	Brazil	**Chennai**	
Abu Dhabi	United Arab Emirates	**Belfast**	UK	**(Madras)**	India
		Belize City	Belize	**Cherbourg**	France
Acajutla	El Salvador	**Benghazi**	Libya	**Chiba**	Japan
Acapulco	Mexico	**Bergen**	Norway	**Chicago**	USA
Accra	Ghana	**Bilbao**	Spain	**Chittagong**	Bangladesh
Adelaide	Australia	**Bissau**	Guinea-Bissau	**Cienfuegos**	Cuba
Aden	Yemen	**Bizerta**	Tunisia	**Cleveland**	USA
Agadir	Morocco	**Bordeaux**	France	**Coatzacoalcos**	Mexico
Ajaccio	Corsica	**Boston**	USA	**Cochin**	India
Alcudia	Majorca	**Boulogne**	France	**Cologne**	Germany
Alexandria	Egypt	**Bourgas**	Bulgaria	**Colombo**	Sri Lanka
Algeciras	Spain	**Brazzaville**	Congo	**Conakry**	Guinea
Algiers	Algeria	**Bremen**	Germany	**Constanta**	Romania
Alicante	Spain	**Brest**	France	**Copenhagen**	Denmark
Almeria	Spain	**Bridgetown**	Barbados	**Corinth**	Greece
Amsterdam	Netherlands	**Brindisi**	Italy	**Corinto**	Nicaragua
Anchorage	USA	**Brisbane**	Australia	**Cork**	Ireland
Ancona	Italy	**Bristol**	UK	**Cotonou**	Benin
Annaba	Algeria	**Buena Ventura**	Colombia	**Dakar**	Senegal
Antofagasta	Chile	**Buenos Aires**	Argentina	**Dalian**	China
Antwerp	Belgium	**Buffalo**	USA	**Dammam**	Saudi Arabia
Apia	Samoa	**Busan**	Korea, Republic of (South Korea)	**Dampier**	Australia
Aqaba	Jordan			**Dar es Salaam**	Tanzania
Archangel	Russia			**Darwin**	Australia
Arica	Chile	**Cabinda**	Angola	**Davao**	Philippines
Ashdod	Israel	**Cadiz**	Spain	**Detroit**	USA
Asunción	Paraguay	**Caen**	France	**Dieppe**	France
Auckland	New Zealand	**Cagliari**	Sardinia	**Djibouti**	Djibouti
Aveiro	Portugal	**Calabar**	Nigeria	**Doha**	Qatar
Aviles	Spain	**Calais**	France	**Dordrecht**	Netherlands
Bahia Blanca	Argentina	**Caldera**	Costa Rica	**Douala**	Cameroon
Baku	Azerbaijan	**Calicut**	India	**Douglas**	Isle of Man
Balboa	Panama	**Callao**	Peru	**Dover**	UK
Baltimore	USA	**Cannes**	France	**Dubai**	United Arab Emirates
Bandar Abbas	Iran	**Cape Town**	South Africa		
Bangkok	Thailand	**Cap Haitian**	Haiti	**Dublin**	Ireland
Banjul	The Gambia	**Cardiff**	UK	**Dubrovnik**	Croatia
Barcelona	Spain	**Cartagena**	Colombia	**Duisburg**	Germany
Bari	Italy	**Cartagena**	Spain	**Duluth**	USA
Barranquilla	Colombia	**Casablanca**	Morocco	**Dundee**	UK

Dunedin	New Zealand
Dunkirk	France
Durban	South Africa
Durres	Albania
East London	South Africa
Elat	Israel
Emden	Germany
Esbjerg	Denmark
Europoort	Netherlands
Famagusta	Cyprus
Faro	Portugal
Felixstowe	UK
Flensburg	Germany
Flushing	Netherlands
Folkestone	UK
Fortaleza	Brazil
Fort de France	Martinique
Frankfurt	Germany
Fray Bentos	Uruguay
Fredericia	Denmark
Frederikshavn	Denmark
Fredrikstad	Norway
Freeport	The Bahamas
Freeport	USA
Freetown	Sierra Leone
Fremantle	Australia
Funchal	Madeira
Galveston	USA
Galway	Ireland
Gateshead	UK
Gavle	Sweden
Gdańsk	Poland
Gdynia	Poland
Geelong	Australia
Genoa	Italy
Georgetown	Cayman Is
Georgetown	Guyana
Ghent	Belgium
Gibraltar	Gibraltar
Gijon	Spain
Glasgow	UK
Godthaab	Greenland
Goole	UK
Gothenburg	Sweden
Grangemouth	UK
Gravesend	UK
Great Yarmouth	UK
Greenock	UK
Grimsby	UK
Guayaquil	Ecuador
Haifa	Israel
Hakodate	Japan
Halifax	Canada
Halmstad	Sweden
Hamburg	Germany
Hamilton	Bermuda
Hamilton	Canada
Harstad	Norway
Hartlepool	UK
Harwich	UK
Havana	Cuba
Hay Point	Australia
Helsingborg	Sweden
Helsinki	Finland
Hiroshima	Japan
Hobart	Australia
Ho Chi Minh City	Vietnam
Hodeida	Yemen
Holyhead	UK
Hong Kong	Hong Kong
Honiari	Solomon Is
Honolulu	Hawaii
Houston	USA
Hull	UK
Ibiza	Ibiza
Inchon	Korea, Republic of (South Korea)
Iskenderun	Turkey
Istanbul	Turkey
Izmir	Turkey
Jacksonville	USA
Jakarta	Indonesia
Jarrow	UK
Jeddah	Saudi Arabia
Juneau	USA
Kagoshima	Japan
Kalmar	Sweden
Kandla	India
Kaohsiung	Taiwan
Karachi	Pakistan
Kawasaki	Japan
Khulna	Bangladesh
Kiel	Germany
Kingston	Jamaica
Kirkcaldy	UK
Kitakyushu	Japan
Klaipeda	Lithuania
Kobe	Japan
Kolkata (Calcutta)	India
Kompong Som	Cambodia
Koper	Slovenia
Kota Kinabalu	Malaysia
Kowloon	Hong Kong
Kristiansand	Norway
Kuching	Malaysia
Kushiro	Japan
Kuwait	Kuwait
Lagos	Nigeria
La Guaira	Venezuela
Langesund	Norway
La Plata	Argentina
Larnaca	Cyprus
Larne	UK
Las Palmas	Grand Canary
La Spezia	Italy
Lattakia	Syria
La Coruña	Spain
Launceton	Australia
La Union	El Salvador
Le Havre	France
Leith	UK
Libreville	Gabon
Liège	Belgium
Limassol	Cyprus
Limerick	Ireland
Lisbon	Portugal
Liverpool	UK
Livingstone	Guatemala
Livorno	Italy
Lobito	Angola
Lomé	Togo
London	UK
Long Beach	USA
Los Angeles	USA
Lowestoft	UK
Luanda	Angola
Lübeck	Germany
Lüda	China
Macao	China
Malaga	Spain
Malmö	Sweden
Manama	Bahrain
Manaus	Brazil
Manchester	UK
Manila	Philippines
Mannheim	Germany
Manzanillo	Mexico
Maputo	Mozambique
Mar del Plata	Argentina
Maracaibo	Venezuela
Mariehamn	Finland
Marsala	Sicily
Marseilles	France
Masan	Korea, Republic of (South Korea)
Matanzas	Cuba
Melbourne	Australia
Mersin	Turkey
Messina	Sicily
Miami	USA
Middlesbrough	UK
Milwaukee	USA
Mina Qaboos	Oman
Mina Sulman	Bahrain
Mindelo	Cape Verde
Mizushima	Japan
Mobile	USA
Mogadishu	Somalia
Mombasa	Kenya
Monrovia	Liberia
Montego Bay	Jamaica
Montevideo	Uruguay
Montreal	Canada
Mormugao	India
Moulmein	Myanmar (Burma)
Mumbai (Bombay)	India
Murmansk	Russia
Muscat	Oman
Nacala	Mozambique
Nagasaki	Japan
Nagoya	Japan
Nampo	Korea, Democratic People's Republic of (North Korea)
Nantes	France
Napier	New Zealand
Naples	Italy
Narvik	Norway
Nassau	The Bahamas
Natal	Brazil
Nelson	New Zealand
New Amsterdam	Guyana
Newcastle	Australia
Newcastle	UK
New Haven	USA
New Mangalore	India
New Orleans	USA
New Plymouth	New Zealand
Newport	UK
New York	USA
Nice	France
Nouakchott	Mauritania
Noumea	New Caledonia
Novorossiysk	Russia
Nukualofa	Tonga
Nyborg	Denmark
Oakland	USA
Odense	Denmark
Odessa	Ukraine
Oporto	Portugal
Oran	Algeria
Osaka	Japan
Oslo	Norway
Ostend	Belgium
Oulu	Finland

Communication

Pago Pago	Samoa	**Rostock**	Germany	**Sydney**	Canada
Palermo	Sicily	**Rotterdam**	Netherlands	**Syracuse**	Sicily
Palma	Majorca	**Rouen**	France	**Szczecin**	Poland
Palm Beach	USA	**Sacramento**	USA	**Tacoma**	USA
Panama Canal	Panama	**Safi**	Morocco	**Takamatsu**	Japan
Papeete	Tahiti	**St George's**	Grenada	**Takoradi**	Ghana
Paradip	India	**St Helier**	Jersey	**Tallinn**	Estonia
Paramaribo	Suriname	**St John**	Canada	**Tampa**	USA
Paranagua	Brazil	**St John's**	Antigua	**Tampico**	Mexico
Paris	France	**St John's**	Canada	**Tanga**	Tanzania
Pasajes	Spain	**St Malo**	France	**Tangier**	Morocco
Pasir Gudang	Malaysia	**St Nazaire**	France	**Taranto**	Italy
Penang	Malaysia	**St Petersburg**	Russia	**Tarragona**	Spain
Philadelphia	USA	**Sakai**	Japan	**Tauranga**	New Zealand
Phnom Penh	Cambodia	**Salerno**	Italy	**Three Rivers**	
Piraeus	Greece	**Salina Cruz**	Mexico	**(Trois Rivières)**	Canada
Plymouth	UK	**Salonica**	Greece	**Thunder Bay**	Canada
Point-a-Pitre	Guadeloupe	**Salvador**	Brazil	**Timaru**	New Zealand
Pointe-Noire	Congo	**Samsun**	Turkey	**Tianjin**	China
Pondicherry	India	**San Diego**	USA	**Toamasina**	Madagascar
Ponta Delgada	Azores	**San Francisco**	USA	**Tokyo**	Japan
Poole	UK	**San José**	Guatemala	**Toledo**	USA
Port Adelaide	Australia	**San Juan**	Puerto Rico	**Toronto**	Canada
Port-au-Prince	Haiti	**San Juan del Sur**	Nicaragua	**Torshavn**	Faroes
Port Cartier	Canada	**San Lorenzo**	Argentina	**Toulon**	France
Port Elizabeth	South Africa	**San Pedro**	Côte d'Ivoire	**Townsville**	Australia
Port Georgetown	Guyana	**San Remo**	Italy	**Toyama**	Japan
Port Gentil	Gabon	**San Sebastián**	Spain	**Trebizond**	Turkey
Port Harcourt	Nigeria	**Santa Cruz de**		**Trieste**	Italy
Port Hedland	Australia	**Tenerife**	Tenerife	**Tripoli**	Lebanon
Pork Kelang	Malaysia	**Santa Fé**	Argentina	**Tripoli**	Libya
Port Kembla	Australia	**Santa Marta**	Colombia	**Trondheim**	Norway
Portland	USA	**Santander**	Spain	**Tunis**	Tunisia
Port Limon	Costa Rica	**Santiago de**		**Turku**	Finland
Port Louis	Mauritius	**Cuba**	Cuba	**Tuticorin**	India
Port Moresby	Papua New	**Santo Domingo**	Dominican	**Tyre**	Lebanon
	Guinea		Republic	**Ulsan**	Korea,
Port of Spain	Trinidad	**Santos**	Brazil		Republic
Port Said	Egypt	**SãoTomé**	SãoTomé and		of (South
Port Sudan	The Sudan		Príncipe		Korea)
PortTalbot	UK	**Sasebo**	Japan	**Vaasa**	Finland
Port Victoria	Seychelles	**Sassandra**	Côte d'Ivoire	**Valencia**	Spain
Porto Alegre	Brazil	**Savannah**	USA	**Valetta**	Malta
Portsmouth	UK	**Savona**	Italy	**Valparaíso**	Chile
Prince Rupert	Canada	**Seattle**	USA	**Vancouver**	Canada
Providence	USA	**Sevastopol**	Ukraine	**Varna**	Bulgaria
Puerto Cortés	Honduras	**Seville**	Spain	**Venice**	Italy
Pula	Croatia	**Sfax**	Tunisia	**Velsen**	Netherlands
Punta Arenas	Chile	**Shanghai**	China	**Veracruz**	Mexico
Pusan	Korea,	**Shimizu**	Japan	**Vigo**	Spain
	Republic	**Singapore**	Singapore	**Visakhapatnam**	India
	of (South	**Sitra**	Bahrain	**Vitoria**	Brazil
	Korea)	**Sittwe**	Myanmar	**Vlaardingen**	Netherlands
Quebec	Canada		(Burma)	**Vladivostok**	Russia
Ramsgate	UK	**Sousse**	Tunisia	**Volgograd**	Russia
Rangoon	Myanmar	**Southampton**	UK	**Walvis Bay**	Namibia
	(Burma)	**Split**	Croatia	**Wellington**	New Zealand
Ravenna	Italy	**Stavanger**	Norway	**Willemstad**	Netherlands
Recife	Brazil	**Stockholm**	Sweden		Antilles
Reykjavik	Iceland	**Stockton**	USA	**Wilmington**	USA
Richards Bay	South Africa	**Stralsund**	Germany	**Xingang**	China
Richmond	USA	**Suez**	Egypt	**Yangon**	Myanmar
Riga	Latvia	**Sunderland**	UK		(Burma)
Rijeka	Croatia	**Sundsvall**	Sweden	**Yokohama**	Japan
Rimini	Italy	**Surabaya**	Indonesia	**Zamboanga**	Philippines
Rio de Janeiro	Brazil	**Suva**	Fiji	**Zanzibar**	Tanzania
Rio Grande	Brazil	**Swansea**	UK	**Zeebrugge**	Belgium
Rosaria	Argentina	**Sydney**	Australia	**Zhdanov**	Ukraine

Map of Europe

Europe

ATLANTIC
OCEAN

ICELAND
Reykjavik

SWEDEN

FINLAND

NORWAY
Oslo
Helsinki

Stockholm
Tallinn
Baltic
Sea
ESTONIA

RUSSIA

NORTHERN
IRELAND

North Sea

Riga
LATVIA

SCOTLAND
Edinburgh

DENMARK

Copenhagen

LITHUANIA
Vilnius

Minsk

Moscow

Belfast

ENGLAND
The
Hague

Berlin

POLAND

BELARUS

Dublin

London

Warsaw

Kiev

WALES

IRELAND

Cardiff

Brussels

1

GERMANY

Prague

Bratislava

UKRAINE

Paris

2

3
Luxembourg

4

5

Liechtenstein
Berne

Vienna

Budapest

17
Kishinev

6
Ljubljana

7

8

FRANCE

ITALY

9

Zagreb

10

Belgrade

ROMANIA

Sarajevo

11

12

Bucharest

Andorra

Corsica

Rome

Tirana

16
Sofia

Black Sea

PORTUGAL

Madrid

Sardinia

14
Skopje

Ankara

SPAIN

Sicily

15

GREECE

TURKEY

Lisbon

Mediterranean Sea

Athens

Gibraltar

Nicosia
CYPRUS

1 THE NETHERLANDS	7 AUSTRIA	12 SERBIA AND
2 BELGIUM	8 HUNGARY	MONTENEGRO
3 LUXEMBOURG	9 SLOVENIA	14 MACEDONIA
4 CZECH REPUBLIC	10 CROATIA	15 ALBANIA
5 SLOVAKIA	11 BOSNIA-	16 BULGARIA
6 SWITZERLAND	HERZEGOVINA	17 MOLDOVA

SCIENCE AND TECHNOLOGY

Scientists

Airy, Sir George Biddell (1802–92) English astronomer and geophysicist, born Alnwick. Astronomer Royal (1835–81) who reorganized the Greenwich Observatory. Initiated measurement of Greenwich Mean Time, determined the mass of the Earth from gravity experiments in mines, and carried out extensive work in optics.

Alzheimer, Alois (1864–1915) German psychiatrist and neuropathologist, born Markbreit. Gave full clinical and pathological description of presenile dementia (Alzheimer's disease) (1907).

Ampère, André Marie (1775–1836) French mathematician and physicist, born Lyons. Laid the foundations of the science of electrodynamics. His name is given to the basic SI unit of electric current (ampere, amp).

Appleton, Sir Edward Victor (1892–1965) English physicist, born Bradford. Researched propagation of wireless waves, and discovered the existence of a layer of electrically charged particles in the upper atmosphere (the Appleton layer) which plays an essential role in radio communication. Received the Nobel prize for physics (1947) for studies of Earth's atmosphere.

Archimedes (c.287–212BC) Greek mathematician, born Syracuse. Discovered formulae for the areas and volumes of plane and solid geometrical figures using methods which anticipated theories of integration to be developed 1800 years later. Also founded the science of hydrostatics; in popular tradition remembered for the cry of 'Eureka' when he discovered the principle of upthrust on a floating body.

Aristotle (384–322BC) Greek philosopher and scientist, born Stagira. One of the most influential figures in the history of Western thought and scientific tradition. Wrote enormous amounts on biology, zoology, physics and psychology.

Avogadro, Amedeo (1776–1856) Italian physicist, born Turin. Formulated the hypothesis (Avogadro's law) that equal volumes of gas contain equal numbers of molecules, when at the same temperature and pressure.

Axelrod, Julius (1912–) US pharmacologist, born New York City. Discovered the substance which inhibits neural impulses, laying the basis for significant advances in the treatment of disorders such as schizophrenia. Joint winner of the 1970 Nobel prize for physiology or medicine.

Babbage, Charles (1791–1871) English mathematician, born Teignmouth. Attempted to build two calculating machines — the 'difference engine', to calculate logarithms and similar functions by repeated addition performed by trains of gear wheels, and the 'analytical engine', to perform much more varied calculations. Babbage is regarded as the pioneer of modern computers.

Bacon, Francis, Baron Verulam of Verulam, Viscount St Albans (1561–1626) English statesman and natural philosopher, born London. Creator of scientific induction; stressed the importance of experiment in interpreting nature, giving significant impetus to future scientific investigation.

Baird, John Logie (1888–1946) Scottish engineer, born Helensburgh. Gave first demonstration of a television image in 1926. Also researched radar and infrared television, and succeeded in producing 3-D and colour images (1944), as well as projection onto a screen and stereophonic sound.

Barnard, Christiaan Neethling (1922–2001) South African surgeon, born Beaufort West. Performed first successful heart transplant in December 1967 at Groote Schuur Hospital. Although the recipient died 18 days later from pneumonia, a second patient operated on in January 1968 survived for 594 days.

Beaufort, Sir Francis (1774–1857) Irish naval officer and hydrographer, born Navan, County Meath. Devised the Beaufort scale of wind force and a tabulated system of weather registration.

Becquerel, Antoine Henri (1852–1908) French physicist, born Paris. While researching fluorescence (the ability of substances to give off visible light), discovered radioactivity in the form of rays emitted by uranium salts, leading to the beginnings of modern nuclear physics. For this he shared the 1903 Nobel prize for physics with Marie and Pierre Curie.

Bell, Alexander Graham (1847–1922) Scottish–US inventor, born Edinburgh. After researching and teaching methods in speech therapy and experimenting with various acoustical devices, produced the first intelligible telephonic transmission on 5 June 1875, and patented the telephone in 1876. Founded the Bell Telephone Company in 1877.

Bishop, (John) Michael (1936–) US molecular biologist and virologist, born York, Pennsylvania. Awarded 1989 Nobel prize for physiology or medicine (jointly with Harold Varmus), for their discovery of oncogenes. This discovery is crucial to the understanding of cancer mechanisms.

Bohr, Niels Henrik David (1885–1962) Danish physicist, born Copenhagen. Greatly extended the theory of atomic structure by explaining the spectrum of hydrogen by means of an atomic model and quantum theory (1913). Awarded the Nobel prize for physics in 1922. Assisted in atom bomb research in America during World War II.

Boltzmann, Ludwig Eduard (1844–1906) Austrian physicist, born Vienna. Carried out important work on the kinetic theory of gases and established Boltzmann's law, or the principle of equipartition of energy.

Boyle, The Hon Robert (1627–91) Irish physicist and chemist, born Munster. One of the first members of the Royal Society. Carried out experiments on air, vacuum, combustion and respiration, and in 1662 arrived at Boyle's law, which states that the pressure and volume of a gas are inversely proportional at constant temperature.

Brahe, Tycho or **Tyge** (1546–1601) Danish astronomer, born Knudstrup, Sweden (then under Danish crown). After seeing the partial solar eclipse of 1569, became obsessed with astronomy. Accurately measured and compiled catalogues of the positions of stars, providing vital information for later astronomers and recorded unique observations of a new star in Cassiopeia in 1572 (a nova now known as Tycho's star).

Brunel, Isambard Kingdom (1806–59) English engineer and inventor, born Portsmouth. Helped to plan the Thames Tunnel and later planned the Clifton Suspension Bridge. Designed the first steamship to cross the Atlantic, the first ocean screw-steamer. In 1833 appointed engineer to the Great Western Railway and constructed all tunnels, bridges and viaducts on that line; also constructed and improved many docks.

Celsius, Anders (1701–44) Swedish astronomer, born Uppsala. Devised the centigrade, or 'Celsius', scale of temperature. Also advocated the introduction of the Gregorian calendar, and made observations of the aurora borealis, or northern lights.

Chadwick, Sir James (1891–1974) English physicist, born near Macclesfield. Studied radioactivity and as a result of the Curies' work was able to confirm the existence of the neutron which Rutherford had postulated in 1920. Built Britain's first cyclotron in 1935 and assisted in atomic bomb research in America during World War II.

Chandrasekhar, Subrahmanyan (1910–95) Indian–US astrophysicist, born Lahore (now in Pakistan). Showed that at the end of their lives, stars of less than a certain critical mass will collapse to form white dwarfs. Shared the 1983 Nobel Prize for physics with William Fowler (1911–95).

Copernicus, Nicolaus (1473–1543) Polish astronomer, born Torún. Studied mathematics, optics, perspective and canon law before a varied career involving law, medicine and astronomy. Published theory in 1543 that the Sun is at the centre of the Universe; this was not initially accepted due to opposition from the Church which held that the Universe was Earth-centred.

Coulomb, Charles Augustin de (1736–1806) French physicist, born Angoulême. Experimented on friction, and invented the torsion balance for measuring the force of magnetic and electrical attraction. The unit of electric charge (coulomb) is named after him.

Crick, Francis Harry Compton (1916–) English biologist, born Northampton. Constructed a molecular model of the complex genetic material deoxyribonucleic acid (DNA). Later research on nucleic acids led to far-reaching discoveries concerning the genetic code. Joint winner of the Nobel prize for physiology or medicine in 1962 with James Watson (1928–).

Curie, Marie (originally **Manya**) née **Sklodowska** (1867–1934) Polish–French physicist, born Warsaw. After graduating from the Sorbonne worked on magnetism and radioactivity, isolating radium and polonium. Shared the Nobel prize for physics in 1903 with her husband, Pierre Curie, and Antoine Henri Becquerel. Became professor of physics at the Sorbonne in 1906; awarded the Nobel prize for chemistry in 1911. Element 96 is named curium after the Curies.

Curie, Pierre (1859–1906) French chemist and physicist, born Paris. Carried out research on magnetism and radioactivity with his wife, Marie Curie, for which they were jointly awarded the Nobel prize for physics in 1903, with Antoine Henri Becquerel.

Cuvier, Georges (Léopold Chrétien Frédéric Dagobert) (1769–1832) French anatomist, born Montbéliard. Known as the father of comparative anatomy and palaeontology. Opponent of the Theory of Descent, and originated the natural system of animal classification. Linked comparative anatomy and palaeontology through studies of animal and fish fossils.

Dalton, John (1766–1844) English chemist, born Eaglesfield, near Cockermouth. Researched mixed gases, the force of steam, the elasticity of vapours and deduced the law of partial pressures, or Dalton's law. Also made important contributions in atomic theory.

Darwin, Charles Robert (1809–82) English naturalist, born Shrewsbury. Recommended as naturalist for a scientific survey of South American waters (1831–6) on HMS *Beagle*, during which he made many geological and zoological discoveries which led him to speculate on the origin of species. In 1859 published theory of evolution in *The Origin of Species by Means of Natural Selection*.

Davy, Sir Humphry (1778–1829) English chemist, born Penzance. Experimented with newly discovered gases, and discovered the anaesthetic effect of laughing gas. Discovered the new metals potassium, sodium, barium, strontium and magnesium and the metallic element calcium. Also investigated volcanic action, devised safety lamps for use in mining and was important in promoting science within industry.

Dawkins, Richard (1941–) British zoologist, born Nairobi, Kenya. Developed views on evolution in books such as *The Selfish Gene* (1976), *The Blind Watchmaker* (1986) and *Climbing Mount Improbable* (1996). Introduced the concept of the 'meme', a unit of cultural transmission. Well known in the popular media for his scientific atheism.

Delbrück, Max (1906–81) German–US biophysicist, born Berlin. Made significant contributions in the creation of bacterial and bacteriophage genetics, and in 1946 showed that viruses can recombine genetic material. Joint winner of the 1969 Nobel prize for physiology or medicine for his work in viral genetics.

Descartes, René (1596–1650) French philosopher and mathematician, born near Tours. Creator of analytical or co-ordinate geometry, also named after him as Cartesian geometry. Also theorized extensively in physics and physiology, and is regarded as the father of modern philosophy.

Dirac, Paul Adrien Maurice (1902–84) English mathematical physicist, born Bristol. Published complete mathematical formulation of the relativity theory of Albert Einstein after work on quantum mechanics. Joint winner of the Nobel prize for physics in 1933.

Doherty, Peter Charles (1940–) Australian immunologist, born Brisbane. Joint winner of 1996 Nobel prize for physiology or medicine (with Swiss immunologist Rolf M Zinkernagel, 1944–), for his research into the human immune system. Also received the Paul Ehrlich prize in 1983 and became FRS in 1987.

Doppler, Christian Johann (1803–53) Austrian physicist, born Salzburg. The Doppler effect, described in a paper in 1842, explains the increase and decrease of wave frequency observed when a wave source and the observer respectively approach or recede from one another.

Duchenne, Guillaume Benjamin Amand (1806–75) French physician, born Boulogne. Pioneer in electrophysiology and founder of electrotherapeutics. First to describe locomotor ataxia, in 1858.

Dulbecco, Renato (1914–) Italian–US biologist, born Catanzaro. Showed how certain viruses can transform some cells into a cancerous state, giving a valuable simple model system for which he

Science and Technology

Science and Technology

shared the 1975 Nobel prize for physiology or medicine.

Edison, Thomas Alva (1847–1931) US inventor and physicist, born Milan, Ohio. Took out more than 1 000 patents, including the gramophone (1877), the incandescent light bulb (1879) and an improved microphone for Bell's telephone. Also discovered thermionic emission, formerly called the Edison effect.

Ehrlich, Paul (1854–1915) German bacteriologist, born Strehlen (now Strzelin), Silesia. Pioneer in haematology and chemotherapy, he synthesized salvarsan as a treatment for syphilis and propounded the side-chain theory in immunology. Joint winner of the 1908 Nobel prize for physiology or medicine.

Einstein, Albert (1879–1955) German–Swiss–US mathematical physicist, born Ulm, Bavaria. Achieved world fame through his special and general theories of relativity; also studied gases and discovered the photoelectric effect, for which he was awarded the Nobel prize for physics in 1921. Element 99 was named einsteinium after him.

Ernst, Richard Robert (1933–) Swiss physical chemist, born Winterthur. Awarded 1991 Nobel prize for chemistry for innovations in nuclear magnetic resonance (NMR) spectroscopy. Also received the 1986 Benoist prize and the 1990 Ampère prize.

Euclid (fl.300BC) Greek mathematician who taught in Alexandria, where he appears to have founded a mathematical school. His *Elements of Geometry* is the earliest substantial Greek mathematical treatise to have survived, and probably the most widely known mathematical work.

Euler, Leonhard (1707–83) Swiss mathematician, born Basel. Published over 800 different books and papers on mathematics, physics and astronomy, introducing many new functions and carrying out important work in calculus. Introduced the notations e and gp, still used today. Also studied motion and celestial mechanics.

Eysenck, Hans Jurgen (1916–97) German–British psychologist, born Berlin. Researched the variations in human personality and intelligence, and frequently championed the view that genetic factors are to a large extent responsible for psychological differences between people.

Fahrenheit, Gabriel Daniel (1686–1736) German physicist, born Danzig. Devised the alcohol thermometer (1709) and later invented the mercury thermometer (1714). Also devised the temperature scale named after him, and was the first to show that the boiling point of liquids varies at different atmospheric pressures.

Faraday, Michael (1791–1867) English chemist and physicist, born Grenoble. Discovered electromagnetic induction (1831), the laws of electrolysis (1833) and the rotation of polarized light by magnetism (1845). First to isolate benzene and to synthesize chlorocarbons.

Fermat, Pierre de (1601–65) French mathematician, born Beaumont. Made many discoveries about the properties of numbers, probability, geometry and optics. A proof of his so-called 'last theorem' was announced in 1993.

Fermi, Enrico (1901–54) Italian–US nuclear physicist, born Rome. Published method of calculating atomic particles, and in 1943 succeeded in splitting the nuclei of uranium atoms, producing artificial radioactive substances. Awarded the 1938 Nobel prize for physics, and constructed the first US nuclear reactor at Chicago (1942). Element 100 was named fermium after him.

Feynman, Richard Phillips (1918–88) US physicist, born New York City. Made considerable theoretical advances in quantum electrodynamics, for which he was joint winner of the Nobel prize for physics in 1965. Involved in building the first atomic bomb during World War II.

Fleming, Sir Alexander (1881–1955) Scottish bacteriologist, born Loudoun, Ayrshire. First to use anti-typhoid vaccines on humans and pioneered the use of salvarsan to treat syphilis. In 1928 discovered penicillin by chance, for which he was joint winner of the 1945 Nobel prize for physiology or medicine.

Foucault, Jean Bernard Léon (1819–68) French physicist, born Paris. Determined the velocity of light by the revolving mirror method and proved that light travels more slowly in water than in air (1850). In 1851 by means of a freely suspended pendulum, he proved that the Earth rotates. In 1852 constructed the gyroscope and in 1857 the Foucault prism.

Freud, Sigmund (1856–1939) Austrian neurologist and founder of psychoanalysis, born Freiburg. Developed the technique of conversational 'free association' in place of hypnosis, and refined psychoanalysis as a method of treatment. Argued that dreams are disguised manifestations of repressed sexual desires, and propounded theories of infantile sexuality and the division of the unconscious mind into the 'Id', the 'Ego' and the 'Super-Ego'.

Frisch, Karl von (1886–1982) Austrian ethologist and zoologist, born Vienna. Developed ethology using field observation of animals combined with ingenious experiments. Showed that forager bees communicate information (on the location of food sources) in part by use of coded dances. Joint winner of the Nobel prize for physiology or medicine in 1973.

Gadolin, Johan (1760–1852) Finnish chemist, born Turku. He is remembered for his investigations of the rare earth elements, analysing a new black mineral from Ytterby, Sweden, and isolating from it a rare earth mineral, yttria, in 1794. This was an important step towards identifying the remaining undiscovered elements. Element 64 was named gadolinium after him.

Gajdusek, (Daniel) Carleton (1923–) US virologist, born Yonkers, New York. Studied the origin and dissemination of infectious diseases amongst the Fore people of Papua New Guinea. Joint winner of the 1976 Nobel prize for physiology or medicine.

Galen (c.130–c.201) Greek physician, born Pergamum. Wrote on medical and philosophical subjects, collated all the medical knowledge of his time, and was an active experimentalist. Venerated for many centuries as the standard authority on medical matters.

Galilei, Galileo, known as **Galileo** (1564–1642) Italian astronomer, mathematician and natural philosopher, born Pisa. Inferred the value of a pendulum for exact measurement of time, proved that all falling bodies, great or small, descend due to gravity at the same rate. Perfected the refracting telescope and pursued astronomical observations which revealed mountains and valleys on the Moon, four satellites of Jupiter, and sunspots, convincing him of the correctness of the Copernican theory. His advocation of the Copernican theory led to his imprisonment by the Inquisition; he remained under house arrest until his death.

Galvani, Luigi (1737–98) Italian physiologist, born Bologna. Proposed the theory of 'animal electricity' or 'galvanism', later shown to be attributable to other sources. Gave his name to the galvanometer, used from 1820 to detect electric current.

Gauss, Carl Friedrich (1777–1855) German mathematician, astronomer and physicist, born Brunswick. Made significant new advances in number theory, studied errors of observation and devised the method of least squares. Also carried out much work on pure mathematics, studied the Earth's magnetism and was involved in the development of the magnetometer, as well as giving a mathematical theory of optical systems of lenses.

Geiger, Hans Wilhelm (1882–1945) German physicist, born Neustadt-an-der-Haart. Investigated beta-ray radioactivity and, with Walther Müller, devised a counter to measure it.

Gell-Mann, Murray (1929–) US theoretical physicist, born New York City. Developed the theory of 'strangeness' to explain the behaviour of subatomic particles. With George Zweig introduced the concept of quarks as the basic building blocks of hadrons. Awarded the 1969 Nobel prize for physics.

Gould, Stephen Jay (1941–2002) US palaeontologist, born New York City. His ideas on evolution, history and culture appeared in popular collections of essays such as *Bully for Brontosaurus* (1991). He became best known for his theory of 'punctuated equilibrium', or rapid evolutionary change followed by stasis.

Halley, Edmond (1656–1742) English astronomer and mathematician, born London. Studied the Solar System and correctly predicted the return (in 1758, 1835 and 1910) of a comet that had been observed in 1583, and is now named after him.

Harvey, William (1578–1657) English physician, born Folkestone. Discovered the circulation of the blood.

Hawking, Stephen William (1942–) English theoretical physicist, born Oxford. Research on relativity led him to study gravitational singularities such as the 'big bang', out of which the Universe originated, and 'black holes', which result from the death of stars. His book *A Brief History of Time* is a popular account of modern cosmology. Since the 1960s he has suffered from a highly disabling progressive neuromotor disease.

Heisenberg, Werner Karl (1901–76) German theoretical physicist, born Würzburg. Developed quantum mechanics and formulated the principle of indeterminacy (uncertainty principle). Awarded the 1932 Nobel prize for physics. In 1958, with Wolfgang Pauli, announced the formulation of a unified field theory.

Helmholtz, Hermann (Ludwig Ferdinand von) (1821–94) German physiologist and physicist, born Potsdam. Researched physiology of vision, the ear and the nervous system as well as making important contributions in fluid dynamics, studies of vibrations and the spectrum, and studies of the development of electric current within a galvanic battery.

Henle, Friedrich Gustav Jakob (1809–85) German anatomist, born Fürth. Discovered the tubules in the kidney which are named after him and wrote treatises on systematic anatomy.

Herschel, Sir John Frederick William (1792–1871) English astronomer, born Slough. Son of Sir William Herschel; continued his father's research and discovered 525 nebulae and clusters. Pioneered celestial photography and researched photoactive chemicals and the wave theory of light.

Herschel, Sir (Frederick) William (1738–1822) German–British astronomer, born Hanover. Made a reflecting telescope (1773–4) with which he discovered the planet Uranus in 1781. Also discovered satellites of Uranus and Saturn, the rotation of Saturn's rings and Saturn's rotation period. Researched binary stars, nebulae and the Milky Way.

Hertz, Heinrich Rudolph (1857–94) German physicist, born Hamburg. Confirmed James Clerk Max-

well's predictions in 1887 by his discovery of invisible electromagnetic waves, of the same fundamental form as light waves.

Hippocrates (d.377 or 359BC) Greek physician, born Cos. Known as the 'father of medicine', and revered as the most celebrated physician of antiquity. His followers developed his theories that four fluids or 'humours' of the body are the primary seats of disease. His name is remembered in the 'Hippocratic oath'.

Hooke, Robert (1635–1703) English chemist, physicist and architect, born Freshwater, Isle of Wight. Anticipated the invention of the steam engine, formulated Hooke's Law of the extension and compression of elastic bodies, and anticipated Isaac Newton's inverse square law of gravitation. Constructed first Gregorian telescope and inferred rotation of Jupiter. Materially invented the microscope, the quadrant and a marine barometer.

Hubble, Edwin Powell (1889–1953) US astronomer, born Marshfield, Missouri. Demonstrated that some nebulae are independent galaxies, and in 1929 discovered galaxy 'redshift': distant galaxies are receding from us and the apparent speed of recession of a galaxy is proportional to its distance from us.

Hutton, James (1726–97) Scottish geologist, born Edinburgh. Formed the basis of modern geology with the Huttonian theory, emphasizing the igneous origin of many rocks and deprecating the assumption of causes other than those still seen at work.

Huxley, Thomas Henry (1825–95) English biologist, born Ealing. Assistant surgeon on surveying expedition to the South Seas (1846–50), during which he collected marine animal specimens; became foremost scientific supporter of Charles Darwin's theory of evolution. Also studied fossils and later turned to philosophy.

Huygens, Christiaan (1629–93) Dutch physicist, born The Hague. Made pendulum clock (1657), and developed the doctrine of accelerated motion under gravity. Discovered the rings and fourth satellite of Saturn, and the laws of collision of elastic bodies.

Jansky, Karl Guthe (1905–50) US radio engineer, born Norman, Oklahoma. Discovered astronomical radio sources by chance while investigating interference on short-wave radio telephone transmissions, initiating the science of radio astronomy. The SI unit of radio emission strength, the jansky, is named after him.

Jeans, Sir James Hopwood (1877–1946) English physicist and astronomer, born Ormskirk, near Southport. Made important contributions to the dynamical theory of gases, radiation, quantum theory and stellar evolution; best known for his role in popularizing physics and astronomy.

Jenner, Edward (1749–1823) English physician, born Berkeley. In 1796 made the revolutionary discovery of vaccination by inoculating a child with cowpox, then later with smallpox, finding that the child failed to develop the disease. Within five years vaccination was being practised in many parts of the world.

Joule, James Prescott (1818–89) English physicist, born Salford. Showed experimentally that heat is a form of energy and established the mechanical equivalent of heat; this became the basis for the theory of conservation of energy. With Lord Kelvin he studied temperatures of gases and formulated the absolute scale of temperature. The joule, a unit of work or energy, is named after him.

Jung, Carl (Gustav) (1875–1961) Swiss psychiatrist, born Kesswil. After collaborating with Sigmund

Freud, went on to develop his own theories of 'analytical psychology'. Described psychological types ('extraversion/introversion'), propounded the concepts of the 'collective unconscious' and the psyche as a 'self-regulating system', expressing itself in the process of 'individuation'.

Kant, Immanuel (1724–1804) German philosopher, born Königsberg, Prussia (now Kaliningrad, Russia). Researched astronomy and geophysics, and predicted the existence of the planet Uranus before its discovery. Philosophical works had enormous influence.

Katz, Sir Bernard (1911–2003) German–British biophysicist, born Leipzig. Discovered how the neural transmitter acetylcholine is released by neural impulses. Joint winner of the 1970 Nobel prize for physiology or medicine.

Kelvin, William Thomson, 1st Baron (1824–1907) Irish–Scottish physicist and mathematician, born Belfast. Solved important problems in electrostatics, proposed the absolute, or Kelvin, temperature scale and established the second law of thermodynamics simultaneously with Rudolf Clausius. Also investigated geomagnetism and hydrodynamics, and invented innumerable instruments.

Kepler, Johannes (1571–1630) German astronomer, born Weil der Stadt, Württemberg. Formulated laws of planetary motion describing elliptical orbits and forming the starting point of modern astronomy. Also made discoveries in optics, general physics and geometry.

Kirchhoff, Gustav Robert (1824–87) German physicist, born Königsberg. Carried out important research in electricity, heat, optics and spectrum analysis, his work leading to the discovery of caesium and rubidium (1859).

Krebs, Sir Edwin Gerhard (1918–) US biochemist, born Lansing, Iowa. Elected FRS in 1947. Researched the activation of glycogen enzymes together with Edmond Fischer (1920–), for which they were awarded the 1992 Nobel prize for physiology or medicine. Krebs later studied the structure of the kinases and the properties of phosphatases.

Krebs, Sir Hans Adolf (1900–81) German–British biochemist, born Hildesheim. Discovered the series of chemical reactions known as the urea cycle (1932). Joint winner of the 1953 Nobel prize for physiology or medicine for research into metabolic processes, particularly the 'Krebs cycle'.

Kroto, Sir Harold Walter (1939–) English chemist, born Wisbech, Cambridgeshire. Distinguished for his work in detecting unstable molecules, interstellar poly-yne molecules and the third allotrope of carbon C. Joint winner of the 1996 Nobel prize for chemistry (with Robert Curl, 1933– , and Richard Smalley, 1943–).

Lamarck, Jean (Baptiste Pierre Antoine de Monet) Chevalier de (1744–1829) French naturalist, born Bazentin. Made the basic distinction between vertebrates and invertebrates. On evolution he postulated that acquired characteristics can be inherited by later generations, preparing the way for the Darwinian theory of evolution.

Langmuir, Irving (1881–1959) US physical chemist, born New York City. He worked at the General Electric Company for 41 years, and his many inventions include the gas-filled tungsten lamp and an improved vacuum pump. He was awarded the 1932 Nobel prize for chemistry for his work on solid and liquid surfaces.

Laplace, Pierre Simon, Marquis de (1749–1827) French mathematician and astronomer, born Beaumont-en-Auge. Researched the stability of planetary orbits and developed the nebular hypothesis of planetary origin. Also formulated the fundamental differential equation in physics which bears his name, and the modern form of probability theory.

Lavoisier, Antoine Laurent (1743–1794) French chemist, born Paris. Showed that air is a mixture of gases, identifying both oxygen and nitrogen. Devised the modern method of naming chemical compounds, and helped to introduce the metric system. Guillotined in revolutionary Paris for his role as a government tax-collector.

Lawrence, Ernest Orlando (1901–58) US physicist, born Canton, South Dakota. Constructed the first cyclotron for the production of artificial radioactivity (1929), fundamental to the development of the atomic bomb. Became the first director of the radiation laboratory at Berkeley, California, in 1936 and received the Nobel prize for physics in 1939. Element 103 was named lawrencium after him.

Leibniz, Gottfried Wilhelm (1646–1716) German mathematician and philosopher, born Leipzig. Discovered calculus around the same time as Isaac Newton; also made original contributions in the fields of optics, mechanics, statistics, logic and probability, and laid the foundations of 18c philosophy.

Leishman, Sir William Boog (1865–1926) Scottish bacteriologist, born Glasgow. Discovered an effective vaccine for inoculation against typhoid and was first to discover the parasite of the disease kala-azar.

Linnaeus, Carolus (Carl von Linné) (1707–78) Swedish naturalist and physician, born Raceshult. Founder of modern scientific nomenclature for plants and animals.

Lister, Joseph, Lord (1827–1912) English surgeon, born Upton. Professor in Glasgow, Edinburgh and London. Greatest work was the introduction of the antiseptic system (1867), which revolutionized modern surgery. First medical man to be elevated to the peerage.

Lorentz, Hendrik Antoon (1853–1928) Dutch physicist, born Arnhem. Carried out important work in electromagnetism; joint winner of the Nobel prize for physics in 1902 for explaining the effect whereby atomic spectral lines are split in the presence of magnetic fields.

Lorenz, Konrad Zacharias (1903–89) Austrian zoologist and ethologist, born Vienna. Regarded as the father of ethology, favouring the study of the instinctive behaviour of animals in the wild. In 1935 published observations on imprinting in young birds by which hatchlings 'learn' to recognize substitute parents, and argued that while aggressive behaviour in humans is inborn, it may be channelled into other forms of activity, whereas in other animals it is purely survival-motivated.

Lyell, Sir Charles (1797–1875) Scottish geologist, born Kinnordy, Fife. Established the principle of uniformitarianism in geology: geological changes have been gradual and produced by forces still at work, not catastrophic changes. His work significantly influenced Charles Darwin, although Lyell never accepted the theory of evolution by natural selection.

Mach, Ernst (1838–1916) Austrian physicist and philosopher, born Turas, Moravia. Carried out experimental work on projectiles and the flow of gases. His name has been given to the ratio of the speed of flow of a gas to the speed of sound (Mach number) and to the angle of a shock wave to the direction of motion (Mach angle).

Malpighi, Marcello (1628–94) Italian anatomist, born near Bologna. Discovered capillary blood vessels and made many pioneering discoveries in microscopic anatomy.

Marconi, (Marquis) Guglielmo (1874–1937) Italian physicist and inventor, born Bologna. Experimented with converting electromagnetic waves into electricity and achieved wireless telegraphy in 1895. In 1898 transmitted signals across the English Channel and in 1901 succeeded in sending Morse code signals across the Atlantic. Joint winner of the 1909 Nobel prize for physics. Later developed short-wave radio equipment and established a worldwide radio telegraph network for the British government.

Maxwell, James Clerk (1831–79) Scottish physicist, born Edinburgh. Produced mathematical theory of electromagnetism and identified light as electromagnetic radiation. Also suggested that invisible electromagnetic waves could be generated in a laboratory, as later carried out by Hertz. Other research included the kinetic theory of gases, the nature of Saturn's rings, colour perception and colour photography.

Medawar, Sir Peter Brian (1915–87) British zoologist and immunologist, born Rio de Janeiro. Pioneered experiments in skin grafting and the prevention of rejection in transplant operations. Joint winner of the Nobel prize for physiology or medicine in 1960.

Mendel, Gregor Johann (1822–84) Austrian biologist and botanist, born near Udrau, Silesia. Became abbot in 1868. Researched inheritance characteristics in plants leading to the formulation of Mendel's law of segregation and the law of independent assortment; his principles became the basis of modern genetics.

Mendeleyev, Dmitri Ivanovich (1834–1907) Russian chemist, born Tobolsk. Formulated the periodic law from which he predicted the existence of several elements which were subsequently discovered. Element 101 was named mendelevium after him.

Michaelis, Leonor (1875–1949) German–US biochemist, born Berlin. Made early deductions on enzyme action and is best known for the Michaelis–Menten equation on enzyme-catalyzed reactions.

Michelson, Albert Abraham (1852–1931) German–US physicist, born Strelno (now Strzelno, Poland). Carried out famous Michelson–Morley experiment which confirmed the non-existence of 'ether', a result which set Einstein on the road to the theory of relativity. First American scientist to win a Nobel prize (physics) in 1907.

Millikan, Robert Andrews (1868–1953) US physicist, born Illinois. Awarded the Nobel prize for physics in 1923 for determining the charge on the electron, and carried out important work on cosmic rays.

Mullis, Kary Banks (1944–) US biochemist, born Lenoir, North Carolina. Discovered 'polymerase chain reaction' technique, which allows tiny amounts of DNA to be copied millions of times. This has many analytical uses, including HIV virus tests. Joint winner of the 1993 Nobel prize for chemistry (with Michael Smith 1932–2000).

Napier, John (1550–1619) Scottish mathematician, born Edinburgh. He is famous for the invention of logarithms to simplify computation, and for devising a calculating machine using a set of rods, known as 'Napier's Bones'.

Newton, Sir Isaac (1642–1727) English scientist and mathematician, born Woolsthorpe, Lincolnshire. Formulated complete theory of gravitation by 1684; also carried out important work in optics, concluding that the different colours of light making up white light have different refrangibility, developed the reflecting telescope, and invented calculus around the same time as Leibniz.

Ohm, Georg Simon (1787–1854) German physicist, born Erlangen. In 1827 published 'Ohm's law', relating voltage, current and resistance in an electrical circuit. The SI unit of electrical resistance is named after him.

Oppenheimer, (Julius) Robert (1904–67) US nuclear physicist, born New York City. During World War II led the atomic bomb development project at Los Alamos, and after the war continued to play an important role in US atomic energy policy. Opposed the development of the hydrogen bomb, and was suspended from secret nuclear research in 1953.

Parkinson, James (1755–1824) English physician, born London. Gave first description of paralysis agitans, or Parkinson's disease. Described appendicitis and perforation, and was first to recognize perforation as a cause of death.

Pascal, Blaise (1623–62) French mathematician and physicist, born Clermont-Ferrand. Carried out important work in geometry, invented a calculating machine, demonstrated that air pressure decreases with altitude as previously predicted and developed probability theory. The SI unit of pressure (pascal) and the modern computer programming language, Pascal, are named after him.

Pasteur, Louis (1822–95) French chemist, born Dôle. Father of modern bacteriology. Discovered possibility of attenuating the virulence of injurious micro-organisms by exposure to air, by variety of culture, or by transmission through various animals, and demonstrated that the attenuated organisms could be used for immunization. From this he developed vaccinations against anthrax and rabies. Also introduced pasteurization (moderate heating) to kill disease-producing organisms in wine, milk and other foods, and disymmetry in molecules.

Pauli, Wolfgang (1900–58) Austrian–US theoretical physicist, born Vienna. Formulated the exclusion principle (1924), that no two electrons can be in the same energy state, producing important advances in the application of quantum theory to the periodic table of elements; for this he was awarded the Nobel prize for physics in 1945.

Pauling, Linus (1901–94) US chemist, born Portland, Oregon. He made important discoveries concerning chemical bonding and complex molecular structures; this led him into work on the chemistry of biological molecules and the chemical basis of hereditary disease. He was awarded the 1954 Nobel prize for chemistry, and also the 1962 Nobel peace prize.

Pavlov, Ivan Petrovich (1849–1936) Russian physiologist, born near Ryazan. Studied physiology of circulation, digestion and 'conditioned' or acquired reflexes, believing the brain's only function to be to couple neurones to produce reflexes. Awarded the Nobel prize for physiology or medicine in 1904.

Perutz, Max Ferdinand (1914–2002) Austrian–British biochemist, born Vienna. Studied the structure of haemoglobin. Joint winner of the 1962 Nobel prize for chemistry.

Planck, Max Karl Ernst (1858–1947) German theoretical physicist, born Kiel. Researched thermodynamics and black-body radiation, leading him to formulate quantum theory (1900), which assumes energy changes take place in abrupt instalments or quanta. Awarded the Nobel prize for physics in 1918.

Ptolemy or **Claudius Ptolemaeus** (c.90–168) Egyptian astronomer and geographer, believed born Ptolemaeus Hermion. Corrected and improved the astronomical work of his predecessors to form the Ptolemaic System, described by Plato and Aristotle, with the Earth at the centre of the Universe and heavenly bodies revolving round it; beyond this lay the sphere of the fixed stars. Also compiled geographical catalogues and maps.

Purkinje, Jan Evangelista (1787–1869) Czech physiologist, born Libochowitz. Carried out research on the eye, brain, muscles, embryology, digestion and sweat glands, studying 'Purkinje's figure', an effect by which one can see in one's own eye the shadows of the retinal blood vessels, and 'Purkinje's cells', cells in the middle layer of the cerebellar cortex.

Pythagoras (6c BC) Greek mathematician and philosopher, born Samos. Associated with mathematical discoveries involving the chief musical intervals, the relations of numbers and the relations between the lengths of sides of right-angled triangles (Pythagoras's theorem). Profoundly influenced Plato and later astronomers and mathematicians.

Ramón y Cajal, Santiago (1852–1934) Spanish physician and histologist, born Petilla de Aragon. Carried out important work on the brain and nerves, isolated the neuron and discovered how nerve impulses are transmitted to brain cells. Joint winner of the 1906 Nobel prize for physiology or medicine.

Rathke, Martin Heinrich (1793–1860) German biologist, born Danzig (now Gdańsk, Poland). Discovered gill-slits and gill-arches in embryo birds and mammals. 'Rathke's pocket' is the name given to the small pit on the dorsal side of the oral cavity of developing vertebrates.

Rayleigh, John William Strutt, 3rd Baron (1842–1919) English physicist, born near Maldon, Essex. Carried out valuable research on vibratory motion, the theory of sound and the wave theory of light. With Sir William Ramsay (1852–1916) discovered argon (1894). Awarded the Nobel prize for physics in 1904.

Réaumur, René Antoine Ferchault de (1683–1757) French natural philosopher, born La Rochelle. Developed methods for producing iron, steel and porcelain, and became a leading naturalist. His alcohol and water thermometer (1731) introduced the Réaumur temperature scale.

Richter, Charles Francis (1900–85) US seismologist, born near Hamilton, Ohio. Devised the scale of earthquake strength which bears his name (1927–35).

Röntgen, Wilhelm Konrad von (1845–1923) German physicist, born Lennep, Prussia. Discovered the electromagnetic rays which he called X-rays (also known as Röntgen rays) in 1895. For his work on X-rays he was joint winner of the Rumford medal in 1896 and winner of the 1901 Nobel prize for physics. Also carried out important work on the heat conductivity of crystals, the specific heat of gases, and the electromagnetic rotation of polarized light.

Rutherford, Ernest Rutherford, 1st Baron Rutherford of Nelson (1871–1937) New Zealand–British physicist, born Spring Grove, near Nelson. Made first successful wireless transmissions over two miles, discovered the three types of uranium radiations, formulated a theory of atomic disintegration and determined the nature of alpha particles; this led to a new atomic model in which the mass is concentrated in the nucleus. Also discovered that alpha-ray bombardment could produce atomic transformation and predicted the existence of the neutron. Awarded the Nobel prize for chemistry in 1908.

Schrödinger, Erwin (1887–1961) Austrian physicist, born Vienna. Originated the study of wave mechanics as part of the quantum theory with the celebrated Schrödinger wave equation, for which

he was joint winner of the 1933 Nobel prize for physics. Also made contributions to field theory.

Schwann, Theodor (1810–82) German physiologist, born Neuss. Discovered the enzyme pepsin, investigated muscle contraction, demonstrated the role of micro-organisms in putrefaction and extended the cell theory, previously applied to plants, to animal tissues.

Sharp, Phillip Allen (1944–) US molecular biologist, born Kentucky. Invented the mapping technique used in the analysis of RNA molecules, leading to the discovery that genes are split into several sections, separated by stretches of DNA ('introns') which appear to carry no genetic information. Received the 1993 Nobel prize for physiology or medicine, which he shared with Richard Roberts (1943–).

Sörensen, Sören Peter Lauritz (1868–1939) Danish biochemist, born Havrabjerg, Slagelsi. Carried out pioneering research on hydrogen concentration and invented the pH scale for measuring acidity in 1909.

Szent-Györgyi, Albert von Nagyrapolt (1893–1986) Hungarian–US biochemist, born Budapest. Discovered actin, isolated vitamin C and was awarded the Nobel prize for physiology or medicine in 1937. Also made important studies of biological combustion, muscular contraction and cellular oxidation.

Tesla, Nikola (1856–1943) Yugoslav–US physicist and electrical engineer, born Smiljan (now in Croatia). His many inventions included improved dynamos, transformers, electric bulbs, and the high-frequency coil which now bears his name; he also did much to promote the use of alternating current electricity supply.

Thomson, Sir Joseph John (1856–1940) English physicist, born Cheetham Hill, near Manchester. Studied gaseous conductors of electricity and the nature of cathode rays; this led to his discovery of the electron. Also pioneered mass spectrometry and discovered the existence of isotopes of elements. Awarded the Nobel prize for physics in 1906.

Thomson, Sir William ► Kelvin, 1st Baron

Tinbergen, Nikolaas (1907–88) Dutch ethologist, born The Hague. Co-founder with Konrad Lorenz of the science of ethology (study of animal behaviour in natural surroundings). Analysed social behaviour of certain animals and insects as an evolutionary process with considerable relevance to human behaviour, especially courtship and aggression. Joint winner of the 1973 Nobel prize for physiology or medicine.

Van de Graaff, Robert Jemison (1901–67) US physicist, born Tuscaloosa, Alabama. Conceived of an improved type of electrostatic generator, in which electric charge could be built up on a hollow metal sphere; constructed first model, later to be known as the Van de Graaff generator, giving possibility of generating potentials of over a million volts. Developed the generator for use as a particle accelerator for atomic and nuclear physicists. Generator was also adapted to produce high-energy X-rays for cancer treatment and examination of the interior structure of heavy ordnance.

Varmus, Harold (1939–) US molecular biologist, born New York. Awarded the 1989 Nobel prize for physiology or medicine (jointly with Michael Bishop) for the discovery of oncogenes.

Volta, Alessandro Giuseppe Anastasio, Count (1745–1827) Italian physicist, born Como. Developed the theory of current electricity, discovered the electric composition of water, invented an electric battery, the electrophorus, an electroscope, and made investigations into heat and gases. His name is given to the SI unit of electric potential difference, the volt.

Von Neumann, John (1903–57) Hungarian–US mathematician, born Budapest. Worked on the atomic bomb project at Los Alamos during World War II and later designed some of the earliest computers. Went on to invent the idea of self-replicating machines.

Waals, Johannes Diderik van der (1837–1923) Dutch physicist, born Leiden. Formulated van der Waals equation, defining the physical state of a gas or liquid, and investigated the weak attractive forces (van der Waals forces) between molecules. Awarded the Nobel prize for physics in 1910.

Warburg, Otto Heinrich (1883–1970) German biochemist, born Freiburg, Baden. Carried out important cancer research. Awarded the 1931 Nobel prize for physiology or medicine, and in 1944 was offered a second Nobel prize which, as a Jew, he was prevented from accepting by Hitler.

Watson, James Dewey (1928–) US biologist, born Chicago. Deduced with Francis Crick the two-stranded helical structure of DNA, for which they shared the 1962 Nobel prize for physiology or medicine. Later became professor at Harvard and Director of the Cold Spring Harbor Laboratory in New York.

Watt, James (1736–1819) Scottish engineer and inventor, born Greenock. Developed and improved early models of the steam engine, and manufactured it from 1774. The watt, a unit of power, is named after him, and the term horsepower was first used by him.

Weinberg, Steven (1933–) US physicist, born New York City. In 1967 produced the 'electroweak' theory of atomic interaction and shared the 1979 Nobel Prize for physics with Abdus Salam and Sheldon Glashow. Published *The First Three Minutes* (about the early history of the universe) in 1977.

Wien, Wilhelm (1864–1928) German physicist, born Gaffken, East Prussia. Awarded the Nobel prize for physics in 1911 for work on the radiation of energy from black bodies. Research also included investigation of X-rays and hydrodynamics.

Young, Thomas (1773–1829) English physicist and physician, born Milverton, Somerset. Expounded the phenomenon of interference, which established the undulatory theory of light. Also made valuable contributions in insurance, haemodynamics and deciphering the inscriptions on the Rosetta Stone.

Scientific terms

Bold type indicates that a definition of a word or phrase in an entry is given elsewhere in the glossary.

In this glossary 10^{12} is used to mean 1 followed by 12 zeros and 10^{-27} is used to mean 1 occurring 27 places after a decimal point.

aberration In an image-forming system, such as a curved mirror or lens, the failure to produce a true image when different colours of light or light incident on different parts of the mirror or lens are focused to different positions.

absolute alcohol Water-free **ethanol**.

absolute zero The least possible temperature for all substances, when the **molecules** of any substance possess no heat energy. A figure of $-273.15°C$ is generally accepted as the value of absolute zero.

ac ▸ alternating current

acid Normally, a substance which (a) dissolves in water with the formation of hydrogen **ions**, (b) dissolves metals with the liberation of hydrogen gas, or (c) more generally, a substance which tends to lose a **proton** or to accept an **electron** pair.

acid rain Rain that is unnaturally **acid** as a result of pollution of the atmosphere with oxides of nitrogen and sulphur from the burning of coal and oil.

acoustic imaging Determination of distance and direction of objects, such as submarines, by the reception of the reflection of a sound pulse. Also known as sonar.

acquired character In zoology, a modification of an organ during the lifetime of an individual due to use or disuse, and not inherited from a previous generation. ▸ **natural selection**.

adaptation In zoology, any structural, physiological or behavioural characteristic which fits an organism to the conditions under which it lives; the genetic or developmental processes by which such characteristics arise. ▸ **natural selection**.

adiabatic process In physics, a process which occurs without interchange of heat with surroundings.

adsorption In chemistry, the taking up of one substance at the surface of another.

aerosol (1) A system in the form of a **colloid**, such as a mist or a fog, in which the dispersion medium is a gas. (2) Pressurized container with built-in spray mechanism used for packaging insecticides, deodorants, paints, etc.

aerospace The Earth's atmosphere together with the space beyond; the branch of technology or of industry concerned with the flight of spacecraft through this.

algae A group of simple plants containing **chlorophyll** but without roots, stems or leaves, which live in aquatic conditions.

alkali A substance which, when dissolved in water, forms a solution containing hydroxyl **ions**, negatively charged ions containing oxygen and hydrogen, and with a **pH value** of more than 7.

allotropy The existence of two or more forms of an **element** in one phase of matter (ie solid, liquid or gas), called allotropes.

alloy A mixture of metals, or of a metal with a non-metal in which the metal is the major component.

alpha particle The **nucleus** of a helium **atom**, emitted from natural or radioactive **isotopes**. Often written α-particle. ▸ **radioactivity**.

alternating current Generally abbreviated to ac. An electric **current** whose flow alternates in direction.

AM (amplitude modulation) ▸ modulation

amino acid A fatty acid in which an amino group (NH_2) and a carboxyl group (COOH) are attached to an **organic molecule**. They play an important part in the bodies of animals and plants, often combining in different forms to produce **protein**.

amorphous Non-crystalline.

amu ▸ atomic mass unit

anaerobic Living in the absence of oxygen. Anaerobic respiration is the liberation of energy which does not require the presence of oxygen.

anion A negative **ion**, ie **atom** or **molecule** which has gained one or more **electrons**.

anisotropic Said of crystalline material for which physical properties, such as its ability to conduct electrical **current**, depend on the direction relative to the crystal axes.

annihilation Spontaneous conversion of a particle and its **antiparticle** into **radiation**.

Science and Technology

annual A plant that flowers and dies within a period of one year from germination.

annulus A plane surface bounded by two concentric circles, like a washer.

anode A positively charged **conductor** used in conjunction with a **cathode** to lead an electric current into or out of a solid, liquid or gas.

antibody A defensive substance produced in an organism in response to the action of a foreign body, such as the toxin of a **parasite**.

anticyclone A distribution of atmospheric pressure in which the pressure increases towards the centre. Winds in such a system circulate in a clockwise direction in the northern hemisphere and in a counterclockwise direction in the southern hemisphere.

antigen A substance which stimulates the production of an **antibody**.

antiparticle The antiparticle of a given particle has the same mass but opposite values for all its other properties, such as charge. A particle and its antiparticle, eg the **electron** and **positron**, destroy each other on contact in the process of **annihilation**.

aperture (1) The opening, usually circular, through which light enters an optical system, such as a camera lens; its area may be varied by an iris diaphragm to control the amount of light passing. ▶ **f-number**. (2) The rectangular opening at which motion picture film is exposed in a camera or projector.

Archimedes' principle The principle that when a body is wholly or partly immersed in a fluid it experiences an upwards force equal to the weight of fluid it displaces.

aromatic compounds Organic compounds containing **benzene** or with similar chemical properties.

asteroid One of thousands of rocky objects found in the **solar system**, normally between the orbits of Mars and Jupiter, ranging in size from 1 to 1 000km.

astigmatism (1) In medicine, unequal curvature of the focusing surfaces of the eye, which prevents incident light rays from reaching a common focus point on the retina, resulting in blurred eyesight. (2) In physics, a defect in an optical system on account of which, instead of a point image being formed of a point object, two short line images (focal lines) are produced at slightly different positions and at right angles to each other.

astronomical unit The mean distance of the Earth from the Sun, about 149 600 000km or 93 000 000mi.

atom The smallest particle of an element which can take part in a chemical reaction. A central nucleus containing **protons** and **neutrons** is surrounded by shells of **electrons**.

atomic mass unit Exactly one twelfth the mass of a neutral **atom** of the most abundant **isotope** of carbon (1.660×10^{-27} kg).

aurora Luminous curtains or streamers of light seen in the night sky at high latitudes, caused when electrically charged particles from the Sun are guided by the Earth's magnetic field to the polar regions, there colliding with atoms in the upper atmosphere. In the northern hemisphere known as aurora borealis and in the southern as aurora australis.

background radiation **Radiation** which causes **ionization** coming from natural sources such as the Earth's rocks, soil and atmosphere.

bacteriophage A **virus** which infects bacteria.

benthos Collectively, the immobile animal and plant life living on the sea bottom.

benzene A **molecule** consisting of a ring or closed chain of six carbon **atoms** each with a hydrogen atom attached.

beta decay The radioactive disintegration with the emission of an **electron** or **positron**. ▶ **radioactivity**.

biennial A plant that flowers and dies between its first and second years from germination and which does not flower in its first year.

Big Bang Hypothetical model of the universe which postulates that all matter and energy were once concentrated into an unimaginably dense state, from which it has been expanding from a creation event between 13 000 000 000 and 20 000 000 000 years ago.

bioassay The quantitative determination of a substance by measuring its biological effect on eg growth, ie the use of an organism to test the environment.

biogenesis The formation of living organisms from their ancestors and of minute **cell** structures from their predecessors.

bioluminescence The production of light by living organisms, such as glow-worms, some deep-sea fish, some bacteria and some fungi.

biosphere The part of the Earth (upwards at least to a height of 10 000m, and downwards to the depths of the ocean, and a few hundred metres below the land surface) and the atmosphere surrounding it, which is able to support life. The term may be expanded theoretically to other planets.

bit In computer science, a digit in binary notation, ie 0 or 1. It is the smallest unit of storage (from *Binary* dig*IT*).

black hole A region in space from which matter and energy cannot escape. A black hole could be a **star** or the central part of a **galaxy** which has collapsed in on itself to the point where the speed required for matter to escape exceeds the speed of light.

buckyballs **Molecules** consisting of 60 carbon **atoms** arranged symmetrically. Familiar name for buckminsterfullerene.

byte In computer science, a fixed number of **bits**, often corresponding to a single character and operated on as a unit.

calculus The branch of mathematics dealing with continuously varying quantities or functions.

carat or **karat** (1) A standard weight for precious stones equal to 200 milligrams. (2) The standard of fineness for gold, such that 24 carats represents pure gold, and 23 carat gold has $\frac{1}{24}$ part impurity.

carbohydrates Compounds of carbon, hydrogen and oxygen, the last two being in the same proportion as in water. Form the main source of energy in food as sugars and starches.

carbon dating or **radiocarbon dating** The estimation of the date of death of an **organic** material from the amount of a radioactive **isotope** of carbon in it. The quantity of the radioactive carbon naturally decreases with time. ▶ **radioactivity**.

carcinogen Substance which encourages the growth of cancer.

carnivore A flesh-eating mammal.

catalysis The acceleration or retardation of a chemical reaction by a substance, a catalyst, which itself undergoes no permanent chemical change, or which can be recovered when the chemical reaction is completed.

cathode A negatively charged **conductor** used in conjunction with an **anode** to lead an electric current into or out of a solid, liquid or gas.

caustic Said of a material which is destructive or corrosive to living tissue; an agent which burns or destroys living tissue.

cell In biology, the unit from which plants and animals are composed.

cellulose A **carbohydrate** forming the chief component of **cell** walls in plants and in wood.

Celsius scale The **SI** name for centigrade scale. Temperature scale in which the freezing point of water is 0°C and the boiling point is 100°C.

centigrade scale ▶ **Celsius scale**

centrifuge Machine which uses the force produced by rotation to separate molecules from solution, particles and solids from liquids, and liquids which do not mix from each other.

CGS unit Abbreviation for Centimetre-Gram-Second unit, based on the centimetre, the gram and the second as the fundamental units of length, mass and time. For most purposes superseded by **SI units**. (p621)

chaos theory The theory which describes how the behaviour of a system which obeys well-known physical laws can become unpredictable if a very large number of accurately known quantities or a very extensive description of its initial state is required to predict its development. This leads to unpredictability in eg weather forecasting.

chip The popular name for an **integrated circuit**.

chlorophylls Green pigments involved in the process of **photosynthesis**. *Chlorophyll a* is the primary photosynthetic pigment in all organisms that release oxygen, ie all plants and **algae**.

cholesterol A white crystalline solid found in nerve tissues, gall stones, and in other tissues of the body.

chromosome Rod-like structures found in the **nucleus** of a **cell**, which perform an important role in cell division and transmission of hereditary features.

clone Organisms, **cells** or micro-organisms all derived from a single progenitor. They have therefore an almost identical **genotype**.

colloid A solid dispersed through a liquid such that, though apparently dissolved, it cannot pass through a membrane.

comet A small member of the solar system, made of ice, dust and gas, becoming visible as it approaches the Sun. A bright nucleus is often seen, and sometimes a tail which points away from the Sun.

conductor A material used for the transference of heat or electrical energy.

congenital Said of diseases or deformities dating from birth, but not passed on from a previous generation.

continental drift A hypothesis to explain the distribution of the continents and oceans and the structural, geological and physical similarities which exist between them. The continents were believed to have been formed from one large land mass and to have drifted apart. ▸ **plate tectonics**.

convection The transfer of heat in a fluid by the circulation flow due to temperature differences. The regions of higher temperature, being less dense, rise, while the regions of lower temperature move down to take their place.

Coriolis effect The effect whereby an object falling freely towards the Earth is slightly deviated from a straight line and will fall to a point east of the point directly below its initial position, due to the rotation of the Earth underneath as it falls.

cosmic rays Highly penetrating rays from interstellar space, consisting of particles such as **protons, electrons** and **positrons**.

cracking The breaking down of heavier crude-oil **molecules** to form lighter molecules by heat, pressure and the use of **catalysis**.

current The flow of electric charge in a substance, solid, liquid or gas.

cyclone (1) A region of low pressure, or depression. (2) A tropical revolving storm in the Arabian Sea, Bay of Bengal and South Indian Ocean.

Darwinian theory ▸ **natural selection**

desertification Formation of deserts from zones previously supporting plant life by the action of drought and/or increased populations of humans and grass-eating animals.

diffraction The spreading of light or other waves passing through a narrow opening or by the edge of an opaque body.

diffusion General transport of matter whereby **molecules** or **ions** mix through normal movement of particles due to their heat energy.

dimorphism (1) In chemistry, the crystallization into two distinct forms of an **element** or compound, eg carbon as diamond and graphite. (2) In biology, the condition of having two different forms, as animals which show marked differences between male and female (sexual dimorphism), animals which have two different kinds of offspring, and colonial animals in which the members of the colony are of two different kinds.

direct current Generally abbreviated to dc. An electric current which flows in one direction only.

dispersion The separation of visible light into its various colours when passing between media of different density, such as air and glass. Occurs because light passing between the media is deviated from a straight path by an amount which depends on the wavelength, ie the colour.

diurnal During a day. The term is used in astronomy and meteorology to indicate the variations of an astronomical quantity or weather phenomenon during an average day.

DNA or **deoxyribonucleic acid** In its double-stranded form the genetic material of organisms. Usually, two strands of DNA form a double-helix, the strands running in opposite directions.

dominant Of a **gene** which shows its effect in those individuals who received it from only one parent. Also describes an inherited feature due to a dominant gene.

Doppler effect The apparent change of frequency of light or sound because of the relative motion of the source of radiation and the observer, eg the change in frequency of sound heard when a train or aircraft is moving towards or away from an observer.

dry ice Solid (frozen) carbon dioxide, used in refrigeration (storage) and engineering.

dwarf star The name given to a small low-luminosity star. ▸ **white dwarf**.

ecosystem Conceptual view of a plant and animal community, emphasizing the interactions between living and non-living parts, and the flow of materials and energy between these parts.

El Niño An occasional warm tropical ocean current that moves from the East Indies to the South American coast, sometimes causing devastating changes in weather patterns leading to torrential The region in which forces are exerted on any electric charge present.

electrode A **conductor** whereby an electric current is led into or out of a solid, liquid or gas.

electrolysis Chemical change, generally decomposition of a compound, effected by a flow of current through a solution of the chemical, or its molten state, based on **ionization**.

electromagnetic wave A wave comprising two interdependent mutually perpendicular transverse waves of **electric** and **magnetic fields**. The spectrum of electromagnetic waves comprises **gamma-radiation, X-rays, ultraviolet radiation**, visible light, **infrared radiation, microwaves** and **radio waves**. The speed in free space for all such waves is around 300 000km (186 000 mi) per sec.

electron A subatomic particle with negative electric charge, which with the **proton** and **neutron**, is a basic constituent of the **atom**.

element A simple substance, composed of **atoms**, which cannot be resolved into simpler substances by normal chemical means.

emulsion (1) In chemistry, a suspension in the form of a **colloid** of one liquid in another. (2) In photography, a suspension of finely divided crystals in a medium such as gelatine which provides the light-

Science and Technology

sensitive coating on film, glass plates and paper.

endothermic Said of a chemical reaction which is accompanied by the absorption of heat.

entropy In thermal processes, a quantity which measures the extent to which the energy of a system is available for conversion to work.

enzyme A protein which provides **catalysis**, which is restricted to a limited set of reactions.

epicentre That point on the surface of the Earth lying immediately above the focus of an earthquake or nuclear explosion.

equinox Either of the two instants of time at which the Sun crosses the projected plane of the Earth's equator, around 21 March and 23 September.

ethanol or **ethyl alcohol** An alcohol with chemical formula C_2H_5OH, the active substance in alcoholic drinks.

evolution In biology, changes in the genetic composition of a population during successive generations. The gradual development of more complex organisms from simpler ones.

exothermic Said of a chemical reaction which is accompanied by the evolution of heat.

f-number A measure of the **aperture** of a lens, representing its light transmission; it expresses the diameter of the lens diaphragm as a fraction of its focal length, eg f/8, also written f:8 or f8.

Fahrenheit scale The temperature scale in which the freezing point of water is 32°F and the boiling point is 212°F.

fault A fracture in rocks along which some displacement has taken place. The displacement may vary from a few millimetres to thousands of metres. Movement along faults is the most common cause of earthquakes.

feedback Occurs when part of an output signal is fed back into the input of the system, which often occurs in electro-acoustic systems in which the microphone and loudspeaker are in the same room.

fermentation A slow decomposition process of **organic** substances induced by micro-organisms or **enzymes**. An important fermentation process is the alcoholic fermentation of sugar.

fibre optics ▸ **optical fibre**

field theory As yet an unverified attempt to link the properties of all force fields in physics into a unified system.

fission (1) In biology, the reproduction of some single-cell organisms from a single parent in which the **cell** divides into two more or less equal parts. (2) In physics, the spontaneous or induced disintegration of a heavy atomic **nucleus** into two or more lighter fragments. The energy released in the process is referred to as **nuclear energy**.

fossil The relic or trace of some plant or animal which has been preserved by natural processes in rocks of the past.

fractal A geometrical entity characterized by a basic pattern that is repeated at ever decreasing sizes.

fraternal twins ▸ **twins**

fusion (1) The process of forming a new atomic **nucleus** by combining lighter ones. The energy released in the process is referred to as **nuclear energy** or fusion energy. (2) The conversion of a solid into a liquid state. ▸ **atom**.

Galaxy (1) The name given to the belt of faint stars which encircles the heavens and which is known as the Milky Way. (2) The name is also used for the entire system of dust, gases and stars within which the Sun moves. (3) More generally, galaxy is used to mean any extra-galactic nebula, each being a vast collection of stars, dust and gas.

galvanized iron Iron which has been subjected to galvanizing, eg zinc coating, to prevent corrosion due to moisture.

gamma-radiation **Electromagnetic waves** of high energy emitted after **nuclear reactions** or by radioactive atoms during the process of radioactive decay. ▸ **radioactivity.**

gene One of the units of **DNA**, arranged in linear fashion on the **chromosomes**, responsible for passing on specific features from parents to offspring.

genetic code The system by which **genes** pass on instructions that ensure transmission of features inherited from previous generations.

genetic engineering Biological science whose aims include the control of hereditary defects by the modification or elimination of certain **genes**, and the mass production of useful biological substances (eg insulin) by the transplanting of genes.

genome The full set of **chromosomes** of an individual; the total number of **genes** in such a set.

genotype The genetic constitution of an individual; a group of individuals all of which possess the same genetic constitution.

genus In biology, a taxonomic rank of closely related forms, which is lower than family and is further subdivided into species.

geomorphology The structure and development of land forms, including those under the sea; the study of this.

geostationary Said of an orbit lying above the equator, in which an artificial satellite moves at the same speed as the Earth rotates, thus maintaining position above a fixed point on the Earth's surface. Such a satellite would have an altitude of 35 800km (22 200mi) above the Earth's surface.

geothermal power Power generated by using the heat energy of rocks in the Earth's crust.

gestation In mammals, the act of retaining and nourishing the young in the uterus; pregnancy.

giant star A large and luminous star with low average density.

gravitational waves Waves which move through a gravitational field. Accelerating masses are expected to radiate gravitational waves, but so far this has not been observed directly.

greenhouse effect The phenomenon by which thermal radiation from the Sun is trapped by water vapour and carbon dioxide on a planet's surface. This leads to the temperature at the planet's surface being considerably higher than would otherwise be the case.

gyroscope or **gyro** An apparatus in which a heavy flywheel or top rotates at high speed, the turning movement resisting change of direction of axis.

herbaceous A soft and green plant organ or a plant without persistent woody tissues above ground.

herbivore A grass-eating animal.

hermaphrodite A person whose reproductive organs are anatomically ambiguous, so that they are not exclusively male or female.

histamine A substance present in all tissues of the body, being liberated into the blood, eg when the skin is cut or burnt or during allergic reactions, eg hay fever; large releases cause the contraction of nearly all smooth muscle, a fall of arterial blood pressure and shock.

hologram A photograph made without use of a lens by means of interference between two parts of a split **laser** beam, which when suitably illuminated shows as a three-dimensional image.

hormone A substance released by glands into the bloodstream which carries it to remote sites in the body where it has a specific physiological activating or repressing function.

hybrid In biology, the offspring of a cross between two different strains, varieties, races or species.

identical twins ► **twins**

igneous rocks Rock masses generally accepted as being formed by the solidification of the Earth's internal molten **magma**.

immunity The state of having a high resistance to a disease due to the formation of **antibodies** in response to the presence of **antigens**.

imprinting In biology, an aspect of learning in some species, through which attachment to the important parental figure develops and their social preferences become restricted to their own species.

in vitro fertilization The reproduction of the natural process of fertilization outside the living body, in laboratory apparatus.

indigenous Native; not imported.

inertia The property of a body, proportional to its mass, which opposes a change in the motion of the body.

infinity A number which is larger than any quantified concept. For many purposes it may be considered as one divided by zero.

infrared radiation Electromagnetic waves in the wavelength range from 0.000075 to 0.1cm, approximately, lying between the visible and **microwave** regions of the spectrum.

infrasound The sound of frequencies below the usual audible limit, ie of less than around 20 cycles per sec or hertz.

inorganic Said of chemical **elements** and their compounds, other than the compounds of carbon.

integrated circuit A very small circuit consisting of interconnected **semiconductor** devices in a single structure which cannot be subdivided without destroying its intended function.

ion Strictly, any **atom** or **molecule** which has resultant electric charge due to loss or gain of **electrons**. Free electrons are sometimes loosely classified as negative ions.

ionization The formation of **ions** by separating **molecules**, or adding or subtracting **electrons** from **atoms** by various methods.

isobar A line drawn on a map through places having the same atmospheric pressure at a given time.

isomerism The existence of more than one substance having a given molecular composition and molecular mass but differing in constitution or structure.

isotope One of a set of chemically identical species of **atom** which have the same number of **protons**, but different numbers of **neutrons**.

jet stream A fairly well-defined core of strong wind, around 200–300mi (320–480km) wide with wind speeds up to around 200mph (320kph) occurring more than 20 000ft (7 000m) above the Earth.

Kelvin scale Temperature scale in which **absolute zero** is assigned the value zero and the temperature interval is the same as that of the Celsius scale. The unit is abbreviated as K; the freezing point of water (0°C) on this scale is 273.15 K.

La Niña An occasional cold ocean current that moves westerly along the equator, sometimes causing devastating changes in weather patterns leading to torrential rain and flooding in some areas, and drought in others.

laser Light Amplification by Stimulated Emission of Radiation. A source of intense light of a very narrow wavelength range in the ultraviolet, visible or infrared region of **electromagnetic waves**.

LED ► **light-emitting diode**

light-emitting diode A **semiconductor** device which emits light when an electric current is passed through it, as used eg for displays in digital clocks and electronic calculators. Abbreviated as LED.

light-year An astronomical measure of distance, being the distance travelled by light in space during

a year, which is approximately $9.46 \times 1\,012$km or $5.88 \times 1\,012$mi.

lipids or **lipoids** General terms for oils, fats, waxes and related products found in living tissues.

litmus A material of **organic** origin used as an indicator; its colour changes to red in the presence of **acids**, and to blue in the presence of **alkalis**.

luminescence The emission of light otherwise than due to heating, and so at a relatively cool temperature.

Mach number The ratio of the speed of a body, or of the flow of a fluid, to the speed of sound in the same medium. At Mach 1, the speed of the body is that of sound; below Mach 1, it is **subsonic**; above Mach 1, it is **supersonic**.

magma Molten rock, including dissolved water and other gases. It is formed by melting at depth in the Earth and rises either to the surface, as lava, or to whatever level it can reach before crystallizing again.

magnetic field A field of force which exists around a magnetized body. Also associated with electric **currents** and the motions of **electrons** in **atoms**.

magnetic tape Flexible plastic tape, typically 6 to 50mm wide, coated on one side with magnetic material, in which signals are registered for subsequent reproduction. Used for storing television images, sound or computer data.

magnetism The science which covers **magnetic fields** and their effects on materials.

magnitude A measure of the apparent or absolute brightness of an astronomical object. The brightest naked-eye stars are of around first magnitude and the dimmest around the sixth.

matrix A system of numbers arranged in a square or rectangular formation.

metamorphic rocks Rocks formed by alteration of existing rocks by heat, pressure or other processes in the Earth's crust.

meteor A 'shooting star'. A small body which enters the Earth's atmosphere from the space between the planets and burns up due to friction, flashing across the sky and generally ceasing to be visible before it falls to Earth.

microwave background A weak **radio wave** signal which is detectable in every direction in the sky with almost identical intensity. It is believed to be the relic of the early hot phase in the **Big Bang** universe.

microwaves Those electromagnetic waves with wavelengths between 1mm and 30cm, lying between **radio waves** and **infrared radiation** in the spectrum.

Milky Way ► **Galaxy**

minor planet A term used generally in professional astronomy for **asteroid**. Also known as planetoid.

MKSA Metre-Kilogram(me)-Sec-Ampere system of units, adopted by the International Electrotechnical Commission, in place of all other systems of units. ► **SI units**.

modulation The process of impressing information (code, speech, video, data, etc) onto a higher frequency carrier wave. In frequency modulation (FM) the information is recorded as a variation in frequency, with constant amplitude, and in amplitude modulation (AM) as a variation in amplitude at constant frequency. Used in radio broadcasting.

mole The amount of substance that contains as many entities (**atom**, **molecules**, **ions**, **electrons**, **photons**, etc) as there are atoms in 12 of a certain **isotope** of carbon.

molecule An **atom** or a finite group of atoms which is capable of independent existence and has properties characteristic of the substance of which it is the basic unit. Molecular substances are those which have discrete molecules, such as water. Diamond and sodium chloride are examples of non-molecular substances.

Science and Technology

Science and Technology

mutation In biology, a genetic change that can be transmitted to offspring as an inheritable divergence from previous generations.

natural selection An evolutionary theory which postulates the survival of the best-adapted forms of a species, with the inheritance of those characteristics wherein their fitness lies, and which arise as random variations due to **mutation**; it was first propounded by Charles Darwin, and is often referred to as Darwinism or the Darwinian Theory.

neap tides High tides occurring when the Sun's tidal influence is working against that of the Moon.

nebula A term applied to any astronomical object which appears as a hazy smudge of light in an optical telescope, its usage predating photographic astronomy. It is now more properly restricted to true clouds of interstellar medium. **Galaxies** are sometimes referred to as extra-galactic nebulae.

neuron or **neurone** A nerve cell and its processes.

neutrino A fundamental particle with zero charge and zero mass which only interacts weakly with matter and is therefore difficult to detect.

neutron star A small body of very high density resulting from a **supernova** explosion in which a massive **star** collapses under its own gravitational forces, the **electrons** and **protons** combining to form **neutrons**.

neutron An uncharged subatomic particle, with mass approximately equal to that of the **proton**, which is found in the **nucleus** of the **atom**.

noble gases The elements helium, neon, argon, krypton, xenon and radon, which due to their stable structures do not take part in all the usual chemical reactions. Also known as inert gases, rare gases.

node The location of a minimum in the sound, pressure or particle motion when waves superimpose and result in standing waves.

nova Classically, any new star which suddenly becomes visible to the unaided eye. In modern astronomy, a star late in its evolutionary track which suddenly brightens by a factor of 10 000 or more.

nuclear energy In principle, the energy stored in an atomic **nucleus** which binds together the constituent particles. More usually, the energy released during nuclear reactions involving regrouping of such particles (eg **fission** or **fusion** processes).

nuclear fission The spontaneous or induced disintegration of the **nucleus** of a heavy **atom** into two lighter atoms. The process involves a loss of mass which is converted into **nuclear energy**.

nuclear fusion The process of forming **atoms** of new elements by the fusion of atoms of lighter ones. Usually the formation of helium by the fusion of hydrogen and its **isotopes**. The process involves a loss of mass which is converted into **nuclear energy**.

nuclear reaction A process in which an atomic **nucleus** interacts with another nucleus or particle, producing changes in energy and nuclear structure.

nucleon A general name for a **neutron** or proton.

nucleus (1) In biology, the compartment within a **cell** bounded by a double membrane and containing the genomic **DNA**. (2) In physics, the structure within an **atom** composed of **protons** and **neutrons** which constitutes almost all the mass of the atom.

omnivore An animal which eats both plants and animals.

oncogene A type of **gene** involved in the onset and development of cancer.

optical fibre Fibres of ultra-pure glass, having properties such that light can be transmitted through them by continuously reflecting round bends. Used eg in some communications systems.

order of magnitude The approximate size or number of something, usually measured in a scale from one value to ten times that value.

organic Said of the compounds of carbon. Owing to the ability of carbon atoms to combine together in long chains, these compounds are far more numerous than those of other elements and are the basis of living matter.

orogenesis The tectonic process whereby mountain chains are formed through movement of the Earth's crust.

orthogenesis The evolution of organisms systematically in definite directions and not accidentally in many directions; determinate variation.

osmosis Diffusion of a solvent through a semipermeable membrane into a more concentrated solution, tending to equalize the concentrations on both sides of the membrane.

oxidation The addition of oxygen to a compound. More generally, any reaction involving the loss of **electrons** from an **atom**. It is always accompanied by reduction.

ozone layer The region of the Earth's atmosphere, between about 20 and 40km (12.5 and 25mi) above the surface, where ozone makes up a greater proportion of the air than at any other height. This layer exerts a vital influence by absorbing much of the **ultraviolet radiation** in sunlight and preventing it from reaching the Earth's surface where it has considerable biological effect.

parasite An organism which lives in or on another organism and derives subsistence from it without rendering it any service in return.

parsec The unit of length used for distances beyond the solar system, approximately equal to 3.26 **light-years**.

parthenogenesis The development of a new individual from a single, unfertilized reproductive cell, often an egg.

pasteurization Reduction of the number of microorganisms in milk by maintaining it in a holder at a temperature of from 62.8° to 65.5°C for 30 minutes.

pathogen An organism, eg **parasite**, bacterium or **virus**, which causes disease.

perennial A plant that lives for more than two years.

periodic table A table displaying classification of chemical **elements** into periods (corresponding to the filling of successive shells of electrons in the atom) and groups (corresponding to the number of outer electrons present).

pH value A number used to express degrees of acidity or alkalinity in solutions, where a pH above 7 indicates alkalinity and below 7 indicates acidity. ► **acid** and **alkali**.

phage ► **bacteriophage**

phosphorescence (1) In biology, the production of light, usually (in animals) with little production of heat, as in glow-worms. (2) ► **luminescence.**

photochemical reaction The chemical reaction brought about by light or **ultraviolet radiation**.

photoelectric effect Any phenomenon resulting from the absorption of **photon** energy by **electrons**, leading to their release from a surface, when the photon energy exceeds that binding the electron to the surface, or otherwise allowing conduction when the photon energy exceeds the amount of energy binding an electron to the **atom**.

photon A unit of radiation in the **quantum theory** of light in which light is required to have particle character. May also be regarded as a unit of energy. Photons travel at the speed of light.

photosensitive Sensitive to the action of visible or invisible radiation.

photosynthesis The use of energy from light to drive chemical reactions, most notably the building-up of complex compounds by the **chlorophyll** apparatus of plants.

plankton Animals and plants floating in the waters of seas, rivers, ponds and lakes, as distinct from animals which are attached to, or crawl upon, the bottom; especially minute organisms and forms, possessing weak powers of motion.

plasma (1) In physics, a gaseous discharge containing **ions** in which there is no resultant charge, the number of positive and negative ions being equal, in addition to unionized **molecules** or **atoms**. (2) In biology, the bounding membrane of **cells** which controls the entry of molecules and the interaction of cells with their environment.

plate tectonics The interpretation of the Earth's structures and processes (including midocean ridges, mountain building, earthquake zones and volcanic belts) in terms of the movements of large plates of the Earth's crust acting as rigid slabs floating on the layer beneath.

polarization (1) In chemistry, the separation of the positive and negative charges of a molecule by an external agent. (2) In physics, non-random orientation of electric and magnetic fields of an **electromagnetic wave**, ie the restriction of the vibrations of light in certain planes.

Polaroid® The trademark for a range of photographic and optical products, including a transparent light-polarizing plastic sheet and methods of instant photography in black-and-white and colour. ▸ **polarization**.

polymer A plastic material built up from a series of smaller units. The molecular size of the polymer helps to determine the mechanical properties of the plastic material and ranges from a few hundred of the basic units to perhaps hundreds of thousands.

polymorphism (1) The presence in a population of two or more forms of a particular gene. (2) The occurrence of different structural forms at different stages of the life-cycle of the individual.

positron A particle of the same mass as and opposite charge to the (negative) **electron**. The **antiparticle** to the electron.

precession of the equinoxes The variation in the direction of the Earth's axis of rotation caused mainly by the attraction of the Sun and Moon on the equatorial bulge of the Earth, the change describing a full cone with a period of around 25 800 years.

primary colours Colours from which all other colours can be derived; red, yellow and blue.

protein Any member of a group of complex substances containing nitrogen that play an important part in the bodies of plants and animals.

proton The **nucleus** of the hydrogen **atom**, of positive charge. With **neutrons**, protons form the nuclei of all atoms.

quantum mechanics A branch of mechanics based on the **quantum theory**, used in predicting the behaviour of elementary particles.

quantum theory The theory of emission and absorption of energy not in continuous measures but in finite steps, applied to elementary particles.

quark A fundamental subatomic particle, currently seen as any of six types: bottom, top, up, down, charmed and strange. Although not yet observed directly, these are suggested to be the units out of which all other subatomic particles are formed.

quasar A distant, compact object far beyond our **Galaxy** which looks star-like on a photograph but appears to be much more distant than a star that we would be able to observe. The word is a contraction of quasi-stellar object. Thought to be the most luminous objects in the universe, their mechanisms are possibly related to **black holes**.

radar In general, a system using pulsed **radio waves** to measure the distance and direction of a target (from *RA*dio *D*etection *A*nd *R*anging).

radiation The dissemination of energy from a source. The term is applied to **electromagnetic waves** and to emitted particles (**protons**, **neutrons**, etc).

radio galaxy A **galaxy** emitting a particularly high amount of **radio waves**.

radio waves Electromagnetic waves of frequency suitable for radio transmission, of wavelength greater than around 10cm, ie of longer wavelength than **microwaves**.

radioactivity Spontaneous disintegration of certain natural heavy **elements** (eg radium, actinium, uranium, thorium). The ultimate end-product of radioactive disintegration is an **isotope** of lead.

rational number A number which can be expressed as the ratio of two integers, eg $\frac{3}{4}$.

recessive Of a **gene**, showing its effect only in individuals that received it from both parents. Also describes an inheritable feature due to a recessive gene.

recombination Reassortment of genes or inheritable features in combinations different from what they were in the parents.

red giant A large, cool, luminous star with its hydrogen exhausted by **nuclear reaction** to helium.

redshift Generally, the decrease in frequency of light observed when a light source moves away from an observer due to the **Doppler effect**. Often referred to in the sense of redshifts observed in light from distant galaxies, indicating the expansion of the universe.

reduction Any process in which an electron is added to an **atom** or an **ion**. Always occurs accompanied by **oxidation**.

refraction Deflection of waves (light, sound, etc) which occurs when passing from one medium to another of different density.

relative atomic mass The mass of atoms of an element given on the scale where 1 unit is equal to 1.660×10^{-27} kg. Devised by assigning the value 12 to a specific **isotope** of carbon.

relativity Einstein's Special Theory of Relativity (1905) postulates that all motion is relative and that the velocity of light is the same for all observers, and predicts the effects of these assumptions, including variations in the size and mass of objects and in the rate of passage of time, depending on the speed of the observer. His General Theory of Relativity (1916) predicts the variations involved due to acceleration and gravitation.

remote sensing A method in which remote detectors are used to collect data for transmission to a central computer; observation and collection of scientific data without direct contact, especially observation of the Earth's surface from the air or from space using **electromagnetic waves**.

resonance If a vibrating system is set into forced vibrations by a periodic driving force and the applied frequency is at or near the natural vibration frequency of the system, then resonance occurs, producing vibrations of maximum velocity amplitude.

respiration Breathing; the taking in of oxygen and giving out of carbon dioxide, with associated physiological processes.

Richter scale A scale of measurement from 1 to 10, used to indicate the magnitude of an earthquake.

RNA or **ribonucleic acid** Nucleic acid containing ribose, present in the living cells, where it plays an important part in the development of **proteins**. It can hold genetic information as in **viruses**, but is also the primary agent for transferring information from the **genome** to the protein synthetic machinery of the cell.

saprophyte A plant that feeds on dead organic matter.

saturated compounds Compounds to which no hydrogen atoms or their equivalent can be added, ie

Science and Technology

which contain neither a double nor a triple bond.

sedimentary rocks All those rocks which result from the wastage of pre-existing rocks. They include the fragments of rocks deposited as sheets of sediment on the floors of seas, lakes and rivers and on land, and also deposits formed of the hard parts of organisms. **Igneous** and **metamorphic** rocks are excluded.

semiconductor Said of a material (an **element** or a compound) having higher resistance to the flow of electricity than a **conductor**, but lower resistance than an insulator.

sex determination In many organisms (including vertebrates) sex is determined by the possession of a particular combination of **chromosomes**. In mammals, the female's chromosomes are designated XX and the male's are known as XY.

SI The system of coherent metric units (Système International d'Unités) proposed for international acceptance in 1960.

sidereal time Time measured by considering the rotation of the Earth relative to the distant stars (rather than the Sun, which is the basis of civil time).

silicon chip ▶ chip

sine wave A mathematical function which describes a waveform of a single frequency, indefinitely repeated in time. Its displacement can be expressed as the sine (or cosine) of a linear function of time or distance, or both.

software package A fully documented computer program, or set of programs, designed to perform a particular task.

solar system The term designating the Sun and the attendant bodies moving about it under gravitational attraction; comprises nine major planets, and a vast number of **asteroids**, **comets** and **meteors**.

solstice One of the two instants in the year when the Sun reaches its greatest excursion north or south of the equator, or the point reached then. The summer solstice occurs around 21 June, when the Sun reaches the tropic of Cancer, and the winter solstice occurs around 21 December, when the Sun reaches the tropic of Capricorn.

sonar ▶ acoustic imaging

sonic boom A noise phenomenon due to the shock waves projected from an aircraft travelling at **supersonic** speed. The waves create pressures which may be of sufficient intensity to cause damage to buildings, etc.

species A group of individuals that actually or potentially interbreed with each other but not with other such groups and show continuous **variation** within the group but which is distinct from other such groups.

spore A single-cell asexual reproductive body, sometimes extended to other reproductive bodies.

spring tides High tides occurring when the Sun and Moon are acting together to produce a maximum tide.

stalactite A deposit of calcium carbonate which hangs icicle-like from the roofs of limestone caverns.

stalagmite An upward-growing conical formation of calcium carbonate, precipitated from dripping solutions on the floors and walls of limestone caverns.

star A sphere of matter held together entirely by its own gravitational field and generating energy by means of **nuclear fusion** reactions in its deep interior.

stellar evolution The sequence of events and changes covering the entire life-cycle of a star.

subsonic Said of an object or flow which moves with a speed less than that of sound. ▶ **Mach number, supersonic.**

superconductivity The property of some pure metals and metallic alloys at very low temperature of having negligible resistance to the flow of an electric current. Each material has its own critical temperature above which it is a normal conductor. When a current is established, it persists almost indefinitely.

supergiant star A star of very high luminosity, enormous size and low density.

supernova A very bright **nova** resulting from an explosion which blows a star's material into space, leaving an expanding cloud of gas and sometimes a central compact object.

supersonic Faster than the speed of sound in that medium. Erroneously used for ultrasonic. ▶ **Mach number, subsonic, ultrasonic.**

symbiosis A mutually beneficial partnership between organisms of different kinds, especially such an association where one lives within the other.

Système International d'Unités ▶ SI

thermonuclear energy Energy released by a nuclear **fusion** reaction that occurs because of the high thermal energy of the interacting particles.

tornado An intensely destructive, advancing whirlwind formed from strongly ascending air current; also, in West Africa, the squall following thunderstorms between the wet and dry seasons.

transition metal One of the group which have an incomplete inner electron shell. Also known as transition element. ▶ **atom**

transuranic elements Elements of atomic number greater than that of uranium, ie with 93 or more protons in the atomic nuclei. These do not occur naturally but more than 12 have been artificially produced, including neptunium, plutonium, curium and lawrencium.

tsunami A series of waves produced in the ocean by violent movement of the sea floor, most commonly submarine faulting accompanied by an earthquake. Its amplitude in mid-ocean is very small; as it approaches land, the amplitude builds up and all the energy of the original disturbance is concentrated with devastating results. Erroneously called a tidal wave.

turbulence Particle motion which at any point varies rapidly in magnitude and direction.

twins (1) Identical twins arise from the same fertilized egg which has subsequently divided into two, each half developing into a separate individual. (2) In mammals, non-identical twins are produced from separate eggs fertilized at the same time.

typhoon A tropical revolving storm in the China Sea and western North Pacific.

ultrasonic Sound frequencies above the upper limit of the normal range of hearing, at or about 20 000 cycles per sec, or 20 kilohertz. Ultrasonics is the general term for the study and application of ultrasonic sound and vibrations.

ultrasound Ultrasonic sound used by some animals (eg bats, dolphins) for localization and communication, and in a variety of industrial applications.

ultraviolet radiation Electromagnetic waves in a wavelength range from 0.00004 to 0.000001 cm approximately, ie between the visible and X-ray regions of the spectrum.

uncertainty principle The principle that there is a fundamental limit to the precision with which a position co-ordinate of a particle and its momentum in that direction can be simultaneously known. Also, there is a fundamental limit to the knowledge of the energy of a particle when it is measured for a finite time.

unified field theory ▶ field theory

valency A measure of the combining power of an **atom, molecule** or **ion**; the valency of an ion is equal to its charge.

Van Allen radiation belts Two belts encircling the Earth within which electrically charged particles from the Sun are trapped.

variation In biology, the differences between the offspring of a single mating; the differences between the individuals of a race, subspecies, or species; the differences between analogous groups of higher rank.

vector In mathematics, a vector or vector quantity is one which has magnitude and direction, eg force or velocity.

very high frequencies Those between 30 000 000 and 300 000 000 cycles per sec or between 30 and 300 megahertz. Abbreviated as VHF.

virtual reality Computer simulation which takes into account the motion of an observer to produce the illusion of reality in a computer-created situation, using complex graphics and sound reproduction.

virus A **pathogen**, usually protein-coated particles of **DNA** or **RNA**, capable of increasing rapidly inside a living cell.

vitamins Organic substances required in relatively small amounts in the diet for the proper functioning of the organism, comprising vitamins A, C, D, E, K and the vitamins of the B complex.**white dwarf** A small dim star in the final stages of its evolution. The masses of known white dwarfs do not exceed 1.4 times that of the Sun, with a typical diameter about the same as that of the Earth.

X-chromosome ▸ sex determination

X-rays Electromagnetic waves in a wavelength range from 0.0000000001 to 0.000001cm approximately, ie between the ultraviolet and gamma-ray regions of the spectrum.

Y-chromosome ▸ sex determination

zenith In astronomy, the point on the celestial sphere vertically above the observer's head.

zodiac A name, of Greek origin, given to the belt of stars, about 18° wide, through which the Sun appears to pass through the year. The zodiac lies approximately in the plane of the motions of the Sun, Moon and planets.

Fields of scientific study

acoustics The science of mechanical waves including production and propagation properties.

actinobiology The study of the effects of radiation upon living organisms.

aerodynamics That part of the mechanics of fluids that deals with the dynamics of gases, particularly the study of forces acting upon bodies in motion in air.

aerology The study of the free atmosphere.

aeronautics All activities concerned with aerial locomotion.

aerothermodynamics The branch of thermodynamics relating to the heating effects associated with the dynamics of a gas; in particular the physical effects produced in the air flowing over a vehicle during launch and re-entry.

aetiology or **etiology** The medical study of the causation of disease.

algology The study of algae.

angiology The study or scientific account of the anatomy of blood and lymph vascular systems.

astronautics The science of space flight.

astronomy The study of all classes of celestial object and the universe as a whole.

astrophysics That branch of astronomy which applies the laws of physics to the study of inter-stellar matter and the stars, their constitution, evolution, luminosity, etc.

autecology The study of the ecology of any individual species. **▸ synecology.**

autonomics Study of self-regulating systems for process control, optimizing performance.

autoradiography Originally used to show the distribution of radioactive molecules in cells and tissues after injecting the organism with, or growing the cells in a medium containing, a radioactive precursor. It is now widely used to show the distribution of radio-labelled molecules separated on the basis of size, charge, etc. Photographic film or emulsion is exposed after applying it to the section, fixed cell or separating medium and the distribution of developed grains viewed directly or under the microscope. Similar procedures exist for fluorescent and other labels.

bacteriology The scientific study of bacteria.

ballistics The study of the dynamics of the path taken by an object moving under the influence of a gravitational field.

balneology The scientific study of baths and bathing, and of their application to disease.

bioclimatology The study of the effects of climate on living organisms.

biology The study of living organisms and systems; the life sciences collectively, including botany, anatomy, physiology, zoology, etc.

biometeorology The study of the effects of atmospheric conditions on living things.

biophysics The physics of vital processes; the study of biological phenomena in terms of physical principles.

biosystematics The study of relationships with reference to the laws of classification of organisms; taxonomy.

biotechnology The use of organisms or their components in industrial or commercial processes, which can be aided by the techniques of genetic manipulation in developing eg novel plants for agriculture or industry.

botany The study of living organisms and systems.

bronchography The radiological examination of the trachea, bronchi, or the bronchial tree after the introduction of a contrast medium.

cardiology That part of medical science concerned with the function and diseases of the heart.

chemistry The study of the composition of substances and the changes that they undergo.

chromatics The science of colours as affected by phenomena determined by their differing wavelengths.

cladistics A method of classifying organisms into groups (taxa) based on 'recency of common descent' as judged by the possession of shared derived (ie not primitive) characteristics.

climatology The study of climate and its causes.

cosmology The study of the universe on the largest scales of length and time, particularly the propounding of theories concerning its origin, nature, structure and evolution. A cosmology is any model said to represent the observed universe. Western cosmology is entirely scientific in its approach, and has produced two famous models, the Big Bang and steady-state cosmology.

cryogenics The study of materials at very low temperatures.

crystallography The study of internal arrangements (ionic and molecular) and external forms of crystal species, and their classification into types.

cybernetics The study of control and communications in complex electronic systems and in animals, especially humans.

cytogenetics The study of the chromosomal complement of cells, and of chromosomal abnormalities and their inheritance.

Science and Technology

Science and Technology

cytology The study of the structure and functions of cells.

dendrochronology The science of reconstructing past climates from the information stored in tree trunks as annual radial increments of growth.

dermatology That branch of medical science which deals with the skin and its diseases.

dynamics That branch of applied mathematics which studies the way in which force produces motion.

ecology The scientific study of the interrelations between living organisms and their environment, emphasizing both relations between species and within species; the scientific study of the distribution and abundance of living organisms (ie exactly where they occur and precisely how many there are).

econometrics The application of statistical methods to economic phenomena.

ecophysiology The branch of physiology concerned with how organisms are adapted to their natural environment.

electrocardiography The study of electric currents produced in cardiac muscular activity.

electrokinetics The science of electric charges in motion, without reference to the accompanying magnetic field.

electromagnetics or **electromagnetism** The science of the properties of, and relationships between, magnetism and electric currents.

electromyography The study of electric currents set up in muscle fibres by bodily movement.

electronics The study and application of the movement of electrons.

electrophysiology The study of electrical phenomena associated with living organisms, particularly nervous conduction.

electrostatics That section of the science of electricity which deals with the phenomenon of electric charges substantially at rest.

embryology The study of the formation and development of embryos.

endocrinology The study of the internal secretory glands.

energetics The abstract study of the energy relations of physical and chemical changes. ▸ **thermodynamics**.

entomology The branch of zoology which deals with the study of insects.

epidemiology The study of disease in the population, defining its incidence and prevalence, examining the role of external influences such as infection, diet or toxic substances, and examining appropriate preventive or curative measures.

epistemics The scientific study of the perceptual, intellectual and linguistic processes by which knowledge and understanding are acquired and communicated.

ergonomics The application of various human studies to the area of work and leisure; includes anatomy, physiology and psychology.

ethology An approach to the study of animal behaviour in which attempts to explain behaviour combine questions about its immediate causation, development, function and evolution.

etiology ▸ **aetiology**

eugenics The study of the means whereby the characteristics of human populations might be improved by the application of genetics.

exobiology The study of (possible) living systems which probably must exist elsewhere in the universe.

fluidics The science of liquid flow in tubes etc which strongly simulates electron flow in conductors and conducting plasma. The interaction of streams of

fluid can be used for the control of instruments or industrial processes without the use of moving parts.

fractography The microscopic study of fractures in metal surfaces.

genecology The branch of ecology which seeks genetic explanations of the patterns of distribution of plants and animals in time and space.

genetics The study of heredity; of how differences between individuals are passed on from one generation to the next; and of how the information in the genes is used in the development and functioning of the adult organism.

geochronology The study of time with respect to the history of the Earth, primarily through the use of absolute and relative age-dating methods.

geology The study of the planet Earth. It embraces mineralogy, petrology, geophysics, geochemistry, physical geology, palaeontology and stratigraphy. It increasingly involves the use of the chemical, physical, mathematical and biological sciences.

geophysics The study of physical properties of the Earth; it makes use of the data available in Earth measurement, seismology, meteorology and oceanography, as well as that relating to atmospheric electricity, terrestrial magnetism and tidal phenomena.

gerontology The scientific study of the processes of ageing.

gynaecology or **gynecology** That branch of medical science which deals with the functions and diseases peculiar to women's reproductive organs.

histology The study of the minute structure of tissues in organisms.

horology The science of time measurement, or of the construction of timepieces.

hydraulics The science relating to the flow of fluids.

hydrodynamics That branch of dynamics which studies the motion produced in fluids by applied forces.

hydrogeology The study of the geological aspects of the Earth's water.

hydrography The study, determination and publication of the conditions of seas, rivers and lakes, which involves surveying and charting of coasts, rivers, estuaries and harbours, and supplying particulars of depth, bottom, tides, currents, etc.

hydrology The study of water, including rain, snow and water on the Earth's surface, with reference to its properties, distribution, utilization, etc.

hydroponics The technique of growing plants without soil. The roots can be in either a nutrient solution or in an inert medium percolated by such a solution.

hydrostatics The branch of statics which studies the forces arising from the presence of fluids.

immunology The study of the biological responses of a living organism to its invasion by living bacteria, viruses or parasites, and its defence against these; also the study of the body's reaction to foreign substances.

kinematics That branch of applied mathematics which studies the way in which velocities and accelerations of various parts of a moving system are related.

kinetics The study of the rates at which chemical reactions and biological processes proceed.

laryngology That branch of medical science which treats diseases of the larynx and adjacent parts of the upper respiratory tract.

limnology The study of lakes.

lithology The systematic description of rocks, more especially sedimentary rocks. ▸ **petrology**.

magnetohydrodynamics The study of the motions of an electrically conducting fluid in the presence of a magnetic field. The motion of the fluid gives rise to induced electric currents which interact with the magnetic field which in turn modifies the motion. The phenomenon has applications both to magnetic fields in space and to the possibility of generating electricity.

magnetostatics The study of steady-state magnetic fields.

malacology The study of molluscs.

mathematics The study of the logical consequences of sets of axioms. Pure mathematics, roughly speaking, comprises those branches studied for their own sake or their relation to other branches. The most important of these are algebra, analysis and topology. The term applied mathematics is usually restricted to applications in physics. Applications in other fields, eg economics, mainly statistical, are sometimes referred to as applicable mathematics.

mechanics The study of forces on bodies and of the motions they produce. ▸ **dynamics, kinematics, statics.**

metallography The study of metals and their alloys with the aid of various procedures, eg microscopy, X-ray diffraction, etc.

meteorology The study of the Earth's atmosphere in its relation to weather and climate.

metrology The science of measuring.

micropalaeontology The study of microfossils.

mineralogy The study of the chemical composition, physical properties and occurrence of minerals.

morphology The study of the structure and forms of organisms, as opposed to the study of their functions.

mycology The study of fungi.

myology The study of muscles.

neuroendocrinology The study of interactions between the nervous system and endocrine organs, particularly pituitary gland and hypothalamic region of the brain.

neurology The study of the nervous system.

neuropathology The study of pathology of diseases of the nervous system.

nosology The systematic classification of diseases; the branch of medical science which deals with this.

nucleonics The science and technology of nuclear studies.

obstetrics That branch of medical science which deals with the problems and management of pregnancy and labour.

oceanography The study of the oceans, including geological, chemical, physical and biological processes.

odontology The study of the physiology, anatomy, pathology, etc of the teeth.

oncology That part of medical science dealing with new growths (tumours) of body tissue.

oölogy The study of ova.

ophthalmology The study of the eye and its diseases.

optics The study of light. Physical optics deals with the nature of light and its wave properties; geometrical optics ignores the wave nature of light and treats problems of reflection and refraction from the ray aspect.

organography A descriptive study of the external form of plants, with relation to function.

ornithology The study of birds.

orthopaedics or **orthopedics** That branch of surgery which deals with deformities arising from injury or disease of bones or of joints.

osteology The study of bones.

otology That part of surgical science dealing with the organ of hearing and its diseases.

otorhinolaryngology That part of surgical science which deals with diseases of the ear, nose and throat.

palaeoclimatology The study of climatic conditions in the geological record, using evidence from fossils, sediments and their structures, geophysics and geochemistry.

palaeoecology The study of fossil organisms in terms of their mode of life, their interrelationships, their environment, their manner of death and their eventual burial.

palaeogeography The study of the relative positions of land and water at particular periods in the geological past.

palaeontology The study of fossil animals and plants.

palaeopathology The study of disease of previous eras from examination of bodily remains or evidence from ancient writings.

palaeozoology The study of fossil animals. ▸ **palaeontology.**

palynology The study of fossil spores and pollen. They are very resistant to destruction and in many sedimentary rocks are the only fossils that can be used to determine the relationships of strata.

parapsychology The study of certain alleged phenomena, the paranormal, that are beyond the scope of ordinary psychology, eg ESP, psychokinesis, etc.

parasitology The study of parasites and their habits (usually confined to animal parasites).

pathology That part of medical science which deals with the causes and nature of disease, and with the bodily changes brought about by disease.

pedology The study of soil.

petrology That study of rocks which includes consideration of their mode of origin, present conditions, chemical and mineral composition, their alteration and decay.

pharmacodynamics The science of the action of drugs; pharmacology.

pharmacology The scientific study of the action of chemical substances on living systems.

phenology The study of plant development in relation to the seasons.

phenomenology In philosophy, the study of the psychic awareness that accompanies experience and that is the source of all meaning for the individual. In psychiatry, it refers to the description and classification of an individual's mental activity, including subjective experience and perceptions, mental performance (eg memory) and the somatic accompaniments of mental events (eg heart rate).

phonetics Study of speech and vocal acoustics. Used to describe the system of symbols which uniquely represent the spoken word of any language in writing, enabling the reader to pronounce words accurately in spite of spelling irregularities.

photobiology The study of light as it affects living organisms.

phycology The study of algae.

physics The study of electrical, luminescent, mechanical, magnetic, radioactive and thermal phenomena with respect to changes in energy states without change of chemical composition.

physiography The science of the surface of the Earth and the inter-relations of air, water and land.

phytology ▸ **botany**

phytopathology Plant pathology. The study of plant diseases, especially of plants in relation to their parasites.

phytosociology The study of the association of plant species.

planetology The study of the composition, origin and distribution of matter in the planets of the solar system.

prosthetics That branch of surgical science involved in supplying artificial parts to the body.

Science and Technology

Science and Technology

proxemics The study of the spatial features of human social interaction, eg personal space.

psychodynamics A theory of the workings of the mind.

psychometrics The application of mathematical and statistical concepts to psychological data, particularly in the areas of mental testing and experimental data.

psychopathology The study of psychological disorders.

psychopharmacology The study and use of drugs that influence behaviour, emotions, perception and thought, by acting on the central nervous system.

psychophysics The branch of psychology that studies the relationship between characteristics of physical stimuli and the psychological experiences they produce.

radiobiology The branch of science involving study of the effect of radiation and radioactive materials on living matter.

radiology or **röntgenology** The science and application of X-rays, gamma-rays and other penetrating ionizing or non-ionizing radiations.

rheology The science of the flow of matter. The critical study of elasticity, viscosity and plasticity.

robotics The study of the design and use of robots, particularly for their use in manufacturing and related processes.

röntgenology ▸ **radiology**

seismology The study of earthquakes, particularly their shock waves. Studies of the speed and refraction of seismic waves enable the deeper structure of the Earth to be investigated.

semiology The branch of medical science which is concerned with the symptoms of disease.

semiotics The study of communication.

serology The study of serums.

sonics A general term for the study of mechanical vibrations in matter.

spelaeology or **speleology** The study of the fauna and flora of caves.

statics That branch of applied mathematics which studies the way in which forces combine with each other usually so as to produce equilibrium. Until the

early part of the 20c the term also embraced the study of gravitational attractions, but this is now normally regarded as a separate subject.

statistics The branch of mathematics which deals with the collection and analysis of numerical data.

stratigraphy The definition and description of the stratified rocks of the Earth's crust, their relationships and structure, their arrangement into chronological groups, their mineral mass and the conditions of their formation, and their fossil contents.

superaerodynamics Aerodynamics at very low air densities occurring above 30 480m/100 000ft, ie for spacecraft on ascending and re-entry trajectories.

symptomatology The study of symptoms; a discourse or treatise on symptoms; the branch of medical science concerning symptoms of disease.

synecology The study of relationships between communities and their environment. ▸ **autecology.**

systematics The branch of biology which deals with classification and nomenclature.

tectonics The study of the major structural features of the Earth's crust.

teleology The interpretation of animal or plant structures in terms of purpose and utility.

teratology The study of monstrosities, as an aid to the understanding of normal development.

thermionics The study of the processes involved in the emission of electrons from hot bodies.

thermodynamics The study of heat and heat-related phenomena.

topology The study of those properties of shapes and space that are independent of distance.

toxicology The branch of medical science dealing with the nature and effects of poisons.

urodynamics The study of urine flow.

urology That part of medical science which deals with diseases and abnormalities of the urinary tract and their treatment.

virology The study of viruses.

zoogeography The study of animal distribution.

zoology The study of all aspects of animals.

zootaxy The science of the classification of animals.

Table of elements

Atomic weights are taken from the 1983 list of the International Union of Pure and Applied Chemistry. For radioactive elements, the mass number of the most stable isotope is given in square brackets.

Symbol	Element	Derived from	Atomic No.	Weight	Discovered by	Date
Ac	actinium	Greek, *aktis* = ray	89	[227]	André-Louis Debierne (1874–1949)	1899
Ag	silver	Anglo-Saxon, *seolfor*	47	107.8682	Prehistoric	—
Al	aluminium	Latin, *alumen* = alum	13	26.98154	Friedrich Wöhler (1800–82)	1828
Am	americium	America	95	[243]	Glenn Theodore Seaborg (1912–99), Ralph James and others	1944
Ar	argon	Greek, *argos* = inactive	18	39.948	John Rayleigh (1842–1919) and William Ramsay (1852–1916)	1894
As	arsenic	Latin, *arsenicum*	33	74.9216	Prehistoric	—
At	astatine	Greek, *astatos* = unstable	85	[210]	Emilio Segrè (1905–89), Dale Corson and Mackenzie	1940
Au	gold	Anglo-Saxon, *gold*	79	196.9665	Prehistoric	—
B	boron	*Bor*ax + car*bon*	5	10.811	Humphry Davy (1778–1829)	1808
Ba	barium	Greek, *barys* = heavy	56	137.33	Humphry Davy (1778–1829)	1808
Be	beryllium	Greek, *beryllion* = beryl	4	9.01218	Friedrich Wöhler (1800–82)	1828
Bh	bohrium	Niels Bohr	107	[262]	Joint Insititute for Nuclear Research Dubna, USSR	1976
Bi	bismuth	German (origin unknown)	83	208.9804	Basil Valentine	1450
Bk	berkelium	Berkeley, California	97	[247]	Glenn Theodore Seaborg (1912–99) and others	1950
Br	bromine	Greek, *bromos* = stench	35	79.904	Antoine Jérôme Balard (1802–76)	1826
C	carbon	Latin, *carbo* = charcoal	6	12.011	Prehistoric	—
Ca	calcium	Latin, *calx* = lime	20	40.078	Humphry Davy (1778–1829)	1808
Cd	cadmium	Greek, *kadmeia* = calamine	48	112.41	Friedrich Stromeyer (1776–1848)	1817
Ce	cerium	Planet Ceres	58	140.12	Jöns Jacob Berzelius (1779–1848)	1803
Cf	californium	California	98	[251]	Glenn Theodore Seaborg (1912–99) and others	1950
Cl	chlorine	Greek, *chloros* = green	17	35.453	Carl Wilhelm Scheele (1742–86)	1774
Cm	curium	Pierre and Marie Curie	96	[249]	Glenn Theodore Seaborg (1912–99), Ralph James and others	1944
Co	cobalt	German, *Kobold* = goblin	27	58.9332	Georg Brandt (1694–1768)	1739
Cr	chromium	Greek, *chroma* = colour	24	51.9961	Nicolas-Louis Vauquelin (1763–1829)	1797
Cs	cesium/caesium	Latin, *caesium* = bluish-grey	55	132.9054	Robert Wilhelm Bunsen (1811–99)	1860
Cu	copper	Cyprus	29	63.546	Prehistoric	—
Db	dubnium	Dubna, a Russian town	105	[261]	Joint Institute for Nuclear Research, Dubna, USSR	1967
Dy	dysprosium	Greek, *dysprositos*	66	162.50	Paul Émile Lecoq de Boisbaudran (1838–1912)	1886
Er	erbium	Ytterby, a Swedish town	68	167.26	Carl Gustaf Mosander (1797–1858)	1843
Es	einsteinium	Albert Einstein	99	[252]	Albert Ghiorso and others	1952
Eu	europium	Europe	63	151.96	Eugène Anatole Demarcay (1852–1903)	1896
F	fluorine	Latin, *fluo* = flow	9	18.998403	Carl Wilhelm Scheele (1742–86)	1771
Fe	iron	Anglo-Saxon, *iren*	26	55.847	Prehistoric	—
Fm	fermium	Enrico Fermi	100	[257]	Albert Ghiorso and others	1952
Fr	francium	France	87	[223]	Marguerite Catherine Perey (1909–75)	1939
Ga	gallium	Latin, *Gallia* = France	31	69.723	Paul Émile Lecoq de Boisbaudran (1838–1912)	1875
Gd	gadolinium	Johan Gadolin	64	157.25	Jean Charles Galissard de Marignac (1817–94)	1880
Ge	germanium	Latin, *Germania*	32	72.59	Clemens Alexander Winkler (1838–1904)	1886
H	hydrogen	Greek, *hydor* = water + *gen*	1	1.00794	Henry Cavendish (1766–1810)	1766
He	helium	Greek, *helios* = sun	2	4.002602	William Ramsay (1852–1916)	1895
Hf	hafnium	*Hafnia* = Copenhagen	72	178.49	Dirk Coster (1889–1950) and Georg Hevesey (1885–1966)	1923
Hg	mercury	Mercury (myth)	80	200.59	Prehistoric	—
Ho	holmium	*Holmia* = Stockholm	67	164.9304	Per Teodor Cleve (1840–1905)	1879
Hs	hassium	Latin, Hassius = Hess, state in Germany	108	[265]	GSI, Darmstadt, Germany	1984
I	iodine	Greek, *iodes* = violet	53	126.9045	Bernard Courtois (1777–1838)	1811
In	indium	Its indigo spectrum	49	114.82	Ferdinand Reich (1799–1882) and Hieronymous Theodor Richter (1824–98)	1863
Ir	iridium	Latin, *iris* = rainbow	77	192.22	Smithson Tennant (1761–1815)	1803

Symbol	Element	Derived from	Atomic No.	Weight	Discovered by	Date
K	potassium	English, *potash*	19	39.0983	Humphry Davy (1778–1829)	1807
Kr	krypton	Greek, *kryptos* = hidden	36	83.80	William Ramsay (1852–1916) and Morris William Travers (1872–1961)	1898
La	lanthanum	Greek, *lanthanō* = conceal	57	138.9055	Carl Gustaf Mosander (1797–1858)	1839
Li	lithium	Greek, *lithos* = stone	3	6.941	Johan August Arfvedson	1817
Lr	lawrencium	Ernest Lawrence	103	[260]	Albert Ghiorso and others	1961
Lu	lutetium	*Lutetia*, ancient name of Paris	71	174.967	Georges Urbain (1872–1938) and Karl Auer, Baron von Welsbach (1858–1929)	1907
Md	mendelevium	Dmitri Mendeleyev	101	[258]	Glenn Theodore Seaborg (1912–99) and others	1955
Mg	magnesium	Magnesia, district in Thessaly	12	24.305	Antoine Alexandre Brutus Bussy (1794–1882)	1829
Mn	manganese	Latin, *magnes* = magnet	25	54.9380	Johan Gottlieb Gahn (1745–1818)	1774
Mo	molybdenum	Greek, *molybdos* = lead	42	95.94	Peter Jacob Hjelm (1746–1813)	1782
Mt	meitnerium	Lise Meitner	109	[266]	GSI, Darmstadt, Germany	1982
N	nitrogen	Greek, *nitron* = salpetre	7	14.0067	Daniel Rutherford (1749–1819)	1772
Na	sodium	English, *soda*	11	22.98977	Humphry Davy (1778–1829)	1807
Nb	niobium	Niobe (Greek myth)	41	92.9064	Charles Hatchett (1765–1847)	1801
Nd	neodymium	Greek, *neos* = new and *didymos* = twin	60	144.24	Karl Auer, Baron von Welsbach (1858–1929)	1885
Ne	neon	Greek, *neos* = new	10	20.179	William Ramsay (1852–1916) and Morris William Travers (1872–1961)	1898
Ni	nickel	Swedish, abbreviation of *kopparnickel*	28	58.69	Baron Axel Fredrik Cronstedt (1722–65)	1751
No	nobelium	Alfred Nobel	102	[259]	Albert Ghiorso, Glenn Theodore Seaborg (1912–99) and others	1957
Np	neptunium	Planet Neptune	93	[237]	Edwin Mattison McMillan (1907–91) and Philip Hauge Abelson (1913–)	1940
O	oxygen	Greek, *oxys* = acid + *gen*	8	15.9994	Joseph Priestley (1733–1804)	1774
Os	osmium	Greek, *osme* = odour	76	190.2	Smithson Tennant (1761–1815)	1803
P	phosphorus	Latin, from Greek 'light-bearing'	15	30.97376	Hennig Brand	1669
Pa	protactinium	Greek, *protos* = first + *actinium*	91	[231]	Otto Hahn (1879–1968) and Lise Meitner (1878–1968)	1917
Pb	lead	Anglo-Saxon, *lead*	82	207.2	Prehistoric	—
Pd	palladium	Planet Pallas	46	106.42	William Hyde Wollaston (1766–1828)	1804
Pm	promethium	Prometheus, stealer of fire from heaven (Greek myth)	61	[145]	Clinton Laboratories, Oak Ridge, Tennessee	1940
Po	polonium	Poland	84	[209]	Marie Curie (1867–1934)	1898
Pr	praseodymium	Greek, *prasios* = green and *didymos* = twin	59	140.9077	Karl Auer, Baron von Welsbach (1858–1929)	1885
Pt	platinum	Spanish, *platina* = silver	78	195.08	Antonio de Ulloa	1735
Pu	plutonium	Planet Pluto	94	[244]	Glenn Theodore Seaborg (1912–99), Edwin Mattison McMillan (1907–91), Wahl and Kennedy	1940
Ra	radium	Latin, *radius* = ray	88	[226]	Marie (1867–1934) and Pierre (1859–1906) Curie	1898
Rb	rubidium	Latin, *rubidus* = red	37	85.4678	Robert Wilhelm Bunsen (1811–99)	1860
Re	rhenium	German, *Rhein*	75	186.207	Walter Karl Friedrich Noddack (1893–1960) and Ida Eva Tacke (1896–1978)	1925
Rf	rutherfordium	Ernest Rutherford	104	[262]	Joint Institute for Nuclear Research, Dubna, USSR	1964
Rh	rhodium	Greek, *rhodon* = rose	45	102.9055	William Hyde Wollaston (1766–1828)	1804
Rn	radon	Radium emanation	86	[222]	Friedrich Ernst Dorn (1848–1916)	1901
Ru	ruthenium	Latin, *Ruthenia* = Russia	44	101.07	Carl Ernst Claus (1796–1864)	1845
S	sulphur/sulfur	Latin, *sulfur*	16	32.066	Prehistoric	—
Sb	antimony	Latin, *antimonium*	51	121.75	Prehistoric	—
Sc	scandium	Scandinavia	21	44.95591	Lars Fredrik Nilson (1840–99)	1879
Se	selenium	Greek, *selene* = moon	34	78.96	Jöns Jacob Berzelius (1779–1848)	1817
Sg	seaborgium	Glenn Seaborg	106	[263]	Joint Institute for Nuclear Research, Dubna, USSR	1974
Si	silicon	Latin, *silex* = flint	14	28.0855	Jöns Jacob Berzelius (1779–1848)	1823
Sm	samarium	Samarski, a Russian savant	62	150.36	Paul Émile Lecoq de Boisbaudran (1838–1912)	1879
Sn	tin	Anglo-Saxon, *tin*	50	118.710	Prehistoric	—
Sr	strontium	Strontian, a Scottish village	38	87.62	Humphry Davy (1778–1829)	1808
Ta	tantalum	Tantalus (Greek myth)	73	180.9479	Anders Gustaf Ekeberg (1767–1813)	1802
Tb	terbium	Ytterby, a Swedish town	65	158.9254	Carl Gustaf Mosander (1797–1858)	1843

Symbol	Element	Derived from	Atomic No.	Weight	Discovered by	Date
Tc	technetium	Greek, *technetos* = artificial	43	[99]	Emilio Segrè (1905–89) and Carlo Perrier	1937
Te	tellurium	Latin, *tellus* = earth	52	127.60	Franz Joseph Müller, Baron von Reichenstein (1740–1825)	1782
Th	thorium	God Thor	90	232.0381	Jöns Jacob Berzelius (1779–1848)	1828
Ti	titanium	Latin, *Titanes* = sons of the earth	22	47.88	William Gregor (1761–1817)	1789
Tl	thallium	Greek, *thallos* = budding twig	81	204.383	William Crookes (1832–1919)	1862
Tm	thulium	Greek and Roman *Thule* = Northland	69	168.9342	Per Teodor Cleve (1840–1905)	1879
U	uranium	Planet Uranus	92	238.0289	Martin Heinrich Klaproth (1743–1817)	1789
V	vanadium	Goddess Vanadis (Freya)	23	50.9415	Nils Gabriel Sefström (1765–1829)	1830
W	tungsten	Swedish, heavy stone	74	183.85	Don Fausto d'Elhujar (1755–1833)	1781
Xe	xenon	Greek, *xenos* = stranger	54	131.29	William Ramsay (1852–1916) and Morris William Travers (1872–1961)	1898
Y	yttrium	Ytterby, a Swedish town	39	88.9059	Johan Gadolin (1760–1852)	1794
Yb	ytterbium	Ytterby, a Swedish town	70	173.04	Jean Charles Galissard de Marignac (1817–94)	1878
Zn	zinc	German, *zink*	30	65.39	—	c.1500
Zr	zirconium	Persian, *zargun* = gold-coloured	40	91.224	Jöns Jacob Berzelius (1779–1848)	1824

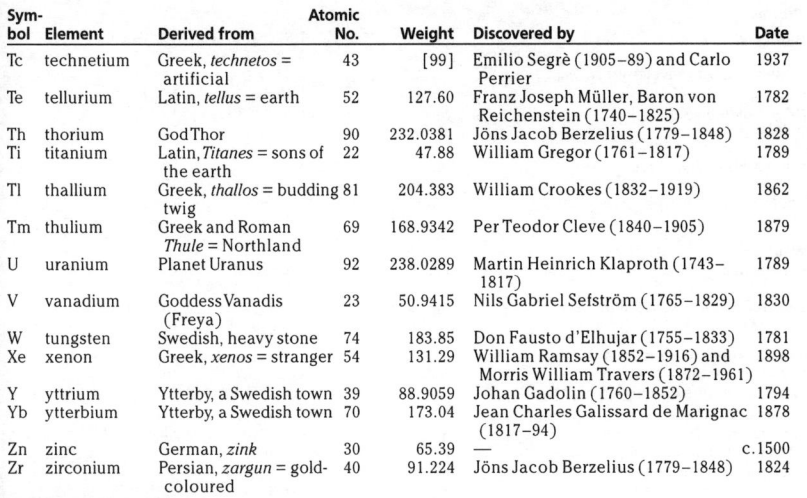

Physical constants

1986 recommended values of the main fundamental physical constants of physics and chemistry.

Quantity	Symbol	Value	Units
■ Universal constants			
speed of light in vacuum	c	299 792 458	$m\ s^{-1}$
permeability of vacuum	μ_0	$4\pi \times 10^{-7}$	$N\ A^{-2}$
		= 12.566370614...	$10^{-7}\ N\ A^{-2}$
permittivity of vacuum, $1/\mu_0\gamma^2$	ε_0	8.854187817...	$10^{-12}\ F\ m^{-1}$
Newtonian constant of gravitation	G	6.67259	$10^{-11}\ m^3\ kg^{-1}\ s^{-2}$
Planck constant	h	6.6260755	$10^{-34}\ J\ s$
$h/2\pi$	$\hbar$	1.05457266	$10^{-34}\ J\ s$
■ Electromagnetic constants			
elementary charge	e	1.60217733	$10^{-19}\ C$
	e/h	2.41798836	$10^{14}\ A\ J^{-1}$
magnetic flux quantum, $h/2e$	Φ_0	2.06783461	$10^{-15}\ Wb$
Josephson frequency-voltage quotient	$2e/h$	4.8359767	$10^{14}\ 14HzV^{-1}$
Bohr magneton, $e\hbar/2m_e$	μ_B	9.2740154	$10^{-24}\ J\ T^{-1}$
nuclear magneton, $e\hbar/2m_p$	μ_N	5.0507866	$10^{-27}\ J\ T^{-1}$
■ Atomic constants			
fine-structure constant, $\mu_0 ce^2/2h$	α	7.29735308	10^{-3}
	α^{-1}	137.0359895	
Rydberg constant, $m_e c\alpha^2 2h$	R_∞	10 973 731.534	m^{-1}
Bohr radius, $\alpha/4\pi R_\infty$	a_0	0.529177249	$10^{-10}\ m$
quantum of circulation	$h/2m_e$	3.63694807	$10^{-4}\ m^2\ s^{-1}$
	h/m_e	7.27389614	$10^{-4}\ m^2\ s^{-1}$
■ Electron			
electron mass	m_e	9.1093897	$10^{-31}\ kg$
		5.48579903	$10^{-4}\ u$
electron-muon mass ratio	m_e/m_μ	4.83633218	10^{-3}
electron-proton mass ratio	m_e/m_p	5.44617013	10^{-4}
electron specific charge	$-e/m_e$	−1.75881962	$10^{11}\ C\ kg^{-1}$
Compton wavelength, $h/m_e c$	λ_C	2.42631058	$10^{-12}\ m$
$\lambda_C/2\pi = \alpha a_0 = \alpha^2/4\pi R_\infty$	$\bar{\lambda}_C$	3.86159323	$10^{-13}\ m$
classical electron radius, $\alpha^2 a_0$	r_e	2.81794092	$10^{-15}\ m$
electron magnetic moment	μ_e	928.47701	$10^{-26}\ J\ T^{-1}$
electron g factor, $2(1+a_e)$	g_e	2.002319304386	
electron-proton magnetic moment ratio	μ_e/μ_p	658.2106881	
■ Muon			
muon mass	m_μ	1.8835327	$10^{-28}\ kg$
		0.113428913	u
muon magnetic moment	μ_μ	4.4904514	$10^{-26}\ J\ T^{-1}$
muon g factor, $2(1+a_\mu)$	g_μ	2.002331846	
muon-proton magnetic moment ratio	μ_μ/μ_p	3.18334547	

■ **Proton**

proton mass	m_p	1.6726231	10^{-27} kg
		1.007276470	u
proton Compton wavelength, $h/m_p c$	$\lambda_{C,\,p}$	1.32141002	10^{-15} m
$\lambda_{C,\,p}/2\pi$	$\lambdabar_{C,\,p}$	2.10308937	10^{-6} m
proton magnetic moment	μ_p	1.41060761	10^{-26} J T^{-1}
in Bohr magnetons	μ_p/μ_B	1.521032202	10^{-3}
in nuclear magnetons	μ_p/μ_N	2.792847386	
proton gyromagnetic ratio	γ_p	26 752.2128	10^4 s^{-1} T^{-1}
	$\gamma_p/2\pi$	42.577469	MHz T^{-1}
uncorrected (H$_2$O, sph., 25°C)	γ'_p	26 751.5255	10^4 s^{-1} T^{-1}
	$\gamma'_p/2\pi$	42.576375	MHz T^{-1}

■ **Neutron**

neutron mass	m_n	1.6749286	10^{-27} kg
		1.008664904	u
neutron Compton wavelength, $h/m_n c$	$\lambda_{C,\,n}$	1.31959110	10^{-15} m
$\lambda_{C,\,n}/2\pi$	$\lambdabar_{C,\,n}$	2.10019445	10^{-16} m

■ **Physico-chemical constants**

Avogadro constant	N_A, L	6.0221367	10^{23} mol^{-1}
atomic mass constant, $m_u = \frac{1}{12}m(^{12}C)$	m_u	1.6605402	10^{-27} kg
Faraday constant, $N_A e$	F	96 485.309	C mol^{-1}
molar gas constant	R	8.314510	J mol^{-1} K^{-1}
Boltzmann constant, R/N_A	k	1.380658	10^{-23} J K^{-1}
molar volume (ideal gas), RT/p			
T=273.15 K, p=101 325 Pa	V_m	0.02241410	m^3 mol^{-1}
Stefan-Boltzmann constant, $(\pi^2/60)\,k^4/\hbar^3 c^2$	σ	5.67051	10^{-8} W m^{-2} K^{-4}
first radiation constant, $2\pi hc^2$	c_1	3.7417749	10^{-16} W m^2
second radiation constant, hc/k	C_2	0.01438769	m K

Radiation

Radiation	Approximate wavelengths	Discovered by	Date	Uses
Radio waves	>10 cm	Heinrich Hertz (German)	1888	communications; radio and TV broadcasting
Microwaves	1mm–10 cm	Heinrich Hertz (German)	1886	communications; radar; microwave ovens
Infrared	$10^{-3}-7.8\times10^{-7}$ m	William Herschel (German–British)	1800	night and smoke vision systems; intruder alarms; weather forecasting; missile guidance systems
Visible	$7.8\times10^{-7}-3\times10^{-7}$ m —	—	—	human eyesight
Ultraviolet	$3\times10^{-7}-10^{-8}$ m	Johann Ritter (German)	1801	forensic science; medical treatment
X-rays	$10^{-8}-3\times10^{-11}$ m	Wilhelm Röntgen (German)	1895	medical X-ray photographs; material structure analysis
Gamma rays	$<3\times10^{-11}$ m	Ernest Rutherford (British)	1902	medical diagnosis

Decibel scale

Source	Decibel level (dB)	Source	Decibel level (dB)
Breathing	10	Traffic	60–90
Whisper	20	Pneumatic drill	110
Conversation	50–60	Jet aircraft	120
Vacuum cleaner	80	Space vehicle launch	140–170

Periodic table

Key:
element symbol — atomic number
element name

1 H hydrogen																	2 He helium
3 Li lithium	4 Be beryllium											5 B boron	6 C carbon	7 N nitrogen	8 O oxygen	9 F fluorine	10 Ne neon
11 Na sodium	12 Mg magnesium											13 Al aluminium	14 Si silicon	15 P phosphorus	16 S sulphur	17 Cl chlorine	18 Ar argon
19 K potassium	20 Ca calcium	21 Sc scandium	22 Ti titanium	23 V vanadium	24 Cr chromium	25 Mn manganese	26 Fe iron	27 Co cobalt	28 Ni nickel	29 Cu copper	30 Zn zinc	31 Ga gallium	32 Ge germanium	33 As arsenic	34 Se selenium	35 Br bromine	36 Kr krypton
37 Rb rubidium	38 Sr strontium	39 Y yttrium	40 Zr zirconium	41 Nb niobium	42 Mo molybdenum	43 Tc technetium	44 Ru ruthenium	45 Rh rhodium	46 Pd palladium	47 Ag silver	48 Cd cadmium	49 In indium	50 Sn tin	51 Sb antimony	52 Te tellurium	53 I iodine	54 Xe xenon
55 Cs caesium	56 Ba barium	57–71 *	72 Hf hafnium	73 Ta tantalum	74 W tungsten	75 Re rhenium	76 Os osmium	77 Ir iridium	78 Pt platinum	79 Au gold	80 Hg mercury	81 Tl thallium	82 Pb lead	83 Bi bismuth	84 Po polonium	85 At astatine	86 Rn radon
87 Fr francium	88 Ra radium	89–103 **	104 Rf rutherfordium	105 Db dubnium	106 Sg seaborgium	107 Bh bohrium	108 Hs hassium	109 Mt meitnerium	110 Uun ununnilium	111 Uuu unununium	112 Uub ununbium						

* Lanthanide series

57 La lanthanum	58 Ce cerium	59 Pr praseodymium	60 Nd neodymium	61 Pm promethium	62 Sm samarium	63 Eu europium	64 Gd gadolinium	65 Tb terbium	66 Dy dysprosium	67 Ho holmium	68 Er erbium	69 Tm thulium	70 Yb ytterbium	71 Lu lutetium

** Actinide series

89 Ac actinium	90 Th thorium	91 Pa protactinium	92 U uranium	93 Np neptunium	94 Pu plutonium	95 Am americium	96 Cm curium	97 Bk berkelium	98 Cf californium	99 Es einsteinium	100 Fm fermium	101 Md mendelevium	102 No nobelium	103 Lr lawrencium

Properties of metals

Name	Symbol	Valence no.	Atomic no.	Melting point (°C)
Aluminium	Al	3	13	660.37
Antimony (stibium)	Sb	3 or 5	51	630.74
Barium	Ba	2	56	725
Beryllium	Be	2	4	1278±5
Bismuth	Bi	3 or 5	83	271.3
Cadmium	Cd	1 or 2	48	320.9
Caesium	Cs	1	55	28.40±0.01
Calcium	Ca	2	20	839±2
Cerium	Ce	3 or 4	58	798
Chromium	Cr	2, 3 or 6	24	1857±20
Cobalt	Co	2 or 3	27	1495
Copper (cuprum)	Cu	1 or 2	29	1083.4±0.2
Gallium	Ga	3	31	29.78
Gold (aurum)	Au	1 or 3	79	1064.43
Iridium	Ir	2 or 4	77	2410
Iron (ferrum)	Fe	2 or 3	26	1535
Lanthanum	La	3	57	918
Lead (plumbum)	Pb	2 or 4	82	327.5
Lithium	Li	1	3	180.5
Magnesium	Mg	2	12	648.8±0.5
Manganese	Mn	2, 3, 4, 6 or 7	25	1244±3
Mercury (hydrargyrum)	Hg	1 or 2	80	−38.87
Molybdenum	Mo	2 or 6	42	2617
Nickel	Ni	2 or 3	28	1453
Osmium	Os	2 or 8	76	3045±30
Palladium	Pd	2 or 4	46	1554
Platinum	Pt	3 or 4	78	1772
Plutonium	Pu	—	94	641
Potassium (kalium)	K	1	19	63.25
Rubidium	Rb	1	37	38.89
Silver (argentum)	Ag	1	47	961.93
Sodium (natrium)	Na	1	11	97.81±0.03
Tin (stannum)	Sn	2 or 4	50	231.97
Titanium	Ti	3 or 4	22	1660±10
Tungsten (wolfram)	W	4 or 6	74	3410±20
Uranium	U	2 or 6	92	1132±0.8
Vanadium	V	5	23	1890±10
Zinc	Zn	2	30	419.58

Properties of polymers

Polymer	Density (kg m^{-3})	Tensile strength (MN m^{-2})	Heat capacity (J g^{-1} K^{-1})	Resistivity (Ω cm)
Acetals	1420	65	1.46	10^{15}
Cellulose	1480–1530	80–240	1.3–1.5	$10^7 - 10^{14}$
Cellulose acetate				
Moulded	1220–1340	12–58	1.26–1.8	$10^{10} - 10^{14}$
Sheet	1280–1320	30–52	1.26–2.1	$10^{11} - 10^{15}$
Cellulose nitrate (celluloid)	1350–1400	50	1.3–1.7	10^{10}
Epoxy cast resins	1110–1400	26–85	1.0	$10^{12} - 10^{17}$
Nylon–6 (Poly-E-caprolactam)	1120–1170	45–90	1.6	$10^{12} - 10^{15}$
Nylon–66 (Polyhexa-methylene-adipamide)	1130–1150	60–80	1.7	$10^{14} - 10^{15}$
Polyacrylonitrile	1160–1180	200	—	10^{14}
Polycarbonates	1200	52–62	1.17–1.25	10^{16}
Polyethylene				
Low density	910–925	4–15	—	$10^{15} - 10^{18}$
Medium density	926–940	8–22	—	$10^{15} - 10^{18}$
High density	940–965	20–36	—	$10^{15} - 10^{18}$
Polyisoprene				
Natural rubber	906–913	—	1.88	10^6
Hard rubber	1130–1180	39	1.38	10^{16}
Polypropylene	902–906	28–36	1.92	$>10^{16}$
Polystyrene	1040–1090	30–100	1.3–1.5	$>10^{16}$
Polyurethane				
Cast liquid	1100–1500	1–65	1.8	$10^{11} - 10^{15}$
Elastomer	1110–1250	29–55	1.8	$10^{11} - 10^{13}$
Polyvinylchloride	1300–1400	50	0.84–1.17	10^{16}
Silicone cast resin	1300	—	—	$10^{14} - 10^{15}$

SI units (International system of units)

Concept	Symbol	Name of Unit	Abbreviation of Unit Name
Length	l	metre	m
Mass	m	kilogramme	kg
Time	t	second	s
Electric current	l	ampere	A
Thermodynamic temperature	T	kelvin	K
Luminous intensity	l	candela	cd
Amount of substance		mole	mol
Plane angle	α, β, θ, etc	radian	rad
Solid angle	Ω, ω	steradian	sr
Area	A, a	square metre	m^2
Volume	V, v	cubic metre	m^3
Velocity	v, u	metre/second	$m\ s^{-1}$
Acceleration	a	metre/second^2	$m\ s^{-2}$
Density	ρ	kilogramme/metre^3	$kg\ m^{-3}$
Mass rate of flow	m, M	kilogramme/sec	$kg\ s^{-1}$
Volume rate of flow	V	cubic metre/sec	$m^3\ s^{-1}$
Moment of inertia	l	kilogramme metre^2	$kg\ m^2$
Momentum	p	kilogramme metre/sec	$kg\ m\ s^{-1}$
Angular momentum	$l\ \omega$	kilogramme metre^2/sec	$kg\ m^2\ s^{-1}$
Force	F	newton	N
Torque (moment of force)	$T (M)$	newton metre	N m
Work (energy, heat)	$W (E)$	joule	J
Potential energy	V	joule	J
Kinetic energy	$T (W)$	joule	J
Heat (enthalpy)	$Q (H)$	joule	J
Power	P	watt	W
Pressure (stress)	$p\ (\sigma, f)$	newton/metre^2	$N\ m^{-2}$
Surface tension	$\gamma\ (\sigma)$	newton/metre	$N\ m^{-1}$
Viscosity, dynamic	η, μ		$N\ s\ m^{-1}$
Viscosity, kinematic	v		$m^2\ s^{-1}$
Temperature	θ, T	degree Celsius, kelvin	°C, K
Velocity of light	c	metre/sec	$m\ s^{-1}$
Permeability of vacuum	μ_0	henry/metre	$H\ m^{-1}$
Permittivity of vacuum	ε_0	farad/metre	$F\ m^{-1}$
Electric charge	Q	coulomb	C
Electric potential (potential difference)	V	volt	V
Electric field strength (electric force)	E	volt/metre	$V\ m^{-1}$
Electric resistance	R	ohm	Ω
Conductance	G	siemens	S
Electric flux	Ψ	coulomb	$\Psi = Q$
Electric flux density (displacement)	D	coulomb/metre^2	$C\ m^{-2}$
Frequency	f	hertz	Hz
Permittivity	ε	farad/metre	$F\ m^{-1}$
Relative permittivity	ε_r		
Magnetic field strength	H	amp. turn/metre	$At\ m^{-1}$
Magnetic flux	Φ	weber	Wb
Magnetic flux density	B	tesla	T
Permeability	μ	henry/metre	$H\ m^{-1}$
Relative permeability	μ_r		
Mutual inductance	M	henry	H
Self inductance	L	henry	H
Capacitance	C	farad	F
Reactance	X	ohm	Ω
Impedance	Z	ohm	Ω
Susceptance	B	siemens	S
Admittance	Y	siemens	S
Total voltamperes	S	volt amp	VA
Reactive voltamperes	Q	volt amp reactive	VAr
Power factor	p.f.	—	—
Luminous flux	Φ	lumen	lm
Illumination	E	lux	lx

SI conversion factors

This table gives the conversion factors for many British and other units which are still in common use, showing their equivalents in terms of the international system of units (SI). The column labelled 'SI equivalent' gives the SI value of one unit of the type named in the first column, eg 1 calorie is 4.186 J.

Unit name	Symbol	Quantity	SI equivalent	Unit
acre		area	0.405	hm^2
ångström[1]	Å	length	0.1	nm
astronomical unit	AU	length	0.150	Tm
atomic mass unit	amu	mass	1.661×10^{-27}	kg
bar[1]	bar	pressure	0.1	MPa

621

Science and Technology

Unit name	Symbol	Quantity	SI equivalent	Unit
barn[1]	b	area	100	fm^2
barrel (US) = 42 US gal	bbl	volume	0.159	m^3
British thermal unit	Btu	energy	1.055	kJ
calorie	cal	energy	4.186	J
cubic foot	ft^3	volume	0.028	m^3
cubic inch	in^3	volume	16.387	cm^3
cubic yard	yd^3	volume	0.765	m^3
curie[1]	Ci	activity of radionuclide	37	GBq
degree = 1/90 rt angle	°	plane angle	$\pi/180$	rad
degree Celsius	°C	temperature	1	K
degree Centigrade	°C	temperature	1	K
degree Fahrenheit	°F	temperature	5/9	K
degree Rankine	°R	temperature	5/9	K
dyne	dyn	force	10	μN
electronvolt	eV	energy	0.160	aJ
erg	erg	energy	0.1	μJ
fathom (6ft)		length	1.829	m
fermi		length	1	fm
foot	ft	length	30.48	cm
foot per second	ft s^{-1}	velocity	$\begin{cases} 0.305 \\ 1.097 \end{cases}$	m s^{-1} km h^{-1}
gallon (UK)[1]	gal	volume	4.546	dm^3
gallon (US)[1] = 231 in^3	gal	volume	3.785	dm^3
gallon (UK) per mile		consumption	2.825	dm^3 km^{-1}
gauss	Gs, G	magnetic flux density	100	μT
grade = 0.01 rt angle		plane angle	$\pi/200$	rad
grain	gr	mass	0.065	g
hectare[1]	ha	area	1	hm^2
horsepower	hp	energy	0.746	kW
inch	in	length	2.54	cm
kilogram-force	kgf	force	9.807	N
knot[1]		velocity	1.852	km h^{-1}
light year	l.y.	length	9.461×10^{15}	m
litre	l	volume	1	dm^3
maxwell	Mx	magnetic flux	10	nWb
metric carat		mass	0.2	g
micron	μ	length	1	μm
mile (nautical)[1]		length	1.852	km
mile (statute)		length	1.609	km
mile per hour (mph)	mile h^{-1}	velocity	1.609	km h^{-1}
minute = (1/60)°	'	plane angle	$\pi/10\,800$	rad
oersted	Oe	magnetic field strength	$1/(4\pi)$	kA m^{-1}
ounce (avoirdupois)	oz	mass	28.349	g
ounce (troy) = 480 gr		mass	31.103	g
parsec	pc	length	30 857	Tm
phot	ph	illuminance	10	klx
pint (UK)	pt	volume	0.568	dm^3
poise	p	viscosity	0.1	Pa s
pound	lb	mass	0.454	kg
pound-force	lbf	force	4.448	N
pound-force/in^{-2}		pressure	6.895	kPa
poundal	pdl	force	0.138	N
pounds per square inch	psi	pressure	6.895×10^3	K Pa
rad[1]	rad	absorbed dose	0.01	Gy
rem[1]	rem	dose equivalent	0.01	Sv
right angle = $\pi/2$ rad		plane angle	1.571	rad
röntgen[1]	R	exposure	0.258	mC kg^{-1}
second = (1/60)″	″	plane angle	$\pi/648$	mrad
slug		mass	14.594	kg
solar mass	M	mass	1.989×10^{30}	kg
square foot	ft^2	area	9.290	dm^2
square inch	in^2	area	6.452	cm^2
square mile (statute)		area	2.590	km^2
square yard	yd^2	area	0.836	m^2
standard atmosphere	atm	pressure	0.101	MPa
stere	st	volume	1	m^3
stilb	sb	luminance	10	kcd m^{-2}
stokes	St	viscosity	1	cm^2 s^{-1}
therm = 10^5 Btu		energy	0.105	GJ
ton = 2 240 lb		mass	1.016	Mg
ton-force	tonf	force	9.964	kN
ton-force/in^{-2}		pressure	15.444	MPa
tonne	t	mass	1	Mg
torr $\big\}$ mmHg	torr	pressure	0.133	kPa
X unit		length	0.100	pm
yard	yd	length	0.915	m

[1] In temporary use with SI.

SI prefixes

Factor	Prefix	Symbol	Factor	Prefix	Symbol	Factor	Prefix	Symbol	Factor	Prefix	Symbol
10^{24}	yotta	Y	10^{9}	giga	G	10^{-1}	deci	d	10^{-12}	pico	p
10^{21}	zetta	Z	10^{6}	mega	M	10^{-2}	centi	c	10^{-15}	femto	f
10^{18}	exa	E	10^{3}	kilo	k	10^{-3}	milli	m	10^{-18}	atto	a
10^{15}	peta	P	10^{2}	hecto	h	10^{-6}	micro	μ	10^{-21}	zepto	z
10^{12}	tera	T	10^{1}	deca	da	10^{-9}	nano	n	10^{-24}	yocto	y

Temperature conversion

To convert	To	Equation
°Fahrenheit	°Celsius	$-32, \times 5, \div 9$
°Fahrenheit	°Rankine	$+459.67$
°Fahrenheit	°Réaumur	$-32, \times 4, \div 9$
°Celsius	°Fahrenheit	$\times 9, \div 5, +32$
°Celsius	Kelvin	$+273.15$
°Celsius	°Réaumur	$\times 4, \div 5$
Kelvin	°Celsius	-273.15
°Rankine	°Fahrenheit	-459.67
°Réaumur	°Fahrenheit	$\times 9, \div 4, +32$
°Réaumur	°Celsius	$\times 5, \div 4$

Carry out operations in sequence.

Degrees Fahrenheit (F) → Degrees Celsius (Centigrade) (C)

°F → °C		°F → °C		°F → °C		°F → °C		°F → °C	
1	−17.2	42	5.5	83	28.3	124	51.1	165	73.9
2	−16.7	43	6.1	84	28.9	125	51.7	166	74.4
3	−16.1	44	6.7	85	29.4	126	52.2	167	75.0
4	−15.5	45	7.2	86	30.0	127	52.8	168	75.5
5	−15.0	46	7.8	87	30.5	128	53.3	169	76.1
6	−14.4	47	8.3	88	31.1	129	53.9	170	76.7
7	−13.9	48	8.9	89	31.7	130	54.4	171	77.2
8	−13.3	49	9.4	90	32.2	131	55.0	172	77.8
9	−12.8	50	10.0	91	32.8	132	55.5	173	78.3
10	−12.2	51	10.5	92	33.3	133	56.1	174	78.9
11	−11.6	52	11.1	93	33.9	134	56.7	175	79.4
12	−11.1	53	11.7	94	34.4	135	57.2	176	80.0
13	−10.5	54	12.2	95	35.0	136	57.8	177	80.5
14	−10.0	55	12.8	96	35.5	137	58.3	178	81.1
15	−9.4	56	13.3	97	36.1	138	58.9	179	81.7
16	−8.9	57	13.9	98	36.7	139	59.4	180	82.2
17	−8.3	58	14.4	99	37.2	140	60.0	181	82.8
18	−7.8	59	15.0	100	37.8	141	60.5	182	83.3
19	−7.2	60	15.5	101	38.3	142	61.1	183	83.9
20	−6.7	61	16.1	102	38.9	143	61.7	184	84.4
21	−6.1	62	16.7	103	39.4	144	62.2	185	85.0
22	−5.5	63	17.2	104	40.0	145	62.8	186	85.5
23	−5.0	64	17.8	105	40.5	146	63.3	187	86.1
24	−4.4	65	18.3	106	41.1	147	63.9	188	86.7
25	−3.9	66	18.9	107	41.7	148	64.4	189	87.2
26	−3.3	67	19.4	108	42.2	149	65.0	190	87.8
27	−2.8	68	20.0	109	42.8	150	65.5	191	88.3
28	−2.2	69	20.5	110	43.3	151	66.1	192	88.8
29	−1.7	70	21.1	111	43.9	152	66.7	193	89.4
30	−1.1	71	21.7	112	44.4	153	67.2	194	90.0
31	−0.5	72	22.2	113	45.0	154	67.8	195	90.5
32	0	73	22.8	114	45.5	155	68.3	196	91.1
33	0.5	74	23.3	115	46.1	156	68.9	197	91.7
34	1.1	75	23.9	116	46.7	157	69.4	198	92.2
35	1.7	76	24.4	117	47.2	158	70.0	199	92.8
36	2.2	77	25.0	118	47.8	159	70.5	200	93.3
37	2.8	78	25.5	119	48.3	160	71.1	201	93.9
38	3.3	79	26.1	120	48.9	161	71.7		
39	3.9	80	26.7	121	49.4	162	72.2		
40	4.4	81	27.2	122	50.0	163	72.8		
41	5.0	82	27.8	123	50.5	164	73.3		

Science and Technology

Science and Technology

Degrees Celsius (Centigrade) (C) → Degrees Fahrenheit (F)

°C → °F		°C → °F		°C → °F
1	33.8	35	95.0	69	156.2
2	35.6	36	96.8	70	158.0
3	37.4	37	98.6	71	159.8
4	39.2	38	100.4	72	161.6
5	41.0	39	102.2	73	163.4
6	42.8	40	104.0	74	165.2
7	44.6	41	105.8	75	167.0
8	46.4	42	107.6	76	168.8
9	48.2	43	109.4	77	170.6
10	50.0	44	111.2	78	172.4
11	51.8	45	113.0	79	174.2
12	53.6	46	114.8	80	176.0
13	55.4	47	116.6	81	177.8
14	57.2	48	118.4	82	179.6
15	59.0	49	120.2	83	181.4
16	60.8	50	122.0	84	183.2
17	62.6	51	123.8	85	185.0
18	64.4	52	125.6	86	186.8
19	66.2	53	127.4	87	188.6
20	68.0	54	129.2	88	190.4
21	69.8	55	131.0	89	192.2
22	71.6	56	132.8	90	194.0
23	73.4	57	134.6	91	195.8
24	75.2	58	136.4	92	197.6
25	77.0	59	138.2	93	199.4
26	78.8	60	140.0	94	201.2
27	80.6	61	141.8	95	203.0
28	82.4	62	143.6	96	204.8
29	84.2	63	145.4	97	206.6
30	86.0	64	147.2	98	208.4
31	87.8	65	149.0	99	210.2
32	89.6	66	150.8	100	212.0
33	91.4	67	152.6		
34	93.2	68	154.4		

Numerical equivalents

Arabic	Roman	Greek	Binary numbers
1	I	α'	1
2	II	β'	10
3	III	γ'	11
4	IV	δ'	100
5	V	ε'	101
6	VI	ς'	110
7	VII	ζ''	111
8	VIII	η'	1000
9	IX	θ'	1001
10	X	ι'	1010
11	XI	$\iota\alpha'$	1011
12	XII	$\iota\beta'$	1100
13	XIII	$\iota\gamma'$	1101
14	XIV	$\iota\delta'$	1110
15	XV	$\iota\varepsilon'$	1111
16	XVI	$\iota\varsigma'$	10000
17	XVII	$\iota\zeta''$	10001
18	XVIII	$\iota\eta'$	10010
19	XIX	$\iota\theta'$	10011
20	XX	κ'	10100
30	XXX	λ'	11110
40	XL	μ'	101000
50	L	ν'	110010
60	LX	ξ'	111100
70	LXX	o'	1000110
80	LXXX	π'	1010000
90	XC	$.o'$	1011010
100	C	ρ'	1100100
200	CC	σ'	11001000
300	CCC	τ'	100101100
400	CD	υ'	110010000

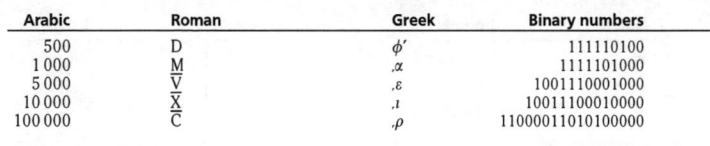

Arabic	Roman	Greek	Binary numbers
500	D	ϕ'	111110100
1 000	$\overline{M}$	$,\alpha$	1111101000
5 000	$\overline{V}$	$,\varepsilon$	1001110001000
10 000	$\overline{X}$	$,\iota$	10011100010000
100 000	$\overline{C}$	$,\rho$	11000011010100000

%	D¹	F²	%	D	F	%	D	F	%	D	F	%	D	F	%	D	F
1	0.01	$\frac{1}{100}$	12½	0.125	$\frac{1}{8}$	24	0.24	$\frac{6}{25}$	36	0.36	$\frac{9}{25}$	49	0.49	$\frac{49}{100}$			
2	0.02	$\frac{1}{50}$	13	0.13	$\frac{13}{100}$	25	0.25	$\frac{1}{4}$	37	0.37	$\frac{37}{100}$	50	0.50	$\frac{1}{2}$			
3	0.03	$\frac{3}{100}$	14	0.14	$\frac{7}{50}$	26	0.26	$\frac{13}{50}$	38	0.38	$\frac{19}{50}$	55	0.55	$\frac{11}{20}$			
4	0.04	$\frac{1}{25}$	15	0.15	$\frac{3}{20}$	27	0.27	$\frac{27}{100}$	39	0.39	$\frac{39}{100}$	60	0.60	$\frac{3}{5}$			
5	0.05	$\frac{1}{20}$	16	0.16	$\frac{4}{25}$	28	0.28	$\frac{7}{25}$	40	0.40	$\frac{2}{5}$	65	0.65	$\frac{13}{20}$			
6	0.06	$\frac{3}{50}$	16⅔	0.167	$\frac{1}{6}$	29	0.29	$\frac{29}{100}$	41	0.41	$\frac{41}{100}$	70	0.70	$\frac{7}{10}$			
7	0.07	$\frac{7}{100}$	17	0.17	$\frac{17}{100}$	30	0.30	$\frac{3}{10}$	42	0.42	$\frac{21}{50}$	75	0.75	$\frac{3}{4}$			
8	0.08	$\frac{2}{25}$	18	0.18	$\frac{9}{50}$	31	0.31	$\frac{31}{100}$	43	0.43	$\frac{43}{100}$	80	0.80	$\frac{4}{5}$			
8⅓	0.083	$\frac{1}{12}$	19	0.19	$\frac{19}{100}$	32	0.32	$\frac{8}{25}$	44	0.44	$\frac{11}{25}$	85	0.85	$\frac{17}{20}$			
9	0.09	$\frac{9}{100}$	20	0.20	$\frac{1}{5}$	33	0.33	$\frac{33}{100}$	45	0.45	$\frac{9}{20}$	90	0.90	$\frac{9}{10}$			
10	0.10	$\frac{1}{10}$	21	0.21	$\frac{21}{100}$	33⅓	0.333	$\frac{1}{3}$	46	0.46	$\frac{23}{50}$	95	0.95	$\frac{19}{20}$			
11	0.11	$\frac{11}{100}$	22	0.22	$\frac{11}{50}$	34	0.34	$\frac{17}{50}$	47	0.47	$\frac{47}{100}$	100	1.00	1			
12	0.12	$\frac{3}{25}$	23	0.23	$\frac{23}{100}$	35	0.35	$\frac{7}{20}$	48	0.48	$\frac{12}{25}$						

¹Decimal   ²Fraction

Fraction	Decimal	Fraction	Decimal
$\frac{1}{2}$	0.5000	$\frac{6}{11}$	0.5454
$\frac{1}{3}$	0.3333	$\frac{7}{11}$	0.6363
$\frac{2}{3}$	0.6667	$\frac{8}{11}$	0.7272
$\frac{1}{4}$	0.2500	$\frac{9}{11}$	0.8181
$\frac{3}{4}$	0.7500	$\frac{10}{11}$	0.9090
$\frac{1}{5}$	0.2000	$\frac{1}{12}$	0.0833
$\frac{2}{5}$	0.4000	$\frac{5}{12}$	0.4167
$\frac{3}{5}$	0.6000	$\frac{7}{12}$	0.5833
$\frac{4}{5}$	0.8000	$\frac{11}{12}$	0.9167
$\frac{1}{6}$	0.1667	$\frac{1}{16}$	0.0625
$\frac{5}{6}$	0.8333	$\frac{3}{16}$	0.1875
$\frac{1}{7}$	0.1429	$\frac{5}{16}$	0.3125
$\frac{2}{7}$	0.2857	$\frac{7}{16}$	0.4375
$\frac{3}{7}$	0.4286	$\frac{9}{16}$	0.5625
$\frac{4}{7}$	0.5714	$\frac{11}{16}$	0.6875
$\frac{5}{7}$	0.7143	$\frac{13}{16}$	0.8125
$\frac{6}{7}$	0.8571	$\frac{15}{16}$	0.9375
$\frac{1}{8}$	0.1250	$\frac{1}{20}$	0.0500
$\frac{3}{8}$	0.3750	$\frac{3}{20}$	0.1500
$\frac{5}{8}$	0.6250	$\frac{7}{20}$	0.3500
$\frac{7}{8}$	0.8750	$\frac{9}{20}$	0.4500
$\frac{1}{9}$	0.1111	$\frac{11}{20}$	0.5500
$\frac{2}{9}$	0.2222	$\frac{13}{20}$	0.6500
$\frac{4}{9}$	0.4444	$\frac{17}{20}$	0.8500
$\frac{5}{9}$	0.5556	$\frac{19}{20}$	0.9500
$\frac{7}{9}$	0.7778	$\frac{1}{32}$	0.0312
$\frac{8}{9}$	0.8889	$\frac{3}{32}$	0.0937
$\frac{1}{10}$	0.1000	$\frac{5}{32}$	0.1562
$\frac{3}{10}$	0.3000	$\frac{7}{32}$	0.2187
$\frac{7}{10}$	0.7000	$\frac{9}{32}$	0.2812
$\frac{9}{10}$	0.9000	$\frac{11}{32}$	0.3437
$\frac{1}{11}$	0.0909	$\frac{13}{32}$	0.4062
$\frac{2}{11}$	0.1818	$\frac{15}{32}$	0.4687
$\frac{3}{11}$	0.2727	$\frac{17}{32}$	0.5312
$\frac{4}{11}$	0.3636	$\frac{19}{32}$	0.5937
$\frac{5}{11}$	0.4545	$\frac{21}{32}$	0.6562

Science and Technology

Fraction	Decimal		Fraction	Decimal
$\frac{23}{32}$	0.7187		$\frac{29}{32}$	0.9062
$\frac{25}{32}$	0.7812		$\frac{31}{32}$	0.9687
$\frac{27}{32}$	0.8437			

Multiplication table

	2	3	4	5	6	7	8	9	10	11	12	13	14	15	16	17	18	19	20	21	22	23	24	25
2	4	6	8	10	12	14	16	18	20	22	24	26	28	30	32	34	36	38	40	42	44	46	48	50
3	6	9	12	15	18	21	24	27	30	33	36	39	42	45	48	51	54	57	60	63	66	69	72	75
4	8	12	16	20	24	28	32	36	40	44	48	52	56	60	64	68	72	76	80	84	88	92	96	100
5	10	15	20	25	30	35	40	45	50	55	60	65	70	75	80	85	90	95	100	105	110	115	120	125
6	12	18	24	30	36	42	48	54	60	66	72	78	84	90	96	102	108	114	120	126	132	138	144	150
7	14	21	28	35	42	49	56	63	70	77	84	91	98	105	112	119	126	133	140	147	154	161	168	175
8	16	24	32	40	48	56	64	72	80	88	96	104	112	120	128	136	144	152	160	168	176	184	192	200
9	18	27	36	45	54	63	72	81	90	99	108	117	126	135	144	153	162	171	180	189	198	207	216	225
10	20	30	40	50	60	70	80	90	100	110	120	130	140	150	160	170	180	190	200	210	220	230	240	250
11	22	33	44	55	66	77	88	99	110	121	132	143	154	165	176	187	198	209	220	231	242	253	264	275
12	24	36	48	60	72	84	96	108	120	132	144	156	168	180	192	204	216	228	240	252	264	276	288	300
13	26	39	52	65	78	91	104	117	130	143	156	169	182	195	208	221	234	247	260	273	286	299	312	325
14	28	42	56	70	84	98	112	126	140	154	168	182	196	210	224	238	252	266	280	294	308	322	336	350
15	30	45	60	75	90	105	120	135	150	165	180	195	210	225	240	255	270	285	300	315	330	345	360	375
16	32	48	64	80	96	112	128	144	160	176	192	208	224	240	256	272	288	304	320	336	352	368	384	400
17	34	51	68	85	102	119	136	153	170	187	204	221	238	255	272	289	306	323	340	357	374	391	408	425
18	36	54	72	90	108	126	144	162	180	198	216	234	252	270	288	306	324	342	360	378	396	414	432	450
19	38	57	76	95	114	133	152	171	190	209	228	247	266	285	304	323	342	361	380	399	418	437	456	475
20	40	60	80	100	120	140	160	180	200	220	240	260	280	300	320	340	360	380	400	420	440	460	480	500
21	42	63	84	105	126	147	168	189	210	231	252	273	294	315	336	357	378	399	420	441	462	483	504	525
22	44	66	88	110	132	154	176	198	220	242	264	286	308	330	352	374	396	418	440	462	484	506	528	550
23	46	69	92	115	138	161	184	207	230	253	276	299	322	345	368	391	414	437	460	483	506	529	552	575
24	48	72	96	120	144	168	192	216	240	264	288	312	336	360	384	408	432	456	480	501	528	552	576	600
25	50	75	100	125	150	175	200	225	250	275	300	325	350	375	400	425	450	475	500	525	550	575	600	625

Science and Technology

Mathematical signs and symbols

Symbol	Meaning	Symbol	Meaning
+	plus; positive; underestimate	∞	infinity
−	minus; negative; overestimate	$\rightarrow$	approaches the limit
±	plus or minus; positive or negative; degree of accuracy	$\sqrt{}$	square root
∓	minus or plus; negative or positive	$\sqrt[3]{}, \sqrt[4]{}$	cube root, fourth root, etc.
x	multiplies (colloq. 'times') (6x 4)	!	factorial ($4! = 4 \times 3 \times 2 \times 1$)
·	multiplies (colloq. 'times') (6.4); scalar product of two vectors ($A \cdot B$)	%	percent
÷	divided by (6÷4)	′	prime; minute(s) of arc; foot/feet
/	divided by; ratio of (6/4)	″	double prime; second(s) of arc; inch(es)
—	divided by; ratio of ($\frac{6}{4}$)	$\frown$	arc of circle
=	equals	°	degree of arc
≠, ≠	not equal to	∠, ∠s	angle(s)
≡	identical with	⋛	equiangular
≢, ≢	not identical with	⊥	perpendicular
:	ratio of (6 : 4); scalar product of two tensors ($X : Y$)	∥	parallel
::	proportionately equals (1 : 2 :: 2 : 4)	○, Ⓢ	circle(s)
≈	approximately equal to; equivalent to; similar to	△, ⚠	triangle(s)
>	greater than	□	square(s)
≫	much greater than	▭	rectangle
≯	not greater than	▱	parallelogram
<	less than	≅	congruent to
≪	much less than	∴	therefore
≮	not less than	∵	because
≥, ≧ ≷	equal to or greater than	m̲	measured by
≤, ≦ ≷	equal to or less than	△	increment
∝	directly proportional to	Σ	summation
( )	parentheses	Π	product
[ ]	brackets	∫	integral sign
{ }	braces	∇	del: differential operator
—	vinculum: division (a̅−b̅); chord of circle or length of line (A̅B̅); arithmetic mean (X̅)	∩	union
		∪	interaction

Squares and roots

No.	Square	Cube	Square root	Cube root	No.	Square	Cube	Square root	Cube root
1	1	1	1.000	1.000	13	169	2 197	3.606	2.351
2	4	8	1.414	1.260	14	196	2 744	3.742	2.410
3	9	27	1.732	1.442	15	225	3 375	3.873	2.466
4	16	64	2.000	1.587	16	256	4 096	4.000	2.520
5	25	125	2.236	1.710	17	289	4 913	4.123	2.571
6	36	216	2.449	1.817	18	324	5 832	4.243	2.621
7	49	343	2.646	1.913	19	361	6 859	4.359	2.668
8	64	512	2.828	2.000	20	400	8 000	4.472	2.714
9	81	729	3.000	2.080	25	625	15 625	5.000	2.924
10	100	1 000	3.162	2.154	30	900	27 000	5.477	3.107
11	121	1 331	3.317	2.224	40	1 600	64 000	6.325	3.420
12	144	1 728	3.464	2.289	50	2 500	125 000	7.071	3.684

Science and Technology

Areas of common shapes

The Greek letter π is used in some of the formulae below, and represents the ratio of the circumference of a circle to its diameter. Its value is approximately equal to 3.14159.

Triangle

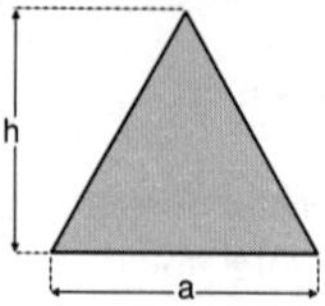

$$A = \frac{ah}{2}$$

Square

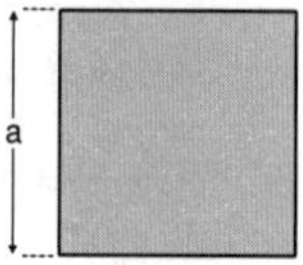

$$A = a^2$$

Rectangle

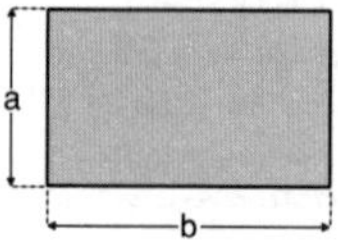

$$A = ab$$

Rhombus

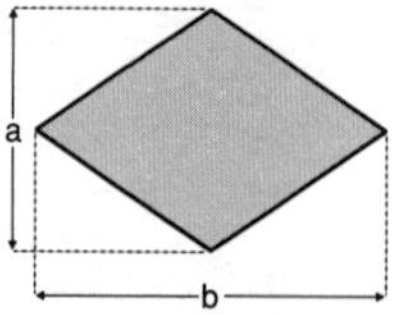

$$A = \frac{ab}{2}$$

Parallelogram

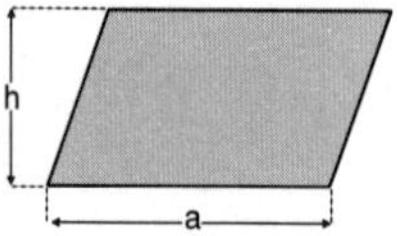

$$A = ah$$

Trapezium

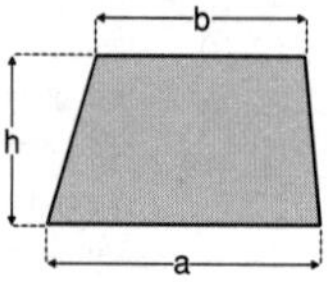

$$A = \frac{a+b}{2} h$$

Regular polygon

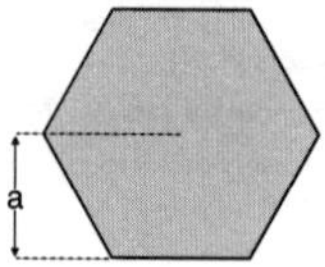

$$A = p \times \frac{a}{2}$$

Circle

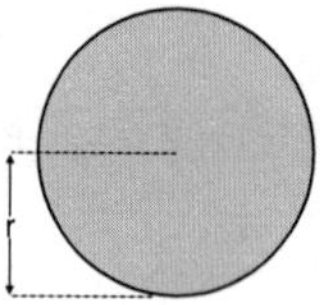

$$A = \pi r^2$$

Ellipse

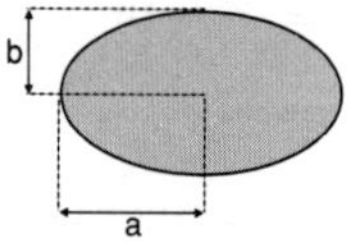

$$A = \pi ab$$

Cone

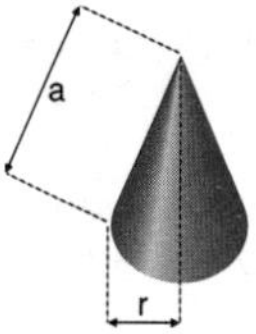

$$A = \pi ra$$

Sphere

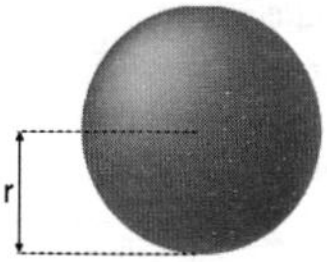

$$A = 4 \pi r^2$$

Spherical section

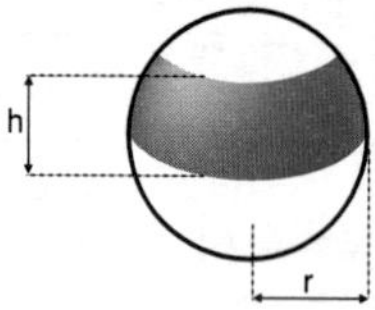

$$A = 2 \pi rh$$

Torus

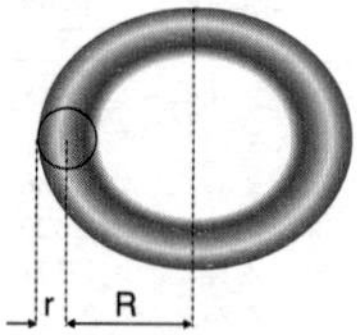

$$A = 4 \pi^2 Rr$$

Cylinder

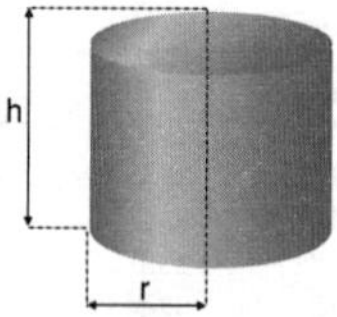

$$A = 2 \pi rh$$

Conic sections

A conic section is the curved figure produced when a plane (flat surface) intersects a cone. Depending on the angle at which it cuts through the cone, it may be a circle, ellipse, hyperbola or parabola. V is the vertex of the right cone.

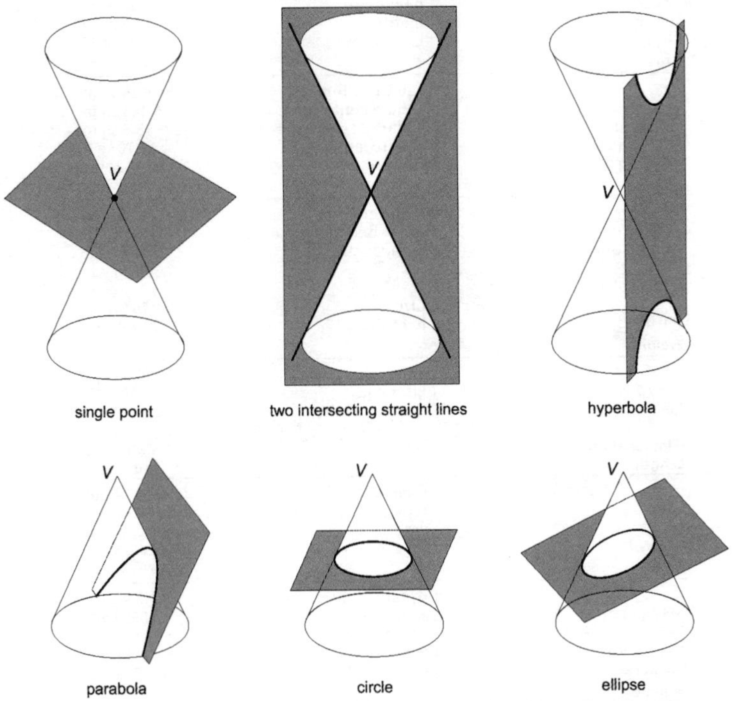

single point

two intersecting straight lines

hyperbola

parabola

circle

ellipse

Pythagoras' theorem

Named after the Greek philosopher and mathematician Pythagoras, the theorem states that, in a right-angled triangle, the square of the length of the hypotenuse (the longest side) is equal to the sum of the squares of the two other sides. It can be used to calculate the length of any side of such a triangle if the lengths of the other sides are known.

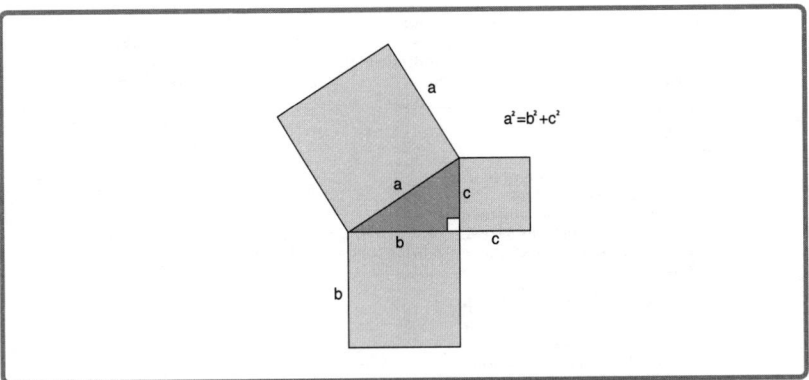

$$a^2 = b^2 + c^2$$

Science and Technology

Common measures

■ Metric units

	Length	Imperial equivalent
10 mm	1 millimetre	0.03937 in
10 cm	1 centimetre	0.39 in
100 cm	1 decimetre	3.94 in
1 000 m	1 metre	39.37 in
	1 kilometre	0.62 mile

	Area	
	1 square millimetre	0.0016 sq in
	1 square centimetre	0.155 sq in
100 sq cm	1 square decimetre	15.5 sq in
10 000 sq cm	1 square metre	10.76 sq ft
10 000 sq m	1 hectare	2.47 acres

	Volume	
	1 cubic centimetre	0.016 cu in
1 000 cu cm	1 cubic decimetre	61.024 cu in
1 000 cu dm	1 cubic metre	35.31 cu ft
		1.308 cu yds

Liquid volume

	1 litre	1.76 pints
100 litres	1 hectolitre	22 gallons

	Weight	
	1 gram	0.035 oz
1 000 g	1 kilogram	2.2046 lb
1 000 kg	1 tonne	0.9842 ton

■ Imperial units

	Length	Metric equivalent
	1 inch	2.54 cm
12 in	1 foot	30.48 cm
3 ft	1 yard	0.9144 m
1 760 yd	1 mile	1.6093 km

	Area	
	1 square inch	6.45 sq cm
144 sq in	1 square foot	0.0929 m^2
9 sq ft	1 square yard	0.836 m^2
4 840 sq yd	1 acre	0.405 ha
640 acres	1 square mile	259. ha

	Volume	
	1 cubic inch	16.3871 cm^3
1 728 cu in	1 cubic foot	0.028 m^3
27 cu ft	1 cubic yard	0.765 m^3

Liquid volume

	1 pint	0.57 litre
2 pints	1 quart	1.14 litres
4 quarts	1 gallon	4.55 litres

	Weight	
	1 ounce	28.3495 g
16 oz	1 pound	0.4536 kg
14 lb	1 stone	6.35 kg
8 stones	1 hundredweight	50.8 kg
20 cwt	1 ton	1.016 tonnes

Other measures

Nautical

1 span = 9 inches = 23 centimetres
8 spans = 1 fathom = 6 feet
1 cable's length = 1/10 nautical mile
1 nautical mile (old) = 6 080 feet
1 nautical mile (international) = 6 076.1 feet = 1.151 statute miles (= 1 852 metres)
60 nautical miles = 1 degree
3 nautical miles = 1 league (nautical)
1 knot = 1 nautical mile per hour
1 ton (shipping) = 42 cubic feet
1 ton (displacement) = 35 cubic feet
1 ton (register) = 100 cubic feet

Crude oil (petroleum)

1 barrel = 35 imperial gallons = 42 US gallons

Paper (writing)

25 sheets = 1 quire
20 quires = 1 ream = 500 sheets

Printing

1 point = 0.3515 millimetres
1 pica = 4.2175 millimetres = 12 points

Timber

1 000 millisteres = 1 stere = 1 cubic metre
1 board foot = 144 cubic inches ($12 \times 12 \times 1$ inch)
1 cord foot = 16 cubic feet
1 cord = 8 cord feet
1 hoppus foot = $4/\pi$ cubic feet (round timber)
1 Petrograd standard = 165 cubic feet

Cloth

1 ell = 45 inches
1 bolt = 120 feet = 32 ells

Brewing

4.5 gallons = 1 pin
2 pins = 9 gallons = 1 firkin
4 firkins = 1 barrel = 36 gallons
6 firkins = 1 hogshead = 54 gallons
4 hogsheads = 1 tun

Horses (height)

1 hand = 4 inches = 10 centimetres

Conversion factors

■ **Imperial to metric**

Length			Multiply by
inches	→	millimetres	25.4
inches	→	centimetres	2.54
feet	→	metres	0.3048
yards	→	metres	0.9144
statute miles	→	kilometres	1.6093
nautical miles	→	kilometres	1.852

Area			
square inches	→	square centimetres	6.4516
square feet	→	square metres	0.0929
square yards	→	square metres	0.8361
acres	→	hectares	0.4047
square miles	→	square kilometres	2.5899

Volume			
cubic inches	→	cubic centimetres	16.3871
cubic feet	→	cubic metres	0.0283
cubic yards	→	cubic metres	0.7646

Capacity			
UK fluid ounces	→	litres	0.0284
US fluid ounces	→	litres	0.0296
UK pints	→	litres	0.5682
US pints	→	litres	0.4732
UK gallons	→	litres	4.546
US gallons	→	litres	3.7854

Weight			
ounces (avoirdupois)	→	grams	28.3495
ounces (troy)	→	grams	31.1035
pounds	→	kilograms	0.4536
tons (long)	→	tonnes	1.016

■ **Metric to imperial**

Length			
millimetres	→	inches	0.0394
centimetres	→	inches	0.3937
metres	→	feet	3.2808
metres	→	yards	1.0936
kilometres	→	statute miles	0.6214
kilometres	→	nautical miles	0.54

Science and Technology

Science and Technology

Area			Multiply by
square centimetres	→	square inches	0.155
square metres	→	square feet	10.764
square metres	→	square yards	1.196
hectares	→	acres	2.471
square kilometres	→	square miles	0.386

Volume			
cubic centimetres	→	cubic inches	0.061
cubic metres	→	cubic feet	35.315
cubic metres	→	cubic yards	1.308

Capacity			
litres	→	UK fluid ounces	35.1961
litres	→	US fluid ounces	33.8150
litres	→	UK pints	1.7598
litres	→	US pints	2.1134
litres	→	UK gallons	0.2199
litres	→	US gallons	0.2642

Weight			
grams	→	ounces (avoirdupois)	0.0353
grams	→	ounces (troy)	0.0322
kilograms	→	pounds	2.2046
tonnes	→	tons (long)	0.9842

Conversion tables: length

in	cm	in	cm	cm	in
$\frac{1}{8}$	0.3	16	40.6	1	0.39
$\frac{1}{4}$	0.6	17	43.2	2	0.79
$\frac{3}{8}$	1	18	45.7	3	1.18
$\frac{1}{2}$	1.3	19	48.3	4	1.57
$\frac{5}{8}$	1.6	20	50.8	5	1.97
$\frac{3}{4}$	1.9	21	53.3	6	2.36
$\frac{7}{8}$	2.2	22	55.9	7	2.76
1	2.5	23	58.4	8	3.15
2	5.1	24	61	9	3.54
3	7.6	25	63.5	10	3.94
4	10.2	26	66	11	4.33
5	12.7	27	68.6	12	4.72
6	15.2	28	71.1	13	5.12
7	17.8	29	73.7	14	5.51
8	20.3	30	76.2	15	5.91
9	22.9	40	101.6	16	6.30
10	25.4	50	127	17	6.69

cm	in	in	mm	mm	in
24	9.45	$\frac{1}{8}$	3.2	1	0.04
25	9.84	$\frac{1}{4}$	6.4	2	0.08
26	10.24	$\frac{3}{8}$	9.5	3	0.12
27	10.63	$\frac{1}{2}$	12.7	4	0.16
28	11.02	$\frac{5}{8}$	15.9	5	0.20
29	11.42	$\frac{3}{4}$	19	6	0.24
30	11.81	$\frac{7}{8}$	22.2	7	0.28
31	12.20	1	25.4	8	0.31
32	12.60	2	50.8	9	0.35
33	12.99	3	76.2	10	0.39
34	13.39	4	101.6	11	0.43
35	13.78	5	127	12	0.47
36	14.17	6	152.4	13	0.51
37	14.57	7	177.8	14	0.55
38	14.96	8	203.2	15	0.59
39	15.35	9	228.6	16	0.63
40	15.75	10	254	17	0.67

Exact conversions 1 in = 2.54 cm 1 cm = 0.3937 in 1 in = 25.40 mm 1 mm = 0.0394 in

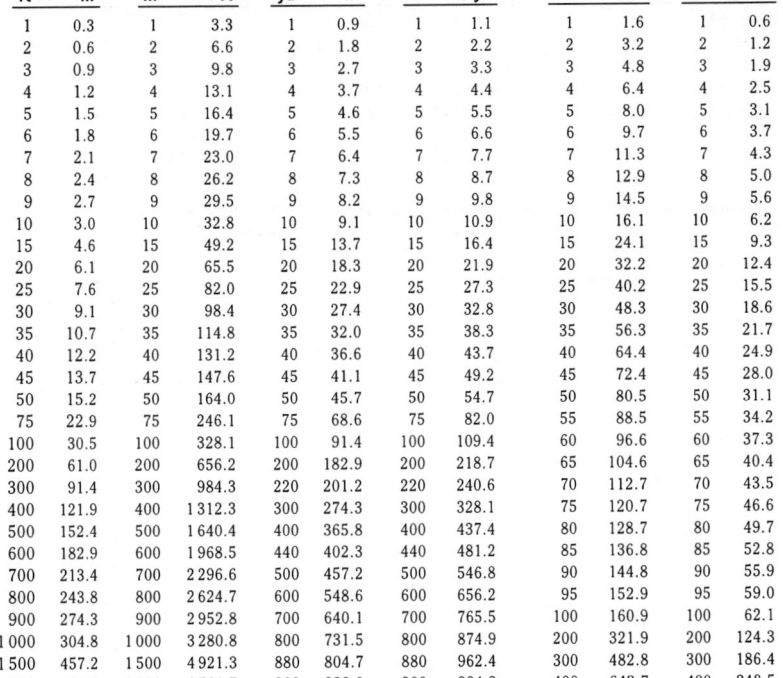

ft	m	m	ft	yd	m	m	yd	mi	km	km	mi*
1	0.3	1	3.3	1	0.9	1	1.1	1	1.6	1	0.6
2	0.6	2	6.6	2	1.8	2	2.2	2	3.2	2	1.2
3	0.9	3	9.8	3	2.7	3	3.3	3	4.8	3	1.9
4	1.2	4	13.1	4	3.7	4	4.4	4	6.4	4	2.5
5	1.5	5	16.4	5	4.6	5	5.5	5	8.0	5	3.1
6	1.8	6	19.7	6	5.5	6	6.6	6	9.7	6	3.7
7	2.1	7	23.0	7	6.4	7	7.7	7	11.3	7	4.3
8	2.4	8	26.2	8	7.3	8	8.7	8	12.9	8	5.0
9	2.7	9	29.5	9	8.2	9	9.8	9	14.5	9	5.6
10	3.0	10	32.8	10	9.1	10	10.9	10	16.1	10	6.2
15	4.6	15	49.2	15	13.7	15	16.4	15	24.1	15	9.3
20	6.1	20	65.5	20	18.3	20	21.9	20	32.2	20	12.4
25	7.6	25	82.0	25	22.9	25	27.3	25	40.2	25	15.5
30	9.1	30	98.4	30	27.4	30	32.8	30	48.3	30	18.6
35	10.7	35	114.8	35	32.0	35	38.3	35	56.3	35	21.7
40	12.2	40	131.2	40	36.6	40	43.7	40	64.4	40	24.9
45	13.7	45	147.6	45	41.1	45	49.2	45	72.4	45	28.0
50	15.2	50	164.0	50	45.7	50	54.7	50	80.5	50	31.1
75	22.9	75	246.1	75	68.6	75	82.0	55	88.5	55	34.2
100	30.5	100	328.1	100	91.4	100	109.4	60	96.6	60	37.3
200	61.0	200	656.2	200	182.9	200	218.7	65	104.6	65	40.4
300	91.4	300	984.3	220	201.2	220	240.6	70	112.7	70	43.5
400	121.9	400	1 312.3	300	274.3	300	328.1	75	120.7	75	46.6
500	152.4	500	1 640.4	400	365.8	400	437.4	80	128.7	80	49.7
600	182.9	600	1 968.5	440	402.3	440	481.2	85	136.8	85	52.8
700	213.4	700	2 296.6	500	457.2	500	546.8	90	144.8	90	55.9
800	243.8	800	2 624.7	600	548.6	600	656.2	95	152.9	95	59.0
900	274.3	900	2 952.8	700	640.1	700	765.5	100	160.9	100	62.1
1 000	304.8	1 000	3 280.8	800	731.5	800	874.9	200	321.9	200	124.3
1 500	457.2	1 500	4 921.3	880	804.7	880	962.4	300	482.8	300	186.4
2 000	609.6	2 000	6 561.7	900	823.0	900	984.2	400	643.7	400	248.5
2 500	762.0	2 500	8 202.1	1 000	914.4	1 000	1 093.6	500	804.7	500	310.7
3 000	914.4	3 000	9 842.5	1 500	1 371.6	1 500	1 640.4	750	1 207.0	750	466.0
3 500	1 066.8	3 500	11 482.9	2 000	1 828.8	2 000	2 187.2	1 000	1 609.3	1 000	621.4
4 000	1 219.2	4 000	13 123.4	2 500	2 286.0	2 500	2 734.0	2 500	4 023.4	2 500	1 553.4
5 000	1 524.0	5 000	16 404.2	5 000	4 572.0	5 000	5 468.1	5 000	8 046.7	5 000	3 106.9

* Statute miles

Exact conversions 1 ft = 0.3048 m   1 m = 3.2808 ft   1 yd = 0.9144 m
1 m = 1.0936 yd   1 mi = 1.6093 km   1 km = 0.6214 mi

Conversion tables: area

sq in	sq cm	sq cm	sq in	sq ft	sq m	sq m	sq ft	acres	hectares	hectares	acres
1	6.45	1	0.16	1	0.09	1	10.8	1	0.40	1	2.5
2	12.90	2	0.31	2	0.19	2	21.5	2	0.81	2	4.9
3	19.35	3	0.47	3	0.28	3	32.3	3	1.21	3	7.4
4	25.81	4	0.62	4	0.37	4	43.1	4	1.62	4	9.9
5	32.26	5	0.78	5	0.46	5	53.8	5	2.02	5	12.4
6	38.71	6	0.93	6	0.56	6	64.6	6	2.43	6	14.8
7	45.16	7	1.09	7	0.65	7	75.3	7	2.83	7	17.3
8	51.61	8	1.24	8	0.74	8	86.1	8	3.24	8	19.8
9	58.06	9	1.40	9	0.84	9	96.9	9	3.64	9	22.2
10	64.52	10	1.55	10	0.93	10	107.6	10	4.05	10	24.7
11	70.97	11	1.71	11	1.02	11	118.4	11	4.45	11	27.2
12	77.42	12	1.86	12	1.11	12	129.2	12	4.86	12	29.7
13	83.87	13	2.02	13	1.21	13	139.9	13	5.26	13	32.1
14	90.32	14	2.17	14	1.30	14	150.7	14	5.67	14	34.6
15	96.77	15	2.33	15	1.39	15	161.5	15	6.07	15	37.1
16	103.23	16	2.48	16	1.49	16	172.2	16	6.47	16	39.5
17	109.68	17	2.64	17	1.58	17	183	17	6.88	17	42
18	116.13	18	2.79	18	1.67	18	193.8	18	7.28	18	44.5
19	122.58	19	2.95	19	1.77	19	204.5	19	7.69	19	46.9
20	129.03	20	3.10	20	1.86	20	215.3	20	8.09	20	49.4
25	161.29	25	3.88	25	2.32	25	269.1	25	10.12	25	61.8

Science and Technology

sq in	sq cm	sq cm	sq in	sq ft	sq m	sq m	sq ft	acres	hectares	hectares	acres
50	322.58	50	7.75	50	4.65	50	538.2	50	20.23	50	123.6
75	483.87	75	11.63	75	6.97	75	807.3	75	30.35	75	185.3
100	645.16	100	15.50	100	9.29	100	1 076.4	100	40.47	100	247.1
125	806.45	125	19.38	250	23.23	250	2 691	250	101.17	250	617.8
150	967.74	150	23.25	500	46.45	500	5 382	500	202.34	500	1 235.5
				750	69.68	750	8 072.9	750	303.51	750	1 853.3
				1 000	92.90	1 000	10 763.9	1 000	404.69	1 000	2 471.1
								1 500	607.03	1 500	3 706.6

Exact conversions $1\,in^2 = 6.4516\,cm^2$ $1\,cm^2 = 0.155\,in^2$ $1\,ft^2 = 0.0929\,m^2$
$1\,m^2 = 10.7639\,ft^2$ $1\,acre = 0.4047\,hectares$ $1\,hectare = 2.471\,acres$

sq mi*	→	sq km		sq km	→	sq mi*
1		2.6		1		0.39
2		5.2		2		0.77
3		7.8		3		1.16
4		10.4		4		1.54
5		12.9		5		1.93
6		15.5		6		2.32
7		18.1		7		2.70
8		20.7		8		3.09
9		23.3		9		3.47
10		25.9		10		3.86
20		51.8		20		7.72
21		54.4		21		8.11
22		57.0		22		8.49
23		59.6		23		8.88
24		62.2		24		9.27
25		64.7		25		9.65
30		77.7		30		11.58
40		103.6		40		15.44
50		129.5		50		19.31
100		259.0		100		38.61
200		518.0		200		77.22
300		777.0		300		115.83
400		1 036.0		400		154.44
500		1 295.0		500		193.05
600		1 554.0		600		231.66
700		1 813.0		700		270.27
800		2 072.0		800		308.88
900		2 331.0		900		347.49
1 000		2 590.0		1 000		386.1
1 500		3 885.0		1 500		579.2
2 000		5 180.0		2 000		772.2

* Statute miles

Exact conversions 1 sq mi = 2.589999 sq km 1 sq km = 0.3861 sq mi

Conversion tables: volume

cu in	cu cm	cu cm	cu in	cu ft	cu m	cu m	cu ft	cu yd	cu m	cu m	cu yd
1	16.39	1	0.06	1	0.03	1	35.3	1	0.76	1	1.31
2	32.77	2	0.12	2	0.06	2	70.6	2	1.53	2	2.62
3	49.16	3	0.18	3	0.08	3	105.9	3	2.29	3	3.92
4	65.55	4	0.24	4	0.11	4	141.3	4	3.06	4	5.23
5	81.93	5	0.30	5	0.14	5	176.6	5	3.82	5	6.54
6	93.32	6	0.37	6	0.17	6	211.9	6	4.59	6	7.85
7	114.71	7	0.43	7	0.20	7	247.2	7	5.35	7	9.16
8	131.10	8	0.49	8	0.23	8	282.5	8	6.12	8	10.46
9	147.48	9	0.55	9	0.25	9	317.8	9	6.88	9	11.77
10	163.87	10	0.61	10	0.28	10	353.1	10	7.65	10	13.08
15	245.81	15	0.92	15	0.42	15	529.7	15	11.47	15	19.62
20	327.74	20	1.22	20	0.57	20	706.3	20	15.29	20	26.16
50	819.35	50	3.05	50	1.41	50	1765.7	50	38.23	50	65.40
100	1638.71	100	6.10	100	2.83	100	3531.5	100	76.46	100	130.80

Exact conversions

$1\ in^3 = 16.3871\ cm^3$ $1\ ft^3 = 0.0283\ m^3$ $1\ yd^3 = 0.7646\ m^3$

$1\ cm^3 = 0.0610\ in^3$ $1\ m^3 = 35.3147\ ft^3$ $1\ m^3 = 1.3080\ yd^3$

Conversion tables: capacity

■ Liquid measure

UK fluid ounces	litres	US fluid ounces	litres	litres	UK fluid ounces	US fluid ounces
1	0.0284	1	0.0296	1	35.2	33.8
2	0.0568	2	0.0592	2	70.4	67.6
3	0.0852	3	0.0888	3	105.6	101.4
4	0.114	4	0.118	4	140.8	135.3
5	0.142	5	0.148	5	176.0	169.1
6	0.170	6	0.178	6	211.2	202.9
7	0.199	7	0.207	7	246.4	236.7
8	0.227	8	0.237	8	281.6	270.5
9	0.256	9	0.266	9	316.8	304.3
10	0.284	10	0.296	10	352.0	338.1
11	0.312	11	0.326	11	387.2	372.0
12	0.341	12	0.355	12	422.4	405.8
13	0.369	13	0.385	13	457.5	439.6
14	0.397	14	0.414	14	492.7	473.4
15	0.426	15	0.444	15	527.9	507.2
20	0.568	20	0.592	20	703.9	676.3
50	1.42	50	1.48	50	1759.8	1690.7
100	2.84	100	2.96	100	3519.6	3381.5

Exact conversions

1 UK fl oz = 0.0284 l   1 l = 35.1961 UK fl oz

1 US fl oz = 0.0296 l   1 l = 33.8140 US fl oz

Science and Technology

UK pints	litres	US pints	litres	litres	UK pints	US pints
1	0.57	1	0.47	1	1.76	2.11
2	1.14	2	0.95	2	3.52	4.23
3	1.70	3	1.42	3	5.28	6.34
4	2.27	4	1.89	4	7.04	8.45
5	2.84	5	2.37	5	8.80	10.57
6	3.41	6	2.84	6	10.56	12.68
7	3.98	7	3.31	7	12.32	14.79
8	4.55	8	3.78	8	14.08	16.91
9	5.11	9	4.26	9	15.84	19.02
10	5.68	10	4.73	10	17.60	21.13
11	6.25	11	5.20	11	19.36	23.25
12	6.82	12	5.68	12	21.12	25.36
13	7.38	13	6.15	13	22.88	27.47
14	7.95	14	6.62	14	24.64	29.59
15	8.52	15	7.10	15	26.40	31.70
20	11.36	20	9.46	20	35.20	105.67
50	28.41	50	23.66	50	87.99	211.34
100	56.82	100	47.32	100	175.98	422.68

Exact conversions   1 UK pt = 0.5682 l   1 US pt = 0.4732 l   1 l = 1.7598 UK pt, 2.1134 US pt
                    1 UK pt = 1.20 US pt   1 US pt = 0.83 UK pt   1 US cup = 8 fl oz

UK gallons	litres	US gallons	litres	litres	UK gallons	US gallons
1	4.55	1	3.78	1	0.22	0.26
2	9.09	2	7.57	2	0.44	0.53
3	13.64	3	11.36	3	0.66	0.79
4	18.18	4	15.14	4	0.88	1.06
5	22.73	5	18.93	5	1.10	1.32
6	27.28	6	22.71	6	1.32	1.58
7	31.82	7	26.50	7	1.54	1.85
8	36.37	8	30.28	8	1.76	2.11
9	40.91	9	34.07	9	1.98	2.38
10	45.46	10	37.85	10	2.20	2.64
11	50.01	11	41.64	11	2.42	2.91
12	54.55	12	45.42	12	2.64	3.17
13	59.10	13	49.21	13	2.86	3.43
14	63.64	14	52.99	14	3.08	3.70
15	68.19	15	56.78	15	3.30	3.96
16	72.74	16	60.57	16	3.52	4.23
17	77.28	17	64.35	17	3.74	4.49
18	81.83	18	68.14	18	3.96	4.76
19	86.37	19	71.92	19	4.18	5.02
20	90.92	20	75.71	20	4.40	5.28
25	113.65	25	94.63	25	5.50	6.60
50	227.30	50	189.27	50	11.00	13.20
75	340.96	75	283.90	75	16.50	19.81
100	454.61	100	378.54	100	22.00	26.42

Exact conversions   1 UK gal = 4.546 l   1 US gal = 3.7854 l   1 l = 0.220 UK gal, 0.2642 US gal

■ **Conversion tables: capacity**

UK gal	US gal		US gal	UK gal
1	1.2		1	0.8
2	2.4		2	1.7
3	3.6		3	2.5
4	4.8		4	3.3
5	6		5	4.2
6	7.2		6	5
7	8.4		7	5.8
8	9.6		8	6.7
9	10.8		9	7.5
10	12		10	8.3
11	13.2		11	9.2
12	14.4		12	10

UK gal	US gal		US gal	UK gal
13	15.6		13	10.8
14	16.8		14	11.7
15	18		15	12.5
20	24		20	16.6
25	30		25	20.8
50	60		50	41.6

Exact conversions   1 UK gal = 1.200929 US gal   1 US gal = 0.832688 UK gal

■ **Dry capacity measures**

UK bushels	cu m	litres	US bushels	cu m	litres
1	0.037	36.4	1	0.035	35.2
2	0.074	72.7	2	0.071	70.5
3	0.111	109.1	3	0.106	105.7
4	0.148	145.5	4	0.141	140.9
5	0.184	181.8	5	0.175	176.2
10	0.369	363.7	10	0.353	352.4

Exact conversions   1 UK bushel = 0.0369 m^3 1 US bushel = 0.9353 m^3
                    1 UK bushel = 36.3677 l   1 US bushel = 35.2381 l

cu m	UK bushels	US bushels	litres	UK bushels	US bushels
1	27.5	28.4	1	0.027	0.028
2	55.0	56.7	2	0.055	0.057
3	82.5	85.1	3	0.082	0.085
4	110	113	4	0.110	0.114
5	137	142	5	0.137	0.142
10	275	284	10	0.275	0.284

Exact conversions   1 m^3 = 27.4962 UK bu   1 l = 0.0275 UK bu
                    1 m^3 = 28.3776 US bu   1 l = 0.0284 US bu

UK pecks	litres	US pecks	litres	UK litres	US pecks	pecks
1	9.1	1	8.8	1	0.110	0.113
2	18.2	2	17.6	2	0.220	0.226
3	27.3	3	26.4	3	0.330	0.339
4	36.4	4	35.2	4	0.440	0.454
5	45.5	5	44	5	0.550	0.567
10	90.9	10	88.1	10	1.100	1.135

Exact conversions   1 UK pk = 9.0919 l   1 l = 0.1100 UK pk = 0.1135 US pk
                    1 US pk = 8.8095 l

US quarts	cu m	litres	US pints	cu m	litres
1	1 101	1.1	1	551	0.55
2	2 202	2.2	2	1 101	1.10
3	3 304	3.3	3	1 652	1.65
4	4 405	4.4	4	2 202	2.20
5	5 506	5.5	5	2 753	2.75
10	11 012	11	10	5 506	5.51

Exact conversions   1 US qt = 1 101.2209 cm^3 1 US pt = 550.6105 cm^3
                    1 US qt = 1.10121 l   1 US pt = 0.55061 l

Science and Technology

Conversion tables: tyre pressures

lb per sq in	kg per sq cm	lb per sq in	kg per sq cm
10	0.7	26	1.8
15	1.1	28	2
20	1.4	30	2.1
24	1.7	40	2.8

Conversion tables: weight

ounces*	grams	grams	ounces*	pounds	kilo-grams	pounds	kilo-grams	kilo-grams	pounds	kilo-grams	pounds
1	28.3	1	0.04	1	0.45	19	8.62	1	2.2	19	41.9
2	56.7	2	0.07	2	0.91	20	9.07	2	4.4	20	44.1
3	85	3	0.11	3	1.36	25	11.34	3	6.6	25	55.1
4	113.4	4	0.14	4	1.81	30	13.61	4	8.8	30	66.1
5	141.7	5	0.18	5	2.27	35	15.88	5	11	35	77.2
6	170.1	6	0.21	6	2.72	40	18.14	6	13.2	40	88.2
7	198.4	7	0.25	7	3.18	45	20.41	7	15.4	45	99.2
8	226.8	8	0.28	8	3.63	50	22.68	8	17.6	50	110.2
9	255.1	9	0.32	9	4.08	60	27.24	9	19.8	60	132.3
10	283.5	10	0.35	10	4.54	70	31.78	10	22	70	154.4
11	311.7	20	0.71	11	4.99	80	36.32	11	24.3	80	176.4
12	340.2	30	1.06	12	5.44	90	40.86	12	26.5	90	198.5
13	368.5	40	1.41	13	5.90	100	45.36	13	28.7	100	220.5
14	396.9	50	1.76	14	6.35	200	90.72	14	30.9	200	440.9
15	425.2	60	2.12	15	6.80	250	113.40	15	33.1	250	551.2
16	453.6	70	2.47	16	7.26	500	226.80	16	35.3	500	1 102.3
		80	2.82	17	7.71	750	340.19	17	37.5	750	1 653.5
		90	3.18	18	8.16	1 000	453.59	18	39.7	1 000	2 204.6
		100	3.53								

* avoirdupois

Exact conversions 1 oz (avdp) = 28.3495 g 1 g = 0.0353 oz (avdp) 1 lb = 0.454 kg 1 kg = 2.205 lb

Tons: long, UK 2 240lb; short, US 2 000lb

UK tons	tonnes	US tons	tonnes	UK tons	US tons	tonnes	UK tons	US tons	US tons	UK tons
1	1.02	1	0.91	1	1.12	1	0.98	1.10	1	0.89
2	2.03	2	1.81	2	2.24	2	1.97	2.20	2	1.79
3	3.05	3	2.72	3	3.36	3	2.95	3.30	3	2.68
4	4.06	4	3.63	4	4.48	4	3.94	4.40	4	3.57
5	5.08	5	4.54	5	5.6	5	4.92	5.50	5	4.46
10	10.16	10	9.07	10	11.2	10	9.84	11.02	10	8.93
15	15.24	15	13.61	15	16.8	15	14.76	16.53	15	13.39
20	20.32	20	18.14	20	22.4	20	19.68	22.05	20	17.86
50	50.80	50	45.36	50	56	50	49.21	55.11	50	44.64
75	76.20	75	68.04	75	84	75	73.82	82.67	75	66.96
100	101.60	100	90.72	100	102	100	98.42	110.23	100	89.29

Exact conversions   1 UK ton = 1.0160 tonnes   1 US ton = 0.9072 tonne   1 UK ton = 1.1199 US tons
1 tonne = 0.9842 UK ton = 1.1023 US tons   1 US ton = 0.8929 UK ton

Hundredweights: long, UK 112lb; short, US 100lb

UK cwt	kilo-grams	US cwt	kilo-grams	UK cwt	US cwt	kilo-grams	UK cwt	US cwt	US cwt	UK cwt
1	50.8	1	45.4	1	1.12	1	0.0197	0.022	1	0.89
2	102	2	90.7	2	2.24	2	0.039	0.044	2	1.79
3	152	3	136	3	3.36	3	0.059	0.066	3	2.68
4	203	4	181	4	4.48	4	0.079	0.088	4	3.57
5	254	5	227	5	5.6	5	0.098	0.11	5	4.46
10	508	10	454	10	11.2	10	0.197	0.22	10	8.93
15	762	15	680	15	16.8	15	0.295	0.33	15	13.39
20	1016	20	907	20	22.4	20	0.394	0.44	20	17.86
50	2540	50	2268	50	56	50	0.985	1.10	50	44.64
75	3810	75	3402	75	84	75	1.477	1.65	75	66.96
100	5080	100	4536	100	102	100	1.970	2.20	100	89.29

Exact conversions 1 UK cwt = 50.8023 kg 1 US cwt = 45.3592 kg 1 UK cwt = 1.1199 US cwt
1 kg = 0.0197 UK cwt = 0.0220 US cwt 1 US cwt = 0.8929 UK cwt

stones	pounds	stones	pounds	stones	kilograms
1	14	11	154	1	6.35
2	28	12	168	2	12.70
3	42	13	182	3	19.05
4	56	14	196	4	25.40
5	70	15	210	5	31.75
6	84	16	224	6	38.10
7	98	17	238	7	44.45
8	112	18	252	8	50.80
9	126	19	266	9	57.15
10	140	20	280	10	63.50

1 st = 14 lb 1 lb = 0.07 st 1 st = 6.350 kg 1 kg = 0.1575 st

International clothing sizes

Size equivalents are approximate, and may display some variation between manufacturers.

■ **Women's suits/dresses**

UK	USA	UK/ Continent
8	6	36
10	8	38
12	10	40
14	12	42
16	14	44
18	16	46
20	18	48
22	20	50
24	22	52

■ **Adults' shoes**

UK	USA	UK/ Continent
4	$5\frac{1}{2}$	37
$4\frac{1}{2}$	6	38
5	$6\frac{1}{2}$	38
$5\frac{1}{2}$	7	39
6	$7\frac{1}{2}$	39
$6\frac{1}{2}$	8	40
7	$8\frac{1}{2}$	41
$7\frac{1}{2}$	$8\frac{1}{2}$	42
8	$9\frac{1}{2}$	42
$8\frac{1}{2}$	$9\frac{1}{2}$	43
9	$10\frac{1}{2}$	43
$9\frac{1}{2}$	$10\frac{1}{2}$	44
10	$11\frac{1}{2}$	44
$10\frac{1}{2}$	$11\frac{1}{2}$	45
11	12	46

■ **Children's shoes**

UK/USA	UK/Continent
0	15
1	17
2	18
3	19
4	20
5	22
6	23
7	24
8	25
$8\frac{1}{2}$	26
9	27
10	28
11	29
12	30
13	32

■ **Women's hosiery**

UK/USA	UK/Continent
8	0
$8\frac{1}{2}$	1
9	2
$9\frac{1}{2}$	3
10	4
$10\frac{1}{2}$	5

Science and Technology

■ Men's suits and overcoats

UK/USA	Continent
36	46
38	48
40	50
42	52
44	54
46	56

■ Men's shirts

UK/USA	UK/Continent
12	30–31
$12\frac{1}{2}$	32
13	33
$13\frac{1}{2}$	34–35
14	36
$14\frac{1}{2}$	37
15	38
$15\frac{1}{2}$	39–40
16	41
$16\frac{1}{2}$	42
17	43
$17\frac{1}{2}$	44–45

■ Men's socks

UK/USA	UK/Continent
$9\frac{1}{2}$	38–39
10	39–40
$10\frac{1}{2}$	40–41
11	41–42
$11\frac{1}{2}$	42–43

International pattern sizes

■ Young junior/teenage

Size	Bust cm	in	Waist cm	in	Hip cm	in	Back waist length cm	in
5/6	71	28	56	22	79	31	34.5	$13\frac{1}{2}$
7/8	74	29	58	23	81	32	35.5	14
9/10	78	$30\frac{1}{2}$	61	24	85	$33\frac{1}{2}$	37	$14\frac{1}{2}$
11/12	81	32	64	25	89	35	38	15
13/14	85	$33\frac{1}{2}$	66	26	93	$36\frac{1}{2}$	39	$15\frac{3}{8}$
15/16	89	35	69	27	97	38	40	$15\frac{3}{4}$

■ Misses

	Bust cm	in	Waist cm	in	Hip cm	in	Back waist length cm	in
6	78	$30\frac{1}{2}$	58	23	83	$32\frac{1}{2}$	39.5	$15\frac{1}{2}$
8	80	$31\frac{1}{2}$	61	24	85	$33\frac{1}{2}$	40	$15\frac{1}{4}$
10	83	$32\frac{1}{2}$	64	25	88	$34\frac{1}{2}$	40.5	16
12	87	34	67	$26\frac{1}{2}$	92	36	41.5	$16\frac{1}{4}$
14	92	36	71	28	97	38	42	$16\frac{1}{2}$
16	97	38	76	30	102	40	42.5	$16\frac{3}{4}$
18	102	40	81	32	107	42	43	17
20	107	42	87	34	112	44	44	$17\frac{1}{4}$

■ Half-sizes

	Bust cm	in	Waist cm	in	Hip cm	in	Back waist length cm	in
$10\frac{1}{2}$	84	33	69	27	89	35	38	15
$12\frac{1}{2}$	89	35	74	29	94	37	39	$15\frac{1}{4}$
$14\frac{1}{2}$	94	37	79	31	99	39	39.5	$15\frac{1}{2}$
$16\frac{1}{2}$	99	39	84	33	104	41	40	$15\frac{3}{8}$
$18\frac{1}{2}$	104	41	89	35	109	43	40.5	$15\frac{7}{8}$
$20\frac{1}{2}$	109	43	96	$37\frac{1}{2}$	116	$45\frac{1}{2}$	40.5	16
$22\frac{1}{2}$	114	45	102	40	122	48	41	$16\frac{1}{8}$
$24\frac{1}{2}$	119	47	108	$42\frac{1}{2}$	128	$50\frac{1}{2}$	41.5	$16\frac{1}{4}$

■ Women's

	Bust cm	in	Waist cm	in	Hip cm	in	Back waist length cm	in
38	107	42	89	35	112	44	44	$17\frac{1}{4}$
40	112	44	94	37	117	46	44	$17\frac{3}{8}$
42	117	46	99	39	122	48	44.5	$17\frac{1}{2}$
44	122	48	105	$41\frac{1}{2}$	127	50	45	$17\frac{5}{8}$
46	127	50	112	44	132	52	45	$17\frac{3}{4}$
48	132	52	118	$46\frac{1}{2}$	137	54	45.5	$17\frac{7}{8}$
50	137	54	124	49	142	56	46	18

International paper sizes

▪ A series

	mm	in
A0	841 × 1 189	33.11 × 46.81
A1	594 × 841	23.39 × 33.1
A2	420 × 594	16.54 × 23.39
A3	297 × 420	11.69 × 16.54
A4	210 × 297	8.27 × 11.69
A5	148 × 210	5.83 × 8.27
A6	105 × 148	4.13 × 5.83
A7	74 × 105	2.91 × 4.13
A8	52 × 74	2.05 × 2.91
A9	37 × 52	1.46 × 2.05
A10	26 × 37	1.02 × 1.46

▪ B series

	mm	in
B0	1 000 × 1 414	39.37 × 55.67
B1	707 × 1 000	27.83 × 39.37
B2	500 × 707	19.68 × 27.83
B3	353 × 500	13.90 × 19.68
B4	250 × 353	9.84 × 13.90
B5	176 × 250	6.93 × 9.84
B6	125 × 176	4.92 × 6.93
B7	88 × 125	3.46 × 4.92
B8	62 × 88	2.44 × 3.46
B9	44 × 62	1.73 × 2.44
B10	31 × 44	1.22 × 1.73

▪ C series

	mm	in
C0	917 × 1 297	36.00 × 51.20
C1	648 × 917	25.60 × 36.00
C2	458 × 648	18.00 × 25.60
C3	324 × 458	12.80 × 18.00
C4	229 × 324	9.00 × 12.80
C5	162 × 229	6.40 × 9.00
C6	114 × 162	4.50 × 6.40
C7	81 × 114	3.20 × 4.50
DL	110 × 220	4.33 × 8.66
C7/6	81 × 162	3.19 × 6.38

All sizes in these series have sides in the proportion of $1:\sqrt{2}$.
A series is used for writing paper, books and magazines; B series for posters; C series for envelopes.

Engineering: bridges

When a single date is given it is the date for completion of construction.

Name	Location	Length (m)[1]	Type	Date
Akashi-Kaikyo	Honshu–Shikoku, Japan	1 990	(longest) suspension	1978–98
Alex Fraser (previously called Annacis)	Vancouver, Canada	465	cable-stayed	1986
Ambassador	Detroit, Michigan, USA	564	suspension	1929
Angostura	Ciudad Bolivar, Venezuela	712	suspension	1967
Astoria	Astoria, Oregon, USA	376	truss	1966
Bayonne (Kill van Kull)	New Jersey–Staten Island, USA	504	steel arch	1932
Bendorf	Rhine River, Coblenz, Germany	1 030	cement girder	1965
Benjamin Franklin	Philadelphia–Camden, USA	534	suspension	1926
Bosporus	Istanbul, Turkey	1 074	suspension	1973
Bosporus II	Istanbul, Turkey	1 090	suspension	1986–8
Bridge of Sighs	Doge's Palace–Pozzi Prison, Venice, Italy	c.5	enclosed arch	16c
Britannia tubular rail	Menai Strait, Wales	420	plate girder	1845–50
Brooklyn	Brooklyn–Manhattan Island, New York City, USA	486	suspension	1869–83
Chao Phraya	Bangkok, Thailand	450	(longest single-plane) cable-stayed	1989
Commodore Barry	Chester, Pennsylvania, USA	501	cantilever	1974
Cooper River	Charleston, S Carolina, USA	488	truss	1989
Delaware River	Chester, Pennsylvania, USA	501	cantilever	1971
Evergreen	Seattle, Washington, USA	longest span 2 293	floating pontoon	1963

Science and Technology

Name	Location	Length (m)[1]	Type	Date
Forth (rail)	Firth of Forth, South Queensferry, Scotland	1 658 (spans 521)	cantilever	1882–90
Forth Road Bridge (road)	Firth of Forth, South Queensferry, Scotland	1 006	suspension	1958–64
George Washington	Hudson River, New York City, USA	1 067	suspension	1927–31
Gladesville	Sydney, Australia	305	(longest) concrete arch	1964
Golden Gate	San Francisco, California, USA	1 280	suspension	1937
Grand Trunk rail-road	Niagara Falls, New York, USA	250	suspension	1855 (survived until 1897)
Great Belt (Storebælt) East	Halsskov–Kudshoved, Denmark	1 624	suspension	1998
Greater New Orleans	Mississippi River, Louisiana, USA	480	cantilever	1958
High Coast	Västernorrland, Sweden	1 210	suspension	1997
Howrah (railroad)	Hooghly River, Kolkata (formerly Calcutta), India	457	cantilever	1936–43
Humber Estuary	Hull–Grimsby, England	1 410	suspension	1973–81
Humen	Humen, China	888	suspension	1996
Jiangsu Yangtze	Jiangsu Province, China	1 385	suspension	1999
Kap Shui Mun	Lantau I–Ma Wan I, Hong Kong	430	cable-stayed (double-deck road/rail)	1997
Kincardine	Forth River, Scotland	822 (swing span 111)	movable	1936
Lake Pontchartrain Causeway	Maudeville–Jefferson, Louisiana, USA	38km	twin concrete trestle	1963
Lion's Gate	Vancouver, Canada	473	suspension	1938
London	Southwark–City of London	centre span 46	concrete arch	1973
Mackinac	Michigan, USA	1 158	suspension	1957
McCall's Ferry	Susquehanna River, Lancaster, Pennsylvania, USA	110	wooden covered	1815
Meiko Chuo	Tokyo Bay, Japan	590	cable-stayed	1997
Menai Strait	Menai Strait, N Wales	177	suspension	1820–6 (reconstructed 1940)
Minami Bisan-Seto	Honshu–Shikoku, Japan	1 118	suspension	1988
New River Gorge	Fayetteville, West Virginia, USA	518	(longest) steel arch	1977
Nord Sundet	Norway	223	lattice	1989
Normandie	Le Havre, France	856	cable-stayed	1995
Øresund	Flinterenden, Denmark–Malmö, Sweden	7.8km (main span 490)		2000
Plauen	Plauen, Germany	span 90	(longest) masonry arch	1903
Pont d'Avignon	Rhône River, France	c.60	arch	1177–87
Pontypridd	S Wales	43	single-span arch	1750
Quebec (railroad)	St Lawrence, Canada	549	(largest-span) cantilever	1918
Rainbow	Canada–USA, Niagara Falls	300	steel arch	1941
Ravenswood	West Virginia, USA	525	cantilever	1981
Rialto	Grand Canal, Venice, Italy	25	single-span arch	1588–92
Rio-Niteroi	Guanabara Bay, Brazil	centre span 300, length 14km	box and plate girder	1972
Salazar	Tagus River, Lisbon, Portugal	1 014	suspension	1966
Severn	Ironbridge, Shropshire, England	31	(first) cast-iron arch	1779
Severn	Beachley, England	988	suspension	1961–6
Severn II	Severn Estuary, England	456	cable-stayed	1996
Skarnsundet	Norway	530	cable-stayed	1991
Sky Train Bridge (rail)	Vancouver, Canada	340	cable-stayed	1989
Sydney Harbour	Sydney, Australia	503	steel arch	1923–32
Tacoma Narrows II	Puget Sound, Washington, USA	854	suspension	1950
Tagus II	Lisbon, Portugal	420	cable-stayed	1997
Tatara, Great	Japan	890	cable-stayed	1999
Tay (road)	Dundee, Scotland	2 246	box girder	1966
Thatcher Ferry	Panama Canal, C America	344	arch	1962
Tower	Thames River, London	76	movable	1886–94
Transbay	San Francisco, California, USA	705	suspension	1933
Trans-Tokyo Bay Highway	Kawasaki–Kisarazu, Japan	590	box girder	1997
Trois-Rivières	St Lawrence River, Quebec, Canada	336	steel arch	1962
Tsing Ma	Tsing Yi I–Ma Wan I, Hong Kong	1 377	suspension (double deck)	1997
Verrazano Narrows	Brooklyn–Staten Island, New York Harbour, USA	1 298	suspension	1959–64
Victoria Jubilee	St Lawrence River, Montreal, Canada	2 742	open steel	1854–9
Wheeling	Wheeling, Virginia, USA	308	suspension	1849
Xiling Yangtze	Three Gorges Dam, China	900	suspension	1996
Yokohama Bay (road)	Japan	855	suspension	1989
Zoo	Cologne, Germany	259	steel box girder	1966

[1] To convert m to ft, multiply by 3.2808.

Engineering: tunnels

When a single date is given it is the date for completion of construction.

Name	Use	Location	Length[1]	Date
Aki	rail	Japan	13km	1975
Box	rail	Wiltshire, England	3km	1841
Cascade	rail	Washington, USA	13km	1929
Channel	rail	Cheriton, England–Sargette, France	50km	1987–94
Chesapeake Bay Bridge-Tunnel	road	USA	28km	1964
Chesbrough	water supply	Chicago, USA	3km	1867
Cumberland Mountain	underground parking	Cumberland Gap, USA	1 402m	1996
Dai-shimizu	rail	Honshu, Japan	22km	1979
Delaware Aqueduct	water supply	Catskill Mts, New York, USA	169km	1937–44
Detroit River	rail	Detroit, Michigan, USA–Windsor, Ontario, Canada	2km	1910
Eupalinus	water supply	Samos, Greece	1 037m	c.525BC
FATIMA (Magerøy)	road	Norway	6 820m	1998
		(longest undersea road)		
Flathead	rail	Washington, USA	13km	1970
Fréjus	rail	Modane, France–Bardonecchia, Italy	13km	1857–71
Fucino	drainage	Lake Fucino, Italy	6km	41
Great Apennine	rail	Vernio, Italy	19km	1934
Hokuriku	rail	Japan	15km	1962
Holland	road	Hudson River, New York City–Jersey City, New Jersey, USA	3km	1927
Hoosac	rail	Massachusetts, USA	8km	1876
Hyperion	sewer	Los Angeles, California, USA	8km	1959
Kanmon	rail	Kanmon Strait, Japan	19km	1975
Keijo	rail	Japan	11km	1970
Kilsby Ridge	rail	London–Birmingham line, England	2km	1838
Languedoc (Canal du Midi)	canal	Malpas, France	157m	1666–92
Lierasen	rail	Norway	11km	1973
London and Southwark Subway	rail	London, England	11km	1890
Lötschberg	rail	Switzerland	15km	1913
Mersey	road	Mersey River, Birkenhead–Liverpool, England	4km	1934
Moffat	rail	Colorado, USA	10km	1928
Mont Blanc	road	France–Italy	12km	1965
Mt MacDonald	rail	Canada	15km	1989
NEAT (St Gotthard)	rail	Switzerland	57km	under construction
NEAT (Bern–Lötschberg–Simplon)	rail	Switzerland	38km	under construction
Orange-Fish River	irrigation	South Africa	82km	1975
		(longest irrigation tunnel)		
Øresund	road-rail	Copenhagen, Denmark–Malmö, Sweden	3 750m (longest immersed tube)	2000
Owingsburg Landing	canal	Pennsylvania, USA	137m	1828
Posilipo	road	Naples–Pozzuoli, Italy	6km	c.36BC
Rogers Pass	rail	Calgary–Vancouver, Canada	15km	1982–8
Rogers Pass	road	British Columbia, Canada	35km	1989
Rokko	rail	Ōsaka–Kōbe, Japan	16km	1972
Seikan	rail	Tsugaru Strait, Honshu–Hokkaido, Japan (longest undersea rail)	54km	1964–88
Shin-shimizu	rail	Japan	13km	1961
Simplon I and II	rail	Brigue, Switzerland–Iselle, Italy	20km	1906 and 1922
St Gotthard	rail	Switzerland	15km	1882
St Gotthard	road	Göschenen, Switzerland–Airolo, Italy	16km	1980
(First) Thames	pedestrian; rail after 1865	Wapping–Rotherhithe, London, England	366m	1825–43
Tower Subway	rail	London, England	411m	1869–70
Tronquoy	canal	France	1 099m	1810

[1] To convert m to ft, multiply by 3.2808; to convert km to mi, multiply by 0.6214.

Science and Technology

Engineering: dams

When a single date is given it is the date for completion of construction.

Name	River, country	Height (m)[1]	Date
Afsluitdijk Sea	Zuider Zee, Netherlands	20 (largest sea dam, length 31km)	1927–32
Aswan High	Nile, Egypt	111	1970
Atatürk	Euphrates, Turkey	184	1990
Bakun	Rajang, Malaysia	204	2002
Chicoasén	Grijalva, Mexico	263	1980
Chivor	Cundinamarca, Colombia	237	1975
Cipasang	Cimanuk, Indonesia	200	under construction
Daniel Johnson	Manicouagan, Canada	214	1968
Ertan	Yalong, China	240	1998
Grand Coulee	Columbia (Franklin D Roosevelt Lake), USA	168	1933–42
Grand Dixence	Dixence, Switzerland	285	1961
Guavio	Guaviare, Colombia	245	1989
Hoover	Colorado (Lake Mead), USA	221	1931–6
Inguri	Inguri, Georgia	272	1980
Itaipú	Paraná, Paraguay/Brazil border	189; length 8km (world's largest hydroelectric complex)	opened 1982, completed 1991
Kambarantinsk	Naryn, Kyrgyzstan	255	under construction
Katse	Malibamatso, Lesotho	182	1996
Kiev	Dneiper, Ukraine	256	1964
Kishau	Tons, India	253	under construction
La Grande 2A	La Grande, Canada	168	under construction
Longtan	Hongshui, China	285	under construction
Mauvoisin	Drance de Bagnes, Switzerland	237	1957
Mica	Columbia, Canada	244	1973
New China (Three Gorges	Chang Jiang (Yangzte), China	175	2009
Nurek	Vakhsh, Tajikistan	310	1980
Oroville	Feather, California, USA	235	1968
Poti	Paraná, Argentina	109 (most massive: volume 238 180 000 m^3)	under construction
Rogun	Vakhsh, Tajikistan	335 (tallest)	1973–96
San Roque	Agno, Philippines	210	under construction
Sardar Sarovar	Narmada, India	163	1994
Sayansk	Yenisey, Russia	236	1980
Tehri	Bhagirathi, India	261	1997
Thames Barrier	Thames, England	spans 520 (largest tidal barrier)	1984
Vaiont	Vaiont, Italy	265	1961 (damaged by landslide 1963)
Xiaolangdi	Huang He, China	154	2001

[1] To convert m to ft, multiply by 3.2808.

Engineering: tallest buildings

Name	Location	Height (m)[1] of construction	Date
Petronas I	Kuala Lumpur, Malaysia	452	1996
Petronas II	Kuala Lumpur, Malaysia	452	1996
Sears Tower	Chicago, USA	443	1974
Jin Mao Building	Shanghai, China	420	1998
World Trade Center, One[2]	New York City, USA	417	1972
World Trade Center, Two[2]	New York City, USA	415	1973
Empire State Building	New York City, USA	381	1931
Central Plaza	Hong Kong	374	1992
Bank of China	Hong Kong	368	1989
T & C Tower	Kaohsiung, Taiwan	347	1989

[1] To convert m to ft, multiply by 3.2808.
[2] Destroyed by terrorists, September 2001.

Inventions

Name	Date	Inventor (nationality)*
adding machine	1642	Blaise Pascal (Fr)
adhesive (rubber-based glue)	1850	anon
adhesive (epoxy resin)	1958	Certas Co
aeroplane (steam powered)	1886	Clement Ader (Fr)
aeroplane	1903	Orville and Wilbur Wright (US)
aeroplane (swing-wing)	1954	Barnes Wallis (UK)
aerosol	1926	Erik Rotheim (Nor)
airship (non-rigid)	1851	Henri Giffard (Fr)
airship (rigid)	1900	Graf Ferdinand von Zeppelin (Ger)
ambulance	1792	Jean Dominique Larrey (Fr)
aspirin (synthesization)	1859	Heinrich Kolbe (Ger)
aspirin (introduction into medicine)	1899	Felix Hoffmann (Ger)
atomic bomb	1939–45	Otto Frisch (Aus), Niels Bohr (D) and Rudolf Peierls (Ger)
balloon	1783	Jacques and Joseph Montgolfier (Fr)
barbed wire (first patent)	1867	Lucien B Smith (US)
barbed wire (manufacture)	1874	Joseph Glidden (US)
barbiturates (preparation of barbituric acid)	1863	Adolf von Baeyer (Pruss)
barometer	1643	Evangelista Torricelli (Ital)
battery (electric)	1800	Alessandro Volta (Ital)
bicycle	1839–40	Kirkpatrick MacMillan (UK)
bifocal lens	1780	Benjamin Franklin (US)
blood (artificial)	1966	Clark and Gollan (US)
bronze (copper with tin)	c.3700BC	Pre-dynastic Egypt
bunsen burner	1855	Robert Wilhelm Bunsen (Pruss)
burglar alarm	1858	Edwin T Holmes (US)
cable-car	1866	W Ritter (Ger) or anon (US)
calendar (modern)	525	Dionysius Exiguus (Scythian)
camera (polaroid)	1947	Edwin Land (US)
canning	1810	Nicolas Appert (Fr)
cannon	2c BC	Archimedes (Gr)
car (three-wheeled steam tractor)	1769	Nicolas Cugnot (Fr)
car (internal combustion)	1884	Gottlieb Daimler (Ger)
car (petrol)	1886	Karl Benz (Ger)
car (air-conditioning)	1902	J Wilkinson (US)
car (disc brakes)	1902	Frederick W Lanchester (UK)
car (speedometer)	1902	Thorpe and Salter (UK)
carbon fibres	1964	Courtaulds Ltd (UK)
carburettor	1876	Gottlieb Daimler (Ger)
carpet sweeper	1876	Melville Bissell (US)
cash register	1892	William Burroughs (US)
celluloid	1870	John W Hyatt (US)
cement (Portland)	1824	Joseph Aspdin (UK)
chocolate (solid)	1819	François-Louis Cailler (Swiss)
chocolate (solid, milk)	1875	Daniel Peter (Swiss)
chronometer	1735	John Harrison (UK)
cinema	1895	Auguste and Louis Lumière (Fr)
cinema (wide screen)	1900	Raoul Grimoin-Sanson (Fr)
clock (mechanical)	725	I-Hsing (Chinese)
clock (pendulum)	1657	Christiaan Huygens (NL)
clock (quartz)	1929	Warren Alvin Marrison (US)
coffee (instant)	1937	Nestlé (Swiss)
compact disc	1979	Philips (NL) and Sony (Japanese)
compass (discovery of magnetite)	1c	China
compass (first record of mariner's compass)	1187	Alexander Neckam (UK)
computer	1835	Charles Babbage (UK)
computer (electronic, digital)	1946	J Presper Eckert and John W Mauchly (US)
concrete	1c	Rome
concrete (reinforced)	1892	François Hennebique (Fr)
contact lenses	1887	Adolph E Fick (Ger)
contraceptive pill	1950	Gregor Pincus (US)
corrugated iron	1853	Pierre Carpentier (Fr)
credit card	1950	Ralph Scheider (US)
crossword	1913	Arthur Wynne (US) in New YorkWorld
crystal	c.1450	anon, Venice
decompression chamber	1929	Robert H Davis (UK)
dental plate	1817	Anthony A Plantson (US)
dental plate (rubber)	1854	Charles Goodyear (US)
detergents	1916	anon, Germany
diesel engine	1892	Rudolf Diesel (Ger)
dishwasher (automatic)	1889	Mrs W A Cockran (US)
drill (pneumatic)	1861	Germain Sommelier (Fr)
drill (electric, hand)	1895	Wilhelm Fein (Ger)
electric chair	1888	Harold P Brown and E A Kenneally (US)

Name	Date	Inventor (nationality)*
electric flat iron	1882	Henry W Seeley (US)
electric generator	1831	Michael Faraday (UK)
electric guitar	1931	Adolph Rickenbacker, Barth and Beauchamp (US)
electric heater	1887	W Leigh Burton (US)
electric light bulb	1879	Thomas Alva Edison (US)
electric motor (AC)	1888	Nikola Tesla (US)
electric motor (DC)	1870	Zenobe Gramme (Belg)
electric oven	1889	Bernina Hotel, Switzerland
electrocardiography	1903	Willem Einthoven (NL)
electromagnet	1824	William Sturgeon (UK)
encyclopedia	c.47BC	Marcus Terentius Varro (Roman)
endoscope	1827	Pierre Segalas (Fr)
escalator	1892	Jesse W Reno (US)
explosives (nitroglycerine)	1847	Ascanio Sobrero (Ital)
explosives (dynamite)	1866	Alfred Nobel (Swed)
extinguisher	1866	François Carlier (Fr)
facsimile machine (fax)	1907	Arthur Korn (Ger)
ferrofluids	1968	Ronald Rosensweig (US)
film (moving outlines)	1874	Jules Janssen (Fr)
	1888	Louis Le Prince (Fr)
	1891	Thomas Alva Edison (US)
film (with soundtrack)	1896	Lee De Forest (US)
forceps (obstetric)	c.1630	Peter Chamberlen (UK)
freeze-drying	1906	Arsene D'Arsonval and Georges Bordas (Fr)
galvanometer	1834	André Marie Ampère (Fr)
gas lighting	1792	William Murdock (UK)
gearbox (automatic)	1910	Hermann Fottinger (Ger)
glass (heat-resistant)	1884	Carl Zeiss (Ger)
glass (stained)	pre-850	Europe
glass (toughened)	1893	Leon Appert (Fr)
glass fibre	1713	René de Réamur (Fr)
glass fibre (industrial)	1931	Owens Illinois Glass Co (US)
glassware	c.2600BC	Egypt
glider	1853	George Cayley (UK)
gramophone	1877	Thomas Alva Edison (US)
gun	245BC	Ctesibius (Gr)
gyro-compass	1911	Elmer A Sperry (US)
heart (artificial)	1937	Vladimir P Demikhov (USSR)
	1982	Robert Jarvik (US)
heat pump	1851	William Thompson, Lord Kelvin (UK)
helicopter	1907	Louis and Jacques Breguet (Fr)
holography	1948	Denis Gabor (Hung/UK)
hovercraft	1955	Christopher Cockerell (UK)
integrated circuit (concept)	1952	Geoffrey Dummer (UK)
interferometry	1802	Thomas Young (UK)
interferometer	1856	J-C Jamin (Fr)
iron (working of)	c.1323BC	Hittites, Anatolia
jeans	1872	Levi-Strauss (US)
kidney (artificial)	1945	Willem Kolff (NL)
laser	1960	Theodore Maiman (US)
launderette	1934	J F Cantrell (US)
lawnmower	1830	Edwin Beard Budding (UK)
lift (mechanical)	1851	Elisha G Otis (US)
lightning conductor	1752	Benjamin Franklin (US)
linoleum	1860	Frederick Walton (UK)
lithography	1796	Aloys Senefelder (Bav)
locomotive (railed)	1804	Richard Trevithick (UK)
lock	c.4000BC	Mesopotamia
loom (power)	1785	Edmund Cartwright (UK)
loudspeaker	1900	Horace Short (UK)
machine gun	1718	James Puckle (UK)
maps	c.2250BC	Mesopotamia
margarine	1868	Hippolyte Mergé-Mouriès (Fr)
match	1680	Robert Boyle (UK)
match (safety)	1845	Anton von Schrotter (Ger)
microchip	1958	Jack Saint Clair Kilby (US)
microphone	1876	Alexander Graham Bell and Thomas Alva Edison (US)
microprocessor	1971	Marcian E Hoff (US)
microscope	1590	Zacharias Janssen (NL)
microscope (electron)	1933	Max Knoll and Ernst Ruska (Ger)
microscope (scanning tunnelling)	1982	Gerd Binnig and Heinrich Rohrer (Swiss)
microscope (atomic force)	1985	Gerd Binnig and Heinrich Rohrer (Swiss)
microwave oven	1945	Percy Le Baron Spencer (US)
missile (air-to-air)	1943	Herbert Wagner (Ger)
motorcycle	1885	Gottlieb Daimler (Ger)

Science and Technology

Name	Date	Inventor (nationality)*
neon lamp	1910	Georges Claude (Fr)
newspaper	59BC	Julius Caesar (Roman)
non-stick pan	1954	Marc Grégoir (Fr)
novel (serialized)	1836	Charles Dickens, Chapman and Hall Publishers (UK)
nylon	1937	Wallace H Carothers (US)
optical fibres	c.1955	Navinder S Kapany (Ind)
optical sound recording	1920	Lee De Forest (US)
pacemaker (implantable)	1956	Wilson Greatbach (US)
paint (fluorescent)	1933	Joe and Bob Switzer (US)
paint (acrylic)	1964	Reeves Ltd (UK)
paper	AD105	Ts'ai Lun (Chinese)
paper clip	1900	Johann Vaaler (Nor)
parachute	c.2c BC	China
parachute (jump)	1797	André-Jacques Garnerin (Fr)
parachute (patent)	1802	André-Jacques Garnerin (Fr)
parchment	2c BC	Eumenes II of Pergamum (reigned 197–159BC)
parking meter	1932	Carlton C Magee (US)
pasteurization	1863	Louis Pasteur (Fr)
pen (fountain)	1884	Lewis Waterman (US)
pen (ball-point)	1938	Laszlo Biro (Hung)
pencil	1795	Nicholas Jacques Conté (Fr)
pentium processor	1995	Intel (US)
phonograph	1877	Thomas Alva Edison (US)
photoelectric cell	1896	Julius Elster and Hans F Geitel (Ger)
phototypesetting	1894	Eugene Porzott (Hung)
photographic lens (for camera obscura)	1812	William H Wollaston (UK)
photographic film	1889	George Eastman (US)
photography (on metal)	1816	Joseph Nicéphore Niepce (Fr)
photography (on paper)	1838	William Henry Fox Talbot (UK)
photography (colour)	1861	James Clerk Maxwell (UK)
pianoforte	1720	Bartolomeo Cristofori (Ital)
plastics	1868	John W Hyatt (US)
pocket calculator	1972	Jack Saint Clair Kilby, James Van Tassell and Jerry D Merryman (US)
porcelain	c.960	China
pressure cooker	1679	Denis Papin (Fr)
printing press (wooden)	c.1450	Johannes Gutenberg (Ger)
printing press (rotary)	1845	Richard Hoe (US)
propeller (boat, hand-operated)	1775	David Bushnell (US)
propeller (ship)	1844	Isambard Kingdom Brunel (UK)
radar (theory)	1900	Nikola Tesla (Croat)
radar (theory)	1922	Guglielmo Marconi (Ital)
radar (application)	c.1930	A Hoyt Taylor and Leo C Young (US)
radio telegraphy (discovery and production of sound waves)	1888	Heinrich Hertz (Ger)
radio (transatlantic)	1901	Guglielmo Marconi (Ital)
rails (iron)	1738	Abraham Barby (UK)
railway (underground)	1843	Charles Pearson (UK)
railway (electric)	1878	Ernst Werner von Siemens (Ger)
rayon	1883	Joseph Swan (UK)
razor (safety)	1895	King Camp Gillette (US)
razor (electric)	1928	Jacob Schick (US)
record (flat disc)	1888	Emil Berliner (Ger)
record (long-playing microgroove)	1948	Peter Goldmark (US)
refrigerator (compressed ether)	1855	James Harrison (UK)
refrigerator (absorption)	1857	Ferdinand Carré (Fr)
revolver	1835	Samuel Colt (US)
Richter seismographic scale	1935	Charles Francis Richter (US)
rocket (missile)	1232	Mongols, China
rubber (latex foam)	1929	E A Murphy, W H Chapman and John Dunlop (US)
rubber (butyl)	1937	Robert Thomas and William Sparks, Exxon (US)
rubber (vulcanized)	1939	Charles Goodyear (US)
Rubik cube	1975	Erno Rubik (Hung)
safety-pin	1849	Walter Hunt (US)
satellite (artificial)	1957	USSR
saw	c.4000BC	Egypt
scanner	1973	Godfrey N Hounsfield (UK)
scotch tape	1930	Richard Drew (US)
screw	3c BC	Archimedes (Gr)
serotherapy	1890	Emil von Behring (Ger)
sewing machine	1830	Barthelemy Thimonnier (Fr)
ship (steam)	1775	Jacques C Perier (Fr)
ship (turbine)	1894	Charles Parsons (UK)
ship (metal hull and propeller)	1844	Isambard Kingdom Brunel (UK)

Name	Date	Inventor (nationality)*
silicon chip	1961	Texas Instruments (US)
silk (reeling)	c.2640BC	Hsi Ling Shi (Chinese)
skin (artificial)	c.1980	John Tanner (US), Bell (US), Neveu (Fr), Ioannis Yannas (Gr), Howard Green (US) and Jacques Thivolet (Fr)
skyscraper	1882	William Le Baron Jenney (US)
slide rule	1621	William Oughtred (UK)
soap	c.2500BC	Sumer, Babylonia
soda (extraction of)	c.16c BC	Egypt
space shuttle	1981	NASA (US)
spectacles	c.1280	Alessandro della Spina and Salvino degli Armati (Ital)
spinning frame	1768	Richard Arkwright (UK)
spinning jenny	c.1764	James Hargreaves (UK)
spinning-mule	1779	Samuel Crompton (UK)
stapler	1868	Charles Henry Gould (UK)
starter motor	1912	Charles F Kettering (US)
steam engine	1698	Thomas Savery (UK)
steam engine (condenser)	1769	James Watt (UK)
steam engine (piston)	1705	Thomas Newcomen (UK)
steel (production)	1854	Henry Bessemer (UK) and William Kelly (US)
steel (stainless)	1913	Henry Brearley (UK)
stethoscope	1816	René Théophile Hyacinthe Laennec (Fr)
stereotype	1725	William Ged (UK)
submarine	c.1620	Cornelis Brebbel or Van Drebbel (NL)
sun-tan cream	1936	Eugène Schueller (Fr)
suspension bridge	25BC	China
syringe (scientific)	1646	Blaise Pascal (Fr)
syringe (hypodermic)	c.1835	Charles Gabriel Pravaz (Fr)
table tennis	1890	James Gibb (UK)
tampon	1930	Earl Hass (US)
tank	1916	Ernest Swinton (UK)
telegraph (electric)	1774	Georges Louis Lesage (Swiss)
telegraph (transatlantic cable)	1866	William Thompson, Lord Kelvin (UK)
telegraph code	1837	Samuel F B Morse (US)
telephone (first practical)	1876	Alexander Graham Bell (US)
telephone (automatic exchange)	1889	Alman B Strowger (US)
telescope (refractor)	1608	Hans Lippershey (NL)
telescope (space)	1990	Edwin Hubble (US)
television (mechanical)	1926	John Logie Baird (UK)
television (colour)	1940	Peter Goldmark (US)
tennis	1873	Walter G Wingfield (UK)
thermometer	3c BC	Ctesibius (Gr)
thermometer (mercury)	1714	Gabriel Fahrenheit (Ger)
timeclock	1894	Daniel M Cooper (US)
toaster	1927	Charles Strite (US)
traffic lights	1868	J P Knight (UK)
traffic lights (automatic)	1914	Alfred Benesch (US)
transformer	1831	Michael Faraday (UK)
tranquillizers	1952	Henri Laborit (Fr)
transistor	1948	John Bardeen, Walter Brattain and William Shockley (US)
travel agency	1841	Thomas Cook (UK)
traveller's cheques	1891	American Express Travel Agency (US)
turbojet	1928	Frank Whittle (UK)
typewriter	1829	William Burt (US)
typewriter (electric)	1872	Thomas Alva Edison (US)
tyre (pneumatic, coach)	1845	Robert William Thomson (UK)
tyre (pneumatic, bicycle)	1888	John Boyd Dunlop (UK)
ultrasonography (obstetric)	1958	Ian Donald (UK)
universal joint	c.140BC	Fang Feng (Chinese)
vacuum cleaner (steam powered)	1871	Ives W McGaffrey (US)
vacuum cleaner (electric)	1901	Hubert Cecil Booth (UK)
vending machine	1883	Percival Everitt (UK)
ventilator	1858	Théophile Guibal (Fr)
videophone	1927	American Telegraph and Telephone Co
video recorder	1956	Ampex Co (US)
washing machine (electric)	1907	Hurley Machine Co (US)
watch	1462	Bartholomew Manfredi (Ital)
watch (waterproof)	1927	Rolex (Swiss)
wheel	c.3500BC	Mesopotamia
windmill	c.600	Syria
word processor	1965	IBM (US)
writing (pictography)	c.3000BC	Egypt
xerography	1938	Chester Carlson (US)
zip-fastener	1893	Whitcomb L Judson (US)

*Aus: Austrian	Fr: French	Ital: Italian
Bav: Bavarian	Ger: German	NL: Dutch
Belg: Belgian	Gr: Greek	Nor: Norwegian
Croat: Croatian	Hung: Hungarian	Pruss: Prussian
D: Danish	Ind: Indian	Swed: Swedish

Industrialists and entrepreneurs

Agnelli, Giovanni (1866–1945) Italian, born Villa Perosa, Piedmont. Founder of Fiat (Fabbrica Italiana Automobili Torino) in 1899. Appointed as a senator in 1923 and mobilized Italian industry in World War II.

Astor, John Jacob, 1st Baron Astor of Hever (1886–1971) Anglo-American, born New York City. Elected MP for Dover (1922) and chairman of the Times Publishing Company.

Astor, William Waldorf, 1st Viscount Astor (1848–1919) Anglo-American, born New York City. After period as US minister to Italy, emigrated to Britain to become newspaper proprietor, acquiring the *Pall Mall Gazette, Pall Mall Magazine* and in 1911, the *Observer.*

Austin, Herbert, 1st Baron Austin of Longbridge (1866–1941) English, born Buckinghamshire. After working in engineering shops in Australia, returned to England and produced his first three-wheel car with the Wolseley Co in 1895, forming his own company in 1905. Conservative MP from 1918 to 1924.

Barclay, Robert (1843–1913) English. Founder of Barclay and Co Ltd with the merger of 20 banks in 1896. In 1917 the name was changed to Barclay's Bank Limited.

Beaverbrook, Max (William Maxwell Aitken), 1st Baron (1879–1964) Anglo-Canadian, born Maple, Ontario. Originally stockbroker, before entering British parliament (1911–16); became minister of information (1918). Later acquired a number of major British newspapers, including the *Daily Express.*

Benz, Karl Friedrich (1844–1929) German, born Karlsruhe. Engineer and car manufacturer who developed two-stroke engine. Founded Benz & Co and produced one of the earliest petrol-driven vehicles; company later merged to become Daimler-Benz.

Birdseye, Clarence (1886–1956) American, born Brooklyn, New York City. Co-founder of the General Seafoods Co in 1924, after developing a process for freezing foods in small packages. Later president of Birdseye Frosted Foods (1930–4) and Birdseye Electric Company (1935–8). He is credited with around 300 patents.

Boeing, William Edward (1881–1956) American, born Detroit, Michigan. Formed Pacific Aero Products Co in 1916 to build seaplanes. Renamed as the Boeing Airplane Co in 1917; it became the largest aircraft manufacturer in the world. Also formed civilian airline Boeing Air Transport Co in 1927.

Bond, Alan (1938–) Anglo-Australian, born London. At the age of 19 established his own company; the Bond Corporation developed extensive interests in Australian newspapers, television, brewing, oil and gas, and gold mining.

Branson, Sir Richard Charles Nicholas (1950–) English entrepreneur and businessman. Started Virgin mail-order business in 1969. Opened first branch of record chain in 1971 and founded record label 1973. Founded Virgin Atlantic Airlines 1984, and sold Virgin Music in 1992 for £560m to expand airline. Launched Virgin Radio in 1993 (sold to Chris Evans's Ginger Productions in 1997) and bought MGM UK high-street cinemas in 1995. Introduced personal banking services and Virgin Trains into the Virgin Group in the 1990s. By 1998 the Virgin Group consisted of 200 companies, with an annual turnover of £1.8 billion.

Brierley, Sir Ron(ald Alfred) (1937–) New Zealand entrepreneur, born Wellington. Founded Brierley Investments in 1961. Sold Industrial Equities conglomerate just before 1987 crash and became chairman of Guinness Peat Group in 1990.

Burrell, Sir William (1861–1958) Scottish, born Glasgow. Ship-owner and art collector. Accumulated 8 000 works of art from all over the world, which he donated to the city of Glasgow in 1944.

Butlin, Sir William Edmund (1899–1980) English, born South Africa. Holiday camp promoter; opened first camp at Skegness in 1936 and expanded business in the UK and abroad after World War II.

Cadbury, George (1839–1922) English, born Birmingham. Quaker businessman, son of John Cadbury. Took over father's business in 1861 and established for the workers the model village of Bournville, near Birmingham. Became proprietor of the *Daily News* in 1902.

Cadbury, John (1801–89) English, born Birmingham. Quaker businessman, founder of Cadbury's cocoa and chocolate business.

Carnegie, Andrew (1835–1918) Scottish, born Dunfermline. Invested in oil lands and a business which grew into the largest iron and steel works in America. Retired in 1901, a multimillionaire.

Chandos, Oliver Lyttelton, 1st Viscount (1893–1972) English, born London. Managing director of the British Metal Corporation from 1928. In 1940 entered the House of Commons and was made President of the Board of Trade. Resigned from politics to return to business in 1954.

Christie, James (1730–1803) English, born London. Founder of Christie's auctioneers in 1766.

Citroën, André Gustave (1878–1935) French, born Paris. Responsible for mass production of armaments during World War I. Later manufacturer of small low-priced cars but in 1934 lost control of the Citroën company.

Conran, Sir Terence Orby (1931–) English, born Esher, Surrey. Businessman and designer who founded and ran the Habitat Company (1971). Has since been involved in management of Richard Shops, Conran Stores, Mothercare and several restaurants.

Cunard, Sir Samuel (1787–1865) Canadian, born Halifax. Merchant and ship-owner who emigrated to Britain in 1838 to found the British and North American Royal Mail Steam Packet Company, later known as the Cunard Line, for the new steam mail service between Britain and America.

du Pont Nemours, Eleuthère Irénée (1771–1834) French–American, born Paris. Worked in father's printing plant until 1797. Emigrated to USA and in 1802 established a gunpowder factory which developed into one of the world's largest chemical concerns.

du Pont, Pierre Samuel (1870–1954) American, born Wilmington, Delaware. Joined family gunpowder company. As its president (1915–20) introduced and developed many new industrial management techniques. Became president of General Motors in 1920.

Science and Technology

Science and Technology

Dunlop, John Boyd (1840–1921) Scottish, born Dreghorn, Ayrshire. Credited with inventing the pneumatic tyre. In 1889 formed business which became the Dunlop Rubber Company Ltd; produced pneumatic tyres for bicycles, and later for cars.

Firestone, Harvey Samuel (1868–1938) American, born Columbiana, Ohio. Sold solid rubber carriage tyres in Chicago and in 1900 founded Firestone Tire and Rubber Company, which grew to be one of the biggest industrial corporations in the USA. Pioneered pneumatic tyres for Ford Model T, and non-skid treads. Started rubber plantations in Liberia in 1924.

Ford, Henry (1863–1947) American, born Greenfield, Michigan. Apprentice to a machinist at the age of 15, produced his first petrol-driven car in 1893. In 1903 founded Ford Motor Company and pioneered mass-production techniques.

Ford, Henry II (1917–87) American, born Dearborn, Michigan. Seized control of the Ford Motor Company from his grandfather Henry Ford in 1945. Stepped down as chief executive officer in 1979 and as chairman in 1980, but remained as member of the board of directors.

Frick, Henry Clay (1849–1919) American, born West Overton, Pennsylvania. Millionaire at 30 after forming company to supply the Pittsburgh steelworks with coke. Became chairman of the Carnegie steel company in 1889. A ruthless employer, he was shot and stabbed after forcefully breaking a strike in 1892, but subsequently recovered. Became a director of United States Steel in 1901.

Gates, Bill (William Henry) (1955–) American, born Seattle. Founded Microsoft Corporation in 1975 and licensed computer operating system (MS-DOS) to IBM in 1980. This system and their applications software have been phenomenally successful. Gates was a billionaire by 1986. By the turn of the century, Microsoft earned revenues in excess of $19 billion, with over 32 000 employees in 60 countries. In recent years the company has faced anti-trust litigation over its perceived monopoly in the market.

Getty, Jean Paul (1892–1976) American, born Minneapolis, Minnesota. Entered oil business in his early twenties and went on to acquire and control more than 100 companies. Also acquired an enormous and valuable art collection.

Guinness, Sir Benjamin Lee (1798–1868) Irish, born Dublin. Inherited Guinness's Brewery (1759) and made it the largest business of its kind in the world. First Lord Mayor of Dublin (1851) and MP (1865–8).

Gulbenkian, Calouste Sarkis (1869–1955) British–Ottoman–Turkish, born Scutari. Entered father's oil business in Baku in 1888. Later organized international oil company mergers and negotiated oil concessions between USA and Saudi Arabia.

Hammer, Armand (1899–1990) American, born New York City. Exported grain to the USSR in exchange for furs, dealing with Lenin and subsequent Soviet leaders. Founded the A Hammer Pencil Company in 1925 and maintained strong connections with the USSR, occasionally acting as intermediary between Soviet and American governments. Bought and expanded the small Occidental Petroleum Corporation in 1957, and founded Hammer Galleries Inc in New York in 1930.

Harmsworth, Harold Sydney, 1st Viscount Rothermere (1868–1940) Irish, born London. Newspaper magnate, founder of the *Glasgow Daily Record* and the *Sunday Pictorial*. Also controlled the *Daily Mail*, *Sunday Dispatch* and the *Daily Mirror*, for which he developed a circulation of three million in 1922.

Heinz, Henry John (1844–1919) American, born Pittsburgh, Pennsylvania. Co-founder of food manufacturing and packing company F & J Heinz, and president of the reorganized business H J Heinz Co from 1905 to 1919. Promoted pure food movement in the USA, and pioneered staff welfare work.

Hilton, Conrad Nicholson (1887–1979) American, born San Antonio, New Mexico. Took over family inn in 1918, then built up a chain of hotels in major cities in the USA. Formed Hilton Hotels Corporation in 1946 and Hilton International in 1948, and continued to expand until 1966 when his son became president.

Honda, Soichiro (1906–91) Japanese, born Iwata Gun. Became garage apprentice in 1922 and opened his own garage in 1928. By 1934 had opened a piston-ring production factory and later produced motor cycles. President of Honda Corporation (1948–73), remaining as a director, and appointed supreme advisor in 1983.

Hoover, William Henry (1849–1932) American, born Ohio. After running a tannery business, bought patent of an electric cleaning machine from a janitor and formed Electric Suction Sweeper Co in 1908 (later renamed Hoover) to manufacture and market it throughout the world.

Hughes, Howard Robard (1905–76) American, born Houston, Texas. Inherited father's oil-drilling equipment company and used profits to make Hollywood films. After working as a pilot, became involved in designing, building and flying aircraft, then abruptly returned to filmmaking. From 1966 lived in complete seclusion but continued to control his vast business interests.

Iacocca, Lee (Lido Anthony) (1924–) American, born Allentown, Pennsylvania. Worked for Ford Motor Co, rising to become president in 1970. In 1978 joined Chrysler Corporation as president and chief executive officer, restoring profitability during serious financial difficulties.

Jobs, Steven (1955–) American, born San Fransisco. Together with Stephen Wozniak (1950–) he set up Apple Computer Co in 1976, which became the fastest-growing company in USA. Jobs left Apple in 1985 and founded NeXT Inc, and co-founded Pixar the following year, the computer animation studio responsible for *Toy Story* (1995), *A Bug's Life* (1998) and *Toy Story 2* (1999). Jobs rejoined Apple in 1997 as CEO, and oversaw the production of the *iMac* and *iBook*.

King (of Wartnaby), John Leonard King, Baron (1917–) English industrialist. Became chairman of Dennis Motor Holdings in 1970 and Babcock and Wilcox Ltd in 1972. He was appointed chairman of British Airways in 1981 and then life president in 1993.

Krupp, Alfred (1812–87) German, born Essen. Inherited father's iron forge and began manufacturing arms in 1837. Established a steel plant and became an international arms supplier. Also acquired large mines, collieries and docks.

Lyons, Sir Joseph (1848–1917) English, born London. Starting with a teashop in Piccadilly, made J Lyons and Co Ltd one of the largest catering businesses in Britain.

Marks, Simon, 1st Baron Marks of Broughton (1888–1964) English, born Leeds. Son of a Jewish immigrant from Poland from whom he inherited 60 Marks and Spencer 'penny bazaars'. With Israel (later Lord) Seif, established Marks and Spencer as a major high-quality retail chain.

Maxwell, (Ian) Robert (1923–91) English, born Czechoslovakia. Founder of Pergamon Press and Labour MP (1964–70). As well as controlling Mirror Group Newspapers and the Maxwell Communication Corporation, he had extensive private business interests. After his death massive debts were revealed.

Morita, Akio (1921–99) Japanese, born Nagoya. Founded Sony electronics firm together with Masaru Ibuka (1908–97) in 1958. Among Sony's most important products have been early tape recorders (c.1950) and the 'Walkman' (1980).

Murdoch, (Keith) Rupert (1931–) Australian–American, born Melbourne. After becoming Australia's second largest publisher, expanded abroad acquiring newspapers in London and New York, including the *Sun*, the *Times* and the *New York Post*. Expanded communications empire in 1989 with the purchase of Collins the publishers and the inauguration of Sky Television. Later bought 20th Century-Fox film studios and New World Communications, and created the Fox Network, becoming the owner of television stations that reached up to 40 per cent of viewership.

Nobel, Alfred (1833–96) Swedish, born Stockholm. Explosives expert who invented dynamite and gelignite. Created an industrial empire to manufacture his many inventions and left his fortune to endow annual Nobel prizes. Element 102 was named nobelium after him.

Nuffield, William Richard Morris, 1st Viscount (1877–1963) English, born Worcester. Started in bicycle repair business and by 1910 was manufacturing prototypes of Morris Oxford cars at Cowley in Oxford. First British manufacturer to develop mass production of cheap cars.

Olivetti, Adriano (1901–60) Italian, born Ivrea. Vastly increased and developed father's typewriter firm. Widely noted for his social concerns.

Onassis, Aristotle Socrates (1906–75) Greek, born Smyrna, Turkey. Made fortune in tobacco trade and built up one of the world's largest independent fleets of ships. Also pioneer in construction of supertankers. Married Jacqueline Kennedy, widow of American president John F Kennedy.

Packer, Kerry Francis Bullmore (1937–) Australian, born Sydney. Inherited from his father the Australian Consolidated Press, newspaper publisher with television and radio interests. Involved in disputes and legal battles with national cricket bodies due to his creation and broadcasting of 'World Series Cricket'.

Pilkington, Sir Lionel Alexander Bethune (Sir Alastair) (1920–95) English, born Calcutta (now Kolkata). Member of family firm of glass-makers, who researched and developed methods of producing defect-free plate glass.

Pulitzer, Joseph (1847–1911) Hungarian–American, born Makó, Hungary. Emigrated to USA in 1864 and joined the army. Later in St Louis he became a reporter, then began to acquire and revitalize old newspapers, including the *New York World* (1883). Established in his will annual Pulitzer prizes for literature, drama, music and journalism.

Rockefeller, John Davison (1839–1937) American, born Richford, New York. Founded the Standard Oil Co in 1870 and through it secured control of the oil trade of America. Gave over $500 million in aid of medical research, universities and Baptist churches; in 1913 established Rockefeller Foundation 'to promote the well-being of mankind'.

Roddick, Anita Lucia (1942–) English, born Brighton. Founded the Body Shop International plc to sell natural cosmetics. Company has around 1900 stores in 50 countries.

Rolls, Charles Stewart (1877–1910) English, born London. Motor car manufacturer, founded C S Rolls & Co in 1902, and later Rolls-Royce Ltd with Sir Henry Royce. In 1910 made first non-stop double crossing of the English Channel by aeroplane.

Rowntree, Joseph (1836–1925) English, born York. With his brother became a partner in a cocoa factory in York in 1869, and built up welfare organizations for employees.

Royce, Sir (Frederick) Henry (1863–1933) English, born near Peterborough. Founder of electrical and mechanical engineering firm Royce Ltd (1884) and co-founder of Rolls-Royce Ltd, manufacturer of car and aeroplane engines. Designed engines used in Spitfires and Hurricanes in World War II.

Sainsbury, Alan John, Baron Sainsbury of Drury Lane (1902–98) English, born Hornsey, Middlesex. Joined family grocery business in 1921 and from 1967 was joint president of major supermarket chain J Sainsbury plc.

Selfridge, Harry Gordon (1858–1947) Anglo-American, born Ripon, Wisconsin. Chicago trader who in 1906 on a visit to London initiated the Selfridge business; the Oxford Street store opened in 1909.

Sieff, Israel Moses, Baron Sieff of Brimpton (1889–1972) English, born Manchester. With Simon Marks, developed Marks and Spencer. Joint managing director from 1926 to 1967 and succeeded Lord Marks as chairman (1964–7).

Sinclair, Sir Clive (Marles) (1940–) English, born Surrey. Launched electronics company which has developed and successfully marketed calculators, miniature televisions and personal computers. Also manufactured Sinclair C5 'personal transport' vehicle powered by a washing-machine motor and rechargeable batteries.

Sugar, Alan Michael (1947–) English, born London. Founded AMSTRAD (the name is a contraction of Alan M Sugar Trading) in 1968. The company expanded rapidly during the personal computer boom of the 1980s, but ran into problems with the slump at the end of that decade, losing, at one stage, £1 million per week. As a result, Sugar bought the company back into private ownership. He was chairman of Tottenham Hotspur football club from 1991 to 2001.

Tate, Sir Henry (1819–99) English, born Chorley, Lancashire. Patented method for cutting sugar cubes (1872) and formed major sugar refinery. Gave nation Tate Gallery (1897) containing his own valuable private collection.

Tiffany, Charles Lewis (1812–1902) American, born Killingby, Connecticut. Goldsmith and jeweller who began dealing in 1837, and by 1883 was one of the largest silverware manufacturers in USA. Held appointments to 23 royal patrons, including the Tsar of Russia and Queen Victoria.

Turner, Ted (Robert Edward) (1938–) American, born Cincinnati. Created the first 'superstation', WTBS, in the mid-1970s and created Cable News Network (CNN) in 1980. In 1985 he bought MGM and established a movie channel on television in 1988. Time Warner Inc merged with Turner Broadcasting System in 1996, creating the world's largest media company, with Turner as its vice-chairman, and in 2001 Time Warner merged with America Online (AOL), the internet provider. Turner stood down in 2003.

Wang, An (1920–89) American–Chinese, born Shanghai. Graduated in science from Shanghai, then studied applied physics at Harvard. Invented the magnetic core memory and founded Wang Laboratories in Boston in 1951, now one of the world's largest automation systems firms. Also introduced desktop computers and calculators.

Woolworth, Frank Winfield (1852–1919) American, born Rodman, Jefferson County, New York. From inexpensive fixed-price goods stores built up a chain of over a thousand stores controlled from a New York headquarters. Most development outside USA was after the death of the founder.

Science and Technology

Nobel prizes

Nobel prizes for Chemistry, Physics and Physiology or Medicine were first awarded in 1901.

Year	Chemistry	Physics	Physiology/Medicine
1935	Frédéric Joliot, Irène Joliot-Curie	Sir James Chadwick	Hans Spemann
1936	Petrus Josephus Wilhelmus Debye	Vincent Franz Hess, Carl David Anderson	Sir Henry Hallett Dale, Otto Loewi
1937	Sir Walter Norman Haworth, Paul Karrer	Clinton Joseph Davisson, Sir George Paget Thomson	Albert von Szent-Györgyi
1938	Richard Kuhn	Enrico Fermi	Corneille Jean François Heymans
1939	Adolf Friedrich Johann Butenandt, Leopold Ruzicka	Ernest Orlando Lawrence	Gerhard Domagk
1940	No award	No award	No award
1941	No award	No award	No award
1942	No award	No award	No award
1943	George de Hevesy	Otto Stern	Henrik Carl Peter Dam, Edward Adelbert Doisy
1944	Otto Hahn	Isidor Isaac Rabi	Joseph Erlanger, Herbert Spencer Gasser
1945	Artturi Ilmari Virtanen	Wolfgang Pauli	Sir Ernst Boris Chain, Sir Alexander Fleming, Lord Howard Walter Florey
1946	James Batcheller Sumner, John Howard Northrop, Wendell Meredith Stanley	Percy Williams Bridgman	Hermann Joseph Muller
1947	Sir Robert Robinson	Sir Edward Victor Appleton	Carl Ferdinand Cori, Gerty Theresa Cori, Bernardo Alberto Houssay
1948	Arne Wilhelm Kaurin Tiselius	Lord Patrick Maynard Stuart Blackett	Paul Hermann Müller
1949	William Francis Giauque	Hideki Yukawa	Walter Rudolf Hess, Antonio Caetano de Abreu Freire Egas Moniz
1950	Otto Paul Hermann Diels, Kurt Alder	Cecil Frank Powell	Philip Showalter Hench, Edward Calvin Kendall, Tadeus Reichstein
1951	Edwin Mattison McMillan, Glenn Theodore Seaborg	Sir John Douglas Cockcroft, Ernest Thomas Sinton Walton	Max Theiler
1952	Archer John Porter Martin, Richard Laurence Millington Synge	Felix Bloch, Edward Mills Purcell	Selman Abraham Waksman
1953	Hermann Staudinger	Frederik Zernike	Sir Hans Adolf Krebs, Fritz Albert Lipmann
1954	Linus Carl Pauling	Max Born, Walther Bothe	John Franklin Enders, Frederick Chapman Robbins, Thomas Huckle Weller
1955	Vincent du Vigneaud	Willis Eugene Lamb, Polykarp Kusch	Axel Hugo Theodor Theorell
1956	Sir Cyril Norman Hinshelwood, Nikolay Nikolaevich Semenov	William Shockley, John Bardeen, Walter Houser Brattain	André Frédéric Cournand, Werner Forssmann, Dickinson W Richards
1957	Lord Alexander R Todd	Chen Ning-Yang, Tsung-Dao Lee	Daniel Bovet
1958	Frederick Sanger	Pavel Alekseyevich Cherenkov, Il'ja Mikhailovich Frank, Igor Yevgenyevich Tamm	George Wells Beadle, Edward Lawrie Tatum, Joshua Lederberg
1959	Jaroslav Heyrovsky	Emilio Gino Segrè, Owen Chamberlain	Arthur Kornberg, Severo Ochoa
1960	Willard Frank Libby	Donald A Glaser	Sir Frank Macfarlane Burnet, Sir Peter Brian Medawar
1961	Melvin Calvin	Robert Hofstadter, Rudolf Ludwig Mössbauer	Georg von Békésy
1962	Max Ferdinand Perutz, Sir John Cowdery Kendrew	Lev Davidovich Landau	Francis Harry Compton Crick, James Dewey Watson, Maurice Hugh Frederick Wilkins
1963	Karl Ziegler, Guilio Natta	Eugene P Winger, Maria Goeppert-Mayer, J Hans D Jensen	Sir John Carew Eccles, Sir Alan Lloyd Hodgkin, Sir Andrew Fielding Huxley
1964	Dorothy Crowfoot Hodgkin	Charles H Townes, Nicolay Gennadiyevich Basov, Aleksandr Mikhailovich Prokhorov	Konrad Bloch, Feodor Lynen
1965	Robert Burns Woodward	Sin-itiro Tomonaga, Julian Schwinger, Richard P Feynman	François Jacob, André Lwoff, Jacques Monod
1966	Robert S Mulliken	Alfred Kastler	Peyton Rous, Charles Brenton Huggins
1967	Manfred Eigen, Ronald George Wreyford Norrish, Lord George Porter	Hans Albrecht Bethe	Ragnar Granit, Haldan Keffer Hartline, George Wald

Science and Technology

Year	Chemistry	Physics	Physiology/Medicine
1968	Lars Onsager	Luis W Alvarez	Robert W Holley, Har Gobind Khorana, Marshall W Nirenberg
1969	Sir Derek H R Barton, Odd Hassel	Murray Gell-Mann	Max Delbrück, Alfred D Hershey, Salvador E Luria
1970	Luis Federico Leloir	Louis Eugène Néel, Hannes Olof Alfvén	Sir Bernard Katz, Ulf von Euler, Julius Axelrod
1971	Gerhard Herzberg	Dennis Gabor	Earl W Sutherland, Jr
1972	Stanford Moore, William H Stein, Christian B Anfinsen	John Bardeen, Leon N Cooper, J Robert Schrieffer	Gerald M Edelman, Rodney R Porter
1973	Ernst Otto Fischer, Sir Geoffrey Wilkinson	Leo Esaki, Ivar Giaever, Brian D Josephson	Karl von Frisch, Konrad Lorenz, Nikolaas Tinbergen
1974	Paul J Flory	Sir Martin Ryle, Antony Hewish	Albert Claude, Christian de Duve, George E Palade
1975	Sir John Warcup Cornforth, Vladimir Prelog	Aage N Bohr, Ben R Mottelson, L James Rainwater	David Baltimore, Renato Dulbecco, Howard Martin Temin
1976	William N Lipscomb	Burton Richter, Samuel Chao Chung Ting	Baruch S Blumberg, D Carleton Gajdusek
1977	Ilya Prigogine	Philip W Anderson, Sir Neville F Mott, John H van Vleck	Roger Guillemin, Andrew V Schally, Rosalyn Yalow
1978	Peter D Mitchell	Pyotr L Kapitsa, Arno A Penzias, Robert W Wilson	Werner Arber, Daniel Nathans, Hamilton O Smith
1979	Herbert C Brown, Georg Wittig	Steven Weinberg, Sheldon L Glashow, Abdus Salam	Allan M Cormack, Sir Godfrey N Hounsfield
1980	Paul Berg, Walter Gilbert, Frederick Sanger	James W Cronin, Val L Fitch	Baruj Benacerraf, George D Snell, Jean Dausset
1981	Kenichi Fukui, Roald Hoffmann	Nicolaas Bloembergen, Arthur L Schawlow, Kai M Siegbahn	Roger W Sperry, David H Hubel, Torsten N Wiesel
1982	Sir Aaron Klug	Kenneth G Wilson	Sune K Bergström, Bengt I Samuelsson, Sir John R Vane
1983	Henry Taube	Subramanyan Chandrasekhar, William A Fowler	Barbara McClintock
1984	Robert B Merrifield	Carlo Rubbia, Simon van der Meer	Niels K Jerne, Georges J F Köhler, César Milstein
1985	Herbert A Hauptman, Jerome Karle	Klaus von Klitzing	Joseph L Goldstein, Michael S Brown
1986	Dudley R Herschbach, Yuan Tseh Lee, John C Polanyi	Gerd Binnig, Heinrich Rohrer, Ernst Ruska	Stanley Cohen, Rita Levi-Montalcini
1987	Charles J Pedersen, Donald J Cram, Jean-Marie Lehn	J Georg Bednorz, K Alexander Müller	Susumu Tonegawa
1988	Johann Deisenhofer, Robert Huber, Hartmut Michel	Leon M Lederman, Melvin Schwartz, Jack Steinberger	Sir James W Black, Gertrude B Elion, George H Hitchings
1989	Sidney Altman, Thomas R Cech	Hans G Dehmelt, Wolfgang Paul, Norman F Ramsey	J Michael Bishop, Harold E Varmus
1990	Elias James Corey	Jerome I Friedman, Henry W Kendall, Richard E Taylor	Joseph E Murray, E Donnall Thomas
1991	Richard R Ernst	Pierre-Gilles de Gennes	Erwin Neher, Bert Sakmann
1992	Rudolph A Marcus	Georges Charpak	Edmond H Fischer, Edwin G Krebs
1993	Kary Banks Mullis, Michael Smith	Russell A Hulse, Joseph H Taylor Jr	Richard J Roberts, Phillip A Sharp
1994	George Olah	Clifford G Shull, Bertram N Brockhouse	Alfred G Gilman, Martin Rodbell
1995	F Sherwood Roland, Mario J Molina, Paul J Crutzen	Martin L Perl, Frederick Reines	Edward B Lewis, Christiane Nüsslein-Volhard, Eric F Wieschaus
1996	Sir Harold W Kroto, Robert F Curl, Jr, Richard E Smalley	David M Lee, Douglas D Osheroff, Robert C Richardson	Peter C Doherty, Rolf M Zinkernagel
1997	Jens C Skou, John E Walker, Paul D Boyer	Steven Chu, William D Phillips, Claude Cohen-Tannoudji	Stanley B Prusiner
1998	Walter Kohn, John A Pople	Robert B Laughlin, Horst L Störmer, Daniel C Tsui	Robert F Furchgott, Louis J Ignarro, Ferid Murad
1999	Ahmed H Zewail	Gerardus 't Hooft, Martinus J G Veltman	Günter Blobel
2000	Alan J Heeger, Alan G MacDiarmid, Hideki Shirakawa	Zhores I Alferov, Herbert Kroemer, Jack S Kilby	Arvid Carlsson, Paul Greengard, Eric Kandel
2001	William S Knowles, Ryoji Noyori, K Barry Sharpless	Eric A Cornell, Wolfgang Ketterle, Carl E Wieman	Leland H Hartwell, R Timothy Hunt, Sir Paul M Nurse
2002	John B Fenn, Koichi Tanaka, Kurt Wüthrich	Raymond Davis Jr, Masatoshi Koshiba, Riccardo Giacconi	Sydney Brenner, H Robert Horvitz, John E Sulston

ARTS AND CULTURE

Arts and Culture (side text)

Novelists

Selected works are listed.

Abrahams, Peter (Henry) (1919–) South African novelist, born Vrededorp, near Johannesburg; *The View from Coyaba* (1985).

Achebe, Chinua (originally **Albert Chinualumogu**) (1930–) Nigerian novelist, born Ogidi; *Things Fall Apart* (1958), *Anthills of the Savannah* (1987).

Ackroyd, Peter (1949–) English novelist, poet, critic, born London; *Notes for a New Culture* (1976), *The Last Testament of Oscar Wilde* (1983), *Hawksmoor* (1985), *Chatterton* (1987), *First Light* (1989), *English Music* (1992), *Milton in America* (1996), *London: The Biography* (2002).

Adams, Douglas (Noël) (1952–2001) English novelist, short-story writer, born Cambridge; *The Hitch Hiker's Guide to the Galaxy* (1979), *Life, the Universe and Everything* (1982), *Mostly Harmless* (1992).

Adams, Richard (George) (1920–) English novelist, short-story writer, born Newbury, Berkshire; *Watership Down* (1972), *Shardik* (1974), *The Girl in a Swing* (1980), *The Day Gone By* (autobiography) (1990).

Alcott, Louisa May (1832–88) US children's writer, born Germantown, Philadelphia; *Little Women* (1868–9), *Little Men* (1871), *Jo's Boys* (1886).

Aldiss, Brian (Wilson) (1925–) English novelist, poet, short-story writer, playwright, critic, born Dereham, Norfolk; *Helliconia Spring* (1982), *Helliconia Summer* (1983), *Helliconia Winter* (1985), *Forgotten Life* (1988), *Dracula Unbound* (1991), *Remembrance Day* (1993).

Aldridge, (Harold Edward) James (1918–) Australian novelist, short-story writer, playwright, born White Hills, Victoria; *The Diplomat* (1949), *The Hunter* (1950), *The Last Exile* (1961), *The True Story of Spit MacPhee* (1986), *The True Story of Lola MacKellar* (1993).

Alvarez, Al(fred) (1929–) English novelist, poet, critic, born London; *The Savage God: A Study of Suicide* (non-fiction) (1971), *Hers* (1974), *Day of Atonement* (1991), *Night* (1995), *Where Did It All Go Right?* (1999).

Ambler, Eric (1909–98) English novelist, playwright screenwriter, born London; *The Mask of Dimitrios* (1939), *The Intercom Conspiracy* (1970), *The Care of Time* (1981), *The Story So Far* (1993).

Amis, Sir Kingsley (William) (1922–95) English novelist, poet, born London; *Lucky Jim* (1954), *That Uncertain Feeling* (1955), *Jake's Thing* (1978), *The Old Devils* (1986, Booker Prize).

Amis, Martin (Louis) (1949–) English novelist, short-story writer, born Oxford; *The Rachel Papers* (1973), *Money* (1984), *London Fields* (1989), *Time's Arrow* (1991), *The Information* (1995), *Experience* (2000).

Anand, Mulk Raj (1905–) Indian novelist, short-story writer, born Peshawar; *Untouchable* (1935), *The Big Heart* (1945).

Angelou, Maya (**Marguerite Annie**) (née **Johnson**) (1928–) US novelist, poet, playwright, born St Louis, Missouri; *I Know Why The Caged Bird Sings* (1970), *All God's Children Need Travelling Shoes* (1986), *Wouldn't Take Nothing for My Journey Now* (1993), *Even the Stars Look Lonesome* (1998).

Apuleius, Lucius (c.123–after 161) Roman writer, born Madaura, Numidia, Africa; *Golden Ass* (the only Roman novel to survive complete), *Apologia*.

Archer, Jeffrey (Howard) Archer, Baron (1940–) English novelist, short-story writer, born London; *Not a Penny More, Not a Penny Less* (1975), *Kane and Abel* (1979), *First Among Equals* (1984), *Honour Among Thieves* (1993), *The Fourth Estate* (1996), *The Eleventh Commandment* (1998).

Asimov, Isaac (1920–92) US novelist, short-story writer, born Petrovichi, Russia; *I Robot* (1950), *Foundation* (1951), *The Disappearing Man and Other Stories* (1985), *Nightfall* (1990).

Atwood, Margaret (Eleanor) (1939–) Canadian novelist, poet, short-story writer, born Ottawa; *Bluebeard's Egg* (1983), *The Handmaid's Tale* (1985), *Cat's Eye* (1989), *The Robber Bride* (1993), *The Blind Assassin* (2000, Booker Prize).

Auchincloss, Louis (Stanton) (1917–) US novelist, short-story writer, born Lawrence, New York; *The Great World and Timothy Colt* (1957), *A World of Profit* (1968), *Diary of a Yuppie* (1986), *Fellow Passengers* (1990), *Lady of Situations* (1991), *Tales of Yesteryear* (1994).

Austen, Jane (1775–1817) English novelist, born Steventon, Hampshire; *Sense and Sensibility* (1811), *Pride and Prejudice* (1813), *Mansfield Park* (1814), *Emma* (1816), *Persuasion* (1818).

Bainbridge, Dame Beryl (Margaret) (1934–) English novelist, born Liverpool; *The Dressmaker* (1973), *The Bottle Factory Outing* (1974), *Injury Time* (1977), *An Awfully Big Adventure* (1989), *Every Man for Himself* (1996), *Master Georgie* (1998).

Baldwin, James Arthur (1924–87) US novelist, playwright, born Harlem, New York City; *Go Tell it on the Mountain* (1954), *Tell Me How Long the Train's Been Gone* (1968), *Just Above My Head* (1979).

Ballantyne, R(obert) M(ichael) (1825–94) Scottish novelist, born Edinburgh; *The Coral Island* (1857), *The Gorilla Hunters* (1862).

Ballard, J(ames) G(raham) (1930–) English novelist, born Shanghai, China; *The Drowned World* (1962), *The Terminal Beach* (1964), *Empire of the Sun* (1984), *The Kindness of Women* (1991), *A User's Guide to the Millennium* (1996).

Balzac, Honoré de (1799–1850) French novelist, born Tours; *Comédie humaine* (1827–47), *Illusions perdues* (1837–43).

Banks, Iain (Menzies) (1954–) Scottish novelist, born Dunfermline; *The Wasp Factory* (1984), *The Bridge* (1995), *Whit* (1995), *Excession* (1996), *A Song of Stone* (1997), *Look to Windward* (2000).

Banks, Lynne Reid (1929–) English novelist, playwright, born London; *The L-Shaped Room* (1961),

The Adventures of King Midas (1976), *Defy the Wilderness* (1981), *The Warning Bell* (1987), *The Magic Hare* (1992), *Harry the Poisonous Centipede* (1996).

Barker, Pat (Patricia Margaret) (1943–) English novelist, short-story writer, born Thornaby-on-Tees; *Union Street* (1982), *Blow Your House Down* (1984), *The Century's Daughter* (1986), *The Man Who Wasn't There* (1989), *Regeneration* (1991), *The Eye in the Door* (1993), *The Ghost Road* (1995, Booker Prize), *Another World* (1998), *Border Crossing* (2001).

Barnes, Julian (Patrick) (1946–) English novelist, born Leicester; *Flaubert's Parrot* (1984), *Staring at the Sun* (1986), *A History of the World in 10½ Chapters* (1989), *Love, Etc* (1992), *Cross Channel* (short stories) (1996), *Something to Declare* (2002).

Barstow, Stan(ley) (1928–) English novelist, short-story writer, playwright, born Horbury, Yorkshire; *A Kind of Loving* (1960), *A Raging Calm* (1968), *Just You Wait and See* (1986), *Next of Kin* (1991), *In My Own Good Time* (2001).

Barth, John (Simmons) (1930–) US novelist, short-story writer, born Cambridge, Maryland; *The Floating Opera* (1956), *Chimera* (1974), *The Tidewater Tales* (1987), *The Last Voyage of Somebody the Sailor* (1991), *Further Fridays* (1995).

Bates, H(erbert) E(rnest) (1905–74) English novelist, short-story writer, born Rushden, Northamptonshire; *Fair Stood the Wind for France* (1944), *The Jacaranda Tree* (1949), *Love for Lydia* (1952), *The Darling Buds of May* (1958).

Bawden, Nina (Mary) (née **Mabey**) (1925–) English writer, born London; *The Birds on the Trees* (1970), *The Peppermint Pig* (children's) (1975), *Walking Naked* (1981), *The Ice House* (1983), *Circles of Deceit* (1987), *Family Money* (1991), *A Nice Change* (1997).

Bedford, Sybille (née **von Schoenebeck**) (1911–) British novelist, born Charlottenburg, Germany; *A Legacy* (1956), *Jigsaw: An Unsentimental Education* (1989), *As It Was* (essays) (1990).

Beerbohm, Sir (Henry) Max(imilian) (1872–1956) English novelist, born London; *Zuleika Dobson* (1912).

Behn, Aphra (1640–89) English novelist, playwright, born Wye, Kent; *The Rover* (play) (1678), *Oroonoko* (1688).

Bellow, Saul (1915–) American novelist, born Quebec, Canada; *Henderson the Rain King* (1959), *Herzog* (1964), *Humboldt's Gift* (1975, Pulitzer Prize 1976) *The Dean's December* (1982), *The Actual* (1997), *Ravelstein* (2000); Nobel Prize for Literature 1976.

Bely, Andrei (pseudonym of **Boris Nikolayvich Bugayev**) (1880–1934) Russian novelist, poet, born Moscow; *The Silver Dove* (1910), *Petersburg* (1913).

Benedictus, David (Henry) (1938–) English novelist, playwright, born London; *The Fourth of June* (1962), *A World of Windows* (1971), *Local Hero* (novelization of screenplay) (1983), *The Stamp Collector* (1994).

Bennett, (Enoch) Arnold (1867–1931) English novelist, born Hanley, Staffordshire; *Anna of the Five Towns* (1902), *The Old Wives' Tale* (1908), *Clayhanger* series (1910–18).

Berger, John (Peter) (1926–) English novelist, playwright, born London; *A Painter of Our Time* (1958), *A Fortunate Man* (non-fiction) (1967), *G* (1972, Booker Prize), *To The Wedding* (1995), *Photocopies* (1996).

Berger, Thomas (Louis) (1924–) US novelist, born Cincinnati, Ohio; *Reinhart in Love* (1962), *Arthur Rex* (1978), *The Houseguest* (1988), *Suspects* (1996).

Binchy, Maeve (1940–) Irish novelist, short-story writer, born Dublin; *Light a Penny Candle* (1982), *Echoes* (1985), *Firefly Summer* (1987), *Circle of Friends* (1990), *Copper Beech* (1992), *The Glass Lake* (1994), *Evening Class* (1996), *Tara Road* (1998).

Blackmore, R(ichard) D(oddridge) (1825–1900) English novelist, born Longworth, Berkshire; *Lorna Doone* (1869).

Bleasdale, Alan (1946–) English novelist, playwright, born Liverpool; *Scully* (1975), *The Boys from the Blackstuff* (TV series) (1982), *Are You Lonesome Tonight?* (musical) (1985), *GBH* (TV series) (1991), *Jake's Progress* (TV series) (1995).

Blyton, Enid (Mary) (1897–1968) English children's writer, born London; best-known characters include Noddy, the Famous Five, and the Secret Seven. Published over 600 books.

Böll, Heinrich (1917–85) German novelist, born Cologne; *And Never Said a Solitary Word* (1953), *The Unguarded House* (1954), *The Bread of Our Early Years* (1955); Nobel Prize for Literature 1972.

Borges, Jorge Luis (1899–1986) Argentinian poet, short-story writer, born Buenos Aires; *Ficciones* (1944), *El Aleph* (1949), *Labyrinths* (1962).

Bowen, Elizabeth (Dorothea Cole) (1899–1973) Anglo-Irish novelist, short-story writer, born Dublin; *The Death of the Heart* (1938), *The Heat of the Day* (1949).

Bowles, Paul (Frederick) (1910–99) US novelist, short-story writer, born New York City; *The Sheltering Sky* (1949), *Pages from Cold Point and Other Stories* (1968), *Midnight Mass* (stories) (1981).

Boyd, William (Andrew Murray) (1952–) Scottish novelist, short-story writer, born Accra, Ghana; *A Good Man in Africa* (1981), *An Ice-Cream Man* (1982), *Brazzaville Beach* (1990), *The Blue Afternoon* (1993), *The Destiny of Nathalie X* (stories) (1995), *Nat Tate: an American Artist* (1998), *Armadillo* (1998).

Bradbury, Sir Malcolm (Stanley) (1932–2000) English novelist, born Sheffield; *Eating People is Wrong* (1959), *The History Man* (1975), *Dr Criminale* (1992).

Bradbury, Ray(mond) (Douglas) (1920–) US novelist, short-story writer, born Waukegan, Illinois; *The Martian Chronicles* (short stories) (1950), *Fahrenheit 451* (1953), *Something Wicked this Way Comes* (1962), *A Graveyard for Lunatics* (1990).

Bradford, Barbara Taylor (1933–) English novelist, born Leeds; *A Woman of Substance* (1979), *Hold the Dream* (1985), *Love in Another Town* (1995).

Bragg, Melvin Bragg, Baron (1939–) English novelist, playwright, short-story writer, born Carlisle; *The Hired Man* (1969), *A Time to Dance* (1991), *The Soldier's Return* (1999).

Braine, John (Gerard) (1922–86) English novelist, born Bradford; *Room at the Top* (1957).

Brink, André (Philippus) (1935–) South African novelist, short-story writer, playwright, born Vrede, Orange Free State; *Looking on Darkness* (1974), *Rumours of Rain* (1978), *A Dry White Season* (1979), *States of Emergency* (1988), *On the Contrary* (1993), *Imaginings of Sand* (1996).

Brittain, Vera (Mary) (1893–1970) English novelist, poet, born Newcastle-under-Lyme, Staffordshire; *Testament of Youth* (1933), *Testament of Friendship* (1940), *Testament of Experience* (1957) (all autobiographies).

Bromfield, Louis (1896–1956) US novelist, short-story writer, born Mansfield, Ohio; *Early Autumn* (1926), *Until the Day Break* (1942).

Brontë, Anne (1820–49) English novelist, poet, born Thornton, Yorkshire; *Agnes Grey* (1847), *The Tenant of Wildfell Hall* (1848).

Arts and Culture

Brontë, Charlotte (1816–55) English novelist, poet, born Thornton, Yorkshire; *Jane Eyre* (1847), *Shirley* (1849), *Villette* (1853).

Brontë, Emily (1818–48) English novelist, poet, born Thornton, Yorkshire; *Wuthering Heights* (1847).

Brooke-Rose, Christine (1926–) English novelist, born Geneva, Switzerland; *The Languages of Love* (1957), *Thru* (1975), *Amalgamemnon* (1984), *Textermination* (1991), *Remake* (1996).

Brookner, Anita (1928–) English novelist, born London; *Hotel du Lac* (1984, Booker Prize), *Family and Friends* (1985), *Brief Lives* (1990), *Altered States* (1996), *Visitors* (1997).

Brophy, Brigid (Antonia) (1929–95) English novelist, short-story writer, playwright, born London; *The Crown Princess and Other Stories* (1953), *The King of a Rainy Country* (1956), *In Transit* (1969).

Brown, George Douglas (1869–1902) Scottish novelist, born Ochiltree, Ayrshire; *The House with the Green Shutters* (1901).

Brown, George Mackay (1921–96) Scottish novelist, poet, short-story writer, playwright, born Orkney; *Greenvoe* (1972), *Beside the Ocean of Time* (1994).

Buchan, John (1875–1940) Scottish novelist, poet, born Perth; *The Thirty-Nine Steps* (1915), *Greenmantle* (1916), *Sir Walter Scott* (biography) (1932).

Buck, Pearl (née **Sydenstricker**) (1892–1973) US novelist, born Hillsboro, West Virginia; *The Good Earth* (1913), *Pavilion of Women* (1946); Nobel Prize for Literature 1938.

Bulgakov, Mikhail (Afanasievich) (1891–1940) Russian novelist, short-story writer, born Kiev; *Diavoliada* (1925), *The Master and Margarita* (1967).

Bunyan, John (1628–88) English novelist, born Elstow, near Bedford; *Pilgrim's Progress* (1678).

Burgess, Anthony (pseudonym of **John Anthony Burgess Wilson**) (1917–93) English novelist, born Manchester; *A Clockwork Orange* (1962), *The Malayan Trilogy* (1972), *Earthly Powers* (1980), *Kingdom of the Wicked* (1985), *Any Old Iron* (1989).

Burnett, Frances Hodgson (1849–1924) Anglo-US children's writer, playwright, born Manchester; *Little Lord Fauntleroy* (1886), *The Little Princess* (1905), *The Secret Garden* (1909).

Burney, Fanny (Frances, later **Mme d'Arblay)** (1752–1840) English novelist, born King's Lynn; *Evelina* (1778), *Cecilia* (1782).

Burroughs, Edgar Rice (1875–1950) US novelist, born Chicago; *Tarzan of the Apes* (1914), *The Land that Time Forgot* (1924).

Burroughs, William S(eward) (1914–97) US novelist, born St Louis, Missouri; *The Naked Lunch* (1959), *The Soft Machine* (1961), *The Wild Boys* (1971), *Exterminator!* (1974), *My Education: a Book of Dreams* (1995).

Byatt, Dame A(ntonia) S(usan) (1936–) English novelist, born Sheffield; *The Shadow of a Sun* (1964), *The Virgin in the Garden* (1978), *Possession* (1990, Booker Prize), *Babel Tower* (1996), *Elementals: stories of Fire and Ice* (short stories) (1998), *The Biographer's Tale* (2000).

Calvino, Italo (1923–87) Italian novelist, short-story writer, born Santiago de Las Vegas, Cuba; *Invisible Cities* (1972), *The Castle of Crossed Destinies* (1969), *If on a Winter's Night a Traveller* (1979).

Camus, Albert (1913–60) French novelist, playwright, born Mondovi, Algeria; *The Outsider* (1942), *The Plague* (1948), *The Fall* (1957); Nobel Prize for Literature 1957.

Canetti, Elias (1905–94) Bulgarian novelist, born Russe, Bulgaria; *Auto da Fé* (1935, trans 1946), *Crowds and Power* (1960, trans 1962); Nobel Prize for Literature 1981.

Capote, Truman (1924–84) US playwright, novelist, short-story writer, born New Orleans; *Other Voices, Other Rooms* (1948), *Breakfast at Tiffany's* (1958).

Carey, Peter (Philip) (1943–) Australian novelist, short-story writer, born Bacchus Marsh, Victoria; *Illywhacker* (1985), *Oscar and Lucinda* (1988, Booker Prize), *The Tax Inspector* (1991), *True History of the Kelly Gang* (2001, Booker Prize).

Carr, Philippa ► **Holt, Victoria**

Carroll, Lewis (pseudonym of **Charles Lutwidge Dodgson**) (1832–98) English children's writer, nonsense poet and mathematician, born Daresbury, near Warrington; *Alice's Adventures in Wonderland* (1865), *Through the Looking-Glass and What Alice Found There* (1871).

Carter, Angela (1940–92) English novelist, poet, playwright, born London; *The Magic Toyshop* (1967), *The Infernal Desire Machines of Dr Hoffman* (1972), *Nights at the Circus* (1984), *Wise Children* (1991).

Cartland, (Mary) Barbara (Hamilton) (1901–2000) English novelist, born Birmingham; *Wings on My Heart* (1954), *The Husband Hunters* (1976), *The Castle Made for Love* (1985), *Love Solves the Problem* (1995).

Carver, Raymond (1939–88) US short-story writer, poet, born Clatskanie, Oregon; story collections: *Will You Please Be Quiet, Please?* (1976), *What We Talk About When We Talk About Love* (1981), *Cathedral* (1983); poetry collections: *Where Water Comes Together with Other Water* (1985), *Ultramarine* (1985).

Cather, Willa (Silbert) (1876–1947) US novelist, poet, born near Winchester, Virginia; *O Pioneers!* (1913), *My Antonia* (1918), *One of Ours* (1922), *The Professor's House* (1925), *My Mortal Enemy* (1926), *Death Comes for the Archbishop* (1927), *Sapphira and the Slave Girl* (1940).

Cela, Camilo José (1916–2002) Spanish novelist, born Iria Flavia; *La familia de Pascual Duarte* (1942), *La Colmena* (1951), *Mazurca para dos muertos* (1984); Nobel Prize for Literature 1989.

Cervantes (Saavedra), Miguel de (1547–1616) Spanish novelist and poet, born Alcala de Henares; *La Galatea* (1585), *Don Quixote* (1605–15).

Chandler, Raymond (1888–1959) US novelist, born Chicago; *The Big Sleep* (1939), *Farewell, My Lovely* (1940), *The High Window* (1942), *The Lady in the Lake* (1943), *The Long Goodbye* (1953).

Chatwin, Bruce (1940–89) English novelist, born Sheffield; *In Patagonia* (1977), *The Viceroy of Ouidah* (1980), *On The Black Hill* (1982), *The Songlines* (1987), *Utz* (1988).

Chesterton, G(ilbert) K(eith) (1874–1936) English novelist, poet, born London; *The Napoleon of Notting Hill* (1904), *The Innocence of Father Brown* (1911).

Christie, Dame Agatha (Mary Clarissa) (née **Miller**) (1890–1976) English novelist, born Torquay, Devon; *Murder on the Orient Express* (1934), *Death on the Nile* (1937), *A Murder is Announced* (1950), *Curtain* (1975).

Clarke, Sir Arthur C(harles) (1917–) English novelist, short-story writer, born Minehead, Somerset; *Childhood's End* (1953), *2001: A Space Odyssey* (1968), *The Fountains of Paradise* (1979), *The Garden of Rama* (1991), *The Hammer of God* (1993).

Clavell, James (du Maresq) (1922–94) US novelist, playwright, born England; *King Rat* (1962), *Tai-Pan* (1966), *Shogun* (1975).

Cleary, Jon (Stephen) (1917–) Australian novelist, born Sydney; *You Can't See Around Corners* (1947), *The Safe House* (1975), *Pride's Harvest* (1991), *Dark Summer* (1992), *Autumn Maze* (1994), *Winter Chill* (1995), *Endpeace* (1996), *Dilemma* (1999).

Coetzee, J(ohn) M(ichael) (1940–) South African novelist, born Cape Town; *Life and Times of Michael K* (1983, Booker Prize), *The Master of Petersburg* (1994), *Disgrace* (1999, Booker Prize).

Colette, Sidonie Gabrielle (1873–1954) French novelist, born Saint-Sauveur-en-Puisaye, Burgundy; *Claudine à l'école* (1900), *Chéri* (1920), *La Fin de Chéri* (1926), *Gigi* (1943).

Collins, (William) Wilkie (1824–89) English novelist, born London; *The Woman in White* (1860), *No Name* (1862), *Armadale* (1866), *The Moonstone* (1868).

Compton-Burnett, Dame Ivy (1884–1969) English novelist, born Pinner, Middlesex; *A House and its Head* (1935), *A Family and a Fortune* (1939), *Manservant and Maidservant* (1947).

Condon, Richard (Thomas) (1915–96) US novelist, born New York City; *The Manchurian Candidate* (1959), *Winter Kills* (1974), *Prizzi's Honor* (1982).

Connell, Evan S(helby) (1924–) US novelist, born Kansas City, Missouri; *Mrs Bridge* (1958), *The Diary of a Rapist* (1966), *Mr Bridge* (1969), *The Alchymist's Journal* (1991).

Conrad, Joseph (originally **Jozef Teodor Konrad Nalecz Korzeniowski**) (1857–1924) Anglo-Polish novelist, short-story writer, born Berdichev, Poland (now Ukraine); *Lord Jim* (1900), *Heart of Darkness* (1902), *Nostromo* (1904), *The Secret Agent* (1907), *Chance* (1914).

Cookson, Dame Catherine (Ann) (1906–98) English novelist, born Tyne Dock, County Durham; *Tilly Trotter* (1956), *The Glass Virgin* (1969), *The Black Candle* (1989).

Cooper, Jilly (1937–) English novelist, born Hornchurch, Essex; *Men and Supermen* (1972), *Class* (1979), *Riders* (1985), *Rivals* (1988), *Polo* (1990), *The Man who made Husbands Jealous* (1993), *Appassionata* (1996), *Score* (1999).

Cooper, William (pseudonym of **Harry Summerfield Hoff**) (1910–2002) English novelist, born Crewe, Cheshire; *Scenes from Provincial Life* (1950), *Disquiet and Peace* (1956), *Immortality At Any Price* (1991).

Crane, Stephen (1871–1900) US novelist, born New Jersey; *The Red Badge of Courage* (1895).

Dahl, Roald (1916–90) Welsh children's writer, short-story writer, playwright, born Llandaff, Glamorgan; *Over to You* (1946), *Someone Like You* (1954), *Kiss, Kiss* (1960) (all short stories), *James and the Giant Peach* (1961), *Charlie and the Chocolate Factory* (1964), *You Only Live Twice* (screenplay) (1967), *Matilda* (1988).

Davidson, Lionel (1922–) English novelist, born Hull, Yorkshire; *The Rose of Tibet* (1962), *Smith's Gazelle* (1971), *The Chelsea Murders* (1978).

Davies, (William) Robertson (1913–95) Canadian novelist, playwright, born Thamesville, Ontario; *The Rebel Angels* (1981), *The Deptford Trilogy* (1970–5), *What's Bred in the Bone* (1985).

de Beauvoir, Simone (1908–86) French novelist, born Paris; *The Second Sex* (1949, trans 1953), *Les Mandarins* (1954), *Memoirs of a Dutiful Daughter* (1959).

Defoe, Daniel (1660–1731) English novelist, born Stoke Newington, London; *Robinson Crusoe* (1719), *Moll Flanders* (1722), *A Journal of the Plague Year* (1722).

Deighton, Len (Leonard Cyril) (1929–) English novelist, born London; *The Ipcress File* (1962), *Spy Hook* (1988), *Spy Line* (1989), *Spy Sinker* (1990), *Faith* (1994), *Hope* (1995), *Charity* (1996).

Delafield, E M (pseudonym of **Edmée Elizabeth Monica Dashwood**) (née **de la Pasture**) (1890–1943) English novelist, born Llandogo, Monmouth, Wales; *The Diary of a Provincial Lady* (1931).

DeLillo, Don (1936–) US novelist, born New York City; *End Zone* (1972), *Ratner's Star* (1976), *The Names* (1982), *White Noise* (1985), *Mao II* (1991), *The Body Artist* (2001).

de Quincey, Thomas (1785–1859) English novelist, born Manchester; *Confessions of an English Opium Eater* (1822).

Desai, Anita (née **Mazumbar**) (1937–) Indian novelist, short-story writer, born Mussoorie; *Cry, The Peacock* (1963), *Clear Light of Day* (1980), *In Custody* (1984), *Baumgartner's Bombay* (1988), *Journey to Ithaca* (1995), *Fasting, Feasting* (1999).

De Vries, Peter (1910–93) US novelist, born Chicago; *The Tunnel of Love* (1954), *The Meckerel Plaza* (1958), *Slouching Towards Kalamazoo* (1983).

Dickens, Charles (1812–70) English novelist, born Landport, Portsmouth; *Oliver Twist* (1837–9), *David Copperfield* (1849–50), *Bleak House* (1852–3), *Great Expectations* (1860–1).

Dickens, Monica (1915–92) English novelist, born London; *One Pair of Hands* (1939), *Spring Comes to the World's End* (1973).

Didion, Joan (1934–) US novelist, born Sacramento, California; *Run River* (1963), *A Book of Common Prayer* (1977), *Democracy* (1984), *The Last Thing He Wanted* (1996).

Dinesen, Isak (pseudonym of **Baroness Karen Blixen**) (1885–1962) Danish novelist, born Rungsted; *Seven Gothic Tales* (1934), *Out of Africa* (1937).

Disraeli, Benjamin (1804–81) English novelist, born London; *Coningsby* (1844), *Sybil* (1846), *Tancred* (1847).

Donleavy, J(ames) P(atrick) (1926–) Irish–US novelist, playwright, born Brooklyn, New York City; *The Ginger Man* (1955), *Schultz* (1980), *Are You Listening, Rabbi Low?* (1987), *The Lady Who Liked Clean Rest Rooms* (1995).

Dos Passos, John Roderigo (1896–1970) US novelist, born Chicago; *Manhattan Transfer* (1925), *USA* (1930–6).

Dostoevsky, Fyodor Mikhailovich (1821–81) Russian novelist, born Moscow; *Notes from the Underground* (1864), *Crime and Punishment* (1866), *The Brothers Karamazov* (1880).

Doyle, Sir Arthur Conan (1859–1930) Scottish novelist, short-story writer, born Edinburgh; *The Memoirs of Sherlock Holmes* (1894), *The Hound of the Baskervilles* (1902), *The Lost World* (1912).

Doyle, Roddy (1958–) Irish novelist, born Dublin; *The Commitments* (1987), *Paddy Clarke, Ha Ha Ha* (1993, Booker Prize), *The Woman Who Walked into Doors* (1996), *A Star Called Henry* (1999).

Drabble, Margaret (1939–) English novelist, short-story writer, born Sheffield; *The Millstone* (1965), *Jerusalem the Golden* (1967), *The Ice Age* (1977), *The Gates of Ivory* (1991), *The Witch of Exmoor* (1996).

Duffy, Maureen (Patricia) (1933–) English novelist, playwright, born Worthing, Sussex; *That's How It Was* (1962), *The Microcosm* (1966), *The Paradox Players* (1967), *Occam's Razor* (1993).

Arts and Culture

Dumas, Alexandre (in full **Alexandre Dumas Davy de la Pailleterie**), known as **Dumas père** (1802–70) French novelist, playwright, born Villers-Cotterets, Aisne; *The Three Musketeers* (1844–5).

Dumas, Alexandre, known as **Dumas fils** (1824–95) French novelist, playwright, born Paris; *La Dame aux camélias* (1848).

du Maurier, Dame Daphne (1907–89) English novelist, born London; *Jamaica Inn* (1936), *Rebecca* (1938), *Frenchman's Creek* (1942), *My Cousin Rachel* (1951).

Dunn, Nell (Mary) (1936–) English novelist, playwright, born London; *Poor Cow* (1967), *Tears His Head Off His Shoulders* (1974), *The Only Child* (1978).

Durrell, Gerald Malcolm (1925–95) English writer, born Jamshedpur, India; *The Overloaded Ark* (1953), *My Family and Other Animals* (1956).

Durrell, Lawrence George (1912–90) English novelist, poet, born Julundur, India; *The Alexandria Quartet* (1957–60).

Eco, Umberto (1932–) Italian novelist, born Alessandria, Piedmont; *The Name of the Rose* (1980), *Foucault's Pendulum* (1989), *The Island of the Day Before* (1995).

Edgeworth, Maria (1767–1849) Irish novelist, born Blackbourton, Oxfordshire; *Castle Rackrent* (1800), *The Absentee* (1809).

Eliot, George (originally **Mary Ann**, later **Marian Evans**) (1819–80) English novelist, born Arbury, Warwickshire; *Adam Bede* (1858), *The Mill on the Floss* (1860), *Middlemarch* (1871–2), *Daniel Deronda* (1874–6).

Elkin, Stanley (Lawrence) (1930–95) US novelist, short-story writer, born Brooklyn, New York City; *Criers and Kibitzers, Kibitzers and Criers* (1966), *The Living End* (1979), *George Mills* (1982), *The Magic Kingdom* (1985).

Ellis, Alice Thomas (pseudonym of **Anna Margaret Haycraft**) (née **Lindholm**) (1932–) English novelist, born Liverpool; *The Sin Eater* (1977), *The 27th Kingdom* (1982), *The Inn at the Edge of the World* (1990), *Fairy Tale* (1996).

Elton, Ben (Benjamin Charles) (1959–) English novelist, born Catford, South London; *Stark* (1989), *Gridlock* (1991), *Popcorn* (1996), *Inconceivable* (1999).

Fairbairns, Zoë (Ann) (1948–) English novelist, born Tunbridge Wells, Kent; *Stand We At Last* (1983), *Daddy's Girls* (1991), *Other Names* (1998).

Farmer, Philip José (1918–) US novelist, short-story writer, born Indiana; *To Your Scattered Bodies Go* (1977), *The Magic Labyrinth* (1980), *Nothing Burns in Hell* (1998).

Fast, Howard (Melvin) (1914–2003) US novelist, playwright, born New York City; *The Last Frontier* (1941), *Spartacus* (1951), *The Immigrants* (1977).

Faulkner, William Harrison (1897–1962) US novelist, born near Oxford, Mississippi; *Sartoris* (1929), *The Sound and the Fury* (1929), *Absalom, Absalom!* (1936); Nobel Prize for Literature 1949.

Feinstein, Elaine (1930–) English novelist, poet, born Bootle, Lancashire; *The Circle* (1970), *The Border* (1984), *All You Need* (1989), *Dark Inheritance* (2001).

Fielding, Henry (1707–54) English novelist, born Sharpham Park, near Glastonbury, Somerset; *Joseph Andrews* (1742), *Tom Jones* (1749).

Figes, Eva (née **Unger**) (1932–) British novelist, born Berlin, Germany; *Winter Journey* (1967), *Light* (1983), *The Tree of Knowledge* (1990), *The Tenancy* (1993), *Tales of Innocence and Experience* (2003).

Fitzgerald, F(rancis) Scott (Key) (1896–1940) US novelist, short-story writer, born St Paul, Minnesota; *The Great Gatsby* (1925), *Tender is the Night* (1934).

Fitzgerald, Penelope (Mary) (née **Knox**) (1916–2000) English novelist, born Lincoln; *The Bookshop* (1978), *Offshore* (1979, Booker Prize), *The Gate of Angels* (1990), *The Blue Flower* (1995).

Flaubert, Gustave (1821–80) French novelist, born Rouen; *Madame Bovary* (1857), *Salammbo* (1862).

Fleming, Ian (Lancaster) (1908–64) English novelist, born London; author of the 'James Bond' novels, eg *Casino Royale* (1953), *From Russia with Love* (1957), *Dr No* (1958), *Goldfinger* (1959), *The Man with the Golden Gun* (1965).

Ford, Ford Madox (originally **Ford Hermann Hueffer**) (1873–1939) English novelist, poet, born Merton, Surrey; *The Fifth Queen* (1906), *The Good Soldier* (1915), *Parade's End* (1924–8).

Ford, Richard (1944–) US novelist, born Jackson, Mississippi; *A Piece of My Heart* (1976), *The Sportswriter* (1986), *Independence Day* (1995, Pulitzer Prize 1996).

Forester, C(ecil) S(cott) (1899–1966) British novelist, born Cairo, Egypt; *Payment Deferred* (1926), *The African Queen* (1935), *The Happy Return* (1937).

Forster, E(dward) M(organ) (1879–1970) English novelist, short-story writer, born London; *A Room with a View* (1908), *Howards End* (1910), *A Passage to India* (1922–4).

Forsyth, Frederick (1938–) English novelist, short-story writer, born Ashford, Kent; *The Day of the Jackal* (1971), *The Odessa File* (1972), *The Fourth Protocol* (1984), *The Fist of God* (1993), *Icon* (1996).

Fowles, John (Robert) (1926–) English novelist, born Leigh-on-Sea, Essex; *The Magus* (1965, revised 1977), *The French Lieutenant's Woman* (1969), *The Ebony Tower* (1974), *The Tree* (1992).

Frame, Janet Paterson (1924–) New Zealand novelist, short-story writer, born Dunedin; *The Lagoon: Stories* (1951), *Scented Gardens for the Blind* (1963), *Living in the Maniototo* (1979), *The Carpathians* (1988); autobiography: *To the Island* (1982), *An Angel at My Table* (1984), *The Envoy from Mirror City* (1985).

Francis, Dick (Richard Stanley) (1920–) English novelist, born Tenby, Pembrokeshire; *Dead Cert* (1962), *Slay-Ride* (1973), *The Edge* (1988), *Comeback* (1991) *To The Hilt* (1996), *10 lb Penalty* (1997).

Fraser, Lady Antonia (née **Pakenham**) (1932–) English novelist, born London; *Mary, Queen of Scots* (1969), *Quiet as a Nun* (1977), *A Splash of Red* (1981), *Have a Nice Death* (1983), *Political Death* (1994).

Frayn, Michael (1933–) English novelist, playwright, born Mill Hill, London; *The Tin Men* (1965), *A Very Private Life* (1968), *Sweet Dreams* (1973), *A Landing on the Sun* (1990), *Headlong* (1999), *Spies* (2002).

Freeling, Nicholas (1927–) English novelist, born London; *Love in Amsterdam* (1962), *Tsing-Boum* (1969), *Sand Castles* (1990), *A Dwarf Kingdom* (1996).

French, Marilyn (1929–) US novelist, born New York City; *The Women's Room* (1977), *The Bleeding Heart* (1980), *Her Mother's Daughter* (1987), *The War Against Women* (1992).

Fuller, Roy (Broadbent) (1912–91) English novelist, poet, born Failsworth, Lancashire; *The Second Curtain* (1953), *The Ruined Boys* (1959), *My Child, My Sister* (1965).

Gaddis, William (1922–98) US novelist, born New

York City; *The Recognitions* (1955), *JR* (1976), *Carpenter's Gothic* (1985), *A Frolic of His Own* (1994).

Galsworthy, John (1867–1933) English novelist, playwright, born Coombe, Surrey; *The Man of Property* (1906), *The Forsyte Saga* (1906–31); Nobel Prize for Literature 1932.

García Márquez, Gabriel (1928–) Colombian novelist, born Aracataca; *One Hundred Years of Solitude* (1970), *Chronicle of a Death Foretold* (1982), *Love in the Time of Cholera* (1985), *The General in His Labyrinth* (1991), *Of Love and Other Demons* (1995); Nobel Prize for Literature 1982.

Garner, Helen (1942–) Australian novelist, born Geelong; *Monkey Gripp* (1977), *The Last Days of Chez Nous* (screenplay) (1993), *Cosmo Cosmolino* (1993).

Gaskell, Mrs Elizabeth (Cleghorn) (née **Stevenson**) (1810–65) English novelist, born Cheyne Row, Chelsea, London; *Mary Barton* (1848), *Cranford* (1853), *North and South* (1855), *Sylvia's Lovers* (1863).

Gerhardie, William Alexander (1895–1977) English novelist, born St Petersburg, Russia; *The Polyglots* (1925), *Resurrection* (1934).

Gibbon, Lewis Grassic (pseudonym of **James Leslie Mitchell**) (1901–35) Scottish novelist, born near Auchterless, Aberdeenshire; *Sunset Song* (1932), *Cloud Howe* (1933), *Grey Granite* (1934).

Gibbons, Stella (Dorothea) (1902–89) English novelist, born London; *Cold Comfort Farm* (1933).

Gide, André (Paul Guillaume) (1869–1951) French novelist, born Paris; *The Immoralist* (1902), *The Vatican Cellars* (1914).

Gilliat, Penelope (Ann Douglas, née **Conner)** (1932–93) English novelist, short-story writer, born London; *One by One* (1965), *The Cutting Edge* (1978), *Mortal Matters* (1983).

Gissing, George Robert (1857–1903) English novelist, short-story writer, born Wakefield, Yorkshire; *New Grub Street* (1891), *The Private Papers of Henry Ryecroft* (1902).

Glasgow, Ellen (1873–1945) US novelist, born Richmond, Virginia; *Barren Ground* (1925), *The Sheltered Life* (1932), *In This Our Life* (1941).

Godden, (Margaret) Rumer (1907–98) English novelist, poet, children's author, born Eastbourne, Sussex; *Black Narcissus* (1939), *Breakfast with the Nikolides* (1942), *The Greengage Summer* (1958), *Coromandel Sea Change* (1991), *Pippa Passes* (1994).

Godwin, William (1756–1836) English novelist, born Wisbech, Cambridgeshire; *Caleb Williams* (1794), *Mandeville* (1817).

Goethe, Johann Wolfgang von (1749–1832) German novelist, poet, born Frankfurt am Main; *The Sorrows of Young Werther* (1774).

Gogol, Nikolai Vasilievich (1809–52) Russian novelist, short-story writer, playwright, born Sorochinstsi, Poltava; *The Overcoat* (1835), *Diary of a Madman* (1835), *Dead Souls* (1842), *The Odd Women* (1893).

Gold, Herbert (1924–) US novelist, born Cleveland, Ohio; *Birth of a Hero* (1951), *The Man Who Was Not With It* (1956), *My Last Two Thousand Years* (autobiography) (1972), *She Took My Arm as if She Loved Me* (1997).

Golding, (Sir) William (Gerald) (1911–93) English novelist, born St Columb Minor, Cornwall; *Lord of the Flies* (1954), *The Inheritors* (1955), *Pincher Martin* (1956), *The Spire* (1964), *Darkness Visible* (1979), *Rites of Passage* (1980, Booker Prize), *The Paper Men* (1984), *Close Quarter* (1987), *Fire Down Below* (1989); Nobel Prize for Literature 1983.

Goldman, William (1931–) US novelist, playwright, born Chicago; *Boys and Girls Together* (1964), *The Princess Bride* (1973), *The Silent Gondoliers* (1984), *Misery* (screenplay) (1990), *Absolute Power* (1997).

Goldsmith, Oliver (1728–74) Anglo-Irish playwright, novelist, poet, born Pallasmore, County Longford; *The Vicar of Wakefield* (1766).

Gordimer, Nadine (1923–) South African novelist, short-story writer, born Springs, Transvaal; *Occasion for Loving* (1963), *A Guest of Honour* (1970), *The Conservationist* (1974, Booker Prize), *A Sport of Nature* (1987), *None to Accompany Me* (1994); Nobel Prize for Literature 1991.

Gorky, Maxim (pseudonym of **Aleksei Maksimovich Peshkov**) (1868–1936) Russian novelist, short-story writer, born Nizhni Novgorod (New Gorky); *The Mother* (1906–7), *Childhood* (1913), *The Life of Klim Samgin* (1925–36).

Gosse, Sir Edmund William (1849–1928) English novelist, poet, born London; *Father and Son* (1907).

Graham, Winston (Mawdsley) (1911–) English novelist, born Victoria Park, Manchester; *Ross Poldark* (1945), *The Little Walls* (1955), *Marnie* (1961), *Poldark's Cornwall* (1983), *The Ugly Sister* (1998).

Grahame, Kenneth (1859–1932) Scottish children's writer, born Edinburgh; *Dream Days* (1898), *The Wind in the Willows* (1908).

Grass, Günter (Wilhelm) (1927–) German novelist, born Danzig; *The Tin Drum* (1962), *The Meeting at Telgte* (1981), *A Broad Field* (1995), *My Century* (1999); Nobel Prize for Literature 1999.

Graves, Robert (Ranke) (1895–1985) English novelist, poet, born London; *I Claudius* (1934), *Claudius the God* (1934).

Gray, Alasdair (James) (1934–) Scottish novelist, short-story writer, poet, born Glasgow; *Lanark* (1981), *Unlikely Stories, Mostly* (stories) (1983), *Janine* (1984), *Poor Things* (1992), *A History Maker* (1994).

Greene, (Henry) Graham (1904–91) English novelist, playwright, born Berkhamstead, Hertfordshire; *Brighton Rock* (1938), *The Power and the Glory* (1940), *The Third Man* (1950), *The Honorary Consul* (1973).

Grossmith, George (1847–1912) and **Weedon** (1852–1919) English writers, entertainers, both born London; *The Diary of a Nobody* (1892).

Guterson, David (1956–) US novelist, short-story writer, born Seattle, Washington; *The Country Ahead of Us, The Country Behind* (stories) (1989), *Snow Falling on Cedars* (1995), *East of the Mountains* (1999).

Haggard, Sir (Henry) Rider (1856–1925) English novelist, born Bradenham Hall, Norfolk; *King Solomon's Mines* (1885), *She* (1887), *Allan Quatermain* (1887).

Hailey, Arthur (1920–) Canadian novelist, playwright, born Luton, Bedfordshire; *Flight into Danger* (1958), *Airport* (1968), *The Evening News* (1990), *Detective* (1997).

Hammett, (Samuel) Dashiell (1894–1961) US novelist, born St Mary's County, Maryland; *Red Harvest* (1929), *The Maltese Falcon* (1930), *The Glass Key* (1931), *The Thin Man* (1934).

Hammond Innes, (Ralph) (1913–98) English novelist, playwright, born Horsham, Sussex; *The Trojan Horse* (1940), *Atlantic Fury* (1962), *Isvik* (1991), *Delta Connection* (1996).

Hardy, Thomas (1840–1928) English novelist, poet, born Higher Bockhampton, Dorset; *Far from the Madding Crowd* (1874), *The Mayor of Casterbridge*

(1886), *Tess of the D'Urbervilles* (1891), *Jude the Obscure* (1895).

Hartley, L(eslie) P(oles) (1895–1972) English novelist, short-story writer, born near Peterborough; *The Shrimp and the Anemone* (1944), *The Go-Between* (1953), *The Hireling* (1957).

Hawthorne, Nathaniel (1804–64) US novelist, short-story writer, born Salem, Massachusetts; *The Scarlet Letter* (1850), *The House of the Seven Gables* (1851).

Hazzard, Shirley (1931–) US novelist, short-story writer, born Sydney, Australia; *People in Glass Houses* (1967), *The Transit of Venus* (1980), *Countenance of Truth* (1990), *Greene on Capri: A Memoir* (2000).

Heinlein, Robert A(nson) (1907–88) US novelist, born Missouri; *Stranger in a Strange Land* (1962), *The Moon is a Harsh Mistress* (1967).

Heller, Joseph (1923–99) US novelist, born Brooklyn, New York City; *Catch-22* (1961), *Something Happened* (1974), *Picture This* (1988), *Closing Time* (1994).

Hemingway, Ernest (Millar) (1899–1961) US novelist, short-story writer, born Oak Park (Chicago), Illinois; *A Farewell to Arms* (1929), *For Whom the Bell Tolls* (1940), *The Old Man and the Sea* (1952); Nobel Prize for Literature 1954.

Hesse, Hermann (1877–1962) German novelist, born Calw, Württemberg; *Rosshalde* (1914), *Steppenwolf* (1927), *The Glass Bead Game* (1943); Nobel Prize for Literature 1946.

Heyer, Georgette (1902–74) English novelist, born London; *The Black Moth* (1929), *Footsteps in the Dark* (1932), *Regency Buck* (1935), *The Corinthian* (1940), *Friday's Child* (1944), *The Grand Sophy* (1950), *Bath Tangle* (1955), *Venetia* (1958), *The Nonesuch* (1962), *Frederica* (1965).

Highsmith, (Mary) Patricia (née **Plangman**) (1921–95) US novelist, short-story writer, born Fort Worth, Texas; *This Sweet Sickness* (1960), *The Cry of the Owl* (1962), *The Boy Who Followed Ripley* (1980).

Hill, Susan (Elizabeth) (1942–) English novelist, short-story writer, born Scarborough, Yorkshire; *I'm the King of the Castle* (1970), *Strange Meeting* (1972), *The Woman in Black* (1983), *Mrs de Winter* (1993), *The Service of Clouds* (1998).

Hilton, James (1900–54) English novelist, born Leigh, Lancashire; *Lost Horizon* (1933), *Goodbye Mr Chips* (1934).

Hines, (Melvin) Barry (1939–) English novelist, playwright, born Barnsley, Yorkshire; *A Kestrel for a Knave* (1968), *The Gamekeeper* (1975), *The Heart of It* (1994).

Hoban, Russell (Conwell) (1925–) US novelist, playwright, children's writer, born Lansdale, Pennsylvania; *Turtle Diary* (1975), *Riddley Walker* (1980), *Pilgermann* (1983), *The Trokeville Way* (1996).

Hogg, James, 'the Ettrick Shepherd' (1770–1835) Scottish novelist, poet, born Ettrick, Selkirkshire; *Confessions of a Justified Sinner* (1824).

Holt, Victoria (pseudonym of **Eleanor Alice Burford Hibbert**) (1906–93) English novelist, born London, also wrote as Philippa Carr, Jean Plaidy; *Catherine de' Medici* (1969, as JP), *Will You Love Me in September* (1981, as PC), *The Captive* (1989, as VH).

Holtby, Winifred (1898–1935) English novelist, born Rudston, Yorkshire; *The Crowded Street* (1924), *The Land of Green Ginger* (1927), *South Riding* (1936).

Horgan, Paul (1903–95) US novelist, poet, short-story writer, born Buffalo, New York; *The Fault of Angels* (1933), *Rome Eternal* (1957), *Mexico Bay* (1982).

Howard, Elizabeth Jane (1923–) English novelist,

born London; *The Sea Change* (1959), *After Julius* (1965), *The Light Years* (1990), *Marking Time* (1991), *Casting Off* (1995), *Slipstream* (autobiography, 2002).

Hughes, Thomas (1822–96) English novelist, born Uffington, Berkshire; *Tom Brown's Schooldays* (1857).

Hugo, Victor (Marie) (1802–85) French novelist, dramatist, poet, born Besançon; *Notre Dame de Paris* (1831), *Les Misérables* (1862).

Hulme, Keri (Ann Ruhi) (1947–) New Zealand novelist, born Christchurch; *The Bone People* (1983, Booker Prize 1985), *Lost Possessions* (1985), *Bait* (1992).

Hunter, Evan (originally **Salvatore A Lambino**) (1926–) US novelist, playwright, short-story writer, born New York City; *The Blackboard Jungle* (1954), *Strangers When We Meet* (1958), *The Paper Dragon* (1966), *Last Summer* (1968), *Privileged Conversation* (1996); also writes as Ed McBain.

Hurston, Zora Neale (1903–60) US novelist, born Eatonville, Florida; *Their Eyes Were Watching God* (1937), *Moses, Man of the Mountain* (1939).

Huxley, Aldous (Leonard) (1894–1963) English novelist, born Godalming, Surrey; *Brave New World* (1932), *Eyeless in Gaza* (1936), *Island* (1962).

Innes, Michael ► Stewart , J I M

Irving, John (Winslow) (1942–) US novelist, short-story writer, born Exeter, New Hampshire; *The World According to Garp* (1978), *The Hotel New Hampshire* (1981), *A Prayer for Owen Meany* (1989), *A Son of the Circus* (1994).

Isherwood, Christopher (William Bradshaw) (1904–86) Anglo-US novelist, born Disley, Cheshire; *Mr Norris Changes Trains* (1935), *Goodbye to Berlin* (1939), *Down There on a Visit* (1962).

Ishiguro, Kazuo (1954–) British novelist, short-story writer, born Nagasaki, Japan; *The Remains of the Day* (1989, Booker Prize), *The Unconsoled* (1995), *When We Were Orphans* (2000).

James, Henry (1843–1916) US novelist, born New York City; *Portrait of a Lady* (1881), *The Bostonians* (1886), *The Turn of the Screw* (1889), *The Awkward Age* (1899), *The Ambassadors* (1903).

James, P(hyllis) D(orothy) (1920–) English novelist, born Oxford; *Cover Her Face* (1962), *Taste for Death* (1986), *Devices and Desires* (1989), *Original Sin* (1994).

Jhabvala, Ruth Prawer (1927–) British novelist, born Cologne, Germany; *Heat and Dust* (1975, Booker Prize), *In Search of Love and Beauty* (1983), *Poet and Dancer* (1993).

Jong, Erica (née **Mann**) (1942–) US novelist, poet, born New York City; *Fear of Flying* (1973), *Fanny* (1980), *Serenissima* (1987), *Any Woman's Blues* (1990), *Fear of Fifty* (1994).

Joyce, James (Augustine Aloysius) (1882–1941) Irish novelist, poet, born Dublin; *Dubliners* (1914), *A Portrait of the Artist as a Young Man* (1914–15), *Ulysses* (1922), *Finnegan's Wake* (1939).

Kafka, Franz (1883–1924) Austrian novelist, short-story writer, born Prague (now in Czech Republic); *Metamorphosis* (1916), *The Trial* (1925), *The Castle* (1926), *America* (1927).

Kaplan, Johanna (1942–) US novelist, short-story writer, born New York City; *Other People's Lives* (1975), *O My America!* (1980).

Kazantazakis, Nikos (1883–1957) Greek novelist, poet, playwright, born Heraklion, Crete; *Zorba the Greek* (1946).

Keane, Molly (1904–96) Anglo-Irish novelist, born

County Kildare, Ireland; *Devoted Ladies* (1934), *Good Behaviour* (1981), *Time After Time* (1983).

Kelman, James (Alexander) (1946–) Scottish novelist, short-story writer, playwright, born Glasgow; *The Busconductor Hines* (1984), *A Chancer* (1985), *Greyhound for Breakfast* (stories) (1987), *A Disaffection* (1989), *How late it was, how late* (1994, Booker Prize), *Translated Accounts* (2001).

Keneally, Thomas (Michael) (1935–) Australian novelist, short-story writer, playwright, born Sydney; *Bring Larks and Heroes* (1967), *Three Cheers for a Paraclete* (1968), *The Survivor* (1969), *Schindler's Ark* (1982, Booker Prize), *Woman of the Inner Sea* (1992), *A River Town* (1995).

Kennedy, Margaret (Moore) (1896–1967) English novelist, playwright, born London; *The Ladies of Lyndon* (1923), *The Constant Nymph* (1924), *The Fool of the Family* (1930).

Kerouac, Jack (Jean-Louis) (1922–69) US novelist, born Lowell, Massachusetts; *On the Road* (1957), *The Dharma Bums* (1958).

Kesey, Ken (Elton) (1935–2001) US novelist, short-story writer, born La Junta, Colorado; *One Flew Over the Cuckoo's Nest* (1962), *Demon Box* (stories) (1987), *Sailor Song* (1992), *Last Go Round* (1994).

King, Francis (Henry) (1923–) English novelist, short-story writer, born Adelboden, Switzerland; *To the Dark Tower* (1946), *The Widow* (1957), *The Custom House* (1961), *Visiting Cards* (1990), *Ash on an Old Man's Sleeve* (1996), *Prodigies* (2001).

King, Stephen (Edwin) (1947–) US novelist, short-story writer, born Portland, Maine; *Carrie* (1974), *The Shining* (1977), *Christine* (1983), *Pet Sematary* (1983), *Misery* (1988), *Four Past Midnight* (1990), *The Plant* (Internet novel) (2000).

Kingsley, Charles (1819–75) English novelist, born Holne vicarage, Dartmoor; *Westward Ho!* (1855), *The Water-Babies* (1863), *Hereward the Wake* (1866).

Kipling, Rudyard (1865–1936) English novelist, poet, short-story writer, born Bombay (now Mumbai), India; *Barrack-room Ballads* (1892), *The Jungle Book* (1894), *Kim* (1901), *Just So Stories* (1902); Nobel Prize for Literature 1907.

Kundera, Milan (1929–) French novelist, born Brno, Czechoslovakia (now Czech Republic); *Life is Elsewhere* (1973), *The Farewell Party* (1976), *The Unbearable Lightness of Being* (1984), *Immortality* (1991), *Testaments Betrayed* (1995), *Slowness* (1996).

Laclos, Pierre (Ambroise François) Choderlos de (1741–1803) French novelist, born Amiens; *Les Liaisons Dangereuses* (Dangerous Liaisons) (1782).

La Fayette, Marie Madeleine Pioche de Lavergne, Comtesse de (1634–93) French novelist, born Paris; *Zaïde* (1670), *La Princesse de Clèves* (1678).

Lamming, George (Eric) (1927–) Barbadian novelist, born Carrington Village; *In the Castle of My Skin* (1953), *Season of Adventure* (1960), *Natives of My Person* (1972).

Lampedusa, Giuseppe Tomasi di (1896–1957) Italian novelist, born Palermo, Sicily; *Il Gattopardo* (The Leopard) (1958).

Lawrence, D(avid) H(erbert) (1885–1930) English novelist, poet, short-story writer, born Eastwood, Nottinghamshire; *Sons and Lovers* (1913), *The Rainbow* (1915), *Women in Love* (1920), *Lady Chatterley's Lover* (1928).

Le Carré, John (pseudonym of **David John Moore Cornwell**) (1931–) English novelist, born Poole, Dorset; *Tinker, Tailor, Soldier, Spy* (1974), *Smiley's People* (1980), *The Little Drummer Girl* (1983), *A Per-* *fect Spy* (1986), *The Russia House* (1989), *The Secret Pilgrim* (1991), *The Night Manager* (1993), *Our Game* (1995), *The Tailor of Panama* (1996).

Lee, (Nelle) Harper (1926–) US novelist, born Monroeville, Alabama; *To Kill a Mockingbird* (1960, Pulitzer Prize 1961).

Lee, Laurie (1914–97) English novelist, poet, born Slad, Gloucestershire; *Cider with Rosie* (1959), *As I Walked Out One Midsummer Morning* (1969).

Le Fanu, (Joseph) Sheridan (1814–73) Irish novelist, short-story writer, born Dublin; *Uncle Silas* (1864), *In a Glass Darkly* (1872).

Le Guin, Ursula K(roeber) (1929–) US novelist, poet, short-story writer, born Berkeley, California; *Rocannon's World* (1966), *The Left Hand of Darkness* (1969), *Searoad* (1991), *Fish Soup* (1992), *Unlocking the Air and Other Stories* (1996), *The Telling* (2000).

Lehmann, Rosamond (Nina) (1903–90) English novelist, born London; *Dusty Answer* (1927), *Invitation to the Waltz* (1932), *The Ballad and the Source* (1944).

Lessing, Doris (May) (née **Tayler**) (1919–) Rhodesian novelist, short-story writer, born Kermanshah, Iran; *The Grass is Singing* (1950), *The Golden Notebook* (1962), *Canopus in Argus Archives* (1979–83), *The Good Terrorist* (1985), *Playing the Game* (1996).

Levi, Primo (1919–87) Italian novelist, born Turin; *If this is a Man* (1947), *The Periodic Table* (1984).

Lewis, (Harry) Sinclair (1885–1951) US novelist, born Sauk Center, Minnesota; *Main Street* (1920), *Babbitt* (1922), *Martin Arrowsmith* (1925), *Elmer Gantry* (1927); Nobel Prize for Literature 1930.

Lively, Penelope (Margaret) (née **Low**) (1933–) English novelist, born Cairo, Egypt; *The Road to Lichfield* (1977), *Moon Tiger* (1987, Booker Prize), *City of the Mind* (1991), *Heat Wave* (1996).

Lodge, David (John) (1935–) English novelist, born London; *The British Museum is Falling Down* (1965), *Changing Places* (1975), *Small World* (1984), *Nice Work* (1988), *Paradise News* (1991), *Therapy* (1995).

London, Jack (John) Griffith (1876–1916) US novelist, born San Francisco; *Call of the Wild* (1903), *White Fang* (1907), *Martin Eden* (1909).

Lowry, (Clarence) Malcolm (1909–57) English novelist, born New Brighton, Merseyside; *Under The Volcano* (1947).

Lurie, Alison (1926–) US novelist, born Chicago; *Love and Friendship* (1962), *The War Between the Tates* (1974), *Foreign Affairs* (1984, Pulitzer Prize 1985), *The Truth about Lorin Jones* (1988), *Women and Ghosts* (short stories) (1994).

Macaulay, Dame (Emilie) Rose (1881–1958) English novelist, born Rugby, Warwickshire; *Dangerous Ages* (1921), *The World, My Wilderness* (1950), *The Towers of Trebizond* (1956).

MacDonald, George (1824–1905) Scottish novelist, born Huntly, Aberdeenshire; *Robert Falconer* (1868), *The Princess and the Goblin* (1872), *Lilith* (1895).

McEwan, Ian (Russell) (1948–) English novelist, short-story writer, playwright, born Aldershot, Hampshire; *The Cement Garden* (1978), *The Child in Time* (1987), *The Innocent* (1990), *Amsterdam* (1998, Booker Prize), *Atonement* (2001).

McIlvanney, William (Angus) (1936–) Scottish novelist, poet, born Kilmarnock, Ayrshire; *Remedy is None* (1966), *Docherty* (1975), *The Big Man* (1985), *Strange Loyalties* (1991).

MacInnes, Colin (1914–76) English novelist, born London; *City of Spades* (1959), *Absolute Beginners* (1959).

Arts and Culture

Arts and Culture

MacKenzie, Sir (Edward Montague) Compton (1883–1972) English novelist, born West Hartlepool, Cleveland; *Whisky Galore* (1942).

MacKenzie, Henry (1745–1831) Scottish novelist, born Edinburgh; *The Man of Feeling* (1771).

MacLean, Alistair (1922–87) Scottish novelist, born Glasgow; *The Guns of Navarone* (1957), *Ice Station Zebra* (1963), *Where Eagles Dare* (1967), *Force Ten from Navarone* (1968).

Mahfouz, Naguib (1911–) Egyptian novelist, born Cairo; *The Cairo Trilogy* (1956–7), *The Thief and the Dogs* (1961), *Adrift on the Nile* (1966), *God's World* (1973), *Arabian Nights and Days* (1995); Nobel Prize for Literature 1988.

Mailer, Norman (Kingsley) (1923–) US novelist, born Long Branch, New Jersey; *The Naked and the Dead* (1948), *Barbary Shore* (1951), *An American Dream* (1965), *Armies of the Night* (1968, Pulitzer Prize 1969), *The Executioner's Song* (1979, Pulitzer Prize 1980), *Oswald's Tale* (1995).

Malamud, Bernard (1914–86) US novelist, born Brooklyn, New York City; *The Fixer* (1966), *The Tenants* (1971).

Malouf, David (1934–) Australian novelist, poet, born Brisbane; *An Imaginary Life* (1978), *Harland's Half Acre* (1984), *Remembering Babylon* (1993), *The Conversations at Curlow Creek* (1996).

Mankowitz, (Cyril) Wolf (1924–98) English novelist, short-story writer, playwright, born London; *Make Me an Offer* (1952), *The Bespoke Overcoat* (play) (1954), *A Kid for Two Farthings* (1953), *My Old Man's a Dustman* (1956), *Exquisite Cadaver* (1990).

Mann, Thomas (1875–1955) German novelist, born Lübeck; *Death in Venice* (1912), *The Magic Mountain* (1924).

Manning, Olivia (1908–80) English novelist, short-story writer, born Portsmouth; *The Balkan Trilogy* (1960–5), *The Levant Trilogy* (1977–80).

Mansfield, Katherine (pseudonym of **Katherine Mansfield Beauchamp**) (1888–1923) New Zealand short-story writer, born Wellington; *Prelude* (1918), *Bliss and Other Stories* (1920), *The Garden Party and Other Stories* (1922).

Markandaya, Kamala (pseudonym of **Kamala Purnaiya Taylor**) (1924–) Indian novelist, born Madras (now Chennai); *Nectar in a Sieve* (1954), *A Silence of Desire* (1960), *The Coffer Dams* (1969).

Mars-Jones, Adam (1954–) English short-story writer, critic, born London; *Lantern Lecture and Other Stories* (1981), *The Darker Proof; Stories From a Crisis* (with Edmund White) (1987), *The Waters of Thirst* (1993), *Blind Bitter Happiness* (1997).

Marsh, Ngaio (1899–1982) New Zealand novelist, born Christchurch; *Death in a White Tie* (1958), *A Grave Mistake* (1978).

Massie, Allan (Johnstone) (1938–) Scottish novelist, journalist, born Singapore; *Change and Decay in All Around I See* (1978), *The Last Peacock* (1980), *A Question of Loyalties* (1989), *The Sins of the Fathers* (1991), *King David* (1995), *Nero's Heirs* (1999).

Maugham, (William) Somerset (1874–1965) English novelist, born Paris; *Of Human Bondage* (1915), *The Moon and Sixpence* (1919), *The Razor's Edge* (1945).

Maupassant, Guy de (1850–93) French short-story writer, novelist, born Miromesnil; *Claire de Lune* (1884), *Bel Ami* (1885).

Mauriac, François (1885–1970) French novelist, born Bordeaux; *Le Baiser au Lépreux* (1922); Nobel Prize for Literature 1952.

Melville, Herman (1819–1909) US novelist, poet, born New York City; *Moby Dick* (1851).

Meredith, George (1828–1909) English novelist, poet, born Portsmouth; *The Egoist* (1879), *Diana of the Crossways* (1885).

Michener, James A(lbert) (1907–97) US novelist, short-story writer, born New York City; *Tales of the South Pacific* (1947, Pulitzer Prize 1948), *Hawaii* (1959), *Chesapeake* (1978), *Miracle in Seville* (1995).

Miller, Henry Valentine (1891–1980) US novelist, born New York City; *Tropic of Cancer* (1934), *Tropic of Capricorn* (1938), *The Rosy Crucifixion Trilogy* (1949–60).

Milne, A(lan) A(lexander) (1882–1956) English children's writer, born London; *Winnie-the-Pooh* (1926), *Now We are Six* (1927), *The House at Pooh Corner* (1928).

Mishima, Yukio (pseudonym of **Hiraoka Kimitake**) (1925–70) Japanese novelist, born Tokyo; *Confessions of a Mask* (1960), *The Temple of the Golden Pavilion* (1959), *The Sea of Fertility* (1969–71).

Mitchell, (Charles) Julian (Humphrey) (1935–) English novelist, playwright, born Epping, Essex; *The White Father* (1964), *The Undiscovered Country* (1968), *Another Country* (play) (1981), *Falling Over England* (play) (1994).

Mitchell, Margaret (1900–49) US novelist, born Atlanta, Georgia; *Gone with the Wind* (1936).

Mitchison, Naomi (Margaret) (née **Haldane**) (1897–1999) Scottish novelist, poet, playwright, born Edinburgh; *The Corn King and The Spring Queen* (1931), *The Big House* (1950); memoirs: *Small Talk* (1973), *All Change Here* (1975), *You May Well Ask* (1979).

Mitford, Nancy (1904–73) English novelist, born London; *Love in a Cold Climate* (1949), *Don't Tell Alfred* (1960).

Mo, Timothy (Peter) (1950–) British novelist, born Hong Kong; *The Monkey King* (1978), *Sour Sweet* (1982), *An Insular Possession* (1986), *The Redundancy of Courage* (1991), *Brownout on Breadfruit Boulevard* (1995).

Monsarrat, Nicholas (John Turney) (1910–79) English novelist, born Liverpool; *The Cruel Sea* (1951), *The Story of Esther Costello* (1953).

Moorcock, Michael (1939–) English novelist, short-story writer, born London; *Gloriana* (1978), *Byzantium Endures* (1983), *The City in the Autumn Stars* (1986), *Stormbringer* (1993), *Silverheart* (2000).

Moore, Brian (1921–99) Irish–Canadian novelist, born Belfast, Northern Ireland; *The Luck of Ginger Coffey* (1960), *The Temptation of Eileen Hughes* (1981), *The Colour of Blood* (1987), *Lies of Silence* (1990), *The Statement* (1995).

Morrison, Toni (Chloe Anthony) (née **Wofford**) (1931–) US novelist, born Lorain, Ohio; *The Bluest Eye* (1970), *Sula* (1973), *Song of Solomon* (1977), *Tar Baby* (1981), *Beloved* (1987, Pulitzer Prize 1988), *Jazz* (1992), *Paradise* (1998); Nobel Prize for Literature 1993.

Mortimer, Sir John (Clifford) (1923–) English novelist, short-story writer, playwright, born London; *A Cat Among the Pigeons* (1964), *Rumpole of the Bailey* (1978), *Paradise Postponed* (1985), *Under the Hammer* (1994).

Mortimer, Penelope (Ruth) (née **Fletcher**) (1918–99) Welsh novelist, playwright, born Rhyl; *A Villa in Summer* (1954), *The Pumpkin Eater* (1962), *My Friend Says It's Bullet-Proof* (1967), *The Home* (1971), *About Time* (autobiography) (1993).

Mosley, Nicholas (3rd Baron Ravensdale) (1923–) English novelist, born London; *Spaces of the Dark* (1951), *Accident* (1965), *Hopeful Monsters* (1991), *Children of Darkness and Light* (1996), *The Hesperides Tree* (2001).

Murdoch, Dame (Jean) Iris (1919–99) Irish novelist, philosopher, born Dublin; *The Bell* (1958), *The Sea, The Sea* (1978, Booker Prize), *The Philosopher's Pupil* (1983), *The Green Knight* (1993).

Nabokov, Vladimir Vladimirovich (1899–1977) Russian–US novelist, poet, born St Petersburg; *Lolita* (1955), *Look at the Harlequins!* (1974).

Naipaul, Sir V(idiadhar) S(urajprasad) (1932–) Trinidadian novelist, born Chaguanas; *A House for Mr Biswas* (1961), *In a Free State* (1971, Booker Prize), *A Bend in the River* (1979), *A Way in the World* (1994); Nobel Prize for Literature 2001.

Nesbit, Edith (1858–1924) English children's writer, born London; *The Story of the Treasure Seekers* (1899), *The Would-Be-Goods* (1901), *Five Children and It* (1902), *The Railway Children* (1906), *The Enchanted Castle* (1907).

Newby, P(ercy) H(oward) (1918–97) English novelist, born Crowborough, Sussex; *The Picnic at Sakkara* (1955), *Revolution and Roses* (1957), *The Barbary Light* (1962), *Something About Women* (1995).

Ngugi wa Thiong'o (formerly wrote as James T Ngugi) (1938–) Kenyan novelist, short-story writer, playwright, born Kamiriithu; *The River Between* (1963), *Weep Not, Child* (1964), *A Grain of Wheat* (1967), *Petals of Blood* (1977), *Moving the Centre* (1994).

Nye, Robert (1939–) English novelist, poet, short-story writer, playwright, born London; *Falstaff* (1976), *Merlin* (1978), *The Life and Death of My Lord Gilles de Rais* (1990), *Mrs Shakespeare: the complete works* (1993), *The Late Mr Shakespeare* (1998).

Oates, Joyce Carol (1938–) US novelist, short-story writer, born Millersport, New York; *A Garden of Earthly Delights* (1967), *Them* (1969), *Wonderland* (1971), *What I Lived For* (1994), *I'll Take You There* (2002).

O'Brien, Edna (1932–) Irish novelist, short-story writer, born Tuamgraney, County Clare; *The Country Girls* (1960), *August is a Wicked Month* (1964), *A Pagan Place* (1971), *Lantern Slides* (stories) (1990), *Time and Tide* (1992), *Wild Decembers* (1999).

Oë Kenzaburo (1935–) Japanese novelist, born Shikoku; *A Personal Matter* (1968), *The Silent Cry* (1974), *Hiroshima Notes* (1981); Nobel Prize for Literature 1994.

O'Flaherty, Liam (1897–1984) Irish novelist, short-story writer, born Inishmore, Aran Islands; *The Informer* (1926), *Two Lovely Beasts* (1948).

O'Hara, John (Henry) (1905–70) US novelist, short-story writer, born Pottsville, Pennsylvania; *Spring Sowing* (1924), *Appointment in Samarra* (1934), *The Doctor's Son* (1935), *Butterfield 8* (1935), *Pal Joey* (1940).

Okri, Ben (1959–) Nigerian novelist, born Minna; *The Famished Road* (1991, Booker Prize), *Dangerous Love* (1996), *Mental Fight* (1999).

Oliphant, Margaret (1828–97) Scottish novelist, born Wallyford, Midlothian; *The Athelings* (1857), *Salem Chapel* (1863).

Ondaatje, (Philip) Michael (1943–) Canadian novelist, poet, born Ceylon (now Sri Lanka); *Coming Through Slaughter* (1976), *In the Skin of a Lion* (1987), *The English Patient* (1991, Booker Prize 1992), *Anil's Ghost* (2000).

Orwell, George (pseudonym of **Eric Arthur Blair**) (1903–50) English novelist, born Bengal, India; *Down and Out in Paris and London* (1933), *The Road*

to Wigan Pier (1937), *Animal Farm* (1945), *Nineteen Eighty-Four* (1949).

Ouida (pseudonym of **Marie-Louise de la Ramée**) (1839–1908) English novelist, born Bury St Edmunds; *Held in Bondage* (1865), *Under Two Flags* (1867), *Folle-Farine* (1871).

Ozick, Cynthia (1928–) US novelist, short-story writer, born New York City; *Trust* (1966), *The Pagan Rabbit and Other Stories* (1971), *The Cannibal Galaxy* (1983), *The Messiah of Stockholm* (1987), *The Puttermesser Papers* (1997).

Pasternak, Boris (Leonidovich) (1890–1960) Russian novelist, born Moscow; *Doctor Zhivago* (1957); Nobel Prize for Literature 1958.

Paton, Allan (Stewart) (1903–88) South African novelist, short-story writer, born Pietermaritzburg, Natal; *Cry, the Beloved Country* (1948).

Peacock, Thomas Love (1785–1866) English novelist, poet, born Weymouth; *Melincourt* (1817), *Nightmare Abbey* (1818).

Peake, Mervyn (Laurence) (1911–68) English novelist, poet, born Kuling, China; *Titus Groan* (1946), *Gormenghast* (1950), *Titus Alone* (1959).

Plaidy, Jean ▶ Holt, Victoria

Poe, Edgar Allan (1809–49) US short-story writer, poet, born Boston, Massachusetts; *Tales of the Grotesque and Arabesque* (eg 'The Fall of the House of Usher') (1840), *The Pit and the Pendulum* (1843).

Porter, Harold (Hal) (1911–84) Australian novelist, playwright, poet, short-story writer, born Melbourne; *A Handful of Pennies* (1958), *The Right Thing* (1971).

Porter, Katherine Anne (Maria Veronica Callista Russell) (1890–1980) US novelist, short-story writer, born Indian Creek, Texas; *Pale Horse, Pale Rider* (1939), *Ship of Fools* (1962).

Powell, Anthony (Dymoke) (1905–2000) English novelist, born London; *A Dance to the Music of Time* (1951–75), *The Fisher King* (1986).

Powys, John Cowper (1872–1963) English novelist, born Shirley, Derbyshire; *Wolf Solent* (1929), *Owen Glendower* (1940).

Pratchett, Terry (1948–) English novelist, born Beaconsfield, Buckinghamshire; *The Colour of Magic* (1983), *Only You Can Save Mankind* (1992), *Carpe Jugulum* (1998).

Priestley, J(ohn) B(oynton) (1894–1984) English novelist, playwright, born Bradford, Yorkshire; *The Good Companions* (1929), *Angel Pavement* (1930).

Pritchett, Sir V(ictor) S(awdon) (1900–97) English novelist, short-story writer, playwright, born Ipswich, Suffolk; *Nothing like Leather* (1935), *Dead Man Leading* (1937), *Mr Beluncle* (1951), *The Key to My Heart* (1963), *Man of Letters* (essays) (1985).

Proulx, E Annie (1935–) US novelist, short-story writer, born Connecticut; *Postcards* (1993), *The Shipping News* (1993, Pulitzer Prize 1994), *Accordion Crimes* (1996), *That Old Ace in the Hole* (2002).

Proust, Marcel (1871–1922) French novelist, born Paris; *Remembrance of Things Past* (1913–27).

Puzo, Mario (1920–99) US novelist, born New York City; *The Godfather* (1969), *The Last Don* (1996), *Omerta* (2000).

Pynchon, Thomas (1937–) US novelist, born Long Island, New York; *V* (1963), *Gravity's Rainbow* (1973), *Vineland* (1990), *Mason & Dixon* (1997).

Queen, Ellery (pseudonym of **Patrick Dannay** (1905–82) and his cousin **Manfred B Lee** (1905–71)) US novelists and short-story writers, both born Brooklyn, New York City; *The French*

Arts and Culture

Powder Mystery (1930), *The Tragedy of X* (1940), *The Glass Village* (1954).

Radcliffe, Ann (1764–1823) English novelist, born London; *The Mysteries of Udolpho* (1794), *The Italian* (1797).

Ransome, Arthur (Mitchell) (1884–1967) English children's writer, born Leeds; *Swallows and Amazons* (1930), *Peter Duck* (1932).

Rao, Raja (1909–) Indian novelist, short-story writer, born Hassan, Mysore; *Kanthapura* (1938), *The Serpent and the Rope* (1960), *The Cat and Shakespeare* (1965).

Raphael, Frederic (Michael) (1931–) US novelist, short-story writer, playwright, born Chicago; *The Earlsdon Way* (1958), *The Limits of Love* (1960), *Lindmann* (1963), *Heaven and Earth* (1985), *Old Scores* (1995).

Read, Piers Paul (1941–) English novelist, born Beaconsfield, Buckinghamshire; *The Junkers* (1968), *Monk Dawson* (1969), *The Villa Golitsyn* (1981), *A Season in the West* (1988), *A Patriot in Berlin* (1995), *Alice in Exile* (2001).

Remarque, Erich Maria (1898–1970) German novelist, born Osnabrück; *All Quiet on the Western Front* (1929), *The Road Back* (1931), *The Black Obelisk* (1957).

Renault, Mary (pseudonym of **Eileen Mary Challans**) (1905–83) English novelist, born London; *The King Must Die* (1958), *Fire from Heaven* (1969), *The Persian Boy* (1972).

Rendell, Ruth (Barbara) Rendell, Baroness (1930–) English novelist, born London, also writes as Barbara Vine; *A Judgement in Stone* (1977), *The Killing Doll* (1980), *Heartstones*, (1987), *Blood Linen* (short stories) (1995); as Barbara Vine: *The House of Stairs* (1989), *The Brimstone Wedding* (1996).

Rhys, Jean (pseudonym of **Ella Gwendolyn Rees Williams**) (1894–1979) British novelist, short-story writer, born Dominica, West Indies; *After Leaving Mackenzie* (1930), *Wide Sargasso Sea* (1966), *Tigers are Better Looking* (1968).

Richardson, Dorothy M(iller) (1873–1957) English novelist, born Abingdon, Berkshire; *Pilgrimage* (12 vol, 1915–38).

Richardson, Harry Handel (pseudonym of **Ethel Florence Lindesay Richardson**) (1870–1946) Australian novelist, born Melbourne; *The Getting of Wisdom* (1910), *Ultima Thule* (1929).

Richardson, Samuel (1689–1761) English novelist, born near Derby; *Pamela* (1740), *Clarissa* (1747–8), *Sir Charles Grandison* (1753–4).

Richler, Mordecai (1931–2001) Canadian novelist, born Montreal, Quebec; *The Apprenticeship of Duddy Kravitz* (1959), *St Urbain's Horseman* (1971), *Solomon Gursky Was Here* (1990), *This Year in Jerusalem* (1994).

Robbins, Harold (pseudonym of **Francis Kane**) (1916–97) US novelist, born Hell's Kitchen, New York City; *Never Love a Stranger* (1948), *A Stone for Danny Fisher* (1951), *The Carpetbaggers* (1961), *The Betsy* (1971), *Tycoon* (1996).

Rolfe, Frederick William (styled **Baron Corvo**) (1860–1913) English novelist, born London; *Hadrian the Seventh* (1904), *The Desire and Pursuit of the Whole* (1934).

Roth, Henry (1906–95) US novelist, short-story writer, born Tysmenica, Austro-Hungary (now Ukraine); *Call It Sleep* (1934).

Roth, Philip Milton (1933–) US novelist, short-story writer, born Newark, New Jersey; *Goodbye Columbus* (1959), *Portnoy's Complaint* (1969), *The Great*

American Novel (1973), *My Life as a Man* (1974), *Patrimony* (1991), *Sabbath's Theater* (1995), *American Pastoral* (1997, Pulitzer Prize 1998).

Rowling, J(oanne) K(athleen) (1965–) English children's writer, born Chipping Sodbury, Bristol; *Harry Potter and the Philosopher's Stone* (1997), *Harry Potter and the Goblet of Fire* (2000).

Rushdie, (Ahmed) Salman (1947–) British novelist, short-story writer, born Bombay (now Mumbai), India; *Midnight's Children* (1981, Booker Prize), *Shame* (1983), *The Satanic Verses* (1988), *Haroun and the Sea of Stories* (1990), *The Moor's Last Sigh* (1995), *The Ground Beneath Her Feet* (1999).

Sackville-West, Vita (Victoria May) (1892–1962) English poet, novelist, short-story writer, born Knole, Kent; *The Edwardians* (1930), *All Passion Spent* (1931).

Sade, Donatien Alphonse François, Comte de, (known as **Marquis**) (1740–1814) French novelist, born Paris; *Les 120 Journées de Sodome* (1784), *Justine* (1791), *La Philosophie dans le boudoir* (1793), *Juliette* (1798), *Les Crimes de l'amour* (1800).

Saint-Exupéry, Antoine de (1900–44) French novelist, born Lyons; *Flight to Arras* (1942), *The Little Prince* (1943).

Saki (pseudonym of **Hector Hugh Munro**) (1870–1916) British novelist, short-story writer, born Akyab, Burma (now Myanmar); *The Chronicles of Clovis* (1912), *The Unbearable Bassington* (1912).

Salinger, J(erome) D(avid) (1919–) US novelist, born New York; *The Catcher in the Rye* (1951), *Franny and Zooey* (1961), *Hapworth 16, 1924* (1997).

Sand, George (pseudonym of **Amandine Aurore Lucille Dupin, Baronne Dudevant**) (1804–76) French novelist, born Paris; *Lélia* (1833), *La Petite Fadette* (1849).

Saroyan, William (1908–81) US novelist, playwright, short-story writer, born Fresno, California; *The Daring Young Man on the Flying Trapeze* (1934), *My Name is Aram* (1940), *The Human Comedy* (1942).

Sartre, Jean-Paul (1905–80) French novelist, playwright, born Paris; *Nausea* (1949), *The Roads to Freedom* (1945–7); Nobel Prize for Literature 1964.

Sayers, Dorothy L(eigh) (1893–1957) English novelist, short-story writer, born Oxford; *Lord Peter Views the Body* (1928), *Gaudy Night* (1935).

Schreiner, Olive (1855–1920) South African novelist, born Wittebergen Mission Station, Cape of Good Hope; *The Story of an African Farm* (1883), *Trooper Peter Halkett of Mashonaland* (1897).

Scott, Sir Walter (1771–1832) Scottish novelist, poet, born Edinburgh; *Waverley* (1814), *Rob Roy* (1817), *The Heart of Midlothian* (1818), *The Bride of Lammermoor* (1819), *Ivanhoe* (1820).

Selby, Hubert, Jr (1928–) US novelist, short-story writer, born Brooklyn, New York City; *Last Exit to Brooklyn* (1964), *The Room* (1971), *Requiem for a Dream* (1978), *Song of the Silent Snow* (1986), *The Willow Tree* (1998).

Seth, Vikram (1952–) Indian novelist, poet, born Calcutta (now Kolkata); *The Golden Gate* (1986), *A Suitable Boy* (1993), *An Equal Music* (1999).

Sharpe, Tom (Thomas Ridley) (1928–) English novelist, born London; *Riotous Assembly* (1971), *Porterhouse Blue* (1973), *Blott on the Landscape* (1975), *Wilt* (1976), *Grantchester Grind* (1995), *The Midden* (1996).

Shelley, Mary (Wollstonecraft) (née **Godwin**) (1797–1851) English novelist, born London; *Frankenstein* (1818), *The Last Man* (1826), *Perkin Warbeck* (1830).

Shields, Carol (Ann) (née **Warner**) (1935–) Canadian novelist, born Illinois, USA; *Small Ceremonies* (1976), *Happenstance* (1980), *Swann: A Mystery* (1987), *The Republic of Love* (1992), *The Stone Diaries* (1993, Pulitzer Prize 1995), *Larry's Party* (1997, Orange Prize 1998), *Dressing Up for the Carnival* (2000).

Sholokhov, Mikhail Alexandrovich (1905–84) Russian novelist, born near Veshenskayal; *And Quiet Flows the Don* (1928–40), *The Upturned Soil* (1940); Nobel Prize for Literature 1965.

Shute, Nevil (pseudonym of **Nevil Shute Norway**) (1899–1960) Anglo-Australian novelist, born Ealing, London; *The Pied Piper* (1942), *A Town Like Alice* (1950), *On the Beach* (1957).

Sillitoe, Alan (1928–) English novelist, poet, short-story writer, born Nottingham; *Saturday Night and Sunday Morning* (1958), *The Loneliness of the Long Distance Runner* (1959), *The Broken Chariot* (1998).

Simenon, Georges (1903–89) French writer, born Liège, Belgium; almost 100 novels featuring Jules Maigret, and 400 other novels: *The Death of Monsieur Gallet* (1932), *The Crime of Inspector Maigret* (1933).

Simon, Claude (Henri Eugène) (1913–) French novelist, born Tananarive, Madagascar; *The Wind* (1959), *The Flanders Road* (1962), *Triptych* (1977); Nobel Prize for Literature 1985.

Singer, Isaac Bashevis (1904–91) US novelist, playwright, born Radzymin, Poland; *The Family Moskat* (1950), *The Satan in Goray* (1955); Nobel Prize for Literature 1978.

Smith, Iain Crichton (Gaelic **Iain Mac A'Ghobhainn**) (1928–98) Scottish novelist, poet, short-story writer, playwright, born Glasgow; *Consider the Lilies* (1968), *Murdo and Other Stories* (1981), *The Dream* (1990).

Smollett, Tobias George (1721–71) Scottish novelist, born Dalquharn, Dunbartonshire; *Roderick Random* (1748), *The Adventures of Peregrine Pickle* (1751), *The Expedition of Humphrey Clinker* (1771).

Snow, C(harles) P(ercy) (1905–80) English novelist, born Leicester; *Strangers and Brothers* (1940–70).

Solzhenitsyn, Aleksandr Isayevich (1918–) Russian novelist, born Kislovodsk, Caucasus; *One Day in the Life of Ivan Denisovich* (1963), *Cancer Ward* (1968), *The First Circle* (1969), *The Gulag Archipelago 1918–56* (3 vols 1974–8); Nobel Prize for Literature 1970.

Spark, Dame Muriel (Sarah) (née **Camberg**) (1918–) Scottish novelist, short-story writer, poet, born Edinburgh; *The Ballad of Peckham Rye* (1960), *The Prime of Miss Jean Brodie* (1961), *The Girls of Slender Means* (1963), *The Mandelbaum Gate* (1965), *A Far Cry from Kensington* (1988), *Reality and Dreams* (1996), *Aiding and Abetting* (2000).

Spring, Howard (1889–1965) Welsh novelist, born Cardiff; *Oh Absalom* (1938).

Stead, C(hristian) K(arlson) (1932–) New Zealand novelist, poet, born Auckland; *Smith's Dream* (1971), *All Visitors Ashore* (1984), *Sister Hollywood* (1990), *The Singing Whalcapapa* (1994), *Kin of Place* (2002).

Stein, Gertrude (1874–1946) US novelist, short-story writer, born Allegheny, Pennsylvania; *Three Lives* (1909), *Tender Buttons* (1914).

Steinbeck, John Ernest (1902–68) US novelist, born Salinas, California; *Of Mice and Men* (1937), *The Grapes of Wrath* (1939), *Cannery Row* (1945), *East of Eden* (1952); Nobel Prize for Literature 1962.

Stendhal (pseudonym of **Henri Marie Beyle**) (1788–1842) French novelist, born Grenoble; *Le Rouge et le noir* (1830), *La Chartreuse de Parme* (1839).

Sterne, Lawrence (1713–68) Irish novelist, born Clonmel, Tipperary; *Tristram Shandy* (1759–67), *A Sentimental Journey* (1768).

Stevenson, Robert Louis (Balfour) (1850–94) Scottish novelist, short-story writer, poet, born Edinburgh; *Travels with a Donkey* (1879), *Treasure Island* (1883), *Kidnapped* (1886), *The Strange Case of Dr Jekyll and Mr Hyde* (1886), *Weir of Hermiston* (1896).

Stewart, J(ohn) I(nnes) M(ackintosh) (1906–94) Scottish novelist, born Edinburgh; *A Use of Riches* (1957), *The Last Tresilians* (1963); as Michael Innes: *Hamlet, Revenge!* (1937), *Appleby and the Ospreys* (1986).

Stewart, Mary (Florence Elinor) (1916–) English novelist, born Sunderland; *This Rough Magic* (1964), *The Last Enchantment* (1979), *The Prince and the Pilgrim* (1995).

Stoker, Bram (Abraham) (1847–1912) Irish novelist, short-story writer, born Dublin; *Dracula* (1897).

Stone, Robert (Anthony) (1937–) US novelist, born Brooklyn, New York City; *Dog Soldiers* (1974), *A Flag for Sunrise* (1982), *Outerbridge Reach* (1992).

Storey, David (Malcolm) (1933–) English novelist, playwright, born Wakefield, Yorkshire; *This Sporting Life* (1960), *Radcliffe* (1963), *Saville* (1976, Booker Prize), *A Prodigal Child* (1982), *Phoenix* (1993).

Stowe, Harriet (Elizabeth) Beecher (1811–96) US novelist, born Litchfield, Connecticut; *Uncle Tom's Cabin* (1852).

Styron, William (Clark) (1925–) US novelist, born Newport News, Virginia; *Lie Down in Darkness* (1951), *The Confessions of Nat Turner* (1967), *Sophie's Choice* (1979), *A Tidewater Morning* (1993).

Swift, Graham (Colin) (1949–) English novelist, born London; *The Sweet Shop Owner* (1980), *Waterland* (1983), *Out of This World* (1988), *Ever After* (1992), *Last Orders* (1996, Booker Prize).

Swift, Jonathan (1667–1754) Irish novelist, poet, born Dublin; *A Tale of a Tub* (1704), *Gulliver's Travels* (1726).

Symons, Julian (Gustave) (1912–94) English novelist, poet, short-story writer, playwright, born London; *The Thirty-First of February* (1950), *The Colour of Murder* (1957), *Sweet Adelaide* (1980).

Tennant, Emma (Christina) (1937–) English novelist, born London; *Hotel de Dream* (1978), *Alice Fell* (1980), *Pemberley* (1993), *Elinor and Marianne* (1996).

Thackeray, William Makepeace (1811–63) English novelist, born Calcutta (now Kolkata), India; *Vanity Fair* (1847–8), *Pendennis* (1848–50).

Theroux, Paul (Edward) (1941–) US novelist, short-story writer, travel writer, born Medford, Massachusetts; *The Mosquito Coast* (1981), *The Kingdom by the Sea* (travel) (1983), *Doctor Slaughter* (1984), *Riding the Iron Rooster* (travel) (1988), *My Secret History* (1989), *My Other Life* (1996).

Thomas, D(onald) M(ichael) (1935–) English novelist, poet, born Redruth, Cornwall; *The White Hotel* (1981); *Russian Nights* (quintet): *Ararat* (1983), *Swallow* (1984), *Sphinx* (1986), *Summit* (1987), *Lying Together* (1990); *Eating Pavlova* (1994).

Tolkien, J(ohn) R(onald) R(euel) (1892–1973) English novelist, born Bloemfontein, South Africa; *The Hobbit* (1937), *The Lord of the Rings* (1954–5).

Tolstoy, Count Leo Nikolayevich (1828–1910) Russian novelist, born Yasnaya Polyana, Central Russia; *War and Peace* (1863–9), *Anna Karenina* (1873–7), *Resurrection* (1899).

Arts and Culture

Tranter, Nigel Godwin (1909–99) Scottish novelist, born Glasgow; over 100 novels including *The Steps to the Empty Throne* (1969), *The Path of the Hero King* (1970), *The Price of the King's Peace* (1971), *Honours Even* (1995).

Tremain, Rose (née **Thomson**) (1943–) English novelist, short-story writer, playwright, born London; *The Cupboard* (1981), *The Colonel's Daughter and Other Stories* (1984), *Restoration* (1989), *Sacred Country* (1992), *The Way I Found Her* (1997), *Music and Silence* (1999).

Trevor, William (properly **William Trevor Cox**) (1928–) Irish novelist, short-story writer, born Mitchelstown, County Cork; *Fools of Fortune* (1983), *The Silence in the Garden* (1988), *Two Lives* (1991), *Felicia's Journey* (1994), *The Story of Lucy Gault* (2002).

Trollope, Anthony (1815–82) English novelist, born London; *Barchester Towers* (1857), *Can You Forgive Her?* (1864), *The Way We Live Now* (1875).

Trollope, Joanna (1943–) English novelist, born Gloucestershire; *Eliza Stanhope* (1978), *The Choir* (1988), *A Village Affair* (1989), *The Rector's Wife* (1991), *Next of Kin* (1996).

Tuohy, Frank (John Francis) (1925–99) English novelist, short-story writer, born Uckfield, Sussex; *The Animal Game* (1957), *The Warm Nights of January* (1960), *The Ice Saints* (1964), *Fingers in the Door* (stories) (1970), *Collected Stories* (1984).

Turgenev, Ivan Sergeevich (1818–83) Russian novelist, born province of Oryel; *Sportsman's Sketches* (1952), *Fathers and Children* (1862).

Tutuola, Amos (1920–97) Nigerian novelist, short-story writer, born Abeokuta; *The Palm-Wine Drinkard and His Dead Palm-Wine Tapster in the Deads' Town* (1952), *The Wild Hunter in the Bush of the Ghosts* (1982), *Pauper, Brawler and Slanderer* (1987), *The Village Witchdoctor and Other Stories* (1990).

Twain, Mark (pseudonym of **Samuel Langhorne Clemens**) (1835–1910) US novelist, born Florida, Missouri; *The Celebrated Jumping Frog of Calaveras County* (1865), *The Adventures of Tom Sawyer* (1876), *The Prince and the Pauper* (1882), *The Adventures of Huckleberry Finn* (1884), *A Connecticut Yankee in King Arthur's Court* (1889).

Tyler, Anne (1941–) US novelist, short-story writer, born Minneapolis, Minnesota; *If Morning Ever Comes* (1964), *Morgan's Passing* (1980), *The Accidental Tourist* (1985), *Breathing Lessons* (1988, Pulitzer Prize 1989), *Ladder of Years* (1995), *A Patchwork Planet* (1998).

Updike, John (Hoyer) (1932–) US novelist, short-story writer, born Shillington, Pennsylvania; *Rabbit, Run* (1960), *Pigeon Feathers and Other Stories* (1962), *Rabbit is Rich* (1982, Pulitzer Prize), *The Witches of Eastwick* (1984), *Rabbit at Rest* (1990, Pulitzer Prize 1991), *In the Beauty of the Lilies* (1996).

Upward, Edward (Falaise) (1903–) English novelist, born Romford, Essex; *Journey to the Border* (1938), *In the Thirties* (1962), *The Rotten Elements* (1969), *An Unmentionable Man* (1994).

Uris, Leon (Marcus) (1924–) US novelist, born Baltimore, Maryland; *Battle Cry* (1953), *Exodus* (1958), *The Haj* (1984), *Redemption* (1995).

Van der Post, Sir Laurens (Jan) (1906–96) South African novelist, playwright, born Philippolis; *Flamingo Feather* (1955), *Journey into Russia* (1964), *A Far-Off Place* (1974).

Vansittart, Peter (1920–) English novelist, born Bedford; *Quintet* (1976), *The Death of Robin Hood* (1981), *Parsifal* (1988), *In the Fifties* (1995).

Vargas Llosa, Mario (1936–) Peruvian novelist, born Arequipa; *The Time of the Hero* (1962), *Aunt Julia and the Scriptwriter* (1977), *The War at the End of the World* (1981), *The Green House* (1986).

Verne, Jules (1828–1905) French novelist, born Nantes; *Voyage to the Centre of the Earth* (1864), *Twenty Thousand Leagues under the Sea* (1870).

Vidal, Gore (Eugene Luther, Jr) (1925–) US novelist, short-story writer, playwright, born West Point, New York; *Williwaw* (1946), *The City and the Pillar* (1948), *The Judgement of Paris* (1952), *Myra Breckenridge* (1968), *Creation* (1981), *Lincoln* (1984), *Empire* (1987), *Hollywood* (1989), *The Season of Conflict* (1996).

Vine, Barbara ▸ Rendell, Ruth

Voltaire, François-Marie Arouet de (1694–1778) French novelist, poet, born Paris; *Zadig* (1747), *Candide* (1759).

Vonnegut, Kurt, Jr (1922–) US novelist, short-story writer, born Indianapolis, Indiana; *Cat's Cradle* (1963), *Slaughterhouse-Five* (1969), *Hocus Pocus* (1990), *Timequake* (1997).

Wain, John (Barrington) (1925–94) English novelist, poet, short-story writer, playwright, born Stoke-on-Trent, Staffordshire; *Hurry on Down* (1953), *The Young Visitors* (1965), *Where the Rivers Meet* (1988).

Walker, Alice (Malsenior) (1944–) US novelist, short-story writer, born Eatonville, Georgia; *The Third Life of Grange Copeland* (1970), *Meridian* (1976), *The Color Purple* (1982, Pulitzer Prize 1983), *Everyday Use* (1994).

Walpole, Horace (1717–97) English novelist, poet, born London; *Letter from Xotto to his Friend Lien Chi at Pekin* (1757), *Anecdotes of Painting in England* (1761–71), *The Castle of Otranto* (1764), *The Mysterious Mother* (1768), *Historic Doubts on the Life and Reign of King Richard the Third* (1768).

Warner, Marina (Sarah) (1946–) English novelist, born London; *In a Dark Wood* (1977), *The Skating Party* (1982), *The Lost Father* (1988), *The Mermaids in the Basement* (1993), *The Leto Bundle* (2001).

Warren, Robert Penn (1905–89) US novelist, poet, born Guthrie, Kentucky; *Night Rider* (1939), *All the King's Men* (1943).

Waterhouse, Keith (Spencer) (1929–) English novelist, playwright, born Leeds, Yorkshire; *Billy Liar* (1959), *Office Life* (1978), *Bimbo* (1990), *Unsweet Charity* (1992).

Waugh, Evelyn (Arthur St John) (1903–66) English novelist, born Hampstead, London; *Decline and Fall* (1928), *A Handful of Dust* (1934), *Brideshead Revisited* (1945).

Weldon, Fay (originally **Franklin Birkinshaw**) (1931–) English novelist, born Alvechurch, Worcestershire; *Down Among the Women* (1971), *Female Friends* (1975), *Life and Loves of a She-Devil* (1983), *Worst Fears* (1996).

Wells, H(erbert) G(eorge) (1866–1946) English novelist, born Bromley, Kent; *The Time Machine* (1895), *The War of the Worlds* (1898), *The History of Mr Polly* (1910).

Welty, Eudora (1909–2001) US novelist, short-story writer, born Jackson, Mississippi; *A Curtain of Green* (1941), *The Robber Bridegroom* (1944), *The Golden Apples* (1949), *The Ponder Heart* (1954), *The Optimist's Daughter* (1972, Pulitzer Prize 1973), *A Writer's Eye: Collected Book Reviews* (1994).

Wesley, Mary (pseudonym of **Mary Aline Siepmann**) (née **Farmar**) (1912–2002) English novelist, born Englefield Green, Berkshire; *The Camomile Lawn* (1984), *A Sensible Life* (1990), *Part of the Furniture* (1997).

West, Morris (Langlo) (1916–99) Australian novelist, playwright, born Melbourne, Victoria; *Children of* the Sun (non-fiction) (1957), *The Devil's Advocate* (1959), *Summer of the Red Wolf* (1971), *The Clowns of God* (1981), *The World is Made of Glass* (1983), *The Ringmaster* (1991), *Vanishing Point* (1996).

West, Dame Rebecca (pseudonym of **Cecily Isabel Andrews**) (née **Fairfield**) (1892–1983) Irish novelist, born County Kerry; *The Harsh Voice* (1935), *The Mountain Overflows* (1957).

Wharton, Edith (Newbold) (1862–1937) US novelist, short-story writer, born New York; *The House of Mirth* (1905), *Ethan Frome* (1911), *The Age of Innocence* (1920).

White, Antonia (pseudonym of **Eirene Adeline Botting**) (1899–1980) English novelist, born London; *Beyond the Glass* (1954), *Frost in May* (1983).

White, Patrick Victor Martindale (1912–90) Australian novelist, playwright, short-story writer, born London; *Voss* (1957), *The Vivisector* (1970), *A Fringe of Leaves* (1976); Nobel Prize for Literature 1973.

White, T(erence) H(anbury) (1906–64) English novelist, poet, born Bombay (now Mumbai), India; *Darkness at Pemberley* (1932), *The Once and Future King* (1958).

Wilde, Oscar (Fingal O'Flahertie Wills) (1854–1900) Irish novelist, short-story writer, playwright, poet, born Dublin; *The Happy Prince and Other Tales* (1888), *The Picture of Dorian Gray* (1890), *The Importance of Being Earnest* (play) (1895).

Wilder, Thornton Niven (1897–1976) US novelist, playwright, born Madison, Wisconsin; *The Bridge of San Luis Rey* (1927), *The Woman of Andros* (1930), *Heaven's My Destination* (1935).

Wilding, Michael (1942–) Australian novelist, short-story writer, born Worcester, England; *Living Together* (1974), *The West Midland Underground* (1975), *Pacific Highway* (1982), *Under Saturn* (1988).

Wilson, A(ndrew) N(orman) (1950–) English novelist, born London; *Kindly Light* (1979), *Wise Virgin* (1982), *Daughters of Albion* (1991), *A Watch in the Night* (1996).

Winterson, Jeanette (1959–) English novelist, born Manchester; *Oranges Are Not the Only Fruit* (1985), *The Passion* (1987), *Sexing the Cherry* (1989), *Gut Symmetries* (1997).

Wodehouse, Sir P(elham) G(renville) (1881–1975) English novelist, short-story writer, born Guildford, Surrey; *The Inimitable Jeeves* (1923), *Carry on, Jeeves* (1925).

Wolfe, Thomas Clayton (1900–38) US novelist, born Asheville, North Carolina; *Look Homeward, Angel* (1929), *Of Time and the River* (1935), *From Death to Morning* (1935).

Wolfe, Tom (Thomas Kennerly) (1931–) US novelist, journalist, born Richmond, Virginia; *The Kandy-Kolored Tangerine-Flake Streamline Baby* (1965), *The Electric Kool-Aid Acid Test* (1968), *The Right Stuff* (1979), *The Bonfire of the Vanities* (1st novel) (1988), *A Man in Full* (1998).

Wolff, Tobias (1945–) US novelist, short-story writer, born Birmingham, Alabama; *In the Garden of the North American Martyrs* (stories) (1981), *The Barracks Thief* (1984), *Back in the World* (stories) (1985), *The Night in Question* (stories) (1996).

Woolf, (Adeline) Virginia (1882–1941) English novelist, born London; *Mrs Dalloway* (1925), *To The Lighthouse* (1927), *Orlando* (1928), *A Room of One's Own* (1929), *The Waves* (1931).

Wouk, Herman (1915–) US novelist, playwright, born New York City; *The Caine Mutiny* (1951), *The Winds of War* (1971), *War and Remembrance* (1978), *Inside, Outside* (1985), *The Hope* (1993), *The Glory* (1994).

Wright, Richard Nathaniel (1908–60) US novelist, short-story writer, born Mississippi; *Native Son* (1940), *Eight Men* (1961).

Wyndham, John (pseudonym of **John Wyndham Parkes Lucas Beynon Harris**) (1903–69) English novelist, born Knowle, Warwickshire; *The Day of the Triffids* (1951), *The Kraken Wakes* (1953), *The Chrysalids* (1955), *The Midwich Cuckoos* (1957), *The Trouble with Lichen* (1960), *Consider Her Ways* (1961) (short stories), *Chocky* (1968).

Yerby, Frank (Garvin) (1916–91) US novelist, born Augusta, Georgia; *The Golden Hawk* (1948), *The Dahomean* (1971), *A Darkness at Ingraham's Crest* (1979).

Yourcenar, Marguerite (pseudonym of **Marguerite de Crayencour**) (1903–87) French novelist, poet, born Brussels; *Memoirs of Hadrian* (1941).

Zamyatin, Evgeny Ivanovich (1884–1937) Russian novelist, short-story writer, born Lebedyan; *We* (1921), *The Dragon: Fifteen Stories* (1966).

Zola, Émile (1840–1902) French novelist, born Paris; *Thérèse Raquin* (1867), *Les Rougon-Macquart* (1871–93), *Germinal* (1885).

Poets

Selected volumes of poetry are listed.

Abse, Dannie (Daniel) (1923–) Welsh, born Cardiff; *After Every Green Thing* (1948), *Tenants of the House* (1957), *There Was a Young Man from Cardiff* (1991), *Arcadia, One Mile* (1998).

Adcock, (Kareen) Fleur (1934–) New Zealander, born Papakura; *The Eye of the Hurricane* (1964), *In Focus* (1977), *The Incident Book* (1986), *Poems 1960–2000* (2000).

Aiken, Conrad (Potter) (1889–1973) American, born Georgia; *Earth Triumphant* (1914), *Preludes for Memnon* (1931).

Akhmatova, Anna (pseudonym of **Anna Andreevna Gorenko**) (1889–1966) Russian, born Odessa; *Evening* (1912), *Poem without a Hero* (1940–62), *Requiem* (1963).

Angelou, Maya (**Marguerite Annie**) (née **Johnson**) (1928–) American, born St Louis, Missouri; *And Still I Rise* (1978), *I Shall Not Be Moved* (1990), *The Complete Collected Poems of Maya Angelou* (1995).

Apollinaire, Guillaume (pseudonym of **Wilhelm Apollinaris de Kostrowitzky**) (1880–1918) French, born Rome; *Alcools* (1913), *Calligrammes* (1918).

Ariosto, Ludovico (1474–1535) Italian, born Reggio; *Orlando Furioso* (1532).

Auden, W(ystan) H(ugh) (1907–73) British, naturalized US citizen, born York; *Another Time* (1940), *The Sea and the Mirror* (1944), *The Age of Anxiety* (1947).

Baudelaire, Charles (Pierre) (1821–67) French, born Paris; *Les Fleurs du mal* (1857).

Beer, Patricia (1919–99) English, born Exmouth, Devon; *The Loss of the Magyar* (1959), *The Lie of the Land* (1983), *Friend of Heraclitus* (1993).

Belloc, (Joseph) Hillaire (Pierre) (1870–1953) British, born St Cloud, France; *Cautionary Tales* (1907), *Sonnets and Verse* (1923).

Berryman, John (1914–72) American, born McAl-

Arts and Culture

ester, Oklahoma; *Homage to Mistress Bradsheet* (1966), *Dream Songs* (1969).

Betjeman, Sir John (1906–84) English, born Highgate, London; *Mount Zion* (1931), *New Bats in Old Belfries* (1945), *A Nip in the Air* (1972).

Bishop, Elizabeth (1911–79) American, born Worcester, Massachusetts; *North and South* (1946), *Geography III* (1978).

Blake, William (1757–1827) English, born London; *The Marriage of Heaven and Hell* (1793), *The Visions of the Daughters of Albion* (1793), *Songs of Innocence and Experience* (1794), *Vala, or The Four Zoas* (1800), *Milton* (1810).

Blunden, Edmund (Charles) (1896–1974) English, born Yalding, Kent; *The Waggoner and Other Poems* (1920).

Brodsky, Joseph (originally **Iosif Aleksandrovich Brodsky**) (1940–96) Russian–American, born Leningrad (now St Petersburg); *Longer and Shorter Poems* (1965), *To Urania: Selected Poems* 1965–1985 (1988); Nobel Prize for Literature 1987.

Brooke, Rupert (Chawner) (1887–1915) English, born Rugby; *Poems* (1911); *1914 and Other Poems* (1915), *New Numbers* (1915).

Brooks, Gwendolyn (Elizabeth) (1917–2000) American, born Topeka, Kansas; *A Street in Bronzeville* (1945), *Annie Allen* (1949, Pulitzer Prize 1950), *In The Mecca* (1968), *Blacks* (1987).

Browning, Elizabeth Barrett (née **Barrett**) (1806–61) English, born Coxhoe Hall, near Durham; *Sonnets from the Portuguese* (1850), *Aurora Leigh* (1855).

Browning, Robert (1812–89) English, born Camberwell, London; *Bells and Pomegranates* (1841–6), *Men and Women* (1855), *The Ring and the Book* (1868–9).

Burns, Robert (1759–96) Scottish, born Alloway, Ayr; *Poems, Chiefly in the Scottish Dialect* (1786), *Tam o'Shanter* (1790).

Byron (of Rochdale), George Gordon, 6th Baron (1788–1824) English, born London; *Hours of Idleness* (1807), *Childe Harolde's Pilgrimage* (1817), *Don Juan* (1819–24).

Catullus, Gaius Valerius (c.84–c.54BC) Roman, born Verona; lyric poet, over 100 poems survive.

Causley, Charles (1917–) English, born Launceston, Cornwall; *Union St* (1957), *Johnny Alleluia* (1961), *Underneath the Water* (1968), *All Day Saturday* (1994), *Collected Poems for Children* (1996).

Chaucer, Geoffrey (c.1343–1400) English, born London; *Book of the Duchess* (1370), *Troilus and Cressida* (c.1385), *The Canterbury Tales* (1387–1400).

Clampitt, Amy (1920–94) American, born Iowa; *The Kingfisher* (1983), *Archaic Figure* (1987), *Westward* (1990).

Clare, John (1773–1864) English, born Helpstone, Northamptonshire; *Poems Descriptive of Rural Life* (1820), *The Shepherd's Calendar* (1827).

Coleridge, Samuel Taylor (1772–1834) English, born Otterly St Mary, Devon; *Poems on Various Subjects* (1796), *'Kubla Khan'* (1797), *'The Rime of the Ancient Mariner'* (1798), *Christabel and Other Poems* (1816), *Sybylline Leaves* (1817).

Cowper, William (1731–1800) English, born Great Berkhampstead, Hertfordshire; *The Task* (1785).

Crabbe, George (1754–1823) English, born Aldeburgh, Suffolk; *The Village* (1783).

cummings, e(dward) e(stlin) (1894–1962) American, born Cambridge, Massachusetts; *Tulips and Chimneys* (1923), *XLI Poems* (1925), *is 5* (1926).

Dante, Alighieri (1265–1321) Italian, born Florence; *Vita Nuova* (1294), *Divine Comedy* (1321).

Day-Lewis, Cecil (1904–72) Irish, born Ballintubbert, Laois; *Overtures to Death* (1938), *The Aeneid of Virgil* (1952).

de la Mare, Walter (1873–1956) English, born Charleston, Kent; *The Listeners* (1912), *The Burning Glass and Other Poems* (1945).

Dickinson, Emily (Elizabeth) (1830–86) American, born Amherst, Massachusetts; only 7 poems published in her lifetime; posthumous publications, eg *Poems* (1890).

Donne, John (c.1572–1631) English, born London; *Satires & Elegies* (1590s), *Holy Sonnets* (1610–11), *Songs and Sonnets*; most verse published posthumously.

Doolittle, Hilda (known as **H D**) (1886–1961) American, born Bethlehem, Pennsylvania; *Sea Garden* (1916), *The Walls Do Not Fall* (1944), *Helen in Egypt* (1961).

Dryden, John (1631–1700) English, born Adwinckle All Saints, Northamptonshire; *Astrea Redux* (1660), *Absalom and Achitophel* (1681), *'Mac Flecknoe'* (1684).

Duffy, Carol Ann (1955–) Scottish, born Glasgow; *Standing Female Nude* (1985), *Mean Time* (1993), *The World's Wife* (1999).

Dunbar, William (c.1460–c.1520) Scottish, birthplace probably E Lothian; *'The Thrissill and the Rois'* (1503), *'Lament for the Makaris'* (c.1507).

Dunn, Douglas (Eaglesham) (1942–) Scottish, born Inchinnan, Renfrewshire; *Love or Nothing* (1974), *Elegies* (1985), *Dante's Drum-kit* (1993), *The Year's Afternoon* (2000).

Dutton, Geoffrey (Piers Henry) (1922–98) Australian, born Kapunda; *Antipodes in Shoes* (1958), *Poems, Soft and Loud* (1968), *A Body of Words* (1977), *New and Selected Poems* (1993).

Eliot, T(homas) S(tearns) (1888–1965) American (British citizen 1927), born St Louis, Missouri; *Prufrock and Other Observations* (1917), *The Waste Land* (1922), *Ash Wednesday* (1930), *Four Quartets* (1944).

Eluard, Paul (pseudonym of **Eugène Grindel**) (1895–1952) French, born Saint-Denis; *La Vie immédiate* (1934), *Poésie et vérité* (1942).

Emerson, Ralph Waldo (1803–84) American, born Boston, Massachusetts; poems published posthumously in *Complete Works* (1903–4).

Empson, Sir William (1906–84) English, born Yokefleet, E Yorkshire; *Poems* (1935), *The Gathering Storm* (1940).

Fitzgerald, Edward (1809–83) English, born near Woodbridge, Suffolk; translator of *The Rubaiyat of Omar Khayyam* (1859).

Frost, Robert (Lee) (1874–1963) American, born San Francisco; *North of Boston* (1914), *Mountain Interval* (1916), *New Hampshire* (1923), *In the Clearing* (1962).

Ginsberg, Allen (1926–97) American, born Newark, New Jersey; *Howl and Other Poems* (1956), *Empty Mirror* (1961), *The Fall of America* (1973).

Graves, Robert (Ranke) (1895–1985) English, born London; *Fairies and Fusiliers* (1917).

Gray, Thomas, (1716–71) English, born London; *'Elegy Written in a Country Churchyard'* (1751), *Pindaric Odes* (1757).

Gunn, Thom(son William) (1929–) English, born Gravesend, Kent; *The Sense of Movement* (1957), *Touch* (1967), *Jack Straw's Castle* (1976), *The Passages of Joy* (1982), *The Man with Night Sweats* (1992), *Boss Cupid* (2000).

Heaney, Seamus (Justin) (1939–) Northern Irish, born Castledawson, County Derry; *Death of a Naturalist* (1966), *Door into the Dark* (1969), *Field Work* (1979), *Seeing Things* (1991), *Spirit Level* (1995), *Beowulf: A New Translation* (2000); Nobel Prize for Literature 1995.

Henri, Adrian (Maurice) (1932–2000) English, born Birkenhead; *The Mersey Sound: Penguin Modern Poets 10* (with Roger McGough and Brian Patten) (1967), *Tonight at Noon* (1968), *From the Loveless Motel* (1980), *Wish You Were Here* (1990), *Not Fade Away* (1994), *Robocat* (1998).

Henryson, Robert (c.1430–1506) Scottish, birthplace unknown; *Testament of Cresseid, Morall Fables of Esope the Phrygian*.

Herbert, George (1593–1633) English, born Montgomery, Wales; *The Temple* (1633).

Herrick, Robert (1591–1674) English, born London; *Hesperides* (1648).

Hill, Geoffrey (William) (1932–) English, born Bromsgrove, Worcestershire; *King Log* (1968), *Mercian Hymns* (1971), *Tenebrae* (1978), *Canaan* (1996).

Hodgson, Ralph (Edwin) (1871–1962) English, born Yorkshire; *Poems* (1917), *The Skylark and Other Poems* (1958).

Homer (10c–8c BC) Greek, birthplace and existence disputed; he is credited with the writing or writing down of *The Iliad* and *The Odyssey*.

Hopkins, Gerard Manley (1844–89) English, born Stratford, London; *'The Wreck of the Deutschland'* (1876), posthumously published *Poems* (1918).

Horace, Quintus Horatius Flaccus (65–8BC) Roman, born Venusia, Apulia; *Epodes* (30BC), *Odes* (23–13BC).

Housman, A(lfred) E(dward) (1859–1936) English, born Flockbury, Worcestershire; *A Shropshire Lad* (1896), *Last Poems* (1922).

Hughes, Ted (1930–98) English, born Mytholmroyd, Yorkshire; *The Hawk in the Rain* (1957), *Lupercal* (1960), *Wodwo* (1967), *Crow* (1970), *Cave Birds* (1975), *Season Songs* (1976), *Gaudete* (1977), *Moortown* (1979), *Wolfwatching* (1989), *Birthday Letters* (1998).

Jennings, Elizabeth (Joan) (1926–2001) English, born Boston, Lincolnshire; *Poems* (1953), *The Mind Has Mountains* (1966), *The Animals' Arrival* (1969), *Relationships* (1972), *Praises* (1998).

Johnson, Samuel (1709–84) English, born Lichfield, Staffordshire; *The Vanity of Human Wishes* (1749).

Kavanagh, Patrick (1905–67) Irish, born Inniskeen; *Ploughman and Other Poems* (1936), *The Great Hunger* (1942).

Keats, John (1795–1821) English, born London; *Endymion* (1818), *Lamia and Other Poems* (1820).

Keyes, Sidney (Arthur Kilworth) (1922–43) English, born Dartford, Kent; *The Iron Laurel* (1942), *The Cruel Solstice* (1943).

La Fontaine, Jean de (1621–95) French, born Chateau-Thierry, Champagne; *Contes et nouvelles en vers* (1665), *Fables choisies mises en vers* (1668).

Langland or **Langley, William** (c.1332–c.1400) English, birthplace uncertain, possibly Ledbury, Herefordshire; *Piers Plowman* (1362–99).

Larkin, Philip (Arthur) (1922–85) English, born Coventry; *The North Ship* (1945), *The Whitsun Weddings* (1964), *High Windows* (1974).

Lear, Edward (1812–88) English, born London; *Book of Nonsense* (1846).

Longfellow, Henry (Wadsworth) (1807–82) American, born Portland, Maine; *Voices of the Night* (1839), *Ballads and Other Poems* (1842), *Hiawatha* (1855).

Lowell, Amy (Laurence) (1874–1925) American, born Brookline, Massachusetts; *A Dome of Many-Colored Glass* (1912), *Legends* (1921).

Lowell, Robert (Traill Spence, Jr) (1917–77) American, born Boston, Massachusetts; *Lord Weary's Castle* (1946), *Life Studies* (1959), *Prometheus Bound* (1967).

Macaulay, Thomas (Babington) (1800–59) English, born Rothey Temple, Leicestershire; *The Lays of Ancient Rome* (1842).

MacCaig, Norman (Alexander) (1910–96) Scottish, born Edinburgh; *Far Cry* (1943), *Riding Lights* (1955), *A Round of Applause* (1962), *A Man in My Position* (1969), *Voice-Over* (1988).

MacDiarmid, Hugh (pseudonym of **Christopher Murray Grieve**) (1892–1978) Scottish, born Langholm, Dumfriesshire; *A Drunk Man Looks at the Thistle* (1926).

McGough, Roger (1937–) English, born Liverpool; *The Mersey Sound: Penguin Modern Poets 10* (with Adrian Henri and Brian Patten) (1967), *Gig* (1973), *Waving at Trains* (1982), *An Imaginary Menagerie* (1988), *The Spotted Unicorn* (1998), *The Way Things Are* (1999).

MacLean, Sorley (Gaelic **Somhairle Macgill-Eain**) (1911–96) Scottish, born Isle of Raasay, off Skye; *Reothairt is Contraigh* (Spring Tide and Neap Tide) (1977).

MacNeice, (Frederick) Louis (1907–63) Irish, born Belfast; *Blind Fireworks* (1929), *Solstices* (1961).

Mallarmé, Stéphane (1842–98) French, born Paris; *L'Après-midi d'un faune* (1876), *Poésies* (1899).

Marvell, Andrew (1621–78) English, born Winestead, near Hull; *Miscellaneous Poems by Andrew Marvell, Esq.* (1681).

Masefield, John (Edward) (1878–1967) English, born Ledbury, Herefordshire; *Salt-Water Ballads* (1902).

Millay, Edna St Vincent (1892–1950) American, born Rockland, Maine; *A Few Figs from Thistles* (1920), *The Ballad of Harp-Weaver* (1922).

Milton, John (1608–74) English, born London; *Lycidas* (1637), *Paradise Lost* (1667), *Samson Agonistes* (1671).

Moore, Marianne (Craig) (1887–1972) American, born Kirkwood, Missouri; *The Pangolin and Other Verse* (1936).

Motion, Andrew (1952–) English, born London; *The Pleasure Steamers* (1978), *Love in a Life* (1991), *Salt Water* (1997), *Public Property* (2002).

Muir, Edwin (1887–1959) Scottish, born Deerness, Orkney; *First Poems* (1925), *Chorus of the Newly Dead* (1926), *Variations on a Time Theme* (1934), *The Labyrinth* (1949), *New Poems* (1949–51).

Nash, (Frederick) Ogden (1902–71) American, born Rye, New York; *Free Wheeling* (1931).

Ovid (in full **Publius Ovidius Naso**) (43BC–c.17AD) Roman, born Sulmo; *Amores* (c.16BC), *Metamorphoses*, *Ars Amatoria*.

Owen, Wilfred (Edward Salter) (1893–1918) English, born Oswestry, Shropshire; most poems published posthumously, 1920, by Siegfried Sassoon; *'Dulce et decorum est'*.

Patten, Brian (1946–) English, born Liverpool; *Penguin Modern Poets 10* (1967), *Notes to the Hurrying Man* (1969), *Grinning Jack* (1990), *Armada* (1996), *The Blue and Green Ark* (1999).

Paz, Octavio (1914–98) Mexican, born Mexico City; *Sun Stone* (1963), *The Bow and the Lyre* (1973), *Col-*

Arts and Culture

lected Poems 1957–87 (1987), Glimpses of India (1995); Nobel Prize for Literature 1990.

Petrarch (in full **Francesco Petrarca**) (1304–74) Italian, born Arezzo; Canzoniere.

Plath, Sylvia (1932–63) American, born Boston, Massachusetts; The Colossus and Other Poems (1960), Ariel (1965), Crossing the Water (1971), Winter Trees (1972).

Pope, Alexander (1688–1744) English, born London; An Essay on Criticism (1711), The Rape of the Lock (1712), The Dunciad (1728–42), Essay on Man (1733–4).

Porter, Peter (Neville Frederick) (1929–) Australian, born Brisbane; Poems, Ancient and Modern (1964), English Subtitles (1981), The Automatic Oracle (1987), Millennial Fables (1994), Max is Missing (2001).

Pound, Ezra (Weston Loomis) (1885–1972) American, born Haile, Idaho; The Cantos (1917, 1948, 1959).

Pushkin, Aleksandr (Sergeyevich) (1799–1837) Russian, born Moscow; Eugene Onegin (1828), Ruslam and Lyudmilla (1820).

Raine, Kathleen (Jessie) (1908–) English, born London; Stone and Flower (1943), The Hollow Hill (1965), Living with Mystery (1992).

Rich, Adrienne (Cecile) (1929–) American, born Baltimore, Maryland; The Diamond Cutters and Other Poems (1955), Snapshots of a Daughter-in-Law (1963), The Will to Change (1971), Dark Fields of the Republic (1995), Fox (2001).

Riding, Laura (née **Reichenfeld**) (1901–91) American, born New York; The Close Chaplet (1926).

Rilke, Rainer Maria (1875–1926) Austrian, born Prague; Die Sonnette an Orpheus (1923).

Rimbaud, (Jean Nicholas) Arthur (1854–91) French, born Charleville, Ardennes; Le Bateau ivre (1871), Les Illuminations (1886).

Rochester, John Wilmot, Earl of (1647–80) English, born Ditchley, Oxfordshire; A Satyre Against Mankind (1675).

Roethke, Theodore Huebner (1908–63) American, born Saginaw, Michigan; Open House (1941), The Lost Son and Other Poems (1948).

Rosenberg, Isaac (1890–1918) English, born Bristol; Night and Day (1912), Youth (1915), Poems (1922).

Saint-John Perse (pseudonym of **Marie René Auguste Alexis Saint-Léger Léger**) (1887–1975) French, born St Léger des Feuilles; Anabase (1924), Exil (1942), Chroniques (1960); Nobel Prize for Literature 1960.

Sassoon, Siegfried (Lorraine) (1886–1967) English, born Brenchley, Kent; Counter-Attack and Other Poems (1917), The Road to Ruin (1933).

Schwarz, Delmore (1913–66) American, born New York City; In Dreams Begin Responsibilities (1938), Vaudeville for a Princess and Other Poems (1950).

Seifert, Jaroslav (1901–86) Czech, born Prague; City of Tears (1921), All Love (1923), A Helmet of Earth (1945); Nobel Prize for Literature 1984.

Shelley, Percy Bysshe (1792–1822) English, born Field Place, Horsham, Sussex; Alastor (1816), The Revolt of Islam (1818), Julian and Maddalo (1818), The Triumph of Life (1822).

Sidney, Sir Philip (1554–86) English, born Penshurst, Kent; Arcadia (1580), Astrophel and Stella (1591).

Sitwell, Dame Edith (Louisa) (1887–1964) English, born Scarborough; Façade (1922), Colonel Fantock (1926).

Smart, Christopher (1722–71) English, born Shipbourne, Kent; Jubilate Agno (first published 1939).

Smith, Stevie (pseudonym of **Florence Margaret**

Smith) (1902–71) English, born Hull; Not Waving but Drowning: Poems (1957).

Spender, Sir Stephen (Harold) (1909–95) English, born London; Poems (1933).

Spenser, Edmund (1552–99) English, born London; The Shepheardes Calender (1579), The Faerie Queene (1590, 1596).

Stevens, Wallace (1879–1955) American, born Reading, Pennsylvania; Harmonium (1923), Transport to Summer (1947).

Swinburne, Algernon Charles (1837–1909) English, born London; Poems and Ballads (1866), Songs before Sunrise (1871), Tristram of Lyonesse (1882).

Szymborska, Wislawa (1923–) Polish, born Kórnik; A Great Number (1976), People on a Bridge (1986), View with a Grain of Sand (1996), Poems New and Collected 1957–1997 (1998); Nobel Prize for Literature 1996.

Tennyson, Alfred, Lord (1809–92) English, born Somersby Rectory, Lincolnshire; Poems (1832) (eg 'The Lotus-Eaters' and 'The Lady of Shalott'), The Princess (1847), In Memoriam (1850), Idylls of the King (1859), Maud (1856).

Thomas, Dylan (Marlais) (1914–53) Welsh, born Swansea; Twenty-five Poems (1936), Deaths and Entrances (1946), In Country Sleep and Other Poems (1952).

Thomas, (Philip) Edward (1878–1917) English, born London; Six Poems (1916), Last Poems (1918).

Thomas, R(onald) S(tuart) (1913–2000) Welsh, born Cardiff; Stones of the Field (1947), Song at the Year's Turning (1955), The Bread of Truth (1963), Between Here and Now (1981), Counterpoint (1990), No Truce with the Furies (1995).

Thomson, James (1700–48) Scottish, born Ednam, Roxburghshire; The Seasons (1730), The Castle of Indolence (1748).

Verlaine, Paul (1844–96) French, born Metz; Fêtes galantes (1869), Sagesse (1881).

Virgil, Publius Vergilius Maro (70–19BC) Roman, born near Mantua; Eclogues (37BC), Georgics (29BC), The Aeneid (19BC).

Walcott, Derek Alton (1930–) West Indian, born St Lucia; Castaway (1965), Fortunate Traveller (1981), Selected Poetry (1993), The Bounty (1997); Nobel Prize for Literature 1992.

Webb, Francis Charles (1925–73) Australian, born Adelaide; A Drum for Ben Boyd (1948), The Ghost of the Cock (1964).

Whitman, Walt (1819–92) American, born West Hills, Long Island, New York; Leaves of Grass (1855–89).

Wordsworth, William (1770–1850) English, born Cockermouth; Lyrical Ballads (with S T Coleridge, 1798), The Prelude (1799, 1805, 1850), The Excursion (1814).

Wright, Judith (Arundell) (1915–2000) Australian, born Armidale, New South Wales; The Moving Image (1946), Birds (1962), Alive (1973), The Cry for the Dead (1981), Collected Poems 1942–1985 (1994).

Wyatt, Sir Thomas (1503–42) English, born Allington Castle, Kent; poems first published in Tottel's Miscellany (1557).

Yeats, W(illiam) B(utler) (1865–1939) Irish, born Sandymount, County Dublin; The Wanderings of Oisin and Other Poems (1889), The Wind Among the Reeds (1894), The Wild Swans at Coole (1917), Michael Robartes and the Dancer (1921), The Winding Stair and Other Poems (1933); Nobel Prize for Literature 1923.

Poets laureate

1617	Ben Jonson[1]	1813	Robert Southey
1638	Sir William Davenant[1]	1843	William Wordsworth
1668	John Dryden	1850	Alfred, Lord Tennyson
1689	Thomas Shadwell	1896	Alfred Austin
1692	Nahum Tate	1913	Robert Bridges
1715	Nicholas Rowe	1930	John Masefield
1718	Laurence Eusden	1968	Cecil Day-Lewis
1730	Colley Cibber	1972	Sir John Betjeman
1757	William Whitehead	1984	Ted Hughes
1785	Thomas Warton	1999	Andrew Motion
1790	Henry Pye		

[1] The post was not officially established until 1668.

Playwrights

Selected plays are listed.

Aeschylus (c.525–c.456BC) Athenian; *The Oresteia trilogy (Agamemnon, Choephoroe, Eumenides)* (458BC), *Prometheus Bound, Seven Against Thebes.*

Albee, Edward Franklin, III (1928–) American, born Washington, DC; *The American Dream* (1960), *Who's Afraid of Virginia Woolf?* (1962), *A Delicate Balance* (1966, Pulitzer Prize), *Seascape* (1974), *Three Tall Women* (1991, Pulitzer Prize 1994), *Fragments* (1993).

Anouilh, Jean (1910–87) French, born Bordeaux; *Antigone* (1944), *Médée* (1946), *L'Alouette* (1953), *Beckett, or the Honour of God* (1960).

Aristophanes (c.448—c.385BC) Athenian; *The Acharnians* (425BC), *The Knights* (424BC), *The Clouds* (423BC), *The Wasps* (422BC), The Birds (414BC), *Lysistrata* (411BC), *The Frogs* (405BC).

Ayckbourn, Sir Alan (1939–) English, born London; *Absurd Person Singular* (1973), *Absent Friends* (1975), *Joking Apart* (1979), *Way Upstream* (1982), *Woman in Mind* (1985), *Henceforward* (1987), *Man of the Moment* (1988), *Wildest Dreams* (1991), *Communicating Doors* (1994), *The Champion of Paribanou* (1996), *The Boy Who Fell Into a Book* (1998).

Beaumont, Sir Francis (1584–1616) English, born Grace-Dieu, Leicestershire, and **John Fletcher**; *Philaster* (1609), *The Maid's Tragedy* (1610).

Beckett, Samuel (Barclay) (1906–89) Irish, born Foxrock, near Dublin; *Waiting for Godot* (1955), *Endgame* (1958), *Krapp's Last Tape* (1958), *Happy Days* (1961), *Not I* (1973); Nobel Prize for Literature 1969.

Behan, Brendan (Francis) (1923–64) Irish, born Dublin; *The Quare Fellow* (1956), *The Hostage* (1958).

Bond, (Thomas) Edward (1934–) English, born North London; *Early Morning* (1969), *Lear* (1971), *Summer* (1982), *The War Plays* (1985), *Olly's Prison* (1992), *Coffee: a tragedy* (1995), *Eleven Vests* (1997), *The Crime of the 21st Century* (2001).

Brecht, (Eugen) Bertolt (Friedrich) (1898–1956) German, born Augsburg; *Galileo* (1938–9), *Mutter Courage and ihre Kinder* (Mother Courage and Her Children) (1941), *Der Gute Mensch von Setzuan* (The Good Woman of Setzuan) (1943), *Der Kaukasische Kreidekreis* (The Caucasian Chalk Circle) (1949).

Brieux, Eugène (1858–1932) French, born Paris; *Les Trois Filles de M Dupont* (1897), *The Red Robe* (1900).

Chapman, George (c.1559–1634) English, born near Hitchin, Hertfordshire; *Bussy D'Ambois* (1607).

Chekhov, Anton Pavlovich (1860–1904) Russian, born Taganrog; *The Seagull* (1895), *Uncle Vanya* (1900), *Three Sisters* (1901), *The Cherry Orchard* (1904).

Congreve, William (1670–1729) English, born Bardsey, near Leeds; *Love for Love* (1695), *The Way of the World* (1700).

Corneille, Pierre (1606–84) French, born Rouen; *Le Cid* (1636), *Horace* (1639), *Polyeucte* (1640).

Coward, Sir Noël Peirce (1899–1973) English, born Teddington, Middlesex; *Hay Fever* (1925), *Private Lives* (1933), *Blithe Spirit* (1941).

Dekker, Thomas (c.1570–1632) English, born London; *The Whore of Babylon* (1606).

Dryden, John (1631–1700) English, born Aldwinkle; *The Indian Queen* (1664), *Marriage à la Mode* (1672), *All for Love* (1678), *Amphitryon* (1690).

Eliot, T(homas) S(tearns) (1888–1965) American, naturalized British, born St Louis, Missouri; *Murder in the Cathedral* (1935), *The Family Reunion* (1939), *The Cocktail Party* (1950).

Esson, (Thomas) Louis (Buvelot) (1879–1943) Australian, born Edinburgh; *The Drovers* (1920), *Andeganora* (1937).

Euripides (c.480–406BC) Athenian; *Medea* (431BC), *Electra* (413BC), *The Bacchae* (407BC).

Fletcher, John (1579–1625) English, born Rye, Sussex, *The Faithful Shepherdess* (1610), *A Wife for a Month* (1624).

Fo, Dario (1926–) Italian, born Lombardy; *Accidental Death of an Anarchist* (1970), *Can't Pay! Won't Pay!* (1974), *The Pope and the Witch* (1989), *The Tricks of the Trade* (1991), *The Devil in Drag* (1997); Nobel Prize for Literature 1997.

Ford, John (1586–c.1640) English, born Devon; *'Tis Pity She's a Whore* (1633), *Perkin Warbeck* (1634).

Galsworthy, John (1867–1933) English, born Coombe, Surrey; *Strife* (1909), *Justice* (1910); Nobel Prize for Literature 1932.

Genet, Jean (1910–86) French, born Paris; *The Maids* (1948), *The Balcony* (1956), *The Screens* (1961).

Giraudoux, (Hippolyte) Jean (1882–1944) French, born Bellac; *Judith* (1931), *Ondine* (1939).

Goethe, Johann Wolfgang von (1749–1832) German, born Frankfurt am Main; *Faust* (1808, 1832).

Gogol, Nikolai (Vasilievich) (1809–52) Russian, born Ukraine; *The Inspector General* (1836).

Goldsmith, Oliver (1728–74) Irish, born Pallas, County Longford; *She Stoops to Conquer* (1773).

Greene, Robert (1558–92) English, born Norwich; *Orlando Furioso* (1594), *James the Fourth* (1598).

Arts and Culture

Arts and Culture

Hare, David (1947–) English, born London; *Slag* (1970), *Plenty* (1978), *Pravda* (1985, with Howard Brenton), *The Secret Rapture* (1988), *Amy's View* (1997), *The Breath of Life* (2002).

Hauptmann, Gerhart Johann Robert (1862–1946) German, born Obersalzbrunn, Silesia; *Before Sunrise* (1889), *The Weavers* (1892); Nobel Prize for Literature 1912.

Hayes, Alfred (1911–85) American, born England; *The Girl on the Via Flaminia* (1954).

Hebbel, (Christian) Friedrich (1813–63) German, born Wesselburen, Dithmarschen; *Judith* (1841), *Maria Magdalena* (1844).

Hewett, Dorothy (Coade) (1923–2002) Australian, born Wickepin, West Australia; *The Chapel Perilous* (1972), *This Old Man Comes Rolling Home* (1976), *Golden Valley* (1984), *Nowhere* (2001).

Heywood, Thomas (c.1574–1641) English, born Lincolnshire; *A Woman Killed with Kindness* (1603), *The Fair Maid of the West* (1631), *The English Traveller* (1633).

Hibberd, Jack (1940–) Australian, born Warracknabeal, Victoria; *Dimboola* (1969), *White with Wire Wheels* (1970), *A Stretch of the Imagination* (1973), *Squibs* (1984), *The Prodigal Son* (1997).

Howard, Sidney (Coe) (1891–1939) American, born Oakland, California; *They Knew What They Wanted* (1924), *The Silver Cord* (1926).

Ibsen, Henrik (1828–1906) Norwegian, born Skien; *Peer Gynt* (1867), *A Doll's House* (1879), *The Pillars of Society* (1880), *The Wild Duck* (1884), *Hedda Gabler* (1890), *The Master Builder* (1892).

Inge, William Motter (1913–73) American, born Kansas; *Picnic* (1953), *Where's Daddy?* (1966).

Ionesco, Eugène (1912–94) French, born Romania; *The Bald Prima Donna* (1948), *The Picture* (1958), *Le Rhinocéros* (1960).

Jonson, Ben(jamin) (c.1572–1637) English, born Westminster, London; *Every Man in His Humour* (1598), *Sejanus* (1603), *Volpone* (1606), *The Alchemist* (1610), *Bartholomew Fair* (1614).

Kaiser, Georg (1878–1945) German, born Magdeburg; *The Burghers of Calais* (1914), *Gas* (1920).

Kushner, Tony (1956–) American, born New York City; *Yes, Yes, No, No* (1985), *Angels in America* (1992, Pulitzer Prize 1993), *Slavs!* (1995), *Henry Box Brown* (1997), *Homebody/Kabul* (2001).

Kyd, Thomas (1558–94) English, born London; *The Spanish Tragedy* (1587).

Lawler, Ray(mond Evenor) (1922–) Australian, born Melbourne; *The Summer of the Seventeenth Doll* (1955), *The Man Who Shot the Albatross* (1970), *Kid Stakes* (1975), *Other Times* (1976), *Godsend* (1982).

Lorca, Federico García (1899–1936) Spanish, born Fuente Vaqueros; *Blood Wedding* (1933), *The House of Bernarda Alba* (1945).

Maeterlinck, Maurice, Count (1862–1949) Belgian, born Ghent; *La Princesse Maleine* (1889), *Pélleas et Mélisande* (1892), *The Blue Bird* (1909).

Mamet, David Alan (1947–) American, born Chicago; *Sexual Perversity in Chicago* (1974), *Duck Variations* (1974), *American Buffalo* (1975), *Edmond* (1982), *Glengarry Glen Ross* (1984, Pulitzer Prize), *Oleanna* (1992), *Death Defying Acts* (1996), *Wag the Dog* (screenplay) (1997).

Marlowe, Christopher (1564–93) English, born Canterbury; *Tamburlaine the Great* (in two parts, 1587), *Dr Faustus* (1588), *The Jew of Malta* (c.1589), *Edward II* (1592).

Marston, John (1576–1634) English, born Wardington, Oxfordshire; *Antonio's Revenge* (1602), *The Malcontent* (1604).

Miller, Arthur (1915–) American, born New York City; *All My Sons* (1947), *Death of a Salesman* (1949), *The Crucible* (1952), *A View from the Bridge* (1955), *The Misfits* (1961), *After the Fall* (1964), *The Creation of the World and Other Business* (1972), *Playing for Time* (1981), *Danger: Memory!* (1987), *The Ride Down Mount Morgan* (1991), *The Last Yankee* (1992), *Broken Glass* (1994), *Homely Girl* (1995), *Mr Peter's Connections* (1998).

Molière (pseudonym of **Jean-Baptiste Poquelin**) (1622–73) French, born Paris; *Le Bourgeois Gentilhomme* (The Bourgeois Gentleman) (1660), *Tartuffe* (1664), *Le Misanthrope* (The Misanthropist) (1666), *Le Malade Imaginaire* (The Hypochondriac) (1673).

Oakley, Barry (1931–) Australian, born Melbourne; *The Feet of Daniel Mannix* (1975), *Bedfellows* (1975).

O'Casey, Sean (originally **John Casey**) (1880–1964) Irish, born Dublin; *Juno and the Paycock* (1924), *The Plough and the Stars* (1926).

O'Neill, Eugene Gladstone (1888–1953) American, born New York City; *Beyond the Horizon* (1920), *Desire under the Elms* (1924), *Mourning Becomes Electra* (1931), *Long Day's Journey into Night* (1941), *The Iceman Cometh* (1946); Nobel Prize for Literature 1936.

Orton, Joe (John Kingsley) (1933–67) English, born Leicester; *Entertaining Mr Sloane* (1964), *Loot* (1965), *What the Butler Saw* (1969).

Osborne, John (James) (1929–94) Welsh, born Fulham, London; *Look Back in Anger* (1956), *The Entertainer* (1957), *Inadmissible Evidence* (1965), *The Hotel in Amsterdam* (1968), *West of Suez* (1971), *Almost a Vision* (1976), *Déja Vu* (1989).

Otway, Thomas (1652–85) English, born Milland, Sussex; *Don Carlos* (1676), *The Orphan* (1680), *Venice Preserv'd* (1682).

Patrick, John (1905–95) American, born Louisville, Kentucky; *The Teahouse of the August Moon* (1953).

Pinter, Harold (1930–) English, born East London; *The Birthday Party* (1958), *The Caretaker* (1960), *The Homecoming* (1965), *Landscape* (1967), *Old Times* (1970), *No Man's Land* (1974), *Betrayal* (1978), *A Kind of Alaska* (1982), *One for the Road* (1984), *Party Time* (1991), *Ashes to Ashes* (1996), *Celebration* (1999), *Remembrance of Things Past* (2000).

Pirandello, Luigi (1867–1936) Italian, born near Agrigento, Sicily; *Six Characters in Search of an Author* (1921), *Henry IV* (1922); Nobel Prize for Literature 1934.

Plautus, Titus Maccius (c.250–184BC) Roman; *Menachmi, Miles Gloriosus.*

Porter, Hal (1911–84) Australian, born Melbourne; *The Tower* (1963), *The Professor* (1966), *Eden House* (1969).

Potter, Dennis (Christopher George) (1935–94) English, born Forest of Dean; *Vote, Vote, Vote for Nigel Barton* (1965), *Pennies from Heaven* (1978), *The Singing Detective* (1986), *Lipstick on Your Collar* (1993), *Karaoke* (1994).

Racine, Jean (1639–99) French, born near Soissons; *Andromaque* (1667), *Phèdre* (1677), *Bajazet* (1672), *Esther* (1689).

Rattigan, Sir Terence (1911–77) English, born London; *French without Tears* (1936), *The Winslow Boy* (1946), *The Browning Version* (1948), *Separate Tables* (1954).

Romeril, John (1945–) Australian, born Melbourne; *Chicago, Chicago* (1970), *I Don't Know Who to Feel*

Sorry For (1973), *The Kelly Dance* (1986), *Love Suicides* (1997).

Russell, Willy (William) (1947–) English, born Whiston, Merseyside; *Educating Rita* (1979), *Blood Brothers* (1983), *Shirley Valentine* (1986).

Sackville, Thomas (1553–1608) English, born Buckhurst, Sussex; *Gorboduc* (1592).

Sartre, Jean-Paul (1905–80) French, born Paris; *The Flies* (1943), *Huis Clos* (1945), *The Condemned of Altona* (1961).

Schiller, Johann Christoph Friedrich von (1759–1805) German, born Marbach; *The Robbers* (1781), *Wallenstein* (1799), *Maria Stuart* (1800).

Seneca, Lucius Annaeus (c.4BC–AD65) Roman, born Cordoba; *Hercules, Medea, Thyestes.*

Seymour, Alan (1927–) Australian, born Perth; *The One Day of the Year* (1962), *Swamp Creatures* (1958), *Danny Johnson* (1960).

Shaffer, Sir Peter (Levin) (1926–) English, born Liverpool; *The Royal Hunt of the Sun* (1964), *Equus* (1973), *Amadeus* (1979), *Yonadab* (1985), *The Gift of the Gorgon* (1992).

Shakespeare, William ▸ Plays of Shakespeare below

Shaw, George Bernard (1856–1950) Irish, born Dublin; *Arms and the Man* (1894), *Man and Superman* (1903), *Pygmalion* (1913), *Saint Joan* (1924); Nobel Prize for Literature 1925.

Shepard, Sam (originally **Samuel Shepard Rogers**) (1943–) American, born Fort Sheridan, Illinois; *La Turista* (1967), *The Tooth of Crime* (1972), *Buried Child* (1978), *True West* (1979), *Fool for Love* (1983), *A Lie of the Mind* (1985), *Simpatico* (1993), *Eyes for Consuela* (1998).

Sheridan, Richard Brinsley (1751–1816) Irish, born Dublin; *The Rivals* (1775), *The School for Scandal* (1777), *The Critic* (1779).

Sherwood, Robert (Emmet) (1896–1955) American, born New Rochelle, New York; *Idiot's Delight* (1936), *Abe Lincoln in Illinois* (1938), *There Shall Be No Night* (1940).

Sophocles (496–406BC) Athenian, born Colonus; *Antigone, Oedipus Rex, Oedipus at Colonus.*

Soyinka, Wole (in full **Akinwande Oluwole Soyinka**) (1934–) Nigerian, born Abeokuta, West Nigeria; *The Swamp Dwellers* (1958), *The Strong Breed* (1962), *The Road* (1964), *The Bacchae of Euripides* (1973), *Opera Wonyosi* (1978), *From Zia, with Love* (1991), *The Beatification of Area Boy* (1995), *King Baabu* (2001); Nobel Prize for Literature 1986.

Stoppard, Sir Tom (Thomas Straussler) (1937–) English, born Czechoslovakia (now Czech Republic); *Rosencrantz and Guildenstern are Dead* (1966), *The Real Inspector Hound* (1968), *Travesties* (1974), *New-Found-Land* (1976), *Undiscovered Country* (1980), *Rough Crossing* (1984), *Arcadia* (1993), *Indian Ink* (1995), *Shakespeare in Love* (screenplay) (1998).

Strindberg, (Johan) August (1849–1912) Swedish, born Stockholm; *Master Olof* (1877), *Miss Julie* (1888), *The Dance of Death* (1901).

Synge, (Edmund) J(ohn) M(illington) (1871–1909) Irish, born near Dublin; *The Well of Saints* (1905), *The Playboy of the Western World* (1907).

Webster, John (c.1578–c.1632) English, born London; *The White Devil* (1612), *The Duchess of Malfi* (1614).

Wesker, Arnold (1932–) English, born London; *Chicken Soup with Barley/Roots/I'm Talking about Jerusalem* (trilogy) (1959–60), *The Kitchen* (1959), *Chips with Everything* (1962), *The Friends* (1970), *Tokyo* (1994), *Denial* (1997).

Wilde, Oscar (Fingal O'Flahertie Wills) (1854–1900) Irish, born Dublin; *Lady Windermere's Fan* (1892), *The Importance of Being Earnest* (1895).

Wilder, Thornton (Niven) (1897–1975) American, born Wisconsin; *Our Town* (1938), *The Merchant of Yonkers* (1938), *The Skin of Our Teeth* (1942), *The Matchmaker* (1954, later a musical *Hello, Dolly!*, 1964).

Williams, Tennessee (originally **Thomas Lanier Williams**) (1911–83) American, born Mississippi; *The Glass Menagerie* (1944), *A Streetcar Named Desire* (1947), *Cat on a Hot Tin Roof* (1955), *Sweet Bird of Youth* (1959).

Williamson, David Keith (1942–) Australian, born Melbourne; *The Removalists* (1971), *The Club* (1977), *The Perfectionist* (1981), *Sons of Cain* (1985), *Money & Friends* (1991), *Up For Grabs* (2000).

Wycherly, William (1641–1715) English, born Clive, near Shrewsbury; *The Gentleman Dancing-Master* (1672), *The Country Wife* (1675).

Plays of Shakespeare

William Shakespeare (1564–1616), English playwright and poet, born Stratford-upon-Avon.

Title	Date	Category	Title	Date	Category
The Two Gentlemen of Verona	1590–1	comedy	As You Like It	1599–1600	comedy
Henry VI Part One	1592	history			
Henry VI Part Two	1592	history	Hamlet, Prince of Denmark	1600–1	tragedy
Henry VI Part Three	1592	history	Twelfth Night, or What You Will	1601	comedy
Titus Andronicus	1592	tragedy	Troilus and Cressida	1602	tragedy
Richard III	1592–3	history	Measure for Measure	1603	dark comedy
The Taming of the Shrew	1593	comedy			
The Comedy of Errors	1594	comedy	Othello	1603–4	tragedy
Love's Labour's Lost	1594–5	comedy	All's Well That Ends Well	1604–5	dark comedy
Richard II	1595	history			
Romeo and Juliet	1595	tragedy	Timon of Athens	1605	romantic drama
A Midsummer Night's Dream	1595	comedy			
King John	1596	history	The Tragedy of King Lear	1605–6	tragedy
The Merchant of Venice	1596–7	comedy	Macbeth	1606	tragedy
Henry IV Part One	1596–7	history	Antony and Cleopatra	1606	tragedy
The Merry Wives of Windsor	1597–8	comedy	Pericles	1607	romance
Henry IV Part Two	1597–8	history	Coriolanus	1608	tragedy
Much Ado About Nothing	1598	dark comedy	The Winter's Tale	1609	romance
			Cymbeline	1610	comedy
Henry V	1598–9	history	The Tempest	1611	comedy
Julius Caesar	1599	tragedy	Henry VIII	1613	history

Film and TV actors

Selected films and television productions are listed. Original and full names of actors are given in parentheses.

Arts and Culture

Adams, Brooke (1949–) American, born New York City; *Invasion of the Body Snatchers* (1978), *A Man, a Woman, and a Bank* (1980), *Dead Zone* (1983), *Lace* (TV 1984), *Lace 2* (TV 1985), *Moonlighting* (TV 1987), *The Babysitter's Club* (1995).

Adjani, Isabelle (1955–) French, born Paris; *The Story of Adele H* (1975), *Nosferatu* (1978), *Possession* (1980), *Quartet* (1981), *One Deadly Summer* (1983), *Subway* (1985), *Ishtar* (1987), *Camille Claudel* (1988), *La Reine Margot* (1992), *Diabolique* (1996).

Agutter, Jenny (1952–) British, born Taunton; *The Railway Children* (1970), *Walkabout* (1971), *Logan's Run* (1976), *The Eagle Has Landed* (1977), *Equus* (1977), *The Man in the Iron Mask* (1977), *An American Werewolf in London* (1981), *Silas Marner* (TV 1985), *Child's Play 2* (1990), *Blue Juice* (1995).

Aiello, Danny (1935–) American, born New York City; *Fort Apache The Bronx* (1981), *Once Upon a Time in America* (1984), *The Purple Rose of Cairo* (1984), *Moonstruck* (1987), *Do the Right Thing* (1988), *Harlem Nights* (1989), *Leon* (1994), *Dinner Rush* (2000).

Aimée, Anouk (Françoise Sorya) (1934–) French, born Paris; *Les Amants de Verone* (1949), *La Dolce Vita* (1960), *Lola* (1961), *Un Homme et une Femme* (1966), *Justine* (1969), *Flagrant Desire* (1985), *Scar* (1994), *Prêt-À-Porter* (1994), *Une pour toutes* (1999).

Albert, Eddie (Eddie Albert Heimberger) (1908–) American, born Rock Island, Illinois; *Brother Rat* (1938), *Four Wives* (1939), *Smash Up* (1947), *Carrie* (1952), *Roman Holiday* (1953), *Oklahoma!* (1955), *I'll Cry Tomorrow* (1955), *Attack!* (1956), *The Roots of Heaven* (1958), *Orders to Kill* (1958), *The Miracle of the White Stallions* (1962), *Green Acres* (TV 1965–70), *The Longest Yard* (1974), *Escape to Witch Mountain* (1975), *Switch* (TV 1975–6), *Yes, Giorgio* (1982), *Dreamscape* (1984), *Deadly Illusion* (1987), *The Big Picture* (1989).

Alda, Alan (1936–) American, born New York City; *Paper Lion* (1968), *Catch-22* (1970), *M*A*S*H* (TV 1972–83), *California Suite* (1978), *Same Time Next Year* (1978), *The Four Seasons* (1981), *Sweet Liberty* (1986), *A New Life* (1988), *Crimes and Misdemeanors* (1989), *Betsy's Wedding* (1990), *Manhattan Murder Mystery* (1993), *Mad City* (1997), *What Women Want* (2000).

Allen, Karen (1951–) American, born Carrollton, Illinois; *Animal House* (1978), *The Wanderers* (1979), *East of Eden* (TV 1980), *Raiders of the Lost Ark* (1981), *Shoot the Moon* (1981), *Starman* (1984), *The Glass Menagerie* (1987), *Scrooged* (1988), *Secret Weapon* (TV, 1990), *Sweet Talker* (1991), *Malcolm X* (1992), *The Turner* (1994), *Falling Sky* (1998), *The Perfect Storm* (2000).

Allen, Nancy (1950–) American, born New York City; *Carrie* (1976), *I Wanna Hold Your Hand* (1978), *1941* (1979), *Dressed to Kill* (1980), *Blow Out* (1981), *The Philadelphia Experiment* (1984), *The Gladiator* (TV 1986), *Robocop* (1987), *Poltergeist III* (1988), *Robocop 2* (1990), *Robocop 3* (1994), *Les Patriotes* (1994), *Out of Sight* (1998).

Allen, Woody (Allen Stewart Konigsberg) (1935–) American, born Brooklyn, New York City; *What's New, Pussycat?* (1965), *Casino Royale* (1967), *Bananas* (1971), *Play it Again Sam* (1972), *Sleeper* (1973), *Annie Hall* (1977), *Manhattan* (1979), *Hannah and Her Sisters* (1986), *New York Stories* (1989), *Crimes and Misdemeanors* (1989), *Shadows and Fog* (1992), *Husbands and Wives* (1992), *Manhattan Murder Mystery* (1993), *Mighty Aphrodite* (1995), *Anna Oz* (1996), *Deconstructing Harry* (1997), *The Curse of the Jade Scorpion* (2001).

Alley, Kirstie (1955–) American, born Wichita, Kansas; *Star Trek II: The Wrath of Khan* (1982), *Blind Date* (1983), *Champions* (1983), *Runaway* (1984), *North and South* (TV 1986), *Summer School* (1987), *Cheers* (TV 1987–93), *Shoot to Kill* (1988), *Look Who's Talking* (1989), *Madhouse* (1990), *Loverboy* (1990), *Sibling Rivalry* (1990), *Look Who's Talking Too* (1991), *Look Who's Talking Now* (1993), *It Takes Two* (1995), *Drop Dead Gorgeous* (1999).

Allyson, June (Ella Geisman) (1917–) American, born Westchester, New York; *Two Girls and a Sailor* (1944), *Music for Millions* (1944), *Little Women* (1949), *The Glen Miller Story* (1954), *The Shrike* (1955), *The June Allyson Show* (TV 1959–61).

Ameche, Don (Dominic Felix Amici) (1908–93) American, born Kenosha, Wisconsin; *Ramona* (1936), *In Old Chicago* (1938), *The Three Musketeers* (1939), *Midnight* (1939), *The Story of Alexander Graham Bell* (1939), *Swanee River* (1939), *Four Sons* (1940), *Down Argentine Way* (1940), *That Night in Rio* (1941), *Heaven Can Wait* (1943), *Happy Land* (1943), *Trading Places* (1983), *Cocoon* (1985), *Coming to America* (1988), *Things Change* (1988), *Cocoon: The Return* (1988), *Oscar* (1991), *Corrina, Corrina* (1994).

Anderson, Dame Judith (Frances Margaret Anderson) (1898–1992) Australian, born Adelaide; *Rebecca* (1940), *The Ten Commandments* (1956), *Cat on a Hot Tin Roof* (1958), *A Man Called Horse* (1970), *Star Trek III: The Search for Spock* (1984).

Andress, Ursula (1936–) Swiss, born Berne; *Dr No* (1963), *She* (1965), *What's New, Pussycat?* (1965), *Casino Royale* (1967), *The Clash of the Titans* (1981).

Andrews, Anthony (1948–) British, born London; *Danger UXB* (TV 1978), *Brideshead Revisited* (TV 1981), *The Scarlet Pimpernel* (TV 1982), *Under the Volcano* (1984), *The Lighthorsemen* (1987), *Lost in Siberia* (1991), *Haunted* (1995).

Andrews, Dame Julie (Julia Elizabeth Wells) (1935–) British, born Walton-on-Thames, Surrey; *Mary Poppins* (1964), *The Americanization of Emily* (1964), *The Sound of Music* (1965), *Torn Curtain* (1966), *Thoroughly Modern Millie* (1967), *Star!* (1968), *SOB* (1981), *Victor/Victoria* (1982), *The Man Who Loved Women* (1983), *Tchin Tchin* (1990), *Relative Values* (2000), *The Princess Diaries* (2001).

Ann-Margret (Ann-Margret Olsson) (1941–) Swedish-American, born Valsobyn, Jamtland, Sweden; *State Fair* (1962), *Bye Bye Birdie* (1963), *The Cincinnati Kid* (1965), *Carnal Knowledge* (1971), *Tommy* (1975), *52 Pick-Up* (1986), *A New Life* (1988), *Newsies* (1991), *Grumpy Old Men* (1994), *Grumpier Old Men* (1996), *Any Given Sunday* (1999).

Anthony, Lysette (1963–) British, born London; *Krull* (1983), *Three Up, Two Down* (TV 1987–8), *Jack the Ripper* (TV 1988), *Without a Clue* (1988), *The Lady and the Highway Man* (1989), *Campion* (TV 1989–90), *Dracula: Dead and Loving It* (1995).

Archer, Anne (1947–) American, born Los Angeles; *Bob and Carol and Ted and Alice* (TV 1973), *Paradise Alley* (1978), *Green Ice* (1980), *Fatal Attraction* (1987), *Love at Large* (1990), *Narrow Margin* (1990), *Body of Evidence* (1992), *Patriot Games*

(1992), *Short Cuts* (1993), *Clear and Present Danger* (1994), *The Rules of Engagement* (2000).

Arquette, Rosanna (1959–) American, born New York City; *Shirley* (1979 TV), *SOB* (1981), *Johnny Belinda* (TV 1982), *The Executioner's Song* (TV 1982), *Desperately Seeking Susan* (1983), *Silverado* (1985), *After Hours* (1985), *Nobody's Fool* (1985), *Eight Million Ways to Die* (1987), *The Big Blue* (1988), *New York Stories* (1989), *The Black Rainbow* (1990), *The Player* (1992), *Nowhere to Run* (1993), *Pulp Fiction* (1994), *Crash* (1996), *The Whole Nine Yards* (2000).

Ashcroft, Dame Peggy (1907–91) British, born Croydon, Greater London; *The Thirty-Nine Steps* (1935), *Quiet Wedding* (1940), *Edward and Mrs Simpson* (TV 1978), *A Passage to India* (1984), *The Jewel in the Crown* (TV 1984), *Madame Sousatzka* (1988), *She's Been Away* (TV 1990).

Asher, Jane (1946–) British, born London; *The Masque of the Red Death* (1964), *Deep End* (1971), *Dreamchild* (1985), *Paris by Night* (1988).

Astaire, Fred (Frederick Austerlitz) (1899–1987) American, born Omaha, Nebraska; *Flying Down to Rio* (1933), *The Gay Divorcee* (1934), *Top Hat* (1935), *Funny Face* (1957), *It Takes a Thief* (TV 1965–9), *Finian's Rainbow* (1968).

Astor, Mary (Lucille Langhanke) (1906–87) American, born Quincy, Illinois; *Beau Brummell* (1924), *Don Juan* (1926), *Dodsworth* (1936), *The Prisoner of Zenda* (1937), *The Great Lie* (1941), *The Maltese Falcon* (1941), *The Palm Beach Story* (1942), *Meet Me in St Louis* (1944), *Act of Violence* (1948), *Little Women* (1949), *Return to Peyton Place* (1961).

Atkinson, Rowan (1955–) British, born Newcastle upon Tyne; *The Black Adder* (TV 1984), *Blackadder II* (TV 1985), *Blackadder III* (TV 1986), *Blackadder Goes Forth* (TV 1989), *The Tall Guy* (1989), *The Witches* (1990), *Mr Bean* (TV 1990–4), *Bean: The Ultimate Disaster Movie* (1997), *Maybe Baby* (2000).

Attenborough, Richard Samuel Attenborough, Baron (1923–) British, born Cambridge; *In Which We Serve* (1942), *The Man Within* (1942), *Brighton Rock* (1947), *The Guinea Pig* (1949), *The Great Escape* (1963), *Brannigan* (1975), *Jurassic Park* (1993), *Miracle on 34th Street* (1994), *E=MC²* (1995), *The Lost World: Jurassic Park* (1997), *Elizabeth* (1998).

Avalon, Frankie (Francis Thomas Avallone) (1940–) American, born Philadelphia, Pennsylvania; *The Alamo* (1960), *Voyage to the Bottom of the Sea* (1962), *Beach Blanket Bingo* (1965), *Fireball 500* (1966), *Grease* (1978), *Blood Song* (1982).

Aykroyd, Dan (1952–) Canadian, born Ottawa, Ontario; *1941* (1979), *The Blues Brothers* (1980), *Neighbors* (1981), *Twilight Zone* (1983), *Ghostbusters* (1984), *Spies Like Us* (1986), *Dragnet* (1987), *The Couch Trip* (1988), *The Great Outdoors* (1988), *Caddyshack II* (1968), *Ghostbusters II* (1989), *My Stepmother is an Alien* (1989), *Driving Miss Daisy* (1989), *Loose Cannons* (1990), *My Girl* (1991), *Chaplin* (1992), *Sneakers* (1992), *Coneheads* (1993), *My Girl 2* (1994), *Getting Away With Murder* (1995), *Casper* (1995), *Sgt Bilko* (1996), *Blues Brothers 2000* (1998), *Crossroads* (2002).

Bacall, Lauren (Betty Joan Perske) (1924–) American, born New York City; *To Have and Have Not* (1944), *The Big Sleep* (1946), *How to Marry a Millionaire* (1953), *The Fan* (1981), *Mr North* (1988), *Misery* (1990), *Prêt-À-Porter* (1994), *The Mirror Has Two Faces* (1996).

Bacon, Kevin (1958–) American, born Philadelphia, Pennsylvania; *Animal House* (1978), *Friday the 13th* (1980), *Diner* (1982), *Footloose* (1984), *She's Having a Baby* (1988), *Tremors* (1989), *Flatliners* (1990), *The*

Big Picture (1990), *JFK* (1991), *He Said She Said* (1991), *A Few Good Men* (1992), *The River Wild* (1994), *Apollo 13* (1995), *Sleepers* (1996), *Stir of Echoes* (1999).

Baker, Joe Don (1936–) American, born Groesbeck, Texas; *Cool Hand Luke* (1967), *Mongo's Back in Town* (TV 1971), *Charley Varrick* (1972), *Walking Tall* (1972), *Mitchell* (1974), *The Natural* (1984), *Fletch* (1984), *Getting Even* (1985), *The Living Daylights* (1987), *The Killing Time* (1987), *Cape Fear* (1991), *Reality Bites* (1994), *Golden Eye* (1995), *Mars Attacks!* (1996), *Tomorrow Never Dies* (1997).

Baker, Tom (1935–) British, born Liverpool; *Nicholas and Alexandra* (1971), *Doctor Who* (TV 1975–81), *The Life and Loves of a She-Devil* (TV 1987), *The Chronicles of Narnia* (TV 1990).

Baldwin, Alec (1958–) American, born Massapequa, New York; *Sweet Revenge* (TV 1984), *She's Having a Baby* (1988), *Beetlejuice* (1988), *Working Girl* (1988), *Married to the Mob* (1988), *The Hunt for Red October* (1989), *Miami Blues* (1990), *Alice* (1991), *Glengarry Glen Ross* (1992), *Malice* (1993), *The Shadow* (1994), *Bookworm* (1997), *Notting Hill* (1999), *Pearl Harbor* (2001).

Ball, Lucille (1910–89) American, born Celaron, New York; *Top Hat* (1935), *Stage Door* (1937), *The Affairs of Annabel* (1938), *Five Came Back* (1939), *The Big Street* (1942), *Du Barry was a Lady* (1943), *Without Love* (1945), *Ziegfeld Follies* (1946), *Her Husband's Affairs* (1947), *Fancy Pants* (1950), *I Love Lucy* (TV 1951–5), *The Long Long Trailer* (1954), *The Facts of Life* (1956), *The Lucy Show* (TV 1962–8), *Yours Mine and Ours* (1968), *Here's Lucy* (TV 1968–73), *Life with Lucy* (TV 1976).

Bancroft, Anne (Anna Maria Italiano) (1931–) American, born The Bronx, New York City; *The Miracle Worker* (1962), *The Graduate* (1968), *Silent Movie* (1976), *The Elephant Man* (1980), *84 Charing Cross Road* (1986), *Torch Song Trilogy* (1988), *The Assassin* (1992), *Malice* (1993), *How To Make an American Quilt* (1995), *Dracula: Dead and Loving It* (1995), *Great Expectations* (1998).

Bankhead, Tallulah (1902–68) American, born Huntsville, Texas; *Tarnished Lady* (1931), *A Royal Scandal* (1945).

Bardot, Brigitte (Camille Javal) (1934–) French, born Paris; *And God Created Woman* (1956), *En Cas de Malheur* (1958), *Viva Maria!* (1965).

Barkin, Ellen (1959–) American, born The Bronx, New York City; *Diner* (1982), *The Adventures of Buckeroo Banzai* (1984), *The Big Easy* (1987), *Siesta* (1987), *Sea of Love* (1990), *Johnny Handsome* (1990), *Switch* (1991), *Mac* (1993), *Trigger Happy* (1996), *Drop Dead Gorgeous* (1999).

Barrymore, Drew (1975–) American, born Los Angeles; *ET* (1982), *Firestarter* (1984), *Irreconcilable Differences* (1984), *Cat's Eye* (1984), *Poison Ivy* (1992), *Wayne's World 2* (1993), *Batman Forever* (1995), *Never Been Kissed* (1999), *Charlie's Angels* (2000), *Riding in Cars with Boys* (2001), *Confessions of a Dangerous Mind* (2002).

Barrymore, Ethel (Edith Blythe) (1879–1959) American, born Philadelphia, Pennsylvania; *Rasputin and the Empress* (1932), *None but the Lonely Heart* (1944), *The Farmer's Daughter* (1947), *Young at Heart* (1954).

Barrymore, John (John Blythe) (1882–1942) American, born Philadelphia, Pennsylvania; *Dr Jekyll and Mr Hyde* (1920), *Show of Shows* (1929), *Rasputin and the Empress* (1932), *Dinner at 8* (1933), *Midnight* (1939), *The Great Profile* (1940).

Barrymore, Lionel (Lionel Blythe) (1878–1954) American, born Philadelphia, Pennsylvania; *Peter Ibbetson* (1917), *The Copperhead* (1918), *The Bells* (1926), *Sadie Thompson* (1928), *A Free Soul* (1931), *The Man I Killed* (1932), *Arsène Lupin* (1932), *Rasputin and the Empress* (1932), Grand Hotel (1932), *Dinner at 8* (1933), *David Copperfield* (1934), *Captains Courageous* (1937), *A Family Affair* (1937), *Young Dr Kildare* (1938), *Calling Dr Gillespie* (1942), *On Borrowed Time* (1939), *Three Wise Fools* (1946), *It's a Wonderful Life* (1946), *Duel in the Sun* (1946), *Key Largo* (1948).

Basinger, Kim (1953–) American, born Athens, Georgia; *From Here to Eternity* (TV 1980), *Hard Country* (1981), *Never Say Never Again* (1983), *The Natural* (1984), *9½ Weeks* (1985), *No Mercy* (1986), *Blind Date* (1987), *Nadine* (1987), *Batman* (1989), *My Stepmother is an Alien* (1989), *The Marrying Man* (1990), *Wayne's World 2* (1993), *Prêt-À-Porter* (1994), *Kansas City* (1996), *LA Confidential* (1997), *8 Mile* (2002).

Bates, Alan (1934–) British, born Allestree, Derbyshire; *A Kind of Loving* (1962), *Whistle Down the Wind* (1962), *Zorba the Greek* (1965), *Far from the Madding Crowd* (1967), *Women in Love* (1969), *The Rose* (1979), *A Prayer for the Dying* (1987), *We Think the World of You* (1988), *Hamlet* (1990), *Grotesque* (1995), *Gosford Park* (2001).

Béart, Emmanuelle (1965–) French, born Gassin; *Manon des Sources* (1986), *Mission: Impossible* (1996), *8 Women* (2002).

Beatty, Ned (1937–) American, born Louisville, Kentucky; *Deliverance* (1972), *Nashville* (1975), *Network* (1976), *All the President's Men* (1976), *Superman* (1978), *Friendly Fire* (TV 1979), *Incredible Shrinking Woman* (1981), *Superman II* (1981), *The Toy* (1983), *Hopscotch* (1983), *Stoker Ace* (1983), *Restless Natives* (1986), *The Big Easy* (1987), *The Fourth Protocol* (1987), *Switching Channels* (1988), *The Unholy* (1988), *Midnight Crossing* (1988), *After the Rain* (1988), *Purple People Eater* (1988), *Just Cause* (1995), *Cookie's Fortune* (1999).

Beatty, Warren (Henry Warren Beaty) (1937–) American, born Richmond, Virginia; *Splendor in the Grass* (1961), *The Roman Spring of Mrs Stone* (1961), *All Fall Down* (1962), *Bonnie and Clyde* (1967), *The Parallax View* (1974), *Shampoo* (1975), *Heaven Can Wait* (1978), *Reds* (1981), *Ishtar* (1987), *Dick Tracy* (1990), *Bugsy* (1991), *Love Affair* (1994), *Bulworth* (1998), *Town and Country* (2001).

Bedelia, Bonnie (1952–) American, born New York City; *They Shoot Horses Don't They?* (1969), *Love and Other Strangers* (1970), *Heart Like a Wheel* (1983), *The Prince of Pennsylvania* (1988), *Die Hard* (1988), *Die Hard II: Die Harder* (1990), *Presumed Innocent* (1990).

Belmondo, Jean-Paul (1933–) French, born Neuilly-sur-Seine, Paris; *À Bout de Souffle* (1959), *Moderato Cantabile* (1960), *Un Singe en Hiver* (1962), *That Man from Rio* (1964).

Belushi, James (1954–) American, born Chicago; *Trading Places* (1983), *Salvador* (1986), *About Last Night* (1987), *Red Heat* (1988), *Only the Lonely* (1991), *Curly Sue* (1991), *Last Action Hero* (1993), *Separate Lives* (1995), *Jingle All The Way* (1996).

Belushi, John (1949–82) American, born Chicago; *Animal House* (1978), *1941* (1979), *The Blues Brothers* (1981), *Neighbors* (1981).

Berenger, Tom (1950–) American, born Chicago; *The Big Chill* (1983), *Platoon* (1987), *Shoot to Kill* (1988), *Betrayed* (1988), *Last Rites* (1988), *Born On The Fourth Of July* (1990), *Sliver* (1993), *The Substitute* (1996), *Training Day* (2001).

Bergen, Candice (1946–) American, born Beverly

Hills, California; *The Group* (1966), *The Magus* (1969), *Carnal Knowledge* (1971), *Rich and Famous* (1981), *Gandhi* (1982), *Miss Congeniality* (2000).

Bergman, Ingrid (1915–82) Swedish, born Stockholm; *Intermezzo* (1939), *Dr Jekyll and Mr Hyde* (1941), *Casablanca* (1943), *For Whom the Bell Tolls* (1943), *Gaslight* (1943), *Spellbound* (1945), *Anastasia* (1946), *Notorious* (1946), *Stromboli* (1950), *Indiscreet* (1958), *Cactus Flower* (1969), *Murder on the Orient Express* (1974), *Autumn Sonata* (1978).

Berkoff, Stephen (1937–) British, born London; *Octopussy* (1983), *Beverly Hills Cop* (1984), *Rambo* (1985), *War and Remembrance* (TV 1989).

Bernhardt, Sarah (Henriette Rosine Bernhardt) (1884–1923) French, born Paris; *Queen Elizabeth* (1912).

Bisset, Jacqueline (1944–) British, born Weybridge, Surrey; *Cul-de-Sac* (1966), *Casino Royale* (1967), *Bullitt* (1968), *The Grasshopper* (1970), *Murder on the Orient Express* (1974), *The Deep* (1977), *Rich and Famous* (1981), *Class* (1983), *Under the Volcano* (1984), *High Season* (1987), *Scenes from the Class Struggle in Beverly Hills* (1989), *Wild Orchid* (1990), *Joan of Arc: The Virgin Warrior* (2000).

Blessed, Brian (1936–) British, born Mexborough, South Yorkshire; *Z Cars* (TV 1962–5), *I, Claudius* (TV 1976), *Flash Gordon* (1980), *Henry V* (1989), *Robin Hood: Prince of Thieves* (1991), *Much Ado About Nothing* (1993), *Macbeth* (1997).

Bloom, Claire (1931–) British, born London; *Look Back in Anger* (1959), *The Haunting* (1963), *The Spy who Came in from the Cold* (1966), *Clash of the Titans* (1981), *Crimes and Misdemeanors* (1989), *Daylight* (1996).

Bogarde, Sir Dirk (Derek Niven Van Den Bogaerde) (1921–99) Anglo-Dutch, born Hampstead, London; *A Tale of Two Cities* (1958), *Victim* (1961), *The Servant* (1963), *Darling* (1965), *Death in Venice* (1971), *Providence* (1977), *These Foolish Things* (1990).

Bogart, Humphrey (De Forest) (1899–1957) American, born New York City; *Broadway's Like That* (1930), *The Petrified Forest* (1936), *High Sierra* (1941), *The Maltese Falcon* (1941), *Casablanca* (1942), *To Have and Have Not* (1944), *The Big Sleep* (1946), *The Treasure of the Sierra Madre* (1947), *The African Queen* (1952), *The Barefoot Contessa* (1954), *The Caine Mutiny* (1954).

Bonham-Carter, Helena (1966–) British, born London; *Oxford Blues* (1984), *Lady Jane* (1985), *A Room with a View* (1985), *Hamlet* (1990), *Where Angels Fear to Tread* (1991), *Howards End* (1992), *Frankenstein* (1994), *Twelfth Night* (1996), *Wings of the Dove* (1997), *Fight Club* (1999), *Planet of the Apes* (2001).

Borgnine, Ernest (Ermes Borgnino) (1918–) American, born Hamden, Connecticut; *From Here to Eternity* (1953), *Bad Day at Black Rock* (1954), *Marty* (1955), *The Catered Affair* (1956), *The Best Things in Life Are Free* (1956), *The Vikings* (1958), *Pay or Die* (1960), *McHale's Navy* (TV 1962–5), *The Dirty Dozen* (1967), *Ice Station Zebra* (1968), *The Wild Bunch* (1969), *The Poseidon Adventure* (1972), *Convoy* (1978), *The Black Hole* (1979), *Escape from New York* (1981), *Deadly Blessing* (1981), *Codename: Wildgeese* (1984), *Airwolf* (TV 1984–6), *Mel* (1999).

Bow, Clara (1905–65) American, born Brooklyn, New York City; *Mantrap* (1926), *It* (1927), *Wings* (1927).

Bowie, David (David Robert Jones) (1947–) British, born Brixton, South London; *The Man Who Fell to Earth* (1976), *Cat People* (1982), *The Hunger* (1983), *Merry Christmas Mr Lawrence* (1983), *Into the Night*

(1985), *Labyrinth* (1986), *The Last Temptation of Christ* (1988), *Twin Peaks: Fire Walk With Me* (1992), *Basquiat* (1996).

Branagh, Kenneth (1960–) British, born Belfast; *High Season* (1987), *A Month in the Country* (1988), *Henry V* (1989), *Dead Again* (1991), *Peter's Friends* (1992), *Much Ado About Nothing* (1993), *Frankenstein* (1994), *In the Bleak Midwinter* (1995), *Othello* (1995), *Hamlet* (1996), *Love's Labour's Lost* (2000), *Rabbit-Proof Fence* (2002), *Harry Potter and the Chamber of Secrets* (2002).

Brandauer, Klaus Maria (1944–) Austrian, born Alt Aussee; *Mephisto* (1980), *Never Say Never Again* (1983), *Colonel Redl* (1984), *Out of Africa* (1985), *Streets of Gold* (1986), *The Russia House* (1990), *White Fang* (1991), *Becoming Colette* (1991).

Brando, Marlon (1924–) American, born Omaha, Nebraska; *A Streetcar Named Desire* (1951), *Viva Zapata* (1952), *Julius Caesar* (1953), *The Wild One* (1953), *On the Waterfront* (1954), *Guys and Dolls* (1955), *The Teahouse of the August Moon* (1956), *One-Eyed Jacks* (1961), *Mutiny on the Bounty* (1962), *The Chase* (1966), *The Godfather* (1972), *Last Tango in Paris* (1972), *Superman* (1978), *Apocalypse Now* (1979), *A Dry White Season* (1988), *The Freshman* (1990), *Don Juan de Marco* (1995).

Bridges, Jeff (1949–) American, born Los Angeles; *The Last Picture Show* (1971), *Hearts of the West* (1975), *Stay Hungry* (1976), *King Kong* (1976), *Somebody Killed Her Husband* (1978), *Winter Kills* (1979), *Tron* (1982), *Against All Odds* (1983), *Starman* (1984), *Jagged Edge* (1985), *8 Million Ways to Die* (1985), *The Morning After* (1986), *Nadine* (1987), *Tucker: The Man and His Dream* (1987), *The Fabulous Baker Boys* (1989), *Texasville* (1990), *The Fisher King* (1991), *The Vanishing* (1992), *Fearless* (1993), *The Mirror Has Two Faces* (1996), *Arlington Road* (1999).

Bridges, Lloyd (1913–98) American, born San Leandro, California; *Home of the Brave* (1949), *Try and Get Me* (1951), *The Rainmaker* (1956), *Sea Hunt* (TV 1957–60), *The Goddess* (1958), *The Love War* (TV 1970), *Roots* (TV 1977), *Airplane* (1980), *Hot Shots!* (1991), *Honey, I Blew Up the Kid* (1992), *Hot Shots! Part Deux* (1993).

Broderick, Matthew (1963–) American, born New York City; *War Games* (1983), *Ladyhawke* (1984), *Ferris Bueller's Day Off* (1986), *Biloxi Blues* (1988), *Torch Song Trilogy* (1988), *Family Business* (1989), *Glory* (1989), *The Freshman* (1990), *The Cable Guy* (1996), *Inspector Gadget* (1999).

Bronson, Charles (Charles Buchinski) (1920–) American, born Ehrenfield, Pennsylvania; *Drumbeat* (1954), *Vera Cruz* (1954), *The Magnificent Seven* (1960), *This Property is Condemned* (1966), *The Dirty Dozen* (1967), *Chato's Land* (1972), *The Mechanic* (1972), *The Valachi Papers* (1972), *Death Wish* (1974), *Hard Times* (1975), *Telefon* (1977), *Death Wish II* (1982), *Death Wish III* (1985), *Death Wish IV* (1987), *Murphy's Law* (1987), *Messenger of Death* (1988), *Kinjite: Forbidden Subjects* (1989), *The Indian Runner* (1991), *Death Wish V* (1993).

Brooks, Louise (Leslie Gettman) (1906–85) American, born Cherryvale, Kansas; *Pandora's Box* (1929), *Diary of a Lost Girl* (1930).

Brooks, Mel (Melvin Kaminski) (1926–) American, born New York City; *The Twelve Chairs* (1969), *Blazing Saddles* (1974), *Silent Movie* (1976), *High Anxiety* (1978), *History of the World Part One* (1981), *Spaceballs* (1987), *Robin Hood: Men in Tights* (1993), *Dracula: Dead and Loving It* (1995), *Svitati* (1999).

Brown, Bryan (1947–) Australian, born Panania; *A Town Like Alice* (TV 1981), *The Thorn Birds* (TV 1983), *Eureka Stockade* (TV 1985), *F/X: Murder by Illusion* (1985), *Rebel* (1985), *Taipan* (1985), *The Shiralee* (TV 1987), *Cocktail* (1988), *Gorillas in the Mist* (1988), *Dead Heart* (1996), *Risk* (2000).

Brynner, Yul (1915–85) Swiss–Russian, naturalized American, born Sakhalin, Siberia; *The King and I* (1956), *The Brothers Karamazov* (1958), *The Magnificent Seven* (1960), *Return of the Seven* (1966).

Burton, Richard (Richard Walter Jenkins) (1925–84) British, born Pontrhydfen, S Wales: *My Cousin Rachel* (1952), *Alexander the Great* (1956), *Look Back in Anger* (1959), *Cleopatra* (1962), *The Night of the Iguana* (1964), *The Spy Who Came in from the Cold* (1965), *Who's Afraid of Virginia Woolf?* (1966), *The Taming of the Shrew* (1967), *Where Eagles Dare* (1969), *Equus* (1977), *Exorcist II: The Heretic* (1977), *Absolution* (1979), *1984* (1984).

Caan, James (1939–) American, born The Bronx, New York City; *Brian's Song* (TV 1971), *The Godfather* (1972), *The Godfather, Part II* (1974), *Rollerball* (1975), *A Bridge Too Far* (1977), *Alien Nation* (1989), *Dick Tracy* (1990), *Misery* (1990), *Eraser* (1996), *Mickey Blue Eyes* (1999).

Cage, Nicolas (Nicholas Coppola) (1964–) American, born Long Beach, California; *Fast Times at Ridgemont High* (1982), *Rumblefish* (1983), *Racing with the Moon* (1984), *The Cotton Club* (1984), *Birdy* (1985), *Peggy Sue Got Married* (1986), *Raising Arizona* (1987), *Moonstruck* (1987), *Vampire's Kiss* (1988), *Wild at Heart* (1990), *Wings of the Apache* (1990), *Leaving Las Vegas* (1995), *The Rock* (1996), *Face Off* (1997), *Snake Eyes* (1998), *Gone in Sixty Seconds* (2000), *Captain Corelli's Mandolin* (2001), *Adaptation* (2002).

Cagney, James (Francis Jr) (1899–1986) American, born New York City; *Public Enemy* (1931), *Lady Killer* (1933), *A Midsummer Night's Dream* (1935), *The Roaring Twenties* (1939), *Yankee Doodle Dandy* (1942), *White Heat* (1949), *Love Me or Leave Me* (1955), *Mister Roberts* (1955), *One, Two, Three* (1961), *Ragtime* (1981).

Caine, Sir Michael (Maurice Micklewhite) (1933–) British, born London; *Zulu* (1963), *The Ipcress File* (1965), *Alfie* (1966), *The Italian Job* (1969), *Sleuth* (1972), *The Man Who Would Be King* (1975), *The Eagle Has Landed* (1976), *California Suite* (1978), *Beyond the Poseidon Adventure* (1979), *Dressed to Kill* (1980), *Death Trap* (1983), *Educating Rita* (1983), *Hannah and Her Sisters* (1986), *The Whistle Blower* (1987), *Without a Clue* (1988), *Bullseye* (1990), *Shock to the System* (1990), *Mr Destiny* (1990), *Noises Off* (1992), *Blue Ice* (1992), *Blood and Wine* (1996), *Little Voice* (1998), *The Quiet American* (2002).

Callow, Simon (1949–) British, born London; *Amadeus* (1984), *A Room With a View* (1985), *Maurice* (1987), *Four Weddings and a Funeral* (1994), *Shakespeare in Love* (1998).

Candy, John (1950–94) Canadian, born Toronto, Ontario; *Stripes* (1981), *Splash!* (1984), *Summer Rental* (1984), *Brewster's Millions* (1985), *Little Shop of Horrors* (1986), *Spaceballs* (1987), *Planes, Trains, and Automobiles* (1988), *The Great Outdoors* (1988), *Who's Harry Crumb?* (1989), *Uncle Buck* (1989), *Only the Lonely* (1991), *JFK* (1991), *Cool Runnings* (1993).

Cardinale, Claudia (1939–) Italian, born Tunis, Tunisia; *The Pink Panther* (1963), *Once Upon a Time in the West* (1969), *Escape to Athena* (1979), *Fitzcarraldo* (1982), *A Man in Love* (1987), *Torrents of Spring* (1988), *Son of the Pink Panther* (1993).

Carlyle, Robert (1961–) British, born Glasgow; *Riff Raff* (1990), *Priest* (1994), *Hamish Macbeth* (TV 1994–7), *Carla's Song* (1996), *Trainspotting* (1996),

Arts and Culture

Arts and Culture

The Full Monty (1997), *Face* (1997), *Angela's Ashes* (1999), *The Beach* (2000), *Once Upon A Time in the Midlands* (2002).

Caron, Leslie (Claire Margaret) (1931–) French, born Boulogne-Billancourt, near Paris; *An American in Paris* (1951), *Lili* (1953), *The Glass Slipper* (1954), *Daddy Long Legs* (1955), *Gigi* (1958), *Fanny* (1961), *The L-Shaped Room* (1962), *Father Goose* (1964), *QB VII* (TV 1974), *The Reef* (1997).

Carradine, John (Richmond Reed Carradine) (1906–88) American, born New York City; *Five Came Back* (1939), *Stagecoach* (1939), *The Grapes of Wrath* (1940), *Bluebeard* (1944), *House of Frankenstein* (1945), *The Man Who Shot Liberty Valance* (1962), *Peggy Sue Got Married* (1986).

Carrera, Barbara (1945–) Nicaraguan–American, born Managua, Nicaragua; *The Master Gunfighter* (1975), *Embryo* (1976), *The Island of Dr Moreau* (1977), *Condorman* (1981), *Never Say Never Again* (1983), *Dallas* (TV 1984–5), *Codename: Wildgeese II* (1986), *Loverboy* (1990), *Love Is All There Is* (1996).

Carrey, Jim (James Eugene) (1962–) Canadian, born Newmarket, Ontario; *Earth Girls Are Easy* (1989), *The Mask* (1994), *Ace Ventura: Pet Detective* (1994), *Dumb and Dumber* (1994), *Batman Forever* (1995), *Liar Liar* (1997), *The Truman Show* (1998), *Man on the Moon* (1999), *Me, Myself and Irene* (2000).

Cassavetes, John (1929–89) American, born New York City; *Johnny Staccato* (TV 1959), *The Dirty Dozen* (1967), *Rosemary's Baby* (1969), *The Fury* (1978), *Minnie and Moskovitz* (1979), *Whose Life is it Anyway?* (1981), *Tempest* (1982).

Cates, Phoebe (1963–) American, born New York City; *Fast Times at Ridgemont High* (1982), *Paradise* (1982), *Private School* (1983), *Gremlins* (1984), *Lace* (TV 1984), *Lace 2* (TV 1985), *Bright Lights, Big City* (1988), *Shag* (1988), *Gremlins 2: The New Batch* (1990), *Heart of Dixie* (1990), *Drop Dead Fred* (1991), *Princess Caraboo* (1994).

Chamberlain, Richard (1935–) American, born Beverly Hills, California; *Dr Kildare* (TV 1961–6), *The Music Lovers* (1970), *Lady Caroline Lamb* (1972), *The Slipper and the Rose* (1976), *The Man in the Iron Mask* (1977), *The Last Wave* (1978), *Shogun* (TV 1980), *The Thorn Birds* (TV 1983).

Chaplin, Charlie (Sir Charles Spencer) (1889–1977) British, born London; *The Champion* (1915), *The Tramp* (1915), *Easy Street* (1917), *A Dog's Life* (1918), *Shoulder Arms* (1918), *The Kid* (1920), *The Idle Class* (1921), *The Gold Rush* (1924), *City Lights* (1931), *Modern Times* (1936), *The Great Dictator* (1940), *Limelight* (1952), *A King in New York* (1957).

Chaplin, Geraldine (1944–) American, born Santa Monica, California; *Doctor Zhivago* (1965), *The Three Musketeers* (1974), *Nashville* (1975), *Hidden Talent* (1984), *White Mischief* (1987), *The Moderns* (1988), *Mama Turns 100* (1988), *Chaplin* (1992), *The Age of Innocence* (1993), *Jane Eyre* (1996).

Charisse, Cyd (Tula Ellice Funklea) (1922–) American, born Amarillo, Texas; *Ziegfeld Follies* (1945), *The Unfinished Dance* (1947), *Singin' in the Rain* (1952), *The Band Wagon* (1953), *Brigadoon* (1954), *It's Always Fair Weather* (1955), *Invitation to the Dance* (1957), *Two Weeks in Another Town* (1962).

Chase, Chevy (Cornelius Crane Chase) (1943–) American, born New York City; *Caddyshack* (1980), *Seems Like Old Times* (1980), *Vacation* (1983), *European Vacation* (1984), *Fletch* (1985), *Spies Like Us* (1985), *The Three Amigos* (1986), *The Couch Trip* (1988), *Caddy Shack II* (1988), *Funny Farm* (1988), *Fletch Lives* (1988), *Christmas Vacation* (1989), *LA*

Story (1991), *Hero* (1992), *Last Action Hero* (1993), *Vegas Vacation* (1997).

Cher (Cherilyn Sarkisian La Pier) (1946–) American, born El Centro, California; *Silkwood* (1983), *Mask* (1985), *Moonstruck* (1987), *Suspect* (1987), *The Witches of Eastwick* (1987), *Mermaids* (1990), *Faithful* (1995), *Tea with Mussolini* (1999).

Chevalier, Maurice (1888–1972) French, born Paris; *The Innocents of Paris* (1929), *One Hour with You* (1932), *Love Me Tonight* (1932), *The Love Parade* (1932), *Gigi* (1958).

Christie, Julie (1941–) British, born Chukua, Assam, India; *The Fast Lady* (1963), *Billy Liar* (1963), *Doctor Zhivago* (1965), *Darling* (1965), *Farenheit 451* (1966), *Far from the Madding Crowd* (1967), *The Go-Between* (1971), *Don't Look Now* (1974), *Shampoo* (1975), *Heaven Can Wait* (1978), *Heat and Dust* (1982), *Power* (1985), *The Gold Diggers* (1988), *Dragon Heart* (1996), *Hamlet* (1996), *Afterglow* (1997).

Clark, Petula (1932–) British, born Epsom, Surrey; *Finian's Rainbow* (1968), *Goodbye Mr Chips* (1969).

Cleese, John (Marwood) (1939–) British, born West-on-super-Mare; *The Frost Report* (TV 1966), *At Last the 1948 Show* (TV 1967), *Monty Python's Flying Circus* (TV 1969–74), *Monty Python and the Holy Grail* (1974), *Fawlty Towers* (TV 1975, 1979), *Life of Brian* (1979), *The Meaning of Life* (1983), *Clockwise* (1985), *A Fish Called Wanda* (1988), *Splitting Heirs* (1993), *Frankenstein* (1994), *Fierce Creatures* (1996), *The World is Not Enough* (1999), *Harry Potter and the Philosopher's Stone* (2001), *Harry Potter and the Chamber of Secrets* (2002), *Die Another Day* (2002).

Clift, (Edward) Montgomery (1920–66) American, born Omaha, Nebraska; *Red River* (1946), *The Search* (1948), *A Place in the Sun* (1951), *From Here to Eternity* (1953), *Suddenly Last Summer* (1959), *Freud* (1962).

Close, Glenn (1947–) American, born Greenwich, Connecticut; *The World According to Garp* (1982), *The Big Chill* (1983), *The Natural* (1984), *Jagged Edge* (1985), *Maxie* (1985), *Fatal Attraction* (1987), *Dangerous Liaisons* (1988), *Immediate Family* (1989), *Reversal of Fortune* (1990), *Hamlet* (1990), *Meeting Venus* (1991), *Hook* (1991), *The Paper* (1994), *Mary Reilly* (1996), *101 Dalmatians* (1996), *Mars Attacks!* (1996), *Cookie's Fortune* (1999).

Cobb, Lee J (Lee Jacoby) (1911–76) American, born New York City; *Golden Boy* (1939), *The Moon is Down* (1943), *Anna and the King of Siam* (1946), *The Dark Past* (1948), *On the Waterfront* (1954), *The Man in the Grey Flannel Suit* (1956), *Twelve Angry Men* (1957), *The Brothers Karamazov* (1958), *The Virginian* (TV 1962–6), *Come Blow Your Horn* (1963), *Death of a Salesman* (TV 1966), *Coogan's Bluff* (1968), *They Came to Rob Las Vegas* (1968), *The Young Lawyers* (TV 1970–1), *The Exorcist* (1973).

Coburn, James (1928–2002) American, born Laurel, Nebraska; *The Magnificent Seven* (1960), *The Great Escape* (1963), *Charade* (1963), *Our Man Flint* (1966), *In Like Flint* (1966), *A Fistful of Dynamite* (1971), *California Suite* (1978), *Loving Couples* (1980), *Young Guns II* (1990), *Sister Act 2: Back in the Habit* (1993), *Maverick* (1995), *Eraser* (1996).

Collins, Joan (Henrietta) (1933–) British, born London; *Lady Godiva Rides Again* (1951), *The Virgin Queen* (1955), *The Bitch* (1979), *Dynasty* (TV 1981–9), *Decadence* (1993), *In the Bleak Midwinter* (1995).

Coltrane, Robbie (Robin McMillan) (1950–) British, born Rutherglen, near Glasgow; *Mona Lisa* (1986),

The Fruit Machine (1987), *Tutti Frutti* (TV 1987), *Henry V* (1989), *Nuns on the Run* (1990), *The Pope must Die* (1991), *Cracker* (TV 1993–6), *Golden Eye* (1995), *The World is Not Enough* (1999), *Harry Potter and the Philosopher's Stone* (2001), *Harry Potter and the Chamber of Secrets* (2002).

Connery, Sir Sean (Thomas Connery) (1930–) British, born Edinburgh; *Dr No* (1963), *Marnie* (1964), *From Russia With Love* (1964), *Goldfinger* (1965), *Thunderball* (1965), *A Fine Madness* (1966), *You Only Live Twice* (1967), *The Molly Maguires* (1969), *The Anderson Tapes* (1970), *Diamonds are Forever* (1971), *The Offence* (1972), *Zardoz* (1973), *Murder on the Orient Express* (1974), *The Man Who Would Be King* (1975), *Robin and Marian* (1976), *Meteor* (1979), *Outland* (1981), *Time Bandits* (1981), *Never Say Never Again* (1983), *Highlander* (1985), *The Name of the Rose* (1986), *The Untouchables* (1987), *The Presidio* (1988), *Indiana Jones and the Last Crusade* (1989), *The Hunt for Red October* (1990), *The Russia House* (1990), *Highlander II: The Quickening* (1991), *Robin Hood: Prince of Thieves* (1991), *Medicine Man* (1991), *Rising Sun* (1992), *Dreadnought* (1992), *Broken Dreams* (1992), *First Knight* (1995), *Dragon Heart* (1996), *Entrapment* (1999).

Conti, Tom (1941–) British, born Paisley; *Merry Christmas Mr Lawrence* (1983), *Reuben Reuben* (1983), *Saving Grace* (1984), *Miracles* (1985), *Heavenly Pursuits* (1985), *Shirley Valentine* (1989), *Out of Control* (1998).

Cooper, Gary (Frank J Cooper) (1901–61) American, born Helena, Montana; *The Winning of Barbara Worth* (1926), *The Virginian* (1929), *A Farewell to Arms* (1932), *City Streets* (1932), *The Lives of a Bengal Lancer* (1935), *Sergeant York* (1941), *For Whom the Bell Tolls* (1943), *The Fountainhead* (1949), *High Noon* (1952), *Friendly Persuasion* (1956).

Costner, Kevin (1955–) American, born Los Angeles; *American Flyers* (1984), *Silverado* (1985), *The Untouchables* (1987), *No Way Out* (1987), *Bull Durham* (1988), *Field of Dreams* (1989), *Revenge* (1990), *Dances with Wolves* (1990), *Robin Hood: Prince of Thieves* (1991), *JFK* (1991), *The Bodyguard* (1992), *A Perfect World* (1993), *The War* (1994), *Waterworld* (1995), *Tin Cup* (1996), *Message in a Bottle* (1999).

Cotten, Joseph (1905–94) American, born Petersburg, Virginia; *Citizen Kane* (1941), *The Magnificent Ambersons* (1942), *Journey into Fear* (1942), *Shadow of a Doubt* (1943), *I'll Be Seeing You* (1945), *Portrait of Jennie* (1948), *The Third Man* (1949), *Niagara* (1952), *Tora! Tora! Tora!* (1971).

Courtenay, Tom (1937–) British, born Hull; also stage; *The Loneliness of the Long Distance Runner* (1962), *Billy Liar* (1963), *Doctor Zhivago* (1965), *The Dresser* (1983), *Let Him Have It* (1991), *Last Orders* (2001).

Cox, Ronny (1938–) American, born Cloudcroft, New Mexico; *Deliverance* (1972), *The Onion Field* (1978), *Taps* (1981), *Vision Quest* (1985), *Beverly Hills Cop* (1984), *Beverly Hills Cop II* (1987), *Robocop* (1987), *St Elsewhere* (TV 1989), *Total Recall* (1990).

Crawford, Joan (Lucille Le Sueur) (1906–77) American, born San Antonio, Texas; *Our Dancing Daughters* (1928), *Our Blushing Brides* (1933), *Dancing Lady* (1933), *The Women* (1939), *Mildred Pierce* (1945), *Possessed* (1947), *What Ever Happened to Baby Jane?* (1962), *Trog* (1970).

Crenna, Richard (1926–2003) American, born Los Angeles; *Pride of St Louis* (1952), *Star!* (1968), *Body Heat* (1981), *Death Ship* (1981), *First Blood* (1982), *Breakheart Pass* (1983), *Table for Five* (1983), *The Flamingo Kid* (1984), *Summer Rental* (1985), *Rambo* (1986), *Rambo III* (1988), *Leviathan* (1989), *Hot Shots! Part Deux* (1993).

Crosby, Bing (Harry Lillis Crosby) (1904–77) American, born Tacoma, Washington; *King of Jazz* (1930), *Mississippi* (1935), *Anything Goes* (1936), *Road to Singapore* (1940), *Road to Zanzibar* (1941), *Holiday Inn* (1942), *Road to Morocco* (1942), *Going My Way* (1944), *The Bells of St Mary's* (1945), *Blue Skies* (1946), *A Connecticut Yankee in King Arthur's Court* (1949), *White Christmas* (1954), *The Country Girl* (1954), *High Society* (1956), *Road to Hong Kong* (1962).

Cruise, Tom (Tom Cruise Mapother IV) (1962–) American, born Syracuse, New York; *The Outsiders* (1983), *Legend* (1984), *Risky Business* (1984), *Top Gun* (1985), *The Color of Money* (1986), *Cocktail* (1988), *Rain Man* (1988), *Born on the Fourth of July* (1989), *Days of Thunder* (1990), *Far and Away* (1992), *A Few Good Men* (1992), *The Firm* (1993), *Interview with the Vampire* (1994), *Mission: Impossible* (1996), *Jerry Maguire* (1996), *Eyes Wide Shut* (1999), *Mission: Impossible 2* (2000), *Vanilla Sky* (2001), *Minority Report* (2002).

Crystal, Billy (1947–) American, born Long Beach, New York; *This Is Spinal Tap* (1984), *Throw Momma from the Train* (1987), *The Princess Bride* (1988), *When Harry met Sally ...* (1989), *City Slickers* (1991), *Mr Saturday Night* (1992), *Hamlet* (1996), *Analyze This* (1999), *Analyze That* (2002).

Culp, Robert (1930–) American, born Oakland, California; *I Spy* (TV 1965–7), *Bob and Carol and Ted and Alice* (1969), *The Greatest American Hero* (TV 1981–2), *The Gladiator* (TV 1986), *The Pelican Brief* (1994), *Spy Hard* (1996).

Curtis, Jamie Lee (1958–) American, born Los Angeles; *Operation Petticoat* (TV 1978), *Halloween* (1979), *The Fog* (1980), *Halloween II* (1981), *Love Letters* (1983), *Trading Places* (1983), *Perfect* (1985), *A Fish Called Wanda* (1988), *Dominick and Eugene* (1988), *Blue Steel* (1990), *My Girl* (1991), *Forever Young* (1992), *My Girl 2* (1994), *Fierce Creatures* (1996), *Virus* (1999), *The Tailor of Panama* (2001).

Curtis, Tony (Bernard Schwarz) (1925–) American, born New York City; *Houdini* (1953), *Trapeze* (1956), *The Vikings* (1958), *Some Like it Hot* (1959), *Spartacus* (1960), *The Boston Strangler* (1968), *The Persuaders* (TV 1971–2).

Cusack, Cyril (James) (1910–93) Irish, born Durban, South Africa; *Odd Man Out* (1947), *The Blue Lagoon* (1949), *Jacqueline* (1965), *The Spy Who Came in From the Cold* (1965), *Fahrenheit 451* (1966), *Day of the Jackal* (1973), *1984* (1984), *Little Dorrit* (1987), *My Left Foot* (1989), *The Fool* (1990).

Cushing, Peter (1913–94) British, born Kenley, Surrey; *The Man in the Iron Mask* (1939), *Hamlet* (1947), *1984* (TV 1955), *The Curse of Frankenstein* (1957), *Dracula* (1958), *The Mummy* (1959), *The Hound of the Baskervilles* (1959), *Cash on Demand* (1963), *Dr Who and the Daleks* (1965), *Sherlock Holmes* (TV 1968), *Tales from the Crypt* (1972), *Horror Express* (1972), *Star Wars* (1977), *Biggles* (1988).

Dafoe, Willem (1955–) American, born Appleton, Wisconsin; *Platoon* (1986), *The Last Temptation of Christ* (1988), *Mississippi Burning* (1988), *Triumph of the Spirit* (1989), *Wild At Heart* (1990), *Flight of the Intruder* (1990), *Light Sleeper* (1992), *Body of Evidence* (1992), *Tom and Viv* (1994), *Clear and Present Danger* (1994), *The English Patient* (1996), *Bullfighter* (2001), *eXistenZ* (1999), *Spider-Man* (2002).

Dalton, Timothy (1946–) British, born Wales; *The Lion in Winter* (1968), *Wuthering Heights* (1970),

Arts and Culture

Mary Queen of Scots (1971), *Agatha* (1979), *Flash Gordon* (1980), *Centennial* (TV 1981–2), *The Living Daylights* (1987), *License to Kill* (1989), *The Rocketeer* (1991).

Dance, Charles (1946–) British, born Rednal, Worcestershire; *For Your Eyes Only* (1981), *The Jewel in the Crown* (TV 1984), *The Golden Child* (1985), *Plenty* (1985), *Good Morning Babylon* (1987), *White Mischief* (1987), *Pascali's Island* (1988), *Phantom of the Opera* (TV 1990), *Last Action Hero* (1993), *Hilary and Jackie* (1998), *Gosford Park* (2001).

D'Angelo, Beverly (1953–) American, born Columbus, Ohio; *First Love* (1977), *Every Which Way But Loose* (1978), *Hair* (1979), *Coal Miner's Daughter* (1980), *Paternity* (1981), *Honky Tonk Freeway* (1981), *Vacation* (1984), *European Vacation* (1985), *Aria* (1987), *High Spirits* (1988), *Christmas Vacation* (1989), *The Pope Must Die* (1991), *Judgement Day* (1993), *American History X* (1998).

Daniels, William (1927–) American, born Brooklyn, New York City; *Captain Nice* (TV 1966), *The Graduate* (1967), *1776* (1972), *The Parallax View* (1974), *The Blue Lagoon* (1981), *Reds* (1981), *St Elsewhere* (TV 1982–9), *Blind Date* (1987).

Danson, Ted (1947–) American, born Flagstaff, Arizona; *The Onion Field* (1979), *Body Heat* (1981), *Cheers* (TV 1982–93), *Creepshow* (1982), *Something About Amelia* (TV 1984), *Three Men and a Baby* (1988), *Cousins* (1989), *Dad* (1990), *Three Men and a Little Lady* (1990), *Made In America* (1993), *Loch Ness* (1995), *Saving Private Ryan* (1998).

Darren, James (James Ercolani) (1936–) American, born Philadelphia, Pennsylvania; *Gidget* (1959), *The Guns of Navarone* (1961), *For Those Who Think Young* (1964), *Time Tunnel* (TV 1966), *T J Hooker* (TV 1983–6).

Davenport, Nigel (1928–) British, born Shelford, Cambridge; *A Man for All Seasons* (1966), *The Virgin Soldiers* (1969), *Living Free* (1972), *The Island of Dr Moreau* (1977), *Longitude* (2000).

Davis, Bette (Ruth Elizabeth Davis) (1908–89) American, born Lowell, Massachusetts; *Bad Sister* (1931), *Dangerous* (1935), *Jezebel* (1938), *The Great Lie* (1941), *All About Eve* (1950), *What Ever Happened to Baby Jane?* (1962), *Strangers* (TV 1979), *The Whales of August* (1987).

Davis, Geena (1957–) American, born Wareham, Massachusetts; *Tootsie* (1982), *Fletch* (1985), *The Fly* (1986), *Beetlejuice* (1988), *The Accidental Tourist* (1989), *Earth Girls Are Easy* (1989), *Thelma and Louise* (1991), *A League of Their Own* (1993), *The Long Kiss Goodnight* (1996).

Davis, Judy (1956–) Australian, born Perth; *My Brilliant Career* (1979), *Who Dares Wins* (1982), *A Passage to India* (1987), *High Tide* (1987), *Naked Lunch* (1991), *Barton Fink* (1991), *Husbands and Wives* (1992), *Anna Oz* (1996), *Deconstructing Harry* (1997).

Day, Doris (Doris von Kappelhoff) (1924–) American, born Cincinnati, Ohio; *Romance on the High Seas* (1948), *Storm Warning* (1950), *Calamity Jane* (1953), *Young at Heart* (1954), *Love Me or Leave Me* (1955), *The Pajama Game* (1957), *Pillow Talk* (1959), *That Touch of Mink* (1962), *With Six You Get Egg Roll* (1968), *The Doris Day Show* (TV 1968–73).

Day-Lewis, Daniel (1958–) Irish, born London; *Gandhi* (1983), *My Beautiful Laundrette* (1985), *Room with a View* (1985), *The Unbearable Lightness of Being* (1988), *Stars and Bars* (1988), *Nanou* (1988), *My Left Foot* (1989), *The Last of the Mohicans* (1992), *The Age of Innocence* (1993), *In the Name of the Father* (1993), *The Crucible* (1996), *The Boxer* (1998), *Gangs of New York* (2002).

Dean, James (Byron) (1931–55) American, born Fairmount, Indiana; *East of Eden* (1955), *Rebel without a Cause* (1955), *Giant* (1956).

De Havilland, Olivia (1916–) British, born Tokyo, Japan; *Midsummer Night's Dream* (1935), *The Adventures of Robin Hood* (1938), *Gone with the Wind* (1939), *The Dark Mirror* (1946), *To Each His Own* (1946), *The Heiress* (1949), *My Cousin Rachel* (1952).

De Mornay, Rebecca (1962–) American, born Los Angeles; *Risky Business* (1984), *Runaway Train* (1985), *And God Created Woman* (1988), *Dealers* (1988), *Feds* (1988), *Backdraft* (1991), *The Hand that Rocks the Cradle* (1993), *The Winner* (1996).

Dench, Dame Judi (Judith Olivia Dench) (1934–) British, born York; *A Fine Romance* (TV 1981–4), *A Room With a View* (1985), *84 Charing Cross Road* (1987), *A Handful of Dust* (1988), *Henry V* (1989), *Behaving Badly* (TV 1989), *Jack and Sarah* (1995), *Hamlet* (1996), *Mrs Brown* (1997), *Shakespeare in Love* (1998), *Tea with Mussolini* (1999), *Chocolat* (2000), *Iris* (2001), *The Shipping News* (2001).

Deneuve, Catherine (Catherine Dorleac) (1943–) French, born Paris; *Les Parapluies de Cherbourg* (1964), *Repulsion* (1965), *Belle de Jour* (1967), *Tristana* (1970), *The Hunger* (1983), *Indochine* (1991), *Les Voleurs* (1996), *Dancer in the Dark* (2000), *8 Women* (2002).

De Niro, Robert (1943–) American, born New York City; *Mean Streets* (1973), *The Godfather, Part II* (1974), *1900* (1976), *Taxi Driver* (1976), *The Deer Hunter* (1978), *Raging Bull* (1980), *King of Comedy* (1982), *Brazil* (1985), *Angel Heart* (1987), *The Untouchables* (1987), *Midnight Run* (1988), *Jacknife* (1989), *Stanley & Iris* (1989), *We're No Angels* (1990), *Goodfellas* (1990), *Awakenings* (1990), *Backdraft* (1991), *Cape Fear* (1991), *The Mistress* (1992), *Mad Dog and Glory* (1992), *Night and The City* (1992), *This Boy's Life* (1992), *Frankenstein* (1994), *Casino* (1995), *Heat* (1995), *Sleepers* (1996), *Jackie Brown* (1998), *Ronin* (1998), *Analyze This* (1999), *Meet the Parents* (2000), *Analyze That* (2002).

Dennehy, Brian (1940–) American, born Bridgeport, Connecticut; *Foul Play* (1978), *Butch and Sundance* (1979), *Big Shamus Little Shamus* (TV 1979), *First Blood* (1982), *Gorky Park* (1983), *Cocoon* (1985), *Silverado* (1985), *Legal Eagles* (1986), *Belly of an Architect* (1987), *Best Seller* (1987), *Miles from Home* (1988), *Cocoon: The Return* (1988), *Return to Snowy River Part II* (1988), *Presumed Innocent* (1990), *Romeo and Juliet* (1996).

Depardieu, Gérard (1948–) French, born Châteauroux; *Get Out Your Handkerchiefs* (1977), *The Last Metro* (1980), *The Return of Martin Guerre* (1981), *Danton* (1982), *The Moon in the Gutter* (1983), *Police* (1985), *Jean de Florette* (1986), *Streets of Departure* (1986), *Under the Sun of Satan* (1987), *The Woman Next Door* (1987), *Cyrano de Bergerac* (1990), *Green Card* (1990), *Uranus* (1991), *Merci la Vie* (1991), *Mon Père, Ce Héros* (1991), *Tous les Matins du Monde* (1991), *Christopher Columbus* (1992), *Germinal* (1992), *Le Colonel Chabert* (1994), *Les Anges Gardiens* (1995), *Unhook the Stars* (1996), *Hamlet* (1996), *The Man in the Iron Mask* (1998), *The Closet* (2001).

Depp, Johnny (1963–) American, born Owensboro, Kentucky; *Nightmare on Elm Street* (1984), *Platoon* (1986), *Cry Baby* (1990), *Edward Scissorhands* (1990), *What's Eating Gilbert Grape?* (1993), *Ed Wood* (1994), *Don Juan de Marco* (1995), *Sleepy Hollow* (1999), *Blow* (2001).

Derek, Bo (Mary Cathleen Collins) (1956–) American, born Long Beach, California; *Orca* (1977), *'10'* (1979), *Tarzan, the Ape Man* (1981), *Bolero* (1984), *Ghosts Can't Do It* (1990), *Tommy Boy* (1995).

Dern, Bruce (MacLeish) (1936–) American, born Chicago; *Marnie* (1964), *They Shoot Horses Don't They?* (1969), *Silent Running* (1972), *The Great Gatsby* (1974), *Family Plot* (1975), *Coming Home* (1978), *The Driver* (1978), *Tattoo* (1981), *Middle Age Crazy* (1981), *That Championship Season* (1982), *Big Town* (1987), *1969* (1988), *World Gone Wild* (1988), *The 'Burbs* (1989), *After Dark My Sweet* (1990), *Last Man Standing* (1996), *The Haunting* (1999).

Dern, Laura (Elizabeth) (1966–) American, born California; *Mask* (1985), *Smooth Talk* (1986), *Blue Velvet* (1986), *Wild at Heart* (1990), *Jurassic Park* (1993), *Citizen Ruth* (1996), *Dr T and the Women* (2000).

De Vito, Danny (1944–) American, born Neptune, New Jersey; *One Flew Over the Cuckoo's Nest* (1975), *Taxi* (TV 1978–82), *Romancing the Stone* (1983), *Terms of Endearment* (1984), *The Jewel of the Nile* (1985), *Ruthless People* (1986), *Tin Men* (1987), *Throw Momma from the Train* (1987), *Twins* (1988), *War of the Roses* (1989), *Batman Returns* (1992), *Renaissance Man* (1994), *Junior* (1994), *Get Shorty* (1995), *Matilda* (1996), *LA Confidential* (1997), *Man on the Moon* (1999).

Dietrich, Marlene (Maria Magdalena von Losch) (1901–92) German–American, born Berlin; *The Blue Angel* (1930), *Morocco* (1930), *Blond Venus* (1932), *Shanghai Express* (1932), *The Scarlett Empress* (1934), *The Devil is a Woman* (1935), *Desire* (1936), *Destry Rides Again* (1939), *A Foreign Affair* (1948), *Rancho Notorious* (1952), *Judgement at Nuremberg* (1961).

Dillon, Matt (1964–) American, born Larchmont, New York; *Tex* (1982), *The Outsiders* (1983), *Rumble Fish* (1983), *The Flamingo Kid* (1984), *Target* (1985), *Big Town* (1987), *Kansas* (1988), *Drugstore Cowboy* (1989), *A Kiss Before Dying* (1991), *Singles* (1992), *Malcolm X* (1992), *Golden Gate* (1994), *Mr Wonderful* (1994), *Albino Alligator* (1996), *Wild Things* (1998), *One Night At McCool's* (2001).

Donat, Robert (1905–58) British, born Manchester; *The Count of Monte Cristo* (1934), *The Thirty-Nine Steps* (1935), *The Ghost Goes West* (1936), *The Citadel* (1938), *Goodbye Mr Chips* (1939), *The Winslow Boy* (1948), *The Inn of the Sixth Happiness* (1958).

Donohoe, Amanda (c.1965–) British; *Castaway* (1987), *The Lair of the White Worm* (1988), *The Rainbow* (1989), *LA Law* (TV 1990–2), *Paper Mask* (1990), *The Madness of King George* (1994), *The Last Day* (1996), *Liar Liar* (1997).

Dors, Diana (Diana Fluck) (1931–84) British, born Swindon, Wiltshire; *Oliver Twist* (1948), *Yield to the Night* (1956), *Deep End* (1970), *There's a Girl in My Soup* (1970), *The Amazing Mr Blunden* (1972), *Theatre of Blood* (1973), *Steaming* (1984).

Douglas, Kirk (Issur Danielovitch Demsky) (1916–) American, born Amsterdam, New York; *The Strange Love of Martha Ivers* (1946), *Lust for Life* (1956), *Gunfight at the OK Corral* (1957), *Paths of Glory* (1957), *The Vikings* (1958), *Spartacus* (1960), *The Man from Snowy River* (1982), *Oscar* (1991), *Greedy* (1994), *Diamonds* (1999).

Douglas, Michael (1944–) American, born New Brunswick, New Jersey; *The Streets of San Francisco* (TV 1972–5), *The China Syndrome* (1980), *The Star Chamber* (1983), *Romancing the Stone* (1984), *The Jewel of the Nile* (1985), *Fatal Attraction* (1987), *Wall Street* (1987), *Black Rain* (1989), *War of the Roses* (1989), *Shining Through* (1991), *Basic Instinct*

(1992), *Falling Down* (1993), *Disclosure* (1994), *The Ghost in the Darkness* (1996), *The Game* (1997), *A Perfect Murder* (1998), *Traffic* (2000), *One Night at McCool's* (2001).

Dreyfuss, Richard (1947–) American, born Brooklyn, New York City; *American Graffiti* (1973), *Jaws* (1975), *Close Encounters of the Third Kind* (1977), *The Goodbye Girl* (1977), *Whose Life is it Anyway?* (1981), *Down and Out in Beverly Hills* (1986), *Stakeout* (1987), *Tin Men* (1987), *Always* (1989), *The Proud and the Free* (1991), *What About Bob?* (1991), *Prisoners of Honor* (1991), *Rosencrantz and Guilderstern are Dead* (1991), *Lost in Yonkers* (1993), *Another Stakeout* (1993), *The American President* (1995), *Trigger Happy* (1996).

Dunaway, (Dorothy) Faye (1941–) American, born Bascom, Florida; *Bonnie and Clyde* (1967), *Little Big Man* (1970), *The Getaway* (1972), *Chinatown* (1974), *The Towering Inferno* (1974), *Network* (1976), *The Eyes of Laura Mars* (1978), *The Champ* (1979), *Mommie Dearest* (1981), *Barfly* (1987), *Midnight Crossing* (1988), *Burning Secret* (1988), *The Handmaid's Tale* (1990), *Scorchers* (1991), *Silhouette* (TV 1991), *Three Weeks in Jerusalem* (1991), *American Dreamers* (1992), *Don Juan de Marco* (1995), *Albino Alligator* (1996), *The Thomas Crown Affair* (1999).

Durbin, Deanna (Edna Mae Durbin) (1921–) Canadian, born Winnipeg, Manitoba; *Three Smart Girls* (1936), *One Hundred Men and a Girl* (1937), *Mad About Music* (1938), *That Certain Age* (1938), *Three Smart Girls Grow Up* (1939), *It Started With Eve* (1941), *Christmas Holiday* (1944), *Lady on a Train* (1945).

Duvall, Robert (1930–) American, born San Diego, California; *To Kill a Mockingbird* (1963), *The Godfather* (1972), *The Godfather, Part II* (1974), *Ike* (TV 1979), *Apocalypse Now* (1979), *The Great Santini* (1980), *Tender Mercies* (1983), *The Natural* (1984), *Colors* (1988), *The Handmaid's Tale* (1990), *Days of Thunder* (1990), *Convicts* (1991), *Newsies* (1992), *An American Legend* (1993), *The Paper* (1994), *The Scarlet Letter* (1995), *Phenomenon* (1996), *The Apostle* (1997), *John Q* (2002).

Duvall, Shelley (1949–) American, born Houston, Texas; *Thieves Like Us* (1974), *Annie Hall* (1977), *The Shining* (1980), *Popeye* (1980), *Roxanne* (1987), *Suburban Commando* (1991), *The Portrait of a Lady* (1996), *Home Fries* (1998).

Eastwood, Clint (1930–) American, born San Francisco, California; *Rawhide* (TV 1958–65), *A Fistful of Dollars* (1964), *For a Few Dollars More* (1965), *The Good, The Bad, and the Ugly* (1966), *Coogan's Bluff* (1968), *Paint Your Wagon* (1969), *Where Eagles Dare* (1969), *Play Misty for Me* (1971), *Dirty Harry* (1972), *High Plains Drifter* (1973), *Magnum Force* (1973), *The Enforcer* (1976), *Every Which Way But Loose* (1978), *Escape from Alcatraz* (1979), *Honky Tonk Man* (1982), *Sudden Impact* (1983), *Heartbreak Ridge* (1986), *The Dead Pool* (1989), *White Hunter Black Heart* (1990), *The Rookie* (1990), *Unforgiven* (1992), *In the Line of Fire* (1993), *A Perfect World* (1993), *The Bridges of Madison County* (1995), *Absolute Power* (1997), *True Crime* (1999).

Eden, Barbara (Barbara Huffman) (1934–) American, born Tucson, Arizona; *Voyage to the Bottom of the Sea* (1961), *I Dream of Jeannie* (TV 1965–70), *Harper Valley PTA* (1978), *Harper Valley PTA* (TV 1981).

Ekberg, Anita (1931–) Swedish, born Malmö; *La Dolce Vita* (1959), *The Summer is Short* (1962), *Bambols* (1996).

Arts and Culture

Ekland, Britt (Britt-Marie Ekland) (1942–) Swedish, born Stockholm; *The Man with the Golden Gun* (1974), *Casanova* (1977), *Scandal* (1989), *Beverly Hills Vamp* (1989).

Elliott, Denholm (1922–92) British, born London; *Nothing but the Best* (1964), *Here We Go Round the Mulberry Bush* (1967), *A Bridge too Far* (1977), *Raiders of the Lost Ark* (1981), *Brimstone and Treacle* (1982), *Trading Places* (1983), *The Razor's Edge* (1984), *A Private Function* (1984), *A Room with a View* (1985), *Defence of the Realm* (1985), *Maurice* (1987), *Indiana Jones and the Last Crusade* (1989), *Toy Soldiers* (1991).

Estevez, Emilio (1962–) American, born New York City; *The Outsiders* (1983), *Repo Man* (1984), *Breakfast Club* (1984), *St Elmo's Fire* (1985), *Stakeout* (1987), *Young Guns* (1988), *Young Guns 2* (1990), *Freejack* (1991), *The Mighty Ducks* (1992), *Another Stakeout* (1993), *Judgement Night* (1993).

Evans, Dame Edith (1888–1976) British, born London; *The Queen of Spades* (1948), *The Importance of Being Earnest* (1951).

Everett, Rupert (1960–) British, born Norfolk; *Another Country* (1984), *Dance with a Stranger* (1985), *The Comfort of Strangers* (1990), *Prêt-À-Porter* (1994), *The Madness of King George* (1994), *My Best Friend's Wedding* (1997), *An Ideal Husband* (1999), *A Midsummer Night's Dream* (1999), *The Importance of Being Earnest* (2002).

Fairbanks, Douglas, Jr (1909–2000) American, born New York City; *Catherine the Great* (1934), *The Prisoner of Zenda* (1937), *Sinbad the Sailor* (1947).

Fairbanks, Douglas, Sr (Douglas Elton Ullman) (1883–1939) American, born Denver, Colorado; *The Mark of Zorro* (1920), *The Three Musketeers* (1921), *Robin Hood* (1922), *The Thief of Baghdad* (1924), *The Black Pirate* (1926).

Falk, Peter (1927–) American, born New York City; *It's a Mad, Mad, Mad, Mad World* (1963), *The Great Race* (1965), *Columbo* (TV 1971–8), *The Princess Bride* (1987), *Cookie* (1988), *Vibes* (1988), *Wings of Desire* (1988), *Aunt Julia and the Scriptwriter* (1991), *The Player* (1992).

Farrow, Mia (Maria Farrow) (1945–) American, born Los Angeles; *Peyton Place* (TV 1964–7), *Rosemary's Baby* (1968), *Blind Terror* (1971), *The Great Gatsby* (1973), *Death on the Nile* (1978), *A Wedding* (1978), *A Midsummer Night's Sex Comedy* (1982), *The Purple Rose of Cairo* (1985), *Hannah and Her Sisters* (1986), *Another Woman* (1988), *New York Stories* (1989), *Alice* (1991), *Shadows and Fog* (1992), *Husbands and Wives* (1992), *Wolf* (1993), *Reckless* (1995), *Coming Soon* (1999).

Fell, Norman (1924–98) American, born Philadelphia, Pennsylvania; *The Graduate* (1967), *Bullitt* (1968), *The Man from UNCLE* (TV 1968), *Three's Company* (TV 1977–8), *The Ropers* (TV 1979–80), *Paternity* (1981).

Field, Sally (1946–) American, born Pasadena, California; *Gidget* (TV 1965), *The Flying Nun* (TV 1967–9), *Sybil* (TV 1976), *Stay Hungry* (1976), *Heroes* (1977), *Smokey and the Bandit* (1977), *Hooper* (1978), *Norma Rae* (1979), *Beyond the Poseidon Adventure* (1979), *Smokey and the Bandit II* (1980), *Absence of Malice* (1981), *Places in the Heart* (1984), *Punchline* (1988), *Steel Magnolias* (1990), *Not Without my Daughter* (1991), *Soapdish* (1991), *Mrs Doubtfire* (1993), *Forrest Gump* (1994), *A Cooler Climate* (1999).

Fields, W C (William Claude Dukenfield) (1879–1946) American, born Philadelphia, Pennsylvania; *Pool Sharks* (1915), *International House*

(1933), *It's a Gift* (1934), *The Old Fashioned Way* (1934), *David Copperfield* (1935), *My Little Chickadee* (1940), *The Bank Dick* (1940), *Never Give a Sucker an Even Break* (1941).

Fiennes, Ralph (Ralph Nathanial Fiennes) (1962–) British; *Wuthering Heights* (1992), *Schindler's List* (1994), *Quiz Show* (1994), *The English Patient* (1996), *Oscar and Lucinda* (1998), *The End of the Affair* (1999), *Red Dragon* (2002).

Finch, Peter (Frederick George Peter Ingle Finch) (1916–77) British, born London; *The Shiralee* (1957), *The Nun's Story* (1959), *No Love for Johnnie* (1961), *Far from the Madding Crowd* (1967), *Sunday, Bloody Sunday* (1971), *Network* (1976).

Finney, Albert (1936–) British, born Salford, Lancashire; *The Entertainer* (1960), *Saturday Night and Sunday Morning* (1960), *Tom Jones* (1963), *Charlie Bubbles* (1968), *Murder on the Orient Express* (1974), *Shoot the Moon* (1981), *Annie* (1982), *The Dresser* (1983), *Under the Volcano* (1984), *The Green Man* (TV 1990), *Miller's Crossing* (1990), *The Playboys* (1992), *Karaoke* (TV 1996), *Washington Square* (1997), *Erin Brockovich* (2000), *Traffic* (2000).

Firth, Peter (1953–) British, born Bradford, Yorkshire; *Equus* (1973), *Tess* (1980), *Life Force* (1985), *Letter to Brezhnev* (1985), *A State of Emergency* (1986), *Shadowlands* (1993), *Amistad* (1997), *Mighty Joe Young* (1998).

Fisher, Carrie (1956–) American, born Beverly Hills, California; *Shampoo* (1975), *Star Wars* (1977), *The Blues Brothers* (1980), *The Empire Strikes Back* (1980), *Under the Rainbow* (1981), *Return of the Jedi* (1983), *The Man With One Red Shoe* (1985), *Hannah and Her Sisters* (1986), *The 'Burbs* (1989), *When Harry Met Sally …* (1989), *Loverboy* (1990), *Sibling Rivalry* (1990), *Drop Dead Fred* (1991), *Soapdish* (1991), *This is My Life* (1991), *So I Married an Axe Murderer* (1992), *Scream 3* (2000).

Fletcher, Louise (1934–) American, born Birmingham, Alabama; *One Flew Over the Cuckoo's Nest* (1975), *Exorcist II: The Heretic* (1977), *The Cheap Detective* (1978), *Brainstorm* (1983), *Firestarter* (1984), *The Boy Who Could Fly* (1985), *Two Moon Junction* (1988), *Cruel Intentions* (1999).

Flynn, Errol (1909–59) Australian–American, born Hobart, Tasmania; *In the Wake of the Bounty* (1933), *Captain Blood* (1935), *The Charge of the Light Brigade* (1936), *The Adventures of Robin Hood* (1938), *The Sea Hawk* (1940), *The Sun Also Rises* (1957).

Fonda, Henry (James) (1905–82) American, born Grand Island, Nebraska; *The Moon's Our Home* (1936), *A Farmer Takes A Wife* (1938), *Young Mr Lincoln* (1939), *The Grapes of Wrath* (1940), *The Lady Eve* (1941), *The Oxbow Incident* (1943), *My Darling Clementine* (1946), *Twelve Angry Men* (1957), *Stage Struck* (1957), *Fail Safe* (1964), *The Boston Strangler* (1968), *On Golden Pond* (1981).

Fonda, Jane (Seymour) (1937–) American, born New York City; *Walk on the Wild Side* (1961), *Barbarella* (1968), *They Shoot Horses Don't They?* (1969), *Klute* (1971), *Julia* (1977), *Coming Home* (1978), *The Electric Horseman* (1979), *The China Syndrome* (1980), *Nine to Five* (1981), *On Golden Pond* (1981), *The Dollmaker* (TV 1983), *The Morning After* (1986), *Old Gringo* (1989), *Stanley and Iris* (1989).

Fonda, Peter (1939–) American, born New York City; *Easy Rider* (1969), *Futureworld* (1976), *Cannonball Run* (1981), *Mercenary Fighters* (1988), *Escape From LA* (1996), *The Laramie Project* (2002).

Fontaine, Joan (Joan de Havilland) (1917–) British, born Tokyo, Japan; *Rebecca* (1940), *Suspicion*

(1941), *Jane Eyre* (1943), *Frenchman's Creek* (1944), *From This Day Forward* (1946), *Letter from an Unknown Woman* (1948), *Born to Be Bad* (1950).

Ford, Harrison (1942–) American, born Chicago; *American Graffiti* (1974), *Star Wars* (1977), *Heroes* (1977), *Force 10 from Navarone* (1978), *The Frisco Kid* (1979), *Hanover Street* (1979), *Apocalypse Now* (1979), *The Empire Strikes Back* (1980), *Raiders of the Lost Ark* (1981), *Blade Runner* (1982), *Return of the Jedi* (1983), *Indiana Jones and the Temple of Doom* (1984), *Witness* (1985), *Mosquito Coast* (1986), *Frantic* (1988), *Working Girl* (1988), *Indiana Jones and the Last Crusade* (1989), *Presumed Innocent* (1990), *Regarding Henry* (1991), *Patriot Games* (1992), *The Fugitive* (1993), *Clear and Present Danger* (1994), *The Devil's Own* (1996), *Random Hearts* (1999), *What Lies Beneath* (2000), *K-19: The Widowmaker* (2002).

Foster, Jodie (Ariane Munker) (1962–) American, born The Bronx, New York City; *Alice Doesn't Live Here Anymore* (1974), *Bugsy Malone* (1976), *Taxi Driver* (1976), *The Little Girl Who Lives Down the Lane* (1976), *Candleshoe* (1977), *Freaky Friday* (1977), *Siesta* (1987), *The Accused* (1988), *5 Corners* (1988), *Stealing Home* (1988), *Catchfire* (1990), *Silence of the Lambs* (1991), *Little Man Tate* (1991), *Shadows and Fog* (1992), *Sommersby* (1993), *Maverick* (1994), *Nell* (1994), *Contact* (1997), *Anna and the King* (1999), *Panic Room* (2002).

Fox, James (1939–) British, born London; *The Magnet* (1950), *The Loneliness of the Long Distance Runner* (1963), *Those Magnificent Men in Their Flying Machines* (1965), *Thoroughly Modern Millie* (1967), *Performance* (1970), *A Passage to India* (1984), *Greystoke* (1984), *The Whistle Blower* (1987), *High Season* (1987), *She's Been Away* (TV 1990), *Hostage* (1992), *Never Ever* (1996), *Mickey Blue Eyes* (1999).

Fox, Michael J (1961–) Canadian, born Edmonton, Alberta; *Letters from Frank* (TV 1979), *Family Ties* (TV 1982–9), *Poison Ivy* (TV 1985), *Back to the Future* (1985), *Teenwolf* (1985), *The Secret of My Success* (1987), *Bright Lights Big City* (1988), *Casualties of War* (1989), *Back to the Future II* (1989), *Back to the Future III* (1990), *The Hard Way* (1991), *Doc Hollywood* (1991), *For Love or Money* (1993), *Life with Mikey* (1993), *Don't Drink the Water* (TV 1994), *The American President* (1995), *Blue in the Face* (1995), *Mars Attacks!* (1996) .

Freeman, Morgan (1937–) American, born Memphis, Tennessee; *The Electric Company* (TV 1971–6), *Street Smart* (1987), *Driving Miss Daisy* (1989), *Glory* (1989), *The Bonfire of the Vanities* (1990), *Robin Hood: Prince of Thieves* (1991), *Unforgiven* (1992), *The Shawshank Redemption* (1994), *Seven* (1995), *Deep Impact* (1998), *The Sum of All Fears* (2002).

Fry, Stephen (John) (1957–) English, born London; *A Handful of Dust* (1988), *A Fish Called Wanda* (1988), *A Bit of Fry and Laurie* (TV 1989–95), *Jeeves and Wooster* (TV 1990–3), *Peter's Friends* (1992), *Cold Comfort Farm* (TV 1995), *Wilde* (1997), *Gosford Park* (2001).

Gabin, Jean (Jean-Alexis Moncorgé) (1904–76) French, born Paris; *Chacun Sa Chance* (1930), *Pépé le Moko* (1936), *La Grande Illusion* (1937), *Quai des Brumes* (1938), *Le Jour se lève* (1939), *Touchez Pas Au Grisbi* (1953), *Archimède Le Clochard* (1958), *Un Singe en Hiver* (1962), *Le Chat* (1971), *L'Année Sainte* (1976).

Gable, (William) Clark (1901–60) American, born Cadiz, Ohio; *Red Dust* (1932), *It Happened One Night* (1934), *Mutiny on the Bounty* (1935), *San Francisco* (1936), *Gone with the Wind* (1939), *The Hucksters* (1947), *Mogambo* (1953), *Never Let Me Go* (1953), *Teacher's Pet* (1958), *The Misfits* (1961).

Gabor, Zsa Zsa (Sari Gabor) (1918–) Hungarian, born Budapest; *Lovely to Look at* (1952), *Moulin Rouge* (1952), *Lili* (1953), *Public Enemy Number One* (1954), *Queen of Outer Space* (1959), *Up the Front* (1972).

Gambon, Sir Michael (1940–) Irish, born Dublin; *Turtle Diary* (1985), *The Singing Detective* (TV 1986), *Paris by Night* (1989), *The Cook, The Thief, His Wife and Her Lover* (1989), *The Wings of the Dove* (1997), *Sleepy Hollow* (1999), *Gosford Park* (2001).

Garbo, Greta (Greta Lovisa Gustafsson) (1905–90) Swedish–American, born Stockholm; *Flesh and the Devil* (1927), *Anna Christie* (1930), *Grand Hotel* (1932), *Queen Christina* (1933), *Anna Karenina* (1935), *Camille* (1936), *Ninotchka* (1939).

Gardner, Ava (Lucy Johnson) (1922–90) American, born Smithfield, North Carolina; *The Killers* (1946), *The Hucksters* (1947), *Show Boat* (1951), *Pandora and the Flying Dutchman* (1951), *The Snows of Kilimanjaro* (1952), *Mogambo* (1953), *The Barefoot Contessa* (1954), *The Sun Also Rises* (1957), *The Night of the Iguana* (1964).

Garland, Judy (Frances Gumm) (1922–69) American, born Grand Rapids, Minnesota; *The Wizard of Oz* (1939), *Babes in Arms* (1939), *For Me and My Gal* (1942), *Meet Me in St Louis* (1944), *Ziegfeld Follies* (1945), *The Clock* (1945), *Easter Parade* (1948), *Summer Stock* (1950), *A Star is Born* (1954).

Garner, James (James Scott Baumgarner) (1928–) American, born Norman, Oklahoma; *Maverick* (TV 1957–62), *The Great Escape* (1963), *The Americanization of Emily* (1964), *The Skin Game* (1971), *Rockford Files* (TV 1974–80), *The Fan* (1980), *Victor/Victoria* (1982), *Maverick* (1994), *My Fellow Americans* (1996), *Space Cowboys* (2000).

Garr, Teri (1949–) American, born Lakewood, Ohio; *Young Frankenstein* (1974), *Oh God* (1977), *Close Encounters of the Third Kind* (1977), *The Black Stallion* (1978), *Honky Tonk Freeway* (1981), *One from the Heart* (1982), *Tootsie* (1982), *The Sting II* (1982), *The Black Stallion Returns* (1983), *Mr Mom* (1983), *First Born* (1984), *After Hours* (1985), *Full Moon in Blue Water* (1988), *Perfect Alibi* (1994), *Prêt-À-Porter* (1994), *Dumb and Dumber* (1994), *Michael* (1996), *Dick* (1999).

Gassman, Vittorio (1922–2000) Italian, born Genoa; *Il Cavaliere Misterioso* (1948), *Riso Amaro* (1948), *La Vie est un Roman* (1983), *Sleepers* (1996).

Gere, Richard (1949–) American, born Philadelphia, Pennsylvania; *American Gigolo* (1980), *An Officer and a Gentleman* (1982), *Breathless* (1983), *The Cotton Club* (1984), *No Mercy* (1986), *Miles from Home* (1988), *Internal Affairs* (1990), *Pretty Woman* (1990), *Final Analysis* (1992), *Sommersby* (1993), *First Knight* (1995), *Primal Fear* (1996), *The Jackal* (1997), *Runaway Bride* (1999), *Dr T and the Women* (2000), *The Mothman Prophecies* (2002).

Gibson, Mel (1956–) American–Australian, born Peekshill, New York; *Tim* (1979), *Mad Max* (1979), *Gallipoli* (1981), *Mad Max 2: The Road Warrior* (1982), *The Year of Living Dangerously* (1982), *Mad Max Beyond Thunderdome* (1985), *Lethal Weapon* (1987), *Tequila Sunrise* (1988), *Lethal Weapon 2* (1989), *Bird on a Wire* (1990), *Air America* (1990), *Hamlet* (1990), *Lethal Weapon 3* (1992), *Forever Young* (1992), *The Man Without A Face* (1993), *Braveheart* (1995), *Ransom* (1996), *Conspiracy Theory* (1997), *The Patriot* (2000), *What Women Want* (2000), *Signs* (2002).

Arts and Culture

Gielgud, Sir John (Arthur) (1904–2000) British, born London; also stage; *Julius Caesar* (1953), *The Charge of the Light Brigade* (1968), *Oh What a Lovely War* (1969), *Murder on the Orient Express* (1974), *Providence* (1977), *Brideshead Revisited* (TV 1981), *Arthur* (1981), *Gandhi* (1982), *The Whistle Blower* (1987), *Loser Takes All* (1989), *Prospero's Books* (1991), *First Knight* (1995), *Haunted* (1995), *Hamlet* (1996), *Elizabeth* (1998).

Gish, Lillian (Diana) (Lillian de Guiche) (1896–1993) American, born Springfield, Ohio; *An Unseen Enemy* (1912), *Birth of a Nation* (1914), *Intolerance* (1916), *Broken Blossoms* (1919), *Way Down East* (1920), *Duel in the Sun* (1946), *Night of the Hunter* (1955), *The Whales of August* (1987).

Glover, Danny (1947–) American, born San Francisco, California; *Silverado* (1985), *Witness* (1985), *Lethal Weapon* (1987), *Bat 21* (1988), *Lethal Weapon 2* (1989), *Predator 2* (1990), *Lethal Weapon 3* (1992), *The Saint of Fort Washington* (1993), *Bopha!* (1993), *Lethal Weapon 4* (1998), *The Patriot* (2000), *The Royal Tenenbaums* (2001).

Goldberg, Whoopi (Caryn Johnson) (1949–) American, born Manhattan, New York City; *The Color Purple* (1985), *Burglar* (1985), *Jumping Jack Flash* (1986), *Clara's Heart* (1988), *The Telephone* (1988), *Ghost* (1990), *Soapdish* (1991), *Sister Act* (1992), *Change of Heart* (1992), *The Player* (1992), *Made in America* (1993), *Sister Act 2: Back in the Habit* (1993), *Corrina Corrina* (1994), *Star Trek: Generations* (1994), *Girl Interrupted* (1999).

Goldblum, Jeff (1952–) American, born Pittsburgh, Pennsylvania; *California Split* (1974), *Death Wish* (1974), *Nashville* (1975), *Invasion of the Body Snatchers* (1978), *Escape from Athena* (1979), *The Big Chill* (1983), *Silverado* (1985), *The Fly* (1985), *Vibes* (1988), *The Tall Guy* (1989), *Earth Girls Are Easy* (1989), *Mister Frost* (1990), *The Player* (1992), *Fathers and Sons* (1992), *Jurassic Park* (1993), *Nine Months* (1995), *Independence Day* (1996), *The Lost World: Jurassic Park* (1997), *Cats and Dogs* (2001).

Goodman, John (1953–) American, born St Louis, Missouri; *True Stories* (1986), *The Big Easy* (1987), *Roseanne* (TV 1988–97), *Punchline* (1988), *Sea of Love* (1990), *Always* (1990), *Stella* (1990), *Arachnophobia* (1990), *King Ralph* (1991), *The Flintstones* (1994), *Pie in the Sky* (1996), *The Borrowers* (1997), *Blues Brothers 2000* (1998), *The Big Lebowski* (1998), *O Brother Where Art Thou?* (2000), *One Night At McCool's* (2001).

Gossett, Louis Jr (1936–) American, born Brooklyn, New York City; *Travels with My Aunt* (1972), *The Lazarus Syndrome* (TV 1979), *An Officer and a Gentleman* (1982), *The Powers of Matthew Starr* (TV 1982), *Jaws 3D* (1983), *Iron Eagle* (1985), *Iron Eagle II* (1988), *Cover Up* (1991), *Aces: Iron Eagle III* (1992), *Keeper of the City* (1992), *The Highwayman* (1999).

Granger, Stewart (James Lablanche Stewart) (1913–93) British, born London; *The Man in Grey* (1943), *Waterloo Road* (1944), *Love Story* (1944), *Caesar and Cleopatra* (1945), *Captain Boycott* (1947), *King Solomon's Mines* (1950), *Scaramouche* (1952), *The Prisoner of Zenda* (1952), *Beau Brummell* (1954), *The Wild Geese* (1977).

Grant, Cary (Archibald Alexander Leach) (1904–86) Anglo-American, born Bristol, England; *This is the Night* (1932), *The Awful Truth* (1937), *Bringing Up Baby* (1938), *His Girl Friday* (1940), *Arsenic and Old Lace* (1944), *Notorious* (1946), *To Catch a Thief* (1953), *North by Northwest* (1959).

Grant, Hugh (1960–) British, born London; *Maurice* (1987), *The Lair of the White Worm* (1988), *Impromptu* (1991), *Bitter Moon* (1992), *Four Weddings and a Funeral* (1994), *Nine Months* (1995), *An Awfully Big Adventure* (1995), *Sense and Sensibility* (1995), *Extreme Measures* (1996), *Notting Hill* (1999), *Mickey Blue Eyes* (1999), *Bridget Jones's Diary* (2001), *About A Boy* (2002), *Two Week's Notice* (2002).

Grant, Lee (Lyova Rosenthal) (1930–) American, born New York City; *Detective Story* (1951), *The Landlord* (1970), *Shampoo* (1975), *The Voyage of the Damned* (1976), *Damien: Omen II* (1978), *Big Town* (1987), *It's My Party* (1996), *Dr T and the Women* (2000).

Greenwood, Joan (1921–87) British, born Chelsea, London; *Whisky Galore* (1949), *Kind Hearts and Coronets* (1949), *The Man in the White Suit* (1951), *The Importance of Being Earnest* (1952), *Tom Jones* (1963), *Little Dorrit* (1987).

Griffith, Melanie (1957–) American, born New York City; *Something Wild* (1987), *Cherry 2000* (1988), *Working Girl* (1988), *Stormy Monday* (1988), *Pacific Heights* (1990), *Bonfire of the Vanities* (1990), *Paradise* (1991), *Shining Through* (1992), *Close to Eden* (1992), *Born Yesterday* (1993), *Nobody's Fool* (1994), *Lolita* (1996), *Forever Lulu* (2000).

Guinness, Sir Alec (1914–2000) British, born London; *Oliver Twist* (1948), *Kind Hearts and Coronets* (1949), *The Lavender Hill Mob* (1951), *The Man in the White Suit* (1951), *The Card* (1952), *Father Brown* (1954), *The Ladykillers* (1955), *The Bridge on the River Kwai* (1957), *The Horse's Mouth* (1958), *Our Man in Havana* (1960), *Tunes of Glory* (1962), *Lawrence of Arabia* (1962), *Doctor Zhivago* (1966), *Star Wars* (1977), *Tinker, Tailor, Soldier, Spy* (1979), *Smiley's People* (TV 1981), *Return of the Jedi* (1983), *A Passage to India* (1984), *Little Dorrit* (1987), *A Handful of Dust* (1988), *Kafka* (1991).

Guttenberg, Steve (1958–) American, born Massapequa, New York; *Diner* (1981), *Police Academy* (1984), *Police Academy II* (1985), *Cocoon* (1985), *Short Circuit* (1986), *The Bedroom Window* (1986), *Three Men and a Baby* (1988), *High Spirits* (1988), *Cocoon: The Return* (1988), *Three Men and a Little Lady* (1990), *Airborne* (1998).

Gwynne, Fred (1926–93) American, born New York City; *Car 54 Where are You?* (TV 1961–2), *The Munsters* (TV 1964–5), *On the Waterfront* (1954), *Munster Go Home* (1966), *The Cotton Club* (1984), *Fatal Attraction* (1987), *Kane and Abel* (TV 1988), *Pet Sematary* (1989), *Shadows and Fog* (1992), *My Cousin Vinny* (1992).

Hackman, Gene (1931–) American, born San Bernardino, California; *Bonnie and Clyde* (1967), *I Never Sang for My Father* (1969), *French Connection* (1971), *The Poseidon Adventure* (1972), *Young Frankenstein* (1974), *French Connection II* (1975), *A Bridge Too Far* (1977), *Superman* (1978), *Superman II* (1981), *Target* (1985), *Superman IV* (1987), *Bat 21* (1988), *Full Moon in Blue Water* (1988), *Split Decisions* (1988), *Mississippi Burning* (1989), *The Package* (1989), *Loose Cannons* (1990), *Postcards from the Edge* (1990), *Narrow Margin* (1990), *Class Action* (1990), *Company Business* (1991), *Unforgiven* (1992), *The Firm* (1993), *Geronimo: An American Legend* (1993), *Get Shorty* (1995), *The Birdcage* (1996), *The Chamber* (1996), *Extreme Measures* (1996), *Absolute Power* (1997), *Enemy of the State* (1999), *The Royal Tenenbaums* (2001).

Hagman, Larry (Larry Hageman) (1931–) American, born Weatherford, Texas; *Ensign Pulver* (1964), *I Dream of Jeannie* (TV 1965–70), *The Eagle Has Landed* (1976), *Superman* (1978), *Dallas* (TV 1978–90), *Nixon* (1995), *Primary Colors* (1998).

Hamill, Mark (1952–) American, born Oakland, California; *Star Wars* (1977), *The Big Red One* (1979), *The Empire Strikes Back* (1980), *The Night the Lights Went out in Georgia* (1981), *Return of the Jedi* (1983), *Slipstream* (1988), *Flash II* (1991), *Village of the Damned* (1995).

Hamlin, Harry (1951–) American, born Pasadena, California; *Clash of the Titans* (1981), *Dragonslayer* (1981), *Space* (TV 1985), *LA Law* (TV 1986–92).

Hanks, Tom (1957–) American, born Oakland, California; *Bachelor Party* (1983), *Splash!* (1984), *Dragnet* (1987), *Big* (1988), *Punchline* (1988), *The 'Burbs* (1989), *Turner and Hooch* (1990), *Bonfire of the Vanities* (1991), *A League of Their Own* (1992), *Benny and Joon* (1992), *Sleepless in Seattle* (1993), *Philadelphia* (1993), *Forrest Gump* (1994), *Apollo 13* (1995), *That Thing You Do* (1996), *Saving Private Ryan* (1998), *You've Got Mail* (1998), *The Green Mile* (1999), *Cast Away* (2000), *Road to Perdition* (2002).

Hannah, Daryl (1960–) American, born Chicago; *Blade Runner* (1982), *Splash!* (1984), *Clan of the Cave Bear* (1986), *Legal Eagles* (1986), *Roxanne* (1987), *Wall Street* (1987), *High Spirits* (1988), *Steel Magnolias* (1989), *Crazy People* (1990), *At Play in the Fields of the Lord* (1991), *Memoirs of an Invisible Man* (1992), *The Last Days of Frankie the Fly* (1997), *Run for the Money* (2002).

Hardy, Oliver (Norvell Hardy Junior) (1892–1957) American, born near Atlanta, Georgia; *Putting Pants on Philip* (1927), *The Battle of the Century* (1927), *Two Tars* (1928), *The Perfect Day* (1929), *Laughing Gravy* (1931), *The Music Box* (1932), *Babes in Toyland* (1934), *Bonnie Scotland* (1935), *Way Out West* (1937), *The Flying Deuces* (1939), *Atoll K* (1950).

Harlow, Jean (Harlean Carpentier) (1911–37) American, born Kansas City, Missouri; *Red Dust* (1932), *Hell's Angels* (1930), *Platinum Blonde* (1931), *Red-Headed Woman* (1932), *Bombshell* (1933), *Dinner at 8* (1933), *Libelled Lady* (1936).

Harrelson, Woody (1961–) American, born Midland, Texas; *Harper Valley PTA* (1978), *Wildcats* (1986), *LA Story* (1991), *Doc Hollywood* (1991), *Ted and Venus* (1991), *White Men Can't Jump* (1992), *Indecent Proposal* (1993), *Natural Born Killers* (1994), *Kingpin* (1996), *The People vs Larry Flynt* (1996), *The Thin Red Line* (1998), *EdTV* (1999).

Harris, Julie (Julia Harris) (1925–) American, born Grosse Point, Michigan; *The Member of the Wedding* (1953), *East of Eden* (1955), *The Haunting* (1963).

Harris, Richard (1930–2002) Irish, born County Limerick; *The Guns of Navarone* (1961), *Mutiny on the Bounty* (1962), *This Sporting Life* (1963), *Camelot* (1967), *A Man Called Horse* (1969), *Cromwell* (1970), *The Cassandra Crossing* (1977), *Orca — Killer Whale* (1977), *The Wild Geese* (1978), *The Field* (1990), *Gladiator* (2000), *Harry Potter and the Philosopher's Stone* (2001), *Harry Potter and the Chamber of Secrets* (2002).

Harrison, Sir Rex (Reginald Carey Harrison) (1908–90) British, born Huyton, Lancashire; *Major Barbara* (1940), *Blithe Spirit* (1945), *Anna and the King of Siam* (1946), *The Ghost and Mrs Muir* (1947), *The Reluctant Debutante* (1958), *The Constant Husband* (1955), *Cleopatra* (1962), *My Fair Lady* (1964), *Dr Doolittle* (1967).

Hauer, Rutger (1944–) Dutch, born Amsterdam; *Nighthawks* (1981), *Blade Runner* (1982), *Eureka* (1983), *The Osterman Weekend* (1983), *The Hitcher* (1985), *Flesh and Blood* (1985), *Wanted Dead or Alive* (1986), *The Legend of the Holy Drinker* (1989), *Blind Fury* (1990), *Ocean Point* (1991), *On a Moonlit*

Night (1991), *Split Second* (1992), *Buffy the Vampire Slayer* (1992), *Past Midnight* (1992), *Nostradamus* (1994), *Crossworlds* (1996), *Confessions of a Dangerous Mind* (2002).

Hawn, Goldie (Jeanne) (1945–) American, born Washington DC; *Laugh In* (TV 1968–73), *Cactus Flower* (1969), *There's a Girl in My Soup* (1970), *Butterflies are Free* (1971), *Sugarland Express* (1974), *Shampoo* (1975), *Foul Play* (1978), *Seems Like Old Times* (1980), *Private Benjamin* (1980), *Best Friends* (1982), *Swing Shift* (1984), *Bird on a Wire* (1990), *CrissCross* (1991), *Deceived* (1991), *Housesitter* (1992), *Death Becomes Her* (1992), *The First Wives Club* (1996), *The Banger Sisters* (2002).

Hawthorne, Sir Nigel (Barnard) (1929–2001) British, born Coventry; *Yes Minister* (TV 1980–92), *Yes, Prime Minister* (TV 1986–8), *The Madness of King George* (1994), *Richard III* (1995), *Twelfth Night* (1996), *A Reasonable Man* (1999).

Hay, Will (1889–1949) British, born Stockton-on-Tees; *Good Morning Boys* (1937), *Old Bones of the River* (1938), *Oh Mr Porter* (1938), *Ask a Policeman* (1939), *The Ghost of St Michaels* (1941), *My Learned Friend* (1944).

Hayward, Susan (Edythe Marrenner) (1917–75) American, born Brooklyn, New York City; *Smash-Up: The Story of a Woman* (1947), *With a Song In My Heart* (1952), *I'll Cry Tomorrow* (1955), *I Want to Live!* (1958), *Where Love Has Gone* (1964), *Valley of the Dolls* (1967), *The Revengers* (1972).

Hayworth, Rita (Margarita Carmen Cansino) (1918–87) American, born New York City; *Only Angels Have Wings* (1939), *The Lady in Question* (1940), *The Strawberry Blonde* (1940), *Blood and Sand* (1941), *You'll Never Get Rich* (1941), *Cover Girl* (1944), *Gilda* (1946), *The Lady from Shanghai* (1948), *Separate Tables* (1958).

Hepburn, Audrey (Audrey Hepburn-Ruston) (1929–93) Anglo-Dutch, born Brussels, Belgium; *Roman Holiday* (1953), *War and Peace* (1956), *Funny Face* (1957), *The Nun's Story* (1959), *Breakfast at Tiffany's* (1961), *My Fair Lady* (1964), *How to Steal a Million* (1966), *Wait Until Dark* (1967), *Robin and Marian* (1976), *Always* (1989).

Hepburn, Katharine (1907–) American, born Hartford, Connecticut; *A Bill of Divorcement* (1932), *Morning Glory* (1933), *Stage Door* (1937), *Bringing Up Baby* (1938), *Holiday* (1938), *The Philadelphia Story* (1940), *Woman of the Year* (1942), *Adam's Rib* (1949), *The African Queen* (1951), *Long Day's Journey into Night* (1962), *Guess Who's Coming to Dinner* (1967), *Suddenly Last Summer* (1968), *The Lion in Winter* (1968), *Rooster Cogburn* (1975), *On Golden Pond* (1981), *Love Affair* (1994).

Hershey, Barbara (formerly Barbara Seagull, originally Herzstein) (1948–) American, born Hollywood, California; *Last Summer* (1968), *Diamonds* (1975), *The Flood* (TV 1976), *The Stunt Man* (1978), *Angel on My Shoulder* (TV 1980), *The Entity* (1983), *The Right Stuff* (1983), *The Natural* (1984), *Passion Flower* (TV 1985), *Hannah and Her Sisters* (1986), *Tin Men* (1987), *A World Apart* (1988), *The Last Temptation of Christ* (1988), *Beaches* (1988), *Barton Fink* (1990), *Naked Lunch* (1991), *The Public Eye* (1991), *A Dangerous Woman* (1993), *Splitting Heirs* (1993), *The Portrait of a Lady* (1996), *Passion* (1999).

Heston, Charlton (John Charlton Carter) (1922–) American, born Evanston, Illinois; *Arrowhead* (1953), *The Ten Commandments* (1956), *Touch of Evil* (1958), *Ben-Hur* (1959), *El Cid* (1961), *The Greatest Story Ever Told* (1965), *The War Lord* (1965), *Khartoum* (1966), *Planet of the Apes* (1968), *Will Pen-*

Arts and Culture

Arts and Culture

ny (1968), *Earthquake* (1973), *Airport* (1975), *The Four Musketeers* (1975), *Almost an Angel* (1990), *Wayne's World 2* (1993), *Tombstone* (1993), *Hamlet* (1996), *Any Given Sunday* (1999).

Hiller, Dame Wendy (1912–) British, born Bramhall, Cheshire; also stage; *Major Barbara* (1940), *I Know Where I'm Going* (1945), *Separate Tables* (1958), *Sons and Lovers* (1960), *A Man for All Seasons* (1966), *Murder on the Orient Express* (1974), *Voyage of the Damned* (1976), *The Elephant Man* (1980), *The Lonely Passion of Judith Hearne* (1987).

Hoffman, Dustin (1937–) American, born Los Angeles; *The Graduate* (1967), *Midnight Cowboy* (1969), *Little Big Man* (1970), *Papillon* (1973), *Lenny* (1974), *All the President's Men* (1976), *Kramer vs Kramer* (1979), *Tootsie* (1982), *Death of a Salesman* (TV 1984), *Rain Man* (1988), *Dick Tracy* (1990), *Hook* (1991), *Hero* (1992), *Outbreak* (1995), *Sleepers* (1996), *Wag The Dog* (1997), *Sphere* (1998).

Hogan, Paul (1939–) Australian, born New South Wales; *Crocodile Dundee* (1986), *Crocodile Dundee II* (1988), *Almost an Angel* (1990), *Lightning Jack* (1994), *Flipper* (1996), *Crocodile Dundee in Los Angeles* (2001).

Holbrook, Hal (Harold Holbrook) (1925–) American, born Cleveland, Ohio; *The Group* (1966), *The Bold Ones* (1970–1), *That Certain Summer* (TV 1972), *Magnum Force* (1973), *All the President's Men* (1976), *Capricorn One* (1976), *Julia* (1977), *The Fog* (1980), *Creepshow* (1982), *The Star Chamber* (1982).

Holden, William (William Franklin Beedle, Jr) (1918–82) American, born O'Fallon, Illinois; *Golden Boy* (1939), *Rachel and the Stranger* (1948), *Sunset Boulevard* (1950), *Born Yesterday* (1950), *Stalag 17* (1953), *Love is a Many-Splendored Thing* (1955), *Picnic* (1955), *The Bridge on the River Kwai* (1957), *Casino Royale* (1967), *The Wild Bunch* (1969), *The Towering Inferno* (1974), *Network* (1976), *Damien: Omen II* (1978), *Escape to Athena* (1979), *The Earthling* (1980), *SOB* (1981), *When Time Ran Out* (1981).

Hope, Bob (Leslie Townes Hope) (1903–) Anglo-American, born Eltham, London; *Thanks for the Memory* (1938), *The Cat and the Canary* (1939), *Road to Singapore* (1940), *The Ghost Breakers* (1940), *Road to Zanzibar* (1941), *My Favorite Blonde* (1942), *Road to Morocco* (1942), *The Paleface* (1948), *Fancy Pants* (1950), *The Facts of Life* (1960), *Road to Hong Kong* (1961), *How to Commit Marriage* (1969).

Hopkins, Anthony (1941–) Welsh–American, born Port Talbot, Wales; *The Lion in Winter* (1968), *When Eight Bells Toll* (1971), *War and Peace* (TV 1972), *Magic* (1978), *The Elephant Man* (1980), *The Bounty* (1983), *84 Charing Cross Road* (1986), *Desperate Hours* (1991), *Silence of the Lambs* (1991), *Spotswood* (1991), *Freejack* (1992), *Howards End* (1992), *Charlie* (1992), *The Innocent* (1992), *Dracula* (1992), *The Remains of the Day* (1993), *Shadowlands* (1993), *The Road to Wellville* (1994), *Legends of the Fall* (1994), *Nixon* (1995), *Surviving Picasso* (1996), *Bookworm* (1997), *Meet Joe Black* (1998), *Hannibal* (2001), *Red Dragon* (2002).

Hopper, Dennis (1936–) American, born Dodge City, Kansas; *Rebel Without a Cause* (1955), *Giant* (1956), *Cool Hand Luke* (1967), *Easy Rider* (1969), *Apocalypse Now* (1979), *Blue Velvet* (1986), *River's Edge* (1986), *Blood Red* (1990), *Catchfire* (1990), *Paris Trout* (1991), *The Indian Runner* (1991), *Money Men* (1992), *True Romance* (1993), *Speed* (1994), *Basquiat* (1996), *Bad City Blues* (1999).

Hordern, Sir Michael (1911–95) British, born Berkhampstead, Hertfordshire; *The Constant Husband*

(1955), *The Spanish Gardener* (1956), *Dr Syn — Alias the Scarecrow* (1963), *A Funny Thing Happened on the Way to the Forum* (1966), *The Bed-Sitting Room* (1969), *The Slipper and the Rose* (1976), *The Missionary* (1982), *Paradise Postponed* (TV 1986), *The Fool* (1990).

Hoskins, Bob (Robert William) (1942–) British, born Bury St Edmunds, Suffolk; *Pennies from Heaven* (TV 1978), *The Long Good Friday* (1980), *The Honorary Consul* (1983), *The Cotton Club* (1984), *Brazil* (1985), *Mona Lisa* (1986), *A Prayer for the Dying* (1987), *Who Framed Roger Rabbit?* (1988), *Heart Condition* (1990), *Mermaids* (1990), *Shattered* (1991), *Hook* (1991), *The Favour, the Watch and the very Big Fish* (1991), *The Inner Circle* (1992), *Rainbow* (1995), *Nixon* (1995), *The Secret Agent* (1996), *Parting Shots* (1998), *Last Orders* (2001).

Howard, Leslie (Leslie Howard Stainer) (1890–1943) British, born London; *Of Human Bondage* (1934), *The Scarlet Pimpernel* (1935), *Pygmalion* (1938), *Gone with the Wind* (1939).

Howard, Trevor (Wallace) (1916–88) British, born Cliftonville, Kent; *The Way Ahead* (1944), *Brief Encounter* (1946), *Green for Danger* (1946), *The Third Man* (1949), *The Heart of the Matter* (1953), *The Key* (1958), *Sons and Lovers* (1960), *Mutiny on the Bounty* (1962), *The Charge of the Light Brigade* (1968), *Ryan's Daughter* (1970), *The Night Visitor* (1971), *Catholics* (TV 1973), *Conduct Unbecoming* (1975), *Meteor* (1979), *Staying On* (TV 1980), *Gandhi* (1982), *White Mischief* (1987), *The Unholy* (1988).

Hudson, Rock (Roy Scherer, Jr) (1925–85) American, born Winnetka, Illinois; *Magnificent Obsession* (1954), *Giant* (1956), *Written on the Wind* (1956), *The Tarnished Angel* (1957), *Pillow Talk* (1959), *Send Me No Flowers* (1964), *Seconds* (1966), *Darling Lili* (1969), *McMillan and Wife* (TV 1971–5), *McMillan* (TV 1976), *Embryo* (1976), *The Martian Chronicles* (TV 1980), *Dynasty* (TV 1985).

Hulce, Tom (1953–) American, born Plymouth, Michigan; *September 30, 1955* (1977), *Animal House* (1978), *Amadeus* (1984), *Dominick and Eugene* (1988), *Parenthood* (1989), *Shadow Man* (1990), *The Inner Circle* (1991), *Fearless* (1993), *Wings of Courage* (1995).

Hunter, Holly (1958–) American, born Conyers, Georgia; *Raising Arizona* (1987), *Once Around* (1990), *The Piano* (1993), *The Firm* (1993), *The Positively True Adventures of the Alleged Texas Cheerleader-Murdering Mom* (TV 1993), *Copycat* (1995), *Crash* (1996), *A Life Less Ordinary* (1997), *O Brother Where Art Thou?* (2000), *Moonlight Mile* (2002).

Hunter, Kim (Janet Cole) (1922–2002) American, born Detroit, Michigan; *A Matter of Life and Death* (1945), *A Streetcar Named Desire* (1951), *Deadline USA* (1952), *The Swimmer* (1968), *Planet of the Apes* (1968), *Beneath the Planet of the Apes* (1970), *Escape from the Planet of the Apes* (1971).

Huppert, Isabelle (1955–) French, born Paris; *César et Rosalie* (1972), *La Dentellière* (1977), *Heaven's Gate* (1980), *The Possessed* (1987), *Une Affaire des Femmes* (1988), *Madame Bovary* (1991), *Pas de scandale* (1999), *8 Women* (2002).

Hurt, John (1940–) British, born Chesterfield, Derbyshire; *A Man for All Seasons* (1966), *10 Rillington Place* (1971), *The Naked Civil Servant* (TV 1975), *Midnight Express* (1978), *Alien* (1979), *The Elephant Man* (1980), *History of the World Part One* (1981), *Champions* (1983), *1984* (1984), *Spaceballs* (1987), *White Mischief* (1987), *Scandal* (1989), *Frankenstein Unbound* (1990), *King Ralph* (1991), *Dark at Noon* (1992), *Rob Roy* (1995), *Darkening* (1996), *New*

Blood (1999), Captain Corelli's Mandolin (2001).

Hurt, William (1950–) American, born Washington, DC; Altered States (1981), The Janitor (1981), Body Heat (1981), Gorky Park (1983), Kiss of the Spider Woman (1985), Children of a Lesser God (1986), Broadcast News (1987), The Accidental Tourist (1989), Love You to Death (1990), Alice (1990), Until the End of the World (1991), The Doctor (1991), The Plague (1992), Second Best (1994), Smoke (1995), Jane Eyre (1995), Michael (1996), Lost in Space (1998), Artificial Intelligence: AI (2001).

Hussey, Olivia (1951–) British, born Buenos Aires, Argentina; Romeo and Juliet (1968), Lost Horizon (1973), Jesus of Nazareth (TV 1977), Death on the Nile (1978), The Man with Bogart's Face (1980), Ivanhoe (TV 1982), El Grito (2000).

Huston, Anjelica (1952–) Irish–American, born Ireland; The Last Tycoon (1976), Frances (1982), This is Spinal Tap (1984), Prizzi's Honor (1985), The Dead (1987), Gardens of Stone (1987), A Handful of Dust (1988), Mr North (1988), The Witches (1990), The Grifters (1990), The Addams Family (1991), Bitter Moon (1992), Addams Family Values (1993), Manhattan Murder Mystery (1994), The Crossing Guard (1995), Agnes Browne (1999), The Royal Tenenbaums (2001).

Hyde-White, Wilfrid (1903–91) British, born Gloucester; The Third Man (1949), My Fair Lady (1964), The Associates (TV 1979), Buck Rogers (TV 1980–2), Oh God Book Two (1980), The Fog (1982).

Irons, Jeremy (1948–) British, born Cowes; The French Lieutenant's Woman (1981), Brideshead Revisited (TV 1981), Swann in Love (1984), The Mission (1985), Dead Ringers (1988), Reversal of Fortune (1990), Kafka (1991), Waterland (1992), Damage (1992), M Butterfly (1992), Die Hard with a Vengeance (1995), Stealing Beauty (1996), Lolita (1996), The Fourth Angel (2001).

Jackson, Glenda (1936–) British, born Liverpool; Women in Love (1969), Sunday, Bloody Sunday (1971), Mary Queen of Scots (1971), Elizabeth R (TV 1971), A Touch of Class (1972), Hedda (1975), Stevie (1978), Turtle Diary (1985), Business as Usual (1987), Salome's Last Dance (1988), The Rainbow (1989), Doombeach (1990).

Jackson, Gordon (1923–89) British, born Glasgow; Whisky Galore (1948), Tunes of Glory (1960), The Great Escape (1963), The Ipcress File (1965), The Prime of Miss Jean Brodie (1969), Upstairs Downstairs (TV 1970–5), Kidnapped (1972), The Medusa Touch (1977), The Professionals (TV 1977–81), A Town Like Alice (TV 1980), The Shooting Party (1984), The Whistle Blower (1987), Beyond Therapy (1987).

Jacobi, Sir Derek (1938–) British, born Leytonstone, London; The Odessa File (1964), I Claudius (TV 1976), Burgess and MacLean (TV 1977), Mr Pye (TV 1986), Little Dorrit (1987), The Fool (1990), Hamlet (1996), Gladiator (2000), Gosford Park (2001).

Johnson, Don (1950–) American, born Flatt Creek, Missouri; From Here to Eternity (1979), Miami Vice (TV 1984–90), The Long Hot Summer (TV 1985), Dead Bang (1988), The Hot Spot (1990), Harley Davidson and the Marlboro Man (1991), Paradise (1991), Born Yesterday (1993), Guilty as Sin (1993), Tin Cup (1996).

Jones, James Earl (1931–) American, born Tate County, Missouri; The Great White Hope (1970), Jesus of Nazareth (TV 1977), Exorcist II: The Heretic (1977), Roots II (TV 1979), Conan the Barbarian (1982), Beastmaster (1982), Coming to America (1988), Field of Dreams (1988), Three Fugitives

(1988), The Hunt for Red October (1989), Best of the Best (1990), Clear and Present Danger (1994).

Jones, Jennifer (Phyllis Isley) (1919–) American, born Tulsa, Oklahoma; The Song of Bernadette (1943), Duel in the Sun (1946), Portrait of Jennie (1948), Carrie (1951), Love is a Many-Splendored Thing (1955), A Farewell to Arms (1958), Tender is the Night (1961), The Towering Inferno (1974).

Julia, Raul (1940–94) Puerto Rican, born San Juan; The Eyes of Laura Mars (1978), One From the Heart (1982), Tempest (1982), Kiss of the Spider Woman (1985), The Morning After (1986), Moon over Parador (1988), The Penitent (1988), Tequila Sunrise (1989), Romero (1990), Presumed Innocent (1990), The Rookie (1990), Frankenstein Unbound (1990).

Karloff, Boris (William Henry Pratt) (1887–1969) Anglo-American, born London; Frankenstein (1931), The Mask of Fu Manchu (1931), The Lost Patrol (1934), The Raven (1935), The Bride of Frankenstein (1935), The Body Snatcher (1945).

Kaye, Danny (David Daniel Kominski) (1913–87) American, born New York City; Up in Arms (1944), The Secret Life of Walter Mitty (1947), Hans Christian Andersen (1952), White Christmas (1954), The Court Jester (1956), The Five Pennies (1959).

Keaton, Buster (Joseph Francis Keaton) (1895–1966) American, born Piqua, Kansas; Our Hospitality (1923), The Navigator (1924), The General (1927), San Diego I Love You (1944), Sunset Boulevard (1950), Limelight (1952), It's a Mad, Mad, Mad, Mad World (1963).

Keaton, Diane (Diane Hall) (1946–) American, born Los Angeles, California; The Godfather (1972), The Godfather, Part II (1974), Sleeper (1973), Annie Hall (1977), Manhattan (1979), Reds (1981), Shoot the Moon (1982), Mrs Soffel (1984), Baby Boom (1987), The Good Mother (1988), The Godfather, Part III (1990), Success (1991), Father of the Bride (1991), Manhattan Murder Mystery (1993), Father of the Bride II (1995), The First Wives Club (1996), Marvin's Room (1996), The Other Sister (1999).

Keaton, Michael (Michael Douglas) (1951–) American, born Carapolis, Pennsylvania; Night Shift (1982), Mr Mom (1983), Beetlejuice (1988), Batman (1989), The Dream Team (1989), Clean and Sober (1989), Pacific Heights (1990), Batman Returns (1992), Much Ado About Nothing (1993), My Life (1993), The Paper (1994), Desperate Measures (1997), Jack Frost (1998).

Keitel, Harvey (1947–) American, born Brooklyn, New York City; Mean Streets (1973), Taxi Driver (1976), Bad Timing (1980), The Men's Club (1986), The Last Temptation of Christ (1988), The January Man (1989), Bugsy (1991), Thelma and Louise (1991), Reservoir Dogs (1992), The Bad Lieutenant (1992), Sister Act (1992), The Piano (1993), Pulp Fiction (1994), Smoke (1995), Clockers (1995), Blue in the Face (1995), Get Shorty (1995), Head Above Water (1996), Copland (1997), Holy Smoke (1999), Red Dragon (2002).

Kelly, Gene (Eugene Curran Kelly) (1912–96) American, born Pittsburgh, Pennsylvania; For Me and My Girl (1942), Cover Girl (1944), Anchors Aweigh (1945), Ziegfeld Follies (1946), The Pirate (1948), The Three Musketeers (1948), Take Me Out to the Ball Game (1949), On the Town (1949), Summer Stock (1950), An American in Paris (1951), Singin' in the Rain (1952), Brigadoon (1954), Invitation to Dance (1956), Les Girls (1957), Marjorie Morningstar (1958), Inherit the Word (1960), Sins (TV 1987).

Kelly, Grace (Patricia) (1928–82) American, born Philadelphia, Pennsylvania; High Noon (1952), Mogambo (1953), *Dial M for Murder* (1954), *Rear Window* (1954), *The Country Girl* (1954), *To Catch a Thief* (1955), *High Society* (1956).

Kennedy, George (1925–) American, born New York City; *Charade* (1963), *The Flight of the Phoenix* (1967), *The Dirty Dozen* (1967), *Cool Hand Luke* (1967), *Sarge* (TV 1971), *Thunderbolt and Lightfoot* (1974), *Earthquake* (1974), *The Blue Knight* (TV 1975–6), *The Eiger Sanction* (1977), *Death on the Nile* (1979), *Bolero* (1984), *Delta Force* (1985), *Creepshow 2* (1987), *Dallas* (TV 1988–91), *Naked Gun* (1989), *Naked Gun 2½: The Smell of Fear* (1991), *Naked Gun 33⅓: The Final Insult* (1994).

Kerr, Deborah (Deborah Jane Kerr-Trimmer) (1921–) British, born Helensburgh, Scotland; *Major Barbara* (1940), *Love on the Dole* (1941), *The Life and Death of Colonel Blimp* (1943), *Perfect Strangers* (1945), *I See a Dark Stranger* (1945), *Black Narcissus* (1947), *From Here to Eternity* (1953), *The King and I* (1956), *Tea and Sympathy* (1956), *An Affair to Remember* (1957), *Separate Tables* (1958), *The Sundowners* (1960), *The Innocents* (1961), *The Night of the Iguana* (1964), *Casino Royale* (1967), *Prudence and the Pill* (1968), *The Assam Garden* (1985).

Kidman, Nicole (1968–) Australian–American, born Honolulu, Hawaii; *Days of Thunder* (1990), *To Die For* (1995), *The Portrait of a Lady* (1996), *Practical Magic* (1998), *Eyes Wide Shut* (1999), *Moulin Rouge!* (2001), *Birthday Girl* (2001), *The Hours* (2002).

Kingsley, Ben (Krishna Banji) (1943–) Anglo-Indian, born Snaiton, Yorkshire; *Gandhi* (1982), *Betrayal* (1982), *Turtle Diary* (1985), *Testimony* (1987), *Pascali's Island* (1988), *Without a Clue* (1988), *Slipstream* (1989), *Bugsy* (1991), *Sneakers* (1992), *Schindler's List* (1994), *Death and the Maiden* (1994), *Species* (1996), *Parting Shots* (1998).

Kinski, Klaus (Claus Gunther Nakszynski) (1926–94) Polish, born Sopot (Zoppot), Danzig; *For a Few Dollars More* (1965), *Dr Zhivago* (1965), *Aguirre: Wrath of God* (1972), *Nosferatu* (1978), *Fitzcarraldo* (1982), *Codename: Wildgeese* (1984).

Kinski, Nastassja (Nastassja Nakszynski) (1960–) German, born Berlin; *Tess* (1979), *Cat People* (1982), *One from the Heart* (1982), *Paris, Texas* (1984), *Maria's Lovers* (1985), *Revolution* (1985), *Magdalane* (1988), *Torrents of Spring* (1989), *On a Moonlit Night* (1991), *The Secret* (1991), *Night Sun* (1992), *Terminal Velocity* (1994), *One Night Stand* (1997), *Town and Country* (2001).

Kline, Kevin (1947–) American, born St Louis, Missouri; *Sophie's Choice* (1983), *The Big Chill* (1983), *Silverado* (1985), *Cry Freedom* (1987), *A Fish Called Wanda* (1988), *January Man* (1989), *Love You to Death* (1990), *Soap Dish* (1991), *Dave* (1993), *Princess Caraboo* (1994), *Paris Match* (1995), *Fierce Creatures* (1996), *The Ice Storm* (1998), *Wild Wild West* (1999).

Ladd, Alan (1913–64) American, born Hot Springs, Arkansas; *This Gun for Hire* (1942), *The Glass Key* (1942), *The Blue Dahlia* (1946), *The Great Gatsby* (1949), *Shane* (1953), *The Carpetbaggers* (1964).

Lamarr, Hedy (Hedwig Eva Maria Kiesler) (1913–2000) Austrian, born Vienna; *Algiers* (1938), *White Cargo* (1942), *Samson and Delilah* (1949).

Lambert, Christopher (1957–) French, born New York City; *Greystoke* (1984), *Subway* (1985), *Highlander* (1985), *The Sicilian* (1987), *Why Me?* (1990), *Highlander II: The Quickening* (1991), *Knight Moves* (1993), *Gunmen* (1994), *The Hunted* (1994), *Mortal Kombat* (1995), *Highlander III: The Sorcerer* (1995), *Highlander: Endgame* (2000).

Lamour, Dorothy (Mary Leaton Dorothy Slaton) (1914–96) American, born New Orleans, Louisiana; *The Jungle Princess* (1936), *The Hurricane* (1937), *Road to Singapore* (1940), *Road to Zanzibar* (1941), *Manhandled* (1948), *Creepshow 2* (1987).

Lancaster, Burt (Stephen Burton) (1913–94) American, born New York City; *Brute Force* (1947), *The Flame and the Arrow* (1950), *Come Back Little Sheba* (1953), *From Here to Eternity* (1953), *Vera Cruz* (1954), *Gunfight at the OK Corral* (1957), *Elmer Gantry* (1960), *Birdman of Alcatraz* (1962), *The Professionals* (1966), *The Swimmer* (1968), *1900* (1976), *Atlantic City* (1980), *Local Hero* (1983), *Rocket Gibraltar* (1988), *Field of Dreams* (1988).

Lange, Hope (1933–) American, born Redding Ridge, Connecticut; *Bus Stop* (1956), *Peyton Place* (1957), *Death Wish* (1974), *Nightmare on Elm Street II* (1985), *Blue Velvet* (1986), *Tune in Tomorrow* (1990), *Clear and Present Danger* (1994), *Just Cause* (1995).

Lange, Jessica (1949–) American, born Cloquet, Minnesota; *King Kong* (1976), *All That Jazz* (1979), *The Postman Always Rings Twice* (1981), *Tootsie* (1982), *Frances* (1982), *Country* (1984), *Sweet Dreams* (1985), *Crimes of the Heart* (1986), *Far North* (1988), *Music Box* (1989), *Men Don't Leave* (1990), *Blue Sky* (1991), *Cape Fear* (1991), *Night and The City* (1992), *Losing Isaiah* (1995), *Rob Roy* (1995), *Titus* (1999), *Prozac Nation* (2001).

Lansbury, Angela (Brigid) (1925–) American, born London; *National Velvet* (1944), *Gaslight* (1944), *The Picture of Dorian Gray* (1945), *The Private Affairs of Bel Ami* (1947), *The Three Musketeers* (1948), *The Reluctant Debutante* (1958), *The Long Hot Summer* (1958), *The Dark at the Top of the Stairs* (1960), *The Manchurian Candidate* (1962), *The Greatest Story Ever Told* (1965), *Bedknobs and Broomsticks* (1971), *Death on the Nile* (1978), *The Lady Vanishes* (1979), *Lace* (TV 1984), *Company of Wolves* (1984), *Murder She Wrote* (TV series 1984–96).

Laughton, Charles (1899–1962) British, born Scarborough; *The Sign of the Cross* (1932), *The Private Life of Henry VIII* (1932), *The Barretts of Wimpole Street* (1934), *Ruggles of Red Gap* (1935), *Mutiny on the Bounty* (1935), *Les Misérables* (1935), *Rembrandt* (1936), *The Hunchback of Notre Dame* (1939), *Hobson's Choice* (1954), *Witness for the Prosecution* (1957), *Advise and Consent* (1962).

Laurel, Stan (Arthur Stanley Jefferson) (1890–1965) Anglo-American, born Ulverston, Lancashire; *Nuts in May* (1917), *Monsieur Don't Care* (1925); for films with Hardy ▶ **Hardy, Oliver**.

Laurie, Piper (Rosetta Jacobs) (1932–) American, born Detroit, Michigan; *The Hustler* (1961), *Carrie* (1976), *Tim* (1979), *The Thorn Birds* (TV 1983), *Tender is the Night* (TV 1985), *Return to Oz* (1985), *Children of a Lesser God* (1986), *Twin Peaks* (TV 1991), *Other People's Money* (1991), *Storyville* (1992), *Wrestling Ernest Hemingway* (1993), *The Crossing Guard* (1995), *The Faculty* (1998).

Law, Jude (1973–) British, born London; *Wilde* (1997), *The Wisdom of Crocodiles* (1998), *Onegin* (1999), *The Talented Mr Ripley* (1999), *Artificial Intelligence: AI* (2001), *Road to Perdition* (2002).

Lee, Christopher (1922–) British, born London; *The Curse of Frankenstein* (1956), *Dracula* (1958), *The Man Who Could Cheat Death* (1959), *The Mummy* (1959), *The Face of Fu Manchu* (1965), *Rasputin the Mad Monk* (1965), *Horror Express* (1972), *The Three Musketeers* (1973), *The Man With the Golden Gun* (1974), *Return from Witch Mountain* (1976), *Howling II* (1985), *The Land of Faraway* (1988), *Gremlins 2: The*

New Batch (1990), *Police Academy 7: Mission to Moscow* (1994), *The Knot* (1996), *Ivanhoe* (TV 1997), *Sleepy Hollow* (1999), *The Lord of the Rings: The Fellowship of the Ring* (2001), *Star Wars: Attack of the Clones* (2002), *The Lord of the Rings: The Two Towers* (2002).

Lee, Spike (Shelton Jackson Lee) (1957–) American, born Atlanta, Georgia; *She's Gotta Have It* (1986), *School Daze* (1988), *Do the Right Thing* (1989), *Mo' Better Blues* (1990), *Lonely in America* (1990), *Jungle Fever* (1991), *Malcolm X* (1992), *Summer of Sam* (1999), *The 25th Hour* (2002).

Leigh, Janet (Jeanette Helen Morrison) (1927–) American, born Merced, California; *Little Women* (1949), *That Forsyte Woman* (1949), *Houdini* (1953), *My Sister Eileen* (1955), *The Vikings* (1958), *Psycho* (1960), *The Manchurian Candidate* (1962), *The Fog* (1980).

Leigh, Vivien (Vivien Hartley) (1913–67) British, born Darjeeling, India; *Dark Journey* (1937), *A Yank at Oxford* (1938), *Gone with the Wind* (1939), *Lady Hamilton* (1941), *Caesar and Cleopatra* (1945), *Anna Karenina* (1948), *A Streetcar Named Desire* (1951), *The Roman Spring of Mrs Stone* (1961), *Ship of Fools* (1965).

Lemmon, Jack (John Uhler Lemmon III) (1925–2001) American, born Boston, Massachusetts; *It Should Happen to You* (1953), *Mister Roberts* (1955), *Some Like It Hot* (1959), *The Apartment* (1960), *Irma La Douce* (1963), *The Great Race* (1965), *The Odd Couple* (1968), *The Prisoner of Second Avenue* (1975), *The China Syndrome* (1979), *Missing* (1982), *Dad* (1990), *JFK* (1991), *The Player* (1992), *Glengarry Glen Ross* (1992), *Short Cuts* (1993), *The Grass Harp* (1995), *Hamlet* (1996), *The Odd Couple II* (1998).

Lewis, Jerry (Joseph Levitch) (1926–) American, born Newark, New Jersey; *My Friend Irma* (1949), *The Bellboy* (1960), *Cinderfella* (1960), *The Nutty Professor* (1963), *It's a Mad, Mad, Mad, Mad World* (1963), *The Family Jewels* (1965), *King of Comedy* (1983), *Smorgasbord* (1983), *Cookie* (1988), *Funny Bones* (1995).

Lithgow, John (1945–) American, born Rochester, New York; *Blow Out* (1973), *High Anxiety* (1978), *The World According to Garp* (1982), *Twilight Zone* (1983), *Terms of Endearment* (1983), *The Day After* (TV 1983), *2010* (1984), *Footloose* (1984), *Distant Thunder* (1988), *Memphis Belle* (1990), *Ricochet* (1991), *Raising Cain* (1992), *Cliffhanger* (1993), *The Pelican Brief* (1993), *Homegrown* (1998).

Lloyd, Christopher (1938–) American, born Stanford, Connecticut; *Star Trek III: The Search for Spock* (1984), *Back to the Future* (1985), *Who Framed Roger Rabbit?* (1988), *Track 29* (1988), *Eight Men Out* (1988), *Back to the Future II* (1989), *Back to the Future III* (1990), *Why Me?* (1990), *The Addams Family* (1991), *Addams Family Values* (1993), *My Favourite Martian* (1999).

Lloyd, Emily (1970–) British, born London; *Wish You Were Here* (1987), *Cookie* (1988), *In Country* (1989), *Chicago Joe and the Showgirl* (1989), *Scorchers* (1992), *The Poet* (1996), *Welcome to Sarajevo* (1997), *The Honeytrap* (2002).

Lloyd, Harold (Clayton) (1893–1971) American, born Burchard, Nebraska; *High and Dizzy* (1920), *Grandma's Boy* (1922), *Safety Last* (1923), *Why Worry?* (1923), *The Freshman* (1925), *The Kid Brother* (1927), *Feet First* (1930), *Movie Crazy* (1932).

Lockwood, Margaret (Margaret Day) (1916–90) British, born Karachi, India; *Lorna Doone* (1934), *The Beloved Vagabond* (1936), *The Lady Vanishes* (1938), *Night Train to Munich* (1940), *The Man in Grey* (1943), *The Wicked Lady* (1945), *Cast a Dark Shadow* (1947), *The Slipper and the Rose* (1976).

Loggia, Robert (1930–) American, born Staten Island, New York; *THE Cat* (TV 1966), *First Love* (1977), *SOB* (1981), *An Officer and a Gentleman* (1982), *Psycho 2* (1982), *Scarface* (1983), *Jagged Edge* (1985), *Over the Top* (1987), *Big* (1988), *Prizzi's Honor* (1988), *Mancuso FBI* (TV 1989–90), *The Marrying Man* (1991), *Innocent Blood* (1992), *Independence Day* (1996).

Lollobrigida, Gina (1927–) Italian, born Subiaco; *Belles de Nuit* (1952), *Bread, Love and Dreams* (1953), *Beautiful but Dangerous* (1955), *Trapeze* (1956), *Woman of Straw* (1964).

Lom, Herbert (Herbert Charles Angelo Kuchacevich ze Schluderpacheru) (1917–) Czech, born Prague; *The Seventh Veil* (1946), *Duel Alibi* (1947), *State Secret* (1950), *The Ladykillers* (1950), *El Cid* (1961), *Phantom of the Opera* (1962), *A Shot in the Dark* (1964), *Murders in the Rue Morgue* (1972), *The Return of the Pink Panther* (1974), *The Pink Panther Strikes Again* (1977), *Revenge of the Pink Panther* (1978), *The Lady Vanishes* (1979), *Whoops Apocalypse* (1986), *Going Bananas* (1988), *Ten Little Indians* (1989), *The Pope Must Die* (1991), *Son of the Pink Panther* (1993).

Loren, Sophia (Sofia Scicolone) (1934–) Italian, born Rome; *Woman of the River* (1955), *Boy on a Dolphin* (1957), *The Key* (1958), *El Cid* (1961), *Two Women* (1961), *The Millionairess* (1961), *Marriage Italian Style* (1964), *Cinderella Italian Style* (1967), *A Special Day* (1977), *Prêt-À-Porter* (1994), *Grumpier Old Men* (1995), *Between Strangers* (2002).

Lorre, Peter (Laszlo Lowenstein) (1904–64) Hungarian, born Rosenberg; *M* (1931), *Mad Love* (1935), *Crime and Punishment* (1935), *The Maltese Falcon* (1941), *Casablanca* (1942), *The Mask of Dimitrios* (1944), *Arsenic and Old Lace* (1944), *The Beast With Five Fingers* (1946), *20 000 Leagues Under the Sea* (1954), *The Raven* (1963).

Lowe, Rob (1964–) American, born Charlottesville, Virginia; *Class* (1983), *Oxford Blues* (1984), *St Elmo's Fire* (1985), *Youngblood* (1985), *About Last Night* (1987), *Illegally Yours* (1987), *Masquerade* (1988), *Bad Influence* (1990), *Wayne's World* (1991), *The Finest Hour* (1992), *Tommy Boy* (1995), *Austin Powers: The Spy Who Shagged Me* (1999), *The West Wing* (TV series, 1999–2003), *Austin Powers in Goldmember* (2002).

Lugosi, Bela (Bela Ferenc Denzso Blasko) (1882–1956) Hungarian–American, born Lugos (now Romania); *Dracula* (1930), *The Murders in the Rue Morgue* (1931), *White Zombie* (1932), *International House* (1933), *The Black Cat* (1934), *Son of Frankenstein* (1939), *Abbott and Costello Meet Frankenstein* (1948), *Plan 9 from Outer Space* (1956).

Lumley, Joanna (1946–) British, born Kashmir, India; *On Her Majesty's Secret Service* (1969), *General Hospital* (TV 1974–5), *The New Avengers* (TV 1976–7), *Sapphire and Steel* (TV 1979), *Trail of the Pink Panther* (1982), *Curse of the Pink Panther* (1983), *Shirley Valentine* (1989), *Absolutely Fabulous* (TV series 1992–7), *Maybe Baby* (2000).

McCallum, David (1933–) British, born Glasgow; *The Great Escape* (1963), *The Man From UNCLE* (TV 1964–7), *The Greatest Story Ever Told* (1965), *Colditz* (TV 1972), *The Invisible Man* (TV 1975), *Sapphire and Steel* (TV 1979), *The Watcher in the Woods* (1980), *Return of the Man from UNCLE* (TV 1983), *Mother Love* (1989), *Cherry* (1999).

McCarthy, Andrew (1962–) American, born New York City; *Class* (1983), *Pretty in Pink* (1986), *Mannequin* (1987), *Less Than Zero* (1987), *Fresh Horses*

(1988), *Kansas* (1988), *Weekend at Bernie's* (1989), *Only You* (1992), *Dead Funny* (1994), *New World Disorder* (1999).

McCarthy, Kevin (1914–) American, born Seattle, Washington; *Death of a Salesman* (1952), *Invasion of the Body Snatchers* (1956), *The Misfits* (1961), *The Prize* (1963), *Invasion of the Body Snatchers* (1978), *Piranha* (1978), *Flamingo Road* (TV 1980–1), *The Howling* (1981), *SOB* (1981), *Private Benjamin* (1982), *My Tutor* (1983), *Twilight Zone* (1983), *Innerspace* (1987), *Love or Money* (1990), *The Distinguished Gentleman* (1992), *Just Cause* (1995).

McCowen, Alec (Alexander Duncan) (1925–) British, born Tunbridge Wells; *The Cruel Sea* (1953), *The One That Got Away* (1957), *The Loneliness of the Long Distance Runner* (1962), *The Witches* (1966), *Frenzy* (1972), *Never Say Never Again* (1983), *Forever Young* (1984), *The Assam Garden* (1985), *Cry Freedom* (1987), *Henry V* (1989), *The Age of Innocence* (1993), *Gangs of New York* (2002).

MacDowell, Andie (Rosalie Anderson MacDowell) (1958–) American, born Gaffney, South Carolina; *St Elmo's Fire* (1985), *Sex, Lies and Videotape* (1990), *Green Card* (1990), *The Player* (1992), *Groundhog Day* (1993), *Short Cuts* (1993), *Four Weddings and a Funeral* (1993), *Michael* (1996), *Town and Country* (2001).

McGoohan, Patrick (1928–) Irish–American, born Long Island, New York; *The Dam Busters* (1954), *Hell Drivers* (1957), *Danger Man* (TV 1960–7), *The Prisoner* (TV 1968–9), *Ice Station Zebra* (1968), *Escape from Alcatraz* (1979), *A Time to Kill* (1996).

McGregor, Ewan (1971–) British, born Crieff; *Lipstick on Your Collar* (TV1993), *Shallow Grave* (1994), *Blue Juice* (1995), *The Pillow Book* (1995), *Emma* (1995), *Trainspotting* (1996), *Brassed Off* (1996), *A Life Less Ordinary* (1997), *Little Voice* (1998), *Star Wars: The Phantom Menace* (1999), *Moulin Rouge!* (2001), *Star Wars: Attack of the Clones* (2002).

McKern, Leo (Reginald) (1920–2002) Australian, born Sydney; *Time without Pity* (1957), *The Mouse That Roared* (1959), *A Jolly Bad Fellow* (1964), *A Man for All Seasons* (1966), *Ryan's Daughter* (1970), *The Omen* (1976), *Candleshoe* (1977), *Rumpole of the Bailey* (TV 1978–92), *The Blue Lagoon* (1980), *The French Lieutenant's Woman* (1981), *Ladyhawke* (1984), *Monsignor Quixote* (TV 1986), *Travelling North* (1986), *Good King Wenceslas* (TV 1994).

MacLaine, Shirley (Shirley Beaty) (1934–) American, born Richmond, Virginia; *The Trouble with Harry* (1955), *Ask any Girl* (1959), *The Apartment* (1959), *Irma La Douce* (1963), *Sweet Charity* (1968), *Terms of Endearment* (1983), *Madame Sousatzka* (1988), *Postcards from the Edge* (1990), *Defending Your Life* (1991), *Used People* (1992), *Guarding Tess* (1994), *The Evening Star* (1996), *Bruno* (2000).

Macnee, (Daniel) Patrick (1922–) British, born London; *The Life and Death of Colonel Blimp* (1943), *Hamlet* (1948), *Scrooge* (1951), *Les Girls* (1957), *The Avengers* (TV 1960–8), *The New Avengers* (TV 1977–8), *The Sea Wolves* (1980), *This is Spinal Tap* (1984), *A View to a Kill* (1985), *Chill Factor* (1990).

McQueen, Steve (Terence Steven McQueen) (1930–80) American, born Slater, Missouri; *Wanted Dead or Alive* (TV 1958), *The Blob* (1958), *The Magnificent Seven* (1960), *The Great Escape* (1962), *Love with the Proper Stranger* (1963), *The Cincinnatti Kid* (1965), *Bullitt* (1968), *Le Mans* (1971), *Getaway* (1972), *Papillon* (1973), *The Towering Inferno* (1974), *An Enemy of the People* (1977).

Madonna (Madonna Louise Veronica Ciccone)

(1958–) American, born Bay City, Michigan; *Desperately Seeking Susan* (1985), *Shanghai Surprise* (1986), *Who's That Girl?* (1987), *Dick Tracy* (1990), *A League of Their Own* (1992), *Body of Evidence* (1993), *Blue in the Face* (1995), *Four Rooms* (1995), *Girl 6* (1996), *Evita* (1996), *The Next Best Thing* (2000), *Swept Away* (2002).

Malkovich, John (1953–) American, born Christopher, Illinois; *The Killing Fields* (1984), *Places in the Heart* (1984), *Empire of the Sun* (1987), *Miles from Home* (1988), *Dangerous Liaisons* (1988), *Crazy People* (1990), *The Sheltering Sky* (1990), *Of Mice and Men* (1992), *In the Line of Fire* (1993), *Mary Reilly* (1996), *Being John Malkovich* (1999), *Je rentre à la maison* (2001).

Mansfield, Jayne (Vera Jayne Palmer) (1933–67) American, born Bryn Mawr, Pennsylvania; *The Girl Can't Help It* (1957), *The Sheriff of Fractured Jaw* (1959), *Too Hot to Handle* (1960), *The Challenge* (1960), *Promises! Promises!* (1965).

Martin, Steve (1945–) American, born Waco, Texas; *Sgt Pepper's Lonely Hearts Club Band* (1978), *The Jerk* (1978), *Muppet Movie* (1979), *Pennies from Heaven* (1981), *Dead Men Don't Wear Plaid* (1982), *The Man With Two Brains* (1983), *The Lonely Guy* (1984), *All of Me* (1984), *The Three Amigos* (1986), *The Little Shop of Horrors* (1986), *Planes, Trains and Automobiles* (1987), *Roxanne* (1987), *Dirty, Rotten Scoundrels* (1989), *Parenthood* (1989), *My Blue Heaven* (1990), *LA Story* (1991), *Father of the Bride* (1991), *Housesitter* (1992), *A Simple Twist of Faith* (1994), *Sgt Bilko* (1995), *Bowfinger* (1999).

Marvin, Lee (1924–87) American, born New York City; *The Wild One* (1954), *Attack* (1957), *The Killers* (1964), *Cat Ballou* (1965), *The Dirty Dozen* (1967), *Paint Your Wagon* (1969), *Gorky Park* (1983), *Dirty Dozen 2: The Next Mission* (TV 1985).

Marx Brothers, The: Chico (Leonard Marx) (1886–1961); **Harpo** (Adolph Marx) (1888–1964); **Groucho** (Julius Henry Marx) (1890–1977); **Zeppo** (Herbert Marx) (1901–79) all American, born New York City; (joint) *The Cocoanuts* (1929), *Monkey Business* (1931), *Horse Feathers* (1932), *Duck Soup* (1933), *A Night at the Opera* (1935), *A Day at the Races* (1937), *A Night in Casablanca* (1946).

Mason, James (1909–84) British, born Huddersfield; *I Met a Murderer* (1939), *The Night Has Eyes* (1942), *The Man in Grey* (1943), *Fanny by Gaslight* (1944), *The Seventh Veil* (1945), *The Wicked Lady* (1946), *Odd Man Out* (1946), *Pandora and the Flying Dutchman* (1951), *The Desert Fox* (1951), *Five Fingers* (1952), *The Prisoner of Zenda* (1952), *Julius Caesar* (1953), *20 000 Leagues Under the Sea* (1954), *A Star is Born* (1954), *Journey to the Center of the Earth* (1959), *Lolita* (1962), *The Pumpkin Eater* (1964), *Georgy Girl* (1966), *The Blue Max* (1966), *The Deadly Affair* (1967), *Voyage of the Damned* (1976), *Heaven Can Wait* (1978), *The Boys from Brazil* (1978), *Murder by Decree* (1979), *Evil Under the Sun* (1982), *The Verdict* (1982), *Yellowbeard* (1983), *The Shooting Party* (1984).

Massey, Raymond (1896–1983) American, born Toronto, Canada; *The Old Dark House* (1932), *The Scarlet Pimpernel* (1934), *Things to Come* (1936), *The Prisoner of Zenda* (1937), *Abe Lincoln in Illinois* (1940), *Arsenic and Old Lace* (1944), *The Fountainhead* (1949), *East of Eden* (1955), *I Spy* (TV 1955), *Dr Kildare* (TV 1961–6).

Mastroianni, Marcello (1924–96) Italian, born Fontana Liri, near Frosinone; *I Miserabili* (1947), *White Nights* (1957), *La Dolce Vita* (1959), *Divorce Italian Style* (1962), *Yesterday, Today and Tomorrow* (1963), *8½* (1963), *Casanova* (1970), *Diamonds for*

Breakfast (1968), *Ginger and Fred* (1985), *Black Eyes* (1987), *The Two Lives of Mattia Pascal* (1988), *Traffic Jam* (1988), *Used People* (1992), *Prêt-À-Porter* (1994), *Beyond the Clouds* (1996).

Matthau, Walter (Matuschanskavasky) (1920–2000) American, born New York City; *A Face in the Crowd* (1957), *King Creole* (1958), *Charade* (1963), *Mirage* (1965), *The Fortune Cookie* (1966), *A Guide to the Married Man* (1967), *The Odd Couple* (1968), *Hello Dolly* (1969), *Cactus Flower* (1969), *Kotch* (1971), *Earthquake* (1974), *The Taking of Pelham One Two Three* (1974), *Hopscotch* (1980), *Pirates* (1986), *The Couch Trip* (1988), *JFK* (1991), *Grumpy Old Men* (1993), *Grumpier Old Men* (1995), *Out to Sea* (1997).

Mature, Victor (1913–99) American, born Louisville, Kentucky; *One Million BC* (1940), *My Darling Clementine* (1946), *Kiss of Death* (1947), *Samson and Delilah* (1949), *The Robe* (1953), *The Egyptian* (1954), *Safari* (1956), *The Long Haul* (1957), *After the Fox* (1966).

Maura, Carmen (1945–) Spanish, born Madrid; *Dark Habits* (1983), *What Have I Done to Deserve This?* (1984), *Law of Desire* (1987), *Women on the Verge of a Nervous Breakdown* (1988), *Baton Rouge* (1988), *How to Be a Woman and Not Die Trying* (1991), *Lisboa* (1999).

Mercouri, Melina (1923–94) Greek, born Athens; *Stella* (1954), *Never on Sunday* (1960), *Topkapi* (1964).

Midler, Bette (1945–) American, born Honolulu, Hawaii; *The Rose* (1979), *Down and Out in Beverly Hills* (1986), *Ruthless People* (1986), *Outrageous Fortune* (1987), *Beaches* (1988), *Big Business* (1988), *Stella* (1989), *Scenes from a Mall* (1991), *For the Boys* (1991), *Hocus Pocus* (1993), *Gypsy* (1993), *Get Shorty* (1995), *The First Wives Club* (1996), *Bette* (TV 2000).

Mills, Hayley (1946–) British, born London; *Tiger Bay* (1959), *Pollyanna* (1960), *The Parent Trap* (1961), *Whistle Down the Wind* (1961), *The Moonspinners* (1965), *Forbush and the Penguins* (1971), *Deadly Strangers* (1974), *After Midnight* (1989).

Mills, Sir John (Lewis Ernest Watts) (1908–) British, born Felixstowe, Suffolk; *Those Were the Days* (1934), *Cottage to Let* (1941), *In Which We Serve* (1942), *Waterloo Road* (1944), *The Way to the Stars* (1945), *Great Expectations* (1946), *The October Man* (1947), *Scott of the Antarctic* (1948), *The History of Mr Polly* (1949), *The Rocking Horse Winner* (1950), *The Colditz Story* (1954), *Hobson's Choice* (1954), *Town on Trial* (1957), *Tiger Bay* (1959), *Swiss Family Robinson* (1959), *Tunes of Glory* (1960), *Ryan's Daughter* (1970), *Lady Caroline Lamb* (1972), *The Big Sleep* (1978), *The 39 Steps* (1978), *Quatermass* (TV 1979), *Young at Heart* (TV 1980–1), *Gandhi* (1982), *Sahara* (1983), *Who's That Girl?* (1987), *Hamlet* (1996).

Minnelli, Liza (1946–) American, born Los Angeles; *Cabaret* (1972), *New York New York* (1977), *Arthur* (1981), *Stepping Out* (1991).

Mirren, Helen (1945–) British, born London; *Miss Julie* (1973), *Excalibur* (1981), *Cal* (1984), *2010* (1985), *Heavenly Pursuits* (1985), *White Nights* (1986), *Mosquito Coast* (1986), *Pascali's Island* (1988), *The Cook, The Thief, His Wife and Her Lover* (1989), *The Comfort of Strangers* (1990), *Where Angels Fear to Tread* (1991), *Prime Suspect* (TV 1991–5), *The Hawk* (1993), *The Madness of King George* (1994), *Gosford Park* (2001).

Mitchum, Robert (1917–97) American, born Bridgeport, Connecticut; *The Story of GI Joe* (1945), *Pursued* (1947), *Crossfire* (1947), *Out of the Past* (1947), *The Big Steal* (1949), *Night of the Hunter* (1955), *Home from the Hill* (1960), *The Sundowners* (1960),

Cape Fear (1962), *The List of Adrian Messenger* (1963), *Ryan's Daughter* (1970), *Farewell My Lovely* (1975), *The Big Sleep* (1978), *The Winds of War* (TV 1983), *War and Remembrance* (TV 1987), *Mr North* (1988), *Scrooged* (1988), *Cape Fear* (1991), *Tombstone* (1993), *Backfire* (1994).

Modine, Matthew (1959–) American, born Utah; *Private School* (1983), *Streamers* (1983), *Birdy* (1984), *Mrs Soffel* (1984), *Vision Quest* (1985), *Full Metal Jacket* (1988), *Married to the Mob* (1989), *Memphis Belle* (1990), *Pacific Heights* (1990), *Short Cuts* (1993), *Any Given Sunday* (1999).

Monroe, Marilyn (Norma Jean Mortenson or Baker) (1926–62) American, born Los Angeles; *How to Marry a Millionaire* (1953), *Gentlemen Prefer Blondes* (1953), *The Seven Year Itch* (1955), *Bus Stop* (1956), *Some Like It Hot* (1959), *The Misfits* (1960).

Montand, Yves (Ivo Levi) (1921–91) French, born Monsumagno, Italy; *The Wages of Fear* (1953), *Let's Make Love* (1962), *Jean de Florette* (1986), *Manon des Sources* (1986).

Moore, Demi (Demi Guines) (1962–) American, born Roswell, New Mexico; *St Elmo's Fire* (1986), *About Last Night* (1987), *The Seventh Sign* (1988), *We're No Angels* (1990), *Ghost* (1990), *The Butcher's Wife* (1991), *A Few Good Men* (1992), *Indecent Proposal* (1993), *Disclosure* (1994), *The Scarlet Letter* (1995), *Striptease* (1996), *GI Jane* (1997), *Deconstructing Harry* (1997), *Passion of Mind* (2000).

Moore, Dudley (1935–2002) British, born Dagenham, Essex; *Bedazzled* (1967), *Foul Play* (1978), *'10'* (1979), *Arthur* (1981), *Lovesick* (1983), *Unfaithfully Yours* (1983), *Micki and Maude* (1984), *Best Defense* (1985), *Santa Claus* (1985), *Arthur 2: On the Rocks* (1988), *Like Father, Like Son* (1989), *Crazy People* (1990), *Blame it on the Bellboy* (1992).

Moore, Roger (George) (1927–) British, born London; *Ivanhoe* (TV 1957), *The Saint* (TV 1963–8), *The Persuaders* (TV 1971–2), *Live and Let Die* (1973), *The Man with the Golden Gun* (1974), *Shout at the Devil* (1976), *The Spy Who Loved Me* (1977), *The Wild Geese* (1978), *Escape to Athena* (1979), *Moonraker* (1979), *For Your Eyes Only* (1981), *The Cannonball Run* (1981), *Octopussy* (1983), *A View to a Kill* (1985), *The Quest* (1996).

Moorehead, Agnes (1906–74) American, born Chinton, Massachusetts; *Citizen Kane* (1941), *The Magnificent Ambersons* (1942), *Jane Eyre* (1943), *The Lost Moment* (1947), *The Woman in White* (1948), *Johnny Belinda* (1948), *Summer Holiday* (1948), *The Bat* (1959), *How the West was Won* (1963), *Bewitched* (TV 1964–71).

Moranis, Rick (1953–) Canadian, born Toronto, Ontario; *Strange Brew* (1984), *Ghostbusters* (1984), *Brewster's Millions* (1985), *Little Shop of Horrors* (1986), *Spaceballs* (1987), *Ghostbusters II* (1989), *Parenthood* (1989), *Honey, I Shrunk the Kids* (1990), *My Blue Heaven* (1990), *LA Story* (1991), *Honey, I Blew Up the Kid* (1992), *The Flintstones* (1994).

Moreau, Jeanne (1928–) French, born Paris; *Les Amants* (1958), *Ascenseur Pour L'Echafaud* (1957), *Jules et Jim* (1961), *Eva* (1962), *The Trial* (1963), *Journal d'une Femme de Chambre* (1964), *Viva Maria* (1965), *Nikita* (1990), *La Vieille Qui Marchait Dans La Mer* (1991), *Ever After* (1998).

Morgan, Frank (Francis Phillip Wupperman) (1890–1949) American, born New York City; *Hallelujah I'm a Bum* (1933), *Bombshell* (1933), *The Affairs of Cellini* (1934), *The Great Ziegfeld* (1936), *Trouble for Two* (1936), *Piccadilly Jim* (1936), *Dimples* (1936), *The Last of Mr Cheyney* (1937), *The Wizard of Oz* (1939), *Boom Town* (1940), *The Vanishing Vir-*

ginian (1942), *Tortilla Flat* (1942), *The Human Comedy* (1943), *The Three Musketeers* (1948).

Morgan, Harry (Harry Bratsburg) (1915–) American, born Detroit, Michigan; *High Noon* (1952), *December Bride* (TV 1954–8), *The Teahouse of the August Moon* (1956), *Dragnet* (TV 1969), *M*A*S*H* (TV 1976–83), *Aftermash* (TV 1983), *Dragnet* (TV 1987).

Murphy, Eddie (1961–) American, born Brooklyn, New York City; *48 Hours* (1982), *Trading Places* (1983), *Beverly Hills Cop* (1985), *The Golden Child* (1986), *Beverly Hills Cop II* (1987), *Coming to America* (1988), *Harlem Nights* (1989), *Another 48 Hours* (1990), *Boomerang* (1992), *Distinguished Gentleman* (1992), *Beverly Hills Cop III* (1994), *The Nutty Professor* (1995), *Doctor Dolittle* (1998), *Bowfinger* (1999), *Nutty Professor II: The Klumps* (2000).

Murray, Bill (1950–) American, born Evanston, Illinois; *Meatballs* (1977), *Caddyshack* (1980), *Stripes* (1981), *Tootsie* (1982), *Ghostbusters* (1984), *Razor's Edge* (1984), *Little Shop of Horrors* (1986), *Scrooged* (1988), *Ghostbusters II* (1989), *What About Bob?* (1991), *Mad Dog and Glory* (1992), *Groundhog Day* (1993), *Ed Wood* (1994), *Kingpin* (1996), *Cradle Will Rock* (1999), *The Royal Tenenbaums* (2001).

Neal, Patricia (1926–) American, born Packard, Kentucky; *The Fountainhead* (1949), *The Hasty Heart* (1950), *Diplomatic Courier* (1952), *Breakfast at Tiffany's* (1961), *Hud* (1963), *A Face in the Crowd* (1957), *All Quiet on the Western Front* (TV 1980), *Cookie's Fortune* (1999).

Neeson, Liam (1952–) British, born Ballymena, Northern Ireland; *Excalibur* (1981), *Suspect* (1987), *Satisfaction* (1988), *High Spirits* (1988), *The Good Mother* (1988), *The Dead Pool* (1988), *The Big Man* (1990), *Dark Man* (1990), *Husbands and Wives* (1992), *Schindler's List* (1994), *Nell* (1994), *Rob Roy* (1995), *Michael Collins* (1996), *Star Wars: The Phantom Menace* (1999), *Star Wars: Attack of the Clones* (2002), *K-19: The Widowmaker* (2002).

Neill, Sam (1947–) New Zealander, born Northern Ireland; *The Final Conflict* (1982), *Reilly: Ace of Spies* (TV 1983), *Robbery Under Arms* (TV 1985), *Plenty* (1985), *Kane and Abel* (TV 1988), *A Cry in the Dark* (1988), *Evil Angels* (1988), *The Hunt for Red October* (1990), *Jurassic Park* (1993), *The Horse Whisperer* (1998), *The Dish* (2000).

Newman, Paul (1925–) American, born Cleveland, Ohio; *Somebody Up There Likes Me* (1956), *The Long Hot Summer* (1958), *The Hustler* (1961), *Hud* (1963), *The Prize* (1963), *Cool Hand Luke* (1967), *Butch Cassidy and the Sundance Kid* (1969), *Judge Roy Bean* (1972), *The Sting* (1973), *Absence of Malice* (1981), *The Verdict* (1982), *The Color of Money* (1986), *Blaze* (1990), *Mr and Mrs Bridge* (1990), *The Hudsucker Proxy* (1994), *Nobody's Fool* (1994), *Twilight* (1998), *Road to Perdition* (2002).

Nicholson, Jack (1937–) American, born Neptune, New Jersey; *The Little Shop of Horrors* (1960), *Easy Rider* (1969), *Five Easy Pieces* (1970), *Carnal Knowledge* (1971), *The Last Detail* (1974), *Chinatown* (1974), *One Flew Over the Cuckoo's Nest* (1975), *Tommy* (1975), *The Shining* (1980), *The Postman Always Rings Twice* (1981), *Reds* (1981), *Terms of Endearment* (1983), *Prizzi's Honor* (1985), *The Witches of Eastwick* (1987), *Batman* (1989), *The Death of Napoleon* (1991), *Man Trouble* (1992), *A Few Good Men* (1992), *Hoffa* (1992), *Wolf* (1994), *The Crossing Guard* (1995), *Blood and Wine* (1996), *Mars Attacks!* (1996), *As Good as it Gets* (1997), *About Schmidt* (2002).

Nielsen, Leslie (1926–) Canadian, born Regina, Saskatchewan; *Forbidden Planet* (1956), *Incident in San Francisco* (TV 1970), *The Poseidon Adventure* (1972), *Airplane* (1980), *Prom Night* (1980), *Police Squad* (TV 1982), *Soul Man* (TV 1986), *The Patriot* (TV 1987), *Fatal Confession* (TV 1987), *Naked Gun* (1988), *Repossessed* (1990), *Naked Gun 2½: The Smell of Fear* (1991), *Naked Gun 33⅓: The Final Insult* (1994), *Dracula: Dead and Loving It* (1995), *Spy Hard* (1996), *2001: A Space Travesty* (2000).

Nimoy, Leonard (1931–) American, born Boston, Massachusetts; *Star Trek* (TV 1966–8), *Mission Impossible* (TV 1970–2), *Invasion of the Body Snatchers* (1978), *Star Trek: The Motion Picture* (1979), *Star Trek II: The Wrath of Khan* (1982), *Star Trek III: The Search for Spock* (1984), *Star Trek IV: The Voyage Home* (1986), *Star Trek V: The Final Frontier* (1989), *Star Trek VI: The Undiscovered Country* (1991).

Niven, David (James David Graham Niven) (1910–83) British, born London; *The Prisoner of Zenda* (1937), *Wuthering Heights* (1939), *Bachelor Mother* (1939), *Raffles* (1940), *The Way Ahead* (1944), *A Matter of Life and Death* (1946), *Carrington VC* (1955), *Around the World in Eighty Days* (1956), *Separate Tables* (1958), *The Guns of Navarone* (1961), *The Pink Panther* (1964), *Casino Royale* (1967), *Candleshoe* (1977), *Death on the Nile* (1978), *Escape to Athena* (1979), *Trail of the Pink Panther* (1982), *Curse of the Pink Panther* (1982).

Nolte, Nick (1940–) American, born Omaha, Nebraska; *Rich Man Poor Man* (TV 1976), *Cannery Row* (1982), *48 Hours* (1982), *Down and Out in Beverly Hills* (1986), *Weeds* (1987), *New York Stories* (1989), *Three Fugitives* (1989), *Another 48 Hours* (1990), *Cape Fear* (1991), *Prince of Tides* (1991), *The Player* (1992), *Lorenzo's Oil* (1992), *Blue Chips* (1993), *I'll Do Anything* (1994), *I Love Trouble* (1994), *Jefferson in Paris* (1995), *Nightwatch* (1996), *The Thin Red Line* (1998).

Oberon, Merle (Estelle Merle O'Brien Thompson) (1911–79) Anglo-Indian, born Bombay (now Mumbai), India; *The Dark Angel* (1935), *The Scarlet Pimpernel* (1935), *The Divorce of Lady X* (1938), *Wuthering Heights* (1939), *That Uncertain Feeling* (1941), *Forever and a Day* (1943), *A Song to Remember* (1943), *The Oscar* (1966), *Hotel* (1967), *Interval* (1973).

Oldman, Gary (1959–) British, born New Cross, South London; *Sid and Nancy* (1986), *Prick Up Your Ears* (1987), *Track 29* (1988), *Rosencrantz and Guildenstern are Dead* (1990), *JFK* (1991), *Bram Stoker's Dracula* (1992), *True Romance* (1993), *Leon* (1994), *The Scarlet Letter* (1995), *The Fifth Element* (1996), *Lost in Space* (1998), *Hannibal* (2001).

Olivier, Sir Laurence (Kerr) (1907–89) British, born Dorking; *The Divorce of Lady X* (1938), *Wuthering Heights* (1939), *Rebecca* (1940), *Pride and Prejudice* (1940), *Henry V* (1944), *Hamlet* (1948), *Richard III* (1956), *The Prince and the Showgirl* (1958), *The Devil's Disciple* (1959), *The Entertainer* (1960), *Sleuth* (1972), *Marathon Man* (1976), *A Bridge Too Far* (1977), *Brideshead Revisited* (TV 1981), *A Voyage Round My Father* (TV 1982), *The Last Days of Pompeii* (1984), *The Jigsaw Man* (1984), *The Bounty* (1984), *A Talent for Murder* (TV 1986), *War Requiem* (1988).

O'Neal, Ryan (Patrick Ryan O'Neal) (1941–) American, born Los Angeles; *Peyton Place* (TV 1964–8), *Love Story* (1970), *What's Up, Doc?* (1972), *Paper Moon* (1973), *Nickelodeon* (1976), *A Bridge Too Far* (1977), *Green Ice* (1980), *Fever Pitch* (1985), *Tough Guys Don't Dance* (1987), *Chances Are* (1989), *Zero Effect* (1998).

O'Neal, Tatum (1963–) American, born Los Angeles; *Paper Moon* (1973), *Nickelodeon* (1976), *International Velvet* (1978), *Little Darlings* (1980), *Little Noises* (1991), *Basquiat* (1996), *The Scoundrel's Wife* (2002).

O'Sullivan, Maureen (1911–98) Irish, born Boyle; *Tarzan the Ape Man* (1932), *Tarzan and His Mate* (1934), *The Barretts of Wimpole Street* (1934), *Pride and Prejudice* (1940), *Never Too Late* (1965), *Hannah and Her Sisters* (1986), *Peggy Sue Got Married* (1986), *Stranded* (1987).

O'Toole, Peter (Seamus) (1932–) Irish, born Kerry, Connemara; *Lawrence of Arabia* (1962), *How to Steal a Million* (1966), *The Lion in Winter* (1968), *Goodbye Mr Chips* (1969), *The Ruling Class* (1972), *The Stunt Man* (1980), *My Favourite Year* (1982), *The Last Emperor* (1987), *High Spirits* (1988), *Wings of Fame* (1989), *Isabelle Eberhardt* (1990), *King Ralph* (1991), *Worlds Apart* (1992), *Phantoms* (1998).

Pacino, Al (Alfredo Pacino) (1940–) American, born New York City; *The Godfather* (1972), *The Godfather, Part II* (1974), *Dog Day Afternoon* (1975), *Scarface* (1983), *Revolution* (1984), *Sea of Love* (1990), *Dick Tracy* (1990), *The Godfather, Part III* (1990), *Frankie and Johnny* (1991), *Glengarry Glen Ross* (1992), *Scent of a Woman* (1992), *Damon* (1992), *Carlito's Way* (1993), *Heat* (1995), *Donnie Brasco* (1997), *The Insider* (1999), *Insomnia* (2002).

Page, Geraldine (1924–87) American, born Kirksville, Missouri; *Summer and Smoke* (1961), *Sweet Bird of Youth* (1962), *Dear Heart* (1965), *The Happiest Millionaire* (1966), *Interiors* (1978), *Harry's War* (1980), *Honky Tonk Freeway* (1981), *The Pope of Greenwich Village* (1984), *The Trip to Bountiful* (1985).

Palance, Jack (Walter Palanuik) (1919–) American, born Lattimer, Pennsylvania; *Panic in the Streets* (1950), *Shane* (1953), *The Big Knife* (1953), *Arrowhead* (1953), *They Came to Rob Las Vegas* (1968), *Oklahoma Crude* (1973), *Ripley's Believe It or Not* (TV 1982–6), *Gor* (1988), *Batman* (1988), *Young Guns* (1988), *Tango and Cash* (1989), *City Slickers* (1991), *Tombstone* (1993), *The Incredible Adventures of Marco Polo* (1998).

Palin, Michael (1943–) British, born Sheffield; *Monty Python's Flying Circus* (TV 1969–74), *And Now for Something Completely Different* (1970), *Monty Python and the Holy Grail* (1974), *Three Men in a Boat* (TV 1975), *Jabberwocky* (1976), *Ripping Yarns* (TV 1976–80), *The Life of Brian* (1978), *The Meaning of Life* (1982), *The Missionary* (1982), *Brazil* (1985), *A Fish Called Wanda* (1988), *Around the World in 80 Days* (TV 1990), *American Friends* (1990), *GBH* (TV 1991), *Pole to Pole* (TV 1992), *Fierce Creatures* (1996), *Full Circle* (TV 1997), *Hemingway Adventure* (TV 1999), *Sahara* (TV 2002).

Paltrow, Gwyneth (1973–) American, born Los Angeles, California; *Jefferson in Paris* (1995), *Emma* (1996), *Sliding Doors* (1998), *Shakespeare in Love* (1998), *The Talented Mr Ripley* (1999), *The Royal Tenenbaums* (2001), *Possession* (2002).

Peck, Gregory (Eldred) (1916–) American, born La Jolla, California; *The Keys to the Kingdom* (1944), *Spellbound* (1945), *Duel in the Sun* (1946), *Gentleman's Agreement* (1947), *The Macomber Affair* (1947), *The Paradine Case* (1947), *Twelve O'Clock High* (1949), *The Gunfighter* (1950), *Captain Horatio Hornblower* (1951), *The Million Pound Note* (1954), *The Purple Plain* (1955), *The Man in the Grey Flannel Suit* (1956), *The Big Country* (1958), *The Guns of Navarone* (1961), *Cape Fear* (1962), *To Kill a Mockingbird* (1963), *The Omen* (1976), *Old Gringo* (1989), *Other People's Money* (1991), *Cape Fear* (1991).

Penn, Sean (1960–) American, born Burbank, California; *Fast Times at Ridgemont High* (1982), *Racing with the Moon* (1984), *The Falcon and the Snowman* (1985), *At Close Range* (1986), *Shanghai Surprise* (1986), *Colors* (1988), *Casualties of War* (1989), *We're No Angels* (1989), *State of Grace* (1990), *Carlito's Way* (1993), *Dead Man Walking* (1995), *The Thin Red Line* (1998), *I Am Sam* (2001).

Perkins, Anthony (1932–92) American, born New York City; *The Actress* (1953), *Desire Under the Elms* (1957), *Fear Strikes Out* (1957), *This Angry Age* (1958), *Psycho* (1960), *Five Miles to Midnight* (1962), *Murder on the Orient Express* (1974), *For the Term of His Natural Life* (TV 1982), *Psycho II* (1983), *Crimes of Passion* (1985), *Psycho III* (1986), *Destroyer* (1988), *Edge of Sanity* (1989), *Naked Target* (1991).

Pesci, Joe (1943–) American, born Newark, New Jersey; *Raging Bull* (1980), *Lethal Weapon 2* (1989), *Goodfellas* (1990), *Home Alone* (1990), *JFK* (1991), *My Cousin Vinny* (1992), *Lethal Weapon 3* (1992), *Home Alone 2* (1992), *A Bronx Tale* (1993), *Jimmy Hollywood* (1994), *Casino* (1995), *Lethal Weapon 4* (1998).

Pfeiffer, Michelle (1957–) American, born Santa Ana, California; *Grease 2* (1982), *Scarface* (1983), *Sweet Liberty* (1982), *Into the Night* (1985), *The Witches of Eastwick* (1987), *Dangerous Liaisons* (1988), *Tequila Sunrise* (1988), *Married to the Mob* (1989), *The Fabulous Baker Boys* (1989), *The Russia House* (1990), *Frankie and Johnny* (1991), *Batman Returns* (1992), *The Age of Innocence* (1993), *Wolf* (1994), *Up Close and Personal* (1995), *A Midsummer Night's Dream* (1999), *What Lies Beneath* (2000), *I Am Sam* (2001).

Philipe, Gérard (1922–59) French, born Cannes; *The Idiot* (1946), *Le Diable au Corps* (1947), *Une Si Jolie Petite Plage* (1949), *Fanfan la Tulipe* (1951), *Les Belles de Nuit* (1952), *Knave of Hearts* (1954), *Montparnasse* (1957), *Les Liaisons Dangereuses* (1959).

Phoenix, River (1970–93) American, born Madras, Oregon; *Mosquito Coast* (1986), *Running on Empty* (1988), *Little Nikita* (1988), *Indiana Jones and the Last Crusade* (1989), *I Love You to Death* (1990), *Dogfight* (1991), *My Own Private Idaho* (1991), *Sneakers* (1992), *The Thing Called Love* (1993).

Pickford, Mary (Gladys Mary Smith) (1893–1979) Canadian, born Toronto, Ontario; *The Violin Maker of Cremona* (1909), *Rebecca of Sunnybrook Farm* (1917), *Poor Little Rich Girl* (1917), *Pollyanna* (1919), *Little Lord Fauntleroy* (1921), *Tess of the Storm Country* (1922), *The Taming of the Shrew* (1929), *Coquette* (1929), *Secrets* (1933).

Pickup, Ronald (Alfred) (1940–) British, born Chester; *Day of the Jackal* (1973), *The 39 Steps* (1978), *Nijinski* (1980), *Never Say Never Again* (1983), *Fortunes of War* (TV 1987), *Testimony* (1987), *Bring Me the Head of Mavis Davis* (1998).

Pitt, Brad (William Bradley Pitt) (1963–) American, born Shawnee, Oklahoma; *Thelma and Louise* (1991), *A River Runs Through It* (1992), *Kalifornia* (1993), *True Romance* (1993), *Interview with the Vampire* (1994), *Legends of the Fall* (1994), *Seven* (1995), *Twelve Monkeys* (1995), *Sleepers* (1996), *Seven Years in Tibet* (1997), *Fight Club* (1999), *The Mexican* (2001), *Ocean's Eleven* (2001).

Pleasence, Donald (1919–95) British, born Worksop; *Robin Hood* (TV 1955–7), *Battle of the Sexes* (1959), *Dr Crippen* (1962), *The Great Escape* (1963), *The Caretaker* (1964), *Cul-de-Sac* (1966), *Fantastic Voyage* (1966), *You Only Live Twice* (1967), *Escape to Witch Mountain* (1975), *The Eagle Has Landed* (1977), *Oh God* (1977), *Telefon* (1977), *Halloween*

(1978), *Sgt Pepper's Lonely Hearts Club Band* (1979), *Escape from New York* (1981), *Halloween 4* (1988), *Hanna's War* (1988), *Ground Zero* (1988), *Halloween 5* (1989), *Ten Little Indians* (1989), *Shadows and Fog* (1992), *Halloween 6* (1995).

Plowright, Joan (1929–) British, born Brigg, Lincolnshire; *The Entertainer* (1960), *Drowning by Numbers* (1988), *Love You to Death* (1990), *Tea with Mussolini* (1999), *Callas Forever* (2002).

Plummer, Christopher (1927–) Canadian, born Toronto, Ontario; *The Fall of the Roman Empire* (1964), *The Sound of Music* (1965), *Waterloo* (1970), *The Man Who Would Be King* (1975), *The Return of the Pink Panther* (1975), *International Velvet* (1978), *Hanover Street* (1979), *Somewhere in Time* (1980), *The Janitor* (1981), *Dreamscape* (1984), *Where the Heart Is* (1990), *Liar's Edge* (1992), *Impolite* (1992), *Malcolm X* (1992), *Twelve Monkeys* (1995), *Crackerjack* (1996), *The Insider* (1999), *A Beautiful Mind* (2001).

Poitier, Sidney (1927–) American, born Miami, Florida; *No Way Out* (1950), *Cry, the Beloved Country* (1952), *The Blackboard Jungle* (1955), *The Defiant Ones* (1958), *Porgy and Bess* (1959), *Lilies of the Field* (1963), *To Sir with Love* (1967), *In the Heat of the Night* (1967), *Guess Who's Coming to Dinner* (1967), *Little Nikita* (1988), *Shoot to Kill* (1988), *Separate But Equal* (TV 1991), *Sneakers* (1992), *To Sir with Love II* (1996), *The Jackal* (1997).

Powell, Robert (1944–) British, born Salford, Lancashire; *The Italian Job* (1969), *Jesus of Nazareth* (TV 1977), *The 39 Steps* (1978), *Pygmalion* (TV 1981), *Frankenstein* (TV 1984), *Hannay* (TV 1988).

Powers, Stefanie (Stefania Federkiewicz) (1942–) American, born Hollywood, California; *Experiment in Terror* (1962), *Fanatic* (1964), *Stagecoach* (1966), *The Girl from UNCLE* (TV 1966), *Herbie Rides Again* (1973), *Escape to Athena* (1979), *Hart to Hart* (TV 1979–83), *Family Secrets* (TV 1984), *Someone is Watching* (2000).

Presley, Elvis (Aaron) (1935–77) American, born Tupelo, Mississippi; *Love Me Tender* (1956), *Jailhouse Rock* (1957), *King Creole* (1958), *GI Blues* (1960), *Girl Happy* (1965), *That's the Way It Is* (1971).

Price, Vincent (1911–93) American, born St Louis, Missouri; *Tower of London* (1940), *Dragonwyck* (1946), *His Kind of Woman* (1941), *House of Wax* (1953), *The Story of Mankind* (1957), *The Fly* (1958), *The Fall of the House of Usher* (1961), *The Raven* (1963), *The Tomb of Ligeia* (1964), *City Under the Sea* (1965), *House of a Thousand Dolls* (1967), *The House of Long Shadows* (1983), *Dead Heat* (1988), *Edward Scissorhands* (1991).

Pryor, Richard (1940–) American, born Peoria, Illinois; *Busy Body* (1967), *Lady Sings the Blues* (1972), *Silver Streak* (1976), *Blue Collar* (1978), *Stir Crazy* (1980), *Superman III* (1982), *Brewster's Millions* (1985), *Jo Jo Dancer Your Life is Calling* (1986), *Harlem Nights* (1989), *Lost Highway* (1997).

Quaid, Dennis (1954–) American, born Houston, Texas; *Breaking Away* (1978), *Caveman* (1980), *The Night the Lights Went Out in Georgia* (1980), *Bill* (TV 1981), *All Night Long* (1981), *Johnny Belinda* (TV 1982), *The Right Stuff* (1983), *Jaws 3D* (1983), *Dreamscape* (1984), *The Big Easy* (1986), *Innerspace* (1987), *Suspect* (1987), *DOA* (1988), *Great Balls of Fire* (1989), *Come See the Paradise* (1990), *Postcards from the Edge* (1990), *Wilder Napalm* (1992), *Undercover Blues* (1993), *Wyatt Earp* (1995), *Dragon Heart* (1996), *Any Given Sunday* (1999), *Traffic* (2000), *Far From Heaven* (2002).

Quaid, Randy (1950–) American, born Houston,

Texas; *The Last Picture Show* (1971), *What's Up, Doc?* (1972), *Paper Moon* (1973), *Midnight Express* (1978), *Vacation* (1983), *Parents* (1988), *Caddyshack II* (1988), *Christmas Vacation* (1989), *Days of Thunder* (1990), *Texasville* (1990), *Kingpin* (1996), *Hard Rain* (1998).

Quayle, Sir Anthony (1913–89) British, born Ainsdale, Lancashire; *Ice Cold in Alex* (1958), *The Guns of Navarone* (1961), *Lawrence of Arabia* (1962).

Quinn, Anthony (Rudolph Oaxaca) (1915–2001) Irish–American, born Chihuahua, Mexico; *Viva Zapata* (1952), *La Strada* (1954), *Lust for Life* (1956), *The Guns of Navarone* (1961), *Zorba the Greek* (1964), *The Shoes of the Fisherman* (1968), *Revenge* (1989), *Ghosts Can't Do It* (1990), *Jungle Fever* (1991), *Mobsters* (1991), *Last Action Hero* (1993).

Rampling, Charlotte (1946–) British, born Sturmer; *Georgy Girl* (1966), *The Damned* (1969), *Zardoz* (1973), *Orca* (1977), *Stardust Memories* (1980), *The Verdict* (1982), *Max mon Amour* (1986), *Angel Heart* (1987), *Paris by Night* (1988), *DOA* (1988), *Head Games* (1996), *Wings of the Dove* (1997), *Sous le Sable* (2000).

Rathbone, Basil (Philip St John) (1892–1967) British, born Johannesburg, South Africa; *David Copperfield* (1935), *Anna Karenina* (1935), *Captain Blood* (1935), *Romeo and Juliet* (1936), *The Adventures of Robin Hood* (1938), *The Hound of the Baskervilles* (1939), *The Adventures of Sherlock Holmes* (1939), *Spider Woman* (1944), *Heartbeat* (1946), *The Court Jester* (1956).

Reagan, Ronald (Wilson) (1911–) American, born Tampico, Illinois; *King's Row* (1941), *Desperate Journey* (1942), *The Hasty Heart* (1949), *Bedtime for Bonzo* (1951), *The Killer* (1964).

Redford, (Charles) Robert (1937–) American, born Santa Monica, California; *Barefoot in the Park* (1967), *Butch Cassidy and the Sundance Kid* (1969), *The Candidate* (1972), *The Great Gatsby* (1973), *The Sting* (1973), *The Way We Were* (1973), *All the President's Men* (1976), *The Natural* (1984), *Out of Africa* (1985), *Legal Eagles* (1986), *Havana* (1990), *Sneakers* (1992), *Indecent Proposal* (1993), *Up Close and Personal* (1995), *The Horse Whisperer* (1998).

Redgrave, Sir Michael (Scudamore) (1908–85) British, born Bristol; *The Lady Vanishes* (1938), *The Way to the Stars* (1945), *The Browning Version* (1951), *The Importance of Being Earnest* (1952), *The Dam Busters* (1955), *The Quiet American* (1958), *The Innocents* (1961), *Nicholas and Alexandra* (1971).

Redgrave, Vanessa (1937–) British, born London; *Morgan!* (1965), *Blow-Up* (1966), *Camelot* (1967), *Mary, Queen of Scots* (1971), *Julia* (1977), *Playing for Time* (TV 1980), *The Bostonians* (1984), *Wetherby* (1985), *Three Sovereigns for Sarah* (TV 1985), *Prick Up Your Ears* (1987), *Consuming Passions* (1988), *The Ballad of The Sad Café* (1991), *What Ever Happened to Baby Jane?* (1991), *Howards End* (1992), *Little Odessa* (1994), *Mission: Impossible* (1996), *Deep Impact* (1998), *Girl, Interrupted* (1999).

Reed, Oliver (Robert Oliver Reed) (1938–99) British, born Wimbledon, London; *The Damned* (1962), *The Jokers* (1966), *Women in Love* (1969), *The Brood* (1980), *Condorman* (1981), *Castaway* (1987), *Gor* (1988), *Return of the Musketeers* (1989), *The Pit and the Pendulum* (1991), *Severed Ties* (1992), *Funny Bones* (1995), *Gladiator* (2000).

Reeve, Christopher (1952–) American, born New York City; *Superman* (1978), *Superman II* (1980), *Somewhere in Time* (1980), *Monsignor* (1982), *Death Trap* (1982), *Superman III* (1983), *The Bostonians* (1984), *Superman IV* (1987), *Switching Channels*

(1988), *Noises Off* (1992), *The Remains of the Day* (1993), *Morning Glory* (1993), *Speechless* (1994), *Village of the Damned* (1995), *Rear Window* (1998).

Reeves, Keanu (1964–) American, born Beirut, Lebanon; *River's Edge* (1986), *The Night Before* (1988), *Dangerous Liaisons* (1988), *Bill and Ted's Excellent Adventure* (1989), *Parenthood* (1989), *Love You to Death* (1990), *Bill and Ted's Bogus Journey* (1991), *My Own Private Idaho* (1991), *Dracula* (1992), *Much Ado About Nothing* (1993), *Little Buddha* (1993), *Speed* (1994), *Even Cowgirls Get the Blues* (1994), *A Walk in the Clouds* (1995), *Feeling Minnesota* (1995), *The Matrix* (1999), *Hard Ball* (2001).

Reynolds, Burt (1935–) American, born Waycross, Georgia; *Gunsmoke* (TV 1965–7), *Deliverance* (1972), *Nickelodeon* (1976), *Smokey and the Bandit* (1977), *Hooper* (1978), *Starting Over* (1979), *Smokey and the Bandit II* (1980), *The Cannonball Run* (1981), *Sharkey's Machine* (1981), *The Best Little Whorehouse in Texas* (1982), *Stroker Ace* (1983), *The Man Who Loved Women* (1983), *City Heat* (1984), *Switching Channels* (1988), *Breaking In* (1989), *Evening Shade* (TV 1990–4), *Modern Love* (1990), *Cop-and-a-Half* (1992), *The Player* (1992), *The Maddening* (1995), *Striptease* (1996), *Trigger Happy* (1996), *Boogie Nights* (1997), *Driven* (2001).

Richardson, Miranda (1958–) British, born Liverpool; *Dance with a Stranger* (1984), *The Innocent* (1985), *Blackadder II* (TV 1986), *Empire of the Sun* (1987), *A Month in the Country* (1988), *Die Kinder* (TV 1990), *The Fool* (1990), *Enchanted April* (1991), *Damage* (1992), *The Crying Game* (1992), *Tom and Viv* (1994), *Paradise Pages* (1995), *Kansas City* (1996), *Sleepy Hollow* (1999), *The Hours* (2002).

Richardson, Sir Ralph (1902–83) British, born Cheltenham; *Bulldog Jack* (1935), *Q Planes* (1939), *The Four Feathers* (1939), *Anna Karenina* (1948), *The Fallen Idol* (1948), *The Heiress* (1949), *Richard III* (1956), *Oscar Wilde* (1960), *Long Day's Journey into Night* (1962), *Dr Zhivago* (1966), *The Wrong Box* (1967), *A Doll's House* (1973), *The Man in the Iron Mask* (1977), *Time Bandits* (1980), *Dragonslayer* (1981), *Greystoke* (1984).

Rickman, Alan (1947–) British, born London; *Die Hard* (1988), *Robin Hood: Prince of Thieves* (1991), *Truly, Madly, Deeply* (1991), *Close My Eyes* (1991), *Sense and Sensibility* (1995), *Michael Collins* (1996), *Rasputin* (TV 1996), *Galaxy Quest* (1999), *Harry Potter and the Philosopher's Stone* (2001), *Harry Potter and the Chamber of Secrets* (2002).

Rigg, Dame Diana (1938–) British, born Doncaster, Yorkshire; *The Avengers* (TV 1965–7), *On Her Majesty's Secret Service* (1969), *Theatre of Blood* (1973), *Diana* (TV 1973–4), *Evil Under the Sun* (1981), *Mother Love* (TV 1989), *Snow White* (1989), *The Mrs Bradley Mysteries* (TV 1998–9).

Ringwald, Molly (1968–) American, born Rosewood, California; *The Facts of Life* (TV 1979–80), *Tempest* (1982), *Space Hunter 3D: Adventures in the Forbidden Zone* (1983), *Packin' It In* (TV 1983), *Sixteen Candles* (1984), *The Breakfast Club* (1985), *Pretty in Pink* (1986), *Maybe Baby* (1987), *The Pick-up Artist* (1987), *Fresh Horses* (1988), *For Keeps?* (1988), *Loser Takes All* (1989), *Betsy's Wedding* (1990), *Seven Sundays* (1994), *Malicious* (1995), *Office Killer* (1996), *The Giving Tree* (2000).

Robards, Jason (Jr) (1922–2000) American, born Chicago; *Tender is the Night* (1961), *Long Day's Journey into Night* (1962), *The Hour of the Gun* (1967), *Once Upon a Time in the West* (1969), *Tora! Tora! Tora!*

(1970), *All the President's Men* (1976), *Julia* (1977), *Melvin and Howard* (1980), *The Legend of the Lone Ranger* (1981), *The Day After* (1983), *Sakharov* (TV 1984), *The Long Hot Summer* (TV 1985), *Bright Lights, Big City* (1988), *The Good Mother* (1988), *Parenthood* (1989), *Reunion* (1989), *Storyville* (1992), *Philadelphia* (1993), *The Trial* (1993), *The Paper* (1994), *Beloved* (1998).

Robbins, Tim (Timothy Francis) (1958–) American, born New York City; *Bull Durham* (1988), *Cadillac Man* (1990), *Jacob's Ladder* (1990), *The Player* (1992), *Bob Roberts* (1992), *Short Cuts* (1993), *The Hudsucker Proxy* (1994), *The Shawshank Redemption* (1994), *Nothing to Lose* (1996), *Arlington Road* (1999), *High Fidelity* (2000).

Roberts, Julia (1967–) American, born Smyrna, Georgia; *Mystic Pizza* (1988), *Steel Magnolias* (1989), *Flatliners* (1990), *Pretty Woman* (1990), *Sleeping with the Enemy* (1991), *Hook* (1991), *The Player* (1992), *The Pelican Brief* (1993), *I Love Trouble* (1994), *Prêt-À-Porter* (1994), *Michael Collins* (1996), *My Best Friend's Wedding* (1997), *Notting Hill* (1999), *Runaway Bride* (1999), *Erin Brockovich* (2000), *The Mexican* (2001), *Ocean's Eleven* (2001), *Confessions of a Dangerous Mind* (2002).

Robinson, Edward G (Emanuel Goldenberg) (1893–1973) American, born Bucharest, Romania; *Little Caesar* (1930), *Five Star Final* (1931), *The Whole Town's Talking* (1935), *The Last Gangster* (1937), *A Slight Case of Murder* (1938), *The Amazing Dr Clitterhouse* (1938), *Dr Ehrlich's Magic Bullet* (1940), *Brother Orchid* (1940), *The Sea Wolf* (1941), *Double Indemnity* (1944), *The Woman in the Window* (1944), *Scarlet Street* (1945), *All My Sons* (1948), *Key Largo* (1948), *House of Strangers* (1949), *Two Weeks in Another Town* (1962), *The Cincinnati Kid* (1965), *Soylent Green* (1973).

Rogers, Ginger (Virginia Katherine McMath) (1911–95) American, born Independence, Missouri; *Young Man of Manhattan* (1930), *42nd Street* (1933), *Flying Down to Rio* (1933), *The Gay Divorcee* (1934), *Top Hat* (1935), *Follow the Fleet* (1936), *Stage Door* (1937), *Bachelor Mother* (1939), *Kitty Foyle* (1940), *Roxie Hart* (1942), *Lady in the Dark* (1944).

Rogers, Will (William Penn Adair) (1879–1935) American, born Colagah, Indian Territory (now Oklahoma); *Jubilo* (1919), *State Fair* (1933), *Judge Priest* (1934), *David Harum* (1934), *Handy Andy* (1934), *Life Begins at Forty* (1935), *Steamboat Round the Bend* (1935).

Rooney, Mickey (Joe Yule, Jr) (1920–) American, born Brooklyn, New York City; *A Midsummer Night's Dream* (1935), *Ah Wilderness* (1935), *A Family Affair* (1937), *Judge Hardy's Children* (1938), *Boys' Town* (1938), *Babes in Arms* (1939), *The Human Comedy* (1943), *National Velvet* (1944), *Summer Holiday* (1948), *The Bold and the Brave* (1956), *Breakfast at Tiffany's* (1961), *It's a Mad, Mad, Mad, Mad World* (1963), *Leave 'Em Laughing* (TV 1980), *Bill* (TV 1981), *Erik the Viking* (1989), *Home for Christmas* (TV 1990), *The Toy Maker* (1991), *The Legend of Wolf Mountain* (1992), *That's Entertainment! III* (1994), *Heidi* (1996), *The First of May* (1999).

Rossellini, Isabella (1952–) Italian, born Rome; *White Nights* (1985), *Blue Velvet* (1986), *Siesta* (1987), *Zelly and Me* (1988), *Cousins* (1989), *Wild at Heart* (1990), *Death Becomes Her* (1992), *Fearless* (1993), *Wyatt Earp* (1994), *The Funeral* (1996), *Left Luggage* (1998).

Roth, Tim (1962–) British, born London; *A World Apart* (1988), *The Cook, The Thief, His Wife and Her*

Arts and Culture

Lover (1989), *Vincent and Theo* (1990), *Rosencrantz and Guildenstern are Dead* (1990), *Backsliding* (1991), *Jumpin' at the Boneyard* (1991), *Reservoir Dogs* (1992), *Bodies Rest and Motion* (1993), *Pulp Fiction* (1994), *Rob Roy* (1995), *Deceiver* (1997), *Planet of the Apes* (2001).

Rourke, Mickey (1956–) American, born Schenectady, New York; *Body Heat* (1981), *Rumble Fish* (1983), *9½ Weeks* (1985), *The Year of the Dragon* (1985), *Angel Heart* (1987), *A Prayer for the Dying* (1987), *Johnny Handsome* (1990), *Wild Orchid* (1990), *Harley Davidson and the Marlboro Man* (1991), *Desperate Hours* (1991), *White Sands* (1992), *Bullet* (1995), *Exit in Red* (1996), *The Rainmaker* (1997).

Russell, Jane (1921–) American, born Bemidji, Minnesota; *The Outlaw* (1943), *The Paleface* (1948), *Gentlemen Prefer Blondes* (1953).

Russell, Kurt (1951–) American, born Springfield, Massachusetts; *The Quest* (TV 1976), *Elvis* (TV 1979), *Escape from New York* (1981), *The Thing* (1982), *Silkwood* (1983), *Swing Shift* (1984), *Big Trouble in Little China* (1986), *Tequila Sunrise* (1988), *Tango and Cash* (1990), *Backdraft* (1991), *Unlawful Entry* (1992), *Tombstone* (1993), *Escape from LA* (1996), *Breakdown* (1997), *Vanilla Sky* (2001).

Rutherford, Dame Margaret (1892–1972) British, born London; *Blithe Spirit* (1945), *The Happiest Days of Your Life* (1950), *The Importance of Being Earnest* (1952), *The Smallest Show on Earth* (1957), *Murder She Said* (1961), *The VIPs* (1963), *Murder Most Foul* (1964), *Murder Ahoy* (1964).

Ryan, Meg (1962–) American, born Fairfield, Connecticut; *Rich and Famous* (1981), *Top Gun* (1985), *Innerspace* (1987), *DOA* (1988), *Promised Land* (1988), *The Presidio* (1988), *When Harry Met Sally …* (1989), *Joe Versus the Volcano* (1990), *The Doors* (1991), *Prelude to a Kiss* (1992), *Sleepless in Seattle* (1993), *Flesh and Bone* (1993), *French Kiss* (1995), *Courage Under Fire* (1996), *Easy Women* (1996), *You've Got Mail* (1998), *Hanging Up* (2000).

Ryan, Robert (1909–73) American, born Chicago; *Gangway for Tomorrow* (1943), *Crossfire* (1947), *The Set-Up* (1949), *Clash by Night* (1952), *God's Little Acre* (1958), *Odds Against Tomorrow* (1959), *Billy Budd* (1962), *The Dirty Dozen* (1967), *The Wild Bunch* (1969).

Ryder, Winona (1971–) American, born Winona, Michigan; *Beetlejuice* (1988), *1969* (1988), *Heathers* (1989), *Great Balls of Fire* (1989), *Mermaids* (1990), *Night on Earth* (1992), *Dracula* (1992), *The Age of Innocence* (1993), *Reality Bites* (1994), *Little Women* (1994), *How to Make an American Quilt* (1995), *The Crucible* (1996), *Alien: Resurrection* (1997), *Girl, Interrupted* (1999), *Mr Deeds* (2002).

Sabu (Sabu Dastagir) (1924–63) Indian, born Karapur, Mysore; *Elephant Boy* (1937), *The Thief of Baghdad* (1940), *The Jungle Book* (1942), *The End of the River* (1947), *Black Narcissus* (1947).

Sanders, George (1906–73) British, born St Petersburg, Russia; *Lancer Spy* (1937), *Rebecca* (1940), *The Saint's Double Trouble* (1940), *The Moon and Sixpence* (1942), *The Picture of Dorian Gray* (1944), *Scandal in Paris* (1946), *The Ghost and Mrs Muir* (1947), *Forever Amber* (1947), *The Private Affairs of Bel Ami* (1947), *Lady Windermere's Fan* (1949), *All About Eve* (1950), *Village of the Damned* (1960), *A Shot in the Dark* (1964).

Sands, Julian (1958–) British, born Yorkshire; *Oxford Blues* (1982), *The Killing Fields* (1984), *A Room with a View* (1985), *Gothic* (1987), *Siesta* (1987),

Vibes (1988), *Warlock* (1989), *Arachnophobia* (1990), *Impromptu* (1990), *Grand Isle* (1991), *Naked Lunch* (1991), *Husbands and Lovers* (1992), *Boxing Helena* (1993), *Warlock, Part II* (1993), *Leaving Las Vegas* (1995), *One Night Stand* (1997), *The Scoundrel's Wife* (2002).

Sarandon, Susan (Susan Abigail Tomalin) (1946–) American, born New York City; *Dragonfly* (1977), *Atlantic City* (1981), *The Hunger* (1983), *The Witches of Eastwick* (1987), *Bull Durham* (1988), *A Dry White Season* (1989), *White Palace* (1991), *Thelma and Louise* (1991), *Light Sleeper* (1991), *Lorenzo's Oil* (1992), *The Client* (1994), *Little Women* (1995), *Dead Man Walking* (1995), *Stepmom* (1998).

Savalas, Telly (Aristotle Savalas) (1924–94) Greek-American, born Garden City, New York; *Birdman of Alcatraz* (1962), *The Battle of the Bulge* (1965), *The Dirty Dozen* (1967), *On Her Majesty's Secret Service* (1969), *Horror Express* (1972), *Visions of Death* (1972), *Kojak* (TV 1973–7), *Escape to Athena* (1979), *Kojak* (TV 1989–90), *Backfire* (1994).

Scheider, Roy (1932–) American, born Orange, New Jersey; *French Connection* (1971), *Jaws* (1975), *Jaws 2* (1978), *All That Jazz* (1979), *Blue Thunder* (1982), *Still of the Night* (1982), *2010* (1984), *52 Pick-Up* (1986), *Night Game* (1989), *The Russia House* (1990), *Naked Lunch* (1991), *Romeo Is Bleeding* (1994), *The Rainmaker* (1997).

Schwarzenegger, Arnold (1947–) American, born Thal, near Graz, Austria; *Conan the Barbarian* (1982), *Conan the Destroyer* (1984), *The Terminator* (1984), *Red Sonja* (1985), *Commando* (1985), *Raw Deal* (1986), *Predator* (1987), *The Running Man* (1987), *Twins* (1988), *Red Heat* (1989), *Total Recall* (1990), *Kindergarten Cop* (1990), *Terminator 2: Judgement Day* (1991), *The Last Action Hero* (1993), *True Lies* (1994), *Junior* (1994), *Jingle All the Way* (1996), *Eraser* (1996), *Batman and Robin* (1997), *Collateral Damage* (2002).

Scofield, (David) Paul (1922–) British, born Hurstpierpoint, Sussex; *That Lady* (1955), *A Man for All Seasons* (1966), *Henry V* (1989), *Hamlet* (1990), *Quiz Show* (1994), *The Crucible* (1996).

Scott, George C (1927–99) American, born Wise, Virginia; *Anatomy of a Murder* (1959), *The Hustler* (1962), *The List of Adrian Messenger* (1963), *Dr Strangelove* (1963), *Patton* (1970), *The Hospital* (1972), *Fear on Trial* (TV 1976), *The Changeling* (1980), *Taps* (1981), *Oliver Twist* (1982), *Firestarter* (1984), *A Christmas Carol* (TV 1984), *The Last Days of Patton* (TV 1986), *The Exorcist III* (1990), *Malice* (1993), *Family Rescue* (TV 1996).

Selleck, Tom (1945–) American, born Detroit, Michigan; *Coma* (1977), *Magnum* (TV 1981–9), *High Road to China* (1983), *Lassiter* (1984), *Runaway* (1984), *Three Men and a Baby* (1988), *Three Men and a Little Lady* (1990), *Christopher Columbus: The Discovery* (1992), *Mr Baseball* (1992), *Open Season* (1994), *The Love Letter* (1999).

Sellers, Peter (1925–80) British, born Southsea; *The Smallest Show on Earth* (1957), *The Ladykillers* (1959), *I'm Alright Jack* (1959), *Only Two Can Play* (1962), *Lolita* (1962), *Dr Strangelove* (1963), *The Pink Panther* (1963), *A Shot in the Dark* (1964), *Return of the Pink Panther* (1975), *The Pink Panther Strikes Again* (1976), *Revenge of the Pink Panther* (1978), *Being There* (1979).

Seymour, Jane (Joyce Frankenberg) (1951–) British, born Hillingdon, Middlesex; *Live and Let Die* (1972), *Battle Star Galactica* (TV 1978), *East of Eden* (TV 1981), *Somewhere in Time* (1980), *The Scarlet Pimpernel* (TV 1982), *War and Remembrance* (TV

1987–9), *Matters of the Heart* (1991), *Angel of Death* (1991), *Dr Quinn, Medicine Woman* (TV 1992–3).

Sharif, Omar (Michael Shalhouz) (1932–) Egyptian, born Alexandria; *Lawrence of Arabia* (1962), *Genghis Khan* (1965), *Doctor Zhivago* (1965), *Che!* (1969), *Green Ice* (1980), *The 13th Warrior* (1999).

Shatner, William (1931–) Canadian, born Montreal, Quebec; *Star Trek* (TV 1966–8), *Horror at 37 000 Feet* (TV 1974), *Big Bad Mama* (1974), *Star Trek: The Motion Picture* (1979), *The Kidnapping of the President* (1980), *Star Trek II: The Wrath of Khan* (1982), *T J Hooker* (TV 1982–6), *Star Trek III: The Search for Spock* (1984), *Star Trek IV: The Voyage Home* (1987), *Star Trek V: The Final Frontier* (1989), *Star Trek VI: The Undiscovered Country* (1991), *Star Trek: Generations* (1994), *Miss Congeniality* (2000).

Sheedy, Ally (1962–) American, born New York City; *Wargames* (1983), *The Breakfast Club* (1985), *St Elmo's Fire* (1986), *Short Circuit* (1986), *Heart of Dixie* (1990), *Betsy's Wedding* (1990), *Only the Lonely* (1991), *Man's Best Friend* (1993).

Sheen, Charlie (Carlos Irwin Estevez) (1965–) American, born Santa Monica, California; *Ferris Bueller's Day Off* (1986), *Wall Street* (1987), *Platoon* (1987), *Eight Men Out* (1988), *Major League* (1989), *The Rookie* (1990), *Catchfire* (1990), *Navy Seals* (1990), *Back Track* (1991), *Hot Shots!* (1991), *Hot Shots! Part Deux* (1993), *The Three Musketeers* (1993), *Terminal Velocity* (1994), *Being John Malkovich* (1999).

Sheen, Martin (Ramon Estevez) (1940–) American, born Dayton, Ohio; *Catch-22* (1970), *Badlands* (1973), *The Execution of Private Slovik* (TV 1974), *The Little Girl Who Lives Down the Lane* (1976), *Apocalypse Now* (1979), *Gandhi* (1982), *That Championship Season* (1982), *The Dead Zone* (1983), *Firestarter* (1984), *Wall Street* (1987), *Siesta* (1987), *Da* (1988), *Judgement in Berlin* (1988), *Stockade* (1990), *JFK* (1991), *Gettysburg* (1993), *Finnegan's Wake* (1993), *Hot Shots! Part Deux* (1993), *A Hundred and One Nights* (1994), *The American President* (1995), *The West Wing* (TV 1999–2002).

Shepard, Sam (Samuel Shepard Rogers) (1943–) American, born Fort Sheridan, Illinois; *The Right Stuff* (1983), *Country* (1984), *Crimes of the Heart* (1986), *Baby Boom* (1987), *Steel Magnolias* (1989), *Bright Angel* (1990), *Voyager* (1990), *Thunderheart* (1992), *The Pelican Brief* (1993), *Swordfish* (2001), *Black Hawk Down* (2001).

Shepherd, Cybill (1950–) American, born Memphis, Tennessee; *The Last Picture Show* (1971), *Taxi Driver* (1976), *The Lady Vanishes* (1979), *The Long Hot Summer* (TV 1985), *Moonlighting* (TV 1985–9), *Texasville* (1990), *Alice* (1991), *Married to It* (1991), *Once Upon a Crime* (1992), *Cybill* (TV 1995–8).

Sim, Alastair (1900–76) British, born Edinburgh; *Inspector Hornleigh* (1939), *Green for Danger* (1946), *The Happiest Days of Your Life* (1950), *Scrooge* (1951), *Laughter in Paradise* (1951), *The Bells of St Trinians* (1954).

Simmons, Jean (1929–) British, born London; *Great Expectations* (1946), *Black Narcissus* (1946), *Hamlet* (1948), *The Blue Lagoon* (1948), *The Big Country* (1958), *Elmer Gantry* (1960), *Spartacus* (1960), *The Grass is Greener* (1961), *The Thorn Birds* (TV 1982), *Going Undercover* (1988), *Great Expectations* (TV 1991), *Sense and Sensibility* (TV 1990), *How to Make an American Quilt* (1995).

Sinatra, Frank (Francis Albert Sinatra) (1915–98) American, born Hoboken, New Jersey; *Anchors Aweigh* (1945), *On the Town* (1949), *From Here to Eternity* (1953), *The Man With the Golden Gun* (1955), *Pal Joey* (1957), *The Manchurian Candidate*

(1962), *The Detective* (1963).

Sinden, Sir Donald (1923–) British, born Plymouth; *Doctor in the House* (1954), *The National Health* (1973), *The Day of the Jackal* (1973), *The Island at the Top of the World* (1973), *Two's Company* (TV 1977–80), *Never the Twain* (TV 1981–91), *The Canterville Ghost* (TV 1996).

Singer, Marc (1948–) Canadian, born Vancouver, British Columbia; *Beast Master* (1982), *If You Could See What I Hear* (1982), *V* (TV 1983), *V — The Final Battle* (TV 1984–5), *Dallas* (TV 1986), *Born to Race* (1988).

Skerritt, Tom (1933–) American, born Detroit, Michigan; *M*A*S*H* (1970), *Big Bad Mama* (1974), *Run, Joe* (TV 1974), *The Devil's Rain* (1975), *Up in Smoke* (1978), *Alien* (1979), *Ice Castles* (1979), *The Dead Zone* (1983), *Top Gun* (1986), *Wisdom* (1986), *Cheers* (TV 1987–8), *Space Camp* (1988), *Poltergeist III* (1988), *Steel Magnolias* (1989), *Knight Moves* (1991), *A River Runs Through It* (1992), *Singles* (1992), *Smoke Signals* (1998), *Changing Hearts* (2002).

Slater, Christian (1969–) American, born New York City; *The Name of the Rose* (1986), *Tucker: The Man and His Dream* (1988), *Heathers* (1989), *Young Guns II* (1990), *Pump Up the Volume* (1990), *Robin Hood: Prince of Thieves* (1991), *Kuffs* (1992), *Where the Day Takes You* (1992), *True Romance* (1993), *Jimmy Hollywood* (1994), *Interview with the Vampire* (1994), *Broken Arrow* (1996), *Very Bad Things* (1998), *The Contender* (2000).

Smith, Sir C Aubrey (Charles Aubrey Smith) (1863–1948) British, born London; *Love Me Tonight* (1932), *Morning Glory* (1933), *Lives of a Bengal Lancer* (1935), *The Prisoner of Zenda* (1937), *The Four Feathers* (1939), *Rebecca* (1940), *And Then There Were None* (1945), *An Ideal Husband* (1947), *Little Women* (1949).

Smith, Dame Maggie (1934–) British, born Ilford, Essex; *The VIPs* (1963), *The Pumpkin Eater* (1964), *The Prime of Miss Jean Brodie* (1969), *Travels with My Aunt* (1972), *California Suite* (1978), *A Private Function* (1984), *A Room With a View* (1985), *The Lonely Passion of Judith Hearne* (1987), *Hook* (1991), *Sister Act* (1992), *The Secret Garden* (1993), *Sister Act 2: Back in the Habit* (1993), *Richard III* (1995), *The First Wives Club* (1996), *Washington Square* (1997), *Tea with Mussolini* (1999), *Gosford Park* (2001).

Smith, Will (Willard Christopher Smith Jr) (1968–) American, born Philadelphia, Pennsylvania; *The Fresh Prince of Bel-Air* (TV 1990–96), *Six Degrees of Separation* (1993), *Bad Boys* (1995), *Independence Day* (1996), *Men in Black* (1997), *Enemy of the State* (1998), *Ali* (2001), *Men in Black II* (2002).

Spacey, Kevin (1959–) American, born South Orange, New Jersey; *Glengarry Glen Ross* (1992), *The Usual Suspects* (1995), *Seven* (1995), *LA Confidential* (1997), *American Beauty* (1999), *K-PAX* (2001), *The Shipping News* (2001), *The Life of David Gale* (2003).

Spader, James (1960–) American, born Boston, Massachusetts; *Pretty in Pink* (1986), *Jack's Back* (1988), *Sex, Lies and Videotape* (1989), *The Rachel Papers* (1989), *Bad Influence* (1990), *White Palace* (1991), *True Colors* (1991), *Storyville* (1992), *Bob Roberts* (1992), *The Music of Chance* (1993), *Wolf* (1994), *Stargate* (1994), *Crash* (1996), *Curtain Call* (1999).

Stallone, Sylvester (1946–) American, born New York City; *Rocky* (1976), *Paradise Alley* (1978), *Rocky II* (1979), *Nighthawks* (1981), *First Blood* (1981), *Rocky III* (1981), *Rambo* (1985), *Rocky IV* (1985), *Rambo II* (1986), *Over the Top* (1987), *Rambo*

Arts and Culture

III (1988), *Lock Up* (1989), *Tango and Cash* (1990), *Rocky V* (1990), *Oscar* (1991), *Stop, Or My Mom Will Shoot* (1992), *Bartholomew vs Neff* (1992), *Cliffhanger* (1992), *Demolition Man* (1993), *The Specialist* (1994), *Judge Dredd* (1995), *Daylight* (1996), *Copland* (1997).

Stamp, Terence (1939–) British, born Stepney, London; *The Collector* (1965), *Far from the Madding Crowd* (1967), *Superman* (1978), *Superman II* (1981), *Company of Wolves* (1985), *Legal Eagles* (1986), *Wall Street* (1987), *The Sicilian* (1988), *Alien Nation* (1988), *Young Guns* (1988), *Genuine Risk* (1990), *Stranger in the House* (1991), *Priscilla Queen of the Desert* (1994), *Star Wars: The Phantom Menace* (1999).

Stanton, Harry Dean (1926–) American, born Kentucky; *How the West Was Won* (1962), *Cool Hand Luke* (1967), *The Godfather, Part II* (1974), *Alien* (1979), *The Rose* (1979), *Private Benjamin* (1980), *Young Doctors in Love* (1982), *Christine* (1983), *Repo Man* (1984), *Paris, Texas* (1984), *Pretty in Pink* (1986), *Mr North* (1988), *Stars and Bars* (1988), *The Last Temptation of Christ* (1988), *Twister* (1989), *Wild at Heart* (1990), *Twin Peaks: Fire Walk With Me* (1992), *Fear and Loathing in Las Vegas* (1998).

Stanwyck, Barbara (Ruby Shaw) (1907–90) American, born Brooklyn, New York City; *Broadway Nights* (1927), *Miracle Woman* (1931), *Night Nurse* (1931), *The Bitter Tea of General Yen* (1933), *Baby Face* (1933), *Annie Oakley* (1935), *Stella Dallas* (1937), *Union Pacific* (1939), *The Lady Eve* (1941), *Meet John Doe* (1941), *Ball of Fire* (1941), *Double Indemnity* (1944), *The Strange Love of Martha Ivers* (1946), *Sorry Wrong Number* (1948), *The Furies* (1950), *Executive Suite* (1954), *Walk on the Wild Side* (1962), *The Big Valley* (TV 1965–9), *The Thorn Birds* (TV 1983).

Steiger, Rod (Rodney Stephen Steiger) (1925–2002) American, born Westhampton, New York; *On the Waterfront* (1954), *Oklahoma!* (1955), *The Court Martial of Billy Mitchell* (1955), *The Harder They Fall* (1956), *Al Capone* (1958), *The Pawnbroker* (1964), *Doctor Zhivago* (1965), *In the Heat of the Night* (1967), *A Fistful of Dynamite* (1971), *The Amityville Horror* (1979), *Hollywood Wives* (TV 1984), *American Gothic* (1988), *The January Man* (1988), *Tennessee Nights* (1989), *Men of Respect* (1990), *Guilty as Charged* (1991), *The Player* (1992), *Genghis Khan* (1992), *Taking Liberties* (1993), *The Specialist* (1994), *Mars Attacks!* (1996), *End of Days* (1999).

Stewart, James (Maitland) (1908–97) American, born Indiana, Pennsylvania; *Seventh Heaven* (1937), *You Can't Take It With You* (1938), *Mr Smith Goes to Washington* (1939), *Destry Rides Again* (1939), *The Shop around the Corner* (1940), *The Philadelphia Story* (1940), *It's a Wonderful Life* (1946), *Harvey* (1950), *Broken Arrow* (1950), *The Glen Miller Story* (1953), *Rear Window* (1954), *The Man from Laramie* (1955), *Vertigo* (1958), *Anatomy of a Murder* (1959), *Mr Hobbs Takes a Vacation* (1962), *Shenandoah* (1965), *The Big Sleep* (1978), *North and South II* (TV 1986).

Stockwell, Dean (1936–) American, born Hollywood, California; *The Green Years* (1946), *The Boy with Green Hair* (1948), *Kim* (1950), *Compulsion* (1959), *Sons and Lovers* (1959), *McCloud: Twas the Fight Before Christmas* (TV 1977), *Paris, Texas* (1984), *Dune* (1984), *The Legend of Billie Jean* (1985), *Blue Velvet* (1986), *Gardens of Stone* (1987), *Tucker: The Man and His Dream* (1988), *The Blue Iguana* (1988), *Married to the Mob* (1988), *Quantum Leap* (TV 1989–93), *Smokescreen* (1990), *Back Track* (1991), *The Player* (1992), *Chasers* (1994), *Midnight Blue* (1996).

Stoltz, Eric (1961–) American, born California; *Fast Times at Ridgemont High* (1982), *Mask* (1985), *Some Kind of Wonderful* (1987), *Sister Sister* (1988), *Haunted Summer* (1988), *Fly II* (1989), *Memphis Belle* (1990), *The Waterdance* (1992), *Bodies Rest and Motion* (1993), *Killing Zoë* (1993), *Pulp Fiction* (1994), *Little Women* (1994), *Rob Roy* (1995), *The Rules of Attraction* (2002).

Stone, Sharon (1964–) American, born Meadsville, Pennsylvania; *Deadly Blessing* (1981), *Action Jackson* (1987), *Total Recall* (1990), *He Said She Said* (1991), *Basic Instinct* (1992), *Diary of a Hitman* (1992), *Sliver* (1993), *Last Action Hero* (1993), *Intersection* (1994), *Casino* (1995), *Diabolique* (1996), *The Mighty* (1998), *Gloria* (1999).

Streep, Meryl (Mary Louise Streep) (1949–) American, born Summit, New Jersey; *Julia* (1977), *The Deer Hunter* (1978), *Kramer vs Kramer* (1979), *Manhattan* (1979), *The French Lieutenant's Woman* (1981), *Sophie's Choice* (1982), *Still of the Night* (1982), *Silkwood* (1983), *Plenty* (1985), *Out of Africa* (1986), *Ironweed* (1987), *A Cry in the Dark* (1988), *Evil Angels* (1988), *She-Devil* (1989), *Postcards from the Edge* (1990), *Defending Your Life* (1991), *Death Becomes Her* (1992), *The River Wild* (1994), *The Bridges of Madison County* (1995), *Music of the Heart* (1999), *Adaptation* (2002), *The Hours* (2002).

Streisand, Barbra (Joan) (1942–) American, born Brooklyn, New York City; *Funny Girl* (1968), *Hello Dolly* (1969), *On a Clear Day You Can See Forever* (1970), *What's Up, Doc?* (1972), *The Way We Were* (1973), *A Star is Born* (1976), *Yentl* (1983), *Nuts* (1987), *Prince of Tides* (1991), *The Mirror Has Two Faces* (1996).

Sutherland, Donald (1935–) Canadian, born St John, New Brunswick; *The Dirty Dozen* (1967), *M*A*S*H* (1970), *Klute* (1971), *Casanova* (1976), *1900* (1976), *The Eagle Has Landed* (1977), *Animal House* (1978), *Invasion of the Body Snatchers* (1978), *Ordinary People* (1980), *Apprentice to Murder* (1988), *A Dry White Season* (1989), *Backdraft* (1991), *Buffy the Vampire Slayer* (1992), *Benefit of the Doubt* (1993), *The Shadow Conspiracy* (1995), *The Poet* (1996), *Instinct* (1999), *Space Cowboys* (2000).

Sutherland, Kiefer (1967–) American, born Los Angeles; *Bright Lights, Big City* (1985), *Stand By Me* (1987), *The Lost Boys* (1987), *The Killing Time* (1987), *1969* (1988), *Promised Land* (1988), *Young Guns* (1988), *Renegades* (1989), *Chicago Joe and the Showgirl* (1989), *Flatliners* (1990), *Young Guns II* (1990), *Article 99* (1991), *A Few Good Men* (1992), *Twin Peaks: Fire Walk With Me* (1992), *The Vanishing* (1992), *The Three Musketeers* (1993), *Double Cross* (1995), *Truth or Consequences* (1996), *Ground Control* (1998), *24* (TV 2001).

Swanson, Gloria (Gloria May Josephine Svensson) (1897–1983) American, born Chicago; *Male and Female* (1919), *The Affairs of Anatol* (1921), *Manhandled* (1924), *Sadie Thompson* (1928), *Queen Kelly* (1928), *The Trespasser* (1929), *Sunset Boulevard* (1950).

Swayze, Patrick (1954–) American, born Houston, Texas; *The Outsiders* (1983), *Red Dawn* (1984), *Young Blood* (1986), *North and South* (TV 1986), *North and South II* (TV 1986), *Dirty Dancing* (1987), *Tiger Warsaw* (1988), *Road House* (1989), *Next of Kin* (1989), *Ghost* (1990), *Point Break* (1991), *City of Joy* (1992), *Father Hood* (1993), *Tall Tale* (1995), *Three Wishes* (1995), *Donnie Darko* (2001).

Tandy, Jessica (1909–94) British, born London; *Dragonwyck* (1946), *The Birds* (1963), *Honky Tonk Freeway* (1981), *The World According to Garp* (1982), *Still* of the Night (1982), The Bostonians (1984), Cocoon (1985), The House on Carroll Street (1988), Cocoon: The Return (1988), Driving Miss Daisy (1989), Fried Green Tomatoes (1991), Used People (1992).

Taylor, Dame Elizabeth (Rosemond) (1932–) British, born London; National Velvet (1944), Little Women (1949), The Father of the Bride (1950), A Place in the Sun (1951), Giant (1956), Raintree Country (1957), Cat on a Hot Tin Roof (1958), Butterfield 8 (1960), Cleopatra (1962), Who's Afraid of Virginia Woolf? (1966), Reflections in a Golden Eye (1967), The Taming of the Shrew (1967), Suddenly Last Summer (1968), A Little Night Music (1977), The Mirror Crack'd (1981), Malice in Wonderland (TV 1985), Poker Alice (TV 1986), Young Toscanini (1988), Sweet Bird of Youth (TV 1989), Faithful (1992), The Flintstones (1994).

Taylor, Robert (Spangler Arlington Brugh) (1911–69) American, born Filley, Nebraska; Magnificent Obsession (1935), Camille (1936), Three Comrades (1938), A Yank at Oxford (1938), Waterloo Bridge (1940), Bataan (1943), Song of Russia (1943), Quo Vadis (1951), Ivanhoe (1952), Knights of the Round Table (1953), Party Girl (1958), The Detectives (TV 1959–61), The Miracle of the White Stallions (1962).

Taylor, Rod (Robert Taylor) (1929–) Australian, born Sydney; The Time Machine (1960), The Birds (1963), The VIPs (1963), Thirty-Six Hours (1964), The Glass Bottom Boat (1966), A Rage in Harlem (1991), Open Season (1995).

Tearle, Sir Godfrey (1884–1953) British, born New York City; also stage; Romeo and Juliet (1908), The Thirty-Nine Steps (1935), One of Our Aircraft is Missing (1942), The Titfield Thunderbolt (1953).

Temple, Shirley (1928–) American, born Santa Monica, California; Little Miss Marker (1934), Curly Top (1935), Dimples (1936), Heidi (1937), The Little Princess (1939).

Terry-Thomas (Thomas Terry Hoar-Stevens) (1911–90) British, born Finchley, London; Private's Progress (1956), Carleton Browne of the FO (1958), The Naked Truth (1958), I'm All Right, Jack (1959), It's a Mad, Mad, Mad, Mad World (1963), How to Murder Your Wife (1965), Those Magnificent Men in Their Flying Machines (1965), Don't Look Now (1968).

Thompson, Emma (1959–) British, born Cambridge; The Tall Guy (1989), Henry V (1989), Dead Again (1989), Impromptu (1991), Howards End (1992), Peter's Friends (1992), Much Ado About Nothing (1993), The Remains of the Day (1993), In the Name of the Father (1993), Junior (1994), My Father the Hero (1994), Carrington (1995), Sense and Sensibility (1995), The Well of Loneliness (1997), Maybe Baby (2000).

Thompson, Lea (1961–) American, born Minneapolis, Minnesota; Jaws 3D (1983), Red Dawn (1984), Back to the Future (1985), Howard: A New Breed of Hero (1985), Space Camp (1986), The Wizard of Loneliness (1988), Casual Sex? (1988), Going Undercover (1988), Back to the Future II (1989), Article 99 (1991), Dennis the Menace (1993), The Unknown Cyclist (1997).

Tierney, Gene (Eliza) (1920–91) American, born Brooklyn, New York City; The Return of Frank James (1940), Tobacco Road (1941), Belle Starr (1941), Heaven Can Wait (1943), Laura (1944), Leave Her to Heaven (1945), The Ghost and Mrs Muir (1947), Whirlpool (1949), Toys in the Attic (1963), The Pleasure Seekers (1964).

Tilly, Meg (1960–) Canadian, born Texada; Fame

(1980), The Big Chill (1983), Psycho II (1983), Agnes of God (1985), Masquerade (1988), Valmont (1989), The Two Jakes (1991), Leaving Normal (1992), Body Snatchers (1994), Double Cross (1994), Journey (TV 1995).

Tomlin, Lily (1939–) American, born Detroit, Michigan; Nine to Five (1980), The Incredible Shrinking Woman (1981), All of Me (1984), Big Business (1988), Shadows and Fog (1992), The Beverly Hillbillies (1993), Short Cuts (1993), Even Cowgirls Get the Blues (1993), Blue in the Face (1995), Flirting with Disaster (1996), Tea with Mussolini (1999).

Tracy, Spencer (1900–67) American, born Milwaukee, Wisconsin; Twenty Thousand Years in Sing Sing (1932), The Power and the Glory (1933), A Man's Castle (1933), Fury (1936), San Francisco (1936), Libeled Lady (1936), Captains Courageous (1937), Boys' Town (1938), Stanley and Livingstone (1939), Northwest Passage (1939), Edison the Man (1940), Dr Jekyll and Mr Hyde (1941), Woman of the Year (1942), The Seventh Cross (1944), State of the Union (1948), Adam's Rib (1949), Father of the Bride (1950), Bad Day at Black Rock (1955), The Last Hurrah (1958), Inherit the Wind (1960), Judgement at Nuremberg (1961), It's a Mad, Mad, Mad, Mad World (1963), Guess Who's Coming to Dinner (1967).

Travolta, John (1954–) American, born Englewood, New Jersey; Welcome Back Kotter (TV 1975–8), Carrie (1976), Saturday Night Fever (1977), Grease (1978), Blow Out (1981), Staying Alive (1983), Two of a Kind (1984), Perfect (1985), Look Who's Talking (1989), Look Who's Talking Too (1991), Chains of Gold (1991), Pulp Fiction (1994), White Man's Burden (1995), Get Shorty (1995), Broken Arrow (1996), Phenomenon (1996), Michael (1996), The Thin Red Line (1998), Swordfish (2001).

Turner, Kathleen (1954–) American, born Springfield, Missouri; The Doctors (TV 1977–8), Body Heat (1981), The Man With Two Brains (1983), Romancing the Stone (1984), Crimes of Passion (1984), The Jewel of the Nile (1985), Prizzi's Honor (1985), Peggy Sue Got Married (1986), Switching Channels (1988), Julia and Julia (1988), The Accidental Tourist (1989), War of the Roses (1989), V I Warshawski (1991), House of Cards (1992), Serial Mom (1994), Moonlight and Valentino (1995), The Virgin Suicides (1999).

Turner, Lana (Julia Jean Mildred Frances Turner) (1920–95) American, born Wallace, Indiana; Dr Jekyll and Mr Hyde (1940), Somewhere I'll Find You (1942), The Three Musketeers (1948), Peyton Place (1957).

Turturro, John (1957–) American, born Brooklyn, New York City; Raging Bull (1980), Hannah and Her Sisters (1986), Do the Right Thing (1989), Miller's Crossing (1990), Barton Fink (1991), Mac (1992), Fearless (1993), O Brother, Where art Thou? (2000).

Tushingham, Rita (1942–) British, born Liverpool; A Taste of Honey (1961), Girl with Green Eyes (1964), The Knack (1965), Dr Zhivago (1965), Judgement in Stone (1986), Resurrected (1988), Paper Marriage (1992), An Awfully Big Adventure (1995), Swing (1999).

Ullmann, Liv (1938–) Norwegian, born Tokyo, Japan; Persona (1966), The Emigrants (1972), Face to Face (1975), Autumn Sonata (1978), Dangerous Moves (1983), Gaby — The True Story (1987), La Amiga (1988), The Rose Garden (1989), Mindwalk (1990), The Ox (1991), The Long Shadow (1992).

Ustinov, Sir Peter (Alexander) (1921–) British, born London; Private Angelo (1949), Hotel Sahara (1951), Quo Vadis (1951), Beau Brummell (1954), The Sundowners (1960), Spartacus (1960), Romanoff and Ju-

Arts and Culture

liet (1961), *Topkapi* (1964), *Logan's Run* (1976), *Death on the Nile* (1978), *Evil Under the Sun* (1982), *Appointment with Death* (1988), *Lorenzo's Oil* (1992), *Stiff Upper Lips* (1997), *The Bachelor* (1999).

Valentino, Rudolph (Rodolpho Alphonso Guglielmi di Valentina d'Antonguolla) (1895–1926) Italian–American, born Castellaneta, Italy; *The Four Horsemen of the Apocalypse* (1921), *The Sheikh* (1921), *Blood and Sand* (1922), *The Young Rajah* (1922), *Monsieur Beaucaire* (1924), *The Eagle* (1925), *The Son of the Sheikh* (1926).

Van Cleef, Lee (1925–89) American, born Somerville, New Jersey; *High Noon* (1952), *For a Few Dollars More* (1967), *The Good, the Bad and the Ugly* (1967), *Return of Sabata* (1971), *The Magnificent Seven Ride* (1972), *Escape from New York* (1981), *Codename: Wildgeese II* (1986), *The Heist* (1988).

Van Damme, Jean-Claude (1961–) Belgian, born Brussels; *No Retreat No Surrender* (1985), *Kickboxer* (1989), *Universal Soldier* (1992), *Nowhere to Run* (1993), *Last Action Hero* (1993), *Timecop* (1994), *Streetfighter* (1994), *The Quest* (1996), *Legionnaire* (1998), *Derailed* (2002).

Van Dyke, Dick (1925–) American, born West Plains, Missouri; *The Dick Van Dyke Show* (TV 1961–6), *Mary Poppins* (1964), *Chitty Chitty Bang Bang* (1968), *The Comic* (1969), *Dropout Father* (TV 1982), *Dick Tracey* (1990).

Vaughn, Robert (Francis Vaughn) (1932–) American, born New York City; *The Magnificent Seven* (1960), *The Man from UNCLE* (TV 1964–7), *The Towering Inferno* (1974), *Superman III* (1983), *Delta Force* (1985), *Black Moon Rising* (1986), *The Sender* (1997).

Vincent, Jan-Michael (1944–) American, born Denver, Colorado; *The Mechanic* (1972), *The World's Greatest Athlete* (1973), *Bite the Bullet* (1974), *Hooper* (1978), *Hard Country* (1981), *Airwolf* (TV 1982–6), *The Winds of War* (TV 1983), *Alienator* (1989), *Beyond the Call of Duty* (1992), *Extreme* (1993), *Redline* (1995), *Russian Roulette* (1996), *White Boy* (2002).

von Stroheim, Erich (Hans Erich Maria Stroheim von Nordenwall) (1885–1957) Austrian, born Vienna; *Foolish Wives* (1921), *La Grande Illusion* (1937), *Five Graves to Cairo* (1943), *Sunset Boulevard* (1950).

von Sydow, Max (Carl Adolf) (1929–) Swedish, born Lund; *The Seventh Seal* (1956), *The Face* (1959), *The Greatest Story Ever Told* (1965), *Hawaii* (1966), *Through a Glass Darkly* (1966), *Hour of the Wolf* (1967), *The Emigrants* (1972), *The Exorcist* (1973), *Exorcist II: The Heretic* (1977), *Flash Gordon* (1980), *Never Say Never Again* (1983), *Hannah and Her Sisters* (1986), *Pelle, the Conquerer* (1988), *Awakenings* (1990), *Dr Grassler* (1990), *The Father* (1990), *The Ox* (1991), *The Touch* (1992), *Needful Things* (1993), *Judge Dredd* (1995), *Snow Falling on Cedars* (1999), *Minority Report* (2002).

Wagner, Robert (John Jr) (1930–) American, born Detroit, Michigan; *The Silver Whip* (1953), *Prince Valiant* (1954), *A Kiss Before Dying* (1956), *The True Story of Jesse James* (1957), *All the Fine Young Cannibals* (1959), *The Condemned of Altona* (1963), *The Pink Panther* (1963), *It Takes a Thief* (TV 1965–9), *Colditz* (TV 1972–3), *The Towering Inferno* (1974), *Switch* (TV 1975–7), *Hart to Hart* (TV 1979–84), *Trail of the Pink Panther* (1982), *Curse of the Pink Panther* (1983), *Delirious* (1993), *The Bruce Lee Story* (1993), *Austin Powers: International Man of Mystery* (1997), *Austin Powers: The Spy Who Shagged Me* (1999), *Austin Powers in Goldmember* (2002).

Walken, Christopher (1943–) American, born As-

toria, New York; *Annie Hall* (1977), *The Deer Hunter* (1978), *The Dogs of War* (1981), *Pennies from Heaven* (1981), *The Dead Zone* (1983), *Brainstorm* (1983), *A View to a Kill* (1984), *At Close Range* (1986), *The Milagro Beanfield War* (1987), *Biloxi Blues* (1988), *Puss in Boots* (1988), *The Comfort of Strangers* (1990), *Batman Returns* (1992), *True Romance* (1993), *Wayne's World 2* (1993), *Pulp Fiction* (1994), *Things to Do in Denver When You're Dead* (1995), *Darkening* (1996), *Sleepy Hollow* (1999).

Walters, Julie (1950–) British, born Birmingham; *Educating Rita* (1983), *She'll Be Wearing Pink Pajamas* (1984), *Car Trouble* (1986), *Prick Up Your Ears* (1987), *Personal Services* (1987), *Buster* (1987), *Killing Dad* (1989), *Stepping Out* (1991), *Sister My Sister* (1995), *Intimate Relations* (1996), *Billy Elliott* (2000).

Wanamaker, Sam (1919–93) American, born Chicago; *Those Magnificent Men in Their Flying Machines* (1965), *The Spy Who Came in from the Cold* (1965), *Voyage of the Damned* (1976), *Death on the Nile* (1978), *Private Benjamin* (1980), *Raw Deal* (1986), *Superman IV* (1986), *Baby Boom* (1987), *Judgement in Berlin* (1988), *Guilty by Suspicion* (1991).

Warner, David (1941–) British, born Manchester; *Morgan* (1966), *The Bofors Gun* (1968), *The Engagement* (1970), *The Omen* (1976), *Holocaust* (TV 1978), *The 39 Steps* (1978), *Time Bandits* (1981), *The French Lieutenant's Woman* (1981), *Tron* (1982), *The Man with Two Brains* (1983), *Company of Wolves* (1984), *Mr North* (1988), *Hanna's War* (1988), *Star Trek V: The Final Frontier* (1989), *The Secret Life of Ian Fleming* (1990), *Star Trek VI: The Undiscovered Country* (1991), *The Unnameable Returns* (1992), *Tryst* (1994), *Darkening* (1996), *Titanic* (1997).

Washington, Denzel (1954–) American, born Mt Vernon, New York; *St Elsewhere* (TV 1982–9), *Cry Freedom* (1987), *Queen and Country* (1988), *Glory* (1989), *Mo' Better Blues* (1990), *Mississippi Masala* (1991), *Ricochet* (1991), *Malcolm X* (1992), *Philadelphia* (1993), *The Pelican Brief* (1993), *Much Ado About Nothing* (1993), *Devil in a Blue Dress* (1995), *Crimson Tide* (1995), *Courage Under Fire* (1996), *The Preacher's Wife* (1996), *Training Day* (2001), *John Q* (2002), *Antwone Fisher* (2002).

Wayne, John (Marion Michael Morrison) (1907–79) American, born Winterset, Iowa; *The Big Trail* (1930), *Stagecoach* (1939), *The Long Voyage Home* (1940), *Red River* (1948), *She Wore a Yellow Ribbon* (1949), *Sands of Iwo Jima* (1949), *The Quiet Man* (1952), *The High and the Mighty* (1954), *The Searchers* (1956), *Rio Bravo* (1959), *The Alamo* (1960), *True Grit* (1969), *The Shootist* (1976).

Weaver, Sigourney (Susan Weaver) (1949–) American, born New York City; *Alien* (1979), *The Janitor* (1981), *The Year of Living Dangerously* (1982), *Ghostbusters* (1984), *Aliens* (1986), *Gorillas in the Mist* (1988), *Working Girl* (1988), *Ghostbusters II* (1989), *Alien 3* (1992), *1492* (1992), *Dave* (1993), *Death and The Maiden* (1994), *Copycat* (1995), *Ice Storm* (1996), *Alien: Resurrection* (1997), *Galaxy Quest* (1999).

Welch, Raquel (Raquel Tejada) (1940–) American, born Chicago; *Fantastic Voyage* (1966), *One Million Years BC* (1967), *Myra Breckenridge* (1970), *The Three Musketeers* (1974), *The Four Musketeers* (1975).

Welles, Orson (1915–85) American, born Kenosha, Wisconsin; *Citizen Kane* (1941), *Journey into Fear* (1942), *The Stranger* (1945), *The Lady from Shanghai* (1947), *The Third Man* (1949), *The Trial* (1962), *Touch of Evil* (1965), *A Man For All Seasons* (1966),

Casino Royale (1967), Voyage of the Damned (1976), History of the World Part One (1981).

West, Mae (1892–1980) American, born Brooklyn, New York City; She Done Him Wrong (1933), I'm No Angel (1933), My Little Chickadee (1939), Myra Breckenridge (1970).

Widmark, Richard (1914–) American, born Sunrise, Minnesota; Kiss of Death (1947), Night and the City (1950), How the West Was Won (1963), The Bedford Incident (1965), Madigan (1968), Madigan (TV 1972), Murder on the Orient Express (1974), Who Dares Wins (1982), Hanky Panky (1982), Against all Odds (1983), True Colors (1991).

Wilder, Gene (Jerome Silberman) (1935–) American, born Milwaukee, Wisconsin; Bonnie and Clyde (1967), The Producers (1967), Willy Wonka and the Chocolate Factory (1971), Blazing Saddles (1974), Young Frankenstein (1974), The Frisco Kid (1979), Stir Crazy (1982), Hanky Panky (1982), The Woman in Red (1984), Haunted Honeymoon (1986), See No Evil Hear No Evil (1989), Funny About Love (1991).

Williams, Kenneth (1926–88) British, born London; Carry on Sergeant (1958), Carry on Dick (1974), Follow that Camel (1968).

Williams, Robin (1952–) American, born Chicago; Mork and Mindy (TV 1978–82), Popeye (1980), The World According to Garp (1982), Good Morning Vietnam (1987), Dead Poets Society (1989), Cadillac Man (1990), Awakenings (1990), Dead Again (1991), The Fisher King (1991), Hook (1991), Toys (1992), Ferngully (1992), Being Human (1992), Mrs Doubtfire (1993), Jumanji (1995), Hamlet (1996), Father's Day (1997), Good Will Hunting (1997), Bicentennial Man (1999), One Hour Photo (2002), Insomnia (2002).

Williams, Treat (Richard Williams) (1951–) American, born Rowayton, Connecticut; The Eagle Has Landed (1977), Hair (1977), 1941 (1979), Once Upon a Time in America (1984), Dempsey (TV 1985), Smooth Talk (1985), A Streetcar Named Desire (1986), The Men's Club (1986), Dead Heat (1988), Heart of Dixie (1990), The Phantom (1995), Deep Rising (1997).

Williamson, Nicol (1938–) British, born Hamilton, near Glasgow; Inadmissible Evidence (1967), The Bofors Gun (1968), The Reckoning (1969), Excalibur (1981), Sakharov (TV 1985), Return to Oz (1985), Black Widow (1986), The Exorcist III (1990).

Willis, Bruce (1955–) American, born Penns Grove, New Jersey; Moonlighting (TV 1985–9), Blind Date (1987), Die Hard (1988), Sunset (1988), In Country (1989), Die Hard 2: Die Harder (1990), Bonfire of the Vanities (1991), Hudson Hawk (1991), Billy Bathgate (1991), The Last Boy Scout (1991), Death Becomes Her (1992), Striking Distance (1993), Pulp Fiction (1994), Nobody's Fool (1994), Die Hard with a Vengeance (1995), Twelve Monkeys (1995), The Fifth Element (1996), The Jackal (1997), The Sixth Sense (1999), Hart's War (2002).

Winger, Debra (1955–) American, born Columbus, Ohio; Urban Cowboy (1980), Cannery Row (1981), An Officer and a Gentleman (1982), Terms of Endear-

ment (1983), Legal Eagles (1985), Black Widow (1987), Made in Heaven (1987), Betrayed (1988), The Sheltering Sky (1990), Wilder Napalm (1992), A Dangerous Woman (1993), Shadowlands (1993), Forget Paris (1995).

Winters, Shelley (Shirley Schrift) (1922–) American, born St Louis, Missouri; A Double Life (1948), The Big Knife (1955), The Night of the Hunter (1955), The Diary of Anne Frank (1959), Lolita (1962), A Patch of Blue (1965), Alfie (1966), The Poseidon Adventure (1972), SOB (1981), Purple People Eater (1988), Stepping Out (1991), Backfire (1994), The Portrait of a Lady (1996), Gideon (1999).

Wisdom, Norman (1915–) British, born London; Trouble in Store (1955), Man of the Moment (1955), Just My Luck (1958), There was a Crooked Man (1960), On the Beat (1962), A Stitch in Time (1963), Sandwich Man (1966), The Night They Raided Minsky's (1968), What's Good for the Goose (1969).

Wood, Natalie (Natasha Gurdin) (1938–81) American, born San Francisco, California; Miracle on 34th Street (1947), The Ghost and Mrs Muir (1947), Rebel Without a Cause (1955), The Searchers (1956), Marjorie Morningstar (1958), All The Fine Young Cannibals (1959), Splendor in the Grass (1961), West Side Story (1961), Love with the Proper Stranger (1964), The Great Race (1965), This Property is Condemned (1966), Bob and Carol and Ted and Alice (1969), From Here to Eternity (TV 1979), Meteor (1979), Brainstorm (1983).

Woods, James (1947–) American, born Vernal, Utah; The Choirboys (1977), Videodrome (1983), Salvador (1986), Best Seller (1987), Cop (1988), The Boost (1988), The Getaway (1994), Nixon (1995), Contact (1997), John Q (2002).

Woodward, Joanne (1930–) American, born Thomasville, Georgia; Three Faces of Eve (1957), No Down Payment (1957), The Long Hot Summer (1958), The Stripper (1963), A Big Hand for the Little Lady (1966), Rachel, Rachel (1968), Summer Wishes, Winter Dreams (1973), The Glass Menagerie (1987), Mr and Mrs Bridge (1990), Philadelphia (1993), Breathing Lessons (TV 1994).

York, Michael (1942–) British, born Fulmer; Accident (1967), Romeo and Juliet (1968), Cabaret (1972), Lost Horizon (1973), The Three Musketeers (1973), The Four Musketeers (1974), Jesus of Nazareth (TV 1977), The Island of Dr Moreau (1977), The White Lions (1980), Space (TV 1985), The Far Country (TV 1986), Sword of Gideon (TV 1986), Return of the Musketeers (1989), The Four Minute Mile (1992), The Ring (1996), Austin Powers: International Man of Mystery (1997), Austin Powers: The Spy Who Shagged Me (1999), Austin Powers in Goldmember (2002).

Young, Sean (1959–) American, born Louisville, Kentucky; Blade Runner (1982), Dune (1984), Baby ... Secret of the Lost Legend (1985), Wall Street (1987), The Boost (1988), Cousins (1989), Wings of the Apache (1990), Hold Me Thrill Me Kiss Me (1993), Ace Ventura: Pet Detective (1994), Special Delivery (1999).

Arts and Culture

Motion picture Academy Awards

Awarded by the Academy of Motion Picture Arts and Sciences; popularly known as Oscars.

Year	Best film	Best actor	Best actress
1927/8	*Wings* (William A Wellman)	Emil Jannings *The Last Command, The Way of All Flesh*	Janet Gaynor *7th Heaven, Street Angel, Sunrise*
1928/9	*The Broadway Melody* (Harry Beaumont)	Warner Baxter *In Old Arizona*	Mary Pickford *Coquette*
1929/30	*All Quiet on the Western Front* (Lewis Milestone)	George Arliss *Disraeli*	Norma Shearer *The Divorcee*
1930/1	*Cimarron* (Wesley Ruggles)	Lionel Barrymore *A Free Soul*	Marie Dressler *Min and Bill*
1931/2	*Grand Hotel* (Edmund Goulding)	Wallace Beery *The Champ*; Fredric March *Dr Jekyll and Mr Hyde*	Helen Hayes *The Sin of Madelon Claudet*
1932/3	*Cavalcade* (Frank Lloyd)	Charles Laughton *The Private Life of Henry VIII*	Katharine Hepburn *Morning Glory*
1934	*It Happened One Night* (Frank Capra)	Clark Gable *It Happened One Night*	Claudette Colbert *It Happened One Night*
1935	*Mutiny on the Bounty* (Frank Lloyd)	Victor McLaglen *The Informer*	Bette Davis *Dangerous*
1936	*The Great Ziegfeld* (Robert Z Leonard)	Paul Muni *The Story of Louis Pasteur*	Luise Rainer *The Great Ziegfeld*
1937	*The Life of Émile Zola* (William Dieterle)	Spencer Tracy *Captains Courageous*	Luise Rainer *The Good Earth*
1938	*You Can't Take It with You* (Frank Capra)	Spencer Tracy *Boys' Town*	Bette Davis *Jezebel*
1939	*Gone with the Wind* (Victor Fleming)	Robert Donat *Goodbye Mr Chips*	Vivien Leigh *Gone with the Wind*
1940	*Rebecca* (Alfred Hitchcock)	James Stewart *The Philadelphia Story*	Ginger Rogers *Kitty Foyle*
1941	*How Green Was My Valley* (John Ford)	Gary Cooper *Sergeant York*	Joan Fontaine *Suspicion*
1942	*Mrs Miniver* (William Wyler)	James Cagney *Yankee Doodle Dandy*	Greer Garson *Mrs Miniver*
1943	*Casablanca* (Michael Curtiz)	Paul Lukas *Watch on the Rhine*	Jennifer Jones *The Song of Bernadette*
1944	*Going My Way* (Leo McCarey)	Bing Crosby *Going My Way*	Ingrid Bergman *Gaslight*
1945	*The Lost Weekend* (Billy Wilder)	Ray Milland *The Lost Weekend*	Joan Crawford *Mildred Pierce*
1946	*The Best Years of Our Lives* (William Wyler)	Fredric March *The Best Years of Our Lives*	Olivia de Havilland *To Each His Own*
1947	*Gentleman's Agreement* (Elia Kazan)	Ronald Colman *A Double Life*	Loretta Young *The Farmer's Daughter*
1948	*Hamlet* (Laurence Olivier)	Laurence Olivier *Hamlet*	Jane Wyman *Johnny Belinda*
1949	*All the King's Men* (Robert Rossen)	Broderick Crawford *All the King's Men*	Olivia de Havilland *The Heiress*
1950	*All About Eve* (Joseph L Mankiewicz)	Jose Ferrer *Cyrano de Bergerac*	Judy Holliday *Born Yesterday*
1951	*An American in Paris* (Vincente Minnelli)	Humphrey Bogart *The African Queen*	Vivien Leigh *A Streetcar Named Desire*
1952	*The Greatest Show on Earth* (Cecil B DeMille)	Gary Cooper *High Noon*	Shirley Booth *Come Back, Little Sheba*
1953	*From Here to Eternity* (Fred Zinnemann)	William Holden *Stalag 17*	Audrey Hepburn *Roman Holiday*
1954	*On the Waterfront* (Elia Kazan)	Marlon Brando *On the Waterfront*	Grace Kelly *The Country Girl*
1955	*Marty* (Delbert Mann)	Ernest Borgnine *Marty*	Anna Magnani *The Rose Tattoo*
1956	*Around the World in 80 Days* (Michael Anderson)	Yul Brynner *The King and I*	Ingrid Bergman *Anastasia*
1957	*The Bridge on the River Kwai* (David Lean)	Alec Guinness *The Bridge on the River Kwai*	Joanne Woodward *The Three Faces of Eve*
1958	*Gigi* (Vincente Minnelli)	David Niven *Separate Tables*	Susan Hayward *I Want to Live!*
1959	*Ben-Hur* (William Wyler)	Charlton Heston *Ben-Hur*	Simone Signoret *Room at the Top*
1960	*The Apartment* (Billy Wilder)	Burt Lancaster *Elmer Gantry*	Elizabeth Taylor *Butterfield 8*
1961	*West Side Story* (Jerome Robbins, Robert Wise)	Maximilian Schell *Judgement at Nuremberg*	Sophia Loren *Two Women*
1962	*Lawrence of Arabia* (David Lean)	Gregory Peck *To Kill a Mockingbird*	Anne Bancroft *The Miracle Worker*
1963	*Tom Jones* (Tony Richardson)	Sidney Poitier *Lilies of the Field*	Patricia Neal *Hud*
1964	*My Fair Lady* (George Cukor)	Rex Harrison *My Fair Lady*	Julie Andrews *Mary Poppins*
1965	*The Sound of Music* (Robert Wise)	Lee Marvin *Cat Ballou*	Julie Christie *Darling*

Year	Best film	Best actor	Best actress
1966	*A Man for All Seasons* (Fred Zinnemann)	Paul Scofield *A Man for All Seasons*	Elizabeth Taylor *Who's Afraid of Virginia Woolf?*
1967	*In the Heat of the Night* (Norman Jewison)	Rod Steiger *In the Heat of the Night*	Katharine Hepburn *Guess Who's Coming to Dinner*
1968	*Oliver!* (Carol Reed)	Cliff Robertson *Charly*	Katharine Hepburn *The Lion in Winter*; Barbra Streisand *Funny Girl*
1970	*Patton* (Franklin J Schaffner)	George C Scott *Patton*	Glenda Jackson *Women in Love*
1971	*The French Connection* (William Friedkin)	Gene Hackman *The French Connection*	Jane Fonda *Klute*
1972	*The Godfather* (Francis Ford Coppola)	Marlon Brando *The Godfather*	Liza Minnelli *Cabaret*
1973	*The Sting* (George Roy Hill)	Jack Lemmon *Save the Tiger*	Glenda Jackson *A Touch of Class*
1974	*The Godfather, Part II* (Francis Ford Coppola)	Art Carney *Harry and Tonto*	Ellen Burstyn *Alice Doesn't Live Here Anymore*
1975	*One Flew Over the Cuckoo's Nest* (Miloš Forman)	Jack Nicholson *One Flew Over the Cuckoo's Nest*	Louise Fletcher *One Flew Over the Cuckoo's Nest*
1976	*Rocky* (John G Avildsen)	Peter Finch *Network*	Faye Dunaway *Network*
1977	*Annie Hall* (Woody Allen)	Richard Dreyfuss *The Goodbye Girl*	Diane Keaton *Annie Hall*
1978	*The Deer Hunter* (Michael Cimino)	Jon Voight *Coming Home*	Jane Fonda *Coming Home*
1979	*Kramer vs Kramer* (Robert Beaton)	Dustin Hoffman *Kramer vs Kramer*	Sally Field *Norma Rae*
1980	*Ordinary People* (Robert Redford)	Robert de Niro *Raging Bull*	Sissy Spacek *Coal Miner's Daughter*
1981	*Chariots of Fire* (Hugh Hudson)	Henry Fonda *On Golden Pond*	Katharine Hepburn *On Golden Pond*
1982	*Gandhi* (Richard Attenborough)	Ben Kingsley *Gandhi*	Meryl Streep *Sophie's Choice*
1983	*Terms of Endearment* (James L Brooks)	Robert Duvall *Tender Mercies*	Shirley MacLaine *Terms of Endearment*
1984	*Amadeus* (Miloš Forman)	F Murray Abraham *Amadeus*	Sally Field *Places in the Heart*
1985	*Out of Africa* (Sydney Pollack)	William Hurt *Kiss of the Spider Woman*	Geraldine Page *The Trip to Bountiful*
1986	*Platoon* (Oliver Stone)	Paul Newman *The Color of Money*	Marlee Matlin *Children of a Lesser God*
1987	*The Last Emperor* (Bernardo Bertolucci)	Michael Douglas *Wall Street*	Cher *Moonstruck*
1988	*Rain Man* (Barry Levinson)	Dustin Hoffman *Rain Man*	Jodie Foster *The Accused*
1989	*Driving Miss Daisy* (Bruce Beresford)	Daniel Day-Lewis *My Left Foot*	Jessica Tandy *Driving Miss Daisy*
1990	*Dances with Wolves* (Kevin Costner)	Jeremy Irons *Reversal of Fortune*	Kathy Bates *Misery*
1991	*The Silence of the Lambs* (Jonathan Demme)	Anthony Hopkins *The Silence of the Lambs*	Jodie Foster *The Silence of the Lambs*
1992	*Unforgiven* (Clint Eastwood)	Al Pacino *Scent of a Woman*	Emma Thompson *Howards End*
1993	*Schindler's List* (Steven Spielberg)	Tom Hanks *Philadelphia*	Holly Hunter *The Piano*
1994	*Forrest Gump* (Robert Zemeckis)	Tom Hanks *Forrest Gump*	Jessica Lange *Blue Sky*
1995	*Braveheart* (Mel Gibson)	Nicolas Cage *Leaving Las Vegas*	Susan Sarandon *Dead Man Walking*
1996	*The English Patient* (Anthony Minghella)	Geoffrey Rush *Shine*	Frances McDormand *Fargo*
1997	*Titanic* (James Cameron)	Jack Nicholson *As Good as it Gets*	Helen Hunt *As Good as it Gets*
1998	*Shakespeare in Love* (Guy Madden)	Roberto Benigni *Life is Beautiful*	Gwyneth Paltrow *Shakespeare in Love*
1999	*American Beauty* (Sam Mendes)	Kevin Spacey *American Beauty*	Hilary Swank *Boys Don't Cry*
2000	*Gladiator* (Ridley Scott)	Russell Crowe *Gladiator*	Julia Roberts *Erin Brockovich*
2001	*A Beautiful Mind* (Ron Howard)	Denzel Washington *Training Day*	Halle Berry *Monster's Ball*
2002	*Chicago* (Rob Marshall)	Adrien Brody *The Pianist*	Nicole Kidman *The Hours*

Arts and Culture

Film directors

Selected films are listed.

Aldrich, Robert (1918–83) American, born Cranston, Rhode Island; *Apache* (1954), *Vera Cruz* (1954), *Kiss Me Deadly* (1955), *Attack!* (1957), *What Ever Happened to Baby Jane?* (1962), *The Dirty Dozen* (1967).

Allen, Woody (Allen Stewart Konigsberg) (1935–) American, born Brooklyn, New York City; *What's Up, Tiger Lily?* (1966), *Bananas* (1971), *Everything You Wanted to Know About Sex, But Were Afraid to Ask* (1972), *Play it Again, Sam* (1972), *Sleeper* (1973), *Love and Death* (1975), *Annie Hall* (1977), *Interiors* (1978), *Manhattan* (1979), *A Midsummer Night's Sex Comedy* (1982), *Hannah and Her Sisters* (1986), *Radio Days* (1987), *Crimes and Misdemeanors* (1990), *Alice* (1991), *Shadows and Fog* (1992), *Husbands and Wives* (1992), *Manhattan Murder Mystery* (1993), *Bullets Over Broadway* (1994), *Mighty Aphrodite* (1996), *Anna Oz* (1996), *Deconstructing Harry* (1997), *Celebrity* (1998), *Sweet and Lowdown* (1999), *The Curse of the Jade Scorpion* (2001).

Almodóvar, Pedro (1951–) Spanish, born Calzada de Calatrava; *Women on the Verge of a Nervous Breakdown* (1988), *Tie Me Up! Tie Me Down!* (1990), *High Heels* (1991), *Kika* (1993), *Live Flesh* (1997), *All About My Mother* (1999), *Talk to Her* (2002).

Altman, Robert (1925–) American, born Kansas City, Missouri; *The James Dean Story* (1957), *M*A*S*H* (1970), *McCabe and Mrs Miller* (1971), *The Long Goodbye* (1973), *Nashville* (1975), *Popeye* (1980), *Come Back to the 5 & Dime Jimmy Dean Jimmy Dean* (1982), *Fool for Love* (1985), *Aria* (1987), *Vincent and Theo* (1990), *The Player* (1992), *Short Cuts* (1993), *Prêt-À-Porter* (1994), *Kansas City* (1996), *The Gingerbread Man* (1998), *Cookie's Fortune* (1999), *Gosford Park* (2001).

Antonioni, Michelangelo (1912–) Italian, born Ferrara; *L'Avventura* (1959), *La Notte* (1960), *L'Eclisse* (1962), *Blow-Up* (1966), *The Passenger* (1975), *Beyond the Clouds* (1995).

Asquith, Anthony (1902–68) British, born London; *Underground* (1930), *Pygmalion* (1937), *French without Tears* (1939), *Quiet Wedding* (1940), *The Demi-Paradise* (1943), *Fanny by Gaslight* (1944), *The Way to the Stars* (1945), *The Browning Version* (1950), *The Importance of Being Earnest* (1952), *Orders to Kill* (1958), *The VIPs* (1963).

Attenborough, Richard Samuel Attenborough, Baron (1923–) British, born Cambridge; *Oh! What a Lovely War* (1968), *A Bridge Too Far* (1977), *Gandhi* (1982), *A Chorus Line* (1985), *Cry Freedom* (1987), *Chaplin* (1992), *Shadowlands* (1993), *In Love and War* (1996), *Grey Owl* (1998).

Badham, John (1939–) American, born Luton, England; *The Law* (TV 1974), *Saturday Night Fever* (1977), *Whose Life is it Anyway?* (1981), *Blue Thunder* (1982), *War Games* (1983), *American Flyers* (1984), *Short Circuit* (1986), *Stakeout* (1987), *Bird on a Wire* (1989), *The Assassin* (1992), *Another Stakeout* (1993), *Floating Away* (1998).

Beatty, Warren (Henry Warren Beaty) (1937–) American, born Richmond, Virginia; *Heaven Can Wait* (1978), *Reds* (1981), *Dick Tracy* (1990), *Bulworth* (1998).

Bergman, (Ernst) Ingmar (1918–) Swedish, born Uppsala; *Crisis* (1945), *Prison* (1948), *Sawdust and Tinsel* (1953), *The Face* (1955), *Smiles of a Summer Night* (1955), *The Seventh Seal* (1957), *Wild Strawberries* (1957), *The Virgin Spring* (1959), *Through a Glass Darkly* (1961), *The Silence* (1963), *Shame* (1968), *Cries and Whispers* (1972), *The Magic Flute* (1974), *Autumn Sonata* (1978), *Fanny and Alexander* (1983).

Bertolucci, Bernardo (1940–) Italian, born Parma; *Love and Anger* (1969), *The Conformist* (1970), *Last Tango in Paris* (1972), *1900* (1976), *The Last Emperor* (1987), *The Sheltering Sky* (1990), *Little Buddha* (1993), *Stealing Beauty* (1996), *Besieged* (1998).

Besson, Luc (1959–) French, born Paris; *The Last Battle* (1983), *Subway* (1985), *The Big Blue* (1988), *Nikita* (1990), *Leon* (1994), *The Fifth Element* (1997), *The Messenger: The Story of Joan of Arc* (1999).

Bogdanovich, Peter (1939–) American, born Kingston, New York; *Targets* (1967), *The Last Picture Show* (1971), *Paper Moon* (1973), *What's Up, Doc?* (1972), *Nickelodeon* (1976), *Mask* (1985), *Illegally Yours* (1987), *Texasville* (1990), *Noises Off* (1992), *The Thing Called Love* (1993).

Boorman, John (1933–) English, born Epsom, Surrey; *Point Blank* (1967), *Hell in the Pacific* (1969), *Deliverance* (1972), *Zardoz* (1974), *Excalibur* (1981), *The Emerald Forest* (1984), *Hope and Glory* (1987), *Where the Heart Is* (1990), *Beyond Rangoon* (1995), *The Tailor of Panama* (2001).

Bresson, Robert (1901–99) French, born Bromont-Lamothe; *Les Dames du Bois de Boulogne* (1946), *Journal d'un Curé de Campagne* (1950), *Pickpocket* (1959), *Au hasard, Balthazar* (1966), *Une Femme douce* (1969), *L'Argent* (1983).

Brook, Peter (Stephen Paul) (1925–) British, born London; *Lord of the Flies* (1963), *King Lear* (1971), *Carmen* (1983).

Brooks, Mel (Melvin Kaminski) (1926–) American, born Brooklyn, New York City; *The Producers* (1966), *Blazing Saddles* (1974), *Young Frankenstein* (1974), *High Anxiety* (1978), *History of the World Part One* (1981), *Spaceballs* (1987), *Life Stinks* (1991), *Robin Hood: Men in Tights* (1993), *Dracula: Dead and Loving It* (1995).

Buñuel, Luis (1900–83) Spanish, born Calanda; *Un Chien Andalou* (with Salvador Dalí) (1928), *L'Age d'Or* (1930), *Los Olvidados* (1950), *Robinson Crusoe* (1952), *El* (1953), *Nazarin* (1958), *Viridiana* (1961), *The Exterminating Angel* (1962), *Belle de Jour* (1967), *The Discreet Charm of the Bourgeoisie* (1972), *The Phantom of Liberty* (1974), *That Obscure Object of Desire* (1977).

Burton, Tim (1958–) American, born Burbank, California; *Beetlejuice* (1988), *Batman* (1989), *Edward Scissorhands* (1990), *Batman Returns* (1992), *Ed Wood* (1994), *Mars Attacks!* (1996), *Sleepy Hollow* (1999), *Planet of the Apes* (2001).

Capra, Frank (1897–1991) Italian–American, born Bisacquino, Sicily; *Platinum Blonde* (1932), *American Madness* (1932), *Lady for a Day* (1933), *It Happened One Night* (1934), *Mr Deeds Goes to Town* (1936), *Lost Horizon* (1937), *You Can't Take It With You* (1938), *Mr Smith Goes to Washington* (1939), *Meet John Doe* (1941), *Arsenic and Old Lace* (1944), *It's a Wonderful Life* (1946).

Carné, Marcel (1909–96) French, born Batignolles, Paris; *Quai des Brumes* (1938), *Le Jour se lève* (1939), *Les Enfants du Paradis* (1944).

Carpenter, John (1948–) American, born Carthage, New York; *Dark Star* (1974), *Assault on Precinct 13* (1976), *Halloween* (1978), *The Fog* (1979), *Escape from New York* (1981), *The Thing* (1982), *Christine* (1983), *Starman* (1984), *Big Trouble in Little China* (1986), *Prince of Darkness* (1987), *Memoirs of an Invisible Man* (1992), *Escape From LA* (1996), *Vampires* (1998).

Chabrol, Claude (1930–) French, born Paris; *Beau*

Serge (1958), *Les Cousins* (1959), *Les Biches* (1968), *La Femme Infidèle* (1969), *Le Boucher* (1969), *Les Noces rouges* (1973), *Masques* (1987), *Une Affaire des Femmes* (1989), *The Swindle* (1997), *Merci pour le Chocolat* (2000).

Clair, René (René Lucien Chomette) (1891–1981) French, born Paris; *An Italian Straw Hat* (1927), *Sous Les Toits de Paris* (1929), *Le Million* (1931), *À Nous la liberté* (1931), *I Married a Witch* (1942), *It Happened Tomorrow* (1944), *And Then There Were None* (1945), *Les Belles de Nuit* (1952), *Porte des Lila* (1956), *Tout l'or du Monde* (1961).

Cocteau, Jean (1889–1963) French, born Maisons-Lafitte; *Le Sang d'un poète* (1930), *La Belle et La Bête* (1946), *Orphée* (1950), *Le Testament d'Orphée* (1959).

Coen, Ethan (1958–) and **Joel** (1955–) American, both born St Louis Park, Minnesota; *Blood Simple* (1984), *Raising Arizona* (1987), *Miller's Crossing* (1990), *Barton Fink* (1991), *The Hudsucker Proxy* (1994), *Fargo* (1995), *The Big Lebowski* (1998), *O Brother, Where Art Thou?* (2000), *The Man Who Wasn't There* (2001).

Coppola, Francis Ford (1939–) American, born Detroit, Michigan; *The Godfather* (1972), *The Godfather, Part II* (1974), *Apocalypse Now* (1979), *One from the Heart* (1982), *The Outsiders* (1983), *Rumble Fish* (1983), *The Cotton Club* (1984), *Peggy Sue Got Married* (1987), *Gardens of Stone* (1987), *Tucker: The Man and His Dream* (1988), *The Godfather, Part III* (1991), *Dracula* (1992), *The Rainmaker* (1997).

Corman, Roger (1926–) American, born Detroit, Michigan; *Not of This Earth* (1957), *Bucket of Blood* (1960), *Fall of the House of Usher* (1960), *The Little Shop of Horrors* (1960), *The Intruder* (1961), *The Raven* (1963), *The Man with the X-ray Eyes* (1963), *The Masque of the Red Death* (1964), *The Tomb of Ligeia* (1965), *Frankenstein Unbound* (1990), *The Pit and the Pendulum* (1990).

Cronenberg, David (1943–) Canadian, born Toronto, Ontario; *Shivers* (1976), *Rabid* (1977), *The Brood* (1978), *Scanners* (1980), *Videodrome* (1983), *The Dead Zone* (1983), *The Fly* (1985), *Dead Ringers* (1988), *Naked Lunch* (1991), *M Butterfly* (1992), *Crash* (1996), *eXistenZ* (1999), *Spider* (2002).

Curtiz, Michael (Mihály Kertész) (1888–1962) American-Hungarian, born Budapest, Hungary; *Noah's Ark* (1929), *Mammy* (1930), *Doctor X* (1932), *The Mystery of the Wax Museum* (1933), *British Agent* (1934), *Black Fury* (1935), *Captain Blood* (1935), *Charge of the Light Brigade* (1936), *The Adventures of Robin Hood* (1938), *Angels with Dirty Faces* (1938), *The Sea Hawk* (1940), *The Sea Wolf* (1941), *Yankee Doodle Dandy* (1942), *Casablanca* (1943), *Mildred Pierce* (1945), *White Christmas* (1954), *We're No Angels* (1955), *King Creole* (1958).

Dante, Joe (1946–) American, born Moristown, New Jersey; *Piranha* (1978), *The Howling* (1980), *Gremlins* (1984), *Explorers* (1985), *Innerspace* (1987), *The 'Burbs* (1989), *Amazon Women on the Moon* (1987), *Gremlins 2: The New Batch* (1990), *Small Soldiers* (1998).

de Mille, Cecil B(lount) (1881–1959) American, born Ashfield, Massachusetts; *Male and Female* (1919), *King of Kings* (1927), *The Ten Commandments* (1923 & 1956), *The Greatest Show on Earth* (1952).

Demme, Jonathan (1944–) American, born Long Island, New York; *Citizens Band* (1977), *Swing Shift* (1984), *Swimming to Cambodia* (1987), *Married to the Mob* (1988), *The Silence of the Lambs* (1991), *Philadelphia* (1993), *Beloved* (1998).

de Palma, Brian (1940–) American, born Newark, New Jersey; *Greetings* (1968), *Carrie* (1976), *The Fury* (1978), *Dressed to Kill* (1980), *Blow Out* (1981),

Scarface (1983), *Body Double* (1984), *The Untouchables* (1987), *Casualties of War* (1989), *Bonfire of the Vanities* (1990), *Carlito's Way* (1993), *Mission: Impossible* (1996), *Mission to Mars* (2000).

Donner, Richard (1930–) American, born New York City; *The Omen* (1976), *Superman* (1978), *Inside Moves* (1980), *The Final Conflict* (1981), *Ladyhawke* (1984), *The Goonies* (1985), *Lethal Weapon* (1987), *Scrooged* (1988), *Lethal Weapon 2* (1989), *Lethal Weapon 3* (1992), *Maverick* (1994), *Conspiracy Theory* (1997), *Lethal Weapon 4* (1998).

Eastwood, Clint (1930–) American, born San Francisco, California; *Play Misty for Me* (1971), *The Outlaw Josey Wales* (1976), *Pale Rider* (1985), *Birdy* (1988), *Unforgiven* (1992), *The Bridges of Madison County* (1995), *Absolute Power* (1997), *True Crime* (1999), *Space Cowboys* (2000).

Eisenstein, Sergei Mikhailovich (1898–1948) Russian, born Riga; *Stride* (1924), *Battleship Potemkin* (1925), *Alexander Nevsky* (1938), *Ten Days that Shook the World* (1928), *The Magic Seed* (1941), *Ivan the Terrible* (1942–6).

Fassbinder, Rainer Werner (1946–82) German, born Bad Worishofen; *Warnung von einer heiligen Nutte* (1971), *Satan's Brew* (1976).

Fellini, Federico (1920–93) Italian, born Rimini; *I Vitelloni* (1953), *La Strada* (1954), *La Dolce Vita* (1960), *8½* (1963), *Satyricon* (1969), *Fellini's Rome* (1972), *Casanova* (1976), *Orchestra Rehearsal* (1979), *City of Women* (1981), *The Ship Sails On* (1983), *Ginger and Fred* (1986).

Fleming, Victor (1883–1949) American, born Pasadena, California; *Mantrap* (1926), *The Virginian* (1929), *The Wet Parade* (1932), *Red Dust* (1932), *Treasure Island* (1934), *Test Pilot* (1938), *Gone with the Wind* (1939), *The Wizard of Oz* (1939), *Dr Jekyll and Mr Hyde* (1941), *A Guy Named Joe* (1943).

Forbes, Bryan (John Theobald Clarke) (1926–) British, born London; *The Angry Silence* (1960), *The Slipper and the Rose* (1976), *International Velvet* (1978).

Ford, John (1895–73) American, born Cape Elizabeth, Maine; *The Tornado* (1917), *The Iron Horse* (1924), *Arrowsmith* (1931), *The Informer* (1935), *Stagecoach* (1939), *Young Mr Lincoln* (1939), *The Grapes of Wrath* (1940), *My Darling Clementine* (1946), *The Quiet Man* (1952), *The Searchers* (1956), *The Man Who Shot Liberty Valance* (1962).

Forman, Miloš (1932–) Czech, born Kaslov; *Taking Off* (1971), *One Flew Over the Cuckoo's Nest* (1975), *Amadeus* (1984), *The People vs Larry Flynt* (1996), *Man on the Moon* (1999).

Frears, Stephen (1941–) British, born Leicester; *The Hit* (1984), *My Beautiful Laundrette* (1985), *Prick Up Your Ears* (1987), *Sammy and Rosie Get Laid* (1987), *Dangerous Liaisons* (1988), *The Grifters* (1990), *The Snapper* (1993), *Mary Reilly* (1995), *High Fidelity* (2000), *Dirty Pretty Things* (2002).

Friedkin, William (1939–) American, born Chicago; *The French Connection* (1971), *The Exorcist* (1973), *The Guardian* (1990), *Rules of Engagement* (2000).

Gilliam, Terry (1940–) American, born Minneapolis, Minnesota; *Jabberwocky* (1977), *Time Bandits* (1980), *Brazil* (1985), *The Adventures of Baron Munchausen* (1988), *The Fisher King* (1991), *Twelve Monkeys* (1995), *Fear and Loathing in Las Vegas* (1998).

Godard, Jean-Luc (1930–) French, born Paris; *À Bout de Souffle* (1960), *Alphaville* (1965), *Le Plus Vieux Métier du Monde* (1967), *Sauve Qui Peut La Vie* (1980), *Hail Mary* (1985), *Nouvelle Vague* (1990), *The Old Place* (1998).

Greenaway, Peter (1942–) British, born London; *The Draughtman's Contract* (1982), *The Belly of an Architect* (1987), *Drowning by Numbers* (1988), *The Cook, The Thief, His Wife and Her Lover* (1989), *Prospero's Books* (1991), *The Baby of Macon* (1993), *The Pillow Book* (1995), *8½ Women* (1999).

Griffith, D(avid) W(ark) (1875–1948) American, born La Grange, Kentucky; *Judith of Bethulia* (1913), *The Birth of a Nation* (1915), *Intolerance* (1916), *Hearts of the World* (1918), *Broken Blossoms* (1919), *Orphans of the Storm* (1922).

Hall, Sir Peter (Reginald Frederick) (1930–) British, born Bury St Edmunds, Suffolk; *Work is a Four Letter Word* (1968), *Perfect Friday* (1971), *Akenfield* (1974), *Never Talk to Strangers* (1995).

Hawks, Howard Winchester (1896–1977) American, born Goshen, Indiana; *The Dawn Patrol* (1930), *Scarface* (1932), *Twentieth Century* (1934), *Barbary Coast* (1935), *Bringing Up Baby* (1938), *His Girl Friday* (1940), *To Have and Have Not* (1944), *The Big Sleep* (1946), *Red River* (1948), *Gentlemen Prefer Blondes* (1953), *Rio Bravo* (1959).

Hill, George Roy (1921–2002) American, born Minneapolis, Minnesota; *The World of Henry Orient* (1964), *Thoroughly Modern Millie* (1967), *Butch Cassidy and the Sundance Kid* (1969), *Slaughterhouse 5* (1972), *The Sting* (1973), *The World According to Garp* (1982), *Funny Farm* (1988).

Hitchcock, Sir Alfred Joseph (1899–1980) British, born Leytonstone, London; *The Lodger* (1926), *Blackmail* (1929), *Murder* (1930), *The Thirty-Nine Steps* (1935), *The Lady Vanishes* (1938), *Rebecca* (1940), *Spellbound* (1945), *Notorious* (1946), *The Paradine Case* (1947), *Strangers on a Train* (1951), *Rear Window* (1954), *Dial M for Murder* (1955), *Vertigo* (1958), *North by Northwest* (1959), *Psycho* (1960), *The Birds* (1963), *Marnie* (1964), *Frenzy* (1972), *Alfred Hitchcock Presents* (TV 1955–61).

Huston, John Marcellus (1906–87) Irish–American, born Nevada, Missouri; *Murders in the Rue Morgue* (1932), *Juarez* (1939), *High Sierra* (1941), *The Maltese Falcon* (1941), *Key Largo* (1948), *The Treasure of the Sierra Madre* (1948), *The Asphalt Jungle* (1950), *The African Queen* (1951), *Moulin Rouge* (1952), *The Misfits* (1960), *Freud* (1962), *Night of the Iguana* (1964), *Casino Royale* (1967), *Fat City* (1972), *The Man Who Would Be King* (1975), *Annie* (1982), *Prizzi's Honor* (1985), *The Dead* (1987).

Ivory, James Francis (1928–) American, born Berkeley, California; *Shakespeare Wallah* (1965), *Heat and Dust* (1982), *The Bostonians* (1984), *A Room with a View* (1985), *Maurice* (1987), *Mr and Mrs Bridge* (1990), *Howards End* (1992), *The Remains of the Day* (1993), *Jefferson in Paris* (1995), *Surviving Picasso* (1996), *The Golden Bowl* (2000).

Jarman, (Michael) Derek (1942–94) British, born Northwood, Middlesex; *Sebastiane* (1976), *Jubilee* (1977), *The Tempest* (1979), *Caravaggio* (1985), *The Last of England* (1987), *The Garden* (1990), *Edward II* (1991), *Wittgenstein* (1993).

Jarmusch, Jim (1953–) American, born Akron, Ohio; *Stranger than Paradise* (1984), *Down by Law* (1986), *Mystery Train* (1989), *Night on Earth* (1991), *Dead Man* (1995), *Ghost Dog: Way of the Samurai* (1999).

Jordan, Neil (1950–) Irish, born Sligo; *Angel* (1982), *The Company of Wolves* (1984), *Mona Lisa* (1986), *High Spirits* (1988), *The Crying Game* (1992), *Interview with the Vampire* (1994), *Michael Collins* (1996), *The Butcher Boy* (1997), *The End of the Affair* (1999), *The Good Thief* (2002).

Kasdan, Lawrence (1949–) American, born Miami Beach, Florida; *Body Heat* (1981), *The Big Chill* (1983), *Silverado* (1985), *The Accidental Tourist* (1989), *Love You to Death* (1990), *Wyatt Earp* (1994), *French Kiss* (1995), *Mumford* (1999).

Kaufman, Philip (1936–) American, born Chicago; *Invasion of the Body Snatchers* (1978), *The Wanderers* (1979), *The Right Stuff* (1983), *The Unbearable Lightness of Being* (1988), *Henry and June* (1990), *Quills* (2000).

Kazan, Elia (Elia Kazanjoglou) (1909–) American, born Istanbul, Turkey; *Boomerang* (1947), *Gentleman's Agreement* (1947), *Pink* (1949), *A Streetcar Named Desire* (1951), *Viva Zapata* (1952), *On the Waterfront* (1954), *East of Eden* (1955), *Baby Doll* (1956), *A Face in the Crowd* (1957), *Splendor in the Grass* (1962), *America, America* (1963), *The Arrangement* (1969), *The Visitors* (1972), *The Last Tycoon* (1976).

Kieslowski, Krzystof (1941–96) Polish, born Warsaw; *Camera Buff* (1979), *A Short Film About Killing* (1988), *The Double Life of Veronique* (1991), *Three Colours: Blue* (1993), *White* (1993), *Red* (1994).

Kubrick, Stanley (1928–99) American, born The Bronx, New York City; *The Killing* (1956), *Paths of Glory* (1957), *Spartacus* (1960), *Lolita* (1962), *Dr Strangelove* (1964), *2001: A Space Odyssey* (1968), *A Clockwork Orange* (1971), *Barry Lyndon* (1975), *The Shining* (1980), *Full Metal Jacket* (1987), *Eyes Wide Shut* (1999).

Kurosawa, Akira (1910–98) Japanese, born Tokyo; *Rashomon* (1950), *The Idiot* (1951), *Living* (1952), *The Seven Samurai* (1954), *Throne of Blood* (1957), *The Lower Depths* (1957), *The Hidden Fortress* (1958), *Dersu Uzala* (1975), *The Shadow Warrior* (1981), *Ran* (1985), *Dreams* (1990), *Rhapsody in August* (1991).

Landis, John (1950–) American, born Chicago; *Schlock* (1971), *Kentucky Fried Movie* (1977), *Animal House* (1978), *The Blues Brothers* (1980), *An American Werewolf in London* (1981), *Twilight Zone* (1983), *Trading Places* (1983), *Into the Night* (1985), *Spies Like Us* (1985), *The Three Amigos* (1986), *Coming to America* (1988), *Oscar* (1991), *Innocent Blood* (1992), *Beverly Hills Cop III* (1994), *Blues Brothers 2000* (1998).

Lang, Fritz (1890–1976) German, born Vienna, Austria; *Destiny* (1921), *Dr Mabuse the Gambler* (1922), *Siegfried* (1923), *Metropolis* (1926), *Spies* (1927), *M* (1931), *The Testament of Dr Mabuse* (1932), *You Only Live Once* (1937), *The Return of Frank James* (1940), *The Woman in the Window* (1944), *The Big Heat* (1953), *Beyond a Reasonable Doubt* (1956), *While the City Sleeps* (1955).

Lean, Sir David (1908–91) British, born Croydon; *Pygmalion* (1938), *In Which We Serve* (1942), *Blithe Spirit* (1945), *Brief Encounter* (1946), *Great Expectations* (1946), *The Sound Barrier* (1952), *Hobson's Choice* (1954), *Summer Madness* (1955), *Bridge on the River Kwai* (1957), *Lawrence of Arabia* (1962), *Doctor Zhivago* (1965), *Ryan's Daughter* (1970), *A Passage to India* (1984).

Lee, Spike (Shelton Jackson Lee) (1957–) American, born Atlanta, Georgia; *She's Gotta Have It* (1986), *School Daze* (1988), *Do the Right Thing* (1989), *Mo' Better Blues* (1990), *Jungle Fever* (1991), *Malcolm X* (1992), *Crooklyn* (1994), *Clockers* (1995), *Girl 6* (1996), *He Got Game* (1998), *Summer of Sam* (1999), *The 25th Hour* (2002).

Leigh, Mike (1943–) British, born Salford; *Bleak Moments* (1971), *Nuts in May* (1976), *Abigail's Party* (1977), *High Hopes* (1988), *Life is Sweet* (1990), *Naked* (1993), *Secrets and Lies* (1996), *Career Girls* (1997), *Topsy-Turvy* (1999), *All or Nothing* (2002).

Leone, Sergio (1922–89) Italian, born Rome; *A Fistful of Dollars* (1964), *For a Few Dollars More* (1965), *The Good the Bad and the Ugly* (1967), *Once upon a Time* *in the West* (1969), *A Fistful of Dynamite* (1972), *Once upon a Time in America* (1984).

Levinson, Barry (1942–) American, born Baltimore, Maryland; *Diner* (1982), *The Natural* (1984), *The Young Sherlock Holmes* (1985), *Tin Men* (1987), *Good Morning Vietnam* (1987), *Rain Man* (1988), *Avalon* (1990), *Bugsy* (1991), *Toys* (1992), *Disclosure* (1994), *Sleepers* (1996), *Wag the Dog* (1997), *Sphere* (1998), *Bandits* (2001).

Lucas, George (1944–) American, born Modesto, California; *THX-1138: 4EB/Electronic Labyrinth* (1965), *American Graffiti* (1973), *Star Wars* (1977), *Star Wars: The Phantom Menace* (1999), *Star Wars: Attack of the Clones* (2002).

Lumet, Sidney (1924–) American, born Philadelphia, Pennsylvania; *The Pawnbroker* (1965), *Serpico* (1974), *Dog Day Afternoon* (1975), *Network* (1976), *The Verdict* (1982), *Night Falls on Manhattan* (1994), *Gloria* (1999).

Lynch, David K (1946–) American, born Missoula, Montana; *Eraserhead* (1976), *The Elephant Man* (1980), *Dune* (1984), *Blue Velvet* (1986), *Wild at Heart* (1990), *Twin Peaks* (TV 1990–1), *Twin Peaks: Fire Walk With Me* (1992), *Lost Highway* (1997), *Mulholland Drive* (2001).

McBride, Jim (1941–) American, born New York City; *Breathless* (1983), *The Big Easy* (1986), *Great Balls of Fire* (1989), *The Wrong Man* (1992), *The Informant* (1997), *Six Feet Under* (TV 2001).

Mankiewicz, Joseph Leo (1909–93) American, born Wilkes-Barre, Pennsylvania; *All About Eve* (1950), *The Barefoot Contessa* (1954), *Guys and Dolls* (1954), *Suddenly Last Summer* (1959), *Sleuth* (1972).

Miller, George (1945–) Australian, born Brisbane; *Mad Max* (1979), *Mad Max 2: The Road Warrior* (1982), *Mad Max Beyond Thunderdome* (1985), *The Witches of Eastwick* (1987), *Lorenzo's Oil* (1992), *Babe: Pig in the City* (1998).

Miller, Jonathan Wolfe (1934–) British, born London; *The Magic Flute* (1986), *The Tempest* (1988).

Minnelli, Vincente (1913–86) American, born Chicago; *Ziegfeld Follies* (1946), *An American in Paris* (1951), *Lust for Life* (1956), *Gigi* (1958).

Nichols, Mike (Michael Igor Peschkowsky) (1931–) American–German, born Berlin, Germany; *Who's Afraid of Virginia Woolf?* (1966), *The Graduate* (1967), *Catch-22* (1970), *Working Girl* (1988), *Postcards from the Edge* (1990), *Wolf* (1994), *The Birdcage* (1996), *Primary Colors* (1998).

Olivier, Laurence Kerr Olivier, Baron (1907–89) British, born Dorking, Surrey; *Henry V* (1944), *Hamlet* (1948), *Richard III* (1956), *The Prince and the Showgirl* (1958), *The Entertainer* (1960).

Parker, Alan (1944–) British, born London; *Bugsy Malone* (1976), *Midnight Express* (1978), *Fame* (1980), *Shoot the Moon* (1981), *Pink Floyd: The Wall* (1982), *Angel Heart* (1987), *Mississippi Burning* (1988), *Come See the Paradise* (1990), *The Commitments* (1991), *Evita* (1996), *Angela's Ashes* (1999).

Pasolini, Pier Paolo (1922–75) Italian, born Bologna; *Accatone!* (1961), *The Gospel According to St Matthew* (1964), *Oedipus Rex* (1967), *Medea* (1970).

Peckinpah, Sam (1925–84) American, born Fresno, California; *The Deadly Companions* (1961), *Major Dundee* (1965), *The Wild Bunch* (1969), *Straw Dogs* (1971), *Bring Me the Head of Alfredo Garcia* (1974), *Cross of Iron* (1977).

Polanski, Roman (1933–) Polish, born Paris; *Knife in the Water* (1962), *Repulsion* (1965), *Cul-de-Sac* (1966), *Rosemary's Baby* (1968), *Macbeth* (1971), *Chinatown* (1974), *Tess* (1979), *Pirates* (1985), *Fran-*

tic (1988), *Bitter Moon* (1992), *Death and the Maiden* (1994), *The Ninth Gate* (1999), *The Pianist* (2002).

Pollack, Sydney (1934–) American, born South Bend, Indiana; *They Shoot Horses Don't They?* (1969), *The Electric Horseman* (1979), *Absence of Malice* (1981), *Tootsie* (1982), *Out of Africa* (1985), *Havana* (1990), *The Firm* (1993), *Random Hearts* (1999).

Powell, Michael Latham (1905–90) British, born Bekesbourne, near Canterbury; with **Emeric Pressburger** (1902–88) Hungarian–British, born Miskolc, Hungary; *The Spy in Black* (1939), *The Thief of Baghdad* (1940), *The Life and Death of Colonel Blimp* (1943), *Black Narcissus* (1946), *A Matter of Life and Death* (1946), *The Red Shoes* (1948).

Ray, Satyajit (1921–92) Indian, born Calcutta (now Kolkata); *Pather Panchali* (1954), *The Music Room* (1958), *The World of Apu* (1959), *The Kingdom of Diamonds* (1980), *Pickoo* (1982), *The Home and The World* (1984).

Redford, (Charles) Robert (1937–) American, born Santa Monica, California; *Ordinary People* (1980), *The Milagro Beanfield War* (1987), *A River Runs Through It* (1992), *Quiz Show* (1994), *The Horse Whisperer* (1998), *The Legend of Bagger Vance* (2000).

Reed, Sir Carol (1906–76) British, born London; *The Young Mr Pitt* (1942), *The Way Ahead* (1944), *The Fallen Idol* (1948), *The Third Man* (1949), *An Outcast of the Islands* (1952), *The Man Between* (1953), *Our Man in Havana* (1959), *Oliver!* (1968).

Reiner, Carl (1922–) American, born The Bronx, New York City; *Oh God* (1977), *The Jerk* (1979), *Dead Men Don't Wear Plaid* (1982), *The Man with Two Brains* (1983), *Summer School* (1987), *That Old Feeling* (1997).

Reiner, Rob (1945–) American, born The Bronx, New York City; *This is Spinal Tap* (1984), *Stand by Me* (1987), *The Princess Bride* (1988), *When Harry Met Sally ...* (1989), *Misery* (1990), *A Few Good Men* (1992), *North* (1994), *The American President* (1995), *The Story of Us* (1999).

Renoir, Jean (1894–1979) French, born Paris; *Une Partie de Campagne* (1936), *La Règle du Jeu* (1939), *The Southerner* (1945).

Robbins, Tim (Timothy Francis) (1958–) American, born West Covina, California; *No Small Affair* (1984), *Bob Roberts* (1992), *Dead Man Walking* (1995), *The Cradle Will Rock* (1999).

Roeg, Nicolas Jack (1928–) British, born London; *Performance* (1970), *Walkabout* (1971), *Don't Look Now* (1973), *The Man Who Fell to Earth* (1976), *Bad Timing* (1979), *Eureka* (1983), *Insignificance* (1985), *Castaway* (1986), *Black Widow* (1988), *Track 29* (1988), *The Witches* (1990), *Heart of Darkness* (1995), *Two Deaths* (1995).

Rossellini, Roberto (1906–77) Italian, born Rome; *The White Ship* (1940), *Rome, Open City* (1945), *Paisan* (1946), *Germany, Year Zero* (1947), *Stromboli* (1950), *Voyage to Italy* (1953), *General Della Rovera* (1959).

Russell, Ken (Henry Kenneth Alfred Russell) (1927–) British, born Southampton; *Women in Love* (1969), *The Devils* (1971), *Crimes of Passion* (1984), *Gothic* (1987), *Lair of the White Worm* (1989), *The Rainbow* (1989), *Whore* (1991), *Tales of Erotica* (1996).

Schlesinger, John Richard (1926–) British, born London; *A Kind of Loving* (1962), *Billy Liar!* (1963), *Midnight Cowboy* (1969), *Sunday, Bloody Sunday* (1971), *Marathon Man* (1976), *Honky Tonk Freeway* (1981), *An Englishman Abroad* (TV 1982), *Madame Sousatzka* (1988), *Pacific Heights* (1990), *The Innocent* (1993), *The Next Best Thing* (2000).

Scorsese, Martin (1942–) American, born Queens, New York; *Mean Streets* (1973), *Alice Doesn't Live*

Arts and Culture

Here Any More (1974), *Taxi Driver* (1976), *Raging Bull* (1980), *King of Comedy* (1982), *After Hours* (1985), *The Color of Money* (1986), *The Last Temptation of Christ* (1988), *GoodFellas* (1990), *Cape Fear* (1991), *The Age of Innocence* (1992), *Casino* (1995), *Kundun* (1997), *Gangs of New York* (2002).

Scott, Ridley (1937–) British, born South Shields; *Alien* (1979), *Blade Runner* (1982), *Black Rain* (1989), *Thelma and Louise* (1991), *1492* (1992), *G I Jane* (1997), *Gladiator* (2000), *Hannibal* (2001), *Black Hawk Down* (2001).

Siegel, Don (1912–91) American, born Chicago; *Riot in Cell Block 11* (1954), *Invasion of the Body Snatchers* (1956), *Baby Face Nelson* (1957), *Coogan's Bluff* (1968), *Two Mules for Sister Sara* (1969), *Dirty Harry* (1971), *Charley Varrick* (1973), *The Shootist* (1976), *Telefon* (1977), *Escape from Alcatraz* (1979).

Spielberg, Steven (1946–) American, born Cincinnati, Ohio; *Duel* (TV 1972), *Sugarland Express* (1973), *Jaws* (1975), *Close Encounters of the Third Kind* (1977), *Raiders of the Lost Ark* (1981), *ET* (1982), *Twilight Zone* (1983), *The Color Purple* (1985), *Indiana Jones and the Temple of Doom* (1984), *Empire of the Sun* (1987), *Indiana Jones and the Last Crusade* (1989), *Hook* (1992), *Jurassic Park* (1993), *Schindler's List* (1993), *The Lost World: Jurassic Park* (1997), *Amistad* (1997), *Saving Private Ryan* (1998), *Artificial Intelligence: AI* (2001), *Minority Report* (2002).

Stevenson, Robert (1905–86) British, born Buxton, Derbyshire; *King Solomon's Mines* (1937), *Mary Poppins* (1964), *The Love Bug* (1968), *Bedknobs and Broomsticks* (1971).

Stone, Oliver (1946–) American, born New York City; *Platoon* (1987), *Wall Street* (1987), *Born on the Fourth of July* (1989), *The Doors* (1991), *JFK* (1991), *Heaven and Earth* (1993), *Natural Born Killers* (1994), *Nixon* (1995), *Any Given Sunday* (1999).

Tarantino, Quentin (1963–) American, born Knoxville, Tennessee; *Reservoir Dogs* (1993), *Pulp Fiction* (1994), *Jackie Brown* (1998).

Tati, Jacques (Jacques Tatischeff) (1908–82) French, born Le Pecq; *Jour de fête* (1947), *Monsieur Hulot's Holiday* (1952), *Mon Oncle* (1958), *Playtime* (1968), *Traffic* (1981).

Tavernier, Bertrand (1941–) French, born Lyons; *L'Horloger de Saint-Paul* (1973), *Dimanche à la Campagne* (1984), *La Mort en direct* (1979), *La Vie et rien d'autre* (1989), *Daddy Nostalgie* (1990), *L 627* (1992), *Capitaine Conan* (1996), *It All Starts Today* (1999), *Safe Conduct* (2002).

Truffaut, François (1932–84) French, born Paris; *Jules et Jim* (1961), *The Bride Wore Black* (1967), *Baisers volés* (1968), *L'Enfant Sauvage* (1969), *Day for Night* (1973), *The Last Metro* (1980).

Visconti, Luchino (Count Don Luchino Visconti Di Morone) (1906–76) Italian, born Milan; *The Leopard* (1963), *Ossessione* (1942), *The Damned* (1969), *Death in Venice* (1971).

Weir, Peter (1944–) Australian, born Sydney; *The Cars That Ate Paris* (1974), *Picnic at Hanging Rock* (1975), *Gallipoli* (1981), *The Year of Living Dangerously* (1982), *Witness* (1985), *Mosquito Coast* (1986), *Dead Poets Society* (1989), *Green Card* (1990), *Fearless* (1993), *The Truman Show* (1998).

Welles, (George) Orson (1915–85) American, born Kenosha, Wisconsin; *Citizen Kane* (1941), *The Magnificent Ambersons* (1942), *Jane Eyre* (1943), *Macbeth* (1948), *Othello* (1951), *Touch of Evil* (1958), *The Trial* (1962), *Chimes at Midnight* (1966).

Wenders, Wim (1945–) German, born Düsseldorf; *Summer in the City* (1970), *Alice in the Cities* (1974), *Kings of the Road* (1976), *Paris, Texas* (1984), *Wings of Desire* (1987), *Until the End of the World* (1991), *Faraway, So Close* (1993), *Beyond the Clouds* (co-director 1995), *The End of Violence* (1997), *Buena Vista Social Club* (1999), *The Million Dollar Hotel* (2000).

Wilder, Billy (1906–2002) Austrian–American, born Sucha, Austria; *Double Indemnity* (1944), *The Lost Weekend* (1945), *Sunset Boulevard* (1950), *The Seven Year Itch* (1955), *Some Like It Hot* (1959), *The Apartment* (1960), *Avanti!* (1972).

Wise, Robert (1914–) American, born Winchester, Indiana; *The Body Snatcher* (1945), *The Day the Earth Stood Still* (1951), *West Side Story* (1961), *The Sound of Music* (1965), *Star Trek: The Motion Picture* (1979).

Wyler, William (1902–1981) German–American, born Mulhouse, Alsace; *The Little Foxes* (1941), *Mrs Miniver* (1942), *The Best Years of Our Lives* (1946), *Friendly Persuasion* (1956), *Ben-Hur* (1959), *Funny Girl* (1968).

Zeffirelli, Franco (Gianfranco Corsi) (1922–) Italian, born Florence; *The Taming of the Shrew* (1966), *Romeo and Juliet* (1968), *Brother Sun, Sister Moon* (1973), *Jesus of Nazareth* (TV 1977), *The Champ* (1979), *Endless Love* (1981), *La Traviata* (1982), *Otello* (1986), *Hamlet* (1990), *Jane Eyre* (TV 1995), *Tea with Mussolini* (1999).

Zemeckis, Robert (1951–) American, born Chicago; *I Wanna Hold Your Hand* (1978), *Romancing The Stone* (1984), *Back to the Future* (1985), *Who Framed Roger Rabbit?* (1988), *Back to the Future II* (1989), *Back to the Future III* (1990), *Death Becomes Her* (1992), *Forrest Gump* (1994), *Contact* (1997), *What Lies Beneath* (2000), *Cast Away* (2000).

Zinnemann, Fred (1907–97) Austrian–American, born Vienna, Austria; *High Noon* (1952), *From Here to Eternity* (1953), *A Man for All Seasons* (1966), *Five Days One Summer* (1982).

Composers

Selected works are listed.

Adams, John Coolidge (1947–) American, born Worcester, Massachusetts; works include opera (eg *Nixon in China*) and compositions for chorus and orchestra (eg *Harmonium*).

Albéniz, Isaac (1860–1909) Spanish, born Camprodón, Catalonia; works include operas and works for piano based on Spanish folk music (eg *Iberia*).

Arnold, Sir Malcolm Henry (1921–) English, born Northampton; works include concertos, ballets, operas, vocal, choral, chamber and orchestral music (eg *Tam O'Shanter*) and film scores (eg *Bridge over the River Kwai*).

Bach, Johann Sebastian (1685–1750) German, born Eisenach; prolific composer, works include over 190 cantatas and oratorios, concertos, chamber music, keyboard music, and orchestral works (eg *Toccata and Fugue in D minor*, *The Well-tempered Clavier*, *Six Brandenburg Concertos*, *St Matthew Passion*, *Mass in B minor*, *Goldberg Variations*, *The Musical Offering*, *The Art of Fugue*).

Bartók, Béla (1881–1945) Hungarian, born Nagyszentmiklós; works include six string quartets, *Sonata for 2 pianos and percussion*, concertos (for piano, violin, viola and notably the *Concerto for Orches-*

tra), opera (*Duke Bluebeard's Castle*), two ballets (*The Wooden Prince, The Miraculous Mandarin*), songs, choruses, folksong arrangements.

Beethoven, Ludwig van (1770–1827) German, born Bonn; works include 33 piano sonatas (eg the 'Pathétique', 'Moonlight', *Waldstein, Appassionata*), nine symphonies (eg *Eroica*, 'Pastoral', *Choral Symphony No.9*), string quartets, concertos, *Lebewohl* and the opera *Fidelio*.

Berg, Alban (1885–1935) Austrian, born Vienna; works include songs (*Four Songs*), operas (*Wozzeck, Lulu*, unfinished), a violin concerto and a string quartet (*Lyric Suite*).

Berio, Luciano (1925–) Italian, born Oneglia; works include compositions using tapes and electronic music (eg *Mutazioni, Omaggio a James Joyce*), works for solo instruments (*Sequenzas*), stage works (eg *Laborintus II, Opera*) and symphonies (*Synfonia*).

Berlioz, (Louis) Hector (1803–69) French, born Côte St André, near Grenoble; works include the overture *Le carnival romain*, the cantata (*La Damnation de Faust*), symphonies (eg *Symphonie Fantastique, Romeo et Juliette*) and operas (eg *Béatrice et Bénédict, Les Troyens*).

Bernstein, Leonard (1918–90) American, born Laurence, Massachusetts; works include ballets (*Jeremiah, The Age of Anxiety, Kaddish*), symphonies (eg *Fancy Free, The Dybbuk*), and musicals (eg *Candide, West Side Story, On The Town, Songfest, Halil*).

Birtwistle, Sir Harrison (1934–) English, born Accrington, Lancashire; works include operas (eg *The Mask of Orpheus*), 'dramatic pastorals' (eg *Down by the Greenwood Side*) and orchestral pieces (eg *The Triumph of Time*).

Bizet, Georges (1838–75) French, born Paris; works include opera (eg *Carmen, Les Pêcheurs de Perles, La Jolie Fille de Perth*), incidental music to Daudet's play *L'Arlésienne* and a symphony.

Boulez, Pierre (1925–) French, born Montbrison; works include three piano sonatas, and works for piano and flute (eg *Sonatine*).

Brahms, Johannes (1833–97) German, born Hamburg; works include songs, four symphonies, two piano concertos, choral work (eg *German Requiem*), orchestral work (eg *Variations on a Theme of Haydn*), programme work (eg *Tragic Overture*), also the *Academic Festival Overture* and *Hungarian Dances*.

Bruckner, Anton (1824–96) Austrian, born Ansfelden; works include nine symphonies, a string quartet, choral-orchestral Masses and other church music (eg *Te Deum*).

Cage, John (1912–92) American, born Los Angeles; works include unorthodox modern compositions, eg *Sonatas and Interludes for the Prepared Piano*.

Carter, Elliott Cook, Jr (1908–) American, born New York City; works include quartets, symphonies, concertos, songs and chamber music.

Chabrier, Emmanuel (1841–94) French, born Ambert; works include operas (*Gwendoline, Le Roi malgré lui, Briséis*) and an orchestral rhapsody (*España*).

Chausson, Ernest (1855–99) French, born Paris; works include songs and orchestral works (eg *Poème*).

Chopin, Frédéric François (1810–49) Polish, born Zelazowa Wola, near Warsaw; wrote almost exclusively for piano – nocturnes, polonaises, mazurkas, preludes, concertos, and a funeral march.

Copland, Aaron (1900–90) American, born Brooklyn, New York City; ballets (eg *Billy The Kid, Appalachia*

Spring), film scores (eg *Our Town, The Heiress*), symphonies (eg *Symphonie Ode, Connotations, Clarinet Concerto*).

Corelli, Arcangelo (1653–1713) Italian, born Fusignano, near Bologna; works include 12 concertos (eg *Concerto for Christmas Night*), and solo and trio sonatas for violin.

Couperin, François (1668–1733) French, born Paris; works include chamber music, four books containing 240 harpsichord pieces, motets and other church music.

Debussy, Claude Achille (1862–1918) French, born St Germaine-en-Laye, near Paris; songs (eg the cantata *L'Enfant prodigue*), opera (*Pelléas et Mélisande*), orchestral works (eg *Prélude a l'après-midi d'un faune, La Mer*), chamber and piano music (eg *Feux d'artifice, La Cathédrale engloutie*).

Delius, Frederick (1862–1934) English (of German Scandinavian descent), born Bradford; works include songs (eg *A Song of Summer, Idyll, Songs of Farewell*), concertos, operas (eg *Koanga, A Village Romeo and Juliette*), chamber music and orchestral variations (eg *Appalachia, Sea Drift, A Mass of Life*).

Dukas, Paul (1865–1935) French, born Paris; works include a symphonic poem (*L'Apprenti sorcier*) and opera (*Ariane et Barbe-Bleue*).

Dutilleux, Henri (1916–) French, born Angers; works include a piano sonata, two symphonies, a violin concerto, a string quartet (*Ainsi la nuit*), compositions for two pianos and other orchestral works.

Dvořák, Antonin Leopold (1841–1904) Czech, born near Prague; works include songs, concertos, choral (eg *Hymnus*) and chamber music, symphonies (notably 'From the New World'), operas (eg *Rusalka, Armida, Slavonic Dances*).

Elgar, Sir Edward (William) (1857–1934) English, born Broadheath, near Worcester; works include chamber music, two symphonies, oratorios (eg *The Dream of Gerontius, The Apostles, The Kingdom*), and the orchestral work *Enigma Variations*.

Falla, Manuel de (1876–1946) Spanish, born Cádiz; works include opera (eg *La Vida Breve, Master Peter's Puppet Show*), ballet (eg *The Three-Cornered Hat, Love the Magician*) and orchestral suites (eg *Nights in the Gardens of Spain*).

Fauré, Gabriel Urbain (1845–1924) French, born Pamiers; works include songs (eg *Après un rêve*), chamber music, choral music (eg the *Requiem*), operas and orchestral music (eg *Masques et bergamasques*).

Franck, César Auguste (1822–90) naturalized French, born Liège, Belgium; works include tone-poems, (eg *Les Béatitudes*), sonatas for violin and piano, *Symphony in D minor* and *Variations symphoniques* for piano and orchestra.

Gershwin, George (1898–1937) American, born Brooklyn, New York City; Broadway musicals (eg *Lady Be Good, Of Thee I Sing*), symphonies, songs (notably 'I Got Rhythm', 'The Man I Love'), operas (eg *Porgy and Bess*), and concert works (eg *Rhapsody in Blue, Concerto in F, An American in Paris*).

Glass, Philip (1937–) American, born Baltimore, Maryland; works include stage pieces (eg *Einstein on the Beach*), film scores (eg *Hamburger Hill*) and the opera *Orphee*.

Gluck, Christoph (Willibald) (1714–87) Austro-German, born Erasbach, Bavaria; operas include *Orfeo ed Euridice, Iphigénie en Auilide, Alceste, Paride ed Elena, Iphigénie en Tauride*.

Gounod, Charles (François) (1818–93) French, born

Arts and Culture

Paris; works include operas (eg *Le Médecin malgré lui*, *Faust*, *Philémon et Baucis*, *Roméo et Juliette*), masses, hymns, anthems and songs.

Grainger, Percy Aldridge (1882–1961) Australian, born Melbourne; works include songs, piano and chamber music (eg *Molly on the Shore*, *Mock Morris*, *Shepherd's Hey*).

Grieg, Edvard Hagerup (1843–1907) Norwegian, born Bergen; works include songs, a piano concerto, orchestral suites, violin sonatas, choral music, and incidental music for *Peer Gynt* and *Sigurd Jorsalfar*.

Handel, George Friederic (1685–1759) naturalized English, born Halle, Saxony; prolific output including over 27 operas (eg *Almira*, *Rinaldo*), 20 oratorios (eg *The Messiah*, *Saul*, *Israel in Egypt*, *Samson*, *Jephthah*), orchestral suites (eg the *Water Music* and *Music for the Royal Fireworks*), organ concertos and chamber music.

Haydn, (Franz) Joseph (1732–1809) Austrian, born Rohrau, Lower Austria; prolific output including 104 symphonies (eg the 'Salomon' or 'London' Symphonies), string quartets and oratorios (notably *The Creation*, *The Seasons*).

Holst, Gustav Theodore (originally **von Holst**) (1874–1934) English of Swedish origin, born Cheltenham; works include choral and ballet music, operas (eg *The Perfect Fool*, *At the Boar's Head*), orchestral suites (eg *The Planets*, *St Paul's Suite for Strings*), choral music (eg *The Hymn of Jesus*, *Ode to Death*), and *Concerto for Two Violins*.

Honegger, Arthur (1892–1955) French, born Le Havre; works include five symphonies and dramatic oratorios (*King David*, *Joan of Arc at the Stake*).

Ireland, John Nicholson (1879–1962) English, born Bowden, Cheshire; works include sonatas (eg *Violin Sonata in A*), piano music, songs (eg 'Sea Fever'), the rhapsody *Mai-dun* and orchestral works (eg *The Forgotten Rite*, *These Things Shall Be*).

Ives, Charles (1874–1954) American, born Danbury, Connecticut; works include five symphonies, chamber music (eg *Concord Sonata*) and many songs.

Janáček, Leoš (1854–1928) Czech, born Hukvaldy, Moravia; works include chamber, orchestral and choral music (eg the song cycle *The Diary of One Who Has Vanished*), operas (eg *Janufa*, *The Cunning Little Vixen*, *The Excursions of Mr Brouček*, *From the House of the Dead*), two string quartets and a mass.

Lalo, (Victor Antoine) Édouard (1823–92) French, born Lille. Works include compositions for violin (eg *Symphonie espagnole*), opera (eg *Le Roi d'Ys*) and ballet (*Namouna*).

Ligeti, Györgi Sándor (1923–) Hungarian, born Dicsöszentmárton; works include orchestral compositions (eg *Apparitions*, *Lontano*, *Double Concerto*), choral works (eg *Requiem*) and music for harpsichord, organ, and wind and string ensembles.

Liszt, Franz (1811–86) Hungarian, born Raiding; 400 original compositions including symphonic poems, piano music and masses (eg *The Legend of St Elizabeth*, *Christus*).

Lloyd-Webber, Andrew Lloyd Webber, Baron (1948–) English, born London; works include the 'rock opera' *Jesus Christ Superstar* and the musicals *Cats*, *Evita*, *Aspects of Love* and *Whistle Down the Wind*.

Mahler, Gustav (1860–1911) Austrian, born Kalist, Bohemia; works include 10 symphonies, songs, the cantata *Das klagende Lied*, and the song-symphony *Das Lied von der Erde* (The Song of the Earth).

Maxwell Davies, Sir Peter (1934–) English, born Manchester; works include operas (eg *Taverner*), songs (eg *Eight Songs for a Mad King*), symphonies, concertos and chamber ensembles.

Mendelssohn, (Jacob Ludwig) Felix (1809–47) German, born Hamburg; prolific output, including concerto overtures (eg *Fingal's Cave*, *A Midsummer Night's Dream*, *Hebrides*), symphonies (*Symphony in C minor*, *Scottish*, *Italian*), quartets (*B minor Quartet*), operas (eg *Camacho's Wedding*), and oratorios (eg *Elijah*).

Messiaen, Olivier Eugène Prosper Charles (1908–92) French, born Avignon; works include compositions for piano (*Vingt regards sur l'enfant Jésus*, *Catalogue d'oiseaux*), the symphony *Turangalila*, an oratorio (*La Transfiguration de Notre Seigneur Jésus-Christ*) and an opera (*St François d'Assisi*).

Milhaud, Darius (1892–1974) French, born Aix-en-Provence; works include several operas, incidental music for plays, ballets (eg the jazz ballet *La Création du monde*), symphonies and orchestral, choral and chamber works.

Monteverdi, Claudio (Giovanni Antonio) (1567–1643) Italian, born Cremona; works include masses (eg *Mass* and *Vespers* of the Virgin), cantatas and operas (eg *Orfeo*, *Il Ritorno d'Ulisse*, *L'Incoronazione di Poppea*).

Mozart, (Johann Chrysostom) Wolfgang Amadeus (1756–91) Austrian, born Salzburg; 600 compositions including symphonies (eg 'Jupiter', *Linz*, *Prague*), concertos, string quartets, sonatas, operas (eg *Marriage of Figaro*, *Don Giovanni*, *Così fan tutte*) and the Singspiels *The Abductions from the Seraglio*, *Die Zauberflöte*.

Mussorgsky, Modeste (1839–81) Russian, born Karevo; works include operas (eg *Boris Godunov*), song cycles and instrumental works (eg *Pictures from an Exhibition*, *Night on the Bare Mountain*).

Nielsen, Carl August (1865–1931) Danish, born Furen; works include operas (eg *Saul and David*, *Masquerade*), symphonies (eg 'The Four Temperaments'), string quartets, choral and piano music.

Offenbach, Jacques (1819–80) German, born Cologne; works include operettas (eg *Orphée aux enfers*, *La Belle Hélène*, *La Barbe bleu*, *La Grande Duchesse*, *La Vie Parisienne*) and the grand opera *Les Contes d'Hoffman*.

Orff, Carl (1895–1982) German, born Munich; works include the scenic cantata *Carmina Burana* and the operatic pieces *Antigone*, *Oedipus* and *Prometheus*.

Palestrina, Giovanni Pierluigi da (c.1525–1594) Italian, born Palestrina, near Rome; works include chamber music and the organ work *Commotion*, masses, choral music (eg *Song of Songs*), madrigals.

Parry, Sir (Charles) Hubert (Hastings) (1848–1918) English, born Bournemouth, Hampshire; works include three oratorios, an opera, five symphonies, and many other pieces. Best-known work is the unison chorus *Jerusalem*.

Pendericki, Krzysztof (1933–) Polish, born Debica; works include compositions for strings (eg *Trenofiarom Hiroszimy*), operas (eg *Die schwarze Maske*) and concertos (eg *Flute Concerto*).

Poulenc, Francis (1899–1963) French, born Paris; works include much chamber music and the ballet *Les Biches*. Best known for his considerable output of songs, such as *Fêtes Galantes*.

Prokofiev, Sergei (1891–1953) Russian, born Sontsovka, Ukraine; works include 11 operas (eg *The Gambler*, *The Love for Three Oranges*, *The Fiery An-*

gels, *Semyon Kotko, Betrothal in a Monastery, War and Peace, The Story of a Real Man*), ballets (eg *Romeo and Juliet, Cinderella*), concertos, sonatas, cantatas (eg *We are Seven, Hail to Stalin*), film scores (eg *Alexander Nevsky*), and the 'children's piece' *Peter and the Wolf*.

Puccini, Giacomo (Antonio Domenico Michele Secondo Maria) (1858–1924) Italian, born Lucca; 12 operas (eg *Manon Lescaut, La Bohème, Tosca, Madama Butterfly, Turandot*).

Purcell, Henry (1659–95) English, born London; works include songs (eg 'Nymphs and Shepherds', 'Arise, ye Subterranean Winds'), sonatas, string fantasies, church music and opera (eg *Dido and Aeneas*).

Rachmaninov, Sergei Vasilyevich (1873–1943) Russian, born Nizhny Novgorod; works include operas, three symphonies, four piano concertos (eg *Prelude in C Sharp Minor*), the tone-poem *The Isle of the Dead*, and *Rhapsody on a Theme of Paganini* for piano and orchestra.

Rameau, Jean Philippe (1683–1764) French, born Dijon; works include over 30 ballets and operas (eg *Hippolyte et Aricie, Castor et Pollux*) and harpsichord pieces.

Ravel, Maurice (1875–1937) French, born Ciboure; works include piano compositions (eg *Sonatina, Miroirs, Ma Mère L'Oye, Gaspard de la nuit*), string quartets, operas (eg *L'Heure espagnol, L'Enfant et les sortilèges*), ballets (eg *Daphnis and Chloé*), the 'choreographic poem' *La Valse* and the miniature ballet *Boléro*.

Rimsky-Korsakov, Nikolai Andreyevich (1844–1908) Russian, born Tikhvin, Novgorod; works include orchestral music (eg the symphonic suite *Sheherazade, Capriccio Espagnol, Easter Festival*) and 15 operas (eg *Sadko, The Snow Maiden, The Tsar Sultan, The Invisible City of Kitesh, The Golden Cockerel*).

Rossini, Gioacchino Antonio (1792–1868) Italian, born Pesaro; works include many operas (eg *Il Barbiere de Seviglia, Otella, Guillaume Tell*) and a number of vocal and piano pieces.

Roussel, Albert (1869–1937) French, born Tourcoing; works include four symphonies, numerous choral works (eg *Évocations*), ballets (eg *Bacchus and Ariane, Le Festin de l'araignée*) and an opera (*Padmâvati*).

Saint-Saëns, (Charles) Camille (1835–1921) French, born Paris; works include four symphonic poems (eg *Danse macabre*), piano (*Le Rouet d'Omphale, Phaëton, La Jeunesse d'Hercule*), violin and cello concertos, symphonies, the opera *Samson et Dalila*, church music (eg *Messe solennelle*), and *Carnival des animaux* for two pianos and orchestra.

Satie, Erik Alfred Leslie (1866–1925) French, born Honfleur; works include ballets (eg *Parade*), lyric dramas and whimsical pieces.

Scarlatti, (Guiseppe) Domenico (1685–1757) Italian, born Naples; works include over 600 harpsichord sonatas.

Schönberg, Arnold (1874–1951) naturalized American, born Vienna, Austria; works include chamber music (eg *Chamber Symphony*), concertos (eg *Piano Concerto*), and symphonic poems (eg *Pelleas and Melisande*), the choral-orchestral *Gurrelieder*, string quartets, the oratorio *Die Jacobsiter*, and opera (*Von Heute auf Morgen, Moses and Aaron*).

Schubert, Franz Peter (1797–1828) Austrian, born Vienna; prolific output, works include symphonies, piano sonatas, string quartets and songs (eg *Gretchen am Spinnrade, Erlkönig, Die schöne Müllerin, Winterreise, Who is Sylvia?, Hark, Hark the Lark, Schwanengesang*).

Schumann, Robert Alexander (1810–56) German, born Zwickau, Saxony; works include piano music (eg *Fantasiestücke*), songs (eg 'The Fool's Song' in *Twelfth Night*, the Chamisso songs *Frauenliebe und Leben* or 'Woman's Love and Life'), chamber music, and four symphonies (eg the *Rhenish*).

Scriabin, Alexander (1872–1915) born Moscow; works include a piano concerto, three symphonies, two tone-poems (eg *Poem of Ecstasy*), 10 sonatas, studies and preludes.

Shostakovich, Dmitri (1906–75) Russian, born St Petersburg; works include 15 symphonies, operas (eg *The Nose, A Lady Macbeth of Mtensk*), concertos, string quartets and film music.

Sibelius, Jean (1865–1957) Finnish, born Tavastehus; works include symphonic poems (eg *Swan of Tuonela, En Saga*), songs, a violin concerto, and seven symphonies.

Simpson, Robert Wilfred Levick (1921–97) English, born Leamington Spa, Warwickshire; works include 11 symphonies; concertos for violin, piano, flute and cello; 15 string quartets; other chamber pieces; brass band music and two choral compositions; also wrote on music, eg *The Essence of Bruckner* (1966).

Stockhausen, Karlheinz (1928–) German, born Mödrath, near Cologne; works include orchestral music (eg *Gruppen*), choral and instrumental compositions.

Strauss, Johann, (the Younger) (1825–99) Austrian, born Vienna; works include over 400 waltzes (eg *The Blue Danube, Wine, Women, and Song, Perpetuum Mobile, Artist's Life, Tales from the Vienna Woods, Voices from Spring, The Emperor*), and operettas (eg *Die Fledermaus, A Night in Venice*).

Strauss, Richard (1864–1949) German, born Munich; works include symphonic poems (eg *Don Juan, Till Eulenspiegels lustige Streiche, Also Sprach Zarathustra, Tod und Verklärung* ('Death and Transfiguration'), *Don Quixote, Ein Heldenleben*) and operas (eg *Der Rosenkavalier, Ariadne auf Naxos, Capriccio*).

Stravinsky, Igor (1882–1971) Russian, born Oranienbaum, near St Petersburg (naturalized French, then American); works include operas (eg *The Rake's Progress*), oratorios (eg *Oedipus Rex, Symphony of Psalms*), concertos, ballets (eg *The Firebird, The Rite of Spring, Petrushka, Pulcinella, Apollo Musogetes, The Card Game, Orpheus, Agon*), and a musical play *Elegy for JFK* for voice and clarinets.

Tavener, John (Kenneth) (1944–) English, born London; works include the cantata *The Whale*, the choral-orchestral work *Ultimos ritos*, the sacred opera *Thérèse*, as well as pieces such as *The Protecting Veil* for cello and strings, and *The Repentant Thief* for clarinet, percussion and strings.

Tchaikovsky, Piotr Ilyich (1840–93) Russian, born Kamsko-Votkinsk; works include 10 operas (eg *Eugene Onegin, The Queen of Spades*), a violin concerto, six symphonies, two piano concertos, three ballets (*The Nutcracker, Swan Lake, The Sleeping Beauty*) and tone-poems (eg *Romeo and Juliet, Italian Capriccio*).

Telemann, George Philipp (1681–1767) German, born Magdeburg; prolific composer, works include 600 overtures, 40 operas, 200 concertos, sonatas, suites, and overtures (eg *Der Tag des Gerichts, Die Tageszeiten*).

Tippett, Sir Michael Kemp (1905–98) English, born London; works include operas (eg *The Midsummer Marriage, King Priam, The Knot Garden, The Ice Break*), concertos, symphonies, cantatas and oratorios (eg *A Child of Our Time, The Vision of St Augustine*).

Arts and Culture

Arts and Culture

Varèse, Edgard (1883–1965) American, born Paris; works are almost entirely orchestral (eg *Metal, Ionization, Hyperprism*).

Vaughan Williams, Ralph (1872–1958) English, born Down Ampney, Gloucestershire; works include songs, symphonies (eg *London Symphony, Pastoral Symphony*), choral-orchestral works (eg *Sea Symphony, Magnificat*), operas (eg *Hugh the Drover, The Pilgrim's Progress*), a ballet *Job*, and film music (eg *Scott of the Antarctic*).

Verdi, Giuseppe (1813–1901) Italian, born le Roncole, near Busseto; works include church music (eg *Requiem*) and operas (eg *Oberto, Nabucco, Rigoletto, Il Trovatore, La Traviata, Un Ballo in Maschera, La Forza del Destino, Aïda, Otello, Falstaff*).

Vivaldi, Antonio (1678–1741) Italian, born Venice; prolific output, works include over 400 concertos (eg *L'Estro Armonico, The Four Seasons*), 40 operas and an oratorio, *Juditha Triumphans*.

Wagner, (Wilhelm) Richard (1813–83) German, born Leipzig; operas include *Lohengrin, Rienzi*, the *Ring* cycle (*Das Rheingold, Die Walküre, Siegfried, Götterdämmerung*), *Die Meistersinger, Tristan und Isolde, Parsifal*.

Walton, Sir William Turner (1902–83) English, born Oldham; works include concertos, operas (*Troilus and Cressida, The Bear*), a cantata (*Belshazzar's Feast*), ballet music for *The Wise Virgins*, a songcycle (*Anon in Love*) and film music.

Weber, Carl Maria Friedrich von (1786–1826) German, born Eutin, near Lübeck; works include operas (eg *Oberon, Euryanthe, Silvana*), concertos, symphonies, sonatas, scenas, cantatas (eg *Kampf und Sieg*) and songs.

Webern, Anton Friedrich Wilhelm von (1883–1945) Austrian, born Vienna; works include a symphony, three cantatas, *Four Pieces for Violin and Pianoforte, Five Pieces for Orchestra*, and a concerto for nine instruments and songs.

Whitehead, Gillian (1941–) New Zealand, born Whangerei; works include compostitions for choir and chamber orchestra (eg *Inner Harbour*), for soprano and instrumental ensemble (eg *Hotspur*) for opera (eg *Eleanor of Aquitaine*) and for strings (eg *Pakuru*).

Xenakis, Iannis (1922–2001) French, born Romania; works include compositions for piano and orchestra (eg *Erikhthon*), *Shaar* for strings, *Tetras* for string quartet and solo pieces (eg *Nomos Alpha* for cello, *Herma* for piano), and *Pithoprakta* for 50 instruments.

Songwriters

A selection of songs is listed. Original and full names of songwriters are given in parentheses.

Arlen, Harold (Hyman Arluck) (1905–86) US composer, lyricist, born Buffalo, New York; over 500 songs, including 'Between the Devil and the Deep Blue Sea', 'Stormy Weather', 'Get Happy' (lyrics by Ted Koehler), *A Star is Born* (1953) ('The Man that Got Away') (lyrics by Ira Gershwin); *The Wizard of Oz* (1939) ('Over the Rainbow') (lyrics by E Y Harburg, 1896–1981).

Berlin, Irving (originally **Israel Baline**) (1888–1989) US composer, lyricist, born Temus, Siberia; composer; *Annie Get Your Gun* (1946), *Call Me Madam* (1950); over 900 songs, including 'There's No Business Like Show Business', 'White Christmas', 'God Bless America', 'Oh, How I Hate to Get Up in the Morning'.

Bernstein, Leonard (1918–90) US composer, lyricist, born Laurence, Massachusetts; composer of opera, symphonies, songs; *West Side Story* (1958) (lyrics by Stephen Sondheim); songs include 'You Got Me', 'New York, New York'.

Britten, Baron (Edward) Benjamin, of Aldeburgh (1913–76) English, born Lowestoft; composer of choral symphonic works, opera, song cycles, eg *Our Hunting Fathers, On This Island* (text by W H Auden).

Brown, Nacio Herb (1896–1954) US composer, lyricist, born Deming, New Mexico; composer; *Broadway Melody* (lyrics by Arthur Field, 1894–1973); *Singin' in the Rain* (1952); songs include 'You were Meant for Me'.

Cahn, Sammy (Samuel) (1913–93) US lyricist, born New York; 'I've Heard That Song Before', 'I'll Walk Alone', 'It's Magic' (with Julie Styne); 'All the Way', 'High Hopes' (with Jimmy van Heusen).

Carmichael, Hoagy (Hoagland Howard) (1899–1981) US songwriter and pianist, born Bloomington Indiana; wrote many popular and enduring songs, eg 'Riverboat Shuffle', 'Stardust', 'Georgia on My Mind', 'Lazy River', 'I Get Along Without You Very Well', 'Lamplighter's Serenade' (Frank Sinatra's first recording).

Cohan, George M(ichael) (1878–1942) US composer, lyricist, born Providence, Rhode Island; *Little Johnny Jones* (1904) ('Give My Regards to Broadway'); 'The Talk of the Town' (1907).

Coward, Sir Noël Pierce (1899–1973) English composer, lyricist, playwright, born Teddington; *Words and Music* (revue) (1932) ('Mad Dogs and Englishmen', 'Someday I'll Find You').

Dylan, Bob (Robert Allen Zimmerman) (1941–) US songwriter, musician, born Duluth, Minnesota; 'Blowin' in the Wind', 'With God on Our Side', 'The Times They are A-Changin'', 'It's Alright Ma, I'm Only Bleeding', 'Mr Tambourine Man', 'Subterranean Homesick Blues', 'Like a Rolling Stone', 'Leopard-Skin Pill-Box Hat', 'Knockin' on Heaven's Door'.

Ellington, (Edward Kennedy) 'Duke' (1899–1974) US pianist, composer, bandleader, born Washington, DC; 2 000 works, including songs, instrumentals, film music; 'It Don't Mean a Thing if it Ain't Got That Swing' (lyrics Irving Mills), 'Best Wishes' (lyrics Ted Koehler), 'Creole Love Call' (vocal, no lyrics).

Fields, Dorothy (1905–74) US lyricist, born Allenhurst, New Jersey; 'I Can't Give You Anything But Love' (with Jimmy McHugh, from *Blackbirds*, 1928), 'On the Sunny Side of the Street' (with Jimmy McHugh), 'Exactly Like You', 'Lovely to Look At' and 'The Way You Look Tonight' (with Jerome Kern); *Stars in Your Eyes* (1939) (with Arthur Schwartz); *Sweet Charity* (1966) ('Big Spender') (with Cy Coleman).

Gershwin, George (originally **Jacob Gershvin**) (1898–1937) US composer, born Brooklyn, New York City; and **Ira Gershwin** (originally **Israel Gershvin**) (1896–1983) US lyricist, born New York City; *Lady, Be Good!* ('The Man I Love', 'How Long Has This Been Going On?'), *Girl Crazy, Porgy and Bess* ('Summertime') (lyrics by Ira Gershwin and Du Bose Heyward); songs include 'You Can't Take That Away from Me', 'Nice Work if You Can Get It', 'Love Walked In', 'They All Laughed'.

Gilbert, Sir William Schwenck (1836–1911) Englishlibrettist, born London; and **Sir Arthur Seymour Sullivan** (1842–1900) English composer, born London; operettas and songs include *HMS Pinafore* (1878), *The Mikado* (1885), *The Gondoliers* (1889).

Herman, Jerry (1932–) US composer, lyricist, born New York City; *Hello Dolly!* (1964), *Mame* (1966).

Kern, Jerome (David) (1885–1945) US composer, born New York City; 'The Way You Look Tonight' (lyrics Dorothy Fields); 'Ol' Man River', 'They Didn't Believe Me' (lyrics Herbert Reynold); *Show Boat* (1927) (lyrics Oscar Hammerstein II (1895–1960) US lyricist, born New York City).

Lennon, John Winston (1940–80) English songwriter, musician, born Liverpool; and **(James) Paul McCartney** (1942–) English songwriter, musician, born Liverpool; 'Please Please Me', 'Yesterday', 'All You Need is Love', 'Strawberry Fields Forever', 'I Want to Hold Your Hand', 'Michelle', 'Eleanor Rigby', 'Ticket to Ride', 'Dear Prudence', 'Help'.

Lerner, Alan Jay (1918–86) US librettist, lyricist, playwright, born New York City; and **Frederick Loewe** (1904–88) German–American composer, born Berlin; *Brigadoon* (1947), *Paint Your Wagon* (1951), *My Fair Lady* (1956), *Gigi* (1958) (film).

Livingston, Jay (1915–2001) US composer, lyricist, born McDonald, Pennsylvania; and **Ray Evans** (1915–) US lyricist, born Salamanca, New York; 'The Cat and the Canary', 'Mona Lisa', 'Whatever Will Be, Will Be (Que Sera Sera)', 'Dear Heart'.

Lloyd-Webber, Andrew Lloyd Webber, Baron (1948–) English composer, born London, with **Tim Rice** (1944–) English lyricist, born Amersham, Buckinghamshire; *Joseph and the Amazing Technicolor Dreamcoat* (1968) ('Any Dream Will Do'); *Jesus Christ Superstar* (1970) ('Jesus Christ Superstar', 'I Don't Know How to Love Him'), *Evita* (1978) ('Don't Cry for Me, Argentina'); *Cats* (1981) (libretto T S Eliot), *Phantom of the Opera* (1986), *Aspects of Love* (1989), *Whistle Down the Wind* (1996).

Loesser, Frank (Henry) (1910–69) US composer, lyricist, born New York City; *Guys and Dolls* (1950) ('I've Never Been in Love Before', 'Luck Be a Lady'); *The Perils of Pauline* (1947) (words and music); lyrics for 'The Boys in the Back Room' (music by Frederick Hollander); lyrics for 'The Lady's in Love with You' and 'Some Like it Hot', from the film *Some Like it Hot* (1959).

MacColl, Ewan (originally **James Miller**) (1915–89) Scottish folk-singer, composer, collector, born Salford, Lancashire; 'The Shoals of Herring', 'Dirty Old Town', 'Freeborn Man', 'The First Time Ever I Saw Your Face'.

McHugh, Jimmy (James Frances McHugh) (1896–1969) US composer, born Boston, Massachusetts; with Dorothy Fields, as above; 'I'm Shooting High' (with Ted Koehler); 'Exactly Like You' (with Al Dubin).

Mancini, Henry (1924–94) US composer of songs and film music, born Cleveland, Ohio; over 80 films, eg *Breakfast at Tiffany's* (1961); songs include 'Moon River' (lyrics Johnny Mercer), 'Days of Wine and Roses', 'Charade'.

Mercer, Johnny H (1909–76) US lyricist, born Savannah, Georgia; 1 500 songs for over 70 films and seven Broadway musicals; songs with Henry Mancini, as above; 'Blues in the Night' (music by Harold Arlen), 'That Old Black Magic' (music by Harold Arlen), 'Jeepers Creepers' (music by Henry Warren); lyrics for *Seven Brides for Seven Brothers*.

Novello, Ivor (originally **David Ivor Davies**) (1893–1951) Welsh composer, songwriter, born Cardiff; 'Keep the Home Fires Burning', musical plays including *Glamorous Night* (1935), *The Dancing Years* (1939), *King's Rhapsody* (1949).

Porter, Cole (1891–1964) US composer, lyricist, born Peru, Indiana; *Gay Divorcee* (1932), *Anything Goes* (1934), *Du Barry Was a Lady* ('Well, Did You Evah!') (1939), *Kiss Me Kate* (1948) ('So in Love'); songs include 'I'm in Love Again', 'Let's Do It, Let's Fall in Love', 'Just One of Those Things'.

Rodgers, Richard (1902–79) US composer, born Long Island, New York; with **Lorenz Hart** (1895–1943) US lyricist, born New York City; *The Girl Friend* (1926), *Babes in Arms* (1937), 'Manhattan'; with **Oscar Hammerstein II** (1895–1960) US lyricist, born New York City; *Oklahoma!* (1943) ('Oh, What a Beautiful Morning'), *South Pacific* (1949), *The King and I* (1959) ('Shall We Dance?'), *The Sound of Music* (1959) ('Do-Re-Mi', 'Edelweiss').

Romberg, Sigmund (1887–1951) US composer, born Nagykanizsa, Hungary; *The Desert Song* (1926), *The New Moon* (1928), ('Lover Come Back to Me'), *The Student Prince* (1924), *Girl of the Golden West* (1938).

Schubert, Franz (Peter) (1797–1828) Austrian composer, born Vienna; works include 145 songs, texts by Schiller and Goethe, among others.

Schumann, Robert (Alexander) (1810–56) German composer, born Zwickau; songs to texts by Heine, among others.

Simon, Paul (1942–) US songwriter, musician, born Newark, New Jersey; 'I am a Rock', 'Bridge over Troubled Water', 'Mrs Robinson', 'Cecilia', 'Keep the Customer Satisfied', 'Homeward Bound', 'The Boxer', 'The Sound of Silence', 'You Can Call Me Al'.

Sondheim, Stephen (Joshua) (1930–) US composer, lyricist, born New York City; lyrics for Bernstein's *West Side Story* (1958), *A Funny Thing Happened on the Way to the Forum* (1962), *A Little Night Music* (1973) ('Send in the Clowns') (lyrics and music).

Styne, Jule (1905–94) US composer, born London, England; 'There Goes That Song Again', 'I'll Walk Alone', 'It's Magic' (with Sammy Cahn); *Gentlemen Prefer Blondes* (1949) ('Diamonds are a Girl's Best Friend') with Leo Robin.

Warren, Harry (1893–1981) US composer of songs, film scores, born Brooklyn, New York City; 'You're My Everything', 'We're in the Money', 'Chattanooga Choo-Choo', 'Jeepers Creepers' (with Johnny H Mercer); with **Al Dubin** (1891–1945) US lyricist, born Zurich, Switzerland; *42nd Street* (1932), 'The Boulevard of Broken Dreams', 'I Only Have Eyes for You'.

Weill, Kurt (1900–50) German composer, born Dessau; songs, opera, with **(Eugen) Bertolt Friedrich Brecht** (1898–1956) German lyricist, playwright, born Augsburg; *Threepenny Opera* (1928) ('Mack the Knife'); *Lady in the Dark* (1941) (lyrics Ira Gershwin), *Street Scene* (1947) (lyrics Langston Hughes), *Lost in the Stars* (1949) (lyrics Maxwell Anderson).

Operas and operettas

Name	Composer	Date
Aïda	Verdi	1871
Akhnaten	Philip Glass	1984
Albert Herring	Britten	1947
Alceste	Gluck	1767
Andrea Chénier	Umberto Giordano	1896
Ariadne auf Naxos	Richard Strauss	1916
Armide et Rénaud	Lully	1686
Un Ballo in Maschera	Verdi	1859
The Barber of Seville	Rossini	1816
The Bartered Bride	Smetana	1866
Béatrice et Bénédict	Berlioz	1862
The Beggar's Opera	Pepusch	1728
Billy Budd	Britten	1951
La Bohème	Puccini	1896
Boris Godunov	Mussorgsky	1874
Capriccio	Richard Strauss	1942
Carmen	Bizet	1875
Cavalleria Rusticana	Mascagni	1890
La Cenerentola (Cinderella)	Rossini	1817
La Clemenza di Tito	Mozart	1791
The Consul	Gian-Carlo Menotti	1950
Così Fan Tutte	Mozart	1790
The Cunning Little Vixen	Janáček	1924
The Damnation of Faust	Berlioz	1846
Death in Venice	Britten	1973
Dido and Aeneas	Purcell	1689
Don Carlos	Verdi	1867
Don Giovanni	Mozart	1787
Don Pasquale	Donizetti	1843
Duke Bluebeard's Castle	Bartók	1918
The Egyptian Helen	Richard Strauss	1928
Einstein on the Beach	Philip Glass	1976
Elegy for Young Lovers	Hans Werner Henze	1961
Elektra	Richard Strauss	1909
Eugene Onegin	Tchaikovsky	1879
The Fair Maid of Perth	Bizet	1867
Falstaff	Verdi	1893
Faust	Gounod	1859
La Fille du Régiment	Donizetti	1840
Fidelio	Beethoven	1814
Die Fledermaus	Johann Strauss	1874
The Flying Dutchman	Wagner	1843
La Gioconda	Amilcare Ponchielli	1876
The Golden Cockerel	Rimsky-Korsakov	1909
The Gondoliers	Gilbert and Sullivan	1889
Le Grand Macabre	Ligeti	1978
Hansel and Gretel	Humperdinck	1893
HMS Pinafore	Gilbert and Sullivan	1878
Hugh the Drover	Vaughan Williams	1924
The Ice Break	Tippett	1977
Idomeneo	Mozart	1781
L'Incoronazione di Poppea	Monteverdi	1642
Iphigénie en Tauride	Gluck	1779
Jenufa	Janáček	1904
Katya Kabanova	Janáček	1921
King Priam	Tippett	1962
Lady Macbeth of Mtsensk	Shostakovich	1934
Lohengrin	Wagner	1850
The Love for Three Oranges	Prokofiev	1920
Lucia di Lammermoor	Donizetti	1835
Lucrezia Borgia	Donizetti	1833
Lulu	Berg	1937
Macbeth	Verdi	1847
Madama Butterfly	Puccini	1904
The Magic Flute	Mozart	1791
Les Mamelles de Tirésias	Poulenc	1947
Manon	Massenet	1884
Manon Lescaut	Puccini	1893
The Marriage of Figaro	Mozart	1786
Maskarade	Nielsen	1906
Mask of Orpheus	Harrison Birtwistle	1986
Der Meistersinger von Nürnberg	Wagner	1868
The Merry Wives of Windsor	Otto Nicolai	1849
The Midsummer Marriage	Tippett	1955
The Mikado	Gilbert and Sullivan	1885
Moses und Aron	Schönberg	1954
Nabucco	Verdi	1842
Nixon in China	Peter Adams	1990
Norma	Bellini	1831
Noye's Fludde	Britten	1958
Oedipus Rex	Stravinsky	1927
Orfeo ed Euridice	Gluck	1762
Orpheus in the Underworld	Offenbach	1858
Otello	Verdi	1887
Pagliacci	Leoncavallo	1892
Parsifal	Wagner	1882
The Pearl Fishers	Bizet	1863
Pelléas et Mélisande	Debussy	1902
Peter Grimes	Britten	1945
Porgy and Bess	Gershwin	1935
Punch and Judy	Harrison Birtwistle	1968
I Puritani	Bellini	1835
The Rake's Progress	Stravinsky	1951
The Rape of Lucretia	Britten	1946
Rigoletto	Verdi	1851
The Ring	Wagner	1876
Der Rosenkavalier	Richard Strauss	1911
Le Rossignol	Stravinsky	1914
Salome	Richard Strauss	1911
Samson et Dalila	Saint-Saëns	1877
Semele	Handel	1744
Simon Boccanegra	Verdi	1857
La Sonnambula	Bellini	1831
The Tales of Hoffman	Offenbach	1881
Tannhäuser	Wagner	1845
The Threepenny Opera	Weill	1928
Tosca	Puccini	1900
La Traviata	Verdi	1853
Tristan und Isolde	Wagner	1865
The Trojans	Berlioz	1863
Il Trovatore	Verdi	1853
Turandot	Puccini	1926
The Turn of the Screw	Britten	1954

Name	Composer	Date	Name	Composer	Date
I Vespri Siciliani	Verdi	1855	William Tell	Rossini	1829
Werther	Massenet	1892	Wozzeck	Berg	1925
Where the Wild Things Are	Oliver Knussen	1980			

Opera singers

Allen, Sir Thomas (Boaz) (1944–) English baritone, born Seaham.

Anderson, Marian (1902–93) US contralto, born South Philadelphia.

Austral, Florence (originally **Florence Wilson**) (1892–1968) Australian soprano, born Richmond, West Melbourne.

Bailey, Norman (Stanley) (1933–) English baritone, born Birmingham.

Baker, Dame Janet (Abbott) (1933–) English mezzo-soprano, born Hatfield, Yorkshire.

Barstow, Dame Josephine (Clare) (1940–) English soprano, born Sheffield.

Bartoli, Cecilia (1966–) Italian mezzo-soprano, born Rome.

Battistini, Mattia (1856–1928) Italian baritone, born Rome.

Berganza, Teresa (1935–) Spanish mezzo-soprano, born Madrid.

Bergonzi, Carlo (1924–) Italian tenor, born Polisene.

Björling, Jussi (1911–60) Swedish tenor, born Stora Tuna.

Bonci, Alessandro (1870–1940) Italian tenor, born Cesena.

Borgatti, Giuseppe (1871–1950) Italian tenor, born Cento.

Borgioli, Dino (1891–1960) Italian tenor, born Florence.

Bowman, James (1941–) English countertenor, born Oxford.

Brannigan, Owen (1908–73) English, bass baritone, born Annitsford, Northumberland.

Butt, Dame Clara (1872–1936) English contralto, born Southwick, Sussex.

Caballé, Montserrat (1933–) Spanish soprano, born Barcelona.

Callas, Maria (originally **Maria Anna Sofia Cecilia Kalogeropoulos**) (1923–77) US soprano of Greek parents, born New York City.

Carden, Joan Maralyn (1937–) Australian soprano, born Melbourne.

Carreras, José (1947–) Spanish tenor, born Barcelona.

Caruso, Enrico (1873–1921) Italian tenor, born Naples.

Charles, Craig (1922–) English tenor, born London.

Collier, Maria (1926–71) Australian soprano, born Ballarat.

Crossley, Ada (Jessica) (1874–1929) Australian mezzo-soprano, born Tarraville, Gippsland.

Davies, Arthur (1950–) Welsh tenor, born Wrexham.

Davies, Ryland (1943–) Welsh tenor, born Cwym, Ebbw Vale.

de Luca, Giuseppe (1876–1950) Italian baritone, born Rome.

De Lucia, Fernando (1860–1925) Italian tenor, born Naples.

de Reszke, Jean (originally **Jan Mieczislaw**) (1850–1925) Polish tenor, born Warsaw.

Del Monaco, Mario (1915–82) Italian tenor, born Florence.

Deller, Alfred (George) (1912–79) English countertenor, born Margate.

Domingo, Placido (1941–) Spanish tenor, born Madrid.

Evans, Sir Geraint (Llewellyn) (1922–92) Welsh baritone, born Pontypridd, South Wales.

Ewing, Maria (Louise) (1950–) US mezzo-soprano, born Detroit.

Farrar, Geraldine (1882–1967) US soprano, born Melrose, Massachusetts.

Farrell, Eileen (1920–2002) US soprano, born Willimantic, Connecticut.

Ferrier, Kathleen (1912–53) English contralto, born Higher Walton, Lancashire.

Field, Helen (1951–) Welsh soprano, born Awyd, North Wales.

Fischer-Dieskau, Dietrich (1925–) German baritone, born Zehlendorf, Berlin.

Flagstad, Kirsten (1895–1962) Norwegian soprano, born Hamar.

Forrester, Maureen (1930–) Canadian contralto, born Montreal.

Fremstad, Olive (1871–1951) US soprano, born Stockholm.

Freni, Mirella (1936–) Italian soprano, born Modena.

Galli-Curci, Amelita (1882–1963) Italian soprano, born Milan.

Galli-Marie, Celestine (1840–1905) French mezzo-soprano, born Paris.

Garrett, Lesley (1955–) English soprano, born Thorne, Doncaster.

Gedda, Nicolai (1925–) Swedish tenor, born Stockholm.

Gigli, Beniamino (1890–1957) Italian tenor, born Recanati.

Gobbi, Tito (1913–84) Italian baritone, born Bassano del Grappa.

Harper, Heather (1930–) Northern Irish soprano, born Belfast.

Hendricks, Barbara (1948–) US soprano, born Stephens, Arizona.

Hotter, Hans (1909–) Austrian bass-baritone, born Offenbach-am-Main, Germany.

Jurinac, Sena (1921–) Yugoslav (now Bosnian) soprano, born Travnik.

Kollo, René (1937–) German tenor, born Berlin.

Kraus, Alfredo (1927–99) Spanish tenor, born Las Palmas, Canary Islands.

Lanza, Mario (originally **Alfredo Arnold Coccozza**) (1921–59) US tenor, born Philadelphia, Pennsylvania.

Lehmann, Lilli (1848–1929) German soprano, born Würzburg.

Lehmann, Lotte (1888–1976) German soprano, born Perleberg.

Arts and Culture

Lind, Jenny ('the Swedish Nightingale') (1820–87) Swedish soprano, born Stockholm.

Los Angeles, Victoria de (originally **Victoria Gómez Cima**) (1923–) Spanish soprano, born Barcelona.

Ludwig, Christa (Deiber) (1928–) German mezzo-soprano, born Berlin.

Luxon, Benjamin (1937–) English baritone, born Redruth, Cornwall.

McCormack, John (1884–1945) Irish tenor, born Athlone.

Major, Dame Malvina (Lorraine) (1943–) New Zealand soprano, born Hamilton.

Mangin, Noel (1931–95) New Zealand bass, born Wellington.

Martinelli, Giovanni (1885–1969) Italian tenor, born Montagnana.

Meier, Johanna (1938–) US soprano, born Chicago.

Melba, Dame Nellie (originally **Helen Mitchell**) (1861–1931) Australian soprano, born Burnle, near Richmond, Melbourne.

Melchior, Lauritz (1890–1973) Danish tenor, born Copenhagen.

Migenes-Johnson, Julia (1945–) US soprano, born New York City.

Milanov, Zinka (1906–89) Croatian soprano, born Zagreb.

Nash, Heddle (1896–1961) English tenor, born London.

Nilsson, Birgit (1918–) Swedish soprano, born near Karup.

Norman, Jessye (1945–) US soprano, born Augusta, Georgia.

Patti, Adelina (Adela Juana Maria) (1843–1919) Italian soprano, born Madrid.

Pavarotti, Luciano (1935–) Italian tenor, born Modena.

Pears, Sir Peter (1910–86) English tenor, born Farnham, Surrey.

Pinza, Ezio (1892–1957) Italian bass, born Rome.

Ponselle, Rosa (Melba) (1897–1981) US soprano, born Meriden, Connecticut.

Popp, Lucia (1939–93) Czech soprano, born Llhorsaká.

Prey, Hermann (1929–98) German baritone, born Berlin.

Price, (Mary Violet) Leontyne (1927–) US soprano, born Laurel, Mississippi.

Schumann, Elisabeth (1889–1952) US soprano, born Merseburg, Germany.

Schwarzkopf, Dame Elisabeth (1915–) Austrian-British soprano, born Jarotschin, near Poznan, Poland.

Scotto, Renata (1934–) Italian soprano, born Savona.

Shirley-Quirk, John (1931–) English bass-baritone, born Liverpool.

Siepi, Cesare (1923–) Italian bass, born Milan.

Smirnov, Dimitri (1882–1944) Russian tenor, born Moscow.

Söderström, Elisabeth (1927–) Swedish soprano, born Stockholm.

Stratas, Teresa (1938–) Canadian soprano, born Toronto.

Studer, Cheryl (1955–) US soprano, born Midland, Michigan.

Sutherland, Dame Joan (1926–) Australian soprano, born Sydney.

Tauber, Richard (1891–1948) Austrian-British tenor, born Linz.

Tear, Robert (1939–) Welsh tenor, born Barry, South Wales.

Tebaldi, Renata (1922–) Italian soprano, born Pesaro.

Te Kanawa, Dame Kiri (1944–) New Zealand soprano, born Gisborne.

Terfel, Bryn (1965–) Welsh bass-baritone, born Pwllheli, Gwynedd.

Tetrazzini, Luisa (1871–1940) Italian soprano, born Florence.

Teyte, Dame Maggie (1888–1976) English soprano, born Wolverhampton.

Tibbett, Lawrence Mervil (1896–1960) US baritone, born Bakersfield, California.

Turner, Dame Eva (1892–1990) English soprano, born Oldham.

Van Dam, José (1940–) Belgian bass-baritone, born Brussels.

Vickers, Jon(athan) Stewart (1926–) Canadian tenor, born Prince Albert.

Wiener, Otto (1911–2000) Austrian baritone, born Vienna.

Layout of an orchestra

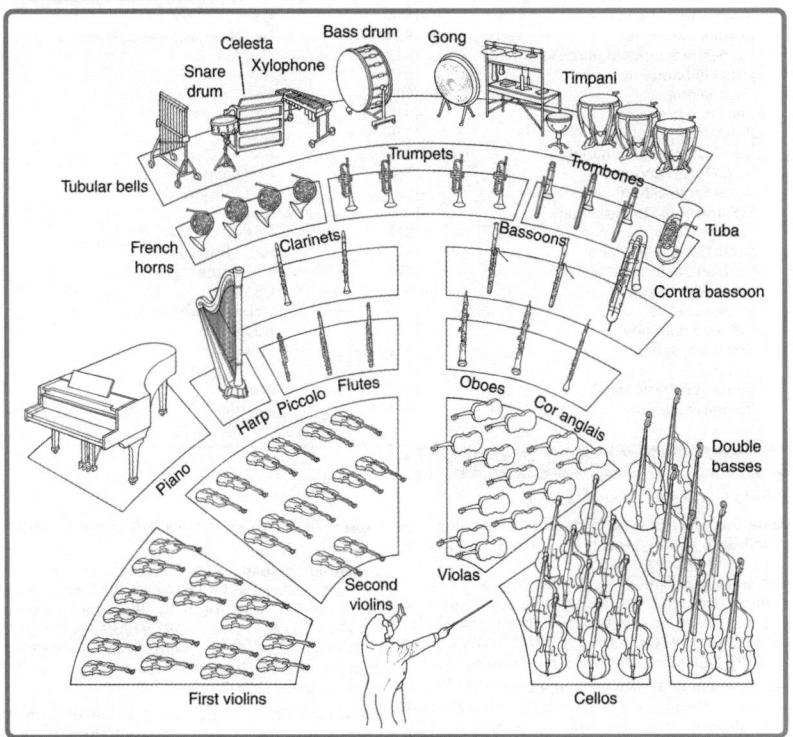

Orchestras

Name	Date founded	Location
Academy of Ancient Music	1973	UK (London)
Academy of St Martin-in-the-Fields	1959	UK (London)
Australian Chamber	1975	Sydney
BBC Philharmonic	1934	UK (Manchester)
BBC Scottish Symphony	1935	UK (Glasgow)
BBC Symphony	1930	UK (London)
BBC Welsh Symphony	1935	UK (Cardiff)
Berliner Philharmonic	1882	Germany
Boston Symphony	1881	USA
Bournemouth Symphony	1893	UK
Chicago Symphony	1891	USA
City of Birmingham Symphony	1920	UK
City of Glasgow Philharmonic	1990	UK
Cleveland Symphony	1918	USA
Concertgebouw	1888	Netherlands (Amsterdam)
Detroit Symphony	1914	USA
English Chamber	1948	UK (London)
Hallé	1858	UK (Manchester)
Israel Philharmonic	1936	Israel (Tel Aviv)
London Philharmonic	1904	UK
London Symphony	1904	UK
Los Angeles Philharmonic	1904	USA
Melbourne Symphony	1906	Australia
Milan La Scala	1778	Italy
Minnesota	1903	USA (Minneapolis)
National Symphony	1931	USA (Washington DC)
NBC Symphony	1937–54	USA (New York)
New Orleans Philharmonic Symphony	1936	USA
New York Philharmonic	1842	USA

Name	Date founded	Location
New York Symphony	1878	USA
Northern Sinfonia	1958	UK (Newcastle-upon-Tyne)
Orchestre Symphonique de Montréal	1842	Canada
Oslo Philharmonic	1919	Norway
Philadelphia	1900	USA
The Philharmonia	1945	UK (London)
Pittsburgh Symphony	1926	USA
Royal Liverpool Philharmonic	1840	UK
Royal Philharmonic	1946	UK (London)
Royal Scottish National	1891	UK (Glasgow)
St Petersburg Philharmonic	1921	Russia
San Francisco	1911	USA
Santa Cecelia Academy	1895	Italy (Rome)
Scottish Chamber	1974	UK (Edinburgh)
Seattle Symphony	1903	USA
Staatskapelle	1923	Germany (Dresden)
Sydney Symphony	1934	Australia
Toronto Symphony	1922	Canada
Ulster	1966	UK (Belfast)
Vienna Philharmonic	1842	Austria
Vienna Symphony	1900	Austria

Pop and rock musicians and singers

Selected singles and albums are listed.

Abba Swedish group, 1970s to early 1980s; members include Bjorn Ulvaeus (1945–) singer, guitarist, born Gothenburg; Agnetha Faltskog (1950–) singer, born Jankoping; Anni-Frid Lyngstad (1945–) singer, born Narvik, Norway; Benny Andersson (1946–) singer, keyboardist, born Stockholm; *Waterloo* (1974), *Arrival* (1976), *Voulez-Vous* (1979), *Super Trouper* (1980), *The Visitors* (1981).

AC/DC Australian heavy metal group, mid-1970s to present; members include Bon Scott (originally Ronald Belford Scott) (1946–80) vocalist, born Kirriemuir, Scotland; Brian Johnson (1947–) vocalist, born North Shields, England; Angus Young (1959–) guitarist, born Glasgow, Scotland; Malcolm Young (1953–) guitarist, born Glasgow, Scotland; Phil Rudd (1954–) drummer, born Melbourne, Australia; *High Voltage* (1976), *If you want blood, you've got it* (1978), *Highway to Hell* (1979), *Dirty Deeds Done Dirt Cheap* (1981), *For Those About to Rock* (1981), *Blow Up Your Video* (1988), *Stiff Upper Lip* (2000).

Adams, Bryan (1959–) Canadian singer, guitarist, songwriter, born Vancouver, British Columbia; 'Everything I Do', *Cuts Like a Knife* (1983), *You Want It, You Got It* (1984), *Reckless* (1985), *Into the Fire* (1987), *Waking Up The Neighbours* (1991), *So Far So Good* (1993), *LIVE! LIVE! LIVE!* (1994), *18 'Til I Die* (1997), *Spirit: Stallion of the Cimarron* (2002).

Aerosmith US group, 1970s to present; members include Steve Tyler (1948–) vocalist, born New York City; Joe Perry (1950–) guitarist, born Boston, Massachusetts; Tom Hamilton (1951–) bassist, born Colorado Springs; Joey Kramer (1950–) drummer, born New York City; 'Come Together', 'Dream On', 'Angel', 'Dude Looks Like a Lady', 'Love in an Elevator', 'Jamie's Got a Gun', *Aerosmith* (1973), *Toys in the Attic* (1975), *Permanent Vacation* (1987), *Pump* (1989), *Get a Grip* (1993), *Big Ones* (1994), *Just Push Play* (2001).

The Animals British group, 1960s; split up in 1960s, reformed 1983; members include Eric Burdon (1941–) vocalist, born Newcastle upon Tyne; Alan Price (1942–) keyboardist, born Fairfield, County Durham; 'House of the Rising Sun', 'We've Gotta Get Out of this Place', *Animals* (1964), *Ark* (1983), *Rip It To Shreds — The Animals Greatest Hits Live* (1995).

Armatrading, Joan (1950–) British singer, guitarist, born St Kitts Island, Caribbean; *Joan Armatrading* (1976), *To the Limit* (1978), *Walk Under Ladders* (1981), *The Key* (1983), *Sleight of Hand* (1986), *The Shouting Stage* (1988), *Hearts and Flowers* (1990), *Square the Circle* (1992), *What's Inside* (1995), *Lovers Speak* (2003).

Baez, Joan (1941–) US singer, guitarist, born Staten Island, New York; 'The Night They Drove Ol' Dixie Down' (1972), *Any Day Now* (1968), *Farewell, Anjelica* (1975), *Diamonds and Rust* (1975), *Recently* (1987), *Gone from Danger* (1997).

Bassey, Dame Shirley (1937–) British singer, born Tiger Bay, Cardiff, Wales; 'Goldfinger', 'Big Spender', 'Diamonds are Forever', *The Birthday Concert* (1998).

The Beach Boys US group, 1960s to 1990s; members include Brian (1942–) bassist, vocalist; Dennis (1944–83) drummer, vocalist; and Carl (1946–98) Wilson guitarist, vocalist; all born Hawthorne, California; Mike Love (1941–) vocalist; 'Surfin' USA', 'Help Me Rhonda', 'Barbara Ann', 'Good Vibrations', 'Fun, Fun, Fun', 'I Get Around', 'California Girls', 'Little Deuce Coupe', 'God Only Knows', 'Wouldn't It Be Nice'.

The Beatles British group, 1960s; John (Winston) Lennon (1940–80) singer/songwriter, guitarist; (James) Paul McCartney (1942–) singer/songwriter, guitarist; George Harrison (1943–) singer/songwriter, guitarist; Ringo Starr (originally Richard Starkey) (1940–) singer/songwriter, drummer; all born Liverpool; 'Love Me Do', 'She Loves You', 'From Me to You', 'I Want to Hold Your Hand', 'Yesterday', 'Day Tripper', 'Paperback Writer', 'I am the Walrus', 'Penny Lane', 'Strawberry Fields Forever', 'Hey Jude', *Please Please Me* (1963), *With the Beatles* (1963), *A Hard Day's Night* (1964), *Beatles for Sale* (1964), *Help!* (1965), *Rubber Soul* (1965), *Revolver* (1966), *Sergeant Pepper's Lonely Hearts Club Band* (1967), *Magical Mystery Tour* (1967), *Yellow Submarine* (1968), *The White Album* (1968), *Abbey Road* (1969), *Let It Be* (1970).

The Bee Gees Anglo-Australian group, 1960s to

present; members include Barry (1946–), Robin (1949–), and Maurice (1949–2003) Gibb; all born Isle of Man; 'Massachusetts', 'Jive Talkin'', 'How Deep is Your Love?', 'Staying Alive', 'Night Fever', *Children of the World* (1976), *ESP* (1987), *Size Isn't Everything* (1993), *Still Waters* (1997), *This is Where I Came In* (2001).

Berry, Chuck (originally **Charles Edward Anderson Berry**) (1926–) US singer/songwriter, guitarist; born St Louis, California; 'Maybellene', 'Sweet Little Sixteen', 'Too Much Monkey Business', 'Rock and Roll Music', 'School Days', 'No Particular Place to Go', 'Johnny B Goode', 'Nadine', 'My Ding-a-Ling'.

B52s US group, 1970s to present; members include Cindy Wilson (1957–) vocalist; Ricky Wilson (1953–85) guitarist; Keith Strickland (1953–) drummer; all born Athens, Georgia; Fred Schneider (1954–) vocalist, born Newark, Georgia; Kate Pierson (1948–) vocalist, keyboardist, born Weehawken, New Jersey; 'Rock Lobster', 'Love Shack', 'Roam', 'Deadbeat Club', *Wild Planet* (1980), *Mesopotamia* (1982), *Whammy* (1983), *Bouncing off the Satellites* (1986), *Cosmic Thing* (1989), *Good Stuff* (1992).

Black Sabbath British heavy rock group, 1970s to present; members include Ozzy Osbourne (1948–) vocalist; Tony Iommi (1948–) guitarist; both born Birmingham; *Paranoid* (1971), *Sabbath Bloody Sabbath* (1973), *Dehumanizer* (1992), *Cross Purposes* (1994), *Forbidden* (1995), *Reunion* (1998).

Blondie US group, 1970s to present; members include Deborah Harry (1945–) vocalist, born Miami, Florida (solo 'Island of Lost Souls', 'French Kissin' in the USA', 'Free to Fall', 'I Want That Man'); Chris Stein (1950–) guitarist, born Brooklyn, New York City; 'Denis', 'Heart of Glass', 'Union City Blue', 'Call Me', 'The Tide is High', *Blondie* (1976), *Plastic Letters* (1977), *Parallel Lines* (1978), *Auto American* (1980), *The Hunter* (1982), *No Exit* (1999).

Blur British group, formed Colchester, late 1980s to present; members include Damon Albarn (1968–) singer, born London; Graham Coxon (1969–) guitarist, born Bournemouth; Alex James (1968–) bassist, born Hanover, Germany, vocalist; Dave Rowntree (1963–) drummer, born Colchester, Essex; 'Parklife', 'For Tomorrow', 'Beetlebum', *Leisure* (1991), *Modern Life is Rubbish* (1993), *Parklife* (1994), *The Great Escape* (1995), *Blur* (1997), *13* (1999), *Think Tank* (2003).

Bolan, Marc (and T Rex) (originally **Mark Feld**) (1947–77) British singer/songwriter, guitarist, born London; 'Get It On', 'Metal Guru', 'Children of the Revolution', 'Jeepster', *Unicorn* (1970).

Bon Jovi, Jon (originally **John Francis Bongiovi**) (1962–) US lead singer and guitarist of Bon Jovi, 1980s to present; group members include David Bryan (1962–) keyboardist; Richie Sambora (1959–) lead guitarist; Alec John Such (1956–) bassist; Tico 'Tour Monster' Torres (1953–) drummer; *Bon Jovi* (1984), *Slippery When Wet* (1986), *New Jersey* (1988), *Keep The Faith* (1992), *These Days* (1995), *Destination Anywhere* (1997), *Bounce* (2002).

Booker T and the MGs US group, 1960s; Booker T Jones (1944–) vocalist, organist, born Memphis, Tennessee; Donald 'Duck' Dunn (1941–) bassist, born Memphis; Steve Cropper (1941–) guitarist, born Willow Springs, Missouri; 'To be a Lover', *Green Onions* (1962).

Bowie, David (originally **David Robert Jones**) (1947–) British singer/songwriter, guitarist, born Brixton, London; 'The Laughing Gnome', 'Space Oddity', 'Life on Mars', 'Jean Genie', 'Andy War-hol', 'Rebel Rebel', 'Ashes to Ashes', 'Blue Jean', 'China Girl', 'Let's Dance', 'Modern Love', *The Man who Sold the World* (1970), *Hunky Dory* (1971), *The Rise and Fall of Ziggy Stardust and the Spiders from Mars* (1972), *Diamond Dogs* (1974), *Heroes* (1977), *Scary Monsters* (1980), *Let's Dance* (1983), *Tonight* (1984), *Never Let Me Down* (1987), *Black Tie White Noise* (1993), *Earthling* (1997), *Hours* (1999).

Brown, James (1928–) US singer/songwriter, drummer, pianist, born Barnwell, South Carolina; 'Papa's Got a Brand New Bag', 'It's a Man's Man's Man's World', 'Ain't It Funky Now', 'Sex Machine', 'Get Up Offa That Thing'.

Bush, Kate (1958–) British singer/songwriter, keyboardist, born Plumstead; 'Wuthering Heights', 'The Man with the Child in His Eyes', 'Wow', 'Running Up That Hill', *Never Forever* (1980), *The Dreaming* (1982), *Hounds of Love* (1986), *The Sensual World* (1989), *The Red Shoes* (1993).

The Byrds US group, 1960s to 1970s; Roger McGuinn (1942–) guitarist, born Chicago; Chris Hillman (1942–) bassist, mandolin player, vocalist, born Los Angeles; David Crosby (1941–) vocalist, guitarist; Michael Clarke (1943–93) drummer, born New York City; 'Mr Tambourine Man', 'Eight Miles High', *Mr Tambourine Man* (1965), *Turn, Turn, Turn* (1966), *Fifth Dimension* (1966).

Carey, Mariah (1969–) US singer, born New York City; *Mariah Carey* (1990), *Emotions* (1991), *MTV Unplugged EP* (1992), *Music Box* (1993), *Merry Christmas* (1994), *Daydream* (1995), *Butterfly* (1997).

The Carpenters US group, 1970s to 1980s; members include Karen Carpenter (1950–83) vocalist, drummer; Richard Carpenter (1946–) vocalist, keyboardist; both born New Haven, Connecticut; *Close to You* (1970), *Yesterday Once More* (1974), *Voice of the Heart* (1983), *Only Yesterday* (1990), *Interpretations* (tribute album) (1994).

Cash, Johnny (1932–) US singer/songwriter, guitarist, born Kingsland, Arkansas; 'Don't Take Your Guns to Town', 'Ring of Fire', 'A Boy Named Sue', 'The Man in Black', 'A Thing Called Love', *The Man In Black — The Definitive Collection* (1994).

Charles, Ray (originally **Ray Charles Robinson**) (1930–) US singer/songwriter, pianist, born Albany, Georgia; 'I Got a Woman', 'Lonely Avenue', 'You Are My Sunshine', 'Crying Time', 'Hit the Road, Jack', *The Genius of Ray Charles* (1959), *Heart to Heart — 20 Hot Hits* (1980), *The Collection* (1990).

Cher (originally **Cherilyn Sarkasian La Pierre**) (1946–) US singer/songwriter, born El Centro, California; (with Sonny Bono) 'I Got You Babe', 'Just You', 'All I Ever Need Is You'; 'Gypsys, Tramps and Thieves', 'Half Breed', 'The Shoop Shoop Song', *Love Hurts* (1991), *It's a Man's World* (1995), *Believe* (1998), *Living Proof* (2003).

Clapton, Eric (1945–) British singer/songwriter, guitarist, born Ripley, Surrey; (was in 1960s groups The Yardbirds and Cream); 'Layla', 'Lay Down Sally', 'Wonderful Tonight', 'I Shot the Sheriff', 'Tulsa Time', 'Cocaine', 'I've Got a Rock 'n Roll Heart', *Derek and the Dominos* (with Duane Allman) (1970); *461 Ocean Boulevard* (1974), *Slowhand* (1977), *Just One Night* (1980), *Money and Cigarettes* (1983), *August* (1986), *Journey Man* (1989), *24 Nights* (1991), *Unplugged* (1992), *From The Cradle* (1994), *Reptile* (2001).

The Clash British group, late 1970s to 1980s; members include Joe Strummer (originally John Mellors) (1952–2002) guitarist, vocalist, born Ankara, Turkey; Mick Jones (1955–) guitarist, vocalist, born London; Paul Simonon (1956–) bassist, born Lon-

Arts and Culture

don; 'Topper' Headon (1956–) drummer, born Dover; 'I Fought the Law', 'Rock the Casbah', 'Should I Stay or Should I Go', *The Clash* (1977), *Cost of Living* (1979), *London Calling* (1979), *Combat Rock* (1982), *Cut the Crap* (1985).

Cochran, Eddie (1938–60) US singer, guitarist, born Oklahoma City; 'Three Steps to Heaven', 'Summertime Blues', 'C'mon Everybody', 'Something Else'.

Cocker, Joe (1944–) British singer/songwriter, born Sheffield; 'With a Little Help from My Friends', 'You Are So Beautiful', 'Up Where We Belong' (with Jennifer Warnes), *Mad Dogs and Englishmen* (1970), *I Can Stand a Little Rain* (1974), *Unchain My Heart* (1987), *Night Calls* (1992), *Have a Little Faith* (1997), *Respect Yourself* (2002).

Cohen, Leonard (1934–) Canadian singer/songwriter, guitarist, born Montreal, Quebec; 'Suzanne', 'Famous Blue Raincoat', *Songs of Leonard Cohen* (1968), *Songs of Love and Hate* (1970), *Various Positions* (1984), *I'm Your Man* (1988), *The Future* (1992), *Cohen Live* (1994), *Ten New Songs* (2001).

Cooke, Sam (originally **Sam Cook**) (1935–64) US singer/songwriter, born Chicago, Illinois; 'You Send Me', 'A Change Is Gonna Come', 'Wonderful World', *Sam Cooke at the Copa* (1964).

Cooper, Alice (originally **Vincent Furnier**) (1948–) US singer/songwriter, born Detroit, Michigan; 'School's Out', 'Poison', 'Hey Stoopid', *Love it to Death* (1971), *School's Out* (1972), *Trash* (1989), *Hey Stoopid* (1991), *The Last Temptation* (1994), *Dragontown* (2001).

Costello, Elvis (originally **Declan Patrick McManus**) (1955–) British singer/songwriter, guitarist, born Paddington, London; 'Watching the Detectives', '(I Don't Want To Go To) Chelsea', 'Accidents Will Happen', 'Alison', 'Shipbuilding', 'Every Day I Write the Book', 'Don't Let Me Be Misunderstood', *My Aim is True* (1977), *This Year's Model* (with The Attractions) (1978), *Armed Forces* (1979), *Almost Blue* (1981), *Imperial Bedroom* (1982), *Punch the Clock* (1983), *Goodbye Cruel World* (1984), *King of America* (1986), *Spike* (1989), *Mighty Like a Rose* (1991), *When I Was Cruel* (2002).

Cream British group, late 1960s; members include Eric Clapton (1945–) singer, guitarist; Jack Bruce (1943–) singer, bassist; Ginger Baker (1939–) drummer; 'I Feel Free', 'Sunshine of Your Love', 'Strange Brew', 'Badge', 'Crossroads', *Fresh Cream* (1966), *Disraeli Gears* (1967), *Wheels of Fire* (1968), *Goodbye* (1969).

Creedence Clearwater Revival US group, late 1960s to early 1970s; members include John Cameron Fogerty (1945–) (solo 'Rockin' All Over the World', *Centerfield* (1985)), Tom Fogerty (1941–90), both guitarists and vocalists, born Berkeley, California; Doug Clifford (1945–) drummer, born Palo Alto; Stu Cook (1945–) bassist, born Oakland; 'Susie Q', 'Proud Mary', 'Bad Moon Risin'', 'Green River', 'Born on the Bayou', 'Down on the Corner', 'I Heard it through the Grapevine', 'Fortunate Son', 'Travellin' Band', 'Up, around the Bend', *Creedence Clearwater Revival* (1968), *Pendulum* (1970), *Mardi Gras* (1972).

Crosby, Bing (originally **Harry Lillis**) (1903–77) US singer, born Spokane, Washington; 'Swingin' on a Star', 'White Christmas', 'True Love' (with Grace Kelly).

Crosby, Stills, Nash and Young US group, late 1960s to present; David Crosby (originally David van Cortland) (1941–) guitarist, vocalist, born Los Angeles; Graham Nash (1942–) vocalist, born Blackpool, England; Stephen Stills (1945–) guitarist, vocalist, pianist; Neil Young (1945–) guitarist,

vocalist, pianist; 'Ohio', *Déjà vu* (1970), *Four Way Street* (1971), *Allies* (1983).

Crow, Sheryl (1962–) US singer/songwriter, born Kennett, Missouri; 'Every Day is a Winding Road', 'All I Wanna Do', *Tuesday Night Music Club* (1993), *Sheryl Crow* (1996), *C'mon C'mon* (2002).

Culture Club British group, 1980s; split up 1987, re-formed in 1998; members include Boy George (originally George O'Dowd) (1961–) vocalist, born Eltham; Jon Moss (1957–) drummer, born London; 'Karma Chameleon', *Colour By Numbers* (1983), *Don't Mind if I Do* (1999).

The Cure British group, mid-1970s to present; members include Robert Smith (1957–) guitarist, singer/songwriter, born Crawley, Sussex; Laurence Tolhurst (1959–) drummer, keyboardist; 'Killing an Arab', 'Boys Don't Cry', 'Love Cats', 'The Caterpillar', 'Close to Me', 'Standing on the Beach', 'In Between Days', *Boy's Don't Cry* (1980), *Faith* (1981), *Pornography* (1982), *The Head on the Door* (1985), *Disintegration* (1989), *Mixed Up* (1990), *Entreat* (1991), *Wish* (1992), *Paris* (1993), *Bloodflowers* (2000).

Davis, Sammy, Jr (1925–90) American singer, born New York City; 'Something's Gotta Give', 'That Old Black Magic', 'Candy Man', *Starring Sammy Davis Jr* (1955), *Just for Lovers* (1955), *The Wham of Sam* (1960).

The Dead Kennedys American group, late 1970s to 1980s; members include Jello Biafra (originally Eric Boucher) (1958–) vocalist; East Bay Ray (aka Ray Valium) guitarist; Klaüs Flouride bassist; Ted drummer; 'California Über Alles', 'Kill the Poor', 'Too Drunk to Fuck', 'Holiday in Cambodia', *Fresh Fruit for Rotten Vegetables* (1980), *Plastic Surgery Disaster* (1982), *Frankenchrist* (1985).

Deep Purple British heavy rock group, late 1960s to present; members include Ian Gillan (1945–) vocalist, born Hounslow; David Coverdale (1951–) vocalist, born Saltburn; Ritchie Blackmore (1945–) guitarist, born Weston-super-Mare; Jon Lord (1941–) keyboardist, born Leicester; Roger Glover (1945–) bassist; Ian Paice (1948–) drummer; 'Black Night', 'Smoke on the Water', *Shades of Deep Purple* (1968), *Deep Purple* (1969), *Deep Purple In Rock* (1970), *Machine Head* (1972), *Made in Japan* (1972), *Perfect Strangers* (1984), *The Battle Rages On* (1993), *Abandon* (1998).

Denver, John (originally **John Henry Deutschendorf**) (1943–97) US singer/songwriter, born New Mexico; 'Take Me Home Country Roads', 'Annie's Song', 'I'm Sorry', *Back Home Again* (1974), *An Evening With John Denver* (1975), *Perhaps Love* (1981), *One World* (1986).

Depeche Mode British group, 1980s to present; Andy Fletcher (1961–); Martin Gore (1961–); Vince Clark (1960–); Alan Wilder (1963–) keyboardist; *Speak and Spell* (1981), *Black Celebration* (1986), *Music for the Masses* (1987), *Violator* (1990), *Songs of Faith and Devotion* (1993), *Exciter* (2001).

Devo American group, 1970s to 1980s; Jerry Casale bassist, singer/songwriter; Bob Casale and Mark Mothersbaugh keyboardists, guitarists, vocalists; Bob Mothersbaugh guitarist, vocalist; Alan Myers drummer; 'Satisfaction', 'Whip It', *Q: Are We Not Men? A: We Are Devo!* (1978), *Shout* (1984).

Diamond, Neil (Leslie) (1941–) US singer/songwriter, guitarist, born Coney Island, New York; 'Song Sung Blue', 'You Don't Bring Me Flowers' (with Barbra Streisand), 'Love on the Rocks', *Beautiful Noise* (1976), *The Jazz Singer* (1980), *Heartlight* (1982), *Headed for the Future* (1986), *Lovescape* (1991), *Up On The Roof — Songs From The Brill Building* (1993), *Three Chord Opera* (2001).

Diddley, Bo (originally **Ellas McDaniel**) (1928–) US singer, guitarist, born McComb, Mississippi; 'Bo Diddley'/'I'm a Man', 'Road Runner', 'Do Wah Diddy Diddy', *Got My Own Bag of Tricks* (1971).

Dire Straits British group, late 1970s to 1990s; members include Mark Knopfler (1949–) singer/songwriter, guitarist, born Glasgow (solo soundtrack *Local Hero*); David Knopfler (1951–) guitarist, replaced by Hal Lindes (1953–); John Illsley (1949–) bassist, born London; Pick Withers (1948–) drummer; Alan Clark (1952–) keyboardist; 'Romeo and Juliet', 'Tunnel of Love', 'So Far Away', 'Money for Nothing', 'Walk of Life', *Dire Straits* (1978), *Communiqué* (1979), *Making Movies* (1981), *Love Over Gold* (1983), *Alchemy* (1984), *Brothers in Arms* (1985), *Money for Nothing* (1988), *On Every Street* (1991), *On The Night* (1993).

Domino, Fats (originally **Antoine Domino**) (1928–) US singer, pianist, born New Orleans, Louisiana; 'Every Night About This Time', 'It's Midnight', 'Ain't That a Shame', 'Blue Monday', 'Blueberry Hill'.

The Doors US group, late 1960s to early 1970s; members include Jim Morrison (1943–71), singer/songwriter, born Melbourne, Florida; Ray Manzarek (1939–) keyboardist, born Chicago; Robby Krieger (1946–) guitarist, born Los Angeles; John Densmore (1945–) drummer, born Los Angeles; 'Light My Fire', 'The End', 'When the Music's Over', 'LA Woman', 'Hello, I Love You', 'Five To One', 'Touch Me', 'Riders on the Storm', *The Doors* (1967), *Strange Days* (1967), *Waiting for the Sun* (1968), *LA Woman* (1970), *An American Prayer* (1978), *Alive, She Cried* (1983), *In Concert* (1991).

Duran Duran British group, 1980s to present; members include Simon Le Bon (1958–) vocalist, born Watford, Hertfordshire; Nick Rhodes (originally Nicholas Bates) (1962–) keyboardist, born Birmingham; John Taylor (1960–) bassist, born Birmingham; Roger Taylor (1960–) drummer; Andy Taylor (1961–) guitarist; 'Planet Earth', 'Hungry Like the Wolf', 'Save a Prayer', 'Rio', 'Union of the Snake', 'Wild Boys', *Duran Duran* (1981), *Rio* (1982), *Seven and the Ragged Tiger* (1983), *Arena* (1984), *Notorious* (1986), *Decade* (1989), *Liberty* (1990), *Thankyou* (1995), *Pop Trash* (2000).

Dury, Ian (1942–2000) British singer/songwriter, born Upminster, Essex; (with the Blockheads) 'Sex & Drugs & Rock 'n' Roll', 'Hit Me with your Rhythm Stick', *New Boots and Panties* (1977), *Do It Yourself* (1979), *Laughter* (1980), *Mr Love Pants* (1998).

Dylan, Bob (originally **Robert Allen Zimmerman**) (1941–) US singer/songwriter, guitarist, born Duluth, Minnesota; 'Blowin' in the Wind', 'Mr Tambourine Man', 'Desolation Row', 'Like a Rolling Stone', 'Maggie's Farm', 'All Along the Watchtower', 'Lay Lady Lay', *The Freewheelin' Bob Dylan* (1963), *The Times They Are A-Changin'* (1963), *Another Side of Bob Dylan* (1964), *Bringing It All Back Home* (1965), *Blonde on Blonde* (1966), *John Wesley Harding* (1968), *Nashville Skyline* (1969), *Blood on the Tracks* (1974), *The Basement Tapes* (1975), *Slow Train Coming* (1979), *Infidels* (1983), *World Gone Wrong* (1993), *Time Out of Mind* (1997), *Love and Theft* (2001).

The Eagles US group, 1970s; members include Glenn Frey (1948–) singer, guitarist, born Detroit, Michigan; Don Henley (1947–) singer, drummer, born Texas (solo 'Dirty Laundry', 'Boys of Summer', *Building the Perfect Beast* (1984)); Bernie Leadon (1947–) guitarist replaced by Joe Walsh (1947–) guitarist, singer/songwriter, born Wichita, Kansas (solo 'Life's Been Good', *But Seriously Folks* (1976), *Got Any Gum?* (1987)); Randy Meisner (1946–) bassist, born Nebraska; 'Best of My Love', 'Lyin' Eyes', 'New Kid in Town', 'Heartache Tonight', *Eagles* (1972), *Desperado* (1973), *One of these Nights* (1975), *Hotel California* (1976), *The Long Run* (1979), *Eagles Live* (1980), *Hell Freezes Over* (1994).

Earth, Wind and Fire US group, 1970s to present; Maurice White (1941–) vocalist, drummer, born Memphis, Tennessee; Verdine White (1951–) bassist; Philip Bailey (1951–) vocalist, born Denver, Colorado; Larry Dunn (1953–) keyboardist, born Colorado; Johnny Graham (1951–) guitarist, born Kentucky; Al McKay (1948–) guitarist, born Louisiana; Andre Woolfolk (1950–) reeds, born Texas; Ralph Johnson (1951–) drummer, born California; 'Shining Star', 'Got to Get you into My Life', 'Boogie Wonderland', *Open Our Eyes* (1974), *That's The Way of the World* (1975), *In the Name of Love* (1997).

Electric Light Orchestra British group, 1970s to 1980s; members include Jeff Lynne (1947–) guitarist, vocalist; Roy Wood (1946–) guitarist, vocalist; Bev Bevan (1946–) drummer; all born Birmingham; 'Roll Over Beethoven', 'Evil Woman', 'Hold On Tight', 'Mr Blue Sky', 'Last Train to London', 'Calling America', *Xanadu* (1980), *Balance Of Power* (1986).

Eno, Brian (1948–) British singer/songwriter, keyboardist, born Woodbridge, Suffolk (was in early 1970s Roxy Music line-up); *My Life In the Bush Of Ghosts* (with David Byrne) (1981), *More Net* (1992), *Wah Wah* (1994), *Spinner* (1995), *Sonora Portraits* (1999).

Eurythmics British group, 1980s to present; members include David Allan Stewart (1952–) songwriter, keyboardist, guitarist, born Sunderland, England; Annie Lennox (1954–) singer/songwriter, born Aberdeen, Scotland; 'Love is a Stranger', 'Who's that Girl?', 'Here Comes the Rain Again', 'Sexcrime', 'Thorn in My Side', 'It's Alright (Baby's Coming Back)', 'Sisters are Doin' it for Themselves' (with Aretha Franklin), 'When Tomorrow Comes', *Sweet Dreams are Made of This* (1982), *Touch* (1983), *1984* (1984), *Be Yourself Tonight* (1985), *Revenge* (1986), *Savage* (1987), *We Too are One* (1989), *Peace* (1999).

The Everly Brothers US group, 1960s; Don (1937–), Phil (1939–), born Brownie, Kentucky; 'Bye Bye Love', 'Little Susie', 'Dream', *EB 84* (1984).

Ferry, Bryan (1945–) British singer, born Washington, County Durham (was founder-member of Roxy Music, 1970); 'Tokyo Joe', 'The Price of Love', 'Slave to Love', 'Don't Stop the Dance', *Boys and Girls* (1985), *Bête Noire* (1987), *Taxi* (1993), *Mamouna* (1994), *Frantic* (2002).

Flack, Roberta (1939–) US singer/songwriter, pianist; 'Killing Me Softly With His Song', 'Back Together Again', 'Tonight I Celebrate My Love', *And Donny Hathaway* (1972), *Killing Me Softly* (1973), *Born To Love* (1983).

Fleetwood Mac Anglo-US group, late 1960s to present; members include Peter Green (originally Peter Greenbaum) (1946–) singer/songwriter, guitarist, born London; Mick Fleetwood (1942–) drummer, born Redruth, Cornwall; John McVie (1945–) bassist; Christine McVie (1943–) singer, keyboardist; Lindsey Buckingham (1947–) singer, guitarist, born Palo Alto, California; Stevie (Stephanie) Nicks (1948–) singer/songwriter, born Phoenix, Arizona (solo *Bella Donna* (1982), *The Wild Heart* (1983), *Rock A Little* (1985)); 'Albatross', 'Oh Well', 'Big Love', 'Little Lies', *Fleetwood Mac* (1975), *Rumours* (1977), *Mirage* (1982), *Tango in*

Arts and Culture

the Night (1987), Behind The Mask (1990), Time (1995), The Dance (1997), Say You Will (2003).

Frankie Goes to Hollywood British group, early 1980s; Holly Johnson (1960–) and Paul Rutherford (1959–) vocalists; Mark O'Toole (1964–) bassist; Peter Gill (1960–) drummer; Brian Nash (1963–) guitarist; 'Relax!', 'Two Tribes', 'The Power of Love', 'Ferry Across the Mersey', Welcome to the Pleasure Dome (1984).

Franklin, Aretha (1942–) US singer, born Memphis, Tennessee; 'Think', 'Respect', I Never Loved A Man The Way I Love You (1967), Lady Soul (1968), Amazing Grace (1972), Everything I Feel in Me (1974), Almighty Fire (1978), Aretha (1980), Love All The Hurt Away (1981), Get It Right (1983), Through The Storm (1989), Love Songs (2001).

Gaye, Marvin (Pentz) (1939–84) US singer/songwriter, pianist, drummer, born Washington, DC; 'Hitch Hike', 'Can I Get a Witness', 'I Heard it through the Grapevine', 'What's Goin' On', 'Sexual Healing', What's Goin' On (1971), Let's Get it On (1973), Here My Dear (1979), In Our Lifetime (1981), Midnight Love (1982).

Genesis British group, late 1960s to present; members include (at various times) Peter Gabriel (1950–) singer/songwriter, born Cobham, Surrey (solo 'Games without Frontiers', 'Sledgehammer', So (1986)); Phil Collins (1951–) singer/songwriter, drummer, born London (solo 'You Can't Hurry Love', 'One More Night', Face Value (1981), No Jacket Required (1985)); Tony Banks (1950–) keyboardist; Michael Rutherford (1950–) guitarist, bassist, vocalist; Selling England by the Pound (1973), Nursery Cryme (1971), The Lamb Lies Down on Broadway (1974), Duke (1980), Abacab (1981), Genesis (1983), Invisible Touch (1986), We Can't Dance (1991), Turn it On Again (1999).

The Grateful Dead US group, late 1960s to present; members include Jerry Garcia (originally Jerome Garcia) (1942–95) guitarist, born San Francisco, California; 'Dark Star', Live Dead (1970), Europe (1972), Blues for Allah (1975), In the Dark (1987), Dylan and the Dead (with Bob Dylan) (1988).

Guns n' Roses US group, late 1980s to present; W Axl Rose (1962–) singer; Slash (1965–) guitarist; Matt Sorum (1960–) drummer; 'Sweet Child O' Mine', 'Welcome to the Jungle', 'Night Train', 'Patience', 'You Could Be Mine', Appetite for Destruction (1987), G N' R Lies (1988), The Spaghetti Incident? (1993), Live Era '87–'93 (1999).

Haley, Bill (1925–81) US singer/songwriter, guitarist, born Highland Park, Michigan; (with The Comets) 'Crazy Man Crazy', 'Shake Rattle and Roll', 'Rock Around the Clock', 'See You Later, Alligator', 'Rudy's Rock'.

Harrison, George (1943–2001) British singer/songwriter, guitarist, born Liverpool; 'My Sweet Lord', 'All Those Years Ago', 'Got My Mind Set On You', 'When We Was Fab', All Things Must Pass (1970), Cloud Nine (1987), Brainwashed (posthumously, 2002).

Hendrix, Jimi (originally **James Marshall Hendrix**) (1942–70) US singer/songwriter, guitarist, born Seattle, Washington; (with the Experience) 'Voodoo Chile', 'Hey Joe', 'Purple Haze', 'The Wind Cries Mary', 'Crosstown Traffic', 'All Along the Watchtower', Are You Experienced? (1967), Axis: Bold As Love (1968), Electric Ladyland (1968).

The Hollies British group, 1960s to present; members include Allan Clarke (1942–) vocalist, born Salford; Graham Nash (1942–) guitarist, vocalist, born Blackpool replaced by Terry Sylvester (1945–) born Liverpool; Tony Hicks (1943–) gui-

tarist, born Nelson; Eric Haydock (1943–) bassist, born Stockport replaced by Bernie Calvert (1943–) born Burnley; Bobby Elliott (1943–) drummer, born Burnley; 'Searchin', 'Just One Look', 'He Ain't Heavy, He's My Brother', 'The Air That I Breathe', 'Stop In the Name of Love'.

Holly, Buddy (originally **Charles Hardin Holley**) (1936–59) US singer/songwriter, guitarist, violinist, born Lubbock, Texas; (with The Crickets) 'That'll Be the Day', 'Oh Boy!', 'Not Fade Away', 'Peggy Sue', 'Every Day', 'Rave On', 'Peggy Sue Got Married'.

Houston, Whitney (1963–) US singer, born Newark, New Jersey; 'Saving All My Love For You', 'How Will I Know', 'Greatest Love', 'I Wanna Dance With Somebody (Who Loves Me)', 'Where Do Broken Hearts Go', 'My Name is Not Susan', Whitney Houston (1985), Whitney (1987), I'm Your Baby Tonight (1990), The Bodyguard (1992) (soundtrack), The Preacher's Wife (1996) (soundtrack), My Love is Your Love (1998), Just Whitney (2002).

The Human League British group, late 1970s to present; members include Philip Oakey (1955–) singer; Susanne Sully (1963–) singer; Joanne Catherall (1962–) singer; Ian Burden (1957–) bassist; Jo Callis (1951–) guitarist; 'Don't You Want Me' (1981), '(Keep Feeling) Fascination', 'Mirror Man', 'Louise', Dare (1981), Crash (1986), Romantic? (1990), Octopus (1995).

INXS Australian group, 1980s to 1990s; Michael Hutchence (1960–97) singer, born Sydney; Andrew Farriss (1959–) keyboardist; John Farriss (1961–) drummer; Tim Farriss (1957–) guitarist; Kirk Pengilly (1958–) guitarist, saxophonist; Garry Beers (1957–) drummer; 'Original Sin', 'This Time', 'Never Tear Us Apart', 'Need You Tonight', Shabooh Shoobah (1982), The Swing (1984), Listen Like Thieves (1985), Kick (1987), X (1990), Live Baby Live (1991), Welcome To Wherever You Are (1992), Full Moon, Dirty Hearts (1993).

Iron Maiden British heavy metal group, mid-1970s to present; members include Steve Harris (1957–) bassist, born Leytonstone, London; Dave Murray (1958–) guitarist, born Clapham, London; Adrian Smith (1957–) guitarist, born London; Paul Di'Anno (1959–) singer, born Chingford, Essex replaced by Bruce Dickinson (1958–) born Sheffield; Nicko McBain (1954–) drummer, born London; 'Running Free', 'Run to the Hills', Iron Maiden (1980), The Number of the Beast (1982), Power Slave (1984), Live After Death (1985), Somewhere In Time (1986), Seventh Son of a Seventh Son (1988), Running Free/Sanctuary (1990), Fear of the Dark (1992), The X Factor (1995), Brave New World (2000).

The Isley Brothers US group; Kelly (originally O'Kelly) (1937–86), Rudolph (1939–), Ronald (1941–) Isley; all born Cincinnati, Ohio; 'Shout', 'Twist and Shout', 'This Old Heart of Mine (Is Weak For You)', Harvest for the World (1976).

Jackson, Michael (Joe) (1958–) US singer/songwriter, born Gary, Indiana; (was in The Jacksons, American group, 1960s to 1970s); 'Billy Jean', 'Beat It', 'The Girl is Mine', 'Say Say Say' (with Paul McCartney); 'I Can't Stop Loving You' (with Siedah Garrett), Ben (1972), Off the Wall (1979), Thriller (1982), Bad (1987), Dangerous (1991), History — Past Present and Future Book 1 (1995), Blood on the Dancefloor (2000).

The Jam British group, mid-1970s to early 1980s; members include Paul Weller (1958–) singer/songwriter, guitarist, born Woking, Surrey (solo Stanley Road (1995), Heliocentric (2000)); Bruce

Foxton (1955–) bassist, born Woking; Rick Butler (1955–) drummer; 'Going Underground', 'Eton Rifles', 'Town Called Malice', 'Beat Surrender', 'Dream of Children'.

Jarre, Jean-Michel (1948–) French keyboardist, composer, born Lyons; *Oxygène* (1977), *Equinoxe* (1978), *Magnetic Fields* (1981), *The Concerts In China* (1982), *Rendez Vous* (1986), *Revolutions* (1988), *Waiting For Cousteau* (1990), *Chronologie* (1993), *Chronologie Part 6* (1994), *Metamorphoses* (2000).

Joel, Billy (originally **William Martin Joel**) (1949–) US singer/songwriter, pianist, born Hicksville, Long Island, New York; 'Say Goodbye to Hollywood', 'Just The Way You Are', 'My Life', 'It's Still Rock 'n' Roll to Me', 'Tell Her About it', 'Uptown Girl', 'We Didn't Start the Fire', *The Stranger* (1977), *52nd Street* (1978), *Glass House* (1980), *The Nylon Curtain* (1982), *An Innocent Man* (1983), *The Bridge* (1986), *Storm Front* (1989), *River of Dreams* (1993).

John, Sir Elton (originally **Reginald Kenneth Dwight**) (1947–) British singer/songwriter, pianist, born Pinner, Middlesex; 'Your Song', 'Crocodile Rock', 'Don't Go Breakin' My Heart' (with Kiki Dee), 'Little Jeannie', 'Candle In The Wind', 'Wrap Her Up', 'Nikita', 'Sacrifice', 'Candle In The Wind' (rewritten version for the late Princess Diana's funeral), *Tumbleweed Connection* (1970), *Don't Shoot Me, I'm Only The Piano Player* (1973), *Goodbye Yellow Brick Road* (1973), *A Single Man* (1979), *Too Low for Zero*, *Ice on Fire* (1985), *Sleeping With The Past* (1989), *The One* (1992), *Duets* (1993), *Made In England* (1995), *One Night Only* (2000).

Jones, Grace (1952–) Jamaican singer/songwriter, born Jamaica, West Indies; 'Private Life', 'Love is the Drug', 'Pull up to the Bumper', 'Slave to the Rhythm', *Island Life* (1983), *Inside Story* (1986).

Jones, Tom (originally **Thomas Jones Woodward**) (1940–) British singer, drummer, born Pontypridd, S Wales; 'It's Not Unusual', 'What's New, Pussycat?', 'Green Green Grass of Home', 'I'll Never Fall In Love Again', 'Delilah', *After Dark* (1989), *Carrying a Torch* (1991), *The Lead and How To Swing It* (1994), *Reload* (1999), *Mr Jones* (2002).

Joplin, Janis (1943–70) US singer/songwriter, born Port Arthur, Texas; 'Piece of My Heart', *Cheap Thrills* (1968), *I Got Dem Ol' Kozmic Blues Again, Mama!* (1969), *Pearl* (1971).

Khan, Chaka (originally **Yvette Marie Stevens**) (1953–) US singer/songwriter, born Great Lakes, Illinois; (with Rufus) *Rags to Rufus* (1974); *Chaka* (1978), *I Feel For You* (1984), *Destiny* (1986), *Life is a Dance — The Remix Project* (1989).

King, B B (originally **Riley B King**) (1925–) US guitarist, singer/songwriter, born Itta Bena, near Indianola, Mississippi; *Live at the Regal* (1965), *Confessin' the Blues* (1966), *Blues Is King* (1967), *Indianola Mississippi Seeds* (1970), *Live in Stock County Jail* (1971), *There Must Be A Better World Somewhere* (1981), *Six Silver Strings* (1985).

King, Ben E (originally **Benjamin Earl Nelson**) (1938–) US singer, born Henderson, North Carolina; 'Stand By Me'.

King, Carole (originally **Carole Klein**) (1942–) US singer/songwriter; 'It Might As Well Rain Until September', 'It's Too Late', 'You've Got A Friend', 'Will You Love Me Tomorrow', *Tapestry* (1971), *Wrap Around Joy* (1974), *Pearls* (1980).

The Kinks British group, 1960s to 1980s; Ray Davies (1944–) singer/songwriter, guitarist (solo 'A Quiet Life'); Dave Davies (1947–) singer, guitarist; both born Muswell Hill, London; Mike Avory (1944–) drummer, born Hampton, Middlesex; Peter Quaife (1943–) bassist, born Tavistock, Devon; 'You Really Got Me', 'All Day and All of the Night', 'Dedicated Follower of Fashion', 'Sunny Afternoon', 'Waterloo Sunset', 'Autumn Almanac', 'Lola', 'Come Dancing', 'Don't Forget to Dance', *Village Green Preservation Society* (1968), *Lola vs Powerman & The Moneyground Pt 1* (1970), *State of Confusion* (1983).

Kiss US group, 1970s to present; members include Paul Stanley (originally Paul Stanley Eisen) (1952–) guitarist, born New York City; Gene Simmons (originally Gene Klein) (1949–) bassist, born Haffa, Israel; Peter Criss (originally Peter Crisscoula) (1947–) drummer, born New York City; Ace (Paul) Frehley (1951–) guitarist, born New York City; 'Rock and Roll All Nite', 'Beth', 'I was Made for Lovin' You', 'Tears are Fallin'', *Dressed to Kill* (1975), *Double Platinum* (1978), *Lick It Up* (1983), *Crazy Nights* (1987), *Revenge* (1992), *Alive* (1993).

Knight, Gladys (1944–) US singer, band leader (The Pips, American group, late 1960s), born Atlanta, Georgia; (with The Pips) 'I Heard It Through The Grapevine', 'Help Me Make It Through The Night', 'Midnight Train To Georgia', 'On And On', *Imagination* (1973), *Visions* (1983), *Life* (1985).

Kraftwerk German group, 1970s to present; Ralph Hutter (1946–) and Florian Schneider (1947–); 'Radio Activity', 'The Model', 'Trans Europe Express', 'Computer Love', 'Tour de France', *Autobahn* (1975), *Man Machine* (1978), *Computer World* (1981), *Trans Europe Express* (1982), *The Mix* (1991).

lang, k d (Katheryn Dawn) (1962–) Canadian singer, born Alberta; *A Truly Western Experience* (1983); *Shadowland* (1988); *Absolute Torch and Twang* (1989), *Ingenue* (1992), *Even Cowgirls Get The Blues* (1993, soundtrack), *All You Can Eat* (1995), *Drag* (1997), *Invincible Summer* (2000).

Led Zeppelin British group, late 1960s to 1980s; members include Jimmy Page (1944–) guitarist, born Heston, London; Robert Plant (1948–) vocalist, born Bromwich, Staffordshire; John Paul Jones (originally John Baldwin) (1946–) bassist, born Sidcup; John Bonham (1948–80) drummer, born Redditch; *Led Zeppelin I* (1969), *Led Zeppelin II* (1970), *Led Zeppelin III* (1970), *Led Zeppelin IV* (1971), *Houses of the Holy* (1973), *Physical Graffiti* (1975), *In Through The Out Door* (1979), *Coda* (1982), *Remasters* (1990), *BBC Sessions* (1997).

Lee, Peggy (originally **Norma Delores Egstrom**) (1920–2002) US singer, born Jamestown, North Dakota; 'Manana', 'Fever'.

Lennon, John Winston (1940–80) British singer/songwriter, guitarist, keyboardist, born Liverpool; 'Give Peace A Chance', 'Working Class Hero', 'Jealous Guy', 'Merry Xmas (War Is Over)', 'Whatever Gets You Through The Night', *Imagine* (1971), *Rock 'n' Roll* (1975), *Double Fantasy* (1980).

Lewis, Jerry Lee (1935–) US pianist, singer, born Ferriday, Louisiana; 'Great Balls of Fire', 'Whole Lotta Shakin' Goin' On', 'High School Confidential', 'Breathless'.

Little Richard (originally **Richard Wayne Penniman**) (1935–) US singer/songwriter, pianist, born Macon, Georgia; 'Tutti Frutti', 'Long Tall Sally', 'Rip It Up', 'The Girl Can't Help It', 'Lucille', 'Jenny, Jenny', 'Good Golly, Miss Molly', 'Lawdy Miss Clawdy', *Life Time Friend* (1986).

Lynyrd Skynyrd US group, 1970s; reformed late 1990s; members include Ronnie Van Zandt (1949–77) vocalist, born McCombe, Minnesota;

Arts and Culture

'Sweet Home Alabama', 'Freebird', *Pronounced Leh-nerd Skin-nerd* (1973), *Second Helping* (1974), *Street Survivors* (1977), *Gold and Platinum* (1979), *Edge of Forever* (1999).

McCartney, Sir Paul (1942–) British singer/songwriter, guitarist, born Liverpool; 'Wonderful Christmastime', 'Coming Up', 'Ebony and Ivory' (with Stevie Wonder), 'No More Lonely Nights', *Tug of War* (1982), *Pipes of Peace* (1983), *Give My Regards To Broad Street* (1984), *Flowers In The Dirt* (1989), *Off The Ground* (1993), *Flaming Pie* (1997), *Driving Rain* (2001).

McLean, Don (1945–) US singer/songwriter, born New Rochelle, New York; 'And I Love You So', 'Vincent', 'Castles in the Air', *American Pie* (1971), *Chain Lightning* (1981), *Dominion* (1983).

Madness British group, late 1970s to 1990s; members include Graham 'Suggs' McPherson (1961–) vocalist, born Hastings, Sussex; Mike Barson (1958–) keyboardist, Lee Thompson (1957–) saxophonist; Chris Foreman (1958–) guitarist; Mark Bedford (1961–) bassist; Daniel 'Woody' Woodgate (1960–) drummer; Chas Smash (originally Carl Smith) (1959–) vocalist, trumpeter; 'House Of Fun', 'Our House', 'Baggy Trousers', 'Ghost Train', *One Step Beyond* (1979), *Complete Madness* (1982), *Mad Not Mad* (1985), *Utter Madness* (1986).

Madonna (originally **Madonna Louise Veronica Ciccone**) (1958–) US singer/songwriter, born Rochester, Michigan; 'Holiday', 'Crazy For You', 'Gambler', 'Into The Groove', 'Live To Tell', 'Vogue', *Madonna* (1983), *Like a Virgin* (1984), *True Blue* (1986), *Who's that Girl?* (1987), *Like a Prayer* (1989), *The Immaculate Collection* (1990), *Erotica* (1992), *Bedtime Stories* (1994), *Something to Remember* (1995), *Ray of Light* (1998), *Music* (2000).

The Mamas and the Papas US group, late 1960s; members include John Philips (1935–) singer/songwriter, guitarist, born Parris Island, South Carolina; Dennis Doherty (1941–) born Halifax, Nova Scotia; Michelle Phillips (originally Holly Michelle Gilliam) (1944–) born Long Beach, California; 'Mama' Cass Elliot (originally Ellen Naomi Cohen) (1943–74) vocalist, born Baltimore, Maryland; 'California Dreamin'', 'Monday, Monday', 'Dedicated to the One I Love', 'San Francisco'.

Manfred Mann British group, 1960s to 1980s; members include Manfred Mann (originally Michael Lubowitz) (1940–) keyboardist, born Johannesburg, South Africa; Paul Jones (originally Paul Pond) (1942–) vocalist, harmonica player, born Portsmouth; '5-4-3-2-1', 'Do Wah Diddy Diddy', 'If You Gotta Go, Go Now', 'The Mighty Quinn', 'Pretty Flamingo', 'Blinded By The Light', *The Roaring Silence* (1986), *Ages of Mann* (1993).

Manilow, Barry (originally **Barry Alan Pincus**) (1946–) US singer/songwriter, pianist, born Brooklyn, New York City; 'Mandy', 'I Write the Songs', 'Looks Like We Made It', 'Copacabana (At the Copa)', *Barry Manilow* (1974), *Barry Manilow II* (1975), *Barry Manilow Live* (1977), *Even Now* (1978), *A Touch More Magic* (1983), *Showstoppers* (1991), *Summer of '78* (1996), *Ultimate Manilow* (2002).

Marley, Bob (originally **Robert Nesta Marley**) (1945–81) Jamaican singer/songwriter, guitarist, born Rhoden Hall, St Ann's Parish, Jamaica; (with The Wailers) 'No Woman, No Cry', 'I Shot the Sheriff', 'Exodus', 'Buffalo Soldier', *Catch a Fire* (1972), *Rastaman Vibration* (1976), *Uprising* (1980).

Mayall, John (1933–) British singer/songwriter, guitarist, harmonica player, born Macclesfield; *Bluesbreakers — John Mayall with Eric Clapton* (1965), *Crusader* (1967), *A Hard Road* (1967), *The Turning Point* (1970), *Wake Up Call* (1993), *Stories* (2002).

Michael, George (originally **Yorgos Kyriatou Panayiotou**) (1963–) British singer/songwriter (was in Wham!, British 1980s group), born Finchley, London; 'Careless Whisper', 'Different Corner', 'I Want Your Sex', *Faith* (1987), *Listen Without Prejudice Vol 1* (1990), *Older* (1996), *Songs from the Last Century* (1999).

Midler, Bette (1945–) US singer, born Honolulu, Hawaii; 'From A Distance', *The Divine Miss M* (1972), *The Rose* (1979), *No Frills* (1983), *Bette of Roses* (1995), *Bette* (2000).

Miller, Steve (1943–) US singer/songwriter, guitarist, born Milwaukee, Wisconsin; 'Rock'n' Me', *The Joker* (1973), *Fly Like An Eagle* (1976), *Abracadabra* (1982), *Living In The 20th Century* (1986).

Minogue, Kylie (1968–) Australian singer, born Melbourne; 'I Should Be So Lucky', 'Spinning Around', *Kylie* (1987), *Enjoy Yourself* (1989), *Rhythm of Love* (1990), *Kylie Minogue* (1994), *Light Years* (2000), *Fever* (2001).

Mitchell, Joni (originally **Roberta Joan Anderson**) (1943–) Canadian singer/songwriter, guitarist, born McLeod, Alberta; 'Big Yellow Taxi', 'Help Me', *Joni Mitchell* (1968), *Clouds* (1969), *Ladies of the Canyon* (1970), *Blue* (1971), *Dog Eat Dog* (1986), *Chalk Mark in a Rain Storm* (1988), *Night Ride Home* (1991), *Turbulent Indigo* (1994), *Travelogue* (2002).

The Monkees US group, late 1960s; members include Mickey Dolenz (1945–) vocalist, drummer, born Los Angeles; Davy Jones (1946–) vocalist, born Manchester, England; Peter Tork (originally Peter Torkelson) (1944–) bassist, born Washington, DC; Mike Nesmith (1942–) guitarist; 'I'm a Believer', 'Daydream Believer', *Pool It* (1987).

The Moody Blues British group, mid-1960s to 1990s; members include Justin Hayward (1946–) guitarist, John Lodge (1945–) bassist; Mike Pinder (1941–) keyboardist; Graeme Edge (1941–) drummer; Ray Thomas (1941–) flautist, saxophonist, vocalist; 'Nights in White Satin', *Days of Future Passed* (1967), *Keys To The Kingdom* (1991).

Morrison, Van (originally **George Ivan Morrison**) (1945–) Northern Irish singer/songwriter, guitarist, born Belfast; (with Them Irish group, 1960s) 'Baby Please Don't Go', 'Brown Eyed Girl', *Blowin' Your Mind* (1967), *Enlightenment* (1990), *Hymns To The Silence* (1991), *Too Long in Exile* (1993), *Days Like This* (1995), *Down the Road* (2002).

Motörhead British heavy metal group, late 1970s to present; members include Lemmy (originally Ian Kilminster) (1945–) vocalist, born Stoke-on-Trent; *Overkill* (1979), *Bomber* (1979), *Ace of Spades* (1980), *No Sleep 'Til Hammersmith* (1981), *Orgasmatron* (1986), *No Sleep At All* (1988), *1916* (1991), *Everything Louder than Everyone Else* (1999).

Nelson, Ricky (originally **Eric Hilliard Nelson**) (1940–85) US singer, guitarist, born Teaneck, New Jersey; 'Travelin' Man', 'Hello Mary Lou', *Garden Party* (1972).

Newman, Randy (originally **Randolph Newman**) (1944–) US singer/songwriter, pianist, born Los Angeles; 'I Love LA', 'Gone Dead Train', *Sail Away* (1972), *Trouble In Paradise* (1983), *The Natural* (1984) (soundtrack), *Parenthood* (1990) (soundtrack), *Awakenings* (1991) (soundtrack), *Toy Story* (1996) (soundtrack), *Meet the Parents* (2000) (soundtrack).

Nirvana US group, late 1980s to mid-1990s; members include Kurt Cobain (1967–94) vocalist, guitarist, born Aberdeen, Washington; Krist Novoselic (1965–) bassist, born Croatia; Dave Grohl

(1969–) drummer, born Warren, Ohio; 'Smells like Teen Spirit', *Nevermind* (1991), *Unplugged in New York* (1994).

Oasis British group, formed Manchester 1992 as Rain; members include Liam Gallagher (1972–) vocalist; Noel Gallagher (1967–) guitarist; Paul 'Bonehead' Arthurs (1965–) guitarist; Paul McGuigan (1971–) guitarist; Tony McCarroll drummer; *Definitely Maybe* (1994), *(What's The Story) Morning Glory* (1995), *Be Here Now* (1997), *Heathen Chemistry* (2002).

Oldfield, Mike (1953–) British multi-instrumentalist, composer, born Reading, Berkshire; 'Blue Peter', 'Moonlight Shadow', *Tubular Bells* (1973), *Hergest Ridge* (1974), *Ommadawn* (1975), *Killing Fields* (1984), *Islands* (1987), *The Songs of Distant Earth* (1994), *Voyager* (1996), *Tres Lunas* (2002).

Orbison, Roy (1936–88) US singer/songwriter, guitarist, born Vernon, Texas; 'Only the Lonely', 'Crying', 'Dream Baby', '(Oh) Pretty Woman', 'In Dreams', 'Blue Bayou'.

The Osmonds US group, 1970s; members include Alan (1949–), Wayne (1951–), Merrill (1953–), Jay (1955–), Donny (originally Donald Clark Osmond) (1957–), and Marie Osmond (1959–); all born Ogden, Utah; Jimmy (1963–) born Canoga Park, California, 'Crazy Horses'.

Palmer, Robert (1949–) British singer, born W Yorkshire, England; 'Every Kinda People', 'Bad Case Of Loving You (Doctor Doctor)', 'Some Guys Have All The Luck', 'Addicted To Love', 'She Makes My Day', *Riptide* (1985).

Peter, Paul and Mary US trio, 1960s to 1980s; Peter Yarrow (1938–) guitarist, vocalist, born New York City; Paul Stookey (1937–) guitarist, vocalist, born Baltimore, Maryland; Mary Travers (1937–) vocalist, born Louisville, Kentucky; 'If I Had A Hammer', 'Blowin' In The Wind', 'Puff The Magic Dragon', 'Leavin' On A Jet Plane', *Peter, Paul & Mary* (1962), *In The Wind* (1963), *Peter, Paul & Mommy* (1969), *No Easy Walk To Freedom* (1986).

Pickett, Wilson (1941–) US singer, born Prattville, Alabama; 'In The Midnight Hour', '634-5789', 'Hey Jude'.

Pink Floyd British group, late 1960s to present; members include 'Syd' (Roger Keith) Barrett (1946–) singer/songwriter, guitarist; Roger Waters (1944–) singer/songwriter; David Gilmour (1944–) singer/songwriter, guitarist; all born Cambridge; *The Piper at the Gates of Dawn* (1967), *A Saucerful of Secrets* (1968), *Ummagumma* (1969), *Meddle* (1971), *Dark Side of the Moon* (1973), *Wish You Were Here* (1975), *The Wall* (1979), *The Final Cut* (1983), *A Momentary Lapse of Reason* (1987), *A Delicate Sound of Thunder* (1988), *The Division Bell* (1994), *Pulse* (1995), *Echoes* (2001).

Pitney, Gene (1941–) US singer, born Hartford, Connecticut; 'The Man Who Shot Liberty Valance', '24 Hours From Tulsa'.

The Pogues Anglo-Irish group, 1980s to 1990s; members include Shane MacGowan vocalist, Philip Chevron (originally Philip Ryan) (1957–) guitarist, born Dublin; James Fearnley (1954–) accordionist, born Manchester; Andrew Ranken (1953–) drummer, born London; Jem Finer (originally Jeremy Max Finer) (1955–) banjo player, born Dublin; Spider Stacy (originally Peter Richard Stacy) (1958–) tin whistle player, born Eastbourne; 'Dirty Old Town', 'Sally Maclennane', 'A Pair of Brown Eyes', 'Irish Rover' (with the Dubliners), *Red Roses For Me* (1984), *Rum, Sodomy & The Lash* (1985), *If I Should Fall From Grace With God* (1988), *Peace and Love*

(1989), *Hell's Ditch* (1990), *Waiting For Herb* (1993).

The Pointer Sisters US group, 1970s to 1980s; Ruth (1946–), Anita (1948–), Bonnie (1950–), June (1954–) Pointer; all born Oakland, California; 'Fairy Tale', 'Fire', 'Slow Hand', 'Jump (For My Love)', 'Automatic', 'Neutron Dance', *So Excited!* (1982), *Break Out* (1983), *Serious Slammin'* (1988).

The Police British group, late 1970s to 1980s; members include Sting (originally Gordon Sumner) (1951–), singer/songwriter, bassist, born Wallsend, Northumberland (solo 'Set Them Free', 'Russians', 'Desert Rose', *The Dream of the Blue Turtles* (1985), *Nothing Like The Sun* (1987), *Brand New Day* (1999)); Stewart Copeland (1952–) drummer, born Alexandria, Virginia; Andy Summers (1942–) guitarist, born Lancaster; 'Can't Stand Losing You', 'Roxanne', 'Message In A Bottle', 'Walking On The Moon', 'Don't Stand So Close To Me', 'Every Little Thing She Does Is Magic', 'Every Breath You Take', *Outlandos d'Amour* (1978), *Regatta de Blanc* (1979), *Zenyatta Mondatta* (1980), *Ghost in the Machine* (1981), *Synchronicity* (1983).

Pop, Iggy (originally **James Newell Osterburg**) (1947–) US singer/songwriter, drummer, born Ypsilanti, Michigan; 'I Wanna Be Your Dog', *The Stooges* (1969), *Raw Power* (1973) (with the Stooges); 'Nightclubbing', 'The Passenger', 'Real Wild Child', 'Well Did You Evah' (with Deborah Harry), *The Idiot* (1976), *Lust for Life* (1977), *Blah Blah Blah* (1986), *Instinct* (1988), *Brick By Brick* (1990), *American Caesar* (1993), *A Damned Stooge With A Pistol* (1997).

Presley, Elvis (Aaron) (1935–77) US singer, guitarist, born Tupelo, Mississippi; 'Heartbreak Hotel', 'Hound Dog', 'Love Me Tender', 'All Shook Up', 'Jailhouse Rock', 'One Night', 'A Fool Such as I', 'It's Now or Never', 'Are You Lonesome Tonight', *G I Blues* (1961), *Blue Hawaii* (1961), *Roustabout* (1964), *From Elvis in Memphis* (1969).

The Pretenders British group, late 1970s to present; members include Chrissie Hynde (1951–) singer/songwriter, guitarist, born Akron, Ohio; 'Back on the Chain Gang', 'Brass in Pocket', *Pretenders* (1979), *Single Records* (1988), *Packed!* (1990), *Last Independents* (1994), *The Isle Of View* (1995), ¡Viva El Amor! (1999).

Prince (originally **Prince Rogers Nelson**) (1958–) US singer/songwriter, guitarist, keyboardist, drummer, born Minneapolis, Minnesota; 'Little Red Corvette', 'Delirious', 'When Doves Cry', 'Let's Go Crazy', 'Raspberry Beret', 'Kiss', *Prince* (1979), *Dirty Mind* (1980), *Controversy* (1981), *1999* (1982), *Purple Rain* (with The Revolution) (1984), *Around The World In A Day* (1985), *Parade* (1986), *Sign o' the Times* (1987), *Love Sexy* (1988), *Batman* (1989) (soundtrack), *Diamonds and Pearls* (1991), *Symbol* (1992), *Come* (1994), *The Gold Experience* (1995).

Public Enemy US group, 1980s to present; members include Chuck D (originally Carlton Ridenhour) (1960–) vocalist; Flavor Flav (originally William Drayton) (1959–) vocalist, instrumentalist; Terminator X (originally Norman Rogers) (1966–) DJ; Professor Griff (originally Richard Griffin) (1960–) vocalist; *Yo! Bum Rush the Show* (1987), *Fear of a Black Planet* (1990), *He Got Game* (soundtrack) (1998).

Public Image Limited (PIL) British group, late 1970s to present; members include John Lyndon (1956–); 'This Is Not A Love Song', 'Rise', *Flowers Of Romance* (1981), *Album* (1986), *The Greatest Hits So Far* (1990), *That What Is Not* (1992).

Pulp British group, formed Sheffield 1981 as Arabacus Pulp; members include Jarvis Cocker (1962–) vocalist, guitarist, pianist; Simon Hinkler, keyboardist; Peter Broam, bassist; David Hinkler, keyboardist; Gary Wilson, trombonist; guest vocalists Saskia Cocker and Gill Taylor; guest keyboardist Tim Allcard; 'Common People', 'Underwear', 'Disco 2000', *IT* (1983), *Freaks* (1987), *Separations* (1991), *His 'n' Hers* (1994), *Different Class* (1995), *This is Hardcore* (1998), *We Love Life* (2001).

Queen British group, 1970s to present; members include Freddie Mercury (originally Frederick Bulsara) (1946–91) singer/songwriter, born Zanzibar; Brian May (1947–) guitarist, born Hampton, Middlesex; John Deacon (1951–) bassist, born Leicester; Roger Taylor (originally Roger Meadows-Taylor) (1949–) drummer, born Norfolk; 'Seven Seas of Rhye', 'Killer Queen', 'Bohemian Rhapsody', 'We are the Champions', 'Somebody to Love', 'Another one Bites the Dust', 'Crazy Little Thing Called Love', 'Under Pressure' (with David Bowie), 'Radio Ga-Ga', *Queen II* (1974), *Sheer Heart Attack* (1974), *A Night at the Opera* (1975), *A Day at the Races* (1976), *The Game* (1980), *Hot Space* (1982), *The Works* (1984), *A Kind of Magic* (1986), *The Miracle* (1989), *Innuendo* (1991), *Made In Heaven* (1995).

Radiohead British group, late 1980s to present; members include Thom Yorke, vocalist, guitarist; Ed O'Brien, guitarist, vocalist; Jon Greenwood, guitarist; Colin Greenwood, bassist; Phil Selway, drummer; *The Bends* (1995), *OK Computer* (1997), *Kid A* (2000).

Ray, Johnnie (1927–90) US singer, born Rosebud, Oregon; 'Cry'/'The Little White Cloud That Cried', 'Walkin' My Baby Back Home', 'Just Walking In The Rain', 'You Don't Owe Me A Thing', 'I'll Never Fall In Love Again', *The Big Beat* (1957).

Redding, Otis (1941–67) US singer/songwriter, born Dawson, Georgia; 'I've Been Loving You Too Long', 'Try a Little Tenderness', 'Mr Pitiful', 'Satisfaction', '(Sittin' On The) Dock of the Bay', 'Respect', *The Otis Redding Story* (1968).

Reed, Lou (originally **Louis Firbank**) (1944–) US singer/songwriter, born Long Island, New York (was founder-member of The Velvet Underground in 1965) 'Walk On The Wild Side', 'I Love You Suzanne', *Lou Reed* (1972), *Transformer* (1972), *Rock 'n' Roll Animal* (1974), *Coney Island Baby* (1976), *Street Hassle* (1978), *New Sensations* (1984), *New York* (1989), *Magic and Loss* (1992), *The Best of Lou Reed and The Velvet Underground* (1995), *Ecstasy* (2000).

Martha Reeves and The Vandellas US group, 1960s; members include Martha Reeves (1941–) singer; Rosalind Ashford (1943–) singer; Betty Kelly (1944–) singer; all born Detroit, Michigan; 'Nowhere To Run', 'I'm Ready For Love', 'Jimmy Mack', 'Dancing In The Street'.

REM US group, 1980s to present; members include Michael Stipe (1960–) vocalist; Peter Buck (1956–) guitarist; Michael Mills (1958–) bassist; Bill Berry (1958–) drummer; 'World Leader Pretend', 'The One I Love', 'Stand', 'Superman', 'Orange Crush', 'Losing my Religion', 'Shiny Happy People', *Murmur* (1983), *Reckoning* (1984), *Life's Rich Pageant* (1986), *Number 5: Document* (1987), *Green* (1989), *Out of Time* (1991), *Automatic For The People* (1992), *Monster* (1994), *Reveal* (2001).

Richard, Sir Cliff (originally **Harry Rodger Webb**) (1940–) British singer/songwriter, guitarist, born Lucknow, India; over 100 hits including 'Livin' Doll', 'The Young Ones', 'Summer Holiday', 'Congratulations', *21 Today* (1961), *Rock & Roll Juvenile* (1971), *Love Songs* (1981), *Wired For Sound* (1981), *Now You See Me, Now You Don't* (1982), *Dressed For The Occasion* (1983), *Always Guaranteed* (1987), *Private Collection* (1988), *The Album* (1993), *Songs From Heathcliff* (1995), *Wanted* (2001).

Richie, Lionel (originally **Lionel Brockman Richie, Jr**) (1949–) US singer/songwriter, pianist, born Tuskegee, Alabama; 'All Night Long', 'Say You', *Can't Slow Down* (1983), *Dancing On The Ceiling* (1986), *Back To Front* (1992).

The Righteous Brothers US duo, 1960s to 1970s; Bobby Hatfield (1940–) singer, born Beaver Dam, Wisconsin; Bill Medley (1940–) singer, born Los Angeles; 'You've Lost That Lovin' Feelin'', 'Just Once In My Life', 'Unchained Melody', 'Ebb Tide', 'Rock And Roll Heaven'.

Robinson, Smokey (originally **William Robinson, Jr**) (1940–) US singer/songwriter, born Detroit, Michigan; (with The Miracles, American group, 1960s) 'Shop Around', 'The Tracks Of My Tears', 'I Second That Emotion'; 'Being With You', *Where There's Smoke* (1979), *Smoke Signals* (1986).

The Rolling Stones British group, 1960s to present; members include 'Mick' (Michael Philip) Jagger (1943–) vocalist, harmonica-player, born Dartford, Kent (solo 'Just Another Night', 'Dancing In The Street' (with David Bowie), *She's The Boss* (1985)); Keith Richards (1943–) guitarist, born Dartford, Kent; Bill Wyman (originally William Perks) (1936–) bassist, born Penge, London, replaced by Darryl Jones; Charlie Watts (1941–) drummer, born Neasden, London; Brian Jones (originally Lewis Brian Hopkin-Jones) (1942–69) guitarist, born Cheltenham, replaced by Mick Taylor (1948–) born Hertfordshire, replaced by Ron Wood (1947–) born Hillingdon, Middlesex; Ian Stewart (1938–85) keyboardist; 'It's All Over Now', 'Little Red Rooster, 'The Last Time', '(I Can't Get No) Satisfaction', 'Get Off My Cloud', '19th Nervous Breakdown', 'Paint It Black', 'Mother's Little Helper', 'Let's Spend The Night Together', 'Jumpin' Jack Flash', 'Sympathy For The Devil', 'Honky Tonk Women', 'You Can't Always Get What You Want', 'Brown Sugar', 'Miss You', *The Rolling Stones* (1964), *Aftermath* (1966), *Beggar's Banquet* (1968), *Let it Bleed* (1969), *Get Yer Ya-Ya's Out* (1970), *Sticky Fingers* (1971), *Exile on Main Street* (1972), *Goat's Head Soup* (1973), *Some Girls* (1978), *Emotional Rescue* (1980), *Tattoo You* (1981), *Undercover* (1983), *Dirty Work* (1986), *Steel Wheels* (1989), *Flashpoint* (1990), *Voodoo Lounge* (1994), *Stripped* (1995), *Bridges to Babylon* (1997), *Forty Licks* (2002).

Ross, Diana (1944–) US singer, born Detroit, Michigan; with the Supremes, 1960s group; 'Ain't No Mountain High Enough', 'Baby Love', 'Stop! In the Name of Love', 'You Can't Hurry Love', 'You Keep Me Hangin' On', 'Where Did Our Love Go', 'I'm Gonna Make You Love Me'; with Lionel Richie: 'Endless Love'; 'Upside Down', 'I'm Coming Out', 'My Old Piano', 'Chain Reaction', *Diana* (1980), *Eaten Alive* (1985) *Red Hot Rhythm 'n' Blues* (1987), *The Force Behind The Power* (1991), *Take Me Higher* (1995), *Love and Life* (2001).

Roxy Music British group, 1970s to early 1980s; members include Bryan Ferry (1945–) singer, born Washington, County Durham; Brian Eno (1948–) songwriter, keyboardist, born Woodbridge, Suffolk; Phil Manzanera (originally Philip Targett-Adams) (1941–) guitarist, born London; Andy Mackay (1946–) saxophonist; 'Virginia Plain', 'Do The Strand', 'Street Life', 'Love is the Drug', 'Dance Away', 'Angel Eyes', 'Jealous Guy', 'My Only Love', *Roxy Music* (1972), *Stranded* (1973), *Siren* (1975), *Manifesto* (1980), *Avalon* (1982).

Santana, Carlos (1947–) Mexican guitarist, vocalist, born Autlan de Novarra, Jalisco, Mexico; (with

band Santana, late 1960s to present) 'Black Magic Woman', *Santana* (1969), *Abraxas* (1970), *Amigos* (1976), *Moonflower* (1977), *Zebop!* (1981), *Freedom* (1987), *Supernatural* (1999).

Sedaka, Neil (1939–) US singer/songwriter; 'Breaking Up Is Hard To Do', 'Laughter In The Rain', 'Bad Blood', *Laughter And Tears: Best of Neil Sedaka Today* (1976).

The Sex Pistols British punk group, 1970s; members include Johnny Rotten (originally John Lydon) (1956–) vocalist; Steve Jones (1955–) guitarist; Paul Cook (1956–) drummer; Sid Vicious (originally John Simon Ritchie) (1958–79) singer, bassist; 'Anarchy in the UK', 'God Save The Queen', 'Pretty Vacant', 'Holidays In The Sun', 'My Way', 'Something Else', 'C'mon Everybody', 'Silly Thing', *Never Mind the Bollocks — Here's The Sex Pistols* (1977), *Some Product* (1978), *Flogging a Dead Horse* (1979), *The Great Rock 'n' Roll Swindle* (1980), *Kiss This* (1992), *Filthy Lucre Live* (1996).

The Shadows British group, late 1950s to present; members include Hank Marvin (originally Brian Rankin) (1941–) guitarist, born Newcastle upon Tyne; Bruce Welch (1941–) guitarist, born Newcastle upon Tyne; Jet Harris (originally Terry Harris) (1939–) bassist, born London; Tony Meehan (1943–) drummer, born London; 'Apache', 'Kon Tiki', 'Wonderful Land', 'Dance On', 'Foot Tapper', 'Don't Cry For Me Argentina', *Moonlight Shadows* (1986), *Reflection* (1990), *Shadows In The Night* (1993).

The Shangri-las US group, mid-1960s; Betty Weiss singer; Mary Weiss; Marge and Mary Ann Ganser; 'Leader of the Pack', 'Past, Present and Future'.

Shannon, Del (1939–90) US singer, born Coopersville, Michigan; 'Runaway', *Little Town Flirt* (1963), *Drop Down And Get Me* (1983).

Shaw, Sandie (originally **Sandra Goodrich**) (1947–) British singer, born Dagenham, Essex; 'There's Always Something There To Remind Me', 'Long Live Love', 'Puppet on a String', 'Hand In Glove', 'Are You Ready To Be Heartbroken?', *Nothing Less Than Brilliant* (1994).

Simon, Carly (1945–) US singer/songwriter, born New York City; 'You're So Vain', 'Nobody Does It Better', 'Coming Round Again', 'Let The River Run', *No Secrets* (1972).

Simon, Paul (1941–) US singer/songwriter, guitarist, born Newark, New Jersey; with Art Garfunkel (1942–) singer, born Forest Hills, New York; 'The Sound of Silence', 'Mrs Robinson', 'Bridge over Troubled Water', 'The Boxer', 'Scarborough Fair', 'Homeward Bound', *Bridge over Troubled Water* (1970); 'You Can Call Me Al', *Paul Simon* (1972), *Graceland* (1986), *Rhythm of the Saints* (1990), *Greatest Hits: Shining Like a National Guitar* (2000).

Simply Red British group, 1980 to present; members include Mick Hucknall (1960–) singer/songwriter; Tony Bowers (1952–) bassist; Chris Joyce (1957–) drummer; Fritz McIntyre (1956–) keyboardist; Sylvan Richardson guitarist; 'Money's Too Tight To Mention', 'Holding Back The Years', *Picture Book* (1985), *Men And Women* (1987), *A New Flame* (1989), *Stars* (1991), *Life* (1995), *Blue* (1998), *Home* (2003).

Sinatra, Frank (Francis Albert) (1915–98) US singer, born Hoboken, New Jersey; 'I've Got You Under My Skin', 'Strangers In The Night', 'The Lady Is A Tramp', 'Theme From New York, New York', 'My Way', *Songs For Swingin' Lovers* (1956), *Come Fly with Me* (1962).

Sly and the Family Stone US funk and soul group, 1960s to 1970s; members include Sly Stone (originally Sylvester Stewart) (1944–) vocalist, guitarist, keyboardist; Freddie Stone (1946–) guitarist; Cynthia Robinson (1946–) trumpeter; Larry Graham (1946–) guitarist; Rosemary Stone (1945–) vocalist, pianist; 'Dance To The Music', 'Everyday People', *Greatest Hits* (1970), *There's A Riot Goin' On* (1971).

Smith, Patti (1946–) US singer/songwriter, born Chicago; 'Because the Night', *Horses* (1976), *Easter* (1978), *Dream Of Life* (1988).

The Smiths British group, 1980s; members include (Steven Patrick) Morrissey (1959–) singer/songwriter (solo 'Everyday Is Like Sunday', *Viva Hate* (1988)); Johnny Marr (1963–) guitarist, songwriter; both born Manchester; 'Hand In Glove', 'Bigmouth Strikes Again', 'Boy With The Thorn In His Side', 'Panic', *The Smiths* (1984), *Meat Is Murder* (1985), *Hatful of Hollow* (1985), *The Queen Is Dead* (1986), *Strangeways, Here We Come* (1987).

Spears, Britney (Jean) (1981–) US singer, born Kentwood, Louisiana; *Baby One More Time* (1999), *Oops!... I Did It Again* (2000), *Britney* (2001).

The Spice Girls British group, 1990s to 2000; Posh Spice (Victoria Adams) (1975–); Sporty Spice (Melanie Chisholm) (1974–); Ginger Spice (Geri Halliwell) (1972–); Scary Spice (Melanie Brown) (1975–) and Baby Spice (Emma Bunton) (1976–); 'Say You'll Be There', '2 Become 1', 'Spice Up Your Life', *Spice* (1996), *Forever* (2000).

Springfield, Dusty (originally **Mary O'Brien**) (1939–99) British singer, born Hampstead, London; 'I Only Want To Be With You', 'You Don't Have To Say You Love Me', *Dusty In Memphis* (1969), *Reputation* (1990), *A Very Fine Love* (1995).

Springsteen, Bruce (Frederick Joseph) (1949–) US singer/songwriter, guitarist, born Freehold, New Jersey; 'Hungry Heart', 'Dancing In The Dark', 'Brilliant Disguise', *Greetings from Ashbury Park, NJ* (1973), *Born to Run* (1975), *Darkness on the Edge of Town* (1978), *The River* (1980), *Nebraska* (1982), *Born in the USA* (1985), *Tunnel of Love* (1987), *Human Touch* (1992), *Lucky Town* (1992), *In Concert — MTV Plugged* (1993), *The Ghost of Tom Joad* (1995), *The Rising* (2002).

Status Quo British group, 1970s to present; members include Francis Rossi (1949–) guitarist, vocalist; Richard Parfitt (1948–) guitarist, vocalist; Alan Lancaster (1949–) bassist; John Coghland (1946–) drummer; all born London; 'Down, Down', 'Caroline', 'You're in the Army Now', *Piledriver* (1973), *Hello* (1973), *On The Level* (1975), *Blue For You* (1976), *Rockin' All Over the World* (1978), *Back To Back* (1983), *In The Army Now* (1986), *Rocking All Over The Years* (1990), *Live Alive Quo* (1992), *Thirsty Work* (1994), *Famous in the Last Century* (2000).

Steely Dan US group, 1970s to present; Walter Becker (1950–) bassist, guitarist; Donald Fagen (1948–) keyboardist; 'Reelin' In The Years', *Aja* (1977), *Gaucho* (1980), *Gold* (1982), *Alive In America* (1995), *Two Against Nature* (2000).

Stevens, Cat (originally **Steven Demitri Georgiou**) (1947–) British singer/songwriter, born London; 'Lady D'Arbanville', 'Wild World', 'Peace Train', 'Morning Has Broken', *Tea For The Tillerman* (1971), *Teaser & The Firecat* (1971), *Catch Bull At Four* (1972), *Foreigner* (1973), *Buddha And The Chocolate Box* (1974).

Stewart, Rod(erick David) (1945–) British singer/songwriter, guitarist, born London; *Long Player* (1971) (with the Faces); 'Maggie May', 'You Wear It Well', 'Sailing', 'Do Ya Think I'm Sexy?', 'I Don't

Arts and Culture

Want To Talk About It', 'Passion', 'Baby Jane', 'Stay with Me', 'Young Turks', 'The Motown Song', *Every Picture Tells A Story* (1971), *Atlantic Crossing* (1975), *Blondes Have More Fun* (1978), *Tonight I'm Yours* (1981), *Body Wishes* (1983), *Every Beat Of My Heart* (1986), *Out Of Order* (1988), *Vagabond Heart* (1991), *Unplugged And Seated* (1993), *A Spanner In The Works* (1995).

The Stranglers British group, mid-1970s to present; members include Hugh Cornwell (1949–) vocalist, guitarist; Jean-Jacques Burnel (1952–) vocalist, bassist; 'Peaches', 'Walk On By', 'Golden Brown', 'Always The Sun', '96 Tears', *Rattus Norvegicus* (1977), *No More Heroes* (1977), *Feline* (1983), *Aural Structure* (1984), *Dreamtime* (1986), *Ten* (1990), *Stranglers In The Night* (1992), *About Time* (1992), *Coup de Grace* (1998).

Streisand, Barbra (Joan) (1942–) US singer/songwriter, born Brooklyn, New York City; (with Neil Diamond) 'You Don't Bring Me Flowers'; 'Guilty', *Stoney End* (1971), *The Way We Were* (1974), *Streisand Superman* (1977), *Emotion* (1984), *One Voice* (1987), *A Love Like Ours* (1999).

Summer, Donna (originally **Donna Adrian Gaines**) (1948–) US singer, born Boston, Massachusetts; 'Love To Love You Baby', 'I Feel Love', 'Last Dance', 'Hot Stuff', 'Highway Runner', 'He's A Rebel', 'Forgive Me', 'Dinner With Gershwin', *Live And More* (1978), *Bad Girls* (1979), *The Wanderer* (1980), *She Works Hard For The Money* (1983), *All Systems Go* (1987), *Another Place and Time* (1989).

Talking Heads US group, mid-1970s to present; members include David Byrne (1952–) singer/songwriter, guitarist, born Dumbarton, Scotland; Chris Frantz (1951–) drummer, born Fort Campbell, Kentucky; Martina 'Tina' Weymouth (1950–) bassist, born Coronado, California; Jerry Harrison (1949–) keyboardist, born Milwaukee, Wisconsin; 'Psycho Killer', 'Burning Down the House', 'Road to Nowhere', 'And She Was', *Talking Heads* (1977), *Fear of Music* (1979), *Remain in Light* (1980), *Speaking In Tongues* (1983), *Little Creatures* (1985), *True Stories* (1986), *Naked* (1988), *Once In a Lifetime/Sand In The Vaseline* (1992).

Taylor, James (1948–) US singer/songwriter, guitarist, born Boston, Massachusetts; 'You've Got A Friend', *Mud Slide Slim And The Blue Horizon* (1971), *One Man Dog* (1972), *Gorilla* (1975), *That's Why I'm Here* (1986), *Never Die Young* (1988).

The Temptations US group, 1960s to present; members have included David Ruffin (1941–91) singer; Eddie Kendricks (1939–92) singer; Dennis Edwards (1943–) singer; Melvin Franklin (1942–95) singer; Otis Williams (1941–); Damon Harris (1950–); over 80 hit singles since 1962; 'Just My Imagination (Running Away With Me)', 'Treat Her Like a Lady', 'Papa Was A Rolling Stone', *Diana Ross & The Supremes Join The Temptations* (1968), *All Directions* (1972), *Truly For You* (1984).

Thin Lizzy Irish heavy rock group, 1970s to mid-1980s; members include Phil Lynott (1951–86) vocalist, bassist (solo 'Yellow Pearl', 'Nineteen'); Brian Downey (1951–) drummer; Eric Bell (1947–) guitarist, born Belfast; Gary Moore vocalist, guitarist, born Dublin; Brian Robertson (1956–) guitarist, born Glasgow; Scott Gorham (1951–) guitarist, born Santa Monica, California; 'Whiskey In The Jar', 'The Boys Are Back In Town', *Jailbreak* (1976), *Live And Dangerous* (1978), *Black Rose* (1979), *China Town* (1980), *Adventures of Thin Lizzy* (1981), *Thunder and Lightning* (1983).

Turner, Tina (originally **Annie Mae Bullock**) (1938–) US singer/songwriter, born Nutbush, Tennessee; (with Ike Turner 1931–) singer, pianist, born Clarksdale, Mississippi) 'River Deep, Mountain High', 'Nutbush City Limits', *The Best of Ike and Tina Turner* (1976); 'Let's Stay Together', 'What's Love Got to Do with It', 'Better Be Good To Me', 'We Don't Need Another Hero', *Private Dancer* (1984), *Break Every Rule* (1986), *Live In Europe* (1988), *Foreign Affair* (1989), *Simply The Best* (1991), *What's Love Got To Do With It* (1993) (soundtrack), *Twenty Four Seven* (2000).

Twain, Shania (originally **Eileen Regina Edwards**) (1965–) Canadian singer/songwriter, born Windsor, Ontario; 'That Don't Impress Me Much', 'Man! I Feel Like a Woman', *The Woman in Me* (1995), *Come on Over* (1997), *Up!* (2002).

UB40 British group, 1980s to present; members include Ali Campbell (1959–) singer, guitarist; Robin Campbell (1954–) guitarist; Jim Brown (1957–) drummer; Brian Travers (1959–) saxophonist; Earl Falconer (1959–) bassist; Norman Hassan (1958–) percussionist; Mickey Virtue (1957–) keyboardist; 'Red Red Wine', 'I Got You Babe', 'Don't Break My Heart', 'Sing Our Own Song', *Signing Off* (1982), *Labour Of Love* (1983), *Baggaridim* (1985), *Rat In The Kitchen* (1986), *Labour of Love II* (1989), *Promises and Lies* (1993).

U2 Irish group, 1980s to present; members include Bono (originally Paul Hewson) (1960–) vocalist, born Dublin; The Edge (originally David Evans) (1961–) guitarist; Larry Mullen (1961–) drummer; Adam Clayton (1960–) bassist; 'New Year's Day', 'Pride (In The Name of Love)', 'Sunday, Bloody Sunday', 'With Or Without You', 'Desire', *War* (1983), *Live Under a Blood Red Sky* (1983), *The Unforgettable Fire* (1984), *The Joshua Tree* (1987), *Rattle and Hum* (1988), *Achtung Baby* (1991), *Zooropa* (1993), *Pop* (1997), *All That You Can't Leave Behind* (2000).

Valens, Ritchie (originally **Richard Valenzuela**) (1941–59) US singer/songwriter, guitarist, born Pacoima, California; 'Come On, Let's Go', 'Donna', 'La Bamba'.

Vandross, Luther (1951–) US soul singer; 'Never Too Much', 'Here And Now', *Give Me The Reason* (1986), *Any Love* (1988).

Van Halen US group, late 1970s to present; members include David Lee Roth (1955–) vocalist, born Bloomingdale, Indiana (solo 'California Girls', 'Yankee Rose', *Eat 'Em and Smile* (1986), *Skyscraper* (1987)); Sammy Hagar (1951–) singer/songwriter, guitarist, born Monterey, California (solo 'I've Done Everything For You', 'You're Love is Driving Me Crazy', 'Two Sides of Love', 'I Can't Drive 55', *Three Lock Box* (1983), *Voice of America* (1984)); Eddie Van Halen (1955–) guitarist; Alex Van Halen (1953–) drummer; both born the Netherlands; Michael Anthony (1955–) bassist; 'You Really Got Me', 'Jump', 'Panama', 'Hot For Teacher', 'Why Can't This Be Love', *Van Halen* (1978), *Van Halen II* (1979), *Women And Children First* (1980), *Fair Warning* (1981), *Diver Down* (1982), *1984* (1984), *5150* (1986), *OU812* (1988), *For Unlawful Carnal Knowledge* (1991), *Live — Right Here Now* (1993), *Balance* (1995), *Van Halen III* (1998).

Vega, Suzanne (1959–) US singer/songwriter, guitarist, born Santa Monica, California; 'Marlene On The Wall', 'Small Blue Thing', 'Left Of Center', 'Luka', 'Tom's Diner', *Suzanne Vega* (1985), *Solitude Standing* (1987), *Days of Open Hand* (1990), *99.9°F* (1992).

The Velvet Underground US group, late 1960s; members include John Cale (1940–) guitarist, viola player, born Garnant, Wales; Nico (originally Christa Paffgen) (1938–88) vocalist, born Cologne, Germany; Lou Reed (originally Louis Firbank) (1944–) singer/songwriter, guitarist, born Long Island, New York; *The Velvet Underground & Nico* (1967), *White Light, White Heat* (1968), *The Velvet Underground* (1969), *Loaded* (1970), *Live at Max's Kansas City* (1972), *1969 Velvet Underground Live* (1974), *VU* (1985), *Live MCMXCIII* (1993).

The Verve British group, 1990s; members include Richard Ashcroft (1971–) vocalist; Nick McCabe, guitarist; Simon Jones, bassist; Peter Salisbury, drummer; *A Storm In Heaven* (1993), *A Northern Soul* (1995), *Urban Hymns* (1997).

Vincent, Gene (originally **Vincent Eugene Craddock**) (1935–71) US singer, born Norfolk, Virginia; (with the Blue Caps) 'Be-Bop-a-Lula', 'Pistol Packin' Mama', 'Bird Doggin''.

Waits, Tom (1949–) US singer/songwriter, pianist, born Pamona, California; *Small Change* (1976), *Swordfishtrombone* (1983), *The Asylum Years* (1984), *Rain Dogs* (1985), *Frank's Wild Years* (1987), *Big Time* (1988), *Bone Machine* (1992), *The Black Rider* (1993), *Mule Variations* (1999).

Warwick, Dionne (also **Marie Dionne Warwicke**) (1940–) US singer/songwriter, pianist, born East Orange, New Jersey; 'There Came You' (with The Spinners); (Dionne & Friends) 'That's What Friends Are For'; *Dionne* (1979), *Heartbreaker* (1982), *So Amazing* (1983), *Without Your Love* (1985), *Love Songs* (1990), *Christmas In Vienna II* (1994).

Wham! British group, 1980s; George Michael (originally Yorgos Kyriatou Panayiotou) (1963–) singer/songwriter, born Finchley, London; Andrew Ridgely (1963–) singer, guitarist, born Bushey, Hertsfordshire; 'Young Guns (Go For It)', 'Club Tropicana', 'Wake Me Up Before You Go-Go', 'Freedom', 'Last Christmas', 'I'm Your Man', 'Edge of Heaven', *Fantastic* (1983), *Make It Big* (1984), *The Final* (1986).

White, Barry (1944–) US singer/songwriter, born Galveston, Texas; 'Can't Get Enough Of Your Love, Babe', *Can't Get Enough* (1974), *Right Now Barry White* (1987), *The Right Night And Barry White* (1987), *The Icon Is Love* (1995), *Staying Power* (1999).

The Who British group, late 1960s to present; members include Pete Townshend (1945–) singer/songwriter, guitarist (solo *Who Came First* (1972)); Roger Daltry (1944–) vocalist, born London (solo *After The Fire* (1985)); John Entwhistle (1944–2002) bassist, French horn player; Keith Moon (1947–78) drummer; all born London; 'Substitute', 'Won't Get Fooled Again', 'You Better You Bet', *My Generation* (1966), *The Who Sell Out* (1967), *Tommy* (1969), *Who's Next* (1971), *Quadrophenia* (1973), *Face Dances* (1981), *It's Hard* (1982), *Who's Last* (1984), *Who's Better Who's Best* (1988), *Join Together* (1990), *30 Years of Maximum R&B* (1994).

Williams, Robbie (1974–) British singer/songwriter, born Stoke-on-Trent (with Take That, 1990s) 'It Only Takes a Minute', 'Back for Good'; 'Angels', 'She's the One', 'Millennium', *Life Thru a Lens*

(1997), *Sing When You're Winning* (2000), *Escapology* (2002).

Wings British group, 1970s to 1980s; members include Paul McCartney (1942–) singer/songwriter, guitarist; 'Give Ireland Back to the Irish', 'Venus and Mars', 'Live and Let Die', 'Crossroads', 'Mull of Kintyre', *Band On The Run* (1973), *Wild Life* (1973), *Wings over America* (1976).

Wonder, Stevie (originally **Steveland Judkins** or **Steveland Morris**) (1950–) US singer/songwriter, harmonica player, keyboardist, born Saginaw, Michigan; 'Fingertips', 'Superstition', 'You Are The Sunshine Of My Life', 'Isn't She Lovely', 'Master Blaster', 'Happy Birthday', 'I Just Called to Say I Love You', 'Part-Time Lover', 'Ebony and Ivory' (with Paul McCartney), *Stevie Wonder/The 12 Year Old Genius* (1961), *Music of My Mind* (1972), *Talking Book* (1972), *Innervisions* (1973), *Songs in the Key of Life* (1976), *Hotter than July* (1980), *In Square Circle* (1985), *Characters* (1987), *Jungle Fever* (1991) (soundtrack), *Conversation Peace* (1995), *At the Close of A Century* (1999).

Yardbirds British group, 1960s; members include Keith Relf (1943–76) singer, harmonica player, born Richmond, Surrey; Paul Samwell-Smith (1943–) bassist, born Twickenham, Middlesex; Chris Dreja (1946–) guitarist, born Surbiton, Surrey; Eric Clapton (1945–) guitarist; Jeff Beck (1944–) guitarist; Jimmy Page (1944–) bassist, guitarist; 'Good Morning Little Schoolgirl', 'For Your Love', 'I'm A Man', 'Happening Ten Years Time Ago'.

Yes British group, 1970s to present; members include Jon Anderson (1944–) vocalist, born Lancashire; Rick Wakeman (1949–) keyboardist, born London; Steve Howe (1947–) guitarist, born London; Chris Squire (1948–) bassist, born London; 'Owner of a Lonely Heart', *Fragile* (1972), *Close to the Edge* (1972), *90125* (1983), *Big Generator* (1987), *Union* (1991), *Talk* (1994), *Magnification* (2001).

Young, Neil (1945–) Canadian singer/songwriter, guitarist, born Toronto; 'Heart Of Gold', *After the Gold Rush* (1970), *Harvest* (1972), *Tonight's the Night* (1975), *Zuma* (1975), *Rust Never Sleeps* (1979), *Reactor* (1981), *Landing On Water* (1986), *Freedom* (1989), *Ragged Glory* (1990), *Harvest Moon* (1992), *Unplugged* (1993), *Sleeps With Angels* (1994), *Mirror Ball* (1995), *Are You Passionate?* (2002).

Zappa, Frank (originally **Francis Vincent Zappa, Jr**) (1940–93) US singer/songwriter, guitarist, bandleader (The Mothers of Invention, American 1970s group), born Baltimore, Maryland; 'Valley Girl', *Apostrophe* (1974), *Joe's Garage* (1979), *Ship Arriving Too Late To Save A Drowning Witch* (1982), *The Perfect Stranger And Other Works* (1985), *Guitar* (1988).

ZZ Top US group, 1970s to present; Billy Gibbons vocalist, guitarist; Dusty Hill vocalist, bassist; Frank Beard drummer; 'Gimme All Your Lovin'', 'Sharp Dressed Man', 'Legs', 'Sleeping Bag', *Tres Hombres* (1973), *Tejas* (1976), *Deguello* (1979), *Eliminator* (1983), *Afterburner* (1985), *Recycler* (1990), *Antenna* (1994), *XXX* (1999).

Arts and Culture

Arts and Culture

Grammy awards

Grammy awards are awarded annually, in a number of categories, by the US National Academy of Recording Arts and Sciences. They were first awarded in 1958.

Year	Best record	Best album
1958	Domenico Modugno 'Nel Blu Dipinto Di Blu (Volare)'	Henry Mancini *Peter Gunn*
1959	Bobby Darin 'Mack the Knife'	Frank Sinatra *Come Dance with Me*
1960	Percy Faith 'Theme from *A Summer Place*'	Bob Newhart *Button Down Mind*
1961	Henry Mancini 'Moon River'	Judy Garland *Judy at Carnegie Hall*
1962	Tony Bennett 'I Left My Heart in San Francisco'	Vaughn Meader *The First Family*
1963	Henry Mancini 'The Days of Wine and Roses'	Barbra Streisand *The Barbra Streisand Album*
1964	Stan Getz, Astrud Gilberto 'The Girl from Ipanema'	Stan Getz, João Gilberto *Getz/Gilberto*
1965	Herb Alpert 'A Taste of Honey'	Frank Sinatra *September of My Years*
1966	Frank Sinatra 'Strangers in the Night'	Frank Sinatra *A Man and His Music*
1967	5th Dimension 'Up, Up and Away'	The Beatles *Sgt Pepper's Lonely Hearts Club Band*
1968	Simon and Garfunkel 'Mrs Robinson'	Glen Campbell *By the Time I Get to Phoenix*
1969	5th Dimension 'Aquarius/Let the Sunshine In'	Blood, Sweat and Tears *Blood, Sweat and Tears*
1970	Simon and Garfunkel 'Bridge Over Troubled Water'	Simon and Garfunkel *Bridge Over Troubled Water*
1971	Carole King 'It's Too Late'	Carole King *Tapestry*
1972	Roberta Flack 'The First Time Ever I Saw Your Face'	Various *The Concert for Bangladesh*
1973	Roberta Flack 'Killing Me Sofly with His Song'	Stevie Wonder *Innervisions*
1974	Olivia Newton-John 'I Honestly Love You'	Stevie Wonder *Fulfillingness' First Finale*
1975	Captain and Tennille 'Love Will Keep Us Together'	Paul Simon *Still Crazy After All These Years*
1976	George Benson 'This Masquerade'	Stevie Wonder *Songs in the Key of Life*
1977	Eagles 'Hotel California'	Fleetwood Mac *Rumours*
1978	Billy Joel 'Just the Way You Are'	Bee Gees *Saturday Night Fever*
1979	The Doobie Brothers 'What a Fool Believes'	Billy Joel *52nd Street*
1980	Christopher Cross 'Sailing'	Christopher Cross *Christopher Cross*
1981	Kim Carnes 'Bette Davis Eyes'	John Lennon, Yoko Ono *Double Fantasy*
1982	Toto 'Rosanna'	Toto *Toto IV*
1983	Michael Jackson 'Beat It'	Michael Jackson *Thriller*
1984	Tina Turner 'What's Love Got to Do with It'	Lionel Richie *Can't Slow Down*
1985	USA for Africa 'We Are the World'	Phil Collins *No Jacket Required*
1986	Steve Winwood 'Higher Love'	Paul Simon *Graceland*
1987	Paul Simon 'Graceland'	U2 *The Joshua Tree*
1988	Bobby McFerrin 'Don't Worry, Be Happy'	George Michael *Faith*
1989	Bette Midler 'Wind Beneath My Wings'	Bonnie Raitt *Nick of Time*
1990	Phil Collins 'Another Day in Paradise'	Quincy Jones *Back on the Block*
1991	Natalie Cole with Nat 'King' Cole 'Unforgettable'	Natalie Cole with Nat 'King' Cole *Unforgettable*
1992	Eric Clapton 'Tears in Heaven'	Eric Clapton *Unplugged*
1993	Whitney Houston 'I Will Always Love You'	Whitney Houston *The Bodyguard*
1994	Sheryl Crow 'All I Wanna Do'	Tony Bennett *MTV Unplugged*
1995	Seal 'Kiss From a Rose'	Alanis Morissette *Jagged Little Pill*
1996	Eric Clapton 'Change the World'	Celine Dion *Falling into You*
1997	Shawn Colvin 'Sunny Came Home'	Bob Dylan *Time Out of Mind*
1998	Celine Dion 'My Heart Will Go On'	Lauryn Hill *The Miseducation of Lauryn Hill*
1999	Santana, featuring Rob Thomas 'Smooth'	Santana *Supernatural*
2000	U2 'Beautiful Day'	Steely Dan *Two Against Nature*
2001	U2 'Walk On'	Various *O Brother, Where Art Thou?*
2002	Norah Jones 'Don't Know Why'	Norah Jones *Come Away With Me*

Jazz and blues musicians and singers

Selected songs, compositions and albums are listed.

Adderley, 'Cannonball' (Julian Edwin) (1928–75) US alto saxophonist, bandleader and composer, born Tampa, Florida. Played blues and funk, one of the first to electrify the saxophone; made hits out of Afro-American themes; 'Sermonette', 'This Here', 'Work Song'.

Armstrong, Louis (Daniel) ('Satchmo') (1900–71) US trumpeter and singer, born New Orleans. First major jazz virtuoso and exponent of 'scat' singing (vocal imitation of an instrument); appeared in more than 50 films, also very successful commercially; 'Mack the Knife', 'Blueberry Hill', 'Hello Dolly!'.

Ayler, Albert (1936–70) US tenor saxophonist, born Cleveland, Ohio. Influenced from youth by gospel and religious bands; début at 16 with Little Walter as sax player; developed Free Jazz style; 'Bells', 'Ghosts'.

Baker, Chet (Chesney H) (1929–88) US trumpeter and singer, born Yale, Oklahoma. One of the most lyrical trumpeters in jazz history, at centre of West Coast 'cool jazz' scene; had success with Gerry Mulligan's pianoless quartet with 'My Funny Valentine'.

Barbieri, Gato (Leandro J) (1934–) Argentinian clarinettist, tenor saxophonist and composer, born Rosario, Argentina. Made début playing the requinto (clarinet) in the 'milonga' bands, then developed own styles, from Free Jazz to Latin; tenor player of tropical alcoves and clubs; won Grammy for film soundtrack *Last Tango in Paris* (1972).

Basie, 'Count' (William Allen) (1904–84) US pianist and bandleader, born Red Bank, New Jersey. Major big band (16-piece) leader of the swing era; Kansas City style music; compositions include 'One O'Clock Jump' and 'Jumpin' at the Woodside'.

Bechet, Sidney (Joseph) (1897–1959) US clarinettist and soprano saxophonist, born New Orleans. Began in New Orleans style; contributed to the popularization of jazz, mingling tradition with accessible tunes; 'Les Oignons', 'Petite Fleur', 'Dans les Rues d'Antibes'; music for ballet *La Nuit est une Sorcière*.

Beiderbecke, Bix (Leon) (1903–31) US cornettist and pianist, born Davenport, Iowa. First great white jazz musician, characterized by his richly harmonic tone and soft, warm sonority; 'I'm Comin' Virginia', 'In the Dark', 'In a Mist' (piano solo).

Bennett, Tony (Anthony Dominick Benedetto) (1926–) US jazz and popular singer, born New York. Established reputation as singer in 1950s, graduating towards jazz in the 1960s; 'I Left My Heart in San Francisco'. Recorded two albums with pianist Bill Evans in the 1970s.

Blakey, Art ('Bu') (Buhaina, Abdullah ibn) (1919–90) US drummer and bandleader, born Pittsburgh, Pennsylvania. Leading exponent of 'hard bop' style; played in double time; studied African rhythms; leader of The Jazz Messengers; composed score for 1985 film *Des Femmes Disparaissent; Oh, By the Way, New York Scene*.

Bley, Carla (née **Borg**) (1938–) US pianist, bandleader and composer, born Oakland, California. Elegant rhythm 'n' blues, blended bebop and folk; leader of own band and record company; compositions include 'Ida Lupina', 'Sing Me Softly of the Blues' and Gary Burton's masterpiece 'A Genuine Tong Funeral'.

Broonzy, Big Bill (Conley, William Lee) (1893–1958) US singer, musician and composer, born Scott, Mississippi. Guitar accompanist and composer to the great blues players of his generation; played in ragtime style, also encompassing folksong, rural and urban blues; 'See See Rider', 'Trouble in Mind', his own 'Texas Tornado' and 'Bossie Woman' and recordings of John Hampton's 1938–9 *Spirituals to Sing* concerts.

Brown, Sandy (Alexander) (1929–75) Anglo-Indian clarinettist, bandleader and composer, born Izatnagar, India. Outstanding blues player. Originally influenced by Louis Armstrong's Hot Five and the New Orleans style, then by West Indian calypso and African folk.

Brubeck, Dave (David Warren) (1920–) US pianist, bandleader and composer, born Concord, California. Pupil of Schoenberg and Milhaud; uses odd rhythms, the rondo form, fugue-like passages; made popular by Paul Desmond's 'Take Five'; compositions include 'The Duke', 'In Your own Sweet Way', 'Unsquare Dance'.

Burton, Gary (1943–) US vibraphonist and bandleader, born Anderson, Indiana. Has habit of 'discovering' new talent, eg Tommy Smith. Also involved in music education and publishing. Many successful album recordings, including Carly Bley's *A Genuine Tong Funeral* and *Alone at Last*.

Byrd, Charlie (1925–99) US guitarist, born Chuckatuck, Virginia. Specialist on nylon string guitar; very versatile; played jazz, classical and South American in the same concerts; prolific recordings include *Jazz/Samba* with Stan Getz.

Calloway, Cab(ell) (1907–94) US bandleader and singer, born Rochester, New York. His band succeeded Duke Ellington's at Harlem's Cotton Club in 1931. Known for his signature tune *Minnie the Moocher* and his scat-style catchphrases.

Carter, Betty (Lillie Mae Jones) (1930–98) US singer, born Flint, Michigan. Sang with bebop musicians, including Charlie Parker and Dizzie Gillespie. A brilliant vocal improviser, who was popular in the 1950s. Rediscovered in the 1970s after setting up own record label, Bet-Car.

Charles, Ray ('The Genius') (Robinson, Ray Charles) (1930–) US singer, pianist and composer, born Albany, Georgia. Successful soul artist (despite blindness) with sensitive, vibrant voice and sincere, expressive preacher's tone; often accompanied by big bands; 'Sewanee River Rock', 'What'd I Say', 'Georgia on My Mind', 'Hit the Road Jack', 'I Can't Stop Loving You', film theme 'Ruby'.

Cherry, Don(ald Eugene) (1936–95) US trumpeter, cornetist, bandleader and composer, born Oklahoma City. Exponent of improvised music; considered himself not playing the trumpet but singing with it; came to prominence in Ornette Coleman's Free Jazz quartet and on the John Coltrane quartet album *The Avant-Garde*.

Christian, Charlie (1916–42) US guitarist, born Dallas, Texas. Electric guitar pioneer, establishing it as a solo instrument; helped lay basis of bebop revolution in Minton's Playhouse; played with Benny Goodman. Early death due to TB. Shared composer credit with Goodman for 'Solo Flight' and 'Seven Come Eleven'; also 'Blues in C', 'Waitin' for Benny'.

Clarke, Kenny ('Klook') (Kenneth Spearman) (1914–85) US drummer, bandleader and composer, born Pittsburgh, Pennsylvania. Inventor of bebop drums; father of modern percussionists; co-led Clarke–Boland big band. Compositions include 'Epistrophy' with Thelonious Monk, 'Salt Peanuts' with Dizzy Gillespie.

Cole, Nat 'King' (Coles, Nathaniel Adams) (1919–65) US singer, pianist and composer, born Montgomery, Alabama. Inventor of modern concept of trio, using piano, guitar and double bass. Won popularity as a singer; 'Straighten up and Fly Right', 'Too Young', 'Unforgettable', 'Answer Me, My Love', 'Ballerina', 'Stardust'.

Coleman, Ornette (1930–) US alto and tenor saxophonist, trumpeter and composer, born Fort Worth, Texas. Experimented in free-form jazz and atonality to mixed acclaim; now regarded as major innovator; invented word 'harmelodic' (improvised coloration). Albums include *Something Else!* and *The Shape of Jazz to Come*.

Collins, Albert (1932–93) US blues guitarist and singer, born Leona, Texas. A cousin of Lightnin' Hopkins, he inherited the Texas blues guitar tradition of Hopkins and T-Bone Walker. He had a regional hit in 1958 with 'The Freeze', and became known for an 'icy', spare guitar sound. He recorded in a crossover blues-funk style in the late 1960s, but did little more of real note until he signed with Alligator Records in 1977. Both he and the label flourished in the blues revival of the 1980s, and his distinctive guitar style has influenced younger players like Robert Cray. He joined Cray and Johnny Copeland on the best-selling *Showdown*

Arts and Culture

Arts and Culture

(1985), one of several records for which he received Grammy award nominations.

Coltrane, John (William) (1926–67) US tenor and soprano saxophonist, bandleader and composer, born Hamlet, North Carolina. One of the most influential performers of the post-bebop era. Developed and experimented with improvisation, influenced by Indian ragas, African pentatonic scales and the polyphonic music of the Pygmys; 'Giant Steps', 'A Love Supreme'.

Corea, Chick (Corea, Armando Anthony) (1941–) Italian–US pianist and composer, born Chelsea, Massachusetts. His taste for diversity makes him hard to classify; plays from acoustics to electronics and from Latin rhythms to bebop, Free Jazz to classical; replaced Herbie Hancock in Miles Davis's group for *In a Silent Way* and *Bitches Brew*; 'Return to Forever', 'Crystal Silence', 'Armando's Rhumba', *Now He Sings, Now He Sobs*.

Cray, Robert (1953–) US singer, blues guitarist, born Columbus, Georgia. One of the most successful blues artists of the last 20 years, Cray's clean guitar style is coupled with a soul-infused singing voice. Frontman with the Robert Cray Band since 1974, recordings include *Don't Be Afraid of the Dark* (1988) and *Shoulda Been Home* (2001).

Dankworth, John (Philip William) (1927–) English alto saxophonist, bandleader and composer, born London. A student of the Royal Academy of Music, he later converted stables at his home to be a workshop for young musicians. Hits include novelty 'Experiments with Mice', 'African Waltz'; ballet *Lysistrata*; film score *Saturday Night and Sunday Morning*; piece for orchestra *What the Dickens*.

Davis, Miles (Dewey III) ('Prince of Darkness') (1926–91) US trumpeter and bandleader, born Alton, Illinois. One of the most popular and adaptable jazz musicians of all time. Recording début with 'Now's the Time', 'Billie Bounce', 'Koko'. Working with Gil Evans, he led a nonet that inspired the 'cool jazz' school. Albums include *The Birth of the Cool* (a turning point in jazz history), *Kind of Blue*; recorded music for Louis Malle's film *Ascenseur pour l'Echafaud* (1957).

Dolphy, Eric (Allan) (1928–64) US alto saxophonist, clarinettist, flautist and composer, born Los Angeles. Music rooted in Afro-American tradition but with birdsong-like improvisation comprising screeches, airiness and wild escapades, eg in 'Gazelloni' on *Out to Lunch* and 'Jim Crow' on *Other Aspects*.

Dorsey, Tommy (Thomas Francis) ('The Sentimental Gentleman of Swing') (1905–56) US trombonist and big-band leader, born Shenandoah, Pennsylvania. Characteristic sweet-toned instrumental style with seamless legato; formed Dorsey Brothers Orchestra in 1928 with brother Jimmy, one of the most popular swing dance bands. Nearly 200 hits 1935–53 including 'Treasure Island', 'Marie', 'Satan Takes a Holiday', 'Indian Summer', 'In the Blue of Evening' (with Frank Sinatra), 'Boogie Woogie'.

Eldridge, Roy (David Roy) ('Little Jazz') (1911–89) US trumpeter, pianist, drummer, bass player and bandleader, born Pittsburgh, Pennsylvania. Virtuoso who influenced Louis Armstrong and Dizzy Gillespie. Famous trumpet soloist, often playing in the high register; played with top bands, eg McKinney's Cotton Pickers and the Fletcher Henderson Orchestra; vocal duet hit with Anita O'Day 'Let Me Off Uptown', also countless recordings, including *Dale's Wail* with Oscar Peterson, *The Trumpet Battle* with Charlie Shavers and Lester Young.

Elis, Don(ald Johnson) (1934–78) US trumpeter, bandleader and composer, born Los Angeles. Worked in both jazz and contemporary music, experimenting with oriental instruments and compositions, and incorporating string quartets; music full of virtuosity collages and improvisation, but poorly represented on disc.

Ellington, 'Duke' (Edward Kennedy) (1899–1974) US pianist, bandleader and composer, born Washington, DC. One of the most important jazz composers and players. Produced about 2 000 works including 'Mood Indigo', 'Sophisticated Lady', 'Take the A Train', film music for *Anatomy of a Murder* (1959) and *Paris Blues* (1961).

Evans, Bill (William John) (1929–80) US pianist and composer, born Plainfield, New Jersey. Most influential pianist of his generation. Won several Grammies, eg for *Conversations with Myself*; 'Waltz for Debby', 'N Y C's No Lark' (for Sonny Clark).

Evans, Gil (Green, Ian Ernst Gilmore) (1912–88) Canadian composer, pianist and bandleader, born Toronto. Collaboration with Miles Davis led to emergence of 'cool jazz' style; one of the first modern jazz arrangers to combine electronics and rock influences with bebop and swing. Compositions include 'Boplicity' and 'Moon Dreams' for Davis's *Birth of the Cool*, 'Concierto de Aranjuez' for *Sketches of Spain*, electric album *Svengali*.

Fitzgerald, Ella (1917–96) US singer, born Newport News, Virginia. Talented jazz singer; famous for scat singing (vocal imitation of an instrument) and improvisation; starred in drummer Chick Webb's orchestra; sang with Duke Ellington's and Count Basie's bands; performed *Porgy and Bess* with Louis Armstrong; 'Stone Cold Dead in the Market', 'Mack the Knife', 'Party Blues'.

Franklin, Aretha ('Lady Soul', 'Queen of Soul') (1942–) US singer, born Memphis, Tennessee. Daughter of Detroit preacher and gospel singer; many million-selling singles; recorded 'Respect' with Ray Charles and 'Lady Soul' with Otis Redding; masterpiece album *Amazing Grace*; *Love All the Hurt Away*, *One Lord, One Faith, One Baptism*.

Garbarek, Jan (1947–) Norwegian saxophonist, born Mysen, Norway. Despite being inspired by Coltrane, his influence is very much European, drawing on the moods and haunting melodies from his Scandinavian roots; has played and recorded with George Russell's sextet and orchestra in Sweden, and with the medieval folk group the Hilliard Ensemble (*Officium*, 1996); style described as 'distilled thought'.

Garner, Erroll (1921–77) US pianist, born Pittsburgh, Pennsylvania. Self-taught artist with a gift for melody; combined old and new styles; his own lingering style became known as the 'Garner amble'; known for 'Play Piano Play', 'Laura', 'Misty'; awarded gold disc for *Concert by the Sea* (1958).

Getz, Stan(ley) ('The Sound') (1927–91) US tenor saxophonist and bandleader, born Philadelphia. Most important white jazz saxophonist for 40 years of his life. Characteristic smooth, light tone and articulate phrasing. Popularized bossa nova jazz style in the 1960s; 'Focus', 'Desafinado', 'The Girl from Ipanema'.

Gillespie, 'Dizzy' (John Birks) (1917–93) US trumpeter, bandleader and composer, born Cheraw, South Carolina. Great pioneering virtuoso and innovator; created bebop style (with Charlie Parker); introduced African rhythms into jazz; compositions include classics 'Night in Tunisia', 'Groovin' High', 'Dizzy Atmosphere', 'Anthropology'.

Goodman, Benny (Benjamin David) ('The King of Swing') (1909–86) US clarinettist, bandleader and composer, born Chicago. The first white performer to integrate black musicians into his own band; in 1962 played in first American jazz band to perform in the Soviet Union; clean, joyful style; sextet recordings include 'Six Appeal', 'Seven Come Eleven', 'Wholly Cats', 'Breakfast Feud'; 'Jersey Bounce', 'Why Don't You Do Right' (sung by Peggy Lee).

Gordon, Dexter (Keith) (1923–90) US tenor saxophonist, born Los Angeles. One of the first to play bop tenor; developed modern ballad style and keen harmonic tone (which Coltrane and Rollins studied); 'The Chase', 'The Duel', 'Daddy Plays the Horn', *Gotham City*; also acted in play *The Connection* and film *Round Midnight* (1986).

Grapelli, Stephane (1908–97) French violinist, born Paris. Founder member (with Django Reinhardt) of Quintette du Hot Club de France, which had a European influence on jazz in the 1930s. Adapted violin to jazz; master of swing-based style; recorded swing versions of the 'Marseillaise' called 'Echoes of France', and of J S Bach's *Concerto in D Minor*. Duets with Yehudi Menuhin include *Tea for Two* and *Strictly for the Birds*.

Guy, Buddy (1936–) US singer and guitarist, born Lettsworth, Louisiana. Began at 13 with homemade guitar and progressed to centre of Chicago blues scene in the 1950s and 1960s; 'Stone Crazy', début album *A Man And His Blues*, compilation with other Chicago bands *In The Beginning*.

Hampton, Lionel ('Hamp') (1909–2002) US vibraphonist, born Louisville, Kentucky. Made vibraphone a solo instrument, first recording with Louis Armstrong; played in Benny Goodman's band before forming own big band in 1940; 'Flyin' Home' (famous solo by Illinois Jacquet).

Hancock, Herbie (Herbert Jeffrey) (1940–) US pianist and composer, born Chicago. Child classical musician, but dedicated to jazz; played in Miles Davis's quintet for five years, seeing developments towards jazz rock; with own band turned to electric and electronic means. Music blends rhythm 'n' blues and soul blues, or blues and swing; 'Watermelon Man', 'Rock It'; soundtrack of Bertrand's Tavernier's film *Round Midnight* (1986) won an Oscar.

Handy, W(illiam) C(hristopher) (1873–1958) US musician and composer, born Florence, Alabama. Despite the opposition of his Methodist preacher father to his choice of a musical career, he joined a minstrel show as a cornet player. In 1903 he formed his own band in Memphis, Tennessee, and drew on various genres of African-American music, including spirituals, folk ballads, work songs and early jazz, to develop the form of music known as the blues. His earliest known composition 'The Memphis Blues', was followed by 'St Louis Blues', 'Beale Street Blues', 'Yellow Dog Blues', 'Careless Love' and many others. He was the first to introduce the blues style to printed music, founding a music publishing company with a partner in Memphis in 1913 and continuing to run the firm independently in New York City in the 1920s and afterwards. Long known as the 'father of the blues', he used that epithet as the title of his autobiography, published in 1958.

Hawkins, Coleman (Randolph) ('Bean', 'Hawk') (1904–69) US tenor saxophonist, born St Joseph, Missouri. Elevated tenor sax to status of solo instrument, hence title 'father of the saxophone'. Abandoned staccato style to develop melodic fluid tone. Compositions include 'Queer Notions'. Hits include masterpiece 'Body and Soul', 'The Man I Love', 'Picasso'.

Henderson, (James) Fletcher ('Smack') (1897–1952) US bandleader, pianist and arranger, born Cuthbert, Georgia. Pioneer of the big band formation. Perfected technique of writing for separate sections and set standard for the swing era. Joined Benny Goodman's band as pianist and arranger and contributed to its success with 'King Porter Stomp' and 'Blue Skies'.

Henderson, Joe (Joseph) (1937–2001) US saxophonist, bandleader and composer, born Lima, Ohio. Established reputation as a sideman, most notably to Herbie Hancock. Recorded under own name for Blue Note from 1963 onwards. In the 1990s recorded a series of award-winning records for the Verve label.

Herman, Woody (Woodrow Charles) (1913–87) US clarinettist, saxophonist, singer, bandleader and composer, born Milwaukee, Wisconsin. A forerunner of 'cool jazz', his first band, The Band That Plays The Blues, had 1939 hit 'Woodchopper's Ball'. His first Herd band was famous: Igor Stravinsky composed *Ebony Concerto* for him; the second had 'Four Brothers' reed section and recorded 'Early Autumn', which includes Stan Getz's influential solo.

Hines, Earl (Kenneth) ('Fatha') (1903–83) US pianist and bandleader, born Duquesne, Pennsylvania. Often associated with trumpeter Louis Armstrong (they had an influential duet recording 'Weather Bird'), Hines's trumpet-style of piano playing was a significant development among jazz pianists. His big band had a 12-year residency at the *Grand Terrace Ballroom*. One of the first jazz pianists to play and record solo; 'Boogie Woogie on St Louis Blues', 'Jelly Jelly', 'Second Balcony Jump', 'The Earl', 'Rosetta'.

Hodges, Johnny ('Jeep', 'Rabbit') (Hodge, Cornelius) (1906–70) US alto and soprano saxophonist, born Cambridge, Massachusetts. Dominant in alto scene before Charlie Parker; constant member of Duke Ellington's band (except 1951–5); technically orthodox but aesthetically inimitable, known for 'I Got It Bad', 'On the Sunny Side of the Street', 'Warm Valley' and 'In a Sentimental Mood' (later recorded by Coltrane in his honour).

Holiday, Billie ('Lady Day') (Fagan, Eleanora) (1915–59) US singer, born Baltimore, Maryland. Talented singer with a tragic destiny; noticed as a cabaret singer, she became famous alongside Benny Goodman and Lester Young, toured with Artie Shaw and made a film *New Orleans* with Louis Armstrong before drug addiction killed her; 'Strange Fruit', 'Lover Man', 'God Bless the Child'.

Hooker, John Lee (1917–2001) US singer and guitarist, born Clarksdale, Mississippi. Popular blues musician with relaxed vocal style; often sang alone and accompanied himself on guitar; began in gospel choirs and became one of the most influential of trad bluesmen; 'Boogie Chillen', 'Boogie With the Hook', 'It Serves Me Right to Suffer'; made *Hooker and Heat* with band Canned Heat; own albums include *Do the Boogie* and *Sittin' Here Thinkin'*.

Hopkins, Lightnin' (Sam) (1912–82) US blues singer and guitarist, born Centerville, Texas. He began to perform blues as a child, and toured the South with his cousin, singer Texas Alexander. He cut his first record in 1946, and is thought to be the most recorded of all blues artists, although his use of pseudonyms to avoid contractual problems has made an accurate count difficult. He was 'rediscovered' singing in clubs in 1959, and his acoustic country

Arts and Culture

blues style won favour with the folk revival audiences of the early 1960s. He was an inimitable raconteur as well as an idiosyncratic singer and guitarist, and he is one of the most important artists to have worked in the country blues tradition.

Howlin' Wolf (Burnett, Chester Arthur) (1910–76) US blues singer, guitarist and harmonica player, born West Point, Mississippi. He began playing blues as a child, and was able to amalgamate several strains of country and urban blues into a distinctive, individual style. He was already a mature artist before recording his first record in Memphis in 1951, and settled in Chicago in 1953, where he was a giant (physically as well as metaphorically) of the emerging electric blues scene. He was one of the most intensely exciting of all blues performers, and recorded a number of classics of the genre, many of which were later covered by rock bands like The Rolling Stones and The Doors in the 1960s. Despite failing health after a car crash in 1970, he continued to perform until shortly before his death.

Ibrahim, Abdullah (Dollar Brand) (1934–) South African pianist, born Cape Town. Formed the Jazz Epistles group, recording the country's first black jazz album. Worked with Duke Ellington in America in the 1960s. Also plays cello, soprano saxophone and flute. Known for jazz interpretations of melodies and rhythms of his African childhood.

Jackson, 'Milt' (Milton) ('Bags') (1923–99) US vibraphonist, born Detroit, Michigan. Most important vibraphonist of the bebop era. Co-founder with John Lewis of Modern Jazz Quartet, with which his career is linked; 'La Ronde' and 'Vendome' are the MJQ's mascots.

James, Elmore (Brooks, Elmore) (1918–63) US blues guitarist and singer, born Richmond, Mississippi. He taught himself to play on a homemade guitar, and was profoundly influenced by meeting Robert Johnson in 1937. He began performing with Sonny Boy Williamson (originally Rice Miller, 1910–65), and went on to establish the most important slide guitar style in modern blues. He made his first recording in 1952, and had an immediate hit with his adaptation of a Robert Johnson song, 'Dust My Broom', which became his best-known record. He moved to Chicago, but always remained in touch with his roots in the Mississippi Delta. Ironically, he died just as blues music was beginning to find a wider white audience.

Jarrett, Keith (1945–) US pianist and composer, born Allentown, Pennsylvania. With his idiosyncratic style of playing, going wild on the keys and embellishing his solos with big 'free' lyrical passages, he became very popular; played with Miles Davis, among others; *Facing You, Sun Bear Concerts*.

Jefferson, Blind Lemon (1897–1929) US blues guitarist and singer, born Couchman, Texas. He was one of seven children, and was born blind. He performed locally in and around Worthman, Texas, then moved to Dallas in 1917, where he played on the streets for small change. His recorded legacy of almost 100 songs was made between 1926 and his death (including some gospel and spiritual material using the pseudonym Deacon L J Bates). He was the first blues singer to establish a repertoire of his own songs, rather than buying from commercial songwriters, and his performing style, notably his intricate, improvisational guitar playing, was enormously influential in the development of the music.

Johnson, J J (James Louis) (1924–2001) US trombonist, pianist, baritone saxophonist and composer, born Indianapolis, Indiana. Father of the modern jazz trombone who invented bebop trombone playing, being the first slide trombonist to match the requirements of speed and articulation, as shown when he played with Charlie Parker; compositions include 'Rodeo for Quartet and Orchestra'; *All-Star Jam, The Eminent J J Johnson, The Bosses*.

Johnson, James P(rice) (1894–1955) US pianist and composer, born New Brunswick, New Jersey. Pioneer of stride with 'Carolina Shout'; often accompanied the great female blues singers; swinging style influential on eg Duke Ellington and Thelonious Monk; composer of symphonic works and hits 'Old Fashioned Love', 'Charleston' (with Cecil Mack).

Johnson, Robert (1911–38) US blues singer and guitarist, born Hazelhurst, Mississippi. He is perhaps the most famous name in blues, and his story has attained a semi-legendary status in the mythology of the music. He was a virtuoso self-taught guitarist, and although he recorded only 29 songs, their impact on the development of blues has been incalculable. Little is known of his life, but the legend that he acquired his skills by selling his soul to the Devil has taken root in blues mythology. His real impact is due not only to his musical skills, but also to the passionate, haunted intensity of his singing and playing. Most of his surviving songs, recorded in only two sessions in 1936 and 1937, have acquired classic status.

Johnston, Lonny (Alonzo) (1889–1970) US guitarist, born New Orleans. Major blues figure in New Orleans, introduced guitar in its modern form as a solo instrument; invented style of playing note by note; 'Stardust', 'Confused', 'Swinging with Lonnie'.

Jones, Elvin (Ray) (1927–) US drummer, born Pontiac, Michigan. Versatile, inventive, self-taught drummer who eschewed the restrictions of continuous tempo and created complicated polyrhythms, producing the river, a new tornado of sound in jazz. Played in Coltrane's quartet for six years; *Live at the Village Vanguard, Heart to Heart* (with Davis); appeared in film dedicated to him *Different Drummer*.

Jones, Quincy (Delight) (1933–) US trumpeter, bandleader, composer and arranger, born Illinois. Famous as arranger and producer, but also successful solo musician. Michael Jackson's mentor and producer of the *Thriller* album; 'Killer Joe '70', 'Just Once', 'Summer in the City' (Grammy winner).

Joplin, Scott (1866–1917) US ragtime pianist and composer, born Texarkana, Texas. Originator and exponent of 'Ragtime' music. First score *Multiple Leaf Rag* sold more than a million copies, but he died unfulfilled; Gunther Schiller made *Treemonisha* into a Broadway hit in the 1970s; 'The Entertainer' was used in the soundtrack of the film *The Sting* (1973).

Kenton, Stan(ley Newcomb) (1912–79) US pianist, composer and bandleader, born Wichita, Kansas. Exponent of 1950s big band 'progressive' jazz style; later bands had unusual five-trombone sections. Music considered loud and pretentious by some, but innovative by others; won Grammy 1961 for *West Side Story*.

Kidd, Carol (1944–) Scottish singer, born Glasgow. Formed permanent trio at the age of 17. Became known in London clubs in late 1970s and later appeared in radio and television. Won various awards in the 1980s.

King, B B (Riley B) (1925–) US blues singer and guitarist, born Itta Bena, Mississippi. Famous as singer and influential for economical guitar style. Prolific recording success includes 'Three O'Clock Blues',

'Sweet Black Angel' and 1981 Grammy-winner *There Must be a Better World Somewhere*.

Kirk, (Rhasaan) Roland (1936–77) US multi-instrumentalist, born Columbus, Ohio. Music rooted in gospel and blues; polyinstrumentalist despite blindness; could play three saxophones at once, sang into his flute and played whistle, siren, bagpipes, etc.

Krupa, Gene (1909–73) US drummer and bandleader, born New York City. Exuberant soloist who made the drummer a solo instrumentalist; played with Benny Goodman; formed own band; had hit 'Sing Sing Sing' with Goodman small group, and 'Rockin' Chair' with trumpeter Roy Eldridge; also 'Chickery Chick', 'Bonaparte's Retreat' and compilation *World's Greatest Drummer*; appeared in several films, eg *Some Like It Hot* (1939) and *The Benny Goodman Story* (1956).

Lacy, Steve (Lackritz, Steven) (1934–) US soprano saxophonist and composer, born New York City. Concentrated on soprano sax and developed own rough-edged tone; in the 1950s was sideman to the best soloists of the revival and Swing, then was partner to Cecil Taylor (*In Transition*), then to Thelonious Monk; first record in his own name, *Soprano Today*, included some of Monk's music, as did much of his work.

Leadbelly or **Lead Belly (Ledbetter, Huddie William)** (1888–1949) US folk and blues singer and guitarist, born Mooringsport, Louisiana. Little is known of his early life, but at 15 he could play several instruments. He was twice sentenced to long prison terms, for murder in 1917 and intent to murder in 1930, but received an early pardon on each occasion. While serving the second sentence, he was heard by folk researcher Alan Lomax, who helped secure his release. He moved to New York, where he became a seminal figure in the burgeoning folk scene, alongside Woody Guthrie and Pete Seeger. His rough-hewn vocals and blues-soaked 12-string guitar style was hugely influential into the rock era, while songs like 'Good Night Irene' and 'The Midnight Special' became folk-blues standards.

Lewis, John (Aaron) (1920–2001) US pianist and composer, born LaGrange, Illinois. Succeeded Monk as pianist in Dizzy Gillespie's big band; influential in the first bebop era; recorded with Charlie Parker and Miles Davis; formed the Modern Jazz Quartet in 1951; uncluttered, confident yet bluesy style; celebrated Monk with version of 'Round Midnight'; also composed 'Toccata for Trumpet' which shows Bach's influence, 'Move' and 'Rouge' in Davis's *Birth of the Cool*.

Lunceford, Jimmie (James Melvin) (1902–47) US alto saxophonist and bandleader, born Fulton, Missouri. His band, the Chickasaw Syncopaters, was a great addition to the history of big bands, playing music by Sy Oliver and having outstanding success with 'Tain't What You Do (It's The Way That You Do It)', 'Rhythm is our Business' and 'Blues in the Night'; 'Honeydripper', 'Got a Right to Cry', 'Rag Mop', 'Pink Champagne'.

Lyttelton, Humphrey ('Humph') (1921–) English trumpeter and bandleader, born Eton, Berkshire. Mainstream jazz musician; celebrated 40 continuous years as bandleader in 1988; pioneer in the British revivalist movement; introduced three-saxophone section and original tunes from English and West Indian folk roots; albums include *Bad Penny Blues*.

McLaughlin, John (1942–) English electric guitarist and bandleader, born Doncaster. Impressive speed and rhythm technique; music developed into synthesis of Afro-American and Indian music. Took part in birth of jazz-rock with Miles Davis; formed Mahavishnu Orchestra; first album *Extrapolation*; plays one track in 1986 film soundtrack *Round Midnight*.

Marsalis, Wynton (1961–) US trumpeter and bandleader, born New Orleans. Classical soloist and jazz performer; played Haydn's *Concerto for Trumpet* at age 14; joined Art Blakey's Jazz Messengers at 18; first recording was with the 'giants' Herbie Hancock, Ron Carter and Tony Williams; style combines extension of bebop with sense of swing; won Grammy 1984 as both best classical and jazz soloist. Albums include 1987 *Standard Time*.

Metheny, Pat (1954–) US guitarist and composer, born Lee's Summit, Missouri. Musically open-minded, appeals to bebop, rock and Free Jazz fans; blends acoustics and electronics; composed music for John Schlesinger's *The Falcon and the Snowman* (sung by David Bowie); *Song X* (with Ornette Coleman), *Bright Side of Life*, *American Garage*, *Offramp*.

Mezzrow, Mezz (Mesirow, Milton) (1899–1972) US reeds player (especially clarinet), born Chicago. Began playing sax in jail; played as a professional musician with eg Eddie Condon, Sidney Bechet; *Paris* and two volumes of *The King Jazz Story* with Bechet.

Miller, (Alton) Glenn (1904–44) US bandleader and trombonist, born Clarinda, Iowa. Very popular as dance band leader, especially during war years. Characteristic style was produced by doubling the lead tenor with a clarinet; 'In the Mood', 'Moonlight Serenade'.

Mingus, Charles (Jr) (1922–79) US double bassist, pianist, composer and bandleader, born Nogales, Arizona. One of the most important composers in 20c black music; 'Pussy Cat Dues', 'Boogie Stop Shuffle', 'Jelly Roll', 'Goodbye Pork Pie Hat', *Tijuana Moods*.

Monk, Thelonious (Sphere) (1917–82) US pianist and composer, born Rocky Mount, North Carolina. Famous 'Prophet' or 'High Priest' of bebop, with which he experimented at Minton's Playhouse in Harlem. Leading composer in jazz history; 'Round Midnight' and 'Straight No Chaser' are classics.

Montgomery, Wes (John Lesley) (1923–68) US guitarist, born Indianapolis, Indiana. Influential, innovative and versatile self-taught guitarist; worked with Lionel Hampton; mellow sound due to plucking strings with thumb instead of plectrum; *The Incredible Jazz Guitar of Wes Montgomery*.

Morton, Jelly Roll (LaMenthe, Ferdinand-Joseph) (1890–1941) US bandleader, composer and pianist, born New Orleans. First great composer in jazz, and a link between ragtime and jazz; formed successful band the Red Hot Peppers, who may have been the first to combine arranged ensemble pieces with improvisation; 'Georgia Stomp', 'Grandpa's Spells', 'Wolverine Blues', 'King Porter Stomp'.

Mulligan, Gerry (Gerald Joseph) ('Jeru') (1927–96) US baritone saxophonist, born New York City. Talented arranger and popular musician who made the baritone saxophone a solo instrument; wrote 'Jeru', 'Boplicity', 'Venus de Milo' and 'Godchild' for Davis's *Birth of the Cool*.

Oliver, King (Joseph) (1885–1938) US cornettist and bandleader, born New Orleans. By the collective improvisation of Oliver's 'Dippermouth Blues', jazz was freed from the polyphonic concept of the New Orleans style; the Chicago style developed which retained swing but had many elements (marches,

Arts and Culture

melodies, polkas, etc). Oliver thus one of the 'fathers' of jazz; innovative cornet player, using newly invented mute; 'landmark' hits include 'West End Blues', 'Canal Street Blues' and 'Doctor Jazz'.

Ory, Kid (Edward) (1886–1973) US trombonist, singer, bandleader and composer, born La Prince, Louisiana. A master of New Orleans 'tailgate' trumpet style, playing rhythmic bass as well as solo; led and played in various successful bands, eg Kid Ory's Sunshine Orchestra, the first black jazz band to record, and Louis Armstrong's Hot Five. From 1942 he was active in the New Orleans Revival, though he'd been there from the start. Compositions include 'Muskrat Ramble'; appeared as bandleader in *The Benny Goodman Story* (1956); albums include *Kid Ory's Creole Jazz Band 1944–45*.

Parker, Charlie (Charles Christopher) ('Bird', 'Yardbird') (1920–55) US alto saxophonist, bandleader and composer, born Kansas City, Missouri. Influential modern jazz performer in post-1940s, whose ideas formed the basis of the bebop style; innovative association with trumpeter Dizzy Gillespie in bebop quintets; compositions include 'Now's the Time' and 'Ornithology'.

Pass, Joe (Passalaqua, Giuseppe) (1929–94) US guitarist, born New Brunswick, New Jersey. Most influential swing guitarist since Wes Montgomery, comparable to pianist Oscar Peterson in speed and vigour; world-famous as sideman with eg Peterson, Count Basie, Ella Fitzgerald, Duke Ellington; own albums include *Virtuoso* and *University of Akron Concert*.

Pedersen, Niels-Henning Ørsted (1946–) Danish pianist and bassist, born Osted. Established reputation as one of the top jazz bassists in the world. Flexible in style, he could play mainsteam to avantgarde. Much in demand with touring soloists. Has played extensively with pianist Oscar Peterson.

Peterson, Oscar (Emmanuel) (1925–) Canadian pianist and composer, born Montreal. Reliable accompanist and flamboyant soloist; permanent member of Jazz at the Philharmonic; also performed with double-bass player Niels-Henning Ørsted Pedersen and guitarist Joe Pass; solo albums include *My Favourite Instrument*, *At Salle Playel*, *Affinity* and *Jazz Portrait of Frank Sinatra*.

Pine, Courtney (1964–) English tenor and soprano saxophonist and bass clarinettist, bandleader and composer, born London. Originally Coltrane-inspired, this talented saxophonist of Jamaican origin has formed two bands, The Jazz Warriors and The World's First Saxophone Posse; 1986 album *Journey to the Urge Within* includes tune 'Miss Interpret'; also contributed to soundtrack of film *Angel Heart* (1987).

Portal, Michel (1935–) US soprano, alto and tenor saxophonist and clarinettist, born Bayonne, New Jersey. Jazz and classical, uses different instruments for each style; a pioneer of Free Jazz in France; founded 'Unit', an open, informed group where American and European guests were welcomed; film music includes *La Cecilia* and *L'Ombre Rouge*.

Powell, Bud (Earl) (1924–66) US pianist and composer, born New York City. A great virtuoso, very important in bebop movement, and in jazz history generally; encouraged by Thelonious Monk in the 1940s, he made many recordings with other virtuosos and solo, including 'Cheryl', 'Dana Lee', 'Chasin' the Bird', 'Un Poco Loco', 'Passion Thoroughfare', 'Bouncing With Bud'; the character

Gordon in 1986 film *Round Midnight* is based on Powell.

Rainey, Gertrude Pridgett ('Ma Rainey') (1886–1939) US blues singer, born Columbus, Georgia. She began her career as a singer with the Rabbit Foot Minstrels, and claimed that she first introduced blues into her act in 1902, after hearing a girl in Missouri sing a song about the man who had deserted her. She won a large following among African-American Southerners and toured with Bessie Smith, who was her protégée. From 1923 to 1928 she made a series of recordings on the Paramount label, which won her an audience in the North. Often called the 'Mother of the Blues', she is considered to be the first of the great black blues singers, with a style of singing that preserves the continuity from early African-American music to jazz. Her best-known songs include 'See See Rider' and 'Slow Driving Moan'.

Reinhardt, Django (Jean-Baptiste) (1910–53) Belgian guitarist, born Liverchies, Belgium. Self-taught musician of gypsy background and the first European to have an influence on swing-style American guitarists, despite losing two fingers in a caravan fire; joined with Stephane Grapelli (1908–97) to form the Quintette du Hot Club de France, which inaugurated a French-style jazz; toured with the Duke Ellington orchestra, changing from acoustic to electric guitar; produced swing version of Bach's *First Movement of the Concerto in D Minor*; compositions include 'Love's Melody' and 'Improvisation', also (with Grapelli) 'HQC Strut', 'Daphne', 'Djangology'.

Roach, Max(well) (1924–) US drummer, bandleader and composer, born New York City. Key member of bebop movement and a 'giant' of modern jazz; being the first to 'swing' on the drums and use them for 'melody', he created the very influential legato rhythmic feeling; *The Freedom Suite* (waltzes), *We Insist — Freedom Now Suite*, *Money Jungle* (with Duke Ellington), *Drums Unlimited*.

Rollins, Sonny (Theodore Walter) ('Newk') (1930–) US tenor saxophonist and composer, born New York City. Powerful improviser and important voice in the 'hard bop' movement, joining Clifford Brown and Max Roach; used Caribbean calypso eg in 'Saint Thomas' and 'Don't Stop the Carnival'; 'Tenor Madness', 'Olea', 'Airegin', *Saxophone Colossus*.

Shaw, Artie (Arshawsky, Arthur Jacob) (1910–) US clarinettist, bandleader and composer, born Norwalk, Connecticut. Like Benny Goodman in tone and innovation, he was also one of the first to present a mixed black and white band, which had a 'cooler' atmosphere due to its reliance on strings; 'Begin the Beguine', 'Summit Ridge Drive', 'Frenesi', 'Dancing in the Dark'.

Shepp, Archie (1937–) US saxophonist, pianist, singer and bandleader, born Fort Lauderdale, Florida. Created formula of three horns, bass and drums which became the Free Jazz standard; developed frantic solo style in orchestral context; jazz for him was 'Great Black Music'; faithful to blues and gospel traditions and embraced West African trends eg in *Mama Too Tight* and *Magic of Ju-Ju*; also *Four for Trane* and *Ascension* with Coltrane.

Shorter, Wayne (1933–) US tenor and soprano saxophonist, bandleader and composer, born Newark, New Jersey. Played in Art Blakey's Jazz Messengers and Miles Davis's quintet (whose development towards jazz rock he helped); formed own group Weather Report, then continued in electric jazz style; the ethereal 'Mysterious Traveller' and dance-like 'Heavy Weather' contributed to *Round Midnight* (1986) film soundtrack.

Silver, Horace (Ward Martin Tavares) (1928–) US bandleader and composer, born Norwalk, Connecticut. Leading figure, with Art Blakey, of the hard bop style, and main exponent of funky jazz; first pianist and musical director of The Jazz Messengers; compositions have flavour of blues and gospel; 'Doodlin', 'The Preacher', 'Senor Blues' and 'Opus de Funk'.

Simone, Nina (Wayman, Eunice) (1933–2003) US singer, pianist and composer, born North Carolina. Performance varied from gospel through blues and soul to modern jazz, excelling in all registers; repertoire included Gershwin; best known composition 'To Be Young, Gifted and Black'; 'I Loves You Porgy', 'Mississippi Goddam', 'Central Park Blues', 'My Baby Just Cares For Me'.

Smith, Bessie (1894–1937) US singer, born Chattanooga, Tennessee. Advertised as 'The Empress of the Blues'; hers was a blues-based repertoire including recordings accompanied by leading musicians (eg Louis Armstrong). Realistic songs depict poverty and love pains often flavoured by angry feminism, eg 'Downhearted Blues'; made short film *St Louis Blues* (1929).

Smith, Tommy (1967–) Scottish saxophonist and composer, born Luton, Bedfordshire. Cosmopolitan musician with broad ideas and lavish tonality; disciple of John Coltrane, with a 'European' feeling for textures and moods in his playing; in his first album *Step By Step* he plays his own compositions, with John Scofield and Jack De Johnette; also *Peeping Tom*.

Solal, Martial (1927–) Algerian pianist, composer and bandleader, born Algiers. Improviser with boundless imagination who defies classification, and who can render standard pieces unrecognizable by his artistry; compositions include *Suite in D Flat* for jazz quartet, and for the film *A Bout De Souffle*.

Sun Ra (Blount, Herman or **Lee, Sonny)** (1914–93) US pianist, composer and bandleader, born Birmingham, Alabama. Pioneer of electronic music, little is known of him before the 1950s; his influential Arkestra functioned as a cooperative, and combined the traditions of the swing era with the freedom of improvisation and the rhythmic agility of bop; dedicated his music 'to the Creator of the Universe'.

Surman, John (1944–) English multi-instrumentalist, composer and bandleader, born Tavistock, Devon. Emerging from a classical background with folk, ethnic and church music roots. He was sideman of French-born bluesman Alexis Korner before becoming world famous as soloist; *The Trio, The Amazing Adventures of Simon Simon.*

Taylor, Cecil (Percival) (1933–) US pianist, bandleader and composer, born New York City. An exponent of the avant-garde due to his powerful free style of improvisation; very energetic and fast player who treats his piano like a percussion instrument; worked with saxophonist Jimmy Lyons for many years; *Conquistador, Unit Structures, For Olim*.

Teagarden, Jack ('Mr T') (1905–64) US trombonist and bandleader, born Texas. Great classical jazz figure with warm, natural tone; inventor of jazz trombone; also sang with Louis Armstrong; 'That's an Awful Serious Thing', 'I'm Gonna Stomp Mr Henry Lee' (with Eddie Condon), 'You Rascal You', 'Chances Are', 'Someone Stole Gabriel's Horn', 'A Hundred Years From Today'.

Tatum, Art(hur, Jr) (1909–56) US pianist, born Toledo, Ohio. The most influential of the swing-style pianists, and considered unequalled; despite near-blindness from birth his technique was astonishing and he became famous as the greatest in the history of jazz; 'Body and Soul', 'Tea For Two', 'Tiger Rag'.

Thielemans, 'Toots' (Jean-Baptiste) (1922–) Belgian guitarist and harmonica player, born Brussels. Converted from the accordian to the guitar and harmonica by Django Reinhardt, he also played with Benny Goodman, Lester Young, Count Basie and Stan Getz in America and Europe; Quincy Jones's favourite soloist; played film soundtrack *Midnight Cowboy* (1969); successes include album *Affinity*, and 'Bluesette', a composition which followed an evening improvising with Stephane Grapelli.

Tormé, Mel(vin Howard) (1925–99) US jazz and popular singer, born Chicago. He studied piano and drums as a youngster, and cut his professional teeth touring with Chico Marx in 1943, then led his own pop group, The Mel-Tones. He worked as an arranger after leaving the army in 1946, and began to build his reputation as a sophisticated singer of both jazz and pop music. His soft, slightly husky voice earned him the unwelcome nickname of 'The Velvet Fog', but his impeccable control of phrasing, pitch and expression were much admired by musicians. He recorded classic albums with arranger Marty Paitch throughout his career, and worked regularly with pianist George Shearing from the early 1980s. He wrote hundreds of songs, as well as novels and books on music, including an autobiography, and a biography of drummer Buddy Rich.

Tracey, Stan (1926–) English pianist, bandleader and composer, born London. Important contributor to European jazz scene; being self-taught meant an unconventional and individual technique; percussive piano style; compositions include jazz suites *Under Milk Wood, The Bracknell Connection, Genesis*, also for album *We Love You Madly*.

Tristano, Lennie (Leonard Joseph) (1919–78) US pianist and composer, born Chicago. Blind by age 11; 'Pianist of the Year' 1948; great jazz teacher and 'father confessor to all the avant-garde musicians in the city (Chicago)'; anticipated the 1960s Free Jazz movement in eg 'Intuition', 'Digression', 'Yesteryear'.

Tyner, McCoy (Alfred) (1938–) US pianist and composer, born Philadelphia, Pennsylvania. Part of epochal Coltrane quartet, where the calmness of his playing was a background to the furious solos; later joined Ike and Tina Turner for *Sahara*; 1973 best record prize for *Enlightenment; Double Trios* includes revived standard and classic bebop numbers, eg 'Lover Man'.

Vaughan, Sarah (Lois) ('Sassy', 'The Divine One') (1924–90) US singer, born Newark, New Jersey. Encouraged by Ella Fitzgerald, she began her career in Earl Hines's and Billy Eckstein's bands; wide vocal range, keen sense of improvisation; attracted by new bebop, she recorded with its inventors, eg Dizzy Gillespie and Charlie Parker; 'Things Must Change', 'Make Yourself Comfortable', 'Whatever Lola Wants', 'Broken-Hearted Melody'.

Walker, T-Bone (Aaron Thibeaux) (1910–75) US guitarist, singer and songwriter, born Linden, Texas. One who achieved perfect cohesion between voice and electric sound; teenage friends with Charlie Christian (both were influential in guitar-playing field); made name as blues player with 'T-Bone Blues' in 1939; 'Call It Stormy Monday'; won Grammy 1968 for *Good Feelin'*.

Waller, Fats (Thomas Wright) (1904–43) US pianist, singer, bandleader and composer, born New York City. Professional musician at 15 and master of the New York 'Stride' piano style; talented musician but popular for singing and humour; prolific composer; 'Honeysuckle Rose', 'Ain't Misbehavin'', 'Black and Blue', 'I'm Crazy Bout My Baby', 'Two Sleepy People'; appeared in films eg, *Stormy Weather* (1943).

Washington, Dinah (Jones, Ruth Lee) (1924–63) US singer, born Tuscaloosa, Alabama. Originally 'discovered' by Lionel Hampton, she became the 'Queen of the Blues' whose vibrato voice expressed the aspirations and disappointments of the Black community; 'Baby, Get Lost', 'This Bitter Earth', 'What a Difference a Day Makes', 'Baby (You've Got What It Takes)', 'It Could Happen To You'.

Waters, Ethel (1900–77) US singer, born Chester, Pennsylvania. Began in blues style and became a highly regarded 1930s pop singer; also worked in cabaret and film; 'Stormy Weather', 'A Hundred Years From Today' (with Benny Goodman and Jack Teagarden), 'Come Up and See Me Sometime' (from Mae West film).

Waters, Muddy (Morganfield, McKinley) (1915–83) US singer, guitarist, bandleader and composer, born Rolling Fork, Mississippi. Popular blues player from 1943; sang with passionate gravelly voice; achieved fame worldwide and his pupils too are many of the 'greats' in jazz; 'Rolling Stone', 'I've Got My Mojo Working', 'Hoochie Coochie Man', 'She's 19 Years Old'.

Weber, Eberhard (1940–) German bass player, bandleader and composer, born Stuttgart. Exponent of European (rather than American) music. Plays with five-string 'electro-bass', having made it a front-line instrument for rhythm to melody and improvisation; eschews American blues roots and, like Jan Garbarek, blends romanticism with evocative or moody sounds; successful first album *The Colours of Chloe*.

Webster, Ben(jamin Francis) (1909–1973) US saxophonist, born Kansas City, Missouri. Leading instrumentalist of the swing era. Worked with many of leading musicians of the period including Duke Ellington. Went on to become much sought after soloist.

Williams, Tony (1945–97) US drummer and composer, born Chicago. Contributed to evolution of jazz-rock; percussionist in Miles Davis's quartet; made fame as 1970s symbol of modern drumming; drummer for Eric Dolphy's *Out to Lunch* and Davis's *Filles de Kilimanjaro*; latterly played modern jazz and jazz fusion; *Spring, Lifetime, Emergency, Turn It Over, The Joy of Flying*.

Winding, Kai (1922–83) Danish–US trombonist, born Aarhus, Denmark. Played with many of the jazz 'greats', eg co-leading quintet with J J Johnson, restoring trombone to important position; toured with Gillespie, Monk and Hampton; played on Davis's *Birth of the Cool*; had hit with 'More' (*Mondo Cane* (1963) film theme), also *More Brass, Betwixt And Between Jazz Showcase*.

Young, Lester (Willis) ('Prez') (1909–59) US tenor saxophonist, born Woodville, Mississippi. A forerunner of 'cool jazz', which was the opposite of the 1930s saxophone style (eg Coleman Hawkins); pioneer of linear improvisation (J J Johnson); eschewed accepted concepts of melody, rhythm and swing; made reputation with Count Basie's Band; recordings with them include 'Tickle Toe', 'Every Tub', 'One O'Clock Jump'; also 'Lady Be Good', 'Taxi War Dance', 'Rock-A-Bye Basie'.

Musical symbols, terms and abbreviations

▪ Symbols

The staff or stave

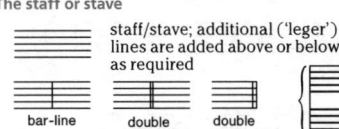

staff/stave; additional ('leger') lines are added above or below as required

bar-line double bar-line double bar-line (conclusion) brace, joining staves; read staves simultaneously

Clefs

These are in common use (the note Middle C is shown in each case):

treble (G) clef bass (F) clef alto or viola (C) clef tenor (C) clef

In older music the C clef is found on any of the five lines of the staff.

Accidentals

♯	sharp, raising the pitch of a note by a semitone
𝄪	double sharp, raising the pitch of a note by two semitones
♭	flat, lowering the pitch of a note by a semitone
♭♭	double flat, lowering the pitch of a note by two semitones
♮	natural, cancelling the effect of a previous accidental

Note lengths

⊏⊐ (or ⊟)	breve (double whole-note)
o	semibreve (whole-note)
d	minim (half-note)
	crotchet (quarter-note)
	quaver (eighth-note)
	semiquaver (1/16 note)
	demisemiquaver (1/32 note)
	hemidemisemiquaver (1/64 note)

chord: two or more notes sounded simultaneously

Ties (⌒, ⌣) are used to combine the lengths of two or more notes of the same pitch; dots are used to extend the length of a note by one-half, eg:

Beams are often used to group together quavers (eighth-notes) or shorter notes into larger units, eg:

Time signatures

The lower figure indicates the unit of measurement, the upper figure the number of these units in a bar, eg:

$\frac{2}{2}$ (or 𝄵)	two minims (half-notes) or their equivalent in a bar
$\frac{4}{4}$ (or 𝄴)	four crotchets (quarter-notes) or their equivalent in a bar
$\frac{3}{8}$	three quavers (eighth-notes) or their equivalent in a bar
$\frac{9}{16}$	nine semiquavers (1/16-notes) or their equivalent in a bar

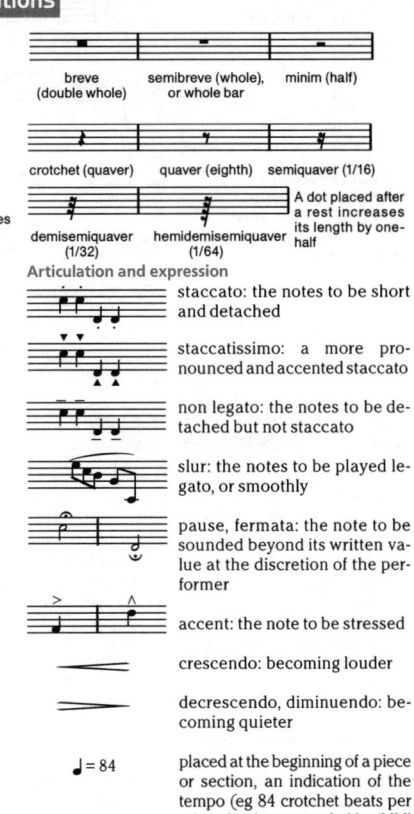

breve (double whole) semibreve (whole), or whole bar minim (half)

crotchet (quaver) quaver (eighth) semiquaver (1/16)

demisemiquaver (1/32) hemidemisemiquaver (1/64)

A dot placed after a rest increases its length by one-half

Articulation and expression

staccato: the notes to be short and detached

staccatissimo: a more pronounced and accented staccato

non legato: the notes to be detached but not staccato

slur: the notes to be played legato, or smoothly

pause, fermata: the note to be sounded beyond its written value at the discretion of the performer

accent: the note to be stressed

crescendo: becoming louder

decrescendo, diminuendo: becoming quieter

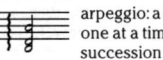

♩ = 84 placed at the beginning of a piece or section, an indication of the tempo (eg 84 crotchet beats per minute); often preceded by 'MM' (Metronom Maelzel)

Ornaments

arpeggio: a chord whose notes are played one at a time in rapid (normally upward) succession rather than simultaneously

acciaccatura: a short grace note, that does not take any time from the note on which it leans

appoggiatura: an ornamental note, that is not essential to the melody but which leans on the following note, taking half its time from it

mordent ('lower' mordent): sounding approximately

pralltriller, inverted (or 'upper') mordent: sounding approximately

trill, shake: the rapid and continuous alternation of the written note and the note immediately above it

turn: sounding (depending on tempo and context) approximately

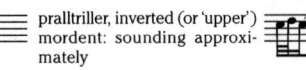

Arts and Culture

Key signatures
(Major keys: capital letters;
minor keys: lower-case
letters)

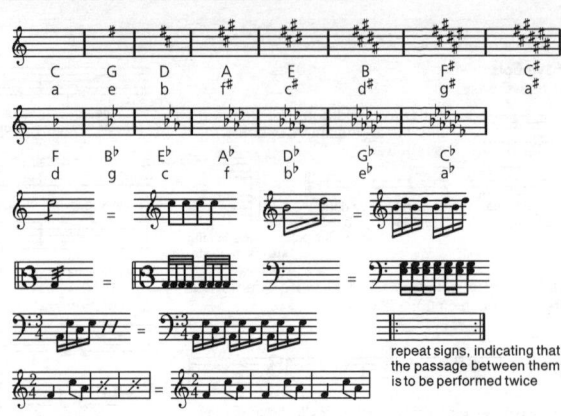

C	G	D	A	E	B	F#	C#
a	e	b	f#	c#	d#	g#	a#

F	Bb	Eb	Ab	Db	Gb	Cb
d	g	c	f	bb	eb	ab

Repetition
In instrumental music
repeated notes, figures
and even whole sections
are sometimes shown in
abbreviated form, eg:

repeat signs, indicating that
the passage between them
is to be performed twice

Tempo and expression marks

Italian terms placed at the head of a piece or section to indicate its tempo and general expression have changed in meaning over the years and are rarely precise. The following list gives some indication of how the more common terms are generally understood today.

adagio slow

agitato agitated

allegro quick and lively

allegretto fairly quick and lively

andante 'going'; slow and steady

andantino a little quicker than **andante**

animato animated, lively appasionato impassioned

assai 'very' (**allegro assai** very fast)

brio 'spirit', 'fire' (**allegro con brio** fast and energetic)

cantabile flowing and melodious

dolente sadly

energico energetic, vigorous

espressivo expressive

feroce fierce

fuoco 'fire' (**con fuoco** with fire)

furioso furious

giocoso lively or humorous

grave slow, solemn

grazioso graceful

larghetto fairly slow

largo slow and dignified

legato smooth and flowing

leggiero light

lento slow

maestoso majestic

marciale in the style of a march

marziale in a military style

meno 'less' (**meno mosso** slower)

moderato moderate, at a moderate pace

molto 'much', 'very' (**molto lento** very slow)

moto 'motion' (**con moto** quickly)

pesante heavy, ponderous

piacevole pleasant or playful

più 'more' (**più mosso** faster)

poco 'little' (**poco adagio** rather slowly)

prestissimo faster than **presto**

presto very fast

quasi 'as if', 'almost' (**andante, quasi allegretto**)

risoluto with emphasis, boldly

scherzando playful

semplice simple, in an unforced style

sotto voce very softly

strepitoso loud, noisy, boisterous

tanto, troppo 'so much', 'too much' (**allegro non tanto** fast but not very fast; **lento ma non troppo** slow, but not becoming too slow)

veloce with great rapidity

vivace lively

vivo vigorous, brisk

Other terms and abbreviations

This section lists symbols and terms that might be found in a musical score.

a tempo in time (ie revert to the previous or original tempo)

accel. (**accelerando**) with increasing speed

alla breve played quickly with two beats to the bar instead of four

allarg. (**allargando**) slowing

arco with the bow

cal. (**calando**) dying away

colla voce 'with the voice'; follow closely the singer's tempo

col legno 'with the wood'; play a string instrument with the stick of the bow

con sordino with the mute

cres. (**crescendo**) becoming louder

DC, da capo (**al fine**) go back to the beginning of the piece or movement (and play to the end marked **Fine**)

decresc. (**decrescendo**) becoming quieter

dim. (**diminuendo**) becoming quieter

dol (**dolce**) gently or sweetly

DS, dal segno go back to the sign 𝄋

f (**forte**) loud; **ff** (**fortissimo**), **fff** increasing degrees of loudness

Fine see **DC**

fz (**forzato**) with sudden emphasis

gliss. (**glissando**) slide quickly from one note to another

GP 'general pause'; a rest for the whole ensemble

MM metronom Maelzel

marc. (**marcato**) emphatic, accented

mf (**mezzo forte**) moderately loud

mp (**mezzo piano**) moderately quiet

ossia 'or', 'alternatively'

ottava, 8va, 8 play a passage an octave higher or lower; **coll ottava, col 8va, col 8** play the written notes together with their octaves

p (**piano**) quiet, soft; **pp** (**pianissimo**), **ppp** increasing (but imprecise) degrees of softness

ped. depress the sustaining (loud) pedal on a piano, release indicated by *

pizz. (**pizzicato**) played using the fingers to pluck the strings

rall. (**rallentando**) becoming gradually slower

rinf., rfz, rf getting suddenly louder

rit., ritard. (**ritardando**) becoming gradually slower

rubato with a freedom of tempo, but not impairing the overall flow of the music

segno see **DS**

senza sordino without the mute

sf., sfz., (sforzando, sforzato) with sudden emphasis

simile play in the same manner as before

smorz. (**smorzando**) gradually fading away, growing slower and softer

sost. (**sostenuto**) steady and sustained

stacc. (**staccato**) short and abrupt

string. (**stringendo**) with increasing speed and excitement

ten (**tenuto**) in a sustained manner

tre corde release the soft pedal on the piano

una corda play using the soft pedal on the piano

VS (**volti subito**) turn the page quickly

Ballet and modern dancers

Ashley, Merrill (Linda Michelle Merrill) (1950–) American, born St Paul, Minnesota.

Baker, Josephine (Freda Josephine McDonald) (1906–75) American, born St Louis, Missouri.

Baryshnikov, Mikhail (Nikolaievich) (1948–) Russian, born Riga.

Bausch, Pina (1940–) German, born Solingen.

Bessmertnova, Natalia (1941–) Russian, born Moscow.

Bujones, Fernando (1955–) American, born Florida.

Bull, Deborah (Clare) (1963–) English, born London.

Bussell, Darcey (Andrea) (1969–) English, born London.

Camargo, Maria Anna de (1710–70) French, born Brussels.

Carlson, Carolyn (1943–) American, born California.

Chauviré, Yvette (1917–) French, born Paris.

Clark, Michael (1962–) Scottish, born Kintore, near Aberdeen.

Danilova, Alexandra (Dionysievna) (1903–97) Russian–American, born Peterhof.

De Keersmaeker, Anne Teresa (1906–) Belgian, born Mechelen.

Dolin, Sir Anton (Sydney Francis Patrick Chippendall Healey-Kay) (1904–83) English, born Slinfold, Sussex.

Dowell, Sir Anthony (1943–) English, born London.

Duncan, Isadora (1878–1927) American, born San Francisco.

Dunham, Katherine (1909–) American, born Chicago.

Dunn, Douglas (1942–) American, born Palo Alto, California.

Dupond, Patrick (1959–) French, born Paris.

Eglevsky, André (1917–77) Russian–American, born Moscow.

Elssler, Fanny (Franziska Elssler) (1810–84) Austrian, born Gumpendorf.

Farrell, Suzanne (1945–) American, born Cincinnati, Ohio.

Fonteyn, Dame Margot (Peggy Hookham) (1919–91) English, born Reigate, Surrey.

Fracci, Carla (1936–) Italian, born Milan.

Genée, Dame Adelin (Anina Jensen) (1878–1970) Danish, born Hinnerup.

Gilpin, John (1930–83) English, born Southsea.

Gore, Walter (1910–79) Scottish, born Waterside.

Gorsky, Alexander Alexeivich (1871–1924) Russian, born St Petersburg.

Gregory, Cynthia (1946–) American, born Los Angeles.

Grey, Dame Beryl (Beryl Svenson) (1927–) English, born London.

Grisi, Carlotta (1819–99) Italian, born Visinada.

Hamilton, Gordon (1918–59) Australian, born Sydney.

Haydée, Marcia (Marcia Haydee Salaverry Pereira de Silva) (1939–) Brazilian, born Niteroi.

Helpmann, Sir Robert (1909–86) Australian, born Mount Gambier.

Jasinski, Roman (Roman Czeslaw) (1907–91) Polish–American, born Warsaw.

Kain, Karen (1951–) Canadian, born Hamilton, Ontario.

Karsavina, Tamara Platonovna (1885–1978) Russian–British, born St Petersburg.

Kaye, Nora (Nora Koreff) (1920–87) American, born New York.

Kent, Allegra (1938–) American, born Los Angeles.

Kirkland, Gelsey (1952–) American, born Bethlehem, Pennsylvania.

Lichine, David (David Lichenstein) (1910–72) Russian–American, born Rostov-na-Donu.

Makarova, Natalia (1940–) Russian, born St Petersburg.

Markova, Dame Alicia (Lilian Alicia Marks) (1910–) English, born London.

Martins, Peter (1946–) Danish, born Copenhagen.

Mauri, Rosita (1849–1923) Spanish, born Tarragona.

Neary, Patricia (1942–) American, born Miami, Florida.

Nemchinova, Vera (Nicolayevna) (1899–1984) Russian, born Moscow.

Nijinsky, Vaslav Fomich (1889–1950) Russian, born Kiev.

Nureyev, Rudolf Hametovich (1938–93) Russian–British, born on a train between Lake Baikal and Irkutsk, Siberia.

Page, Ruth (1899–1991) American, born Indianapolis.

Panov, Valery (Matvevich) (1938–) Russian, born Vitebsk.

Panova, Galina (1949–) Russian, born Archangel.

Petipa, Lucien (1815–98) French, born Marseilles.

Petipa, Marie (Mariusovna II) (1857–1930) Russian, born St Petersburg.

Petronio, Stephen (1956–) American, born Nutley, New Jersey.

Plisetskaya, Maya Mikailovna (1925–) Russian, born Moscow.

Rambert, Dame Marie (Cyvia Rambam, then Miriam Ramberg) (1888–1982) Polish–British, born Warsaw.

Riabouchinska, Tatiana (1917–2000) Russian–American, born Moscow.

Arts and Culture

Rubinstein, Ida Lvovna (1885–1960) Russian, born St Petersburg.

Seymour, Lynn (Lynn Springbett) (1939–) Canadian, born Wainwright.

Shearer, Moira (Moira King) (1926–) Scottish, born Dunfermline.

Shearer, Sybil (1918–) American, born Toronto.

Sibley, Dame Antoinette (1939–) English, born Bromley.

Sleep, Wayne (1948–) English, born Plymouth.

Somes, Michael (1917–94) British, born Horsley.

Spessivtseva, Olga Alexandrovna (1895–1991) Russian–American, born Rostov.

Taglioni, Marie (1804–84) Swedish–Italian, born Stockholm.

Tallchief, Maria (1925–) American, born Fairfax, Oklahoma.

Trefilova, Vera Alexandrovna (1875–1943) Russian, born St Petersburg.

Ulanova, Galina (Sergeyevna) (1910–98) Russian, born St Petersburg.

Villella, Edward (1936–) American, born Bayside, New York.

Ballet and modern dance companies

Name	Date founded	Location
Alvin Ailey American Dance Theater	1958	New York
American Ballet Theater	1940	New York
Australian Ballet	1962	Melbourne
Australian Dance Theatre	1965	Adelaide
Ballet Gulbenkian	1965	Lisbon
Ballet Jooss	1933	Cambridge
Ballet Rambert	1926	London
Ballet Russe de Monte Carlo	1938	Monte Carlo
Ballets des Champs Élysées	1944	Paris
Ballets de Paris	1948	France
Ballets Russes de Sergei Diaghilev (now Kirov Ballet)	1909–29	Paris and St Petersburg
Ballets Trockadero de Monte Carlos	1974	New York
Ballet-Théâtre Contemporain	1968	Amiens
Ballet West	1963	Salt Lake City, Utah
Béjart Ballet Lausanne (formerly Ballet du XXe siècle, 1960)	1987	Lausanne
Birmingham Royal Ballet (formerly Sadler's Wells Royal Ballet)	1946	Birmingham
Bolshoi Ballet	1776	Moscow
Borovansky Ballet	1942	Melbourne
Boston Ballet	1963	USA
Central Ballet of China	1959	Beijing
Cholmondeleys, The	1984	London
City Ballet of London	1996	London
Dance Theater of Harlem	1961	New York
Dutch National Ballet	1986	Amsterdam
DV8 Physical Theatre	1986	London
English National Ballet (formerly London Festival Ballet)	1950	London
Feld Ballet NY	1974	New York
Grands Ballets Canadiens de Montreal	1957	Montreal
Hong Kong Ballet	1979	Hong Kong
Houston Ballet	1968	Houston
Joffrey Ballet of Chicago (formerly Joffrey Ballet)	1956	Chicago
José Limón Dance Company	1946	New York
Kirov Ballet	1935	St Petersburg
Lar Lubovitch Dance Company	1968	New York
London Festival Ballet (originally Festival Ballet)	1949	London
Maly Ballet	1915	St Petersburg
Mark Morris Dance Group	1980	New York
Martha Graham Dance Company	1927	New York
Merce Cunningham Dance Company	1953	New York
Miami City Ballet	1986	Miami
Murray Louis and Nikolais Dance Company	1989	New York
National Ballet	1948	Maryland
National Ballet of Canada	1951	Toronto
National Ballet of Cuba (formerly Ballet Alicia Alonso, 1948)	1959	Havana
National Ballet of Mexico	1949	Mexico City
Netherland Dance Theatre	1959	The Hague
New York City Ballet	1948	New York
Northern Ballet Theatre (formed from part of Western Theatre Ballet)	1969	Manchester
Paris Opéra Ballet	1669	Paris

Name	Date founded	Location
Pennsylvania Ballet	1964	Philadelphia
Pilobolus Dance Theater	1971	Washington, Connecticut
Pittsburgh Ballet Theater	1970	Pittsburgh
Richard Alston Dance Company	1994	London
Royal Ballet (formerly Sadler's Wells Ballet)	1936	London
Royal Danish Ballet	ballets from second half 16c	Copenhagen
Royal New Zealand Ballet	1953	Wellington
Royal Swedish Ballet	1st court ballet 1638	Stockholm
Royal Winnipeg Ballet	1938	Canada
San Francisco Ballet (formerly San Francisco Opera Ballet)	1933	San Francisco
Scottish Ballet (formed from part of Western Theatre Ballet)	1969	Glasgow
Stanislavsky Ballet (Stanislavsky and Nemirovich-Danchenko Music Theatre Ballet)	1929	Moscow
Stuttgart Ballet	court ballets from 1609	Germany
Sydney Dance Company	1971	Sydney
Western Theatre Ballet (divided 1969 to form Northern Ballet, Scottish Ballet)	1957	Bristol

Ballets

Ballet	Composer	Choreographer	First performance
Anastasia	Tchaikovsky, Martinu	MacMillan	1971
Apollon Musagète	Stravinsky	Bolm	1928
Appalachian Spring	Copland	Graham	1944
L'Après-midi d'un faune	Debussy	Nijinsky	1912
La Bayadère	Minkus	Petipa	1877
Les Biches	Poulenc	Nijinska	1924
Billy the Kid	Copland	Loring	1938
Bolero	Ravel	Bejart	1961
La Boutique Fantasque	Rossini, arr. Respighi	Massine	1919
The Burrow	Martin	MacMillan	1958
Cain and Abel	Panufnik	MacMillan	1968
Carmen	Bizet	Petit	1949
Le Chant du rossignol	Stravinsky	Massine	1920
Checkmate	Bliss	de Valois	1937
Cinderella	Prokofiev	Ashton	1948
Concerto Barocco	Bach	Balanchine	1940
Coppélia	Delibes	St Léon	1870
Don Quixote	Minkus	Petipa	1869
Duo Concertant	Stravinsky	Balanchine	1972
Ebony Concerto	Stravinsky	Carter	1957
Elite Syncopations	Joplin	MacMillan	1974
Enigma Variations	Elgar	Ashton	1968
Façade	Walton	Ashton	1931
Fall River Legend	Gould	de Mille	1948
Fancy Free	Bernstein	Robbins	1944
La Fille mal gardée	Various (French popular songs and airs)	Dauberval	1789
The Firebird	Stravinsky	Fokine	1910
The Four Seasons	Verdi	MacMillan	1975
The Four Temperaments	Hindemith	Balanchine	1946
Giselle	Adam	Coralli and Perro (later revised by Petipa)	1841
The Gods Go A-Begging	Handel	Balanchine	1928
Hamlet	Tchaikovsky	Helpmann	1942
Harlequinade	Drigo	Balanchine	1965
Las Hermanas	Martin	MacMillan	1963
Illumination	Britten	Ashton	1950
The Invitation	Seiber	MacMillan	1960
Isadora	Rodney Bennett	MacMillan	1981
Ivan the Terrible	Prokofiev, arr. Chulaki	Grigorovich	1975

Arts and Culture

Ballet	Composer	Choreographer	First performance
Jeu de cartes	Stravinsky	Balanchine	1937
Le Jeune homme et la mort	Bach	Petit	1946
The Judas Tree	Elias	MacMillan	1992
Jewels	Fauré, Stravinsky and Tchaikovsky	Balanchine	1967
Knight Errant	Richard Strauss	Tudor	1968
The Lady and the Fool	Verdi, arr. Mackerass	Cranko	1954
Lady of Shallot	Sibelius	Ashton	1931
Lament of the Waves	Masson	Ashton	1970
Legend of Joseph	Richard Strauss	Fokine	1914
Legend of Judith	Mordecai	Graham	1962
La Luna	Bach	Béjart	1991
Le Malade imaginaire	Rota	Béjart	1976
Manon	Massenet	MacMillan	1974
The Masques	Poulenc	Ashton	1933
Mathilde	Wagner	Béjart	1965
Mayerling	Liszt	MacMillan	1978
A Midsummer Night's Dream	Mendelssohn	Balanchine	1962
A Month in the Country	Chopin, arr. Lanchbery	Ashton	1976
Monumentum pro Gesualdo	Stravinsky	Balanchine	1960
The Moor's Pavane	Purcell	Limón	1949
Night Journey	Schuman	Graham	1947
Night Shadow	Rieti	Balanchine	1946
Les Noces	Stravinsky	Nijinska	1923
Nocturne	Delius	Ashton	1936
The Nutcracker	Tchaikovsky	Ivanov	1892
Ondine	Henze	Ashton	1958
Onegin	Tchaikovsky, arr. Stolze	Cranko	1965
Orpheus	Stravinsky	Balanchine	1948
Les Papillons	Schumann, arr. Tcherepnin	Fokine	1913
Parade	Satie	Massine	1917
Les Patineurs	Mayerbeer, arr. Lambert	Ashton	1937
Petroushka	Stravinsky	Fokine	1911
Pineapple Poll	Sullivan, orch. Mackerras	Cranko	1951
Present Histories	Schubert	Tuckett	1991
Prince Igor	Borodin	Fokine	1909
The Prince of the Pagodas	Britten	Cranko	1957
The Prodigal Son	Prokofiev	Balanchine	1929
The Rake's Progress	Gordon	de Valois	1935
Raymonda	Glazunov	Petipa	1898
Le Renard	Stravinsky	Nijinska	1922
Les Rendezvous	Auber, arr. Lambert	Ashton	1933
Requiem	Fauré	MacMillan	1976
Rhapsody	Rachmaninov	Ashton	1980
Rituals	Bartók	MacMillan	1975
Rodeo	Copland	de Mille	1942
Romeo and Juliet	Prokofiev	Lavrovsky	1940
Rooms	Hopkins	Sokolow	1955
Russian Soldier	Prokofiev	Fokine	1942
Les Saisons	Glazunov	Petipa	1900
Le Sacré du printemps (The Rite of Spring)	Stravinsky, Roerich	Nijinsky	1913
Scènes de ballet	Stravinsky	Dolin	1944
Schéhérazade	Rimsky-Korsakov	Fokine	1910
Scotch Symphony	Mendelssohn	Balanchine	1952
Serenade	Tchaikovsky	Balanchine	1934
The Seven Deadly Sins	Weill	Balanchine	1933
The Sleeping Beauty	Tchaikovsky	Petipa	1890
Song of the Earth	Mahler	MacMillan	1965
Spartacus	Khachaturian	Grigorovich	1968
Le Spectre de la Rose	Weber	Fokine	1911
Stoics Quartet	Mendelssohn	Burrows	1991
Summerspace	Feldman	Cunningham	1958
Swan Lake	Tchaikovsky	Petipa and Ivanov	1895
La Sylphide	Løvenskjold	Bournonville	1836
Les Sylphides (Chopiniana)	Chopin, variously orchestrated	Fokine	1909
Symphonic Variations	Franck	Ashton	1946
Symphonie fantastique	Berlioz	Massine	1936
Symphony in C	Bizet	Balanchine	1947

Ballet	Composer	Choreographer	First performance
Symphony in Three Movements	Stravinsky	Blanchine	1972
Tales of Hoffman	Offenbach, arr. Lanchberg	Darrell	1973
The Taming of the Shrew	Scarlatti-Stolze	Cranko	1969
The Three-Cornered Hat	de Falla	Massine	1919
Les Vainqueurs	Wagner, and Indian and Tibetan music	Béjart	1969
La Valse	Ravel	Nijinska	1929
Variations	Stravinsky	Balanchine	1966
La Ventana	Lumbye and Holm	Bournonville	1854
Voluntaries	Poulenc	Tetley	1973
The Walk to the Paradise Garden	Delius	Ashton	1972
A Wedding Bouquet	Berners	Ashton	1937

Ballet and modern dance choreographers

Selected ballets are listed.

Alston, Richard John William (1948–) English, born Stoughton, Sussex; *Something to Do* (1969), *Rumours, Visions* (1969), *Red Rum* (1998).

Ashton, Sir Frederick William Mallandaine (1904–88) English, born Guayaquil, Ecuador; *Façade* (1931), *Les Rendezvous* (1933), *Cinderella* (1948), *Daphnis and Chloe* (1951), *Ondine* (1958), *The Two Pigeons* (1961), *The Dream* (1964), *Rhapsody* (1980).

Balanchine, George (Georgi Balanchivadze) (1904–83) Russian–American, born St Petersburg; *Apollo* (1928), *The Prodigal Son* (1929), *Bourrée Fantasque* (1949), *Jeu de cartes* (1937), *Agon* (1957), *The Seven Deadly Sins* (1958), *Davidsbundlertazue* (1980).

Béjart, Maurice (Maurice Jean Berger) (1928–) French, born Marseilles; *The Firebird* (1970), *Notre Faust* (1975), *Choreographic Offering* (1971), *Kabuki* (1986), *MutationX* (1998).

Bournonville, August (1805–79) Danish, born Copenhagen; *La Sylphide* (1836), *Napoli* (1842), *La Ventana* (1854).

Bruce, Christopher (1945–) English, born Leicester; *Ancient Voices of Children* (1975), *Ghost Dances* (1981), *Swansong* (1987), *Four Scenes* (1998).

Childs, Lucinda (1940–) American, born New York City; *Einstein on the Beach* (1976), *Relative Calm* (1981), *Available Light* (1983), *Premier Orange* (1984), *Rhythm Plus* (1991), *One and One* (1992).

Cranko, John (1927–73) South African, born Rustenburg; *Beauty and the Beast* (1949), *Pineapple Doll* (1951), *The Prince of the Pagodas* (1957), *Jeu de Cartes* (1965), *Onegin* (1965), *Taming of the Shrew* (1969), *Traces* (1973).

Cunningham, Merce (1919–) American, born Centralia, Washington; *Suite for Five* (1956), *Antic Meet* (1958), *Aeon* (1961), *Scramble* (1967), *Duets* (1980), *Loosestrife* (1991), *Occasion Piece* (1999).

Darrell, Peter (1929–87) English, born Richmond, Surrey; *A Wedding Present* (1962), *Beauty and the Beast* (1969), *Tales of Hoffman* (1972), *Swan Lake* (1977).

Davies, Siobhan (Susan Davies) (1950–) English, born London; *New Galileo* (1984), *Bridge the Distance* (1985), *Different Trains* (1990), *Winnsboro Cotton Mill Blues* (1992), *Plants and Ghosts* (2002).

de Mille, Agnes George (1905–93) American, born New York City; *Three Virgins and a Devil* (1941), *Rodeo* (1942), *Fall River Legend* (1948), and for Broadway, *Oklahoma!* (1943), *Gentlemen Prefer Blondes* (1949).

de Valois, Dame Ninette (Edris Stannus) (1898–2001) Irish, born Baltiboys, County Wicklow; *Job* (1931), *La Création du monde* (1931), *The Rake's Progress* (1935), *Checkmate* (1937), *Don Quixote* (1950).

Diaghilev, Sergei Pavlovich (1872–1929) Russian, born Selistchev barracks, province of Novgorod; producer, impressario, and founder of Ballet Russes; not a choreographer himself, he fostered the talents of Balanchine, Fokine, Nijinsky.

Fokine, Michel (Mikhail Mikhaylovich Fokine) (1880–1942) Russian–American dancer and choreographer, born St Petersburg; *Les Sylphides* (1907), *Petroushka* (1911).

Graham, Martha (1894–1991) American, born Pittsburgh; *Lamentation* (1930), *Frontier* (1935), *Appalachian Spring* (1958).

Ivanov, Lev (Ivanovich) (1834–1901) Russian, born Moscow; *The Enchanted Forest* (1887), *The Nutcracker* (1892), *Swan Lake* (with Petipa, 1895).

Jooss, Kurt (1901–79) German, born Waaseralfingen; *Petrushka* (1930), *The Green Table* (1932), *Pulcinella* (1932), *The Mirror* (1935).

Limón, José (1908–72) American, born Culiacan, Mexico; *La Malinche* (1949), *The Moor's Pavane* (1949), *The Traitor* (1954), *Miss Brevis* (1958), *Carlotta* (1972).

Loring, Eugene (1914–82) American, born Milwaukee; *Yankee Clipper* (1937), *Billy the Kid* (1938).

Macmillan, Sir Kenneth (1929–92) Scottish, born Dunfermline, Fife; *The Rite of Spring* (1962), *Las Hermanas* (1963), *Romeo and Juliet* (1965), *Anastasia* (1971), *The Four Seasons* (1975), *Mayerling* (1978), *Isadora* (1981).

Massine, Léonide (Fedorovich) (1895–1979) Russian–American, born Moscow; *Parade* (1917), *La Boutique Fantasque* (1919), *The Three-Cornered Hat* (1919), *Bachanale* (1939).

Morris, Mark (William) (1956–) American, born Seattle, Washington; *Il Penseroso ed il Moderato* (1988), *Dido and Aeneas* (1989), *The Hard Nut* (1991), *Resurrection* (2002).

Nijinska, Bronislova (Fominitshna) (1891–1972) Russian–Polish–American, born Minsk, Russia; *Le Renard* (1922), *Les Noces* (1923, 1966), *Les Biches* (1924, 1964), *La Valse* (1929), *The Snow Maiden* (1942).

Arts and Culture

Nikolais, Alwin (1910–93) American, born Southington, Connecticut; *Noumenon* (1953), *Kaleidoscope* (1956), *Imago* (1963), *Sanctum* (1964), *Gallery* (1978), *Schema* (1980), *Arc-en-Ciel* (1987).

Perrot, Jules (Joseph) (1810–94) French, born Lyons; *Ondine* (1843), *Les Eléments* (1847), *Faust* (1848), *Markobomba* (1854).

Petipa, Marius (1818–1910) French, born Marseilles; *Pharoah's Daughter* (1862), *La Bayadère* (1877), *The Sleeping Beauty* (1890), *Cinderella* (1893), *Swan Lake* (1895), *Raymonda* (1898).

Petit, Roland (1924–) French, born Paris; *Le Rossignol et la rose* (1944), *Les Forains* (1945), *Le Jeune homme et la mort* (1946), *Nana* (1976), *Marcel Proust Remembered* (1980), *Clavigo* (1999).

Robbins, Jerome (Jerome Rabinowitz) (1918–98) American, born New York; *Fancy Free* (1944), *Interplay* (1945), *The Pied Piper* (1951), *Afternoon of a* *Fawn* (1953), *West Side Story* (1957, musical), and for Broadway, eg *The King and I* (1951).

St-Léon, Arthur (1821–70) French, born Paris; *Le Violon du diable* (1849), *La Fille mal gardée* (1866), *La Source* (1866), *Coppélia* (1870).

Tetley, Glen (1926–) American, born Cleveland, Ohio; *Pierrot lunaire* (1962), *Voluntaries* (1973), *The Tempest* (1979), *La Ronde* (1987), *Oracle* (1994).

Tharp, Twyla (1941–) American, born Portland, Indiana; *Eight Jelly Rolls* (1971), *Push Comes to Shove* (1976), *Hair* (1978, film), *The Catherine Wheel* (1983, musical), *White Nights* (1985, film), *Jump Start* (1995), *Movin' Out* (2002, musical).

Tudor, Antony (William Cook) (1908–87) English, born London; *Undertow* (1945), *Lady of the Camellias* (1951), *Shadowplay* (1967), *The Tiller in the Field* (1978).

Major painting styles

Abstract Art A non-representational 20c style developed as a means of expressing inner reality in pictorial form. Some abstract pictures bear no resemblance to reality, whereas others feature a highly subjective treatment or 'abstraction' of recognizable subjects (as in Cubism). The earliest consciously abstract paintings were by Wassily Kandinsky (1910) and Frantisek Kupka (*Amorpha: Fugue in Two Colours*, 1912), both inspired by music, the universal abstract language. Abstract art led to other movements such as Neo-Plasticism, Constructivism and American Abstract Expressionism.

Abstract Expressionism A term relating to the vivid, non-representational work of a group of artists in 1940s New York, who were united by their emphasis on the expression inherent in the texture and colour of the paint itself, and the interaction of artist, paint and canvas; eg work by Mark Rothko, Arshile Gorky, Franz Kline, Jackson Pollock.

Action Painting A form of Abstract Expressionism; the technique of creating a picture that emphasizes the physical process of painting eg by throwing, splashing, dribbling or pouring on the paint. Its early exponents included Jackson Pollock, who also used knives on his canvases, dragged things across them and rode a bicycle on them, and Willem de Kooning.

Baroque An extravagant, confident and highly decorative style (c.1600–1720) which inherited movement from Mannerism and a sense of grandeur and solidity from High Renaissance. It was associated with the reinvigorated Catholic Church in Europe and often expressed intense religious emotion. In secular art, such as that commissioned by Louis XIV for Versailles, it served to express the glory of royalty; eg work by Rubens.

Buddhist Buddhism (founded 6c BC, India's national religion 3c BC), coupled with the patronage of such rulers as the Mauryan emperor Asoka and the Kushan ruler Kanishka, had a major influence on Indian art and architecture. From 1c AD Buddha, previously represented by the lotus flower, a wheel, or by his throne, could be shown in human form, which gave rise to many highly ornate statues.

Constructivism A term usually applied to a form of abstract art that began in Russia c.1917, using machine-age materials such as steel, glass and plastic. Leading practitioners included Vladimir Tatlin, and the brothers Antoine Pevsner and Naum Gabo. In Russia this impetus was channelled into industrial design (Soviet Constructivism). Pevsner and Gabo left Russia in the early 1920s, and their ideas subsequently influenced abstract artists in the West (International Constructivism).

Cubism A radical movement founded 1908 by Georges Braque and Pablo Picasso which revolutionized European painting and sculpture and continued in its purest form until the 1920s. Objects were no longer depicted from a single, fixed viewpoint, but were broken up into a multiplicity of facets, so that several different aspects of an object could be seen simultaneously; eg also work by Juan Gris, Fernand Léger, Stuart Davis.

Dada and **Surrealism** Two important, closely related movements in Europe and America. Both were pointedly anti-rationalist, laying emphasis on incongruous or shocking effects, but a key difference was that Dada (1916–22), arising from the mood of despair following World War I, was predominantly nihilistic, while Surrealism (1924–c.1940), which aimed to release and explore the creative powers of the subconscious mind using dreamlike effects, was much more positive in spirit; eg work by Ernst, Duchamp, Man Ray, Schwitters (Dada); Dalí, Magritte (Surrealism).

Dutch Art, 17c The golden age in Dutch art (c.1609–70) began when the Netherlands gained its freedom from Spain; its subjects tended to celebrate the country's hard-won peace and prosperity, eg seascapes, landscapes, portraits of successful merchants, domestic scenes, and still lifes. There was little religious art because of the Protestant ethos; eg work by Frans Hals, Vermeer, Rembrandt.

Egyptian Painting and sculpture were mainly for decoration of tombs and temples, and figures were shown in static poses, expressing a schematic idea of their essence rather than depicting how they appeared to the eye.

Expressionism The communication of the internal emotional realities of a situation, rather than its external 'realistic' aspect. Traditional ideas of beauty and proportion are disregarded, so that artists can express their feelings more strongly by means of distortion, exaggeration and jarring colours. The term was first used in Germany in 1911, but the trend began with Van Gogh and Gauguin in the 1880s; eg work by the groups known as *Die Brücke* (incl Ernst Kirchner) and *Der Blaue Reiter* (incl Wassily Kandinsky) in Germany.

Fauvism An early 20c movement by a group of French painters dubbed *les Fauves* ('wild beasts'). Their work was characterized by the use of brilliant colours, distorted shapes and flat composition, without regard to realism or perspective; eg work by Matisse, André Derain, Maurice de Vlaminck.

Feminist Art Art not simply made by women, but exploring issues specifically relating to women's identity and experience. The movement began in the 1960s and involved reviving the reputations of neglected women artists of the past as well as promoting the work of contemporary women artists; eg Judy Chicago, Miriam Schapiro.

Gothic A style of Christian art (12–16c) characterized by stylized figures wearing flowing garments.

Greek Greek painters and sculptors were the first to master naturalistic depiction of the human body. Most of the surviving painting is on vases or wall fragments. Greek art is broken down into four periods: Geometric (9c–8c BC, named after a style of vase decoration); Archaic (700–480BC); Classical (480–323BC, when Greek art reached its greatest harmony and majesty); and Hellenistic (323–27BC).

High Renaissance The period c.1490–1520 in Rome, Florence and Venice, during which the ideals of the Renaissance are thought to have been given most complete expression in art; eg work by Leonardo da Vinci, Michelangelo, Raphael, Titian, Andrea del Sarto.

Impressionism A style which aims to give a general impression of feelings and events rather than a formal or structural treatment of them. It was born in 1874 when a number of French artists who had difficulty in having their work accepted for the official Paris Salon organized their own group exhibition. Impressionist pictures are typically bright and cheerful, depicting contemporary life in a fresh and immediate way, and conveying the impression of a scene without minute detail; eg work by Monet, Manet, Pissarro, Renoir, Sisley, Degas, Cassatt.

International Gothic A style of art which flourished in W Europe (c.1375–c.1425), characterized by jewel-like colour, graceful shapes and realistic details. The style was seen especially in miniature paintings, drawings, and tapestries, often representing secular themes from courtly life.

Islamic Despite vast regional variations, there is an underlying unity in Islamic art, which reflects the main features of Islam (founded 7c AD): Mecca and the ornate niche in every mosque showing its direction; mosques; minarets, from which the faithful are called to prayer; and domes, symbolizing the heavens. Islamic theology forbids representation of the human figure in religious art, so decoration is abstract, eg complex geometrical patterns incorporating flowing Arabic script. However, in secular art illuminated manuscripts were produced showing hunting scenes and courtly life.

Mannerism A form of art and architecture prevalent in France, Spain, and especially Italy during the 16c. It is characterized by the playful use of Classical elements and *trompe l'oeil* effects in bizarre or dramatic compositions; eg work by Giulio Romano, Jacopa da Pontormo, Francesco Parmigianino, Giambologna.

Medieval The Middle Ages were dominated by Romanesque and Gothic architecture, and large-scale painting and sculpture existed mainly as adjuncts to these styles. Otherwise, painting mainly appeared as stained glass, which reached its zenith in 12c France.

Neoclassicism A movement (late 18c–early 19c) which arose partly as a reaction to Rococo and Baroque excesses in decoration, and partly from a renewed interest in the antique, especially the simplicity and grandeur of Greek and Roman art. Centred in Rome, it later spread throughout W Eur-

ope and N America. In painting, the classical themes and subjects were powerfully and dramatically represented in works by Jacques Louis David (eg *The Oath of the Horatii*, 1784).

Neo-Expressionism A term used to describe an international representational style which arose in the late 1970s. Works are sometimes abstract, sometimes figurative and sometimes bordering between the two, but are usually large in scale and tend to go to extremes of aggressive rawness in technique and feeling. They are characterized by a theatrical, melodramatic flavour conveyed by strong brushstrokes and colours, and distorted shapes; eg work by Julian Schnabel, Anselm Kiefer.

Neo-Plasticism A style of abstract painting in which geometrical patterns are formed of patches of pure flat colour enclosed by intersecting vertical and horizontal lines. It encompasses the 1920s style and theories of Dutch painter and theosophist Piet Mondrian, who tried to express an ideal of universal harmony in his austerely geometrical works.

Pop Art A modern art form based on the commonplace and ephemeral aspects of 20c urban life, such as soup cans, comics, movies and advertising. Pioneer British Pop Artists in the mid-1950s include Peter Blake, Eduardo Paolozzi, Richard Hamilton; leading American contributors in the 1960s included Jasper Johns, Andy Warhol, Roy Lichtenstein.

Post-Impressionism An umbrella term (coined 1910 by Roger Fry) for a number of trends in French painting that developed in the wake of Impressionism c.1880–1905. Its features included focus on structure and renewed importance of the subject; the decorative and symbolic, rather than naturalistic, use of colour and line; and emotional intensity conveyed by brilliant colour and swirling brushstrokes; eg work by Cézanne, Gauguin, Van Gogh.

Post-Modernism Most commonly an architectural or literary term, Post-Modernist refers to art works that blend disparate styles and make knowing use of cultural references, as in Pop Art.

Pre-Raphaelite A highly symbolic style characterizing the work of a group of mid-19c artists in London (the Pre-Raphaelite Brotherhood). Rejecting the formal academic art and neoclassicism prevalent at the time, they turned for inspiration to the brightly coloured work of Italian artists active before Raphael (1483–1520), and painted historical, literary and religious subjects with moral fervour, vivid colour, rich detail and elaborate symbolism; eg work by Holman Hunt, Dante Gabriel Rossetti, John Everett Millais.

Primitivism The result of the influence on modern artists of the art of the indigenous peoples of Africa, Oceania, and the Americas, which was seen to contain a sense of vitality and truth that had been polished out of western painting and sculpture; eg work by Ernst Kirchner, Modigliani, Picasso, Gauguin.

Realism A term which until the end of the 19c referred to naturalism, or the true-to-life depiction of subjects, eg late 16c work by Caravaggio. In France c.1840–80 it was a specific term relating to the depiction of unidealized subject-matter taken from everyday life, deliberately chosen to make a social or political point; eg work by Gustave Courbet and Honoré Daumier. In the late 20c, realism may refer simply to the move away from abstract art towards a more representational style, though it may also refer to the kind of abstract art that opposes superficial appearances and focuses on inner truth as 'reality'.

Arts and Culture

Renaissance A style prevalent in Europe (14–16c) reflecting classical Greek and Roman styles. Little Roman painting had survived to be copied, but the ancient artists' fidelity to nature became a basic tenet of the Renaissance style; eg work by Masaccio (the first to master perspective), Albrecht Dürer, Pieter Brueghel.

Rococo A florid European style born in France (c.1700). Partly a development from Baroque art and partly a reaction against it, Rococo art is characterized by elaborate ornamental details and asymmetrical patterns, and was most successful as a style of interior decoration. Whereas Baroque art is sometimes sombre and often religious, it is much lighter (often intentionally playful) in spirit and usually secular. It flourished until the 1760s in France and the late 18c elsewhere; eg work by Watteau, Boucher and Fragonard.

Romanticism An intellectual trend (late 18c–mid-19c) that regarded the emotions and self-expression, rather than beauty of form or structure, as the basis of composition. Typical themes were wild or mysterious landscapes and dramatic scenes from literature; there was also interest in dreams and nightmares and in extremes of feelings and behaviour; eg work by Delacroix, Caspar David Friedrich, J M W Turner, Goya.

Artists

Selected paintings are listed.

Altdorfer, Albrecht (c.1480–1538) German, born Regensburg; *Danube Landscape* (1520), *Alexander's Victory* (1529).

Andrea del Sarto (properly **Andrea d'Agnolo di Francesco**) (1486–1530) Italian, born Florence; *Miracles of S Filippo Benizzi* (1509–10), *Madonna del Saeco* (1525).

Angelico, Fra (real name **Guido di Pietro**) (c.1400–55) Italian, born Vicchio, Tuscany; *Coronation of the Virgin* (1430–5), *San Marco altarpiece* (c.1440).

Auerbach, Frank (1931–) Anglo-German, born Berlin; *Mornington Crescent* (1967), *Jake* (1990).

Bacon, Francis (1909–92) British, born Dublin; *Three Figures at the Base of a Crucifixion* (1945), *Two Figures with a Monkey* (1973), *Triptych Inspired by the Oresteia of Aeschylus* (1981).

Beardsley, Aubrey (Vincent) (1872–98) British, born Brighton; illustrations to Malory's *Morte d'Arthur* (1893), Wilde's *Salome* (1894).

Bell, Vanessa (1879–1961) British, born Kensington, London; *Still Life on Corner of a Mantlepiece* (1914).

Bellini, Gentile (c.1429–1507) Italian, born Venice; *Procession of the Relic of the True Cross* (1496), *Miracle at Ponte di Lorenzo* (1500).

Blackadder, Elizabeth (1931–) British, born Falkirk; *Interior with Self-Portrait* (1972), *White Anemones* (1983), *Texas Flame* (1986), *Still Life with Pagoda* (1998).

Blake, Peter (1932–) British, born Dartford, Kent; *On the Balcony* (1955–7), design for the Beatles' album *Sergeant Pepper's Lonely Hearts Club Band* (1967), *The Meeting* (1981).

Blake, William (1757–1827) British, born London; illustrations for his own *Songs of Innocence and Experience* (1794), *Newton* (1795), illustrations for the *Book of Job* (1826).

Böcklin, Arnold (1827–1901) Swiss, born Basel; *Pan in the Reeds* (1857), *The Island of the Dead* (1880).

Bomberg, David (1890–1957) British, born Birmingham; *In the Hold* (1913–14), *The Mud Bath* (1913–14).

Bonnard, Pierre (1867–1947) French, born Paris; *Young Woman in Lamplight* (1900), *Dining Room in the Country* (1913), *Seascape of the Mediterranean* (1941).

Bosch, Hieronymus (real name **Jerome van Aken**) (c.1460–1516) Dutch, born 's-Hertogenbosch, Brabant; *The Temptation of St Anthony*, *The Garden of Earthly Delights* (work undated).

Botticelli, Sandro (originally **Alessandro di Mariano Filipepi**) (1444–1510) Italian, born Florence; *Primavera* (c.1478), *The Birth of Venus* (c.1485), *Mystic Nativity* (1500).

Boucher, François (1703–70) French, born Paris; *Reclining Girl* (1751), *The Rising* and *The Setting of the Sun* (1753).

Braque, Georges (1882–1963) French, born Argenteuil-sur-Seine; *Still Life with Violin* (1910), *The Portuguese* (1911), *Blue Wash-Basin* (1942).

Brueghel, Pieter, (the Elder) (c.1525–69) Dutch, born Bruegel, near Breda; *Road to Calvary* (1564), *Massacre of the Innocents* (c.1566), *The Blind Leading the Blind* (1568), *The Peasant Wedding* (1568), *The Peasant Dance* (1568).

Burne-Jones, Sir Edward (Coley) (1833–98) British, born Birmingham; *The Beguiling of Merlin* (1874), *The Arming of Perseus* (1877), *King Cophetua and the Beggar Maid* (1880–4).

Burra, Edward (1905–76) British, born London; *Dancing Skeletons* (1934), *Soldiers* (1942), *Scene in Harlem (Simply Heavenly)* (1952).

Canaletto (properly **Giovanni Antonio Canal**) (1697–1768) Italian, born Venice; *Stone Mason's Yard* (c.1730).

Caravaggio (properly **Michelangelo Merisi da Caravaggio**) (1573–1610) Italian, born Caravaggio, near Burgamo; *The Supper at Emmaus* (c.1598–1600), *Martyrdom of St Matthew* (1599–1600), *The Death of the Virgin* (1605–6).

Cassatt, Mary (1844–1926) American, born Pittsburgh, Pennsylvania; *The Blue Room* (1878), *Lady at the Tea Table* (1885), *Morning Toilette* (1886), *The Tramway* (1891), *The Bath* (1892).

Cézanne, Paul (1839–1906) French, born Aix-en-Provence; *The Black Marble Clock* (c.1869–70), *Maison du Pendu* (c.1873), *Bathing Women* (1900–5), *Le Jardinier* (1906).

Chagall, Marc (1887–1985) Russian–French, born Vitebsk; *The Musician* (1912–13), *Bouquet of Flying Lovers* (1947).

Chicago, Judy (originally **Judy Gerowitz**) (1939–) American, born Chicago; *The Dinner Party* (1974–9).

Chirico, Giorgio de (1888–1978) Italian, born Volos, Greece; *Portrait of Guillaume Apollinaire* (1914), *The Jewish Angel* (1916), *The Return of Ulysses* (1968).

Christo (originally **Christo Javacheff**) (1935–) American, born Gabovra, Bulgaria, and **Jean-Claude** (originally **Jean-Claude de Guillebon**) (1935–) American, born Casablanca, Morocco; *Surrounded Islands* (1980–3), *Wrapped Reichstag* (1995).

Cimabue (originally **Bencivieni di Pepo**) (c.1240–c.1302) Italian, born Florence; *Crucifix* (date unknown), *Saint John the Evangelist* (1302).

Claude Lorraine (in full Claude Le Lorrain) (real name Claude Gêllée) (1600–82) French, born near Nancy; *The Mill* (1631), *The Embarkation of St Ursula* (1641), *Ascanius Shooting the Stag of Silvia* (1682).

Constable, John (1776–1837) British, born East Bergholt, Suffolk; *A Country Lane* (c.1810), *The White Horse* (1819), *The Hay Wain* (1821), *Stonehenge* (1835).

Corot, Jean Baptiste Camille (1796–1875) French, born Paris; *Bridge at Narni* (1827), *Souvenir de Marcoussis* (1869), *Woman Reading in a Landscape* (1869).

Correggio (Antonio Allegri da) (c.1494–1534) Italian, born Correggio; *The Agony in the Garden* (c.1528).

Courbet, (Jean Désiré) Gustave (1819–77) French, born Ornans; *The After-Dinner at Ornans* (1848–9), *The Bathers* (1853), *The Painter's Studio* (1855), *The Stormy Sea* (1869).

Cranach, Lucas, (the Elder) (1472–1553) German, born Kronach, near Bamberg; *The Crucifixion* (1503), *The Fountain of Youth* (1550).

Dalí, Salvador (Felipe Jacinto) (1904–89) Spanish, born Figueras, Gerona; *The Persistence of Memory* (1931), *The Transformation of Narcissus* (1934), *Christ of St John of the Cross* (1951).

Daumier, Honoré (1808–78) French, born Marseilles; many caricatures and lithographs; *The Legislative Paunch* (1834), *The Third Class Carriage* (1840s), paintings on the theme of *Don Quixote*.

David, Jacques Louis (1748–1825) French, born Paris; *Death of Socrates* (1788), *The Death of Marat* (1793), *The Rape of the Sabines* (1799), *Madame Récamier* (1800).

Davis, Stuart (1894–1964) American, born Philadelphia; *The President* (1917), *House and Street* (1931), *Visa* (1951), *Premiere* (1957).

Degas, (Hilaire Germain) Edgar (1834–1917) French, born Paris; *Cotton-brokers Office* (1873), *L'Absinthe* (1875–6), *Little Fourteen-year-old Dancer* (sculpture) (1881), *Dancer at the Bar* (c.1900).

de Kooning, Willem (1904–97) American, born Rotterdam, the Netherlands; *Woman I–V* (1952–3), *Montauk Highway* (1958), *Pastorale* (1963).

Delacroix, (Ferdinand Victor) Eugène (1798–1863) French, born St-Maurice-Charenton; *Dante and Virgil in Hell* (1822), *Liberty Guiding the People* (1831), *Jacob and the Angel* (1853–61).

Derain, André Louis (1880–1954) French, born Chatou; *Mountains at Collioure* (1905), *Westminster Bridge* (1907), *The Bagpiper* (1910–11).

Dix, Otto (1891–1969) German, born Gera-Unternhaus; *The Match Seller* (1920), *The War* (1924).

Doré, (Louis Auguste) Gustave (1832–83) French, born Strasbourg; Illustrations to Dante's *Inferno* (1861), Milton's *Paradise Lost* (1866).

Duccio di Buoninsegna (c.1260–c.1320) Italian; *Maesta* (Siena Cathedral altarpiece) (1308–11).

Duchamp, (Henri Robert) Marcel (1887–1968) French–American, born Blainville, Normandy; *Nude Descending a Staircase* (1912), *The Bride Stripped Bare by Her Bachelors, Even* (1915–23).

Dufy, Raoul (1877–1953) French, born Le Havre; *Posters at Trouville* (1906), illustrations to Guillaume Apollinaire's *Bestiary* (1911), *Riders in the Wood* (1931).

Dürer, Albrecht (1471–1528) German, born Nuremberg; *Adam and Eve* (1507), *Adoration of the Magi* (1504), *Adoration of the Trinity* (1511).

Eardley, Joan (1921–63) British, born Warnham, Sussex; *Winter Sea IV* (1958), *Two Children* (1962).

Emin, Tracey (1964–) English, born London; *Everyone I Have Ever Slept With* (1995), *My Bed* (1998).

Ernst, Max(imillian) (1891–1976) German–American–French, born Brühl, near Cologne, Germany; *Europe After the Rain* (1940–2), *The Elephant Célèbes* (1921), *Moonmad* (1944) (sculpture), *The King Playing with the Queen* (1959) (sculpture).

Escher, M(aurits) C(ornelis) (1898–1972) Dutch, born Leeuwarden; *Day and Night* (1938), *Convex and Concave* (1955).

Eyck, Jan van (c.1389–1441) Dutch, born Maaseyck, near Maastricht; *The Adoration of the Holy Lamb* (Ghent altarpiece) (1432), *Man in a Red Turban* (1433), *Arnolfni Marriage Portrait* (1434), *Madonna by the Fountain* (1439).

Fini, Léonor (1908–96) Italian–Argentinian, born Buenos Aires; *The End of the World* (1944).

Fragonard, Jean Honoré (1732–1806) French, born Grasse; *Coroesus Sacrificing Himself to Save Callirhoe* (1765), *The Swing* (c.1766), four canvases for Mme du Barry entitled *The Progress of Love* (1771–3).

Freud, Lucian (1922–) German–British, born Berlin; *Woman with a Daffodil* (1945), *Interior in Paddington* (1951), *Hotel Room* (1953–4).

Friedrich, Caspar David (1774–1840) German, born Pomerania; *The Cross in the Mountains* (1807–8).

Fuseli, Henri (originally Johann Heinrich Füssli) (1741–1825) Anglo-Swiss, born Zurich; *The Nightmare* (1781), *Appearance of the Ghost* (1796).

Gainsborough, Thomas (1727–88) British, born Sudbury, Suffolk; *Peasant Girl Gathering Sticks* (1782), *The Watering Place* (1777).

Gauguin, (Eugène Henri) Paul (1848–1903) French, born Paris; *The Vision After the Sermon* (1888), *Still Life with Three Puppies* (1888), *The White Horse* (1898), *Women of Tahiti* (1891), *Tahitian Landscape* (1891), *Where Do We Come From? What Are We? Where Are We Going?* (1897–8), *Golden Bodies* (1901).

Géricault, Théodore (1791–1824) French, born Rouen; *Officer of Light Horse* (c.1812), *Raft of the Medusa* (1819).

Ghirlandaio, Domenico (properly Domenico diTommaso Bigordi) (1449–94) Italian, born Florence; *Virgin of Mercy* (1472), *St Jerome* (1480), *Nativity* (1485).

Giorgione (da Castelfranco) or Giorgio Barbarelli (c.1478–1511) Italian, born Castelfranco; *The Tempest* (c.1508), *Three Philosophers* (c.1508), *Portrait of a Man* (1510).

Giotto (di Bondone) (c.1266–1337) Italian, born near Florence; frescoes in *Arena Chapel*, Padua (1304–12), *Ognissanti Madonna* (1311–12).

Goes, Hugo van der (c.1440–82) Dutch, born probably Ghent; *Portinari Altarpiece* (1475).

Gorky, Arshile (originally Vosdanig Manoog Adoian) (1905–48) American, born Khorkom Vari, Turkish Armenia; *The Artist and His Mother* (c.1926–36), series *Image in Xhorkam* (from 1936), *The Liver is the Cock's Comb* (1944), *The Betrothal II* (1947).

Goya (y Lucientes), Francisco (José) de (1746–1828) Spanish, born Fuendetotos; *Family of Charles IV* (1799), *Los Desastres de la Guerra* (1810–14), *Black Paintings* (1820s).

Greco, El (properly Domenico Theotocopoulos) (1541–1614) Greek, born Candia, Crete; *Lady in Fur Wrap* (c.1577–8), *El Espolio* ('The Disrobing of Christ') (1577–9), *The Saviour of the World* (1600), *Portrait of Brother Hortensio Felix Paravicino* (1609), *Toledo Landscape* (c.1610).

Arts and Culture

Gris, Juan (pseudonym of **José Victoriano González**) (1887–1927) Spanish, born Madrid; *Sunblind* (1914), *Still Life with Dice* (1922), *Violin and Fruit Dish* (1924).

Grosz, George (1893–1959) German–American, born Berlin; *Fit for Active Service* (1918), *The Face of the Ruling Class* (1921), *Ecce Homo* (1927).

Grünewald, Matthias (originally **Mathis Nithardt or Gothardt**) (c.1480–1528) German, born probably Würzburg; *Isenheim Altarpiece* (1515).

Hals, Frans (c.1580–1666) Dutch, born Antwerp; *The Laughing Cavalier* (1624), *Banquet of the Company of St Adrian* (1627), *Gypsy Girl* (c.1628–30), *Man in a Slouch Hat* (c.1660–6).

Hamilton, Richard (1922–) British, born London; *Hommage a Chrysler Corp* (1952), *Just what is it that makes today's homes so different, so appealing?* (1956), *Study of Hugh Gaitskell as a Famous Monster of Film Land* (1964).

Hilliard, Nicholas (c.1547–1619) British, born Exeter; miniature of *Queen Elizabeth I* (1572), *Henry Wriothesley* (1594).

Hirst, Damien (1965–) British, born Bristol; *The Physical Impossibilty of Death in the Mind of Someone Living* (1991), *The Asthmatic Escaped* (1991), *Mother and Child, Divided* (1993).

Hockney, David (1937–) British, born Bradford, Yorkshire; *We Two Boys Together Clinging* (1961), *The Rake's Progress* (1963), *A Bigger Splash* (1967), *Invented Man Revealing a Still Life* (1975), *Dancer* (1980).

Hodgkin, Sir Howard (1932–) English, born London; *Dinner at Smith Square* (1975–9), *Goodbye to the Bay of Naples* (1980–2).

Hogarth, William (1697–1764) British, born Smithfield, London; *Before and After* (1731), *A Rake's Progress* (1733–5).

Hokusai, Katsushika (1760–1849) Japanese, born Tokyo; *Tametomo and the Demon* (1811), *Mangwa* (1814–19), *Hundred Views of Mount Fuji* (1835).

Holbein, Hans, (the Younger) (1497–1543) German, born Augsburg; *Bonifacius Amerbach* (1519), *Solothurn Madonna* (1522), *Anne of Cleves* (1539).

Hundertwasser, Friedensreich (Friedrich Stowasser) (1928–2000) Austrian, born Vienna; *Many Transparent Heads* (1949–50), *The End of Greece* (1963), *The Court of Sulaiman* (1967).

Hunt, (William) Holman (1827–1910) British, born London; *Our English Coasts* (1852), *Claudio and Isabella* (1853), *The Light of the World* (1854), *Isabella and the Pot of Basil* (1867).

Ingres, Jean August Dominique (1780–1867) French, born Montauban; *Gilbert* (1805), *La Source* (1807–59), *Bather* (1808), *Turkish Bath* (1863).

John, Augustus (Edwin) (1878–1961) British, born Tenby; *The Smiling Woman* (1908), *Portrait of a Lady in Black* (1917).

John, Gwen (1876–1939) British, born Haverfordwest, Pembrokeshire; *Girl with Bare Shoulders* (1909–10).

Johns, Jasper (1930–) American, born Allendale, South Carolina; *Target with Four Faces* (1955), *Beer Cans* (1961) (sculpture).

Kandinsky, Wassily (1866–1944) Russian–French, born Moscow; *Kossacks* (1910–11), *Swinging* (1925), *Two Green Points* (1935), *Sky Blue* (1940).

Kiefer, Anselm (1945–) German, born Donaueschingen, Baden; *Parsifal III* (1973), *Innenraum* (1982), *Lilith* (1989).

Kirchner, Ernst Ludwig (1880–1938) German, born Aschaffenburg; *Recumbent Blue Nude with Straw Hat* (1908–9), *The Drinker* (1915), *Die Amselfluh* (1923).

Kitaj, R(onald) B(rooks) (1932–) American, born Cleveland, Ohio; *The Ohio Gang* (1964), *If Not, Not* (1975–6).

Klee, Paul (1879–1940) Swiss, born Münchenbuchsee, near Berne; *Der Vollmond* (1919), *Rosegarden* (1920), *Twittering Machine* (1922), *A Tiny Tale of a Tiny Dwarf* (1925), *Fire in the Evening* (1929).

Klimt, Gustav (1862–1918) Austrian, born Baumgarten, near Vienna; *Music* (1895), *The Kiss* (1907–8), *Judith II (Salome)* (1909).

Kline, Franz Joseph (1910–62) American, born Wilkes-Barre, Pennsylvania; *Orange and Black Wall* (1939), *Chief* (1950), *Mahoning* (1956).

Kokoschka, Oskar (1886–1980) Anglo-Austrian, born Pochlarn; *The Dreaming Boys* (1908).

Kupka, Frantisek (1871–1957) Czech, born in Opocno, East Bohemia; *Girl with a Ball* (1908), *Amorpha: Fugue in Two Colours* (1912), *Working Steel* (1921–9).

Landseer, Sir Edwin (Henry) (1803–73) British, born London; *The Old Shepherd's Chief Mourner* (1837), *The Monarch of the Glen* (1850).

La Tour, Georges (Dumesnil) de (1593–1652) French, born Vic-sur-Seille, Lorraine; *St Jerome Reading* (1620s), *The Denial of St Peter* (1650).

Léger, Fernand (1881–1955) French, born Argentan; *Contrast of Forms* (1913), *Black Profile* (1928), *The Great Parade* (1954).

Lely, Sir Peter (originally **Pietar van der Faes**) (1618–80) Anglo-Dutch, born Soest, Westphalia; *The Windsor Beauties* (1668), *Admirals* series (1666–7).

Leonardo da Vinci (Leonardo di Ser Piero da Vince) (1452–1519) Italian, born Vinci; *The Last Supper* (1495–7), *Madonna and Child with St Anne* (begun 1503), *Mona Lisa* (1500–6), *The Virgin of the Rocks* (c.1508).

Lichtenstein, Roy (1923–97) American, born New York City; *Whaam!* (1963), *As I Opened Fire* (1964).

Lippi, Fra Filippo, called **Lippo** (c.1406–69) Italian, born Florence; *Tarquinia Madonna* (1437), *Barbadori Altarpiece* (begun 1437).

Lochner, Stefan (c.1400–51) German, born Meersburg am Bodensee; *The Adoration of the Magi* (c.1448), triptych in Cologne Cathedral.

Lowry, L(aurence) S(tephen) (1887–1976) English, born Manchester; *Salford Street Scene (*1928), *Coming from the Mill* (1930), *Industrial Landscape* (1955).

Macke, August (1887–1914) German, born Meschede; *Greeting* (1912), *The Zoo* (1912), *Girls Under Trees* (1914).

Magritte, René (François Ghislain) (1898–1967) Belgian, born Lessines, Hainault; *The Menaced Assassin* (1926), *Loving Perspective* (1935), *Presence of Mind* (1960).

Manet, Edouard (1932–83) French, born Paris; *Le Déjeuner sur l'herbe* (1863), *La Brioche* (1870), *A Bar at the Folies-Bergères* (1882).

Mantegna, Andrea (1431–1506) Italian, born Vicenza; *Madonna of Victory* (altarpiece), *San Zeno Altarpiece* (1457–9), *Triumphs of Caesar* (c.1486–94).

Martin, John (1789–1854) British, born Haydon Bridge; *Joshua Commanding the Sun to Stand Still* (1816), *The Last Judgement* (1851–4).

Martini or **Memmi, Simone** (c.1284–1344) Italian, born Siena; *S Caterina Polyptych* (1319), *Annunciation* (1333).

Masaccio (real name Tommaso di Giovanni di Simone Guidi) (1401–28) Italian, born Castel San Giovanni di Val d'Arno; *polyptych* for the *Carmelite Church* in Pisa (1426), frescoes in *Sta Maria del Carmine*, Florence (1424–7).

Masson, André (Aimé René) (1896–1987) French, born Balgny, Oise; *Massacres* (1933), *The Labyrinth* (1939).

Matisse, Henri (Emile Benot) (1869–1954) French, born Le Cateau-Cambrésis; *La Desserte* (1908), *Notre Dame* (1914), *The Large Red Studio* (1948), *L'Escargot* (1953).

Michelangelo (in full Michelangelo di Lodovico Buonarroti) (1475–1564) Italian, born Caprese, Tuscany; *The Pietà* (1497) (sculpture), *David* (1501–4) (sculpture), *Madonna* (c.1502), ceiling of the *Sistine Chapel*, Rome (1508–12), *The Last Judgement* (begun 1537).

Millais, Sir John Everett (1829–96) British, born Southampton; *Ophelia* (1851–2), *The Bridesmaid* (1851), *Tennyson* (1881), *Bubbles* (1886).

Millet, Jean-François (1814–75) French, born Grouchy; *Sower* (1850), *The Gleaners* (1857).

Miro, Joán (1893–1983) Spanish, born Montroig; *Catalan Landscape* (1923–4), *Maternity* (1924).

Modigliani, Amedeo (1884–1920) Italian, born Leghorn (Livorno), Tuscany; *The Jewess* (1908), *Moise Kisling* (1915), *Reclining Nude* (c.1919), *Jeanne Hébuterne* (1919).

Mondrian, Piet (properly Pieter Cornelis Mondriaan) (1872–1944) Dutch, born Amersfoort; *Still Life with Gingerpot II* (1911), *Composition with Red, Black, Blue, Yellow, and Grey* (1920), *Broadway Boogie-Woogie* (1942–3).

Monet, Claude (1840–1926) French, born Paris; *Impression: Sunrise* (1872), *Haystacks* (1890–1), *Rouen Cathedral* (1892–5), *Waterlilies* (1899 onwards).

Moreau, Gustave (1826–98) French, born Paris; *Oedipus and the Sphinx* (1864), *Apparition* (1876), *Jupiter and Semele* (1889–95).

Morisot, Berthe (Marie Pauline) (1841–95) French, born Bourges; *The Harbour at Cherbourg* (1874), *In the Dining Room* (1886).

Morris, William (1834–96) British, born Walthamstow, London; *Queen Guinevere* (1858).

Motherwell, Robert (Burns) (1915–91) American, born Aberdeen, Washington; *Gauloises* (1967), *Opens* (1968–72).

Munch, Edvard (1863–1944) Norwegian, born Löten; *The Scream* (1893), *Mother and Daughter* (c.1897), *Self-Portrait between the Clock and the Bed* (1940–2).

Nash, Paul (1899–1946) British, born London; *We Are Making a New World* (1918), *Menin Road* (1919).

Newman, Barnett (1905–70) American, born New York; *The Moment* (1946), *Onement I* (1948), *Vir Heroicus Sublimis* (1950–1).

Nicholson, Ben (1894–1982) British, born Denham, London; *White Relief* (1935), *November 11, 1947* (1947).

Nicholson, Winifred (1893–1981) British, born Oxford; *Honeysuckle and Sweet Peas* (1950), *The Copper and Capari* (1967), *The Gate to the Isles* (1980).

Nolde, Emil (pseudonym of Emil Hansen) (1867–1956) German, born Nolde; *The Missionary* (1912), *Candle Dancers* (1912).

Oliver, Isaac (c.1560–1617) Anglo-French, born Rouen; *Self-Portrait* (c.1590), *Henry, Prince of Wales* (c.1612).

Palmer, Samuel (1805–81) British, born London; *Repose of the Holy Family* (1824), *The Magic Apple Tree* (1830), *Opening the Fold* (1880).

Parmigiano or **Parmigianino** (properly Girolamo Francesco Maria Mazzola) (1503–40) Italian, born Parma; frescoes in *S Giovanni Evangelista*, Parma (c.1522), *Self-Portrait in a Convex Mirror* (1524), *Vision of St Jerome* (1526–7), *Madonna Altarpiece*, Bologna (c.1528–30), *The Madonna of the Long Neck* (c.1535).

Pasmore, (Edwin John) Victor (1908–98) British, born Chelsham, Surrey; *The Evening Star* (1945–7), *Black Symphony — the Pistol Shot* (1977).

Peploe, S(amuel) J(ohn) (1871–1935) British, born Edinburgh; one of the 'Scottish colourists'; *Boats of Royan* (1910).

Perugino (properly Pietro di Cristoforo Vannucci) (c.1450–1523) Italian, born Città della Pieve, Umbria; *Christ Giving the Keys to Peter* (fresco in the Sistine Chapel) (c.1483).

Pevsner, Antoine (1886–1962) French, born Orël, Russia; *Torso* (1924–6), *Development Column* (1942).

Picabia, Francis (Marie) (1879–1953) French, born Paris; *I See Again in Memory My Dear Undine* (1913), *The Kiss* (1924).

Picasso, Pablo (Ruiz) (1881–1973) Spanish, born Malaga; *Mother and Child* (1921), *Three Dances* (1925), *Guernica* (1937), *The Charnel House* (1945), *The Artist and His Model* (1968).

Piero della Francesca (c.1420–92) Italian, born Borgo san Sepolcro; *Madonna of the Misericordia* (1445–8), *Resurrection* (c.1450).

Piper, John (1903–92) British, born Epsom; *Windsor Castle* watercolours (1941–2), *Council Chamber, House of Commons* (1941); also stage designs and illustrated publications.

Pissarro, Camille (Jacob) (1830–1903) French, born St Thomas, West Indies; *Landscape at Chaponval* (1880), *The Boieldieu Bridge at Rouen* (1896), *Boulevard Montmartre* (1897).

Pollock, (Paul) Jackson (1912–56) American, born Cody, Wyoming; *No 14* (1948), *Guardians of the Secret* (1943).

Pontormo, Jacopo da (1494–1552) Italian; frescoes eg of the *Passion* (1522–5), *Deposition* (c.1525).

Poussin, Nicolas (1594–1665) French, born Les Andelys, Normandy; *The Adoration of the Golden Calf* (1624), *Inspiration of the Poet* (c.1628), *Seven Sacraments* (1644–8), *Self-Portrait* (1650).

Raeburn, Sir Henry (1756–1823) British, born Edinburgh; *Rev Robert Walker Skating* (1784), *Isabella McLeod, Mrs James Gregory* (c.1798).

Ramsay, Allan (1713–84) British, born Edinburgh; *The Artist's Wife* (1754–5).

Raphael (properly Raffaello Santi or Sanzio) (1483–1520) Italian, born Urbino; *Assumption of the Virgin* (1504), *Madonna of the Meadow* (1505–6), *Transfiguration* (1518–20).

Redon, Odilon (1840–1916) French, born Bordeaux; *Woman with Outstretched Arms* (c.1910–14).

Redpath, Anne (1895–1965) British, born Galashiels; *Pinks* (1947).

Rembrandt (properly Rembrandt Harmenszoon van Rijn) (1606–69) Dutch, born Leiden; *Anatomy Lesson of Dr Tulp* (1632), *Blinding of Samson* (1636),

Arts and Culture

Arts and Culture

The Night Watch (1642), *The Conspiracy of Claudius* (1661–2).

Renoir, (Jean Pierre) Auguste (1841–1919) French, born Limoges; *Woman in Blue* (1874), *Woman Reading* (1876), *The Bathers* (1887).

Reynolds, Sir Joshua (1723–92) British, born Plympton Earls, near Plymouth; *Portrait of Miss Bowles with Her Dog* (1775), *Master Henry Hoare* (1788).

Riley, Bridget (Louise) (1931–) British, born London; *Pink Landscapes* (1959–60), *Zig-Zag* (1961), *Fall* (1963), *Apprehend* (1970).

Rivera, Diego (1886–1957) Mexican, born Guanajuato; *Man at the Crossroads* (1933), *Detroit Industry* (1932–3), *Man, Controller of the Universe* (1934).

Rosa, Salvator (1615–73) Italian, born Arenella, near Naples; *Self-Portrait with a Skull* (1656), *Humana Fragilitas* (c.1657).

Rossetti, Dante Gabriel (1828–82) British, born London; *Beata Beatrix* (1849–50), *Ecce Ancilla Domini!* (1850), *Astarte Syriaca* (1877).

Rothko, Mark (Marcus Rothkovitch) (1903–70) Latvian–American, born Dvinsk; *The Omen of the Eagle* (1942), *Red on Maroon* (1959).

Rousseau, Henri (Julien Félix), known as **Le Douanier** (1844–1910) French, born Laval; *Monsieur et Madame Stevene* (1884), *Sleeping Gipsy* (1897), *Portrait of Joseph Brunner* (1909).

Rubens, Sir Peter Paul (1577–1640) Flemish, born Siegen, Westphalia; *Marchesa Brigida Spinola-Doria* (1606), *Hélène Fourment with Two of Her Children* (c.1637).

Sargent, John Singer (1856–1925) American, born Florence; *Madame X* (1884), *Lady Agnew* (1893), *Gassel* (1918).

Schiele, Egon (1890–1918) Austrian, born Tulln; *Autumn Tree* (1909), *Pregnant Woman and Death* (1911), *Edith Seated* (1917–18).

Schnabel, Julian (1951–) American, born New York City; *The Unexpected Death of Blinky Palermo in the Tropics* (1981), *Humanity Asleep* (1982).

Seurat, Georges (Pierre) (1859–91) French, born Paris; *Bathers at Asnières* (1884), *Sunday on the Island of La Grande Jatte* (1885–6), *Le Cirque* (1891).

Sickert, Walter (Richard) (1860–1942) British, born Munich; *La Hollandaise* (1905–6), *Ennui* (c.1914).

Sisley, Alfred (1839–99) French, born Paris; *Avenue of Chestnut Trees near La Celle Saint-Cloud* (1868), *Mosley Weir, Hampton Court* (1874).

Spencer, Sir Stanley (1891–1959) British, born Cookham-on-Thames, Berkshire; *The Resurrection* (1927), *The Leg of Mutton Nude* (1937).

Steen, Jan (Havicksz) (1627–79) Dutch, born Leiden; *A Woman at Her Toilet* (1663), *The World Upside Down* (1663).

Stubbs, George (1724–1806) British, born Liverpool; *James Stanley* (1755), *Anatomy of the Horse* (1766), *Hambletonian, Rubbing Down* (1799).

Sutherland, Graham (Vivian) (1903–80) British, born London; *Entrance to a Lane* (1939), *Crucifixion* (1946), *A Bestiary and some Correspondences* (1968).

Tanguy, Yves (1900–55) French–American, born Paris; *He Did What He Wanted* (1927), *The Invisibles* (1951).

Tatlin, Vladimir Yevgrafovich (1885–1953) Russian, born Moscow; painted reliefs, relief constructions, corner reliefs (all 1914 onwards); design for *Monument to the Third International* (1920).

Tintoretto (properly **Jacopo Robusti**) (1518–94) Italian, born probably Venice; *The Miracle of the*

Slave (1548), *St George and the Dragon* (c.1558), *The Golden Calf* (c.1560).

Titian (properly **Tiziano Veccellio**) (c.1488–1576) Italian, born Pieve di Cadore; *The Assumption of the Virgin* (1516–18), *Bacchus and Ariadne* (1522–3), *Pesaro Madonna* (1519–26), *Crowning with Thorns* (c.1570).

Toulouse-Lautrec, Henri (Marie Raymond de) (1864–1901) French, born Albi; *The Jockey* (1899), *At the Moulin Rouge* (1895), *The Modiste* (1900).

Turner, Joseph Mallord William (1775–1851) British, born London; *Frosty Morning* (1813), *The Shipwreck* (1805), *Crossing the Brook* (1815), *The Fighting Téméraire* (1839), *Rain, Steam and Speed* (1844).

Uccello, Paolo (originally **Paolo di Dono**) (c.1396–1475) Italian, born Pratovecchio; *The Flood* (c.1445), *The Rout of San Romano* (1454–7).

Utamaro, Kitagawa (1753–1806) Japanese, born Edo (modern Tokyo); *Ohisa* (c.1788), *The Twelve Hours of the Green Houses* (c.1795).

Van Dyck, Sir Anthony (1599–1641) Flemish, born Antwerp; *Marchesa Elena Grimaldi* (c.1625), *The Deposition* (1634–5), *Le Roi a la chasse* (c.1638).

Van Gogh, Vincent (Willem) (1853–90) Dutch, born Groot-Zundert, near Breda; *The Potato Eaters* (1885), *Self-Portrait with Bandaged Ear* (1888), *The Harvest* (1888), *The Sunflowers* (1888), *Starry Night* (1889), *Cornfields with Flight of Birds* (1890).

Velázquez, Diego (Rodríguez de Silva y) (1599–1660) Spanish, born Seville; *The Immaculate Conception* (c.1618), *The Waterseller of Seville* (c.1620), *The Surrender of Breda* (1634–5), *Pope Innocent X* (1650), *Las Meninas* (c.1656).

Vermeer, Jan (Johannes) (1632–75) Dutch, born Delft; *The Astronomer* (1668), *Christ in the House of Mary and Martha* (date unknown), *A Lady with a Gentleman at the Virginals* (c.1665), *The Lacemaker* (date unknown).

Veronese (pseudonym of **Paolo Caliari**) (1528–88) Italian, born Verona; *The Feast in the House of Levi* (1573), *Marriage at Cana* (1573), *Triumph of Venice* (c.1585).

Verrocchio, Andrea del (properly **Andrea del 'Cioni**) (c.1435–c.1488) Italian, born Florence; *Baptism of Christ* (c.1470), *David* (c.1475) (sculpture).

Vlaminck, Maurice de (1876–1958) French, born Paris; *The Red Trees* (1906), *Tugboat at Chatou* (1906).

Warhol, Andy (originally **Andrew Warhola**) (1928–87) American, born McKeesport, Pennsylvania; *Marilyn* (1962), *Electric Chair* (1963).

Watteau, (Jean) Antoine (1684–1721) French, born Valenciennes; *The Pilgrimage to the Island of Cythera* (1717), *L'Enseigne de Gersaint* (1721).

Whistler, James (Abbott) McNeill (1834–1903) American, born Lowell, Massachusetts; *The Artist's Mother* (1871), *Nocturne in Blue and Silver: Old Battersea Bridge* (1872–5), *Falling Rocket* (1875).

Wilkie, Sir David (1785–1841) British, born Cults, Fife; *The Village Politicians* (1806), *Chelsea Pensioners Reading the Waterloo Despatch* (1822).

Wood, Grant (1891–1942) American, born Iowa; *American Gothic* (1930), *Spring Turning* (1936).

Wright, Joseph, (of Derby) (1734–97) British, born Derby; *Experiment with an Air Pump* (1766), *The Alchemist in Search of the Philosopher's Stone Discovers Phosphorus* (1795).

Wyeth, Andrew (Newell) (1917–) American, born Chadds Ford, Pennsylvania; *Christina's World* (1948).

Turner prize

TheTurner Prize was founded in 1984 by the Patrons of New Art. It is an award of £20 000 given to contemporary British artists under the age of 50 for an outstanding exhibition of work in the past 12 months.

Year	Winners	Year	Winners
1984	Malcolm Morley, painter	1995	Damien Hirst, painter and conceptual and installation artist
1985	Sir Howard Hodgkin, painter		
1986	Gilbert and George; Gilbert Proesch and George Passmore, performance artists	1996	Douglas Gordon, video artist
		1997	Gillian Wearing, photographer and video artist
1987	Richard Deacon, sculptor	1998	Chris Ofili, painter
1988	Tony Cragg, sculptor	1999	Steve McQueen, video artist
1989	Richard Long, land artist	2000	Wolfgang Tillmans, photographer
1990	no prize awarded	2001	Martin Creed, conceptual and installation artist
1991	Anish Kapoor, sculptor		
1992	Grenville Davey, sculptor	2002	Keith Tyson, conceptual and installation artist
1993	Rachel Whiteread, sculptor		
1994	Antony Gormley, sculptor		

Major architectural styles

Art Nouveau A deliberately new style, c.1890–1910, uninfluenced by past art, characterized mainly by undulating plant-like forms (particularly as surface decoration) and coloured materials; eg *Glasgow School of Art* by Charles Rennie Mackintosh.

Baroque The dominant European style of the 17c and early 18c, typically bold and exuberant, using Renaissance forms with a new freedom; eg gardens, fountains and palace at *Versailles*, France; Early Baroque: façade for *St Peter's* by Carlo Moderno; High Baroque: work by Gian Lorenzo Bernini and Francesco Borromini in Italy; Late Baroque: work by Balthasar Neumann and Johann Bernhard Fischer von Erlach.

Brutalism A reaction in the 1950s against the sleek sophistication of the International Modern style, characterized by chunky forms and exposed concrete; eg *Chandigarh,* the new capital of the Punjab, India, by Le Corbusier.

Byzantine The style of the Byzantine empire, which flourished 4–15c, its capital being Constantinople (originally Byzantium, now Istanbul). It blends Roman and eastern influences and its most typical form is the large domed church, lavishly decorated with mosaics; eg *Hagia Sophia,* Istanbul.

Gothic The style that succeeded Romanesque throughout Europe, characterized most obviously by the use of pointed arches and also by rib vaults, flying buttresses and elaborate window tracery. It began in France in the 1140s and flourished in many places into the 16c, windows generally becoming an increasingly prominent feature; eg *Cathedrals of Lincoln* and *Salisbury,* England; *Cathedral of Chartres,* France.

Gothic Revival A revival of the Gothic style of the Middle Ages, beginning in the 18c and flourishing in the 19c, particularly in Britain; it was used in buildings of all kinds — religious, civil, commercial and domestic; eg *Houses of Parliament,* London, by Sir Charles Barry and August W N Pugin; *Grace Church,* New York City, by James Renwick.

Greek The style charlacteristic of ancient Greece and its Mediterranean colonies from the 7 BC, when stone building was revived, to the 1c BC, when Greece was absorbed into the Roman Empire. The most important Greek buildings were temples, and the beautifully proportioned columns that became typical of them were immensely influential on Roman and on much subsequent European architecture; eg *Parthenon,* Athens.

High Tech An approach popular since the 1970s in which architects stress the technological aspects of a building, typically by giving dramatic visual expression to structural elements or services (pipes, air ducts and so on) that are usually hidden from view; eg *Pompidou Centre,* Paris, and the *Lloyds Building,* London, both by Richard Rogers.

International Modern or **International Style** A sleek, functional style that dominated progressive architecture in Europe and America in the 1930s and 1940s; eg *Bauhaus,* Dessau, Germany, by Walter Gropius; *Falling Water,* Mill Run, Pennsylvania by Frank Lloyd Wright.

Neoclassicism A revival of the styles of ancient Greece and Rome in the late 18c and early 19c; eg *Charlotte Square,* Edinburgh, by Robert Adam; *Hôtel Dieu,* Lyons, by Jacques Soufflot.

Post-Modernism A trend, beginning in the 1970s, in which the cool rationalism of International Modern style was abandoned in favour of stylistic eclecticism; eg *Brant-Johnson House* in Vail, Colorado, by Robert Venturi; *Piazza d'Italia,* New Orleans, by Charles Willard Moore.

Renaissance A revival or 'rebirth' of the classical art of ancient Rome, beginning in Italy in the early 15c and spreading over Europe until the advent of Baroque; eg the circular *Tempietto of S Pietro,* Montoria, Rome, by Donato Bramante; *Banqueting House,* Whitehall, London, by Inigo Jones.

Rococo A style that emerged from Baroque in the early 18c; like Baroque, it tended to make vigorous use of curved forms, but it was lighter and more playful; eg *Residenztheater,* Munich, by François de Cuvilliés.

Roman The style of the ancient Romans, which spread over their empire, at its peak 1–4c AD; the Romans took much of the 'vocabulary' of classical architecture from the Greeks (particularly the systematic use of columns), but added many features of their own, and excelled in the sheer size of their buildings and engineering projects; eg *Pantheon,* Rome; *Colosseum,* Rome.

Romanesque The style prevailing in most of Europe in the 11c and 12c, characterized by massive strength of construction, and the use of round-headed arches and windows (as opposed to the pointed arches of the Gothic style that succeeded it); eg *San Miniato al Monte,* Florence.

Architects

Selected works are listed.

Aalto, (Hugo) Alvar (Henrik) (1898–1976) Finnish, born Kuortane; *Convalescent Home*, Paimio, near Turku (1929–30), *Town Hall*, Saynatsab (1950–2), *Finlandia Concert Hall*, Helsinki (1971).

Adam, Robert (1728–92) Scottish, born Kirkcaldy; *Adelphi*, London (1769–71, demolished 1936), *General Register House* (begun 1774), *Charlotte Square* (1791), *University of Edinburgh, Old College* (1789–94), all Edinburgh; *Culzean Castle*, Ayrshire (1772–92).

Adam, William (1689–1748) Scottish, born Maryburgh; *Hopetoun House*, near Edinburgh (1721).

Alberti, Leon Battista (1404–72) Italian, born Genoa; façade of the *Palazzo Recellai*, Florence (1460), *San Andrea*, Mantua (1470).

Anthemias of Tralles (dates unknown) Greek, born Tralles, Lydia; *Hagia Sophia*, Constantinople (now Istanbul) (532–7).

Apollodorus of Damascus (dates unknown) Greek, born Syria; *Trajan's Forum*, Rome, *The Baths of Trajan*, Rome.

Arnolfo di Cambio (1232–1302) Italian, born Colle di Val d'Elsa, Tuscany; *Florence Cathedral* (1299–1310).

Asplund, Erik Gunnar (1885–1940) Swedish, born Stockholm; *Stockholm City Library* (1924–7), *Law Courts*, Gothenburg (1934–7).

Baker, Sir Herbert (1862–1946) English, born Kent; *Groote Schuur*, near Cape Town (1892–1902), *Union Government Buildings*, Pretoria (1907).

Barry, Sir Charles (1795–1860) English, born London; *Royal Institution of the Arts*, Manchester (1824), *Houses of Parliament*, London (opened 1852).

Behrens, Peter (1868–1940) German, born Hamburg; *Turbine Assembly Works*, Berlin (1909), *German Embassy*, St Petersburg (1912).

Berlage, Hendrick Petrus (1856–1934) Dutch, born Amsterdam; *Amsterdam Bourse* (1903), *Holland House*, London (1914), *Gemeente Museum*, The Hague (1934).

Bernini, Gian Lorenzo (1598–1680) Italian, born Naples; *St Peter's Baldacchino* (1625), *Cornaro Chapel* in the Church of Santa Maria della Vittoria (1645–52), both Rome.

Borromini, Francesco (1599–1667) Italian, born Bissone, on Lake Lugano; *S Carlo alle Quattro Fontane* (1637–41), *S Ivo della Sapienza* (1642–61), both Rome.

Boullée, Etienne-Louis (1728–99) French, born Paris; *Hôtel de Brunoy*, Paris (1772), *Monument to Isaac Newton* (never built) (1794).

Bramante, Donato (originally **Donato di Pascuccio d'Antonio**) (1444–1514) Italian, born near Urbino; *San Maria presso S Satiro*, Milan (begun 1482), *Tempietto of S Pietro*, Rome (1502).

Breuer, Marcel Lajos (1902–81) Hungarian–American, born Pécs, Hungary; *UNESCO Building*, Paris (1953–8).

Brosse, Salomon de (1565–1626) French, born Verneuil-sur-Oise; *Luxembourg Palace*, Paris (1615–20), *Louis XIII's Hunting Lodge*, Versailles (1624–6).

Brunelleschi, Filippo (1377–1446) Italian, born Florence; *San Lorenzo*, Florence (begun 1418), Dome of *Florence Cathedral* (begun 1420), *Ospedale degli Innocenti*, Florence (1419).

Bryce, David (1803–76) Scottish, born Edinburgh; *Fettes College* (1863–9), *Royal Infirmary* (begun 1870), both Edinburgh.

Burnham, David Hudson (1846–1912) American, born Henderson, New York; *Reliance Building*, Chicago (1890–5), *Monadnock Building*, Chicago (1890–1), *Selfridge Building*, London (1908).

Burton, Decimus (1800–81) English, born London; *Regent's Park Colosseum* (1823), *Arch at Hyde Park Corner* (1825), both London.

Butterfield, William (1814–1900) English, born London; *Keble College*, Oxford (1866–86), *St Augustine's College*, Canterbury (1844–73), *All Saints'*, Margaret Street, London (1849–59).

Campen, Jacob van (1595–1657) Dutch, born Haarlem; *Maurithuis*, The Hague (1633), *Amsterdam Theatre* (1637), *Amsterdam Town Hall* (1647–55).

Candela, Felix (1910–97) Spanish–Mexican, born Madrid; *Sports Palace* for Olympic Games, Mexico City (1968).

Chambers, Sir William (1726–96) Scottish, born Stockholm; *Somerset House* (1776), pagoda in *Kew Gardens* (1757), both London.

Chermayeff, Serge (1900–96) American, born the Caucasus Mountains, Russia; *De La Warr Pavilion*, Bexhill (1933–5).

Churriguera, Don José (1650–1725) Spanish, born Salamanca; *Salamanca Cathedral* (1692–4).

Coates, Wells Wintemute (1895–1958) English, born Tokyo; *BBC Studios* (1932), *EKCO Laboratories* (1936), *Cinema*, Festival of Great Britain Exhibition (1951).

Cockerell, Charles Robert (1788–1863) English, born London; *Taylorian Institute*, Oxford (1841–5), *Fitzwilliam Museum*, Cambridge (1837–40).

Cortona, Pietro Berrettini da (1596–1669) Italian, born Cortona; *Villa Sacchetti*, Castel Fusano (1626–7), *San Firenze*, Florence (1645).

Cuvilliés, François de (1695–1768) Bavarian, born Belgium; *Amelienburg Pavilion* at Schloss Nymphenburg, near Munich (1734–9), *Residenztheater*, Munich (1750–3).

Dance, George, (the Elder) (1700–68) English, born London; *Mansion House*, London (1739).

Dance, George, (the Younger) (1741–1825) English, born London; rebuilt *Newgate Prison* (1770–83).

Delorme, Philibert (c.1510–70) French, born Lyons; *Tuileries* (1565–70), *Châteaux of Anet, Meudon, Saint Germain-en-Laye* (1547–55).

Doesburg, Theo van (originally **Christian Emil Marie Kupper**) (1883–1931) Dutch, born Utrecht; *L'Art Nouveau Shop*, Paris (1896), *Keller und Reiner Art Gallery*, Berlin (1898).

Doshi, Balkrishna Vithaldas (1927–) Indian, born Poona; *City Hall*, Toronto (1958), *Indian Institute of Management*, Ahmedabad (1951–7).

Dudok, Willem Marinus (1884–1974) Dutch, born Amsterdam; *Hilversum Town Hall* (1928–30), *Bijenkorf Department Store*, Rotterdam (1929).

Engel, Johann Carl Ludwig (1778–1840) Finnish, born Berlin; layout of Helsinki (1818–26).

Erickson, Arthur Charles (1924–) Canadian, born Vancouver; *Simon Fraser University Buildings*, British Columbia (1963), *Lethbridge University*, Alberta (1971).

Fischer von Erlach, Johann Bernard (1656–1723) Austrian, born Graz; *Karlskirche*, Vienna (1716), *Hofbibliotek*, Vienna (1723), *Kollegienkirche*, Salzburg (1707).

Foster, Norman Foster, Baron (1935–) English, born Manchester; *Willis Faber Dumas Building*, Ipswich (1975), *Sainsbury Centre*, University of East Anglia (1978), *Hong Kong and Shanghai Bank*, Hong Kong (1979–85), *Hong Kong Airport*, Hong Kong (1992–8), *Millennium Bridge*, London (1996–2000).

Francesco di Giorgio (1439–1501/2) Italian, born Siena; *Church of San Bernardino all'Osservanza*, Siena (1474–84), *Palazzo Ducale*, Gubbio (1476–82).

Gabriel, Ange-Jacques (1698–1782) French, born Paris; *Pavillon de Pompadour*, Fontainebleau (begun 1749), Paris; layout of *Place de la Concorde*, Paris (1753), *Petit Trianon*, Versailles (1761–8).

Garnier, Tony (Antoine) (1869–1948) French, born Lyons; *Grange Blanche Hospital*, Lyons (1911–27), *Stadium*, Lyons (1913–18), *Hôtel de Ville*, Boulogne-Bilancourt (1931–3).

Gaudí (i Cornet), Antoni (1852–1926) Spanish, born Reus, Tarragona; *Casa Vicens* (1878–80), *Sagrada Familia* (1884 onwards), *Casa Batlló* (1904–17), *Casa Milá* (1905–9), all Barcelona.

Geddes, Sir Patrick (1854–1932) Scottish, born Perth; *Ramsay Garden*, Edinburgh (1892), *Edinburgh Zoo* (1913), *Scots College*, Montpelier, France (1924).

Gibbs, James (1682–1754) Scottish, born Aberdeen; *St-Martin-in-the-Fields*, London (1722–6), *King's College Fellows' Building*, Cambridge (1724–49).

Gilbert, Cass (1859–1934) American, born Zanesville, Ohio; *Woolworth Building*, New York City (1913).

Gilly, Friedrich (1772–1800) German, born Berlin; *Funerary Precinct and Temple* to Frederick II, the Great of Prussia (1796), *Prussian National Theatre*, Berlin (1798).

Giotto (di Bondone) (c.1266–1337) Italian, born Vespignano, near Florence; *Campanile*, Florence Cathedral (from 1334).

Giulio Romano (properly **Giulio Pippi de' Gianuzzi**) (c.1492–1546) Italian, born Rome; *Palazzo del Tè*, Mantua (1526), *Church of S Petronio* façade, Bologna (1546).

Greenway, Francis Howard (1777–1837) Anglo-Australian, born Bristol; *Macquarie Lighthouse*, Sydney Harbour (1818), *St James' Church*, Sydney (1824).

Gropius, Walter (1883–1969) German–American, born Berlin; *Fagus Shoe Factory*, Alfeld (1911), *The Bauhaus*, Dessau (1925), both Germany; *Harvard University Graduate Centre* (1950), Massachusetts.

Guarini, Guarino (originally **Camillo**) (1624–83) Italian, born Modena; *San Lorenzo* church, Turin (1668–80), *Capella della SS Sindone* church, Turin (1668), *Palazzo Carignano*, Racconigi (1679).

Hamilton, Thomas (1784–1858) Scottish, born Glasgow; *Royal High School* (1825–9), *Royal College of Physicians Hall* (1844–5), *George IV Bridge* (1827–34), all Edinburgh.

Haussmann, Georges Eugène (1809–91) French, born Paris; layout of *Bois de Boulogne, Bois de Vincennes*, Paris (1853–70).

Hawksmoor, Nicholas (1661–1736) English, born Nottinghamshire; *St Mary Woolnoth Church* (1716–24), *St George's*, Bloomsbury (1716–30), both London.

Hildebrandt, Johann Lukas von (1668–1745) Austrian, born Genoa; *Lower and Upper Belvedere*, Vienna, (1714–15, 1720–3).

Hoffmann, Josef (1870–1956) Austrian, born Pirnitz; *Purkersdorf Sanatorium* (1903–5), *Stociet House*, Brussels (1905–11).

Holland, Henry (1746–1806) English, born London; *Carlton House*, London (1783–96), *Brighton Pavilion* (1787).

Howard, Sir Ebenezer (1850–1928) English, born London; *Letchworth Garden City* (1903).

Itkinos and **Callicrates** (dates and place of birth unknown) Greek; *The Parthenon*, Athens (447/6–438BC).

Jacobsen, Arne (1902–71) Danish, born Copenhagen; *Town Hall of Aarhus* (with Erik Moller, 1938–42), *Town Hall of Rodovre* (1955–6), *SAS Tower*, Copenhagen (1960), all Denmark; new *St Catherine's College*, Oxford (1959).

Jefferson, Thomas (1743–1826) American, born Shadwell, Virginia; *Monticello*, Albemarle County (1769), *Virginia State Capitol* (1796).

Johnson, Philip Cortelyou (1906–) American, born Cleveland, Ohio; *Glass House*, New Canaan, Connecticut (1949–50), *Seagram Building*, New York City (1945), *Amon Carter Museum of Western Art*, Texas (1961), *New York State Theater*, Lincoln Center (1964).

Jones, Inigo (1573–1652) English, born London; *The Queen's House*, Greenwich (1616–18, 1629–35), *Banqueting House*, Whitehall, London (1619–22).

Kahn, Louis Isadore (1901–74) American architect, born Osel (now Saaremaa), Estonia; *Richards Medical Research Building*, Pennsylvania (1957–61), *City Tower Municipal Building*, Philadelphia (1952–7).

Kent, William (1685–1748) English, born Bridlington, *Holkham Hall* (begun 1734).

Labrouste, (Pierre François) Henri (1801–75) French, born Paris; *Bibliothèque Sainte Geneviève* (1838–50), *Bibliothèque Nationale* reading room (1860–7), both Paris.

Lasdun, Sir Denys Louis (1914–2001) English, born London; *Royal College of Musicians* (1958–64), *National Theatre* (1965–76), both London.

Le Corbusier (pseudonym of **Charles Édouard Jeanneret**) (1887–1965) French, born La Chaux-de-Fonds, Switzerland; *Salvation Army Hostel*, Paris (begun 1929), *Chapel of Ronchamp*, near Belfort (1950–4), *Chandigarh*, Punjab (1951–6), *Museum of Modern Art*, Tokyo (1957).

Ledoux, Claude Nicolas (1736–1806) French, born Dormans, Champagne; *Château*, Louveciennes (1771–3), *Theatre*, Besançon (1771–3).

Leonardo da Vinci (1452–1519) Italian, born Vinci; *Mariolo de Guiscardi House*, Milan (1497), *La Veruca Fortress*, near Pisa (1504), *Villa Melzi*, Vaprio, Milan (1513).

Lescot, Pierre (c.1510–78) French, born Paris; rebuilt one wing of the *Louvre*, Paris (1546), screen of *St Germain l'Auxerrois* (1541–4).

Lethaby, William Richard (1857–1931) English, born Barnstaple; *Avon Tyrell*, Christchurch, Hampshire (1891–2), *Eagle Insurance Buildings*, Birmingham (1899–1900).

Le Vau or **Levau, Louis** (1612–70) French, born Paris; *Hôtel Lambert*, Paris (1640–4), part of *Palace of Versailles* (from 1661), *Collège des Quatre Nations*, Paris (1661).

Loos, Adolf (1870–1933) Austrian, born Bruno, Moravia; *Steiner House*, Vienna (1910).

Lorimer, Sir Robert Stodart (1864–1929) Scottish, born Edinburgh; *Thistle Chapel, St Giles*, Edinburgh (1909–11), *Scottish National War Memorial*, Edinburgh Castle (1923–8).

Arts and Culture

Lutyens, Sir Edwin Landseer (1869–1944) English, born London; *Cenotaph*, Whitehall, London (1919–20), *Liverpool Roman Catholic Cathedral* (1929–c.1941), *Viceroy's House*, New Delhi (1921–5).

Mackintosh, Charles Rennie (1868–1928) Scottish, born Glasgow; *Glasgow School of Art* (1897–9), *Hill House*, Helensburgh (1902–3).

Mackmurdo, Arthur Heygate (1851–1942) English, born London; *Gordon Institute for Boys*, St Helens (1890).

Maderna or **Maderno, Carlo** (1556–1629) Italian, born Capalago; façade of *St Peter's* (1606–12), *S Susanna* (1597–1603), *Palazzo Barberini* (1628–38), all Rome.

Mansard or **Mansart, François** (1598–1666) French, born Paris; north wing of *Château de Blois* (1635), *Sainte-Marie de la Visitation*, Paris (1632).

Mansard or **Mansart, Jules Hardouin** (1645–1708) French, born Paris; *Grand Trianon, Palace of Versailles* (1678–89).

Mendelsohn, Eric (1887–1953) German, born Allenstein; *De La Warr Pavilion*, Bexhill (1933–5), *Anglo-Palestine Bank*, Jerusalem (1938).

Michelozzo di Bartolommeo (1396–1472) Italian, born Florence; *Villa Medici*, Fiesole (1458–61), *San Marco*, Florence (begun 1437).

Mies van der Rohe, Ludwig (1886–1969) German–American, born Aachen; *Seagram Building*, New York City (1956–8), *Public Library*, Washington (1967).

Moore, Charles Willard (1925–93) American, born Benton Harbor, Michigan; *Sea Ranch Condominium Estate*, Glendale, California (1965), *Kresge College*, Santa Cruz, California (1974), *Piazza d'Italia*, New Orleans (1975–8), *Civic Center*, Beverly Hills, California (1990).

Nash, John (1752–1835) English, born London; layout of *Regent's Park* and *Regent Street*, London (1811 onwards), *Brighton Pavilion* (1815).

Nervi, Pier Luigi (1891–1979) Italian, born Sondrio; *Berta Stadium*, Florence (1930–2), *Olympic Stadia*, Rome (1960), *San Francisco Cathedral* (1970).

Neumann, (Johann) Balthasar (1687–1753) German, born Eger; *Würzburg Palace* (1730–43), *Schloss Bruchsal* (1738–53).

Niemeyer, Oscar (1907–) Brazilian, born Rio de Janeiro; *Church of St Francis of Assisi*, Pampúlha, Belo Horizonte, Brazil (1942–4), *Niemeyer House*, Rio de Janeiro (1953).

Oud, Jacobus Johann Pieter (1890–1963) Dutch, born Purmerend; *Alida Hartog-Ond House*, Purmerend (1906), *Café de Unie*, Rotterdam (1924), *Convention Centre*, The Hague (1957–63).

Palladio, Andrea (1508–80) Italian, born Padua; *Godi-Porto* (villa at Lonedo) (1540), *La Malcontenta* (villa near Padua) (1560), *San Giorgio Maggiore*, Venice (begun 1566).

Paxton, Sir Joseph (1801–65) English, born Milton-Bryant, near Woburn; building for *Great Exhibition* of 1851, later re-erected as the *Crystal Palace*, Sydenham (1852–4).

Pei, Ieoh Ming (1917–) Chinese–American, born Canton; *Mile High Center*, Denver (1954–9), *John Hancock Tower*, Boston (1973), *Glass Pyramids*, the Louvre, Paris (1983–9).

Perret, Auguste (1874–1954) French, born Brussels; *Théatre des Champs Elysées*, Paris (1911–13), *Musée des travaux publics*, Paris (1936).

Piranesi, Giambattista (1720–78) Italian, born Ve-

nice; *Santa Maria Arentina*, Rome (1764–6).

Pisano, Nicola (c.1225–c.1284) Italian, born Tuscany; *Pisa Baptistry* (1260), façade renovation of *Pisa Cathedral* (1260–70).

Playfair, William Henry (1789–1857) Scottish, born London; *National Gallery of Scotland* (1850–7), *Royal Scottish Academy* (1832–5), *Surgeon's Hall* (1829–32), all Edinburgh.

Poelzig, Hans (1869–1936) German, born Berlin; *Exhibition Hall*, Posen (1910–11), *Salzburg Festival Theatre* (1920–2).

Pugin, Augustus Welby Northmore (1812–52) English, born London; drawings, decorations and sculpture for the *Houses of Parliament*, London (1836–7), *Birmingham Cathedral* (1839–41).

Renwick, James (1818–95) American, born New York; *Smithsonian Institution*, Washington (1844–55), *Grace Church*, New York (1846), *St Patrick's Cathedral*, New York (1858–79).

Rietveld, Gerrit Thomas (1888–1964) Dutch, born Utrecht; *Schröder House*, Utrecht (1924), *Van Gogh Museum*, Amsterdam (1963–4).

Rogers, Richard George Rogers, Baron (1933–) English, born Florence; *Pompidou Centre*, Paris (1971–9), *Lloyds*, London (1979–85), *Millennium Dome*, London (1996–9), *Princeton Campus Centre*, New Jersey (1996–2000).

Saarinen, Eero (1910–61) Finnish–American, born Kirkknonummi; *Jefferson Memorial Arch*, St Louis (1948–64), *American Embassy*, London (1955–60).

Saarinen, (Gottlieb) Eliel (1873–1950) Finnish–American, born Rantasalmi; *Cranbrook Academy of Art*, Michigan (1934–40).

Sanmichele, Michele (c.1484–1559) Italian, born Verona; *Capella Pelegrini*, Verona (1527–57), *Palazzo Grimani*, Venice (1551–9).

Sansovino, Jacopo (1486–1570) Italian, born Florence; *Library* and *Mint*, Venice.

Schinkel, Karl Friederich (1781–1841) German, born Neurippen, Brandenburg; *Old Museum*, Berlin (1823–30), *War Memorial on the Kreuzberg* (1818).

Scott, Sir George Gilbert (1811–78) English, born Gawcott, Buckinghamshire; *Albert Memorial*, London (1862–3), *St Pancras station and hotel*, London (1865), *Glasgow University* (1865).

Serlio, Sebastiano (1475–1554) Italian, born Bologna; *Grand Ferrare*, Fontainebleau (1541–8), *Château*, Ancy-le-Franc, Tonnerre (from 1546).

Shaw, (Richard) Norman (1831–1912) English, born Edinburgh; *Old Swan House*, Chelsea (1876), *New Scotland Yard*, London (1888).

Smirke, Sir Robert (1781–1867) English, born London; *Covent Garden Theatre*, London (1809), *British Museum*, London (1823–47).

Smythson, Robert (c.1535–1614) English, place of birth unknown; *Wollaton Hall*, Nottingham (1580–8), *Hardwick Hall*, Derbyshire (1591–7).

Soane, Sir John (1753–1837) English, born near Reading; altered interior of *Bank of England* (1788–1833), *Dulwich College Art Gallery* (1811–14).

Sottsass, Ettore, Jr (1917–) Italian, born Innsbruck; *Apartment Building*, Turin (1934), *Galleria del Cavalliro*, Venice (1956).

Soufflot, Jacques Germain (1713–80) French, born Irancy; *Hôtel Dieu*, Lyons (1741), *St Geneviève* (Panthéon), Paris (begun 1757).

Spence, Sir Basil Urwin (1907–76) Scottish, born India; Pavilions for *Festival of Britain* (1951), *Coventry Cathedral* (1951).

Stirling, Sir James (1926–92) Scottish, born Glasgow; *Department of Engineering*, Leicester University (1959–63) (with James Gowan), *History Faculty*, Cambridge (1965–8), *Florey Building*, Queen's College, Oxford (1966), *Neue Staatsgalerie*, Stuttgart (1980–4).

Street, George Edmund (1824–81) English, born Woodford, Essex; *London Law Courts* (1870–81).

Stuart, James (1713–88) English, born London; rebuilt interior of *Chapel of Greenwich Hospital* (1779).

Sullivan, Louis Henry (1856–1924) American, born Boston, Massachusetts; *Wainwright Building*, St Louis (1890), *Carson, Pirie and Scott Store*, Chicago (1899–1904).

Tange, Kenzo (1913–) Japanese, born Tokyo; *Hiroshima Peace Centre* (1949–55), *Shizoka Press and Broadcasting Centre*, Tokyo (1966–7).

Utzon, Jørn (1918–) Danish, born Copenhagen; *Sydney Opera House* (1956–68), *Kuwait House of Parliament* (begun 1972).

Vanbrugh, Sir John (1664–1726) English, born London; *Castle Howard* (1699–1726), *Blenheim Palace* (1705–20).

Velde, Henri Clemens van de (1863–1957) Belgian, born Antwerp; *Werkbund Theatre*, Cologne (1914), *Museum Kröller-Muller*, Otterloo (1937–54).

Venturi, Robert Charles (1925–) American, born Philadelphia, Pennsylvania; *Brant-Johnson House*, Vail, Colorado (1976), *Sainsbury Wing* of the National Gallery, London (1986–91).

Vignola, Giacomo Barozzi da (1507–73) Italian, born Vignola; *Villa di Papa Giulio* (1550–5), church of the *Il Gesu*, Rome (1586–73).

Viollet-le-Duc, Eugène Emmanuel (1814–79) French, born Paris; restored cathedral of *Notre Dame*, Paris (1845–64), *Château de Pierrefonds* (1858–70).

Vitruvius (in full **Marcus Vitruvius Pollio**) (1c BC) Roman; wrote the 10-volume *De Architectura* (35BC), the only extant Roman treatise on architecture.

Voysey, Charles Francis Annesley (1857–1941) English, born London; *Grove Town Houses*, Kensington (1891–2), *Sanderson's Wallpaper Factory*, Chiswick (1902).

Wagner, Otto (1841–1918) Austrian, born Penzing, near Vienna; stations for *Vienna Stadtbahn* (1894–7), *Post Office Savings Bank*, Vienna (1904–6).

Waterhouse, Alfred (1830–1905) English, born Liverpool; *Manchester Town Hall* (1867–77), *Natural History Museum*, South Kensington, London (1873–81).

Webb, Sir Aston (1849–1930) English, born London; eastern façade of *Buckingham Palace* (1912), *Admiralty Arch* (1903–10), *Imperial College of Science* (1906), all London.

Webb, Philip (1831–1915) English, born Oxford; *Red House*, Bexley (1859), *Clouds*, Wiltshire (1881–6), *Standen*, East Grinstead (1891).

Wood, John, (the Elder) (1704–54) English. *Queen Square*, Bath (1729–36).

Wood, John, (the Younger) (1728–82) English. *Royal Crescent*, Bath (1767–75), *Assembly Rooms*, Bath (1769–71).

Wren, Sir Christopher (1632–1723) English, born East Knoyle, Wiltshire; *Pembroke College Chapel*, Cambridge (1663–5), *The Sheldonian Theatre*, Oxford (1664), *Royal Greenwich Observatory* (1675–6), *St Paul's*, London (1675–1710), *Greenwich Hospital* (1696).

Wright, Frank Lloyd (1869–1959) American, born Richland Center, Wisconsin; *Larkin Building*, Buffalo (1904), *Robie House*, Chicago (1908), *Johnson Wax Factory*, Racine, Wisconsin (1936–9), *Falling Water*, Mill Run, Pennsylvania (1936), *Guggenheim Museum*, New York (begun 1942).

Wyatt, James (1746–1813) English, born Staffordshire; *London Pantheon* (1772), *Gothic Revival Country House*, Fonthill Abbey, Wiltshire (1796–1813).

Sculptors

Selected works are listed.

Andre, Carl (1935–) American, born Quincy, Massachusetts; *144 Magnesium Square* (1969), *Twelfth Copper Corner* (1975), *Bloody Angle* (1985), *Armadillo* (1998).

Armitage, Kenneth (1916–2002) British, born Leeds; *People in the Wind* (1950), *Sprawling Woman* (1958), *Figure and Clouds* (1972), *Richmond Oak* (1985–90).

Arp, Hans (Jean) (1887–1966) French, born Strasbourg; *Eggboard* (1922), *Kore* (1958).

Barlach, Ernst (1870–1938) German, born Wedel; *Moeller-Jarke Tomb* (1901), *Have Pity!* (1919).

Bernini, Gianlorenzo (1598–1680) Italian, born Naples; *Neptune and Triton* (1620), *David* (1623), *Ecstasy of St Theresa* (1640s), *Fountain of the Four Rivers* (1648–51).

Beuys, Joseph (1921–86) German, born Kleve; *Fat Chair* (1964), *Snowfall* (1965).

Bologna, Giovanni da (also called **Giambologna**) (1529–1608) French, born Douai; *Mercury* (1564–5), *Rape of the Sabines* (1579–83).

Bourgeois, Louise (1911–) American, born Paris; *Labyrinthine Tower* (1963), *Destruction of the Father* (1974), *Spiders* (1995).

Brancusi, Constantin (1876–1957) Romanian–French, born Hobitza, Gorj; *The Kiss* (1909), *Torso of a Young Man* (1922).

Calder, Alexander (1898–1976) American, born Philadelphia, Pennsylvania; *Stabiles and Mobiles* (1932), *A Universe* (1934).

Canova, Antonio (1757–1822) Italian, born Possagno; *Theseus* (1782), *Cupid and Psyche* (1787), *Pauline Borghese as Venus* (1805–7).

Caro, Sir Anthony (1924–) British, born London; *Sailing Tonight* (1971–4), *Veduggio Sound* (1973), *Ledge Piece* (1978), *Night Movements* (1987–90).

Cellini, Benvenuto (1500–71) Italian, born Florence; salt cellar of *Neptune and Ceres* (1543), *Cosimo de' Medici* (1545–7), *Perseus with the Head of Medusa* (1564).

Deacon, Richard (1949–) British, born Bangor, Wales; *Double Talk* (1987), *Kiss and Tell* (1989), *Never Mind* (1993), *Show and Tell* (1997).

Donatello (originally **Donnato di Niccolo di Betto Bardi**) (c.1386–1466) Italian, born Florence; *St Mark* (1411–12), *St George Killing the Dragon* (c.1417), *Feast of Herod* (1423–37), *David, Judith and Holofernes*, Piazza della Signoria, Florence.

Epstein, Sir Jacob (1880–1959) Anglo-American, born New York City; *Rima* (1925), *Genesis* (1930), *Ecce Homo* (1934–5), *Adam* (1939), *Christ in Majesty*

(Llandaff Cathedral), *St Michael and the Devil* (on the façade of Coventry Cathedral) (1958–9).

Frink, Dame Elisabeth (1930–93) British, born Thurlow, Suffolk; *Horse Lying Down* (1975), *Running Man* (1985), *Seated Man* (1986).

Gabo, Naum (originally **Naum Neemia Pevsner**) (1890–1977) American, born Bryansk, Russia; *Kinetic Construction* (1920), *No.1* (1943).

Gaudier-Brzeska, Henri (1891–1915) French, born St Jean de Braye, near Orléans; *Red stone dancer* (1913).

Ghiberti, Lorenzo (c.1378–1455) Italian, born in or near Florence; *St John the Baptist* (1412–15), *St Matthew* (1419–22), *The Gates of Paradise* (1425–52).

Giacometti, Alberto (1901–66) Swiss, born Bogonova, near Stampa; *Head* (c.1928), *Woman with Her Throat Cut* (1932).

Goldsworthy, Andy (1956–) British, born Cheshire; *Hazel Stick Throws* (1980), *Slate Cone* (1988), *The Wall* (1988–9).

González, Julio (1876–1942) Spanish, born Barcelona; *Angel* (1933), *Woman Combing Her Hair* (1936), *Cactus People* (1930–40).

Gormley, Antony (1950–) English, born London; *Natural Selection* (1981), *Angel of the North* (1997).

Hepworth, Dame (Jocelyn) Barbara (1903–75) British, born Wakefield, Yorkshire; *Figure of a Woman* (1929–30), *Large and Small Forms* (1945), *Single Form* (1963).

Leonardo da Vinci (1452–1519) Italian, born Vinci, between Pisa and Florence; *St John the Baptist*.

Michelangelo (in full **Michelangelo di Lodovico Buonarotti**) (1475–1564) Italian, born Caprese, Tuscany; *Cupid* (1495), *Bacchus* (1496), *Pieta* (1497), *David* (c.1500).

Moore, Henry (Spencer) (1898–1986) British, born Castleford, Yorkshire; *Recumbent Figure* (1938), *Fallen Warrior* (1956–7).

Oldenburg, Claes Thure (1929–) American, born Stockholm, Sweden; *Giant Clothespin* (1975), *The Course of the Knife* (1985), *Match Cover* (1992).

Paolozzi, Sir Eduardo Luigi (1924–) British, born Leith, Edinburgh; *Krokodeel* (c.1956–7), *Japanese War God* (1958), *Medea* (1964), *Piscator* (1981), *Manuscript of Monte Cassino*, Edinburgh (1991), *Daedalus* (1993).

Pheidias (c.490–c.417BC) Greek, born Athens; *Athena Promachos* (460–450BC), marble sculptures of the *Parthenon* (447–432BC).

Pisano, Andrea (c.1270–1349) Italian, born Pontedera; bronze doors of the *Baptistry* of Florence (1330–6).

Pisano, Giovanni (c.1248–c.1320) Italian, born Pisa; *Fontana Magiore*, Perugia (1278), *Duomo pulpit*, Pisa (1302–10).

Pisano, Nicola (c.1225–c.1284) Italian, birthplace unknown; *Baptistry* at Pisa (1260).

Praxiteles (5c BC) Greek, born probably Athens; *Hermes Carrying the Boy Dionysus* (date unknown).

Robbia, Luca della (in full **Luca di Simone di Marco della Robbia**) (c.1400–1482) Italian, born Florence; *Cantoria* (1432–7).

Rodin, (François) Auguste (René) (1840–1917) French, born Paris; *The Age of Bronze* (1875–6), *The Gates of Hell* (1880–1917), *The Burghers of Calais* (1884), *The Thinker* (1904).

Schwitters, Kurt (1887–1948) German, born Hannover; *Merzbau* (1920–43).

Tinguely, Jean (1925–91) Swiss, born Fribourg; *Baluba No 3* (1959), *Métamécanique No 9* (1959), *Homage to New York* (1960), *EOSX* (1967).

Whiteread, Rachel (1963–) British, born London; *Torso* (1991), *House* (1993), *Orange Bath* (1996), *Water Tower* (1998).

Photographers

Adams, Ansel (Easton) (1902–84) American, born San Francisco. Notable for broad landscapes of western America, especially the Yosemite in the 1930s. One of the founders of Group f/64 (1932). Publications include *Taos Pueblo* (1930) and *Born Free and Equal* (1944).

Adams, Marcus Algernon (1875–1959) English, born Southampton. Portrait photographer who established studio in 1919 specializing in formal children's portraits with soft-focus style. His portraits of three generations of the British royal family, taken from 1926 until his retirement in 1957, were published worldwide.

Adamson, Robert (1821–48) Scottish, born Berunside. Pioneer in photography. With David Octavius Hill applied the calotype process of making photographic prints on silver chloride paper for a commission to portray the founders of the Free Church of Scotland in 1843.

Akiyama, Shotaro (1920–2003) Japanese, born Tokyo. Worked for a Japanese motion picture company before becoming a freelance photographer for a number of publishers in 1951.

Anschütz, Ottomar (1846–1907) German, born Lissa (now in Poland). Pioneer of instantaneous photography and one of the first to make a series of pictures of moving animals and people, making a substantial contribution to the invention of the cinematograph.

Arbus, Diane (née **Nemerov**) (1923–71) American,

born New York City. After work in conventional fashion photography, sought to portray people 'without their masks'. Achieved fame in the 1960s with ironic studies of social poses and the deprived classes, but became increasingly depressed, eventually committing suicide.

Arnold, Eve (1913–) American photojournalist, born Philadelphia. First woman to photograph for Magnum Photos in 1951. Famous for pictures of women, the poor and the elderly, as well as celebrities such as Marilyn Monroe.

Atget, (Jean) Eugène (Auguste) (1856–1927) French, born Libourne, near Bordeaux. Studied at the Conservatoire d'Art Dramatique, Paris (1879–81), before working as a stage actor, comedian and painter. His photographic work (1898–1925) was discovered in 1926 in Paris by Berenice Abbott.

Avedon, Richard (1923–) American, born New York City. Studied photography at the New School for Social Research, New York and served in the photography section of the US merchant navy (1942–4). Established his own studio in New York and worked freelance for *Harper's Bazaar*, *Vogue* and *Life*. Received Photographer of the Year award from the American Society of Magazine Photographers in 1985, and worked for the *New Yorker* from 1992.

Bailey, David (Royston) (1938–) English, born London. Originally specialized in freelance fashion photography from 1959, later extending to portraits expressing the spirit of the 1960s and to studies of the nude. Also writes extensively on photography and has been director of television commercials and documentaries since the 1970s.

Beaton, Sir Cecil (Walter Hardy) (1904–80) English, born London. Outstanding photographer of fashion and celebrities, including royalty. Also designed scenery and costumes for ballet, operatic, theatrical and film productions. Publications include *My Royal Past* (1939), *The Glass of Fashion* (1959), *The Magic Image* (1975), as well as several volumes of autobiography (1961–78).

Bischof, Werner (1916–54) Swiss, born Zurich. Freelance graphic artist and photographer in Zurich (1932–6) and later magazine photographer for *Life*, *Picture Post* and *Paris Match*.

Blumenfeld, Erwin (1897–1969) American, born Berlin, Germany. Self-taught photographer, associated with Dadaist artists in Amsterdam (1918–23). Worked as a fashion photographer for *Verve* and *Vogue* in Paris before opening a studio in New York in 1943.

Bourke-White, Margaret (White, Margaret) (1904–71) American, born New York City. Photo-journalist for *Fortune* magazine (1929) and later *Life* magazine from 1936, for which she covered World War II. First woman photographer to be attached to US armed forces. Also produced reports of the siege of Moscow (1941) and opening of the concentration camps in 1944, later covering troubles around the world. Books include *Eyes on Russia* (1931), *Halfway to Freedom* (1946) and an autobiography, *Portrait of Myself* (1963).

Brady, Matthew B (1823–96) American, born near Lake George, New York. Operated portrait studio in New York using daguerrotype from 1844, and later recorded the American Civil War with the Union armies, an effort which ruined him financially so that he died in poverty in a New York almshouse.

Brandt, Bill (1904–83) English, born London. Studied with Man Ray in Paris in 1929. In 1930s produced striking social records and during World War II worked for ministry of information recording conditions in London in the Blitz. Subsequently turned to landscape and studies of the nude. Collections include *The English at Home* (1936), *A Night in London* (1938), *Perspective of Nudes* (1961), *Shadows of Light* (1966).

Brassaï (Halász, Gyula) (1899–1984) French, born Brasso, Transylvania, Hungary (now Romania). From 1930 recorded underworld and nightlife of Paris. Refused to photograph during the German occupation, but worked in Picasso's studios, returning to photography after World War I.

Bullock, Wynn (Percy Wingfield Bullock) (1902–75) American, born Chicago. Studied photography at the Art Center School, Los Angeles (1938–40). Worked in commercial postcard photography and later taught at the Institute of Design at the University of California.

Burgin, Victor (1941–) English, born Sheffield. Influenced by conceptual art of the 1960s. Concentrates on black-and-white images with text superimposed onto them, forcing the viewer to participate. Publications include *Some Cities* (1996) and *Relocating: Victor Burgin* (2002).

Cameron, Julia Margaret (née **Pattle**) (1815–79) British, born Calcutta (now Kolkata), India. Became outstanding amateur photographer in the 1860s, and received permanent acclaim for close-up portraits of Victorian celebrities.

Capa, Robert (Friedmann, André) (1913–54) American, born Budapest, Hungary. Recorded the Span-ish Civil War (1935–7), China under Japanese attack (1938), World War II in Europe and subsequently the early days of the state of Israel. Killed by a land mine in the Indo-China fighting.

Cartier-Bresson, Henri (1908–) French, born Paris. Presented his first photographic exhibition in 1933; later visited Mexico and America and worked as assistant to film director Jean Renoir. After World War II developed his human interest style of black-and-white photography worldwide travels. Was a co-founder of Magnum Photos. Publications include *Images à la sauvette* (The Decisive Moment, 1952), *The Europeans* (1955).

Chim, David Seymour (David Szymin) (1911–56) American, born Warsaw, Poland. Freelance photographer who worked for *Vu* and *Ce Soir* in Paris, and throughout Europe and N Africa. Established his own studio in New York (1940–2) and was a co-founder of Magnum Photos, Paris and New York.

Clergue, Lucien (Georges) (1934–) French, born Arles. Self-taught freelance teacher at Arles from 1960. Founder of Recontres Internationales de la Photographie, Arles (1970).

Coburn, Alvin Langdon (1882–1966) British, born Boston, Massachusetts. Established a studio in New York (1901–2) and worked as an independent photographer in Boston, London, California and Wales. Associated with the Vorticist Group in London (1917–18).

Cosindas, Marie (1925–) American, born Boston, Massachusetts. Attended photography workshops under Ansel Adams in Boston in 1961 and has worked as a freelance photographer since 1960. Received Guggenheim Fellowship in 1967.

Crawford, Osbert Guy Stanhope (1886–1957) British, born Bombay (now Mumbai), India. Identified potential of aerial photography in archaeology, resulting in the collection *Wessex from the Air* (1928).

Cunningham, Imogen (1883–1976) American, born Portland, Oregon. Opened portrait studio in Seattle (1910) specializing in soft-focus sentimental-style portraits and still-life flower studies. Later converted to sharply defined images, and was still teaching at the Art Institute in San Francisco in her nineties.

Curtis, Edward Sheriff (1868–1952) American, born Madison, Wisconsin. From 1896 recorded the North American Indian tribes and their way of life, publishing first 20 volumes in 1907. Took around 40 000 negatives, stressing the Indians' peaceful arts and culture.

Daguerre, Louis Jacques Mandé (1787–1851) French, born Cormeilles. Inventor of the 'daguerrotype', a process in which a photographic image is obtained on a copper plate coated with a layer of metallic silver sensitized to light by iodine vapour.

Davidson, Bruce (1933–) American, born Chicago. Studied photography at Rochester Institute of Technology and since 1958 has worked freelance for *Life*, *Queen*, *Vogue* and other magazines in New York, Paris and Los Angeles. Received Guggenheim Fellowship in 1962.

DeCarava, Roy (1919–) African–American, born New York City. His work includes pictures of life in Harlem, jazz musicians and civil rights protests. Received Guggenheim Fellowship in 1952.

Dodgson, Charles Lutwidge (Carroll, Lewis) (1832–98) English, born Daresbury, near Warrington. Pioneer photographer, mainly interested in portrait photography.

Doisneau, Robert (1912–94) French, born Gentilly, Seine. Studied lithography in Paris (1926–9) and

Arts and Culture

worked as a photographer from 1930, including industrial photography and as a photojournalist. Awarded the Kodak Prize (1947) and the Niepce Prix (1956).

Draper, Henry (1837–82) American, born Prince Edward County, Virginia. Pioneer of astronomical photography who produced photographs of the Orion nebula and over 100 stellar spectra.

Duclos du Hauron, Louis (1837–1920) French, born Langon. Outlined principles of additive and subtractive colour separation in *Les Couleurs en Photographie* (1869). Described practical photographic methods which he patented in *Photographie en Couleur* (1878), and proposed the anaglyph method of viewing stereoscopic images.

Eakins, Thomas (1844–1916) American, born Philadelphia, Pennsylvania. Extended advances made by Muybridge in his studies of figures in motion. His composite plates inspired Duchamp's *Nude Descending the Staircase*.

Eastman, George (1854–1932) American, born Waterville, New York. Produced a successful rollfilm (1884), the 'Kodak' box camera (1888) and pioneered experiments which made possible the moving-picture industry. Formed the Eastman Kodak Co in 1892 and produced the Brownie camera in 1900.

Edgerton, Harold Eugene (1903–90) American, born Fremont, Nebraska. Engineer who specialized in high-speed photography. Produced a krypton–xenon gas arc which was employed in photographing the capillaries in the white of the eye without harming the patient.

Eisenstaedt, Alfred (1898–1995) American, born Dirschau, West Prussia (now Tczew, Poland). One of the original photojournalists on *Life* magazine (1936–72). Voted Photographer of the Year in 1951. Publications include *Witness to Our Time* (1966), *The Eye of Eisenstaedt* (1969) and *Photojournalism* (1971).

Evans, Walker (1903–75) American, born St Louis, Missouri. Architectural and social photographer who recorded rural life in the Southern states and people in New York City subways. Publications include *American Photographs* (1938) and *Many Are Called* (1966).

Feininger, Andreas (Bernhard Lyonel) (1906–99) American, born Paris. Self-taught photographer, involved in industrial and architectural photography in Stockholm (1933–9). Worked as a freelance photographer in New York and as a war photographer for the US Office of War Information (1941–2).

Fenton, Roger (1819–69) English, born Lancashire. Photographed in Russia in 1852 and was a founder of the Photographic Society (later the Royal) in 1953; Queen Victoria became its patron and Fenton photographed the royal family at Balmoral and Windsor. In 1855 went to the Crimea as the world's first accredited war photographer. Later travelled in Britain producing architectural and landscape studies.

Firth, Francis (1822–98) English, born Chesterfield. Topographical photographer who produced the first photographic traveller's records to be seen in Britain during travel in Egypt and the Near East between 1856 and 1859. Established nationwide service of photographs of local scenes as prints in Britain, a business which survived commercially until 1971.

Frank, Robert (1924–) Swiss, born Zurich. After working as a photographer in Zurich (1943–4) moved to America in 1947 and worked freelance

for *Harper's Bazaar* and *Life* in New York. Later worked in film-making and received the Guggenheim Fellowship (1955).

Genthe, Arnold (1869–1942) American, born Berlin. Commercial portrait photographer who emigrated to America in 1896 and established a studio in San Francisco (1897–1906). Concentrated on dance and theatrical portraits.

Gill, Sir David (1843–1914) Scottish, born Aberdeen. Astronomer who pioneered use of photography for charting the heavens.

Godwin, Fay Simmonds (1931–) English, born Berlin. Best known for landscape photography, including Welsh and Scottish scenes. Publications include *The Oldest Road* (1975, co-authored with J R C Anderson), *Glassworks and Secret Lives* (1999) and *Landmarks* (2001).

Haas, Ernst (1921–86) Austrian, born Vienna. Studied photography in Vienna and worked freelance for *Vogue* and *Life* in Paris (1948–50) before moving to America in 1950.

Halsman, Philippe (1906–79) American, born Riga, Latvia. Self-taught photographer who established a studio in Paris and worked for *Vogue* and *Voila* (1931–40). Emigrated to America in 1940 and became President of the American Society of Magazine Photographers, New York (1944, 1954) and received a Life Achievement Award (1975).

Hardy, Bert (1913–95) English, born London. Photojournalist on staff of *Picture Post* until 1957, except for service as Army photographer from 1942 to 1946, during which he recorded concentration camps. Later assignments took him to the Korean and Vietnam wars. Became involved in advertising until his retirement in 1967.

Hill, David Octavius (1802–70) Scottish, born Perth. Pioneer in photography. With Robert Adamson applied the calotype process of making photographic prints on silver chloride paper for a commission to portray the founders of the Free Church of Scotland in 1843.

Hine, Lewis W(ickes) (1874–1940) American, born Oshkosh, Wisconsin. Expressed social concern through photographic studies of Ellis Island immigrants and child labour. During World War I documented the plight of refugees for the American Red Cross and recorded the construction of the Empire State Building in *Men at Work* (1932). Later registered the effects of the Depression for a US government project.

Hiro (Yasuhiro Wakabayashi) (1930–) Japanese, born Shanghai, China. Moved to New York in 1954 and established a studio there in 1958. Worked freelance for *Harper's Bazaar* from 1958, and received the Photographer of the Year award from the American Society of Magazine Photographers.

Karsh, Yousuf (1908–2002) Canadian, born Mardin, Turkey. Apprenticed to a Boston portraitist (1928–31) and in 1932 opened a studio in Ottawa. Appointed official portrait photographer to the Canadian government in 1935. Produced wartime studies of national leaders and continued to portray statesmen, artists and writers throughout the world.

Kertész, André (1894–1985) Hungarian–American, born Budapest. Photographer with Hungarian army during World War I and later an acclaimed reporter of the 'human condition' in Paris. Worked for Condé-Nast publications and other magazines in New York in the 1930s and 1940s. After a major retrospective exhibition at the New York Museum of Modern Art in 1964 received belated official recognition.

Lange, Dorothea (originally **Nutzhorn**) (1895–1965) American, born Hoboken, New Jersey. Established studio in San Francisco in 1919, and later recorded rural life in the south and west of America during the depression years from 1935. With her husband collaborated on the book *An American Exodus: A Record of Human Erosion* (1939). After World War II worked as a freelance reporter in Asia, South America and the Middle East.

Lartigue, Jacques-Henri (Charles Auguste) (1894–1986) French, born Courbvoie, Seine. Adopted informal approach to photography, elevating the snapshot into a creative art form. *Diary of a Century* is a collection recording the elegance of the inter-war years in France.

Leibovitz, Annie (1949–) American, born Connecticut. Known for photographs of celebrities. Worked for *Rolling Stone* in the 1970s and has been chief photographer for *Vanity Fair* since 1983. Won Innovation in Photography Award in 1987. Publications include *Photographs 1970–90* in 1992, and *Women* in 1999.

Levitt, Helen (1913–) American, born New York City. Known for documentation of urban life. Work published in *Time*, the *New York Post* and *Harper's Bazaar*. Also worked in film during the 1940s and 1950s.

Lichfield, Patrick, 5th Earl of (1939–) English. After working as an assistant opened his own studio and since 1981 has achieved success in travel and publicity photography and royal portraits.

Marey, Etienne Jules (1830–1903) French, born Beaune. Physiologist who pioneered scientific cinematography in studies of animal movement (1887–1900). Improved camera design and reduced exposure time to around 1/25 000 of a second to photograph insect flight.

Martin, Paul (1864–1942) Anglo-French, born Herbenville, France. Made use of a disguised camera to record working people in the streets of London and on holiday at the seaside (1888–98), recording the realities of late-Victorian everyday life in *London by Gaslight* (1896). Turned professional in 1899.

McBean, Angus Rowland (1904–90) Welsh, born Newbridge, Monmouth. Theatrical photographer from 1934, noted for an individualistic approach to portraiture, use of photographic montage, collage and double-exposure to achieve surrealistic effects. Later photographed in the world of pop music and withdrew from professional photography after 1969.

McCullin, Don(ald) (1935–) English, born London. Studied painting (1948–50) and later became a photographic assistant in aerial reconnaissance with the RAF (1953–5). Worked abroad as freelance photographer and as staff photographer for the *Sunday Times* (1964–84). Publications include *A Life's Work in Photography* (1995) and *Don McCullin* (2001).

Miller, Lee (1907–77) American, born Poughkeepsie, New York. Known for her documentary work and fashion photography. Photographer for *Vogue* before and after World War II. During war worked as official war correspondent for the US forces.

Moholy-Nagy, László (Nagy, László) (1895–1946) American, born Bucsborsod, near Mohol, south Hungary. Produced first 'photograms' (non-representational photographic images made directly without a camera) in 1923 and later became recognized as a leading avant-garde artist in Germany in the European New Photographers movement (1925–35), his work including film-making and typography integrated with photographic illustration. Moved to the USA in 1937.

Mountford, Charles Percy (1890–1976) Australian, born Hallett, South Australia. Ethnologist who wrote a series of books, illustrated with his own photographs, about Aboriginal Australians and their culture. Later directed feature films on Aboriginal life from 1950.

Muybridge, Eadweard (Muggeridge, Edward James) (1830–1904) Anglo-American, born Kingston-on-Thames. Became professional photographer in 1866 and later chief photographer to the American government. In 1880 devised the zoopraxiscope to show picture sequences, achieving a rudimentary kind of cinematography. *Animal Locomotion* (1887) gives the results of his extensive survey of animal and human movement.

Nadar (Tournachon, Gaspard-Felix) (1820–1910) French, born Paris. Photographer, artist and journalist who produced lively portraits of distinguished literary and artistic contemporaries and the first 'photo-interview', series of photographs captioned with the sitter's replies to his questions. Proposed the use of aerial photographs for map-making and in 1858 took the first photographs from a balloon, of Paris.

Newman, Arnold (Abner) (1918–) American, born New York City. Assistant portrait photographer (1938–9) and later Director of the Newman Portrait Studio, Miami Beach (1942–5). Worked freelance for publications including the *New Yorker*; books include *Arnold Newman* (2000). Recipient of the gold medal, Biennale Internazionale della Fotografica, Venice (1963).

Newton, Helmut (1920–) Australian, born Berlin, Germany. Apprentice to a theatre and fashion photographer in Berlin (1936–40) and freelance photographer for *Elle, Queen, Marie-Claire* and *Vogue* since 1958. Received the Best Photography Award, Art Directors Club, Tokyo (1976).

Niepce, Joseph Nicéphore (1765–1833) French, born Chalon-sur-Saône. Chemist who succeeded in producing a photograph on metal (1826), said to be the world's first. Later cooperated with others in further research.

Nilsson, Lennart (1922–) Swedish, born Rome. Freelance press photographer, acclaimed for several portraits such as *Sweden in Profiles* (1954) who later pioneered microfilm showing the anatomy of plants and animals. Perfected special lenses to film inside the human body, enabling him to produce pictures of the human foetus in the womb from conception to birth. *Ett barn blir till* (1965, The Everyday Miracle: A Child is Born) won the American National Press Association Picture of the Year Award.

Parer, Damien (1912–44) Australian, born Malvern, Victoria. Official cameraman with the 2nd Australian Imperial Forces. Filmed action at the siege of Tobruk in the Middle East, later working in Greece, Syria and New Guinea. His documentary film *Kokoda Front* was the first Australian film to win an Oscar. Killed while filming American troops landing at Peleliu, Caroline Islands.

Parkinson, Norman (originally **Parkinson Smith, Ronald William**) (1913–90) English, born London. Opened studio in 1934 and became a well-known portrait and fashion photographer, his work being used widely in quality magazines. Later advertising work in the 1950s involved worldwide travel. Settled in Tobago in 1963.

Parks, Gordon (Alexander Buchanan) (1912–) American, born Fort Scott, Kansas. Self-taught photogra-

Arts and Culture

pher; worked for the US Office of War Information (1943–5) and as a freelance fashion photographer in Minneapolis (1937–42). After working as a documentary film-maker in America and Saudi Arabia, became an independent photographer, film writer and director for Warner Brothers, MGM and Paramount Pictures (1962–71).

Penn, Irving (1917–) American, born Plainfield, New Jersey. Served as an ambulance driver and documentary photographer in the American Field Service in Italy and India (1944–5). Later worked for *Vogue* in New York (1943–4) and as a freelance advertising photographer from 1952.

Porter, Eliot (Furness) (1901–90) American, born Winnetka, Illinois. Self-taught photographer who concentrated on his photographic career from 1939, in particular in landscape and wildlife photography. Received the Conservation Award from the US Department of the Interior (1967).

Rankin (originally **Rankin Waddell**) (1966–) Scottish, born Glasgow. Co-founded *Dazed and Confused* style magazine (1991) and is known for celebrity and fashion work; books include *Nudes* (1999).

Ray, Man (Rabinovich, Emanuel) (1890–1976) American, born Philadelphia, Pennsylvania. After making a number of Surrealist films in Paris, published and exhibited many photographs and 'rayographs' (photographic images made without a camera) in the 1930s, returning to America in 1940. Awarded the gold medal at the Biennale of Photography in Venice (1961). Published his autobiography, *Self Portrait*, in 1963.

Robinson, Henry Peach (1830–1901) English, born Ludlow. Opened studio in Leamington Spa in 1857, but moved from formal portraiture to 'high art photography', often creating scenes using composites of several separate images of costumed models and painted settings in the mid-Victorian style. A founder member of The Linked Ring (1892), an association of photographers seeking artistic creation, which developed into the international Photo-Secession Group. Wrote *Pictorial Effect in Photography* (1869).

Rodchenko, Alexander Mikhailovich (1891–1956) Russian, born St Petersburg. Photographer, painter and designer whose most original photographic works were documentary photographs of the new communist society.

Rosenblum, Walter (1919–) American, born New York City. After studying photography in New York, worked as a photographer for the US army in Europe (1943–5), becoming the most decorated photographer in the army. Editor of *Photo Notes* (1939–41) and chairman of the Exhibition Committee (1941–2) in New York. Awarded the Guggenheim Fellowship in 1979.

Rothstein, Arthur (1915–85) American, born New York City. Photo officer for the US army in India, Burma and China (1943–6) and picture editor for the Office of War Information, New York (1942–3). Founder of the American Society of Magazine Photographers (1941) and recipient of the Lifetime Arts Achievement award from the New York Council of the Arts (1985).

Saint Joseph, John Kenneth Sinclair (1912–94) English, born Worcestershire. Professor of aerial photographic studies at Cambridge (1948–80), developing large photographic archive with emphasis on systematic reconnaissance, and low-level oblique photography of natural landscapes and of archaeological monuments in their landscape setting. *Monastic Sites from the Air* (1952), *Medieval England: An Aerial Survey* (1958, 1979), *Roman Britain from the Air* (1983) are collections of some of the results.

Salgado, Sebastião Ribeiro, Jr (1944–) Brazilian, born Aimorés, Minas Gerais. Photo-reporter in the 1970s, for Magnum from 1979. Works include *Migrations: Humanity in Transition* (1993–99).

Salomon, Erich (1886–1944) German, born Berlin. Prisoner-of-war in France (1915–18). Began freelance photographic career in 1927, working for *L'Illustration* of Paris and *Fortune* of New York. Died at Auschwitz with his wife and son.

Sander, August (1876–1964) German, born Herdorf am Sieg. Planned a massive photographic documentary study, *Men in the* 20th Century, but only the first part *Faces of Our Times* (1929) was published as his social realism was discouraged by the Nazi Ministry of Culture after 1934. Surviving material has provided penetrating portraits of all levels of German life in the early part of the century.

Sheeler, Charles (1883–1965) American, born Philadelphia, Pennsylvania. Worked as industrial photographer from 1912, producing creative industrial records, especially the skyscrapers of Manhattan in *Mannahatta* (1920). Commissioned to record the building of the Ford Motor installation at River Rouge, Michigan (1927), and staff photographer at the New York Museum of Modern Art (1942–5).

Sielmann, Heinz (1917–) German, born Königsberg. Interested in animal photography, started making films in 1938, for which he won three German Oscars (1953–5). Developed techniques enabling photography in inaccessible animal lairs which revolutionized the study of animal behaviour.

Siskind, Aaron (1903–91) American, born New York City. Self-taught freelance photographer from 1932. Member of Film and Photo League of New York and later photography teacher. Co-editor of the Chicago poetry and photographic magazine *Choice* (1961–70). Received Guggenheim Fellowship (1966).

Smith, W(illiam) Eugene (1918–78) American, born Wichita, Kansas. Staff photographer for *Newsweek* in New York (1937–8) and later freelance for magazines including *Harper's Bazaar* and *Life*. Pacific war correspondent (1942–5) and photographer for Hitachi in New York and Japan (1959–77). Received Honor Award from the American Society of Magazine Photographers (1959).

Smythe, Francis Sydney (1900–49) English, born Maidstone. Mountaineer whose many books, including *Kamet Conquered* (1932), *Camp Six* (1937), *Adventures of a Mountaineer* (1940), *Over Welsh Hills* (1941) contain acclaimed mountain photography.

Snowdon, Antony Charles Robert Armstrong-Jones, 1st Earl of (1930–) English, born London. Freelance photographer from 1951 and artistic adviser for many publications. Famous for informal portraits of the famous, he has also photographed disabled people and has produced documentaries for television on similar themes.

Steichen, Edward Jean (1879–1973) American, born Luxembourg. Practised painting and photography in Europe until 1914. Member of The Linked Ring in England and noted for his studies of the nude. A founder of the American Photo-Secession Group, he later served in the photographic division of the US army during World War I, and in the 1920s achieved success in fashion photography. Head of US Naval Film Services during World War II and director of photography at the New York Museum of Modern Art (1945–62), organizing the world-famous exhibition *The Family of Man* (1945).

Stieglitz, Alfred (1864–1946) American, born Hoboken, New Jersey. Studied engineering and photography in Berlin and later was a founder of the Photo-Secession Group in 1902, devoted to artistic expression in photography. Exerted great influence through his magazine *Camera Work* (1903–17) and his gallery of modern art. Other work includes studies of New York architecture, clouds and portraits.

Strand, Paul (1890–1976) American, born New York City. Became commercial photographer in 1912, committed to 'straight' photography of precision and clarity. Produced documentary films during the 1920s and 1930s, but from the 1940s concentrated on still photography for records of his life in many different parts of the world.

Sutcliffe, Frank Meadow (1853–1941) English, born near Whitby, Yorkshire. Received numerous international awards for studies of the vanishing world of English farmhands and fisher-folk in the local country and seacoast between 1881 and 1905. From late 1890s made use of new lightweight cameras to obtain natural snapshots rather than formal poses. A fully illustrated account of his work was published in 1974.

Talbot, William Henry Fox (1800–77) English, born Melbury, Dorset. Announced his invention of photography, a system of making photographic prints on silver chloride paper, in 1839. In 1841 patented the calotype, the first process for photographic negatives from which prints could be made and was awarded the Rumford Medal of the Royal Society in 1842. Also discovered a method of instantaneous flash photography and his *Pencil of Nature* (1844) was the first photographically illustrated book to be published.

Van der Elsken, Ed(uard) (1925–90) Dutch, born Amsterdam. Self-taught freelance photographer in Amsterdam (1947–50), Paris (1950–5) and Edam, the Netherlands since 1955. Also freelance filmmaker.

Weston, Edward (Henry) (1886–1958) American, born Highland Park, Illinois. Became recognized as modernist, emphasizing sharp images and precise definition in landscapes, portraits and still-life. Member of Group f/64 in California from 1932. First photographer to receive a Guggenheim Fellowship with which he travelled widely throughout the American West. Illustrated an edition of Walt Whitman's *Leaves of Grass*.

White, Minor (Martin) (1908–76) American, born Minneapolis, Minnesota. Developed the realism of the photographic sequence and the abstraction of the 'equivalent', the visual metaphor in which he continued Stieglitz's symbolism of natural formations. In 1946 moved to San Francisco and worked with Ansel Adams. Founded the periodicals *Aperture* (1952) and *Image* (1953–7) and was appointed Professor of Creative Photography at the Massachusetts Institute of Technology (1965–76).

Winogrand, Garry (1928–84) American, born New York. Studied photography in New York from 1951. Received Guggenheim Fellowship (1964, 69 and 78).

Fashion designers

Amies, Sir (Edwin) Hardy (1909–2003) English, born London. Couturier and dressmaker by appointment to Queen Elizabeth II. Renowned especially for tailored suits for women. Founded his own fashion house in 1946 and started designing for men also in 1959.

Armani, Giorgio (1935–) Italian, born Piacenza. Became designer for Nino Cerruti in 1961 and also freelanced before setting up the Giorgio Armani company in 1975. Designed first for men, then women, including loose-fitting jackets and blazers.

Ashley, Laura (née **Mountney**) (1925–85) Welsh, born Merthyr Tydfil. Started business with husband Bernard Ashley in 1953, manufacturing furnishing materials and wallpapers with patterns based mainly on 19th-century document sources. Later experimented with designing and making clothes, transforming the business from one shop to an international chain of boutiques.

Balenciaga, Cristóbal (1895–1972) Spanish, born Guetaria. Opened dressmaking and tailoring shops in Madrid and Barcelona in 1915. Moved to Paris in 1937 because of the Spanish Civil War. His clothes were noted for dramatic simplicity and elegant design.

Balmain, Pierre Alexandre (1914–82) French, born St Jean-de-Maurienne. Worked for Edward Molyneux and Lucien Lelong before opening his own house in 1945. Famous for elegant simplicity, his designs included evening dresses, tailored suits, sportswear and stoles. Also designed for the theatre and cinema.

Cardin, Pierre (1922–) French, born Venice, Italy. Worked in fashion houses and on costume design in Paris after World War II and opened his own house in 1953. Since then has been prominent in fashion for both women and men.

Chanel, Gabrielle (known as **Coco**) (1883–1971) French, born Saumur. Orphaned at an early age, she worked with her sister as a milliner until 1912, when she opened a shop of her own. Later opened couture houses in Deauville and Paris, producing designs combining simple elegance and comfort. Also introduced the vogue for costume jewellery and the evening scarf. Retired in 1938, but made a successful comeback in 1954.

Claiborne, Liz (1929–) Belgian–American, born Brussels. Designed for Youth Guild Inc, New York City, before founding own company in 1976. Her designs are targeted at the working woman. She retired in 1989, though the company continues.

Conran, Jasper (1959–) English, born London. Son of Sir Terence Conran, he trained in art and design in New York before joining Fiorucci briefly as a designer in 1977. Produced his first collection of easy-to-wear, quality clothes in London in 1978.

Courrèges, André (1923–) French, born Pau. Trained by Balenciaga from 1952 to 1960, he opened his own house in 1961. Famous for stark, futuristic, 'Space Age' designs, he introduced the miniskirt (1964) and has featured white boots and trouser suits for women.

De la Renta, Oscar (1932–) American, born Santo Domingo, Dominican Republic. Worked at Balenciaga's couture house in Madrid, joined the house of Lanvin-Castillo in Paris (1961) then Elizabeth Arden in New York (1963), before starting his own company in 1965. Has reputation for opulent, ornately trimmed clothes, particularly evening dresses, but also designs daywear and accessories.

Dior, Christian (1905–57) French, born Granville, Normandy. Began designing clothes in 1935, and founded his own Paris house in 1947. Achieved worldwide fame with his long-skirted 'New Look' and subsequently the 'A-line' and 'the Sack'.

Farhi, Nicole (1946–) Anglo-French, born Nice, France. Started working in London on French Connection and the Stephen Marks label. Launched own company in 1983 and became well known for simple, comfortable, but elegant clothing.

Galliano, John (originally **Galliano, Juan Carlos**) (1960–) Gibraltan, born Gibraltar. Graduated from St Martin's School of Art and Design, London in 1984. Inspired by a range of cultural and historical references. Became designer-in-chief at Givenchy in 1995. Left in 1996 to become designer-in-chief at the House of Dior.

Gaultier, Jean-Paul (1952–) French, born Paris. Worked with Cardin for two years (1969–71), then at Patou. In 1976, began working as a freelance designer, drawing inspiration from the London streetscene, which he glamorized for the Paris market. He is now one of the most influential Paris designers.

Givenchy, Hubert James Marcel Taffin de (1927–) French, born Beauvais. After training and working with a number of well-known designers, opened his own house in 1952. His Bettina blouse in white cotton became internationally famous, and his clothes are noted for their elegance and quality. He retired in 1995.

Hamnett, Katharine (1952–) English, born Gravesend, Kent. After studying fashion at St Martin's School of Art and Design in London, worked as a freelance designer, setting up a short-lived company (1969–74) and then her own business in 1979. Draws inspiration for designs from workwear and from movements such as the peace movement.

Hartnell, Sir Norman (Bishop) (1901–78) English, born Honiton, Devon. Started his own couturier business in 1923, receiving the Royal Warrant in 1940. Produced costumes for leading actresses, wartime 'utility' dresses, the WRAC uniform and Princess Elizabeth's wedding and coronation gowns.

Hulanicki, Barbara (1936–) Born Palestine of Polish parents. Launched Biba's Postal Boutique in 1963. Opened three stores in London which became fashion mecca of the 1960s. Biba closed in 1973.

Karan, Donna (originally **Donna Faske**) (1948–) American, born Forest Hills, New York. Became Director of Design at Anne Klein in 1974. Launched Donna Karan Company in 1984, which became Donna Karan International in 1996. She sold the company in 2001 for a reported £250 million.

Kenzo Takada (1940–) Japanese, born Kyoto. After studying art, worked in Japan before producing freelance collections in Paris from 1964. Started a shop called Jungle Jap in 1970. Creates clothes with both oriental and western influences, and is a trendsetter in the field of knitwear.

Klein, Anne Hannah (née **Hannah Golofski**) (1921–74) American, born New York City. Started as sketcher on Seventh Avenue in 1938, and established Anne Klein & Co in 1968. Designed practical sportswear for women.

Klein, Calvin Richard (1942–) American, born New York City. Graduated from New York's Fashion Institute of Technology in 1962, and set up his own firm in 1968. Quickly achieved recognition and is known for understatement and the simple but sophisticated style of his clothes, including 'designer jeans'.

Lacroix, Christian (1951–) French couturier, born Arles, Provence. After studying fashion history, worked for a leather firm with Guy Paulin, a ready-to-wear designer. In 1981 joined Jean Patou; in 1987 opened the House of Lacroix in Paris. Made his name with ornate and frivolous clothes.

Lagerfeld, Karl (1938–) German, born Hamburg. Won an International Wool Secretariat competition in 1954 and worked with Balmain in Paris. After three years he left to begin freelance work with a number of design houses, including Chloë, Ballantyne, Fendi and Valentino. His talents lie particularly in meticulous cut, extravagant beading, furs and knitwear. He is renowned for his flamboyant fashion shows.

Lang, Helmut (1956–) Austrian, born Vienna. From 1979 has owned made-to-measure shop in Vienna. Launched his first ready-to-wear collection in 1984. Won Council of American Fashion Designers of the Year Award in 1996.

Laroche, Guy (1923–89) French, born La Rochelle, near Bordeaux. Worked in millinery, first in Paris then on Seventh Avenue, New York, before returning to Paris where he worked for Dessès for eight years; started his own business in 1957, achieving a reputation for skilful cutting. From 1966 his designs included menswear.

Lauren, Ralph (originally **Ralph Lipschitz**) (1939–) American, born The Bronx, New York City. In 1967 joined Beau Brummel Neckwear and created the Polo range for men, later including womenswear. Famous for his American styles, such as the 'prairie look' and 'frontier fashions'.

McCartney, Stella (Nina) (1971–) English, born London. At age 15 she worked for Christian Lacroix, and then spent a number of years on Savile Row. Graduated from St Martin's School of Art and Design, London in 1995, with her entire final collection bought by a London boutique. Succeeded Karl Lagerfeld as chief designer for Chloë in 1997, leaving in 2001 to found her own house.

McQueen, Alexander (1970–) British, born London. Showed final collection at St Martin's School of Art and Design, London in 1992. From 1996 to 2001 he was Chief Designer at Givenchy. In 1996 won Designer of the Year, London Fashion Awards.

Mainbocher (originally **Main Rousseau Bocher**) (1891–1976) American, born Chicago. After service in World War I stayed on in Paris, eventually becoming a fashion artist with *Harper's Bazaar* and later editor of French *Vogue* until 1929. Started his couture house in Paris in 1930; created the Duchess of Windsor's wedding dress (1937).

Missoni, Tai Ottavio (1921–) Italian, born Dubrovnik, Yugoslavia (now Croatia). Founded the Missoni company in Milan with his wife, Rosita, in 1953. At first manufactured knitwear to be sold under other labels, but later created, under their own label, innovative knitwear notable for its sophistication and distinctive colours and patterns.

Miyake, Issey (1938–) Japanese, born Hiroshima. Spent six years in Paris and New York fashion houses before showing his first collection in Tokyo in 1963. Distinctive style combines eastern and western influences in garments which have an almost theatrical quality, frequently in subdued colours.

Molyneux, Edward Henry (1891–1974) English, born London. After studying art, worked for Lucile. Opened his own couture house in Paris in 1919 with branches in London, Monte Carlo, Cannes and Biarritz, and became famous for the elegant simplicity of tailored suits with pleated skirts, and evening wear.

Montana, Claude (1949–) French, born Paris. Began designing jewellery in London, and then moved to leather and knitwear companies. Designed his first ready-to-wear collection in 1976.

Mortensen, Erik (1926–98) Danish. From 1948, attached to the Balmain fashion house in Paris, becoming artistic director in 1960 and taking over the management after the death of Pierre Balmain in 1982. Awarded the Golden Thimble of the French Haute Couture in 1983 and 1987. Left Balmain in 1992 and worked for Jean-Louis Scherrer until 1994.

Muir, Jean Elizabeth (1928–95) English, born London. Started as sales assistant with Liberty's in London, then moved to Jaeger in 1956. In 1961 started on her own as Jane & Jane and in 1966 established her company Jean Muir. Her clothes are noted for their classic shapes, softness and fluidity.

Oldfield, Bruce (1950–) English, born London. As a freelance designer sold sketches to Yves Saint Laurent and designed for Bendel's store in New York. Showed his first collection in 1975 in London. His designs include evening dresses for royalty and screen stars and ready-to-wear clothes.

Ozbek, Rifat (1953–) Turkish, born Istanbul. Beginning with small collections, now has multi-million pound business. Awarded Designer of the Year twice (1989 and 1992). His designs cover many styles and display cross-cultural references.

Patou, Jean (1880–1936) French, born Normandy. In 1912 opened Maison Parry in Paris and in 1913 sold his collection outright to an American buyer. After war service he successfully opened again as couturier in 1919. Noted for his designs for sports stars and actresses and for his perfume 'Joy'.

Poiret, Paul (1879–1944) French, born Paris. Worked for Jacques Doucet and Worth before opening his own fashion house in 1904. Influenced by the exotic oriental costumes of the Ballets Russes, his designs featured turbans and harem pants and he became a leader of fashion rather than a designer for individual clients. After World War I did not re-establish his prominence and died in poverty.

Pucci, Emilio, Marchese di Barsento (1914–92) Italian, born Naples, Member of Italy's Olympic ski team (1933–4) and later member of the Italian parliament (1963–72), he started designing ski clothes in 1947 and in 1950 opened his own couture house, creating print dresses for women. Became renowned for use of bold patterns and brilliant colour.

Quant, Mary (1934–) English, born London. Began fashion design when she opened a small boutique in Chelsea in 1955. Her clothes became extremely fashionable in the 1960s when the geometric simplicity of her designs and the originality of her colours became an essential feature of the 'swinging Britain' era.

Rhodes, Zandra (1940–) English, born Chatham, Kent. After studying art, designed and printed textiles and, with others, opened The Fulham Road Clothes Shop, afterwards setting up on her own. Showed her first dress collection in 1969, and is noted for distinctive, exotic designs in chiffons and silks.

Saint Laurent, Yves (originally **Henri Donat Mathieu**) (1936–) French, born Oran, Algeria. Employed by Christian Dior in 1955 after winning an International Wool Secretariat design competition. Took over the house on Dior's death in 1957. In 1962 opened his own house and launched the first of his 160 Rive Gauche boutiques in 1966, selling ready-to-wear clothes, a trend which many other designers were to follow. He retired in 2002.

Schiaparelli, Elsa (1890–1973) Italian–French, born Rome. After living in America, moved to Paris and started business in 1929. Her designs were inventive and sensational, and she was noted for her use of bright colour and traditional fabrics, featuring zippers and buttons, and outrageous hats. Opened a salon in New York in 1949, and retired in 1954.

Ungaro, Emanuel Maffeoliti (1933–) French, born Aix-en-Provence. Worked for small Paris tailoring firm and later with Balenciaga, before opening his own house in 1965, with Sonia Knapp designing his fabrics. Initially featured rigid lines, but later produced softer styles. Produced his first ready-to-wear lines in 1968.

Valentino (originally **Valentino Garavani**) (1933–) Italian, born Rome. Studied fashion in Milan and Paris, then worked for Jean Dessès and Guy Laroche in Paris. Opened his own house in Rome in 1959, and achieved worldwide recognition with his 1962 show in Florence. Opened numerous ready-to-wear boutiques. Sold the House of Valentino for over £200 million in 1998.

Versace, Gianni (1946–97) Italian, born Calabria. Launched first women's wear collection in 1978. Opened boutique and designed first menswear collection in 1979. Has designed for various ballet productions. Won many awards including the CDFA in 1992 and the Golden Eye in 1982, 1984 and 1997. Was shot dead outside American home.

Westwood, Vivienne (1941–) English, born London. Began clothes design on meeting Malcolm McLaren, manager of The Sex Pistols. They established a shop in London and became known as the leading creators of punk clothing. Since her split from McLaren in 1983, has become accepted by the mainstream, and was Designer of the Year in 1990 and 1991.

Worth, Charles Frederick (1825–95) Anglo-French, born Bourn, Lincolnshire. Achieved success as a fashion designer in Paris, gaining the patronage of the Empress Eugénie. His establishment in the Rue de la Paix became the centre of the fashion world.

Yamamoto, Yohji (1943–) Japanese, born Tokyo. Started his own company in 1972 producing his first collection in 1976 in Tokyo. After some time in Paris, opened a new headquarters in London in 1987. Designs loose, functional clothes for men and women, which conceal rather than emphasize the body.

Philosophers

Anaxagoras (500–428BC) Greek, born Clazomenae. Believed that matter is infinitely divisible into particles containing a mixture of all qualities and that mind is a pervasive formative agency in the creation of material objects.

Anaximander (611–547BC) Greek, born Miletus. Proposed that basic matter is the *apeiron*, the infinite or indefinite. Speculated that the Earth is unsupported at the centre of the Universe and that human beings developed from another species.

Arts and Culture

Aristotle (384–322BC) Greek, born Stagira, Macedonia. One of the most important philosophers and scientists in the history of Western thought, writing extensively on logic, metaphysics, ethics, politics, rhetoric, poetry, biology, zoology, physics and psychology. Best-known works include the *Metaphysics*, *Nicomachean Ethics*, *Politics*, *Poetics*, the *De Anima*, the *Organon*.

Austin, John L(angshaw) (1911–60) English, born Lancaster. Professor at Oxford University and leading figure in 'Oxford Philosophy' movement. Examined ordinary linguistic usage to resolve philosophical perplexities. Best-known works: *Philosophical Papers* (1961), *Sense and Sensibilia* (1962), *How to Do Things with Words* (1962).

Averroës, Ibn Rushd (1126–98) Muslim, born Cordova, Spain. Famous medieval Islamic philosopher who also wrote on jurisprudence and medicine. Most important works were the *Commentaries on Aristotle* which offered a partial synthesis of Greek and Arabic philosophical traditions.

Ayer, Sir Alfred (Jules) (1910–89) English, born London. Professor at London and Oxford Universities. *Language, Truth and Logic* (1936) gives an account of the logical positivist, anti-metaphysical doctrines with which he became involved in the 1930s, and aroused great hostility when published. Later publications include *The Problem of Knowledge* (1956), *The Central Questions of Philosophy* (1972). Knighted in 1970.

Bacon, Francis, Viscount St Albans (1561–1626) English, born London. Important philosopher and statesman, knighted in 1603. Abandoned deductive logic of Aristotle and stressed the importance of experiment in interpretation of nature. Philosophical works include *The Advancement of Learning* (1605), *De Augmentis Scientiarum* (1623), *Novum Organum* (1620). He also wrote many religious and professional works.

Bacon, Roger (c.1214–92) English, born probably Ilchester, Somerset. Philosopher, scientist and Franciscan monk with reputation for unconventional learning in magic and alchemy, and imprisoned for heresy. Also published many works on mathematics, philosophy, and logic whose importance was recognized in later centuries.

Bentham, Jeremy (1748–1832) English, born London. Philosopher, jurist and social reformer: advocated utilitarianism in *A Fragment on Government* (1776) and *Introduction to the Principles of Morals and Legislation* (1789). Published many works on penal and social reform, economics and politics.

Berkeley, Bishop George (1685–1753) Irish, born near Kilkenny. Developed the belief that the contents of the material world are 'ideas' that only exist when perceived by a mind in *Essay towards a New Theory of Vision* (1709), *A Treatise concerning the Principles of Human Knowledge* (1710), *Three Dialogues between Hylas and Philonous* (1713). Expressed concern about social corruption and national decadence and wrote on social reform and religion.

Berlin, Sir Isaiah (1909–97) British, born Riga, Russia. Oxford professor whose philosophical works include *Karl Marx* (1939), *Historical Inevitability* (1954), *Two Concepts of Liberty* (1953), *Vico and Herder* (1976) and four volumes of essays.

Boethius, Anicius Manlius Severinus (c.475–524) Roman, born probably Rome. Produced translations of and commentaries on Aristotle. During a period of imprisonment for treason for which he was later executed, he wrote *De Consolatione Philosophiae*, which explains the mutability of all earthly fortune and demonstrates that happiness can only be attained by virtue.

Burke, Edmund (1729–87) Irish, born Dublin. Statesman and philosopher whose political thought has become the philosophy of modern Conservatism. Works include *Observations on the Present State of the Nation* (1769), *On the Causes of the Present Discontents* (1770).

Carnap, Rudolf (1891–1970) German–American, born Wuppertal. Leading member of the 'Vienna Circle' of logical positivists who dismissed most traditional metaphysics as a source of meaningless answers to pseudo-problems. Works include *Der logische Aufbau der Welt* (1928), *Logische Syntax der Sprache* (1934), *Meaning and Necessity* (1947), *The Logical Foundations of Probability* (1950).

Comte, Auguste (1798–1857) French, born Montpelier. Usually regarded as the founder of sociology. His 'positivism' sought to expound the laws of social evolution, to describe the organization of all branches of human knowledge, and to establish a science of society as a basis for social planning. Works include *Cours de Philosophie positive* (1830–42), *Système de Politique positive* (1851–4).

Copleston, Frederick (Charles) (1907–93) English, born near Taunton, Somerset. Catholic philosopher; published many critical studies of philosophers and wrote *A History of Philosophy* (1946–66).

Cousin, Victor (1792–1867) French, born Paris. An eclectic in philosophy; published many historical studies and commentaries on other philosophers. Most original work is *Du Vrai, du Beau, et du Bien* (1854).

Croce, Benedetto (1866–1952) Italian, born Pescasserolli. Developed phenomenology of the mind in which four principle activities, art and philosophy (theoretical), political economy and ethics (practical), complement each other. His theory of aesthetics is described in *Lo Spirito* and his opposition to totalitarianism is expressed in *History as the Story of Liberty* (1941).

Cudworth, Ralph (1617–88) English, born Aller, Somerset. Leading member of the Cambridge Platonists. *The True Intellectual System of the Universe* (1678) aimed to refute determinism and materialism and to establish the reality of a supreme divine intelligence; *Treatise concerning Eternal and Immutable Morality* is a posthumous publication discussing ethics.

Davidson, Donald Herbert (1917–) American, born Springfield, Massachusetts. One of the most influential recent analytical philosophers, who has made contributions to the philosophy of language, mind and action in *Essays on Action and Events* (1980) and *Structure and Content of Truth* (1990).

de Beauvoir, Simone (1908–80) French, born Paris. Sorbonne professor, novelist and feminist who contributed substantially to the existentialist movement. Works include *Le Deuxième Sexe* (1949), translated as *The Second Sex* (1953).

Democritus (c.460–370BC) Greek, born Abdera, Thrace. Prolific ancient philosopher publishing works on ethics, physics, mathematics, cosmology and music, although only fragments of his writings remain. Best known for physical speculations, in particular the belief that the world consists of an infinite number of minute particles whose different combinations account for different properties.

Derrida, Jacques (1930–) French, born El Biar, Algeria. Work spans literary criticism, psychoanalysis, linguistics and philosophy. Founded the school of criticism known as 'deconstruction'.

Descartes, René (1596–1650) French, born La Haye, near Tours. Usually regarded as the founder of modern philosophy. *Discourse de la Méthode* (1637), *Meditationes de Prima Philosophia* (1641) and *Principia Philosophiae* (1644) set out his ideas on philosophical methods, propositions and religious beliefs. Famous for the dictum, 'I think, therefore I am' (cogito ergo sum) and for his dualism of mind and body, he also made important contributions in astronomy and mathematics.

Dewey, John (1859–1952) American, born Burlington, Vermont. Exponent of pragmatism whose philosophy stressed the instrumental function of ideas and judgements in problem solving. Also published widely on psychology and education. Works include *The School and Society* (1899), *Reconstruction in Philosophy* (1920), *Experience and Nature* (1925), *The Quest for Certainty* (1929), *Experience and Education* (1938).

Diogenes (412–323BC) Greek, born Sinope, Pontus. Continued the pre-Socratic tradition of speculation about the primary constituent of the world, which he identified as air, operating as an active and intelligent life-force.

Duns Scotus, John (c.1266–1308) Scottish, born probably Duns, Berwickshire. Philosopher whose beliefs represented a strong reaction against Aristotle and Aquinas; he propounded the primacy of the individual and the freedom of the individual will. His writings were mainly commentaries on the Bible and other philosophers.

Empedocles (490–430BC) Greek, born Acragas, Sicily. Philosopher, poet, doctor, statesman and soothsayer who described a cosmic cycle in which earth, air, fire and water periodically combine and separate under the forces of Love and Hate as well as beliefs on the transmigration and redemption of souls.

Epicurus (341–270BC) Greek, born Samos. Advocated a philosophy designed to promote detachment, serenity and freedom from fear, and the belief that pleasure is the only good and the only goal of morality.

Feuerbach, Ludwig (Andreas) (1804–72) German, born Landshut, Bavaria. Attacked conventional Christianity in *Das Wesen des Christentums* (1847), translated as *The Essence of Christianity*, arguing that God is the projection of human ideals and human nature.

Fichte, Johann Gottlieb (1762–1814) German, born Rammenau, Saxony. Posited the Ego as the basic reality, affirming itself in the act of consciousness and constructing the external world as its field of action. He elaborates this system in *Grundlage des Naturrechts* (1796) and *System der Sittenlehre* (1798).

Foucault, Michel (1926–84) French, born Poitiers. Believed that prevailing social attitudes are manipulated by those in power to define such categories as insanity, illness, sexuality and criminality and these are used to identify and oppress 'deviants'. Translations of his work include *The Order of Things* (1970), *Madness and Civilization* (1971), *The Archaeology of Knowledge* (1972), *The History of Sexuality* (1984).

Frege, (Friedrich Ludwig) Gottlob (1848–1925) German, born Wismar. Regarded as the founder of modern mathematical logic and the philosophy of language. Main works are *Begriffschrift* (1879), *Die Grundlagen der Arithmetik* (1884) and *Die Grundgesetze der Arithmetik* (1893, 1903).

Gödel, Kurt (1906–78) American, born Brünn, Austria-Hungary (now Brno, Czechoslovakia). Logician and mathematician whose theorem, published in 1931, demonstrated the existence of formally undecidable elements in any formal system of arithmetic.

Gorgias (c.485–380BC) Greek, born Leontini, Sicily. Advocated a philosophy which was an extreme form of scepticism or nihilism; that nothing exists, that if it did it would be unknowable, that if it were knowable it would be incommunicable to others. He is portrayed in Plato's dialogue, the *Gorgias*.

Hamilton, Sir William (1788–1856) Scottish, born Glasgow. Philosopher whose main work *Lectures on Metaphysics and Logic*, published posthumously (1856–60), presented views on perception and knowledge. Important figure in the revival of philosophy in Britain at this time.

Hegel, Georg Wilhelm Friedrich (1770–1831) German, born Stuttgart. Idealist philosopher whose major works include *Phänomenologie des Geistes* (1807), *Wissenschaft der Logik* (1812, 1816), *Encyclopadie der philosophischen Wissenschaften in Grundrisse* (1817). Although his philosophy is difficult and obscure it has remained influential until the present.

Heidegger, Martin (1889–1976) German, born Messkirch, Baden. Philosopher whose writings examine the nature and predicament of human existence, classify modes of 'Being' and discuss the human mode of existence characterized by participation and involvement in the world of objects. His major work is *Sein und Zeit* (*Being and Time*, 1927).

Heraclitus (c.540–460BC) Greek, born Ephesus. Believed that everything is in a state of flux and that fire is the ultimate constituent of the world. Only fragments remain of his book *On Nature*.

Herbert of Cherbury, Edward, (1st Baron) (1583–1648) English, born Eyton, Shropshire. Soldier, statesman and philosopher who argued in *De Religione Gentilum* (1645) that all religions recognize five main articles, from the acknowledgement of a supreme God to the concept that there are rewards and punishments in a future state.

Hobbes, Thomas (1588–1679) English, born Malmesbury. Political philosopher whose major work *Leviathan* (1651) presented and connected his thoughts on metaphysics, psychology and political philosophy. His materialistic philosophy described how the world is a mechanical system consisting of bodies in motion in which human beings are wholly selfish and enlightened self-interest explains the existence of the sovereign state and prevents 'a war of every man against every man'. He was banned from publishing in England in 1666 after being accused of being an atheist.

Hume, David (1711–76) Scottish, born Edinburgh. Philosopher and historian whose beliefs concerning perception, causation, personal identity, and ethics are still influential. Most important works include *A Treatise of Human Nature* (1739–40), *Essays Moral and Political* (1741, 1742), *Enquiry concerning Human Understanding* (1748), *Political Discourses* (1752), *Dialogues concerning Natural Religion* (published posthumously, 1779).

Husserl, Edmund (Gustav Albrecht) (1859–1938) - German, born Prossnitz, Austrian Empire. Defender of philosophy as an *a priori* discipline and founder of Phenomenology: the systematic investigation of consciousness and its objects by suspending belief in the empirical world.

James, William (1842–1910) American, born New York City. Philosopher and psychologist who de-

Arts and Culture

veloped the pragmatist ideas of Charles Peirce; beliefs are true because they work, not vice versa. These ideas, and discussions of ethics and religion are given in *The Will to Believe* (1907), *Pragmatism* (1907), *The Varieties of Religious Experience* (1902), *The Meaning of Truth* (1909).

Jaspers, Karl (Theodor) (1883–1969) German, born Oldenburg. One of the founders of existentialism; his beliefs are developed in *Philosophie* (1932).

Kant, Immanuel (1724–1804) German, born Konigsberg, Prussia. Influential scientist and philosopher, whose main interest was in the role of reason. He argued that the immediate objects of perception depend not only on our sensations but also on our perceptual equipment and that some properties we observe in objects are due to the nature of the observer. Ethics, aesthetics and politics are also discussed in *Critique of Pure Reason* (1781), *Critique of Practical Reason* (1788), *Critique of Judgement* (1790), *Perpetual Peace* (1795).

Kierkegaard, Søren Aabye (1813–55) Danish, born Copenhagen. A founder of existentialism who tried to reinstate the central importance of the individual and the significant choices each of us makes informing our future selves, and wrote in many works about the necessity for individual choice rather than prescribed dogma.

Langer, Suzanne K(nauth) (1895–1985) American, born New York City. Published important works in linguistic analysis and aesthetics; *Philosophy in a New Key* (1942), *Feeling and Form* (1953), *Problems of Art* (1957), *Mind: an Essay on Human Feeling* (1967–82).

Leibniz, Gottfried Wilhelm (1647–1716) German, born Leipzig. Mathematician and philosopher who believed that the world is composed of an infinity of simple immaterial 'monads' which form a hierarchy, the highest of which is God. Had greatest influence as a mathematician.

Locke, John (1632–1704) English, born Wrington, Somerset. Philosopher who defended natural rights, constitutional law and the liberty of the individual. *Essay concerning Human Understanding* (1690) explores the nature and scope of human reason and seeks to establish that 'all knowledge is founded on and ultimately derives from sense ... or sensation'.

Lukacs, George (1885–1971) Hungarian, born Budapest. Marxist philosopher who wrote prolifically on literature and aesthetics. His major work on Marxism was *History and Class Consciousness* (1923).

Mach, Ernst (1838–1916) Austrian, born Turas, Moravia. Physicist and philosopher whose writings laid the foundations of logical positivism.

Maimonides, Moses (Moses ben Maimon) (1135–1204) Jewish, born Córdoba, Spain. Physician and philosopher who tried to harmonize the thought of Aristotle and Judaism in *Guide to the Perplexed* (1190).

Marcuse, Herbert (1898–1979) American, born Berlin. Radical political theorist who analysed the repressions imposed by the unconscious mind in *Eros and Civilization* (1955) and condemned the 'repressive tolerance' of modern industrial society which both stimulated and satisfied superficial material desires of the masses at the cost of more fundamental needs and freedoms in *One Dimensional Man* (1964).

Marx, Karl (1818–83) German, born Trier. Social, political and economic philosopher in the German idealistic tradition. Founded the theory of historical materialism, and in his *Economic and Philoso-*

phical Manuscripts of 1844 (posthumously published, 1932), developed the notion of the alienation of man under capitalism. His most famous publication *Das Kapital* (Vol 1 1867, Vols 2 & 3 posthumously published 1884, 1894) was one of the most influential works of the 19th century.

Merleau-Ponty, Maurice (1908–61) French, born Rochefort-sur-mer. Philosopher who rejected extremes of both behaviouristic psychology and subjectivist accounts; the world is neither wholly 'given', nor wholly 'constructed' for the perceiving subject, but is essentially ambiguous and enigmatic. Major works are *La Structure du Comportement* (1942) and *Phénoménologie de la Perception* (1945).

Mill, J(ohn) S(tuart) (1806–73) English, born London. Philosopher and social reformer, leading exponent of the British empiricism and utilitarian traditions who also restored the importance of cultural values. Active in politics, he campaigned for women's suffrage and supported the Advanced Liberals. Major works include *A System of Logic* (1843), *On Liberty* (1859), *The Subjection of Women* (1869).

Montesquieu, Charles-Louis de Secondat, Baron de la Brède et de (1689–1755) French, born near Bordeaux. Became an advocate, but turned to scientific research and literary work. Best known for his comparative study of legal and political issues, *De l'ésprit des lois* (1748), which was a major influence on 18c Europe.

Moore, George (Edward) (1873–1958) English, born London. Cambridge professor of mental philosophy and logic who emphasized the intellectual virtues of clarity, precision and honesty, identifying as a principal task of philosophy the analysis of ordinary concepts and arguments. Works include *Principia Ethica* (1903), *Ethics* (1916).

More, Henry, ('the Cambridge Platonist') (1614–87) English, born Grantham, Lincolnshire. Followed the philosophies of Plato, Plotinus and Descartes and attempted to demonstrate the compatibility of reason and faith. Later became interested in occultism and mysticism. Main works: *Philosophical Poems* (1647), *An Antidote against Atheism* (1653), *The Immortality of the Soul* (1659), *Enchiridion Ethicum* (1666), *Divine Dialogues* (1668).

Murdoch, Dame (Jean) Iris (1919–99) Irish novelist, playwright and philosopher. Published three important philosophical works in the Platonic tradition: *The Sovereignty of the Good* (1970), *The Fire and the Sun* (1977) and *Metaphysics as a Guide to Morals* (1992). These deal with the relationships between art and philosophy, and between love, freedom, knowledge and morality.

Nietzsche, Friedrich (Wilhelm) (1844–1900) German, born Röcken, Saxony. Philosopher who produced many unconventional works expressing repudiation of Christian and liberal ethics, detestation of democratic ideals, the celebration of the *Übermensch* (superman) who can create and impose his own law, and the death of God. Best-known writings include *Unzeitgemässe Betrachtungen* (Untimely Meditations, 1873–6), *Die Fröliche Wissenschaft* (The Gay Science, 1882), *Also Sprach Zarathustra* (Thus Spake Zarathustra, 1883–92), *Jenseits von Gut and Böse* (Beyond Good and Evil, 1886).

Ockham, William of (1285–1349) English, born Ockham, Surrey. Philosopher, theologian and political writer whose controversial religious views led to disputes with the Catholic church. Defended no-

minalism against realism and introduced 'Ockham's razor'; the belief that a theory should not propose the existence of anything more than is needed for its explanation. Works include *Summa Logicae, Quodlibta Septem*.

Ortega y Gasset, José (1883–1955) Spanish, born Madrid. Argued that great philosophies demarcate the cultural horizons of their epochs. Works include *Meditaciones del Quijote* (1914), *Tema de nuestro tiempa* (1923), *La Rebelión de Las Masas* (1930).

Parmenides (c.515–c.445BC) Greek, born Elea, S Italy. Argued in *On Nature* for the impossibility of motion, plurality and change, and set an agenda of problems for subsequent pre-Socratic philosophers.

Peirce, Charles (Sanders) (1839–1914) American, born Cambridge, Massachusetts. Philosopher, logician and mathematician, best known as the founder of pragmatism.

Philo Judeaus (c.20BC–c.40AD) Hellenistic Jew, born Alexandria. Prolific author who attempted to synthesize Greek philosophy and Jewish scripture.

Plato (c.428–c.348BC) Greek, born probably Athens. One of the most important philosophers of all time. Pupil of Socrates and teacher of Aristotle, his writings consist of philosophical dialogues and letters discussing the definition of moral virtues, the theory of knowledge as recollection, the immortality of the soul, and contrasts of transient and timeless aspects of the world. The *Republic* presents Plato's political utopia.

Plotinus (c.205–70) Greek, born possibly Lycopolis, Egypt. Neoplatonist philosopher who advocated asceticism and the contemplative life, and greatly influenced early Christian theology.

Popper, Sir Karl (Raimund) (1902–94) Austrian, born Vienna. Rejected philosophical systems with totalitarian political implications from Plato to Marx and stressed the importance of 'falsifiability'; true scientific theories must specify in advance the conditions under which they could be tested and refuted. Main works include *Die Logik der Forschung* (1934, trans *The Logic of Scientific Discovery*, 1959), *The Open Society and its Enemies* (1945), *The Poverty of Historicism* (1957).

Protagoras (c.490–c.420BC) Greek, born Abdera. Sophist philosopher, with a sceptical or relativistic view of human knowledge; his many works are lost and most information about him comes from Plato's dialogues.

Pythagoras (6c BC) Greek, born Samos. Philosopher and mathematician whose life is surrounded in myth and legend. Emphasized moral asceticism and purification; also associated with mathematical discoveries involving musical intervals and relations of numbers. He had a profound influence on later philosophers and scientists.

Quine, Willard van Orman (1908–2000) American, born Akron, Ohio. Influential professor of philosophy who challenged the standard sharp distinctions between analysis and synthetic truths and between science and metaphysics; also presented a systematic linguistic philosophy. Best-known works: *Two Dogmas of Empiricism* (1951), *From a Logical Point of View* (1953), *Word and Object* (1960), *The Roots of Reference* (1973).

Rawls, John (1921–2002) American, born Baltimore, Maryland. Social and political philosopher concerned mainly with the question of justice in publications including *A Theory of Justice* (1962), *Justice as Fairness* (1991), *Political Liberalism* (1993).

Reichenbach, Hans (1891–1953) German, born Hamburg. Made important contributions to technical probability theory and wrote widely on logic and the philosophical bases of science in *Philosophie der Raum-Zeit-Lehre* (1927–8), *Elements of Symbolic Logic* (1947), *The Rise of Scientific Philosophy* (1951).

Ricoeur, Paul (1913–) French, born Valence, Drôme. Influential figure in both French and Anglo-American philosophy, covering a wide range of problems on the nature of language, interpretation, human action and will, freedom and evil. Major works include *Philosophy of the Will* (1950–60), *The Living Metaphor* (1975).

Rousseau, Jean Jacques (1712–78) French–Swiss, born Geneva, Switzerland. Largely self-taught, he wrote *Discours sur l'origine de l'inégalité parmi les hommes* (1755), which emphasizes the essential goodness of humankind. His masterpiece was *Du contrat social* (1762), which introduced the slogan 'Liberty, Equality, Fraternity'. Fled to England in 1762, where he wrote most of his *Confessions* (published posthumously, 1782).

Russell, Bertrand (Arthur William, 3rd Earl) (1872–1970) English, born Trelleck, Monmouthshire. Philosopher, mathematician, prolific author and controversial figure, who was imprisoned in 1918 during World War I as an active pacifist and in 1961 for taking part in a sit-down demonstration in Whitehall, London. Wrote wide-ranging literature on mathematics, philosophy, politics, education and morals, such as *The Principles of Mathematics* (1903), *The Problems of Philosophy* (1912), *Theory and Practice of Bolshevism* (1919), *On Education* (1926), *Marriage and Morals* (1932).

Ryle, Gilbert (1900–76) English, born Brighton, Sussex. Influential exponent of linguistic philosophy. *The Concept of Mind* (1949) was directed against the traditional theory that mind and matter were distinct and problematically related. Other works: *Dilemmas* (1954), *Plato's Progress* (1966).

Santayana, George (Jorge Augustin Nicola Ruiz de Santayana) (1863–1952) Spanish–American, born Madrid. Naturalistic and materialistic critic of the transcendental claims of religion and German idealism, who believed that our knowledge of the external world depends on an act of 'animal faith'. Main philosophical works: *The Sense of Beauty* (1896), *The Life of Reason* (1905–6), *Scepticism and Animal Faith* (1923), *Realms of Being* (1927–40), *Platonism and the Spiritual Life* (1927).

Sartre, Jean-Paul (1905–80) French, born Paris. Philosopher, dramatist and novelist who developed characteristic atheistic existentialist doctrines from an early anarchistic tendency; these are expressed in the autobiographical novel *La Nausée* (1938) and in *Le Mur* (1938). Awarded, but declined to accept, the Nobel prize for literature in 1964.

Schelling, Friedrich (Wilhelm Joseph) von (1775–1854) German, born Leonburg. Idealist philosopher who examined the relation of the self to the objective world and argued that consciousness itself is the only immediate object of knowledge and that only in art can the mind become fully aware of itself. Works include *Ideen zur einer Philosophie der Natur* (1797), *System des transzendentalen Idealismus* (1800).

Schlick, Moritz (1882–1936) German, born Berlin. Leader of the 'Vienna Circle' of logical positivists who wrote on ethics, which he argued was a factual science of the causes of human actions. Main publications: *Allgemeine Erkenntnislehre* (General

Arts and Culture

Theory of Knowledge, 1918), *Fragen der Ethik* (Problems of Ethics, 1930).

Schopenhauer, Arthur (1788–1860) German, born Danzig. Philosopher who emphasized the active role of Will as the creative but covert and irrational force in human nature and argued that art represented the sole kind of knowledge that was not subservient to the Will; his work is often characterized as a systematic philosophical pessimism. Major work: *Die Welt als Wille und Vorstellung* (The World as Will and Idea, 1819).

Shaftesbury, Anthony Ashley Cooper, 3rd Earl of (1671–1713) English, born London. Moral philosopher and politician who argued that we possess natural 'moral sense' and affections directed to the good of the species and in harmony with the larger cosmic order in *Characteristics of Men, Manners, Opinions, Times* (1711).

Socrates (469–399BC) Greek, born Athens. One of the most important philosophers in history, responsible for a decisive shift of philosophical interest from speculation about the natural world and cosmology to ethics and conceptual analysis. His reputation for eliciting contradictions in the philosophies of others may have contributed to demands for his conviction for 'impiety' and 'corrupting the youth'; he was sentenced to die by drinking hemlock.

Spencer, Herbert (1820–1903) British, born Derby. Philosopher with interest in evolutionary theory which he expounded in *Principles of Psychology* (1855). Also applied his evolutionary theories to ethics and sociology and became an advocate of 'Social Darwinism', the view that societies naturally evolve in competition for resources and that the 'survival of the fittest' is therefore morally justified. Works include *System of Synthetic Philosophy* (1862–93), *Social Statistics* (1851), *Education* (1861), *The Man Versus the State* (1884).

Spinoza, Baruch (Benedict de) (1632–77) Dutch, born Amsterdam. Rationalist philosopher who advocated a strictly historical approach to the interpretation of biblical sources and argued that complete freedom of philosophical and scientific speculation was appropriate. His major work, the *Ethics* (1677, posthumous) described a complete, deductive metaphysical system intended to be a proof derived with mathematical certainty of what is good for human beings.

Tarski, Alfred (1902–83) Polish, born Warsaw. Logician and mathematician who gave a definition of 'truth' in formal logical languages in *Der Wahrheitsbetriff in den Formalisierten Sprachen* (The Concept of Truth in Formalized Languages, 1933).

Thales (c.620–c.555BC) Greek, born Miletus. Traditionally the founder of European philosophy. Proposed the first natural cosmology, identifying water as the original substance and the basis of the universe. Also had wide-ranging practical and scientific interests.

Weil, Simone (1909–43) French, born Paris. Combined sophisticated scholarly and philosophical interests with dedicated involvement and interest in the oppressed and exploited. Translated philosophical and spiritual works include *Gravity and Grace* (1952), *The Need for Roots* (1952), *Waiting for God* (1951), *Oppression and Liberty* (1958).

Whitehead, A(lfred) N(orth) (1861–1947) English, born Ramsgate. Mathematician and idealist philosopher. *Process and Reality* (1929) attempted a metaphysics comprising psychological as well as physical experience, with events as the ultimate component of reality. Other works include *Adventures of Ideas* (1933) and *Modes of Thought* (1938).

Williams, Sir Bernard Arthur Owen (1929–) English, born Essex. Philosopher whose work has been wide-ranging. Particularly influential in his contributions to moral philosophy, including *Morality: an introduction to Ethics* (1972), *Ethics and the Limits of Philosophy* (1985), *Shame and Necessity* (1993), and *Truth and Truthfulness* (2002).

Wittgenstein, Ludwig (Josef Johann) (1889–1951) Austrian, born Vienna. Philosopher who studied the nature and limits of language. *Logisch-philosophische Abhandlung* (1921) describes how meaningful language must consist in propositions that are 'pictures' of the facts of which the world is composed and therefore many claims of speculative philosophy must be rejected. *Philosophical Investigations* (1953, posthumous) comes to different conclusions, pointing to the variety and subtlety in language and exploring its functions.

Zeno of Elea (c.490–c.420BC) Greek, born Elea, Italy. A disciple of Parmenides who devised famous paradoxes which purported to show the impossibility of motion and spatial division.

Literary prizes 1982–2002

▪ Booker Prize (UK)

1982 Thomas Keneally, *Schindler's Ark*
1983 J M Coetzee, *Life and Times of Michael K*
1984 Anita Brookner, *Hotel du Lac*
1985 Keri Hulme, *The Bone People*
1986 Kingsley Amis, *The Old Devils*
1987 Penelope Lively, *Moon Tiger*
1988 Peter Carey, *Oscar and Lucinda*
1989 Kazuo Ishiguro, *The Remains of the Day*
1990 A S Byatt, *Possession*
1991 Ben Okri, *The Famished Road*
1992 Michael Ondaatje, *The English Patient;* Barry Unsworth, *Sacred Hunger*
1993 Roddy Doyle, *Paddy Clarke, Ha Ha Ha*
1994 James Kelman, *How late it was, how late*
1995 Pat Barker, *The Ghost Road*
1996 Graham Swift, *Last Orders*
1997 Arundhati Roy, *The God of Small Things*
1998 Ian McEwan, *Amsterdam*

1999 J M Coetzee, *Disgrace*
2000 Margaret Atwood, *The Blind Assassin*
2001 Peter Carey, *True History of the Kelly Gang*
2002 Yann Martel, *Life of Pi*

▪ Orange Prize for Fiction (women writers)

1996 Helen Dunmore, *A Spell of Winter*
1997 Anne Michaels, *Fugitive Pieces*
1998 Carol Shields, *Larry's Party*
1999 Suzanne Berne, *A Crime in the Neighborhood*
2000 Linda Grant, *When I Lived in Modern Times*
2001 Kate Grenville, *The Idea of Perfection*
2002 Ann Patchett, *Bel Canto*

▪ Prix Goncourt (France)

1982 Dominique Fernandez, *Dans la Main de l'ange*
1983 Frédérick Tristan, *Les Égarés*
1984 Marguerite Duras, *L'Amant*

1985 Yann Queffelec, *Les Noces barbares*
1986 Michel Host, *Valet de Nuit*
1987 Tahar ben Jalloun, *La Nuit sacrée*
1988 Erik Orsenna, *L'Exposition coloniale*
1989 Jean Vautrin, *Un Grand Pas vers le Bon Dieu*
1990 Jean Rouaud, *Les Champs d'Honneur*
1991 Pierre Combescot, *Les Filles du Calvaire*
1992 Patrick Chamoiseau, *Texaco*
1993 Amin Maalouf, *Le Rocher de Tanios*
1994 Didier van Cauwelaert, *Un Aller simple*
1995 Andréï Makine, *Le Testament français*
1996 Pascale Roze, *Le Chasseur Zéro*
1997 Patrick Rambaud, *La Bataille*
1998 Paule Constant, *Confidence pour confidence*
1999 Jean Echenoz, *Je m'en vais*
2000 Jean-Jacques Schuhl, *Ingrid Caven*
2001 Jean-Christophe Rufin, *Rouge Brésil*
2002 Pascal Quignard, *Les ombres errantes*

■ **Pulitzer Prize in Letters: Fiction (USA)**
1982 John Updike, *Rabbit is Rich*
1983 Alice Walker, *The Color Purple*
1984 William Kennedy, *Ironweed*

1985 Alison Lurie, *Foreign Affairs*
1986 Larry McMurtry, *Lonesome Dove*
1987 Peter Taylor, *A Summons to Memphis*
1988 Toni Morrison, *Beloved*
1989 Anne Tyler, *Breathing Lessons*
1990 Oscar Hijuelos, *The Mambo Kings Play Songs of Love*
1991 John Updike, *Rabbit at Rest*
1992 Jane Smiley, *A Thousand Acres*
1993 Robert Olen Butler, *A Good Scent From A Strange Mountain*
1994 E Annie Proulx, *The Shipping News*
1995 Carol Shields, *The Stone Diaries*
1996 Richard Ford, *Independence Day*
1997 Steven Millhauser, *Martin Dressler: The Tale of an American Dreamer*
1998 Philip Roth, *American Pastoral*
1999 Michael Cunningham, *The Hours*
2000 Jhumpa Lahiri, *Interpreter of Maladies*
2001 Michael Chabon, *The Amazing Adventures of Kavalier & Clay*
2002 Richard Russo, *Empire Falls*

Arts and Culture

Nobel prizes

Year	Peace	Literature	Economic Science
1901	Jean Henri Dunant, Frédéric Passy	Sully Prudhomme	
1902	Élie Ducommun, Charles Albert Gobat	Theodor Mommsen	
1903	Sir William Randall Cremer	Bjørnstjerne Bjørnson	
1904	Institut de Droit International	Frédéric Mistral, José Echegaray y Eizaguirre	
1905	Baroness Bertha Sophie Felicita von Suttner	Henryk Sienkiewicz	
1906	Theodore Roosevelt	Giosuè Carducci	
1907	Ernesto Moneta, Louis Renault	Rudyard Kipling	
1908	Klas Arnoldson, Fredrik Bajer	Rudolf Eucken	
1909	August Beernaert, Paul Henri Benjamin Balluet (Baron de Constant de Rebecque)	Selma Lagerlöf	
1910	Bureau International Permanent de la Paix	Paul von Heyse	
1911	Tobias Asser, Alfred Fried	Maurice Maeterlinck	
1912	Elihu Root	Gerhart Hauptmann	
1913	Henri La Fontaine	Rabindranath Tagore	
1914	No award	No award	
1915	No award	Romain Rolland	
1916	No award	Verner von Heidenstam	
1917	Comité International de la Croix-Rouge	Karl Gjellerup, Henrik Pontoppidan	
1918	No award	No award	
1919	Thomas Woodrow Wilson	Carl Spitteler	
1920	Léon Bourgeois	Knut Hamsun	
1921	Karl Branting, Christian Lange	Anatole France	
1922	Fridtjof Nansen	Jacinto Benavente y Martinez	
1923	No award	William Butler Yeats	
1924	No award	Wladslaw Reymont	
1925	Sir Austen Chamberlain, Charles Dawes	George Bernard Shaw	
1926	Aristide Briand, Gustav Stresemann	Grazia Deledda Madesani	
1927	Ferdinand Buisson, Ludwig Quidde	Henri Bergson	
1928	No award	Sigrid Undset	
1929	Frank B Kellogg	Thomas Mann	
1930	Nathan Söderblom	Sinclair Lewis	
1931	Jane Addams, Nicholas Butler	Erik Axel Karlfeldt	
1932	No award	John Galsworthy	
1933	Sir Norman Angell	Ivan Bunin	

Arts and Culture

Year	Peace	Literature	Economic Science
1934	Arthur Henderson	Luigi Pirandello	
1935	Carl von Ossietzky	No award	
1936	Carlos Saavedra Lamas	Eugene O'Neill	
1937	Viscount Cecil of Chelwood	Roger Martin du Gard	
1938	Office International Nansen pour les Réfugiés	Pearl Buck	
1939	No award	Frans Emil Sillanpää	
1940	No award	No award	
1941	No award	No award	
1942	No award	No award	
1943	No award	No award	
1944	Comité International de la Croix-Rouge	Johannes Vilhelm Jensen	
1945	Cordell Hull	Gabriela Mistral	
1946	Emily Balch, John R Mott	Hermann Hesse	
1947	The Friends Service Council, The American Friends Service Committee (the Quakers)	André Gide	
1948	No award	T S Eliot	
1949	Baron Boyd Orr of Brechin	William Faulkner	
1950	Ralph Bunche	Bertrand Russell	
1951	Léon Jouhaux	Pär Lagerkvist	
1952	Albert Schweitzer	François Mauriac	
1953	George C Marshall	Sir Winston Churchill	
1954	Office of the United Nations High Commissioner for Refugees	Ernest Hemingway	
1955	No award	Halldór Laxness	
1956	No award	Juan Ramón Jiménez	
1957	Lester B Pearson	Albert Camus	
1958	Georges Pire	Boris Pasternak	
1959	Philip Noel-Baker	Salvatore Quasimodo	
1960	Albert Lutuli	Saint-Jean Perse	
1961	Dag Hammarskjöld	Ivo Andric	
1962	Linus Pauling	John Steinbeck	
1963	Comité International de la Croix-Rouge, Ligue des Sociétés de la Croix-Rouge	George Seferis	
1964	Martin Luther King, Jr	Jean-Paul Sartre (declined)	
1965	United Nations Children's Fund	Mikhail Sholokhov	
1966	No award	Shmuel Yosef Agnon, Nelly Sachs	
1967	No award	Miguel Angel Asturias	
1968	René Cassin	Kawabata Yasunari	
1969	International Labour Organization	Samuel Beckett	Ragnar Frisch, Jan Tinbergen
1970	Norman Borlaug	Aleksandr Solzhenitsyn	Paul Samuelson
1971	Willy Brandt	Pablo Neruda	Simon Kuznets
1972	No award	Heinrich Böll	Sir John Hicks, Kenneth Arrow
1973	Henry Kissinger, Le Duc Tho (declined)	Patrick White	Wassily Leontief
1974	Seán MacBride, Eisaku Sato	Eyvind Johnson, Harry Martinson	Gunnar Myrdal, Friedrich von Hayek
1975	Andrei Sakharov	Eugenio Montale	Leonid Kantorovich, Tjalling Koopmans
1976	Mairead Corrigan, Betty Williams	Saul Bellow	Milton Friedman
1977	Amnesty International	Vicente Alexandre	James Meade, Bertil Ohlin
1978	Menachem Begin, Anwar al-Sadat	Isaac Bashevis Singer	Herbert Simon
1979	Mother Teresa	Odysseus Elytis	Sir Arthur Lewis, Theodore Schultz
1980	Adolfo Pérez Esquivel	Czesław Miłosz	Lawrence Klein
1981	Office of the UN High Commissioner for Refugees	Elias Canetti	James Tobin
1982	Alfonso García Robles, Alva Myrdal	Gabriel García Márquez	George Stigler
1983	Lech Wałesa	William Golding	Gerard Debreu
1984	Desmond Tutu	Jaroslav Seifert	Sir Richard Stone
1985	International Physicians for the Prevention of Nuclear War	Claude Simon	Franco Modigliani
1986	Elie Wiesel	Wole Soyinka	James Buchanan, Jr

Year	Peace	Literature	Economic Science
1987	Oscar Arias Sánchez	Joseph Brodsky	Robert Solow
1988	United Nations Peacekeeping Forces	Naguib Mahfouz	Maurice Allais
1989	Tenzin Gyatso (Dalai Lama)	Camilo José Cela	Trygve Haavelmo
1990	Mikhail Gorbachev	Octavio Paz	Harry Markowitz, Merton Miller, William Sharpe
1991	Aung San Suu Kyi	Nadine Gordimer	Ronald Coase
1992	Rigoberta Menchú Tum	Derek Walcott	Gary Becker
1993	Nelson Mandela, F W de Klerk	Toni Morrison	Robert Fogel, Douglass North
1994	Yasser Arafat, Shimon Peres, Yitzhak Rabin	Kenzaburo Ōe	John Harsanyi, John Nash, Reinhard Selten
1995	Joseph Rotblat and the Pugwash Conferences on Science and World Affairs	Seamus Heaney	Robert Lucas, Jr
1996	Carlos Filipe Ximenes Belo, José Ramos-Horta	Wislawa Szymborska	James Mirrlees, William Vickrey
1997	Jody Williams and the International Campaign to Ban Landmines	Dario Fo	Robert Merton, Myron Scholes
1998	John Hume, David Trimble	José Saramago	Amartya Sen
1999	Medécins Sans Frontières	Günter Grass	Robert Mundell
2000	Kim Dae Jung	Gao Xingjian	James Heckman, Daniel McFadden
2001	United Nations, Kofi Annan	V S Naipaul	George A Akerlof, A Michael Spence, Joseph E Stiglitz
2002	Jimmy Carter	Imre Kertész	Daniel Kahneman, Vernon L Smith

Arts and Culture

Museums and art galleries — Europe

A selection of the most important museums and galleries is given.

Amsterdam, Netherlands
Anne Frank's House
Museum of Amsterdam
Rijksmuseum,
Stedelijk Museum of Modern Art
Van Gogh Museum

Ankara, Turkey
Archaeological Museum

Antwerp, Belgium
Folklore Museum
Maritime Museum
Royal Museum of Fine Art
Rubens's House

Athens, Greece
Acropolis Museum
Byzantine Museum
Goulandris Natural History Museum
National Archaeological Museum
Museum of Decorative Arts
Museum of Modern Art

Barcelona, Spain
Catalan Museum of Art
Joán Miró Foundation
Museum of Costume
Picasso Museum

Basle, Switzerland
Basle Historical Museum
Basle Art and Contemporary Art Museum

Berlin, Germany
The Bauhaus Archives and Museum of Design
Berlin Museum
Memorial Museum of the German Resistance
Museum of German Ethnology
Museum of Transport and Technology
New National Gallery
Old National Gallery

Bruges, Belgium
Folklore Museum

Brunswick, Germany
Museum of Brunswick

Brussels, Belgium
Museum of Brussels
Museum of Modern Art
Railway Museum
Royal Museum of the Army

Budapest, Hungary
Hungarian National Museum

Cologne, Germany
Cologne Art Collective
Diocesan Museum
Museum of the City of Cologne
Schnütgen Museum

Copenhagen, Denmark
Copenhagen City Museum
National Museum
State Museum of Art
Theatre Museum

Delphi, Greece
Archaeological Museum

Dresden, Germany
Semper Gallery
State Gallery of Art
Grünes Gewölbe

Dublin, Ireland
Dublin Civic Museum
Guinness Museum
National Gallery of Ireland
National Museum of Ireland
National Transport Museum

Essen, Germany
Folkwang Museum

Figueres, Spain
Dalí Museum

Florence, Italy
Accademia Gallery
Bardini Museum
Bargello Museum
Museum of the History of Science
Uffizi Gallery

Arts and Culture

Frankfurt, Germany
Goethe Museum
Historical Museum
Modern Art Gallery

Freiburg im Breisgau, Germany
Augustiner Museum
Museum of Modern Art
Museum of Natural History

Geneva, Switzerland
Museum of Art and History
Voltaire Museum

Genoa, Italy
Gallery of Modern Art
Palazzo Bianco
Palazzo Rosso

Hamburg, Germany
Altona Museum
Hamburg Art Gallery
Museum of Art and History

Helsinki, Finland
Helsinki City Museum
Museum of Applied Arts
Museum of Finnish Architecture
Sports Museum of Finland

Istanbul, Turkey
Archaeological Museum
Hagia Sophia Museum
Museum of the Ancient Orient
Topkapi Palace Museum

Leipzig, Germany
Museum of Art

Liège, Belgium
Museum of Firearms
Museum of Modern Art
Museum of Walloon Life

Lisbon, Portugal
Calouste Gulbenkian Museum
Museum of Archaeology and Ethnology
Museum of Art
Museum of Contemporary Art
Museum of Decorative Arts

Madrid, Spain
Museum of Madrid
National Archaeological Museum
National Museum of Ethnology
National Museum of Decorative Arts
Palace of El Pardo
The Prado Museum
Reina Sofia

Milan, Italy
Castle of the Sforzas
Gallery of Modern Art
La Scala Museum of Theatre History
Leonardo da Vinci Museum of Science and
    Technology

Moscow, Russia
Armory Museum
Central Lenin Museum
Pushkin Museum of Fine Arts
Tretyakov Art Gallery

Munich, Germany
Bavarian National Museum
City Museum
Deutsches Museum
Folklore Museum
Residence Museum
State Collection of Minerals

Naples, Italy
Archaeological Museum
Palazzo Capodimonte

Olympia, Greece
Museum of Ancient Olympia

Oslo, Norway
Edvard Munch Museum
National Gallery
Norwegian Folk Museum
Ski Museum

Paris, France
Auguste Rodin Museum
Carnavalet Museum
The Louvre
Musée d'Orsay
Museum of Modern Art at the Pompidou Centre
Museum of Technology

Prague, Czech Republic
National Museum
State Jewish Museum

Rome, Italy
Borghese Gallery
National Gallery of Ancient Art
National Museum of Popular Art
Vatican Museums

Rotterdam, The Netherlands
Rotterdam Museum: The Double Palmtree
Rotterdam Museum: Schielandshuis

St Petersburg, Russia
Museum of the History of Religion and Atheism
Russian Museum
State Hermitage Museum

Salzburg, Austria
Mozart's Birthplace
Residence Gallery

Siena, Italy
Siena Art Gallery
Siena Museum

Stockholm, Sweden
National Museum of Antiquities
Nordic Museum
Stockholm City Museum

The Hague, The Netherlands
Netherlands Costume Museum
Sikkens Museum of Signs

Thessaloniki, Greece
Archaeological Museum
Macedonian Folk Art Museum

Toledo, Spain
El Greco Museum
Museum of the Alcazar of Toledo

Utrecht, The Netherlands
Catharine Convent State Museum
Netherlands Railway Museum

Venice, Italy
Accademia Gallery
Correr Museum
Treasury of St Mark's

Versailles, France
Château de Versailles
Lambinet Museum

Vienna, Austria
Belvedere Gallery
Museum of the History of Art
Museum of Lower Austria
Treasury of the Holy Roman Empire

Warsaw, Poland
National Museum

Zürich, Switzerland
House for Art
Swiss National Museum

Museums and art galleries — UK

Aberdeen, Scotland
  Aberdeen Art Gallery
Bangor, Wales
  Museum of Welsh Antiquities
  Bangor Art Gallery
Bath, England
  Museum of East Asian Art
  Victoria Art Gallery
Belfast, Northern Ireland
  Ulster Museum
Birmingham, England
  The Barber Institute of Fine Arts
  Birmingham Museum and Art Gallery
  National Motorcycle Museum
Bristol, England
  Arnolfini Gallery
  Blaise Castle House Museum
  Bristol Industrial Museum
  Bristol City Museums and Art Gallery
Cambridge, England
  The Fitzwilliam Museum
  Imperial War Museum
  Kettle's Yard
  Museum of Classical Archaeology
Cardiff, Wales
  National Museum and Gallery
  Museum of Welsh Life (at St Fagans)
Edinburgh, Scotland
  City Art Centre
  Gladstone's Land
  Museum of Childhood
  Museum of Scotland
  National Gallery of Scotland (previously the Royal
    Scottish Museum and the National Museum of
    Antiquities of Scotland)
  Royal Museum of Scotland
  Scottish National Gallery of Modern Art
  Scottish National Portrait Gallery
Glasgow, Scotland
  Kelvingrove Art Gallery and Museum
  The Burrell Collection
  Hunterian Art Gallery and Museum
  McLellan Galleries
  Museum of Transport
  People's Palace Museum
Leeds, England
  City Art Gallery
  Leeds Industrial Museum
Leicester, England
  Leicester Gas Museum
Liverpool, England
  Liverpool Museum
  Merseyside Maritime Museum
  Museum of Liverpool Life
  Tate Gallery, Liverpool
  Walker Art Gallery

London, England
  The British Museum
  Courtauld Gallery
  Design Museum
  Dulwich Picture Gallery
  Imperial War Museum
  Institute of Contemporary Arts
  London Transport Museum
  Museum of Instruments
  Museum of London
  Museum of the Moving Image
  The National Gallery
  National Maritime Museum
  The National Portrait Gallery
  Natural History Museum
  Pollock's Toy Museum
  Science Museum
  The Serpentine Gallery
  Tate Britain
  Tate Modern
  Victoria and Albert Museum
  The Wallace Collection
  The Wellcome Museum of the History of Medicine
Manchester, England
  Museum of Science and Industry in Manchester
  Manchester City Art Gallery
  Manchester Jewish Museum
  The Manchester Museum
  Whitworth Art Gallery
Newcastle upon Tyne, England
  Laing Art Gallery
  Museum of Antiquities
  Newcastle Discovery Museum
Oxford, England
  Ashmolean Museum of Art and Archaeology
  The Bate Collection of Historical Instruments
  Museum of Modern Art
  Museum of the History of Science
  Pitt Rivers Museum
Reading, England
  Museum of English Rural Life
Sheffield, England
  Abbeydale Industrial Hamlet
  Kelham Island Museum
  Sheffield City Museum and Mappin Art Gallery
Southampton, England
  Southampton City Art Gallery
  Southampton Maritime Museum
Swansea, Wales
  Glynn Vivian Art Gallery
  Swansea Maritime and Industrial Museum
York, England
  National Railway Museum
  York Castle Museum
  York City Art Gallery
  Yorkshire Museum

Museums and art galleries — USA

Atlanta, Georgia
  High Museum of Art
Baltimore, Maryland
  Baltimore Museum of Art
  Walters Art Gallery
Boston, Massachusetts
  Isabella Stewart Gardner Museum
  Museum of Fine Arts
  Museum of Science and Hayden Planetarium
Buffalo, New York

  Albright-Knox Art Gallery
Cambridge, Massachusetts
  Fogg Art Museum
  MIT Museum
  Arthur M Sackler Museum
Charleston, South Carolina
  Charleston Museum
Chicago, Illinois
  Art Institute of Chicago
  Museum of Contemporary Art

Arts and Culture

Cincinnati, Ohio
Cincinnati Art Museum
Museum Center at Union Terminal

Cleveland, Ohio
Cleveland Museum of Art

Dallas, Texas
Dallas Museum of Art

Denver, Colorado
Denver Art Museum
Museum of Natural History

Des Moines, Iowa
Living History Farms (at Urbandale)

Detroit, Michigan
Detroit Institute of Arts
Henry Ford Museum

Dodge City, Kansas
Boot Hill Museum

Fort Lauderdale, Florida
Museum of Discovery and Science

Fort Myers, Florida
Edison Winter Home

Gainsville, Florida
Florida State Museum

Hartford, Connecticut
Wadsworth Museum

Honolulu, Hawaii
Honolulu Academy of Arts

Houston, Texas
Baker Planetarium, and the Museum of Medical
Science
Burke Museum of Fine Arts
The Contemporary Arts Museum
Menil Collection

Indianapolis, Indiana
Children's Museum
Indianapolis Museum of Art

Jackson, Mississippi
Mississippi Museum of Art

Kansas City, Missouri
The Kemper Museum of Contemporary Art and
Design
Nelson Atkins Museum of Art

Los Angeles, California
California Museum of Science and Industry
George C Page Museum of La Brea Discoveries
Jean Paul Getty Museum (at Malibu)
Los Angeles County Museum of Art
Museum of Contemporary Art
Natural History Museum

Memphis, Tennessee
Memphis Brooks Museum of Art

Minneapolis, Minnesota
Minneapolis Institute of Arts
Walker Art Center

New Haven, Connecticut
The Yale Art Gallery

New Orleans, Louisiana
Delgado Museum of Art
Louisiana State Museum

New York City, New York
American Museum of the Moving Image
American Museum of Natural History
Brooklyn Museum
Frick Collection
Gallery of Modern Art
Metropolitan Museum of Art and the Cloisters
Morgan Library
Museum of Holography
Museum of Modern Art
Museum of the American Indian

Museum of the City of New York
Solomon R Guggenheim Museum
Whitney Museum of American Art

Oklahoma City, Oklahoma
National Cowboy Hall of Fame

Pasadena, California
Norton Simon Museum

Philadelphia, Pennsylvania
Academy of Natural Sciences
Barnes Foundation Collection (in Merion,
Pennsylvania)
Franklin Institute Science Museum
Museum of American Art
Philadelphia Museum of Art
Rodin Museum
Rosenbach Museum
University Museum of Archaeology and
Anthropology

Pittsburgh, Pennsylvania
Carnegie Museum of Art
Carnegie Museum of Natural History

Plymouth, Massachusetts
Plymouth Plantation

Portland, Oregon
Oregon Art Institute

Reno, Nevada
Harrah's Auto Collection

Rochester, New York
Rochester Memorial Art Gallery

Salt Lake City, Utah
The Museum of Church History and Art

San Francisco, California
Asian Art Museum
California Academy of Sciences
California Palace of the Legion of Honor
M H DeYoung Memorial Museum
San Francisco Museum of Art

Santa Fé, California
El Rancho de las Golondririas (at Cienega)
Museum of Indian Art and Culture
Museum of International Folk Art

San Marino, California
Huntington Library and Art Gallery

Sarasota, Florida
Ringling Museum of Art

Seattle, Washington
Seattle Art Museum

Toledo, Ohio
Toledo Museum of Art

Tulsa, Oklahoma
Philbrook Art Centre

Washington, District of Columbia
Corcoran Gallery of Art
Dumbarton Oaks Collection
Freer Gallery of Art
Museum of Modern Art of Latin America
National Air and Space Museum
National Archives
National Gallery of Art
National Museum of American Art
National Museum of American History
Smithsonian Institute
Washington Gallery of Modern Art

Williamsburg, Virginia
Abby Aldrich
Rockefeller Folk Art Collection
Colonial Williamsburg

Williamstown, Massachusetts
Sterling and Francine Clark Art Institute

SPORTS AND GAMES

Olympic Games

First Modern Olympic Games took place in 1896, founded by Frenchman Baron de Coubertin (1863–1937); held every four years; women first competed in 1900; first separate Winter Games celebrations in 1924.

Venues

- **Summer Games**

1896 Athens, Greece	1960 Rome, Italy
1900 Paris, France	1964 Tokyo, Japan
1904 St Louis, USA	1968 Mexico City, Mexico
1908 London, UK	1972 Munich, W Germany
1912 Stockholm, Sweden	1976 Montreal, Canada
1920 Antwerp, Belgium	1980 Moscow, USSR
1924 Paris, France	1984 Los Angeles, USA
1928 Amsterdam, Netherlands	1988 Seoul, South Korea
1932 Los Angeles, USA	1992 Barcelona, Spain
1936 Berlin, Germany	1996 Atlanta, USA
1948 London, UK	2000 Sydney, Australia
1952 Helsinki, Finland	2004 Athens, Greece
1956 Melbourne, Australia	2008 Beijing, China

- **Winter Games**

1924 Chamonix, France	1972 Sapporo, Japan
1928 St Moritz, Switzerland	1976 Innsbruck, Austria
1932 Lake Placid, New York, USA	1980 Lake Placid, New York, USA
1936 Garmisch-Partenkirchen, Germany	1984 Sarajevo, Yugoslavia
	1988 Calgary, Canada
1948 St Moritz, Switzerland	1992 Albertville, France
1952 Oslo, Norway	1994 Lillehammer, Norway
1956 Cortina, Italy	1998 Nagano, Japan
1960 Squaw Valley, California, USA	2002 Salt Lake City, USA
1964 Innsbruck, Austria	2006 Turin, Italy
1968 Grenoble, France	

The 1956 equestrian events were held at Stockholm, Sweden, due to quarantine laws in Australia.

Olympic Games were also held in 1906 in Athens, Greece, to commemorate the tenth anniversary of the birth of the modern Games.

In 1994, the Winter Games celebrations were re-adjusted to take place every four years between the Summer Games years.

Sports and Games

Leading medal winners

Summer Games

(including 2000)	Gold	Silver	Bronze	Total
1 USA	862	652	576	2 090
2 Russia[1]	499	410	369	1 278
3 Germany[2]	217	258	286	761
4 Great Britain	180	233	222	635
5 France	172	182	200	554
6 Sweden	137	154	171	462
7 Italy	172	136	153	461
8 Hungary	148	130	153	431
9 East Germany	153	129	127	409
10 Australia	103	110	136	349

Winter Games

(including 2002)	Gold	Silver	Bronze	Total
1 Russia[1]	113	83	78	274
2 Norway	94	92	75	261
3 USA	69	72	51	192
4 Germany[2]	68	68	52	188
5 Austria	42	57	64	163
6 Finland	41	52	49	142
7 East Germany	39	36	35	110
8 Sweden	36	30	38	104
9 Switzerland	33	33	38	104
10 Canada	30	28	37	95

[1] Includes medals won by the former USSR team, and by the Unified Team (Armenia, Azerbaijan, Belarus, Georgia, Kazakhstan, Kyrgyzstan, Moldova, Russia, Tajikistan, Turkmenistan, Ukraine and Uzbekistan) in 1992.

[2] Includes medals won as West Germany 1968–88.

Paralympic Games

Summer Games first held in Stoke Mandeville, England, in 1952 (solely for competitors from the UK and the Netherlands), then once every four years from 1960; Winter Games first held in Örnsköldsvik, Sweden, in 1976, then once every four years until 1992, after which they were held once every four years from 1994, to coincide with the Winter Olympic Games.

Leading medal winners

Summer Games

(1984–2000)	Gold	Silver	Bronze	Total
1 USA	381	352	364	1 097
2 Great Britain	284	305	292	881
3 Germany	274	287	267	828
4 Canada	227	191	197	615
5 France	217	209	187	613
6 Australia	199	191	184	574
7 Spain	151	113	140	404
8 Sweden	145	123	80	348
9 Netherlands	124	108	92	324
10 Poland	105	104	82	291

Winter Games

(1984–2002)	Gold	Silver	Bronze	Total
1 Germany	89	80	78	247
2 Austria	92	76	76	244
3 Norway	102	74	62	238
4 USA	85	91	61	237
5 Switzerland	35	53	47	135
6 Finland	54	31	39	124
7 France	36	39	37	112
8 Russia[1]	39	39	27	105
9 Canada	19	30	33	82
10 Sweden	13	22	22	57

[1] Includes medals won by the former USSR team, and by the Unified Team (Armenia, Azerbaijan, Belarus, Georgia, Kazakhstan, Kyrgyzstan, Moldova, Russia, Tajikistan, Turkmenistan, Ukraine and Uzbekistan) in 1992.

SOURCE: INTERNATIONAL PARALYMPIC COMMITTEE

Commonwealth Games

First held as the British Empire Games in 1930; take place every four years and between Olympic celebrations; became the British Empire and Commonwealth Games in 1954; current title adopted in 1970.

Venues

1930	Hamilton, Canada
1934	London, England
1938	Sydney, Australia
1950	Auckland, New Zealand
1954	Vancouver, Canada
1958	Cardiff, Wales
1962	Perth, Australia
1966	Kingston, Jamaica
1970	Edinburgh, Scotland
1974	Christchurch, New Zealand
1978	Edmonton, Canada
1982	Brisbane, Australia
1986	Edinburgh, Scotland
1990	Auckland, New Zealand
1994	Victoria, Canada
1998	Kuala Lumpur, Malaysia
2002	Manchester, England
2006	Melbourne, Australia

Leading medal winners

	Nation	Gold	Silver	Bronze	Total
1	Australia	646	551	488	1 685
2	England	542	513	528	1 583
3	Canada	388	413	430	1 231
4	New Zealand	118	156	221	495
5	Scotland	71	87	142	300
6	South Africa	80	79	83	242
7	India	80	79	63	222
8	Wales	46	64	85	195
9	Kenya	53	42	49	144
10	Nigeria	35	41	50	126

Sports

aikido Ancient Japanese art of self-defence; combination of karate and judo deriving from ancient jujitsu; two main systems; *tomiki* and *uyeshiba*.

American football ▶ football

angling Fishing with rod, line and hook in the form of freshwater, fly, game and deep-sea fishing. Rules govern time of year when different types of fishing take place, and type and amount of bait used. Oldest fishing club is in Ellem, Scotland.

archery Shooting with a bow and arrow at a circular target divided into 10 scoring zones, the smallest of which is coloured gold and worth 10 points; popular as sport from 17c. In competition, arrows are fired from 30, 50, 70 and 90 metres (men), and 30, 50, 60 and 70 metres (women).

athletics Tests of running, jumping, throwing and walking skills. The running or **track** events range from the 100m (328ft) sprint to the 42.2km/26.2mi marathon; jumping and throwing or **field** events consist of high jump, long jump, triple jump and pole vault, and the discus throw, shot put, javelin throw and hammer throw (men only). Multi-event competitions are the **decathlon** (10) for men and the **heptathlon** (7) for women. Athletics dates to c.3800BC Egypt; International Amateur Athletic Federation founded 1912.

badminton Indoor game, two or four players, played on court 13.4m/44ft long and 5.2m/17ft wide (6.1m/20ft wide for doubles), using rackets, a shuttlecock (cork or plastic half sphere with 'feathers') and a raised central net; object is to volley the shuttlecock over the net so that the opponent is unable to return it; name derives from Badminton House, the seat of the Duke of Beaufort, where game played 19c, but it dates from China over 2 200 years ago.

bagatelle Restricted form of billiards, played on a table with nine numbered cups instead of pockets; takes many different forms which vary according to local conditions.

baseball Team game played by two sides of 25 possible players on a diamond-shaped field which has bases at the corners each 27.43m/90ft apart. Essential pieces of equipment are long cylindrical bats, the solid ball 'pitched' from the 'mound',

and the glove worn by each fielder; team 'at bat' tries to score most runs by having its players circle the three bases and touch home plate before being put out by the team 'in the field'; players out if their hit is caught, if they are tagged with the ball when 'off-base', if the base is touched by the ball before they arrive at it, or if they 'strike out', ie fail to hit the ball after three pitches have been judged strikes by the umpire; 'home run' scored when player hits ball, circles all three bases and crosses home plate; game popularly believed to have been invented in 1839 by a West Point cadet, Abner Doubleday, at Cooperstown, NY.

basketball Five-a-side team ball game played on a hard surface court approx 26m/84ft by 14m/45ft 9in, with a bottomless basket 3.05m/10ft above the ground at each end; object is to move the ball by a series of passing and bouncing moves and throw it through the opponent's basket; invented by James Naismith in 1891 at Springfield, Massachusetts, but similar game believed to have been played in 10c Mexico.

biathlon Combined test of cross-country skiing and rifle shooting. It is used as a form of military training, based on the old military patrol race. Men's individual competitions are over 10 and 20km (6.2 and 12.4mi), and women's over 5 and 10km (3.1 and 6.2mi). At designated points on the course, competitors have to fire either standing or prone at a fixed target.

billiards Indoor table game played in many different forms. The standard green baize-covered table measures 3.66m/12ft by 1.83m/6ft and has six pockets into which the players use a tapered pole or *cue* to 'pot' the one red or two white balls to score, the balls going in off another ball. Scoring also achieved by making 'cannons' (hitting the white ball so that it successively hits the two others). Originally an outdoor game, its origins are uncertain; an early reference is 1429 when Louis XI of France owned a billiard table.

bobsledding Propelling oneself along snow or ice on a sledge, popular as a sport since 19c; special luge run was created at Davos, Switzerland, in 1879.

Sports and Games

Most popular competitive forms; **luge tobogganing** on a small sledge and **bobsleighing** in a steel-bodied two- or four-person toboggan down special tracks at speeds of up to 130kph/80mph; earliest known sledge dates to c.6500BC Finland.

bowling Delivering a rubber or plastic ball along a 18.3m/60ft wooden lane to knock down pins; in **tenpin bowling** these are often mechanically replaced; popularized by third- and fourth-century German churchgoers, who would roll a ball at a *kegel*, a club used for protection; a hit would absolve them from sin. The game of nine pins was taken to the USA by Dutch and German immigrants; when outlawed, 10th pin introduced as a way around the legislation.

bowls Indoor or outdoor game played as singles, pairs, triples or fours. **Lawn bowls** ('flat green') is played on a flat level rink; **crown green bowls** is played on an uneven green raised at the centre (usually singles and pairs only); object is to deliver your bowl nearest to the *jack*, a small target ball; similar game believed to have been played by the Egyptians in c.5200BC. Glasgow solicitor William Mitchell drew up rules for modern bowls in 1848.

boxing Fist-fighting between two people, usually men, in a roped ring 4.3–6.1m/14–20ft square. Professional championship bouts constitute 12 three-minute rounds; amateur bouts three rounds, unless one fighter is knocked out or retires, the referee halts the fight, or a fighter is disqualified. The 17 weight divisions range from straw-weight for fighters under 48kg/105lb to heavyweight, normally over 88kg/195lb. Boxing dates from Greek and Roman times; first known match in Britain 1681 when Duke of Albemarle organized one between his butler and butcher in New Hall, Essex. First rules drawn up 1743, when each round lasted until one fighter was knocked down; gloves and three-minute rounds introduced 1867.

bull-fighting National sport in Spain, where it is called *corrida de toros* and the leading *matadors* are national heroes. *Picadors* are sent into the bull ring to weaken the bull before the matador enters the arena to make the final killing.

caber tossing Throwing a 3–4m/10–13ft tree trunk or *caber*, often practised in Highland Games gatherings in Scotland. The competitor has the caber placed vertically in his hands; he runs with it and tosses it so that it revolves longitudinally and lands with the base as near to the 12 o'clock position from him as possible.

canoeing Water sport practised by one to four people in canoes, developed 1865 by the British barrister John Macgregor. Competition usually consists of a river slalom course using poles suspended between the river banks to mark out the gates. Two types of competition canoe: the *kayak*, which has a keel (the canoeist sits in the boat), and the *Canadian canoe*, which has no keel (the canoeist kneels).

clay-pigeon shooting or **trap shooting** Pastime and sport in which shotguns are fired at clay targets (*clays*) in the air; these simulate birds in flight and are launched by an automatic or manually operated machine.

cricket Bat and ball 11-a-side team game. A wicket consisting of three stumps (wooden sticks) surmounted by a pair of bails (smaller sticks) is placed at each end of a grassy pitch 20.1m/22yd in length. Each team takes it in turn to bat (with long flat-sided wooden bats) and bowl (with a solid ball), the object being to defend the two wickets while trying to score as many runs as possible.

A bowler delivers an 'over' of six balls to a batsman standing in front of one of the wickets before a different bowler attacks the other wicket. If the batsman hits a ball (and in certain other circumstances), he may exchange places with the other batsman, thus scoring at least one run. A ball reaching the boundary of the field scores four runs automatically, and six if it has not bounced on the way. A batsman can be got out by being 'caught' (a fielder catches the ball before it reaches the ground), 'bowled' (the ball from the bowler knocks the bails off the stumps), 'stumped' (the wicket-keeper knocks the bails off the stumps with the ball while the defending batsman is standing outside his 'safe ground' or 'crease'), 'run out' (the bails on the wicket towards which one of the batsmen is running are knocked off before the safe ground is reached), 'leg before wicket' or 'lbw' (when the lower part of the batsman's leg prevents the ball from the bowler reaching the wicket) and 'hit wicket' (the batsman accidentally knocks the bails off the stumps). Once 10 batsmen have been dismissed, the innings comes to a close, but a team can stop its innings or 'declare' if it thinks it has made enough runs. Each team has two innings, and the one with the greater number of runs at the end of the match wins. A similar game was played in the mid-16c; first known county match 1719; test matches usually last five days; county championship three or four, and limited-over competitions normally concluded in one day, lasting for a specific number of overs per side. Earliest known laws: 1744; Marylebone Cricket Club (MCC) founded 1787; first test match: Melbourne 1877.

croquet A ball-and-mallet game for two to four players, played on a lawn about 32m/35yd long and 25m/28yd wide, on which six hoops have been arranged, with a small stake in the centre of the lawn. The object is to strike your own ball (blue, red, yellow or black) through the hoops in a prescribed order, a process which can be delayed by an opponent's ball hitting your ball out of the way. The central peg marks the finish and the first to hit it with his/her ball is the winner.

curling Similar to bowls but played on ice using special smooth, heavy round stones fitted with handles. The object is to slide the stones, which curl in different directions depending on the twist as they are released, near to a circular target or *house* marked on the ice, the centre of which is called the *tee*. A match lasts for a certain number of *heads* or shots, or by time. Sweeping the ice in front of a stone can make it travel further.

cycling Bicycle riding as a sport can take several forms: *time trials* are raced against the clock; *cyclocross* is a mixture of cycling and cross-country running, carrying the bike; *track racing* takes place on purpose-built concrete or wooden velodromes; *criteriums* are races around town or city centres; *road races* are normally in excess of 150km/100mi in length, between two points or several circuits of a predetermined course; *stage races* involve many days' racing over more than 150km/100mi. First cycle race Paris 1868, won by James Moore of England.

cyclocross ▸ cycling

darts Indoor game of throwing three 13cm/5in darts from a distance of 2.4m/8ft at a circular board which has its 'bull' or centre 1.7m/5ft 8in from the floor. The standard board is divided into 20 segments numbered 1–20 (not in numerical order); each contains smaller segments which either double or treble that number's score if hit. The centre ring (the bull) is worth 50 points, and

Sports and Games

the area around it (the outer) is worth 25 points. Most popular game '501': players start at that figure and deduct all scores from it, aiming to reduce the starting score exactly to zero; final shot must consist of a double.

decathlon Ten-event track-and-field competition held over two days, usually for men: 100m, long jump, shot put, high jump, 400m, 110m hurdles, discus, pole vault, javelin, and 1500m. Points are awarded in each event.

discus throw Athletics field event using a circular disc of wood with metal plates, weighing 2kg/4.4lb for men and 1kg/2.2lb for women. It is thrown with one hand from within the confines of a circle 2.5m/8ft 2in in diameter.

diving Jumping from an elevated rigid or sprung board into a swimming pool, often performing a variety of twists and somersaults. Style gains marks, as does successfully completing the dive, based on the level of difficulty of each attempt (which is used as a multiplying factor). Springboard events take place from a board 3m/9ft 10in above the water; platform diving from a rigid board 10m/32ft 10in above the water.

falconry Sport in which birds of prey are trained to hunt animals and other birds, also known as **hawking**. Two kinds of falcon: *long-winged* birds (eg the peregrine), used in open country, which swoop on their prey from a great height, and *short-winged* birds, or accipiters, which perch on the falconer's gloved fist or tree branch until they see their prey, and then rely on speed. The birds are hooded until such time as they are ready to 'work'.

fencing Sword fighting, using a light *foil*, heavier *épée*, or *sabre* (curved handle, narrow blade). Different target areas exist for each weapon, and protective clothing registers hit electronically. It can be traced back to the Egyptians of c.1300BC and was popular in the Middle Ages.

fishing ▸ **angling**

fives A handball game played on a three or four-walled court (which in Rugby fives is 5.49m/18ft wide, 8.54m/28ft long, with front wall 4.57m/15ft high, back wall 1.83m/6ft high and side walls sloping) by two or four players with a hard white ball, hit with gloved hands. It is derived from the French game *jeu de paume*. First recorded game 1825 at Eton College; another variation is Winchester fives.

football A field team game using an inflated ball, which has developed several forms: **1 Association football** or **soccer**. An 11-a-side team game played on a grass or synthetic pitch measuring 90–120m/100–130yd in length, and 45–90m/50–100yd wide; goal nets measure 7.3m/8yd wide by 2.4m/8ft high; object is to move the ball around using the foot or head until it can be put into the net, thus scoring a goal. Only the goalkeeper within a specific area is allowed to touch the ball with the hand while it is in play. Ancient Greeks, Chinese, Egyptians and Romans all played a form of football; it became an organized game in 19c Britain, in schools and universities; standard rules drawn up 1848; Football Association formed 1863; first FA Cup final played 1872; first World Cup Uruguay 1930. **2 American football**. Players wear heavy padding and helmets, and passing of the ball by hand, including forward passing, is permitted; played on a rectangular field 91m/100yd by 49m/53yd, divided gridiron-like into 4.6m/5yd segments; object is to score 'touchdowns' by moving the ball into the opposing team's 'end zone' (area behind the posts), but progress has to be made upfield by a series of 'plays': a team must make 9.1m/10yd of ground within four plays, otherwise they lose possession of the ball. Six points are awarded for a touchdown and one for an 'extra point', for kicking the ball between the posts and over the crossbar — the equivalent of a conversion in rugby. A goal kicked from anywhere on the field (a 'field goal') is worth three points. Teams consist of more than 40 members, but only 11 are allowed on the field at any one time; special units of players have different roles so they change eg when the team changes from attacking to defending. First intercollegiate game 1869. **3 Australian Rules football**. A handling and kicking game with few rules, a cross between Association football and rugby, with 18 players on an oval pitch measuring c.165m/180yd long by c.137m/150yd wide. The object is to score by kicking the ball between the opponent's goal posts (six points). Smaller posts are positioned either side of the main goal: a ball kicked through that area scores one point; first recorded game played 1858. **4 Gaelic football**. Mixture of rugby, soccer and Australian Rules football, played by teams of 15 on a rectangular pitch 77–91m/84–100yd wide and 128–146m/140–160yd long with goals resembling rugby posts with soccer-style nets attached; points scored by either putting the ball into the goal net (three), or over the crossbar and between the uprights (one); first game resembling Gaelic football took place 1712 at Slane, Ireland. **5 rugby football** ▸ **rugby**.

foxhunting Mounted blood sport involving chasing and killing a wild fox using foxhounds (similar to the beagle); hunt is controlled by a Master of Hounds, the hounds by the Huntsman; season lasts November to April. It developed in the UK in the late 17c. Since 1949 there has been a movement to try to get the sport banned in the UK; hunting with dogs was outlawed in Scotland in 2002.

golf Outdoor sport played on a course 4500–6500m/5000–7000yd long, usually with 18 but sometimes 9 holes; object is to hit a small rubber-cored ball using a long-handled iron or wooden-faced club from a flat starting point or *tee* along a *fairway* to a hole positioned on an area of smooth grass or *green*; additional hazards: trees, bushes, streams, sand-filled bunkers and the *rough*, or uncut grass beside the fairway; winner completes the course using the lowest number of strokes. The *par* is the expected number of strokes a good player needs to complete a hole; one stroke above par is called a *bogey*; one stroke below par is a *birdie*; two strokes below an *eagle*; three strokes below an *albatross*; a hole completed in one stroke is a *hole in one*. A similar game was played by the Dutch c.1300, known as *kolf* or *colf*. *Gouf* was definitely played in Scotland in the 15c; world's first club, the Gentleman Golfers of Edinburgh, formed 1744.

greyhound racing Spectator sport which takes place on an enclosed circular or oval track where greyhound dogs (on whose success bets are usually placed) are lured to run by a mechanical hare; invented California 1919.

gymnastics Physical exercises. Men compete on the parallel bars, pommel horse, high bar, rings, horse vault and floor exercise, and women on the asymmetrical bars, beam, horse vault and floor exercise. Judges award marks out of 10, looking for control, suppleness, balance and ingenuity. The ancient Greeks and Romans performed such exercises for health purposes; modern techniques date from late 18c Germany.

hammer throw Athletics field event; hammer weighing 7.6kg/16lb is thrown using one hand from within the confines of a circle 2.13m/7ft in diameter (protected by a wire cage). Six throws are allowed, the object being to attain the greatest distance.

handball Indoor and outdoor game first played in Germany c.1890; resembles Association football, but played with the hands. Indoor game played seven-a-side on a court 40m/43.8yd long and 20m/21.9yd wide, with goals 2m/6ft 6in high and 3m/9ft 9in wide; outdoor game (**field handball**) played on a field with 11 on each side.

hang gliding Flying in a glider with a delta-shaped wing, usually having launched from a high place. The pilot is suspended by a harness from the light frame holding the wing, and controls the direction of the craft by body movement. Providing the angle of attack is maintained, lift is generated. A hang glider with a motor and wing span increased to 10m/33ft is called a *micro-light*, which typically has a speed of 90kph/55mph. Hang gliding was pioneered in the 1890s in Germany.

harness racing Horse race with rider seated in a small two-wheeled cart or *sulky*; horses trot or pace; races run on an oval dirt track measuring 800–1500m/0.5–1mi in circumference; first introduced 1554 Holland, popularized mid-19c USA.

hawking ▸ falconry

heptathlon Seven-event track-and-field competition held over two days, usually for women: 100m hurdles, shot put, high jump, 200m, long jump, javelin and 800m; replaced pentathlon in 1981.

high jump Athletics field event; competitors attempt to clear a bar without any aids; height increased gradually; three failed attempts means disqualification. The winner clears the greatest height, or has the fewest failures.

hockey or (USA) **field hockey** Stick-and-ball game played by two teams of 11 on a pitch 91m/100yd long and 54m/60yd wide, the object being to move the ball around with the sticks until a player can score from within the semicircle of radius 14.64m/16yd in front of the opposing side's goal; game is split into two halves of 35 minutes; ancient Greeks played a similar game c.2500BC; modern hockey dates from 1875.

horse racing Racing of horses against one another, each ridden by a jockey. Two categories: **flat racing** for thoroughbred horses on a flat grass or dirt surface over a predetermined distance from 1 to 4km/5 furlongs to 2.5mi, and **national hunt racing** in which the horses negotiate either movable hurdles or fixed fences over a distance up to 6.5km/4.5mi. The ancient Egyptians took part in horse races in c.1200BC; popularized in 12c England. Most monarchs have supported the sport, hence name the 'sport of kings'. ▸ **harness racing, hurdles** and **steeplechase**.

hurdles Horse race in which the horses jump hurdles of at least 106.7cm/3ft 6in in height; hurdles are easily knocked down so that horses can continue the race.

hurdling Athletics event in which the competitors race to clear 10 obstacles (hurdles) placed on the track; race distances: 110m and 400m for men, 100m and 400m for women; hurdle height varies: 106.7cm/3ft 6in for the 110m; 91.4cm/3ft for the 400m and 84cm/2ft 9in for the 100m.

hurling or **hurley** Irish 15-a-side field game played with curved sticks and a ball; object to hit ball into opposing team's goal: under the crossbar scores three points; above the crossbar but between the posts scores one; played since 1800BC;

standardized in 1884 following the formation of the Gaelic Athletic Association.

ice hockey Fast game played by two teams of six on an ice rink 56–61m/184–200ft long and 26–30m/85–98ft wide with sticks and a small rubber *puck*; aim is to score goals by using the stick to hit the puck into the opposing team's goal; players wear ice skates and protective clothing; possibly first played 1850s Canada.

ice skating 1 figure skating. Artistic dancing on ice for individuals and pairs; first known skating club formed mid-18c London; first artificial rink opened 1876 Baker Street. **2 speed skating**. Competitors race against one another on an oval ice track over distances between 500 and 10000m/550 and 11000yd.

javelin throw Athletics field event; throwing a spear-like javelin which consists of three parts: pointed metal head, shaft and grip; men's javelin is 2.6–2.7m/8ft 6in–8ft 10in in length and weighs 800g/1.8lb; women's is 2.2–2.3m/7ft 2in–7ft 6in and weights at least 600g/1.3lb; the competitor runs to a specified mark with the javelin in one hand, and throws it; for throw to count, metal head must touch ground before any other part; first mark made by the head is the point used for measuring the distance achieved.

judo Unarmed combat sport of late 19c Japanese origin. Contestants wear a *judogi* or loose-fitting suit and compete on a mat which breaks their falls. When one cannot break a hold, surrender is signalled by slapping the mat; ability is graded from fifth to first Kyu, and then first to 12th Dan — only Dr Jigoro Kano, who devised the sport, has been awarded 12th Dan. Different coloured belts indicate grades; eg white for novice, brown (three degrees) and black (nine degrees).

jujitsu Japanese art of unarmed offence and self-defence used by the Samurai; forms basis of judo, aikido and karate; thought to have been introduced early 17c by Chinese monk, Chen Yuan-ping.

karate Martial art of unarmed combat, dating from 17c; developed Japan 20c; name adopted 1930s; aim is to be in total control of the body's muscular power, so it can be used with great force and accuracy at any instant. Experts may show their mental and physical training by eg breaking various thicknesses of wood, but in fighting an opponent, blows do not actually make contact; levels of prowess symbolized by coloured belts.

kendo Japanese martial art of sword fighting, now practised with *shiani*, or bamboo swords; object is to land two scoring blows on opponent's target area. *Kendokas* (participants) wear traditional dress of the Samurai period, including face masks and aprons; grades according to ability are from sixth to first Kyu, then from first to 10th Dan; earliest reference is AD789.

kung fu Chinese unarmed combat dating from the sixth century, when it was practised at the Shaolin Temple; best known form is *wing chun*.

lacrosse Stick-and-ball field game; teams of 10 (men's) or 12 (women's) play on a pitch measuring about 100–110m/110–120yd by 55–75m/60–85yd; stick measures at least 90cm/3ft and has thongs forming a triangular net at one end in which ball is caught and carried, and thrown into opponents' goal (just under 2m/6ft square); derived from Native American game of *baggataway*; stick supposedly resembled a bishop's crozier, so French settlers called it *la crosse*; played since 15c; spread to Europe early 19c, and to Britain 1867.

long jump Athletics field event; contestant runs up

to the take-off mark and leaps into a sandpit; length of the jump measured from front of take-off line to nearest break in the sand made by any part of the competitor's body; also called **broad jump** in North America.

lugeing Travelling across ice on a toboggan sled, usually made of wood with metal runners; rider sits upright or lies back (but lies on the stomach in tobogganing). Competitors in single or two-seater luges race against time on a predetermined run of at least 1 000m/1 094yd; luge is approximately 1.5m/5ft in length, steered by the feet and a hand rope. ▸ **bobsledding**.

marathon Long-distance running race, normally on open roads, over 42km 195m/26mi 385yd (distance first used at 1908 London Olympics so competitors could finish exactly in front of the royal box); race introduced at the 1896 Olympic Games to commemorate the run of the Greek courier (according to legend, Pheidippides) who ran the c.24mi/39km from Marathon to Athens in 490BC with the news of a Greek victory over the Persian army. In the 1980s the **half marathon** over 21km/13mi 194yd also became popular.

martial arts ▸ **aikido, judo, jujitsu, karate, kendo, kung fu, taekwondo**

moto-cross or **scrambling** Motorcycle racing over a circuit of rough terrain, taking advantage of natural hazards eg streams and hills; uses sturdier motorcycles than those for road use; competitions usually categorized by engine size; first moto-cross race held 1924 at Camberley, Surrey.

motorcycle racing Speed competitions for motorcycles which for the annual season-long grand prix are categorized by the engine sizes 80cc, 125cc, 250cc, 500cc, Superbike and Sidecar. Other forms include speedway, moto-cross and motorcycle trials riding.

motor racing Racing finely-tuned motor cars, either purpose-built or modified production vehicles; season-long (Mar–Nov) Formula One world championship involves usually 16 races at different venues worldwide; other popular forms include stock-car racing, hill-climbing, sports-car racing and rallying; first race 1894, between Paris and Rouen.

mountaineering Climbing a mountain aided by ropes and other accessories, which for tall peaks can take weeks; most popular form in UK is **rock climbing**; in higher places elsewhere the form is **snow and ice climbing**.

netball Women's seven-a-side court game invented in the USA and developed from basketball; court is 30.5m/100ft long and 15.25m/50ft wide; object is to score goals by passing the inflated ball between players and throwing it through opponent's hoop suspended on a post 3.05m/10ft high. Players must not touch each other or run with the ball.

octopush A form of hockey played underwater, first introduced 1960s in South Africa; teams of six; players use miniature hockey sticks and a *puck* or *squid*, which must hit the opposing team's end of the swimming pool to score a goal.

orienteering Cross-country running and route-finding aided by map and compass; competitors set off at intervals and have to find their way to offical check-points; devised as a sport in Sweden in 1918, based on military training techniques; became an international sport 1960s.

paddle tennis Bat-and-ball game for two or four people, invented USA c.1920; rules similar to lawn tennis, but court is half the size; bat wooden and ball made of sponge.

parachuting Jumping out of an aircraft and landing with the aid of a parachute; competitions involve landing within a specific area; participant can choose to freefall for a few thousand feet before opening the chute, normally c.750m/2 500ft.

pelota Generic name for various hand, glove, racket or bat-and-ball games, all developed from French *jeu de paume*; most popular form **Pelote Basque**: it uses a walled court (*trinquete*), players wear a shaped wicker basked attached to their forearm in which they catch and propel the ball. Pelota is one of the world's fastest games.

pentathlon 1 Five-event track-and-field competition, usually for women: 100m hurdles, shot put, high jump, long jump, and 800m; replaced by **heptathlon** in 1981. **2** modern pentathlon. Five-sport competition based on military training, comprising cross-country riding, épée fencing, pistol shooting, swimming and cross-country running.

point-to-point Horse races for amateur riders over a cross-country course, normally farmland; organized by hunts; horses used are regular hunting horses; original courses went from one point to another (hence name), but are now often over circular or oval courses with mixture of artificial and natural fences.

pole vault Athletics field event; jumping contest for height using fibreglass pole for leverage to clear a bar, which is raised progressively; three attempts may be made to clear the height before attempting a new one.

polo Stick-and-ball game; played by teams of four on horseback on a pitch measuring 274m/300yd by 146m/160yd; object is to hit the ball into the opposing team's 7.3m/8yd-wide and 3m/10ft-high goal using a long-handled mallet; match lasts about an hour, divided into seven-minute *chukkas*, the number of which varies according to competition; a pony is not expected to play more than two chukkas; game derives its name from Tibetan *pulu*; first played in C Asia c.500BC.

pool US table game played in many forms, using 15 balls, a *cue* similar to that used in billiards and snooker, and a table half the size of a standard billiard table, with six round pockets; in UK most popular form is eight-ball pool, where the object is to pot all balls of your colour and finally the black (or No. 8) ball.

potholing or (USA) **spelunking** Exploration and study of caves and other underground features, originally to survey extent, physical history and structure, and natural history. When practised as a hobby people descend through access points (potholes) to follow courses of underground rivers and streams; scientific term: **speleology**.

powerboat racing Inshore and offshore racing of boats fitted with high-powered and finely-tuned engines; first race of note Calais to Dover 1903.

quoits Outdoor game demanding great accuracy; metal ring is thrown at a peg; became popular mid-14c England; horseshoe pitching developed from quoits.

rackets or (USA) **raquets** Racket-and-ball game; played by two or four players on walled court; probably forerunner to many racket-and-ball games; thought to have originated Middle Ages, and to have developed 18c at the Fleet debtors' prison, London.

rallying Motor racing on open roads and in forests, sometimes lasting several days; driver and navigator require skill and endurance; uses modified production cars.

real tennis Indoor racket-and-ball game similar to rackets; played on walled court with specifically designed hazards; derivation of the 11c *jeu de paume*;

racket developed 16c and the game became very popular in the 17c; also known as 'royal' or 'court' tennis, and a minority sport today.

rodeo US sport; mainly competitive riding and a range of skills deriving from cowboy ranching practices; events include bronco riding with and without saddle (where the cowboy must stay on a wild bucking horse for a set time holding on with only one hand, points being awarded for style to the horse and rider), bull riding, steer wrestling, calf roping and team roping.

roller skating First seen 1760 in Liège, Belgium; developed as a sport late 19c, following invention of the modern four-wheeled skate in 1863. Competitions exist as for ice skating; individual, pairs, dancing and speed skating on a track.

rounders Outdoor bat-and-ball game; baseball may derive from it; teams of nine players; object, after hitting the ball, which is bowled from the centre of the pitch, is to score a rounder by running around the outside of the four posts without being put out (by the ball being caught, the batter being tagged between posts, or the post ahead of the batter being 'stopped' by a fielder touching it with the hand holding the ball); first reference to rounders 1774.

rowing Propulsion of a boat by oars; involves two or more rowers, each with an oar, and often with a coxswain; **sculling** involves one rower with two oars; rowing as an organized sport dates from 1715 (first rowing of the Doggetts Coat and Badge race on the R Thames, London).

rugby Team ball game played with oval ball on a pitch 68.62m/75yd wide and 100m/110yd long; developed 1823 from football (when William Webb Ellis of Rugby school picked up the ball and ran with it); H-shaped goalposts at each end of field are 5.6m/18ft 6in wide, with a crossbar 3m/10ft above the ground; object is to score a *try* by grounding ball in opposing team's scoring area behind goal line. The 15-a-side **Rugby Union** game and 13-a-side **Rugby League** are now both professional games, with some rule differences: eg the scoring (League in brackets): try 5 (4), conversion 2 (2), penalty 3 (2), dropped goal 3 (1). Rugby League was formed by the breakaway Northern Union after a dispute with the Rugby Football Union about pay in 1895.

sailing Travelling over water in a suitable craft, usually a small single or double-sided dinghy, often with outboard motor or auxiliary engine for use in no wind; **yachting** involves racing small, light sailing vessels with crews of one, two or three; large ocean-going yachts may be 25m/80ft or more in length; several classes of racing yacht in Olympic and international competitions — eg the Admiral's Cup and Americas Cup.

scrambling ▸ motocross

sculling ▸ rowing

sepek takrow Three-a-side court game played on badminton court with ball made from rattan palm; ball is propelled over centre net (lower than in badminton) by players using any part of the body other than arms or hands; popular in SE Asia, particularly Philippines, Malaysia (as 'kick') and Thailand (as 'rattan ball').

shinty Twelve-a-side stick-and-ball game originating in Ireland more than 1 500 years ago, now popular in the Scottish Highlands; played on pitch up to 155m/170yd long and 73m/80yd wide; aim is to score goals by propelling the leather-covered cork and worsted ball, using curved sticks or *camans*, into the opposing team's goal or *hail*.

shooting Competitive shooting takes many forms and uses different types of weapon; most popular weapons: the standard pistol, small bore rifle, full bore rifle, air rifle and air pistol. All events involve shooting at still or moving targets (▸ **clay pigeon shooting**). Using firearms for sport developed in 15c. Hunting for game, eg grouse or pheasant shooting, has specifically defined seasons.

shot put Athletics field event; the shot is a brass or iron sphere weighing 7.26kg/16 lb for men and 4kg/8 lb 13oz for women. It is propelled, using only one hand, from a starting position under the chin. The thrower must not leave the 2.1m/7ft diameter throwing circle. In competition six throws are allowed.

skiing Propelling oneself along snow while standing on skis, aided by poles; named from Norwegian *ski*, 'snowshoe'; two forms of competition skiing: **alpine skiing**, consisting of the downhill, slalom (zigzag courses through markers) and ski-jumping, and **Nordic skiing** or **langlaufing** (on narrower skis to which only the toe is attached), incorporating cross-country skiing and the **biathlon**. Other forms: **ski-flying** (ski-jumping from a high take-off point), **skijoring** (being towed behind a vehicle or horse), hang gliding on skis and parapenting on skis.

skydiving or **freefalling** Jumping from an aircraft and freefalling, often performing a wide range of stunts or forming patterns by holding hands with other skydivers, to a height of 600m/2 000ft, when the parachute must be opened.

snooker Indoor game played on a standard billiard table by two (or occasionally four) players; aim is to 'pot' the 21 coloured balls (arranged on the table at the start) by hitting them with the white ball, itself hit using a tapered pole or *cue*. Fifteen of the balls are red; these must be potted alternately with the coloured ones. This sequence is called a *break* and continues until a mistake is made; reds remain in pockets but coloureds are returned to the table until no reds are left, when they are potted in ascending order; game ends when the black is finally potted. Points 1–7 relate to colours, in order: red, yellow, green, brown, blue, pink, black.

soccer ▸ football

softball Smaller version of **baseball**, played on diamond-shaped pitch of sides measuring 18.3m/60ft; ball is larger as well as softer; teams of nine; game lasts for nine innings per team, each innings lasting until a team has three players out; object is to complete a circuit of the diamond without being put out, eg by being caught out, struck out, or tagged between bases by a player with the ball. Pitching is underarm in softball, overarm in baseball; two forms: *fast pitch* and *slow pitch*; in the latter the bowler must deliver ball in arc at least 2.4m/8ft high.

speedway Motorcycle racing on machines with no brakes and only one gear, usually on an oval track and involving four riders at once. Other forms include *long track* racing and *ice speedway*.

squash or **squash rackets** Strenuous indoor racket-and-ball game played (in English singles) on an enclosed court measuring 9.75m/32ft long by 6.4m/21ft wide; small rubber ball is hit alternately by players against the front wall, so that it cannot be returned; developed 1817 from **rackets** at Harrow school.

steeplechase 1 National hunt horse racing; horses negotiate fixed fences normally 0.9–1.2m/3–4ft high; first one in Ireland in 1752; most famous is Grand National. ▸ **horse racing. 2** Track race, usually for men, run over 3 000m and comprising 28 0.9m/3ft hurdles and seven waterjumps.

stock-car racing Motor racing; in USA highly supercharged production cars race around a concreted track; in UK 'bangers' (old cars) race on a round or oval track; the aim is to be the last car still moving at the end of the race; some 'rough' tactics are allowed to try to eliminate other drivers.

street hockey Hockey played on roller skates, popular in USA and Europe; five members to each team play on an enclosed rink.

sumo wrestling A Japanese national sport; competition takes place in a 3.66m/12ft diameter circle; object is to force opponent out of ring or to ground; sumo wrestlers are very heavy and eat vast amounts of food to increase weight and body size.

surfing Riding waves, either with the body alone, or with the aid of a board; object is to ride along the face of a wave before it breaks; board is usually about 1.8m/6ft long, but a longer one is used for competition; originated in Oceania, developed in Hawaii and has flourished in modern times there and in California and Australia.

swimming Propelling oneself through water without mechanical aids. Four strokes: *breast stroke*, the slowest stroke, developed in the 16c; *front crawl* or *freestyle*, the fastest stroke; *backstroke*; and *butterfly*, developed in the USA in the 20c. In competitions there are also relays, involving four swimmers, and medley races, combining all four strokes. Olympic-size pool is 50m/55yd long, with eight lanes; race lengths from 50m/55yd to 1 500m/1 640yd; earliest reference to swimming as a sport is 36BC Japan.

table tennis or **ping pong** Indoor bat-and-ball game played by two or four players; uses small wooden bats covered in rubber or sponge and a hollow plastic ball; table measures 2.75m/9ft by 1.52m/5ft and has a 15.25cm/6in-high net across it; ball must be hit over the net and into opposing half of table, to be returned without volleying; object is to play unreturnable shots; in doubles, players must hit ball alternately; winner is first to reach 21 points with at least a two-point lead; thought to have been first played 1880s.

taekwondo Martial art developed in Korea by General Choi Hong Hi; officially part of Korean tradition and culture since 1955, now popular as a sport.

tennis, lawn Racket-and-ball game for two or four players; court measures 23.77m/78ft long by 8.23m/27ft wide (singles), or 10.97m/36ft wide (doubles); net 0.9m/3ft high is stretched across centre; rackets have oval heads strung with nylon or gut; playing surface can be grass, clay, shale, concrete, wood, or other man-made materials; object is to play unreturnable strokes, thus scoring points; progression of scoring is 15, 30, 40, deuce if both reach 40, and game; set won by winning six games with a two-game lead (or one in a 'short' set); a very close match can be decided using a tie-break. In doubles, players may hit the ball in any order, but must serve in rotation. 'Field tennis' was played 18c but game similar to modern game was invented 1873 as *sphairstike* in Wales by Walter Wingfield.

tenpin bowling ► **bowling**

tobogganing ► **bobsledding** and **lugeing**

trampolining Performing acrobatics on a sprung canvas sheet stretched across a frame, first used at turn of 20c as a circus attraction; developed as a sport following design of modern trampoline in 1936. In competition, marks gained for performing difficult manoeuvres; popular forms are synchronized trampolining and tumbling.

trap shooting ► **clay pigeon shooting**

triple jump Athletics field event; takes place in same place as long jump, governed by same rules. After the run-up, competitors must take off and hop on the same foot; second phase is a step onto the other foot, followed by a jump; previously called the *hop, step and jump*.

tug of war Athletics event of strength; two teams (normally eight men) pull against each other from opposite ends of a long thick rope; aim is to pull the opponents over a predetermined mark. Ancient Chinese and Egyptians participated in similar events; first rules drawn up 1879.

volleyball Indoor court game; two teams of six play on a court measuring 18m/59ft by 9m/29ft which has a raised net stretched across the centre; aim is to score points by grounding the inflated ball on opponent's side after hitting it over net with the arms or hands; ball may not be hit more than three times on one team's side of the net.

walking Either a leisurely pursuit (eg **fell walking**) or a competitive sport on roads or tracks which has strict rules; eg raised foot must touch ground before the other leaves it.

water polo Sport played by two seven-a-side teams in a swimming pool; aim is to score by propelling inflated ball into opposing team's goal at end of the pool, without touching the bottom; developed in Britain in 1869; originally called 'football in water'.

water skiing Being towed by a motor boat on one or two skis, using a 23m/75ft-long rope. Competitions held for jumping, slalom and acrobatics.

weightlifting Test of strength by lifting weights attached to both ends of a metal pole or *barbell*. Competitors have to make two successful lifts: the *snatch*, taking the bar to an outstretched position above the head in one movement (held for two seconds), and the *clean and jerk* or *jerk* which is achieved in two movements, first onto the chest, then above the head with outstretched arms; aggregate weight of the two lifts gives a competitor's total, and the weights are gradually increased. Another form is *powerlifting*, which calls for sheer strength rather than technique, and takes three forms: the *squat*, *dead lift* and *bench press*. Weightlifting was part of Ancient Olympic Games; introduced as sport c.1850.

wrestling Fighting person to person without using fists; aim is to throw opponent to the ground; most popular forms are *freestyle*, where the legs can be used to hold and trip, and *Graeco-Roman* where holds below the waist are not allowed. Ten weight divisions, from 55kg to 120kg. Other forms: *sumo*, the national sport in Japan; *Sambo* in Russia; *Kushti* in Iran; *Glima* in Iceland; *Schwingen* in Switzerland; and *Yagli*, the national sport in Turkey; also UK variations *Devon and Cornwall* and *Cumberland and Westmoreland*.

yachting ► **sailing**

100 Champions in Sport

Sports and Games

Aaron, Hank (Henry Lewis) (1934–) US baseball player, born Mobile, Alabama. Regarded as one of the greatest batters ever, he set almost every batting record in his 23-season career with the Milwaukee Braves and the Milwaukee Brewers: 2 297 runs batted in, 1 477 extra-base hits, and 755 home runs (he broke **Babe Ruth**'s long-standing record of 714 in 1974). Named the Most Valuable Player in 1957, he led the Braves to the World Series Championship.

Ali, Muhammad, formerly **Cassius Marcellus Clay** (1942–) US boxer, born Louisville, Kentucky. Won Olympic amateur light-heavyweight title in Rome (1960); turned professional and won world heavyweight title (1964). Stripped of title 1967 for refusing military service on religious grounds, but returned 1970. Made history by regaining the world heavyweight title twice — lost 1971, regained 1974; lost 1978, regained later 1978.

Anquetil, Jacques (1934–87) French racing cyclist, born Normandy. Winner of Tour de France five times (1957, 1961–4); see also **Bernard Hinault, Miguel Indurain** and **Eddy Merckx**; also won Tour of Spain (1963) and of Italy (1964).

Aouita, Said (1960–) Moroccan athlete, born Rabat. Set world records at 1 500m and 5 000m in 1985 — the first man for 30 years to hold both records. Later broke world records at 2 miles, 2 000m, and 3 000m. Also Olympic champion (1984), overall Grand Prix winner (1986) and world 5 000m champion (1987).

Beamon, Bob (Robert) (1946–) US athlete, born New York City. Broke world long jump record by 55cm (21½ins) at the 1968 Olympic Games in Mexico City, with a jump of 8.90m (29ft 2½ins). His record held until broken by Mike Powell in Tokyo (1991).

Beckenbauer, Franz, nicknamed **Kaiser Franz** (1945–) German footballer, coach, manager and administrator, born Munich. European Footballer of the Year in 1972, he captained the West German national side to success in the European Nations Cup (1972) and in the World Cup (1974); he also won three successive European Cup winner's medals with Bayern Munich (1974–6). After retiring from playing in 1983, he coached the West German team (1984–90) and as manager of West Germany from 1986 took them to consecutive World Cup finals — as runners up in 1986 and then as winners (for Germany) in 1990.

Best, George (1946–) Northern Irish footballer, born Belfast. Northern Ireland's greatest individual footballing talent; leading scorer for Manchester United in the Football League First Division (1967–8), and in 1968 winner of a European Cup medal and the title of European Footballer of the Year. Immense career success dwindled early due to pressures of top-class football.

Biondi, Matt(hew) (1965–) US swimmer, born Morego, California. Winner of record seven medals at the 1986 world championships, including three golds; of seven medals at the 1988 Olympics, including five golds; and a silver in the 50m freestyle at the 1992 Olympics. Set 100m freestyle world record of 48.74 seconds in Orlando, Florida (1986).

Border, Allan (1955–) Australian cricketer, born Cremorne, Sydney. Made Test debut for Australia in 1978; team captain 1984–94. Set world records for most Test match and one-day international appearances, and for runs scored in Test matches when his career total reached 10 161 (1993). Played county cricket in England for Gloucestershire and Essex.

Borg, Bjorn Rune (1956–) Swedish tennis player. Swedish Davis Cup team member aged 15, and Wimbledon junior champion aged 16. Winner of five consecutive Wimbledon singles titles (1976–80), two Italian championship titles and six French Open titles (1974–5, 1978–81).

Botham, Ian Terence (1955–) English cricketer, born Heswall, Merseyside. Played for England in 102 Test matches, took 383 wickets, and scored 5 200 runs. Held record number of Test wickets (373 wickets at an average of 27.86 runs) until overtaken by **Richard Hadlee**, and four times took 10 wickets in a match. Played county cricket in England for Somerset (1974–87), Worcestershire (1987–91) and Durham (1992–3).

Bradman, Don (Sir Donald George) (1908–2001) Australian cricketer, born Cootamundra, New South Wales, regarded as one of the greatest batsmen ever. Played for Australia from 1928 to 1948 (captain 1936–48); made highest aggregate and largest number of centuries in Tests against England, and set record for the highest Australian Test score against England (334 at Leeds in 1930); batting average in Test matches was 99.94 runs per innings.

Bubka, Sergei (1963–) Ukrainian field athlete, born Donetsk. Won gold medal for pole-vaulting at the 1983 world championship, retaining title 1987, 1991, 1993, 1995 and 1997; also won gold at the 1988 Olympics. Broke 35 world records and in 1993 took the world pole-vault record to 6.15m.

Carson, Willie (William Hunter Fisher) (1942–) Scottish jockey, born Stirling. Rode 17 Classic winners and is fourth in the all-time winners table. First Classic success was on High Top in the 2 000 Guineas (1972); recorded a notable royal double for Queen Elizabeth II by winning the Oaks and the St Leger on Dunfermline (1977); won Derby first on Troy (1979), then Henbit (1980).

Charlton, Bobby (Sir Robert) (1937–) English footballer, born Ashington, Northumberland. He played with Manchester United (1954–73), winning three League championship medals (1956–7, 1964–5, 1966–7) and an FA Cup winner's medal (1963), and captained Manchester United to victory in the 1968 European Cup. Also played 106 games for England between 1957 and 1973, scoring a record 49 goals, and was a member of the victorious World Cup team (1966). In all he played 754 games, scoring 245 goals.

Clark, Jim (James) (1936–68) Scottish racing driver, born Berwickshire. Won first motor race in 1956; Scottish Speed Champion 1958–9. Joined Lotus team as a Formula One driver 1960, and won world championship 1963, 1965; also in 1965 became the first non-American since 1916 to win the Indianapolis 500. Won 25 of his 72 Grand Prix races, breaking Juan Fangio's record of 24, and took pole position 33 times.

Cobb, Ty(rus Raymond), nicknamed **the Georgia Peach** (1886–1961) US baseball player, born Narrows, Georgia. Regarded as outstanding offensive player of all time; played for the Detroit Tigers (1905–26) and the Philadelphia Athletics (1926–8), and until Pete Rose in 1985 was the only player with more than 4 000 hits in major league baseball. Career batting average was .367, (ie he had a hit more than once every three times at bat).

Coe, Sebastian (1956–) English athlete, born Chiswick, London. Winner of 1500m Olympic gold medal and 800m silver medal at both Moscow (1980) and Los Angeles (1984). Broke world record for the 800m, 1000m and the mile in 1981. Between Sep 1976 and June 1983 he did not lose the final of any race over 1500m or a mile.

Comaneci, Nadia (1961–) Romanian gymnast, born Onesti, Moldavia. Winner at the 1976 Olympic Games (aged 14) of gold medals in the parallel bars and beam disciplines and a bronze in the floor, becoming the first to obtain a perfect score of 10 for performance on the bars and beam; also won gold medals in the beam at the 1978 world championships and in the beam and the floor exercise at the 1980 Olympics.

Connors, Jimmy (James Scott) (1952–) US tennis player, born East St Louis, Illinois. Winner of the men's singles competition at Wimbledon (1974, 1982), the Australian Open (1974), and the US Open (1974, 1976, 1978, 1982–3). With Ilie Nastase, he won the men's doubles at Wimbledon (1973) and the US Open men's doubles (1975). He was World Championship Tennis champion (1977, 1980), Masters champion (1978), and a US team member in the Davis Cup (1976; 1981 victory).

Court, Margaret Jean Smith, née **Smith** (1942–) Australian tennis player, born Albury, New South Wales. Winner of more Grand Slam events (66) than any other player: 10 Wimbledon titles (including the singles — the first Australian to do so — in 1963, 1965, 1970), 22 US titles (singles in 1962, 1965, 1968–70, 1973), 13 French (singles 1962, 1964, 1969–70, 1973), and 21 Australian (singles 1960–66, 1969–71, 1973). In 1970 she became the second woman (after Maureen Connolly) to win all four major titles in one year.

Davis, Joe (1901–78) English billiards and snooker champion, born Whitwell, near Chesterfield. Made first break of 100 aged 12. World professional snooker champion (1927–46), and billiards champion (1928–33). Attained maximum snooker break of 147 in 1955, later officially recognized as the world record.

Davis, Steve (1957–) English snooker player, born London. World's leading player during the 1980s, and world champion six times (1981, 1983–4, 1987–9).

DiMaggio, Joe (Joseph Paul), nicknamed **Joltin' Joe** and **the Yankee Clipper** (1914–99) US baseball player, born Martinez, California. Played entire career (1936–51) with the New York Yankees. Greatest achievement was hitting safely (recording a hit) at least once in 56 consecutive games in the 1941 season. Was the American League's Most Valuable Player three times and winner of the batting championship twice (1939, 1940). Career total was 361 home runs, with a batting average of .325.

Eddery, Pat(rick James John) (1952–) Irish jockey, born Newbridge, Kildare. Champion jockey 11 times between 1974 and 1996; Classics victories include the Derby (1975, 1982, 1990), the Oaks (1979, 1996), the St Leger (1986, 1991, 1994, 1997), 1000 Guineas (1996), 2000 Guineas (1983–4, 1993); also had four Prix de l'Arc de Triomphe wins (1980, 1985–7).

Edwards, Gareth Owen (1947–) Welsh rugby player, born Gwaun-cae-Gurwen, near Swansea. First capped for Wales aged 19 (1967), and became their youngest-ever captain (1968). His 53 consecutive caps set a Welsh record; also played in 10 Lions Tests.

Evert, Chris(tine) Marie (1954–) US tennis player, born Fort Lauderdale, Florida. Winner of 157 professional titles, and undefeated on clay from Aug 1973 to May 1979. Her 18 singles Grand Slam titles were: the Australian Open (1982, 1984), the French Open (1974–5, 1979–80, 1983, 1985–6), the All-England Championship at Wimbledon (1974, 1976, 1981) and the US Open (1975–78, 1980, 1982).

Faldo, Nick (Nicholas Alexander) (1957–) English golfer, born Welwyn Garden City, Hertfordshire. Early in career won the Professional Golfers' Association (PGA) championships (1978, 1980–1). Reworked swing and then won the Open championship (1987, 1990, 1996) and the Masters (1989, 1990, 1996). Ryder Cup team member from 1977 to 1997.

Fischer, Bobby (Robert James) (1943–) US chess player, born Chicago. Winner of both US junior and senior chess titles aged 14; later world champion (1972–5). He won the title from Boris Spassky in 1972, but was stripped of it in 1975 for failing to agree conditions to defend it against **Anatoliy Karpov**. He achieved the highest results rating (Elo 2785) in the history of chess.

Fitzpatrick, Sean (Brian Thomas) (1963–) New Zealand rugby union player, born Auckland. New Zealand's most capped player, and the world's most capped hooker. Set world record of 63 consecutive caps (1986–95). Captained New Zealand from 1992 and played 33 caps as captain (1992–5).

Gavaskar, Sunil Manohar, nicknamed **the Little Master** (1949–) Indian cricketer, born Bombay (now Mumbai). Became one of the most prolific run-scorers in Test cricket history. Played for India in 125 Test matches from 1971 to 1997, scoring 10122 runs, including a record 34 test centuries. Was the first player to score more than 10000 Test runs.

Girardelli, Marc (1963–) Luxembourg skier, born Lustenau, Austria. Winner of overall World Cup title more times than any other skier; also 11 world championship medals (four gold, four silver, three bronze) and two Olympic silver medals.

Gooch, Graham (1953–) English cricketer, born London. Made debut for Essex 1973, first capped for England 1975; played in over 100 Test matches, recording his highest score of 333 runs against India in 1990. Captained England 34 times, but resigned July 1993. Scored over 100 centuries, and when he retired from English Test cricket in 1995 had made a career total of 8900 runs.

Grace, W(illiam) G(ilbert) (1848–1915) English cricketer, born Downend, near Bristol. Made first-class debut with Gloucestershire aged 16 (1864) and remained in first-class cricket until 1908, making 126 centuries, scoring 54896 runs and taking 2864 wickets, becoming a national hero. He scored 2739 runs in a season in 1871, 344 runs in an innings in 1876 for MCC, and 100 first-class centuries by 1895.

Graf, Steffi (1969–) German tennis player, born Bruehl. In 1988 she won a Golden Grand Slam — the US, French, Australian and Wimbledon singles titles — as well as the gold medal at the Seoul Olympics. Singles wins include the French Open (1987–8, 1993, 1995–6, 1999), the Australian Open (1988–90, 1994), the US Open (1988–9, 1993, 1995–6) and the All-England championship at Wimbledon (1988–9, 1991–3, 1995–6).

Green, Lucinda, née **Prior-Palmer** (1953–) English three-day eventer, born London. She won the Badminton Horse Trials a record six times (1973,

1976–7, 1979, 1983–4) and the Burghley Horse Trials twice (1977, 1981). In the European championships she won an individual gold medal (1975, 1977), a team gold (1977, 1985, 1987), and an individual and team silver (1983). In 1982 she was world champion and won another team gold.

Gretzky, Wayne (1961–) Canadian ice-hockey player, born Brantford, Ontario. Played for the Edmonton Oilers (1978–88), the Los Angeles Kings (1988–96), the St Louis Blues briefly and the New York Rangers (1996–9). He set numerous records including the most goals scored in a season (92 in 1981–2) and most career points (he scored his 2 500th point in 1995 and retired with a total of 2 857). National Hockey League's Most Valuable Player nine times (1980–7, 1989).

Griffith-Joyner, Florence, known as **Flo-Jo** (1959–98) US track and field sprinter, born Los Angeles, California. Winner of National Collegiate Athletic Association 200m title (1982), an Olympic silver medal in the 200m (1984), and three Olympic gold medals (1988): for the 100m and 200m — setting world records of 10.54 seconds for the former and 21.34 seconds for the latter — and for the 4 × 400m relay.

Hagen, Walter Charles, nicknamed **the Haig** (1892– 1969) US golfer, born Rochester, New York State. First US-born winner and four-times winner of the British Open championship (1922, 1924, 1928–9); also won the US Open (1914, 1919), the US Professional Golfers' Association (PGA) a record five times (1921, 1924–7), and captained the first six US Ryder Cup teams (1927–37), which won in 1927, 1931, 1935 and 1937.

Hendry, Stephen (1969–) Scottish snooker player, born Edinburgh. Professional from age 16, became youngest-ever winner of a professional title at the Rothmans Grand Prix (1987). Gained several titles in 1989, including the British Open and, with Mike Hallett, the Fosters World Doubles. Winner of Embassy World Championship (1990, 1992–6, 1999).

Hinault, Bernard, known as **Le Blaireau (the badger)** (1954–) French cyclist, born Yffiniac. Winner of the Tour de France five times (1978–9, 1981–2, 1985). (Only Hinault, **Jacques Anquetil, Miguel Indurain** and **Eddy Merckx** have won five times.) Won Tour of Italy three times and Tour of Spain twice.

Holyfield, Evander (1962–) US boxer, born Alabama. Undisputed heavyweight world champion in 1990–2, 1993–4 and 1996–7. In 2000 he won the WBA belt, becoming the first boxer to become world champion on four separate occasions.

Hutton, Len (Sir Leonard) (1916–90) English cricketer, born Fulneck, Yorkshire. Played for Yorkshire; made debut for England 1937, scoring a century in his first Test against Australia (1938), and in the Oval Test against Australia (also 1938) scored a world record of 364 runs, which stood for 20 years until it was exceeded by one run by **Gary Sobers**. He made 129 first-class centuries, and captained England in 23 Test matches after World War II.

Indurain, Miguel (1964–) Spanish cyclist, born Villava, Navarre. He is the fourth cyclist to win five Tours de France (1991–5), largely thanks to his invincibility in the Tour's time trials (see **Jacques Anquetil, Bernard Hinault** and **Eddy Merckx**). Retired 1997.

Johnson, Magic (Earvin) (1959–) US basketball player, born Lansing, Michigan. Played with the Los Angeles Lakers (1979–91 as a guard, 1996 as a forward), when they won five National Basketball Association (NBA) championships (1980, 1982, 1985, 1987–8), and in the 1992 gold medal-winning US Olympic basketball team ('Dream Team'). A member of the NBA All-Star team (1980, 1982–92), he was named NBA Most Valuable Player in 1987, 1989 and 1990.

Johnson, Michael (1967–) US track athlete, born Dallas. He won world championship races in the 200m (1991, 1995) and in the 400m (1993, 1995, 1997, 1999), and at the 1996 Olympics in Atlanta won gold medals in both 200m and 400m events, the first man ever to do so; he also set a new world 200m record.

Jones, Bobby (Robert Tyre) (1902–71) US amateur golfer, born Atlanta, Georgia. He won the US Open four times (1923, 1926, 1929, 1930), the British Open three times (1926, 1927, 1930), the US Amateur championship five times and the British Amateur championship once. In 1930 he won the Grand Slam of the US and British Open and Amateur championships. Later he was responsible for the founding of the US Masters in Augusta.

Jones, Marion (1975–) US athlete, born Los Angeles, California. Set new world record for 100m at 1997 world championships and at the 2000 Olympics won 3 golds and 2 bronzes, becoming the first female athlete to win 5 track and field medals at a single Olympics.

Jordan, Michael Jeffrey (1963–) US basketball player, born Brooklyn, New York City. Played for Chicago Bulls (1984–93, 1995–8), and set many records, including most consecutive seasons leading the league in scoring (1986–7 to 1992–3); also played in US Olympic gold medal-winning basketball teams (1984, 1992). As member of National Basketball Association (NBA) All-Star team (1985–93, 1996–8), was NBA Most Valuable Player in 1988, 1991, 1992, 1996 and 1998.

Kapil Dev, (Nihanj) (1959–) Indian cricketer, born Chandigarh, Punjab. Made first-class debut for Haryana aged 16, and played county cricket in England for Northamptonshire and Worcestershire. Led India to victory in the 1983 World Cup, and set a competition record score of 175 not out against Zimbabwe. In 1983 became youngest player (at 24 years 68 days) to perform a Test double of 2 000 runs and 200 wickets (surpassing **Ian Botham**). In Feb 1994 he set a new world record of 432 Test wickets, surpassing **Richard Hadlee**'s 431.

Karpov, Anatoliy Yevgenevich (1951–) Soviet chess player, born Zlatoust, in the Urals. Became world champion by default in 1975 after **Bobby Fischer** refused to defend his title; defeated 1985 by **Garry Kasparov**, but won title back 1993. He held the FIDE (Fédération Internationale des Échecs) world championship from 1994, but lost his title to Alexander Khalifman in 1999.

Kasparov, Garry Kimovich, originally **Gary Weinstein** (1963–) Soviet chess player, born Baku, Azerbaijan. He won the USSR under-18 championship aged 12 and became world junior champion at 16. He was world champion from 1985, when he defeated **Anatoliy Karpov**, until 1993, when Karpov won the title back. In 1994 he won the Professional Chess Association world championship, losing the title to Vladimir Kramnik in 2000.

Khan, Jahangir (1963–) Pakistani squash player, born Karachi. Winner of three world amateur titles (1979, 1983, 1985), a record six World Open titles (1981–5, 1988), and nine consecutive British Open titles (1982–90). He was undefeated from

Apr 1981 until the World Open final in Nov 1986.

Killy, Jean-Claude (1943–) French ski racer, born St-Cloud. Winner of the downhill and combined gold medals at the world championship in Chile (1966), and of three gold medals for slalom, giant slalom and downhill at the Winter Olympics (1968).

King, Billie Jean, née **Moffitt** (1943–) US tennis player, born Long Beach, California. She won the ladies doubles title at Wimbledon in 1961 (with Karen Hantze) at her first attempt, and between 1961 and 1979 won a record 20 Wimbledon titles, including the singles in 1966–8, 1972–3 and 1975, and four mixed doubles. She also won 13 US titles (including four singles in 1967, 1971–2, 1974), four French titles (one singles in 1972), and two Australian titles (one singles in 1968).

Klammer, Franz (1953–) Austrian alpine skier, born Mooswald. Olympic downhill champion (1976), and World Cup downhill champion five times (1975–78, 1983). Between 1974 and 1984 he won a record 25 World Cup downhill races.

Koch, Marita (1957–) German athlete, born Wismar. She won the Olympic 400m title in 1980 and the European title three times, remaining undefeated over 400m between 1977 and 1981. In the 200m race, she won three indoor European championship titles and a World Student Games title. She set 16 world records, including the 400m seven times (which still stands) and the 200m four times.

Korbut, Olga Valentinovna (1956–) Soviet gymnast, born Grodno, Belorussia. In the 1972 Olympic Games she won a gold medal as a member of the winning Soviet team, as well as individual golds in the beam and floor exercises and silver for the parallel bars.

Leonard, Sugar Ray (1956–) US boxer, born South Carolina. In 1976 he won an Olympic gold, starting a professional career in which he fought 12 world title fights at various weights and won world titles in each weight. In 35 fights (1977–87) he was beaten once (by Roberto Duran, welterweight title 1980). He became undisputed world welterweight champion again in 1981.

Lewis, Carl (1961–) US track and field athlete, born Birmingham, Alabama. He won four gold medals at the 1984 Olympics (100m, 200m, 4 × 100m relay and long jump), emulating **Jesse Owens**'s achievement of 1936. In 1988 he won an Olympic gold in the long jump and was awarded the 100m gold after Ben Johnson was stripped of the title. In 1992 he won two more Olympic golds in the long jump and the 4 × 100m relay, and in 1996 he earned his ninth and final Olympic gold medal in the long jump.

Louis, Joe, professional name of **Joseph Louis Barrow** (1914–81) US boxer, born Lexington, Alabama. He won the US amateur light-heavyweight title in 1934 and turned professional. He won the world championship in 1937, and held it for a record 12 years, defending his title 25 times. In all he won 68 of his 71 professional fights.

McBride, Willie (William) John (1940–) Irish rugby player, born Toomebridge, County Antrim. He played mostly with the Ballymena team from 1962. A lock forward, he won 45 caps, made a record 17 appearances for the British Lions on five tours, and played for Ireland 63 times.

McEnroe, John Patrick (1959–) US tennis player, born Wiesbaden, Germany. He won the Wimbledon singles title three times (1981, 1983–4), the US Open singles four times (1979–81, 1984), and eight Grand Slam doubles events, seven of them with Peter Fleming, and one at Wimbledon in 1992, with Michael Stich. He was Grand Prix winner in 1979 and 1984–5, and world championship winner in 1979, 1981 and 1983–4.

Maradona, Diego (1960–) Argentine footballer, born Lanús. One of the best players of his generation, he won over 80 international caps. He played in the 1982 World Cup in Spain, and captained the Argentine side to World Cup victory in 1986. He played for Boca Juniors, Barcelona, then Naples (1984–91), leading them to their first-ever Italian championship (1987). After leaving Naples, he played for Seville, Argentina and Boca Juniors again.

Marciano, Rocky, originally **Rocco Francis Marchegiano** (1923–69) US boxer, born Brockton, Massachusetts. Made his name in 1951 by defeating former world champion **Joe Louis** and won world title from Jersey Joe Walcott in 1952; on retiring in 1956 he was undefeated as world champion with a professional record of 49 bouts and 49 victories.

Matthews, Sir Stanley (1915–2000) English footballer, born Hanley. Joined Stoke City as a winger 1931, made debut for England aged 20, and over 22 years won 54 international caps. He played for Blackpool (1947–61), winning an FA Cup winner's medal in 1953, then returned to Stoke (1961), playing First Division football until after the age of 50. He was Footballer of the Year twice (1948, 1963), and the inaugural winner of the European Footballer of the Year award (1956).

Merckx, Eddy, known as **the Cannibal** (1945–) Belgian racing cyclist, born Woluwe St Pierre, near Brussels. In the 1969 Tour de France he won the major prize in all three sections — overall, points classification and King of the Mountains. He won the Tour de France five times (1969–72, 1974, now sharing the record with **Jacques Anquetil**, **Bernard Hinault** and **Miguel Indurain**); also won Tour of Italy five times, and all the major classics, including the Milan–San Remo race seven times. World professional road race champion three times, he won more races (445) and more classics than any other rider. Retired 1978.

Montana, Joe (1956–) US American football player, born New Eagle, Pennsylvania. Played as quarterback with San Francisco 49ers (1979–93), then Kansas City Chiefs (1993–5). Member of victorious San Francisco 49ers Super Bowl teams in 1982, 1985, 1989, and 1990; Most Valuable Player in 1982, 1985 and 1990.

Moore, Bobby (Robert) (1941–93) English footballer, born Barking, Essex. With West Ham (1958–74) and later Fulham (1974–7), he played 1 000 matches at senior level, winning an FA Cup winner's medal in 1964 and a European Cup-Winners' Cup medal in 1965. He was capped a record 108 times (107 in succession), 90 of them as captain. He played in the World Cup finals in Chile in 1962 and captained the victorious England side in the 1966 World Cup.

Moser-Proll, Annemarie, née **Proll** (1953–) Austrian alpine skier, born Kleinarl. Winner of a women's record 62 World Cup races (1970–9), she was overall champion (1979), downhill champion (1978, 1979), Olympic downhill champion (1980), world combined champion (1972, 1978), and world downhill champion (1974, 1978, 1980). Retired 1980.

Moses, Ed(win Corley) (1955–) US track athlete, born Dayton, Ohio. The greatest 400m hurdler

Sports and Games

ever, he was unbeaten from Aug 1977 to June 1987, was Olympic champion twice (1976, 1984) and four times world record holder. Missed 1980 Moscow Olympics due to US boycott.

Navratilova, Martina (1956–) US tennis player, born Prague, Czechoslovakia (Czech Republic). In 1975 she defected to the USA and turned professional. She won a record nine singles titles at Wimbledon (1978–9, 1982–7, 1990) and the US Open four times (1983–4, 1986–7). Her 100-plus tournament wins include two Golden Grand Slams. She retired from regular competitive singles play after reaching the Wimbledon final in 1994.

Nicklaus, Jack, known as **the Golden Bear** (1940–) US golfer, born Columbus, Ohio. His first professional victory was the US Open (1962), which he also won 1967, 1972 and 1980. Of the other Majors, he won the Masters a record six times (1963, 1965–6, 1972, 1975, 1986); the Open championship three times (1966, 1970, 1978); and the US Professional Golfers' Association (PGA) a record-equalling five times (1963, 1971, 1973, 1975, 1980). He also set a record total of 20 Major victories (including two US Amateurs pre-1962).

Nurmi, Paavo Johannes, known as **the Flying Finn** (1897–1973) Finnish athlete, born Turku. He won nine gold medals at three Olympic Games (1920, 1924, 1928). From 1922 to 1926 he set four world records at 3 000m, bringing the time down to 8 minutes 20.4 seconds. He also established world records at six miles (1921, 29:7.1), one mile (1923, 4:10.4) and two miles (1931, 8:59.5).

Oerter, Al(fred) (1936–) US athlete and discusthrower, born Astoria, New York State. An outstanding Olympic competitor, he won four consecutive gold medals for the discus, at Melbourne (1956), Rome (1960), Tokyo (1964) and Mexico (1968), breaking the Olympic record each time.

Owens, Jesse James Cleveland (1913–80) US athlete, born Danville, Alabama; considered the greatest sprinter of his generation. In 1935, while in Ohio State University team, he set three world records and equalled another, including the long jump (26ft 8$\frac{1}{4}$in/8.13m), which lasted 25 years. In 1936 he won four Olympic gold medals (100m, 200m, long jump, and 4 × 100m relay).

Palmer, Arnold (1929–) US golfer, born Youngstown, Pennsylvania. After a brilliant amateur career he turned professional 1955, but won only eight Majors: the US Amateur (1954), US Masters (1958, 1960, 1962, 1964), US Open (1960) and the Open championship (1961, 1962). He was twice captain of the American Ryder Cup team.

Payton, Walter, nicknamed **Sweetness** (1954–99) US American football player, born Columbia, Mississippi. He played with the Chicago Bears as a running back (1975–87), establishing a National Football League rushing record of 16 726 yards (15 294m), scoring 125 touchdowns, and winning the Super Bowl in 1986. In one game (1977) he rushed for a record 275 yards (251m).

Pelé, pseudonym of **Edson Arantes do Nascimento** (1940–) Brazilian footballer, born Três Corações, Minas Gerais. He made his international debut for Brazil aged 16, played in four World Cup competitions (1958–70), and led Brazil to victory in 1958, 1962 and 1970. For most of his senior career he played for Santos. Regarded as one of the finest inside-forwards in football history, he attained 1 000 goals in first-class football (Nov 1969); his career total was 1 281 in 1 363 games.

Perry, Fred(erick John) (1909–95) English tennis player, born Stockport, Cheshire. World singles

table tennis champion in 1929, he took up lawn tennis aged 19. He won the Wimbledon singles three times (1934–6), the US Open singles three times (1933–4, 1936), and the Australian (1934) and French (1935) championships, and helped to keep the Davis Cup in Great Britain for four years (1933–6). He was the first man to win all four major titles.

Piggott, Lester Keith (1935–) English jockey, born Wantage. Rode his first winner in 1948, was champion jockey in England on 11 occasions, and in all rode 30 Classic winners, including the Derby nine times. Retired 1995.

Player, Gary (1935–) South African golfer, born Johannesburg. He won the British Open three times (1959, 1968, 1974), the US Masters three times (1961, 1974, 1978), the US Open once (1965), and the US Professional Golfers' Association (PGA) title twice (1962, 1972). He also won the South African Open 13 times, and the Australian Open seven times.

Prost, Alain (1955–) French racing driver, born St Chamond. Won his first Grand Prix in 1981, was world champion four times (1985, 1986, 1989 and 1993), and Runner-Up four times (1983, 1984, 1988, 1990). Surpassed **Jackie Stewart**'s record of 27 Grand Prix wins in 1987, becoming the most successful driver in the history of the sport. Retired 1994.

Redgrave, Steve (Sir Steven Geoffrey) (1962–) English oarsman and sculler, born Marlow, Buckinghamshire. He has won five successive Olympic gold medals (coxed four 1984, coxless pairs 1988, 1992, 1996, coxless four 2000). Nine times world champion, he also won a record three gold medals in the 1986 Commonwealth Games. Together he and Matthew Pinsent (1970–) have been world coxless pairs champions (1991, 1993, 1994, 1995), world coxless four champions (1997, 1998, 1999), and Olympic champions (1992, 1996, 2000).

Ruth, Babe, properly **George Herman Ruth** (1895–1948) US baseball player, born Baltimore. Started career as a left-handed pitcher with the Boston Red Sox (1914–19), and became famous for his powerful hitting with the New York Yankees (1920–34); also played for Boston Braves (1935). Considered the greatest all-rounder in baseball history, he scored a record 60 home runs in 1927. In all he played in 10 World Series, and hit 714 home runs, a record that stood unsurpassed until **Hank Aaron** broke it in 1974.

Sampras, Pete (1971–) US tennis player, born Washington DC. Four times winner of the US Open singles title (1990, 1993, 1995–96) and seven times winner of All-England singles title at Wimbledon (1993–95, 1997–2000); with 13 Grand Slam Championships he is the game's most successful player.

Sella, Philippe (1962–) French rugby union player, born Clairac. First capped aged 20, he succeeded Serge Blanco in 1993–4 as the most capped international player of all time with a record 111 caps. During the period 1982–95 he scored 30 international test tries and was France's most capped centre.

Shoemaker, Willie (William Lee) (1931–) US jockey, born Fabens, Texas. In the USA his major successes included four Kentucky Derbies, five Belmont Stakes, and two Preakness event wins at Baltimore; later, he was successful in Europe too. In 1953 he rode a record 485 winners in a season. The first jockey to saddle more than 8 000 winners, he was one of the most successful in racing history and retired in 1990 with 8 833 wins.

Smetanina, Raisa Petrovna (1952–) Soviet cross-country skier, born Mokhcha. She won 23 medals between 1974 and 1992, including a record 10 Olympic skiing medals: four gold, five silver and one bronze.

Sobers, Gary, properly **Sir Garfield St Auburn Sobers** (1936–) West Indian cricketer, born Bridgetown, Barbados. In 93 Test matches for the West Indies (captain 1965–74), he scored more than 8 000 runs (including 26 centuries), and took 235 wickets and 110 catches. In county cricket he played for Nottinghamshire (captain 1968–74), and in 1968 scored the maximum of 36 runs (six sixes) off one over against Glamorgan at Swansea, a feat equalled by Ravi Shastri in the 1984–5 season.

Spitz, Mark (Andrew) (1950–) US swimmer, born Modesto, California. Winner of seven gold medals at the 1972 Olympics, achieving a world record time in each event, and of two golds in the 1968 Games. He set 26 world records between 1967 and 1972.

Stenmark, Ingemar (1956–) Swedish champion skier, born Tarnaby. In the 1974–5 World Cup he won the slalom and was second overall; he then won the World Cup (1976–8) and became the most successful competitor ever in slalom and grand slalom. He was World Master in 1978 and 1982 and won the Olympic gold medal at Lake Placid in 1980. The first man to win three consecutive slalom titles (1980–2), he won a record 86 World Cup races between 1974 and 1989, when he retired.

Stewart, Jackie (John Young) (1939–) Scottish racing driver, born Dunbartonshire, he won the Dutch, German and US Grand Prix in 1968. World champion in 1969, 1971 and 1973.

Thompson, Daley (Frances Morgan) (1958–) English athlete, born London. He won Olympic gold medals for decathlon (1980, 1984) and won the world championship (1983), also breaking the world record four times between 1980 and 1984. Retired 1992.

Tyson, Mike (Michael Gerald) (1966–) US boxer, born New York City. Professional from 1985, he knocked out 15 of his first 25 opponents in the first round. In 1986 he beat Trevor Berbick in the World Boxing Council (WBC) world heavyweight contest, becoming the youngest heavyweight champion (20 yrs 145 days). In 1987 he defeated James

Smith to gain the World Boxing Association title, and then beat Tony Tucker to become world champion. He held the title until defeated by James 'Buster' Douglas in Feb 1990. In 1996 he beat Frank Bruno to reclaim the WBC title, but later gave it up, and in 1997 was disqualified in his WBA world heavyweight fight against Evander Holyfield for biting his opponent's ear.

Underwood, Rory (1963–) English rugby union player, born Middlesbrough. He was England's most-capped player, and most-capped wing, with 85 caps from 1985 to 1996. Toured Australia (1989) and New Zealand (1993) with the British Lions. At club level he has represented Middlesbrough, Durham, Leicester, Newcastle, and Bedford.

Watson, Tom (Thomas Sturges) (1949–) US golfer, born Kansas City, Missouri. Through the mid-1970s and early 1980s he and **Jack Nicklaus** dominated world golf; Watson won the US Open, two Masters tournaments and five British Opens. He was the US Player of the Year six times and in 1993 captained the US Ryder Cup team to victory.

Woods, Tiger (1976–) US golfer, born Cypress, California. He became the first golfer to win the US junior amateur and US amateur titles, and retained his amateur title for a record three years in a row. Having turned professional in 1996, he became the first player to record five top-ten finishes in a row on the US Tour, and in 1997 became the youngest, as well as the first black winner of the US Masters. In 2000 he became only the second player to win three majors in a single year.

Zatopek, Emil (1922–2000) Czech athlete and middle-distance runner, born Moravia, Czechoslovakia (Czech Republic). He won an Olympic gold medal for the 10 000m in the 1948 Olympics and over the next six years broke 13 world records. In the 1952 Olympics he achieved a remarkable golden treble: he retained his gold medal in the 10 000m, and also won the 5 000m and the marathon.

Zurbriggen, Pirmin (1963–) Swiss skier, born Saas Almagell. Winner of a record number of victories in the downhill during the 1980s, and a total of 40 World Cup victories. In the 1987 World Cup at Crans-Montana he won two gold medals (giant slalom and super G) and two silver medals (downhill and combined) within five days, and in the 1988 Winter Olympics he won a gold in the downhill and a bronze in the giant slalom.

Champions 1985–2002

For 1992 Summer Olympic events the designation (UT) is given for members of the Unified Team (Armenia, Azerbaijan, Belarus, Georgia, Kazakhstan, Kyrgyzstan, Moldova, Russia, Tajikistan, Turkmenistan, Ukraine and Uzbekistan).

Angling

■ **World Fresh Water Championship**
First held in 1957; takes place annually.

Individual

1985	David Roper (England)
1986	Lud Wever (Holland)
1987	Clive Branson (Wales)
1988	Jean-Pierre Fouquet (France)
1989	Tom Pickering (England)
1990	Bob Nudd (England)
1991	Bob Nudd (England)
1992	David Wesson (Australia)
1993	Mario Barras (Portugal)
1994	Bob Nudd (England)
1995	Pierre Jean (France)
1996	Alan Scotthorne (England)
1997	Alan Scotthorne (England)
1998	Alan Scotthorne (England)
1999	Bob Nudd (England)
2000	Jacobo Falsini (Italy)
2001	Umberto Ballabeni (Italy)
2002	Juan Blasco (Spain)

Team

1985	England
1986	Italy
1987	England
1988	England
1989	Wales
1990	France

Sports and Games

1991	England
1992	Italy
1993	Italy
1994	England
1995	France
1996	Italy
1997	Italy
1998	England
1999	Spain
2000	Italy
2001	England
2002	Spain

■ World Fly Fishing Championship
First held in 1981; takes place annually.

Individual

1985	Leslaw Frasik (Poland)
1986	Slivoj Svoboda (Czechoslovakia)
1987	Brian Leadbetter (England)
1988	John Pawson (England)
1989	Wladyslaw Trzebuinia (Poland)
1990	Franciszek Szajnik (Poland)
1991	Brian Leadbetter (England)
1992	Pierluigi Cocito (Italy)
1993	Russell Owen (Wales)
1994	Pascal Cognard (France)
1995	Jeremy Herrmann (England)
1996	Pierluigi Cocito (Italy)
1997	Pascal Cognard (France)
1998	Tomas Starychfojtu (Czech Republic)
1999	Ross Stewart (Australia)
2000	Pascal Cognard (France)
2001	Vladimir Sedivy (Czech Republic)
2002	Jerome Brossutti (France)

Team

1985	Poland
1986	Italy
1987	England
1988	England
1989	Poland
1990	Czechoslovakia
1991	New Zealand
1992	Italy
1993	England
1994	Czech Republic
1995	England
1996	Czech Republic
1997	France
1998	Czech Republic
1999	Australia
2000	France
2001	France
2002	France

Archery

■ World Championships
First held in 1931; took place annually until 1959; since then, every two years.

Individual (Men)

1985	Richard McKinney (USA)
1987	Vladimir Yesheyev (USSR)
1989	Stanislav Zabrodsky (USSR)
1991	Simon Fairweather (Australia)
1993	Kyung-Mo Park (South Korea)
1995	Kyung-Chul Lee (South Korea)
1997	Kim Kyung-Ho (South Korea)

1999	Hong Sung-Chil (South Korea)
2001	Jung Ki Yeon (South Korea)

Team (Men)

1985	South Korea
1987	South Korea
1989	USSR
1991	South Korea
1993	France
1995	South Korea
1997	South Korea
1999	Italy
2001	South Korea

Individual (Women)

1985	Irina Soldatova (USSR)
1987	Ma Xiaojun (China)
1989	Kim Soo-Nyung (South Korea)
1991	Kim Soo-Nyung (South Korea)
1993	Kim Hyo-Jung (South Korea)
1995	Natalia Valeyeva (Moldova)
1997	Kim Du-Ri (South Korea)
1999	Lee Eun-Kyung (South Korea)
2001	Sung Hyun Park (South Korea)

Team (Women)

1985	USSR
1987	USSR
1989	South Korea
1991	South Korea
1993	South Korea
1995	South Korea
1997	South Korea
1999	Italy
2001	China

Athletics

■ World Championships
First held in Helsinki, Finland in 1983, then in Rome, Italy in 1987; since 1995 every two years.

Event (Men)	Winners
1995	
100m	Donovan Bailey (Canada)
200m	Michael Johnson (USA)
400m	Michael Johnson (USA)
800m	Wilson Kipketer (Denmark)
1500m	Noureddine Morceli (Algeria)
5000m	Ismael Kirui (Kenya)
10000m	Haile Gebrselassie (Ethiopia)
Marathon	Martin Fiz (Spain)3000m
steeplechase	Moses Kiptanui (Kenya)
110m hurdles	Allen Johnson (USA)
400m hurdles	Derrick Adkins (USA)
20km walk	Michele Didoni (Italy)
50km walk	Valentin Kononen (Finland)
4 × 100m relay	Canada
4 × 400m relay	USA
High jump	Troy Kemp (Bahamas)
Long jump	Ivan Pedroso (Cuba)
Triple jump	Jonathan Edwards (Great Britain)
Pole vault	Sergei Bubka (Ukraine)
Shot	John Godina (USA)
Discus	Lars Riedel (Germany)
Hammer	Andrei Abduvaliyev (Tajikistan)
Javelin	Jan Zelezny (Czech Republic)
Decathlon	Dan O'Brien (USA)

1997

100m	Maurice Greene (USA)
200m	Ato Boldon (Trinidad)
400m	Michael Johnson (USA)
800m	Wilson Kipketer (Denmark)
1500m	Hicham El Guerrouj (Morocco)
5000m	Daniel Komen (Kenya)
10000m	Haile Gebrselassie (Ethiopia)
Marathon	Abel Antón (Spain)
3000m steeplechase	Wilson Kipketer (Denmark)
110m hurdles	Allen Johnson (USA)
400m hurdles	Stephane Diagana (France)
20km walk	Daniel Garcia (Mexico)
50km walk	Robert Korzeniowski (Poland)
4 × 100m relay	Canada
4 × 400m relay	USA
High jump	Javier Sotomayor (Cuba)
Long jump	Ivan Pedroso (Cuba)
Triple jump	Yoelvis Quesada (Cuba)
Pole vault	Sergei Bubka (Ukraine)
Shot	Aleksandr Bagach[1] (Ukraine)
Discus	Lars Riedel (Germany)
Hammer	Heinz Weis (Germany)
Javelin	Marius Corbett (South Africa)
Decathlon	Tómas Dvorák (Czech Republic)

1999

100m	Maurice Greene (USA)
200m	Maurice Greene (USA)
400m	Michael Johnson (USA)
800m	Wilson Kipketer (Denmark)
1500m	Hicham El Guerrouj (Morocco)
5000m	Salah Hissou (Morocco)
10000m	Haile Gebreselassie (Ethiopia)
Marathon	Abel Antón (Spain)
3000m steeplechase	Christopher Koskei (Kenya)
110m hurdles	Colin Jackson (Great Britain)
400m hurdles	Fabrizio Mori (Italy)
20km walk	Ilya Markov (Russia)
50km walk	German Skurygin (Russia)
4 × 100m relay	USA
4 × 400m relay	USA
Long jump	Ivan Pedroso (Cuba)
High jump	Vyacheslav Voronin (Russia)
Triple jump	Charles Michael Friedek (Germany)
Pole vault	Maksim Tarasov (Russia)
Shot	C J Hunter (USA)
Discus	Anthony Washington (USA)
Hammer	Karsten Kobs (Germany)
Javelin	Aki Parviainen (Finland)
Decathlon	Tomás Dvorák (Czech Republic)

2001

100m	Maurice Greene (USA)
200m	Konstantinos Kederis (Greece)
400m	Avard Moncur (Bahamas)
800m	André Bucher (Switzerland)
1500m	Hicham El Guerrouj (Morocco)
5000m	Richard Limo (Kenya)
10000m	Charles Kamathi (Kenya)
Marathon	Gezahegne Abera (Ethiopia)
3000m steeplechase	Reuben Kosgei (Kenya)
110m hurdles	Allen Johnson (USA)
400m hurdles	Felix Sanchez (Dominican Republic)
20km walk	Roman Rasskazov (Russia)
50km walk	Robert Korzeniowski (Poland)

4 × 100m relay	USA
4 × 400m relay	Jamaica
High jump	Buss Martin (Germany)
Long jump	Ivan Pedroso (Cuba)
Triple jump	Jonathan Edwards (Great Britain)
Pole vault	Dmitry Markov (Russia)
Shot	John Godina (USA)
Discus	Lars Riedel (Germany)
Hammer	Szymon Ziólkowski (Poland)
Javelin	Jan Zelezný (Czech Republic)
Decathlon	Tomás Dvorák (Czech Republic)

[1] Stripped of gold medal following positive drugs test; medal awarded to John Godina (USA).

Event (Women)	Winners

1995

100m	Gwen Torrence (USA)
200m	Merlene Ottey (Jamaica)
400m	Marie-José Pérec (France)
800m	Ann Quirot (Cuba)
1500m	Hassiba Boulmerka (Algeria)
5000m	Sonia O'Sullivan (Ireland)
10000m	Fernanda Ribeiro (Portugal)
Marathon	Manuela Machado (Portugal)
100m hurdles	Gail Devers (USA)
400m hurdles	Kim Batten (USA)
10km walk	Irina Stankina (Russia)
4 × 100m relay	USA
4 × 400m relay	USA
High jump	Stefka Kostadinova (Bulgaria)
Long jump	Fiona May (Italy)
Shot	Astrid Kumbernuss (Germany)
Discus	Ellina Zvereva (Belarus)
Javelin	Natalya Shikolenko (Belarus)
Heptathlon	Natalya Shikolenko (Belarus)

1997

100m	Marion Jones (USA)
200m	Zhanna Pintussevich (Ukraine)
400m	Cathy Freeman (Australia)
800m	Ana Fidelia Quirot (Cuba)
1500m	Carla Sacramento (Portugal)
5000m	Gabriela Szabo (Romania)
10000m	Sally Barsosio (Kenya)
Marathon	Hiromi Suzuki (Japan)
100m hurdles	Ludmila Engquist (Sweden)
400m hurdles	Nezha Bidouane (Morocco)
10km walk	Annarita Sidoti (Italy)
4 × 100m relay	USA
4 × 400m relay	Germany
High jump	Hanne Haugland (Norway)
Long jump	Lyudmila Galkina (Russia)
Triple jump	Sarka Kasparkova (Czech Republic)
Shot put	Astrid Kumbernuss (Germany)
Discus	Beatrice Faumuina (New Zealand)
Javelin	Trine Hattestad (Norway)
Heptathlon	Sabina Braun (Germany)

1999

100m	Marion Jones (USA)
200m	Inger Miller (USA)
400m	Cathy Freeman (Australia)
800m	Ludmilla Formanova (Czech Republic)
1500m	Svetlana Masterkova (Russia)
5000m	Gabriela Szabo (Romania)
10000m	Gete Wami (Ethiopia)
Marathon	Jong Song-Ok (North Korea)
100m hurdles	Gail Devers (USA)
400m hurdles	Daimi Pernia (Cuba)

Sports and Games

20km walk	Liu Hongyu (China)
4 × 100m relay	Bahamas
4 × 400m relay	Russia
High jump	Inga Babakova (Ukraine)
Long jump	Niurka Montalvo (Spain)
Triple jump	Paraskevi Tsiamita (Greece)
Pole vault	Stacy Draglia (USA)
Shot	Astrid Kumbernuss (Germany)
Discus	Franka Dietzsch (Germany)
Hammer	Michaela Melinte (Romania)
Javelin	Mirela Manjani-Tzelili (Greece)
Heptathlon	Eunice Barber (France)

2001

100m	Zhanna Pintusevich-Block (Ukraine)
200m	Marion Jones (USA)
400m	Amy Mbacke Thiam (Senegal)
800m	Maria Mutola (Mozambique)
1500m	Gabriela Szabo (Romania)
5000m	Olga Yegorova (Russia)
10000m	Derartu Tulu (Ethiopia)
Marathon	Lidia Simon (Romania)
100m hurdles	Anjanette Kirkland (USA)
400m hurdles	Nezha Bidouane (Morocco)
20km walk	Olimpiada Ivanova (Russia)
4 × 100m relay	USA
4 × 400m relay	USA
High jump	Hestrie Cloete (South Africa)
Triple jump	Tatyana Lebedeva (Russia)
Long jump	Fiona May (Italy)
Shot	Yanina Korolchik (Belarus)
Discus	Natalya Sadova (Russia)
Javelin	Osleidys Menéndez (Cuba)
Pole vault	Stacy Dragila (USA)
Hammer	Yipsi Moreno (Cuba)
Heptathlon	Yelena Prokhorova (Russia)

Badminton

▪ World Championships

First held in 1977; initially took place every three years; since 1983 every two years.

Men

1985	Han Jian (China)
1987	Yang Yang (China)
1989	Yang Yang (China)
1991	Zhao Jianhua (China)
1993	Joko Suprianto (Indonesia)
1995	Heryanto Arbi (Indonesia)
1997	Peter Rasmussen (Denmark)
1999	Sun Jun (China)
2001	Hendra Wan (Indonesia)

Women

1985	Han Aiping (China)
1987	Han Aiping (China)
1989	Li Lingwei (China)
1991	Tang Jiuhong (China)
1993	Susi Susanti (Indonesia)
1995	Ye Zhaoying (China)
1997	Ye Zhaoying (China)
1999	Camilla Martin (Denmark)
2001	Gong Ruina (China)

▪ Thomas Cup

An international team event for men's teams; inaugurated 1949, now held every two years.

1986	China
1988	China
1990	China
1992	Malaysia
1994	Indonesia
1996	Indonesia
1998	Indonesia
2000	Indonesia
2002	Indonesia

▪ Uber Cup

An international event for women's teams; first held in 1957; now held every two years.

1986	China
1988	China
1990	China
1992	China
1994	Indonesia
1996	Indonesia
1998	China
2000	China
2002	China

▪ All-England Championship

Badminton's premier event prior to the inauguration of the World Championships; first held in 1899.

Men

1985	Zhao Jianhua (China)
1986	Morten Frost (Denmark)
1987	Morten Frost (Denmark)
1988	Ib Frederikson (Denmark)
1989	Yang Yang (China)
1990	Zhao Jianhua (China)
1991	Ardi Wiranata (Indonesia)
1992	Liu Jun (China)
1993	Heryanto Arbi (Indonesia)
1994	Heryanto Arbi (Indonesia)
1995	Poul-Erik Hoyer-Larsen (Denmark)
1996	Poul-Erik Hoyer-Larsen (Denmark)
1997	Dong Jiong (China)
1998	Sun Jun (China)
1999	Peter Gade Christensen (Denmark)
2000	Xia Xuanze (China)
2001	Pulella Gopichand (India)
2002	Chen Hong (China)

Women

1985	Han Aiping (China)
1986	Yun-Ja Kim (Korea)
1987	Kirsten Larsen (Denmark)
1988	Gu Jiaming (China)
1989	Li Lingwei (China)
1990	Susi Susanti (Indonesia)
1991	Susi Susanti (Indonesia)
1992	Tang Jiuhong (China)
1993	Susi Susanti (Indonesia)
1994	Susi Susanti (Indonesia)
1995	Lim Xiao Qing (Sweden)
1996	Bang Soo Hyun (South Korea)
1997	Ye Zhaoying (China)
1998	Ye Zhaoying (China)
1999	Ye Zhaoying (China)
2000	Zichao Gong (China)
2001	Zichao Gong (China)
2002	Camilla Martin (Denmark)

Baseball

▪ World Series

First held in 1903; takes place each October, the best of seven matches; professional baseball's

Baseball field

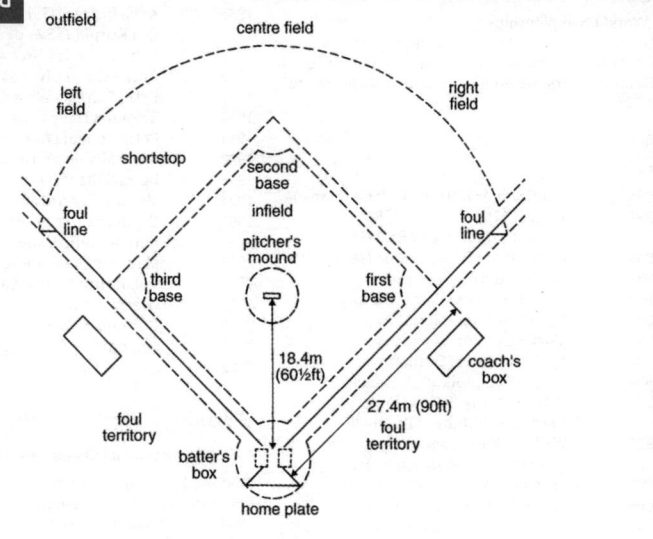

leading event, the end-of-season meeting between the winners of the two major baseball leagues in the USA, the National League (NL) and American League (AL).

1985	Kansas City Royals (AL)
1986	New York Mets (NL)
1987	Minnesota Twins (AL)
1988	Los Angeles Dodgers (NL)
1989	Oakland Athletics (AL)
1990	Cincinatti Reds (NL)
1991	Minnesota Twins (AL)
1992	Toronto Blue Jays (AL)
1993	Toronto Blue Jays (AL)
1994	*not held*
1995	Atlanta Braves (NL)
1996	New York Yankees (AL)
1997	Florida Marlins (NL)
1998	New York Yankees (AL)
1999	New York Yankees (AL)
2000	New York Yankees (AL)
2001	Arizona Diamondbacks (NL)
2002	Anaheim Angels (AL)

■ World Cup
Instituted in 1938; since 1990 held every four years.

1986	Cuba
1988	Cuba
1990	Cuba
1994	Cuba
1998	Cuba
2001	Cuba

Basketball

■ World Championship
First held 1950 for men, 1953 for women; takes place approximately every four years.

Men

1986	USA
1990	Yugoslavia
1994	USA
1998	Yugoslavia
2002	Yugoslavia

Women

1987	USA
1991	USA
1994	Brazil
1998	USA
2002	USA

■ National Basketball Association Championship
First held in 1947; the major competition in professional basketball in the USA, end-of-season NBA Play-off involving the champion teams from the Eastern (EC) Conference and Western Conference (WC).

1985	Los Angeles Lakers (WC)
1986	Boston Celtics (EC)
1987	Los Angeles Lakers (WC)
1988	Los Angeles Lakers (WC)
1989	Detroit Pistons (EC)
1990	Detroit Pistons (EC)
1991	Chicago Bulls (EC)
1992	Chicago Bulls (EC)
1993	Chicago Bulls (EC)
1994	Houston Rockets (WC)
1995	Houston Rockets (WC)
1996	Chicago Bulls (EC)
1997	Chicago Bulls (EC)
1998	Chicago Bulls (EC)
1999	San Antonio Spurs (WC)
2000	Los Angeles Lakers (WC)
2001	Los Angeles Lakers (WC)
2002	Los Angeles Lakers (WC)

Sports and Games

Biathlon

■ **World Championships**
First held in 1958; take place annually; the Olympic champion is the automatic world champion in Olympic years; women's championship first held in 1984.

Men

10km

1985	Frank-Peter Rötsch (East Germany)
1986	Valeriy Medvetsev (USSR)
1987	Frank-Peter Rötsch (East Germany)
1988	Frank-Peter Rötsch (East Germany)
1989	Frank Luck (East Germany)
1990	Mark Kirchner (East Germany)
1991	Mark Kirchner (Germany)
1992	Mark Kirchner (Germany)
1993	Mark Kirchner (Germany)
1994	Serguei Tchepikov (Russia)
1995	Patrice Bailly-Salins (France)
1996	Vladimir Dratchev (Russia)
1997	Wilfried Pallhuber (Italy)
1998	Ole Einar Bjoerndalen Norway)
1999	Frank Luck (Germany)
2000	Frode Andresen (Norway)
2001	Paul Rostovtsev (Russia)
2002	Ole Einar Bjoerndalen (Norway)

20km

1985	Yuriy Kashkarov (USSR)
1986	Valeriy Medvetsev (USSR)
1987	Frank-Peter Rötsch (East Germany)
1988	Frank-Peter Rötsch (East Germany)
1989	Eiric Kvalfoss (Norway)
1990	Valeriy Medvetsev (USSR)
1991	Mark Kirchner (Germany)
1992	Yevgeny Redkine (CIS)
1993	Franz Zingerle (Austria)
1994	Sergei Tarasov (Russia)
1995	Tomaz Sikora (Poland)
1996	Sergei Tarasov (Russia)
1997	Ricco Gross (Germany)
1998	Halvard Hanevold (Norway)
1999	Ricco Gross (Germany)
2000	Wolfgang Rottman (Austria)
2001	Paavo Puurunen (Finland)
2002	Ole Einar Bjoerndalen (Norway)

Women

7.5km

1985	Sanna Gronlid (Norway)
1986	Kaya Parva (USSR)
1987	Yelena Golovina (USSR)
1988	Petra Schaaf (West Germany)
1989	Anne-Elinor Elvebakk (Norway)
1990	Anne-Elinor Elvebakk (Norway)
1991	Ingeborg Nykelmo (Norway)
1992	Anfissa Restzova (CIS)
1993	Myriam Bedard (Canada)
1994	Myriam Bedard (Canada)
1995	Anne Briand (France)
1996	Olga Romansko (Russia)
1997	Olga Romansko (Russia)
1998	Galina Koukleva (Russia)
1999	Martina Zellner (Germany)
2000	Liv Grete Skjelbreid (Norway)
2001	Kati Wilhelm (Germany)
2002	Kati Wilhelm (Germany)

15km

1985	Kaya Parva (USSR)
1986	Eva Korpela (Sweden)
1987	Sanna Gronlid (Norway)
1988	Anne-Elinor Elvebakk (Norway)
1989	Petra Schaaf (West Germany)
1990	Svetlana Davydova (USSR)
1991	Petra Schaaf (Germany)
1992	Antje Misersky (Germany)
1993	Petra Schaaf (Germany)
1994	Myriam Bedard (Canada)
1995	Corinne Niogret (France)
1996	Emmanuelle Claret (France)
1997	Magdalena Forsberg (Sweden)
1998	Yekaterina Dafovska (Bulgaria)
1999	Olena Zubrilova (Ukraine)
2000	Corinne Niogret (France)
2001	Magdalena Forsberg (Sweden)
2002	Andrea Henkel (Germany)

Billiards

■ **World Professional Championship**

First held in 1870, organized on a challenge basis; became a knockout event in 1909; discontinued in 1934; revived in 1951 as a challenge system; reverted to a knockout event in 1980.

1985	Ray Edmonds (England)
1986	Robbie Foldvari (Australia)
1987	Norman Dagley (England)
1988	Norman Dagley (England)
1989	Mike Russell (England)
1990	*not held*
1991	Mike Russell (England)
1992	Geet Sethi (India)
1993	Geet Sethi (India)
1994	Peter Gilchrist (England)
1995	Geet Sethi (India)
1996	Mike Russell (England)
1997	*not held*
1998	Geet Sethi (India)
1999	Mike Russell (England)
2000	Mike Russell (England)
2001	Peter Gilchrest (England)
2002	Mike Russell (England)

Bobsleighing and tobogganing

■ **World Championships**
First held in 1930 (four-man) and in 1931 (two-man); Olympic champions automatically become world champions.

Two-man

1985	Wolfgang Hoppe/Dietmar Schauerhammer (East Germany)
1986	Wolfgang Hoppe/Dietmar Schauerhammer (East Germany)
1987	Ralf Pichler/Celest Poltera (Switzerland)
1988	Janis Kipurs/Vladimir Kozlov (USSR)
1989	Wolfgang Hoppe/Bogdan Musiol (East Germany)
1990	Gustav Weder/Bruno Gerber (Switzerland)
1991	Rudi Lochner/Markus Zimmermann (Germany)
1992	Gustav Weder/Donat Acklin (Switzerland)

1993	Christoph Langen/Peer Joechel (Germany)
1994	Gustav Weder/Donat Acklin (Switzerland)
1995	Christoph Langen/Olaf Hampel (Germany)
1996	Christoph Langen/Markus Zimmermann (Germany)
1997	Reto Goetschi/Guido Acklin (Switzerland)
1998	Guenther Huber/Antonio Tartaglia (Italy)
1999	Guenther Huber/Ubaldo Ranzi (Italy)
2000	Christoph Langen/Markus Zimmermann (Germany)
2001	Christoph Langan/Marco Jacobs (Germany)
2002	Christoph Langan/Markus Zimmermann (Germany)

Four-man

1985	East Germany
1986	Switzerland
1987	Switzerland
1988	Switzerland
1989	Switzerland
1990	Switzerland
1991	Germany
1992	Austria
1993	Switzerland
1994	Germany
1995	Germany
1996	Germany
1997	Germany
1998	Germany
1999	France
2000	Germany
2001	Germany
2002	Germany

■ Luge World Championships

First held in 1955; annually until 1981, then every two years until 1989, then annually. Not held in Olympic years.

Men's single-seater

1985	Michael Walter (East Germany)
1987	Markus Prock (Austria)
1989	Georg Hackl (West Germany)
1990	Georg Hackl (West Germany)
1991	Arnold Huber (Italy)
1993	Werdel Suckow (USA)
1995	Armin Zoeggeler (Italy)
1996	Jana Bode (Germany)
1997	Georg Hackl (Germany)
1999	Armin Zoeggeler (Italy)
2000	Jens Müller (Germany)
2001	Armin Zoeggeler (Italy)

Women's single-seater

1985	Steffi Martin (East Germany)
1987	Cerstin Schmidt (East Germany)
1988	Susi Erdmann (East Germany)
1989	Susi Erdmann (East Germany)
1990	Gabriele Kohlisch (East Germany)
1993	Gerda Weissensteiner (Italy)
1995	Gabriele Kohlisch (Germany)
1996	Susi Erdmann (Germany)
1997	Susi Erdmann (Germany)
1999	Sonja Wiedemann (Germany)

| 2000 | Sylke Otto (Germany) |
| 2001 | Sylke Otto (Germany) |

Bowls

■ World Outdoor Championships

Instituted for men in 1966 and for women in 1969; held every four years.

Men's Singles

1988	David Bryant (England)
1992	Tony Allcock (England)
1996	Tony Allcock (England)
2000	Jeremy Henry (Ireland)

Men's Pairs

1988	New Zealand
1992	Scotland
1996	Ireland
2000	Scotland

Men's Triples

1988	New Zealand
1992	Israel
1996	Scotland
2000	New Zealand

Men's Fours

1988	Ireland
1992	Scotland
1996	England
2000	Wales

■ Leonard Trophy

Team award, given to the nation with the best overall performances in the men's world championship.

1988	England
1992	Scotland
1996	Scotland
2000	Australia

Women's Singles

1985	Merle Richardson (Australia)
1988[1]	Janet Ackland (Wales)
1992	Margaret Johnston (Ireland)
1996	Carmen Anderson (Norfolk Is)
2000	Margaret Johnston (Ireland)

Women's Pairs

1985	Australia
1988[1]	Ireland
1992	Ireland
1996	Ireland
2000	Scotland

Women's Triples

1985	Hong Kong
1988[1]	Australia
1992	Scotland
1996	South Africa
2000	New Zealand

Women's Fours

1985	Scotland
1988[1]	Australia
1992	Scotland

Sports and Games

| 1996 | Australia |
| 2000 | New Zealand |

Women's Team

1985	Australia
1988[1]	England
1992	Scotland
1996	South Africa
2000	England

[1]The women's event was advanced to Dec 1988 (Australia).

■ **World Indoor Championships**
First held in 1979; take place annually.

Men's singles

1985	Terry Sullivan (Wales)
1986	Tony Allcock (England)
1987	Tony Allcock (England)
1988	Hugh Duff (Scotland)
1989	Richard Corsie (Scotland)
1990	John Price (Wales)
1991	Richard Corsie (Scotland)
1992	Ian Schuback (Australia)
1993	Richard Corsie (Scotland)
1994	Andy Thomson (England)
1995	Andy Thomson (England)
1996	David Gourlay, Jr (Scotland)
1997	Hugh Duff (Scotland)
1998	Paul Foster (Scotland)
1999	Alex Marshall (Scotland)
2000	Robert Weale (Wales)
2001	Darren Burnett (Scotland)
2002	Tony Allcock (England)

■ **Waterloo Handicap**
First held in 1907 and annually at Blackpool's Waterloo Hotel; the premier event of Crown Green Bowling.

1985	Tommy Johnstone
1986	Brian Duncan
1987	Brian Duncan
1988	Ingham Gregory
1989	Brian Duncan
1990	John Bancroft
1991	John Eccles
1992	Brian Duncan
1993	Alan Broadhurst
1994	Bill Hilton
1995	Ken Strutt
1996	Lee Heaton
1997	Andrew Cairns
1998	Michael Jagger
1999	Ivan Smout
2000	Carl Armitage
2001	Glynn Cookson
2002	Stan Frith

Boxing

■ **World Heavyweight Champions**
The first world heavyweight champion under Queensbury Rules with gloves was James J Corbett in 1892.

		Recognizing Body
1985	Michael Spinks (USA)	IBF
1985	Tony Tubbs (USA)	WBA
1986	Tim Witherspoon (USA)	WBA
1986	Trevor Berbick (Canada)	WBC
1986	Mike Tyson (USA)	WBC

1986	James Smith (USA)	WBA
1987	Tony Tucker (USA)	IBF
1987	Mike Tyson (USA)	WBA/WBC
1987	Mike Tyson (USA)	UND
1989	Francesco Damiani (Italy)	WBO
1990	James (Buster) Douglas (USA)	WBA/WBC/IBF
1990	Evander Holyfield (USA)	WBA/WBC/IBF
1991	Ray Mercer (USA)	WBO
1992	Riddick Bowe (USA)[1]	WBA/WBC/IBF
1992	Michael Moorer (USA)	WBO
1993	Evander Holyfield (USA)	WBA/IBF
1993	Lennox Lewis (UK)	WBC
1993	Tommy Morrison (USA)	WBO
1993	Michael Bentt (USA)	WBO
1994	Herbie Hide (UK)	WBO
1994	Michael Moorer (USA)	WBA/IBF
1994	Oliver McCall (USA)	WBC
1994	George Foreman (USA)[2][3]	WBA/IBF
1995	Riddick Bowe (USA)	WBO
1995	Bruce Seldon (USA)	WBA
1995	Frank Bruno (UK)	WBC
1995	Frans Botha (South Africa)[4]	IBF
1996	Mike Tyson (USA)[5]	WBA/WBC
1996	Henry Akinwande (UK)	WBO
1996	Michael Moorer (USA)	IBF
1996	Evander Holyfield (USA)	WBA
1997	Evander Holyfield (USA)	WBA/IBF
1997	Lennox Lewis (UK)	WBC
1997	Herbie Hide (UK)	WBO
1999	Vitali Klitschko (Ukraine)	WBO
1999	Lennox Lewis (UK)[6]	UND (WBA/WBC/IBF)
2000	Chris Byrd (USA)	WBO
2000	Evander Holyfield (USA)	WBA
2000	Lennox Lewis (UK)	WBC, IBF
2001	John Ruiz (USA)	WBA
2001	Wladimir Klitschko (Ukraine)	WBO
2001	Hashim Rahman (USA)	WBC, IBF
2001	Lennox Lewis (UK)[7]	WBC, IBF
2001	John Ruiz (USA)	WBA

[1] stripped of WBC title in 1992;

[2] gave up IBF title in 1995;

[3] stripped of WBA title in 1995;

[4] stripped of IBF title in 1996;

[5] gave up WBC title in 1996;

[6] stripped of WBA title in 2000;

[7] gave up IBF title in 2002;

UND = Undisputed Champion; WBC = World Boxing Council; WBA = World Boxing Association; IBF = International Boxing Federation; WBO = World Boxing Organization.

Canoeing

■ **Olympic Games**
The most prestigious competition in the canoeing calendar, included at every Olympic celebration since 1936; the Blue Riband event in the men's competition is the Kayak Singles over 1 000 metres, and in the women's the Kayak Singles over 500 metres.

Single kayak (Men)

| 1988 | Greg Barton (USA) |
| 1992 | Clint Robinson (Australia) |

| 1996 | Knut Holman (Norway) |
| 2000 | Knut Holman (Norway) |

Single kayak (Women)

1988	Vania Guecheva (USSR)
1992	Birgit Schmidt (Germany)
1996	Rita Koban (Hungary)
2000	Josefa Guerrini (Italy)

Chess

▪ World Champions (FIDE)
World Champions have been recognized since 1886. The first international tournament was held in London in 1851, and won by Adolf Anderssen (Germany); first women's champion recognized in 1927.

Men

1985–93	Gary Kasparov (USSR)
1993–8	Anatoliy Karpov (Russia)
1999–2000	Alexander Khalifman (Russia)
2000	Vishwanathan Anand (India)
2001–2	Ruslan Ponomariov (Ukraine)

Women

1978–91	Maya Chiburdanidze (USSR)
1991–6	Xie Jun (China)
1996–8	Zsuzsa Polgar (Hungary)
1999–2000	Xie Jun (China)
2001–2	Zhu Chen (China)

Contract bridge

▪ World Team Championship
The game's biggest championship; men's contest (The Bermuda Bowl) first held in 1950, and now takes place every two years, with the exception of 1999; women's contest (The Venice Cup) first held in 1974, and since 1985 has been concurrent with the men's event.

Men

1985	USA
1987	USA
1989	Brazil
1991	Iceland
1993	Netherlands
1995	USA
1997	France
2000	USA
2001	USA II

Women

1985	UK
1987	Italy
1989	USA
1991	USA
1993	USA
1995	Germany
1997	USA
2000	Netherlands
2001	Germany

▪ World Team Olympiad
First held in 1960; since then, every four years.

Men

| 1988 | USA |
| 1992 | France |

| 1996 | France |
| 2000 | Italy |

Women

1988	Denmark
1992	Austria
1996	USA
2000	USA

Cricket

▪ World Cup
First played in England in 1975; usually held every four years; the 1987 competition, held in India and Pakistan, was the first to be played outside England.

1987	Australia
1992	Pakistan
1996	Sri Lanka
1999	Australia

▪ County Championship
The oldest cricket competition in the world; first won by Sussex in 1827; not officially recognized until 1890, when a proper points system was introduced.

1985	Middlesex
1986	Essex
1987	Nottinghamshire
1988	Worcestershire
1989	Worcestershire
1990	Middlesex
1991	Essex
1992	Essex
1993	Middlesex
1994	Warwickshire
1995	Warwickshire
1996	Leicestershire
1997	Glamorgan
1998	Leicestershire
1999	Surrey
2000	Surrey
2001	Yorkshire
2002	Surrey

▪ Norwich Union League
First held in 1969; known as the John Player League until 1987, the Refuge Assurance League until 1991, the Axa Equity and Law League until 1999 and the CGU League until 2000.

1985	Essex
1986	Hampshire
1987	Worcestershire
1988	Worcestershire
1989	Lancashire
1990	Derbyshire
1991	Nottinghamshire
1992	Middlesex
1993	Glamorgan
1994	Warwickshire
1995	Kent
1996	Surrey
1997	Warwickshire

Sports and Games

1998	Lancashire
1999	Lancashire
2000	Gloucestershire
2001	Kent
2002	Glamorgan

■ Cheltenham & Gloucester Trophy

First held in 1963; known as the Gillette Cup until 1981 and the NatWest Bank Trophy until 2000.

1985	Essex
1986	Sussex
1987	Nottinghamshire
1988	Middlesex
1989	Warwickshire
1990	Lancashire
1991	Hampshire
1992	Northamptonshire
1993	Warwickshire
1994	Worcestershire
1995	Warwickshire
1996	Lancashire
1997	Essex
1998	Lancashire
1999	Gloucestershire
2000	Gloucestershire
2001	Somerset
2002	Yorkshire

■ Benson and Hedges Cup

First held in 1972.

1985	Leicestershire
1986	Middlesex
1987	Yorkshire
1988	Hampshire
1989	Nottinghamshire
1990	Lancashire
1991	Worcestershire
1992	Hampshire
1993	Derbyshire

1994	Warwickshire
1995	Lancashire
1996	Lancashire
1997	Surrey
1998	Essex
1999	Gloucestershire
2000	Gloucestershire
2001	Surrey
2002	Warwickshire

■ Pura Milk Cup

Australia's leading domestic competition; contested inter-state since 1891–2; known as the Sheffield Shield until 1999.

1985	New South Wales
1986	New South Wales
1987	Western Australia
1988	Western Australia
1989	Western Australia
1990	New South Wales
1991	Victoria
1992	Western Australia
1993	New South Wales
1994	New South Wales
1995	Queensland
1996	South Australia
1997	Queensland
1998	Western Australia
1999	Western Australia
2000	Queensland
2001	Queensland
2002	Queensland

Croquet

■ MacRobertson Shield

Croquet's leading tournament; held spasmodically since 1925; contested by teams from Great Britain, New Zealand, Australia and, since 1993, the USA.

Cricket field positions

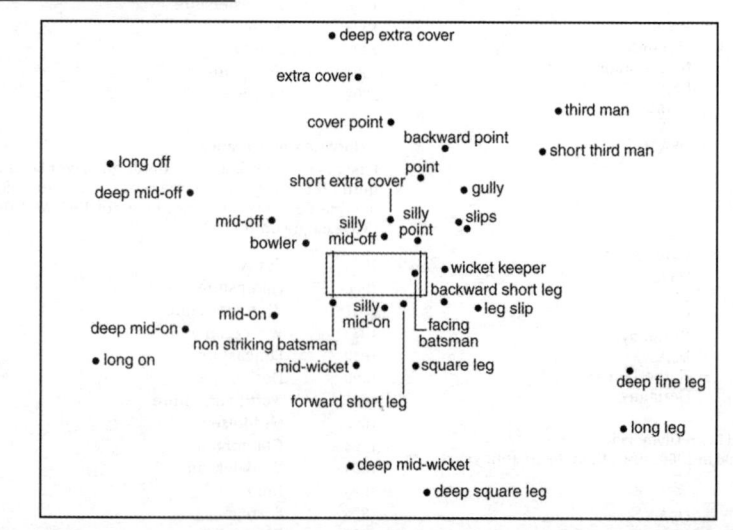

1986	New Zealand
1990	Great Britain
1993	Great Britain
1996	Great Britain
2000	Great Britain

Cross country running

■ **World Championships**

First international championship held in 1903, but only included runners from England, Ireland, Scotland and Wales; recognized as an official world championship from 1973; first women's race in 1967.

Individual (Men)

1985	Carlos Lopes (Portugal)
1986	John Ngugi (Kenya)
1987	John Ngugi (Kenya)
1988	John Ngugi (Kenya)
1989	John Ngugi (Kenya)
1990	Khalid Skah (Morocco)
1991	Khalid Skah (Morocco)
1992	John Ngugi (Kenya)
1993	William Sigei (Kenya)
1994	William Sigei (Kenya)
1995	Paul Tergat (Kenya)
1996	Paul Tergat (Kenya)
1997	Paul Tergat (Kenya)
1998	Paul Tergat (Kenya)
1999	Paul Tergat (Kenya)
2000	Mohammed Mourhit (Belgium)
2001	Mohammed Mourhit (Belgium)
2002	Kenenisa Bekele (Ethiopia)

Team (Men)

1985	Ethiopia
1986	Kenya
1987	Kenya
1988	Kenya
1989	Kenya
1990	Kenya
1991	Kenya
1992	Kenya
1993	Kenya
1994	Kenya
1995	Kenya
1996	Kenya
1997	Kenya
1998	Kenya
1999	Kenya
2000	Kenya
2001	Kenya
2002	Kenya

Individual (Women)

1985	Zola Budd (England)
1986	Zola Budd (England)
1987	Annette Sergent (France)
1988	Ingrid Kristiansen (Norway)
1989	Annette Sergent (France)
1990	Lynn Jennings (USA)
1991	Lynn Jennings (USA)
1992	Lynn Jennings (USA)
1993	Albertina Dias (Portugal)
1994	Helen Chepngeno (Kenya)
1995	Derartu Tulu (Ethiopia)
1996	Gete Wami (Ethiopia)
1997	Derartu Tulu (Ethiopia)
1998	Sonia O'Sullivan (Ireland)
1999	Gete Wami (Ethiopia)
2000	Derartu Tulu (Ethiopia)
2001	Paula Radcliffe (England)
2002	Paula Radcliffe (England)

Team (Women)

1985	USA
1986	England
1987	USA
1988	USSR
1989	USSR
1990	USSR
1991	Ethiopia and Kenya (shared)
1992	Kenya
1993	Kenya
1994	Portugal
1995	Kenya
1996	Kenya
1997	Ethiopia
1998	Kenya
1999	France
2000	Ethiopia
2001	Kenya
2002	Kenya

Curling

■ **World Championships**

First men's championship held in 1959; first women's championship in 1979; takes place annually.

Men

1985	Canada
1986	Canada
1987	Canada
1988	Norway
1989	Canada
1990	Canada
1991	Scotland
1992	Switzerland
1993	Canada
1994	Canada
1995	Canada
1996	Canada
1997	Sweden
1998	Canada
1999	Scotland
2000	Canada
2001	Sweden
2002	Canada

Women

1985	Canada
1986	Canada
1987	Canada
1988	West Germany
1989	Canada
1990	Norway
1991	Norway
1992	Sweden
1993	Canada
1994	Canada
1995	Sweden
1996	Canada
1997	Canada
1998	Sweden
1999	Sweden
2000	Canada
2001	Canada
2002	Scotland

Cycling

■ Tour de France
World's premier cycling event; first held in 1903.

1985	Bernard Hinault (France)
1986	Greg LeMond (USA)
1987	Stephen Roche (Ireland)
1988	Pedro Delgado (Spain)
1989	Greg LeMond (USA)
1990	Greg LeMond (USA)
1991	Miguel Indurain (Spain)
1992	Miguel Indurain (Spain)
1993	Miguel Indurain (Spain)
1994	Miguel Indurain (Spain)
1995	Miguel Indurain (Spain)
1996	Bjarne Riis (Denmark)
1997	Jan Ullrich (Germany)
1998	Marco Pantani (Italy)
1999	Lance Armstrong (USA)
2000	Lance Armstrong (USA)
2001	Lance Armstrong (USA)
2002	Lance Armstrong (USA)

■ World Road Race Championships
Men's race first held in 1927; first women's race in 1958; takes place annually.

Professional Men

1985	Joop Zoetemelk (Holland)
1986	Moreno Argentin (Italy)
1987	Stephen Roche (Ireland)
1988	Maurizio Fondriest (Italy)
1989	Greg LeMond (USA)
1990	Rudy Dhaenens (Belgium)
1991	Gianni Bugno (Italy)
1992	Gianni Bugno (Italy)
1993	Lance Armstrong (USA)
1994	Luc Leblanc (France)
1995	Abraham Olano (Spain)
1996	Johan Museeuw (Belgium)
1997	Laurent Brochard (France)
1998	Oskar Camenzind (Switzerland)
1999	Oscar Freire Gomez (Spain)
2000	Romans Vainsteins (Latvia)
2001	Oscar Freire Gomez (Spain)
2002	Mario Cipollini (Italy)

Women

1985	Jeannie Longo (France)
1986	Jeannie Longo (France)
1987	Jeannie Longo (France)
1988	Jeannie Longo (France)
1989	Jeannie Longo (France)
1990	Catherine Marsal (France)
1991	Leontien van Moorsel (Holland)
1992	Kathryn Watt (Australia)
1993	Leontien van Moorsel (Holland)
1994	Monica Valvik (Norway)
1995	Jeannie Longo (France)
1996	Barbara Heeb (Switzerland)
1997	Alessandra Cappellotto (Italy)
1998	Diana Ziliute (Lithuania)
1999	Edita Pucinskaite (Lithuania)
2000	Zinaida Stahurskaia (Belarus)
2001	Rosa Polikeviciute (Lithuania)
2002	Susanne Ljungskog (Sweden)

Cyclocross

■ World Championships
First held in 1950 as an open event; separate professional and amateur events from 1967 to 1993. Since 1994 held as an open event, known as the Elite.

Professional

1985	Klaus-Peter Thaler (West Germany)
1986	Albert Zweifel (Switzerland)
1987	Klaus-Peter Thaler (West Germany)
1988	Pascal Richard (Switzerland)
1989	Danny De Bie (Belgium)
1990	Henk Baars (Holland)
1991	Radomir Simunek (Czechoslovakia)
1992	Mike Kluge (Germany)
1993	Dominique Arnould (France)

Amateur

1985	Mike Kluge (West Germany)
1986	Vito di Tano (Italy)
1987	Mike Kluge (West Germany)
1988	Karol Camrola (Czechoslovakia)
1989	Ondrej Glaja (Czechoslovakia)
1990	Andreas Buesser (Switzerland)
1991	Thomas Frischknecht (Switzerland)
1992	Daniele Pontoni (Italy)
1993	Henrik Djernis (Denmark)

Open

1994	Paul Herijgers (Belgium)
1995	Dieter Runkel (Switzerland)

Elite

1996	Adri van der Poel (Netherlands)
1997	Daniele Pontoni (Italy)
1998	Mario de Clerq (Belgium)
1999	Mario de Clerq (Belgium)
2000	Richard Groenendaal (Netherlands)
2001	Erwin Vervecken (Belgium)
2002	Mario de Clerq (Belgium)

Darts

■ Embassy World Professional Championship
Run by the British Darts Organisation and first held at Nottingham in 1978.

1985	Eric Bristow (England)
1986	Eric Bristow (England)
1987	John Lowe (England)
1988	Bob Anderson (England)
1989	Jocky Wilson (Scotland)
1990	Phil Taylor (England)
1991	Dennis Priestley (England)
1992	Phil Taylor (England)
1993	John Lowe (England)
1994	John Part (Canada)
1995	Richie Burnett (Wales)
1996	Steve Beaton (England)
1997	Les Wallace (Scotland)
1998	Raymond Barneveld (Netherlands)
1999	Raymond Barneveld (Netherlands)
2000	Ted Hankey (England)
2001	John Walton (England)
2002	Tony David (Australia)

▪ World Cup

A team competition first held at Wembley in 1977; takes place every two years.

Team (Men)

1985	England
1987	England
1989	England
1991	England
1993	England
1995	England
1997	Wales
1999	England
2001	England

Individual (Men)

1985	Eric Bristow (England)
1987	Eric Bristow (England)
1989	Eric Bristow (England)
1991	John Lowe (England)
1993	Roland Schollen (Denmark)
1995	Martin Adams (England)
1997	Raymond Barneveld (Netherlands)
1999	Raymond Barneveld (Netherlands)
2001	Martin Adams (England)

▪ World Championship

Run by the World Darts Council (now Professional Darts Corporation) since 1994.

1994	Dennis Priestley (England)
1995	Phil Taylor (England)
1996	Phil Taylor (England)
1997	Phil Taylor (England)
1998	Phil Taylor (England)
1999	Phil Taylor (England)
2000	Phil Taylor (England)
2001	Phil Taylor (England)
2002	Phil Taylor (England)

Draughts

▪ British Open Championship

The leading championship in Britain; first held in 1926; now takes place every two years.

1986	H Devlin (Great Britain)
1988	D E Oldbury (Great Britain)
1990	T Watson (Great Britain)
1992	H Devlin (Great Britain)
1994	W J Edwards (Great Britain)
1996	J Francis (Barbados)
1998	Pat McCarthy (Republic of Ireland)
2000	William Docherty (Scotland)
2002	Ron King (Barbados)

Equestrian events

▪ World Championships

Show Jumping championships first held in 1953 (for men) and 1965 (for women); since 1978 they have competed together and on equal terms; team competition introduced in 1978; Three Day Event and Dressage championships introduced in 1966; all three now held every four years. Renamed the World Equestrian Games in 1990.

Show Jumping (Individual)

1986	Gail Greenough (Canada)
1990	Eric Navet (France)
1994	Franke Sloothaak (Germany)
1998	Rodrigo Pessoa (Brazil)
2002	Dermott Lennon (Ireland)

Show Jumping (Team)

1986	USA
1990	France
1994	Germany
1998	Germany
2002	France

Three Day Event (Individual)

1986	Virginia Leng (Great Britain)
1990	Blyth Tait (New Zealand)
1994	Vaughn Jefferis (New Zealand)
1998	Blyth Tait (New Zealand)
2002	Jean Teulere (France)

Three Day Event (Team)

1986	Great Britain
1990	New Zealand
1994	Great Britain
1998	New Zealand
2002	USA

Dressage (Individual)

1986	Anne Grethe Jensen (Denmark)
1990	Nicole Uphoff (West Germany)
1994	Anky van Grunsven (Netherlands)
1998	Isabell Werth (Germany)
2002	Nadine Capellmann (Germany)

Dressage (Team)

1986	West Germany
1990	West Germany
1994	Germany
1998	Germany
2002	Germany

Fencing

▪ World Championships

Held annually since 1921 (between 1921–35, known as European Championships). Not held in Olympic years. Women's Sabre was introduced in 1999.

Foil Individual (Men)

1985	Mauro Numa (Italy)
1986	Andrea Borella (Italy)
1987	Mathias Gey (West Germany)
1989	Alexander Koch (West Germany)
1990	Philippe Omnès (France)
1991	Ingo Weissenborn (Germany)
1993	Alexander Koch (Germany)
1994	Rolando Tuckers (Cuba)
1995	Dimitriy Chevtchenko (Russia)
1997	Sergei Golubitsky (Ukraine)
1998	Sergei Golubitsky (Ukraine)
1999	Sergei Golubitsky (Ukraine)
2001	Salvatore Sanzo (Italy)
2002	Simone Vanni (Italy)

Foil Team (Men)

1985	Italy
1986	Italy
1987	USSR
1989	USSR
1990	Italy
1991	Cuba
1993	Germany
1994	Italy
1995	Cuba
1997	France
1998	Poland
1999	France
2001	Italy
2002	Germany

Sports and Games

Foil Individual (Women)

1985	Cornelia Hanisch (West Germany)
1986	Anja Fichtel (West Germany)
1987	Elisabeta Tufan (Romania)
1989	Olga Velitchko (USSR)
1990	Anja Fichtel (West Germany)
1991	Giovanna Trillini (Italy)
1993	Francesca Bortolozzi (Italy)
1994	Reka Szabo-Lazar (Romania)
1995	Laura Badea (Romania)
1997	Giovanna Trillini (Italy)
1998	Sabine Bau (Germany)
1999	Valentina Vezzali (Italy)
2001	Valentina Vezzali (Italy)
2002	Svetlani Bojko (Russia)

Foil Team (Women)

1985	West Germany
1986	USSR
1987	Hungary
1989	West Germany
1990	Italy
1991	Hungary
1993	Germany
1994	Romania
1995	Italy
1997	Italy
1998	Italy
1999	Germany
2001	Japan
2002	Russia

Épée Individual (Men)

1985	Philippe Boisse (France)
1986	Philippe Riboud (France)
1987	Volker Fischer (West Germany)
1989	Manuel Pereira (Spain)
1990	Thomas Gerull (West Germany)
1991	Andrei Shovalov (USSR)
1993	Pavel Kolobkov (Russia)
1994	Pavel Kolobkov (Russia)
1995	Eric Srecki (France)
1997	Eric Srecki (France)
1998	Hughes Obry (France)
1999	Arnd Schmitt (Germany)
2001	Paulo Milanoli (Italy)
2002	Pavel Kolobkov (Russia)

Épée Team (Men)

1985	West Germany
1986	West Germany
1987	West Germany
1989	Italy
1990	Italy
1991	USSR
1993	Italy
1994	France
1995	Germany
1997	Cuba
1998	Hungary
1999	France
2001	Switzerland
2002	France

Épée Individual (Women)

1989	Anja Straub (Switzerland)
1990	Taime Chappe (Cuba)
1991	Mariann Horvath (Hungary)
1993	Oksana Jermakova (Estonia)
1994	Laura Chiesa (Hungary)
1995	Joanna Jakimiuk (Poland)
1997	Miraide Garcia-Soto (Cuba)
1998	Laura Flessel (France)
1999	Laura Flessel-Colovic (France)
2001	Claudia Bokel (Germany)
2002	Hee Hyun (Korea)

Épée Team (Women)

1989	Hungary
1990	West Germany
1991	Hungary
1993	Hungary
1994	Spain
1995	Hungary
1997	Hungary
1998	France
1999	Hungary
2001	Estonia
2002	Hungary

Sabre Individual (Men)

1985	György Nebald (Hungary)
1986	Sergey Mindirgassov (USSR)
1987	Jean-François Lamour (France)
1989	Grigory Kirienko (USSR)
1990	Gyorgy Nebald (Hungary)
1991	Grigory Kirienko (USSR)
1993	Grigory Kirienko (Russia)
1994	Felix Becker (Germany)
1995	Grigory Kirienko (Russia)
1997	Stanislav Pozdniakov (Russia)
1998	Luigi Tarantino (Italy)
1999	Damien Touya (France)
2001	Stanislav Pozdniakov (Russia)
2002	Stanislav Pozdniakov (Russia)

Sabre Team (Men)

1985	USSR
1986	USSR
1987	USSR
1989	USSR
1990	USSR
1991	Hungary
1993	Hungary
1994	Russia
1995	Italy
1997	France
1998	Hungary
1999	France
2001	Ukraine
2002	Russia

Sabre Individual (Women)

1999	Elena Jemayeva (Azerbaijan)
2000	Elena Jemayeva (Azerbaijan)
2001	Anne Lise Touya (France)
2002	Xue Tan (China)

Sabre Team (Women)

1999	Italy
2000	USA
2001	Russia
2002	Russia

Football pitch

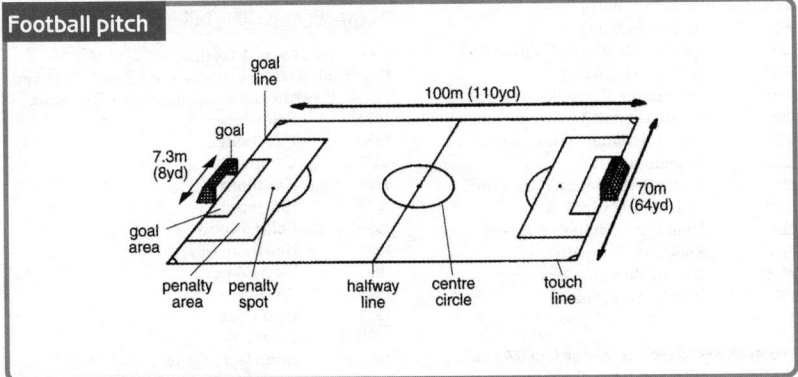

Football pitch diagram with labels: goal line, goal, 7.3m (8yd), goal area, 100m (110yd), 70m (64yd), penalty area, penalty spot, halfway line, centre circle, touch line

Football, American

■ Super Bowl
First held in 1967; takes place each January; an end-of-season meeting between the champions of the two major US leagues, the National Football Conference (NFC) and the American Football Conference (AFC).

1985	San Francisco 49ers (NFC)
1986	Chicago Bears (NFC)
1987	New York Giants (NFC)
1988	Washington Redskins (NFC)
1989	San Francisco 49ers (NFC)
1990	San Francisco 49ers (NFC)
1991	New York Giants (NFC)
1992	Washington Redskins (NFC)
1993	Dallas Cowboys (NFC)
1994	Dallas Cowboys (NFC)
1995	San Francisco 49ers (NFC)
1996	Dallas Cowboys (NFC)
1997	Green Bay Packers (NFC)
1998	Denver Broncos (AFC)
1999	Denver Broncos (AFC)
2000	St Louis Rams (NFC)
2001	Baltimore Ravens (AFC)
2002	New England Patriots (AFC)

Football, Association

■ FIFA World Cup
Association Football's premier event; first contested for the Jules Rimet Trophy in 1930; Brazil won it outright after winning for the third time in 1970; since then teams have competed for the FIFA (*Féderation Internationale de Football Association*) World Cup; held every four years.

Post-war winners

1950	Uruguay
1954	West Germany
1958	Brazil
1962	Brazil
1966	England
1970	Brazil
1974	West Germany
1978	Argentina
1982	Italy
1986	Argentina
1990	West Germany
1994	Brazil
1998	France
2002	Brazil

■ European Championship
Held every four years since 1960; qualifying group matches held over the two years preceding the final.

All winners

1960	USSR
1964	Spain
1968	Italy
1972	West Germany
1976	Czechoslovakia
1980	West Germany
1984	France
1988	Netherlands
1992	Denmark
1996	Germany
2000	France

■ South American Championship
Known as Copa de América; first held in 1916, for South American national sides; there were two tournaments in 1959, won by Argentina and Uruguay; discontinued in 1967, but revived eight years later; now played every two years.

1987	Uruguay
1989	Brazil
1991	Argentina
1993	Argentina
1995	Uruguay
1997	Brazil
1999	Brazil
2001	Colombia

■ European Champions Cup
The leading club competition in Europe; open to the League champions of countries affiliated to UEFA (Union of European Football Associations); commonly known as the 'European Cup'; inaugurated in the 1955–6 season; played annually.

1985	Juventus (Italy)
1986	Steaua Bucharest (Romania)
1987	FC Porto (Portugal)
1988	PSV Eindhoven (Holland)

1989	AC Milan (Italy)
1990	AC Milan (Italy)
1991	Red Star Belgrade (Yugoslavia)
1992	Barcelona (Spain)
1993	Olympique Marseille (France)
1994	AC Milan (Italy)
1995	Ajax Amsterdam (Holland)
1996	Juventus (Italy)
1997	Borussia Dortmund (Germany)
1998	Real Madrid (Spain)
1999	Manchester United (England)
2000	Real Madrid (Spain)
2001	Bayern Munich (Germany)
2002	Real Madrid (Spain)

■ **Football Association Challenge Cup (FA Cup)**

The world's oldest club knockout competition (the 'FA cup'), held annually; first contested in the 1871–2 season; first final at the Kennington Oval on 16 March 1872; first winners were The Wanderers.

1985	Manchester United
1986	Liverpool
1987	Coventry City
1988	Wimbledon
1989	Liverpool
1990	Manchester United
1991	Tottenham Hotspur
1992	Liverpool
1993	Arsenal
1994	Manchester United
1995	Everton
1996	Manchester United
1997	Chelsea
1998	Arsenal
1999	Manchester United
2000	Chelsea
2001	Chelsea
2002	Arsenal

■ **Football League (Premier League)**

The oldest league in the world, and regarded as the toughest; founded in 1888; consists of four divisions; the current complement of 92 teams achieved in 1950.

1984–5	Everton
1985–6	Liverpool
1986–7	Everton
1987–8	Liverpool
1988–9	Arsenal
1989–90	Liverpool
1990–1	Arsenal
1991–2	Leeds United
1992–3	Manchester United
1993–4	Manchester United
1994–5	Blackburn Rovers
1995–6	Manchester United
1996–7	Manchester United
1997–8	Arsenal
1998–9	Manchester United
1999–2000	Manchester United
2000–1	Manchester United
2001–2	Arsenal

Football, Australian Rules

■ **Australian Football League**

First held in 1897 as the Victoria Football League (1897–1989); inaugural winners were Essendon.

1985	Essendon
1986	Hawthorn
1987	Carlton
1988	Hawthorn
1989	Hawthorn
1990	Collingwood
1991	Hawthorn
1992	West Coast
1993	Essendon
1994	West Coast
1995	Carlton
1996	North Melbourne
1997	Adelaide
1998	Adelaide
1999	North Melbourne
2000	Essendon
2001	Brisbane
2002	Brisbane

Football, Gaelic

■ **All-Ireland Championship**

First held in 1887; takes place in Dublin on the third Sunday in September each year.

1985	Kerry
1986	Kerry
1987	Meath
1988	Meath
1989	Cork
1990	Cork
1991	Down
1992	Donegal
1993	Derry
1994	Down
1995	Dublin
1996	Meath
1997	Kerry
1998	Galway
1999	Meath
2000	Kerry
2001	Galway
2002	Armagh

Gliding

■ **World Championships**

First held in 1937; current classes are Open, Standard and 15m; the Open class is the principal event, held every two years until 1978 and again since 1981.

1985	Ingo Renner (Australia)
1987	Ingo Renner (Australia)
1989	Robin May (Great Britain)
1991	Janusz Centka (Poland)
1993	Andy Davis (Great Britain)
1995	Raymond Lynskey (New Zealand)
1997	Gerard Lherm (France)
1999	Holger Karow (Germany)
2001	Oscar Goudriaan (South Africa)

Golf

■ British Open

First held at Prestwick in 1860, and won by Willie Park; takes place annually; regarded as the world's leading golf tournament.

1985	Sandy Lyle (Great Britain)
1986	Greg Norman (Australia)
1987	Nick Faldo (Great Britain)
1988	Severiano Ballesteros (Spain)
1989	Mark Calcavecchia (USA)
1990	Nick Faldo (Great Britain)
1991	Ian Baker-Finch (Australia)
1992	Nick Faldo (Great Britain)
1993	Greg Norman (Australia)
1994	Nick Price (Zimbabwe)
1995	John Daly (USA)
1996	Tom Lehman (USA)
1997	Justin Leonard (USA)
1998	Mark O'Meara (USA)
1999	Paul Lawrie (Great Britain)
2000	Tiger Woods (USA)
2001	David Duval (USA)
2002	Ernie Els (South Africa)

■ United States Open

First Held at Newport, Rhode Island, in 1895, and won by Horace Rawlins; takes place annually.

1985	Andy North (USA)
1986	Ray Floyd (USA)
1987	Scott Simpson (USA)
1988	Curtis Strange (USA)
1989	Curtis Strange (USA)
1990	Hale Irwin (USA)
1991	Payne Stewart (USA)
1992	Tom Kite (USA)
1993	Lee Janzen (USA)
1994	Ernie Els (South Africa)
1995	Corey Pavin (USA)
1996	Steve Jones (USA)
1997	Ernie Els (South Africa)
1998	Lee Janzen (USA)
1999	Payne Stewart (USA)
2000	Tiger Woods (USA)
2001	Retief Goosen (South Africa)
2002	Tiger Woods (USA)

■ US Masters

First held in 1934; takes place at the Augusta National course in Georgia every April.

1985	Bernhard Langer (West Germany)
1986	Jack Nicklaus (USA)
1987	Larry Mize (USA)
1988	Sandy Lyle (Great Britain)
1989	Nick Faldo (Great Britain)
1990	Nick Faldo (Great Britain)
1991	Ian Woosnam (Great Britain)
1992	Fred Couples (USA)
1993	Bernhard Langer (Germany)
1994	José-María Olazábal (Spain)

1995	Ben Crenshaw (USA)
1996	Nick Faldo (Great Britain)
1997	Tiger Woods (USA)
1998	Mark O'Meara (USA)
1999	José-María Olazábal (Spain)
2000	Vijay Singh (Fiji)
2001	Tiger Woods (USA)
2002	Tiger Woods (USA)

■ United States PGA Championship

The last of the season's four 'Majors'; first held in 1916, and a match-play event until 1958; takes place annually.

1985	Hubert Green (USA)
1986	Bob Tway (USA)
1987	Larry Nelson (USA)
1988	Jeff Sluman (USA)
1989	Payne Stewart (USA)
1990	Wayne Grady (Australia)
1991	John Daly (USA)
1992	Nick Price (Zimbabwe)
1993	Paul Azinger (USA)
1994	Nick Price (Zimbabwe)
1995	Steve Elkington (Australia)
1996	Mark Brooks (USA)
1997	Davis Love III (USA)
1998	Vijay Singh (Fiji)
1999	Tiger Woods (USA)
2000	Tiger Woods (USA)
2001	David Toms (USA)
2002	Rich Beem (USA)

■ Ryder Cup

The leading international team tournament; first held at Worcester, Massachusetts in 1927; takes place every two years between teams from the USA and Europe (Great Britain 1927–71; Great Britain and Ireland 1973–7).

1985	Europe	$16\frac{1}{2}$–$11\frac{1}{2}$
1987	Europe	15–13
1989	Drawn	14–14
1991	USA	$14\frac{1}{2}$–$13\frac{1}{2}$
1993	USA	15–13
1995	Europe	$14\frac{1}{2}$–$13\frac{1}{2}$
1997	Europe	$14\frac{1}{2}$–$13\frac{1}{2}$
1999	USA	$14\frac{1}{2}$–$13\frac{1}{2}$
2002	Europe	$15\frac{1}{2}$–$12\frac{1}{2}$

Greyhound racing

■ Greyhound Derby

The top race of the British season, first held in 1927; run at the White City every year (except 1940) until its closure in 1985; since then all races run at Wimbledon.

1985	Pagan Swallow
1986	Tico
1987	Signal Spark
1988	Hit the Lid
1989	Lartigue Note
1990	Slippy Blue
1991	Ballinderry Ash
1992	Farloe Melody
1993	Ringa Hustle

1994	Moral Standards
1995	Moaning Lad
1996	Shanless Slippy
1997	Some Picture
1998	Tom's the Best
1999	Chart King
2000	Rapid Ranger
2001	Rapid Ranger
2002	Allen Gift

Gymnastics

■ **World Championships**
First held in 1903.

Individual (Men)

1985	Yuri Korolev (USSR)
1987	Dmitri Belozerchev (USSR)
1989	Igor Korobichensky (USSR)
1991	Vitaly Scherbo (USSR)
1993	Vitaly Scherbo (Belarus)
1994	Ivan Ivankov (Belarus)
1995	Li Xianoshuang (China)
1997	Ivan Ivankov (Belarus)
1999	Nikolay Krukov (Russia)
2001	Jing Feng (China)

Team (Men)

1985	USSR
1987	USSR
1989	USSR
1991	USSR
1993	*no team prize*
1994	China
1995	China
1997	China
1999	China
2001	Belarus

Individual (Women)

1985	Yelena Shoushounova (USSR) and Oksana Omeliantchuk (USSR)
1987	Aurelia Dobre (Romania)
1989	Svetlana Boginskaya (USSR)
1991	Kim Zmeskal (USA)
1993	Shannon Miller (USA)
1994	Shannon Miller (USA)
1995	Lilia Podkopayeva (Ukraine)
1997	Svetlana Khorkina (Russia)
1999	Maria Olaru (Romania)
2001	Svetlana Khorkina (Russia)

Team (Women)

1985	USSR
1987	Romania
1989	USSR
1991	USSR
1993	*no team prize*
1994	Romania
1995	Romania
1997	Romania

1999	Romania
2001	Romania

Handball

■ **World Championships**
First men's championships held in 1938, both indoors and outdoors (latter discontinued in 1966); first women's outdoor championships in 1949 (discontinued in 1960); first women's indoor championships in 1957; take place every two years.

Men

1986	Yugoslavia
1990	Sweden
1993	Russia
1995	France
1997	Russia
1999	Sweden
2001	France

Women

1986	USSR
1990	USSR
1993	Germany
1995	Germany
1997	Denmark
1999	Norway
2001	Russia

Hang gliding

■ **World Championships**
First held officially in 1976; since 1979, take place every two years.

Individual: Class 1

1985	John Pendry (Great Britain)
1987	Rich Duncan (Australia)
1989	Robert Whittall (Great Britain)
1991	Tomás Suchanek (Czechoslovakia)
1993	Tomás Suchanek (Czech Republic)
1995	Tomás Suchanek (Czech Republic)
1997	John Pendry (Great Britain)
1999	Manfred Ruhmer (Austria)
2001	Manfred Ruhmer (Austria)

Team

1985	Great Britain
1987	Australia
1989	Great Britain
1991	Great Britain
1993	USA
1995	Australia
1997	Switzerland
1999	Brazil
2001	Austria

Hockey

▪ World Cup
Men's tournament first held in 1971, and every four years since 1978; women's tournament first held in 1974, and now takes place every three or four years.

Men

1986	Australia
1990	Netherlands
1994	Pakistan
1998	Netherlands
2002	Germany

Women

1986	Netherlands
1990	Netherlands
1994	Australia
1998	Australia
2002	Argentina

▪ Olympic Games
Regarded as hockey's leading competition; first held in 1908; included at every celebration since 1928; women's competition first held in 1980.

Men

1988	Great Britain
1992	Germany
1996	Netherlands
2000	Netherlands

Women

1988	Australia
1992	Spain
1996	Australia
2000	Australia

Horse racing

▪ The Derby
The 'Blue Riband' of the Turf; run at Epsom over $1\frac{1}{2}$ miles; first run in 1780.

Horse (Jockey)

1985	Slip Anchor (Steve Cauthen)
1986	Shahrastani (Walter Swinburn)
1987	Reference Point (Steve Cauthen)
1988	Kahyasi (Ray Cochrane)
1989	Nashwan (Willie Carson)
1990	Quest For Fame (Pat Eddery)
1991	Generous (Alan Munro)
1992	Dr Devious (John Reid)
1993	Commander in Chief (Michael Kinane)
1994	Erhaab (Willie Carson)
1995	Lammtarra (Walter Swinburn)
1996	Shaamit (Michael Hills)
1997	Benny the Dip (Willie Ryan)
1998	High Rise (Olivier Peslier)
1999	Oath (Kieren Fallon)
2000	Sinndar (John Murtagh)
2001	Galileo (Michael Kinane)
2002	High Chaparral (John Murtagh)

▪ The Oaks
Raced at Epsom over $1\frac{1}{2}$ miles; for fillies only; first run in 1779.

Horse (Jockey)

1985	Oh So Sharp (Steve Cauthen)
1986	Midway Lady (Ray Cochrane)
1987	Unite (Walter Swinburn)
1988	Diminuendo (Steve Cauthen)
1989	Aliysa (Walter Swinburn)
1990	Salsabil (Willie Carson)
1991	Jet Ski Lady (Christy Roche)
1992	User Friendly (George Duffield)
1993	Intrepidity (Michael Roberts)
1994	Balanchine (Frankie Dettori)
1995	Moonshell (Frankie Dettori)
1996	Lady Carla (Pat Eddery)
1997	Reams of Verse (Kieren Fallon)
1998	Shahtoush (Michael Kinane)
1999	Ramruma (Kieren Fallon)
2000	Love Divine (Richard Quinn)
2001	Imagine (Michael Kinane)
2002	Kazzia (Frankie Dettori)

▪ OneThousand Guineas
Run over 1 mile at Newmarket; for fillies only; first run in 1814.

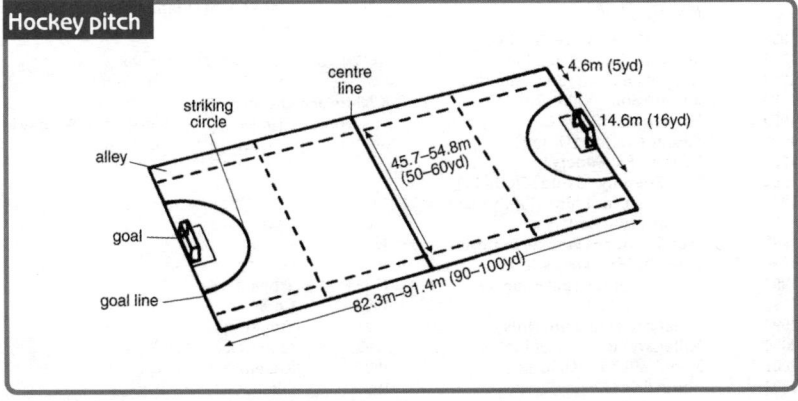

Hockey pitch

centre line

striking circle

4.6m (5yd)

14.6m (16yd)

alley

45.7–54.8m (50–60yd)

goal

goal line

82.3m–91.4m (90–100yd)

Sports and Games

	Horse (Jockey)
1985	Oh So Sharp (Steve Cauthen)
1986	Midway Lady (Ray Cochrane)
1987	Miesque (Freddy Head)
1988	Ravinella (Gary Moore)
1989	Musical Bliss (Walter Swinburn)
1990	Salsabil (Willie Carson)
1991	Shadayid (Willie Carson)
1992	Hatoof (Walter Swinburn)
1993	Sayyedati (Walter Swinburn)
1994	Las Meninas (John Reid)
1995	Harayir (Richard Hills)
1996	Bosra Sham (Pat Eddery)
1997	Sleepytime (Kieren Fallon)
1998	Cape Verdi (Frankie Dettori)
1999	Wince (Kieren Fallon)
2000	Lahan (Richard Hills)
2001	Ameerat (Philip Robinson)
2002	Kazzia (Frankie Dettori)

■ **TwoThousand Guineas**
Run at Newmarket over 1 mile; first run in 1809.

	Horse (Jockey)
1985	Shadeed (Lester Piggott)
1986	Dancing Brave (Greville Starkey)
1987	Don't Forget Me (Willie Carson)
1988	Doyoun (Walter Swinburn)
1989	Nashwan (Willie Carson)
1990	Tirol (Michael Kinane)
1991	Mystiko (Michael Roberts)
1992	Rodrigo de Traiano (Lester Piggott)
1993	Zafonic (Pat Eddery)
1994	Mister Baileys (Jason Weaver)
1995	Pennekamp (Thierry Jarnet)
1996	Mark of Esteem (Frankie Dettori)
1997	Entrepreneur (Michael Kinane)
1998	King of Kings (Michael Kinane)
1999	Island Sands (Frankie Dettori)
2000	King's Best (Kieren Fallon)
2001	Golan (Kieren Fallon)
2002	Rock of Gibraltar (John Murtagh)

■ **St Leger**
The oldest of the five English classics; first run in 1776; raced at Doncaster annually over 1 mile 6 furlongs 127 yards.

	Horse (Jockey)
1985	Oh So Sharp (Steve Cauthen)
1986	Moon Madness (Pat Eddery)
1987	Reference Point (Steve Cauthen)
1988	Minster Son (Willie Carson)
1989	Michelozzo (Steve Cauthen)
1990	Snurge (Richard Quinn)
1991	Toulon (Pat Eddery)
1992	User Friendly (George Duffield)
1993	Bob's Return (Philip Robinson)
1994	Moonax (Pat Eddery)
1995	Classic Cliche (Frankie Dettori)
1996	Shantou (Frankie Dettori)
1997	Silver Patriarch (Pat Eddery)
1998	Nedawi (John Reid)
1999	Mutafaweq (Richard Hills)
2000	Millenary (Richard Quinn)
2001	Milan (Michael Kinane)
2002	Bollin Eric (Kevin Darley)

■ **Grand National**
Steeplechasing's most famous race; first run at Maghull in 1836; at Aintree since 1839; war-time races at Gatwick 1916–18.

	Horse (Jockey)
1985	Last Suspect (Hywel Davies)
1986	West Tip (Richard Dunwoody)
1987	Maori Venture (Steve Knight)
1988	Rhyme 'N' Reason (Brendan Powell)
1989	Little Polveir (Jimmy Frost)
1990	Mr Frisk (Marcus Armytage)
1991	Seagram (Nigel Hawke)
1992	Party Politics (Carl Llewellyn)
1993	*race declared void* Esha Ness (John White) first past the post
1994	Minnehoma (Richard Dunwoody)
1995	Royal Athlete (Jason Titley)
1996	Rough Quest (Mick Fitzgerald)
1997	Lord Gyllene (Tony Dobbin)
1998	Earth Summit (Carl Llewelyn)
1999	Bobbyjo (Paul Carberry)
2000	Papillon (Ruby Walsh)
2001	Red Marauder (Richard Guest)
2002	Bindaree (Jim Culloty)

■ **Prix de l'Arc de Triomphe**
The leading end of season race in Europe; raced over 2 400 metres at Longchamp; first run in 1920.

	Horse (Jockey)
1985	Rainbow Quest (Pat Eddery)
1986	Dancing Brave (Pat Eddery)
1987	Trempolino (Pat Eddery)
1988	Tony Bin (John Reid)
1989	Caroll House (Michael Kinane)
1990	Suamarez (Gerard Mosse)
1991	Suave Dancer (Cash Asmussen)
1992	Subotica (Thierry Jarnet)
1993	Urban Sea (Eric Saint-Martin)
1994	Carnegie (Thierry Jarnet)
1995	Lammtarra (Frankie Dettori)
1996	Helissio (Olivier Peslier)
1997	Peintre Celebre (Olivier Peslier)
1998	Sagamix (Olivier Peslier)
1999	Montjeu (Michael Kinane)
2000	Sinndar (John Murtagh)
2001	Sakhee (Frankie Dettori)
2002	Marienbard (Frankie Dettori)

Hurling

■ **All-Ireland Championship**
First contested in 1887; played on the first Sunday in September each year.

1985	Offaly
1986	Cork
1987	Galway
1988	Galway
1989	Tipperary
1990	Cork
1991	Tipperary
1992	Limerick
1993	Kilkenny
1994	Offaly

1995	Clare
1996	Wexford
1997	Clare
1998	Offaly
1999	Cork
2000	Kilkenny
2001	Tipperary
2002	Kilkenny

Ice hockey

▪ World Championship
First held in 1930; takes place annually (except 1980); up to 1968 Olympic champions also regarded as world champions.

1985	Czechoslovakia
1986	USSR
1987	Sweden
1988	USSR
1989	USSR
1990	USSR
1991	Sweden
1992	Sweden
1993	Russia
1994	Canada
1995	Finland
1996	Czech Republic
1997	Canada
1998	Sweden
1999	Czech Republic
2000	Czech Republic
2001	Czech Republic
2002	Slovakia

▪ Stanley Cup
The most sought-after trophy at club level; the end-of-season meeting between the winners of the two conferences in the National Hockey League in the USA and Canada.

1985	Edmonton Oilers
1986	Montreal Canadiens
1987	Edmonton Oilers
1988	Edmonton Oilers
1989	Calgary Flames
1990	Edmonton Oilers
1991	Pittsburgh Penguins
1992	Pittsburgh Penguins
1993	Montreal Canadiens
1994	New York Rangers
1995	New Jersey Devils
1996	Colorado Avalanche
1997	Detroit Red Wings
1998	Detroit Red Wings
1999	Dallas Stars
2000	New Jersey Devils
2001	Colorado Avalanche
2002	Detroit Red Wings

Ice skating

▪ World Championships
First men's championships in 1896; first women's event in 1906; pairs first contested in 1908; Ice Dance officially recognized in 1952.

Men

1985	Alexander Fadeyev (USSR)
1986	Brian Boitano (USA)
1987	Brian Orser (Canada)
1988	Brian Boitano (USA)
1989	Kurt Browning (Canada)
1990	Kurt Browning (Canada)
1991	Kurt Browning (Canada)
1992	Viktor Petrenko (CIS)
1993	Kurt Browning (Canada)
1994	Elvis Stojko (Canada)
1995	Elvis Stojko (Canada)
1996	Todd Eldredge (USA)
1997	Elvis Stojko (Canada)
1998	Alexei Yagudin (Russia)
1999	Alexei Yagudin (Russia)
2000	Alexei Yagudin (Russia)
2001	Evgeny Plushenko (Russia)
2002	Alexei Yagudin (Russia)

Ice hockey rink

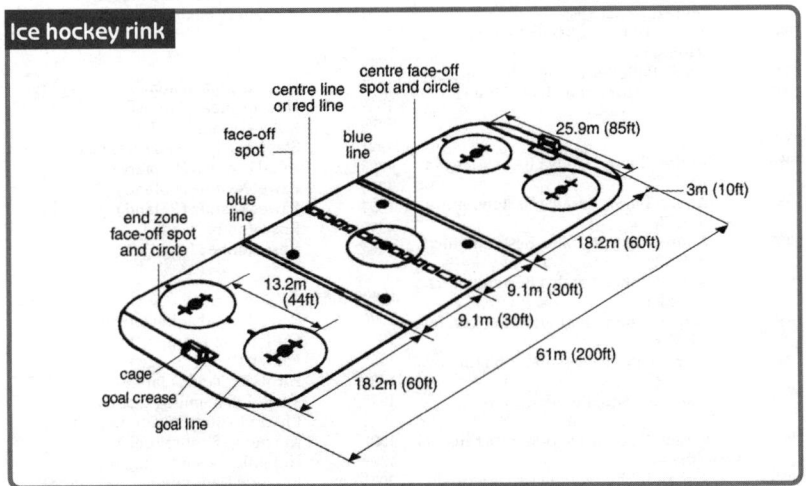

centre face-off spot and circle

centre line or red line

face-off spot

blue line

25.9m (85ft)

3m (10ft)

18.2m (60ft)

end zone face-off spot and circle

blue line

13.2m (44ft)

9.1m (30ft)

9.1m (30ft)

61m (200ft)

cage

goal crease

goal line

18.2m (60ft)

Sports and Games

Women

1985	Katarina Witt (East Germany)
1986	Debbie Thomas (USA)
1987	Katarina Witt (East Germany)
1988	Katarina Witt (East Germany)
1989	Midori Ito (Japan)
1990	Jill Trenary (USA)
1991	Kristi Yamaguchi (USA)
1992	Kristi Yamaguchi (USA)
1993	Oksana Baiul (Ukraine)
1994	Yuka Sato (Japan)
1995	Lu Chen (China)
1996	Michelle Kwan (USA)
1997	Tara Lipinski (USA)
1998	Michelle Kwan (USA)
1999	Maria Butyrskaya (Russia)
2000	Michelle Kwan (USA)
2001	Michelle Kwan (USA)
2002	Irina Slutskaya (Russia)

Pairs

1985	Oleg Vasiliev/Yelena Valova (USSR)
1986	Sergei Grinkov/Yekaterina Gordeeva (USSR)
1987	Sergei Grinkov/Yekaterina Gordeeva (USSR)
1988	Oleg Vasiliev/Yelena Valova (USSR)
1989	Sergei Grinkov/Yekaterina Gordeeva (USSR)
1990	Sergei Grinkov/Yekaterina Gordeeva (USSR)
1991	Artur Dmtriev/Natalya Mishkutienok (USSR)
1992	Artur Dmtriev/Natalya Mishkutienok (USSR)
1993	Lloyd Eisler/Isabelle Brasseur (Canada)
1994	Vadim Naumov/Evgenia Shiskova (Russia)
1995	Rene Novotny/Radka Kovarikova (Czech Republic)
1996	Andrei Bushkov/Marina Eltsova (Russia)
1997	Ingo Steuer/Mandy Woetzel (Germany)
1998	Anton Sikharulidze/Elena Berezhnaya (Russia)
1999	Anton Sikharulidze/Elena Berezhnaya (Russia)
2000	Alexei Tikhonov/Maria Petrova (Russia)
2001	David Pelletier/Jamie Sale (Canada)
2002	Xue Shen/Hongbo Zhao (China)

Ice Dance

1985	Andrei Bukin/Natalya Bestemianova (USSR)
1986	Andrei Bukin/Natalya Bestemianova (USSR)
1987	Andrei Bukin/Natalya Bestemianova (USSR)
1988	Andrei Bukin/Natalya Bestemianova (USSR)
1989	Sergei Ponomarenko/Marina Klimova (USSR)
1990	Sergei Ponomarenko/Marina Klimova (USSR)
1991	Paul and Isabelle Duchesnay (France)
1992	Sergei Ponomarenko/Marina Klimova (CIS)
1993	Alesandr Zhulin/Maia Usova (Russia)
1994	Yevgeni Platov/Oksana Gritschuk (Russia)
1995	Yevgeni Platov/Oksana Gritschuk (Russia)
1996	Yevgeni Platov/Oksana Gritschuk (Russia)
1997	Yevgeni Platov/Oksana Gritschuk (Russia)
1998	Oleg Ovsyannikov/Anjelika Krylova (Russia)
1999	Oleg Ovsyannikov/Anjelika Krylova (Russia)
2000	Gwendal Peizerat/Marina Anissina (France)
2001	Maurizio Margaglio/Barbara Fusar-Poli (Italy)
2002	Ilia Averbukh/Irina Lobacheva (Russia)

Judo

■ **World Championships**

First held in 1956, now contested every two years; current weight categories established in 1999; women's championship instituted in 1980.

Men

Open Class

1985	Yoshimi Masaki (Japan)
1987	Naoya Ogawa (Japan)
1989	Naoya Ogawa (Japan)
1991	Naoya Ogawa (Japan)
1993	Rafael Kubacki (Poland)
1995	David Douillet (France)
1997	Rafael Kubacki (Poland)
1999	Shinichi Shinohara (Japan)
2001	Alexandre Mikhaylin (Russia)

Over 100kg

1985	Yung-Chul Cho (Korea)
1987	Grigori Vertichev (USSR)
1989	Naoya Ogawa (Japan)
1991	Sergey Kosorotov (USSR)
1993	David Douillet (France)
1995	David Douillet (France)
1997	David Douillet (France)
1999	Shinichi Shinohara (Japan)
2001	Alexandre Mikhaylin (Russia)

Under 100kg

1985	Hitoshi Sugai (Japan)
1987	Hitoshi Sugai (Japan)
1989	Koba Kurtanidze (Japan)
1991	Stephane Traineau (France)
1993	Antal Kovacs (Hungary)
1995	Pawel Nastula (Poland)
1997	Pawel Nastula (Poland)
1999	Kosei Inoue (Japan)
2001	Kosei Inoue (Japan)

Under 90kg

1985	Peter Seisenbacher (Austria)
1987	Fabien Canu (France)
1989	Fabien Canu (France)
1991	Hirotaka Okada (Japan)
1993	Yoshoi Nakamura (Japan)
1995	Chun Ki Young (South Korea)
1997	Ki Young (South Korea)
1999	Hidehiko Yoshida (Japan)
2001	Frederic Demoutfaucon (France)

Under 81kg

1985	Nobutoshi Hikage (Japan)
1987	Hirotaka Okada (Japan)
1989	Byung-ju Kim (South Korea)
1991	Daniel Lascau (Germany)
1993	Chun Ki Young (South Korea)
1995	Toshihiko Koga (Japan)
1997	Chul Cho In (South Korea)
1999	Graeme Randall (Great Britain)
2001	Chul Cho In (South Korea)

Under 78kg

1986	Irene de Kok (Netherlands)
1987	Irene de Kok (Netherlands)
1989	Ingrid Berghmans (Belgium)
1991	Kim Mi-Jeong (South Korea)
1993	Chun Huileng (China)
1995	Castellano Luna (Cuba)
1997	Noriko Anno (Japan)
1999	Noriko Anno (Japan)
2001	Noriko Anno (Japan)

Under 73kg

1985	Byeong-Keun Ahn (Korea)
1987	Mike Swain (USA)
1989	Toshihiko Koga (Japan)
1991	Toshihiko Koga (Japan)
1993	Yung Chung Hoon (South Korea)
1995	Daisuke Hideshima (Japan)
1997	Kenzo Nakamura (Japan)
1999	Jimmy Pedro (USA)
2001	Vital Makarov (Russia)

Under 70kg

1986	Brigitte Deydier (France)
1987	Alexandra Schreiber (West Germany)
1989	Emanuela Pierantozzi (Italy)
1991	Emanuela Pierantozzi (Italy)
1993	Cho Min Sun (South Korea)
1995	Cho Min Sun (South Korea)
1997	Kate Howey (Great Britain)
1999	Sibelis Veranes (Cuba)
2001	Masae Ueno (Japan)

Under 66kg

1985	Yuriy Sokolov (USSR)
1987	Yosuke Yamamoto (Japan)
1989	Drago Becanovic (Yugoslavia)
1991	Udo Quellmalz (Germany)
1993	Yukimasa Nakamura (Japan)
1995	Udo Quellmalz (Germany)
1997	Hyuk Kim (Korea)
1999	Larbi Benboudaoud (France)
2001	Arashi Miresmaeli (Iran)

Under 63kg

1986	Diane Bell (Great Britain)
1987	Diane Bell (Great Britain)
1989	Catherina Fleury (France)
1991	Frauke Eickhoff (Germany)
1993	Gella van de Cayeve (Belgium)
1995	Jung Sung Sook (South Korea)
1997	Servenr Vandenhende (France)
1999	Keiko Maedo (Japan)
2001	Gella van de Cayeve (Belgium)

Under 60kg

1985	Shinji Hosokawa (Japan)
1987	Kim Jae-Yup (South Korea)
1989	Amiran Totikashvili (USSR)
1991	Tadanori Koshino (Japan)
1993	Ryudi Sanoda (Japan)
1995	Nikolai Ojeguine (Russia)
1997	Tadahiro Nomura (Japan)
1999	Manuelo Poulot (Cuba)
2001	Anis Lounifi (Tunisia)

Under 57kg

1986	Ann Hughes (Great Britain)
1987	Catherine Arnaud (France)
1989	Catherine Arnaud (France)
1991	Miriam Blasco (Spain)
1993	Nicola Fairbrother (Great Britain)
1995	Driulis González (Cuba)
1997	Isabel Fernandez (Spain)
1999	Driulis González (Cuba)
2001	Yourisledes Lupety (Cuba)

Women

Open Class

1986	Ingrid Berghmans (Belgium)
1987	Fenglian Gao (China)
1989	Estela Rodriguez (Cuba)
1991	Zhuang Xiaoyan (China)
1993	Beata Maksymow (Poland)
1995	Monique van der Lee (Netherlands)
1997	Daina Beltran (Cuba)
1999	Daina Beltran (Cuba)
2001	Celine Lebrun (France)

Under 52kg

1986	Dominique Brun (France)
1987	Sharon Rendle (Great Britain)
1989	Sharon Rendle (Great Britain)
1991	Alessandra Giungi (Italy)
1993	Rodriguez Verdecia (Cuba)
1995	Marie-Claire Restoux (France)
1997	Marie-Claire Restoux (France)
1999	Noriko Narasaki (Japan)
2001	Sun-Hui Kye (North Korea)

Over 78kg

1986	Gao Fengliang (China)
1987	Gao Fengliang (China)
1989	Gao Fengliang (China)
1991	Moon Ji-Yoon (South Korea)
1993	Johanna Hagen (Germany)
1995	Angelique Seriese (Netherlands)
1997	Christine Cicot (France)
1999	Beata Maksymow (Poland)
2001	Yuan Hua (China)

Under 48kg

1986	Karen Briggs (Great Britain)
1987	Zangyun Li (China)
1989	Karen Briggs (Great Britain)
1991	Cécile Nowak (France)
1993	Ryoko Tamura (Japan)
1995	Ryoko Tamura (Japan)
1997	Ryoko Tamura (Japan)
1999	Ryoko Tamura (Japan)
2001	Ryoko Tamura (Japan)

Karate

■ **World Championships**

First held in Tokyo in 1970; taken place every two years since 1980, when women first competed; there are team competitions plus individual competitions at Kumite and Kata. Since 1992 there have been separate men's and women's teams.

Kumite

Men		Women	
1992	Spain	1992	Great Britain
1994	France	1994	Spain
1996	France	1996	Great Britain
1998	France	1998	Turkey
2000	France	2000	France
2002	France	2002	France

Kata

Men		Women	
1992	Japan	1992	Japan
1994	Japan	1994	Japan
1996	Japan	1996	Japan
1998	Japan	1998	Japan
2000	Japan	2000	France
2002	Japan	2002	France

Lacrosse

■ **World Championships**

First held for men in 1967; for women in 1969; taken place every four years since 1974; since 1982 the women's event has been called the World Cup.

Men

1986	USA
1990	USA
1994	USA
1998	USA
2002	USA

Women

1986	Australia
1990	USA
1993	USA
1997	USA
2001	USA

■ **Iroquois Cup**

The sport's best known trophy; contested by English club sides annually since 1890.

1985	Cheadle
1986	Heaton Mersey
1987	Stockport
1988	Mellor
1989	Stockport
1990	Cheadle
1991	Cheadle
1992	Cheadle
1993	Heaton Mersey
1994	Cheadle
1995	Cheadle
1996	Stockport
1997	Mellor
1998	*not held*
1999	*not held*
2000	Cheadle
2001	*not held*
2002	Heaton Mersey

Modern Pentathlon

■ **World Championships**

Held annually since 1949 with the exception of Olympic years, when the Olympic champions automatically become world champions.

Individual

1985	Attila Mizser (Hungary)
1986	Carlo Massullo (Italy)
1987	Joel Bouzou (France)
1988	Janos Martinek (Hungary)
1989	Laszlo Fabien (Hungary)
1990	Gianluca Tiberti (Italy)
1991	Arkadiusz Skrzypaszek (Poland)
1992	Arkadiusz Skrzypaszek (Poland)
1993	Richard Phelps (Great Britain)
1994	Dmitri Svatovski (Russia)
1995	Dmitri Svatovski (Russia)
1996	Alexander Parygin (Kazakhstan)
1997	Sebastien Deleigne (France)
1998	Sebastien Deleigne (France)
1999	Gabor Balogh (Hungary)
2000	Dmitri Svatovski (Russia)
2001	Gabor Balogh (Hungary)
2002	Michal Sedlecky (Czech Republic)

Team

1985	USSR
1986	Italy
1987	Hungary
1988	Hungary
1989	Hungary
1990	USSR
1991	USSR
1992	Poland
1993	Hungary
1994	France
1995	Poland
1996	Poland
1997	Hungary
1998	Mexico
1999	Hungary
2000	*not held*
2001	Hungary
2002	Germany

Motor cycling

■ **World Championships**

First organized in 1949; current titles for Superbike, 500cc, 250cc, 125cc, 80cc and Sidecar; Formula One and Endurance world championships also held annually; the most prestigious title is the 500cc category.

500cc

1985	Freddie Spencer (USA)
1986	Eddie Lawson (USA)
1987	Wayne Gardner (Australia)
1988	Eddie Lawson (USA)
1989	Eddie Lawson (USA)
1990	Wayne Rainey (USA)
1991	Wayne Rainey (USA)
1992	Wayne Rainey (USA)
1993	Kevin Schwantz (USA)
1994	Michael Doohan (Australia)
1995	Michael Doohan (Australia)
1996	Michael Doohan (Australia)
1997	Michael Doohan (Australia)
1998	Michael Doohan (Australia)
1999	Alex Criville (Spain)
2000	Kenny Roberts (USA)
2001	Valentino Rossi (Italy)
2002	Valentino Rossi (Italy)

■ Isle of ManTT Races

The most famous of all motor cycle races; take place each June; first held 1907; principal race is the Senior TT.

SeniorTT

1985	Joey Dunlop (Ireland)
1986	Roger Burnett (Great Britain)
1987	Joey Dunlop (Ireland)
1988	Joey Dunlop (Ireland)
1989	Steve Hislop (Great Britain)
1990	Carl Fogarty (Great Britain)
1991	Steve Hislop (Great Britain)
1992	Steve Hislop (Great Britain)
1993	Phil McCallen (Ireland)
1994	Steve Hislop (Great Britain)
1995	Joey Dunlop (Ireland)
1996	Phil McCallen (Ireland)
1997	Phil McCallen (Ireland)
1998	Ian Simpson (Great Britain)
1999	David Jefferies (Great Britain)
2000	David Jefferies (Great Britain)
2001	*not held*
2002	David Jefferies (Great Britain)

Motor Racing

■ World Championship

A Formula One drivers' world championship instituted in 1950; constructor's championship instituted in 1958.

1985	Alain Prost (France)	*McLaren*
1986	Alain Prost (France)	*McLaren*
1987	Nelson Piquet (Brazil)	*Williams*
1988	Ayrton Senna (Brazil)	*McLaren*
1989	Alain Prost (France)	*McLaren*
1990	Ayrton Senna (Brazil)	*McLaren*
1991	Ayrton Senna (Brazil)	*McLaren*
1992	Nigel Mansell (Great Britain)	*Williams*
1993	Alain Prost (France)	*Williams*
1994	Michael Schumacher (Germany)	*Benetton*
1995	Michael Schumacher (Germany)	*Benetton*
1996	Damon Hill (Great Britain)	*Williams*
1997	Jacques Villeneuve (Canada)	*Williams*
1998	Mika Hakkinen (Finland)	*McLaren*
1999	Mika Hakkinen (Finland)	*McLaren*
2000	Michael Schumacher (Germany)	*Ferrari*
2001	Michael Schumacher (Germany)	*Ferrari*
2002	Michael Schumacher (Germany)	*Ferrari*

■ Le Mans 24-Hour Race

The greatest of all endurance races; first held in 1923.

1985	Klaus Ludwig (West Germany)
	'John Winter'[1] (West Germany)
	Paolo Barilla (Italy)
1986	Hans Stuck (West Germany)
	Derek Bell (Great Britain)
	Al Holbert (USA)
1987	Hans Stuck (West Germany)
	Derek Bell (Great Britain)
	Al Holbert (USA)
1988	Jan Lammers (Netherlands)
	Johnny Dumfries (Great Britain)
	Andy Wallace (Great Britain)
1989	Jochen Mass (West Germany)
	Manuel Reuter (West Germany)
	Stanley Dickens (Sweden)
1990	John Nielsen (Denmark)
	Price Cobb (USA)
	Martin Brundle (Great Britain)
1991	Volker Weidler (Germany)
	Johnny Herbert (Great Britain)
	Bertrand Gachot (Belgium)
1992	Derek Warwick (Great Britain)
	Mark Blundell (Great Britain)
	Yannick Dalmas (France)
1993	Geoff Brabham (Australia)
	Christophe Bouchut (France)
	Eric Helary (France)
1994	Yannick Dalmas (France)
	Hurley Haywood (USA)
	Mauro Baldi (Italy)
1995	Yannick Dalmas (France)
	J J Lehto (Finland)
	Masanori Sekiya (Japan)
1996	Manuel Reuter (Germany)
	Davy Jones (USA)
	Alexander Wurz (Austria)
1997	Michele Alboreto (Italy)
	Stefan Johansson (Sweden)
	Tom Kristensen (Denmark)
1998	Allan McNish (Great Britain)
	Laurent Aiello (France)
	Stephane Ortelli (France)
1999	Pierluigi Martini (Italy)
	Joachim Winkelhock (Germany)
	Yannick Dalmas (France)
2000	Frank Biela (Germany)
	Tom Kristensen (Denmark)
	Emanuele Pirro (Italy)
2001	Frank Biela (Germany)
	Tom Kristensen (Denmark)
	Emanuele Pirro (Italy)
2002	Frank Biela (Germany)
	Tom Kristensen (Denmark)
	Emanuele Pirro (Italy)

■ Indianapolis 500

First held in 1911; raced over the Indianapolis Raceway as part of the Memorial Day celebrations at the end of May each year.

1985	Danny Sullivan (USA)
1986	Bobby Rahal (USA)
1987	Al Unser (USA)
1988	Rick Mears (USA)

1989	Emerson Fittipaldi (Brazil)
1990	Arie Luyendyk (Netherlands)
1991	Rick Mears (USA)
1992	Al Unser (USA)
1993	Emerson Fittipaldi (Brazil)
1994	Al Unser (USA)
1995	Jacques Villeneuve (Canada)
1996	Buddy Lazier (USA)
1997	Arie Luyendyk (Netherlands)
1998	Eddie Cheever (USA)
1999	Kenny Brack (USA)
2000	Juan Montoya (Colombia)
2001	Helio Castroneves (Brazil)
2002	Helio Castroneves (Brazil)

▪ Monte Carlo Rally
The world's leading rally; first held in 1911.

1985	Ari Vatanen (Finland)
	Terry Harryman (Great Britain)
1986	Henri Toivonen (Finland)
	Sergio Cresto (Italy)
1987	Miki Biasion (Italy)
	Tiziano Siviero (Italy)
1988	Bruno Saby (France)
	Jean-François Fauchille (France)
1989	Miki Biasion (Italy)
	Tiziano Siviero (Italy)
1990	Didier Auriol (France)
	Bernard Occelli (France)
1991	Carlos Sainz (Spain)
	Luis Moya (Spain)
1992	Didier Auriol (France)
	Bernard Occelli (France)
1993	Didier Auriol (France)
	Bernard Occelli (France)
1994	François Delecour (France)
	Daniel Grataloup (France)
1995	Carlos Sainz (Spain)
	Luis Moya (Spain)
1996	Patrick Bernardini (France)
	Bernard Occelli (France)
1997	Piero Liatti (Italy)
	Fabrizia Pons (Italy)
1998	Carlos Sainz (Spain)
	Luis Moya (Spain)
1999	Tommi Mäkinen (Finland)
	Risto Mannisenmäki (Finland)
2000	Tommi Mäkinen (Finland)
	Risto Mannisenmäki (Finland)
2001	Tommi Mäkinen (Finland)
	Risto Mannisenmäki (Finland)
2002	Tommi Mäkinen (Finland)
	Kaj Lindstrom (Finland)

Netball

▪ World Championships
First held in 1963, then every four years.

1987	New Zealand
1991	Australia
1995	Australia
1999	Australia

Orienteering

▪ World Championships
First held in 1966; takes place every two years (to 1978, and since 1979).

Individual (Men)

1985	Kari Sallinen (Finland)
1987	Kent Olsson (Sweden)
1989	Peter Thoresen (Norway)
1991	Jörgen Mårtensson (Sweden)
1993	Alan Mogensen (Denmark)
1995	Jörgen Mårtensson (Sweden)
1997	Peter Thoresen (Denmark)
1999	Bjornar Valstad (Norway)
2001	Jörgen Rostup (Finland)

Individual (Women)

1985	Annichen Kringstad Svensson (Norway)
1987	Arja Hannus (Sweden)
1989	Marita Skogum (Sweden)
1991	Katalin Olah (Hungary)
1993	Marita Skogum (Sweden)
1995	Katalin Olah (Hungary)
1997	Hanne Staff (Norway)
1999	Kirsi Bostrom (Finland)
2001	Simone Luder (Switzerland)

Relay (Men)

1985	Norway
1987	Norway
1989	Norway
1991	Switzerland
1993	Switzerland
1995	Switzerland
1997	Denmark
1999	Norway
2001	Finland

Relay (Women)

1985	Sweden
1987	Norway
1989	Sweden
1991	Sweden
1993	Sweden
1995	Finland
1997	Sweden
1999	Norway
2001	Finland

Polo

▪ Veuve Clicquot Gold Cup
First held in 1956, replacing the Champion Cup; the British Open Championship for club sides, played at Cowdray Park, Sussex; formerly called the Cowdray Park Gold Cup.

1985	Maple Leafs
1986	Tramontona
1987	Tramontona

Polo field

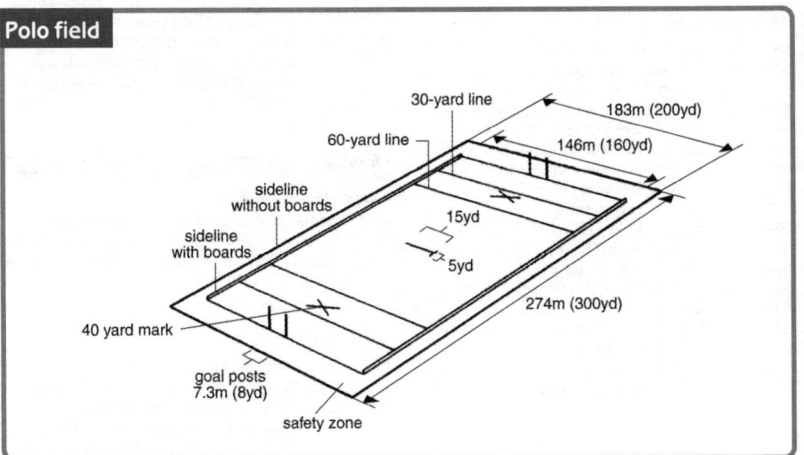

1988	Tramontona
1989	Tramontona
1990	Tramontona
1991	Tramontona
1992	Black Bears
1993	Alcatel
1994	Ellerston Blacks
1995	Ellerston Whites
1996	C S Brooks
1997	Labegorce
1998	Ellerston
1999	Pommery
2000	Geebung
2001	Dubai
2002	Black Bears

Powerboat racing

■ **World Championships**
Instituted in 1982; held in many categories, with Formula One and Formula Two being the principal competitions; Formula One was not held between 1987 and 1989; Formula Two was discontinued in 1989 and revived for one year in 1997.

Formula One

1985	Bob Spalding (Great Britain)
1986	Gene Thibodaux (USA)
1990	John Hill (Great Britain)
1991	Jonathan Jones (Great Britain)
1992	Fabrizio Bocca (Italy)
1993	Guido Cappellini (Italy)
1994	Guido Cappellini (Italy)
1995	Guido Cappellini (Italy)
1996	Guido Cappellini (Italy)
1997	Scott Gilman (USA)
1998	Jonathan Jones (Great Britain)
1999	Guido Cappellini (Italy)
2000	Scott Gilman (USA)
2001	Guido Cappellini (Italy)
2002	Guido Cappellini (Italy)

Formula Two

1985	John Hill (Great Britain)

1986	Jonathan Jones (Great Britain) and Buck Thornton (USA) (*shared*)
1987	Bill Seebold (USA)
1988	Chris Bush (USA)
1989	Jonathan Jones (Great Britain)
1997	Mark Rolls (Great Britain)

Real tennis

■ **World Championship**
Organized on a challenge basis; the first world champion was M Clerge (France) c.1740, regarded as the first world champion of any sport.

1981–7	Chris Ronaldson (Great Britain)
1987–94	Wayne Davies (Australia)
1994–	Robert Fahey (Australia)

Roller skating

■ **World Championships**
Figure skating world championships were first organized in 1947.

Men Combined

1985	Michele Biserni (Italy)
1986	Michele Tolomini (Italy)
1987	Kevin Carroll (USA)
1988	Sandro Guerra (Italy)
1989	Sandro Guerra (Italy)
1990	Samo Kokorovec (Italy)
1991	Sandro Guerra (Italy)
1992	Sandro Guerra (Italy)
1993	Samo Kokorovec (Italy)
1994	Steven Findlay (USA)
1995	Jason Sutcliffe (Australia)
1996	Francesco Ceresola (Italy)
1997	Mauro Mazzoni (Italy)
1998	Daniel Tofani (Italy)
1999	Adrian Stolzenberg (Germany)
2000	Adrian Stolzenberg (Germany)
2001	Leonardo Pancani (Italy)
2002	Frank Albiez (Germany)

Sports and Games

Women Combined

1985	Chiara Sartori (Italy)
1986	Chiara Sartori (Italy)
1987	Chiara Sartori (Italy)
1988	Rafaela Del Vinaccio (Italy)
1989	Rafaela Del Vinaccio (Italy)
1990	Rafaela Del Vinaccio (Italy)
1991	Rafaela Del Vinaccio (Italy)
1992	Rafaela Del Vinaccio (Italy)
1993	Letitia Tinghi (Italy)
1994	April Dayney (USA)
1995	Letitia Tinghi (Italy)
1996	Giusy Loncani (Italy)
1997	Sabrina Tomasini (Italy)
1998	Elke Dederichs (Germany)
1999	Elisa Facciotti (Italy)
2000	Elisa Facciotti (Italy)
2001	Elisa Facciotti (Italy)
2002	Tania Romano (Italy)

Pairs

1985	John Arishita/Tammy Jeru (USA)
1986	John Arishita/Tammy Jeru (USA)
1987	Fabio Trevisani/Monica Mezzardi (Italy)
1988	Fabio Trevisani/Monica Mezzardi (Italy)
1989	David De Motte/Nicky Armstrong (USA)
1990	Larry McGrew/Tammy Jeru (USA)
1991	Larry McGrew/Tammy Jeru (USA)
1992	Patrick Venerucci/Maura Ferri (Italy)
1993	Patrick Venerucci/Maura Ferri (Italy)
1994	Patrick Venerucci/Beatrice Pallazzi Rossi (Italy)
1995	Patrick Venerucci/Beatrice Pallazzi Rossi (Italy)
1996	Patrick Venerucci/Beatrice Pallazzi Rossi (Italy)
1997	Patrick Venerucci/Beatrice Pallazzi Rossi (Italy)
1998	Patrick Venerucci/Beatrice Pallazzi Rossi (Italy)
1999	Patrick Venerucci/Beatrice Pallazzi Rossi (Italy)
2000	Patrick Venerucci/Beatrice Pallazzi Rossi (Italy)
2001	Patrick Venerucci/Beatrice Pallazzi Rossi (Italy)
2002	Patrick Venerucci/Beatrice Pallazzi Rossi (Italy)

Dance

1985	Martin Hauss/Andrea Steudte (West Germany)
1986	Scott Myers/Anna Danks (USA)
1987	Rob Ferendo/Lori Walsh (USA)
1988	Peter Wulf/Michela Mitzlaf (West Germany)
1989	Greg Goody/Jodee Viola (USA)
1990	Greg Goody/Jodee Viola (USA)
1991	Greg Goody/Jodee Viola (USA)
1992	Doug Wait/Deanna Monaham (USA)
1993	Doug Wait/Deanna Monaham (USA)
1994	Tim Patten/Lisa Friday (USA)
1995	Tim Patten/Lisa Friday (USA)
1996	Axel Haber/Swansi Gebauer (Germany)
1997	Axel Haber/Swansi Gebauer (Germany)
1998	Ronald Brenn/Candi Powderly (USA)
1999	Tim Patten/Tara Graney (USA)
2000	Adam White/Melissa Quinn (USA)
2001	Adam White/Melissa Quinn (USA)
2002	Marco Bornati/Emanuela Bornati (Italy)

Rowing

▪ World Championships

First held for men in 1962 and for women in 1974; Olympic champions assume the role of world champion in Olympic years; principal event is the single sculls.

Single Sculls (Men)

1985	Perrti Karppinen (Finland)
1986	Peter-Michael Kolbe (West Germany)
1987	Thomas Lange (East Germany)
1988	Thomas Lange (East Germany)
1989	Thomas Lange (East Germany)
1990	Yuri Janson (USSR)
1991	Thomas Lange (Germany)
1992	Thomas Lange (Germany)
1993	Derek Porter (Canada)
1994	Andre Wilms (Germany)
1995	Iztok Cop (Slovenia)
1996	Xeno Müller (Switzerland)
1997	Jamie Koven (USA)
1998	Rob Waddell (New Zealand)
1999	Rob Waddell (New Zealand)
2000	Rob Waddell (New Zealand)
2001	Olaf Tufte (Norway)
2002	Marcel Hacker (Germany)

Single Sculls (Women)

1985	Cornelia Linse (East Germany)
1986	Jutta Hampe (East Germany)
1987	Magdelena Georgieva (Bulgaria)
1988	Jutta Behrendt (East Germany)
1989	Elisabeta Lipa (Romania)
1990	Brigit Peter (East Germany)
1991	Silke Laumann (Canada)
1992	Elisabeta Lipa (Romania)
1993	Jana Phieme (Germany)
1994	Trine Hansen (Denmark)
1995	Maria Brandin (Sweden)
1996	Ekaterina Khodotovich (Belarus)
1997	Ekaterina Khodotovich (Belarus)
1998	Irina Fedotova (Russia)
1999	Ekaterina Karsten (Belarus)
2000	Ekaterina Karsten (Belarus)
2001	Katrin Rutschow-Stomporowski (Germany)
2002	Rumyana Neykova (Bulgaria)

▪ The Boat Race

An annual contest between the crews from the Oxford and Cambridge University rowing clubs; first contested in 1829; the current course is from Putney to Mortlake.

1985	Oxford
1986	Cambridge
1987	Oxford
1988	Oxford
1989	Oxford

1990	Oxford
1991	Oxford
1992	Oxford
1993	Cambridge
1994	Cambridge
1995	Cambridge
1996	Cambridge
1997	Cambridge
1998	Cambridge
1999	Cambridge
2000	Oxford
2001	Cambridge
2002	Oxford

■ Diamond Sculls
Highlight of Henley Royal Regatta held every July; first contested in 1884.

1985	Steve Redgrave (Great Britain)
1986	Bjarne Eltang (Denmark)
1987	Peter-Michael Kolbe (West Germany)
1988	Hamish McGlashan (Australia)
1989	Vaclav Chlupa (Czechoslovakia)
1990	Erik Verdonk (New Zealand)
1991	Wim van Belleghem (Belgium)
1992	Rorie Henderson (Great Britain)
1993	Thomas Lange (Germany)
1994	Xeno Müller (Switzerland)
1995	Juri Jaanson (Estonia)
1996	Merlin Vervoorn (Netherlands)
1997	Greg Searle (Great Britain)
1998	Jamie Koven (USA)
1999	Marcel Hacker (Germany)
2000	Aquil Abdullah (USA)
2001	Duncan Free (Australia)
2002	Peter Wells (Great Britain)

Rugby league

■ Challenge Cup Final
First contested in 1897 and won by Batley; first final at Wembley Stadium in 1929.

1985	Wigan
1986	Castleford
1987	Halifax
1988	Wigan
1989	Wigan
1990	Wigan
1991	Wigan
1992	Wigan
1993	Wigan
1994	Wigan
1995	Wigan
1996	St Helens
1997	St Helens
1998	Sheffield
1999	Leeds
2000	Bradford
2001	St Helens
2002	Wigan

■ Premiership Trophy
End-of-season knockout competition involving the top eight teams in the first division; first contested at the end of the 1974–5 season; discontinued in 1997.

1985	St Helens
1986	Warrington

1987	Wigan
1988	Widnes
1989	Widnes
1990	Widnes
1991	Hull
1992	Wigan
1993	St Helens
1994	Wigan
1995	Wigan
1996	Wigan
1997	Wigan

■ Regal Trophy
A knockout competition, first held in 1971–2. Known as the John Player Special Trophy until 1989–90; discontinued in 1996.

1985	Hull
1986	Wigan
1987	Wigan
1988	St Helens
1989	Wigan
1990	Wigan
1991	Warrington
1992	Widnes
1993	Wigan
1994	Castleford
1995	Wigan
1996	Wigan

■ Tetley's Super League
First held in 1996. The top five teams in the league at the end of the season play off for the title; known as the JJB Super League from 1996 to 1999.

1996	St Helens
1997	Bradford
1998	Wigan
1999	St Helens
2000	St Helens
2001	Bradford
2002	St Helens

Rugby union

■ World Cup
The first Rugby Union World Cup was staged in 1987; takes place every four years.

1987	New Zealand
1991	Australia
1995	South Africa
1999	Australia

■ Six Nations' Championship
A round robin competition involving England, Ireland, Scotland, Wales, France, and from 2000, Italy; first contested in 1884.

1985	Ireland
1986	France and Scotland
1987	France
1988	France and Wales
1989	France
1990	Scotland

1991	England
1992	England
1993	France
1994	Wales
1995	England
1996	England
1997	France
1998	France
1999	Scotland
2000	England
2001	England
2002	France

■ County Championship
First held in 1889.

1985	Middlesex
1986	Warwickshire
1987	Yorkshire
1988	Lancashire
1989	Durham
1990	Lancashire
1991	Cornwall
1992	Lancashire
1993	Lancashire
1994	Yorkshire
1995	Warwickshire
1996	Gloucestershire
1997	Cumbria
1998	Cheshire
1999	Cornwall
2000	Yorkshire
2001	Yorkshire
2002	Gloucestershire

■ Powergen Cup
An annual knockout competition for English Club sides; first held in the 1971–2 season; known as the John Player Special Cup until 1988, the Pilkington Cup until 1997, and the Tetley's Bitter Cup until 2000.

1985	Bath
1986	Bath
1987	Bath
1988	Harlequins
1989	Bath

1990	Bath
1991	Harlequins
1992	Bath
1993	Leicester
1994	Bath
1995	Bath
1996	Bath
1997	Leicester
1998	Saracens
1999	Wasps
2000	Wasps
2001	Newcastle Falcons
2002	London Irish

■ Principality Cup
The knockout tournament for Welsh clubs; first held in 1971–2; formerly known as the Schweppes Welsh Cup and the Swalec Cup.

1985	Llanelli
1986	Cardiff
1987	Cardiff
1988	Llanelli
1989	Neath
1990	Neath
1991	Llanelli
1992	Llanelli
1993	Llanelli
1994	Cardiff
1995	Swansea
1996	Pontypridd
1997	Cardiff
1998	Llanelli
1999	Swansea
2000	Llanelli
2001	Newport
2002	Pontypridd

Shinty

■ Camanachd Cup
The sport's principal trophy, it was first held in 1896 and won by Kingussie. Shinty is the popular name for the original game of Camanachd.

1985	Newtonmore
1986	Newtonmore
1987	Kingussie

Rugby Union pitch

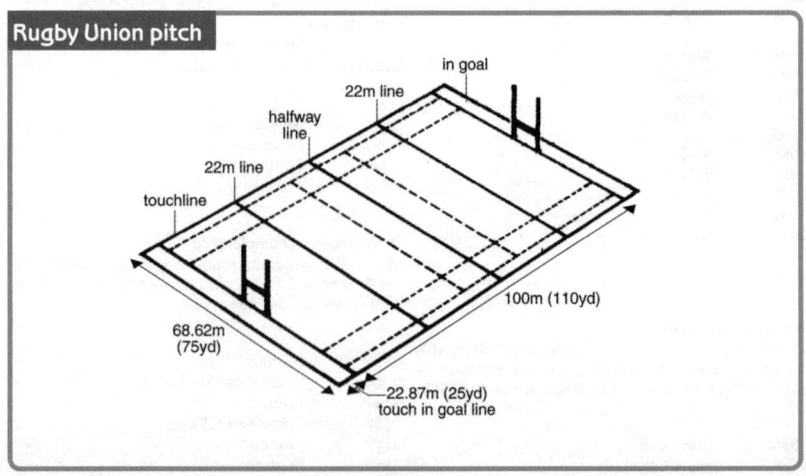

in goal
22m line
halfway line
22m line
touchline
68.62m (75yd)
100m (110yd)
22.87m (25yd) touch in goal line

1988	Kingussie
1989	Kingussie
1990	Skye
1991	Kingussie
1992	Fort William
1993	Kingussie
1994	Kyles Athletic
1995	Kingussie
1996	Oban
1997	Kingussie
1998	Kingussie
1999	Kingussie
2000	Kingussie
2001	Kingussie
2002	Kingussie

Shooting

■ Olympic Games

The Olympic competition is the highlight of the shooting calendar; winners in all categories since 1988 are given below.

Free Pistol (Men)

1988	Sorin Babil (Romania)
1992	Konstantine Loukachik (UT)
1996	Boris Kokorev (Russia)
2000	Tanyu Kiriakov (Bulgaria)

Rapid Fire Pistol (Men)

1988	Afanasi Kouzmine (USSR)
1992	Ralf Schumann (Germany)
1996	Ralf Schumann (Germany)
2000	Sergei Alifirenko (Russia)

Small Bore Rifle (Three Position) (Men)

1988	Malcolm Cooper (Great Britain)
1992	Grachya Petikiane (UT)
1996	Jean-Pierre Amat (France)
2000	Rajmond Debevec (Slovenia)

Running Game Target (Men)

1988	Tor Heiestad (Norway)
1992	Michael Jakosits (Germany)
1996	Ling Yang (China)
2000	Ling Yang (China)

Trap (Men)

1988	Dmitri Monakov (USSR)
1992	Petr Hrdlicka (Czechoslovakia)
1996	Michael Diamond (Australia)
2000	Michael Diamond (Australia)

Double Trap (Men)

1988	*not held*
1992	*not held*
1996	Russell Mark (Australia)
2000	Richard Faulds (Great Britain)

Skeet (Men)

1988	Axel Wegner (East Germany)
1992	Zhang Shan (China)
1996	Ennio Falco (Italy)
2000	Mykola Milchev (Ukraine)

Small Bore Rifle (Prone) (Men)

1988	Miroslav Varga (Czechoslovakia)
1992	Lee Eun-chul (South Korea)
1996	Christian Klees (Germany)
2000	Jonas Edmans (Sweden)

Air Rifle (Men)

1988	Goran Maksimovic (Yugoslavia)
1992	Yuri Fedkin (UT)
1996	Artem Khadzhibekov (Russia)
2000	Yalin Cai (China)

Air Pistol (Men)

1988	Tariou Kiriakov (USSR)
1992	Wang Yifu (China)
1996	Roberto di Donna (Italy)
2000	Franck Dumoulin (France)

Sport Pistol (Women)

1988	Nino Saloukvadze (USSR)
1992	Marina Logvinenko (UT)
1996	Li Duihong (China)
2000	Maria Grozdeva (Bulgaria)

Air Rifle (Women)

1988	Irina Chilova (USSR)
1992	Yeo Kab Soon (South Korea)
1996	Renata Mauer (Poland)
2000	Nancy Johnson (USA)

Small Bore Rifle (Three Position) (Women)

1988	Silvia Sperber (West Germany)
1992	Launa Meili (USA)
1996	Alexandra Ivosev (Yugoslavia)
2000	Renata Mauer-Rozanska (Poland)

Air Pistol (Women)

1988	Jasna Sekuric (Yugoslavia)
1992	Marina Logvinenko (UT)
1996	Olga Klochneva (Russia)
2000	Luna Tao (China)

Double Trap (Women)

1988	*not held*
1992	*not held*
1996	Kim Rhode (USA)
2000	Pia Hansen (Sweden)

Trap (Women)

1988	*not held*
1992	*not held*
1996	*not held*
2000	Daina Gudzineviciute (Lithuania)

Skeet (Women)

1988	*not held*
1992	*not held*
1996	*not held*
2000	Zemfira Meftakhetdinova (Azerbaijan)

Skiing

World Cup
A season-long competition first organized in 1967; champions are declared in downhill, slalom, giant slalom and super-giant slalom, as well as the overall champion; points are obtained for performances in each category.

Overall winners

Men

1985	Marc Girardelli (Luxembourg)
1986	Marc Girardelli (Luxembourg)
1987	Pirmin Zurbriggen (Switzerland)
1988	Pirmin Zurbriggen (Switzerland)
1989	Marc Girardelli (Luxembourg)
1990	Pirmin Zurbriggen (Switzerland)
1991	Marc Girardelli (Luxembourg)
1992	Paul Accola (Switzerland)
1993	Marc Girardelli (Luxembourg)
1994	Kjetil-Andre Aamodt (Norway)
1995	Alberto Tomba (Italy)
1996	Lasse Kjus (Norway)
1997	Luc Alphand (France)
1998	Hermann Maier (Austria)
1999	Lasse Kjus (Norway)
2000	Hermann Maier (Austria)
2001	Hermann Maier (Austria)
2002	Stephan Eberharter (Austria)

Women

1985	Michela Figini (Switzerland)
1986	Maria Walliser (Switzerland)
1987	Maria Walliser (Switzerland)
1988	Michela Figini (Switzerland)
1989	Vreni Schneider (Switzerland)
1990	Petra Kronberger (Austria)
1991	Petra Kronberger (Austria)
1992	Petra Kronberger (Austria)
1993	Anita Wachter (Austria)
1994	Vreni Schneider (Switzerland)
1995	Vreni Schneider (Switzerland)
1996	Katja Seizinger (Germany)
1997	Pernilla Wiberg (Sweden)
1998	Katja Seizinger (Germany)
1999	Alexandra Meissnitzer (Austria)
2000	Renate Götschl (Austria)
2001	Janica Kostelic (Croatia)
2002	Michaela Dorfmeister (Austria)

Snooker

World Professional Championship
Instituted in the 1926–7 season; a knockout competition open to professional players who are members of the World Professional Billiards and Snooker Association; played at the Crucible Theatre, Sheffield.

1985	Dennis Taylor (Northern Ireland)
1986	Joe Johnson (England)
1987	Steve Davis (England)
1988	Steve Davis (England)
1989	Steve Davis (England)
1990	Stephen Hendry (Scotland)
1991	John Parrott (England)
1992	Stephen Hendry (Scotland)
1993	Stephen Hendry (Scotland)
1994	Stephen Hendry (Scotland)
1995	Stephen Hendry (Scotland)
1996	Stephen Hendry (Scotland)
1997	Ken Doherty (Ireland)
1998	John Higgins (Scotland)
1999	Stephen Hendry (Scotland)
2000	Mark Williams (Wales)
2001	Ronnie O'Sullivan (England)
2002	Peter Ebdon (England)

World Doubles
First played in 1982; discontinued after 1987.

All winners

1982	Steve Davis (England)/Tony Meo (England)
1983	Steve Davis (England)/Tony Meo (England)
1984	Alex Higgins (Ireland)/Jimmy White (England)
1985	Steve Davis (England)/Tony Meo (England)
1986	Steve Davis (England)/Tony Meo (England)
1987	Mike Hallett (England)/Stephen Hendry (Scotland)

World Team Championship
Also known as the World Cup; first held in 1979.

1985	Ireland 'A'
1986	Ireland 'A'
1987	Ireland 'A'
1988	England
1989	England
1990	Canada
1991	*not held*
1992	*not held*
1993	*not held*
1994	*not held*
1995	*not held*
1996	Scotland
1997	*not held*
1998	*not held*
1999	*not held*
2000	*not held*
2001	*not held*
2002	*not held*

World Amateur Championship
First held in 1963; originally took place every two years, but annual since 1984.

1985	Paul Mifsud (Malta)
1986	Paul Mifsud (Malta)
1987	Darren Morgan (Wales)
1988	James Wattana (Thailand)
1989	Ken Doherty (Republic of Ireland)
1990	Stephen O'Connor (Republic of Ireland)
1991	Noppodol Noppajorn (Thailand)
1992	Neil Mosley (England)
1993	Chuchat Triratanapradit (Thailand)
1994	Mohamed Yusuf (Pakistan)
1995	Sakchai Sim-Nhan (Thailand)
1996	Stuart Bingham (England)
1997	Marco Fu (China/Hong Kong)
1998	Luke Simmonds (England)
1999	Ian Preece (Wales)
2000	Stephen Maguire (Scotland)
2001	*not held*
2002	Steve Mifsud (Australia)

Softball

■ **World Championships**
First held for women in 1965 and for men the following year; now held every four years.

Men

1988	USA
1992	Canada
1996	New Zealand
2000	New Zealand

Women

1986	USA
1990	USA
1994	USA
1998	USA
2002	USA

Speedway

■ **Grand Prix**
Individual World Championships inaugurated in 1936; replaced by Grand Prix season in 1995. Team championship (the World Team Cup) instituted in 1960; first official World Pairs Championship in 1970 (threes from 1991); World Team Cup and World Pairs Championship amalgamated in 1994 to become World Team Championship; replaced by Speedway World Cup in 2001.

Individual Grand Prix

1985	Erik Gundersen (Denmark)
1986	Hans Nielsen (Denmark)
1987	Hans Nielsen (Denmark)
1988	Erik Gundersen (Denmark)
1989	Hans Nielsen (Denmark)
1990	Per Jonsson (Sweden)
1991	Jan Pedersen (Denmark)
1992	Gary Havelock (England)
1993	Sam Ermolenko (USA)
1994	Tony Rickardsson (Sweden)
1995	Hans Nielsen (Denmark)
1996	Billy Hamill (USA)
1997	Greg Hancock (USA)
1998	Tony Rickardsson (Sweden)
1999	Tony Rickardsson (Sweden)
2000	Mark Loram (England)
2001	Tony Rickardsson (Sweden)
2002	Tony Rickardsson (Sweden)

Pairs/Threes

1985	Erik Gunderson/Tommy Knudsen (Denmark)
1986	Erik Gundersen/Hans Nielsen (Denmark)
1987	Erik Gundersen/Hans Nielsen (Denmark)
1988	Erik Gundersen/Hans Nielsen (Denmark)
1989	Jeremy Doncaster/Paul Thorp (Great Britain)
1990	Sam Ermolenko/Rick Miller (USA)
1991	Hans Nielsen/Jan Pedersen/Tommy Knudsen (Denmark)
1992	Greg Hancock/Sam Ermolenko/Ronnie Correy (USA)
1993	Greg Hancock/Sam Ermolenko (USA)

■ **World Cup**

1994	Per Gustaffson/Tony Rickardsson/Michael Karlsson (Sweden)
1995	Hans Nielsen/Tommy Knudsen/Brian Carger (Denmark)
1996	Tomasz Gollob/ Piotr Protasiewicz/Slawomir Drabik (Poland)
1997	Hans Neilsen/Tommy Knudsen/Jesper Jensen (Denmark)
1998	Greg Hancock/Sam Ermolenko/ Billy Hamill (USA)
1999	Jason Crump/Jason Lyons/Leigh Adams/Ryan Sullivan/Todd Wiltshire (Australia)
2000	Tony Rickardsson/Mikael Karlsson/Henrik Gustafsson/Peter Karlsson/Niklas Klingberg (Sweden)
2001	Jason Crump/Leigh Adams/Ryan Sullivan/Todd Wiltshire/Craig Boyce (Australia)
2002	Jason Crump/Leigh Adams/Jason Lyons/Ryan Sullivan/Todd Wiltshire (Australia)

Squash

■ **World Open Championship**
First held in 1976; takes place annually for men and women; every two years for women 1976–89.

Men

1985	Jahangir Khan (Pakistan)
1986	Ross Norman (New Zealand)
1987	Jansher Khan (Pakistan)
1988	Jahangir Khan (Pakistan)
1989	Jansher Khan (Pakistan)
1990	Jansher Khan (Pakistan)
1991	Rodney Martin (Australia)
1992	Jansher Khan (Pakistan)
1993	Jansher Khan (Pakistan)
1994	Jansher Khan (Pakistan)
1995	Jansher Khan (Pakistan)
1996	Jansher Khan (Pakistan)
1997	Rodney Eyles (Australia)
1998	Jonathon Power (Canada)
1999	Peter Nicol (Great Britain)
2000	*not held*
2001	*not held*
2002	David Palmer (Australia)

Women

1985	Sue Devoy (New Zealand)
1987	Sue Devoy (New Zealand)
1989	Martine Le Moignan (Great Britain)
1990	Sue Devoy (New Zealand)
1991	*not held*
1992	Sue Devoy (New Zealand)
1993	Michelle Martin (Australia)
1994	Michelle Martin (Australia)
1995	Michelle Martin (Australia)
1996	Sarah Fitz-Gerald (Australia)
1997	Sarah Fitz-Gerald (Australia)
1998	Sarah Fitz-Gerald (Australia)
1999	Cassie Campion (Great Britain)
2000	Carol Owens (Australia)
2001	Sarah Fitz-Gerald (Australia)
2002	Sarah Fitz-Gerald (Australia)

Surfing

■ **World Professional Championship**
A season-long series of Grand Prix events; first held in 1970.

Men

1985	Tom Carroll (Australia)

Squash court

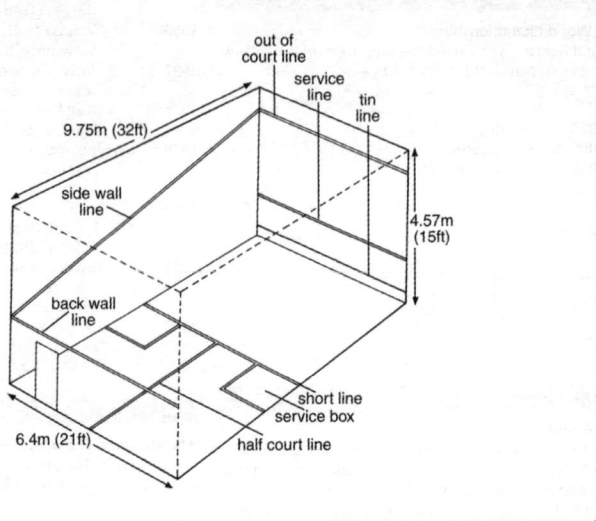

out of
court line

service
line

tin
line

9.75m (32ft)

side wall
line

4.57m
(15ft)

back wall
line

short line
service box

6.4m (21ft)

half court line

1986	Tommy Curren (USA)
1987	Damien Hardman (Australia)
1988	Barton Lynch (Australia)
1989	Martin Potter (Great Britain)
1990	Tommy Curren (USA)
1991	Damien Hardman (Australia)
1992	Kelly Slater (USA)
1993	Derek Ho (USA)
1994	Kelly Slater (USA)
1995	Kelly Slater (USA)
1996	Kelly Slater (USA)
1997	Kelly Slater (USA)
1998	Kelly Slater (USA)
1999	Mark Occhilupo (Australia)
2000	Sunny Garcia (USA)
2001	CJ Hobgood (USA)
2002	Andy Irons (USA)

Women

1985	Frieda Zamba (USA)
1986	Frieda Zamba (USA)
1987	Wendy Botha (South Africa)
1988	Frieda Zamba (USA)
1989	Wendy Botha (South Africa)
1990	Pam Burridge (Australia)
1991	Wendy Botha (Australia)
1992	Wendy Botha (Australia)
1993	Pauline Menczer (Australia)
1994	Lisa Andersen (USA)
1995	Lisa Andersen (USA)
1996	Lisa Andersen (USA)
1997	Lisa Andersen (USA)
1998	Layne Beachley (Australia)
1999	Layne Beachley (Australia)
2000	Layne Beachley (Australia)
2001	Layne Beachley (Australia)
2002	Layne Beachley (Australia)

Swimming and diving

■ **World Championships**

First held in 1973 and again in 1975; from 1978 held
approximately every four years; since 2001 held

every two years; the complete list of 2001 world
champions is given below.

Men

50m freestyle	Anthony Ervin (USA)
100m freestyle	Anthony Ervin (USA)
200m freestyle	Ian Thorpe (Australia)
400m freestyle	Ian Thorpe (Australia)
1 500m freestyle	Grant Hackett (Australia)
100m backstroke	Matt Welsh (Australia)
200m backstroke	Aaron Peirsol (USA)
100m breaststroke	Roman Sloudnov (Russia)
200m breaststroke	Brendan Hansen (USA)
100m butterfly	Lars Frolander (Sweden)
200m butterfly	Michael Phelps (USA)
200m individual medley	Massimiliano Rosolini (Italy)
400m individual medley	Alessio Boggiatto (Italy)
4 × 100m freestyle relay	Australia
4 × 200m freestyle relay	Australia
4 × 100m medley relay	Australia
3m springboard diving	Dimitry Saoutine (Russia)
1m springboard diving	Feng Wang (China)

Women

50m freestyle	Inge de Bruijn (Netherlands)
100m freestyle	Inge de Bruijn (Netherlands)
200m freestyle	Giaan Rooney (Australia)
400m freestyle	Yana Klochova (Ukraine)
800m freestyle	Hannah Stockbauer (Germany)
100m backstroke	Natalie Coughlin (USA)
200m backstroke	Diana Iuliana Mocanu (Romania)
100m breaststroke	Xuejuan Luo (China)
200m breaststroke	Agnes Kovacs (Hungary)
100m butterfly	Petria Thomas (Australia)
200m butterfly	Petria Thomas (Australia)

200m individual medley	Martha Bowen (USA)
400m individual medley	Yana Klochova (Ukraine)
4 × 100m freestyle relay	Germany
4 × 200m freestyle relay	Great Britain
4 × 100m medley relay	Australia
1m springboard diving	Blythe Hartley (Canada)
3m springboard diving	Mian Xu (China)
Synchronized swimming	
Solo	Olga Brusnikina (Russia)
Duet	Japan
Team	Russia

Table tennis

■ World Championships
First held in 1926 and every two years since 1957, with the exception of 1999.

Swaythling Cup (Men's Team)

1985	China
1987	China
1989	Sweden
1991	Sweden
1993	Sweden
1995	China
1997	China
1999	*not held*
2000	Sweden
2001	China

Corbillon Cup (Women's Team)

1985	China
1987	China
1989	China
1991	Unified Korea
1993	China
1995	China
1997	China
1999	*not held*
2000	China
2001	China

Men's Singles

1985	Jiang Jialiang (China)
1987	Jiang Jialiang (China)
1989	Jan-Ove Waldner (Sweden)
1991	Jorgen Persson (Sweden)
1993	Jean-Philippe Gatien (France)
1995	Kong Linghui (China)
1997	Jan-Ove Waldner (Sweden)
1999	Liu Guoliang (China)
2001	Wang Liqin (China)

Women's Singles

1985	Cao Yanhua (China)
1987	He Zhili (China)
1989	Qiao Hong (China)
1991	Deng Yaping (China)
1993	Hyun Jung-Hwa (South Korea)
1995	Deng Yaping (China)
1997	Deng Yaping (China)
1999	Wang Nan (China)
2001	Wang Nan (China)

Men's Doubles

1985	Mikael Applegren/Ulf Carlsson (Sweden)
1987	Chen Longcan/Wei Quinguang (China)
1989	Jaerg Rosskopf/Stefen Fetzner (West Germany)
1991	Peter Karlsson/Tomas von Scheele (Sweden)
1993	Wang Tao/Lu Lin (China
1995	Wang Tao/Lu Lin (China)
1997	Jan-Ove Waldner/Jorgen Persson (Sweden)
1999	Liu Guoliang/Kong Linghui (China)
2001	Liu Guoliang/Kong Linghui (China)

Women's Doubles

1985	Dai Lili/Geng Lijuan (China)
1987	Yang Young-Ja/Hyun Jung-Hwa (Korea)
1989	Qiao Hong/Deng Yaping (China)
1991	Chen Zhie/Gao Jun (China)
1993	Liu Wei/Qiao Yunping (China)
1995	Qiao Hong/Deng Yaping (China)
1997	Li Ju/Wang Nan (China)
1999	Wang Nan/Li Ju (China)
2001	Li Ju/Wang Nan (China)

Mixed Doubles

1985	Cai Zhenua/Cao Yanhua (China)
1987	Hui Jun/Geng Lijuan (China)
1989	Yoo Nam-Kyu/Hyun Jung-Hwa (South Korea)
1991	Wang Tao/Liu Wei (China)
1993	Wang Tao/Liu Wei (China)
1995	Wang Tao/Liu Wei (China)
1997	Kong Linghui/Deng Yaping (China)
1999	Zhang Yingying/Ma Lin (China)
2001	Qin Zhijian/Yang Yin (China)

Tennis (lawn)

■ All-England Championships at Wimbledon
The All-England Championships at Wimbledon are Lawn Tennis's most prestigious championships; first held in 1877.

Men's Singles

1985	Boris Becker (West Germany)
1986	Boris Becker (West Germany)
1987	Pat Cash (Australia)
1988	Stefan Edberg (Sweden)
1989	Boris Becker (West Germany)
1990	Stefan Edberg (Sweden)
1991	Michael Stich (Germany)
1992	André Agassi (USA)
1993	Pete Sampras (USA)
1994	Pete Sampras (USA)
1995	Pete Sampras (USA)
1996	Richard Krajicek (Netherlands)
1997	Pete Sampras (USA)
1998	Pete Sampras (USA)
1999	Pete Sampras (USA)
2000	Pete Sampras (USA)
2001	Goran Ivanisevic (Croatia)
2002	Lleyton Hewitt (Australia)

Women's Singles

1985	Martina Navratilova (USA)
1986	Martina Navratilova (USA)
1987	Martina Navratilova (USA)

Sports and Games

1988	Steffi Graf (West Germany)
1989	Steffi Graf (West Germany)
1990	Martina Navratilova (USA)
1991	Steffi Graf (Germany)
1992	Steffi Graf (Germany)
1993	Steffi Graf (Germany)
1994	Conchita Martínez (Spain)
1995	Steffi Graf (Germany)
1996	Steffi Graf (Germany)
1997	Martina Hingis (Switzerland)
1998	Jana Novotna (Czech Republic)
1999	Lindsay Davenport (USA)
2000	Venus Williams (USA)
2001	Venus Williams (USA)
2002	Serena Williams (USA)

Men's Doubles

1985	Heinz Gunthardt (Switzerland)/ Balazs Taroczy (Hungary)
1986	Joakim Nystrom/Mats Wilander (Sweden)
1987	Ken Flach/Robert Seguso (USA)
1988	Ken Flach/Robert Seguso (USA)
1989	John Fitzgerald (Australia)/Anders Jarryd (Sweden)
1990	Rick Leach/Jim Pugh (USA)
1991	John Fitzgerald (Australia)/Anders Jarryd (Sweden)
1992	John McEnroe (USA)/Michael Stich (Germany)
1993	Todd Woodbridge/Mark Woodforde (Australia)
1994	Todd Woodbridge/Mark Woodforde (Australia)
1995	Todd Woodbridge/Mark Woodforde (Australia)
1996	Todd Woodbridge/Mark Woodforde (Australia)
1997	Todd Woodbridge/Mark Woodforde (Australia)
1998	Jacco Eltingh/Paul Haarhuis (Netherlands)
1999	Mahesh Bhupathi/Leander Paes (India)
2000	Todd Woodbridge/Mark Woodforde (Australia)
2001	Donald Johnson/Jared Palmer (USA)

| 2002 | Todd Woodbridge (Australia)/Jonas Bjorkman (Sweden) |

Women's Doubles

1985	Kathy Jordan/Elizabeth Smylie (Australia)
1986	Martina Navratilova/Pam Shriver (USA)
1987	Claudia Kohde-Kilsch (West Germany)/ Helena Sukova (Czechoslovakia)
1988	Steffi Graf (West Germany)/Gabriela Sabatini (Argentina)
1989	Jana Novotna/Helena Sukova (Czechoslovakia)
1990	Jana Novotna/Helena Sukova (Czechoslovakia)
1991	Natalya Zvereva/Larissa Savchenko (USSR)
1992	Gigi Fernandez (USA)/Natalya Zvereva (CIS)
1993	Gigi Fernandez (USA)/Natalya Zvereva (CIS)
1994	Gigi Fernandez (USA)/Natalya Zvereva (CIS)
1995	Arantxa Sanchez Vicario (Spain)/ Jana Novotna (Czech Republic)
1996	Helena Sukova (Czech Republic)/ Martina Hingis (Switzerland)
1997	Gigi Fernandez (USA)/Natalya Zvereva (Belarus)
1998	Jana Novotna (Czech Republic) Martina Hingis (Switzerland)
1999	Lindsay Davenport/Corina Morariu (USA)
2000	Serena Williams/Venus Williams (USA)
2001	Lisa Raymond (USA)/Rennae Stubbs (Australia)
2002	Serena Williams/Venus Williams (USA)

Mixed Doubles

1985	Martina Navratilova (USA)/Paul McNamee (Australia)
1986	Kathy Jordan/Ken Flach (USA)
1987	Jo Durie/Jeremy Bates (Great Britain)

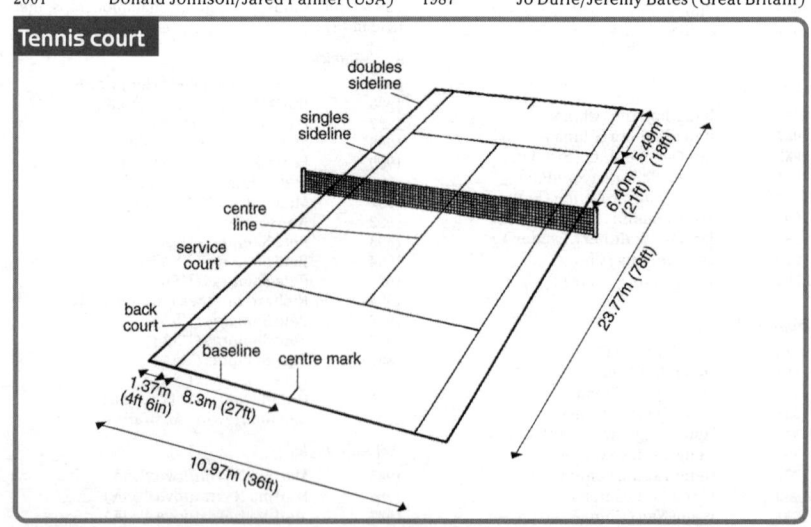

Tennis court

doubles sideline
singles sideline
centre line
service court
back court
baseline
centre mark

5.49m (18ft)
6.40m (21ft)
23.77m (78ft)
1.37m (4ft 6in)
8.3m (27ft)
10.97m (36ft)

1988	Zina Garrison/Sherwood Stewart (USA)
1989	Jana Novotna (Czechoslovakia)/ Jim Pugh (USA)
1990	Zina Garrison/Rick Leach (USA)
1991	Elizabeth Smylie/John Fitzgerald (Australia)
1992	Larissa Savchenko-Neiland (Latvia)/ Cyril Suk (Czechoslovakia)
1993	Martina Navratilova (USA)/Mark Woodforde (Australia)
1994	Helena Sukova (Czech Republic)/ Todd Woodbridge (Australia)
1995	Martina Navratilova/Jonathan Stark (USA)
1996	Helena Sukova/Cyril Suk (Czech Republic)
1997	Helena Sukova/Cyril Suk (Czech Republic)
1998	Serena Williams (USA)/Max Mirnyi (Belarus)
1999	Lisa Raymond (USA)/Leander Paes (India)
2000	Kimberly Po/Donald Johnson (USA)
2001	Daniela Hantuchova (Slovakia)/Leos Friedl (Czech Republic)
2002	Elena Likhovtseva (Russia)/Mahesh Bhupathi (India)

■ **United States Open**
First held in 1891 as the United States Championship; became the United States Open in 1968.

Men's Singles

1985	Ivan Lendl (Czechoslovakia)
1986	Ivan Lendl (Czechoslovakia)
1987	Ivan Lendl (Czechoslovakia)
1988	Mats Wilander (Sweden)
1989	Boris Becker (West Germany)
1990	Pete Sampras (USA)
1991	Stefan Edberg (Sweden)
1992	Stefan Edberg (Sweden)
1993	Pete Sampras (USA)
1994	Andre Agassi (USA)
1995	Pete Sampras (USA)
1996	Pete Sampras (USA)
1997	Pat Rafter (Australia)
1998	Pat Rafter (Australia)
1999	Andre Agassi (USA)
2000	Marat Safin (Russia)
2001	Lleyton Hewitt (Australia)
2002	Pete Sampras (USA)

Women's Singles

1985	Hana Mandlikova (Czechoslovakia)
1986	Martina Navratilova (USA)
1987	Martina Navratilova (USA)
1988	Steffi Graf (West Germany)
1989	Steffi Graf (West Germany)
1990	Gabriela Sabatini (Argentina)
1991	Monica Seles (Yugoslavia)
1992	Monica Seles (Yugoslavia)
1993	Steffi Graf (Germany)
1994	Arantxa Sanchez Vicario (Spain)
1995	Steffi Graf (Germany)
1996	Steffi Graf (Germany)
1997	Martina Hingis (Switzerland)
1998	Lindsay Davenport (USA)

1999	Serena Williams (USA)
2000	Venus Williams (USA)
2001	Venus Williams (USA)
2002	Serena Williams (USA)

■ **Davis Cup**
International team competition organized on a knockout basis; first held in 1900; contested on a challenge basis until 1972.

1985	Sweden
1986	Australia
1987	Sweden
1988	West Germany
1989	West Germany
1990	USA
1991	France
1992	USA
1993	Germany
1994	Sweden
1995	USA
1996	France
1997	Sweden
1998	Sweden
1999	Australia
2000	Spain
2001	France
2002	Russia

Tenpin bowling

■ **World Championships**
First held in 1923 by the International Bowling Association; since 1954 organized by the Fédération Internationale des Quillieurs (FIQ); since 1963, when women first competed, held every four years.

Men

1987	Rolland Patrick (France)
1991	Jon Juneau (USA)
1995	Marc Doi (Canada)
1999	Gery Verbuggen (Belgium)

Women

1987	Edda Piccini (Italy)
1991	Asa Larsson (Sweden)
1995	Debby Ship (Canada)
1999	Kelly Kulick (USA)

Trampolining

■ **World Championships**
First held in 1964 and annually until 1968; since then, every two years until 1998, when the competition was put forward one year.

Men

1986	Lionel Pioline (France)
1988	Vadim Krasnoshapka (USSR)
1990	Aleksandr Moskalenko (USSR)
1992	Aleksandr Moskalenko (Russia)
1994	Aleksandr Moskalenko (Russia)
1996	Dimitri Poliarauch (Belarus)
1998	German Khanytchve (Russia)
1999	Aleksandr Moskalenko (Russia)
2001	Alexsandr Moskalenko (Russia)

Sports and Games

Women

1986	Tatyana Lushina (USSR)
1988	Rusadan Khoperia (USSR)
1990	Elena Merkulova (USSR)
1992	Elena Merkulova (Russia)
1994	Irina Karavaeva (Russia)
1996	Tatyana Kovaleva (Russia)
1998	Irina Karavaeva (Russia)
1999	Irina Karavaeva (Russia)
2001	Irina Karavaeva (Russia)

Tug of war

■ World Outdoor Championships
Instituted in 1975, now usually held every two years; contested at 560kg from 1982.

	720kg	640kg	560kg
1985	Switzerland	Switzerland	Switzerland
1986	Ireland	Ireland	England
1988	Ireland	England	England
1990	Ireland	Ireland	Switzerland
1992	Switzerland	Switzerland	Spain
1994	Switzerland	Switzerland	Spain
1996	Netherlands	Switzerland	Ireland
1998	Netherlands	England	Spain
2000	Switzerland	Switzerland	Switzerland
2002	Netherlands	Switzerland	Switzerland

Volleyball

■ World Championships
Inaugurated in 1949; first women's championships in 1952; now held every four years, but Olympic champions are also world champions in Olympic years.

Men

1986	USA
1988	USA
1990	Italy
1992	Brazil
1994	Italy
1996	Netherlands

| 1998 | Italy |
| 2000 | Yugoslavia |

Women

1986	China
1988	USSR
1992	Cuba
1994	Cuba
1996	Cuba
1998	Cuba
2000	Cuba

Walking

■ Race Walking World Cup
Team competitions for both distances introduced in 1993; contested every two years by men's national teams.

	20km
1993	Mexico
1995	China
1997	Russia
1999	Russia
2002	Russia

	50km
1993	Mexico
1995	Mexico
1997	Russia
1999	Russia
2002	Russia

■ Eschborn Cup
The women's equivalent of the Lugano Trophy; first held in 1979; takes place every two years.

1985	China
1987	USSR
1989	USSR
1991	USSR
1993	Italy

Volleyball court

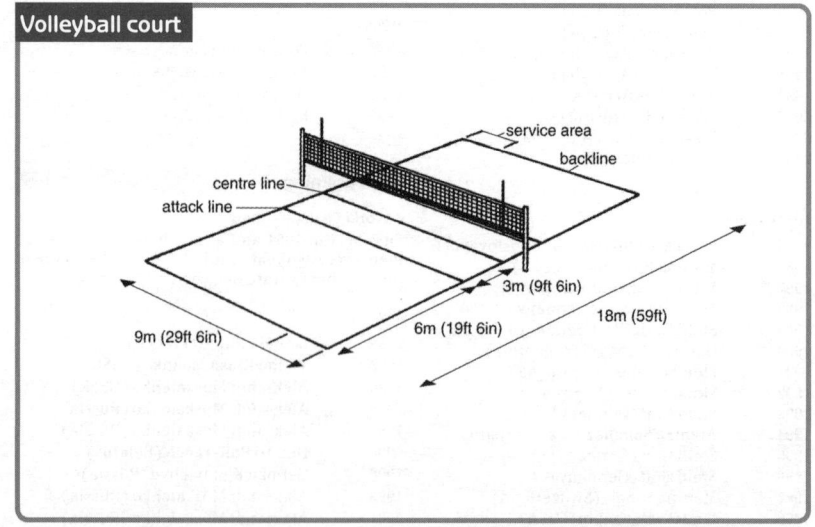

1995	China
1997	Russia
1999	China
2002	Russia

Water polo

▪ World Championships
First held in 1973, and sporadically since 1978; formerly included in the World Swimming Championships, now held separately; first women's event in 1986.

Men

1986	Yugoslavia
1990	Italy
1994	Italy
1998	Spain
2001	Spain

Women

1986	Australia
1990	USSR
1994	Hungary
1998	Italy
2001	Italy

▪ World Cup
Inaugurated in 1979 and held every two years. Women's event unofficial until 1989.

Men

1985	West Germany
1987	Yugoslavia
1989	Yugoslavia
1991	USA
1993	Italy
1995	Hungary
1997	United States
1999	Hungary
2001	Spain

Women

1988	Netherlands
1989	Netherlands
1991	Netherlands
1993	Netherlands
1995	Australia
1997	Netherlands
1999	Netherlands
2001	Italy

Water skiing

▪ World Championships
First held in 1949; take place every two years; competitions for Slalom, Tricks, Jumps, and the Overall Individual title.

Overall (Men)

1985	Sammy Duvall (USA)
1987	Sammy Duvall (USA)
1989	Patrice Martin (France)
1991	Patrice Martin (France)
1993	Patrice Martin (France)
1995	Patrice Martin (France)

1997	Patrice Martin (France)
1999	Patrice Martin (France)
2001	Jaret Llewellyn (Canada)

Overall (Women)

1985	Karen Neville (Australia)
1987	Deena Brush (USA)
1989	Deena Mapple (née Brush) (USA)
1991	Karen Neville (Australia)
1993	Natalia Rumiantseva (Russia)
1995	Judy Messer (Canada)
1997	Elena Milakova (Russia)
1999	Elena Milakova (Russia)
2001	Elena Milakova (Russia)

Weightlifting

▪ World Championships
First held in 1898; 11 weight divisions; the most prestigious is the 105kg-plus category (formerly known as Super Heavyweight, then 110kg-plus; in 1993 changed to 108kg-plus; in 1998 reduced to current weight); Olympic champions are automatically world champions in Olympic years.

105kg-plus

1985	Antonio Krastev (Bulgaria)
1986	Antonio Krastev (Bulgaria)
1987	Aleksandr Kurlovich (USSR)
1988	Aleksandr Kurlovich (USSR)
1989	Stefan Botev (Bulgaria)
1990	Stefan Botev (Bulgaria)
1991	Aleksandr Kurlovich (USSR)
1992	Aleksandr Kurlovich (UT)
1993	Ronnie Weller (Germany)
1994	Aleksandr Kurlovich (Belarus)
1995	Andrey Chemerkin (Russia)
1996	Andrey Chemerkin (Russia)
1997	Andrey Chemerkin (Russia)
1998	Andrey Chemerkin (Russia)
1999	Andrey Chemerkin (Russia)
2000	Hossein Rezazadeh (Iran)
2001	Saeed Salem Jaber (Qatar)
2002	Hossein Rezazadeh (Iran)

Wrestling

▪ World Championships
Graeco-Roman world championships first held in 1921; first freestyle championships in 1951; each style contests 10 weight divisions, the heaviest being the 120kg (formerly over 100kg, and until December 2001 130kg) category; Olympic champions become world champions in Olympic years.

Super-heavyweight/120kg

Freestyle

1985	David Gobedzhishvilli (USSR)
1986	Bruce Baumgartner (USA)
1987	Aslam Khadartsev (USSR)
1988	David Gobedzhishvilli (USSR)
1989	Ali Reiza Soleimani (Iran)
1990	David Gobedzhishvilli (USSR)
1991	Andreas Schroder (Germany)
1992	Bruce Baumgartner (USA)
1993	Bruce Baumgartner (USA)
1994	Mahmut Demir (Turkey)
1995	Bruce Baumgartner (USA)
1996	Mahmut Demir (Turkey)

Sports and Games

1997	Zekeriya Güglü (Turkey)
1998	Alexis Rodriguez (Cuba)
1999	Stephen Neal (USA)
2000	David Moussoulbes (Russia)
2001	David Moussoulbes (Russia)
2002	David Moussoulbes (Russia)

Graeco-Roman

1985	Igor Rostozotskiy (USSR)
1986	Thomas Johansson (Sweden)
1987	Igor Rostozotskiy (USSR)
1988	Aleksandr Karelin (USSR)
1989	Aleksandr Karelin (USSR)
1990	Aleksandr Karelin (USSR)
1991	Aleksandr Karelin (USSR)
1992	Aleksandr Karelin (UT)
1993	Aleksandr Karelin (Russia)
1994	Aleksandr Karelin (Russia)
1995	Aleksandr Karelin (Russia)
1996	Aleksandr Karelin (Russia)
1997	Aleksandr Karelin (Russia)
1998	Aleksandr Karelin (Russia)
1999	Aleksandr Karelin (Russia)
2000	Rulon Gardner (USA)
2001	Rulon Gardner (USA)
2002	Dremiel Byers (USA)

Yachting

▪ America's Cup

One of sport's famous trophies; first won by the schooner *Magic* in 1870; now held approximately every four years, when challengers compete in a series of races to find which of them races against the holder; all 25 winners up to 1983 were from the USA.

Winning Yacht (Skipper)

1987	Stars & Stripes (USA) (Dennis Conner)
1988	Stars & Stripes (USA) (Dennis Conner)[1]
1992	America (USA) (Bill Koch)
1995	Black Magic (New Zealand) (Russell Coutts)
2000	Black Magic (New Zealand) (Russell Coutts)

[1] Stars and Stripes (USA) skippered by Dennis Conner won a special challenge match but on appeal the race was awarded to the New Zealand boat. However the decision was reversed by the New York Appeals court in 1989.

▪ Admiral's Cup

A two-yearly series of races, originally held in the English Channel, around Fastnet rock and at Cowes; originally four national teams of three boats per team, now nine teams of three boats per team; first held in 1957.

1985	West Germany
1987	New Zealand
1989	Great Britain
1991	France
1993	Germany
1995	Italy
1997	USA
1999	Netherlands
2001	*not held*

Card, board and other indoor games

baccarat Casino card game; most popular version **baccarat banque**, in which bank plays against players; in another, **chemin de fer**, all players take turns to hold the bank; object is to assemble, either with two or three cards, a points value of nine: picture cards and the 10 = 0; ace = one; other cards face value; if total is a double figure then the first figure is ignored, eg 18 would count as 8. Of 15c derivation, thought to have been introduced into France from Italy during reign of Charles VIII.

backgammon Board game for two players; each has 15 round counters which are moved around the *outer* and *inner tables* on the throw of two dice; aim is to be first to return one's pieces home to inner table and remove them from the board. Equipment similar to backgammon was found in Tutankhamen's tomb; introduced to Britain by the Crusaders; known as backgammon from c.1750.

bézique Card game played with at least two players; each has a pack but with 2s, 3s, 4s, 5s and 6s taken out; object is to win tricks (rounds of play) and score points on the basis of the cards won. Believed to have originated in Spain and brought to England in 1861; first rules drawn up 1861; a variation is **rubicon bézique**.

blackjack Casino card game with object of accumulating score of 21 (with two cards this is a *blackjack*). Ace = one or 11; picture cards = 10; others according to face value. Normally four packs of cards are shuffled together and dealt from a wooden 'shoe' by a banker; bets placed before first card is dealt; all cards dealt face up.

bridge Card game developed from whist, using full set of 52 playing cards, played by two pairs of players; thought to have originated in either Greece or India, introduced into Britain in 1880. Most popular forms: **auction bridge** and **contract bridge**. In the former, trumps are decided by preliminary bid or auction. In contract bridge, the most widely played form, trumps are nominated by the highest bidder. Scoring uses chart designed by US inventor, Harold Stirling Vanderbilt, based on tricks (rounds of play) contracted for and won.

canasta Card game similar to rummy, where cards are picked up and discarded; uses two packs, including four jokers; object is to collect as many of same denomination as possible. All have points value, but jokers and deuces (2s) are 'wild' (can take any value). Originated in Uruguay in the 1940s, the name deriving from the Spanish word *canasta* ('basket'), probably referring to tray where cards were discarded.

checkers ▶ draughts

chemin de fer or **'chemmy'** Casino card game; variant of **baccarat banque**, played by up to nine players; object is to obtain total near as possible to nine with two or three cards; if total is a double figure then the first figure is ignored; 16 would count as 6. Ace = 1; picture cards = 10; others face value.

chess Game of strategy for two players using chequered board of 64 squares. Each player has 16 pieces: eight pawns, two castles or rooks, two knights, two bishops, queen and king; object is to capture or *checkmate* opponent's king; all pieces have set moves, queen is most versatile. Played in ancient India as *chaturanga*; earliest reference c.600AD; current pieces have existed in standard form for over 500 years.

Cluedo ® Board game where board is divided into 'rooms' and the players, who are each dealt a few person, place, and implement cards, are characters who must find out the facts concerning a murder (ie murderer, implement used and scene of the crime), which are on cards seen by no-one and hidden in an envelope at the start. Detective work is done by deduction, arranging meetings in the rooms and asking the other character involved to reveal his or her relevant cards.

contract bridge ▶ bridge

craps Casino dice game of US origin, adapted from game 'hazard' in 1813. Using two dice, a player loses throwing 2, 3, and 12, but wins with 7 or 11.

cribbage Card game played with two, three or four people with pack of 52 cards and a holed board, the *peg board*, used for scoring. Number of cards dealt to each player is five, six or seven, depending on number of players; cards are discarded into a dummy hand, which each player has in turn; points are scored according to cards dropped (ie for playing a card that makes a pair, a run of three or more, etc); cards are discarded in each round until total of 31 is reached; play continues until the players have discarded all their cards; value of hand then calculated.

dominoes Indoor game, various forms, played by two or more players; dominoes are either wooden or plastic rectangular blocks, with the face of each divided into two halves, each half containing a number of spots, no two identical. In a double-six set of dominoes, every combination between 6–6 and 0–0 is marked on the 28 dominoes. Object of basic game is to lay out sequence or 'line' of dominoes, each player in turn having to put down a domino of the same value as the one at either end of the line.

draughts or **(USA) checkers** (Game played on chess board by two players, each with 12 small, flat, round counters or *pieces*, which are lined up on alternate squares on the first three rows at either side of the board; object is to remove opponent's pieces from board by jumping over them into a vacant diagonal square, having got in a position to do so by moving only forward (until a piece reaches back row of opponent's 'territory', thus becoming a two-piece *king* and permitted to move backwards and forwards) and always on squares of the same colour; believed to have been played in ancient Egypt; first book about draughts published Spain 1547.

gin rummy ▶ rummy

go National game of Japan; first played China c.1500BC; board game for two players played on grid of 19 vertical and 19 horizontal lines (361 intersections); each player has supply of counters and play alternates beginning with black; object is to conquer territory by both encircling vacant intersections and surrounding opponent's counters which are then removed from board; handicapping system exists.

hazard Card game for four players in pairs; similar to **solo**, but to make 25 cards, all cards with face value of two to eight are discarded, and joker is added.

mah-jong Chinese game, originally played with cards, introduced to the West under its present name after World War I; usually played by four people using 144 small tiles divided into six suits. (Sets containing 136 tiles and five suits are also used.) Aim is to collect sequences of tiles. Name means 'sparrow', a bird of mythical great intelligence, which appears on one tile.

Monopoly ® Board game for two or more players; aim is acquisition of property; players move a counter each around a board which has some of a capital city's streets, stations and public utility companies on it, which can be bought, built upon, mortgaged etc and for which rent must be paid (using Monopoly money) when landed on as a non-owner. Game ends when all but one player are bankrupt.

pinochle Card game derived from **bézique**; uses two packs of 24 cards, all cards from two to eight having been discarded; object is to win tricks, as in whist, and to score points according to cards won: ace = 11; ten = 10; king = 4; queen = 3; jack = 2; nine = 0.

poker Gambling card game for two to eight players; object is to get a better hand than opponents (or convince them that you have one). Hands are ranked: best hand is *royal flush* ie 10, Jack, Queen, King, Ace, all of the same suit. Most popular varieties: five-card draw, five-card stud and seven-card stud. Poker started in 19c USA.

pontoon or **vingt-et-un** Card game; a variation of **blackjack**, played by any number of players, but ideally six. Object is to try to obtain a total of 21. A *royal pontoon* consists of a picture card and an ace (ace = 11 or 1). Bets are placed and bank held by any player (usually latest royal pontoon winner).

roulette Casino game played with ball and spinning wheel, which is divided into 37 alternately either red or black segments numbered 0 to 36, but not in numerical order. Bets are placed (before the wheel is spun) on where ball will come to rest, and can take several forms — on a single number, any two numbers, or any three numbers etc, and on whether winning one will be odd or even.

rummy Domestic card game; possibly derived from **mah-jong**; cards picked up and discarded with object of forming two *hands* of three and four cards, or one of seven; hand obtained must consist of cards of same denomination, or sequence in same

suit. A variation is **gin rummy**, where hands are laid face upwards and can be added to by any player during the game. Points are obtained for each card dropped according to its face value, and deducted according to cards remaining in hand when one player wins game by disposing of all his or her cards.

Scrabble ® Word game on special board for two to four players; points scored by placing letter tiles of different values crossword-fashion to form interlocking words; each player has choice of seven tiles until none remain. Scores can be doubled or trebled by making use of premium squares on the board.

shogi Japanese form of **chess**, believed to have originated in India; played on square board with pieces (of which each player has 20) of different powers; object is to *checkmate* king.

solo Card game; a form of **whist**, and similar to **bridge**; players must declare how many tricks they will win before each game; tricks won as in whist.

Trivial Pursuit ® Board game in which players make progress by giving correct answers to general knowledge questions on eg art and literature, entertainment, geography, history, science and nature, and sport and leisure, which are written on special cards. Coloured wedges corresponding to all topics have to be won and the middle space reached to win the game.

whist Non-gambling card game; normally played with four people in pairs; each player receives 13 cards; object is to win more *tricks*, or rounds of play, than the opposing pair; trumps (suit of which cards can win against any card of any other suit) are decided before each game; at *whist drives* trumps are normally played in the following order: hearts, clubs, diamonds, spades; a round of 'no trumps' (where all suits have equal power) is also common.

Hobbies and pastimes

abseiling Descending a steep slope or mountainside; used in mountaineering but now recognized as pursuit in itself. A rope is attached either around the body or through *karabiners* (steel links with spring clips in one side) and is secured from above so that speed of downwards climb can be safely controlled.

aerobics System of exercises which are designed to increase oxygen consumption and speed blood circulation, thereby increasing fitness.

ballooning ▸ **hot-air ballooning**

batik Ancient folk art of fabric design using a basic wax-resist technique; warm wax is painted onto light-coloured fabric, according to a chosen design, and then dipped into a solution of dye and water — only unwaxed fabric takes dye so when wax is removed design appears against coloured background.

bell-ringing or **campanology** Ringing church bells; two popular forms; *change ringing* (handpulled method) and *carillon* (uses keyboard connected to the clapper of the bells).

birdwatching or **ornithology** Study and observation of birds in their natural habitat; may involve recording details concerning bird anatomy, behaviour, song and flight patterns.

brass-rubbing Duplicating designs on ornamental brass plate, such as is found in churches; brass is covered with paper and then rubbed over with coloured crayons or chalk until copy is produced.

bungee-jumping Leaping from river-crossing bridges; person's legs are tied together, covered with protective material, and then clipped with a strong elastic (bungee) rope (adapted to their

weight and height), and secured firmly to the bridge; the jumper 'dives for the horizon' from a platform on top of the bridge and freefalls, before hanging suspended by the elastic rope, experiencing a series of bouncing movements; jumps also made from cranes, towers, etc.

butterfly-collecting or **lepidoptery** Obtaining butterflies either by catching them in their natural environment or purchasing them already preserved; insects are identified and mounted, usually in a glass display unit.

calligraphy Penmanship, or writing at its most formal; a major art form in many countries of E Asia and in Arabic-speaking countries; revival of interest in Europe and USA since the 19c; special pen nibs, brushes, ink and paper usually required.

campanology ▸ **bell-ringing**

candle-making Producing candles by repeatedly dipping a prepared wick into wax, pouring wax over a wick or pouring wax into moulds; paraffin wax is most often used; candles can be created in any colour, shape, size or fragrance.

climbing Generally refers to scaling anything from a 15m/50ft wall to an assault on the Himalayas, although there should be some level of difficulty in reaching highest point; as well as the physical aspect, climbing also involves psychological thrills of discovery, exploration and avoidance of danger.

coin-collecting ▸ **numismatics**

cookery Preparing and cooking food; may involve production of exotic and speciality dishes and creation of new recipes.

crochet Making a variety of textile items; uses a special hook to loop yarn in a number of different stitches according to pattern requirements.

dancing The following are just a few of the many forms that dancing takes: **1 ballroom** Social dance form; developed early 20c, revealing strong influence of American ragtime, syncopated rhythms producing the foxtrot, quickstep and tango; also popular were animal dances (eg Turkey Trot, Bunny Hug) and Latin-American dances (cha-cha-cha and samba). **2 country** Historic social dances began to spread across Europe in the 17c, taught by travelling dancing masters, adding 19c forms such as the waltz, quadrille and polka; emphasis on spatial design, with couples in long or circular sets, using simple walking steps. **Traditional dance** In *England*, began 16c; lines, circles, and square sets are common patterns; steps based on simple walking and skipping. In *Ireland*, early forms share the European history of country and court dance; jigs and reels typical, resembling English and Scottish stepping; competitive high stepping form is a 20c creation; arms are held stiffly to the sides; body is erect; there is rapid, complex rhythmic use of the feet; and the knees are sharply lifted. In *Scotland* some country dances are commonly known as **Scottish reels**, but strictly, the reel is an indigenous form of stepping dance performed to bagpipes and showing French aristocratic connections; originally performed in circles as in 'round reels' (threesome, foursome, eightsome etc) and later in lines, 'longwise forms'; feet are in balletic positions with the weight on the balls of the feet; typical steps include slip step, pas de basque, strathspey, and schottische; men's costume is the kilt; women wear dresses with a tartan sash. Other country dances in Scotland also progress in two long lines of male/female couples, and there are square dances (eg quadrille), and circle dances (eg Circassian circle); dances take place to traditional tunes, formerly played on the fiddle, and now also on the accordion; nowadays reels danced to these instruments too. In *Wales*, due to former religious disapproval, there are few traces of traditional dance, but there are some reels and country dances similar to those in England. **3 disco** Popular form of dance mainly for young people, originating 1960s; accompanying music is usually contemporary, often loud, with a rhythmic beat. Definite fashions eg new romantic style, soul, punk, break dancing, robotics, and gothic style. It takes account of Black music, particularly rapping, and heavy rock. **4 jazz** N American form of vernacular dancing performed to jazz rhythms; a style that swings, owing its origins to African and Caribbean forms of dance, blended with European influences; also used in musical shows on Broadway and in the UK (eg *Cats*). **5 Morris** Ceremonial form of traditional dance found in England. Distinctive features: stamping and hopping; files of performers usually dressed in white and always carrying a stick, handkerchief or garland; some wear bells; accordion or concertina with brass drum accompaniment. Originally exclusively a male domain, women can now take part. **6 step** Social and often competitive form of dance relying on rhythmically complex footwork using parts of the foot, heel, and toe beats, often performed in clogs; maintained through folk festivals both as social and exhibition dance; structure in performance is part fixed and part improvised.

dressmaking Pastime usually undertaken to make low-cost clothes, using a bought tissue-paper pattern and a length of material, but also a creative hobby lending itself to sophisticated fashion design.

electronic games Games programmed and controlled by a small microprocessor; most connected to visual display unit and known as **video games**; many have war themes, others simulate sports; some board games (eg Monopoly®, Scrabble®, Trivial Pursuit®) are available in electronic form; all operated by using a computer keyboard, joystick or joypad attached to a games console or home computer. Larger versions are produced for use in eg amusement arcades.

embroidery Ornamentation of fabric with decorative stitching; dates from very early times, when designs were sewn on to a base fabric by hand; became highly developed eg for rich garments and furnishings, and church vestments in the Middle East, India and Europe; famous example is 11c Bayeux tapestry. Hand embroidery still exists as a craft, but today computer-controlled sewing machines are also used.

fell-walking Trekking on hills or moorland, wearing specialized walking boots and using map and compass to find direction in otherwise desolate tracts of land.

gardening Laying out and cultivating plants on a piece of ground for ornamental purposes, rather than for economic gain; type of garden depends not only on gardener's tastes and space available, but also on soil type and fertility, climate, air pollution, and shelter from wind and sun, provided by eg existing trees and rocks. Some special garden types and techniques are: **1 espalier** Technique involving the training of trees on a lattice-work of wood flat against a wall; tree is carefully tied to the trellis and pruned to control its shape, often creating a decorative effect in limited space. **2 herb garden** Usually includes shrubs as well as herbs, all mostly perennial. The herbs are used primarily for cooking, either fresh or dried (see p429). **3 Japanese-style garden** Maximum use is made of evergreen plants, the only colour being eg spring-flowering azaleas, and autumn berries; features include stone lanterns, walkways, natural or simulated streams and waterfalls, and occasional stones; **bonsai** technique is associated with Japanese style, though it originated in China; involves dwarfing plants by shallow planting in containers, starvation, root and soil pruning, and the twisting of new shoots with wire to give plants gnarled, aged appearance; pine, fir and maple trees often used. **4 rock garden** or **rockery** Man-made or natural heap of soil and rock fragments in a garden for growing rock plants, usually flowering, hardy perennials, and dwarf trees; rock gardens are often terraced to prevent the topsoil being washed away by rain. **5 water garden** Plants arranged in and around natural or artificial pools and streams, eg water lilies and marsh marigolds. **6 wild-flower garden** Often includes native marsh or bog plants as well as forest-floor wild flowers; usually requires a rich, acid soil.

go-kart racing Driving and racing small, single-seated, motorized vehicles around outdoor tracks; originated USA; has gained a popular following in the UK.

hatha yoga ▸ **yoga**

horse-riding Involves acquisition of specialized skills learned in order to control the horse from a seated position on its back. Commands are signalled by hand, leg and voice instruction, sometimes reinforced by the use of whip and spurs.

Sports and Games

Sports and Games

hot-air ballooning Being carried as a passenger through the air by hot-air balloon; may involve navigating the balloon, the mechanics of getting the balloon airborne, and following the balloon in road vehicles.

ikebana Formal Japanese style of flower arrangement; a few blooms or leaves are selected and placed in very careful relationship to one another; popular 1950s and 1960s pastime in W Europe.

kite-flying Flying a light frame covered with paper, cloth or plastic at the end of a length of string, usually requiring windy conditions. Kites can be brightly coloured and of various different shapes; simplest form has only one string, but with two strings, one attached to each side, it can be more easily controlled from the ground and made to do complicated loops and dives in the air.

knitting Ancient craft used for making fabric; loops of yarn are linked together using two or three hand-held needles; machines are now used to produce complex knitted garments and fabrics of many kinds, but they cannot create all the intricate designs commonly produced by skilled hand knitters.

lace-making Most popular method (especially in Europe) of lace production is *bobbin* or *pillow* lace. As many as 1 100 bobbins are wound with thread and hung on pins which are inserted, according to the design required, into the small holes on a piece of stiff paper attached to a pillow, cushion or polystyrene base; bobbins then looped, plaited and twisted following pattern instructions until the desired item is produced.

lepidoptery ▸ butterfly-collecting

macramé Making a type of coarse lace by knotting and plaiting; widespread revival in mid-19c; used to make decorative fringed borders for costumes as well as furnishings eg window blinds, antimacassars, and cushions.

model-making Mainly the construction of cars, ships, trains and aeroplanes by gluing together pre-shaped plastic or wooden parts from specialized kits. Some enthusiasts design and produce the parts for their own models.

numismatics Studying and collecting coins, notes and other similar objects, eg medals; dates from Italian Renaissance; 17c collectors were first to catalogue their collections.

origami Making models of animals or other objects by folding sheets of paper into shapes, with minimum use of scissors or other implements; often used as an educational aid for young children; originated 10c Japan.

ornithology ▸ birdwatching

paintball Simulation of military combat; involves firing paint pellets which splatter on contact with clothing to indicate a hit; played by two or more teams; popular in the USA, UK and parts of Europe; believed to be beneficial in the reduction of stress.

panelology Carving thin, wooden panels which may be either framed or lodged between other upright and cross pieces normally stretching across the surface of a wall; pictures are often painted onto these panels; most effective results achieved on panels made from chestnut, oak or white poplar.

paragliding Being towed through the air by a plane whilst wearing an adapted parachute and then being separated in order to glide to the ground.

philately Collecting stamps; one of the world's most popular hobbies; often involves documentation in special books or albums; stamps issued and stamped by the post office on their first day of issue (*first-day covers*) increasingly popular; first philatelist said to have been John Tomlinson, who started collecting the day after the issue of the first postage stamp (the *penny black*) in 1840.

pigeon-fancying Breeding pigeons to exhibit or race, popular in the USA, UK and France.

pigeon racing Pigeons are taken from their loft and released at a starting point that may be hundreds of miles away; their homing instinct takes them back to their loft where a special clock times their arrival, thus establishing the fastest pigeon.

pottery or **potting** Forming clay objects; moist clay is shaped and then dried, usually by *firing* in a *kiln* or oven. Shaping by hand may be aided by using a *potter's wheel*, on which a lump of clay is rotated so it can be *thrown* by the potter's hands; moulding may involve either pressing soft clay into a mould and allowing it to dry, or *slip moulding*, where liquid clay or *slip* is poured into a mould that absorbs the moisture; shaped or moulded objects can be decorated by etching and painted with a colour *glaze*. Pottery tends to be porous and so is protected by a second glaze, which may be transparent or opaque and also gives shiny decorative appearance. Glaze is applied after first firing (when the pottery is called *biscuit*); then object is placed in kiln a second time at a lower temperature.

scuba diving Underwater swimming with the aid of *scuba* (self-contained underwater breathing apparatus) or *aqualung*, first developed in 1942 by Jacques Cousteau and Émil Gagnan; equipment consists of air tank(s), face mask, air regulator, depth gauge, weight belt and buoyancy compensator; divers propel themselves with the legs, wearing large *fins* or *flippers*.

shuffleboard or **shovelboard** Deck game played aboard ship; a larger version of the popular shove-halfpenny; wooden discs, usually c.15cm/6in in diameter, are pushed along deck with long-handled drivers into scoring area.

skateboarding Riding on a single flexible board, longer and wider than the foot, fixed with four small wheels on the underside; speeds of over 100kph/60mph are possible and difficult jumps performed; developed as a way of experiencing surfing thrills on land; became popular in 1960s USA and in UK in 1970s and again in late 1980s.

skin-diving Underwater swimming, popularized in the 1930s. Skin-divers use only goggles, face mask, flippers, and short breathing tube or *snorkel*.

skipping Making jumps over a rope, the ends of which are held in each hand so that it can be twirled over the head and under the feet; often thought of as a child's pastime; recognized as good form of exercise and keep-fit.

skittles Game played in several different forms; object is to knock down nine pins with a ball. **Alley skittles** is played in long alleys and **table skittles** is played indoors on a specially constructed table with a swivelled ball attached to a mast by means of a chain; pins are much smaller than those used in tenpin bowling, and are replaced manually, rather than mechanically.

spinning Converting fibres into yarns, originally using distaff and later the spinning wheel, and now often using methods such as friction and rotor spinning; two types of yarn traditionally produced were *woollen* (fibres are randomly arranged), and *worsted* (fibres lie parallel to the length of the yarn).

stamp-collecting ▸ philately

tapestry Creation of decorative textiles, originally hand woven, with multi-coloured pictorial designs, made by passing coloured threads among fixed warp threads; Oriental in origin, used for wall hangings, furniture and floor coverings.

taxidermy Preparation and practice of creating life-like replicas of animals and birds from their treated skins and the careful use of celluloids and other plastics.

train-spotting Identifying locomotives by their numbers or names and ticking them off in special, collectable notebooks.

video games ▸ electronic games

weaving Ancient fabric-producing craft; warp (lengthwise) and weft (crosswise) threads are interlaced on machines called *looms*; hand looms known from very early times; modern industry uses modern weaving looms which have dispensed with shuttles — 'bullets', 'rapiers', water jets and air jets now carry the weft across the warp, with 1 500 picks per minute being possible on some machines.

yoga In Indian religious tradition, any of various physical and contemplative techniques designed to free the superior, conscious element in a person from involvement with the inferior material world. **Hatha yoga** most common form in W Hemisphere; importance of physical exercises and positions and breathing-control is stressed in promoting physical and mental well-being.

Sports and Games

THOUGHT AND BELIEF

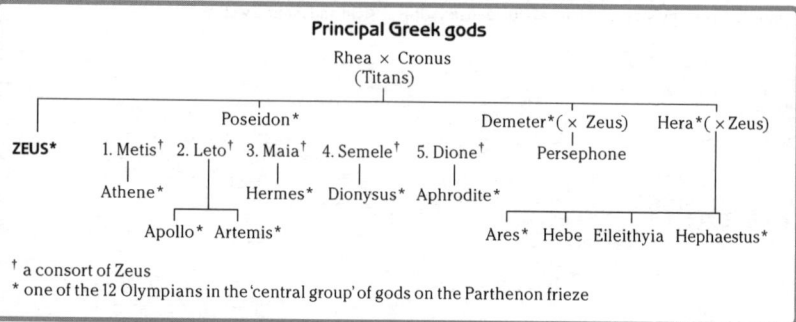

Principal Greek gods

Rhea × Cronus
(Titans)

Poseidon*   Demeter*(× Zeus)   Hera*(× Zeus)

ZEUS*   1. Metis† 2. Leto† 3. Maia† 4. Semele† 5. Dione†   Persephone

Athene*   Hermes* Dionysus* Aphrodite*

Apollo* Artemis*   Ares* Hebe Eileithyia Hephaestus*

† a consort of Zeus
* one of the 12 Olympians in the 'central group' of gods on the Parthenon frieze

Greek gods of mythology

Adonis	God of vegetation and rebirth
Aeolus	God of the winds
Alphito	Barley goddess of Argos
Aphrodite	Goddess of love and beauty
Apollo	God of prophecy, music, youth, archery and healing
Ares	God of war
Arethusa	Goddess of springs and fountains
Artemis	Goddess of fertility, chastity and hunting
Asclepius	God of healing
Athene	Goddess of prudence and wise council; protectress of Athens
Atlas	A Titan who bears up the earth
Attis	God of vegetation
Boreas	God of the north wind
Cronus	Father of Zeus
Cybele	Goddess of the earth
Demeter	Goddess of the harvest
Dionysus	God of wine, vegetation and ecstasy
Eos	Goddess of the dawn
Eros	God of love
Gaia	Goddess of the earth
Ganymede	God of rain
Hades	God of the underworld
Hebe	Goddess of youth

Hecate	Goddess of the moon
Helios	God of the sun
Hephaestus	God of fire
Hera	Goddess of marriage and childbirth; queen of heaven
Hermes	Messenger of the gods
Hestia	Goddess of the hearth
Hypnos	God of sleep
Iris	Goddess of the rainbow
Morpheus	God of dreams
Nemesis	God of destiny
Nereus	God of the sea
Nike	Goddess of victory
Oceanus	God of the river Oceanus
Pan	God of male sexuality and of herds
Persephone	Goddess of the underworld and of corn
Poseidon	God of the sea
Rhea	The original mother goddess; wife of Cronus
Selene	Goddess of the moon
Thanatos	God of death
Zeus	Overlord of the Olympian gods and goddesses; god of the sky and all its properties

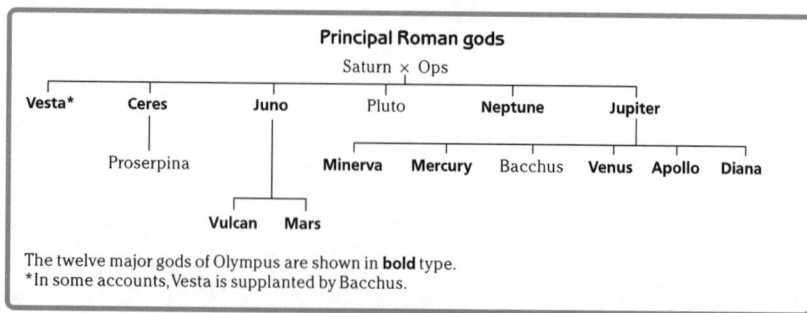

Principal Roman gods

Saturn × Ops

Vesta*   Ceres   Juno   Pluto   Neptune   Jupiter

Proserpina   Minerva   Mercury   Bacchus   Venus   Apollo   Diana

Vulcan   Mars

The twelve major gods of Olympus are shown in **bold** type.
*In some accounts, Vesta is supplanted by Bacchus.

Roman gods of mythology

Apollo	God of the sun	**Maia**	Goddess of fertility
Bacchus	God of wine and ecstasy	**Mars**	God of war
Bellona	Goddess of war	**Mercury**	Messenger of the gods; also god of merchants
Ceres	Goddess of corn		
Consus	God of seed sowing	**Minerva**	Goddess of war, craftsmen, education and the arts
Cupid	God of love		
Diana	Goddess of fertility and hunting	**Mithras**	The sun god; god of regeneration
Egreria	Goddess of fountains and childbirth	**Neptune**	God of the sea
Epona	Goddess of horses	**Ops**	Goddess of the harvest
Fauna	Goddess of fertility	**Orcus**	God of death
Faunus	God of crops and herbs	**Pales**	Goddess of flocks
Feronia	Goddess of spring flowers	**Penates**	Gods of food and drink
Fides	God of honesty	**Picus**	God of woods
Flora	Goddess of fruitfulness and flowers	**Pluto**	God of the underworld
Fortuna	Goddess of chance and fate	**Pomona**	Goddess of fruit trees
Genius	Protective god of individuals, groups and the state	**Portunus**	God of husbands
		Proserpina	Goddess of the underworld
Janus	God of entrances, travel, the dawn	**Rumina**	Goddess of nursing mothers
Juno	Goddess of marriage, childbirth, light	**Saturn**	God of fertility and agriculture
Jupiter	God of the sky and its attributes (sun, moon, thunder, rain, etc)	**Silvanus**	God of trees and forests
		Venus	Goddess of spring, gardens and love
Lares	Gods of the house	**Vertumnus**	God of fertility
Liber Pater	God of agricultural and human fertility	**Vesta**	Goddess of the hearth
Libitina	Goddess of funeral rites	**Victoria**	Goddess of victory
Luna	Goddess of the moon	**Vulcan**	God of fire

Norse gods of mythology

Aegir	God of the sea	**Mimir**	God of wisdom
Aesir	Race of warlike gods, including Odin, Thor, Tyr	**Nanna**	Goddess wife of Balder
		Nehallenia	Goddess of plenty
Alcis	Twin gods of the sky	**Nerthus**	Goddess of earth
Balder	Son of Odin and favourite of the gods	**Njord**	God of ships and the sea
Bor	Father of Odin	**Norns**	Goddesses of destiny
Bragi	God of poetry	**Odin,**	Chief of the Aesir family of gods, the
Fafnir	Dragon god	**(Woden,**	'father' god; the god of battle,
Fjorgynn	Mother of Thor	**Wotan)**	death, inspiration
Frey	God of fertility	**Otr**	Otter god
Freyja	Goddess of libido	**Ran**	Goddess of the sea
Frigg	Goddess of fertility; wife of Odin	**Sif**	Goddess wife of Thor
Gefion	Goddess who received virgins after death	**Sigyn**	Goddess wife of Loki
		Thor	God of thunder and sky; good crops
Heimdall	Guardian of the bridge Bifrost	**(Donar)**	
Hel	Goddess of death; Queen of Niflheim, the land of mists	**Tyr**	God of battle
		Ull	Stepson of Thor, an enchanter
Hermod	Son of Odin	**Valkyries**	Female helpers of the gods of war
Hoder	Blind god who killed Balder	**Vanir**	Race of benevolent gods, including Njord, Frey, Freyja
Hoenir	Companion to Odin and Loki		
Idunn	Guardian goddess of the golden apples of youth; wife of Bragi	**Vidar**	Slayer of the wolf, Fenrir
		Weland,	Craftsman god
Kvasir	God of wise utterances	**(Volundr,**	
Logi	Fire god	**Wayland,**	
Loki	God of mischief	**Weiland)**	

Egyptian gods of mythology

Amun-Re	Universal god	**Khonsou**	Son of Amun-Re
Anubis	God of funerals	**Maat**	Goddess of order
Apis	God of fertility	**Nephthys**	Goddess of funerals
Aten	Unique god	**Nut**	God of the sky
Geb	God of the earth	**Osiris**	God of vegetation
Hathor	Goddess of love	**Ptah**	God of creation
Horus	God of light	**Sekhmet**	Goddess of might
Isis	Goddess of magic	**Seth**	God of evil
Khnum	Goddess of creation	**Thoth**	Supreme scribe

Thought and Belief

Thought and Belief

Figures of myth and legend

Selected figures from religion, myth and legend are given. **Bold** type indicates that a figure is described elsewhere in the list.

Achilles Greek hero; son of **Peleus** and the goddess **Thetis**; his body invulnerable to injury, except his ankle, due to being held by the ankles when he was dipped in the R Styx (in another version **Cheiron** replaced his ankle bone with one taken from the fast-running giant Damysos); killed with an arrow in the heel by **Paris** or **Apollo**.

Actaeon Greek hero; a hunter who came upon **Artemis**, the goddess of chastity, while she was bathing and therefore naked; she threw water at him, changing him into a stag, so that he was pursued and then killed by his own hounds.

Adad Mesopotamian god of storms; known throughout the area of Babylonian influence; the Assyrians called him **Hadad**, and in the Bible he is Rimmon, the god of thunder; helped to cause the Great Flood in Gilgamesh; his symbol was the lightning held in his hand and his animal the bull.

Adapa Akkadian hero; one of the seven Apkallu, beings of great brilliance and genius, and envoy of the god **Ea**, the divine creator of Man, who lost the opportunity of immortality due to disagreements between Ea and **Anu**, the god of heaven.

Aditi Indian goddess; mother of the gods and all beings, and the guardian of childbirth; outwith the divine world, she represented *everything* at the same time, being the total, the beginning, the end and the opposites; adopted by Buddhist tradition.

Adonis God of Phoenician origin; son of Myrrha, the daughter of the king of Syria who had been turned into a tree; spent one third of the year with **Persephone**, goddess of hell, and two thirds with **Aphrodite** after a decision by **Zeus**; mortally wounded by a wild boar in a battle.

Aegir Norse god of the sea; a giant, who collected dead sailors in his hall on the island of Hlesey; here also he sometimes gave banquets to the gods.

Aegisthus Greek hero; son of **Thyestes**; while **Agamemnon** was absent at Troy he became the lover of **Clytemnestra**; together they killed Agamemnon on his return to Argo; later killed by **Orestes**.

Aeneas Greek hero; son of **Aphrodite**, and bravest of the Trojans after **Hector** whose command he replaced in the fight against the Greeks; sailed to coast of Italy and is said to have given Rome its divine origin; subject of the *Aeneid* by Virgil.

Aeolus Greek god of the winds; in the *Odyssey*, Aeolus lived on an island, and gave **Odysseus** the winds tied in a bag so that his ship would not be blown off course; the ship had nearly reached Ithaca when Odysseus's men opened the bag, thinking it contained treasure; as a result, the ship was blown far away.

Aesculapius ▶ Asclepius

Agamemnon Greek king of Argos; commander of the Greek army in the Trojan War; Homer calls him 'king of men'; on his return he was murdered by his wife **Clytemnestra**.

Agni Indian god of fire; immortal god, regarded as the guide and protector of men; had two faces, one calm, one terrible, and gave both life and death.

Ahura Mazda Indo-Iranian god; had the form of the sun and nine wives; creator of other living beings and formed the world by his thought; his powers made plants grow and allowed fire to give its heat, water to quench thirst, animals to reproduce and armies to be victorious.

Ajax Two Greek heroes of the Trojan War; one was the son of Telamon, king of Salamis, therefore known as Telamonian Ajax and was proverbial for his size and strength; in all the worst situations he 'stood like a tower'; when the armour of the dead **Achilles** was not given to him, he went mad and killed himself. The second was the son of Oileus, king of Locris; returning from Troy, he provoked the anger of the gods, and was killed by **Poseidon** as he reached the shore of Greece.

Alcestis Greek heroine; she saved her husband, Admetus, who was doomed to die, by offering to die in his place; the action so impressed **Heracles** that he wrestled with the messenger of death and brought her back to life.

Alcmaeon Greek hero; to avenge the death of his father, Amphiaros, he killed his mother, and was pursued by the **Erinyes** until he came to a land which had not seen the sun at the time of his mother's death; he found this recently emerged land at the mouth of the R Achelous; **Apollo** commanded him to lead the expedition of the **Epigoni** against Thebes.

Alcyone ▶ Halcyone

Alexander ▶ Paris

Amaterasu Japanese goddess of the sun and light; considered to be the divine origin of the imperial dynasty; shut herself in a cave after a conflict with her brother Susa-no-o, plunging the world into darkness; returned light to the world when the gods managed to tempt her out.

Amazons Warrior-women of Greek myth; people of the Amazon state, where men were only tolerated for work of a servile nature; removed one breast so that they would not be restricted in the practice of archery and spear-throwing; said to be descendants of the god of war, **Ares**, and the **Nymph**, Harmony; crushed the Atlantians, occupied Gorgon and the greater part of Libya, fought with **Priam** during the Trojan war and invaded Attica; their leader, Hippolyta, married **Theseus**.

Amen ▶ Amun-Re

Amitabha The divine Buddha; one of five 'meditation Buddhas' sent by Adi Buddha, the original Buddha; wished to gather together all those who would pray to him with faith, to enjoy perfect happiness until they entered Nirvana.

Amma Dogon god; origin of all creation; with the earth gave birth to twins who were sacrificed to make the earth fertile, then brought back to life in the form of a human couple; created the sun and divided the world into two domains; his myth led to the practice of male circumcision.

Ammon, Amon ▶ Amun-Re

Amphitrite Greek goddess of the sea; married to **Poseidon**; the mother of **Triton** and other minor deities.

Amphitryon In Greek mythology, the husband of Alcmene; in his absence, **Zeus** took his shape and so became the father of **Heracles**.

Amun-Re (Amen, Ammon, Amon) Egyptian god; Amun was the local god of Thebes, considered as the god of air or fertility, who had the form of a man, but sometimes also the head of a ram; was likened to the sun-god Re, thus becoming Amun-Re; the pharaohs developed his cult.

Anahita Persian goddess of dawn and fertility; became a spirit of prosperity, collaborating in the work of creation, fighting for justice and initiating men into religious rites.

Anchises In Roman mythology, the Trojan father of **Aeneas**; the *Aeneid* gives an account of Aeneas's piety in carrying Anchises on his shoulders out of the blazing city of Troy.

Androcles Roman slave; escaped from his master, met a lion, and extracted a thorn from its paw; when recaptured, he was made to confront a lion in the arena, and found it was the same animal, so that his life was spared.

Andromache In Greek mythology, the wife of **Hector**, the hero of Troy; after the fall of the city she became the slave of **Neoptolemus**.

Andromeda In Greek mythology, the daughter of Cepheus, king of the Ethiopians; to appease **Poseidon**, she was fastened to a rock by the seashore as an offering to a sea-monster; rescued by **Perseus**, who used the **Gorgon's** head to change the monster to stone; the persons named in the story were all turned into constellations.

Angels Messengers of God; nine choirs were divided into three ranks; the seraphim, cherubim and thrones; the dominions, powers and virtues; and the principalities, archangels and angels. The first class was to praise and worship God, and the last was to assist the course of the stars, nations and people; angels or lesser gods would pass on messages, give orders or bring help to men.

Angra Mainyu Persian **demon**; creator of darkness and of evil things; belonged to death, filth and rottenness, inspiring disgust.

Anna Perenna Roman goddess; represented as an old woman, and worshipped in a sacred wood situated north of Rome; named Perenna, meaning eternity, when she became a **Nymph**; approached by Mars (► **Ares**) when she was old and asked to be an intermediary between himself and Minerva (► **Athene**); realizing

Angra Mainyu

this was impossible, she substituted herself for the chaste goddess and made fun of Mars.

Antigone Greek heroine; the guardian of the family; defied the dictator **Creon** to follow the wishes of the gods to fulfil the rite of burial for warriors considered as traitors, and for this was buried alive by Creon in the family tomb, where she hanged herself.

Anu Sumerian god of heaven; earthly royalty was descended from him, and as the god of Uruk, he gave back the city to Rim-Sin of the Larsa dynasty, who later conquered the neighbouring cities by Anu's strength.

Anubis Egyptian god; guide of souls to the world beyond; often represented with a human body and the head of a jackal or dog.

Aphrodite (Venus) Greek goddess of love who reigned over the hearts and senses of men; a proud and cruel goddess who punished all those who would not succumb to her; as a bribe, offered **Paris** the most beautiful mortal, **Helen**, causing the Trojan war; her worship was assimilated by the Romans with that of Venus, a goddess of ancient Italy.

Apis Egyptian god of strength and fecundity; represented as a bull for whom divine honours were reserved; Menes, the first Egyptian pharaoh, was said to have started the cult of Apis about 3000BC.

Apollo Greek and Roman god; son of **Zeus**; young and handsome, seer, poet and musician, he was said to be the most powerful of the gods; often identified with the sun, his nature also had a terrifying side and even his friends were afraid of him; said to have been responsible for the death of **Achilles**.

Arachne In Greek mythology, a weaver from Lydia; challenged **Athene** to a contest; when Arachne's work was seen to be superior, Athene destroyed the web and Arachne hanged herself; Athene saved her, but changed her into a spider.

Ares (Mars) Greek god of war; a supreme fighter who cared little for the interests he defended, and de-

lighted in bloody massacres; fought with **Athene**, the sons of **Poseidon** and **Heracles**; identified with the Roman god Mars, said to be the father of **Romulus**, the founder of Rome.

Arethusa Greek **Nymph**; pursued by the river-god Alpheus from Arcadia in Greece to Ortygia in Sicily; the myth attempts to account for the freshwater fountain which appears in the harbour of Syracuse and is believed to have flowed under the Ionian Sea.

Argonauts Greek heroes; sailed in the *Argo* to find the Golden Fleece; under **Jason's** leadership they sailed through the Symplegades (presumably the Dardanelles) and along the Black Sea coast to Colchis; their return is variously described, and may have included a river-passage to the North Sea.

Argus Greek watchman with a hundred eyes, appointed by **Hera** to watch over **Io**; after Argus was killed by **Hermes**, the eyes were placed in the tail of the peacock; also the name of **Odysseus's** dog.

Ariadne In Greek mythology, the daughter of King **Minos** of Crete; enabled **Theseus** to escape from the labyrinth by giving him a ball of thread; he fled with her, but deserted her on the island of Naxos; there she eventually became the wife of **Dionysus**.

Aristaeus Greek god of the countryside; a minor deity who introduced bee-keeping, vines, and olives; pursued **Eurydice**, the wife of **Orpheus**, who trod on a snake and died; in revenge her sister **dryads** killed his bees; **Proteus** told him to sacrifice cattle to appease the dryads, and in nine days he found bees generated in the carcasses.

Arjuna Indian hero; in the *Bhagavadgita*, a poem in the *Mahabharata*, he hesitates before entering the battle, knowing the killing which will ensue; his charioteer, Krishna, urges him to fulfil the action which is his duty as a warrior, explaining that the whole universe needs the fulfilment of actions which advance God's will.

Artemis (Diana) Greek goddess; daughter of **Zeus** and sister of **Apollo**; defender of virginity and modesty, and warrior who turned against anyone who attempted to force her against her will; also the protectress of women in labour and newborn children; identified with the Roman goddess Diana, a huntress.

Arthur Celtic medieval hero; brought up by **Merlin** and crowned king of Britain, King

Artemis

Arthur; armed with his magical sword Excalibur, he rid his country of monsters and giants, drove out the invaders, conquered the continent to reach Rome and in some stories as far as Palestine, from where he brought back the Cross of Christ.

Asclepius (Aesculapius) Greek and Roman god of the earth; son of **Apollo**, he acquired the magic powers to cure and revitalize from **Cheiron** the **Centaur**; used his powers to serve mortals, curing the sick and bringing the dead back to life; became a god when killed by **Zeus**, who was enraged that Asclepius had upset the natural order by restoring **Hippolytus** to life.

Astarte ► **Ishtar**

Atalanta Greek heroine; nurtured by a she-bear and grew up to be a strong huntress; refused to marry any man who would not take part in a foot-race with her; those who lost were killed; eventually Hippomenes (or Milanion) threw three golden apples of the **Hesperides** at her feet, so that her attention was diverted and she lost.

Aten Egyptian god; showed himself to mankind in the form of the solar disc, gave life, was the creator of all

Thought and Belief

Thought and Belief

things, and all things depended on him; had no connection with the other, numerous gods.

Athene (Minerva) Greek goddess of restraint and forethought; daughter of **Zeus**, virgin and warrior, whose protégés were **Odysseus**, **Heracles** and **Achilles**; fought with the Achaeans in the Trojan war, and enemy of **Ares**; in competition with **Poseidon**, won the possession of Attica, beginning the era of civilization for the city of Athens; identified with the Roman god Minerva.

Atlas Greek **Titan**; made to hold up the heavens with his hands, as a punishment for taking part in the revolt against the Olympians; when books of maps came to be published, he was often portrayed as a frontispiece, hence the term atlas.

Atreus Greek king of Argos; quarrelled with his brother **Thyestes**, and placed the flesh of Thyestes' children before him at a banquet; the father of **Agamemnon** and **Menelaus**.

Atropos ▸ **Moerae**

Attis (Atys) Greek god of vegetation; connected with the Asiatic cult of **Cybele**; died after castrating himself, and was resurrected; the story was later associated with the spring festival.

Aurora ▸ **Eos**

Autolycus In Greek mythology, the maternal grandfather of **Odysseus**, who surpassed all men in thieving; he was said to be a son of **Hermes**.

Baal Phoenician god of fertility and fecundity; known as king of the gods, and with his sister Anat was responsible for the universal prosperity of people and animals; his victory over the god of the sea gave sailors the courage to set their boats on water.

Bacchus ▸ **Dionysus**

Balder Norse god of sovereignty and power; son of **Odin** and **Frigg**; unlike the other power gods, he was kind and pleasant; a jealous god **Loki** conspired to kill him, and on death

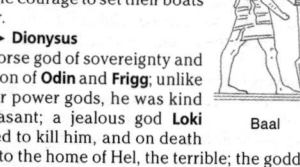

Baal

he went to the home of Hel, the terrible; the goddess of hell agreed to free him on condition that every creature would weep for him; all did, except an old woman (Loki in disguise), so that Balder would have to remain in hell until the battle (*Ragnarok*) which will bring about the end of the world.

Basilisk (Cockatrice) Greek monster; a small dragon-like creature combining features of the snake and the cockerel; its eye could freeze and kill, hence the expression: 'If looks could kill'; equivalent to the Cockatrice, which was hatched by a serpent from the egg of a cock.

Bellerophon Greek hero; sent to Lycia with a letter telling the king to put him to death; the king set him impossible adventures, notably the killing of the **Chimera**; in later accounts it is said that **Athene** helped him to tame **Pegasus**.

Berserker Norse warrior; fought in a 'bear-shirt' in such a frenzy that he was impervious to wounds; the name is the origin of the phrase 'to go berserk'.

Bes Egyptian god; depicted as a bandy-legged dwarf who was horrific in appearance, but congenial in temperament; the protector in childbirth, and guardian of the family.

Bladud Legendary king of Britain; discovered the hot spring at Bath and founded the city; one story is that he was a leper who found that the mud cured him.

Brahma Indian god; the creator; divided himself into two to make a couple bringing **Sarasvati**, feminine energy, into existence; he then developed four heads so that he could always see Sarasvati as she constantly circled him; he was also given four arms to

show his power; organized the world, and laid down the rules of *karma*, the standard of reward for one's actions.

Bran Celtic hero; known as Bendigeid Vran, the son of Llyr; invaded Ireland to help his sister, and died there; his seven followers cut off his head and buried it on the site of the Tower of London, from where it protects the whole island of Britain. In another legend, he was an Irish voyager who set out to find the Other World with 27 companions; on their return, as they approached the shore, people asked who they were, and said that the only Bran they knew was the hero of the ancient tale of *The Voyages of Bran*, so Bran wandered away forever.

Brigit (Brighid) Irish goddess of fire and the hearth; also of poetry and handicrafts; in the Christian era a number of her attributes were taken over by St Brigid.

Brunhild (Brunhilde, Brynhild) Norse **Valkyrie** who has assumed human form; **Odin** places her behind a wall of flame where she lies in an enchanted sleep; she is woken by **Sigurd**, who is able to leap the barrier on his horse Grani; tricked into marrying Gunnar, she finally kills herself on Sigurd's funeral pyre; in the similar Nibelungen legend, she is the wife of Gunther.

Bunyip In Australian aboriginal mythology, the source of evil; not to be thought of as a spirit or as a human; the **Rainbow Snake**, the mother of life, confined Bunyip to a waterhole; it haunts dark and gloomy places.

Cadmus Greek hero; son of Agenor, king of Tyre; set off in pursuit of his sister **Europa**, arrived in Greece, and founded the city of Thebes, teaching the natives to write; sowed dragon's teeth, from which armed men sprang up.

Calchas Greek seer; advised that **Iphigeneia** should be sacrificed at Aulis; at Troy he told **Agamemnon** to return Chryseis, the daughter of the priest of **Apollo**, to stop the plague; died in a combat of 'seeing'.

Calliope Greek **Muse** of epic poetry; sometimes said to be the mother of **Orpheus**.

Callisto Arcadian **Nymph**; attendant upon **Artemis**; loved by **Zeus**, she became pregnant, and was sent away from the virgin band; **Hera** changed her into a she-bear and after 15 years had passed, her son tried to spear her; taking pity on them, Zeus changed her into the constellation Ursa Major.

Cassandra Greek heroine; daughter of **Priam**, king of Troy; favoured by **Apollo**, who gave her the gift of prophecy; because she did not return his love, he decreed that while she would always tell the truth, she would never be believed; at the fall of Troy she was allotted to **Agamemnon**, and murdered on her arrival in Argos.

Castor and **Pollux** Greek heroes; twin sons of **Leda**; Pollux the son of **Zeus** and Castor the son of Tyndareus, king of Sparta, but both born at the same time; Castor was a good fighter and Pollux a skilled boxer, and the twins were inseparable; during their search for the Golden Fleece with the **Argonauts**, they saved the ship, the *Argos*, from a storm; when Castor was killed in a fight, Zeus agreed to Pollux's pleas for Castor to share his immortality so that he would not be separated from his brother.

Cecrops (Kekrops) Greek ancestor and first king of the Athenians; born from the earth, and formed with snakelike appendages instead of legs; during his reign, **Athene** and **Poseidon** fought for the possession of Athens; buried in the Erechtheum.

Centaurs Mythical Greek monsters; half man, half horse, aggressive and unintelligent with reputations for raping and kidnapping, with two exceptions: **Cheiron**, tutor of **Apollo**, **Jason** and **Achilles**, and Pholus, friend of **Heracles**, who were kindly Centaurs.

Cerberus Greek dog; guards the entrance to the underworld; originally fifty-headed, later with three heads; any living souls visiting hell gave 'a sop to Cerberus', ie a honey-cake, to quieten him; **Heracles** carried him off as one of his labours.

Ceres ▸ Demeter

Cernunnos Celtic god of plenty; represented with the ears and antlers of a stag, often accompanied by a serpent with the head of a ram; master of wild, earthly and aquatic animals.

Chac Mayan rain-god; characterized by two wide eyes, a long turned-up nose and two curved fangs; in the East he was red, in the North, white, in the West, black and in the South, yellow; made thunder and rain and was regarded as beneficent and friend of man.

Cernunnos

Charon Greek ferryman of the underworld; carried the shades or souls of the dead across the R Styx; sometimes other rivers are substituted in literature, such as Acheron and Lethe; the Greeks placed a small coin in the mouth of a corpse as Charon's fee.

Cheiron Greek **Centaur**; son of **Cronus** and Philyra the **Oceanid**, who kept a school for princes in Thessaly; educated **Asclepius** in the art of medicine and music, **Jason** the **Argonaut**, **Odysseus** and **Achilles**; wounded by one of **Heracles's** poisoned arrows, he gladly gave up his immortality to be rid of pain.

Chimera (Chimaera) Greek monster; had the head of a lion, the body of a goat (the name means 'she-goat'), and the tail of a serpent, which breathed fire.

Circe Greek enchantress; in the *Odyssey*, detained **Odysseus** and his followers on the island of Aeaea; her house was full of wild beasts; transformed Odysseus's men into swine with a magic drink, but he was able to defeat her charms through the protection of the herb moly.

Clio Greek **Muse** of history and lyre-playing.

Clotho ▸ Moerae

Clytemnestra (Clytemestra) In Greek mythology, the twin sister of **Helen** and the wife of **Agamemnon**; murdered her husband on his return from Troy, assisted by her lover, **Aegisthus**; killed in revenge by her son, **Orestes**.

Cockatrice ▸ Basilisk

Consentes Dii (Di) Twelve Roman gods; their statues, grouped in male/female pairs, stood in the Forum; probably Jupiter/Juno, Neptune/Minerva, Mars/Venus, Apollo/Diana, Volcanus/Vesta and Mercury/Ceres (▸ **Zeus/Hera, Poseidon/Athene, Ares/Aphrodite, Apollo/Artemis, Hephaestus/Vesta** and **Hermes/Demeter**).

Creon (Kreon) Greek kings; the name (meaning 'ruler') is applied especially to the brother of **Jocasta**, regent of Thebes, who awarded the throne to **Oedipus**; later, after the siege of the city by the seven Champions, he commanded that **Polynices** should not be buried, and condemned **Antigone** for disobedience.

Cressida In medieval accounts of the Trojan War, the daughter of Calchas, a Trojan priest; beloved by **Troilus**, a Trojan prince, she deserted him for **Diomedes** when transferred to the Greek camp.

Cronus (Kronos) Greek ruler of the universe (the second ruler); a **Titan**, the youngest son of **Uranus**, who rebelled against his father; during his rule people lived in the Golden Age; probably a pre-Greek deity, he is incorrectly, but popularly, confused with Chronos 'Time', because he too devoured his children.

Cu Chulainn Irish hero and supreme warrior; halted the progress of enemies united against his country; finally killed by Lugaid, the son of one of his victims.

Cupid ▸ Eros

Cybele Phrygian goddess of the earth; made through the mutilation of a hermaphrodite monster by the gods, she lived in forests and mountains.

Cyclopes Greek mythological monsters; one-eyed giants who worked as smiths and were associated with volcanic activity; the Cyclops **Polyphemus** was outwitted and blinded by **Odysseus**.

Daedalus Athenian inventor; worked for King **Minos** in Crete and constructed the labyrinth; later he escaped to Sicily with wings he had made for himself and **Icarus**; there he made the golden honeycomb kept at Mt Eryx; any archaic work of skill was ascribed to him, and he was a patron saint of craftsmen in Ancient Greece.

Danaans (Danaoi) Collectively, the Greeks who joined together in the expedition to Troy.

Danae Greek heroine; daughter of King Acrisius of Argos; when an oracle prophesied that her son would kill his grandfather, Acrisius imprisoned her in a bronze tower, where **Zeus** visited her in the form of a golden shower; gave birth to a son, **Perseus**, who accidentally killed Acrisius with a discus.

Danaoi ▸ Danaans

Danu Celtic mother-goddess; associated with hills and the earth.

Daphne Greek heroine; daughter of a river-god, Ladon (or, in another story, Peneios); pursued by the god **Apollo**, she was saved by being turned into a laurel, which became Apollo's sacred tree.

Daphnis Sicilian shepherd; half-brother of **Pan**, who was loved by a **Nymph**; he did not return her love, so she blinded him; became the inventor of pastoral poetry; in another story he would love nobody; when he died, all the beings of the island mourned him.

Deirdre In Irish legends, a girl destined to cause evil; grew up to be the most beautiful girl in Ireland; although intended for King Conchobhar, she was abducted by Naoise, a young king, and lived with him for seven years; when Naoise was killed by treachery, she was forced to marry Conchobhar, and killed herself.

Demeter (Ceres) Greek goddess of corn; presided over the interplay between life and death, and provided food; forced a compromise after **Hades** imprisoned her daughter **Persephone** in the underworld allowing her to return to the world above between spring and autumn; identified with the Roman goddess Ceres.

demons Evil celestial beings who force men to do evil and also do harm to men themselves, taking on the appearance of foreign gods, led by Satan; invisible and innumerable, they originally preferred to live in isolated and unclean places like deserts and ruins, and were greatly feared, especially at night; exorcisms are religious rites to remove demonic influences when a demon is thought to inhabit the body of a person, stripping him or her of self control and moral awareness.

Deucalion Greek hero; son of **Prometheus**; when **Zeus** flooded the world, Deucalion and his wife Pyrrha built an 'ark' which grounded on the top of Parnassus; as the only survivors, they asked how the human race was to be restored; an oracle told them 'to throw the bones of their mother over their shoulders'; they correctly interpreted this oracle, and threw stones (the bones of their mother Earth) which turned into human beings.

Diana ▸ Artemis

Dido Greek heroine; in the *Aeneid*, the daughter of the king of Tyre, who founded Carthage; **Aeneas** was diverted to Africa by storms, and told her his story; they fell in love, but when Aeneas deserted her she committed suicide by throwing herself upon a pyre.

Thought and Belief

Diomedes (Diomede) Greek hero; fought in the Trojan War, even taking on the gods in battle; also a wise counsellor, the partner of **Odysseus** in various schemes; in the medieval version of the story, he became the lover of **Cressida**.

Dionysus (Bacchus) Greek god of wine and the vine; lord of exuberance and drunkenness, he upset everything that got in his way, did not respect laws or customs and wandered about in caves; said to have made his followers coarse and vulgar, taught them to drink wine and caused madness.

Dragons Legendary animals present in Chinese, Greek and Indian mythology, and medieval Christian legends; had the claws of a lion, the wings of an eagle, a powerful serpent's tail and breathed fire; sometimes represented as the guardian of treasure, eg guarding the Golden Fleece, as an incarnation of Satan, as a primordial principle and as the symbol of the power of the emperor of China.

Dryads Greek mythological **Nymphs**; originally connected with oak-trees, but more usually referring to a wood-nymph, living in or among the trees; were usually friendly, but could frighten travellers.

Durga Indian goddess; wife of **Shiva** and his feminine part, and both the creator and destroyer of the world; a force for leading astray as well as for salvation, and a warrior who enjoyed battle and bloodshed.

Ea ▸ Enki

Echidna Greek monster; half-woman and half-snake, and the mother of various other monsters, eg **Hydra**.

Echo Greek **Nymph**; in one legend, beloved by **Pan**, and torn to pieces, only her voice surviving; in another story, punished by **Hera** so that she could only repeat the last words of another speaker; loved **Narcissus**, who rejected her, so that she wasted away to a voice.

Electra Heroine of Greek tragedies (but not in Homer); daughter of **Agamemnon** and **Clytemnestra**, who assisted her brother **Orestes** when he came to Argos to avenge his father, and who later married his friend Pylades; her personality is developed in different ways by the playwrights.

Endymion Greek shepherd of Mt Latmos; loved by the moon-goddess **Selene**; **Zeus** put him to sleep, while Selene looked after his flocks, and visited him every night; one of the mythological figures who was said to have founded the Olympic Games, as king of Elis.

Enki (Ea) Sumerian god who organized life on earth and developed the world; invented man and made a mould from him so that he could be reproduced, and created plants and livestock.

Enlil Sumerian god and keeper of sovereign power who maintained the order of the world; originally ruled over proletarian gods who became exhausted by their work and rebelled; it was agreed that man should be created to take over a part of the labours necessary for the maintenance of the world; later the prosperity and din of mankind, whose number was steadily increasing, irritated Enlil, who sent epidemics, suffering, death and worldwide flood.

Eos (Aurora) Greek goddess of the dawn; daughter of **Helios**, mother of **Memnon**; abducted various mortals; when she took the mortal Tithonus, **Zeus** granted her request that he should be made immortal, but she forgot to ask for perpetual youth, so he grew older and older, finally shrinking to no more than a voice or, possibly, the cicada insect.

Epigoni Greek heroes; collectively, the 'next generation'; after the failure of the **Seven against Thebes**, their sons made another expedition and succeeded; this was shortly before the Trojan War.

Epona Gallic goddess and guardian of horses; patron of civil and military horsemen, travellers and those on their way to the Great Beyond; sometimes seen

as a goddess of fertility and also identified with **Rhiannon**.

Erato Greek **Muse** of lyric poetry and hymns.

Erechtheus Greek king of Athens; born from the earth and nurtured by **Athene**; sacrificed his daughter Chthonia to secure victory over the Eleusinians, but was killed by **Poseidon**; the Erechtheum, a temple on the Acropolis, is probably on the site of his palace.

Erinyes (Furies) Greek goddesses; inhabitants of hell who were responsible for punishing bloody crimes; named Alecto, Tisiphone and Megara, they were represented as winged spirits who had long hair entwined with snakes, and carried whips and torches; tortured their victims and drove them mad.

Eris Greek heroine; daughter of Night and the sister of **Ares**; a late story tells how she was present at the wedding of **Peleus** and **Thetis** and threw a golden apple 'for the fairest'; this brought **Hera**, **Athene**, and **Aphrodite** into contention, and was the first cause of the Trojan War; the name means 'strife' in Greek.

Eros (Cupid) Greek god, responsible for keeping the world together and for the continuation of the species; his power to inspire sexual desires could make people lose their reason and paralyse their will power; became Cupid for the Romans.

Eteocles Greek hero; elder of **Oedipus**'s two sons, whom he cursed; became king of Thebes after his father's death, and refused to share power with his brother **Polynices**; the **Seven against Thebes** attacked the city, and Eteocles was killed by Polynices.

Eumenides A euphemistic name given to the **Erinyes** after being domesticated at Athens in Aeschylus' play of the same name; the name means 'the kindly ones'.

Europa (Europe) Greek heroine; daughter of Agenor, king of Tyre, who was abducted by **Zeus** in the shape of a bull, and swam with her on his back to Crete; her children were **Minos** and **Rhadamanthus**.

Eurydice Greek **Dryad**; wife of **Orpheus**; after her death, Orpheus went down to the underworld and persuaded **Hades** to let her go by the power of his music; the condition was that she should follow him, and that he should not look at her until they reached the light; not hearing her footsteps, he looked back, and she disappeared back into the underworld.

Euterpe Greek **Muse** of flute-playing.

Fates ▸ Moerae

Faunus Roman god of agriculture; responsible for the fertility of plants and the energy of living nature; reproduced himself in fauns, **satyrs** who were half man, half goat.

Finn mac Cumhal Irish hero; warrior and magician who avenged his father who was killed in battle and reorganized his elite troops, whose qualities were intelligence, cunning, faithfulness, a hatred of money and respect for women; possessed the gift of receiving visions when he bit his thumb.

Flora Roman goddess of flowers and flowering plants; appears with the spring; given a temple in 238BC; her games were celebrated on 28 April.

Fortuna Roman goddess of fortune; introduced by King Servius Tullius (578–534BC); in the Middle Ages was highly revered as a divine and moral figure, redressing human pride; her wheel is frequently referred to and depicted, as at St Etienne in Beauvais, where figures can be seen climbing and falling off

Freyja Norse goddess of love, fertility, fecundity, victory and peace, and sister of **Freyr**; took on the form of a falcon to travel between one world and the other.

Freyr (Frey) Norse god of fertility and fecundity and brother of **Freyja**; presided over love, wealth and orgies, brought sun and rain to make crops grow; mainly worshipped by women.

Frigg (Frigga) Norse goddess of married love; wife of **Odin** (often confused with **Freyja**).

Furies ► Erinyes

Gaea (Gaia, Ge, Tellus) Greek goddess; 'the earth' personified, and later the goddess of the whole earth (not a particular piece of land); came into being after Chaos, and was the wife of **Uranus**, producing numerous children; the Romans identified her with Tellus.

Galahad, Sir One of King **Arthur**'s knights; son of **Lancelot** and Elaine; distinguished for his purity, he alone was able to succeed in the adventures of the Siege Perilous and the Holy Grail.

Galatea Greek **Nymph**; a sea-nymph, wooed by **Polyphemus** the **Cyclops** with uncouth love-songs; in some versions Polyphemus destroys his rival Acis with a rock; in other versions he happily marries Galatea; probably a Sicilian story.

Ganesha Indian god; master of intelligence and the patron of artists and writers who was given by **Brahma** the task of copying the *Mahabharata*; represented with the head of an elephant; a popular god, he put obstacles in the way of those who neglected him, and spared others.

Ganesha

Ganymede In Greek mythology, the son of Tros, a Trojan prince; **Zeus** sent a stormwind, or (later and more usually) an eagle, who carried Ganymede up to Olympus, where he became the cup-bearer; in return his father was given a stud of exceptional horses.

Gawain (Gawayne) One of King **Arthur**'s knights; son of King Lot of Orkney, whose character varies in different accounts; in the medieval *Sir Gawayn and the Grene Knight*, he is a noble hero undergoing a test of faith; in other stories he is a jeering attacker of reputations, especially that of **Lancelot**.

Gawayne ► Gawain

Genii Spirits of mythology throughout the world; their forces were less beneficent than those of **angels**, but less wicked than those of **demons**; regarded as the doubles of objects, beings and events.

Giants Large, strong and often stupid beings from mythology throughout the world; in the Bible, the product of an unnatural union between fallen angels and the daughters of men; taught men the rudiments of the knowledge they had from being able to see from high up; for the Greeks, sons of the earth representing youth, strength and virility, who could only be killed by a god and a man together.

Gigantes Greek giants; sons of earth and Tartaros, with snake-like legs; made war on the Olympian gods, were defeated, and are buried under various volcanic islands; the Gigantomachy ('war of the giants') was the subject of large-scale sculpture, as at Pergamum; a sub-group, the Aloadi, piled Mt Pelion upon Mt Ossa.

Gilgamesh Sumerian hero; tyrannical king of Uruk and intrepid adventurer; began an adventure to search for immortality, but failed, and returned to Uruk to accept his fate and resume his former life.

Gorboduc Legendary king of Britain; first heard about in Geoffrey of Monmouth's *History*; when he grew senile, his two sons Ferret and Porrex quarrelled over the inheritance; he was the subject of an early Elizabethan tragedy in the Senecan style, written by Norton and Sackville (1561).

Gorgons Three mythical Greek monsters; represented with hair made of angry serpents, tusks like a boar's, hands of bronze and golden wings; anyone who looked at them was turned to stone; Euryale represented sexual excess, Stheno, social perversion, and **Medusa**, vanity; Medusa's head was cut off by **Perseus**, and the children of **Poseidon** emerged from the wound.

Graces In Greek mythology, three daughters of **Zeus** and **Hera**; embodied beauty and social accomplishments; sometimes called Aglaia, Euphrosyne and Thalia.

Graiae In Greek mythology, three sisters with the characteristics of extreme old age; had one eye and one tooth between them; **Perseus** took the eye and made them tell the route to the **Gorgons**, who were their sisters.

Griffin (Gryphon) Greek monster; originated in tales of the Arimaspians, who hunted the creature for its gold; had a lion's body, and an eagle's head, wings, and claws; collected fragments of gold to build its nest, and, instead of an egg, laid an agate.

Gryphon ► Griffin

Guan Di (Kuan Ti) Chinese god of war; based on a historical person who died in the 3c AD; made a god in 1594, and greatly revered.

Gudrun Norse heroine; wife of **Sigurd** the Volsung; after his death she married Atli (the legendary Attila) who put her brothers to death; in revenge she served up his sons in a dish, and then destroyed him by fire; in the similar German story she is known as Kriemhild.

Guinevere King **Arthur**'s queen; originally Guanhamara in Geoffrey of Monmouth's *History*, and there are other spellings; in later romances, much is made of her affair with Sir **Lancelot** (an example of courtly love); in Malory's epic poem she survives Arthur's death and enters a nunnery.

Hadad Assyrian god of storms, known as **Adad** by the Mesopotamians; invoked in curses when begged to send torrential rain to the lands of enemies, but also brought agricultural fertility.

Hades (Pluto) Greek god of hell; brother of **Zeus** and **Poseidon**; invisible god who ruled the dead, assisted by **demons**; forbade his subjects to leave his domain and became enraged when anyone tried to steal his prey; the most hated of the gods among mortals; identified by the Romans as Pluto.

Halcyone (Alcyone) In Greek mythology, daughter of **Aeolus**, who married Ceyx, son of the morning star; either for impiety, or because she mourned his death at sea, both were changed into seabirds (halcyons, or kingfishers, who are fabled to calm the sea); sometimes described instead as one of the **Pleiades**.

Hamadryads Greek **Nymphs**; tree-nymphs who were offended or died when the trees containing them were harmed.

Hanuman Indian monkey god, son of the god of the winds, Vayu; as soon as he was born, he rushed towards the sun believing it to be a ripe fruit, crashing into all the planets on the way; as protector, he destroyed the death rays emitted by the planets and was known as the god of athletes and gymnasts.

Hanuman

Harpies Greek genii/spirits; represented as three women with wings or birds with the heads of women; seized children and souls and tortured their victims.

Harpocrates ► Horus

Hathor Egyptian goddess; portrayed as a woman bearing the sun between two cow's horns representing the intoxication of pleasure, love and fertility; identified by the Greeks with **Aphrodite**.

Thought and Belief

Hebe Greek goddess of youth and youthful beauty; daughter of **Zeus** and **Hera**; became cup-bearer to the Olympians, and was married to **Heracles** after he was deified.

Hecabe ▸ Hecuba

Hecate Greek goddess of witchcraft, spooks, and magic; not in Homer, she appears in Hesiod, and seems to represent the powerful mother-goddess of Asia Minor; worshipped with offerings at places where three roads cross, and so given three bodies in sculpture.

Hector Hero of Greek mythology; the bravest Trojan, who led out their army to battle; the son of **Priam**, and married to **Andromache**; **Achilles** killed him and dragged his body behind his chariot; Priam ransomed it at the end of the *Iliad*.

Hecuba (Hecabe) Greek heroine; wife of **Priam**, king of Troy, and mother of 18 children, including **Hector** and **Cassandra**; after the Greeks took Troy, she saw her sons and her husband killed, and was sent into slavery.

Heimdallr Norse god; born of nine mothers, he could see everything and never closed his eyes; the guardian of the gods' abode; at the moment of the end of the world, it was said that he would blow his trumpet to call all the gods to hold a council.

Hel (Hela) In Norse mythology, the youngest child of **Loki**; half her body was living human flesh, the other half decayed; assigned by **Odin** to rule Helheim (the underworld) and to receive the spirits of the dead who do not die in battle.

Helen Greek heroine; daughter of **Zeus** and **Leda**, sister to **Clytemnestra**, **Castor** and **Pollux**; the most beautiful of women who captivated all men, and as a result was the cause of the Trojan War when she was abducted by **Paris**; granted immortality by Zeus and Apollo.

Helios Greek god of the sun; represented as a charioteer with four horses; in early times Helios was not worshipped, except at Rhodes; in the late classical period, there was an Imperial cult of the sun, Sol Invictus.

Hellen In ancient Greek genealogies, the eldest son of **Deucalion**; father of Doros, Xuthos and Aiolos, who were the progenitors of the Dorian, Ionian, and Aeolic branches of the Greek race; the Greeks (or Hellenes) were named after him.

Hephaestus (Volcanus, Vulcan) Greek god of fire; son of **Zeus** and **Hera**; lame (either because his mother dropped him from Olympus when she realized how ugly he was, or because Zeus threw him down onto the island when he took his mother's side in a marital dispute); volcanoes were his workshops and the **Cyclopes** his assistants in his work as a blacksmith and jeweller; identified by the Romans as Vulcan.

Hera (Juno) Greek goddess; married her brother **Zeus**; conceived some of her sons without any male assistance by hitting the ground with her hand or eating a lettuce; pursued with a vengeance Zeus's mistresses and their children, putting enormous snakes into **Heracles**'s cradle forcing Zeus to hide his illegitimate children by transforming them into animals or enclosing them in the earth; identified by the Romans as Juno; her name means 'lady'.

Heracles (Hercules) Greek hero; demonstrated amazing strength from birth, choking the serpents sent to him by the jealous **Hera**; many achievements are attributed to him including the 12 labours of Eurystheus; he delivered Troy from a monster but came back to wreak havoc on the city because it did not pay his salary; succeeded in injuring **Hades** and **Hera** with his arrows and won immortality;

identified by the Romans as Hercules.

Hercules ▸ Heracles

Hermaphroditus Greek god; a minor god with bisexual characteristics, the son of **Hermes** and **Aphrodite**; the **Nymph** Salmacis, unloved by him, prayed to be united with him; this was granted by combining them in one body.

Hermes (Mercury) Greek god of the spoken word and son of **Zeus**; intermediary who went from men to Olympus and Olympus to **Hades**; as the god of commerce, the only person to achieve immortality as a result of a contract; identified by the Romans as Mercury.

Hero and Leander Greek lovers; lived on opposite sides of the Hellespont; Hero was the priestess of **Aphrodite** at Sestos, and Leander, who lived at Abydos, swam across each night guided by her light; when this was extinguished in a storm, he was drowned, and Hero committed suicide by throwing herself into the sea.

Hesperides In Greek mythology, the daughters of the evening star (Hesper); guarded the Golden Apples together with the dragon, Ladon; sang as they circled the tree, which was given by **Gaia** to **Hera** as a wedding-present; when **Heracles** had to fetch the apples, he either killed the dragon, or sent it to sleep, or, more usually, persuaded **Atlas** to get them for him while he took over Atlas' function of holding up the sky.

Hestia (Vesta) Greek goddess of hearth and home; sister of **Zeus** and **Hera**; never intervened in the stormy history of the gods and became the central point, the meeting place; identified by the Romans as Vesta.

Hiawatha Native American hero; appeared in *The Song of Hiawatha*, which retells Native American legends in the manner and metre of the Finnish *Kalevala*; Hiawatha is educated by his grandmother Nokomis, and marries Minnehaha.

Hippolytus Greek hero; son of **Theseus** and Hippolyta, leader of the **Amazons**; Theseus' new wife, **Phaedra**, made advances to Hippolytus, which were refused, so she falsely accused Hippolytus of rape; Theseus invoked a curse, **Poseidon** sent a frightening sea-monster, and Hippolytus was thrown from his chariot and killed.

Horae In Greek mythology, 'the seasons'; implied the right or fitting time for something to happen; given various names either connected with fertility or peace.

Horatii and Curiatii Early Roman legend used to justify appeals; under Tullus Hostilius there was war between Rome and Alba; two groups of three brothers were selected from Rome (the Horatii) and Alba (the Curiatii) to fight, the winners to decide the battle; all were killed except one, Horatius; when his sister, who was betrothed to a Curiatius, abused him, he murdered her, but was acquitted after appealing to the Roman people.

Horus (Harpocrates) Egyptian god; husband of **Hathor**, brother of **Seth** and ancestor of the dynasties of the pharaohs; had a falcon's head and ruled the air, his eyes being the sun and the moon; became universal king of the earth after defeating Seth, who had seized power after murdering Horus's father.

Huang-ti Chinese cultural hero; legendary emperor, patron of alchemists, doctors and seers, and one of the fathers of Taoism; born miraculously after his mother was made pregnant by lightning from the Great Bear; invented chariots, ships and houses, and understood that every activity in the world had to be preceded by putting the individual body in order; discovered the way of the Tao in a dream and searched for ways of attaining immortality.

Huitzilopochtli Aztec god of war and protector of the city; symbolized in the midday sun and represented with hummingbird feathers on his head and left leg, a black face and brandishing a serpent of turquoise or fire; massacred all his brothers and sisters immediately after he was born, as they planned to kill his mother; as a soothsayer he communed with the priests at night and as a cruel god, tore out the hearts of those who disobeyed him.

Huitzilopochtli

Hydra Greek monster; many-headed child of **Typhon** and **Echidna**, which lived in a swamp at Lerna; since the heads grew again when struck off, **Heracles** could kill it only with the assistance of Iolaos, who cauterized the places where the heads grew; the name means 'water-snake'.

Hygeia Greek goddess; the daughter of **Asclepius**; a minor deity, her name was a personification of the word for 'health'.

Hymen Greek god of marriage; in Ancient Greece and Rome, the cry of 'O Hymen Hymenaie' at weddings (later a marriage song) led to the invention of a being called Hymen of Hymenaeus, who was assumed to have been happily married, and therefore suitable for invocation as a god of marriage; depicted as a youth with a torch.

Hyperboreans Greek unvisited people of fabled virtue and prosperity; lived in the land 'beyond the North Wind'; in Herodotus they worshipped **Apollo** and sent offerings to Delos; could refer to a lost Greek colony in what is now Romania, or even to the Swedes at the end of the trans-European amber route.

Hyperion Greek **Titan**; son of **Uranus** and **Gaia**, and father of **Eos** (the Dawn), **Helios** (the sun), and **Selene** (the moon); later, as in Shakespeare and Keats, identified with the sun.

Iapetus Greek **Titan**; father of **Prometheus** and **Atlas**; grandfather of **Deucalion**; the close resemblance to Japhet may indicate borrowing from near Eastern sources.

Icarus In Greek mythology, the son of **Daedalus**; his father made him wings to escape from Crete, but he flew too near the sun; the wax holding the wings melted and he fell into the Aegean at a point now known as the Icarian Sea.

Idomeneus Leader of the Cretans; a descendant of **Minos** who assisted the Greeks at Troy; caught in a storm at sea, he vowed to sacrifice the first thing he met on his safe return; this was his own son; after carrying out the sacrifice he was driven into exile.

Inanna Sumerian goddess of love and war; stole the *me* (meaning everything that makes up civilization) from **Enki** to give to her city, Uruk; attempted to seize power of the underworld from her sister but failed; in rage at her husband's lack of sympathy for her resulting predicament, she ordered the **demons** to torture him and imprison him in hell.

Indra Indian god; an athlete and exemplary warrior who gave life and light, created the ox and the horse, gave the cow milk and made all women fertile; crushed the evil **demon** Vrtra, allowing the dawn and the sunrise to be created.

Io Greek heroine; beloved by **Zeus**, who turned her into a heifer to save her from **Hera**'s jealousy; Hera kept her under the gaze of the **Argus**; but she escaped with **Hermes**'s help; was then punished with a gad-fly which drove her through the world until she arrived in Egypt; there Zeus changed her back into human shape, and she gave birth to Epaphos, ancestor of many peoples.

Iphigeneia Greek priestess; daughter of **Agamemnon** and **Clytemnestra**; was about to be sacrificed at Aulis as the fleet could not sail to Troy, because the winds were against it, but at the last moment was saved by **Artemis**, who made her a priestess in the country of the Tauri (the Crimea); finally her brother **Orestes** saved her.

Irene In Greek mythology, a personification of 'peace'; one of the **Horae**.

Iris Greek goddess of the rainbow; became the messenger of the gods, especially of **Zeus** in Homer, and of **Hera** in later writers; depicted sitting under Hera's throne.

Ishtar (Astarte) Mesopotamian goddess; as the star of the morning, personified war, and as the star of the evening, personified love; came to the aid of the sexually impotent and was cruel and determined as a hostile warrior; established the fame of Assyria and was responsible for the cruelty of its kings.

Isis Egyptian goddess; mother of **Horus**; wore a solar disc and the horns of a cow, and was known as the protectress of love and mistress of destiny; obtained her powers by trickery and as a magician, cured her son who had been bitten by a snake.

Isis

Isolde ▸ **Tristan** and **Isolde**

Itzamma Mayan god of heaven; the creator and civilizer of mankind, with the appearance of an old toothless man with sunken cheeks and a prominent nose, he gave places their names and distributed land between the different tribes; sometimes depicted as an enormous serpent which represented the sky.

Iuppiter ▸ **Zeus**

Ixion Greek king of Thessaly; the first murderer; also the father of the **Centaurs**; for attempting to rape **Hera** he was bound to a wheel of fire, usually located in the underworld.

Izanagi no Mikoto and **Izanami no Mikoto** Japanese male and female gods; in the creation myth these were the first beings who created islands in the water and the other gods; Izanami died when she gave birth to fire; Izanagi followed her to the land of the dead (Yomi), but she turned against him and pursued him; finally he had to block the exit from Yomi with a large rock and Izanami then became the goddess of the underworld.

Janus Roman god of beginnings; a two-faced god who personified clearsightedness; protected **Saturn** when he was being hunted by Jupiter (▸ **Zeus**); invented money, the cultivation of soil and legislation.

Jason Greek hero; son of the king of Iolcus, who was deposed by his half-brother, Pelias; Jason claimed the power from Pelias, who challenged him to demonstrate his worthiness of the crown by bringing back the Golden Fleece, guarded by an ever-wakeful dragon, hoping that Jason would never return from such an impossible mission; a ship, the *Argo*, was built for the mission, and Jason overcame many obstacles to return with the Golden Fleece; the king did not keep his promise, and weary of war, Jason stole the fleece and left.

Jimmu Tenno First emperor of Japan in the Shinto religion; said to be descended from **Amaterasu**, and to have reigned between 660 and 585BC, dying at the age of 127; probably a real person, subsequently deified.

Jocasta In Greek legend, the wife of King Laius of Thebes and mother of **Oedipus**; later unwittingly became the wife of her son; she is called Epikaste in Homer; bore Oedipus four children: **Eteocles, Poly-**

Thought and Belief

nices, **Antigone** and Ismene; killed herself when she discovered her incest.

Julunggul ▸ Rainbow Snake

Juno ▸ Hera

Jupiter ▸ Zeus

Kama Indian god of love; represented with a bow and arrow; as soon as he was born, looked around him and asked who he was going to set on fire; always ready to initiate love in men or in the gods.

Kami Japanese spirits; manifestations of natural forces and superior to men; there were 80 million kami, to personify anything big or inexplicable at a time when animals, rivers, lakes and seas were objects of veneration; the drink saké was the offering preferred by the kami.

Kane ▸ Tane

Kekrops ▸ Cecrops

Kreon ▸ Creon

Krishna Indian god; a lovable child and merciless warrior; endowed with exceptional strength and intelligence, he killed the monster Baku who had taken the form of a crane, and fought with Kaliya, the king of serpents; his life with 16000 wives and 180000 children was interspersed with numerous battles against **demons**; has become the only god in many Hindu sects.

Krishna

Kronos ▸ Cronus

KuanTi ▸ Guan Di

Kumarbi Hurrian god; deposed from the divine throne by the storm-god, **Teshub**; became the father of an enormous stone man in the hope that this son could overthrow the storm-god, but this was prevented by the other gods.

Lachesis ▸ Moerae

Laius Greek king ofThebes; father of **Oedipus**; he married **Jocasta**, and was warned by an oracle that their son would destroy him; this happened when Oedipus, assumed to be dead, returned from Corinth and accidentally killed Laius during a quarrel on the road.

Lakshmi Indian goddess of happiness, beauty and prosperity; the wife of **Vishnu**, she was the incarnation of the great god's power.

Lancelot, Sir (Launcelot du Lac) The most famous of King **Arthur**'s knights, though he is a relatively late addition to the legend; the son of King Ban of Benwick, the courtly lover of **Guinevere**, and the father of **Galahad** by Elaine; in spite of his near-perfection as a knight, he was unable to achieve the Grail adventure; he arrived too late to help Arthur in the last battle.

Lakshmi

Laocoon Trojan prince; a priest of **Apollo**, who objected to the plan to bring the Wooden Horse into Troy; two serpents came out of the sea and killed him, together with his two sons.

Lapiths In Greek mythology, a people of Thessaly; Perithous, king of the Lapiths, invited the **Centaurs** to his wedding with Hippodameia; a terrible fight took place between the two groups, in which the Centaurs were defeated.

Lares Roman gods; protectors of inhabited places; depicted as two boys accompanied by a dog; divided into two groups; *lares compitales* were found in the country, at crossroads and in meeting places; *lares familiares* were guardians of the family home.

Latinus Roman ancestor and eponymous king of the Latins; descended from **Circe** (according to Hesiod) or from **Faunus** (according to Virgil); in the *Aeneid*, Latinus gives his daughter Lavinia to **Aeneas**.

Latona ▸ Leto

Launcelot du Lac ▸ Lancelot, Sir

Leander ▸ Hero and Leander

Lear Legendary king of Britain; son of **Bladud**, who reigned for 60 years; in his old age two of his daughters, Goneril and Regan, conspired against him, but the third daughter, Cordelia, saved him and became queen after his death (the story is changed by Shakespeare, so that she died before his eyes); Leicester is named after him.

Leda In Greek mythology, the wife ofTyndareus, king of Sparta, and mother, either by him or **Zeus**, of **Castor** and **Pollux**, **Helen**, and **Clytemnestra**; a frequent subject in art is Zeus courting Leda in the form of a swan; Helen was believed to have been hatched from an egg, preserved at Sparta into historic times.

Lemminkainen Finnish hero; in the *Kalevala*, has to undertake impossible tasks, such as shooting the swan of Tuonela; this causes his death, and his mother has to reanimate him; his ride through a land of horrors inspired Sibelius.

Lemures Roman ghosts; wandered about outside the house on 9, 11 and 13 May (the Lemuria).

Leto (Latona) GreekTitan; mother by **Zeus** of the twins **Apollo** and **Artemis**; they were born at Delos, because in her jealousy **Hera** would allow no land to harbour Leto; luckily, at that time Delos was a floating island.

Leviathan Phoenician monster; personification of evil, believed to have come out of the primal chaos; sparks of fire shot from his mouth and smoke poured from his nostrils; always present, hidden in each individual.

Lif and **Lifthrasir** In Norse mythology, the mother and father of the new race of human beings after Ragnarok (the last battle); the names presumably mean 'life' and 'strong life'.

Lilith In Jewish legend, the first wife of Adam; or, more generally, a **demon** woman.

Lohengrin In Germanic legend, the son of Parsifal (▸ **Perceval, Sir**); left the temple of the Grail and was carried to Antwerp in a boat drawn by swans; there he saved Princess Elsa of Brabant, and intended to marry her; however, she asked forbidden questions about his origin, and he was forced to leave her, the swan-boat taking him back to the Grail temple.

Loki Norse god; represented deceit, disorder, malevolence and perversity; fathered horrible monsters and put obstacles in the way of happiness; as a magician, had the power to transform himself into different animals and insulted and offended the other gods.

Lotus-eaters (Lotophagi) People encountered by **Odysseus**; lived on 'a flowery food' which makes those who eat it forget their own country, and wish to live always in a dreamy state; Odysseus had to force his men to move on.

Lucretia (Lucrece) Roman wife of Collatinus; raped by Sextus, son ofTarquinius Superbus; after telling her story, she committed suicide; the incident led to the expulsion of theTarquins from Rome.

Lud Legendary king of Britain; first walled the principal city, from that time called Kaerlud after him, and eventually London; buried near Ludgate, which preserves his name.

Lug Irish god; skilled in many arts and fulfilled the office of all gods; proclaimed by the king to be the wisest of the wise and given the task of organizing the battle which conquered the Fomoiri, evil beings who occupied Ireland and oppressed its inhabitants.

Lycurgus Greek king of Thrace; opposed **Dionysus**

and was blinded; his name is shared by the founder of the Spartan constitution, with its military caste-system (the date when this originated has been much disputed, and is now thought to be c.600BC, much too late for the legendary Lycurgus to have participated).

Maat Egyptian goddess; represented the social and cosmic order and the guardian of ethics and rites; there at the beginning of the universe, she maintained order in heaven as on earth, and was responsible for the seasons, night and day, the movement of the stars and rainfall.

Maenads Greek 'mad women'; followed **Dionysus** on his journeys; dressed in animal-skins and so strong that they could uproot trees and kill wild animals, eating the flesh raw; also known as Bacchae or Bacchantes.

Manes In Roman religion, 'the dead'; the concept developed from the spirits of the dead in general, to the gods of the underworld, Di Manes, the ancestors of the family, and the spirits of individuals in gravestone inscriptions.

Marduk Babylonian god; represented life, civilization and progress; created the winds and raised the tempest, distressing the first-born gods who declared war on him but were defeated; Marduk created heaven, earth and man; when the god of death succeeded by a ruse in making him rise from his seat, the sun stopped shining, the roads became infested with brigands, and man ate man until Marduk took his place again.

Marduk

Mars ▸ **Ares**

Marsyas Greek **satyr**; challenged **Apollo** to a flute-contest; defeated and flayed alive by the god, his blood or tears formed a river of the same name.

Medea Greek witch; daughter of Aeetes, the king of Colchis, who assisted **Jason** in obtaining the Golden Fleece; on their return to Iolcos, she renewed the youth of Aeson, and tricked the daughters of Pelias into performing a similar ritual, so that they destroyed their own father; when deserted by Jason at Corinth, she fled in her aerial chariot after killing her children.

Medusa Greek **Gorgon**; depicted with staring eyes and snakes for hair.

Meleager Greek hero; at his birth the **Moerae** appeared and prophesied that he would die when the brand then on the fire had burnt away; his mother, Althaea, removed it and kept it; when the quarrel over the Calydonian boar took place and her brothers were killed, she threw the brand onto the fire, so that he died.

Melias ▸ **Nymphs**

Melpomene Greek **Muse** of tragedy.

Memnon In Greek mythology, a prince from Ethiopia; son of **Eos**; killed at Troy by **Achilles**; the Greeks thought that one of the gigantic statues at Thebes represented him; it gave out a musical sound at sunrise.

Menelaus King of Sparta; younger brother of **Agamemnon**, who married **Helen**; took part in the Trojan War and was delayed in Egypt on his return; finally settled down at Sparta with Helen again.

Mercury ▸ **Hermes**

Merlin Good wizard or sage whose magic was used to help King **Arthur**; son of an incubus and a mortal woman, and therefore indestructible, but was finally entrapped by Vivien, the Lady of the Lake, and bound under a rock for ever; famous for his prophecies.

Mermaid Legendary sea-creature; had the body of a woman and the tail of a fish, a fiction possibly based on early encounters with seals or sea-cows; in stories their singing attracts mortal men to love them; their male counterparts were mermen.

Midas King of Phrygia; as a reward for helping the **Satyr** Silenus, **Dionysus** gave Midas a wish, and he asked that anything he touched should turn to gold; however, this caused so many difficulties (eg in eating and drinking) that he asked to be released; he was told to bathe in the River Pactolus, which thereafter had golden sands.

Minerva ▸ **Athene**

Minos Greek hero; son of **Zeus**, who took the form of a bull in order to impregnate **Europa**; claimed power as king of Crete and took part in military expeditions to avenge the murder of his son and to force Athens to provide men and women to feed to the **Minotaur**; became a judge in hell after being drowned in his bath.

Minotaur Greek monster; son of **Pasiphae** and a bull from the sea, half bull and half human; the name means **Minos's** bull; kept in a labyrinth made by **Daedalus**, and killed by **Theseus** with the help of **Ariadne**.

Mithra Indo-European god; represented friendship, benevolence, non-hostility and compromise; depicted as a 'killer of the bull', plunging a sword into a dying bull's body, from which all herbs and beneficial plants were born; closely associated with the sun.

Mnemosyne Greek **Titan**; daughter of earth and heaven, and mother of all the **Muses**; her name means 'Memory'.

Modimo African god; originally from Zimbabwe, and considered to be the creator; when appearing in the east, he distributed good things and belonged to the element water; appearing in the west, he was a destroyer, responsible for drought, cyclones and earthquakes, and represented the element fire; his name was taboo and spoken only by priests or seers, and he could only be reached by imperfect beings.

Moerae (Fates, Parcae) Three Greek goddesses; named Atropos, Clotho and Lachesis, daughters of **Zeus**; the first spun a thread which signified birth, the second unravelled the thread, symbolizing the unravelling of life, and the third cut the thread, signifying death; they were the personification of inflexible law, representing destiny and the limits which could not be overstepped; in Rome assimilated to the Parcae, who were originally birth **demons**.

Moloch Biblical god of the Canaanites and other peoples; in his cult children were sacrificed by fire; a rebel angel in Milton's *Paradise Lost*, his name is used for any excessive and cruel religion.

Monsters Wild, unmanageable forces which appear as enemies in all mythologies; in general, a mixture of living creatures (eg horse and man for **Centaurs** and fish and woman for **Sirens**); signified irrational forces, the death necessary for new life and the anarchical energy which preceded and produced creation and order.

Morgan le Fay Legendary enchantress; 'Morgan the Fairy', King **Arthur's** sister, and generally hostile towards him; one of the three queens who received him at his death.

Morpheus Roman god of sleep; one of the sons of Somnus ('sleep') who sent or impersonated images of people in the dreamer's mind; later, as in Spenser, the god of sleep.

Muses Nine Greek goddesses; daughters of **Zeus**, each with the vocation to promote an area of the arts: epic poetry, mime, history, the flute, dance, lyric poetry, tragedy, comedy, astronomy; they favoured communication, delighted the gods and inspired poets; ▸ **Calliope, Polyhymnia, Clio, Euterpe, Terpsichore, Erato, Melpomene, Thalia, Urania.**

Thought and Belief

Thought and Belief

Myrmidons Greek band of warriors from Thessaly; went to the Trojan War with **Achilles**.

Naiads Greek **Nymphs**; inhabited springs, rivers, and lakes.

Narcissus Greek hero; the symbol of self-love, he was told by a seer that he would live to a ripe old age as long as he never looked at himself; caring for no one but himself, he drove his friends and those who fell in love with him to despair; the goddess **Nemesis** decided to avenge his victims by leading him to a spring in which he saw his own reflection, which he immediately fell in love with, and moving towards it, he fell into the spring and drowned; from his body was born the flower which bears his name.

Nausicaa Greek heroine; in Homer's *Odyssey*, the daughter of King Alcinous; when **Odysseus** landed in Phaeacia, alone and naked, she was doing the laundry by the sea-shore; she took him home to her father's palace.

Nemesis Greek goddess of moderation; ruled over the distribution of wealth, taking revenge on arrogance and punishing excess; said to have prevented the Persians from seizing the city of Athens.

Neoptolemus Greek warrior; son of **Achilles**, his original name being Pyrrhus; went with **Odysseus** to persuade **Philoctetes** to come to Troy; at the end of the war he killed **Priam** and enslaved **Andromache**; for this, **Apollo** prevented him from reaching his home, and he was killed in a dispute at Delphi.

Nephthys Egyptian goddess; wife of **Seth**; cared for and protected the dead; took sides with her husband's enemies and when he was vanquished, killed and torn to pieces, helped to find the fragments of his body and put them back together, bringing him to life; Nephthys and her sister were the guardians of the tomb.

Neptune ▸ **Poseidon**

Nereids Greek **Nymphs**; 50 or (in some accounts) 100 daughters of **Nereus**; lived with their father in the depths of the sea.

Nereus Greek god of the sea; the wise old man of the sea who always told the truth; Heracles had to wrestle with him to find the location of the Golden Apples.

Nergal Babylonian god of death; son of the god of heaven, he loved catastrophes, epidemics and war, and made death his personal territory; later acquired the power of the ruler of the underworld; tricked **Marduk** into rising up from his seat, resulting in chaos throughout the world, until Marduk regained his position.

Nessus Greek **Centaur**; attacked **Heracles's** wife, Deinira; Heracles shot him, and the dying Centaur told Deinira that his blood would be a cure for infidelity; later, through jealousy, she put the blood on a shirt, or made Heracles wear Nessus' shirt; this coated him with poison, so that he died.

Nestor A Greek leader in the Trojan War; in the *Iliad*, Homer portrays him as a long-winded sage, whose advice is often not taken; in the *Odyssey*, he is still living at Pylos, where a Mycenaean palace was discovered in the 1930s.

Nibelungen Medieval German race of dwarfs; lived in Norway and possessed a famous treasure; the *Nibelungenlied* recounts how Siegfried obtained the treasure and his later misfortunes; Wagner conflated this with other legends for his opera cycle.

Nike (Victoria) Greek goddess of victory, either in war or in an athletic contest; the frequent subject of sculpture, often shown as a winged figure; identified by the Romans as Victoria.

Ninurta Sumerian god of war; chosen by the gods to fight against Anzu, who had stolen the tablets of destiny; on victory, he became champion of the gods.

Niobe Greek heroine; proud of having seven sons and seven daughters, she insulted mothers who had few children; her insults to **Leto** earned the revenge of Leto's son and daughter, **Apollo** and **Artemis**, and their father, **Zeus**, who murdered Niobe's children, left them without burial for nine days and turned her to stone on Mt Sipylus.

Nix (Nixie) European water-sprite; occasionally entrapped people in her pool; not to be confused with the deity **Nyx** in Greek mythology.

Njord Norse god; father of **Freyr** and **Freyja**; succeeded **Odin** as sovereign and maintained peace and prosperity.

Norns Three Norse goddesses; Urdr represented the past, Verdandi, the present, and Skuld, the future; decided the fates of men and gods without reason or interest, dealing out as much good as evil.

Nox, Nux ▸ **Nyx**

Nymphs Greek goddesses; symbolized the beauty and charm of nature; for the most part, Nymphs were daughters of **Zeus** with lives lasting several centuries; dark formidable powers, whose beauty could lead to madness, and provoked sudden terror at midday; grouped into **Melias**, **Naiads**, **Nereids**, **Oreads**, **Dryads** and **Oceanids**.

Nyx (Nox, Nux) Greek goddess; a very ancient deity ('Night'), born of Chaos, and mother of Aither and Day, the **Hesperides**, and the **Moerae**; in the Orphic religion, Night was the original first principle; she laid an egg from which sprang other gods.

Oberon European king of the fairies; appears in European literature such as Shakespeare's *A Midsummer Night's Dream* and Wieland's *Oberon*.

Oceanids Greek **Nymphs**; inhabited the ocean and other watery places; daughters of **Oceanus** and Tethys.

Oceanus Greek **Titan**; son of **Uranus** and **Gaia**; a benign god who personified the stream of Ocean which was assumed to surround the world, as known to the Greeks.

Odin (Woden, Wotan) Norse god; keeper of all knowledge, represented as an old one-eyed bearded man wearing a multicoloured robe and a wide-brimmed hat; his horse had eight legs and galloped through the air, on the ocean as well as on ground; a cruel sovereign, he inspired deceit and was fond of human sacrifices; preserved the head of the decapitated giant Mimir, who was famous for his knowledge, and consulted it whenever he had some mystery to unravel.

Odysseus (Ulysses) Greek hero; a leader of the Achaeans in the Trojan War; returning to Greece, he became separated by a windstorm from his companions and overcame **Cyclopes**, **Sirens**, gods and magicians to return; his adventures are described in Homer's *Odyssey*.

Oedipus Greek hero; afflicted from birth by the curse that he would kill his father, marry his mother and be at the root of an endless series of misfortunes which would lead to the ruin of his family; because of this, his father abandoned him, and he was adopted by King Polybus; when the child was older and learned of the curse, he became frightened for the king, whom he believed to be his father and went into voluntary exile; he later killed his father in a fight when they met coincidentally; after being crowned king, he unknowingly married his mother, widowed by the death of his father.

Ogmios Celtic god; an old wrinkled man who wore a lion's skin and carried a club, a bow and a quiver; could draw or tow men attached by their ears to a gold chain, the end of which passed through the god's pierced tongue; attracted his followers by magic.

Olympians Greek gods and goddesses; collectively,

the major gods and goddesses who were thought to live on Mt Olympus, the highest mountain in Ancient Greece, situated in a range between Macedonia and Thessaly.

Ops Roman goddess of plenty, the consort of **Saturn**, identified with **Rhea**.

Oreads ▸ Nymphs

Orestes In Greek legend, the son of **Agamemnon** and **Clytemnestra**; after his father's murder he went into exile, but returned to kill **Aegisthus** and his mother, for which he was pursued by the **Erinyes**.

Orion Greek gigantic hunter; beloved by **Eos** and killed by **Artemis**; changed into a constellation, and this generated further astronomical stories, for example, that he pursues the **Pleiades**.

Orpheus Greek hero; a musician and poet, he had the power to enchant gods, men, animals and inanimate objects who followed him under his spell; married the **Nymph Eurydice** who was taken to hell after dying from the bite of a serpent; Orpheus charmed the rulers of hell who agreed to release Eurydice on the condition that Orpheus did not turn round to look at her as she followed him out of hell; his doubts that she was following made him eventually turn round, to see Eurydice disappear into the underworld forever.

Osiris Egyptian god of vegetation; provided laws and customs and gave the fruits of the earth; his jealous brother **Seth** conspired to kill him by trapping him in a wooden chest and sinking it in a river; his wife **Isis** recovered the body and managed to make Osiris father a son, to take vengeance on her enemies.

Ouranus ▸ Uranus

Pan Greek god of animal instinct; half man, half goat with a long wrinkled face and two horns on his head; son of **Hermes**, he lived in fields and woods; constantly pursued by **Nymphs** and those who became possessed by him took on his characteristics.

Pandarus Trojan prince; in Homer's *Iliad*, was killed by **Diomedes**; in later developments of the story of **Troilus** and **Cressida**, he became her uncle and their 'go-between' (hence 'pander').

Pandora Greek heroine; the first woman on earth, who led men to their downfall by seduction and entrapment; a gift from **Zeus** to man, made in the form of the immortal goddesses, Pandora was divine in appearance but human in reality; with her she brought a box which she had been forbidden to open; overcome with curiosity, she opened the box and let out all the evils of the world, such as disease, death, lies and theft, which spread throughout nature.

Pan Gu Chinese first being of creation; broke open the primal egg from within, held up the sky, and prevented it from bearing down upon the earth; the world was then made from parts of him, so that his body became the mountains, his hair the stars, and his eyes the sun and moon.

Parasurama Indian hero; united the religious purity of a Brahman with the impurity of a warrior; cut off his mother's head as requested by his father, who believed her to have produced the racial impurity; in 21 battles, freed the world of the kshatriya warriors.

Parcae ▸ Moerae

Paris (Alexander) Greek hero; a prince of Troy, the son of **Priam**; because of a prophecy, he was exposed at birth on Mt Ida, where he was loved by Oenone, a Nymph; there he also chose **Aphrodite** as the fairest of three goddesses; she offered him the most beautiful woman in the world; he abducted **Helen**, causing the Trojan war; wounded by **Philoctetes**, and in his death-agony asked Oenone for help, which she refused.

Parsifal ▸ Perceval, Sir

Pasiphae In Greek mythology, the daughter of **Helios**;

wife of **Minos**, king of Crete; loved a bull sent by **Poseidon**, and became the mother of the **Minotaur**.

Patroclus Greek warrior; faithful follower of **Achilles** at Troy; went into battle wearing Achilles's armour, but was cut down by **Hector**; his death made Achilles return to the battle.

Pegasus Greek winged horse; sprang from the body of the **Medusa** after her death; **Bellerophon** caught it with **Athene's** assistance; various fountains sprang from the touch of its foot, such as Hippocrene on Mt Helicon; finally it was placed in the sky as a constellation.

Peleus Greek king of Phythia in Thessaly; had to capture Thetis, a **Nereid**, before he could marry her; the gods attended the wedding feast; the father of **Achilles**.

Pelops Greek hero; protégé of **Poseidon**; eaten unknowingly by **Demeter** at birth as a result of his father's attempt to test the keenness of the gods; the other gods resurrected him to restore their reputation; protected by Poseidon on Olympus until his father led him to steal the nectar and ambrosia of the gods to give to mortals, for which he was forced to return to earth; drove his chariot drawn by winged horses to win the chance to marry Hippodameia; one of the mythological figures said to have founded the Olympic Games, in memory of his victory.

Penates Roman guardians of the storeroom; '**Lares** and Penates' were the household gods; the *penates publici* were the 'luck' of the Roman state, originally brought by **Aeneas** from Troy and kept at Lavinium.

Penelope In Greek legend, the wife of **Odysseus**; faithfully waited 20 years for his return from Troy; tricked her insistent suitors by weaving her web (a shroud for Odysseus' father, Laertes, which had to be finished before she could marry), and undoing her work every night.

Pentheus In Greek mythology, the king of Thebes; did not welcome **Dionysus**; disguising himself as a woman, he tried to spy on the orgiastic rites of the **Maenads**, who tore him to pieces, his mother leading them on.

Perceval, Sir (Parsifal) One of King **Arthur's** knights; went in quest of the Holy Grail; in the German version (Parzival) his bashfulness prevented him from asking the right questions of the warden of the Grail castle, so that the Fisher King was not healed.

Peri Persian good fairy or genie; Peri-Banou, for example, was the name of a beautiful fairy in the *Arabian Nights*.

Persephone (Proserpina) Greek goddess of the underworld; daughter of **Demeter** and **Zeus**, originally called Kore ('maiden'); while gathering flowers at Enna in Sicily was abducted by **Hades** and made queen of the underworld; there she ate the seeds of the pomegranate, which meant (in fairy lore) that she was bound to stay; however, a compromise was arranged so that she could return for half of every year (an allegory of the return of spring).

Perseus Greek hero; shut in a chest and thrown into the sea by his grandfather; washed up on the island of Seriphos; after he grew up, the island's tyrant demanded that he bring him the gift of the head of a **Gorgon**; with the help of **Hermes** and the **Nymphs**, he slew Medusa and returned with her head; married **Andromeda** after freeing her from the sea-monster to whom she was promised; unknowingly killed his grandfather, fulfilling an oracle which predicted this.

Perun Slavic god of rain and fertility; represented as a human being with a silver head and golden moustache; controlled the seasons and destroyed the countries of wicked men with hail.

Phaedra Greek heroine; daughter of **Minos** and the second wife of **Theseus**; while he was away she fell in

Thought and Belief

Thought and Belief

love with her step-son **Hippolytus**; he rejected her, so she killed herself, but left a note accusing him of trying to rape her; Theseus called on **Poseidon** to grant a promised favour, and punish Hippolytus with death.

Phaethon Greek hero; challenged to prove his ancestry by his friends, he asked to drive his father's chariot for a day; as he was inexperienced in this, the horses bolted, the chariot veered off its route and everything in their path was set on fire; the earth complained to the king of Olympus, and **Zeus** struck down the charioteer.

Phenix ▶ Phoenix

Philemon and **Baucis** Greek old man and wife; the only ones to entertain the Greek gods **Zeus** and **Hermes** when they visited the earth to test people's hospitality; in return they were saved from a flood, made priest and priestess, and allowed to die at the same time, when they were changed into trees.

Philoctetes Greek hero; son of Poeas, who inherited the bow of **Heracles** and its poisoned arrows; on the way to Troy was bitten by a snake, and the wound stank, so that he was left behind on the island of Lemnos; it was prophesied that only with the arrows of Heracles could Troy be taken, so **Diomedes** and **Odysseus** came to find Philoctetes; his wound was healed and he entered the battle, killing **Paris**.

Philomela (Philomel) and **Procne (Progne)** In Greek mythology, daughters of Pandion, king of Athens; Procne married Tereus, king of Thrace, who raped Philomela and removed her tongue; but she was able to tell Procne by a message in her embroidery; Procne served up her son Itys, or Itylos, in a meal to his father; while pursuing the sisters, the gods changed Tereus into the hoopoe, Philomela into the swallow, and Procne into the nightingale; in Latin legend, the birds of the sisters are reversed.

Phoebe Greek **Titan**, identified with the moon; later she was confused with **Artemis**.

Phoenix (Phenix) Legendary bird; lived for a long time; killed itself on a funeral pyre, but was then reborn from the ashes.

Pleiades In Greek mythology, the seven daughters of **Atlas** and **Pleione**; Maia, Taygete, Elektra, Alkyone, Asterope, Kelaino and Merope; after their deaths they were transformed into the star-cluster of the same name.

Pluto ▶ Hades

Pollux ▶ Castor and **Pollux**

Polyhymnia Greek **Muse** of dance, mime and acting.

Polynices (Polyneices) Greek hero; second son of **Oedipus**, who led the **Seven against Thebes**; **Creon's** refusal to bury him led eventually to the death of **Antigone**.

Polyphemus Greek **Cyclops**; imprisoned **Odysseus** and some of his companions in his cave; Odysseus blinded Polyphemus's one eye, and told him that 'No one' had hurt him; as a result, when he called on the other Cyclopes for help, and they asked who had attacked him, they did not understand his answer; Odysseus's band escaped by hiding under the sheep when they were let out of the cave to graze.

Pomona Roman goddess of fruit-trees and their fruit, especially apples and pears.

Poseidon (Neptune) Greek god of the sea; represented wielding a trident and being pulled by monsters in a chariot; could evoke storms and set fire to rocks; took part in the construction of the walls of Troy, then called up a monster to devastate the area when he did not receive payment; Neptune was a Roman water god who was later associated with Poseidon.

Prajapati Indian god; master of creatures and posterity; he was born aged a thousand years from a primordial egg; created the gods, the evil spirits, man,

melodies and the sun, then wasted away, exhausted by his tasks.

Priam In Greek legend, the king of Troy; son of Laomedon, and husband of **Hecuba**; presented in the *Iliad* as an old man; when **Hector** was killed, went secretly to **Achilles** to beg his son's body for burial; at the sack of Troy, he was killed by **Neoptolemus**.

Priapus Greek god; represented as a small bearded man with an oversized penis; in some traditions, the son of **Zeus** and **Aphrodite**; Zeus's jealous wife **Hera** made sure that the child was born with the extraordinary deformity to which he owes his name; Aphrodite abandoned him in the mountains; the guard of the orchard, he scared off thieves and threatened females with sexual violence.

Procrustes Thief of Attica; in the legend of **Theseus**, made travellers lie on his bed, and either cut or lengthened them to fit it; his name means 'the stretcher'; Theseus gave him the same treatment, and killed him.

Prometheus Greek hero; symbolized the revolt of man against the gods and brought to humanity all the good things refused it by the gods; punished for this when **Zeus** sent mankind the gift of **Pandora**, who spread evils throughout the world; became immortal after exchanging death for immortality with **Cheiron** the **Centaur**.

Proserpina ▶ Persephone

Proteus Greek god of the sea; associated with seals, and a shape-changer; he gave answers to questions after a wrestling match; was sometimes to be found on the island of Pharos, in Egypt, where **Menelaus** wrestled with him.

Psyche Greek personification of 'the soul'; usually represented by a butterfly; in the story told by Apuleius, was beloved by Cupid (▶ **Eros**), who hid her in an enchanted palace, and visited her at night, forbidding her to look at him; she saw Cupid, but was separated from him, and given impossible tasks by Venus (▶ **Aphrodite**), who impeded her search for him.

Ptah Egyptian god; principal god of the city of Memphis, known as the creator and master of craftsmen; subsequently regarded as a healing god in the form of a flat-headed dwarf and as a protective spirit.

Ptah

Purusha Primordial being of India; thought to be a gigantic man who covered the earth and went beyond it; heaven made up three-quarters of his being, and the fourth quarter consisted of all mortal creatures.

Pwyll Celtic hero; wise prince of Dyfed who as a service to the king of Annwn killed the king's permanent enemy; courteous and powerful, he emerged victorious from a thousand trials.

Pygmalion In Greek mythology, a king of Cyprus; made a statue of a beautiful woman; he prayed to **Aphrodite**, and the sculptured figure came to life.

Pyramus and **Thisbe** Two lovers; kept apart by their parents, they conversed through a crack in the wall between their houses, and agreed to meet at Ninus's tomb outside the city of Babylon; finding Thisbe's blood-stained cloak, Pyramus thought she had been killed by a lion, and committed suicide; when she found him, Thisbe killed herself on his sword; incorporated into Shakespeare's *A Midsummer Night's Dream*.

Python Greek monster; lived at Delphi and was killed by **Apollo** when he took over the shrine; the name Pythia continued in use, and the Pythian games were celebrated there.

Qat Hero of Oceania; born from a rock which had been hollowed out in the centre to allow his birth; organizer of life, he created man and then death to allow renewal; initiated day and night; canoed away to a far country, taking with him the hopes of mankind.

Querinus Roman god; initially a god of the city who watched over the material well being of the community; also likened to **Ares** by the Greeks, and to **Romulus**, founder of Rome.

Quetzalcoatl Aztec god of vegetation and wind; depicted as a bearded man wearing a mask, earrings and a conical hat; son of the sun-god and one of the five goddesses of the moon; created mankind from the bones of the ancient dead; taught measurement of time and how to discover the movement of the stars.

Quetzalcoatl

Ra ▸ Re

Rainbow Snake (Julunggul) Australian Aboriginal fertility spirit; both male and female, creator and destroyer, known as Julunggul; associated with streams and waterholes, from which it emerges in the creation story and leaves special markings on the ground.

Rama Indian hero; incarnation of the god **Vishnu** on earth; was taught magic spells to allow him to conquer the rakasa, the **demons**; saved his wife from abduction and was made king; after his wife had been swallowed up by the earth, gave up his royal status, and went to the river Sarayu to be carried off to heaven.

Re (Ra) Egyptian god; the ancient sun-god of Heliopolis; as the creator, he emerged from the primeval waters at the beginning of time; depicted as a falcon with the sun's disc on his head; at night he appears as a ram-headed god who sails through the underworld.

Rhadamanthus (Rhadamanthys) In Greek mythology, a Cretan, son of **Zeus** and **Europa**; did not die but was taken to Elisium, where he became the just judge of the dead.

Rhea (Rheia) Greek Titan; sister and wife of **Cronus**, and mother of **Zeus** and other Olympian gods; when Cronus consumed his children, Rhea gave him a stone instead of Zeus, who was saved and later rebelled against his father.

Rhiannon Celtic heroine; mistress of horses and horsemen; refused all her suitors out of love for **Pwyll**, who prepared to marry her; Pwyll, however, agreed to grant a supplicant, Gnawl, any wish, and he claimed Rhiannon; Pwyll later set her free from Gnawl through trickery and became her husband; accused of infanticide after her son mysteriously disappeared, but the child later reappeared.

Roc Arabian mythical creature; an enormous bird encountered by travellers in the Indian Ocean, capable of carrying off an elephant.

Rod Slavic god; initially the god of husbandmen but also a universal god, the god of heaven, the thunderbolt and rain; responsible for the nation's increase and closely linked with the worship of ancestors; later dethroned by **Perun**.

Romulus and **Remus** In Roman legend, the twin sons of Mars (▸ **Ares**) and the Vestal Virgin Rhea Silvia; an example of an invented myth, to explain the name of the city; thrown into the Tiber, which carried them to the Palatine, where they were suckled by a she-wolf; in building the wall of Rome, Remus made fun of the work and was killed by Romulus or one of his followers; having founded Rome, Romulus was later carried off in a thunderstorm.

Rosmerta Gallo-Roman goddess; represented as a woman standing draped in a long robe, holding a cornucopia and a patera; invoked to obtain fertility, fruitfulness and everything essential for a better life.

Rudra Indian god; a being with a thousand eyes and a thousand feet, with plaited hair, a black belly, a red back and armed with a bow and arrows; the great destroyer, he cast evil spells over men and beasts, and spread terror and illness.

Sakhmet ▸ Sekhmet

Sarapis ▸ Serapis

Sarasvati Indian goddess; wife of **Brahma**; personification of the word of the god Veda; carried the book of Veda, a musical instrument and a rosary composed of the letters of the alphabet; mother of the scriptures, the sciences and the arts; also associated with water.

Sarpedon Warrior of Greek mythology; in the *Iliad*, a son of **Zeus**, who led the Lycian troops on the Trojan side, and made an important speech on the duties of a warrior; killed by **Patroclus**, and carried off by Sleep and Death to Lycia.

Saturn Roman god; master of agriculture who invented the dressing of the vine, taught man agricultural methods and provided the first laws; depicted as being armed with a scythe; associated with the Golden Age, synonymous with religious festivals and feasts.

Satyr Greek god; a minor deity associated with **Dionysus**; usually depicted with goat-like ears, tail, and legs; rural, wild and lustful, the satyrs were said to be the brothers of the **Nymphs**.

Scylla Greek sea-monster; usually located in the Straits of Messina opposite to Charybdis; originally a woman, she was changed by **Circe** or **Amphitrite** into a snake with six heads; in the *Odyssey* she snatched six men from **Odysseus's** ships.

Sekhmet (Sakmet, Sakhmet, Sekmet) Egyptian goddess; wife of the god **Ptah**; depicted with the head of a lioness and the body of a woman; a terrible bloodthirsty goddess, responsible for epidemics, death, carnage and war; also had the power of healing.

Selene Greek goddess of the moon; depicted as a charioteer (the head of one of her horses may be seen among the Elgin Marbles).

Semele In Greek mythology, the daughter of Cadmus, and mother by **Zeus** of **Dionysus**; asked Zeus to appear in his glory before her, and was consumed in fire, but it made her son immortal.

Semiramis In Greek mythology, a queen of Assyria; founded many cities, including Nineveh and Babylon.

Serapis (Sarapis) Egyptian god; a compound deity, combining the names and aspects of two Egyptian gods, **Osiris** and **Apis**, to which were further added features of major Greek gods, such as **Zeus** and **Dionysus**; introduced to Alexandria by Ptolemy I in an attempt to unite Greeks and Egyptians in common worship.

Sesostris Egyptian king; alleged to have conquered vast areas of Europe, Asia and N Africa; probably a compound of the three Egyptian pharaohs (20c–19c BC) and Rameses II (13c BC).

Seth Egyptian god; depicted as a strange being with a forked tail, a long gaunt body, huge ears and protruding eyes; represented all evils and caused all disasters; fought the **demon** Apopis every morning and every evening and as a result of this permanent conflict, the equilibrium of forces and universal harmony were born.

Seven against Thebes Seven Greek Champions; attacked Thebes to deprive **Eteocles** of his kingship; led by his brother **Polynices**; the names of the other six were Tydeus, Adrastus (or Eteoklos), Capaneus, Hippomedon, Parthenopaeus and Amphiarus; de-

Thought and Belief

Thought and Belief

feated by another seven champions at the seven gates of Thebes; all were killed in battle, except for Amphiarus, whom the earth swallowed alive, and Adrastus, who escaped; later the sons of the Seven, the **Epigoni**, led by Adrastus, succeeded in destroying the city.

Seven Sleepers of Ephesus In medieval legend, seven persecuted Christians who fled into a cave at the time of the Emperor Decius (AD250); slept for 200 years, emerging in 447 at the time of Theodosius II; the story was thought to confirm the resurrection of Christ.

Shamash Babylonian god; depicted bearing a headdress with four rows of horns and a large beard, wearing a long robe and holding a staff and a hoop; symbolized by a solar disc rising between two mountains or by a spoked wheel; god of light and justice, he gave light to the world and distributed punishment and reward.

Shango African god of thunder; dispensed justice using the thunderbolt which was regarded as the god's punishment; the victim of his punishment was compelled to pay heavy fines and to appease him by means of sacrifices; originally a cruel king whose subjects drove him away; he hanged himself from a tree leaving a hole from which emerged an iron chain; finding the tree without the body, his supporters concluded that he had become a god.

Shiva Indian god; representing darkness, his three eyes are filled with snakes; had four arms and a girdle made of skulls; danced amid devils on cremation sites, representing the world's constructive and destructive periods; withdrew to the mountains after the suicide of his wife but later came back to produce a son to kill a **demon** which threatened the world; carried out many heroic deeds and was regarded as a beneficent force.

Sibyl (Sibylla) Roman prophetess; uttered mysterious wisdom; **Aeneas** met the Cumaean Sibyl, who was inspired by **Apollo** and whose prophecies were written on leaves; she had been given 1 000 years of life, and eventually shrank to a tiny creature hung up in a bottle; later there were said to be 10 Sibyls; the Sibylline Books were nine books of prophecy offered by the Sibyl to Tarquinius Priscus, who refused to pay her price; she destroyed three, and came again, with the same result; she destroyed three more, and then Tarquin bought the remainder for the price originally asked.

Sigurd In Norse mythology, the son of Sigmund the Volsung; killed Fafnir the dragon and won **Brunhild**; married **Gudrun**, having forgotten Brunhild, and was killed by Gudrun's brother Gutthorn; virtually the same story is told of Siegfried in German legends.

Sileni Greek followers of **Dionysus**; depicted with horse ears, tail and legs, or as old men in need of support (Papposileni); could give good advice to humans if captured; plural form of **Silenus**.

Silenus Greek demi-god; fostered and educated **Dionysus**; represented as a festive old man, usually quite drunk.

Silvanus (Sylvanus) Roman god of uncultivated land, especially woodland; he was therefore strange, and dangerous, like **Pan**.

Sin Sumerian god; represented the moon; depicted seated on a throne, with a long beard, holding an axe, a sceptre and a staff; his predictions were binding on the gods and man, and an eclipse was his most formidable sign, announcing catastrophe.

Sirens Three Greek demonesses; became half woman, half bird when they asked the gods for wings, to look for **Persephone** who had been taken to the underworld by **Hades**; one held a lyre, the second sang and the third played the flute; devoured sailors lured to their island by their enchanting sounds.

Sisyphus In Greek mythology, a Corinthian king who was a famous trickster; in one story he caught and bound Thanatos (Death); in the underworld was condemned to roll a large stone up a hill from which it always rolled down again.

Sita Indian heroine; emerged from a furrow in a ploughed field; married **Rama** and was abducted by Ravana; on reunion with her husband, was tested by fire and exiled as he believed she had been unfaithful; requested the earth to open up and swallow her forever.

Skanda Indian hero; son of **Shiva** and chief of the divine armies; killed the **demon** Taraka who threatened the world.

Skyamsen ▸ Thunderbird

Soma Indian moon-god; marked the rhythm of the days and months and was the nectar of immortality, a divine drink essential to the gods.

Sucellus Gallic god; depicted with a tunic, cowl and boots, holding a club or sceptre and a vase, indicating that he was a sovereign and the dispenser of food; married to the river goddess.

Svarog Slavic god of fire; dispenser of all wealth, and judge and protector of monogamy; also a magician and soothsayer.

Sventovit Slavic god of war; depicted with a trumpet and a bow; also the god of fertility, fruitfulness and destiny; his horse had the gift of divination, and its movement could reveal the meaning of oracles it wished to communicate.

Sylvanus ▸ Silvanus

Syrinx Greek **Nymph**; pursued by **Pan**, she called on the earth to help, and so sank down into it and became a reed-bed; Pan cut some of the reeds, and made the panpipes.

Tammuz (Thammuz) Babylonian god of vegetation; beloved by **Ishtar** (in Assyria by Astarte); returned from the dead and died again each year.

Tane (Kane) Divinity from the Pacific Islands; kept heaven and earth apart, permitting the world to exist; misfortune and death were born from his destructive war with his enemy, the god Tangaroa.

Tantalus In Greek mythology, a king of Sisyphos in Lydia; committed terrible crimes; stole the food of the gods, so becoming immortal, and served them his son **Pelops** in a dish; for this he was punished in the underworld; he sits in a pool which recedes when he bends to drink, and the grapes over his head elude his grasp.

Taranis Gallic god; master of the universe, who inspired fear by sending thunder and lightning; at the same time, brought the gentle rain which fed the earth and made crops grow; demanded human sacrifices; his victims were shut in wooden cages which were set alight, and severed heads were offered to him.

Tarpeia Roman woman who betrayed the Capitol to the Sabines, in return for 'what they wore on their left arms' (meaning gold rings); in their disgust, they threw their shields on her and crushed her to death.

Telemachus Greek hero; in the *Odyssey*, the son of **Odysseus** and **Penelope**; set out to find his father, visiting **Nestor** and **Menelaus**; later helped Odysseus fight Penelope's suitors.

Tellus ▸ Gaea

Tengri Mongol god of heaven; imposed the order of the natural world, the organization and movements of the stars and the government of the Mongol empire; distributed good luck and wealth and showed his anger by sending thunderstorms.

Terminus Roman god of boundary marks; his statue or bust was sometimes placed there; his stone on the Capitol was within the temple of Jupiter Optimus

Maximus (▸ **Zeus**), but was not allowed to be covered in.

Terpsichore Greek **Muse** of dance and lyric poetry.

Teshub Hurrian god of the thunderstorm; depicted holding an axe and thunderclouds; dethroned the king of heaven to become the supreme god and battled victoriously against the deposed king who sought his revenge.

Teutates Gallic god; a warrior god, sometimes compared to Mars (**Ares**) and Mercury (**Hermes**); depicted beside a serpent with a ram's head; a cruel god who demanded human sacrifices; the victims were drowned in a vat of water.

Tezcatlipoca Aztec god; depicted in human form with a stripe of black paint across his face and a mirror replacing one of his feet; said to have been mutilated by the mythical crocodile on which the earth was supposed to rest; reigned over the four worlds destroyed prior to the creation of the present one; with his mirror could see everything and was aware of both human actions and thoughts; a malevolent wizard who brought the custom of human sacrifice to Mexico.

Thalia (Thaleia) Greek **Muse** of comedy and idyllic poetry.

Thammuz ▸ **Tammuz**

Themis Greek goddess of established law and justice; a consort of **Zeus**, she was the mother of the **Horae** and the **Moerae**.

Theseus Greek hero; set out for Athens to find his father, the king, and slew many monsters on the way; fought those who tried to depose his father and killed the **Minotaur**; assumed power and defended Attica against the **Amazons** who almost won but in the end were forced to sign a peace treaty (he married their leader, Hippolyta); later became powerless and was forced into exile before being killed when thrown into a ravine.

Thetis Greek goddess; mother of **Achilles**; saved **Zeus** from a conspiracy to remove his power; an oracle predicted that her son would be more powerful than his father, and fearing this, Zeus forced her to marry a mortal; an unhappy goddess, she failed in her determined attempts to make her children immortal.

Thor Nordic god; son of **Odin**; armed with a hammer which returned automatically to the hand of the one who hurled it, and doubled his strength by wearing a magic belt; fond of tricks and practical jokes; killed the serpent of Midgard, but was himself killed by its venom.

Thoth (Hermes) Egyptian god; skilled at calculation, secretary to the gods and master of effective speech; also a magician and capable of providing cures; identified by the Greeks as Hermes.

Thunderbird (Skyamsen) Totem figure of NW Native American religion; lightning flashed from its eye and it fed on killer whales; the chief of the Thunderbirds was Golden Eagle (Keneun).

Thyestes In Greek mythology, a son of **Pelops**; inherited the curse upon that house; his brother **Atreus** set before him a dish made of the flesh of Thyestes's children; later became the father of **Aegisthus**.

Thunderbird

Tiamat Akkadian goddess; a primordial divinity who represented salt water; became angry after an old god was murdered by a younger one; decided to create monsters as gods, and in the resulting confrontation was killed by **Marduk**; from one half of her corpse, heaven was created, and from the other half, Marduk formed dry land.

Tiresias In Greek mythology, a blind Theban prophet; takes a prominent part in Sophocles's plays about

Oedipus and **Antigone**; later legends account for his wisdom by saying that he had experienced the life of both sexes.

Titania Greek female **Titan**; identified with the moon; in Shakespeare's *A Midsummer Night's Dream* she is the queen of the fairies, who is tricked into falling in love with Bottom the Weaver.

Titans Greek gods; members of the older generation of gods, the children of **Uranus** and **Gaia**; after **Zeus** and the Olympians took power, the Titans made war on them; but they were defeated and imprisoned in Tartarus; one or two, notably **Prometheus**, helped Zeus; may represent memories of pre-Greek Mediterranean gods.

Tlaloc Aztec god of mountains, rain and springs; represented as a man painted black with huge round eyes with circles or serpents around them, and long fangs; ordered the distribution of rain and hurricanes; sometimes killed by means of a thunderbolt; his victims were buried with a piece of dry wood which would come back to life in Tlaloc's paradise.

Tlazolteotl Aztec goddess of lust; represented as a young girl wearing a rubber mask and a crescent-shaped ornament in her nose; responsible for conjugal infidelities and at the same time the granter of pardon; also the goddess of renewal.

Triglav Slavic god; had three heads and a golden veil which covered his eyes and mouth, signifying his desire to disregard human faults; a soothsayer, priest, warrior and nourisher.

Tristan and **Isolde** Celtic heroes; Tristan was a master harp-player and huntsman; Isolde was the daughter of the king of Ireland, who was to marry Mark the king of Cornwall, and become queen; through a misunderstanding, Tristan and Isolde drank from the same love potion and became bound by an indissoluble love; discovered to be meeting secretly, Tristan and the queen were condemned to be burned alive, and both fled; King Mark searched for them, and finding them asleep, became seized with pity, leaving his sword between them and replacing a ring on Isolde's finger; moved by his generosity, the lovers returned to the court, where Isolde was accepted, but Tristan was sent into exile.

Triton In Greek mythology, the son of **Poseidon** and **Amphitrite**; depicted in art as a fish from the waist down, and blowing a conch-shell; beings of similar form (mermen) who serve Poseidon are often referred to as Tritons.

Troilus In Greek legend, a prince of Troy; son of **Priam** and **Hecuba**, who was killed by **Achilles**; in medieval stories, the lover of **Cressida**.

Tuatha de Danann Irish race of wise beings; came to Ireland in c.1500BC, and became the ancient gods of the Irish; the name means 'the people of the goddess Danu'; conquered by the Milesians, and retreated into tumuli near the R Boyne.

Tyche Greek goddess of chance or luck; prominent in the Hellenistic period; depicted as blind, or, with a wall, as the luck of a city.

Typhoeus ▸ **Typhon**

Typhon (Typhoeus) Greek monster; had 100 heads and was brought forth by **Gaea**; a serious challenge to **Zeus**, who hurled his thunderbolts and thrust him down into Tartarus; in another story, said to be buried under Etna.

Tyr Nordic god; courageous and bold, he guaranteed right and justice; lost one arm in the courageous act of restraining the horrible wolf Fenrir.

Ulysses ▸ **Odysseus**

Unicorn Creature of medieval legend; a horse with a single horn on its forehead; probably based on stories of the rhinoceros; could be captured only by a virgin putting its head in her lap.

Thought and Belief

Urania Greek **Muse** of astronomy.

Uranus (Ouranus) Greek god of the sky; father of the Titans; a very abstract figure, not the subject of worship or of art, he was displaced by **Cronus**; equivalent to Roman Caelus, 'the heavens'.

Uther Pendragon Legendary king of Britain; father of King **Arthur** by Ygerna, the wife of Duke Gorlois of Cornwall.

Vahagn Armenian deity; born of water and fire, and married to the goddess of the stars; god of victory and destroyer of obstacles; created the Milky Way when he stole some straw one night and fled in haste across the sky, leaving wisps of straw across his path.

Vainamoinen Finnish sage, shaman and bard; dominates the epic *Kalevala*; sought the sampo, the magic cauldron of plenty, and invented the kantele or harp.

Valkyries Nordic goddesses; goddesses of fertility and the angels of battle; 40 are recorded as magicians and combat goddesses who selected those who were doomed to die, apportioning death not as a punishment, but as a reward.

Varuna Indian god and guardian of world order; ordered nature and supervised sacrificial rites; his domain consisted of darkness and the waters, and the stars were his thousand eyes; also producing evil, he caused earthquakes and sent disease, but possessed and provided the remedies.

Venus ▸ **Aphrodite**

Vesta ▸ **Hestia**

Vesta Roman goddess of the hearth; particularly known for the cult dedicated to her; her temple in the Roman Forum was served by virgins who were walled up alive at the Colline Gate if they failed to remain chaste; a fire was kept lit in her honour all year round.

Viracocha Incan god; the creator and civilizer, he created the first men, but disappointed by them, he changed some into stone statues and destroyed the others by fire; recreated humanity, accompanied by the sun and moon, then provided mountains, rivers and farmland to permit them to live in a civilized way; after this mission, disappeared over the horizon, and his return is still awaited; protector of the emperor of the Incas.

Vishnu Indian god; originally a dwarf who wanted to secure dominion over the world, he became the god of space, who gave the world its stability; the origin of the fertility of both nature and man; appeared in the form of heroes and animals each time the world needed him.

Visvamitra Indian hero; tried to equal the Brahman Vasistha by

Vishnu

leading a life of increasing rigid asceticism; finally achieved his aim by stopping eating and breathing for a number of years.

Volcanus ▸ **Hephaestus**

Vulcan ▸ **Hephaestus**

Wak Ethiopian god; kept heaven at a distance from the earth and covered it with stars; created man on the flat earth, then buried him for seven years while he made fire rain down to create the mountains; when after this, man sprang back to life, he said that he had slept only for a brief moment; this was said to be why man is awake for most of the day; later created woman.

Weyland Norse, German, and Old English legend-ary inventor; known as Weyland the Smith; lame, having been maimed by King Nidud; many heroes carry swords made by him; his 'Smithy', is a dolmen on the Berkshire Downs, UK.

Woden, Wotan ▸ **Odin**

Xipe Totec Aztec god of springtime, renewal and nocturnal rain; inspired Mexican ceremonies with human sacrifices and mock battles; during the ceremonies the priests flayed the sacrifices and wore their skins.

Xiuhtecuhtli Aztec god of the hearth, fire, the sun and volcanoes; also associated with peppers and the pine, the tree from which torches were made.

Yama The first Indian man; the first mortal who on death became king of the dead; came to look for those who had used up their lifetimes; produced excessive increases of the human population when one day he became distracted and did not make a single man die.

Yggdrasil In Norse mythology, a giant ash; the World-Tree, which supported the sky, held the different realms of gods and men in its branches, and had its roots in the underworld.

Yu the Great Chinese hero; a thin, ill man who hopped about on one foot; dug out the mountains and allowed waters to flow from a catastrophic flood, working for 13 years without returning home; became a god and travelled the world to plan it; first emperor of the Hsia Dynasty.

Zanhary Madagascan god; creator god and father of heaven; terrifying, and spoke in thunder and lightning; a double god, the Zanhary from below created man and Zanhary from above gave him life; the two gods disagreed over women and became enemies, separating the worlds above and below forever.

Zeus (Jupiter, Iuppiter) Greek god of all gods; god of light and weather, and arbiter among gods and among men; had many wives and affairs with mortal women to whom he appeared in various guises, eg as a shower of gold, a bull or a swan; hanged his jealous wife **Hera** from Olympus with anvils fastened to her ankles.

Patron saints of occupations

Accountants	Matthew	Messengers	Gabriel
Actors	Genesius, Vitus	Metalworkers	Eligius
Advertisers	Bernardino of Siena	Midwives	Raymond Nonnatus
Architects	Thomas (Apostle)	Miners	Anne, Barbara
Artists	Luke, Angelico	Motorists	Christopher
Astronauts	Joseph (Cupertino)	Musicians	Cecilia, Gregory the Great
Astronomers	Dominic	Nurses	Camillus de Lellis, John of God
Athletes	Sebastian	Philosophers	Thomas Aquinas, Catherine of
Authors	Francis de Sales		Alexandria
Aviators	Our Lady of Loreto	Poets	Cecilia, David
Bakers	Honoratus	Police	Michael
Bankers	Bernardino (Feltre)	Politicians	Thomas More
Barbers	Cosmas and Damian	Postal Workers	Gabriel
Blacksmiths	Eligius	Priests	Jean-Baptiste Vianney
Bookkeepers	Matthew	Printers	John of God
Book trade	John of God	Prisoners	Leonard
Brewers	Amand, Wenceslaus	Radio Workers	Gabriel
Builders	Barbara, Thomas (Apostle)	Sailors	Christopher, Erasmus, Francis
Butchers	Luke		of Paola
Carpenters	Joseph	Scholars	Thomas Aquinas
Chemists	Cosmas and Damian	Scientists	Albert the Great
Comedians	Vitus	Sculptors	Luke, Louis
Cooks	Lawrence, Martha	Secretaries	Genesius
Dancers	Vitus	Servants	Martha, Zita
Dentists	Apollonia	Shoemakers	Crispin, Crispinian
Doctors	Cosmas and Damian, Luke	Singers	Cecilia, Gregory
Editors	Francis de Sales	Soldiers	George, Joan of Arc, Martin of
Farmers	Isidore		Tours, Sebastian
Firemen	Florian	Students	Thomas Aquinas
Fishermen	Andrew, Peter	Surgeons	Luke, Cosmas and Damian
Florists	Dorothy, Thérèse of Lisieux	Tailors	Homobonus
Gardeners	Adam, Fiacre	Tax Collectors	Matthew
Glassworkers	Luke, Lucy	Taxi Drivers	Fiacre
Gravediggers	Joseph of Arimathea	Teachers	Gregory the Great, John
Grocers	Michael		Baptiste de la Salle
Hotelkeepers	Amand, Julian the Hospitaler	Theologians	Augustine, Alphonsus Liguori,
Housewives	Martha		Thomas Aquinas
Jewellers	Eligius	Television	
Journalists	Francis de Sales	Workers	Gabriel
Labourers	James, John Bosco	Undertakers	Dismas, Joseph of Arimathea
Lawyers	Ivo, Thomas More	Waiters	Martha
Librarians	Jerome, Catherine of Alexandria	Writers	Lucy
Merchants	Francis of Assisi		

Thought and Belief

Baha'i

Founded 1863 in Persia.
Founder Mirza Husayn Ali (1817–92), known as Baha'u'llah (Glory of God). He declared himself the prophet foretold by Mirza ali Mohammed (1819–50), a direct descendant of Muhammad, who proclaimed himself to be the Bab ('gate' or 'door').
Sacred texts Most Holy Book, The Seven Valleys, The Hidden Words and The Bayan.
Beliefs Baha'i teaches the oneness of God, the unity of all faiths, the inevitable unification of humankind,

the harmony of all people, universal education, and obedience to government. It does not predict an end to this world or any intervention by God but believes there will be a change within man and society.

Organization There is a network of elected local and national level bodies, and an elected international governing body. Although there is little formal ritual (most assemblies are simply gatherings of the faithful), there are ceremonies for marriages and funerals, and there are shrines and temples.

Buddhism

Founded c.500BC in India.
Founder Prince Siddhartha Gautama (c.560–c.480BC) who became Buddha ('the enlightened') through meditation.
Sacred texts The Pali Canon or Tripitaka made up of the Vinaya Pitaka (monastic discipline), Sutta Pitaka (discourses of the Buddha) and the Abhidhamma Pitaka (analysis of doctrines). Other texts: the Mahayana Sutras, the Milindapanha (Questions of Milinda) and the Bardo Thodol (Tibetan Book of the Dead).
Beliefs Buddha's teaching is summarized in the Four

Noble Truths; suffering is always present in life; desire is the cause of suffering; freedom from suffering can be achieved by Nirvana (perfect peace and bliss); the Eightfold Path leads to Nirvana. Karma, by which good and evil deeds result in appropriate reward or punishment, and the cycle of rebirth can be broken by taking the Eightfold Path. All Buddhas are revered but particularly Gautama.

Organization There is a monastic system which aims to create favourable conditions for spiritual development. This involves meditation, personal discipline and spiritual exercises in the hope of liberation from self. Buddhism has proved very flexible in adapting its organization, ceremony and pattern of belief to different cultural and social conditions. There are numerous festivals and ceremonies, and pilgrimage is of great spiritual value.

Divisions There are two main traditions in Buddhism. Theravada Buddhism adheres to the teachings of the earliest Buddhist writings; salvation can be attained only by the few who accept the severe discipline and

effort necessary to achieve it. Mahayana Buddhism developed later and is more flexible and creative, embracing popular piety. It teaches that salvation is possible for everyone and introduced the doctrine of the bodhisattva (one who attains enlightenment but out of compassion forestalls passing into Nirvana to help others achieve enlightenment). As Buddhism spread, other schools sprang up including Zen, Lamaism, Tendai, Nichiren and Soka Gakkai.

Major Buddhist festivals

Weekly Uposatha Days, Buddha's Birth, Enlightenment, First Sermon and Death are observed in the different countries where Buddhism is practised but often on different dates. In some of these countries there are additional festivals in honour of Buddha.

Christianity

Founded 1c AD.

Founder Jesus Christ 'the Son of God' (c.4BC–c.30AD).

Sacred texts The Bible consisting of the Old and New Testaments. The New Testament written between AD30 and AD150 consists of the Gospels, the Acts of the Apostles, the Epistles and the Apocalypse.

Beliefs A monotheistic world religion, centred on the life and works of Jesus of Nazareth in Judaea, who proclaimed the most important rules of life to be love of God, followed by love of one's neighbour. Christians believe that Jesus was the Son of God who was put to death by crucifixion as a sacrifice in order to save humanity from the consequences of sin and death, and was raised from the dead; he makes forgiveness and reconciliation with God possible, and ensures eternal life for the repentant believer. The earliest followers of Jesus were Jews who believed him to be the Messiah or 'Saviour' promised by the prophets in the Old Testament. Christians believe he will come again to inaugurate the 'Kingdom of God'.

Organization Jesus Christ appointed 12 men to be his disciples:

1 Peter (brother of Andrew)
2 Andrew (brother of Peter)
3 James, son of Zebedee (brother of John)
4 John (brother of James)
5 Philip
6 Bartholomew
7 Thomas

8 Matthew
9 James of Alphaeus
10 Simon the Canaanite (in Matthew and Mark) or Simon 'the Zealot' (in Luke and the Acts)
11 Judas Iscariot

(Thaddeus in the book of Matthew and Mark is the twelfth disciple, while in Luke and the Acts the twelfth is Judas or James. Matthias succeeded to Judas's place.) Soon after the resurrection the disciples gathered for the festival of Pentecost and received special signs of the power of God, the Holy Spirit. The disciples became a defined new body, the Church. Through the witness of the Apostles and their successors, the Christian faith quickly spread and in AD315 became the official religion of the Roman Empire. It survived the 'Dark Ages' to become the basis of civilization in the Middle Ages in Europe.

Divisions Major divisions — separated as a result of differences of doctrine and practice — are the Orthodox or Eastern Church, the Roman Catholic Church, acknowledging the Bishop of Rome as head, and the Protestant Churches stemming from the split with the Roman Church in the 16c. All Christians recognize the authority of the Bible, read at public worship, which takes place at least every Sunday, to celebrate the resurrection of Jesus Christ. Most Churches recognize at least two sacraments (Baptism and the Eucharist, Mass, or Lord's Supper) as essential.

Major Christian denominations

Denomination and origins

Baptists In radical Reformation objections to infant baptism, demands for Church–State separation; John Smyth, English Separatist in 1609; Roger Williams, 1638, Providence, Rhode Island.

Church of England Henry VIII separated the English Catholic Church from Rome, 1534, for political reasons.

Lutherans Martin Luther (1483–1546) in Wittenberg, Germany, 1517, objected to Catholic doctrine of salvation by merit and sale of indulgences; break complete by 1519.

Methodists John Wesley (1703–91) began movement, 1738, within Church of England.

Orthodox Original Christian proselytizing in 1c; broke with Rome, 1054, after centuries of doctrinal disputes and diverging traditions.

Denomination and origins

Pentecostal ► **Pentecostalism** on p865.

Presbyterians In Calvinist Reformation in 1500s; differed with Lutherans over sacraments, and church government. John Knox (c.1513–1572) founded Scottish Presbyterian Church about 1560.

Roman Catholic Traditionally in the naming of St Peter as the first vicar by Jesus; historically, in early Christian proselytizing and the conversion of imperial Rome in the 4c.

United Church of Christ Union of the Congregational and Christian Churches with the Evangelical and Reformed Church. An ecumenical Protestant Church, it allows for variation in organization and interpretation of doctrine but reflects its Reformed theological background.

The Ten Commandments

I	I am the Lord your God, who brought you out of the land of Egypt, out of the house of bondage. You shall have no other gods before me.	V	Honour your father and your mother.
		VI	You shall not kill.
II	You shall not make for yourself a graven image. You shall not bow down to them or serve them.	VII	You shall not commit adultery.
		VIII	You shall not steal.
III	You shall not take the name of the Lord your God in vain.	IX	You shall not bear false witness against your neighbour.
IV	Remember the sabbath day, to keep it holy.	X	You shall not covet.

The Ten Commandments appear in two different places in the Bible — Exodus 20:17 and Deuteronomy 5:6–21. Most Protestant, Anglican and Orthodox Christians enumerate the Commandments differently from Roman Catholics and Lutherans.

Major immovable Christian feasts

For Saints' days ▸ pp858–60

1 Jan	Solemnity of Mary, Mother of God	22 Aug	Queenship of Mary
6 Jan	Epiphany	8 Sep	Birthday of the Virgin Mary
7 Jan	Christmas Day (*Eastern Orthodox*)[1]	14 Sep	Exaltation of the Holy Cross
11 Jan	Baptism of Jesus	2 Oct	Guardian Angels
25 Jan	Conversion of Apostle Paul	1 Nov	All Saints
2 Feb	Presentation of Jesus (*Candlemas Day*)	2 Nov	All Souls
22 Feb	The Chair of Peter, Apostle	9 Nov	Dedication of the Lateran Basilica
25 Mar	Annunciation of the Virgin Mary	21 Nov	Presentation of the Virgin Mary
24 Jun	Birth of John the Baptist	8 Dec	Immaculate Conception
6 Aug	Transfiguration	25 Dec	Christmas Day
15 Aug	Assumption of the Virgin Mary	28 Dec	Holy Innocents

[1] Fixed feasts in the Julian Calendar fall 13 days later than the Gregorian Calendar date.

Movable Christian feasts 1995–2015

Year	Ash Wednesday	Easter	Ascension	Whit Sunday (Pentecost)	Trinity Sunday	Sundays after Trinity	Corpus Christi	First Sunday in Advent
1995	1 Mar	16 Apr	25 May	4 Jun	11 Jun	24	15 Jun	3 Dec
1996	21 Feb	7 Apr	16 May	26 May	2 Jun	25	6 Jun	1 Dec
1997	12 Feb	30 Mar	8 May	18 May	25 May	26	29 May	30 Nov
1998	25 Feb	12 Apr	21 May	31 May	7 Jun	24	11 Jun	29 Nov
1999	17 Feb	4 Apr	13 May	23 May	30 May	25	3 Jun	28 Nov
2000	8 Mar	23 Apr	1 Jun	11 Jun	18 Jun	23	22 Jun	3 Dec
2001	28 Feb	15 Apr	24 May	3 Jun	10 Jun	24	14 Jun	2 Dec
2002	13 Feb	31 Mar	9 May	19 May	26 May	26	30 May	1 Dec
2003	5 Mar	20 Apr	29 May	8 Jun	15 Jun	23	19 Jun	30 Nov
2004	25 Feb	11 Apr	20 May	30 May	6 Jun	24	10 Jun	28 Nov
2005	9 Feb	27 Mar	5 May	15 May	22 May	26	26 Jun	27 Nov
2006	1 Mar	16 Apr	25 May	4 Jun	11 Jun	24	15 Jun	3 Dec
2007	21 Feb	8 Apr	17 May	27 May	3 Jun	25	7 Jun	2 Dec
2008	6 Feb	23 Mar	1 May	11 May	18 May	27	22 May	30 Nov
2009	25 Feb	12 Apr	21 May	31 May	7 Jun	24	11 Jun	29 Nov
2010	17 Feb	4 Apr	13 May	23 May	30 May	25	3 Jun	28 Nov
2011	9 Mar	24 Apr	2 Jun	12 Jun	19 Jun	22	23 Jun	27 Nov
2012	22 Feb	8 Apr	17 May	27 May	3 Jun	25	7 Jun	2 Dec
2013	13 Feb	31 Mar	9 May	19 May	26 May	26	30 May	1 Dec
2014	5 Mar	20 Apr	29 May	8 Jun	15 Jun	23	19 Jun	30 Nov
2015	18 Feb	5 Apr	14 May	24 May	31 May	25	4 Jun	29 Nov

Ash Wednesday, the first day of Lent, can fall at the earliest on 4 February and at the latest on 10 March.

Palm (Passion) Sunday is the Sunday before Easter; Good Friday is the Friday before Easter; Holy Saturday (often referred to as Easter Saturday) is the Saturday before Easter; Easter Saturday, in traditional usage, is the Saturday following Easter.

Easter Day can fall at the earliest on 22 March and at the latest on 25 April. Ascension Day can fall at the earliest on 30 April and at the latest on 3 June. Whit Sunday can fall at the earliest on 10 May and at the latest on 13 June. There are not fewer than 22 and not more than 27 Sundays after Trinity. The first Sunday of Advent is the Sunday nearest to 30 November.

Thought and Belief

Thought and Belief

Saints' days

Selected Saints' days are given below. The official recognition of Saints, and the choice of a Saint's Day, varies greatly between different branches of Christianity, calendars and localities. Only major variations are included below, using the following abbreviations:

C Coptic   E Eastern   G Greek   W Western

■ **January**
1   Basil (E), Fulgentius, Telemachus
2   Basil and Gregory of Nazianzus (W), Macarius of Alexandria, Seraphim of Sarov
3   Geneviève
4   Angela of Foligno
5   Simeon Stylites (W)
7   Cedda, Lucian of Antioch (W), Raymond of Penyafort
8   Atticus (E), Gudule, Severinus
9   Hadrian the African
10 Agatho, Marcian
12 Ailred, Benedict Biscop
13 Hilary of Poitiers
14 Kentigern
15 Macarius of Egypt, Maurus, Paul of Thebes
16 Honoratus
17 Antony of Egypt
19 Wulfstan
20 Euthymius, Fabian, Sebastian
21 Agnes, Fructuosus, Maximus (E), Meinrad
22 Timothy (G), Vincent
23 Ildefonsus
24 Babylas (W), Francis de Sales
25 Gregory of Nazianzus (E)
26 Paula, Timothy and Titus, Xenophon (E)
27 Angela Merici
28 Ephraem Syrus (E), Paulinus of Nola, Thomas Aquinas
29 Gildas
31 John Bosco, Marcella

■ **February**
1   Brigid, Pionius
3   Anskar, Blaise (W), Werburga, Simeon (E)
4   Gilbert of Sempringham, Isidore of Pelusium, Phileas
5   Agatha, Avitus
6   Dorothy, Paul Miki and companions, Vedast
8   Theodore (G), Jerome Emiliani
9   Teilo
10 Scholastica
11 Benedict of Aniane, Blaise (E), Caedmon, Gregory II
12 Meletius
13 Agabus (W), Catherine dei Ricci, Priscilla (E)
14 Cyril and Methodius (W), Valentine (W)
16 Flavian (E), Pamphilus (E), Valentine (G)
18 Bernadette (France), Colman, Flavian (W), Leo I (E)
20 Wulfric
21 Peter Damian
23 Polycarp
25 Ethelbert, Tarasius, Walburga
26 Alexander (W), Porphyrius
27 Leander
28 Oswald of York

■ **March**
1   David
2   Chad, Simplicius
3   Ailred
4   Casimir
6   Chrodegang
7   Perpetua and Felicity
8   Felix, John of God, Pontius
9   Frances of Rome, Gregory of Nyssa, Pacian

10 John Ogilvie, Macarius of Jerusalem, Simplicius
11 Constantine, Oengus, Sophronius
12 Gregory (the Great)
13 Nicephorus
14 Benedict (E)
15 Clement Hofbauer
17 Gertrude, Joseph of Arimathea (W), Patrick
18 Anselm of Lucca, Cyril of Jerusalem, Edward
19 Joseph
20 Cuthbert, John of Parma, Martin of Braga
21 Serapion of Thmuis
22 Catherine of Sweden, Nicholas of Flüe
23 Turibius de Mongrovejo
30 John Climacus

■ **April**
1   Hugh of Grenoble, Mary of Egypt (E), Melito
2   Francis of Paola, Mary of Egypt (W)
3   Richard of Chichester
4   Isidore of Seville
5   Juliana of Liège, Vincent Ferrer
7   Hegesippus, John Baptist de la Salle
8   Agabus (E)
10 Fulbert
11 Gemma Galgani, Guthlac, Stanislaus
12 Julius I, Zeno
13 Martin I
15 Aristarchus, Pudus (E), Trophimus of Ephesus
17 Agapetus (E), Stephen Harding
18 Mme Acarie
19 Alphege, Leo IX
21 Anastasius (E), Anselm, Beuno, Januarius (E)
22 Alexander (C)
23 George
24 Egbert, Fidelis of Sigmaringen, Mellitus
25 Mark, Phaebadius
27 Zita
28 Peter Chanel, Vitalis and Valeria
29 Catherine of Siena, Hugh of Cluny, Peter Martyr, Robert
30 James (the Great) (E), Pius V

■ **May**
1   Asaph, Joseph the Worker, Walburga
2   Athanasius
3   Philip and James (the Less) (W)
4   Gotthard
5   Hilary of Arles
7   John of Beverley
8   John (E), Peter of Tarantaise
10 Antoninus, Comgall, John of Avila, Simon (E)
11 Cyril and Methodius (E), Mamertus
12 Epiphanius, Nereus and Achilleus, Pancras
14 Matthias (W)
16 Brendan, John of Nepomuk, Simon Stock
17 Robert Bellarmine, Paschal Baylon
18 John I
19 Dunstan, Ivo, Pudens (W), Pudentiana (W)
20 Bernardino of Siena
21 Helena (E)
22 Rita of Cascia
23 Ivo of Chartres
24 Vincent of Lérins
25 Aldhelm, Bede, Gregory VII, Mary Magdalene de Pazzi

26	Philip Neri, Quadratus
27	Augustine of Canterbury
30	Joan of Arc

■ June

1	Justin Martyr, Pamphilus
2	Erasmus, Marcellinus and Peter, Nicephorus (G), Pothinus
3	Charles Lwanga and companions, Clotilde, Kevin
4	Optatus, Petrock
5	Boniface
6	Martha (E), Norbert
7	Paul of Constantinople (W), Willibald
8	William of York
9	Columba, Cyril of Alexandria (E), Ephraem (W)
11	Barnabas, Bartholomew (E)
12	Leo III
13	Anthony of Padua
15	Orsisius, Vitus
17	Alban, Botulph
19	Gervasius and Protasius, Jude (E), Romuald
20	Alban
21	Alban of Mainz, Aloysius Gonzaga
22	John Fisher and Thomas More, Niceta, Pantaenus (C), Paulinus of Nola
23	Etheldreda
24	Birth of John the Baptist
25	Prosper of Aquitaine
27	Cyril of Alexandria (W), Ladislaus
28	Irenaeus
29	Peter and Paul
30	First Martyrs of the Church of Rome

■ July

1	Cosmas and Damian (E), Oliver Plunkett
3	Anatolius, Thomas
4	Andrew of Crete (E), Elizabeth of Portugal, Ulrich
5	Anthony Zaccaria
6	Maria Goretti
7	Palladius, Pantaenus
8	Kilian, Aquila and Prisca (W)
11	Benedict (W), Pius I
12	John Gualbert, Veronica
13	Henry II, Mildred, Silas
14	Camillus of Lellis, Deusdedit, Nicholas of the Holy Mountain (E)
15	Bonaventure, Jacob of Nisibis, Swithin, Vladimir
16	Eustathius, Our Lady of Mt Carmel
17	Ennodius, Leo IV, Marcellina, Margaret (E), Scillitan Martyrs
18	Arnulf, Philastrius
19	Macrina, Symmachus
20	Aurelius, Margaret (W)
21	Lawrence of Brindisi, Praxedes
22	Mary Magdalene
23	Apollinaris, Bridget of Sweden
25	Anne and Joachim (E), Christopher, James (the Great) (W)
26	Anne and Joachim (W)
27	Pantaleon
28	Innocent I, Samson, Victor I
29	Lupus, Martha (W), Olave
30	Peter Chrysologus, Silas (G)
31	Giovanni Colombini, Germanus, Joseph of Arimathea (E), Ignatius of Loyola

■ August

1	Alphonsus Liguori, Ethelwold
2	Eusebius of Vercelli, Stephen I
4	Jean-Baptiste Vianney

6	Hormisdas
7	Cajetan, Sixtus II and companions
8	Dominic
9	Matthias (G)
10	Laurence, Oswald of Northumbria
11	Clare, Susanna
13	Maximus (W), Pontian and Hippolytus, Radegunde
14	Maximilian Kolbe
15	Arnulf, Tarsicius
16	Roch, Simplicianus, Stephen of Hungary
17	Hyacinth
19	John Eudes, Sebaldus
20	Bernard, Oswin, Philibert
21	Jane Frances de Chantal, Pius X
23	Rose of Lima, Sidonius Apollinaris
24	Bartholomew (W), Ouen
25	Joseph Calasanctius, Louis IX, Menas of Constantinople
26	Blessed Dominic of the Mother of God, Zephyrinus
27	Caesarius, Monica
28	Augustine of Hippo
29	Beheading of John the Baptist, Sabina
30	Pammachius
31	Aidan, Paulinus of Trier

■ September

1	Giles, Simeon Stylites (E)
2	John the Faster (E)
3	Gregory (the Great)
4	Babylas (E), Boniface I
5	Zacharias (E)
9	Peter Claver, Sergius of Antioch
10	Finnian, Nicholas of Tolentino, Pulcheria
11	Deiniol, Ethelburga, Paphnutius
13	John Chrysostom (W)
15	Catherine of Genoa, Our Lady of Sorrows
16	Cornelius, Cyprian of Carthage, Euphemia, Ninian
17	Robert Bellarmine, Hildegard, Lambert, Satyrus
19	Januarius (W), Theodore of Tarsus
20	Agapetus or Eustace (W)
21	Matthew (W)
23	Adamnan, Linus
25	Sergius of Rostov
26	Cosmas and Damian (W), Cyprian of Antioch, John (E)
27	Frumentius (W), Vincent de Paul
28	Exuperius, Wenceslaus
29	Michael (Michaelmas Day), Gabriel and Raphael
30	Jerome, Otto

■ October

1	Remigius, Romanos, Teresa of the Child Jesus
2	Leodegar (Leger)
3	Teresa of Lisieux, Thomas de Cantilupe
4	Ammon, Francis of Assisi, Petronius
6	Bruno, Thomas (G)
9	Demetrius (W), Denis and companions, Dionysius of Paris, James (the Less) (E), John Leonardi
10	Francis Borgia, Paulinus of York
11	Atticus (E), Bruno, Nectarius
12	Wilfrid
13	Edward the Confessor
14	Callistus I, Cosmas Melodus (E)
15	Lucian of Antioch (E), Teresa of Avila
16	Gall, Hedwig, Lullus, Margaret Mary Alacoque
17	Ignatius of Antioch, Victor
18	Luke

Thought and Belief

Thought and Belief

19 John de Bréboeuf and Isaac Jogues and companions, Paul of the Cross, Peter of Alcantara
21 Hilarion, Ursula
22 Abercius
23 John of Capistrano
24 Anthony Claret
25 Crispin and Crispinian, Forty Martyrs of England and Wales, Gaudentius
26 Demetrius (*E*)
28 Firmilian (*E*), Simon and Jude
30 Serapion of Antioch
31 Wolfgang

■ November
1 All Saints, Cosmas and Damian (*E*)
2 Eustace (*E*), Victorinus
3 Hubert, Malachy, Martin de Porres, Pirminius, Winifred
4 Charles Borromeo, Vitalis and Agricola
5 Elizabeth (*W*)
6 Illtyd, Leonard, Paul of Constantinople (*E*)
7 Willibrord
8 Elizabeth (*E*), Willehad
9 Simeon Metaphrastes (*E*)
10 Justus, Leo I (*W*)
11 Martin of Tours (*W*), Menas of Egypt, Theodore of Studios
12 Josaphat, Martin of Tours (*E*), Nilus the Ascetic
13 Abbo, John Chrysostom (*E*), Nicholas I
14 Dubricius, Gregory Palamas (*E*)
15 Albert the Great, Machutus
16 Edmund of Abingdon, Eucherius, Gertrude (the Great), Margaret of Scotland, Matthew (*E*)
17 Elizabeth of Hungary, Gregory Thaumaturgus, Gregory of Tours, Hugh of Lincoln

18 Odo, Romanus
19 Mechthild, Nerses
20 Edmund the Martyr
21 Gelasius
22 Cecilia
23 Amphilochius, Clement I (*W*), Columban, Felicity, Gregory of Agrigentum
25 Clement I (*E*), Mercurius, Mesrob
26 Siricius
27 Barlam and Josaphat
28 Simeon Metaphrastes
29 Cuthbert Mayne
30 Andrew, Frumentius (*G*)

■ December
1 Eligius
2 Chromatius
3 Francis Xavier
4 Barbara, John Damascene, Osmund
5 Clement of Alexandria, Sabas
6 Nicholas
7 Ambrose
10 Miltiades
11 Damasus, Daniel
12 Jane Frances de Chantal, Spyridon (*E*), Vicelin
13 Lucy, Odilia
14 John of the Cross, Spyridon (*W*)
16 Eusebius
18 Frumentius (*C*)
20 Ignatius of Antioch (*G*)
21 Peter Canisius, Thomas
22 Anastasia (*E*), Chrysogonus (*E*)
23 John of Kanty
26 Stephen (*W*)
27 John (*W*), Fabiola, Stephen (*E*)
29 Thomas à Becket, Trophimus of Arles
31 Sylvester

Confucianism

Founded 6c BC in China.
Founder K'ung Fu-tse (Confucius) (c.551–479BC).
Sacred texts Shih Ching, Li Ching, Shu Ching, Chu'un Ch'iu, I Ching.
Beliefs The oldest school of Chinese thought, Confucianism did not begin as a religion. Confucius was concerned with the best way to behave and live in this world and was not concerned with the afterlife. He emerges as a great moral teacher who tried to replace the old religious observances with moral values as the basis of social and political order. He laid particular emphasis on the family as the basic unit in society and the foundation of the whole community. He believed that government was a matter of moral responsibility, not just manipulation of power.

Organization Confucianism is not an institution and has no church or clergy. However, ancestor-worship and veneration of the sky have their sources in Confucian texts.Weddings and funerals follow a tradition handed down by Confucian scholars. Social life is ritualized and colour and patterns of clothes have a sacred meaning.
Divisions There are two ethical strands in Confucianism. One, associated with Confucius and Hsun Tzu (c.298–238BC), is conventionalistic: we ought to follow the traditional codes of behaviour for their own sake. The other, associated with Mencius (c.371–289BC) and medieval neo-Confucians, is intuitionistic: we ought to do as our moral natures dictate.

Major Chinese festivals

January/February	Chinese New Year	August	All Souls' Festival
February/March	Lantern Festival	September	Mid-Autumn Festival
March/April	Festival of Pure Brightness	September/October	Double Ninth Festival
May/June	Dragon Boat Festival	November/December	Winter Solstice
July/August	Herd Boy and Weaving Maid Festival		

Hinduism

Founded c.1500BC by Aryan invaders of India with their Vedic religion.

Sacred texts The Vedas ('knowledge'), including the Upanishads which contain much that is esoteric and mystical. Also included are the epic poems the Ramayana and the Mahabharata. Best known of all is the Bhagavad Gita, part of the Mahabharata.

Beliefs Hinduism emphasizes the right way of living (dharma) and embraces many diverse religious beliefs and practices rather than a set of doctrines. It acknowledges many gods who are seen as manifestations of an underlying reality. Devout Hindus aim to become one with the 'absolute reality' or Brahman. Only after a completely pure life will the soul be released from the cycle of rebirth. Until then the soul will be repeatedly reborn. Samsara refers to the cycle of birth and rebirth. Karma is the law by which consequences of actions within one life are carried over into the next.

Organization There is very little formal structure. Hinduism is concerned with the realization of religious values in every part of life, yet there is a great emphasis on the performance of complex demanding rituals under the supervision of a Brahman priest and teacher. There are three categories of worship: temple, domestic and congregational. The most common ceremony is prayer (puja). Many pilgrimages take place and there is an annual cycle of festivals.

Divisions As there is no concept of orthodoxy in Hinduism, there are many different sects worshipping different gods. The three most important gods are Brahman, the primeval god, Vishnu, the preserver, and Shiva, both destroyer and creator of life. The three major living traditions are those devoted to Vishnu, Shiva and the goddess Shakti. Folk beliefs and practices exist together with sophisticated philosophical schools.

Major Hindu festivals

S = Sukla ('waxing fortnight')   *K* = Krishna ('waning fortnight')

Chaitra S 9	Ramanavami (Birthday of Lord Rama)	Asvina S 1–10	Navaratri (Festival of Nine Nights)
Asadha S 2	Rathayatra (Pilgrimage of the Jagannatha Chariot at Puri)	Asvina S 15	Lakshmi-puja (Homage to Goddess Lakshmi)
Sravana S 11–15	Jhulanayatra (Swinging the Lord Krishna)	Asvina K 15	Diwali, Dipavali (String of Lights)
Sravana S 15	Rakshabandhana (Tying on Lucky Threads)	Kartikka S 15	Guru Nanak Jananti (Birthday of Guru Nanak)
Bhadrapada K 8	Janamashtami (Birthday of Lord Krishna)	Magha K 5	Sarasvati-puja (Homage to Goddess Sarasvati)
Asvina S 7–10	Durga-puja (Homage to Goddess Durga) (*Bengal*)	Magha K 13	Maha-sivaratri (Great Night of Lord Shiva)
		Phalguna S 14	Holi (Festival of Fire)
		Phalguna S 15	Dolayatra (Swing Festival) (*Bengal*)

Islam

Founded 7c AD.

Founder Muhammad (c.570–c.632).

Sacred texts The Koran, the word of God as revealed to Muhammad, and the Hadith, a collection of the prophet's sayings.

Beliefs A monotheistic religion, God is the creator of all things and holds absolute power over man. All persons should devote themselves to lives of grateful and praise-giving obedience to God as they will be judged on the Day of Resurrection. It is acknowledged that Satan often misleads humankind but those who have obeyed God or have repented of their sins will dwell in paradise. Those sinners who are unrepentant will go to hell. Muslims accept the Old Testament and acknowledge Jesus Christ as an important prophet, but they believe the perfect word of God was revealed to Muhammad. Islam imposes five pillars of faith on its followers: belief in one God and his prophet, Muhammad; salat, formal prayer preceded by ritual cleansing five times a day, facing Mecca; saum, fasting during the month of Ramadan; Hajj, pilgrimage to Mecca at least once; zakat, a religious tax on the rich to provide for the poor.

Organization There is no organized priesthood but great respect is accorded to descendants of Muhammad and holy men, scholars and teachers such as mullahs and ayatollahs. The Shari'a is the Islamic law and applies to all aspects of life, not just religious practices.

Divisions There are two main groups within Islam. The Sunni are the majority and the more orthodox. They recognize the succession from Muhammad to Abu Bakr, his father-in-law, and to the next three caliphs. The Shiites are followers of Ali, Muhammad's nephew and son-in-law. They believe in 12 imams, perfect teachers, who still guide the faithful from paradise. Shi'ah practice tends towards the ecstatic. There are many other subsects including the Sufis, the Ismailis and the Wahhabis.

Thought and Belief

Thought and Belief

Major Islamic festivals

1 Muharram	New Year's Day; starts on the day which celebrates Muhammad's departure from Mecca to Medina in AD622.		27 Ramadan	'Night of Power' (Laylat al-Qadr); sending down of the Koran to Muhammad.
12 Rabi I	Birthday of Muhammad (Mawlid al-Nabi) AD572; celebrated throughout month of Rabi I.		1 Shawwal	'Feast of Breaking the Fast' (Id al-Fitr); marks the end of Ramadan.
27 Rajab	'Night of Ascent' (Laylat al-Miraj) of Muhammad to Heaven.		8–13 Dhu-l-Hijja	Annual pilgrimage ceremonies at and around Mecca; month during which the great pilgrimage (Hajj) should be made.
1 Ramadan	Beginning of month of fasting during daylight hours.		10 Dhu-l-Hijja	Feast of the Sacrifice (Id al-Adha).

Jainism

Founded 6c BC in India.
Founder Vardhamana Mahavira (c.540–468BC).
Sacred texts Svetambara canon of scripture and Digambara texts.
Beliefs Jainism is derived from the ancient jinas ('those who overcome'). They believe that salvation consists in conquering material existence through adhering to a strict ascetic discipline, thus freeing the 'soul' from the working of karma for eternal, all-knowing bliss. Liberation requires detachment from worldly existence, an essential part of which is Ahimsa, non-injury to living beings. Jains are also strict vegetarians.
Organization Like Buddhists, the Jains are dedicated to the quest for liberation and the life of the ascetic. However, rather than congregating in monastic cen-

tres, Jain monks and nuns have developed a strong relationship with lay people. There are temple rituals resembling Hindu puja. There is also a series of lesser vows and specific religious practices that give the lay person an identifiable religious career.

Divisions There are two categories of religious and philosophical literature. The Svetambara have a canon of scripture consisting of 45 texts, including a group of 11 texts in which the sermons and dialogues of Mahavira himself are collected. The Digambara hold that the original teachings of Mahavira have been lost but that their texts preserve accurately the substance of the original message. This disagreement over scriptures has not led to fundamental doctrinal differences.

Judaism

Founded c.2000BC.
Founder Abraham (c.2000–1650BC), with whom God made a covenant, and Moses (15c–13c BC), who gave the Israelites the law.
Sacred texts The Hebrew Bible, consisting of 24 books, the most important of which are the Torah or Pentateuch — the first five books. Also the Talmud made up of the Mishna, the oral law, and the Gemara, an extensive commentary.
Beliefs A monotheistic religion, the Jews believe God is the creator of the world, delivered the Israelites out of bondage in Egypt, revealed his law to them, and chose them to be a light to all humankind. However varied their communities, Jews see themselves as members of a community whose origins lie in the patriarchal period. Ritual is very important and the family is the basic unit of ritual.
Organization Originally a theocracy, the basic institution is now the synagogue, operated by the congre-

gation and led by a rabbi of their choice. The chief rabbis in France and Britain have authority over those who accept it; in Israel the two chief rabbis have civil authority in family law. The synagogue is the centre for community worship and study. Its main feature is the 'ark' (a cupboard) containing the hand-written scrolls of the Pentateuch. Daily life is governed by a number of practices and observances: male children are circumcised, the Sabbath is observed, and food has to be correctly prepared. The most important festival is the Passover, which celebrates the liberation of the Israelites from Egypt.
Divisions Today most Jews are descendants of either the Ashkenazim or the Sephardim, each with marked cultural differences. There are also several religious branches of Judaism from ultra-liberal to ultra-conservative, reflecting different points of view regarding the binding character of the prohibitions and duties prescribed for Jews.

Major Jewish festivals

1–2 Tishri	Rosh Hashana (New Year)		10 Tevet	Asara be-Tevet (Fast of 10th Tevet)
3 Tishri	Tzom Gedaliahu (Fast of Gedaliah)		13 Adar	Taanit Esther (Fast of Esther)
10 Tishri	Yom Kippur (Day of Atonement)		14–15 Adar	Purim (Feast of Lots)
15–21 Tishri	Sukkot (Feast of Tabernacles)		15–22 Nisan	Pesach (Passover)
22 Tishri	Shemini Atzeret (8th Day of the Solemn Assembly)		5 Iyar	Israel Independence Day
			6–7 Sivan	Shavuot (Feast of Weeks)
23 Tishri	Simchat Torah (Rejoicing of the Law)		17 Tammuz	Shiva Asar be-Tammuz (Fast of 17th Tammuz)
25 Kislev to 2–3 Tevet	Hanukkah (Feast of Dedication)		9 Av	Tisha be-Av (Fast of 9th Av)

Shintoism

Founded 8c AD in Japan.
Sacred texts Kojiki and Nihon Shoki.
Beliefs Shinto 'the teaching' or 'way of the gods', came into existence independently from Buddhism which was coming to the mainland of Japan at that time. It subsequently incorporated many features of Buddhism. Founded on the nature-worship of Japanese folk religions, it is made up of many elements; animism, veneration of nature and ancestor-worship. Its gods are known as kami and there are many ceremonies appealing to these kami for benevolent treatment and protection. Great stress is laid on the harmony between humans, their kami and nature. Moral and physical purity is a basic law. Death and other pollutions are to be avoided. Shinto is primarily concerned with life and this world and the good of the group. Followers must show devotion and sincerity but aberrations can be erased by purification procedures.

Organization As a set of prehistoric agricultural ceremonies, Shinto was never supported by a body of philosophical or moralistic literature. Shamans originally performed the ceremonies and tended the shrines, then gradually a particular tribe took over the ceremonies. In the 8c Shinto became political when the imperial family were ascribed divine origins and state Shintoism was established.

Divisions In the 19c Shinto was divided into Shrine (jinga) Shinto and Sectarian (kyoko) Shinto. Jinga became a state cult and it remained the national religion until 1945.

Major Japanese festivals

Public holidays in Japan are listed on p423. In addition, the following festivals should be noted:

1–3 Jan	Oshogatsu (New Year)	7 Jul	Hoshi matsuri or Tanabata (Star Festival)
3 Mar	Ohinamatsuri (Doll's or Girls' Festival)	13–31 Jul	Obon (Buddhist All Souls)
5 May	Tango no Sekku (Boys' Festival)		

Sikhism

Founded 15c in India.
Founder Guru Nanak (1469–1539).
Sacred text Adi Granth.
Beliefs Nanak preached tolerance and devotion to one God before whom everyone is equal. Sikh is the Sanskrit word for disciple. Nanak's doctrine sought a fusion of Brahmanism and Islam on the grounds that both were monotheistic. God is the true Guru and his divine word has come to humanity through the 10 historical gurus. The line ended in 1708, since when the Sikh community has been called guru.
Organization There is no priestly caste and all Sikhs are empowered to perform rituals connected with births, marriages, and deaths. Sikhs worship in their own temples but they evolved distinct features like the langar, 'kitchen', a communal meal where people of any religion or caste could eat. Rest houses for travellers were also provided. The tenth guru instituted an initiation ceremony, the Khalsa. Initiates wear the Five Ks (uncut hair, steel bangle, comb, shorts, ceremonial sword) and a turban. Members of the Khalsa add the name Singh (lion) to their name and have to lead pure lives and follow a code of discipline. Sikhs generally rise before dawn, bathe and recite the japji, a morning prayer. Hindu festivals from northern India are observed.
Divisions There are several religious orders of Sikhs based either on disputes over the succession of gurus or points of ritual and tradition. The most important current issue is the number of Khalsa Sikhs cutting off their hair and beards and relapsing into Hinduism.

Taoism

Founded 600BC in China.
Founder Lao-tzu (6c BC).
Sacred texts Chuang-tzu, Lao-tzu (Tao-te-ching).
Beliefs Taoism is Chinese for 'the school of the tao' and the 'Taoist religion'. Tao ('the way') is central in both Confucianism and Taoism. The former stresses the tao of humanity, the latter the tao of nature, harmony with which ensures appropriate conduct. Taoist religion developed later and was probably influenced by Buddhist beliefs. The doctrine emphasizes that good and evil action decide the fate of the soul. The Taoists believe that the sky, the earth and water are deities; that Lao-tzu is supreme master; that the disciple masters his body and puts evil spirits to flight with charms; that body and spirit are purified through meditation and by taking the pill of immortality to gain eternal life; and that the way is handed down from master to disciple. Religious Taoism incorporated ideas and images from philosophical Taoist texts, especially the Tao-te-ching but also the theory of Yin-Yang, the quest for immortality, mental and physical discipline, interior hygiene, internal alchemy, healing and exorcism, a pantheon of gods and spirits, and ideals of theocratic states. The Immortals are meant to live in the mountains far from the tumult of the world.

Organization This is similar to Buddhism in the matter of clergy and temple. The jiao is a ceremony to purify the ground. Zhon-gyual is the only important religious festival, when the hungry dead appear to the living and Taoist priests free the souls of the dead from suffering.

Divisions Religious Taoism emerged from many sects. These sects proliferated between 618 and 1126AD and were described collectively as Spirit Cloud Taoists. They form the majority of Taoist priests in Taiwan, where they are called 'Masters of Methods' or Red-headed Taoists. The more orthodox priests are called 'Tao Masters' or Black-headed Taoists.

Thought and Belief

Thought and Belief

Sacred texts of world religions

Baha'i Most Holy Book, The Seven Valleys, The Hidden Words, The Bayan

Buddhism Tripitaka, Mahayana Sutras, Milindapanha, Bardo Thodol

Christianity Old Testament: Genesis, Exodus, Leviticus, Numbers, Deuteronomy, Joshua, Judges, Ruth, 1 Samuel, 2 Samuel, 1 Kings, 2 Kings, 1 Chronicles, 2 Chronicles, Ezra, Nehemiah, Esther, Job, Psalms, Proverbs, Ecclesiastes, Song of Solomon, Isaiah, Jeremiah, Lamentations, Ezekiel, Daniel, Hosea, Joel, Amos, Obadiah, Jonah, Micah, Nahum, Habakkuk, Zephaniah, Haggai, Zechariah, Malachi. New Testament: Matthew, Mark, Luke, John, Acts of the Apostles, Romans, 1 Corinthians, 2 Corinthians, Galatians, Ephesians, Philippians, Colossians, 1 Thessalonians, 2 Thessalonians, 1 Timothy, 2 Timothy, Titus, Philemon, Hebrews, James, 1 Peter, 2 Peter, 1 John, 2 John, 3 John, Jude, Revelation. Apocrypha (Revised standard version 1957): 1 Esdras, 2 Esdras, Tobit, Judith, Additions to Esther, Wisdom of Solomon, Ecclesiasticus, Epistle of Jeremiah, Baruch, Prayer of Azariah and the Song of the Three Young Men, (History of) Susan-

na, Bel and the Dragon, Prayer of Manasseh, 1 Maccabees, 2 Maccabees. (The Authorized version incorporates Jeremiah into Baruch; The prayer of Azariah is simply called the Song of the Three Holy Children. The Roman Catholic Church includes Tobit, Judith, all of Esther, Maccabees 1 and 2, Wisdom of Solomon, Ecclesiasticus, and Baruch in its canon.)

Confucianism Shih ching, Li ching, Shu ching, Chu'un Ch'iu, I Ching

Hinduism The Vedas (including the Upanishads), Ramayana, Mahabharata and the Bhagavad Gita

Islam The Koran, the Hadith

Jainism Svetambara canon, Digambara texts

Judaism The Hebrew Bible: Torah (Pentateuch): Genesis, Exodus, Leviticus, Numbers, Deuteronomy. Also the books of the Prophets, Psalms, Chronicles and Proverbs. The Talmud including the Mishna and Gemara. The Zohar (Book of Splendour) is a famous Cabalistic book.

Shintoism Kojiki, Nihon Shoki

Sikhism Adi Granth

Taoism Chuang-tzu, Lao-tzu (Tao-te-ching)

Other religions, sects and religious movements

Adventist A member of one of the many Christian groups which believe the second coming of Christ will happen very soon. ▶ **Seventh Day Adventists**

anthroposophy A modern spiritual movement founded in Switzerland in 1912 by Rudolf Steiner (1861–1925). *Anthropos* (meaning 'man') suggests it is more human-centred than God-centred; fundamental to anthroposophy is the aim to develop the whole human being — socially, intellectually and spiritually — and to restore the innate human capacity for spiritual perception, which has been dulled by materialism. Anthroposophy has influenced many areas of activity, particularly the foundation of special schools around the world.

charismatic movement A modern international, transdenominational Christian movement of spiritual renewal, which has its roots in the Pentecostal Church. Taking a variety of forms in Roman Catholic, Protestant, and Eastern Orthodox churches, it emphasizes the present reality and work of the Holy Spirit in the life of the Church and the individual. It may be characterized by the practice of speaking in tongues (glossolalia), prophecy and healing.

Christadelphians A Christian sect, founded in 1848 in the USA by John Thomas (1805–71). They claim that Christ will soon come again to establish a theocracy lasting for a millennium and based in Jerusalem. They are congregational in organization and have no ordained ministers. They believe in the complete accuracy of the Bible, and claim that only true believers will go on to life after death and that adult followers must be baptized to attain full salvation.

ecumenism A movement seeking to unify the different churches and denominations within Christianity. Modern ecumenism stems from the Edinburgh Missionary Conference (1910) and led to the formation in 1948 of the World Council of Churches. It encourages dialogue between churches, unions where possible, joint acts of worship, and joint service in the community.

evangelicalism A term (from Greek 'to announce the good news') which since the Reformation has been applied to the Protestant Churches due to their principles of justification through faith alone, and the su-

preme authority accorded to Scripture (ie not to church tradition or institutional figures). Although the term goes beyond denominational divisions, and has featured throughout the history of the Christian Church, in later years it has been applied more narrowly to Protestant Churches which emphasize biblical authority, and personal experience of conversion, commitment and ongoing relationship with Jesus Christ. Evangelicals believe in and are inspired by the necessity of carrying the Christian faith to those not already within the community of the Christian Church.

Freemasonry An international, secretive adult male fraternity who meet in clubs called lodges for social enjoyment and mutual assistance, united by their belief in a supreme being and in the immortal soul. The organization comes under attack for the secrecy concerning its activities, both towards outsiders and between the different levels of freemasons. Modern Freemasonry in the UK began in the early 18c, and is known for its rituals and signs of recognition that date back to ancient non-Christian religions and to the practices of the medieval craft guild of the stonemasons (in England).

Fundamentalism A conservative theological movement seeking to preserve the essential doctrines of the Christian faith, eg the Virgin birth and the resurrection of Christ. Its roots lie in the 19c when traditional assumptions began to be challenged by the concept of evolution and the growth of biblical criticism. The term dates from a 1920s Protestant movement in the USA which was characterized by a literal interpretation of the Bible. It was revived in the late 20c to describe some Christian and Muslim movements.

Hare Krishna Popular name for a Hindu cult founded in the USA in 1965 by His Divine Grace A C Bhaktivedanta Swami Prabhupada as The International Society for Krishna Consciousness. It focuses on love for Krishna (an incarnation of the god Vishnu) and promotes wellbeing through consciousness of God based on the ancient Vedic texts of India, eg the *Bhagavad Gita*. Its saffron-robed devotees are sometimes seen gathered in town centres chanting the mantra 'Hare Krishna'; they are vegetarians, avoid intoxicants and gambling, and are celibate apart from procreation within marriage.

Jehovah's Witnesses A millenarian movement organized in the USA in 1884 by Charles Taze Russell (1852–1916), then by Joseph Franklin Rutherford (1869–1942). They have their own translation of the Bible, which they interpret literally, and view themselves as entirely distinct from orthodox Christianity. They believe in the imminent second coming of Christ, and that their place in heaven depends on their obedience to God. Expected to 'witness' through house-to-house visiting, they avoid worldly involvement, and refuse to obey laws which they view as a contradiction of the law of God (eg taking oaths and military service). Their newspaper is called *The Watchtower* and their churches 'Kingdom Halls'.

Mormons, properly **The Church of Jesus Christ of Latter-Day Saints** A religious sect which since 1847 has been based in Salt Lake City, Utah. The sect was founded in 1830 by Joseph Smith (d.1844) and was polygamous until 1890. They base their beliefs on *The Book of Mormon* and on Smith's own revelations, *Doctrine and Covenants* and *The Pearl of Great Price*; these texts tell of the coming of a millennium when Christ will rule from a New Jerusalem established in America. Smith claimed to have received visions of the Angel Moroni and a new revelation of the prophet Mormon on golden tablets which he translated as *The Book of Mormon*. Mormons believe that God was a physical being like them, that humans progress from a spiritual state with God, to mortality and then on to an afterlife, that they too can become gods, and that the incarnation of Jesus was unique only because it was the first.

New Age A modern cultural trend encompassing a wide range of concepts concerned with the union of mind, body, and spirit. New Age expresses itself in an interest in a variety of beliefs and disciplines such as mysticism, meditation, astrology, and holistic medicine, including the pseudoscientific application of the 'healing powers' of crystals. Many adherents of New Age anticipate the dawning of an astrological or spiritual age in which humans will realize a 'higher' existence and experience true peace and harmony.

Pentecostalism A Christian renewal movement which began in the early 1900s in the USA — in Topeka, Kansas (1901) and Los Angeles (1906) — inspired by the coming of the Holy Spirit upon the disciples (Acts 2) and in reaction to the loss of evangelical fervour among Methodists and other denominations. Pentecostals believe in the blessing and empowering of Christians through the gifts of the Holy Spirit, eg speaking in tongues, prophecy and healing, and in the literal interpretation of the Bible. Their churches are characterized by missionary zeal, informal worship, enthusiastic singing, and the practice of spiritual gifts.

Plymouth Brethren A fundamentalist Christian sect founded in 1827 by a group of evangelicals in Dublin, Ireland, under John Nelson Darby (1800–82). It spread to England in 1832 and met in Plymouth. Millenarian in outlook, the sect is characterized by a simplicity of belief, practice and style of life based on the New Testament. There are no ordained priests and no maintained church buildings since meetings are held in members' homes.

Quakers, properly **The Society of Friends** A Christian sect rooted in radical Puritanism, founded in England by George Fox (1624–91). A colony for persecuted Quakers was founded in Pennsylvania in 1682 by William Penn (1644–1718). Belief in the 'inner light', a living contact with the divine Spirit, is the basis of its meetings for worship, where Friends gather in silence until moved by the Spirit to speak. Many meetings now have programmed orders of worship. Quakers are often actively involved in promoting tolerance, justice and peace.

Scientology A movement developed in the USA in the 1950s by L Ron Hubbard (1911–86). Based on his *Dianetics: The Modern Science of Mental Health*, which outlines a type of counselling for curing emotional illnesses and for enhancing life, it strives to open the minds of adherents to all great truths and to self-determination. The Church of Scientology (founded 1954) has made several controversial religious and scientific claims.

Seventh Day Adventists A section of the American Adventist movement of 1831 that stemmed from the preaching of William Miller (1782–1849). Many followers left the movement when Miller's prophecy that Christ would return to earth in 1843 or 1844 did not materialize. Some turned to the teaching of Ellen Gould White (1827–1915), particularly the importance of honouring the Sabbath (Friday evening to Saturday evening), and formed the Seventh Day Adventists (1863). They believe Christ's second coming is imminent, but delayed until the Adventist message is preached worldwide. They also observe Old Testament dietary laws, abstain from alcohol, and practise adult baptism by total immersion.

transcendental meditation or TM A meditation technique based in part on Hindu meditation, but with no doctrinal content and practised by both religious and non-religious people. Rediscovered by Guru Dev, it came to prominence after 1958 through Dev's disciple Maharishi Mahesh Yogi, who travelled widely teaching TM. Practitioners are taught to meditate for 20 minutes twice a day, sometimes repeating a silent mantra, as a means of reducing stress, achieving relaxation and gaining self understanding. The ultimate goal is 'god-realization'.

Zoroastrianism An ancient religion of Persian origin founded or reformed by Zoroaster, which teaches the existence of two equally opposed divine beings, one good and the other evil. It was forced out of Persia by the expansion of Islam. Zoroastrians believe that the spirit of evil, Ahriman, will finally be overcome by Ahura Mazda ('Wise Lord') or God, only if individuals play their part in saving the world. Their body of scripture is known as the *Avesta*, and rites of worship are performed by priests.

Thought and Belief

Religious leaders and theologians

Abelard, Peter (1079–1142) French, born near Nantes. Philosopher and theologian. Secretly married his pupil Héloïse, whose relatives exacted revenge by castrating him, after which he became a monk and she a nun. His adversaries, headed by Bernard of Clairvaux, accused him of heresies, and he died on his way to Rome to defend himself. Abelard and Héloïse compiled a famous collection of their correspondence.

Abraham (Abram) (c.2000–1650BC) Biblical character regarded as the ancestor of Israel and of several other nations; also an important figure in Islam. God called him to travel from the Chaldaean town of Ur to Canaan, promising him a land and descendants which would become a great nation (Genesis 12, 15). At 100 years of age he and his previously barren wife Sarah had a son, Isaac, who he nearly had to sacrifice as a test of faith (Genesis 21, 22).

'Ali (d.661) Cousin and son-in-law of Muhammad, and fourth caliph. Married the prophet's daughter Fatima, thus founding the Fatimid Dynasty. Shia Muslims believe him to be the only true successor to Muhammad.

Anselm, St (1033–1109) Italian, born near Aosta. Theologian and philosopher who became abbot of the Abbey of Bec (1078) and later Archbishop of Canterbury (1093). Frequently in conflict with his masters over Church rights, Anselm was a major figure in early scholastic philosophy, remembered especially for his ontological proof for the existence of God.

Aquinas, St Thomas (1225–74) Italian, born Roccasecca, near Aquino. Combined Christian doctrine with the teachings of Aristotle. Wrote on principles of natural religion in *Summa contra Gentiles* (1259–64) and on proving the existence of God in *Summa Theologiae* (1266–73). Had considerable influence on theological thought of following ages.

Arius (c.250–336) Libyan theologian, founder of the heresy known as Arianism. In c.319 he claimed that, in the doctrine of the Trinity, the Son was not co-equal or co-eternal with the Father, but only the first and highest of all finite beings. Fierce controversy followed, resolved at the Council of Nicaea (325), which condemned Arianism and affirmed the equality and unity of the three persons of the Trinity.

Athanasius, St (c.296–373) Greek theologian and prelate, born Alexandria. Distinguished himself at the Council of Nicaea (325) and was chosen Patriarch of Alexandria and Primate of Egypt. As a result of his stand against the heretic Arius, he was dismissed from his See on several occasions by emperors sympathetic to the Arian cause.

Augustine of Hippo, St (354–430) Italian, born North Africa. One of the most influential Christian theologians, he was influenced primarily by Manicheanism, then Neoplatonism, before converting to Christianity in 386. Famous works are the *Confessions* (400), *The City of God* (412–27).

Baha'u'llah (Mirza Husayn Ali) (1817–92) Persian religious leader and founder of the Islamic Baha'i sect. Initially a follower of the Persian Babi sect, he was imprisoned in 1852, then exiled. In 1863 he proclaimed himself to be the prophet foretold by Bab-ed-din, and became the leader of the new Baha'i faith.

Barth, Karl (1886–1968) Swiss, born Basle. Protestant theologian, the major exponent of Reformed theology. His commentary (1919) on St Paul's Epistle to the Romans established his theological reputation, and he became a professor at Göttingen (1921), Münster (1925) and Bonn (1930). After refusing to take an unconditional oath to Hitler he was dismissed, and so became professor at Basle (1935–62). Other works include *Church Dogmatics* (1932–67).

Becket, St Thomas (à) (1118–70) English, born London. Became Chancellor (1155) and Archbishop of Canterbury (1162) but clashed with Henry II over Henry's desire to reduce the power of the Church. Henry's wish to be rid of this 'turbulent priest' led to Becket's murder in Canterbury Cathedral (29 December 1170). Pilgrimages to his burial place in Trinity Chapel are the subject of Chaucer's *Canterbury Tales* (c.1387–1400).

Bede, St ('the Venerable Bede') (c.673–735) Anglo-Saxon historian and theologian, born near Monkwearmonth, Durham. His most valuable work is the *Ecclesiastical History of the English People*, virtually the only source of English history before 731.

Besant, Annie (1847–1933) English, born London. Social reformer who became Vice-President of the National Secular Society (1874), and turned to theosophy after meeting Madame Blavatsky (1889); also championed nationalism and education in India and was President of the Indian National Congress (1917–23).

Blavatsky, Helena Petrovna (1831–91) Russian, born Ekaterinoslav (now Dnepropetrovsk, Ukraine). Helped to found the Theosophical Society in New York (1875), and later carried on her work in India. Her psychic powers were widely acclaimed but did not survive scientific investigation. Writings include *Isis Unveiled* (1877).

Bodhidharma (6c) Indian, born near Madras (now Chennai). Monk and founder of the Ch'an (or Zen) sect of Buddhism. In 520 he travelled to China, where he had a famous audience with the emperor. He argued that merit leading to salvation could not be accumulated through good deeds, and taught meditation as the way to return to Buddha's spiritual precepts.

Boff, Leonardo (1938–) Brazilian, born Concordia. Franciscan liberation theologian, ordained in Brazil in 1964, and Professor of Systematic Theology in Petrópolis, Rio. His best-known work, *Jesus Christ Liberator* (1972), offers hope and justice for the oppressed rather than religious support of the status quo in Church and Society.

Bonhoeffer, Dietrich (1906–45) German, born Breslau. Lutheran pastor and theologian who left Germany in 1933 in protest against Nazi anti-Jewish legislation, then returned (1935) to become head of a pastoral seminary until its closure by the Nazis in 1937. Deeply involved in the German resistance movement, he was arrested (1943), imprisoned and hanged. His most influential works are *Ethics* (1949) and the posthumously published *Letters and Papers from Prison* (1951).

Booth, William (1829–1912) English, born Nottingham. In 1865 he founded the Salvation Army (so named in 1878) to do mission work in London's East End, waging war against such evils as sweated labour and child prostitution. His wife Catherine (1829–90) was an active partner in the work, as were his children Bramwell (1856–1929), Kate (1859–1955) and Evangeline (1865–1950).

Brunner, (Heinrich) Emil (1889–1966) Swiss, born Winterthur. Pastor and theologian, the author of nearly 400 books and articles, notably *The Mediator* (1927) and *The Divine Imperative* (1937). *The Divine–Human Encounter* (1944) reveals his debt to Martin Buber's 'I-Thou' understanding of the relationship between God and Man.

Buber, Martin (1878–1965) Jewish, born Vienna. Published many works on social and ethical problems and is best known for the religious philosophy expounded in *Ich und Du* (1922), contrasting personal relationships of mutuality and reciprocity with utilitarian or objective relationships.

Buddha (Prince Siddhartha Gautama) (c.560–c.480BC) Founder of Buddhism, born the son of the rajah of the Sakya tribe ruling in Kapilavastu, Nepal. Aged about 30 he left the luxuries of the court, his beautiful wife, and all earthly ambitions for the life of an ascetic; after several years of severe austerities he saw in the contemplative life the perfect way to self-enlightenment. Taught for around 40 years, and gained many disciples and followers.

Bultmann, Rudolf Karl (1884–1976) German, born Wiefelstede. Protestant theologian who maintained that it was almost impossible to know anything about the historical Jesus, and that the Gospels needed to be 'de-mythologized' of their supernatural content; faith in a transcendent Christ, however, was still possible. Works include *Jesus and the Word* (1934), *The Gospel of John* (1941), *Theology of the New Testament* (1952–5) and *Jesus Christ and Mythology* (1960).

Calvin, John (1509–64) French, born Noyon. Protestant reformer and theologian active as a preacher and propagandist in France and Switzerland, founding a theocracy in Geneva which controlled most of the city's affairs. He left a double legacy to Protestantism by systematizing its doctrine and organizing its ecclesiastical discipline. Works include the influential *Institutes of the Christian Religion* (1536) and commentaries on most of the Old and New Testaments (published 1617).

Clement of Alexandria, St (Titus Flavius Clemens) (c.150–c.215) Church Father, probably born in Athens, who became head of the catechetical school at Alexandria (c.180–201). His most famous pupil was Origen. His chief surviving works are *Who is the Rich Man that is Saved* and the trilogy of *The Missionary*, *The Tutor* and *The Miscellanies*.

Confucius (K'ung Fu-tse, 'the Master K'ung') (551–479BC) Chinese, born state of Lu (modern Shantung). Moral teacher who tried to replace old religious observances with moral values as the basis of social and political order, emphasizing the importance of respect and benevolence. 'Confucianism' became, and remained until recently, the state religion of China. His teachings are recorded in the *Analects*, written by his pupils after his death.

Cupitt, Don (1934–) English, born Oldham. Theologian and priest best known for the radical views expressed in his book *Sea of Faith* (1984), which became a successful television series. Other works include *Taking Leave of God* (1971) and *Reforming Christianity* (2001).

Dalai Lama (Tenzin Gyatso) (1935–) Spiritual and temporal head of Tibet, born Takster. He was designated the 14th incarnation of the Dalai Lama in 1937, and ruled Tibet from 1940 until 1959, when he fled to exile in India following China's suppression of a Tibetan uprising. Each successive Dalai Lama is held to be a reincarnation of the previous one, and is regarded as a manifestation of the Bodhisattva Avalokiteshvara. He won the Nobel peace prize in 1989.

Eckhart, Johannes (known as **Meister Eckhart**) (c.1260–c.1327) German, born Hochheim. Priest and theologian whose mystic pantheism influenced later religious mysticism and speculative philosophy. In 1325 he was accused of heresy by

the Archbishop of Cologne, and two years after his death his writings were condemned by Pope John XXII.

Erasmus, Desiderius (1466–1536) Dutch, born Rotterdam. Influential Renaissance humanist and scholar who published many popular works including *Adagia* (*Adages*, 1500, 1508), *Enchiridion Militis Christiani* (*Handbook of a Christian Soldier*, 1503) and Encomium Moriae (*In Praise of Folly*, 1509).

Eusebius of Caesarea (c.264–340) Palestinian theologian and Bishop of Caesarea, known as the Father of Church History. His great work, the *Ecclesiastical History*, is a record of the Christian Church down to 324.

Fox, George (1624–91) English, born Fenny Drayton, Leicestershire. Founder of the Society of Friends or 'Quakers', he argued for God-given inward light and against sacerdotalism and all social conventions. His life was a record of persecutions, imprisonments and missionary travel to several parts of the world.

Francis of Assisi, St (originally **Giovanni Bernadone**) (c.1181–1226) Italian, born Assisi. Left a worldly life in 1205 to care for the poor and the sick, and live as a hermit. His followers formed the Franciscan order, which by 1219 had 5000 members. Preached widely in Europe and the Holy Land, and on returning to Italy (1224) is said to have received the stigmata.

Gandhi, Mohandas Karamchand (known as **Mahatma**, 'of great soul') (1869–1948) Indian, born Poorbandar. Studied law in London, but in 1893 went to South Africa, where he opposed discriminatory legislation against Indians. Returned to India in 1914, and as leader of the Indian National Congress advocated a policy of non-violent non-cooperation to achieve independence; jailed for conspiracy (1922–4). After independence (1947) his attempts to stop the Hindu–Muslim conflict in Bengal led to his assassination by a Hindu fanatic. Revered worldwide as a pacifist and moral teacher.

Garvey, Marcus (1887–1940) Jamaican, born St Ann's Bay. Founded the Universal Negro Improvement Association (1914) which promoted worldwide black unity and pride. Wrote and taught in New York from 1916; called for a return to Africa and established the Black Star Line, a steamship line owned and operated by blacks.

Ghazali, Abu Hamid Mohammed al- (1058–1111) Persian, born Tus (near the modern Meshed). Islamic philosopher, theologian and jurist. Following a spiritual crisis (1095) he abandoned his position of Professor of Philosophy at Baghdad for the ascetic life of a mendicant sufi, later founding a monastic community at Tus. Works include *The Intentions of the Philosophers* and *The Revival of the Religious Sciences*.

Gobind Singh (1666–1708) Indian, born Patna. Last of the 10 Sikh Gurus, he completed the process by which the Sikhs developed from the quietist faith of Guru Nanak to a militant creed. Established a small Sikh state in the Punjab foothills by military means, and instituted the Khalsa (a Sikh brotherhood marked by a new code of discipline), the 'Five Ks' regulating personal appearance, and common adoption of the name Singh for males and Kaur for females.

Graham, William Franklin ('Billy') (1918–) American, born Charlotte, North Carolina. Ordained a minister of the Southern Baptist Church in 1940, he quickly gained a reputation as a preacher. Since the 1950s he has conducted a series of highly organized revivalist crusades in the USA, the UK, South America and Europe.

Thought and Belief

Guru Nanak (1469–1539) Indian, born near Lahore, present-day Pakistan. Religious leader and founder of Sikhism. Though originally a Hindu, his doctrine, set out later in the *Adi Granth*, sought a fusion of Brahmanism and Islam on the grounds that both were monotheistic, although Nanak's own ideas leaned rather towards pantheism.

Gutiérrez, Gustavo (1928–) Peruvian, born Lima. Liberation theologian and priest, whose seminal *A Theology of Liberation* (1971) is dedicated to the needs of the poor and oppressed. Other works include *The Power of the Poor in History* (1984) and *Las Casas: In Search of the Poor of Jesus Christ* (1994).

Hick, John Harwood (1922–) English, born Scarborough, North Yorkshire. Theologian and philosopher of religion known for his concern with questions of evil, the soul, eternal life, and the status of Christianity among the world religions, raised in works such as *Faith and Knowledge* (1966) and *God has Many Names* (1982).

Huddleston, Trevor (1913–98) English, born Bedford. Anglican missionary and human rights campaigner. He entered the Community of the Resurrection and in 1943 he went to Johannesburg, where he became provincial of the order (1949–55); from 1960 to 1983 his posts included Bishop of Masasi (in Tanzania) and Archbishop of the Indian Ocean. After retiring he returned to London to become Chairman of the Anti-Apartheid Movement (1981).

Hutter, Jakob (d.1536) Swiss, born Moos. Anabaptist minister who founded the Hutterian Brethren (or Hutterites) in Moravia (1528), but was condemned and burned as a heretic in South Tyrol. The Brethren were organized in communal farms and espoused pacifism, adult baptism and rejection of oaths, and later became widespread in the USA.

Ignatius Loyola, St (originally **Iñigo López de Recalde**) (1491–1556) Spanish, born Loyola Castle, Guipúzcoa. Soldier and founder of the Jesuits. While convalescing he experienced a religious awakening and renounced military life; in 1534 with Frances Xavier he founded the Society of Jesus, establishing schools and sending out missionaries to Japan, India and Brazil. Works include the influential *Spiritual Exercises.*

Irenaeus, St (c.130–c.200) Greek, born Asia Minor. Theologian, bishop and Father of the Greek Church, chiefly remembered for his opposition to Gnosticism (especially the Valentinians), on which he wrote his *Against Heresies.*

Jansen, Cornelius (Otto) (1585–1638) Dutch, born Acquoi. Roman Catholic theologian and Bishop of Ypres, founder of the reform movement known as Jansenism. His major work *Augustinus* (published 1640) sought to prove that St Augustine's teachings were opposed to those of the Jesuit schools, and was condemned by Pope Urban VIII in 1642; controversy raged in France until a large number of Jansenists emigrated to the Netherlands.

Jenkins, David Edward (1925–) English, born Bromley, Kent. Theologian and prelate who was appointed Bishop of Durham (1984–94) amidst controversy over his interpretation of the Virgin Birth and the Resurrection. Writings include *The Contradiction of Christianity* (1976) and *The Calling of a Cuckoo* (2002).

Jesus Christ (Jesus of Nazareth) (c.4BC–c.30AD) Jewish teacher, born Bethlehem, the central figure of Christianity, which holds that he is the Son of God who was crucified and resurrected to redeem humanity from sin. In Islam he is considered a prophet second only to Muhammad. Began his ministry (mainly recorded in the New Testament Gospels) with baptism by John in the River Jordan (Luke 3.1), after which he gathered a group of 12 disciples and began healing the sick and demon-possessed, performing miracles, and proclaiming the coming of the kingdom of God, but was executed by order of the Roman procurator Pontius Pilate.

John of the Cross, St (originally **Juan de Yepes y Álvarez**) (1542–91) Spanish, born Fontiveros. Founded the Discalced Carmelites with St Teresa (1568); imprisoned in Toledo (1577), where he wrote a number of poems highly regarded in Spanish mystical literature. After escaping, he became Vicar Provincial of Andalusia (1585–7).

Kempis, Thomas à (Thomas Hemerken) (1379–1471) German, born Kempen. In 1400 he entered the Augustinian convent of Agnietenberg near Zwolle, was ordained in 1413, chosen sub-prior in 1429, and died there as superior. His many writings include the influential devotional work *The Imitation of Christ* (c.1415–24).

King, Martin Luther (1929–68) American, born Atlanta, Georgia. Minister and civil rights leader who challenged the segregation laws of the Southern states, and after 1965 turned his attention to social conditions in the North. Received the Kennedy peace prize and the Nobel peace prize (both 1964); assassinated in Memphis, Tennessee.

Knox, John (c.1513–72) Scottish, born Haddington, Lothian. Protestant religious reformer and chaplain to Edward VI. On Mary I's accession (1553) he fled to Geneva, where he was much influenced by Calvin. Returned to Scotland permanently in 1559 where he founded the Church of Scotland (1560). Contributed to the Second Book of Common Prayer; other writings include *First Blast of the Trumpet against the Monstrous Regiment of Women* (1558).

Küng, Hans (1928–) Swiss, born Sursee. Roman Catholic theologian whose questioning of Catholic doctrine has found an audience especially among lay people. Works such as *Infallible? An Inquiry* (1971) provoked the Vatican authorities to withdraw his licence to teach as a Catholic theologian in 1979; other writings include *Does God Exist?* (1980).

Lao-tzu (Lao Zi) (6c BC) Chinese philosopher and sage, the founder of Taoism. Probably a legendary figure, he is represented as the older contemporary of Confucius, against whom most of his teaching is directed. *The Tao Te Ching* ('Way of Power'), the most venerated of the three classical texts of Taoism, is attributed to him, though it dates from 300 years after his death.

Luther, Martin (1483–1546) German, born Eisleben. Priest and religious reformer whose notoriety began after a visit to Rome in 1510–11, where he was angered by the sale of indulgences. Drew up 95 theses attacking the papal system (1517), which he nailed on the church door at Wittenberg. Violent controversy followed; the drawing up of the Augsburg Confession, where he was represented by Melanchthon, marked the culmination of the German Reformation (1530). His translation of the Bible is a landmark of German literature.

Maharishi Mahesh Yogi (originally **Mahesh Prasad Varma**) (1911–) Indian, born Jabalpur. Founder of Transcendental Meditation, a relaxation technique which first became popular in the West in the 1950s and 1960s; went on to found the Spiritual Regeneration movement, aimed at solving world problems through meditation.

Mahavira, Vardhamana (c.540–468BC) Indian, born near Vaisali. Founder of Jainism, he renounced the world aged about 30 to lead a severely ascetic life. His sermons and dialogues, stressing non-injury to all living things, are believed by some Jain adherents to be collected in the Svetambara canon of scripture.

Manes (Mani) (c.216–76) Prophet active in Persia from 240, the founder of Manichaeism, which holds that the material world represents an invasion of the realm of light by the powers of darkness. The Zoroastrians condemned the sect and executed Manes, but it spread rapidly in the West, and survived until the 10c.

Mbiti, John Samuel (1931–) Kenyan pastor, theologian and Director of the World Council of Churches Ecumenical Institute (1972–80). His writings maintain that the Christian message can be seen as a fulfilment of traditional African beliefs, and include *African Religions and Philosophy* (1969) and *Bible and Theology in African Christianity* (1987).

Melanchthon, Philip (originally **Philip Schwarzerd**) (1497–1560) German, born Bretten. Protestant reformer who became Luther's fellow-worker and composed the Augsburg Confession (1530). After Luther's death he led the German Reformation movement, but his concessions to the Catholics led to painful controversies. Works include the influential *Loci Communes* (1521).

Mencius (Meng-tzu) (c.372–c.298BC) Chinese, born Shantung. Philosopher who popularized and developed Confucian ideas and made many proposals for social and political reform; his beliefs are recorded in a book compiled after his death, *Book of Meng-tzu*.

Moltmann, Jürgen (1926–) German, born Hamburg. Reformed theologian whose espousal of a theology of hope marked a reaction against the individualistic existential approach of Rudolf Bultmann. Best known for trilogies such as *Theology of Hope* (1967), *The Crucified God* (1974) and *The Church in the Power of the Spirit* (1977).

Moses (c.15c–13c BC) Biblical character, a prophet and lawgiver, who escaped the slaughter of all male Jewish babies and was brought up in the Egyptian court. Was called by God to lead the enslaved Hebrews out of Egypt, which involved the miraculous crossing of the Red Sea (Exodus 14) and the revelation of the Ten Commandments on Mount Sinai (Exodus 20). Traditionally considered the author of the Pentateuch.

Muhammad (Mohammed, Mahomet) (c.570–c.632) Arab prophet and founder of Islam, born Mecca. His teachings were based on revelations of the word of Allah (God), transcribed in the Koran, which holds that God's mercy is principally to be obtained by prayer, fasting and almsgiving. Established a strong following in Medina by 622, and in 629 seized control of Mecca by armed force, thus securing the new religion in Arabia. Died in the home of Ayeshah, the favourite of his nine wives. His tomb in the mosque at Medina is venerated throughout Islam.

Muhammad, Elijah (originally **Elijah Poole**) (1897–1975) American, born near Sandersville, Georgia. Leader of the Black Muslims from 1934, and advocate of racial separation; imprisoned during World War II for discouraging his followers from registering for the draft. His national representative from 1963 was Louis Farrakhan (1933–), who later succeeded him as leader of the Nation of Islam.

Nagarjuna (c.150–c.250) Indian Buddhist monk-philosopher, the founder of the Madhyamika or Middle Path school of Buddhism. His teachings concentrate on the contradictions inherent in

philosophy while stressing the liberating power of enlightenment.

Newman, John Henry, Cardinal (1801–90) English, born London. Prelate and theologian, a vigorous member of the Oxford Movement until its dissolution (1841) and later a convert to Catholicism (1845). Joined the Oratorians in Rome, then established his own community in Birmingham; made cardinal in 1879. Works include the spiritual autobiography *Apologia pro Vita Sua* (1864).

Niebuhr, Reinhold (1892–1971) American, born Wright City, Missouri. Theologian who became an evangelical pastor in working-class Detroit (1915–28) and Professor of Christian Ethics in the Union Theological Seminary, New York (1928–1960). An advocate of Christian Realism, his works include *Moral Man and Immoral Society* (1932), *Faith and History* (1949) and *Structure of Nations and Empires* (1959).

Origen (c.185–c.254) Christian scholar, theologian, and an early Greek Father of the Church, born probably in Alexandria. Head of the catechical school in Alexandria (c.211–232); imprisoned and tortured during the persecution under Decius in 250. His views on the unity of God and speculations about the salvation of the Devil were condemned by Church Councils in the 5c–6c.

Otto, Rudolf (1869–1937) German, born Peine. Theologian and philosopher who, following several journeys to the East, published *The Idea of the Holy* (1923), in which he defines religious experience as a non-rational but objective sense of the 'numinous', inspiring both awe and a promise of exaltation and bliss. Other works include *The Philosophy of Religion* (1931) and *Mysticism East and West* (1932).

Paley, William (1743–1805) English, born Peterborough. Theologian and priest who, in works such as *Evidences of Christianity* (1794) and *Natural Theology* (1802), aimed to derive a proof of Christian belief from the order inherent in creation. Other works such as *Principles of Moral and Political Philosophy* (1785) expounded a form of utilitarianism.

Pannenberg, Wolfhart (1928–) German, born Stettin (now Poland). Lutheran theologian whose best-known work, *Jesus — God and Man* (1964), opposes Bultmann's programme of demythologization with the claim that the resurrection of Jesus is central to the Christian faith. Other works include *Theology and the Philosophy of Science* (1976).

Paul, St (also known as **Saul of Tarsus**) (d.c.64) New Testament figure born of Jewish parents in Tarsus, Cilicia. Originally a fervent Pharisee and persecutor of Christians, he converted to Christianity after a vision of Christ during a journey to Damascus (c.34–5), and became a passionate evangelist and missionary, especially to Gentiles, throughout the Roman world. After imprisonment in Jerusalem and Rome c.60–4 he was probably executed under Nero. Thirteen New Testament letters and some other works are traditionally attributed to him.

Rahner, Karl (1904–84) German, born Freiburg. Roman Catholic theologian and priest whose writings maintain a dialogue between traditional dogma and contemporary existential questions. Advised Vatican Council II. Best known for his *Theological Investigations* (1961–81); other works include *Prayers for a Lifetime* (1984) and the autobiographical interviews *I Remember* (1985).

Rajneesh, Bhagwan Shree (originally **Rajneesh Chandra Mohan**) (1931–90) Indian exponent of yogic spirituality who attracted many Westerners to his ashram in Poona in the 1970s, relocating to Oregon in 1981. His flamboyant lifestyle and advocacy of

Thought and Belief

free sexual expression met with some scepticism, but a nucleus of devotees remained loyal up to his death in 1990.

Ramakrishna Paramahasa (originally **Gadadhar Chattopadhyaya**) (1836–86) Indian, born Hooghly. Hindu religious teacher who formed a religious order which bore his name and established its headquarters in Calcutta (now Kolkata). Among his chief tenets is that all religions are paths to the same goal; his most noteworthy disciple was Swami Vivekananda.

Ramsey, Ian Thomas (1915–72) English, born Kearsley, near Bolton. Theologian and Bishop of Durham (1966–72), respected for his intellectual contribution to the Church of England's stance on educational and social matters. His theological work includes *Models and Mystery* (1964) and *Models for Divine Activity* (1973).

Robinson, J(ohn) A(rthur) T(homas) (1919–83) English, born Canterbury. Theologian and Bishop of Woolwich (1959–69) best known for his bestselling book *Honest to God* (1963), which he described as an attempt to explain the Christian faith to modern man. Other works include *Jesus and His Coming* (1957) and *Redating the New Testament* (1976).

Ruether, Rosemary Radford (1936–) American, born Minneapolis, Minnesota. Theologian who has written extensively on women and the need to affirm the feminine dimension of religion. Works include *New Woman/New Earth* (1975), *Sexism and God-Talk* (1983) and *Women–Church* (1985).

Russell, Charles Taze (known as **Pastor Russell**) (1852–1916) American, born Pittsburgh, Pennsylvania. Founder of the Jehovah's Witnesses movement, a sect with a literalist interpretation of the Bible and an apocalyptic bent.

Sankara (**Samkara, Sankaracharya**) (c.700–c.750) Indian, born Kalati. Philosopher and theologian who is the most famous exponent of Advaita or non-dualistic Vedanta, and is the source of the main currents of modern Hindu thought. His teaching that Brahma alone has true existence, and the goal of the self is to become one with the Divine, influenced Ramakrishna. Founded monastic centres throughout India.

Schleiermacher, Friedrich (Ernst Daniel) (1768–1834) German, born Breslau. Theologian, philosopher and priest widely held to be the founder of modern Protestant theology; led the movement which brought about the union of the Lutheran and Reformed Churches in Prussia (1817). His most important work is *The Christian Faith* (1821–2).

Schweitzer, Albert (1875–1965) German, born Kaysersberg. Medical missionary, theologian, musician and philosopher. Despite his international reputation in music and theology, he turned to studying medicine (1905), and after qualifying (1913) departed with his wife to set up a hospital to fight leprosy and sleeping sickness in Lambaréné, French Equatorial Africa. Awarded the Nobel peace prize in 1952. Religious writings include *The Quest of the Historical Jesus* (1906).

Smith, Joseph (1805–44) American, born Sharon, Vermont. Founder of Mormonism, he was told in a vision of a hidden gospel written on golden plates, the *Book of Mormon*, which was unearthed in 1827. Despite ridicule and hostility, the new 'Church of Jesus Christ of Latter-day Saints' (founded 1830) rapidly gained converts, and continues to be influential in the USA and worldwide.

Steiner, Rudolf (1861–1925) Austrian, born Kraljevec. Social philosopher, the founder of anthroposophy, he established his first 'school of spiritual science' in Dornach, Switzerland (1912),

integrating ideas of psychology, ecology and physical therapy. Many schools and research institutions arose from his ideas, notably the Rudolf Steiner Schools for children with special needs.

Strauss, David Friedrich (1808–74) German, born Ludwigsburg. Theologian who sought to prove in his controversial *Life of Jesus* (1835) that the gospel history is a collection of myths, each containing nevertheless a nucleus of historical truth. Other works include *The Old and New Faiths* (1872), several biographies, and lectures on Voltaire (1870).

Swami Vivekananda (originally **Narendranath Dutt**) (1863–1902) Indian, born Calcutta (now Kolkata). Hindu missionary and chief disciple of Ramakrishna Paramahasa, a persuasive exponent of Hinduism in the West; organized the now worldwide Ramakrishna Mission.

Swedenborg, Emmanuel (originally **Swedberg**) (1688–1772) Swedish, born Stockholm. Mystic and scientist who wrote on algebra, navigation, astronomy and chemistry, but became increasingly convinced that he had direct access to the spiritual world, which he explored in such works as *Heavenly Arcana* (1749–56) and *The New Jerusalem* (1758). In 1787 his followers in London formed the Church of the New Jerusalem.

Teilhard de Chardin, Pierre (1881–1955) French, born Sarcenat. Geologist, palaeontologist, Jesuit priest and philosopher whose unorthodox ideas led to a ban on his teaching and publishing. His major work, *The Phenomenon of Man* (1955), argues that humanity is in a continuous process of evolution towards a perfect spiritual state.

Teresa of Ávila, St (1515–82) Spanish, born Ávila. Carmelite nun noted for her asceticism and ecstatic visions. To re-establish the ancient Carmelite rule, in 1562 she founded the first of her 16 religious houses, and in 1568 she helped St John of the Cross found the first community of reformed Carmelite friars. Among her writings are her autobiography *The Way of Perfection* and the mystical work *The Interior Castle*.

Teresa of Calcutta, Mother (originally **Agnes Gonxha Bojaxhiu**) (1910–97) Albanian, born Skopje (now Macedonia). Roman Catholic nun and missionary in India. Became principal of a convent school in Calcutta (now Kolkata), but in 1948 left to work alone in the slums, especially with destitute children. Opened her House for the Dying in 1952, and in 1957 began work with lepers and in many disaster areas of the world. Awarded the Nobel peace prize in 1979.

Tertullian (c.160–220) Theologian and Father of the Latin Church, born Carthage, whose opposition to worldliness in the Church culminated in his becoming a leader of the Montanist sect (c.207). The first to produce major Christian works in Latin, he had a profound influence on the development of ecclesiastical language, and also wrote against heathens, Jews and heretics.

Tillich, Paul (Johannes) (1886–1965) German, born Starzeddel, Prussia. Protestant theologian and philosopher, an early critic of the Nazis whose main work *Systematic Theology* (1951–63) combines elements of existentialism and the ontological tradition in Christian thought. He explained faith as a reality transcending finite existence rather than a belief in a personal God, leading to oversimplified accusations of atheism. Popular works include *The Courage to Be* (1952), *Dynamics of Faith* (1957).

Tutu, Desmond Mpilo (1931–) South African, born Klerksdorp. Became an Anglican parish priest (1960) and rapidly rose to become Bishop of Lesotho (1977), the first black Bishop of Johannesburg (1984) and Archbishop of Cape Town (1986). A fierce critic of the apartheid system, he has nevertheless condemned the use of violence. Awarded the Nobel peace prize in 1984; chaired the Truth and Reconciliation Commission from 1995.

Wesley, John (1703–91) English, born Epworth, Lincolnshire. Priest and founder of Methodism. His evangelistic zeal led to persecution and isolation from the Church, and he was driven to preach to huge crowds in the open air in Bristol, where he founded the first Methodist chapel (1739). An energetic traveller and prolific writer, he produced grammars, histories, biographies, collections of hymns, his own sermons and journals, and a magazine.

Wycliffe, John (c.1330–1384) English, born near Richmond, North Yorkshire. Religious reformer and rector of Lutterworth who wrote many popular tracts in English (as opposed to Latin) attacking the Church hierarchy, and issued the first English translation of the Bible. His opinions were condemned by the Church and his followers known derisively as 'Lollards'.

Young, Brigham (1801–77) American, born Whitingham, Vermont. Mormon leader who became one of the 12 apostles of the Mormon Church in 1835, and succeeded Joseph Smith as President (1844); later founded Salt Lake City. Appointed Governor of Utah in 1850, but was replaced in 1857 when an army was sent to establish federal law and suppress polygamy in the territory.

Zoroaster (Zarathushtra, Zaradusht) (c.630–c.553BC) Iranian religious leader and prophet, the founder or reformer of the Parsee religion known as Zoroastrianism. His visions of Ahura Mazda led him to preach against polytheism, and as the centre of a group of chieftains, he carried on a struggle for the establishment of a holy agricultural state against Turanian and Vedic aggressors.

Zwingli, Huldreich or **Ulrich** (1484–1531) Swiss, born Wildhaus. Protestant reformer and priest who opposed the selling of indulgences and espoused the Reformed doctrines, but in 1524 disagreed with Martin Luther over the question of the Eucharist. War between the cantons followed, and he was killed in an attack on Zurich.

Thought and Belief

Templeton Prize

Awarded for progress toward research or discoveries about spiritual realities.

1973	Mother Teresa, India
1974	Brother Roger, France
1975	Sir Sarvepalli Radhakrishnan, India
1976	Cardinal Leon Joseph Suenens, Belgium
1977	Chiara Lubich, Italy
1978	Rev Prof Thomas F Torrance, UK
1979	Rev Nikkyo Niwano, Japan
1980	Prof Ralph Wendell Burhoe, USA
1981	Dame Cecily Saunders, UK
1982	Rev Dr Billy Graham, USA
1983	Aleksandr Solzhenitsyn, USSR
1984	Rev Michael Bourdeaux, UK
1985	Sir Alister Hardy, UK
1986	Rev Dr James I McCord, USA
1987	Rev Prof Stanley L Jaki, Hungary/USA
1988	Dr Inamullah Khan, Pakistan
1989	Very Rev Lord MacLeod of Fiunary, UK;

	Prof Carl Friedrich von Weizsäcker, Germany
1990	Baba Amte, India; Prof L Charles Birch, Australia
1991	Rt Hon Lord Jakobovits, UK
1992	Rev Dr Kyung-Chik Han, South Korea
1993	Charles W Colson, USA
1994	Michael Novak, USA
1995	Paul Charles William Davies, UK
1996	William Rohl Bright, USA
1997	Pandurang Shastri Athavale, India
1998	Sir Sigmund Sternberg, Hungary/UK
1999	Ian Graeme Barbour, USA
2000	Prof Freeman J Dyson, USA
2001	Rev Canon Dr Arthur Peacocke, UK
2002	Rev Dr John C Polkinghorne, UK

Population distribution of major beliefs

Figures are for nation states only, and have been compiled from the most accurate recent available information and in most cases are correct to the nearest possible 1%. Where possible, within Islam the relative proportion of Sunnis and Shiites is indicated. No precise information was available for the following: Estonia, Latvia, Lithuania, Mongolia, Nauru, Uzbekistan.

■ Baha'i		Malaysia	17%	Andorra	1%	Brazil	7%
Bolivia	3%	Myanmar (Burma)	89%	Angola	12%	Brunei	8%
Kiribati	3%	Nepal	5%	Antigua and		Bulgaria	80%
Panama	1%	Singapore	28%	Barbuda	87%	Burkina Faso	1%
Tuvalu	1%	Sri Lanka	69%	Argentina	2%	Burundi	7%
		Taiwan	42%	Armenia	94%	Cameroon	18%
■ Buddhism		Thailand	95%	Australia	47%	Canada	42%
Bhutan	73%	Vietnam	55%	Austria	7%	Central African	
Brunei	12%			Azerbaijan	5%	Republic	25%
Cambodia	95%	**■ Chinese folk religion**		Bahamas, The	74%	Chad	5%
China	6%	China	20%	Barbados	67%	Chile	8%
France	1%	Laos	1%	Belarus	64%	Congo, Democratic	
India	1%	Malaysia	12%	Belgium	10%	Republic of	15%
Indonesia	1%	Taiwan	45%	Belize	30%	Côte d'Ivoire	7%
Japan	38%			Benin	3%	Croatia	11%
Korea, Democratic		**■ Christianity**		Bermuda	73%	Cuba	3%
People's Republic		◇ *Protestantism*		Bolivia	5%	Cyprus	78%
of (North Korea)	2%	(includes all non-		Botswana	41%	Czech Republic	8%
Korea, Republic of		Roman Catholic		Bosnia-		Denmark	92%
(South Korea)	47%	denominations and		Herzegovina	35%	Djibouti	2%
Laos	76%	forms of Christianity)					
		Albania	8%				

Thought and Belief

Dominica	16%	Poland	3%	Chile	80%	Samoa	22%

Dominica 16% Poland 3% Chile 80% Samoa 22%
Ecuador 2% Portugal 2% Colombia 95% San Marino 93%
Egypt 6% Romania 88% Comoros 14% São Tomé and
El Salvador 20% Russia 75% Congo 50% Príncipe 80%
Eritrea 50% Rwanda 9% Congo, Democratic Senegal 2%
Ethiopia 42% St Kitts and Nevis 71% Republic of 45% Serbia and
Fiji 37% St Lucia 10% Costa Rica 85% Montenegro 4%
Finland 90% St Vincent and the Côte d'Ivoire 18% Seychelles 90%
France 4% Grenadines 62% Croatia 77% Sierra Leone 3%
Gabon 30% Samoa 78% Cuba 40% Slovakia 59%
Georgia 83% São Tomé and Czech Republic 40% Slovenia 72%
Germany 39% Príncipe 10% Denmark 1% Solomon Islands 19%
Ghana 32% Serbia and Djibouti 4% South Africa 8%
Greece 98% Montenegro 66% Dominica 77% Spain 97%
Grenada 38% Seychelles 8% Dominican Suriname 23%
Guatemala 22% Sierra Leone 6% Republic 92% Swaziland 8%
Guinea 8% Slovakia 10% Ecuador 94% Sweden 2%
Guinea-Bissau 6% Slovenia 1% El Salvador 77% Switzerland 46%
Guyana 36% Solomon Islands 72% Equatorial Guinea 89% Togo 23%
Haiti 15% Somalia 2% Fiji 9% Tonga 16%
Honduras 3% South Africa 54% Finland 1% Trinidad and
Hungary 25% Sri Lanka 8% France 80% Tobago 32%
Iceland 93% Sudan, The 7% Gabon 65% Uganda 33%
India 2% Suriname 25% Germany 37% UK 14%
Indonesia 6% Swaziland 52% Ghana 18% Ukraine 14%
Iraq 3% Sweden 91% Grenada 52% Uruguay 60%
Ireland 3% Switzerland 40% Guatemala 73% USA 28%
Israel 2% Syria 10% Guyana 19% Vanuatu 15%
Jamaica 55% Taiwan 5% Haiti 80% Vatican 100%
Jordan 6% Tanzania 35% Honduras 94% Venezuela 92%
Kazakhstan 46% Togo 7% Hungary 64% Vietnam 7%
Kenya 38% Tonga 63% Iceland 1% Zambia 28%
Kiribati 38% Trinidad and Indonesia 3% Zimbabwe 12%
Korea, Democratic Tobago 28% Ireland 88%
  People's Republic Tunisia 1% Italy 85% **■ Druze**
  of (North Korea) 1% Turkmenistan 9% Jamaica 6% Israel 2%
Korea, Republic of Tuvalu 98% Kenya 28% Lebanon 1%
  (South Korea) 39% Uganda 33% Kiribati 53%
Kyrgyzstan 20% UK 65% Korea, Republic of **■ Hinduism**
Laos 1% Ukraine 79% (South Korea) 12% Bangladesh 12%
Lebanon 30% Uruguay 3% Laos 1% Bhutan 22%
Lesotho 49% USA 56% Lesotho 45% Fiji 38%
Liberia 68% Vanuatu 67% Liechtenstein 80% Guyana 35%
Liechtenstein 8% Zambia 41% Luxembourg 97% India 82%
Luxembourg 2% Zimbabwe 33% Madagascar 24% Indonesia 2%
Macedonia 67%   Malawi 20% Kuwait 2%
Madagascar 18% *◇ Roman Catholicism* Malta 97% Malaysia 7%
Malawi 50% Albania 4% Marshall Islands 7% Mauritius 52%
Malaysia 6% Andorra 94% Mauritius 26% Myanmar (Burma) 1%
Mali 1% Angola 69% Mexico 93% Nepal 90%
Malta 90% Antigua and Micronesia, Federated Oman 13%
Marshall Islands 7% Barbuda 9% States of 50% Pakistan 2%
Mauritius 2% Argentina 90% Monaco 90% Qatar 1%
Mexico 3% Australia 26% Mozambique 25% Seychelles 1%
Micronesia, Federated Austria 77% Namibia 24% Singapore 5%
  States of 47% Bahamas, The 21% Netherlands, The 36% South Africa 2%
Moldova 98% Barbados 4% New Zealand 15% Sri Lanka 15%
Monaco 5% Belarus 8% Nicaragua 95% Suriname 27%
Morocco 1% Belgium 75% Nigeria 12% Trinidad and
Mozambique 3% Belize 62% Norway 1% Tobago 24%
Myanmar (Burma) 6% Benin 19% Palau 66% UK 1%
Namibia 66% Bermuda 14% Panama 84%
Netherlands, The 27% Bolivia 92% Papua New Guinea 22% **■ Islam**
New Zealand 52% Bosnia- Paraguay 90% Afghanistan 99%
Nicaragua 5% Herzegovina 15% Peru 93% (Shiite 25%, Sunni 74%)
Niger 5% Botswana 9% Philippines 83% Albania (Sunni) 60%
Nigeria 28% Brazil 87% Poland 93% Algeria (Sunni) 99%
Norway 88% Burkina Faso 10% Portugal 94% Austria 2%
Pakistan 1% Burundi 63% Romania 6% Azerbaijan (Shiite) 93%
Panama 5% Cameroon 35% Rwanda 65% Bahrain 95%
Papua New Guinea 44% Canada 47% St Kitts and Nevis 7% (Shiite 73%, Sunni 22%)
Paraguay 9% Cape Verde 98% St Lucia 90% Bangladesh 87%
Peru 5% Central African St Vincent and the Belgium 2%
Philippines 9% Republic 25% Grenadines 19% Benin 17%
  Chad 20%   Bhutan 5%
      Bosnia-Herzegovina
      (Sunni) 40%

Brunei	65%
Bulgaria	13%
Burkina Faso	44%
Burundi	1%
Cambodia	2%
Cameroon	22%
Central African Republic	14%
Chad	50%
China	2%
Comoros (Sunni)	86%
Congo	2%
Congo, Democratic Republic of	10%
Côte d'Ivoire	45%
Croatia	1%
Cyprus	18%
Djibouti (Sunni)	94%
Egypt (Sunni)	94%
Equatorial Guinea	1%
Eritrea	50%
Ethiopia	40%
Fiji	8%
France	6%
Gabon	1%
Gambia, The	95%
Georgia	11%
Germany	3%
Ghana	10%
Greece	1%
Guinea	85%
Guinea-Bissau	42%
Guyana	9%
India	12%
Indonesia	87%
Iran	99%
(Shiite 91%, Sunni 8%)	
Iraq	96%
(Shiite 54%, Sunni 42%)	
Israel	14%
Jordan (Sunni)	94%
Kazakhstan	48%
Kenya	7%
Kuwait	85%
(Shiite 40%, Sunni 45%)	
Kyrgyzstan	75%
Laos	1%
Lebanon	69%
Liberia	14%
Libya (Sunni)	97%
Macedonia	30%
Madagascar	6%
Malawi	21%
Malaysia	53%
Maldives (Sunni)	100%
Mali	85%
Mauritania	99%
Mauritius	17%
Morocco (mostly Sunni)	99%
Mozambique	17%
Myanmar (Burma)	4%
Nepal	3%
Netherlands, The	3%
Niger (Sunni)	80%
Nigeria	50%
Oman	86%
Pakistan	97%
(Shiite 20%, Sunni 77%)	
Panama	5%
Philippines	5%
Qatar (mostly Sunni)	95%
Romania	1%
Rwanda	1%
Saudi Arabia (mostly Sunni)	99%
Senegal (Sunni)	92%
Serbia and Montenegro	19%
Sierra Leone (Sunni)	39%
Singapore	16%
Slovenia	1%
Somalia (Sunni)	98%
South Africa	1%
Sri Lanka	8%
Sudan, The	70%
Suriname	21%
Sweden	1%
Switzerland	2%
Syria (mostly Sunni)	90%
Taiwan	1%
Tajikistan	85%
(Shiite 5%, Sunni 80%)	
Tanzania	33%
Thailand	4%
Togo	15%
Trinidad and Tobago	6%
Tunisia (Sunni)	98%
Turkey (Sunni)	99%
Turkmenistan (mostly Sunni)	89%
Uganda	16%
UK	3%
United Arab Emirates	96%
(Shiite 16%, Sunni 80%)	
USA	2%
Yemen	97%
(Shiite 56%, Sunni 41%)	
Zimbabwe	1%

■ **Jainism**

India	1%

■ **Judaism**

Argentina	2%
Bulgaria	1%
France	1%
Hungary	1%
Israel	82%
Luxembourg	1%
Moldova	2%
UK	2%
Ukraine	2%
Uruguay	2%
USA	2%

■ **Non-religious belief/unaffiliated**

Albania	28%
Andorra	5%
Antigua and Barbuda	1%
Australia	17%
Austria	8%
Bahamas, The	3%
Barbados	17%
Belgium	10%
Belize	2%
Bermuda	8%
Bosnia-Herzegovina	1%
Brazil	3%
Bulgaria	5%
Canada	8%
Cape Verde	1%
Central African Republic	1%
Chile	11%
China	59%
Cuba	55%
Czech Republic	40%
Denmark	2%
Dominican Republic	1%
Equatorial Guinea	4%
Finland	9%
France	8%
Germany	15%
Haiti	1%
Hungary	8%
Iceland	6%
Ireland	5%
Italy	14%
Jamaica	18%
Korea, Democratic People's Republic of (North Korea)	67%
Malta	1%
Mexico	1%
Netherlands, The	32%
New Zealand	16%
Norway	6%
Poland	2%
Portugal	3%
Romania	4%
San Marino	3%
Singapore	17%
Slovakia	31%
Slovenia	5%
Sweden	6%
Switzerland	9%
Trinidad and Tobago	5%
UK	14%
Uruguay	35%
USA	10%
Vanuatu	1%
Vietnam	15%

■ **Rastafarianism**

Antigua and Barbuda	1%
Jamaica	6%

■ **Shintoism**

Japan	40%

■ **Sikhism**

Fiji	1%
India	2%
UK	1%

■ **Taoism**

Singapore	13%

■ **Traditional beliefs**

Angola	19%
Benin	61%
Botswana	50%
Brunei	15%
Burkina Faso	45%
Burundi	29%
Cameroon	25%
Central African Republic	22%
Chad	25%
Congo	48%
Congo, Democratic Republic of	30%
Côte d'Ivoire	30%
Cuba	2%
Equatorial Guinea	4%
Ethiopia	14%
Gabon	4%
Gambia, The	1%
Ghana	34%
Guatemala	5%
Guinea	7%
Guinea-Bissau	52%
Kenya	26%
Korea, Democratic People's Republic of (North Korea)	30%
Korea, Republic of (South Korea)	2%
Laos	20%
Lesotho	6%
Liberia	10%
Madagascar	52%
Malawi	9%
Mali	14%
Mozambique	55%
Namibia	10%
Niger	15%
Nigeria	10%
Palau	34%
Papua New Guinea	34%
Rwanda	25%
Senegal	6%
Sierra Leone	52%
Singapore	21%
South Africa	35%
Sudan, The	23%
Suriname	4%
Swaziland	40%
Tanzania	30%
Togo	55%
Uganda	18%
Vanuatu	8%
Zambia	31%
Zimbabwe	40%

■ **Unspecified/others**

Afghanistan	1%
Algeria	1%
Antigua and Barbuda	2%
Argentina	6%
Armenia	6%
Australia	10%
Austria	6%
Azerbaijan	2%
Bahamas, The	2%
Bahrain	5%
Bangladesh	1%
Barbados	12%
Belarus	28%
Belgium	3%
Belize	6%
Bosnia-Herzegovina	9%
Brazil	3%
Bulgaria	1%
Cambodia	3%
Canada	3%
Cape Verde	1%
Central African Republic	13%
Chile	1%
China	13%
Colombia	5%
Costa Rica	15%
Croatia	11%
Cyprus	4%
Czech Republic	12%
Denmark	5%
Dominica	7%
Dominican Republic	7%
Ecuador	4%
El Salvador	3%
Ethiopia	4%

Thought and Belief

Thought and Belief

Fiji	7%	Kuwait	13%	Paraguay	1%	Switzerland	3%
Gambia, The	4%	Kyrgyzstan	5%	Peru	2%	Taiwan	7%
Georgia	6%	Liberia	8%	Philippines	3%	Tajikistan	15%
Germany	6%	Libya	3%	Poland	2%	Tanzania	2%
Ghana	6%	Liechtenstein	12%	Portugal	1%	Thailand	1%
Greece	1%	Macedonia	3%	Qatar	5%	Tonga	21%
Grenada	10%	Malaysia	5%	Romania	1%	Trinidad and Tobago	5%
Guyana	1%	Malta	1%	Russia	25%	Tunisia	1%
Haiti	4%	Marshall Islands	3%	St Kitts and Nevis	22%	Turkey	1%
Honduras	3%	Mauritania	1%	St Vincent and the		Turkmenistan	2%
Hungary	2%	Mauritius	3%	Grenadines	19%	Tuvalu	1%
Indonesia	1%	Mexico	3%	San Marino	4%	Ukraine	5%
Iran	1%	Micronesia, Federated		São Tomé and		United Arab	
Iraq	1%	States of	3%	Príncipe	10%	Emirates	4%
Ireland	4%	Monaco	5%	Saudi Arabia	1%	USA	2%
Italy	1%	Nepal	2%	Serbia and		Vietnam	23%
Jamaica	15%	Netherlands, The	2%	Montenegro	1%	Yemen	3%
Japan	4%	New Zealand	17%	Seychelles	1%	Zambia	1%
Kazakhstan	6%	Norway	5%	Slovenia	21%	Zimbabwe	14%
Kenya	1%	Oman	1%	Solomon Islands	9%		
Kiribati	6%	Panama	5%	Spain	3%		

Religious symbols

The Trinity

Equilateral Triangle · Triangle in circle · Circle within triangle

Father · God Son · Holy Spirit

All-seeing eye · ΙΧΘΥΣ Fish · Sevenfold flame

Seven branch candlestick The Menorah · Abraham

Pentateuch (The Law) · Doorposts and lintel (Passover) · Twelve tribes of Israel · Star of David

Crosses

Barbée · Trefly · Canterbury · Celtic · Cercelée · Cross crosslet

Crux ansata · Globical · Graded (Calvary) · Greek · Iona · Jerusalem

Latin · Maltese · Millvine · Papal · Patée · Patée formée · Patriarchal (or Lorraine)

Potent · Raguly or Ragulée · Russian Orthodox · St Andrew's (Saltire) · St Peter's · Tau (St Anthony's)

| Ankh (Egyptian) | Yin-yang (Taoism) symbol of harmony | torii (shinto) | Om (Hinduism, Buddhism, Jainism; sacred syllable) | Ik-onkar (Sikhism; symbol of God) | Swastika | Yantra: Sri Cakra (wheel of fortune) |

Thought and Belief

Signs of the zodiac

Pisces · Aries · Leo · Scorpio · Sagittarius · Cancer · Capricorn · Gemini · Taurus · Aquarius · Virgo · Libra

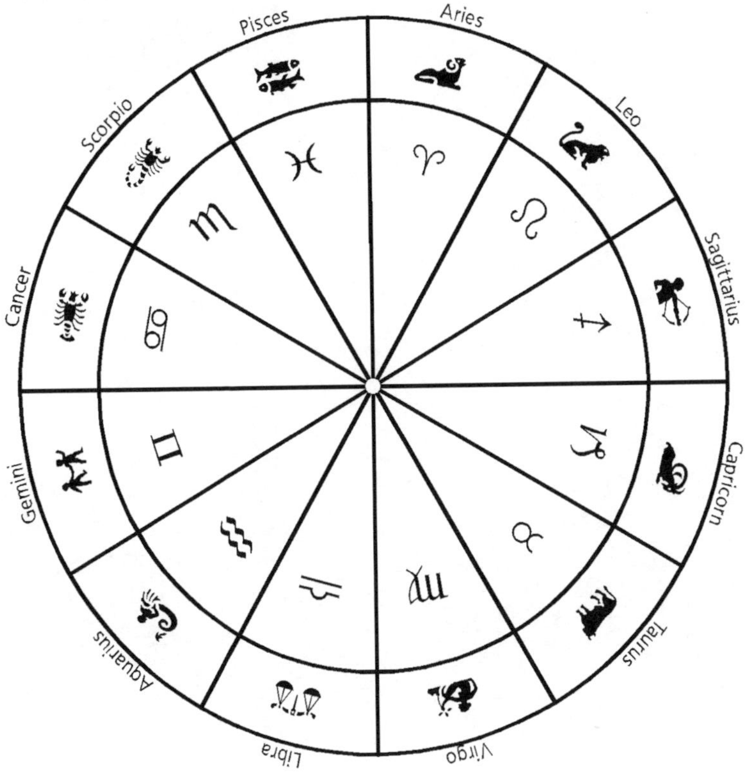

Index

■ Illustrations are indicated in blue

INDEX

897

911

U

Vanbrugh, Sir John *Architects* 757
Van Cleef, Lee *Film and TV actors* 700
Vancouver *Major cities of the world* 274
Vancouver, George *Journeys of exploration* 350
vandalism *Endangered species (Mammals, birds, reptiles)* 480
Van Dam, José *Opera singers* 716
Van Damme, Jean-Claude *Film and TV actors* 700
Van de Graaff, Robert Jemison *Scientists* 602
Vanderbilt, Harold Stirling *Card, board and other indoor games* 831
Van der Elskin, Ed(uard) *Photographers* 763
Van der Meer, Simon *Nobel prizes* 653
Van der Post, Sir Laurens (Jan) *Novelists* 666
Vandross, Luther *Pop and rock musicians and singers* 728
Van Dyck, Sir Anthony *Artists* 752
Van Dyke, Dick *Film and TV actors* 700
Vane, Sir John R *Nobel prizes* 653
Van Gogh, Vincent (Willem) *Artists* 752
Van Gogh Museum *Museums and art galleries — Europe* 773
Vanguard *Significant space missions* 10
Van Halen *Pop and rock musicians and singers* 728
vanilla
  Spices 431
  Spices 430
Vanir *Norse gods of mythology* 837
Vansittart, Peter *Novelists* 666
Vanuatu
  Commonwealth membership 296
  National holidays 426
  Nations of the World A–Z 282
  Political leaders 409
  Speakers of English 542
  United Nations membership 295
  Vanuatu 261
van Vleck, John H *Nobel prizes* 653
vaquita *Endangered species (Mammals, birds, reptiles)* 486
Varanasi *Major cities of the world* 274
Vardhamana Mahavira *Jainism* 862
Varèse, Edgard *Composers* 712
Vargas *Major cities of the world* 274
Vargas Llosa, Mario *Novelists* 666
variation *Scientific terms* 611
Variations *Ballets* 745
varicella *Infectious diseases and infections* 513
varieties of wines and grapes 536
Varmus, Harold E
  Nobel prizes 653
  Scientists 602
Varna *Major cities of the world* 274
Varro, Marcus Terentius *Inventions* 646
Varuna *Figures of myth and legend* 854
Vasistha *Figures of myth and legend* 854
Vatican
  Nations of the World A–Z 282
  Vatican 262
  World Heritage sites 55
Vatican Museums *Museums and art galleries — Europe* 774
Vaughan, Sarah (Lois) ('Sassy', 'The Divine One') *Jazz and blues musicians and singers* 737
Vaughan Williams, Ralph
  Composers 712
  Operas and operettas 714
Vaughn, Robert *Film and TV actors* 700
vault *Terms relating to wine-making and wine-tasting* 539
Vauquelin, Nicolas-Louis *Table of elements* 615
Vautrin, Jean *Literary prizes* 771
Vayu *Figures of myth and legend* 843
VDQS *Terms relating to wine-making and wine-tasting* 539
vector *Scientific terms* 611

Veda, Vedas
  Figures of myth and legend 851
  Hinduism 861
Vedic religion *Hinduism* 861
Vega *The 20 brightest stars* 8
Vega 1 *Significant space missions* 11
Vega, Suzanne *Pop and rock musicians and singers* 728
vegetables
  Dietary recommendations 529
  E numbers 506
  Vegetables 431
  Vegetables 432
Velázquez, Diego (Rodriguez de Silva y) *Artists* 752
Vela *The constellations* 7
Velde, Henri Clemens van de *Architects* 757
velocity
  SI conversion factors 622
  SI units (international system of units) 621
velocity of light *Scientists* 598
velouté *Culinary terms of foreign origin* 533
Veltman, Martinus J G *Nobel prizes* 653
velvet shank *Fungi* 438
Velvet Underground, The *Pop and rock musicians and singers* 728
vending machine *Inventions* 648
Venera *Significant space missions* 11
venereal infection *Infectious diseases and infections* 517
Venezuela
  National holidays 426
  Nations of the World A–Z 282
  Political leaders 409
  United Nations membership 295
  Venezuela 262
  World Heritage sites 55
Venice
  Major cities of the world 274
  Museums and art galleries — Europe 774
  World Heritage sites 52
ventilator *Inventions* 648
ventricles *The heart* 499
Venturi, Robert Charles *Architects* 757
Venus
  Figures of myth and legend 839
  Planetary data 1
  Roman gods of mythology 837
  Significant space missions 10
Venus de Milo *Chronology* 311
Veracruz *Major cities of the world* 274
Verdandi *Figures of myth and legend* 848
Verdi, Giuseppe
  Ballets 743, 744
  Composers 712
  Operas and operettas 714, 715
Verdun, Battle of *Major battles and wars* 353
Verlaine, Paul *Poets* 670
Vermeer, Jan (Johannes) *Artists* 752
vermicelli *Culinary terms of foreign origin* 533
Vermont *States of the USA* 257
vermouth *Terms relating to wine-making and wine-tasting* 539
vernal equinox *The seasons* 419
Verne, Jules *Novelists* 666
Veronese (Paolo Caliari) *Artists* 752
veronica *Flowers (Shrubs)* 437
Verrazano, Giovanni da *Journeys of exploration* 350
Verrazano Narrows *Engineering: bridges* 642
Verrocchio, Andrea del (Andrea de 'Cioni) *Artists* 752
Versace, Gianni *Fashion designers* 765
Versailles
  Museums and art galleries — Europe 774
  World Heritage sites 51
vertebrates *Scientists* 600
Vertumnus *Roman gods of mythology* 837
vervain *Herbs* 430

Verve, The *Pop and rock musicians and singers* 729
very high frequencies *Scientific terms* 611
Very Large Array (VLA) *Largest ground-based telescopes* 10
Vespucci, Amerigo *Journeys of exploration* 350
Vesta
  Figures of myth and legend 844, 854
  Roman gods of mythology 837
Vesterålen *Major island groups* 25
Vestre Mardola *Highest waterfalls* 27
Vesuvius *Major volcanoes* 28
VHF *Scientific terms* 611
viburnum *Flowers (Shrubs)* 437
Vichy *France* 124
Vickers, Jon(athan) Stewart *Opera singers* 716
Vickrey, William *Nobel prizes* 773
Victoria
  Australian states and territories 71
  Figures of myth and legend 848
  Largest lakes 26
  Major cities of the world 274
  Major island groups 22
  Monarchs 359
  Roman gods of mythology 837
Victoria and Albert Museum *Museums and art galleries — UK* 775
Victoria *Largest islands* 22
Victoria Cross, The (VC) *Honours: UK* 302
Victoria Falls
  Journeys of exploration 350
  National parks and nature reserves 57
  World Heritage sites 55
Victoria Jubilee *Engineering: bridges* 642
Vidal, Gore (Eugene Luther, Jr) *Novelists* 666
Vidar *Norse gods of mythology* 837
video games *Hobbies and pastimes* 835
videophone *Inventions* 648
video recorder *Inventions* 648
Vienna
  Major cities of the world 274
  Museums and art galleries — Europe 774
  Orchestras 718
Vientiane *Major cities of the world* 274
Viet Cong *Major battles and wars* 354
Vietnam
  Major battles and wars 354
  National holidays 426
  Nations of the World A–Z 282
  Political leaders 409
  United Nations membership 295
  Vietnam 263
  World Heritage sites 55
Vietnamese *Languages: number of speakers* 541
Vietnam War
  Major battles and wars 354
  Vietnam 264
Vignola, Giacomo Barozzi da *Architects* 757
Vijayawada *Major cities of the world* 274
Viking *Shipping Forecast Areas* 59
Viking 1 *Significant space missions* 11
Viking Raids *Major battles and wars* 351
Vikrama era *Year equivalents* 418
Villella, Edward *Ballet and modern dancers* 742
Vilnius *Major cities of the world* 274
Vina del Mar *Major cities of the world* 274
vinaigrette *Culinary terms of foreign origin* 533
Vinaya Pitaka *Buddhism* 855
Vincent, Gene (Vincent Eugene Craddock) *Pop and rock musicians and singers* 729
Vincent, Jan-Michael *Film and TV actors* 700
vine *Terms relating to wine-making and wine-tasting* 539
vineyard *Terms relating to wine-making and wine-tasting* 539